July 24–28, 2011
Beijing, China

Association for
Computing Machinery

Advancing Computing as a Science & Profession

SIGIR'11

Proceedings of the 34th International ACM SIGIR Conference on
Research and Development in Information Retrieval

Sponsored by:

ACM SIGIR

Supported by:

Microsoft Research, Baidu, EMC^2, Google, SOSO, Yahoo!, eBay, HP Labs, IBM Research, Yandex, CIPS, and Universitité de Montréal

Association for
Computing Machinery

Advancing Computing as a Science & Profession

The Association for Computing Machinery
2 Penn Plaza, Suite 701
New York, New York 10121-0701

Notice to Past Authors of ACM-Published Articles
ACM intends to create a complete electronic archive of all articles and/or other material previously published by ACM. If you have written a work that has been previously published by ACM in any journal or conference proceedings prior to 1978, or any SIG Newsletter at any time, and you do NOT want this work to appear in the ACM Digital Library, please inform permissions@acm.org, stating the title of the work, the author(s), and where and when published.

ISBN: 978-1-4503-0934-9

ISBN Print: 978-1-4503-1250-9

Additional copies may be ordered prepaid from:

ACM Order Department
PO Box 30777
New York, NY 10087-0777, USA

Phone: 1-800-342-6626 (USA and Canada)
+1-212-626-0500 (Global)
Fax: +1-212-944-1318
E-mail: acmhelp@acm.org
Hours of Operation: 8:30 am – 4:30 pm ET

Printed in the USA

Preface from the General Chairs

Welcome to the 34th ACM SIGIR conference on research and development in information retrieval, and welcome to Beijing!

The whole Chinese IR community is delighted to host this year's SIGIR conference for the first time in China in the historical and vibrant city of Beijing. The last decade has witnessed the great surge of China's Internet and search engine industry as one of the largest and most active in the world. The SIGIR conferences have also seen increased Chinese participation: the number of full papers from China has reached a record high of 18 this year, while more than half of them have at least one Chinese name as author. This year's SIGIR conference is a significant opportunity to forge stronger ties between the Chinese IR community and the international SIGIR community. We hope that you will enjoy the great technical program as well as the supporting events in connection with the search engine industry in China.

The conference promises to be a success, with a record number of full papers to be presented. The program committee, chaired by Ricardo Baeza-Yates, Tat-Seng Chua and Bruce Croft and helped by 43 area chairs and many reviewers, did a great job in selecting high quality papers that reflect the latest developments in IR. We are equally grateful to all the other committee members: the Posters and Demos chairs Kevyn Collins-Thompson, Gary Geunbae Lee, and Massimo Melucci; the Tutorial chair Yi Zhang; the Workshops chairs Noriko Kando and Luo Si; the Mentoring Program chair Gareth Jones; the Outstanding Paper Award chair Susan Dumais; the Doctoral Consortium chairs Marteen de Rijke and Paul Thomas; the Industrial Track chairs David Carmel and Haifeng Wang; and the Publication chair Zaiqing Nie. We are especially grateful to Jimmy Huang for his active attraction of corporate sponsorship. The conference also benefits from the great help of the Local Organization Committee, chaired by Xiaoming Li. Special thanks go to Hang Li and Ling Huang for their involvement throughout the preparation of this conference.

SIGIR'11 is sponsored by ACM and has received generous financial support from a large number of companies and organizations. To date, Microsoft Research supports at the *Diamond* level; Baidu, EMC, Google, Tencent and Yahoo! provide *Gold* support; eBay is a *Silver* supporter; HP, IBM Research and Yandex take part at the *Bronze* level; while Springer, Now Publishers and Morgan & Claypool exhibit their products. SIGIR'11 is organized in association with the Chinese Information Processing Society. Finally, we are thankful to the University of Montreal for allowing Jian-Yun Nie to devote himself entirely to this conference during the last 6 months, and we thank ACM and the SIGIR Executive Committee for their constant support.

We hope you will enjoy the conference and your visit to Beijing and China.

Wei-Ying Ma
Microsoft Research Asia

Jian-Yun Nie
University of Montreal

Preface from the Program Committee Chairs

Welcome to the 34th ACM SIGIR International Conference on Research and Development in Information Retrieval. The record number of papers in this year's conference represents both the breadth and depth of the research being done in this vibrant field, both in academia and industry. We have done our best to ensure that these papers meet high standards of quality in terms of presentation, citations, and experimental methodology. At the same time, we have tried to be flexible in the application of these criteria in order to accept papers describing novel and innovative work that may be somewhat unconventional.

The conference received 543 full paper submissions this year, with 240 (44%) coming from Asia and Pacific region, 185 (34%) from the Americas, and 112 (21%) from Europe (the rest were "unknown"). Of these papers, 108 (19.9%) were accepted, up from the acceptance rate of 16.7% in last year's conference. The top five countries in terms of accepted papers were the U.S.A. (52), China (18), Germany (7), and then the U.K. and Spain (both 5). In addition, 274 short papers were submitted to the poster track, of which 89 (32.5%) were accepted. In the other categories, there were 15 (42.8%) demonstrations, 8 workshops, and 11 half-day tutorials accepted. In terms of the technical areas that the accepted papers cover, using the primary keyword assigned by the authors, the top five areas are document representation and content analysis (20%), retrieval models and ranking (17%), users and interactive IR (13%), queries and query analysis (11%), and filtering and recommendation (11%). Perhaps the only surprise there is the increase in the number of papers in filtering and recommendation. We believe that the papers at this year's conference provide an excellent cross-section of what is going on in our field. We hope that you find that reading them and listening to the presenters to be a rewarding experience.

SIGIR uses a two-tier double blind review system. For the full papers, the first step is that at least three first-tier reviewers read every paper and provide ratings and comments. Then two additional reviewers, referred to as the primary or secondary area chairs, study those reviews, and introduce their own opinions and summaries where appropriate by making additional comments. In some cases, the area chairs initiate the discussion among the first-tier reviewers to work out any controversial issues or significant differences of opinion. A new step introduced this year was to request author feedback for specific issues in some papers. Another change this year was that final decisions for nearly all papers were made by the two area chairs together with the reviewers. At the program committee meeting in Barcelona, the program chairs and some area chairs went over the reviews, obtained additional input, and made decisions in the few cases where the area chairs had requested more discussion.

The success of the conference depends entirely on the large number of volunteers that every year devotes large amounts of their time to reviewing and organizing. We are grateful to the more than 200 first-tier reviewers (or general program committee), who performed their tasks very well. We also acknowledge the tremendous job done by the Posters Chairs in handling the short papers, and the great work done by the other Chairs with their tasks. We are particularly indebted to the 43 Area Chairs for their willingness to try a new approach that required more effort from them, and for their responsiveness throughout the reviewing process. We also acknowledge the help of Thomas Preuss with support for the ConfMaster reviewing system. Finally, we extend our best wishes to next year's Program Chairs!

Ricardo Baeza-Yates
Yahoo! Research Barcelona
Africa and Europe

Tat-Seng Chua
National University of Singapore
Asia and Pacific

W. Bruce Croft
University of Massachusetts
Americas

Table of Contents

VOLUME 1

Session 1C: Learning to Rank

Session 2A: Personalization

Session 2B: Retrieval Models I

Session 2C: Social Media

Session 3A: Content Analysis

Session 4B: Query Analysis II

Session 4C: Communities

Session 5A: Classification

Session 5B: Retrieval Models II

Session 5C: Image Search

Session 6A: Indexing

Session 6B: Web Queries

Session 6C: Collaborative Filtering II

VOLUME 2

Session 8B: Query Suggestions

Session 8C: Linguistic Analysis

Session 9A: Clustering

Session 9B: Effectiveness

Session 9C: Multilingual IR

Session 10A: Efficiency

Session 10B: Recommender Systems

Session 10C: Test Collections

Posters Presentations

Demonstrations

Tutorials

Doctoral Consortium

Industrial Track

SIGIR 2011 Organization

General Co-Chairs:	Wei-Ying Ma (*Microsoft Research Asia, China*) Jian-Yun Nie (*University of Montreal, Canada*)
Program Co-Chairs:	Ricardo Baeza-Yates (*Yahoo! Research, Spain*) Tat-Seng Chua (*National University of Singapore*) W. Bruce Croft (*University of Massachusetts, Amherst, USA*)
Posters and Demos Co-Chairs:	Kevyn Collins-Thompson (*Microsoft Research, USA*) Gary Geunbae Lee (*POSTECH, Korea*) Massimo Melucci (*University of Padua, Italy*)
Tutorial Chair:	Yi Zhang (*University of California, Santa Cruz, USA*)
Workshop Co-Chairs:	Noriko Kando (*National Institute of Informatics, Japan*) Luo Si (*Purdue University, USA*)
Mentor Chair:	Gareth Jones (*Dublin City University, Ireland*)
Outstanding Paper Awards Chair:	Susan Dumais (*Microsoft Research, USA*)
Doctoral Consortium Co-Chairs:	Maarten de Rijke (*University of Amsterdam, The Netherlands*) Paul Thomas (*CSIRO, Australia*)
Industrial Track Co-Chairs:	David Carmel (*IBM Research, Haifa, Israel*) Haifeng Wang (*Baidu, China*)
Sponsorship Chair:	Jimmy Huang (*York University, Canada*)
Publicity Chair:	Kam-Fai Wong (*Chinese University of Hong Kong, China*)
Local Organization Chair:	Xiaoming Li (*Peking University, China*)
Finance Chair:	Hang Li (*Microsoft Research Asia, China*)
Proceedings Chair:	Zaiqing Nie (*Microsoft Research Asia, China*)
Chair of Coordination with Local Societies:	Sheng Li (*Harbin Institute of Technology, China*)
Conference Management:	Racemind (*China*)

SIGIR 2011 Area Chairs

Ricardo Baeza-Yates (*Yahoo! Research, Spain*) - Chair
Tat-Seng Chua (*National University of Singapore, Singapore*) - Chair
W. Bruce Croft (*University of Massachusetts, Amherst, USA*) – Chair

1. Document Representation and Content Analysis
James Allan (*University of Massachusetts Amherst, USA*)
Jamie Callan (*CMU, USA*)
Fernando Diaz (*Yahoo! Research, USA*)
Wessel Kraaij (*Radboud University Nijmegen, The Netherlands*)
Douglas Oard (*University of Maryland, USA*)
Maarten de Rijke (*Universiteit van Amsterdam, The Netherlands*)

2. Queries and Query Analysis
Eugene Agichtein (*Emory University, USA*)
Nick Craswell (*Microsoft Research, USA*)
Evgeniy Gabrilovich (*Yahoo! Research, USA*)
Rosie Jones (*Akamai, USA*)

3. Users and Interactive IR
Nick Belkin (*Rutgers, The State University of New Jersey, USA*)
Susan Dumais (*Microsoft Research, USA*)
Diane Kelly (*University of North Carolina, Chapel Hill, USA*)
Ryen White (*Microsoft Research, USA*)

4. Retrieval Models and Ranking
Norbert Fuhr (*Universität Duisburg-Essen, Germany*)
Djoerd Hiemstra (*University of Twente, The Netherlands*)
Oren Kurland (*Technion, Israel*)
Hang Li (*Microsoft Research Asia, China*)
Tie-Yan Liu (*Microsoft Research Asia, China*)
Donald Metzler (*USC/ISI, USA*)
Luo Si (*Purdue University, USA*)
ChengXiang Zhai (*University of Illinois at Urbana-Champaign, USA*)

5. Search Engine Architectures and Scalability
Alistair Moffat (*University of Melbourne, Australia*)
Fabrizio Silvestri (*ISTI-CNR, Italy*)

6. Filtering and Recommendion
David Carmel (*IBM Research, Israel*)
John Riedl (*University of Minnesota, USA*)
Yi Zhang (*UC Santa Cruz, USA*)

7. Evaluation
Ben Carterette (*University of Delaware, USA*)
Mark Sanderson (*RMIT, Australia*)
Ian Soboroff (*NIST, USA*)
Justin Zobel (*University of Melbourne, Australia*)

8. Web IR and Social Media Search
Soumen Chakrabarti (*Indian Institute of Technology, Bombay, India*)
Yoelle Maarek (*Yahoo! Research, Israel*)
Marc Najork (*Microsoft Research, USA*)
Iadh Ounis (*University of Glasgow, UK*)
Berthier Ribeiro-Neto (*Federal University of Minas Gerais, Brazil*)

9. IR and Structured Data
Mounia Lalmas (*Yahoo! Research, Spain*)
Andrew Trotman (*University of Otago, New Zealand*)
Arjen de Vries (*Centrum Viskunde & Informatica and Delft University of Technology, The Netherlands*)

10. Multimedia IR
Xian-Sheng Hua (*Microsoft Research Asia, China*)
R. Manmatha (*University of Massachusetts Amherst, USA*)

11. Other Applications
Charlie Clarke (*University of Waterloo, Canada*)
Edward Fox (*Virginia Tech, USA*)

SIGIR 2011 Program Committee

Maristella Agosti (*University of Padua, Italy*)
Omar Alonso (*Microsoft, USA*)
Ismail Altingovde (*Bilkent University, Turkey*)
Gianni Amati (*Fondazione Ugo Bordoni, Italy*)
Avi Arampatzis (*Democritus University of Thrace, Greece*)
Paavo Arvola (*University of Tampere Finland, Finland*)
Javed Aslam (*Northeastern University, USA*)
Leif Azzopardi (*University of Glasgow, United Kingdom*)
Ricardo Baeza-Yates (*Yahoo! Research, Spain*)
Peter Bailey (*Microsoft, USA*)
Niranjan Balasubramanian (*University of Massachusetts Amherst, USA*)
Timothy Baldwin (*University of Melbourne, Australia*)
Krisztian Balog (*Norwegian University of Science and Tech., Norway*)
Roberto Basili (*University of Roma, Tor Vergata, Italy*)
Steve Beitzel (*Telcordia Technologies, USA*)
Michael Bendersky (*University of Massachusetts Amherst, USA*)
Paul Bennett (*Microsoft, USA*)
Mikhail Bilenko (*Microsoft Research, USA*)
Gloria Bordogna (*National Research Council of Italy, Italy*)
Mohand Boughanem (*IRIT, University Paul Sabatier, Toulouse, France*)
Giorgio Brajnik (*University of Udine, Italy*)
Martin Braschler (*Zurich University of Applied Sciences, Switzerland*)
Eric Brown (*IBM Research, USA*)
Peter Bruza (*Queensland University of Technology, Australia*)
Chris Buckley (*Sabir Research, USA*)
Stefan Buettcher (*Google, USA*)
Fazli Can (*Bilkent University, Turkey*)
Guihong Cao (*Microsoft, USA*)
Robert Capra (*University of North Carolina at Chapel Hill, USA*)
Ben Carterette (*University of Delaware, USA*)
Vitor Carvalho (*Microsoft, USA*)
Carlos Castillo (*Yahoo! Research, Spain*)
Raman Chandrasekar (*Evri, USA*)
Yi Chang (*Yahoo! Labs, USA*)
Kevin Chang (*University of Illinois at Urbana-Champaign, USA*)
Francine Chen (*FX Palo Alto Laboratory, USA*)
Pu-Jen Cheng (*National Taiwan University, Taiwan*)
Jean-Pierre Chevallet (*Université Grenoble, France*)
Abdur Chowdhury (*Twitter, USA*)
Paul Clough (*University of Sheffield, United Kingdom*)
Jack Conrad (*Thomson Reuters, USA*)
Gordon V. Cormack (*University of Waterloo, Canada*)
Hang Cui (*Google, USA*)
Brian Davison (*Lehigh University, USA*)
Debora Donato (*Yahoo! Labs, USA*)
Antoine Doucet (*University of Caen, France*)
Georges Dupret (*Yahoo! Labs, USA*)
Koji Eguchi (*Kobe University, Japan*)
David Eichmann (*U. Iowa, USA*)
Jonathan Elsas (*CMU, USA*)
David Elsweiler (*Friedrich-Alexander Universitaet Erlangen, Germany*)
Jianping Fan (*UNC-Charlotte, USA*)
Hui Fang (*U. of Delaware, USA*)
Henry Feild (*University of Massachusetts Amherst, USA*)
Shaolei Feng (*Siemens Corporate Research Labs, USA*)
Radu Florian (*IBM Research, USA*)
Martin Franz (*IBM, USA*)
Jim French (*Corporation for National Research Initiatives, USA*)
Luanne Freund (*University of British Columbia, Canada*)
Evgeniy Gabrilovich (*Yahoo, USA*)
Patrick Gallinari (*Université Pierre et Marie Curie - Paris 6, France*)
Bin Gao (*Microsoft Research Asia, China*)
Eric Gaussier (*Université Joseph Fourier, France*)
Fredric Gey (*University of California, Berkeley, USA*)
C. Lee Giles (*Pennsylvania State University, USA*)
Ayse Goker (*City University London, United Kingdom*)
Marcos Goncalves (*UFMG, Brazil*)
Gregory Grefenstette (*Exalead, France*)
Jacek Gwizdka (*Rutgers University, USA*)
Sanda Harabagiu (*USA*)
Donna Harman (*NIST, USA*)
David Harper (*Google Switzerland, Switzerland*)
Ahmed Hassan (*University of Michigan Ann Arbor, USA*)
Claudia Hauff (*TU Delft, Netherlands*)
Daqing He (*University of Pittsburgh, USA*)
William Hersh (*Oregon Health and Science University, USA*)
Timo Honkela (*Helsinki University of Technology, Finland*)
Eric Horvitz (*Microsoft Research, USA*)
Xuanjing Huang (*Fudan University, China*)
Jimmy Huang (*York University, Canada*)
Panos Ipeirotis (*New York University, USA*)
CV Jawahar (*IIIT Hyderabad, India*)
Jiwoon Jeon (*Google, USA*)
Daxin Jiang (*Microsoft Research Asia, China*)
Hideo Joho (*University of Tsukuba, Japan*)
Gareth Jones (*Dublin City University, Ireland*)
Joemon Jose (*University of Glasgow, United Kingdom*)
Vanja Josifovski (*Yahoo! Research, USA*)

Ralf Schenkel (*Saarland University, Germany*)
Hinrich Schuetze (*University of Stuttgart, Germany*)
Jangwon Seo (*University of Massachusetts Amherst, USA*)
Chirag Shah (*Rutgers University, USA*)
Rao Shen (*Yahoo!, USA*)
Jialie Shen (*Singapore Management University, Singapore*)
Dou Shen (*Buzz Labs, USA*)
Milad Shokouhi (*Microsoft, United Kingdom*)
David Smith (*University of Massachusetts Amherst, USA*)
Mark Smucker (*University of Waterloo, Canada*)
Aya Soffer (*IBM, Israel*)
Dawei Song (*The Robert Gordon University, United Kingdom*)
Ruihua Song (*Microsoft Research Asia, China*)
Eero Sormunen (*Finland*)
Torsten Suel (*Polytechnic Institute of NYU, USA*)
Krysta Svore (*Microsoft Research, USA*)
John Tait (*Information Retrieval Facility, Austria*)
Simone Teufel (*University of Cambridge, United Kingdom*)
Martin Theobald (*Max-Planck Institute Informatics, Germany*)
James Thom (*RMIT, Australia*)
Paul Thomas (*CSIRO, Australia*)
Paul Thompson (*Dartmouth College, USA*)
Anastasios Tombros (*Queen Mary University of London, United Kingdom*)
Elaine Toms (*Dalhousie University, Canada*)
Andrew Turpin (*University of Melbourne, Australia*)
Howard Turtle (*Syracuse University, USA*)
Antti Ukkonen (*Yahoo! Research Barcelona, Spain*)
Pertti Vakkari (*University of Tampere, Finland*)
Olga Vechtomova (*University of Waterloo, Canada*)
Nina Wacholder (*Rutgers University, USA*)
Jingdong Wang (*Microsoft Research Asia, China*)
Meng Wang (*National University of Singapore, Singapore*)
Kai Wang (*Institute for Infocom Research (I2R), Singapore*)
Qiuyue Wang (*Renmin Univ. of China, China*)
William Webber (*University of Melbourne, Australia*)
Ingmar Weber (*Yahoo! Research Barcelona, Spain*)
Xing Wei (*Microsoft Corp., USA*)
Gerhard Weikum (*Max-Planck Institute for Informatics, Germany*)
Thijs Westerveld (*Teezir Search Solutions, Netherlands*)
Gu Xu (*Microsoft Research Asia, China*)
Xiaobing Xue (*University of Massachusetts, USA*)
Yiming Yang (*Carnegie Mellon University, USA*)
Linjun Yang (*Microsoft Research Asia, China*)
Xing Yi (*University of Massachusetts Amherst, USA*)
Emine Yilmaz (*Microsoft Research Cambridge, United Kingdom*)
Elad Yom-Tov (*Yahoo! Research, USA*)
Masaharu Yoshioka (*Hokkaido University, Japan*)
Markus Zanker (*Alpen-Adria-Universitaet Klagenfurt, Austria*)
Lei Zhang (*Microsoft Research Asia, China*)
Shenghuo Zhu (*NEC Labs America, USA*)
Nivio Ziviani (*Federal University of Minas Gerais, Brazil*)

Posters Committee

Kevyn Collins-Thompson (*Microsoft Research, USA*) - Chair
Gary Geunbae Lee (*POSTECH, Korea*) - Chair
Massimo Melucci (*University of Padua, Italy*) - Chair

Eugene Agichtein (*Emory University, USA*)
Alnur Ali (*Microsoft, USA*)
Omar Alonso (*Microsoft, USA*)
Robin Aly (*University of Twente, The Netherlands*)
Jaime Arguello (*Carnegie Mellon University, USA*)
Azin Ashkan (*University of Waterloo, Canada*)
Javed Aslam (*Northeastern University, USA*)
Hany Azzam (*Queen Mary, University of London, UK*)
Niranjan Balasubramanian (*University of Massachusetts, Amherst, USA*)
Alberto Barrón-Cedeño (*University of Valencia, Spain*)
Michael Bendersky (*University of Massachusetts, Amherst, USA*)
Roi Blanco (*Yahoo! Research, Spain*)
Rui Cai (*Microsoft Research Asia, China*)
Silvia Calegari (*University of Milan-Bicocca, Italy*)
Annalina Caputo (*University of Bari, Italy*)
Ben Carterette (*University of Delaware, USA*)
Marc-Allen Cartright (*University of Massachusetts, Amherst, USA*)
Carlos Castillo (*Yahoo! Research Barcelona, Spain*)
Khe Chai Sim (*National University of Singapore, Singapore*)
Yi Chang (*Yahoo! Research, USA*)
Francine Chen (*FXPAL, USA*)
Yi Chen (*Dublin City University, Ireland*)
Yun Chi (*NEC Laboratories, USA*)
Paul Clough (*University of Sheffield, UK*)
Gao Cong (*Nanyang Technological University, Singapore*)
Bin Cui (*Peking University, China*)
Tonya Custis (*Thomson Reuters, USA*)
Na Dai (*Lehigh University, USA*)
Lorand Dali (*Jozef Stefan Institute, Slovenia*)
Kareem Darwish (*Microsoft, Egypt*)

Emanuele Di Buccio (*University of Padua, Italy*)
Debora Donato (*Yahoo! Labs, USA*)
Georges Dupret (*Yahoo! Labs, USA*)
Miles Efron (*University of Illinois, Urbana-Champaign, USA*)
Koji Eguchi (*Kobe University, Japan*)
Jonathan Elsas (*Carnegie Mellon University, USA*)
Tamer Elsayed (*University of Maryland, USA*)
Jianping Fan (*UNC Charlotte, USA*)
Hui Fang (*University of Delaware, USA*)
Fabio Faria (*University of Campinas, Brazil*)
Ingo Frommholz (*University of Glasgow, UK*)
Xin Fu (*Microsoft, USA*)
Atsushi Fujii (*Tokyo Institute of Technology, Japan*)
Bin Gao (*Microsoft Research Asia, China*)
Wei Gao (*The Chinese University of Hong Kong, China*)
Susan Gauch (*University of Arkansas, USA*)
Shima Gerani (*University of Lugano, Switzerland*)
Brigitte Grau (*LIMSI, France*)
Mark Greenwood (*University of Sheffield, UK*)
Gregory Grefenstette (*Exalead, France*)
Daniel Gruhl (*IBM, USA*)
Guihong Cao (*Microsoft, USA*)
Karl Gyllstrom (*Katholieke Universiteit Leuven, Belgium*)
Preben Hansen (*Swedish Institute of Computer Science, Sweden*)
Donna Harman (*NIST, USA*)
Morgan Harvey (*Strathclyde University, Glasgow, UK*)
Claudia Hauff (*University of Twente, The Netherlands*)
Ben He (*Chinese Academy of Sciences, China*)
Jiyin He (*University of Amsterdam, The Netherlands*)
Andreas Henrich (*University of Bamberg, Germany*)
Katja Hofmann (*University of Amsterdam, The Netherlands*)
Frank Hopfgartner (*University of Glasgow, UK*)
Vivian (Qinmin) Hu (*York University, Canada*)
Meishan Hu (*Nanyang Technological University, Singapore*)
Jimmy Huang (*York University, Canada*)
Yoshiyuki Inagaki (*Yahoo! Labs, USA*)
Giacomo Inches (*UNISI, Switzerland*)
Jagadeesh Jagarlamudi (*University of Maryland, USA*)
Adam Jatowt (*Kyoto University, Japan*)
Daxin Jiang (*Microsoft Research Asia, China*)
Jing Jiang (*Singapore Management University, Singapore*)
Gareth Jones (*Dublin City University, Ireland*)
Joemon Jose (*University of Glasgow, UK*)
Leszek Kaliciak (*Robert Gordon University, UK*)
Jaap Kamps (*University of Amsterdam, The Netherlands*)
Nattiya Kanhabua (*Norwegian University of Science and Technology, Norway*)
Evangelos Kanoulas (*University of Sheffield, UK*)
Maryam Karimzadehgan (*University of Illinois, Urbana-Champaign, USA*)
Mostafa Keikha (*University of Lugano, Switzerland*)
Jin-Dong Kim (*University of Tokyo, Japan*)
Jinyoung Kim (*University of Massachusetts, Amherst, USA*)
Seokhwan Kim (*Pohang University of Science and Technology, Korea*)
Jonathan Koren (*University of California, Santa Cruz, USA*)
Alexander Kotov (*University of Illinois, Urbana-Champaign, USA*)
Donald Kraft (*Louisiana State University, USA*)
Anagha Kulkarni-Joshi (*Carnegie Mellon University, USA*)
Giridhar Kumaran (*Microsoft, USA*)
Oren Kurland (*Technion, Israel*)
Ni Lao (*Carnegie Mellon University, USA*)
Guy Lapalme (*Université de Montréal, Canada*)
Neal Lathia (*University College London, UK*)
Matthew Lease (*University of Texas at Austin, USA*)
Jung-Tae Lee (*Korea University, Korea*)
Yeha Lee (*Pohang University of Science and Technology, Korea*)
Teerapong Leelanupab (*University of Glasgow, UK*)
Xiao Li (*Microsoft Research, USA*)
Elizabeth Liddy (*Syracuse University, USA*)
Xia Lin (*Drexel University, USA*)
Nathan Liu (*Hong Kong University of Science and Technology, China*)
Yi Liu (*Microsoft Research Asia, China*)
Robert Luk (*The Hong Kong Polytechnic University, China*)
Yuanhua Lv (*University of Illinois, Urbana-Champaign, USA*)
Hao Ma (*The Chinese University of Hong Kong, China*)
Craig Macdonald (*University of Glasgow, UK*)
Andrew MacFarlane (*City University London, UK*)
Takuya Maekawa (*NTT, Japan*)
Prasenjit Majumder (*Dhirubhai Ambani Institute of Information and Communication Technology, India*)
Yi Mao (*Microsoft, USA*)
Giorgio Maria Di Nunzio (*University of Padua, Italy*)
Ilya Markov (*UNISI, Switzerland*)
Paul McNamee (*Johns Hopkins University, USA*)
Tao Mei (*Microsoft Research Asia, China*)
Edgar Meij (*University of Amsterdam, The Netherlands*)
Donald Metzler (*University of Southern California, USA*)
Natasa Milic-Frayling (*Microsoft Research Cambridge, UK*)
Zhao-Yan Ming (*National University of Singapore, Singapore*)
Einat Minkov (*University of Haifa, Israel*)
Riccardo Miotto (*University of Padua, Italy*)

Nicola Montecchio (*University of Padua, Italy*)
Yashar Moshfeghi (*University of Glasgow, UK*)
Seung-Hoon Na (*National University of Singapore, Singapore*)
Preslav Nakov (*National University of Singapore, Singapore*)
Michael Nelson (*Old Dominion University, USA*)
Charles Nicholas (*University of Maryland, USA*)
Tae-Gil Noh (*Kyungpook National University, Korea*)
Virgil Pavlu (*Northeastern University, USA*)
Fuchun Peng (*Microsoft, USA*)
Jeremy Pickens (*Catalyst Repository Systems, USA*)
Karen Pinel-Sauvagnat (*IRIT, France*)
Benjamin Piwowarski (*University of Glasgow, UK*)
Tamara Polajnar (*University of Glasgow, UK*)
Luca Pretto (*University of Padua, Italy*)
Diego Puppin (*Google, USA*)
Xiaoguang Qi (*Lehigh University, USA*)
Kira Radinsky (*Technion, Israel*)
Hema Raghavan (*IBM, USA*)
Edie Rasmussen (*University of British Columbia, Canada*)
Henning Rode (*CWI Amsterdam, The Netherlands*)
Haggai Roitman, (*IBM Research – Haifa, Israel*)
Jun Sakuma (*Tokyo Institute of Technology, Japan*)
Kazuhiro Seki (*Kobe University, Japan*)
Jangwon Seo (*University of Massachusetts, Amherst, USA*)
Pavel Serdyukov (*Delft University of Technology, The Netherlands*)
James Shanahan (*Church and Duncan Group, USA*)
Jialie Shen (*Singapore Management University, Singapore*)
Milad Shokouhi (*Microsoft Research, UK*)
Gianmaria Silvello (*University of Padua, Italy*)
Mark Smucker (*University of Waterloo, Canada*)
Vassilios Stathopoulos (*University of Glasgow, UK*)
J. Stephen Downie (*University of Illinois, Urbana-Champaign, USA*)
Juliane Stiller (*Humboldt University, Germany*)
Aixin Sun (*Nanyang Technological University, Singapore*)
Mingxuan Sun (*Georgia Institute of Technology, USA*)
Shanu Sushmita (*University of Glasgow, UK*)
S.M.M. Tahaghoghi (*Microsoft, USA*)
John Tait (*Information Retrieval Facility, Austria*)
Bin Tan (*Amazon, USA*)
Michael Taylor (*Microsoft Research Cambridge, UK*)
Carla Teixeira Lopes (*University of Porto, Portugal*)
Martin Theobald (*Max-Planck Institute Informatics, Germany*)
Ulrich Thiel (*IPSI-Darmstadt, Germany*)
James Thom (*RMIT, Australia*)
Paul Thomas (*CSIRO Australian National University, Australia*)
Paul Thompson (*Dartmouth College, USA*)
Qi Tian (*University of Texas at San Antonio, USA*)
Anastasios Tombros (*Queen Mary, University of London, UK*)
Ricardo Torres (*University of Campinas, Brazil*)
Andrew Trotman (*University of Otago, New Zealand*)
Sarah Tyler (*University of California, Santa Cruz, USA*)
Eduardo Valle (*University of Campinas, Brazil*)
Sumithra Velupillai (*Stockholm University, Sweden*)
Xiaojun Wan (*Peking University, China*)
Changhu Wang (*Microsoft Research Asia, China*)
Jun Wang (*University College London, UK*)
Lidan Wang (*University of Maryland, USA*)
Mengqiu Wang (*Stanford University, USA*)
Taifeng Wang (*Microsoft Research Asia, China*)
Xin-Jing Wang (*Microsoft Research Asia, China*)
William Webber (*University of Melbourne, Australia*)
Wouter Weerkamp (*University of Amsterdam, The Netherlands*)
Tak-Lam Wong (*The Chinese University of Hong Kong, China*)
Jun Xu (*Microsoft Research Asia, China*)
Xiaobing Xue (*University of Massachusetts, Amherst, USA*)
Murat Yakici (*Strathclyde University, Glasgow, UK*)
Hui Yang (*Carnegie Mellon University, USA*)
Jiang-Ming Yang (*Microsoft, China*)
Emine Yilmaz (*Microsoft Research Cambridge, UK*)
Elad Yom-Tov (*Yahoo! Research, USA*)
Minoru Yoshida (*University of Tokyo, Japan*)
Xiaojun Yuan (*SUNY Albany, USA*)
Dell Zhang (*Birkbeck University of London, UK*)
Lei Zhang (*Microsoft Research Asia, China*)
Min Zhang (*Tsinghua University, China*)
Peng Zhang (*Robert Gordon University, Aberdeen, UK*)
Zhongfei Zhang (*SUNY Binghamton, USA*)
Le Zhao (*Carnegie Mellon University, USA*)
Dong Zhou, (*Trinity College Dublin, Ireland*)
Guido Zuccon (*University of Glasgow, UK*)

Demonstrations Committee

Kevyn Collins-Thompson (*Microsoft Research, USA*) - Chair
Gary Geunbae Lee (*POSTECH, Korea*) - Chair
Massimo Melucci (*University of Padua, Italy*) - Chair

Omar Alonso (*Microsoft, USA*)
Steve Beitzel (*Telcordia Technologies, USA*)
Mikhail Bilenko (*Microsoft Research, USA*)
Gloria Bordogna (*CNR - National Research Council of Italy, Italy*)
Mohand Boughanem (*IRIT, University Paul Sabatier, Toulouse, France*)
Carlos Castillo (*Yahoo! Research, Spain*)
Silviu Cucerzan (*Microsoft Research, USA*)
Emanuele Di Buccio (*University of Padua, Italy*)
Giorgio Maria Di Nunzio (*University of Padua, Italy*)
Debora Donato (*Yahoo! Labs, USA*)
Georges Dupret (*Yahoo! Labs, USA*)
Jiwoon Jeon (*Google, USA*)
Joemon Jose (*University of Glasgow, UK*)
Giridhar Kumaran (*Microsoft, USA*)
Jochen Leidner (*Thomson Reuters, Switzerland*)
Chin-Yew Lin (*Microsoft Research Asia, China*)
Ting Liu (*Harbin Institute of Technology, China*)
Vibhu Mittal (*Root-1, USA*)
John Prager (*IBM Research, USA*)
Filip Radlinski (*Microsoft, Canada*)
Hema Raghavan (*IBM Research, USA*)
Chirag Shah (*Rutgers University, USA*)
Rao Shen (*Yahoo!, USA*)
Milad Shokouhi (*Microsoft, UK*)
Anastasios Tombros (*Queen Mary University of London, UK*)
Antti Ukkonen (*Yahoo! Research, Spain*)
Lei Zhang (*Microsoft Research Asia, China*)

Tutorials Committee

Yi Zhang (*UC Santa Cruz, USA*) – Chair

Jing Bai (*Microsoft, USA*)
Xueqi Cheng (*Institute of Computing Technology, Chinese Academy of Science, China*)
Nick Craswell (*Microsoft, USA*)
Cai Deng (*Zhejiang University, China*)
Byron Dom (*Yahoo! Lab, USA*)
Tao Hong (*University of California Santa Cruz, USA*)
Jussi Karlgren (*Swedish Institute of Computer Science, Sweden*)
Birger Larsen (*Royal School of Library and Information Science, Denmark*)
Donald Metzler (*ISI, University of South California, USA*)
Marie-Francine Moens (*Katholieke Universiteit Leuven, Belgium*)
Paul Ogilvie (*LinkedIn, USA*)
Tao Qin (*Microsoft, China*)
Maarten de Rijke (*University of Amsterdam, The Netherlands*)
Ian Ruthven (*University of Strathclyde, UK*)
James G. Shanahan (*Church and Duncan Group, USA*)
Min Zhang (*Tsinghua University, China*)

Workshops Committee

Noriko Kando (*National Institute of Informatics, Japan*) – Chair
Luo Si (*Purdue University, USA*) – Chair

Omar Alonso (*Microsoft, USA*)
Kuang-hua Chen (*National Taiwan University, Taiwan*)
Hazem Elmeleegy (*AT&T Research, USA*)
Hui Fang (*University of Delaware, USA*)
Gareth Jones (*Dublin City University, Ireland*)
Jaana Kekäläinen (*University of Tampere, Finland*)
Mounia Lalmas (*Yahoo! Research, Spain*)
Tetsuya Sakai (*Microsoft Research Asia, China*)
Mark Smucker (*University of Waterloo, Canada*)
Andrew Trotman (*University of Otago, New Zealand*)

Outstanding Paper Awards Committee

Susan T. Dumais (*Microsoft Research, USA*) – Chair

Javed A. Aslam (*Northeastern University, USA*)
Gordon V. Cormack (*University of Waterloo, Canada*)
Brian D. Davison (*Lehigh University, USA*)
David Hawking (*Funnelback and Australian National University, Australia*)
Rong Jin (*Michigan State University, USA*)
Thorsten Joachims (*Cornell University, USA*)
Jussi Karlgren (*Swedish Institute of Computer Science, Sweden*)
Daniel M. Russell (*Google, USA*)
Howard Turtle (*Syracuse University, USA*)

Doctoral Consortium Committee

Maarten de Rijke (*University of Amsterdam, The Netherlands*) - Chair
Paul Thomas (*CSIRO, Australia*) - Chair

Maristella Agosti (*University of Padua, Italy*)
Jamie Callan (*Carnegie Mellon University, USA*)
Charles L.A. Clarke (*University of Waterloo, Canada*)
Julio Gonzalo (*UNED, Spain*)
Franciska de Jong (*University of Twente, The Netherlands*)
Diane Kelly (*University of North Carolina at Chapel Hill, USA*)
Mounia Lalmas (*Yahoo! Research, Spain*)
Marie-Francine Moens (*Katholieke Universiteit Leuven, Belgium*)
Ian Ruthven (*University of Strathclyde, UK*)
Tetsuya Sakai (*Microsoft Research Asia, China*)
Mark Sanderson (*RMIT University, Australia*)
Howard Turtle (*Syracuse University, USA*)
Arjen de Vries (*Centrum Wiskunde & Informatica, The Netherlands*)
ChengXiang Zhai (*University of Illinois at Urbana-Champaign, USA*)
Min Zhang (*Tsinghua University, China*)

Mentoring Committee

Gareth Jones (*Dublin City University, Ireland*) - Chair

B. Barla Cambazoglu (*Yahoo! Research, Spain*)
David Elsweiler (*University of Erlangen, Germany*)
Oren Kurland (*Technion, Israel*)
David Losada (*University of Santiago de Compostela, Spain*)
Jahna Otterbacher (*Illinois Institute of Technology, USA*)
Le Sun (*Institute of Software, Chinese Academy of Sciences, China*)
Bin Wang (*Institute of Computing Technology, Chinese Academy of Sciences, China*)

Local Organization Committee

Xiaoming Li (*Peking University, China*) - Chair

Xueqi Cheng (*Institute of Computing Technology, Chinese Academy of Sciences, China*)
Ling Huang (*Microsoft Research Asia, China*)
Ting Liu (*Harbin Institute of Technology, China*)
Le Sun (*Institute of Software, Chinese Academy of Sciences, China*)
Min Zhang (*Tsinghua University, China*)

SIGIR 2011 Sponsor and Supporters

Sponsor

SIGIR
Special Interest Group
on Information Retrieval

Association for
Computing Machinery

Corporate Supporters

Microsoft Research

Baidu 百度 EMC² Google
SOSO 搜搜 YAHOO!

eBay Research Labs

HP Labs IBM Research
Yandex

Associated Organization

CIPS

Also supported by

Université
de Montréal

Exhibitors

Morgan & Claypool Publishers

now
the essence of knowledge

Springer
the language of science

Keynote Talk

Future of the Web and Search

Qi Lu
Microsoft
Bellevue, WA, USA
qilu@microsoft.com

Abstract

No one doubts that we have only scratched the surface of what is possible with the Web. The day is coming fast when the Web will become almost a virtual mind reader. Your intent, interests, and needs will be instantly perceived and the information you want will be promptly delivered -- whether you ask for it directly or not -- based on a deep understanding of the meaning of words in your query, knowledge of your preferences and patterns, what others have done before you, your location, and more. In this talk, I will share some of my thoughts about where the Web is heading and how search will be transformed to align to this new Web, laying out some specifics behind Microsoft's vision to empower people with knowledge.

Categories & Subject Descriptors: H3.3 Information Search and Retrieval, H4 Information System Applications

General Terms: Algorithms

Bio

As president of Microsoft's Online Services Division (OSD), Dr. Qi Lu leads the company's search and online advertising efforts. Dr. Lu oversees the OSD Research & Development team which has responsibility for the evolution of Microsoft's search, portal and advertising services; the Online Audience Business Group; and the Advertiser and Publisher Solutions Business Group. Dr. Lu reports to Microsoft chief executive officer Steve Ballmer.

Prior to joining Microsoft, Dr. Lu spent 10 years as a Yahoo! senior executive. His roles included serving as the executive vice president of engineering for the company's Search and Advertising Technology Group where he oversaw the development of Yahoo!'s Web search and monetization platforms and vice president of engineering responsible for the technology development of Yahoo!'s search, e-commerce and local listings of businesses and products.

Before joining Yahoo!, Dr. Lu worked as a research staff member at IBM's Almaden Research Center and Carnegie Mellon University and was a faculty member at Fudan University in China. He received his bachelor of science and master of science in computer science from Fudan University and his Ph.D. in computer science from Carnegie Mellon University. Dr. Lu holds 20 U.S. patents.

SIGIR'11, July 24-28, 2011, Beijing, China.
ACM 978-1-4503-0757-4/11/07.

Keynote Talk

Beyond Search: Statistical Topic Models for Text Analysis

ChengXiang Zhai
Department of Computer Science
University of Illinois at Urbana-Champaign
Urbana, IL, USA
czhai@illinois.edu

Abstract

Search is generally a means to the end of finishing a task. While the current search engines are useful to users for finding relevant information, they offer little help to users for further digesting and analyzing the overwhelming found information needed for finishing a complex task. In this talk, I will discuss how statistical topic models can be used to help users analyze and digest the found relevant information and turn search results into actionable knowledge needed to complete a task. I will present several general statistical topic models for extracting and analyzing topics and their patterns in text, and show sample applications of such models in tasks such as opinion integration, comparative summarization, contextual topic trend analysis, and event impact analysis. The talk will conclude with a discussion of novel challenges raised in extending a search engine to an analysis engine that can go beyond search to provide more complete support for users to finish their tasks.

Categories & Subject Descriptors: H3.3 Information Search and Retrieval, H4 Information System Applications

General Terms: Algorithms

Bio

ChengXiang Zhai is an Associate Professor of Computer Science at the University of Illinois at Urbana-Champaign, where he also holds a joint appointment at the Graduate School of Library and Information Science, Institute for Genomic Biology, and Department of Statistics. He received a Ph.D. in Computer Science from Nanjing University in 1990, and a Ph.D. in Language and Information Technologies from Carnegie Mellon University in 2002. He worked at Clairvoyance Corp. as a Research Scientist and a Senior Research Scientist from 1997 to 2000. His research interests include information retrieval, text mining, natural language processing, machine learning, and bioinformatics. He is an Associate Editor of ACM Transactions on Information Systems, and Information Processing and Management, and serves on the editorial board of Information Retrieval Journal. He is a program co-chair of ACM CIKM 2004, NAACL HLT 2007, and ACM SIGIR 2009. He is an ACM Distinguished Scientist and the recipient of an Alfred P. Sloan Research Fellowship, IBM Faculty Award, ACM SIGIR 2004 Best Paper Award, and a Presidential Early Career Award for Scientists and Engineers (PECASE).

SIGIR'11, July 24–28, 2011, Beijing, China.
ACM 978-1-4503-0757-4/11/07.

Modeling and Analysis of Cross-Session Search Tasks

Alexander Kotov[1], Paul N. Bennett[2], Ryen W. White[2], Susan T. Dumais[2], and Jaime Teevan[2]
[1] Department of Computer Science, University of Illinois at Urbana-Champaign, Urbana, IL 61801, USA
[2] Microsoft Research, One Microsoft Way, Redmond, WA 98052, USA
akotov2@illinois.edu, {pauben, ryenw, sdumais, teevan}@microsoft.com

ABSTRACT
The information needs of search engine users vary in complexity, depending on the task they are trying to accomplish. Some simple needs can be satisfied with a single query, whereas others require a series of queries over a longer period of time. While search engines effectively satisfy many simple needs, searchers receive little support when their information needs span sessions. In this work, we propose methods for modeling and analyzing user search behavior that extends over multiple search sessions. We focus on two problems: (i) given a user query, identify all related queries from previous sessions that the user has issued, and (ii) given a multi-query task for a user, predict whether the user will return to this task in the future. We model both problems within a classification framework that uses features of individual queries and long-term user search behavior at different granularity. Experimental evaluation of the proposed models for both tasks indicates that it is possible to effectively model and analyze cross-session search behavior. Our findings have implications for improving search for complex information needs and designing search engine features to support cross-session search tasks.

Categories and Subject Descriptors
H.3.3 [**Information Storage and Retrieval**]: Information Search and Retrieval – *search process, selection process*

General Terms
Algorithms, Experimentation, Human Factors

Keywords
Cross-session search tasks, machine learning, user behavior.

1. INTRODUCTION
Web searchers perform a broad range of information seeking tasks, from figuring out how to spell a word to researching cancer treatment options. Correspondingly, the information needs of search engine users vary in complexity. Some simple information needs, like finding a person's home page or navigating to a social networking site, can be unambiguously expressed as keyword queries and have distinct answers. Other, more complicated needs, like planning a wedding or vacation, have multiple aspects and cannot be satisfied by the results shown on a single search result page. Addressing complex information needs requires a user to issue a series of queries, potentially spanning a long period of time and multiple search sessions. In doing so, searchers may collect, filter, and summarize information from many Web pages. In previous work [9], it has been estimated through manual analysis of query logs that approximately 10% of search sessions include queries on such longitudinal tasks and 25% of the overall query volume corresponds to this type of search task.

While modern search engines effectively serve many of the individual queries that correspond to simple information needs, users get little or no help when their information needs transcend the boundary of a single search session. A *search session*, as defined by Boldi *et al.* [5], is a *sequence of queries issued by a single user within a specific time limit*. In this work, we model and analyze complex, multi-session information needs, which we call *cross-session search tasks*. Cross-session tasks are related to research missions and goals [9][16], as we describe in more detail below, but we explicitly focus on tasks that extend across sessions. We assume that an individual cross-session task consists of a series of queries that corresponds to a distinct high-level information need. The queries related to the task are not necessarily consecutive, and a single search session may contain interleaved queries from multiple cross-session tasks, as well as shorter, within-session tasks. Cross-session tasks may evolve over time, with users starting with only a general idea of what they are searching for and progressively refine their need over time. During a single session, a user may find some results of interest, disregard others and continue exploring, try related queries, or interleave one task with other tasks. They may then drop the task before returning to it at a later time [17][19][20].

Since Web search is currently stateless, the cognitive burden of keeping track of complex search tasks is placed on the searcher. Incorporating the analysis and prediction of long-term user search behavior into search engine infrastructure could improve the search experience for searchers in many ways. For example, Web search traditionally only considers a user's current query when identifying relevant search results. If a search engine were able to identify past queries and interactions related to the searcher's current long-term intent, this information could be used to improve search quality. Past information could also be retained and displayed to help the user re-establish the context of a long-term search task, relieving the user from the burden of recalling past queries and pages visited (e.g., [9]). Similarly, if a search engine could predict that a user was going to return to a task that has only been temporarily suspended, the search engine could help support future related searches by, for example, pre-identifying and pre-caching relevant documents, or soliciting user assistance to archive the current search session for future use.

In this paper, we explore how effectively cross-session search tasks can be modeled. Specifically, we focus on two related problems: (i) identify all previous queries by a user on the same search task, and (ii) given a search task for a user, predict whether the user will return to this task in the future. After a discussion of recent work in modeling user search behavior, we formally define the specific aspects of the challenge of modeling and analyzing cross-session search tasks that we address. We next discuss the formulation of the two research problems as classification tasks, and describe the classification models used. We then present the experimental setup and results for both problems. Finally, we summarize our findings and discuss future work.

2. RELATED WORK

User search behavior has been actively studied in recent years, primarily using search logs as a valuable resource to understand people's interactions with Web search engines. Earlier work on understanding search behavior focused on methods for classifying queries into high-level search goals, such as informational, navigational and transactional [8][18][29]. Downey *et al.* [10] studied the relationship between information needs and their formulation as search queries. Recent work indicates that, in addition to queries themselves, long-term and short-term search contexts can be effectively leveraged to predict user interests [34], search success [14], and improve search result ranking [1].

Search behavior can be analyzed over time to identify queries that express the same underlying information need. Most previous work has focused on search behavior analysis and prediction within a single search session. Related queries within a session have been referred to as being part of a *query chain* [26] or *search goal* [14][16][24]. He *et al.* [15] proposed an algorithm to segment a query stream into sessions by detecting topical shifts between the queries. Hassan *et al.* [14] modeled session-level search goals using hidden Markov models. They experimentally demonstrated that models that took into account users' search behavior were more predictive of session success than those that relied on document relevance. Piwowarski *et al.* [24] used a layered Bayesian network to model a hierarchy of user search actions, with the goal of identifying distinct patterns of user search behavior that correspond to the latent states of the Bayesian network. They used a classifier to learn the mapping from the distribution of latent states for a clicked document to the relevance assessment of that document in the absence of document content models. Mei *et al.* [21] proposed a general framework to study sequences of search activities and focused on simple prediction and classification tasks, ranging from predicting if the next click will be on an algorithmic result to segmenting the query stream into goals and missions. Single-session analyses have also been used for various search-related tasks such as query suggestion [6][7], interactive feeback [30], and query disambiguation [22].

In this paper we focus on tasks that extend across sessions. There has been some work on characterizing such tasks using log or survey data, and on automatically identifying queries on the same task. Teevan *et al.* [32] showed, via query log analysis, that nearly 40% of queries were attempts to re-find previously encountered results. Using a survey methodology, Aula *et al.* [2] studied the search and information re-access strategies of experienced Web users. They found that people often have difficulty remembering the queries they used originally to discover information of interest. In a field study of 21 people, MacKay and Watters [20] explored a variety of Web-based information seeking tasks. They found that information gathering tasks accounted for 13.4% of tasks, and that 58.8% of these tasks continued across sessions. Information gathering tasks were complex and people used a variety of browser tools and actions to help complete these tasks. Liu and Belkin [19] examined the structure (parallel or dependent) of tasks that extend across different sessions. Jones and Klinker [16] proposed methods to partition a query stream into research missions and goals, where each mission corresponds to a set of related information needs and may include multiple search goals. This work is closely related to our problem of identifying previous queries on the same search task. However, we do not decompose tasks into a hierarchical structure of missions and goals, we examine tasks that extend over a longer time period (up to a week) and we study an order of magnitude more users. We also propose many new features and experiment with different classification models.

Several algorithms and tools have been developed to support the resumption of search tasks. Morris *et al.* [23] developed *SearchBar*, a system that proactively and persistently stores query histories, browsing histories, and users' notes and ratings. SearchBar supports multi-session investigations by assisting with task context resumption and information re-finding. However, instead of determining the search tasks automatically, SearchBar requires users to explicitly identify them, thus creating additional user overhead. Donato *et al.* [9] developed *SearchPad*, a system which automatically identifies research missions and presents a search workspace comprising previous queries and results related to the mission. SearchPad uses measures of topic coherence between pairs of consequtive queries and user engagement to identify such research missions. Although Donato and colleagues describe a method and architecture for detecting research missions, the system evaluation presented in [9] focused primarily on systems issues (triggering without influencing latency and using online evaluation to set application-specific parameters). They did not compare alternative classification algorithms or consider the problem of predicting whether users will return to the same task in the future.

The research presented here addresses two important problems in modeling cross-session information needs: (i) identifying all previous queries in a user's search history on the same task as the current query, and (ii) predicting whether a user will return to the task in future sessions. We formalize these problems as classification tasks within a supervised learning framework. Our work differs from prior work in several ways:

- We formalize and evaluate the problem of predicting search task continuation. Predicting whether a search task will be resumed in the future is new, as far as we know.
- We extend previous work on same-task detection (notably that on research missions) by examining tasks that extend over longer time periods, studying many more searchers, and evaluating new features and classification models.
- We describe a new method for automatically and semi-automatically creating labeled data sets that can be used for both problems addressed in this work.
- We experiment with different feature sets and classifiers to identify the most informative features and the best-performing classifiers for the two problems addressed here.

In the following section, we formally define the two problems that we address and the context from which they arise.

3. PROBLEM DEFINITION

User search behavior has been modeled at different levels of granularity, ranging from eye fixations on search results [11] to information needs underlying a set of queries [16][26]. Different sources of data can be used depending on the particular modeling task. An important data source for many high-level modeling tasks is search logs, traditionally defined as follows:

DEFINITION 1 SEARCH LOG $\mathcal{L}$ *is a temporally-ordered set of quintuples* $(u_i, t_i, q_i, \mathcal{R}_i, \mathcal{C}_i)$, *associated with user queries, where* u_i *is the identifier of the user,* t_i *is the time of user action,* q_i *is the query submitted by the user,* $\mathcal{R}_i$ *is the set of results returned for* q_i *and* $\mathcal{C}_i$ *is the set of clicks on results* $\mathcal{R}_i$.

Time	Query	Automatic Label	Labeled Dominant	
			Automatically	By a Human
1/22/2011 1:10pm	peanut butter recipes	peanut butter recipes	×	×
1/22/2011 1:13pm	peanut butter cookies	peanut butter recipes	×	×
1/22/2011 1:25pm	calories peanut butter cookies	peanut butter recipes	×	
1/22/2011 3:10pm	weather nyc	weather nyc		
1/22/2011 3:11pm	nyc 10-day weather forecast	weather nyc		
1/22/2011 3:15pm	peanut butter sandwiches	peanut butter recipes	×	×
1/22/2011 3:16pm	pb&j			×
1/22/2011 3:18pm	fluffanutter			×
1/22/2011 3:19pm	fluffernutter			×
1/22/2011 6:15pm	sigir 2011	sigir 2011		
1/22/2011 6:17pm	sigir 2010 schedule	sigir 2011		
1/23/2011 3:17pm	nytimes			
1/24/2011 3:00pm	flight status united 123			
1/24/2011 3:31pm	peanut butter cookies low calorie	peanut butter recipes	×	×
1/24/2011 3:33pm	peanut butter cookies foodtv	peanut butter recipes	×	×
1/24/2011 4:10pm	weather forecast nyc	weather nyc		
1/25/2011 3:05pm	nytimes			
1/25/2011 3:29pm	foodtv			×
1/25/2011 3:31pm	famous pb&j drop recipe			×
1/25/2011 3:31pm	famous pb&j drop cookie recipe			×
1/25/2011 3:33pm	pb&j drop cookie recipe foodtv			×
1/25/2011 3:43pm	peanut butter cookies foodtv	peanut butter recipes	×	×

Table 1. Example of automatically and manually assigned cross-session and early-dominant tasks labels.

Queries from the search logs can be aggregated for each user to create a user search history:

DEFINITION 2 SEARCH HISTORY $\mathcal{H}_u = \{(a_1, t_1), \dots, (a_n, t_n)\}$ *for a particular user u is a temporally-ordered sequence* $(t_1 < \dots < t_n)$ *of pairs of user search actions (such as issuing a query, clicking on a search result URL and navigating back to search results) and time stamps associated with each action.*

The search history provides rich sequences of observations for making inferences about search behavior, including what intent motivated the user to search and whether that intent was satisfied. In order to simplify the analysis of user search history, it is typically partitioned into units, called search sessions:

DEFINITION 3 SEARCH SESSION $\mathcal{S} = \{(a_i, t_i), \dots, (a_j, t_j)\}$ *is a maximal subset of user search history* $\mathcal{S} \subset \mathcal{H}_u$*, such that* $\forall k: k = i, \dots, j$ $t_{k+1} - t_k < \Theta$ *, where* Θ *is a threshold for a period of user inactivity.*

In query log analysis, sesson timeouts are often used as boundaries to demarcate the sessions. The session threshold is typically set to 30 minutes [25][26][32]. Since search sessions include user actions other than queries, the time interval between two successive queries in one session can be more than 30 minutes. A sequence of queries forms a *user query stream*:

DEFINITION 4 QUERY STREAM $\mathcal{Q}_u = \{(q_1, t_1), \dots, (q_n, t_n)\}$ *is a temporally-ordered sequence of queries, submitted by a particular user u during the course of user search history.*

The first two columns in Table 1 show an example of a query stream for a fictitious user. In this example, more than 20 queries (related to several intents) are issued over the course of four days.

DEFINITION 5 CROSS-SESSION SEARCH TASK

$$\mathcal{T} = \{(q_i, t_i, l_i), \dots, (q_j, t_j, l_j)\}$$

is a subset of a query stream $\mathcal{T} \subset \mathcal{Q}_u$*, corresponding to a certain high-level intent that motivated search. Each query* q_i *is automatically or semi-automatically assigned a label* l_i*. When a labeled task extends over multiple sessions, we designate this as a cross-session search task.*

Cross-session tasks typically correspond to high level information needs, which may not be directly reflected in the queries. For example, queries corresponding to the same task may not have any terms in common. Such tasks represent a level of abstraction above the stream of queries. For the purpose of modeling, all queries about the same cross-session task can be assigned a label, representing such a task. The third column of Table 1 provides examples of automatic labels, assigned to the queries in the second column, according to the method presented in Section 4.2. As can be seen from this example, automatic labeling is effective when there is significant term overlap between the queries or when the inference step needed to relate one query to another query is fairly simple. However, our automatic labeling method was unable to infer the meaning of the acronym "pb&j" and connect it to the task labeled as "peanut butter recipes."

In order to identify previous queries on the same task or predict if a task is going to continue in the future, we must first define the task of interest. Because our search log data covered a limited period of time, we chose to focus our labeling efforts on the tasks that occurred early in the observation period and thus have the potential to be continued in the future. We designated those tasks as *early-dominant tasks*, and formally define them as follows:

Definition 6 Early-dominant task: *given a query stream $\hat{Q}_u = \{(q_1, t_{11}, l_1), \ldots, (q_n, t_{nd}, l_n)\}$, in which the queries are labeled with the tasks they correspond to, for a particular user u over d days, an early-dominant task is the first task that spans at least k distinct queries with the same label that occur within the first m days of the user search history. When multiple task labels meet the threshold criterion, the first such task is taken as the early-dominant task.*

The goal of identifying the early-dominant task is to create a data set for the problem of predicting whether the user will return to the task, given search log data covering a limited period of time. Parameters k and m can be set depending on the length of the available search history. The fourth column in Table 1 shows the queries that were automatically labeled as corresponding to the early-dominant task, based on the criteria that there should be at least two distinct queries automatically labeled with the same task (peanut butter recipes) in the first two days of the observed user search history. By requiring two distinct queries on the same task we omit most repeat navigational tasks, which are easy to identify and have been studied by others [32].

Query streams containing automatically-identified early-dominant tasks can be post-processed by humans to add additional queries that were missed by the labeling method or remove incorrectly labeled queries. As can be seen from the fifth column of Table 1, human annotators added queries on "pb&j drop cookie recipe," "fluffernutter," and "foodtv" to the automatically-identified early-dominant task.

In this work, we focus on two specific practical problems arising in the context of *cross-session search tasks*:

1. **SameTask:** Given a user query, *identify all previous queries on the same early-dominant search task* in the query stream of the user;
2. **TaskContinuation:** Given an early-dominant task for a user and the last query of the user on the early-dominant search task, *predict whether the user will return to this task in a future session.*

Methods that effectively solve the above two problems can be applied in a range of search scenarios. We describe some specific application scenarios for cross-session tasks later in the paper.

Having introduced the two problems in the context of analysis of *cross-session search tasks* addressed in the present work, we now discuss our approach to solving them. For both tasks we adopt a machine learning methodology by learning a classifier on a catalog of features. In the following section we describe the experimental setup for both problems.

4. EXPERIMENTAL METHODOLOGY

The most important and challenging aspect of an experimental evaluation of models for the analysis of cross-session tasks is generating a training set, in which the queries are labeled with the corresponding long-term tasks. In this section, we discuss the data that we used for evaluating the models proposed in this work as well as the semi-supervised process for generating training labels.

4.1 Dataset

We used a dataset containing the anonymized logs of URLs visited by users who consented to provide interaction data through a widely-distributed browser plug-in. The data set contained browser-based logs with both searching and browsing episodes from which we extract search-related data. These data provide us with examples of real-world searching behavior that are useful in understanding and modeling natural search behavior. Log entries include a timestamp for each Web page view, and the URL of the Web page visited. To remove variability caused by geographic and linguistic variation in search behavior, we only include log entries generated in the English-speaking United States locale. The results described in this paper are based on URL visits during the last week of February 2010 representing billions of Web page visits from hundreds of thousands of unique users. From these data we extracted search sessions that started with a query to Bing using a session extraction methodology similar to [35]. After the initial query, search sessions include subsequent clicked results and queries occurring in the same browser/tab instance, and ending after 30 minutes of inactivity.

Number of users	**3k**	**10k**	**Human**
Total	3,376	10,852	1,218
Return to dominant task	1,688	1,694	701
Number of queries	**3k**	**10k**	**Human**
Total	66,219	119,814	28,474
Query pairs	866,860	1,486,492	660,120

Table 2. Statistics of data set used in experiments.

4.2 Labeling

Labeling queries with long-term search tasks is challenging, since it requires an abstraction from the query stream to the level of information needs. The mapping from queries to information needs is perhaps best performed by human annotators, who are better able than machines to understand the relationship between the queries and visited URLs. However, manual labeling of a large data set is cognitively demanding and time consuming. To address this, we examine both fully automatic initial labeling (for more than ten thousand users) and additional human annotation for a subset of these data (more than one thousand users).

4.2.1 Automatic labeling

The automatic labeling process comprises four stages:

In the **first stage**, a subset of users, who are likely to be involved in some long-term task, were selected using a simple heuristic: a user must have at least five search sessions with at least 10 queries in their search history during the week covered by our log. This resulted in a set of 270,470 users.

In the **second stage**, queries in the original query stream were expanded using two query association resources:

1. A list of queries, in which each query is associated with a set of clusters computed using query reformulation and click data via the method described by Radlinski *et al.* [27]. Each cluster is assigned a score, reflecting the frequency of a particular intent in the data set;
2. A list of pairs of related queries, with the strength of association between the queries derived using query-click data in a manner similar to what has been described in previous work [4][33]. A query may be part of many pairs.

The representation of a query was expanded with queries from the top-scoring query cluster, and with related queries from the query graph. Each expanded query was then divided into terms to create a bag-of-words representation for the query.

In the **third stage**, in order to automatically identify and label queries that are on the same task, all pairs of queries in the user's query steam were enumerated and two similarity measures were calculated for each query pair, using the bag-of-words query representations. We used the size of the intersection and the Jaccard coefficient between the term sets of two queries as similarity measures and experimented with different thresholds for both measures. If a similarity measure exceeded a threshold, the queries were labeled as belonging to the same long-term task. The labels were assigned to the pair of queries exceeding the threshold according to the following rules: (i) if one of the queries has already been labeled before, the other query is assigned the same label; (ii) if neither query has been labeled before, the first query in the pair is used as the label for both queries.

In addition to automatically assigning labels corresponding to search tasks, we determined whether there was an *early-dominant task* in each user's search history. An early-dominant task was previously defined as the first task during the first two days of the search history that was associated with at least two unique queries. The early-dominant task labels were used to evaluate predictions of whether a user will return to a task in a future session. Focusing labeling efforts on a single task per user (namely the early-dominant task) simplifies the human editorial task labeling process and, as we show in the next section, leads to high inter-judge agreement.

We experimented with all combinations of query expansion strategies and similarity measures and evaluated each combination in terms of the proportion of queries with automatically assigned cross-session task labels, the total number of users who have early-dominant task labels, and the proportion of users who return to the early-dominant task. The best performing automatic labeling method expanded queries using both the top scoring query cluster and a one-step walk on the query graph, and used the Jaccard coefficient with threshold 0.5.

In the **fourth stage**, from the set of 270,470 users selected in the first stage, we selected a subset of 10,852 users who had an early-dominant task and issued at least one query after the first two days. Of these people, 1,694 (15.6%) issued at least one query on the dominant task after the first two days and the remaining 9,158 (84.4%) did not. We will refer to this data set as *10k* and it represents an 85-15 split between the (automatically labeled) negative and positive examples of returning to the dominant task. In order to create a training set with a balanced number of positive and negative examples, we included all users who returned to the early-dominant task and randomly subsampled 1,688 of the 9,164 users who did not return to the early-dominant task. We will refer to the resulting data set with a 50-50 split between the positive and negative examples as *3k*.

4.2.2 Human labeling

From the *3k* data set we randomly selected 1,250 users and three annotators manually modified the automatic labels. Annotators were instructed to start with the automatically-identified early-dominant task and find other queries by the same user that were on the same task. This typically involved identifying additional queries that were missed by the automatic algorithm, but sometimes also involved removing queries that were not on the same task. As a result, 1,218 users had an early-dominant task and 701 (57.6%) of these users returned to the task in a subsequent session. Table 2 summarizes the statistics of the data sets used for experiments. The numbers presented for the 3k and 10k data sets are for the fully automatic labels, and the Human set represents the human augmentation.

Automatic labeling identified 7,038 queries corresponding to the early-dominant task (for the 1,250 users). The human labeling process identified more than 7,500 additional queries on the early-dominant task, for a total of 14,549 such queries. Examples of additions include: adding *angelcare deluxe* to a task about *baby monitors*, and adding *princesspeach* to a task about *mariotoys*. The labelers also removed 232 of the queries that the automatic method had identified as dominant. Examples include: removing *map of south carolina* from a task about visiting haiti which included the query *map of haiti,* and correcting some labeling errors. Overall the agreement was 96.7% for automatic postive labels and 79.2% for automatic negative labels.

All annotators also labeled queries from 100 additional users which we used to measure inter-labeler agreement. Cohen's kappa showed high inter-annotator agreement, ranging from 0.86 to 0.92 for the three pairs of annotators.

4.2.3 Task characteristics

Recall that we required two distinct queries on the early-dominant task in an effort to omit simple repeat navigational tasks. In order to verify this, the query sessions used to assess inter-labeler agreement were also annotated as to whether the early-dominant task was navigational or informational. The majority (88%) of the tasks identified by the method described above were indeed informational. The remaining 12% of the tasks were navigational and were included because of spelling errors, word boundary differences (*mc gilvery oil* vs. *mcgillvery oil*), or different query formulations to find items of interest *(drudgereport com, matt drudge report, drudge report*). As intended, the vast majority of tasks identified were informational needs such as research, school work, shopping, travel planning, and general topic search [20].

4.3 Classifiers

We used two different classifiers to address the two problems of multi-session search tasks outlined earlier: (i) identifying all previous queries on the same early-dominant task (*SameTask*), and (ii) given an early-dominant task for a user, predicting whether the task will be continued in subsequent sessions (*TaskContinuation*). The two classifiers that we used were Logistic Regression (LR) and Multiple Additive Regression Trees (MART) [13]. MART is a boosted tree algorithm that uses gradient descent for regression and classification. Logistic regression has previoulsy been used for similar task-modeling problems [16]. MART allows us to model conditional interactions so that we can evaluate the importance of richer feature combinations.

For all experiments, we used z-score normalization for feature values and performed 10-fold cross validation.

4.4 Performance measures

To compare the performance of the classification methods we look at the standard performance measures of accuracy and F1 [28]. We also display precision, recall, and the contingency tables for each method. By analogy to topic classification, we look at both the *macro* average of F1 which weights the F1 for each query equally and *micro* average which weights each binary prediction (for the current query to all previous queries) equally 0. We look at only the micro averages for the problem of predicting whether the user will return to the task, as there is only one example per user and thus macro and micro are the same. Significance between approaches is calculated using two-tailed independent samples t-tests.

In the following sections, we discuss in detail our approaches to solve the *SameTask* and *TaskContinuation* problems in the context of modeling cross-session tasks.

Query-Based Features	
NUMQUERYCHARS	The number of characters in the query.
NUMQUERYTERMS	The number of terms in the query.
NUMTOP10CLICKS	The number of clicks on the top 10 search results for the query.
MINCLICKPOS	The minimum position of a clicked result for the query.
MAXCLICKPOS	The maximum position of a clicked result for the query.
SPELLSUGGEST	Whether a spelling suggestion was shown for the query.
Session-Based Features	
NUMQUERIESSESS	The number of queries since the beginning of the session.
NUMCLICKSSESS	The number of clicks on search results since the beginning of the session.
TIMESINCESESS	The amount of time from the beginning of the session to the query.
SAMEQUERYSESS	Whether the same query appeared earlier in the same session.
SUBQUERYSESS	Whether a query with a subset of the query's terms appeared in the same session.
SUPQUERYSESS	Whether a query with a superset of the query's terms appeared in the same session.
History-Based Features	
NUMSESSHIST	The number of sessions in the user's search history.
NUMQUERIESHIST	The number of queries in the user's search history.
NUMCLICKSHIST	The number of clicks on search results in the user's search history.
SAMEQUERYHIST	Whether the same query appeared in the user's search history.
SUBQUERYHIST	Whether a query with a subset of the query's terms appeared in the user's history.
SUPQUERYHIST	Whether a query with a superset of the query's terms appeared in the user's history.
Pair-Wise Features	
NUMTERMSOVER	The number of overlapping terms between the two queries.
QUERYTERMSJAC	Jaccard coefficient between the term sets of two queries.
LEVENDIST	Levenshtein edit distance between the two queries.
TIMEBETWEEN	The time between the two queries.
SAMESESS	Whether the two queries occurred in the same session.
QUERIESSAME	Whether the two queries are identical.
QUERYSUBSET	Whether one query's terms are a subset of the other's.
HAVECOCLICKURLS	Whether the two queries have co-clicked URLs.
HAVECOCLICKDOM	Whether the two queries have co-clicked URLs with the same domain.

Table 3. Features for identifying whether two queries relate to the same long-term task. Except for the pair-wise features, every feature is calculated individually for each query in a pair and thus occur twice. Session and history features are computed over all actions *before* the current query.

5. SAME-TASK QUERY IDENTIFICATION

We begin by addressing the first problem of detecting queries on the same long-term task. Specifically: *for a given query, find all previous queries in the user's search history that are on the same long-term task*. We formulated this as a classification problem. Given a set of users, whose queries have been manually or automatically labeled with the early-dominant task, train a classification model that will classify each pair of user queries as either on the same task or not.

5.1 Formal definition

Formally, given a history of automatically or manually labeled queries $\mathcal{H} = \{(q_1, t_{11}, l_1), \dots, (q_n, t_{nd}, l_n)\}$, where $l_i = \{d, \neg d\}$ is a label that indicates whether the query is part of the early-dominant task, we create a set of all possible pairs of queries:

$$\{(q_1, q_2, l_{12}'), \dots, (q_1, q_n, l_{1n}'), \dots, (q_{n-1}, q_n, l_{n-1,n}')\}$$

in which each pair is labeled as either a positive or negative example as follows:

$$l_{i,j}' = \begin{cases} 1, & \text{if } l_i = d \text{ and } l_j = d \\ 0, & \text{if } l_i = \neg d \text{ or } l_j = \neg d \end{cases} \quad (1)$$

A query pair is labeled as a positive example if both queries are related to the early-dominant task, and as a negative example if one of the queries is not related to the early-dominant task. We do not consider instances where neither query is labeled as being related to the early-dominant, since the queries might be on the same long-term task (but not labeled as the early-dominant task). The numbers of query pairs given in Table 2 were calculated *after* dropping such pairs. Because queries are only compared with queries that occur earlier in the user's history, the later in time that a query occurs, the more pairs it will be involved in.

5.2 Features

Since the *SameTask* problem involves predicting the similarity relationship between pairs of queries, we extracted pair-wise features as well as features for the individual queries. Individual query features are computed at different levels of granularity for historical information of a user: ranging from the session in which a query occurred, to the entire search history of a user. The 18 single-query and nine pair-wise features extracted to identify queries on the same long-term task are summarized in Table 3.

As a baseline (BASE), we use logistic regression to learn a model using only Levenshtein edit distance between the current (given) query and all previous queries. This is a reasonable baseline under the assumption that an intelligently-chosen threshold applied to the dissimilarity between two queries could provide an accurate prediction of whether two queries are on the same task.

	3k			10k			Human		
	BASE	LR	MART	BASE	LR	MART	BASE	LR	MART
Micro statistics									
TP	57,273	86,673	97,870	66,175	112,081	126,369	78,084	194,126	166,438
FP	14,262	20,913	23,260	16,582	25,293	28,971	52,322	52,032	65,310
TN	717,120	710,469	708,122	1,298,996	1,290,285	1,286,607	309,972	310,262	296,984
FN	78,205	48,805	37,608	104,739	58,833	44,545	219,742	103,700	131,388
Recall	0.4157	0.6431	0.7258	0.4300	0.6693	0.7556	0.3267	0.6067	0.5617
Precision	0.8382	0.8135	0.8183	0.8240	0.8268	0.8233	0.6138	0.7857	0.7325
Accuracy	0.8970	0.9227	**0.9331**	0.9245	**0.9646**	0.9534	0.6104	**0.7629**	0.7118
F1	0.5495	0.7160	**0.7681**	0.5520	0.7383	**0.7876**	0.3957	**0.6670**	0.6156
Macro statistics									
Recall	0.8520	0.9243	0.9440	0.8205	0.9288	0.9507	0.7329	0.8440	0.8277
Precision	0.8746	0.9134	0.9218	0.8406	0.9183	0.9284	0.6661	0.7781	0.7944
Accuracy	0.9540	0.9569	**0.9597**	0.9612	0.9646	**0.9661**	0.7139	**0.8196**	0.8133
F1	0.8419	0.8904	**0.9063**	0.8131	0.8982	**0.9146**	0.5676	0.7164	**0.7265**

Table 4. Experimental results for identifying queries on the same cross-session task. The best result for F1 and accuracy in each dataset is in bold. Significant differences relative to BASE are indicated by underline ($p < .01$). TP = Num. true positives, FP = Num. false positives, TN = Num. true negatives, FN = Num. false negatives.

5.3 Results

The results of classification experiments with features specified in Table 3 on three experimental data sets are reported in Table 4. Several conclusions can be made from the findings presented in Table 4. First, both classifiers (LR and MART) consistently outperform the baseline (BASE), which is not surprising. The two classifiers show similar levels of accuracy especially for the automatically-labeled data. Second, for the automatically-labeled data, classication results improve as more data is observed, but this is difficult to interpret since the ratio of positive to negative examples changed from 50-50 to 15-85. Third, classification performance decreases on the task labels that have been assigned by human annotators. This suggests that the human-labeled data provides a more challenging learning problem. This is expected since the human labels were intended to capture task structure that was not already captured automatically, and this often involved identifying related queries that were not lexically similar.

The micro precision-recall curves for the two classifiers for the task of identifying queries on the same cross-session task on different data sets are shown in Figure 1 (aggregated over all test splits). Performance at default thresholds is indicated by markers.

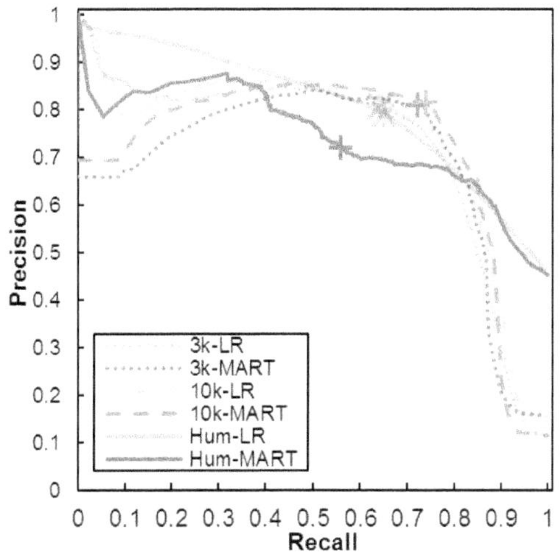

Figure 1. Micro precision/recall curves for LR and MART for identifying queries on the same task.

Both classifiers show good performance. However, for all three dataets, LR dominates at the low recall/high precision end of the curves. This suggests that the LR model might be more applicable for high-precision tasks such as suggesting related queries. As in Table 4, LR has notably better micro performance over the human-labeled data in the area of optimal F1 (upper right) although this does not translate to higher macro performance. Understanding the relationship between micro and macro performance for this domain is an area of future work.

5.3.1 Feature Importance Analysis

Feature weights from the logistic regression model for the identification of queries on the same long-term task, trained on the manually annotated data, are summarized in Table 5. Both single and pair-wise features are important in identifying queries on the same task. But, pair-wise features are more prevalent, meaning that understanding the relationship between the queries is more valuable than understanding either query in isolation. This is not surprising given that the goal is to understand if both queries are on the same task. Similarity features, such as whether the queries are identical and term overlap measures between the bag-of-words representations for a pair of queries (NUMTERMSOVER and

Feature	Feature Type	Weight
QUERYTERMSJAC	Pair-wise	1.44
NUMQUERYCHARS_1	Query-based	1.05
NUMTERMSOVER	Pair-wise	0.93
QUERYSUBSET	Pair-wise	0.88
NUMCLICKSHIST_2	History-based	0.81
NUMQUERYCHARS_2	Query-based	0.79
SAMESESS	Pair-wise	0.52
HAVECOCLICKDOM	Pair-wise	0.40
NUMCLICKSHIST_1	History-based	0.39
NUMQUERIESSESS_1	Session-based	0.31
SUBQUERYSESS_2	Session-based	-0.30
NUMQUERYTERMS_2	Query-based	-0.47
NUMQUERIESHIST_1	History-based	-0.52
NUMQUERYTERMS_1	Query-based	-0.68
LEVENDIST	Pair-wise	-0.84

Table 5. The top 15 (absolute magnitude) feature weights for the logistic regression model to identify queries on the same cross-session task. Features related to the first query are marked with a 1 and to the second query with a 2.

Session-Based Features	
AVGINTERQTIMESESS	The average time between all sequential pairs of queries in the session.
AVGINTERDOMQTIMESESS	The average time between sequential pairs of dominant queries in the session.
NUMDWELL30SESS	The number of queries in the session with a dwell time more than 30 seconds.
AVGNUMQTERMSSESS	The average number of unique terms per query within the session.
NUMDOMQUERIESSESS	The number of queries on the dominant task in the session.
PCTDOMQUERIESSESS	The number of queries on the dominant task divided by the number of queries in the session.
PCTCLICKQUERIESSESS	The number of the queries with clicked results divided by the number queries in the session.
NUMCOCLICKDOMSESS	The number of co-clicked URLs with the same domain in the session.
History-based features	
AVGINTERQTIMEHIST	The average time between all sequential pairs of queries in the user's search history.
AVGINTERDOMQTIMEHIST	The average time between sequential pairs of dominant queries in the user's search history.
NUMDWELL30HIST	The number of queries with dwell time more than 30 seconds in the user's history.
AVGNUMQTERMSHIST	The average number of unique terms per query in the user's search history.
NUMDOMQUERIESHIST	The number of queries on the dominant task in the user's search history.
PCTDOMQUERIESHIST	The number of queries on the dominant task divided by the number of queries in the user's history.
PCTCLICKQUERIESHIST	The number of queries with clicked results divided by the number of queries in the user's history.
NUMCOCLICKDOMHIST	The number of co-clicked URLs with the same domain in the user's search history.

Table 6. Additional features to those shown in Table 3 that are used for predicting whether a user will return to the early-dominant long-term task. The pair-wise features from Table 3 are not relevant for this task.

QUERYTERMJAC) are among the strongest signals. The high negative weight of the LEVENDIST feature shows that most queries on the same task are morphologically similar. Features related to the length of each individual query in characters (NUMQUERYCHARS) receive high positive weights, while features related to the length in terms (NUMQUERYTERMS) receive negative weights. This suggests that long, descriptive query terms are particularly indicative of cross-session tasks. This seems reasonable since longer terms may be associated with complex information needs spanning multiple search sessions.

6. TASK CONTINUATION PREDICTION

We next consider the second problem of predicting whether a user will return to a task. Specifically: *given an early-dominant task for a user and the user's last query on the early-dominant task, predict whether the user will return to this task in a future session.*

6.1 Formal definition

Given a stream of user queries and a target date, features are computed up to the end of the session containing the last early-dominant query on the target date. The feature vector is assigned a positive label, if there are queries on the early-dominant task after the target date, and a negative label if there are no such queries.

6.2 Features

The nature of the *TaskContinuation* problem suggests that the most predictive features should reflect two aspects of a cross-session task: (i) user satisfaction with the presented search results, and (ii) the difficulty of the task itself. The most frequently-used feature to capture user satisfaction is click-through rate on search results (e.g., [1]). The intuition behind this is that if a user issued a series of queries and clicked on at least one search result for most or all of these queries, she is likely to have obtained useful information that allowed her to make progress on the task and, hence, is less likely to return to it. Similarly, the dwell time on results has been shown to reflect satisfcation (e.g., Fox et al. [12]). The difficulty of the task can be reflected by several patterns of user behavior including the number of queries issued, the time between successive queries, etc. [3][17]. Individual query features, reflecting these interaction patterns, are computed at different levels of granularity (ranging from the session where a query occurred to the entire search history of a user). Features summarizing the user's history with the early-dominant task are also included. These additional features are shown in Table 6. The features in Tables 3 and 6 are used together to predict whether the user will return to the early-dominant task.

As a baseline (BASE), we use logistic regression to learn a model using the number of queries in the user's history before the cutoff date (NUMQUERIESHIST). This is a reasonable baseline under the assumption that an intelligently-chosen threshold applied to the level of user activity in a short window of time around the task could provide an accurate prediction of task continuation.

	3k			10k			Human		
	BASE	LR	MART	BASE	LR	MART	BASE	LR	MART
TP	680	1,112	1,106	14	470	523	569	514	489
FP	477	360	327	12	226	211	391	169	141
TN	1,211	1,328	1,361	9,146	8,932	8,947	126	348	376
FN	1,008	576	582	1,680	1,224	1,171	132	187	212
Recall	0.4038	0.6593	0.6546	0.0084	0.2777	0.3096	0.8154	0.7342	0.6971
Precision	0.5906	0.7555	0.7708	0.675	0.6784	0.7219	0.5961	0.7538	0.7766
Accuracy	0.5601	0.7228	**0.7308**	0.8441	0.8664	**0.8726**	0.5706	0.7074	**0.7100**
F1	0.4775	0.7029	**0.7072**	0.0166	0.3933	**0.4305**	0.6844	**0.7428**	0.7326

Table 7. Experimental results for predicting whether the user will return to the early-dominant task. The best result for F1 and accuracy in each dataset is in bold. Significance relative to BASE indicated by underline ($p < .01$).

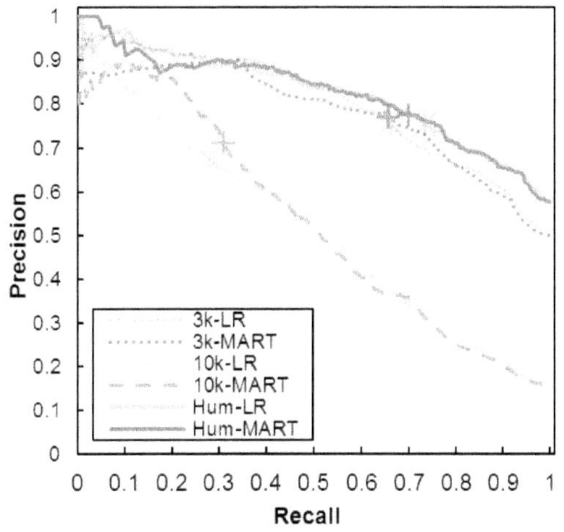

Figure 2. Precision/recall curves for LR and MART for predicting return to the early-dominant task.

6.3 Results

Experimental results for predicting whether the user will return to the early-dominant task with features specified in Tables 3 and 6 on three data sets are reported in Table 7. Several major conclusions can be drawn from Table 7. First, again we see that both classifiers improve over the baseline in all datasets and perform similarly to each other overall. Additionally, recall and precision substantially decrease when moving from a smaller balanced dataset (*3k*) to a larger unbalanced one with more negative examples (*10k*). However, both LR and MART still classify a large number of negative examples correctly, as evidenced by the fact that the accuracy increases for both classifiers. Next, recall significantly improves for both classifiers on manually corrected labels, which can be attributed to the fact that this data set is less sparse. There are more positive examples, because human annotators assign the missing early-dominant task labels to some queries.

Precision-recall curves for the classifiers for *TaskContinuation* are shown in Figure 2 (aggregated over all test splits). Performance at default thresholds is indicated by markers. Both models perform very similar for each dataset. There are some differences across datasets, with overall performance being worse on the *10k* set. MART has a slight advantage over LR for the low recall/high precision region of the curves for the human dataset.

6.3.1 Feature Importance Analysis

Weights of the LR model for predicting whether the user will return to the early-dominant task, trained on the editorially-corrected data set, are summarized in Table 8. From the table, it appears that the most important feature is whether the query has ever occurred in the user's history (SAMEQUERYHIST). All identical queries were labeled as being from the same task, both automatically and by human labelers. The importance of this feature is consistent with previous research that suggests re-finding is very common [32]. Although most of the early-dominant tasks are informational (as described in 4.2.3), queries are sometimes repeated as part of such tasks.

Features of the user's history with the dominant task were also important. If many of their past queries (NUMDOMQUERIESHIST) or a high proportion of them (PCTDOMQUERIESHIST) were related to the dominant task, they appeared particularly likely to return to the task again at a later date. This suggests that intense interest in a topic at one point in time is likely to lead to returning to the task at a later point (during the week).

Feature	Feature Type	Weight
SAMEQUERYHIST	History-based	1.11
NUMSESSHIST	History-based	0.60
NUMDOMQUERIESHIST	History-based (Table 6)	0.39
AVGINTERQTIMEHIST	History-based (Table 6)	0.24
FREQDOMQUERIESHIST	History-based (Table 6)	0.24
NUMDWELL30HIST	History-based (Table 6)	0.22
NUMQUERYHIST	History-based	0.21
NUMTOP10CLICKS	Query-based	-0.16
AVGINTERQTIMESESS	Session-based (Table 6)	-0.17
NUMCLICKSHIST	History-based	-0.18
NUMQUERYCHARS	Query-based	-0.21
SUBQUERYHIST	History-based	-0.23
SUPQUERYSESS	Session-based	-0.40
SUPQUERYHIST	History-based	-0.40
SUBQUERYSESS	Session-based	-0.49

Table 8. Top 15 (absolute magnitude) feature weights for the logistic regression model which predicts return to the early-dominant task.

In the previous section we observed that past queries on the dominant task could be identified in part by complex queries. Here again we see that the complexity of the user's dominant information need, as indicated by the high weight on longer queries (NUMQUERYCHARS) and deeper examination in result lists (NUMTOP10CLICKS), suggests that it is more likely that the user will return to the task. The predictive value of NUMTOP10CLICKS provides evidence to support similar claims by Donato *et al.* [9].

Features related to the user's intensity of search engine use (e.g., AVGINTERQTIMEHIST, NUMSESSHIST) are among the most important. This is not surprising, since people who search more are more likely to search again on all tasks, including both the early-dominant task and other tasks. However, not only the absolute frequency of searches, but also the deeper engagement with past search results (NUMDWELL30HIST) appear to be important, suggesting that people who use search deeply may also use search for more extended tasks.

7. CONCLUSIONS AND FUTURE WORK

As the importance of a deeper understanding of user search behavior continues to grow, it becomes necessary to develop models that consider complex long-term information needs and effectively incorporate them into existing search engine infrastructures. In this work, we introduced and addressed the two problems in the context of analysis of cross-session search tasks: (i) identifying queries from earlier sessions on the same task, and (ii) predicting whether a user will return to the same task during a later session, formulating both problems as supervised machine learning tasks. We proposed a method for creating a semi-automatically labeled data set that can be used for both problems and developed feature sets, tailored for each of the individual problems. Experimental results using two classifiers (logistic regression and MART) for both problems indicate that we can effectively model and analyze cross-session information needs.

Our research is an important first step in helping searchers more effectively manage long-term information needs. Knowledge of previous user queries on the same long-term task enables a search engine to provide support for task resumption. For example, if it is known that a user has previously been undertaking a vacation-planning task and has issued queries about airline tickets, whenever the user comes back to this task, a search engine can show pertinent updates in the time since the last query (e.g., ticket price drops) or suggest queries to re-find useful past results. By using a model that can accurately predict continuation of a cross-session task, a search engine can determine whether it is necessary to retain the task context, start monitoring Web content (e.g., during Web crawls or others' queries) for information pertaining to the task, and use the task model for query suggestions or search result suggestions.

There are several directions for future work, including using richer prediction models and alternative feature sets, exploring new prediction and classification problems in the context of cross-session information needs, and incorporating our models into commerical search engines.

8. REFERENCES

[1] E. Agichtein, E. Brill and S. Dumais. Improving Web search ranking by incorporating user behavior information. *SIGIR '06*, 19–26, 2006.

[2] A. Aula, N. Jhaveri and M. Käki. Information search and re-access strategies of experienced Web users. *WWW '05*, 583–592, 2005.

[3] A. Aula, R. M. Kahn and Z. Guan. How does search behavior change as search behavior becomes more difficult. *CHI '10*, 35–44, 2010.

[4] D. Beeferman and A. Berger. Agglomerative clustering of a search engine query log. *KDD '00*, 407–416, 2000.

[5] P. Boldi, F. Bonchi, C. Castillo, D. Donato, A. Gionis and S. Vigna. The query-flow graph: Model and applications. *CIKM '08*, 609–618, 2008.

[6] H. Cao, D.H. Hu, D. Shen, D. Jiang, J.-T. Sun, E. Chen and Q. Yang. Context-aware query classification. *SIGIR '09*, 3–10, 2009.

[7] H. Cao, D. Jiang, J. Pei, Q. He, Z. Liao, E. Chen and H. Li. Context-aware query suggestion by mining click-through and session data. *KDD '08*, 875–883, 2008.

[8] Y.-S. Chang, K.-Y. He, S. Yu and W.-H. Lu. Identifying user goals from Web search results. *WWW '06*, 1038–1041, 2006.

[9] D. Donato, F. Bonchi, T. Chi and Y. Maarek. Do you want to take notes? Identifying research missions in Yahoo! Search Pad. *WWW '10*, 321-330, 2010.

[10] D. Downey, S. Dumais, D. Liebling and E. Horvitz. Understanding the relationship between searchers' queries and information goals. *CIKM '08*, 449–458, 2008.

[11] S. Dumais, G. Buscher and E. Cutrell. Individual differences in gaze patterns for web search. *IIiX '10*, 185–194.

[12] S. Fox, K. Karnawat, M. Mydland, S. T. Dumais and T. White. Evaluating implicit measures to improve the search experience, *TOIS, 23(2),* 147–168.

[13] J. Friedman, T. Hastie and T. Tibshirani. Additive logistic regression: A statistical view of boosting. *Annals of Statistics*, *28(2)*, 337–407, 2000.

[14] A. Hassan, R. Jones and K. Klinkner. Beyond DCG: User behavior as a predictor of a successful search.*WSDM '09*, 221–230, 2010.

[15] D. He, A. Göker, and D.J. Harper. Combining evidence for automatic Web session identification. *Information Processing & Management*, 38(5):727–742, 2002.

[16] R. Jones and K. Klinkner. Beyond the session timeout: Automatic hierarchical segmentation of search topics in query logs. *CIKM '08*, 699–708, 2008.

[17] M. Kellar, C. Watters, and M. Shepherd. A field study characterizing Web-based information-seeking tasks. *JASIST, 58(7),* 999–1018, 2007.

[18] U. Lee, Z. Liu and J. Cho. Automatic indetification of user goals in Web search. *WWW '05*, 391–400, 2005.

[19] J. Liu and N.J. Belkin. Personalizing information retrieval for multi-session tasks: The roles of task stage and task type. *SIGIR '10*, 26–33, 2010.

[20] B. MacKay and C. Watters. Exploring multi-session Web tasks. *CHI '08*, 1187–1196, 2008.

[21] Q. Mei, K. Klinkner, R. Kumar and A. Tomkins. An analysis framework for search sequences. *CIKM '09*, 1991–1994, 2009.

[22] L. Mihalkova and R. Mooney. Learning to disambiguate search queries from short sessions. *ECML '09*, 111–127, 2009.

[23] D. Morris, M. Ringel Morris and G. Venolia. SearchBar: A search-centric Web history for task resumption and information re-finding. *CHI '08*, 1207–1216, 2008.

[24] B. Piwowarski, G. Dupret and R. Jones. Mining user Web search activity with layered Bayesian networks or how to capture a click in its context. *WSDM '09*, 162–171, 2009.

[25] B. Piwowarski and H. Zaragoza. Predictive user click models based on click-through history. *CIKM '07*, 175–182, 2007.

[26] F. Radlinski and T. Joachims. Query chains: Learning to rank from implicit feedback. *KDD '05*, 239–248, 2005.

[27] F. Radlinski, M. Szummer and N. Craswell. Inferring query intent from reformulations and clicks. *WWW '10*, 1171–1172, 2010.

[28] C. J. van Rijsbergen. *Information Retrieval*. Butterworths, London, 1979.

[29] D.E. Rose and D. Levinson. Understanding user goals in Web search. *WWW '04*, 13–19, 2004.

[30] X. Shen, B. Tan and C. Zhai. Context-sensitive information retrieval using implicit feedback. *SIGIR '05*, 43–50, 2005.

[31] B. Tan, X. Shen and C. Zhai. Mining long-term search history to improve search accuracy. *KDD '06*, 718–723, 2006.

[32] J. Teevan, E. Adar, R. Jones and M.A.S. Potts. Information re-retrieval: Repeat queries in Yahoo's logs. *SIGIR '07*, 151–158, 2007.

[33] J.-R. Wen, J.-Y. Nie and H.-J. Zhang. Clustering user queries of a search engine. *WWW '01*, 162–168, 2001.

[34] R.W. White, P. Bailey and L. Chen. Predicting user interests from contextual information. *SIGIR '09*, 363–370, 2009.

[35] R.W. White and S.M. Drucker. Investigating behavioral variability in Web search. *WWW '07*, 21–30, 2007.\

[36] Y.Yang and Z. Liu. A re-examination of text categorization methods. *SIGIR '99*, 42-49, 1999.

The Economics in Interactive Information Retrieval

Leif Azzopardi
School of Computing Science, University of Glasgow
Glasgow, United Kingdom
Leif.Azzopardi@glasgow.ac.uk

ABSTRACT

Searching is inherently an interactive process usually requiring numerous iterations of querying and assessing in order to find the desired amount of relevant information. Essentially, the search process can be viewed as a combination of inputs (queries and assessments) which are used to "produce" output (relevance). Under this view, it is possible to adapt microeconomic theory to analyze and understand the dynamics of Interactive Information Retrieval. In this paper, we treat the search process as an economics problem and conduct extensive simulations on TREC test collections analyzing various combinations of inputs in the "production" of relevance. The analysis reveals that the total Cumulative Gain obtained during the course of a search session is functionally related to querying and assessing. Furthermore, this relationship can be characterized mathematically by the Cobbs-Douglas production function. Subsequent analysis using cost models, that are grounded using cognitive load as the cost, reveals which search strategies minimize the cost of interaction for a given level of output. This paper demonstrates how economics can be applied to formally model the search process. This development establishes the theoretical foundations of Interactive Information Retrieval, providing numerous directions for empirical experimentation that are motivated directly from theory.

Categories and Subject Descriptors

H.3.3 [**Information Storage and Retrieval**]: Information Search and Retrieval:Search Process; H.3.4 [**Information Storage and Retrieval**]: Systems and Software:Performance Evaluation

General Terms

Theory, Experimentation, Economics, Human Factors

Keywords

Retrieval Strategies, Production Theory, Prosumer Theory, Consumer Theory, Simulation, Evaluation

SIGIR'11, July 24–28, 2011, Beijing, China.

1. INTRODUCTION

Interaction in the search process is usually required in order to find the desired amount of relevant information, especially in the context of topic retrieval. Often the user will need to pose a number of queries and examine numerous documents before their underlying information need is satisfied [6, 18]. Given that searching for information requires user effort (and thus a cost), it is interesting to consider what kinds of *search strategies* a user could or should employ to efficiently undertake their search task. Broadly speaking, we can think of search strategies as different ways to interact with an Information Retrieval (IR) system. So, for example, to obtain the desired amount of relevant information in a cost efficient manner, what search strategy should a user employ? Should they:

1. pose a handful of queries and assess deeply into the ranks,
2. pose numerous queries and assess only the top ranks,
3. or, invoke some other combination of interactions?

In this paper, we aim to examine such strategies by applying microeconomic theory to Interactive Information Retrieval (IIR). We argue that the process of interaction between a user and a system can be modeled as a series of inputs (queries, assessments, etc) that "produce" an output (utility/gain from finding relevant items). Under this view, we can adapt techniques from microeconomics, in particular, production theory to analyze the interaction in the search process using formal methods. By framing the search process as an economics problem, it is possible to ask questions such as, what search strategy (i.e. *combination of inputs*) will minimize user effort (i.e. *cost*) for a given level of utility/gain (i.e. *output*) when using a particular retrieval system (i.e. *technology*)?

Being able to answer such questions is important for IIR because while numerous behavioural and observational studies have been conducted, there is a lack of any formal theory to explain why such behaviours and observations are witnessed [5]. For example, in practice users often issues short queries [22], but longer queries have been shown to be more effective [14]. Kestalous *et al* [16] tried to justify this strategy empirically, and showed that a series of extremely short queries can be quite effective for finding one highly relevant document. But searching for a number of relevant documents often requires numerous queries to be posed during the search session [15]. And generally, users will usually only examine the first page or so of the result list [22, 17]. However, users of Boolean systems will often examine up to 200 documents [17, 11]. The variation in search strategy is believed to be, in part, due to user adaption. Cantor and Smith [19] showed that users can adapt to degraded systems by modifying their search strategy. In their experiments, users increased the number of queries they issued to compensate for a poor system. While, this enabled the users to find relevant material, it did come at a greater cost. While these are interesting observations, is it possible to explain why users interact and behave in such a manner? To understand why, and perhaps show that these observed behaviors are optimal or justified in some way, we need to be able to formally model the search process. By applying microeconomic theory to IIR it may be possible to: (i) develop such formal models, (ii) provide arguments for particular courses of interaction, and (iii) suggest alternative ways for users to interact with systems, such that they minimize their effort/cost. To this end, we describe how microeconomic theory can be applied to model the search process. Then, we explore its application by performing a large scale simulation that evaluates an array of search strategies on various retrieval systems to determine which strategies are feasible and which are cost efficient.

2. THE ECONOMICS IN IIR

Economics provides a series of tools and techniques for analyzing social phenomena [23], and can be applied to IR in a number of different ways. Varian in his SIGIR 1999 keynote address "Economics and Search" presented three suggestions on how economics could be useful in IR [24]: (1) to examine the economic value of information using consumer theory, "where a consumer is making a choice to maximize expected utility or minimize expected cost", (2) to obtain better estimates of the probability of relevance, and (3) to apply Stigler's theory on Optimal Search Behavior to IR. Despite these promising suggestions, little research has been undertaken investigating the use of economics and economic theory within IR. However, in line with (2), Wang and Zhu [25] used mean-variance analysis from economics to develop Modern Portfolio Theory to obtain better estimates of document relevance. While, the work in [2] employed methods from economics to conduct an analysis of query length showing that the law of diminishing returns applies to querying. These past works provide the inspiration and motivation for this research. In particular, we follow Varian's first suggestion on applying consumer theory in IR. However, here, we shall apply production theory, instead (for reasons which we shall explain later). Thus, in the remainder of this section, we shall describe how the theory of production can be adapted to model the search process.

2.1 Modeling the Search Process

Interactive Information Retrieval is a non-trivial process consisting of a multitude of factors, interactions and variables, from user context to system configurations [10]. Trying to incorporate all of these complexities would result in a rather unwieldy model. Since one of the goals of this paper is to inform on the cost efficiency of different search strategies, then we shall concentrate on the main interactions between a user and a system.

The model that we shall be defining is based upon production theory [23]. In production theory, a firm produces an output (such as goods or services), and to do so requires *inputs* to the process (usually termed, capital and labour) [23]. The firm will utilize some form of *technology* to then produce the *output* given the inputs. The process of production is similar to the search process, which we model as follows: the output of the search process is the utility or gain obtained from the relevant documents found, and the inputs to the process we have chosen consist of: (i) the number of queries, (ii) the length of queries, and (iii) the depth of assessment per query. Each of these inputs will directly influence the number of relevant documents found during the search process. For example, query length has been shown to directly relate to performance [2], while the number of documents that are assessed provides an upper bound on the total number of relevant documents which could be found. Given this abstraction of the search process, we can define a search strategy as a combination of inputs $(\mathbf{Q}, \mathbf{D})$ for a given query length L, which a user could employ, where:

Q the number of queries that the user will issue,

D how many documents the user will assess per query.

So the particular combinations of inputs describe potential user search strategies. Then the technology engaged by the user to produce/find relevant documents is, of course, a particular retrieval system. Through the course of interacting with the system the output of the search process, unlike production theory, is not a good or service, but a certain amount of utility. Here we consider the total Cumulative Gain acquired over the search session as a measure of utility/output. This abstraction reduces the search process down to the core variables which directly influence how much utility a user receives through the course of interaction with the system.

Now, depending on the particular retrieval system employed, different **technological constraints** will be imposed upon the search process such that only certain combinations of inputs will produce a given or specified amount of gain. In economic terminology, the set of all combinations of inputs and outputs that are technologically feasible can be referred to as the **production set**. However, for the purposes of analysis what is of interest is the boundary case given this production set which is defined by the maximum possible output for a given level of input. The function describing this boundary case is referred to as the **production function**. Applied to search, where we consider the two inputs Q and D for a given L, we can devise a search production function $f(Q, D)$ which will quantify the maximum amount of Cumulative Gain that could be obtained if the user issued Q queries, and assessed D documents per query for a given L using a particular retrieval system[1].

Figure 1 provides an example of the production set for BM25 on the Associated Press Collection for the different input combinations. The upper right hand region enclosed by the black dotted line denotes the set of combinations of Q and D which could be issued to obtain a particular level of gain (i.e. this is the production set). The boundary case denoted by the dotted line is referred to as an isoquant in microeconomics, and denotes the minimum amount of the inputs required to produce the particular level of gain. Note the isoquant represents the most efficient usage given the inputs. Using the isoquant it is possible to estimate the search production function.

[1]While, we could devise a function using all three inputs (Q, D and L), but this would be add a lot more complexity to the model. In order to facilitate explanation and to concentrate on introducing the economic concepts to IR, we shall leave such formulations to future work.

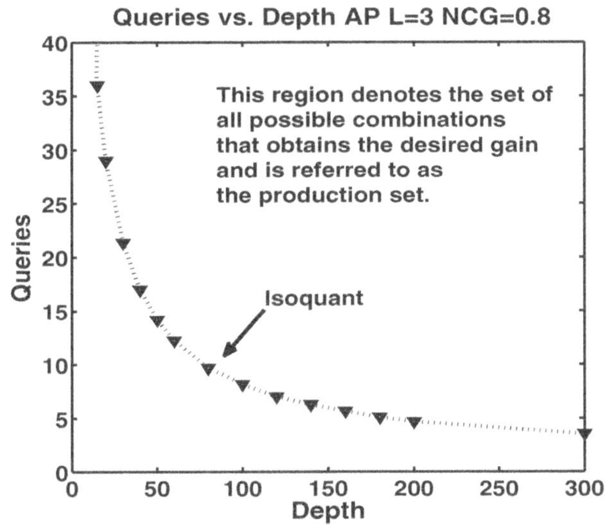

Figure 1: Example: Queries vs Depth on Aquaint collection for BM25. The isoquant denotes the minimum amount of the inputs to produce the specified level of gain.

2.2 Model Limitations and Caveats

Firstly, in terms of the analogy with production theory, it should be noted that the search process is not exactly like the production process. This is because relevance is not really produced, so to speak, it is found within documents. However, the relevant documents found provide the user with some utility or gain. In our formulation the gain is considered the output of the search process. In mapping the search process as an economics problems we also considered using consumer theory as suggested by Varian [24]. In consumer theory, a consumer receives utility from the bundles of the goods that they consume [23]. However, this analogy was less intuitive because searchers do not buy goods or services in the search process. Instead, they exert effort like labour in a production process when they query and assess. While neither production theory nor consumer theory exactly fits the search process[2]: the techniques used in both consumer and production theory are similar i.e. they derive a utility or production function that characterizes the consumer or production process, and then examine the rates of change, maximize utility/profit, minimize expense/cost, etc, see [23] for more details). So either way we shall be applying similar techniques.

Secondly, in terms of IIR, our abstraction of the search process makes a number of assumptions about possible interactions. In reality, users are likely to vary the depth of assessment, the length of queries, and the number of queries that they pose depending on how (un)successful their queries are at returning relevant results given the retrieval system. While, we assume the search strategies denoted by (Q, D) are fixed for a given L, i.e. the user will issue Q queries, each of length L, and assess D documents per query, this helps constrain and reduce the possibilities to a manageable size so that we can perform the analysis. Rather than thinking that these are fixed, if we consider that these variables reflect how a user would search on average, i.e. if a user on average examined D per query, and issued on average Q queries with an average length of L, then this model provides a reasonable approximation of usage. Nonetheless, this abstraction still provides a sufficiently rich representation of the search process which can still provide interesting insights and explanations.

[2] Actually, the process appears to be an example of "prosumer theory", where the producer and the consumer are one and the same.

2.3 Research Objectives and Questions

Given this view of the search process, our main objective is to estimate or describe the search production function for interactive topic retrieval mathematically; and in doing so provide a formal model for IIR. During the course of this research we shall also consider the following research questions:

- What combination of inputs are required to achieve a particular level of utility?
- What is the trade-off between querying and assessing? Or, what is the rate of change between querying and assessing? and,
- Given a cost function, which search strategy or strategies minimize the cost of searching?

3. EXPERIMENTAL METHODOLOGY

For the purposes of this study, three TREC test collections were used: the AP 88-89 collection with TREC 1, 2 and 3 Topics (AP), the LA Times collection (LA) with TREC 6, 7, and 8 Topics, and the Aquaint collection (AQ) with TREC 2005 Robust Topics (See Table 1). Each test collection was indexed using the Lemur toolkit[3], where the documents were preprocessed using Porter Stemming and a standard stop list. Since we are interested in interactive ad-hoc querying and retrieval, where the goal is to retrieve a number of relevant documents, we have selected only those topics that have at least 50 relevant documents in Aquaint and AP, and at least 40 relevant documents in LA. We used these cut offs to ensure that there were enough relevant documents to produce sensible values when we examined the various levels of gain. Also, in terms of examining interaction, if we only had a few of relevant documents per topic, then it is likely that only one query would be needed, which would not be particularly interesting.

[3] http://www.lemurproject.org

Collections	AP	LA	Aqaint
Docs	164,597	131,896	1,033,461
Topic Set	TREC 123	TREC 678	Robust 05
No. of Topics Used	87	43	26
Avg. Query Len.	3.3	2.5	2.6
	Mean Average Precision		
BM25	0.2966	0.2145	0.2021
LM2K	0.2967	0.2143	0.2043
BM25AND	0.2038	0.1094	0.1331
TFIDF	0.1867	0.0683	0.0803
TF	0.1435	0.0501	0.0598
BOOL	0.1202	0.0683	0.0460

Table 1: TREC Collection and Topic Statistics for Associated Press (AP), LA Times (LA) and Aquaint (AQ), along with the Mean Average Precision for the retrieval models used in this study.

To explore the influence of different retrieval systems on search behavior we employed six different retrieval systems: two probabilistic systems, BM25 and a Language Model with Dirichlet Prior Smoothing (LM2K). The modified Okapi BM25 function was used with $b = 0.75$, while the Dirichlet Prior was set to 2000 for LM2K. Two vector space systems were also employed one with TF.IDF weightings and other TF weightings. These were included to contrast the probabilistic models as TFIDF and TF usually perform poorly in comparison. We also used two Boolean systems: one which was configured to be Boolean with an implicit AND, sorted by date order (referred to as BOOL), and another which was Boolean with implicit AND, ranked by BM25 (referred to as BM25AND). We used the implicit AND, because according to [17], over 90% of searches under taken using Boolean based models are AND queries, while other operators are rarely used. As previously mentioned, for our experiments we used session based Cumulative Gain (CG) as a measure of the utility/output. However, during the analysis, we also used normalized session based Cumulative Gain (NCG) so that we could aggregate the results across topics.

3.1 Simulated Interaction

Simulation in Information Retrieval has recently attracted a lot of attention, especially in Interactive IR [4]. Simulation enables researchers to conduct carefully designed and controlled experiments to elicit precise answers to research questions and obtain novel insights into the retrieval process [3, 20, 21, 27, 26]. In these studies, the simulations were designed to replicate and mimic the different aspects of the retrieval process as realistically as possible. In this paper, we also employ simulation as part of the experimental methodology but to explore an array of *possible* search strategies that *could* be employed. For example, it is unlikely that a web user would, on average, examine hundreds of documents per query, but it is of interest to see whether this strategy is better or worse than other strategies. In the following paragraphs we shall detail and justify the simulated querying and interaction that was employed to generate the data used in the analysis.

Querying: To provide the queries that will be issued during simulated search sessions, we needed to generate a number of queries per topic. In this paper, we adopt the approach taken in [12], where controlled queries are created, as opposed to probabilistically generating random queries as suggested in [3]. The reason is that we wish to generate high quality queries, as opposed to queries of varying quality. The query generation process was as follows: (1) given a document or set of documents d: construct a weighted term vector $w(t, d)$, (2) rank $w(t, d)$ from highest to lowest, and (3) select the top k terms to be the query q. For our experiments, the weighted term vector is simply the number of times a term appears in d. This is referred to as the popular sampling strategy, which for generating queries in English was shown to produce queries akin to real queries [3]. For our experiments, we generated one query per relevant document and an additional query given all the relevant documents[4]. By generating queries in the manner we should obtain high quality queries that provide the "best case" scenario. This should enable us to obtain a reasonable approximation of the isoquant i.e. boundary case. However, it is interesting to note that the quality of queries produced by the query generation method, far from being complete unrealistic, is in line with the performance of the TREC title queries. For example, when using BM25 the TREC short queries for the AP, LA, and AQ collections resulted in a MAP of 0.297, 0.215, and 0.202, respectively. While, for generated queries of length 3, the performance, in terms of MAP was 0.30, 0.1950 and 0.266, respectively. Also, on the whole the queries generated appeared quite sensible: and reflected the querying behavior observed in the study by Keskustalo *et al* [16], referred to as S3. S3 was the most common strategy they observed, and was where users would issue multiple queries of length three: pivoting on two key words, and then varying the third query term. See Table 2 for examples of some generated queries.

AP Topic 52	LA Topic 313	AQ Topic 303
TREC Title Query		
south african sanction	magnet levit maglev	hubble telescop achiev
Generated Queries		
group south govern	rail line studi	astronom galaxi univers
south govern state	rail line metro	galaxi astronom light
south africa sanction	line rail vallei	galaxi matter star
south africa apartheid	train french speed	telescop studi galaxi
south africa human	train tgv engin	telescop studi space
south jackson africa	train public counti	hubbl star dust

Table 2: TREC Title queries for topics 52, 313 and 303, along with the generated queries of length 3.

Interacting To build up the sequence of interactions we used a greedy best-first approach to select the subset of queries required to obtain the desired level of Cumulative Gain utility. While this might not always achieve the optimal subset of queries it should provide a good approximation for the analysis. Thus, we assumed that the user will issue the best possible query out of all the generated queries first, then issued the next best, and so on until they have found the desired amount of relevant material. The best or next best query is determined by selecting the query which provided the largest increase to the total Cumulative Gain at the given depth D. If the desired level of total Cumulative Gain was not been reached, then the process is repeated until the desired level of total Cumulative Gain has been reached, or all queries were posed. For the total Cumulative Gain during the search session the query had to retrieve relevant documents which had not been seen at previous query iterations. Once the desired level of utility had been reached, the number of queries required Q was recorded for the given assessment depth D and query length L. The number of queries was a free parameter which was determined through the simulated interaction - and averaged over all topics, so from here on when we refer to Q as the number of queries, strictly speaking we mean the average number of queries, and similarly with (normalized) Cumulative Gain, we mean the average (normalized) Cumulative Gain over all topics.

3.2 Experimental Setup

For each topic, we generated a series of queries of length $L = 3$ which is a typical length for user queries [1, 17]. The assessment depths D considered were $D = \{5, 10, 15, 20, 25, 30, 40, 50, 60, 80, 100, 120, 140, 160, 180, 200, 300, 400, 500, 700, 1000\}$ documents per query. We selected this subset to cover the top ranks, and first few pages of search results (where it is typical for search results to be dispatched in groups of 10 to 25) [17]. Also, we consider significantly deeper depths (or multiple pages of search results) up to

[4]The query generation software was written using the Lemur 4.10 Toolkit and the code is available on request.

the typical depth of assessment used at TREC (i.e. 1000). While, most studies report that users only examine the top ranks or first page or two of results [22, 17], it is of interest to determine whether there are alternative strategies which are more cost effective. As stated above, given the depth D and length L, the number of queries Q required to obtain Normalized Cumulative Gain levels of $NCG = \{0.2, 0.4, 0.6, 0.8, 1.0\}$ was determined according to the interaction algorithm employed. For each level of output NCG the corresponding inputs D and Q which were needed to obtain that output given length L were recorded and used in the analysis.

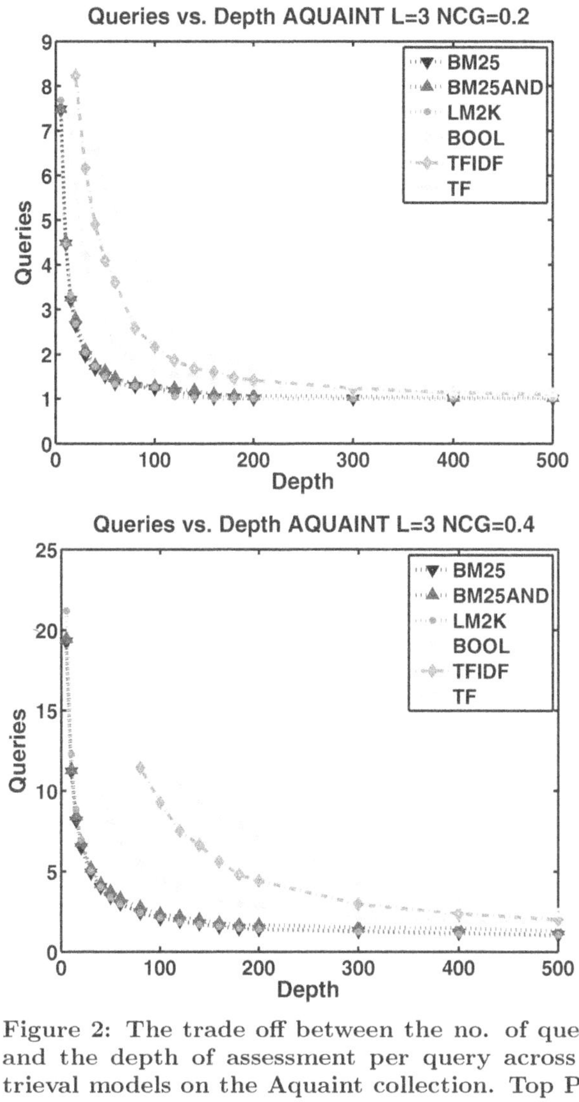

Figure 2: The trade off between the no. of queries and the depth of assessment per query across retrieval models on the Aquaint collection. Top Plot: NCG = 0.2, Bottom Plot: NCG=0.4.

4. ECONOMIC ANALYSIS

In this section, we shall focus mainly on presenting the analysis using the simulated interaction data from the Aquaint collection. However, the general findings, trend and patterns observed were also obtained on the two other collections (see Figure 4 for examples on these collections). We shall start the analysis by examining the production set and estimating the search production function. The two input variables which we shall pay most attention to is the number of queries issued Q and the number of documents assessed per query D (or assessment depth).

Production Set: Figure 2 shows the isoquants for each of the different retrieval models for two gain levels. Combinations where Q and D are greater than the boundary case will yield similar or greater utility. The top plot shows the combinations required to yield an NCG of 0.2, whereas the bottom plot shows the combinations required to yield an NCG of 0.4 for each retrieval model on the Aquaint collection (where $L = 3$). On inspection of these two plots, there are a number of interesting observations to be made:

- As the gain level is increased from 0.2 to 0.4, more queries are required and/or more assessments per query. Naturally, this is to be expected because more documents need to be examined in order to achieve a higher gain. For example, with BM25 it is possible to obtain NCG=0.2 with a combination of $Q = 2$ and $D = 25$, whereas to obtain NCG=0.4 while keeping one of the inputs fixed then either: (a) $Q = 2$ and D increases to 75, or (b) $D = 25$ and Q increases to 5.
- For particular retrieval models some combinations do not yield the desired level of gain. That is, given a particular depth there is no subset of queries which will obtained the specified gain. For example, in the bottom plot, the Boolean Model, TFIDF, and TF do not provide complete sets of feasible combinations over the range of depths examined i.e. their production sets contain fewer technically feasible input combinations than the other retrieval models. For example, using the TF model, a user would have to examine to a depth of at least 140, before they could find a viable search strategy where they could pose enough queries to obtain an NCG of 0.4.
- On the other hand, BM25, BM25AND, and LM2K provide a greater number of combinations ranging from $D = 5$ up to $D = 1000$. This means that BM25, LM2K and BM25AND provide more search strategies to the user, such that: if a user prefers to issue many queries or only a few queries, then provided they examine deeply enough, there are combinations which could yield the desired gain.
- Also, the plots graphically show the trade-off between querying and assessing: as depth D increases, we see that the number of queries required decreases. Whereas, if the number of queries is increased, then the depth can be decreased. We shall examine this phenomena in more detail later in our analysis.

With regards to standard IR evaluation, it is interesting to note the difference between retrieval models. In Table 1 we reported the standard measure of retrieval performance, mean average precision, for each of the different retrieval models. The results, not surprisingly, show that BM25 and LM2K deliver substantially greater retrieval performance than TFIDF, TF, BM25AND and BOOL. However, the graphs of the production set for these retrieval models are far more illuminating: they show the array of search strategies that are possible. Specifically, the plots show how much querying and/or assessing is required in order to obtain the same level of gain. These plots also show

			NCG=0.2			NCG=0.6			NCG =1.0		
Col.	Model	L	K	α	r^2	K	α	r^2	K	α	r^2
AP	**BM25**	3	5.118	0.608	0.952	6.161	0.566	0.996	4.417	0.586	0.998
	LM2K	3	5.126	0.607	0.9501	5.921	0.563	0.994	3.918	0.565	0.999
	BM25AND	3	5.105	0.612	0.9523	6.062	0.585	0.99	4.365	0.6457	0.994
	BOOL	3	4.027	0.598	0.965	4.563	0.585	0.986	4.025	0.680	0.991
	TFIDF	3	3.928	0.559	0.981	3.693	0.523	0.997	2.127	0.512	0.999
	TF	3	3.704	0.571	0.968	2.998	0.501	0.992	2.246	0.479	0.998
AQ	**BM25**	3	4.819	0.624	0.943	5.394	0.576	0.995	3.733	0.606	0.999
	LM2K	3	4.741	0.618	0.947	5.033	0.562	0.998	3.223	0.586	0.999
	BM25AND	3	4.808	0.634	0.946	5.232	0.581	0.992	3.824	0.689	0.989
	BOOL	3	3.114	0.589	0.963	3.471	0.607	0.997	-	-	-
	TFIDF	3	2.466	0.569	0.984	1.694	0.503	0.996	-	-	-
	TF	3	1.989	0.556	0.981	1.445	0.500	0.979	-	-	-
LA	**BM25**	3	4.008	0.718	0.812	3.82	0.603	0.998	2.876	0.686	0.989
	LM2K	3	3.223	0.585	0.999	3.463	0.611	0.995	2.413	0.645	0.994
	BM25AND	3	4.021	0.747	0.794	3.501	0.68	0.978	2.543	0.799	0.969
	BOOL	3	2.805	0.871	0.977	2.443	0.663	0.986	2.805	0.871	0.978
	TFIDF	3	1.962	0.653	0.991	1.377	0.553	0.977	-	-	-
	TF	3	1.686	0.636	0.992	1.145	0.541	0.989	-	-	-

Table 3: Cobbs-Douglas Production Function Fitting Parameters (K,α) and the r^2 value for 3 gains levels across all models and collections. (-) indicates when no combinations were found for that gain level.

what kind of adaption is required to adjust to systems of varying performance. We know from the work of Smith and Cantor [19] that users can adapt to degraded systems, and in their study they observed users compensating for a degraded system by issuing more queries. If we examine the top plot in Figure 3, then we can see, for example, that for BM25 $Q = 2$ and $D = 25$ to obtain an NCG=0.2, but for TFIDF, if the user fixes D equal to 25, then they need to posed 4 additional queries, i.e. $Q = 6$ to obtain the same gain. These findings are consistent with the work in [19]. However, here we are enable to examine more precisely the differences between systems, and predict how much more interaction is required to compensate for degraded systems.

Search Production Function: While the plots are quite illustrative showing the relationship between querying and assessing, it is our objective to try and characterize this relationship mathematically. Given the shape of the plots, the data appears to be in the form of a Cobbs-Douglas production function (which is one of several types of production functions often used in microeconomics, see [23] for others). Thus, we hypothesize that the *search production function* would take the following form:

$$f(Q, D) = K.Q^{\alpha}.D^{(1-\alpha)} \qquad (1)$$

where $f(Q, D)$ is the function that quantifies the total cumulative gain given the inputs Q and D (conditioned on query length L and retrieval system), K provides an indication of the efficiency of the technology (i.e. a greater K will result in more gain), and α is a mixing parameter determined by the technology used. If $\alpha = 0.4$, a 10% increase in querying would lead to approximately a 4% increase in output.

To determine whether the isoquants could be modeled by the Cobbs-Douglas search production function described in Equation 1, we tried to estimate the parameters K and α using the Curve Fitting tool provided in Matlab's statistics toolbox. Table 3 shows the fits for each model, for each collection, when the query length was three and for the NCG values 0.2, 0.6 and 1.0. The K and α values are shown along with the coefficient of determination (i.e. the r^2 value) for each fit. The closer the r^2 value is to 1 the better the fit is to the data, given the specified parameters. For the particular retrieval models and gain levels, which have incomplete isoquants across the range of D explored, then the estimate of $f(Q, D)$ will only hold where D is greater than or equal to the depth at which a combination is technically feasible. For example, when $NCG = 0.4$, TFIDF and TF in Figure 2 both have incomplete isoquants and so their production function is constrained.

For each model and collection, we can see that r^2 for most of the models is quite close to one, indicating that the Cobbs-Douglas function is quite a good fit to the data, and a reasonably good characterization of the gain produced through querying and assessing. This is an important finding because it means that instead of empirically estimating the rates of changes we can use differentiation to obtain the marginal product of querying and assessing, and the marginal rate of technical substitution (see below). If we consider the results for different retrieval models, we note that (1) TFIDF and TF tend to have the lowest values of K indicating these technologies are rather inefficient, while (2) BM25 and LM2K have the highest values indicating that they are more efficient at producing gain. While, this is consistent with the retrieval models retrieval effectiveness (i.e. MAP), the search production function quantifies the retrieval models performance under interaction (and across various possible ways in which the system could be used).

4.1 Marginals or Rates of Change

Of particular interest in microeconomics is the rates of change between the inputs and output (and are often referred to as marginals). Here we describe the *marginal product of querying* and the *marginal product of assessing*. These describe how much the output changes, when an additional query is submitted or an additional document is assessed (i.e. how much more Cumulative Gain do we obtain if we pose one more query, or assess one more document). Given these marginals, then it is possible to determine the *rate of technical substitution*. This would allow us to determine how much more assessing is required if one less query was posed, in the case where we substitute queries for assessments.

The **Marginal Product of Querying** is the increase in output given an increase in querying i.e. if we issue another querying how much more gain will we get for each additional query. Given the search production function defined in Equation 1 the marginal product of querying can be obtained by differentiating with respect to Q:

$$MP_Q = \frac{\delta CG}{\delta Q} = K.\alpha.Q^{(1-\alpha)}.D^{(1-\alpha)} \quad (2)$$

Similarly the **Marginal Product of Assessing** is the increase in output given an increase in assessing: and is obtained by differentiating with respect to D:

$$MP_D = \frac{\delta CG}{\delta D} = K.(1-\alpha).Q^{\alpha}.D^{-\alpha} \quad (3)$$

The marginal products of querying and assessing result in diminishing marginal returns; where the gain gets smaller if you hold one of the inputs constant while increasing the other. So, if querying is held constant, and the depth of assessment is increased then each additional document that is assessed will add less and less to the Cumulative Gain. This is consistent with what we would expect during search because documents are usually ranked in decreasing order of relevance [8]. One of the possible uses of the Marginal Product of Assessing would be to predict when a user would stop examining the ranked list. For example, if we assumed that the user would like to obtain at least an additional g of gain for every n documents that they assess, then we could determine at what depth D the rate of change equals g/n. Beyond that D the rate of change would be lower than the desired and so the user would stop at depth D. While this would be very interesting to determine and empirically test, we shall leave such a direction to future work, and focus on quantifying the relationship between querying and assessing.

The Technical Rate of Substitution: Instead of considering how much output changes by, the technical rate of substitution considers how much of one input we need to increase or decreases, if we decrease or increase the other input in order to hold output at the same level. So for example, how many more documents would we need to assess per query, if we issued one less query. The technical rate of substitution can be defined as:

$$TRS(Q, D) = \frac{\Delta D}{\Delta Q} = -\frac{MP_Q}{MP_D} \quad (4)$$

and it measures the rate at which querying can be substituted for assessing. While, $TRS(D, Q)$ measures the rate at which assessments can be substituted for querying. Note that the TRS is the slope of the line of the search production function. For convenience, we shall not report $-MP_Q/MP_D$, but MP_Q/MP_D, so that it can be intuitively interpreted as the number of additional documents that would have to be assessed per query, if one query was given up.

In Table 4, we report the technical rate of substitution of querying for assessing for BM25, TFIDF and Boolean at several different levels of gain and at particular depths[5]. If we take BM25 for example when the $NCG = 0.2$, then when $D = 5$, a user would have to assess, on average, 1.1 extra documents per query, if they give up one query. Whereas when $D = 30$, they would have to assess, on average, approximately 25 extra documents per query, if they forgo one query. Overall, the trend is that as depth increases, the TRS also increases, and this appears to be at an increasing rate. Essentially the technical rate of substitution enables us to quantify the trade-off between querying and assessing. Next we examine the cost of the different strategies to determine which strategy is the most cost-efficient.

[5] Note, we have not displayed the TRS value when the average number of queries is less than two . This is because the search process requires at least one query to be posed - i.e. it does not make any sense to pose less than one query.

4.2 Cost of Interaction

In order to determine what search strategies minimize the cost to the user, we have constructed a cost function to measure the effort required to obtain the desired level of output for the given inputs. The **user cost function** we shall employ is a linear combination of querying and assessing, and is defined as follows:

$$c(Q, D) = \beta.Q + Q.D \quad (5)$$

where the cost is composed of two parts: the total cost of querying, and the total cost of assessing i.e. the total number of documents examined[6]. Here, the total querying cost is proportional to the number of queries issued Q. And the relative cost of a document versus a query is dictated by the parameter β. If β is greater than one than it is relatively more expensive to pose a query than to assess a document, and vice versa. For these experiments, we determined β by drawing upon the user experiments conducted in [9], where the cognitive load of various interactions in the information seeking process were measured. In these experiments, a dual-task method was used which measured how long it takes for the participant to respond to a secondary task (in milliseconds). It was found, on average, that assessing documents placed a load of 2266 ms on the user, while posing queries was somewhat more taxing with a load of 2628 ms (values taken from Table 11 in [9]). Since we need a relative cost between querying and assessing then we assigned $\beta = 2628/2266 = 1.1598$. This estimate provides a reasonable indication of the relative costs based on the available data which provides some grounding for our analysis. Essentially, this user cost function estimates the relative cognitive effort of querying and assessing. Given that we are examining various search strategies under similar circumstances it should be adequate to make a reasonably fair comparison between strategies. However, in the future it would be interesting to explore alternative cost functions and different parameterizations.

Search Strategy Cost Efficiency: For each input combination, we calculated the cost to the user and we have reported the costs for various combinations in Table 4. The asterisk indicates if the combination was the minimum cost in the set. In Figure 3, for BM25, TFIDF and Boolean retrieval models, we have also plotted Q vs. D for each gain level in the top plots, whilst in the bottom plots we show the corresponding cost across the depths at each level. From inspecting the plots, we can see that as the gain increases so does the cost. For a given level of gain, we can also see that the most cost efficient strategies tend to be the ones where

[6] We acknowledge that this is a rather simple user cost function, but it does capture the main elements of interest and is similar to the cost function proposed in [13] for evaluating faceted browsing strategies. We shall leave the development of non-linear cost models, which cater for other factors like user frustration and fatigue when assessing [7], or the increasing costs of generating queries [18] to future work.

	NCG=0.2				NCG=0.4				NCG=0.6			
Model	Q	D	Cost	TRS	Q	D	Cost	TRS	Q	D	Cost	TRS
BM25	7.5	5	63	1.1	19.3	5	163	0.4	41.1	5	348	0.2
	4.5	10	60	3.7	11.2	10	151	1.2	24.7	10	333	0.5
	3.2	15	59*	7.8	8.1	15	150*	2.5	17.6	15	326*	1.1
	2.7	20	62	12.5	6.5	20	152	4.2	14	20	328	1.9
	2	30	66	25.2	4.9	30	164	8.3	10.2	30	343	3.8
TFIDF	8.2	20	193*	3.2	11.4	80	955	7	14.9	180	2731	12.1
	6.2	30	206	6.4	9.3	100	958	10.9	14.2	200	2882*	14.1
	4.9	40	213	10.8	7.5	120	928*	16.1	9.5	300	2887	31.4
	4.1	50	219	16.2	6.6	140	951	21.3	6.9	400	2787	57.7
	3.6	60	229	22	5.6	160	916	28.7	5.4	500	2705	92.8
BOOL	7.3	15	135*	2.9	9.8	40	428*	5.5	9.3	120	1154*	19.1
	5.7	20	135	5.0	8.3	50	442	8.2	8.2	140	1181	25.3
	4.2	30	140	10.3	6.9	60	440	11.7	7.3	160	1186	32.8
	3.1	40	137	18.3	5.4	80	452	19.9	6.8	180	1246	39.4
	2.7	50	144	26.6	4.5	100	464	30.1	6.3	200	1292	46.8

Table 4: Costs and Rate of Technical Substitutions: For each retrieval model, shown for the first five combinations of Q and D that result in the specified NCG, along with the cost $c(Q, D)$, TRS of Q for D (which is how many more documents would need to be assessed if one query was given up at the given depth). * indicate the depth length which obtains the overall minimum for a given level of gain.

less documents are assessed (i.e. assessing lots of documents imposes a high cost to the user). However, to get the most out of each query usually a number of documents need to be assessed, and of course, the strategy needs to be technically feasible. We can see from the top plots in Figure 3, that for TFIDF and BOOL, in particular, that not all combinations are possible. In these cases, it is the combination with the lowest depth that minimizes costs (usually around a depth of 100-200 documents). For BM25, which provides the user with a greater array of strategies to choose from, we see that the minimum cost is around a depth of 10 to 20 documents. If we inspect the costs in the Table 4, then we see that for BM25 the depth that, on average, provides the lowest cost to the user is examining 15 documents per query[7]. Recall, that this depth is approximately the number of documents a user typically examines [22, 17]. This suggests that state of the art systems which deliver reasonably good performance (like BM25 on these collections) may induce similar behavior in users (i.e. an emphasis on querying more, rather than assessing deeply). For TFIDF and BOOL, however, the strategies that minimized cost varied across the levels of gain. Essentially, as the desired gain increased, more queries and greater depths were required. Interestingly, for the Boolean retrieval model for higher gain levels, the user would have to examine up to 120 documents per query to reach an NCG of 0.6. According to the studies in [17] and [11], this statistic reflects the number of documents users typically examine when using Boolean systems. While for TFIDF, these results show that, a user may be able to adapt to a degraded system (i.e. BM25 vs TFIDF) but this is going to substantially increase the cost to the users. These findings are not definitive explanations for observed user behavior, but they do provide some credence to observed behaviors. Nonetheless, the application of economic theory to IIR process has thrown up a number of possibilities to hypothesize about and test search strategies: and this analysis shows that for a reasonably good retrieval system, like BM25 on these collections, then examining only the top 15 or documents, and posing as many queries as needed to obtain the desired level of gain is a viable and cost efficient strategy to employ.

[7]This was observed for gain levels up to 0.8. To obtain $NCG = 1.0$ then at least 50 documents needed to be examined per query.

What happens when β changes? On a hypothetical note it is interesting to consider what would happen if we varied the relative cost β. For example, let's assume that the search system employed provides query assistance functionality like query suggestion [15], which reduces the effort of posing queries (i.e. β decreases). In this case, queries become cheaper, and the preferred search strategy would tend to towards strategies where more queries are posed and less documents examined. While, if queries were more costly to pose (i.e. β increases), perhaps because there was no automatic spelling corrections or exact matching was enforced, then the preferred search strategy would would tend towards strategies where less queries were issued, but more documents examined. This is because assessing documents, under this condition, would be relatively cheaper than posing additional queries. This example shows how a formal model for IIR can be used to better understand and explain the dynamics within the search process.

5. DISCUSSION AND CONCLUSION

In this paper, we have shown how production theory from microeconomics can be applied to IIR by modeling the searching process as if it were a production process. Then, through the course of the analysis we have shown how the tools and techniques from microeconomics can used to describe the dynamics of querying and assessing on various test collections and retrieval models. For instance, we found that BM25 supported a greater variety of search strategies when compared to TFIDF and BOOL. A result that would not have otherwise been found through standard evaluations. We also found that it was possible to mathematically describe the search process through the Cobbs-Douglas production function. From this, we were able to derive the technical rate of substitution from the search production function in order to calculate the trade-off between querying and assessing. After we mapped the inputs to a cost function, we were able to show that for BM25 the search strategy that minimized the cost was when D was around 15. This suggests that a user would only need to examine the first page or so of re-

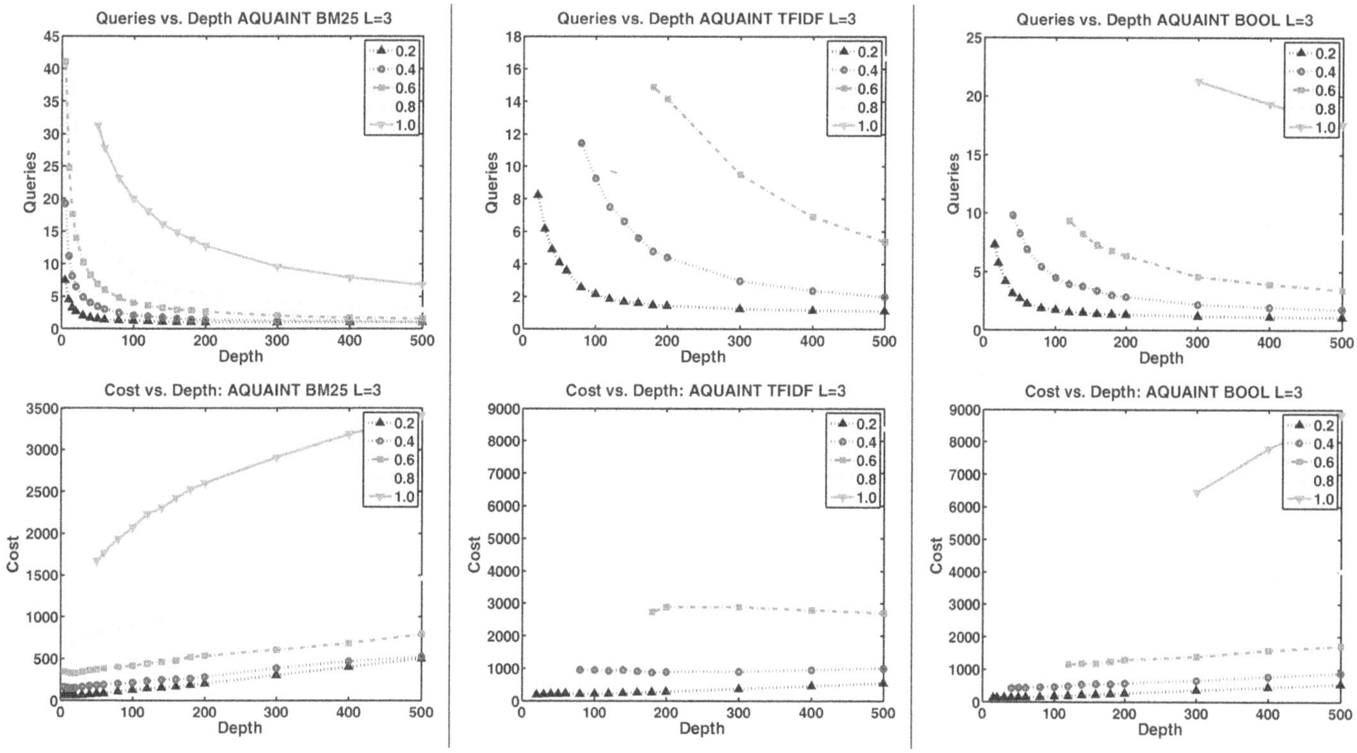

Figure 3: Top: Query vs. Depth, and Bottom: Cost vs. Depth, for the different levels of gain. From Left to Right: BM25, TFIDF and Boolean retrieval models.

sults per query, and continue to pose queries until they reach their desired level of gain to operate the retrieval system efficiently. On the other hand, for retrieval models like TFIDF and BOOL, our study suggests that users would needs to delve deeper into the rankings and issue substantially more queries in order to achieve the same level of gain. These findings are consistent with previous findings obtained from studying users [22, 17, 19] suggesting that there is an economic justification for such search strategies. In our final example, we showed how the theory can be used to generate hypotheses about how users would change their search strategy depending on whether the cost of a query increased or decreased. This work demonstrates that the formal models and methods from microeconomic theory are useful for describing, explaining and hypothesizing about IIR. However, further research is required to empirically explore and test the models and theory developed here, and to address the limitations of this work.

During the course of this research we have tried to point out the main limitations. In particular, we mentioned that the abstraction of the search process could be improved to include more variables and factors (such as query length, and interactions which are not fixed). However, given the initial model of the search process, we were still able to reveal a number of interesting findings regarding the economics of interaction. When we applied production theory to IIR we had to re-consider what the output was – and what was "produced" by the search process. However, this was overcome by considering the gain obtained from finding the relevant documents as the output of the process. Another limitation at the modeling level was that we employed a linear user cost function. However, there is a growing body of work examining the cost of interaction, which has begun to emerge over the past couple of years [20, 7, 9, 13]. As this area develops then the findings from such studies will enable the development of more accurate cost functions, so that search strategies can be evaluated more precisely.

To sum up, we have shown that microeconomic theory provides a number of valuable tools and techniques for understanding IIR. The mapping of production theory to the search process provided a novel way in which we can formally model IIR. Thus, this work provides the foundations on which to build formal models for describing, understanding and explaining the interactions between a user and system, i.e. we can explore the economics of IIR. Clearly, there are a number of ways in which we can develop this work further, from refining the initial models of the search process to applying the theory in practice. In future work we shall:

(i) develop production functions that incorporate other inputs such as query length,

(ii) refine the model of the search process to introduce other variations in interaction, for example, examining snippets in the results list, and then selectively picking documents to assess,

(iii) given the Marginal Product of Assessing predict when users will stop examining the ranked list,

(iv) develop non-linear user cost functions which incorporate factors like user fatigue and frustration, as well as the factor in the costs involved when trying to formulate the nth query on a particular topic, and

(v) investigate how the quality, length and order of the queries affects interaction.

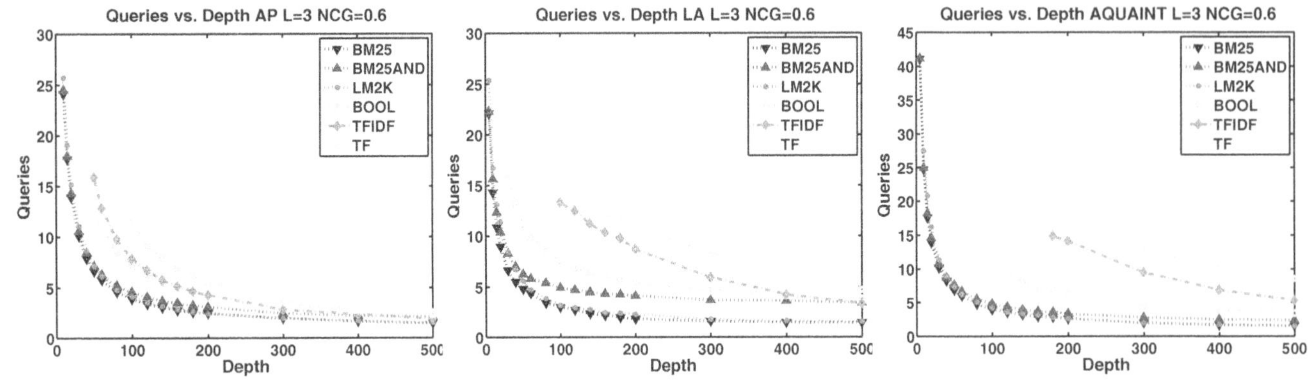

Figure 4: The trade off between No. of Queries and Assessment Depth across the different retrieval models on AP (Left), LA (Middle) and Aquaint (Right). Note how BM25 and LM2K require less input to obtain the desired gain. They also provide more possible combinations to obtain the desired gain compared to the other retrieval models.

Acknowledgments I would like to thank Richard Glassey and Guido Zuccon for the numerous discussions we had on this topic and for their useful comments and suggestions. Their feedback greatly improved the clarity of this work.

6. REFERENCES

[1] A. Arampatzis and J. Kamps. A study of query length. In *Proceedings of the 31st ACM SIGIR conference*, pg 811–812, 2008.

[2] L. Azzopardi. Query side evaluation: an empirical analysis of effectiveness and effort. In *Proceedings of the 32nd ACM SIGIR conference*, pg 556–563, 2009.

[3] L. Azzopardi, M. de Rijke, and K. Balog. Building simulated queries for known-item topics In *SIGIR '07*, pg 455–462, 2007.

[4] L. Azzopardi, K. Järvelin, J. Kamps, and M. D. Smucker. Sigir 2010 workshop report on the simulation of interaction. *SIGIR Forum*, 44:35–47, 2011.

[5] N. J. Belkin. Some(what) grand challenges for information retrieval. *SIGIR Forum*, 42:47–54, 2008.

[6] N. J. Belkin, R. N. Oddy, and H. M. Brooks. Ask for information retrieval: part i: background and theory; part ii: results of a design study. *Journal of Documentation*, 38(2) 61-71 and 38(3) 145-164, 1982.

[7] H. A. Feild, J. Allan, and R. Jones. Predicting searcher frustration. In *Proceeding of the 33rd ACM SIGIR conference*, pg 34–41. ACM, 2010.

[8] N. Fuhr. A probability ranking principle for interactive information retrieval. *Inf. Retr.*, 11:251–265, June 2008.

[9] J. Gwizdka. Distribution of cognitive load in web search. *J. Am Soc Inf Sci Tech*, 61:2167–2187, 2010.

[10] P. Ingwersen and K. Järvelin. *The Turn: Integration of Information Seeking and Retrieval in Context (The Information Retrieval Series)*. Springer-Verlag, 2005.

[11] H. Joho, L. Azzopardi, and W. Vanderbauwhede. A survey of patent users. In *3rd IIiX*, pg 13–24, 2010.

[12] C. Jordan, C. Watters, and Q. Gao. Using controlled query generation to evaluate blind relevance feedback algorithms. In *6th JCDL*, pg 286–295, 2006.

[13] A. Kashyap, V. Hristidis, and M. Petropoulos. Facetor: cost-driven exploration of faceted query results. In *Proceedings of the 19th ACM CIKM conference*, pg 719–728. ACM, 2010.

[14] D. Kelly, V. D. Dollu, and X. Fu. The loquacious user In *Proc. of the 28th ACM SIGIR*, pg 457–464, 2005.

[15] D. Kelly, K. Gyllstrom, and E. W. Bailey. A comparison of query and term suggestion features for interactive searching. In *Proceedings of the 32nd ACM SIGIR conference* , pg 371–378. ACM, 2009.

[16] H. Keskustalo, K. Järvelin, A. Pirkola, T. Sharma, and M. Lykke. Test collection-based ir evaluation needs extension toward session, In *Proc. of the 5th AIR Symp.*, pg 63–74. 2009.

[17] K. Markey. Twenty-five years of end-user searching, part 1: Research findings. *J. Am. Soc. Inf. Sci. Technol.*, 58:1071–1081, June 2007.

[18] I. Ruthven. Interactive information retrieval. *Annual Review of Inf. Sci. and Technol*, 42:43–92, 2008.

[19] C. L. Smith and P. B. Kantor. User adaptation: good results from poor systems. In *Proceedings of the 31st ACM SIGIR conference*, pg 147–154, 2008.

[20] M. D. Smucker. Towards timed predictions of human performance for IIR evaluation. In *Proc. of the 3rd Workshop on HCIR*, 2009.

[21] M. D. Smucker and J. Allan. Find-similar: similarity browsing as a search tool. In *Proceedings of the 29th ACM SIGIR*, pg 461–468, 2006.

[22] A. Spink, D. Wolfram, M. B. J. Jansen, and T. Saracevic. Searching the web *J. Am. Soc. Inf. Sci. Technol.*, 52:226–234, Feb. 2001.

[23] H. R. Varian. *Intermediate microeconomics : a modern approach.* W.W. Norton, New York, 1987.

[24] H. R. Varian. *Economics and search. SIGIR Forum*, 33:1-5, 1999.

[25] J. Wang and J. Zhu. Portfolio theory of information retrieval. In *Proceedings of the 32nd ACM SIGIR conference*, pg 115–122. ACM, 2009.

[26] R. W. White. Using searcher simulations to redesign a polyrepresentative implicit feedback interface. *Inf. Process. Manage.*, 42:1185–1202, Sept. 2006.

[27] R. W. White, I. Ruthven, J. M. Jose, and C. J. van Rijsbergen. Evaluating implicit feedback models using searcher simulations. *ACM TOIS*, 23(3):325–361, 2005.

Seeding Simulated Queries with User-study Data for Personal Search Evaluation

David Elsweiler[1], David E. Losada[2], José Carlos Toucedo[2], Ronald T. Fernández[2]
[1]Department of Computer Science (8 AI), University of Erlangen, Germany
david@elsweiler.co.uk
[2]Departmento de Electrónica y Computación, Universidad de Santiago de Compostela, Spain
{ david.losada, josecarlos.toucedo, ronald.teijeira }@usc.es

ABSTRACT

In this paper we perform a lab-based user study (n=21) of email re-finding behaviour, examining how the characteristics of submitted queries change in different situations. A number of logistic regression models are developed on the query data to explore the relationship between user- and contextual- variables and query characteristics including length, field submitted to and use of named entities. We reveal several interesting trends and use the findings to seed a simulated evaluation of various retrieval models. Not only is this an enhancement of existing evaluation methods for Personal Search, but the results show that different models are more effective in different situations, which has implications both for the design of email search tools and for the way algorithms for Personal Search are evaluated.

Categories and Subject Descriptors

H.3.3 [**Information Search and Retrieval**]:

General Terms

Measurement,Experimentation, Human Factors

Keywords

Personal Search, Email Re-finding, User Study, Evaluation

1. INTRODUCTION

It is well documented in the literature that people regularly need to re-access and re-use information that they have created or accessed in the past [11, 27, 29] and that existing desktop management and search tools are inadequate to support this activity effectively, resulting in huge frustration and waste of resources [1, 4, 5, 28]. Personal Information Access (PIA) as a research area focuses on providing search solutions to help people re-find information they have seen or accessed previously or information relating to themselves [16]. The need for better tools to support PIA is clear. However, there are two main research issues that must be addressed to facilitate progress in this area:

First, little is known about the behaviour of users in response to information re-access needs, i.e. the behaviour that search tools should support. An understanding of what people need and how they act in order to achieve those aims is essential to know how to best support user behaviour, either through algorithmic or interface support.

Second, new tools and algorithms are difficult to evaluate scientifically given a lack of open and accepted test collections and evaluation frameworks for Personal Search. Although progress in this area has been made [3, 20, 21], the current state of the art approach suffers from a number of limitations and is not widely used as a result.

In this paper we contribute to resolving these issues. First, we perform a user study to learn about the characteristics of user querying behaviour when re-finding email messages and the factors which can influence the types of queries people submit. We examine the relationship between user and contextual variables and query characteristics including the length of the query, the field submitted on and the use of named entities. Second, we utilize the findings of this study to improve the query simulation process as applied in the literature [20, 21]. We analyse the performance of several retrieval algorithms based on simulated query profiles generated from the user study data. Taking this approach allows us to investigate and understand the relationship between user behaviour and algorithmic support for re-finding.

The remainder of the paper is structured as follows: Section 3 presents the user study, detailing the study design and data analyses; Section 4 describes the seeded evaluation process, explaining the choice of collections, the query generation method, and the retrieval models tested; Section 5 presents the experimental results; Section 6 discusses the scope and limitations of our work. Finally, Section 7 outlines our main conclusions and plans to extend the work in the future. First, to motivate the work and provide a platform to discuss our findings, we summarize appropriate related work.

2. RELATED WORK

2.1 An Overview of Re-finding behaviour

Previous work has shown people to re-access and re-find information regularly. For example, 60-80% of web page visits are re-accesses [23] and roughly 40% of web searches are performed with the aim of re-finding something seen before [27]. Desktop search tool logs show that on average

SIGIR'11, July 24–28, 2011, Beijing, China.
Copyright 2011 ACM 978-1-4503-0757-4/11/07 ...$10.00.

users submit over 4 queries per day and email is the type of media people re-find most often [11, 10].

Re-finding queries tend to be much shorter than typical web queries. Dumais and her colleagues [11] and Cutrell and his colleagues [10] both report average queries lengths of 1.6 terms compared to the well documented 2.3 for web search. Tyler and Teevan [29] found that web re-finding queries had on average 12.1 characters compared to 18.9 for queries to find new results. Desktop search logs show that re-finding queries rarely contain advanced query operators with as little as 7.5% of the queries containing features, such as boolean operators, phrases, or field restrictions specified [11]. Named entities play an important role in re-finding with queries often containing references to people. A quarter of queries in [11], for example, contained people's names.

Context is another important aspect of re-finding. What people tend to remember [13] and how difficult they perceive re-finding tasks to be [15] both vary in different situations. Given these relationships, it is possible that different behaviour will be exhibited in these situations as has been shown previously for web search engine behaviour. In web search, when users are faced with a difficult task, they start to formulate more diverse queries, use advanced operators more, and spend longer examining result pages [2]. If similar behavioural changes occur when performing difficult re-finding tasks then it would important consequences for the way behaviour is simulated in automated evaluation approaches for Personal Search. Here we seek to identify important situational variations to inform the choice of tasks in simulated evaluations.

2.2 Evaluating Personal Search

The difficulties in evaluating Personal Search behaviour are well-documented [17, 19]. In addition to major privacy and participation issues, there is a lack of shared resources, such as test collections and tasks. The main approaches to date have been naturalistic investigations with specific tools [11, 10, 9], case studies for particular scenarios [19] and lab-based user studies [7, 25, 17]. While all of these approaches offer advantages, none are suited to the controlled, repeatable evaluation of search algorithms.

Methods for automated evaluation have also been proposed. For example, Chernov and colleagues [8] suggested that researchers volunteer their own personal data to create a shared test collection for research purposes. Kim and Croft use pseudo-desktop collections that share the properties of personal collections to avoid privacy issues[20]. Three separate collections were created from the TREC Enterprise Track's W3C dataset, by taking the email messages for three prominent people in the collection and augmenting them by gathering related documents of various types from the Web. A further collection was created by using public university documents relating to individuals. These datasets have since been publicly released.

Using their collections, Kim and Croft create known-item retrieval tasks based on simulated queries [3]. Simulated queries are a potentially powerful method of scientific evaluation for Personal Search. However, there are problems with current implementations, which are over-simplified and make assumptions about user behaviour that are not necessarily true. For example, query terms are typically drawn independently from the document and either do not make use of field information [3] or assume that all fields are equally likely to be queried on [20]. Further, current implementations do not incorporate what we already know about user behaviour (e.g. that people often make use of named entities in queries).

It seems likely to us that the kinds of queries submitted will change in different scenarios. Re-finding behaviour is guided by user recollections [6] and people remember different things in different situations, with this being heavily influenced by contextual factors [13]. We hypothesize that the types of queries submitted will change in different situations. If this is the case, not only should this be incorporated in simulations, but it may mean that the type of algorithmic support required will also vary situationally, with obvious implications for search tools.

To test this hypothesis we performed a controlled user study to examine re-finding behaviour for email messages. We analyse some of the data collected to learn about the characteristics of the queries submitted and how these can change in different situations.

3. A STUDY OF EMAIL QUERY BEHAVIOUR

3.1 Study Design

We decided to focus on email search tasks because looking for different types of documents may lead to different behaviour and therefore require a larger-scale study to investigate properly. As email is the type of object re-found most often and there are appropriate collections available, we felt this would be a good starting point for research of this kind.

Our study population included 21 participants from a well-known British university, consisting of a mix of academic and research staff, undergraduate computer science students and a post-graduate class with a variety of undergraduate academic backgrounds, including former business, geography, modern-languages and philosophy students. The participants had been using their collections for varying time periods, with the post-grads having relatively new collections (the average age of collection was less than 3 months) and the academic staff comparatively older collections (avg. age ~3years). Reflecting this, some of the collections contained few messages (min = 95) and others several thousand (max =8954, median = 5132). The participants also reported using email for different purposes. While the students tended to use email mainly for class announcements and collaborative working, the academics used email for a wide range of purposes, including task and contact management, data storage, version control, collaborative authoring, as well as simple communication.

We went to great lengths to establish realistic re-finding tasks for participants that could be performed on their own personal collections without invading individual privacy. This was achieved following the methodology proposed by [17] and involved performing a number of preliminary studies with the participants and their peers, including interviews, collection tours and diary studies of the re-finding tasks people in these groups perform. This work allowed us to establish a pool of experimental tasks suitable for each groups of users. These pools reflected the contents of their collections and simulating the kinds of re-finding tasks they may perform in a naturalistic setting. The task pools contained example tasks of each of the three types identified in [17]: Lookup tasks involved finding specific pieces of information, such as passwords or phone numbers from an email; Item tasks involved finding complete emails perhaps to print out or forward to someone else; and multi-item tasks involved re-finding multiple email messages and sometimes processing to content of those mails to complete the task[1].

Each participant was allocated 9 tasks from these pools to complete on 3 systems (3 tasks per system - 1 of each type), 2 search-based interfaces and a third interface where the participants could only browse through their folders to find the information required to complete tasks. Here, we only study the queries submitted to the search systems because we were interested in understanding how the characteristics of submitted queries changed in different situations. Both search interfaces provided an interface widget to select the field that the query would be submitted to, but it is important to acknowledge that the search systems were not the same, differing in the way queries were submitted and in the way that results were presented. The main difference was in the way results were presented. The first system presented results as a standard list, while in the second system results were clustered graphically by date received. Full details of the systems can be found in [12]. We account for differences in the systems in our data analyses below.

The responses from pre- and post-task questionnaires combined with the demographic data and collection statistics for the experimental population provided a rich basis to investigate the variables influencing the querying behaviour[2]. Further details of the experimental design and user population can be found in our previous publications [13, 14], which analysed different aspects of participant behaviour.

3.2 Data Analyses

In total 347 queries were submitted. The mean length of the queries was 1.48 words (max = 7). A good mixture of fields were queried on. The most commonly queried on field was the sender field (39.48% of queries contained at least one clause on sender field), the least common field was "to or cc", which only featured in 7.5% of queries. Only 13.3% of queries were submitted against all fields. Named Entities (NEs) were heavily used with 60.5% of queries containing a reference to the name of a person, place, event or thing. Peoples names were most common, featuring in 40% of all queries and 24.21% of all queries contained a NE other than a person's name.

To understand the influence various contextual factors had on the characteristics of submitted queries we developed a number of logistic regression models. Logistic regression is a useful way of describing the relationship between one or more independent variables (e.g., the number of emails in a collection or the user filing strategy) and a binary response variable that has only two possible values expressed as a probability, such as ("contains a NE" or "does not contain a NE"). We were interested in several query characteristics including, the field the query was applied to (e.g. "contains a clause for Sender field"), types of named entities contained within the query and query length (i.e, whether the query is longer or shorter than the mean value). There were other factors of interest in the logs. For example, spelling mistakes were obviously present in some queries and expert query syntax was sometimes used to exploit email etiquette, e.g. "Fwd" or "Re" in the subject line. However, examples of these kinds were too rare to be considered in the analyses.

In total 7 models were generated. All available factors (24 in total) collated from the user study were analysed initially using a stepwise procedure in order to isolate any significant relationships. The stepwise procedure automatically enters and removes factors at each step assessing the overall goodness of fit of the linear regression model ([22] provide an overview on generalized linear models and the stepwise procedure). As an example, Table 1 presents the regression model associated with the length of the query in words. The remaining models can be found in the Appendix. These other models are associated with the following query characteristics: hasSender (whether or not the query contains a clause on the Sender field), hasSubj (whether or not the query contains a clause on the Subject field), hasBody (whether or not the query contains a clause on the Body field), NE (whether or not the query contains a NE), Person_NE (whether or not the query contains a NE person), and Other_NE (whether or not the query contains a NE -other than person-). Examining these tables shows a number of contextual variables, some of which are highlighted in bold. While all of these variables contribute to the model's predictive power, the significant factors (marked in bold), are those that exert the biggest influence. For instance, the query length model (Table 1) shows that, in our study, having an old collection significantly influenced the length of queries submitted, while other variables, such performing the task frequently did not.

The generated models indicate that several variables had an influence on the users' querying behaviour. Here we focus on variables that featured significantly in several of the models developed: Collection age (whether the collection was new (< 1 year old), medium (up to 2 years old) or old (> 2 years old); Task temperature [26](if the sought-after information was hot (had been accessed in the last week), warm (accessed in the last month), cold (had not been accessed for over 1 month) or range, where multiple emails needed to be re-found and no temperature category fitted; Task difficulty (high vs medium vs low); User experience (high vs low); and User filing strategy (filers vs no filers vs spring-cleaners [30])[3].

Table 2 summarizes the important findings for all of the models generated, showing the contextual variables that were significant factors in many models and how these factors influenced the characteristics of submitted queries.

Examining these variables reveals several interesting trends:

- Participants with older collections tended to submit longer queries and were more likely to query on the subject field. The age of the collection also seemed to influence the way NEs were used in the queries. For example, queries submitted against older collections were much more likely to contain a NE than those submitted against newer collections.

- Experienced participants were more likely to query on the subject field than less-experienced participants, but were less likely to query on the sender field.

[1]The exact experimental tasks can be found in [12].
[2]The full questionnaires can be found in [12].

[3]Task difficulty and user experience were derived from the participants' responses in the questionnaire.

Variable of Interest		length	hasSender	hasSubj	hasBody	NE	Person_NE	Other_NE
General profile		1.48	0.39	0.31	0.24	0.61	0.39	0.24
Collection Age	new	1.37	-	0.33	-	0.55	-	-
	medium	1.47	-	0.23	-	0.58	-	-
	old	1.64	-	0.42	-	0.71	-	-
Task Temperature	Hot	1.68	-	0.43	0.16	-	0.27	0.4
	Warm	1.29	-	0.34	0.16	-	0.46	0.28
	Cold	1.47	-	0.28	0.39	-	0.43	0.15
User Experience	high	-	0.39	0.34	-	-	-	-
	low	-	0.4	0.26	-	-	-	-
Task Difficulty	difficult	1.47	0.28	-	-	-	-	-
	medium	1.53	0.48	-	-	-	-	-
	easy	1.46	0.46	-	-	-	-	-
Filing Strategy	Filers	-	-	-	0.29	-	-	0.08
	no filers	-	-	-	0.31	-	-	0.3
	spring cleaners	-	-	-	0.09	-	-	0.21

Table 2: A summary of the main findings of modelling process. The main variables of interest are shown with their influence on various query characteristics. The figures represent the mean value of the query characteristic (- means the variable did not significantly influence the characteristic so the general profile value is used when generating queries).

	Est.	Std.Error	t value	Pr(> $\|t\|$)
(Intercept)	-2.72579	1.77215	-1.538	0.12497
Collection age:new	0.08563	0.12551	0.682	0.49556
Collection age:old	**0.25779**	**0.12418**	**2.076**	**$<$0.05**
Avg.#emails/day	**0.03421**	**0.01307**	**2.617**	**$<$0.01**
Task-type:item	-0.06530	0.13495	-0.484	0.62880
Task-type:multi	0.24317	0.16124	1.508	0.13248
Temperature:hot	0.11253	0.16204	0.694	0.48787
Temperature:range	-0.25784	0.20498	-1.258	0.20932
Temperature:warm	-0.25499	0.14462	-1.763	0.07879
Task Freq:infreq.	0.05257	0.12724	0.413	0.67977
Task Freq:freq.	-0.26170	0.14921	-1.754	0.08038
Difficulty:hard	**3.81902**	**1.66846**	**2.289**	**$<$0.05**
Difficulty:easy	**3.70450**	**1.66782**	**2.221**	**$<$0.05**
Difficulty:medium	**3.78639**	**1.65860**	**2.283**	**$<$0.05**
Sender	0.18179	0.12036	1.510	0.13189
Reason	0.20308	0.13210	1.537	0.12518

Table 1: Regression Model for Query Length

- When the participants were looking for older information they were much more likely to query on the body field. When they were looking for newer information the queries submitted were less likely to contain a reference to a person, but more likely to include other NEs such as organisations, books, groups or programming languages. This situation was reversed for older information with queries submitted in these situations more likely to contain references to people.

- There was a correlation between the task difficulty rating and the probability of the query including a reference to a person with easier tasks more likely to have such a reference. Difficult tasks were much less likely to be on the sender field. There was the unusual finding that tasks rated as being of medium difficulty tended to have some different characteristics to those rated as easy or difficult. For example, tasks of medium difficulty tended to be longer (mean =1.53 words) than easy tasks (mean =1.46) and difficult tasks (mean =1.47).

- The filing strategy that the participant applied also seemed to influence their querying behaviour. Participants with more than 1 folder were much less likely to query on the body of an email than those who kept all of their messages in the inbox. Further, of those participant who did use folders, those who tended to tidy up their folders occasionally (spring-cleaners), were less likely to query on the body of the email than those who filed emails regularly.

The main conclusions from these analyses are that: 1) querying behaviour changes in different situations, and 2) clear relationships exist between certain variables and the query submitted in terms of length, field to which the terms were submitted and the use of NEs in the query.

In the next part of the paper we use these results as the basis of what we argue is an improved query simulation process to better understand how different retrieval algorithms perform in the various situations shown to be important in these analyses.

4. QUERY SIMULATION FOR PERSONAL SEARCH

4.1 Email Collections

The simulated evaluation process requires the selection of an appropriate collection. Here we use four such collections. The first collection is the set of emails contained in the CS collection described in [21]. This is a collection of 806 emails from a computer science department's mailing list. Three further collections were generated from TREC Enterprise track dataset by following the methodology used in [20]. This involved filtering the W3C mailing list collection where the name of each person was tagged, enabling us to identify prominent individuals. We chose three such individuals and isolated the messages sent and received by them to create three unique collections (W3C_U1: 3943 emails, W3C_U2: 3152 emails, and W3C_U3: 1892 emails). These collections share many of the properties of personal collections and thus seem a reasonable way to simulate personal collections without compromising privacy.

4.2 Query simulation

Strategies for building simulated queries have been proposed for known-item web page search [3] and for desktop search [20]. Essentially, they are based on randomly selecting a document (known-item) from the collection and algorithmically selecting query terms from the target document. This leads to the automatic generation of simulated queries and relevance judgments. These methods have been shown to be very effective and have been evaluated successfully under different dimensions (i.e predictive and replicative validity [3, 20]). This simulation approach is appropriate in our case because we work with email re-finding queries, which are typically known-item queries [17] and are a sub-problem of desktop search [20].

We have adapted and improved these techniques in a number of ways. Current simulations are over-simplified and make assumptions about user behaviour that are not necessarily true. For example, query terms are typically drawn independently from the document and either do not make use of field information [3] or assume that all fields are equally likely to be queried on [20]. Our analysis in Section 3.2 demonstrates that the presence of fields in real queries is not uniform and the resulting statistical models allow the generation of queries incorporating appropriate statistics for the presence of terms from different fields. A further problem with current implementations is that they do not incorporate other important aspects of user behaviour (e.g. that people often make use of named entities in queries). Neither [3] nor [20] consider any kind of named entity information to guide the query production process. We claim that this is problematic because the literature shows that queries for known-item tasks contain a high number of named entities [11, 10], a fact that is further evidenced in our data. Therefore, biasing the query generation towards named entities is likely to produce more realistic queries.

4.2.1 Simulating email re-finding queries

The data analyses in Section 3 revealed that a number of variables influenced the characteristics of submitted queries [See Table 2]. For instance, different collection ages led to different patterns in variables, such as query length or presence of named entities. In contrast, other query characteristics were unaffected by this contextual variable. The data show, for instance, that different collection ages did not influence the probability that the query contained a clause submitted to the Sender or Body fields, nor whether the query was more likely to contain a person or another kind of NE. The simulation process has to account for this.

Another important point to note is that we aim to compare an assorted set of retrieval models. This means our simulation should generate flat queries, consistent with the approaches in the literature [3, 20]. The fact that the trends in Section 3 come from analyses of query logs where the queries are often structured is not a problem because these trends can be used to infer the fields at which particular terms were targeted and, therefore, help us to produce simulated flat queries with query terms in a way that reflects real-life behaviour.

In order to replicate queries associated to the situations described in Table 2 our simulation proceeds as follows:

a) Obtain a *general model* from the complete query log that reflects the general statistics found empirically for all the target variables (length, hasSender, hasSubj, hasBody, NE, Person_NE, Other_NE). For instance, if we randomly draw a one-item sample from this general model we could obtain $(3, 1, 0, 1, 1, 1, 0)$, which essentially says that we need to produce a 3-term query the terms for which should come from multiple fields (Sender+Body fields). The query should also contain a named entity that refers to a person.

b) For each situation (i.e. each potential value for each of the variables of interest), obtain a *situation-dependent model* that biases the query generation process towards the pattern determined by the situation. For instance, the value of the collection age variable strongly influences the following query variables: length, hasSubj, and NE. Therefore, for the three possible values of the collection age variable (old, medium, new) we obtain three situation-dependent models that give us proper statistics for the three query variables. Again, this is computed from the distribution obtained empirically from our user study query logs.

Next, we produce artificial queries for each situation of interest by repeating the following process:

1. randomly draw one item from the situation-dependent model
2. obtain a random item from the general model whose *situation-influenced variables* fit the pattern extracted in 1. This gives us the statistics needed for the query to be generated (*target query*).
3. initialise an empty query.
4. randomly select a document d_i from the collection as a known-item.
5. if the target query demands a NE then randomly extract a NE from any of the target fields of d_i (fields set to 1 in the target query statistics)[4]. If there are no NEs in the target fields or the number of terms in all possible NEs exceeds the target query length then go back to 2.
6. complete the query (up to the target length) with (non NE) terms extracted randomly (popularity selection as described in [3]) from the target fields. This completion should ensure that all target fields set to 1 are satisfied (i.e. they all contribute at least one term to the query). If this is not possible then go back to 2.
7. record the query-doc pair in the relevance judgments file and store the query in the query file for proper evaluation.

For each situation (i.e for each possible value of the variables of interest [See Table 2]) we generated and evaluated 10 sets of 100 simulated queries and we report the average performance obtained over the 10 query sets.

4.3 Retrieval models

In our experiments we evaluated an assorted set of retrieval algorithms: a) the well-known **bm25**, which ignores any document structure and represents the email as a flat bag of words; b) Language Models (LMs) based on Query likelihood [32]. Here, we considered both Jelinek-Mercer and Dirichlet smoothing and tested the following alternatives: **lm email**, where the document LM is constructed from all document fields (considering the doc as plain text), and **lm body**, **lm from**, **lm to**, and **lm subject** where the models are constructed from a single field of the document (and the remaining fields are ignored); c) a well-known mixture-based model (**lmmix**), as described in [24]. This defines the

[4]The collections were preprocessed using the Stanford Name Entity Recognizer, which automatically detects NEs and distinguishes between particular types of NEs (including person, location and organization) and is available at http://nlp.stanford.edu/software/CRF-NER.shtml

document's LM as a a combination LMs associated to every document representation:

$$P(w|d) = \sum_i \lambda_i \cdot P(w|d_i) \quad (1)$$

where $P(w|d_i)$ is the i-th representation's LM, and λ_i is the weight on the i-th model, with $\sum_i \lambda_i = 1$. In our case, we build one LM for every field plus one LM for the document as a whole. This leads to a document model based on combining five different representations. Again, these models are smoothed with Dirichlet or Jelinek-Mercer smoothing.

5. EXPERIMENTS

We experimented with the four collections described in Section 4. For training purposes, for each collection, we generated 140 simulated queries and relevance judgments by taking account each of the variables of interest (10 queries for each of the 14 situations [see 2nd column in Table 2]). This provides a diverse training set and avoids over-fitting to any particular situation (the parameters are tuned from generic queries). Training was done by parameter sweeping[5], where we optimized for Mean Reciprocal Rank (MRR), which is a standard measure to evaluate known-item search algorithms. For simplicity, the smoothing configuration was fixed for each situation after training (i.e. the performance reported for the LMs refers to the LMs with the smoothing configuration, Dirichlet or Jelinek-Mercer, that was optimal in the training for the given situation).

Once the parameters for each model were fixed, the testing stage was done with new simulated queries (100 queries for each situation). To account for the randomness within the query simulation process we repeated the testing process 10 times (with 10 different 100-query sets) and we report the average MRR obtained. The collections were indexed with Indri and we removed 733 common words from the emails. No stemming was applied.

The results are presented in Table 3. For each situation, the values for the best performing model and all models that did not perform statistically poorer than the best are highlighted in bold[6].

Despite different query profiles being used, the results show that overall lm email and lmmix were the best performing models. In each of the investigated situations one of these models (and often both) was (were) in the the set of best performing models. For some situations the model bm25 was included in the set of best performing models. Overall, however, bm25 is not able to compete with lm email or lmmix. The models lm email and bm25 are similar in the sense that both of them represent the document as a whole. Still, the evolved term weighting incorporated within bm25 does not seem to offer added value wrt the simpler weighting schemes implemented by LM approaches [32]. This might be due to the characteristics of our retrieval task, where lengths of documents and term statistics deviate strongly from those found in more standard document retrieval scenarios.

Despite many of the queries consisting of single terms and many of these being NEs, the models that represent the emails with a single field (i.e. lm from, lm to, lm subject and lm body) perform poorly and are never as effective as the best models. Overall, the results clearly indicate that lm email or lmmix are optimal for re-finding email messages. Nevertheless, there are some trends in the results that, depending on the contextual situation, could help us decide which of these two models to use. For instance, if the collection is old then we should select lm email because it is always among the best performing models whereas lmmix is not. In constrast, for new or medium collection ages we should go for lmmix, which performs stronger overall than lm email in these contexts. Similar analyses lead us to conclude that a) lm email is preferable when the user does not use folders, while lmmix is better for spring cleaners; b) lm email performs more consistently for difficult tasks and lmmix is better choice for tasks with easy or medium difficulty, and c) lm email is a good choice for re-finding messages that have not been accessed for long time periods (cold temperature tasks) whereas lmmix is better for re-finding messages that have been accessed more recently (warm or hot temperature tasks).

Summing up, our findings reveal a quite interesting trend. It seems that when conditions are somehow difficult (the sought-after email has not been accessed for a long time, the task is perceived as difficult, users who do not file messages, or the collection is old) then we should go for a simple model that does not take into account structure and simply represents the document as a bag of words (lm email). In contrast, when conditions are somehow easier, then lmmix, which is a more evolved model that considers weights for the email fields, seems to be a more suitable choice.

We would also like to note that many of these scenarios can be automatically detected (e.g. the age of the collection or the user filing strategy) and, therefore, search applications can directly adapt their behaviour depending on the context. Some situations, such as the temperature of the task or the task difficulty, are more difficult to infer. Our findings seem to endorse further research on methods of automatically detecting such contextual variables. This could be achieved based on learning from the user interactions with the system including factors, such as the type and number of queries submitted, query sessions, etc.

6. LIMITATIONS AND DISCUSSION

The approach taken in this paper is extremely novel. We used user study data analyses to directly seed the query simulation process for evaluating retrieval models for email search. Ideally, however, before evaluating the performance of the models, we should try to establish the validity of the simulated queries. According to Zeigler [31], there are three kinds of validation that can be performed on a simulation; predictive, structural and replicative. A model has predictive validity if it can produce the same data output as the real system (i.e. comparing the query terms for a given known-item from the simulated model and a real system). A model has structural validity if the way it operates is a reflection of how the real system operates. Finally, replicative validity is achieved if the model produces output that

[5]For BM25, we fixed k_3 to 1000 (the effect of k_3 is negligible for short queries like ours) and varied k_1 (from 0 to 10 in steps of 0.2) and b (from 0 to 1 in steps of 0.1). For the LMs, we varied the smoothing parameters as follows: μ (Dirichlet smoothing parameter) from 0 to 5000 in steps of 500, and λ (Jelinek-Mercer smoothing parameter) from 0 to 1 in steps of 0.1. For lmmix we also varied the λ_i's between 0 and 1 in steps of 0.1

[6]Statistical significance was estimated with a paired t-test (p-value=0.05)

		Collection Age			User Experience		Filing Strategy			Task Difficulty			Task Temperature		
		new	medium	old	high	low	filers	no filers	spring	easy	medium	difficult	cold	warm	hot
CS	bm25	**0.438**	**0.430**	0.468	**0.472**	0.473	**0.468**	0.468	0.445	0.437	0.477	0.449	0.457	**0.480**	**0.450**
	lm from	0.221	0.264	0.213	0.247	0.267	0.239	0.216	0.233	0.239	0.285	0.156	0.187	0.283	0.210
	lm to	0.074	0.060	0.034	0.066	0.068	0.046	0.033	0.054	0.072	0.041	0.053	0.053	0.057	0.062
	lm subject	0.211	0.159	0.246	0.233	0.179	0.185	0.171	0.257	0.163	0.225	0.249	0.186	0.199	0.283
	lm body	0.278	0.295	0.330	0.304	0.289	0.336	0.333	0.299	0.281	0.308	0.321	0.331	0.322	0.296
	lm email	**0.439**	**0.433**	**0.479**	**0.471**	**0.481**	**0.474**	**0.484**	**0.455**	**0.446**	**0.493**	**0.459**	**0.468**	**0.484**	**0.454**
	lmmix	**0.439**	**0.433**	**0.479**	**0.471**	**0.481**	**0.474**	**0.484**	**0.455**	**0.446**	**0.493**	**0.459**	**0.468**	**0.484**	**0.454**
W3C-U1	bm25	0.201	0.175	0.262	0.231	0.197	0.206	0.188	0.203	0.209	0.203	0.219	0.199	0.186	0.262
	lm from	0.102	0.111	0.111	0.120	0.097	0.104	0.091	0.115	0.124	0.147	0.068	0.067	0.131	0.108
	lm to	0.072	0.055	0.054	0.081	0.082	0.053	0.045	0.068	0.075	0.045	0.073	0.057	0.051	0.092
	lm subject	0.126	0.098	0.162	0.137	0.101	0.115	0.091	0.147	0.095	0.138	0.159	0.112	0.118	0.173
	lm body	0.149	0.136	0.204	0.161	0.153	0.156	0.164	0.136	0.162	0.143	0.177	0.166	0.138	0.198
	lm email	0.219	0.201	**0.287**	0.249	**0.223**	**0.235**	**0.224**	0.223	0.238	0.236	**0.259**	**0.230**	0.204	0.303
	lmmix	**0.249**	**0.221**	**0.271**	**0.279**	**0.239**	**0.235**	**0.215**	**0.277**	**0.271**	**0.261**	0.237	0.209	**0.256**	**0.332**
W3C-U2	bm25	0.178	0.173	0.221	0.193	0.175	0.215	0.204	0.178	0.190	0.192	0.225	0.193	0.175	0.232
	lm from	0.054	0.071	0.047	0.069	0.076	0.067	0.052	0.072	0.069	0.078	0.043	0.048	0.061	0.061
	lm to	0.024	0.023	0.013	0.024	0.028	0.020	0.014	0.022	0.027	0.010	0.020	0.020	0.025	0.028
	lm subject	0.114	0.099	0.137	0.125	0.094	0.104	0.097	0.155	0.088	0.144	0.163	0.110	0.127	0.166
	lm body	0.111	0.121	0.165	0.120	0.122	0.157	0.172	0.107	0.142	0.124	0.179	0.152	0.129	0.136
	lm email	0.186	**0.182**	**0.249**	0.210	0.190	**0.232**	**0.216**	0.191	**0.204**	0.206	**0.241**	**0.212**	0.189	**0.240**
	lmmix	**0.199**	**0.194**	0.213	**0.224**	**0.206**	**0.217**	0.198	**0.219**	**0.219**	**0.237**	**0.232**	**0.211**	**0.207**	**0.251**
W3C-U3	bm25	0.205	0.209	0.270	0.251	0.230	0.219	0.229	0.235	0.222	0.241	0.246	0.203	0.216	0.259
	lm from	0.102	0.120	0.097	0.121	0.119	0.101	0.077	0.119	0.123	0.131	0.065	0.069	0.119	0.104
	lm to	0.042	0.015	0.025	0.046	0.020	0.035	0.023	0.021	0.026	0.030	0.029	0.019	0.028	0.040
	lm subject	0.144	0.096	0.177	0.150	0.122	0.129	0.093	0.173	0.110	0.149	0.174	0.114	0.136	0.188
	lm body	0.149	0.142	0.220	0.164	0.164	0.175	0.183	0.144	0.174	0.157	0.185	0.155	0.157	0.189
	lm email	**0.221**	**0.228**	**0.297**	**0.259**	**0.240**	**0.237**	**0.256**	**0.249**	**0.235**	**0.256**	**0.268**	**0.221**	**0.230**	**0.272**
	lmmix	**0.221**	**0.228**	**0.297**	**0.259**	**0.240**	**0.237**	**0.256**	**0.249**	**0.235**	**0.256**	**0.268**	**0.221**	**0.230**	**0.272**

Table 3: Mean Reciprocal Rank of the retrieval models in the 14 different situations. For each situation, the bolded figures refer either to the highest performing model or to those models whose difference wrt to the highest performing model is not statistically significant.

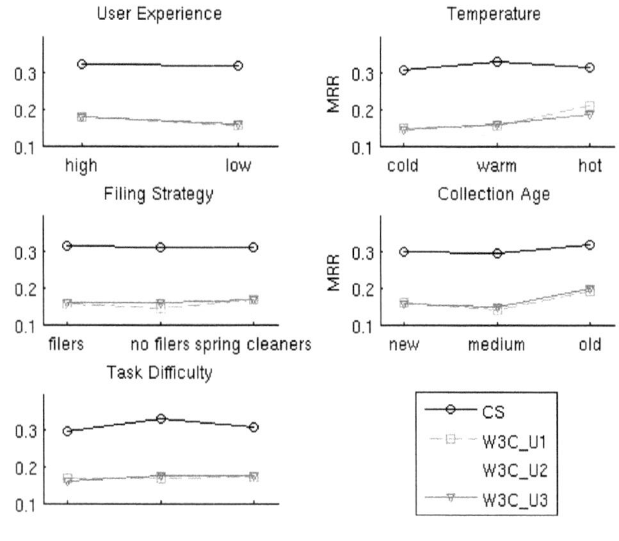

Figure 1: Mean performance of the retrieval models for different values of the contextual variables

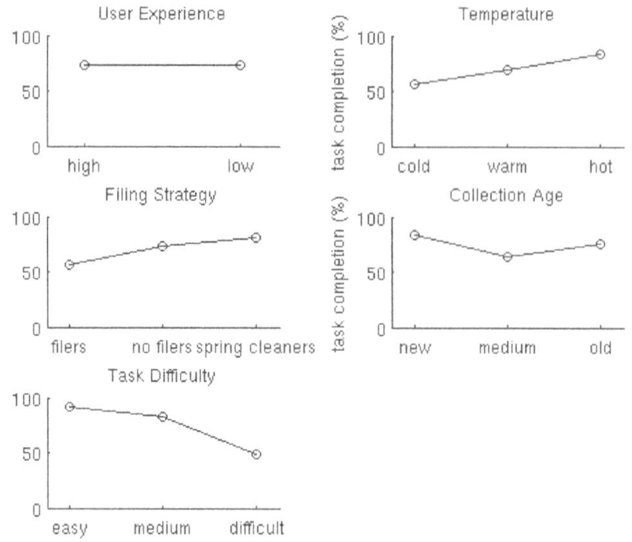

Figure 2: User Study Performance in terms of percentage of task completion.

is similar to the output of the real system (e.g. equivalent retrieval performance).

Previous work on query simulation for known-item tasks has established validity using both predictive [20] and replicative approaches [3, 20]. As our simulations build on the approaches used in these studies and in the case of [20] we make use of the same datasets, it is likely that the queries generated as a whole will be similarly valid. Nevertheless, it would be nice to have been able to validate our approach at the level of situation. Unfortunately, we are restricted in terms of what we can do to validate our simulated queries. We cannot perform predictive or replicative validity because these approaches require real queries along with an appropriate test collections.

In our case, we have real queries (from the user study) but do not have appropriate collection data (privacy concerns mean we cannot access user study participant collections). We also have publicly available test collections, but unfortunately for these collections we do not have suitable real queries against which to validate our simulated queries. What we can do with respect to replicative validity is compare the average performance of the evaluated models with the performance in the user study. Figure 1 shows the trends for the systems evaluation and Figure 2 provides the user study performance in terms of rate of task completion.

The results for the User experience and Task Temperature variables follow similar trends in both the system and user evaluations. This suggests that our simulations are most accurate in these situations. Also, for the filing strategy variable, in both evaluations, the spring-cleaners were the best performing group. The final two variables, Collection Age and Task Difficulty have trends that do not at all match the user study performance. It is important to note, however, that the user study results are user performance figures and do not necessarily reflect query performance. Although the quality of query will likely be a good indicator of overall performance, if the user is skilled at looking through lots of messages or in recognising relevant results this will skew the results.

It is also possible that for the Collection Age variable, the size of collection may be a larger factor in overall performance than the query generated. Older collections will most likely be larger in size and our results in Section 5 demonstrate how collection size can influence performance. The CS dataset (806 emails) was associated with much higher performance than the other collections (1892-3943 emails). This underlines the need for other ways of validating queries. It also suggests that bigger test collections are needed for this kind of work. The collections we used are equivalent in size to typical email collections [30, 13]. However, collections can be much bigger [18]. It is important that automated experiments reflect this.

There are other limitations to our work that we should mention. Although we extend previous simulations to incorporate fields and NEs, we do not consider how discriminative the selected terms or queries are. In the past, some effective simulations [3] have been based on selecting discriminative terms from the documents (tf/idf-like term selection). Nevertheless, our documents tend to be short, we remove common words and NEs make up a significant number of our query terms. Therefore, it is unlikely that further extending our simulations to consider the discriminative power of the terms would improve the realism of our simulation.

Another limitation of our work is that our simulation (as in [3, 20, 21]) only draws terms, named entities etc. from within the target document so the simulation does not account for user error. It would be relatively simple to include terms outside the document, for instance by interpolating terms with a collection language model, but we felt it would beyond the scope of this paper to do this. Similarly, we do not consider spelling mistakes or the fact that often multi-term queries will be phrases.

7. CONCLUSIONS AND FUTURE WORK

This paper has made two main contributions by first, investigating email re-finding queries and then second, by using the findings to seed a simulated evaluation of retrieval models for email search. The main findings can be summarised as follows:

- There was clear evidence in the user study of relationships existing between situational variables and query characteristics.
- We discovered that the age of the collection, the time that had elapsed since last accessing the email, the perceived difficulty of the task, the experience of the user, and the filing strategy the user adopted all had some influence on one or more of the following characteristics: the length of the query, the field submitted to, and the use of named-entities.
- We incorporated the trends as they appeared in the user study data in a simulated evaluation of retrieval models for email search.
- We learned about the performance of various models for email search. The results showed that models that make use of the whole document (lm email and lmmix and sometimes bm25) achieved the best performance.
- We uncovered situations when it is more sensible to make use of structural information of the document. A pattern emerged indicating that in more difficult situations it best to use a simple model that ignores structure, whereas in easier situations better performance can be achieved by taking structure into account.

Although we feel that the presented work is an important starting point for the fusion of user and systems IR approaches, it is important to acknowledge that it is only the starting point. Currently we are working on ways to improve the methodology in order to incorporate a means of validating simulated queries. We are also looking to extend the approach to look at other kinds of personal data including visited web pages, personal files, and calender entries. In other related work we are looking at ways of implicitly detecting contextual variables from live re-finding behaviour so that search applications can make use of different retrieval models appropriately depending on the contextual situation.

Acknowledgments

The first author was supported by the Alexander von Humboldt Foundation, Germany. The last three authors thank the financial support given by Ministerio de Ciencia e Innovación through research project ref. TIN2010-18552-C03-03. We would also like to thank Jinyoung Kim for providing us with the test collections.

8. REFERENCES

[1] A. Aula, N. Jhaveri, and M. Käki, *Information search and reaccess strategies of experienced web users*, Proc. Int. Conf. World Wide Web, 2005, pp. 583–592.

[2] A. Aula, R. M. Khan, and Z. Guan, *How does search behavior change as search becomes more difficult?*, Proc. SIGCHI conference on Human factors in computing systems, 2010, pp. 35–44.

[3] L. Azzopardi, M. de Rijke, and K. Balog, *Building simulated queries for known-item topics: an analysis using six european languages*, Proc. ACM SIGIR conference on Research and development in information retrieval, 2007, pp. 455–462.

[4] R. Boardman and M. A. Sasse, *"stuff goes into the computer and doesn't come out": a cross-tool study of personal information management*, CHI '04: Proc. SIGCHI, 2004, pp. 583–590.

[5] H. Bruce, W. Jones, and S. Dumais, *Keeping and re-finding information on the web: What do people do and what do they need?*, ASIST 2004: Proceedings of the 67th ASIST annual meeting, October 2004.

[6] R. G. Capra and M. A. Perez-Quinones, *Re-finding found things: An exploratory study of how users re-find information*, Tech. report, Computer Science Dept., Virginia Tech, 2003.

[7] R. G. Capra and M. A. Perez-Quinones, *Using web search engines to find and refind information*, Computer **38** (2005), no. 10, 36–42.

[8] S. Chernov, P. Serdyukov, P. Chirita, G. Demartini, and W. Nejdl, *Building a desktop search test-bed*, ECIR'07: Proceedings of the 29th European conference on IR research (Berlin, Heidelberg), Springer-Verlag, 2007, pp. 686–690.

[9] S. Cohen, C. Domshlak, and N. Zwerdling, *On ranking techniques for desktop search*, ACM Trans. Inf. Syst. **26** (2008), 11:1–11:24.

[10] E. Cutrell, D. Robbins, S. Dumais, and R. Sarin, *Fast, flexible filtering with phlat*, Proc. SIGCHI conference on Human Factors in computing systems, 2006, pp. 261–270.

[11] S. Dumais, E. Cutrell, J. Cadiz, G. Jancke, R. Sarin, and D.C. Robbins, *Stuff i've seen: a system for personal information retrieval and re-use*, Proc. ACM SIGIR '03:, 2003, pp. 72–79.

[12] D. Elsweiler, *Supporting human memory in personal information management*, Ph.D. thesis, Department of Computer and Information Sciences, University of Strathclyde, 2007.

[13] D. Elsweiler, M. Baillie, and I. Ruthven, *Exploring memory in email refinding*, ACM Trans. Inf. Syst. **26** (2008), no. 4, 1–36.

[14] D. Elsweiler, M. Baillie. and I. Ruthven, *On understanding the relationship between recollection and refinding*, Journal of Digital Information (JoDI) **10** (2009), no. 5.

[15] D. Elsweiler, M. Baillie, and I. Ruthven, *What makes re-finding information diffcult? a study of email re-finding*, Proc. ECIR 2011, 2011.

[16] D. Elsweiler, G. Jones, L. Kelly, and J. Teevan, *Workshop on desktop search*, SIGIR Forum **44** (2010), 28–34.

[17] D. Elsweiler and I. Ruthven, *Towards task-based personal information management evaluations*, Proc. ACM SIGIR conference on Research and development in information retrieval, 2007, pp. 23–30.

[18] D. Fisher, A. J. Brush, E. Gleave, and M. A. Smith, *Revisiting whittaker & sidner's "email overload" ten years later*, Proc. Conference on Computer supported cooperative work, 2006, pp. 309–312.

[19] D. Kelly and J. Teevan, *Personal information management*, ch. Understanding what works: Evaluating personal information management tools, pp. 190–204, Seattle: University of Washington Press., 2007.

[20] J. Kim and W. B. Croft, *Retrieval experiments using pseudo-desktop collections*, CIKM '09: Proceeding of the 18th ACM conference on Information and knowledge management (New York, NY, USA), ACM, 2009, pp. 1297–1306.

[21] J. Kim and W. B. Croft, *Ranking using multiple document types in desktop search*, Proceeding of the 33rd international ACM SIGIR conference on Research and development in information retrieval (New York, NY, USA), SIGIR '10, ACM, 2010, pp. 50–57.

[22] P. McCullagh and J. A. Nelder, *Generalized linear models (second edition)*, Chapman and Hall, 1989.

[23] B. McKenzie and A. Cockburn, *An empirical analysis of web page revisitation*, Proc. of the HICSS34, 2001.

[24] P. Ogilvie and J. Callan, *Combining document representations for known item search*, Proc. ACM SIGIR '03:, 2003, pp. 143–150.

[25] M. Ringel, E. Cutrell, S. Dumais, and E. Horvitz, *Milestones in time: The value of landmarks in retrieving information from personal stores.*, Proc. INTERACT 2003, 2003, pp. 184–191.

[26] A. J. Sellen and R. H. R. Harper, *The myth of the paperless office*, MIT Press, Cambridge, MA, USA, 2003.

[27] J. Teevan, E. Adar, R. Jones, and M. Potts, *Information re-retrieval: Repeat queries in yahoo's logs*, Proc. SIGIR '07, 2007.

[28] J. Teevan, C. Alvarado, M. S. Ackerman, and D. R. Karger, *The perfect search engine is not enough: a study of*

orienteering behavior in directed search, Proc. SIGCHI conference on Human factors in computing systems, 2004, pp. 415–422.

[29] S. K. Tyler and J. Teevan, *Large scale query log analysis of re-finding*, Proc. WSDM '10, 2010.

[30] S. Whittaker and C. Sidner, *Email overload: exploring personal information management of email*, Proc. SIGCHI conference on Human factors in computing systems, 1996, pp. 276–283.

[31] Bernard P. Zeigler, *Theory of modelling and simulation*, Krieger Publishing Co., Inc., Melbourne, FL, USA, 1984.

[32] C. Zhai and J. Lafferty, *A study of smoothing methods for language models applied to information retrieval*, ACM Transactions on Information Systems **22** (2004), no. 2, 179–214.

APPENDIX

	Est.	Std.Error	t value	Pr(> |t|)
(Intercept)	-1.418e+00	9.404e-01	-1.508	0.132622
Collection Size	-4.007e-05	2.727e-05	-1.469	0.142716
number_folders	3.580e-03	1.886e-03	1.898	0.058533
Avg.#emails/day	**3.351e-02**	**1.366e-02**	**2.452**	**<0.05**
User experience:low	**1.339e-01**	**5.751e-02**	**2.329**	**<0.05**
Difficulty:hard	**1.705e+00**	**8.590e-01**	**1.985**	**<0.05**
Difficulty:easy	**1.784e+00**	**8.591e-01**	**2.077**	**<0.05**
Difficulty:medium	**1.880e+00**	**8.528e-01**	**2.205**	**<0.05**
When	**2.405e-01**	**5.535e-02**	**4.345**	**<0.01**
Sender	**2.203e-01**	**5.926e-02**	**3.718**	**<0.01**
Topic	**-3.110e-01**	**7.839e-02**	**-3.968**	**<0.01**

Table 4: Regression Model for hasSender

	Est.	Std.Error	t value	Pr(> |t|)
(Intercept)	2.283e+00	1.139e+00	2.004	<0.05
Collection size	1.055e-05	1.696e-05	0.622	0.53421
number_folders	7.031e-04	2.190e-03	0.321	0.74843
Collection age:new	**2.563e-01**	**1.009e-01**	**2.539**	**<0.05**
Collection age:old	**1.890e-01**	**8.176e-02**	**2.311**	**<0.05**
User experience:low	**-2.508e-01**	**8.440e-02**	**-2.971**	**<0.01**
Task-type:item	-9.696e-02	7.429e-02	-1.305	0.19273
Task-type:multi	1.306e-01	9.198e-02	1.420	0.15654
Filing:no filer	-4.944e-02	9.931e-02	-0.498	0.61893
Filing:spring	-1.219e-01	1.142e-01	-1.067	0.28659
pre_contains:not sure	-3.169e-01	1.741e-01	-1.820	0.06967
pre_contains:yes	-2.739e-01	1.462e-01	-1.874	0.06186
Temperature:hot	1.653e-01	9.604e-02	1.721	0.08623
Temperature:Range	-2.481e-01	1.129e-01	-2.198	**<0.05**
Temperature:warm	2.453e-02	8.752e-02	0.280	0.77945
Task Freq:infreq.	7.729e-03	7.004e-02	0.110	0.91220
Task Freq:freq.	-4.040e-02	8.853e-02	-0.456	0.64845
Task difficulty:hard	-1.532e+00	1.068e+00	-1.435	0.15216
Task difficulty:easy	-1.510e+00	1.061e+00	-1.423	0.15567
Task difficulty:medium	-1.596e+00	1.056e+00	-1.510	0.13192
When	-2.291e-02	6.678e-02	-0.343	0.73180
Sender	-2.184e-01	6.714e-02	-3.253	**<0.01**
Topic	8.805e-02	1.111e-01	0.793	0.42846
Reason	-4.873e-02	9.431e-02	-0.517	0.60570
Other.recp	-4.206e-02	6.660e-02	-0.632	0.52816

Table 5: Regression Model for hasSubject

	Est.	Std.Error	t value	Pr(> |t|)
(Intercept)	0.619595	0.139081	4.455	<0.01
Avg.#emails/day	**-0.024198**	**0.005725**	**-4.227**	**<0.01**
number_folders	**0.003369**	**0.001199**	**2.810**	**<0.01**
Filing:no filer	**0.158860**	**0.072745**	**2.184**	**<0.05**
Filing:spring	**-0.152566**	**0.068970**	**-2.212**	**<0.05**
pre_contains:not sure	-0.269388	0.146071	-1.844	0.066029
pre_contains:yes	-0.114047	0.124052	-0.919	0.358573
Temperature:hot	**-0.276521**	**0.064366**	**-4.296**	**<0.01**
Temperature:range	**-0.264592**	**0.068707**	**-3.851**	**<0.01**
Temperature:warm	**-0.361725**	**0.064131**	**-5.640**	**<0.01**
When	**-0.095110**	**0.030288**	**-3.140**	**<0.01**

Table 6: Regression Model for hasBody

	Est.	Std.Error	t value	Pr(> |t|)
(Intercept)	c	0.47430	0.07363	6.442 <0.01
Collection age:new	-0.02863	0.06374	-0.449	0.65360
Collection age:old	**0.19052**	**0.07288**	**2.614**	**<0.01**
Filing:no filer	0.15413	0.08061	1.912	0.05669
Filing:spring	0.02966	0.08650	0.343	0.73185

Table 7: Regression Model for hasNamedEntity

	Est.	Std.Error	t value	Pr(> |t|)
(Intercept)	8.077e-01	3.529e-01	2.289	<0.05
Collection size	-1.674e-05	1.142e-05	-1.465	0.1437
Collection age:new	-6.605e-02	7.705e-02	-0.857	0.3919
Collection age:old	1.283e-01	7.260e-02	1.768	0.0780
User experience:low	1.253e-01	6.630e-02	1.889	0.0597
pre_contains:not sure	1.777e-01	1.708e-01	1.040	0.2989
pre_contains:yes	2.788e-01	1.519e-01	1.836	0.0673
Temperature:hot	**-1.730e-01**	**7.830e-02**	**-2.210**	**<0.05**
Temperature:range	-4.201e-03	8.737e-02	-0.048	0.9617
Temperature:warm	1.339e-02	7.903e-02	0.169	0.8656
Task difficulty:hard	-7.429e-01	3.805e-01	-1.952	0.0517
Task difficulty:easy	-5.788e-01	3.763e-01	-1.538	0.1249
Task difficulty:medium	-6.862e-01	3.813e-01	-1.800	0.0728

Table 8: Regression Model for hasPerson

	Est.	Std.Error	t value	Pr(> |t|)
(Intercept)	0.067843	0.079382	0.855	0.393358
number_folders	0.001858	0.001143	1.625	0.105018
User experience:low	-0.094082	0.048853	-1.926	0.054966
Filing:no filer	**0.208101**	**0.075727**	**2.748**	**<0.01**
Filing:spring	0.004585	0.076354	0.060	0.952148
Temperature:hot	**0.238175**	**0.061590**	**3.867**	**<0.01**
Temperature:range	-0.035453	0.063167	-0.561	0.574990
Temperature:warm	0.098244	0.062560	1.570	0.117258

Table 9: Regression Model for hasOtherNamedEntity

Understanding Re-finding Behavior in Naturalistic Email Interaction Logs

David Elsweiler
Department of Computer Science (8 AI), University of Erlangen, Germany
david@elsweiler.co.uk

Morgan Harvey
Department of Computer and Information Sciences, University of Strathclyde, Scotland
morgan@cis.strath.ac.uk

Martin Hacker
Department of Computer Science (8 AI), University of Erlangen, Germany
Martin.Hacker@informatik.uni-erlangen.de

ABSTRACT

In this paper we present a longitudinal, naturalistic study of email behavior (n=47) and describe our efforts at isolating re-finding behavior in the logs through various qualitative and quantitative analyses. The presented work underlines the methodological challenges faced with this kind of research, but demonstrates that it is possible to isolate re-finding behavior from email interaction logs with reasonable accuracy. Using the approaches developed we uncover interesting aspects of email re-finding behavior that have so far been impossible to study, such as how various features of email-clients are used in re-finding and the difficulties people encounter when using these. We explain how our findings could influence the design of email-clients and outline our thoughts on how future, more in depth analyses, can build on the work presented here to achieve a fuller understanding of email behavior and the support that people need.

Categories and Subject Descriptors

H3.3 [**Information Search and Retrieval**]:

General Terms

Measurement,Management,Experimentation, Human Factors

Keywords

Personal Information Management, Re-finding, Naturalistic User Evaluation, Query Log Analysis

1. INTRODUCTION

There is an increasing body of evidence showing that people regularly require to re-find and re-use information they create, acquire or receive [9, 23, 25]. The tools used to do this, however, such as web-browsers, email-clients, search engines etc., are often not designed with re-finding in mind and, as a result, re-finding is frequently difficult, time-consuming and frustrating [1, 5, 24]. Designing better tools or improving the tools that we already have requires knowledge of what people need, how they behave and the reasons for their behavior. Currently our knowledge about these aspects is very limited and most of what we do know comes from studies of re-finding either files or web pages.

Despite evidence showing that email is the information type re-found most often [9] and for many users the hub of their information space [27], there have been no naturalistic investigations of how people interact with email-clients to re-find, how and when the strategies change and how these behaviors may be supported. Naturalistic investigations of web page re-finding, e.g. [23, 25], on the other hand, have provided key insights into the behavior people employ when re-finding. These include discovering that different types of re-finding occur within and across sessions and that strategies converge for regularly accessed items. Similar approaches for email would allow researchers to discover if these behaviors transfer or if the varied uses of email and many differences in form and function between web pages and email messages mean that people behave differently and need alternative re-finding support.

One of the principal reasons that naturalistic approaches have not been used to analyze email behavior is that email-clients are not like search engines. They are used for several purposes and many user interactions will have nothing at all to do with re-finding i.e. checking, reading, sending, organizing mails. This leads to a large amount of noise in the logs and difficulties in drawing conclusions about re-finding behavior. In this paper, we present a naturalistic study of email behavior and describe our efforts at isolating re-finding behavior in the logs through various qualitative and quantitative analyses. The presented work underlines the methodological challenges faced with this kind of research, but shows that by using a specific logistic regression model developed as part of this work, that it is possible to isolate re-finding behavior from email-client interaction logs with reasonable accuracy. By demonstrating that re-finding interactions can be successfully and reliably isolated within log-data, we make it possible to study email re-finding behavior in the same way that web page re-finding can currently be studied with Search Engine (SE) logs. Using the approaches developed we uncover interesting aspects of email re-finding behavior that have so far been impossible to study. We also outline our thoughts on how future, more in depth analyses can build on the work presented here to achieve a fuller un-

SIGIR'11, July 24–28, 2011, Beijing, China.

derstanding of email behavior and the support that people need.

The paper is structured as follows: Section 3 describes the main study methodology; Section 4 outlines additional experiments used to create an annotated dataset for training and testing models for isolating re-finding behavior. Section 5 details the modeling work and model performance. Sections 6 and 7 use the modeling work as a means to analyze re-finding behavior and discuss the main findings with respect to previous work. Finally, we conclude in Section 8 by summarizing the main contributions and outlining our plans for extending the work in the future. First, to motivate the work and provide a platform to discuss our findings, we summarize appropriate related work.

2. BACKGROUND LITERATURE

Personal Information Management (PIM) is the research domain interested in learning about and supporting the behavior people exhibit to acquire, store, organize and re-find information [15]. Re-accessing information has been shown to be an activity people undertake regularly. For example, 60-80% of web-page visits are re-accesses [18] and approx. 40% of web searches are performed with the aim of re-finding something seen before [23, 25]. Similar access patterns have been observed for many other information types, including Unix commands, borrowed library books, and human recollections [9]. Analyses of desktop-search tools show that email is the type of media people re-find most often [9]. Email has historically been an important topic within PIM, with numerous studies investigating the different uses of email (e.g. for collaborative working [8], management of contacts [28], tasks [29], and documents [29, 2]) and how collections are organized to account for these uses [29].

To date there has been limited focus on the methods people employ to re-find email messages and the studies which have been performed have been laboratory-based and have focused on behavior with novel tools [21] or specific aspects relating to behavior (e.g. user recollections [10]). The lack of research on email re-finding contrasts that of files and web pages, from which we know about preferences for browse over search in different scenarios [3, 4]; particular seeking tactics [24, 6]; that re-finding tends to be performed in bursts [25]; that strategies are honed over time for regularly re-found objects [25] and that different behavior is exhibited for within and between session searches [25].

We believe that complementing this work with research on email re-finding behavior is important given the differences between email messages and other types of information objects in terms of the way they are acquired and used, as well as the frequency with which people have been shown to re-find information within their email collections. There are several unanswered research questions that could be answered by a naturalistic examination of email behavior.

- How often do people re-find and how much time do they spend doing this?
- What strategies do people use to re-find and how do strategies change for in different situations? Do different people use different strategies or are relatively homogeneous approaches applied? Do individual users employ different strategies to re-find the same messages? Do email re-finding strategies converge over time as [25] found with web-page re-finding?
- Are there indicators of people having difficulty when re-finding and can we learn what these difficulties are and how to resolve them?
- Are there patterns in the emails that people tend to re-find and can these be used to predict which messages may need to be re-found in the future?

Answering such questions could potentially have a huge impact on the way we design email-clients. A prerequisite to answering these and similar questions, however, is the ability to isolate the interactions associated with re-finding behavior within naturalistic log files. In the following sections we outline our efforts at achieving this and evaluate the performance of our methods.

3. NATURALISTIC STUDY

We performed a naturalistic investigation by developing an extension for the popular, open-source email-client Mozilla Thunderbird[1], which captured user interactions with the client during the course of normal usage. We recorded interactions such as opening folders, selecting messages, sort operations, changing views (e.g. to show only unread messages), submitting queries etc.. The query strings and information about the results were also recorded. Further, events such as opening and closing Thunderbird's specialist search facilities, as well as queries submitted to these facilities and actions performed with the found messages were recorded. For privacy reasons no data relating to message content was stored but message senders and subjects were given an identifier and particular message properties (timestamp information, read before flag, message size etc.) were noted.

By utilizing Mozilla mailing lists and user fora we were able to recruit a diverse study population. 47 participants (37 male, 10 female, aged 21-49), from 7 countries volunteered to take part over a period of 4 months. The population included people with a broad range of occupations from a film-festival organizer, a lab-technician and software engineers to teachers, lawyers and consultants, although academics and students were particularly well represented. The academic participants had backgrounds stretching across the sciences and humanities.

Analyzing the log data revealed large differences in email usage. For example, some participants interacted with their email-clients regularly throughout the day, while others checked email less often. Some collections were well established (up to 15 years old) and had several hundred thousand messages and other collections were only a few months old and contained less than 100 messages (median 3,892). As our study was longitudinal in nature, it provides the possibility to determine how email usage in such new collections developed over time. The collected log files consisted of 205,742 interactions. The vast majority of interactions (~80%) were message selects, ~14% were folder opened, ~2% were keyword search queries and ~1% were sort operations. The advanced searching features were rarely used, only being opened 83 times and with 139 queries being submitted. Only 14 out of the 47 participants made use of these facilities.

Despite relatively few search operations being performed, breaking the select-message interactions down reveals considerable re-accessing behavior. ~55% of the messages that were selected had been previously read and as Table 1 shows, many of re-accessed messages were quite old with ~7% of

[1]See http://www.mozilla.org. We used version 2.3

the re-accessed messages being received over a year previously. The oldest message accessed was 6.65 years old. These statistics are similar to those for other types of information as noted in Section 2.

Message Originally Received	Count	Percentage
Over 1 year previously	6936	~7%
Over 180 days previously	2627	2%
Over 90 days previously	2793	3%
Over 60 days previously	2097	2%
Over 30 days previously	3398	3%
Over 1 week previously	9859	10%
Over 1 day previously	16984	18%
Over 1 hour previously	32777	36%

Table 1: Re-accessed Messages Over Time

Although generating statistics about the frequency of interactions can provide an interesting overview of re-accessing behavior and suggests that the participants have been re-finding, to learn about user strategies in greater detail requires the isolation of re-finding interactions. What we need is to establish chains (sequences) of interactions representing only re-finding behavior and relating to a single task. This would allow us to perform analyses similar to those performed with search engine logs. The following sections outline our efforts at achieving this.

4. FURTHER DATA COLLECTION

4.1 Manual Analyses

As a first step in the process, we analyzed a subset of the logs manually to determine if features existed in the logs that may indicate that a re-finding task was being performed. We divided the dataset into interaction chains by looking for hard and soft boundaries. A hard boundary was defined as a new start of the email client and following previous work [22, 7], a soft boundary was defined as a gap greater than 5 minutes between interactions.

We randomly chose ~1% of the dataset (250 chains) and also took the chains before and after these for manual analysis. These ~750 chains were color-coded and printed, with each interaction being represented by one line of text including important meta-data and each interaction type having a unique color. A manual analysis of these chains by three researchers (separately marking each chain positively or negatively depending on whether they believed it to contain re-finding behavior or neutral if they were unsure) revealed high overlap across researchers. The researchers achieved a very high agreement (96%), with 21% being marked positive and 8% neutral. As a result of this process several chain features were identified that the researchers believed helped indicate whether or not a re-finding task was present in the chain. These are shown in Table 2.

As the features used to manually determine re-finding behavior were relatively straightforward and experimenters achieved a high-level of agreement, we attempted to recreate our coding behavior automatically with a heuristic-based algorithm. By utilizing the indicators listed in Table 2, we were able to calculate an overall score for each chain. We applied weights to the features as they occurred in the logs and normalized the score by the number of interactions. At this stage the weights (see Table 2) were derived from our impression of their importance in our own personal classification process and adjusted by trial and error to achieve

Indicator	Sign	Weight
Quicksearch Query submitted	+	20
Advanced search facilities opened	+	30
Query to advanced search submitted	+	30
Particularly old, previously read message access	+	20
Messages in folder sorted	+	8
Folder opened	+	0
New message access	-	10
Message re-access shortly after accessing	-	0
Short-duration chains	-	NI

Table 2: Indicators of Re-finding behavior (NI = not implemented in algorithm)

best results against our judgements. To account for situations where the user returned to read emails more thoroughly shortly after they had been originally received, we assigned a neutral weight to selected messages that had been accessed recently (in the previous 48 hours). We chose this value because although it is certainly feasible that people may have to re-find something they have accessed or read less than two days previously, in particular people who receive large amounts of mail, it is possible that the message could be clicked on without involving any re-finding behavior, which would lead to the detection of many chains that do not contain tasks. Given the frequency with which we observed this behavior in the logs without any other hints of re-finding behavior in the chains, we felt it better to make a trade off in terms of small loss of recall in favor of a large benefit in precision. After some experimentation we settled on an overall threshold score of 1.8, i.e, if a chain had a score of 1.8 or higher based on the weights in Table 2, the algorithm classified the chain as containing re-finding behavior.

4.2 Creating an Annotated Dataset

To evaluate the performance of the algorithm we performed a small additional user study to create an annotated dataset. In a second step we used what we learned from this study to create a fuller dataset more suitable for training models by performing a second critical incident study where the participants confirmed or rejected chains classified by a version of our algorithm optimized for recall. The following subsections outline this work in detail.

4.2.1 Critical Incident Study 1: Manual Logging

We performed a critical-incident study where 5 of the original participants repeated their participation, but used a modified version of the extension that allowed them to indicate when re-finding tasks started and ended. The only difference between this version and the original, which used the standard Thunderbird interface, was a button located in the top-right corner of the window that the participants were to click before they started and after they completed re-finding tasks. To help remind the participants that they should log their tasks, a pop-up message appeared every time the email client window was refocused. Upon marking a task as complete, a pop-up electronic form queried the participant regarding some simple information about the task (what they were looking for, if they were successful, how difficult the task was and how often they need to re-find this information).

We collected data for approximately 2 weeks. The outcome of this additional experiment was a dataset of naturalistic logs – as in the original study – but this dataset was annotated with interactions we knew to be associated with re-finding tasks. We refer to this as dataset 1 (DS1). Running the heuristic algorithm on DS1 achieved relatively high recall (0.77), although precision was lower (0.62). The algorithm marked 11.5% of the interaction chains as re-finding tasks, which was slightly higher than the percentage annotated by the participants themselves.

To optimize performance we wanted to train a model using a machine learning approach. There were, however, a number of problems with our annotated dataset that made it unsuitable for this purpose. First, the population was small and relatively homogeneous. Second, one user was dominant in the logs, which was fine for testing the performance of the heuristic model, but not for training a new model. Third, we had concerns about the use of the log button approach. It is possible that despite giving frequent reminders that participants may have forgotten to log re-finding tasks. To deal with these issues and provide a dataset suitable for training and testing an improved model, we designed and performed a second critical-incident study, which exploited what we had learned so far and the heuristic algorithm we had tested on the first dataset.

4.2.2 Critical Incident Study 2: Automatic Detection

We integrated a version of our algorithm into the Thunderbird extension, allowing re-finding behavior to be detected live as the user interacted with their messages and providing the opportunity to question the participants on their behavior when the algorithm estimated a re-finding task to have taken place. We chose a version of our algorithm with high recall by weighting all re-accessed messages equally, regardless if they had been recently accessed. This naturally meant sacrificing precision. On DS1 this algorithm achieved a recall of 0.93 and precision of 0.18.

Another change we had to make for this study was respect to soft chain boundaries. In a live re-finding setting, a gap of 5 minutes would have been impractical as we needed to detect re-finding tasks as close as possible to them happening in order to avoid the forgetting problems we believe may have occurred during the manual-logging study. Consequently, the algorithm was run on chains that preceded gaps in interactions lasting 40 seconds or longer (which after piloting we found to be an appropriate time gap) or preceding the user switching the focus to another window. When a re-finding task was detected, the participant was asked whether or not they had been attempting to re-find. If the response was positive we questioned them on the task they were trying to perform. If the response was negative, we asked about the participants' activities, i.e. what was the behavior which the algorithm had detected as re-finding.

9 participants, only one of whom did not take part in the initial study, responded to the algorithm's prompts for a period of between 7 and 14 days during normal email usage. This approach allowed 118 re-finding chains to be detected and confirmed by the participants. We refer to this as dataset 2 (DS2). To achieve the largest possible dataset for training and testing models, we combined DS1 and DS2 (removing the interactions from the dominant participant in DS1). Although there will be some noise in the collection (e.g. we suspect some missing (forgotten to be recorded) tasks in the first dataset and there was a possibility that a 40 sec interaction gap may have meant missing interactions from tasks in the second collection), attaining a perfect set is almost impossible for this problem and the combined dataset provides a solid basis from which to train and test models.

The combined dataset (DS3) was generated from relatively heterogeneous sample of the original population and is of sufficient size for a problem of this nature. Using a soft-boundary of 5 minutes the dataset consists of 1,124 chains, 162 of which contain re-finding. Also, from the questionnaire responses in the critical incident studies, we know the dataset contains a broad range of re-finding tasks, task difficulties, familiarity with tasks and time-lapses between accessing and re-accessing the sought-after message.

5. MODELLING WORK

5.1 Model Selection

Our problem can be defined as one of identifying whether a chain contains or does not contain a re-finding task. Our evidence to base this decision on is a set of numerical features. We decided that it would be advantageous to focus the model on achieving high precision scores so as to gain the most accurate understanding of re-finding behavior possible. While there are a large number of classification models available, due to the binary nature of the class and our requirement for high precision, the most natural choice is a logistic regression model. In such a model the class of the dependent variable y_i (in this case, whether a chain contains or does not contain a re-finding behavior) is assumed to be drawn independently from a Bernoulli distribution. The probability of "success" of each Bernoulli trial is assumed to be related to the explanatory variables.

This model is a special case of the class of models known as generalized linear models as the explanatory variables are each multiplied by their own coefficient and then combined linearly. If there are n features in the data then we typically have a coefficient vector θ of size $n+1$ in order to allow for an intercept in the linear equation. This also requires that the feature vector be augmented by adding a value of 1 in the first position. Given our vector of coefficients and a new data point x^i we calculate the output of the linear model as follows:

$$\hat{y^i} = \sum_{j=1}^{n+1} \theta_j \times x^i_j = \theta^T x^i \quad (1)$$

In the case of logistic regression we wish to bound the output of the linear model to be between 0 and 1 (i.e. to ensure the output is a valid probability). To achieve this we apply the logistic function to the output from the linear equation above:

$$P(y^i = 1 | x^i; \theta) = \frac{1}{1 + e^{-\hat{y^i}}} \quad (2)$$

The values of the coefficients in the vector θ are trained by maximizing the log likelihood over the training set using iteratively re-weighted least squares (IRLS) [17]. This algorithm will return a close approximation to the best coefficient values in order to minimize the classification error given the observed data. However due to the relative sparsity and high-dimensionality of the data and the potential for collinearity between the explanatory variables this model is prone to over-fitting. In order to prevent such over-fitting we can add regularization terms to the end of the linear model. These regularization terms are added to penalize large parameter values and "shrink" the estimates of these coefficients towards zero, relative to the maximum likelihood estimate. It has been shown by experiment that L1 regularization works well for such models [19]. In L1 regularization (also known as "Lasso" regularization) the penalty term encourages the sum of the absolute values of the coefficients to be small. As mentioned earlier, we can fit the parameters of the model by maximizing the log likelihood of the data:

$$argmax_{\theta} \sum_{i=1}^{m} logP(y^i = 1|x^i; \theta) - \alpha R(\theta) \quad (3)$$

In the above optimization problem we have added a function $R(\theta)$ which is the regularization term and a constant α which can be varied and allows us to control how much regularization to apply. Note that if either $R(\theta)$ or α are 0 then the models decompose back to the un-regularized version. In L1 regularization the term function $R(\theta)$ is simply: $\sum_{j=1}^{n+1} |\theta_j|$.

To optimize the value of α we train a model over a range of values and then test each model on held-out testing data over a number of folds (cross-validation). To choose the optimal value of α we simply choose the value which maximizes an objective function, in this case the log likelihood of the held-out data.

5.2 Feature selection and model parameters

The manual analyses above form the basis for the model feature selection. In addition to the set of features listed in Table 2 we also examined a number of features that were impossible to detect accurately by a human assessor (e.g., the maximum time gap between interactions in the chain, the average age of messages and the number of unique messages).

While L1 regularization has the proven ability to automatically select relevant features it is still sensible to first perform some manual exploratory data analysis to identify useful features. By comparing each feature individually in the training data over the 2 classes we can gain an understanding of which will be useful as predictors in the model. In particular, if the feature values are significantly different when conditioned on each of the 2 class labels then it is likely that they will be useful indicators. We can then rely on the regularization to deal with issues of over-fitting and collinearity.

This analysis can be performed by either visually comparing plots as shown in Figure 1 or by using an appropriate statistical test. For example, the MaxInteractionGap feature shown in the figure visually appears longer on average for re-finding tasks and this observation is confirmed by a highly significant Wilcoxon signed-rank test ($p \ll 0.01$)

Using this methodology we created a series of competing models and tested their performance over the datasets obtained from the critical incident studies. The results from this are presented in Table 3. Since we are most interested in the accuracy of our predictions rather than coverage we chose $F_{0.5}$ as the metric on which to determine the utility of each model. The $F_{0.5}$ score is the harmonic mean of the precision and recall where the precision is given twice the relative weight of the recall. The results show that model 3 returns consistently the best score over the labelled datasets and we therefore use that for the analysis of our larger dataset.

It turns out in evaluating these models that the more parsimonious models perform better overall. This is preferable

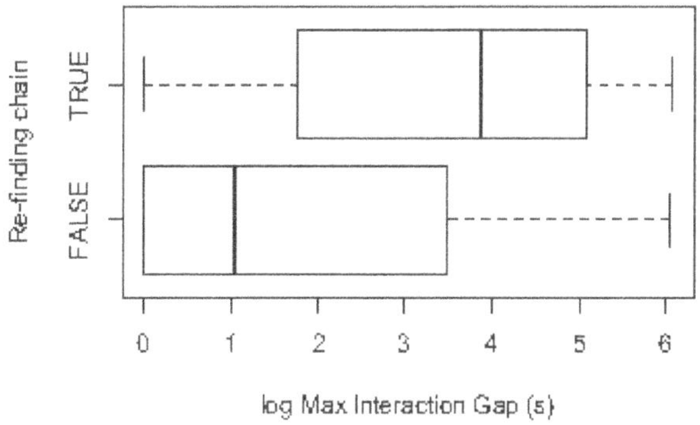

Figure 1: Boxplots of Max Interaction Gap conditioned on whether it is a re-finding chain. Note that in this case we have taken the log of the interaction gap in order to make the plot clearer.

Model	$F_{0.5}$ DS1	$F_{0.5}$ DS2	$F_{0.5}$ DS3	P DS3	R DS3
fitted 1	0.7849	0.6605	0.6469	0.72	0.46
fitted 2	0.7452	0.6801	0.6467	0.74	0.43
fitted 3	**0.8615**	**0.6803**	**0.7200**	**0.9**	0.4
heuristic	0.6451	0.6582	0.5993	0.61	0.56

Table 3: Fitted logistic regression model performance

as they are also less likely to be over-fit when compared to models that make use of more factors and are on the whole more generalizable. Fitted model 3 uses the number of old messages which have not recently been reaccessed (*noOld*), the number of times search facilities were used (*search*), the maximum gap between interactions (*maxGap*) and the length of the chain (*length*) as indicators of re-finding behavior as follows:

$$P(y|x;\theta) = logit(1.689 + 0.365noOld + 1.763search$$
$$+2.44 \times 10^{-5}maxGap - 3.18 \times 10^{-3}length)$$

It is interesting to note that the model fitting process has utilized features in a similar way to the earlier heuristic approach. This suggests that many of the assumptions made in that algorithm based on manual analysis of logs were correct. Full details of all models will be published in a technical report.

5.3 Scope and limitations of these analyses

Although our best model (fitted 3) is only able to detect approximately 40% of re-finding tasks, we argue that, from the perspective of our research aims, the tasks that the model is able to detect are those most important and interesting to analyze. Wilcoxon SR tests on the training data show that the tasks missed by the model were significantly shorter than those detected both in terms of number of interactions (median = 3 , IQR = 6 vs 10, IQR = 12, $p \ll 0.01$) and in terms of time (median time in mins= 0.37, IQR 3.05 vs 3.31, IQR 7.75, $p \ll 0.01$). These tasks also contained far fewer non-recently accessed messages that were received more than two days previously (median = 0, IQR 1 vs median = 2, IQR 3, $p \ll 0.01$). All of this evidence combines to suggest that the tasks our model misses are those which are fairly straightforward to complete and less interesting to study in terms of learning about the problems people have and the behavior people employ to resolve these problems.

It is also worth noting that all models showed better performance on dataset 1 (DS1). We believe that the tasks that were difficult to detect in DS2 would have been less likely to cue the participant to log the task for DS1. In the creation of DS2 the participants were provided with an active cue i.e. they were directly asked if they were re-finding something, explaining the presence of such tasks in the collection and accounting for the lower precision scores for DS2.

We must acknowledge that it is possible that multiple re-finding tasks could be present within a single detected chain and / or re-finding tasks could cross chains. Analyzing the manually annotated logs in dataset 1 shows that this happened in 6% and 12% of chains respectively. Additionally, we also need to concede that there will be interactions in some chains not to do with re-finding. Analyzing DS1 where the annotations will be most accurate, shows that there is a median of 3.5 (IQR=4.75) non-re-finding interactions (that occur before and / or after re-finding) for chains correctly identified as containing re-finding behavior. Both of these points should be taken into account when reading the analyses in the following section.

In the remainder of this paper we analyze the chains classified as re-finding using fitted model 3 on the full unannotated dataset. We refer to such chains as re-finding chains. We start by looking at general characteristics of re-finding behavior, looking at how prevalent re-finding is and what the associated behavior looks like. We then look at how specific features of the email client were used during re-finding, providing a better understanding of how people re-find, as well as the problems encountered during re-finding. Finally, we examine the distribution of re-finding over time to establish how often the same messages are re-found and present some initial analyses regarding how the frequency of re-access and the time between accessing and re-accessing influence behavior.

6. ANALYSING RE-FINDING BEHAVIOR

6.1 Overview of Re-finding

Although previous studies of re-finding behavior have shown re-finding to be prevalent (e.g. approx. 40% of search engine queries are re-finding queries [23] and on average 4.4 queries per day are submitted to desktop search engines [9]), the metrics used in these studies are inappropriate to gauge the frequency of re-finding in the context of email use. Instead we look at more useful metrics for our purpose – the percentage of chains that contain re-finding and how frequently these chains occur with respect to the number of days email was used.

According to our best model, 6.08% of interaction chains contain re-finding [95%CI = 5.78-6.39][2] and this increases to 15.2% [95%CI = 14.45-15.96] if we adjust the figure to account for the training data recall score of 0.4. Examining the regularity of tasks across participants showed huge variance. Cluster analysis[3] revealed two clear groups of users. The first group (n=33) re-found relatively infrequently (median = 0.25 tasks per day of email use[4]). The second group (n=14) re-found much more regularly (median = 2.193 tasks per day). The cluster of users who frequently re-found had significantly more mails overall but made use of email on a very similar number of days during the study period as the users in the other cluster.

There is very little in the literature regarding how much time people spend re-finding, but to help understand the cost of re-finding on the lives of the participants, we felt it important to look at the lengths of the re-finding chains in minutes.

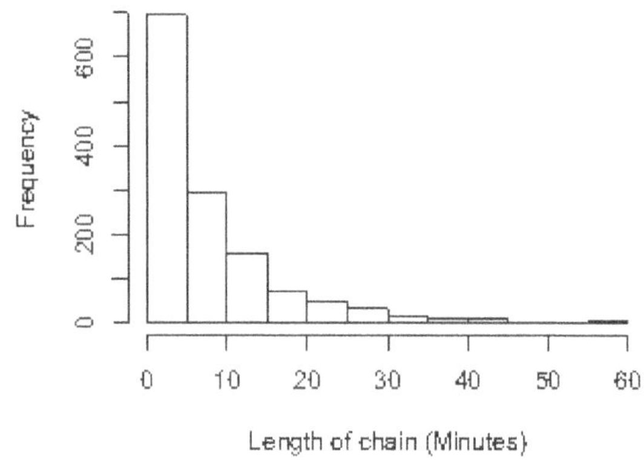

Figure 2: The distribution of re-finding chain lengths in minutes

There was no significant difference between the time taken to complete tasks for the two clusters of users. The distribution of chain lengths was Zipfian for both groups with both distributions exhibiting a long and heavy tail. Figure 2 shows the distribution for all re-finding chains, the median chain length was 4.05 minutes, with the longest chain lasting 71.7 minutes. The number of interactions in the re-finding chains follows a similar pattern. Again, the distribution is Zipfian with the median interaction count being 11 interactions and the longest chain containing 501 interactions. These findings suggest that the majority of re-finding tasks seem to be quite short, mostly taking a few minutes. On occasion, however, our data suggest people can spend much longer looking for emails they need. The Zipfian distribution is extremely important with respect to this work with nearly all of the analyses we perform conforming to this distribution (inverse power law). Both the median age of messages re-finding chains and the number of messages viewed within these chains follow this distribution and both exhibit long and heavy tails. The median age of messages is 14.7 days (max = 2,430) and the median number of messages viewed is 4 (max = 290).

All of the statistical analyses in this section indicate that the majority of re-finding tasks are short and straight-forward. Nevertheless, there is evidence that some tasks cause problems. Just how problematic re-finding emails can be is underlined by examining the Message Uncertainty Ratio (MUR) for re-finding chains, i.e. the ratio of unique messages viewed to the total number of messages viewed. Only 34.07% of chains have MUR of 1, i.e. that all of the messages were viewed only once. 13.02% have an MUR greater than or equal to 2. This suggests that people are pretty regularly

[2]using binomial proportion confidence intervals [95%] assuming a normal approximation

[3]We used hierarchical agglomerative clustering using Ward's method, which looks at cluster analysis as an analysis of variance problem, instead of using distance metrics or measures of association. Analyzing the resulting dendrogram showed many sub-clusters, but in order to keep analyses simple we chose to look at the two main clusters.

[4]These figures are recall adjusted

getting lost, viewing on average every message in the chain at least twice in over 13% of re-finding tasks. The maximum MUR is 12, which is incredibly high.

As a next step we examine the re-finding chains to establish the approaches taken and the features of the email client people use in order to re-find. First, we examine the use of folders in re-finding before moving to analyze the use of sorting and finally the search queries submitted. The analyses help build up an understanding of the way people use the features of current email clients to re-find and reveals some problems they have.

6.2 The Use of Folders in Re-finding

While there is considerable literature on how and why people create folder organizations [16, 29], there has been no work on how people tend to use folders when re-finding content. Our data allows us to investigate this issue. Out of our population, 14 participants described themselves as being no-filers, 16 described themselves as Filers and 17 described themselves as Spring-cleaners. The median number of folders (other than the "default" folders, i.e. inbox, outbox, drafts and trash) was 13 with counts ranging from 0 all the way up to 192.

Our data indicate that when the participants had folders, these folders tended to be used regularly during re-finding. 71.07% of re-finding chains for users with folders involved opening a folder other than the inbox. If we look at the proportion of re-finding chains where folders other than the inbox were opened we can see (as would be expected) that people with more folders are more likely to look in folders other than the inbox when re-finding. Figure 3 shows how folder usage increases with the number of folders in the user's collection. As we expected, there appears to be a strong linear relationship between the number of folders a users has and how many folders they look at when re-finding. This visual relationship is confirmed by the linear model of folder usage given folder count having an adjusted R^2 statistic of 0.9162 (F-statistic=318.2, $p \ll 0.05$).

For users with more than the default folders, the median number of unique folders (other than the inbox) in re-finding chains involving folders is 2 (IQR 2), suggesting that people are quite good at using folders to re-find. Nevertheless, the data show that 38.17% of these chains contained 2 or more unique folders (other than the inbox) indicating that they regularly first look in an incorrect folder before moving to the correct one. In 21.86% of chains they look at 3 or more folders. Again this follows an Zipfian distribution, with the maximum number of unique folders in a chain being 26. 145 (10.7%) chains involved 5 or more unique folders and 36 (2.7%) instances of chains involved 10 or more unique folders. This indicates that there are certainly situations where individuals are very poor at judging which folder to look in and must check many folders before locating the correct one or giving up.

Further, when we examine Folder Uncertainty Ratio (FUR), i.e. the number of folders opened with respect to the number of unique folders opened, there is evidence that the participants were occasionally becoming disorientated when looking within their folders to re-find. 29.5% of chains involving folders other than the inbox had an FUR score >1 and 8.67% had an FUR score ≥ 2. The maximum FUR score was 4.67. All of this evidence combines to show that quite often the participants were looking in the same folders multiple times when re-finding, suggesting disorientation.

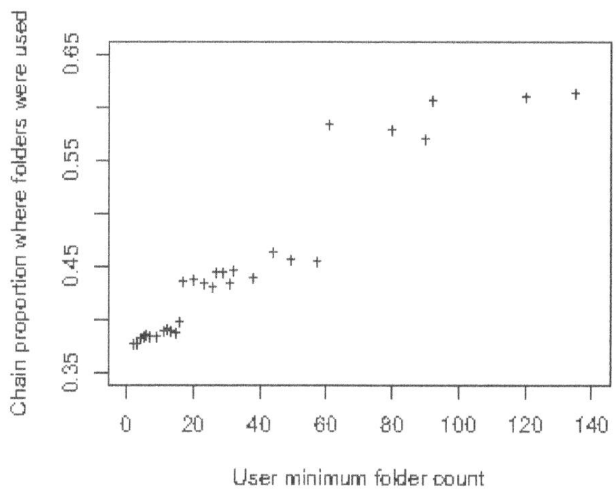

Figure 3: Plot of folder usage against number of folders in the collection

6.3 The Use of Sorting in Re-finding

Our data shows surprisingly little use of sorting during re-finding tasks. Only 1.4% of the detected re-finding chains contained a sort operation[5]. This contrasts with the findings of investigations of desktop search tool usage, which have shown users to like sorting the results of desktop searches [9, 7]. It also contrasts with the findings of Elsweiler and colleagues [12], who performed a laboratory-based study to investigate email re-finding behavior. In their study sorting was a popular means of narrowing the information space to facilitate re-access by browsing. Nevertheless, there was no inline "quick-search" facility available in their interface and as this was the only difference between their interface and ours, this could mean that searching is a preferable means to narrow down the search space.

Of the 492 total instances of sorting within re-finding chains, 318 (64.6%) were sorts on the date column and 72 (14.6%) were on the sender column. Again this contrasts with the study in [12] where the sender was the most common attribute to sort on. As we show in the following section this is the most frequently queried on attribute, perhaps indicating that people like to re-find based on the sender of the message, but prefer to use a search query to facilitate this when the option is available.

6.4 Analyzing Submitted Queries

Searching seems to be an extremely popular re-finding tactic. 93.8 % of re-finding chains contained at least one search query. The mean number of queries per re-finding chain was 2.29 (max=21) with the distribution again reflecting the basic Zipfian trend reported above.

The queries submitted were extremely short. Most (90.88%) were single words and only 0.8% had a length greater than

[5]This finding is not an artifact of the model as the number of sorting interactions in the dataset as a whole was also extremely low

2 terms, with the mean number of terms in the queries being 1.10. The mean character length of all queries was 5.87 and many of the queries were partial words. This is much shorter than reported in the literature with 1.6 words being reported for desktop search [9, 7] and 12.1 characters for webpage re-finding [25]. We found a trend that the length of the query in words increased the later in the re-finding chain they appeared, perhaps indicating that after failing with shorter queries, the queries tended to be reformulated by appending characters or terms. This result aligns with previous work by [25] who found that web re-finding queries tended to get longer later in the session.

Table 4 shows the frequency with which queries were submitted to different fields. As would be expected the default option, i.e. to submit queries to both the "subject" or "sender" fields, was the most common option. Like previous work, people's names were highly prevalent in the queries, although the "to or cc" field was very infrequently chosen. We thought that some fields may be used as a backup strategy after an initial strategy had failed e.g. that the user may start by trying to search using the default "subject" and "sender" option and if this failed try to search on the entire message. Examining the query position in the chain against the field, however, failed to provide any evidence to support this hypothesis.

Field	Count	Percentage
subject	231	7.49
sender	585	18.97
subject or send (default)	1677	54.38
entire message	412	13.36
to or cc	179	5.8

Table 4: Distribution of Query Fields

In terms of query performance, over one quarter of all queries (25.17%) failed i.e. returned no hits at all. Contrastingly, many queries returned a large number of hits. Over one third (33.78%) returned over 20 results (median = 7 and the maximum 17110). 8.09% of queries returned a single hit. To examine what these outcomes mean in terms of performance we looked at whether or not they tended to represent the last query submitted in a chain (a possible indicator of satisfaction with the outcome). Of the queries returning 0 hits only 12.85% were the last query in the chain. In other words, the user tended to reformulate the query afterwards. However, only 40.78% of those queries with 1 hit were the last query in the chain, a lower percentage than those returning >1 hits (51.57%). This suggests that returning 1 hit is not a good indicator of query success.

The median message click/query ratio was 3 with most chains having a ratio of 1 (32.44%). However, in 15.3% of chains containing queries this ratio was greater than 10, again indicating that there are many instances where re-finding is not straightforward and people are resorting to orienteering strategies [24] in order to find their emails. This behavior is different from that for web-page re-finding where the majority of re-finding queries are single click queries [25].

6.5 Re-finding Over Time

In line with previous work on web-page re-finding with search engines [25], we looked at how individual messages were re-found over time. We used an equivalent definition of re-finding to that used in this previous work, defining a re-found message to be any message viewed that has been read before and appears within a chain classified as re-finding.

Using this definition we found that only 3.59% of all messages received by participants were later re-found. However, 39.1% of all re-found messages were re-found again within the 4 month study period. Although this may sound reasonably high, it is in fact much lower than the figure reported for web-page re-finding (66.1% for 1 month of data)[25].

The vast majority of emails were only re-found relatively infrequently (85% were re-found less than 6 times (median=2). Nevertheless, this again followed the familiar long and heavy tailed Zipfian distribution, with messages being re-found up to 75 times within the study period. This demonstrates how email messages can stay in regular active use over long time periods. Tyler and Teevan discovered a similar long-tailed distribution for re-re-finding web-pages [25]. They also found that re-finding tends to happen in bursts, with most re-finding occurring only a short time after another instance of re-finding. We found similar burstiness in email re-finding behavior. Out of all of the re-found messages that would be later re-re-found 70.09% were re-found again within 24 hours and 87.41% were re-found again within 1 week.

Intuitively, our data suggest that the participants became better at re-finding the more often they had to re-find a message. For messages which are frequently re-found the length of chains are significantly shorter. For example if we compare the median length of chains containing emails re-found more than the median number of times (median times re-found = 2) with the length of chains for emails re-found the median number of times or less we can see a large difference (55 against 43). The two distributions of chain lengths are confirmed to be significantly different according to a Wilcoxon SR test ($p \ll 0.01$). We found a very similar relationship between the length of chains and the time gap between re-finding and re-finding again. In a similar vain to the previous analysis we use the median gap length as a divider, in this case a gap of 3.4 hours. We found that the mean chain length for emails with a time gap less than the median was significantly shorter than for emails with a gap larger than the median (52 against 57). This finding is backed-up by a highly significant Wilcoxon SR test ($p=0.0008$) and concurs with evidence from the literature [13, 11].

7. SUMMARY AND DISCUSSION

7.1 Summary of main finding

Our findings with respect to the re-finding chains can be summarized as follows:

- The frequency of re-finding behavior varies greatly

We found 2 main clusters of users: 1 cluster tended to re-find relatively infrequently (on average once every 4 days) and the other much more regularly (on average more than 2 times per day).

- Email re-finding can be very challenging

Many re-finding tasks were short and straight-forward, but there was also strong evidence for tasks being difficult and in some cases very difficult. Indicators for this included longer chains, looking at more messages and in more folders, as well as disorientation (MUR and FUR).

- Orienteering was a common email re-finding strategy

Orienteering behavior was a common re-finding strategy for our participants. Most queries were very short and often consisted of partial words or names. Further, the number of hits returned by the query was not a good indicator of performance, and there tended to be a large number of message clicks per query submitted. All of this suggests that the preferred method of re-finding was to narrow the search space with a short query and browse for clues that facilitated navigating to the email required. This combination of searching and browsing distinguishes email re-finding behavior from file re-finding where there is strong evidence that people prefer to navigate purely spatially to their information [3, 4] and web page re-finding where although orienteering is a common tactic [24], the evidence shows that people prefer to use search engines rather than use spatial-navigation facilities, such as bookmark organizations [5, 14].

- The same messages tend to re-found time and again

When analyzing re-finding over time, we found that many (39%) re-found emails were re-found again, most of which (70%) within a day. There was also evidence that re-finding messages becomes easier with frequency and becomes more difficult the longer the time gap between accessing and re-accessing.

7.2 Design Implications

Although our findings suggest that much of email re-finding is straight-forward, there are many occasions when it can be hard. We found evidence for people spending long time periods re-finding, submitting long query chains and getting very lost. It is clear that extra help would be beneficial in such situations. Whilst we have only performed initial, high-level analyses on the dataset, there are a number of ways the understanding of re-finding developed in this paper can be used to improve the re-finding experience in email clients.

- Minimizing Disorientation

We discovered that a real problem people seem to have when performing difficult email re-finding tasks is that they become disorientated and look in the same folders multiple times and repeatedly check the same messages. One way email interfaces could provide support in such situations would be to offer a search-trail metaphor. The system could keep a record of folders and messages that have been viewed within a chain and these could be highlighted in some way, perhaps by using color. Another solution could be to provide the user with the option to filter out folders already viewed within a search, i.e remove them from view. Both the highlighting and filtering concepts could be toggled on / off by the user as required.

- Supporting Orienteering behavior

Our findings suggest that people tend to prefer orienteering strategies when re-finding email messages. There was also evidence that users regularly require to view the content of numerous messages before finding what they need. Perhaps this is an indication that the standard representation of messages, message meta-data in columns, may not be enough for the user to judge the relevance of a message. To facilitate better message previewing, we may need to provide summary snippets for emails similar to those used by web search engines. The number of clicks per query is much lower for web-page re-finding with search engines and better document representations may be one reason for this.

Incorporating landmarks, which are an important part of how people orientate themselves in physical environments, may be another interface feature that could assist orienteering behavior. Our findings endorse the approach taken by Ringel and her colleagues [21] who investigated how temporal landmarks could be incorporated into email re-finding interfaces. Other interface features, similar to those suggested in [20], could allow the user to manually annotate connections between messages to allow them to be identified and used as landmarks. However, given the existing costs of processing email messages and the problems this causes [29], it seems an automatic means of achieving this would be preferable. Our dataset could be used to analyze if certain messages are used as landmarks i.e. if re-accessing particular emails lead to re-accessing others. If this is the case, annotating these messages automatically may assist the user to successfully navigate their collection.

- Highlighting Re-found messages

We showed that messages that were re-found tended to be re-found again, most within short time periods. It may, therefore, be worthwhile highlighting messages that have recently been re-found to make them easier to locate or by providing a means to filter to these messages, given that people are normally able to identify when they last accessed a message [10]. A useful extension of this work would be try and predict more accurately which messages might be likely to be re-found again. We talk about this idea in more detail below.

8. CONCLUSIONS AND FUTURE WORK

In this paper we have presented a naturalistic study of email re-finding and described our efforts at isolating re-finding behavior from the logs. By performing two additional user studies we were able to create an annotated dataset and train and test various models, showing that re-finding could be detected with good accuracy. Examining the resulting re-finding chains allowed us to uncover interesting aspects of email re-finding behavior that until now had been been impossible to study.

The ability to accurately isolate re-finding behavior from email interaction logs opens up the possibility to learn about many aspects of behavior using datasets such as ours. We are currently applying for ethics permission to release an anonymous version of our dataset to the research community. Below we outline some of our ideas of how our work could be extended.

Here we presented some initial high-level analyses that looked at the use of specific email client features (e.g. folders, sorting, searching) in isolation. It would be useful to investigate behavior at chain level to determine how different features are used in combination and to determine how strategies evolve over time. For example, do users converge on an optimal approach to re-finding when a particular message is regularly re-found? This could be analyzed in a number of ways, e.g. by employing search trails [26] or modeling behavior as a probabilistic model [12].

The logs could also be used to better understand when and why re-finding tasks are difficult. This could be achieved by looking for relationships between context and user variables and the indicators that we uncovered for task difficulty (chain length, message and folder uncertainty etc.). This kind of analysis on naturalistic data would complement similar analyses that have been performed on lab-study data [6, 11].

We mentioned above the potential benefit of being able to predict which messages are likely to be re-found in the future. In this paper we identified two factors which may influence the probability of a message needing to be re-found in the future - whether or not the message had been re-found before and the time that had elapsed since re-finding. We are currently building on these findings to learn if other message or user properties can help predict if and when a message may be needed again in the future.

Acknowledgments

The first author was supported by the Alexander von Humboldt Foundation, Germany.

9. REFERENCES

[1] A. Aula, N. Jhaveri, and M. Käki. Information search and reaccess strategies of experienced web users. In *Proc. 14th IntŠl Conf. World Wide Web*, pages 583–592. ACM Press, 2005.

[2] O. Bälter. Keystroke level analysis of email message organization. In *Proc. SIGCHI conference on Human factors in computing systems*, pages 105–112, 2000.

[3] D. K. Barreau and B. Nardi. Finding and reminding: File organization from the desktop. *ACM SIGCHI Bulletin*, 27(3):39–43, 1995.

[4] O. Bergman, R. Beyth-Marom, R. Nachmias, N. Gradovitch, and S. Whittaker. Improved search engines and navigation preference in personal information management. *ACM Trans. Inf. Syst.*, 26(4):1–24, 2008.

[5] R. Boardman and M. A. Sasse. "stuff goes into the computer and doesn't come out": a cross-tool study of personal information management. In *CHI '04: Proc. SIGCHI*, pages 583–590, 2004.

[6] R. G. Capra and M. A. Perez-Quinones. Using web search engines to find and refind information. *Computer*, 38(10):36–42, 2005.

[7] E. Cutrell, D. Robbins, S. Dumais, and R. Sarin. Fast, flexible filtering with phlat. In *Proc. SIGCHI conference on Human Factors in computing systems*, pages 261–270, 2006.

[8] N. Ducheneaut and V. Bellotti. E-mail as habitat: an exploration of embedded personal information management. *interactions*, 8(5):30–38, 2001.

[9] S. Dumais, E. Cutrell, J. Cadiz, G. Jancke, R. Sarin, and D.C. Robbins. Stuff i've seen: a system for personal information retrieval and re-use. In *Proc. ACM SIGIR '03:*, pages 72–79, 2003.

[10] D. Elsweiler, M. Baillie, and I. Ruthven. Exploring memory in email refinding. *ACM Trans. Inf. Syst.*, 26(4):1–36, 2008.

[11] D. Elsweiler, M. Baillie, and I. Ruthven. What makes re-finding information diffcult? a study of email re-finding. In *Proc. ECIR 2011*, 2011.

[12] D. Elsweiler, M. Hacker, and S. Mandl. Visualising pim behaviour with markov chains. In *Personal Information Management Workshop at Annual Meeting of American Society for Information Science (ASIST 2009)*, 2009.

[13] D. Elsweiler and I. Ruthven. Towards task-based personal information management evaluations. In *Proc. ACM SIGIR conference on Research and development in information retrieval*, pages 23–30, 2007.

[14] W. Jones, H. Bruce, and S. Dumais. How do people get back to information on the web? how can they do it better? *Proc. INTERACT*, 2003.

[15] W. Jones and J. Teevan, editors. *Personal Information Management.* Seattle: University of Washington Press, 2007.

[16] T. W. Malone. How do people organize their desks?: Implications for the design of office information systems. *ACM Trans. Inf. Syst.*, 1(1):99–112, 1983.

[17] P. McCullagh and J. A. Nelder. *Generalized Linear Models (Second Edition).* Chapman and Hall, 1989.

[18] B. McKenzie and A. Cockburn. An empirical analysis of web page revisitation. In *Proc. of the HICSS34*, 2001.

[19] A. Y. Ng. Feature selection, l1 vs. l2 regularization, and rotational invariance. In *Proceedings of the twenty-first international conference on Machine learning*, ICML '04, pages 78–, New York, NY, USA, 2004. ACM.

[20] V. L. O'Day and R. Jeffries. Orienteering in an information landscape: How information seekers get from here to there. In *Proceedings of INTERCHI '93*, pages 438–445, 1993.

[21] M. Ringel, E. Cutrell, S. Dumais, and E. Horvitz. Milestones in time: The value of landmarks in retrieving information from personal stores. In *Proc. INTERACT 2003*, pages 184–191, 2003.

[22] C. Silverstein, M. Henzinger, H. Marais, and M. Moricz. Analysis of a very large alta vista query log. Technical report, SRC, 1998. Technical Note 1998-014.

[23] J. Teevan, E. Adar, R. Jones, and M. Potts. Information re-retrieval: Repeat queries in yahoo's logs. In *Proc. SIGIR '07*, 2007.

[24] J. Teevan, C. Alvarado, M. S. Ackerman, and D. R. Karger. The perfect search engine is not enough: a study of orienteering behavior in directed search. In *Proc. SIGCHI conference on Human factors in computing systems*, pages 415–422, 2004.

[25] S. K. Tyler and J. Teevan. Large scale query log analysis of re-finding. In *Proc. WSDM '10*, 2010.

[26] R. W. White and S. M. Drucker. Investigating behavioral variability in web search. In *Proc. international conference on WWW*, pages 21–30, New York, NY, USA, 2007. ACM.

[27] S. Whittaker, V. Bellotti, and J. Gwizdka. *Personal Information Management*, chapter Everything through Email, pages 167–189. Seattle: University of Washington Press., 2007.

[28] S. Whittaker, Q. Jones, and L. Terveen. Contact management: Identifying contacts to support long term communication. In *Proc. CSCW'02*, pages 216–225, 2002.

[29] S. Whittaker and C. Sidner. Email overload: exploring personal information management of email. In *CHI '96: Proc SIGCHI conference on Human factors in computing systems*, pages 276–283, 1996.

People Searching for People: Analysis of a People Search Engine Log

Wouter Weerkamp
ISLA, University of Amsterdam
w.weerkamp@uva.nl

Richard Berendsen
ISLA, University of Amsterdam
r.w.berendsen@uva.nl

Bogomil Kovachev
ISLA, University of Amsterdam
b.k.kovachev@uva.nl

Edgar Meij
ISLA, University of Amsterdam
edgar.meij@uva.nl

Krisztian Balog
NTNU Trondheim
krisztian.balog@idi.ntnu.no

Maarten de Rijke
ISLA, University of Amsterdam
derijke@uva.nl

ABSTRACT

Recent years show an increasing interest in vertical search: searching within a particular type of information. Understanding what people search for in these "verticals" gives direction to research and provides pointers for the search engines themselves. In this paper we analyze the search logs of one particular vertical: people search engines. Based on an extensive analysis of the logs of a search engine geared towards finding people, we propose a classification scheme for people search at three levels: (a) queries, (b) sessions, and (c) users. For queries, we identify three types, (i) event-based high-profile queries (people that become "popular" because of an event happening), (ii) regular high-profile queries (celebrities), and (iii) low-profile queries (other, less-known people). We present experiments on automatic classification of queries. On the session level, we observe five types: (i) family sessions (users looking for relatives), (ii) event sessions (querying the main players of an event), (iii) spotting sessions (trying to "spot" different celebrities online), (iv) polymerous sessions (sessions without a clear relation between queries), and (v) repetitive sessions (query refinement and copying). Finally, for users we identify four types: (i) monitors, (ii) spotters, (iii) followers, and (iv) polymers.

Our findings not only offer insight into search behavior in people search engines, but they are also useful to identify future research directions and to provide pointers for search engine improvements.

Categories and Subject Descriptors

H.3.3 [**Information Storage and Retrieval**]: Search process

General Terms

Experimentation, Measurement, Theory

Keywords

People search, query log analysis, classification

1. INTRODUCTION

As a result of the growth of the amount of online information, search has become one of the most important online activities. Major web search engines are among the most visited web pages,[1] with Google, Yahoo!, and Baidu in the global top six. An important aspect of research related to search is understanding how users deploy a search engine: What is it they are looking for? Who is using the search engine? How do they use it? Answering such questions leads to new research directions and, in the end, helps to improve the user experience.

Much of the research in understanding search behavior exploits the log files of search engines. Query (or transaction) logs contain information about the query a user issued, and the subsequent actions (result pages viewed, results clicked, etc.), if any. Early work by Broder [6] shows that there is a fair correlation between findings from query log analysis and user surveys and, in the same paper, he also proposes an influential taxonomy of web queries.

Much of the work on query log analysis was, and still is, focused around web search (see Section 2), despite the increase in so-called *vertical* search engines. Instead of relying on a single general web search engine to provide information on specific queries, users use a search engine specialized in a single domain or segment of online content. Well-known examples of vertical search engines include scientific literature search [21], medical IR [11], patent retrieval [20], search in cultural heritage [27], and book search [18]. Although previous work on query log analysis has provided us with general insights in users' search behavior, this behavior might change when searching for a particular type of information. For this reason, research is now also focusing on query log analysis for particular information objects. For example, Jones et al. [17] look at how users search digital libraries, Ke et al. [19] explore search behavior in scientific literature, Mishne and de Rijke [26] analyze blog search, and Huurnink et al. [13] do so for search in an audio-visual archive.

One type of information users frequently look for is *people*. It is estimated that 11–17% of web queries contain a person name, and, more so, 4% of web queries are person name queries only [1]. No fewer than 57% of adult internet users uses a search engine to search for their own name [23]. In addition to these "vanity searches," many internet users search for (i) information on people from their past (46%), (ii) their friends (38%), and (iii) business-related persons, like colleagues and competitors (31% of employed internet users). These numbers have increased by 10% in a period of four years, indicating the importance of people search in an online setting.

In this paper, we analyse the query logs of a people search engine. These logs offer us information at three levels: queries, sessions, and users (see Section 3), and we are interested in the structure we can identify within each of these levels. More specifically,

[1] `http://www.alexa.com/topsites`

SIGIR'11, July 24–28, 2011, Beijing, China.

we seek to answer the following research questions: (A) What are the general usage statistics of a people search engine? (B) Can we identify different types for each of our information objects (queries, sessions, users)? (C) Can we automatically classify queries into the proposed types? (D) What are interesting findings in people search that indicate future research directions?

The paper makes the following contributions: (1) We describe how a people search engine is being used. (2) We propose a classification scheme for queries, sessions, and users in a people search engine. (3) We identify features to allow for automatic classification of person name queries. (4) We offer recommendations as to future research in, and implementation of, people search technology. To the best of our knowledge, our study is the first to provide a detailed log analysis in the emerging area of entity search.

In Section 2 we discuss previous work on query log analysis and query classification. Section 3 defines the information objects we explore in the paper. In Section 4 we introduce the search system and interface from which our logs originate, and offer insights in the general statistics of our log data. We propose our classification scheme in Section 5 and experiment with automatic classification. Finally, we discuss further observations in Section 6 and conclude in Section 7.

2. RELATED WORK

One of the first large scale query log analysis papers explores search logs of AltaVista [30]. The authors perform a descriptive analysis of the (almost) 1 billion queries in the log, indicating query length (mostly 1–3 term queries), session length (mostly one query sessions), popular query terms (sex related), the number of result pages a user looks at (mostly one page), and how queries are modified within a session. Following several other studies of web search engine logs, Jansen and Spink [15] compare analyses of nine search engine logs between 1997 and 2002. They conclude that most findings are stable over time, but that, e.g., the percentage of users that only looks at the first result page increases. They also show that the percentage of queries related to people, places or things ("entities") increases from 21% in 2001 to over 41% in 2002, clearly indicating the importance of people search.

When it comes to people search and query log analysis, not much work has been done. Guo et al. [10] propose a method to recognize named entities in queries by learning context for these entities. Although their work shows promise, it focuses on entities like books, movies and music, rather than people. More closely related work is done by Pound et al. [28] and looks at ad-hoc object retrieval; the authors show that over 40% of queries in their dataset is of type "entitiy" and they specify methods for dealing with such queries in a "web of data" setting.

Queries. What is it users are searching for in a particular search environment? This question is the rationale behind many papers covering queries and query types. Classification of queries is often based on (i) query intent or (ii) query semantics. An influential paper of the former type by Broder [6] looks at queries in a web search engine. An exploration of query log data reveals three types of query: informational, navigational, and transactional. Most queries in a web search engine are informational (40–50%), followed by transactional (30–36%). Later work by Rose and Levinson [29] extends this taxonomy with subclasses. A manual classification of 1,500 web queries shows that the percentage of informational queries is higher than in the original paper (about 60%), at the cost of both other types.

The rise of verticals leads to users interacting with specialized search systems, which in turn might lead to different types of queries and different behavior. Mishne and de Rijke [26] acknowledge this and look at query types in a blog search engine. Since almost all blog queries are informational they propose two new query types: concept and context queries—both of which are informational but quite distinctive in blog search. Another type of vertical search that is explored using query logs are audiovisual archives [13]. Here, the authors do not classify queries, but show general statistics of the logs, indicating that users mainly look for program titles and entities (organizations, people). These two papers show that, by moving towards more specialized search engines, the query typology needs refinement too.

Looking at query classification research based on query semantics, there exists a large body of related work that considers queries that a given query co-occurs with (see "Sessions"). One example is the classification of query refinements, addressed in [12]. A different classification task is proposed by Cao et al. [9], who state that query context (i.e., previous queries in the same session) is needed to classify queries into categories. A similar notion is used by Meij et al. [25], who aim at identifying concepts in queries.

Sessions. Sessions are an important aspect in query log analysis, and various ways of detecting sessions have been proposed. According to Jansen et al. [14], session duration is the interval between the user submitting the first query and the user "leaving" the search engine, resulting in sessions varying from several seconds to a few hours. Most time-based session detection approaches group logged actions by some user id, sort the actions chronologically for each user, and split sessions on intervals longer than a certain cutoff value. The choice of cutoff value is dependent on the goal of the analysis. For example, based on a manual examination Mishne and de Rijke [26] use very small cutoff values between 10 and 30 seconds and show that these values mimic sessions based on query reformulation. Longer sessions (e.g., 30 minutes [16]) allow one to explore the different queries and query types a user issues.

Although the time-based approach is a commonly used definition of sessions, there are alternatives. Huang and Efthimiadis [12] use query reformulations to identify session boundaries. Here, sessions consist of consecutive queries by the same user, where each query is a reformulation of the previous query (e.g., adding or deleting words). The idea is that all reformulated queries address a single underlying information need and should be in one session. Jansen et al. [16] compare query reformulations for session detection to the time-based detection; they conclude that query reformulation results in more detected sessions.

A different approach has been proposed by Lucchese et al. [22], who try to detect sessions based on a user's task. Since multitasking is very common in web search, they conclude that time-based techniques fail at task-dependent session detection; instead, they propose to cluster queries and use the clusters for session detection.

Users. Research into user behavior from query logs can be challenging, since it can be hard to determine which queries and sessions belong to the same user. White and Drucker [34] counter this issue by using a set of volunteer users. They collect search data from these users over a five month period. From this data, they identify two user types: navigators (users with consistent search behavior) and explorers (variable behavior). A different approach (in the setting of searching literature in CiteSeer) by Manavoglu et al. [24] tries to model user behavior and predicts actions by similar users, based on previous users' actions.

Where the two studies just mentioned model users based on their actions, Weber and Jaimes [33] describe users' demographics. For this, they use characteristics per ZIP code, and election results per county. Combining demographics with what users are searching for and how they do so, allows them to gain insight in the behavior of users with specific characteristics.

3. INFORMATION OBJECTS

In the analysis of our people search query logs, we use four types of information object present in the logs. Here, we detail what we consider these objects to be and how they relate to previous work.

Query A query is a search instance in the query logs. A query consists of a name and possibly a keyword (see Section 4 for a discussion of the interface), and a timestamp. The timestamp is important in that the query type can change over time: a person can be "just anyone" at time t, but could become a main player in a news event at time $t+n$, or a celebrity could become "just anyone" after disappearing from television for a while.

Session As mentioned in Section 2, the way to detect sessions is dependent on the type of search system, the goal of the research, and the data available. Since this paper is the first to analyze people search, we take a high-level view of sessions to see how users combine person name queries. For this, we take a long interval (40 minutes) between two actions to signal a session boundary and construct sessions accordingly. Sessions can be characterized by their length (i.e., the number of queries in one session) and their duration (i.e., the time interval between the first and last action within one session). In Section 6 we return to the issue of session detection for people search.

User Identifying users over time can be difficult. We use a persistent cookie to assign a user id to queries, and although different users might use the same computer and browser, it is a fairly accurate way of identifying returning users.

Out click A user clicks on one of the search results; these out clicks are identified by their URL and type (e.g., Facebook, LinkedIn, images, or Blogger).

In the next section we go into details regarding the search system and interface and describe the collected data for each of the objects just mentioned.

4. SEARCH SYSTEM AND DATA

The main data source for this paper is a large sample of queries, issued to a Dutch language commercial people search engine. This search engine allows users to submit a person name query and offers search results in four different categories:

- social media,
- web search,
- multimedia, and
- miscellaneous.

Social media results consist of profiles from social networking sites like Facebook and LinkedIn, and other social media sites like Twitter, Blogger, Digg, and Last.fm. The web search category returns search results from major web search engines like Google, Yahoo!, and Bing, and vertical search engines for news and blogs. Multimedia results look for images and video about the person, and the miscellaneous category lists related persons (based on last name), facts about the person (e.g., "John Irving is a writer"), tags, and documents (PDF or Word documents).

The people search engine offers two search interfaces. First, the standard (simple) search interface consists of just one search box, in which the user is supposed to type the first and last name of the person she is looking for (Figure 1). The advanced search interface

Figure 1: Simple search interface: a single search box with a search button.

is somewhat hidden and it presents the user with three search boxes: The first box is used for the first name, the second for the last name, and the third can be used to supply the search engine with additional keywords (Figure 2). Besides adding a keyword to the person name

Figure 2: Advanced search interface: a first name, last name and keyword search box with the search button.

query using the advanced search interface, a user can also click on one of the suggested tags after the initial search using the first and last name only. The clicked tag is then added to the query as a keyword. We provide a detailed analysis of the keywords in Section 6.

From the simple interface, the search engine extracts a first and last name, whereas this segmentation is explicitly given by the user in the advanced interface. In cases where a user only enters one name (simple interface) or leaves one of the name fields empty (advanced interface), we end up with a single name query. This happens in 4% of the queries.

4.1 Query logs

The query log data was collected between September 1, 2010 and December 31, 2010. During this period there were no major updates to the search interface, to allow log entries to be comparable. Entries in the query log consist of a number of fields, listed in Table 1. The three query fields (first and last name, and keyword) have been discussed above; Timestamp indicates the date and time when the query was issued, the SearchID can be used to match a query to out clicks, and finally, the UserID is our indication of the user, as explained before. For out clicks, similar fields are available, indicating the URL of the click, the type, and the date and time when the user clicked the result.

Table 1: Fields in the query logs.

Queries	
SearchID	unique identifier for the query
First name	part of the query
Last name	part of the query
Keyword	optional; part of the query
Timestamp	date and time of the query
UserID	unique identifier using a cookie
Out clicks	
SearchID	connect out click with query
Type	name of the result category
URL	URL of the clicked result
Timestamp	date and time of the click

In the remainder of this section we give a high-level description of the data in our query logs. Section 4.2 offers insights in individual queries, Section 4.3 details sessions in the data, Section 4.4 looks at users of the people search engine, and finally, Section 4.5 explores out clicks after a search.

4.2 Query characteristics

Table 2 lists the characteristics of the individual queries in our log data. Our full dataset consists of over 13m person name queries, issued in a four month period, of which over 4m are unique queries. Figure 4 (left) shows the query frequency distribution of the log data, which follows a power law (with slope $\alpha = 2.0$). As we can see, most queries are issued only once. On average, users issued over 110,000 queries per day. In the left plot of Figure 3 we show the number of queries for each day in the dataset. We see a clear cyclic pattern (indicated by the red line), which is due to the popularity of searching on working days compared to weekends. This is clarified in the center plot, which shows the distribution of queries over days of the week. We observe a drop in the number of queries during the weekend; for this plot we looked at the 16 full weeks within our data preventing certain weekdays to occur more often.

Table 2: Characteristics of individual queries.

Number of queries	13,331,417	
Number of unique queries	4,221,556	
Number of single-term queries	537,365	(4.0%)
Average number of queries per day	110,177	
Busiest day in number of queries	144,309	
Number of queries with keyword	514,850	(3.9%)

In about 4% of the queries the user submitted only one term (i.e., only a first or last name), and non of these single-term queries is accompanied by a keyword, making it hard to retrieve relevant results for these queries. In Section 6 we get back to single-term queries and their impact on out clicks. In general, keyword usage is low, as only 3.9% of the person name queries contain an additional keyword. The absence of this field in the standard interface is most likely the cause of this. Again, we revisit the issue of keyword usage in Section 6.

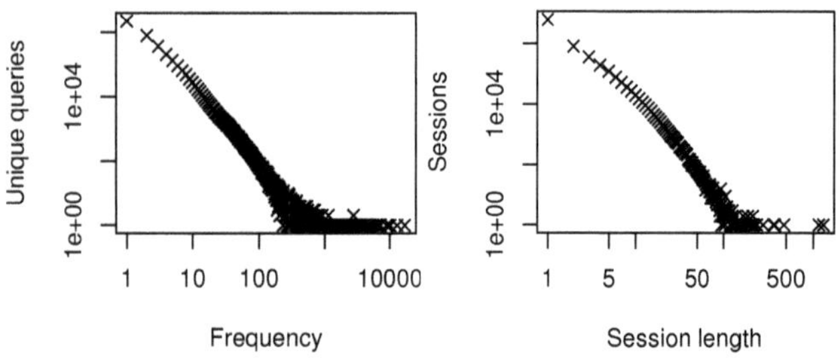

Figure 4: Distribution of (Left:) query frequencies, and (Right:) session length in number of queries. Both follow a power law for slope $\alpha = 2.0$ and $\alpha = 2.6$.

Zooming in on the most popular queries, we list the 10 most frequently queried names, the query counts, the number of unique users searching for these names, and a description of who they are in Table 3. The top 10 shows a mixture of celebrities (persons known to most users), like *Geert Wilders* and *Lieke van Lexmond*, and (previously) non-famous people who gained attention through some event. Ranking queries by their frequency or by the number of unique users results in almost the same list, which indicates that, even without user information, we can assume that popular queries are issued by many different users.

Table 3: 10 most popular queries during Sep. 1–Dec. 31, 2010, in terms of query counts and unique users.

Name	Count	Users	Gloss
Suze van Rozelaar	16,929	15,373	mistress of soccer player
Kelly Huizen	13,005	11,706	teenage girl with sex tape
Ben Saunders	10,074	9,145	participant of talent show
Barbara van der Vegte	9,879	8,256	mistress of tv host
Geert Wilders	8,990	8,483	politician
Lieke van Lexmond	7,774	6,368	actress
Quincy Schumans	7,266	6,315	murdered teenage boy
Joyce Exalto	6,656	5,584	murdered teenage girl
Aa Aa	6,457	6,442	test query
Sietske Hoekstra	6,088	5,323	mother, killed her babies

4.3 Session characteristics

As mentioned in Section 3, we detect sessions using a time-out between two subsequent actions by the same user in the log. Applying this detection method to our log data leaves us with over 8m sessions. Characteristics of the sessions are listed in Table 4. We observe that most sessions, over 6m (78.1%), contain only one query, and that the distribution of session length follows a power law (see Figure 4, right plot) with slope $\alpha = 2.6$. Compared to sessions in web search engines, we find that our people search engine has a much higher percentage of one-query sessions (web search engine logs contain 50–60% one-query sessions [15]). Sessions that do consist of multiple queries, contain on average almost four queries, and these sessions last, on average, just over six minutes. It seems most users use a people search engine to quickly find information on one particular person, and leave after the information has been found.

Table 4: Characteristics of sessions.

Number of sessions	8,125,695
Number of sessions with > 1 query	1,775,880
Average number of sessions per day	67,155
Longest session in hours	08h25m
Average session duration	
all sessions	1m21s
sessions with > 1 query	6m9s
Longest session in number of queries	1,302
Average session length	
all sessions	1.64
sessions with > 1 query	3.93

4.4 User characteristics

The log data offers us close to 7m different users (see Table 5) and, similar to sessions, most users only issue one query (and therefore interact in only one session). Still, we have about 500,000 users that use the people search engine in more than one session. These returning users instigate, on average, 3.5 sessions in the four month period: roughly one session each month. Figure 5 shows the distribution of queries over users (on the left), and of sessions over users (on the right). Both distributions follow a power law, with slope $\alpha = 2.5$ for queries and $\alpha = 3.8$ for sessions.

To get a sense of when users deploy the people search engine, we look at the distribution of searches over hours of the day in Figure 3 (right plot). Here, the dashed, red line indicates working days, and the solid, green line weekend days. We see that, for

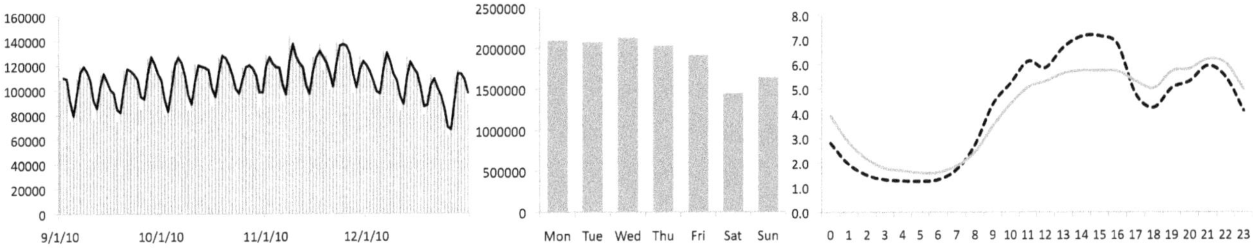

Figure 3: Distribution of queries over time. (Left:) Number of queries per day during Sep. 1–Dec. 31, 2010, with a black trend line. (Center:) Distribution of queries over weekdays. (Right:) Distribution of queries over hours of the day. In the right plot, the y-axis indicates the percentage of queries submitted in an hour; the black, dashed line are working days, the gray, solid line weekend days.

Table 5: Characteristics of users.

Number of users	6,841,442
Number of users with > 1 query	1,481,377
Number of users with > 1 session	514,042
Busiest day in unique users	11/24/2010 90,799
Average number of queries per user	
all users	1.95
users with > 1 query	5.38
Average number of sessions per user	
all users	1.19
users with > 1 session	3.50

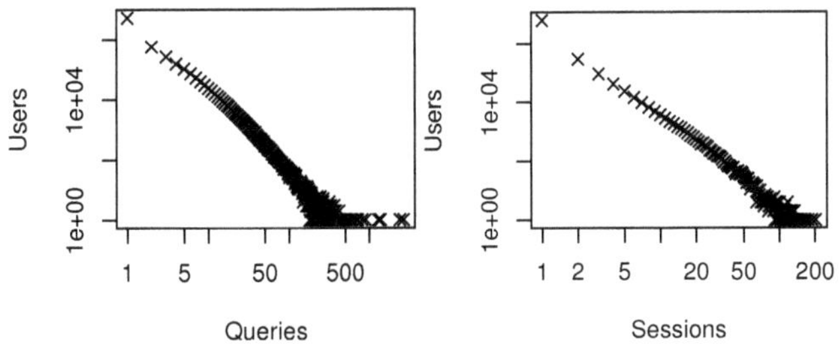

Figure 5: Distribution over users of (Left:) queries, and (Right:) sessions. Both distributions follow a power law for slope $\alpha = 2.5$ and $\alpha = 3.8$.

working days, peaks exist in the afternoon (around 2–3pm) and in the evening (around 9pm), while usage drops during lunch (11am–12pm) and dinner (5–7pm); there is a large drop during the night. When we compare this to weekends, we observe that usage shifts several hours: there are more searches during early night (1–4am) in weekends, but fewer during the morning and afternoon. The highest peak shifts from around 2–3pm for working days to 9–10pm during weekends.

4.5 Out click characteristics

The final information object we explore in our log data are the out clicks: do users click on results after a query? If so, where do they click to? Table 6 shows that about 4m clicks are recorded, of which almost 3m unique ones. About 17% of the queries in the logs are followed by an out click, and for sessions this is 20%. Once again, the distribution of out clicks over both queries and sessions (Figure 6) follows a power low. When we compare the percentage of queries with at least one out click to out clicks in web search, we notice that the percentages in people search are much lower. Numbers for web search vary greatly, but are consistently higher than the 17% for our data: Callan et al. [8] report on 50% of queries with out click(s), followed by 73% [32], and more than 87% [31]. We identify two reasons for the low out click ratio in people search: (i) People search is still a challenging problem, and it is not easy to find relevant results for all person queries, and (ii) the interface already displays information about the person (e.g., related news articles, images, and facts).

Table 6: Characteristics of out clicks.

Number of out clicks	3,965,462	
Number of unique out clicks	2,883,230	
Number of queries followed by out click	2,351,848	17.6%
Number of sessions that include out click	1,625,817	20.0%

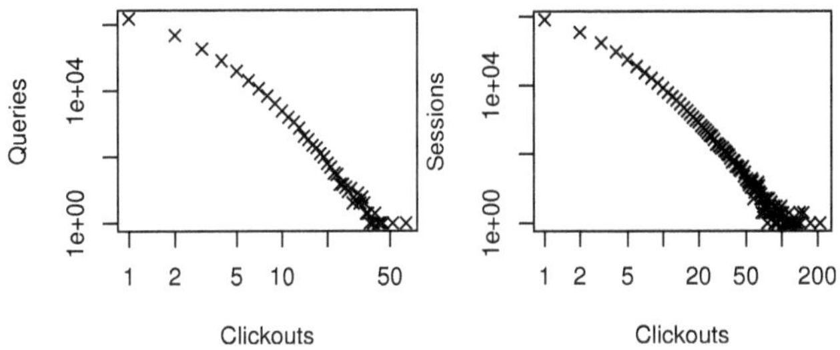

Figure 6: Distribution of (Left:) out clicks over queries, and (Right:) out clicks over sessions. Both follow a power law for slope $\alpha = 2.4$ and $\alpha = 2.0$.

More interesting than the overall numbers are the details of the out clicks. We can categorize the out clicks according to the search result interface category they belong to. From this categorization, we obtain the percentages as listed in Table 7. Social media results are the most popular and make up 66% of all out clicks, followed by search engine results. Besides the interface result categories explicitely mentioned in the interface, we identify an additional category that attracts many out clicks: the "alternative sources" area at

Table 7: Interface result categories and number of out clicks.

Social media	2,625,500	66.2%
Search engines	674,079	17.0%
Multimedia	120,874	3.1%
Miscellaneous	337,104	8.5%
"Alternative sources"	187,098	4.7%

the bottom of the initial result page. Here, users can click on (sponsored) links to external sites, mainly dating sites and web shops, to look for this person. The links to dating sites are particularly popular, receiving 154,419 out clicks.

We zoom in on individual result types, and plot the number of out clicks per site in Figure 7. Social networking site Hyves is by far the most popular result type in number of clicks, and it is followed by fellow networking sites Facebook, Schoolbank (to find old school friends), and LinkedIn. All of these result types are displayed on the first result page. Web search engines Google, Yahoo!, and Bing are also among the most popular result types, as are dating sites. The first site-specific result type is "related," which refers to a click on a related person. We see that users prefer to find pages

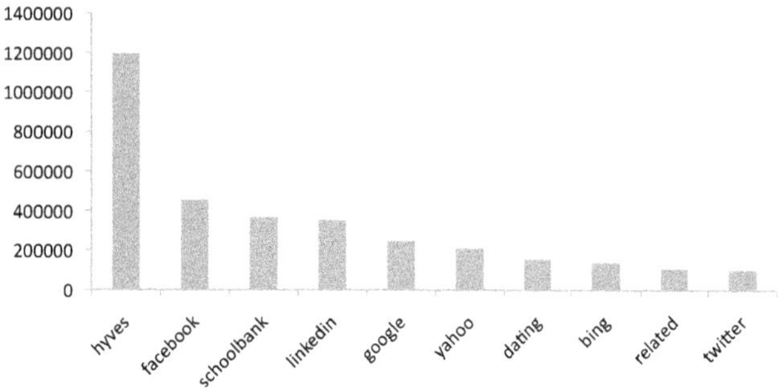

Figure 7: Number of out clicks per result type.

that are directly linked to the person they are looking for (answering the question "Who is this?"), profiles being by far the most popular result type. Multimedia results are not very popular, however, the interface already shows these results without a click necessary and, hence, it is likely that users see many more multimedia results than can be concluded from the log data. Finally, dating sites appear to be a particular popular result type.

5. OBJECT CLASSIFICATIONS

In the previous section we performed a high-level exploration of the logs of a people search engine. In this section we add more context to the contents of these logs. More specifically, for each of the information objects (see Section 3), we propose a classification scheme. This exercise resembles work we discussed in Section 2 but has a specific focus on people search. Section 5.1 introduces the query types we identified for people search; in Section 5.2 we explore session types in people search and in Section 5.3 we propose different types of users of people search engines.

To come to our classification schemes, we sampled random queries from our log data. After assigning the query to one of our query types, we continued to annotate all queries in the same session (in case the session contains more than one query), and annotate the session as a whole. The annotation system that we designed for this purpose then allowed us to annotate all other queries and sessions by the same user, resulting in a user annotation. In total we manually annotated 3,281 queries, 1,005 sessions, and 412 users.

5.1 Queries

Based on an initial exploration of the data, we propose the following query types for people search:

High-profile queries These queries involve people that stand out in some way and denote people that are known to a relatively large group of users. We distinguish two types of high-profile people:

Event-based People of this type get a boost in attention based on an event that is either currently happening or took place shortly before the query was submitted. In most cases, these events are news-related and are reported either in traditional media or in social media. This type also includes events not related to world news, like recurring cultural events (e.g., Christmas, Easter).

Regular People that are continuously at the center of attention, like celebrities and public persons. In principle, event-based high-profile people can, in time, turn into regular high-profile people, but our period of data collection is too short to be able to observe this phenomenon.

Low-profile queries These queries involve people that are "just anyone": users can be looking for their own name, names of relatives, friends, or other "unknown" persons. We consider all of these queries low-profile queries.

To further explain the difference between the two high-profile query types, we plot the query volume of three example queries in Figure 8. Note that the y-axis has a different scale for each of the

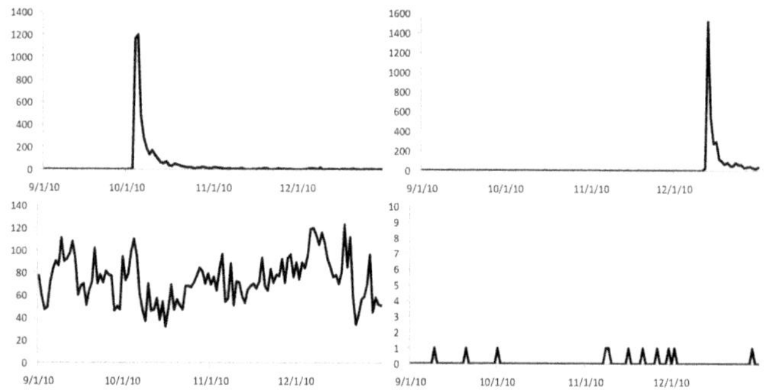

Figure 8: Examples of query volume per day for the two high-profile query types (Top:) event-based queries (Derck Stabler and Nathalie Weinreder, respectively), and (Bottom:) a regular query (Geert Wilders). For comparison, we have included a random low-profile query (Yucel Ugur).

plots. We can clearly see a peak in query volume for the two event-based high-profile queries. For both queries we can identify related (news) events that led to this peak: Derck Stabler was the main suspect in the murder of his mother (on October 4); Nathalie Weinreder is a murder victim (on December 12). On the other hand, the query volume for the regular high-profile query is relatively stable, with about 100 queries per day over the whole period. The low-profile query has no peaks, and search volume is very modest (one search on a few days).

During the annotation of queries, we came across instances that could not be classified, mainly because they contained only one query term. After removing these 285 queries, we are left with 2,995 annotated queries. Table 8 lists the counts for each of our query types in our sample. By far most of the queries in our sample are of the low-profile type, and only 6.6% of the queries involves high-profile people. Of the 199 high-profile queries, almost 75% is related to some event, leaving only 1.8% of all queries for regular high-profile people ("celebrities"). We explore the event-based high-profile queries in more detail, and distinguish between six common classes (and one miscellaneous class). Table 9 lists the sub-classes and the percentage of queries belonging to them.

Users mostly deploy the people search engine to search for, e.g., relatives, co-workers, neighbors, friends, the guy from the pub last

Table 8: Query types and their frequency in a sample.

Query type	Count	
Low-profile	2,796	93.4%
High-profile	199	6.6%
Event-based	144	72.4%
Regular	55	27.6%

Table 9: Subclasses of the event-based high-profile queries and their percentage.

Event-based subclass	Percentage
Deaths	33.3%
Criminals	22.9%
Related to celebrities	9.7%
Related to other high-profiles	9.7%
Television	9.0%
Sex related	6.3%
Miscellaneous	9.0%

night, or themselves: low-profile people. Occasionally they search for information on high-profile people, and here we notice that event-based queries are about three times as common as "celebrity" queries. One of the reasons for this could be that general search engines already allow us to get easy access to information about celebrities, but this might be harder for people that were low-profile up to the point they became part of an event. An in-depth analysis shows that users are mainly attracted by "sensational" events, related to murders, child abuse, and fatal crashes.

Automatic classification. Being able to automatically classify queries as high-profile or low-profile is useful, both for investigating sessions/users and for a people search system. Based on this classification, the system might prioritize different result types or show additional information sources. For query classification, we use the following features: (i) search volume in the logs over the previous week; (ii) number of mentions in the Dutch news from September 2010 onwards; (iii) number of mentions in the Dutch news in the previous week; and result counts for the query in (iv) social media (using Topsy[2]) and (v) the Dutch Wikipedia (using Yahoo!). We train a J48 decision tree algorithm on a sample of our annotated set of queries. To counter class distribution skewedness, we downsample the more common classes to the size of the least common class, leaving us with 162 annotated queries. We use 10-fold cross-validation, and present results in Table 10.

Table 10: Results of automatic query classification using the J48 decision tree algorithm.

Query type	Precision	Recall
Event-based high-profile	0.745	0.759
Regular high-profile	0.739	0.630
Low-profile	0.820	0.926
Low-profile	0.911	0.879
High-profile	0.883	0.914

The results of the automatic query classification show our features are sufficient to classify low-profile queries with good accuracy. Distinguishing between the two high-profile query types proves to be challenging. Taking one step back, and trying to classify high-profile vs. low-profile queries (downsampled to the number of high-profile queries; 396 queries in total), we improve accuracy on both types: see the bottom half of Table 10. An analysis of the contribution of the individual features shows that search volume in the logs, and result counts for Wikipedia and social media are most important, while the Dutch news mentions are ignored.

[2]http://www.topsy.com

5.2 Sessions

Based on our query types and initial data observations, we propose four different session types:

Family session In a family session, a user issues several queries trying to find information about relatives. This session type will mainly consist of low-profile queries, with repetitive use of the same last name(s).

Event session Events (e.g., in the news) usually have several main players involved. The event session is centered around an event, and its queries relate to this event. Most of the queries in this session will be of the event-based high-profile type.

Spotting session Users try to "spot" celebrities in the real world, and do the same in an online environment. When trying to spot several celebrities in one session, we have a spotting session. Here, most queries in the session are of the regular high-profile type.

Polymerous session For sessions that show a mixture of the three above mentioned types, or that contain various low-profile queries without clear relation between them, we have a polymerous session type.

We manually annotated 1,005 sessions. Since we are unable to determine a session type for one query sessions, we remove the 540 sessions that contain just one query, leaving us with 465 annotated multiple query sessions. The counts and percentages of the session types in our sample are listed in Table 11. Most users engage in a polymerous session, consisting of either multiple low-profile queries without a clear relation or a mixture of session types. Family sessions are frequent too, taking up about 13% of all multiple query sessions. Event and celebrity sessions are rare, as these query types are mostly used in combination with other, low-profile queries, leading to a polymerous session.

Table 11: Session types and their frequency in a sample of 465 sessions.

Query type	Count	
Family session	59	12.7%
Event session	2	0.4%
Spotting session	2	0.4%
Polymerous session	239	51.4%
Repetitive session	163	35.1%

We introduced a fifth session type during annotations: the *repetitive session*. Sessions of this type consist of either a sequence of identical queries or queries with small corrections in one of the names (which is similar to query refinement in web search). About 35% of the sessions in our sample are of this type, and this high percentage could indicate the need for "person name suggestion" techniques. The system suggests a person name either when no results are found or when the queried name is very similar to another popular person name.

We are interested in the type of results users click on for the various session types. For the spotting and event session, there is not enough data available to perform this analysis. For the remaining three session types we plot the percentage of out clicks per result type in Figure 9. We observe some interesting differences: In family sessions, users are more likely to click a "related" result, and focus less on Hyves results. In repetitive sessions, users click more often on search engine results. Polymerous sessions follow roughly the same distribution as all queries (Figure 7).

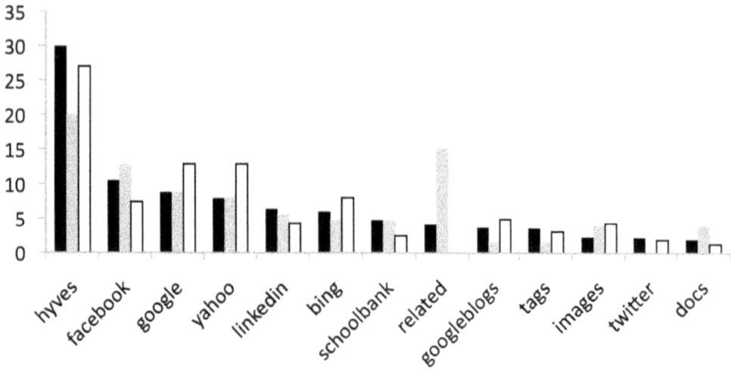

Figure 9: Percentage of out clicks per result type for polymerous (black), family (gray), and repetitive (white) sessions.

5.3 Users

We select a random sample of 412 users and manually look at their characteristics and typology. We discern the following types.

Monitor To track their own (or someone else's) web presence, monitors regularly return to the people search engine with the same query (associated characteristics: recurring queries, large interval between queries, few out clicks).

Spotter Based on the physical activity of spotting celebrities in cities, spotters use people search engines to spot celebrities online (characteristics: high frequency queries, high-profile queries, out clicks to social media and multimedia).

Follower Inspired by news events, followers look for what is happening right now (characteristics: high-profile queries, high frequency peaks, low frequency before or after each peak, out-clicks to social media).

Polymer Has no clear-cut behavior; combines various session and query types.

In our annotated sample, we observe that for 320 users we cannot determine their type. As indicated in Table 5, we can only ascertain more than one query for 21.7% percent of the users. So, for the bulk of the users we observe a single query, making the classification of these difficult if not impossible. For the remainder we find that 69 users are polymers, 22 are monitors, and 1 is a follower.

6. DISCUSSION AND IMPLICATIONS

In this section we take the results of our people search log analysis, and discuss observations with regard to people search aspects, and pointers to interesting research directions.

Keywords. As mentioned in Section 4, the search engine offers users the opportunity to add keywords to their search. Since this field is not part of the standard search interface, its usage is limited: about 4% of all person queries contain keywords, the bulk of which are single terms. Table 12 shows the ten most popular keywords; a quick look reveals that many of the keywords are Dutch cities or keywords indicating the type of result the searches wants to see.[3]

Table 12: 10 most popular keywords.

Keyword	Count	Gloss
Amsterdam	4,733	Dutch city
Com	3,451	top level domain
Jan	3,009	January
Rotterdam	2,782	Dutch city
Foto	2,519	photo
Facebook	2,411	social networking site
Anonymous	2,377	name of the search engine
Www	2,265	
Profiel	2,135	profile
Groningen	2,069	Dutch city

To investigate the use of the keyword field in more detail, we take a sample of 250 keywords and manually classify these. Table 13 lists the classes we identified from this sample. We see that most keywords are *locations*; these consist mostly of cities, although more specific locations are found as well (streets, neighborhoods). Users also enter *person names* in the keyword field. Although these can be errors, they may be examples of users searching for combinations of names (i.e., relation-finding) or users adding names for disambiguation purposes. The third class, *result types*, is used to point the search engine to a particular type of result; here, we mostly see names of social platforms (Facebook, Hyves) or genre or document types (pictures, news, profiles). The final major class is *activities*. Here, searchers add an activity related to the person they are looking for. These activities include job descriptions, hobbies, and other characteristics of people. Many of the keywords are hard to classify, either because they are hard to understand or because there is no obvious relation to people search or search in general (e.g., licensed, excel, or surprise).

Table 13: Keyword classes for people search, their frequency, and examples.

Keyword class	Percentage	Examples
Locations	22.8%	*Amsterdam, Rotterdam, ...*
Person names	15.6%	*Maaike, Peter, Snelders, ...*
Result types	13.6%	*Facebook, pictures, website, ...*
Activities	10.4%	*gardener, swindler, soccer, ...*
Date	3.2%	*November, Monday, jan, ...*
Miscellaneous	34.4%	

Person name disambiguation. The task of person name disambiguation is an interesting and active research topic (see, e.g., [1–3]), and it is an important and very challenging aspect of people search. The same name can refer to many different persons: data from 1990 suggests that in the U.S., only 90,000 different names are shared by 100 million persons [3]. Clearly, returning relevant results for person name queries is the challenging.

Our analysis so far revealed several aspects to person name disambiguation: First, as we saw in the previous paragraph, users use the keyword field to give pointers on how to disambiguate people sharing the same name. To this end they mainly enter a location or activity (job, hobby); these two types of keywords combined cover 33% of all keywords. Second, we find evidence of person name

[3]The name of the search engine in Table 12 has been hidden to preserve anonymity.

disambiguation in the out clicks. Consider the number of different profiles users go to after searching for the same name; Table 14 shows the person names with the largest number of different profiles clicked (Facebook profiles left, LinkedIn profiles right). Except for "Joran van der Sloot" (a high-profile person with many fake profiles and hate groups), all names are very common Dutch names. To support this claim, Table 15 lists the most common Dutch last names:[4] almost all last names in our outclick tables are listed in the top 10.

Table 14: Person names with most unique Facebook (left) and LinkedIn (right) results clicked.

Name	Count	Name	Count
Joran van der Sloot	18	Herman de Vries	11
Jeroen de Vries	14	Michiel Bakker	11
Rob van Dijk	14	Nicole Bakker	11
Marieke de Jong	14	Nynke de Vries	10
Peter de Vries	13	Mirjam de Vries	10
Peter van Dijk	13	Marjan de Jong	10
Peter Visser	12	Annemieke de Vries	10
Saskia de Vries	12	Arjan Visser	10
Karin de Jong	12	Bas Alberts	10
Marieke de Vries	12	Frank Driessen	10

Table 15: Ten most common last names in the Netherlands.

Name	Percentage
De Jong	0.53%
Jansen	0.46%
De Vries	0.45%
Van der Berg	0.37%
Van Dijk	0.35%
Bakker	0.35%
Janssen	0.34%
Visser	0.31%
Smit	0.27%
Meijer	0.25%

Relationship finding. Current research in entity retrieval focuses, among other things, on finding relationships between entities, or finding related entities [4, 5, 7]. Our analysis of people search logs show that users are indeed interested in finding combinations of people or finding the relationship between people. As observed in the "keyword" paragraph, users of the people search engine currently use the keyword field to achieve this goal. An interesting example is the female first name "Maaike," which is frequently used as a keyword. Table 16 shows person name queries with which this keyword is being used, and explains the relation between the two people. Note that, although we are looking at the same name (Maaike), searchers seem to be referring to different people. Improvements in the interface and in search algorithms should, in the future, facilitate searching for combinations of people or for relationships between persons.

Single-term queries. As mentioned in Section 4.2, we encountered many log entries with only one term in the query (4% of all queries). These single-term queries are likely to be used in two ways: (i) last name search, where the goal is to explore people that share the same last name, and (ii) first name search, aimed at finding the right person and thus that person's full name.

[4]http://en.wikipedia.org/wiki/List_of_most_common_surnames_in_Europe

Table 16: Queries issued with person (first) name "Maaike" as keyword, and the relation between query and keyword.

Queried person	Relation
Ben Saunders	Maaike is ex-girlfriend of talent show participant Ben
Sietske Hoekstra	Maaike and Sietske are relatives
Jaap Siewertsz van Reesema	Jaap and Maaike were both finalists of a talent show

About 16.6% of the single-term queries have at least one out click, which is one percent lower than for all queries (17.6%). However, when we look at the top 10 queries with most out clicks, six of these queries are single-term queries. To explore this finding in more detail, we plot the percentage of queries with their number of out clicks (Figure 10); we binned the out clicks to make the difference apparent, and split the data over two plots for the same reason: The left plot shows bins for 2, 3–5, and 6–10 out clicks, and the right plot those for 11–20, 21–30, and > 30. As we can see, the tail of the single-term queries (gray columns) is "fatter" than for multiple term queries, indicating that users are more likely to try various results for single-term query than for multiple term queries. Users seem to use just one term, to start an exploration of the results. Future work on interfaces and algorithms should account for the fact that users use exploratory search for people search too, and again, person name disambiguation is an important aspect here.

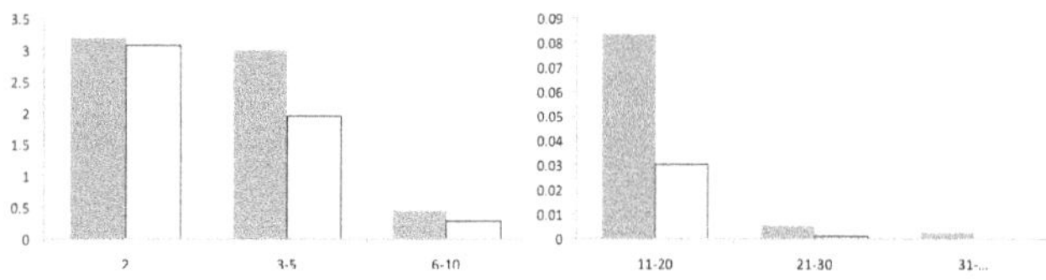

Figure 10: Percentage of queries (y-axis) with their number of out clicks (binned, x-axis) for single-term queries (gray) and multiple term queries (white).

Session detection. In our current setup, we used a (rather long) time-out between actions to detect sessions. From our analysis at the session level (Section 5.2) we observe that we have many polymerous, and a significant portion of these sessions contain "subsessions" (e.g., a sequences of (almost) identical person names, or some event-related queries, followed by searches for relatives). It would be interesting to apply more advanced session detection methods, based on, for example, query types or overlap in content, to the log data. Offering smarter session detection also allows research into session prediction (i.e., given an initial observation of two or more queries, can be predict the session type and suggest follow-up queries).

7. CONCLUSION

In this paper we performed an analysis of query log data from a commercial people search engine, consisting of 13m queries submitted over a four month period. It is the first time a query log analysis is performed on a people search engine, in order to investigate search behavior for this particular type of information object. Our results provide hints for future research in terms of both algorithms and interfaces for people search (or entity search in general).

We focused our analysis on four information objects: queries, sessions, users, and out clicks. The most interesting findings include (i) a significant number of users type just one term (i.e., only a first or last name) and start exploring results; (ii) we observe a much higher percentage of one query sessions in people search as compared to web search; (iii) we observe a low click-through ratio as compared to web search; (iv) social media results are the most popular result type. Furthermore, we have proposed classification schemes for queries, sessions, and users, and shown, through an initial experiment, that automatic classification of queries is doable. Analysis of the features shows the usefulness of social media reports in identifying high-profile queries.

Our analysis of search behavior in people search has revealed many directions for future work, including (i) improved session detection methods for people search, (ii) person name disambiguation, (iii) query prediction within sessions, and (iv) a longitudinal study of users.

Acknowledgments This research was partially supported by the European Union's ICT Policy Support Programme as part of the Competitiveness and Innovation Framework Programme, CIP ICT-PSP under grant agreement nr 250430, the PROMISE Network of Excellence co-funded by the 7th Framework Programme of the European Commission, grant agreement no. 258191, the DuOMAn project carried out within the STEVIN programme which is funded by the Dutch and Flemish Governments under project nr STE-09-12, the Netherlands Organisation for Scientific Research (NWO) under project nrs 612.061.814, 612.061.815, 640.004.802, 380-70-011, the Center for Creation, Content and Technology (CCCT), the Hyperlocal Service Platform project funded by the Service Innovation & ICT program, the WAHSP project funded by the CLARIN-nl program, and under COMMIT project Infiniti.

References

[1] J. Artiles. *Web People Search*. PhD thesis, UNED University, 2009.

[2] J. Artiles, A. Borthwick, J. Gonzalo, S. Sekine, and E. Amigó. Weps-3 evaluation campaign: Overview of the web people search clustering and attribute extraction tasks. In *CLEF 2009 Working Notes*, 2009.

[3] J. Artiles, J. Gonzalo, and S. Sekine. Weps 2 evaluation campaign: overview of the web people search clustering task. In *WePS 2009*, 2009.

[4] K. Balog, A. P. de Vries, P. Serdyukov, P. Thomas, and T. Westerveld. Overview of the TREC 2009 entity track. In *TREC 2009*. NIST, 2010.

[5] K. Balog, P. Serdyukov, and A. de Vries. Overview of the trec 2010 entity track. In *TREC 2010*. NIST, 2011.

[6] A. Broder. A taxonomy of web search. *SIGIR Forum*, 36(2): 3–10, 2002.

[7] M. Bron, K. Balog, and M. de Rijke. Ranking related entities: Components and analyses. In *CIKM 2010*, pages 1079–1088. ACM, 2010.

[8] J. Callan, J. Allan, C. L. Clarke, S. Dumais, D. A. Evans, M. Sanderson, and C. Zhai. Meeting of the minds: An information retrieval research agenda. *ACM SIGIR Forum*, 41(2):25–34, 2007.

[9] H. Cao, D. H. Hu, D. Shen, D. Jiang, J.-T. Sun, E. Chen, and Q. Yang. Context-aware query classification. In *SIGIR 2009*, pages 3–10. ACM, 2009.

[10] J. Guo, G. Xu, X. Cheng, and H. Li. Named entity recognition in query. In *SIGIR 2009*, pages 267–274, 2009.

[11] W. Hersh, C. Buckley, T. J. Leone, and D. Hickam. Ohsumed: an interactive retrieval evaluation and new large test collection for research. In *SIGIR 1994*, pages 192–201, 1994.

[12] J. Huang and E. Efthimiadis. Analyzing and evaluating query reformulation strategies in web search logs. In *CIKM 2000*, pages 77–86. ACM, 2009.

[13] B. Huurnink, L. Hollink, W. van den Heuvel, and M. de Rijke. Search Behavior of Media Professionals at an Audiovisual Archive: A Transaction Log Analysis. *Journal of the American Society for Information Science and Technology*, 61(6):1180–1197, June 2010.

[14] B. Jansen, A. Spink, and I. Taksai. *Handbook of research on web log analysis*. Information Science Reference, 2009.

[15] B. J. Jansen and A. Spink. How are we searching the world wide web? a comparison of nine search engine transaction logs. *Information Processing and Management*, 42(1): 248–263, 2006.

[16] B. J. Jansen, A. Spink, C. Blakely, and S. Koshman. Defining a session on web search engines. *Journal of the American Society for Information Science and Technology*, 58:862–871, 2007.

[17] S. Jones, S. J. Cunningham, R. Mcnab, and S. Boddie. A transaction log analysis of a digital library. *International Journal on Digital Libraries*, 3(2):152–169, 2000.

[18] G. Kazai and A. Doucet. Overview of the INEX 2007 book search track: Booksearch '07. *SIGIR Forum*, 42:2–15, 2008.

[19] H.-R. Ke, R. Kwakkelaar, Y.-M. Tai, and L.-C. Chen. Exploring behavior of e-journal users in science and technology: Transaction log analysis of elsevier's sciencedirect onsite in taiwan. *Library & Information Science Research*, 24(3):265–291, 2002.

[20] L. S. Larkey. A patent search and classification system. In *DL 1999*, pages 179–187. ACM, 1999.

[21] S. Lawrence, K. D. Bollacker, and C. L. Giles. Indexing and retrieval of scientific literature. In *CIKM 1999*, pages 139–146. ACM, 1999.

[22] C. Lucchese, S. Orlando, R. Perego, F. Silvestri, and G. Tolomei. Identifying task-based sessions in search engine query logs. In *WSDM 2011*, 2011.

[23] M. Madden and A. Smith. Reputation management and social media: How people monitor their identity and search for others online. Technical report, PewResearchCenter, 2010.

[24] E. Manavoglu, D. Pavlov, and C. L. Giles. Probabilistic user behavior models. In *ICDM 2003*, pages 203–210, 2003.

[25] E. Meij, M. Bron, B. Huurnink, L. Hollink, and M. de Rijke. Learning semantic query suggestions. In *ISWC 2009*, pages 424–440, 2009.

[26] G. Mishne and M. de Rijke. A study of blog search. In *ECIR 2006*, volume 3936 of *LNCS*, pages 289–301. Springer, 2006.

[27] W. E. Moen. Accessing distributed cultural heritage information. *Communications of the ACM*, 41:44–48, 1998.

[28] J. Pound, P. Mika, and H. Zaragoza. Ad-hoc object retrieval in the web of data. In *WWW 2010*, pages 771–780, 2010.

[29] D. E. Rose and D. Levinson. Understanding user goals in web search. In *WWW 2004*, pages 13–19, 2004.

[30] C. Silverstein, H. Marais, M. Henzinger, and M. Moricz. Analysis of a very large web search engine query log. *SIGIR Forum*, 33:6–12, 1999.

[31] S. Stamou and E. N. Efthimiadis. Queries without clicks: Successful or failed searches? In *Proceedings of the SIGIR 2009 Workshop on the Future of IR Evaluation*, 2009.

[32] S. Stamou and E. N. Efthimiadis. Interpreting user inactivity on search results. In *ECIR 2010*, pages 100–113, 2010.

[33] I. Weber and A. Jaimes. Who uses web search for what? and how? In *WSDM 2011*, 2011.

[34] R. W. White and S. M. Drucker. Investigating behavioral variability in web search. In *WWW 2007*, pages 21–30, 2007.

Learning Search Tasks in Queries and Web Pages via Graph Regularization

Ming Ji[†*], Jun Yan[‡], Siyu Gu[§], Jiawei Han[†], Xiaofei He[¶], Wei Vivian Zhang[♯], Zheng Chen[‡]
[†]Department of Computer Science, University of Illinois at Urbana-Champaign, Urbana, IL, USA
[‡]Microsoft Research Asia, Beijing, China
[§]Department of Computer Science, Beijing Institute of Technology, Beijing, China
[¶]State Key Lab of CAD&CG, College of Computer Science, Zhejiang University, China
[♯]Microsoft Corporation, Redmond, WA, USA
[†]{mingji1, hanj}@illinois.edu, [‡]{junyan, zhengc}@microsoft.com
[§]gusuperstar@gmail.com, [¶]xiaofeihe@cad.zju.edu.cn, [♯]wzha@microsoft.com

ABSTRACT

As the Internet grows explosively, search engines play a more and more important role for users in effectively accessing online information. Recently, it has been recognized that a query is often triggered by a *search task* that the user wants to accomplish. Similarly, many web pages are specifically designed to help accomplish a certain task. Therefore, learning hidden tasks behind queries and web pages can help search engines return the most useful web pages to users by task matching. For instance, the search task that triggers query "thinkpad T410 broken" is to maintain a computer, and it is desirable for a search engine to return the Lenovo troubleshooting page on the top of the list. However, existing search engine technologies mainly focus on topic detection or relevance ranking, which are not able to predict the *task* that triggers a query and the *task* a web page can accomplish.

In this paper, we propose to simultaneously classify queries and web pages into the popular search tasks by exploiting their content together with click-through logs. Specifically, we construct a task-oriented heterogeneous graph among queries and web pages. Each pair of objects in the graph are linked together as long as they potentially share similar search tasks. A novel graph-based regularization algorithm is designed for search task prediction by leveraging the graph. Extensive experiments in real search log data demonstrate the effectiveness of our method over state-of-the-art classifiers, and the search performance can be significantly improved by using the task prediction results as additional information.

Categories and Subject Descriptors

H.3.3 [**Information Storage and Retrieval**]: Information Search and Retrieval—*search process*; I.2.6 [**Artificial Intelligence**]: Learning

*This work was done when the first author was visiting Microsoft Research Asia.

SIGIR'11, July 24–28, 2011, Beijing, China.

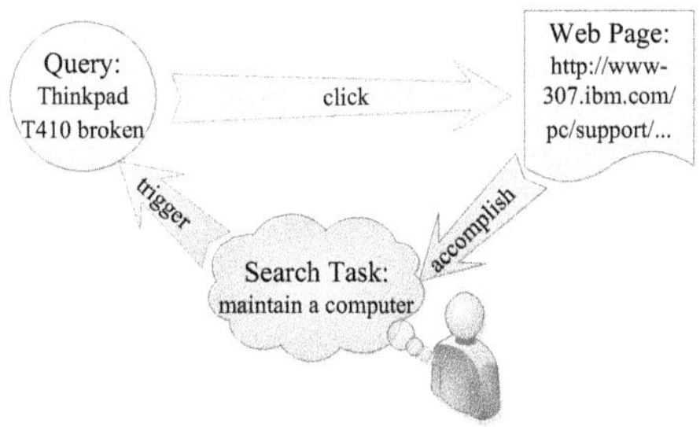

Figure 1: The user is searching for a web page which can effectively accomplish the search task that triggers the query.

General Terms

Algorithms

Keywords

Web search task, classification, graph regularization

1. INTRODUCTION

Until a few years ago, most search engine technologies focus on how to ideally rank web pages according to the relevance to a given query. Although this has been very successful, merely measuring topic relevance is not precise enough to capture the actual *search task* that the user wants to accomplish by issuing a query. Taking the situation in Figure 1 as an example, it can be inferred that the user's search task that triggers query "thinkpad T410 broken" is to "maintain a computer". The Lenovo troubleshooting page[1] might be the most useful to help accomplish this task, and the user would like to click it to obtain information. However, without search task detection, it is difficult for current search engines to return this web page or similar pages in the top few results of relevance ranking. As shown in Figure 2, Bing search and Yahoo! return some reviews about thinkpad T410, while Google finds some forum discussions and other general information. Although these web pages returned by search engines are very relevant to thinkpad T410, they cannot accomplish the right search task in the users' mind. In addition, the search task of "maintain a computer" is actually very popular. According to our analysis of the search log of a commercial search engine, about 14% of the queries related to computers are triggered

[1]http://www-307.ibm.com/pc/support/site.wss/document.do?sitestyle=lenovo&lndocid=MIGR-4YRRG6

(a) Search results of Bing

(b) Search results of Google

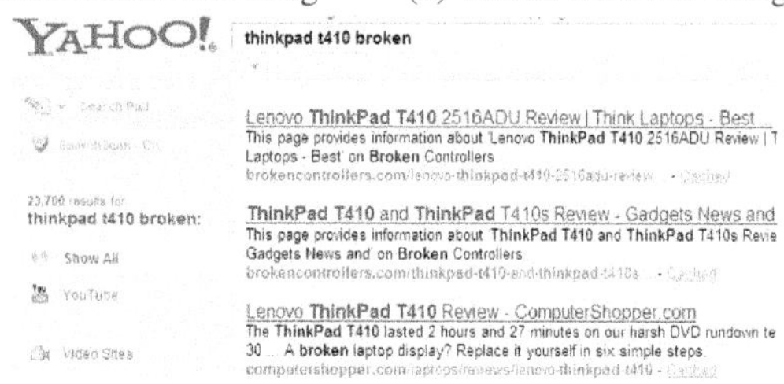

(c) Search results of Yahoo!

Figure 2: The result pages of query "thinkpad T410 broken"

by this task. Therefore, it is crucial to learn the popular search tasks behind queries and web pages in order to return the most useful web pages to users by task matching.

Given some queries and web pages labeled by several pre-defined popular search tasks, together with large amounts of unlabeled queries and web pages, the purpose of our study is to learn two content-based search task predictors for queries and web pages, respectively. A natural idea for learning popular search tasks behind queries and web pages is to cast it as a semi-supervised classification problem, so as to make use of both labeled and unlabeled data. Current query or web page classification methods usually exploit the content together with click-through information [12] [16]. However, most of the algorithms work on one side of the query-page click graph [12], collecting discriminative information either centering around queries, or around web pages. And general classifiers including Support Vector Machines, Maximum Entropy [14], logistic regression, etc., only work with one type of data. Therefore, directly applying existing approaches can either classify queries and web pages separately, or treat queries and web pages as the same type of data and train one unified classifier to handle both of them. These two simple solutions are likely to be suboptimal due to the following challenges:

1. *Close interrelationship between data.* Queries and web pages are two counterparts in the search scenario. As illustrated in Figure 1, the reason why a user clicks certain web pages lies in that these pages might be useful in accomplishing the search task that triggers the query. In other words, a query and a web page linked together by the click relationship are likely to share similar search tasks. So the task predictions of queries and web pages provide good knowledge in understanding each other. Classifying queries and web pages separately fails to make use of the close interrelationship between the two sets of data.

2. *Different types of data.* Queries and web pages are essentially two different types of data, whose content are represented by different kinds of languages. Particularly, queries and web pages often have very different terms to describe the same search task. Taking the search task "maintain a computer" in Figure 1 as an example, not all the users can come up with the term "troubleshooting" which precisely matches the term representing the same search task in the desirable web page. Therefore, we should design two classifiers to fit queries and web pages respectively rather than building a unified classifier to handle both of them.

In this paper, we propose to predict the search tasks behind queries and web pages simultaneously by designing a novel semi-supervised classification framework which addresses both challenges. Specifically, we organize the content and click-through information of both sides of the query-page click relationship into a task-oriented heterogeneous graph among queries and web pages as shown in Figure 3, where each pair of objects are linked together according to task similarity. Through constructing two content-based affinity subgraphs among queries and web pages, respectively, we fully exploit the content information of both labeled and unlabeled data. Meanwhile, the semantic gap between queries and web pages is bridged by the click-through subgraph. Then we perform graph-based regularization over the heterogeneous graph to let the intermediate task predictions of queries and web pages mutually enhance each other throughout the learning process. We further incorporate a linear regression model to directly train two content-based search task predictors for queries and web pages, respectively. By employing our method, we can return web pages to users that are not only relevant, but are also effective in accomplishing the right tasks.

The rest of our paper is structured as follows. We go over the related work in Section 2. Then we formally define the problem of search task classification in Section 3. Section 4 introduces our construction of the graph among queries and web pages. In Section 5, we propose our novel semi-supervised classification framework to train two search task predictors for queries and web pages, respectively. Section 6 provides the experimental results on the real data set of click-through logs. Finally, we conclude this work in Section 7.

2. RELATED WORK

Query classification has received substantial interest in literature. Many existing approaches try to combine the click-through information centering around queries together with the query content to boost the classification performance. Shen et al. [18] enrich the feature representation of queries by using search snippets and similar queries discovered from click-through data. Li et al. [12] use content-based classification to regularize the learning process on click graphs. They essentially transform the bipartite click graph into a homogeneous graph among queries for label propagation. Different from these methods, we aim to directly exploit the content and click-through information on both sides of the bipartite click graph, so that the prediction results of queries and web pages can mutually enhance each other.

On the other hand, extensive research has been dedicated to classifying web pages into given topics [16]. Existing methods exploit the textual content [13], hyperlinks [3] and other information of web pages to improve the classification results. Although hyperlinks are often useful when grouping web pages according to different topics, in our problem of search task classification, however, hyperlinks may be not that helpful, or even be misleading. The reason is that web pages linked by hyperlinks are very likely to aim at accomplishing different tasks. For example, web pages for search tasks like "purchase computers", "maintain hardware" and "download software" are all linked with the Lenovo homepage [2], and hyperlinks are also built among these web pages for users to jump from one task to another conveniently. Shen et al. [19] leverage the click-through information by drawing implicit links between web pages that are clicked after the same query. Moreover, recent years have witnessed a surge of interest in mining multi-typed web objects concurrently by exploiting their interrelationships, with the

[2] http://www.lenovo.com

effectiveness widely recognized [22]. Xue et al. [20] design an iterative reinforcement categorization algorithm which initializes the label prediction via a content-based classifier and then propagates the category information between web pages and queries through the click graph. Ji et al. [10] perform transductive classification over heterogeneous networked data without content features. One key distinction of our work is that we unify the content and click-through information into a data-dependent regularization framework. In addition, we aim to directly build two content-based classifiers which not only give prediction for the data already seen in the training phase, but are also defined everywhere in the ambient feature space.

Meanwhile, it is worth noticing that many research efforts are devoted to learning the user goals in web search. Broder et al. [2] divide the web queries into three main categories, namely *navigational*, *informational* and *transactional*. Rose et al. [17] build a search goal taxonomy with a similar top level except that the *transactional* category is replaced by *resource*. This three-class based web search taxonomy has been widely employed and triggered many follow-up studies [11, 9]. Recent works start discovering some other goals, or in other words, query intents, which are useful for commercial search engines. Proposed intents include product intent, job intent [12], vertical search intent [8], etc. These approaches make binary predictions that a query has a general intent or not. Our goal is significantly different from the previous work since we try to directly understand the *search task* that the user wants to accomplish. Queries and web pages with different topics (such as computers or cars) naturally have different search tasks, thus making our task definition at a finer scale than the existing binary or three-class web search taxonomy. Yin et al. [21] build a hierarchical taxonomy of the generic search intents for a class of named entities by analyzing the relationships between queries and grouping them into a tree structure, which is essentially data-driven. On the contrary, we focus on classifying queries and web pages into several pre-defined tasks that are of special interest among search engine users. To the best of our knowledge, our work is one of the first to study the search task that a web page can accomplish.

Another group of related work is graph-based semi-supervised learning. Most of these methods construct an affinity graph over both labeled and unlabeled examples based on data features to encode the similarity between instances. They then design a learner which preserves the smoothness and consistency over the intrinsic geometry of the data, which is modeled by the affinity graph [10] [6]. Zhu et al. [24] formulate the problem using a Gaussian random field model defined with respect to the graph. Zhou et al. [23] propose to let each point iteratively spread its label information to neighbors so as to ensure both local and global consistency. Our algorithm is closely related to manifold regularization [1], which is a framework for data-dependent regularization that exploits the geometry of the probability distribution on the labeled and unlabeled data. However, traditional graph-based learning mainly works on one type of data, and thus cannot distinguish the multi-typed data. In this paper, we extend the manifold regularization framework to study queries and web pages simultaneously.

3. PROBLEM DEFINITION

Our study is about the *search task* that triggers a query, and the *task* a web page can accomplish. As discussed in [21], the content in a query can be divided into two parts: named entities[3] and other terms. In this paper, we define the search task to be the action that the user wants to perform towards the entities. For instance, the entity in query "thinkpad T410 broken" is "thinkpad T410", while the search task can be described as "maintain a computer" which is inferred from the word "broken". The search task behind a web page is defined similarly. The Lenovo troubleshooting web page can help accomplish the search task of "maintain a computer", regardless of the named entities involved such as "thinkpad" and "Lenovo". Queries only containing named entities can be filtered out from the data that we study, since their search tasks cannot be inferred even manually. We use the word "entity" and "named entity" interchangeably in this paper to refer to the same concept.

Moreover, we focus on classifying queries with a certain category of named entities and the related web pages. A named entity category is a set of entities that are usually considered to be of the same kind, such as computers, cars, cities, etc. Instead of studying all the queries as a whole, it is more appropriate to work on queries with the same category of entities because they are likely to have the same possible tasks, while the search tasks of queries with different categories of entities can vary greatly. For example, the entity category of "computers" can have search tasks like "purchase computers", "download software", "find reviews", etc. And the popular tasks of the entity category of "cars" include "rent a car", "purchase a used car", etc. It is often easy to group entities into categories by using some state-of-the-art methods [15] or through parsing Wikipedia categories/lists.

Now the problem we are going to address can be formally defined as follows. The input data contain a set of queries $\mathcal{Q} = \{q_1, \ldots, q_{|\mathcal{Q}|}\}$ with entities of the same category, a set of web pages $\mathcal{P} = \{p_1, \ldots, p_{|\mathcal{P}|}\}$ clicked by different users after issuing these queries, and a set of search tasks $\mathcal{T} = \{t_1, \ldots, t_{|\mathcal{T}|}\}$ that we want to predict. A subset of queries $\{q_1, \ldots, q_n\}$ and a subset of web pages $\{p_1, \ldots, p_m\}$ are labeled by the search tasks, $n < |\mathcal{Q}|$, $m < |\mathcal{P}|$. Given any query q and any web page p, we aim at computing a task indicator vector $\mathbf{f}(q) = [f^{(1)}(q), \ldots, f^{(|\mathcal{T}|)}(q)]^T \in \mathbb{R}^{|\mathcal{T}|}$, and a task indicator vector $\mathbf{g}(p) = [g^{(1)}(p), \ldots, g^{(|\mathcal{T}|)}(p)]^T \in \mathbb{R}^{|\mathcal{T}|}$. Each $f^{(t)}(q)$ measures the confidence that query q is triggered by task t, and each $g^{(t)}(p)$ measures the confidence that web page p can accomplish task t, $1 \leq t \leq |\mathcal{T}|$. Then we can predict the most probable task behind each query and each web page by finding the maximum value in $\mathbf{f}(q)$ and $\mathbf{g}(p)$:

$$task(q) = \arg\max_{1 \leq t \leq |\mathcal{T}|} f^{(t)}(q) \text{ and } task(p) = \arg\max_{1 \leq t \leq |\mathcal{T}|} g^{(t)}(p)$$

Non-goals. In this paper, we do *not* study the following problems:

1. How to recognize the named entities in queries or web pages and group the entities into categories. This is a well-studied problem which can be solved effectively by employing some state-of-the-art methods, as discussed above.

2. How to define the popular search tasks to be learned. In this paper, the popular search tasks we want to predict are already defined by manual study of the statistics of query logs, just like in other studies of query/web page classification. In fact, the popular search tasks related to an entity category can also be easily specified by common sense.

4. TASK-ORIENTED GRAPH

In this section, we try to unify the content and the click-through information of both sides of the query-page click relationship into

[3]Here we mainly work with named entity queries and related web pages, since named entity queries are the most popular which account for about 71% of all the search queries as reported in [7].

a task-oriented heterogeneous graph among queries and web pages, as illustrated in Figure 3. The principle is to link two objects if and only if they are likely to share similar search tasks. The whole graph over all the objects can be divided into three subgraphs, which are explained in detail in the following subsections.

4.1 Homogeneous subgraph construction

As discussed in Section 3.1, the search tasks can be inferred from the content of queries and web pages excluding the named entities. Similar to [21], we extract the *task phrases* from queries as the substring left after removing the terms corresponding to named entities. For instance, for query "thinkpad T410 broken", the named entity is "thinkpad T410", and "broken" is the task phrase. We consider a task phrase representing the same task for entities of the same category, where a category is composed of a set of entities that people usually consider them to be of the same kind. Examples include computers, cars, cities, actors, movies, etc. It is usually easy to obtain entity categories with the help of Wikipedia or by employing algorithms such as [15].

After extracting entities and task phrases from queries, we merge queries with the same task phrases to clusters because they share the same search tasks. For example, queries "thinkpad T410 broken", "MacBook Pro broken" and " HP Pavilion dv6z broken" are grouped into a single node represented by task phrase "$*$ broken" in the graph, where we use "$*$" to denote a named entity. As long as the search task of a query is predicted, the task of all the other queries sharing the same task phrase is known. In this way, task classification in queries is equivalent to classifying query task phrases. For convenience, we still use $\mathcal{Q} = \{q_1, \ldots, q_{|\mathcal{Q}|}\}$ to represent the set of query task phrases, and let n denote the number of labeled task phrases.

We use the words of the task phrases as the task-oriented content features of the query side, which can be extracted as a term-frequency vector. Task phrases containing similar words are likely to share similar tasks. Then the content-based task similarity between two query clusters represented by task phrases can be computed by any distance measurement in the task-oriented feature space. We use cosine similarity here for simplicity. A k-nearest neighbor subgraph $\mathcal{G}_q$ over queries can be built, with $\mathbf{W}_q$ denoting the adjacency matrix as follows:

$$W_{q,ij} = \begin{cases} sim(q_i, q_j) & \text{if } q_i \in N_k(q_j) \text{ or } q_j \in N_k(q_i) \\ 0 & \text{otherwise.} \end{cases}$$

where $W_{q,ij}$ denotes the element at the i-th row and j-th column of matrix $\mathbf{W}_q$. $N_k(q)$ denotes the set of k nearest neighbors of query q, and $sim(q_i, q_j)$ denotes the similarity between q_i and q_j measured by the given distance measurement (here cosine similarity).

Similarly, we can extract the task-oriented terms for each web page after removing the terms representing named entities in the content. But the web pages are not clustered as queries are, since the terms of web pages after removing named entities still vary drastically. Then a k-nearest neighbor subgraph $\mathcal{G}_p$ can be built over web pages according to the similarity between the task-oriented content features. We let $\mathbf{W}_p$ denote the corresponding adjacency matrix.

Recently, the local consistency idea has received substantial interest [1]. It assumes that two nearby data points in the feature space tend to have the same label. In our problem, it is also natural to assume that two nearby web pages or queries in the content feature space have the same task. Following this idea, we construct the two nearest neighbor subgraphs for queries and web pages in order to ensure the local consistency in their feature spaces. In each subgraph, two objects are connected according to task similarity measured by the lexical content. However, the disadvantage of using all the words is that the search tasks are likely to be overwhelmed by the entity names. For instance, the named entities like "thinkpad", "MacBook" and "HP Pavilion" are not helpful in revealing the hidden search tasks. Our method avoids the influence of named entities by simply filtering them out in the content features.

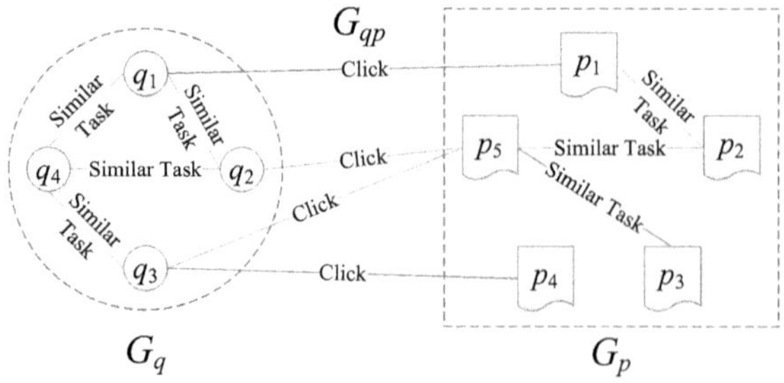

Figure 3: The heterogeneous graph among queries and web pages.

4.2 Bipartite subgraph construction

According to the click-through logs, we assume that a web page p *clicked* by the user after issuing query q is likely to be useful in accomplishing the search task behind q. Therefore, we build a bipartite subgraph $\mathcal{G}_{qp}$ between queries and web pages, where the task similarity between a query and a web page is measured by the click-through relationship. In this subgraph, each edge connects a query q and a web page p if and only if p is clicked by a user after issuing q, with the edge weight being the total number of clicks. Similar as before, queries containing the same *task phrases* are clustered with the click counts added up accordingly. Since $\mathcal{G}_{qp}$ is bipartite, there are no edges between query task phrases or between web pages. $\mathcal{G}_{qp}$ is often called the click graph in literature [12]. We let $\mathbf{R}_{qp}$ be a $|\mathcal{Q}| \times |\mathcal{P}|$ adjacency matrix corresponding to $\mathcal{G}_{qp}$, and $R_{qp,ij}$ denote the element at the i-th row and j-th column of matrix $\mathbf{R}_{qp}$.

It is worth noticing that because queries are often very short, some query task phrases only consist of a single word, such as "$*$ broken", which will not link to any other task phrase in $\mathcal{G}_q$. However, by constructing $\mathcal{G}_{qp}$, these task phrases are linked to some web pages so that we can still make inference on them.

5. GRAPH-BASED REGULARIZATION

As mentioned in the introduction, our ultimate goal is to learn two content-based search task predictors for queries and web pages, respectively. In other words, our final task predictor should be able to correctly classify a query or a web page into one of the $|\mathcal{T}|$ search tasks given its content-based feature representation. In this work, we consider a simple linear regression model for predicting the confidence measure of each query and web page having task t, $1 \leq t \leq |\mathcal{T}|$. Let $\mathbf{q}_i$ denote the d_q-dimensional content-based feature vector of a query task phrase q_i, as discussed in section 4.1. Similarly, we let $\mathbf{p}_j$ denote the d_p-dimensional task-oriented content feature of a web page p_j. Then we have:

$$f^{(t)}(q_i) = \mathbf{w}_q^{(t)T}\mathbf{q}_i \text{ and } g^{(t)}(p_j) = \mathbf{w}_p^{(t)T}\mathbf{p}_j$$

where $\mathbf{w}_q^{(t)}$ and $\mathbf{w}_p^{(t)}$ are the two weight vectors to be estimated for queries and web pages, respectively. Let $\mathbf{u}_i = [u_i^{(1)}, \ldots, u_i^{(|\mathcal{T}|)}]^T \in \mathbb{R}^{|\mathcal{T}|}$ denote the task indicator vector for a labeled query task phrase q_i, and $\mathbf{v}_j = [v_j^{(1)}, \ldots, v_j^{(|\mathcal{T}|)}]^T \in \mathbb{R}^{|\mathcal{T}|}$ denote the task indicator vector for a labeled web page p_j. Then it is natural to define:

$$u_i^{(t)} = \begin{cases} 1 & \text{if } q_i \text{ is labeled to have task } t \\ 0 & \text{otherwise.} \end{cases}$$

$$v_j^{(t)} = \begin{cases} 1 & \text{if } p_j \text{ is labeled to have task } t \\ 0 & \text{otherwise.} \end{cases}$$

Now our problem becomes: given $\{\mathbf{u}_i\}_{i=1}^n$, $\{\mathbf{v}_i\}_{i=1}^m$, $n < |\mathcal{Q}|$, $m < |\mathcal{P}|$, and the constructed heterogeneous graph $\mathcal{G}$ composed of $\mathcal{G}_{qp}$, $\mathcal{G}_p$ and $\mathcal{G}_q$, how to estimate $\mathbf{w}_q^{(t)}$ and $\mathbf{w}_p^{(t)}$, for all $1 \leq t \leq |\mathcal{T}|$.

According to the construction of the task-oriented heterogeneous graph in Section 4, we have the assumption that the confidence estimations of each query task phrase q_i and web page p_j having task t, denoted by $f^{(t)}(q_i)$ and $g^{(t)}(p_j)$, respectively, should be as consistent as possible with the graph structure. And the task prediction on labeled queries and web pages should be similar to their labels. We formulate the *consistency assumption* as follows:

1. Within each subgraph, the confidence estimations of two objects having each task should be similar if they are linked together, with the edge weight measuring the similarity.
2. The confidence estimations of the labeled query task phrases and web pages having task t should be similar to their labels encoded in $\{u_1^{(t)}, \ldots, u_n^{(t)}\}$ and $\{v_1^{(t)}, \ldots, v_m^{(t)}\}$.

For the adjacency matrix $\mathbf{R}_{qp}$ corresponding to $\mathcal{G}_{qp}$, we further define two diagonal matrices $\mathbf{D}_{qp}$ and $\mathbf{D}_{pq}$, whose entries are the row sums and column sums of $\mathbf{R}_{qp}$:

$$\mathbf{D}_{qp} \in \mathbb{R}^{|\mathcal{Q}| \times |\mathcal{Q}|}, D_{qp,ii} = \sum_{j=1}^{|\mathcal{P}|} R_{qp,ij}$$

$$\mathbf{D}_{pq} \in \mathbb{R}^{|\mathcal{P}| \times |\mathcal{P}|}, D_{pq,ii} = \sum_{j=1}^{|\mathcal{Q}|} R_{qp,ji}$$

Since $\mathbf{W}_q$ and $\mathbf{W}_p$ are symmetric matrices whose row sums and column sums are the same, we only need to define one diagonal matrix for each of them:

$$\mathbf{D}_q \in \mathbb{R}^{|\mathcal{Q}| \times |\mathcal{Q}|}, D_{q,ii} = \sum_{j=1}^{|\mathcal{Q}|} W_{q,ij} = \sum_{j=1}^{|\mathcal{Q}|} W_{q,ji}$$

$$\mathbf{D}_p \in \mathbb{R}^{|\mathcal{P}| \times |\mathcal{P}|}, D_{p,ii} = \sum_{j=1}^{|\mathcal{P}|} W_{p,ij} = \sum_{j=1}^{|\mathcal{P}|} W_{p,ji}$$

Then the consistency assumption discussed before leads to minimizing the following objective function:

$$\begin{aligned} & J(\mathbf{w}_q^{(t)}, \mathbf{w}_p^{(t)}) \\ = \; & \lambda_{qp} \sum_{i=1}^{|\mathcal{Q}|} \sum_{j=1}^{|\mathcal{P}|} R_{qp,ij} \left(\frac{\mathbf{w}_q^{(t)T} \mathbf{q}_i}{\sqrt{D_{qp,ii}}} - \frac{\mathbf{w}_p^{(t)T} \mathbf{p}_j}{\sqrt{D_{pq,jj}}} \right)^2 \\ & + \lambda_q \sum_{i,j=1}^{|\mathcal{Q}|} W_{q,ij} \left(\frac{\mathbf{w}_q^{(t)T} \mathbf{q}_i}{\sqrt{D_{q,ii}}} - \frac{\mathbf{w}_q^{(t)T} \mathbf{q}_j}{\sqrt{D_{q,jj}}} \right)^2 \\ & + \lambda_p \sum_{i,j=1}^{|\mathcal{P}|} W_{p,ij} \left(\frac{\mathbf{w}_p^{(t)T} \mathbf{p}_i}{\sqrt{D_{p,ii}}} - \frac{\mathbf{w}_p^{(t)T} \mathbf{p}_j}{\sqrt{D_{p,jj}}} \right)^2 \\ & + \alpha_q \sum_{i=1}^{n} (\mathbf{w}_q^{(t)T} \mathbf{q}_i - u_i^{(t)})^2 + \alpha_p \sum_{i=1}^{m} (\mathbf{w}_p^{(t)T} \mathbf{p}_i - v_i^{(t)})^2 \\ & + \beta_q ||\mathbf{w}_q^{(t)}||^2 + \beta_p ||\mathbf{w}_p^{(t)}||^2 \qquad (1) \end{aligned}$$

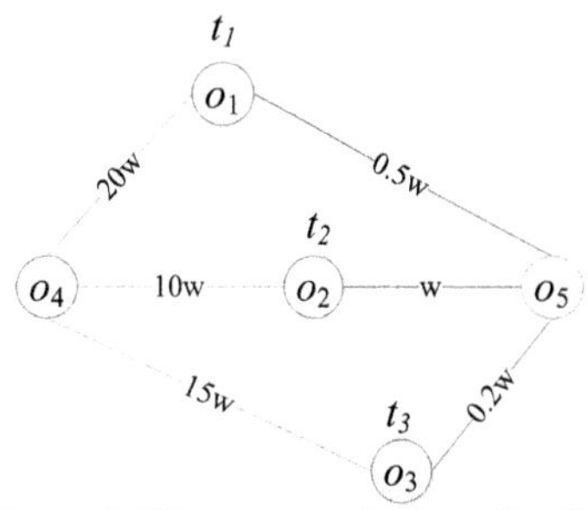

Figure 4: The reason of normalization.

for $t \in \{1, \ldots, |\mathcal{T}|\}$. $||.||$ denotes the L2 norm. The first three terms encode the consistency assumption in the three subgraphs $\mathcal{G}_{qp}$, $\mathcal{G}_q$ and $\mathcal{G}_p$ among query task phrases and web pages. These terms are normalized by $\sqrt{D_{qp,ii}}$, $\sqrt{D_{pq,jj}}$, $\sqrt{D_{p,ii}}$ and $\sqrt{D_{q,ii}}$, respectively, in order to reduce the impact of popularity of objects. For example, the subgraph in Figure 4 contains five objects denoted as $\{o_1, \ldots, o_5\}$, each of which is either a query task phrase or a web page. Suppose o_1, o_2 and o_3 are labeled to have tasks t_1, t_2 and t_3, respectively. The edge between o_5 and o_2 weighs w, while the edge between o_4 and o_2 has the weight of $10w$. However, this does not mean that the confidence of o_4 having task t_2 should be 10 times higher than that of o_5. In fact, the confidence of o_4 triggered by task t_2 should be the lowest among all the three tasks, since the edges between o_4 and objects having tasks t_1 and t_3 weigh more than the edge between o_4 and o_2 does. Similarly, the confidence of o_5 having t_2 should be the highest among the three tasks. Therefore, we normalize the weight of each edge by the sum of the weight on all the edges connected to the two objects at the end of the edge in order to prevent the confidence of popular objects having each task from increasing incorrectly. This normalization technique is adopted in traditional graph-based learning and its effectiveness is well proved [23]. The fourth and fifth terms ensure the consistency between the estimated results and the given labels. Finally, the last two terms are two Tikhonov regularizers imposed on $\mathbf{w}_q^{(t)}$ and $\mathbf{w}_p^{(t)}$ in order to ensure the stableness of the obtained solution [1].

The trade-off among these terms is controlled by the parameters λ_{qp}, λ_q, λ_p, α_q, α_p, β_q and β_p in the range of $(0, 1]$. Note that λ_{qp}, λ_q, λ_p, α_q and α_p encode the relative importance of five different types of information, namely the click-through information, the content of queries and web pages, the labels of queries and web pages, respectively. The larger the corresponding parameter, the more value is placed on certain type of information. For instance, if the user believes that the click-through information is more trustworthy and influential than the content-based features, then λ_{qp} can be set larger than λ_q and λ_p. However, we will show in Section 6 that the parameter setting will not influence the performance of our algorithm dramatically.

We then generate the normalized form of $\mathbf{R}_{qp}$, $\mathbf{W}_q$ and $\mathbf{W}_p$ as follows:

$$\mathbf{S}_{qp} = \mathbf{D}_{qp}^{-1/2} \mathbf{R}_{qp} \mathbf{D}_{pq}^{-1/2}$$

$$\mathbf{S}_q = \mathbf{D}_q^{-1/2} \mathbf{W}_q \mathbf{D}_q^{-1/2}$$

$$\mathbf{S}_p = \mathbf{D}_p^{-1/2} \mathbf{W}_p \mathbf{D}_p^{-1/2}$$

We further make the following notations:

$$\mathbf{w}^{(t)} = [\mathbf{w}_q^{(t)T}, \mathbf{w}_p^{(t)T}]^T$$

$$\mathbf{Q} = [\mathbf{q}_1, \ldots, \mathbf{q}_{|\mathcal{Q}|}] \quad , \quad \mathbf{P} = [\mathbf{p}_1, \ldots, \mathbf{p}_{|\mathcal{P}|}]$$

$$\mathbf{Q}_L = [\mathbf{q}_1, \ldots, \mathbf{q}_n] \quad , \quad \mathbf{P}_L = [\mathbf{p}_1, \ldots, \mathbf{p}_m]$$

$$\mathbf{u}^{(t)} = [u_1^{(t)}, \ldots, u_n^{(t)}]^T \in \mathbb{R}^n \quad , \quad \mathbf{v}^{(t)} = [v_1^{(t)}, \ldots, v_m^{(t)}]^T \in \mathbb{R}^m$$
$$\mathbf{L}_q = \mathbf{I}_{|\mathcal{Q}|} - \mathbf{S}_q \quad , \quad \mathbf{L}_p = \mathbf{I}_{|\mathcal{P}|} - \mathbf{S}_p$$
$$\mathbf{L}_{qp} = \begin{bmatrix} \mathbf{I}_{|\mathcal{Q}|} & -\mathbf{S}_{qp} \\ -\mathbf{S}_{qp}^T & \mathbf{I}_{|\mathcal{P}|} \end{bmatrix}$$

where $\mathbf{I}_n$ is the identity matrix of size $n \times n$. Note that $\mathbf{L}_q$, $\mathbf{L}_p$ and $\mathbf{L}_{qp}$ are the *normalized graph Laplacians* [5] of the three subgraphs $\mathcal{G}_q$, $\mathcal{G}_p$ and $\mathcal{G}_{qp}$, respectively.

Then with simple algebraic formulations, the first term of objective function (1) can be rewritten as:

$$\begin{aligned}
&\lambda_{qp} \sum_{i=1}^{|\mathcal{Q}|} \sum_{j=1}^{|\mathcal{P}|} R_{qp,ij} \left(\frac{\mathbf{w}_q^{(t)T}\mathbf{q}_i}{\sqrt{D_{qp,ii}}} - \frac{\mathbf{w}_p^{(t)T}\mathbf{p}_j}{\sqrt{D_{pq,jj}}} \right)^2 \\
=\ & \lambda_{qp} \sum_{i=1}^{|\mathcal{Q}|} \sum_{j=1}^{|\mathcal{P}|} R_{qp,ij} \Big(\frac{(\mathbf{w}_q^{(t)T}\mathbf{q}_i)^2}{D_{qp,ii}} - 2\frac{(\mathbf{w}_q^{(t)T}\mathbf{q}_i)(\mathbf{w}_p^{(t)T}\mathbf{p}_j)}{\sqrt{D_{qp,ii}D_{pq,jj}}} \\
&+ \frac{(\mathbf{w}_p^{(t)T}\mathbf{p}_j)^2}{D_{pq,jj}} \Big) \\
=\ & \lambda_{qp} \Big(\sum_{i=1}^{|\mathcal{Q}|} (\mathbf{w}_q^{(t)T}\mathbf{q}_i)^2 + \sum_{i=1}^{|\mathcal{P}|} (\mathbf{w}_p^{(t)T}\mathbf{p}_i)^2 \\
&-2 \sum_{i=1}^{|\mathcal{Q}|} \sum_{j=1}^{|\mathcal{P}|} \left(\mathbf{w}_q^{(t)T}\mathbf{q}_i S_{qp,ij} \mathbf{w}_p^{(t)T}\mathbf{p}_j \right) \Big) \\
=\ & \lambda_{qp} \left(\mathbf{w}_q^{(t)T}\mathbf{Q}\mathbf{Q}^T\mathbf{w}_q^{(t)} + \mathbf{w}_p^{(t)T}\mathbf{P}\mathbf{P}^T\mathbf{w}_p^{(t)} \right. \\
&\left. -2\mathbf{w}_q^{(t)T}\mathbf{Q}\mathbf{S}_{qp}\mathbf{P}^T\mathbf{w}_p^{(t)} \right) \\
=\ & \lambda_{qp} \left(\mathbf{w}^{(t)T} \begin{bmatrix} \mathbf{Q} & \mathbf{0} \\ \mathbf{0} & \mathbf{P} \end{bmatrix} \mathbf{L}_{qp} \begin{bmatrix} \mathbf{Q}^T & \mathbf{0} \\ \mathbf{0} & \mathbf{P}^T \end{bmatrix} \mathbf{w}^{(t)} \right) \qquad (2)
\end{aligned}$$

Following similar derivations, the second and third terms can be rewritten as:

$$\lambda_q \sum_{i,j=1}^{|\mathcal{Q}|} W_{q,ij} \left(\frac{\mathbf{w}_q^{(t)T}\mathbf{q}_i}{\sqrt{D_{q,ii}}} - \frac{\mathbf{w}_q^{(t)T}\mathbf{q}_j}{\sqrt{D_{q,jj}}} \right)^2 = 2\lambda_q \mathbf{w}_q^{(t)T}\mathbf{Q}\mathbf{L}_q\mathbf{Q}^T\mathbf{w}_q^{(t)}$$
$$\lambda_p \sum_{i,j=1}^{|\mathcal{P}|} W_{p,ij} \left(\frac{\mathbf{w}_p^{(t)T}\mathbf{p}_i}{\sqrt{D_{p,ii}}} - \frac{\mathbf{w}_p^{(t)T}\mathbf{p}_j}{\sqrt{D_{p,jj}}} \right)^2 = 2\lambda_p \mathbf{w}_p^{(t)T}\mathbf{P}\mathbf{L}_p\mathbf{P}^T\mathbf{w}_p^{(t)}$$

Then we can rewrite objective function (1) in the following matrix-vector form:

$$\begin{aligned}
J(\mathbf{w}_q^{(t)}, \mathbf{w}_p^{(t)}) =\ & \lambda_{qp} \left(\mathbf{w}^{(t)T} \begin{bmatrix} \mathbf{Q} & \mathbf{0} \\ \mathbf{0} & \mathbf{P} \end{bmatrix} \mathbf{L}_{qp} \begin{bmatrix} \mathbf{Q}^T & \mathbf{0} \\ \mathbf{0} & \mathbf{P}^T \end{bmatrix} \mathbf{w}^{(t)} \right) \\
&+2\lambda_q \mathbf{w}_q^{(t)T}\mathbf{Q}\mathbf{L}_q\mathbf{Q}^T\mathbf{w}_q^{(t)} + 2\lambda_p \mathbf{w}_p^{(t)T}\mathbf{P}\mathbf{L}_p\mathbf{P}^T\mathbf{w}_p^{(t)} \\
&+\alpha_q(\mathbf{Q}_L^T\mathbf{w}_q^{(t)} - \mathbf{u}^{(t)})^T(\mathbf{Q}_L^T\mathbf{w}_q^{(t)} - \mathbf{u}^{(t)}) \\
&+\alpha_p(\mathbf{P}_L^T\mathbf{w}_p^{(t)} - \mathbf{v}^{(t)})^T(\mathbf{P}_L^T\mathbf{w}_p^{(t)} - \mathbf{v}^{(t)}) \\
&+\beta_q\mathbf{w}_q^{(t)T}\mathbf{w}_q^{(t)} + \beta_p\mathbf{w}_p^{(t)T}\mathbf{w}_p^{(t)} \qquad (3)
\end{aligned}$$

We further define

$$\begin{aligned}
\widehat{\mathbf{L}} &= \begin{bmatrix} \lambda_{qp}\mathbf{I}_{|\mathcal{Q}|} + 2\lambda_q\mathbf{L}_q & -\lambda_{qp}\mathbf{S}_{qp} \\ -\lambda_{qp}\mathbf{S}_{qp}^T & \lambda_{qp}\mathbf{I}_{|\mathcal{P}|} + 2\lambda_p\mathbf{L}_p \end{bmatrix} \\
\mathbf{y}^{(t)} &= [\mathbf{u}^{(t)T}, \mathbf{v}^{(t)T}]^T \\
\widehat{\mathbf{X}} &= \begin{bmatrix} \mathbf{Q} & \mathbf{0} \\ \mathbf{0} & \mathbf{P} \end{bmatrix}, \widehat{\mathbf{X}}_L = \begin{bmatrix} \mathbf{Q}_L & \mathbf{0} \\ \mathbf{0} & \mathbf{P}_L \end{bmatrix} \\
\boldsymbol{\alpha} &= \begin{bmatrix} \alpha_q\mathbf{I}_n & \mathbf{0} \\ \mathbf{0} & \alpha_p\mathbf{I}_m \end{bmatrix}, \boldsymbol{\beta} = \begin{bmatrix} \beta_q\mathbf{I}_{d_q} & \mathbf{0} \\ \mathbf{0} & \beta_p\mathbf{I}_{d_p} \end{bmatrix}
\end{aligned}$$

Finally, objective function (3) is equivalent to the following:

$$\begin{aligned}
J(\mathbf{w}^{(t)}) =\ & \mathbf{w}^{(t)T}\widehat{\mathbf{X}}\widehat{\mathbf{L}}\widehat{\mathbf{X}}^T\mathbf{w}^{(t)} \\
&+(\widehat{\mathbf{X}}_L^T\mathbf{w}^{(t)} - \mathbf{y}^{(t)})^T\boldsymbol{\alpha}(\widehat{\mathbf{X}}_L^T\mathbf{w}^{(t)} - \mathbf{y}^{(t)}) \\
&+\mathbf{w}^{(t)T}\boldsymbol{\beta}\mathbf{w}^{(t)} \qquad (4)
\end{aligned}$$

5.1 Closed form solution

It is easy to check that $\mathbf{L}_q$, $\mathbf{L}_p$ and $\mathbf{L}_{qp}$, which are the three *normalized graph Laplacians* [5] over the three subgraphs, $\mathcal{G}_q$, $\mathcal{G}_p$ and $\mathcal{G}_{qp}$, are positive semi-definite. $\widehat{\mathbf{L}}$ is the weighted summation of $\mathbf{L}_q$, $\mathbf{L}_p$ and $\mathbf{L}_{qp}$, which is also positive semi-definite. $\boldsymbol{\alpha}$ and $\boldsymbol{\beta}$ are diagonal matrices whose entries are all positive, therefore are both positive definite. We then check the Hessian matrix of the objective function (1), which is easy to derive from equation (4):

$$H\big(J(\mathbf{w}^{(t)})\big) = 2\widehat{\mathbf{X}}\widehat{\mathbf{L}}\widehat{\mathbf{X}}^T + 2\widehat{\mathbf{X}}_L\boldsymbol{\alpha}\widehat{\mathbf{X}}_L^T + 2\boldsymbol{\beta} \qquad (5)$$

Since $\widehat{\mathbf{X}}\widehat{\mathbf{L}}\widehat{\mathbf{X}}^T$ and $\widehat{\mathbf{X}}_L\boldsymbol{\alpha}\widehat{\mathbf{X}}_L^T$ are positive semi-definite and $\beta_q, \beta_p > 0$, we conclude that $H\big(J(\mathbf{w}^{(t)})\big)$ is positive definite. Therefore, the objective function (4) is strictly convex. The unique global minimum is obtained by differentiating (4) with respect to $\mathbf{w}^{(t)T}$ and letting $\frac{\partial J(\mathbf{w}^{(t)})}{\partial \mathbf{w}^{(t)T}} = 0$:

$$\frac{\partial J(\mathbf{w}^{(t)})}{\partial \mathbf{w}^{(t)T}} = 2\widehat{\mathbf{X}}\widehat{\mathbf{L}}\widehat{\mathbf{X}}^T\mathbf{w}^{(t)} + 2\widehat{\mathbf{X}}_L\boldsymbol{\alpha}(\widehat{\mathbf{X}}_L^T\mathbf{w}^{(t)} - \mathbf{y}^{(t)}) + 2\boldsymbol{\beta}\mathbf{w}^{(t)} = 0$$

Finally, we give the closed form solution of $\mathbf{w}^{(t)} = [\mathbf{w}_q^{(t)T}, \mathbf{w}_p^{(t)T}]^T$ as follows:

$$\mathbf{w}^{(t)} = (\widehat{\mathbf{X}}\widehat{\mathbf{L}}\widehat{\mathbf{X}}^T + \widehat{\mathbf{X}}_L\boldsymbol{\alpha}\widehat{\mathbf{X}}_L^T + \boldsymbol{\beta})^{-1}\widehat{\mathbf{X}}_L\boldsymbol{\alpha}\mathbf{y}^{(t)} \qquad (6)$$

for $t \in \{1, \ldots, |\mathcal{T}|\}$.

5.2 Theoretical interpretations

Equations (4) and (6) show that our proposed algorithm has a consistent form with Laplacian Regularized Least Squares (LapRLS) [1], which is a semi-supervised manifold regularization framework on homogeneous data. If we set $\lambda_{qp} = \lambda_p = \alpha_p = \beta_p = 0$, our algorithm reduces to LapRLS on queries only. Similarly, letting $\lambda_{qp} = \lambda_q = \alpha_q = \beta_q = 0$ reduces to LapRLS on web pages. Under the assumption that data reside on or close to an underlying submanifold in the ambient feature space, LapRLS makes use of both labeled and unlabeled examples to learn a regression model whose prediction result is locally consistent along the geodesics of the data manifold. However, as discussed before, queries and web pages essentially have different feature spaces, therefore reside on two different pieces of submanifold in the ambient word space. We thus construct two homogeneous graphs $\mathcal{G}_q$ and $\mathcal{G}_p$ to ensure the local consistency of queries and web pages, respectively. And the bipartite graph $\mathcal{G}_{qp}$ is built to let the task prediction results on queries and web pages mutually enhance each other in the whole learning process.

6. EXPERIMENTS

In this section, we present an empirical study of the effectiveness of our Graph-based Regularization framework for Search Task Classification in queries and web pages simultaneously (denoted by GRSTC) on the click-through data over a continuous period of time from the search log of a commonly used commercial search engine. As discussed before, we try to classify each query and each web page to one of the pre-defined search tasks.

Table 1: Statistics of the data sets

Entity category	Computers	Cars
# of named entities	7.5k	20k
# of distinct queries	780k	7,600k
# of query task phrases	2,268	3,308
# of web pages	36,890	33,039
# of edges in the click graph	190k	340k
Total click count	1,100k	2,800k

6.1 Data set

We use two real click-through data sets of queries containing the entity categories of computers and cars, respectively, from a commonly used commercial search engine. Some statistics of the two data sets are listed in Table 1. We ignore queries involving entities belonging to more than one category.

For the computer category, we collect 780k distinct queries from which 2,268 *task phrases* are extracted. Among all the web pages clicked by these queries, we select 36,890 web pages which received totally no less than 5 clicks over all of these queries, since these web pages are the most popular and the most important to study. Then we extract the lexical features from the task phrases, which have totally 3,210 dimensions. And the content-based lexical features for web pages extracted in the same way have totally 8,532 dimensions. From the different numbers of dimensions of the content-based features, we can see that queries and web pages do have very different feature spaces. Many terms contained in web pages never appear in the query task phrases.

For the car category, we obtain 3,308 task phrases covering totally 7,600k distinct queries. Although the number of task phrases is similar to the computer category, the number of queries covered is significantly larger. This is because the car category involves many more named entities than the computer category, as observed in the first row of Table 1. Moreover, the large number of queries leads to many more web pages clicked. Then we select totally 33,039 web pages which received no less than 20 clicks from all the queries as our experimental data, while our learned classifier can actually work on all the web pages. Similar as before, we extract the 2,997-dimensional lexical features of the query task phrases, and the 11,926-dimensional lexical features of the web pages.

6.2 Algorithms for comparison

Since we are trying to predict search tasks of queries and web pages based on the textual content and the click-through information, the problem can also be cast as a traditional classification task, as discussed above. We compare our proposed method with several state-of-the-art classification approaches as follows:

- Maximum Entropy (ME): Train *two* maximum entropy classifiers for queries and web pages, respectively, using the content-based features only.
- LapRLS-content: Train *two* LapRLS classifiers for queries and web pages, respectively, using the content-based features only.
- LapRLS-click: Train *one* LapRLS classifier by treating queries and web pages as homogeneous data. We use the click graph to play the role of the nearest-neighbor graph in the algorithm.

Maximum Entropy (ME) [14] is a supervised content-based classifier widely used in web mining and information retrieval. We use the same content-based features extracted from query task phrases and web pages for all the algorithms. Since our algorithm belongs to the category of semi-supervised learning, which has been reported to perform generally better than purely supervised methods [4], we tried several supervised classifiers including Support Vector Machines, Regularized Least Squares, ME, etc., and present the best results generated by ME. LapRLS [1] is a semi-supervised manifold regularization framework preserving local consistency in the feature space of the data, which is the homogeneous reduction of our algorithm as discussed in Section 5.2. Here we try two versions of LapRLS: (1) LapRLS-content, the original version running on homogeneous data, where a nearest-neighbor graph is constructed based on local features[4]; and (2) LapRLS-click, which considers queries and web pages as the the same type of data. However, since queries and web pages have different feature spaces, we can no longer build a feature-based nearest-neighbor graph over all the data. Then we use the click graph to play the role of the affinity graph. The idea of LapRLS-click is similar to [20], with an out-of-sample extension performed by incorporating linear regression.

The original LapRLS algorithm [1] works on homogeneous data, therefore has only one α, one λ and one β. And α is fixed to be 1 since only the ratio between the three parameters matters in the model selection. In our experiments, we follow this configuration and search λ and β in the grid $\{10^{-5}, 2\times10^{-5}, 5\times10^{-5}, 10^{-4}, 2\times10^{-4}, 5\times10^{-4}, 0.001, 0.002, 0.005, 0.01, 0.02, 0.05, 0.1, 0.2, 0.5, 1, 2, 5, 10\}$, where the best results for LapRLS are obtained by $\lambda = 0.5$ and $\beta = 10^{-4}$. It has been reported that the performance of LapRLS is generally not very sensitive to the parameter setting. In order to have a fair comparison, we treat the three subgraphs $\mathcal{G}_{qp}$, $\mathcal{G}_q$ and $\mathcal{G}_p$ in GRSTC as equally important and use the same set of parameters as LapRLS, i.e., $\lambda_{qp} = \lambda_q = \lambda_p = 0.5$, $\beta_q = \beta_p = 10^{-4}$. This may not be the best choice for GRSTC, but it is good enough to show the effectiveness of this method. We also fix $\alpha_q = 1$ in GRSTC. But for α_p, since many web pages can help accomplish more than one search task, therefore strictly labeling a web page to one most relevant search task is not very accurate. In this way, we slightly reduce α_p and empirically set it to 0.2. The number of nearest neighbors k is empirically set to 15 for LapRLS-content and GRSTC.

Finally, we use the F_1 measure to evaluate the classification performance of different algorithms, which is computed as follows:

$$F_1 = \frac{2 \times precision \times recall}{precision + recall}$$

6.3 Prediction performance

6.3.1 *Computer category*

We try to classify the query task phrases and web pages of the computer category into 7 popular search tasks as listed in Table 2, which are discovered according to manual study of the search log summary.

For performance evaluation, we manually labeled all the 2,268 *task phrases* and 1,634 web pages with the largest number of clicks. In the following sections, we randomly choose $l\%(= 5\%, 10\%, \ldots, 70\%)$ of the labeled queries and web pages and use their label information as prior knowledge. The search task prediction performance is evaluated by comparing with manually labeled results on the rest of the labeled queries and web pages. For each given $l\%$, we average the results over 10 random splits. We show the F_1 measure of

[4]We also tried transforming the query-page bipartite graph into homogeneous graphs among queries and among web pages to play the role of the nearest-neighbor graphs, which is similar to the idea of [12]. But this implementation did not outperform LapRLS-content in our experiments and therefore we do not present the results.

Table 2: Popular search tasks to be discovered in the computer category (%)

No.	Search task	Description	Example task phrases
1	Purchase computer	Buy a computer	* amazon, coupon *, * deal
2	Find review	Find the reviews or general information of a computer	* reviews, * desktop, * models
3	Compare	Compare two computers on various aspects	* versus *, * or *
4	System help	Find out about how to use a system	* tech support, * configuration, * recovery
5	Download software	Download or update software, especially drivers	* driver download, * audio driver, * media
6	Maintain hardware	Repair or upgrade hardware	* broken, * memory upgrade, upgrade * hard drive
7	Purchase accessories	Buy a printer/scanner/camera or other accessories	* printer, * bag, * camera

Table 3: F_1 measure on queries of the computer category

% labeled queries	5	10	20	30	40	50	60	70	average
ME	0.59	0.62	0.66	0.69	0.70	0.71	0.72	0.73	0.68
LapRLS-content	0.66	0.69	0.73	0.75	0.75	0.76	0.77	0.78	0.73
LapRLS-click	0.62	0.67	0.71	0.74	0.76	0.77	0.78	0.78	0.73
GRSTC	**0.67**	**0.70**	**0.75**	**0.77**	**0.78**	**0.79**	**0.80**	**0.81**	**0.76**

Table 4: F_1 measure on web pages of the computer category

% labeled web pages	5	10	20	30	40	50	60	70	average
ME	0.39	0.40	0.41	0.41	0.43	0.43	0.43	0.43	0.42
LapRLS-content	0.45	0.46	0.48	0.46	0.50	0.50	0.51	0.52	0.49
LapRLS-click	0.53	0.57	0.60	0.61	0.63	0.64	0.64	0.65	0.61
GRSTC	**0.58**	**0.62**	**0.64**	**0.65**	**0.67**	**0.67**	**0.67**	**0.68**	**0.65**

queries and web pages with different percentage of labeled data of different algorithms in Table 3 and Table 4, respectively.

When classifying queries, LapRLS-content and LapRLS-click perform comparably to each other and better than ME, verifying the effectiveness of learning from both labeled and unlabeled data. When classifying web pages, LapRLS-content still outperforms ME. And it is interesting to note that LapRLS-click performs much better than LapRLS-content. This is because that the content-based features of web pages are noisier than those of queries, therefore merely relying on content is not very accurate, as reported in many past studies in web page classification [16]. LapRLS-click takes the advantage of learning from labeled queries by exploiting the click-through information, while LapRLS-content can only use the labels on web pages even if some labels on queries are also available. However, LapRLS-click fails to consider the local consistency in the content feature space of the data.

Overall, our proposed GRSTC algorithm performs the best in both queries and web pages. Even though GRSTC uses the same set of parameters as its homogeneous reduction, LapRLS, GRSTC still outperforms the two versions of LapRLS by unifying the content and click-through information of both queries and web pages in an organized way. We also performed the two-tailed t-test over the F_1 measure of the experimental results. All the p-values between the results of GRSTC and other algorithms with varying percentage of labeled data are less than 0.05. Therefore, the improvements of our GRSTC algorithm are statistically significant.

6.3.2 Car category

The pre-defined search tasks to be classified in the car category are listed in Table 5. Similar as the computer category, these popular search tasks discovered by manual study of the search log summary are of special interest to the search engine users. Notice that several tasks of the car category are very different from those of the computer category, such as search tasks "purchase a used car", "rent a car", etc. That is the reason why we work on queries containing named entities of the same category and related web pages.

Similar as before, we manually labeled all the 3,308 *task phrases* and 1,434 web pages with the largest number of clicks. We then randomly choose $l\%(= 5\%, 10\%, \ldots, 70\%)$ of the labeled queries and web pages as prior knowledge, and evaluate the performance of search task prediction by comparing with manually labeled results on the rest of the labeled data. The results for each $l\%$ are averaged over 10 random splits. The F_1 measure of queries and web pages with different portions of labeled data are shown in Table 6 and Table 7, respectively.

As can be observed, the semi-supervised LapRLS-content and LapRLS-click still generally outperform the supervised ME method. It is interesting to note that when classifying web pages in this category, the F_1 measure of LapRLS-click drops below that of LapRLS-content, although LapRLS-click uses additional labels of the queries. This indicates that we need to handle the label information on queries carefully when it is used to study web pages. After all, queries and web pages are two different types of data with different semantic meanings, therefore it is inappropriate to treat them equally as LapRLS-click does. Our proposed GRSTC consistently outperforms all the other algorithms by well respecting the semantic differences between queries and web pages through making full use of their content information, while letting their classification results mutually enhance each other at the same time.

Finally, we performed the two-tailed t-test over the F_1 measure of the experimental results. All the p-values between the results of GRSTC and other algorithms with different portions of labeled data are less than 0.05, indicating that the improvements of our GRSTC method are statistically significant.

6.4 Task-oriented re-ranking

In order to verify the usefulness of search task prediction in search ranking, here we test a simple task-oriented re-ranking scheme by directly incorporating our search task classification results as additional information. This may not be the optimal solution to consider search tasks in ranking, but it is good enough to show the benefit of employing our algorithm.

The basic idea is to use search task prediction as an additional feature to re-evaluate the relevance between the query and the web pages to rank. Given a query q, the search engine can retrieve the top-k relevant web pages $\{p_1, \ldots, p_k\}$ using its original ranking function. Then we can use the query classifier trained by our GRSTC algorithm to predict the search task t_q behind the query. On the other hand, the web page classifier trained by GRSTC can estimate the confidence that each web page p_j could accomplish t_q,

Table 5: Popular search tasks to be discovered in the car category (%)

No.	Search task	Description	Example task phrases
1	Purchase a new car	Buy a new car	* price, * dealer, * retail
2	Purchase a used car	Buy a second-hand car	used *, pre-owned *, second hand *
3	Find reviews	Find the reviews or general information of a car	* reviews, * new model, * cars
4	Compare	Compare two cars on various aspects	compare * and *, * vs *, difference between * and *
5	Rent a car	Rent a car	* rental, rent a *, cheap * rental
6	Maintain a car	Repair a broken car	* repair, * problems, * oil leak
7	Purchase accessories	Buy a wheel/headlight/diesel or other accessories	wheels for *, * engine, * parts
8	Troubleshooting	General questions about cars	* insurance, * manuals, * troubleshooting

Table 6: F_1 measure on queries of the car category

% labeled queries	5	10	20	30	40	50	60	70	average
ME	0.50	0.55	0.60	0.62	0.63	0.64	0.65	0.66	0.61
LapRLS-content	0.69	0.72	0.76	0.77	0.78	0.79	0.79	0.80	0.76
LapRLS-click	0.68	0.72	0.77	0.79	0.79	0.81	0.81	0.81	0.77
GRSTC	**0.70**	**0.74**	**0.78**	**0.80**	**0.81**	**0.81**	**0.82**	**0.82**	**0.79**

Table 7: F_1 measure on web pages of the car category

% labeled web pages	5	10	20	30	40	50	60	70	average
ME	0.74	0.77	0.78	0.79	0.80	0.80	0.81	0.81	0.79
LapRLS-content	0.74	0.76	0.79	0.81	0.81	0.81	0.82	0.82	0.79
LapRLS-click	0.66	0.71	0.75	0.78	0.79	0.80	0.81	0.83	0.77
GRSTC	**0.75**	**0.78**	**0.80**	**0.82**	**0.83**	**0.83**	**0.84**	**0.84**	**0.81**

which is viewed as the task-oriented relevance score (scaled into the range $[0, 1]$). Then the web pages that have high confidence in accomplishing t_q are promoted in the ranking list, with a parameter μ controlling the weight of the task-oriented relevance score. We summarize our task-oriented re-ranking scheme in Algorithm 1.

To test the effectiveness of the task-oriented re-ranking scheme, we design the following experiment. For each entity category, we sample 40% of the labeled query task phrases and web pages and use GRSTC to train two classifiers for queries and web pages, respectively. Then we sample 500 of the rest of the task phrases and randomly choose one query containing each task phrase as testing data. For each of the 500 queries, we submit it to the search engine and crawl the top-50 returned web pages. Then we run Algorithm 1 to re-rank these web pages, where μ is empirically set to 0.1 in our experiments. The web pages clicked by the user are regarded as relevant (ground truth). We measure the ranking performance before and after re-ranking using the Mean Average Precision (MAP) metric. For the totally 1000 queries in the computer category and the car category, the MAP increases by 4.87% after employing the task-oriented re-ranking scheme, indicating that taking the search tasks into consideration can improve the search quality.

Algorithm 1. Task-oriented re-ranking for search.

Input: query q, weight parameter μ.
Output: re-ranked web pages $\{p'_1, \ldots, p'_k\}$.
Procedure:

1. Retrieve k relevant web pages $\{p_1, \ldots, p_k\}$ of q using the search engine's original retrieval function. The k relevant web pages are ranked according to their relevance scores $\{r_1, \ldots, r_k\}$.
2. Run the classifiers trained by GRSTC to predict the search task t_q behind query q, and the confidence estimation $g^{(t_q)}(p_j)$ that each web page p_j can accomplish task t_q, $1 \leq j \leq k$.
3. For each $j = 1, \ldots, k$, do:

   Normalize $g^{(t_q)*}(p_j) = \frac{g^{(t_q)}(p_j)}{max\{g^{(t_q)}(p_1),\ldots,g^{(t_q)}(p_k)\}}$.

   $r'_j = r_j + \mu g^{(t_q)*}(p_j)$.
4. Re-rank $p_1, \ldots, p_k$ in the descending order of r'_j.

6.5 Model selection

Following the manifold regularization framework [1], we fix parameter α_q which controls the confidence of labels of queries, and let the other parameters vary to perform model selection. Therefore, the rest of the parameters λ_q, λ_p, λ_{qp}, α_p, β_q and β_p are essential in our GRSTC algorithm which control the relative importance of different terms. We empirically set $\lambda_q = \lambda_p = \lambda_{qp} = 0.5$, $\alpha_p = 0.2$, and $\beta_q = \beta_p = 10^{-4}$ in the previous experiments. In this subsection, we try to study the impact of parameters on the performance of GRSTC. Empirically, parameters β_q and β_p for the two Tikhonov regularizers [1] imposed on $\mathbf{w}_q$ and $\mathbf{w}_p$ are less important than other parameters, λ_q, λ_p, λ_{qp}, α_p, which control the importance of the three subgraphs and the confidence of the labels of web pages. So we mainly evaluate the sensitivity of our model with parameters λ_q, λ_p, λ_{qp}, and α_p by fixing all the other parameters and letting one of $\{\lambda_q, \lambda_p, \lambda_{qp}, \alpha_p\}$ vary. We also change λ and α in LapRLS-content and LapRLS-click accordingly. Figure 5 shows the average F_1 measure of queries and web pages in the two categories as a function of the parameters, with 20% of the data labeled. Parameter sensitivity curves of other percentages of labeled data are similar to Figure 5 and therefore omitted due to lack of space.

It can be observed that over a large range of parameters, GRSTC achieves significantly better performance than all the other algorithms, including two versions of its homogeneous reduction, LapRLS-content and LapRLS-click, with the parameters varying the same way. So the parameter selection will not critically affect the performance of GRSTC.

7. CONCLUSIONS

In this work, we propose to classify queries and web pages into the popular search tasks. One key distinction of our study is that the search tasks are defined as the specific action that the user wants to perform towards the entity in the query, which is at a finer scale than existing binary or three-class taxonomy of user goals or intents. We then organize the content and click-through information of both sides of the query-page click relationship into a heterogeneous graph, where each pair of objects are connected according to

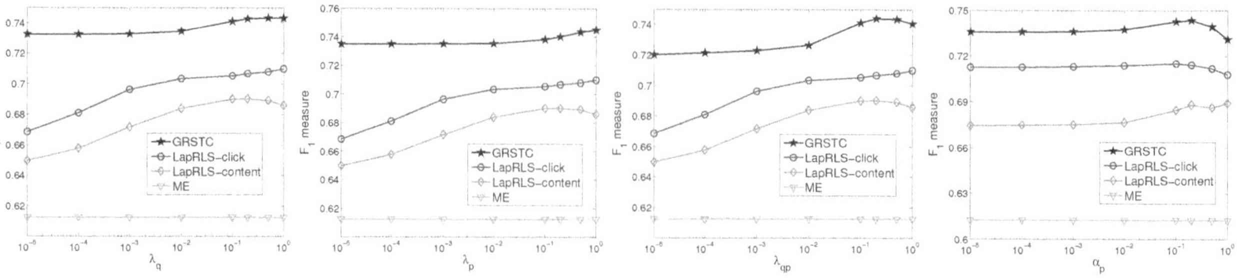

(a) Varying λ_q (b) Varying λ_p (c) Varying λ_{qp} (d) Varying α_p

Figure 5: Model selection when 20% of queries and web pages are labeled

task similarity. By designing a novel semi-supervised classification framework based on the task-oriented graph, we not only preserve the local consistency in the content feature spaces of queries and web pages, but also make full use of the close interactions between the two sets of data to let their task predictions mutually enhance each other. Through employing the content-based task classifiers trained by our algorithm, we can predict the search tasks of future queries and web pages so as to return the most useful information to users by task matching.

In the future, we plan to study how to automatically discover what are the popular search tasks among queries instead of manual study. One possible solution is to develop some task-oriented clustering methods. Another promising direction is how to better consider search tasks in ranking. Besides directly using the search task prediction results as an additional feature, it is also interesting to design some task-oriented ranking models.

8. ACKNOWLEDGEMENTS

The work was supported in part by the U.S. National Science Foundation under grant IIS-09-05215, and by the U.S. Army Research Laboratory under Cooperative Agreement No. W911NF-09-2-0053 (NS-CTA). The views and conclusions contained in this document are those of the authors and should not be interpreted as representing the official policies, either expressed or implied, of the Army Research Laboratory or the U.S. Government. The U.S. Government is authorized to reproduce and distribute reprints for Government purposes notwithstanding any copyright notation here on.

9. REFERENCES

[1] M. Belkin, P. Niyogi, and V. Sindhwani. Manifold regularization: A geometric framework for learning from examples. *Journal of Machine Learning Research*, 7:2399–2434, 2006.

[2] A. Broder. A taxonomy of web search. *SIGIR Forum*, 36(2):3–10, 2002.

[3] S. Chakrabarti, B. Dom, and P. Indyk. Enhanced hypertext categorization using hyperlinks. In *SIGMOD Conference*, pages 307–318, 1998.

[4] O. Chapelle, B. Schölkopf, and A. Zien, editors. *Semi-Supervised Learning*. MIT Press, 2006.

[5] F. R. K. Chung. *Spectral Graph Theory*, volume 92 of *Regional Conference Series in Mathematics*. AMS, 1997.

[6] Q. Gu and J. Zhou. Transductive classification via dual regularization. In *ECML/PKDD (1)*, pages 439–454, 2009.

[7] J. Guo, G. Xu, X. Cheng, and H. Li. Named entity recognition in query. In *SIGIR*, pages 267–274, 2009.

[8] J. Hu, G. Wang, F. H. Lochovsky, J.-T. Sun, and Z. Chen. Understanding user's query intent with wikipedia. In *WWW*, pages 471–480, 2009.

[9] B. J. Jansen, D. L. Booth, and A. Spink. Determining the informational, navigational, and transactional intent of web queries. *Information Processing and Management*, 44(3):1251–1266, 2008.

[10] M. Ji, Y. Sun, M. Danilevsky, J. Han, and J. Gao. Graph regularized transductive classification on heterogeneous information networks. In *ECML/PKDD (1)*, pages 570–586, 2010.

[11] U. Lee, Z. Liu, and J. Cho. Automatic identification of user goals in web search. In *WWW*, pages 391–400, 2005.

[12] X. Li, Y.-Y. Wang, and A. Acero. Learning query intent from regularized click graphs. In *SIGIR*, pages 339–346, 2008.

[13] D. Mladenic. Turning yahoo to automatic web-page classifier. In *European Conference on Artificial Intelligence*, pages 473–474, 1998.

[14] K. Nigam, J. Lafferty, and A. McCallum. Using maximum entropy for text classification. In *IJCAI Workshop on Machine Learning for Information Filtering*, pages 61–67, 1999.

[15] M. Paşca. Organizing and searching the world wide web of facts – step two: harnessing the wisdom of the crowds. In *WWW*, pages 101–110, 2007.

[16] X. Qi and B. D. Davison. Web page classification: Features and algorithms. *ACM Computing Surveys*, 41(2):1–31, 2009.

[17] D. E. Rose and D. Levinson. Understanding user goals in web search. In *WWW*, pages 13–19, 2004.

[18] D. Shen, Y. Li, X. Li, and D. Zhou. Product query classification. In *CIKM*, pages 741–750, 2009.

[19] D. Shen, J.-T. Sun, Q. Yang, and Z. Chen. A comparison of implicit and explicit links for web page classification. In *WWW*, pages 643–650, 2006.

[20] G.-R. Xue, D. Shen, Q. Yang, H.-J. Zeng, Z. Chen, Y. Yu, W. Xi, and W.-Y. Ma. Irc: An iterative reinforcement categorization algorithm for interrelated web objects. In *ICDM*, pages 273–280, 2004.

[21] X. Yin and S. Shah. Building taxonomy of web search intents for name entity queries. In *WWW*, pages 1001–1010, 2010.

[22] Z. Yin, R. Li, Q. Mei, and J. Han. Exploring social tagging graph for web object classification. In *KDD*, pages 957–966, 2009.

[23] D. Zhou, O. Bousquet, T. N. Lal, J. Weston, and B. Schölkopf. Learning with local and global consistency. In *NIPS*, 2003.

[24] X. Zhu, Z. Ghahramani, and J. D. Lafferty. Semi-supervised learning using gaussian fields and harmonic functions. In *ICML*, pages 912–919, 2003.

Intentions and Attention in Exploratory Health Search

Marc-Allen Cartright
Department of Computer Science
University of Massachusetts Amherst
Amherst, MA 01003
irmarc@cs.umass.edu

Ryen W. White
Microsoft Research
One Microsoft Way
Redmond, WA 98052
ryenw@microsoft.com

Eric Horvitz
Microsoft Research
One Microsoft Way
Redmond, WA 98052
horvitz@microsoft.com

ABSTRACT
We study information goals and patterns of attention in exploratory search for health information on the Web, reporting results of a large-scale log-based study. We examine search activity associated with the goal of diagnosing illness from symptoms versus more general information-seeking about health and illness. We decompose exploratory health search into *evidence-based* and *hypothesis-directed* information seeking. Evidence-based search centers on the pursuit of details and relevance of signs and symptoms. Hypothesis-directed search includes the pursuit of content on one or more illnesses, including risk factors, treatments, and therapies for illnesses, and on the discrimination among different diseases under the uncertainty that exists in advance of a confirmed diagnosis. These different goals of exploratory health search are not independent, and transitions can occur between them within or across search sessions. We construct a classifier that identifies medically-related search sessions in log data. Given a set of search sessions flagged as health-related, we show how we can identify different intentions persisting as foci of attention within those sessions. Finally, we discuss how insights about foci dynamics can help us better understand exploratory health search behavior and better support health search on the Web.

Categories and Subject Descriptors
H.3.3 [**Information Storage and Retrieval**]: Information Search and Retrieval – *search process, information filtering.*

General Terms
Experimentation, Human Factors.

Keywords
Health search, medical search, diagnosis, cyberchondria.

1. INTRODUCTION
Search engines are an important resource in locating medical information online. A December 2009 poll found that 66% of Internet users have pursued online information about health or medicine [20]. The Web has become a primary source of information about illnesses or treatments and a first stop for many when concerning symptoms emerge. Exploratory search describes a class of search activities that move beyond fact retrieval toward fostering learning, investigation, and information use [19]. Previous studies have shown that people use search engines to perform *exploratory health search* (EHS), where they diagnose medical conditions or perform informational health-related searches [23][28].

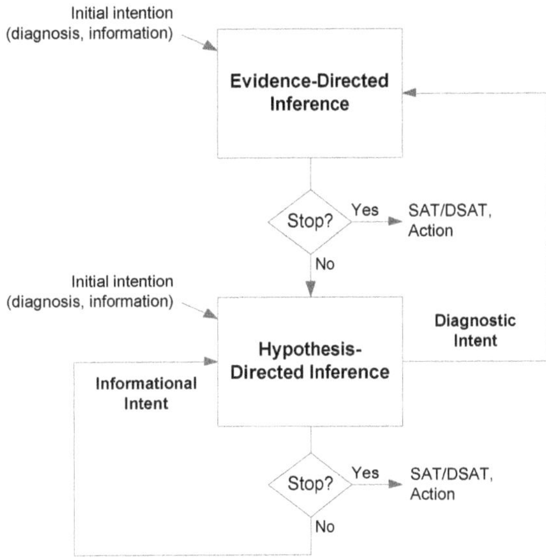

Figure 1. Intentions and flow of attention in exploratory health search.

We consider different informational goals associated with exploratory health search. In particular, we consider *diagnostic search* versus more general information-seeking about health and illness. We further partition diagnostic search into *evidence-directed* and *hypothesis-directed* information seeking. Evidence-based search focuses on the relevance of signs and symptoms to the potential existence of one of more medical disorders. With hypothesis-directed search, information is sought specifically about one or more illnesses. Hypothesis-directed information seeking plays a role in diagnostic search, where searchers pursue information about confirming or ruling out of potential disorders. However, hypothesis-directed search also describes the pursuit of information such as risk factors and therapies for illnesses, including the search for information on disorders that have been previously diagnosed by professionals.

We borrow the concepts of evidence-directed and hypothesis-directed phases of analysis from studies of diagnostic problem solving in medicine, which have demonstrated that physicians often employ an approximation of hypothetico-deductive reasoning [10], a method that involves a volley between two phases of analysis. In an *evidence-directed* phase, findings are fused to construct a list of potential explanatory diagnoses ranked by likelihood. In a *hypothesis-directed* phase, the current list of diagnoses ranked by likelihood is used to guide the collection of additional evidence, centering on discriminating among the competing hypotheses. The additional evidence collected via this phase is then considered, along with the evidence collected earlier, in a revised evidence-directed phase. Several automated decision-support systems for diagnosis and triage have been developed that employ the hypothetico-deductive cycle [11][13][17].

We believe that it can be useful to view diagnostic health search as a coarse form of hypothetico-deductive reasoning, where searchers harness Web search and browsing to guide the iterative cycle of hypotheses about wellness and disease being formulated from evidence and those hypotheses individually or together then guiding the collection of additional discriminating evidence. People performing diagnostic search may branch out of diagnostic goals and focus on general information about particular illnesses or symptoms. Also, people may initiate search without intention to perform diagnosis and flow into a diagnostic session. We consider non-diagnostic health search as being largely hypothesis-directed, focused on learning more about the nature and treatment of illnesses. Figure 1 captures key intentions and flow of attention in exploratory health search, where a searcher's initial intention may be diagnostic or informational. For diagnostic search, the user may cycle between evidence-directed and hypothesis-directed phases as their information needs evolve. At some point the searching will come to an end or be suspended, and the searcher will be either satisfied (SAT) or dissatisfied (DSAT) with the information acquired. At times, the searching will lead to actions in the world. Such actions include seeking healthcare services, evidence of which may be observable in log data as healthcare utilization intent (HUI) [29].

We explore in this paper intentions and the dynamics of attention in exploratory health search. Our work relates to prior work on understanding how users' cognitive states and information needs evolve during search as they discover new information [3]. An improved understanding of the processes by which people use Web search to explore health issues online and act on the information gathered can guide refinements of medical search systems.

To better understand exploratory health search, we analyze a set of filtered logs from a toolbar deployed by the Windows Live search engine. To perform the filtering, we first construct a statistical classifier that can identify EHS sessions from general search and browsing logs. Then, we extract terms in queries representing potential causes and symptoms, treating each of these distinct entities as a *focus*, capturing the current focus of attention of the searcher. Finally, we investigate two applications of medical foci for information retrieval (IR): (i) clustering EHS sessions based on the extracted attributes, helping us better understand foci dynamics during EHS, and (ii) predicting a searcher's likely next focus in EHS sessions given their recent foci.

The remainder of the paper is structured as follows. In Section 2, we describe related work on medical IR, with a particular focus on studies of health-related information seeking and medical search. Section 3 describes the data set that we use, including the definitions of evidence-directed and hypothesis-directed activities that we adopt, and a classifier trained to automatically label diagnostic search sessions given human labeled data. Section 4 describes our work on extracting and analyzing foci dynamics from search sessions. In Section 5, we describe work on clustering sessions to identify common patterns of EHS behavior and in predicting future foci given recent search history. We discuss our findings and their implications in Section 6 and conclude in Section 7.

2. RELATED WORK

Web interaction logs have been used previously to study medical Web search behavior. Bhavnani *et al.* [6] demonstrated that term co-occurrence counts for medical symptoms and disorders on Web pages can reasonably predict the degree of influence on search behavior. Spink *et al.* [23] characterized healthcare-related queries issued to Web search engines, and showed that users were gradually shifting from general-purpose search engines to specialized Web sites for medical- and health-related queries. Ayers and Kronenfeld [1] also utilized log data on Web use, and perform a multiple regression analysis to explore the relationship between chronic medical conditions and frequency of Web use, as well as changes in health behavior due to frequency of Web use. Their findings suggest that it was not the presence of one particular chronic illness, but rather the total number of chronic conditions that determines the nature of Web use. They also found that the more frequently someone uses the Web as a source of health information, the more likely that person is to alter their health behavior. White and Horvitz [28] used a log-based methodology to study escalations in medical concerns during Web search from rudimentary symptoms to serious ailments, a behavior that they call *cyberchondria*. They found that users frequently escalated from basic medical concerns to more serious concerns based on exposure to Web content. In a follow-up study, White and Horvitz [29] also examined the occurrence of escalation from symptoms to searches for real-world medical resources, informational goals (HUIs, defined earlier). We seek to more broadly characterize the dynamics of focus of attention to a larger set of actions, including escalations from queries on basic symptoms to rare and frightening diseases and to searches for local medical expertise.

Researchers have investigated the search behavior of medical domain experts [5][15][16][31] with a view to better understanding the search behavior of those with specialist domain knowledge. Hersh *et al.* [15] review research in the medical informatics and information science literature on how physicians use IR tools to support clinical question answering and decision making. They found that retrieval technology was inadequate for this purpose and generally retrieved less than half of the relevant articles on a given topic. They follow up this review with a study of how medical and nurse practitioner students use MEDLINE to gather evidence for clinical question-answering [16]. Their findings show that these users were only moderately successful at answering clinical questions with the help of literature searching. Bhavnani [5] observed healthcare and online shopping experts while they performed search tasks inside and outside their domains of expertise, and identified domain-specific search strategies in each domain, and that such search knowledge is not automatically acquired from general-purpose search engines. Wildemuth [31] performed a longitudinal study examining the tactics of medical students searching a database in microbiology. Findings showed that over the course of the study changes in students' search tactics were observed as domain knowledge increased.

Several researchers have also noted a need for improved information services to the medical information consumer. Cline and Haynes [8] present a review of work in this area that suggests that public health professionals should be concerned about online health seeking, consider potential benefits, synthesize quality concerns, and identify criteria for evaluating online health information. Eysenbach and Kohler [12] used focus groups and naturalistic observation to study users attempting assigned search tasks on the Web. They found that the credibility of Web sites (in terms of source, design, scientific or official appearance, language used, and ease of use) was important in the focus group setting, but in practice, many participants largely ignored the source of their medical information. Baker *et al.* [2] examined the effects that Web and email use has on users' knowledge about health care matters and their use of the health care system. They found that users rarely use email to communicate with physicians and that the Web's influence of healthcare utilization is uncertain. Sillence and colleagues [22] studied the influence of design and information content on the trust and mistrust of online health sites. Through observational study of a small number of subjects engaged in structured and unstructured search sessions they found that aspects of design appeal engendered mistrust, whereas the credibility of information and personalization of content engendered user trust. Eastin and Guinsler [10] investigated the relationship between online health information seeking and healthcare utilization such as visiting a general practitioner. Their findings suggest that an individual's level of health anxiety moderates the relationship between online health information seeking and health care utilization decisions. Lewis [18] performed a qualitative study into young peoples' use of the Web for health material that showed that in fact they are often skeptical consumers of the material they encounter. The findings of these studies demonstrate some of the conflicting opinions around the effect of healthcare information on human behavior. This may be attributable to differences in the goals of the studies, the samples used, and the experimental methodologies. In response to these issues, some organizations have already started efforts to improve general quality of medical information on the Web, such as the Health on the Net Foundation [14]. Others have studied augmenting Web pages or search results with tools to support credibility assessment [21].

Previous work in this area has focused on general medical search behavior, and either performed relatively simple analyses of query logs, or more in-depth studies across small focused groups. The large-scale log-based methodology that we employ enables observation of many searchers' naturalistic information-seeking behaviors at *the session level*, rather than at the query level as in previous studies [23], affording a detailed analysis of how people perform exploratory health search on the Web.

3. DATA SET

We now describe the data that we used in this study and the classifier we developed to identify exploratory health search sessions.

3.1 Sessions

We began with anonymized logs of URLs visited by users who consented to provide data through a widely-distributed browser toolbar. We gathered data over six months during early 2009. Log entries include a user identifier, a timestamp for each page view, and the URL of the page visited. We excluded intranet and secure (https) URL visits at the source. Only entries generated in the English speaking regions of the United States were included. From these logs we extracted search sessions on Google, Yahoo, and Microsoft's Live Search via a methodology similar to White and Drucker [26]. Sessions comprised queries, hyperlink clicks on search engine results, and pages visited during post-result-page navigation. Sessions began with a query to one of the three search engines and terminated following a period of user inactivity of over 30 minutes, suggesting that the current search episode has ended. We filtered these logs to retain only sessions that had at least one query containing a term in a wordlist extracted from a list of symptoms from the Merck medical dictionary. To improve session coverage, synonyms of Merck symptoms were also used. Synonyms for each symptom were identified through a two-step walk on the search engine click graph with an approach similar to [4]. Statistics about the constructed data set are shown in Table 1. *Action* is used for a query or URL (page view) within a session.

Table 1. Characterization of the data set.

Statistic	Value
Number of unique users	660,219
Number of sessions	1,237,737
Total number of actions	26,983,597
Average number of actions per session	21.8
Average number of queries per session	10.4
Min / Max / StDev num. actions per session	1 / 968 / 27.7

We randomly sampled 0.1% of the sessions in the data set (1,238 instances) and annotated them manually. The annotation procedure is described in more detail in the next section.

3.2 Labeling Exploratory Health Sessions

We sought to construct and use a statistical classification following the filtering based on medical keywords to remove sessions that were tagged as medical erroneously (e.g., those containing queries such as [*saturday night fever*] and [*red eye xbox*]). The goal was to classify each session into one of two classes: *EHS* (positive class), and *non-EHS* (negative class). An exploratory health search session is one where the searcher performed, at some point in the session, one or more actions indicating that they were either engaged in some evidence-directed (i.e., to understand the relevance of a set of observed symptoms) or hypothesis-directed strategy. We focused in this study on the pursuit of information on the causes or remedies for a set of observed symptoms). A session may contain activities suggesting that a searcher is engaged in one or both of these types of pursuits. We now describe the criteria that we used to manually label evidence-directed and hypothesis-directed events in search sessions.

3.2.1 Evidence-Directed

During evidence-directed exploratory health search, users seek to understand the relevance of symptoms. A canonical example of an evidence-directed search is the query [*what causes dizziness and nausea?*]. Observing such a query in a log of search activity suggests that the user seeks to understand the relevance to disease of observing these two symptoms. We identified several criteria for identifying exploratory health queries as being evidence-directed. These criteria required that queries contain the following:

- combinations of symptoms via connectives, e.g., [*back pain, nausea, dizziness*], [*dry cough with chest pain*];
- the word "symptom" and/or the word "pain", and;
- symptom or condition in conjunction with a specific entity, i.e., [*diarrhea in 2 year olds*].

Although this list is not exhaustive, it provides a simple set of rules for identifying instances of evidence-directed search that can be easily applied by human judges as they inspect a session.

3.2.2 Hypothesis-Directed

As displayed in Figure 1, hypothesis-directed search includes both diagnostic and informational intents. We now describe each type of informational goal.

3.2.2.1 Diagnostic Intent

During the hypothesis-directed phase of diagnostic search, users seek information that can help to refine uncertainty about the hypotheses under consideration, including information that can rule out, raise or lower the likelihood of one or more hypotheses, or to identify new hypotheses. We use the presence of queries with reference to benign or serious medical conditions (using the list of conditions from [28]) as evidence of diagnostic intent.

3.2.2.2 Informational Intent

Hypothesis-directed searches also include the non-diagnostic pursuit of information about a condition, such as seeking details on potential hypotheses, including treatments and outcomes, e.g., pages on exercises to alleviate back pain. The primary focus of attention is obtaining information about conditions or treatment. We use the following features as evidence of informational intent:

- queries about treatment, including those with advanced syntax, e.g., [*whooping cough more:condition_treatment*];
- use of 'for' in query as the connective between entities: [*ointments for eczema*];
- query contains the terms 'treatment' or 'cure';
- queries for exercises or medications, particularly in reference to a specific condition, e.g., [*back stretching exercises*];
- user performs an HUI action [29], e.g., searching for an in-world medical resource such as a clinic or hospital.

We focus on the search for treatments as a class of hypothesis-directed informational queries that could be distinguished easily from evidence-directed diagnostic search. Queries on treatments are clearly a subset of the larger space of hypothesis-directed search with informational goals, and do not addresses hypothesis-directed search with diagnostic goals. We pursue the basic partition of intentions into hypothesis-directed search for treatments and evidence-directed diagnostic search as an initial analysis of the study of intentions and attention in EHS.

One of authors (MAC) reviewed the 1,238 sessions, applied the criteria listed above, and assigned the labels *evidence-directed*, *hypothesis-directed*, or *both* to each of the sessions.

3.3 Classifying Exploratory Health Sessions

Search sessions may contain actions that are both evidence- and hypothesis-directed. We developed separate classifiers for identifying evidence-directed, hypothesis-directed, as well as the joint appearance in sessions of both phases of analysis.

Table 2 shows the features used in our classification. We identified a set of features about each of the sessions that captures elements of evidence-directed and hypothesis-directed phases (e.g., *HasCausePatterns*, *HasMedications*), as well as features that might help with selecting medical sessions and filtering out noise (e.g., *HasMedicalSites*, *HasSocialSites*). Many of the feature names listed in Table 2 are self-explanatory. Of the others, *HasListElements* is true if a query appears to contain a list (detected by splitting on "and", "or", or commas, and counting the number of resultant items). *HasNLElements* is true if the query contains connective stopwords, e.g., "by", "with", "for", etc. *HasObservations* is true if the query contains terms such as "feeling", "pain", and "hurt" that may indicate an observed medical symptom. We use "Portion" as a prefix of features to denote the fraction of all actions in the session where a feature was observed.

We trained a logistic regression classifier for each class (*evidence-only* or *hypothesis-only*) as well as for *both*. We repeated the following process for each experimental run: (i) randomly permute the 1,238 labeled sessions; (ii) split the 1,238 sessions into five equally-sized sets, and; (iii) perform five-fold cross-validation, using four folds for training and the remaining fold for testing. Since logistic regression provides probabilities that each test case is an instance of the positive class, we set a threshold value (α). If the probability exceeds that threshold, we consider the instance to be in the positive class, and negative class otherwise. For any given threshold, performance is averaged over the five runs.

Table 2. Feature names and weights for the three classifiers. Sorted in descending order by the absolute values for *Both*.

Feature Name	Evidence	Hypothesis	Both
HasMedicalSites	+1.396	−0.803	+1.682
HasObservations	+0.992	−0.444	+1.135
HasCausePatterns	+0.282	+0.901	+0.973
HasListElements	+0.431	+0.330	+0.700
HasBodyParts	+0.772	+0.129	+0.696
PortionQueries	+0.396	−1.384	+0.543
NumTreatPatternsURL	−0.067	+0.107	+0.474
HasNLElements	+0.525	−0.589	+0.458
PortionRepeatQueries	+0.230	−0.128	+0.339
HasSymptomPatterns	+0.427	−0.523	+0.287
PortionImages	−0.095	−0.182	−0.156
HasMedications	+0.200	+0.025	+0.129
HasTreatmentPatterns	−0.060	+1.770	+0.123
NumYoutubeViews	−0.086	−0.083	−0.116
HasSocialSites	+0.068	−0.340	+0.114
NumSearches	−0.108	+0.052	−0.103
NumRepeatedQueries	+0.084	+0.008	+0.074
PortionHealthRelated	+0.051	−0.099	+0.072
HasAdultContent	−0.049	+0.196	−0.042
NumActions	−0.002	−0.040	−0.003
AvgPageDwellTime	+0.002	−0.007	+0.002

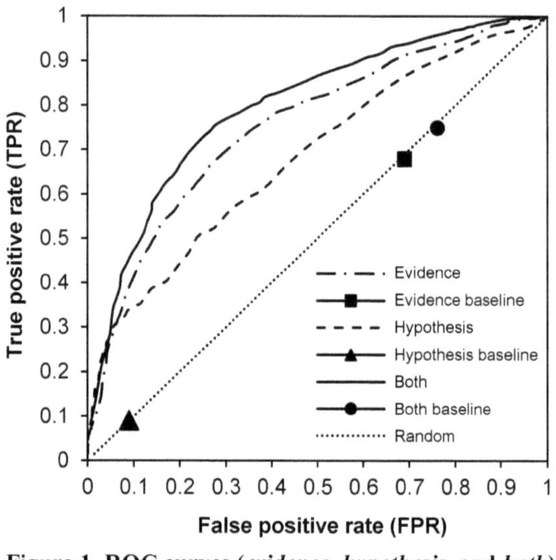

Figure 1. ROC curves (*evidence, hypothesis*, and *both*).

Figure 1 shows the receiver-operator characteristic (ROC) curves as we reduce α for *evidence-only*, *hypothesis-only*, and *either* classes. A threshold of 0.0 corresponds to the upper right corner of the figure, where all instances are classified as true. Conversely, a threshold of 1.0 corresponds to the lower left corner, where all instances are classified as false. Baselines are determined using the maximum likelihood estimator (MLE) of the positive class from the training data, and then using the MLE as the threshold value of a random roll for each instance. Therefore the baseline estimator uses only frequency information in the training data, and no instance-specific features. The false-positive and true-positive rates of the baseline estimator are averaged over five runs, which results in a single point on the curve: a single (false positive rate, true positive rate) coordinate, shown for each method in Figure 1.

Table 2 shows the weights assigned by the classifier to each of features used in the classifying whether a session is evidence-directed, hypothesis-directed, or both per the definitions of these categories for the study. We focus on the sessions identified as EHS-related by the *Both* classifier for the remainder of the paper as it had the highest accuracy and allowed us to extract and study examples of hypothesis- and evidence-directed search behaviors.

The presence of medical Websites (*HasMedicalSites*) such as WebMD and PubMed is the most predictive feature of EHS sessions, followed by queries associated with pain or feelings (*HasObservations*). Other features such as *NumYoutubeViews* and the fraction of the session that are image searches (*PctImages*) are negatively correlated with the search session being medically-oriented. Features such as the average amount of time users spend on a page (*AvgPageDwellTime*) and the number of actions in a session (*NumActions*) had little predictive value for this task.

Using the *Both* classifier, we automatically labeled the original full data set described in Table 1, setting α to 0.95. We did this to increase classification precision, and to help ensure that the recovered set contains few false positives at the cost of missing a portion of the EHS sessions. Following automatic labeling, we obtained 249,833 sessions (from 94,498 users) that we considered as EHS-related. Hereafter we refer to these EHS sessions as M, and we use them for the analysis performed in the rest of the paper.

4. DYNAMICS OF ATTENTION

We have focused on the automated classification of EHS sessions. This is necessary to create a subset of all sessions that we can use to study the dynamics of the focus of attention in exploratory health search. We now turn to extracting foci from those sessions and characterize focus of attention during health searches.

4.1 Extracting Intentional Foci

Beyond focusing on evidence- and hypothesis-directed phases of EHS, we magnified our analytic resolution to the sub-session level, to examine user behavior at each step in sessions. To better understand user activity within a single session, we define several concepts and provide a formulation for investigating the flow of intentions during exploratory health search. As mentioned above, we consider actions to only be queries submitted to a search engine. We consider sessions to be temporally ordered sets of actions. For any action, we attempt to extract a *focus* associated with that action. We shall focus here only on actions that are search queries as: (i) extracting information from the URL string itself provides only partial coverage of the remaining actions and we have no gauge of how well these extractions correlate to current intent, and; (ii) content analysis of Web pages may introduce significant noise into the process of extracting foci. Web pages containing medical content may cover many topics on a single page, raising the likelihood of making erroneous extractions of foci.

4.1.1 Defining Medical Foci

During our analysis of the 1,238 labeled sessions, we identify three types of foci. These include the pursuit of information on symptoms, causes, and remedies, corresponding to evidence-directed, hypothesis-directed (diagnostic intent), and hypothesis-directed (informational intent) behaviors respectively. For the focus of attention study, we take as *causes* conditions that explain one or more symptoms. A *symptom* is a physical manifestation that is seen as a departure from normal function, even if the underlying cause may not be a malady. A *remedy* is a step taken to treat a cause. Symptoms expressed in queries likely indicate evidence-directed phases, and causes input as queries likely indicate hypothesis-directed phases. Remedies in queries are indications of users seeking treatment information and are likely indications of users with non-diagnostic, hypothesis directed goals.

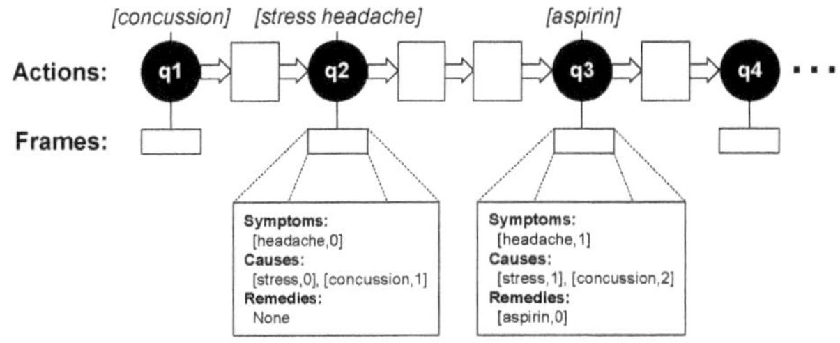

Figure 2. Generating references and frames for foci.

When we extract a focus from an action, we consider that instance to be a *reference* to that focus. We may extract any number of foci from a given action, for example a query for [*exercises for chronic back pain*] is identified as the symptom "back pain" and remedy "exercise." We define a *frame* to be the representation of the user's focus of attention over a single action. Each frame consists of three ordered lists, one each for symptoms, causes, and remedies, respectively. Each item in a list maintains the number of times that particular cause or symptom has been referenced thus far in the session and the number of steps since the last reference (which is zero if the item is first seen in the current frame).

Figure 2 shows an example of a medically focused search session, with queries (black circles) and page views (rectangles) as the actions. The figure shows how we extract frames from the queries of these sessions and how the frames evolve over the course of the search session as more queries are issued by the searcher.

4.1.2 Identifying Medical Foci in Sessions

Identifying diagnostic foci from search sessions is challenging. We see large variations in users' search behaviors, including how they specify their information needs and the strategies they employ in exploratory health search. To identify symptoms, causes, and remedies in the context of a medically relevant query, we use methods similar to those described earlier for labeling EHS sessions. For each focus type, we employ a set of rules, partly based on compiled dictionaries of potentially salient terms and phrases identified via a manual review of query logs. We formulate a set of regular expressions based on common patterns for each focus type that appeared in the log data. Some examples are as follows:

- Symptoms (evidence directed):
  - o rules such as <body part> pain, where body part is derived from lists of major appendages, organs, etc.;
  - o terms/phrases such as "ache" and "dizziness", and;
  - o expressions (e.g., query starts "pain in" or "causes of").
- Causes (hypothesis-directed – *diagnostic* intent):
  - o rules such as <body part> failure;
  - o terms/phrases such as "acid reflux" and "sinusitis", and;
  - o expressions (e.g., "symptoms of" or "diagnosis of").
- Remedies (hypothesis-directed – *informational* intent):
  - o terms such as "treatment", "clinic", and "doctor", and;
  - o expressions (e.g., "cure for" or "treatment for").

These rules and resources are used to extract foci automatically from all queries in all sessions in M. Although the generalizability of this methodology is limited, we believe that the labels can provide the basis for generating initial insights about patterns of activity in exploratory health search. We believe that there is promise in the longer term with refining the labeling methodology using of machine learning.

4.1.3 Extracting Medical Foci

The set of sessions in *M* comprised 5,292,871 actions. We labeled 370,498 (7%) of these actions as "non-medical," meaning either the query or URL contained strong indicators of non-medical intent in the action. We used two types of indicators: (i) we maintained a list of popular socially-oriented websites that occurred often in our log data (e.g., Facebook, MySpace), and excluded any actions with a URL from any of these domains, and; (ii) we also maintained a keyword list containing words that indicated a completely different intent than medical search. For example the word "lyrics" was in this list, meaning a query such as "headache lyrics" would be excluded. An initial list was generated and this list was updated during the analysis as false positives emerged. An examination of a random sampling of excluded actions revealed that no actions were falsely excluded.

Of the remaining actions, 2,329,231 (44%) contain queries that we consider as serving as strong signals of search intent from the user, from we may be able to directly extract medical foci. Of this number, we are able to extract at least one cause focus from 652,180 (28%), at least one symptom focus from 1,213,529 (52%), and at least one remedy focus from 92,169 (4%). 141,660 (49%) of all EHS search sessions in *M* contain at least one non-medical query. Non-medical queries are ignored for our analysis. The remaining 2,593,142 (49%) of actions in *M* are URL visits that may offer evidence of medical intent. However, as stated earlier, we only use queries in this work.

4.2 Characterizing Foci Dynamics

We now present an analysis of the characteristics of the foci extracted from *M*, specifically examining the three focus categories and the transitions among those categories during sessions. We begin by looking at how health search sessions start, how they end, and transitions that occur within them.

4.2.1 Starts, Ends, and Transitions

Table 3 displays how often each of the medical foci types appears at the outset and conclusion of sessions. The table also shows the percentages for each of the start and end points.

Table 3. Start and end states of health search sessions.

Session starts			Session ends		
Symptom	*Cause*	*Remedy*	*Symptom*	*Cause*	*Remedy*
157,433	62,785	7,528	164,218	68,312	9,346
69.1%	27.6%	3.3%	66.5%	29.7%	3.8%

The EHS sessions identified primarily begin and end with symptoms, highlighting the prominence of evidence-directed reasoning in the data. Hypothesis-directed foci (causes and remedies) tend to occur toward the ends of EHS sessions, suggesting a shift between evidence-directed and hypothesis-directed phases over the course of sessions. We shall examine such transitions later in this section. We note that the total number of references within and across foci types increases from session start to session end. This finding suggests that the average density of types (the number of different foci in one session start/end) increases. There could be many reasons for this including exposure to Web content stimulating users to become more medically focused as the session proceeds [28].

We were interested in the number of focus types that occur in a given session. In most sessions in *M* (68%), searchers stay with the same focus type for the duration of the session, even though the specific symptom or condition being pursued might change. The distribution of focus categories is shown in Table 4. Focus categories can include multiple foci, e.g., *SymptomCause* means that the focus is on symptoms and causes together for the duration of the session (e.g., query for [*chest pain heart attack*], [*chest pain indigestion*], etc.). *Other* refers to queries that were identified as being non-medical.

Table 4. Number of sessions with single focus of attention.

Focus type	Count	% sessions
Symptom	125,232	63.8%
SymptomCause	44,365	22.6%
Cause	10,433	5.3%
Other	7,564	3.9%
SymptomRemedy	3,879	2.0%
Remedy	2,241	1.1%
SymptomCauseRemedy	1,641	0.8%
CauseRemedy	829	0.4%

The findings of our analysis shows that sticking with symptoms is particularly common. Non-medical sessions (labeled as *Other*) were initially labeled as EHS sessions by the classifier described in Section 3, but were not found to be associated with medical intent per the rules used in the focus extraction. One explanation for the difference in label is that the classifier was based on all actions in the session (including URLs visited, e.g., the *HasMedicalSites* feature was important in EHS session labeling), whereas the focus extraction phase was based only on query actions.

92,934 (32%) health search sessions contained a transition among different focus types. A transition involves the expansion of an existing type to include another (e.g., symptom → symptom + cause), or a complete change in the type (e.g., symptom → cause). In Table 5, we summarize the frequency of each transition type.

Table 5. Frequency of occurrence of types of transitions among categories.

Transition type	Count	% transitions
Symptom→Cause	40,618	43.4%
Cause→Symptom	35,779	38.6%
Symptom→Remedy	6,628	7.2%
Remedy→Symptom	4,240	4.7%
Cause→Remedy	3,559	3.7%
Remedy→Cause	2,110	2.3%

The statistics on transitions show that transitions between symptoms and causes are most common. Searchers' exposure to Web content may lead them to link their perceived symptoms with causes. We found that transitions from causes to symptoms occurred almost as frequently as transitions from symptoms to causes. This implies the existence of oscillations or loops among these categories, perhaps in the spirit of the hypothetico-deductive cycle described earlier. We examine such cycling later in the paper.

4.2.2 Pursuits

We now move to characterizing sequences of foci, and define a *pursuit* as a series of consecutive queries within a search session. There are two types of pursuit: (i) *full pursuits* over all session actions, and (ii) *sub-pursuits* on particular foci types (e.g., symptoms) over a subset of actions in the session. A typical set of pursuits for a search session is illustrated in Figure 3. The duration of each sub-pursuit is marked above its session actions. For completeness, the figure contains both queries and page views, but our analysis was performed using only queries.

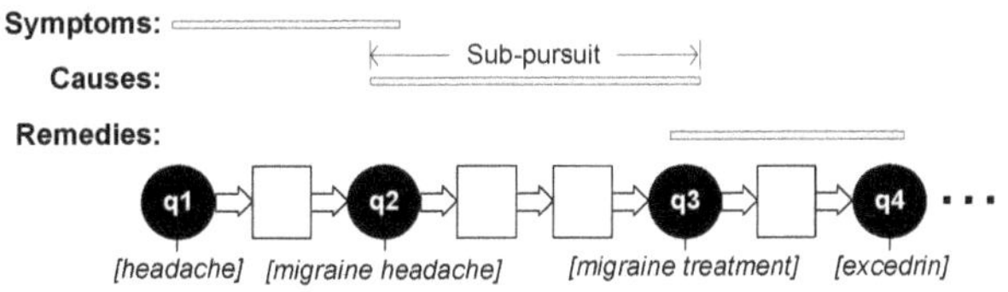

Figure 3. Pursuits and sub-pursuits within a search session.

We sought to characterize the differences in the length of pursuits by focus type. A better understanding of the length of time that searchers pursue on each condition can be useful for understanding differences in search strategies for different foci or for predicting when transitions among pursuits are going to occur. Table 6 shows the mean average number of queries associated with pursuits for each type. For example, the average length of a *SymptomCause* pursuit (symptoms *and* causes) was 8.33 queries.

Table 6. Average pursuit length for each focus type.

Focus type	Pursuit length
SymptomCauseRemedy	13.46
CauseRemedy	11.98
Symptom	11.69
SymptomRemedy	10.43
Remedy	10.27
SymptomCause	8.33
Other	8.20
Cause	7.91

As shown in Table 6, the average lengths depending on the focus type. We find that the pursuit lengthens with increases in the number of focus types included in the pursuit. We note that when remedy foci are involved, the pursuit length tends to be longer than in pursuits without remedy foci. For example, symptom/cause pursuits average a little over eight steps in length. If we add remedies to the pursuits, the number jumps to over 13. Indeed, if we focus only on the length of the sub-pursuits for each of the three main focus types (for sessions with at least one transition so we can focus on sub-pursuits), we see that remedy-related pursuits contain more user actions on average (Table 7).

Table 7. Average sub-pursuit length for each focus type.

Focus type	Sub-pursuit length
Symptom	4.49
Cause	5.08
Remedy	5.94

The pursuit of remedies may indicate a desire to address a known condition. We speculate that searchers appear to be more engaged in that task than in symptom or cause searching, or may experience more difficulty in finding relevant search results and hence need to revise their query statements more frequently.

4.2.3 Oscillations

As mentioned earlier an oscillation instance involves the transition from one focus type to another and then back to the original type (e.g., *Symptom→Cause→Symptom* describes an oscillation instance where the focus is symptom, then cause, and then returning to symptom). We mined the foci extracted from our EHS sessions, extracted oscillations, and obtained the distribution among oscillation types (summarized in Table 8). Such oscillations were observed in the EHS sessions of 16.2% of the users in *M*.

Table 8. Frequency of occurrence for oscillation types.

Oscillation type	Count	% oscillations
Symptom→Cause→Symptom	10,034	51.4%
Cause→Symptom→Cause	7,490	38.4%
Symptom→Remedy→Symptom	989	5.1%
Remedy→Symptom→Remedy	526	2.7%
Cause→Remedy→Cause	301	1.5%
Remedy→Cause→Remedy	171	0.9%

As noted in our earlier analysis, transitions between causes and symptoms occur often, and more frequently than any other type of transition. This evidence supports the hypothesis that searchers engage in forms of hypothetico-deductive searching as part of diagnostic search. We now explore this hypothesis in more detail.

4.2.4 Diagnostic Cycles

As discussed earlier, the hypothetico-deductive method [25] has been proposed as a description of an iterative process of medical diagnosis involving a cycling between evidence-directed and hypothesis-directed phases, with an ongoing revision of the diagnoses under consideration and information being pursued. We sought to better understand potential cycles of revision in diagnostic search. We were particularly interested in *cycles* where users were observed to repeat a search for symptoms but pursue different causes or remedies with the progression of a session. Although the average number of new foci per session is around one (suggesting that if users do oscillate, they do not do so repeatedly), we find evidence that diagnostic cycles occur. Table 9 presents the frequencies with which we observed cycles with different numbers of iterations. A cycle with two iterations means that the user searched for a symptom, a cause, then returned to the original symptom, and proceeded to search for a different cause.

Table 9. Frequency of cycles with different iteration counts.

Num. iterations	Count	% iterations
2	2,122	88.4%
3	229	9.5%
4	43	1.8%
5	4	0.2%
6	3	0.1%

Cycles were observed in the EHS sessions of 3.1% of the users in *M*. An example of such a cycle taken from the logs is a user searching for [*stomach pain*], who first considered [*irritable bowel syndrome*], then [*appendicitis*], before settling on [*gallstones*] and proceeding to explore treatment options ([*gallstone surgery*], [*cholecystectomy*], etc.). Although our rule-based detection mechanism is limited (e.g., we identify users returning to the exact same symptom (and associated synonyms) following each iteration), we find that diagnostic cycles appear in Web search, and are likely to occur even more frequently than we found with our limited methodology for identifying actions.

5. CLUSTERING AND PREDICTING

We now describe two applications that demonstrate the potential value of harnessing representations of searcher focus of attention to understand and support exploratory health search behaviors.

The two applications are (i) clustering EHS sessions to better understand the health-related search strategies that users employ, and (ii) predicting future foci given a recent history of exploratory health searching. These applications seek to identify common patterns of exploratory health search sessions.

5.1 Generalizing Sessions for Analysis

Extracting the foci from various sessions provides a microscopic view of EHS search behavior. However, to represent sessions in a way that allows comparability among the sessions, we seek to create a more macroscopic view of user behavior. To do this, we represent an EHS session in M as a character sequence and depict each action in the session with a character. Such a mapping affords easy manipulation and analysis, and also removes identifying information, further preserving user privacy without destroying the salient aspects of search behavior that are necessary for sequence clustering and prediction. Downey *et al.* [9] introduced formal models and languages that encode search behavior as character sequences, with a view to comparing search behavior in different scenarios. In a similar manner, we formulated an alphabet designed to represent the focus of attention at each query in the session. The alphabet appears in Table 10. Each symbol represents a set of foci, e.g., 'A' is used to represent a query that has both symptom and cause elements, such as [*headache migraine*].

Table 10. Symbols assigned to queries based on medical foci.

Symbol	Focus type
S	Symptom
C	Cause
R	Remedy
A	SymptomCause
B	SymptomRemedy
D	CauseRemedy
E	SymptomCauseRemedy
N	Non-medical

If a user searched for symptoms across multiple queries, pursued a cause, returned to the symptom, and ended up querying for a remedy, the session would be represented as "SSSCSR." We created a sequence representation for each of the sessions in M, hereafter referred to as M_S. We use these sequences for the analysis presented in the remainder of this section. For the purposes of this analysis, we exclude the non-medical actions ('N' in Table 10) as they were not pertinent to either of our application scenarios. We now describe the first application: session clustering.

5.2 Clustering Exploratory Health Sessions

Clustering exploratory health search sessions based on the sequences described in the previous section promises to be useful for understanding foci dynamics. Clusters emerging from this analysis could help inform the design of tools to support medical search. We clustered the sessions using the approach described by Cadez *et al.* [7], which was used to cluster users' browsing categories of a popular news website (msnbc.com) by learning a mixture of first-order Markov models using the Expectation-Maximization procedure. We ran the clustering algorithm (which has a built-in model-selection procedure) across all character sequences in M_S. This yielded a set of 12 clusters that represented different aspects of diagnostic search strategies. Since the clusters were based on sets of symbols rather than the detailed search strategies themselves, there was some redundancy across the set of clusters generated. For example, although one cluster comprised only sessions with all symptoms, and another cluster comprised sessions with all causes, both had consistent foci *types* that were unchanged over the course of the session. To remove redundancy and to simplify our analysis of the clusters, we manually grouped the clusters into five distinct cluster categories. The goal of the re-grouping was only to remove redundancy, and no other manipulation of the clusters was performed during this procedure.

We assigned names to each of the categories and list them below. For each category, we indicate whether the pursuit is evidence-driven, hypothesis-driven, or some combination of the two. We also show the percentage of all sequences in M_S that each category comprises, and provide a canonical example to clarify the nature of the search strategies observed in each category:

1. **Constant (mostly evidence-directed) (75%)**: Foci (cause, symptom, or some combination, sometimes remedy) remain the same for the entire session. For example, a user searching for symptoms of headache persists with headache-related symptom searches over all queries in the duration of their session.
2. **Incremental (evidence-directed) (10%)**: Assuming a natural progression from symptom, to cause, to remedy, searches searchers transition among each of these foci types in that order. For example, a searcher first searches on headache symptoms, then headache causes, and then headache medication.
3. **Incremental (hypothesis-directed) (7%)**: Searches do not conform to the natural progression described above, and instead progress in opposite direction (i.e., from remedies/causes to symptoms). For example, searches may start with a possible explanation for experienced symptoms and end with the searcher seeking more information about these symptoms.
4. **Oscillating (both evidence- and hypothesis- directed) (5%)**: Searches alternate among categories. For example, a searcher may seek causes for a symptom and then search for a different symptom.
5. **Cyclic (evidence- and hypothesis- directed) (3%)**: Searches anchor on symptom and explore related causes and remedies. For example, search for a symptom, identify a cause, return to the same symptom, then search for an alternative cause.

Through sequence clustering, we could summarize and distill exploratory health search strategies into five key elements. Such analyses can provide search engines with insight about the evolving informational goals and intentions of searchers pursuing health information, and to ultimately inform the design of more effective search engines.

5.3 Predicting Foci in EHS Sessions

Rather than considering the character sequence holistically across a session, we can consider transitions among foci. We can seek to predict whether a searcher will stick with a current set of foci or to transition to new foci. Being able to predict such transitions in real-time based on interaction history could enable search providers to offer proactive support or intervene if transitions to causes are anticipated (especially if those causes could be identified as inappropriately escalatory [30]).

We generated a state transition diagram, displayed in Figure 4, using all sequences in M_S, given the frequency with which foci-foci transitions are observed. The symbols in each of the nodes correspond to Table 10. The darker the node, the more occurrences there are of that state (foci) in our data. Also shown are the empirically based probabilities of remaining in each state, and the probability of starting or ending an EHS session in each state.

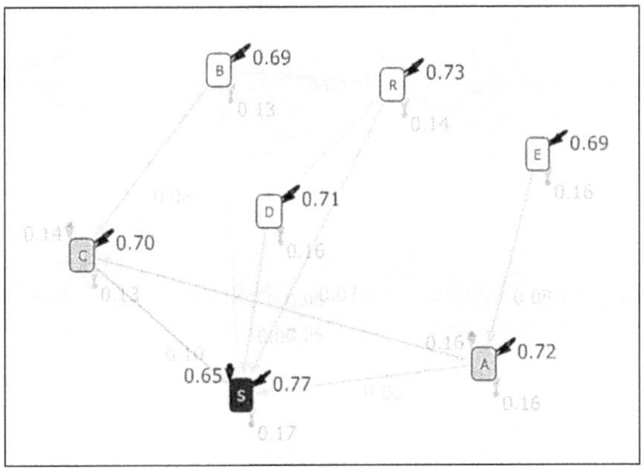

Figure 4. State transition diagram across all sequences in M_S.

The transition diagram illustrates that once users get into a particular state they do not usually leave. The diagram also shows that although all states have a similar chance of being the last state in the session, EHS sessions primarily start with symptoms (65% of the time), causes (14%), or a combination of symptoms and causes (16%). It is less common for medical sessions to begin with a remedy-oriented query (also supported by the data in Table 3). From these statistics, it also seems that evidence-driven pursuits occur more frequently than hypothesis-driven search.

We applied the sequence prediction algorithm from [7] to the character sequences in M_S. The task was to predict the next symbol in sequence given the previous sequence. We used five-fold cross validation and varied the size of the window w containing the sequence of symbols preceding the predicted symbol (foci), and used this window in both training and testing. We measured the accuracy with which we were able to predict the next state, given the previous w symbols in the sequence, averaged across 100 randomized runs and within each run across the five folds. The findings show that we are able to predict the next state with accuracies ranging from 86% (w=2) to 92% (when w=8). A default strategy of always predicting that users remain in the same state as the last action in w has an accuracy of 74%. Performance degraded when w exceeded eight steps, perhaps because of the diminished amount of training data.

6. DISCUSSION AND IMPLICATIONS

We presented log-based analyses of the dynamics of focus of attention in exploratory health search. The analyses provide views into the behaviors of people searching for health information on the Web. We first presented a schema for categorizing the informational goals behind exploratory health search, touching on informational and diagnostic intentions, and on evidence- and hypothesis-directed strategies. We then reviewed methods for classifying sessions as being medically focused, studied the dynamics of foci (symptoms, causes, remedies) in those sessions, and highlighted patterns of activity demonstrated by searchers, such as the prevalence of symptom-oriented search, and the tight interplay between searchers for symptoms and causes when transitions are observed. We identified the existence of cycles and oscillations among foci that indicate that users may employ patterns of medical search that can be viewed as a rough approximation to hypothetico-deductive reasoning, using the Web as a source of information, in lieu of probabilistic inference.

Our analyses also reveal that users tend to remain in a single state during exploratory health search. Further study is needed to determine whether such search behavior is associated with EHS or is simply an indication of the persistence of a goal in the absence of satisfaction. The log-based nature of the study means that we cannot validate searchers' true intentions. Beyond consumer health search, sessions under consideration in our study likely also included professional medical searches including those by practitioners and students among numerous user cohorts searching for different purposes. Another concern is that since users use various search engines, sites, and other non-Web resources as they perform exploratory health searches, our approach may be unable to detect all of the nuances of such searching amidst the larger information context and motivations of searchers. We are interested in further investigating the underlying causes and intentions behind the observed behaviors via user studies.

The work presented here can be extended in several ways. First and foremost, we note that the current implementation uses a restricted set of ad hoc rules to label medical sessions, as well as to extract foci. We believe that the rules and terms being considered can be expanded and that potential biases in the existing set need to be explored and characterized. Machine-learning methods could be used to learn features of foci and to more robustly label sessions and identify foci in EHS sessions. Our analyses were also limited to within-session analysis. Although this scope provided a significant cache of information on searchers' activities, we believe that extending the analysis beyond the boundaries of a single session will provide even richer information concerning the user's intentions, enabling us to form a more accurate model of their reasoning process. For example, our earlier studies in this area revealed trends in how users re-access medical information over time [28], and significant benefit from multi-session features in predicting real world healthcare utilization [29]. In an attempt to reduce noise, we solely considered queries in search sessions. However, we know that a significant portion of the actions in each session were post-query browsing of web pages. These actions include navigating to pages on social networking sites that support groups for specific diseases. Future work will extend our analysis to include these and other post-query browsing actions.

The clustering and prediction tasks suggest directions for potential uses of information on the dynamics of focus of attention. The clustering provides a way to group individual searches so as to identify predominant exploratory health search strategies. Search systems or medical websites could make use of this kind of information to better understand how people perform health search. For example, a search system may expand queries using symptoms that a user has previously searched on so as to focus the search (potentially while sharing this strategy with the user) on the larger set of symptoms. Likewise, our ability to predict user actions (at a coarse level, in the form of foci) suggests that a search service might accurately anticipate shifts and more complex patterns of the users focus of attention during the course of a session. Such competencies demonstrate the potential utility of extracting foci from raw search logs, and have several implications in the design of search systems for medically-focused search. The use of representations of foci can provides useful handles on the structure and flow of a user's search session; search engines could provide an advanced search interface that exposes additional controls for users. Prediction could be used to anticipate forthcoming states of a user and search, such as an understanding of when a searcher might soon become inappropriately anxious based on the content of search results [28], enabling a system to act to provide guidance to users. Search systems could support medical searchers by pre-fetching results of possible interest or suggesting useful search strategies. In other approaches, search engines could be linked to more formal diagnostic decision support based on probabilistic and decision-theoretic inference [17].

7. CONCLUSIONS

We explored patterns of behavior of users searching for health information online. We sought insights on varying intentions and on the dynamics of focus of attention in search. As part of this work, we demonstrated that it is possible to extract search sessions that contain medically oriented searches. We demonstrated a simple mechanism to mine foci from a set of sessions that were extracted automatically. These sessions were used in analyses of user behavior during exploratory health search. The analyses included the generation of encodings of foci sequences that were used to discover common search strategies that people employ during health search. We showed that we were able to predict transitions among different focus types based on a recent sequence of user actions. There is much to be done to refine and extend the methods that we have presented. However, we are heartened by the initial results and believe that continuing this line of research will ultimately lead to new methods and tools that assist people with finding answers to their questions about illness and health.

REFERENCES

[1] S. Ayers and J. Kronenfeld. (2007). Chronic illness and health-seeking information on the Internet. *Health*, 11(3): 327–347.

[2] L. Baker, T.H. Wagner, S. Singer, and M.K. Bundorf. (2003). Use of internet and e-mail for health care information. *J. Amer. Med. Assoc.*, 289(18): 2401–2406.

[3] M.J. Bates. (1989). The design of browsing and berrypicking techniques for the online search interface. *Online Review*, 13 (5): 407–424.

[4] D. Beeferman and A. Berger. (2000). Agglomerative clustering of a search engine query log. *KDD*, 407–416.

[5] S.K. Bhavnani. (2002). Domain-specific search strategies for the effective retrieval of healthcare and shopping information. *SIGCHI*, 610–611.

[6] S.K. Bhavnani, R.T. Jacob, J. Nardine, and F.A. Peck. (2003). Exploring the distribution of online healthcare information. *SIGCHI*, 816–817.

[7] I.V. Cadez, D. Heckerman, C. Meek, P. Smyth, and S. White. (2001). Model-based clustering and visualization of navigation patterns on a web site. *MSR-TR-00-18.*

[8] R.J. Cline and K.M. Haynes. (2001). Consumer health information seeking on the Internet; the state of the art. *Health Education Research*, 16(6): 671–692.

[9] D. Downey, S.T. Dumais, and E. Horvitz. (2007). Models of searching and browsing: Languages, studies and applications. *IJCAI*, 2740–2747.

[10] M.S. Eastin and N.M. Guinsler. (2006). Worried and wired: effects of health anxiety on information-seeking and health care utilization behaviors. *Cyber. and Behav.*, 9(4): 494–498.

[11] A.S. Elstein, L.S. Shulman, and S.A. Sprafka. (1978). *Medical Problem Solving: An Analysis of Clinical Decision Making*. Harvard University Press.

[12] G. Eysenbach and C. Kohler. (2002). How do consumers search for and appraise health information on the world wide web? Qualitative studies using focus groups, usability test, and in-depth interviews. *Brit. Med. J.*, 324: 573–577.

[13] G.A. Gorry and G.O. Barnett. (1968). Sequential diagnosis by computer. *J. Amer. Med. Assoc.*, 12(205): 849–854.

[14] Health on the Net Foundation. www.hon.ch/HONcode/Pro.

[15] W.R. Hersh and D.H. Hickam. (1998). How well do physicians use electronic information retrieval systems? A framework for investigation and systematic review. *J. Amer. Med. Assoc.*, 280: 1347.

[16] W.R. Hersh et al. (2002). Factors associated with success in searching MEDLINE and applying evidence to answer clinical questions. *J. Amer. Med. Inform. Assoc.*, 9: 283–293.

[17] E.J. Horvitz, D.E. Heckerman, B.N. Nathwani, and L.M. Fargan. (1984). Diagnostic strategies in the hypothesis-directed pathfinder system. *First Conference on Artificial Intelligence Applications*, 630–636.

[18] T. Lewis. (2006). Seeking health information on the Internet: lifestyle choice of bad attack of cyberchondria? *Media, Culture, and Society*, 28(4): 521–539.

[19] Marchionini, G. Exploratory search: From finding to understanding. *Communications of the ACM 49*, 4, (2006), 41-46.

[20] K. Purcell, L. Rainie, A. Mitchell, T. Rosenstiel, and K. Olmstead. (2010). Understanding the participatory news consumer. *Pew Internet and American Life Project*, March 1.

[21] J. Schwarz and M.R. Morris. (2011). Augmenting web pages and search results to support credibility assessment. *SIGCHI*, 1245–1254.

[22] E. Sillence, P. Briggs, L. Fishwick, and P. Harris. (2004). Trust and mistrust of online health sites. *SIGCHI*, 663–670.

[23] A. Spink, Y. Yang, J. Jansen, P. Nykanen, D.P. Lorence, S. Ozmutlu, and H.C. Ozmutlu. (2004). A study of medical and health queries to Web search engines. *Health Information and Libraries Journal*, 21: 44–51.

[24] S.M. Weiss, C.A. Kulikowski, S. Amarel, and A. Safir. (1978). A model-based method for computer-aided medical decision-making *Artificial Intelligence*, 11(1-2): 145–172.

[25] W. Whewell. (1837). *History of the Inductive Sciences*. Parker and Deighton. Cambridge, UK.

[26] R.W. White and S.M. Drucker. (2007). Investigating behavioral variability in web search. *WWW*, 21–30.

[27] R.W. White and E. Horvitz. (2009). Experiences with web search on medical concerns and self-diagnosis. *AMIA*, 696–700.

[28] R.W. White and E. Horvitz. (2009). Cyberchondria: studies of the escalation of medical concerns in web search. *ACM Transactions on Information Systems*, 27(4), Article: 23.

[29] R.W. White and E. Horvitz. (2010). Web to World: Predicting transitions from self-diagnosis to the pursuit of local medical assistance in web search. *AMIA*, 882–886.

[30] R.W. White and E. Horvitz. (2010). Predicting escalations of medical queries based on web page structure and content. *SIGIR*, 769–770.

[31] B.M. Wildemuth. (2004). The effects of domain knowledge on search tactic information. *JASIST*, 55(3): 246–258.

User Behavior in Zero-Recall eCommerce Queries

Gyanit Singh[1], Nish Parikh[1] and Neel Sundaresan[1]
[1]eBay Research Labs, 2065 Hamilton Ave, San Jose, CA, USA
[1]{gysingh, nparikh, nsundaresan}@ebay.com

ABSTRACT

User expectation and experience for web search and eCommerce (product) search are quite different. Product descriptions are concise as compared to typical web documents. User expectation is more specific to find the right product. The difference in the publisher and searcher vocabulary (in case of product search the seller and the buyer vocabulary) combined with the fact that there are fewer products to search over than web documents result in observable numbers of searches that return no results (zero recall searches). In this paper we describe a study of zero recall searches. Our study is focused on eCommerce search and uses data from a leading eCommerce site's user click stream logs. There are 3 main contributions of our study: 1) The cause of zero recall searches; 2) A study of user's reaction and recovery from zero recall; 3) A study of differences in behavior of power users versus novice users to zero recall searches.

Categories and Subject Descriptors

H.3.3 [**Information Storage and Retrieval**]: Information Search and Retrieval—*search process, query formulation*

General Terms

Experimentation, Human Factors, Measurement

Keywords

Zero recall, e-Commerce search, User studies

1. INTRODUCTION

The challenges faced by typical search engines are different from those faced by eCommerce search engines. Product descriptions are shorter and less redundant and less abundant as compared to other web documents. Further, transience of the content (as items or products sell out they may not be available for search) and the difference in the vocabulary between the sellers or retailers and potential buyers can result in zero recall. Consider the following example: A seller selling a travel power adapter that works world-wide may describe it as a "*Universal Travel Adapter*". A buyer traveling to Europe and looking to buy a travel adapter might search for "*Travel Adapter for Europe*". More specifically, recently the query "*Oblong Shipping Boxes*" on eBay returned no results. The query "*Vintage Silvertone Frog Bracelet*" on Amazon and the query "*Wooden carom board*" on craigslist returned no results. For online businesses when a buyer sees no result it causes buyer frustration and implies potential loss of revenue. Novice users may walk away from such situations while experienced or persistent users might try variations on the queries to get what they came looking for. Table 1 shows the trail of a user looking for a "*boiler condensate disposal unit*". Differences in buyer and seller vocabulary led to zero recall searches for this user. User had to go through 2 zero recall searches and various modifications of her original query to get to an item of interest. For example in the first search "*boiler neutralization unit*" the searcher used the wrong keyword to describe the unit, i.e. *neutralization* and not *trap*.

Table 1: Example trail from logs where the user was looking for "*Boiler condensate disposal unit*". The time flows from top to bottom. Difference in buyer and seller vocabulary resulted in 2 zero recall searches. The tenacious buyer reformulated her query 3 times before she found the product she was interested in.

Action	Query/Title	Recall
Homepage	-	-
Search	boiler neutralization unit	0
Search	neutralization unit	0
Search	condensate	370
Search	condensate trap	32
View	Evaporator coil condensate drain trap	-

If we were to mine the intelligence buried in such trails, assistive tools can be provided that direct novice users to a path of potential purchase.

In this paper we focus our discussion on the analysis of user click stream data for a large sample of users for zero recall queries. The data is obtained from user click-stream logs of a leading eCommerce site. We focus on the following research questions and attempt to provide answers for these.

1. How do users get to a zero recall situation?

SIGIR'11, July 24–28, 2011, Beijing, China.

2. How do they react, and how this impacts their path to success?

3. How do power users differ from novice users in such situations?

Rest of the paper is organized as follows. Related work is described in Section 2. In Section 3 we describe the dataset used for our study and we also define the terminology used in the rest of the paper. In Section 4 we discuss first order analysis, linguistic characteristics and temporal volatility of zero recall queries. In Section 5 we study major mechanisms for the cause of zero recall searches. We show how different users (Power users vs. Novices) react to and recover from zero recall searches. In Section 6 we summarize our key contributions and indicate plans for future work.

2. RELATED WORK

User behavior in web search has been well studied. In [6], Granka et al. use eye-tracking to investigate how users interact with the results page of a WWW search engine. They describe the amount of time users spend viewing the abstracts, the amount of abstracts they view as well as measures of how thoroughly searchers evaluate their results set. Recently in [18] White and Huang presented a log-based study estimating the value of search trails to users. In [2], Baeza-Yates et al. model user's search behavior using query log data.

User variability in search has also been extensively studied. In [3] Bhavnani describes a study in which healthcare and online shopping experts were observed when they performed search tasks within and outside their domain of expertise. The study showed that non-domain experts could benefit from Search Strategy portals that provide domain specific knowledge to help with searching in unfamiliar domains. In [10] Lazonder et al. describe a study conducted on 25 Dutch students. The results showed that subjects with WWW-experience were more proficient in locating web-sites than novice WWW-users. In [8] Hölscher and Strube highlight the variability in the web search behavior of Internet experts and newbies. In a recent study [9] Kang and Fu conducted an experiment comparing search behavior of experts and novices when they searched using a traditional search engine and a social tagging system. Results from the experiment showed that experts relied more on their own domain knowledge to generate search queries while novices were influenced more by social cues in the social tagging system.

Large-scale studies based on looking at trails in logs have also been conducted to investigate the differences in behaviors of users in different search situations. In [16] White and Drucker find that there are dramatic differences in variability in key aspects of the interaction within and between users, and within and between the search queries they submit. Most research has suggested that domain experts search differently than people with little or no domain knowledge. Domain experts employ different search strategies and are more successful in finding what they are looking for than non-experts. In [17], White et al. present a large-scale, longitudinal, log-based analysis of the effect of domain expertise on web search behavior in four different domains (medicine, finance, law and computer science). They characterize the nature of the queries, search sessions, web sites visited, and search success for users identified as experts and non-experts within those domains. They also show how domain expertise can be used to help non-experts gain expertise.

User behavior can also be used to enhance search features. In [14] Singla et al. demonstrate value in user trails, highlight interesting differences in the performance of trail-finding algorithms and show how to find best trails for a query that can outperform the trails that most users follow. In [1] Agichtein et al. show how web search ranking can be improved by incorporating user behavior information.

In [4] Blair and Maron describe detailed evaluation of a full text document retrieval system. They show how the system does not perform satisfactorily and suffers from problems related to poor recall. Zero recall queries have also been described in literature. In [13] Pera describes how a shortcoming of existing library systems is the generation of a large percentage of zero-hits, i.e. no library records are retrieved for the corresponding library patron's queries. In [11] Parikh and Sundaresan describe how product searches can often return null results due to buyer-seller vocabulary mismatch or over-specialization of queries. They propose the use of a Semantic Query Network to help the users reformulate their query or to recommend queries which are likely to return inventory and are related to the user's intent. In [5] Broder et al. describe rare queries. They mention that rare web query sets contain 8-15% of queries which lead to zero recall.

Although user behavior in search has been studied in various domains, to the best of our knowledge not many large scale studies have been done for eCommerce search. Also, not much work has been done around understanding user reaction to zero recall queries. Our work focuses on bridging this gap.

3. DATASET

For our study we used click-stream logs from eBay. The dynamic nature of inventory poses unique challenges for search in a marketplace like eBay. Search on eBay is predominantly boolean. Based on partially typed queries, query completions are shown in the auto-complete dropdown box. Other searches related to the user typed-in query are shown below the search box as "Related Searches". As query suggestion features use algorithms based on mining query logs, for a minority of tail traffic, the algorithm [7] may be unable to compute and display suggestions. In case of zero recall, an option to retry the search with fewer keywords is shown at the bottom of the interface. The search interface offers the users features to constrain the product results and navigate to the inventory of interest. If product matches are found across multiple categories in the taxonomy tree, the matching categories are displayed on the left side of the interface for narrowing the search. Both navigation filters and query suggestions are displayed at the onset of the interaction. The interface also provides an option to the users to further constrain their search based on price range, condition of item (new or used), reputation of seller and format of item (fixed price or auction). The user has the option to sort the matching product set based on different factors like expiry time, price or BestMatch (eBay's multi-factor ranking, which is the default). By default products are displayed in a list view. Users can optionally select a grid view. In list view a short product title, thumbnail image and other meta-data like price, shipping charges and expiry time are displayed. We used a large sample from click-stream logs gathered over a 12 month period.

3.1 Terminology

Query: User typed in terms which are used as input to look up matching items in a product inventory.

Search: Using query and other constraints namely price, item condition specifics, shipping information, color and categorical constraints (for example Electronics) to find matching inventory.

Recall of query: Number of items matched to that query.

Zero recall search (ZRS): Searches which return no matching items.

Non-zero recall search (NZRS): Searches which return at least one matching item.

3.2 Logs

The data used for our study comprises of 16 million unique users performing 2.2 billion searches. The dataset comprises of 140 million search trails. We compute cumulative price for all the historical purchase activity of the user with in last 365 days. We classify users as novice users and power users based upon the money they spend on the site. Users who spend more than a predefined threshold (δ_1) are considered *power users* and those that spend less than a predefined threshold (δ_2) are considered *novice users*. Threshold used for definition for power users is magnitude of order greater than the threshold used for definition of novice users ($\delta_1 \gg \delta_2$).

All pages visited and all interactions on the site are logged in click-stream logs. We assigned each page visit and user interaction into one of the below mentioned classes. This set of page and user interaction classes are highly relevant and generic to most eCommerce platforms. *Homepage (H)* is the main landing page of the website. *Search (S)* pages are the pages on which user can provide a query and other parameters to perform a search. A search not only involves the query typed in by the user but also may contain other constraints like price, location or category (for example Electronics or Clothing & Shoes). *Detail (V)* pages are the pages on which inventory details are presented to the user. Links to these pages are provided as a response to the search done by the user. *Purchase (P)* pages are the pages associated with the purchase activity done by the user. For example, the page that confirms price and shipping address is one of these pages. *Account information (A)* pages are the pages which deal with account management. *Log in (L)* pages are the pages on which a user signs in. This page has been separated as users are usually forced to sign in for purchase pages but not for search pages.

3.3 Browse and Search Trails

Click stream logs collected from user browsing on the website are represented as continuous paths which we refer to as *browser trails*. Each node in the path is a web-page visited by the user. All pages visited by the user are grouped into various categories as described in Section 3.2.

Search trails in our logs are analogous to search trails described by White et al. in [18]. Search trails begin with a search being issued by the user and terminate at a point where user has finished her searching activity. We approximate the termination point by occurrence of certain activities in the browser trail. For example if a user visits purchase page then the search trail is assumed to have ended. Page timeouts and closing of browser window are also considered as the end of search trail. We define a search trail as being *successful* if the search trail ends in the purchase page.

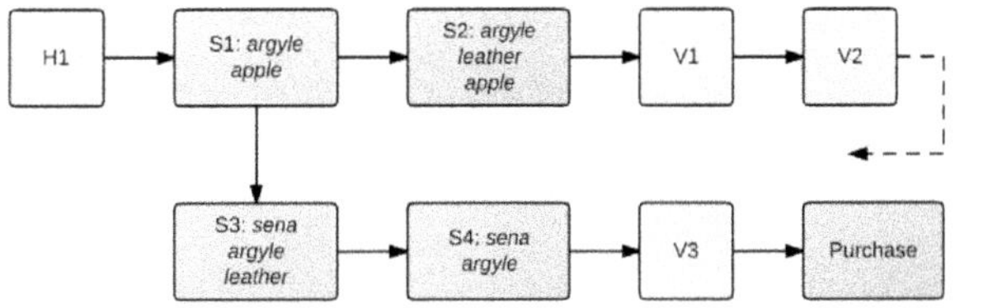

Figure 1: Example browser trail from click stream logs. Search block are tagged using following convention name:query. For example S1 event was search done using query "argyle apple". The back arrow means that user went back to S1 (or branching point). Time increases from left to right and from top to bottom.

Figure 1 displays an example browse trail and its corresponding search trail. This trail depicts a user entering the web site at *Homepage*($H1$) and then performing a search "*argyle apple*" ($S1$). She changes the query and reissues the search "*argyle leather apple*" ($S2$). On this search result page the user clicked on two results and went to detail pages of those two items ($V1, V2$). User reissued the search with a different query "*sena argyle leather*" ($S3$). She then generalizes the query to "*sena argyle*" in ($S4$) and views detail page of an item ($V3$) in the result set. The user then purchases the item by visiting purchase pages (*Purchase*). In the example described above the search trail would be $S1 \rightarrow S2 \rightarrow V1 \rightarrow V2 \rightarrow S3 \rightarrow S4 \rightarrow V3 \rightarrow Purchase$.

Zero recall search trail (ZRST) is defined as search trails with at least one zero recall search in them.

Non-zero recall search trail (NZRST) is defined as search trails with no zero recall search in them.

We also define notion of *post zero-recall search trails (PZR search trails)*. PZR search trails are sub trails of search trails but they start with the first zero-recall search encountered in the search trail. These trails denote the user activity after the user has seen the zero-recall search to the end of the trail. Let's say that $S3$ in search trail in Figure 1 was a zero recall search, then the PZRS trail would be given by; $S3 \rightarrow S4 \rightarrow V3$.

Defining trail end point as purchase or timeout has advantages. Firstly the quest to find the right item to purchase is an activity which involves multiple searches. By defining trail endpoint this way we are also able to include all the activity done by the user in other open tabs and windows of the browser. Since this patching is browser cookie based it can only stitch activity done by the user on the same browser. It also provides a holistic view of the user experience on the website. The search trail of a user who had to stumble through many searches and item detail pages has a different finger-print than the trail of a user who was able to succeed in one step.

Search trails are encoded to a string for studying various patterns in the trail. For this we encode a zero-recall search to alphabet Z and non-zero recall search to alphabet S. Detail page view obtained by click on a search result is converted to V whereas purchases are encoded to P.

Closing of the page or time outs are encoded as E. For example the trail in the example will be encoded to the string $SSVVSSVP$. This helps us encode certain type of trails as a regular expression over an alphabet. Alphabet set $\Sigma = \{Z, S, V, P, E\}$. For example a trail starting with zero-recall query and ending with exit are encoded as $Z\Sigma * E$. Here $\Sigma*$ encodes any alphabet with repetition count of zero or more.

4. CHARACTERISTICS OF ZERO RECALL SEARCHES

In this we section we present the general first order characteristic of zero recall queries. We compare and contrast the characteristics of these queries with those of non-zero recall queries. We find some interesting differences in query distributions and patterns. We examine statistics of zero recall queries such as the length of an individual query, the number of terms per query and the query distribution and repetition pattern.

4.1 Linguistic Analysis

The quality of experience that can be provided to users is dependent on the amount of understanding about queries the engine possesses. We studied characteristics of zero recall queries along different dimensions and the information around extracted attributes is shown in Figure 2.

In order to detect adjectives, conjunctions, prepositions and articles we used the Stanford NLP Group's POS Tagger trained on an English language corpus [15]. We also used human generated lists for celebrity and brand names. As the tagger was trained on a different corpus and the extraction of attributes was done based on simple string match algorithms, the results are conservative estimates of the actual percentages. All possible nick names of the celebrity or all abbreviations of the brand may not be present in the list hence making these percentages conservative estimates. If the brand or celebrity name to which the query pertains can be known, it can be effectively used for query suggestions and merchandising (even if the query cannot be matched to any relevant inventory).

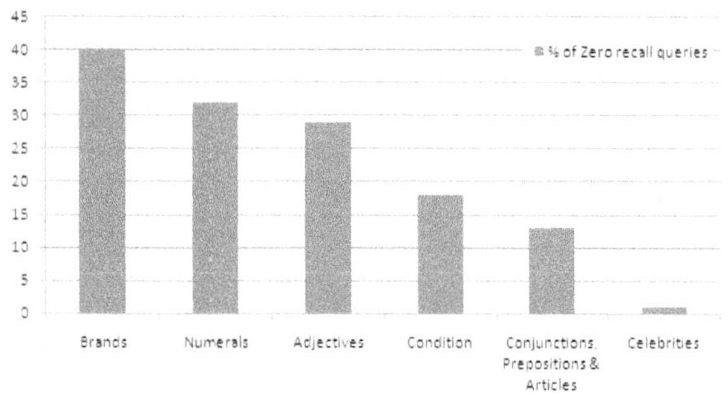

Figure 2: Zero recall searches covered by various attributes.

Being able to extract properties such as numerals, adjectives, conjunctions from queries can be useful in devising a strategy to predict the necessity of a query term to search for desired items along the lines of work described by Zhao and Callan in [19].

4.2 First Order Analysis, Uniqueness and Temporal Volatility

In this section we provide first order analysis of zero recall queries and non-zero recall queries. We compare character lengths, term lengths, repetition factor and uniqueness of these queries.

Term length analysis of queries is provided in Table 2. Zero recall queries tend to be longer. Number of terms used on average is 3.8 compared to 2.3 terms used for non-zero recall queries. Zero recall queries are more verbose than non-zero recall queries by 1.5 terms on average. Zero recall queries tend to be longer in number of characters as well. Average characters used for zero recall queries are 21 compared to 13 for non-zero recall queries. Users can do *negation* and *disjunction* through query. For example, *"father's day (gift, product) -old"*. The term *old* should not appear in any result and atleast one of the words *gift* or *product* should appear. We refer them as advanced queries. Advanced query length can be large.

Table 2: First order analysis of zero recall queries and non zero recall queries with respect to (a) Number of terms. (b) Number of characters

Terms per query		Zero recall	Non zero recall
All searches	Avg	3.83	2.37
	Median	3	2
	StdDev	2.56	1.82
	Max	1971	1286
Unique queries	Avg	4.65	3.8
	Median	3	3
	StdDev	3.47	2.74
	Max	1971	1286

Characters per query		Zero recall	Non zero recall
All searches	Avg	21.68	13.24
	Median	21	13
	StdDev	13.7	11.9
	Max	4484	4292
Unique queries	Avg	21.3	21.5
	Median	20	20
	StdDev	14.4	15.3
	Max	4484	4292

The zero recall queries are close to being unique. As shown in Table 3 zero recall queries have a repetition factor of 1.4. Non-zero recall queries on the other hand have a repetition factor of 20. Even the most popular zero recall queries do not repeat more than tens of thousands of times within a month. But the most popular non-zero recall query repeats more than millions of times.

Table 3: Repetition factor for zero recall queries and non-zero recall queries. Zero recall queries are almost unique (1.45 repetition factor); whereas non-zero recall queries have a heavy head.

	Repetition count
Zero recall queries	1.45
Non-zero recall queries	19.57

Figure 3(a) describes the quantity of search traffic covered by only top-k most popular queries. Top 10% most popular

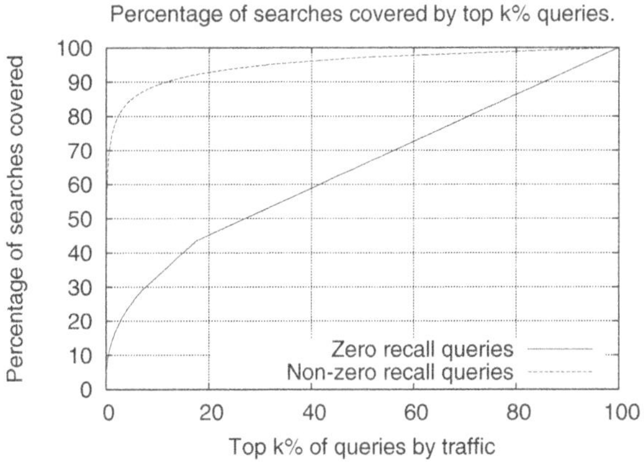

(a)

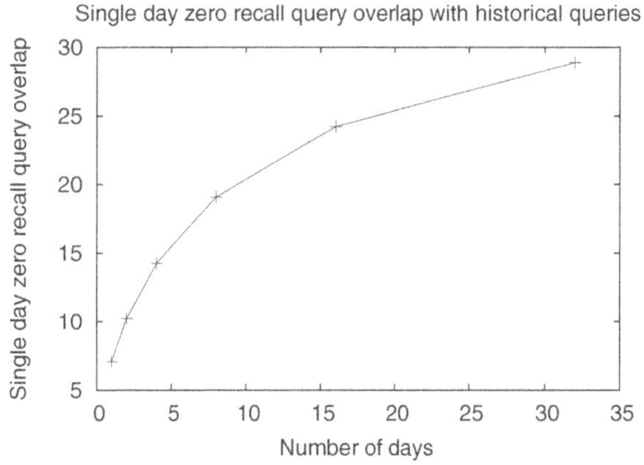

(b)

Figure 3: (a)Search traffic coverage of top k% most popular queries. Only 30% of zero recall searches are covered by 10% most popular zero-recall queries. But 90% of non-zero recall search traffic is generated by 10% most popular queries. (b) Overlap of single day zero recall queries with historical queries.

queries only cover 30% of zero recall search traffic. But for non-zero recall queries top 10% most popular queries cover 90% of the search traffic. This shows that the zero recall search traffic has extremely thin head and long tail. Further more Figure 3(b) describes day over day over lap of zero recall queries. For this all zero recall queries that appeared in a single day were taken. Then overlap was computed over historically occurring queries. It was observed that any two separate days have only 7% zero recall queries in common. When the historical zero recall queries time period is increased to 32 days then also the overlap only increases to 28%. As can be seen in the figure adding more historical data has diminishing returns with respect to amount of queries overlapping.

Zero recall queries have a long tail and do not repeat so often over time. Hence it is not practical to apply techniques that rely on query specific models to zero recall searches.

5. ZERO RECALL SEARCHES AND USER BEHAVIOR

In this section we describe how and when zero recall searches are generated. We also study the effect they have on the users and how the search trails are impacted due to zero recall searches. We also discuss the variability of effect of zero recall searches on power users and novice users.

5.1 Generation of Zero Recall Searches

Zero recall searches are caused because of various reason. The zero-recall queries are much longer than non-zero recall queries. In eCommerce domain as the documents are shorter and far less than web domain, query verbosity is the major reason for search being a zero-recall search. For example the following query *"aquasource kitchen faucet with sprayer 2 chrome handle"* likely leads to no results on major commerce search engines. The faucet might match but the color chrome may not match leading to a zero recall search. For users who have a strong preference for a specific color, ignoring color information and showing relevant items may not be the best strategy.

Another reason for zero recall search is the temporal volatility of the document space. As the items are being sold they are being removed from the marketplace. Non-zero recall queries may turn into zero recall queries due to this reason. Some zero recall queries also transition to non-zero recall queries. Queries have seasonal (for example Christmas, Thanksgiving) and buzz [12] (for example world cup) properties. Just like queries item corpora (supply) in the eCommerce market place also has seasonal and buzz properties. That is items being sold in holiday season may not be available during summer, Valentine's day based inventory is only available close to valentine's day. The queries (demand) are also seasonal in their peaks. But many queries do not go down to zero in off season. At that time it can lead to zero-recall searches.

Figure 3(b) shows the magnitude of volatility among zero recall queries. To compute the volatility in the inventory-document space we conducted an experiment. Instead of performing search over products currently being sold in the market place we performed the search over inventory that was available even once in previous year.For this we indexed historical inventory from previous year.We randomly sampled 500k queries from the set of current zero recall queries. We ran these queries on the historical cumulative index and found that 22% of queries became non-zero recall. Another reason for zero recall searches is difference in vocabulary between seller and buyers.

We also notice a considerable difference in fraction of zero recall search trails to non-zero recall search trails per user between novice and power users. Table 4 shows the fraction of zero recall search trails to non-zero recall search trails per user for different segment. The ratio of ZRST to NZRST per user is 81% higher for novice users as compared to power users.

Zero recall searches are more likely to occur in the beginning of the search trails. Figure 4 shows the fraction of zero recall searches as a function of position of zero recall

Table 4: **Fraction of zero recall search trails to non-zero recall search trails per user for different segments. The ratio of ZRST to NZRST per user is 81% higher for novice users as compared to power users.**

User segment	$\frac{ZRST\ per\ user}{NZRST\ per\ user}$	Normalized rate of ZRST per NZRST per user
All users	0.35	1
Power	0.22	0.64
Novice	0.4	1.12

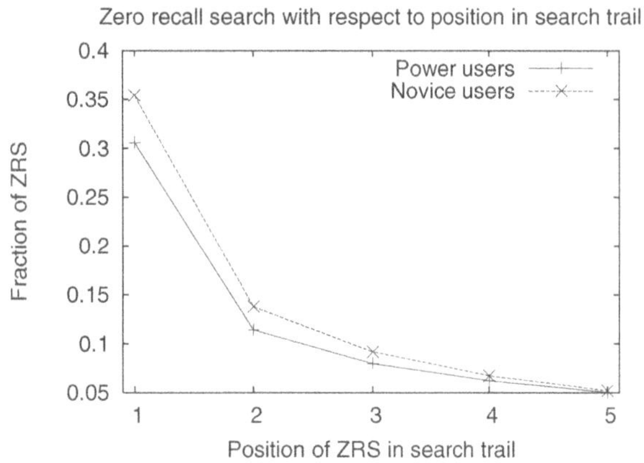

Figure 4: Zero recall searches are plotted with respect to their position in the search trail. Novice users do more zero recall searches in beginning of search trail (35%) than power users (30%). Half of the zero-recall searches occur within first 3 searches in search trails.

search in the trail. Novice users are more likely to perform ZRS in the first position than power users. Moreover 50% of ZRS done by power users occur within first 3 searches of search trail whereas for the same three position novice users do 58% of zero recall search.

Both of the above mentioned facts namely novice users do more ZRS per NZRS per user compared to power users and they are more likely to do them early in the search trail can be explained due to the fact that power users have more prior information in the domain than novice users. This puts novice users at much bigger disadvantage. Hence more coping strategies needed to be provided by the search engine to novice users, especially at the beginning of the search trails.

5.2 Effect of Zero Recall Searches on Users

Zero recall searches are a common phenomenon in the user's quest to find a relevant item for purchase. But zero recall searches present themselves as a big hindrance in the user's quest. Some users end their searching as soon as they experience zero recall searches. Others tend to reformulate their query to search for the relevant items. In this section we show the effect of zero recall searches on various user segments.

We notice that the purchase rate drops when the users experience a zero recall search in their search trail. A user with zero-recall search in her search trail has a purchase rate which is 0.64 times the purchase rate of user who did not experience zero recall search. Table 5 describes this factor for various user segments. Power users who have seen a ZRS in their search trails have a purchase rate (probability) of 0.68 time the purchase rate of power users which have not seen a ZRS. Similarly for novice users this factor is 0.61. That is power users who see a ZRS see a degradation of 32% in purchase rate but for novice users the degradation is 39%. Hence ZRS have more detrimental effect on novice users than on power users. Power users are more familiar with the domain and the search engine and marketplace. Hence they are able to reformulate queries efficiently and successfully.

Table 5: **For a user segment compares degradation of purchase rate for zero recall search trails from non-zero recall search trails. Purchase rate for power users degrades by a lower amount (0.32) when compared to novice users (0.39)**

User segment	$\frac{Purchase\ rate\ for\ ZRST}{Purchase\ rate\ for\ NZRST}$
All users	0.63
Power users	0.68
Novices	0.61

Zero recall searches experienced early in search trails are more damaging to purchase probability when compared with zero-recall searches experienced later in the search trail. Figure 5 presents the normalized purchase probability as a function of the position of zero recall searches in the search trail. A power user is able to overcome zero recall search with a much higher probability if it occurs late in the searching experience. Novice users on the other hand cannot cope with zero recall searches. They are most negatively affected if they experience it early in their interaction. As majority of ZRS happen early for novice users it is more damaging for eCommerce marketplaces.

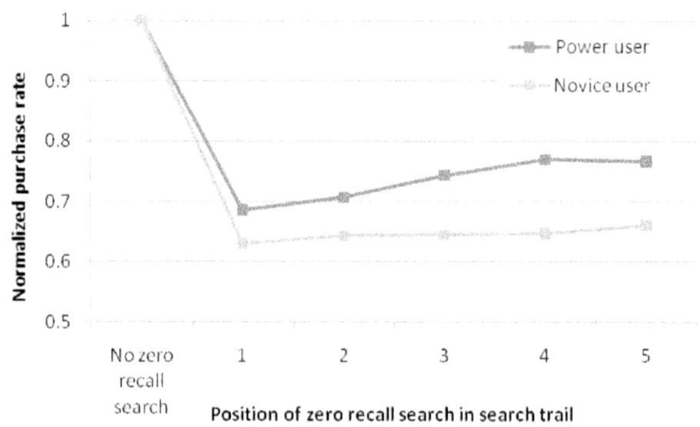

Figure 5: Normalized purchase probability as a function of the position of zero recall search in the search trail. Early zero recall searches are more damaging than later zero recall searches and they are more damaging for novice users than power users.

Novice users are twice as likely to give up immediately when they see ZRS as compared to power users. 16% of novice users exit the site without doing any other search after ZRS compared to only 8% of power users. Many users interpret zero recall search as no items of relevance present in the marketplace. Also they are not sophisticated enough in reformulating the query to represent the same intention.

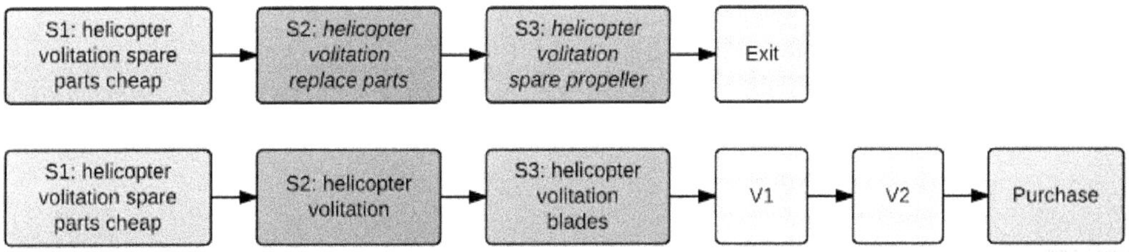

Figure 7: Two PZRS trails which start with same zero-recall search. The top one is done by a novice user and the bottom one is done by a power user. The novice stumbles 2 times $S2, S3$ before exiting. She is never able to reformulate the query to get desired results. Whereas power user stumbles once and then is able to move to a desirable search $S3$ leading to purchase.

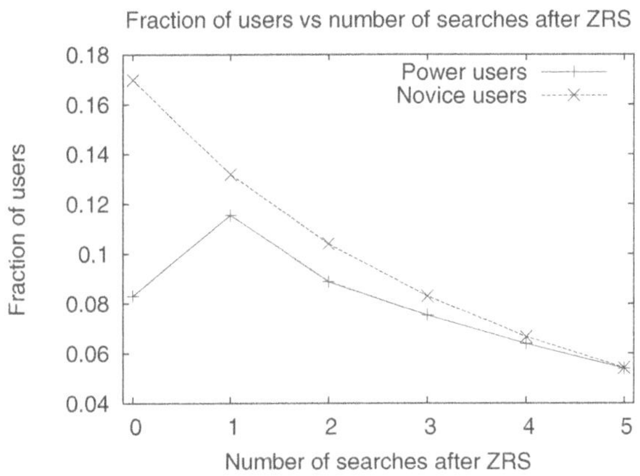

Figure 6: Fraction of zero recall search trails as a function of length of the search trail after the user experienced zero recall search. 0 corresponds to user giving up immediately and not doing any more searches which is twice as large for novice user (17%) compared to power users (8%). Power users are doing more searches after ZRS which shows they are persistent and not giving up easily.

Hence features like query suggestions and product merchandising become extremely important for these users.

For studying the effect of zero recall searches given the same intent of the user we collected set of trails which have same zero recall search in them. These zero recall searches were done by at least one power user and one novice user. To remove the effect of inventory volatility we only considered searches not more than a few days apart. Just in these set of trails we evaluated the difference of effect of zero recall searches on power users and novice users. Figure 7 shows one such pair of post zero recall search trail. Top PZR search trail is done by a novice user whereas the lower PZR search trail is done by a power user. Both start with a zero recall search *"helicopter volitation spare parts cheap"*. These users are searching for spare parts for *Volitation* brand toy helicopter. The novice user reformulated the query to *"helicopter volitation replace parts"* ($S2$) which also returned zero results. This user did another query ($S3$) which returned zero results and at this time user gave up. On the other hand power user (bottom trail) reformulates the zero recall search ($S1$) to *"helicopter volitation"* ($S2$) from where she learned the most appropriate refinement query *"helicopter volitation blades"* ($S3$). On this page she views two item details ($V1, V2$) and proceeds to purchase one of those.

Table 6 compares the purchase rates for novice users and power users when they are put into same scenarios. Power users succeed in purchasing with a 53% higher rate than novice users.

Table 6: Given set of zero recall search trails with same intent, purchase rate for user segment normalized by purchase rate for novice. Purchase rate for power users is 53% higher than of the novice users.

User segment	Normalized purchase rate
Novice	1
Power users	1.53
Average user	1.1

Table 7: Table of comparison between Power users and Novice users. It compares generation of zero recall search trails, effect of ZRS on purchase activity and browsing .

Metric	Power	Novice
ZRST per NZRST per user	0.22	0.4
Degradation of purchase rate due to ZRS	0.68	0.61
Exit rates in PZRST	15%	20%
Weak recovery in PZRST	85%	80%
Strong recovery in PZRST	68%	62%

5.3 User Recovery

In this subsection we discuss how users cope with and recover from zero-recall searches. We define two concepts of recovery from zero-recall searches. User is defined to have *weak recovered* or just *recovered* if she does a search with non zero recall after the zero-recall search. A *strong recovery* is defined as user doing a search with non-zero recall on which she clicks on at least one result item after the zero recall search is done. Strong recovery is a more stronger definition of recovery than the weak recovery because in the case of strong recovery a user not only performs a search with non-zero recall after the ZRS, but that search also return relevant items that user gets interested enough to click on them. Hence a strong recovery always imply a weak recovery but a weak recovery may not lead to strong recovery.

Post zero recall search trails ending at weak recovery point are called *weak recovery trail*. PZR search trails ending in

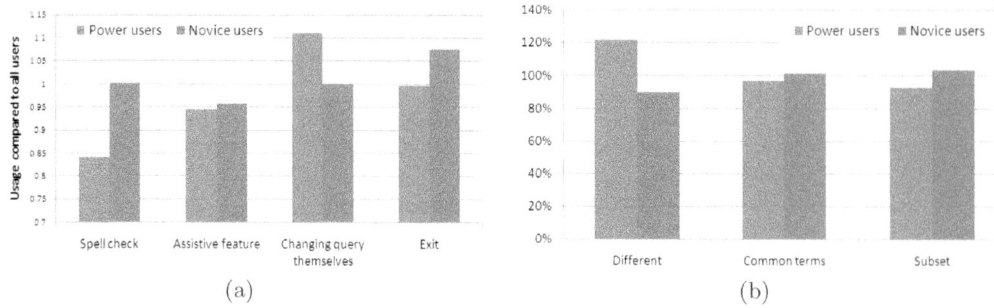

Figure 8: Different strategies used by power users and novice users to recover from zero recall searches (a) Usage of mechanisms normalized by average usage. (b) Recovery query comparison with zero recall query.

strong recovery point are called *strong recovery trails*. For example a search trail of $S1 \rightarrow S2 \rightarrow S3 \rightarrow S4 \rightarrow S5 \rightarrow V \rightarrow Exit$ where $S2$ and $S3$ were zero recall searches and $S1$, $S4$, $S5$ were non-zero recall searches would give us following PZR search trail: $S2 \rightarrow S3 \rightarrow S4 \rightarrow S5 \rightarrow V \rightarrow Exit$ and weak recovery trail: $S2 \rightarrow S3 \rightarrow S4$ and following strong recovery trail $S2 \rightarrow S3 \rightarrow S4 \rightarrow S5 \rightarrow V$.

Many PZR search trails do not end in recovery, i.e. non-zero recall searches or a click on the search result to item detail page. These recovery trails end with an exit and correspond to users who failed to recover. For example the search trail $S1 \rightarrow S2 \rightarrow S3 \rightarrow Exit$. Where $S1$ is a non-zero recall search and $S2$, $S3$ are zero recall searches the recovery trail is $S2 \rightarrow S3 \rightarrow Exit$.

Figure 6 showed that 16% of novice and 8% of power users give up without any other search after the zero recall search. In general we observed that 15% of power users exit the site without doing weak recovery whereas 20% novice users exit the site without doing weak recovery.

5.3.1 Weak Recovery and Strategies Used

We analyzed the mechanisms used by users to recover from zero recall queries. Users either tend to use assistive features provided by the site (for example, query suggestions, query reduction by dropping terms etc.) or undertake the effort to reformulate their queries in order to recover. We observed a considerable difference in PZR search trails of novice and power users. Novices tend to use assistive features more whereas power users tend to reformulate queries themselves in order to recover. We also studied query reformulation i.e. how different are the reformulated queries as compared to the original zero recall queries.

Figure 8 compares the strategy used by two user segments to perform weak recovery. Figure 8(a) compares the site features used by different user segments. The usage is normalized with respect to an average user. Power users wrongly spell queries 0.84 times that of an average user where as novice users wrongly spell queries at par with average user. This is due to the fact that novice users commit more spelling mistakes than power user.

Usage of assistive features like query suggestions, recommendation of dropping of terms etc. is used at a smaller rate than of average user in both segments. Power user change the query terms themselves at a 1.11 factor larger than the average user. Whereas novice user changes the query themselves at the similar rate of that of an average user. This implies that power users change the query themselves at 10% higher rate than novice users and weak recover.

In those cases we compared the terms of the recovering query with the zero recall query. Figure 8(b) provides the results of this analysis. Novice users tend to drop terms and do queries which are subset of the zero recall queries at a 13% higher rate than the power user. The disadvantage of doing this is that they will not be able to represent all the constraint represented by the terms that were relevant to them. Also shorter sub queries are more likely to return a large recall set and overwhelm the user. Power users are more likely to change the query terms. This can be due to the much richer knowledge of domain vocabulary possessed by the power users.

For example in eBay category for chandeliers we found that sellers use "*unique*", "*antique*" and "*vintage*" to describe the same style of chandeliers. One of the power buyers after doing a search of "*crystal chandelier one of kind*" which gives a zero recall changed it to "*crystal chandelier unique*" and then "*crystal chandelier antique*" both of them are non-zero recall searches and highly relevant to the power buyers intent.

5.3.2 Strong Recovery

Although 85% of power users weak recover, only 68% strong recover. This implies that PZR search trails reaching to a non-zero recall search does not necessarily imply that the results returned were relevant to the user. Table 8 provide a detail view of the number of users strong recovering. Only 62% of novice users are able to strong recover. This number is lower than the average recovery rate of 64.2%.

5.4 Recovery Analysis

In this subsection we describe the analysis of recovery. We measure it along two dimensions namely user frustration and effort and recovery quality.

5.4.1 User Frustration and Effort to Recovery

User frustration and effort is approximated by the amount of time spent and the number of searches user has to do to recover. These numbers encapsulate user frustration and effort because for every additional search user is paying a price both in terms of effort and time. It requires time to enter a new query and also effort is required in coming up with new relevant keywords to express the same buying intent. As the effort required in finding relevant items increases so does the frustration level of the user. We define

$$User\ effort = \#\ searches\ to\ recovery$$

Figure 9 provides the breakdown of fraction of recovery trails as a function of number of searches in them. It can be seen that that 66% strong recovery trail contain more than or equal to 2 searches.

Table 8 below provides with further high level break down into interesting recovery trail patterns. Half of the users who end their trails without recovery do so by performing at least 2 searches. Also 2 out of 3 strong recoveries require at least 2 searches by the user after the zero-recall search is performed. All these users are stumbling to find the right search query that will return relevant results.

A more continuous measure of effort is presented in Figure 9. The recovery trails ending in strong recovery are broken down into various chunks based on number of searches they did after a ZRS to achieve strong recovery. Only 1 in 3 strong recoveries happen in 1 search. All other strong recovery require user to perform at least 2 searches. This can weigh heavily on user patience and lead to a bad user experience.

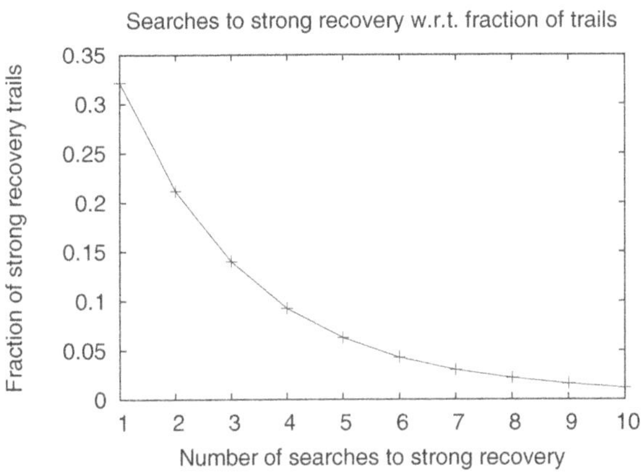

Figure 9: Number of searches it takes to strong recovery. Only 32% ($\frac{1}{3}$) of strong recoveries happen with one search. Remaining 66% strong recovery take two or more searches. This can lead to lot of user effort and frustration.

5.4.2 Recovery Quality

Although users search trail might be returning to non-zero recall searches but those searches may not be good with respect to user intent. For example a user doing a query "adidas originals women tracksuit bottoms large" which leads to zero recall due to over-specialization dropped terms "women", "large", "tracksuit" to get to non-zero recall query "adidas originals bottoms". However, there are lot of key aspects which are missing in the result set for this new query.

We define the quality of recovery as a function of quality of searches performed by the user in the recovery trail. The quality of a search is defined as probability of the event that user clicks on a search result presented to her as the answer to the search. For this we measure the click through percentage of search. We compare the searches that happen after the zero recall search with searches happening in search trails in which zero-recall searches never happened.

Figure 10 describes the quality of searches performed after the zero-recall search in the PZR search trail. It also

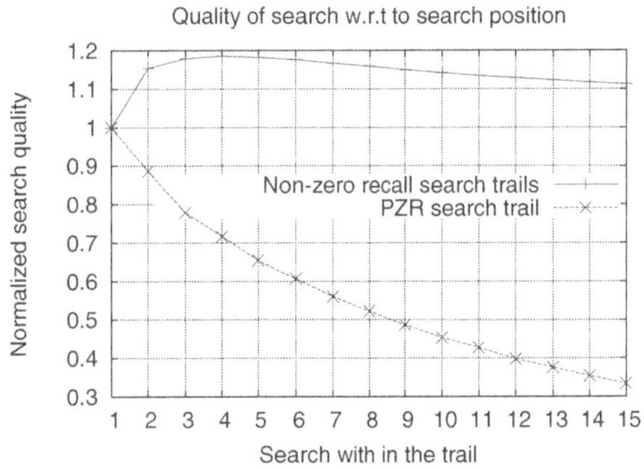

Figure 10: Normalized quality of search as position of search in trail. The normalization is done by the first search in the trail. The search quality (Pr[search will get a click]) in post zero-recall search trail detoriates with position. Although for non-zero recall search trail the quality improves initially and then slightly decreases.

compares the quality with the searches in the non-zero recall search trails. The quality numbers are normalized by the quality of first search in the trail. Probability[search getting click] or quality increases in non-zero recall search trails. This can be explained by the fact that as users perform more searches, they change their queries to be more relevant to their intent. After five searches it starts dropping as users start dropping off.

For PZR search trails the quality of searches keep on degrading with the search count within the trail. Normalized view probability (search quality) for searches in PZRS reduces to $\frac{1}{3}$ value of the corresponding searches in non-zero recall search trails. Although users are able to get to non-zero recall searches in their recovery trails, but those non zero-recall searches are of much lower relevance to the user on average. This conveys a lack of discovery of right inventory by that user in PZR search trails. Hence, tools and features to enable these users in discovering exciting and relevant inventory are necessary.

6. DISCUSSION

Concise product descriptions, stricter user expectations and volatile inventory collections differentiate eCommerce search from web search. In this paper, we described user behavior in zero recall searches, a common and important phenomenon in the eCommerce domain. Our contributions are an analysis of the following:

- Cause of Zero Recall Searches: We studied how zero recall is cause by differences in buyer and seller vocabulary and limited and dynamic inventory described by short descriptions.

- User Reaction to Zero Recall: We discussed how zero recall queries lead to user frustration and a degradation in purchase rates. We also saw how most users try to recover from such situations through query reformulation.

Table 8: Various post zero recall (PZR) search trail patterns. The PZR trails are segmented into those which exited and those which strong recovered by getting to an item detail view page from search.

Trail Path	Explanation		Power	Novice	All
ZΣ+	All trails		100%	100%	100%
Z(Z|S)*E	No strong recovery	All trails with no strong recovery	**29.76%**	**36.64%**	**34.26%**
ZE		Exit with no other searches	7.53%	9.66%	8.82%
Z(S|Z)E		Exit with 1 more search	7.31%	7.94%	7.46%
Z(Z|S)(Z|S)+E		Exit with ≥ 2 more search	14.93%	19.05%	17.98%
Z(Z|S)*V	Strong recovery	All trails with strong recovery	**68.09%**	**61.95%**	**64.24%**
ZSV		1 search to strong recovery	21.87%	20.56%	21.07%
Z(Z|S)(Z|S)+V		≥ 2 searches to strong recovery	46.22%	41.39%	43.18%
ZZΣ*	Users who do zero recall searches twice		21.71%	22.15%	21.45%

- Variability in behavior of novices and power users: We discussed that power users are less impacted as compared to novices (see Table 7). Power users seem to be able to reformulate queries more intelligently in order to recover as compared to novices. Under zero recall situations for the same task and query, power users are 50% more likely to be eventually successful as compared to novice users.

Zero recall searches have negative effects on user conversion. Also, user variability poses unique challenges for an eCommerce search engine. Variability also implies that the engine has to offer features which can cater to all segments of users. Some of these issues can be tackled by personalization in search engines. As power users tend to react to difficult situations better and possess unique knowledge of the domain, intelligence from power trails can be used to learn and help other users. We would like to address this as part of future work.

7. REFERENCES

[1] E. Agichtein, E. Brill, and S. T. Dumais. Improving web search ranking by incorporating user behavior information. In *Proceedings of SIGIR*, pages 19–26, 2006.

[2] R. A. Baeza-Yates, C. A. Hurtado, M. Mendoza, and G. Dupret. Modeling user search behavior. In *LA-WEB*, pages 242–251, 2005.

[3] S. Bhavnani. Domain-specific search strategies for the effective retrieval of healthcare and shopping information. In *CHI Extended Abstracts*, pages 610–611, 2002.

[4] D. C. Blair and M. E. Maron. An evaluation of retrieval effectiveness for a full-text document-retrieval system. In *Commun. ACM*, 1985.

[5] A. Z. Broder, M. Fontoura, E. Gabrilovich, A. Joshi, V. Josifovski, and T. Zhang. Robust classification of rare queries using web knowledge. In *Proceedings of SIGIR*, pages 231–238, 2007.

[6] L. A. Granka, T. Joachims, and G. Gay. Eye-tracking analysis of user behavior in www search. In *Proceedings of SIGIR*, pages 478–479, 2004.

[7] M. A. Hasan, N. Parikh, G. Singh, and N. Sundaresan. Query suggestion for e-commerce sites. In *Proceedings of the WSDM*, 2011.

[8] C. Hölscher and G. Strube. Web search behavior of internet experts and newbies. computer networks. In *Computer Networks*, volume 33, pages 337–346, 2000.

[9] R. Kang and W.-T. Fu. Exploratory information search by domain experts and novices. In *Proceedings of IUI*, pages 329–332, 2010.

[10] A. W. Lazonder, H. J. A. Biemans, and I. G. J. H. Wopereis. Differences between novice and experienced users in searching information on the world wide web. In *JASIS*, volume 51, pages 576–581, 2000.

[11] N. Parikh and N. Sundaresan. Inferring semantic query relations from collective user behavior. In *Proceedings of CIKM*, pages 349–358, 2008.

[12] N. Parikh and N. Sundaresan. Buzz-based recommender system. In *Proceedings of WWW*, 2009.

[13] M. S. Pera. Improving library searches using word-correlation factors and folksonomies. In *Master of Science Thesis, Department of Computer Science, Brigham Young University*, 2009.

[14] A. Singla, R. White, and J. Huang. Studying trailfinding algorithms for enhanced web search. In *Proceedings of SIGIR*, pages 443–450, 2010.

[15] K. Toutanova. Enriching the knowledge sources used in a maximum entropy part-of-speech tagger. In *EMNLP/VLC*, 2000.

[16] R. W. White and S. M. Drucker. Investigating behavioral variability in web search. In *Proceedings of WWW*, pages 21–30, 2007.

[17] R. W. White, S. T. Dumais, and J. Teevan. Characterizing the influence of domain expertise on web search behavior. In *Proceedings of WSDM*, pages 132–141, 2009.

[18] R. W. White and J. Huang. Assessing the scenic route: measuring the value of search trails in web logs. In *Proceedings of SIGIR*, pages 587–594, 2010.

[19] L. Zhao and J. Callan. Term necessity prediction. In *CIKM*, pages 259–268, 2010.

Bagging Gradient-Boosted Trees for High Precision, Low Variance Ranking Models

Yasser Ganjisaffar
School of Information & Computer Sciences
University of California, Irvine
Irvine, CA, USA
yganjisa@ics.uci.edu

Rich Caruana
Microsoft Research
One Microsoft Way
Redmond, WA 98052
rcaruana@microsoft.com

Cristina Videira Lopes
School of Information & Computer Sciences
University of California, Irvine
Irvine, CA, USA
lopes@ics.uci.edu

ABSTRACT

Recent studies have shown that boosting provides excellent predictive performance across a wide variety of tasks. In Learning-to-rank, boosted models such as RankBoost and LambdaMART have been shown to be among the best performing learning methods based on evaluations on public data sets. In this paper, we show how the combination of bagging as a variance reduction technique and boosting as a bias reduction technique can result in very high precision and low variance ranking models. We perform thousands of parameter tuning experiments for LambdaMART to achieve a high precision boosting model. Then we show that a bagged ensemble of such LambdaMART boosted models results in higher accuracy ranking models while also reducing variance as much as 50%. We report our results on three public learning-to-rank data sets using four metrics. Bagged LamdbaMART outperforms all previously reported results on ten of the twelve comparisons, and bagged LambdaMART outperforms non-bagged LambdaMART on all twelve comparisons. For example, wrapping bagging around LambdaMART increases NDCG@1 from 0.4137 to 0.4200 on the MQ2007 data set; the best prior results in the literature for this data set is 0.4134 by RankBoost.

Categories and Subject Descriptors

H.3.3 [**Information Systems**]: Information Search and Retrieval; H.4.m [**Information Systems**]: Miscellaneous—*Machine Learning*

General Terms

Algorithms, Experimentation

Keywords

Learning-to-rank, Tree Ensembles, Bagging

1. INTRODUCTION

The general problem of ranking, and in particular ranking of web search results, has received significant attention. Given the large amount of training data now available it has become possible to learn effective ranking models using machine learning. Methods that learn how to combine predefined features for ranking are called "Learning-to-rank" methods. A large number of learning-to-rank algorithms have been proposed, such as [8, 7, 9, 21, 28, 30] (see [22] for a more complete list).

Recent studies have shown that tree models combined with ensemble techniques provide excellent predictive performance. In the recent Yahoo! learning-to-rank challenge [10], the top ranked teams all used tree ensemble methods. The winning entry in this competition used an ensemble of LambdaMART [32] models.

In this work, we study the effectiveness of bagged ensembles of ranking models to achieve higher prediction accuracy. We train multiple independent ranking models on different samples of the training data and combine the outputs of these models to get improved prediction accuracy. In our experiments, we use LambdaMART, which is a boosted ensemble of trees, as the baseline model. Thus we are forming bagged ensembles of boosted ensembles of trees. Our approach is motivated by Breiman's Bagging [3], so we call this method *BL-MART* for *B*agged Lambda*MART*. Since sub-models are independent they can be trained in parallel and the training time is not more than training time of a single LambdaMART model. In fact, because we perform sampling without replacement, each of the LambdaMART models is trained on a smaller training set and therefore the training time is less than training a single LambdaMART model on the full train set.

We summarize the main contributions of this paper as follows:
(a) We perform thousands of parameter tuning experiments for the LambdaMART algorithm to find near optimal parameter configurations for it and also study its sensitiveness to its parameters (section 3.4).
(b) We show that adding randomness during the training of LambdaMART models can improve the accuracy of these models. We introduce randomness by sub-sampling queries that are available to the algorithm during each of the training iterations. We also use feature sampling as another method for increasing randomness of the algorithm (section 3.3).
(c) We study the effectiveness of bagging ensembles of Lamb-

daMART models to both increase the prediction accuracy of the ranking model and reduce the model variance.
(d) We show that bagged ensembles of overfitted base-level models (overfitted boosted tree models) result in higher prediction accuracy than bagging optimally generated base-level models and we explain why this happens.

2. BACKGROUND AND RELATED WORK

LambdaMART [32] is a ranking algorithm that uses Gradient boosting [15] to optimize a ranking cost function similar to the LambdaRank [7] cost function. Readers can refer to [6] for details of this algorithm. However, since it is our base model, we briefly describe some of the important concepts that are referenced in the reminder of this paper.

Gradient boosting produces an ensemble of weak models (typically regression trees) that together form a strong model. The ensemble is built in a stage-wise process by performing gradient descent in function space. The final model maps an input feature vector $x \in R^d$ to a score $F(x) \in R$:

$$F_m(x) = F_{m-1}(x) + \gamma_m h_m(x)$$

where each h_i is a function modeled by a single regression tree and the $\gamma_i \in R$ is the weight associated with the i-th regression tree. Both the h_i and the γ_i are learned during training. A given tree h_i maps a given feature vector x to a real value by passing x down the tree, where the path (left or right) at a given node is determined by the value of a particular feature in the feature vector and the output is a fixed value associated with the leaf that is reached by following the path.

Gradient boosting usually requires regularization to avoid overfitting. In an overfitted model, the model's generalization ability degrades because of fitting too closely to the training data. Different kinds of regularization techniques can be used to reduce overfitting in boosted trees. One common regularization parameter is the number of trees in the model, M. Increasing M reduces the error on training set, but setting it too high often leads to overfitting. An optimal value of M often is selected by monitoring prediction error on a separate validation data set.

Another regularization approach is to control the complexity of the individual trees via a number of user-chosen parameters. For example, *Max Number of Leaves per tree* limits the size of individual trees thus preventing them from overfitting to the training data. Another user–set parameter for controlling tree size is the minimum number of observations allowed in leaves. This parameter is used in the tree building process by ignoring splits that lead to nodes containing fewer than this number of training set observations. This prevents adding leaves that contain statistically small samples of training data.

Another important regularization technique is shrinkage which modifies the boosting update rule as follows:

$$F_m(x) = F_{m-1}(x) + \eta\gamma_m h_m(x), \quad 0 < \eta \leq 1,$$

where parameter η is called the *learning rate*. Small learning rates can dramatically improve a model's generalization ability over gradient boosting without shrinkage ($\eta = 1$), however they result in more boosting iterations and therefore larger models.

Bias-Variance Decomposition of Error

According to the bias-variance decomposition of error [16], the squared error of a single example x can be decomposed into the sum of three non-negative terms: *noise*, *bias*, and *variance*. The first term, Noise, is the irreducible error which cannot be avoided regardless of the learning algorithm. In learning-to-rank domain, it can be interpreted as the noise in relevance judgments of query-url pairs. The second term, Bias, measures how closely the average prediction of the learning algorithm (considering all possible training sets of a fixed size) matches the optimal prediction (the Bayes rate prediction). Finally, the Variance of an algorithm is how much the algorithm's prediction fluctuates over different possible training sets of a given size.

Ensemble methods such as Gradient Boosting [15] reduce bias by increasing the expressive power of the base learner and by forcing learning to attend to training cases that consistently are mispredicted. Because boosting combines the predictions of multiple trees it also can reduce variance, but boosted trees are so powerful that regularization usually is needed to prevent overfitting. Other ensemble methods such as Bagging [3] mainly reduce variance by averaging outputs of several models trained on different samples of training data. Because bagging usually does not significantly increase expressive power and often yields large reductions in variance, it is a relatively *safe* procedure that usually does not require regularization or careful parameter tuning. In fact, bagging can be used as an effective regularization method when wrapped around other high-variance learning methods that are prone to overfitting such as boosting. There has been attempts for combining bias and variance reduction techniques for classification [31, 29] and regression [5, 14, 26, 27] problems. In this work, we combine bagging and boosting for improved learning-to-rank.

Similar to us, BagBoo [23] wraps Bagging around Boosting for improved learning-to-rank. However, there are several fundamental differences that make our work different from BagBoo. The most important difference is the size of the final model. On two public data sets that BagBoo reports its results, our BL-MART models are approximately 250 times smaller and also more accurate on most metrics (section 4). BagBoo is training more than a million trees on these data sets which makes its size infeasible for real time applications. In addition, the boosting algorithm that is used in BagBoo is a pointwise method, while BL-MART uses LambdaMART for boosting which is a listwise algorithm. Pointwise methods such as [12, 21] do not exploit relative rank information between documents, instead attempting to directly create a scoring function. In contrast, listwise methods such as [7, 9, 30] use lists of ranked documents as instances during training, and learn a ranking model by minimizing a listwise loss function. In addition, we also show that bagging boosted ensembles that are mildy overfitted to their training data gives better results.

3. METHODS

3.1 Data sets

For our experiments we work with three public data sets: TD2004 and MQ2007 from LETOR data sets [24] and the recently published MSLR-WEB10K data set from Microsoft Research [1]. Table 1 summarizes the properties of these data sets. The TD2004 and MQ2007 data sets have been used many times for evaluating new learning-to-rank algorithms. This provides a baseline for comparing our method with other state-of-the-art learning-to-rank algorithms. MSLR-WEB10K is a large data set which is more similar to commercial search data sets. Because it is larger it should provide results that are more reliable. All three data sets are pre-folded and come with evaluation scripts that allow fair comparison of different ranking algorithms.

3.2 Evaluation Metrics

For model comparison we use two information retrieval metrics: Normalized Discounted Cumulative Gain (NDCG) [19] and Mean Average Precision (MAP) [2]. NDCG@k is a measure for evaluating top k positions of a ranked list using multiple levels of relevance judgment. It is defined as follows,

$$NDCG@k = N^{-1} \sum_{j=1}^{k} g(r_j) d(j),$$

where N^{-1} is a normalization factor chosen so that a perfect ordering of the results will receive the score of one; r_j denotes the relevance level of the document ranked at the j-th position; $g(r_j)$ is a gain function:

$$g(r_j) = 2^{r_j} - 1;$$

and $d(j)$ denotes a discount function. The evaluation scripts that come with the three data sets use the following discount function:

$$d(j) = \begin{cases} 1 & \text{for j = 1,2} \\ \frac{1}{\log_2(j)} & \text{otherwise.} \end{cases}$$

We use the same scripts for fair comparison of our final models with other algorithms. However in our implementation of the LambdaMART algorithm and in all of our training and parameter tuning experiments, we optimize for the following discount function which places stronger emphasis on higher positions:

$$d(j) = \frac{1}{\log_2(1+j)}$$

Also, based on whether we assign NDCG values of zero or one to a query where all of the documents are assigned non-relevant labels, the scale of NDCG values will change.

3.3 Randomization for LambdaMART

In [14], Friedman proposed a modification of the gradient boosting algorithm which was motivated by Breiman's bagging method. He proposed that at each iteration of the algorithm, a base learner should be fit on a sub-sample of the training set drawn at random without replacement. Friedman observed a substantial improvement in gradient boosting's accuracy with this modification. Sub-sample size is some constant fraction s of the size of the training set. When $s = 1$, the algorithm is deterministic. Smaller values of s introduce randomness into the algorithm and help prevent overfitting, acting as a kind of regularization. The algorithm also becomes faster, because regression trees have to be fit to smaller data sets at each iteration.

Also similar to Random Forests [4], more randomness can be introduced by sampling features that are available to the algorithm on each tree split. On each split, the algorithm selects the best feature from a random subset of features instead of the best overall feature.

Table 2: Values used in grid search for parameter tuning

(a) TD2004 and MQ2007 data sets

Parameter	Values
Max Number of Leaves	2, 4, 7, 10, 15, 20, 25
Min Percentage of Obs. per Leaf	0.12, 0.25, 0.50
Learning rate	0.05, 0.1, 0.2, 0.3
Sub-sampling rate	0.3, 0.5, 1.0
Feature Sampling rate	0.1, 0.3, 0.5, 1.0

(b) MSLR-WEB10K data set

Parameter	Values
Max Number of Leaves	10, 40, 70
Min Percentage of Obs. per Leaf	0.12, 0.25, 0.50
Learning rate	0.05, 0.1, 0.2
Sub-sampling rate	0.5, 1.0
Feature Sampling rate	0.3, 0.5, 1.0

In our experiments, we add both observation sub-sampling and feature sampling as two new parameters that need to be tuned for the LambdaMART algorithm. These parameters can take values between 0 and 1, where 1 means no sampling and values less than 1 introduce sampling randomness.

3.4 Parameter Tuning

The original LambdaMART algorithm has three parameters that need to be tuned to achieve the best results: "Max number of leaves", "Min percentage of observations per leaf", and "Learning rate". These were described in section 2. As mentioned above, to these we have added two new parameters: "Sub-sampling rate" and "Feature sampling rate". We use grid search to test 1,008 different combination of parameters on the smaller data sets and 162 combinations on the larger data set. Table 2 shows the values we tried for each of the parameters. Since MSLR-WEB10K contains more features for each query-url pair, we need more complex trees (trees with more leaves) on this data set.

Each combination of parameters is tested on 5 folds of each data set. On each fold we use 3 different random seeds to get more accurate results. This requires $1,008 \times 5 \times 3 = 15,120$ experiments on each of the smaller data sets and $162 \times 5 \times 3 = 2,430$ experiments on MSLR-WEB10K. We used a MapReduce cluster of 40 nodes for these experiments. Map tasks receive experiments as input and compute validation and test NDCG for the configuration specified by that experiment. Reduce tasks perform NDCG averaging over different folds and random seeds for each parameters combination. It takes about 8 hours to run this portion of our experiments once on this cluster.

Table 3 shows the best configurations based on Validation NDCG@3 on each data set. The best performing configurations on all three data sets use feature sampling. The smaller data sets also get better results by sub-sampling of training queries on each iteration. We conjecture that sub-sampling queries helps when the training data is small because it helps avoid overfitting by not allowing trees to see all queries on each iteration of boosting. This adds diversity to the individual trees which is then reduced when boosting averages

Table 1: **Properties of data sets used for experiments**

Data set	Queries	Query–URL Pairs	Features	Relevance Labels
TD2004	75	74,146	64	{0, 1}
MQ2007	1,692	69,623	46	{0, 1, 2}
MSLR-WEB10K	10,000	1,200,192	136	{0, 1, 2, 3, 4}

Table 3: Best combinations of parameters found after parameter tuning.

(a) TD2004 data set

Validation NDCG@3	Max Leaves	Min Obs. Per Leaf	Learning Rate	Sub-sampling	Feature Sampling
0.5113	20	0.25	0.1	0.5	0.1
0.5105	10	0.50	0.05	0.3	0.1
0.5061	10	0.12	0.05	0.5	0.3
0.5056	10	0.50	0.1	0.3	0.1
0.5055	15	0.25	0.05	0.5	0.1

(b) MQ2007 data set

Validation NDCG@3	Max Leaves	Min Obs. Per Leaf	Learning Rate	Sub-sampling	Feature Sampling
0.5647	7	0.25	0.05	0.3	0.3
0.5643	4	0.25	0.1	1.0	0.1
0.5643	10	0.25	0.05	0.5	0.3
0.5635	7	0.50	0.05	0.5	0.5
0.5633	7	0.25	0.05	0.5	0.3

(c) MSLR-WEB10K data set

Validation NDCG@3	Max Leaves	Min Obs. Per Leaf	Learning Rate	Sub-sampling	Feature Sampling
0.4873	40	0.25	0.1	1.0	0.5
0.4872	70	0.50	0.05	1.0	0.3
0.4870	40	0.25	0.05	1.0	0.5
0.4867	40	0.50	0.1	1.0	0.3
0.4865	40	0.50	0.05	0.5	1.0

tree predictions. With very large data sets this is less critical because individual trees cannot themselves significantly overfit a large data set when tree size is limited.

Grid search for parameter tuning is computationally expensive and becomes prohibitive as the data sets become large. Because of this it is useful to study the sensitivity of the LambdaMART algorithm to its parameters to have a better understanding of the number of training experiments needed on a new data set. We use the results of our parameter tuning experiments to study the effect of number of experiments on improvement in NDCG. For each dataset, we create a pool of configurations that we evaluated during parameter tuning experiments. Then we randomly select different numbers of these configurations. On each random selection, we pick the config with best validation NDCG@3 and then record validation and test NDCG@3 for that config. To get more accurate results, we repeat this random process 10K times and report average NDCG@3. Figure 1 shows the results.

As expected, for all three data sets, validation NDCG improves monotonically as we perform more experiments. On MSLR-WEB10K, the largest data set, there is less discrepancy between validation and test scores. The discrepancy between validation and test is largest on TD2004, the smallest data set, because the validation sets which are held aside form the training data must also be small.

Given that the parameter values we had chosen for grid search where chosen based on our experiments with LambdaMART on different data sets, we were expecting the parameter tuning experiments to reach to the pick value on test set after trying few combinations. On TD2004, the data set with the smallest validation sets, accuracy on the test set peaks after only about 100 parameter configurations, and then slowly drops. Accuracy on the validation set is still rising at 100 iterations, suggesting that hyperparameter optimization is overfitting to the validation sets. A similar effect is observed on MQ2007, but overfitting does not begin on this problem until about 400 parameter configurations have been tried. And on MSLR-WEB10K, we again observe overfitting to the validation sets after fewer than 25 configurations have been tested.

When there is randomness in the algorithm and the validation sets are not infinite, as more parameter combinations are tried search begins to find parameter combinations that look better on the validation set because of this randomness. If one is not careful, the computational power provided by MapReduce Clusters is so great that it is possible to overdo parameter tuning and find parameter combinations that work not better than the hyperparameters that would have been found by less thorough search. One way to avoid overfitting at the hyperparameter learning stage is to use a 2nd held-out validation set to detect when parameter tuning begins to overfit and early-stop the parameter optimization. Holding out a 2nd validation set will reduce the size of the primary hyperparameter tuning validation sets, making overfitting more likely. But as we have seen, even large cross-validated validation sets do not completely protect from overfitting when hyperparameter optimization is

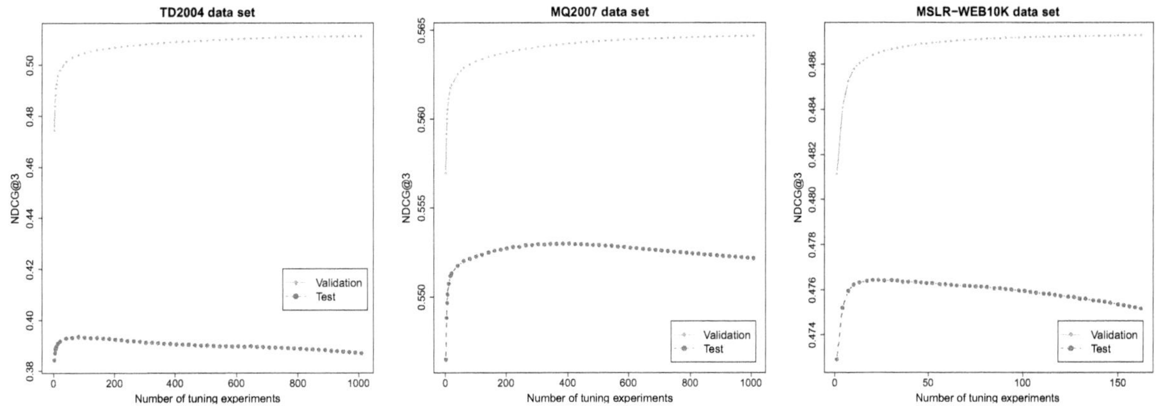

Figure 1: As more combinations of parameters are tested during parameter tuning of LambdaMART, NDCG@3 improves on the validation sets, but the test set curves show overfitting of the hyperparameters eventually occurs.

exhaustive, so care must be exercised to prevent hyperparameter optimization from becoming counterproductive.

We do not directly control the best number of trees for the LambdaMART models via a user-set parameter. Instead, as iterations of boosting continue, the prediction accuracy of the model is checked on a separate validation set. Boosting continues until there has been no improvement in accuracy for 250 iterations. The algorithm then returns the number of iterations that yielded maximum accuracy on the validation set.

Figure 2 shows two sample runs on MQ2007 and MSLR-WEB10K data sets. While NDCG@3 continues to improve on the training set, it reaches its maximum on validation sets after a few hundred iterations on both data sets. It is also interesting that we do not see significant drop in NDCG on validation sets even after 2000 iterations. This suggests that the combination of regularization techniques we use is sufficient to prevent models from overfitting on these datasets.

3.5 BL-MART details

As mentioned before, for bagged LambdaMART we train many LambdaMART models in parallel and then aggregate their outputs for improved accuracy. In order to have more diverse models in the final ensemble, we randomly sample training data (without replacement) for training each of the LambdaMART sub-models. The randomization techniques discussed in section 3.3 also contribute additional diversity to the models.

3.5.1 Combining Scores

For combining scores of the sub-models, one can simply take average of their scores. However, the scale and distribution of the scores generated from LambdaMART algorithm is dependent on the training data and on smaller training data can be very different for models trained on different sub-samples. Because of this, simply averaging LambdaMART scores may not give the best results. As an example, Figure 3 shows the distributions of validation scores generated from two models that are trained on different random samples of MQ2007 and MSLR-WEB10K training data. While on the larger data set, the output scores have very similar distributions, on the smaller data set we observe difference distributions and different scales of the scores. Note that even on the MSLR-WEB10K data set the output score of individual queries do not necessarily have the same scales across different models. The reason that we see a final normal-like distribution on this data set is that scores of individual queries have close to uniform distributions with different scales and result in a normal-like distribution once aggregated.

Since scores of different sub-models are on different scales, we initially tried using Borda count [18] as a rank aggregation technique. Each of the LambdaMART sub-models is used for generating a ranking of the test data. For each ranking, a score of 0 is assigned to the lowest ranked result, 1 to the next-to-lowest result, and so forth; then the total score of each result is computed over all the sub-models and the ensemble orders documents by this score. However, since Borda count converts real valued scores of documents to integer value ranks and then combines these ranks, the possibility of having ties increases significantly when averaging only have a few LambdaMART sub-models. Since tied documents would have to be ordered arbitrarily, this can significantly reduce the performance of the bagged model. Our experiments showed that Borda count works well when used to aggregate ranks of many model, but performs even worse than a single model when applied to only a few sub-models.

A better approach for combining the outputs of different sub-models is to normalize the scores of documents generated by each sub-model for each query. For each query we linearly scale the scores of its corresponding documents such that the document with the highest score will have a score of 1.0 and the document with the lowest score will have a score of 0.

3.5.2 Overfitting Tolerance

As mentioned in section 2, prediction error can be reduced by reducing both bias and variance. When bagging single decision or regression trees, bagging typically results in higher accuracy if applied to unpruned trees. The reason is that unpruned trees are overfitted to their training data and therefore have low bias and high variance. Since bagging is a variance reduction technique, it can reduce this variance so that the final bagged model has both low bias and low variance and thus lower total prediction error. Similarly, we may get better results by bagging boosted tree

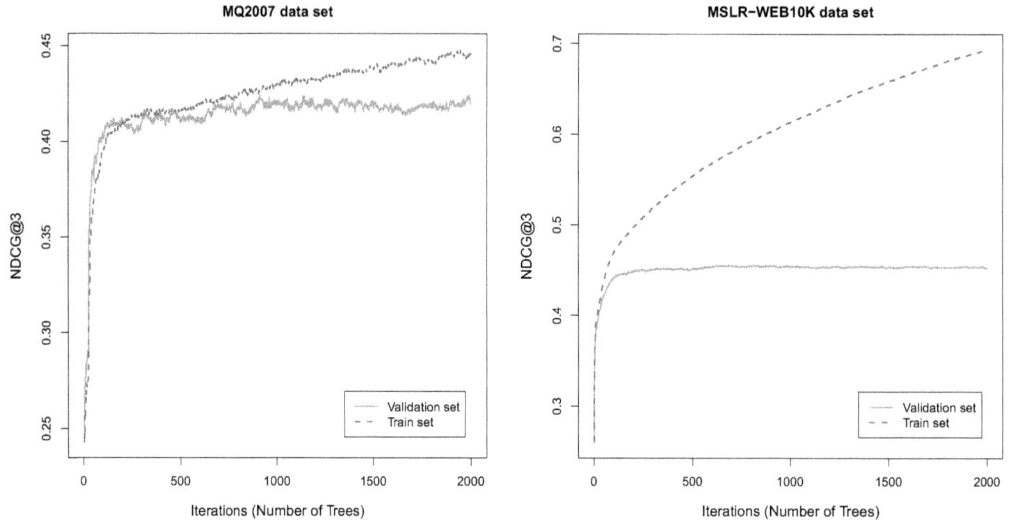

Figure 2: As more trees are added to the LamdaMART model train set accuracy begins to deviate from validation set accuracy. The appropriate number of iterations is determined by monitoring performance on the validation set.

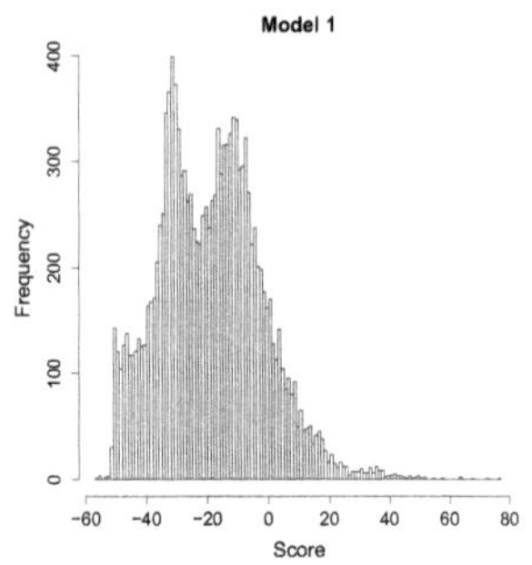

(a) MQ2007 data set

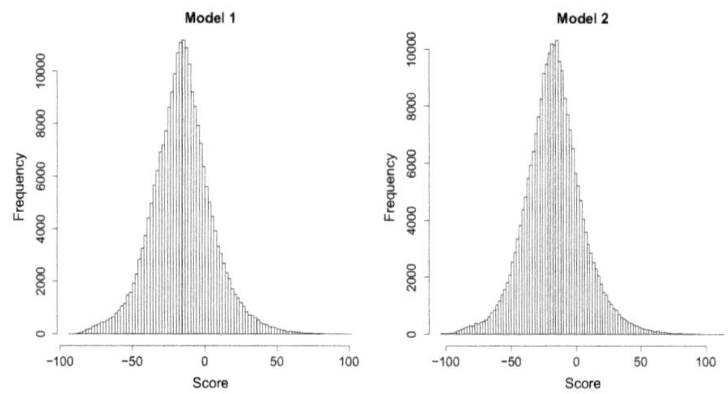

(b) MSLR-WEB10K data set

Figure 3: Distributions of validation scores generated from two models (per data set) that are trained on different random samples of training data.

models that have less bias but more variance. We test the effectiveness of this idea by adding an overfitting tolerance as a new parameter to the LamdaMART algorithm.

To generate overfitted LambdaMART models, we monitor the prediction accuracy on a separate validation set. Without overfitting, we would select the first N trees that results in the maximum prediction accuracy on the validation set. With overfitting tolerance, we add more trees after this maximum point until accuracy drop is more than a threshold value. We experimented with different threshold values and found that 2% worked well across the three data sets. As Figure 2 shows, it is possible that even after adding hundreds of additional trees, the drop in prediction accuracy on validation set is small. To prevent the size of the overfitted model from growing excessively large in this situation we allow a maximum of 250 trees to be added after the maximum point has been reached on the validation set. It is possible that allowing more overfitting would further improve the results from bagging, but at the expense of a much larger model.

4. RESULTS

BL-MART combines LambdaMART sub-models in order to achieve higher accuracy. There is a trade-off between increasing accuracy and model complexity: as we add more sub-models, the gain in accuracy is offset by the final model becoming too complex. It is important to balance the number of sub-models needed to achieve a reasonable gain in accuracy with the need to control complexity so that the models are still feasible to use in practice. To do this, we train BL-MART with different number of sub-models and evaluate its performance on the validation sets. We first create pools of LambdaMART models for each of the folds of the three data sets and then use these pools of models during the bagging process. We used pools of size 1000 models for TD2004 and MQ2007 data sets and 50 models for MSLR-WEB10K data set. The reason is that on the smaller data sets variance is higher and bagging needs to add more models before accuracy asymptotes.

We create different pools for overfitted and non-overfitted models. Overall, we need to train 10,000 LambdaMART models on each of the smaller data sets and 500 models on MSLR-WEB10K data set. We used a MapReduce cluster for this purpose. Each mapper task is assigned a fold in one of the data sets. It then randomly selects 67% of the training queries from that fold and generates a LambdaMART model on this random sample. Once the model is created, it evaluates the scores of validation and test data corresponding to that fold and passes these scores to reducer tasks. Reducer tasks just dump the scores that they receive. It takes about 18 hours to generate output scores for these models on a cluster of 40 nodes.

To study the effectiveness of using overfitted models in the bagging process, we create bagged models of different sizes from overfitted and non–overfitted models and then compare their MAP. Since we use a pool of models and each bagged model is created by randomly selecting a subset of models from these pools, we repeat the random process of bagged model creation 100 times and compute average validation MAP of these bagged models to have more reliable results. Figure 4 shows the results confirming that using overfitted models results in better accuracy for the final bagged ensemble. On MSLR-WEB10K data set, we need to include more models in the bagged ensemble before overfitted models show better results.

We use the same results of Figure 4 for determining the number of models that should be included in the bagged ensemble. In order to have a balance between accuracy and model complexity, we picked 45 models on smaller data sets and 20 models on the larger data set.

To compare the performance of BL-MART model with the original LambdaMART model and other learning-to-rank algorithms, we create BL-MART models for each of the data sets. Since, we create bagged models by random selection of sub-models from our model pools, we repeat this process for 20 times and report average results. Similarly, we use 20 different random seeds for "LambdaMART with randomization" and report average results. The original LambdaMART algorithm is deterministic and we only need to run it once. Since LambdaMART code is not publicly available, we re-implemented it for our experiments.

4.1 Accuracy Analysis

Table 4 summarizes the results of our experiments analyzing the accuracy of BL-MART models in comparison to LambdaMART and other learning-to-rank algorithms. On TD2004 and MQ2007 all prior published results are included in the table for four metrics. For the new MSLR-WEB10K data set no other results have yet been published.

On TD2004 data set, BL-MART significantly outperforms LambdaMART on all four metrics. Also bagging overfitted models results in better performance on this data set. In comparison to other learning-to-rank algorithms, BL-MART performs best in terms of MAP and NDCG@5, but on NDCG@1 and NDCG@3 RankBoost and BagBoo are slightly better. It should be noted that we have limited the size of BL-MART to control complexity. For example, on this data set, BL-MART contains about 4,500 trees while BagBoo is using 1.1 million trees which is 250 times larger than our model.

On MQ2007 data set, BL-MART again significantly outperforms LambdaMART on all metrics and it also achieves the best results compared to other learning-to-rank algorithms which have reported their results on this data set.

On the new MSLR-WEB10K data set, BL-MART again improves LambdaMART performance on all of the metrics. However, on this data set the difference between bagging of overfitted and non–overfitted models is not statistically significant.

Across the three problems and four metrics, BL-MART with overfitting improves accuracy an average of 2.6% when compared to LambdaMART with randomization.

While we have reported the best results (as far as we know) compared to other ranking algorithms on TD2004 and MQ2004 data sets, it should be noted that we did not tune the LamdaMART models for bagging. We tuned a single LambdaMART model and then used the same set of best parameters in the bagged model. It might be possible to get better results by bagging LambdaMART models which are generated from different set of parameters. For example, using more complex trees in sub-models might lead to overfitting which shows to be a desirable property for sub-models of a bagged ensemble. However, tuning the bagged model would have required much more experiments.

4.2 Variance Analysis

Variance can hurt in several ways: 1) by increasing the variance term in the bias/variance decomposition it reduces the expected accuracy of the trained models; 2) by increasing uncertainty it increases the number of experiments that must be run to determine which learning method and parameters yield the best results; and 3) it creates risk when a final model must be selected to deploy. All other things being equal (e.g. expected accuracy across multiple trials), the lower-variance learning method is prefered. For example, reducing variance by half reduces the number of experiments that must be run to pass a t-test by $\sqrt{2}$, and reduces the expected loss of the single deployed model compared to the expected loss of a typical model by a factor of 2. Because of this, learning methods that exhibit high variance can be difficult to work with, and learning methods that have lower variance are safer to deploy and easier to use for new feature development. Boosting often has relatively high variance. Bagging, however, is an effective variance reduction method. Thus we expect BL-MART to have significantly lower variance than LambdaMART.

In order to compare the variance of LambdaMART and BL-MART models, we use the MSLR-WEB10K data set. We randomly select 10 samples from the training data of Fold1 of this data set. Each sample contains a random selection of 67% of the training queries in this fold. We then train LambdaMART and BL-MART models on each of these samples and evaluate these models on the test data of this fold.

Table 5 shows the NDCG and MAP scores and their corresponding variance for each of the models. If we compare "LambdaMART with randomization" with "BL-MART with overfitting", the following would be the reduction in variance for different metrics:

- NDCG@1: −67.3%
- NDCG@3: −18.8%
- Mean NDCG: −40.2%
- MAP: −57.1%

5. DISCUSSION

Wrapping bagging around LambdaMART boosting yields two distinct benefits: 1) it achieves accuracy comparable to

Table 4: Evalutation results on three public learning-to-rank data sets.

(a) TD2004 data set

	NDCG@1	NDCG@3	NDCG@5	MAP
SVMmap [34]	0.2933	0.3035	0.3007	0.2049
RankSVM-Struct [20]	0.3467	0.3371	0.3192	0.2196
ListNet [9]	0.3600	0.3573	0.3325	0.2231
SmoothRank [11]	0.4000	0.3832	0.3555	0.2326
RankSVM [17]	0.4133	0.3467	0.3240	0.2237
AdaRank-MAP [33]	0.4133	0.3757	0.3602	0.2189
AdaRank-NDCG [33]	0.4267	0.3688	0.3514	0.1936
BoltzRank [30]	0.4767	0.3902	0.3635	0.2390
FRank [28]	0.4933	0.3875	0.3629	0.2388
RankBoost [13]	**0.5067**	**0.4295**	0.3878	0.2614
BagBoo [23]	**0.5067**	0.4080	0.3898	0.2499
LambdaMART	0.4267	0.3584	0.3266	0.2378
LambdaMART with randomization	0.4560	0.4033	0.3722	0.2513
BL-MART without overfitting	0.4947	0.4217	0.3886	0.2649
BL-MART with overfitting	0.4947	0.4270	**0.3948**	**0.2684**

(b) MQ2007 data set

	NDCG@1	NDCG@3	Mean NDCG	MAP
RankSVM-Struct [20]	0.4096	0.4063	0.4966	0.4645
ListNet [9]	0.4002	0.4091	0.4988	0.4652
AdaRank-MAP [33]	0.3821	0.3984	0.4891	0.4577
AdaRank-NDCG [33]	0.3876	0.4044	0.4914	0.4602
RankBoost [13]	0.4134	0.4072	0.5003	0.4662
CRR [25]	–	–	0.5000	0.4660
BagBoo [23]	0.4071	0.4176	–	0.4676
LambdaMART	0.4147	0.4119	0.5011	0.4660
LambdaMART with randomization	0.4137	0.4157	0.5035	0.4684
BL-MART without overfitting	0.4197	0.4217	0.5079	0.4726
BL-MART with overfitting	**0.4200**	**0.4224**	**0.5093**	**0.4731**

(c) MSLR-WEB10K data set

	NDCG@1	NDCG@3	Mean NDCG	MAP
LambdaMART	0.4580	0.4467	0.5693	0.3670
LambdaMART with randomization	0.4628	0.4487	0.5706	0.3684
BL-MART without overfitting	0.4640	0.4514	0.5720	0.3696
BL-MART with overfitting	**0.4642**	**0.4516**	**0.5729**	**0.3705**

Table 5: Variance reduction in BL-MART models compared to LambdaMART models. The first column in each group is the mean accuracy. The second column in the variance of this accuracy measured across the trials.

	NDCG@1		NDCG@3		Mean NDCG		MAP	
	Mean	Variance	Mean	Variance	Mean	Variance	Mean	Variance
LambdaMART	0.4484	18×10^{-6}	0.4395	9.1×10^{-6}	0.5640	1.2×10^{-6}	0.3657	0.9×10^{-6}
LambdaMART with randomization	0.4492	22×10^{-6}	0.4421	5.4×10^{-6}	0.5647	1.4×10^{-6}	0.3665	1.3×10^{-6}
BL-MART without overfitting	0.4516	10×10^{-6}	0.4468	7.8×10^{-6}	0.5675	1.5×10^{-6}	0.3690	0.9×10^{-6}
BL-MART with overfitting	0.4528	7×10^{-6}	0.4471	4.4×10^{-6}	0.5686	0.8×10^{-6}	0.3703	0.5×10^{-6}

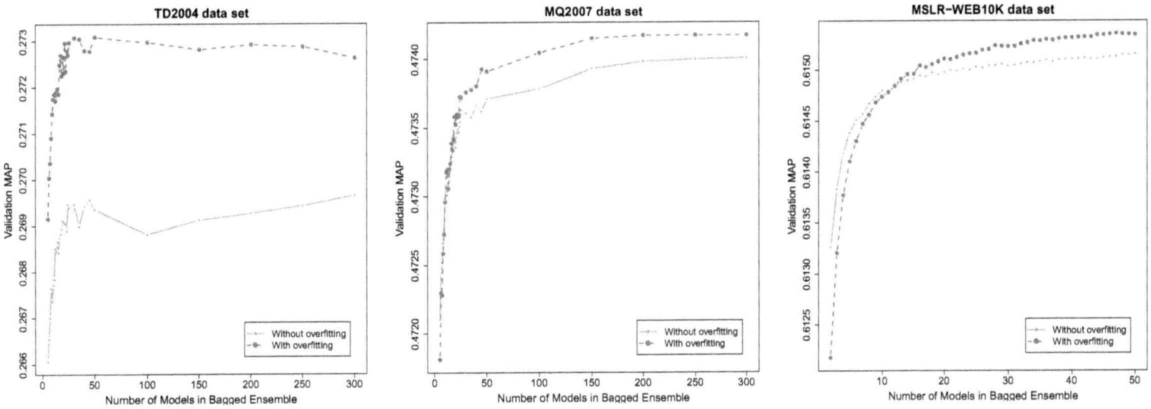

Figure 4: The effect of overfitting tolerance

and often better than the current state of the art in learning-to-rank; and 2) it achives this very high accuracy while simultaneously reducing variance. Taken individually, each of these is a reason to be interested in BL-MART. Together, however, they represent a substantial step forward.

For those interested in delivering high accuracy search results at commercial search engines, the reduction in variance may be the more important result. In commercial search engines most gains come not from improved learning methods, but from developing new or improved features (and data) to feed into learning. Feature and data refinement requires frequent experimentation to determine if the refinement is better and should be released. Reduced learning variance makes these experiments easier and more reliable. Because bagging can easily be parallelized across multiple computers, it allows one to obtain low variance experimental results with little increase in wall clock time. That these results also will have state-of-the-art accuracy makes the method even more appealing.

The final output of our BL-MART method is a high precision and low variance bagged ensemble of models. However, in real-time applications such as search engines, it may not be feasible to use such large models. We are currently working on compression pruning techniques that allow dropping a large fraction of trees from the final model without significantly impacting the accuracy. This is possible because we find empirically that large shrinkage is necessary to prevent massive overfitting in LambdaMART models. When shrinkage is high, boosting sometimes needs to generate a sequence of nearly identical trees to do what it might have accomplished with one tree without shrinkage. Yet in other places shrinkage is critical and subsequent trees are quite different from each other. By deleting and reweighting trees *after* the full LambdaMART ensemble has been grown, we can determine post-facto which trees are redundant and contribute little to the model, and which trees are critical for the model to have high accuracy. The method is currently under development, but it looks like we can also exploit the fact that bagging boosted trees generates even more reduntant trees that can safely be eliminated afterwards with little or no loss in accuracy. For example, in one set of experiments we are able to prune away 40–80% of the trees without significant loss in NDCG.

To run experiments, we developed a platform called *jforests* that not only implements LambdaMART and BL-MART, but which supports many tree-based learning methods such as bagging, boosting, regression, classification, ranking, etc. The platform is written in such a way to make it easy to code additional tree-based methods with minimum effort. For example, AdaRank and RankBoost can each be implemented in less than a dozen lines of new code. Our code platform including the implementations of LamdaMART and BL-MART will be made publicly available. The jforests platform also supports running on MapReduce environments to allow parallelization of methods such as bagging.

6. CONCLUSIONS

We present new results for LambdaMART, a state-of-the-art learning-to-rank algorithm, on three public data sets. We show that wrapping bagging around a boosting-based ranking model can improve its performance while also significantly reducing model variance. In our experiments, bagged LambdaMART (BL-MART) increased NDCG@1, NDCG@3, Mean NDCG, and MAP on all three test problems compared to un-bagged LambdaMART. Moreover, bagging reduced variance an average of 46% across all metrics on the MSLR-WEB10K data set on which we measured variance. Most of the ideas and methods reported in this paper are general and not limited specifically to ranking. For example, our finding that overfitting boosted models that will be bagged improves accuracy can be used in other classification and regression problems to further improve performance.

Acknowledgments

Authors would like to thank Amazon for a research grant that allowed us to use their MapReduce cluster. This work has been also partially supported by NSF grant OCI-074806.

7. REFERENCES

[1] Microsoft learning to rank datasets. http://research.microsoft.com/en-us/projects/mslr/.

[2] R. Baeza-Yates and B. Ribeiro-Neto. *Modern Information Retrieval.* Addison-Wesley Longman Publishing Co., Inc., Boston, MA, USA, 1999.

[3] L. Breiman. Bagging predictors. *Mach. Learn.*, 24:123–140, August 1996.

[4] L. Breiman. Random forests. *Machine Learning*, 45:5–32, 2001. 10.1023/A:1010933404324.

[5] L. Breiman. Using iterated bagging to debias regressions. *Mach. Learn.*, 45:261–277, December 2001.

[6] C. Burges. From RankNet to LambdaRank to LambdaMART: An overview. Technical report, Microsoft Research Technical Report MSR-TR-2010-82, 2010.

[7] C. J. C. Burges, R. Ragno, and Q. V. Le. Learning to rank with nonsmooth cost functions. In *NIPS*, pages 193–200, 2006.

[8] C. J. C. Burges, T. Shaked, E. Renshaw, A. Lazier, M. Deeds, N. Hamilton, and G. N. Hullender. Learning to rank using gradient descent. In *ICML*, pages 89–96, 2005.

[9] Z. Cao, T. Qin, T.-Y. Liu, M.-F. Tsai, and H. Li. Learning to rank: from pairwise approach to listwise approach. In *ICML '07: Proceedings of the 24th international conference on Machine learning*, pages 129–136, New York, NY, USA, 2007. ACM.

[10] O. Chapelle, Y. Chang, and T.-Y. Liu. The Yahoo! learning to rank challenge. http://learningtorankchallenge.yahoo.com, 2010.

[11] O. Chapelle and M. Wu. Gradient descent optimization of smoothed information retrieval metrics. *Inf. Retr.*, 13:216–235, June 2010.

[12] K. Crammer and Y. Singer. Pranking with ranking. In *Advances in Neural Information Processing Systems 14*, pages 641–647. MIT Press, 2001.

[13] Y. Freund, R. Iyer, R. E. Schapire, and Y. Singer. An efficient boosting algorithm for combining preferences. *J. Mach. Learn. Res.*, 4:933–969, 2003.

[14] J. H. Friedman. Stochastic gradient boosting. Technical report, Technical report, Dept. Statistics, Stanford Univ., 1999.

[15] J. H. Friedman. Greedy function approximation: A gradient boosting machine. *Annals of Statistics*, 29:1189–1232, 2000.

[16] S. Geman, E. Bienenstock, and R. Doursat. Neural networks and the bias/variance dilemma. *Neural Comput.*, 4:1–58, January 1992.

[17] R. Herbrich, T. Graepel, and K. Obermayer. Large margin rank boundaries for ordinal regression. In A. Smola, P. Bartlett, B. Schölkopf, and D. Schuurmans, editors, *Advances in Large Margin Classifiers*, pages 115–132, Cambridge, MA, 2000. MIT Press.

[18] T. K. Ho, J. Hull, and S. Srihari. Decision combination in multiple classifier systems. *Pattern Analysis and Machine Intelligence, IEEE Transactions on*, 16(1):66 –75, Jan. 1994.

[19] K. Järvelin and J. Kekäläinen. IR evaluation methods for retrieving highly relevant documents. In *SIGIR '00: Proceedings of the 23rd annual international ACM SIGIR conference on Research and development in information retrieval*, pages 41–48, New York, NY, USA, 2000. ACM.

[20] T. Joachims. Training linear SVMs in linear time. In *Proceedings of the 12th ACM SIGKDD international conference on Knowledge discovery and data mining*, KDD '06, pages 217–226, New York, NY, USA, 2006. ACM.

[21] P. Li, C. J. C. Burges, and Q. Wu. Mcrank: Learning to rank using multiple classification and gradient boosting. In *NIPS*, 2007.

[22] T.-Y. Liu. Learning to rank for information retrieval. *Foundations and Trends in Information Retrieval*, 3(3):225–331, 2009.

[23] D. Y. Pavlov, A. Gorodilov, and C. A. Brunk. BagBoo: a scalable hybrid bagging-the-boosting model. In *Proceedings of the 19th ACM international conference on Information and knowledge management*, CIKM '10, pages 1897–1900, New York, NY, USA, 2010. ACM.

[24] T. Qin, T.-Y. Liu, J. Xu, and H. Li. LETOR: A benchmark collection for research on learning to rank for information retrieval. *Information Retrieval*, 13:346–374, 2010. 10.1007/s10791-009-9123-y.

[25] D. Sculley. Combined regression and ranking. In *Proceedings of the 16th ACM SIGKDD international conference on Knowledge discovery and data mining*, KDD '10, pages 979–988, New York, NY, USA, 2010. ACM.

[26] D. Sorokina, R. Caruana, and M. Riedewald. Additive groves of regression trees. In *Proceedings of the 18th European conference on Machine Learning*, ECML '07, pages 323–334, Berlin, Heidelberg, 2007. Springer-Verlag.

[27] Y. L. Suen, P. Melville, and R. J. Mooney. Combining bias and variance reduction techniques for regression trees. In *In Proceedings of the European Conference on Machine Learning (ECML'05)*, pages 741–749, 2005.

[28] M.-F. Tsai, T.-Y. Liu, T. Qin, H.-H. Chen, and W.-Y. Ma. FRank: a ranking method with fidelity loss. In *SIGIR '07: Proceedings of the 30th annual international ACM SIGIR conference on Research and development in information retrieval*, pages 383–390, New York, NY, USA, 2007. ACM.

[29] G. Valentini and T. G. Dietterich. Low bias bagged support vector machines. In *Proceedings of the International Conference on Machine Learning, ICML'03*, pages 752–759. Morgan Kaufmann, 2003.

[30] M. N. Volkovs and R. S. Zemel. Boltzrank: learning to maximize expected ranking gain. In *Proceedings of the 26th Annual International Conference on Machine Learning*, ICML '09, pages 1089–1096, New York, NY, USA, 2009. ACM.

[31] G. I. Webb. Multiboosting: A technique for combining boosting and wagging. *Mach. Learn.*, 40:159–196, August 2000.

[32] Q. Wu, C. Burges, K. Svore, and J. Gao. Ranking, boosting and model adaptation. Technical report, Microsoft Technical Report MSR-TR-2008-109, 2008.

[33] J. Xu and H. Li. AdaRank: a boosting algorithm for information retrieval. In *SIGIR '07: Proceedings of the 30th annual international ACM SIGIR conference on Research and development in information retrieval*, pages 391–398, New York, NY, USA, 2007. ACM.

[34] Y. Yue, T. Finley, F. Radlinski, and T. Joachims. A support vector method for optimizing average precision. In *Proceedings of the 30th annual international ACM SIGIR conference on Research and development in information retrieval*, SIGIR '07, pages 271–278, New York, NY, USA, 2007. ACM.

Learning to Rank for Freshness and Relevance

Na Dai
Computer Sci. & Engr.
Lehigh University, PA, USA
nad207@cse.lehigh.edu

Milad Shokouhi
Microsoft Research
Cambridge, UK
milads@microsoft.com

Brian D. Davison
Computer Sci. & Engr.
Lehigh University, PA, USA
davison@cse.lehigh.edu

ABSTRACT

Freshness of results is important in modern web search. Failing to recognize the temporal aspect of a query can negatively affect the user experience, and make the search engine appear stale. While freshness and relevance can be closely related for some topics (e.g., news queries), they are more independent in others (e.g., time insensitive queries). Therefore, optimizing one criterion does not necessarily improve the other, and can even do harm in some cases.

We propose a machine-learning framework for simultaneously optimizing freshness and relevance, in which the trade-off is automatically adaptive to query temporal characteristics. We start by illustrating different temporal characteristics of queries, and the features that can be used for capturing these properties. We then introduce our supervised framework that leverages the temporal profile of queries (inferred from pseudo-feedback documents) along with the other ranking features to improve both freshness and relevance of search results. Our experiments on a large archival web corpus demonstrate the efficacy of our techniques.

Categories and Subject Descriptors

H.3.3 [**Information Storage and Retrieval**]: Information Search and Retrieval

General Terms

Algorithms, Performance

Keywords

Temporal profiles, Query classification, Freshness ranking

1. INTRODUCTION

The query stream seen by a web search engine and the interpretation of those queries change over time. Previous analysis has shown that web logs clearly reflect daily events in user queries [6]. For example, during seasonal events such as Halloween, there are always spikes in the frequency of related queries such as "halloween", "halloween costumes" and "pumpkins". For many of the queries that correspond to events, the best answer may change over time (e.g., the latest SIGIR conference homepage for the query "sigir conference"). In more extreme cases, the major intent behind the same query can temporally vary; for instance, the query "US open" is more likely to be targeting the tennis open in September, and the golf tournament in June. Kulkarni et al. [22] referred to this class of temporally ambiguous queries as *shift* topics.

News events, depending on their significance, can cause enormous growth in frequency of related queries.[1] It is also not uncommon for news events to change the general meaning of a query. For example, the query "ipad" which could be treated as a misspelling for "ipod" in 2009, suddenly turned into a valid query with several related websites in 2010.[2] Therefore, making search engine results appear current and fresh is important to satisfy users' ever-changing information needs.

In this paper, we focus on improving the ranking of results for queries based on their temporal profiles. Of course, the importance of the temporal profiles of queries extends beyond web result ranking; advertisement rankers have to address similar problems; related search and auto-complete suggestions must provide users with fresh and relevant alternatives to their queries; vertical search [11] ranking and triggering can be affected by temporal changes, and in general, the entire search experience can be influenced according to the temporal aspect of a query.

Learning ranking functions that can respond effectively to diverse temporal dynamics of queries is challenging. One of the difficulties is that traditional machine learning ranking algorithms fail to consider the interaction between freshness and relevance. While relevance clearly quantifies the topical matchability between query and web pages, freshness can be interpreted in different ways. For certain *temporal* queries such as breaking news, freshness is more meaningful when the actual page content reflects new information. Whereas, for *non-temporal* (time-insensitive) queries, it makes more sense to interpret freshness as the recency of page maintenance with respect to the time point of generating ranking lists (suppose web pages contain such information). Therefore, these two interpretations for freshness may be correlated to some extent but are not the same, considering that pages updated recently tend to record fresh information. It is worthwhile pointing out that both explanations can be part of the overall quality of search results that influences user search experience. In this work, the definition of freshness is sensitive to query temporal characteristics, varying

SIGIR'11, July 24–28, 2011, Beijing, China.
Copyright 2011 ACM 978-1-4503-0757-4/11/07...$10.00.

[1]For example, the traffic caused by queries related to Michael Jackson's death in 2009, was so huge that Google mistook it as an attack (Source: Google Blog, 26 Jun 2009).

[2]It is probably still the case that some people mistype ipod as ipad. However, this group no longer represents the majority.

on whether human editors (judges) can identify temporal intents concealed within queries. (See Section 4 for details.)

For certain *temporal* queries such as breaking news, relevance and freshness are highly correlated. Therefore, a ranker optimized for returning fresh documents may produce satisfactory results. However, for queries that are not usually time-sensitive (e.g., "facebook", "machine learning"), paying too much attention to freshness may significantly hurt ranking effectiveness in terms of relevance. Among common ranking features, clicks, anchor-text and historical data might be the most powerful for answering time-insensitive queries. For temporal queries however, other features such as the rate of content change in documents may provide better signals [22]. Therefore, a ranker optimizing either freshness or relevance only may not be flexible enough to deal with the temporal dynamics of queries effectively.

To address this issue, previous work [3, 12] suggested training separate rankers for different classes of queries. The query is first classified according to its temporal profile, and then is sent to the appropriate ranker that has been optimized for either relevance or freshness. The main disadvantage of classification-based techniques is that selecting a wrong ranker due to misclassification can significantly degrade the performance.

We propose a machine learning model that optimizes freshness and relevance simultaneously. Our flexible framework allows training multiple rankers with different optimization functions, and runs each query against all rankers with the weights varying according to the query's temporal profile. This is in contrast with existing solutions that suggest selecting one ranker per query, and consequently has a lower risk of poor performance when queries are misclassified. In addition, instead of splitting the labeled data to train separate rankers, our technique leverages the entire data in training all rankers. To the best of our knowledge, this is the first attempt to incorporate the trade-off between freshness and relevance into a single ranking framework.

Our work can be regarded as an extension to the family of *divide and conquer* (DAC) techniques for ranking [2]. In DAC, queries are clustered based on their feature representations, and separate rankers are trained with each for one cluster simultaneously. At test time, the query is compared against the generated cluster centroids and is ranked under all rankers with the weights depending on query-cluster similarity values. We follow a similar path since DAC enables specialized ranker training by considering query features, but we incorporate multiple criteria (freshness and relevance) into ranking optimization. We also modify the DAC loss function by introducing a new query-document importance factor that emphasizes certain documents during training, and leads to further improvements in the results. Our experiments on a large web archive demonstrate that the rankers trained by our techniques can achieve better relevance and freshness compared to state-of-the-art alternatives. The contributions of this paper are four-fold:

1. We extend an existing learning to rank framework to optimize for both freshness and relevance.

2. We introduce a new loss function that emphasizes certain query-document pairs for better optimization.

3. We investigate the correlation between freshness and relevance and compare it across temporal and non-temporal queries.

4. We introduce *hybrid NDCG*, a new variant of NDCG that considers both freshness and relevance labels in evaluation.

The remainder of this paper is organized as follows. We review prior work in Section 2, and continue by introducing our criteria-sensitive ranking specialization framework in Section 3. Features are summarized in Section 4. We describe our experimental results in Section 5 followed by a more thorough discussion in Section 6. Section 7 concludes the paper and suggests directions for future research.

2. RELATED WORK

Pairwise learning to rank techniques have been widely studied in recent years [5, 15, 19]. They cast learning to rank as a preferential relation learning problem. Given a query and a pair of associated documents, if one is more relevant than the other, then it is boosted in the training process to get a higher rank. In most early work, the query type information was ignored in ranking, which limits the effectiveness of ranking functions. For instance, navigational queries target specific websites, while informational queries have a broader range of relevant answers. Hence, their ranking models could be optimized in different ways that depend on query intent [21].

Query-dependent loss/ranking functions were introduced to address these issues [2, 3, 16]. The general idea is to adopt a query-dependent loss or ranking function based on the query type (class). Geng et al. [16] proposed a k-Nearest Neighbor based method which trains a query-dependent ranking function for each query based on its nearest neighbors in the training set.

Bian et al. [3] achieved better results by learning both multiple ranking functions (by minimizing query-dependent ranking risks) and query categorization (navigational, informational, transactional) simultaneously. Although the query-dependent loss function has been found superior to the query-dependent ranking method of Geng et al. [16], it still leaves a few issues unaddressed: (1) query categorization and taxonomies may not be available or could be too noisy; (2) external taxonomies may not necessarily provide the best way of splitting queries for training specialized rankers; and (3) such categories may not be fine-grained enough for training and ranking purposes. To overcome these problems, Bian et al. [2] proposed a *divide-and-conquer* framework (DAC) for ranking specialization and instantiated it on RankSVM [19].

Divide and conquer for ranking. The DAC ranking framework [2] can be summarized in three main steps: (1) identifying ranking-sensitive query categories, (2) learning topic-specific ranking models via minimizing a global ranking risk, and (3) running each unseen query against all ranking models and merging the outputs to produce the final ranked list.

In the first step (divide), queries are categorized (clustered) in a soft way to form ranking-sensitive topics. The queries in each cluster have similar ranking characteristics and similar ranking feature discriminativity. Bian et al. [2] suggested using the ranking features aggregated from the top-ranked pseudo-feedback documents that are generated by a reference ranking model to represent queries for clustering. In this way, the queries that have similar features are clustered together. The number of query clusters (topics) can be pre-defined or could be determined according to gap statistics [27].

In the second step (*conquer*), a unified learning method is used to train multiple ranking models, one for each cluster (topic). The authors applied a global loss aggregated across all ranking topics, and trained multiple rankers simultaneously by minimizing the global ranking risk. Each query contributes to training all ranking models though with the different weights that are determined by the probabilities of belonging to each cluster.

In the last step, each unseen query is submitted to all ranking models and a weighted combination is used to merge the final results.

While most previous work focused on optimizing relevance, we propose an extended framework which optimizes freshness and relevance simultaneously in a more adaptive way. We enhance query representations by adding *criteria-sensitive* features that can capture different aspects (relevance, freshness) of query-document pairs. Each query is categorized according to both temporal and relevance features, and the final ranking is produced by merging the results generated from several different ranking models.

Multiple criteria ranking. Training ranking models for multiple criteria beyond relevance, such as diversity, freshness, and efficiency, has been the subject of many recent papers [12, 13, 17, 28]. Dong et al.'s work on recency ranking [12, 13] is among the closest to our work; they consider freshness in instance labeling for training effective ranking models. They argued that freshness is especially important for breaking news queries and demoted the relevance labels of stale pages for training. Empirical experiments demonstrated that such demotion can result in significant improvements on both relevance and freshness. We similarly generate hybrid labels for documents based on their relevance and freshness grades, and show that the labels generated by our strategy are more effective than those demoted for training. Despite this resemblance, our optimization tasks are fundamentally different; Dong et al. [12, 13] studied learning single *adaptive* or *over-weighting* rankers that can be trained with an imbalanced amount of training data for freshness and relevance primarily from the perspective of ranking adaptation. We investigate multi-criteria ranking problem in a *divide and conquer* framework with balanced distribution of training data, and emphasize adaptive balance between different criteria.

Temporal signals for ranking. Exploiting temporal signals that capture the dynamics of queries, web pages, hyperlinks, and user interaction to improve search quality has been widely studied. Several methods focused on complementing content-based matching by utilizing the knowledge of query temporal characteristics [1, 10, 20, 23, 24]. Typically this includes: (1) profiling query temporal characteristics, e.g., generating a temporal distribution over pseudo-feedback documents or based on query popularity over time; and (2) emphasizing documents whose temporal characteristics are close to the query's temporal profile, e.g., enhancing document representation by adding temporal dimension and then incorporating temporal based matching into search process.

Elsas and Dumais [14] incorporated the dynamics of content changes into document language models and showed that their enhanced representations can improve retrieval effectiveness. Dai and Davison [8] exploited the frequency of web content and hyperlink changes over time for better estimation of web authorities. Dong et al. [13] used Twitter data to detect and rank fresh documents.

3. CRITERIA-SENSITIVE RANKING

In this section, we introduce our *criteria-sensitive* divide-and-conquer ranking framework (denoted as CS-DAC) that incorporates the balance between relevance and freshness into training customized rankers that optimize both freshness and relevance.

CS-DAC framework. A typical ranking function f with ω parameters takes a query-document feature vector $\mathbf{X}$ as input and produces ranking scores of documents.

$$\hat{\mathbf{y}} = f(\mathbf{X}, \omega)$$

The common goal of learning to rank systems is to find a ranking model f^* that takes query-document feature vectors as input, and produces a document ranking—as close as possible to the *oracle* ranking of documents according to their relevance labels $\mathbf{y}$—by minimizing the ranking risk aggregated from the loss $\mathcal{L}$ of all training queries.

$$f^* = \arg\min_f \sum_q \mathcal{L}(f(\mathbf{X}_q, \omega), \mathbf{y}_q) = \arg\min_f \sum_q \mathcal{L}(\hat{\mathbf{y}}_q, \mathbf{y}_q)$$

By considering query differences in the DAC framework, we essentially *cluster*[3] training queries based on their ranking characteristics, and train one ranker per cluster. Each query contributes to learning all rankers with different importance based on its topical affinity to query clusters. Each ranker f_i^* is learned via:

$$f_i^* = \arg\min_{f_i} \sum_{q \in \mathcal{Q}} \mathcal{I}(q, i) \mathcal{L}_i(\hat{\mathbf{y}}_q, \mathbf{y}_q) \quad (1)$$

where $\mathcal{Q}$ is the training query set, and $\mathcal{I}(q, i)$ is the importance of query q with respect to the ith ranking model.

To account for relevance and freshness simultaneously, we propose to use hybrid labels that are generated based on freshness and relevance judgments.[4] For this purpose, we exploit a weighted harmonic mean function which maps relevance and freshness grades (i.e., $y_{q,d}^R$ and $y_{q,d}^F$ on the query-document pair $<q, d>$) to a single equivalent numerical score $\widetilde{y}_{q,d}$ for training f_i^*. We believe harmonic mean is appropriate here since (1) it heavily biases towards the minimum score; (2) it is more sensitive when $y_{q,d}^R$ and $y_{q,d}^F$ are close; and (3) it has been shown as a good optimization metric for tasks such as learning to rank for efficiency [28] and classification. Formally, $\widetilde{y}_{q,d,i}$ is defined as:

$$\widetilde{y}_{q,d,i} = \frac{(1 + \beta_i^2) \cdot y_{q,d}^R \cdot y_{q,d}^F}{y_{q,d}^R + \beta_i^2 \cdot y_{q,d}^F} \quad (2)$$

where parameter β_i sets the trade-off between relevance and freshness for each ranker, and is learned during training. Allowing different values of β for rankers enables a flexible framework where each ranker can assign different weights to freshness and relevance. It also means that each query-document pair may affect the pairwise learning of each ranker differently.[5] Therefore, we factorize query-document pair importance as follows:

$$f_i^* = \arg\min_{f_i} \sum_{q \in \mathcal{Q}} \mathcal{I}(q, i) \times$$

$$\sum_{<d_1, d_2> \in \mathcal{D}_q} \mathcal{U}'(q, i, d_1, d_2) \mathcal{L}_i\left(\begin{bmatrix} \hat{y}_{q,d_1,i} \\ \hat{y}_{q,d_2,i} \end{bmatrix}, \begin{bmatrix} \widetilde{y}_{q,d_1,i} \\ \widetilde{y}_{q,d_2,i} \end{bmatrix}\right) \quad (3)$$

where, $\mathcal{D}_q$ is the set of preferential query-document pairs with respect to query q, and $\mathcal{U}'(q, i, d_1, d_2)$ is the importance of $<d_1, d_2>$ in training for query q with respect to the ith ranking model. For simplicity, we assume $<q, d_1>$ and $<q, d_2>$ are independent, and so factorize the importance of the preferential pair $\mathcal{U}'(q, i, d_1, d_2)$ as follows.

$$\mathcal{U}'(q, i, d_1, d_2) = \mathcal{U}(q, i, d_1) \cdot \mathcal{U}(q, i, d_2)$$

where $\mathcal{U}(q, i, d_1)$ is the importance of query-document pair

[3] We use query cluster, topic and category interchangeably.

[4] Generating hybrid labels (single aggregate objective functions), is a simple form of multi-criteria optimization [26].

[5] Similar ideas can be applied to list-wise and point-wise ranking learning algorithms.

<q, d_1> in training for query q with respect to the ith ranking model.[6]

Ensemble ranking. Given an unseen query q', we first profile its query characteristics, and then calculate its distances to the centroids of existing query clusters $\mathbf{c}_1, \mathbf{c}_2, \ldots, \mathbf{c}_n$. The trained ranking functions are then scored according to the normalized distance between the query and their corresponding clusters (a.k.a. query importance $\mathcal{I}$), given by:

$$W_i = \frac{\mathcal{I}(q', i)}{\sum_{i'=1}^{n} \mathcal{I}(q', i')}$$

The query q' is run against all n rankers (one for each cluster), and the final results $\theta_{q'}$ are produced according to the ensemble ranking of their outputs. That is,

$$\theta_{q'} = \sum_{i=1}^{n} W_i f_i^*(\mathbf{X}_{q'}, \omega_i)$$

where f_i^* is the ith ranking model, $\mathbf{X}_{q'}$ is the query-document feature vectors for query q', and ω_i is the feature weights.

The CS-DAC framework summarized in Equation 3 consists of three main factors: query importance ($\mathcal{I}$), ranker-specific query-document importance ($\mathcal{U}$), and the loss function ($\mathcal{L}$). We continue by describing each of these items.

Query importance ($\mathcal{I}$). In the *divide* step of the DAC framework, the query space is split into a few clusters based on *criteria-sensitive* features. These are the features that are extracted from the top-ranked documents of a basic reference ranker (BM25 [25] in our work) for the query. We will provide more details about these features in Section 4.

The $\mathcal{I}(q, i)$ values provide a Binomial distribution over each of criteria-sensitive query clusters, and specify the importance of different ranking functions. We use Gaussian Mixture model as soft k-means clustering to group queries into clusters. The importance of query q with respect to the ith cluster is thus given by:

$$\mathcal{I}(q, i) = 1 - \frac{\|\mathbf{p}_q - \mathbf{c}_i\|^2}{\max_{q' \in \mathcal{Q}} \|\mathbf{p}_{q'} - \mathbf{c}_i\|^2} \quad (4)$$

where $\mathbf{p}_q$ and $\mathbf{c}_i$ respectively denote the feature vectors of query q and the centroid of the ith cluster, and $\mathcal{Q}$ represents the set of training queries. Therefore, $\mathcal{I}(q, i)$ is scaled between $[0, 1]$, and is inversely proportional to the distance between query feature vector $\mathbf{p}_q$ and cluster centroid $\mathbf{c}_i$.

Document importance ($\mathcal{U}$). In pairwise learning to rank methods, the importance of a document with label $\mathbf{y}$ during training depends on the number of times it is compared to other documents with different labels. Due to the ranker-specific value of β which is set during training, a query-document pair with the same relevance and freshness grades can get unequal hybrid labels under different rankers, and hence may contribute unequally in training various rankers. Besides, centralizing hybrid label distribution within each query cluster stabilizes the correlation between freshness and relevance, which further emphasizes the effect of β_i in Equation 2. To factorize these impacts, we introduced the $\mathcal{U}$ component in Equation 3. We estimate the importance of a query-document pair with label $\mathbf{y}_{q,d}$ by the likelihood of visiting that label in the training dataset, under the assumption that the importance of a hybrid label is proportional to the ratio of query-document pairs with that label in the training dataset. We define the document importance $\mathcal{U}$ as below.

$$\mathcal{U}(q, i, d) = \frac{\sum_{q' \in \mathcal{Q}} N(q', i, \mathbf{y}_{q,d}) \cdot N(q', i, \neg \mathbf{y}_{q,d})}{\sum_{\mathbf{y'} \in \mathcal{Y}_i} \sum_{q' \in \mathcal{Q}} N(q', i, \mathbf{y'}) \cdot N(q, i, \neg \mathbf{y'})} \quad (5)$$

where $\mathcal{Y}_i$ is the space of labels for ranker i, and $\mathcal{Q}$ denotes the training query set. The number of documents with and without label $\mathbf{y}$ are represented by $N(q, i, \mathbf{y})$ and $N(q, i, \neg\mathbf{y})$. Equation 5 can be regarded as a function of the unique hybrid label $\mathbf{y}_{q,d}$, and is denoted as $w(\mathbf{y}_{q,d})$ for short.

There are two potential problems with this type of normalization: (1) additional inter-label dependencies may arise from comparing common labels (e.g., $\mathbf{y}_a$ and $\mathbf{y}_b$, versus $\mathbf{y}_b$ and $\mathbf{y}_c$), and, (2) overemphasizing certain documents inevitably introduces bias in ranking. To overcome these issues, we exploit a random walk approach to determine $\mathcal{U}$ (instead of Equation 5) that has the effect of smoothing document importance values.

To perform a random walk, we first construct a fully connected bipartite graph $G(V, E)$ (one graph per ranker) in which each node (state) v stands for a unique *hybrid* label $\mathbf{y}$ (associated with the weight $w(\mathbf{y})$), and each edge e is associated with a weight computed according to the number of times the labels of the connected nodes compare with each other during training. At each step, the random walk surfer jumps to a random node with probability d (selection among random nodes is proportional to $w(\mathbf{y})$ values) or follows some connected edge with probability $1 - d$ (the selection among connected edges is proportional to the weights on edges). The value of d can be pre-defined or set during the training and validation. When d equals 1, the probability that the random surfer reaches every node (state) is proportional to the direct comparison between preferential query-document pairs with different hybrid labels. Whereas, $d = 0$ suggests document importance entirely propagates through indirect comparison between preferential query-document pairs. Parameter d actually controls the extent that such propagation (from indirect comparison) influences the computation of document importance. We analyze the importance of $\mathcal{U}$, with and without smoothed probabilities in Section 6.

Loss function ($\mathcal{L}$). The core of each ranker in our CS-DAC framework is a loss function that is trained for hybrid labels (Equation 2). We follow Bian et al. [3] and use RankSVM [19] as our basic learning algorithm although it is important to note that the framework is flexible and not restricted to any particular learning technique.

RankSVM [19] is designed to maximize the margin between positively and negatively labeled documents in the training data by minimizing the number of discordant pairs. The RankSVM optimization problem is defined as:

$$\arg\min_{\omega, \xi_{q,i,j}} \frac{1}{2}\|\omega\|^2 + C \sum_{q,i,j} \xi_{q,i,j} \quad \textit{subject to}$$

$$\forall y_i^q \succeq y_j^q : \quad \omega^T X_i^q \geq \omega^T X_j^q + 1 - \xi_{q,i,j},$$
$$\forall_q \forall_i \forall_j : \quad \xi_{q,i,j} \geq 0$$

where the non-negative slack variable $\xi_{q,i,j}$ is used to approximate the NP-hard optimization solution by minimizing the upper bound $\sum \xi_{q,i,j}$. Parameter C sets the trade-off between the training error and the margin size. The query-document feature vectors for documents i and j are respectively represented by X_i^q and X_j^q. The notation $y_i^q \succeq y_j^q$ implies that the document i is ranked higher than

[6]The independence assumption is unrealistic, but we believe it is not unreasonable because if two query-documents pairs are important, then so is their preferential pair.

document j with respect to query q in the training dataset (i has the same or higher relevance than j).

CS-DAC modified the RankSVM loss function by incorporating query importance ($\mathcal{I}$) and document importance ($\mathcal{U}$). Formally, the ith ranking model of CS-DAC is optimized via:

$$\arg\min_{\omega_i, \xi_{q,j,k}} \frac{1}{2}\|\omega_i\|^2 + C\sum_{q,j,k} \xi_{q,j,k} \tag{6}$$

$$\textit{subject to,} \quad \forall \widetilde{y}_{q,j,i} \succeq \widetilde{y}_{q,k,i} : \mathcal{I}(q,i)\mathcal{U}(q,i,j)\omega_i^T X_j^q$$
$$\geq \mathcal{I}(q,i)\mathcal{U}(q,i,k)\omega_i^T X_k^q + 1 - \xi_{q,j,k},$$
$$\forall_q \forall_i \forall_j : \quad \xi_{q,i,j} \geq 0$$

where $\xi_{q,j,k}$ is the slack variable and parameter C sets the trade-off between training error and the margin size.

In CS-DAC, several rankers are trained simultaneously, and each ranking function f_k^* (see Equation 3) is optimized using the CS-DAC loss function and hybrid labels. The β values are tuned via hill climbing based on the *hybrid NDCG* values of the final ranking lists merged from different rankers. That is, each ranker is trained on different values of β and the best combination of rankers is chosen by hill climbing on the training and validation data. Here, *hybrid NDCG* extends the commonly used evaluation metric NDCG [18] to take hybrid labels for evaluation, since this new freshness-sensitive metric can take into account both freshness and relevance into a single measurement, aiming to quantify the overall search quality. Formally, we define *hybrid NDCG* as below:

$$\textit{hybrid NDCG}(n) = Z_n \sum_{j=1}^{n} \frac{2^{(\gamma \mathbf{y}_R + (1-\gamma)\mathbf{y}_F)} - 1}{\log_2(j+1)} \tag{7}$$

where Z_n is the oracle *discounted cumulative gain* at ranking cut-off n, that bounds the NDCG values between 0 and 1. The $\mathbf{y}_R$, and $\mathbf{y}_F$ values—also known as *gains*—are assigned according to the relevance and freshness labels of documents. Parameter γ specifies the trade-off between relevance and freshness and is set to 0.5 in our experiments. Note that $\gamma = 1$ turns hybrid NDCG into typical relevance-based NDCG, while setting γ to zero, makes it the same as the NDCF metric [13]. Dai and Davison [8] also adopted NDCG with freshness labels, although they did not refer to it as NDCF. While other combination forms may better fit the search utility that quantifies comprehensive users' satisfaction, we leave the best definition of *hybrid NDCG* for future work.

4. EXPERIMENTAL SETUP

Testbed data. Standard learning to rank datasets only contain relevance judgments for query-document pairs without any information regarding their freshness.

Therefore, we built a new testbed based on a large archival web corpus. Our dataset contains 158 million unique URLs and 12 billion links from the `.ie` domain, covering the time span from January 2000 to December 2007 (one snapshot per month and 88 in total). We removed pages with less than five snapshots, and only kept the remaining 3.8 million unique pages with 435 million links in total.

We choose *April 2007* as our time point of interest for ranking evaluation. We constructed two *temporal* and *non-temporal* query sets, each containing 90 queries. While the query size is small, the queries in the temporal set are manually selected from Google Trends suggestions for Ireland, which were popular during *April 2007*.[7] For the non-temporal set, we first randomly sampled queries

[7] `www.google.com/trends`

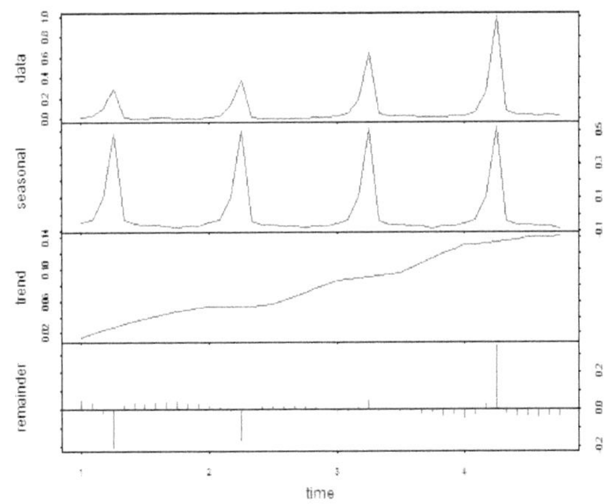

Figure 1: The STL decomposition [7] of a time series into seasonal, trend and remainder components. The data is generated from the click histogram of the query *jingle bells* in a commercial search engine.

from a 2006 MSN query log (i.e., generating a representative query sample from a real-world search log), and then automatically filtered out about 10% of them that were detected as *potentially temporal* by a commercial classifier. The classifier has high precision (almost all Google Trend queries are detected as temporal), and uses several years of the query-frequency history extracted from the query logs of a major commercial search engine.

Judgments and metrics. We have an average of 71 URLs per query judged by one or more participants from Amazon Mechanical Turk.[8] Given a query-URL pair, the judges were instructed to assess the quality of the URL with respect to both relevance and freshness. For relevance, the selection was among *highly relevant*, *relevant*, *borderline*, *not relevant* and *not related*, which was further translated to integer gains ranging from 4 to 0. For freshness, editors were instructed to judge the URL freshness for the given query according to our chosen point in time (April 2007).[9] Judges could select between *very fresh*, *fresh*, *borderline*, *stale*, and *very stale*, which we transferred into $\{4, 3, 2, 1, 0\}$. Judges were also required to provide the confidence of their judgements by choosing between *high*, *medium* and *low*. Table 2 shows the guideline of query-URL pair judgments used by Mturk workers. Judgments with low confidence were resubmitted for labeling. The standard deviations of relevance and freshness judgements on a random sample of 76 query URL pairs among three judgers are 0.88 and 1.02 respectively.

Freshness and relevance are evaluated by *hybrid NDCG*, and so when $\gamma = 0$ or $\gamma = 1$, this corresponds to NDCF [13] and NDCG, respectively.

Ranking features. The features used by RankSVM for ranking can be grouped into non-temporal and temporal features. The non-temporal features (summarized in Table 1) include several commonly used text-similarity scores such as BM25 [25], and language

[8] `http://www.mturk.com`

[9] Admittedly, judging for freshness according to an arbitrary time in past could be a difficult task. However, the choice was dictated to us by the time span of our dataset.

Table 1: Non-temporal ranking features used by RankSVM in the CS-DAC framework and baseline methods. Body, title, heading and anchor-text fields are respectively represented by B, T, H and A.

Feature name	Feature description	Feature name	Feature Description
Okapi(B)	Okapi BM25 score [25] for body-text.	RQT(B)	Ratio of covered terms in body-text.
RQT(H)	Ratio of covered terms in heading-text.	LM.JM(B)	body-text language modeling (Jelinek-Mercer) score [31].
LM.Dir(B)	Body-text language modeling (Dirichlet) score [31].	RQT(T)	Ratio of covered terms in title-text.
InNum	Number of inlinks.	TF(B)	Term frequency in body-text.
AvgNTF(B)	Average normalized TF in body-text.	LM.JM(T)	title-text language modeling (Jelinek-Mercer) score
STFIDF(H)	Sum of term TFIDF in heading-text.	NumQT(A)	Number of covered terms in anchor-text.
MaxNTF(B)	Maximum normalized TF in body-text.	PR	PageRank score [4].
AvgNTF(T)	Avgerage normalized TF for title-text.	LM.Dir(T)	title-text language modeling (Dirichlet) score.
MxTFIDF(T)	Maximum term TFIDF in title-text.	MaxNTF(T)	Maximum normalized TF in title-text.
LM.Dir(H)	heading-text language modeling (Dirichlet) score	MaxTF(T)	Maximum query term frequency in title-text.
ATFIDF(T)	Average term TFIDF in title-text.	AvgTF(T)	Average query term frequency in title-text.
SumTF(T)	Sum of term frequency in title-text.	LM.JM(H)	heading-text language modeling (Jelinek-Mercer) score.
L(B)	Body-text length.	AvgTF(H)	Average query term frequency in heading-text.
SumTF(H)	Sum of term frequency in heading-text.		

Table 2: Relevance and freshness judging guidelines for mechanical turk editors.

1. Relevance Evaluation.

Imagine you searched for "Mechanical Turk" in Google and got back a list of URLs in your results.

- A result of "www.mturk.com" would be a **highly relevant** match.
- A blog entry or news about working on Mechanical Turk would be **relevant**.
- A story about a person's daily life in which Mechanical Turk is mentioned in one sentence is treated as **borderline**.
- A story about an airplane in Turkey having had mechanical problems shortly after take off is **not relevant**.
- A story about a child eating fruits is considered **not related**.

2. Freshness Evaluation.

Use your knowledge about the query, combined with the time clues on the web page, including the time that the author wrote the story, the timestamp in copyright areas, etc., to judge whether the page is fresh or not, suppose you are in around April 2007.

Imagine you searched for "2007 cricket world cup" in Google around April 2007 and got back a list of URLs in your results.

- A news reporting the story of 2007 cricket world cup on previous one day would be **very fresh**.
- A critique about the fact that the ireland cricket coach is murdered in April 2007 is **fresh**.
- An introduction about the preparation of ireland cricket team for the world cup written in September 2006 is treated as **borderline**.
- A comment about stories in 2003 cricket world cup written in 2004 is **stale**.
- The introduction about the schedule of 2003 cricket world cup is **very stale**.

modeling [31], computed over different fields of documents (heading, title, body). The list also includes a few well-known link-based static features such as the number of inlinks and PageRank [4].

The temporal ranking features are generated by measuring the changes in the contents of documents with respect to their previous snapshots. For this purpose, we build a time series of each document's content changes, by going through the entire time span and comparing the TFIDF similarity of the document at each point with the previous and next versions. We generate separate time series for different document fields (heading, title, body), and use *STL seasonal-trend decomposition* [7] to decompose each time series τ into trend ($\mathcal{T}$), seasonal ($\mathcal{S}$) and remainder ($\mathcal{R}$) components.

$$STL(\tau) = \mathcal{T}_\tau + \mathcal{S}_\tau + \mathcal{R}_\tau$$

The same steps are repeated to decompose the time series generated based on link and page activities (create, remove, update) [8]. Figure 1 depicts an example of STL decomposition on a time series. In this instance, the time series (data) is generated from the frequency distribution of the query *jingle bells* in the logs of a commercial search engine. The same decomposition can be applied to a sequence of TFIDF scores, PageRank values or any other type of time series data. We use the output of STL decomposition for different time series to generate our temporal ranking features as summarized in Table 3. The slope of τ captures the speed of content changes, and has been suggested to be an effective feature for ranking [9]. The amplitude feature can measure the scale of content changes, and the position feature $Rp(\tau)$ is calculated with respect to the distance to the nearest peak in the time series. The confidence features are computed according to the distribution of $\mathcal{S}_\tau$ and $\mathcal{T}_\tau$ values after decomposition. We also employ the *Timed PageRank* of Yu et al. [30] as our temporally-sensitive static-rank feature.

Query clustering features. The query importance $\mathcal{I}$ features are used to cluster queries and assign the weights in each corresponding ranking function. We follow the approach taken by Bian et al. [2] and used the η top-ranked documents returned by a reference ranker (BM25 [25]) to generate our clustering features. We set the value of η to 15 in all our experiments. Once the pseudo-feedback documents are gathered, we compute the average value of each *ranking feature* over them and use the final mean value as a clustering feature. The feature importance is computed by training a reference RankSVM model for hybrid NDCG ($\gamma = 0.5$) on the training dataset.

Baseline methods. We compare the effectiveness of our CS-DAC with four baselines:

- Single ranker (SinR).
- Separate ranker training and selection (SepR).
- Over-weighting model [12].
- TopicalSVM [2].

In SinR, we train a single RankSVM ranker with all features. This could be regarded as a *weak* baseline that has no form of query categorization, and has been shown to perform more poorly than the

Table 3: **Temporal ranking features used by RankSVM in the CS-DAC framework and baseline methods. The features (except for TPR) are produced from the STL decomposition [7] of time series generated from the content changes in title, body, heading, anchor, and page/link activities [8].**

Feature name	Feature description
Slp(τ)	Slope of trend component T_τ.
Amp(τ)	Amplitude of seasonal component S_τ.
Rp(τ)	Relative position in S_τ.
Cs(τ)	Confidence of seasonality.
Cr(τ)	Confidence of regularity.
TPR	Timed PageRank [30].

other baselines in previous work [2, 16]. Nevertheless, we report its results because it represents one of the most common learning to rank architectures.

The SepR baseline is representative for the family of query-dependent loss function methods [2, 3, 16], in which the loss function is determined according to the temporal aspect of the query. Separate RankSVM rankers are trained for temporal and non-temporal queries, and each query is tested on the *correct* ranker for its type. Note that using the correct query type information—which is generally unavailable without manual effort—means that the performance numbers for this baseline are unaffected by potential query type misclassification, and therefore are overstated.

Dong et al. [12] investigated several techniques for ranking optimization with imbalanced amount of training data for freshness and relevance. Among their methods the *over-weighting* approach was most effective. The over-weighting model combines relevance and freshness labeled data to train a single ranker. This is similar to SepR except that the training pairs of the criterion with fewer labels are over-weighted. Dong et al. [12] used GBrank [32] as their ranking model. However, we modify the over-weighting loss function to RankSVM for consistency with the other methods in our experiments as follows:

$$\arg \min_{\omega,\xi_{q,i,j}} \frac{1}{2}\|\omega\|^2 + C\sum_{q,i,j} \xi_{q,i,j} \quad \textit{subject to}$$

$$\forall y_i^q \succeq y_j^q : \begin{cases} \frac{\alpha}{N_T}\omega^T X_i^q \geq \frac{\alpha}{N_T}\omega^T X_j^q + 1 - \xi_{q,i,j} & q \in \mathcal{Q}_T \\ \frac{1-\alpha}{N_N}\omega^T X_i^q \geq \frac{1-\alpha}{N_N}\omega^T X_j^q + 1 - \xi_{q,i,j} & q \in \mathcal{Q}_N \end{cases}$$

$$\forall_q \forall_i \forall_j : \qquad \xi_{q,i,j} \geq 0$$

where $\mathcal{Q}_T$ and $\mathcal{Q}_N$ denote the sets of queries from Google Trends and MSN query log. N_T and N_N are respectively the number of preferential pairs of query-documents in each of those sets. α is a parameter that controls the balance of Google Trends queries vs. MSN queries, ranging over [0,1]. ω represents the feature weights within the ranking model.

Our last experimental baseline is TopicalSVM [2] which is the state-of-the-art in the family of divide and conquer techniques. TopicalSVM trains all rankers using a global loss function, and does not factorize the query-document importance $\mathcal{U}$ in contrast to CS-DAC.

5. EXPERIMENTS

We start our experiments by investigating the performance of our baseline techniques optimized for different goals. We then pick the best-performing baselines and compare them against CS-DAC. In all our experiments we run 5-fold cross-validation in which the first three folds are used for training, and the remaining two folds are used for validation and testing. The number of ranking functions (clusters) in CS-DAC and TopicalSVM to are set to three ($k = 3$), since preliminary results demonstrate CS-DAC and TopicalSVM perform the best when $k = 3$ and $k = 4$ (slightly outperforms the case when $k = 3$) respectively.

Table 4: Freshness comparison on the *temporal* (top) and *non-temporal* (bottom) query sets. All methods are trained using the hybrid labels and the evaluation is based on the freshness ratings ($\mathbf{y}^F$). Symbols †, §, and ‡ respectively denote statistically significant differences according to a single-tailed student t-test (p-value<0.05) over the SepR, TopicalSVM and Over-weighting baselines.

	Temporal Queries (Google Trends)			
	NDCF1	NDCF3	NDCF5	NDCF10
SepR	0.378	0.360	0.372	0.408
TopicalSVM	0.365	0.355	0.365	0.402
Over-weighting	0.340	0.348	0.363	0.404
CS-DAC	0.398‡	0.364	0.376	0.411
CS-DAC($\mathcal{U}$)	0.416†§‡	0.379‡	0.388	0.400
	Non-Temporal Queries (MSN logs)			
	NDCF1	NDCF3	NDCF5	NDCF10
SepR	0.348	0.411	0.434	0.475
TopicalSVM	0.355	0.408	0.430	0.485
Over-weighting	0.335	0.408	0.434	0.480
CS-DAC	0.427†§‡	0.454†§‡	0.473†§‡	0.510§‡
CS-DAC($\mathcal{U}$)	0.452†§‡	0.466†§‡	0.488†§‡	0.527†§‡

Performance analysis for experimental baselines. We investigate the performance of baseline techniques when trained for one of four optimization goals:

1. Relevance (Rel): The baselines are trained using relevance labels only.
2. Freshness (Fre): The baselines are trained using freshness labels only.
3. Hybrid labels (Hyb): The baselines are trained using hybrid labels (Equation 2).
4. Demoted labels (Dem): Dong et al. [12, 13] suggested *demoting* the the relevance grades of outdated documents. They suggested that if a document is somewhat outdated, then its relevance label should be demoted by one grade. For totally outdated documents the relevance labels are demoted by two grades. We followed the same strategy to compute our demoted labels. In essence, this is a special case of hybrid labeling.

The final results of each optimized ranker are evaluated separately for freshness and relevance using NDCG with corresponding labels.

Figure 2 shows the performance of baseline techniques on the *non-temporal* query set (sampled from the MSN logs). As expected, when evaluating using the relevance labels ($\mathbf{y}^R$), it is more effective to optimize for relevance (Rel) rather than freshness (Fre). Similarly, optimizing for freshness produces results that have better NDCF values. The methods optimized for demoted (Dem) and hybrid (Hyb) labels consistently outperform those that are optimized for either freshness or relevance. The results also suggest that our hybrid labels are better for improving both relevance and freshness compared to the demoted labels of Dong et al. [12, 13].

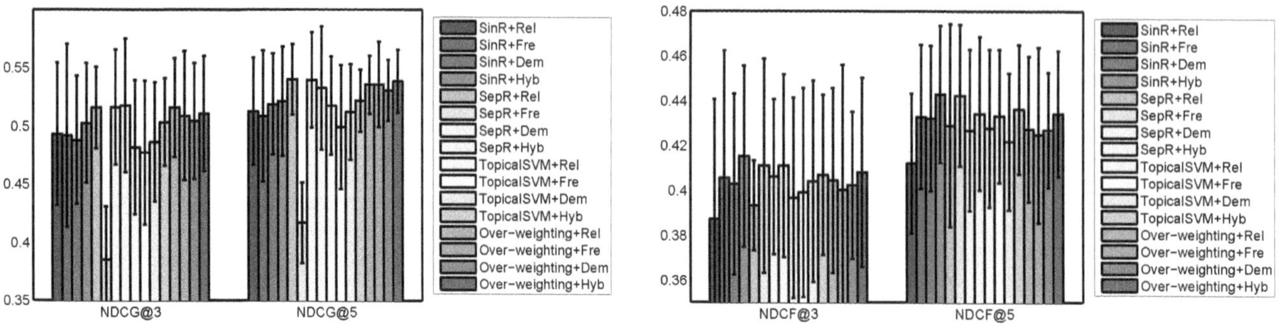

(a) *Relevance labels* ($\mathbf{y}^R$) (b) *Freshness labels* ($\mathbf{y}^F$)

Figure 2: Ranking performance of baseline systems on relevance (left) and freshness (right) for the *non-temporal* query set. Error bars are the standard deviations of performance across five cross-validation folds.

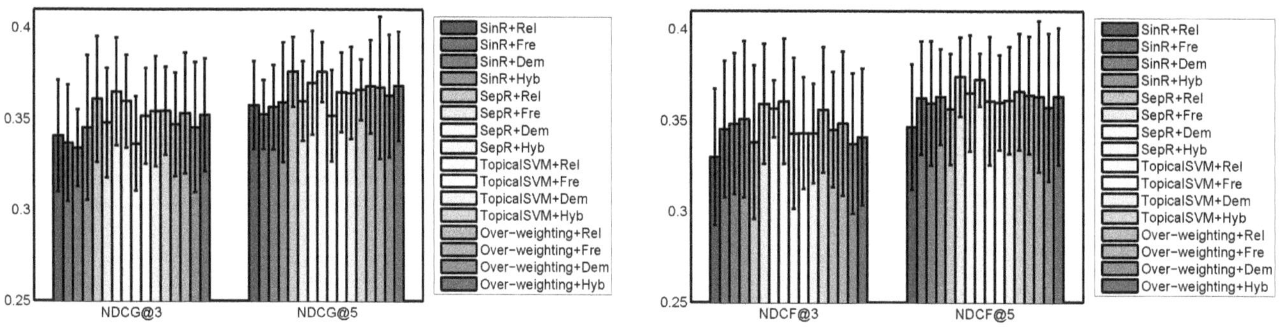

(a) *Relevance labels* ($\mathbf{y}^R$) (b) *Freshness labels* ($\mathbf{y}^F$)

Figure 3: Ranking performance of baseline systems on relevance (left) and freshness (right) for the *temporal* query set. Error bars are the standard deviations of performance across five cross-validation folds.

Among the baselines, SinR has overall the poorest performance which is consistent with previous observations [3]. TopicalSVM, over-weighting and SepR show similar effectiveness while the latter might be considered marginally better—not surprising given that we use correct query type information in SepR.

We repeat the analysis on the *temporal* query set and the results are illustrated in Figure 3; as in the previous experiment, SinR has the lowest performance on both sets of labels while the other methods show similar effectiveness. Compared to the experiments on the non-temporal query set, there is less variation in performance when optimized for different types of labels. Our investigations revealed that this is due to high correlation between relevance and freshness labels on the temporal set. The Pearson's correlation between relevance and freshness labels on the temporal query set is 0.912 ± 0.004, statistically significantly higher than 0.429 ± 0.021 for the non-temporal set.

Based on the summarized results, we choose hybrid labels for training rankers in our remaining experiments. We also drop SinR as it consistently showed inferior effectiveness compared to all other methods.

Comparative performance on freshness. We use NDCG with freshness $\mathbf{y}^F$ labels (NDCF [13]) to compare the performance of CS-DAC with the baselines on both temporal (Google Trends) and non-temporal (MSN logs) query sets. We report the results for CS-DAC in the presence and absence of the query-document importance factor ($\mathcal{U}$) described in Equations 3 and 5. We respectively refer to these two versions as CS-DAC($\mathcal{U}$) and CS-DAC.

Table 4 includes the NDCF results on both query sets. The over-weighting baseline performs worst than the other methods. This is not surprising given that over-weighting is originally designed for scenarios with imbalanced training data [12], and the fact that it does not leverage any type of query classification or clustering. Consistent with the observations in the previous section, SepR and TopicalSVM produce similar results on the temporal queries, while they are both outperformed by CS-DAC. Introducing the $\mathcal{U}$ factor leads to further improvements in performance particularly at higher cutoffs. On non-temporal queries, TopicalSVM and SepR and over-weighting show similar effectiveness while CS-DAC consistently outperforms all baselines significantly. It is interesting to observe that CS-DAC improvements over the baselines are larger on the non-temporal query set. This can be explained by two reasons: (1) the documents returned for temporal queries tend to be fresher on average than those returned for the non-temporal ones, and (2) the high correlation between relevance and freshness labels in this set leads to more effective learning by reducing impact of potential noise in clustering and hybrid labels.

Comparative performance on relevance. We run a similar analysis, and compare the NDCG values of different techniques as

Table 5: Relevance comparison on the *temporal* (top) and *non-temporal* (bottom) query sets. All methods are trained using the hybrid labels and the evaluation is based on the freshness ratings (y^R). Symbols †, §, and ‡ respectively denote statistically significant differences according to a single-tailed student t-test (p-value<0.05) over the SepR, TopicalSVM and Over-weighting baselines.

	Temporal Queries (Google Trends)			
	NDCG1	NDCG3	NDCG5	NDCG10
SepR	0.373	0.359	0.375	0.411
TopicalSVM	0.342	0.354	0.365	0.408
Over-weighting	0.355	0.351	0.368	0.411
CS-DAC	0.385	0.365	0.377	0.417
CS-DAC($\mathcal{U}$)	0.401†‡	0.375	0.389	0.426†
	Non-Temporal Queries (MSN logs)			
	NDCG1	NDCG3	NDCG5	NDCG10
SepR	0.481	0.517	0.532	0.562
TopicalSVM	0.490	0.508	0.521	0.566
Over-weighting	0.476	0.510	0.538	0.570
CS-DAC	0.493	0.520	0.541	0.574
CS-DAC($\mathcal{U}$)	0.509	0.522	0.541	0.574

measured by the relevance labels (y^R) in Table 5. For non-temporal queries, the CS-DAC results are marginally better than the baselines, although none of the differences are statistically significant. On the temporal query set, SepR has the edge over the other baselines while CS-DAC outperforms the three of them at all cutoff values. Adding the $\mathcal{U}$ factor significantly improves the results for NDCG@1 and NDCG@10. As in the NDCF numbers on this query set, the NDCG values could be also affected by the high correlation between freshness and relevance.

6. DISCUSSION

We showed that our CS-DAC method could significantly improve both freshness and relevance of the results compared to state-of-the-art baselines. In this section, we investigate the impact of random walk smoothing in improving the query-document factor $\mathcal{U}$ for training. We also compare CS-DAC and the baselines in terms of hybrid NDCG by assigning various weights to relevance and freshness. Finally, we report the most effective features according to our experiments for ranking temporal and non-temporal queries.

Smoothing query-document importance. We described earlier how original query-document importance values can be smoothed by random walk, where the probability d of random jumping can be tuned during training and validation. Figure 4 shows how choosing different fixed values for d may affect the results. On the non-temporal query set, different degrees of smoothing have little advantage over no smoothing ($d = 0$). On the temporal query set however, random-walk helps to smooth inter-label dependencies, and hence improves the results on both freshness and relevance.

Hybrid labels for evaluation. In Section 5 we showed that training for hybrid NDCG ($\gamma = 0.5$) was effective for improving both freshness and relevance. Here, we provide the evaluation results on hybrid NDCG, the metric we used for optimizing the ensemble ranking. Although we used $\gamma = 0.5$ for training, we report the evaluation results for different values of γ in Figure 5 to account for scenarios where freshness and relevance are

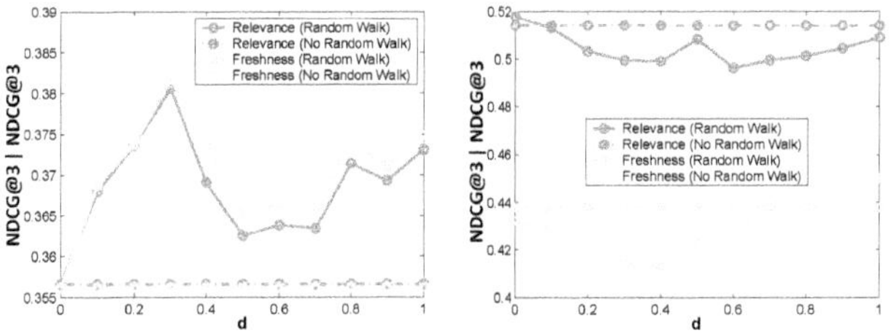

(a) *Temporal queries* (b) *Non-temporal queries*

Figure 4: The impact of changing the random jump probability d during smoothing of the query-document importance values $\mathcal{U}$. The results are evaluated on temporal (left) and non-temporal (right) queries using both relevance and freshness labels.

weighted differently. The results are consistent with our previous experiments; CS-DAC outperforms the baselines, and the weighting between freshness and relevance is less important for temporal queries. Increasing the γ value grows the overall hybrid NDCG almost monotonically because the relevance-based NDCG values are generally greater than those computed based on the freshness labels. It is worthwhile of pointing out that this observation does not suggest that ranking performance benefits the most when only optimizing for relevance.

Feature Analysis. CS-DAC relies on several temporal and non-temporal features for query clustering and document ranking. We examined all cross-validation folds to find the features that are assigned with highest weights during training. Among the temporal features, the confidence values for the seasonality CS(τ), and regularity Cr(τ) of STL decompositions were generally the most effective. Furthermore, the features generated from the time-series decomposition of changes in anchor-text and inlinks were more successful than those similarly produced based on other fields (e.g., title, body, heading). The effectiveness of temporal link-based features for improving relevance and freshness has been also acknowledged previously by Dai and Davison [8].

Between the non-temporal features, BM25 and language modeling scores had the highest weights and were most effective when computed over the body and title text.

7. CONCLUSIONS AND FUTURE WORK

In this paper, we proposed a learning to rank approach (CS-DAC) for optimizing for relevance and freshness simultaneously. We extended the state-of-the-art in divide and conquer ranking [3] by adding two new key elements; first, instead of optimizing for relevance labels, we generated and used hybrid labels based on relevance and freshness grades. Second, we introduced a new query-document importance factor ($\mathcal{U}$) that allows each ranker to set different importance to relevance and freshness. Compared with traditional metasearch engines, divide-and-conquer ranking frameworks generate merged ranking lists on the model level instead of the result level. It enables automatic identification of effective ranking features for individual type of queries. Our experiments on a large web archive demonstrated that CS-DAC can improve both relevance and freshness compared to existing baselines. In the future, we plan to compare with data fusion methods, i.e, training two separate rankers with each utilizing judgments based on one criterion (relevance or freshness), and then merging results into a single ranking list. We also plan to consider the document diversity

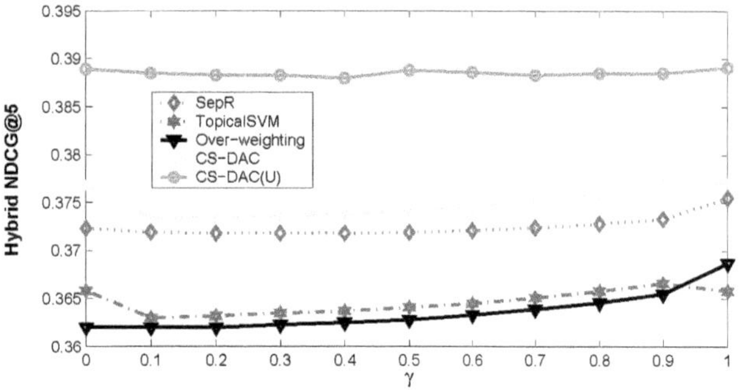

(a) *Temporal queries*

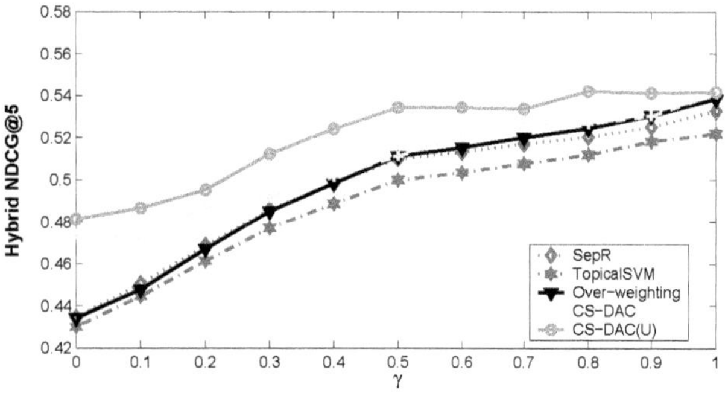

(b) *Non-temporal queries*

Figure 5: Hybrid NDCG5 values for different values of γ on the *temporal* (top) and *non-temporal* (bottom) query set. Similar trends were found for NDCG at different cutoff values.

problem that is especially important for answering time-sensitive queries, e.g, a news-related query may have many news articles which may incur document duplication.

We studied the correlation between relevance and freshness grades, and its implications on the training effectiveness. Our results revealed high correlation between relevance and freshness labels in temporal queries, suggesting that the choice of document labels is less important for training on that set. We modeled document importance by the likelihood of visiting each unique hybrid label, and surprisingly found that it can improve ranking performance, especially for temporal queries. However, in what way that such document weighting strategies influence ranking performance is still unclear. We will leave it as one of our future work.

Our work can be considered as the simplest form of *multi-objective (multiple-criteria) optimization* [26], where multiple objective functions (freshness, relevance) are combined to form a single optimization goal (hybrid labels). These kinds of *aggregated* functions require the weight of each objective to be known in advance (γ in our case), and are incapable of finding all optimal solutions. Deploying more sophisticated multi-objective optimization techniques may lead to more significant improvements in relevance and freshness. Further work includes adopting other learning to rank architectures such as boosted decision trees [29] for multi-objective optimization of freshness and relevance.

Acknowledgments

We thank the anonymous reviewers for their useful comments. We also thank Jiang Bian for valuable discussion on TopicalSVM model and Jingjing Liu for helpful comments on the judgments for ranking evaluation. This work was supported in part by a grant from the National Science Foundation under award IIS-0803605.

8. REFERENCES

[1] K. Berberich, S. J. Bedathur, O. Alonso, and G. Weikum. A language modeling approach for temporal information needs. In *Proc. of ECIR*, pages 13–25, 2010.

[2] J. Bian, X. Li, F. Li, Z. Zheng, and H. Zha. Ranking specialization for web search: a divide-and-conquer approach by using topical RankSVM. In *Proc. of WWW*, pages 131–140, 2010.

[3] J. Bian, T.-Y. Liu, T. Qin, and H. Zha. Ranking with query-dependent loss for web search. In *Proc. of WSDM*, pages 141–150, 2010.

[4] S. Brin and L. Page. The anatomy of a large-scale hypertextual Web search engine. In *Proc. of WWW*, pages 107–117, Apr. 1998.

[5] C. Burges, T. Shaked, E. Renshaw, M. Deeds, N. Hamilton, and G. Hullender. Learning to rank using gradient descent. In *Proc. of ICML*, pages 89–96, 2005.

[6] S. Chien and N. Immorlica. Semantic similarity between search engine queries using temporal correlation. In *Proc. of WWW*, pages 2–11, 2005.

[7] R. B. Cleveland, W. S. Cleveland, J. E. Mcrae, and I. Terpenning. STL: A seasonal-trend decomposition procedure based on loess. *Journal of Official Statistics*, 6(1):3–73, 1990.

[8] N. Dai and B. D. Davison. Freshness matters: In flowers, food, and web authority. In *Proc. of SIGIR*, pages 114–121, 2010.

[9] N. Dai and B. D. Davison. Mining anchor text trends for retrieval. In *Proc. of ECIR*, pages 127–139, 2010.

[10] W. Dakka, L. Gravano, and P. G. Ipeirotis. Answering general time sensitive queries. In *Proc. of CIKM*, pages 1437–1438, 2008.

[11] F. Diaz. Integration of news content into web results. In *Proc. of WSDM*, pages 182–191, 2009.

[12] A. Dong, Y. Chang, Z. Zheng, G. Mishne, J. Bai, R. Zhang, K. Buchner, C. Liao, and F. Diaz. Towards recency ranking in web search. In *Proc. of WSDM*, pages 11–20, 2010.

[13] A. Dong, R. Zhang, P. Kolari, J. Bai, F. Diaz, Y. Chang, Z. Zheng, and H. Zha. Time is of the essence: improving recency ranking using twitter data. In *Proc. of WWW*, pages 331–340, 2010.

[14] J. L. Elsas and S. T. Dumais. Leveraging temporal dynamics of document content in relevance ranking. In *Proc. of WSDM*, pages 1–10, 2010.

[15] Y. Freund, R. Iyer, R. E. Schapire, and Y. Singer. An efficient boosting algorithm for combining preferences. *Journal of Machine Learning Research*, 4:933–969, December 2003.

[16] X. Geng, T.-Y. Liu, T. Qin, A. Arnold, H. Li, and H.-Y. Shum. Query dependent ranking using k-nearest neighbor. In *Proc. of SIGIR*, pages 115–122, 2008.

[17] S. Gollapudi and A. Sharma. An axiomatic approach for result diversification. In *Proc. of WWW*, pages 381–390, 2009.

[18] K. Jarvelin and J. Kekalainen. IR evaluation methods for retrieving highly relevant documents. In *Proc. of SIGIR*, pages 41–48, 2000.

[19] T. Joachims. Optimizing search engines using clickthrough data. In *Proc. of SIGKDD*, pages 133–142, 2002.

[20] R. Jones and F. Diaz. Temporal profiles of queries. *ACM Transactions on Information Systems*, 25(3):14, 2007.

[21] I. Kang and G. Kim. Query type classification for web document retrieval. In *Proc. of SIGIR*, pages 64–71, 2003.

[22] A. Kulkarni, J. Teevan, K. Svore, and S. Dumais. Understanding temporal query dynamics. In *Proc. of WSDM*, pages 167–176, 2011.

[23] L. Li, F. Liu, and W. Chou. An information theoretic approach for using word cluster information in natural language call routing. Technical Report ALR-2003-014, Avaya Labs Research, 2003.

[24] D. Metzler, R. Jones, F. Peng, and R. Zhang. Improving search relevance for implicitly temporal queries. In *Proc. of SIGIR*, pages 700–701, 2009.

[25] S. Robertson, H. Zaragoza, and M. Taylor. Simple BM25 extension to multiple weighted fields. In *Proc. of CIKM*, pages 42–49, 2004.

[26] R. Steuer. *Multiple Criteria Optimization: Theory, Computation and Application*. John Wiley, 546 pp, 1986.

[27] R. Tibshirani, G. Walther, and T. Hastie. Estimating the Number of Clusters in a Dataset via the Gap Statistic. *Journal of the Royal Statistical Society, Series B*, 63:411–423, 2000.

[28] L. Wang, J. Lin, and D. Metzler. Learning to efficiently rank. In *Proc. of SIGIR*, pages 138–145, 2010.

[29] Q. Wu, C. Burges, K. Svore, and J. Gao. Adapting boosting for information retrieval measures. *Information Retrieval*, 13, 2010.

[30] P. S. Yu, X. Li, and B. Liu. On the temporal dimension of search. In *Proc. of WWW*, pages 448–449, 2004.

[31] C. Zhai and J. Lafferty. A study of smoothing methods for language models applied to information retrieval. *ACM Transactions on Information Systems*, 22:179–214, 2004.

[32] Z. Zheng, H. Zha, T. Zhang, O. Chapelle, K. Chen, and G. Sun. A general boosting method and its application to learning ranking functions for web search. In *Advances in NIPS 20*, 2008.

A Cascade Ranking Model for Efficient Ranked Retrieval

Lidan Wang
Dept. of Computer Science
University of Maryland
College Park, MD
lidan@cs.umd.edu

Jimmy Lin
The iSchool
University of Maryland
College Park, MD
jimmylin@umd.edu

Donald Metzler
Information Sciences Institute
Univ. of Southern California
Marina del Rey, CA
metzler@isi.edu

ABSTRACT

There is a fundamental tradeoff between effectiveness and efficiency when designing retrieval models for large-scale document collections. Effectiveness tends to derive from sophisticated ranking functions, such as those constructed using learning to rank, while efficiency gains tend to arise from improvements in query evaluation and caching strategies. Given their inherently disjoint nature, it is difficult to jointly optimize effectiveness and efficiency in end-to-end systems. To address this problem, we formulate and develop a novel cascade ranking model, which unlike previous approaches, can simultaneously improve both top k ranked effectiveness and retrieval efficiency. The model constructs a cascade of increasingly complex ranking functions that progressively prunes and refines the set of candidate documents to minimize retrieval latency and maximize result set quality. We present a novel boosting algorithm for learning such cascades to directly optimize the tradeoff between effectiveness and efficiency. Experimental results show that our cascades are faster *and* return higher quality results than comparable ranking models.

Categories and Subject Descriptors: H.3.3 [Information Storage and Retrieval]: Information Search and Retrieval

General Terms: Algorithms, Performance

Keywords: learning to rank, effectiveness, efficiency

1. INTRODUCTION

There is often a tension between effectiveness and efficiency when building information retrieval systems. To achieve greater effectiveness (i.e., to deliver higher quality results), system designers are driven towards complex ranking functions that may combine evidence from dozens, hundreds, or even thousands of relevance signals, typically using sophisticated machine learning techniques [16]. This frequently comes at a cost in efficiency (i.e., a slower system), since complex ranking functions are computationally expensive, thus requiring more resources to achieve the same level of service. On the other hand, efficiency can be enhanced through a variety of approaches such as index pruning, feature pruning, approximate query evaluation, and systems engineering. However, most of these approaches degrade effectiveness, typically in ways that are difficult to control.

With the goal of achieving a better balance between retrieval effectiveness and efficiency, recent work has explored approaches to ranking that exhibit good tradeoff characteristics [27, 28]. In general, they work by eliminating features that are costly to compute and not predicted to contribute much to the quality of the results. While efficiency-minded feature selection is a natural way to make existing models faster, such pruning may negatively affect retrieval effectiveness. This problem is exacerbated for very large collections under tight efficiency constraints. In this setting, only a small handful of cheap features can be used for ranking, which can result in poor retrieval effectiveness.

We introduce a novel *cascade ranking model* for efficient ranked retrieval. Unlike previous approaches, the cascade uses a sequence of increasingly complex ranking functions to progressively prune documents and refine the rank order of non-pruned documents. Thus, the cascade model views retrieval as a multi-stage progressive refinement problem, where each stage considers successively richer and more complex ranking models, but over successively smaller candidate document sets. The intuition is that although complex features are generally more time-consuming to compute, additional overhead is offset by the fact that fewer documents are examined. This type of ranking paradigm is well-suited for large document collections, because the number of relevant documents is very small compared to the collection size. Hence, the ability to quickly hone in on a small set of candidate documents, via the cascade, can yield higher quality results *and* faster query execution times.

To achieve a desired efficiency-effectiveness tradeoff, we describe a novel boosting algorithm, a generalization of AdaRank [30], that jointly learns the model structure (i.e., optimal sequence of ranking stages) and the set of documents to prune at each stage. Experiments show that our cascade model can simultaneously improve effectiveness and efficiency compared to non-cascade feature-based models.

This paper has three major contributions. The first is the cascade model itself. Although similar coarse-to-fine-grained models have been used in other disciplines, to our knowledge this is the first application of this principle for learning an efficient ranking model. Second, we introduce a novel boosting algorithm for learning ranking cascades,

SIGIR'11, July 24–28, 2011, Beijing, China.

complete with a theoretical analysis. Finally, we carry out an extensive evaluation of our proposed model on several web collections. Results show that the cascade model consistently outperforms current state-of-the-art models, both in terms of efficiency and effectiveness.

The remainder of the paper is organized as follows: Section 2 describes related work. Section 3 details our proposed cascade ranking model, and Section 4 presents how cascade models can be learned. Next, Section 5 describes experimental results. Finally, Section 6 concludes the paper and outlines possible directions for future work.

2. RELATED WORK

In recent years, we have witnessed the success of machine learning approaches to the document ranking problem, as a whole known as learning to rank (e.g., [6, 17, 9, 30, 16], just to name a few). For the most part, however, these approaches have focused exclusively on effectiveness, sometimes leading to ranking functions that deliver high quality results, but are unbearably slow. Recently, however, a thread of work has emerged, dubbed learning to *efficiently* rank, that adopts an efficiency-minded approach. For example, regularization is useful for "encouraging" models to have few non-zero parameters, thereby serving as a crude form of feature pruning [24, 11]. More recently, Wang et al. [27, 28], in two separate studies, proposed linear ranking models that explicitly account for feature costs: the first is able to discover a more optimal point in the tradeoff space between efficiency and effectiveness, while the second is able to perform feature pruning to meet an externally-imposed time constraint. With feature pruning, the retrieval engine still implements a single monolithic ranking function—and thus it remains necessary to compute complex features for many documents (which is especially problematic for large web collections). In addition, since the number of non-relevant documents is significantly larger than the number of relevant documents in web-scale collections [8], applying a monolithic ranking model (even if used with a fast query evaluation engine) may waste computations, because a large number of the documents examined are non-relevant. In contrast, the cascade model considers increasingly complex features/ranking models on progressively fewer candidate documents. This approach, as we will show in the experiments, results in ranking functions that are simultaneously effective and efficient.

Our work is complementary to query evaluation [5, 25, 23]. Query evaluation focuses on how to efficiently evaluate a *given* ranking model, where we aim to *learn* an efficient ranking model in the first place. Along a similar direction, Cambazoglu et al. [8] explored early-exit strategies for additive ensembles. Although this approach bears some superficial resemblance to our cascade model, it is in fact completely different. They focus on optimizing the query evaluation process *given* a particular additive ensemble—and not about learning the ensemble. In contrast, our proposed model is accompanied by a boosting algorithm for learning optimal cascades according to a tradeoff metric.

A complementary approach to fast query evaluation is index pruning [10, 20]. Since query evaluation time monotonically increases with length of postings lists, shorter postings lists translate into faster queries. While discarding postings help reduce query latency, it does not directly optimize the underlying effectiveness and efficiency tradeoffs.

Finally, a variety of system engineering strategies exist to increase search efficiency, especially in operational settings. Caching [2, 21] reduces query latency significantly. Partitioning the document collection reduces latency, while replication of services increases throughout [12, 3]. These strategies are not IR-specific, but represent general principles for building large-scale distributed systems. In particular, we are not concerned with the system engineering aspects of efficiency (caching, partitioning, and replication), since these techniques can be applied to the cascade model just as they can be applied to any retrieval algorithm. These system engineering aspects can be viewed as orthogonal to our learning framework; their effects are captured by our analytical model of query execution time, which simply serves as an input to our task of learning an efficient ranking model.

The idea of progressive refinement in the cascade model is related to the general class of coarse-to-fine models that have been successfully applied in computer vision and machine learning [26, 29]. Most notably, Viola and Jones [26] tackled the problem of real-time face detection in images by a sequence of binary classifiers of increasing complexity, such that the most unlikely images are rejected early by simple classifiers, and the more promising object-like regions are passed to more complex classifiers for further consideration. However, these models are for high recall/precision applications and cannot be used for ranked retrieval, since they can only filter, but not *rank* items. As we will show, our proposed cascade is specifically built for achieving high top k *ranked* effectiveness in a very efficient manner.

3. CASCADE MODEL

In web search, there are significantly more non-relevant documents than relevant documents and most users only browse the top few results. Applying a monolithic ranking model for each query, even if used in conjunction with fast query evaluation techniques (e.g., [5, 25, 23]), may not be very efficient because a large number of scored documents are likely to be non-relevant and/or will not appear in the top k. Our proposed cascade model leverages these facts to achieve high *top k ranked* effectiveness in a highly efficient manner by constructing ranking models from simple to complex, applying the simple ones first, and pruning documents at each subsequent stage so that more complex (and better) ranking models are computed over fewer documents.

The cascade model consists of an additive sequence of stages $\{S_1 ... S_T\}$, where each stage S_t is associated with a pruning function J_t and a local ranking function H_t. Each stage receives as input the set of ranked documents from the previous stage and applies two sequential operations: first, the pruning function J_t is used to remove a number of documents from the input set (thus reducing the amount of effort involved in document scoring); then, the score contribution of the local ranking function H_t is added to the candidate documents still under consideration (to improve top k quality of the remaining documents). The results are forwarded to the next cascade stage for further pruning and re-ranking.

By construction, the cascade is arranged so that the local ranking functions increase in cost (and thus, complexity). Early stages take advantage of "cheap" ranking models to rank documents; the pruning functions discard documents that are unlikely to appear in the final top k. As a result, each successive stage is presented with a smaller candidate set, which enables the cascade to exploit more complex

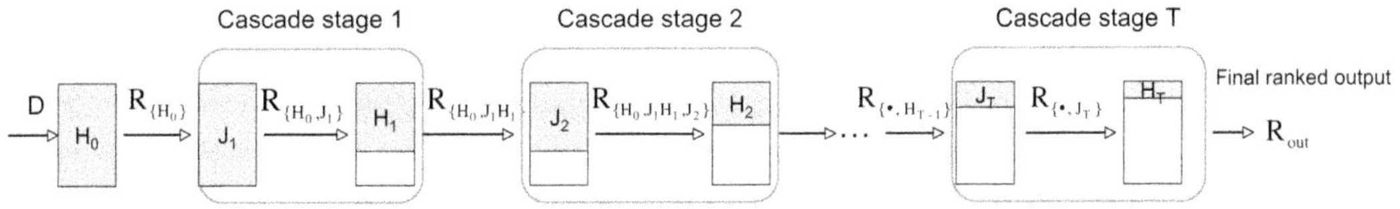

Figure 1: An example cascade. After an initial ranking function H_0, each stage consists of two sequential operations: J_t prunes the input ranked documents, then a local ranking function H_t refines the rank order of the retained documents. The new ranked list is passed to the next stage. The size of the shaded area denotes the size of the candidate documents. Subscripts for each ranked list denotes the sequence of actions applied.

and costly ranking models—hence improving effectiveness—without sacrificing efficiency.

As an example, Figure 1 presents a cascade model. The input to the cascade is a set of documents for a given query, and the final output is a ranked list of k documents (where k is specified in advance). An initial ranking function H_0 is applied to obtain an initial ranked list, $R_{\{H_0\}}$, which is then passed as input to the first stage. At the first cascade stage, the pruning function J_1 prunes documents in $R_{\{H_0\}}$ based on features of these documents (details in Section 3.1). The output from the pruning operation, denoted by $R_{\{H_0,J_1\}}$, is re-ranked by adding the contribution of H_1 to the document scores. This process repeats for the next cascade stage.

The overall score of a *non-pruned* document d_i at the end of a cascade model with T stages has the following form:

$$f_T(d_i) = \sum_{t=1}^{T} \alpha_t \cdot H_t \tag{1}$$

where α_t denotes the importance of the local model H_t. Following previous work in learning to rank, each H_t is a "weak ranker". We postpone discussing the actual ranking functions and our feature set until Section 4.

The iterative pruning and scoring mechanisms of the cascade provide a way to explicitly control the tradeoff between retrieval efficiency and ranked effectiveness. In terms of efficiency, the cascade aims to reduce the number of candidate documents at each stage:

$$|R_{\{\cdot,J_t\}}| \leq |R_{\{\cdot,J_{t-1}\}}| \leq \ldots |R_{\{\cdot,J_1\}}| \tag{2}$$

where each $|R_{\{\cdot,J_t\}}|$ denotes the resulting size of the documents after pruning at stage t, and the $\cdot$ abbreviates the previous sequence of pruning and re-ranking actions that have been applied to the input ranked documents R. In terms of effectiveness, the cascade aims to achieve the following:

$$E(R_{\{\cdot,H_t\}}) \geq E(R_{\{\cdot,H_{t-1}\}}) \geq \ldots E(R_{\{H_0\}}) \tag{3}$$

where $E(R_{\{\cdot,H_t\}})$ denotes the resulting top k effectiveness from applying H_t to refine the overall scores of the non-pruned documents that have reached S_t.

We can trivially obtain the most desirable outcome for either Equation (2) or Equation (3) at the expense of the other. If we set the pruning functions to never discard any documents, then the final ranked effectiveness $E(R_{\{\cdot,H_t\}})$ will be as high as possible since there will be no "loss" due to pruning. However, the cascade will likely be inefficient. Alternatively, if we prune every document, the result will almost certainly be fast, but ineffective. Thus, the objective is to design a well-balanced cascade by jointly learning the local ranking and pruning functions, guided by a tradeoff metric. We describe exactly such an algorithm in Section 4.

Before proceeding, a comment about the order in which pruning and re-ranking is performed at each stage: the pruning function is applied on the ranked documents produced from the *previous* stage, i.e., J_t reduces the size of the output documents from stage $t-1$. The reason behind this ordering is that while the local ranking function H_{t-1} used at the previous stage helps to refine the top k ranked effectiveness, pruning its re-ranked documents has a direct impact on the efficiency of stages $t, t+1, \ldots, T$. If the pruning is aggressive, then fewer documents will reach $t, t+1, \ldots, T$, thereby improving efficiency. Therefore, when learning the cascade, the pruning function defined for output documents from $t-1$ should (ideally) be jointly selected with the ranking functions at $t, t+1, \ldots, T$. For example, if H_t is complex, then pruning documents from $t-1$ must be aggressive to make it feasible to apply H_t; on the other hand, if H_t is simple, then more documents from $t-1$ may be kept and scored. While it would be ideal to jointly consider the pruning function with all subsequent ranking functions, this significantly complicates learning. Instead, we only consider the pruning function for documents produced from $t-1$ with the current ranking model H_t at stage t. To instantiate a cascade, we need to define the pruning functions, discussed next.

3.1 Pruning functions

At the input of each cascade stage t, we receive a set of ranked documents $R_{\{\cdot,H_{t-1}\}}$ passed from the previous stage, which are then filtered by the pruning function J_t. Since we have complete rank and score information for these input documents (up to stage $t-1$), the pruning function J_t can utilize their global rank and score. There are many ways to prune documents based on such global information: both rank-based [8] and score-based pruning methods [8, 1] have been proposed in the past. A key benefit of our model is that it is highly modular and flexible—the cascade is not restricted to a single pruning technique, but different stages can use different pruning functions J_t, which may be better suited to work with its corresponding local model H_t. This allows us to simply treat the different pruning methods as "pruning features", which can be selected at each stage. Our goal is not to develop novel pruning methods, but rather to use existing methods as building blocks within our model.

In this section, we present three pruning methods (J_t) that we have found to work well in our experiments. Each of these methods is parameterized by a pruning threshold β_t. The first two use document rank and score information to prune, while the third also considers the score distribution.

Rank-based. This pruning method uses document rank to eliminate a desired proportion of the input documents at each stage. The rank-based cutoff is defined as follows:

$$\textsc{RankCutoff}(\beta_t) : (1-\beta_t) \cdot |R_{\{\cdot,H_{t-1}\}}|$$

A document is pruned if it ranks below this cutoff value,

where β_t here is the pruning parameter, and $|R_{\{\cdot,H_{t-1}\}}|$ is the size of input documents at stage t. Large values of β_t lead to more aggressive pruning, i.e., $\beta_t = 1$ means all documents are discarded.

Score-based. Document scores provide another signal for pruning. Document scores for different queries are different, so enforcing a common score threshold is unlikely to work well. Instead, the score threshold is defined relative to the score range in each input document set:

$$\text{SCORECUTOFF}(\beta_t) : \beta_t \cdot \text{SCORERANGE}_{t-1} + \text{MINS}_{t-1}$$

Where SCORERANGE_{t-1} is defined to be the difference between the maximum and minimum scores in input $R_{\{\cdot,H_{t-1}\}}$ and MINS_{t-1} is the minimum score in $R_{\{\cdot,H_{t-1}\}}$. This is equivalent to normalizing each score into [0, 1] by using the maximum and minimum scores in the candidate set. A document is pruned if it scores less than this threshold, where β_t is the pruning parameter. As before, large value of β_t leads to more aggressive pruning.

Mean-Max threshold. Often it is useful to consider the document score distribution for pruning. Several previous studies [14, 1] have considered the problem of inferring the score distributions of relevant and non-relevant documents, which are then used to help identify the best cutoff threshold for the top k documents in the ranked list to optimize a given evaluation metric. However, these methods only work for *set-based* measures such as F-measure and precision/recall, and do not work for top k ranked effectiveness measures.

We instead adopt a variant of this approach, and use a mean-max threshold function to capture characteristics of the score distribution, defined as a combination of the mean and the max of the input document scores:

$$\text{MEANMAX}(\beta_t) : \beta_t \cdot \text{MAXS}_{t-1} + (1 - \beta_t) \cdot \text{MEANS}_{t-1}$$

Where MAXS_{t-1} and MEANS_{t-1} are the maximum and mean scores in input $R_{\{\cdot,H_{t-1}\}}$, respectively. A document is pruned if it scores less than this mean-max threshold. Similar approaches for using a mean-max threshold to control runtime scoring/prediction complexity have been used in the NLP task of structured prediction [29]. This formulation has the advantage that the pruning function can be better suited for each individual ranked list of documents.

4. LEARNING THE CASCADE

We now turn to the problem of learning a well-balanced cascade that optimizes a desired tradeoff between retrieval efficiency and ranked effectiveness. The entire cascade is defined by $\{<J_t(\beta_t), H_t, \alpha_t>\}$, for $t = 1, \ldots, T$: $J_t(\beta_t)$ is the pruning function and associated parameter (Section 3.1), and H_t is the local ranking model (described below) with its associated weight α_t.

Before we can learn a cascade, we must define how we measure top k ranked effectiveness and retrieval efficiency. For effectiveness, our primary measure is NDCG at k, although other metrics defined over top k rankings can easily be used instead. For retrieval efficiency, we use a cost model to estimate the execution cost of a given cascade. Retrieval engine details, such as query evaluation and caching strategies, are orthogonal to our general framework since their effects on query execution are captured by our cost model and simply serve as input to our learning algorithm.

4.1 Cost estimation

The total cost of cascade $\mathbf{S} = \{S_t\}$, $t = 1, \ldots, T$ for query q_i, denoted by $C(\mathbf{S}, q_i)$, is the sum of individual stage costs:

$$C(\mathbf{S}, q_i) = \sum_{t=1}^{T} C(S_t, q_i) \tag{4}$$

The cost of each stage is determined by the complexity of H_t and how many documents will be evaluated by H_t. We let U_t denote the unit cost of evaluating H_t over each document. The total cost of H_t at stage S_t is given by:

$$C(S_t, q_i) = U_t \cdot |R_{i\{\cdot,J_t\}}| \tag{5}$$

where $|R_{i\{\cdot,J_t\}}|$ denotes the size of the non-pruned documents after applying J_t. Intuitively, this cost model captures the fact that evaluating a more complex model over a large number of documents will result in greater time complexity.

The exact value of U_t depends on the implementation details of the search engine. Several previous studies have proposed strategies for estimating retrieval costs [7, 25]. The most common approach is directly fitting U_t to the actual query execution time of the ranking model [7]. We use this common approach for estimating U_t, where we run each H_t on the set of training queries, record its time, and set U_t to be the total time taken divided by the number of documents evaluated by H_t. For convenience, we normalize the unit costs so that the cheapest feature has a cost of one.

Finally, the query execution costs are unbounded, which makes them difficult to work with when learning a model. Therefore, we need to map the costs into the range [0, 1]. This is accomplished by using an exponential decay function $\exp(-\delta\ C(\mathbf{S}, q_i))$ to transform the cost into the [0, 1] interval ($\delta = 0.01$ in our experiments). Other normalization techniques, such as computing the maximum cost (e.g., cost of applying the most expensive feature to every document in the collection) and then using it as a normalization factor, are also possible. However, this particular alternative may not differentiate costs very well since the cost distribution is likely to be skewed.

4.2 Tradeoff metric

The cascade learning problem is a multi-objective optimization problem [22]. The final objective metric is obtained by linearly combining the multiple objectives, which, in our case are the top k ranked effectiveness and the cost of the cascade model $\mathbf{S}$. For a given query q_i, the tradeoff is defined as follows:

$$\mathrm{T}(\mathbf{S}, q_i) = E(\mathbf{S}, q_i) - \gamma \cdot C(\mathbf{S}, q_i)$$

where $E(\mathbf{S}, q_i)$ represents ranked effectiveness, $C(\mathbf{S}, q_i)$ is the computational cost (Equation 4), and $\gamma \in [0, 1]$ is a parameter that controls the relative importance between effectiveness and efficiency. Note that $E(\mathbf{S}, q_i)$ and $E(f_T, q_i)$ mean the same thing, i.e., the effectiveness achieved by a cascade $\mathbf{S}$ with T stages (by Equation 1); in cases where we wish to draw attention to the ranking of the cascade, we use f_T for convenience. From the tradeoff definition, it should be clear that as we add more stages to a cascade, the total cost will increase. Therefore, in order to improve the tradeoff metric, the effectiveness gain from adding extra stages must counteract their costs.

Algorithm 1: Boosting algorithm for cascade learning

Initialize distribution $P_1(q_i) = 1/N$, where N is the number of queries and q_i denotes a query;

Initialize cascade model $\mathbf{S} = \{\}$;

for $t = 1, \ldots, T$ **do**

- Select a cascade stage $S_t = <J_t(\beta_t), H_t, \cdot>$ over the training instances weighted by P_t
- Set feature weight α_t for H_t: $\alpha_t = \frac{1}{2} ln \frac{\sum_{q_i} \frac{P_t(q_i)}{1-\gamma \cdot C(S_t, q_i)} \cdot (1+E(S_t, q_i))}{\sum_{q_i} \frac{P_t(q_i)}{1-\gamma \cdot C(S_t, q_i)} \cdot (1-E(S_t, q_i))}$;
- Add full stage $<J_t(\beta_t), H_t, \alpha_t>$ to $\mathbf{S}$;
- Update distribution P_{t+1}: $P_{t+1}(q_i) = \frac{exp(-E(\mathbf{S}, q_i)) exp(\gamma \cdot C(\mathbf{S}, q_i))}{\sum_{q_i} exp(-E(\mathbf{S}, q_i)) exp(\gamma \cdot C(\mathbf{S}, q_i))}$;

end

return cascade model $\mathbf{S}$

4.3 Learning

We now turn to the problem of learning the best cascade model. The general setup is that given a set of ranking features (described later in Section 4.4), pruning functions (Section 3.1), and training queries with their associated relevance judgments, we want to learn a cascade to optimize a given tradeoff metric, where the cascade model is characterized by $\{<J_t(\beta_t), H_t, \alpha_t>\}$, $t = 1, \ldots, T$.

We propose a novel boosting algorithm, a generalization of AdaRank [30], that jointly learns the cascade structure and parameters. It is important to note that we can not simply use AdaRank to optimize our tradeoff metric because AdaRank assumes linearity of its optimization metric O, i.e., $O(\mathbf{S}_{t-1} + \alpha_t S_t, q_i) \approx O(\mathbf{S}_{t-1}, q_i) + \alpha_t O(S_t, q_i)$, where $\mathbf{S}_{t-1}$ denotes the additive model up to stage $t-1$, S_t is a stage and α_t is the local weight [30, 16]. Note that each AdaRank stage consists of only H_t (a weak learner), since it does not perform document pruning. The tradeoff metric T does *not* satisfy the assumption because α_t in our case is not defined over the *entire* stage S_t, since in addition to H_t, the stage has a pruning function J_t for document reduction as well.

Our boosting algorithm for jointly optimizing top k ranked effectiveness *and* retrieval efficiency in a unified framework is shown in Algorithm 1. The algorithm proceeds in rounds to sequentially learn a set of cascade stages to optimize over weighted training instances. Each training instance (a query q_i) has an associated importance weight, denoted by $P_t(q_i)$. Initially, the weight distribution is set to uniform, and is updated at the end of each iteration. At each iteration, the parameterized pruning function $J_t(\beta_t)$ and the weak ranker H_t are first constructed based on the weighted training data. We describe this construction in more detail in Section 4.4.

Once $J_t(\beta_t)$ and H_t are chosen, the algorithm selects the local weight $\alpha_t > 0$ for the ranker H_t, where $E(S_t, q_i)$ and $C(S_t, q_i)$ in the formula denote the effectiveness and cost, respectively, from evaluating H_t on the *reduced* set of documents (after J_t). Intuitively, α_t captures the effectiveness of H_t over weighted training instances.

Once α_t is selected, we add the fully constructed stage to the current cascade model. The weight distribution P_{t+1} is then updated using the cost and effectiveness from the *overall* cascade (as defined in the previous section). The weights on the underperforming queries (i.e., queries that have poor ranked effectiveness, yet are expensive to compute) are increased, so the subsequent iteration can focus more on improving those hard queries. Note that H_0, the first stage in the cascade, is not associated with any pruning. Stage H_0 simply scores and passes a set of top hits $R_{\{H_0\}}$ to the first cascade stage (in our experiments, $|R_{\{H_0\}}| = 20,000$).

4.4 Cascade Stage Construction

In this paper, we use single features as weak rankers H_t, as in AdaRank [30]. Table 2 provides a summary of the features, which are similar to those in previous work (e.g., [18]). We use two families of scoring functions, based on the Dirichlet score from language modeling and BM25. Each family consists of a unigram feature, a bigram proximity feature that takes term order into account (parameterized with a window $S \in \{1, 2, 4\}$), and a bigram feature score for unordered terms (parameterized with a window $S' \in \{2, 4, 8\}$).

Typically, bigram features are computed over the entire query, which is problematic, as pointed out in Wang et al. [28]. Consider the query "white house rose garden": intuitively, the bigram "white house" is more important than "house rose". Computing features for *all* bigrams would be wasteful, so we need a mechanism to capture the importance of different query bigrams. It is accomplished by parameterizing bigram features with an "importance bin". Each query bigram occupies a bin, sorted by concept importance as measured by the *weighted sequential dependence* model [4]. Therefore, selecting the first bin amounts to selecting the most important query bigram. The cross of the feature and the bin is available to the learner to independently select from, thus allowing the cascade to selectively add query bigrams. Note that unigram features are *not* binned.

We note that our cascade model and learning algorithm can work with other ranking features beyond those defined here. Our approach can easily handle hundred or even thousands of features, the scale at which commercial search engines operate. The contribution of this work is not feature engineering, but rather the novel cascade ranking model and learning algorithm.

Let S_t denote the pair $< J_t(\beta_t), H_t >$, where J_t is a pruning function as defined in Section 3.1 and H_t is a weak ranker drawn from one of the features described above. At each boosting iteration, we select a stage S_t according to the following formula:

$$S_t = \arg\max_{S_t} \varphi_t^2 - \left[\sum_{q_i} \frac{P_t(q_i)}{1 - \gamma \cdot C(S_t, q_i)} \right]^2$$

$$\text{where } \varphi_t = \sum_{q_i} \frac{P_t(q_i)}{1 - \gamma \cdot C(S_t, q_i)} E(S_t, q_i) \qquad (6)$$

where $E(S_t, q_i)$ and $C(S_t, q_i)$ are effectiveness and cost, respectively, from computing H_t over the *reduced* set of documents (after pruning).[1] The goal of this optimization is to find the optimal combination of $J_t(\beta_t)$ and H_t that best balances cost and effectiveness over the weighted training data. Several methods can be used for this optimization, and in

[1]Note that for the purposes of the above arg max computation, α_t is irrelevant.

$$f_{T,Dir}(q,D) = \log\left[\frac{\text{tf}(q,D) + \frac{\mu}{|C|}\text{cf}(q)}{|D| + \mu}\right]$$

$$f_{T,BM25}(q,D) = \frac{(k_1+1)\cdot\text{tf}(q,D)}{K + \text{tf}(q,D)}\log\left[\frac{N - \text{df}(q) + 0.5}{\text{df}(q) + 0.5}\right]$$

$$f_{O,Dir,S}(q_j,q_{j+1},D) = \log\left[\frac{\text{tf}(\text{OD}(S,q_j,q_{j+1}),D) + \frac{\mu}{|C|}\text{cf}(\text{OD}(S,q_j,q_{j+1}))}{|D| + \mu}\right]$$

$$f_{O,BM25,S}(q_j,q_{j+1},D) = \frac{(k_1+1)\cdot\text{tf}(\text{OD}(S,q_j,q_{j+1}),D)}{K + \text{tf}(\text{OD}(S,q_j,q_{j+1}),D)}\log\left[\frac{N - \text{df}(\text{OD}(S,q_j,q_{j+1})) + 0.5}{\text{df}(\text{OD}(S,q_j,q_{j+1})) + 0.5}\right]$$

$$f_{U,Dir,S'}(q_j,q_{j+1},D) = \log\left[\frac{\text{tf}(\text{UW}(S',q_j,q_{j+1}),D) + \frac{\mu}{|C|}\text{cf}(\text{UW}(S',q_j,q_{j+1}))}{|D| + \mu}\right]$$

$$f_{U,BM25,S'}(q_j,q_{j+1},D) = \frac{(k_1+1)\cdot\text{tf}(\text{UW}(S',q_j,q_{j+1}),D)}{K + \text{tf}(\text{UW}(S',q_j,q_{j+1}),D)}\log\left[\frac{N - \text{df}(\text{UW}(S',q_j,q_{j+1})) + 0.5}{\text{df}(\text{UW}(S',q_j,q_{j+1})) + 0.5}\right]$$

Figure 2: Definition of features used in our cascade model. $\text{tf}(e, D)$ **is the count of concept** e **in** D, $\text{df}(e)$ **is the document frequency of concept** e, $\text{cf}(e)$ **is the collection frequency of concept** e, **where** e **is defined as follows:** q **is a query term;** $\text{OD}(S, q_j, q_{j+1})$ **is an ordered phrase, span of** S ($S \in \{1, 2, 4\}$); $\text{UW}(S', q_j, q_{j+1})$ **is an unordered phrase, span of** S' ($S' \in \{2, 4, 8\}$). N **is the number of documents in the collection;** $|D|$ **is the length of document** D; $|D|'$ **is the average document length in the collection;** $|C|$ **is the total length of the collection; for Dirichlet features,** μ **is a smoothing parameter; for BM25,** $K = k_1[(1-b) - b \cdot (|D|/|D|')]$, **and** k_1, b **are free parameters.**

this work, we employ grid search [19] to find the set of H_t, J_t and β_t that maximizes the equation.

A formal analysis of the boosting algorithm is presented in Section 4.5 and the proof is provided in the Appendix. For now, we note that when the tradeoff parameter $\gamma = 0$ (i.e., efficiency is ignored), the model simplifies to AdaRank. However, our algorithm can produce *both* effective and efficient ranking models and can be viewed as a generalization of AdaRank's effectiveness-only approach.

4.5 Analysis

In this section, we show how our boosting algorithm can continuously improve the tradeoff metric over the training data. We want to maximize the tradeoff metric T over the training queries:

$$\max_{\mathbf{S}} \sum_{q_i} \text{T}(\mathbf{S}, q_i) \quad (7)$$

which is equivalent to:

$$\min_{\mathbf{S}} \sum_{q_i} (1 - \text{T}(\mathbf{S}, q_i)) \quad (8)$$

Because $1 - x \le e^{-x}$ for any real value x, we minimize an exponential upper-bound of above expression:

$$\min_{\mathbf{S}} \sum_{q_i} exp(-\text{T}(\mathbf{S}, q_i)) \quad (9)$$

In our case, a linear combination of weak rankers is used to score the documents, with pruning performed at each stage. The optimization in Equation 9 is the same as:

$$\min_{S_t} \sum_{q_i} exp(-\text{T}(\mathbf{S}_{t-1} \cup S_t, q_i)) \quad (10)$$

where $\mathbf{S}_{t-1}$ denotes the cascade up to stage $t-1$. For determining a single stage S_t, our boosting algorithm takes the approach of "forward stage-wise selection" [13], i.e., successively adding each cascade stage to improve the overall tradeoff metric. It can be proved that there exists a lower bound on the tradeoff metric over the training data:

$$T \ge 1 - \prod_{t=1}^{T} e^{-\delta^t_{min}} \sqrt{\left[\sum_{q_i} \frac{P_t(q_i)}{1 - \gamma \cdot C(S_t, q_i)}\right]^2 - \varphi_t^2} \quad (11)$$

where φ_t is given in Equation 6, and let

$$\delta^t_i = E(f_{t-1} + \alpha_t H_t, q_i) - E(f_{t-1}) - \alpha E(H_t, q_i)$$

where f_{t-1} denotes the linear combination of weak rankers up to $t-1$ (applied to the *non-pruned* documents only) and $\delta^t_{min} = \min_{i=1,\dots,N} \delta^t_i$, where N denotes the number of queries. This means that the tradeoff metric can be continuously improved as long as the following holds:

$$e^{-\delta^t_{min}} \sqrt{\left[\sum_{q_i} \frac{P_t(q_i)}{1 - \gamma \cdot C(S_t, q_i)}\right]^2 - \varphi_t^2} < 1 \quad (12)$$

That is, this condition is satisfied as long as the gain in effectiveness from additional stages is not outweighed by its cost. A detailed proof can be found in the Appendix.

5. EXPERIMENTS

This section presents experimental results: we first describe the experimental setup and implementation details, and then present an evaluation using TREC data.

5.1 Experiment Setup

Our cascade model was evaluated on three TREC web test collections: Wt10g, Gov2, and Clue (first English segment of ClueWeb09). Details for these collections are provided in Table 1. The topic titles were used as queries, split equally into a training and a test set. Model parameters were tuned on the training set; reported results are from the test set.

We compare our cascade model against a set of strong baselines in terms of top k ranked effectiveness and retrieval efficiency. Effectiveness is measured in terms of NDCG20 and precision at 20 (P20), while retrieval efficiency is measured in terms of average query execution time. Our cascade model is compared against three others: AdaRank [30],

Name	Number of Docs	TREC Topics
Wt10g	1,692,096	451-550
Gov2	25,205,179	701-850
Clue	50,220,423	1-50

Table 1: Summary of TREC collections and topics used in our experiments.

which can be seen as a special case of the cascade model (i.e., optimized for effectiveness only with no efficiency considerations); a previously best-known model that jointly optimizes for both ranked effectiveness and efficiency by reducing the number of features computed at query time (which we call "FeaturePrune") [27]; and the basic query-likelihood model (QL). For fairness of comparison, "FeaturePrune" re-implements the approach and training method (greedy line search) described by Wang et al. [27], using the exact same feature set and objective function as our cascade model. As previously noted, since Cambazoglu et al. [8] focuses on early-exit strategies given a particular additive ensemble, it is difficult to meaningfully compare with our approach.

For training, we used NDCG20 as the effectiveness measure (E) in our tradeoff metric T, with γ set to 0.1. Both the cascade structure and the cascade parameters are automatically learned by directly optimizing the tradeoff metric over the training set. All results are reported over the test set. The Wilcoxon signed rank test with $p < 0.05$ was used to test for statistical significance.

Experiments were performed on a server running Red Hat Linux, with dual Intel Xeon quad-core processors (E5620 2.4GHz), 64GB RAM, and six 2TB 7.2K RPM SATA drives in RAID-6 configuration.

5.2 Implementation Details

All models were implemented in the Ivory open-source retrieval toolkit [15]. Baseline QL, AdaRank, and FeaturePrune work exactly as one might expect: by traversing postings in an inverted index and performing document-at-a-time scoring with max-score optimization [25]. The first stage of our cascade H_0 also works in the same way, using the weak learner that was selected by our boosting algorithm (retaining the top 20,000 hits). However, the remaining stages in the cascade adopt a different architecture. For stage H_1 and subsequent stages, we construct a forward index, which is essentially a list of pairs consisting of a document and a query term, grouped by the document. This structure can be efficiently built on the fly as we traverse postings in the initial cascade stage, by retaining the top documents as determined by the pruning function used in the first cascade stage. The forward index is small enough to be stored in memory and query evaluation for the subsequent stages is performed by iterating over the forward index. The reported retrieval efficiency of our cascade model accounts for the overall time taken by the cascade to return results, including the first stage. Other than this architectural difference, all models share exactly the same code, which makes for a fair comparison. Note that in all cases we used a single monolithic inverted index (i.e., no document partitioning). Based on the method described in Section 4.1, we computed U_T to be 1 for unigram and 20 for bigram features. This empirically matches actual retrieval times well.

One final implementation detail: to speed up pruning, our cascade allows pruning J_t to be performed "on-the-fly" within the computation of H_t, and so it incurs no additional cost. To see this, we observe that all three pruning methods prune input documents based on their rank order, i.e., a document with low score will be pruned before a document with high score. Thus, we simply iterate over the input documents in rank order, checking if each document d_i passes J_t, and if so, H_t is evaluated; else, the pruning/scoring process at stage t terminates (because if d_i does not pass pruning, any document ranked below it will not either). Note that descriptive statistics such as minimum, maximum, mean, etc. can be computed at the previous stage and passed to the pruning function. Coupling pruning J_t with H_t makes pruning extremely efficient.

5.3 Effectiveness vs. Efficiency

Table 2 reports NDCG20, P20, and average query evaluation time for our cascade model, QL, AdaRank, and the FeaturePrune method. For all three datasets, percentage improvements for both NDCG20 and P20 are shown in parentheses: over QL for AdaRank, and over QL/AdaRank for FeaturePrune and the cascade model. Statistical significance is denoted by special symbols in the table.

In all datasets, the cascade model achieves similar (and many times slightly better) effectiveness compared to AdaRank in both NDCG20 and P20, while being much faster. For instance, the cascade is 32.7%, 48.7%, and 34.7% faster than AdaRank on Wt10g, Gov2, and Clue, respectively. This means that our cascade model can equal or beat an effectiveness-only boosting model, while also being much faster. This illustrates that using a monolithic ranking function, as has been common practice for *ad hoc* retrieval, trades a great deal of efficiency for effectiveness. Such costly monolithic models are *not* more effective either since most of the documents they score are not relevant anyway. This also highlights the advantage of the cascade: by progressively reducing the size of candidate documents, it allows for the use of more complex ranking functions for high effectiveness without sacrificing efficiency.

Furthermore, we observe that the efficiency improvement of the cascade over AdaRank is greater for the two larger datasets (Gov2 and Clue) than Wt10g. This makes sense: compared to smaller document collections, larger collections contain more non-relevant documents. Thus, by filtering out these documents early in the ranking process, the cascade drastically improves efficiency and avoids evaluating documents that have little chance of appearing in the top k.

The cascade model also outperforms the feature pruning method in all evaluation measures across all datasets. In terms of retrieval time, the cascade is 12.9%, 44.5%, and 24.9% faster than the feature prune method on Wt10g, Gov2, and Clue, respectively. In terms of ranked effectiveness, the feature pruning method is slightly worse than AdaRank, likely due to removing ranking features for efficiency considerations. The FeaturePrune method behaves exactly as described in Wang et al. [27], discovering a better tradeoff point by giving up a bit of effectiveness for a gain in efficiency. However, the cascade model is able to obtain the best of both worlds: it can achieve better top k effectiveness *and* return results in a shorter amount of time.

Finally, compared to QL, which only uses simple term-based features for ranking and hence is very efficient, we observe that the cascade model is only slightly slower, but achieves much better top k effectiveness. Our cascade model

	Wt10g			Gov2			Clue		
	Time	NDCG20	P20	Time	NDCG20	P20	Time	NDCG20	P20
QL	0.080	34.07	32.40	1.15	44.57	50.93	2.60	27.50	34.20
AdaRank	0.260	35.49 (+4.2)	33.50 (+3.4)	3.90	47.37* (+6.3)	53.60 (+5.2)	6.55	**30.94*** (+12.5)	**37.40** (+9.4)
FeaturePrune	0.201	34.86 (+2.3/-1.8)	33.10 (+2.2/-1.2)	3.61	47.16 (+5.8/-0.7)	51.87 (+1.8/-2.1)	5.70	29.66 (+7.9/-4.1)	36.20 (+5.8/-3.2)
Cascade	0.175	**35.60** (+4.5/+0.3)	**33.80** (+4.3/+0.9)	2.00	**47.44*** (+6.4/0.1)	**54.47*** (+7.0/1.6)	4.28	30.60* (+11.3/-1.1)	**37.40** (+9.4/-)

Table 2: Comparison of retrieval time and effectiveness between query likelihood (QL), AdaRank, a feature-pruning method (FeaturePrune) and our cascade model. Effectiveness/efficiency tradeoff parameter γ is set to 0.1. Symbol * denotes sig. difference over QL. % improvement shown in parentheses: over QL for AdaRank, and over QL/AdaRank for FeaturePrune and Cascade. Time is measured in seconds.

	Wt10g			Gov2			Clue		
	NDCG20	Filtered	Filter loss	NDCG20	Filtered	Filter loss	NDCG20	Filtered	Filter loss
Stage 0	34.07	—	—	44.57	—	—	27.60	—	—
Stage 1	34.91	91.2%^{S}	0.09%	46.34	95.1%^{M}	0.15%	30.05	97.7%^{S}	0.09%
Stage 2	35.23	0.0%	0.0%	46.53	50.0%^{R}	1.6%	30.53	68.3%^{R}	0.18%
Stage 3	35.60	20.2%^{R}	0.04%	47.44	0.0%	0.0%	30.60	10.7%^{R}	0.0%

Table 3: For each stage of the cascade models in Table 2, we compute NDCG20, % documents filtered from the previous stage, and filter loss (% documents incorrectly pruned out of all documents passed from the *previous* stage). Values in the "Filtered" column are annotated with the pruning function that was learned: R for rank-based pruning, S for score-based pruning, and M for the mean-max threshold.

outperforms QL by 4.5%, 6.4% and 11.3% in NDCG20 on Wt10g, Gov2, and Clue, respectively, with the improvements on Gov2 and Clue statistically significant. Similar gains are also observed for P20.

5.4 Cascade Analysis

For the cascades learned in the previous section, we examine their behavior on a stage-by-stage basis in terms of effectiveness and efficiency. A detailed analysis is shown in Table 3: for each cascade stage, we present NDCG20 achieved up to that stage and the percentage of documents filtered from the *previous* stage. The values are annotated with the pruning function J learned by our boosting algorithm at each stage. We also compute filter loss, defined as the percentage of documents incorrectly filtered (i.e., relevant documents which are pruned) out of all documents passed from the *previous* stage. For all three collections, a tradeoff parameter of $\gamma = 0.1$ yields four stages. This is because the cost from adding additional stages outweighs the marginal gain in effectiveness, even with document pruning.

We see from Table 3 that in most cases, each cascade stage processes a substantially smaller set of documents than the previous stage, but always improves ranked effectiveness. As an example, by Stage 1, the cascade reduces the document set size by more than 90% in all three test collections, however, NDCG20 continues to improve in subsequent stages, due to using high quality/expensive ranking features over the small number of retained documents. For instance, our boosting algorithm learns to use simple term-based features in the initial stage for all three datasets, and uses term-proximity features (which are more costly) in subsequent stages to further improve the model's retrieval effectiveness. It is also interesting to see in all three datasets, the first stage prunes much more aggressively than subsequent stages. Because the input document set size is the largest at the first stage, the efficiency of the cascade can be significantly improved by eliminating a large number of documents early.

Also interesting is that in comparison to the NDCG20 achieved by FeaturePrune in Table 2 (which optimizes the same tradeoff), the cascade quickly achieves comparable effectiveness, and then surpasses it in subsequent stages. For instance, in comparison to Table 2, by stage 1, the cascade begins to surpass the final NDCG20 score achieved by FeaturePrune (Wt10g and Clue). By the final stage, the cascade NDCG20 scores surpass that achieved by AdaRank (Wt10g and Gov2). This illustrates that document pruning performed by the cascade improves efficiency while having minimal impact on effectiveness, compared to the monolithic ranking models. This is confirmed by the very low filter loss reported in the table (nearly zero for all stages).

We also observe that at stage 2 for Wt10g and stage 3 for Gov2, the cascade does not prune any input documents. This behavior can be explained by the tradeoff metric—the effectiveness gain from applying the ranking feature on all input documents outweighs its cost, and therefore the optimal pruning parameters at these stages are zero (i.e., no pruning). However, interestingly, the learned cascade for Clue, the largest collection, *always* prunes at all stages, and much more aggressively (e.g., at 97.7%, 68.3% and 10.7%) than the same stages for the two smaller collections. This is because web-scale collections contain a greater proportion of non-relevant documents; to combat this, the model learns that more aggressive pruning is necessary.

Finally, further analysis reveals that relevant documents that are filtered by our cascade are not ranked in the top k documents by AdaRank either, i.e., these documents have no chance of entering the top k even if an effectiveness-centric model is used. The cascade model is able to obtain the best of both worlds: it can achieve better top k effectiveness *and* return results in a shorter amount of time, compared to both AdaRank and the feature-pruning approach.

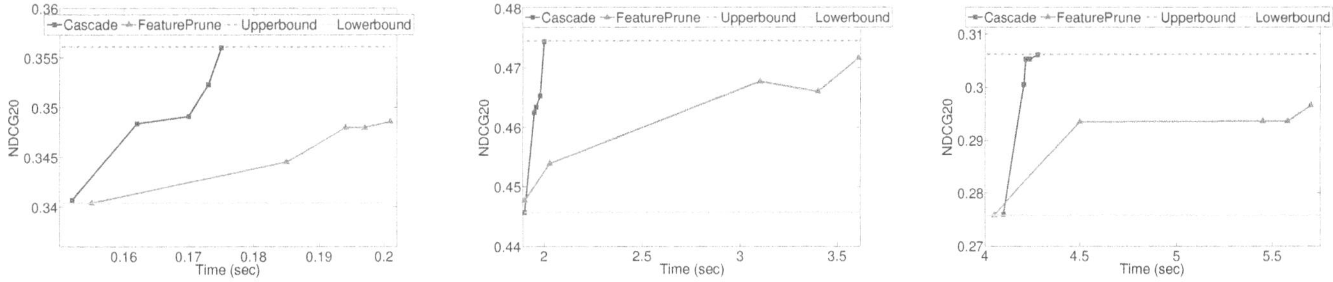

(i) Wt10g (ii) Gov2 (iii) Clue

Figure 3: NDCG20 as a function of time, generated by varying $\gamma \in \{0.1, 0.3, 0.5, 0.7, 0.9\}$.

5.5 Parameter Variations

Our final set of experiments explores the effects of varying γ, the tradeoff parameter that balances effectiveness E and cost C in our objective function T. The setting of γ affects the cascade model and the feature pruning method, but not AdaRank (since it does not take into account efficiency) or the QL baseline (since no training is involved). Figure 3 shows NDCG20 of our cascade model and the feature-pruning method as function of average query evaluation time for each of the three collections, where each point represents a setting of γ, selected from the set $\{0.1, 0.3, 0.5, 0.7, 0.9\}$. Different values of γ produce different effectiveness/efficiency tradeoffs: a high value penalizes costly ranking functions, thus yielding faster models, whereas a smaller value yields more effective models. In each graph, the effectiveness lower bound, defined as the minimum effectiveness achieved under any condition, is plotted as the lower solid line, and the effectiveness upper bound, defined as the maximum effectiveness achieved, is plotted as the upper dotted line.

While in general effectiveness improves for both the cascade and the feature-pruning method when given more time for ranking, the cascade model consistently achieves equal or better NDCG20 across all conditions. It also approaches the upper bound more rapidly as time increases. Although both the cascade model and the feature-pruning method are able to realize different effectiveness/efficiency tradeoffs, these results show that the cascade model is superior in being able to return higher quality results much faster.

We also note that for Gov2 and Clue, the cascade tradeoff curve rises more steeply than for Wt10g. This bolsters our argument that the cascade model works particularly well for large collections. From the point of view of top k ranked effectiveness and efficiency, applying ranking features on a small number of documents is considerably more efficient but can also be more effective (by eliminating many non-relevant documents from consideration).

6. CONCLUSIONS AND FUTURE WORK

In this paper, we introduce a cascade ranking model for efficient top k retrieval, where a sequence of increasingly complex ranking functions is used to progressively refine a shrinking set of candidate documents. We propose a novel boosting-based algorithm that jointly learns the model structure (i.e., the optimal sequence of ranking stages) and the pruning criteria at each stage. Experiments show that our cascade model is able to *simultaneously* achieve high effectiveness and fast retrieval.

There are several future directions. We have only begun to explore the design space of machine learning algorithms for multi-objective optimization in the context of learning to rank: possibilities include other types of objectives (beyond linear combinations), other pruning functions (that take into account more than document score and rank), and different types of weak rankers (for example, decision trees). More work along these lines can further contribute to this emerging thread of learning to *efficiently* rank.

7. ACKNOWLEDGMENTS

This work has been supported by NSF under awards IIS-0836560, IIS-0916043, and CCF-1018625. Any opinions, findings, conclusions, or recommendations expressed are the authors' and do not necessarily reflect those of the sponsors. The second author is grateful to Esther and Kiri for their loving support and dedicates this work to Joshua and Jacob.

8. REFERENCES

[1] A. Arampatzis, J. Kamps, and S. Robertson. Where to stop reading a ranked list? *SIGIR 2009*.

[2] R. Baeza-Yates, A. Gionis, F. Junqueira, V. Murdock, V. Plachouras, and F. Silvestri. The impact of caching on search engines. *SIGIR 2007*.

[3] L. Barroso and U. Hölzle. *The Datacenter as a Computer: An Introduction to the Design of Warehouse-Scale Machines*. Morgan & Claypool, 2009.

[4] M. Bendersky, D. Metzler, and W. Croft. Learning concept importance using a weighted dependence model. *WSDM 2010*.

[5] E. Brown. Fast evaluation of structured queries for information retrieval. *SIGIR 1995*.

[6] C. Burges, T. Shaked, E. Renshaw, A. Lazier, M. Deeds, N. Hamilton, and G. Hullender. Learning to rank using gradient descent. *ICML 2005*.

[7] F. Cacheda, V. Plachouras, and I. Ounis. A case study of distributed information retrieval architectures to index one terabyte of text. *IP&M*, 41:1141–1161, 2005.

[8] B. Cambazoglu, H. Zaragoza, O. Chapelle, J. Chen, C. Liao, Z. Zheng, and J. Degenhardt. Early exit optimizations for additive machine learned ranking systems. *WSDM 2010*.

[9] Y. Cao, J. Xu, T.-Y. Liu, H. Li, Y. Huang, and H.-W. Hon. Adapting ranking SVM to document retrieval. *SIGIR 2006*.

[10] D. Carmel, D. Cohen, R. Fagin, E. Farchi, M. Herscovici, Y. Maarek, and A. Soffer. Static index pruning for information retrieval systems. *SIGIR 2001*.

[11] K. Collins-Thompson. Reducing the risk of query expansion via robust constrained optimization. *CIKM 2009.*
[12] J. Hamilton. On designing and deploying Internet-scale services. *LISA 2007.*
[13] T. Hastie, R. Tibshirani, and J. Friedman. *The Elements of Statistical Learning.* Springer, 2009.
[14] E. Kanoulas, V. Pavlu, K. Dai, and J. Aslam. Modeling the score distribution of relevant and non-relevant documents. *ICTIR 2009.*
[15] J. Lin, D. Metzler, T. Elsayed, and L. Wang. Of Ivory and Smurfs: Loxodontan MapReduce experiments for web search. *TREC 2009.*
[16] T.-Y. Liu. Learning to rank for information retrieval. *FnTIR*, 3(3), 2009.
[17] I. Matveeva, C. Burges, T. Burkard, A. Laucius, and L. Wong. High accuracy retrieval with multiple nested ranker. *SIGIR 2007.*
[18] D. Metzler. Automatic feature selection in the Markov random field model for information retrieval. *CIKM 2007.*
[19] J. Nocedal and S. Wright. *Numerical optimization.* Springer, 2006.
[20] A. Ntoulas and J. Cho. Pruning policies for two-tiered inverted index with correctness guarantee. *SIGIR 2007.*
[21] G. Skobeltsyn, F. Junqueira, V. Plachouras, and R. Baeza-Yates. ResIn: A combination of results caching and index pruning for high-performance web search engines. *SIGIR 2008.*
[22] R. Steuer. *Multiple Criteria Optimization: Theory, Computation and Application.* John Wiley, 1986.
[23] T. Strohman, H. Turtle, and W. Croft. Optimization strategies for complex queries. *SIGIR 2005.*
[24] R. Tibshirani. Regression shrinkage and selection via the lasso. *Journal of the Royal Statistical Society*, 58(1):267–288, 1996.
[25] H. Turtle and J. Flood. Query evaluation: Strategies and optimizations. *IP&M*, 31(6):831–850, 1995.
[26] P. Viola and M. Jones. Robust real-time object detection. *International Journal of Computer Vision*, 57(2):137–154, 2002.
[27] L. Wang, J. Lin, and D. Metzler. Learning to efficiently rank. *SIGIR 2010.*
[28] L. Wang, D. Metzler, and J. Lin. Ranking under temporal constraints. *CIKM 2010.*
[29] D. Weiss and B. Taskar. Structured prediction cascades. *13th Conference on AI and Statistics*, 2010.
[30] J. Xu and H. Li. AdaRank: A boosting algorithm for information retrieval. *SIGIR 2007.*

Appendix

Here we prove Equation 11. For notational clarity, let $E(f_T, q_i)$ and $E(H_T, q_i)$ denote the effectiveness of cascade $\mathbf{S}_T$ and a stage S_T, respectively.

PROOF. Let: $Z_T = \sum_{q_i} exp(-E(f_T, q_i))exp(\gamma C(\mathbf{S}_T, q_i))$, $\phi_T = \frac{\sum_{q_i} \frac{P_T(q_i)}{1-\gamma C(S_T, q_i)} + \varphi_T}{2}$. Using definitions of $P_T(q_i)$, φ_T, and α_T in Section 4, we get $e^{\alpha_T} = \sqrt{\frac{2\phi_T}{2(\phi_T - \varphi_T)}} = \sqrt{\frac{\phi_T}{(\phi_T - \varphi_T)}}$.

$$
\begin{aligned}
Z_T = & \sum_{q_i} exp(-(E(f_T, q_i) - \gamma C(\mathbf{S}_T, q_i))) \\
= & \sum_{q_i} exp\{-E(f_{T-1}, q_i) - \alpha_T E(H_T, q_i) - \delta_i^T \\
& +\gamma C(\mathbf{S}_{T-1}, q_i) + \gamma C(S_T, q_i)\} \\
\leq & e^{-\delta_{min}^T} \sum_{q_i} exp(-E(f_{T-1}, q_i))exp(-\alpha_T E(H_T, q_i)) \\
& \cdot exp(\gamma C(\mathbf{S}_{T-1}, q_i))exp(\gamma C(S_T, q_i)) \\
= & e^{-\delta_{min}^T} Z_{T-1} \sum_{q_i} P_T(q_i) exp(-\alpha_T E(H_T, q_i)) \\
& \cdot exp(\gamma C(S_T, q_i))
\end{aligned}
$$

Since $e^x \leq \frac{1}{1-x}$ for any real x we have:

$$
Z_T \leq e^{-\delta_{min}^T} Z_{T-1} \sum_{q_i} \frac{P_T(q_i)}{1 - \gamma C(S_T, q_i)} exp(-\alpha_T E(H_T, q_i))
$$

Since $E(H_T, q_i) \in [-1, 1]$ we have:

$$
\begin{aligned}
Z_T \leq & e^{-\delta_{min}^T} Z_{T-1} \sum_{q_i} \frac{P_T(q_i)}{1 - \gamma C(S_T, q_i)} \{\frac{1 + E(H_T, q_i)}{2} e^{-\alpha_T} \\
& + \frac{1 - E(H_T, q_i)}{2} e^{\alpha_T}\} \\
= & e^{-\delta_{min}^T} Z_{T-1} \left(\phi_T e^{-\alpha_T} + (\phi_T - \varphi_T) e^{\alpha_T}\right) \\
= & Z_1 \prod_{t=2}^{T} e^{-\delta_{min}^t} \sqrt{4\phi_t(\phi_t - \varphi_t)} \\
= & N \sum_{q_i} \frac{1}{N} exp(-E(f_1, q_i))exp(\gamma C(S_1, q_i)) \\
& \cdot \prod_{t=2}^{T} e^{-\delta_{min}^t} \sqrt{4\phi_t(\phi_t - \varphi_t)} \\
\leq & N\ e^{-\delta_{min}^1} \sum_{q_i} exp(-E(f_1, q_i))exp(\gamma C(S_1, q_i)) \\
& \cdot \prod_{t=2}^{T} e^{-\delta_{min}^t} \sqrt{4\phi_t(\phi_t - \varphi_t)} \\
\leq & N\ e^{-\delta_{min}^1} \sqrt{4\phi_1(\phi_1 - \varphi_1)} \prod_{t=2}^{T} e^{-\delta_{min}^t} \sqrt{4\phi_t(\phi_t - \varphi_t)} \\
= & N \prod_{t=1}^{T} e^{-\delta_{min}^t} \sqrt{4\phi_t(\phi_t - \varphi_t)}
\end{aligned}
$$

Substitute in ϕ_t and φ_t:

$$
\leq N \prod_{t=1}^{T} e^{-\delta_{min}^t} \sqrt{\left[\sum_i \frac{P_t(q_i)}{1 - \gamma C(S_t, q_i)}\right]^2 - \varphi_t^2}
$$

So we have:

$$
\begin{aligned}
T = & \frac{1}{N} \sum_{q_i} E(f_T, q_i) - \gamma C(\mathbf{S}_T, q_i) \\
\geq & \frac{1}{N} \sum_{q_i} 1 - exp(1 - (E(f_T, q_i) - \gamma C(\mathbf{S}_T, q_i))) \\
\geq & 1 - \prod_{t=1}^{T} e^{-\delta_{min}^t} \sqrt{\left[\sum_i \frac{P_t(q_i)}{1 - \gamma C(S_t, q_i)}\right]^2 - \varphi_t^2}
\end{aligned}
$$

A special case is when $\gamma = 0$ (effectiveness-only), this bound is exactly the same as AdaRank's. However, non-zero γ values will induce cascades of various tradeoff behaviors.

Relevant Knowledge Helps in Choosing Right Teacher: Active Query Selection for Ranking Adaptation

Peng Cai[1], Wei Gao[2], Aoying Zhou[1], Kam-Fai Wong[2,3]

[1]East China Normal University, Shanghai, China
pengcai2010@gmail.com, ayzhou@sei.ecnu.edu.cn
[2]The Chinese University of Hong Kong, Shatin, N.T., Hong Kong
{wgao, kfwong}@se.cuhk.edu.hk
[3]Key Laboratory of High Confidence Software Technologies, Ministry of Education, China

ABSTRACT

Learning to adapt in a new setting is a common challenge to our knowledge and capability. New life would be easier if we actively pursued supervision from the right mentor chosen with our relevant but limited prior knowledge. This variant principle of active learning seems intuitively useful to many domain adaptation problems. In this paper, we substantiate its power for advancing automatic ranking adaptation, which is important in web search since it's prohibitive to gather enough labeled data for every search domain for fully training domain-specific rankers. For the cost-effectiveness, it is expected that only those most informative instances in target domain are collected to annotate while we can still utilize the abundant ranking knowledge in source domain. We propose a unified ranking framework to mutually reinforce the active selection of informative target-domain queries and the appropriate weighting of source training data as related prior knowledge. We select to annotate those target queries whose documents' order most disagrees among the members of a committee built on the mixture of source training data and the already selected target data. Then the replenished labeled set is used to adjust the importance of source queries for enhancing their rank transfer. This procedure iterates until labeling budget exhausts. Based on LETOR3.0 and Yahoo! Learning to Rank Challenge data sets, our approach significantly outperforms the random query annotation commonly used in ranking adaptation and the active rank learner on target-domain data only.

Categories and Subject Descriptors

H.3.3 [**Information Storage and Retrieval**]: Information Search and Retrieval

General Terms

Algorithms, Experimentation

Keywords

Ranking adaptation, active learning, query by committee

1. INTRODUCTION

In recent years, a lot of learning to rank (or rank learning) algorithms have been proposed for information retrieval (IR) as an effective relevance ranking approach to ordering search results [27]. Other than document ranking, learning to rank was also widely applied to many real-world domains of application such as online computational advertisement [26], recommendation [41], key phrase extraction [23] and question and answering [37].

General rank learning algorithms follow the supervised learning paradigm which requires large amount of training data that are usually expensive and time-consuming to obtain. This limit is striking in particular for ranking because relevance judgment is query dependent in terms of multiple ratings, requiring annotators to carefully assess not only the similarity between each retrieved document and the query but also the preference order among different documents. Giving a new ranking field, therefore, it is often desperately desired that somehow we can keep the work of annotation minimum while maximizing the effectiveness of learning at same time. Such kind of effort is especially beneficial to the quick deployment of ranking model into different search domains for applications such as vertical search and cross-language search towards different markets.

Domain adaptation and active learning are two general learning paradigms that are proposed to save labeling costs from fundamentally different perspectives. Each of them has been successfully applied in rank learning. Ranking adaptation [8, 9, 10, 11, 17, 18, 19, 40] focuses on the exploration of cross-domain relatedness of ranking knowledge by reusing the training data in large amount from another domain (i.e. source domain) to help the rank learning in the designated domain (i.e. target domain) where no or just a few labeled data is available. Active rank learning [2, 15, 16, 28, 45] is motivated to proactively select and annotate those most informative set of examples, which are expected that, if labeled, they can maximize the information value to the ranking function.

Despite of their different motivations and mechanisms, the two approaches seem to be inherently complementary in a sense that the deficiency of one method can be naturally remedied by the strengths of another. Active rank learning is characterized as the proactive seeking for feedback from domain expert (e.g. an oracle), and it prevents from using prior knowledge that sometimes is abundantly in existence elsewhere. In contrast, ranking adaptation advocates the cross-domain transfer of prior ranking knowledge from a related domain, which is controlled by resorting to merely a small random set of labeled examples in target domain, not allowing for any feedback for receiving more informative supervision. Therefore, we may take advantage of both approaches for the cost-effective rank learning.

There is little research on combining the two paradigms even in the general machine learning study. For this purpose, we need to conquer two obvious challenges: (1) how to effectively bridge the shift of data across domains in terms of different joint distributions of rank features and rank labels; (2) how to select the minimum set of target-domain examples to label that can well represent the ranking information of the target domain. In this work, we propose to combine the utilization of relevant knowledge in source-domain training data and the active selection of informative queries from target domain, where the performance of these two components can be mutually reinforced within a unified iterative framework. Specifically, we first select those target-domain queries whose document order most disagree among the members of a committee, which is built on the mixture of source-domain training data and the already selected target data. Then the replenished labeled set is used to adjust the importance weights of source-domain queries for boosting the transfer of prior ranking knowledge. The two components proceed alternately until the labeling budget exhausts. With the experiments on LETOR3.0 and Yahoo! Learning to Rank Challenge data sets, the results show that our method outperforms two strong baselines: one is based on the random query annotation commonly used in ranking adaptation and the other is the active rank learning on target-domain data only. Note that our method, although discussed in particular for ranking problem herein, can be generalized to other learning scenarios.

The rest of the paper is organized as follows: We review the related work in Section 2; Section 3 introduces the concept of informative knowledge for adaptation; Section 4 describes active rank learning algorithm using query-by-committee; Section 5 presents the unified learning framework of active query selection for ranking adaptation; Section 6 discusses experiments and results; Finally, we conclude in Section 7.

2. RELATED WORK

In this section, we outline the literature related to ranking adaptation and active rank learning. The fundamentals of learning to rank can be found in the comprehensive survey [27], which are not reviewed here due to space limit.

2.1 Ranking Adaptation

In essence, domain adaptation deals with the learning setting where the training and test examples are drawn from different distributions, which is referred to as dataset shift problem [31]. It is hypothesized that common information between two domains can be found and used to bridge the shift across domains in learning. Most domain adaptation studies are focused on classifier adaptation [3, 13, 14, 22, 46]. The main concentration of rank learning is the preference order or the full order of multiple documents instead of absolute class label. It is thus not straightforward to directly apply classifier adaptation for ranking. Therefore, ranking adaptation was received more and more attention.

Usually we have large amount of source-domain training examples, but have only a small set of training examples in target domain. Various ranking adaptation algorithms have been proposed under this setting [8, 9, 10, 11, 17, 18, 19, 40]. In [11, 19], the parameters of ranking model trained on source-domain data was adjusted with the target-domain labeled data. [9, 10] presented instance-based and feature-based adaptation approaches with the help of a few target-domain training data. [40] focused on ranking adaptation among heterogeneous domains. [17] learned ranking models on two domains separately and then constructed a stronger model by interpolating them. [18] proposed a ranking adaptation framework based on instance weighting in a more relaxed setting where target-domain data need not be labeled. [8] modeled a multi-task learning algorithm based on boosted decision trees, where the commonalities among different ranking tasks were leveraged to enhance those specific tasks with only few training examples.

Existing methods assume that the small set of target-domain training examples carry domain-specific information that can be used to guide the identification of relevant examples in source domain and the transfer of their ranking knowledge to target domain. However, this is often invalid since the target training set is commonly very small and is predetermined randomly rather than purposefully. Therefore, it can hardly well characterize the target domain. In this work, we intend to find those most specific target-domain examples to annotate for ranking adaptation.

2.2 Active Rank Learning

The motivation of active learning is to put limited human resource on annotating most informative examples. Many strategies were proposed to measure the informativeness of unlabeled examples. The simplest one is uncertainty sampling [24], where the examples whose predicted label is the most uncertain are deemed informative. Another typical strategy is the query-by-committee (QBC) algorithm [34], where a committee is formed by a set of *diverse* hypotheses trained on currently labeled data. The informative examples are the ones whose labels most disagree among committee members. Expected model change is yet another active learning framework where an example is labeled if knowing its label tends to incur some significant change on the current model. Similarly, expected error reduction assesses the expected generalization error reduced if the label is obtained for an example. The comprehensive survey of active learning is given in [33].

Active learning has been actively extended to rank learning [2, 15, 16, 28, 45]. Based on uncertainty sampling, [45] selected the most ambiguous document pairs, in which two documents received close scores predicted by the current model, as informative examples. [15] chose those document pairs, which if labeled could change the current model parameters significantly. [16] addressed active rank learning based on expected hinge rank loss minimization criterion. Inspired by expected loss reduction strategy, [28] recently introduced an expected loss optimization framework for ranking, where the selection of query and documents were integrated in a principled manner.

A closely related problem to active rank learning is the

active feedback for ad-hoc information retrieval [35, 42]. [35] presented a general framework for active feedback based on diversity-based selection algorithm, which outperformed traditional relevance feedback that simply selects the top K documents. [42] described a Bayesian logistic regression model for active feedback using the variance reduction approach to capture relevance, diversity and uncertainty of the unlabeled documents.

2.3 The Hybrid Approach

The combination of domain adaptation and active learning is potentially more powerful and cost-effective, but so far has not been well studied. In natural language processing, [6] used naive Bayes classifier with active leaning based on uncertainty sampling for word sense disambiguation in a domain adaptation setting. The selection was made in the entire set of target-domain instances. For sentiment classification, [32] leveraged the source-domain information to learn a best initial hypothesis for active selection and ruled out target instances on the source side using the domain separator hypothesis. [36] presented an active transfer learner, where a few labeled examples must be provided initially for training a target-domain classifier which is the basis of active knowledge transfer. In cross-domain video concept detection, [25] proposed a hybrid selection strategy by combining discriminative strategy that selected target instances near the decision boundary and generative strategy that chose target samples unlikely generated by the source distribution. The intent of the two strategies was to deal with the different extent of distribution divergence between the domains. To our best knowledge, there is no hybrid approach studied for rank learning.

3. INFORMATIVE KNOWLEDGE TO SELECT FOR ADAPTATION

Domain adaptation aims to use source-domain training data as prior knowledge to help construct a model for target domain tasks by leveraging the common information to bridge the gap between two domains. Figure 1 conceptually illustrates the high-level data distribution in two related domains. As we can understand, the instances in between (in the blue ellipse) may contain some general cross-domain knowledge and the other two groups of instances fallen apart (in the green and red ellipses) only encode the specific knowledge of their own domains, thus referred to as cross-domain instances and domain-specific instances, respectively.

Note that the source-domain instances (red circles and rectangles) are assumed as all labeled, in which those cross-domain instances (red rectangles) tend to be more useful than domain-specific instances (red circles) for the training of adaptation model. Meanwhile, to annotate those cross-domain instances in target domain (green rectangles) is largely not required because such equivalent knowledge can be obtained from the cross-domain instances in source domain. As a result, no matter there is labeled instances in target domain or not, the most critical issue is how to obtain the domain-specific knowledge of target domain (green circles). If no target-domain instances are labeled, it is reasonable to selectively label some of them for bridging the distribution gap between two domains. On the other hand, even if a small set of training data are available in target domain, it is still unknown whether they can provide important domain-specific knowledge because they are usually *randomly* sampled for annotation. Therefore, it is necessary to *purposefully* select and annotate those most informative instances in target domain for providing domain-specific knowledge which is not contained in the source-domain training data.

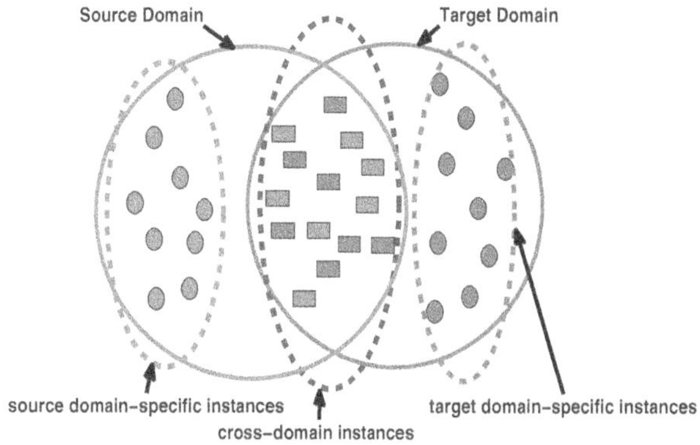

Figure 1: A conceptual illustration of data distribution of two domains. The cross-domain instances from source domain can help in learning the ranking model for target domain. Proactively selecting to label the target domain-specific instances is important to the success of adaptation.

One is likely to argue that with the initial set of labeled data in target domain people can simply perform in-domain active learning with no need of adaptation. We emphasize, however, that since the initial set is usually small and random, one must be dedicated to select wide spectrum of instances to strengthen the diversity of the labeled set. With the out-of-domain training data, it is expected that we need not label the cross-domain instances in target domain as the equivalent relevant knowledge can be acquired from the cross-domain instances in source domain, and thus can only focus on selecting and labeling those most specific target-domain instances for acquiring the informative knowledge useful for adaptation. Therefore, the overall labeling cost can be saved as compared to in-domain active learning.

4. QBC-BASED ACTIVE RANK LEARNING

Before elaborating our entire active rank learning framework in the next section, we discuss some essential issues on how pure active learning is applied to ranking. As compared to active classification, one of the most important differences is that in active rank learning it can be more flexible to choose informative examples at various levels such as query level [43, 44], document level [5, 15, 16, 45] or the combination of both [28]. Both query-level and document-level selection strategies have their own drawbacks. Query-level selection tends to waste labeling effort on non-informative documents when the number of documents for each query is large. Document-level selection assumes unrealistically that the documents or document pairs are independent of queries and may lead to the missing of informative queries or undesirable labeling results for rank learning [28]. For example, only one document is selected in a query or all the documents selected in a query have the same rating. Without the loss of generality, we adopt query-level selection because of three reasons: (1) The generation of preference order patterns are prescribed within the scope of queries. The preference order of documents across queries are meaningless for web search ranking; (2) The informativeness of a selected query is more straightforward to measure with various rank evaluation criteria based on the list of its documents; (3) It is easy to extend query-level selection by further considering the informative documents associated with the query.

In this section, we present active query selection for ranking based on the typical query-by-committee (QBC) technique [34]. The QBC-based algorithm is implemented with two necessary components. The first is to build a committee of ranking models that are well diversified and compatible with the currently labeled data. The second is to measure the informativeness of queries by calculating the disagreement among the committee members on their ranking of search results, which aims at the selection of optimal queries. We describe the two components in Section 4.1 and 4.2.

4.1 Construct the Committee

A committee consists of multiple ranking models as committee members. Previously, different methods for building the committee have been proposed according to the genre of committee members. For generative model, the members can be obtained by randomly sampling the posterior distribution of model parameters [29]. For discriminative model, Abe and Mamitsuka [1] proposed two algorithms called query-by-boosting and query-by-bagging based on the ensemble leaning methods boosting and bagging [4]. We use query-by-bagging considering that most ranking algorithms are discriminative and bagging is a more general and flexible in this setting. Given the set of currently labeled instances D_l, bagging generates T partitions of sub-samples by sampling uniformly from D_l with replacement, and then the committee can be constructed by training each of its members on one portion of the sub-sample partitions.

Algorithm 1 details our QBC-based active selection algorithm using bagging. Suppose we initially have a small base set of queries and their labeled documents (*labeled queries* for short throughout the rest of paper). Similarly, we sample with replacement for T times in the set of labeled queries and train a ranking model on each subset of queries. In step 3, we set the size of each subset to be $m\%$ of $|D_l|$ and m is fixed so that the size of subsets keeps growing with the increase of $|D_l|$. In step 5, the informative query q_i is selected for annotation whose document ranking most disagrees among the T members (see Section 4.2 for the measurement on ranking disagreement). With the required number of informative queries being selected and annotated, the final ranking model H is trained on D_l in step 9.

4.2 Measure Ranking Disagreement

Given a query q, the committee members $h_1, h_2, \ldots, h_T$ return T ranked lists. We need to measure the inconsistency of these different rankings. The query whose documents are the most inconsistently ranked by the members is considered as informative query. All the traditional disagreement measures used by QBC are for classification purpose. Two well-known measures are vote entropy [12] and average KL-divergence [29]. For the KL-divergence-based metrics, the probability distribution of instance labels need be accurately estimated, and it cannot be directly extended to ranked list

Algorithm 1 Active rank learning based on bagging

Input:
N: The number of queries to be labeled
T: The size of committee
D_b: The base set of queries initially labeled, $|D_b| > 0$
D_l: Labeled queries, $|D_l| = 0$
D_u: Unlabeled queries, $|D_u| > 0$

Output:
Ranking model H derived from D_l;

1: $D_l \leftarrow D_b$;
2: **for** $i = 1$; $i \leq N$; $i++$ **do**
3: Sample queries in D_l uniformly with replacement, obtain subsets $S_1, S_2, \ldots, S_T$, each with size $|D_l| \times m\%$;
4: Train on each subset and obtain ranking models $h_1, h_2, \ldots, h_T$;
5: Find $q_i \in D_u$ whose ranking list most disagree among $h_1, h_2, \ldots, h_T$;
6: Obtain the rank label of each document in q_i;
7: $D_l \leftarrow D_l + q_i$, $D_u \leftarrow D_u - q_i$;
8: **end for**
9: Training H on D_l;
10: **return** H;

for the popular pairwise or listwise algorithms. Inspired by vote entropy, we find that the members can vote on each partial order of any document pair $\langle d_i \succ d_j \rangle$, where d_i has a higher ranking score than d_j. Given q and its corresponding ranked list D_q, the vote entropy of q can be defined as follows:

$$VE(q) = -\frac{1}{T} \sum_{d_i, d_j \in D_q} V(\langle d_i \succ d_j \rangle) \log \frac{V(\langle d_i \succ d_j \rangle)}{T} \quad (1)$$

where $V(\langle d_i \succ d_j \rangle)$ denotes the number of votes given by committee members who agree that d_i is ranked higher than d_j, and T is the size of committee. The query with maximum vote entropy will be selected from the unlabeled set for annotation. That is, $q^* = \operatorname{argmax}_q \{VE(q)\}$.

5. ACTIVE RANKING ADAPTATION

Ranking adaptation requires finding the most informative target-domain knowledge as the right teacher for guiding the cross-domain transfer of ranking knowledge. As discussed in Section 3, the cross-domain instances from source domain shown in Figure 1 carry the common knowledge relevant to target domain. Such kind of common knowledge from source domain only need to be identified for reuse but not to be taught de novo since their rank labels already exist. Once identified, such kind of information can be used to choose those most domain-specific instances in target domain for annotation so that the transfer of ranking knowledge can take place. Clearly, two important problems need to be solved: (1) How to identify the cross-domain instances from source domain? (2) How could the identified cross-domain knowledge be exploited to choose target domain-specific instances for annotation?

We address the first problem by query weighting scheme where an appropriate importance or commonality measure is introduced to evaluate the degree of relevance of each source-domain query instance relative to the target domain. It can be expected that the cross-domain queries receive higher weights than domain-specific queries. Inspired by QBC, we approach the second problem by selecting those informative queries from target domain with the help of cross-domain queries that are appropriately weighted. In return, with more target domain-specific queries labeled, it is expected to benefit the weighting of source queries in the first problem.

In this section, we model these two problems in a unified framework to mutually reinforce the source query weighting and the active selection of informative target queries by leveraging their reciprocal nature.

5.1 The Framework

Our ranking adaptation framework is built on the mixture of training data consisting of two parts: one is the source-domain training data appropriately weighted so that the cross-domain queries can be emphasized; another is the actively selected queries from target domain which tend to be those most domain-specific queries with rank labels assigned by an oracle (e.g. human annotator). Note that our method does not distinguish whether some labeled data is initially available or not in target domain. Let f denote ranking function, and based on RankSVM [20], the overall active ranking adaptation framework incorporating the mixed training data is formulated as to minimize the $L2$ norm of hyperplane parameter $\vec{w}$ and the Hinge loss on pairs:

$$\begin{aligned}\underset{\vec{w}}{\operatorname{argmin}} & \left\{ \frac{1}{2}||\vec{w}||^2 \right.\\ &+ \lambda_s \sum_{q_s \in D_s} \sum_{i=1}^{\ell_{q_s}} W(q_s) * \left[1 - z_i * f\left(\vec{w}, \vec{x}_i^{(1)} - \vec{x}_i^{(2)}\right)\right]^+ \\ &\left. + \lambda_t \sum_{q_t \in D_t} \sum_{j=1}^{\ell_{q_t}} \left[1 - z_j * f\left(\vec{w}, \vec{x}_j^{(1)} - \vec{x}_j^{(2)}\right)\right]^+ \right\} \end{aligned} \quad (2)$$

where $z_i = \begin{cases} +1, & \text{if } x_i^{(1)} \succ x_i^{(2)}; \\ -1, & \text{otherwise} \end{cases}$ is the binary value depending on the ground-truth order of two documents in the i-th pair, the Hinge loss terms in $[.]^+$ correspond to the source-part loss and target-part loss based on source training queries in D_s and the actively selected target training queries in D_t ($|D_s| \gg |D_t|$), respectively, $W(q_s)$ is the importance weight of source query q_s, ℓ_{q_s} and ℓ_{q_t} are respectively the number of document pairs in source query q_s and target query q_t, and λ_s and λ_t are free coefficients balancing the volumes of the two sets. Generally, we set $\lambda_t \gg \lambda_s$ because $|D_t|$ is much less than $|D_s|$ and the training should focus on the ranking accuracy of target domain.

We first describe our query weighting scheme in Section 5.2, and then present our framework to combine adaptation with active selection in Section 5.3.

5.2 Query Weighting

Intuitively, if the retrieved documents associated with a source query q_s can be ranked well by the target ranking model which is learned on target training data only, it implies that the document information in q_s is more likely to be consistent to the target domain, thus should be deemed as more important. Otherwise q_s may be incompatible with target domain. Based on this intuition, $W(q_s)$ can be estimated with the ranking performance on q_s produced by the target ranking model. Since the source data are all labeled, we can directly use Normalized Discounted Cumulative Gain (NDCG) [21] as performance measure, which is calculated

Algorithm 2 Ranking adaptation based on query weighting

Input:

D_s: Training data in source domain, $|D_s| > 0$

D_t: Training data in target domain, $|D_t| > 0$

λ_s, λ_t: The free balance coefficients

Output:

Ranking model H for target domain;

1: Learn ranking model H_t on D_t;
2: **for** $i = 1$; $i \le |D_s|$; $i{+}{+}$ **do**
3: Calculate $W(q_s^i)$ by H_t using Equation 3;
4: **end for**
5: Train H on D_s and D_t with $W(.)$, λ_s and λ_t;
6: **return** H;

as follows:

$$W(q_s) = \frac{1}{Z_n} \sum_{i=1}^{n} \frac{2^{r(i)} - 1}{\log(1+i)} \quad (3)$$

where $r(i)$ denotes the rank label of the i-th document in the ranked list, n is length of the ranked list and Z_n is a normalization constant which is chosen so that the perfect list gets score of 1. The procedure of ranking adaptation based on query weighting is given in Algorithm 2.

Note that in query weighting we assume certain labeled queries in target domain have been available for training the target ranking model. In practice, however, there can be no training data in target domain at the beginning, which is to be selected actively from scratch using the source-domain data (see the next Section).

5.3 Active Adaptation

Active adaptation algorithm should select the most informative target queries to annotate for obtaining domain-specific knowledge. Interestingly, we find the selection can be done with the help of source training queries that are weighted properly as discussed earlier. The soundness of our approach is due to the following. Note that the cross-domain queries in source domain are highlighted by weighting. It can be expected that the model built on these weighted training data can rank the cross-domain queries in target domain much better than the target domain-specific queries. In other words, the rank of target domain-specific queries (the queries we attempt to identify) tend to be less predictable, therefore leading to greater disagreement among the committee members. Therefore, the committee encourages the selection of these informative queries with domain-specific knowledge. The details of the procedure are presented in Algorithm 3.

For building the committee, which exhibits adequate diversity in terms of different generalization power of its member models, we need to resample the two sets in step 2 and 3. And then we train a ranking model on each combined subset in step 4, which makes the committee covered at utmost by the training patterns in D_s and D_t. The informative query q_i is selected in step 5. Since D_t is augmented stepwise and each committee member is built on D_s and the up-to-date D_t, the information of each new labeled q_i does not overlap with that in D_s and D_t. Finally, the final ranking model H is trained in step 9. Note that the committee is trained on the mixture of subsets of two domains, which does not change its tendency of choosing domain-specific queries from target domain.

Algorithm 3 Active query selection for ranking model adaptation

Input:

D_s: Training data in source domain, $|D_s| > 0$
D_t: Training data in target domain, $|D_t| \geq 0$
D_u: Unlabeled queries in target domain
N: The number of queries need to be labeled
T: The size of committee

Output:

Ranking model H for target domain;

```
for i = 1; i ≤ N; i++ do
    Sample D_s uniformly with replacement, obtain subsets S_{s_1}, S_{s_2}, ..., S_{s_T} ;
    Sample D_t uniformly with replacement, obtain subsets S_{t_1}, S_{t_2}, ..., S_{t_T} ;
    Train on each S_{s_i} + S_{t_i} using Algorithm 2 and obtain committee members h_1, h_2, ..., h_T;
    Find q_i ∈ D_u whose ranking most disagree among h_1, h_2, ..., h_T;
    Obtain the rank label of each document in q_i;
    D_t ← D_t + q_i,  D_u ← D_u − q_i.
end for
Train H on D_s and D_t using Algorithm 2;
return H;
```

Table 1: The statistics of the two data sets used for adaptation experiments according to different domains

Data set	Domains	# queries	# docs/query
LETOR3.0	HP03	150	1000
	NP03	150	1000
	NP04	75	1000
	TD04	75	1000
Yahoo!	Y!Large	29,921	22.7
	Y!Small	6,330	26.3

The main differences between the in-domain active rank learning (see Algorithm 1) and the active ranking adaptation (see Algorithm 3) are twofold. First, the former needs a set of initially labeled target queries to start the active learning process, and this is not necessary for the latter. Second, in contrast to the in-domain active rank learning, active ranking adaptation can make full use of the prior knowledge from source training data. At a high level, the relationship between ranking adaptation based on query weighting (see Algorithm 2) and active ranking adaptation resembles the connection between general supervised learning and active learning in that the former randomly selects instances to label and the latter only selects the informative ones.

6. EXPERIMENTS AND RESULTS

6.1 Data Sets

We used two data sets for our experiments: LETOR3.0[1] and Yahoo! Learning to Ranking Challenge[2] data sets. The statistics of two data sets are summarized in Table 1.

[1] `http://research.microsoft.com/en-us/um/beijing/projects/letor/`
[2] `http://learningtorankchallenge.yahoo.com/datasets.php`

LETOR3.0 was constructed from the raw document collections of TREC 2003 and 2004 Web track. The raw data were preprocessed into the standard format for learning to rank [30]. In LETOR3.0, each query-document pair is represented by 64 features, including both low-level features such as term frequency, inverse document frequency and document length, and high-level features such as BM25, language-modeling, PageRank and HITS. The relevance judgments take binary values, i.e., 1 (relevant) and 0 (irrelevant). In TREC's Web track, three ranking tasks were defined, namely Home Page Finding (HP), Named Page Finding (NP) and Topic Distillation (TD) [38, 39]. HP aims to return the homepage of the specific organization or person. NP is required to return the page whose name is exactly the query. TD is to return a list of entry points of good websites that contain the contents relevant to the topic. We regard each query task as a different but related domain.

Yahoo! Learning to Ranking Challenge held a track for transfer ranking. This track provided two sets of rank training data of search engines, each from a different country. The larger set (denoted as Y!Large) serves as source domain, and the smaller one (denoted as Y!Small) as target domain. There are total 700 features provided, but the feature definition is not disclosed to public. Some of the features are defined for source or target domain only while some others are defined for both. The relevance judgment of each query-document pair takes 5 levels from 0 (irrelevant) to 4 (perfectly relevant).

6.2 Setup

With LETOR data, since HP and NP are similar tasks but TD is rather different, we conducted experiments on HP03-to-NP04 and NP03-to-TD04 adaptation, where the former setting is for adapting to a similar domain and the latter for adapting to a distinct one. The aim is not only to compare the effectiveness of different algorithms, but also to examine whether the adaptation can be done between domains with various degree of divergence. With Yahoo! data, we simply follow the original setting of the Challenge, i.e. Yahoo!Large as source and Yahoo!Small as target.

We partitioned each set of the data in target domain into two parts, one part as the unlabeled pool for active query selection and the other used for evaluation only. In each round of active selection, we set the sample size as the number of currently labeled queries, i.e. $m\% = 100\%$. For efficiency, we constructed only 2 members in a committee. The free parameters λ_s and λ_t were set such that $\frac{\lambda_s}{\lambda_t}$ is inversely proportional to $\frac{|D_s|}{|D_t|}$.

Three baselines were studied comparatively. The first is the most fundamental one that *randomly* selects *target* queries for annotation, denoted as `Random-T`. This is the classical passive rank learning setting. The second is the pure active rank learning in a single domain, which *actively* selects *target* queries based on QBC using Algorithm 1, denoted as `Active-T`. Note that the first two baselines did not exploit source-domain prior knowledge. The third one is a typical ranking adaptation approach that is trained on *source* training data and the *randomly* sampled *target* training queries for *adaptation* based on the proposed query weighting scheme using Algorithm 2, denoted as `RandomAda-S-T`. Our proposed active ranking adaptation in Algorithm 3 is also trained and denoted by `ActiveAda-S-T`. Additionally, the *super-naive* adaptation method is performed for reference where the model trained on source data is directly used for target domain.

The ranking performance was measured by NDCG@10 (see Equation 3) and Expected Reciprocal Rank (ERR) [7]. ERR is computed as follows:

$$ERR = \sum_{i=1}^{n} \frac{1}{i} R(r_i) \prod_{j=1}^{i-1} (1 - R(r_j)) \quad (4)$$

where r_i is the relevance level of document ranked at the i-th position, $R(r) = \frac{2^r - 1}{2^{r_{max}}}$ is a mapping from relevance level to probability of relevance (r_{max} is the maximum relevance level), and n is the length of document list.

6.3 Results and Discussions

In this section, we present and discuss the experimental results on the three ranking adaptation settings. The learning curves of different algorithms on HP03-to-NP04, NP03-to-TD04 and Y!Large-to-Y!Small ranking adaptation are shown in Figure 2, 3 and 4, respectively. As we can see, there are some general observations based on all three sets of results shown in the figures.

1. Including more training data from target domain is clearly more helpful to all the algorithms except for the super-naive adaptation (the straight lines in each figure) which does not use any target data. However, with more and more training data selected from target domain, different selection strategies tend to converge to some similar effectiveness. We are particularly concerned with their performance gap when not many queries are selected, which manifests the advantage of active selection that focuses on obtaining minimum number of examples.

2. `Active-T` consistently outperforms `Random-T`. T-test demonstrates that the improvement is statistically significant at most of the check points (p-value less than 0.03). This indicates that our query selection strategy based on query-by-bagging using vote entropy as ranking disagreement measure can choose informative queries much more effectively than the random selection. Note that `Active-T` must start from some initial set of labeled queries, for which we randomly choose 5 labeled queries.

3. `RandomAda-S-T` and `ActiveAda-S-T` respectively outperform `Random-T` and `Active-T`. T-test indicates that both of the improvements are significant most of the times with $p < 0.03$ and $p < 0.05$, respectively. This implies that the relevant ranking knowledge from the related domain is helpful to improve the ranking tasks in target domain, which can be successfully achieved by using our proposed source query weighting measure based on NDCG that reflects how well the source queries can be ranked by the target model.

4. `RandomAda-S-T` and `Active-T` are basically comparable. Either one is not consistently better or worse than the other. This implies that the contribution of random in-domain ranking knowledge plus out-of-domain knowledge, which are largely imprecise but abundant, tends to be equivalent to that of using a small amount of accurate in-domain knowledge.

5. Most importantly, `ActiveAda-S-T` outperforms all other algorithms and the trend is evident especially when not so many target queries are selected. T-tests shows that it significantly outperforms `Random-T` ($p < 0.01$), `Active-T` ($p < 0.03$) and `RandomAda-S-T` ($p < 0.05$) most of the times. This implies the cost-effectiveness of our active ranking adaptation approach using out-of-domain relevant knowledge to help the selection of target domain-specific queries. That is, with limited amount of budget for annotating the selected queries, our method performs the most effectively.

Our underlying assumption is that the prior training data is freely available from source domain. This follows the general presupposition of domain adaptation that ignores the original expense on collecting source data. However, from the perspective of active learning practitioners, the cost of out-of-domain training data seems not completely negligible as they might be purchased or built-in-house with initial expenses. How to take into account such cost is an open question. We believe that the initial cost is dissolved gradually as the data are reused repeatedly. Therefore, it's fair for us to ignore it here and leave the issue for future study.

6.3.1 HP03-to-NP04 Adaptation

The learning curves of the algorithms under HP03-to-NP04 setting are shown in Figure 2(a) and Figure 2(b) based on NDCG@10 and ERR, respectively. Several particular observations in this setting are noteworthy.

Indeed the two domains are similar evidenced as the generally large NDCG@10 and ERR scores even with the super-naive adaptation method. This suggests that the model trained only using HP03 performs not so bad for ranking on NP04 as compared to ranking model trained directly on NP04 using limited number (say around 15) of randomly sampled queries. Furthermore, because of the close similarity between the two domains, randomly introducing new queries from target domain does not significantly disturb the original data distribution of source domain. As we can observe, therefore, the increasing trend of the performance of `RandomAda-S-T` keeps relatively smooth and is almost always superior than `Active-T` because the purposeful selection is not an advantage under this situation.

6.3.2 NP03-to-TD04 Adaptation

The learning curves of the algorithms under NP03-to-TD04 setting are shown in Figure 3(a) and Figure 3(b) based on NDCG@10 and ERR, respectively.

Compared to HP03-to-NP04 adaptation above, the two domains here have large data distribution gap. Therefore, it is more difficult for adaptation algorithms to achieve high NDCG@10 and ERR scores. Meanwhile, due to the large distribution gap, randomly introducing new queries from TD04 tends to disturb the distribution of NP03 rendering its predictive power unstable. This is clearly visible when not many random TD04 queries are used. In Figure 3(a) and Figure 3(b), the performance of `RandomAda-S-T` demonstrates some large variations when less than 15 TD04 queries are selected. Since this small number of instances are randomly chosen which may not be the domain-specific ones, they may not be able to help positively the weighting of source queries, which further harms the adaptation. As a consequence, `RandomAda-S-T` occasionally performs even worse than `Random-T`.

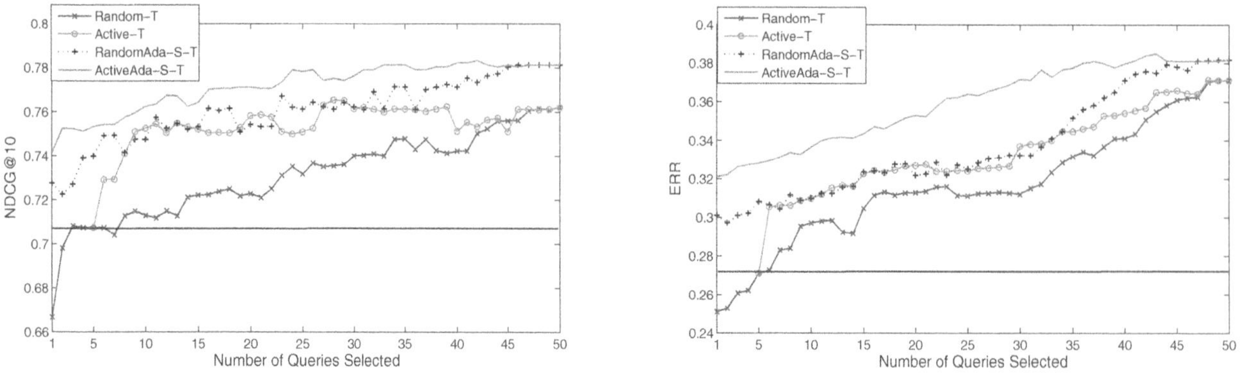

(a) NDCG@10 results (b) ERR resutls

Figure 2: The performance comparison of different algorithms for HP03-to-NP04 ranking adaptation using LETOR3.0 dataset. The source domain is Home Page finding task in TREC-2003 (HP03) and the target domain is Named Page finding task in TREC-2004 (NP04). `Random-T`**: Random query selection in target domain only;** `Active-T`**: Active query selection in target domain only;** `RandomAda-S-T`**: Random selection of target queries for ranking adaptation;** `Active-S-T`**: Active selection of target queries for ranking adaptation. The horizontal straight line is the performance of super-naive adaptation method which is trained only with source-domain training data.**

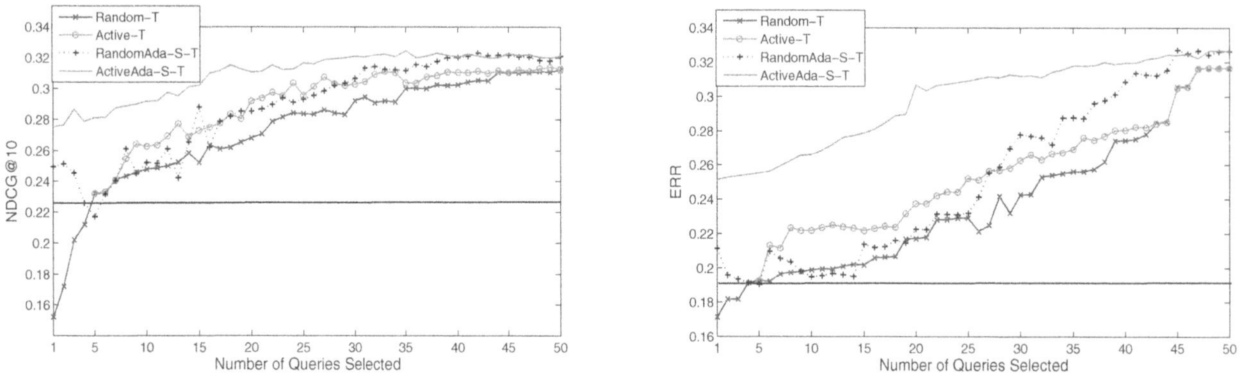

(a) NDCG@10 results (b) ERR results

Figure 3: The performance comparison of different algorithms for NP03-to-TD04 ranking adaptation using LETOR3.0 dataset. The source domain is Named Page Finding task in TREC-2003 (NP03) and the target domain is Topic Distillation task in TREC-2004 (TD04).

However, with more and more queries in target domain used, the target ranking model for query weighting can be radically enhanced, which then boosts the power of adaptation with the relevant prior ranking knowledge. With more than 30 target queries selected, `RandomAda-S-T` can outperform `Active-T` since `Active-T` cannot take advantage of source queries.

`ActiveAda-S-T` does not suffer from this random factor since the target queries are selected purposefully to provide the domain-specific knowledge, which aims to reinforce the weighting of source queries so as to boost up adaptation performance very quickly with minimum cost.

6.3.3 Y!Large-to-Y!Small Adaptation

This set of experiments examine the ranking performance in the Y!Large-to-Y!Small adaptation setting. Note that the feature space of the two domains are different. We did not particularly deal with the feature difference since our method is instance-based adaptation focusing on the selection of instances. We just naively expanded the feature space to include all features of both domains where the missing features were given as 0. We leave the feature-based study for future work. The learning curves of the algorithms are shown in Figure 3(a) and Figure 3(b) based on NDCG@10 and ERR, respectively. Here we discuss some particular observations with this setting.

On Yahoo! data set, we find that `RandomAda-S-T` outperforms `Active-T` most of the times. This data set is characterized as the large scale source training data whose size is approximately 5 times of the target data. The results indicate that the large source data is very useful for the ranking adaptation as well as query selection in the target domain.

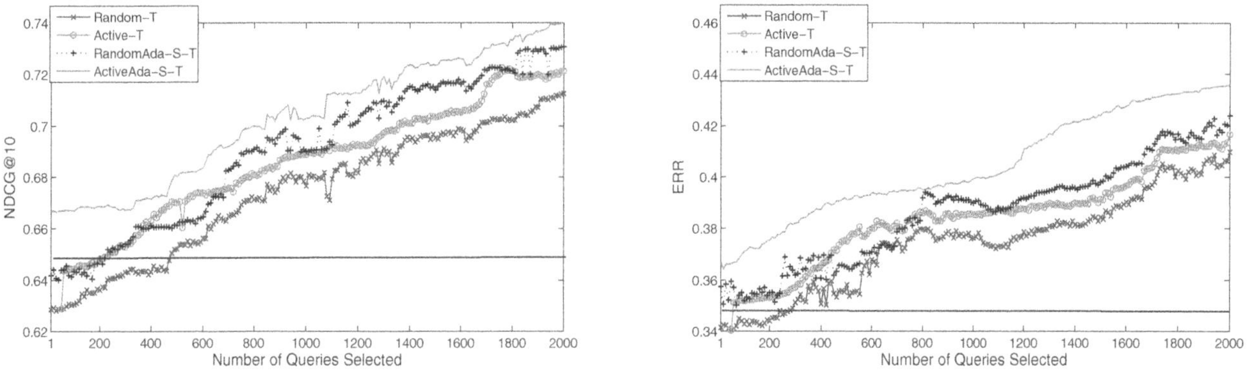

(a) NDCG results

(b) ERR resutls

Figure 4: The performance comparison of different algorithms for Y!Large-to-Y!Small ranking adaptation using Yahoo! Learning to Rank Challenge dataset. The source domain is the large set (Y!Large) and the target domain is the small set (Y!Small).

The explanation is that with lots of labeled data, more cross-domain knowledge can be encoded in the source domain. It is more likely that these cross-domain relevant knowledge in source domain are even more helpful than those most informative target queries identified by `Active-T`.

Furthermore, unlike on LETOR where the performance of `ActiveAda-S-T` converges more quickly than others, we do not observe any trend of convergence up to the point with 2000 selected queries. This is because even the smaller target domain on Yahoo data (Y!Small) contains a lot more queries than LETOR does. Therefore, we can deduce that if with very limited budget, a small unlabeled pool of target data is a reasonable choice to do active adaptation, but if with some large budget, we should use a large unlabeled pool to take the most advantage out of active adaptation.

7. CONCLUSION AND FUTURE WORK

We propose a general rank learning framework by using the combination of active query selection and ranking model adaptation that are rooted from inherently complementary learning paradigms. The idea is that active selection focuses on providing concise knowledge while adaptation encourages the transfer of prior relevant knowledge, and the combination leverages both to improve the overall cost-effectiveness of rank learning. Specifically, we extend and incorporate the essential techniques commonly used in active sampling (e.g. query-by-committee) and domain adaptation (e.g instance weighting) into our unified iterative framework so that the two components are mutually reinforced to boost up the overall ranking performance. Experiment results show that our active ranking adaptation approach not only saves considerable amount of labeling effort but also significantly improves ranking effectiveness.

Our framework provides a general approach that can be used to combine various specific active ranking and ranking adaptation algorithms for cost-effective rank learning. Our algorithm did not outperform the champion of the Yahoo! Learning to Rank Challenge because we just applied the essential ranking techniques such as RankSVM rather than the sophisticated ones such as rank boosting trees used by others. However, the sophisticated ranking algorithms can be tried in a trivial manner. Also, we merely investigated query selection and weighting in this work, but it is expected that our method can be extended without difficulty to document level which will be studied in the future.

Acknowledgement

P. Cai and A. Zhou are supported by NSFC grant (Grant No. 60925008) and 973 program (Grant No. 2010CB731402) of China. W. Gao and K.-F. Wong are supported by national 863 program (Grant No. 2009AA01Z150) of China. We thank anonymous reviewers for their helpful comments.

8. REFERENCES

[1] N. Abe and H. Mamitsuka. Query learning strategies using boosting and bagging. In *Proceedings of ICML*, pages 1–9, 1998.

[2] M. Amini, N. Usunier, F. Laviolette, A. Lacasse, and P. Gallinari. A selective sampling strategy for label ranking. In *Proceedings of ECML*, pages 18–29. 2006.

[3] J. Blitzer, R. Mcdonald, and F. Pereira. Domain adaptation with structural correspondence learning. In *Proceedings of EMNLP*, pages 120–128, 2006.

[4] L. Breiman. Bagging predictors. *Machine Learning*, 24:123–140, August 1996.

[5] B. Carterette, J. Allan, and R. Sitaraman. Minimal test collections for retrieval evaluation. In *Proceedings of SIGIR*, pages 268–275, 2006.

[6] Y. S. Chan and H. T. Ng. Domain adaptation with active learning for word sense disambiguation. In *Proceedings of ACL*, pages 49–56, 2007.

[7] O. Chapelle, D. Metzler, Y. Zhang, and P. Grinspan. Expected reciprocal rank for graded relevance. In *Proceedings of CIKM*, pages 621–630, 2009.

[8] O. Chapelle, P. K. Shivaswamy, S. Vadrevu, K. Q. Weinberger, Y. Zhang, and B. L. Tseng. Multi-task learning for boosting with application to web search ranking. In *Proceedings of SIGKDD*, pages 1189–1198, 2010.

[9] D. Chen, Y. Xiong, J. Yan, G.-R. Xue, G. Wang, and

Z. Chen. Knowledge transfer for cross domain learning to rank. *Information Retrieval*, 13(3):236–253, 2009.

[10] D. Chen, J. Yan, G. Wang, Y. Xiong, W. Fan, and Z. Chen. Transrank: A novel algorithm for transfer of rank learning. In *IEEE International Conference on Data Mining Workshops*, pages 106–115, 2008.

[11] K. Chen, R. Lu, C. Wong, G. Sun, L. Heck, and B. Tseng. Trada: Tree based ranking function adaptation. In *Proceedings of CIKM*, pages 1143–1152, 2008.

[12] I. Dagan and S. P. Engelson. Committee-based sampling for training probabilistic classifiers. In *Proceedings of ICML*, pages 150–157, 1995.

[13] H. Daumé III. Frustratingly easy domain adaptation. In *Proceedings of ACL*, pages 256–263, 2007.

[14] H. Daumé III and D. Marcu. Domain adaptation for statistical classifiers. *Journal of Artificial Intelligence Research*, 26(1):101–126, 2006.

[15] P. Donmez and J. G. Carbonell. Optimizing estimated loss reduction for active sampling in rank learning. In *Proceedings of ICML*, pages 248–255, 2008.

[16] P. Donmez and J. G. Carbonell. Active sampling for rank learning via optimizing the area under the roc curve. In *Proceedings of ECIR*, pages 78–89, 2009.

[17] J. Gao, Q. Wu, C. Burges, K. Svore, Y. Su, N. Khan, S. Shah, and H. Zhou. Model adaptation via model interpolation and boosting for web search ranking. In *Proceedings of EMNLP*, pages 505–513, 2009.

[18] W. Gao, P. Cai, K.-F. Wong, and A. Zhou. Learning to rank only using training data from related domain. In *Proceedings of SIGIR*, pages 162–169, 2010.

[19] B. Geng, L. Yang, C. Xu, and X.-S. Hua. Ranking model adaptation for domain-specific search. In *Proceedings of CIKM*, pages 197–206, 2009.

[20] R. Herbrich, T. Graepel, and K. Obermayer. *Large Margin Rank Boundaries for Ordinal Regression*. MIT Press, Cambridge, 2000.

[21] K. Jarvelin and J. Kekalainen. IR evaluation methods for retrieving highly relevant documents. In *Proceedings of SIGIR*, pages 41–48, 2000.

[22] J. Jiang and C. Zhai. Instance weighting for domain adaptation in nlp. In *Proceedings of ACL*, pages 264–271, 2007.

[23] X. Jiang, Y. Hu, and H. Li. A ranking approach to keyphrase extraction. In *Proceedings of SIGIR*, pages 756–757, 2009.

[24] D. D. Lewis and W. A. Gale. A sequential algorithm for training text classifiers. In *Proceedings of SIGIR*, pages 3–12, 1994.

[25] H. Li, Y. Shi, M.-Y. Chen, A. G. Hauptmann, and Z. Xiong. Hybrid active learning for cross-domain video concept detection. In *Proceedings of the International Conference on Multimedia*, pages 1003–1006, 2010.

[26] N. Liu, J. Yan, D. Shen, D. Chen, Z. Chen, and Y. Li. Learning to rank audience for behavioral targeting. In *Proceedings of SIGIR*, pages 719–720, 2010.

[27] T.-Y. Liu. Learning to rank for information retrieval. *Foundations and Trends in Information Retrieval*, 3(3):225–331, 2009.

[28] B. Long, O. Chapelle, Y. Zhang, Y. Chang, Z. Zheng, and B. L. Tseng. Active learning for ranking through expected loss optimization. In *Proceedings of SIGIR*, pages 267–274, 2010.

[29] A. McCallum and K. Nigam. Employing EM in pool-based active learning for text classification. In *Proceedings of ICML*, pages 350–358, 1998.

[30] T. Qin, T.-Y. Liu, J. Xu, and H. Li. LETOR: A benchmark collection for research on learning to rank for information retrieval. *Information Retrieval*, 2010.

[31] J. Quiñonero-Candela, M. Sugiyama, A. Schwaighofer, and N. Lawrence. *Dataset Shift in Machine Learning*. MIT Press, Cambridge, 2009.

[32] P. Rai, A. Saha, H. Daumé III, and S. Venkatasubramanian. Domain adaptation meets active learning. In *Proceedings of the NAACL HLT 2010 Workshop on Active Learning for Natural Language Processing*, 2010.

[33] B. Settles. Active learning literature survey. Technical report, Technical Report, Computer Sciences 1648, University of Wisconsin, Madison, 2010.

[34] H. S. Seung, M. Opper, and H. Sompolinsky. Query by committee. In *Proceedings of the Fifth Annual Workshop on Computational Learning Theory*, pages 287–294, 1992.

[35] X. Shen and C. Zhai. Active feedback in ad hoc information retrieval. In *Proceedings of SIGIR*, pages 59–66, 2005.

[36] X. Shi, W. Fan, and J. Ren. Actively transfer domain knowledge. In *Proceedings of ECML and KDD*, pages 342–357, 2008.

[37] M. Surdeanu, M. Ciaramita, and H. Zaragoza. Learning to rank answers on large online QA collections. In *Proceedings of ACL*, pages 719–727, 2008.

[38] E. M. Voorhees. Overview of TREC 2003. In *Proceedings of TREC 2003*, pages 1–13, 2003.

[39] E. M. Voorhees. Overview of TREC 2004. In *Proceedings of TREC 2004*, pages 1–12, 2004.

[40] B. Wang, J. Tang, W. Fan, S. Chen, Z. Yang, and Y. Liu. Heterogeneous cross domain ranking in latent space. In *Proceedings of CIKM*, pages 987–996, 2009.

[41] Z. Wang, J. Feng, C. Zhang, and S. Yan. Learning to rank tags. In *Proceedings of the ACM International Conference on Image and Video Retrieval*, pages 42–49, 2010.

[42] Z. Xu and R. Akella. A bayesian logistic regression model for active relevance feedback. In *Proceedings of SIGIR*, pages 227–234, 2008.

[43] L. Yang, L. Wang, B. Geng, and X.-S. Hua. Query sampling for ranking learning in web serach. In *Proceedings of SIGIR*, pages 754–755, 2009.

[44] E. Yilmaz and S. Robertson. Deep versus shallow judgments in learning to rank. In *Proceedings of SIGIR*, pages 662–663, 2009.

[45] H. Yu. Svm selective sampling for ranking with application to data retrieval. In *Proceedings of SIGKDD*, pages 354–363, 2005.

[46] B. Zadrozny. Learning and evaluating classifiers under sample selection bias. In *Proceedings of ICML*, pages 114–121, 2004.

SCENE : A Scalable Two-Stage Personalized News Recommendation System

Lei Li, Dingding Wang, Tao Li
School of Computing and Information Sciences
Florida International University
Miami, FL 33199
{lli003, dwang003, taoli}@cs.fiu.edu

Daniel Knox, Balaji Padmanabhan
DailyMe, Inc.
4000 Hollywood Blvd. Suite 745-S
Hollywood, FL 33021
daniel@dailyme.com, bp@usf.edu

ABSTRACT

Recommending news articles has become a promising research direction as the Internet provides fast access to real-time information from multiple sources around the world. Traditional news recommendation systems strive to adapt their services to individual users by virtue of both user and news content information. However, the latent relationships among different news items, and the special properties of new articles, such as short shelf lives and value of immediacy, render the previous approaches inefficient.

In this paper, we propose a scalable two-stage personalized news recommendation approach with a two-level representation, which considers the exclusive characteristics (e.g., news content, access patterns, named entities, popularity and recency) of news items when performing recommendation. Also, a principled framework for news selection based on the intrinsic property of user interest is presented, with a good balance between the novelty and diversity of the recommended result. Extensive empirical experiments on a collection of news articles obtained from various news websites demonstrate the efficacy and efficiency of our approach.

Categories and Subject Descriptors: H.3.3[Information Search and Retrieval]: Information filtering

General Terms: Algorithms, Design, Experimentation

Keywords: Multi-level News Recommendation, News Entity, Personalization, Submodularity, User Profile

1. INTRODUCTION

Web-based news reading services, like Google News and Yahoo! News, have become increasingly prevalent as the Internet provides fast access to news articles from various information sources around the world. With the gigantic amount of news articles, a key issue of online news services is how to help users find interesting articles that match the users' preference as much as possible, by making use of both news content and user information. This is the problem of personalized news recommendation.

Despite a few recent advances, personalized news recommendation remains challenging for at least three reasons. First, the scalability of most news recommendation services needs more research for fast and real-time processing; Second, news articles are not independent in most scenarios, i.e., browsing one news item may affect the subsequent news reading; Third, the popularity and recency of news articles change dramatically over time, which differentiates news items from other web objects, such as products and movies, rendering traditional recommendation methods ineffective. As a result, many critical issues of news recommendation have not been explored in previous studies. These issues include news selection (i.e., how to effectively select news articles for recommendation considering their unique characteristics?), news representation (i.e., how to effectively present the recommended new articles to facilitate user navigation and exploration?), news processing (i.e., how to efficiently handle large scale news collection?), and user profiling (i.e., how to construct high-quality user profiles?).

In our work, to address the issues mentioned above, we propose *SCENE*, a SCalable two-stage pErsonalized News rEcommendation system with a two-level representation, where the first level contains various topics relevant to users' preference, and the second level includes specific news articles. In our system, we explore the intrinsic relation between users and news articles, along with the special properties (e.g., popularity and recency) of news items when recommending to individual users. Also, the system is capable of efficiently dealing with large scale news corpus.

Specifically, *SCENE* consists of three major components – *Newly-Published News Articles Clustering*, *User Profile Construction* and *Personalized News Items Recommendation*. For news articles clustering, we initially partition newly-published news articles into small groups by making use of *Locality Sensitive Hashing* [10], and then hierarchically separate these groups into intermediate clusters, each of which is summarized using probabilistic language models (e.g., *Probabilistic Latent Semantic Indexing* (PLSI) [12] and *Latent Dirichlet Allocation* (LDA) [3]). For personalization, the user's profile is constructed in three different yet related dimensions – news topic distribution, similar access patterns and news entity preference. Based on the generated topic distribution, we sequentially select news clusters similar to the profile of a given user as the first level of the result representation. In each news cluster, the submodularity hidden in different dimensions of news articles motivates us to incorporate this property into our solution to the second level of the representation. Extensive empirical experiments on a collection of news articles obtained from various news websites demonstrate the efficacy of our approach, in terms of the accuracy of selected top ranking news items and the diversity of the recommended news list.

In summary, the contribution of this paper is three-fold:

- **A novel two-level representation** (see Section 4 and 6): Unlike prior approaches simply providing a list of news items, our system generates a two-level representation, where the first level contains general topics *summarized* from news clusters similar to the user's profile, and the second level includes *representative* items within each cluster. Such a representation can help users easily navigate their preferred articles.

- **A principled framework for news selection** (see Section 6): We observe that the interestingness of news articles with respect to a user could be *regressive*, and based on this "submodularity" property, we model the news selection problems as a budgeted maximum coverage problem [16], which is more realistic than independently selecting news items. The proposed framework achieves a good balance between the *novelty* and *diversity* of the recommendation result.

- **Multi-factor high-quality user profile construction** (see Section 5): We explore the feasibility of incorporating various properties of news articles – *news content*, *access patterns* and *named entities* – into the construction of user profiles. Our work provides the first systematic study on constructing high-quality user profiles using these dimensions. It is with great benefit of using such enriched profile to capture the exact reading interest of users.

In addition, we integrate locality sensitive hashing and hierarchical clustering to address the scalability issue in news processing (See Section 4). The rest of this paper is organized as follows. Section 2 presents a brief summary of prior work relevant to personalized news recommendation. In Section 3, the system framework will be introduced, and the detailed algorithmic descriptions for major components in our framework are presented in Section 4, Section 5,and Section 6, respectively. Extensive experimental results are reported in Section 7. Finally Section 8 concludes the paper.

2. RELATED WORK

Recently, recommending news articles or other document-format web objects has attracted more research attention. Several adaptive news recommending systems, such as Google News and Yahoo! News provide personalized news recommendation services for a substantial amount of online users. Existing news recommender systems can be roughly categorized into two different groups: content-based and collaborative filtering.

Content-based: The systems try to sequentially find newly-published articles similar to the user's reading history in terms of content. Generally speaking, news content is often represented using vector space model (e.g., TF-IDF) [15], or topic distributions obtained by language models (e.g., PLSI and LDA), and specific similarity measurements are adopted to evaluate the relatedness between news articles. For example, News Dude [2], is a personal news recommender agent that utilizes TF-IDF combined with the K-Nearest Neighbor algorithm to recommend news items to individual users. Another content-based method is Newsjunkie [8], which filters news stories by formal measures of information novelty, and shows how the techniques can be used to custom-tailor newsfeeds based on a user's reading history. Content-based recommender systems are easy to implement; however, in some scenario, simply representing the user's profile information by a bag of words is insufficient to capture the exact reading interest of the user.

Collaborative filtering: The systems make use of news ratings by users to provide recommendation services, and in general, they are content-free. Note that news ratings are typically binary; a click on a piece of news corresponds to a 1 rating, whereas a non-click is represented as a 0 rating [7]. In practice, most collaborative filtering systems are constructed based on users' past rating behaviors, either using a group of users "similar" to the given user to predict news ratings [22, 23], or modeling users' behaviors in a probabilistic way [13, 21]. Collaborative filtering systems can efficiently capture users' behaviors in case where overlap in historical consumption across users is relatively high and the content universe is almost static [24]; however, in many web-based scenarios, the content universe undergoes frequent changes, with content popularity changing over time as well [18]. Moreover, many online users do not have enough historical consumption record, which is known as a *cold-start* problem [25]. These issues render collaborative filtering ineffective.

As discussed above, content-based and collaborative filtering systems can provide meaningful recommendation and in case also have some disadvantages. To get more reasonable results, many researchers investigate the feasibility of combining these two types of methods, and propose hybrid solutions to news recommendation. Representative examples include [4, 5], in which the inability of collaborative filtering to recommend news items is commonly alleviated by combining it with content-based filtering.

Our work is essentially a hybrid recommendation approach. What differentiates our work from prior methods is that we model personalized news recommendation as a budgeted maximum coverage problem, i.e., the selection of one news item will influence the selection of the following news items. From this perspective, our work is similar to [18], in which personalized recommendation of news articles is modeled as a contextual bandit problem, where a learning algorithm sequentially selects articles to serve users based on contextual information about users and articles, while simultaneously adapting its article-selection strategy based on user-click feedback to maximize total user clicks. Our work is orthogonal to theirs in terms of news articles selection, since they focus on the long-term effect of recommendation, whereas our concern is located on single-session recommendation.

Our SCENE system is also closely related to EMM News Explorer [1] and Newsjunike [8] in the use of news content and named entities for news recommendation. However, EMM Newsexplorer does not provide personalized services and Newsjunike does not address the news selection, news presentation and scalability issues as we do.

3. RECOMMENDATION FRAMEWORK

Figure 1 depicts a brief framework of our proposed system, *SCENE*. The recommendation is performed by following a two-stage procedure, where the first stage serves to divide news collection into groups, and the second stage aims to

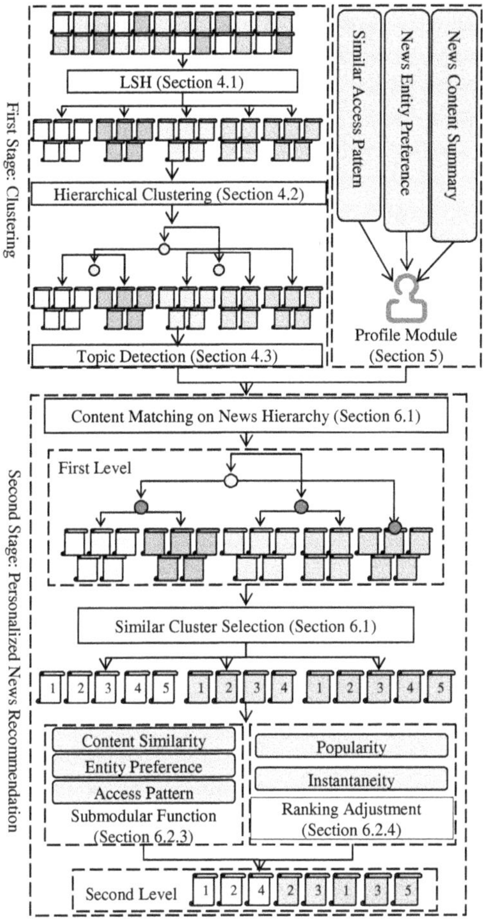

Figure 1: System Framework of *SCENE*.

recommend news items. The three major components in our framework are described as follows.

I. **News articles clustering**: Newly-published news collection is initially divided into small groups using LSH purely based on news content. In order to quickly navigate to specific groups, we employ hierarchical clustering with average-link on these small groups. Then, probabilistic language models are applied to summarizing news articles in each intermediate cluster and small news groups within the cluster. By doing this, a two-layer news hierarchy can be obtained, where leaf nodes denote small groups accompanied by their topic distributions, and internal nodes contain a couple of news groups, representing more general news topics.

II. **User profile construction**: A user's profile is represented as an integrated information capsule, in which three different yet related aspects – accessed news content, similar access patterns and preferred name entities – are combined. All these three factors are extracted from the user's reading history. Specifically, news content is denoted as a topic distribution of the reading history; similar access patterns are generated by analyzing click behaviors of different users; and preferred named entities are extracted from the history using open source NLP tools, e.g., GATE [6].

III. **Personalized News recommendation**: We compare the topic distributions of each intermediate cluster and news content in the user's profile, and then sequentially select the intermediate clusters based on the similarity score, as the first level of the recommendation result. Within each cluster, we continue to compare the similarities between each small news group and the user's accessed news content, and select the most similar group as the base of the second recommendation level. In the selected group, we model personalized news recommendation as a budgeted maximum coverage problem [16], and solve it by selecting news items in a greedy way. Note that when recommending specific news items within each group, the entire user profile is utilized. Moreover, the exclusive properties of news articles, such as popularity and recency, are synthesized into the final news ranking as adjustment factors.

4. NEWS ARTICLES CLUSTERING

Formally, given a set of news articles $\mathcal{N} = \{n_1, n_2, \cdots, n_M\}$, where $|\mathcal{N}| = M$, our goal is to generate a hard clustering result $\mathcal{C} = \{\mathcal{C}_1, \mathcal{C}_2, \cdots, \mathcal{C}_K\}$ on $\mathcal{N}$, where K is a predefined cluster number. Each cluster $\mathcal{C}_i$ is composed of a list of news groups $\mathcal{G}_i = \{G_1, G_2, \cdots\}$, and each news group G_j ($|G_j| = t_j$) contains t_j news articles. Each cluster and its news groups are associated with a topic distribution $\mathcal{T}$ respectively, to describe the latent topics hidden in news articles. The intuition of this representation is simple: news recommendation requires fast response to immediately show the result to users; representing news articles in such way can help quickly navigate to news articles that the user prefers. In *SCENE*, the clustering component lies in the first stage.

4.1 Clustering over News Articles

In reality, large volume of newly-published news corpus requires substantial computational power. For instance, a news corpus with 100,000 news items requires ten billion pairwise comparisons. To tackle this issue, we propose to employ LSH to eliminate unnecessary similarity computations between unrelated articles, and get a rough separation on the original news corpus. In our system, we use a standard Jaccard-based hashing method to find similar news articles. The procedure can be divided into three modules.

I. **Decompose news articles to shingles**: To overcome the disadvantages of the traditional bag-of-words model, we use "shingles" to represent news articles. A k-shingle for an article is a sequence of k continuous words that appear in the article. Before decomposing news articles into shingles, a sequence of preprocessing steps, such as removing stop words, tokenizing and stemming, are executed on the original articles. Since typical news articles are in moderate length, we empirically choose $k = 10$ to guarantee that the probability of any given shingle appearing in any article is low. By shingling, original news corpus can be quantified as a shingle-article matrix $\mathcal{M}$, where rows represent shingles and columns represent news articles.

II. **Minhashing**: In general, $\mathcal{M}$ may still not fit into memory, since the number of news articles tends to be substantial. To handle this issue, we use Minhashing technique to generate a succinct signature for each column in $\mathcal{M}$, such that the probability that two articles have the same signature is equal to the Jaccard similarity between these two. In our system, we construct a length-100 Minhash signature using the technique detailed in [14]. Note that the randomized nature of the Minhash generation method requires further checks to increase the probability of uncovering all pairs of related articles in terms of the signature. Thus, we utilize LSH to increase such probability.

III. **Locality Sensitive Hashing**: LSH [10] is employed to reduce the comparisons, where the generated Minhash signatures are initially decomposed into multiple bands, and for each band, we adopt a standard hash function to hash it into a big hash table. In our experiment, we choose empirically the band length as 5. We treat columns (or news articles) that are hashed into the same bucket[1] at least once as the similar ones. Finally, the original news corpus can be separated into multiple small news groups.

4.2 Clustering over News Groups

When dealing with large news corpus, the number of generated news groups by LSH are still substantial, ranging from hundreds to even thousands. To further speed up the selection of news articles, we propose to hierarchically cluster news groups based on the average-link cross-cluster measurement to provide an elegant global representation of the latent structure of news corpus. Formally, given a number of news groups $\mathcal{G} = \{G_1, G_2, \cdots\}$, hierarchical clustering produces a dendrogram $\mathcal{H}$ of $\mathcal{G}$. With a predefined cluster number K, our system automatically cut $\mathcal{H}$ to get K clusters. The generated clusters serve to be the base of the first level of news recommendation result.

Discussion: As introduced above, we use "LSH + hierarchical" clustering to to separate the original news set into multiple clusters. One may argue that such strategy might result in poor performance in terms of accuracy. Alternative ways of grouping news articles involve the standard K-means and hierarchical clustering directly on the original news corpus. However, these two clustering techniques are not efficient when dealing with large text corpus, and their performance on accuracy cannot be guaranteed when the dataset becomes larger. Also, when recommending news items, we cannot quickly navigate to a small news group that the user might be interested in by using these two clustering techniques. In the experiment, we will verify our claim.

4.3 News Topic Detection

A natural way to explore the correlations between intermediate clusters (or news groups) and the given user's profile is to compare the similarity of latent topics underlying their news articles. In general, detecting latent topics of a text corpus is typically done using probabilistic language models, such as PLSI and LDA, by extracting a list of representative words from the original corpus along with the corresponding weights. In our system, we employ LDA as the language model to detect latent topics, and represent the topic distribution of each news collection located at intermediate clusters (or news groups) as a topic vector, each entry of which denotes the weight of the corresponding word.

Discussion: The PLSI model and the LDA model are similar, except that in LDA the topic distribution is assumed to have a *Dirichlet prior*. Note that the PLSI model is equivalent to the LDA model under a uniform *Dirichlet prior* information, whereas the LDA model is essentially the *Bayesian* version of the PLSI model [11]. *Bayesian* formulation tends to perform better on small datasets because *Bayesian* methods can avoid overfitting. In a very large dataset, the results are probably the same. One difference is that PLSI uses a variable d to represent a document in the training set. As discussed in [3], when a model representing a document has not seen before, PLSI fixes $Pr(w|z)$ – the probability of words under topics – to be that learned from the training set and infers $Pr(z|d)$ – the topic distribution under d. Blei argues that this step is cheating because the model is essentially refitted to the new data [3]. To get a more robust representation of topic distribution, we choose LDA as our language model. A comparison on recommendation results of using LDA and PLSI is provided in Section 7.

[1]In the experiment, we set the size of the hash table to be 1000, which is large enough to distinguish news articles.

5. USER PROFILE CONSTRUCTION

In order to capture a user's reading interests on news articles, news recommendation systems start with constructing the user's profile. Traditionally, a user's profile can be defined by keeping track of what articles the user has read so far (or called consumption history), mainly based on news content. A comprehensive survey of various user profile construction techniques is provided in [9]. However, simply representing a user's profile as a weighted topic distribution cannot effectively capture the user's exact reading preference, as the user's interest might be affected by other users. Another reason of the insufficiency of topic representation is that many news readers tend to glance at news articles, interested in some named entities, such as what happened, who involved, when it happened and so on.

Based on the above analysis, we propose to build users' profiles by the exploration on three different yet related dimensions – news content, similar access patterns and preferred news entities. Each user's profile can be parameterized with a three-attribute tuple $\mathcal{U} = <\mathcal{T}, \mathcal{P}, \mathcal{E}>$, where

- $\mathcal{T}$ represents the topic distribution of news articles the user accessed in the past, in the format of a topic vector $\{<t_1, w_1>, <t_2, w_2>, \cdots\}$, where each entry consists of a representative word and the corresponding weight;
- $\mathcal{P}$ denotes a list of users $<u_1, u_2, \cdots>$ that have similar access patterns with the given user;
- $\mathcal{E}$ is a list of named entities $<e_1, e_2, \cdots>$ extracted from the user's reading history, associated with the corresponding entity type.

Clearly, these three dimensions have mutual interaction with each other. The topic distribution learned from the reading history is likely to be related to the list of entities in the profile, whereas these two dimensions might contribute to the similar access patterns that the two users have. In the following, we will introduce the detailed techniques adopted to construct different aspects of users' profiles.

5.1 News Content Summarization

In our recommendation system, news articles in users' consumption history are summarized as a topic distribution, by making use of the same strategy employed in Section 4.3. The way that we represent users' reading history as the same as the representations for intermediate clusters (or news groups), guarantees that news content matching is applicable to the first level recommendation.

5.2 Access Pattern Analysis

In reality, many online news readers may exhibit similar reading preference. A user's profile information can be enriched in a way of analyzing other users' reading preference similar to the given user, which is essentially collaborative filtering. Under such intuition, we propose to integrate similar access patterns from other users into the given user's profile. Specifically, each user's reading history is maintained. Suppose the news collection read by user A and B are $\mathcal{N}_A$ and $\mathcal{N}_B$, their pairwise similarity of access patterns is defined as the Jaccard similarity of $\mathcal{N}_A$ and $\mathcal{N}_B$. By calculating pairwise user similarities, a similarity matrix can be obtained, each entry of which is the Jaccard similarity between two users' access patterns. The calculation is done offline. Given a specific user u, any other user can be said to be similar with u if their pairwise similarity score is above a predefined threshold τ_u[2]. By doing this, all the users similar to u are stored in u's profile.

5.3 Named Entities Extraction

Typically, in news articles, named entities include when, where, what happened, who are involved, and so on. News readers might have special preference on some particular named entities contained in news articles. Therefore, named entities are important when recommending news items to individual users. To extract named entities, we employ an open source NLP tool – GATE[6], which is capable to automatically identify named entities in texts by predefining a couple of entity rules. By default, we use the rules provided in GATE. After entity detection, each news article is associated with a list of named entities along with their corresponding entity types.

6. PERSONALIZED RECOMMENDATION

Personalized news recommendation is oriented from exploring the relations between newly-published news articles and the user's profile. In this paper, what we proposed is essentially a hybrid recommendation method; however, different from prior approaches, we provide a two-level recommendation hierarchy, where the first level shows a brief summary for each topic category the user might prefer, and the second level gives a specific list of news articles similar to the user's reading interest. In our system, this component lies in the second recommendation stage.

6.1 Interest Matching for Representation Lv.1

Once we generate the news hierarchy and the user's profile, the first representation level can be obtained by sequentially matching the user's profile onto the news hierarchy, and selecting appropriate intermediate clusters. Note that each cluster corresponds to a topic category. For simplicity, we only consider the similarity between topic distributions of each intermediate cluster and the user's reading history.

Formally, the topic distribution is represented as a topic vector $\mathcal{T} = \{<t_1, w_1>, <t_2, w_2>, \cdots\}$. To ensure that all the topic vectors are within the same dimensionality, we create a topic vocabulary $\mathcal{V}$ based on the existing topics, where $|\mathcal{V}|$ is the total number of representative words. When comparing the similarity between the topic distribution of each cluster, $\mathcal{T}_C$, and the one of the user's profile, $\mathcal{T}_U$, we adopt the cosine similarity:

$$Sim(\mathcal{T}_C, \mathcal{T}_U) = \frac{\mathcal{T}_C \cdot \mathcal{T}_U}{||\mathcal{T}_C||\,||\mathcal{T}_U||}, \qquad (1)$$

where $|\mathcal{T}_C| = |\mathcal{T}_U| = |\mathcal{V}|$, and $||\mathcal{T}_C||$, $||\mathcal{T}_U||$ are the l_2 norms.

[2]In the experiment, τ_u is tuned to be an optimal value.

The ranking of intermediate clusters is based on the similarity score calculated by Eq.(1). In general, people tend to have their preference on topic categories, i.e., not interested in all the topics. Therefore, we choose the clusters with the similarity greater than a dynamic threshold[3]. After selecting the appropriate clusters, we dig into each cluster and choose the news group most similar to the user's interest using the same strategy for selecting clusters. By doing this, a list of news groups will be selected, as the recommendation base of the second level.

6.2 News Selection for Representation Lv.2

After obtaining news groups that the user might be interested in, the subsequent step is to select specific news articles to present to the user. We initially maintain a news profile for each news article, and then model personalized recommendation as a budgeted maximum coverage problem, and solve it by a greedy algorithm.

6.2.1 *News Profile Construction*

A news profile includes static descriptors (e.g., topic distribution, named entities) and dynamic characteristics (e.g., accessed users, popularity, recency). Continuous refinement on the news profile will help to optimize the use of the news corpus. For the popularity, it is computed as the ratio of the number of users accessing to the article and the size of the users' pool. For the recency, the score is represented as $(CurrentTime - PublishedTime)/(24 * 60)$.

In *SCENE*, news profiles are helpful to compare two news articles, and to evaluate how the news item can satisfy the user's reading preference. These two types of comparisons are calculated under the same setup. Given a news profile $\mathcal{F}_n = <\mathcal{T}_n, \mathcal{P}_n, \mathcal{E}_n>$ and a user's profile $\mathcal{F}_u = <\mathcal{T}_u, \mathcal{P}_u, \mathcal{E}_u>$, the similarity between $\mathcal{F}_n$ and $\mathcal{F}_u$ is computed as

$$Sim(\mathcal{F}_n, \mathcal{F}_u) = \frac{\alpha Sim(\mathcal{T}_n, \mathcal{T}_u) + \beta Sim(\mathcal{P}_n, \mathcal{P}_u) + \gamma Sim(\mathcal{E}_n, \mathcal{E}_u)}{\sqrt{\alpha^2 + \beta^2 + \gamma^2}}, \qquad (2)$$

where α, β and γ are parameters to control how we trust the corresponding components. $Sim(\mathcal{T}_n, \mathcal{T}_u)$ is computed by Eq.(1), whereas $Sim(\mathcal{P}_n, \mathcal{P}_u)$ and $Sim(\mathcal{E}_n, \mathcal{E}_u)$ are calculated by the Jaccard similarity.

Discussion: As noted, three components in Eq.(2) evaluate the similarities of news content, access patterns and preferred named entities, respectively. In prior approaches, either news content, or access pattern, or their combination is considered. Comparatively, we assign equal importance to these three factors in our recommender system, since they represent different yet related aspects of news articles or users' profiles. In Section 7, we present our evaluation on the effects of different combinations of these three factors.

6.2.2 *Introduction to Submodularity*

Let E be a finite set and f be a real valued nondecreasing function defined on the subsets of E that satisfies

$$f(T \cup \{\varsigma\}) - f(T) \leqslant f(S \cup \{\varsigma\}) - f(S), \qquad (3)$$

where $S \subseteq T$, S and T are two subsets of E, and $\varsigma \in E \setminus T$. Such a function f is called a **submodular** function [20]. Intuitively, by adding one element to a larger set T, the value increment of f can never be larger than that by adding

[3]The dynamic threshold is set to be the median of all similarity scores with respect to a specific user's profile.

one element to a smaller set S. This intuitive diminishing property exists in different areas, e.g., in social network, adding one new friend cannot increase more social influence for a more social group than for a less social group.

The budgeted maximum coverage problem is then described as: given a set of elements E where each element is associated with an influence and a cost defined over a domain of these elements and a budget B, the goal is to find out a subset of E which has the largest possible influence while the total cost does not exceed B. This problem is NP-hard [16]. However, [16] proposed a greedy algorithm which sequentially picks up the element that increases the largest possible influence within the cost limit and it guarantees the influence of the result subset is $(1-1/e)$-approximation. Submodularity resides in each "pick up" step. A key observation is that submodular functions are closed under non-negative linear combinations [17].

6.2.3 Submodularity Model for Recommendation

In a particular news group, most of news articles concentrate on similar or even the same topic, with minor difference on major aspects of the corresponding topic. For example, given a news group talking about a popular movie "*Inception*", one piece of news may focus on the actor cast of this movie, while another may describe the high-end techniques used in this movie. Typically, a news reader is interested in some specific aspects of the given topic, but not all of them. Based on this intuition, our news selection strategy can be described as follows (note that $\mathcal{N}$ denotes the original news group, $\mathcal{S}$ represents the selected news set, and ς is the news item being selected). After selecting ς,

- $\mathcal{S}$ should be similar to the general topic in $\mathcal{N} \setminus \mathcal{S}$;
- The topic diversity should not deviate much in $\mathcal{S}$;
- $\mathcal{S}$ should provide more satisfaction to the given user's reading preference.

Per the above strategy, we define a quality function f to evaluate the current selected news set $\mathcal{S}$ over the entire news group $\mathcal{N}$ as

$$f(\mathcal{S}) = \frac{1}{|\mathcal{N}\setminus\mathcal{S}|\cdot|\mathcal{S}|}\sum_{n_1\in\mathcal{N}\setminus\mathcal{S}}\sum_{n_2\in\mathcal{S}} sim(n_1,n_2) + \frac{1}{\binom{|\mathcal{S}|}{2}}\sum_{\substack{n_1,n_2\in\mathcal{S}\\ n_1\neq n_2}} -sim(n_1,n_2) + \frac{1}{|\mathcal{S}|}\sum_{n_1\in\mathcal{S}} sim(u,n_1), \quad (4)$$

where n_1 and n_2 denote news items, u represents the given user, and $sim(\cdot,\cdot)$ represents the similarity between two profiles, either the user profile or the news profile.

In Eq.(4), three components are involved, corresponding to the news selection strategy we list above. The first one aims to evaluate the quality of how representative that the selected news set $\mathcal{S}$ is over the original news set; the second one provides a perspective on how diverse that the topics underlying the selected news articles are; and the last component gives us the evidence that how much the user's preference is satisfied by the selected news set $\mathcal{S}$. $f(\mathcal{S})$ balances the contributions of different components. Note that all these three components are naturally submodular functions. Based on the non-negative linear invariability of the submodular function, $f(\mathcal{S})$ is also a submodular function. Suppose ς is the candidate news article, the quality increase is therefore represented as follows:

$$I(\varsigma) = f(\mathcal{S}\cup\{\varsigma\}) - f(\mathcal{S}). \quad (5)$$

The goal is to select a list of news articles which provide the largest possible quality increase within the budget[4]. Hence, personalized news recommendation is transformed to the budgeted maximum coverage problem.

In each news group, a greedy algorithm is employed to solve the budgeted maximum coverage problem, by sequentially selecting the news article providing the largest quality increase based on the selected news set until the budget is reached. To integrate recommended news items from different news groups into the final recommendation list, we select top ranking items within each group, where the number of items selected in one group is proportional to the interest weight of the user on the corresponding topic category.

Discussion: The submodularity-based news selection strategy provides us a diverse news recommendation list within each topic category. In addition, multiple topic categories are recommended to individual users, by which the diversity of the final recommendation result is explicitly enriched to a great extent. In Section 7, we will present detailed evaluation to verify our claim.

6.2.4 Ranking Adjustment

By adopting the greedy algorithm introduced above, we can obtain a list of news articles for each topic category. Taking into account the exclusive characteristics of news articles, e.g., the popularity and the recency, the ranking of the selected news articles needs to be adjusted in order to make the recommendation result more reasonable.

In our system, the popularity and the recency of news articles are maintained in news profiles, as described in Section 6.2.1. When doing adjustment on the selected news list, we combine the normalized values of these two types of properties. Formally, given a news article n, the popularity $n_{\mathcal{P}}$ and the recency $n_{\mathcal{I}}$ can be combined as

$$n_\phi = \frac{n_{\mathcal{P}} - n_{\mathcal{P}_{min}}}{n_{\mathcal{P}_{max}} - n_{\mathcal{P}_{min}}} - \frac{n_{\mathcal{I}} - n_{\mathcal{I}_{min}}}{n_{\mathcal{I}_{max}} - n_{\mathcal{I}_{min}}}. \quad (6)$$

Note that the recency is restricted by time; the smaller it is, the higher ranking the article is. Given a ranking list of news articles, we sequentially select two adjacent news items n_i and n_j from top to bottom, and compare their dynamic score n_ϕ. If $n_{\phi_j} - n_{\phi_i}$ is larger than 0, we swap the order of n_i and n_j; otherwise, we skip them and continue to compare the next article pair. By such minor adjustment, the generated ranking can emphasize more popular and fresh news items, as well as concentrating on news articles that satisfy the user's reading preference.

7. EXPERIMENTAL EVALUATION

In this section, we provide a comprehensive experimental evaluation to show the efficacy and efficiency of our proposed news recommendation system, *SCENE*. We start with an introduction to a real-world news collection obtained from multiple news service websites, and then describe the experimental design based on the recommendation framework introduced in Section 3.

[4]Here the budget can be regarded as the maximum number of recommended items in each news group.

7.1 Real World Dataset

For experiments, we gather news articles along with users' access history from popular news websites which contain multiple news topic categories, such as sports, movies and politics. We gather the news data for 9 categories on purpose, where the data collection ranges from Aug 15th, 2010 to Nov 16th, 2010. In order to embody the role of similar access patterns in users' profiles, we preprocess the data by removing news articles that are rarely accessed (i.e., the accessed frequency is less than 10 times per day) and by storing users with frequent online reading behaviors (i.e., users who read news articles every day and read more than 10 pieces of news each day). After preprocessing, 112,380 news items are stored, with 4,630 users, each day in average with 1,221 news articles.

7.2 Experiments

SCENE contains three major components: (a) An offline component responsible for periodically clustering news articles published within a time range; (b) An online component of dynamically constructing and updating user profiles; and (c) An online component capable to recommend news articles to individual users based on the generated cluster hierarchy and user profiles. From the experimental perspective, we verify our system components separately, where Component a is tested in an offline manner, and Component b and c are tested under a unified online environment. In the following we will describe the detailed experiments, along with a user study to evaluate the real-world users' satisfaction.

7.2.1 Clustering Evaluation

To evaluate the performance of the clustering component, we provide three different comparisons: (i) "LSH + Hierarchical" clustering against direct clustering on news articles; (ii) hierarchical clustering against K-means on news groups; and (iii) LDA against PLSI on topic detection.

I : *"LSH + Hierarchical" Clustering* V.S. *Direct Clustering*

We select multiple time ranges with different intervals and run the clustering procedure on news articles from these time ranges. We also implement the general K-means and hierarchical clustering with average-link, to compare the F-measure and the time cost. All the clustering algorithms are implemented using Java and tested under the same experimental environment. For K-means and hierarchical clustering, we represent each news article using vector space model, each entry of which is denoted by TF-IDF value of the corresponding term. For each time range, we execute different algorithms 10 times respectively, except hierarchical clustering, and compare micro-averaging $F1$ and macro-averaging $F1$ to evaluate the average performance across multiple clusters with different cardinality. The number of clusters is set to be the number of categories introduced in Section 7.1.

Table 1 lists the clustering evaluation results. Statistical significance test is performed on $F1$ scores and shows the significance of the combined clustering technique; however, due to the space limit, the test is not reported. Based on the comparison, we observe that: (i) Our proposed "LSH + Hierarchical" clustering on news collection significantly outperforms the general K-means and hierarchical clustering techniques in terms of accuracy and efficiency. A straightforward explanation for the accuracy increase is that *SCENE* uses shingles to represent news articles. Shingling aims to separate articles into shingles where the probability of any given shingle appearing in any article is low. In this way, similar articles will have more shingles in common, whereas dissimilar articles share rarely few shingles. (ii) The accuracy of K-means and hierarchical clustering on news corpus decreases when the volume of the dataset increases.

II : *Hierarchical Clustering* V.S. *K-means Clustering*

An alternative approach to divide the news corpus into news groups is K-means clustering. In this section, we provide comparison between K-means and hierarchical clustering on news groups. We select 10 time ranges with 3-days interval, and run LSH on news articles located in these ranges. Then we apply K-means and hierarchical clustering with average-link on small news groups, respectively. For evaluation purpose, we randomly select 100 users and recommend news articles to them. The recommendation result consists of top 30 news articles. We evaluate the averaged *precision*, *recall* and *F-score* based on the 100 users' actual reading history in these time ranges. Table 2 represents the comparison results. We can observe that hierarchical clustering based system outperforms its rival to a great extent, which verifies our claim in Section 4.2. Statistical significance test is performed on F-scores and demonstrates the qualification of hierarchical clustering on news groups.

Time Range	# of Articles	K-means			Hierarchical(average-link)		
		P	R	F	P	R	F
08/20–08/22	3,340	0.1892	0.3115	0.2241	0.2935	0.4073	0.3406
09/06–09/08	2,985	0.2031	0.3230	0.2408	0.3016	0.4252	0.3512
09/23–09/25	3,920	0.1938	0.2988	0.2376	0.2863	0.3908	0.3389
10/18–10/20	2,807	0.2101	0.3296	0.2492	0.2997	0.4186	0.3557
11/03–11/05	3,742	0.1834	0.3053	0.2283	0.2874	0.3922	0.3392
Average	3.305	0.1959	0.3136	0.2360	**0.2937**	**0.4068**	**0.3451**

Table 2: Comparison between K-means based and hierarchical clustering based systems.

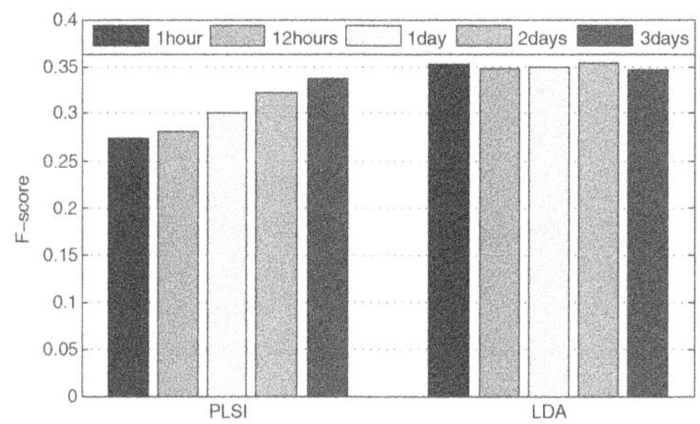

Figure 2: Recommendation F-score of different time periods for PLSI-based and LDA-based systems.

III : *LDA* V.S. *PLSI*

In reality, news article clustering happens per day, or even per hour. The number of news events happened in a small time range may be at a scale of hundreds or thousands, but not more in regular. Based on our analysis in Section 4.3, LDA tends to perform better than PLSI in terms of topic detection when the dataset is relatively small. In order to verify this claim, we design the experiment as follows: (1) use 1 hour, 12 hours, 1 day, 2 days, and 3 days as the time periods; (2) for each time period, randomly select 10 time ranges, and extract news articles in these time ranges; (3) perform PLSI and LDA on these news sets respectively; (4) perform top 30 news recommendation to 100 users randomly

Time Range	# of Articles	K-means			Hierarchical(average-link)			"LSH + Hierarchical"		
		Micro-F1	Macro-F1	Time Cost	Micro-F1	Macro-F1	Time Cost	Micro-F1	Macro-F1	Time Cost
08/15–08/16	2,340	0.4530	0.3744	3min	0.4398	0.3551	5min	0.5016	0.4622	2min
08/19–08/22	5,572	0.4365	0.3653	5min	0.4207	0.3506	9min	0.4897	0.4406	4min
08/23–08/31	10,985	0.4227	0.3421	10min	0.4156	0.3412	15min	0.4902	0.4535	7min
09/01–09/15	18,841	0.3962	0.3302	21min	0.3820	0.3409	25min	0.4830	0.4480	10min
09/01–09/30	35,920	0.3783	0.3153	38min	0.3777	0.3344	50min	0.5128	0.4598	15min
10/01–11/16	63,659	0.3529	0.2976	59min	0.3755	0.3220	78min	0.5239	0.4679	25min
08/15–11/16	112,380	0.3217	0.2711	121min	0.3622	0.3118	152min	0.5093	0.4506	38min
Average	–	0.3945	0.3280	–	0.3962	0.3367	–	**0.5015**	**0.4547**	–

Table 1: "LSH + Hierarchical" Clustering V.S. Direct Clustering.

selected from the users' pool; and (5) compute the average F-score for PLSI-based and LDA-based systems. The result is shown as in Figure 2.

From the result, we have the following observations: (i) LDA-based recommender system has stable recommendation performance in terms of F-score, regardless of different size of news corpus; and (ii) PLSI-based recommender system has comparable results when the news corpus becomes larger. However, when the dataset is relatively small, the performance of PLSI-based system is comparatively lower than LDA-based system. Essentially, it results from overfitting when the dataset is small, and verifies our claim in Section 4.3. Therefore, the probabilistic language model LDA is more applicable to our news recommendation system.

7.2.2 Profile Evaluation

In our system, we propose to utilize three different yet relevant types of information to construct users' profiles – *news content*, *similar access pattern* and *named entities preference*. Prior approaches often use one or both of "news content" and "similar access pattern" to fulfill the recommendation requirement. However, based on our analysis in Section 5, news readers might have more interest on named entities appeared in news articles. In order to evaluate the performance of our hybrid approach, we test the effect of each possible combination of the three factors to the recommendation results[5]. Specifically, we select 100 users from the users' pool, randomly pick up 10 time ranges with 3-day interval from our news dataset, and recommend news items (top @10, @20 and @30) to these users based on different aspect combinations. For comparison, we compute the averaged F-score of recommendation results for the 100 selected users over 10 time ranges. Figure 3 depicts the result.

From the comparison, we observe that: (i) our hybrid approach that considers all the three aspects always performs the best. (ii) recommendation purely based on one single aspect cannot outperform the system based on the combinations. The reason is straightforward: more intrinsic properties of news articles and users' profiles can be revealed as we take more aspects into account. (iii) recommender systems with preferred named entities involved perform better than the ones without considering named entities. This observation verifies our claim that news readers tend to show more interest on simple but representative named entities contained in news articles.

In order to find similar access patterns for a given user, we use a threshold τ_u to eliminate irrelevant users. To find an optimal value for τ_u, we adopt the same experimental setup with the above procedure, except that when selecting

[5]For simplicity, we set $\alpha = \beta = \gamma = 1$ in Eq.(2).

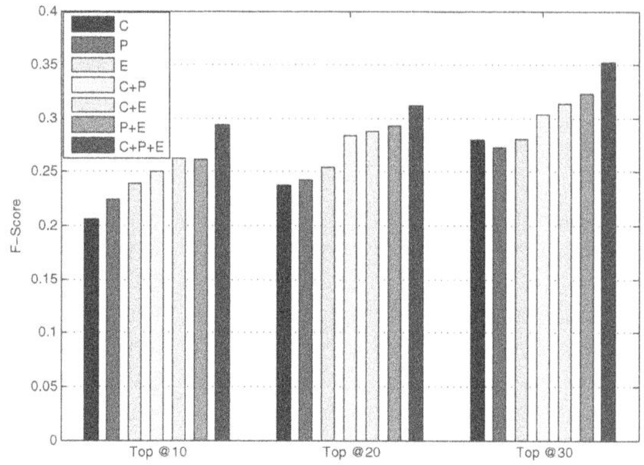

Figure 3: Recommendation F-score of different combinations of profile factors. Remark: C – News Content; P – Similar Access Pattern; E – Preferred Named Entities.

news articles, we only consider the effect of similar access pattern. As we change the value of τ_u, averaged F-scores of the recommendation results are observed. The tuning result is shown in Figure 4. As is depicted, for top @10, @20, @30 recommended news articles, the performance achieves the best when $\tau_u = 0.25$. Therefore, we set τ_u as 0.25 for *SCENE*.

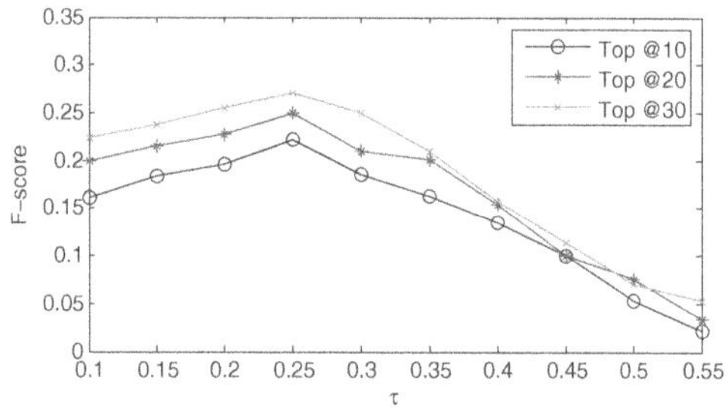

Figure 4: τ_u tuning curve.

7.2.3 Selection Strategy Evaluation

In order to verify the effectiveness of our proposed news selection strategy, we provide detailed comparison between ours and the general greedy selection strategy simply based on pairwise similarities. Also, we implement a recommender system that models the recommendation as a contextual bandit problem [18], as the comparison base. For each approach, we randomly select 100 users to provide recommendations for them. We plot the precision and recall pair for each user on top @10, @20, and @30 news items recommended to these users. Figure 5 shows the comparison results. From Figure 5, we observe that besides the higher precision and recall, the performance distribution of *SCENE* is more compact than the other methods, which demonstrates the stability of our proposed news selection strategy.

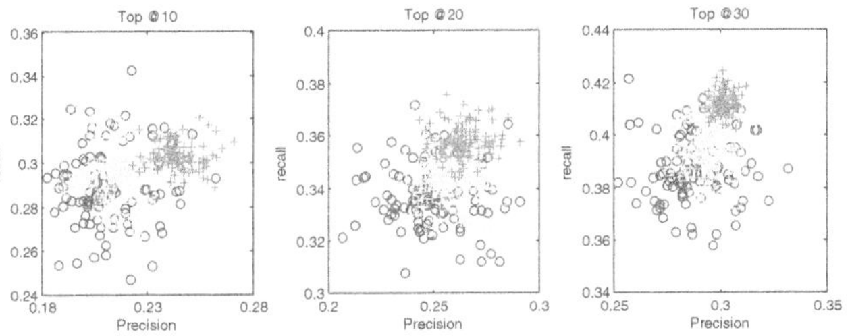

Figure 5: Precision-recall plot for different news selection strategies. Remark: "◯" represents users using the general greedy-based recommender system; "□" denotes users using the bandit-based recommender system; and "+" represents users using *SCENE*.

In the above experiments, all the users are equally treated as the experimental subject. In reality, users with different news access patterns, such as different reading frequency every day, may have distinct patterns of news topic preference, and therefore the dynamic interest on news articles may vary a lot. In addition, many news recommendation systems cannot address the so-called "cold-start" problem. In order to verify the performance of our proposed algorithm on different user groups, we separate the selected users into three groups based on their reading habits. Suppose a user reads N news articles per day, then the three groups are: (i) $N \leq 10$; (ii) $10 < N \leq 50$; (iii) $N > 50$. We apply different algorithms on these three users groups with top @10, top @20 and top @30 recommended news, and record the F1-score respectively. Here, the comparison base includes two existing approaches: [7] (Goo) and [19] (ClickB). The former is a collaborative filtering based method, whereas the latter is a content-based method. Figure 6 shows the comparison results. From the comparison, we observe that our system *SCENE* can achieve a reasonable recommendation result when it is subject to the "cold-start" problem. The reason is that besides considering similar access patterns when recommending news articles to individual users, we also measure the importance of news content and named entities preferred by news readers.

7.2.4 Diversity Evaluation

The recommendation news list provided by *SCENE* shows a great diversity on both topic categories and topic aspects. Such diversity is oriented from two sparkles of our two-stage recommender system: the "LSH + Hierarchical" clustering component and the news selection strategy based on "submodularity". "LSH + Hierarchical" clustering provides a diverse list of topic categories as the first level of recommendation, whereas the "submodularity" model increases the diversity of the result in terms of news content. To evaluate how diverse our recommendation result is, we compare the set diversity described in [26] between the results of *SCENE* and other recommender systems. The news set diversity is

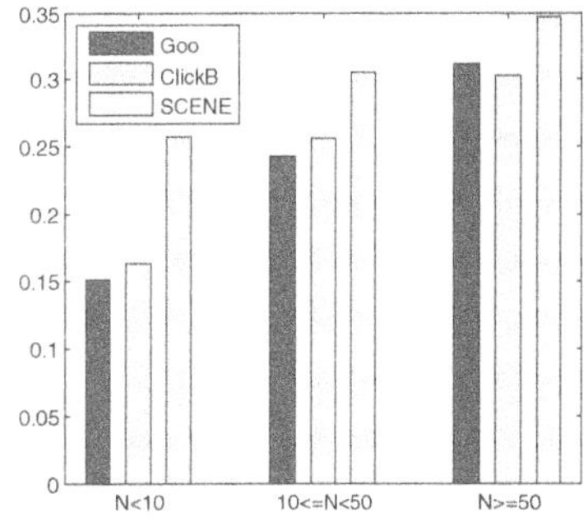

Figure 6: Comparison on F-score of different algorithms for three distinct user groups.

defined as the *average dissimilarity* of all pairs of news items in the recommendation list. Specifically, given a news set $\mathcal{N}$, the *average dissimilarity* of $\mathcal{N}$, $f_d(\mathcal{N})$, is defined as

$$f_d(\mathcal{N}) = \frac{2}{p(p-1)} \sum_{n_i \in \mathcal{N}} \sum_{n_j \in \mathcal{N}, n_j \neq n_i} (1 - Sim(n_i, n_j)) \quad (7)$$

where $|\mathcal{N}| = p$, and the dissimilarity of a news pair is represented as $1 - Sim(n_i, n_j)$, in which $Sim(n_i, n_j)$ denotes the news profile similarity between the news item n_i and n_j.

For diversity evaluation, we choose [7] (Goo), [19] (ClickB), [5] (Bilinear) and [18] (Bandit) as the comparison baselines. We employ the same experiment setup described in Section 7.2.2, to compare the diversities of recommendation lists with different cardinalities. Table 3 shows the averaged diversity result for 10 time ranges.

Methods	Top @10	Top @20	Top @30
Goo	0.4101	0.3074	0.1105
ClickB	0.4329	0.3128	0.1562
Bilinear	0.4234	0.2517	0.0933
Bandit	0.5056	0.4126	0.2925
SCENE	**0.6930**	**0.6671**	**0.6059**

Table 3: Diversity evaluation on the result list.

From the result, we observe that: (i) The diversity decreases as the recommendation news list enlarges. It is straightforward that when more news articles are selected, the topic distribution of the news list becomes closer to the user's reading interest, and therefore the selected news items are more similar. (ii) The diversity of the recommendation list provided by the baseline methods drops dramatically as the list size increases, since they did not take the diversity into account. (iii) *SCENE* outperforms the others very significantly, and since we intentionally consider the requirement of news readers, the diversity decreases very smoothly when we recommend more news items to individual users.

7.2.5 A User Study on *SCENE*

In order to verify the efficacy of our proposed recommender system, we implement a prototype system of *SCENE* and conduct a user study on it. Specifically, *SCENE* gathers newly-published news articles from popular news websites per day, as the news articles pool for recommendation. Then 50 volunteers are hired to experience *SCENE* in 15 days. Most of them have online news reading hobbies. For the first 5 days, we collect the users' accessing news articles as the reading history; for the successive 10 days, we recommend news items to the volunteers. For evaluation purpose, we define several indexes to measure the satisfaction of user experience. Each experience index is rated by the volunteers in a range of 1 to 5, where 1 – "Execrable", 2 – "Below Average", 3 – "Average", 4 – "Above Average", and 5 – "Exceptional". The experience indexes include: (i) The response time once a user logs onto the system; (ii) The preference on the recommended news articles; (iii) The diversity of the recommended news list; and (iv) The ordering of the recommended news articles.

We collect all the volunteers' ratings on these four experience indexes at the end of the testing period. To analyze the investigation result, we plot the number of users with different ratings on the four indexes, and get a histogram as shown in Figure 7. From the result, we observe that all the four aspects of *SCENE* can satisfy the requirements of the majority users. Particularly for the diversity of the recommended news list, most volunteers thumb up towards our prototype system. This also verifies our claim in Section 6.2.3.

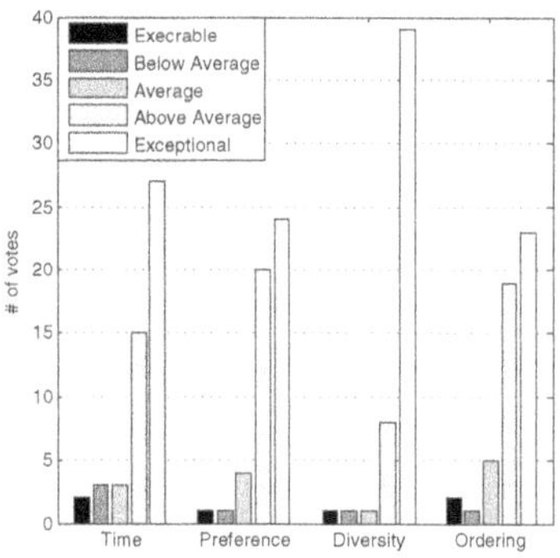

Figure 7: User experience on different indexes.

8. CONCLUDING REMARKS

In this paper, we propose *SCENE* to tackle personalized news recommendation. We explore the intra relations among news articles, along with different characteristics of news items, including news content, similar access patterns and named entities preferred by users. Our system supports efficient clustering on newly-published news articles, as well as high quality of recommendation results. Extensive evaluation has demonstrated the efficacy and efficiency of *SCENE*.

For future work, to handle high volume press releases, we plan to deploy the offline clustering component onto the Map-Reduce framework. It requires careful investigation on the seamless integration of LSH on news articles and hierarchical clustering on news groups. Another remarkable point is the interest evolution of users, which is able to provide insights on the exploration of users' reading behaviors.

ACKNOWLEDGEMENTS

The work is partially supported by US National Science Foundation under grants IIS-0546280 and CCF-0830659.

9. REFERENCES

[1] C. Best, E. van der Goot, M. de Paola, T. Garcia, and D. Horby. Europe media monitor–emm. *JRC Technical Note No.I*, 2, 2002.

[2] D. Billsus and M.J. Pazzani. A personal news agent that talks, learns and explains. In *Proceedings of the 3rd Annual Conference on Autonomous Agents*, pages 268–275, 1999.

[3] D.M. Blei, A.Y. Ng, and M.I. Jordan. Latent dirichlet allocation. *Journal of Machine Learning Research*, 3:993–1022, 2003.

[4] R. Burke. Hybrid systems for personalized recommendations. *Intelligent Techniques for Web Personalization*, pages 133–152, 2005.

[5] W. Chu and S.T. Park. Personalized recommendation on dynamic content using predictive bilinear models. In *WWW 2009*, pages 691–700.

[6] D.H. Cunningham, D.D. Maynard, D.K. Bontcheva, and M.V. Tablan. GATE: A framework and graphical development environment for robust NLP tools and applications. In *ACL*, 2002.

[7] A.S. Das, M. Datar, A. Garg, and S. Rajaram. Google news personalization: scalable online collaborative filtering. In *WWW 2007*, pages 271–280.

[8] E. Gabrilovich, S. Dumais, and E. Horvitz. Newsjunkie: providing personalized newsfeeds via analysis of information novelty. In *WWW 2004*, pages 482–490.

[9] S. Gauch, M. Speretta, A. Chandramouli, and A. Micarelli. User profiles for personalized information access. *The adaptive web*, pages 54–89, 2007.

[10] A. Gionis, P. Indyk, and R. Motwani. Similarity search in high dimensions via hashing. In *VLDB 1999*, pages 518–529.

[11] M. Girolami and A. Kabán. On an equivalence between PLSI and LDA. In *SIGIR 2003*, pages 433–434.

[12] T. Hofmann. Probabilistic latent semantic indexing. In *SIGIR 1999*, pages 50–57.

[13] T. Hofmann. Latent semantic models for collaborative filtering. *ACM Transactions on Information Systems*, 22(1):89–115, 2004.

[14] P. Indyk. A small approximately min-wise independent family of hash functions. In *Proceedings of the 10th Annual ACM-SIAM Symposium on Discrete Algorithms*, pages 454–456, 1999.

[15] D. Jurafsky, J.H. Martin, A. Kehler, K. Vander Linden, and N. Ward. *Speech and language processing*. Prentice Hall, 2000.

[16] S. Khuller, A. Moss, and J.S. Naor. The budgeted maximum coverage problem. *Information Processing Letters*, 70(1):39–45, 1999.

[17] J. Leskovec, A. Krause, C. Guestrin, C. Faloutsos, J. VanBriesen, and N. Glance. Cost-effective outbreak detection in networks. In *SIGKDD 2007*, pages 420–429.

[18] L. Li, W. Chu, J. Langford, and R.E. Schapire. A contextual-bandit approach to personalized news article recommendation. In *WWW 2010*, pages 661–670.

[19] J. Liu, P. Dolan, and E.R. Pedersen. Personalized news recommendation based on click behavior. In *Proceedings of the 15th International Conference on Intelligent User Interfaces*, pages 31–40. ACM, 2010.

[20] GL Nemhauser, LA Wolsey, and ML Fisher. An analysis of approximations for maximizing submodular set functions. *Mathematical Programming*, 14(1):265–294, 1978.

[21] D.M. Pennock, E. Horvitz, S. Lawrence, and C.L. Giles. Collaborative filtering by personality diagnosis: A hybrid memory- and model-based approach. In *UAI 2000*, pages 473–480.

[22] P. Resnick, N. Iacovou, M. Suchak, P. Bergstrom, and J. Riedl. GroupLens: an open architecture for collaborative filtering of netnews. In *Proceedings of ACM conference on Computer Supported Cooperative Work*, pages 175–186. ACM, 1994.

[23] B. Sarwar, G. Karypis, J. Konstan, and J. Reidl. Item-based collaborative filtering recommendation algorithms. In *WWW 2001*, pages 285–295.

[24] J.B. Schafer, J. Konstan, and J. Riedi. Recommender systems in e-commerce. In *Proceedings of the 1st ACM Conference on Electronic Commerce*, pages 158–166, 1999.

[25] A.I. Schein, A. Popescul, L.H. Ungar, and D.M. Pennock. Methods and metrics for cold-start recommendations. In *SIGIR 2002*, pages 253–260.

[26] M. Zhang and N. Hurley. Avoiding monotony: improving the diversity of recommendation lists. In *Proceedings of the 2008 ACM Conference on Recommender Systems*, pages 123–130.

Inferring and Using Location Metadata to Personalize Web Search

Paul N. Bennett[1,†], Filip Radlinski[2], Ryen W. White[1], and Emine Yilmaz[3]
[1] Microsoft Research, Redmond, USA; [2] Microsoft, Vancouver, Canada; [3] Microsoft, Cambridge, UK
{pauben,filiprad,ryenw,eminey}@microsoft.com

ABSTRACT
Personalization of search results offers the potential for significant improvements in Web search. Among the many observable user attributes, approximate user location is particularly simple for search engines to obtain and allows personalization even for a first-time Web search user. However, acting on user location information is difficult, since few Web documents include an address that can be interpreted as constraining the locations where the document is relevant. Furthermore, many Web documents – such as local news stories, lottery results, and sports team fan pages – may not correspond to physical addresses, but the location of the user still plays an important role in document relevance. In this paper, we show how to infer a more general location relevance which uses not only physical location but a more general notion of locations of interest for Web pages. We compute this information using implicit user behavioral data, characterize the most location-centric pages, and show how location information can be incorporated into Web search ranking. Our results show that a substantial fraction of Web search queries can be significantly improved by incorporating location-based features.

Categories and Subject Descriptors
H.3.3 [**Information Storage and Retrieval**]: Information Search and Retrieval

General Terms
Algorithms, Measurement.

Keywords
Location metadata, personalization, Web search.

1. INTRODUCTION
Web search personalization has recently received tremendous attention from the information retrieval (IR) research community (e.g. [10][21][22][23]). Among the many approaches to personalization, the location of the user has been explored as an implicit feature of search queries (e.g. [12]). Based on the user's location, search engines commonly select the preferred language of results, adapt suggested spelling corrections, and promote search results that are near the user. In particular, location-based personalization has the benefit that it does not require the IR system to have constructed a model of the user in order to adapt search results.

† Authors are listed in alphabetical order.

SIGIR'11, July 24–28, 2011, Beijing, China.

Identifying local search results usually implies that the documents being ranked (or, occasionally documents dynamically created to represent entities such as restaurants or cinemas) must also be associated with a specific geographic location. The distance between the user's location and that of this document can then be taken as a ranking feature when ordering results. Alternatively, if the user provides an explicit location in a query (such as [*pizza new york*]), the location specified in the query provides a reference point from which locations in documents can be measured.

We propose to address location-based personalization in a more general setting. First, consider the geographic sensitivity of a document. Rather than estimating the location of the document from document content, we propose to observe the locations of users who visit this Web page, similarly to Zhuang *et al.* [35]. However, rather than using this to estimate the geographic sensitivity of the query used to reach this document, we simply learn a distribution over user locations for each document, in the form of a density estimate. This density estimate can then be used to recognize the location interest of each document, rather than assuming that each document is relevant to a single location defined at some fixed level of granularity. This approach is beneficial as not all documents that relate to a specific location are equally location sensitive. For example, if a user searches for [*picturehouse cinema*], they are likely interested in a cinema with that name that is within a short drive of their present location. On the other hand, a user who searches for [*disneyland*] is not necessarily interested in the closest Disneyland theme park. We argue that usage statistics, rather than locations mentioned in document content, best represent where a document is most relevant.

Most importantly, this approach is not limited to Web pages that represent clearly localized entities. For instance, consider the online local news section of the Los Angeles (LA) Times newspaper. As expected, Figure 1c shows that this website is of most interest to users located in the greater Los Angeles area. However, as shown in Figure 1d, the crossword section of the same newspaper website is frequently accessed by users from across the United States. This indicates that should a user in Miami issue the query [*la times*], it is relatively more likely that they in fact want the crossword section instead of the local news section desired by a user in Los Angeles. Even more generally, this geographic distribution can tell us that, for instance, service providers' websites are relevant mostly in the areas which they serve, allowing this service area to be directly inferred from usage behavior. For instance, we see in Figure 1a that Sarasota Memorial Hospital serves customers in all of Florida, while the LA Times reviews and recommendations are most relevant in southern California.

In this paper, we present our approach using generalized Gaussian Expectation Maximization to efficiently learn compact density estimates of the distribution of user locations for each relevant Web site. We then show how to use the estimates obtained in this way for both Web documents and search queries to learn a location-sensitive IR system, demonstrating that this approach can produce substantially improved search result rankings.

We start by presenting related work in depth. Following this, we describe the data and algorithm used to estimate the location-interest distribution for each Web document. We characterize particularly location-sensitive Web documents and demonstrate that different documents exhibit vastly different location-interest properties. Next, we describe how the document density estimates can be used to infer the likely relevance of documents in response to a query, presenting a learning approach to re-rank documents in a location sensitive manner. Finally, our results show that this approach leads to substantially improved retrieval quality.

2. RELATED WORK

Related work can be grouped into three general areas: (i) research on personalization of search results, (ii) geographic information retrieval, and (iii) inference of Web page locations from various sources such as page content and search engine logs.

Personalized search leverages information about an individual to identify the most relevant search results for that person. A large number of personalization techniques have been proposed in IR research. Some of these methods reside on the server [10] and some on the client [22], some leverage long-term query histories [15][23], and some use short-term implicit feedback [20][21]. A challenge for personalization, especially at Web scale, is in collecting user profiles that are sufficiently rich to be useful in settings such as result ranking, while balancing privacy concerns.

One way that an individual's personalized profile can be augmented is by using data from other people. To better understand whether groups of people can be used to benefit personalized search, Teevan *et al.* [25] explored the similarity of query selection, desktop information, and explicit relevance judgments across people grouped in different ways. They found that some groupings provide valuable insight into what members consider relevant to queries related to the group focus, but that it can be difficult to identify valuable groups implicitly. Building on their findings, Teevan and colleagues show that ranking Web search results based on group leads to a significant relevance gains for group-relevant queries. Along similar lines, Mei and Church [17] proposed a new way to personalize search through back-off based on searcher IP address. They suggest that if there are no relevant data for a particular user, then we should back off to increasingly larger classes of similar users. As a proof of concept, they used the first few bytes of the IP address to define classes and estimated the coefficients of each back-off. In their analysis, Mei and Church examined the effects of backing off based on day-of-week and time-of-day. Our work differs from these personalization methods in that we explicitly use location (rather than implicitly via IP address) and personalize based on the location of the search results, estimated based on usage patterns. Using our approach we can infer that proximal users may have similar information needs. Similar functionality can only be obtained via IP address if they back-off to similar values, but IP addresses can be widely varying, even for proximal users, depending on network connection setup, service provider, and similar factors.

Geographic information retrieval (GIR) addresses the retrieval of documents according to geographic criteria of relevance. Previous GIR research has addressed problems such as the recognition and disambiguation of place references in a text [14], the assignment of documents to encompassing geographic scopes [1], or the retrieval of documents considering geographic relevance [2]. Van Kreveld *et al.* [27] retrieved documents by creating a linear combination of textual and geographic similarity. Purves *et al.* [19] extracted location information from documents and linearly interpolated geographic and text-based retrieval scores in the context of free text ranking. GeoCLEF research (e.g., [13]) has used geographic term expansion on the queries and documents and then conventional term matching algorithms on the resulting expanded texts. Jones *et al.* [12] examined the effectiveness of geographic features of the document, the query, and the document-query combined, and trained a ranker to learn to combine textual and geographic similarity features. They trained a relevance model with both a content-based ranking algorithm and geo-spatial features as inputs, and used the learned weights to predict relevance and perform ranking. For queries with *explicit* place names which they could extract and use as the basis for matching to document mentions, they found that the minimum distance between the document locations and query location is the strongest geographical predictor of document relevance, and that combining geographic features with text features yields a 5% improvement in relevance over using text features alone. Yu and Cai [33] proposed a dynamic document ranking scheme to combine the thematic and geographic relevance measures on a per-query basis. They used query specificity to determine how best to combine different sources of ranking evidence for each query, and demonstrated relevance gains. Research on spatial diversity [24] provides search results that are not only relevant but also spatially diversified so that they are from many different locations. The work presented in this paper differs from previous work in that we do not mine locations from Web page or query content, and do not compute distances based on distance estimates between locations in the query and the content. Rather, we build location-interest models, That is, models of the locations from which users view individual Web documents. We then personalize based on properties of these models and how typical the user's location is for each search result.

There has also been work on detecting and using locations in non-retrieval settings. Mehler *et al.* used locations mentioned in online news articles to detect regional biases toward entities such as players in local sports teams and local politicians [16]. Mei *et al.* [18] use the geography of Weblog authors to model spatial patterns of news topics. Zhuang *et al.* [35] use click information in order to determine whether a search query is geo-sensitive, model and detect, disambiguate, and visualize the associated geographical locations. Wang *et al.* [30] present a method to automatically determine the dominant locations of search queries by mining the top search results and/or query logs. Wang *et al.* [28] tackle the problem of detecting provider, content, and serving location based on content features of Web pages, hyperlinks and queries. In our work, rather than modeling locations based on explicit mentions of location names in logs, we use implicit location information inferred from aggregated locations of users accessing pages.

It is clear from this section that there is a substantial amount of related work in areas similar to that covered by our research. However, our work extends previous research in three key ways. First, we perform personalization based on location metadata, showing how to efficiently and compactly maintain this metadata. Second, we use that personalization metadata for the purpose of re-ranking search engine results. Finally, we infer our location-interest models from log data, estimating the location meta-data to associate with results based on the aggregated location information of those who access the pages, rather than based on content of the results or the query itself. It is worth noting that although the framework of inferring metadata to improve rankings that we present in this paper is focused on the use of locations, it generalizes to other problem scenarios where metadata is available for documents (e.g., readability levels).

3. ESTIMATING WEBSITE LOCATION SENSITIVITY

In this section, we present the first stage of our approach, namely efficiently estimating a geographic distribution for each website. In particular, our approach creates a compact model of the locations in which each website is likely of interest. In the following sections, we will then show how this model can be used for information retrieval in particular.

3.1 Data Collection

The primary source of data for this study is a proprietary data set consisting of the anonymized logs of URLs visited by users who consented to provide interaction data through a widely-distributed Web browser add-on. The data set consists of browsing logs (with both Web search and general browsing episodes) consisting of tuples including a random user identifier, the time and date, and the Web page visited. These data provide us with examples of real-world searching behavior that may be useful in understanding and modeling location-based search. Further, each user's IP address is resolved into geographic location information for the user (i.e., city, state, latitude, and longitude) and this geographic location is recorded. All log entries resolving to the same town or city were assigned the same latitude and longitude coordinates. To remove variability caused by cultural and linguistic variation in search behavior, we only include log entries generated by users in the English-speaking United States locale.

The models we construct are based on URL visits during three months from July through September 2010. The evaluation results described in this paper are based on URL visits during the first week of October 2010, representing millions of Web page visits from hundreds of thousands of unique users. From these data we extracted *search sessions* on a commercial Web search engine, using a session extraction methodology similar to [31]. Search sessions begin with a query, occur within the same browser and tab instance (to lessen the effect of any multi-tasking that users may perform), and terminate following 30 minutes of inactivity.

3.2 Location-Interest Models

For each URL with more than 50 visits during the three month period used to collect model data, we infer a location-interest model (referred to as *location model* or *distribution* for brevity). This model estimates the probability of the location of the user given they view this particular URL. For compactness, instead of representing each URL by the particular locations from which it was visited, we learn a mixture of Gaussians[1] that can be written:

$$P(location = x|URL) = \sum_{i=1}^{n} w_i \; N(x; \mu_i, \Sigma_i)$$

$$= \sum_{i=1}^{n} \frac{w_i}{(2\pi)^2 |\Sigma_i|^{1/2}} e^{-\frac{1}{2}(x-\mu_i)^T \Sigma_i^{-1} (x-\mu_i)}$$

where $\{\mu_i\}$ and $\{\Sigma_i\}$ are inferred from the data.

[1] For simplicity, capital "P" is used for (continuous) probability density functions and (discrete) probability mass functions.

(a) Sarasota Memorial Health, http://smh.com/

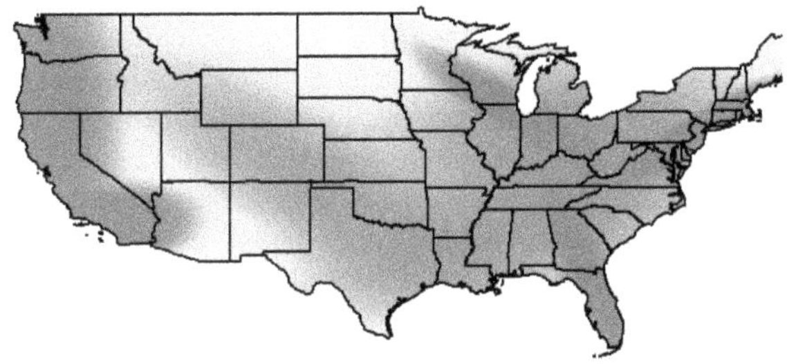

(b) Sydney Morning Herald, http://smh.com.au/

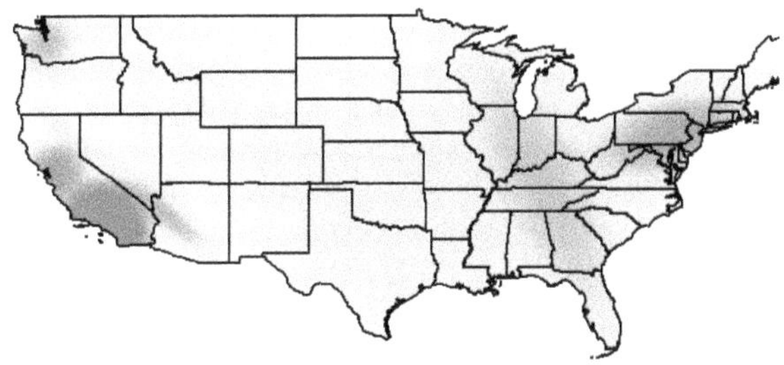

(c) Los Angeles Times: Reviews and Recommendations http://findlocal.latimes.com/

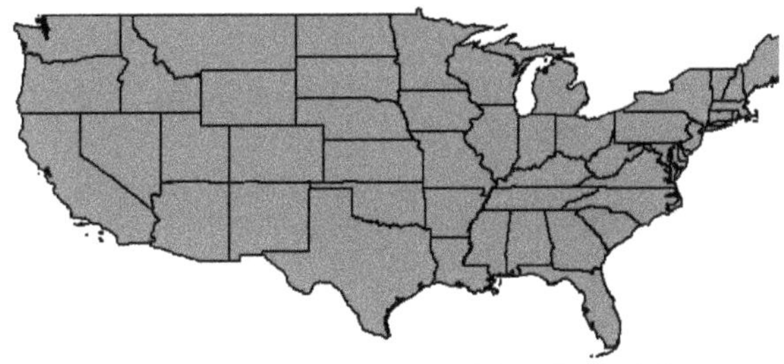

(d) Los Angeles Times: Crossword Puzzles and Games http://games.latimes.com/

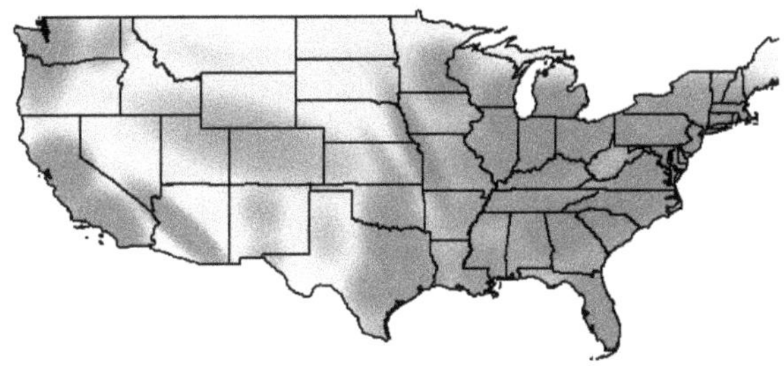

(e) Background Model

Figure 1. Example location density estimates. Red indicates higher density, orange and yellow lower density. (a), (b): For two results returned for the query *[smh]* (c), (d): For two results returned for the query *[la times]* (e) Population background model.

Specifically, for a given URL we start with a set of locations {(latitude, longitude)} from which this URL was viewed. To avoid any one user having a large impact on the model, only one location data point is allowed for each user for each day for each URL. Moreover, if a URL has more than 50,000 (user, day) pairs, we uniformly subsample 50,000 location samples.

Using these location data, we learn a density estimate consisting of between 5 and 25 Gaussians (depending on the amount of location data available for each URL) using Expectation Maximization (EM). The EM algorithm specifically adapted to estimating general two-dimensional Gaussians is presented in Algorithm 1, where $f_g(x)$ is the inner term of $P(location = x|URL)$ and $\beta = 0.9$. Intuitively, the algorithm iterates between estimating the probability that each point belongs to each Gaussian (p_{gx}), and estimating the most likely mean, covariance and weight of each Gaussian (μ_g, Σ_g, w_g). The Gaussian locations are initialized at a random observed location, with a high initial variance of 50 degrees in each direction (about 5,500km). As the algorithm progresses, each Gaussian tends to narrow and migrate to a high density area, or broaden to cover a background probability over large geographic areas. Examples of the output of the algorithm can be seen in Figure 1.

In addition, when working at Web scale it is essential to minimize the size of metadata used for ranking. As such, Algorithm 1 merges Gaussians that are too similar (i.e., those with means that are within one degree of each other and with covariance matrices which are also very similar), modifying the EM algorithm (by setting $\beta = 0.9$ instead of the standard value of 1) to encourage Gaussians to be nearby in the E step.

EM exhibits many additional useful properties making it particularly suitable for this setting – such as being efficient at finding a reliable density estimate that dynamically adapts the complexity of the model to the data. The precise mathematical properties of the algorithm are beyond the scope of this paper. We refer the reader to [8] for further details of Gaussian EM and [26] for details about the modification used.

In addition to learning a density estimate per URL, we also learn a general background model describing the density of all users who have opted to provide these interaction data. Aggregating the location information for all URLs yields the background model ($P(location)$). The background model obtained in this way is shown in Figure 1e. From the figure, it can be clearly seen that this model is reasonably representative of the population distribution in the United States.

Finally, we also learn a location-interest model for each query. For each distinct query observed in our data, we take the locations of the users who issued this query, and use Algorithm 1 in exactly the same way as for URLs. This provides an estimate of $P(location|query)$.

Algorithm 1: Generalized Gaussian EM.

1. $X \leftarrow$ location data; $n \leftarrow$ initial number of Gaussians;
2. For each Gaussian $g_i \in G$ *[Initialize model]*
   1. μ_i = distinct random point $x \in X$
   2. $\Sigma_i = \begin{bmatrix} 50^2 & 0 \\ 0 & 50^2 \end{bmatrix}$
   3. $w_i = \frac{1}{n}$
3. For iteration = 1 to 10
   1. Until convergence
      1. For every $g \in G, x \in X$ *[E step]*

$$p_{gx} = \frac{\left(w_g f_g(x)\right)^\beta}{\sum_{g' \in G} \left(w_{g'} f_{g'}(w)\right)^\beta}$$

      2. For every $g \in G$, update parameters concurrently *[M step]*
         1. $\mu_g = \frac{\sum_x p_{gx} x w_g}{\sum_x p_{gx} w_g}$
         2. $\Sigma_g = \frac{\sum_x p_{gx}(x-\mu_g)(x-\mu_g)^T w_g}{\sum_x p_{gx} w_g}$
         3. $w_g = \frac{\sum_x p_{gx} w_g}{|X|}$
   2. For every $g, g' \in G$ *[Merge near-duplicate Gaussians]*
      If g and g' are too close, merge g and g'

4. LOCATION SENSITIVE FEATURES

Given the location model generated for each URL, as well as for each query and the background model for the entire population, we can now leverage these models for personalized search. We now describe the features we use to represent geographic locality of search results.

4.1 Non-Contextual Features

The first class of features we investigate involve characterizing the query and results without considering the specific user. For example: Is the query issued location sensitive? Are these URLs location sensitive? These are likely to act as indicators as to when location should be taken into account by a ranker.

4.1.1 Features of the URL alone and the query alone

Let M_u be the location model for a given URL u, and M_{bg} be our background model. Our URL features include the aggregate popularity of the URL (n_{URL}, the number of distinct (user, day) pairs observed), as well as the overall entropy of the location distribution and its KL divergence from the background.

As computing the entropy of a mixture of Gaussians exactly is intractable, we computed the entropy by sampling from the location distribution of the URL:

$$Entropy(M_u) = E_{loc}[-\log(P(loc|M_u))] \approx \langle -\log(P(loc|M_u)) \rangle$$

where loc is a location drawn from M_u and $\langle f \rangle$ represents an empirical mean of f across many samples. The KL divergence between the location model for u and the background location model is defined as:

$$KLScore(u, background) = KL(M_u \,||\, M_{bg}) = \int_{loc} P(loc|M_u) \log\left[\frac{p(loc|M_u)}{p(loc|M_{bg})}\right] d\,loc$$

We computed the KL divergence both using sampling for the entropy (*KLScore-Sam*), and using a simple variational upper bound (*KLScore-Var*) [9].

Finally, we also compute the mean width of each URL model, $ModelWidth(u)$, by sampling from the distribution and computing the mean distance from the sampled mean of the distribution. Figure 1a shows an example of a low width model, and Figure 1b shows an example of a high width model.

The same features were also computed for each query.

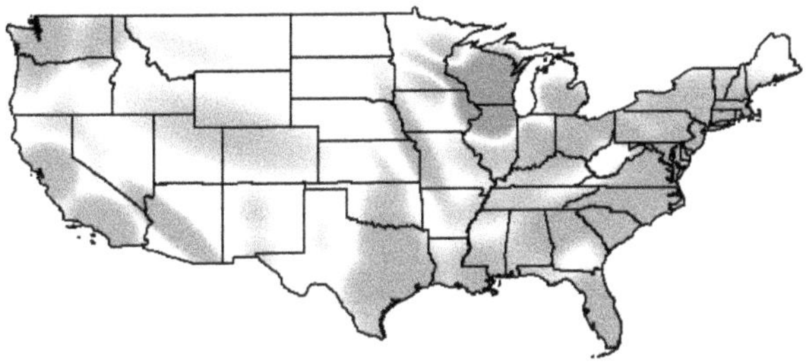

(a) University of Wisconsin homepage

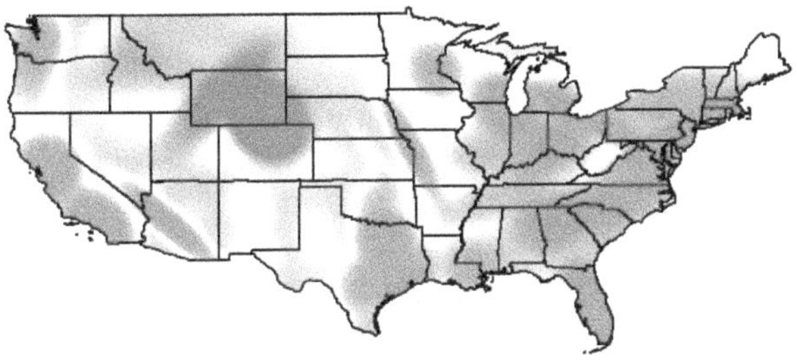

(b) University of Wyoming homepage

Figure 2. *NormLocUrl* for two websites as a function of location. Green (red) indicates that the URL is more (less) likely than predicted by the background (and also non-trivial).

4.1.2 Features of (URL, query) pair

We also compute the KL divergence between the URL and query location distribution, $KL(URL||Query)$, again both using sampling and the variational upper bound. Intuitively, if a query and URL have a very similar distribution, with low KL divergence, we would expect the URL to more likely be relevant to users who issue this query.

4.2 Contextual Features

Contextual features take into account the user's particular location, and we expect them to be particularly important in personalizing search results. We used the following contextual features:

4.2.1 Features of the user

The user's location (latitude, longitude) is included as a feature.

4.2.2 Features of the (user, URL) pair

The simplest interesting contextual feature is the probability of the user's location given the URL *u*, $P(loc|M_u)$, estimated by evaluating the URL location model at the user's location. We call this feature *LocUrl*. If this user is in a location where this URL is popular, the feature would be high.

If the personalization model were a perfect estimator of the location distribution of the URL, and location was the only determining feature (i.e., there were no query), the best we could do would be to rank by $P(u|loc)$, the probability of the URL *u* given the user's location. Using Bayes rule, we can estimate this quantity as follows:

$$P(u|loc) = \frac{P(loc|u)\,P(u)}{P(loc)}$$

Given that the ranking task involves ranking URLs for a user in a particular location, we can ignore the $P(loc)$ term. $P(u)$ can be estimated from the frequency with which this URL was viewed overall. Hence, we use:

$$UrlLoc(u, loc) = n_{URL}\,P(loc|M_u)$$

However, relying on $P(loc|M_u)$ for our features suffers from every large population center having a higher probability of location for all URLs. As such, when training a ranker, this feature will always be large when the user is in a high population region, and always small otherwise. To obtain more useful ranking scores, we also use a normalized probability of location given URL, subtracting the background model:

$$NormLocUrl(u, loc) = \frac{LocUrl(u, loc)}{LocUrl(background, loc)}$$

As an illustration of this feature, consider **Error! Reference source not found.**. It shows the *NormLocUrl* as a function of location for two universities both returned for the query *UW*, namely the University of Wyoming, and the University of Wisconsin. We see that the popularity of the University of Wyoming relative to the background frequency is higher over a larger geographic area than that of the University of Wisconsin. Note that higher popularity relative to the background over a large region does not necessarily imply greater popularity in terms of number of users: the University of Wyoming is popular in less populated areas than the University of Wisconsin.

In addition, we implemented two variants of this feature. The first (*NormLocUrl-Thresh*) thresholds the normalized feature, setting it to 1 whenever the above ratio is less than 1, i.e., whenever the user location is less likely under the URL model than under the background model. This has the effect of emphasizing URLs that are more likely for this query. The second variant (*NormLocUrl-Renorm*) renormalizes the background model so that it sums to 1 over the area where $P(loc|URL) > \epsilon$, for a small ϵ. This in effect allows the background normalization to only take into account the population distribution where this URL has ever been clicked, avoiding URLs that are of limited geographical interest having feature values much larger than URLs that are of broad geographical interest.

Finally, we compute general properties of the URL distribution in the context of the user: (1) *TotalVolume(u,loc,d)*, the percent of the URL *u* probability mass within a particular distance *d* of the user location; (2) *DistMean(u,loc)*, the distance from the user's location to the mean of the URL model; (3) *PeakDist(u,loc)*, the distance from the user's location to the nearest individual Gaussian component of the URL model as well as the weight of this Gaussian in the model (*PeakWeight*). These features attempt to capture features of the neighborhood of the URL location model close to the user.

4.2.3 Features of the (user, query) pair

We also computed exactly the same features taking the query location model instead of the URL location model, naming them equivalently (e.g., *LocQuery* instead of *LocUrl*). These represent how typical the user location is of this query.

4.3 Standard Ranking Features

As our experiments will involve learning a re-ranking of Web results that take user location into account, we also incorporate relevance of the URL to the user's query in the form of two simple features:

1. The rank of the URL in the non-personalized results returned by an underlying ranking function of the Bing search engine.
2. The score of this (query, URL) pair as produced by Bing (monotonically decreasing with the rank of the URL).

5. EXPERIMENTAL METHOD

Having described our data and features in the preceding sections, we now detail the evaluation of our method. We start with an analysis of the properties of our dataset, followed by quantitative experimentation on learning to rank.

5.1 Evaluation Dataset Construction

From the week-long sample of search sessions described in Section 3.1, we generate a dataset for our re-ranking experiments. The dataset comprises a set of approximately one million queries selected uniformly at random from the search sessions. For each query, the top ten search results retrieved by the Bing Web search engine were included, along with the latitude and longitude of the user, any location models available for each of the top ten search results, and the location model built for the query, if available.

For evaluation, we need a personalized relevance judgment for each result. Obtaining many relevance judgments from real users in a wide range of geographic locations is impractical, and there is no known approach to train expert judges to provide reliable location-sensitive judgments that reflect real user preferences. Hence we obtained these judgments using a log-based methodology inspired by [7]. Specifically, we assign a positive judgment to one of the top 10 URLs if it is the last satisfied result click in the session. We define a satisfied result click in a similar way to previous work [23][29], as either a click followed by no further clicks for 30 seconds or more, or the last result click in the session. The remaining top-ranked URLs receive a negative judgment. This gives us one positive judgment and nine negative judgments for each of the top-10 URLs for each session.

The rank position of this single positive judgment is used to evaluate retrieval performance before and after re-ranking. Specifically, we will measure our performance using the inverse of the rank of the relevant document, otherwise known as the mean reciprocal rank (MRR). Queries for which we cannot assign a positive judgment to any top-10 URL are excluded from the evaluation dataset. We also exclude queries for which we cannot assign a location model to at least one of the top-10 results (approximately 16% of queries were removed in this way), or where one of several high precision rich graphical results is shown (for example detailing information about a celebrity, corresponding to approximately 2% of remaining queries). Note that this means that up to nine of the URLs may not have a location model, and thus may have zero values for all location features. Additionally, the query may or may not have a location model depending on the query frequency during the previous three months.

As the correctness of our evaluation relies on the assumption that promoting satisfied click documents improves overall relevance, we consider these labels further. Previous work on inferring relevance from clicks has shown that assuming clicks to indicate relevance does provide reliable evaluation metrics (e.g., [29]). Further, similar models have also been used to infer relevance directly from clicks (e.g., [6][34]). Moreover, even if the assumption that results lacking satisfied clicks are non-relevant does not hold, promoting the satisfied clicked results is still likely to improve relevance by displacing higher ranked skipped results, with skipping followed by clicking having been reliably shown to indicate that the skipped result is less relevant [11]. More generally our labeling method can be considered studying the task of predicting only the *most* relevant item. Furthermore, when we consider all satisfied clicks, 97% of the queries in our evaluation set have two or fewer satisfied clicks. Thus, considering all satisfied clicks does not change a large proportion of the data. Finally, it is also worth noting that our approach does not require training data to come from documents labeled in this way. If personalized relevance judgments were available, our model could be trained from such judgments without any modifications.

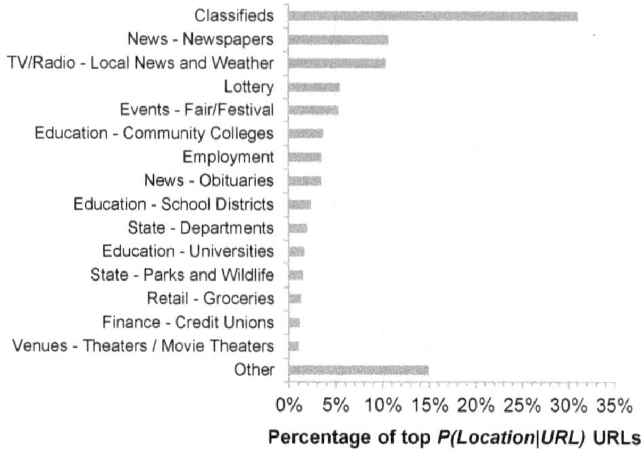

Figure 3. Distribution of topics in most location-centric URLs.

5.2 Labeling Location-Centric Pages

We next studied our dataset to understand which of the visited pages in our sessions are most location centric, and to better understand the nature of these pages.

We first ranked all URLs observed in our week-long evaluation dataset in descending order based on average log-likelihood of the user's actual location given the URL. After we removed pages consisting of search engine result lists and a small number of obviously non-local other URLs (e.g., online gaming sites), the top 750 remaining URLs were manually labeled by one of the authors of this paper, who created a taxonomy to categorize the most location-focused URLs based on their subject matter. This process involved visiting each URL and assigning it to an existing category or creating a new category as appropriate. We iterated and refined the taxonomy, ending up with 56 distinct labels on a broad range of location-centric topics ranging from classifieds to education. In Figure 3, we show the distribution across the 15 most popular categories, capturing 85% of the URLs in the labeled set. Remaining URLs were grouped in the category *Other*.

The figure shows that *Classifieds*, *News* (e.g., online versions of local newspapers, local television and radio stations, obituaries), and *Education* (community/technical colleges, school districts, smaller universities or outreach campuses of larger universities, grade tracking, student portals) are among the most location-centric URLs. Those labeled as *Other* in Figure 3 included pages associated with *Justice* (criminal records, court cases, inmate searches), *Property* (appraisals, auditors), *Transit* (public, traffic, tolls), *Utilities* (power or communication companies) and *Government* (city or state homepage). It is clear from this analysis that $P(location|URL)$ finds pages with a clear local intent.

Interestingly, URLs classified as *Retail* were usually associated with items that shoppers would typically be expected to purchase in person – such as furnishings, groceries, and medication. Stores selling electronics or other items that could easily be obtained online did not emerge in our analysis as strongly location centric.

Also, we observe that knowing the address associated with the URL does not always equate to knowing the locations from which

Table 1. **Summary learning results, split between navigational and other queries as well as by click entropy (CE).**

Queries			Change in MRR	Fraction of queries
All			1.9	100%
Navigational	All		3.5	34%
Navigational	CE Sample	All	4.5	1.2%
Navigational	CE Sample	CE > 3	7.2	3.2%
Navigational	CE Sample	1 < CE < 3	4.6	63.8%
Navigational	CE Sample	CE < 1	3.1	33.0%
Other	All		1.1	66%
Other	CE Sample	All	1.4	1.8%
Other	CE Sample	CE > 3	4.5	22.8%
Other	CE Sample	1 < CE < 3	4.2	55.7%
Other	CE Sample	CE < 1	2.7	21.5%

people would want to access that URL. One solution to identifying locations from URLs would be to simply extract addresses directly from Web page content, and use these to build the location model for the page. For example, from parsing Web pages, we would establish that the Massachusetts Institute of Technology (MIT) is located in Boston, MA. However, that does not tell us whether or not only people located in the Boston area would want to access the MIT page. The website of the university Boston College, which is less than five miles from MIT, has a much different location-interest profile with a much higher proportion of visits being from local users rather than distant users. This demonstrates the value of our method for inferring location metadata for URLs from usage patterns (rather than page content).

5.3 Learning to Rank

We next turn to the motivating task of personalizing Web search results based on the user location. For all the labeled rankings observed during the week of training, we compute all the features described in Section 4. From this dataset we then subsampled approximately half a million queries by uniformly randomly choosing one query per session. This was done to avoid giving extra importance to long sessions where the same user location would be seen repeatedly. The queries were then partitioned into ten parts in order to conduct ten-fold cross validation. For each fold, 10% of the training set is used as a validation set for model selection. All results presented below are the means of performance on the ten folds.

Using this dataset, we train a ranking model using the LambdaMART learning algorithm [32] for re-ranking the top ten results of the query. LambdaMART is an extension LambdaRank [3] based on boosted decision trees. LambdaMART has recently been shown to be one of the best algorithms for learning to rank. Indeed, an ensemble model in which LambdaMART rankers were the key component won Track 1 of the 2010 Yahoo! *Learning to Rank Challenge* [4]. In our experiments, we use LambdaMART with 500 decision trees. However, we also note that the choice of learning algorithm is not central to this work, and any reasonable learning to rank algorithm would likely provide similar results.

Our baseline is the original ranking of the top-10 provided by the Bing search engine, presenting a very competitive baseline. Because of the proprietary nature of its performance, we do not report absolute MRR, but instead we report the change in MRR value in the scale of 0 to 100, i.e., $100 \times (MRR(learned) - MRR(baseline))$.

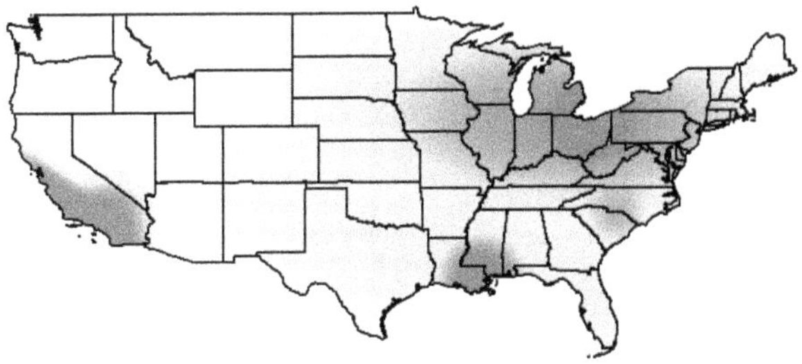

Figure 4. Query location model for the query [*rta bus schedule*]. We see three peaks: in Ohio, Louisiana, and California.

6. RESULTS AND DISCUSSION

We now present results from our learning experiments, both in terms of ranking performance, and analyzing the impact of the different classes of features proposed.

6.1 Ranking Performance

Table 1 shows the summary results for LambdaMART versus the baseline ranker performance. In the first row, we see that the learned model improves by 1.9 (on a scale of 0 to 100) over the baseline ranker in terms of MRR. All the improvements in the table are statistically significant with 95% confidence according to the Wilcoxon sign-rank test. The learned model changes the position of the relevant item for 16.8% of the queries and improves 10.4% of the queries. This shows that the location of the user is important for a substantial fraction of Web search queries. The learned model boosts the position of the relevant item in 61.8% of queries where the relevant item's position changes. On average, over the queries where the relevant item shifts, the learned model boosts the relevant item by 0.54 positions. In other words, every other query experiences an improvement of about one position in rank. Given the importance of the first position on user satisfaction, it is worth considering impact on that position separately. The learned model moves a relevant item out of position one 2.3% of the time and moves a relevant item into position one 4.3% of the time.

6.2 Effect of Query Type

Next, we break down our results by separating out navigational queries. We define navigational queries as queries that are particularly frequent and where one popular URL dominates user clicks. In our dataset, 34% of the queries are marked as navigational in this way. We find more substantial improvements for navigational queries than the remaining queries. This is particularly interesting as most clicks on the navigational queries are the same for all users, suggesting that some of the improvements are on queries issued predominantly in a confined geographic area, where the original ranker is not taking this location into account.

As an example of this, consider the query [*rta bus schedule*]. In our dataset, this query was issued by a user in New Orleans in the state of Louisiana. Figure 4 shows the location distribution of this query. We see that it is most frequently issued in Southern California, in Ohio and in Louisiana. The top result returned by the baseline system for this query was most relevant in Ohio, as can be seen in Figure 5a. However, in this case the user clicked on an

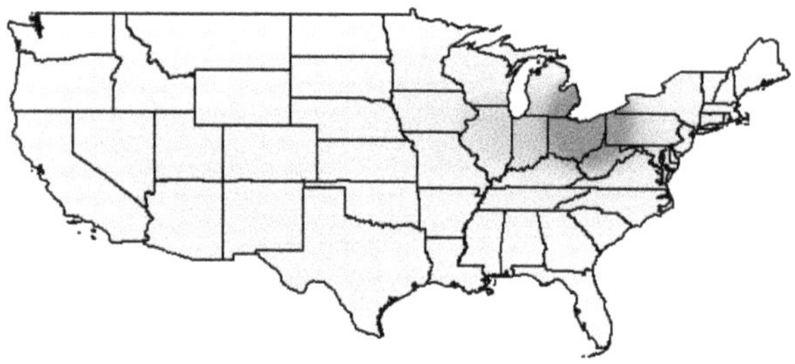
(a) http://www.riderta.com/maps-schedules.asp

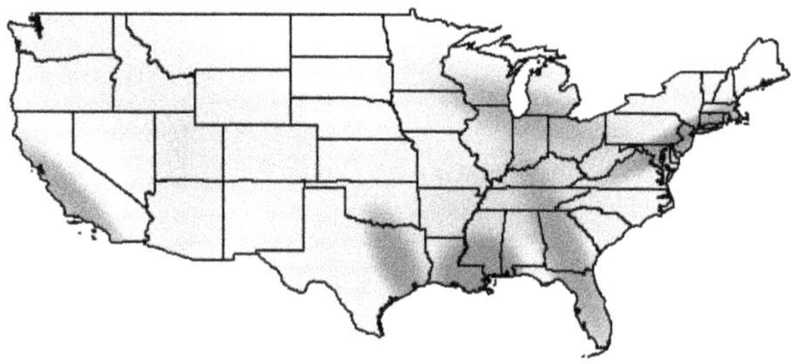
(b) http://www.norta.com/

Figure 5. User location model for (a) the top original result for the query [*rta bus schedule*], and (b) for the result eventually clicked by a particular user in New Orleans, LA.

appropriate result for Louisiana, with the location model shown in Figure 5b. The original ranking for this query, as well as the re-ranked results produced by our learned model are shown in Table 2. For each of the original top ten results, we see the URL, our estimate of the most relevant location (through manual inspection of the page), the approximate location of the largest Gaussian peak in the URL model, as well as the distance between the model peak and the manually determined URL location. We see that overall the URL models reflect the true page location reasonably well. In the case of the user in New Orleans, we also see that the correct result was moved from position 8 to position 2, resulting in a large improvement in the quality of the results for this particular user.

Returning to the summary results in Table 1, we show the results for navigational and other queries broken down further. In particular, we study improvements as a function of query click entropy (CE) [5] over a sample of queries with sufficient frequency to estimate click entropy. This sample constituted 3% of our data. The query click entropy measures the distribution of URLs previously clicked by users, where a high value indicates that many different URLs are frequently clicked by different users, while a low value indicates that the same URL is clicked reliably. Note that the values of click entropy we report have been scaled by a factor of 50 to simplify presentation.

In general, navigational queries are expected to have low click entropy as there is usually one destination URL that is clicked by most users. A navigational query with high click entropy is likely to be affected by user location: the destination URL is different for users from different locations, hence different URLs are clicked by different users. Thus, one would expect the learned model to achieve higher gains for these queries. As expected, we see that queries where many different URLs are frequently clicked show the largest improvement in performance due to location-based personalization.

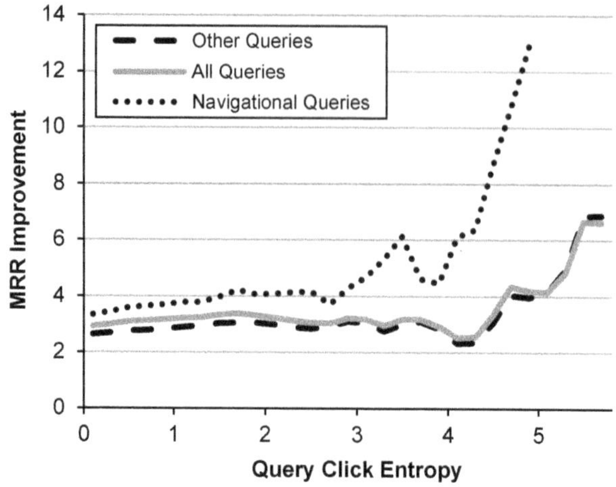

Figure 6. MRR improvement as a function of query click entropy for frequent queries.

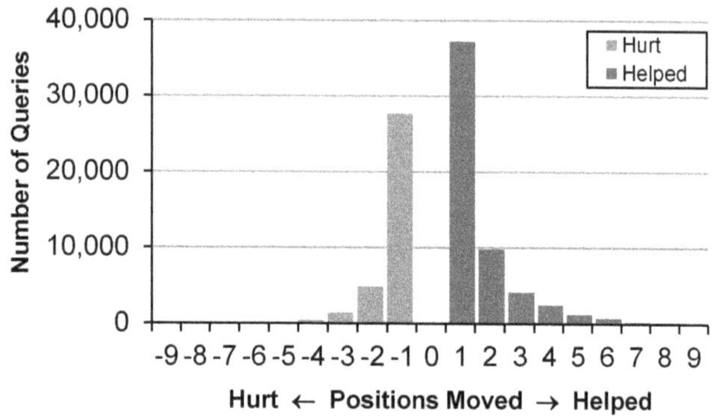

Figure 7. Positions by which clicked item in evaluation data moved up or down due to personalization.

Considering the click entropy in more detail, Figure 6 shows the MRR improvement of the learned model for the same query types as a function of click entropy. Overall, the performance numbers are higher than for all queries due to this analysis being limited to queries with known click entropy. We see that the small fraction of navigational queries improve more at all click entropy levels, but that click entropy is a good indicator of potential for personalization (as also noted by [5]). However, we also see that even queries with little or no variation in the URL clicked (CE $\approx$ 0) benefit from our approach.

As a further analysis, we measure how often location based personalization hurts or helps on a per query basis, across all queries. Figure 7 shows the number of queries for which the satisfied clicked result moved up, or down, by the given number of positions. We see that ranking changes are most often of one or two positions, with improvements substantially more frequent than degradation of performance. We also note that results are sometimes promoted by more than 5 positions, moving search results to substantially more prominent positions. Such high impact changes have a more substantial effect on user satisfaction.

Table 2. Learned re-ranking of results for the query [*rta bus schedule*] from a user in New Orleans, LA. The user's last satisfied click was on the shaded item, which has moved from rank 8 in the baseline to rank 2 in the personalized ranking.

New Rank	**Top 10 Ordered by New Ranking**	**Actual Location** (of resource on page)	**Most Probable Inferred Peak**	**Orig. rank**	**Distance** (inferred to actual)
1	http://www.riderta.com/maps-schedules.asp	Cleveland, OH	Ohio (South of Cleveland)	1	25 km
2	http://www.norta.com/	New Orleans, LA	New Orleans, LA	8	0 km
3	http://www.riderta.com/	Cleveland, OH	Ohio (South of Cleveland)	3	25 km
4	http://www.riversidetransit.com/home/index.htm	Riverside, CA	California (East of Riverside)	2	55 km
5	http://www.rtachicago.com/	Chicago, IL	Chicago, IL	4	0 km
6	http://norta.com/routes/	New Orleans, LA	New Orleans (Lake Pontchartrain)	6	5 km
7	http://www.riversidetransit.com/bus_info/schedules.htm	Riverside, CA	California (East of Riverside)	5	55 km
8	http://slorta.org/	San Luis Obispo, CA	California (Northwest of San Luis Obispo)	9	10 km
9	http://www.cctexas.com/?fuseaction=main.view&page=2847	Corpus Christi, TX	*Insufficient data*	10	–
10	http://gunnisonvalleyrta.org/	Gunnison, Co	Colorado (Between Denver and Gunnison)	7	170 km

6.3 Feature Analysis

Next we turn to analysis of the features contributing to the results in the previous section.

In our ranking model, we found that the most important feature is the initial rank determined by the original ranking function. This may be because the location features do not depend on the match between the query and the URL. The second most important feature is *UrlLoc*, which estimates the probability of the URL given the user's location. This suggests that the feature is indeed providing a reasonable estimate of the utility of each URL at each user location. We also saw that URL popularity plays a strong role, followed by the KL divergence of the URL model from the background model. This indicates that URLs whose popularity merely mirrors the background distribution are less likely to be good candidates for promotion or demotion based on user location.

7. CONCLUSIONS AND FUTURE WORK

In this paper, we presented an approach for inferring the locations of interest for URLs based on user browsing behavior. We showed that these models are more informative than content alone. We showed how locations can be efficiently encoded as a Gaussian model describing the probability of the location given a URL, and further how this basic model can be transformed into a number of informative features. We demonstrated that these features allow location based personalization of search results, leading to significant gains in offline evaluation, changing the position of the relevant item in 16.8% of the queries, improving it for 10.4% of queries, and improving overall MRR by 1.9%.

Natural next steps include a comparison with content-based methods, and further validation of our approach in an online setting by dynamically re-ranking search results, and evaluating with an appropriate online metric. Additionally, although 84% of queries return results where at least one in the top-10 has a location model, smoothing approaches could allow location information to be shared between related URLs and allow this approach to be extended to URLs which are visited less frequently or are entirely new. However, this work also suggests broader applications. Location-based personalization is applicable beyond standard Web search, also encompassing advertising, product recommendation, and social networking. Similar models can also be constructed of locations of interest to individual user or specific user cohorts.

8. ACKNOWLEDGMENTS

We would like to thank Nick Craswell and Tom Minka for helpful comments and advice on this research.

REFERENCES

[1] E. Amitay, N. Har'El, R. Sivan, and A. Soffer. (2004). Web-a-where: geo-tagging web content. In *Proceedings of the ACM SIGIR Conference on Research and Development on Information Retrieval*, pp. 273–280.

[2] L. Andrade and M. Silva. (2006). Relevance ranking for geographic IR. In *Proceedings of the ACM SIGIR Workshop on Geographic Information Retrieval*.

[3] C.J.C. Burges, R. Ragno, and Q.V. Le. (2006). Learning to rank with non-smooth cost functions. *Advances in Neural Information Processing Systems*, pp. 193–200.

[4] O. Chapelle, Y. Chang, and T.-Y. Liu. (2010). The Yahoo! Learning to Rank Challenge. *http://learningtorankchallenge.yahoo.com.*

[5] Z. Dou, R. Song, and J.R. Wen. (2007). A large-scale evaluation and analysis of personalized search strategies. In *Proceedings of the International Conference on the World Wide Web*, 581–590.

[6] G. Dupret and B. Piwowarski. (2008). A user browsing model to predict search engine click data from past observations. In *Proceedings of ACM SIGIR Conference on Research and Development on Information Retrieval*, pp. 331–388.

[7] J. Gao, W. Yuan, X. Li, K. Deng, and J.-Y. Nie. (2009). Smoothing clickthrough data for web search ranking. In *Proceedings of ACM SIGIR Conference on Research and Development on Information Retrieval*, pp. 355–362.

[8] T. Hastie, R. Tibshirani, and J. Friedman. (2001). *Elements of Statistical Learning*. Springer.

[9] J.R. Hershey and P.A. Olsen (2007). Approximating the kullback leibler divergence between gaussian mixture models. In *Proceedings of the IEEE International Conference on Acoustics, Speech and Signal Processing*.

[10] G. Jeh and J. Widom. (2003). Scaling personalized web search. In *Proceedings of the International Conference on the World Wide Web*, pp. 271–279.

[11] T. Joachims, L. Granka, B. Pan, H. Hembrooke, F. Radlinski, and G. Gay. (2007). Evaluating the accuracy of implicit feedback from clicks and query reformulations in web search. *ACM Transactions on Information Systems*, 25(2):7.

[12] R. Jones, A. Hassan, and F. Diaz. (2008). Geographic features in Web search retrieval. In *Proceedings of ACM GIR Workshop on Geographic Information Retrieval*, pp. 57-58.

[13] Y. Li, N. Stokes, L. Cavedon, and A. Moffat. (2006). NICTA I2D2 group at GeoCLEF 2006. In *Proceedings of Cross-Language Evaluation Forum*, pp. 938–945.

[14] B. Martins, I. Anastacio, and P. Calado. (2010). A machine learning approach for resolving place references in text. In *Proceedings of the AGILE Conference on Geographical Information Science*.

[15] N. Matthijs and F. Radlinski. (2011). Personalizing Web search using tong term browsing history. In *Proceedings of the ACM WSDM Conference on Web Search and Data Mining*, pp. 25–34.

[16] A. Mehler, Y. Bao, X. Li, Y. Wang, and S. Skiena. (2006). Spatial analysis of news sources. *IEEE Transactions on Visualization and Computer Graphics*, 12(5): 765–772.

[17] Q. Mei and K. Church. (2008). Entropy of search logs: how hard is search? with personalization? with backoff? In *Proceedings of ACM WSDM Conference on Web Search and Data Mining*, pp. 45–54.

[18] Q. Mei, C. Liu, H. Su, and C. Zhai. (2006). A probabilistic approach to spatiotemporal theme pattern mining on weblogs. In *Proceedings of the International Conference on the World Wide Web*, pp. 533–542.

[19] R. Purves, P. Clough, C. Jones, A. Arampatzis, B. Bucher, D. Finch, G. Fu, H. Joho, A. Syed, S. Vaid, et al. (2007). The design and implementation of SPIRIT: a spatially aware search engine for information retrieval on the internet. *International J. of Geographical Information Science*, 21(7).

[20] F. Radlinski and T. Joachims. Query chains: learning to rank from implicit feedback. (2005). In *Proceedings of the ACM SIGKDD Conference on Knowledge Discovery and Data Mining*, pp. 239–248.

[21] X. Shen, B. Tan, and C. Zhai. (2005). Context-sensitive information retrieval using implicit feedback. In *Proceedings of the ACM SIGIR Conference on Research and Development in Information Retrieval*, pp. 43–50.

[22] X. Shen, B. Tan, and C. Zhai. (2005). UCAIR: A personalized search toolbar. In *Proceedings of the ACM SIGIR Conference on Research and Development in Information Retrieval*, pp. 681–681.

[23] B. Tan, X. Shen, and C. Zhai. (2006). Mining long-term search history to improve search accuracy. In *Proceedings of the ACM SIGKDD Conference on Knowledge Discovery and Data Mining*, pp. 718–723.

[24] J. Tang and M. Sanderson. (2010). Spatial diversity, do users appreciate it? In *Proceedings of the ACM GIR Workshop on Geographic Information Retrieval*.

[25] J. Teevan, M.R. Morris, and S. Bush. (2009). Discovering and using groups to improve personalized search. In *Proceedings of the ACM Conference on Web Search and Data Mining*, pp. 15–24.

[26] N. Ueda and R. Nakano. (1998). Deterministic annealing EM algorithm. *Neural Networks*, 11(2), pp. 271–282.

[27] M. J. van Kreveld, I. Reinbacher, A. Arampatzis, and R. van Zwol. (2005). Multi-dimensional scattered ranking methods for geographic information retrieval. *GeoInformatica*, 9(1): 61–84.

[28] C. Wang, X. Xie, L. Wang, Y. Lu, and W.-Y. Ma. (2005). Web resource geographic location classification and detection. In *Proceedings of the International Conference on the World Wide Web*, pp. 1138–1139.

[29] K. Wang, T. Walker, and Z. Zheng. (2009). PSkip: estimating relevant ranking quality from Web search clickthrough data. In *Proceedings of the ACM SIGKDD Conference on Knowledge Discovery and Data Mining*, pp. 1355–1364.

[30] L. Wang, C. Wang, X. Xie, J. Forman, Y. Lu, W.-Y. Ma, and Y. Li. (2005). Detecting dominant locations from search queries. In *Proceedings of the ACM SIGIR Conference on Research and Development in Information Retrieval*, pp. 424–431.

[31] R.W. White, P.N. Bennett, and S.T. Dumais. (2010). Predicting short-term interests using activity-based search context. In *Proceedings of the ACM CIKM Conference on Information and Knowledge Management*, pp. 1009-1018

[32] Q. Wu, C. J.C. Burges, K. M. Svore and J Gao. (2008). Ranking, Boosting, and Model Adaptation. *Microsoft Research Technical Report MSR-TR-2008-10.*

[33] B. Yu and G. Cai (2007). A query-aware document ranking method for geographic information retrieval. In *Proceedings of the ACM GIR Workshop on Geographical Information Retrieval*.

[34] F. Zhong, D. Wang, G. Wang, W. Chen, Y. Zhang, Z. Chen, and H. Wang. (2010). Incorporating post-click behaviors into a click model. In *Proceeding of the International ACM SIGIR Conference on Research and Development in Information Retrieval*, pp. 355–362.

[35] Z. Zhuang, C. Brunk, and C. L. Giles. (2008). Modeling and visualizing geo-sensitive queries based on user clicks. In *Proceedings of the International Workshop on Location and the Web*, pp. 73–76.

Active Learning to Maximize Accuracy vs. Effort in Interactive Information Retrieval

Aibo Tian
Department of Computer Science
The University of Texas at Austin
atian@cs.utexas.edu

Matthew Lease
School of Information
The University of Texas at Austin
ml@ischool.utexas.edu

ABSTRACT

We consider an interactive information retrieval task in which the user is interested in finding several to many relevant documents with minimal effort. Given an initial document ranking, user interaction with the system produces relevance feedback (RF) which the system then uses to revise the ranking. This interactive process repeats until the user terminates the search. To maximize accuracy relative to user effort, we propose an active learning strategy. At each iteration, the document whose relevance is maximally uncertain to the system is slotted high into the ranking in order to obtain user feedback for it. Simulated feedback on the Robust04 TREC collection shows our active learning approach dominates several standard RF baselines relative to the amount of feedback provided by the user. Evaluation on Robust04 under noisy feedback and on LETOR collections further demonstrate the effectiveness of active learning, as well as value of negative feedback in this task scenario.

Categories and Subject Descriptors

H.3.3 [**Information Search and Retrieval**]: Relevance Feedback; I.2.6 [**Artificial Intelligence**]: Learning

General Terms

Algorithms, Experimentation, Performance

Keywords

Relevance Feedback, Active learning, Personalized Search

1. INTRODUCTION

This paper presents an interactive information retrieval (IR) task [14] based on iterative relevance feedback (RF) [20, 4]. Given an initial document ranking, the user interacts with the system to explicitly or implicitly provide the system with labeled feedback documents. In standard RF fashion, the system then utilizes this feedback to generate an improved ranking. However, our interaction model involves

SIGIR'11, July 24–28, 2011, Beijing, China.
Copyright 2011 ACM 978-1-4503-0757-4/11/07 ...$10.00.

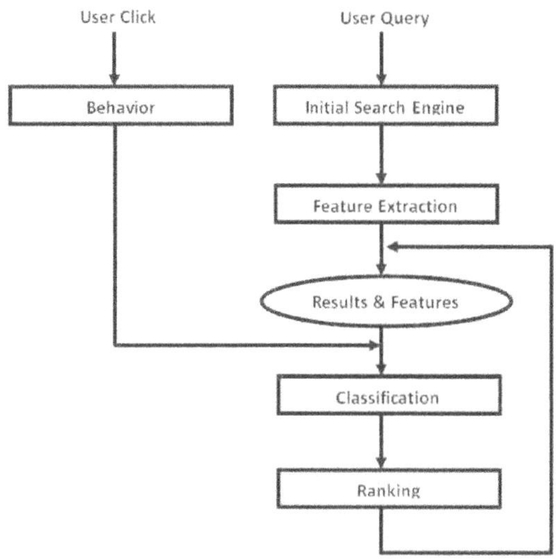

Figure 1: Task scenario and system architecture.

an iterative back-and-forth between user and system, providing the user a natural way to provide feedback and the system with an opportunity to request targeted feedback to improve ranking. User behavior is simulated via a simple model of top-to-bottom search result browsing (§2). Active learning [24, 13] is used to maximize system accuracy while minimizing the amount of feedback required (§4). Figure 1 depicts our overall task scenario and system architecture.

Brandt et al. [3] recently described an interactive IR creating a dynamic ranking tree for user interaction. Ranking is based on recommendations from the history of other users. Radlinski and Joachims [17] also explore use of active learning to quickly learn the document ranking function, focusing on estimating the general relevance measure (and ranking) of documents based on clickthrough data from query logs. Our work is more user-specific in personalizing the ranking based for the current user's interactions.

We investigate two active learning methods for selecting the next document to slot high for feedback. The *Simple Margin* method [24] picks the document lying closest to the decision surface whose relevance is maximally uncertain. We also propose an enhancement, *Local Structure*, which captures the idea that useful examples to label should also be far from already labeled examples and near to other unlabeled examples. We use Laplacian Score feature selection [10] to prune the vocabulary for more tractable learning (§5).

Our iterative RF task scenario presents several challenges to standard evaluation methodology typically used for ad hoc retrieval and single-iteration RF (§6). To address these challenges, we propose a paired approach of *KeepAll* and *TakeOut* evaluation which differ in how feedback documents are treated with regard to evaluation. Both strategies have advantages and disadvantges. In tandem, they provide a useful way to compare relative effectiveness of methods while not having to exclude the full union of feedback documents as typical with *residual* evaluation, something which can be difficult to apply when relevant documents are limited.

Empirical evaluation is conducted on the Robust04 TREC collection, as well as the LETOR 3.0 TD2003 and TD2004 collections [15] (§7). While we primarily assume relevance feedback provided by the user is correct, as in traditional RF settings, we also consider a noisy feedback setting in which the user sometimes provides erroneous feedback. This is simulated through simple false positive and negative rate Bernoulli parameters. Active learning methods are compared to standard RF baselines of Rocchio [20] and model-based feedback [28] (§3). We also evaluate Rocchio using positive-only feedback, and results show negative feedback is quite valuable in this task scenario, something rarely seen in prior work [26]. Overall, learning curves and average performance show active learning methods dominate baseline techniques, maximizing ranking accuracy for users relative to the amount of user feedback provided.

A simple prototype version of our system is available online[1] which reranks search results from Bing[2] using active learning. The interface presents left and right views of search results. The original ranking remains fixed in the left view, while the right view is continually re-ordered based on user feedback. Clicking search results in either views will open the clicked page in a new tab, as well as re-order search results in the view on the right.

Our paper is organized as follows. Our task scenario and user behavior model is introduced in §2. §3 defines the baseline RF methods we employ. Active learning methods are presented in §4. §5 describes feature selection for dimensionality reduction. Evaluation methodology for iterative RF is discussed in §6, and our evaluation of methods is presented in §7. We conclude with discussion of future work in §8.

2. TASK SCENARIO AND USER MODEL

Imagine a user who is interested in finding several to many relevant documents (with minimal effort). Given an initial document ranking, user interaction with the system produces relevance feedback (explicitly or implicitly) which the system then utilizes to improve the ranking. This interactive process repeats iteratively until the user terminates the search. In practice, we expect different information needs, task situations, and users will drive different types of thresholds for stopping. These might include a limited amount of effort the user is willing to invest, a target number of relevant documents to be found, or perhaps a target system accuracy to achieve (e.g. for later use searching the collection as new documents are added to it). Iteration also stops whenever the set of relevant documents available for feedback is exhausted. In all cases, the system goal is to maximize ranking accuracy for any amount of relevance feedback provided. In other words, the system should maximize the *learning curve*.

We generate relevance feedback from a simple model of user behavior. Given a document ranking, the user browses the document ranking from top-to-bottom and clicks on the first relevant document encountered. This interaction generates relevance feedback consisting of both one relevant document (the one clicked) and a set of zero or more non-relevant documents (those ranked above the relevant document). We do not explicitly model the user's stopping criterion for terminating the search (evaluation in §7 will measure system accuracy across varying amounts of user feedback).

Note that the user model just described assumes user feedback is always correct, similar to a traditional RF setting with known relevant and non-relevant documents [4]. We also consider a second, noisy model of user feedback (§7.3). Such noise might arise in practice with either explicit or implicit feedback due to the user's misperceptions of relevance prior to clicking or by simple clicking mistakes. This second user model introduces two Bernoulli parameters, f_p and f_n, which control the user's false positive and negative rates, respectively. As the user browses each non-relevant document, with probability f_p he will mistakenly click on it to indicate it as relevant. Similarly, whenever the user browses a relevant document, with probability f_n he will fail to click on it and instead continue scanning down the results list, providing incorrect negative feedback.

3. RELEVANCE FEEDBACK BASELINES

We evaluate three baseline RF methods for this iterative feedback task: (1) Rocchio feedback [20], (2) Rocchio with positive feedback only, and (3) model-based feedback (language modeling paradigm) [28]. Since prior work has rarely observed benefits from negative feedback [26], we were particularly interested in comparing the relative performance of (1) and (2) for this task scenario.

Let D denote the document collection, D_U the set of unlabeled documents, D_F documents with feedback, D_{F+} positive feedback documents, and D_{F-} the set of negative feedback documents. Let $\mathbf{q}$ and $\mathbf{d}$ denote the query and document vectors. Superscript k represents the kth iteration. $S(\mathbf{d})$ represents $\mathbf{d}$'s final score.

Rocchio [20] performs query expansion based on both positive and negative user feedback. Let $\mathbf{q^k} = \alpha\mathbf{q^0} + (1-\alpha)\mathbf{q_f^{k-1}}$ denote linear interpolation between original query $\mathbf{q^0}$ and feedback vector $\mathbf{q_f^k}$. Using term frequency representation for $\mathbf{q}$ and $\mathbf{d}$ vectors, we compute $\mathbf{q_f^k}$ by:

$$\mathbf{q_f^k} = \frac{\beta}{|D_{F+}^k|} \sum_{\mathbf{d} \in D_{F+}^k} \frac{\mathbf{d}}{|\mathbf{d}|} - \frac{(1-\beta)}{|D_{F-}^k|} \sum_{\mathbf{d_i} \in D_{F-}^k} \frac{\mathbf{d}}{|\mathbf{d}|} \quad (1)$$

The score of $\mathbf{d}$ in iteration k is then computed by cosine similarity between the expanded query and document $\mathbf{d}$'s vector: $S^k(\mathbf{d}) = cos(\mathbf{q^k}, \mathbf{d}) = \mathbf{q^k} \cdot \mathbf{d}$.

Model-based feedback [28] incorporates only positive feedback into the language model. Let Θ_Q, Θ_D, Θ_F, and Θ_d represent the model for query Q, collection D, positive feedback documents F, and given document $\mathbf{d}$. Similar to Rocchio, let $\Theta_Q^k = \alpha\Theta_Q^0 + (1-\alpha)\Theta_F^k$ denote the updated query model computed by linear interpolation of the original query model and the feedback model. To limit the noise of the feedback documents, feedback documents are assumed to be generated based on linear combination of feedback model and the

[1] http://www.cs.utexas.edu/~atian/search

[2] http://www.bing.com

collection model (2). Let $c(w, \mathbf{d})$ denote the frequency of word w in document $\mathbf{d}$. The feedback model is estimated by maximum likelihood (ML) using the EM algorithm where $\log p(D^k_{F+}, \Theta^k_F)$ is computed by:

$$\sum_{\mathbf{d} \in D^k_{F+}} \sum_{w} c(w, \mathbf{d}) \log \left(\lambda p(w|\Theta^k_F) + (1-\lambda) p(w|\Theta_D) \right) \quad (2)$$

We estimate the document model by $\Theta_d = (1-\gamma)\frac{\mathbf{d}}{|\mathbf{d}|} + \gamma \Theta_D$, where smoothing parameter γ mixes $\mathbf{d}$'s ML estimate with the collection model Θ_D. Document relevance to the query is then measured by KL divergence: $S^k(\mathbf{d}) = -\mathcal{D}(\Theta^k_Q || \Theta_\mathbf{d})$.

4. ACTIVE LEARNING

To maximize ranking accuracy with respect to the amount of user effort (i.e. relevance feedback) invested in training the system, we propose an active learning strategy for utilizing feedback. At the core of this active learning is supervised classification: learning to distinguish between relevant and non-relevant classes given training data. Documents are ranked in order of decreasing estimated relevance [19]. We describe two active learning approaches, **Simple Margin** and **Local Structure**, which we later evaluate (§7).

We adopt a support vector machine (SVM) [24] approach to active learning. Training a linear SVM consists of solving a quadratic optimization subject to linear inequality constraints. Optimization maximizes the margin between positive and negative samples so the classifier generalizes well to unseen data. The version (i.e. parameter) space is the dual space of feature space. A point in version space corresponds to a hyperplane in the feature space and vice-versa. SVM optimization in the feature space corresponds to finding the largest sphere in the version space, subject to constraints of the hyperplanes for the current feature points.

An active learning algorithm selects which unlabeled example to be labeled next in order to maximize learning relative to user effort required.The key problem of active learning is estimating the expected benefits of labeling different data points. Tong and Koller [24] find that the best example to label next halves the version space. Unfortunately, explicitly computing the size of version space is computationally infeasible. Consequently, Tong and Koller identify useful approximation criteria for example selection. Their **Simple Margin** criterion requires minimal computational costs so can be practically applied in real-time. It predicts utility of labeling all unlabeled data based on current SVM model, then chooses the example lying nearest to the classification hyperplane via $M(\mathbf{d}, \Theta)$, where d is the document vector in TF-IDF (normalized $\frac{tf}{logdf}$), Θ parameterizes the SVM model trained with all labeled data, and $M(\mathbf{d}, \Theta)$ is the positive distance of $\mathbf{d}$ from the model's hyperplane (capturing uncertainty of $\mathbf{d}$'s classification under the model).

Because this criterion does not require additional training, its computational cost is low. Its effectiveness, however, depends on the shape of the version space. If the version space is far from spherical, this criterion may not perform well. The middle figure in Figure 2 shows such an example failure case of this criterion. Tong and Koller's approximation criteria select which example to label next entirely based upon the learned SVM model [24]. In other words, the structure information of the whole data set is missed in those criteria.

However, often it is the case (as it is here) that we actually know about the entire dataset, including the labeled and

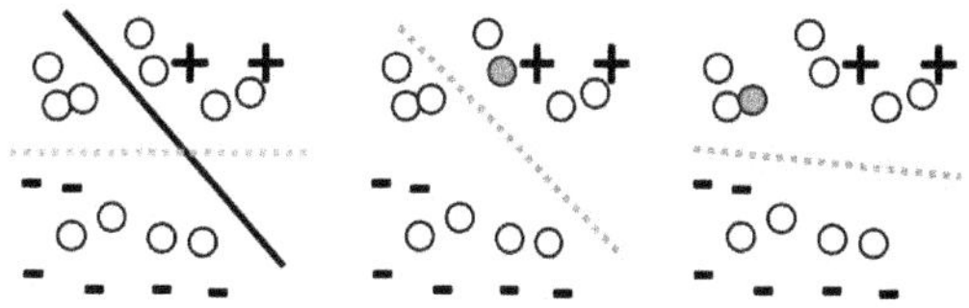

Figure 2: An example illustrating the difference between Simple Margin and Local Structure criteria. "+", "-", and circle represent positive, negative and unlabeled examples. The left figure shows the predicted classification prior to active learning. The black solid line denotes the current hyperplane, while the green dashed line shows the optimal hyperplane. The middle and right figures demonstrate the behavior of Simple Margin and Local Structure criteria, respectively. Red points represent examples selected by active learning for labeling, and the red dashed line shows the updated hyperplane after this labeling. While Simple Margin selects the example closest to the current hyperplane, Local Structure selects an example both close to the hyperplane and away from already labeled examples.

unlabeled. Such additional information can be usefully exploited by the learner. For example, work in semi-supervised learning often exploits the imbalance between plentiful unlabeled data and scarce labeled data by utilizing more accurate estimates of variance on the unlabeled data to improve classifier accuracy. In this case, we propose another selection criterion which considers both the performance of SVM *and* the structure information of the whole data set in tandem.

Intuitively, a useful unlabeled example to label should embody several characteristics. First, the classifier should be uncertain of its label prediction for the example given current model parameters; this is captured by the Simple Margin criterion. A second property, however, is that example should not lie close to already labeled data since close examples are likely to have the same label (e.g. standard nearest neighbor approaches to classification or utilizing unlabeled data in semi-supervised learning). Such close examples are unlikely to improve the performance of the classifier much more than a single, more useful example (e.g. see Figure 2). As a third characteristic, the data should have nearby unlabeled neighbors so knowing the example's label is likely to help us better label other nearby examples.

To capture the three properties above, we propose a new active learning selection criterion we refer to as **Local Structure**. Let $SL(\mathbf{d}) = \max_{\mathbf{d_f} \in D_F} cos(\mathbf{d}, \mathbf{d_f})$ find the maximum cosine similarity between $\mathbf{d}$ and all labeled $\mathbf{d_f} \in D_F$, i.e. how close $\mathbf{d}$ is to another already labeled document. Let $\mathbf{d_m}$ denote $\mathbf{d}$'s mth closest neighboring document, where m is a parameter. $SN(\mathbf{d}) = cos(\mathbf{d}, \mathbf{d_m})$ measures cosine similarity of $\mathbf{d}$ and $\mathbf{d_m}$ to model $\mathbf{d}$'s local neighborhood. The intuition is that smaller values of SN indicate a greater number of nearby documents that might benefit by labeling $\mathbf{d}$. We minimize a linear combination of SL, SN and $M(\mathbf{d}, \Theta)$ to select an example $\mathbf{d}'$ to label capturing the three properties:

$$\mathbf{d}' = \arg\min_{d \in D_U} \alpha M(\mathbf{d}, \Theta) + (1-\alpha)\left(SL(\mathbf{d}) - SN(\mathbf{d})\right) \quad (3)$$

Figure 2 visually compares the differing behaviors of active learning based on Simple Margin and Local Structure criteria. In this figure, Simple Margin criterion is seen to select the point nearest to the hyperplane without considering structure information. The chosen example lies near to an already labeled example, resulting in minimal change to the classification hyperplane and thereby minimal benefit to learning. In contrast, Local Structure criterion chooses the point close to the hyperplane and away from labeled data. In doing so, it thereby avoids the failure case of Simple Margin.

In our iterative RF scenario, the document selected for feedback is "slotted" into the top position in the ranking to guarantee the user provides feedback for it. While this ensures the system obtains the most useful feedback, this will often hurt ranking accuracy (since the maximally uncertain document will be non-relevant roughly half of the time). We discuss this issue further in regard to evaluation methodology (§6.2) and our future work (§8).

5. FEATURE SELECTION

High dimensionality represents a general obstacle to effective machine learning. Natural language learning tasks exhibit an especially visible example of this due to fast vocabulary growth from many words used infrequently. Various prior work in IR has investigated dimensionality reduction methods to mitigate issues of term mismatch between semantically related terms (e.g. LSI [8], pLSI [12], and LDA [27]). Learning to rank methods are also impacted if we use term-level features rather than higher-level aggregate features as used in LETOR [15, 1]. As such, we employ dimensionality reduction methods for more tractable learning.

In particular, we apply a dimensionality reduction technique known as Laplacian score (LS) [10]. This unsupervised technique is attractive due to the sparsity of labeled data available in our task scenario (i.e. relatively few feedback documents in comparison to the size of the feature space). LS is a filter-based method for feature selection, where we refer to the different dimensions of a feature vector as the feature set. Given m input features, LS scores each feature independently and selects the top N features, where N is a parameter. LS is based on Laplacian Eigenmaps and Locality Preserving Projection [2, 11]. The basic assumption of LS is that if two data points are close, they are likely to have the same class label. An effective feature set, therefore, should preserve such proximity for examples belonging to the same class. This is the same property exploited by our Local Structure method for example selection described earlier (§4). LS for the rth feature (LS_r) is computed according to $LS_r = \frac{1}{\sigma_{f_r}} \sum_{i,j} (f_{ri} - f_{rj})^2 S_{ij}$, where $\mathbf{f_r}$ is the rth feature for all examples, f_{ri} is the rth feature for example i, σ is the variance, and S is a sparse, inverse distance matrix over all examples in which only examples in close proximity have non-zero values. S thereby stores the local structure of the whole example space based on all features.

Let $\mathbf{x_i^{1:k}}$ denote the k nearest neighbors to feature vector $\mathbf{x_i}$, where k is a parameter. Non-zero entries in S are given by $(\forall \mathbf{x_i}, \forall \mathbf{x_j} \in \mathbf{x_i^{1:k}})\ S_{ij} = e^{-|\mathbf{x_i} - \mathbf{x_j}|}$, where $\mathbf{x_i}$ and $\mathbf{x_j}$ denote feature vectors for examples i and j along all dimensions.

6. EVALUATION METHODOLOGY

Evaluating iterative RF presents several different challenges from typical Cranfield-style evaluation of ad hoc and single-iteration RF. Acknowledging these challenges directly helps to ensure we establish a solid evaluation framework for measuring accuracy in this setting, comparing methods, and understanding limitations of evaluation methodology used.

6.1 Challenges

Feedback document selection vs. use. Relevance feedback methods can differ in how documents are selected for feedback as well as how those documents are utilized. Recent work in the TREC RF track has sought to isolate this confounding effect to better understand what makes one RF method more effective than another [4]. Our iterative feedback scenario makes it difficult to avoid this confound since each method produces a unique ranking at each iteration which the user then browses to provide feedback (§2).

Scarcity of relevant documents. Multiple RF methods are typically compared via *residual* evaluation in which feedback documents used by any of the methods being compared are excluded from evaluation (i.e. removed from both "gold standard" judgments and system rankings). This yields a single, common document collection for fair comparison of methods. With iterative feedback, ideally the residual collection would be determined by removing all feedback documents used by any method at any iteration considered. Once the residual collection was known, we could "go back in time" to evaluate accuracy of RF methods at earlier iterations.

The problem with this ideal strategy is scarcity of relevant documents in typical test collections available: using assessed documents for feedback often leaves relatively few for evaluation (especially relevant documents). Consequently, we sought an evaluation methodology that would allow us to meaningfully evaluate relevance feedback without the full exclusion required by traditional residual evaluation.

Another challenge due to scarcity of relevant documents lies in computing average system accuracy across topics. Recall our task scenario involves the user selecting a relevant document for feedback at each iteration (§2). Once the set of relevant documents is exhausted for a given topic, iterative RF terminates. However, if RF for a given topic terminates at iteration 8, how do we compute average system accuracy across topics at iteration 9? Do we (a) omit the query from the average or (b) include its accuracy as of iteration 8? Choice (a) would yield increasing error bars across iterations as progressively fewer topics contribute to the computed average, while choice (b) would dampen the learning effects (positive or negative) we are trying to observe. We adopt (a) with awareness of needing to monitor result instability at late iterations of feedback.

6.2 KeepAll and TakeOut Evaluation

To address the challenge of scarce relevant documents, we evaluate accuracy of methods in two distinct ways, which we denote as **KeepAll** and **TakeOut**. Both have strengths and weaknesses, and our general thought is that evaluating methods under both strategies in tandem provides a balanced view for comparing relative accuracy of methods.

KeepAll evaluation compares methods without removal of feedback documents. This means that even after a given document's relevance is made known to the system via user feedback, we continue to include that document in the evaluation set. However, we also follow prior work's strategy [9] of imposing the restriction that systems cannot memorize the list feedback documents, but instead must limit learning to parameter updates. Nonetheless ranking documents that were previously viewed still results in artificially inflated ranking accuracies observed across systems. On the positive side, *KeepAll* evaluation does preserve the expected trend of accuracies rising across systems with increasing feedback.

A possible problem with *KeepAll* in our task scenario is that it could lead to the same document being selected repeatedly for RF across iterations. While such repeated selection is actually a useful property in some learning models such as Boosting [21], it would be odd to the user to keep seeing the same feedback documents over-and-over again in the results list, let alone having to tell the system multiple times that a given document is relevant.

To address this, we distinguish two separate rankings: a *feedback ranking* and an *evaluation ranking*. The evaluation ranking is generated over all documents and is used to evaluate system accuracy. The feedback ranking is presented to the user for feedback and filters out all previous feedback documents from the evaluation ranking. This is similar to a search interface that lets users "bookmark" known relevant webpages in a sidebar and thereafter excludes them from the ranking. Since the user is never presented the same relevant document twice for feedback, RF iteration terminates for each topic once all of its relevant documents are exhausted.

TakeOut evaluation, unlike *KeepAll*, removes feedback documents from evaluation. We do not perform full *residual evaluation*, but rather evaluate each method on a unique residual document subset at each iteration based on feedback documents used up to the current iteration. This means different methods will typically be evaluated on different document subsets in the same iteration, though they will still have the same number of relative documents under the correct user feedback. Moreover, since progressively fewer relevant documents remain to be found as iteration progresses, topics become increasingly difficult. Relevant documents that are easier to find are taken out in earlier iterations, so remaining relevant documents in the pool tend to become progressively more difficult to find individually as well as fewer in number overall. Consequently, we observe a counter-intuitive effect whereby the general trend across systems is for ranking accuracy to decrease rather than increase as iteration proceeds. Nonetheless, we would expect in comparative evaluation of methods to see a stronger RF method to decrease in accuracy more slowly than other methods.

A final challenge with both *KeepAll* and *TakeOut* evaluation is specific to active learning (§4). Recall active learning selects a document whose relevance is maximally uncertain and slots it at the top rank. A practical consequence of evaluating ranking accuracy is that early precision metrics like MRR become entirely dominated by this single document, and so fail to provide any meaningful measure of the actual ranking. To address this artifact, we focus evaluation of active learning on the point at which the user's effort threshold is exceeded. The user then terminates the training phrase and only wants to use the system thereafter. This disables active learning and so eliminates these slotting effects. To model this, we evaluate system accuracy on the *evaluation ranking* (without slotting) rather than the *feedback ranking* (with slotting). User effort is still measured off the feedback ranking, ensuring that slotting any non-relevant documents increases measured user effort since the user must browse more results before finding a relevant document.

7. EVALUATION

Recall our interactive search task involves iterative back-and-forth between system ranking and user feedback (§2). The system goal in this scenario is to maximize ranking accuracy for any amount of relevance feedback provided. Consequently, our evaluation measures ranking accuracy achieved under varying amounts of user feedback in order to compute the *learning curve* of each relevance feedback method. Measuring this curve enables us to compare the relative strength of each method across a range of possible stopping points which might be encountered in practice and suggest different methods being better suited to different use cases. Our main results assume user feedback to the system is always correct, similar to a traditional RF setting with known relevant and non-relevant documents (§7.2). We also present results for a noisy feedback scenario (§7.3) and an alternative learning scenario on LETOR TD2003 and TD2004 collections (§7.4).

7.1 Experimental Setup

Experiments in §7.2 and §7.3 are reported on the TREC[3] Robust04 document collection of newswire articles. Topics 301-450 were used for evaluation during system development and tuning, with topics 601-700 held out for final testing. System queries are taken from title field of each topic. An initial ranking of 200 documents for each query is generated using Indri [23]. This initial ranking provides both a baseline measure of system accuracy as well as the document pool subsequently re-ranked by each RF method. To reduce vocabulary growth from rare words, we prune out any term which does not occur at least twice in some document and at least four times in the entire collection. This reduces the vocabulary size of the query-specific document pools from about 10,000-20,000 terms to about 3,000-4,000 terms.

We compare the relative performance of several RF baseline methods in this task setting of iterative feedback (§3): (1) Rocchio feedback [20] (denoted by "Rocchio"), (2) Rocchio with positive feedback only (denoted by "RocchioPos"), and (3) model-based feedback [28] (denoted by "Language"). Since prior work has only observed modest benefits from negative feedback, we were particularly interested in comparing the relative performance of (1) and (2) in our task setting. Additional details of baseline methods are discussed in §3. For all baselines, parameters are tuned on the development set to maximize the accuracy of each method: Rocchio ($\alpha = 0.05$, $\beta = 0.5$), RocchioPos ($\alpha = 0.05$, $\beta = 1$), and model-based (Language) ($\alpha = 0.05$, $\lambda = 0.8$, and $\gamma = 0.3$).

For active learning, we evaluate both **Simple Margin** and **Local Structure** criteria (§4). Simple Margin has no parameters, while with Local Structure we use $m = 10$ neighbors and $\alpha = 0.5$. LS feature selection (§5) further reduces vocabulary size for active learning using $k = 15$ neighbors and $N = 2500$ features (a modest further reduction from the already reduced vocabulary size). Feature selection is not used with baseline methods. While baselines benefit from interpolating the original query with feedback (an anchoring effect to prevent query drift), active learning methods perform ranking based on feedback documents only. Exploring anchoring between the query model and active learning via rank fusion [6] remains for future work.

Ranking accuracy is measured by three metrics: mean-average precision (MAP), top-10 precision (P@10), and mean

[3]http://trec.nist.gov

	MAP	P10	MRR	MAP_All	P@10_All
RocchioPos	0.3296 ($p < 0.001$)	0.2554 ($p < 0.001$)	0.5437 ($p < 0.001$)	0.6268 ($p < 0.001$)	0.6423 ($p < 0.001$)
Rocchio	0.3449 ($p < 0.001$)	0.2755 ($p < 0.001$)	0.5848 ($p < 0.001$)	0.6846 ($p < 0.001$)	0.6987 ($p < 0.001$)
Language	0.3923 ($p \approx 0.24$)	0.2918 ($p \approx 0.019$)	0.6028 ($p \approx 0.016$)	0.6730 ($p < 0.001$)	0.6754 ($p < 0.001$)
ActiveMargin	0.3952†	0.3116‡	**0.6251‡**	0.7427‡	0.7399‡
ActiveStructure	**0.3978†**	**0.3135‡**	0.6248‡	**0.7475‡***	**0.7525‡**

Table 1: Average accuracy of each method across feedback iterations. Statistical significance is computed by two-sided paired t-test [22]. Significance levels p for ActiveMargin vs. each baseline are included in each baseline's cell. † denotes significant improvement ($p < 0.05$) over at least one baseline, ‡ a significant improvement over all baselines, and * a significant improvement of Local Structure over Simple Margin. MAP_All and P@10_All correspond to *KeepAll* evaluation; other measures correspond to *TakeOut* evaluation.

reciprocal rank (MRR). User effort is measured by the total number of clicks, which equals the number of positive documents with correct feedback and upper-bounds the number of positive documents with noisy feedback. We also tracked the total number of documents viewed by the user in browsing search results but saw the number of clicks and views were very correlated and largely yielded the same learning curve plots. Consequently, we omit these results to simplify presentation. Another related metric we did not measure is Cooper's expected search length: the number of non-relevant documents a user needs to skip over to find some number of relevant documents desired [5].

7.2 Correct Relevance Feedback

Figure 3 presents empirical results for both *TakeOut* and *KeepAll* evaluation conditions (see §6.2) assuming relevance feedback provided by the user is always correct. We also compute the average accuracy of each method across iterations and present this in Table 1, along with results of statistical significance tests. Statistical significance of improvements is determined using a two-sided paired t-test [22] at the 5% significance level over all queries. The proposed active learning methods (Simple Margin and Local Structure) are seen to by-and-large dominate baselines across iterations, metrics, and for both *TakeOut* and *KeepAll* conditions. We omit the plot of MRR due to space limitations, though we do report it for *TakeOut* evaluation in Table 1. MRR is not meaningful for *KeepAll* since the labeled documents are essentially always ranked at the top.

As mentioned earlier (§6), an experimental challenge is that while we expect system accuracy to improve with increasing feedback, we have a confounding factor that tends to work against this: as more relevant documents are "used up" for feedback, fewer remain to be found in subsequent iterations, effectively increasing query difficult. Moreover, documents that are "easier" to find are taken out in earlier iterations, so remaining relevant documents in the pool become progressively more difficult to find individually as well as fewer in number overall. This effect is particularly pronounced in the *TakeOut* condition in which system accuracies tend to decrease due to fewer relevant documents remaining in the residual collection used for evaluation.

With the *KeepAll* condition, *all* documents are reranked and included in evaluation at each iteration. As noted earlier (see §6.2), this system does not "remember" earlier feedback documents and must rerank them like any other document based on learned parameters. However, it is still the case that the system has learned from having seen some of the relevant documents that are now being evaluated on, which tends to introduce the opposite evaluation effect that system accuracy tends to be inflated across methods with increasing feedback. Allowing for this effect, Figure 3(a) shows that under *KeepAll* evaluation, all feedback methods are seen to exhibit the expected (and more intuitive) behavior of achieving increased accuracy with greater feedback. While *TakeOut* and *KeepAll* evaluation conditions each have their own respective limitations, the key point to observe with regard to our evaluation of active learning is that it dominates the other baselines across both methods of evaluation.

Another interesting point to note is the observed value of negative feedback in our results vs. what has traditionally been observed in ad hoc search or single-iteration relevance feedback. The traditional wisdom has been that negative documents have relatively little in common, so learning what one looks like does not help the system avoid ranking another one highly. In our experiments, three methods use both positive and negative feedback: Rocchio, Simple Margin, and Local Structure. RocchioPos and Language only use positive feedback. Of particular note, Rocchio outperforms RocchioPos on nearly all metrics in all iterations. Both active learning methods dominate all baselines, including all methods using only positive feedback, in MAP and P@10. One possible explanation for our findings is that our user model and method for obtaining relevance feedback tend to produce many more non-relevant documents than relevant documents for feedback, thus *en masse*, many examples of non-relevant documents do help to characterize the overall space of non-relevance. Another possible effect we are observing is due the entire document pool coming from the initial Indri ranking, thus the set of non-relevant documents used for feedback might otherwise be highly ranked by the system. The TREC Relevance Feedback track [4] has investigated issues of feedback document selection in recent years, though the question remains open as to what constitutes a useful non-relevant document for negative feedback [26].

7.3 Noisy Relevance Feedback

This section reports relative accuracy achieved by different RF methods under noisy feedback, when the user clicks on non-relevant documents or fails to click on relevant ones. As discussed earlier (§2), noisy feedback is modeled using two Bernoulli parameters, f_p and f_n, to control the false positive and negative rates, respectively. Setting both parameters to zero yields the same correct feedback setting evaluated above. We evaluate methods for three noise conditions: (1) $f_p = 0$ and $f_n = 0.1$, (2) $f_p = 0.1$ and $f_n = 0$, and (3) $f_p = 0.1$ and $f_n = 0.1$. Results of *KeepAll* evaluation are shown in Figure 5.

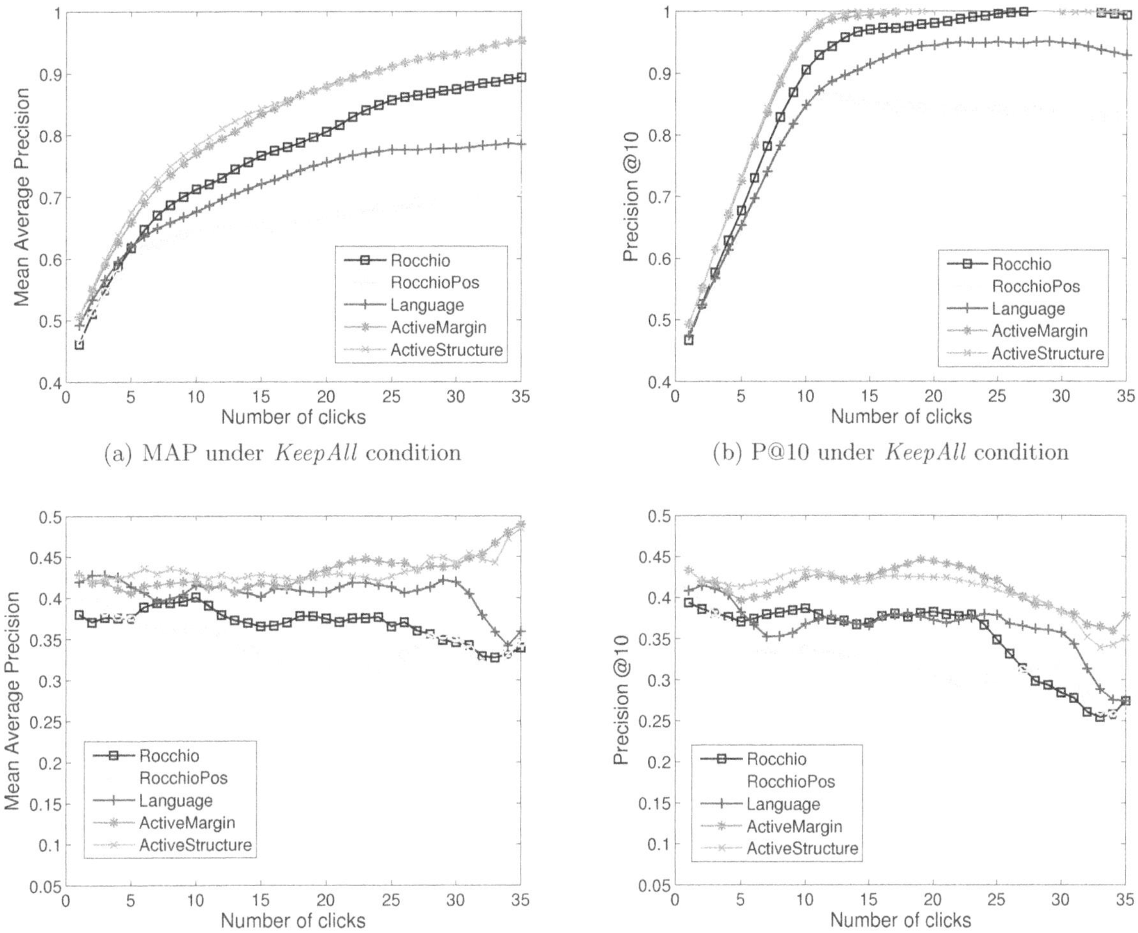

(a) MAP under *KeepAll* condition

(b) P@10 under *KeepAll* condition

(c) MAP under *TakeOut* condition

(d) P@10 under *TakeOut* condition

Figure 3: Learning curve plots depict ranking accuracy on Robust04 of the different feedback methods given a varying number of correct relevance feedback documents provided by the user. The horizontal axis indicates the number of feedback iterations (and by this same token, the number of positive feedback documents used).

While all methods are seen to decrease in accuracy in comparison to the noiseless condition, active learning methods continue to dominate the other baselines. However, results with noise rates of 20% and higher have shown Rocchio to dominate active learning, suggesting a threshold for method selection based upon the level of noise. Our hypothesis for this behavior is that active learning, which updates the decision surface based on feedback, is inherently more sensitive than Rocchio, which simply updates its linear combination of feedback documents. Thus the same virtue which enables active learning to learn more efficiently from correct feedback appears to render it less robust to noisy feedback.

7.4 Relevance Feedback on LETOR

This section presents experimental results conducted on LETOR 3.0 [15]. LETOR defines a standard feature representation of documents for supporting machine learning studies, enabling easier comparison of alternative learning strategies for the same features. In comparison to the term-based features used in our earlier experiments on Robust04, LETOR features are quite different and potentially more powerful, providing another useful benchmark for assessing the relative effectiveness of our active learning methods.

While LETOR includes several document collections, not all are suitable for our study. In particular, because we are interested in RF (which requires many relevant documents), we exclude OHSUMED, as well as Homepage or Named Page Finding collections. Instead, we focus on Topic Distillation: TD2003 and TD2004. These collections are derived from the 2003 and 2004 TREC Web track [7] tasks on the .GOV collection (a 1.25 million web crawl of the .gov domain performed in 2002). No dimensionality reduction is performed.

For LETOR, we do not have the query, so model-based feedback [28] cannot be evaluated. For other methods, we use two positive and two negative documents to form the query for Rocchio, and to initialize the active learning models. Active learning parameters are identical to those used in our earlier experiments on Robust04 with one notable exception: we restrict the ratio of non-relevant feedback to relevant feedback at a heuristic 7:1 ratio. That is, we ignore additional non-relevant documents provided as feedback whenever it would exceed this threshold. While TD2003 and

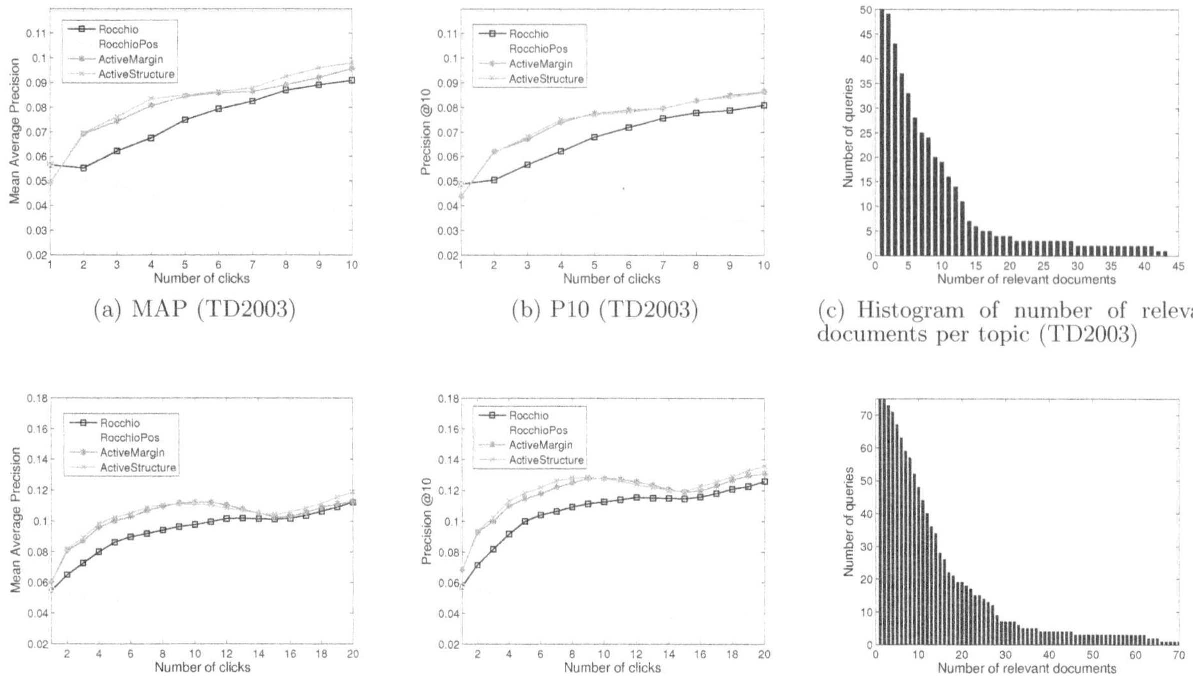

(a) MAP (TD2003) (b) P10 (TD2003) (c) Histogram of number of relevant documents per topic (TD2003)

(d) MAP (TD2004) (e) P10 (TD2004) (f) Histogram of number of relevant documents per topic (TD2004)

Figure 4: Learning curves of RF methods on LETOR's TD2003 (first row) and TD2004 (second row) collections depict ranking accuracy vs. amount of relevance feedback provided. Accuracy levels reflect training on a *single* topic and testing on the remaining topics, repeated round-robin for cross-validation. The horizontal axis indicates the number of feedback iterations (equal to the number of positive feedback documents used). Active learning methods perform as well or better than Rocchio. As the histogram shows, relevant documents per topic are quite sparse, restricting the number of feedback iterations possible with stable evaluation.

TD2004 have more relevant documents per topic than other LETOR collections, relevant documents remain relatively sparse. We found that an excess of non-relevant documents hurt active learning accuracy. Parameters are tuned on TD2003, and tested on TD2004.

A significant difference between our evaluation on LETOR vs. Robust04 stems from the differing nature of features in the two collections. With term-based features (Robust04), RF let us learn term-based weights to improve ranking accuracy for the current query. For example, while the word "dog" might be very important to the current query, RF on this query cannot tell us anything about how important this word should be for other queries. With LETOR, in contrast, features capture general properties of query-document compatibility. This means, for example, that if the PageRank feature is important for the current query, there is a good chance it will be important for other queries as well.

Due to this difference in features, we can simplify our evaluation methodology enormously by adopting a slightly altered task scenario. In this new scenario, training and testing phases are completely distinct: the user trains the system via iterative feedback on *one* topic, then uses the system to rank documents for all other topics. Because the user cannot provide iterative feedback on multiple queries in parallel, we abandon LETOR's standard 5-fold partition of topics. Instead, for each topic we train on it alone and evaluate on all other topics, then we average this over all topics. Since we are only training on a single topic, resulting accuracy is far lower than what typically published LETOR results. As with our first batch of results presented for Robust04, we again assume the user provides correct feedback.

This revised task means that the user no longer cares about finding relevant documents for the current topic. However, he stills terminates iteration whenever either (a) the trained system is "good enough", (b) his effort threshold in training the system is exceeded, or (c) no additional relevant documents remain for feedback. As in earlier experiments on Robust04, once (c) occurs, we exclude the given topic from average accuracy calculations in subsequent iterations. This means that learning curve plots reflect an average over progressively fewer topics as the number of relevant documents is exhausted. As the average is computed over progressively fewer topics, stability decreases, especially at late iterations.

Consequently, we only present results for 10 iterations with TD2003 and 20 iterations with TD2004. These termination points stem from the corresponding histograms for TD2003 and TD2004 indicating number of relevant documents per query (Figures 4(c) and Figure 4(f), respectively). We stop iteration when the number of topics remaining would fall below 20 (a loose threshold for result stability from observation). While the histogram for the Robust04 collection is not shown, the choice of terminating after 35 iterations there is the same: there would be less than 20 topics with any relevant documents left to be found.

Results in Figure 4 show that active learning methods perform as well or better than Rocchio.

8. CONCLUSION AND FUTURE WORK

This paper considers an interactive IR scenario in which the user is interested in finding several to many relevant documents with minimal effort. Given an initial document ranking, the user interacts with the system to provide iterative relevance feedback. Evaluation on the TREC Robust04 collection and LETOR TD2003 and TD2004 collections shows our active learning approach dominates several standard baselines in terms of effectiveness achieved relative to the amount of user effort required.

Future work will continue to develop our active learning methods, evaluate on additional document collections, compare stability of parameters across collections, and evaluate noisy feedback using real user data. We are also interested in modeling and evaluating active learning for diversity ranking [16, 18, 25] with interactive retrieval.

Investigation of the exploration vs. exploitation learning tradeoff represents another interesting direction for future work: varying the rank at which to slot-in an uncertain document for feedback, as well as potentially varying the number of uncertain documents used. While a lower ranking of uncertain documents will increase ranking accuracy at the current iteration, doing so may reduce accuracy at future iterations by increasing the probability of a different relevant document occurring at a higher rank. In that event, the user would never see the uncertain document (under assumptions of the current user model), thereby failing to label the example selected by active learning.

Acknowledgments

We would like to thank the anonymous reviewers for their valuable feedback. This work was partially supported by a John P. Commons Fellowship for the second author.

9. REFERENCES

[1] B. Bai, J. Weston, D. Grangier, R. Collobert, K. Sadamasa, Y. Qi, O. Chapelle, and K. Weinberger. Learning to rank with (a lot of) word features. *Information Retrieval*, 13(3):291–314, 2010.

[2] M. Belkin and P. Niyogi. Laplacian eigenmaps and spectral techniques for embedding and clustering. *NIPS*, 1:585–592, 2002.

[3] C. Brandt, T. Joachims, Y. Yue, and J. Bank. Dynamic ranked retrieval. In *Proc. WSDM*, pages 247–256. ACM, 2011.

[4] C. Buckley and S. Robertson. Relevance feedback track overview. In *17th TREC Notebook*, 2008.

[5] W. Cooper. Expected search length: A single measure of retrieval effectiveness based on the weak ordering action of retrieval systems. *American Documentation*, 19(1):30–41, 1968.

[6] G. Cormack, C. Clarke, and S. Buttcher. Reciprocal rank fusion outperforms condorcet and individual rank learning methods. In *SIGIR*, pages 758–759, 2009.

[7] N. Craswell and D. Hawking. Overview of the TREC-2004 Web track. In *Proc. TREC*, 2005.

[8] S. Deerwester, S. Dumais, G. Furnas, T. Landauer, and R. Harshman. Indexing by latent semantic analysis. *Journal of the American Society for Information Science*, 41(6):391–407, 1990.

[9] F. Diaz and D. Metzler. Improving the estimation of relevance models using large external corpora. In *Proc. SIGIR*, pages 154–161. ACM, 2006.

[10] X. He, D. Cai, and P. Niyogi. Laplacian score for feature selection. *NIPS*, 18:507, 2006.

[11] X. He and P. Niyogi. Locality preserving projections. *NIPS*, 16:153, 2004.

[12] T. Hofmann. Probabilistic latent semantic indexing. In *Proc. SIGIR*, pages 50–57. ACM, 1999.

[13] A. Kapoor, E. Horvitz, and S. Basu. Selective supervision: guiding supervised learning with decision-theoretic active learning. In *IJCAI*, pages 877–882, 2007.

[14] P. Over. The TREC interactive track: an annotated bibliography. *Information Processing & Management*, 37(3):369–381, 2001.

[15] T. Qin, T. Liu, J. Xu, and H. Li. LETOR: A benchmark collection for research on learning to rank for information retrieval. *Information Retrieval*, pages 1–29, 2010.

[16] F. Radlinski and S. Dumais. Improving personalized web search using result diversification. In *Proc. SIGIR*, pages 691–692. ACM, 2006.

[17] F. Radlinski and T. Joachims. Active exploration for learning rankings from clickthrough data. In *Proc. SIGKDD*, pages 570–579. ACM, 2007.

[18] D. Rafiei, K. Bharat, and A. Shukla. Diversifying web search results. In *WWW*, pages 781–790. ACM, 2010.

[19] S. Robertson. The probability ranking principle in IR. *Journal of Documentation*, 33(4):294–304, 1977.

[20] G. Salton and C. Buckley. Improving retrieval performance by relevance feedback. *Journal of the American Society for Information Science*, 41(4):288–297, 1990.

[21] R. Schapire. A brief introduction to boosting. In *Proc. IJCAI*, volume 16, pages 1401–1406, 1999.

[22] M. D. Smucker, J. Allan, and B. Carterette. A comparison of statistical significance tests for information retrieval evaluation. In *Proc. of CIKM*, pages 623–632, 2007.

[23] T. Strohman, D. Metzler, H. Turtle, and W. B. Croft. Indri: A language model-based search engine for complex queries. In *Proceedings of the International Conference on Intelligence Analysis*, 2004.

[24] S. Tong and D. Koller. Support vector machine active learning with applications to text classification. *The Journal of Machine Learning Research*, 2:45–66, 2002.

[25] J. Wang and J. Zhu. Portfolio theory of information retrieval. In *Proc. SIGIR*, pages 115–122. ACM, 2009.

[26] X. Wang, H. Fang, and C. Zhai. A study of methods for negative relevance feedback. In *Proc. SIGIR*, pages 219–226. ACM, 2008.

[27] X. Wei and W. Croft. LDA-based document models for ad-hoc retrieval. In *SIGIR*, pages 178–185, 2006.

[28] C. Zhai and J. Lafferty. Model-based feedback in the language modeling approach to information retrieval. In *Proc. CIKM*, pages 403–410. ACM, 2001.

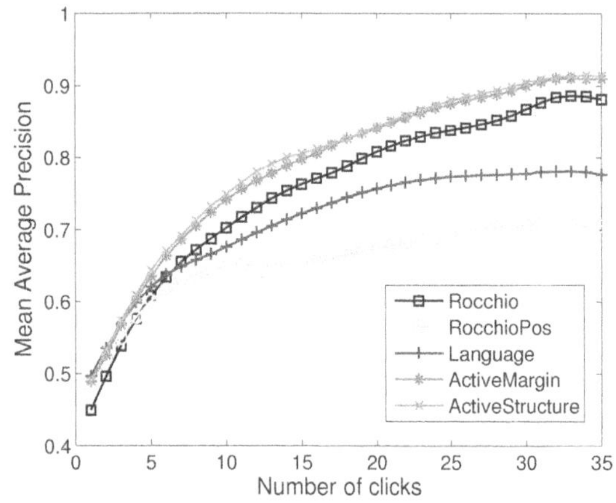

(a) MAP: $f_p = 0$ and $f_n = 0.1$

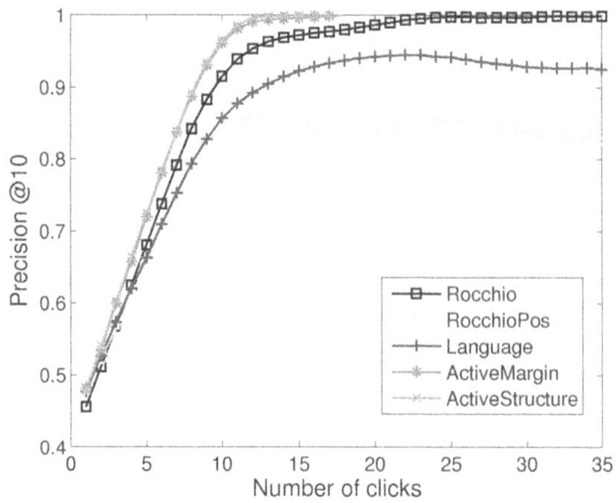

(b) P@10: $f_p = 0$ and $f_n = 0.1$

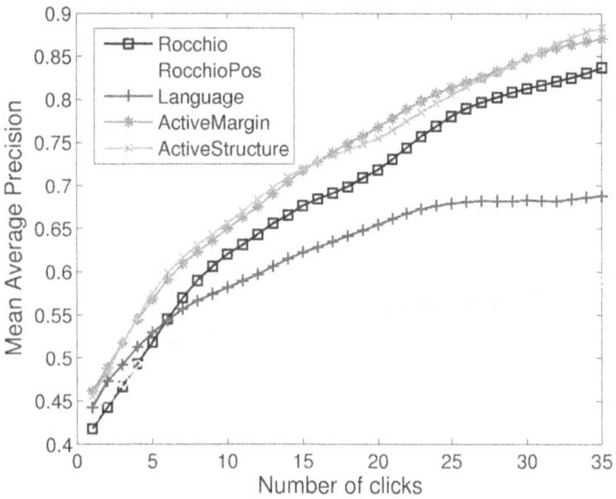

(c) MAP: $f_p = 0.1$ and $f_n = 0$

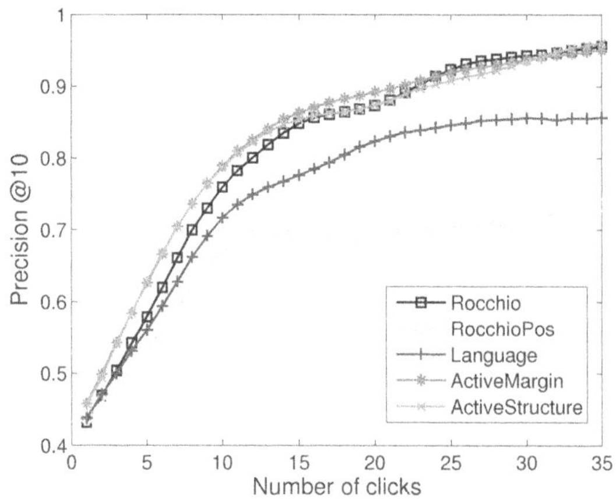

(d) P@10: $f_p = 0.1$ and $f_n = 0$

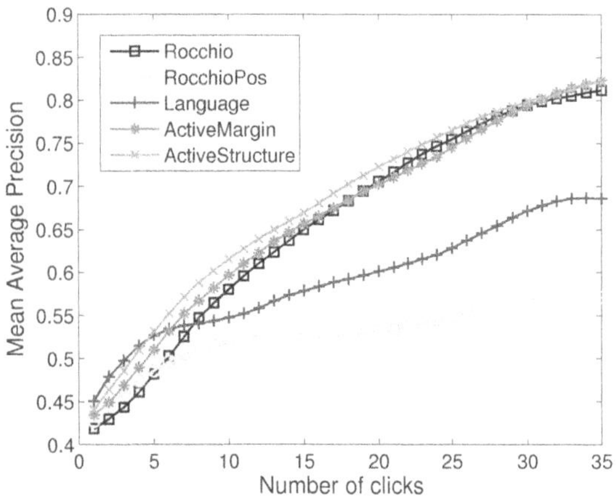

(e) MAP: $f_p = 0.1$ and $f_n = 0.1$

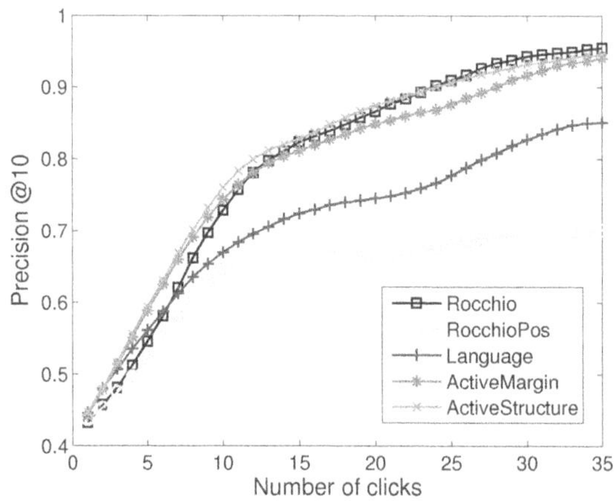

(f) P@10: $f_p = 0.1$ and $f_n = 0.1$

Figure 5: Learning curves for the five relevance feedback methods given noisy user feedback. f_p and f_n denote Bernoulli probabilities of false positives (erroneous clicks) and false negatives (missed relevant documents) by the user, respectively. Evaluation is performed under *KeepAll* condition. The horizontal axis indicates the number of feedback iterations (and by this same token, the number of user clicks). In comparison to earlier results with correct feedback, we see the introduction of noise decreases accuracy, as expected. Active learning methods Simple Margin and Local Structure continue to dominate the baseline methods.

CRTER: Using Cross Terms to Enhance Probabilistic Information Retrieval

Jiashu Zhao
Information Retrieval and Knowledge Management Research Lab
Department of Computer Science & Engineering
York University
Toronto, Canada
jessie@cse.yorku.ca

Jimmy Xiangji Huang, Ben He
Information Retrieval and Knowledge Management Research Lab
School of Information Technology
York University
Toronto, Canada
{jhuang, benhe}@yorku.ca

ABSTRACT

Term proximity retrieval rewards a document where the matched query terms occur close to each other. Although term proximity is known to be effective in many Information Retrieval (IR) applications, the within-document distribution of each individual query term and how the query terms associate with each other, are not fully considered. In this paper, we introduce a pseudo term, namely Cross Term, to model term proximity for boosting retrieval performance. An occurrence of a query term is assumed to have an impact towards its neighboring text, which gradually weakens with the increase of the distance to the place of occurrence. We use a shape function to characterize such an impact. A Cross Term occurs when two query terms appear close to each other and their impact shape functions have an intersection. We propose a CRoss TErm Retrieval (CRTER) model that combines the Cross Terms' information with basic probabilistic weighting models to rank the retrieved documents. Extensive experiments on standard TREC collections illustrate the effectiveness of our proposed CRTER model.

Categories and Subject Descriptors

H.3.3 [**Information Storage & Retrieval**]: Information Search & Retrieval

General Terms

Performance, Experimentation

Keywords

Cross Term, Kernel, BM25, Proximity, Probabilistic IR

1. INTRODUCTION AND MOTIVATION

Most of the traditional Information Retrieval models are based on the assumption that query terms are independent of each other, where a document is represented as a bag of words. Nevertheless this assumption may not hold in practice. There might be some implied associations among them. For example, given a query "Vancouver Olympics", there exists an association between the query terms. Users are not looking for either other events in Vancouver or the Olympic games in other cities.

- The **Vancouver Olympics** draw to a spectacular close after 17 days of intense competition.
- **Vancouver** athletes ... 2012 London **Olympics**.

Given above two documents with both "Vancouver" and "Olympics" occurring once each, a traditional IR model will give them the same weights. Obviously the former document contains more valuable information for users than the later. The association between "Vancouver" and "Olympics" reflects the distance between them. Therefore, it is necessary to reward the document where the matched query terms appear together/close.

Many researchers have been working on proximity metrics in information retrieval [4, 11, 12]. Whereas, the nature of the associations among query terms still awaits further study. Some proximity approaches only considers adjacency [26, 27], while non-adjacent terms may also have associations. N-gram models [1, 17] consider n word sequences, which expand the radius of matching. It is yet hard to determine N, and complexity grows exponentially with the growth of N. Also, redundant proximity information may be led into the model, which may on the other hand decreases the performance of the probabilistic weighting models. Other proximity based probabilistic weighting models, such as [5, 6], add proximity information into their weighting functions in a heuristic manner. However, their experiments are not conclusive and their retrieval functions are not shown to be effective and robust enough [28].

In this paper, we present a Cross Term Retrieval model, denoted as CRTER, to model the associations among query terms in probabilistic retrieval models. A pseudo term, Cross Term, is introduced for boosting retrieval performance. A Cross Term is generated by two closely occurred query terms.

We assume that an occurrence of a query term has an impact towards its neighbouring text. This impact attenuates when a position is farther away. If we try to characterize this impact with a mathematic function, intuitively the function should satisfy the following properties: Non-negative, Continuous, Symmetric, Monotonic, Identity (See detail in Section 3). We use kernel functions that have been brought to proximity retrieval [10, 16] to estimate the query term occurrence's impact. In this paper, we investigated three more kernel functions that satisfy the above properties: Quartic Kernel, Epanechnikov Kernel, and Triweight Kernel. The kernel functions are normalized with a minimum value of 0 and a maximum value of 1. When two query terms, q_i and q_j, occur closely in a document, their impact shape functions will have an intersection. We say q_i and q_j are generating terms of a Cross Term $q_{i,j}$, which occurs when q_i and q_j's impact shape functions intersect.

The corresponding impact shape functions' value at this intersection is Cross Term $q_{i,j}$'s occurrence value, which ranges from 0 to 1. The closer two query terms' occurrences are, their generated Cross Term has higher occurrence value, according to the impact shape function's properties. Therefore, the Cross Term's occurrence value indicates to which extent two query terms are correlated.

The challenge we are facing is how to estimate a Cross Term from a document collection, and integrate the Cross Term into a probabilistic weighting model. In a probabilistic weighting model, some variants change from term to term, namely the within-document Cross Term frequency (tf), the number of documents containing the Cross Term (n), and the within-query Cross Term frequency (qtf), respectively. We define the corresponding variants for Cross Terms: $tf(q_{i,j})$, $n(q_{i,j})$, and $qtf(q_{i,j})$. For $tf(q_{i,j})$, as a pseudo term, the traditional counting method of the occurrences in a document does not make much sense, especially when we aim to reward more on the Cross Terms that the generating query terms are closer. Instead of accumulating the number of occurrences, we accumulate a Cross Term's occurrence value in a document as its $tf(q_{i,j})$, which is small when generating query terms are far away, and large when generating query terms are close to each other. Please note that $tf(q_{i,j})$ is always smaller than the number of occurrences of a Cross Term in the document. In order to balance with $tf(q_{i,j})$, we define $n(q_{i,j})$ and $qtf(q_{i,j})$ correspondingly. $n(q_{i,j})$ is the accumulated Cross Term's average value on each document over the collection. In a query, since it is normally short and only contains query terms, we assume that terms in a query are densely distributed. If two terms exist in a query, they are regarded as being adjacent. Then $qtf(q_{i,j})$ is a simplified case of within-document frequency by treating the query as a document. With the defined Cross Term variants, we integrate Cross Terms into traditional BM25 weighting model [25], by treating them as special terms. Cross Terms' weights are computed and linearly combined with query terms' weights.

The remainder of this paper is organized as follows. In Section 2, we discuss the prior related work. In Section 3, we introduce the concept of Cross Term and define its variants. In Section 4, we propose Cross Term Retrieval (CRTER) model utilizing BM25 as basic weighting function. In Section 5, we set up our experimental environment on six TREC collections, and test the proposed CRTER model and compare it with some existing models. In Section 6, we conclude the paper with a discussion of our findings and future work.

2. RELATED WORK

In the 1990s, some early researchers started to investigate the effectiveness of term proximity in Information Retrieval. Allan and Ballesteros [2] indexed phases instead of terms with InQuery [7], and obtained improvements in TREC campaigns. Clarke and Cormack [9] introduced a "NEAR" operator to quantify the proximity of query terms. Hawking and Thistlewaite [12] evaluated "Span" proximity approaches on TREC data sets, which is the text segments containing all query term instances.

Some studies heuristically integrated word proximity into probabilistic weighting models, such as [5, 6, 24, 28]. However, the nature of query term proximity still awaits further study.

N-gram IR models have been investigated as a proximity approach by researchers for years [1, 17, 18]. They are recognized as having high complexity and may lead to redundant information. Bigram models make a better balance between effectiveness and complexity. Song and Croft [26] proposed a general language model that combines bigram language models with several smoothing techniques including a Good-Turing estimate and corpus-based smoothing of unigram probabilities. The relative contributions of the different models to the query generation probability are determined empirically. Srikanth and Rohini [27] approximated the biterm probabilities using the frequency of occurrence of terms. Biterm language models are similar to bigram language models except that the constraint of order in terms is relaxed. In [3], authors proposed a language modeling approach that incorporates word pairs, without a constraint on adjacency or word order, where word pairs are determined statistical relationships, or lexical affinities, between words. Pickens [23] introduced an approach that uses non-adjacent biterms, but the particular domain, musical documents, requires an emphasis on the order of "words". We also only investigate the proximity between a pair of query terms, whereas, our approach differs from the previous studies that we propose the concept of a pseudo term, Cross Term, generated by two query terms to investigate how two query terms' occurrence change together. Cross Terms are naturally integrated into basic retrieval models as new terms, and therefore incorporate proximity into retrieval process.

Various proximity approaches integrating knowledge from other realms were investigated. [11] introduced the linkage of a query as a hidden variable, which expressed the term dependencies within the query as an acyclic, planar, undirected graph. A method of incorporating term dependence in probabilistic retrieval model was proposed in [8] by adapting Bahadur-Lazarsfeld expansion (BLE), which was originally used in the pattern recognition field. In [4], authors proposed a mathematical model based on a fuzzy proximity degree of term occurrences particularly for boolean queries. A retrieval model based on Markov random field [20] was presented for developing a general framework for modeling term dependencies.

Density functions based on proximity have been adopted to characterize term influence propagation [10, 14, 16, 19, 22]. [10] is early work that proposed to propagate the $tf \cdot idf$ score of each query term to other positions, where triangle, cosine, circle, and arc contribution functions were discussed. The highest accumulated $tf \cdot idf$ score on all the positions is adopted as the document's score. [14] uses hanning (cosine) window function to characterize the density of terms. Lv and Zhai [16] proposed a positional language model that incorporates the term proximity in a model based approach using four term propagation functions: gaussian, triangle, cosine, and circle. We utilize the above term influence propagation functions in measuring Cross Terms, and test more potentially functions.

3. A NEW PSEUDO TERM: CROSS TERM

In this section, formally define the notion of Cross Term and the method of computing a Cross Term. Suppose we have a query, $Q = \{q_1, q_1, ..., q_n\}$ and a document D, where pos is one of the positions of query term q_i in document D. The term q_i will influence the positions between $pos + k$ and $pos - k$.

We assume that the impact of a matching term q_i at position pos can be captured by the value of an impact function $f_i(pos, k)$.

PROPERTY 1. *Let $f_i(pos, k)$ be the impact function of a query term q_i at position $pos + k$. $f_i(pos, k)$ must follow the following 5 properties.*

(1) Non-negative: $f_i(pos, k) > 0$, the impact of a term towards its neighborhood is always non-negative(We only focus on the position influence between query terms).

(2) Continuous: $|f_i(pos, k) - f_i(pos, k+1)|$ is small, i.e., there is a slight difference between two neighboring positions.

(3) Symmetric: $f_i(pos, -k) = f_i(pos, k)$, the term has the same impact towards two equal-distance positions.

(4) Monotonic: $f_i(pos, k) > f_i(pos, k+1)$, where $k > 0$. The influence would decrease with the increasing of $|k|$.

(5) Identity: $f_i(pos, 0) = 1$, set one as standard influence.

Gaussian Kernel, Circle Kernel, and Triangle Kernel are widely used kernel function and satisfy all of above properties [16]. We will discuss more about various kernel function in Section 3.4. When two query terms are close enough, their impact shape functions will join. Their point of intersection reflects the association between these two query terms.

Definition 1. Given two query terms q_i and q_j, if there exists points of intersections for impact functions $f_i(pos_1, k_1)$ and $f_j(pos_2, k_2)$, where $pos_1 + k_1$ equals to $pos_2 - k_2$, we say that a **Cross Term** occurs, denoted as $q_{i,j}$. We call q_i and q_j ***Generating Terms*** of $q_{i,j}$.

Definition 2. When a Cross Term $q_{i,j}$ occurs, the ***Cross Term's value*** is the impact function's value at the intersection.

Without previous domain knowledge of a query and a collection, we assume that the query terms are identically distributed, i.e., the query terms have the same impact shape functions. A Cross Term always locates in the middle of its generating query terms, and has higher value when the query terms occur closer.

Figure 1 shows a Cross Term's example. Two query terms, q_1 and q_2, located at the 8th position and the 12th position in the document. More intuitively, We adopt Gaussian Kernel as impact shape function. Their impact's shape functions are $f_1(pos_1, 2)$ and $f_2(pos_2, -2)$, accordingly. We can see that two shape functions cross over each other, and there exists an intersection at the 10th position. There is no threshold incorporated into the definitions of Cross Term and its value. For a continuous kernel function, there would always be an intersection if two terms occur in one document.

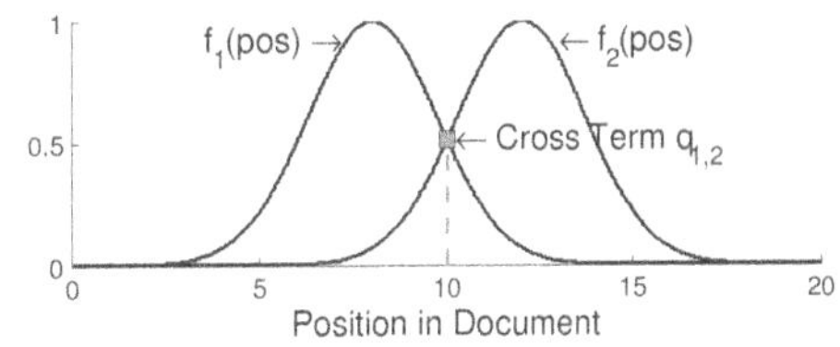

Figure 1: An example of Cross Term

3.1 Within-Document Cross Term Frequency

Here we want to define the counting method for the frequency. The within-document frequency is the rate at which a term occurs in a document. For a single query term, its frequency in document D equals how many times it occurs in D. But for a Cross Term, to simply count its occurrence might overestimate the frequency. We introduce a new estimation of a Cross Term's within-document frequency. As we can see from Figure 1 that $q_{1,2}$'s value becomes higher if q_1 and q_2 are close and lower if there is a farther distance between q_1 and q_2. Naturally we adopt the Cross Term's value in estimating its within-document frequency.

Suppose the positions of q_i in a document are $\{pos_{1,i}, pos_{2,i}, ..., pos_{tf_i,i}\}$, where tf_i is the term frequency of q_i. Correspondingly, the positions of q_j in the document are $\{pos_{1,j}, pos_{2,j}, ..., pos_{tf_j,j}\}$, where tf_j is the term frequency of q_j. Then the within-document term frequency of $q_{i,j}$ is defined as follows.

Definition 3. The frequency of $q_{i,j}$ in D is the accumulation of $q_{i,j}$'s value.

$$tf\,(q_{i,j}, D) = \sum_{k_1=1}^{tf_i} \sum_{k_2=1}^{tf_j} Kernel\left(\frac{1}{2} dist(pos_{k_1,i}, pos_{k_2,j})\right) \quad (1)$$

where tf is the term frequency of $q_{i,j}$ in D, $Kernel(\cdot)$ is the kernel function adopted in query term's impact function, and $dist(\cdot)$ is the distance between two positions

$$dist(pos_{k_1,i}, pos_{k_2,j}) = |pos_{k_1,i} - pos_{k_2,j}|$$

Please note that the frequency of a Cross Term might not be an integer. Meanwhile, various of kernel functions will be studied in 3.4.

3.2 Number of Documents with A Cross Term

To evaluate the number of documents containing a Cross Term $q_{i,j}$, it is not reasonable to simply count how many documents in which $q_{i,j}$ occurs. The contribution from a query term and a Cross Term are different. For a query term q_i, an occurrence means its frequency accumulates 1, and the number of documents containing q_i is

$$n(q_i) = \sum_{D \in Index} \mathbf{1}_{\{qi \in D\}}$$

where $\mathbf{1}_{\{qi \in D\}}$ is an indicator function, which equals to 1 if $q_i \in Doc_i$ and equals to 0 otherwise. On the other hand, an occurrence of a Cross Term adds a value less than 1 to its frequency. A Cross Term's value could be various, and ranges from 0 to 1. Thus the difference of Cross Terms should be shown in its variants.

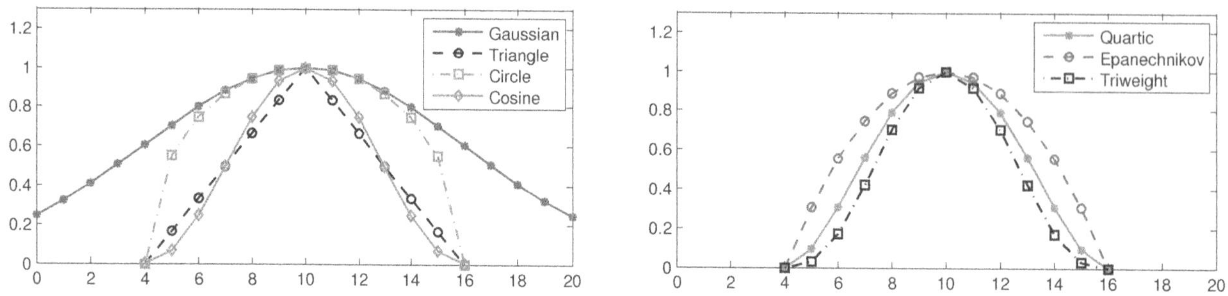

Figure 2: Kernel Functions

Definition 4. The number of documents containing a Cross Term $q_{i,j}$, is the sum of $q_{i,j}$'s average value on each document, shown as follows

$$n(q_{i,j}) = \sum_{D \in Index, Occur(q_{i,j},D) \neq 0} \frac{tf(q_{i,j},D)}{Occur(q_{i,j},D)} \quad (2)$$

where $Occur$ is the number of occurrence of $q_{i,j}$, which is

$$Occur(q_{i,j},D) = \sum_{k_1=1}^{tf_i} \sum_{k_2=1}^{tf_j} \mathbf{1}_{\{Kernel(\frac{1}{2}dist(pos_{k_1,i},pos_{k_2,j})) \neq 0\}}$$

3.3 Within-Query Cross Term Frequency

To evaluate a Cross Term's within-query term frequency, we can track each positions of q_i and q_j the same way as within-document frequency by the sum of all possible intersections. Moreover, different from in documents, query terms distribute densely in a query, so we can assume that query terms are adjacent to each other.

Definition 5. The within-query frequency of $q_{i,j}$ is

$$qtf(q_{i,j}) = Kernel(\frac{1}{2}) \cdot min\,(qtf(q_i), qtf(q_j)) \quad (3)$$

where $qtf(q_i)$ and $qtf(q_j)$ are within query term frequencies of q_i and q_j, and Kernel is the same kernel function utilized in $tf(q_{i,j}, D)$.

3.4 Kernel Functions

We first apply four kernel functions that have been brought into IR applications. Among them, the Gaussian kernel is widely used in statistics and machine learning algorithms such as the Support Vector Machines. Moreover, the Triangle kernel, Circle Kernel, and Cosine Kernel come from basic genomic graphics, which are applied to estimate the proximity-based density distribution for the positional language model [16]. below:

- Gaussian Kernel:

$$Kernel(u) = exp[\frac{-u^2}{2\sigma^2}] \quad (4)$$

- Triangle Kernel:

$$Kernel(u) = (1 - \frac{u}{\sigma}) \cdot \mathbf{1}_{\{u \leq \sigma\}} \quad (5)$$

- Circle Kernel:

$$Kernel(u) = \sqrt{1 - (\frac{u}{\sigma})^2} \cdot \mathbf{1}_{\{u \leq \sigma\}} \quad (6)$$

- Cosine Kernel:

$$Kernel(u) = \frac{1}{2}[1 + cos(\frac{u\pi}{\sigma})] \cdot \mathbf{1}_{\{u \leq \sigma\}} \quad (7)$$

where σ is a normalization parameter, and $\mathbf{1}_{\{u \leq \sigma\}}$ is indicator function, which equals to 1 if $u \leq \sigma$ and equals to 0 otherwise.

Moreover, some other kernel functions satisfy the query term impact function's properties (Property 1). We also introduce them into IR since the kernel functions are not maturely applied in Information Retrieval. They are: Quartic Kernel, Epanechnikov Kernel and Triweight Kernel, shown as the following. The shape of the included kernel functions are shown in Figure 2. The performance of using all the kernel functions will be investigated in the experiments.

- Quartic Kernel:

$$Kernel(u) = (1 - (\frac{u}{\sigma})^2)^2 \cdot \mathbf{1}_{\{u \leq \sigma\}} \quad (8)$$

- Epanechnikov Kernel:

$$Kernel(u) = (1 - (\frac{u}{\sigma})^2) \cdot \mathbf{1}_{\{u \leq \sigma\}} \quad (9)$$

- Triweight Kernel:

$$Kernel(u) = (1 - (\frac{u}{\sigma})^2)^3 \cdot \mathbf{1}_{\{u \leq \sigma\}} \quad (10)$$

4. CROSS TERM RETRIEVAL MODEL

We propose a Cross Term Retrieval (CRTER) model, utilizing the Cross Term as a special term. A new combined weighting model for a document is

$$CRTER(D) = (1-\lambda) \cdot \sum_{1 \leq i \leq K} w(q_i, D) + \lambda \cdot \sum_{1 \leq i < j \leq K} w'(q_{i,j}, D) \quad (11)$$

where w is the weighting function of query terms in Q, w' is the Cross Term $q_{i,j}$'s weight, and λ is a parameter balancing the query terms and Cross Terms. When λ equals to 0, the retrieval model uses query terms only, which is the standard weighting model. When λ equals to 1, the retrieval model uses Cross Terms only. Since the weights of query terms and Cross Terms are normalized independently, the value of λ reflects the influence of using Cross Terms. In this paper, we use BM25 as the basic weighting model in CRTER. BM25 is a classical weighting function employed by the Okapi system [25]. As shown by previous TREC experimentation, BM25 usually provides very effective retrieval performance on the TREC collections that are used in [29]

4.1 BM25

In BM25, the weight of a search term is assigned based on its within-document term frequency and query term frequency. The corresponding weighting function is as follows.

$$w(q_i, D) = \frac{(k_1+1)*tf}{K+tf} * \frac{(k_3+1)*qtf}{k_3+qtf} * \log\frac{N-n+0.5}{n+0.5} \quad (12)$$

where w is the weight of a query term q_i in a document. The variants in the above formula can be grouped into two categories as follows:

- The first category of variants are query independent. In this category, N is the number of indexed documents in the collection. k_1 and k_3 are tuning constants which depend on the dataset used and possibly on the nature of the queries. K equals to $k_1 * ((1-b) + b * dl/avdl)$, dl is the length of the document, and $avdl$ is the average document length. In our experiments, the values of k_1, k_3 are default to 1.2 and 8, respectively, which is the recommended setting in [25].

- Values of the other group of variants change from query to query. In this category, n is the number of documents containing a specific term. tf is within-document term frequency. qtf is within-query term frequency.

Finally, a document's weight for a query is given by the sum of its weight for each terms in the query,

$$BM25(D) = \sum_{i=1}^{i<K} w(q_i, D) \quad (13)$$

where w is the term weight obtained from Equation 12.

4.2 Algorithm and Time Complexity

In this section, we present the CRTER Algorithm with an analysis on tis time complexity. We show that the time complexity of our proposed algorithm is at the same level of the basic weighting model. Figure 3 is the algorithm for Cross Term Retrieval (CRTER) model. In the rest of this section, we will analyze its time complexity.

Suppose the number of terms in a query Q is $|Q|$, the number of documents in an index is $|Index|$, the average document length is $\overline{|D|}$. The first 6 steps are query processing that the within-query term frequency is computed for both query terms and Cross Terms, and the time complexity of this part is $O(|Q|^2)$. The remaining steps are document processing through the index. Also both query terms and Cross Terms are computed separately. For steps 8 to 12, this is standard document processing except storing term positions as well, and the time complexity of this part is $O(|Q| \cdot \overline{|D|})$. In steps 14 to 20, $tf(q_{i,j}, D)$ and $Occur(q_{i,j}, D)$ are accumulated, and it takes $O(\overline{tf}^2)$ time, where $\overline{tf}$ is average within-document term frequency. Thus computing all Cross Terms' variants on one document takes $O(|Q|^2 \cdot \overline{tf}^2)$. From step 24 to step 27, the weights for query terms and Cross Terms are computed and the documents are ranked according to CRTER. This algorithm for CRTER model has the time complexity of the follows

$$O(|Q|^2 + |Index| \cdot (|Q| \cdot \overline{|D|} + |Q|^2 \cdot \overline{tf}^2)) \quad (14)$$

Generally the number of query terms $|Q|$ in a submitted query is far smaller than the number of documents in index, i.e., $|Q| << |Index|$, therefore the first $|Q|^2$ in Forumla 14 could be eliminated. The use of Cross Terms is represented as $|Q|^2 \cdot \overline{tf}^2$ in Formula 14. The percentage of query terms' within-document frequency over the documents' length is normally very low. Formula 14 will become

$$O(|Index| \cdot (|Q| \cdot \overline{|D|})) \quad (15)$$

when $|Q| \cdot \overline{tf}^2 \le \overline{|D|}$. This means the time complexity of CRTER is the same as a basic probabilistic weighting model.

1: **for all** $q_i \in Q$ **do**
2: Compute $qtf(q_i)$
3: **end for**
4: **for all** $q_i, q_j \in Q$ **do**
5: Compute $qtf(q_{i,j})$
6: **end for**
7: **for all** $D \in Index$ **do**
8: **for all** $q_i \in Q$ **do**
9: Compute $tf(q_i, D)$
10: Store q_i's positions on D in an array
11: Compute $n(q_i) = n(q_i) + 1$
12: **end for**
13: **for all** $q_i, q_j \in Q$ **do**
14: **for** $k_1 < tf(q_i, D) \& k_2 < tf(q_j, D)$
15: $Kernel_{temp} = Kernel(\frac{1}{2}|pos_{k_1,i} - pos_{k_2,j}|)$
16: **if** $Kernel_{temp} \neq 0$
17: $tf(q_{i,j}, D) += Kernel_{temp}$
18: $Occur(q_{i,j}, D) += 1$
19: **end if**
20: **end for**
21: Compute $n(q_{i,j}) = n(q_{i,j}) + \frac{tf(q_{i,j}, D)}{Occur(q_{i,j}, D)}$;
22: **end for**
23: **end for**
24: Compute $w(q_i, D)$
25: Compute $w'(q_{i,j}, D)$;
26: Compute $CRTER(D)$
27: Rank documents according to CRTER(D)

Figure 3: Algorithm for CRTER

5. EXPERIMENTAL RESULTS

5.1 Data Sets and Evaluation Metrics

We conduct a series of experiments on six standard TREC collections shown in Table 1. These collections are diverse in both sizes and content, which facilitate a thorough evaluation of our proposed CRTER model. The TREC8 contains newswire articles from various sources, such as Financial Times (FT), the Federal Register (FR) etc., which are usually considered as high-quality text data with little noise. AP88-89 contains articles published by Association Press from the year of 1988 to 1989. The WT2G collection is a 2G size crawl of Web documents. The WT10G collection is a medium size crawl of Web documents, which was used in the TREC 9 and 10 Web tracks. It contains 10 Gigabytes of uncompressed data. The .GOV2 collection, which has 426 Gigabytes of uncompressed data, is a crawl from the .gov domain. This collection has been employed in the TREC 14 (2004), 15 (2005) and 16 (2006) Terabyte tracks. The Blog06 collection includes 100,649 blog feeds collected over an 11 week period from December 2005 to February 2006. Following the official TREC settings [21], we index only the permalinks, which are the blog posts and their associated comments. For all test collections used, each term is stemmed using Porter's English stemmer, and standard English stopwords are removed.

Collection Name	# of Docs	Topics	# of Topics
TREC8	528,155	401-450	50
AP88-89	164,597	51-100	50
WT2G	247,491	401-450	50
WT10G	1,692,096	451-550	100
.GOV2	25,178,548	701-850	150
Blog06	3,215,171	851-950	150

Table 1: Overview of the TREC collections used.

Each topic contains three topic fields, namely title, description and narrative. We only use the title topic field that contains very few keywords related to the topic. The title-only queries are usually short which is a realistic snapshot of real user queries in practice. On each collection, we evaluate our proposed model by a 10-fold cross-validation. The test topics associated to each collection are randomly split into ten equal subsets. In each fold, 9 subsets of the test topics are used for training, and the remaining subset is used for testing. The overall retrieval performance is averaged over all 10 test subsets of topics.

We use the TREC official evaluation measures in our experiments, namely the topical MAP on Blog06 [21], and the Mean Average Precision (MAP) on the other five collections [29]. To emphasize on the top retrieved documents, we also include P@5 and P@20 in the evaluation measures. All statistical tests are based on Wilcoxon Matched-pairs Signed-rank test.

5.2 Effectiveness of CRTER

We first investigate how much our proposed Cross Term Retrieval (CRTER) model can boost BM25. We use optimal BM25 as our baseline. The parameter b is set to be 0.35, which is shown to be optimal in our preliminary experiments (See Figure 7). The related experimental results are presented in Table 2. Seven different kernel functions are applied to instantiate the CRTER model, including: Gaussian, Triangle, Circle, Cosine, Quartic, Epanechnikov, and Triweight kernels. All the results are evaluated by MAP, P@5, and P@20. The percentage of how much CRTER outperforms BM25 is also listed. The best result obtained on each collection is marked bold. As shown by the results, our proposed CRTER model outperforms BM25 on all six collections used. The advantage of CRTER over BM25 is especially evident on the .GOV2 and Blog06 Web collections, where statistically significant improvement is observed with all 7 kernel functions used. Moreover, according to the results in Table 2, each kernel function has its advantage on some aspects. There is no single kernel function can outperform others on all the datasets.

5.3 Parameter Sensitivity

An important issue that may affect the robustness of the CRTER model is the sensitivity of its parameters λ (in Equation 11) and σ (in Equation 4-10) to retrieval performance. The parameter λ balances the query terms and the Cross Terms. When λ equals to 0, the retrieval model uses query terms only, which is the standard BM25 weighting model. When λ equals to 1, the retrieval model uses Cross Terms only. Since the weights of query terms and Cross Terms are normalized independently, the value of λ reflects the influence of using Cross Terms. The kernel parameter σ controls the range of a query term's impact. When σ is small, a Cross Term occurs only if its generating term are very close. When σ is large, query terms far away from each other can generate a Cross Term. But the Cross Term's value will be different according to the distance between query terms.

Figure 4 plots the evaluation metrics MAP, P@5, and P@20 obtained by CRTER over λ values ranging from 0 to 1 on WT2G. In addition, a group of different settings of σ are applied, namely $\sigma = 2, 5, 10, 20, 50, 75, 100$. The general tendency on each evaluation metric is similar. As we can see from Figure 4, CRTER's retrieval performance decreases with large λ values. CRTER generally performs well over different datasets when λ locates between 0 and 0.2. Overall, a λ value between 0 and 0.2 is recommended as it is shown to be reliable. In addition, CRTER's retrieval performance increases with large σ values, and tends to be stable when σ is larger than 20.

Figure 5 plots the CRTER model's performance with all kernel functions against kernel parameter σ on TREC8 dataset. It illustrates the effect of kernel parameters in detail. The increment of σ is 1 at the beginning and becomes larger after 10, because the model is more sensitive when σ is smaller. For a given σ, the range of CRTER's performance under different kernel functions is shown as a segment. The CRTER model overall appears to be effective over a wide range of σ values. When σ becomes larger, CRTER's performance normally increases at the beginning, due to the incorporation of term proximity. However, a larger σ value brings noise to the model and therefore decreases CRTER's performance. A σ value between 20 and 25 is recommended to be a reliable setting.

5.4 Robustness and Generalized Performance

The proposed CRTER model's robustness is important to its applications in practice. Ideally, we would like to have a reliable retrieval performance using CRTER on various datasets with its parameters within a stable safe range. This issue is particularly crucial for a given new dataset without training data.

We first fix BM25's parameter b = 0.35, and evaluate the robustness of CRTER provided by an empirical setting, ob-

	Eval Metric	TREC8	AP88-89	WT2G	WT10G	.GOV2	Blog06
BM25	MAP	0.2561	0.2710	0.3156	0.2119	0.3039	0.3246
	P@5	0.4920	0.4360	0.5280	0.3800	0.6134	0.6400
	P@20	0.4000	0.3860	0.3930	0.2670	0.5426	0.5997
CRTER Gaussian	MAP	0.2604 (+1.679%)	0.2787 (+2.841%)	0.3354 (+6.274%)	0.2213 (+4.436%)	**0.3322** (+9.312%)	0.3484 (+7.332%)
	P@5	0.5040 (+2.439%)	0.4520 (+3.670%)	**0.5480** (+3.788%)	**0.4080** (+7.368%)	**0.6336** (+3.293%)	0.6440 (+0.625%)
	P@20	0.4190 (+4.750%)	0.3900 (+1.036%)	0.4070 (+3.562%)	0.2775 (+3.933%)	**0.5691** (+4.884%)	0.6147 (+2.501%)
CRTER Triangle	MAP	**0.2606** (+1.757%)	**0.2789** (+2.915%)	**0.3359** (+ 6.432%)	0.2207 (+4.153%)	0.3287 (+8.161%)	0.3494 (+7.640%)
	P@5	0.5040 (+2.439%)	0.4520 (+3.670%)	**0.5480** (+3.788%)	**0.4080** (+7.368%)	**0.6336** (+3.293%)	0.6507 (+1.672%)
	P@20	0.4190 (+4.750%)	0.3890 (+0.777%)	**0.4100** (+4.326%)	0.2775 (+3.933%)	0.5671 (+4.515%)	0.6170 (+2.885%)
CRTER Circle	MAP	0.2599 (+1.484%)	0.2783 (+2.694%)	**0.3359** (+ 6.432%)	**0.2227** (+5.97%)	0.3264 (+7.404%)	0.3487 (+7.425%)
	P@5	0.5040 (+2.439%)	**0.4600** (+5.505%)	0.5440 (+ 3.030%)	0.4060 (+6.842%)	0.6282 (+ 2.413%)	0.6453 (+0.828%)
	P@20	0.4190 (+4.750%)	0.3890 (+0.777%)	0.4080 (+ 3.817%)	**0.2785** (+4.307%)	0.5631 (+3.778%)	0.6137 (+2.335%)
CRTER Cosine	MAP	0.2599 (+1.484%)	**0.2789** (+2.915%)	0.3358 (+ 6.401%)	0.2216 (+4.578%)	0.3289 (+8.226%)	0.3501 (+7.856%)
	P@5	0.5040 (+2.439%)	0.4560 (+4.587%)	0.5440 (+3.030 %)	**0.4080** (+7.368%)	**0.6336** (+3.293%)	0.6533 (+2.078%)
	P@20	0.4190 (+4.750%)	**0.3910** (+1.295%)	0.4090 (+ 4.071%)	0.2765 (+3.558%)	0.5668 (+4.460%)	0.6316 (+5.319%)
CRTER Quartic	MAP	0.2599 (+1.484%)	0.2787 (+2.841%)	0.3352 (+6.210 %)	0.2212 (+4.389%)	0.3258 (+7.206%)	0.3497 (+7.733%)
	P@5	0.5040 (+2.439%)	0.4560 (+4.587%)	0.5440 (+ 3.030%)	**0.4080** (+7.368%)	0.6322 (+3.065%)	0.6533 (+2.078%)
	P@20	0.4170 (+4.250%)	0.3920 (+1.554%)	**0.4100** (+ 4.326%)	0.2780 (+4.120%)	0.5658 (+4.276%)	0.6173 (+2.935%)
CRTER Epanechnikov	MAP	0.2602 (+1.601%)	0.2787 (+2.841%)	0.3343 (+ 5.925%)	0.2217 (+4.625%)	0.3277 (+7.832%)	0.3482 (+7.270%)
	P@5	**0.5080** (+3.252%)	0.4520 (+3.670%)	0.5440 (+ 3.030%)	**0.4080** (+7.368%)	**0.6336** (+3.293%)	0.6467 (+1.047%)
	P@20	**0.4200** (+5.000%)	0.3890 (+0.777%)	0.4070 (+ 3.562%)	0.2785 (+4.307%)	0.5654 (+4.202%)	0.6147 (+2.501%)
CRTER Triweight	MAP	0.2601 (+1.562%)	0.2788 (+2.878%)	0.3356 (+ 6.337%)	0.2225 (+5.002%)	0.3293 (+8.358%)	**0.3506** (+8.010%)
	P@5	**0.5080** (+3.252%)	0.4600 (+5.505%)	0.5440 (+ 3.030%)	0.4060 (+6.842%)	**0.6336** (+3.293%)	**0.6587** (+2.922%)
	P@20	0.4180 (+4.500%)	**0.3910** (+1.295%)	0.4070 (+ 3.562%)	0.2780 (+4.120%)	0.5674 (+4.571%)	**0.6187** (+3.168%)

Table 2: Comparison between BM25 baseline and CRTER with different kernel functions. BM25 parameter b is initialized to be 0.35. All the results are evaluated by MAP, P@5, and P@20. CRTER outperforms BM25 on all collections.

tained from previous observations, namely Triangle Kernel, $\sigma = 25$, and $\lambda = 0.2$. We compare this empirical setting with the following optimization strategies: first, optimize each of kernel function, σ or λ while setting the other parameter to the empirical value; second, optimize all of kernel functions, σ and λ. Figure 6 presents the related results on 4 datasets: TREC8, AP88-89, WT2G and WT10G. From this figure, we can see that the performance obtained by the empirical setting is comparable to the retrieval performance obtained by the optimized parameter settings on all datasets used.

We also test CRTER's performance under the same empirical setting with BM25 over different BM25 parameters on all the six collections. In BM25, b ranges from 0.15 to 0.95. In Figure 7, MAP of BM25 changes over different b, and CRTER can boost BM25 under all b's settings and over all the collections. More specifically, for .GOV2 dataset, we can see that BM25's performance is very sensitive to b, its MAP gradually increases with the incrementment of b at the beginning, and sharply decreases later. CRTER, on the other hand, boosts basic BM25 over different b, and tends to stabilize the retrieval performance.

In general, CRTER performs robustly and has strong gen-

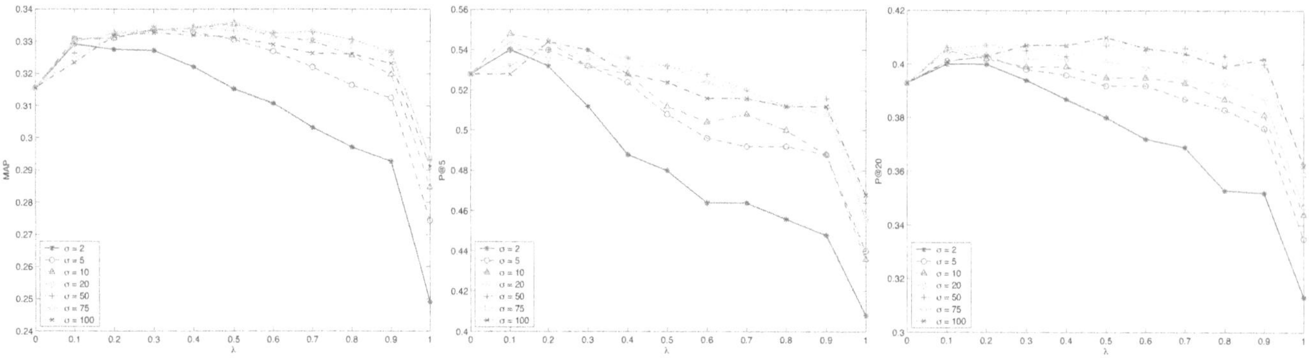

(a) MAP (b) P@5 (c) P@20

Figure 4: Sensitivity to CRTER parameter λ with different kernel parameters on WT2G

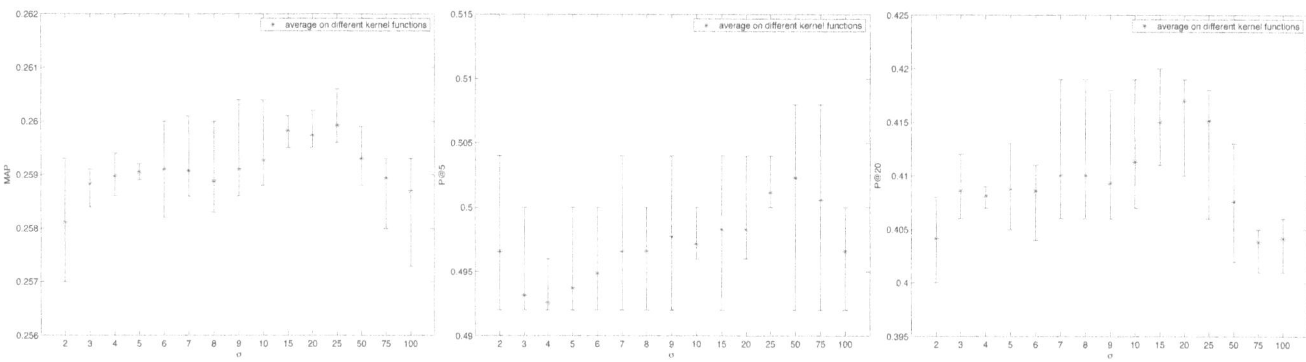

(a) MAP (b) P@5 (c) P@20

Figure 5: Sensitivity to CRTER kernel parameter σ on TREC8 (Each segment gives the range of results using different kernel functions under the given kernel parameter σ. The lowest point is the minimal result, the highest point is the maximal result, and the point in the middle is the average result.)

eralized performance. Without much knowledge of a new dataset, a group of parameters are recommended for CRTER: Triangle Kernel, $\sigma = 25$, and $\lambda = 0.2$.

5.5 Comparison with Positional Language Model

We study how the proposed CRTER model performs compared to the state-of-the-art approaches. In particular, its effectiveness is evaluated over the positional language model proposed by Lv et al. [16]. The positional language model (PLM) estimates a language model for every single position in a document. Among various kernel functions tested, the Gaussian kernel is shown to provide the best retrieval performance [16].

We compare CRTER's results with PLM on the datasets used in [16], including AP88-89, WT2G and TREC 8. As illustrated in Table 3, PLM improves the language model baseline (LM) by 1.3%, 2.0%, and 1.1% on TREC8, AP88-89 and WT2G, respectively, while the corresponding improvement over BM25 by CRTER is 1.8%, 2.9% and 6.4%, respectively. Overall, CRTER's retrieval performance is at least comparable to, if not better than PLM in our experiments.

	TREC8	AP88-89	WT2G
LM	0.2518	0.2154	0.3249
PLM	0.255(1.3%)	0.2198(2.0%)	0.3285(1.1%)
BM25	0.2561	0.2710	0.3156
CRTER	0.2606(1.8%)	0.2789(2.9%)	0.3359(6.4%)

Table 3: Direct MAP Comparison with PLM

What is more, another advantage of CRTER model is that it can be fitted into more basic probabilistic weighting models other than BM25, using defined variants of Cross Term.

5.6 A Case Study

To further analyze the effectiveness of the proposed CRTER model, out of the 550 test topics used in our experiments, we conduct a case study on topic 867 on the Blog06 collection. Using the judged documents, namely the golden standard provided by TREC, we explore the factors that could differentiate relevant documents from non-relevant ones. The statistics about the distribution of the query terms in the

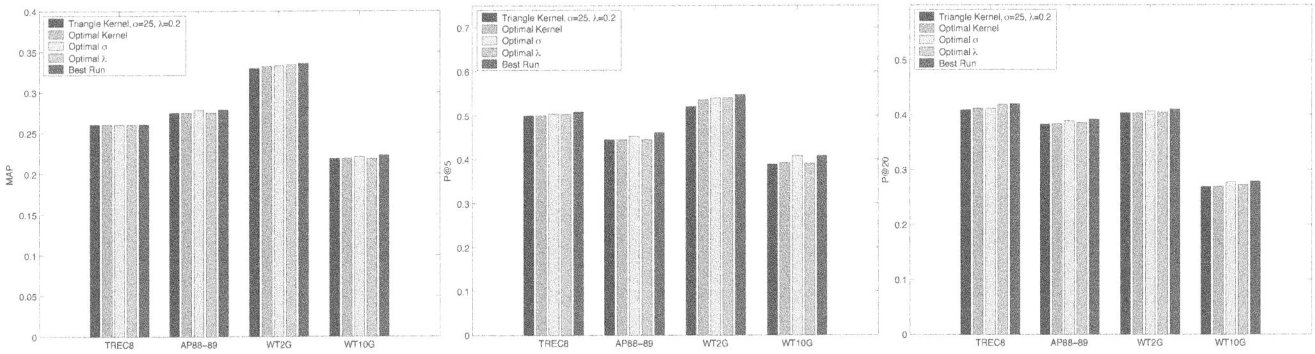

(a) MAP (b) P@5 (c) P@20

Figure 6: Robustness of CRTER:Compare CRTER's retrieval performance provided by an empirical setting, namely Triangle Kernel, $\sigma = 25$, and $\lambda = 0.2$ with the following optimization strategies: first, optimize each of kernel function, σ or λ while setting the other parameter to the empirical value; second, optimize all of kernel functions, σ and λ

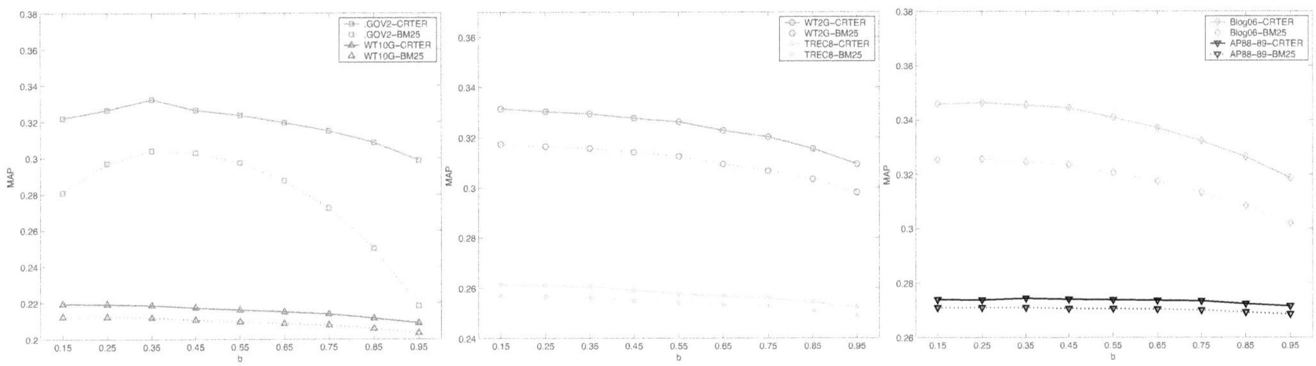

Figure 7: Generalized Performance of CRTER: Compare MAP between CRTER and BM25 with the change of b. (CRTER uses fixed parameter: Triangle Kernel, $\sigma = 25$, $\lambda = 0.2$)

relevant and non-relevant documents is shown in Table 4. The relevant and non-relevant documents cannot be distinguished from each other by neither their average minimum distance nor the average distance (less than 10). Therefore, traditional proximity-based approaches may not be able to boost the relevant documents of this specific topic. However, the average Cross Term's within document frequency (in CRTER model) of the relevant documents is clearly higher than the non-relevant ones, indicating that our proposed CRTER model can effectively identify the relevant documents from the non-relevant ones for this topic.

6. CONCLUSIONS AND FUTURE WORK

In this paper, we introduce the concept of Cross Term to integrate the context of the query term proximity into IR models. The Cross Term measures the association that two terms have in the textual proximity context. A query term's influence to their neighboring text is approximated by a kernel function, which gradually decreases with the distance to the term. The Cross Term is then defined as the overlapped influence of the two terms. Based on this idea, we propose a Cross Term Retrieval (CRTER) model, where within-document, within-query frequency of a Cross Term and the number of documents that contain the Cross Term are well defined. Through extensive experiments on standard TREC collections with various kernel functions, we show that the proposed model outperforms the BM25 baseline, and is at least comparable to the state-of-the-art Positional Language model. Furthermore, how the setting of the balancing parameter in the CRTER model and the shape parameter of kernel function affect CRTER's effectiveness are discussed. Meanwhile, a group of optimal parameters shows the robustness of the CRTER model on all collections used.

Our proposed concept of Cross Term has various promising future research directions. For example, we can apply the CRTER model to other classical IR models, such as language modeling, and the divergence from randomness models. We can also conduct an in-depth study on the Cross Term's distribution in documents collections, and examine which of the kernel functions fits the best to the actual distribution.

	# of Docs	# of Docs containing both terms	Average min dist. between query terms	Average dist. for dist. <10	Average Cross Term Freq. in Docs
Relevant	702	673	2.34	4.45	7.08
Non-Relevant	867	324	2.32	3.84	1.96

Table 4: A Case Study: Distribution of Terms in Relevant and Non-Relevant Documents. (Topic 867 on the Blog06 Collection)

7. ACKNOWLEDGEMENTS

This research is supported by the research grant from the Natural Sciences & Engineering Research Council (NSERC) of Canada and the Early Researcher Award/ Premier's Research Excellence Award. We thank four anonymous reviewers for their thorough review comments on this paper.

8. REFERENCES

[1] F. Ahmed and A. Nurnberger. Evaluation of n-gram conflation approaches for Arabic text retrieval. *Journal of the American Society for Information Science and Technology*, 60(7):1448-1465, 2009.

[2] J. Allan, L. Ballesteros, J.P. Callan, W.B. Croft, and Z. Lu Recent experiments with INQUERY. In *Proc. of the 4th TREC*, pages 49-64, 1995.

[3] C. Alvarez, P. Langlais, and J. Nie. Word pairs in language modeling for information retrieval. In *Proc. 7th International Conference on Computer Assisted Information Retrieval*, pages 686-705. Citeseer, 2004.

[4] M. Beigbeder and A. Mercier. An information retrieval model using the fuzzy proximity degree of term occurences. In *Proc. of the 2005 ACM symposium on Applied computing*, pages 1018-1022. ACM, 2005.

[5] A. Broschart and R. Schenkel. Proximity-aware scoring for XML retrieval. In *Proc. of the 31th ACM SIGIR*, pages 845-846. ACM, 2008.

[6] S. Buttcher, C. Clarke, and B. Lushman. Term proximity scoring for ad-hoc retrieval on very large text collections. In *Proc. of the 29th ACM SIGIR*, page 622-623. ACM, 2006.

[7] J.P. Callan, W.B. Croft, and S.M. Harding. The INQUERY retrieval system. *Proceedings of the 3rd International Conference on Database and Expert Systems Applications*, pages 78-83, Citeseer. 1992

[8] B. Cho, C. Lee, and G. Lee. Exploring term dependences in probabilistic information retrieval model. *Information Processing and Management*, 39(4):505-519, 2003.

[9] C. Clarke, G. Cormack, and F. Burkowski. Shortest substring ranking (MultiText experiments for TREC-4). In *Proc. of the 4th TREC*, pages 295-304, 1996.

[10] O. de Kretser and A. Moffat. Effective document presentation with a locality-based similarity heuristic. In *Proc. of the 22th ACM SIGIR*, pages 113-120. ACM, 1999.

[11] J. Gao, J. Nie, G. Wu, and G. Cao. Dependence language model for information retrieval. In *Proc. of the 27th ACM SIGIR*, page 177. ACM, 2004.

[12] D. Hawking and P. Thistlewaite. Proximity operators - So near and yet so far. In *Proc. of the 4th Text Retrieval Conference*, pages 131-143, 1995.

[13] S. Kirkpatric, C. Gelatt, and M. Vecchi. Optimization by simulated annealing. *Science*, 220(4598):671-680, 1983.

[14] K. Kise, M. Junker, A. Dengel, and K. Matsumoto. Passage retrieval based on density distributions of terms and its applications to document retrieval and question answering. *Lecture notes in computer science*, pages 306-327. Springer, 2004.

[15] E. Krause. Taxicab Geometry. *Mathematics Teacher*, 66(8):695-706, 1973.

[16] Y. Lv and C. Zhai. Positional language models for information retrieval. In *Proc. of the 32th ACM SIGIR*, pages 299-306. ACM, 2009.

[17] J. Mayfield and P. McNamee. Single n-gram stemming. In *Proc. of the 26th ACM SIGIR*, pages 415-416. ACM, 2003.

[18] P. McNamee and J. Mayfield. Character n-gram tokenization for European language text retrieval. *Information Retrieval*, 7(1):73-97, 2004.

[19] A. Mercier and M. Beigbeder. Fuzzy proximity ranking with boolean queries. *Proc. of TREC*, 2005.

[20] D. Metzler and W. Croft. A Markov random field model for term dependencies. In *Proc. of the 28th ACM SIGIR*, pages 472-479. ACM, 2005.

[21] I. Ounis, M. De Rijke, C. Macdonald, G. Mishne, and I. Soboroff. Overview of the TREC-2006 blog track. *Proc. of TREC*, 2006.

[22] D. Petkova and W. Croft. Proximity-based document representation for named entity retrieval. In *Proc. of the 16th ACM CIKM*, pages 731-740. ACM, 2007.

[23] J. Pickens. A comparison of language modeling and probabilistic text information retrieval approaches to monophonic music retrieval. In *Proc. of ISMIR*. Citeseer, 2000.

[24] Y. Rasolofo and J. Savoy. Term proximity scoring for keyword-based retrieval systems. *Lecture Notes in Computer Science*, pages 207-218. Springer, 2003.

[25] S. Robertson, S. Walker, S. Jones, M. Hancock-Beaulieu, and M. Gatford. Okapi at TREC-4. In *Proc. of the 4th TREC*, pages 73-97, 1996.

[26] F. Song and W. Croft. A general language model for information retrieval. In *Proc. of the 8h ACM CIKM*, pages 316–321. ACM, 1999.

[27] M. Srikanth and R. Srihari. Biterm language models for document retrieval. In *Proc. of the 25th ACM SIGIR*, pages 425-426. ACM, 2002.

[28] T. Tao and C. Zhai. An exploration of proximity measures in information retrieval. In *Proc. of the 30th ACM SIGIR*, pages 295-302. ACM, 2007.

[29] E. Voorhees and D. Harman. *TREC: Experiment and evaluation in information retrieval.* Cambridge, Mass. MIT Press, 2005.

A Boosting Approach to Improving Pseudo-Relevance Feedback

Yuanhua Lv
Dept of Computer Science
University of Illinois at Urbana-Champaign
ylv2@uiuc.edu

ChengXiang Zhai
Dept of Computer Science
University of Illinois at Urbana-Champaign
czhai@cs.uiuc.edu

Wan Chen *
Wolfram Research, Inc.
100 Trade Center Drive
Champaign, IL
wanc@wolfram.com

ABSTRACT

Pseudo-relevance feedback has proven effective for improving the average retrieval performance. Unfortunately, many experiments have shown that although pseudo-relevance feedback helps many queries, it also often hurts many other queries, limiting its usefulness in real retrieval applications. Thus an important, yet difficult challenge is to improve the overall effectiveness of pseudo-relevance feedback without sacrificing the performance of individual queries too much. In this paper, we propose a novel learning algorithm, FeedbackBoost, based on the boosting framework to improve pseudo-relevance feedback through optimizing the combination of a set of basis feedback algorithms using a loss function defined to *directly measure both robustness and effectiveness*. FeedbackBoost can potentially accommodate many basis feedback methods as features in the model, making the proposed method a general optimization framework for pseudo-relevance feedback. As an application, we apply FeedbackBoost to improve pseudo feedback based on language models through combining different document weighting strategies. The experiment results demonstrate that FeedbackBoost can achieve better average precision and meanwhile dramatically reduce the number and magnitude of feedback failures as compared to three representative pseudo feedback methods and a standard learning to rank approach for pseudo feedback.

Categories and Subject Descriptors

H.3.3 [**Information Search and Retrieval**]: Retrieval models, query formulation, relevance feedback

General Terms

Algorithms

Keywords

Pseudo-relevance feedback, FeedbackBoost, loss function, robustness, learning, optimization, boosting

*This work was done when Wan Chen was with University of Illinois at Urbana-Champaign.

1. INTRODUCTION

Pseudo-relevance feedback has proven effective for automatically improving the overall retrieval accuracy and average precision for informational queries in many experiments [24, 22, 25, 3, 23, 15, 31, 18]. The basic idea of pseudo feedback is to assume a certain number of top-ranked documents from an initial retrieval run to be relevant and extract useful information from these feedback documents to improve the original query.

However, although traditional pseudo feedback techniques generally improve retrieval performance (e.g., AP) on average, they are not robust in the sense that they tend to help some queries, but hurt other queries [10, 7], limiting its usefulness in real retrieval applications. Thus an important, yet difficult challenge is to *improve the overall effectiveness of pseudo-relevance feedback without sacrificing the performance of individual queries too much.* Although there has been a lot of work on pseudo feedback, little work has been devoted to address this issue, with only a few exceptions, e.g., [7]. In [7], the authors tried to reduce feedback failures in a constrained optimization approach. However their work was only able to optimize an objective function loosely related to the effectiveness and robustness of pseudo feedback.

In this paper, we propose a novel learning algorithm, FeedbackBoost, based on the boosting framework to improve pseudo-relevance feedback through combining a set of basis feedback algorithms optimally using a loss function defined to *directly measure both robustness and effectiveness*, which has not been achieved in any previous work on pseudo feedback. Specifically, like all other boosting algorithms [9, 26, 8, 30], FeedbackBoost iteratively selects and combines basis feedback methods. In each iteration, a basis feedback method is selected to improve those queries on which the already selected basis feedback methods perform poorly in terms of both effectiveness and robustness. At last, FeedbackBoost uses a linear combination of these basis feedback methods as its final feedback model.

There are several important differences between our work and previous work on improving pseudo feedback: (1) we cast the pseudo feedback problem as an optimization problem that can be solved in a supervised way; (2) we propose a novel objective function that directly measures the effectiveness and the number of failure cases of pseudo feedback; (3) FeedbackBoost can incorporate potentially many different basis feedback methods as features in the model, making it a general optimization framework for pseudo feedback; (4) FeedbackBoost does not introduce any extra parameter that needs to be manually tuned.

As an application, we apply FeedbackBoost to improve pseudo feedback based on language models through combining different document weighting strategies. One cause of the low robustness and effectiveness in pseudo feedback is that the feedback documents are simply assumed to be relevant whereas in reality, not all of them are relevant. Thus one way to improve pseudo feedback would be to assign appropriate weights to these documents. Indeed, our previous work [18] has already shown that with relevance-based document weighting, the relevance model [15] tends to be more robust and effective than alternative models for feedback with language models. In the existing work, however, such weighting is generally based on one heuristic or another, and is not optimized directly to improve feedback. Our main idea is to combine a variety of feedback methods each with a different strategy for document weighting under the framework of FeedbackBoost. Although we only try to leverage feedback methods with different document weighting methods in this work, the proposed boosting framework can potentially accommodate many other basis feedback methods.

We evaluate our method using two representative large test sets and compare FeedbackBoost with multiple baseline methods. The experiment results demonstrate that the proposed FeedbackBoost algorithm can improve average precision significantly and meanwhile reduce the number and magnitude of feedback failures dramatically as compared to two representative pseudo feedback methods based on language models, the mixture model and the relevance model. We also compare our algorithm with a recently proposed constrained optimization approach to robust feedback, and the results show that our method is more robust. In addition, we compare FeedbackBoost with a traditional learning to rank approach applied for pseudo feedback and observe that FeedbackBoost works clearly better.

2. RELATED WORK

Pseudo-relevance feedback has been shown to be effective for various retrieval models [24, 22, 25, 3, 23, 15, 31, 18]. In the vector space model, feedback is usually done by using the Rocchio algorithm [24]. The feedback method in classical probabilistic models is to select expansion terms primarily based on the Robertson/Sparck-Jones weight [22]. A number of model-based pseudo feedback techniques have been developed for the language modeling framework, including the relevance model [15] and the mixture-model feedback [31], which will be reviewed in Section 5.1.1 and 5.1.2 respectively. Most existing pseudo feedback algorithms aim at improving average precision alone but rarely address the robustness issue. In contrast, our work attempts to improve both average precision and robustness at the same time.

A few previous studies also attempted to improve the robustness of pseudo feedback [28, 27, 7]. Tao and Zhai [28] used a regularized EM algorithm to reduce the parameter sensitivity of the mixture-model feedback but did not minimize the feedback failures. Soskin et al. [27] leveraged multiple relevance models [15] in a heuristic unsupervised way to improve feedback performance. However, their method is not guaranteed to optimize the combination of feedback algorithms. Collins-Thompson [7] also tried to reduce feedback failures in an optimization framework. However this work was only able to optimize an objective function loosely related to the robustness of pseudo feedback. In contrast, we propose a general machine learning framework to directly optimize both the robustness and effectiveness of pseudo feedback, which can incorporate existing methods, such as [28], [27], and [7], as features. In this sense, our work offers a unified framework that can be used to potentially combine all the existing pseudo feedback methods.

Selective feedback [2] and adaptive feedback [17] are another stream of work to improve the robustness of pseudo feedback, where the idea is to disable query expansion if query expansion is predicted to be detrimental to retrieval [2] or to adaptively set the amount of query expansion in a per-query way [17]. However, these methods are not as general as our proposed framework. Besides, our work and the selective/adaptive feedback method are complementary in the following sense: our work can construct a strong ensemble feedback method, which can be used by selective/adaptive feedback to further improve its performance, while selective/adaptive feedback methods can be incorporated into our framework as features for boosting.

Recently, learning to rank [13, 8, 4, 30, 6, 33, 16] has attracted much attention in IR. Our work can also be regarded a novel use of machine learning to leverage multiple feedback-related features to improve ranking. However, a main difference of our work from traditional work on learning to rank is that we design a novel learning algorithm to directly optimize both robustness and effectiveness of pseudo feedback (novel objective function). Another difference is that most learning to rank work learns optimal ways to combine retrieval functions but fails to improve the query representation. Our work, however, uses machine learning to improve a content-based query representation. Therefore, our study is orthogonal to the existing learning to rank work, and existing learning to rank algorithms can be used to learn a retrieval function on the basis of our improved query representation to further improve retrieval performance.

Machine learning was also introduced to improve pseudo feedback through selecting good expansion terms [5] or good feedback documents [12]. However, neither work attempted to directly optimize robustness of pseudo feedback.

Boosting is a general method for improving the accuracy of supervised learning. The basic idea of boosting is to repeatedly construct "weak learners" by re-weighting training data and form an ensemble of weak learners so that the total performance of the ensemble is "boosted". Freund and Schapire have proposed the first and most popular boosting algorithm called AdaBoost for binary classification [9]. Extensions of boosting have been made to deal with the problems of multi-class classification [26], ranking [8, 30, 33], etc. Our work can be viewed as a novel extension of the boosting framework to improve pseudo-relevance feedback.

3. PROBLEM FORMULATION

Given a query q_i and a document collection C, a retrieval function F returns a ranked list of m documents $\mathbf{d} = \{d_1, \cdots, d_m\}$, where d_j denotes the j-th ranked document in the ranked list. In pseudo feedback, we assume the top-n documents are "relevant", and construct a feedback model $\phi_t(q_i, \mathbf{d}, n, C)$, or $\phi_t(q_i)$ for short, for query q_i by exploiting those assumed "relevant" documents. Here ϕ_t can be any pseudo feedback method that is able to output an improved query representation, and we call it a *weak* or *basis* feedback method; $\phi_t(q_i)$ is essentially an expanded representation of the original query q_i, and we call it a *weak* or *basis* feedback model for q_i. In general, the format of $\phi_t(q_i)$

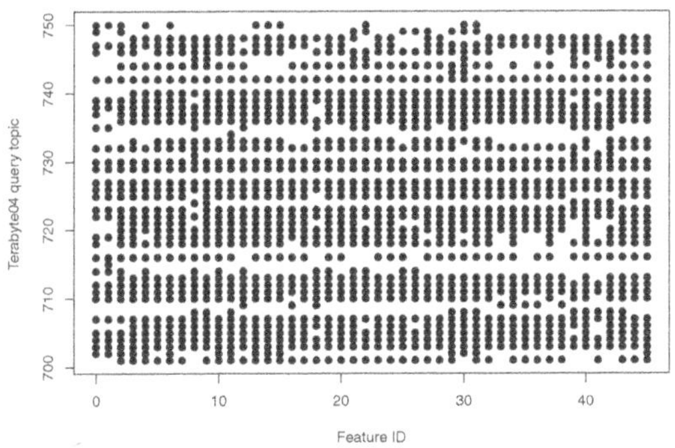

Figure 1: Plot of each query w.r.t. different weak feedback methods, where '•' indicates that the corresponding weak feedback improves performance.

would depend on the retrieval function F; for example, in the vector space model, $\phi_t(q_i)$ is represented as a vector of weighted terms, while in language modeling approaches, it is represented as a word distribution. We can use $\phi_t(q_i)$ as the new query and apply F to retrieve another ranked list of documents $\mathbf{d}'$.

Given a performance measure E and the relevance judgments set $J(q_i)$ for query q_i, we can compute the performance scores for the original query q_i and for the expanded query $\phi_t(q_i)$, which will be denoted as $E(F(q_i), J(q_i))$ and $E(F(\phi_t(q_i)), J(q_i))$, respectively, and will be represented as $E(q_i)$ and $E(\phi_t(q_i))$ in the rest of the paper for conciseness. We choose the widely accepted average precision (AP) as the performance measure E in this paper, though the proposed algorithm can in principle also work with other measures.

Although many pseudo feedback methods have been shown to improve the performance of a retrieval system on average, they all share a common deficiency, i.e., the average performance gain always comes inevitably at the cost of (sometimes significantly) degraded performance of some queries. That is, while on average, $\frac{1}{|Q|}\sum_{i=1}^{|Q|} E(\phi(q_i)) > \frac{1}{|Q|}\sum_{i=1}^{|Q|} E(q_i)$, it is almost always the case that for some queries, $E(\phi(q_j)) < E(q_j)$. Indeed, it has been a long-standing difficult challenge to improve the robustness of pseudo feedback so that we can improve average performance without sacrificing the performance of individual queries too much.

In this paper, we propose to use a learning method to address this problem. Specifically, given a query q_i, we assume there are a variety of basis feedback models $\phi_k(q_i)$ based on different feedback methods $\Phi = \{\phi_1, \cdots, \phi_m\}$, and our main idea is to combine a set of such basis feedback models $\phi_k(q_i)$ into a single feedback model $H(q_i)$ called the *final* or *combined* feedback model to reduce feedback failures:

$$H(q_i) = \sum_{k=1}^{t} \alpha_k \phi_k(q_i) \tag{1}$$

A linear combination is chosen because the final feedback model $H(q_i)$ should be in the same format as that of each basis model $\phi_k(q_i)$; that is, if $\phi_k(q_i)$ is a vector of weighted terms, so is $H(q_i)$, while if $\phi_k(q_i)$ is a language model, $H(q_i)$ should also be a language model by normalizing the learned α_k $(k = 1, \cdots, t)$ to make them sum to 1.

Our main motivation of combining multiple feedback methods is that different basis feedback methods often have relative strengths for different query topics and thus are complementary to each other. To illustrate it, we examine 46 basis feedback methods constructed using methods described in Section 5. The results are presented in Figure 1. We can see that many feedback methods indeed have relative strengths on different queries (e.g., topic 708 and 709). It seems there are only 3 very hard queries that no feedback method can help, while for other queries, there are always some successful feedback methods. Thus, constructing an ensemble feedback method H would be an effective strategy to reduce feedback loss. For example, suppose we have two weak feedback methods ϕ_1 and ϕ_2; ϕ_1 improves 0.2 and -0.1 (i.e., decreases by 0.1) on q_1 and q_2 respectively, while ϕ_2 improves -0.1 and 0.2 on q_1 and q_2 respectively. So the fbloss scores are 0.5 for both ϕ_1 and ϕ_2 on these two queries. However, an ensemble method $\alpha_1\phi_1 + \alpha_2\phi_2$ would probably have 0 fbloss while still achieving better or comparable average improvement if the combination coefficients α_1 and α_2 are chosen appropriately.

Our goal is to minimize the number of query instances for which the retrieval performance is decreased by the final feedback model $H(q_i)$ as compared to the original query q_i. The learning algorithm that we study attempts to find an H with a small number of query failures, a quality called the *feedback loss* and denoted by $\text{fbloss}_D(H)$. Formally,

$$\text{fbloss}_D(H) = \sum_{i=1}^{|Q|} D(q_i) \cdot I\{E(H(q_i)) < E(q_i)\} \tag{2}$$

Here and throughout this paper, the indicator function $I\{\pi\}$ is defined to be 1 if the predicate π holds and 0 otherwise. $D(q_i)$ is the weight of q_i, and we set it initially to uniform, i.e., $D(q_i) = 1/|Q|$ so that all queries are equally important; later the query weights would be updated iteratively in a boosting framework [9] so that queries that do not perform well would contribute more to the loss function more. We will also show later in Section 4.1 that the feedback loss can be bounded by the degradation of retrieval precision, which means that the feedback loss can actually measure both feedback failures and retrieval effectiveness, which is necessary in order to ensure both robustness and effectiveness.

In the following section, we will discuss how to optimize the combination of weak feedback methods so as to minimize fbloss on some training data, formally,

$$\arg\min_{\{\alpha_{1:t}\}} \sum_{i=1}^{|Q|} D(q_i) \cdot I\left\{E(\sum_{k=1}^{t} \alpha_k \cdot \phi_k(q_i)) < E(q_i)\right\} \tag{3}$$

4. A BOOSTING APPROACH TO IMPROVING PSEUDO FEEDBACK

With only a few basis feedback methods, it is possible to optimize their combination through manual parameter tuning. However, manual tuning is infeasible if there are many basis feedback methods as is often the case. Inspired by the AdaBoost [9], we devise a boosting approach, referred to as "FeedbackBoost", to solve this problem.

4.1 Minimizing Feedback Loss via Forward Stagewise Additive Modeling

Ideally we want to minimize the feedback loss on the training data as shown in Equation 3. However, it is difficult to solve this optimization problem because the combination is inside a retrieval function and not differentiable. To simplify this problem, we make an assumption that the feedback loss of the combined feedback H is less than or equal to that of a linear performance combination of the corresponding basis feedback methods. Formally,

$$\sum_{i=1}^{|Q|} D(q_i)\cdot I\left\{E(\sum_{k=1}^{t}\alpha_k\cdot\phi_k(q_i)) < E(q_i)\right\}$$
$$\leq \sum_{i=1}^{|Q|} D(q_i)\cdot I\left\{\left[\sum_{k=1}^{t}\frac{\alpha_k}{\sum_{j=1}^{t}\alpha_j}E(\phi_k(q_i))\right] < E(q_i)\right\} \quad (4)$$

Although we have not found a theoretical proof for the above inequality, we can empirically guarantee this assumption to be true in our algorithms since we can automatically adjust the algorithms to make sure this assumption holds (as shown in the step 5 of the pseudo code of the algorithm). In practice, this assumption turns out to work well. One possible explanation is that different feedback models often complement to each other, so the performance of a mixture model with reasonable coefficients is often better than the performance of any single model and thus also better than the weighted average performance of these single models. An example is that an appropriate interpolation of a pseudo feedback model and the original query model usually works better than either single model [31, 1, 18]. Thus we will minimize the following upper bound of the feedback loss.

$$\arg\min_{\{\alpha_{1:t}\}}\sum_{i=1}^{|Q|} D(q_i) I\left\{\sum_{k=1}^{t}\alpha_k E(\phi_k(q_i)) < \sum_{k=1}^{t}\alpha_k E(q_i)\right\} \quad (5)$$

However the above optimization problem is still hard to handle, because the indicator function I is non-continuous. Fortunately, we know that $I\{x < y\} \leq e^{y-x}$ for all real x and y, so, instead of solving Equation 5 directly, we can alternatively minimize its upper bound below, which is essentially a measure of retrieval performance degradation.

$$\arg\min_{\{\alpha_{1:t}\}}\sum_{i=1}^{|Q|} D(q_i)\exp\left(\sum_{k=1}^{t}\alpha_k E(q_i) - \sum_{k=1}^{t}\alpha_k E(\phi_k(q_i))\right) \quad (6)$$

Now we can address this problem using forward stagewise additive modeling, which is an effective strategy to find an approximate solution to an optimization problem through sequentially adding new basis method without adjusting those already selected methods [11]. By forward stagewise additive modeling, the above formula can be expressed as follows where we would iteratively choose α_t and ϕ_t, as well as adjust $D_t(q_i)$:

$$\arg\min_{\{\alpha_t,\phi_t\}}\sum_{i=1}^{|Q|} D_t(q_i)\cdot\exp\left(\alpha_t\cdot[E(q_i) - E(\phi_t(q_i))]\right) \quad (7)$$

where

$$D_t(q_i) \propto \frac{D_{t-1}(q_i)\cdot\exp\left(\alpha_{t-1}\cdot[E(q_i) - E(\phi_{t-1}(q_i))]\right)}{Z_t} \quad (8)$$

Here, Z_t is a normalization factor to make D_t a distribution; such a normalization operation does not affect the choosing of α_t and ϕ_t, since D_t depends neither on α_t nor ϕ_t in the forward stagewise additive modeling [11]. D_t is defined in a recursive way, where $D_1(q_i) = D(q_i) = 1/|Q|$ is the initial weight for query q_i. After T iterations, we can obtain the desired combined feedback model as $H(q_i) = \sum_{t=1}^{T}\alpha_t\phi_t$.

Algorithm 1 The FeedbackBoost algorithm

Input:

Query set $\{q_i, J(q_i)\}_{i=1}^{|Q|}$, retrieval model F, retrieval performance measure E, and the number of iterations T;
A set of basis feedback methods $\Phi = \{\phi_1, \cdots, \phi_m\}$;
Initial distribution D_1 over training queries: $D_1(i) = 1/|Q|$;

Output:

1: **for** $t = 1, 2, \cdots, T$ **do**
2: Select basis feedback method ϕ_t with weighted distribution D_t on training queries using Formula 14; if there is no ϕ_t selected, break;
3: Compute $\text{Eloss}_t(\phi_t)$ using Formula 9.
4: Choose α_t based on Formula 12 and $\text{Eloss}_t(\phi_t)$.
5: While the inequality in Formula 4 does not hold, goto step 2 and choose the next optimal basis feedback as ϕ_t; if there is no ϕ_t that satisfies the inequality, break;
6: Update D_{t+1} using Formula 8;
7: **end for**
8: Output the final feedback: $H = \sum_{t=1}^{T}\alpha_t\phi_t$;

4.2 FeedbackBoost

FeedbackBoost is designed to find a solution to the optimization problem in Formula 7 using a boosting approach. Specifically, like all other boosting algorithms, FeedbackBoost operates in rounds. At each round, we calculate a distribution of weights over training queries. In fact, D_t can be regarded as a weight that is applied to each query after $t-1$ iterations. From Equation 8, we can see that D_t will put more weights on queries that are hurt more by previously selected basis feedback methods.

We next select a basis feedback method ϕ_t that works well on those highly-weighted queries, and the selection of this basis feedback method is to optimize an objective function that is defined to directly measure the feedback loss. Specifically, we define the weighted performance degradation of ϕ at iteration t as

$$\text{Eloss}_t(\phi) = \sum_{i=1}^{|Q|} D_t(q_i)\cdot(E(q_i) - E(\phi(q_i))) \quad (9)$$

And the feedback method ϕ_t with the minimum Eloss_t will be selected. Theoretical analysis is provided as follows:

The performance measure E, e.g., AP in this paper, is usually within range $[0, 1]$. Even a measure is beyond this range, we can still normalize it to $[0, 1]$. Therefore, for any basis feedback method ϕ_t, we have the performance degradation $E(q_i) - E(\phi_t(q_i)) \in [-1, 1]$. By the convexity of $e^{\alpha x}$ as a function of x when $x \in [-1, 1]$ [8], we thus have

$$\exp\left(\alpha_t[E(q_i) - E(\phi_t(q_i))]\right) \leq \left(\frac{1 + E(q_i) - E(\phi_t(q_i))}{2}\right)\exp(\alpha_t)$$
$$+\left(\frac{1 - E(q_i) + E(\phi_t(q_i))}{2}\right)\exp(-\alpha_t) \quad (10)$$

So Equation 7 can be approximated by

$$\arg\min_{\{\alpha_t,\phi_t\}}\frac{1 + \text{Eloss}_t(\phi_t)}{2}\exp(\alpha_t) + \frac{1 - \text{Eloss}_t(\phi_t)}{2}\exp(-\alpha_t) \quad (11)$$

We can easily minimize this equation by setting

$$\alpha_t^* = \frac{1}{2}\log\frac{1 - \text{Eloss}_t(\phi_t)}{1 + \text{Eloss}_t(\phi_t)} \quad (12)$$

which indeed makes sense since it suggests that a ϕ_t with less performance degradation will receive a larger weight α_t.

Then, by plugging Equation 12 into 11, we obtain the following optimal basis feedback.

$$\phi_t^* = \arg\min_{\{\phi_t\}} \sqrt{(1 - \text{Eloss}_t(\phi_t))(1 + \text{Eloss}_t(\phi_t))} \quad (13)$$

We can see that Equation 13 is minimized when $\text{Eloss}_t(\phi_t)$ is close to 1 or -1. With respect to the former case, we would choose a ϕ_t with the largest weighted performance degradation, and α_t will be negative, which, however, does not make sense: if a pseudo feedback ϕ_t leads to large performance degradation, a negative α_t may not make ϕ_t work well. Therefore, $\text{Eloss}_t(\phi_t)$ should be negative to keep the coefficient α_t positive. So we choose a basis pseudo feedback ϕ_t with the smallest negative Eloss_t so far.

$$\phi_t^* = \arg\min_{\{\phi_t\}} \{\text{Eloss}_t(\phi_t)\} \quad \text{subject to } \text{Eloss}_t(\phi_t) < 0 \quad (14)$$

4.3 Algorithm Summary

To summarize, FeedbackBoost works as follows. The input to the algorithm includes a set of queries and relevance judgments $\{q_i, J(q_i)\}_{i=1}^{|Q|}$, a set of basis feedback methods $\Phi = \{\phi_1, \cdots, \phi_m\}$, a document collection C, a retrieval function F, a retrieval performance measure E, and the iteration number T. FeedbackBoost works in an iterative way: during each iteration t, a basis feedback method ϕ_t is chosen based on its performance on training data with weight distribution D_t, i.e., $\text{Eloss}_t(\phi_t)$. Also the coefficient α_t of ϕ_t is calculated based on $\text{Eloss}_t(\phi_t)$. After that, the query weight distribution D_t is updated by increasing weights on queries for which ϕ_t performs poorly, leading to a new distribution D_{t+1}; D_{t+1} will be used in the next iteration to select ϕ_{t+1} and α_{t+1}. At last, the final feedback model H is created by linearly combining all the selected basis feedback methods. A sketch of the algorithm flow is shown in Algorithm 1.

5. APPLICATION OF FEEDBACKBOOST TO LANGUAGE MODELS

In order to apply FeedbackBoost, the main task is to design appropriate basis feedback methods $\{\phi\}$. A basis feedback method ϕ_k generally consists of three components: a weighting function h_k to assign weights to feedback documents, a weighting function g_k to calculate the importance of different expansion terms, and the retrieval model F to decide the representation format of the feedback model. Formally, $\phi_k = f(h_k, g_k, F)$. Given a retrieval model F, one feedback method differs from others often because it uses different document and/or term weighting functions [18]. We can thus naturally construct many basis feedback methods by varying the document and/or term weighting functions.

5.1 Basis Pseudo Feedback Methods based on Language Models

As a specific application, here we discuss how we can apply FeedbackBoost to improve pseudo feedback under the language modeling framework through combining different document weighting strategies. This application is especially interesting because (1) language models deliver state of the art retrieval performance [21, 14]; (2) feedback document weighting has been shown to be a critical factor affecting robustness and effectiveness of pseudo feedback methods [18]. However, our methodology could be applicable to other retrieval models and to optimizing term weighting methods as well, which we leave as future work.

We use the KL-divergence retrieval method [14] as our retrieval model (i.e., F), which scores a document d with respect to a query q by computing the negative KL divergence between the query and the document language model:

$$S(q, d) = -\sum_{w \in q} P(w|q) \log \frac{P(w|q)}{P(w|d)} \quad (15)$$

Two important instantiations of basis pseudo feedback methods in language models are the relevance model [15] and the mixture model [31], which are among the most effective and robust feedback techniques based on language models [18].

5.1.1 Relevance Model

The relevance model ϕ_r essentially uses the query likelihood as the weight for document d and takes an average of the probability of word w given by each document language model. Formally, let Θ represent the set of smoothed document models in the pseudo feedback collection $\Omega = \{d_1, \cdots, d_n\}$. The formula of the relevance model is:

$$P(w|\phi_r(q)) \propto \sum_{\theta_d \in \Theta} P(w|\theta_d) \prod_{w' \in q} P(w'|\theta_d) \quad (16)$$

Let's denote the original query model as $P(w|q)$. The relevance model $P(w|\phi_r(q))$ can be interpolated with the original query model $P(w|q)$ to improve performance using a interpolation coefficient α. In this paper, we will use the following interpolated model $P(w|\theta_q)$ as the new query model, which is often called RM3 [1]:

$$P(w|\theta_q) = (1 - \alpha)P(w|q) + \alpha P(w|\phi_r(q)) \quad (17)$$

In Equation 16, $h_r(d) = \prod_{w' \in q} P(w'|\theta_d)$ is the query likelihood score of document d, serving for document weighting, and $g_r(w, d) = P(w|\theta_d)$ works for term weighting. If we instantiate the document weighting strategy in a different way, e.g., h'_r, whereas the term weighting strategy is fixed to g_r, it will lead to a different "relevance model" ϕ'_r. Formally

$$P(w|\phi'_r(q)) \propto \sum_{\theta_d \in \Theta} P(w|\theta_d) \cdot h'_r(d) \quad (18)$$

which can also be used for feedback after a similar interpolation. Following this way, we can construct a set of relevance-model style basis feedback methods by varying their document weighting strategies.

5.1.2 Mixture Model

In the simple two-component mixture model (SMM) ϕ_m, the words in Ω are assumed to be drawn from two models: (1) background model $P(w|C)$ and (2) topic model $P(w|\phi_m(q))$. Thus the log-likelihood for the entire set of feedback documents is:

$$\log P(\Omega|\phi_m(q)) = \sum_{w \in V} c(w, \Omega) \log((1 - \lambda)P(w|\phi_m(q)) + \lambda P(w|C)) \quad (19)$$

where V is the word vocabulary, $c(w, \Omega)$ is the count of word w in feedback document set Ω, and $\lambda \in [0, 1]$ is the mixture parameter. The estimate of $\phi_m(q)$ can be computed using the EM algorithm to maximize the log-likelihood. Finally, $\phi_m(q)$ is also interpolated with the original query model $P(w|q)$ to update the query model with a coefficient α. We notice in Formula 19 that

$$c(w, \Omega) = \sum_{d \in \Omega} |d| \cdot P(w|d) \quad (20)$$

It means that the document length $|d|$ is used as a weight of document d (i.e., $h_m(d) = |d|$) to sum over the term evidence from each feedback document. As in the case of the relevance model, we can also use any other document weighting method h'_m to replace h_m while keeping g_m the same, which will lead to a new family of mixture-model style basis feedback method ϕ'_m.

5.2 Document Weighting Strategies

We next introduce a set of document weighting strategies $\{h_t\}$. As we have discussed, each of them can be plugged into the relevance model (Section 5.1.1) or the mixture model (Section 5.1.2), leading to a new basis feedback method ϕ_t.

Relevance Score: Relevance score is shown to be a critical factor for feedback document weighting in a recent work [18]. We explore the use of query likelihood [21] h_1 and BM25 score [23] h_2 for document weighting: w.r.t. the former, the Dirichlet smoothing method [32] with $\mu = 1,000$ is used to smooth the document language model; w.r.t. the latter, we fix $k_1 = 1.2$, $b = 0.5$, and $k3 = 1,000$.

Document Novelty: We estimate a novelty score for each document to reward novel information. Three different methods are proposed: (1) The distance between the centroid of all feedback documents $h_3(d_i) = 1-\text{cosim}(\vec{d_i}, \frac{1}{k}\sum_{j=1}^{k}\vec{d_j})$, where 'cosim' stands for cosine similarity; (2) The distance between the centroid of all feedback documents ranked before the document $h_4(d_i) = 1-\text{cosim}(\vec{d_i}, \frac{1}{i-1}\sum_{j=1}^{i-1}\vec{d_j})$. (3) The distance between the most similar document ranked before the document: $h_5(d_i) = 1 - \max_{j=1}^{i-1}\{\text{cosim}(\vec{d_i}, \vec{d_j})\}$.

Query Term Proximity: Query term proximity has been largely ignored in traditional retrieval models [23, 21]. We use the recently proposed positional language model [19] and the minimum pair distance [29] to capture term proximity for improving document weighting: (1) we compute a positional query likelihood score based on the "best-matching" position [19], i.e., $h_6(d) = \max_{j=1}^{|d_i|}\prod_{w\in q} P(w|d,j)^{c(w,q)}$, where $c(w,q)$ is the count of w in q, and we follow work [17] to estimate the positional language model $P(w|d,j)$; (2) we use the normalized minimum pair-wise distance proposed in [29] by setting $\alpha = 1$ which prevents negative document weights, i.e., $h_7(d) = \log(\alpha + \exp(-\delta(q,d)))$.

Document Length: Though the heuristic of document length normalization has been incorporated into the relevance scores [23, 32], we still list it here because it was explicitly used in some existing pseudo feedback methods [18]: (1) raw document length: $h_8(d) = |d|$; (2) reciprocal of the raw document length: $h_9(d) = 1/h_8(d)$; (3) Dirichlet document length: $h_{10}(d) = |d|/(|d| + \mu)$, where we set $\mu = 1,000$; (4) reciprocal of the Dirichlet document length: $h_{11}(d) = 1/h_{10}(d)$.

Besides the above basic document weighting methods, for each h_t, we also introduce some of their variations as our document weighting, including $\exp(h_t)$, $(h_t)^2$, and $\sqrt{h_t}$. Also we include $\log(h_2)$ and $\log(h_8)$, since the values of h_2 and h_8 are usually larger than 1.0 for top-ranked documents. Overall, there are 46 methods in total, all of which are normalized to sum to 1.0 for each query.

5.3 Implementation Details

We next apply the FeedbackBoost algorithm to learn an ensemble feedback method. We denote $E_d(\phi(q))$ as the score of document d with respect to a basis feedback method ϕ on query q. In fact, with the KL-divergence retrieval method (Equation 15), we only need to retrieve and score documents once for each basis feedback method. Then during the training process, if we need to score a document d using any combined feedback $H' = \sum_{k=1}^{t}\alpha_k\phi_k$, we can do it efficiently by linearly combining the scores of the corresponding basis feedback methods.

$$\begin{aligned}E_d(H'(q)) &\propto \sum_{w\in q} P\left(w|\sum_k^t \frac{\alpha_k}{\sum_j^t \alpha_j}\phi_k(q)\right)\log P(w|d)\\ &= \sum_{w\in q}\left[\sum_{k=1}^{t}\frac{\alpha_k}{\sum_{j=1}^{t}\alpha_j}P\left(w|\phi_k(q)\right)\right]\log P(w|d) \qquad (21)\\ &\propto \sum_{k=1}^{t}\alpha_k E_d(\phi_k(q))\end{aligned}$$

So training FeedbackBoost would be as efficient as training general AdaBoost algorithm [9].

Besides, during the testing phase, $H(q)$ can also be estimated efficiently. For example, for the relevance model, we can plug the ensemble document weighting method used in $H(q)$ into Formula 18 to replace $h'_r(d)$ and estimate $H(q)$ directly; for the mixture model style $H(q)$, we can also replace $|d|$ with the combined document weighting methods in Formula 20, which does not affect feedback performance in the experiments. Hence, the efficiency of $H(q)$ for pseudo feedback would be comparable to that of basis feedback algorithms, which is also confirmed empirically.

6. EXPERIMENTAL SETUP

We evaluate our method using the Terabyte Web dataset and a large news dataset Robust04. Only title portions of the topics are taken as queries. For each dataset, we split the available topics into training, validate and test sets, where the training set is used solely for training the algorithms, the validate set is used for tuning the number of iterations T, and the test set is used for evaluation purposes. Table 1 shows some document set statistics. The preprocessing of the collections includes stemming using the Porter algorithm and stopword removal using a standard InQuery stoplist.

We train two FeedbackBoost models: in the first one, each basis feedback method implements a different document weighting strategy proposed in Section 5.2, while all of them use the same mixture-model style term weighting, and thus we refer to it as **BoostMM**; in the second one, each basis feedback method also implements a different document weighting strategy but all of them share the relevance-model style term weighting, thus the name **BoostRM**. That is, we parameterize Φ in different ways for BoostRM and BoostMM. This design allows us to meaningfully compare BoostMM and BoostRM with the corresponding two baseline feedback methods (i.e., SMM and RM3) and the basic query language model without feedback (labeled as "NoFB"). This set of experiments are mainly to compare FeedbackBoost with traditional pseudo feedback methods. A main hypothesis we would like to test is whether BoostMM and BoostRM are indeed more robust than the corresponding baseline SMM and RM3.

Furthermore, we also compare FeedbackBoost with two other lines of baseline methods. In the first line, we compare FeedbackBoost with another strong baseline representing a recent work on improving robustness of pseudo feedback, i.e., the **REXP-FB** method [7]. In the second line, we are interested in knowing if an existing learning to rank approach can also improve both robustness and effectiveness as much as FeedbackBoost does. So we introduce yet another baseline **AdaRank** [30], which performed well [16]. AdaRank

Collection	Description	#Docs	Training Topics	Validate Topics	Test Topics
Robust04	TREC disk 4&5 (minus CR)	528,155	301-450	601-650	651-700
Terabyte	2004 crawl of .gov domain	25,205,179	701-750	751-800	801-850

Table 1: Overview of TREC collections and topics

BoostMM Versus SMM

Collection		Metric	NoFB	fbDocCount = 20		fbDocCount = 50	
				SMM	BoostMM	SMM	BoostMM
Validate	Robust04	MAP	0.2850	0.3215*	**0.3447***+	0.2973	**0.3468***+
		Pr@20	0.3310	0.3610	**0.3790**	**0.3850**	**0.3850**
		RI	n/a	0.3600	**0.6400** (+77.8%)	0.0400	**0.6000** (+1400%)
		APloss	n/a	0.6191	**0.2877** (−53.5%)	1.3730	**0.2815** (−79.5%)
	Terabyte	MAP	0.3076	0.3477*	**0.3701***+	0.3445*	**0.3669***+
		Pr@20	0.5410	0.5570	**0.5970**	0.5540	**0.5820**
		RI	n/a	0.4400	**0.7200** (+63.6%)	0.3200	**0.6000** (+87.5%)
		APloss	n/a	0.6036	**0.1667** (−72.4%)	0.6963	**0.2433** (−65.1%)
Test	Robust04	MAP	0.2930	0.3265*	**0.3511***+	0.3067	**0.3453***+
		Pr@20	0.3796	0.4041	**0.4143**	0.3867	**0.4082**
		RI	n/a	0.3878	**0.5102** (+31.6%)	0.2653	**0.4286** (+61.6%)
		APloss	n/a	0.7108	**0.3493** (−50.9%)	1.3429	**0.4231** (−68.5%)
	Terabyte	MAP	0.3012	0.3061	**0.3331***+	0.3067	**0.3298***+
		Pr@20	0.4878	0.4765	**0.5255**	0.4663	**0.5112**
		RI	n/a	0.1429	**0.5102** (+257%)	0.1429	**0.5102** (+257%)
		APloss	n/a	0.6438	**0.1499** (−76.7%)	0.7546	**0.2511** (−66.7%)

BoostRM Versus RM3

Collection		Metric	NoFB	fbDocCount = 20		fbDocCount = 50	
				RM3	BoostRM	RM3	BoostRM
Validate	Robust04	MAP	0.2850	0.3431*	**0.3450***	0.3430*	**0.3490***+
		Pr@20	0.3310	**0.3840**	0.3800	0.3800	**0.3880**
		RI	n/a	0.2800	**0.4800** (+71.4%)	0.3600	**0.5200** (+44.4%)
		APloss	n/a	0.7084	**0.5056** (−28.6%)	0.6421	**0.4155** (−35.3%)
	Terabyte	MAP	0.3076	0.3471*	**0.3661***+	0.3466*	**0.3628***+
		Pr@20	0.5410	0.5840	**0.5890**	**0.5770**	0.5740
		RI	n/a	0.5200	**0.6800** (+30.8%)	0.4800	**0.5600** (+16.7%)
		APloss	n/a	0.9042	**0.2946** (−67.4%)	0.9458	**0.4247** (−55.1%)
Test	Robust04	MAP	0.2930	0.3483*	**0.3537***+	0.3462*	**0.3488***+
		Pr@20	0.3796	0.4010	**0.4122**	**0.4082**	**0.4082**
		RI	n/a	0.3061	**0.4286** (+40.0%)	0.3061	**0.4694** (+53.3%)
		APloss	n/a	0.5736	**0.3662** (−36.2%)	0.5184	**0.4261** (−17.8%)
	Terabyte	MAP	0.3012	0.3187	**0.3287***	0.3188	**0.3311***+
		Pr@20	0.4878	0.4939	**0.5010**	0.4980	**0.5173**
		RI	n/a	0.2245	**0.3469** (+54.5%)	0.1837	**0.3469** (+88.8%)
		APloss	n/a	0.6847	**0.2797** (−59.1%)	0.6608	**0.2614** (−60.4%)

Table 2: Comparison of BoostMM and BoostRM with SMM and RM3 respectively. Note that for APloss, lower is better (negative change is good), while for RI, higher is better. '*' and '+' mean the MAP improvement is statistically significant over NoFB and the corresponding baseline feedback method respectively. The improvement of APloss and RI is shown for BoostMM/BoostRM relative to SMM/RM3.

attempts to learn a ranking function through directly optimizing retrieval measures. One variation of AdaRank used in our comparison is **AdaRank.MAP**, which tries to optimize MAP. Since it is non-trivial to directly optimize the proposed fbloss using AdaRank, we further extend AdaRank to optimize a loss function that is similar to fbloss: a novel robustness-related measure E' that measures the performance degradation in feedback: $E'(q_i) = E\left(\sum_{k=1}^{t} \alpha_k \cdot \phi_k(q_i)\right) - E(q_i)$. According to the Formula 6 in [30], AdaRank turns out to minimize an exponential loss function $\sum_{i=1}^{|Q|} \exp\{-E'(q_i)\}$, leading to a new run **AdaRank.FB**. Note that AdaRank.FB is no longer the traditional AdaRank algorithm because the loss function is novel, thus it is a very strong baseline.

We use the Dirichlet smoothing method [32] for all document language models, where we set the $\mu = 1,000$. Besides, as suggested in our previous study [18], we set the mixture noise parameter λ to 0.9 for SMM and all the mixture-model style basis feedback methods. We also set the number of expansion terms to 40. These parameter settings work well and are used in our experiments unless otherwise stated.

It does not make sense to talk about fbloss alone, since we can always get 0 loss for any feedback method by setting the feedback coefficient α to 0. In the traditional evaluation strategy [31, 18], people often tune α to optimize one retrieval precision measure. We thus follow such a strategy to first optimize α in terms of MAP, on the basis of which we then try to reduce fbloss. Specifically, we give a priority to SMM and RM3 to optimize their feedback coefficient α on the training, validate and test sets respectively. However, for all the mixture-model style basis feedback methods, we simply set the feedback coefficients to those optimized for SMM, while for all the relevance-model style basis feedback methods, we use RM3's setting directly.

We are interested in both effectiveness and robustness of pseudo feedback methods, so besides MAP (on top-ranked 1,000 documents) and Pr@20, we also compare all runs in

Metric	fbDocCount = 20			fbDocCount = 50		
	AdaRank.MAP	AdaRank.FB	FeedbackBoost	AdaRank.MAP	AdaRank.FB	FeedbackBoost
MAP	0.3451	0.3535	**0.3537**	0.3418	0.3485	**0.3488**
RI	0.3061	0.3878	**0.4286**	0.3061	0.3469	**0.4694**
APloss	0.9776	0.4333	**0.3662**	1.0033	0.6329	**0.4261**

Table 3: Comparison of FeedbackBoost, AdaRank.MAP, and AdaRank.FB on the test set of Robust04. Note that AdaRank.FB is different from the traditional AdaRank algorithm, since it is armed with a novel robustness-related loss function.

Collection		NoFB-1	REXP-FB	NoFB-2	BoostRM	BoostMM
Robust04	MAP	0.2152	0.2451	0.2502	0.2617^+	0.2752^+
	RI	n/a	0.3773	n/a	0.5100	**0.5221**
Terabyte	MAP	0.2736	0.3004	0.2901	0.3086^+	0.3230^+
	RI	n/a	0.2624	n/a	0.5135	**0.5270**

Table 4: Comparison of FeedbackBoost and REXP-FB on the same collections, where cross-validation is used for training. '+' indicates that the improvement of MAP over NoFB-2 is statistically significant.

terms of two robustness measures, the robustness index (RI) and the accumulative loss of retrieval performance (APloss). $RI = 1 - 2 \cdot fbloss$, is essentially a transformation of the fbloss proposed in our paper; we show RI instead of fbloss mainly because RI was often used in previous studies, e.g., [7]. APloss is to measure the feedback loss in a finer degree, which is the accumulative AP degradation in failure cases (since AP is used as E in our paper), defined as: $APloss = \sum_{i=1}^{|Q|} [E(q_i) - E(H(q_i))] \cdot I\{E(H(q_i)) < E(q_i)\}$

7. EXPERIMENT RESULTS

7.1 Performance of FeedbackBoost

Table 2 compares MAP, Pr@20, RI, and APloss for NoFB, SMM, RMM, BoostMM, and BoostRM on the validate and test sets. Note that each time all runs use the same set of feedback documents to make the comparison fair; that is, we fix the base ranking for all runs. Besides, the iteration number T in FeedbackBoost is chosen to minimize the corresponding fbloss on the validate sets. We also vary the number of feedback documents from 20 to 50.

For all cases, we can see that BoostMM and BoostRM significantly improve the robustness over SMM and RM3 respectively. For example, BoostMM *reduces* APloss as compared with SMM by amounts ranging from 50.9% to 77.8% when using 20 feedback documents and from 65.1% to 79.5% when using 50 feedback documents. Moreover, BoostMM and BoostRM also significantly improve MAP over SMM and RM3 in almost all cases. The results demonstrate that the FeedbackBoost algorithm does a good job to improve robustness while still achieving better effectiveness. Moreover, FeedbackBoost works consistently well when we use different number of feedback documents. The performance of FeedbackBoost shows that it is effective to combine multiple feedback methods using our FeedbackBoost to improve both robustness and effectiveness of pseudo feedback.

We next compare FeedbackBoost with AdaRank.MAP and AdaRank.FB. These three algorithms are all trained on the same set of relevance-model style basis feedback methods. The iteration number for all the algorithms are chosen to minimize fbloss on the validate set. We present the experiment results in Table 3. One interesting observation is that AdaRank.FB is more effective than AdaRank.MAP, suggesting that the proposed robustness-related measure is better than MAP as an objective function to improve pseudo feedback: one possible explanation is that the average precision does not work well to indicate the room for improvement of a query, so focusing on queries with lower average precision may not be a good strategy to fully exploit the potential of different queries; however, our new measure would be able to capture more precisely the potential room of a query through comparing its performance with the baseline performance. Moreover, we also see that FeedbackBoost is clearly better than AdaRank.FB, though they use similar objective functions, sugggesting that our optimization framework is more effective for pseudo feedback.

We finally compare FeedbackBoost with a state-of-the-art feedback method, REXP-FB [7], which attempted to reduce failures of pseudo feedback but was only able to optimize an indirect objective function. They also used Terabyte and Robust04 as their test collections. So we used a 3-fold (701-750, 751-800, and 801-850) and a 2-fold (301-450 and 601-700) cross validation method to evaluate FeedbackBoost on the whole Terabyte and Robust04 topics respectively in order to compare with their reported numbers. In this comparison, we use the same collection and parameter settings as were used in [7]. The comparison is reported in Table 4.

There are clear performance improvements of our baseline runs (NoFB-2) over theirs (NoFB-1), probably because we use a latest version of Indri search engine (2.10) [1]. We still can see that, in terms of relative improvements, BoostMM performs similarly to REXP-FB, although REXP-FB used a lot of constraints to improve the selection of expansion terms while we only use the default term weighting. However, the most interesting observation is from the comparison of RI, which may be more comparable across systems. We can see that our algorithms achieve a significantly *higher RI* in all cases, even though our baseline run is even harder to beat. This finding confirms the conclusion in [18] that document weighting plays a key role in affecting the robustness of feedback. Furthermore, it suggests that our way of directly optimizing robustness indeed works more effectively.

7.2 Robustness Histograms

To examine in details how badly queries are hurt by a pseudo feedback algorithm, we show in Figure 2 the robustness histograms by combining two test sets (query 651-701 and query 801-850). The x-axis represents the individual APloss in percentage (i.e., $[E(q) - E(\phi(q))]/E(q)$, where ϕ is

[1]http://www.lemurproject.org/

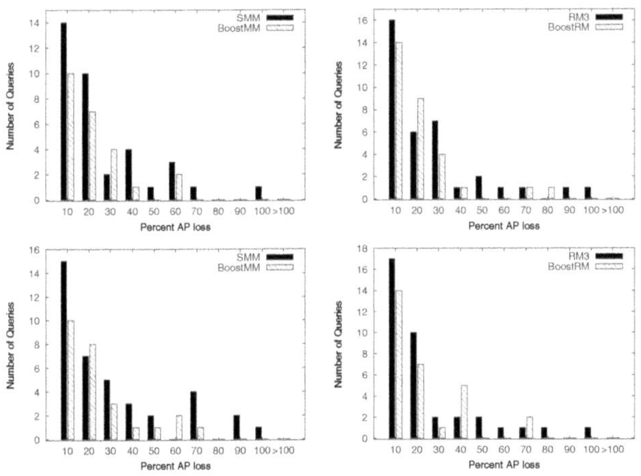

Figure 2: Histograms that compare robustness of SMM vs BoostMM (first and third) and RM3 vs BoostRM (second and fourth) on the combination of two test sets. 20 (50) feedback documents are used in the left (right) two histograms respectively.

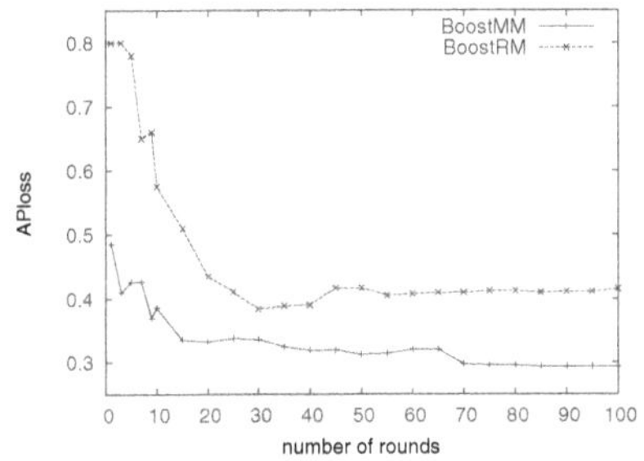

Figure 5: Sensitivity of BoostMM and BoostRM to the iteration number on Robust04 validate set.

the corresponding feedback method) for individual failure queries, and the y-axis stands for the number of queries with the corresponding percentage APloss. We can see that for the worst cases, where a query's AP is decreased by more than 40%, both BoostMM and BoostRM perform much better than SMM and RM3 respectively. It suggests that the proposed FeedbackBoost algorithm indeed concentrates more on difficult queries that are hurt seriously by baseline feedback methods, i.e., SMM and RM3, and the significant reduction of APloss and improvement of RI shown in Table 2 could be mainly due to the elimination of those worst cases.

7.3 Parameter Sensitivity

Usually there is a tradeoff between robustness and effectiveness: if we use a smaller feedback coefficient α, there would be fewer feedback failures, but we may not fully improve the effectiveness; if we increase this α to some appropriate value, the overall retrieval precision could be optimized, which, however, may lead to more feedback failures. Although we have shown that FeedbackBoost improves both robustness and effectiveness at the same time, we are still interested in how the performance of FeedbackBoost interacts with α (where α in FeedbackBoost is used to control the feedback interpolation of each basis feedback method involved.) We thus draw the sensitivity curves for FeedbackBoost in terms of the percentage MAP degradation and the overall MAP improvement in Figure 3 and 4 respectively. The percentage MAP degradation is essentially the relative APloss, i.e., $\text{APloss}/[\sum_i^{|Q|} E(q_i)]$; the overall MAP improvement of ϕ is defined as $[\sum_i^{|Q|} E(\phi(q_i))]/[\sum_i^{|Q|} E(q_i)] - 1.0$. We use 50 feedback documents in all curves. The curves clearly show that FeedbackBoost consistently improves the robustness and effectiveness over two baseline algorithms. Additionally, our algorithm is also less sensitive to α in both curves, and setting α around 0.8 often leads to a large improvement in precision with only a small amount of failures.

Finally, we show in Figure 5 the curves of performance changes as we increase the iteration number T. We see that the APloss decreases steadily and quickly as the training goes on, until it reaches its plateau. In our experiments, we can usually find the best parameter T within 100 rounds.

8. CONCLUSIONS

In this paper, we propose a novel learning algorithm, FeedbackBoost, based on the boosting framework to improve pseudo feedback. A major contribution of our work is to optimize pseudo feedback based on a novel loss function that *directly measures both robustness and effectiveness*, which has not been achieved in any previous work.

The experiment results show that the proposed FeedbackBoost algorithm can improve average precision effectively and meanwhile reduce the number and magnitude of feedback failures dramatically as compared to two representative pseudo feedback methods based on language models, the mixture model and the relevance model. We also compare our algorithm with a recently proposed robust feedback method, and the results show that our method is more robust. In addition, we compare FeedbackBoost with a well-performing learning to rank approach applied for pseudo feedback and observe that FeedbackBoost works clearly better. These results show that the proposed FeedbackBoost is more effective and robust than any of the existing method for pseudo feedback, including both traditional pseudo feedback methods and new learning-based approaches.

Our work can be extended in several ways. First, in our current work, we only use basis feedback methods with different document weighting strategies, so a straightforward future work is to also introduce term weighting methods to construct a larger set of basis feedback methods. Second, we are also interested in combining even more recently proposed pseudo feedback algorithms, e.g., [2, 28, 7, 20], and other families of feedback methods, e.g., [24, 22], to diversify our basis feedback methods. Third, personalized search is another scenario which shares similar effectiveness-robustness tradeoff issues; thus it is also interesting to improve personalized search by exploring the FeedbackBoost framework.

9. ACKNOWLEDGMENTS

We thank the anonymous reviewers for their useful comments. This material is based upon work supported by the National Science Foundation under Grant Numbers IIS-0713581 and CNS-1028381. The first author is also supported by a Yahoo! Key Scientific Challenge Award.

10. REFERENCES

[1] N. Abdul-Jaleel, J. Allan, W. B. Croft, F. Diaz, L. Larkey, X. Li, D. Metzler, M. D. Smucker, T. Strohman, H. Turtle, and C. Wade. Umass at trec 2004: Novelty and hard. In *TREC '04*, 2004.

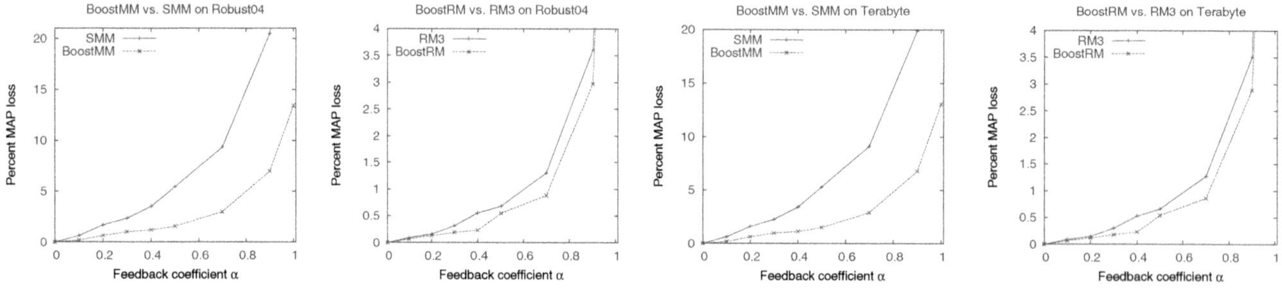

Figure 3: Sensitivity of the percentage degradation of MAP in failure queries to the feedback coefficient α. SMM versus BoostMM and RM3 versus BoostRM are shown in the odd and even-number figures respectively.

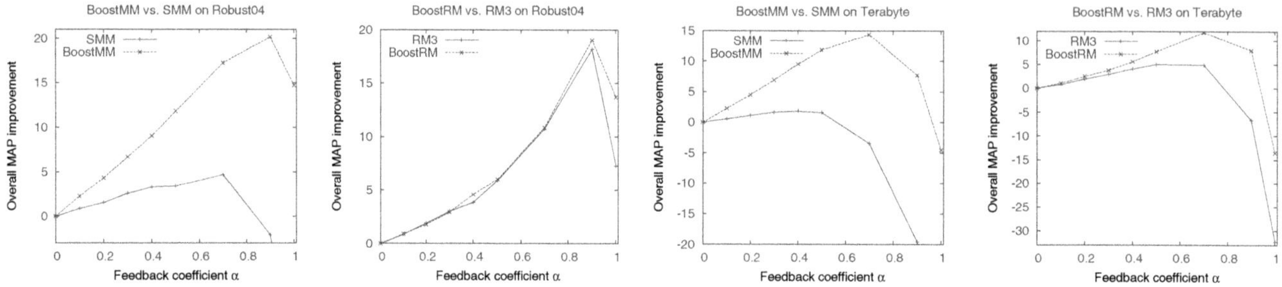

Figure 4: Sensitivity of the average improvement of MAP in all queries to the feedback coefficient α. SMM versus BoostMM and RM3 versus BoostRM are shown in the odd and even-number figures respectively.

[2] G. Amati, C. Carpineto, and G. Romano. Query difficulty, robustness, and selective application of query expansion. In *ECIR '04*, pages 127–137, 2004.

[3] C. Buckley, G. Salton, J. Allan, and A. Singhal. Automatic query expansion using smart: Trec 3. In *TREC '94*, pages 69–80, 1994.

[4] C. Burges, T. Shaked, E. Renshaw, A. Lazier, M. Deeds, N. Hamilton, and G. Hullender. Learning to rank using gradient descent. In *ICML '05*, pages 89–96, 2005.

[5] G. Cao, J.-Y. Nie, J. Gao, and S. Robertson. Selecting good expansion terms for pseudo-relevance feedback. In *SIGIR*, pages 243–250, 2008.

[6] Z. Cao, T. Qin, T.-Y. Liu, M.-F. Tsai, and H. Li. Learning to rank: from pairwise approach to listwise approach. In *Proceedings of ICML*, pages 129–136, 2007.

[7] K. Collins-Thompson. Reducing the risk of query expansion via robust constrained optimization. In *CIKM '09*, pages 837–846, 2009.

[8] Y. Freund, R. Iyer, R. E. Schapire, and Y. Singer. An efficient boosting algorithm for combining preferences. *J. Mach. Learn. Res.*, 4:933–969, 2003.

[9] Y. Freund and R. E. Schapire. A decision-theoretic generalization of on-line learning and an application to boosting. In *EuroCOLT '95*, pages 23–37, London, UK, 1995. Springer-Verlag.

[10] D. Harman and C. Buckley. The nrrc reliable information access (ria) workshop. In *SIGIR '04*, pages 528–529, 2004.

[11] T. Hastie, R. Tibshirani, and J. Friedman. *The Elements of Statistical Learning*. Springer, 2009.

[12] B. He and I. Ounis. Finding good feedback documents. In *CIKM '09*, pages 2011–2014, 2009.

[13] T. Joachims. Optimizing search engines using clickthrough data. In *Proceedings of the ACM KDD 2002*, pages 133–142, 2002.

[14] J. D. Lafferty and C. Zhai. Document language models, query models, and risk minimization for information retrieval. In *SIGIR '01*, pages 111–119, 2001.

[15] V. Lavrenko and W. B. Croft. Relevance-based language models. In *SIGIR '01*, pages 120–127, 2001.

[16] T.-Y. Liu. Learning to rank for information retrieval. *Foundations and Trends in Information Retrieval*, 3(3):225–331, 2009.

[17] Y. Lv and C. Zhai. Adaptive relevance feedback in information retrieval. In *CIKM '09*, 2009.

[18] Y. Lv and C. Zhai. A comparative study of methods for estimating query language models with pseudo feedback. In *Proceedings of CIKM '09*, 2009.

[19] Y. Lv and C. Zhai. Positional language models for information retrieval. In *SIGIR '09*, pages 299–306, 2009.

[20] Y. Lv and C. Zhai. Positional relevance model for pseudo-relevance feedback. In *SIGIR '10*, pages 579–586, 2010.

[21] J. M. Ponte and W. B. Croft. A language modeling approach to information retrieval. In *SIGIR '98*, pages 275–281, 1998.

[22] S. E. Robertson and K. S. Jones. Relevance weighting of search terms. *JASIS*, 27(3):129–146, 1976.

[23] S. E. Robertson, S. Walker, S. Jones, M. Hancock-Beaulieu, and M. Gatford. Okapi at trec-3. In *TREC '94*, pages 109–126, 1994.

[24] J. J. Rocchio. Relevance feedback in information retrieval. In *In The SMART Retrieval System: Experiments in Automatic Document Processing*, pages 313–323. Prentice-Hall Inc., 1971.

[25] G. Salton and C. Buckley. Improving retrieval performance by relevance feedback. *JASIS*, 41(4):288–297, 1990.

[26] R. E. Schapire and Y. Singer. Improved boosting algorithms using confidence-rated predictions. In *COLT' 98*, pages 80–91, 1998.

[27] N. Soskin, O. Kurland, and C. Domshlak. Navigating in the dark: Modeling uncertainty in ad hoc retrieval using multiple relevance models. In *ICTIR '09*, pages 79–91, 2009.

[28] T. Tao and C. Zhai. Regularized estimation of mixture models for robust pseudo-relevance feedback. In *SIGIR '06*, pages 162–169, 2006.

[29] T. Tao and C. Zhai. An exploration of proximity measures in information retrieval. In *SIGIR '07*, pages 295–302, 2007.

[30] J. Xu and H. Li. Adarank: a boosting algorithm for information retrieval. In *SIGIR '07*, pages 391–398, 2007.

[31] C. Zhai and J. D. Lafferty. Model-based feedback in the language modeling approach to information retrieval. In *CIKM '01*, pages 403–410, 2001.

[32] C. Zhai and J. D. Lafferty. A study of smoothing methods for language models applied to ad hoc information retrieval. In *SIGIR '01*, pages 334–342, 2001.

[33] Z. Zheng, K. Chen, G. Sun, and H. Zha. A regression framework for learning ranking functions using relative relevance judgments. In *SIGIR '07*, pages 287–294, 2007.

Enhancing Ad-hoc Relevance Weighting Using Probability Density Estimation

Xiaofeng Zhou
Information Retrieval and Knowledge Management Research Lab
Department of Mathematics and Statistics
York University
Toronto, Canada
bluesky@mathstat.yorku.ca

Jimmy Xiangji Huang, Ben He
Information Retrieval and Knowledge Management Research Lab
School of Information Technology
York University
Toronto, Canada
{jhuang,benhe}@yorku.ca

ABSTRACT

Classical probabilistic information retrieval (IR) models, e.g. BM25, deal with document length based on a trade-off between the Verbosity hypothesis, which assumes the independence of a document's relevance of its length, and the Scope hypothesis, which assumes the opposite. Despite the effectiveness of the classical probabilistic models, the potential relationship between document length and relevance is not fully explored to improve retrieval performance. In this paper, we conduct an in-depth study of this relationship based on the Scope hypothesis that document length does have its impact on relevance. We study a list of probability density functions and examine which of the density functions fits the best to the actual distribution of the document length. Based on the studied probability density functions, we propose a length-based BM25 relevance weighting model, called BM25L, which incorporates document length as a substantial weighting factor. Extensive experiments conducted on standard TREC collections show that our proposed BM25L markedly outperforms the original BM25 model, even if the latter is optimized.

Categories and Subject Descriptors

H.4 [**Information Search and Retrieval**]: Retrieval models

General Terms

Algorithms, Experimentation, Theory

Keywords

Probabilistic IR, BM25, Document length, Normalization

1. INTRODUCTION

An information retrieval system receives a query from user and returns the supposedly relevant documents. A crucial issue underlying an IR system is to rank the returned documents by decreasing order of relevance. Generally, ranking is based on a *weighting model*. The basic probabilistic model proposed in [23] is one of the most popular weighting models in modern IR systems, which is developed from the Probability Ranking Principle [22]. This probabilistic approach is refined based on the Verbosity hypothesis [24] which assumes independence of document length from relevance. In other words, long documents simply use more words than short documents to cover similar scope [24].

An opposite assumption about document length is the so-called Scope hypothesis, which states that some documents may contain more material than others if longer [24]. That is, long documents are more likely to be retrieved. In practice, a document may be considered as a trade-off between the Verbosity hypothesis and the Scope hypothesis. How to balance between these two hypotheses by modeling document length within the basic probabilistic weighting paradigm remains a challenging research issue. The impact of document length on relevance is particularly important for ad-hoc retrieval, where relevance is defined in a binary or graded manner. Compared to a short document, a long document is likely to be relevant if it contains paragraphs that meet the information need of the query, even if a large part of the document is in fact non-relevant.

To address the effect of document length on relevance, the basic probabilistic weighting function takes into account the document length d as follows [24]:

$$w(x, d) = \log \frac{P(\underline{x}, d|R)}{P(\underline{x}, d|\overline{R})} \frac{P(\underline{0}, \Delta|\overline{R})}{P(\underline{0}, \Delta|R)} \tag{1}$$

where $w(x, d)$ is the relevance weight of a given document. d is the document evidence for relevance, which is given by document length. Δ denotes the average document length of the reference vector $\underline{0}$, and $\underline{x}$ represents all other information about the document. $\overline{R}$ and R stand for the non-relevance and relevance, respectively. This function measures the difference between the probabilities of document length and all other information we have for the document when it is relevant and when it is not relevant, respectively, in log scale. The above equation also implies a relevant document should receive a higher weight than a non-relevant document in order to achieve a satisfying retrieval performance.

Equation 1 can be further decomposed into the three components as follows [24]:

$$w(x, d) = w(\underline{x}, d)_1 + w(\underline{0}, d)_{21} + w(\underline{0}, d)_{22} \tag{2}$$

where

$$w(\underline{x}, d)_1 = \log \frac{P(\underline{x}, d|R)}{P(\underline{x}, d|\overline{R})} \frac{P(\underline{0}, d|\overline{R})}{P(\underline{0}, d|R)},$$

SIGIR'11 July 24-28, 2011, Beijing, China

$$w(\underline{0}, d)_{21} = \log \frac{P(\underline{0}|d, R)}{P(\underline{0}|d, \overline{R})} \frac{P(\underline{0}|\Delta, \overline{R})}{P(\underline{0}|\Delta, R)}$$

and

$$w(d, \Delta)_{22} = \log \frac{P(d|R)P(\Delta|\overline{R})}{P(d|\overline{R})P(\Delta|R)}.$$

Under the Verbosity hypothesis, document length has been considered as independent evidence of relevance. This hypothesis nullifies the component $w(d, \Delta)_{22}$ in Equation 2, which as a consequence is set to zero [24]. Thus, the weighting function becomes

$$w(\underline{x}, d) = w(\underline{x}, d)_1 + w(\underline{0}, d)_{21}. \quad (3)$$

The classical BM25 weighting model [10] is derived from Equation 3, more specifically, $w_{BM25} = w(\underline{x}, d)$, where w_{BM25} is the relevance score of BM25, given by the following weighting function [10]:

$$w_{BM25} = \frac{(k_1 + 1)tf}{K + tf} * w^{(1)} * \frac{(k_3 + 1)qtf}{k_3 + qtf} \oplus L \quad (4)$$

where

$$K = k_1 * \left((1 - b) + b * \frac{dl}{avdl}\right),$$

$$w^{(1)} = \log \frac{(r + 0.5)/(R - r + 0.5)}{(n - r + 0.5)/(N - n - R + r + 0.5)},$$

$$L = k_2 * nq * \frac{avdl - dl}{avdl + dl},$$

N is the number of indexed documents in the collection, n is the number of documents containing the query term, R is the number of known relevant documents to a specific topic, r is the number of relevant documents containing the term, tf is within-document term frequency, qtf is within-query term frequency, dl is the document length (i.e. the document evidence d in Equation 2), $avdl$ is the average document length, nq is the number of query terms, $k_i's$ and b are tuning constants (whose setting depends on the dataset used and is usually empirically determined), and $\oplus$ indicates that its following component is added only once per document. Particularly, b functions as a justification factor that adjusts the relative importance between the two hypotheses [25].

The main focus of this research is to study the relationship between document length and relevance in the context of the Scope hypothesis by exploring a list of probability density distribution for document length. The Scope hypothesis suggests the existence of a relationship between document length and relevance. It implies that the component $w(d, \Delta)_{22}$ in Equation 2 may not be zero. In this paper, we consider document length itself as a direct predictor of relevance. Our study of document length is based on the intuition that long documents tend to have high retrieval probabilities, since long documents usually have a large number of unique terms, which are likely to be picked up by the query term matching [28]. Our experiments show that long documents tend to have high frequencies of query terms, which leads to high relevance scores. This provides evidence supporting the Scope hypothesis that there exists a dependency of relevance on document length. Particularly, there are two extreme cases that need to be considered. One is that the relevance of each document in a collection is independent of its length. This is the case of BM11 or $b = 1$ in BM25 [25]. The other one is BM15 or $b = 0$ in BM25 [25], which implies that long documents are likely to be retrieved. To balance between these two extreme cases, Robertson et al. introduce a parameter b in BM25 to control the effect of tf normalization [25]. In our study, we first use statistical tools to learn the pattern of the relationship between the document length and its relevance, investigate the behavior of $w(d, \Delta)_{22}$ in Equation (2), and propose a new weighting function incorporating this relationship, which is the result of a mixture of the two hypotheses. Our results show that the retrieval performance of BM25 can be markedly improved over different settings of the parameter b by exploiting the document length evidence.

The rest of the paper is organized as follows. Section 2 gives a brief survey in previous work. Then Section 3 introduces the datasets and presents the idea of the length-based weighting function, and proposes seven models based on the density analysis. The proposed models are evaluated through extensive experiments in Section 4. Finally, we conclude on the work and suggest future research directions in Section 5.

2. RELATED WORK

The classical probabilistic models for IR rank documents according to their relevance scores, assigned by matching the query terms with adjustment for the relationship between document length and term frequency. This approach is developed based on the Verbosity hypothesis which assumes the document's relevance is independent of its length [24]. However, in practice, the impact of document length on relevance may be a mixture of both the Scope hypothesis and the Verbosity hypothesis [24].

Many previous studies have been conducted to investigate the impact of document length on relevance. Singhal *et al.* [28] suggest that long documents tend to have more unique terms, and consequently, long documents have a better chance to be retrieved than short documents. As the document length increases, the number of times the query terms occur in the documents also increases, which in turn increases the matching score. For instance, Singhal *et al.* illustrate that the probability of a document's relevance increases proportionally with document length in the early TREC test collections [28, 29]. Similar results have also been reported on the later "ad-hoc" test collections [15]. Moreover, a number of empirical studies have provided statistical evidence supporting that the probability of a document's relevance to an information need is considered to be correlated with the length of the document. Kraaij *et al.* show that the probability of relevance is positively correlated with document length on a number of TREC ad-hoc and Web collections [16]. Singhal *et al.* state that the documents retrieved by a model produce a retrieval pattern by the distribution of the document length [28]. Huang *et al.* use functional curve to approximate the distribution of document length on the TREC data sets and conclude that the retrieval system can be improved through an appropriate document length function [12, 13]. Furthermore, proper term weighting strategies based on document length can also improve retrieval performance [31]. For example, normalization techniques have been applied for each term in the query through the length adjustment to avoid the bias introduced by document length. Normalizing the document length within a retrieval system could improve the performance [7]. By applying statistical regression of the similarity scores within the normalizing document length and query size, Lamprier *et al.* show that a significant improvement can be made to IR systems [17]. Blanco *et al.* device a probabilistic document length prior for language modeling [4]. Losada *et al.* apply smoothing techniques for document length in language modeling to show the significant impact of document length on the information retrieval performance [19]. They also argue in [20] that the causal link between document length and its relevance may not exist when incompleteness is taken into account, although the evidence is not concrete enough to nullify the effect of document length on relevance. For the issue addressed in [20], we set up the experiments in this paper using Expectation-maximization (EM) algorithm and bootstrapping method [8] to avoid this problem.

3. DENSITY ANALYSIS AND LENGTH RELEVANCE WEIGHTING

Under the Scope hypothesis, $w(d,\Delta)_{22}$ in Equation 2 is no longer zero since a dependence of relevance on document length is assumed. To add the length information into the weighting function $w(x,d)$, we decompose the $w(d,\Delta)_{22}$ further into

$$w(d,\Delta)_{22} = \log\frac{P(d|R)}{P(d|\overline{R})} + \log\frac{P(\Delta|\overline{R})}{P(\Delta|R)} \quad (5)$$

The second component of Equation 5 is constant over a given document collection. This is because the average document length Δ for the reference vector $\underline{0}$ in a document collection is known and fixed. Therefore, for each document in a collection, the second component of Equation 5 above is the same across the whole document collection and does not affect the document ranking. For simplicity, we refer $w(d,\Delta)_{22}$ to as the first component in the Equation 5. Thus, the relevance weight $w(d,\Delta)_{22}$ is given by the log-odd of the relevance and non-relevance probabilities $P(d|R)$ and $P(d|\overline{R})$. In other words, $w(d,\Delta)_{22}$ measures the difference between the probabilities of given document length condition on relevance and non-relevance in log scale. We name Equation 5 as *length relevance weighting*. Our ultimate goal is to calculate the $w(d,\Delta)_{22}$ in Equation 5, this needs a way to estimate the probabilities $P(d|R)$ and $P(d|\overline{R})$. By adding the measurement of document length itself into the basic weighting function, the retrieval system is expected to achieve high accuracy since the length information brings more evidence of relevance. The estimation of probability distribution function [1] of document length will be discussed in the next subsections.

The density estimation has three parts. First, we study the distributional pattern of document length on standard TREC test collections using kernel density estimation method [3, 27], which gives us a guidance in density estimation. In the second part, we apply data transformation techniques on the document length in order to get a better fitting of the document length distribution. Finally, Maximum Likelihood Estimation (MLE) is applied to obtain the distribution parameters estimates of document length. Length relevance weighting function is then derived based on the above density estimation.

In the rest of this paper, we use **d** to denote the document length. As a general rule, we usually make an assumption about observed d's, *i.e.* $d_1, d_2, ..., d_N$ are independent and identically distributed, N is the number of documents in the collection. We first introduce the test collections we used and then give the details of density estimation in the following subsections.

[1]We use probability distribution function and probability density function interchangeable in the rest of this paper.

3.1 The TREC Test Collections

We examine the impact of document length on relevance using 4 standard TREC test collections. These four test collections are the most recent TREC datasets, and provide a good coverage on the a variety of commonly used datasets in IR evaluation, and are used for different test purposes and vary in size in term of the document length. Basic information about the test collections and topics are given in Table 1.

Table 1: Information about the test collections.

Coll.	TREC Task	Topics	# Docs
disk1&2	1-3, Ad-hoc	51-200	741,856
WT10G	9, 10 Web	451-550	1,692,096
.GOV2	2004-2006 Terabyte Ad-hoc	701-850	25,178,548
ClueWeb B	2009 Relevance Feedback	rf.01-rf.50	49,375,681

The disk1&2 collection contains newswire articles from various sources, such as Association Press (AP), Wall Street Journal (WSJ), Financial Times (FT), etc., which are usually considered as high-quality text data with little noise. It usually used for ad hoc test. The WT10G collection is a medium size crawl of Web documents, which was used in the TREC 9 and 10 Web tracks. It contains 10 Gigabytes of uncompressed data. The .GOV2 collection, which has 426 Gigabytes of uncompressed data, is a crawl from the .gov domain. This collection has been employed in the TREC 14 (2004), 15 (2005) and 16 (2006) Terabyte tracks. The ClueWeb collection is a very large crawl of the Web, and is currently the largest TREC test collection. We use the category B of ClueWeb, which contains about 50 million English Web pages, and its associated topics used in the TREC 2009 Relevance Feedback track. We index all documents in the above four collections. For all four test collections used, each term is stemmed using Porter's English stemmer, and standard English stopwords are removed.

3.2 Kernel Density Analysis

Kernel density estimation (or Parzen window method) is a non-parametric way of estimating the probability density function of a random variable. It can be used to extrapolate the data to the entire population as follows [27]:

$$\widehat{f_h}(d) = \frac{1}{nh}\sum_{i=1}^{n} K(\frac{d-d_i}{h}) \quad (6)$$

where $d_i, i = 1,\ldots,n$ is the independent and identically-distributed sample from some unknown distribution, n is the number of samples we draw from the population, K is the kernel function and h is the bandwidth (also called smoothing parameter). We can obtain the smoothing curve by adjusting the parameter h. Usually K is instantiated by a standard Gaussian function with a mean of zero and a variance of 1:

$$K(\frac{d-d_i}{h}) = \frac{1}{\sqrt{2\pi}}exp(-\frac{(d-d_i)^2}{2h^2}) \quad (7)$$

Kernel density estimation gives us a global picture of the given dataset.

Figure 1 shows the distributional pattern of relevant and non-relevant document length for the test collections disk1&2, .GOV2, WT10G and ClueWeb B respectively using kernel density estimation with the standard normal kernel function. In Figure 1, the length curves have been cut when the document length is large than 1500 in $x-$axis in order to visualize the difference between the relevant and non-relevant document length because the long documents have low frequencies to be emerged in test collections. The length of

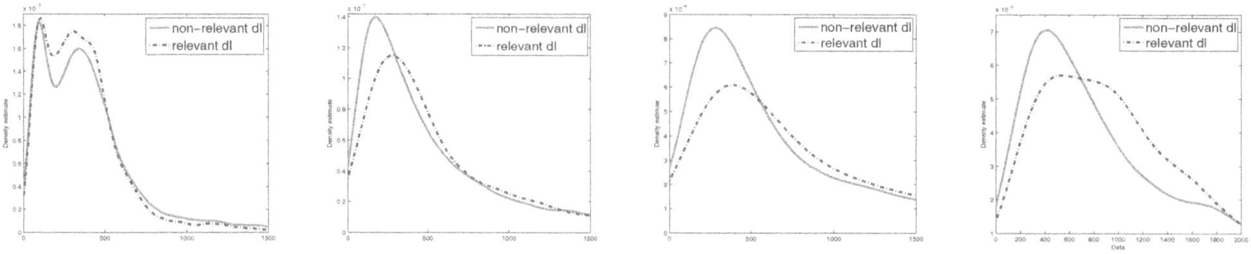

(a) disk1&2 (b) WT10G (c) .GOV2 (d) ClueWeb B

Figure 1: Kernel density estimate constructed from the document length on four test collections. "dl" stands for document length

Table 2: Basic statistical Information about the document length of four test collections. "rel" stands for relevant document length, "non-rel" stands for non-relevant document length.

Dataset	Mean		Standard Deviation		Minimum		Maximum	
	rel	non-rel	rel	non-rel	rel	non-rel	rel	non-rel
disk1&2	534.22	716.16	3960.11	3498.03	4	3	252983	252983
WT10G	1213.29	1165.83	2392.08	3801.12	24	5	48363	214693
.GOV2	3153.02	2821.13	4844.15	5022.19	11	10	47815	59566
ClueWeb B	1563.18	1583.32	1806.17	1888.64	50	52	16088	16087

non-relevant and relevant documents from four test collections are both positively skewed and have a long tail with different tail shapes. Non-relevant document has higher frequency than relevant documents when the document length is relatively short. The curve on disk1&2 appears to have two distinct peaks called bimodality. In contrast, there is only one mode that arises on WT10G, .GOV2 and ClueWeb B.

We also list the basic statistics in Table 2 for the length of relevant and non-relevant documents on each of the four test collections. At first glance, we may not see much difference between relevant and non-relevant documents from these two tables. However, further looking into the Table 2, we observe that disk1&2 has the longest document length in term of maximum and the shortest document length in term of mean and minimum value, but relative high variance, which indicate that document length of disk1&2 is spread out over a large range of values. The .GOV2 has the highest variability and mean value among the four test collections. The length of relevant and the length of non-relevant documents are very close to each other on the ClueWeb B. However, the length of relevant and the length non-relevant documents of WT10G differ most among the four test collections.

We apply the data transformation techniques to visualize the difference between the relevant and non-relevant document length on each test collection used. By applying the data transform technique, we can also obtain higher likelihood distribution function and achieve more accurate estimates of distribution parameters.

3.3 Data Transformation

The data transformation technique is widely used in data processing or pre-processing for stabilizing the variance and make the data more normal distribution-like. In our case, all document lengths are positive, whose distribution is skewed to the right as described in Figure 1, and document length cannot be described by standard statistical methods because of the skewness. Therefore, data transformation is required to extract a better characteristic of the data. We initiate it by applying central limit theory, *i.e.* transformation I, it is also called standardization. By standardizing the data, it forces the data to locate on the common scales to be compared. Secondly, the Power transformation is from the family of functions that are applied to create a rank-preserving transformation of data which improves the correlation between variables and for other data stabilization procedures [5]. Box-Cox power transformation is commonly used to alleviate heteroscedasticity when the distribution of the variable of interest is not known, *i.e* transformations II and III. Transformation II is the special case of transformation III when $\theta = 0$. We also transform the document length to be within the scale of $0 - 1$ using transformation IV. The four types of transformation is described as follows:

- Transformation I: Standardization
$$z = (d - \bar{d})/s_d \tag{8}$$
- Transformation II: Log transformation
$$z = \log(d) \tag{9}$$
- Transformation III: Box-Cox transformation
$$z = (d^{\theta} - 1)/\theta \tag{10}$$
Box-cox transformation is a parametric power transformation technique in order to reduce anomalies such as non-additivity, non-normality and heteroscedasticity, $\theta \neq 0$ is the transformation power.

- Transformation IV: Normalization
$$z = (d - d_{min})/(d_{max} - d_{min}) \tag{11}$$

where z is the document length after the transformation, $\bar{d}$ is the average document length, s_d is the standard deviation of document length, d_{min} denotes the minimum document length and d_{max} is the maximum document length.

Figure 2 plots the distributional pattern of transformed relevant and non-relevant document length on four test collections. In Figure 2, we examine length distribution patterns of relevant and non-relevant documents on the four test

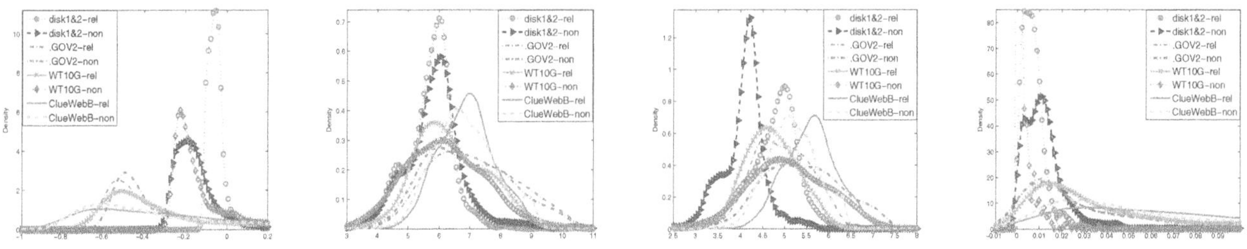

(a) Transformation I (b) Transformation II (c) Transformation III (d) Transformation IV

Figure 2: Kernel density estimates constructed from the transformed document length of four test collections. "rel" stands relevant document length and "non" stands non-relevant document length.

collections used. A major observation is that the the curves of the transformed document length distribution have similar shapes before and after the transformation. That is, the curves on disk1&2 remain bimodal, while the curves on the other three test collections are still left-skewed, but not as much as those of the original document length distribution, thanks to the data transformation. Moreover, the curves on .GOV2 and ClueWeb B become more symmetric after the transformation. On disk1&2, .GOV2 and WT10g, the center of the non-relevant document length distribution shifts far away to the right of the relevant document length distribution. From Figure 2(d), we can clearly see that relevant and non-relevant document length on Clueweb B can be distinguished from their distributional frequencies. Note that similar observations can also be drawn from other three collections used, but the difference between relevant and non-relevance document length distribution is not as obvious as on ClueWeb B. This is an encouraging finding as it gives us clue of differentiating between relevance and non-relevant documents based on their length distribution. In the next section, we propose to fit the document length distribution with a list of statistical distributions, in order to find the distributions that can match the characteristics of relevance and non-relevant documents.

3.4 Distribution of Document Length

The criterion of selecting distributions is that the distribution must be positive skewed with shape and rate parameters. With different shape and rate parameters, the probability distribution can describe as many different shapes as possible that document length may have. It is impossible to use one single distribution to capture all kinds features of all different document collections. The commonly used distributions we applied to fit the transformed document length are as follows:

- Gamma distribution with $(\gamma > 0, \beta > 0)$

$$f(z) = \frac{z^{\gamma-1}e^{-z/\beta}}{\beta^{\gamma}\Gamma(\gamma)} \tag{12}$$

for $z \geq 0$, where γ and β are shape and scale parameters respectively. Varying setting of γ can lead to symmetrical or skewed figures.

- Normal distribution with (μ, σ^2), which is symmetric with respect to its mean value (μ), and the variance (σ^2) measures the width of the distribution. A Normal distribution is bell shaped and the shape is independent of its distribution parameters. The reason of choosing normal distribution is that transformation I try to standardize the document length. The Normal distribution density function is given as follows:

$$f(z) = \frac{1}{\sqrt{2\pi\sigma^2}}\, exp\left\{-\frac{(z-\mu)^2}{2\sigma^2}\right\} \tag{13}$$

where σ is the standard deviation.

- Lognormal distribution with (μ, σ^2)

$$f(z) = \frac{1}{z\sigma\sqrt{2\pi}}\, exp\left\{-\frac{(\log z-\mu)^2}{2\sigma^2}\right\} \tag{14}$$

for $z \geq 0$, where if Z is distributed lognormally with parameters μ and σ, $\log(Z)$ is distributed normally with a mean of μ and a standard deviation of σ. Lognormal and gamma distribution can produce similar graphs, but the curvature of lognormal distribution is more steep than gamma distribution.

- Inverse Gaussian distribution (IGD) with (μ, λ)

$$f(z) = \sqrt{\frac{\lambda}{2\pi z^3}}\, exp\left\{-\frac{\lambda}{2\mu^2 z}(z-\mu)^2\right\} \tag{15}$$

for $z > 0$, where $\mu > 0$ is the mean and $\lambda > 0$ is the shape parameter, changing λ changes the level of the skewness for the IGD.

- Weibull distribution with (a, b)

$$f(z) = \frac{b}{a}\left(\frac{z}{a}\right)^{b-1} exp\left\{-(\frac{z}{a})^b\right\} \tag{16}$$

where $a > 0$ is the scale parameter and $b > 0$ is the shape parameter. Weibull distribution can produce the graph similar to Gamma distribution but with less steep curve.

- Generalized Extreme Value distribution (GEV) (κ, μ, σ),

$$\begin{aligned} f(z) = &\frac{1}{\sigma} * exp\left\{-(1+\kappa\frac{(z-\mu)}{\sigma})^{-\frac{1}{\kappa}}\right\} \\ &* \left(1+\kappa\frac{(z-\mu)}{\sigma}\right)^{(-1-\frac{1}{\kappa})} \end{aligned} \tag{17}$$

where $\kappa \neq 0$ is the shape parameter, μ is the location parameter and $\sigma > 0$ is the scale parameter. Compared to the statistical distributions mentioned above, GEV is a complicated distribution developed within the extreme value theory [9].

Figure 3 illustrates the six distribution fittings for the relevant document length of four test collections using Transformation I. Similar plots can be obtained for the relevant and non-relevant document length of all four test collections

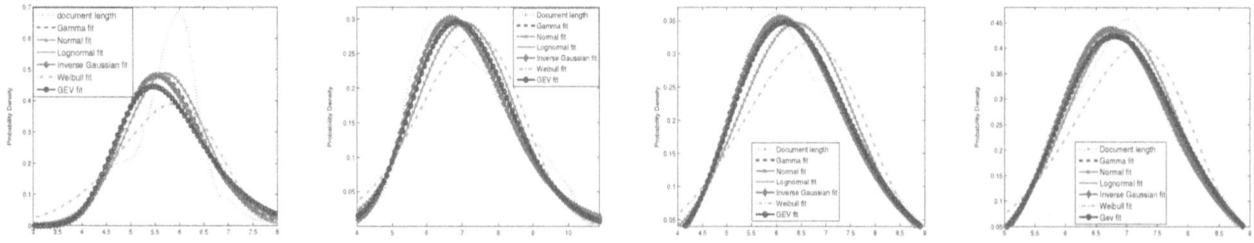

(a) disk1&2 (b) .GOV2 (c) WT10G (d) ClueWebB

Figure 3: Distribution fittings for the relevant document length using transformation two $z = log(d)$.

using Transformation I, Transformation III and Transformation IV respectively. All six distributions fit the .GOV2, WT10G and ClueWebB well, not disk1&2 since the bimodality. Inverse Gaussian ans GEV distribution fit the data best on all test collections, Weibull distribution can preserve the skewness better than the Lognormal, Gamma distribution, but normal distribution performs very badly in this case since skewness of the data. After the density functions are fit to the actual length distribution, it is necessary to use goodness of fit test to determine how well the distributions fit to the actual data.

3.5 Parameter Estimation

We adopt two methods in distribution parameter estimation for $P(d|R)$ and $P(d|\bar{R})$ in the Equation 2: bootstrapping and expectation-maximization(EM) algorithm. These are very simple but powerful statistical methods in parameter estimation.

Bootstrapping is a Monte Carlo method to learn about the sample characteristics to infer the population by resampling. It has been proved effective in reducing the bias of samples [8]. Adèr recommend to use bootstrapping when the sample size is insufficient for straightforward statistical inference [1]. The bootstrapping procedure is described as follows:

1. Construct an empirical probability distribution Ω from the sample by placing a probability of $1/n$ at each point, $z_1, z_2, \ldots, z_n$ of the sample. This is the empirical distribution function of the sample, which is the nonparametric maximum likelihood estimate of the population distribution, ω. Now, each sample's element has the same probability of being drawn.

2. From the empirical distribution function, Ω, draw a random sample of size n with replacement. This step is called resampling.

3. Calculate the statistic of interest, θ, for this resample, yielding $\hat{\theta}^*$.

4. Repeat steps 2 and 3 for B times, where B is a large number, in order to create B resamples. The setting of B depends on the tests to be run on the data.

5. Compute $\bar{\hat{\theta}}^* = \frac{1}{B}\sum_{j=1}^{B}\hat{\theta}_j^*$.

The Expectation-Maximization (EM) algorithm is a general algorithm for maximum-likelihood estimation where the data are "incomplete" [8]. The EM algorithm is an iterative method which seeks to find the MLE of the marginal likelihood by iteratively applying the following two steps:

- Expectation step: Calculate the expected value of the log likelihood function with respect to the conditional distribution of y given z under the current estimate of the parameters $\theta^{(t)}$

$$Q(\theta|\theta^{(t)}) = E_{Y|z,\theta^{(t)}}[\log L(\theta; z, Y)]$$

- Find the parameter which maximizes following:

$$\theta^{(t+1)} = arg\max Q(\theta|\theta^{(t)})$$

where $L(\theta; z)$ is the likelihood function, θ is the parameter vector, z is the transformed document length and y represents the unobserved data.

The estimates from two methods are very close. For simplicity reason, we average the estimates from two methods in the experiments.

3.6 Length Relevance Weighting

After we obtain the distribution function for transformed document length Z, we apply the change variable technique [26] to obtain the distribution function for the original document length D, *i.e.* the document length before transformation. The theorem of change variable we used is as follows

THEOREM 1. *Let Z be a random variable with probability density function (pdf) $f_Z(z)$ and support $\mathcal{S}_Z$. Let $D = g(Z)$, where $g(z)$ is one to one differentiable function, on the support of Z, $\mathcal{S}_Z$. Denote the inverse of g by $z = g^{-1}(d)$ and let $\frac{\partial z}{\partial d} = \frac{\partial[g^{-1}(d)]}{\partial d}$. Then the pdf of D is given by*

$$f_D(d) = f_Z(z^{-1}(d))\left|\frac{\partial z}{\partial d}\right|, \quad for\ d \in \mathcal{S}_D \qquad (18)$$

with the support of D which is the set $\mathcal{S}_D = \{d = g(z) : z \in \mathcal{S}_Z\}$.

Where $z^{-1}(d)$ is equivalent to Equations 8, 9, 10 and 11 when transforming the document length, and $|\frac{\partial z}{\partial d}|$ is the determinant of Jacobian of the transformation [11].

Based on the discussion above, we initiate the pattern of the document length by kernel density estimation. Based on the findings in step one, second, we apply data transformation and the change variable techniques to find the distribution functions of relevant and non-relevant document length and use MLE to obtain the parameter estimators. Two statistical methods, EM and bootstrapping are exploited to prevent potential bias during parameter estimation, such as incomplete test collection, randomness of sampling. Hypothesis test employees to eliminate the distributions at 95%

significant level. Finally Equation 5 is used to construct the following seven models:

1. In this model, transformed relevant and non-relevant document length follow the Normal distribution using same transformation I:standardization in Equation 8. We call it 'Normal'. Together, Using Equation 5 and change variable technique in Equation 18, the length relevance weighting function is as follows

$$w(d,\Delta)_{22} \propto -\frac{1}{2\sigma_1^2}\left[\left(\frac{d-\bar{d}}{s_d}\right)-\mu_1\right]^2+\frac{1}{2\sigma_2^2}\left[\left(\frac{d-\bar{d}}{s_d}\right)-\mu_2\right]^2 \quad (19)$$

where subscript 1 indicates that it is the estimates of distribution for relevant document length, 2 is the estimates of non-relevant document length distribution.

2. In this model, transformed relevant and non-relevant document length follow the Gamma distribution using transformation II:log transformation in Equation 9. We call it 'Log-Gamma'.

$$w(d)_{22} \propto (\gamma_1-\gamma_2)*\log d - \log d/\beta_1 + \log d/\beta_2 \quad (20)$$

3. In this model, transformed relevant and non-relevant document length follow the IGD distribution using transformation II:log transformation in Equation 9. We call it 'Log-IGD'.

$$w(d)_{22} \propto \log\sqrt{\frac{\lambda_1}{2*\pi*(\log d)^3}}-\log\sqrt{\frac{\lambda_2}{2*\pi*(\log d)^3}} - \frac{\lambda_1*(\log d-\mu_1)^2}{2*\mu_1^2*\log d}+\frac{\lambda_2*(\log d-\mu_2)^2}{2*\mu_2^2*\log d} \quad (21)$$

4. In this model, transformed relevant and non-relevant document length follow the Inverse Gaussian distribution distribution using transformation III:Box-Cox transformation in Equation 10. We call it 'Box-Cox-IGD'.

$$w(d)_{22} \propto \log\sqrt{\frac{\lambda_1}{2*\pi*(\frac{d^\theta-1}{\theta})^3}}-\frac{\lambda_1*(\log(\frac{d^\theta-1}{\theta})-\mu_1)^2}{2*\mu_1^2*\log(\frac{d^\theta-1}{\theta})} -\log\sqrt{\frac{\lambda_2}{2*\pi*(\frac{d^\theta-1}{\theta})^3}}+\frac{\lambda_2*(\log(\frac{d^\theta-1}{\theta})-\mu_2)^2}{2*\mu_2^2*\log(\frac{d^\theta-1}{\theta})} \quad (22)$$

5. In this model, transformed relevant and non-relevant document length follow the GEV distribution using transformation III:Box-Cox transformation in Equation 10. We call it 'Box-Cox-GEV'.

$$w(d)_{22} \propto (-1-\frac{1}{\kappa_1})\log(1+\kappa_1\frac{V}{\sigma_1})-(1+\kappa_1\frac{V}{\sigma_1})^{-\frac{1}{\kappa_1}} -(-1-\frac{1}{\kappa_2})\log(1+\kappa_2\frac{V}{\sigma_2})+(1+\kappa_2\frac{V}{\sigma_2})^{-\frac{1}{\kappa_2}} \quad (23)$$

where $V=(d^\theta-1)/\theta$.

6. In this model, transformed relevant and non-relevant document length follow the Lognormal distribution using transformation IV:normalization in Equation 11. We call it 'Lognormal'.

$$w(d)_{22} \propto -\frac{1}{2\sigma_1^2}[\log L-\mu_1]^2+\frac{1}{2\sigma_2^2}[\log L-\mu_2]^2 \quad (24)$$

where $L=(d-d_{min})/(d_{max}-d_{min})$

7. In this model, transformed relevant and non-relevant document length follow the Weibull distribution using transformation IV in Equation 11:normalization. We call it 'Weibull'.

$$w(d,\Delta)_{22} \propto (b_1-b_2)\log L-(\frac{L}{a_1})^{b_1}+(\frac{L}{a_2})^{b_2} \quad (25)$$

where $L=(d-d_{min})/(d_{max}-d_{min})$.

By adding $w(d,\Delta)_{22}$ into the weighting function $w(x,d)$ or BM25, we propose a new length-based weighting function BM25L as follows:

$$w(\underline{x},d)=(1-\beta)\,w_{BM25}\oplus\beta * w(d,\Delta)_{22} \quad (26)$$

where w_{BM25} is the relevance score of BM25, $\oplus$ indicate that the term $w(d,\Delta)_{22}$ is added only once for each document, β is not only the interpolation factor which is empirically determined and highly depends on the dataset used, but also an adjust factor of the mixture of two hypotheses: Verbosity and Scope hypothesis. A document could be either extreme or of mixture of these two hypotheses as discussed in[24]. More over, the reason of adding β here is that we ignore the constant term in the calculation of $\log\frac{P(\Delta|\bar{R})}{P(\Delta|R)}$, we need to adjust the scale for the weights between w_{BM25} and $w(\underline{x},d)$, and the weights between two hypotheses because BM25L consider the situation when both Verbosity and Scope hypothesis are presented in the same document. For a given query, each of the w_{BM25} or $w(\underline{x},d)$ scores is normalized by the maximum w_{BM25} or $w(\underline{x},d)$ score. The parameter β is obtained by Simulated Annealing [14] over a set of training topics.

4. EVALUATION

We introduce our methodology for evaluating the BM25L model in Section 4.1, and present the related evaluation results in Sections 4.2 and 4.3.

4.1 Evaluation Methodology

We evaluate our proposed BM25L model over the 4 test collections used, namely disk1&2, WT10G, .GOV2, and ClueWeb B. Each topic contains three topic fields, namely title, description and narrative. We only use the title topic field that contains very few keywords related to the topic. The title-only queries are usually short which is a realistic snapshot of real user queries in practice.

On each collection, the associated topics are divided into the odd-numbered and even-numbered topics. Over those two topic subsets, our proposed model is evaluated by a 2-fold cross-validation. In each fold, one of the topic subsets is used for training, and the other subset is used for testing purposes. More specifically, the half of the training topics with lower topic numbers are used to train the length distribution estimation parameters, and the other half of the training topics are used to train the score combination parameter β in Equation 26. Finally, our proposed BM25L model is evaluated by its retrieval performance on average over the two subsets of test topics. We use the TREC official evaluation measures in our experiments, namely the statMAP on ClueWeb B [30], and the Mean Average Precision (MAP) on the other three collections [31].

Our evaluation baseline is the classical BM25 model with different settings of its parameter b. By varying the b value, we investigate to which extent BM25L improves the retrieval performance. In particular, we compare the retrieval performance of BM25L to BM25 with $b=0$, that is, BM25 without *tf* normalization, and BM25 with its parameter b optimized. All statistical tests are based on Wilcoxon Matched-pairs Signed-rank test.

4.2 Comparison with BM25

Tables 3 and 4 compare the retrieval performance of BM25L to the original BM25 without tf normalization (i.e. when

$b = 0$), and with the tf normalization with its parameter b optimized, respectively.

From Tables 3 and 4, we see that modeling document length distribution using GEV distribution leads to the most stable retrieval performance of our proposed length-based BM25L model. This is not of a surprise as we have shown that the GEV density fits the best to the actual document length distribution. Using the GEV density fitting of the document length, BM25L appears to outperform the BM25 baseline, and the improvement is statistically significant in most cases on all four test collections except WT10G.

The use of other distribution functions, in particular Gamma distribution, also leads to retrieval performance over the BM25 baseline on some of the test collections. However, their retrieval performance does not appear to be as robust as that obtained by GEV distribution. An extreme case is Normal distribution, which does not improve the BM25 baseline on disk1&2, WT10G, and .GOV2 when the parameter b is optimized. In contrast, on ClueWeb B, it provides an MAP that is as high as 0.6340, which is 173% higher than the BM25 baseline, even if its parameter b is optimized. Similar observation can also be made with Gamma distribution, which leads to a 130% improvement. One possible explanation is that it has lightest skewness among other 3 test collections that could be observed in Figure 3. Another possible reason for BM25L's extremely high retrieval performance with Gamma and Normal distribution on ClueWeb B is the shallow pool depth of this collection. Out of the four test collections used, ClueWeb B has the most incomplete relevance assessments, for which only the top-10 documents returned by the TREC participating runs are judged by human assessors [6]. As the top ranked documents are mostly overlong, the biase towards long documents in the document ranking could be so evident that the length distribution of relevant and non-relevant documents fits very well with the distribution functions on both training and testing topics. As a consequence, BM25L leads to extremely high retrieval performance on ClueWeb B.

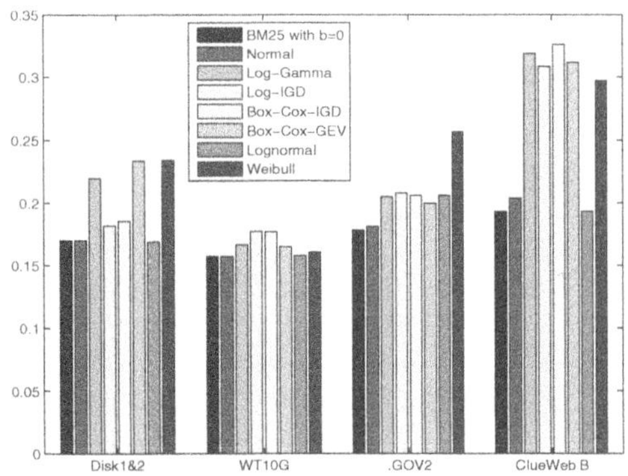

Figure 4: Performance of BM25L over BM25 with b=0

To visualize the improvement brought the proposed length-based BM25L model, we plot the results in Figures 4 and 5 for the comparison to BM25 with $b = 0$ and with b optimized, respectively. As we can see on the WT10G collection, although the improvement is not as much as that obtained on other three test collections using all six distributions, the increase in retrieval performance is the evidence of length ef-

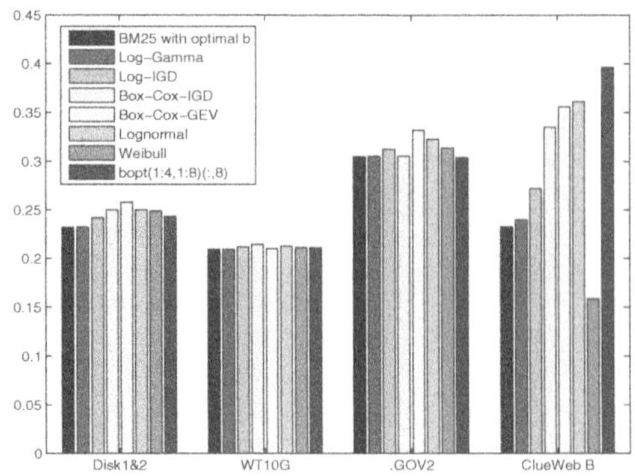

Figure 5: Performance of BM25L over BM25 with optimal b value

fect in information retrieval. Using Weibull distribution and normalization transformation has the best results, this may due to that Weibull distribution does retain the skewness of data between zero and one scale on all collections very well as we can see from Figure 3.

By comparing the performance improvement by BM25L over BM25 with $b = 0$ with the improvement over BM25 with the optimized b, we can see that the improvement over the optimized b is overall of a less scale than that over BM25 without tf normalization. This is because optimizing the parameter b in BM25 has exaggerated the length impact on the relevance weighting of term frequency tf, and in return, it reduces the impact of length relevance weighting itself on improving the document ranking.

When comparing BM25L with the best known results, for the WT10G, BM25L's best MAP is 0.2143, and the best published MAP is 0.2085. A possible explanation of the relatively minor improvement is as follows: the data transformation on WT10G does not show much difference between the length distribution of relevance and non-relevance documents. Compared to large-scale collections such as GOV2 and ClueWeb B, it leaves little room for the BM25L model to further improve the retrieval performance by utilizing such difference (in document length distribution). In other words, the TREC pools are biased by the length distribution. Such bias is minor on WT10G, and becomes evident on heterogeneous collections like GOV2 and ClueWeb B, which is captured by BM25L to boost the ranking effectiveness. For ClueWeb B, we believe the best statMAP in the TREC 2009 Relevance Feedback track, i.e. 0.2638, is achieved by combining BM25 with relevance feedback [32], although the overview paper is not available. Our model BM25L gives an MAP of 0.3963. For GOV2, on top of the retrieval baselines, e.g. BM25 and language model, the best run in TREC 2006 further improved the effectiveness by using pseudo relevance feedback and term dependency [18, 21]. Since our model only considers document length, the best MAP presented in this paper, i.e. 0.3321, is not directly comparable to the best known MAP of 0.3737. For disk1&2, there hasn't been known best result for all 150 topics used in the TREC 1-3 adhoc tasks. According to evaluatir.org, the best known MAP on each task is 0.2062, 0.2475 and 0.3231, respectively, with an average of 0.2589. Note that the above best known results are achieved by stacking additional techniques such as

Table 3: Evaluation results over the BM25 baseline with *b=0*. A star indicates a statistically significant improvement over the baseline.

Coll.	BM25	Normal	Log-Gamma	Log-IGD	Box-Cox-IGD	Box-Cox-GEV	Lognormal	Weibull
disk1&2	0.1698	0.1700	0.2195*	0.1821	0.1856*	0.2336	0.1685	0.2339*
WT10G	0.1571	0.1570	0.1663	0.1772*	0.1769	0.1647	0.1576	0.1604
.GOV2	0.1782	0.1812	0.2051*	0.2079*	0.2058*	0.1995	0.2058*	0.2564*
ClueWeb B	0.1930	0.2035	0.3192*	0.3084*	0.3265*	0.3117*	0.1931	0.2973*

Table 4: Evaluation results over the BM25 baseline with optimized setting of *b*. A star indicates a statistically significant improvement over this baseline.

Coll.	BM25	Normal	Log-Gamma	Log-IGD	Box-Cox-IGD	Box-Cox-GEV	Lognormal	Weibull
disk1&2	0.2324	0.2326	0.2421	0.2504*	0.2579*	0.2501*	0.2491*	0.2432*
WT10G	0.2090	0.2090	0.2115	0.2143	0.2101	0.2125	0.2111	0.2109
.GOV2	0.3044	0.3051	0.3121	0.3056	0.3321*	0.3227*	0.3134	0.3039
ClueWeb B	0.2322	0.2401	0.2722*	0.3350*	0.3561*	0.3612*	0.1586	0.3963*

relevance feedback over the retrieval baseline. Therefore, the results are not directly comparable. Even though, BM25L provides an MAP of 0.2579.

4.3 Impact of Parameters

Experimental results in the previous section shows that, on one hand, BM25L leads to more improvement over BM25 when tf normalization is disabled. This is expected since there is no length information added to BM25 with $b = 0$ when compare to BM25L. On the other hand, BM25L provides higher MAP/statMAP values when the tf normalization parameter b is optimized. From this observation, a question arises: what is the impact of the setting of b on BM25L's effectiveness? To answer this question, Figure 6 plots the MAP/statMAP obtained by BM25L using the 6 different statistics of the document length distribution against different b values, from 0 to 1. BM25L and the original BM25's retrieval performance is seen to be correlated. A better setting of BM25's b leads to a better retrieval performance of BM25L. The document length itself do have a power as a stand-alone factor on the document relevance weighting other than normalization adjustment. The results for the full range of b are illustrated in Figure 6 for all 4 test collections.

Another important factor that could heavily affect BM25L's retrieval performance is the parameter β in Equation 26. Figure 7 plots the MAP/statMAP obtained by BM25L against β on the four collections used. As we can see that length impact on the relevance weighting increase first as β increase, then either decrease or remain flat as β increase. This is no coincidence because with only one factor, *i.e.* length, among other many important factors that can affect document relevance weighting, the improvement would be limited.

Another parameter in Equation 4 is k_1. BM25L outperforms BM25 with different settings of k_1, although the latter's retrieval performance is fairly sensitive to k_1's setting. The related experiments are not included in this paper for brevity, since changing k_1's setting does not affect the conclusions.

In summary, we have shown that the length information can be used for leveraging the bias towards long documents in the document ranking. The retrieval performance of the classical well-established BM25 model can be marked improved by incorporating a length-based weighting component with different settings of BM25's tf normalization parameter, including the optimal setting. Finally, we recommend applying GEV distribution for modeling the document length distribution as it has demonstrated effective and robust retrieval performance in our experiments. In our experiments, all parameters are learned from the training data in the two-fold cross-validation. It is therefore of note that our proposed model is trained and tested with different queries.

5. CONCLUSION AND FUTURE WORK

Our research in this paper is based on the assumption that a document may exhibit both Verbosity and Scope hypotheses. We derive the relationship between document length and its relevance through a list of probability density functions, and propose a BM25L model that incorporates this relationship into the classical BM25 model. The proposed BM25L model is evaluated on standard large-scale TREC collections. Our experiments demonstrate that BM25L is able to markedly outperform the BM25 baseline even with the optimized tf normalization. The results empirically confirm our assumption that the actual relationship between document length and relevance is a mixture and compromise between the Verbosity and Scope hypotheses.

In this paper, we have proposed a general method of utilizing the relationship between document length and relevance for improving retrieval performance. The proposed method is shown to be effective in its application to the classical BM25 weighting model. In the future, we plan to apply our proposed method to other state-of-the-art IR models, such as language modeling, or the PL2 model [2]. In addition, we also plan to investigate possible ways to balance between the effectiveness and efficiency of our proposed method.

6. ACKNOWLEDGMENTS

This research is supported by NSERC of Canada and the Early Researcher Award/Premier's Research Excellence Award. We thank four anonymous reviewers for their excellent comments on this paper.

7. REFERENCES

[1] H. J. Adèr, G. J. Mellenbergh, and D. J. H. Huizen. *Advising on research methods: A consultant's companion.* The Netherlands: Johannes van Kessel, 2008.

[2] G. Amati and C. J. V. Rijsbergen. Probabilistic models for information retrieval based on measuring the divergence from randomness. *ACM Transaction on Information Systems (TOIS)*, 20(4):357-389, 2002.

[3] C. Bishop. *Neural networks for pattern recognition.* Oxford university Press, Oxford, UK, 1996.

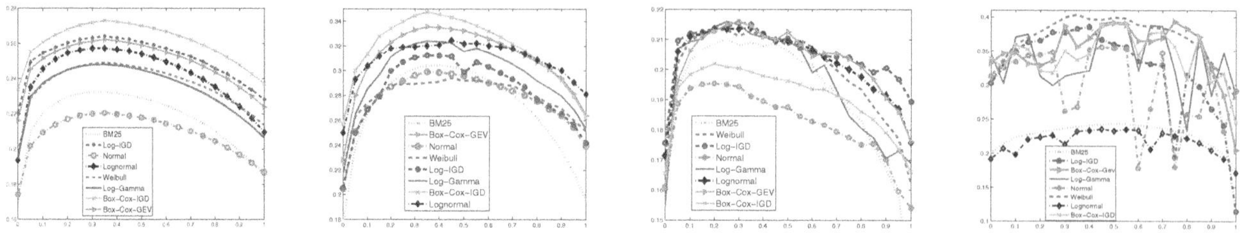

(a) disk1&2 (b) .GOV2 (c) WT10G (d) ClueWeb B

Figure 6: The MAP/statMAP values obtained against the parameter b

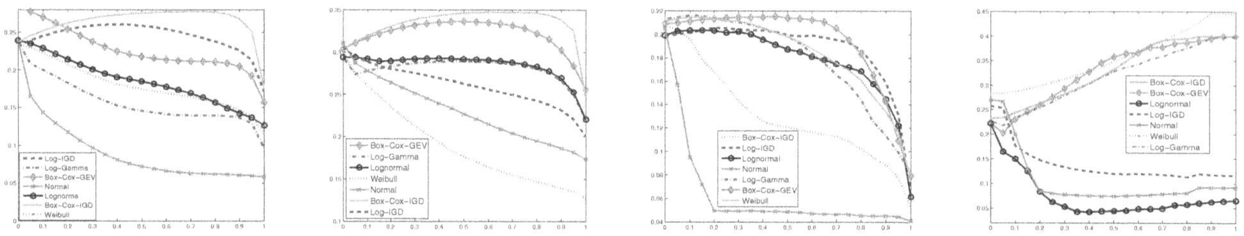

(a) disk1&2 (b) .GOV2 (c) WT10G (d) ClueWeb B

Figure 7: The MAP/statMAP values obtained against the parameter β

[4] R. Blanco and A. Barreiro. Probabilistic document length priors for language models. In *Proc. of 30th ECIR*, pages 394-405, 2008.

[5] G. E. P. Box and D. R. Cox. An analysis of transformations. *Journal of the Royal Statistical Society*, 26(2):211-252, 1964.

[6] C. Buckley and S. E. Robertson. Relevance feedback track overview: TREC 2008. In *Proc. of 17th TREC*, 2008.

[7] A. Chowdhury, M. C. McCabe, D. Grossman, and O. Frieder. Document normalization revisited. In *Proc. of the 25th ACM SIGIR*, pages 381-382, 2002.

[8] J. E. Gentle. *Elements of computational statistics.* Springer, 2002.

[9] E. Gumbel. *Statistics of extremes.* Columbia University Press, 1958.

[10] M. Hancock-Beaulieu, M. Gatford, X. Huang, S. E. Robertson, S. Walker, and P. W. Williams. Okapi at TREC-5. In *Proc. of 5th TREC*, pages 143-165, 1996.

[11] R. V. Hogg, hoseph W. Mckean, and A. T. Craig. *Introduction to mathematical statistics.* Pearson Education, Upper Saddle River, N.J., 2005.

[12] X. Huang, F. Peng, D. Schuurmans, N. Cercone, and S. E. Robertson. Applying machine learing to text segmentation for information retrival. *Information Retrieval*, 6(4):332-362, 2003.

[13] X. Huang, S. E. Robertson, N. Cercone, and A. An. Probability-based Chinese text processing and retrieval. *Computational Intelligence* ,16(4):552-569, 2000.

[14] S. Kirkpatrick, C. D. Gelatt, and M. P. Vecchi. Optimization by simulated annealing. *Science*, 220(4598):671-680, 1983.

[15] W. Kraaij and T. Westerveld. TNO/UT at TREC-9: How different are web documents? In *Proc. of 9th TREC*, 2000.

[16] W. Kraaij, T. Westerveld, and D. Hiemstra. The importance of prior probabilities for entry page search. In *Proc. of 25th ACM SIGIR*, pages 27-34, 2002.

[17] S. Lamprier, T. Amghar, B. Levrat, and F. Saubion. Document length normalization by statistical regression. In *Proceedings of 19th IEEE International Conference on Tools with Artificial Intelligence*, pages 11-18, 2007.

[18] J. Li and H. Yan. Peking university at the TREC 2006 terabyte track. In *Proc. of 15th TREC*, 2006

[19] D. E. Losada and L. Azzopardi. An analysis on document length retrieval trends in language modeling smoothing. *Information Retrieval*, 11(2):109-138, 2008.

[20] D. E. Losada, L. Azzopardi, and M. Baillie. Revisiting the relationship between document length and relevance. In *Proc. of the 17th ACM*, pages 419-428, 2008.

[21] D. Metzler, T. Strohman, and W. Croft. Indri TREC notebook 2006: Lessons learned from three terabyte tracks. In *Proc. of 15th TREC*, 2006

[22] S. E. Robertson. The probability ranking principle in IR. *Journal of Documentation*, 33:294-304, 1977.

[23] S. E. Robertson, C. J. van Rijsbergen, and M. F.Porter. Probabilistic models of indexing and searching. In *Proc. of the 3rd ACM SIGIR*, pages 35-56, 1980.

[24] S. E. Robertson and S. Walker. Some simple effective approximations to the 2-poisson model for probabilistic weighted retrieval. In *Proc. of the 17th ACM SIGIR*, pages 232-241, 1994.

[25] S. E. Robertson, S. Walker, S. Jones, M. Hancock-Beaulieu, and M. Gatford. Okapi at TREC-3. In *Proc. of 3rd TREC*, pages 109-126, 1994.

[26] J. Shao. *Mathematical statistics.* Springer, 2003.

[27] B. Silverman. *Density estimation for statistics and data analysis.* Chapman&Hall, 1986.

[28] A. Singhal, C. Buckley, and M. Mitra. Pivoted document length normalization. In *Proc. of 19th ACM SIGIR*, pages 21-29, 1996.

[29] A. Singhal, G. Salton, M. Mitra, and C. Buckley. Document length normalization. *Information Processing and Management: An International J.*, 32(5):619-633, 1996.

[30] E. M. Voorhees. Overview of TREC 2009. In *Proc. of 18th TREC*, 2009.

[31] E. M. Voorhees and D. K. Harman. *TREC: Experiment and evaluation in information retrieval.* MIT Press, Cambridge, Massachusetts, 2005.

[32] Z. Ye, X. Huang, B. He, and H. Lin. York university at TREC 2009: Relevance feedback track. In *Proc. of 18th TREC*, pages 21-29, *2009.*

Who Should Share What? Item-level Social Influence Prediction for Users and Posts Ranking

Peng Cui
Computer Science Department
Tsinghua University
Beijing, China
cuip@tsinghua.edu.cn

Fei Wang
Healthcare Transformation Group
IBM T J Watson Research Center
Hawthorne, USA
fwang@us.ibm.com

Shaowei Liu
Computer Science Department
Tsinghua University
Beijing, China
liushaowei@sina.com

Mingdong Ou
Computer Science Department
Tsinghua University
Beijing, China
oumingdong@gmail.com

Shiqiang Yang
Computer Science Department
Tsinghua University
Beijing, China
yangshq@tsinghua.edu.cn

Lifeng Sun
Computer Science Department
Tsinghua University
Beijing, China
sunlf@tsinghua.edu.cn

ABSTRACT

People and *information* are two core dimensions in a social network. People sharing information (such as blogs, news, albums, etc.) is the basic behavior. In this paper, we focus on predicting *item-level* social influence to answer the question *Who should share What*, which can be extended into two information retrieval scenarios: (1) Users ranking: given an item, who should share it so that its diffusion range can be maximized in a social network; (2) Web posts ranking: given a user, what should she share to maximize her influence among her friends. We formulate the social influence prediction problem as the estimation of a user-post matrix, in which each entry represents the strength of influence of a user given a web post. We propose a *Hybrid Factor Non-Negative Matrix Factorization* (HF-NMF) approach for item-level social influence modeling, and devise an efficient projected gradient method to solve the HF-NMF problem. Intensive experiments are conducted and demonstrate the advantages and characteristics of the proposed method.

Categories and Subject Descriptors

J.4 [**Social and Behavioral Sciences**]: Sociology; H.1.2 [**Information Systems**]: Models and Principles—*Human factors*

General Terms

Algorithms

Keywords

social influence; matrix factorization; user ranking; web post ranking

1. INTRODUCTION

With the rapid proliferation of social applications, such as Flickr, Facebook, Twitter, etc., more and more user profiles, interactions, and collective intelligence (such as social tags, comments, etc.) are available online, which opens a new perspective for information retrieval applications where more focus should be put on user collaborative information. At the same time, new search scenarios, such as web people search [12] and relationship search [10], also emerged. These scenarios propose a new challenge to traditional information retrieval: *how to effectively handle the social information?*

One key concept related to this challenge is *Social influence*, which has been becoming a prevalent and complex force governing the dynamics of people relationships or social network [20]. It is also a key dimension for modern information retrieval in multiple aspects. To mention a few, (1)each user act as an information source in social network, and the influence of a user is meaningful for the authority of the generated information; (2)in web people search, the social influence is the key indicator for influencer search; (3)as different information varied with the power to affect people to change their actions, they can be recommended by influence ranking for social purpose. Therefore, there is a clear need for techniques to analyze social influence, and more importantly, in information retrieval field. However, to the best of our knowledge, this issue has still not been well studied.

The existing social influence analysis research can be summarized into a diagram: *Who(A) influences Whom(B) given What(C)*. A is often regarded as a single user (or node). For B, previous works can be categorized as *macroscale*, where B is the whole network [2, 20]; *microscale*, where B is a single user [7, 18]; and *mesoscale*, where B is the community or A's friends (neighborhoods) [13, 1]. From the side of C, there are also three lines of research: Structure-level, when

C is empty [14, 17]; Topic-level when C is a topic [18, 8]; and Item-level when C is an item (such as a web page, product, etc.), which is rare in previous research.

In this paper, we focus on measuring item-level social influence in mesoscale to answer the question *Who should share What*, which can be extended into two information retrieval scenarios: (1) Users Ranking: given an item (C), who (A) should share it so that its diffusion range can be maximized in a social network; (2) Web Posts Ranking: given a user (A), what (C) should she share to maximize her influence among her neighbors.

1.1 Motivating Application

In social computing, people and information are two core dimensions and people sharing information (such as blog, news, album, etc.) is the basic behavior. Actually, the spreading out of information is because of the user sharing in social network. The owner of the information, e.g. the advertisers, hope to maximize the diffusion range of the information [4]. This goal makes them desire to target the influencers, who are able to let many friends to click the information they share or even share further to extend the sharing cascades. Psychologically, people share information with their friends mainly because they want to build their reputations and help others, in which *to influence others* is the important motivation for sharing [19].

According to the definition of social influence on Wiki, social influence occurs when "an individual's thoughts, feelings or actions are affected by other people". In the context of online social networks like Facebook and Twitter, when a user share a web post, a portion of her friends (or neighbors) will click, comment, or even forward the post, which are three levels of influence [21]. In this paper, we only consider the first level, click action. That is, the social influence of a user on her friends given a web post is defined as the number of her friends who click the shared web post.

Therefore, the aim of this paper is to predict the number of clicks by friends if a user share a web post. The resulted predictive model can be used in two angles. On one side, given a web post, we can find out the influencers for the diffusion. On the other, given an user, we can recommend a list of web posts to share, which can improve the interactions between the user and her friends.

1.2 Challenges and Contributions

In predicting the item-level social influence, we mainly face the following challenges:

- User-post specific. Item-level social influence is not a general measure on users, but on the interactions of users and posts. That is, we need to discriminate a user's social influences with respect to different web posts. Different from most of the existing research works focusing on users' overall social influence analysis [14, 17] and topical social influence mining [18, 8], the social influence in this paper is a finely grained measure of influence.

- Sparsity. The interactions between users and web posts are extremely sparse compared with the total number of user-post pairs. According to our statistics of 34K users in the website www.renren.com, which is a Facebook style social network site in China, each user only shares 6 web posts in average during a month, compared with a total of 43K web posts; and each post is only shared by 4 users, compared with a total of 34K users. Thus, it is clear that we need subtle and effective prior knowledge for user and post grouping to alleviate the sparsity problem.

- Complex factors. There are a volume of factors that affect how many friends will click a shared post, and provide potential clues for user and post grouping. For example, the total number of friends, the tie strength between the user and her friends, the semantics of web posts, etc., which are often in different scales. How to select the effective factors and integrate these complex factors in one predictive model is also one of the focus of our work.

In this paper, we formulate the social influence prediction problem as the estimation of a user-post matrix, in which each element (i, j) represents the number of clicks by friends of user i on her j-th shared web post. We proposed a *Hybrid Factor Non-negative Matrix Factorization (HF-NMF)* algorithm for item-level social influence modeling. In this model, we try to find out the common hidden vector space for both the users and the posts, where their multiplication can well approximate the observed training interaction matrix. Meanwhile, in order to deal with the sparsity problem, we construct the priors on users and posts by incorporating the user-user similarity matrix and post topic distribution matrix. Also, in order to alleviate the over-fitting problem, we introduce the L2-norm as regulations for the hidden vector space to improve the generalization ability. We apply *Projected Gradient* to solve the HF-NMF problem, and carry out intensive experiments to demonstrate the effectiveness of the proposed method.

It is worthwhile to highlight the key contributions of this paper.

- We formulates the item-level social influence prediction problem formally with HF-NMF, and devise an efficient projected gradient method to solve it.

- The predicted item-level social influence from HF-NMF can support the applications such as influencer ranking and information recommendation by user-post matrix ranking in two directions.

- The strength of social influence in this method is well interpreted, which makes it easy to understand and extendable to higher order social influence, for example, the influence on all the friends and the friends of friends.

- We conducted intensive experiments on real social network datasets, and the results show that the HF-NMF can achieve a better performance compared with other competitors.

The rest of the paper is organized as follows. Section 2 introduces the necessity of item-level social influence and rationality of factor selection. The HF-NMF model and its solution will be proposed in Section 3. The experiment results to validate the proposed method are presented in Section 4, followed by the conclusion in Section 5.

2. PRELIMINARIES

In this section, we will demonstrate the necessity of the item-level social influence, and validate the rationality of predictive factors by preliminary statistical analysis.

2.1 Necessity of Item-level Social Influence

The dataset is acquired from the real social network `http://renren.com/`, which is a Facebook style online social community in China. Till now, the web site already owns more than 150 million active users. In this web site, a user can generate a post or share a web page as a post, and the user's friends will be informed through the news feed mechanism. Then some of the friends will click, comment or share the post. In this paper, we only consider the click action as the manifestation of influence, and the number of clicks corresponds to the strength of influence. As the number of friends is different for each user, the upper bound of users' social influence strengths are also different. In order to make the strength of influence be measured in a unified scale for different users for the sake of observational and modeling study, we use the proportion of friends (of the user who publish a post) who click the shared post as the measure.

Concerning about the influence prediction, we first assume that the influence should be *specific* on each user-post pairs. In order to validate the hypothesis, we randomly select three active users. Given an user, we calculate the proportion of her influenced friends (who clicked the shared post) for each of the shared posts, and plot them as in the first row of Figure 1. Then, we randomly select three popular posts. Given a post, we calculate the proportion of influenced friends when the post is shared by different users, and plot them as in the second row of Figure 1.

As can be observed, the social influence notably varies with different users and posts, which implies that (1) different users have different influence power to their friends; (2) different posts have different influence power (more intuitively, attraction) to users who are interested in; and (3) users' influences manifest differently for different posts. Therefore, only item-level social influence can reveal the users' real influence on friends, and the strength of influence should definitely be user-post specific.

2.2 Predictive Factors

According to Figure 1, the factors that affect the strength of social influence include the following three aspects.

- **User-specific factors**. Although users' social influence vary with the shared posts, the average of the social influences over posts determines the overall social influence of a user. We regard the factors that affect users' overall social influence (excluding the posts) as the user-specific factors.

- **Post-specific factors**. Similar as user-specific factors, we regard the factors affecting posts' overall social influence (excluding the users) as the post-specific factors.

- **User-post specific factors**. As mentioned above, the social influence is user-post specific. The social influence of a user given a post cannot be well approximates only by the user and post-specific factors. The factors indicating the interactions between users and posts are also important for social influence prediction.

One issue that is worthy of emphasizing here is that the user factors and post factors are essential for the predictive modeling. On one hand, the user-post interactions are very sparse. We need to find effective factors to "group" those users and posts to alleviate the sparsity problem. On the other hand, the user and post-specific factors also provide some effective prior knowledge to complement the inference from pure user-post interactions.

In order to find out the effective predictive factors, we first prepared a factor pool, which includes the available potential predictive factors including user profiles, number of users' friends, visiting frequency between users, posts' topic distributions, etc. Given each factor, we measured the correlation between the strength of social influence and the factor value. Finally, we select two user-oriented factors: the percentage of active friends, the average social tie strength (the interaction frequency) between a user and her friends, and one post-specific factor: the topic distribution of a web post's content.

Now we show some statistics to demonstrate the validity of those selected factors. We randomly select 10 users from the dataset. Given each user, we define her social influence as the average percentage of her friends who click the shared post over all shared posts, and calculate the correlation between the selected user factors and this social influence measure. Figure 2 (a)(b) illustrate the correlation between the user factors and the social influence measure on these 10 users, from which we can clearly observe the positive results.

For post topic distribution, our hypothesis is that the posts with similar contents (i.e. similar topic distributions) often induce similar social influences. To validate this assumption, we randomly select ten groups of web posts, where the posts in the same group have similar topic distributions. Given each web post, we define its social influence as the average percentage of users' friends who clicked it over all the users who shared the post. Then we calculate the variances of posts' social influence inside each topic group, and also over all the web posts (i.e. across topic groups). As we can see from Figure 2(c), most variances inside topic groups are smaller than that across the groups, which implies that the introduction of topical grouping is able to reduce down the uncertainty of social influence.

Based on the above analysis, we validate the effective predictive factors and apply them into the predictive modeling in Section 4.

3. THE ALGORITHM

3.1 Problem Formulation

First, we formally define the problem of item-level social influence prediction. Suppose we have M users with the i-th user denoted as u_i and N postings with the j-th post denoted as p_j. We use $\mathcal{N}(u_i)$ to denote the collection of u_i's first-order friends (i.e. the nodes that directly link to u_i). As mentioned in the previous section, two key factors involved in our model are

- **Item-level social influence**: According to the previous presentations, a straightforward way to define the strength of u_i's influence on $\mathcal{N}(u_i)$ given the web post p_j, denoted as f_{ij}, is the number of u_i's friends who clicked post p_j.

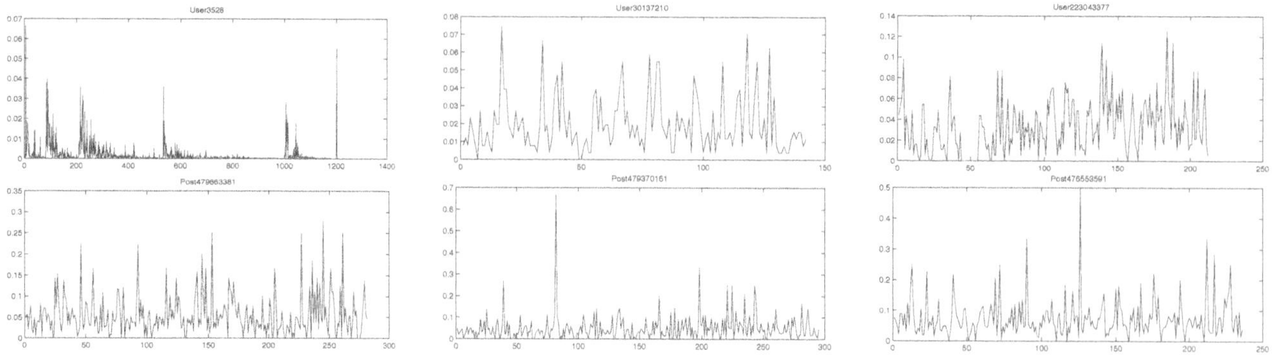

Figure 1: Social influence varies with users and posts.

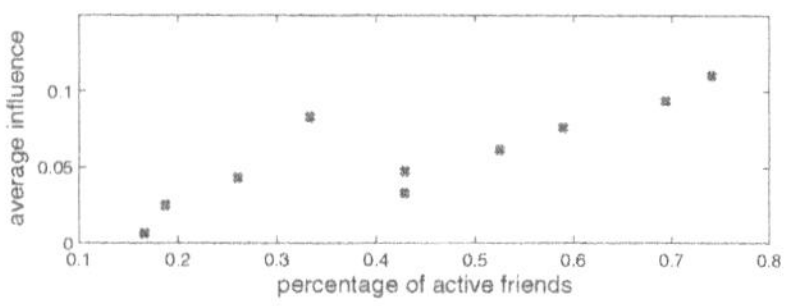

(a) Social influence vs. Active user percentage

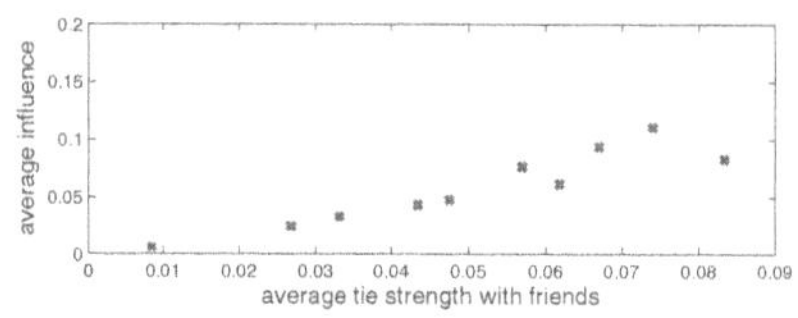

(b) Social influence vs. Average tie strength

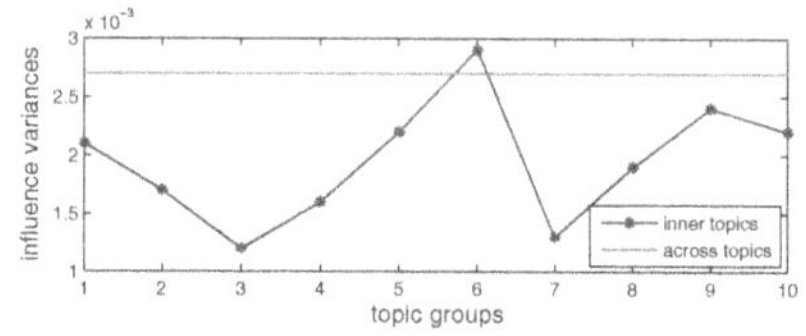

(c) Social influence vs. Post Topic distribution

Figure 2: Predictive factors validation.

- **Social influence prediction**: There are $M \times N$ potential social influences in total. However, in practice, only a tiny fraction of them can be observed. The social influence prediction is to predict the unobserved social influences $\hat{f_{ij}}$ based on the observed f_{ij}'s and those predictive factors.

With the above terminologies, we can formally define the task of item-level social influence prediction. We denote the user-post influence matrix as $\tilde{\mathbf{X}} \in \mathbb{R}^{M \times N}$, with its (i, j)-th entry

$$\tilde{X}_{ij} = \begin{cases} f_{ij} & \text{if } u_i \text{ shared } p_j \\ 0 & otherwise \end{cases} \tag{1}$$

If we use g_i to denote the number of u_i's friends (i.e. $g_i = |\mathcal{N}(u_i)|$, where $|.|$ is the cardinality of a collection), then $f_{ij} \leq g_i$. Also, It should be noted that in the matrix $\tilde{\mathbf{X}}$, there are two cases where an entry $\tilde{X}_{ij}$ is 0. First is that u_i did not share the p_j, and the second is that u_i shared p_j, but no friends of u_i clicked it.

As we mentioned above, different users have different numbers of friends, which makes the strength of social influence (if measured by f_{ij}) for each user-post pair be measured in different scales. To alleviate its effect on the final performance, we propose the following *percentile* influence matrix

$$X_{ij} = \begin{cases} \frac{f_{ij}}{g_i} & \text{if } u_i \text{ shared } p_j \\ 0 & otherwise \end{cases} \tag{2}$$

so that X_{ij}'s are normalized into the range of $[0, 1]$.

The user-post influence matrix $\tilde{X}$ can be reconstructed by

$$\tilde{\mathbf{X}} = Diag(\mathbf{g}) \cdot \mathbf{X} \tag{3}$$

where $\mathbf{g} = [g_1, g_2, \cdots, g_N]^\top \in \mathbb{R}^N$, and $Diag(\mathbf{g})$ is the diagonal matrix with $\mathbf{g}$ on the diagonal line.

In this way, the item-level social influence prediction problem is converted to the problem of predicting the unobserved entries in $\mathbf{X}$.

Our formulation of the item-level social influence prediction problem is quite different from existing works on social network analysis. First, we measure the social influence in item-level, compared with the structure-level analysis [14, 17] and topic-level analysis works [18, 8]. Second, the goal of the problem is to predict the users' social influence for unobserved data, which is in contrast with the majority of existing works to analyze the influence patterns from observed data [2, 3].

In the following section, we will formally present the *Hybrid Factor Nonnegative Matrix Factorization* (HF-NMF) approach to model the problem.

3.2 Hybrid Factor Non-negative Matrix Factorization

We suppose that there exists a joint latent space for both users and posts with dimensionality k, such that the user-post specific social influences are modeled as the inner product between user-post vector pairs in that space. Accordingly, the user u_i is associated with an user vector $\mathbf{u}_i \in \mathbb{R}^k$, and the post p_j is associated with a post vector $\mathbf{v}_j \in \mathbb{R}^k$. Intuitively, the elements in $\mathbf{v}_j$ measures the extent to which the post p_j possess those k factors, and the elements of $\mathbf{u}_i$ measure the extent of social influence the user i has in posts that are high on the corresponding factors.

Now we will formulate the social influence prediction problem mathematically. Suppose that we have M users and N web posts. Let $\mathbf{U} \in \mathbb{R}^{M \times k}$ be the latent user feature matrix, and $\mathbf{V} \in \mathbb{R}^{N \times k}$ be the latent poster feature matrix, where k is the number of latent features. Then given the observed user-post specific social influence matrix $\mathbf{X}$, the objective of this paper is to find the optimal latent user matrix $\mathbf{U}$ and latent post matrix $\mathbf{V}$ by minimizing the following objective.

$$\mathcal{J}_1 = \left\| \mathbf{X} - \mathbf{U}\mathbf{V}^\top \right\|_F^2 \tag{4}$$

where $||.||_F$ denotes the matrix Frobenius Norm.

The objective function $\mathcal{J}_1$ can be regarded as the quality of approximating $\mathbf{X}$ by the inner product of $\mathbf{U}$ and $\mathbf{V}$. However, in real cases, most of the elements in $\mathbf{X}$ are zero because of the sparse interactions between users and posts. Thus, in order to focus more on the valid elements, we propose to only measure the approximation loss on observed elements on $\mathbf{X}$. To formulate this, we introduce the *sharing matrix* $\mathbf{Y} \in \mathbb{R}^{M\times N}$ with its (i, j)-th entry defined as

$$Y_{ij} = \begin{cases} 1 & \text{if } u_i \text{ shared } p_j \\ 0 & otherwise \end{cases} \tag{5}$$

The objective function is converted to

$$\mathcal{J}_2 = \left\| \mathbf{Y} \odot (\mathbf{X} - \mathbf{U}\mathbf{V}^\top) \right\|_F^2 \tag{6}$$

where $\odot$ is the Hadamard product.

As mentioned above, the severe sparsity of $\mathbf{X}$ makes it very challenging to directly learn the latent spaces for users and posts from only observed user-post interaction entries. That's the reason why we need to make full use of the user-specific and post-specific factors to compress the degrees of freedom, so that the correlation within users and web posts can be exploited to alleviate the sparsity problem.

3.2.1 Incorporating User-Specific Factors

As introduced in Section 2, we explored two effective user-oriented predictive factors: the *percentage of active friends*, and the *average friend tie strength*.

In order to calculate the percentage of active friends, we define the activeness of a friend u_r, denoted by $act(u_r)$, as the number of posts she visits during a given time period, so that the percentage of active friends for u_i is calculated by

$$uf_1(u_i) = \frac{\sum_{u_r \in \mathcal{N}(u_i)} \delta(act(u_r) \geq \tau)}{|\mathcal{N}(u_i)|} \tag{7}$$

where τ is the time threshold for active user, and $\delta(.)$ is the Delta function.

Also, we define the *tie strength* between a user u_i and one of her friends u_r as the number of shared posts (by user u_i) friend u_r visits, which is denoted as $tie(u_i, u_r)$. Then, the average friend tie strength is calculated by

$$uf_2(u_i) = \frac{\sum_{u_r \in \mathcal{N}(u_i)} \frac{tie(u_i,u_r)}{\sum_j Y_{ij}}}{|\mathcal{N}(u_i)|}. \tag{8}$$

Then we use these two factors to measure the similarity between u_i and u_j as

$$W_{ij} = \rho_1 |uf_1(u_i) - uf_1(u_j)| + \rho_2 |uf_2(u_i) - uf_2(u_j)| \tag{9}$$

In our case, we set $\rho_1 = \rho_2 = 0.5$.

In this way, we can construct the user-user similarity matrix $\mathbf{W} \in \mathbb{R}^{M\times M}$. We further assume that $\mathbf{W}$ can be approximated by the inner product of the latent user matrix, thus we need to minimize the following objective

$$\mathcal{J}_3 = \left\| \mathbf{W} - \mathbf{U}\mathbf{U}^\top \right\|_F^2 \tag{10}$$

.

3.2.2 Incorporating Post-Specific Factors

As demonstrated in Section 2, the social influence is strongly correlated with the content of the web posts. We denote the post content matrix as $\mathbf{C} \in \mathbb{R}^{N\times d}$, where d is the dimensionality of the posts, which is constructed by implementing *Latent Dirichlet Allocation* (LDA) [6] on the post corpus to discover 100 topics. Then the content of each post is represented as the topic distributions over the 100 topics. Similar to *latent semantic analysis* [9], we assume $\mathbf{C}$ can be factorized by minimizing

$$\mathcal{J}_4 = \left\| \mathbf{C} - \mathbf{V}\mathbf{G}^\top \right\|_F^2 \tag{11}$$

where the matrix $\mathbf{G} \in \mathbb{R}^{k\times M}$ indicates post group identity.

Finally, by combining $\mathcal{J}_2, \mathcal{J}_3, \mathcal{J}_4$ together, we can get the latent user matrix $\mathbf{U}$ and latent post matrix $\mathbf{V}$ by solving the following optimization problem

$$\begin{aligned} \min_{\mathbf{U},\mathbf{V},\mathbf{G}} \quad & \left\| \mathbf{X} - \mathbf{U}\mathbf{V}^\top \right\|_F^2 + \alpha \left\| \mathbf{W} - \mathbf{U}\mathbf{U}^\top \right\|_F^2 + \beta \left\| \mathbf{C} - \mathbf{V}\mathbf{G}^\top \right\|_F^2 \\ & + \gamma \left\| \mathbf{U} \right\|_F^2 + \delta \left\| \mathbf{V} \right\|_F^2 \\ s.t. \quad & \mathbf{U} \geq 0,\ \mathbf{V} \geq 0,\ \mathbf{G} \geq 0 \end{aligned} \tag{12}$$

The last two terms of the objective are penalized for generalization purpose, which is similar to the *Maximum Margin Matrix Factorization* approach in [15] and the *Joint Matrix Factorization* approach in [?].

3.3 Solution

In this section, we will introduce a *Projected Gradient* (PG) method [11] to solve problem (12).

Before going into the details, we first introduce the basic PG algorithm [11]. For notational convenience, we introduce a nonnegativity projection operator $P[\cdot]$ for matrix $\mathbf{A}$ as

$$(P[\mathbf{A}])_{ij} = \begin{cases} A_{ij} & \text{if } A_{ij} \geq 0 \\ 0 & \text{otherwise} \end{cases} \tag{13}$$

Then the PG method for solving the problem

$$\min_{\mathbf{A}\geq 0} f(\mathbf{A}) \tag{14}$$

can be presented in Algorithm 1.

Algorithm 1 Projected Gradient

Require: $0 < \beta < 1$, $0 < \sigma < 1$. Initialization $\mathbf{A}^{(0)}$.
Ensure: $\mathbf{A}^{(0)} \geq 0$
  for $k = 1, 2, \cdots$ **do**
    $\mathbf{A}^{(k)} = P\left[\mathbf{A}^{(k-1)} - \alpha_k \nabla f\left(\mathbf{A}^{(k-1)}\right)\right]$
    where $\alpha_k = \beta^{t_k}$, and t_k is the first nonnegative integer for which

$$f\left(\mathbf{A}^{(k)}\right) - f\left(\mathbf{A}^{(k-1)}\right) \leq \sigma \left\langle \nabla f\left(\mathbf{A}^{(k-1)}\right), \left(\mathbf{A}^{(k)} - \mathbf{A}^{k-1}\right) \right\rangle \tag{15}$$

  end for

In Algorithm 1, $\nabla f(\mathbf{A})$ is the gradient of the objective function with respect to the variable $\mathbf{A}$, $\langle .,. \rangle$ is the sum of the component-wise product of two matrices.

Here condition (15) ensures the sufficient decrease of the function value per iteration, and this rule of determining the stepsize is usually referred to as the *Amijo rule* [5]. However, the Amijo rule is usually time consuming, thus we use the following improved PG method in Algorithm 2 [11].

Algorithm 2 Improved Projected Gratient

Require: $0 < \beta < 1$, $0 < \sigma < 1$. Initialization $\mathbf{A}^{(0)}$, $\alpha_0 = 1$.
Ensure: $\mathbf{A}^{(0)} \geq 0$
for $k = 1, 2, \cdots$ **do**
Assign $\alpha_k = \alpha_{k-1}$
If α_k satisfies condition (15), repeatedly increase it by

$$\alpha_k \leftarrow \alpha_k / \beta$$

until either α_k does not satisfy (15) or $\mathbf{A}(\alpha_k/\beta) = \mathbf{A}(\alpha_k)$
Else repeatedly decrease α_k by

$$\alpha_k \leftarrow \alpha_k \cdot \beta$$

until α_k satisfies condition (15).
Set $\mathbf{A}^{(k)} = P\left[\mathbf{A}^{(k-1)} - \alpha_k \nabla f\left(\mathbf{A}^{(k-1)}\right)\right]$.
end for

Now let's return to problem (12). Although it is not jointly convex with respect to **U**, **V** and **G**, it is convex with each of them with the other two fixed. Therefore we can adopt a *block coordinate descent* scheme to solve the problem [5]. That is, starting from some random initialization on $\mathbf{U}, \mathbf{V}, \mathbf{G}$, we solve each of them alternatively with the other two fixed, and proceed step by step until convergence[1]. Specifically, the gradients of the objective (denoted as $\mathcal{J}$) with respect to the variables are

$$\begin{aligned}\frac{\partial \mathcal{J}}{\partial \mathbf{U}} &= 2\Big(-(\mathbf{Y} \odot \mathbf{X})\mathbf{V} + (\mathbf{Y} \odot \mathbf{U}\mathbf{V}^\top)\mathbf{V} \\ &\quad -2\alpha \mathbf{W}\mathbf{U} + 2\alpha \mathbf{U}\mathbf{U}^\top \mathbf{U} + \gamma \mathbf{U}\Big) \\ \frac{\partial \mathcal{J}}{\partial \mathbf{V}} &= 2\Big(-(\mathbf{Y}^\top \odot \mathbf{X}^\top)\mathbf{U} + (\mathbf{Y}^\top \odot \mathbf{V}\mathbf{U}^\top)\mathbf{U} \\ &\quad -\beta \mathbf{C}\mathbf{G} + \beta \mathbf{V}\mathbf{G}^\top \mathbf{G} + \delta \mathbf{V}\Big) \\ \frac{\partial \mathcal{J}}{\partial \mathbf{G}} &= 2\beta\left(-\mathbf{C}^\top \mathbf{V} + \mathbf{G}\mathbf{V}^\top \mathbf{V}\right)\end{aligned}$$

4. EXPERIMENTS

In this section, we will introduce the experimental results on a real world dataset to demonstrate the effectiveness of the proposed method. First we will introduce the dataset information.

4.1 Experimental Dataset

We perform our experiments on a real online social network dataset, which is crawled from `http://renren.com`, a Facebook style social network web site in China. We have 34k users, and 43k web posts in the dataset, and the basic information we used for each user and post are listed in Table 4.1.

We filter the raw dataset in two aspects: (1) we only use the posts generated at least 6 days before the crawling date, so that the click number of the post is stable; (2) the "dead users" (i.e. users who never shared posts) and "dead posts" (i.e. posts that were never visited) are discarded. After the filtering, we remain 10k users and 10k web posts with 104k user-post sharing interactions for experiments. The sparsity of the dataset (denoted as 10000user dataset) is around 0.1%, which is rather challenging for predictive modeling.

user information	**post information**
user id (UID)	post id
friend links	post content
shared post id list	visiting friend UID list

Table 1: Data set information.

In Figure 3, we show the characteristics of 10000user dataset by plotting (a) histogram of users with respect to the number of shared posts (calculated by $\sum_j Y_{ij}$ for u_i), (b) histogram of posts with respect to the times of being shared (calculated by $\sum_i Y_{ij}$ for p_j), and (c) histogram of percentile item-level social influence (calculated by $\frac{f_{ij}}{g_i}$).

In our experiments, we randomly sample different number of users and select the web posts shared by these sampled users to form datasets with different sizes, including 500users dataset, 2000users dataset, 5000users dataset, and the 10000users dataset. They are used to evaluate the detail performance of the proposed method.

4.2 Comparative Methods

Besides the proposed HF-NMF method, we also implement the following methods for comparison.

- **Logistic Regression** (LR): If we regard the user and post factors as variables, and the strength of social influence as the response, then the prediction of social influence can be formulated as a regression problem. Thus, we firstly use the LR model to linearly combine the user factors and post factors, and learn the regression coefficients of the factors from the observed training data.
- **Cox Proportional Hazards Regression** (CoxPH): Different from LR, the user factors and post factors are combined in an exponential way, as is used in [22], which aims to predict the speed of diffusion of tweets in Twitter.
- **User Averaging Influence** (AvgU): As users have different overall influences regardless of web posts, we can predict unobserved social influence by the average over observed ones, i.e.,

$$f_{i,\cdot} = \frac{\sum_j f_{ij}}{\sum_j Y_{ij}}. \tag{16}$$

- **Post Averaging Influence** (AvgP): As in AvgU, we can also predict the social influence by the web posts' averaging influence regardless of users:

$$f_{\cdot,j} = \frac{\sum_i f_{ij}}{\sum_i Y_{ij}}. \tag{17}$$

- **Basic Non-Negative Matrix Factorization** (bNMF): In this method, we only consider the user-post inter-

[1]Here the objective is obviously lower bounded by 0, and the alternating PG procedure will decrease it monotonically. Thus the algorithm is guaranteed to be convergent.

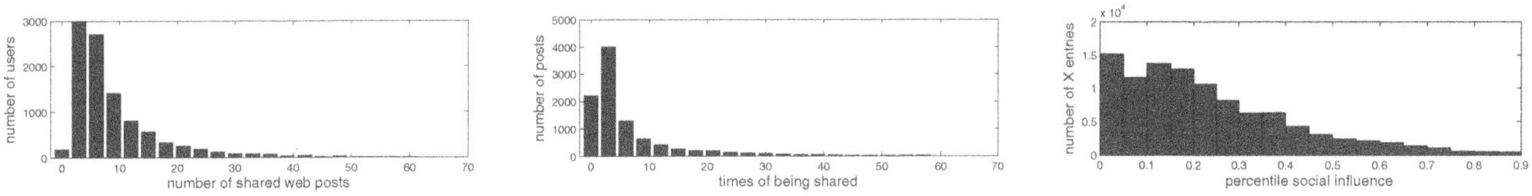

(a) (b) (c)

Figure 3: Statistics of the dataset.

action matrix, and find the joint latent space for users and posts by solving the objective function:

$$\min_{\mathbf{U},\mathbf{V}} \left\|\mathbf{X} - \mathbf{U}\mathbf{V}^\top\right\|_F^2 + \gamma \|\mathbf{U}\|_F^2 + \delta \|\mathbf{V}\|_F^2$$
$$s.t. \mathbf{U} \geq 0,\ \mathbf{V} \geq 0 \qquad (18)$$

- **User Factors Constrained NMF** (bNMF+UF): By incorporating the user factors in to the bNMF, we find the joint latent space for users and posts by solving:

$$\min_{\mathbf{U},\mathbf{V}} \left\|\mathbf{X} - \mathbf{U}\mathbf{V}^\top\right\|_F^2 + \alpha \left\|\mathbf{W} - \mathbf{U}\mathbf{U}^\top\right\|_F^2 + \gamma \|\mathbf{U}\|_F^2 + \delta \|\mathbf{V}\|_F^2$$
$$s.t. \mathbf{U} \geq 0,\ \mathbf{V} \geq 0$$

- **Post Factors Constrained NMF** (bNMF+PF): By incorporating the post factors in to the bNMF, we find the joint latent space for users and posts by solving:

$$\min_{\mathbf{U},\mathbf{V}} \left\|\mathbf{X} - \mathbf{U}\mathbf{V}^\top\right\|_F^2 + \beta \left\|\mathbf{C} - \mathbf{V}\mathbf{G}^\top\right\|_F^2 + \gamma \|\mathbf{U}\|_F^2 + \delta \|\mathbf{V}\|_F^2$$
$$s.t. \mathbf{U} \geq 0,\ \mathbf{V} \geq 0,\ \mathbf{G} \geq 0$$

4.3 Evaluation Measures

The main goal of the paper is to learn the joint latent space for users and posts so that their inner-products can approximate the observed entries in $\mathbf{X}$, and meanwhile, have good prediction performance for unobserved entries. In our experiments, we will hide some observed entries $\mathcal{X}$ by controlling the user sharing matrix $\mathbf{Y}$ in training, and using the learned $\mathbf{U}$ and $\mathbf{V}$ to approximate $\mathcal{X}$. Then the quality of the prediction will be evaluated using the *Root Mean Square Error* (RMSE).

$$RMSE = \sqrt{\frac{\sum_{X_{ij} \in \mathcal{X}} (X_{ij} - \mathbf{U}_i \mathbf{V}_j^\top)^2}{|\mathcal{X}|}} \qquad (19)$$

After predicting the hidden entries, we further rank them along two dimensions (i.e. user dimension and post dimension) according to two application scenarios: influencer ranking and influential post ranking. Here we use two ranking-based evaluation criterions proposed in [16] to measure the ranking performance: (1) T-measure, which simply counts how many of the pairs in the test data are ordered incorrectly, and it is calculated by

$$T = \sum_{i<j} 1(s_i > s_j), \qquad (20)$$

where i, j are the orders in groundtruth, and s_i, s_j are the predicted orders. (2) R-measure, which weights the incorrect ordered pairs by the difference in the testing ranks, and it is calculated by

$$R = \sum_{i<j} (j - i) \cdot 1(s_i > s_j). \qquad (21)$$

These two measures are normalized into [0,1] by

$$\eta = 1 - \frac{2T}{n(n-1)}$$
$$\varrho = 1 - \frac{6R}{n(n-1)(n+1)} \qquad (22)$$

with 1 corresponding to perfect ranking and 0 representing the reverse ranking.

α	β	γ	δ	$RMSE$
0.00001	0.001	0.001	0.001	0.15564
0.0001	0.01	0.01	0.01	0.15234
0.001	0.1	0.1	0.1	0.17742

Table 2: HF-NMF tradeoff parameters setting and evaluation.

4.4 Parameter Settings

In this section, we will investigate the effect of different parameter settings when implementing HF-NMF, include tradeoff parameters, dimension of hidden space, and number of projected gradient iterations, on the performance.

4.4.1 Tradeoff Parameters

The tradeoff parameters $\alpha, \beta, \gamma, \delta$ in HF-NMF play the role of adjusting the strength of different terms in the objective function. As the value range of the 4 components in equation (12) are different, the parameter setting should be consistent with the corresponding component's value range. The component $\left\|\mathbf{W} - \mathbf{U}\mathbf{U}^\top\right\|_F^2$ is the sum of 100 million entries with each entry ranging from 0 to 1. The component $\left\|\mathbf{C} - \mathbf{V}\mathbf{G}^\top\right\|_F^2$ is the sum of 1 million entries with each entry ranging from 0 to 1. Both $\|\mathbf{U}\|_F^2$ and $\|\mathbf{V}\|_F^2$ are the sum of 10k entries with most entries ranging from 0 to 1. Considering the roles of different components, we test the three sets of tradeoff parameters as shown in Table 2, and use the 2000users dataset for validation.

The results in Table 2 show that the parameter set $\alpha = 0.0001, \beta = \gamma = \delta = 0.01$ produce the best performance. In our following experiments, we just use this parameter setting.

4.4.2 *Dimensionality of the Hidden Space*

The goal of HF-NMF is to find a k-dimensional joint latent space for users and web posts. How to set k is important for prediction performance. If k is too small, the users and web posts cannot be well represented and discriminated in the latent space. If k is too large, the computational complexity will be greatly increased. Thus, we conduct 5 experiments with k ranging from 5 to 40 on the 2000users dataset. The results are shown in Figure. 4, from which we can see that with the increase on the dimension k, $RMSE$ will reduce gradually. When $k > 30$, the RMSE reduces rather slow. For the concern of the tradeoff between efficiency and prediction precision, we choose $k = 20$ as the latent space dimension in our experiments.

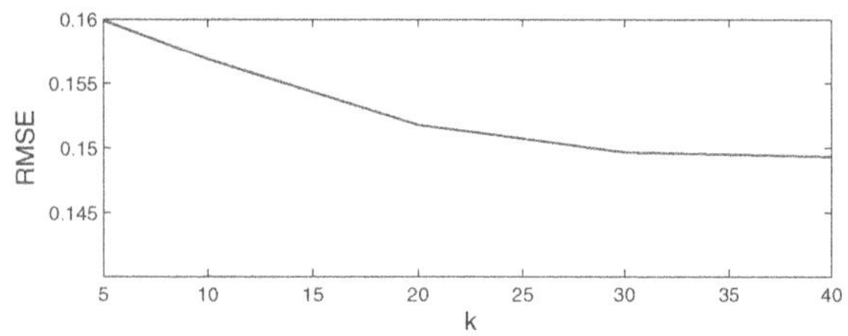

Figure 4: Prediction performance v.s. hidden space dimension.

4.4.3 *Number of Iterations*

When using PG method to solve problem (12), we need to predefine a proper number of updating iterations to get a good performance while avoid overfitting. Here we use 2000users dataset to validat this parameter. We hide 10% entries from matrix $\mathbf{X}$ and run 50 NMF iterations (each NMF iteration corresponds to update the three matrices $\mathbf{U}, \mathbf{V}, \mathbf{G}$ alternatively with). In each iteration, we record the objective function value and RMSE for hidden entries, and simultaneously plot the convergence curve of PG method and the RMSE curve, as shown in Figure 5.

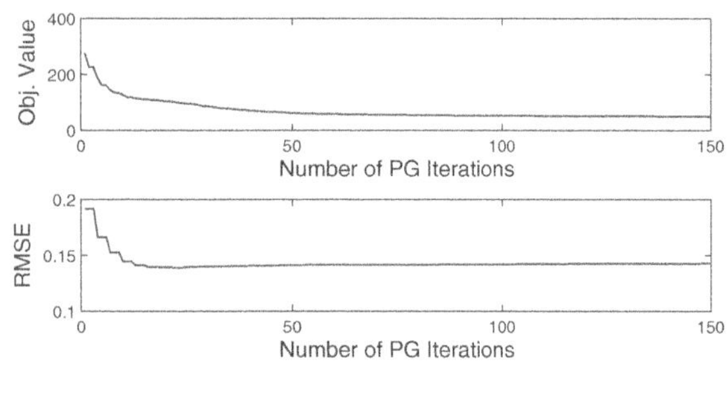

Figure 5: The synchrony between PG convergence curve and prediction performance.

From Figure 5 we can see that the RMSE reduces with the iteration process, as well as the objective function value. Near the 15th PG iteration, the RMSE curve reaches the minimum value. After that, there is a little overfitting effect in RMSE. When the objective function values become stable, the RMSE does not go far away from the minimum value. This demonstrates that the proposed HF-NMF has good generalization ability. Considering the trade-off between the efficiency and prediction precision, we conduct 45 iterations in PG for the solution in the following experiments.

4.5 Prediction Performance

In this section, we will demonstrate the prediction performance of the proposed method, and compare it with other methods.

We randomly select 50%, 70% and 90% of the observed entries in matrix $\mathbf{X}$ of difference sizes of datasets (including 500users dataset, 2000users dataset, 5000users dataset and 10000users dataset) as the training data, and the rest as the testing data. The random selection was carried out 10 times, and the average RMSE is reported. The same experiments are conducted on the proposed method and the 7 comparative methods listed in subsection 4.2. The results are shown in the Table 3.

From the Table 3, we can observe that:

- The proposed HF-NMF algorithm, which incorporates the user, post and the user-post interaction factors together, achieves the best performance in most experimental trials.
- The more entries used for training, the lower RMSE the methods can achieve. This is consistent with the intuitive assumption that the prediction performance depend heavily on the percentage of training data, especially in sparse dataset where the model can be hardly sufficiently trained.
- HF-NMF's advantage over bNMF is more obvious when there are less observed entries (e.g. 50% than 90%) for training . This is because when the matrix is sparse, the matrix factorization has many possible solutions. In this case, the priors on the users and posts are demanded to compress the degrees of freedom. In HF-NMF, by incorporating the hybrid factors into the matrix factorization model, the sparsity problem is effectively alleviated.
- The comparison between bNMF+UF v.s. bNMF and bNMF+PF v.s. bNMF reveals that the user factors are more effective compared with the post factors in our case.
- The two regression models are not fit for this problem. The main reason is that the regression models can only combine the one side factors (i.e. post-specific factors and user-specific factors), but the interaction between the user and post cannot be well incorporated in the model, which is particularly important in this problem.
- The prediction performance of AvgU is better than AvgP, which reveals that the overall social influence of users excluding web posts are more stable than that of web posts. As both of them do not address the user-post specific variances, their prediction performance are worse than all the matrix factorization methods in all the trails.

4.6 Ranking Task Evaluation

After predicting the social influence, we make use of the results in ranking scenarios. One is to rank the influential

	LR	CoxPH	AvgP	AvgU	bNMF	bNMF+PF	bNMF+UF	HF-NMF
500 users								
50%	0.2026	0.202	0.199376	0.159798	0.158551	0.154719	0.153801	**0.152977**
70%	0.2093	0.2089	0.185823	0.150239	0.147858	0.149715	0.149009	**0.146358**
90%	0.1827	0.1822	0.178479	0.145262	0.1416632	0.1420855	**0.1407717**	0.141673
2000 users								
50%	0.266	0.2642	0.226263	0.173654	0.171527	0.17034	0.169171	**0.168771**
70%	0.2304	0.2292	0.204045	0.163817	0.16154	0.161642	0.1597654	**0.15936**
90%	0.1699	0.1742	0.192715	0.1581	0.154478	**0.15044**	0.15273	0.151793
5000 users								
50%	0.2249	0.2241	0.250079	0.185797	0.183837	0.182474	0.179382	**0.177451**
70%	0.2288	0.2206	0.226694	0.1743	0.169922	0.169994	0.170496	**0.169892**
90%	0.2307	0.2324	0.210018	0.170393	0.167686	0.164501	0.164983	**0.164337**
10000 users								
50%	0.2615	0.2591	0.254009	0.189941	0.188926	0.185849	0.182247	**0.181321**
70%	0.2104	0.2073	0.23416	0.175754	0.174362	0.179101	0.172264	**0.170842**
90%	0.2354	0.234	0.210646	0.17097	0.167127	0.167633	0.165806	**0.165159**

Table 3: Prediction performance comparisons.

users given a web post, the other is to rank the web posts given a user.

4.6.1 *User and Post Ranking Performance*

We randomly select 30 web posts. For each post, at least 13 users should have shared it, i.e. at least 13 observed entries correspond to the post in **X**. We hide 10 of the observed entries, and predict the entry values by HF-NMF, and then rank them in a descend order. The top-ranked users are regarded to be more influential with respect to the given post.

An example of user ranking is shown in Table 5. After converting the percentile social influence X_{ij} into $\tilde{X}_{ij}$ by equation 3, the predicted social influence can be well interpreted. For example, given the post4405, we predict that if user1287 share the post, then 27 of her friends will visit it. In groundtruth, 26 of user1287's friends visited the post after she shared the post. Also, given the post, the ranking of the users according to their social influence are mostly consistent with the groundtruth.

We conduct the similar process for post ranking. An example is shown in Table 4.

4.6.2 *Comparison with Other Methods*

In order to compare the proposed method with other comparative methods in ranking performance, we calculate the average η and ϱ over selected users and posts as the comparative measure. The results are shown in Table 6.

We can observe that HF-NMF achieves the best performance in both user ranking and post ranking tasks. bNMF+UF is better than bNMF+PF in user ranking, and bNMF+PF is better than bNMF+UF in post ranking, which demonstrate the effectiveness of the priors on users and posts. Also, by comparing the Table 3 and Table 6, we can see that the advantages of HF-NMF over other comparative methods are more obvious in ranking tasks.

	User Ranking		Post Ranking	
	η	ϱ	η	ϱ
HF-NMF	**0.8942**	**0.9389**	**0.8012**	**0.8697**
bNMF+UF	0.8739	0.9088	0.7423	0.8334
bNMF+PF	0.8236	0.8412	0.7654	0.8548
bNMF	0.813	0.8342	0.7358	0.7926
AvgU	0.7824	0.8056	0.7047	0.7583
AvgP	0.6973	0.7143	0.6746	0.736
CoxPH	0.6596	0.6893	0.659	0.6762
LR	0.6524	0.697	0.6328	0.6593

Table 6: Comparison on user ranking.

5. CONCLUSION

In this paper, we study a novel problem of item-level social influence prediction. We discover the effective user-specific and post-specific predictive factors, and propose a *Hybrid Factor Non-Negative Matrix Factorization* (HF-NMF) method to incorporate these predictive factors for user-post specific social influence prediction. To solve the problem, we devise an efficient Projected Gradient (PG) method for HF-NMF solution. Experimental results on a real social network dataset demonstrate that the proposed method can achieve better performance in social influence prediction compared with baseline methods. Meanwhile, we introduce the item-level social influence into users ranking and web posts ranking, and the experiment results show that the proposed method can effectively recommend the influential users given a web post, and the influential web posts given a user.

6. ACKNOWLEDGEMENTS

This work is supported by National Natural Science Foundation of China, No. 60933013 and No. 61003097; National Basic Research Program of China, No. 2011CB302206; China Postdoctoral Science Foundation, No. 20100470285, and National Key Project Series, No. 2011ZX01042-001-002.

PostIDs	8783	9993	6551	8169	3550	8698	1404	5655	7825	4459
RankOrder(groundtruth)	1	2	3	4	5	6	7	8	9	10
SocialInfluence(groundtruth)	73	53	53	33	13	13	13	13	6	6
RankOrder(Prediction)	1	3	2	4	9	6	7	8	5	10
SocialInfluence(Prediction)	65	43	44	31	12	20	15	14	25	9

Table 4: A web posts ranking example for user 4852.

UserIDs	2627	1287	2336	2952	4466	2764	3052	0893	7666	4909
RankOrder(groundtruth)	1	2	3	4	5	6	7	8	9	10
SocialInfluence(groundtruth)	33	26	19	19	13	13	6	6	6	6
RankOrder(Prediction)	4	1	2	3	5	6	7	8	9	10
SocialInfluence(Prediction)	16	27	19	17	13	11	7	6	6	6

Table 5: A user ranking example for post 4405.

7. REFERENCES

[1] N. Agarwal, H. Liu, L. Tang, and P. S. Yu. Identifying the influential bloggers in a community. In *Proceedings of the international conference on Web search and web data mining*, 2008.

[2] A. Anagnostopoulos, R. Kumar, and M. Mahdian. Influence and correlation in social networks. In *Proceeding of the 14th ACM SIGKDD international conference on Knowledge discovery and data mining*, 2008.

[3] E. Bakshy, B. Karrer, and L. A. Adamic. Social influence and the diffusion of user-created content. In *Proceedings of the 10th ACM conference on Electronic commerce*, 2009.

[4] H. Bao and E. Y. Chang. Adheat: an influence-based diffusion model for propagating hints to match ads. In *Proceedings of the 19th international conference on World wide web*, 2010.

[5] D. P. Bertsekas. *Nonlinear Programming*. MIT Press, MIT, 1999.

[6] D. M. Blei, A. Y. Ng, and M. I. Jordan. Latent dirichlet allocation. *Journal of Machine Learning Research*, 3:993ÍC1022, 2003.

[7] D. Crandall, D. Cosley, D. Huttenlocher, J. Kleinberg, and S. Suri. Feedback effects between similarity and social influence in online communities. In *Proceedings of the 15th ACM SIGKDD international conference on Knowledge discovery and data mining*, 2008.

[8] A. Goyal, F. Bonchi, and L. V. S. Lakshmanan. Learning influence probabilities in social networks. In *Proceedings of the third ACM international conference on Web search and data mining*, 2010.

[9] T. Hofmann. Probabilistic latent semantic indexing. In *Proceedings of the 22nd International conference on Research and development in information retrieval*, 1999.

[10] D. V. Kalashnikov, Z. Q. Chen, S. Mehrotra, and R. Nuray-Turan. Web people search via connection analysis. *IEEE Transactions on Knowledge and Data Engineering*, 20:1550–1565, 2008.

[11] C. J. Lin. Projected gradient methods for nonnegative matrix factorization. *Neural Computation*, 19:2756–2779, 2007.

[12] C. Macdonald and I. Ounis. Voting for candidates: adapting data fusion techniques for an expert search task. In *Proceedings of the 15th ACM international conference on Information and knowledge management*, 2006.

[13] D. W. McMillan and D. M. Chavis. Sense of community: A definition and theory. *Journal of Community Psychology*, 14:6–23, 1986.

[14] M. E. J. Newman. The structure and function of complex networks. *SIAM Reviews*, 45:167–256, 2003.

[15] J. D. M. Rennie and N. Srebro. Fast maximum margin matrix factorization for collaborative prediction. In *Proceedings of the 22nd international conference on Machine learning*, 2005.

[16] S. Rosset, C. Perlich, and B. Zadrozny. Ranking-based evaluation of regression models. *Knowledge and Information Systems*, 12:331–353, 2007.

[17] S. H. Strogatz. Exploring complex networks. *Nature*, 410:268ÍC276, 2003.

[18] J. Tang, J. Sun, C. Wang, and Z. Yang. Social influence analysis in large-scale networks. In *Proceedings of the 15th ACM SIGKDD international conference on Knowledge discovery and data mining*, 2009.

[19] M. M. Wasko and S. Faraj. Why should i share? examining social capital and knowledge contribution in electronic networks of practice. *Management Information System Quarterly*, 29:35–57, 2005.

[20] S. Wasserman and K. Faust. *Social Network Analysis: Methods and Applications*. Cambridge University Press, Cambridge, 1994.

[21] J. S. Weng, E. P. Lim, J. Jiang, and Q. He. Twitterrank: finding topic-sensitive influential twitterers. In *Proceedings of the third ACM international conference on Web search and data mining*, 2010.

[22] J. Yang and S. Counts. Predicting the speed, scale, and range of information diffusion in twitter. In *Proceeding of the international AAAI conference on Weblogs and social media*, 2010.

Mining Tags Using Social Endorsement Networks

Theodoros Lappas
Dept of Computer Science
Univ. of California - Riverside
Riverside, CA 92521
tlappas@cs.ucr.edu

Kunal Punera
Yahoo! Research
701 1st Avenue
Sunnyvale, CA 94089
kpunera@yahoo-inc.com

Tamas Sarlos
Yahoo! Research
701 1st Avenue
Sunnyvale, CA 94089
stamas@yahoo-inc.com

ABSTRACT

Entities on social systems, such as users on Twitter, and images on Flickr, are at the core of many interesting applications: they can be ranked in search results, recommended to users, or used in contextual advertising. Such applications assume knowledge of an entity's nature and characteristic attributes. An effective way to encode such knowledge is in the form of *tags*. An untagged entity is practically inaccessible, since it is hard to retrieve or interact with. To address this, some platforms allow users to manually tag entities. However, while such tags can be informative, they can oftentimes be inadequate, trivial, ambiguous, or even plain false. Numerous automated tagging methods have been proposed to address these issues. However, most of them require pre-existing high-quality tags or descriptive texts for *every* entity that needs to be tagged. In our work, we propose a method based on *social endorsements* that is free from such constraints.

Virtually every major social networking platform allows users to endorse entities that they find appealing. Examples include "following" Twitter users or "favoriting" Flickr photos. These endorsements are abundant and directly capture the preferences of users. In this paper, we pose and solve the problem of using the underlying social endorsement network to extract useful tags for entities in a social system. Our work leverages techniques from topic modeling to capture the interests of users and then uses them to extract relevant and descriptive tags for the entities they endorse. We perform an extensive evaluation of our proposed approach on real large-scale datasets from both Twitter and Flickr, and show that it significantly outperforms meaningful and competitive baselines.

Categories and Subject Descriptors

H.3.3 [**Information Search and Retrieval**]: Information Filtering, Search Process

General Terms

Algorithms, Experimentation

Keywords

Tag extraction, Endorsement networks, Multimodal data mining

1. INTRODUCTION

The "Web 2.0" incarnation of the World Wide Web [26], with its emphasis on user generated content (UGC) and online social interactions, has transformed the way information is accessed by users. The focus of users' attention is now not on webpages managed by a central service provider, but on *entities* that are often uploaded and maintained by other users on social systems like Twitter, Facebook, Flickr, and YouTube. These entities can represent anything that is of interest to users: products, brands, celebrities, pictures, videos, blog posts etc. The lack of a centralized organizing or cataloging authority has both positive implications (e.g. an amazing explosion in content creation by web users) and potentially negative ones as well (e.g. challenges in discovering and recommending relevant content for users.) *Social Tagging* has emerged as an effective way to alleviate some of these challenges. Social Tagging refers to the practice of publicly labeling or categorizing entities in a shared, online environment [31]. The idea is simple: select meaningful tags (keywords) to encode the characteristic attributes of an item, thus making it easily accessible to relevant applications. As cataloged in studies on Flickr [23] and del.icio.us [14], tags can sometimes be a means of information discovery by themselves. However, they typically serve as valuable meta-data that can be used to aid information access mechanisms like recommendation services [7, 16], image search [10], enterprise search [12], and web search [3, 17].

User-Generated Tags. Many social platforms allow users to manually tag entities. Even though these user-generated tags can sometimes be informative, they also present numerous shortcomings. First, as noted by Mathes [24], user-generated tags suffer from problems stemming from an uncontrolled vocabulary, leading to ambiguity and lack of canonicalization. In addition, tags can often be trivial or inadequate, failing to capture all the attributes of entities. Finally, tags can sometimes be false or misleading, submitted either purposefully (e.g. to manipulate the accessibility and reputation of an entity) or simply due to human error.

In addition to the above issues, user-generated tags face the issue of *availability*. Selecting a compact set of high-quality tags for an entity can be a non-trivial and time-consuming task, which requires adequate knowledge of an entity's nature and attributes. This makes tagging less attractive to users, leading to a shortage or even absence of tags for many of the entities. Studies on the "long-tail" of information needs, such as those by Anderson [1] and Goel et al. [13], assert that users would benefit from a system where a large fraction of entities have been assigned high quality tags. In order to address this, some social platforms have been designed explicitly around the Social Tagging paradigm. Examples include the ESP game of Von Ahn et al. [32] and the study by Heymann et al. [17] on del.icio.us. These efforts have demonstrated that useful tags can be obtained for a large fraction of entities. However, in social platforms that do not offer a tagging feature (e.g. Twitter) or when tags are not the central focus (e.g. Flickr), the fraction of entities with useful tags is minimal [23]. Hence, there is a great need of automated support for entity-tagging on such social systems; this is the focus of our work.

AUTOMATED TAGGING METHODS. Automatically extracting tags from text "associated" with entities has been the focus of multiple studies [4, 8, 18, 19, 30]. Past works on social tagging have mostly experimented with the del.icio.us system, where entities (documents) can be robustly represented by their own textual content. However, in scenarios where there is little or no text associated with an entity, such approaches are inapplicable. Consider, for example, a photo on Flickr with no comments or other descriptive text attached to it. One of the primary contributions of our approach is its ability to assign meaningful tags, even to such "cryptic" entities.

Another family of approaches assumes that the social system already has some tags associated with most entities, albeit noisy in nature [7, 18, 19, 30]. These approaches then fall into one of two categories: 1) recommend tags by studying similarities and correlations among entities, and 2) heuristically refine an entity's noisy set of tags. An example of the latter is the work by Krestel et al. [19], who use topic models for tag refinement. Other approaches rely on the historical tagging behavior of users to recommend tags for new documents [4, 8]. All these approaches assume the presence of tags, as well as robust features that allow the comparison and grouping of entities based on notions of similarity. As a result, they have been shown to perform well on social systems like del.icio.us that are built around social tagging of feature-rich entities, i.e. documents. However, we do not expect these approaches to perform well when applied to social systems like Twitter or Flickr that are the focus of our work and include entities with complex non-textual representations and sparse or non-existent tag-sets. In fact, we empirically demonstrate this by comparing our approach to the model of Krestel et al. [19] in the experiments section.

MINING SOCIAL ENDORSEMENT NETWORKS. The relative scarcity of pre-existing tags (and other text content) and their ambiguous nature motivate us to look for an alternative source of information. In this paper we demonstrate that *Social Endorsement Networks* [22] can be used to extract high-quality tags from the noisy and inadequate text associated with entities in social systems like Twitter and Flickr.

Most social systems allow users the option to endorse entities that they find interesting and/or appealing. An endorsement can be expressed in different ways. On Twitter, users have the option to *follow* other users and get updates on their tweets. On Facebook, users can *like* various types of items such as pictures or videos. On Flickr users can *favorite* pictures that they find appealing. In contrast to the often ambiguous and trying task of tagging, endorsements are an intuitive and concise method of expression. *We do not need users to describe an entity or tell us why they like it; we simply need them to tell us that they find it appealing via a single click.* Hence, chiefly due to their inherent simplicity and central role in user activity, endorsements are abundant in social systems. In this work our goal is to develop methods to use these pervasive social endorsements networks to extract meaningful tags from text associated with entities. We still have to deal with the ambiguity associated with the intent behind each endorsement. However, the general abundance of endorsements allows us to leverages techniques from statistical topic modeling to capture user interests and use them to extract meaningful tags for the entities they endorse. At a very high level, the intuition behind our approach is that entities that are frequently co-endorsed by users with the same interests are more likely to have the same or similar tags.

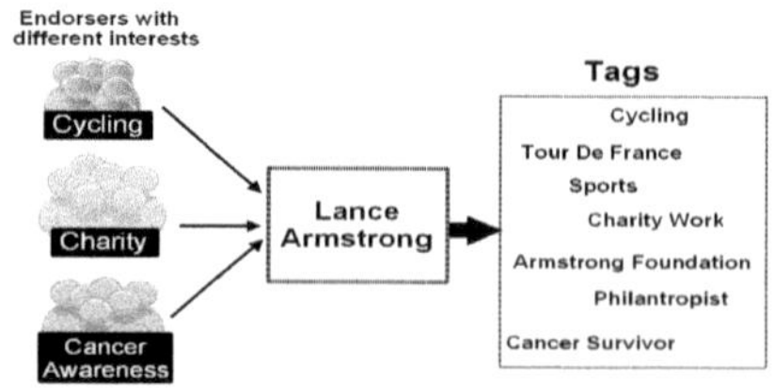

Figure 1: Twitter user Lance Armstrong attracts endorsements due to his various appealing aspects: Pro Cyclist, Philanthropist, Cancer Survivor. Our approach mines these aspects and translates them into meaningful tags.

OUR APPROACH. Our approach works in two phases. The first phase figures out why users choose to endorse the entities that they do. Intuitively, each entity can be mapped to a one or more topics. These topics capture the different aspects that make it appealing to different users. Consider a photograph of a beautiful *landscape* from *Hawaii*. This photo can attract endorsements from nature-lovers who appreciate the beauty of the scenery, or from people who have a particular interest in the island of Hawaii. Another example is given in Figure 1, showing the different aspects of Twitter-user and world-famous cyclist Lance Armstrong.

We uncover the observed endorsements using a generative-model approach based on Latent Dirichlet allocation (LDA) [5]. This allows us to reconstruct the "aspect-space" that the entities reside in. Clearly, not *all* endorsements are due to such coherent topical reasons, and our approach does not require them to be. A user may endorse an entity even if it does not really appeal to her interests, simply because one of her friends did. Such endorsements cannot be translated into meaningful tags; even if we could somehow assign a tag that captures this scenario (e.g. one that encodes the relationship between the user and her friend), it would be of little use to other users or to information retrieval and data mining applications. Thus, while our approach does not explicitly distinguish among endorsements, it is driven by those generated due to aspects of general interest.

The product of the first phase is the set of learned aspects, along with the correlation of each entity with each aspect. In the second phase, these aspects are fleshed out using the text associated with the entities. In practice, this phase translates each aspect into a probability distribution over a vocabulary of terms. Note that we do not require the presence of text for every entity in the network. Instead, we only need enough text to allow us to converge to the distribution of each aspect. We can then use the correlation of an entity with each aspect (learned in the first phase) to extract tags. In the experiments section, we show how one can obtain text for entities in social platforms such as Twitter and Flickr. We also demonstrate how our approach is able to extract high quality tags even when noisy or no text is given as input for some of the entities.

CONTRIBUTIONS.

1. We propose the use of social endorsement networks to extract high quality tags for entities embedded in social systems. To the best of our knowledge, this is the first such application of endorsement networks.
2. We propose an approach that has no requirement for pre-existing tags and can produce high-quality results even when the input consists of *noisy* text that is available for *only a portion* of the entities.
3. We conduct extensive experiments on large scale datasets from two very different social systems -Twitter and Flickr- to demonstrate the efficacy of our approach. Our results indicate that our approach is highly effective at finding high quality tags: in certain cases performing 100% better than the closest baseline.

ORGANIZATION.
The rest of the paper is organized as follows. In Section 2 we motivate the use of social endorsement networks and present our approach. Next, we experimentally demonstrate the merits of our method over a broad set of strong baselines and an extensive evaluation in Section 3. In order to distinguish our work from related existing works, we delay the discussion of related work until Section 4. Finally, we conclude in Section 5.

2. MINING TAGS FROM ENDORSEMENTS

In this section we begin with a formal discussion and motivation of the problem considered in this paper. In Section 2.2, we explore possible approaches and discuss their shortcomings. Finally we present our proposed approach in Section 2.3.

2.1 Motivation

The goal of this work is to devise a method of obtaining high-quality tags for entities embedded in social systems, in order to enhance their accessibility and make them visible to applications such us search and recommendation systems. The scope of the problem is best explained through some examples.

Flickr: On Flickr, the entities to be tagged are pictures. Users have the option to tag pictures with keywords of their own selection. While these manually assigned tags are sometimes informative, they can often be trivial or inadequate. In addition, some pictures are tagged with too few or too many tags. Our study of the pictures uploaded in the group FlickrCentral (the largest user-group on Flickr) showed that 53% of the pictures had either less than 2 or more than 30 tags.

Twitter: The entities of interest on the Twitter platform are the users themselves. Our primary focus is on users with a significant number of followers, since they are more likely to be of interest to other users. Twitter is a particularly challenging scenario, since it does not allow users to tag each other.

One of the primary challenges of automated tag extraction is finding an appropriate source of informative text associated with the entities. This is easier in cases where the entities are documents themselves, as in the case of the del.icio.us platform. However, for entities embedded in social platforms, finding good text can be a non-trivial task. On Twitter, we can consider the tweets of each entity as a source of text. However, as we show in the experiments section, the ambiguous and often irrelevant nature of the tweets often leads to poor results. Another source of text that we explore is the set of results retrieved by issuing the user's name as a query to a major web search engine. However, here we have to deal with issues like the availability of a nickname instead of the user's actual name, ambiguity of results due to common names, and noisy or irrelevant web content. On Flickr, we can use the comments submitted by the users for each picture. Again, we are faced with the issue of dealing with irrelevant or trivial comments or, for some pictures, the complete lack thereof. For the rest of this section, we assume access to a corpus, albeit incomplete and noisy, that associates text with *some* of the entities. We further comment on the specifics of the text we use for each social system in the experiments section.

NOTATION. First, we establish some notation common to the rest of this section. Let $\mathcal{E}$ denote the set of entities we are interested in tagging, with d_e representing the "bag-of-terms" associated with each entity, with terms coming from vocabulary $\mathcal{V}$. Let $n_{t|e}$ denote the number of times term t occurs in d_e, $n_{\cdot|e}$ the total occurrences of terms in d_e, and $n_{t|\cdot}$ the total number of unique entities that have associated text containing t. We will introduce additional notation when needed later in the section.

2.2 Baselines for the Tag Extraction Problem

The earlier examples show that, in order to be effective, an approach has to be able to work with *noisy text* and also tackle cases when text is *unavailable* for some of the entities. To better motivate our approach, we begin by discussing the shortcomings of some intuitive baselines. We then go on to give details of our approach and describe how it overcomes these shortcomings.

2.2.1 *Baseline 1:* TFIDF

A simple method for obtaining tags from the text associated with entities is to treat such text as documents in a information retrieval setting and to use the popular TF-IDF method for scoring words [2]. In terms of our problem, given an entity e from a collection $\mathcal{E}$ and a term t, using the notation from Section 2.1, the measure is defined as follows:

$$TFIDF(t, e) = \frac{n_{t|e}}{n_{\cdot|e}} \log \frac{|E|}{n_{t|\cdot}} \quad (1)$$

While this method has been shown to be highly effective in various information retrieval tasks, it suffers from a number of drawbacks. First, as shown in our experiments, this method often results in extremely obvious or obscure tags. For example, in Twitter, for the entity *Al Gore*, the former vice president of USA, the top two tags obtained by TFIDF were "al gore" and "futurama". The first is trivially the entity's name. The second is a popular TV show that sometimes features Al Gore as a gimmick, hardly one of the entity's most characteristic attributes. Further, if there exist multiple reasons that make an entity appealing in a social system, then it is likely that TFIDF will identify redundant tags from the dominant aspect before identifying tags from any of the others. Finally, this approach depends heavily on the text available for each entity: uninformative text leads to irrelevant tags, and the utter lack of text renders the method inapplicable. All these issues emerged in our experiments, where TFIDF was used as a baseline. In order to address these problems, we clearly need a more sophisticated approach.

2.2.2 *Baseline 2:* TEXTASPECTS

A key insight from the above discussion is that an entity can appeal to users of a social system for multiple distinct reasons.

Examples: *Some Twitter users might follow Lance Armstrong's due to his status as a world-class cyclist, while others choose to follow him for his significant charity work. On Flickr, a picture of the Eiffel tower in Paris may be favorited by people who like Paris in particular, as well by those who care about architecture in general.*

We refer to these different reasons for an entity's appeal as *Aspects*. Using such aspects, we can identify non-redundant tags that are representative of the different facets of an entity and avoid some of the issues that ailed the TFIDF approach. The problem of tag extraction can now be broken down into two distinct steps.

1. Identify the aspects that make each entity appealing and compute a term-based representation of each aspect.

2. Extract high-quality tags, based on each entity's aspects of appeal and each aspect's term-based representation.

Next, we consider an intuitive solution to sub-problem 1 and discuss its shortcomings. Then, we give our own solution to this sub-problem in Section 2.3. A general solution to sub-problem 2 is given in Section 2.4.

A reasonable assumption is that (some of) the aspects of an entity's appeal are represented in the text associated with it.

Examples: *On Twitter, Lance Armstrong's tweets concern his cycling career, as well as his charity work. Hence, both of these central aspects of his appeal are captured in his tweets. Similarly, on Flickr, the comments associated with a picture of the Eiffel Tower may address admiration for Paris, as well as for impressive architecture feats.*

We refer to such aspects that are latent within text as TEXTASPECTS. One principled way to extract TEXTASPECTS is by modeling the text associated with entities using the Latent Dirichlet Allocation (LDA) approach [5]. We use this approach as a baseline.

The LDA generative model states that each word in a document is generated with the document first picking a topic, and then picking a word associated with the topic. The topics are picked from a document-specific distribution. In our *Text Generation Process*, the text associated with an entity is assumed to be generated by the above process, with the topics representing the aspects of an entity's appeal. Let $\mathcal{K}$ be the set of aspects, α and β be the Dirichlet smoothing parameters, Θ the set of aspect-entity distributions, and Φ the set of term-aspect distributions. In the generation process, t_i and z_i indicate a word in a d_e and the topic that generates it, respectively. Given this notation, the text generation process is as follows:

Text Generation Process

1. For all aspects k, sample $\phi_k \sim Dir(\beta)$
2. For all entities e, sample $\theta_e \sim Dir(\alpha)$
3. For each term-slot in d_e
   (a) Sample an aspect $z_i \sim Mult(\theta_e)$
   (b) Sample a term $t_i = w \sim Mult(\phi_{z_i})$

The parameter-sets Θ and Φ can be learned by determining an assignment of term-slots to aspects $\mathbf{z}$, following the collapsed Gibbs sampling method [35]. The core of the method relies on sampling a new value for the aspect z_i that generated the term w at term-slot t_i by using the aspect assignments of all other term-slots (i.e.$\mathbf{z_{-i}}$). Formally,

$$P(z_i = k | t_i = w, \mathbf{t_{-i}}, \mathbf{z_{-i}}) \propto \frac{n_{k|e,-i} + \alpha}{|d_{e,-i}| + \alpha|\mathcal{K}|} \times \frac{n_{t|k,-i} + \beta}{n_{\cdot|k,-i} + \beta|\mathcal{V}|} \quad (2)$$

where $n_{k|e,-i}$ is the number of times aspect k is observed for entity e, $n_{t|k,-i}$ is the number of times term t is sampled from aspect k, $|d_{e,-i}|$ is number of term occurrences associated with e, and $n_{\cdot|k,-i}$ is the total number of terms generated from aspect k, with all these quantities computed over all slots except the ith one.

The learned distributions $\Theta : \{\theta_{ek} = p(k|e), \forall e \in \mathcal{E}, k \in \mathcal{K}\}$ and $\Phi : \{\phi_{kt} = p(t|k), \forall k \in \mathcal{K}, t \in \mathcal{V}\}$ are called the **aspect-entity** and **term-aspect** distributions, respectively. θ_e gives us the probability that the appeal of a given entity e is due to aspect k and ϕ_k represents the probability of a term showing up given an aspect k. Given this knowledge, techniques such as the one we describe in Section 2.4 can be then used to extract tags.

While TEXTASPECTS solves some of the problems with redundancy and coverage of tags, it faces a different issue: the mined TEXTASPECTS are just a *proxy* to the true aspects of an entity's appeal, since they only capture the facets of an entity that are present in the associated text. Let us consider the following examples.

Twitter: While Lance Armstrong's tweets may cover the cycling and philanthropy aspects of his appeal to users, they might not capture his appeal to others who identify with and follow Armstrong because he is a famous American from Texas, or because he is a cancer survivor.

Flickr: On Flickr, a picture of Paris taken by a famous photographer may appeal to people who follow this particular photographer's work. It might be the case, however, that this aspect is not adequately represented in the comments associated with the photograph, and therefore will be erroneously overlooked.

The above examples demonstrate that TEXTASPECTS is still limited by the available text. If the available text is inadequate, some of the entity's appealing aspects will be missed. If the text is uninformative, the produced aspects will lead to inferior tags. Finally, if no text is available at all for an entity, then the approach is not applicable at all. The above analysis motivates us to find a way to disconnect the process of learning the appealing aspects of an entity (i.e., the aspect-entity distribution) from the often inadequate and noisy entity-text.

2.3 Our Approach: ENDORSEASPECTS

In the previous section we discussed the shortcomings of learning aspects directly from text, and motivated the need for an alternative rich and easily accessible data source. In particular, we highlighted the need for an alternative way to estimate the aspect-entity distribution $\theta_{ek}(= p(k|e))$, i.e. the probability that a given entity is appealing due to a specific aspect k. In this section we give an approach for learning this aspect-entity distribution by mining the underlying *social endorsement graph*. Social endorsements are ideal for our purpose since they directly encode the appeal of the entity to the users. In addition, endorsement functionality available in virtually every major social networking platform, ensuring an abundance of endorsement data for almost all entities. On Twitter, the endorsement graph consists of the underlying follower-graph. On Flickr, users endorse pictures by including them to their Favorites. In the context of such a graph, we compute the probability θ_{ek} as follows:

$$\theta_{ek} = p(k|e) = \frac{p(e,k)}{p(e)} \propto \sum_{u \in \mathcal{U}} p(u)p(k|u)p(e|k), \quad (3)$$

where $p(u)$ is the probability that the user u makes an endorsement. This probability can be assumed to be the same for all users in $\mathcal{U}$. In domains where there is reasonable evidence that some users have a stronger propensity to endorsements than others, it can be learned from a training corpus.

Conceptually, $p(k|u)$ is the probability that user u makes an endorsement due to aspect k (**aspect-user** distribution) and $p(e|k)$ is the probability that entity e gets endorsed due to (its association with) aspect k (**entity-aspect** distribution). Hence, our approach computes the required term-aspect distribution by first breaking down social endorsement network into the the aspect-user and entity-aspect distributions.

Examples: *A user who is interested in Cycling is likely to endorse entities based on this aspect. Moreover, most users are likely to have many interests, and will likely have a distribution over these interests ($p(k|u)$). Further, a famous Cyclist such as Lance Armstrong is more likely to be endorsed due to his status in the context of this aspect ($p(e|k)$).*

Since aspects are learned directly through endorsements, our approach gives the appealing aspects even for entities that have no usable text attached to them. Provided that we have enough text from other entities to learn the term distribution of each aspect, we can then still generate high-quality tags. Next, we show how we can learn the aspect-user and entity-aspect distributions by mining the endorsement network.

2.3.1 Learning Appealing Aspects from Endorsements

We learn the appealing aspects from the endorsement network by modeling it using an LDA-like generative process. Informally, the Endorsement Generation Process states that each endorsement made by a user is generated with the user first picking an aspect from his personal distribution of interests, and then picking an entity to endorse based on that aspect. Formally, let $\mathcal{U}$ denote the set of users who endorse entities picked from the set $\mathcal{E}$. For each user u, the set of entities endorsed by her is denoted by $\mathcal{E}(u) \subseteq \mathcal{E}$. Let the set $\mathcal{K}$ be the set of aspects, α' and β' be the Dirichlet smoothing parameters, $\Psi : \{\psi_{uk} = p(k|u), \forall u \in \mathcal{U}, k \in \mathcal{K}\}$ be the set of aspect-user distributions, and $\Xi : \{\xi_{ke} = p(e|k), \forall k \in \mathcal{K}, e \in \mathcal{E}\}$ be the set of entity-aspect distributions. In the generation process, e_i denotes an entity in the endorsed set $\mathcal{E}(u)$ of a user u. Then, y_i denotes the aspect e_i is sampled from. Given this notation, the endorsement generation process is as follows:

Endorsement Generation Process

1. For all aspects k, sample $\xi_k \sim Dir(\beta')$
2. For all entities u, sample $\psi_u \sim Dir(\alpha')$
3. For each endorsement-slot in $\mathcal{E}(u)$
   (a) Sample an aspect $y_i \sim Mult(\psi_u)$
   (b) Sample a entity $e_i = l \sim Mult(\xi_{y_i})$

As in the standard LDA model, the distribution-sets Ψ and Ξ can be learned via the collapsed Gibbs sampling method [35]. This requires an expression that gives the probability that one particular endorsement from a user u to entity $e_i = l$ was due to aspect y_i. This can be derived by following the steps outlined by Griffiths and Steyvers [15]. Due to paucity of space, we skip the derivation and give here the final sampling equation.

$$P(y_i = k|e_i = l, \mathbf{e_{-i}}, \mathbf{y_{-i}}) \propto \frac{n_{k|u,-i} + \alpha'}{|\mathcal{E}(u)| + \alpha'|\mathcal{K}|} \times \frac{n_{e|k,-i} + \beta'}{n_{\cdot|k,-i} + \beta'|\mathcal{E}|} \quad (4)$$

where $n_{k|u,-i}$ is the number of times aspect k is observed for user u, $n_{e|k,-i}$ is the number of times entity e is sampled from aspect k, $|\mathcal{E}(u)|$ is number of entities endorsed by user u, and $n_{\cdot|k,-i}$ is the total number of entities generated from aspect k, with all these quantities computed over all endorsement-slots except the ith one.

The learned aspect-user distributions ψ_u and entity-aspect distributions ξ_k give us the probabilities $p(k|u)$ and $p(e|k)$ that we need to compute Eq. (3) and obtain θ_e, i.e. the distribution over the set of aspects for each entity. We can then plug θ_e into the *Text Generation Process* from Section 2.2.2 and learn the term distribution ϕ_k of each aspect k. The next section describes the details of this learning process. The corresponding plate notation is given in Figure 2. The Endorsement Generation Process follows standard LDA principles. For the Text Generation Process, the θ distribution is now known, which is why it is shown shaded in the plate notation.

2.3.2 *Efficiently Learning the Term-Aspect Distributions*

In the TEXTASPECTS approach discussed in Section 2.2.2, the aspect-entity distribution θ_e of each entity e and the term-aspect distribution ϕ_k of each aspect are learned simultaneously by sampling Eq. 2. In the case of ENDORSEASPECTS, however, θ_e is obtained via an independent mining of the endorsement graph and is thus already known. Therefore, we can re-write Eq. (2) as follows:

$$P(z_i = k|t_i = w, \mathbf{t_{-i}}, \mathbf{z_{-i}}) \propto p(k|e) \times \frac{n_{t|k,-i} + \beta}{n_{\cdot|k,-i} + \beta|\mathcal{V}|} \quad (5)$$

where $p(k|e) = \theta_{ek}$ is already known. Via Gibbs sampling, we can now sample aspects from this equation and infer ϕ_k for each aspect k accordingly.

In their paper on efficient topic model inference [35] Yao et al. introduce SparseLDA, an algorithm for the efficient evaluation of Gibbs sampling distributions. The method is based on the observation that parts of the computations are independent to each other and

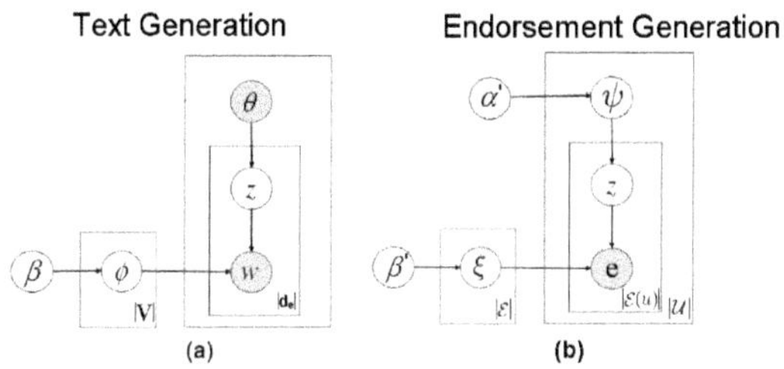

Figure 2: Text and Endorsement Generation in ENDORSEASPECTS.

can thus be cached to reduce the computational cost. Given Eq. (5) we can apply the SparseLDA sampling process to our approach by noticing that the right-hand side of the equation can be re-written as the product of the two following factors:

$$r = \sum_k \frac{p(k|e)\beta}{n_{\cdot|k,-i} + \beta|\mathcal{V}|} \quad , \quad q = \sum_k \frac{p(k|e)n_{t|k,-i}}{n_{\cdot|k,-i} + \beta|\mathcal{V}|}$$

The sampled value $x \sim U(0, r+q)$ can now fall within two buckets, depending on whether $x < r$ or $r < x < q$. The numerator of r is now a constant and can be precomputed for each aspect-entity combination. The denominator can be cached for each aspect and updated by simply subtracting and adding the values of re-sampled aspects. For q, we can cache $\frac{p(k|e)n_{t|k}}{n_{\cdot|k}+\beta|\mathcal{V}|}$ for every aspect k, by remembering the entities for which $p(k|e) \neq 0$. A single multiplication for each aspect k with $n_{t|k} \neq 0$ is then enough to compute q for a given term t.

2.4 From Aspects to Tags

After the appealing aspects of each entity have been extracted and mapped to meaningful term distributions, the final stage consists of assigning useful tags to each entity. We accomplish this via use of the popular *Information Gain measure*. In our context, given a term t and an entity e, we define the measure as follows:

$$\begin{aligned} IG(t|e) &= -p(e)\log p(e) \\ &+p(t)[p(e|t)\log p(e|t) + p(\neg e|t)\log p(\neg e|t)] \\ &+p(\neg t)[p(e|\neg t)\log p(e|\neg t) + p(\neg e|\neg t)\log p(\neg e|\neg t)] \end{aligned} \quad (6)$$

This equation measures the reduction in the entropy associated with entity e, incurred by the presence or absence of term t. The entropy itself is the same for all terms, thus it can be omitted. We compute $p(t)$ as follows:

$$p(t) = \sum_k \sum_e p(e)p(k|e)p(t|k) \quad (7)$$

$p(e) = 1/|\mathcal{E}|$ is assumed to be the same for all entities, $p(k|e)$ is as computed by Eq. (3) and $p(t|k)$ is computed as part of the term distributions learned by the second stage of our approach.

$p(e|t)$ is computed as follows:

$$p(e|t) = p(e,t)/p(t) = \sum_k p(e)p(k|e)p(t|k)/p(t) \quad (8)$$

After computing the information gain scores, we can tag an entity with a fixed number of top-scoring terms, or simply report all terms with a score over a given threshold. Assigned tags need to be good discriminators, in order to be characteristic of the entity. At the same time, tags need to be frequently used terms that are familiar to the users. This is necessary for applications like search, where an entity needs to be matched to user queries based on its tags. We justify our choice of Information Gain by showing in our experiments that it reports terms that satisfy both of these requirements.

3. EXPERIMENTS

In this section, we illustrate the efficacy of our approach through a rigorous experimental evaluation on real data. We begin with a description of the datasets used in the experiments, as well as the baselines that we compare our approach to. We then discuss each experiment in detail.

3.1 Datasets

Each dataset we use in our evaluation consists of a set of users, a set of endorsable entities, the underlying endorsement graph and a piece of textual information associated with each entity.

Twitter: Twitter is a social networking and microblogging website that allows users to broadcast short messages (tweets) to other users that explicitly choose to "follow" them. This act of following a user is interpreted as an endorsement. For our experiments, we used the publicly available crawl of the Twitter graph published by Kwak et al. [21][1]. The crawl consists of 41.7 million user profiles and 1.47 billion social relations. In our experiments, we consider every user with at least 2,000 followers to be an endorsable entity, giving us a total of about 38,400 entities. In order to obtain the text associated with each entity, we harvested all their tweets from July-December of 2009, the same year the graph was crawled.

An inspection of the tweets revealed that the content was often not only sparse, but also very noisy. For example, while an actor may sometimes tweet about his work and projects, the majority of his posts are not related to movies or acting. Hence, we create a second dataset of text associated with entities that was more conducive for the purposes of tagging. We start by making the following useful observation about twitter users: highly-followed entities are often public figures or authorities in some topic of broad interest. Such users use their real name when registering, since they use Twitter as a medium to advertise themselves. First, we extract the real full name of each user. We then submit the name as a query to a major search engine and aggregate the text of the top-5 returned webpages. As we show in our experiments, the data from the search engine turns out to be more useful than the tweets for extracting tags.

Flickr: Flickr is an image hosting website, where users can endorse an entity (image) by including it in their 'Favorites'. Flickr users also have the option to create and join groups, where people can post images and comments. For our experiments, we used the data for all users and images that are affiliated with FlickrCentral, the largest group on Flickr. FlickrCentral consists of users with diverse interests; we collected data for the 370,144 members of the group. After removing images with less than 10 endorsements, we were left with a set of 138,225 distinct images. For each image, we collected the comments attached to it, and, where available, the set of user-assigned tags and descriptive note attached by the image's owner. This comprised the text data associated with each entity. The data was extracted from a complete snapshot of Flickr from 2008.

3.2 Evaluated Approaches

ENDORSEASPECTS: This refers to our own approach of mining aspects from the social endorsement network as described in Section 2.3. The mined aspects are then used to extract tags using the approach outlined in Section 2.4. For Twitter, the number of aspects was set to 400; this was determined via experiments on a validation set of tags of wefollow.com, described in Section 3.3.2. For Flickr, the number of aspects was set to 1000, tuned on a validation subset of images. We implemented our approach by modifying Mallet [2], which also handles hyper-parameter optimizations.

TEXTASPECTS: This baseline refers to the approach of mining aspects from the text associated with each entity (see Section 2.2.2). This can be considered an implementation of an approach proposed by Krestel et al. [19]. As above, the approach in Section 2.4 is used to mine the tags. The number of aspects used were set and hyper-parameter optimization was performed in the same way as for ENDORSEASPECTS.

NN-TEXTASPECTS: For this baseline, the text associated with an entity is enriched with the text associated with its 5 nearest neighbors, selected based on the Jaccard similarity of their endorsement sets. Conceptually, this enriches the text of each entity by taking into consideration the (local) information encoded in the endorsement graph. The TEXTASPECTS approach is then applied on this enriched text representation.

TFIDF: This baseline for mining tags is described in Section 2.2.1.

3.3 Evaluation on Twitter

3.3.1 *Twitter Evaluation via Manual Labeling*

In this section we describe our evaluation of the quality of the tag-sets reported by the different approaches for the Twitter dataset. The study was conducted as follows: first, we separated the entities into 10 groups based on their number of followers. The first group includes all entities with a number of followers in [2000, 4000), the second group those in [4000, 8000), and so on. The purpose of this grouping was to evaluate how the approaches perform for entities of different popularity, as indicated by the number of their followers. We then randomly selected 30 entities from each range, which were then shown to two annotators, along with the tag-sets recommended by each approach. The annotators were asked to pick the approach with the best tag-set; they could also pick multiple winners or no winners at all. For each range, we report the average fraction of wins for each approach, taken over the judgments of both annotators. We quantify the inter-rater agreement by reporting the average Kappa statistic of agreement between each pair of annotators on the wins for each approach; this value was 0.455. To see that this signifies a robust agreement between annotators note that ENDORSEASPECTS outperforms baseline approaches by a wide margin, and hence large values of the Kappa statistic are difficult to obtain as marginal distributions of annotator preferences over approaches are very biased. Another interesting way to visualize results is to group entities by a measure of their activity (number of tweets); we report results this way taking care to avoid biases when estimating the performance of approaches in various ranges.

The fraction of wins of each approach over different groups of users are shown in Figures 3 and 4. As can be seen, our approach (ENDORSEASPECTS) consistently outperforms all others in all specified ranges. For all entities with up to 256K followers, ENDORSEASPECTS is significantly better than the competition. In fact, for some ranges (e.g. 2K-4K and 4K-8K), the achieved score is more than double that of the second best. This gap is reduced for the last three ranges of followers. It is important to observe that this is due to the scores of ENDORSEASPECTS dropping, since the scores of the other methods remain in the same levels as in the other ranges. Considering the nature of ENDORSEASPECTS and its dependence on the underlying endorsement graph, this reduction can be easily explained: users with over 256K followers are very famous public figures, attracting interest from people of different interests. Britney Spears and Ellen Degeneres are both examples of such individuals. Their initial source of fame may have been their achievements in a

[1] http://an.kaist.ac.kr/traces/WWW2010.html

[2] http://mallet.cs.umass.edu/

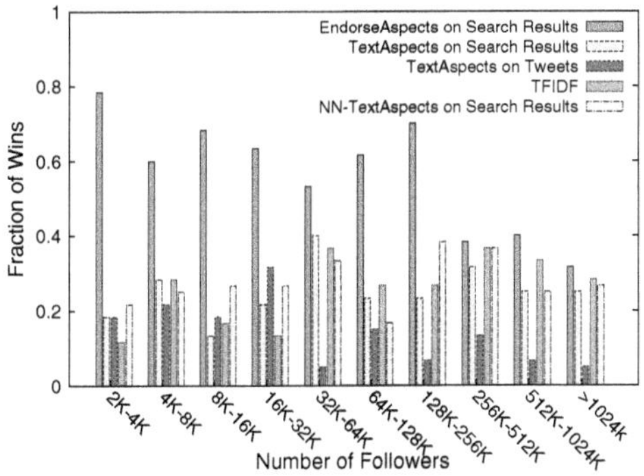

2K-4K	58%
4K-8K	25%
8K-16K	10%
16K-32K	4%
32K-64K	1.4%
64K-128K	0.6%
128K-256K	0.2%
256K-512K	0.2%
512K-1024K	0.4%
>1024K	0.2%

Figure 3: Fraction of wins for each approach with entities grouped by number of followers and the percentage of entities in each group.

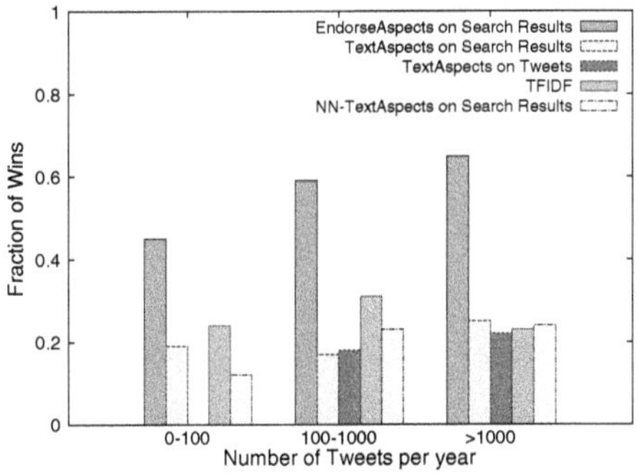

0-100	82.2%
100-1000	14.5%
> 1000	3.3%

Figure 4: Fraction of wins for each approach with entities grouped by activity level and the percentage of entities in each group.

particular area (music and acting, respectively). However, their popularity has grown to a point that they attract followers who may not even have an interest in these areas. This throws off ENDORSEASPECTS, since it cannot easily determine the aspects that attract the entity's endorsements. It is important to note that such entities make up for only small portion of the endorsable population. Moreover, these entities often have name recognition, which reduces the necessity of finding tags. As can be seen in Figure 3, 99.2% percent of the entities have less than 256K followers, and these are the entities that our approach excels at. When grouping entities by activity level as well ENDORSEASPECTS outperforms all competing approaches over all ranges by wide margins (Figure 4).

Overall, our results show three points worth noting. First, it is very clear from the preceding results that using endorsement network information lets us obtain much better tags that simply using text associated with entities (even when applying sophisticated approaches like TEXTASPECTS). Second, we can answer whether it is endorsement information alone that helps or the way ENDORSEASPECTS exploits it. As explained before NN-TEXTASPECTS was designed to enrich the text representation of entities using local information from the endorsement graph. However, we notice that even though NN-TEXTASPECTS improves upon TEXTASPECTS it does come close to ENDORSEASPECTS in terms of performance. This indicates that using text in any form at the first stage of constructing the aspects tends to lead the system astray (in spite of using neighborhood information) and ENDORSEASPECTS is able to exploit the endorsement network information to obtain much cleaner signal. A third point worth noting is that TEXTASPECTS performs much better when run on Search Results as opposed to when run on Tweets, showing that the reasons why users follow entities and hence appropriate tags for them are not very correlated to the tweets produces by these entities.

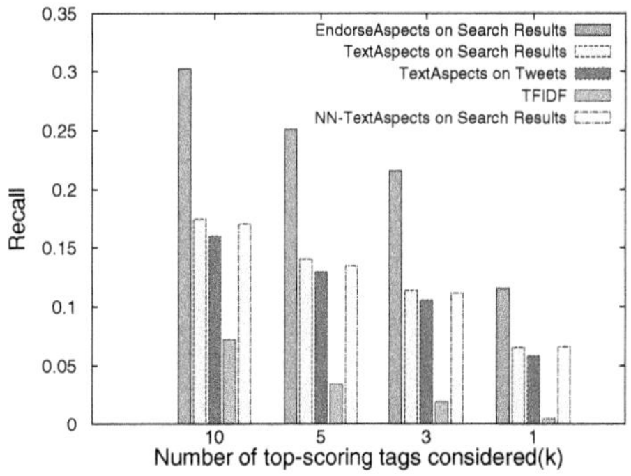

Figure 5: Recall on the wefollow tag-prediction task.

Tagging Entities with Few Followers and No Associated Text: The results so far are reported on entities with at least 2000 followers as we believe that these are of the most interest to Twitter users. However, for some interesting entities - such as new ones - their number of followers may be less than our threshold or there may not be available any text associated with them (they may not tweet much or may resolve to ambiguous search results). Here we report experimental results on such entities.

We conducted this experiment on entities with at least 1000 followers, leading to 146000 entities. Of these, web text was obtained for only those with more than 2000 followers. The goal in this experiment was to then obtain tags for those entities with number of followers between 1000 and 2000 for whom we had no associated text. ENDORSEASPECTS does not require associated text for *every* entity in the corpus, however, the all baselines evaluated in the previous study do, and hence, are no longer applicable. Therefore, we modify the NN-TEXTASPECTS approach to use the 5 nearest neighbors with associated text. For the manual evaluation, we selected 50 entities from the 1000-2000 followers range, uniformly at random. For each entity, the winning approaches were selected by three annotators. The average fraction of wins for ENDORSEASPECTS and modified NN-TEXTASPECTS were **78.6%** and **14%**, respectively. The value of Kappa statistic averaged over annotators pairs and approaches was 0.52. These results show that ENDORSEASPECTS works extremely well for entities that have few followers and no text associated with them. These experiments also show that the impressive performance of ENDORSEASPECTS reported in Figures 3 and 4 is not due to any bias in selecting entities by restricting the number of followers to be at least 2000.

3.3.2 Evaluation with WeFollow Tags

In this experiment we evaluate each approach on the task of predicting tags that Twitter users have assigned to themselves. Even though Twitter does not provide a tagging feature, users can tag themselves by visiting wefollow.com. We found 16,000 entities from our experimental setup that had tagged themselves with at least one tag. An inspection of the data revealed that user-assigned tags can be noisy or irrelevant: single-letter tags, tags with non-letter characters, humorous or inaccurate self descriptions (e.g. "god", "great", "lover", "geek"), misspellings are just some of the factors that make this evaluation particularly challenging. To ameliorate the effects of such factors, we stem the tags, remove stop-words and eliminate tags with less than ten occurrences in the corpus. This brings the total to 32099 (non-distinct) tags for the entities. This experiment measures *Recall@k*: for each approach, we report the percentage of the wefollow tags of each entities found in the top-k tags ($k \in \{1, 3, 5, 10\}$) recommended for it.

As can be seen from Figure 5, ENDORSEASPECTS clearly outperforms the others, for all values of k. Despite the difficulty of pre-

Aspect label	Top-5 Entities				
UK TV Personalities	Chris Moyles	Jonathan Ross	Phillip Schofield	Fearne Cotton	Stephen Fry
Technology People	Leo Laporte	Kevin Rose	Alexal Brecht	John C. Dvorak	Patrick Norton
NBA basketball	Lamar Odom	Derek Fisher	Dwight Howard	Shaquille O'Neal	Baron Davis
US Teen Celebs	Selena Gomez	Miley Cyrus	David Henrie	Mitchel Musso	Emily Osment
Cycling	Lance Armstrong	Levi Leipheimer	George Hincapie	Johan Bruyneel	Dave Zabriskie
Twilight	Peter Facinelli	Twilight Fans	Rachelle Lefevre	Rob Pattinson News	Taylor Lautner
Political Commentators	Rachel Maddow MSNBC	MirHossein Mousavi	Claire McCaskill	TehranBureau.com	HuffingtonPost
Brazilian Celebs	Rafinha Bastos	Marco Luque	Felipe Andreoli	Luciano Huck	Oscar Filho
Country Music	Taylor Swift	Carrie Underwood	Kellie Pickler	Keith Urban	Brad Paisley
Rock Music	Pitchfork	David Lynch	NME Magazine	Sonic Youth	Liam Gallagher

Table 1: Top-5 entities (by $p(e|k)$) for 10 selected aspects

dicting the self-assigned tags, ENDORSEASPECTS achieved a recall as high as 30%. None of the other three TEXTASPECTS based approaches stands out, while TFIDF was consistently last. TFIDF tends to report tags that are more specific to the entity, while users prefer more generic tags to encode themselves and their different characteristics. For example, a famous painter is more likely to choose to tag himself with terms like "artist" and "painter", rather than the name of his wife or his hometown.

Toward a more thorough analysis of the results, we examine the tags that hurt the recall of ENDORSEASPECTS the most. Let *success(t)* be the number of times the wefollow tag t was correctly predicted by ENDORSEASPECTS and *fail(t)* be the number of times it was missed (for k=10). First, we select the 20 wefollow tags with the highest *fail(t)-success(t)* difference. For each selected tag t, we report the seven tags that were most commonly reported for entities tagged with t (the number seven was chosen solely due to space constraints). The results are shown in Table 2. The 1st column holds the tags ENDORSEASPECTS misses. The 2nd column holds the percentage of missed predictions due to each tag. The 3rd column holds the seven most common alternately reported tags.

As shown in the table, these 20 tags alone are responsible for almost 30% of all missed predictions. Note that the reported terms come from the same domain are clearly connected to the missed tag. Another observation is that ENDORSEASPECTS often returns terms that represent more specialized facets of the missed tag. (e.g. see results for "music" and "sports") The consistently high relevance of the tags demonstrates that, even if a tag is missed, the domain and nature of the entity are still correctly identified. This leads to the assignment of appropriate tags that capture the entity's attributes.

3.3.3 Evaluation of Aspects

In this section we evaluate the aspects computed by our approach. Aspect quality is crucial, since it directly affects the tag extraction process in our model. Moreover, good quality of aspects opens the door to using them as browsable pages or for recommendation systems. The experiment is conducted as follows. First, we pick the 50 aspects with the highest $p(k)$ value, which represents the probability that an endorsement made due to aspect k and can be computed as follows $p(k) = \sum_{u \in \mathcal{U}} p(u) * p(k|u)$. Here $\mathcal{U}$ is the set of all users and $p(u)$ encodes the propensity of a user u to make an endorsement. We consider this probability to be equal for all users. $p(k|u)$ is the probability that user u makes an endorsement after picking aspect k from his distribution of interests, as computed by our model.

For each aspect k, we manually assigned a descriptive label, based on the nature of the entities that were given a high probability with respect to k (i.e. $p(e|k)$) by our model. For example, if the entities with high $p(e|k)$ values tend to be basketball players from the NBA, the label "NBA basketball players" was given to the aspect. If the labeling process revealed aspects with the same labels we keep the aspect with the highest $p(k)$ value. This results in 32 distinct aspects.

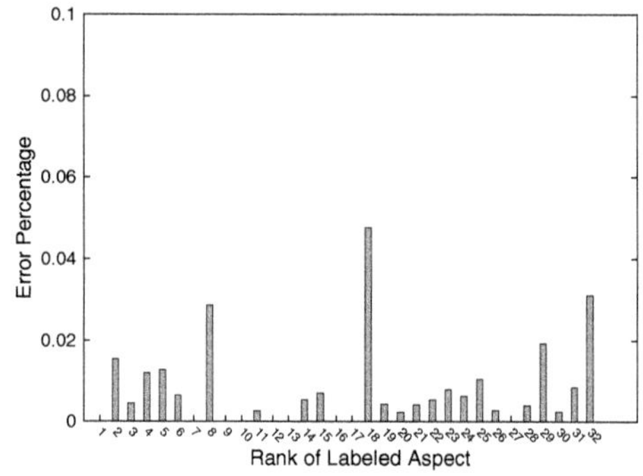

Figure 6: Results of evaluation of aspects on Twitter

Next, we picked the 5 entities with the highest $p(e|k)$ value for each aspect and presented the entire set to three annotators in a randomized order. The annotators were asked to mark from among the 32 labels those that they found appropriate for each entity. The performance of ENDORSEASPECTS for each aspect k was then measured via the following error function:

$$Error(k) = \frac{\sum_{e_1,e_2} I(h(e_1,e_2,k) \neq 0 \text{ and } h(e_1,e_2,k) \neq r(e_1,e_2,k))}{I(h(e_1,e_2,k) \neq 0)} \quad (9)$$

where $h(e_1, e_2, k)$ is equal to 1 if the annotator marked e_1 as relevant to k and e_2 as non-relevant, -1 if she marked e_1 as non-relevant to k and e_2 as relevant and 0 if the marked them both as relevant. Similarly, $r(e_1, e_2, k)$ is 1 if $p(e_1|k) > p(e_2|k)$, -1 if $p(e_1|k) < p(e_2|k)$ and 0 if $p(e_1|k) = p(e_2|k)$, as computed by ENDORSEASPECTS. Conceptually, the error function iterates over all possible entity pairs and adds a penalty point when ENDORSEASPECTS contradicts the annotator. Observe that a penalty can only be incurred for a pair of entities if k was marked by the annotator as relevant for one entity and non-relevant for the other. Thus, the overall error is computed as the percentage of such pairs that actually incurred a penalty. The results are shown in Figure 6. The x-axis holds the selected aspects, in descending order of $p(k)$ from left to right. The y-axis holds the $Error$ values.

The reported $Error$ is consistently low for all aspects. The highest observed value was lower than 5%, while for 9 of the aspects the error was equal to zero. This shows that human annotators agree to a high degree with the assignments of entities to aspects found by ENDORSEASPECTS. As qualitative evidence, we present the top-5 entities (by $p(e|k)$) for 10 of the top-50 aspects. As demonstrated clearly by the error measurements of the previous experiment, any subset of the aspects would produce convincing anecdotal evidence. The aspects were selected purely to maximize the verifiability of the results by the reader. The 1st column of Table 1 holds the labels of the selected aspects, while the selected entities are shown in the 2nd column. The table shows that the reported entities are both famous

wefollow Tag	Fraction of Errors	Reported tags						
social_media	6.3%	marketing	news	business	video	success	internet	music
music	4%	album	band	record	track	news	hip_hop	tour
media	2.7%	obama	politics	republican	elections	marketing	news	music
business	2.1%	marketing	news	social_media	video	blog	media	management
web	1.7%	social_media	marketing	news	media	technology	video	company
sports	1.4%	league	draft	player	basketball	nba	espn	nfl
author	1.3%	marketing	social_media	news	media	business	spiritual	management
technology	1%	marketing	news	social_media	blog	video	media	music
comedy	1%	news	business	home	social_media	starcraft	videos_channel	video
radio	0.9%	music	hiphop	news	obama	rap	mixtape	artist
artist	0.9%	jewelry	handmade	items	art	dollars	shopping	vintage
nonprofit	0.8%	poverty	africa	featured_sponsor	qstring	donate	global	nytimes
actor	0.8%	tv_episode	episode	hollywood	film	movie	trailer	dvd
startup	0.7%	marketing	technology	media	business	company	management	news
geek	0.7%	news	social_media	blog	marketing	video	media	playstation
advertising	0.7%	marketing	social_media	news	business	video	management	media
journalist	0.6%	obama	bbc	social_media	london	politics	british	media
podcast	0.6%	social_media	media	blog	marketing	comment	news	business
consulting	0.6%	marketing	social_media	business	media	success	industry	sales
innovation	0.5%	social_media	marketing	media	management	industry	business	technology
	29.5%							

Table 2: Tags reported most frequently by ENDORSEASPECTS for entities tagged with selected wefollow Tags

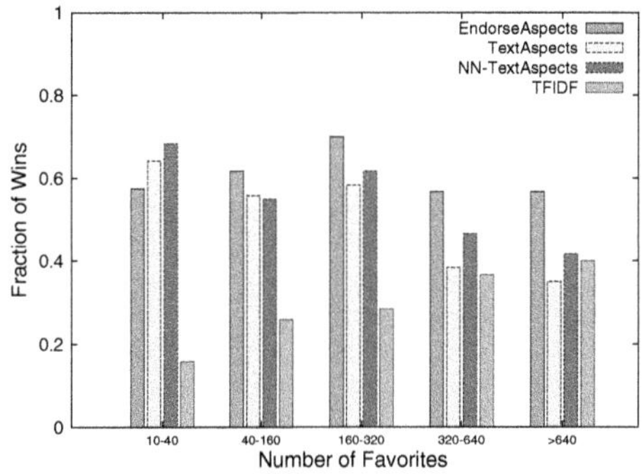

Figure 7: Results of evaluation via manual labeling on Flickr

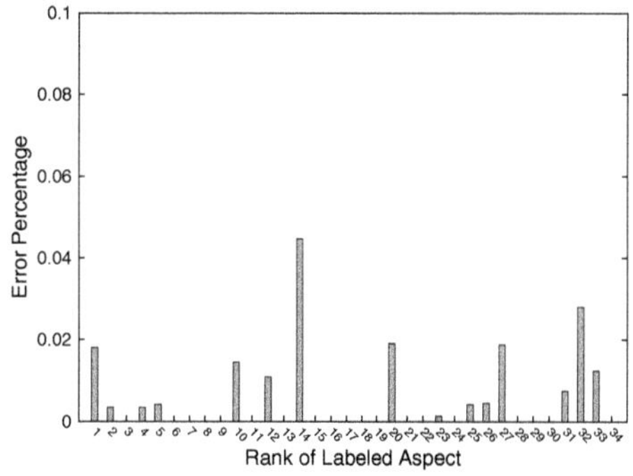

Figure 8: Results of evaluation of aspects on Flickr

individuals (or organizations) and highly relevant to the respective aspects. Just as importantly, the automatically discovered aspects are cohesive and represent interesting concepts.

3.4 Evaluation on Flickr

3.4.1 Flickr Evaluation via Manual Labeling

In this section we describe our evaluation of the quality of the tag-sets reported by the various approaches for the images in the Flickr dataset. The evaluation is conducted in a manner similar to that of the Twitter dataset, described in Section 3.3.1: images are put into 7 groups based on number of endorsements, 30 entities per range are selected, two annotators rate tags for each image. The results are shown in Figure 7. ENDORSEASPECTS consistently reported competitive results, achieving the best score for 4 of the 7 ranges. TEXTASPECTS and NN-TEXTASPECTS were also competitive, especially for images that fall within the first ranges.

Tagging in the Absence of Text: While indicative of the competitiveness of our approach, this experiment does not demonstrate one of its primary advantages: the ability to assign tags to an entity, even when there is no text associated with it. Theoretically, the NN-TEXTASPECTS approach also shares the same advantage, since it can borrow text from the entity's neighbors. To evaluate both methods on this task, we removed all the textual information attached to all the images that were evaluated in the previous study. We then re-applied both approaches to the corpus and generate new sets of tags for each image. A manual inspection of the results verified that the negative effect of removing text on ENDORSEASPECTS was negligible, while NN-TEXTASPECTS failed to produce meaningful results. The outcome of this trial, together with the results of the original user study, indicate the following: the local enhancement offered by the nearest-neighbor approach may help the discovery of appropriate tags, but it fails to produce high-quality results when no text is attached to the entity itself.

3.4.2 Evaluation of Aspects

In this section we evaluate the aspects computed by our approach for the Flickr Dataset. The methodology is the same as for the Twitter dataset (Section 3.3.3). After picking and labeling the 50 aspects with the highest $p(k)$ values, we eliminate those with duplicate labels. This produces a set of 34 distinct aspects. The 5 images with the highest $p(e|k)$ value for each aspect were then presented to a human annotator in randomized order, along with the labels of selected aspects. The annotator was asked to mark the labels that she found appropriate for each image. As we did for the Twitter dataset, we used the error function defined in Eq. (9) to evaluate the results. The produced error values are shown in Figure 8. The x-axis holds the selected aspects, in descending order of $p(k)$ from left to right. The y-axis holds the error percentages. As in the case of Twitter, the observed error percentage was consistently low for all aspects. The highest observed value was lower than 5%. Further, no error was observed for 19 of the 34 aspects. This shows that the computed aspects are cohesive and well-defined.

4. RELATED WORK

Here we review some relevant past works and point out the differences compared to our own work.

SOCIAL TAGGING. With the emergence of Web 2.0, social tagging has attracted much attention. Several approaches [19, 18, 29] assume pre-existing tags. The problem is then formalized as one of re-ranking or propagating existing tags across the entities. This is achieved by utilizing various similarity measures or nearest-neighbor methods [6]. The major shortcoming of such methods is the requirement of a significant number of high-quality tags. However, several major social networking platforms (e.g. Twitter) do not even provide a social tagging feature. Our approach has no requirement for pre-existing tags and thus overcomes this drawback. Chirita et al. [8] mine tags from raw text. However, their approach (which is customized for Web pages) focuses exclusively and depends heavily on text, disregarding the underlying social endorsement graph. In fact, our work is the first to utilize social endorsement data toward improving entity tagging.

ENDORSEMENT NETWORKS. Different facets of social endorsement networks have been considered in the past. Kunegis et al. [20] study a type of endorsement graph from Slashdot.org. In a recent paper [22], Lappas and Gunopulos mine groups of frequently co-endorsed entities toward an interactive recommendation system. As part of their work, the authors apply a very basic group-tagging mechanism that assumes the existence of a piece of text for each entity. Each group is then tagged based on the overlap of the term-sets of its members.

TOPIC MODELING. In their seminal work on topic modeling Blei et al. [5] introduce Latent Dirichlet Allocation (LDA), an unsupervised method to infer latent topics from unlabeled data. The method has been extensively used in several domains, including that of tag recommendation. The approaches by Xu et al. [34] and Krestel et al. [19] are examples of such work, although they both assume pre-existing tags. Si and Sun [28] present an LDA-based approach for tagging documents, making it applicable only to textual entities. Jianshu et al. [33] apply LDA on tweets, toward the identification of topic-sensitive influential Twitter users. We also present experimental results on Twitter data, even though the focus of our work is radically different. In addition, we evaluate the LDA-on-Tweets approach as the baseline (TEXTASPECTS) in our experiments. In our work, we use LDA on the underlying social endorsement graph to mine the topics that drive users to endorse the various entities. While LDA has been applied to graph corpora before [27, 9, 11, 25] in various settings, ours is the first work to apply it to social endorsement graphs toward tag extraction.

5. SUMMARY AND FUTURE WORK

In this work we demonstrated that social endorsement networks can be used to extract high-quality tags from noisy text associated with entities embedded in social systems. Our proposed approach models the reasons why entities appeal to users of social systems and then uses these aspects of appeal to extract tags. Finally, we evaluated our approach against intuitive and competitive baselines on large-scale real-world datasets from Twitter and Flickr. In future work, we would like to evaluate the impact of our extracted tags on tasks such as recommendation systems, contextual advertising, and expert finding.

6. REFERENCES

[1] C. Anderson. *The long tail: Why the future of business is selling less of more*. Hyperion Books, 2008.

[2] R. A. Baeza-Yates and B. Ribeiro-Neto. *Modern Information Retrieval*. Addison-Wesley Longman, Boston, MA, 1999.

[3] S. Bao, G. Xue, X. Wu, Y. Yu, B. Fei, and Z. Su. Optimizing web search using social annotations. In *WWW '07*.

[4] P. Basile, D. Gendarmi, F. Lanubile, and G. Semeraro. Recommending smart tags in a social bookmarking system. In *(SemNet 2007)*, 2007.

[5] D. M. Blei, A. Y. Ng, and M. I. Jordan. Latent dirichlet allocation. *J. Mach. Learn. Res.*, 3:993–1022, 2003.

[6] A. Budura, S. Michel, P. Cudré-Mauroux, and K. Aberer. Neighborhood-based tag prediction. In *ESWC '09*.

[7] A. Byde, H. Wan, and S. Cayzer. Personalized tag recommendations via tagging and content-based similarity metrics. In *ICWSM '07*.

[8] P. A. Chirita, S. Costache, W. Nejdl, and S. Handschuh. P-tag: large scale automatic gen. of pers. annotation tags for the web. In *WWW '07*.

[9] D. Cohn and T. Hofmann. The missing link - a probabilistic model of document content and hypertext connectivity. In *NIPS '01*.

[10] R. Datta, W. Ge, J. Li, and J. Z. Wang. Toward bridging the annotation-retrieval gap in image search by a generative modeling approach. In *MULTIMEDIA '06*.

[11] L. Dietz, S. Bickel, and T. Scheffer. Unsupervised prediction of citation influences. In *ICML '07*.

[12] P. A. Dmitriev, N. Eiron, M. Fontoura, and E. Shekita. Using annotations in enterprise search. In *WWW '06*.

[13] S. Goel, A. Broder, E. Gabrilovich, and B. Pang. Anatomy of the long tail: ordinary people with extraordinary tastes. In *WSDM '10*.

[14] S. Golder and B. A. Huberman. The structure of collaborative tagging systems. Aug. 2005.

[15] T. L. Griffiths and M. Steyvers. Finding scientific topics. *PNAS*, 101(Suppl. 1):5228–5235, April 2004.

[16] C. Hayes and P. Avesani. Using tags and clustering to identify topic-relevant blogs. March 2007.

[17] P. Heymann, G. Koutrika, and H. Garcia-Molina. Can social bookmarking improve web search? In *WSDM '08*.

[18] R. Jäschke, L. Marinho, A. Hotho, L. Schmidt-Thieme, and G. Stumme. Tag recommendations in folksonomies. In *PKDD 2007*.

[19] R. Krestel, P. Fankhauser, and W. Nejdl. Latent dirichlet allocation for tag recommendation. In *RecSys '09*.

[20] J. Kunegis, A. Lommatzsch, and C. Bauckhage. The slashdot zoo: mining a social network with negative edges. In *WWW '09*.

[21] H. Kwak, C. Lee, H. Park, and S. Moon. What is twitter, a social network or a news media? In *WWW '10*.

[22] T. Lappas and D. Gunopulos. Interactive recommendations in social endorsement networks. In *RecSys '10*.

[23] C. Marlow, M. Naaman, D. Boyd, and M. Davis. Ht06, tagging paper, taxonomy, flickr, academic article, to read. In *HYPERTEXT '06*.

[24] A. Mathes. Folksonomies - cooperative classification and communication through shared metadata. Tech. Rep., UIUC, 2004.

[25] R. M. Nallapati, A. Ahmed, E. P. Xing, and W. W. Cohen. Joint latent topic models for text and citations. In *KDD '08*.

[26] T. O'Reilly. What is web 2.0. design patterns and business models for the next generation of software, September 2005.

[27] M. Rosen-Zvi, T. Griffiths, M. Steyvers, and P. Smyth. The author-topic model for authors and documents. UAI '04.

[28] X. Si and M. Sun. Tag-LDA for Scalable Real-time Tag Recommendation. *Journal of Computational Information Sys.*, 2009.

[29] B. Sigurbjörnsson and R. van Zwol. Flickr tag recommendation based on collective knowledge. In *WWW '08*.

[30] Y. Song, Z. Zhuang, H. Li, Q. Zhao, J. Li, W.-C. Lee, and C. L. Giles. Real-time automatic tag recommendation. In *SIGIR '08*.

[31] J. Trant. Studying social tagging and folksonomy: A review and framework. *Journal of Digital Information*, 10(1), 2009.

[32] L. von Ahn and L. Dabbish. Designing games with a purpose. *Commun. ACM*, 51(8):58–67, 2008.

[33] J. Weng, E.-P. Lim, J. Jiang, and Q. He. Twitterrank: finding topic-sensitive influential twitterers. In *WSDM '10*.

[34] H. Xu, J. Wang, X.-S. Hua, and S. Li. Tag refinement by regularized lda. In *MM '09*.

[35] L. Yao, D. Mimno, and A. McCallum. Efficient methods for topic model inference on streaming document collections. In *KDD '09*.

Crowdsourcing for Book Search Evaluation: Impact of HIT Design on Comparative System Ranking

Gabriella Kazai[1] Jaap Kamps[2] Marijn Koolen[2] Natasa Milic-Frayling[1]

[1] Microsoft Research, Cambridge UK, {v-gabkaz,natasamf}@microsoft.com
[2] University of Amsterdam, The Netherlands, {kamps,m.h.a.koolen}@uva.nl

ABSTRACT

The evaluation of information retrieval (IR) systems over special collections, such as large book repositories, is out of reach of traditional methods that rely upon editorial relevance judgments. Increasingly, the use of *crowdsourcing* to collect relevance labels has been regarded as a viable alternative that scales with modest costs. However, crowdsourcing suffers from undesirable worker practices and low quality contributions. In this paper we investigate the design and implementation of effective crowdsourcing tasks in the context of book search evaluation. We observe the impact of aspects of the *Human Intelligence Task* (HIT) design on the quality of relevance labels provided by the crowd. We assess the output in terms of label agreement with a *gold standard* data set and observe the effect of the crowdsourced relevance judgments on the resulting system rankings. This enables us to observe the effect of crowdsourcing on the entire IR evaluation process. Using the test set and experimental runs from the INEX 2010 Book Track, we find that varying the HIT design, and the pooling and document ordering strategies leads to considerable differences in agreement with the gold set labels. We then observe the impact of the crowdsourced relevance label sets on the relative system rankings using four IR performance metrics. System rankings based on MAP and Bpref remain less affected by different label sets while the Precision@10 and nDCG@10 lead to dramatically different system rankings, especially for labels acquired from HITs with weaker quality controls. Overall, we find that crowdsourcing can be an effective tool for the evaluation of IR systems, provided that care is taken when designing the HITs.

Categories and Subject Descriptors: H.3.4 [**Information Storage and Retrieval**]: Systems and Software—*performance evaluation (efficiency and effectiveness)*

General Terms: Experimentation, Measurement, Performance

Keywords: Prove it, Crowdsourcing Quality, Book Search.

1. INTRODUCTION

The evaluation and tuning of Information Retrieval (IR) systems based on the Cranfield paradigm [4, 27] requires purpose-built test collections, at the heart of which lie the human judgments that indicate the relevance of search results to a set of queries. With the ever increasing size and diversity of both the document collections and the query sets, gathering relevance labels by traditional methods, i.e., from a select group of trained experts, has become increasingly challenging [9]. This issue is especially prevalent in specialized search domains such as academic papers or books, which can support a range of tailored search tasks but also present additional complexities in IR evaluation. A good illustration is the INEX Book Track [13] which aims to provide a test bed for the evaluation of book search systems. The track reports on a range of issues related to the gathering of relevance labels [12, 13], one of which is the sheer effort of reviewing whole books and rendering relevance judgments for pages across a large number of retrieved books. While the INEX book collection comprises only 50,000 books, the effort to judge a single topic is estimated at 33 days if the assessor spent 95 minutes a day judging pages on that topic alone [12]. This estimate is based on a relatively shallow pool of 200 books per topic. The issue of scale in collecting human assessments is even more evident in the case of large online repositories that store millions of digitized books such as the Million Books repository[1] and the Google Books Library[2].

Recently, *crowdsourcing* [8] has emerged as a feasible approach to gathering relevance data in the context of IR evaluations [1–3, 7, 11, 15]. As such, it promises to offer a solution to the scalability problem that hinders traditional approaches based on editorial judgments, which has been the cornerstone of the IR evaluation since its conception at Cranfield [4] over 50 years ago. In general, crowdsourcing is a method of outsourcing work through an open call for contributions from members of a *crowd*, who are invited to carry out *Human Intelligence Tasks* (HITs) in exchange for micropayments, social recognition, or entertainment value. Crowdsourcing platforms, such as CrowdFlower[3] or Amazon's Mechanical Turk (AMT)[4] service, enable the gathering of vast amounts of data, such as relevance labels, from a large population of workers within a short period of time and at a relatively low cost.

However, the use of crowdsourcing presents a radical departure from the controlled conditions in which editorial judgments are collected. Thus, its use needs to be carefully examined before it can effectively supplement or replace the traditional methods. Indeed, the literature on crowdsourcing points to the poor quality of the resulting data [16, 22, 23, 30], which is often attributed to sloppy or even malicious workers and suboptimal HIT design [6, 11, 28]. Although best practices are gradually evolving, e.g., providing guidelines for the use of crowdsourcing in relevance as-

[1] `http://www.ulib.org/`
[2] `http://books.google.com/`
[3] `http://crowdflower.com/`
[4] `http://www.mturk.com/`

SIGIR'11, July 24–28, 2011, Beijing, China.

sessments [1, 3, 10, 14], the issues of attracting the 'right' workers and controlling their engagement in the crowdsourcing tasks remain a challenge.

In this paper, we explore the effectiveness of various HIT designs as a means of controlling the crowd workers' engagement and, consequently, the quality of the resulting relevance labels and the reliability of the IR evaluation in terms of the relative system rankings. We use crowdsourcing to collect relevance judgments for book pages, imposing a considerable cognitive effort on the workers, and use the resulting labels to evaluate system performance on a *focused retrieval* task referred to as *Prove It* [13]. We study the elements of the crowdsourcing task design and tackle quality issues by incorporating a range of quality control methods. These include structured questionnaire flows using 'skip-logic' [18] and challenge-response tasks in the form of captchas adopted for digitized books [11]. We evaluate two different HIT designs, comparing how successful they are in motivating productive work behavior and examine the accuracy of the resulting relevance labels based on their agreement with the *gold standard* (GS) label set gathered from the participants of the INEX 2010 Book Track. Furthermore, we observe the relationship between the HIT designs, the label quality, and the resulting system rankings. The latter is motivated by the use of crowdsourcing as a means to an end, to scale up IR evaluation, the conclusions of which are based on the relative rankings of systems by given performance metrics. In our work we take the first step and observe how label accuracy impacts the IR system rankings, providing the basis for future work on quantifying the bias and uncertainty introduced by combining GS and crowd labels. We thus place the crowdsourcing of relevance labels within the larger context of IR evaluation.

We focus our investigation of HIT designs on three aspects: 1) quality control elements, 2) document pooling and sampling for relevance judgments by the crowd, and 3) document ordering within a HIT for presentation to the workers. More specifically, our experiments include two HIT designs, three pooling strategies, and two document ordering methods. Based on the analysis of the collected data, we provide insights on how design decisions influence both the raw label quality, i.e., agreement with GS, and the usefulness of crowdsourced relevance labels in IR evaluation, i.e., their impact on the system rankings. In particular, we study the implications of specific experimental conditions in order to answer the following research questions:

- What is the impact of quality control elements in the HIT design?
- What is the impact of the pooling strategy used to select pages to be judged?
- What is the impact of the ordering of pages in a HIT?
- What is the impact of consensus?
- What is the impact of selecting/rejecting workers based on agreement with the GS labels?

The rest of the paper is structured as follows. Section 2 discusses a use-case scenario for a large repository of scanned books: *Prove It*. We then review two possible strategies to evaluate the *Prove It* task: based on traditional editorial judgments and using crowdsourcing. We detail the design of a large-scale experiment in Section 3, aimed to study the effects of design decisions in crowdsourcing. Then, in Section 4, we analyze the impact of these mechanisms on the quality of the resulting relevance judgments and on the resulting system rankings for the official submissions to the INEX 2010 Book Track's *Prove It* task. Finally, in Section 5 we discuss our findings and draw conclusions.

2. BACKGROUND AND RELATED WORK

2.1 Prove It!

The INEX Book Track provides a forum for researchers to evaluate systems and methods for reading, searching, and navigating the contents of digitized books [13]. Among the IR scenarios supported by the track, since 2010, is the *Prove It* task which explores *focused retrieval* approaches in the context of book search. *Prove It* aims to investigate effective ways to retrieve relevant parts of books that can aid a user *in confirming or refuting a given factual claim*. This scenario is motivated by standard practices in academic authoring where authors use citations to refer to specific chapters or pages in other publications as evidence for an argument or a claim.

Reflecting the nature of the task, the topics of the INEX 2010 Book Track contain general knowledge factual claims. Using these topics, participating systems are required to retrieve and submit a ranked list of book pages per topic, estimated to provide information that can confirm or refute the topic claim or contain information that is related to the topic. Pages in the submitted runs are pooled and presented to assessors, the INEX participants, for relevance judgments using an online assessment system which enables users to browse, search, read and annotate books in the test collection [13]. Assessors are free to choose the topics they judge based on their expertise. For each topic, the system displays a list of books and, for each book, a list of pages compiled from the retrieval results of the participating IR systems. The books are ordered based on their rank positions and number of occurrences in the runs. As with the topics, assessors are free to choose which books to judge from the list. However, once inside a book, assessors are required to judge all listed pages. Assessors are also encouraged to discover further relevant pages, not included in the pools.

In this paper we us the *Prove It* task as the foundation for formulating the crowdsourcing tasks, implementing the crowdsourcing experiments, and analyzing the impact that aspects of the task design have on the evaluation of IR systems.

2.2 Evaluation Strategies

2.2.1 Traditional Editorial Judgments

The standard IR evaluation approach is based on the Cranfield paradigm [4] as adopted by the TREC [27] and other IR forums. This practice relies on test collections built under controlled conditions, consisting a set of documents, topics, and relevance judgments identifying which of the documents are relevant for a topic. The relevance judgments over the set of documents, selected by a given pooling method from the search results of individual systems, are made by (multiple) assessors following precise guidelines [27]. Studies of TREC systems evaluations have shown that relevance assessments are subjective in nature, leading to pairwise agreement levels of 70–80% on average between TREC assessors with high variability across topics [27, p.44]. The evaluation of systems under such variability of assessors and topics requires the use of a large set of topics and the comparison of system rankings under the exact same conditions on the same test collection. This is illustrated by several studies that replicated TREC relevance assessments with different judges [5] and found a significant disagreement on the relevance labels but considerable agreement on the resulting system rankings. Voorhees [26] also explored the impact of variations in relevance judgments on the system rankings. The use of pooling seems an important factor in the relative stability of system rankings, as even a set of randomly selected and labeled documents, assuming a good quality pool with relatively many relevant documents, can lead to a considerable correlation with a system ranking based on the editorial judgments [24].

Recently, there have been concerted efforts to find alternatives to explicit relevance judgments and infer relevance from the user's interaction with the system and the displayed content, e.g., from clicks on search results and hyperlinked pages. Although these approaches show reasonable levels of agreement with explicit judgments [21], it is still uncertain whether they can replace the traditional test collections with editorial relevance labels [9].

2.2.2 *Crowdsourcing*

The popularity and adoption of crowdsourcing have significantly increased with the emergence of widely accessible crowdsourcing platforms on the Internet. This has lowered the barrier for coordinating crowd workers to solve complex problems or engage in tasks that cannot be successfully completed without human intervention. Crowdsourcing has proven particularly useful for labeling large data sets such as acquiring image annotations and relevance assessments for search results [3, 7, 17, 29]. Among the successful examples to harness human resources on the Internet is the ESP game [25], which resulted in a large collection of labeled images by providing entertainment as the main value to its participants. An alternative approach to crowdsourcing is a low cost employment of workers as *mechanized labor* [20]. Crowdsourcing platforms, such as AMT, apply such a micro-payment job market model. Workers can select among a wide range of human intelligence tasks (HITs) that, usually, can be completed quickly for small financial rewards.

While popular, crowdsourcing is increasingly criticized for its poor output quality [16, 23, 30]. Indeed, quality assurance has surfaced as a major challenge and research topic in crowdsourcing [11, 15, 28]. Among main factors contributing to the suboptimal output are (1) workers' dishonest and careless behavior [6] and (2) poor task designs by the task requesters [7, 14]. Clearly, workers motivated by financial gains may aim to complete as many HITs as possible within a given time, which may reflect negatively on the quality of their work. Hence, it is important to devise methods for deterring dishonest and careless workers and detecting suboptimal output among completed tasks. By the same token, conscientious workers who are faced with an ambiguous task or inappropriate HIT design may produce work of inferior quality despite their best intentions. Thus, it is important to understand the principles of good HIT design.

Among quality control methods are tools of defensive task design, such as employing multi-level reviews of workers and leveraging reputation systems [20]. Other such tools include the use of trap questions [30], qualifying questions [6], gold standard data for which agreement can be measured [14, 15, 23], timing controls [10], and challenge-response tests (*captcha*) [11]. A common approach to correcting for unreliable workers is to build redundancy into the task design [20] and collect labels for the same item from different workers and aggregate them by applying a majority or consensus rule [22, 28]. Further steps involve analyzing the individual workers' output for consistency relative to both the label quality and the output of other workers. For example, Sheng et al. [22] model annotators' quality and show that repeated and selective labeling increases the overall quality of the output. Whitehill et al. [29] extend this work by considering the difficulty of the task and the ability of the annotators. Welinder et al. [28] combine both label and annotator quality in a generative Bayesian model.

All the above approaches use quality metrics that are directly focused on the crowdsourced data, such as the label accuracy relative to the GS labels. An exception is the work by Nowak and Rüger [17] who observe the effects of crowdsourced data on the comparative evaluation of systems for concept detection in images. Their study, on a set of 99 images, shows a high level of agreement between the system ranking based on "expert" labels and the ranking based on crowdsourced labels for 53 concepts.

In our research we take a dual approach and consider both the accuracy of the crowdsourced labels and their impact on the system performance rankings in an IR task with informational topics and relevance judgments, at the scale of an IR test collection. Moreover, by varying aspects of the HIT design, we observe the effects of labels from worker groups that are subject to different control mechanisms and thus exhibit different behaviors which may then be associated with different levels of trustworthiness.

3. APPROACH

In this section, we discuss our methodology for investigating the effectiveness of various aspects of HIT design as reflected in the resulting crowdsourced label accuracy and the ranking of IR systems. We devise experiments with different document pooling and ordering strategies and different sets of quality control mechanisms used to direct workers towards effective work practices and to deter dishonest workers. We hypothesize that different HIT designs lead to workers engagements at different levels of trustworthiness. Thus, varying the HIT designs enables us to observe how system rankings differ when we apply relevance labels from workers that are deemed more reliable based on higher accuracy of their labels and participation in more controlled HIT designs.

We use the problem of collecting relevance judgments for the INEX *Prove It* task as a motivation of the HITs for the workers.

3.1 Experiment Data

The data used in our experiments consists of the books, search topics, official runs, and relevance judgments provided by the INEX 2010 Book Track. The corpus comprises 50,239 out-of-copyright books, containing over 17 million pages and amounting to 400GB. There are 15 Best Books runs[5] and 10 *Prove It* runs that were submitted to INEX 2010. Best Books run contain up to 100 books per topic, ranked in the order of estimated relevance. Each *Prove It* run contains a ranked list of up to 1,000 book pages per topic.

From the 83 *Prove It* topics in the 2010 test set, each containing a general knowledge factual claim, 29 topics were assessed by INEX participants. After removing topics with less than 10 known relevant pages, we arrive at the final set of 21 topics with an average of 169 judged pages per topic (total of 3,557 judged pages). This set comprises the GS data set in our experiments. The assigned relevance labels can take one of four values: 3 if the judged page contains information that *confirms* some aspect of the topic claim, 2 if the page contains information that *refutes* some aspect of the claim, 1 if the page contains information that relates to the claim but does not confirm nor refutes the claim explicitly, or 0 if the page is irrelevant. We use 'relevant' to mean labels in $\{1, 2, 3\}$.

3.2 Experiment Design

3.2.1 *Pooling Strategy*

In order to create the pools of book pages for relevance assessment in our HITs, we sample pages from the 10 *Prove It* runs submitted to INEX 2010. We experiment with three pooling strategies, including two approaches to boost the distribution of potentially relevant book pages in the assessment pool. Ensuring that more relevant documents are included has two benefits: it improves the cost effectiveness of obtaining complete relevance judgments for

[5] Ad hoc retrieval of whole books

the collection and improves the experience of the judges by reducing the number of non-relevant documents presented to them.

Top-n pool: We prepare an assessment pool of book pages following a standard top-n round-robin approach [19] to fill a fixed pool size of 100 pages from the *Prove It* runs, removing duplicates in the process.

Rank-boosted pool: We re-rank pages in the *Prove It* runs based on the book's highest rank and *popularity* across all the Best Books and the *Prove It* runs, i.e., the number of runs in which the book containing the page occurs. For *Prove It* runs we determine a book' rank based on the highest ranking page from that book. We order books with the same rank score based on their popularity score. Since in the *Prove It* task, multiple pages from the same book may be returned, they receive additional boost. This is the same method that was used at the INEX Book Track [13].

Answer-boosted pool: We re-rank pages in the *Prove It* runs based on their content similarity to the topic. We employ a simple similarity function based on coordination level or cohort matching to compute the scores and rank individual pages in this pool. We match the terms in the topic claim after removing stopwords and terms occurring in the query and the subject statement parts of the topic.

In the final step, we allocate 9 of the 10 pages per HIT by interleaving the three pooling strategies. This enables us to increase pool diversity and study the effects of pooling in our experiments. Our approach is similar to the interleaving strategies used by Radlinski et al. [21] in the Web context.

Although some overlap already exists between the resulting pools and the GS set due to the above sampling methods, we add to each HIT an additional page with known confirm/refute label (label 2 or 3). Thus, a single HIT of 10 pages includes at least 1 page with a known label, and up to 9 pages sampled from the three interleaved pooling methods. This results into 2,100 pages to be judged by crowd workers: 100 pages per topic with, roughly, 30 unique pages from each pooling method and additional pages with known labels purposely added to the HITs. Pooled pages included in a HIT are unique, but the known relevant page may be repeated across HITs. This leads to the total of 1,918 unique topic-book-page combinations: about 91 pages per 21 topics, covering 759 unique topic-book combinations, i.e., around 36 books per topic. Out of 10 pages per HIT there are, on average, 4.5 pages with a known label among which half, i.e., 2.2 are relevant pages with a known label.

3.2.2 Document Ordering

The study by Le et al. [15] shows that the distribution of relevant documents presented to workers during training affects their behavior later on: workers learn the distribution patterns and apply them in their judgments. Thus, we are interested in whether the ordering of book pages affects the resulting label accuracy and the system rankings. Unlike [15], we do not reveal the ground truth labels to the workers. Nevertheless, it stands to reason that having a relevant page at the top rank of each HIT may bias workers' relevance judgments, creating the expectation that the top document is always relevant. However, since the first page in a HIT may receive more attention by workers, using the first page to filter out dishonest or careless workers may be less effective. In order to study the impact of ordering, we consider two cases:

Biased order: We construct the HITs by preserving the order of pages produced by a given pooling approach, so based on decreasing expected relevance, and by inserting the known relevant page at the first position in the HIT.

Random order: We construct the HITs by first inserting the known relevant pages at any position in the HITs and then randomly distributing pages brought in by the different pooling strategies.

3.2.3 HIT Design and Quality Control

As discussed in Section 2.2.2, quality control is of paramount importance in crowdsourcing. In the context of the *Prove It* task, providing relevance judgments requires workers to (1) read and understand the claim that needs to be confirmed or refuted, (2) read the book page text, (3) identify relevant content, (4) make an inference, and (5) assign the appropriate relevance label from multiple possible labels. A worker's output is likely to be suboptimal if the worker fails to perform well any of the task stages. Thus, we need to devise control mechanisms that verify the proper worker engagement in each stage of the task in order to reduce careless behavior, including the extreme cases of dishonest workers' behavior. In our experiments, we build on established and emerging best practices in crowdsourcing [1, 6, 11, 14] and devise two types of HITs with different sets of quality control mechanisms.

Full design (FullD): This design, see Figure 1, controls all the stages of the task and explicitly pre-qualifies workers, restricting participation to those who completed over 100 HITs at a 95+% approval rate. Following experience that HIT titles influence workers' attention [7], in order to attract workers interested in a given topic, we group FullD HITs into 21 topic-specific batches, and include topic details in the title, description, and the keywords associated with the HITs. With the aim to deter sloppy workers, we explicitly warn workers that at least 60% of their labels need to agree with expert-provided labels in order to qualify for payment. As trap questions are useful for detecting careless workers who miss to read instructions [6], we include two simple trap questions: "Please tick here if you did NOT read the instructions" at the top of the form, and "I did not pay attention" as a relevance label option for each page. To test if workers have read and understood the factual claim for which they are to judge the book pages in the HIT, we ask qualifying questions for which a worker can either find the answer in the claim or respond based on their knowledge of the subject matter. To reduce the effectiveness of random clicking, we devised a structured series of questions based on skip-logic (Flow) to lead the worker through the assignment of relevance labels. The flow of question is such that answering the next question is dependent on the answer given to the previous question. Since only certain combinations of answers make sense, we can use this mechanism to detect careless or random responses. Captcha is commonly used to detect human input in online forms. We adopt it as a way to force workers to perform specific actions, e.g., read the content of a book page, and to verify that the action was indeed completed. For example, we ask workers to enter the first word of the sentence that confirms or refutes the claim. We include a captcha in each possible path of the Flow.

Simple design (SimpleD): This design includes a smaller number of quality control mechanisms and does not impose restrictions on the workers who can participate. Unlike the FullD version, all HITs are packaged into a single batch, using the same generic HIT title, description and keywords. The design includes only one trap question to control for random assignment of relevance labels. No qualifying test is included to check if workers are familiar with the claim. No warning is displayed to workers about the expected quality of their labels. Finally, no captcha is used in this design, also simplifying the structure of the Flow questions from the FullD version, i.e., question D reduces to multiple choice and E is removed.

Common to both designs is that in all the HITs we include pages with known relevance labels. We have the same number of pages with GS labels in both FullD and SimpleD tasks.

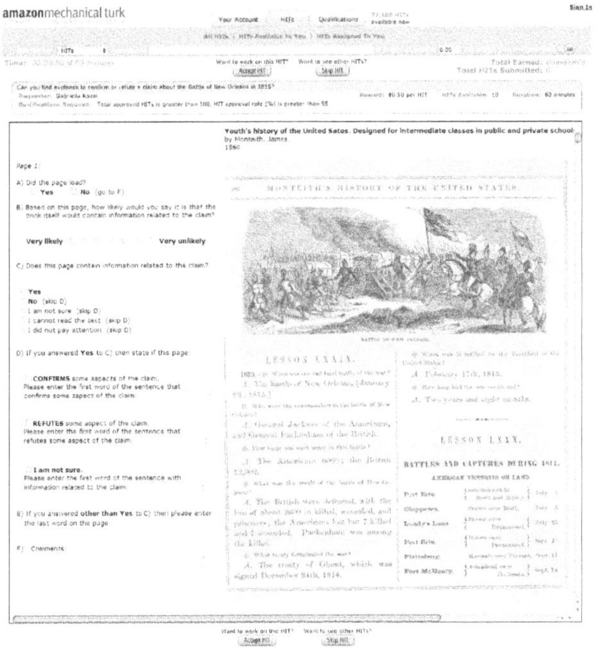

Figure 1: Part of a HIT showing question series to solicit relevance labels for book pages from workers on AMT: Full design.

While pay is an important influencer on workers' participation in AMT [16], in our experiments we aim to keep the pay per unit of effort constant across the designs. Based on our estimate that a FullD HIT requires twice the effort, in terms of time needed to complete, as a SimpleD HIT, we set payment at \$.50 for FullD HITs and \$.25 for SimpleD HITs, each comprising the relevance assessments of 10 pages.

3.2.4 Experiment Grid

Our goal is to investigate the effectiveness of crowdsourcing as we vary the pooling strategy and page ordering on one side and the quality assurance mechanisms that control the workers' engagement on the other. We create four batches of HIT experiments, see Table 1: 1) FullD-bias: Full design with biased ordering of pages; 2) FullD-rand: Full design with random ordering; 3) SimpleD-bias: Simple design with biased ordering; 4) SimpleD-rand: Simple design with random ordering. The interleaved pooling strategy is common across the experiments. We split the topic set between the biased and random batches for the FullD (10 and 11 topics, resp.), but run all 21 topics in the SimpleD task for both page orderings. For each FullD HIT we collect labels from three workers while for the SimpleD HITs we limit to one worker per ordering condition. Thus, we collect two and three labels per page for all 21 topics in SimpleD and FullD, respectively.

3.2.5 Measures

In order to assess the quality of the crowdsourced labels, CS, we rely upon the agreement of the labels with the GS assessments provided by the INEX 2010 Book Track, $GS = \{3,2,1,0\}$. We introduce two measures:

- *Exact Agreement (EA)*: Agreement on the exact degree of relevance, i.e., $CS = GS$,
- *Binary Agreement (BA)*: Either the page is non-relevant ($CS = 0$ and $GS = 0$) or relevant ($CS > 0$ and $GS > 0$) to the topic of the claim.

To investigate the impact on system rankings, we create test collections (qrels) from the sets of labels obtained from the different crowdsourcing experiments and evaluate the *Prove It* runs using standard metrics, e.g., mean average precision (MAP). We compare the resulting system rankings with the system ranking derived using the GS set as our test collection. In our experiment setup, a high correlation between system rankings based on the GS qrel and the qrels derived from the crowdsourced labels over the documents in the rank-boosted pool would mean that crowdsourcing leads to a comparable IR evaluation outcome as traditional methods.

4. ANALYSIS AND DISCUSSION

In this section we analyze the experimental results in two stages. We first observe the label accuracy against the gold set to understand how aspects of the HIT design can affect the accuracy of the crowdsourced labels. In the second stage we consider the comparative system rankings resulting from the crowdsourced relevance judgments, and look at the impact of the HIT design on the resulting test collections.

4.1 Impact on Label Accuracy

4.1.1 Impact of Quality Controls

Table 2 provides statistics on the number and the accuracy of relevance labels obtained under the different experiment conditions. We see that the FullD HITs yield considerably more labels per HIT and per worker than SimpleD (8.72 vs. 7.97 per HIT, and 45 vs. 40 per worker). In addition, the collected labels agree significantly more with the GS labels than those from the SimpleD HITs for both BA and EA measures (e.g., BA is 69% vs. 54% per HIT, and 67% vs. 51% per worker). This is further confirmed in Figure 2, showing the probability density distribution of workers across different agreement levels with the GS labels. We note a striking difference between the FullD and SimpleD HIT designs. The FullD HITs attract workers who achieve significantly higher agreement levels with the GS labels. We, thus, conclude that various aspects of the FullD design, from more informative HIT titles to flow questionnaires, induce more desirable behavior and more trustworthy workers' engagements. This is reflected in the significantly higher percentage of responses to the flow questions (Flow) for workers in FullD than in SimpleD (e.g., 79% vs. 67%), see Table 2.

4.1.2 Refining Relevance Labels

Consolidating multiple relevance judgments. Across HITs, we collected multiple labels per page, with the aim to mitigate possible noise from careless or dishonest workers by establishing internal agreement among workers through a majority vote. Thus, for every page with multiple relevance judgments, we determine the most popular label and, in case of a tie, keep the label with the lowest value among {3-confirms, 2- refutes, 1-relevant, and 0-irrelevant}. Other choices, such as keeping the label with the highest value or a random one, resulted in very similar outcomes.

As before, we use EA and BA to measure the accuracy of the resulting labels. It transpires that the FullD majority vote labels achieve 74% EA and 78% BA accuracy levels with the GS labels. This is significantly higher than the SimpleD majority vote labels with 61% EA and 68% BA levels. We note that these statistics are substantially higher than the mean agreement per HIT in Table 2: 62% EA and 69% BA for FullD and 44% EA and 54% BA for SimpleD.

It is interesting to note that the accuracy of SimpleD labels is improved by the majority rule substantially more than for the FullD design. Furthermore, the accuracy of the consolidated labels of the

Table 1: Batches of HITs with different task parameter settings

Batch	HIT Design	Ordering	#Topics	#Workers per HIT	Total cost (incl. Amazon's 10% commission)
FullD-bias	Full design	Biased	10	3	(10 x 10 x 3 x \$.50 x 1.10)=\$165.00
FullD-rand	Full design	Random	11	3	(11 x 10 x 3 x \$.50 x 1.10)=\$181.50
SimpleD-bias	Simple design	Biased	21	1	(21 x 10 x 1 x \$.25 x 1.10)=\$57.75
SimpleD-rand	Simple design	Random	21	1	(21 x 10 x 1 x \$.25 x 1.10)=\$57.75

Table 2: Statistics per HIT (top) and Worker (bottom) over the batches and designs: number of completed HITs/number of unique workers; the total worker time in seconds; the total number of relevance labels; the exact (EA) and binary agreement (BA) over the GS labels; the fraction of pages respecting the questionnaire flow; and the fraction of pages with a captcha (FullD only). We test for significant differences between pairs of subsets using a two sample t-test (two-tailed, † for $p < 0.05$ and ‡ for $p < 0.01$)

Subset	# HITs or # Workers	Worker Time (s) mean	Worker Time (s) sd	#Labels mean	#Labels sd	%EA mean	%EA sd	%BA mean	%BA sd	%Flow mean	%Flow sd	%Captcha mean	%Captcha sd
FullD	630	876‡	645	8.72‡	2.46	0.62‡	0.32	0.69‡	0.32	0.85‡	0.25	0.26	0.20
SimpleD	420	395‡	432	7.97‡	2.97	0.44‡	0.34	0.54‡	0.33	0.75‡	0.31	–	–
FullD-bias	300	904	674	8.55	2.60	0.60	0.35	0.65‡	0.35	0.83	0.26	0.21‡	0.19
FullD-rand	330	851	618	8.88	2.32	0.65	0.29	0.73‡	0.28	0.86	0.23	0.30‡	0.21
SimpleD-bias	210	394	522	7.71	3.57	0.41	0.34	0.49‡	0.35	0.72	0.36	–	–
SimpleD-rand	210	396	317	8.23	2.19	0.48	0.33	0.58‡	0.31	0.77	0.25	–	–
All	1050	684	616	8.42	2.70	0.55	0.34	0.63	0.33	0.81	0.28	–	–
FullD	121	4562‡	7512	45.41	81.11	0.62‡	0.27	0.67‡	0.28	0.79‡	0.26	0.25	0.19
SimpleD	84	1976‡	2678	39.85	104.91	0.40‡	0.32	0.51‡	0.32	0.67‡	0.32	–	–
FullD-bias	70	3873	4539	36.68	50.38	0.62	0.27	0.66	0.27	0.81	0.23	0.20‡	0.15
FullD-rand	86	3265	4849	34.08	52.24	0.63	0.26	0.69	0.27	0.80	0.26	0.30‡	0.20
SimpleD-bias	42	1972	2849	38.59	130.75	0.36	0.35	0.45	0.33	0.59†	0.34	–	–
SimpleD-rand	45	1847	2298	38.38	69.29	0.45	0.29	0.58	0.30	0.75†	0.26	–	–
All	194	3700	7100	45.56	100.13	0.53	0.31	0.60	0.30	0.74	0.29	–	–

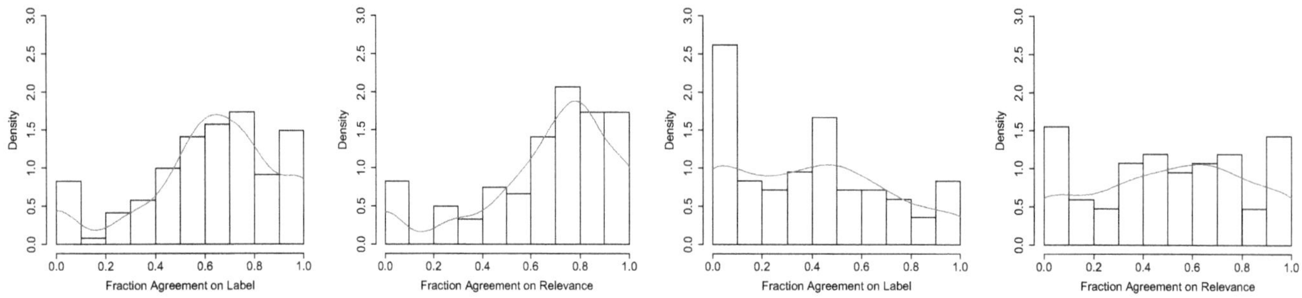

(a) Full Design (EA) (b) Full Design (BA) (c) Simple Design (EA) (d) Simple Design (BA)

Figure 2: Distribution of workers over agreement as histogram and probability density function.

SimpleD HITs almost reaches the average accuracy of the FullD HITs with a single label assignment. This suggests that there might be a cost trade-off that favors the use of simple HITs with multiple labels over the complex HITs with a single label collection. On the other hand, the effectiveness of majority rule is a function of not only the number of labelers but their individual labeling quality [22], which is higher in the FullD HITs. Overall, by collecting multiple relevance labels per page and applying majority voting, we arrive at a highly accurate set of crowdsourced labels.

Removing workers with low label accuracy. In Figure 3 we simulate the effect of rejecting workers below a given level of accuracy over the GS labels. We plot the agreement level for the resulting majority vote labels and show how filtering out workers with low accuracy labels increases the GS agreement for the remaining labels. Essentially, the agreement stays unchanged until the minimal accuracy of the workers reaches 40%. Note that substantially more workers are removed for SimpleD than FullD during this process, see Figure 2. Overall, we see that consensus is an effective way of eliminating potentially suboptimal contributions of low quality workers.

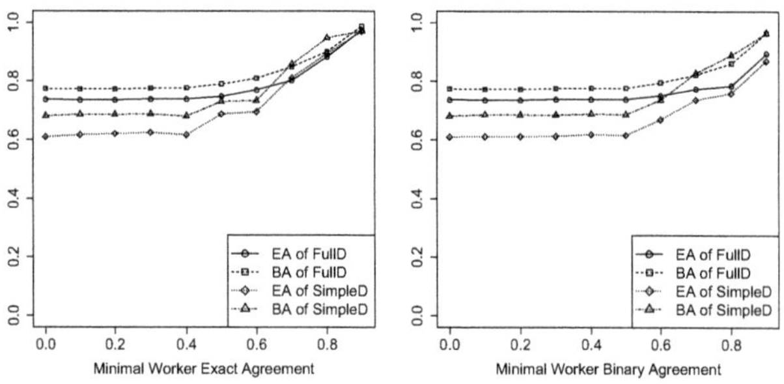

Figure 3: Agreement of majority vote label with the GS labels, after removing workers below n% exact agreement (left) or binary agreement (right).

Table 3: Exact (EA) and binary (BA) agreement across different pooling strategies

Subset	rank-boost		top-n-pages		answer-boost	
	EA	BA	EA	BA	EA	BA
FullD	0.73	0.77	0.74	0.79	0.70	0.77
SimpleD	0.62	0.69	0.56	0.65	0.58	0.68
All	0.75	0.79	0.73	0.80	0.74	0.85

Table 4: Unique pages and unique relevant pages assessed in HITs of different designs

Subset	Pages	rank-boost		top-n-pages		answer-boost	
		Uniq	Rel	Uniq	Rel	Uniq	Rel
FullD	1873	489	66	506	41	554	161
SimpleD	1816	473	168	489	131	531	202
All	1892	489	82	511	56	563	172

4.1.3 *Impact of Pooling and Ordering Strategies*

Comparing the impact of the biased and random order of pages in the FullD and SimpleD (shown in Table 2), we see a higher accuracy of labels for the random order of pages (significantly higher for BA over HITs using two sampled t-test with $p < 0.05$). This suggests that the ranking pattern of relevant pages influences the crowd workers' behavior, even when the known labels of these pages are not revealed (as it was in the study by Le et al. [15]). There were two differences between the ordering strategies. The biased order HITs always start with a page that is relevant according to the GS, which is useful for priming workers. The biased order HITs were extracted in pooling order leading to a decreasing number of relevant pages per HITs. This variation leads to "unexpected" distributions of labels per HIT, ranging from all relevant to only 1 relevant page, which may influence workers' judgments rating less relevant pages as non-relevant, or workers looking for plausible patterns in the label distribution.

Since all the HITs were created by interleaving pages from three different pools, we can consider the accuracy of crowdsourced labels per individual pools. We restrict our attention to the pages that occur among the top 100 pages in the pool. Table 3 shows no substantial difference between label accuracy levels for the three pooling strategies, which could be expected since workers are unaware of the origin of a page. Table 4 shows the number of unique pages contributed by each pooling strategy and the number of relevant pages with labels obtained through majority voting. The number of unique pages from each pool is comparable. The answer-boost pooling leads to the highest number of unique and relevant pages, with a relatively high fraction of the unique pages judged relevant.

4.1.4 *Factors Impacting Accuracy*

The use of GS labels to measure the accuracy of the HITs output and infer the trustworthiness of the workers implies that a substantial effort is spent on the redundant assessment of pages with known relevance labels. Thus, it is of interest to identify other factors that are predictive of the label accuracy.

Table 5 shows the Pearson correlations between the label accuracy, in terms of the exact agreement (EA) with the GS labels, and several characteristics of the crowdsourcing engagement observed in the experiments. Correlations with the binary agreement (BA) are very similar and thus not shown.

We note that the total number of HITs completed by a worker provides no clues about the level of label accuracy ($r = 0.04$). Similarly the average time spent on a HIT is only weakly correlated with accuracy. However, the correlation between the EA and the number of labels produced by the workers ($r = 0.63$) is rather strong, indicating that dishonest and careless workers tend to skip parts of the HITs. As shown in Table 2, that happens significantly more often with the SimpleD HITs than with the FullD. The structure of the flow questionnaires (Flow) has a similarly high correlation with the EA accuracy ($r = 0.65$), implying that workers who respect dependencies among questions provide accurate labels. Interestingly, the captchas that were part of the FullD only, correlates less strongly with the EA. In fact, captchas were filled out only in 26% of the FullD HITs, see in Table 2. We speculate that their frequency and placement in the HIT design is suboptimal and require modifications. Overall, amongst the HIT factors, the completion of the flow questionnaires seems to be the best predictor of the produced label quality. That is expected since, by design, they prevent missing labels and ensure that appropriate logic is applied during label assignments. The latter is hard to mimic by random clicking and careless filling of the HIT forms.

Table 5: Pearson correlations between the label accuracy, in terms of exact agreement (EA) with GS labels, and HIT characteristics: the number of HITs per worker; the average time spent per HIT; the fraction of acquired relevance labels; the fraction of HITs with completed questionnaire flow; and the fraction of filled-in captchas (t-test, two-tailed, † for $p < 0.05$ and ‡ for $p < 0.01$).

Subset	#HITs	Time	Labels	Flow	Captcha
FullD	0.01	0.17	0.72‡	0.71‡	0.29‡
SimpleD	0.06	0.26†	0.55‡	0.57‡	–
FullD-bias	-0.06	0.04	0.64‡	0.65‡	0.30†
FullD-rand	0.03	0.20	0.71‡	0.68‡	0.33‡
SimpleD-bias	0.05	0.29	0.51‡	0.51‡	–
SimpleD-rand	0.05	0.31†	0.55‡	0.62‡	–
All	0.04	0.30‡	0.63‡	0.65‡	–

4.2 Impact on System Rankings

The above analysis shows that differences in the HIT design can lead to considerable variations in the label accuracy. FullD HITs which incorporate multiple control mechanisms to encourage productive worker engagements led to a high label accuracy over the GS set. This suggests that the output of the FullD HITs could be considered more trustworthy than the output of the SimpleD HITs.

We now explore how the use of crowdsourced labels affects the IR system ranking. To each set of labels we apply the majority rule and create a set of relevance judgments, *qrels*, to evaluate and rank the official submissions of the *Prove It* task, performed as part of the INEX 2010 Book Track. We use four performance metrics: MAP, Bpref, P@10, and nDCG@10. MAP and Bpref characterize the overall ranking and their comparison provides insights into the impact of un-judged pages. P@10 and nDCG@10 focus on the search performance in the top 10 retrieved pages. We apply nDCG measure by considering pages labeled 'relevant' as grade 1 and pages labeled 'refutes' and 'confirms' as grade 2. We refer to the system ranking based on the GS labels as the *INEX ranking* and measure its correlation with the rankings generated by other qrels using the Kendall's tau coefficient.

4.2.1 *Quality Control*

In Table 6 we summarize the correlations between the INEX ranking and the rankings based on the qrels from the crowdsourced labels. We note that document sets judged in HITs may be different from the GS documents. Thus, the observed ranking correlations are computed over different document samples in some instances.

Table 6: System rank correlation between the different designs

$Qrels_1$	$Qrels_2$	MAP	Bpref	P@10	nDCG@10
INEX	FullD	0.76	0.45	0.85	0.73
INEX	SimpleD	0.96	0.87	0.34	0.02
FullD	SimpleD	0.81	0.36	0.32	-0.16

Table 7: Impact of biased and random page order on system rank correlations with INEX ranking

Qrels	MAP	Bpref	P@10	nDCG@10
FullD-bias	0.76	0.20	0.62	0.51
FullD-rand	0.78	0.63	0.93	0.81
SimpleD-bias	0.96	0.78	0.16	-0.20
SimpleD-rand	0.94	0.82	0.44	0.24

We observe a relatively high agreement between the FullD ranking and the INEX ranking across all metrics. The SimpleD and INEX rankings based on MAP and Bpref also correlate well (τ of 0.96 and 0.87, respectively), while the P@10 and nDCG@10 lead to poor correlations (τ of 0.34 and 0.02, respectively). In fact, the correlation of INEX and the SimpleD rankings on MAP is remarkably high (τ of 0.96), higher than for the FullD (τ of 0.76). From the distribution of the 'relevant' label across the HITs, we find SimpleD workers to be more lenient, classifying 37% of the judged pages as relevant. On the other hand, the FullD workers regarded only 23% of them as relevant. Since all the HITs involve documents pooled from the results of the participating systems, this observation is in accord with the findings by Soboroff et al. [24]. They noted that by selecting a random set of documents from a high quality pool and treating them as "pseudo-relevant" leads to system ranking that is well correlated with the GS ranking based on MAP.

Comparing the effect of FullD and SimpleD qrels, we see that the system rankings based on P@10 and nDCG@10 disagree considerably and show low correlation for Bpref.

Overall, while the difference in MAP and Bpref indicate some discrepancy in the rankings, the P@10 and the nDCG@10 metrics more strongly differentiate the effects of the two HIT designs on the resulting system rankings, based on the qrels from the SimpleD HITs and the more trusted FullD HITs. The difference due to the lower reliability labels are primarily detected through metrics that focus on the top ranked pages.

4.2.2 *Removing Workers with Low Accuracy*

Earlier, we observed a considerable variation in label accuracy across workers. However, we also saw that removing workers with low accuracy had little effect on the overall accuracy of the majority vote labels. In Figure 4 we show the impact that incrementally filtering out low accuracy workers has on the correlation with the INEX ranking. For FullD we observe the convergence of the resulting system rankings towards the INEX ranking as workers with lower EA or BA are removed. In the case of SimpleD, the trend seems to be opposite. We attribute this to the weakening of the pooling effect as the number of relevant documents is reduced [24].

4.2.3 *Impact of Pooling and Ordering Strategies*

We found that random ordering of documents in the HITs yields higher levels of label accuracy compared to the biased ordering. In Table 7 we show the impact that this has on the system rankings. Overall, the qrels obtained from HITs with random document ordering lead to higher correlation with the INEX ranking.

Finally, we observe the influence that the three pooling strategies have on the system rankings. From Table 8 we see that the rank-

Table 8: Impact of pooling strategy on system rank correlations with INEX ranking

Qrels	MAP	Bpref	P@10	nDCG@10
FullD rank-boost	0.94	0.90	0.91	0.87
FullD top-n-pages	0.89	0.85	0.76	0.82
FullD answer-boost	0.72	0.72	0.59	0.51
SimpleD rank-boost	0.94	0.78	0.88	0.78
SimpleD top-n-pages	0.84	0.47	0.33	0.16
SimpleD answer-boost	0.81	0.64	0.44	0.47

Table 9: System rank correlations with INEX ranking over official submissions (top) and extended set (bottom)

Qrels	MAP	Bpref	P@10	nDCG@10
FullD	0.76	0.45	0.85	0.73
FullD rank-boost	0.94	0.90	0.91	0.87
GS+FullD	0.90	0.73	0.92	0.82
GS+FullD rank-boost	0.96	1.00	0.91	0.82
FullD	0.80	0.34	0.17	0.12
FullD rank-boost	0.90	0.82	0.72	0.71
GS+FullD	0.89	0.63	0.85	0.72
GS+FullD rank-boost	0.92	0.69	0.80	0.84

boosted pool leads to very high correlations with the INEX ranking based on MAP for both the FullD and SimpleD qrels (τ of 0.94). For FullD this is also the case for the Bpref (0.90) and P@10 (0.91) metrics (and to a lesser extent for P@10 with τ of 0.87). Since the GS sample of documents is selected based on the same rank-boosted pooling strategy, these qrels have the highest overlap with the INEX qrels. Thus, the high correlation of system rankings suggests that the qrels comprising crowdsourced labels essentially lead to the same performance evaluation as the GS labels. We note that the more trusted relevance judgments from the FullD HITs lead to higher correlations with the INEX ranking across all the pooling strategies. From Table 4 we learnt that a substantial number of unique relevant pages are brought in by the top-n and answer-boost pools, explaining the increased divergence with the INEX ranking.

4.3 Evaluation of Prove It Systems

Crowdsourcing has a potential to improve evaluation of IR systems by scaling up relevance assessments and creating test collections with more complete judgments. However, as we employ crowd workers, we introduce uncertainty about the quality of the relevance labels. Our experiments were designed to investigate ways of using crowdsourcing to acquire reliable labels for a large portion of the test collection in order to approach the true system ranking based on complete relevance judgments by trusted judges.

In this section we investigate the use of the crowdsourced qrels to evaluate the *Prove It* runs of the INEX 2010 Book Track. We focus on the FullD HIT design where the tighter controls over the crowd engagement led to contributions from more trustworthy workers, with higher label accuracy. We conduct system evaluation (1) with qrels from FullD HITs only and (2) by merging FullD qrels with the GS qrels[6], expanding the GS with reliable labels. We also increase the set of 10 official submissions for the *Prove It* task with variants of the runs generated by re-ranking the retrieved pages based on the rank-boosting method.

Table 9 shows the correlations with the INEX ranking for the 10 official runs and the extended set of 20 runs. We evaluated systems

[6]We merge the qrels where we treat a page as relevant (or confirming/refuting a fact) whenever the INEX judge or the FullD majority vote says so.

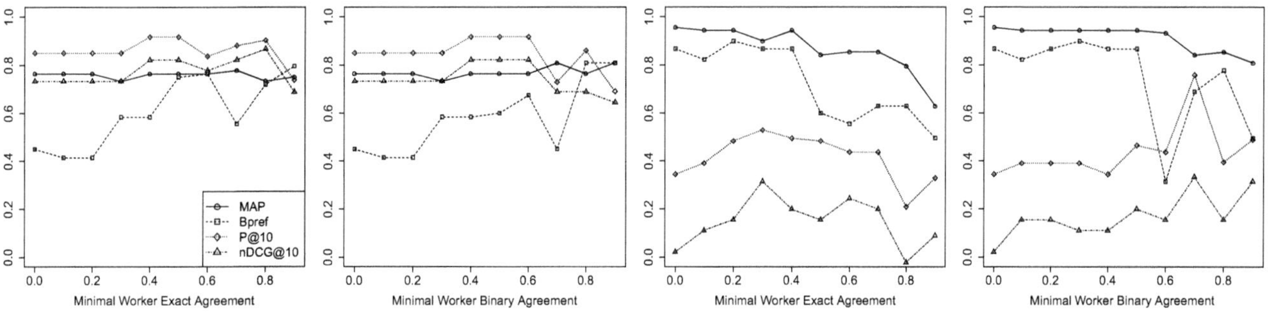

(a) Full Design (EA) (b) Full Design (BA) (c) Simple Design (EA) (d) Simple Design (BA)

Figure 4: System rank correlation with INEX ranking after removing workers below n% exact or binary agreement.

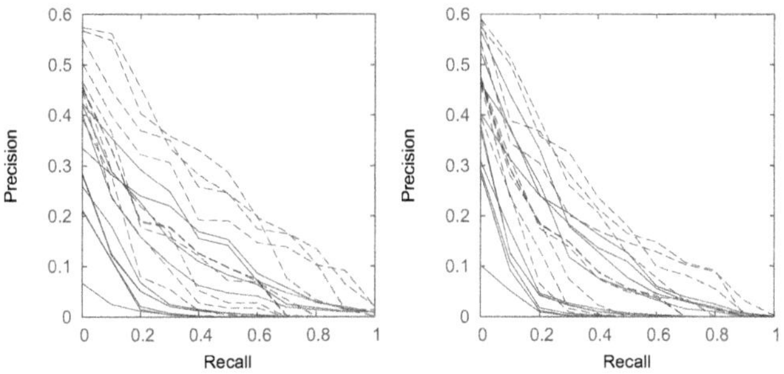

Figure 5: Interpolated precision over recall for the extended set of runs: gold set labels (left) and INEX+FullD labels (right).

using the FullD qrels and with its subset comprising pages from the rank-boosted pool only. As we saw before, the FullD qrels lead to slightly different system rankings from the INEX ranking since, by design, the crowdsourced document pool included pages outside the GS pool. As expected, the combined GS+FullD qrels, comprising the full GS label set leads to better correlation with the INEX ranking.

An interesting outlier is the low correlation of the extended system ranking based on the P@10 (τ of 0.17) and nDCG@10 (τ of 0.12) using the FullD qrels. These result from the additional pages in the FullD qrel that were contributed by the answer-boost and top-n pooling methods, which are ranked lower in the new runs that are based on the rank-boost re-ordering of documents.

Using the GS and the GS+FullD qrels we generate interpolated precision over recall plots in Figure 5, with the official (solid lines) and extended runs (dashed lines). We see that the extended runs dominate the top of the rankings evaluated against the GS labels. This is not surprising, considering that the new runs provide ranking of documents compatible with the pooling used to obtain the GS set. Evaluations using the FullD qrels only (not in Figure 5) and the combined set of GS+FullD qrels show that the performance of the official and the extended runs is closer to each other.

5. CONCLUSIONS

Our research investigates the use of crowdsourcing for collecting relevance judgments in IR tasks, such as book search, where the effort and cost of employing highly skilled editorial staff is prohibitive. While pooling methods reduce the set of documents that need to be judged and make the problem more tractable, crowdsourcing holds the promise of enabling large scale relevance assessments at modest costs. However, the reliability of crowdsourced labels vary and one needs to design HITs to control the engagement of the crowd workers and the quality of their output.

In order to investigate how different aspects of the HIT design influence the label quality and the resulting system rankings, we conducted crowdsourcing experiments that involved: i) various quality control mechanisms embedded in the two HIT designs, FullD and SimpleD, ii) three interleaved pooling strategies for selecting pages to be assessed, and iii) two types of page ordering strategies, the biased and the random ordering within the HITs.

Our quality control approach was tailored to the *Prove It* relevance assessment task which involves several stages, from reading and understanding the topic claim, identifying the supporting or refuting evidence in the text, and then assigning a relevance label. Failing to complete any part of the task properly is likely to lead to suboptimal labels. Thus, we applied combinations of quality control mechanisms in order to encourage productive behavior across all the stages of the task. We characterized the HIT designs based on the label accuracy of the crowd workers over the pages with known relevance labels. This served as an indicator of the design's effectiveness in deterring careless and dishonest behavior, while attracting trustworthy workers who deliver reliable relevance judgments.

From our analysis of the collected labels we found that:

- The full design (FullD), with a rich set of quality control mechanisms, leads to significantly higher label quality in terms of agreement with the gold set labels.
- The random page ordering in the HITs leads to significantly higher label accuracy than the biased order where a known relevant page is likely to be placed at the top.
- Consensus over multiple judgments leads to more reliable labels, while filtering out workers with low accuracy leads only to a small increase in the label quality.
- The completion rate of the questionnaire flow and the fraction of obtained labels provide good indicators of the label quality. Flow is particularly effective in complex tasks since it enables both deterring and detecting suboptimal behavior, such as random clicking or filling of the HIT form.

From our analysis of the system rankings that resulted from the collected relevance judgments we conclude that:

- The choice of HIT design has a significant impact on the system rankings. FullD HITs, with a rich set of quality control mechanisms, lead to the highest correlation with the system ranking based on the gold standard set, the GS system ranking.
- System rankings based on MAP are highly correlated with the GS system ranking across the HIT designs. This suggests that MAP is not a good differentiator of the crowdsourced label quality. Measures like P@10 and nDCG@10 are more susceptible to the varying accuracy of the labels and the resulting qrels. This points to the use of multiple metrics

when evaluating the effectiveness of crowdsourcing through system rankings.

- Filtering out workers with low label accuracy reduces the pooling effect ([24]) that we observed when comparing system rankings based on MAP. By removing workers with low label accuracy, we observe a slight increase in correlation with the GS system ranking based on MAP for the FullD HITs and a decrease in correlation for the SimpleD HITs. The latter is the result of the diminished pooling effect since the number of 'relevant' labels is reduced and, with that, the possibility of achieving high correlation that can be otherwise be attained for any random sample of high-quality pooled documents.

Overall, our research suggests that crowdsourcing provides a useful means of acquiring relevance judgments for the evaluation of IR systems, assuming that reasonable care is taken when designing the HITs and the methods for refining relevance labels, e.g., based on consensus across multiple labels. From the experiments that compare results of crowd workers and editorial judges over the same ranking of pooled documents (rank-boosted), we found that the correlation of resulting system rankings is high for the quality control rich HIT designs across performance metrics. This gives us confidence that the quality of test collections obtained from crowdsourcing can be sufficiently good to enable reliable system evaluation. However, our analysis also highlights the varying quality of the workers' engagement and the resulting labels and a danger of relying upon a single metric in system evaluation, such as MAP, to draw conclusions regarding the success of a crowdsourcing experiment. Thus, crowdsourcing remains an instrument that should be used with due care and that requires further investigation.

Acknowledgments

Jaap Kamps and Marijn Koolen were supported by the Netherlands Organization for Scientific Research (NWO, grant # 639.072.601).

REFERENCES

[1] O. Alonso and R. A. Baeza-Yates. Design and implementation of relevance assessments using crowdsourcing. In *Advances in Information Retrieval – 33rd European Conference on IR Research (ECIR 2011)*, volume 6611 of *LNCS*, pages 153–164. Springer, 2011.

[2] O. Alonso and S. Mizzaro. Can we get rid of TREC assessors? using Mechanical Turk for relevance assessment. In *Proceedings of the SIGIR 2009 Workshop on the Future of IR Evaluation*, pages 15–16, 2009.

[3] O. Alonso, D. E. Rose, and B. Stewart. Crowdsourcing for relevance evaluation. *SIGIR Forum*, 42:9–15, November 2008.

[4] C. W. Cleverdon. The Cranfield tests on index language devices. *Aslib*, 19:173–192, 1967.

[5] G. V. Cormack, C. R. Palmer, and C. L. A. Clarke. Efficient construction of large test collections. In *Proceedings of the 21st annual international ACM SIGIR conference*, SIGIR '98, pages 282–289, 1998.

[6] J. S. Downs, M. B. Holbrook, S. Sheng, and L. F. Cranor. Are your participants gaming the system?: screening mechanical turk workers. In *CHI*, pages 2399–2402. ACM, 2010.

[7] C. Grady and M. Lease. Crowdsourcing document relevance assessment with mechanical turk. In *Proceedings of the NAACL HLT 2010 Workshop on Creating Speech and Language Data with Amazon's Mechanical Turk*, CSLDAMT '10, pages 172–179, 2010.

[8] J. Howe. *Crowdsourcing: Why the Power of the Crowd Is Driving the Future of Business*. Crown Publishing Group, 2008.

[9] J. Kamps, S. Geva, C. Peters, T. Sakai, A. Trotman, and E. Voorhees. Report on the SIGIR 2009 workshop on the future of IR evaluation. *SIGIR Forum*, 43(2):17–36, December 2009.

[10] A. Kapelner and D. Chandler. Preventing satisficing in online surveys: A 'kapcha' to ensure higher quality data. In *The World's First Conference on the Future of Distributed Work (CrowdConf2010)*, 2010.

[11] G. Kazai. In search of quality in crowdsourcing for search engine evaluation. In *Advances in Information Retrieval – 33rd European Conference on IR Research (ECIR 2011)*, volume 6611 of *LNCS*, pages 165–176. Springer, 2011.

[12] G. Kazai, N. Milic-Frayling, and J. Costello. Towards methods for the collective gathering and quality control of relevance assessments. In *Proceedings of the 32nd international ACM SIGIR conference*, SIGIR '09, pages 452–459, 2009. ACM.

[13] G. Kazai, M. Koolen, J. Kamps, A. Doucet, and M. Landoni. Overview of the INEX 2010 book track: Scaling up the evaluation using crowdsourcing. In *Comparative Evaluation of Focused Retrieval : 9th International Workshop of the Initiative for the Evaluation of XML Retrieval (INEX 2010)*, LNCS. Springer, 2011.

[14] A. Kittur, E. H. Chi, and B. Suh. Crowdsourcing user studies with mechanical turk. In *Proceeding of the twenty-sixth annual SIGCHI conference on Human factors in computing systems*, CHI '08, pages 453–456, 2008. ACM.

[15] J. Le, A. Edmonds, V. Hester, and L. Biewald. Ensuring quality in crowdsourced search relevance evaluation: The effects of training question distribution. In *SIGIR 2010 Workshop on Crowdsourcing for Search Evaluation*, pages 21–26, 2010.

[16] W. Mason and D. J. Watts. Financial incentives and the "performance of crowds". In *Proceedings of the ACM SIGKDD Workshop on Human Computation*, HCOMP '09, pages 77–85, 2009. ACM.

[17] S. Nowak and S. Rüger. How reliable are annotations via crowdsourcing: a study about inter-annotator agreement for multi-label image annotation. In *Proceedings of the international conference on Multimedia information retrieval*, MIR '10, pages 557–566, 2010. ACM.

[18] A. N. Oppenheim. *Questionnaire Design, Interviewing and Attitude Measurement*. Pinter Publishers, London, 1992.

[19] B. Piwowarski and M. Lalmas. Providing consistent and exhaustive relevance assessments for XML retrieval evaluation. In *Proceedings of the thirteenth ACM international conference on Information and knowledge management*, CIKM'04, pages 361–370, 2004. ACM.

[20] A. J. Quinn and B. B. Bederson. Human computation: A survey and taxonomy of a growing field. In *Proceedings of CHI 2011*, 2011.

[21] F. Radlinski, M. Kurup, and T. Joachims. How does clickthrough data reflect retrieval quality? In *CIKM*, pages 43–52. ACM, 2008.

[22] V. S. Sheng, F. Provost, and P. G. Ipeirotis. Get another label? improving data quality and data mining using multiple, noisy labelers. In *Proceeding of the 14th ACM SIGKDD international conference*, KDD '08, pages 614–622, 2008. ACM.

[23] R. Snow, B. O'Connor, D. Jurafsky, and A. Y. Ng. Cheap and fast—but is it good?: evaluating non-expert annotations for natural language tasks. In *Proceedings of the Conference on Empirical Methods in Natural Language Processing*, EMNLP '08, pages 254–263, 2008.

[24] I. Soboroff, C. Nicholas, and P. Cahan. Ranking retrieval systems without relevance judgments. In *Proceedings of the 24th annual international ACM SIGIR conference*, SIGIR '01, pages 66–73, 2001.

[25] L. von Ahn and L. Dabbish. Labeling images with a computer game. In *Proceedings of the SIGCHI conference on Human factors in computing systems*, CHI '04, pages 319–326, 2004. ACM.

[26] E. M. Voorhees. Variations in relevance judgments and the measurement of retrieval effectiveness. *Information Processing & Management*, 36(5):697 – 716, 2000.

[27] E. M. Voorhees and D. K. Harman, editors. *TREC: Experimentation and Evaluation in Information Retrieval*. MIT Press, 2005.

[28] P. Welinder, S. Branson, S. Belongie, and P. Perona. The multidimensional wisdom of crowds. In *Advances in Neural Information Processing Systems 23*, pages 2424–2432, 2010.

[29] J. Whitehill, P. Ruvolo, T. Wu, J. Bergsma, and J. Movellan. Whose vote should count more: Optimal integration of labels from labelers of unknown expertise. In *Proceedings of the 2009 Neural Information Processing Systems (NIPS) Conference*, 2009.

[30] D. Zhu and B. Carterette. An analysis of assessor behavior in crowdsourced preference judgments. In *SIGIR 2010 Workshop on Crowdsourcing for Search Evaluation*, pages 17–20, 2010.

A Site Oriented Method for Segmenting Web Pages

David Fernandes
Dep. of Computer Science
Fed. Univ. of Amazonas
Manaus, AM, Brazil
david@dcc.ufam.edu.br

Edleno S. de Moura
Dep. of Computer Science
Fed. Univ. of Amazonas
Manaus, AM, Brazil
edleno@dcc.ufam.edu.br

Altigran S. da Silva
Dep. of Computer Science
Fed. Univ. of Amazonas
Manaus, AM, Brazil
alti@dcc.ufam.edu.br

Berthier Ribeiro-Neto
Dep. of Computer Science
Fed. Univ. of Minas Gerais
Belo Horizonte, MG, Brazil
berthier@dcc.ufmg.br

Edisson Braga
Dep. of Computer Science
Fed. Univ. of Amazonas
Manaus, AM, Brazil
edisson@dcc.ufam.edu.br

ABSTRACT

Information about how to segment a Web page can be used nowadays by applications such as segment aware Web search, classification and link analysis. In this research, we propose a fully automatic method for page segmentation and evaluate its application through experiments with four separate Web sites. While the method may be used in other applications, our main focus in this article is to use it as input to segment aware Web search systems. Our results indicate that the proposed method produces better segmentation results when compared to the best segmentation method we found in literature. Further, when applied as input to a segment aware Web search method, it produces results close to those produced when using a manual page segmentation method.

Categories and Subject Descriptors

H.3.3 [**Information Storage and Retrieval: Information Search and Retrieval**]: Search process

General Terms

Algorithms, Experimentation

Keywords

Page Segmentation, Segment Class

1. INTRODUCTION

Recent work has shown that Web pages can be sub-divided into distinct segments or blocks [5, 10, 21] (such as main content, service channels, decoration skins, navigation bars, copyright and privacy announcements), and that information about these segments can be used to improve information retrieval tasks such as ranking [1, 6, 13, 14, 28], Web link analysis [4], and Web mining [8, 19, 22].

Most of previous segmentation methods we found in literature segment each Web page based on its content only, not considering the content of other pages present in the same Web site. However, since many pages belonging to a same Web site share a common structure and look and feel, we hypothesize that we can achieve a more accurate segmentation by taking all pages of a same Web site into account when dividing them into segments. Based on this idea, we propose and evaluate in this article a segmentation method which segments pages according to properties of the whole Web site, instead of just information obtained from a single page.

Our segmentation method adopts a DOM tree alignment strategy previously proposed in literature to solve the problem of template detection [31, 33]. However, we find no application of such strategy in literature to address the problem of segmenting Web pages. While segmentation of pages and template detection may appear as similar tasks at a first glance, there are important differences between these two tasks. Segmentation consists in dividing a Web page into its structural blocks, each structural block may contain templates or not and may also be part of a template. Further, in a segmentation process an area that does not contain templates may be divided into several blocks.

Our segmentation method is particularly useful to segment the so called *data-intensive* Web sites, such as digital libraries, Web forums, news Web sites, electronic catalogs, or institutional sites, whose main focus is providing access to a large quantity of data and services [9]. These sites usually contain a large set of web pages which can be organized in a few tens of groups according to the regularity of their structure. Our segmentation method takes advantage of such regularity to automatically segment data intensive web sites.

Besides segmenting the Web pages, our algorithm is able to cluster the segments into *segment classes*, which are set of segments that play the same role in a group of pages of a site. Knowledge about the segment classes can be used to estimate a weight for each segment in a Web collection, indicating its importance for ranking purposes [14, 13]. In [13], the authors show how to compute these weights automatically, and then how to estimate term weights according to the weights of the blocks where they occur. The ranking

SIGIR'11, July 24–28, 2011, Beijing, China.

method they proposed is particularly useful for data intensive web sites, where search is an important way of accessing data, given the large amount of information usually provided to their users. This type of Web site is also the main focus of our work here.

Even though this article focus on the use of the segments and their classes as input to segment aware Web search systems, the segmentation method here proposed may be applied to many other applications. For instance, segmentation algorithms can be used to improve the quality of results in many Web mining applications [23]. As another example, segmentation techniques can be also useful for the contextual advertisement problem, in which advertisers often wish to place (or avoid placing) distinct ads on specific regions of a same Web page [35].

To evaluate the performance of our segmentation algorithm, we performed experiments with four distinct Web collections to compare its results with those produced by the Rule-based Block Fusion algorithm — a recently proposed automatic segmentation algorithm that achieves good performance [21]. The results indicate that our algorithm outperforms the baseline for all four Web sites tested and that the results are far superior for two of the sites tested.

We also studied the impact of using our automatic segmentation method with a segment aware ranking search system. For this, we ran experiments to compare such ranking strategy with (i) a traditional ranking function that does not use segment information, (ii) a traditional ranking function applied to pages after template removal, and (iii) a segment aware ranking search system applied to manually segmented Web pages. The experiments indicate that our segmentation method, when combined with the segment aware ranking system, leads to improved results in comparison to the two first baselines. Further, the loss in ranking quality in comparison to the third ranking baseline is not significant in most cases and is small even in the worse results.

The remaining of this paper is organized as follows. Section 2 covers related work. Section 3 presents the model we adopt here to represent Web sites. Section 4 presents the proposed automatic Web page segmentation method. Section 5 reports results we obtained from experiments we run to evaluate the effectiveness of our method in generating suitable segments and the impact of the segmentation it generates in segment aware ranking systems. Finally, Section 6 concludes this article.

2. RELATED WORK

The process of analyzing a Web site to detect structural divisions of its pages has been addressed in several previous research articles [3, 5, 10, 16, 21]. One of the best solutions found in the literature, called Vision-based Page Segmentation algorithm (VIPS) [5], segments a page by simulating the visual perceptions of the users about that page. The VIPS algorithm requires a considerable human effort, since it is necessary to manually set a number parameters to each page to be segmented.

Chakrabarti *et al* [10] also consider the problem of segmenting Web pages into visually and semantically cohesive pieces. This work uses approximation algorithms for clustering problems based on weighted graphs. In the case of the segmentation problem proposed by [10], the weights of edges of the graph capture the likelihood that two regions of the Web page are placed together or apart in the segmentation, and the clusters are the segments occurring in the pages.

Kohlschütter *et al* [21] examined the problem of Web page segmentation from a textual perspective. The key assumption in their work is that the number of tokens in a text fragment (or more precisely, its token density) is a valuable feature for segmentation decisions. Based on this assumption, the authors presented a *Segment Fusion algorithm* for Web page segmentation using text density metrics. The authors show that their method outperforms the method proposed by Chakrabarti *et al.* Given its quite strong results, we decided to use it as the baseline in our experiments. Notice that this method uses less information than ours when segmenting pages, since it segments each page individually and we segment a page based on web site statistics.

Many authors have argued that information present on page templates is noisy and should be disregarded to avoid deteriorating search precision [20, 31]. Such an idea has motivated the proposal of methods for identifying noisy contents or templates based on the structure of the Web pages [3, 15, 20, 24, 31, 33]. However, template extraction is a task different from segmentation. Segmentation consists in dividing a Web page into its structural blocks and each structural block may contain templates or not. Further, in a segmentation process an area that does not contain templates may be divided into several blocks.

Our method aligns the DOM trees of Web pages of a site in order to uncover their implicit structure. Aligning the DOM trees to extract structural information from of Web sites and Web pages is not a new strategy. This idea has been used previously for Web site template identification [31, 33] and web mining [27, 34]. However, we find no application of such strategy in literature to address the problem of segmenting Web pages. The adaptation and heuristics described by us to adopt the DOM tree alignment to the problem of segmenting Web pages constitute the major contribution of our work when compared to the previous application of such strategy. As we show through experiments, the DOM tree alignment strategy is an excellent alternative to solve the problem of segmenting Web pages.

Bar-Yossef and Rajagopalan have also proposed a method that uses the DOM tree of pages in a site to guide the segmentation process [3]. While their proposal can be considered as a segmentation method, their main goal was to detect noisy information in Web pages. As the main heuristic to identify segments, they count the number of links found in each HTML element. If an element contains more than K links it is considered as a segment, otherwise it is counted as part of the element containing it. We have considered the possibility of including their method in our experiments as a segmentation method for sake of completeness, but the method would produce a quite low quality segmentation and we have not reported experiments with it.

In Cai *et al.* [6], the authors proposed a method for taking advantage of the segments generated for pages in a search task. They present a ranking strategy where the segments are processed as semantic passages and then apply previously proposed passage-level ranking strategies [7] to evaluate the possible improvements obtained in ranking quality with their method. Results are superior to other previously studied types of passages, such as paragraphs or fixed size windows.

The method proposed by Song *et al.* in [28] also adopted

the vision based segmentation proposed by [5]. The authors used such a segmentation to compute an importance rank of segments found in a page through a learning approach. Spatial features, such as position and size of segments, and content features, such as the number of images and links on each segment, are extracted from each segment. Two learning algorithms, neural network and SVM, are used to rank the segments according to their importance.

In de Moura *et al.* [13], the authors propose a method for automatically computing segment importance factors to improve Web search. Such a method uses statistical information available in the Web page collection to assign an importance value to all segments of each page found in the collection. Their method produces a significant improvement in the quality of search results when compared to several baselines. However, it requires a complex segmentation mechanism and the authors proposed no fully automatic strategy to generate it.

The segmentation methods found in the literature aim to identify the segment structure of a single page given as input. The method presented in [13] requires the identification of a common structure shared by a large quantity of pages. The purpose of such an identification is to cluster the segments into *segment classes*. A segment class is a set of segments that share a common role on a group of pages of a same site. Although the authors proposed the use of VIPS [5] to guide the segmentation process, the clustering of segments into segment classes requires a manual process even when using VIPS, making the application of the method unfeasible in large Web page collections.

We here propose a novel method for automatically divide Web pages from a collection into segments. This method can be considered as a significant improvement in the proposal of de Moura *et al.*, since our experiments indicate that their segment aware Web search method produces results almost similar in terms of quality either using our new segmentation approach or using the manual approach they originally use.

3. REPRESENTING WEB SITES AS SEGMENT COMPONENTS

Unlike plain text documents, Web pages usually encompass multiple regions such as navigation bars, decoration stuffs, copyrights, advertisements and contact information. Each of these regions play a particular role within the pages and are generically referred to as *segments*. In this Section we present some basic definitions which are useful for better characterizing the problem of dividing the Web pages into segments. Our discussion is based on [13].

DEFINITION 1. *A* segment s *is a self-contained logical region within a Web page that (i) is not nested within any other segment and (ii) is represented by a pair* (l, c)*, where* l *is the label of the segment, represented as the root-to-segment path in the Web page DOM tree, and* c *is the portion of text of the segment.*

It follows that a Web page ρ_n might be represented as a finite set of (non-overlapping) logical segments $\rho_n = \{s_1, ..., s_k\}$, with k varying according to the page structure. The definition of segments we adopt here allows several types of partitions for a given Web page, subject to the interpretation of a human analyst or to the behavior of the segmentation method adopted. Since our segment definition admits that any arbitrary subtree of a DOM structure be assigned as a segment, the decision of how to divide a page into segments should be done by the segmentation algorithm. In this work, we adopt the criterion that the division of a Web page into a set of non-overlapping segments must be performed according to the perception of users about the best logical division of the page.

A Web site $\mathcal{S}$ is represented here as a set of Web pages $\mathcal{S} = \{\rho_1, ..., \rho_m\}$, each of them composed of a set of segments. Given this representation, we can now define the concept of *segment class*. Segments of distinct pages can be clustered into classes as follows:

DEFINITION 2. *A* segment class $\mathcal{C}$ *is a set of segments that belong to distinct pages of a given Web site and that share a same label, i.e.,*

$$\mathcal{C} = \{s_1, s_2, ..., s_{n_\mathcal{C}}\}$$

$$\begin{aligned} s_1 &= (l_\mathcal{C}, c_1) \\ s_2 &= (l_\mathcal{C}, c_2) \\ &\vdots \\ s_{n_\mathcal{C}} &= (l_\mathcal{C}, c_{n_\mathcal{C}}) \end{aligned}$$

where $n_\mathcal{C}$ *is the total number of segments in class* $\mathcal{C}$*,* $l_\mathcal{C}$ *is the common label,* s_i *is the* i_{th} *segment in class* $\mathcal{C}$*, and* c_i *is its corresponding portion of text.*

To illustrate, consider the two news pages depicted on Figure 1. Notice that each page contains a *news title*, which we refer to as *title segments*. Since these title segments are in the same position in both pages, they have a common root-to-segment path and thus, a same label. As a consequence, they are part of a same segment class. We also notice that segments with the same label tend to have the same role within their respective pages. That is, a *segment class* is usually composed of segments that belong to distinct pages of a Web site and that play the same role within the site. Various examples of segments that belong to the same class occur in the news pages depicted in Figure 1, such as segments that represent the menu, the news body, the summary of the news in the page, etc.

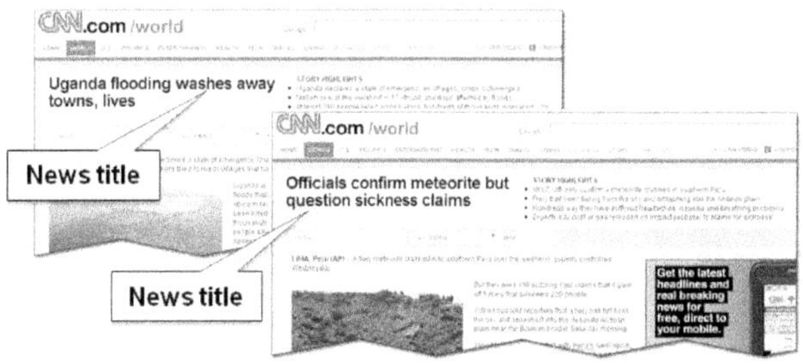

Figure 1: News pages ρ_1 and ρ_2, extracted from CNN Web site.

4. WEB PAGE SEGMENTATION

Algorithm 1 describes the automatic segmentation process, which tries to segment the pages close to the perception of users about how each page should be divided into segments, and how these segments should be clustered into segment classes. It takes the set of pages $\mathcal{S}$ found in the Web site as input and produces as output a set of segment classes. Our segmentation algorithm is divided into three phases, that will be discussed in the following sections.

4.1 Phase 1: Pre-processing Web Pages

The first phase of our algorithm takes as input the pages of the site. In this phase, the DOM trees of the pages are pre-processed to obtain a structural representation that is closer to our definition of segments and segment classes. For instance, we use this phase to identify and remove nodes of the DOM tree that may produce nested segments (that are not allowed by our model). It is also used to aggregate regions of regular structures, such as menus or lists of items, which would be seen by a user as a single segment, but that would be broken into several small segments by the heuristics we adopt in the second phase.

Algorithm 1 *Segment*($\mathcal{S}$)

1: { Phase 1: Pre-processing Web Pages}
2: **for each** $p_i \in \mathcal{S}$ {i is the number of a page} **do**
3: $\quad \rho_i \leftarrow$ preProcess(p_i);
4: **end for**
5: { Phase 2: Constructing the SOM_{tree}}
6: $SOM_{tree} \leftarrow \emptyset$;
7: **for each** $\rho_i \in \mathcal{S}$ {i is the number of a page} **do**
8: $\quad$ **for each** node $N_\rho \in \rho_i$ traversed in pre-order **do**
9: $\quad\quad$ **if** $\exists N_s \in SOM_{tree} \mid N_s.label = N_\rho.label$ **then**
10: $\quad\quad\quad N_s.counter \leftarrow N_s.counter + 1$;
11: $\quad\quad\quad$ **if** $N_\rho.flag$ **then**
12: $\quad\quad\quad\quad$ Append i in $N_s.pageList$;
13: $\quad\quad\quad$ **end if**
14: $\quad\quad$ **else**
15: $\quad\quad\quad$ insertNewNode(SOM_{tree},N_ρ,i);
16: $\quad\quad$ **end if**
17: $\quad$ **end for**
18: **end for**
19: {Phase 3: Refining the SOM_{tree} }
20: **for each** node $N_s \in SOM_{tree}$ traversed in pre-order **do**
21: $\quad$ **if** N_s is an internal node AND $N_s.pageList \neq \emptyset$ **then**
22: $\quad\quad$ **for each** node $n_s \in$ descendants(N_s) traversed in pos-order **do**
23: $\quad\quad\quad$ **if** distance(N_s,n_s)$< \alpha$ AND n_s is a leaf node **then**
24: $\quad\quad\quad\quad$ Append $n_s.pageList$ to $N_s.pageList$;
25: $\quad\quad\quad\quad$ Remove n_s from SOM_{tree};
26: $\quad\quad\quad$ **end if**
27: $\quad\quad$ **end for**
28: $\quad$ **end if**
29: **end for**
30: **for each** node $N_s \in SOM_{tree}$ traversed in pos-order **do**
31: $\quad$ **if** $n_s.counter < \beta, \forall n_s \in children(N_s)$ **then**
32: $\quad\quad$ **for each** $n_s \in children(N_s)$ **do**
33: $\quad\quad\quad$ Remove n_s from SOM_{tree};
34: $\quad\quad\quad$ Add $n_s.pageList$ to $N_s.pageList$;
35: $\quad\quad\quad$ Add $n_s.counter$ value to $N_s.counter$;
36: $\quad\quad$ **end for**
37: $\quad$ **end if**
38: **end for**
39: {Each node N_s of SOM_{tree} represents now a segment class, where $N_s.pageList$ contains the list of segments of N_s, and $N_s.label$ contains the label of the segments}
40: Return the SOM_{tree}

Further, the pre-processing also is used to aggregate further information about each node and adjusts the DOM trees to be used in the second phase of the algorithm. Figure 2 depicts a segment of HTML code and the pre-processed version of its DOM tree. To simplify, only the leftmost node of the DOM tree depicts the additional information introduced by the pre-processing phase. This example is used in the following sections to show how each individual page is pre-processed (see Lines 1–4). The function *PreProcess* of our algorithm consists of four main operations which are described on the following sections.

```
<html>
  <body bgcolor=white>
    <div class=content1>
      Text A
    </div>
    <img src=image.gif>
    <div class=content2>
      <h1>Text B</h1>
      <p>Text C</p>
    </div>
  </body>
</html>
```

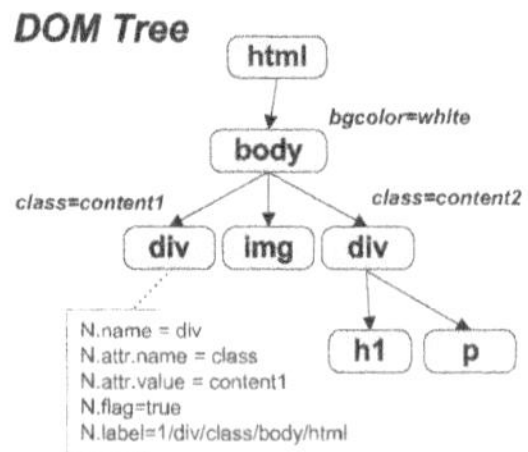

Figure 2: An example of HTML code and the pre-processed version of its DOM tree.

Creating the node labels

Given a page ρ, its DOM tree is a structure that represents the hierarchical relationship between the tags found in the page. Each tag is represented by a node N that contains information about the *name* of the tag ($N.name$) and a list of its *attributes* ($N.attr$), where each attribute is composed by a pair of *name* ($N.attr.name$) and *value* ($N.attr.value$). We use this information to recursively define the *label* of each node N ($N.label$) as the concatenation of its $N.name$, $N.attr.name$ field values and the *label* value of its parent in the DOM tree (considering it as empty when the node is the root of the tree), separating each token in the concatenation by a slash. Whenever two sibling nodes get equal values assigned by this strategy, we distinguish them by adding a sequential number to their *label* values, so that each node has a unique *label*.

For instance, in the leftmost node of Figure 2, the value of *name* is "div" and the only value of attribute name is "class", thus attr.name={"class"}. Its *label* is "1/div/class/body/html". The value "1" is added because there is a second node that would get the same *label* (see the rightmost div tag). This node is the identified by "2/div/class/body/hmtl" in our representation. For the node labelled as "img" in the Figure, the *label* is "img/body/html".

Although information about textual content is not included in DOM tree, it is useful for our segmentation algorithm. Thus, we add to each node N a boolean value ($N.flag$), which indicates whether it has textual content assigned to it ($N.flag = true$) or not ($N.flag = false$).

Dealing with nested content

Our segmentation algorithm assumes that only the leaf nodes of a DOM tree may have textual content assigned to them. This assumption is important in order to avoid the generation of nested segments during the future phases of our algorithm. Thus, whenever we find internal nodes with textual content, we do not represent their children in our DOM tree representation, and thus it becomes a leaf node. The textual content associated to the removed tags is then associated to this new leaf node.

For instance, let us consider the second tag `<div>` in DOM tree of Figure 3. Notice that such a tag contains a text directly attached to it (Last year in Orlando...). Besides, inside this text there is a tag `<a>`, that also has a textual content (anchor text). In this case, we say that the content of `<a>` is nested to the content of `<div>`. As nested contents can generate nested segments in the future phases of our algorithm, the tag `<a>` is removed from our DOM tree representation, and its textual content is associated to the content of `<div>`.

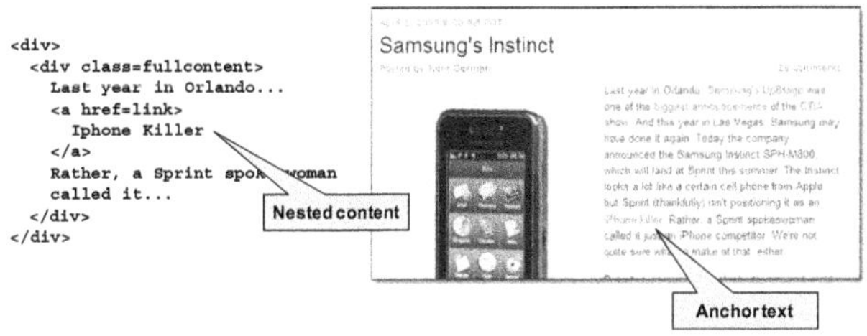

Figure 3: Example of tag with nested content.

Dealing with recurrent regions

Another change we perform in the DOM trees is to remove sequences of tags disposed in a recurrent (or regular) way. In the DOM tree of a typical Web page, it is very common to find regions with a quite regular structure. Let us consider the Web page depicted in Figure 4. Notice that the *menu* signalized by the Arrow 2 is formed by a set of links disposed in a vertical bar. As the set of tags that separate two adjacent links is always the same, we can say these tags are disposed in a regular or recurrent way.

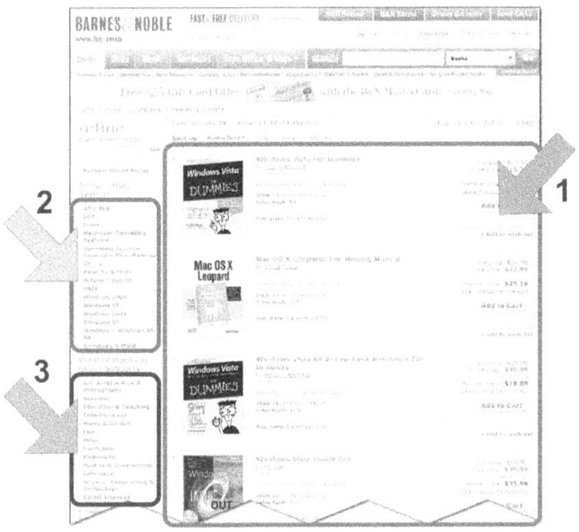

Figure 4: Recurrent structures: the regions pointed by the arrows contain sets of items (links or books) disposed in a regular or recurrent way.

Regions with recurrent structure commonly contain a list of items highly related to each other such as list of links, products, or paragraphs (notice that the regions signalized by the arrows 1 and 3 are also examples of regions with recurrent structures). Thus, each list has a single purpose within their respective pages and then would probably be seen by an user as a single segment. In this way, the DOM subtree of these regions is represented by a single node in our DOM tree representation, in order that all textual content of the subtree with recurrent structure become directly linked to this node. This process is depicted in Figure 5.

Identifying recurrent structures in DOM trees is a procedure commonly executed in methods for extracting data from HTML pages [25, 34]. The motivation is that the information to be extracted is often placed in a particular order, and repetitive patterns can be found in these Web pages when multiple records are aligned together.

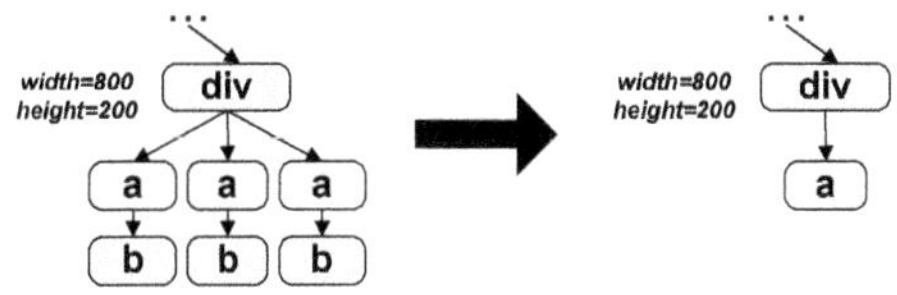

Figure 5: Recurrent substructures of the DOM trees are not represented in our DOM tree representation.

4.2 Phase 2: Constructing the SOM_{tree}

The second phase of the Algorithm 1 creates an auxiliary hierarchical structure named SOM_{tree} (SOM is an acronym to *Site Object Model*) that summarizes the DOM trees of all pages found in a Web site (see Lines 5–18).

Each node N_s of the SOM_{tree} contains the same information found in a node N_ρ of our DOM tree representation, but has two extra fields: $N_s.counter$, with the number of pages where it occurs in the site (i.e., the number of pages that contain a node N_ρ such that $N_\rho.label = N_s.label$); and $N_s.pageList$, with the list of pages where it occurs associated to textual content in the site. Notice that the size of $N_s.pageList$ may be smaller than the value of $N_s.counter$, since only tag occurrences associated with textual content are inserted in $N_s.pageList$. A single tag may occur in a page associated to content and appear in a second page without any content.

As an example of a SOM_{tree} construction, consider a very simple Web site $\mathcal{S}$ formed by only two pages, ρ_1 and ρ_2, depicted in Figure 6. A SOM_{tree} for this site can be constructed by merging ρ_1 and ρ_2 in a single structure. Phase 2 of our algorithm starts by reading page ρ_1, through a pre-order traversal (Lines 8–17). For each node N_ρ of ρ_1, the algorithm checks if the SOM_{tree} already have a node N_s such that $N_s.label = N_\rho.label$ (Line 9). However, since the SOM_{tree} is created empty (Line 6), all nodes N_ρ found in this first page are merged into SOM_{tree} through the function $insertNewNode$, that is called on Line 15, and detailed in Algorithm 2. The insertion point is guided by the value of $N_\rho.label$. Function $insertNewNode$ assigns the value of $N_\rho.label$ to $N_s.label$, and assigns 1 to $N_s.counter$. If N_ρ has textual content ($N_\rho.flag = true$), then function $insertNewNode$ also adds the id of page ρ_1 (value 1) to the pageList of the node N_s.

After that, the algorithm reads the second page of $\mathcal{S}$, ρ_2, to merge it into SOM_{tree}. In Figure 6, we can see that this page starts with the tag `<html>`. In the Line 9, it is verified that the SOM_{tree} has already a node N_s with the label `html`, and thus the algorithm only updates the information of N_s (Lines 10–12): its counter value is incremented.

In Figure 6, we see that the representations of ρ_1 and ρ_2 diverge below the nodes `div` on right. Below this node, page ρ_1 has the nodes `h1` and `pre`, and page ρ_2 has the nodes `h1` and `p`. As the nodes `h1` have the same path in the DOM tree of both pages, then they result in a single node in the SOM_{tree}. On the other hand, the nodes `pre` (in ρ_1) and `p` (in ρ_2) occur only once in their respective pages. Thus, each of them results in a different node in the SOM_{tree}. The counter of these two nodes is 1 in both cases.

4.3 Phase 3: Refining the SOM_{tree}

The third phase of our algorithm has the goal of removing nodes of the SOM_{tree} that would be considered by a human

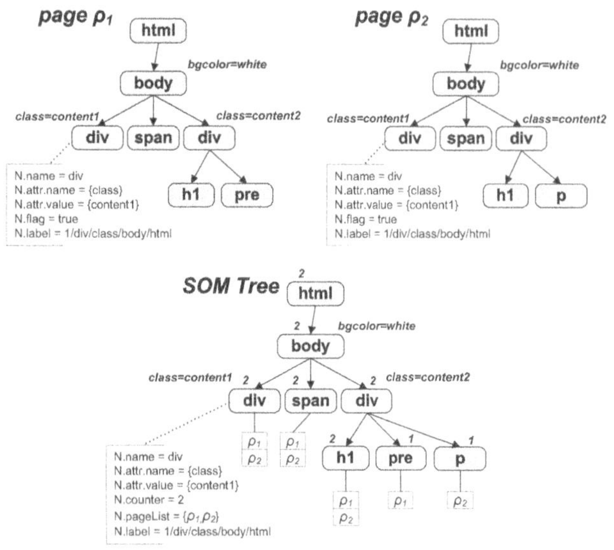

Figure 6: An example of a SOM_{tree} construction. The $pageList$ values are depicted below each node of this structure.

Algorithm 2 insertNewNode(SOM_{tree}, N_ρ, i)

Create an empty node N_s;
$N_s.label = N_\rho.label$;
$N_s.counter = 1$;
if $N_\rho.flag$ **then**
  $N_s.pageList = \{i\}$;
end if
Insert N_s in SOM_{tree} according to $N_s.label$

as internal parts of one or more segments of the site. By removing these nodes, that we refer to as noisy nodes, the SOM_{tree} becomes a structure formed only by nodes that belong to the label (root-to-segment path) of one or more segments, and each each leaf node of this new structure will refer to a distinct segment class of the site.

To better illustrate what is a noisy node, let us consider that there is a table inside the body of a news page. This table would probably be considered by a human as part of a single segment containing the body of the news. However, when including this page in the SOM_{tree}, the content of the table would create new nodes in the structure, and thus would let the segmentation system to consider the table as a separate segment.

When analyzing the results produced by Phase 2 of our segmentation algorithm for several samples, we realized that in general, these noisy segments occur when a given set of pages has a region with pure textual content, while another set of pages has textual content mixed with other type of information in the same region, such as a table containing text, or a different textual style. When humans see such variations, they can easily realize that the region has the same function in both sets of pages. However, the small structural differences introduced affect the representation of the site in the SOM_{tree}. The main goal of the third phase of our algorithm is to remove the noisy nodes, what is done by applying two different heuristics.

The first heuristic performs a join of nested nodes that have textual content and that occur close in the SOM_{tree}. The distance adopted is the difference in the depth between the two nested nodes analyzed. We noticed that as this distance increases, also increases the chance that nodes represent different segment classes of the site. On the other hand, when this distance is small, it is mostly due to small variations in pages, and thus the nodes probably represent the same segment class.

The ideal value for this distance, represented by the threshold α in Algorithm 1, can be empirically set through experiments. An alternative to avoid the necessity of such threshold is to use a clustering algorithm to group the pages of the site according to their templates [11, 12, 30]. After clustering the pages, we can run the algorithm 1 for each cluster. This procedure would avoid the presence of pages with large differences in their structure as input to the segmentation algorithm, and then would allow all nested content to be joined, without a risk of joining segments of pages with distinct structure. On the other hand, the use of clustering would make the segmentation process more expensive and the results we obtained by using our heuristic were good enough for avoiding such extra computational cost.

As an example, consider the SOM_{tree} segment depicted in Figure 7(a). Notice that this segment contains two nodes, `div` and `p`, and that the `p` node is descendant of the `div` node. As one can see, there is a small variation in the structure in this region of the pages, since a set of pages contains textual content connected to the first node (`div`), and another set of pages contain textual content associated to the second node `p`.

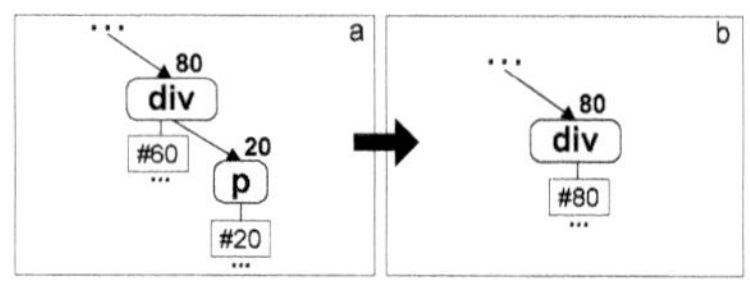

Figure 7: (a) A SOM_{tree} segment example and (b) its pruned version, considering a α threshold equal to 6. Notice that, instead of presenting the list of documents in each leaf element node, this figure presents only the number of documents in each list.

Line 23 of the algorithm 1 verifies whether the distance between these two nodes is smaller than the threshold α or not. If it is smaller, then the pageList of the descendant node is appended to the ancestor, and the descendant node is deleted from the SOM_{tree}(Lines 24–25). On the other side, if this distance is greater than the threshold α, then we assume that these nodes refer to distinct segment classes. In our experiments, we empirically set the value 6 for this threshold based on training experiments. Considering this value for the threshold α, the node `p` depicted in Figure 7(a) must be pruned during the refining process, and its pageList merged to the pageList of the node `div`. The result of this process is depicted in Figure 7(b).

Notice that, although the join can fail in some cases, it does not cause a significant change in the final result of the method, since if we set threshold α too high, the only change is that a few segments with different classes may be joined in a single class. On the other hand, if we set it too low, some small differences in the structure of pages may cause the split of segments considered by humans as single segments. While these changes may contribute to result in a set of segment classes different from the ones produced by humans, the impact of these changes for ranking purposes is expected to be small for Web sites with regular structure, since only a few pages would have a few changes in our proposed term weighting scheme.

The second heuristic joins all the children of a node N to it whenever all of them have counter value smaller than a threshold β (Lines 30–38). This parameter is related to the minimum quantity of elements in a segment class in order to allow safe use of the segment aware ranking method we adopt in the experiments. This parameter is proposed and studied by Moura *et al* [13], where authors suggest to set it as 8.

Notice that the children of a node N_s can be joined to their parent only when all of them have counter value smaller than the threshold β. The purpose of this rule is to avoid the generation, during this stage of the refining process, of new nested nodes with textual content. Thus, even after this second phase of the refining process, some nodes might remain with counter value smaller than the threshold β.

The result of the algorithm after the refining is a set of segment classes that are described by the SOM_{tree}. Each leaf node N of the final SOM_{tree} represents a segment class, with label $N.label$ and occurring in pages $N.pageList$. From the structure of the SOM_{tree} it is possible to define how each page is partitioned into segments by performing a matching between the SOM_{tree} and the DOM tree of the page.

5. EXPERIMENTS

To validate our automatic segmentation method, we performed experiments on 4 real Web collections namely IG, CNN, CNET, and BLOGs. The results for these experiments are discussed in this section.

5.1 Data Sets

The IG collection, which contains 34,460 pages crawled from one of the largest Brazilian Web portals (see www.ig.com.br), is composed of a recipe site, a forum site, and a news Web site, as detailed in Table 1. The set of test queries used in ranking experiments for this collection is composed of 50 popular queries extracted from a log of queries submitted to the IG Web search service. Relevance assessments for these queries were made by 85 volunteers from 5 different Brazilian universities. A pooling method [17] was used to collect relevance judgments. For each of the 50 queries, we composed a query pool formed by the union of the top 20 documents retrieved by each ranking method considered in our experiments, and then presented those documents in random order to the users. To avoid noise and erroneous judgements, each document retrieved by a given query was evaluated by three distinct volunteers. We considered a document as relevant to a query when at least two of the volunteers considered it as relevant to that query.

The second collection is a crawling of the CNN Web site composed of 16,257 Web pages. The queries used for experimentation with this collection were proposed by 50 volunteers, such that each volunteer wrote a single query. We then inspect each one of the proposed queries to ensure that all of them are representative. As in the IG collection, for each query submitted we computed a pool formed by the union of the top 20 results of all the methods we considered.

The third collection was obtained by crawling four Web sites affiliated to the CNET Web portal (see www.cnet.com): CNET News, that provides news, blogs, and special reports about technology; CNET Download, composed by a large set of pages containing free downloads; CNET Shopper, which is a virtual shop of tech products; and CNET Reviews, composed by a set of pages containing reviews of products. This collection contains a total of 352,770 Web pages. The 50 test queries were obtained in similar way as described for the CNN collection.

The fourth collection was obtained by crawling 9 popular blogs from the top popular list presented in Technorati Blog [1]. Table 1 presents the list of the crawled blogs. This collection contains a total of 54,055 blog posts and 50 test queries, which were generated as in the CNN collection.

5.2 Evaluation Metrics and Baselines

To evaluate the results achieved by our segmentation method, we adopted the *Adjusted RAND index (AdjRAND)* metric [18, 21, 32]. The Adjusted RAND index between two partitions measures the fraction of pairs of terms that are either grouped together (in a same segment) or placed in separate segments in both partitions. Hence, the higher the Adjusted RAND index between the segmentation output (obtained by the algorithm we want evaluate) and a manually labeled segmentation, the better the segmentation quality of the algorithm.

We also have performed experiments with a second measure, named as *Average Mutual Information* [29]. Mutual information is a measure of the quantity of information shared between two partitions, and provides an indication of the similarity between the segmentation output of an automatic method and the manual segmentation of a same page. However the conclusions obtained when using this second measure were similar to the ones obtained with AdjRAND and we decided to not include them due to space restrictions.

To conduce this evaluation, we manually segmented the pages of the experimented collections. First, we clustered the pages of each collection according to their internal structure. We asked volunteers to mark one example for each distinct structure of pages they found in the web site, and then clustered the pages based on their structural distance from each structure pointed out by the users.

In the second step, we used the VIPS [6] algorithm to segment the pages of each cluster through a manual selection of parameters. Notice that a single set of parameters can be used to segment all pages of a same cluster, given that these pages have the same internal strucuture. While this fact allows us to perform a human segmentation to produce the reference sets, still the number of structures to be found is high. Further, to assert the quality of the segmentation, we selected three volunteers to analyze the quality of segmentation performed by VIPS. For each distinct structure found in the web sites segmented, we selected one page to be analyzed by a volunteer. Whenever the volunteer did not agree with the segmentation found in a page p, he was able to adapt the segmentation to its perception about how the page p could be segmented. In these cases, we then changed the segmentation of all pages with the same structure of p. Given the necessary manual intervention in the process, we named this approach as *manual segmentation*.

We performed experiments to compare the quality of the segments found by our automatic segmentation algorithm with those found by the algorithm proposed by Kohlschütter and Nejdl [21], referred to as *Rule-based Blockfusion* in

[1] http://technorati.com/blogs/top100

the experiments. The algorithm identifies the segments of Web pages from a textual perspective. It uses the number of tokens in a text fragment (or more precisely, its token density) to segment Web pages (instead of DOM-structural information, as in our method). The segmentation algorithm is based on a merge strategy called *Block-Fusion*, where adjacent text fragments of similar text density (interpreted as "similar class") are iteratively fused until the blocks' densities (and therefore the text classes) are distinctive enough. Using various settings, including a rule-based approach, authors show that the resulting block structure closely resembles a manual segmentation, achieving a segmentation performance better than those achieved by [10], which is another recent work that approached the Web page segmentation problem.

We also studied the impact of using our automatic segmentation method as input to a segment aware ranking system proposed by de Moura *et al.* [13]. This method changes the weight of terms in BM25 ranking model [26] according to the segments where they occur with the goal of improving the search quality. We compared the ranking results obtained when segmenting the Web pages with our method to the results obtained when manually segmenting the pages.

We also report search results obtained when using the BM25 ranking applied to full pages (using no segment information), and the BM25 ranking applied to pages after templates removal. Templates were manually removed to assure a high quality template removal, thus avoiding doubts which could arise when using an automatic method. This last baseline was included to show that using segment information is better than removing templates in search tasks.

To compare the ranking strategies, we adopted two evaluation metrics. The first metric is the traditional mean average precision (MAP) and the second is precision at 10 (P@10), which measures the amount of relevant documents in the top 10 answers provided on each system [2].

5.3 Experimental Results

Table 1 presents the total number of segments and segment classes found by the automatic segmentation approach. The Table also shows the number of segments found in classes with less than β elements. We can see that, despite the number of pages in CNN collection be smaller than the other collections, the number of segment classes found in this collection is relatively high, if compared with those found in other collections. This happens because segments with the same role in the CNN collection may have two or more versions of labels (root-to-segment path), i.e., it is possible to exist two or more segment classes formed by segments with the same function in such collection. For instance, news pages found in the CNN collection usually contain tables, graphics, photos and other illustrative components in different parts of their text. Such characteristic of the CNN collection does not significantly interfere in the results obtained by a segment aware Web search results, since each segment class continues to be formed by segments with the same function.

On the other hand, notice that the number of segment classes found in BLOGS collection is quite small, when compared with those found in other collections. This happens because such collection is formed only by posts of their respective blogs, and the posts of a same blog tend to have the same structure, i.e., they tend to have the same set of segments. Thus, since there is not a big variety of segments from post to post, the number of segment classes found in each blog of this collection tend to be quite small.

An important point to observe in Table 1 is that in all collections just a few segments were grouped into classes with less than β (i.e., 8) elements. For instance, from the total of $1,404,512$ segments found in IG, only $1,109$ were grouped into classes with less than β elements, which is less than 0.08% of the total number of segments found. In CNN the number is less than 0.03%, in CNET less than 0.3%, and in BLOGS it is less than 0.05% of the segments found.

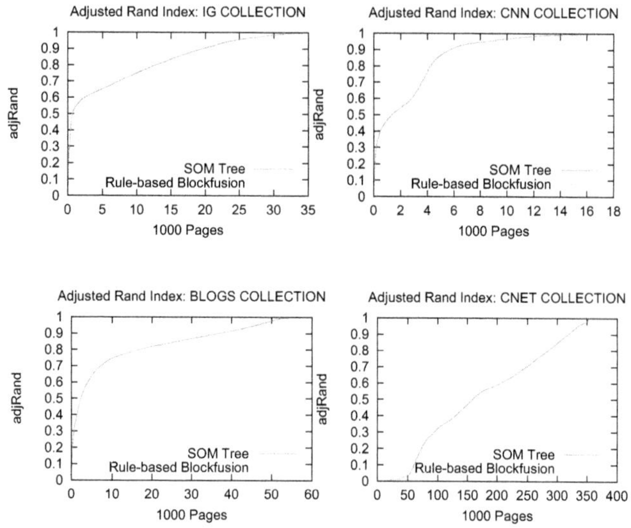

Figure 8: Adjusted RAND Index graphs found for IG, CNN, BLOGs and CNET collections. Due to space constraints, the values in x-axis were divided by 1000.

The results for Adjusted RAND Index is depicted on Figure 8. To compose each curve of the Figure (for instance, the curve SOM Tree in IG collection graph), we computed the Adjusted RAND index achieved by the method of the curve for each page of the collection, and then plotted these values in increasing order. For instance, considering the graphs for IG collection, the k_{th} page of the curve SOM Tree refers to a page segmented by our automatic segmentation method that achieved the k_{th} smaller Adjusted RAND index.

As one can see, these graphs show that our method achieved a segmentation performance better than those achieved by *Rule-based Blockfusion* [21] in all collections. The graphics show that our method outperformed the baseline at all intermediate points, being closer to 1 in all levels. Observing the graphs, we notice that the CNET collection presented the smaller agreement between the manual and the automatic approaches. When checking the results, we realized that this is due to irregularities in the page structures found in CNET which affects the automatic identification of recurrent structures (see Section 4.1). Such irregularities do not affect the manual method since a human can easily deal with them. However, even for this collection, our automatic approach presented a segmentation performance better than *Rule-based Blockfusion*.

To better illustrate the results, in IG collection we have just a few pages with AdjRAND below 0.6, while almost

Site (Domain)	Pages	Classes	Segments	S. Small Classes
IG - Total	34,460	1,095	1,404,512	1,109
News (ultimosegundo.com.br)	26,466	797	1,017,960	887
Forum (jornaldedebates.com.br)	6,389	256	366,202	212
Recipe (panelinha.com.br)	1,605	42	20,350	10
CNN - Total	16,257	1,945	597,301	1,911
News site (cnn.com)	16,257	1,945	597,301	1,911
CNET - Total	352,770	7,587	25,458,565	7,678
News (news.com)	131,474	2,155	6,287,577	5,568
Downloads (downloads.com)	99,186	916	3,182,811	800
Reviews (reviews.cnet.com)	64,142	1,563	6,320,501	620
Shopper (shopper.com)	57,968	2,953	9,667,676	690
BLOGs - Total	54,055	1,383	2,149,039	1,029
B. Boing (boingboing.net)	14,173	59	421,074	9
CNET (news.cnet.comtech-blogs)	8,054	194	415,108	85
Engadget (engadget.com)	6,343	69	282,681	16
Gizmodo (us.gizmodo.com)	4,454	77	119,728	37
Google (googleblog.blogspot.com)	1,050	14	14,503	0
Hacker (lifehacker.com)	3,997	54	93,046	56
Mashable (mashable.com)	7,410	500	560,079	367
S. Film (slashfilm.com)	5,376	213	145,151	283
T. Crunch (techcrunch.com)	3,198	203	97,669	176

Table 1: The set of Web sites crawled for each document collection, and the number of segments and segment classes found by the automatic segmentation process. Table also shows the number of segments found in classes with less than β elements (S. Small Classes).

10,000 are below this threshold when using *Rule-based Blockfusion*. In CNN our method produces less than 4,000 pages with AdjRAND below 0.8, while the baseline produces more than 8,000 pages below this threshold. When taking the average AdjRAND values obtained by each method we can see that our method obtained an average value of 0.83 when processing pages of IG, while the *Rule-based Blockfusion* achieved an average value of 0.72. In CNN the average AdjRAND value obtained by our method was 0.85, while *Rule-based Blockfusion* achieved 0.58.

We also performed some experiments to check whether these results are uniform for Web sites with a small number of pages. For this, we randomly divided the IG collection into subsets containing 1%, 5%, and 10% of the original collection, and then used our method to segment the pages of each subset. Using the AdjRAND metric, we compared the segmentation of each page of the subsets to the segmentation obtained for these pages when processing the whole collection. When checking the results, we realized that the segmentation output obtained for each subset was similar to that obtained for the whole collection (for instance, the average AdjRAND value achieved by the subset containing 1% of the pages of IG was 0.98), which lead us to conclude that our method is able to obtain good segmentation quality even for small Web sites.

Table 2 presents the results obtained when using the segment aware model proposed by de Moura *et al.* [13] with our automatic segmentation method, combination referred to as *AutS*, and with the manual segmentation approach, combination referred to as *ManS*. Notice that we do not perform ranking experiments with *Rule-based Blockfusion* because the search model adopted requires information about segment classes that is not provided by the *Rule-based Blockfusion* method. The Table also shows the ranking quality obtained when using BM25 ranking strategy [26] with no block information, and when using BM25 ranking applied to pages after templates removal. This last baseline method is referred to as BM25NT, which means BM25 without templates.

The first important observation is that the segment aware ranking method yields improved results relative to the BM25 and BM25NT baselines, for both segmentation methods. Further, the results obtained when using our segmentation algorithm are quite close to the ones obtained when using the manual segmentation. When applying the Wilcoxon statistical test with a 95% confidence level, we notice that the differences between our method and *ManS* are not significant in most cases, except for all metrics in CNET and MAP in IG. The differences in the scores obtained by the two methods are not high, being smaller than 1.3% in most cases. Further, the fully automatic method has the advantage of not requiring manual intervention at any point of the segmentation process.

	IG		CNN	
Metric	P@10	MAP	P@10	MAP
BM25	0.594	0.621	0.612	0.691
BM25NT	0.571	0.649	0.602	0.704
ManS	0.667	0.749	0.642	0.786
AutS	0.659	0.733	0.630	0.779
	BLOGs		**CNET**	
Metric	P@10	MAP	P@10	MAP
BM25	0.584	0.644	0.476	0.458
BM25NT	0.594	0.632	0.534	0.481
ManS	0.604	0.678	0.552	0.498
AutS	0.602	0.677	0.512	0.470

Table 2: Ranking quality obtained in four collections when using the BM25 formula, the BM25 without no templates (BM25NT), and the segment aware model applied to manual segmentation (ManS) and to our automatic segmentation (AutS).

6. CONCLUSIONS

In this paper we proposed and evaluated a site oriented segmentation algorithm for Web pages. The method combines the DOM trees of all pages in a site into a single data structure which is called SOM tree. By inserting the individual pages into the SOM Tree, the algorithm performs a clustering-like procedure. By investigating regularities among the pages associated with the leaves of the SOM tree, the algorithm naturally breaks them into segments.

The experiments performed with our segmentation approach indicate it produces quite competitive segmentation results, which opens an opportunity to the use of the method in several Web site segmentation applications.

We show that the method is particularly useful to produce input to a previously proposed segment aware ranking method, since it not only segments the Web pages, but also is able to cluster them into classes. Further, the results obtained by our method in segment aware Web search are close to the ones obtained when using a segmentation approach based on manual intervention.

As future work we plan to study the impact of using our method in large scale Web search systems, where there are usually just a few sample pages of each Web site in the collection. Also, we intend to investigate the application of our segmentation method to mobile applications, including its use in alternative ways of presenting Web search results in mobile devices.

7. REFERENCES

[1] K. Ahnizeret, D. Fernandes, J. M. Cavalcanti, E. S. de Moura, and A. S. da Silva. Information retrieval aware web site modelling and generation. In *ER '04*, pages 402–419, Berlin, Heidelberg, 2004. Springer.

[2] R. A. Baeza-Yates and B. Ribeiro-Neto. *Modern Information Retrieval*. Addison-Wesley Longman Publishing Co., Inc., Boston, MA, USA, 1999.

[3] Z. Bar-Yossef and S. Rajagopalan. Template detection via data mining and its applications. In *WWW '02*, pages 580–591, New York, NY, USA, 2002. ACM.

[4] D. Cai, X. He, J.-R. Wen, and W.-Y. Ma. Block-level link analysis. In *ACM SIGIR '04*, pages 440–447, New York, NY, USA, 2004. ACM.

[5] D. Cai, S. Yu, J.-R. Wen, and W.-Y. Ma. Vips: a vision-based page segmentation algorithm. Microsoft Technical Report, 2003.

[6] D. Cai, S. Yu, J.-R. Wen, and W.-Y. Ma. Block-based web search. In *ACM SIGIR '04*, pages 456–463, New York, NY, USA, 2004. ACM.

[7] J. P. Callan. Passage-level evidence in document retrieval. In *ACM SIGIR '94*, pages 302–310, New York, NY, USA, 1994. Springer-Verlag New York, Inc.

[8] Y. Cao, Z. Niu, L. Dai, and Y. Zhao. Extraction of informative blocks from web pages. In *ALPIT '08*, pages 544–549, Washington, DC, USA, 2008. IEEE Computer Society.

[9] S. Ceri, M. Matera, F. Rizzo, and V. Demaldé. Designing data-intensive web applications for content accessibility using web marts. *Commun. ACM*, 50(4):55–61, 2007.

[10] D. Chakrabarti, R. Kumar, and K. Punera. A graph-theoretic approach to webpage segmentation. In *WWW'08*, pages 377–386, 2008.

[11] V. Crescenzi, P. Merialdo, and P. Missier. Fine-grain web site structure discovery. In *ACM WIDM '03*, pages 15–22, New York, NY, USA, 2003. ACM.

[12] V. Crescenzi, P. Merialdo, and P. Missier. Clustering web pages based on their structure. *Data Knowl. Eng.*, 54(3):279–299, 2005.

[13] E. S. de Moura, D. Fernandes, B. Ribeiro-Neto, A. S. da Silva, and M. A. Gonçalves. Using structural information to improve search in web collections. *JASIST*, 61:2503–2513, December 2010.

[14] D. Fernandes, E. S. de Moura, B. Ribeiro-Neto, A. S. da Silva, and M. A. Gonçalves. Computing block importance for searching on web sites. In *CIKM '07*, pages 165–174, New York, NY, USA, 2007. ACM.

[15] D. Gibson, K. Punera, and A. Tomkins. The volume and evolution of web page templates. In *WWW '05*, pages 830–839, New York, NY, USA, 2005. ACM.

[16] G. Hattori, K. Hoashi, K. Matsumoto, and F. Sugaya. Robust web page segmentation for mobile terminal using content-distances and page layout information. In *WWW '07*, pages 361–370, New York, NY, USA, 2007. ACM.

[17] D. Hawking and N. Craswell. Overview of TREC-7 very large collection track. In *Proc. of the Seventh Text Retrieval Conf.*, pages 91–104, 1998.

[18] L. Hubert and P. Arabie. Comparing partitions. *Journal of Classification*, 2(1):193–218, December 1985.

[19] J. Kang and J. Choi. Detecting informative web page blocks for efficient information extraction using visual block segmentation. pages 306–310, 2007.

[20] C. Kohlschütter, P. Fankhauser, and W. Nejdl. Boilerplate detection using shallow text features. In *WSDM '10*, pages 441–450, New York, NY, USA, 2010. ACM.

[21] C. Kohlschütter and W. Nejdl. A densitometric approach to web page segmentation. In *CIKM '08*, pages 1173–1182, New York, NY, USA, 2008. ACM.

[22] L. Li, Y. Liu, A. Obregon, and M. Weatherston. Visual segmentation-based data record extraction from web documents. In *IRI'07*, pages 502–507, 2007.

[23] S.-H. Lin and J.-M. Ho. Discovering informative content blocks from web documents. In *Proc. of ACM SIGKDD '02*, pages 588–593, New York, NY, USA, 2002. ACM.

[24] A. K. Marco Baroni, Francis Chantree and S. Sharoff. Cleaneval: a competition for cleaning web pages. In *LREC'08*, Marrakech, Morocco, may 2008.

[25] D. C. Reis, P. B. Golgher, A. S. Silva, and A. F. Laender. Automatic web news extraction using tree edit distance. In *WWW'04*, pages 502–511, 2004.

[26] S. E. Robertson and S. Walker. Some simple effective approximations to the 2-poisson model for probabilistic weighted retrieval. In *ACM SIGIR '94*, pages 232–241, New York, NY, USA, 1994. Springer-Verlag New York, Inc.

[27] L. Shi, C. Niu, M. Zhou, and J. Gao. A dom tree alignment model for mining parallel data from the web. In *ACL'06*, pages 489–496, Morristown, NJ, USA, 2006. Association for Computational Linguistics.

[28] R. Song, H. Liu, J.-R. Wen, and W.-Y. Ma. Learning block importance models for web pages. In *WWW '04*, pages 203–211, New York, NY, USA, 2004. ACM.

[29] A. Strehl and J. Ghosh. Cluster ensembles — a knowledge reuse framework for combining multiple partitions. *J. Mach. Learn. Res.*, 3:583–617, 2003.

[30] K. Vieira, A. L. da Costa Carvalho, K. Berlt, E. S. de Moura, A. S. da Silva, and J. Freir. On finding templates on web collections. *World Wide Web*, pages 171–211, 2009.

[31] K. Vieira, A. S. da Silva, N. Pinto, E. S. de Moura, a. M. B. C. Jo and J. Freire. A fast and robust method for web page template detection and removal. In *CIKM '06*, pages 258–267, New York, NY, USA, 2006. ACM.

[32] N. X. Vinh, J. Epps, and J. Bailey. Information theoretic measures for clusterings comparison: is a correction for chance necessary? In *ICML '09*, pages 1073–1080, New York, NY, USA, 2009. ACM.

[33] L. Yi, B. Liu, and X. Li. Eliminating noisy information in web pages for data mining. In *KDD '03*, pages 296–305, New York, NY, USA, 2003. ACM.

[34] Y. Zhai and B. Liu. Web data extraction based on partial tree alignment. In *WWW '05*, pages 76–85, 2005.

[35] Y. Zhang, A. C. Surendran, J. C. Platt, and M. Narasimhan. Learning from multi-topic web documents for contextual advertisement. In *SIGKDD'08*, pages 1051–1059, New York, NY, USA, 2008. ACM.

Composite Hashing with Multiple Information Sources

Dan Zhang
Computer Science Department
Purdue University,
West Lafayette, IN 47907, US
zhang168@cs.purdue.edu

Fei Wang
IBM T. J. Watson Research Lab
Hawthorne, NY 10532
fwang@us.ibm.com

Luo Si
Computer Science Department
Purdue University,
West Lafayette, IN 47907, US
lsi@cs.purdue.edu

ABSTRACT

Similarity search applications with a large amount of text and image data demands an efficient and effective solution. One useful strategy is to represent the examples in databases as compact binary codes through semantic hashing, which has attracted much attention due to its fast query/search speed and drastically reduced storage requirement. All of the current semantic hashing methods only deal with the case when each example is represented by one type of features. However, examples are often described from several different information sources in many real world applications. For example, the characteristics of a webpage can be derived from both its content part and its associated links.

To address the problem of learning good hashing codes in this scenario, we propose a novel research problem – Composite Hashing with Multiple Information Sources (CHMIS). The focus of the new research problem is to design an algorithm for incorporating the features from different information sources into the binary hashing codes efficiently and effectively. In particular, we propose an algorithm CHMIS-AW (CHMIS with Adjusted Weights) for learning the codes. The proposed algorithm integrates information from several different sources into the binary hashing codes by adjusting the weights on each individual source for maximizing the coding performance, and enables fast conversion from query examples to their binary hashing codes. Experimental results on five different datasets demonstrate the superior performance of the proposed method against several other state-of-the-art semantic hashing techniques.

Categories and Subject Descriptors

H.3.1 [**Information Storage and Retrieval**]: Content Analysis and Indexing; H.3.3 [**Information Storage and Retrieval**]: Information Search and Retrieval; I.2.6 [**Artificial Intelligence**]: Learning

General Terms

Algorithms, Performance, Experimentation

Keywords

Composite Hashing, Semantic Hashing, Multiple Information Sources

1. INTRODUCTION

The explosive growth of the internet has generated a huge amount of data such as documents, images and videos. As the data sizes increase, the density of similar objects in the data space also increases. Therefore, nearest neighbor methods for similarity search applications tend to be more reliable than before. However, two key problems for using nearest neighbor search in large datasets are: (1) *Storage challenge*. How to store the training data efficiently? (2) *Retrieval challenge*. How to retrieve the desired data efficiently and effectively? It is clear that the traditional methods, such as TF-IDF for document representations [34, 35], which compare word count vectors, are difficult to be directly used for large datasets, since they need to save the original examples and the computational cost of dealing with floating/integer features is often too high.

A clever way of solving these two challenges is through semantic hashing [17, 33, 47]. By using semantic hashing algorithms, each example in the database is re-represented by a compact binary code, which preserves its semantic meanings in the original feature space. These hashing methods also provide a way to efficiently transform query examples into the corresponding hashing codes. Then, the retrieving process can be simply done by selecting examples within a small Hamming distance of the codes for the query example. This method addresses the two challenges in the following ways: (1) By mapping examples in the database to a low dimensional binary space, it is much more efficient in terms of the storage cost, compared with saving the original examples. (2) The retrieval speed is fast, since an efficient scheme for mapping the query examples to their hashing codes is provided, and the similarity computation can be simply done by using bit XOR operation and counting the number of '0' bits in the low dimensional space. This process is very fast, and nowadays even an ordinary laptop is capable of doing millions of Hamming distance computation in a short time.

Previous semantic hashing methods are successful in addressing the two challenges. However, they do not address the case when examples are described from several different sources. Actually, in many real-world applications, it is often true that examples are derived from several different sources, and therefore are represented by multiple sets of features. For example, in web mining applications, each webpage has disparate descriptions, textual content, in-bound and out-bound links, etc. In image retrieval, each picture can be described by different kinds of features, such as the SIFT features [27], RGB features, texture features, etc. Different sets of features could have different statistical properties. Therefore, designing a hashing algorithm for examples from multiple information sources is necessary. The main challenge for this task is how to incorporate different sets of features together into one set of binary hashing codes.

To address this task, we propose a novel research problem: Composite Hashing with Multiple Information Sources (CHMIS). The basic objective of CHMIS is to design some efficient and effective hashing algorithms that can encode the examples described from several different information sources. An intuitive way of designing a CHMIS method is to simply concatenate the features from several different sources, treat them as if they were from one information source, and apply the previous hashing method to these examples. However, by doing so, the different statistical properties from different individual sources may be lost. This paper proposes an elegant method – CHMIS-AW (CHMIS with Adjusted Weights) to intelligently integrate information from different sources. In particular, CHMIS-AW is an iterative method which preserves the semantic similarities between training examples, and ensures the consistency between the hashing codes and the corresponding hashing functions designed for different information sources. Furthermore, the importance of each individual source is represented as a convex combination coefficient and can be automatically learned through a joint optimization procedure. Our experiments on five real world datasets with different information sources show that the proposed method outperforms state-of-the-art methods substantially.

2. RELATED WORK

Efficiency is a critical issue for many information retrieval applications with a large number of text documents, images or videos. For traditional ad-hoc text search with relatively short user queries, different types of structures and operations of inverted indexing have been proposed [13, 39, 48, 54]. Distributed indexing [2, 3] has also been explored when there is sufficient computing resource. On the other side, similarity search with documents, images, or other entities are typically represented as feature vectors in a space of more than thousands of dimensions [25, 28], which demands different solutions especially when only limited computing resource is available.

The traditional similarity search is conducted based on these feature vectors by space partitioning index structures, like TF-IDF methods [34, 35], KD-tree, or data partitioning index structures, say R-tree [12]. However, when the dimensionality of feature space is too high, traditional similarity search may fail to work efficiently [46]. Semantic hashing [33] is used in the case when the requirement for the exactness of the final results is not high, and the similarity search in the original high dimensional space is not affordable. More precisely, semantic hashing methods try to represent the whole datasets by using a fixed small number of binary bits so that the queries can be answered in a short time (virtually constant time) [41], with some extent of precision being guaranteed. Such hashing based fast similarity search can be considered as a way to embed high dimensional feature vectors into a Hamming space, while preserving the semantic similarity relationship between examples as much as possible. This is different from traditional dimensionality reduction methods, such as Principal Component Analysis (PCA) and Latent Semantic Analysis (LSI) [15, 20]. Hashing methods map original features to low dimensional binary codes, which enables the efficient search in Hamming space.

One of the most well known hashing methods is Locality-Sensitive Hashing (LSH) [1, 14]. It uses random linear projections to map close examples to similar codes. It has already been proved that the Hamming distance between different examples will asymptotically approach their Euclidean distance in the original feature space, with the increase of the hashing bits. Some LSH based methods are also used for near optimal duplicate detection. For example, min-Hash function [8–10] assigns numbers to each example, and, for two documents, the probability of being assigned the same number equals the ratio of the intersection and union of their word representations.

Besides LSH, some machine learning methods can be adapted to solve the hashing problem. The traditional dimensionality reduction methods can be adapted to solve the hashing problem via a simple thresholding [33, 45]. For example, PCA Hashing [26, 45] computes K-bit hashing codes by projecting each example to the K principal components of the training set, and then binarizing the coefficients, by setting each bit to 1 if it exceeds the median value seen for the training set, and -1 otherwise. In [33], the authors use stacked Restricted Boltzman Machine (RBM) [18, 19] to generate compact binary hashing codes, which can be considered as binarlized LSI. Later, in [51], the authors further improve this method. Some traditional classification algorithms can also be adapted. For example, in [4, 37], the authors adapted Adaboost [31] to the hashing method. More precisely, they consider the similar pairs of examples as positive examples, and otherwise negative. Then, a set of classifiers are trained by AdaBoost, the output of all of these weak learners are considered as the binary hashing codes. In [43, 44], the authors solve the problem of semi-supervised semantic hashing. In the following two sections, we mainly discuss two state-of-the-art hashing methods that most related to the proposed method – Spectral Hashing [47] and Self Taught Hashing [52], which have been shown to outperform several other types of hashing methods.

2.1 Spectral Hashing (SH)

As a recently proposed method, Spectral Hashing (SH) [47] was proposed to design compact binary codes for search. This method can be considered as an extension of spectral clustering [49]. Its concrete formulation is as follows:

$$\min \sum_{i,j} \mathbf{S}_{ij} \|\mathbf{y}_i - \mathbf{y}_j\|^2$$
$$s.t. \quad \mathbf{y}_i \in \{-1, 1\}^K, \quad \sum_i \mathbf{y}_i = 0, \quad \frac{1}{n} \sum_i \mathbf{y}_i \mathbf{y}_i^T = \mathbf{I}, \qquad (1)$$

where, $\mathbf{S}_{ij}$ is the similarity measure between the example i and example j, $\mathbf{y}_i$ is the hashing code for the i-th example, K is the number of bits. The basic motivation of this formulation is to preserve the original similarity relationship between examples in the Hamming space. However, solving this above problem is NP hard. After relaxing the discrete constraints to continuous, it can be solved using traditional spectral analysis. Then, the optimal hashing code can be simply obtained by binarizing the solution of the relaxed optimization problem. Moreover, this formulation can be generalized to enable the effective computation for out of sample examples/queries, as introduced in [47].

SH tries to keep the similarity relationships, which are defined in the original feature space, between examples in the hashing codes. However, it is hard to find a good similarity measure which can consider the consistency of the different sources. Actually, some previous works demonstrate an improvement for considering the consistency in multiple source problems [32, 40, 50], in which the authors designed a classifier on each view, and require the outputs from different views should be consistent and not deviate too much.

2.2 Self Taught Hashing (STH)

Self Taught Hashing (STH) [52] can be considered as an extension to SH. To obtain the hashing codes for the training set and the hashing function for efficiently mapping the query examples, STH uses two steps, an unsupervised step and a supervised step. In the unsupervised step, the authors construct a k-nearest-neighbor graph for the given dataset, embed the examples into a K (K is still the number of bits) dimensional space through spectral analysis, and obtain the binary codes for each example through thresholding. In the supervised step, K SVM classifiers are trained based on the training examples, and their binary hashing codes learned from the previous step are used as labels. The hashing codes for the query example can then be obtained through a classification problem and thresholding by using the K classifiers.

Compared with SH, when dealing with query examples, STH does not assume that data are uniformly distributed in a hyper-rectangle, which is restrictive. The maximum margin principle enables a good generalization ability. However, it still cannot avoid the same consistency problem of the similarity measures for different sources as in SH. Different from their method, the method proposed in this paper combines both the unsupervised and supervised steps for intelligently integrating features from multiple sources.

3. PROBLEM STATEMENT

In CHMIS, we are given a set of n training examples from M information sources, represented as: $\{\mathbf{x}_1^{(i)}, \mathbf{x}_2^{(i)}, \ldots, \mathbf{x}_n^{(i)}\} \in \mathbf{R}^{d_i \times 1}$, $i \in \{1, 2, \ldots, M\}$, where d_i is the dimensionality of the i-th information source. The main objective of CHMIS is to find the optimal K binary hashing bits $\mathbf{Y} \in \{-1, 1\}^{K \times n}$ for these training examples, as well as a hashing function $f(\bullet)$ that deals with the query (out-of-sample) examples. The coding optimization criterion is to identify neighbors of the query examples in the training set accurately in a short time. For convenience, throughout this paper, the hashing codes for the i-th training example, i.e., the i-th column of $\mathbf{Y}$, is denoted as $\mathbf{y}_i$. The hashing codes for the p-th hashing bit, which is the p-th row of $\mathbf{Y}$, is denoted as $\mathbf{Y}^p$.

4. COMPOSITE HASHING WITH MULTIPLE INFORMATION SOURCES WITH ADJUSTED WEIGHTS

From the previous presentation, we can see that CHMIS is an important research problem. To solve it, this paper presents a novel optimization formulation – CHMIS-AW (CHMIS with Adjusted Weights).

The main objective of CHMIS-AW is to obtain hashing codes for training examples and to learn the hashing function simultaneously by preserving the similarity relationships between training examples in the original feature space, and generating a consistent hashing function from different information sources. In particular, the objective function of CHMIS-AW is composed of two parts: The first part is a similarity preservation term, which tries to preserve the similarity relationship in the original feature space using the learned hashing codes. The second part ensures the consistency between the learned hashing codes and the corresponding hashing function designed on multiple sources. In the following, we will first introduce how to construct the two parts respectively. Then the joint optimization problem and the corresponding optimization strategy will be provided. Finally, we will discuss the distinctions of the proposed method and some related ones.

4.1 Similarity Preservation

One of the key goals in most state-of-the-art hashing methods, such as [33, 47], is to seek for compact binary codes so that the Hamming distance between codewords correlates with semantic similarity. This indicates that similar data points should be mapped to similar codes within a short Hamming distance. In SH, the authors demonstrated that the problem of finding such an optimal set of codes is closely related to the graph partition methods. They proposed to achieve the goal by using the spectral method.

Different from the previous hashing problems, in CHMIS-AW, we need to deal with multiple information sources. To measure the similarity between examples represented by the binary hashing codes, one natural way is to measure the similarity quantity on each individual source and sum them together as follows:

$$\sum_{t=1}^{M} \sum_{i,j=1}^{n} \mathbf{S}_{ij}^{(t)} \|\mathbf{y}_i - \mathbf{y}_j\|^2. \qquad (2)$$

Here, $\mathbf{S}_{n \times n}^{(t)}$ is the affinity matrix defined on the t-th source. To meet the similarity preservation criterion, we seek to minimize this quantity, because it incurs a heavy penalty if two similar examples are mapped far away on the information source.

There are many different ways of defining the affinity matrix $\mathbf{S}^{(t)}$. In [47], the author used the global similarity structure of all document pairs, while in [52], the local similarity structure, i.e., k-nearest-neighborhood, is used. In this paper, we use the local similarity, due to its nice property in many data mining and information retrieval applications [28]. In particular, the corresponding weights are computed by Gaussian functions, i.e.,

$$\mathbf{S}_{ij}^{(t)} = \begin{cases} e^{-\frac{\|\mathbf{x}_i^{(t)} - \mathbf{x}_j^{(t)}\|^2}{\delta_{ij}^2}} & \text{if } \mathbf{x}_i^{(t)} \in N_k(\mathbf{x}_j^{(t)}) \text{ or } \mathbf{x}_j^{(t)} \in N_k(\mathbf{x}_i^{(t)}) \\ 0 & \text{otherwise} \end{cases}.$$

The variance δ_{ij} is determined automatically by local scaling [49], and $N_k(\mathbf{x})$ represents the set of k-nearest-neighbors of the example $\mathbf{x}$.

By introducing a diagonal $n \times n$ matrix $\mathbf{D}^{(t)}$ for each individual source, whose entries are given by $\mathbf{D}_{ii}^{(t)} = \sum_{j=1}^{n} \mathbf{S}_{ij}^{(t)}$,

Eq.(2) can be rewritten as:

$$tr\left(\mathbf{Y}^T\sum_{t=1}^{M}(\mathbf{D}^{(t)}-\mathbf{S}^{(t)})\mathbf{Y}\right)=tr\left(\mathbf{Y}^T\sum_{t=1}^{M}\mathbf{L}^{(t)}\mathbf{Y}\right), \quad (3)$$

where $\mathbf{L}^{(t)}$ is the graph Laplacian [11] defined on the t-th source, and $tr(\bullet)$ is the trace function. Furthermore, similar to [52], we can replace the graph Laplacian with the normalized graph laplacian due to its superior performance [11, 38] indicated by:

$$\widetilde{\mathbf{L}}^{(t)}=(\mathbf{D}^{(t)})^{-\frac{1}{2}}\mathbf{L}^{(t)}(\mathbf{D}^{(t)})^{-\frac{1}{2}}. \quad (4)$$

Then the objective function that needs to be minimized turns to:

$$\Omega(\mathbf{Y})=tr\left(\mathbf{Y}^T\sum_{t=1}^{M}\widetilde{\mathbf{L}}^{(t)}\mathbf{Y}\right). \quad (5)$$

By minimizing this term, the similarity between different examples can be preserved in the learned hashing codes.

4.2 Consistency

In Section 4.1, our focus is to find the optimal binary hashing matrix $\mathbf{Y}$ that preserves the data similarities in the original feature space. However, this is only a transductive formulation, i.e., $\mathbf{Y}$ cannot be generalized to query examples directly. It is true that we can use the Nyström method [5] to deduct the hashing codes for the query examples from the hashing codes in the training set and the similarity matrix between the query and the training examples, but this operation is as expensive as doing exhaustive nearest neighbor search. We solve this problem by first introducing a linear hash function[1], which is represented as: $f(\mathbf{x}_i)=\sum_{t=1}^{M}\alpha_t(\mathbf{W}^{(t)})^T\mathbf{x}_i^{(t)}$, where $\mathbf{W}^{(t)}\in\mathbf{R}^{d_t\times K}$ is the weight vector for the classifier on the t-th source, and $\alpha=[\alpha_1,\ldots,\alpha_M]^T$ is a M dimensional non-negative convex combination coefficient column vector that balances the outputs from each individual source, and $\sum_{t=1}^{M}\alpha_t=1$.

In this way, the output of this hashing function is a convex combination [7] of the linear hash function outputs on each individual source. A constraint here is that the outputs on the training set should be as close to $\mathbf{Y}$ as possible, i.e., the outputs of the hash functions from different sources should make an "agreement" on the learned binary hashing codes. The importance of each individual source on this agreement is specified by the corresponding convex combination coefficient. In this way, this methodology incorporates the different statistic properties of the different sources. The concrete formulation for the consistency part is given as follows:

$$C_2\sum_{i=1}^{n}\|\mathbf{y}_i-\sum_{t=1}^{M}\alpha_t(\mathbf{W}^{(t)})^T\mathbf{x}_i^{(t)}\|^2+\sum_{t=1}^{M}\|\mathbf{W}^{(t)}\|^2, \quad (6)$$

where, the regularization term $\sum_{t=1}^{M}\|\mathbf{W}^{(t)}\|^2$ is introduced to avoid overfitting [42]. $\sum_{i=1}^{n}\|\mathbf{y}_i-\sum_{t=1}^{M}\alpha_t(\mathbf{W}^{(t)})^T\mathbf{x}_i^{(t)}\|^2$ is a loss function, which measures the difference between the hashing codes and the outputs of the hash functions. C_2 is a trade-off parameter, balancing the loss function and the regularization term.

[1]Although [30, 43, 44, 52] use linear classifiers, as they have claimed, the kernel methods [36] can be easily incorporated into their formulations. So is the proposed method.

For convenience, we introduce the following concatenate matrix:

$$\widetilde{\mathbf{W}}=[(\mathbf{W}^{(1)})^T,(\mathbf{W}^{(2)})^T,\ldots,(\mathbf{W}^{(M)})^T]^T;$$
$$\widetilde{\mathbf{x}}_i^{(t)}=[\mathbf{0},\ldots,(\mathbf{x}_i^{(t)})^T,\ldots,\mathbf{0}]^T. \quad (7)$$

Here, after this concatenation, the new designed $\widetilde{\mathbf{W}}$ is a $(d_1+d_2+\ldots+d_M)\times K$ dimensional matrix, and $\widetilde{\mathbf{x}}_i^{(t)}$ is a one-dimensional column vector with only from the $(d_1+d_2+\ldots,+d_{p-1}+1)$-th to $(d_1+d_2+\ldots,+d_p)$-th elements being nonzero. It is clear that $(\mathbf{W}^{(t)})^T\mathbf{x}_i^{(t)}=\widetilde{\mathbf{W}}^T\widetilde{\mathbf{x}}_i^{(t)}$. Therefore, Eq.(6) can be simplified as:

$$\begin{aligned}J(\mathbf{Y},\widetilde{\mathbf{W}},\alpha)=&C_2\sum_{i=1}^{n}\|\mathbf{y}_i-\sum_{t=1}^{M}\alpha_t(\widetilde{\mathbf{W}})^T\widetilde{\mathbf{x}}_i^{(t)}\|^2+\|\widetilde{\mathbf{W}}\|^2\\ =&C_2\|\mathbf{Y}-\sum_{t=1}^{M}\alpha_t(\widetilde{\mathbf{W}})^T\widetilde{\mathbf{X}}^{(t)}\|^2+\|\widetilde{\mathbf{W}}\|^2, \quad (8)\end{aligned}$$

where $\widetilde{\mathbf{X}}^{(t)}=[\widetilde{\mathbf{x}}_1^{(t)},\widetilde{\mathbf{x}}_2^{(t)},\ldots,\widetilde{\mathbf{x}}_n^{(t)}]$.

4.3 Overall Objective

The overall objective function combines the similarity preservation part given in Eq.(5) and the consistency part in Eq.(8) as follows:

$$\begin{aligned}\min_{\mathbf{Y},\widetilde{\mathbf{W}},\alpha}\quad & T(\mathbf{Y},\widetilde{\mathbf{W}},\alpha)\\ s.t.\quad & \mathbf{Y}\in\{-1,1\}^{K\times n},\\ & \mathbf{Y1}=0,\quad \mathbf{YY}^T=\mathbf{I},\quad \alpha^T\mathbf{1}=1,\quad \alpha\succeq 0, \quad (9)\end{aligned}$$

where $T(\mathbf{Y},\widetilde{\mathbf{W}},\alpha)=tr(C_1\mathbf{Y}^T\sum_{t=1}^{M}\widetilde{\mathbf{L}}^{(t)}\mathbf{Y})+C_2\|\mathbf{Y}-\sum_{t=1}^{M}\alpha_t(\widetilde{\mathbf{W}})^T\widetilde{\mathbf{X}}^{(t)}\|^2+\|\widetilde{\mathbf{W}}\|^2$. Here, $\mathbf{Y1}=0$ requires each bit to fire 50% of the time (with equal probability as positive or negative), and the constraint $\mathbf{YY}^T=\mathbf{I}$ requires the bits to be uncorrelated.

This is a hard optimization problem because of the discrete constraints. We propose to relax this constraint and drop the constraint $\mathbf{Y1}=0$ first. However, even after the relaxation, the objective function $T(\mathbf{Y},\widetilde{\mathbf{W}},\alpha)$ is still nonconvex with respect to $\mathbf{Y}$, $\widetilde{\mathbf{W}}$, α jointly, which makes it difficult to solve.

To solve this problem, we will show the optimal solution of $\widetilde{\mathbf{W}}$ has a closed form solution with respect to $\mathbf{Y}$ and α. For notational convenience, we rewrite $\sum_{t=1}^{M}\alpha_t\widetilde{\mathbf{X}}^{(t)}$ as $\widetilde{\mathbf{X}}_\alpha$. Then, the optimal $\widetilde{\mathbf{W}}$ can be determined by solving the following optimization problem:

$$\min_{\widetilde{\mathbf{W}}}C_2\|\mathbf{Y}-(\widetilde{\mathbf{W}})^T\widetilde{\mathbf{X}}_\alpha\|^2+\|\widetilde{\mathbf{W}}\|^2. \quad (10)$$

This is a standard regularized least square problem [6], and its optimal solution can be obtained by: $\widetilde{\mathbf{W}}=\mathbf{QY}$, where $\mathbf{Q}=C_2(C_2\widetilde{\mathbf{X}}_\alpha\widetilde{\mathbf{X}}_\alpha^T+\mathbf{I})^{-1}\widetilde{\mathbf{X}}_\alpha$. Bringing this solution back to $T(\mathbf{Y},\widetilde{\mathbf{W}},\alpha)$, we can eliminate the optimization variable $\widetilde{\mathbf{W}}$, and problem (9) can be rewritten as:

$$\begin{aligned}\min_{\mathbf{Y},\alpha}\quad & \widetilde{T}(\mathbf{Y},\alpha) \quad (11)\\ s.t.\quad & \mathbf{YY}^T=\mathbf{I},\ \alpha^T\mathbf{1}=1,\quad \alpha\succeq 0,\end{aligned}$$

Algorithm: CHMIS-AW Training
Input: 1. A set of training examples from M information sources: $\{\mathbf{x}_1^{(i)}, \mathbf{x}_2^{(i)}, \ldots, \mathbf{x}_n^{(i)}\}, i \in \{1, 2 \ldots, M\}$. 2. Parameters: Similarity Preservation parameter C_1, and Consistency trade-off parameter C_2, as in Eq.(9).
Output: The hashing code for training examples $\mathbf{Y}$, hashing function weight vector $\widetilde{\mathbf{W}}$, convex combination coefficient α and median vector $\mathbf{m}$

Initialization:
1. Initialize $\alpha_i = \frac{1}{M}$ $(i = 1, \ldots, M)$
2. Construct $\widetilde{\mathbf{X}}^{(\mathbf{t})}$, $t = 1, \ldots, M$ as in Eq.(7)
3. Construct the normalized graph Laplacians $\widetilde{\mathbf{L}}^{(t)}$, $t = 1, \ldots, M$ on each individual view as in Eq.(4).
Repeat
4. Calculate $\widetilde{\mathbf{X}}_\alpha = \sum_{t=1}^{M} \alpha_t \widetilde{\mathbf{X}}^{(t)}$
5. Calculate $\mathbf{Q} = C_2(C_2 \widetilde{\mathbf{X}}_\alpha \widetilde{\mathbf{X}}_\alpha^T + \mathbf{I})^{-1} \widetilde{\mathbf{X}}_\alpha$
6. Calculate the matrix $\mathbf{H}(\alpha)$ as in Eq.(12)
7. Solve the K eigenvectors $\mathbf{Y} = \{\mathbf{v}_1, \mathbf{v}_2, \ldots, \mathbf{v}_K\}$ corresponding to the smallest K eigenvalues of $\mathbf{H}(\alpha)$
8. Solve $\widetilde{\mathbf{W}}$, $\widetilde{\mathbf{W}} = \mathbf{QY}$
9. Compute α by solving problem (13)
Until Convergence
Training Hashing Code Generation:
For $p = 1{:}K$
10. Get the median value for the p-th code by $\mathbf{m}_p = median(\mathbf{Y}^p)$
11. Generating the p-th hashing code by $\mathbf{Y}^p = (\mathbf{Y}^p > \mathbf{m}_p)$
End For

Table 1: Algorithm: CHMIS-AW Training

where,

$$\begin{aligned}\widetilde{T}(\mathbf{Y}, \alpha) =& tr\left(\mathbf{Y}^T (C_1 \sum_{t=1}^{M} \widetilde{\mathbf{L}}^{(t)} + C_2(\mathbf{I} - \mathbf{Q}^T \widetilde{\mathbf{X}}_\alpha \right. \qquad (12)\\ &\left. - \widetilde{\mathbf{X}}_\alpha^T \mathbf{Q} + \mathbf{Q}^T \widetilde{\mathbf{X}}_\alpha \widetilde{\mathbf{X}}_\alpha^T \mathbf{Q}) + \mathbf{Q}^T \mathbf{Q}) \mathbf{Y}\right) \\ =& tr\left(\mathbf{Y}^T \mathbf{H}(\alpha) \mathbf{Y}\right).\end{aligned}$$

Here, $\mathbf{H}(\alpha)$ is a positive semi-definite matrix, which is related to α and is introduced to simplify the formulation. $\mathbf{I}$ is an identity matrix.

The problem (11) is still non-convex, since α and $\mathbf{Y}$ are still coupled together. Fortunately, the problem is convex with respect to either of them, with the other one fixed, and therefore can be solved by alternative optimization with guaranteed convergence. In particular, after initializing α, the optimization problem can be solved by doing the following two steps iteratively, until convergence:

1. Fix α, optimize:

   $$\min_{\mathbf{Y}} \quad \mathbf{Y}^T \mathbf{H}(\alpha) \mathbf{Y}, \quad s.t. \quad \mathbf{Y}\mathbf{Y}^T = \mathbf{I}$$

   The solution of this optimization is given by $\mathbf{Y} = [\mathbf{v}_1, \mathbf{v}_2, \ldots, \mathbf{v}_K]^T$, whose columns are the K eigenvectors corresponding to the smallest eigenvalues of $\mathbf{H}(\alpha)$. Then we calculate $\widetilde{\mathbf{W}} = \mathbf{QY}$.

2. Fix $\mathbf{Y}$, optimize:

   $$\min_{\alpha} \quad \|\mathbf{Y} - \mathbf{O}\alpha\|^2, \quad s.t. \quad \alpha^T \mathbf{1} = 1, \quad \alpha \succeq 0 \quad (13)$$

   where $\mathbf{O} = [\mathbf{o}^{(1)}, \mathbf{o}^{(2)}, \ldots, \mathbf{o}^{(M)}]$, and $\mathbf{o}^{(t)} = (\widetilde{\mathbf{W}})^T \widetilde{\mathbf{X}}^{(t)}$. The combination coefficient α can be solved efficiently by quadratic programming algorithms [7].

After obtaining the optimal $\mathbf{Y}$, we can get the optimal hashing code for the training set by thresholding $\mathbf{Y}$. More specifically, for $\mathbf{Y}^p$, which is the p-th row of $\mathbf{Y}$, if the j-th element $\mathbf{Y}_j^p$ is larger than the specified threshold, $\mathbf{Y}_j^p = +1$, otherwise $\mathbf{Y}_j^p = -1$.

Then, a natural question would be: how to pick these thresholds? In [45], the authors pointed out that a good semantic hashing should also maximize the entropy to ensure efficiency. Using maximum entropy principle, a binary bit that gives balanced partitioning of the whole dataset always provides maximum information. Therefore, we set the threshold for binarising $\mathbf{Y}^p, p \in \{1, 2 \ldots, K\}$ to be the median value of $\mathbf{v}_p, p \in \{1, 2 \ldots, K\}$ (The median value for $\mathbf{Y}^p$ will be denoted as $\mathbf{m}_p$ thereafter). Still, after binarising, since different eigenvectors are mutually orthogonal, the different bits $\mathbf{Y}^p$ will also be uncorrelated. In this way, the binary code achieves the best utilisation of the hash table and the contraint $\mathbf{Y1} = 0$ in Eq.(9) can also be satisfied.

After getting the hashing code for the training set, the hashing code for the query example $\mathbf{q}$ can be computed by first computing the hashing function $f(\mathbf{q}) = \sum_{t=1}^{M} \alpha_t (\widetilde{\mathbf{W}})^T \widetilde{\mathbf{q}}^{(t)}$, where, $\widetilde{\mathbf{q}}^{(t)}$ is derived from $\mathbf{q}^{(t)}$, using exactly the same way as we derive $\widetilde{\mathbf{x}}_i^{(t)}$ from $\mathbf{x}_i^{(t)}$ in Eq.(7). Then, the corresponding binary hashing code can be obtained through thresholding the hashing function output, i.e., the j-th hashing code for $\mathbf{q}$ equals $+1$, if $f(\mathbf{q})_j > \mathbf{m}_j$ and otherwise -1.

4.4 The Whole Algorithm

The training process of the proposed method is described in Table 1. The procedure of deriving hashing codes for query examples is summarized in Table 2. For hashing encoding, the training process is always conducted offline. Therefore, our focus of efficiency is on the prediction process. Since this process only involves some dot products

Algorithm: CHMIS-AW Predicting
Input: 1. A query example $\mathbf{q}$. 2. Hashing function weight vector $\widetilde{\mathbf{W}}$, 3. Convex combination coefficient α, 4. Median vector $\mathbf{m}$. **Output:** The binary hashing code $\mathbf{h} \in \{-1, 1\}^{K \times 1}$ for $\mathbf{q}$
Initialization: 1. Construct $\widetilde{\mathbf{q}}^{(\mathbf{t})}$ similar to Eq.(7) **For** $t = 1{:}M$ 2. Calculate the regression output by $\mathbf{o}^{(t)} = (\widetilde{\mathbf{W}})^T \widetilde{\mathbf{q}}^{(t)}$ **End For** 3. Calculate the balanced output by $\mathbf{h} = f(\mathbf{q}) = \mathbf{O}\alpha$, where $\mathbf{O} = [\mathbf{o}^{(1)}, \mathbf{o}^{(2)}, \ldots, \mathbf{o}^{(M)}]$ **For** $p = 1{:}K$ 4. if $\mathbf{h}_p > \mathbf{m}_p$, $\mathbf{h}_p = +1$, and otherwise $\mathbf{h}_p = -1$ **End For**

Table 2: Algorithm: CHMIS-AW Predicting

and aggregations between two vectors, which can be done in $O(s)$ time. Here, s is the average sparsity for features from the M sources.

4.5 Discussions

The CHMIS problem is related to the traditional multi-view learning [16, 21, 24, 40, 50, 53]. The basic motivation for many previous multi-view learning methods [16, 24, 40, 50] is to design a classifier on each view/source, and requires that the soft labels on these views/sources to be consistent and should not deviate too much. These methods are mainly designed for classification problems. However, in CHMIS, we need to learn two things from the training data, i.e., (1) the hashing codes for the training data, (2) a hashing function that enables efficient mappings of query examples. CHMIS is an unsupervised problem, in which we can consider the hashing codes as unknown labels. Therefore, the traditional multi-view learning methods cannot directly be applied to solve CHMIS.

In CHMIS-AW, we learn both the hashing codes and the hashing functions together in one formulation. They are both considered as optimization objectives in this formulation, so that the solution can be tuned to the best point between good hashing codes that preserves the similarities between examples in the original feature space and a perfect hashing function that approximates hashing codes for queries efficiently, since both of them are vital for efficient and effective retrieval. In contrast, in STH, the hashing codes and hashing functions are optimized in two different steps, which may cause a disconnection between them.

5. EXPERIMENTS

In this section, we will show the effectiveness of the proposed method through an extensive set of experiments[2].

5.1 Dataset

1. **Cora** [29] dataset consists of the abstracts and references of around 34,000 computer science papers. Part of them are categorized into several subfields, such as Data Structure (DS), Hardware and Architecture (HA), Machine Learning (ML), Operation Systems (OS) and Programming Language (PL). We randomly choose OS among them to do comparison experiments. There are 4 topics in this dataset. The tf-idf (normalized term frequency and log inverse document frequency) features of the content part of these webpages are used as the first information source, and the link information is used as the second one. We randomly select 1122 examples as training examples, and another 124 example as testing examples/queries.
2. **Reuters (Reuters21578)**[3] is a collection of documents that appeared on Reuters newswire in 1987. As the name suggests, it contains 21578 documents, with 135 categories. In our experiments, examples corresponding to the top 10 categories are kept, and the documents with more than one of the 10 categories are discarded. There are 7757 documents left. We use the original tf-idf content information, processed by PCA, as one information source, and the hidden topics information obtained from Probabilistic Latent Semantic Analysis (PLSA)[4] of the binary word features as another one. 6982 examples are used as training examples, while 775 for testing.
3. **ReutersV1 (Reuters-Volume I)**: It is an archive of over 800,000 manually categorized newswire stories [23]. There are in total 126 topics in it. A subset of ReutersV1 is used. In experiments, we choose examples from ten categories of them. The documents with more than one category are discarded. There are in total 26161 examples left. 13081 examples are randomly selected as the training examples, while the remaining 13080 examples are used as testing examples. Similar to the Reuters (Reuters21578) dataset, we use the tf-idf features as one information source, and the dimensionality reduction results obtained from the PLSA of the binary word features as another information source.
4. **WebKB**[5] consists of about 7000 webpages, collected from four universities, and is divided into 7 categories. We use content and link information as the two information sources of this dataset, where tf-idf features are used for the content part. 90% examples (6195) are randomly selected as training examples, while the remaining (688) examples are used for testing.
5. **Healthcare** dataset contains the information of 14199 diabetic patients over 1 year. The label of each patient indicates the patient has diabetes or not. We use the CCS hierarchy diagnosis code (where all the codes directly related to diabetic diagnosis have been discarded), CPT procedure code, and NDC drug code information as three different views of patient features

[2]The code and data can be found on the author's homepage.

[3]http://daviddlewis.com/resources/textcollections/reuters21578/.

[4]Actually, PLSA [20] can be considered as a dimensionality reduction method, which maps the documents into some fixed number of hidden topics. The topic distribution for each document can be used as low dimensional features.

[5]CMU world wide knowledge base (WebKB) project. Available at http://www.cs.cmu.edu/ WebKB/.

	Cora			Reuters			ReutersV1			WebKB			Healthcare
	Combined	S1	S2	Combined	S1	S2	Combined	S1	S2	Combined	S1	S2	Combined
CHMIS-AW	**0.978**	N/A	N/A	**0.910**	N/A	N/A	**0.796**	N/A	N/A	**0.993**	N/A	N/A	**0.991**
SH	0.957	0.514	0.329	0.902	0.883	0.820	0.778	0.752	0.718	0.612	0.779	0.584	0.877
STH	0.977	0.976	0.976	0.841	0.847	0.818	0.536	0.529	0.513	0.718	0.849	0.702	0.960
PCAH	0.959	0.861	0.634	0.881	0.862	0.793	0.701	0.674	0.642	0.652	0.809	0.595	0.801
LSH	0.961	0.901	0.718	0.892	0.846	0.820	0.790	0.677	0.620	0.867	0.853	0.647	0.832

Table 3: Precision for examples within Hamming distance 2, with 32 hashing bits. S1: Source 1, S2: Source2.

	Cora			Reuters			ReutersV1			WebKB			Healthcare
	Combined	S1	S2	Combined	S1	S2	Combined	S1	S2	Combined	S1	S2	Combined
CHMIS-AW	**0.495**	N/A	N/A	**0.831**	N/A	N/A	**0.717**	N/A	N/A	0.478	N/A	N/A	**0.795**
SH	0.447	0.468	0.364	0.742	0.723	0.681	0.698	0.653	0.635	0.544	0.537	0.504	0.791
STH	0.468	0.475	0.461	0.784	0.751	0.720	0.554	0.530	0.523	0.407	0.456	0.404	0.766
PCAH	0.431	0.408	0.417	0.769	0.738	0.694	0.569	0.548	0.519	**0.553**	0.538	0.500	0.761
LSH	0.335	0.327	0.340	0.693	0.629	0.652	0.462	0.350	0.384	0.357	0.340	0.373	0.752

Table 4: Precision for the top 100 examples, with 32 hashing bits. S1: Source 1, S2: Source2.

to test our proposed algorithm. In particular, we used the information of 12780 patients as training set, while that of the remaining 1419 patients as testing.

5.2 Evaluation Metric

For each dataset, we use each document in the testing set as a query example to retrieve documents in the training set. We use two different metrics: the precision for the top 100 retrieved documents[6], and the precision for the documents within the Hamming distance 2. Here, precision is defined as follows:

$$precision = \frac{\text{the number of retrieved relevant documents}}{\text{the number of all retrieved documents}}.$$

Throughout this paper, the relevant documents denote the ones with the same topics/labels as the query examples[7]. The averaged precision over all queries are recorded. As claimed in [22], once the number of bits is sufficiently high (e.g. 64), one would expect that distances with a Hamming distance less than or equal to two would correspond to nearest neighbors in the original data embedding.

For Reuters and healthcare dataset, we further report the precision-recall curves, where the recall rate is defined as:

$$recall = \frac{\text{the number of retrieved relevant documents}}{\text{the number of all relevant documents}}.$$

To draw the precision-recall curves, for each query example, we vary the number of retrieved documents from 0 to the number of all training examples, while fixing the number of hashing bits. The final results are the averaged results over all of the testing examples.

5.3 Comparison Methods

The proposed method CHMIS-AW is compared with four different algorithms on these datasets, i.e., Self Taught Hashing (STH), Spectral Hashing (SH), PCA Hashing (PCAH), and Latent Semantic Hashing (LSH).

These four comparison methods cannot be directly used for the multiple information sources. So, when conducting these comparison experiments, we first concatenate the features on different sources, use them as a single set of features and then apply the comparison algorithms. The parameters C_1 and C_2 in CHMIS-AW are tuned by 5-fold cross validation on the training set through the grid $\{0.5, 2, 4, 8, 16, 32, 128\}$.

[6]If there are ties in the desired Hamming distance, some examples are randomly picked.

[7]Please note that the labels are only used for evaluation purpose, but not for training.

When constructing the graph laplacians for both CHMIS-AW and STH, the number of nearest neighbors is fixed to be 7 for all experiments. For LSH, we randomly select projections from a Gaussian distribution with zero-mean and identity covariance to construct the hash tables.

5.4 Results and Discussions

First of all, we evaluate the performances of different algorithms by varying the number of hashing bits in $\{8, 16, 32, 64, 128\}$. The precision for the top 100 retrieved examples with different number of hashing bits is reported in Fig.1. And the precision for examples within hamming distance 2 is reported in Fig.2. From these comparison results, we can see CHMIS-AW shows the best performance among five hashing methods in most of the cases with information from different sources. CHMIS-AW also outperforms the other hashing methods in most cases when they use information from one specific source. In Fig.1(d), the precision of the proposed method is lower than that of SH and PCAH. However, from the perspective of precision within hamming distance 2, as shown in Fig.2(d), it gives the best performance. So, we can conclude that, in WebKB, CHMIS-AW achieves the best performance in retrieving the several most relevant examples, although probably not the top 100. The good performance of the CHMIS-AW is mainly because: (1) CHMIS-AW integrates the different information sources together more naturally; (2) CHMIS-AW learns the hashing codes and hashing functions in one formulation, which effectively avoid the noise that can be caused in a two step's method as in STH.

As claimed in [33, 47], the LSH method is data-oblivious, and may lead to inefficient codes in practice. From the reported results, we can see that, LSH does not perform well in most cases, especially under the criteria of the precision of the top 100 examples. But for the criteria of the precision within Hamming distance 2, LSH does well in some cases. The similar behavior is also observed in [22]. As a spectral based method, SH borrows the idea of spectral analysis. Its basic motivation is reasonable. However, in CHMIS, SH cannot find a good similarity matrix that can be consistent on the different sources. As shown in the experimental results, the performance of SH is worse than that of CHMIS-AW. STH is a two step method. The first step is spectral clustering step, and the second step employs SVM. However, it still cannot integrate the natural of multiple source problem into the algorithm and it needs to prepare the training data in a format for SVM, which may introduce some noise in this

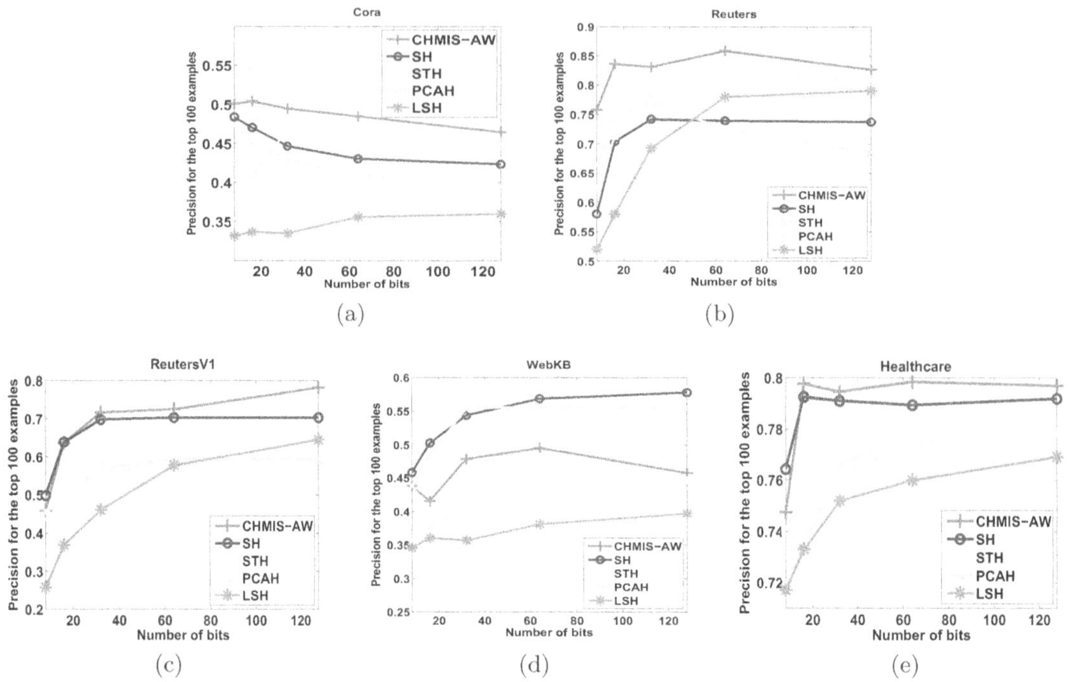

Figure 1: Precision results for the top 100 returned results. It is clear that CHMIS-AW shows the best performance among the five hashing methods in most of the cases.

process. That's why its performance cannot exceed that of CHMIS-AW.

By fixing the number of bits to 32, we further report the corresponding performances on all of the five datasets, along with the performance on each individual source in Tables 3 and 4. It seems that, in some cases, brute force concatenating the features from different sources together may not necessarily improve the hashing performance. It further confirms that we need some more sophisticated algorithms specifically designed for CHMIS. Since the proposed method is specifically for CHMIS, it achieves the best performance in most of scenarios under both of the two criteria. The precision-recall curves with 32 hashing bits on Reuters and healthcare datasets are reported in Fig.3(a) and Fig.3(b) respectively. It is clear that among all of these comparison methods, CHMIS-AW shows the best performance. STH performs better than SH, PCAH and LSH. We have also observed similar results on the other three datasets. But due to the limit of space, they cannot be reported here.

There are two parameters in the proposed method, i.e., C_1 and C_2. To prove the robustness of the proposed method, we conduct some parameter sensitivity experiments on Reuters. For each experiment, we tune only one parameter from the grid $\{0.5, 2, 4, 8, 16, 32, 128\}$, while holding the other one. The results are reported in Fig. 4 and Fig. 5. It is clear from these experimental results that the performance of the proposed method are relatively stable with respect to C_1 and C_2. We have also observed similar patterns of the proposed method in the other four datasets.

The testing process of CHMIS-AW is fast, since the hashing function is a linear mapping and only involves some dot products. On an ordinary PC with Intel Core Duo CPU 2.5 GHZ and 4GB RAM, it takes about 0.0001 second per example for prediction in all datasets, which is similar to the comparison methods.

6. FUTURE WORKS

In this paper, in Eq.(3), we combined the graph Laplacian on each individual source with equal weights. However, a natural question would be: since we are tuning the importance on each individual source by using a balancing factor α, can we do the same thing to combine the different graph Laplacian with different weights? One choice is to change the objective function in Eq.(9) to:

$$tr(C_1\mathbf{Y}^T\sum_{t=1}^{M} g(\alpha_t)\widetilde{\mathbf{L}}^{(t)}\mathbf{Y}) + C_2\|\mathbf{Y} - \sum_{t=1}^{M}\alpha_t(\widetilde{\mathbf{W}})^T\widetilde{\mathbf{X}}^{(t)}\|^2 + \|\widetilde{\mathbf{W}}\|^2,$$

where $g(\bullet) : \mathbf{R} \rightarrow \mathbf{R}$ is a non-decreasing function. We believe this is true. The problem is how to design a reasonable $g(\bullet)$ function for this objective function. It is an intriguing problem that needs to be solved in the future.

Besides the problem of combining graph Laplacians, another future direction is to investigate how to solve the problem when some sources of features are missing for some specific examples.

7. CONCLUSIONS

To enable fast similarity retrieval, semantic hashing methods represent the examples by a small number of binary bits, so that the storage space can be minimized, and the retrieval speed can be accelerated. However, previous hashing methods only consider the case when each example is represented by one type of features. There is no prior work that can incorporate different information sources together and learn the corresponding hashing codes. To address this problem,

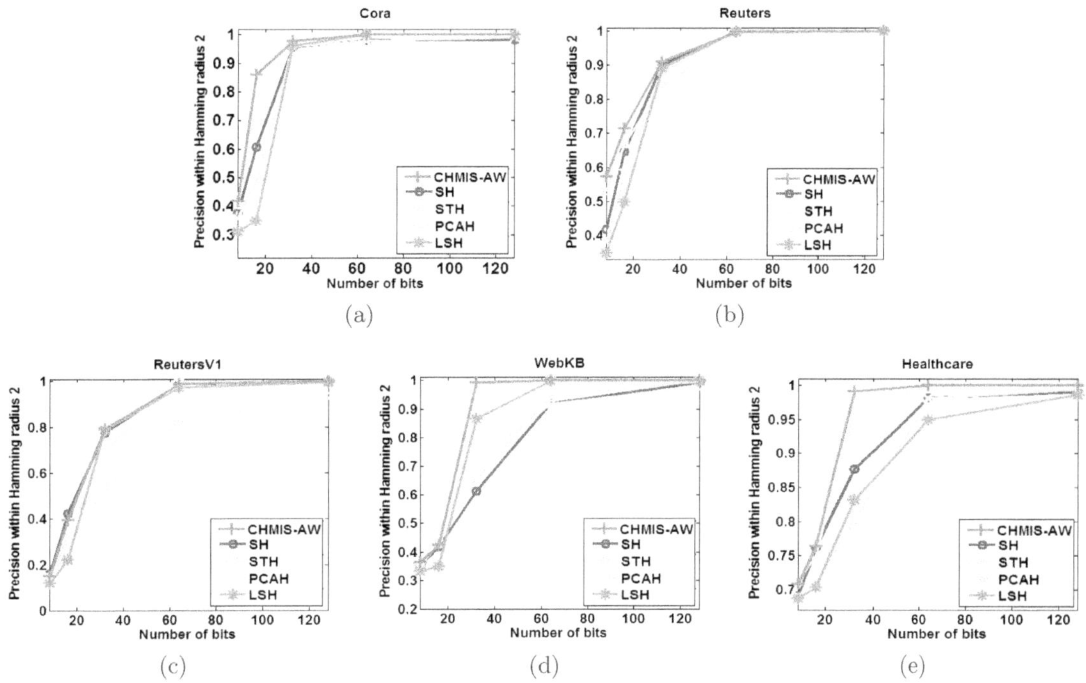

Figure 2: Precision results for the top results within hamming distance 2. It is clear that CHMIS-AW shows the best performance among the five hashing methods in most of the cases.

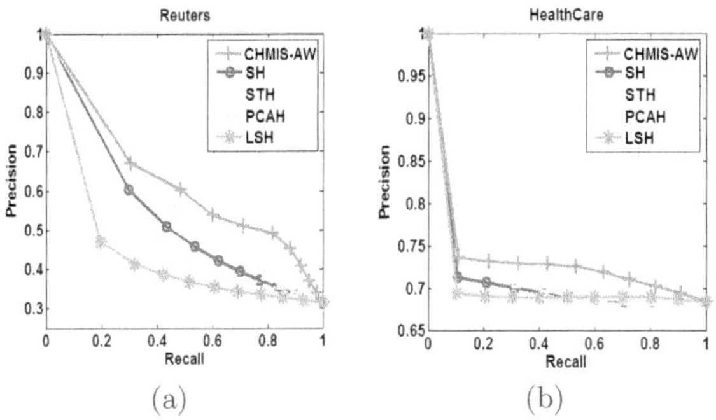

Figure 3: Precision and Recall Curve on Reuters and the healthcare dataset, with fixed bit number 32. CHMIS-AW demonstrates its superior performance over the other three algorithms.

this paper proposes a novel research problem as Composite Hashing with Multiple Information Sources (CHMIS) for intelligently combining information from different sources into final hashing codes. In particular, a method called CHMIS-AW (Adjusted Weights) is proposed to achieve this goal. CHMIS-AW is an iterative method, which optimizes the relaxed hashing codes and the combination coefficients alternatively. An extensive set of experiments clearly demonstrates the superior performance of the proposed method against several state-of-the-art techniques.

8. ACKNOWLEDGEMENT

We thank the anonymous reviewers for valuable comments. This research was partially supported by the NSF research grants IIS-0746830, CNS-1012208, IIS-1017837, CCF- 0939370.

References

[1] A. Andoni and P. Indyk. Near-optimal hashing algorithms for approximate nearest neighbor in high dimensions. In *FOCS*, pages 459–468, 2006.

[2] R. Baeza-Yates, C. Castillo, F. Junqueira, V. Plachouras, and F. Silvestri. Challenges in distributed information retrieval. In *ICDE*, 2007.

[3] R. Baeza-Yates, B. Ribeiro-Neto, et al. *Modern information retrieval*, volume 463. ACM press New York, 1999.

[4] S. Baluja and M. Covell. Learning to hash: forgiving hash functions and applications. *Data Mining and Knowledge Discovery*, 17(3):402–430, 2008.

[5] Y. Bengio, O. Delalleau, N. Roux, J. Paiement, P. Vincent, and M. Ouimet. Learning eigenfunctions links spectral embedding and kernel PCA. *Neural Computation*, 16(10):2197–2219, 2004.

[6] C. Bishop et al. *Pattern recognition and machine learning*. Springer New York, 2006.

[7] S. Boyd and L. Vandenberghe. *Convex optimization*. Cambridge Univ Pr, 2004.

[8] A. Z. Broder. On the resemblance and containment of documents. In *CCS*, pages 21–29. IEEE Computer Society, 1997.

[9] O. Chum, M. Perdoch, and J. Matas. Geometric min-hashing: Finding a (thick) needle in a haystack. In *CVPR*, pages 17–24, 2009.

[10] O. Chum, J. Philbin, and A. Zisserman. Near duplicate image detection: min-hash and tf-idf weighting. In *BMVC*, volume 3, page 4, 2008.

[11] F. Chung and N. Biggs. Spectral graph theory. *American Mathematical Society Providence, RI*, 1997.

[12] T. Cormen, C. Leiserson, R. Rivest, and C. Stein. *Introduction to algorithms*. The MIT press, 2001.

[13] J. S. Culpepper and A. Moffat. Efficient set intersection for inverted indexing. *ACM Trans. Inf. Syst.*, 29:111–125, December 2010.

[14] M. Datar, N. Immorlica, P. Indyk, and V. S. Mirrokni. Locality-sensitive hashing scheme based on p-stable distributions. In *SCG*, pages 253–262, 2004.

[15] S. C. Deerwester, S. T. Dumais, T. K. Landauer, G. W.

Furnas, and R. A. Harshman. Indexing by latent semantic analysis. *JASIS*, 41(6):391–407, 1990.

[16] J. Farquhar, D. Hardoon, H. Meng, J. Shawe-Taylor, and S. Szedmak. Two view learning: SVM-2K, theory and practice. *NIPS*, 18:355, 2006.

[17] A. Gionis, P. Indyk, and R. Motwani. Similarity search in high dimensions via hashing. In *VLDB*, pages 518–529, 1999.

[18] G. E. Hinton, S. Osindero, and Y.-W. Teh. A Fast Learning Algorithm for Deep Belief Nets. *Neural Comp.*, 18(7):1527–1554, July 2006.

[19] G. E. Hinton and R. R. Salakhutdinov. Reducing the Dimensionality of Data with Neural Networks. *Science*, 313(5786):504–507, July 2006.

[20] T. Hofmann. Probabilistic latent semantic indexing. In *SIGIR*, pages 50–57. ACM, 1999.

[21] T. Joachims and N. Cristianini. Composite kernels for hypertext categorisation. In *ICML*, pages 250–257. Morgan Kaufmann Publishers, 2001.

[22] B. Kulis and T. Darrell. Learning to hash with binary reconstructive embeddings. *NIPS*, 2009.

[23] D. D. Lewis, Y. Yang, T. G. Rose, and F. Li. Rcv1: A new benchmark collection for text categorization research. *Journal of Machine Learning Research*, 5:361–397, 2004.

[24] G. Li, S. C. H. Hoi, and K. Chang. Two-view transductive support vector machines. In *SDM*, pages 235–244, 2010.

[25] J. Lin. Brute force and indexed approaches to pairwise document similarity comparisons with mapreduce. In *SIGIR*, pages 155–162. ACM, 2009.

[26] R. Lin, D. Ross, and J. Yagnik. SPEC hashing: Similarity preserving algorithm for entropy-based coding. In *CVPR*, pages 848–854, 2010.

[27] D. Lowe. Object recognition from local scale-invariant features. In *ICCV*, page 1150, 1999.

[28] C. Manning, P. Raghavan, and H. Schutze. An introduction to information retrieval. *Cambridge University Press*, 2008.

[29] A. K. Mccallum, K. Nigam, J. Rennie, and K. Seymore. Automating the construction of internet portals with machine learning. *Information Retrieval*, 3:127–163, 1999.

[30] Y. Mu, J. Shen, and S. Yan. Weakly-supervised hashing in kernel space. In *CVPR*, pages 3344–3351, 2010.

[31] R.E.Schapire. The boosting approach to machine learning: An overview. *Nonlinear Estimation and Classification*, pages 149–172, 2003.

[32] D. Rosenberg, V. Sindhwani, P. Bartlett, and P. Niyogi. A Kernel for Semi-Supervised Learning With Multi-View Point Cloud Regularization. *IEEE Signal Processing Magazine*, 2009.

[33] R. Salakhutdinov and G. Hinton. Semantic hashing. *International Journal of Approximate Reasoning*, 50(7):969–978, 2009.

[34] G. Salton. Developments in automatic text retrieval. *Science*, 253(5023):974–980, 1991.

[35] G. Salton and C. Buckley. Term-weighting approaches in automatic text retrieval. *Information processing and management*, 24(5):513–523, 1988.

[36] B. Scholkopf and A. Smola. *Learning with kernels*. MIT press Cambridge, Mass, 2002.

[37] G. Shakhnarovich, P. A. Viola, and T. Darrell. Fast pose estimation with parameter-sensitive hashing. In *ICCV*, pages 750–759, 2003.

[38] J. Shi and J. Malik. Normalized cuts and image segmentation. *IEEE Transactions on Pattern Analysis and Machine Intelligence*, 22(8):888–905, 2002.

[39] F. Silvestri and R. Venturini. Vsencoding: efficient coding and fast decoding of integer lists via dynamic programming. In *CIKM*, pages 1219–1228, 2010.

[40] V. Sindhwani and P. Niyogi. A co-regularized approach to semi-supervised learning with multiple views. In *ICML Workshop on Learning with Multiple Views*, 2005.

[41] B. Stein. Principles of hash-based text retrieval. In *SIGIR*, page 534. ACM, 2007.

[42] V. Vapnik. *The nature of statistical learning theory*. Springer Verlag, 2000.

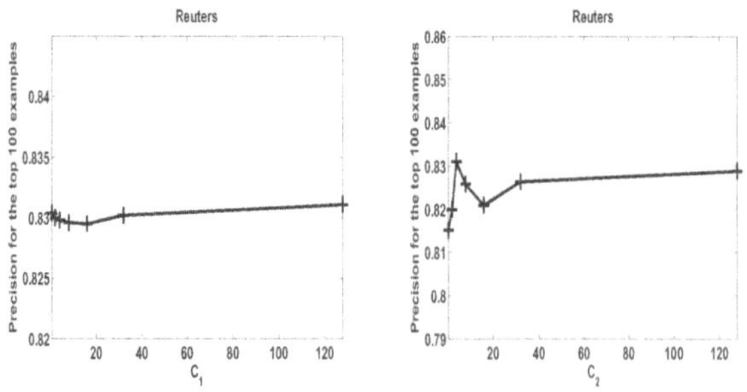

(a) (b)

Figure 4: Parameter Sensitivity for C_1 and C_2, with 32 hashing bits. It shows that the proposed method is relatively stable with the two parameters for the precision of the top 100 retrieved documents.

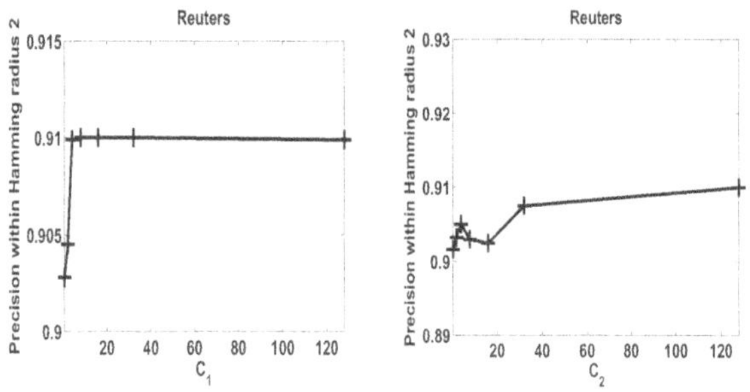

(a) (b)

Figure 5: Parameter Sensitivity for C_1 and C_2, with 32 hashing bits. The proposed method is stable with the two parameters under the precision within hamming distance 2.

[43] J. Wang, O. Kumar, and S.-F. Chang. Semi-supervised hashing for scalable image retrieval. In *CVPR*, pages 3424–3431, 2010.

[44] J. Wang, S. Kumar, and S.-F. Chang. Sequential projection learning for hashing with compact codes. In *ICML*, pages 1127–1134, 2010.

[45] X. Wang, L. Zhang, F. Jing, and W. Ma. Annosearch: Image auto-annotation by search. In *CVPR*, 2006.

[46] R. Weber, H. Schek, and S. Blott. A quantitative analysis and performance study for similarity-search methods in high-dimensional spaces. In *VLDB*, pages 194–205.

[47] Y. Weiss, A. Torralba, and R. Fergus. Spectral hashing. *NIPS*, 21:1753–1760, 2009.

[48] I. H. Witten, I. H. Witten, A. Moffat, and T. C. Bell. *Managing Gigabytes: Compressing and Indexing Documents and Images*. Morgan Kaufmann, May 1999.

[49] L. Zelnik-Manor and P. Perona. Self-tuning spectral clustering. *NIPS*, 17:1601–1608, 2004.

[50] D. Zhang, F. Wang, C. Zhang, and T. Li. Multi-view local learning. In *AAAI*, pages 752–757, 2008.

[51] D. Zhang, J. Wang, D. Cai, and J. Lu. Laplacian co-hashing of terms and documents. *Advances in Information Retrieval*, pages 577–580, 2010.

[52] D. Zhang, J. Wang, D. Cai, and J. Lu. Self-taught hashing for fast similarity search. In *SIGIR*, pages 18–25. ACM, 2010.

[53] T. Zhang, A. Popescul, and B. Dom. Linear prediction models with graph regularization for web-page categorization. In *SIGKDD*, pages 821–826. ACM, 2006.

[54] J. Zobel and A. Moffat. Inverted files for text search engines. *ACM Comput. Surv.*, 38(2), 2006.

Detecting Outlier Sections in US Congressional Legislation

Elif Aktolga
Center for Intelligent Information Retrieval
Department of Computer Science
University of Massachusetts Amherst
Amherst, Massachusetts
elif@cs.umass.edu

Irene Ros, Yannick Assogba
IBM Watson Research Center
Visual Communication Lab
Center for Social Software
Cambridge, Massachusetts
{iros, yannick}@us.ibm.com

ABSTRACT

Reading congressional legislation, also known as bills, is often tedious because bills tend to be long and written in complex language. In IBM Many Bills, an interactive web-based visualization of legislation, users of different backgrounds can browse bills and quickly explore parts that are of interest to them. One task users have is to be able to locate sections that don't seem to fit with the overall topic of the bill. In this paper, we present novel techniques to determine which sections within a bill are likely to be outliers by employing approaches from information retrieval. The most promising techniques first detect the most topically relevant parts of a bill by ranking its sections, followed by a comparison between these topically relevant parts and the remaining sections in the bill. To compare sections we use various dissimilarity metrics based on Kullback-Leibler Divergence. The results indicate that these techniques are more successful than a classification based approach. Finally, we analyze how the dissimilarity metrics succeed in discriminating between sections that are strong outliers versus those that are 'milder' outliers.

Categories and Subject Descriptors: H.3.3 [**Information Search and Retrieval**]: Selection process

General Terms: Experimentation, Measurement, Algorithms

Keywords: Outlier Detection, Language Modeling, Dissimilarity

1. INTRODUCTION

Reading congressional legislation is often tedious and can be demanding to both the expert and average citizen. Bills are often written in complex legalese, which makes reading them a challenging task. Also, the political process of drafting legislation results in new content being added and old content being modified. This sometimes makes the overall gist and structure of a bill difficult to follow. We observe in the legislation data that bills that had content added to them over time are more likely to cover a wider range of topics. Such bills also discuss more varied aspects of the matter and contain sections whose contents represent slight, but still somewhat related shifts from the main topic.

IBM Many Bills [3, 13] is a web based visualization of congressional legislation aiming to make reading bills easier for lay users by providing a visual interface to the various components of a bill. The problem of understanding the structure of a bill is particularly acute in long bills, in which case it would be very helpful for the reader to know exactly where to look for parts of interest within a bill. One way IBM Many Bills supports this is by labeling individual sections with their main topic and color coding these topics to make them easy to identify within a bill. Another region of interest for users such as journalists, watch dog groups and concerned citizens are sections whose content differs from the main topic of the bill. This may indicate that the section is worth paying more attention to.

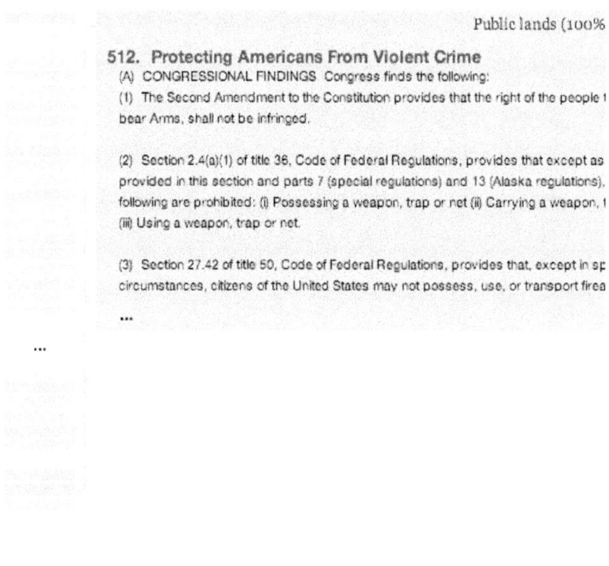

Figure 1: Example of a bill about credit cards with an outlier section about gun control.

To support the latter use case with an example, Figure 1 shows H.R. 627, Credit Card Accountability Responsibility and Disclosure Act of 2009, a bill about credit cards and consumer protection in the IBM Many Bills visualization. Each rectangular bar represents a section, the smallest unit of a bill. Towards the end of this bill there is a section about ensuring the right to carry guns in national parks en-

SIGIR'11, July 24–28, 2011, Beijing, China.

titled 'Protecting Americans from Violent Crime.' This is an unusual section within the context of credit cards, finance and consumer protection and is made particularly interesting because of its existence within this specific bill. We refer to such interesting and unusual sections as *outlier sections*. Our aim in this work is to automatically find such outlier sections in bills.

Unlike the example shown in Figure 1, most bills are consistent in their content and may contain minor topic shifts, or what we identify as *mild outliers*. Whether a section is an outlier or not depends on how important (and how dramatic) its topic shifts in relation to the rest of that bill, as determined by the reader. To illustrate this using the credit card bill described above, a section within it titled 'Privacy Protection for College Students' could be considered a mild outlier or a topic shift, because it still discusses matters related to credit cards and finance, but focuses on a specific target group – college students. This section would not be nearly as interesting to a user looking for anomalies as the one about gun control, but still may be worth noting to some readers. We observe through examples such as this one, that determining whether a section is an outlier is a challenging task because the decision is somewhat subjective, and depends on the context the section appears in, i.e. the content of the bill.

Another issue is that we want to control the number of falsely identified outlier sections shown to the user. The IBM Many Bills application that motivated this work is geared towards members of the general public. Because we do not want them to lose trust in the predictions of our algorithms, we aim at keeping the number of false positives low even at the cost of missing a true positive. We are in effect willing to trade recall for increased precision to a limited extent in order to maintain user expectations in pursuance of our goals.

Given that there is no pre-existing truth data for outliers in US Congressional Legislation, and the fact that outliers are contextual to the bills they appear in, we take a generative approach to detecting outliers within bills. Language models are created from different units of a bill, such as its individual sections, the entire bill text, or even from all the bills within a category, such as all 'Finance' bills. We then apply different dissimilarity measures to compare the section language models of a bill to other language models built from the different units just discussed, from which we obtain a ranking of the sections indicating the probability of each section being an outlier. We apply a threshold to this outlier score for the final decision of whether the section is marked as an outlier or not.

The most promising techniques use a 2-step approach: the main topical sections within a bill are first detected by ranking the top most relevant sections with respect to the bill's title keywords. We then apply dissimilarity measures between section language models of the main sections and remaining sections to obtain the final ranking for outlier sections. We use various dissimilarity metrics based on Kullback-Leibler Divergence [8, 16]. One of them is Kullback-Leibler Divergence Contribution (KLC), which we introduce based on inspiration from Lawrie and Croft's work [19]. The measures aid in distinguishing between outlier and non-outlier sections because they capture the following: (1) terms occurring in potential outlier sections that do not occur in main sections contribute to the outlier score with a positive KL Divergence value; (2) important topical terms contained in main sections that are less frequent in outlier sections contribute to the outlier score with a negative KL Divergence value. By utilizing this information in different ways, some of the dissimilarity metrics are more successful in catching strong outlier sections efficiently, whereas others do better on 'milder' outliers.

We also experiment with an approach that is not based on language modeling: since the category or classification information indicating the main topic for an entire bill (e.g. 'finance' or 'health') is the only truth data we have for the whole dataset, we also compare a classification-based technique to detecting outliers to the language modeling based approaches.

The remainder of this paper is organized as follows: Section 2 details previous and related approaches in the area; Section 3 describes the techniques that we compare to each other for the outlier detection task. In Section 4, we then evaluate the approaches on the 2009 US Congressional Legislation dataset. Section 5 contains an analysis of the KL Divergence Contribution dissimilarity metric that we use and its effect on outlier detection, after which we conclude the work in Section 6.

2. RELATED WORK

Outlier detection first emerged in statistics [4], where the aim is to find data points standing out from a certain distribution — these are typically numeric outliers in data. However, to be able to mine outliers with statistical techniques, characteristics about the distribution of the data must be known in advance, which may be a disadvantage if such information is not available.

Clustering techniques are unsupervised approaches that do not require prior knowledge about the distribution of the data [15, 25]. The aim is to group data into smaller sets that exhibit some structure, for which often a distance measure is required. For example, in flat clustering distance is measured in terms of closeness to the k-nearest neighbor [25]. In such an analysis, data points standing out from the grouped subsets of data would be identified as outliers. The challenge in our task would be to determine k in advance, since it varies depending on the content of the bill itself. Therefore, flat clustering techniques are rather unsuited to our setting. Hierarchical clustering methods are more appropriate in that k is not required [28]. A common technique is to use dendogram cutting for obtaining clusters at a certain similarity level. Still, determining the right similarity level depending on the content of the bill, and identifying which of the clusters constitute outlier sections constitute challenges.

Recently, there has been some research on mining nonnumeric textual outliers from web data [1, 2], in which outliers are mined with more conventional text-mining and n-gram based methods combined with ideas from clustering. These approaches aim at identifying whole documents as outliers within a category both in the presence and absence of a domain dictionary. Our work differs in that: (1) to make conclusions about outlier sections, we do not use any technique requiring prior assumptions about the data such as a domain vocabulary, or any source other than the legislative texts; (2) we detect outliers in the form of sections within a bill, rather than the whole document. The background information we use for making our decisions about outliers come from bill text in different units, but the outliers we detect are at the section level.

In the data mining community, outlier detection research has been done within the context of 'financial fraud detection' [26]. These techniques are mostly machine learning based and target only one type of outliers in text – fraud. Again, such techniques are more suitable when particular outliers are being observed that exhibit a clear pattern which is 'learnable' by such algorithms.

Another related group of work is that on text segmentation [5, 11, 12]. The aim in this research is to identify topic shifts to then break the text down to smaller sentences at such topic boundaries. We do not modify the given section structure of the US Congressional Legislation, but it would be a worthwhile extension of our work to segment long sections further down into smaller subsections to find more fine-grained outliers.

Kullback-Leibler Divergence [8, 16] has widely been applied in information retrieval in the context of language modeling both as a (dis)similarity metric [9, 19] to distinguish between models, as well as a ranking function [17, 22, 30] to rank documents. Inspired by this, we explore KL divergence based dissimilarity metrics for measuring the entropy between different units of language models. One of the metrics we arrive at is called 'KL Divergence Contribution' (Section 3.4.3), which – unlike traditional KL Divergence – measures the undirected weights of the contributions of terms towards the overall KL divergence score. We analyze the measure by means of examples in Section 5.

IBM Many Bills is an example of open government in that it promotes the transparency of bills and the interactivity between citizens and the government. Research in the areas of e-government and e-transparency has shown that this is an important issue [14, 29]. There has been a lot of research in the AI & Law area for tools to assist people and specialists such as lawyers with searching, viewing, and working with government data [18, 24]. We hope that with the addition of this outlier detection feature to the Many Bills system we can further expand the accessibility of these documents to more people outside the legal sphere.

3. OUTLIER DETECTION METHODS

In this section we detail various techniques of outlier detection. The first one described is based on the classification of sections and bills into topics, whereas the remaining methods are based on language modeling [23].

3.1 Classification approach (CL)

For this technique, which serves as our baseline, we utilize categories manually assigned to bills by the Congressional Research Service (CRS) as well as categories automatically assigned to sections by a trained classifier. The classifier is trained as follows: every bill in the original dataset has been assigned a human-determined *top category* describing the main topic of the bill. There is also a given set of categories for other subjects within the bill. Typical examples of categories are 'health', 'finance', 'science & technology' etc. Unfortunately, these categories do not point to specific sections within the bill, so this data strictly refers to the entire bill text. In order to obtain topic categories for sections, we train a multi-class maximum entropy document classifier for 83 of the classes that the CRS assigns as top categories to bills. The classifier is trained over 59552 bills from the past 9 years of congress with 10-fold cross validation. The Mallet [21] toolkit is used to train the classifier and then applied to the sections of bills from the 111th congress (2009-2010) to generate a topic for each section of a bill.

Given a bill D, we determine the probability of a section $s \in D$ being an outlier under the classification approach (CL) as follows: Let s_{class} be the category that was assigned by the classifier to s, further let $D_{cats} = \{d_{c_1}, d_{c_2}, \cdots, d_{c_n}\}$ be the set of categories manually assigned by CRS to D (this set includes the 'top category'). Then:

$$P_{\text{outlier}}(s|D_{cats}, s_{\text{class}}) = 1 - \max_i \text{Popularity}(s_{\text{class}}, d_{c_i}) \quad (1)$$

where i iterates over the elements of D_{cats} and the Popularity measure describes how discriminative this section-bill category pair is with respect to the most common section category seen with this bill's categories in the corpus:

$$\text{Popularity}(s_{\text{class}}, d_c) = \frac{\text{cnt}(s_{\text{class}}, d_c)}{\max_j \text{cnt}(t_{\text{class}_j}, d_c)} \quad (2)$$

where $\text{cnt}(s_{\text{class}}, d_c)$ is the number of times s_{class} occurred in a bill with category d_c with respect to the whole corpus and t_{class} is the category assigned by the classifier to a section t that d_c is seen with. Equation (2) is normalized with $\max_j \text{cnt}(t_{\text{class}_j}, d_c)$, which is the most frequently encountered section-bill category pair with respect to d_c.

The intuition for s being an outlier depends on the degree of inverse popularity of s_{class}: $P_{\text{outlier}}(s|D_{cats}, s_{\text{class}})$ is higher the less popular the co-occurrence of s_{class} is with any element of D_{cats}. We maximize over all the popularity scores of D_{cats} because we want to give each s the greatest chance of not becoming an outlier. This helps in reducing the number of falsely identified outliers found in a bill.

3.2 Language Modeling

The remaining outlier detection techniques described below are based on language modeling [23], i.e. we create a unigram bag-of-words based representation of a unit of text in which the probability of each term in that model is determined by means of maximum likelihood estimation (MLE) as follows:

$$P_{\text{MLE}}(t|\Theta_U) = \frac{\text{cnt}_U(t)}{|U|} \quad (3)$$

where Θ_U is the language model of the unit of text U that token t is sampled from and $\text{cnt}_U(t)$ is the frequency count of t in U. Hence, probabilities for tokens occurring in certain units of text are determined based on their frequency counts with respect to the total number of tokens in those texts. Since the dissimilarity metrics we use for comparing language models are all based on Kullback-Leibler Divergence (KLD) [8, 16], we smooth the language models in an appropriate manner as detailed in Section 3.4.1.

In this work, we infer language models from different units of texts, which are explained in the next section.

3.3 Units of Language Models

We consider three different units of language models for outlier detection: category, document and section. The language models are always built in a unigram MLE fashion as described in Section 3.2. Note that these are independent of the congressional legislation data we are using. They could be applied to any corpus consisting of documents that can be split into sections or paragraphs. The general topic of a document as determined by a classifier or manually is only required for the category model (Section 3.3.2). In all cases we used a 592 term stopword list containing common stopwords as well as a few legislation specific stop terms such as 'act', 'chapter', 'clause' etc. to filter the text of the sections.

3.3.1 Document Model

We infer the language model Θ_D given a document or a bill D. Then the likelihood of a section $s \in D$ being an outlier, given Θ_D, can be stated as:

$$P_{\text{outlier}}(s_{\text{LM}}|\Theta_D) = \text{dissim}_{\text{norm}}(s_{\text{LM}}||\Theta_D) \quad (4)$$

where dissim is any dissimilarity metric described in Section 3.4, and s_{LM} is the language model inferred from s. The dissimilarity scores across all sections s in D are normalized to probabilities between 0 and 1, which is indicated by *norm*.

3.3.2 Category Model

We infer the language model Θ_C given a category C of a document D whose sections are being ranked for outlier probability. This means that all documents $\mathcal{D}$ having category C are included in Θ_C. Then the likelihood of a section $s \in D$ being an outlier, given Θ_C, can be formulated as:

$$P_{\text{outlier}}(s_{\text{LM}}|\Theta_C) = \text{dissim}_{\text{norm}}(s_{\text{LM}}||\Theta_C) \quad (5)$$

where dissim is any dissimilarity metric described in Section 3.4, and s_{LM} is again the language model inferred from s. norm indicates that the scores are normalized between 0 and 1 across all sections s in D.

3.3.3 Section Model

For the section model approach we first infer language models Θ_{S_i} for each section $s_i \in D$. A single comparison between a section $s \in D$ and s_i is then achieved as follows:

$$P_{\text{dsm}}(s_{\text{LM}}|\Theta_{S_i}) = \text{dissim}_{\text{norm}}(s_{\text{LM}}||\Theta_{S_i}) \quad (6)$$

where s_{LM} is the language model inferred from s. More specifically, this denotes the probability of how dissimilar s_{LM} is from Θ_{S_i}. However, for determining the outlier probability of s, we need to know how s compares to each $s_i \in D$ *on average*:

$$P_{\text{outlier}}(s_{\text{LM}}|\Theta_S) = \frac{\sum_{i=1}^{n} P_{\text{dsm}}(s_{\text{LM}}|\Theta_{S_i})}{n} \quad (7)$$

where Θ_S denotes the average section model. Note that in total we perform n comparisons for each section $s \in D$, which altogether take $O(n^2)$. Before summing the comparisons, we normalize the dissimilarity scores for a section s across all section models Θ_{S_i} to probabilities between 0 and 1 as in the other models. $P_{\text{outlier}}(s_{\text{LM}}|\Theta_S)$ thus quantifies how probable s is to be an outlier, given that we have compared it to each other section s_i in D. Finally, we can rank all the sections $s \in D$ in order of their average dissimilarity scores to the section model Θ_S.

3.4 Dissimilarity Metrics

For determining which sections are outliers, we evaluate different dissimilarity metrics with the language models built using the modeling approaches described in Section 3.3. The dissimilarity metrics we choose here are all applicable to the language modeling framework. In fact they are all based on Kullback-Leibler Divergence [8, 16].

3.4.1 KL Divergence (KLD)

Kullback-Leibler Divergence (KLD) is a well-known non-symmetric measure for determining the difference between two probability distributions [8, 16]. In this context, it measures the difference between the two language models P and Q, where Q is the base model:

$$KLD(P||Q) = \sum_{i \in P \wedge Q} P(i) \cdot \log_2 \frac{P(i)}{Q(i)} \quad (8)$$

To be able to apply KLD to language models we smooth the models as follows: (1) If $i \in Q \wedge i \notin P$, then by definition of KLD, this would be $0 \log_2 0 = 0$ for token i, so we do not smooth in this case; (2) If $i \notin Q \wedge i \in P$, then by definition of KLD this would be ∞. For simplicity, we apply Add-1 Smoothing [6] in this case so that i is assumed to occur only once in Q, and the probabilities for other tokens in Q are adjusted accordingly. This prevents the overall KLD score from becoming ∞. With ∞ scores, distinguishing between sections and ranking them would become impossible.

Intuitively, these choices have the following effects on outlier detection: case (1) denotes that the base model Q might include additional tokens that are not contained in the candidate outlier section P that it is being compared to, which has no influence on P's KLD score. For example, for finding outliers in the credit card bill from Figure 1, a typical base model section Q, would discuss finance and credit card related issues with tokens such as 'credit', 'card', 'interest' etc., whereas P, say a section about credit card issues regarding college students, might not use all the credit card related tokens in Q (it might be missing 'interest' for instance). In this case, the mere absence of tokens in P that were present in Q do not make P a stronger outlier according to the choice of smoothing for (1).

Case (2) on the other hand refers to P including a new token previously unseen in Q, resulting in larger relative entropy: this may indicate that the candidate outlier section P discusses other issues than the base model Q, which contributes to its likelihood of being an outlier, resulting in a higher score. To refer back to the credit card example: since section P is about credit card issues regarding college students, it mentions 'college', 'students' and other tokens that do not occur in the base model section Q. These make P distinct from Q, which results in a higher score.

If P includes a token common to Q, the more its usage differs from that in Q, the larger is the impact on the KLD score. This impact is either in a positive direction if $P(token) > Q(token)$, and negative otherwise. In summary, this metric does not 'penalize' a section for missing tokens, but it is penalized for new (previously unseen) tokens and varying usage of previously seen tokens.

3.4.2 JS Divergence (JS)

The symmetric version of KLD, Jensen-Shannon divergence is defined as follows [20]:

$$JS(P||Q) = \frac{1}{2}KLD(P||M) + \frac{1}{2}KLD(Q||M) \quad (9)$$

where $M = \frac{1}{2}(P+Q)$. We apply this measure to the language models P and Q; M is built as a new language model from P and Q accordingly.

3.4.3 KL Divergence Contribution (KLC)

The contribution of a token i towards the KLD score was first characterized in Lawrie and Croft's work [19]: it is 0 if $P(i) = Q(i)$, positive if $P(i) > Q(i)$, and negative if $P(i) < Q(i)$. In previous work it was discovered that tokens with high contributions towards KLD are topical terms, whereas those with low contributions are less likely to be about the topic [10].

tokens	sum of |contributions|
arms	0.099
bear	0.099
firearms	0.099
fish	0.099
land	0.099
protecting	0.099
...	...
payment	8.3
account	8.7
fees	9.3
consumer	19.9
card	24.8
credit	30.3

Table 1: Analysis of token contributions towards the KL Divergence score in all the sections of the credit card bill from Figure 1.

We analyzed the validity of this statement for H.R. 627, the credit card bill from Figure 1. To do so we chose the 10 most representative credit card related sections of the bill as base models Q and compared them to the remaining sections P in the bill. By ignoring the direction of the contributions of tokens (positive or negative), it became evident that topical terms such as 'credit', 'card', 'fees' etc. were present in most of the sections with varying usage, whereas more off topic terms such as 'firearms', 'fish' etc. only occurred in very few sections. By considering the usage of terms across all the sections as a sum of the absolute value contributions as shown in Table 1, we can see this difference.

As emphasized in Section 3.4.1, a section P's outlier probability increases the more the use of language differs from the base model Q. Note that in traditional KL Divergence, positive and negative contributions of different tokens cancel each other out and weaken the overall score of a section. However, the use of language in an outlier section may differ from the base section both in terms of *fewer topical tokens*, such as the sparse usage of tokens like 'credit', 'card', 'account' etc., and in terms of *more off-topic tokens*, such as 'firearms', 'weapons' etc., which is the difference in usage of tokens that we might like to measure. Due to the attenuating effect of KLD with negative scores, this difference is evened out to some regard. We therefore introduce the measure KL Divergence Contribution (KLC) as follows:

$$KLC(P||Q) = \sum_{i \in P \wedge Q} |P(i) \cdot \log_2 \frac{P(i)}{Q(i)}| \quad (10)$$

Note that the only difference to KLD is the absolute value inside the formula. This allows us to keep the weight of each token's contribution regardless of its direction. This measure is one of our contributions in this paper, since we extend the notion of single term contributions towards the KLD score [19] to a measure that captures the sum of absolute value term contributions with respect to two distributions.

3.4.4 Symmetric KL Divergence Contribution (KLC-SYM)

Analogous to Jensen-Shannon divergence (Section 3.4.2), which is a symmetric version of KL Divergence, we can also use a symmetric version of KL Divergence Contribution:

$$KLCSYM(P||Q) = \frac{1}{2}KLC(P||M) + \frac{1}{2}KLC(Q||M) \quad (11)$$

where $M = \frac{1}{2}(P+Q)$. Again, we apply this to the language models P and Q. M is built as a new language model from P and Q accordingly.

3.5 2-step approach (2S)

Among the three models we introduced in Section 3.3, the Section Model is the slowest to compute, since it requires a comparison between all sections in a bill in a quadratic manner. This becomes a problem when the section model is applied to long bills. We propose an alternative 2-step approach that reduces the number of comparisons: instead of applying dissimilarity measures directly to language models, we first locate the main sections in a bill D that are topically representative. For this, we score and rank each section S using the bill's title terms T by means of Okapi BM25:

$$\text{score}(s,T) = \sum_{t \in T} \text{IDF(t)} \cdot \frac{\text{tf}(t,S) \cdot (k_1+1)}{\text{tf}(t,S) + k_1 \cdot (1 - b + b \cdot \frac{|S|}{\text{avgSLength}})} \quad (12)$$

where $\text{tf}(t,S)$ is the frequency of title term t occurring in section S, avgSLength is the average section length in the corpus, and $k_1 = 2, b = 0.75$ are constants. T is usually a fairly long title query despite stopping with the 592 terms stopword list described previously. By scoring sections in this way, we obtain a ranking from which we choose the top m sections as the main sections. The choice of m depends on $|D|$, i.e. #sections in D, which we tuned during training to include between 9% and 55% of sections in a bill. For shorter bills, we include a larger number of sections relative to the length of the bill to reliably capture the main content, whereas for longer bills this percentage is smaller.

The second step then consists of comparing the top m sections in D to the remaining $k = n - m$ sections by employing a dissimilarity measure (Section 3.4), where $n = |D|$ in terms of sections. This is just like using the Section Model (Section 3.3.3) on the m and k sections:

$$P_{\text{outlier}}(s_{\text{LM}}|\Theta_{S^*}) = \frac{\sum_{i=1}^{m} P_{\text{dsm}}(s_{\text{LM}}|\Theta_{S_i})}{m} \quad (13)$$

where s_{LM} is one of the k remaining sections and Θ_{S^*} denotes the average section model built from the main m sections only. $P_{\text{dsm}}(s_{\text{LM}}|\Theta_{S_i})$ is estimated as in Equation (6).

In this comparison, the top m sections are by definition excluded from the candidate outlier sections k and they can therefore never become outlier sections. Intuitively, sections that were determined to be topically representative of a bill should never become outlier sections. So while this approach reduces the number of comparisons between sections, it also protects the main sections from becoming outliers by excluding them.

4. EXPERIMENTS

4.1 Data and Implementation Details

We evaluate the outlier detection methods on several subsets of the 111th Session (2009-2010) of US Congressional Legislation (data obtained from GovTrack [27]), which is a real-world dataset. This includes 7940 bills from 37 categories both from the House of Representatives and from the Senate. These bills have 110,688 sections in total, with the average number of sections per bill approximately equal to 14. The average section length is 2227 characters. Each bill comes with metadata from which we use: the official title (e.g. 'To amend the Internal Revenue Code of 1986 to provide for an extension of the employer wage credit for employees who are active duty members of the Uniformed Services.'), short title (e.g. 'Small Business Supporting our Troops Act of 2009'), the top category assigned to a bill (e.g. 'taxation'), further categories (e.g. 'small business', 'income tax credits'), and the section texts. For the 2-step approach described in Section 3.5, we merge the official and short titles of a bill to generate the query used for ranking the sections in the first step of the process. The titles are stopped using the same 592 term stop list for the language model and contain important key phrases for a bill.

The human-labeled training and test sets were created by randomly choosing bills from the corpus across a number of different categories. The training set consists of 13 bills with a total of 683 sections while the test set consists of 11 bills with 823 sections. We have complete outlier judgments for these sets.

4.2 Evaluation Methods

To evaluate the outlier detection methods we compare against human judgments of bills' sections. The judgments come from three annotators that are not experts in the legislation area, but have extensively dealt with bills in addition to having sufficient familiarity with the outlier detection task. Each section is assigned one of the following labels: **1** for not being an outlier, **2** for a mild outlier, or **3** for being a strong outlier. There are reasons for preferring this scale over a binary one: we observed that annotators tend to be uncertain about some sections since the decision is often based on subjective impressions. Thus, the 'mild outlier' label represents the sections that show topic shifts not deemed completely off-topic. We observed that many bills have mild outliers (around 5%), whereas the annotators' use of the label **3** proved more conservative: only 1% of all ratings were a **3**. To obtain the final judgment for a section we average the judgments from the annotators and round the averages accordingly, so that a section with {1, 1, 3} judgments is assigned a **2**; a section with {1, 1, 2} is assigned a **1**.

We measured inter-annotator agreement for each judgment from the three annotators with Cohen's Kappa (weighted) [7]. Cohen's Kappa is 0 or smaller if there is no agreement between the annotators, and it approaches 1 as agreement becomes perfect. For our judgments, the mean Kappa for 3 pairwise evaluations over the full set is 0.626 with a p-value of < 0.01 using the z-test. This signifies a good agreement between the annotators.

For all results reported on the test set in Section 4.3 we map the truth judgments to outlier scores for sections as follows: a section is counted as a *correct outlier* (true positive) if it was marked as a mild outlier (**2**) or a strong outlier (**3**) in the truth judgments **and** the algorithm being evaluated returns an outlier score of at least 70% for this section. This threshold was determined to be optimal for the algorithms in the training data. If a section has an outlier score of 69% or less and it was judged with a **1** by the annotators, it is interpreted as a correct non-outlier section (true negative).

We evaluate the outlier detection methods using well-known measures: (1) *Precision* measures the percentage of correctly detected outliers among all found by the algorithm; (2) *Recall* measures the percentage of correctly identified outliers among all actual outliers as determined in the truth data; (3) *Accuracy* measures the percentage of correctly marked sections (both true positives and true negatives); (4) *% Sections Predicted to be Outliers* measures the fraction of sections that were detected as outliers versus those that were not. This is with respect to all the bills that a technique examines. Hence, it indicates the percentage of outlier sections found in 'the corpus' by a particular approach. Note that % sections predicted as outliers is inversely proportional to accuracy. This measure is important because precision and recall on their own are not indicative enough of how much noise an approach introduces. We observe that the smaller the % sections predicted as outlier sections by a technique – together with a high precision and accuracy, the more reliably the method finds correct outliers (Table 2). Therefore, in the following section where we look at the results, we will favor techniques that exhibit these characteristics.

4.3 Results

We evaluate each of the techniques considered in Section 3 on the test set. The results are shown in Table 2.

First, we note that the classification approach performs worse than all but the worst performing language modeling based approach, marking 13.1% of sections as outliers, and having low precision (0.368) and accuracy (0.795).

Additionally, we observe that the numbers for precision, accuracy, and % sections predicted to be outliers improve as the unit of the language model used becomes smaller (Category > Document > Section = 2S). This indicates that comparing section language models to larger models is noisy for the outlier detection task. When comparing the two smallest units of language models – Section and 2S – the 2-step approaches perform better than direct application of dissimilarity measures to the section models. 2S-JS achieves the best results in terms of precision (0.542) and accuracy (0.914) *while* maintaining a lower % sections predicted to be outliers in the corpus (2.8%).

When using any of the 2-step approaches the differences between dissimilarity measures are not significant except when using symmetric KLC (KLCSYM), which performs the worst no matter which granularity of language model is used. The section scores are greatly boosted with this

Table 2: Evaluation of Outlier Detection Methods. All results are averages run on the test dataset. CL=Classification approach, Doc=Document Model, Cat= Category Model, Sec=Section Model, 2S= 2-step approach. Significant results (*) between 2S-JS and other methods with p-value < 0.05 using the paired two-sided t-test are marked.

Technique	*% Sections Predicted to be Outliers*	*Precision*	*Recall*	*Accuracy*
CL	13.1	0.368*	0.434	0.795*
Cat-KLD	13.9	0.311*	0.50	0.743*
Cat-JS	18.2	0.294*	0.503	0.657*
Cat-KLC	18.0	0.294*	0.54	0.66*
Cat-KLCSYM	50.0	0.273*	0.661	0.429*
Doc-KLD	11.9	0.271*	0.273	0.808*
Doc-JS	12.5	0.325*	0.436	0.78*
Doc-KLC	16.3	0.316*	0.486	0.743*
Doc-KLCSYM	39.6	0.313*	0.649	0.633*
Sec-KLD	4.2	0.343*	0.271*	0.872*
Sec-JS	3.7	0.35*	0.371*	0.873*
Sec-KLC	8.5	0.34*	0.471	0.842*
Sec-KLCSYM	11.8	0.327*	0.496	0.798*
2S-KLD	3.8	0.528	0.429	0.895*
2S-JS	**2.8**	**0.542**	0.446	**0.914**
2S-KLC	6.1	0.445	0.471	0.858*
2S-KLCSYM	5.2	0.442*	0.471	0.877*

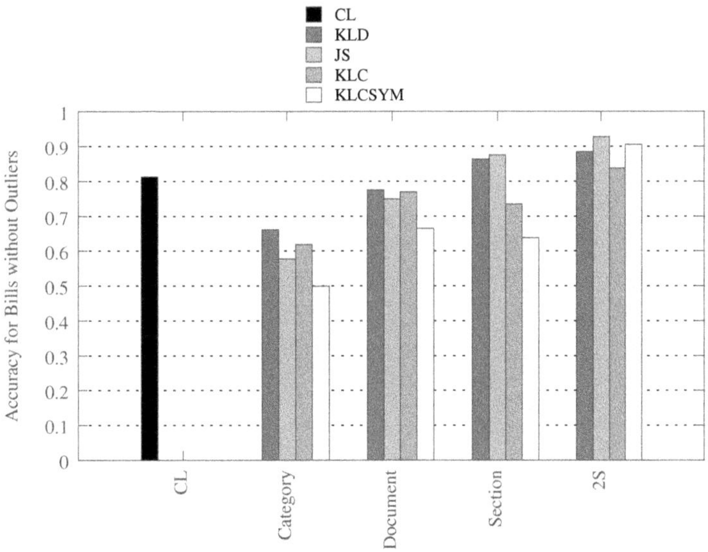

Figure 2: Accuracy for 7 Bills without Outliers. The 2S approaches do the smallest amount of mislabeling (high accuracy scores). 2S-JS is most accurate and statistically significant over all other techniques with p-value < 0.04 using the paired two-sided t-test.

method since it emphasizes differences among the compared models very strongly (half KL contribution to the average model from both sides, see Section 3.4.4), which proves to be too sensitive towards the prediction of outlier sections as it is evident in high recall and low precision and accuracy. This is poor performance according to our aims. We further analyze the differences between the other dissimilarity metrics in Section 5.

We also wanted to know how well the techniques perform when there are *no outliers in a bill.* Our annotators judged 7 bills as not containing outliers. In this case, we want the outlier detection algorithms to produce the fewest false positives. Figure 2 shows the accuracies of the techniques. A high accuracy in labeling sections correctly indicates that the techniques make fewer mistakes. We again observe in the language modeling approaches that the methods become more accurate as the unit of the language model used becomes smaller. The 2S approaches perform best here, with 2S-JS significantly doing the smallest amount of mislabeling of sections (0.92 accuracy) compared to all other techniques. The classification approach performs relatively well with 0.81 accuracy.

Apart from the train and test sets for which we have the judgments, we were also curious to understand how the techniques perform on the larger corpus. Figure 4 gives an overview of the scores assigned to sections by 2S-KLC over the full set of bills from different categories Finance, Health and Economics. The Finance category has 319 bills, Health has 766, and Economics has 123. The red line shows the distribution of the scores across all 37 categories. We were

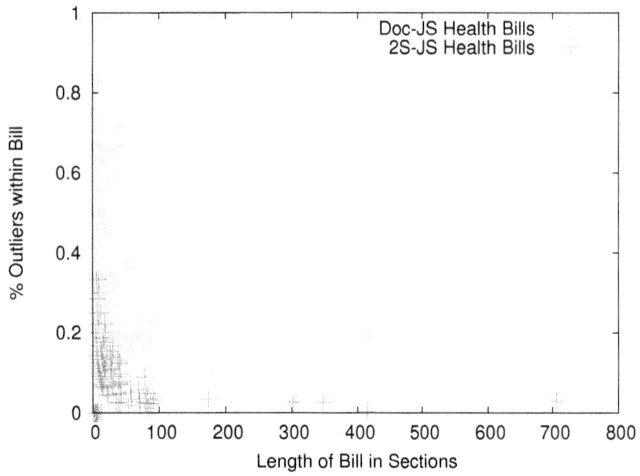

Figure 3: Fraction of sections that are predicted outliers in a bill for 2S-JS and Doc-JS for all Health bills. 2S-JS reduces the % outliers predicted within bills drastically.

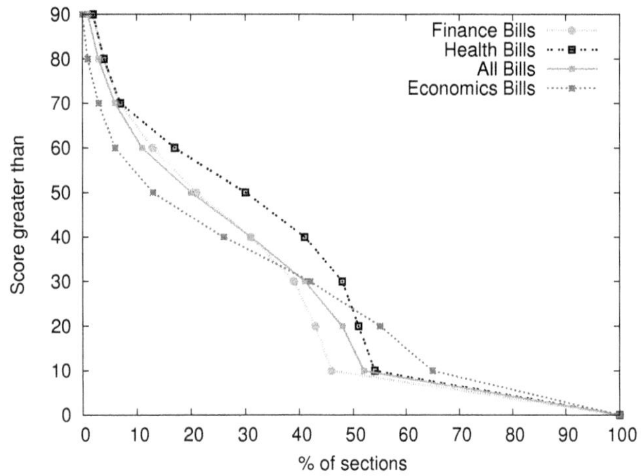

Figure 4: Overview of section scores for all bills in the categories Finance, Health, Economics, and all categories combined. Less than 10% of sections are marked as outliers.

interested in seeing how the outlier detection approaches behave across a wider set of bills without needing to judge them all. One measure that allows us to do that is '% sections predicted to be outliers' with respect to the whole dataset. In Table 2 we observed that approaches with smaller % sections predicted as outliers tend to perform better. We observe that the % sections predicted to be outliers at the outlier threshold ($y \geq 70\%$) is similar to the % sections predicted to be outliers for 2S-KLC reported in Table 2 (6.1%), since not more than about 8% of the sections are marked as outliers across these different categories.

The threshold for marking a section as an outlier is an important parameter. Intuitively, a higher threshold increases precision but hurts recall, while a lower threshold decreases precision and achieves better recall. A lower threshold also results in the % sections predicted as outliers to be increased for most of the techniques. We observed in our training set that increasing the threshold to more than around 70% lead to a large number of false negatives for all the techniques evaluated. Hence, we set the threshold to 70% for all approaches. If our aim was high recall (detecting as many outliers as possible) at the cost of precision, then using a lower threshold would be more appropriate.

We also wanted to verify the superiority of the 2-step approaches over other methods in the larger dataset. Figure 3 shows the performance of 2S-JS versus Doc-JS on all the bills from the 'Health' category in terms of the percentage of sections predicted as outliers *within single bills*: Whereas 2S-Doc marks up to 80% of (shorter) bills as outliers, 2S-JS is more discriminative with up to 30% of bills marked as outliers. Note that '% outliers within a bill' is not the same measure as '% sections predicted as outliers' in the corpus as in Table 2: in Figure 3 we look at the fraction of a bill marked as outliers, whereas the measure '% sections predicted as outliers' was referring to the whole dataset. We obtain similar results with other categories.

5. ANALYSIS OF KL DIVERGENCE CONTRIBUTION MEASURE

The results in Table 2 indicate that for the 2-step approach methods 2S-JS achieves the best performance, although it is not significantly better than 2S-KLD and 2S-KLC. In this section, we want to shed some light on the behavior of our new dissimilarity measure, KL Divergence Contribution (KLC). We do not include KLCSYM in this analysis since the results from Section 4.3 indicated that it is a poor metric.

One way to understand the behavior of KLC is to observe the effect of each term towards the section scores in a bill. Terms that have a high contribution towards each section's score are usually main topical terms (Table 1, [19]), whereas off-topic terms have low contributions. By observing the sum of each term's contribution across all the sections in a bill, we can not only identify the role of the term, but also how differently the measures weight each term. For example, the KLD measure assigns negative scores to terms if they occur more frequently in a main section than in a candidate outlier section. If this is a consistent trend for a term across most of the sections, we can identify this by noting that the sum of that term's scores is negative. Using this we examine the behavior of KLC in two scenarios that we have identified.

5.1 Scenario 1: Mild outliers

Mild outliers are more likely to have a closer distribution of topical terms to non-outlier sections while containing a limited amount of off-topic terms. If we use H.R. 2035 (the Pregnant Women Support Act) as an example, we see a bill that has a single 'mild' outlier. This bill is about pregnancy, support for new parents, and other related issues. The mild outlier in this bill is about monetary aspects of adoption assistance programs and specifically relates to changes in tax credits for the new fiscal year. The outlier is 'mild' because it is still marginally related to the main topic of the bill, yet its topic shifts to the minutiae of appropriations and spending.

In this scenario, Table 4 reveals the following: the top half shows typical off-topic outlier terms such as 'amount', 'dollar', 'taxable', 'adoption', 'inflation', and 'credit'. For these terms, 2S-KLD and 2S-KLC perform similarly, not

Term	sum of JS contributions	sum of KLC |contributions|	sum of KLD contributions
disorders	0.0007	0.001	0.0009
human	0.0007	0.01	0.002
physical	0.04	0.14	0.12
disabilities	0.02	0.07	0.07
care	0.01	0.02	0.02
...	...	...	...
park	1.23	3.06	2.29
river	1.32	3.06	1.99
management	2.09	4.11	1.09
wilderness	5.02	6.39	-3.09
land	5.04	7.71	-2.14
national	5.82	9.75	-3.97

Table 3: Sum of scores of terms for JS, KLC, and KLD across the bill for H.R. 146. KLC is most discriminative, followed by KLD. JS is too weak for this bill.

Term	sum of KLC |contributions|	sum of KLD contributions	sum of JS contributions
inflation	0.013	0.013	0.005
taxable	0.032	0.032	0.012
dollar	0.06	0.06	0.023
credit	0.072	0.035	0.035
amount	0.18	0.18	0.061
adoption	0.26	0.20	0.136
...	...	...	...
pregnant	1.09	-0.62	0.815
women	0.54	-0.48	0.478
services	0.45	-0.27	0.29
support	0.44	-0.23	0.305
assistance	0.15	-0.07	0.131
program	0.11	-0.04	0.105
parents	0.14	-0.03	0.145

Table 4: Differences in term scores across the bill between 2S-KLC, 2S-KLD, and 2S-JS for H.R. 2035.

revealing any differences in handling the outlier. The lower part of Table 4 reveals the scores for main topical terms. In comparing to the other measures, we see that 2S-KLD assigns lower scores to topical terms, while 2S-KLC and 2S-JS assign higher scores. The negative scores for 2S-KLD indicate that in this bill, across all sections, the topical terms occurred slightly more frequently in main sections (Q) than in candidate outlier sections (P), because under KL Divergence a term x with $P(x) < Q(x)$ will have a negative contribution towards the total score. This causes the scores to sufficiently even out for mild outliers. Given that 2S-KLC assigns the highest scores to topical terms, it causes the scores of more non-outlier sections to be pushed towards the outlier threshold. As a result, under 2S-KLC more non-outlier sections are marked as outliers than with 2S-KLD.

5.2 Scenario 2: Strong Outliers

Strong outliers present term distributions that are quite different from topical sections. An example of a strong outlier was mentioned earlier – the gun control section within the credit card bill H.R. 627 from the introduction. Another bill with strong outliers is H.R. 146, The Omnibus Public Land Management Act of 2009, a bill focused on matters pertaining to public lands with several health-related outliers towards the end. These sections contain off-topic terms that do not appear elsewhere in the bill – terms like 'physical', 'disabilities' and 'paralysis'. Table 3 shows the scores for off-topic terms in the top half and topical terms in the bottom half for all three methods. We see that 2S-KLC assigns much higher scores to topical terms with fairly low scores to off-topic terms. Given that a strong outlier will have a high concentration of off-topic terms and very few topical terms, KLC will result in higher contribution scores for the topical terms than it would in a non-outlier section. This is because when such an outlier section is compared to a main section that primarily uses topical terms and very few off-topic terms, then KLC will note both differences in the distributions strongly by means of the absolute value. Combined with higher scores for off-topic terms, in comparison to the other measures, this results in an overall higher section score using 2S-KLC.

From this analysis we conclude that the dissimilarity measures are sensitive with respect to mild outliers versus strong outliers. We also note in the tables that 2S-JS stands in between the two measures 2S-KLC and 2S-KLD, since its scores do not appear as high as KLC, but they do not have the negative dampening effect of KLD. This is also apparent when comparing the formulae of the dissimilarity metrics. Therefore, we conclude that depending on the data and the kind of outliers attempted to be detected, it is worth employing and comparing all these different dissimilarity metrics before making a choice.

6. CONCLUSIONS

We have presented various new ways of approaching outlier detection of sections within documents, which are particularly applicable in the absence of large amounts of truth data. We did this study within the domain of Congressional Legislation. One of the techniques we utilized is classification based, in which the algorithm detects outliers by observing the inverse popularity of a section's category together with its bill's category in the corpus. We also introduced language modeling approaches to outlier detection that differ in the unit of language models used for comparing against sections, and in the dissimilarity measures that they utilize. The dissimilarity measures are based on Kullback-Leibler Divergence. We saw that the language modeling based methods perform better when compared against classification both in terms of precision and accuracy with a smaller fraction of overall outlier sections found. The best performing methods use a 2-step approach, for which first the most topically relevant sections are detected in the bill, after which the remaining sections are compared against the former ones. Sections with an outlier score of 70% or above are marked as outliers. We saw that these techniques perform better than the direct application of dissimilarity measures to the Category, Document, and Section models.

Finally, for the 2-step approach methods, we discovered that the dissimilarity metrics yield different results: the KL Divergence measure works better for bills that have 'mild outliers' which are marginally related to the main topic of the bill. For bills with stronger outliers however, which indicate a very unusual topic shift, KL Divergence Contribution – which we introduce in this paper – is more discriminative because it assigns greater scores to rare terms and less frequently used topical terms in outliers. Our analysis of the term scores does not give us strong indication as to why 2S-JS performs marginally better than the other measures in our evaluation. Given our analysis in Section 5 and the fact that most of the bills in our evaluation set do not contain very strong outliers, we hypothesize that 2S-JS, being a milder measure, does better in the presence of milder outliers.

As for future work, we would particularly be interested in incorporating synonyms into the model comparisons. The current language modeling techniques do a one-by-one comparison of terms, and we believe that the use of synonyms would result in more accurate discrimination between outlier sections and non-outlier sections.

One of the central challenges of this work was to achieve good outlier detection with limited data. We hope to increase the size of our truth-labeled data set in the future, which would enable us to draw further conclusions about the techniques.

7. REFERENCES

[1] M. Agyemang, K. Barker, and R. Alhajj. Framework for mining web content outliers. In *SAC '04: Proc. 2004 ACM symposium on Applied computing*, pages 590–594, New York, NY, USA, 2004. ACM.

[2] M. Agyemang, K. Barker, and R. Alhajj. Hybrid approach to web content outlier mining without query vector. In A. M. Tjoa and J. Trujillo, editors, *Data Warehousing and Knowledge Discovery*, volume 3589 of *Lecture Notes in Computer Science*, pages 285–294. Springer Berlin / Heidelberg, 2005.

[3] Y. Assogba, I. Ros, and M. McKeon. Docblocks: communication-minded visualization of topics in u.s. congressional bills. In *Proc. 28th of the international conference extended abstracts on Human factors in computing systems*, pages 4117–4122, New York, NY, USA, 2010. ACM.

[4] V. Barnett and T. Lewis. *Outliers in statistical data*. John Wiley, 1994.

[5] J. P. Callan. Passage-level evidence in document retrieval. In *Proc. 17th annual international ACM SIGIR conference on Research and development in information retrieval*, SIGIR '94, pages 302–310, New York, NY, USA, 1994. Springer-Verlag New York, Inc.

[6] S. F. Chen and J. Goodman. An empirical study of smoothing techniques for language modeling. In *Proc. 34th annual meeting on Association for Computational Linguistics*, pages 310–318, Morristown, NJ, USA, 1996. Association for Computational Linguistics.

[7] J. Cohen. Weighted kappa: Nominal scale agreement provision for scaled disagreement or partial credit. *Psychological Bulletin*, 70(4):213–220, 1968.

[8] T. M. Cover and J. A. Thomas. *Elements of Information Theory*. Wiley series in Telecommunications. Wiley, New York, NY [u.a.], 1991.

[9] S. Cronen-Townsend and W. B. Croft. Quantifying query ambiguity. In *Proc. second international conference on Human Language Technology Research*, pages 104–109, San Francisco, CA, USA, 2002. Morgan Kaufmann Publishers Inc.

[10] S. Cronen-Townsend and W. B. Croft. Quantifying query ambiguity. In *Proc. second international conference on Human Language Technology Research*, pages 104–109, San Francisco, CA, USA, 2002. Morgan Kaufmann Publishers Inc.

[11] M. A. Hearst. Multi-paragraph segmentation of expository text. In *Proc. 32nd annual meeting on Association for Computational Linguistics*, ACL '94, pages 9–16, Stroudsburg, PA, USA, 1994. Association for Computational Linguistics.

[12] M. A. Hearst and C. Plaunt. Subtopic structuring for full-length document access. In *Proc. 16th annual international ACM SIGIR conference on Research and development in information retrieval*, SIGIR '93, pages 59–68, New York, NY, USA, 1993. ACM.

[13] IBM Many Bills. A Visual Bill Explorer. `http://manybills.researchlabs.ibm.com/`.

[14] P. Jaeger. E-government around the world: lessons, challenges, and future directions. *Government Information Quarterly*, 20(4):389–394, 2003.

[15] E. M. Knorr, R. T. Ng, and V. Tucakov. Distance-based outliers: algorithms and applications. *The VLDB Journal*, 8(3-4):237–253, 2000.

[16] S. Kullback and R. A. Leibler. On information and sufficiency. *The Annals of Mathematical Statistics*, 22(1):79–86, 1951.

[17] J. Lafferty and C. Zhai. Document language models, query models, and risk minimization for information retrieval. In *Proc. 24th annual international ACM SIGIR conference on Research and development in information retrieval*, pages 111–119, New York, NY, USA, 2001. ACM.

[18] G. T. Lau, S. Kerrigan, K. H. Law, and G. Wiederhold. An e-government information architecture for regulation analysis and compliance assistance. In *Proc. 6th international conference on Electronic commerce*, ICEC '04, pages 461–470, New York, NY, USA, 2004. ACM.

[19] D. J. Lawrie and W. B. Croft. Generating hierarchical summaries for web searches. In *Proc. 26th annual international ACM SIGIR conference on Research and development in informaion retrieval*, pages 457–458, New York, NY, USA, 2003. ACM.

[20] J. Lin. Divergence measures based on the shannon entropy. *IEEE Transactions on Information theory*, 37:145–151, 1991.

[21] A. K. McCallum. Mallet: A machine learning for language toolkit. http://mallet.cs.umass.edu, 2002.

[22] D. Metzler, S. Dumais, and C. Meek. Similarity measures for short segments of text. In G. Amati, C. Carpineto, and G. Romano, editors, *Advances in Information Retrieval*, volume 4425 of *Lecture Notes in Computer Science*, pages 16–27. Springer Berlin / Heidelberg, 2007.

[23] J. M. Ponte and W. B. Croft. A language modeling approach to information retrieval. In *Proc. 21st annual international ACM SIGIR conference on Research and development in information retrieval*, pages 275–281, New York, NY, USA, 1998. ACM.

[24] C. Privault, J. O'Neill, V. Ciriza, and J.-M. Renders. A new tangible user interface for machine learning document review. *Artificial Intelligence and Law*, 18:459–479, 2010.

[25] S. Ramaswamy, R. Rastogi, and K. Shim. Efficient algorithms for mining outliers from large data sets. *SIGMOD Rec.*, 29(2):427–438, 2000.

[26] N. T. Roman, C. D. Ferreira, L. A. A. Meira, R. Rezende, L. A. Digiampietri, and J. J. Filho. Attribute-value specification in customs fraud detection: a human-aided approach. In *Proc. 10th Annual International Conference on Digital Government Research*, pages 264–271. Digital Government Society of North America, 2009.

[27] 2009 US Congressional Legislation. Available at GovTrack:. `http://www.govtrack.us/data/us/111/`.

[28] J. Ward, Joe H. Hierarchical grouping to optimize an objective function. *Journal of the American Statistical Association*, 58(301):pp. 236–244, 1963.

[29] E. W. Welch and C. C. Hinnant. Internet use, transparency, and interactivity effects on trust in government. In *Proc. 36th Annual Hawaii International Conference on System Sciences (HICSS'03) - Track 5 - Volume 5*, pages 144.1–, Washington, DC, USA, 2003. IEEE Computer Society.

[30] C. Zhai and J. Lafferty. Model-based feedback in the language modeling approach to information retrieval. In *Proc. tenth international conference on Information and knowledge management*, pages 403–410, New York, NY, USA, 2001. ACM.

DOM Based Content Extraction via Text Density

Fei Sun, Dandan Song* and Lejian Liao*
Lab of High Volume language Information Processing & Cloud Computing
Beijing Lab of Intelligent Information Technology
School of Computer Science, Beijing Institute of Technology
Beijing, China
{ofey, sdd, liaolj}@bit.edu.cn

ABSTRACT

In addition to the main content, most web pages also contain navigation panels, advertisements and copyright and disclaimer notices. This additional content, which is also known as noise, is typically not related to the main subject and may hamper the performance of web data mining, and hence needs to be removed properly. In this paper, we present Content Extraction via Text Density (CETD)—a fast, accurate and general method for extracting content from diverse web pages, and using DOM (Document Object Model) node text density to preserve the original structure. For this purpose, we introduce two concepts to measure the importance of nodes: Text Density and Composite Text Density. In order to extract content intact, we propose a technique called DensitySum to replace Data Smoothing. The approach was evaluated with the CleanEval benchmark and with randomly selected pages from well-known websites, where various web domains and styles are tested. The average F_1-scores with our method were 8.79% higher than the best scores among several alternative methods.

Categories and Subject Descriptors

H.3.3 [**Information Search and Retrieval**]: Information filtering; H.3.1 [**Content Analysis and Indexing**]: Abstracting methods

General Terms

Algorithms, Experimentation

Keywords

Content Extraction, Text Density, Composite Text Density, DensitySum

1. INTRODUCTION

The explosive growth of the Internet has produced a huge number of information sources, and its influence continues to increase. Thus, web data mining has become an important and popular technique for discovering useful information or knowledge. Such research requires *main content* (*e.g.*, an article text) from the web to be gathered, processed and stored quickly and efficiently. However, the main content in web pages is often accompanied by a large amount of additional content such as navigation menus, banner advertisements and copyright notices. Although such information is expected by website owners and benefits user browsing, it is unrelated to the topic of the web pages and not simple enough for computer programs to parse. Thus this information can be treated as noise, hampering information gathering and web mining.

In order to improve the performance of web mining and information retrieval from web pages, content extraction techniques have been developed to remove such noise. Generally, content extraction improves performance, and is essential for many real world applications.

Traditionally, building text corpora was a very expensive and time-consuming process. By automatically downloading textual data from the web, extremely large corpora can be built in a short period, at relatively low cost. Therefore, the idea of *Web as Corpus* has been very attractive for many researchers in Natural Language Processing and related areas. In order to prepare web data for use as a corpus, ACL-SIGWAC held the first CleanEval competition during the summer of 2007 [23].

Additionally, as Pocket-sized devices with small screens such as PDAs and mobile phones have become ubiquitous, adapting web pages for small screens has become an increasingly important and challenging task [3, 8].

However, extracting the main content from the web pages has become more difficult and nontrivial. As early as 2005, Gibson et al. [14] estimated the noise to account for around 40-50% of the data on the web, and predicted correctly that this ratio would go on increasing. Meanwhile, web page layout has become much more complex than before, especially with the development and widespread use of the Cascading Style Sheets (CSS) technique. We find that most of the recent web pages use the style sheets and <div> or <span> tags for structural information to replace structural tags within a web page. Many early content extraction techniques failed to keep up with these changes and performed poorly, because recent web pages no longer include particular HTML cues (*e.g.*, <table>, <td> and fonts) that they used before.

In addition, nowadays most additional web page content, especially advertisements (*e.g.*, Google AdSense), are gen-

*Corresponding authors.

erated dynamically, which means template detection algorithms perform poorly. Moreover, they may also break easily due to the changes in page structure.

In this paper, we propose a highly effective content extraction algorithm to extract the main content from web pages. It can not only extract the main content, but also preserve its original structure information.

Our content extraction technique is based on the following observation: in a typical web page, the noise is usually highly formatted and contain less text and brief sentences, whereas the content is commonly simply formatted and contain more text but far less hyperlinks than in the noise. Furthermore, the content is usually an integral part of a web page and maintains the integrity of the structure, *i.e.* belongs to an ancestor node in the DOM tree.

First, we propose two measures for the importance of the tags in the web pages: *Text Density* and *Composite Text Density*. Once an HTML document is parsed and represented by a DOM tree, we calculate the text density for each node. Higher text density implies the node is more likely to represent a tag with content-text within the web page. In the case of noise the opposite applies. Furthermore, we extend the Text Density to the Composite Text Density by adding statistical information about hyperlinks. To solve the problem of losing low text density nodes in content, a tailored technique called *DensitySum* was designed to extract integral content. The results show that it is a fast, accurate and general content extraction algorithm which outperforms many current content extraction algorithms on large and varied data sets.

One difference between our approach and current methods is that we make no assumptions about the specific structure of an input web page, nor do we look for particular HTML cues. Another is that we can preserve the original structure of the input pages since all operations are performed on their DOM trees. Most existing approaches remove all tags from the HTML document and just output the text of the contents. They are not very user-friendly, and cannot be used to extract structured data from the web pages. In contrast, our method can output cleaned HTML documents instead of unformatted text.

The rest of the paper is organized as follows: after briefly reviewing related work in section 2, we propose two different definitions for text density in section 3. Next, we describe how to choose the threshold and the algorithm to extract content. Then, we describe our evaluation setup and compare the performance of our approach with other content extraction methods, and discuss the results. Finally we offer our conclusions and plans for future research.

2. RELATED WORK

The term *Content Extraction* (CE) was introduced by Rahman et al. in 2001 [25]. In the last decade, extraction of content from web pages has been studied intensively and numerous methods have been developed.

In the early days of content extraction, some handcrafted web scrapers (such as NoDoSE [2] or XWRAP [5]) extracted article text embedded in a common template from web pages by looking for some HTML cues, using regular expressions. These were written in a traditional programming language or with some specialized tools designed for content extraction. The biggest advantage of these methods was their accuracy. Obviously, the disadvantage lies in the fact that different regular expressions need to be manually created for each website. Still, even individual websites employ multiple structures; furthermore, these websites may also change structures or layouts over time. All the above situations mean such approaches require constant updating.

Kushmerick [20] and Davison [9] proposed machine learning mechanisms to recognize banner advertisements, redundant and irrelevant links in web pages. However, these techniques cannot be put to general use because they require a large set of manual-labeled training data and domain knowledge to generate classification rules.

The Vision-based Page Segmentation (VIPS) technique was introduced by Cai et al. [6] in 2003 to divide a web page into a tree, where the nodes are visually grouped blocks. Based on the VIPS method, Song et al. [26] presented an approach to rank block importance for web pages through learning algorithms using spatial features (such as position or size) and content features (such as the number of images and links); and Fernandes et al. [12] developed another way to compute block importance of a web page by means of assigning weights to classes of structurally similar blocks. However, VIPS must partially render a page in order to analyze it. Additionally, if external style sheets are used, they should also be retrieved. Therefore, compared to other techniques, VIPS is resource intensive.

A different approach for content extraction is Template Detection (TD) algorithms [4, 21, 28, 7, 18] in which collections of documents based on the same template are used to learn a common structure. Bar-Yossef et al. presented an approach to automatically detect templates from the largest *pagelet*, *i.e.* self-contained regions in a web page [4]. Lin et al. partitioned a page with <table> tags, and identified redundant blocks using an entropy measure over a set of word-based features [21]. In order to improve the performance of web page clustering and classification, Yi et al. introduced a *site style tree* (SST) structure that labels DOM nodes with similar styles across pages as uninformative [28]. Chen et al. combined template detection and removal with the index building process in large scale search engines to increase accuracy and speed. They segmented pages into blocks and clustered them based upon their styles and positions; then similar clusters among different pages were identified as part of the template [7].

In general, template detection algorithms identify the content by removing identical parts found in all web pages. This is an accurate approach but has been found to be too burdensome. The reason is that models need to be built for each website. This means pages in each site should share the same template. Furthermore, these methods often incorrectly assume that uninformative segments are largely repeated across pages (this is clearly not the case for varying text advertisements or lists of related articles) and any updates of the layout or structure may result in the template's failure.

Conversely, in the CleanEval shared task, only a few pages are available from the same site, thus requiring a more general approach. The winner of the CleanEval task split pages by their tags into a sequence of blocks and then labeled each block as "content" or "noise" using conditional random fields with a number of block-level features [23].

There are sets of content extraction approaches based on statistical information of web pages. In 2001, Finn et al. introduced the Body Text Extraction (BTE) algorithm to improve the accuracy of the content's classifier for digital libraries [13]. They interpreted an HTML document as a sequence of word and tag tokens, and then extracted content by identifying a single, continuous region which contains the most words and the least HTML tags. To overcome the restriction of BTE in discovering only a single continuous block of text, Pinto et al. [24] extended this method to construct Document Slope Curves (DSC), in which a windowing technique is used to locate document regions in which word tokens are more frequent than tag tokens. They used this technique to improve performance and efficiency for answering questions with web data in their QuASM system.

Mantratzis et al. presented an approach named Link Quota Filter (LQF) to identify link lists and navigation elements by identifying DOM elements which have a high ratio of text residing in hyperlink anchors [22]. It can be applied to content extraction by removing the resulting link blocks from the document. The drawback of this method is that it relies on *Structure elements*, and it can only identify hyperlink-type noise.

Debnath et al. proposed the FeatureExtractor (FE) and KFeatureExtractor (KFE) techniques based on block segmentation of the HTML document [10, 11]. Each block is analyzed for particular features such as the amount of text, the presence of images and script code. Content text is extracted by selecting blocks that correspond best to a desired feature, *e.g.* the presence of most text.

The Content Code Blurring (CCB) algorithm was introduced by Gottron in 2008 [16]. Content regions are detected in homogeneously formatted source code character sequences.

Weninger et al. introduced the Content Extraction via Tag Ratios (CETR) algorithm, a method to extract content text from diverse web pages using the HTML document's tag ratios [27]. The approach computes tag ratios on a line-by-line basis and then clusters the resulting histogram into content and noise areas. This is a laconic and efficient algorithm, however vulnerable to the page's source code style changes.

Kohlschütter et al. developed a simple, yet effective technique to classify individual text elements from a web page [19]. They analyzed a small set of shallow text features, which were theoretically grounded by stochastic text generation processes from Quantitative Linguistics, for boilerplate detection. Their study provides theoretical support for the method in this paper.

Gupta et al. attempted to combine different heuristics into one system called the *Crunch* framework [17]. They demonstrated that a well-chosen combination of different content extraction algorithms can provide better results than a single approach on its own. Since Crunch, several new content extraction algorithms have been developed. Then Gottron developed *CombineE* framework, a more recent ensemble method, which made it easier to configure ensembles of content extraction algorithms [15].

3. TEXT DENSITY

Let's take the news article from The New York Times[1] shown in Figure 1 as an example. This page is typical of the web: the banner, navigation and advertisements take up about half space on the page while the content of the page is confined to a relatively small space.

[1]http://www.nytimes.com

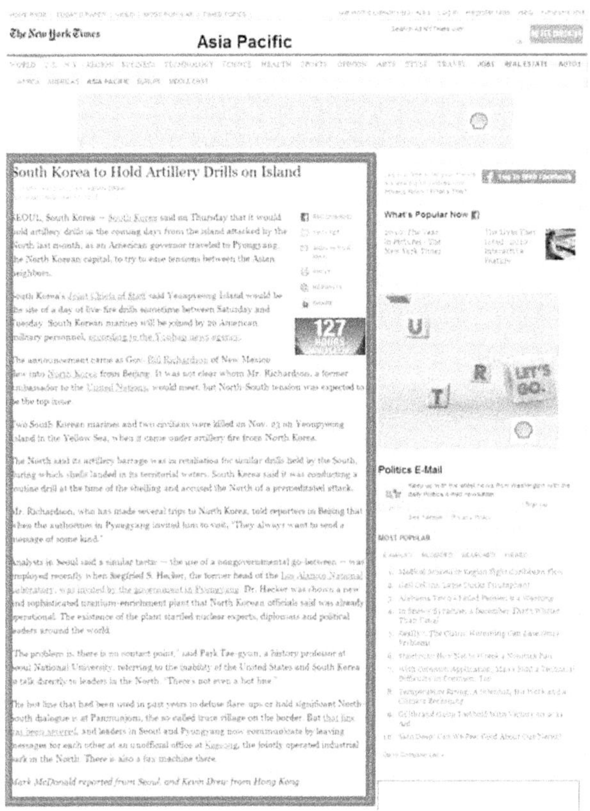

Figure 1: The New York Times web page article

To extract content from this web page, we take advantage of typical text features of content and noise. It was found that the noise in web pages is usually highly formatted and contains less text and brief sentences. On the other hand, the content is commonly lengthy and simply formatted. The example in Figure 1 also supports this observation.

3.1 DOM Tree

Document Object Model (DOM) [1] is a standardized, platform and language independent interface for accessing and updating content, structure and style of documents. Each HTML page corresponds to a DOM tree where tags are internal nodes and the detailed text and images are leaf nodes.

EXAMPLE 1. *Below is a brief segment of HTML code from Figure 1.*

```
<div class="main">
  <div class="article">
    <div class="articleHeadline">
      South Korea to Hold Artillery Drills on Island</div>
    <div class="articleBody">
    ...The announcement came as...
    <a>Bill Richardson</a>...
</div></div></div>
```

Example 1 shows a segment of HTML code from Figure 1, and Figure 2 shows the DOM tree of Example 1.

Notice that our study of HTML web pages begins from the `<body>` tag since all the viewable parts in a web page are within the scope of `<body>`.

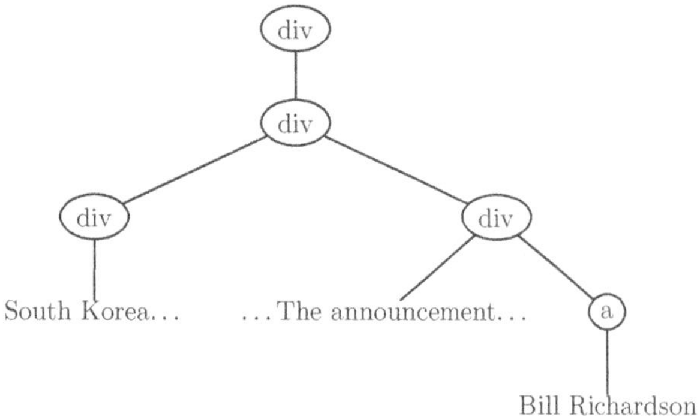

Figure 2: The DOM tree of Example 1

3.2 Text Density

Once an HTML document has been parsed and is represented by a DOM tree, the number of characters and tags that each node contains can be figured out. Then, such statistical information can be added to the node.

- *CharNumber*: number of all characters in its subtree.
- *TagNumber*: number of all tags in its subtree.

Furthermore, we can compute the ratios of the number of characters to the number of tags per node. Now, we define the *Text Density*, the basis of our method, as follows:

Definition 1. If i is a tag (corresponding to an element node in DOM) in a web page, then the tag i's Text Density (TD_i) is the ratio of its CharNumber to its TagNumber:

$$TD_i = \frac{C_i}{T_i}$$

where C_i is the number of all characters under i, T_i is the number of all tags under i. Note that if T_i is 0, it should be set to 1.

TD_i is a measure of the density of each node's text in a web page. It assigns high values for nodes that commonly contain long and simply formatted text and low values for highly formatted nodes containing less, brief text. It is useful for determining whether a part of a web page is meaningful or not. Clearly, content in a web page will be assigned relatively high density.

Before performing the computation, `script`, `comment` and `style` tags are removed from the DOM tree because such information is not visible and would likely skew the results if included in computation. In the likely case where the number of tags under a particular node is 0, the density is set to the number of characters the node contains. The *ComputeDensity* algorithm is described as Algorithm 1 where N is a DOM node being computed.

Computing the text density is a recursive task as evident from the simplicity of Algorithm 1. Example 2 below shows the text density for each node of Example 1.

EXAMPLE 2. *The text density for the five tags in Example 1 are computed as follows:*

1. `<div "main">`: `Chars=85, Tags=4, Density=21.25`
2. `<div "article">`: `Chars=85, Tags=3, Density=28.33`
3. `<div "articleHeadline">`: `Chars=46, Tags=1, Density=46`
4. `<div "articleBody">`: `Chars=39, Tags=1, Density=39`
5. `<a>`: `Chars=15, Tags=1, Density=15`

Algorithm 1 Pseudocode of ComputeDensity(N)

```
INPUT: N
OUTPUT: N
for all child node C in N do
    ComputeDensity(C)
end for
N.CharNumber ← CountChar(N)
N.TagNumber ← CountTag(N)
if N.TagNumber == 0 then
    N.TagNumber ← 1
end if
N.Density ← N.CharNumber/N.TagNumber
```

Figure 3 shows the resulting density-histogram for the page in Figure 1. It can be seen that there are nodes with a relatively high text density. Intuitively, we can take the high text density portion as the web page's content.

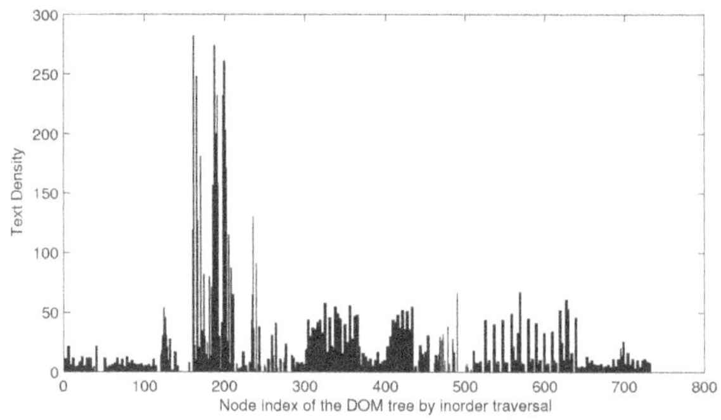

Figure 3: Text density for each node from NYtimes web page

3.3 Composite Text Density

With further study, we find that most of the noise in the web pages consists of hyperlinks. The example web page in Figure 1 supports this observation.

Based on the above discussion, we calculate additional statistical information per node as below:

- *LinkCharNumber*: number of all hyperlink characters in its subtree
- *LinkTagNumber*: number of all hyperlink tags in its subtree

According to the four pieces of statistical information mentioned above, we redefine the *Text Density*. In order to distinguish it from the Text Density defined above, we call it *Composite Text Density*. Unless otherwise specified, we use Text Density to refer to these two densities.

Definition 2. If i is a tag (corresponding to an element node in DOM) in a web page, then its Composite Text Density (CTD_i) is:

$$CTD_i = \frac{C_i}{T_i} \log_{\ln(\frac{C_i}{\neg LC_i} LC_i + \frac{LC_b}{C_b} C_i + e)} \left(\frac{C_i}{LC_i} \frac{T_i}{LT_i}\right)$$

where C_i is the number of all characters under i, T_i is the number of all tags under i, LC_i is the number of all hyperlink characters under i, $\neg LC_i$ is the number of all non-hyperlink characters under i, LT_i is the number of all hyperlink tags under i, LC_b is the number of all hyperlink characters under the `<body>` tag and C_b is the number of all characters under the `<body>` tag. Note that when denominators of the formula are 0, set them to 1.

In Definition 2, $\frac{C_i}{LC_i}$ is a measure of the proportion of hyperlink texts in i; accordingly, $\frac{T_i}{LT_i}$ is a measure of the proportion of hyperlink tags. When tag i contains numerous non-hyperlink characters and few hyperlinks, they will assign high values to it, and vice versa. Meanwhile, $\frac{C_i}{\neg LC_i} LC_i$ would get a low value in this case, and high otherwise. The role of $\frac{LC_b}{C_b} C_i$ is to maintain balance by preventing nodes containing lengthy and homogeneously formatted text from getting an extremely high values, or nodes which contain brief text (*e.g.*, news headlines or one sentence paragraphs) from getting extremely low values.

We argue that a node with too many hyperlinks and less text is less important, thus getting a low density value; and a node that contains much non-hyperlink text and few hyperlinks is more important, and receives a high density value. Clearly, a node's density will be zero if there are only hyperlinks in its subtree. In another extreme case, all tags of a web page which have no hyperlinks will get an infinite density. Thus, we would classify such a page as not containing noise.

Compared to Figure 3, Composite Text Density, shown in Figure 4, is better suited for classification because of the more obvious differences between sections. These two calculation methods of Text Density are discussed further in Section 5.

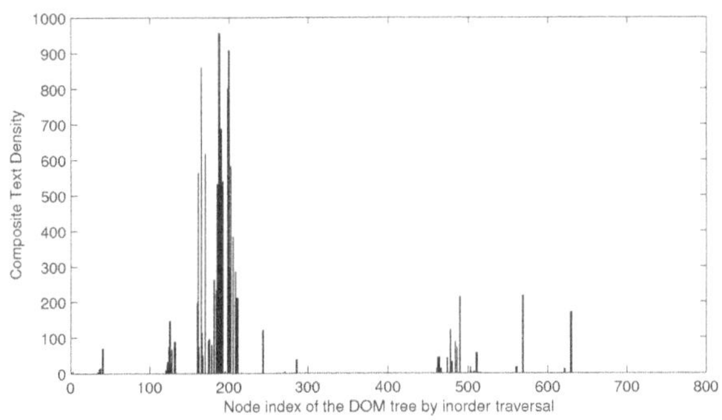

Figure 4: Composite text density for each node from NYtimes web page

4. CONTENT EXTRACTION

In this section we describe the technique used to extract the content. The idea behind this approach is to determine a threshold t which divides nodes into content or noise sections. Simply, any node with text density greater than or equal to t should be labeled as content; and any node should be labeled as noise if its text density is less than t. The problem then becomes a matter of finding the best value of t and a way to extracting the content completely.

4.1 Threshold

Intuitively, since the `<body>` tag is the root node that we compute, therefore it should contains both content and noise. This means that it contains more text than noise, and more hyperlinks than meaningful content. Hence, its text density should be an intermediate value sufficient to distinguish between the two. Empirically, we set the `<body>` tag's text density as the threshold in our study. It must be noted that this criterion is slightly modified in section 4.2.

4.2 DensitySum

It is easy to see that some nodes' text density is abnormally different from the surrounding nodes in Figure 3 and 4. For instance, pictures, hyperlinks, the byline or dateline of news articles, or very short paragraphs in the main article and references of an article may have abnormally low text density; conversely, some noise nodes (*e.g.*, copyright or disclaimer information) may get an abnormally high text density. The authors of [19] also noted this fact. Therefore, many content nodes may be lost if we simply label a node as content or noise just according to the threshold; and some noise nodes may be retained.

To solve this problem, we propose a technique called *DensitySum*. It is known that Data Smoothing can help with this problem to a certain extent by smoothing outlying peaks and valleys, increasing cohesiveness within sections and differences between sections. In general, although data smoothing can achieve good results, it may still lose some low-density content nodes; meanwhile, some noisy nodes may be retained because of text density increase.

DensitySum, is based on the observation that a content block of a web page belongs to an ancestor node in the structure of DOM; and as mentioned before, the text density of content nodes is much higher than that of noise nodes. Therefore, the content block (*i.e.*, a node in DOM) will get a peak value if we add up its children's text densities. Here, we define DensitySum as below:

Definition 3. If N is a tag (corresponding to an element node in DOM) in a web page and i is a child of N, then N's DensitySum is the sum of all its children's text densities:

$$DensitySum_N = \sum_{i \in C} TextDensity_i$$

Where C is the set of N's children and $TextDensity_i$ is the text density of tag i.

Note that $TextDensity$ here is just a general term; we use Text Density or Composite Text Density in practice.

For a simple case, if there exists just one content block, we identify the content by looking for the node under the `<body>` tag with the maximum DensitySum, then mark it as content. Afterwards, we extract the content by keeping its ancestors and subtrees.

Note that in many cases, the web page contains more than one content block. Therefore, for each node in which the text density is greater than the threshold, we apply the same method described above to extract content.

Moreover, in some web pages, the content block's text density may be less than the `<body>`'s text density. This block will be lost if we simply use the `<body>`'s text density as threshold. To resolve this problem, the algorithm first finds the maximum DensitySum tag in the whole page, without thresholding. Next, we set the minimum text density of the node in the path from the maximum DensitySum tag to `<body>` tag as threshold. The simple process of content extraction using DensitySum can be seen in Algorithm 2.

Algorithm 2 Pseudocode of ExtractContent(N)

```
INPUT: N
if N.TextDensity >= threshold then
    T <- FindMaxDensitySumTag(N)
    MarkContent(T)
    for all child node C in N do
        ExtractContent(C)
    end for
end if
```

4.3 Implementation Details

The program is implemented using Tidy[2] and RapidXml[3] in C++. Since there are several types of errors (*e.g.*, non-standard tags, incorrect encoding of HTML files) in web pages, parsing these web pages directly would fail. We use Tidy to correct such errors, and output them as standard X-HTML documents. Afterwards, the XHTML documents are parsed into DOM trees using RapidXml. Before text densities are computed, the algorithm removes invisible parts of an HTML document: `scripts`, `style definitions` and `comments`. Given their similar roles in a webpage, buttons and drop-down lists are treated as hyperlinks.

Three distinct algorithms are implemented. The first is the Text Density with DensitySum method, hereafter referred to as CETD-DS. The second is the Composite Text Density with Data Smoothing method, which, hereafter referred to as CECTD-S; here it is simply weighted averaging with sibling nodes. The last one is the Composite Text Density with DensitySum method, hereafter referred to as CECTD-DS. We use Content Extraction via Text Density (CETD) to refer to the three algorithms collectively.

5. EXPERIMENT

In this section we describe experiments on real world data from various web sites to demonstrate the effectiveness of our method. Data sets used in our experiments and evaluation measures are described first. We then present and discuss our experimental results.

5.1 Data Set

In our experiments we use data from two sources: (1) development and evaluation data sets from the CleanEval competition, and (2) the data sets we gathered from several web sites.

CleanEval: CleanEval is a shared task and competitive evaluation on the topic of cleaning arbitrary web pages [23]. Besides extracting content, the original CleanEval competition also asked participants to annotate the structure of the web pages: identify lists, paragraphs and headers. In this paper, we just focus on extracting content from arbitrary web pages. This data set includes four divisions: a development set and an evaluation set in both English and Chinese languages which are all hand-labeled. It is a diverse data set, only a few pages are used from each site, and the sites use various styles and structures.

However, we found some errors in the data of CleanEval's gold standard in the experiment, for instance, garbled characters or texts clearly not part of the content. Therefore, we manually extracted the main content of these pages using a web browser and saved it into text files (gold standard) in UTF-8. In our experiments, we only use the English data set, and do not distinguish between development and evaluation documents since our approach does not require training.

CETD: In order to evaluate our methods on varied sources, we produced a data set (which can be obtained from the author's website[4]). This data set is separated into two non-overlapping sets. (1) The *Big 5*: Ars Technica, BBC, Yahoo!, New York Times, Wikipedia, and (2) the *Chaos* data set chosen randomly from Google News and the best-known blog platforms such as WordPress and Blogger. For our purposes we arbitrarily selected 100 pages from each of the *Big 5* and 200 pages from *Chaos*. All these pages' contents were labeled manually using a web browser and saved as UTF-8 text files to serve as the gold standard.

5.2 Performance Metrics

Standard metrics were used to evaluate and compare the performance of different approaches. Specifically, precision, recall and F_1-scores were calculated by comparing the results of each method against the hand-labeled gold standard. Let a be the text in the extraction result and b be the text in the gold standard. Precision, recall and F_1-scores then follow from:

$$P = \frac{LCS(a,b).length}{a.length}, R = \frac{LCS(a,b).length}{b.length} \quad (1)$$

$$F_1 = \frac{2 \times P \times R}{P + R} \quad (2)$$

where $LCS(a,b)$ is the longest common subsequence between a and b. It is important to note that every word in the document is considered to be distinct even if two words are lexically the same. However, other methods, such as CETR, treated a and b as a bag of words, *i.e.*, two words are considered the same if they are lexically the same. The bag of words measurement is more lenient, thus the scores of these methods may be further inflated.

CleanEval uses a different metric to evaluate the participants' performance. The scoring method is based on the *Levenshtein Distance* from the output of an extraction algorithm to the gold standard text (the number of insertions and removals of words necessary to align the gold standard text with the output of the extraction algorithm; substitutions are not allowed). The full formula is:

$$Score(a,b) = 1 - \frac{distance(a,b)}{alignmentLength(a,b)} \quad (3)$$

where $alignmentLength(a,b)$ is the number of operations (insert, remove, or align) required to align two word sequences. The Levenshtein distance is relatively expensive to compute, taking $O(|a| \times |b|)$ time, which can be prohibitively large when $|a|$ and/or $|b|$ are sufficiently large. We find that our data sets frequently include documents which are that large (*i.e.*, size greater than 10,000 words). CleanEval's scoring script takes an extremely long time to return results, or even an "out of memory" error.

CleanEval's metric can be transformed into the following formula:

$$Score(a,b) = \frac{LCS(a,b).length}{a.length + b.length - LCS(a,b).length} \quad (4)$$

[2]`http://tidy.sourceforge.net/`

[3]`http://rapidxml.sourceforge.net/`

[4]`http://disnet.cs.bit.edu.cn/`

Therefore, we implemented a test program using *Longest Common Subsequence* instead. In our experiments, it performed very well, and is fast and robust.

5.3 Alternative Approaches

In order to evaluate the performance of our methods, we compare them with several other content extraction algorithms.

Several other algorithms (BTE, DSC, FE, KFE, LQ, C-CB) described in Section 2 have been implemented in Java for the Combine*E* framework [15]. In addition, CETR was also implemented in Java [27]. Evaluation was performed by providing each HTML document as input to each algorithm and collecting the results.

5.4 Result

All results are collected by calculating the average of each metrics over all examples.

Table 1 presents the results of the Content Extraction via Text Density with DensitySum (CETD-DS) method when given the task of extracting contents from the CleanEval, *Big 5* and the *Chaos* data sets.

Table 1: Results for CETD-DS on various domains

Source	Precision	Recall	F_1	Score
CleanEval-Eng	92.96%	94.52%	93.73%	88.96%
NYTimes	98.38%	95.84%	97.09%	94.42%
Yahoo!	83.16%	85.90%	84.51%	72.84%
Wikipedia	98.32%	97.22%	97.77%	95.76%
BBC	84.39%	95.21%	89.48%	80.66%
Ars Technica	97.81%	98.85%	98.33%	96.71%
Chaos	92.23%	94.99%	93.59%	88.76%

Table 2 presents the results of Content Extraction via a Composite Text Density with DensitySum (CECTD-DS) method.

Table 2: Results for CECTD-DS on various domains

Source	Precision	Recall	F_1	Score
CleanEval-Eng	95.87%	97.15%	96.51%	93.87%
NYTimes	99.69%	98.16%	98.92%	97.86%
Yahoo!	84.59%	93.99%	89.04%	80.71%
Wikipedia	98.25%	92.77%	95.43%	91.49%
BBC	86.15%	97.95%	91.67%	84.44%
Ars Technica	98.04%	99.51%	98.76%	97.57%
Chaos	96.21%	96.10%	96.15%	93.47%

Table 1 and 2 clearly show that these two methods perform very well, especially CECTD-DS, which performs better than CETD-DS on the broader corpora. This shows that Composite Text Density is more suitable than Text Density as a measure of the importance of a tag in web pages.

Interestingly, the CETD-DS outperforms CECTD-DS for Wikipedia, especially in recall. The reason for this phenomenon is the high density of in-text hyperlinks and low noise in Wikipedia pages. For the Composite Text Density method, these hyperlink tags in contents may assign their ancestor tags to a low density value, even lower than the threshold. However, the Text Density method could be unaffected.

Table 3 presents the results of Content Extraction via Composite Text Density with Smoothing (CECTD-S) method.

Table 3: Results for CECTD-S on various domains

Source	Precision	Recall	F_1	Score
CleanEval-Eng	90.35%	92.60%	91.46%	87.24%
NYTimes	96.72%	96.56%	96.64%	94.41%
Yahoo!	80.33%	93.34%	86.35%	76.16%
Wikipedia	98.02%	97.61%	97.81%	95.75%
BBC	82.55%	93.77%	87.80%	79.65%
Ars Technica	94.61%	93.56%	94.08%	91.65%
Chaos	89.64%	92.86%	91.22%	86.17%

Clearly, Table 2 and 3 show that CECTD-DS performs far better than CECTD-S for most data sets, again except the Wikipedia site. They demonstrate that DensitySum for deals more effectively than data smoothing with the situation where content nodes' text density is abnormally lower than the threshold, and noisy nodes' text density is abnormally higher than threshold.

Overall, these results show that the CECTD-DS performs far better than CETD-DS and CECTD-S. It is exciting that the CleanEval scores are higher than the winner of CleanEval competition, which only scored 84.1% on the English data set [23].

The results show that the precision of all three methods is relatively lower when applied to Yahoo! and BBC (compared with other sources). For Yahoo!, it is probably because its web pages contain user comments after each article; and these comments' structure hierarchies are very deep and separate from the content. That is why our method cannot extract the whole comments block. It is easy to see more precise results from sources such as Ars Technica which hides comments by default, and NYTimes which does not accept comments at all. As for BBC, the reason is that there are hidden disclaimers at the bottom of each page, with very long text. These disclaimers, which should not be computed because they are not visible in the browser, are included in the results.

5.4.1 Methods Comparison

In order to show the effectiveness of our methods, we compare the above performance with the alternative approaches described earlier in this section. Table 4 presents the results with the best approach for each data source in bold.

Interestingly, the DSC algorithm does not perform better than the BTE algorithm, even though it actually extends the BTE algorithm. We believe this is due to the windowing technique which improves the precision, but reduces the recall rate of the DSC algorithm.

It is noteworthy that CETR is very similar to our approach, whereby content is extracted by tag ratios. However, CETR loses the structural information of web pages, since the tag ratios are computed on a line-by-line basis. The results in Table 4, 5 and 6 show that the Composite Text Density and DensitySum methods outperform CETR.

Table 5 and 6 show that other methods typically achieve either a high recall or a high precision but rarely both. Our CETD performs more consistently than other algorithms with overall high scores in both metrics, and CECTD-DS is the best performing algorithm in most data sets with the

Table 4: F_1-measures for each algorithm in each source. The best scores are marked in bold.

Algorithm	CleanEval-Eng	NYTimes	Yahoo!	Wikipedia	BBC	Ars Technica	Chaos	Average
BTE	92.22%	76.23%	69.64%	82.74%	80.73%	80.44%	83.78%	80.83%
CCB	86.24%	72.03%	62.46%	67.82%	67.72%	76.92%	75.47%	72.66%
DSC	74.07%	91.68%	83.23%	48.62%	83.76%	93.09%	86.79%	80.17%
FE	17.56%	6.98%	9.41%	2.91%	7.15%	0.002%	11.46%	8.97%
KFE	74.13%	72.56%	62.61%	55.59%	64.43%	82.03%	69.78%	68.73%
LQF	91.23%	93.42%	75.40%	79.85%	83.93%	93.15%	88.01%	86.42%
CETR	88.59%	87.80%	73.27%	82.30%	76.76%	88.16%	82.63%	82.78%
CETD-DS	93.73%	97.09%	84.51%	97.77%	89.48%	98.33%	93.59%	93.50%
CECTD-S	91.46%	96.64%	86.35%	**97.81%**	87.80%	94.08%	91.22%	92.24%
CECTD-DS	**96.51%**	**98.92%**	**89.04%**	95.43%	**91.67%**	**98.77%**	**96.15%**	**95.21%**

Table 5: Precision-measures for each algorithm in each source. The best scores are marked in bold.

Algorithm	CleanEval-Eng	NYTimes	Yahoo!	Wikipedia	BBC	Ars Technica	Chaos	Average
BTE	88.87%	62.22%	54.94%	83.91%	69.09%	68.25%	76.36%	71.95%
CCB	80.61%	57.61%	46.90%	63.22%	53.52%	64.05%	64.45%	61.48%
DSC	91.94%	98.58%	96.54%	81.67%	89.27%	95.82%	94.45%	92.61%
FE	73.87%	97.51%	**99.08%**	**98.79%**	**98.95%**	0.005%	72.59%	77.26%
KFE	79.28%	73.82%	69.49%	73.76%	63.84%	81.35%	73.97%	73.64%
LQF	88.60%	90.02%	64.54%	83.60%	77.03%	88.40%	82.76%	82.14%
CETR	91.26%	85.19%	69.36%	94.69%	68.93%	83.06%	78.75%	81.61%
CETD-DS	92.96%	98.38%	83.16%	98.31%	84.39%	97.81%	93.59%	92.66%
CECTD-S	90.35%	96.72%	80.33%	98.02%	82.55%	94.61%	89.64%	90.33%
CECTD-DS	**95.87%**	**99.69%**	84.59%	98.25%	86.15%	**98.04%**	**96.21%**	**94.11%**

Table 6: Recall-measures for each algorithm in each source. The best scores are marked in bold.

Algorithm	CleanEval-Eng	NYTimes	Yahoo!	Wikipedia	BBC	Ars Technica	Chaos	Average
BTE	95.83%	98.38%	**95.06%**	81.60%	97.09%	97.91%	92.80%	94.10%
CCB	92.71%	96.09%	93.45%	73.14%	92.19%	96.27%	91.05%	90.70%
DSC	62.01%	85.67%	73.14%	34.61%	78.89%	90.52%	80.27%	72.16%
FE	9.97%	3.62%	4.94%	1.48%	3.71%	0.001%	6.22%	4.28%
KFE	69.61%	71.35%	56.97%	44.60%	65.02%	82.73%	66.04%	65.19%
LQF	94.02%	97.10%	90.65%	76.41%	92.17%	98.43%	93.98%	91.82%
CETR	86.08%	90.58%	77.65%	72.77%	86.58%	93.93%	86.92%	84.93%
CETD-DS	94.52%	95.84%	85.90%	97.22%	95.21%	98.85%	94.99%	94.65%
CECTD-S	92.60%	96.56%	93.34%	**97.61%**	93.77%	93.56%	91.22%	93.97%
CECTD-DS	**97.15%**	**98.16%**	93.99%	92.77%	**97.95%**	**99.51%**	**96.10%**	**96.52%**

average F_1-score 8.79% higher than the best score among other approaches..

5.5 Discussion

The results show that CETD is an effective and robust content extraction algorithm, which performs relatively well even on non-news web corpora with considerable diversity, such as the CleanEval data set. Note that CETD does not require manual-labeled training examples since it is a completely unsupervised algorithm.

The results also show that CECTD-DS outperforms CETD-DS and CECTD-S on broader corpora. It shows the Composite Text Density and DensitySum techniques are more effective than Text Density and Data Smoothing.

For practical purposes, users usually value recall over precision as a performance metric. Although, CECTD-DS can achieve a very high recall rate, users can still see a marked increase in recall and a sharp decrease in precision by reducing the threshold. This precision/recall tradeoff is shown in Figure 5. We set the threshold in actual use as the base value, and use a coefficient λ to adjust the threshold value in this experiment. Note that the threshold must be lower than the text density of the <body> tag, otherwise the whole page will be viewed as noise. When $\lambda = 0$, the recall is always 100% because all nodes in DOM are included. For the Yahoo! domain, shown in Figure 5, a good tradeoff might be $\lambda = 0.9$. Finding a good threshold value is difficult. In current experiments, we set $\lambda = 1$, which can already achieve very good results on various domains.

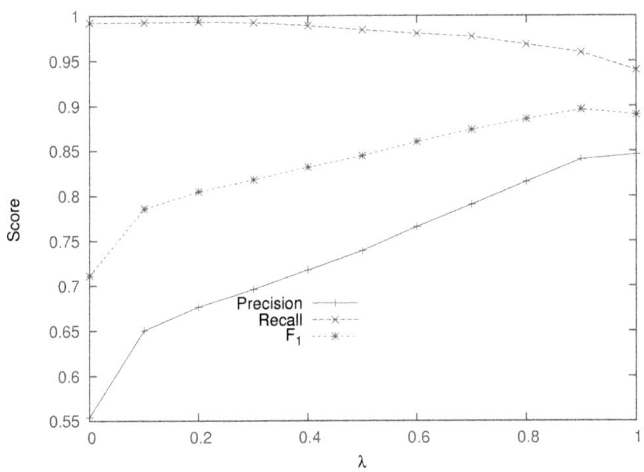

Figure 5: Precision, Recall and F_1 tradeoff for Yahoo! as the threshold coefficient (λ) increases

In contrast to most other methods, which just output unformatted text, content with complete structure information can be obtained by CETD because all operations are done in the DOM tree. Therefore, CETD can be easily integrated with other applications.

Many current methods only extract the most probable content section. However, there is no rule that a web page may only have a single content section. There are many web pages, especially blogs where content is separated by horizontal lines or other delimiters. CETD is not affected by multiple content sections.

Despite many advantages of our algorithm, there are some weaknesses. It does not perform well with some site categories, such as video and picture sites. The contents of such sites are videos or pictures as well as the comments under them. Therefore, our findings do not hold for these sites. For Youtube, CETD can only extract comments. Another situation where CETD does not perform well is portal home pages. These pages usually contain a vast array of menus and news titles or short news descriptions, and most of these are hyperlinks. CETD has problems discerning the content section(s) of these types of web pages. However, in general, these pages have no topic. Therefore, extracting the contents of these pages does not make much sense.

6. CONCLUSIONS

In this paper, we have proposed a method for extracting the contents from web pages by Text Density, based on the observation that the content text is usually lengthy and simply formatted, while noise is usually highly formatted and contain less text with brief sentences. Observing that noise contains many more hyperlinks than meaningful content, we extended Text Density to Composite Text Density by adding statistical information about hyperlinks. In order to extract the content completely, we proposed the DensitySum technique instead of Data Smoothing. The effectiveness of the CETD algorithm has been demonstrated. The results show that CETD performs better than several other content extraction algorithms.

In addition to its effectiveness, the greatest strength of this algorithm over other methods is the simplicity of its concept and implementation. Furthermore, this algorithm just requires a web page as input, and then returns a cleaned page without adjusting parameters, training and building classifier models. CETD can also retain the original structure information of the web pages, which can then be utilized for other applications, such as small screen devices.

6.1 Future Work

In the research for this paper, we found that HTML Tidy was not sufficiently robust since it may sometimes cause some pages to not be properly parsed. In the future, the WebKit[5] Kernel will be incorporated to parse web pages, so that pages rendered normally by a browser can be parsed correctly.

Another area for further investigation is to identify the hidden elements of the pages. In some sites, some of the non-content part (*e.g.*, BBC disclaimers) is not visible. We may achieve better results if we can remove these non-visible elements before the computation of text density, since these elements are meaningless for the end user but treated as non-tag text in the algorithm.

Intuitively, the meaningful content always occupies the center of the screen. Obviously, a web page can be partitioned into multiple segments or blocks, and usually the importance of those blocks on a page is not equivalent. Therefore, spatial information (*e.g.*, position, size) will be added to the density measure to further enhance the performance.

Finally, in this paper, we focused on the comparison between the content extraction methods based on statistical information of web pages. VIPS, on the other hand, is a visual information based method which cannot be compared directly as it outputs a set of page segments rather than ex-

[5] `http://webkit.org/`

tracted text. It can be deduced that CETD performs better than VIPS since CETR outperform VIPS in [27]. In a future study, we will do more experiments to verify this.

7. ACKNOWLEDGMENTS

The authors sincerely thank Tim Weninger, the author of CETR, for the fruitful discussions and data access. We also thank Thomas Gottron, author of the *CombineE* framework, for some of the implementations used in this work; and the CleanEval team for providing a standard evaluation data set. This work is funded by NSFC (Grant Nos.60873237 and 61003168), Beijing Natural Science Foundation (Grant No.4092037), Excellent Researcher Award Program and Basic Research Foundation of Beijing Institute of Technology.

8. REFERENCES

[1] W3C document object model. Website, 2009. http://www.w3.org/DOM.

[2] B. Adelberg. Nodose—a tool for semi-automatically extracting semi-structured data from text documents. In *Proceedings of SIGMOD '98*, pages 283–294, New York, NY, USA, 1998. ACM.

[3] S. Baluja. Browsing on small screens: recasting web-page segmentation into an efficient machine learning framework. In *Proceedings of WWW '06*, pages 33–42, 2006.

[4] Z. Bar-Yossef and S. Rajagopalan. Template detection via data mining and its applications. In *Proceedings of WWW '02*, pages 580–591, New York, NY, USA, 2002.

[5] O. Buyukkokten, H. Garcia-Molina, and A. Paepcke. Accordion summarization for end-game browsing on pdas and cellular phones. In *Proceedings of SIGCHI '01*, pages 213–220, New York, NY, USA, 2001. ACM.

[6] D. Cai, S. Yu, J. Wen, and W. Ma. Extracting content structure for web pages based on visual representation. In *Proceedings of APWeb'03*, pages 406–417, 2003.

[7] L. Chen, S. Ye, and X. Li. Template detection for large scale search engines. In *Proceedings of SAC '06*, pages 1094–1098, New York, NY, USA, 2006.

[8] Y. Chen, P. Fankhauser, and H.-J. Zhang. Detecting web page structure for adaptive viewing on small form factor devices. In *Proceedings of WWW '03*, pages 225–233, 2003.

[9] B. D. Davison. Recognizing nepotistic links on the web. In *AAAI-2000 Workshop On Artificial Intelligence For Web Search*, pages 23–28, Austin, Texas, 2000.

[10] S. Debnath, P. Mitra, and C. L. Giles. Automatic extraction of informative blocks from webpages. In *Proceedings of SAC '05*, pages 1722–1726, 2005.

[11] S. Debnath, P. Mitra, and C. L. Giles. Identifying content blocks from web documents. *ISMIS*, 3488(5):285–293, November 2005.

[12] D. Fernandes, E. S. de Moura, B. Ribeiro-Neto, A. S. da Silva, and M. A. Gonçalves. Computing block importance for searching on web sites. In *Proceedings of CIKM '07*, pages 165–174, 2007.

[13] A. Finn, N. Kushmerick, and B. Smyth. Fact or fiction: Content classification for digital libraries. In *Joint DELOS-NSF Workshop: Personalization and Recommender Systems in Digital Libraries*, 2001.

[14] D. Gibson, K. Punera, and A. Tomkins. The volume and evolution of web page templates. In *WWW '05*, pages 830–839, New York, NY, USA, 2005. ACM.

[15] T. Gottron. Combining content extraction heuristics: the *CombinE* system. In *Proceedings of iiWAS '08*, pages 591–595, 2008.

[16] T. Gottron. Content code blurring: A new approach to content extraction. In *Proceedings of DEXA '08*, pages 29–33, 2008.

[17] S. Gupta, G. Kaiser, and S. Stolfo. Extracting context to improve accuracy for html content extraction. In *Proceedings of WWW '05*, pages 1114–1115, 2005.

[18] H. Kao, S. Lin, J. Ho, and M. Chen. Mining web informative structures and contents based on entropy analysis. In *IEEE Transactions on Knowledge and Data Engineering*, pages 41–55, Piscataway, NJ, USA, 2004.

[19] C. Kohlschütter, P. Fankhauser, and W. Nejdl. Boilerplate detection using shallow text features. In *Proceedings of WSDM '10*, pages 441–450, 2010.

[20] N. Kushmerick. Learning to remove internet advertisements. In *Proceedings of AGENTS '99*, pages 175–181, New York, NY, USA, 1999.

[21] S. Lin and J. Ho. Discovering informative content blocks from web documents. In *Proceedings of SIGKDD '02*, pages 588–593, New York, NY, USA, 2002.

[22] C. Mantratzis, M. Orgun, and S. Cassidy. Separating xhtml content from navigation clutter using dom-structure block analysis. In *Proceedings of HYPERTEXT '05*, pages 145–147, 2005.

[23] M. Marek, P. Pecina, , and M. Spousta. Web page cleaning with conditional random fields. In *Proceedings of the Web as Corpus Workshop (WAC3),Cleaneval Session*, 2007.

[24] D. Pinto, M. Branstein, R. Coleman, W. B. Croft, M. King, W. Li, and X. Wei. Quasm: A system for question answering using semi-structured data. In *Proceedings of JCDL '02*, pages 46–55, 2002.

[25] A. F. R. Rahman, H. Alam, and R. Hartono. Content extraction from html documents. In *WDA2001*, pages 7–10, 2001.

[26] R. Song, H. Liu, J. Wen, and W. Ma. Learning block importance models for web pages. In *Proceedings of WWW '04*, pages 203–211, New York, NY, USA, 2004.

[27] T. Weninger, W. H. Hsu, and J. Han. Cetr - content extraction via tag ratios. In *Proceedings of WWW '10*, pages 971–980, New York, NY, USA, 2010.

[28] L. Yi, B. Liu, and X. Li. Eliminating noisy information in web pages for data mining. In *Proceedings of SIGKDD '03*, pages 296–305, New York, NY, USA, 2003.

Social Context Summarization

Zi Yang*, Keke Cai†, Jie Tang*, Li Zhang†, Zhong Su† and Juanzi Li*

*Department of Computer Science and Technology, Tsinghua University, China
† IBM, China Research Lab
{yangzi, tangjie, ljz}@keg.cs.tsinghua.edu.cn, {caikeke, lizhang, suzhong}@cn.ibm.com

ABSTRACT

We study a novel problem of *social context summarization* for Web documents. Traditional summarization research has focused on extracting informative sentences from standard documents. With the rapid growth of online social networks, abundant user generated content (e.g., comments) associated with the standard documents is available. Which parts in a document are social users really caring about? How can we generate summaries for standard documents by considering both the informativeness of sentences and interests of social users? This paper explores such an approach by modeling Web documents and social contexts into a unified framework. We propose a dual wing factor graph (DWFG) model, which utilizes the mutual reinforcement between Web documents and their associated social contexts to generate summaries. An efficient algorithm is designed to learn the proposed factor graph model. Experimental results on a Twitter data set validate the effectiveness of the proposed model. By leveraging the social context information, our approach obtains significant improvement (averagely +5.0%-17.3%) over several alternative methods (CRF, SVM, LR, PR, and DocLead) on the performance of summarization.

Categories and Subject Descriptors

H.3.1 [**Information Storage and Retrieval**]: Content Analysis and Indexing; H.2.8 [**Database Management**]: Data Mining; J.4 [**Computer Applications**]: Social and Behavioral Sciences

General Terms

Algorithms, Experimentation

Keywords

Document summarization, Social context, Factor graph, Twitter

1. INTRODUCTION

Web document summarization has been widely studied for many years. Existing methods mainly use statistical or linguistic information such as term distribution, sentence position, and topics to extract the most informative sentences from standard (Web) documents. However, these methods only consider the document's content information, but ignore how users (readers) think about the document. With the rapid growth of online social networks, users can freely express what they are thinking about any Web document. For example, many news websites allow the users to directly add comments to each news document. On Twitter[1], many users post the URL address of a news document onto their microblogs, followed by some personal comments. The comments imply the importance of different sentences and can be used to help improve the quality of document summarization. More importantly, the users' comments essentially reflect which part of the document that they are interested in.

In this work, we present a novel problem of *social context summarization*. The question we intend to answer is: how to generate a summary for Web documents by considering both the informativeness of sentences and interests of social users? The concept of "context" for summarization has been previously studied and various approaches have been proposed based on different kinds of context, such as hyperlinks [1, 9], click-through data [29], comments [13, 19], or opinionated text [26, 11, 15]. Most of these methods directly integrate the context information into the target webpage to help estimate the informativeness of sentences. However, in this way, the context information is only considered as textual information. Many important information has been ignored. For example, if a user is an opinion leader, his comments should be more important than others. From a comment's perspective, if a comment has been forwarded or replied by many other users, the comment should be more important than others. One goal of this work is to consider the social influence and the information propagation for document summarization. The problem is referred to as social context summarization. The problem is clearly different from existing research and poses a set of unique challenges:

- First, social context is becoming more and more complicated. There are users, user generated contents, social networks, and implicit networks (such as the forward/reply network). How to formally define the social context is a nontrivial problem.
- Second, in the social environment, the quality of summaries strongly depends on the social context information (such as the social influence between users). How to formalize the problem in a principled framework is a challenging problem.
- Third, the social context contains inevitable noise. How to qualitatively analyze the problem and quantitatively validate

SIGIR'11, July 24–28, 2011, Beijing, China.

[1]http://www.twitter.com, a microblogging system.

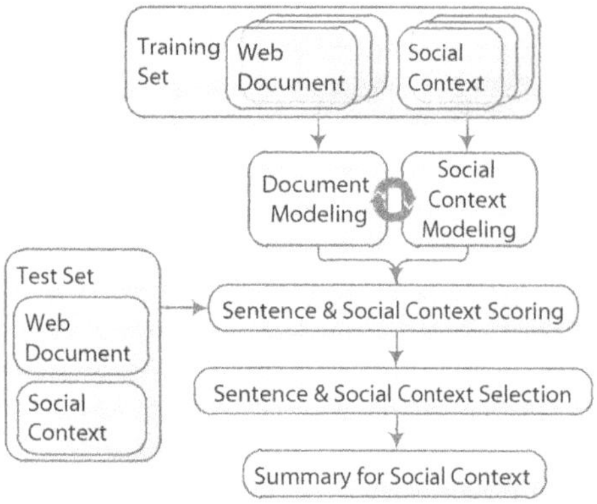

Figure 1: Overview of the proposed approach

the proposed approach on a real-world data set is also a challenging problem.

In this paper, we try to systematically investigate the problem of social context summarization for Web documents. We formulate the problem of social context summarization and propose a dual-wing factor graph (DWFG) model. The DWFG model incorporates the summarization task and the social network analysis into a unified framework. In this way, the two tasks can be mutually reinforced. We employ the Microblogging as an example to quantitatively study the social context summarization problem. In particular, we crawl a data set from Twitter. The user generated content is the tweet posted by the user. The retweeting (forwarding) and replying relationships between tweets form an implicit information network, and the following relationships between users form the user network. Some tweets have the links pointing to standard Web documents (such as news documents). The problem then becomes how to leverage both the information network and the user network to generate high-quality summaries for standard Web documents.

The overview of the proposed method is a supervised framework (as shown in Figure 1). In training, we estimate the importance of defined features and strength of dependencies for identifying key sentences and microblogs in the social contexts. In test, given a new Web document with its social context, we perform collective inference for the importance of each sentence and microblog and select a subset of sentences as the summary according to the trained models. We validate the proposed approach on the Twitter data set. The experiment results show that by leveraging the social context information, our approach can significantly improve (on average +10.8%) the performance of summarization. We also compare with a set of alternative methods (i.e., CRF, SVM, LR, PR, and DocLead), and our approach clearly outperforms (averagely +5.0%-17.3%) the baseline methods.

The paper is organized as follows: in Section 2, we introduce some notations and formally define the problem. In Section 3, we propose the factor graph model to address the problem, and in Section 4, we conduct the experiments on the Twitter data set. Finally, in Section 5 and 6, we summarize related works and conclude.

2. PROBLEM DEFINITION

In this section, we introduce some notations and representations necessary for the problem, and then define the problem of social context summarization.

Definition 1 (Social context). Given a Web document d, its social context C_d is defined as $\langle M_d, U_d \rangle$, where M_d is a set of comments on d written by users U_d in a social network.

In the context of Web 2.0, Web documents, e.g. news or blogs, are freely discussed and commented by users. These comments again spread (e.g., by forwarding between friends) in the social network. The users' activities implicitly reflect the importance of different parts (e.g., sentences) in the document from the user's perspective. We believe that the social context, thus, integrating the document content information and the social context information can disclose a more thorough view of the document. In this paper, we employ Twitter as the basis for our study. Specifically, given a Web document[2] d and its associated social context (tweets M_d containing the URL address of document d and users U_d who posted those tweets), we give the following definition of social context augmented network.

Definition 2 (Social Context Augmented Network, SCAN). Social Context Augmented Network $G_d = (S_d, C_d, E_d)$ is defined as a network that is built upon the sentence set S_d of document d and its social context C_d, where the edge set E_d contains three types of edges: E_d^s, E_d^m, and E_d^u. $E_d^s = \{(s_i, s_j)|s_i, s_j \in S_d\}$ represents the relationships between document sentences, $E_d^m = \{(m_i, m_j)|m_i, m_j \in M_d\}$ represents the relationships between messages, and $E_d^u = \{(u_i, u_j)|u_i, u_j \in U_d\}$ represents the relationships between users.

Compared with traditional contexts that are defined based on textual information, social context need incorporate various dynamic social relationships, such as the *follower-followee relationships* between users, *retweeting relationships* and *replying relationships* between tweets. An example of SCAN is shown in Figure 2(a). In this figure, the upper layer includes two documents d_1 and d_2, and d_1 contains four sentences s_1, s_2, s_3, and s_4. The two documents are respectively associated with two sets of messages $M_1 = \{m_5, m_6, m_7, m_8\}$ and $M_2 = \{m_9, m_{10}\}$ in the middle layer. The lower layer refers to the user layer consisting of users u_1, u_2 and u_3, who are also associated with the messages M_1 and M_2. Besides external relationships between the objects across different layers, SCAN also describes internal relationships between objects within the same layer (as shown in Figure 2(a)).

Given this, we can formally define our problem of *Social Context Summarization*.

Definition 3 (Social Context Summarization). Given a social context augmented network G_d, the goal of social context summarization is to generate a summary which consists of two pieces of information: the most important sentences $S_d^* \subseteq S_d$ and the most representative messages $M_d^* \subseteq M_d$.

The problem of social context summarization contains two subproblems: *Key Sentence Extraction* and *Tweet Summarization*. In the former subproblem, we aim to identify the most important sentences from document d's content, while in the latter subproblem, we intend to find the most representative tweets from the social context C_d of document d. Social context C_d contains rich information about the document d, which is helpful for the Key Sentence Extraction problem, while the important sentences in a document can equally help Tweet Summarization in the social context. The mutual reinforcement between the two subproblems can facilitate generating a high-quality summary. Moreover, social context summarization could also answer a number of related questions, e.g., who are the most experienced users of a specific topic or a fact mentioned in a document.

[2]On Twitter, a Web document (e.g., news document) is often pointed out by a URL address, which might be in some forms of encoded shortened URLs such as by tinyurl.com and bit.ly.

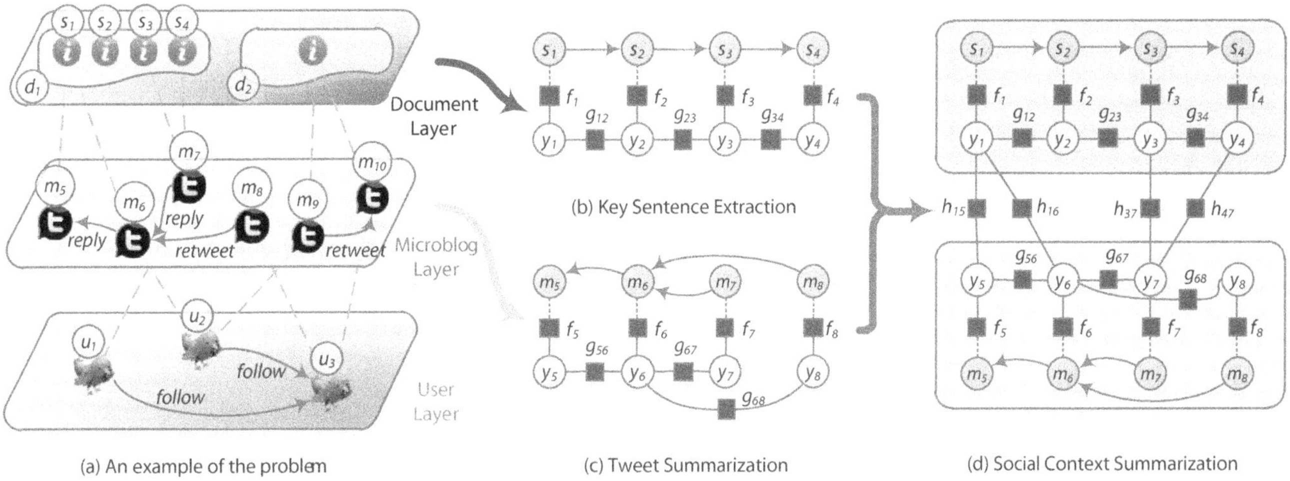

Figure 2: An example of the problem and factor graph representations for summarization tasks. In (b), (c), and (d), each gray circle with s_i indicates a sentence in the Web document; its associated white circle with y_i denotes whether the sentence should be included in the document summary. Each gray circle with m_i indicates a tweet and its associated white circle denotes whether the tweet would be included in the tweet summary.

3. PROBLEM SOLVING

In this section, we propose a dual wing factor graph (DWFG) model, which formulates the social context summarization problem in a unified learning framework. The DWFG model simultaneously incorporates all resources in social context to generate high-quality summaries for Web documents.

3.1 Basic Idea

In our Twitter data set, each Web document is associated with a social context. To generate summaries for Web documents, a straightforward method is to define a set of features to characterize the importance of each sentence, and then use a classification model to identify which sentences should be included into the summary [16, 25, 36]. To further consider the correlation between sentences, we can consider a sequential labeling approach such as conditional random field. Such a method has been studied by [8, 28]. Both of them consider the sentence local features and similarities (correlations) between sentences, and model the sentence extraction task with a linear-chain conditional random field. An example of the graphical representation is shown in Figure 2(b). The method only considers the correlation between sentences (the document layer in Figure 2(a)), but ignores the social context information resided in the microblog and user layers.

To model the tweet network, we design another similar graphical model with structures reflecting the information propagation. Figure 2(c) presents an example. Each gray circle indicates a tweet, the arrow represents the replying/retweeting relationship between two tweets. Based on such a formulation, we can define local features (content-based features) for each tweet, as well as edge features for each replying/retweeting relationship. By learning such a graphical model, we can classify which tweets are important (or informative). Obviously, this model only considers the information from the tweet side and does not consider the Web documents. An ideal way is to incorporate the two tasks together so that they can reinforce each other.

Based on these considerations, we propose a novel dual wing factor graph (DWFG) model. The graphical representation is shown in Figure 2(d). In the DWFG model, the upper layer is used to model the key sentence extraction task and the bottom layer is designed to model the tweet summarization problem. In the middle layer, we design a set of correlation factor functions h to bridge the two tasks. By carefully designing the correlation factor function h, we can elegantly combine the two tasks of key sentence extraction and tweet summarization into a unified framework. In the rest of this section, we will explain in details how we design and learn the dual wing factor graph model.

3.2 Modeling Summarization via Dual Wing Factor Graphs

We model the social context summarization problem in the dual wing factor graph (DWFG) model. Each sentence $s_i \in S_d$ or tweet $m_i \in M_d$ is associated with a binary value y_i indicating the importance of the sentence or tweet (1 representing important, and 0 representing unimportant).

We first collect a set of labeled SCANs (training set) $T = \{G_d\}_{d=1}^{n_T}$, i.e., each sentence $s_i \in S_d$ or tweet $m_i \in M_d$ in each social context C_d is associated with a known binary label y_i, moreover, we also collect the test set S of unlabeled instances, which consists of all the sentences and tweets not yet judged. Our goal is then to learn a DWFG model from the training set and apply it to predict which sentences and tweets are important in the test set S, i.e., to infer the value (label) of y, and then generate a summary for the social context.

We define three types of factor functions associated with individual instances or instance groups: *local attribute factor*, *intra-domain dependency factor*, and *inter-domain dependency factor*.

Local attribute factor. The probability that a sentence or tweet is important could be estimated by some local attributes (represented as $\mathbf{x}$), which refer to features that are inherent to the sentence or tweet itself. In general, we define similar features for sentences and tweets. The features include the average TF-IDF score over words and the log likelihood generated by the context, the position of the sentence in the document, the author's authoritativeness, etc. Details of the defined local features for sentences and tweets are given in Section 4.

To estimate the significance of each feature, we introduce a weight variable λ_c for each feature c, and we define a local attribute factor $f_{i,c}$ for the feature c of each sentence s_i or tweet m_i.

Formally, a factor could be defined as the local entropy:

$$f_{i,c}(\lambda_c, y_i) = \exp(\lambda_c x_{i,c} y_i) \quad (1)$$

where $x_{i,c}$ is the value of the c-th feature extracted from sentence s_i or tweet m_i.

Intra-domain dependency factor. As described in Section 3.1, we introduce factors that are capable of handling multiple instances in either sentence level or tweet level, to characterize the dependencies between sentences and tweets respectively. Intra-domain interaction may promote some sentences to become more important while inhibit others from becoming important. We associate each type of interaction with a weight μ_c indicating the confidence of the corresponding interaction. The interaction has a positive influence only if the weight μ_c is greater than 0. We introduce factor $g_{ij,c}$ to capture the dependency between sentence pair s_i and s_j or tweet pair m_i and m_j.

$$g_{ij,c}(\mu_c, y_i, y_j) = \begin{cases} \exp \mu_c & \text{if some condition holds} \\ 1 & \text{otherwise} \end{cases} \quad (2)$$

A document can be regarded as a sequence of sentences, and thus key sentence extraction could be viewed as a sequence labeling process [28], i.e., the judgment on a certain sentence is affected by the nearby sentences to avoid both sentences of high similarity are chosen simultaneously. Hence, the dependency conditions in Eq. 2 for a sentence pair s_i and s_j can be formalized as follow: the factor takes value $\exp \mu_c$ if $y_i \neq 1$ or $y_j \neq 1$. To avoid high computational complexity, we constrain only consecutive and similar sentences, i.e., establish sentence relation for sentence s_i and s_{i+1} whose mutual similarity (e.g., cosine similarity) exceeds the threshold θ_g.

Moreover, we consider the two interactions between tweets: replying and retweeting. If tweet m_i replies or retweets tweet m_j, then m_j successfully excites and attracts attentions from others, and it is reasonable that m_j is more important than its succeeding tweets in the thread. Formally, for such a tweet pair m_i and m_j, the factor takes value $\exp \mu_c$ if $y_i \leq y_j$.

Inter-domain dependency factor. By leveraging knowledge from both domains, the inter-domain relationships may benefit to the identification of social context summarization. We introduce a set of factors defined on variables across domains, which are able to coordinate the labels of sentences and tweets simultaneously. Specifically, if tweet m_j is considered as a representative tweet, i.e., $y_j = 1$, then a sentence s_i highly similar to m_j (with similarity more than a threshold θ_h) should be biased towards the same label, i.e., $y_i = 1$. Formally, for each sentence-tweet pair (s_i, m_j) of high similarity, we define

$$h_{ij}(\nu, y_i, y_j) = \begin{cases} \exp \nu & \text{if } y_i = y_j \\ 1 & \text{otherwise} \end{cases} \quad (3)$$

where ν is the weight variable that represents the significance of inter-domain dependency factor.

Objective function. Finally, the objective function can be defined as the normalized product of Eqs. 1 - 3 for all the instances. We denote Z as the normalization factor, which sums up the conditional likelihood $P(Y|X, \Theta)$ over all the possible labels of all the instances, where Y contains all the undetermined labels for sentences and tweets, i.e., $Y = \{y_i\}_i$, and Θ is the collection of weights, i.e., $\Theta = \{\lambda_c\}_c \cup \{\mu_c\}_c \cup \{\nu\}$.

We first estimate the parameters Θ with a maximum likelihood procedure on the training instances, i.e.,

$$\max_{\Theta} \frac{1}{Z} \prod_{i,j \in T} \prod_{c \in C} f_{i,c}(\lambda_c, y_i) \cdot g_{ij,c}(\mu_c, y_i, y_j) \cdot h_{ij}(\nu, y_i, y_j) \quad (4)$$

We use L-BFGS, a quasi-Newton method for solving the nonlinear optimization problem (i.e., Eq. 4). To avoid overfitting, we add a penalty term $-\frac{1}{2}||\Theta||^2/\sigma^2$, a spherical Gaussian prior, into the objective function, which is a regularization method commonly used in maximum entropy and conditional random fields [6, 27, 28].

Calculating the marginal distribution for each factor (in deriving the log-gradient of the objective function) requires a loopy sum-product inference algorithm. With the learned parameter Θ, we may summarize an unlabeled social context for a Web document in the test set by extracting important sentences, which are also identified by a similar max-sum inference procedure. The inference algorithm is introduced in the next section.

Connection with existing models. We note that the proposed DWFG model can also be viewed as a model generalized from existing models. In Eq. 4, if parameter ν is fixed as 0, i.e., all factors $\{h_{ij}\}_{i,j}$ take constant values of 1, and factors $\{f_{i,c}\}_{i,c}$ and $\{g_{ij,c}\}_{i,j,c}$ are only defined for sentences, then the simplified model only incorporates sentence local factors and sentence relation factors, and DWFG model is degenerated to a special case: the summarization approach based on linear-chain CRF [28]. Moreover, if all parameters $\{\mu_c\}_c$ are also set as 0, i.e., only the local factors $\{_{i,c}\}_{i,c}$ are non-trivial, then DWFG is turned into the logistic regression classifier [25].

3.3 Inference Algorithm

Since the graphical model DWFG proposed for summarization (cf. Figure 2(d)) contains cycles, we cannot directly employ a forward-backward algorithm like in [28] for exactly inferring the optimal labeling for a test instance. We then propose an approximate inference approach based on the loopy sum-product or max-sum algorithm.

To achieve an approximate inference for predicting labels, the algorithm contains multiple iterations for updating the beliefs, and each iteration is comprised of two phases. Here, we denote the update variables for delivering beliefs between variables and factors by $\{p_{ij}\}_{i,j}$ and $\{q_{ij}\}_{i,j}$, where p_{ij} represents the message propagating from variable (e.g., y_i) to factor (e.g., $g_{ij,c}$ or $h_{ij,c}$), and q_{ij} represents the message propagating from factor to variable. The messages can be formulated as follows:

$$p_{ij} = r_i + \sum_{k \in N(i) \setminus \{j\}} q_{ik} \quad (5)$$

$$\begin{aligned} q_{ij} = &\max\{t_{ij}(1,1) + p_{ji}, t_{ij}(1,0)\} \\ &- \max\{t_{ij}(0,1) + p_{ji}, t_{ij}(0,0)\} \end{aligned} \quad (6)$$

where r_i corresponds to the logarithmic value of the local factor, i.e.,

$$r_i = \sum_{c \in C} (\log f_{i,c}(\lambda_c, y_i = 1) - \log f_{i,c}(\lambda_c, y_i = 0)) \quad (7)$$

Analogously, $t_{ij}(y_i, y_j)$ is the logarithmic value of the dependency factor, i.e.,

$$t_{ij}(y_i, y_j) = \log g_{ij,c}(\mu_c, y_i, y_j) \text{ or } \log h_{ij}(\nu, y_i, y_j) \quad (8)$$

Specific to a particular dependency factors, $f_{i,j}$, $g_{ij,c}$, or h_{ij} (Eq. 1 to 3), the message q_{ij} has a more succinct expression, e.g., the sentence dependency factor $q_{ij} = \max\{p_{ji} - \mu_c, 0\} - \max\{p_{ji}, 0\}$.

We can obtain the label for each sentence s_i or tweet m_i using the variables calculated in the two phases for the last iteration as follows:

$$y_i = \begin{cases} 1 & \text{if } p_{ij} + q_{ij} > 0 \text{ for some } j \\ 0 & \text{otherwise} \end{cases} \quad (9)$$

Algorithm 1: Social context summarization with DWFG

input : A document d with social context C_d and SCAN G_d of d, weight variables Θ, and number of iterations I

output: A summary for social context C_d: important sentences S_d^* and messages M_d^*

// initialization

1 calculate $\{r_i\}_i$ according to Eq. 7;

2 $\{q_{ij}\}_{i,j} \leftarrow 0$;

// update message values

3 **for** $i \leftarrow 1$ *to* I **do**

4   update variables p_{ij} according to Eq. 5;

5   update variables q_{ij} according to Eq. 6;

// output result

6 **foreach** $s_i \in S_d$ *and* $m_i \in M_d$ **do**

7   calculate y_i according to Eq. 9;

8 $S_d^* \leftarrow \{s_i \in S_d | y_i = 1\}$;

9 $M_d^* \leftarrow \{m_i \in M_d | y_i = 1\}$;

The learning algorithm is depicted in Algorithm 1. Initially, we calculate all local variables $\{r_i\}_i$ according to Eq. 7, and initialize all update variables $\{q_{ij}\}_{i,j}$ as 0 (Line 1 and 2). Next, we compute new values for all the update variables $\{p_{ij}\}_{i,j}$ according to Eq. 5. Then we estimate the new values for all $\{q_{ij}\}_{i,j}$ according to Eq. 6. We continue to update the variables for a number of iterations until some termination condition is satisfied (Line 3 - 5). Finally, the summary for the social context is generated according the update variables (Line 6 - 9).

Complexity analysis. If we denote the number of iterations for the inference algorithm as I, then the computational complexity of the algorithm is proportional to $I \cdot (|E^s| + |E^m| + |E^c|)$, where $|E^s|$, $|E^m|$, and $|E^c|$ correspond to the number of sentence relationships, tweet relationships, and inter-domain relationships respectively. They can be varied from zero to many when we tune the thresholds θ_g and θ_h, which is further discussed in Section 4.2.2. In fact, the inference algorithm can be easily parallelized or distributed onto clusters to handle large-scale data set, and the design of distributed algorithm will be reported elsewhere.

4. EXPERIMENT

In this section, we evaluate the proposed summarization method DWFG with manually labeled documents. We firstly introduce the data set, baseline methods that do not incorporate the relationship between the Web document domain and tweet thread domain, the evaluation metrics, and then we give the detailed discussion of the experimental results with the comparison of other approaches. Related support materials (data description and software) of this work can be found at http://arnetminer.org/socialcontext/.

4.1 Settings and Observations

4.1.1 Data Preparation

We aim to find a collection of Web documents with their associated social contexts, and labeled summaries for each document and its social context, so that we can use the data set as the gold-standard to evaluate different approaches for social context summarization. To begin the collection process, we selected the first and also one of the most popular users on Twitter, Jack Dorsey (@jack)[3], and collected his followers. We took these users as seed users and used a crawler to collect all followers of these users by traversing following edges. We continue the traversing process, which produced in total 4,874,389 users. The crawler monitored tweets posted by these users from January 1st 2010 to July 17th 2010. We extracted all tweets posted by these users and in total there are 404,544,462 tweets.

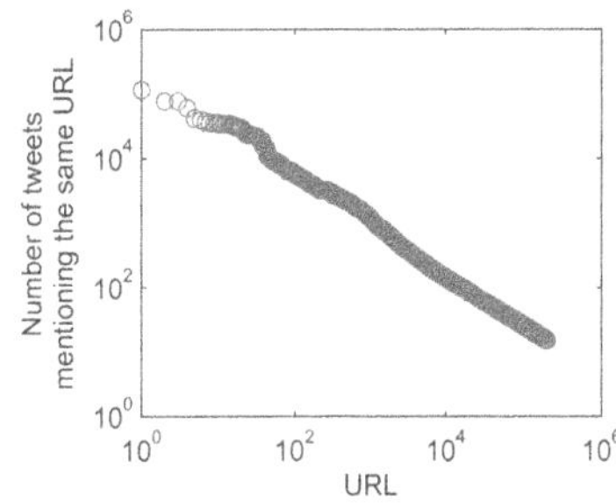

Figure 3: The distribution of URLs carried by the tweets

We use explicit URLs (starting with "http://" or "https://") to identify Web documents from the Twitter data. In some cases, users may shorten the URL addresses via services such as tinyurl.com or bit.ly. We implemented a shorten URL decoder based on a HTTP client to obtain the decoded URLs and finally aligned the obtained URLs.[4] Finally, we use the most frequent (200,000) URLs to constitute the collection of Web documents and employ their associated (12,964,166) tweets to construct the social context. The distribution of frequency for these Web documents (URLs) is plotted in Figure 3 in log-logarithmic scale. We see that the distribution of frequency follows the power law. According to the selected URLs, we crawled the pointed webpages, and then constructed two kinds of data sets (webpages and their corresponding social tweets). The Web documents were then segmented into a set of sentences with the jTokeniser Toolkit[5]. Our summarization algorithm was then performed on both domains.

A preliminary analysis shows that many frequent URLs are advertisement pages. To guarantee the quality of the data set, we restrict ourselves to a few high-quality news websites such as CNN, BBC, Mashable etc., and selected a subset of URLs related to these websites to perform a manual annotation for the summarization. Descriptions of the five selected domains are given in Table 1.

4.1.2 Evaluation Methods

To reduce the possible noise in the manual annotation data, we further manually validated the informativeness of all the selected Web documents by posting both the Web documents and tweets on Amazon Mechanical Turk[6]. We totally issued 1,145 HITs on Mechanical Turk, and for each HIT we asked at least two different workers to read both Web documents and their corresponding tweets. All the HITs were divided into 12 batches with each assignment entitled "Key sentences and tweets extraction from news and related tweets". We gave a detailed description on how to label the sentences and tweets, and also emphasized that the workers should

[3] the creator, co-founder and executive chairman of Twitter.

[4] A Web document might be referred by different URLs, e.g.,
http://news.bbc.co.uk/1/hi/england/8604663.stm,
http://news.bbc.co.uk/2/hi/uk_news/england/8604663.stm,
http://news.bbc.co.uk/2/hi/8604663.stm
correspond to the same document. We further group such Web documents according to the unique document ID: 8604663.

[5] http://code.google.com/p/jtokeniser/

[6] http://mturk.com, an Internet marketplace to use human intelligence to solve various kinds of problems

Table 1: Description on employed domains

Domain	Description	Data Size	
		Doc	Tweet
cnn.com	one of the most popular news websites	1,303	62,225
bbc.co.uk	the most popular news website in the UK	336	10,264
mtv.com	one of the most popular music television networks	176	9,848
espn.go.com	one of the world's leading sports media	171	4,320
mashable.com	the world's largest tech blog	2,940	114,441

Table 2: Feature list

	N°	description
Web documents	1	sentence position in document
	2	sentence position in paragraph
	3	average TF-IDF score of words in sentence
	4	the number of common words to the title
	5	sentence length
	6	the log likelihood generated by the document
Tweets	7	average TF-IDF score of words in post
	8	tweet length
	9	the log likelihood generated by the tweet thread
	10	the number of users following the author
	11	the PageRank score of the post's author

"extract several sentences from news that attract them mostly", and "after reading the news, extract the most interesting tweets that appeal you mostly". We required the workers to label no less than 5 tweets and 10 Web document sentences. Finally, 158 different users have participated in annotating the benchmark for social context summarization task. The labeled sets of sentences and tweets formed the benchmark for evaluation.

In this paper, two performance metrics applied in [29] were adopted to evaluate the proposed approach DWFG. The first is Precision, Recall and F-measure. In the following section, we will report the evaluation on F_1 measure, which is defined as:

$$P = \frac{S_{\text{ref}} \cap S_{\text{cand}}}{S_{\text{cand}}}; R = \frac{S_{\text{ref}} \cap S_{\text{cand}}}{S_{\text{ref}}}; F_1 = \frac{2PR}{P+R}$$

where S_{cand} and S_{ref} denote the sentences contained in the candidate summary and the reference summary respectively.

Another performance metric is ROUGE [18], which measures summarization quality according to the overlap between the units, such as n-gram (referred to as ROUGE-N) etc, of machine generated summary and human generated summary. ROUGE-N is defined as follows:

$$\text{ROUGE-N} = \frac{\sum_{s \in S_{\text{ref}}} \sum_{gram_n \in s} \text{Count}_{\text{match}}(gram_n)}{\sum_{s \in S_{\text{ref}}} \sum_{gram_n \in s} \text{Count}(gram_n)}$$

where n is the length of the n-gram, $\text{Count}_{\text{match}}(gram_n)$ is the maximum number of n-grams co-occurring in a candidate summary and the reference summaries, $\text{Count}(gram_n)$ is the number of n-grams in the reference summaries.

We employ the ROUGE evaluation methods implemented in the Dragon Toolkit[7], and report the experimental results in terms of ROUGE-1 and ROUGE-2 with stop words filtered out. Since ROUGE is a recall-oriented metric, we keep the number of sentences extracted be equal with that of the human summary for fair comparison. Specifically, we select the sentences and tweets with the greatest positive beliefs according to $p(y_i = 1|\mathbf{X})$ (cf. Eq. 9).

4.1.3 Feature Description

Many features have been designed for document summarization in prior literatures. In this paper, we only extract 11 basic and straight-forward features from both domains. Besides some features that are widely used in traditional summarization methods, we also utilize several features extracted from users' online social behaviors, e.g., the number of users following the tweet's author and the PageRank score of the author. Table 2 gives the brief definitions of these features applied in this paper, where some features were represented by nominal values, e.g., Feature 1 will take value 4 if the sentence was extracted from the title of the document, 3 if it was extracted from the subtitle, 2 if the sentence was located in the first paragraph of the original document, 1 if the sentence was located in the last paragraph, and 0 otherwise.

[7]http://dragon.ischool.drexel.edu/

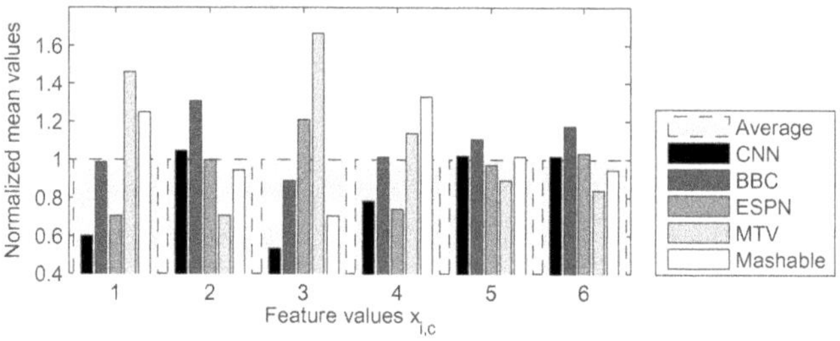

Figure 4: Comparison of feature values for sentence domain on five domains

The feature values extracted from sentence domain and tweet domain are summarized in Figure 4 and 5. Since different features take values in diverse ranges, e.g., the maximum value of Feature 4 is 15, while the maximum value of Feature 6 is 1.495, we normalize the feature values by the mean value of corresponding feature. From Figure 4, we can see that Web documents from different domains exhibit differently. For example, articles in CNN, BBC, and ESPN have smaller values of Feature 1 but greater values of Feature 2 than MTV, which indicates that news websites CNN, BBC, and ESPN have longer articles consisting of a greater number of shorter paragraphs. Therefore, we trained an individual model on each domain respectively to capture the distinctiveness.

4.1.4 Baseline Methods

We compare the proposed DWFG model with six supervised baselines methods. SVM classifiers (SVM) and logistic regression classifiers (LR) are performed for each sentence and tweet only with its local features. Linear-chain and tree-structured CRF models (LC-/TS-CRF) are respectively trained and tested on documents and tweet threads, i.e., inter-domain relationships are considered as a supplement to the basic local features. The linear-chain CRF baseline model employed in the sentence summarizaiton is equivalent to the method proposed in [28].

We also extend the feature list for each sentence and tweet by considering the features of related sentences or tweets extracted from both domains (denoted as SVM+, LR+). Specifically, for each sentence s_i in a document, we append 11 features $(x^s_{i,7}, \ldots, x^s_{i,17})$, where each of $x^s_{i,7}, \ldots, x^s_{i,12}$ adds up the corresponding feature values of its similar sentences, and each of $x^s_{i,13}, \ldots, x^s_{i,17}$ adds up the corresponding feature values of its related tweets. Similarly, for each tweet in the thread, we append 11 features, which are the sums of feature values of its relevant sentences or tweets.

In addition, we also compare DWFG with several unsuper-

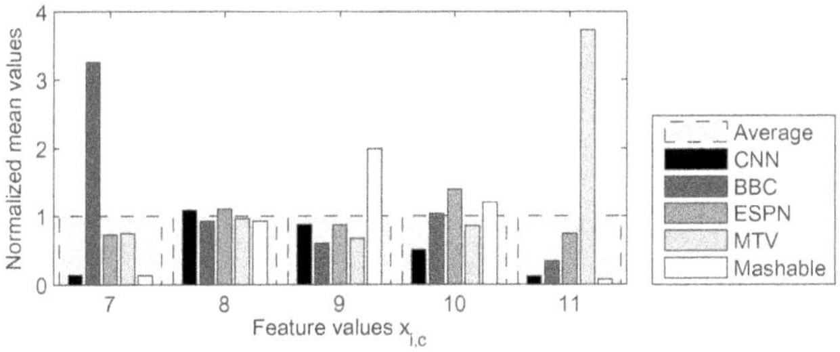

Figure 5: Comparison of feature values for tweet domain on five domains

vised summarization algorithms, i.e., the importance sentences and tweets are selected according to a metric or score. First, we randomly select sentences or tweets (Random) as the basic unsupervised method. Another baseline method for summarization is to select the sentences according to their positions in the document or paragraph (DocLead and ParaLead). Finally, we apply PageRank algorithm for summarization on the whole graph consisting of three types of relationships (PR) [24].

4.2 Results and Analysis

4.2.1 Comparison Results

All experiments were conducted in the 10-fold cross validation procedure, where one fold is for test and the other nine folds for training. The performance results are shown in Table 3 and 4, and the best performances in the comparisons are highlighted in bold. In the following results, we set the similarity threshold for sentence dependency $\theta_g = 0.1$, and the similarity threshold for inter-domain dependency $\theta_h = 0.8$. We will further discuss the variation of performance with different assignment of thresholds in Section 4.2.2.

From Table 3, we see that DWFG clearly outperforms the baseline methods in most cases in terms of both F_1 and ROUGE-N for document summarization. Moreover, we discover that the performances are statistically significantly improved on the MTV and ESPN domains by conducting sign test on the results, where the p values are much smaller than 0.01. In fact, we collect relatively fewer documents and corresponding tweets from MTV and ESPN compared with other domains, and thus, additional dependencies, especially cross-domain dependencies boost the performance by leveraging additional information.

In contrast to the improvements in Web document summarization, DWFG performs comparably to the simpler CRF-based methods for tweet summarization. In fact, the ground truth data are manually annotated from the perspective of readers' interests and focuses, which naturally reveals the users' motivations for writing tweets. Therefore, the identification of important sentences from the Web document domain rarely influences the results for identifying important tweets.

4.2.2 Impact of Thresholds θ_g and θ_h

In this section, we discuss the impact of thresholds θ_g and θ_h to our proposed approach. Although the proposed approach within a supervised framework can automatically learn the optimal model parameters Θ based on the training instances, we still need to predefine the thresholds θ_g and θ_h to control the number of inter-domain and intra-domain dependencies in the factor graph model. Specifically, with larger θ_g or θ_h, we obtain fewer dependencies, and if $\theta_g = 0$, each pair of consecutive sentences will be connected by a inter-domain factor, or if $\theta_h = 0$, all the sentences will be

Table 3: Experimental results for Web documents

		CNN	BBC	MTV	ESPN	Mash	All
F_1	SVM	0.288	0.322	0.490	0.337	0.321	0.351
	LR	0.284	0.340	0.531	0.352	0.297	0.361
	LC-CRF	0.307	0.349	0.596	0.364	0.340	0.391
	SVM+	0.283	0.341	0.476	0.359	0.324	0.357
	LR+	0.277	0.332	0.482	0.366	0.305	0.352
	Random	0.314	0.321	0.455	0.351	0.305	0.349
	DocLead	0.334	0.356	0.441	0.317	**0.415**	0.373
	ParaLead	0.298	0.316	0.508	0.338	0.323	0.356
	PR	**0.354**	0.338	0.453	0.351	0.399	0.379
	DWFG	0.341	**0.450**	**0.642**	**0.518**	0.330	**0.456**
R-1	SVM	0.224	**0.612**	0.392	0.520	0.511	0.452
	LR	0.197	0.599	0.585	0.583	0.599	0.513
	LC-CRF	0.281	0.551	0.667	0.583	**0.618**	0.540
	SVM+	0.176	0.563	0.400	0.635	0.546	0.464
	LR+	0.171	0.610	0.362	0.620	0.605	0.473
	Random	0.429	0.426	0.455	0.470	0.405	0.437
	DocLead	0.410	0.473	0.542	0.372	0.576	0.475
	ParaLead	0.414	0.337	0.629	0.432	0.414	0.445
	PR	**0.433**	0.325	0.563	0.426	0.482	0.446
	DWFG	0.389	0.594	**0.777**	**0.701**	0.613	**0.615**
R-2	SVM	0.151	**0.500**	0.336	0.412	0.412	0.362
	LR	0.131	0.491	0.522	0.481	0.496	0.424
	LC-CRF	0.197	0.496	0.542	0.515	0.516	0.453
	SVM+	0.115	0.463	0.351	0.539	0.449	0.383
	LR+	0.110	0.498	0.310	0.528	0.501	0.390
	Random	0.323	0.325	0.387	0.359	0.301	0.339
	DocLead	0.371	0.424	0.519	0.350	0.525	0.438
	ParaLead	0.363	0.320	0.569	0.370	0.354	0.395
	PR	**0.389**	0.307	0.533	0.387	0.441	0.411
	DWFG	0.228	0.417	**0.687**	**0.612**	**0.557**	**0.500**

connected with all the tweets. To evaluate the impact of thresholds to DWFG and baseline methods (e.g., LC-CRF), we varied θ_g or θ_h from 0 to 1 with step length 0.1 respectively with the other threshold fixed. Due to space limitation, we only report the impact to the performance of DWFG in Figure 6(a) and (b) in terms of F_1, ROUGE-1, and ROUGE-2, and the performances of the baseline methods follow similar trends with different thresholds. We also plot the percentage of consecutive sentence pairs with similarity more than θ_g in Figure 6(a), and the percentage of sentence-tweet relation pairs with similarity more than θ_h in Figure 6(b).

From Figure 6(a), we can see that when θ_g increases from 0.0 to 0.5, the performance drops by $5\% \sim 16\%$ in terms of F_1 and ROUGE, which can be attributed to the lack of a complete view of sentence relations within the document. While with θ_g is 0.7, the performance reaches a local maximum when the retained sentence relations have a relatively higher quality. As shown in Figure 6(b), the performance of sentence identification reaches the global maximum when θ_h is set between 0.5 and 0.6. With smaller or greater θ_h, the extracted relation pairs between sentences and tweets may contain more low-quality relations or lack of high-quality relations. Generally speaking, the performance of important tweet extraction is relatively stable.

4.2.3 Factor Contribution Analysis

We further analyze the contribution or significance of each factor. We show the estimated weights for sentence-level local factors $\lambda_1, \ldots, \lambda_6$ on five domains respectively and calculate their averages in Figure 7, and show the estimated weights with their averages for tweet-level local factors $\lambda_7, \ldots, \lambda_{11}$ in Figure 8.

From Figure 7, we see that most of the local factors have positive contributions to our task except for Feature 4 (the number of common words to the title). On average, it seems that Feature 5 (sentence length) and Feature 2 (sentence position in paragraph)

Table 4: **Experimental results for tweet thread**

		CNN	BBC	MTV	ESPN	Mash	All
F_1	SVM	0.323	0.542	0.640	0.610	0.379	0.499
	LR	0.370	0.531	0.606	0.616	0.408	0.506
	LC-CRF	0.378	0.547	0.637	0.603	**0.417**	0.516
	SVM+	0.378	0.537	0.641	0.607	0.405	0.514
	LR+	0.369	0.537	**0.725**	0.608	0.408	**0.529**
	Random	0.356	0.486	0.665	0.586	0.353	0.489
	PR	0.281	0.428	0.666	0.520	0.327	0.445
	DWFG	**0.380**	**0.547**	0.639	**0.633**	0.380	0.516
R-1	SVM	0.531	0.631	0.670	0.701	0.617	0.630
	LR	0.657	0.618	0.702	0.708	0.737	0.684
	LC-CRF	**0.673**	0.647	0.730	0.703	**0.748**	0.700
	SVM+	0.661	0.659	0.672	0.694	0.740	0.685
	LR+	0.655	**0.660**	0.692	0.756	0.737	0.700
	Random	0.631	0.617	**0.740**	0.704	0.622	0.663
	PR	0.167	0.382	0.522	0.439	0.229	0.348
	DWFG	0.669	0.647	0.731	**0.763**	0.700	**0.702**
R-2	SVM	0.486	0.571	0.661	0.678	0.570	0.593
	LR	0.616	0.556	0.696	0.684	0.698	0.650
	LC-CRF	0.610	0.563	0.708	0.699	0.682	0.653
	SVM+	**0.620**	0.598	0.663	0.671	**0.700**	0.651
	LR+	0.613	**0.601**	0.684	**0.731**	0.698	**0.666**
	Random	0.572	0.533	**0.724**	0.671	0.557	0.611
	PR	0.157	0.356	0.519	0.432	0.218	0.337
	DWFG	0.599	0.563	0.709	0.722	0.631	0.645

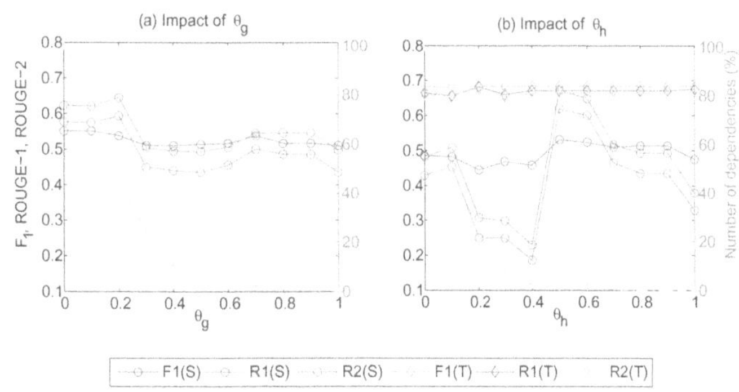

Figure 6: The impact of θ_g and θ_h to the performance of DWFG

are the most important local factors for identifying the important sentences. From Figure 8, we see the two most important local factors for identifying the representative tweets are Feature 8 (tweet length) and Feature 7 (average TF-IDF). In fact, we find that long tweets tend to cover both the main ideas of the Web documents and the personal comments towards them.

4.2.4 *Case Study*

In this section, we demonstrate an example of the inference step for a specific Web document, an article entitled "Women try to take body on plane at Liverpool airport"[8], with its social context. In Figure 9, the left column lists a portion of sentences of the Web document, and the right column lists a portion of tweets containing URLs (or shortened URLs) directing to the article (the selected texts are indicated by bold font). The established inter-domain and intra-domain dependencies are shown in arrows. Furthermore, beliefs propagated from local factors and pair-wise dependency factors in the last iteration of our inference algorithm are partly shown with the associated variables taking values of 1 (in rectangles, rounded rectangles or diamonds). Beliefs taking values

[8]http://news.bbc.co.uk/2/hi/8604663.stm

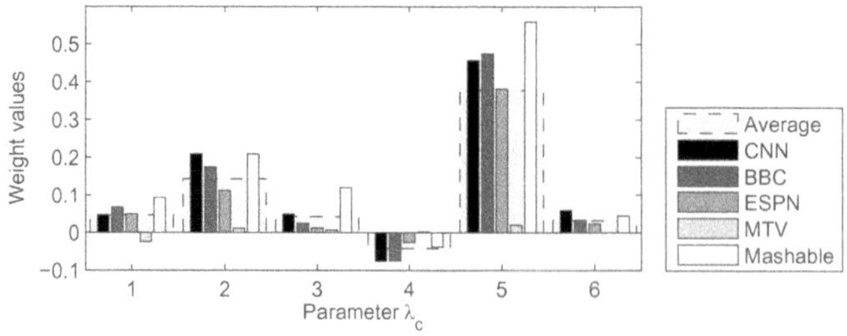

Figure 7: Parameter estimation results for sentence-level local factors on five domains

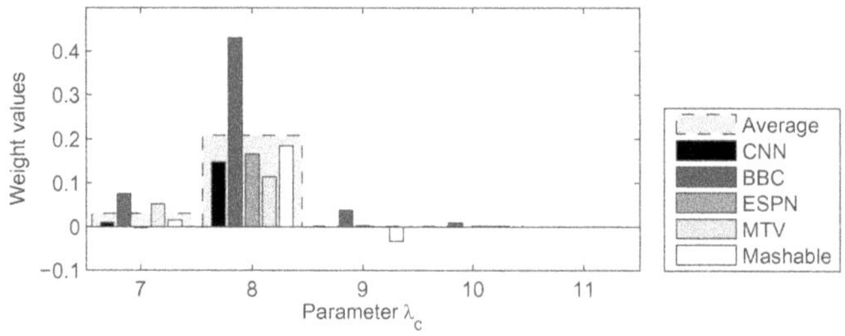

Figure 8: Parameter estimation results for tweet-level local factors on five domains

of 0.5 indicate that the corresponding factors have no preference on whether the sentences are regarded as part of the summary or not. Beliefs taking values greater than 0.5 convey positive attitudes, and the greater the belief values, the stronger the confidence that the associated variables should take values of 1. According to the calculated beliefs, the summary for the social context is generated based on the selected sentences and tweets (in bold).

We can see that the local features, e.g., statistical features, still play a major role for social context summarization. For example, since the most common words or phrases in the Web documents include "women", "dead person", "body", "Liverpool Airport", and those in tweet threads include "Liverpool airport", "Weekend At Bernie's", texts that cover these words or phrases are more likely chosen, and the probability that the relevant sentence-tweet pairs are simultaneously selected is boosted. Moreover, various types of relations also come into play. For example, since the last two tweets shown in the right column form a retweet pair, the content is evaluated more important, and thus the related sentence (the fourth sentence) in the document then receives a higher belief (0.51) of taking a positive decision. As we suggested, in the social context summarization task, the tweet thread contributes additional information (e.g., Weekend At Bernie's[9]) to the original document content, which unveils the users' interests from an alternative angle.

5. RELATED WORK

Web-page summarization techniques have been widely studied for many years and various approaches have been developed. There are two major types of approaches for web-page summarization, i.e., supervised and unsupervised. The supervised summarization approach treats the summarization task as a two-class classification problem [16, 25, 36] or as a sequence labeling problem [8, 28] at the sentence level, where each sentence is represented by

[9]a 1989 American motion picture comedy, which has a similar plot as the news story.

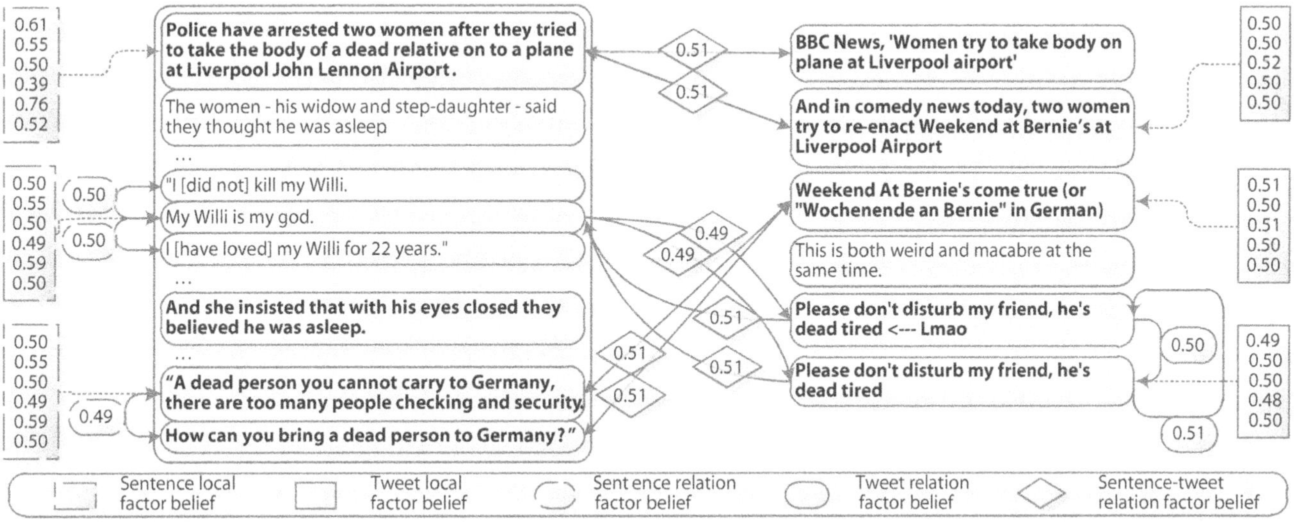

Figure 9: An example of a social context summary with propagated beliefs. Left column is a part of the Web document, and the right column is a portion of tweet thread. Bold texts correspond to the summary for the Web document; colored rectangles, rounded rectangles or diamonds indicate the beliefs propagated in the inference algorithm.

a vector of features. Comparably, the unsupervised approach relies on a set of heuristic rules to develop the summarization. Webpage summarization can also be either generic or query-dependent. Generic summarization targets to cover the main idea of the page while query-oriented summary is to present the information that is most relevant to the given queries [4, 31].

Without consideration of context, the extracted summary is composed of sentences from the Web documents, and thus features from local content of a document is the key to summarization. Traditional document-oriented features can be defined either from linguistic, such as rhetorical structure [22], lexical chains [2] or statistical perspectives, such as term significance [20], sentences similarity [24] and topic detection [12]. Although document-oriented features can disclose most of the basic characteristics of summary sentences, as stated in [29], the textual information of a Web document may be scarce and diverse in topics and, moreover, contain a lot of noise.

Document-oriented features cannot fully capture the main idea of a Web document. In the past few years, some work starts to utilize various kinds of context to assist document summarization, such as external documents or cited articles [23]. User requirement is one of the most important kind of context [10, 32]. In the study of [21], user's needs come from a set of documents selected by user, where the top content words are extracted according to their G^2 score and then treated as users' interests. Hyperlinks among webpages are another kind of context. Based on the text surrounding the hyperlink, summarization of the target webpage can be realized either by extracting the related sentences in surrounding text [1] or by extracting significant sentences from the linked webpage [9]. Similar to the hyperlink context, Sun et al. [29] utilize search-engine clickthrough data to construct the extra knowledge. In their work, webpage and query terms collected from the clickthrough data work together to decide the significance of each word in sentences for summarization. With the rapid growth of social websites, comments-oriented approach is also studied, where the most important comments are selected and leveraged into sentence selection for summarization. Traditional feature-based methods and graph-based methods for sentence extraction have been applied for commented sentence selection [13, 33, 19], or opinionated text [26, 11, 15].

Different from previous works, we study to leverage multifaceted social media information for Web document summarization, especially social influence among users [30] and retweeting relations among messages [35]. However, we adopt a totally different approach to not only incorporate the extra knowledge extracted from microblogs, but also take full advantage of conventional techniques in single document summarization. In recent years, the rapid growth of microblogging services provides an efficient way for information communication. Here, people can freely issue various comments on any topic they interested in. Compared with traditional tightly-coupled relationship between Web document and comments, messages from microblogs can provide more valuable information beneficial for summarization. Microblog has been widely studied in recent years. Some work focuses on investigating the characteristics of Twitter, e.g.,[17], [7], [14], while some work analyzes the patterns of retweets on Twitter, influential twitter and the routines of changes of hashtags, etc., e.g., [34], [5], [3], [35]. To the best of our knowledge, little work in the literature has tried to use microblog data for Web-page summarization.

6. CONCLUSION AND FUTURE WORK

In this paper, we explore a novel problem of social context summarization and aim to utilize the mutual reinforcement between Web document and its associated social data to extract high-quality summaries. In our study, the importance of each document sentence is firstly predicted by considering a series of local features of a document. At the same time, the social context relating to the Web document is associated with it, in which the significant sentences are also identified by taking advantage of various social factors. We formally define the concept of social context for Web document and propose a unified summarization approach through factor graph model. Our experiments are performed on a set of Web documents and associated microblog messages. The experiment results prove that the proposed summarization method shows significant improvement over the baseline approaches on social context summarization task.

To systematically combine the content analysis and social behaviors represents a new and interesting direction for information retrieval. There are many future directions of this work. For example, due to the fact that not only tweets are highly associated with other tweets, users are also connected by the friendship relations, we can extend this work by establishing the connection among users and adding the dependencies between users and their tweets. Intuitively, the influence among users will also affect the identification of important tweets, and subsequently influence the importance of sentences in Web documents.

7. *ACKNOWLEDGMENTS

The work is supported by the Natural Science Foundation of China (No. 61073073, No. 60703059, No. 60973102), Chinese National Key Foundation Research (No. 60933013, No.61035004), National High-tech R&D Program (No. 2009AA01Z138).

8. REFERENCES

[1] E. Amitay. Automatically summarising web sites - is there a way around it? In *CIKM'00*, pages 173–179, 2000.

[2] R. Barzilay and M. Elhadad. Using lexical chains for text summarization. In *ACL Workshop on Intelligent Scalable Text Summarization*, pages 10–17, 1997.

[3] d. boyd, S. Golder, and G. Lotan. Tweet, tweet, retweet: Conversational aspects of retweeting on twitter. In *HICSS'10*, pages 1–10, 2010.

[4] J. Carbonell and J. Goldstein. The use of mmr, diversity-based reranking for reordering documents and producing summaries. In *SIGIR'98*, pages 335–336, 1998.

[5] M. Cha, H. Haddadi, F. Benevenuto, and K. P. Gummadi. Measuring user influence in twitter: The million follower fallacy. In *ICWSM'10*, pages 10–17, 2010.

[6] S. F. Chen and R. Rosenfeld. A gaussian prior for smoothing maximum entropy models. Technical Report CMU-CS-99-108, Carnegie Mellon University, 1999.

[7] M. Cheong and V. Lee. Integrating web-based intelligence retrieval and decision-making from the twitter trends knowledge base. In *SWSM'09*, pages 1–8, 2009.

[8] J. M. Conroy and D. P. O'Leary. Text summarization via hidden markov models. In *SIGIR'01*, pages 406–407, 2001.

[9] J.-Y. Delort, B. Bouchon-Meunier, and M. Rifqi. Enhanced web document summarization using hyperlinks. In *Hypertext'03*, pages 208–215, 2003.

[10] A. Díaz and P. Gervás. User-model based personalized summarization. *Information Processing & Management*, 43(6):1715–1734, 2007.

[11] K. Ganesan, C. Zhai, and J. Han. Opinosis: a graph-based approach to abstractive summarization of highly redundant opinions. In *COLING'10*, pages 340–348, 2010.

[12] Y. Gong and X. Liu. Generic text summarization using relevance measure and latent semantic analysis. In *SIGIR'01*, pages 19–25, 2001.

[13] M. Hu, A. Sun, and E.-P. Lim. Comments-oriented document summarization: understanding documents with readers' feedback. In *SIGIR'08*, pages 291–298, 2008.

[14] A. Java, X. Song, T. Finin, and B. Tseng. Why we twitter: understanding microblogging usage and communities. In *WebKDD/SNA-KDD'07*, pages 56–65, 2007.

[15] H. D. Kim and C. Zhai. Generating comparative summaries of contradictory opinions in text. In *CIKM'09*, pages 385–394, 2009.

[16] J. Kupiec, J. Pedersen, and F. Chen. A trainable document summarizer. In *SIGIR'95*, pages 68–73, 1995.

[17] H. Kwak, C. Lee, H. Park, and S. Moon. What is twitter, a social network or a news media? In *WWW'10*, pages 591–600, 2010.

[18] C.-Y. Lin and E. Hovy. Automatic evaluation of summaries using n-gram co-occurrence statistics. In *NAACL'03*, pages 71–78, 2003.

[19] Y. Lu, C. Zhai, and N. Sundaresan. Rated aspect summarization of short comments. In *WWW'09*, pages 131–140, 2009.

[20] H. P. Luhn. The automatic creation of literature abstracts. *IBM Journal of Research and Development*, 2(2):159–165, 1958.

[21] I. Mani and E. Bloedorn. Machine learning of generic and user-focused summarization. In *AAAI'98/IAAI'98*, pages 820–826, 1998.

[22] D. Marcu. From discourse structures to text summaries. In *ACL Workshop on Intelligent Scalable Text Summarization*, pages 82–88, 1997.

[23] Q. Mei and C. Zhai. Generating impact-cased summaries for scientific literature. In *ACL'08*, pages 816–824, 2008.

[24] R. Mihalcea. Language independent extractive summarization. In *ACL'05*, pages 49–52, 2005.

[25] M. Osborne. Using maximum entropy for sentence extraction. In *ACL Workshop on Automatic Summarization*, pages 1–8, 2002.

[26] M. J. Paul, C. Zhai, and R. Girju. Summarizing contrastive viewpoints in opinionated text. In *EMNLP'10*, pages 66–76, 2010.

[27] F. Sha and F. Pereira. Shallow parsing with conditional random fields. In *NAACL'03*, pages 134–141, 2003.

[28] D. Shen, J. tao Sun, H. Li, Q. Yang, and Z. Chen. Document summarization using conditional random fields. In *IJCAI'07*, pages 2862–2867, 2007.

[29] J.-T. Sun, D. Shen, H.-J. Zeng, Q. Yang, Y. Lu, and Z. Chen. Web-page summarization using clickthrough data. In *SIGIR'05*, pages 194–201, 2005.

[30] J. Tang, J. Sun, C. Wang, and Z. Yang. Social influence analysis in large-scale networks. In *SIGKDD'09*, pages 807–816, 2009.

[31] J. Tang, L. Yao, and D. Chen. Multi-topic based query-oriented summarization. In *SDM'09*, pages 1147–1158, 2009.

[32] C. Teng, N. Xiong, Y. He, L. T. Yang, and D. Liu. A behavioural mode research on user-focus summarization. *Mathematical and Computer Modelling*, 51(7-8):985–994, 2010.

[33] X. Wan and J. Yang. Multi-document summarization using cluster-based link analysis. In *SIGIR'08*, pages 299–306, 2008.

[34] J. Weng, E.-P. Lim, J. Jiang, and Q. He. Twitterrank: Finding topic-sensitive influential twitterers. In *WSDM'10*, pages 261–270, 2010.

[35] Z. Yang, J. Guo, K. Cai, J. Tang, J. Li, L. Zhang, and Z. Su. Understanding retweeting behaviors in social networks. In *CIKM'10*, pages 1633–1636, 2010.

[36] J.-Y. Yeh, H.-R. Ke, W.-P. Yang, and I.-H. Meng. Text summarization using a trainable summarizer and latent semantic analysis. *Inf. Process. Manage.*, 41(1):75–95, 2005.

Probabilistic Factor Models for Web Site Recommendation

Hao Ma*, Chao Liu
Microsoft Research
One Microsoft Way
Redmond, WA 98052
haoma@microsoft.com
chaoliu@microsoft.com

Irwin King†
AT&T Labs Research, USA &
The Chinese University of
Hong Kong, Hong Kong
irwin@research.att.com
king@cse.cuhk.edu.hk

Michael R. Lyu
The Chinese University of
Hong Kong
Shatin, N.T., Hong Kong
lyu@cse.cuhk.edu.hk

ABSTRACT

Due to the prevalence of personalization and information filtering applications, modeling users' interests on the Web has become increasingly important during the past few years. In this paper, aiming at providing accurate personalized Web site recommendations for Web users, we propose a novel probabilistic factor model based on dimensionality reduction techniques. We also extend the proposed method to collective probabilistic factor modeling, which further improves model performance by incorporating heterogeneous data sources. The proposed method is general, and can be applied to not only Web site recommendations, but also a wide range of Web applications, including behavioral targeting, sponsored search, etc. The experimental analysis on Web site recommendation shows that our method outperforms other traditional recommendation approaches. Moreover, the complexity analysis indicates that our approach can be applied to very large datasets since it scales linearly with the number of observations.

Categories and Subject Descriptors

H.3.3 [**Information Search and Retrieval**]: Search Process, Information Filtering

General Terms

Algorithm, Experimentation

Keywords

Probabilistic Factor Modeling, Web Site Recommendation, Matrix Factorization, Recommender Systems

*This work was partially done when the first author was on summer internship at Microsoft Research.

†Irwin King is currently on leave from CUHK to be with AT&T Labs.

SIGIR'11, July 24–28, 2011, Beijing, China.

1. INTRODUCTION

How to find the most relevant search results for Web users has been extensively studied in both academia and industry during the past decade. Traditionally, commercial search engines try to satisfy online users' information needs based on the queries issued by users. By taking advantages of the advanced learning and ranking algorithms, commercial search engine services have already become indispensable in solving Web users' various information needs.

However, due to the rapid growth of information on the Web, especially for the social Web, the traditional search paradigm can no longer meet Web users' ever-growing information needs. The Web is now shifting online users from "search" to "discovery". The current paradigm is that a user who has information needs or questions will search on commercial search engines for related Web sites or answers. Different from "search", the concept of "discovery" refers to the ability to push relevant content to users either based on the meta data that have already been collected about the users, or by exposing their activities that their friends and social networks are engaged in.

From the above definitions, we can see that these two concepts are different but closely related since essentially, the idea of "discovery" is similar to "autonomous search", which helps users search for things when they do not even yet know what they want. Due to its personalized nature, "discovery" or "autonomous search", which combines a person's context with others' past opinions and actions, can therefore create tremendous value and relevance.

In this paper, in order to enhance online users' experience, we investigate a novel application, Web site recommendation, to help users proactively discover relevant Web sites by conducting autonomous search based on their past online behaviors.

Many methods [7, 13, 17, 19, 22, 23, 24, 32] have been proposed to tackle recommendation or collaborative filtering problems in the literature. Typically, in traditional recommender systems, modeling users' interests needs to utilize a user-item rating matrix, which explicitly specifies users' preferences. However, in the scenario of Web site recommendation, it is infeasible to ask Web users to explicitly rate Web sites they like or dislike. Instead, we can only take advantages of implicit user behavior data in the past to make recommendations. Hence, most of the traditional collaborative filtering approaches cannot be directly applied to the Web site recommendation task.

In this work, aiming at solving the Web site recommendation problem effectively and efficiently, we propose a probabilistic factor modeling framework by utilizing implicit user-site frequency data based on the following motivations:

1. A Web user's preference on different Web sites can be represented by how frequently a user visits each Web site;

2. Higher visiting frequency on a site from a user means heavy information need on this site while lower frequency indicates less interest;

3. User-query issuing frequency data can be incorporated to refine a user's preference since normally the user will first issue a query before clicking a Web site.

The first two motivations lead to a Probabilistic Factor Model (PFM) based on dimensionality reduction techniques. More specifically, the user-site frequency matrix is factorized into two low-dimensional factor matrices: user latent matrix and site latent matrix. The value of each dimension in a user factor vector follows a gamma distribution, which indicates a user's preference in a latent topic. A site factor vector also has similar definition. Then, the observed user-site frequency matrix is assumed to follow Poisson distribution with the mean generated by the inner product of the user latent matrix and the item latent matrix. Finally, an efficient multiplicative updating algorithm is proposed to learn the latent factor matrices.

By considering the third motivation, we design a Collective Probabilistic Factor Model (CPFM) which simultaneously factorizes user-site matrix and user-query matrix by sharing the same user latent space. The experimental analysis shows that CPFM model can further improve the recommendation quality.

The remainder of this paper is structured as follows. In Section 2, we provide an overview of several major approaches for recommender systems and some related work. Section 3 details the concept of low-rank matrix factorization. The proposed probabilistic framework and the learning algorithm are presented in Section 4. The results of an empirical analysis is presented in Section 5, followed by the conclusion and future work in Section 6.

2. RELATED WORK

In this section, we review two research topics which are relevant to our work: Web user interests prediction and recommender systems.

2.1 Web User Interests Prediction

In this subsection, we review some closely related tasks in the literature to predict Web user interests.

Personalized search engine is a natural application to Web user interests modeling, which improves the ranking system (ranking problem can also be considered as recommendation problem) by incorporating an individual's historical activities. In [27], Sun et al. conducted sophisticated analysis on the correlation between users, their queries and search results clicked to model user preferences. The experimental results indicate that the proposed CubeSVD approach can significantly improve Web search performance. In [20], Qiu et al. studied how a search engine can learn a user's preference automatically based on her past click history and how it can use the user preference to personalize search results. The experiments show that personalized search based

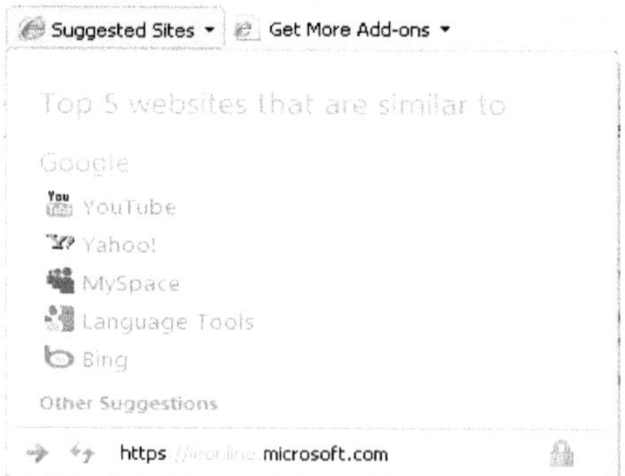

Figure 1: IE8 Site Suggestion for "Google.com"

on user preference yields significant improvements over the best existing ranking mechanism in the literature. Teevan et al. in [28] also utilized implicit information about users' interests to re-rank Web search results within a relevance feedback framework.

Applications of implicit feedback to predict user future visits are also studied in [6, 11]. These systems typically establish historical click trails of a user or a community of users, and assess the accuracy of statistical machine learning models which predict future page visits [29].

Recently, White et al. evaluated how to effectively predict user interests based on five contextual information sources: social, historic, task, collection and user interaction [29]. The user's Web page visits are automatically assigned to Open Directory Project (ODP) categories and then used to predict future visits of sites within a category. Different from this approach, in the work presented in this paper, we focus on predicting a lower granularity of actual frequencies of the visits, as opposed to a category level.

Starting from the release of Internet Explorer 8 (IE8), an important feature was introduced - "Suggested Site". As shown in Figure 1, IE8 lists Top 5 Web sites that are similar to the site a user types in the address bar. So far, this feature makes Web site recommendations based on a single site, which does not include any personalized results. In this paper, we will study how to personalize the suggestion results based on users' past online behaviors.

2.2 Recommender Systems

Our work is closely related to the research of recommender systems. In this subsection, we review several major approaches for recommender systems, especially for collaborative filtering.

A number of algorithms have been proposed to improve both the recommendation quality and the scalability problems. As discussed in [9], one of the most commonly-used and successfully-deployed recommendation approaches is collaborative filtering. These collaborative filtering algorithms can be divided into two main categories: neighborhood-based and model-based approaches. Neighborhood-based methods, or memory-based methods, mainly concentrate on finding the similar users [2, 10] or items [5, 17, 24] for generating recommendations. The neighborhood-based recommendation algorithms are based on the assumption that those who agreed in the past tend to agree again in the future. They usually fall into two classes: user-based approaches and item-based approaches. User-based approaches predict the ratings of active users based on the ratings of similar users found, while item-based approaches predict the ratings of active users based on the computed information of items similar to those chosen by the active user.

In addition to the neighborhood-based approaches, the model-based approaches to collaborative filtering train a predefined model by employing the observed user-item ratings. Algorithms in this category include the clustering model [12], the aspect models [7, 8, 25], the latent factor model [3], the Bayesian hierarchical model [31] and the ranking model [18]. Recently, due to its efficiency in dealing with large datasets, several low-dimensional matrix approximation methods [1, 13, 21, 22, 23, 26] have been proposed. These methods all focus on fitting the user-item rating matrix using low-rank approximations, and employ the matrix to make further predictions. The low-rank matrix factorization methods are very efficient in training since they assume that in the user-item rating matrix, only a small number of factors influence preferences, and that a user's preference vector is determined by how each factor applies to that user. Low-rank matrix approximations based on minimizing the sum-squared errors can be easily solved using Singular Value Decomposition (SVD). In [22], Salakhutdinov et al. proposed a probabilistic graphic model by assuming some Gaussian observation noises on observed user-item ratings. The proposed model achieved promising prediction results. In their following work proposed in [23], the Gaussian-Wishart priors are placed on the user and item hyper-parameters. Since exact inference is intractable in the new model, a Gibbs sampling method is proposed to iteratively learn the user and item latent matrices.

All of the low-dimensional approximation methods mentioned above are based on factorizing the user-item rating matrix. Normally, in a recommender system, users can assign 5-scale integer ratings (from 1 to 5, and 5 indicates "love" while 1 means "dislike") to items[1]. However, in the case of Web site recommendation, the range of the user-site frequency data is much wider than the rating data. A user can visit a site only once, but probably will also visit another site thousands of times or even more. The wide range of the frequency data poses new challenges in modeling the Web site recommendation problem. Some state-of-the-art algorithms based on the rating data may not perform well on the frequency data. For example, in the method proposed in [22], the rating data are modeled as Gaussian distributions with some noises. This assumption is not suitable for modeling the frequency data since the underlying distribution is probably not Gaussian. Hence, most of previous low-dimensional approximation methods cannot generate good recommendation results when they are applied to the Web site recommendation problems.

3. MATRIX FACTORIZATION IN RECOMMENDER SYSTEMS

As mentioned in Section 2, a popular method in recommender systems is to factorize the user-item rating matrix, and to utilize the factorized user-specific and item-specific matrices for further missing data prediction [22, 23, 30]. The premise behind a low-dimensional factor model is that there are only a small number of factors influencing the preferences, and that a user's preference vector is determined by how each factor applies to that user [21].

In recommender systems, considering an $m \times n$ user-item rating matrix R describing m users' numerical ratings on n items, a low-rank matrix factorization approach seeks to approximate the rating matrix R by a multiplication of d-rank factors $R \approx UV^T$, where $U \in \mathbb{R}^{m\times d}$ and $V \in \mathbb{R}^{n\times d}$ with $d << \min(m, n)$. The matrix R in the real-world is usually very sparse since most of the users only rates few items.

The Singular Value Decomposition (SVD) method is employed to estimate a matrix R by minimizing

$$\min_{U,V} \frac{1}{2}\sum_{i=1}^{m}\sum_{j=1}^{n} I_{ij}(R_{ij} - U_i V_j^T)^2, \qquad (1)$$

where U_i and V_j are row vectors with d values, I_{ij} is the indicator function that is equal to 1 if user i rated item j and equal to 0 otherwise.

Another popular method in recommender systems is the Probabilistic Matrix Factorization (PMF) method proposed in [22]. The conditional distribution over the observed ratings is defined as:

$$p(R|U, V, \sigma_R^2) = \prod_{i=1}^{m}\prod_{j=1}^{n}\left[\mathcal{N}\left(R_{ij}|U_i V_j^T, \sigma_R^2\right)\right]^{I_{ij}}, \qquad (2)$$

where $\mathcal{N}(x|\mu, \sigma^2)$ is the probability density function of the Gaussian distribution with mean μ and variance σ^2. The zero-mean spherical Gaussian priors are also placed on user and item feature vectors:

$$p(U|\sigma_U^2)=\prod_{i=1}^{m}\mathcal{N}(U_i|0, \sigma_U^2\mathbf{I}),\ p(V|\sigma_V^2)=\prod_{j=1}^{n}\mathcal{N}(V_j|0, \sigma_V^2\mathbf{I}). \quad (3)$$

Hence, through a Bayesian inference, we have the following objective function:

$$\min_{U,V} \frac{1}{2}\sum_{i=1}^{m}\sum_{j=1}^{n} I_{ij}(R_{ij} - U_i V_j^T)^2 + \frac{\lambda_1}{2}||U||_F^2 + \frac{\lambda_2}{2}||V||_F^2, \quad (4)$$

where $\lambda_1, \lambda_2 > 0$. The optimization problem is to minimize the sum-of-squared-errors objective function with quadratic regularization terms. Gradient based approaches can be applied to find a local minimum. The above algorithm is perhaps one of the most popular methods in collaborative filtering.

Actually, when modeling the observed rating data, both SVD and PMF have the underlying assumption about Gaussian distribution. This assumption may not be appropriate when working on the frequency data. Hence, these models may encounter problems in generating good recommendation results. The experimental analysis conducted in Section 5 demonstrates our concerns. In next section, we propose two probabilistic models which can potentially generate better Web site recommendation results than SVD and PMF.

4. RECOMMENDATION FRAMEWORK

4.1 Problem Definition

The major task studied in this paper is to predict how frequently a user will visit a Web site. In commercial search engines or browser toolbars, query logs record the activities

[1]Different recommender systems adopt different rating scales. Some systems may use 10-scale integer ratings.

Table 1: Samples of Search Engine Query Logs

ID	Query	URL
358	facebook	http://www.facebook.com
358	rww	http://www.readwriteweb.com
3968	iphone4	http://www.apple.com
3968	ipad	http://www.apple.com
...	...	...

Web sites

Web users	v_1	v_2	v_3	v_4	v_5	v_6
u_1		68	1		15	
u_2	42			13		24
u_3		72	12		11	2
u_4	15			33		
u_5		85	45			63

(a) User-Site Matrix

Queries

Web users	z_1	z_2	z_3	z_4	z_5
u_1	12		5	6	
u_2		23		5	1
u_3		14		35	18
u_4	25		11	4	
u_5		12	5		24

(b) User-Query Matrix

Figure 2: Aggregated Data From Query Logs

of Web users, which reflect their interests and the relationships between users and queries, as well as users and clicked Web sites. As shown in Table 1, each line of the data we need includes the following information: a user ID, a query issued by the user, and a Web site on which the user clicked.

By aggregating the data in Table 1, we can construct two matrices, as shown in Figure 2. Figure 2(a) is the user-site frequency matrix, which contains how many times a user visited a Web site. Figure 2(b) gives the user-query frequency matrix, which indicates how frequently a user issued a query.

The problem under investigation is essentially how to effectively and efficiently predict the missing values of the user-site frequency matrix by employing these data sources. To attack this problem, in Section 4.2, we propose a novel probabilistic factor model by using only the user-site frequency matrix, while in Section 4.3, we introduce a collective probabilistic factor model by utilizing both user-site and user-query frequency matrices, which can further improve the model performance.

4.2 Probabilistic Factor Model

Our proposed Probabilistic Factor Model (PFM) is a generative probabilistic model, which can be represented by the graphical model in Figure 3. Let F be an $m \times n$ data matrix whose element f_{ij} is the observed count of event (or feature, or item) j by user i. Y is a matrix of expected counts with the same dimensions as F, and y_{ij} denotes an element in matrix Y. Every observed element f_{ij} in matrix F is assumed to follow Poisson distribution with the mean y_{ij} in matrix Y, respectively. The matrix Y is factorized into two matrices U and V, where U is an $m \times d$ matrix, V is an $n \times d$ matrix and d is the dimensionality. Each element u_{ik} $(k = 1, ..., d)$ in U encodes the preference of user i to latent topic k, and each v_{jk} in V can be interpreted as the affinity of site j to the latent topic k. Finally, u_{ik} and v_{jk} are given the Gamma distributions as the empirical priors.

There are two reasons we use Gamma distributions to model u_{ik} and v_{jk} instead of Gaussian or other distributions: (1) Gamma distribution is suitable for modeling non-negative values, while Gaussian distribution can model both negative and non-negative values. If we allow negative values in u_{ik} and v_{jk}, potentially, the model will generate negative frequency values, which is unreasonable in the real world. (2) The Gamma distribution is already proved to be effective in modeling document latent vectors in text analysis [4], where the document-word relation is also represented as a frequency matrix.

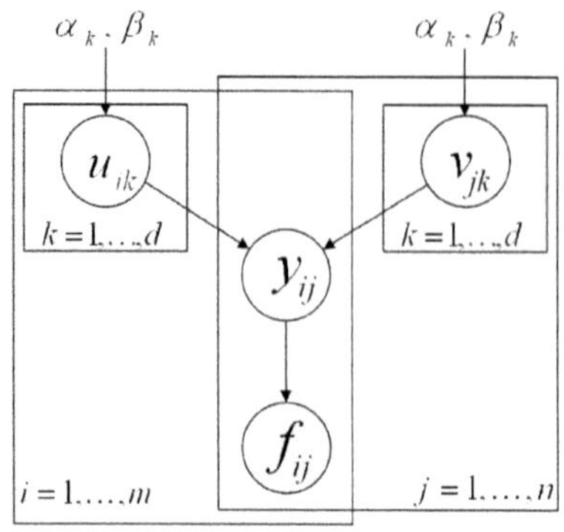

Figure 3: Graphical Model for Probabilistic Factor Modeling

Therefore, the generative process of an observed user-site count f_{ij} in our model follows:

1. Generate $u_{ik} \sim \text{Gamma}(\alpha_k, \beta_k), \forall k$.

2. Generate $v_{jk} \sim \text{Gamma}(\alpha_k, \beta_k), \forall k$.

3. Generate y_{ij} occurrences of item or event j from user i with outcome $y_{ij} = \sum_{k=1}^{d} u_{ik} v_{jk}$.

4. Generate $f_{ij} \sim \text{Poisson}(y_{ij})$.

The gamma distributions of U and V follow the probabilistic functions

$$p(U|\boldsymbol{\alpha}, \boldsymbol{\beta}) = \prod_{i=1}^{m} \prod_{k=1}^{d} \frac{u_{ik}^{\alpha_k - 1} \exp(-u_{ik}/\beta_k)}{\beta_k^{\alpha_k} \Gamma(\alpha_k)}, \tag{5}$$

$$p(V|\boldsymbol{\alpha}, \boldsymbol{\beta}) = \prod_{j=1}^{n} \prod_{k=1}^{d} \frac{v_{jk}^{\alpha_k - 1} \exp(-v_{jk}/\beta_k)}{\beta_k^{\alpha_k} \Gamma(\alpha_k)}, \tag{6}$$

where $\boldsymbol{\alpha} = \{\alpha_1, ..., \alpha_d\}$, $\boldsymbol{\beta} = \{\beta_1, ..., \beta_d\}$, $u_{ik} > 0$, $v_{jk} > 0$, $\alpha_k > 0$ and $\beta_k > 0$, $\Gamma(\cdot)$ is the Gamma function.

The Poisson distribution of F given Y can then be defined as

$$p(F|Y) = \prod_{i=1}^{m} \prod_{j=1}^{n} \frac{y_{ij}^{f_{ij}} \exp(-y_{ij})}{f_{ij}!}, \tag{7}$$

where $y_{ij} = \sum_{k=1}^{d} u_{ik} v_{jk}$.

Since $Y = UV^T$, the posterior distribution of U and V given F can be modeled as

$$p(U, V|F, \boldsymbol{\alpha}, \boldsymbol{\beta}) \propto p(F|Y) p(U|\boldsymbol{\alpha}, \boldsymbol{\beta}) p(V|\boldsymbol{\alpha}, \boldsymbol{\beta}). \tag{8}$$

Hence, we can infer the log of the posterior distribution $p(U, V|F, \boldsymbol{\alpha}, \boldsymbol{\beta})$ as follows

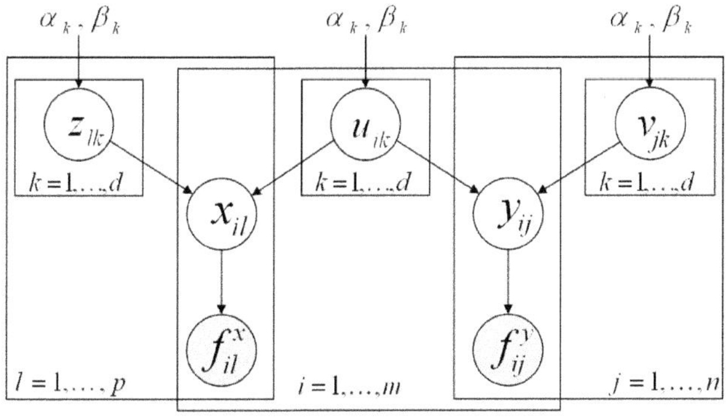

Figure 4: Graphical Model for Collective Probabilistic Factor Modeling

$$\begin{aligned}\mathcal{L}(U,V;F) &= \sum_{i=1}^{m}\sum_{k=1}^{d}((\alpha_k-1)\ln(u_{ik}/\beta_k)-u_{ik}/\beta_k)\\ &+\sum_{j=1}^{n}\sum_{k=1}^{d}((\alpha_k-1)\ln(v_{jk}/\beta_k)-v_{jk}/\beta_k)\\ &+\sum_{i=1}^{m}\sum_{j=1}^{n}(f_{ij}\ln y_{ij}-y_{ij})+\text{const.} \qquad (9)\end{aligned}$$

Taking derivatives on $\mathcal{L}$ with respect to u_{ik} and v_{jk}, we have

$$\begin{aligned}\frac{\partial\mathcal{L}}{\partial u_{ik}} &= \sum_{j=1}^{n}(f_{ij}v_{jk}/y_{ij}-v_{jk})+(\alpha_k-1)/u_{ik}-1/\beta_k,\\ \frac{\partial\mathcal{L}}{\partial v_{jk}} &= \sum_{i=1}^{m}(f_{ij}u_{ik}/y_{ij}-u_{ik})+(\alpha_k-1)/v_{jk}-1/\beta_k. \qquad (10)\end{aligned}$$

Using similar techniques proposed by Lee and Seung in [16], by setting the learning rates to

$$\frac{u_{ik}}{\sum_{j=1}^{n}v_{jk}+1/\beta_k} \text{ and } \frac{v_{jk}}{\sum_{i=1}^{m}u_{ik}+1/\beta_k}$$

respectively, we can obtain the following multiplicative updating rules:

$$\begin{aligned}u_{ik} &\leftarrow u_{ik}\frac{\sum_{j=1}^{n}(f_{ij}v_{jk}/y_{ij})+(\alpha_k-1)/u_{ik}}{\sum_{j=1}^{n}v_{jk}+1/\beta_k},\\ v_{jk} &\leftarrow v_{jk}\frac{\sum_{i=1}^{m}(f_{ij}u_{ik}/y_{ij})+(\alpha_k-1)/v_{jk}}{\sum_{i=1}^{m}u_{ik}+1/\beta_k}. \qquad (11)\end{aligned}$$

4.3 Collective Probabilistic Factor Model

In many Web applications, we have multiple data sources instead of a single data source. In the case of Web site recommendation, the Web users not only browsed many Web sites, but also issued several queries. The queries issued by users can also represent the interests of the users. If we can incorporate this information, we can potentially improve the model performance.

Actually, our proposed model in Section 4.2 can be easily extended to incorporate heterogeneous data sources. When we are observing the example matrices in Figure 2(a) and Figure 2(b), we notice that these two data sources share the same user space. Hence, we propose a Collective Probabilistic Factor Model (CPFM) by sharing the same user latent space. Intuitively, CPFM method should outperform PFM method since the additional user-query matrix can help model users' preferences more accurately. Figure 4 shows the graphical model for mining these two data matrices.

In this graphical model, F^x is an $m\times p$ data matrix whose element f^x_{il} represents how many times user i issued query l. X is a matrix of expected counts with the same dimensions as F^x, and x_{il} denotes an element in matrix X. Every observed element f^x_{il} in matrix F^x is assumed to follow Poisson distribution with the mean x_{il} in matrix X, respectively. The matrix X is factorized into two matrices U and Z, where Z is a $p\times d$ matrix. Each element z_{lk} in Z encodes the affinity of query l to the latent topic k. The definitions of F^y, Y, U, V, u_{ik} and v_{jk} are the same as the definitions in Section 4.2.

Similar to Eq. (8), we have the posterior distribution of U, V and Z, given F^x and F^y:

$$\begin{aligned}&p(U,V,Z|F^x,F^y,\boldsymbol{\alpha},\boldsymbol{\beta})\\ &\quad\propto p(F^x|X)p(F^y|Y)p(U|\boldsymbol{\alpha},\boldsymbol{\beta})p(V|\boldsymbol{\alpha},\boldsymbol{\beta})p(Z|\boldsymbol{\alpha},\boldsymbol{\beta}). \qquad (12)\end{aligned}$$

In this equation, $p(F^x|X)$ and $p(F^y|Y)$ are defined as:

$$p(F^x|X)=\prod_{i=1}^{m}\prod_{l=1}^{p}\frac{x_{il}^{f^x_{il}}\exp(-x_{il})}{f^x_{il}!}, \qquad (13)$$

$$p(F^y|Y)=\prod_{i=1}^{m}\prod_{j=1}^{n}\frac{y_{ij}^{f^y_{ij}}\exp(-y_{ij})}{f^y_{ij}!}, \qquad (14)$$

where $x_{il}=\sum_{k=1}^{d}u_{ik}z_{lk}$ and $y_{ij}=\sum_{k=1}^{d}u_{ik}v_{jk}$.

Moreover, since every element in Z also follows a Gamma distribution, similar to $p(U|\boldsymbol{\alpha},\boldsymbol{\beta})$ and $p(V|\boldsymbol{\alpha},\boldsymbol{\beta})$, $p(Z|\boldsymbol{\alpha},\boldsymbol{\beta})$ can be defined as:

$$p(Z|\boldsymbol{\alpha},\boldsymbol{\beta})=\prod_{l=1}^{p}\prod_{k=1}^{d}\frac{z_{lk}^{\alpha_k-1}\exp(-z_{lk}/\beta_k)}{\beta_k^{\alpha_k}\Gamma(\alpha_k)}. \qquad (15)$$

Hence, by inferring Eq. (12), we have the log of the posterior distribution for CPFM model:

$$\begin{aligned}&\mathcal{L}(U,V,Z;F^x,F^y)\\ &=\sum_{i=1}^{m}\sum_{l=1}^{p}(f^x_{il}\ln x_{il}-x_{il})+\sum_{i=1}^{m}\sum_{j=1}^{n}(f^y_{ij}\ln y_{ij}-y_{ij})\\ &+\sum_{i=1}^{m}\sum_{k=1}^{d}((\alpha_k-1)\ln(u_{ik}/\beta_k)-u_{ik}/\beta_k)\\ &+\sum_{j=1}^{n}\sum_{k=1}^{d}((\alpha_k-1)\ln(v_{jk}/\beta_k)-v_{jk}/\beta_k)\\ &+\sum_{l=1}^{p}\sum_{k=1}^{d}((\alpha_k-1)\ln(z_{lk}/\beta_k)-z_{lk}/\beta_k)+\text{const.} \qquad (16)\end{aligned}$$

Similar to PFM, we can easily obtain the multiplicative updating rules for learning U, V and Z:

$$u_{ik} \leftarrow u_{ik} \frac{\sum_{j=1}^{n}(f_{ij}^{y} v_{jk}/y_{ij}) + \sum_{l=1}^{p}(f_{il}^{x} z_{lk}/x_{il}) + (\alpha_k - 1)/u_{ik}}{\sum_{j=1}^{n} v_{jk} + \sum_{l=1}^{p} z_{lk} + 1/\beta_k},$$

$$v_{jk} \leftarrow v_{jk} \frac{\sum_{i=1}^{m}(f_{ij}^{y} u_{ik}/y_{ij}) + (\alpha_k - 1)/v_{jk}}{\sum_{i=1}^{m} u_{ik} + 1/\beta_k},$$

$$z_{lk} \leftarrow z_{lk} \frac{\sum_{i=1}^{m}(f_{il}^{x} u_{ik}/x_{il}) + (\alpha_k - 1)/z_{lk}}{\sum_{i=1}^{m} u_{ik} + 1/\beta_k}. \quad (17)$$

In Eq. (17), we treat the information from the user-site matrix and the user-query matrix equally. However, sometimes we may want to control how much information to use in each side, and to find a balance between these two data sources. Hence, we add a smoothing parameter θ in order to tune the importance of these two data sources. The updating rules for u_{ik} in Eq. (17) is then changed to

$$u_{ik} \leftarrow u_{ik} \frac{\theta \sum_{j=1}^{n}(f_{ij}^{y} v_{jk}/y_{ij}) + (1-\theta) \sum_{l=1}^{p}(f_{il}^{x} z_{lk}/x_{il}) + (\alpha_k - 1)/u_{ik}}{\theta \sum_{j=1}^{n} v_{jk} + (1-\theta) \sum_{l=1}^{p} z_{lk} + 1/\beta_k}. \quad (18)$$

Our proposed method is general, and can be easily extended to incorporate other contextual information for other research problems. In this section, we utilize the user-query information to improve the PFM method. Actually, in the query logs, every Web site is also associated with some queries. Hence, a natural extension is to further incorporate the site-query frequency matrix by adding another matrix factorization in Figure 4. We hope this can help learn the site latent vectors more accurately. Besides Web site recommendation, many other research problems also have similar frequency data, like sponsored search, behavioral targeting, text mining, etc. Our model can also be easily applied to these problems. We do not discuss the details in this paper since our focus of this paper is to illustrate how to make Web site recommendations.

4.4 Complexity Analysis

The main computation of gradient methods is evaluating the object function $\mathcal{L}$ and its gradients against variables. In PFM model, because of the sparsity of matrix F, the computational complexity of evaluating the object function $\mathcal{L}$ is $O(N_F d)$, where N_F is the number of nonzero entries in matrix F. The computational complexities for gradients $\frac{\partial \mathcal{L}}{\partial U}$ and $\frac{\partial \mathcal{L}}{\partial V}$ in Eq. (10) are also $O(N_F d)$. Therefore, the total computational complexity in one iteration is $O(N_F d)$, which indicates that the computational time of our PFM method is linear with respect to the number of observations in the user-site frequency matrix. The total complexity of PFM is then $O(N_F dr)$, where r is the number of iterations. Similarly, for CPFM, the complexity is $O(N_{F^x} dr + N_{F^y} dr)$, where N_{F^x} and N_{F^y} are the number of nonzero entries in user-query and user-site matrices, respectively. Since our algorithm will converge after 10 to 20 iterations, this complexity analysis shows that our proposed approach is very efficient and can scale up with respect to very large datasets.

Table 2: Statistics of User-Site and User-Query Frequency Matrices

Statistics	User-Site Frequency	User-Query Frequency
Min. Num.	4	10
Max. Num.	9,969	4,693
Avg. Num.	20.33	23.05

5. EXPERIMENTAL ANALYSIS

In this section, we conduct several experiments to compare the recommendation quality of our PFM and CPFM approaches with other baseline and state-of-the-art collaborative filtering or recommendation methods.

Our experiments are intended to address the following questions:

1. How does our approach compare with the baseline and published state-of-the-art algorithms?
2. How do the model parameters α_k and β_k affect the accuracy of prediction?
3. What is the performance difference when we use different dimensions to represent users, sites and queries?
4. How does the smooth parameter θ affect the prediction quality in CPFM?
5. Is our algorithm efficient for large datasets?

5.1 Metrics

We use two metrics, the Normalized Mean Absolute Error (NMAE) and the Normalized Root Mean Square Error (NRMSE), to measure the prediction accuracy.

The metric NMAE is defined as:

$$NMAE = \frac{\sum_{i,j} |(f_{i,j} - \widehat{f}_{i,j})/f_{i,j}|}{N}, \quad (19)$$

where $f_{i,j}$ denotes the frequency user i visited Web site j, $\widehat{f}_{i,j}$ denotes the frequency user i visited Web site j as predicted by a method, and N denotes the number of tested data. The metric NRMSE is defined as:

$$NRMSE = \sqrt{\frac{\sum_{i,j}((f_{i,j} - \widehat{f}_{i,j})/f_{i,j})^2}{N}}. \quad (20)$$

From the definitions, we can see that a smaller NMAE or NRMSE value means a better performance.

5.2 Dataset

The primary source of data for this work is the anonymized logs of Web sites visited by users who opted-in to provide data through a widely-distributed browser toolbar. Each line of the data source may contain a lot of information. We only keep those entries which include a unique identifier for the user, query issued by the user, and the Web sites visited by the user. Similar to the work in [29], in order to remove variability caused by geographic and linguistic variations in search behaviors, we only include those entries generated in the English speaking United States locale.

The experiments conducted in this paper are based on one month browser toolbar data, which represents billions of Web site visits. In order to remove some outliers and

Table 3: **Performance Comparison (Dimensionality = 10)**

Training Data	Metrics	UserMean	SiteMean	SVD	PMF	NMF	GaP	PFM	CPFM
90%	NMAE	2.246	1.094	0.488	0.476	0.465	0.440	0.432	**0.427**
	Improve	80.98%	60.96%	12.50%	10.29%	8.17%	2.95%		
	NRMSE	3.522	2.171	0.581	0.570	0.554	0.532	0.529	**0.520**
	Improve	85.24%	76.05%	10.50%	8.77%	6.14%	2.26%		
80%	NMAE	2.252	1.096	0.490	0.478	0.468	0.441	0.434	**0.428**
	Improve	80.99%	60.95%	12.65%	10.46%	8.55%	2.95%		
	NRMSE	3.714	2.159	0.584	0.571	0.560	0.533	0.530	**0.520**
	Improve	86.00%	75.91%	10.96%	8.93%	7.14%	2.44%		

Table 4: **Performance Comparison (Dimensionality = 20)**

Training Data	Metrics	UserMean	SiteMean	SVD	PMF	NMF	GaP	PFM	CPFM
90%	NMAE	2.246	1.094	0.469	0.460	0.449	0.426	0.413	**0.409**
	Improve	81.79%	62.61%	12.79%	11.09%	8.91%	3.99%		
	NRMSE	3.522	2.171	0.568	0.556	0.542	0.521	0.503	**0.496**
	Improve	85.92%	77.15%	12.68%	10.79%	8.49%	4.80%		
80%	NMAE	2.252	1.096	0.470	0.462	0.451	0.427	0.415	**0.410**
	Improve	81.79%	62.59%	12.77%	11.26%	9.09%	3.98%		
	NRMSE	3.714	2.159	0.570	0.558	0.545	0.522	0.504	**0.498**
	Improve	86.59%	76.93%	12.63%	10.75%	8.62%	4.60%		

clean up the data, we require that every user should at least visited 10 Web sites, and each Web site should at least be visited by 10 users. Moreover, we also constrain that a user should visit each Web site at least four times. URLs of all the Web sites are truncated to the site level. After pruning, we have 165,403 unique users, 265,367 unique URLs and 442,598 unique queries. Totally, the pruned dataset records 53,089,262 Web site visits. In the constructed user-site frequency matrix, 2,612,016 entries are observed, while in the user-query frequency matrix, the number of observed entries is 833,581. Some other statistics are shown in Table 2. From this table, we can see that a user visited a site for 9,969 times in a month, which shows that the range of user-site frequency matrix is very wide.

5.3 Comparison

In this section, in order to show the effectiveness of our proposed recommendation approaches, we compare the recommendation results of the following methods:

1. **UserMean**: this is a baseline method, which uses the mean frequency value of every user to predict the missing values.

2. **SiteMean**: this is also a baseline method, which utilizes the mean frequency value of every site to predict the missing values.

3. **SVD**: this is a well-known method in matrix factorization. We have shown the details of this method in Section 3. It is also been utilized in large scale collaborative filtering tasks [14].

4. **PMF**: this method is proposed by Salakhutdinov and Minh in [22]. The details of this method are also introduced in Section 3.

5. **NMF**: this method is originally proposed in [15, 16] for image analysis. However, it is widely used in collaborative filtering recently. The underlying distribution is also modeled as Poisson distribution.

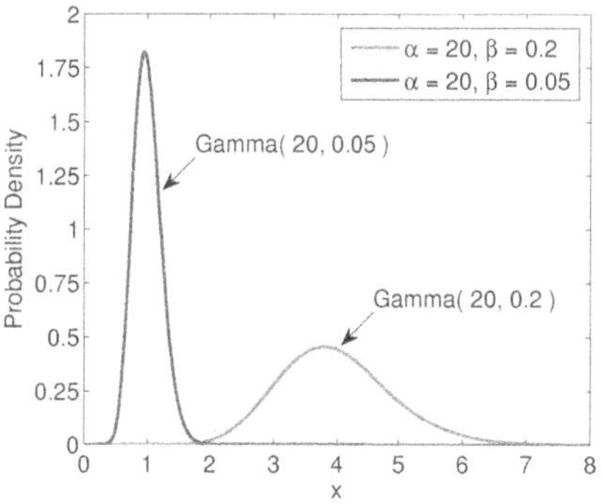

Figure 5: Gamma Distributions

6. **GaP**: this approach is proposed in [4], and it is originally used to model text mining problems. The documents are modeled as a mixture of Gamma distributions.

We use different amounts of training data (90%, 80%) to test the algorithms. Training data 90%, for example, means we randomly select 90% of the observed data as the training data to predict the remaining 10%. The random selection was carried out 5 times independently, and we report the average results. The experimental results using 10 and 20 dimensions to represent the latent features are shown in Table 3 and Table 4, respectively. The standard deviations of the results generated by our methods are all around 0.005. In Table 3, we set all $\alpha_k = 20$, $\beta_k = 0.2$ in our PFM and CPFM models, while in Table 4, we change the settings to $\alpha_k = 20$, $\beta_k = 0.05$ for both PFM and CPFM. In Section 5.4, we will explain why we need to choose different α_k and β_k values when the dimensions are different. In addition, in

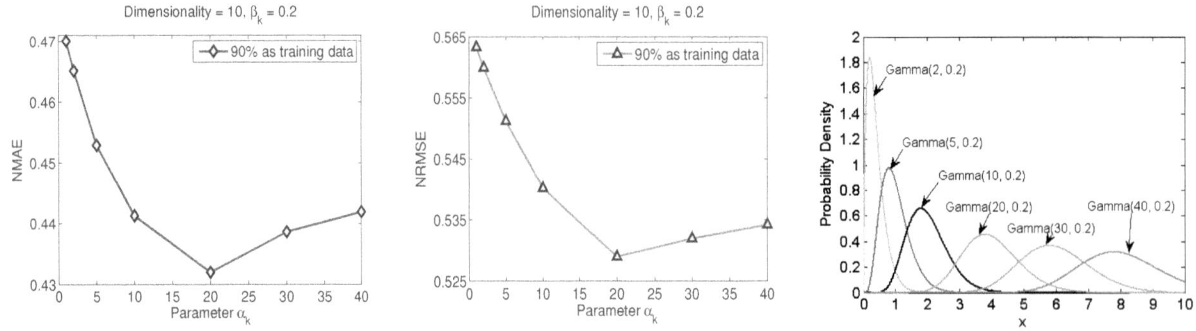

(a) NMAE (b) NRMSE (c) Gamma Distributions

Figure 6: Impact of Parameter α_k in PFM

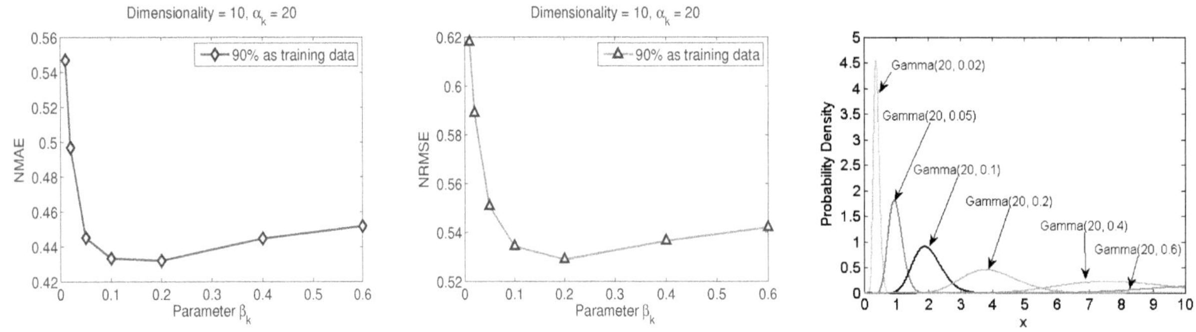

(a) NMAE (b) NRMSE (c) Gamma Distributions

Figure 7: Impact of Parameter β_k in PFM

all the experiments, we set the parameter $\theta = 0.1$ for our CPFM method.

From the results, we can observe that our methods consistently outperform other approaches in all the settings, which shows the promising future of our methods. The percentages in Table 3 and Table 4 are the improvements of our CPFM method over the corresponding approaches.

We observe that the two baseline methods, UserMean and SiteMean, have the worst performance. Among these two methods, SiteMean performs much better than UserMean. This may indicate that users generally have diverse visiting patterns than sites. We also notice that two Gaussian based methods SVD and PMF are not suitable for factorizing frequency data, which coincides with our discussion in Section 2.

5.4 Impact of Dimensionality

From Table 3 and Table 4, we can see that our methods perform better when we choose a larger dimensionality. This is reasonable since more dimensions give us more flexibility to represent both user and site latent vectors. However, this is not always true since in the case we choose a very large dimensionality, we may experience severe overfitting problems.

As we discussed above, we set different α_k and β_k values when choosing different dimensions. This is because we model $\sum_{k=1}^{d} u_{ik}v_{jk}$ as the mean of a Poisson distribution. Since the frequencies are fixed, if we use a larger dimensionality, we need to employ some smaller values of u_{ik} and v_{jk}. That is why in the case of $d = 10$, the optimal parameter settings are $\alpha_k = 20$ and $\beta_k = 0.2$, while in the case where $d = 20$, we set $\alpha_k = 20$ and $\beta_k = 0.05$. We also plot the Gamma probability density functions for these two settings in Figure 5. From this figure, we can see that we will have a very high probability to generate smaller values if we choose the setting $\beta_k = 0.05$. This observation can help guide us to efficiently select appropriate parameters once the dimensionality is decided.

5.5 Impact of Parameters α_k and β_k

Parameters α_k and β_k are two important parameters since they define the shapes and scales of the Gamma distributions. In Figure 6 and Figure 7, we independently study how these two parameters affect the model performance in PFM. Figure 6 shows the impact of parameter α_k, given $\beta_k = 0.2$. We can see that the model achieves the best performance when $\alpha_k = 20$. A larger or smaller α_k value will lead to hurt the model performance.

Figure 6(c) shows some related Gamma distributions with β_k fixed. From this figure, we can easily interpret why different α_k and β_k values can significantly influence the performance. When $\alpha_k = 20$ and $\beta_k = 0.2$, the model has the best performance. At the same time, this Gamma distribution will generate values from 3 to 5 with high probabilities, which also means that these values can best represent user and site latent vectors. However, other parameter settings generate either much smaller or much larger values, which will potentially hurt the model performance.

The impact of parameter β_k is shown in Figure 7, and it shares similar trends as shown in Figure 6.

5.6 Impact of Parameter θ

In our CPFM method proposed in this paper, the parameter θ balances the information from the user-site matrix and

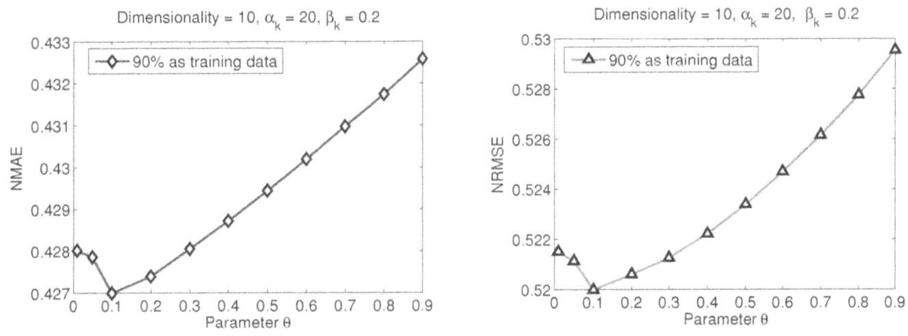

(a) NMAE (b) NRMSE

Figure 8: Impact of Parameter θ in CPFM

Table 5: Efficiency Analysis (90% as Training Data)

PFM				
Dimensions	10D	20D	40D	60D
Seconds per Iteration	6.06	14.73	32.67	53.87
CPFM				
Dimensions	10D	20D	40D	60D
Seconds per Iteration	8.77	20.36	46.13	78.29

the user-query matrix. It controls how much our method should use the information in each matrix. If $\theta = 1$, we only factorize the user-site frequency matrix, and simply employ users' site visiting pattern in learning. If θ equals to a very small value, we will count more on information from the user-query frequency matrix to learn users' interests. For other cases in-between, we fuse information from the user-site matrix and the user-query matrix for collective probabilistic factor modeling and, furthermore, to make Web site recommendation for the users.

The impacts of θ on NMAE and NRMSE are shown in Figure 8. We observe that the value of θ impacts the recommendation results a lot, which illustrates that fusing these two data sources can greatly improve the recommendation quality. As θ increases, the NMAE and NRMSE decrease at first, but when θ surpasses a certain threshold, the NMAE and NRMSE increase with further increase of the value of θ. This phenomenon confirms with our initial intuition that fusing these two data sources together can generate better performance than purely using the user-site frequency matrix for recommendations.

In Figure 8(a) and Figure 8(b), when using 90% as training data, we observe that, our CPFM method achieves the best performance when θ is around 0.1, while smaller values like $\theta = 0.01$ or larger values like $\theta = 0.3$ can potentially hurt the model performance. Also a smaller θ is preferred to a larger θ indicates that we need to use more about user-query information than user-site information. The reason is perhaps the training data of user-site matrix is very sparse, which is less effective in learning the accurate interests of users.

5.7 Efficiency Analysis

The complexity analysis indicates that our method is linear with the observations. We also conduct some experiments on measuring the efficiency of our method. The Seconds-per-Iteration evaluation results are shown in Table 5 for both PFM and CPFM methods. We find that our methods are very efficient since our method will converge after 10 to 20 iterations. Hence, in 10-dimension case, we only need around 2 minutes to learn our PFM and CPFM models. CPFM is generally a little bit slower than PFM since CPFM needs to deal with one extra user-query matrix.

All the experiments are conducted on a workstation containing an *Intel Xeon* CPU (2.5 GHz) with 8G memory.

6. CONCLUSION AND FUTURE WORK

In this paper, aiming at providing personalized, accurate and efficient Web site recommendations for Web users, we propose two novel probabilistic factor models: PFM and CPFM. The experimental analysis on the large browser toolbar data shows the effectiveness and efficiency of our methods. The complexity analysis indicates our methods can be applied to very large datesets since they are linear with the observations in the user-site and user-query matrices.

In order to reduce the model complexity, in our PFM and CPFM methods, we use the same set of α_k and β_k values for both user, site and query latent features. Actually, since users, sites and queries are totally different objects, they may belong to completely different Gamma distributions. Hence, in order to further improve the recommendation performance, in the future, we can slightly modify the model, and allow setting different α_k and β_k values for these three objects.

In all the experiments conducted in this paper, we need to set the values for α_k and β_k. In the future, we will investigate a more intelligent algorithm to automatically determine these values. We may run into some challenges since the data is very sparse, hence, learning α_k and β_k automatically may experience overfitting problems. Another solution is that we can further assume a distribution on top of these two parameters. However, this is also difficult to implement since Gamma distribution does not have a very good conjugate prior distribution.

In our experiment, we only measure how accurate we can predict the user-site visiting frequency. Sometimes, only being accurate cannot meet the application requirements. We also plan to design a prototype for users to use, and ask users to measure the effectiveness of the proposed methods.

For the PFM model itself, we can make further assumption that every user or site is generated from a mixture of Gamma distributions. We can also assume that the mixture coefficients follow a Dirichlet distribution. Since we probably cannot infer the exact form of this model, we need to use sampling or variational approximation methods to solve the problem. This may however increase the complexity of the model.

Our proposed frame work is general; hence, in the future,

we plan to apply our methods to other research problems, such as behavioral targeting and sponsored search. We can use the proposed methods to predict how many times a user will click an advertisement. Finally, we can also apply our methods to many text mining tasks, including clustering, classification, retrieval tasks, etc.

Acknowledgments

The work described in this paper was partially supported by two grants from the Research Grants Council of the Hong Kong Special Administrative Region, China (Project No. CUHK 415210 and Project No. CUHK 415410), and partially supported by a Google Focused Grant Project under "Mobile 2014". The authors also would like to thank the reviewers for their helpful comments.

7. REFERENCES

[1] R. Bell, Y. Koren, and C. Volinsky. Modeling relationships at multiple scales to improve accuracy of large recommender systems. In *Proc. of KDD '07*, pages 95–104, San Jose, California, USA, 2007.

[2] J. S. Breese, D. Heckerman, and C. Kadie. Empirical analysis of predictive algorithms for collaborative filtering. In *Proc. of UAI '98*, 1998.

[3] J. Canny. Collaborative filtering with privacy via factor analysis. In *Proc. of SIGIR '02*, pages 238–245, Tampere, Finland, 2002.

[4] J. Canny. GaP: a factor model for discrete data. In *Proc. of SIGIR '04*, pages 122–129, Sheffield, United Kingdom, 2004.

[5] M. Deshpande and G. Karypis. Item-based top-n recommendation. *ACM Transactions on Information Systems*, 22(1):143–177, 2004.

[6] S. Gündüz and M. T. Özsu. Recommendation models for user accesses to web pages. In *Proc. of ICANN/ICONIP'03*, pages 1003–1010, Istanbul, Turkey, 2003.

[7] T. Hofmann. Collaborative filtering via gaussian probabilistic latent semantic analysis. In *Proc. of SIGIR '03*, pages 259–266, Toronto, Canada, 2003.

[8] T. Hofmann. Latent semantic models for collaborative filtering. *ACM Transactions on Information Systems*, 22(1):89–115, 2004.

[9] Z. Huang, H. Chen, and D. Zeng. Applying associative retrieval techniques to alleviate the sparsity problem in collaborative filtering. *ACM Trans. Inf. Syst.*, 22(1):116–142, 2004.

[10] R. Jin, J. Y. Chai, and L. Si. An automatic weighting scheme for collaborative filtering. In *Proc. of SIGIR '04*, pages 337–344, Sheffield, United Kingdom, 2004.

[11] F. Khalil, J. Li, and H. Wang. Integrating recommendation models for improved web page prediction accuracy. In *Proc. of ACSC '08*, pages 91–100, Wollongong, Australia, 2008.

[12] A. Kohrs and B. Merialdo. Clustering for collaborative filtering applications. In *Proceedings of CIMCA*, 1999.

[13] Y. Koren. Collaborative filtering with temporal dynamics. In *Proc. of KDD '09*, pages 447–456, Paris, France, 2009.

[14] M. Kurucz, A. A. Benczur, and K. Csalogany. Methods for large scale svd with missing values. In *Proceedings of KDD Cup and Workshop*, 2007.

[15] D. D. Lee and H. S. Seung. Learning the parts of objects by non-negative matrix factorization. *Nature*, 401(6755):788–791, 1999.

[16] D. D. Lee and H. S. Seung. Algorithms for non-negative matrix factorization. In *Proc. of NIPS '00*, pages 556–562, 2000.

[17] G. Linden, B. Smith, and J. York. Amazon.com recommendations: Item-to-item collaborative filtering. *IEEE Internet Computing*, pages 76–80, Jan/Feb 2003.

[18] N. N. Liu and Q. Yang. Eigenrank: a ranking-oriented approach to collaborative filtering. In *Proc. of SIGIR '08*, pages 83–90, Singapore, Singapore, 2008.

[19] H. Ma, I. King, and M. R. Lyu. Effective missing data prediction for collaborative filtering. In *Proc. of SIGIR '07*, pages 39–46, Amsterdam, The Netherlands, 2007.

[20] F. Qiu and J. Cho. Automatic identification of user interest for personalized search. In *Proc. of WWW '06*, pages 727–736, Edinburgh, Scotland, 2006.

[21] J. D. M. Rennie and N. Srebro. Fast maximum margin matrix factorization for collaborative prediction. In *Proc. of ICML '05*, pages 713–719, Bonn, Germany, 2005.

[22] R. Salakhutdinov and A. Mnih. Probabilistic matrix factorization. In *Proc. of NIPS '07*, 2007.

[23] R. Salakhutdinov and A. Mnih. Bayesian probabilistic matrix factorization using markov chain monte carlo. In *Proc. of ICML '08*, 2008.

[24] B. Sarwar, G. Karypis, J. Konstan, and J. Reidl. Item-based collaborative filtering recommendation algorithms. In *Proc. of WWW '01*, pages 285–295, Hong Kong, Hong Kong, 2001.

[25] L. Si and R. Jin. Flexible mixture model for collaborative filtering. In *Proc. of ICML '03*, 2003.

[26] N. Srebro and T. Jaakkola. Weighted low-rank approximations. In *Proc. of ICML '03*, pages 720–727, Washington, DC, USA, 2003.

[27] J.-T. Sun, H.-J. Zeng, H. Liu, Y. Lu, and Z. Chen. Cubesvd: a novel approach to personalized web search. In *Proc. of WWW '05*, pages 382–390, Chiba, Japan, 2005.

[28] J. Teevan, S. T. Dumais, and E. Horvitz. Personalizing search via automated analysis of interests and activities. In *Proc. of SIGIR '05*, pages 449–456, Salvador, Brazil, 2005.

[29] R. W. White, P. Bailey, and L. Chen. Predicting user interests from contextual information. In *Proc. of SIGIR '09*, pages 363–370, Boston, MA, USA, 2009.

[30] K. Yu, S. Zhu, J. Lafferty, and Y. Gong. Fast nonparametric matrix factorization for large-scale collaborative filtering. In *Proc. of SIGIR '09*, pages 211–218, Boston, MA, USA, 2009.

[31] Y. Zhang and J. Koren. Efficient bayesian hierarchical user modeling for recommendation system. In *Proc. of SIGIR '07*, pages 47–54, Amsterdam, The Netherlands, 2007.

[32] D. Zhou, S. Zhu, K. Yu, X. Song, B. L. Tseng, H. Zha, and C. L. Giles. Learning multiple graphs for document recommendations. In *Proc. of WWW '08*, Beijing, China, 2008.

Efficiently Collecting Relevance Information from Clickthroughs for Web Retrieval System Evaluation

Jing He*, Wayne Xin Zhao*, Baihan Shu*, Xiaoming Li†, Hongfei Yan*
*Department of Computer Science and Technology, Peking University, China
†State Key Lab of Virtual Reality Technology and Systems, Beihang University, China
*{hj,zhaoxin,sbh,yhf}@net.pku.edu.cn †lxm@pku.edu.cn

ABSTRACT

Various click models have been recently proposed as a principled approach to infer the relevance of documents from the clickthrough data. The inferred document relevance is potentially useful in evaluating the Web retrieval systems. In practice, it generally requires to acquire the accurate evaluation results within minimal users' query submissions. This problem is important for speeding up search engine development and evaluation cycle and acquiring reliable evaluation results on tail queries. In this paper, we propose a *reordering framework* for *efficient evaluation problem* in the context of clickthrough based Web retrieval evaluation. The main idea is to move up the documents that contribute more for the evaluation task. In this framework, we propose four intuitions and formulate them as an optimization problem. Both user study and TREC data based experiments validate that the reordering framework results in much fewer query submissions to get accurate evaluation results with only a little harm to the users' utility.

Categories and Subject Descriptors

H.3.3 [**Information Systems**]: Information Search and Retrieval

General Terms

Algorithms, Experimentation

Keywords

Clickthrough Data, Evaluation, Click Model

1. INTRODUCTION

Evaluation of Web retrieval systems is critical for improving search techniques. So far, the dominant method for evaluation has been the Cranfield evaluation method. However, it may be not so fit for evaluating the Web retrieval systems due to two reasons: 1) judgments become extremely expensive for large and dynamic Web content and variant information needs and 2) it is very difficult for the assessors to understand the needs behind the queries.

It is a promising direction to automatically evaluate Web retrieval systems by using clickthrough data from users. Click models [9, 5, 8] have been validated to be effective to estimate the documents' relevance from the clickthrough data without human judges' effort. One potential application of click models is to evaluate the query-specific retrieval performance with the estimated documents' relevance information. The Web retrieval systems' overall performance can be aggregated by the query-specific performance.

A quick solution [7] that utilizes click models to evaluate IR system on a query works as follows: First, it presents the unchanged ranking for all submissions of a query, and then it can collect the clicks from the users. With these clickthrough data, a click model can be utilized to infer the documents' relevance. The inferred relevance can be considered as an extended graded relevance score, and a graded relevance based IR metrics (such as DCG[12] and RBP[16]) can be used to measure the retrieval system's performance.

However, there are two drawbacks of this quick solution: 1) It is difficult to get reliable evaluation result on tail queries. Besides the popular queries, the performance on tail queries are extremely important for the search engines due to long tail phenomenon [2]. Since a tail query is submitted infrequently, the retrieved documents, especially those ranked lowly, are seldom examined, leading to unreliable relevance estimation about them. Thus the evaluation results based on the unreliable inferred relevance may be questionable. 2) Even for the frequently submitted queries, it may take a long period to collect enough relevance information for the reliable evaluation result, and this slows down the development and evaluation cycle. Therefore, it needs a more efficient way to collect relevance information for evaluation.

In this paper, we propose to study the *efficient evaluation problem* in the context of evaluating Web retrieval systems with clickthrough data. It is to evaluate systems accurately with minimal number of query submissions. For efficient evaluation, it aims at collecting more valuable relevance information to reduce the number of submissions required for accurate evaluation. Generally, retrieved documents contribute differently to Web retrieval evaluation in two aspects. First, the contribution of a document depends on its rank in the result list. For example, a highly ranked document plays a more important role in determining the performance of a Web retrieval system than those documents with lower ranks; Second, with increasing collected clickthrough data, the benefit of collecting more information about a document would change. For example, if the relevance of a document is reliably acquired, it is not so interesting to continue collecting more relevance information about this document.

Therefore, we can selectively collect the relevance information from the documents with most contribution for evaluation.

In this paper, we propose a reordering documents framework to efficiently collect relevance information for Web retrieval evaluation. A key component in this framework is the *reordering function*, which determines how to present the retrieved documents. Generally, the design of reordering functions follows the intuitions of moving up the most contributing documents. However, the decisions based on various intuitions may be inconsistent. A big challenge in designing a reordering function is how these intuitions can be integrated together. To meet this challenge, we formulate these intuitions into an optimization problem. This optimization problem is solved approximately with a greedy algorithm.

The selection of reordering functions depends on the specific evaluation task. There are two important tasks in Web retrieval evaluation: First, given a Web retrieval system, an interesting problem is to measure its performance by some metrics (one-system evaluation task), and the score can be compared with other or future systems (on the same query set); Second, it is also interesting to compare the relative performance of two Web retrieval systems directly (two-system comparison task). In this paper, we propose reordering functions for these two tasks respectively.

To validate our framework, we conduct a user study and the TREC data based experiments. The user study verifies that our proposed reordering framework can collect relevance information more efficiently for evaluation with little harm to the users' utility. To further analyze the performance of the reordering functions on large dataset and more informative scenarios, we conduct a study with TREC data (the submitted runs and the corresponding relevance judgments). The basic experiment shows that the reordering functions generally evaluate much more efficiently than the baselines with the similar user utility. Additional experiments show that the reordering functions are also robust for the performance of the evaluated system, the measure selection and the user click model selection.

The contributions of this papers are:

1. We propose a document reordering framework to solve the *efficient evaluation problem* in the context of Web retrieval evaluation using clickthrough data.
2. We propose four intuitions that can help collecting relevance information more efficiently for evaluation.
3. We integrate these intuitions in an optimization formulation and propose some reordering functions based on the intuitions.
4. We run both real user study and TREC data based experiments to test the proposed method, and find it is very efficient to acquire accurate evaluation results and little harm to the users' utility.

2. RELATED WORK

2.1 IR Evaluation

As a central research topic in Web retrieval, evaluation has been studied extensively. Web retrieval evaluation generally follows the Cranfield paradigm, using a gold standard test collection to evaluate retrieval systems with common retrieval performance measures such as MAP and nDCG [12]. In the context of Cranfield paradigm evaluation, some algorithms have been proposed for reducing the judges' effort, while keeping the evaluation results reliable. Yilmaz et al. [20] proposed to sample some documents for judgment and Carterette et al. [3] proposed to select documents that can distinguish systems best for judgment. We use the similar idea that focus on collecting relevance information of the most contributed documents. However, in the context of clickthrough based evaluation, we cannot ask the assessors to directly judge a document, but can just present a ranked document list to collect relevance information.

Many studies have attempted to leverage implicit feedback information such as clickthroughs to evaluate Web retrieval systems. There are two main categories of methods based on "absolute metric" and "relative comparison test", respectively. In the first category, it predicts the absolute performance of a single Web retrieval system. It is either by inferring absolute relevance of retrieved documents from clickthrough data and then calculating the score for some traditional measures [4, 7], or by some new measures defined on the clickthrough pattern directly [19]. The methods of the second category [13, 18] attempt to compare two systems by leveraging clickthroughs. In this framework, [21] proposed a method to learn powerful test statistics for more efficiently comparing two retrieval systems. Our proposed method is different from [21] that we focus on query-specific evaluation and we can collect relevance information for efficiently estimating absolute metric score and relative comparison adaptively.

2.2 Clickthrough Data Modeling

A fundamental problem of using clickthrough data is that the clicking can not be mapped to relevance directly; for example, it was found that a user's clickthroughs have bias [14]. Some works [14, 1, 6] extract preference relationship between document pairs from query submissions and their corresponding clickthroughs. Radlinski and Joachims [17] proposed a method to actively collect preference relationship between documents by reordering the presented list. In this paper, we also propose a reordering method, but for retrieval evaluation purpose.

Recently, some click models have been proposed to provide a principled approach to infer the document relevance from clickthrough data [9, 5, 8]. These methods model the documents' relevance, user behaviors and their relations in a probability directed graph model. They generally follow some hypotheses such as examination hypothesis (a document is clicked only if its snippet has been examined) and cascade hypothesis (the users examine the snippets in the up-down manner). Based on the clicking information of some sessions about one query, it can infer the distribution of documents' relevance to the corresponding query. Dupret et al. [7] also used click model to infer document relevance for retrieval system evaluation. However, to the best of our knowledge, there has been no work aiming at efficiently collecting document relevance for Web retrieval evaluation purpose based on these click models.

3. EFFICIENT EVALUATION WITH CLICKTHROUGH DATA

The users' click behaviors provide relevance information for the examined documents, and such information can potentially help us to evaluate the retrieval systems. Generally, the clickthrough is very valuable but sparse, so it needs a method to make good use of these clickthrough data to get a reliable evaluation result efficiently, especially for the tail queries. There are generally two styles of Web retrieval evaluation: one-system evaluation and two-system comparison. In both tasks, we expect a method to efficiently collect relevance information to get accuracy results.

For one-system evaluation, it measures the performance of each systems by a score, and then these systems can be compared by their scores. This methodology is commonly used, especially in the test collection based evaluation (like TREC). In this methodology, a key problem is how to predict the absolute performance score of a retrieval system. Given a ranked list and the manual relevance judgments, it usually employs a metric such as MAP and DCG to calculate the score. In the context of evaluation based on clickthrough data, we need to efficiently collect relevance information for reliably predicting a retrieval system's performance. We define *efficient one-system evaluation* problem as follows.

PROBLEM 1. *(Efficient One-system Evaluation Problem): Given a ranked list A and an IR metric S, the efficient one-system evaluation problem is to collect relevance information for predicting A's S score accurately within minimal number of query submissions.*

For two-system comparison, it compares two Web retrieval systems directly. For example, a new invented ranking algorithm is supposed to be compared with the existing algorithms to check whether it can outperform and replace them. They can be compared by the absolute performance scores, but for direct comparison purpose, it usually can be done more efficiently. We define two-system comparison problem as follows.

PROBLEM 2. *(Efficient Two-system Comparison Problem): Given two ranked list A, B and an IR metric S, the efficient two-system comparison problem is to collect relevance information for telling the S based comparison result between A and B accurately within minimal number of query submissions.*

4. REORDERING FUNCTIONS

For efficient evaluation, it is supposed to collect more valuable relevance information at each query submission to reduce the number of submissions needed for accurate evaluation. Generally, retrieved documents contribute differently for evaluating Web retrieval systems, so we can select to collect the relevance information about those most contributed (valuable) documents. Intuitively, we can move them up so that they are more likely to be examined. We study the problem of how to reorder the retrieved documents for more efficiently collecting relevance information for Web retrieval evaluation.

4.1 Framework and Terminology

The reordering function attempts to interact with the retrieval systems and the users for more efficiently collecting relevance information for evaluation. It works as follows:

1. For a query q, a *search engine* returns the ranked document list A.

2. For a query submission by a *user*, a *reordering function* determines the new ranked document list l^* and presents the user the corresponding *query impression* (a ranked list of documents' snippet, URL, etc., following the terminology of Guo et al. [9]), based on the original ranked list and the clickthrough history about the query q.

3. The user examines the *query impression* and clicks some documents (and read the content of document), and the *clicks* (a subset of the ranked list of documents) on this *query impression* is recorded.

Table 1: Terminology

d_i	A retrieved document with identifier i
$\mathring{R}_i$	d_i's actual relevance
R_i	d_i's inferred relevance
E_i	Whether d_i is examined or not
C_i	Whether d_i is clicked or not
A, B	Retrieved ranked lists
A_i, B_i	d_i's rank in list A, B
S	an IR evaluation metric
l, l^*	a reordered list of the retrieval documents

4. It updates the each document's inferred relevance to query q and utilize them for evaluation with a metric S.

5. repeat 2-4 for each submission of the query q

This procedure can be extended to reorder the documents retrieved by two search engines A and B, and thus these two systems can be compared by the collected relevance information. The terminology is summarized in Table 1 briefly.

4.2 Intuitions

The main idea of reordering framework is to move up the documents that are more valuable for evaluation, so that they have larger chance to be examined. In this section, we would detail four intuitions that affect the benefit of a document being examined: relevance uncertainty reduction, document's absolute rank, document's rank difference in two lists, and relevance level for more examination. (In this paper, the "benefit" of a document being examined or of presenting a list are both discussed in terms of the contribution to evaluation)

1. Relevance Uncertainty Reduction. The benefit of a document being examined is affected by its relevance uncertainty reduction. The uncertainty of document relevance is generally reduced when it is examined, but the reductions for documents are different. For example, if we have been very confident about the relevance of a document, it may provide little relevance information by further examining this document. Therefore, it is a good choice to move up the document with large relevance uncertainty reduction.

2. Document Rank. A document's rank affects the benefit of the document being examined. The highly ranked documents usually contribute more to the overall performance score of a retrieval system. Most IR metrics model this rank weight in their formulas. For example, in (the most commonly used version of) *DCG* , the document at rank k can be weighted as $\frac{1}{log_2(k+1)}$. Thus it generally requires to infer relevance of highly ranked document more accurately. With this intuition, it is supposed to keep the original ranking, i.e., keep the document ranked highly in the original list still ranked highly.

3. Document Rank Difference. In the context of comparing two systems, retrieved documents have different effect on distinguishing two systems. For example, if a document is ranked at rank 1 by system A and is ranked 100 by another system B, its relevance information is very helpful to distinguish these two systems. On the contrary, collecting relevance information of a document that is ranked at the same positions by two systems may be not so interesting. Therefore, in addressing the comparison problem, it is supposed to move up the documents that are ranked differently. Carterette et al. [3] used the similar idea for retrieval system comparison, but in the context of constructing minimal test collections for Cranfield paradigm evaluation.

4. More Examination. It can collect more relevance information if encouraging the users to examine deeper. Document relevance information can be collected only if the document is examined, so we can collect more information if the users examine more documents. The users' examination persistence relies on the relevance of the examined documents. The users would generally stop examining when their information need has been satisfied by examining highly relevant documents. To encourage the users to examine deeper, one possible way is to delay the satisfaction by moving the relevant documents down. One concern of using this strategy is that it obviously harms the users' utility. We will carefully test its effect on users' utility and evaluation efficiency, and determine whether it should be used.

These four intuitions are obviously useful for more efficiently collecting relevance information, but it is a challenge to integrate them together into one reordering function. Specifically, they are not consistent to each other well. For example, following intuition 4 requires to rank relevant document lower, but intuition 2 tell us to keep the original ranking, which generally ranks a relevant document highly. We will define the benefit of a document being examined with a *document weight function*, and formulate the document reordering into an optimization problem.

4.3 Formulation

The *efficient evaluation problem* is to find a method that can get accurate absolute or relative metric score of retrieval systems. In the reordering framework, we can estimate documents' relevance distribution. The overall metric score is integrated by relevance of documents in the ranking, so we can also estimate its distribution. Intuitively, the metric score is more reliable once the estimated distribution has a small variance. For each query submission, we would present the retrieved documents in an order so that the expected variance of performance metric score can be maximally reduced, i.e.,

$$l^* = \arg\max_{l} V(S|h) - V(S|l,h) \tag{1}$$

where l is a presented document list, S is the absolute metric score for one ranked list or metric score difference between two lists (e.g., DCG or ΔDCG, etc.), and h is the click-through history about the specific query q. $V(S|h)$ is the variance of the metric score S based on the existing click-through history h, and $V(S|l,h)$ is the expected variance of the metric score S based on the history h and the relevance information newly collected from the clicks on the presented list l.

We have discussed four intuitions that are potentially helpful for *efficient evaluation problem*. In this section, we will integrate them in the formulation of maximizing performance score variance reduction.

4.3.1 Relevance Uncertainty Reduction

The uncertainty of the metric score ($V(S)$) is determined by the uncertainty of the documents' relevance estimation ($V(R_i)$), so a document is valuable if its uncertainty can be largely reduced by a user's examination. We can formulate the inferred relevance variance reduction from examining a document d_i as follows:

$$\Delta V(R_i) = P(C_i = 1|\hat{R}_i)\Delta_1 V(R_i) + P(C_i = 0|\hat{R}_i)\Delta_0 V(R_i) \tag{2}$$

where R_i is the inferred relevance and $\hat{R}_i$ is the actual relevance of d_i; $P(C_i = 1|\hat{R}_i)$ and $P(C_i = 0|\hat{R}_i)$ are its clicked and skipped probability given the actual relevance level $\hat{R}_i$ respectively. In most click models, it assumes that the clicking probability equals to the actual relevance level, i.e., $P(C_i = 1|\hat{R}_i = r) = r$ [9, 10]. Similarly, we use this linear translation assumption between click rate and relevance, and the real relevance can also be inferred from the click rate if other translation function is defined. $\Delta_1 V(R_i)$ and $\Delta_0 V(R_i)$ are variance reduction for clicking and skipping cases respectively. If we observe that d_i is clicked in the next query submission, the click model can update the relevance distribution for d_i and the new variance (denoted as $V(R_i|C_i = 1, E_i = 1)$) is available, so $\Delta_1 V(R_i)$ can be defined by the variance difference. The inferred relevance distribution can be usually formulated as a polynomial [9], so the variance can be calculated by numerical integration with multiple bins. $\Delta_0 V(R_i)$ can be defined in the similar way for the skipping case. Formally, they are defined as:

$$\Delta_1 V(R_i) = V(R_i) - V(R_i|C_i = 1, E_i = 1)$$
$$\Delta_0 V(R_1) = V(R_i) - V(R_i|C_i = 0, E_i = 1)$$

Unfortunately, the actual relevance level $\hat{R}_i$ is unknown, so we approximate it with a document weight function (denoted as w_1) by substituting the actual relevance with the best of our current knowledge, i.e., expected value of inferred relevance distribution (denoted as $\bar{R}_i$). This document weight can reflect the benefit from examining this document in the aspect of document relevance uncertainty reduction.

$$w_1(d_i) = P(C_i = 1|\bar{R}_i)\Delta_1 V(R_i) + P(C_i = 0|\bar{R}_i)\Delta_0 V(R_i) \tag{3}$$

4.3.2 Document Rank

For one-system evaluation problem, the benefit of a document being examined also depends on the document's rank. A higher ranked documents affects the metric score more. The rank effect differs for measures. In this paper, we take DCG as example ($S = DCG$). DCG measures the performance of a ranked list with graded relevance judgments [12]. Though $nDCG$ is more commonly used in test collection based evaluation, we use its unnormalized version for two reasons: 1) the total number of relevant documents in real Web is usually dynamic and unknown, and 2) the precision-based metrics can reflect users' utility well in Web search [11, 16]. Since the inferred relevance is a real value, we extend DCG to handle relevance of real value from 0 to 1. Thus the DCG of a ranked list A can be formulated as

$$DCG_A = \sum_{d_i \in A} \frac{\hat{R}_i}{\log_2(A_i + 1)}$$

Click models can infer a distribution of document relevance, so the expected value and variance of the DCG distribution can be expressed as (assuming the relevance between retrieved documents are independent):

$$E(DCG_A) = \sum_{d_i \in A} \frac{E(R_i)}{\log_2(A_i + 1)}$$
$$V(DCG_A) = \sum_{d_i \in A} \frac{V(R_i)}{\log_2^2(A_i + 1)}$$

In one-system evaluation problem, we can reduce the uncertainty of the absolute metrics score. The contribution of each document does not only depend on its variance reduction but also its original rank. The weight of document at rank k is $1/\log_2^2(k+1)$. Combining both intuition 1 and 2, the benefit of examining document d_i (denoted as $w_{1,2}$) is:

$$w_{1,2}(d_i) = \frac{w_1(d_i)}{\log_2^2(A_i+1)} \quad (4)$$

4.3.3 Document Rank Difference

For two-system comparison problem, the benefit a document being examined also relies on the relative rank difference between these two ranked lists. The documents ranked more differently can distinguish systems better. Again, we take difference between DCGs as example ($S = \Delta DCG$). The expected value and variance of DCG score difference from two ranked lists A and B can be expressed as:

$$E(\Delta DCG_{A,B}) = \sum_{d_i \in A \cup B} (W_A(d_i) - W_B(d_i))E(R_i)$$

$$V(\Delta DCG_{A,B}) = \sum_{d_i \in A \cup B} (W_A(d_i) - W_B(d_i))^2 V(R_i)$$

$$W_L(i) = \begin{cases} \frac{1}{\log_2(L_i+1)} & \text{if } d_i \in L \cdot \\ 0 & \text{otherwise} \end{cases}$$

The positive $E(\Delta DCG_{A,B})$ value indicates that the expected DCG score of list A is higher than that of list B, while negative value indicates that the expected DCG score of list B is higher. We expect to reduce the uncertainty of ΔDCG value, so one document's contribution to the overall performance difference can be formulated as:

$$w_{1,3}(d_i) = (W_A(d_i) - W_B(d_i))^2 w_1(d_i) \quad (5)$$

It is denoted as $w_{1,3}$ for using intuition 1 and 3.

The users are likely to examine the highly ranked documents, so it can collect more valuable relevance information by presenting the more valuable documents higher. We can sort the documents according to their weight of $w_{1,2}$ (Equation 4) for one-system evaluation and $w_{1,3}$ (Equation 5) for two-system comparison. These two reordering functions are denoted as $rf(1,2)$ and $rf(1,3)$ respectively (rf is short for *reordering function*).

4.3.4 More Examination

The benefit of presenting a list can be calculated by aggregating the benefit of the documents in the list being examined, so we expect the users to examine more documents. In the DCG and ΔDCG formulation, the reduction of metric uncertainty is equal to the sum of rank-weighted document relevance uncertainty reduction, so we can define *list benefit* by summing up the benefit of documents a user has examined.

Assuming the ranked list is $(d_1, \ldots, d_n)$, the *list benefit function* $w(d_1, \ldots, d_n)$ can be defined as:

$$w(d_1, \ldots, d_n) = \sum_{i \in \{1,\ldots,n\}} P(e_i = 1) w^*(d_i)$$

where w^* is a *document benefit function* (can be $w_{1,2}$ or $w_{1,3}$, for one-system evaluation and two-system comparison problem respectively). Generally, the users always examine the first ranked document, but the probability of examining deeper documents depends on the relevance of documents ranked above. The above document relevance factor can be plugged in the *list benefit function*.

$$w(d_1, \ldots, d_n) = w^*(d_1) + P(E_2 = 1|\hat{R}_1) w(d_2, \ldots, d_n)$$

Where $P(E_2 = 1|\hat{R}_1)$ is the probability of continuing examining document d_2 given actual relevance $\hat{R}_1$. Again, we don't know the actual relevance $\hat{R}_1$, so we replace it with expected value of d_1's relevance distribution.

$$w(d_1, \ldots, d_n) = w^*(d_1) + P(E_2 = 1|\bar{R}_1) w(d_2, \ldots, d_n) \quad (6)$$

Obviously, an optimal presented document list is to maximize the *list benefit function*. In this way, we have aggregate all intuitions in this optimization framework. Unfortunately, this problem is intractable. We approximate it by a greedy algorithm: at each step, we assign each document a weight that can approximately reflect the benefit of selecting this document and append the document with the largest weight to the end of the presented list. As suggested by Equation 6, the benefit of selecting a document d_i is composed by two parts: the benefit from the document itself ($w^*(d_i)$, can be $w_{1,2}$ or $w_{1,3}$) and the benefit from documents ranked below. The second part can be obtained by multiplying probability of continuing examining at current document and the expected benefit of examining the list below. However, the benefit from the below list is unknown since the below list has not determined when selecting the current document. We approximate the benefit of examining below by the maximal document benefit of the unselected documents. Thus, the weight of a document d_i in an unselected document set D can be formulated as:

$$w(d_i) = w^*(d_i) + P(E_{i+1}|\bar{R}_i) \max_{\substack{d_j \in D \\ i \neq j}} w^*(d_j) \quad (7)$$

Here the probability of examination next document is also be defined in the click model (e.g., the click chain model defines $P(E_{i+1}|R_i) = \alpha_2 R_i + \alpha_3(1 - R_i)$. In this way, the document weight $w(d_i)$ can be denoted as $w_{1,2,4}$ (when $w^* = w_{1,2}$ in Equation 7) and $w_{1,3,4}$ (when $w^* = w_{1,3}$ in Equation 7). With the weight function, the greedy algorithm is presented in Algorithm 1. We select the maximal weighted document from the unselected document set, append it to the presented list, until all documents have been selected or the length of the presented list is enough. This version of reordering functions with two different *document benefit function* ($w_{1,2,4}$ and $w_{1,3,4}$) are denoted as $rf(1,2,4)$ and $rf(1,3,4)$ respectively, for both using intuition 4. Since some click models have online version [9, 10], and the reordering function is fast ($O(n)$ for $rf(1,2)$ and $rf(1,3)$, and $O(n^2)$ for $rf(1,2,4)$ and $rf(1,3,4)$), it can work well online.

Input: Document set $D = \{d_1, \ldots, d_n\}$, list length n
Output: Reordered Ranked List l
begin
  $l = list()$
  while $|D| > 0$ **do**
    $\hat{d} = \arg\max_{d_i \in D} w(d_i)$
    l.append($\hat{d}$)
    $D = D - \{\hat{d}\}$
  end
  return l
end

Algorithm 1: Reordering Algorithm

5. PRELIMINARY USER STUDY

We conducted a user study experiment and a simulation based experiment to verify the usefulness of document reordering framework. In this section, we introduce the user study experiment.

5.1 Experiment Setup

The user study is designed to resemble the common search engine usage. We recruit 50 college students. The users were asked to answer 10 questions with the help of our system. These questions contain both open-information questions (with many answers) and close-information questions (with only one answer) and vary in difficulty and topic. For each question, we designed a query, submitted it to two commercial Web search engines and collected the top 10 results from both engines. The questions and queries were designed according to the guideline that: (1) at least one answer can be found in the results of each search engine; and (2) the performance of these two search engines can be distinguished (relative DCG score difference is larger than 0.1).

In the user study, a user was presented with a question following ten ranked results in a page. The ten presented results are either from one single commercial search engine or interleaved from the two commercial search engines. The snippet of a document is generated by the search engine which returned the corresponding document. In the interleaving case, if these two search engines return an identical document (with the same URL), the snippet is randomly selected from those two corresponding snippets. The user was asked to answer this question with the help of the listed results and she can click the link for browsing the original document. She can continue to the next question once she can answer current question or she found that the presented results can not answer the current question. Since our study aims at the efficient query-specific Web retrieval evaluation, the experimental user interface is a little different from those real search engines that the users can not reformulate their queries for an information need.

We implemented five reordering functions in our user study system: three of them are for one-system evaluation task, and two of them are for two-system comparison task. For one-system evaluation task, the baseline function is *ebase* (short for evaluation baseline) presents the results A unchanged. We tested two reordering functions $rf(1,2)$ and $rf(1,2,4)$ in section 4.3 to reorder the documents from A. For two-system comparison task, the baseline function (*cbase*, short for comparison baseline) and the tested reordering function is $rf(1,3,4)$. *cbase* presents all-A for half query submissions and all-B for other half, e.g., presents A at $2i^{th}$ query submission and another at $(2i+1)^{th}$ query submission (which list was presented at $2i^{th}$ submission is randomly determined for each query). The baselines and tested reordering functions are summarized in Table 2 (it also contains two other reordering functions *balance* and $rf(1,3)$ for two-system comparison task, used in TREC based experiments). Each user submitted a query once, so we can collect 50 submissions for each query. There are 5 tested reordering functions, so each reordering function receives (50 query submissions/5 functions) = 10 submissions of each query. Within the 10 questions each user answers, every reordering function would provide the results of 2 questions to avoid the user bias.

The proposed reordering functions need a click model to estimate the relevance distribution of the retrieved documents. In this experiments, we adopted click chain model [9], which is a state-of-art Bayesian click model for relevance inference. In the model, the parameters were learned from $1M$ sampled click logs of a commercial search engine: $\alpha_1 = 0.97, \alpha_2 = 0.34, \alpha_3 = 0.23$.

5.2 Performance Metrics

The performance of a reordering function can be measured in two dimensions: the evaluation efficiency and the users' utility. For evaluation, as defined in *efficient evaluation problem*, a "good" reordering function is supposed to get the accurate evaluation result with minimal number of query submissions. On the other hand, as discussed in Section 4, the reordering function (especially with intuition 4 – *more examination intuition*) moves up the documents ranked lower by a retrieval system, so it may harm the users' utility. A search engine usually uses only a small volume of traffic for evaluation. Nevertheless, a good reordering function should not hurt the users' utility too much. Therefore, we also need to measure the users' utility of using a reordering function.

Table 2: Reordering Functions

Type	Function	Interpretation
One-system Evaluation	*ebase*	presenting A
	$rf(1,2)$	using intuition 1, 2
	$rf(1,2,4)$	using intuition 1, 2, 4
Two-system Comparison	*cbase*	presenting A, B alternatively
	balance	balanced strategy [13]
	$rf(1,3)$	using intuition 1, 3
	$rf(1,3,4)$	using intuition 1, 3, 4

In our experiment, we asked three assessors to judge of the results' relevance. They judged the results by assigning each of them a relevance level between 0 and 5. We find that the they agree to each other very well (the disagreement is 0.11, according to the disagreement for scalar judgment defined in [15]), and we use the average score as the gold relevance level. The search engine's real performance on a query can be measured by DCG based on the actual relevance judgments (denoted as $\hat{DCG}$).

Evaluation Efficiency. A more efficient evaluation method can get more accurate result with same number of query submissions. So we use evaluation accuracy at N submissions of a query q to measure the efficiency of an evaluation method. The accuracy can be measured by comparing real metric score (denoted as $\hat{DCG}$) calculated by manual judgment and the inferred metric score (denoted as DCG) by estimated document relevance.

Since $\hat{DCG}$ and DCG are of the different value scales, we linearly transform estimated DCG using $DCG = aDCG + b$. For the two-system comparison task, such transformation would not change the comparison result, because it affects two systems scores in the same way. In the one-system evaluation task, though it tries to get an absolute score for a retrieval system, the score is also used for comparing with the score of other or future systems. In conclusion, the transformation can rescale the score values, but it will not change the evaluation result.

For one-system evaluation task, we expect to predict the metric score of a retrieval system. If the performance score from inferred relevance is close to the real performance score, it indicates that the evaluation is accurate. The closeness can be measured by *relative difference* (denoted as $rdiff$) between $\hat{DCG}$ and DCG (see Equation 8). The linear transformation parameters can affect the $rdiff$ value. For each reordering function, we set the parameters a and b to minimize the average relative difference on all queries.

$$rdiff_A = \frac{|DCG_A - \hat{DCG}_A|}{\hat{DCG}_A} \quad (8)$$

For two-system comparison task, we check the correctness of comparison between two retrieval systems. It raises an

Table 3: User Study Results

	Func.	Relative Diff.	Utility
Eval.	cbase	0.34	1.00
	rf(1,2)	**0.14(−58.8%)**	0.95(−5%)
	rf(1,2,4)	0.18(−47.1%)	0.92(−8%)
	Func.	**Error Ratio**	**Utility**
Comp.	cbase	0.30	1.00
	rf(1,3,4)	**0.00(−100.0%)**	0.89(−11%)

error when the sign symbol of the predicted $\Delta DCG_{A,B}$ does not conform to that of real $\Delta D\hat{C}G_{A,B}$, i.e., $\Delta DCG_{A,B} \cdot \Delta D\hat{C}G_{A,B} < 0$. They can be integrated to get the *error ratio* by comparing the predicted comparison results and real comparison results, i.e.,

$$\textit{error ratio} = \frac{\sum_{(A,B)} \mathbf{1}(\Delta DCG_{A,B} \cdot \Delta D\hat{C}G_{A,B} < 0)}{\sum_{(A,B)} 1} \quad (9)$$

where **1** is an indicative function, returning 1 if the input is true and 0 otherwise.

Users' Utility. It is to measure how the users' utility affected by using a reordering function, so we compare the users' utility from the reordered list and that from original list. In our experiment, we measure the users' utility by the relative *DCG* score. For one-system evaluation (for *A*), the users' utility is defined as:

$$\text{Utility} = \frac{\overline{D\hat{C}G_L}}{D\hat{C}G_A} \quad (10)$$

where $\overline{D\hat{C}G_L}$ is the average of real *DCG* value for reordered lists for the query submissions, and $D\hat{C}G_A$ is the real *DCG* score for original retrieved result *A*. For two-system comparison (between *A* and *B*), the users' utility is defined as the ratio between average *DCG* score of reordered lists and average *DCG* score of two compared lists:

$$\text{Utility} = \frac{2\overline{D\hat{C}G_L}}{D\hat{C}G_A + D\hat{C}G_B} \quad (11)$$

5.3 Results

The results from the user study is presented in Table 3. In the table, row 2-4 (*ebase*, $rf(1,2)$ and $rf(1,2,4)$) show the results for one-system evaluation and row 5-6 (*cbase* and $rf(1,3,4)$) show the results for two-system comparison. The second column is the accuracy results: *relative difference* for one-system evaluation and *error ratio* for two-system comparison. The third column is the users' utility results (relative utility to that from original list(s)). The numbers in the brackets are the relative percentage difference compared that of baselines.

In the one-system evaluation results, we can find that the both $rf(1,2)$ and $rf(1,2,4)$ perform much more efficiently than *ebase*. In this experiment, we find that $rf(1,2)$ performs even better than $rf(1,2,4)$, though the improvement is not so obvious on such small dataset. For users' utility, both two reordering functions decrease users' utility, and $rf(1,2)$ harms much less than $rf(1,2,4)$.

In the two-system comparison results, we find that $rf(1,3,4)$ can distinguish two search engines accurately on all questions but *cbase* can distinguish accurately on only 7 of the 10 questions, and the reordering function has little harm to the users' utility.

6. EXPERIMENTS ON TREC DATASET

The preliminary user study shows that reordering functions can more efficiently collect relevance information for Web retrieval evaluation. We further deploy a large scale experiment on the TREC dataset, which contains various types of queries, system retrieval results (runs) and the relevance judgments. We can simulate a user's behavior on the retrieved results of TREC submitted runs, and analyze the performance of reordering functions in multiple scenarios according to retrieval result quality, system similarity, etc.

6.1 Basic Experiment

In the experiment, we need two types of data: 1) the queries, corresponding retrieval results and the relevance judgments, and 2) users' examination and click behavior.

In our experiment, we use the queries, results and judgments of TREC terabyte06 dataset. It contains 50 queries (801-850), 71 runs' results, and three-way scale judgments. In addition, we use the same click chain model [9] as that used in the user study to simulate the users' behavior. Users' behavior is also affected by the documents' relevance. In our basic experiments, we present the results with the empirical setting of $R = 0.9$ for highly relevant documents, $R = 0.6$ for relevant documents, and $R = 0.2$ for non-relevant documents.

The experiment works as follows: 1) For a simulated query submission, a reordering function determines the presented ranking of retrieved documents (from one or two runs); 2) The simulated users would examine and click on the presented results; 3) The estimated relevance information is updated based the collected clickthrough data. 4) The performance of the reordering function is measured by the utility from the presented ranking and the accuracy of the systems' estimated performance. We will reuse the metrics defined in section 5.2.

Besides the reordering functions tested in the user study, we also test *balance* and $rf(1,3)$ in the TREC based experiments (see Table 2). *balance* reordering function was proposed to compare two retrieval systems by Joachims [13], and Radlinski et al.[18] showed that it works better than the methods solely relying on the features of users' implicit feedback. $rf(1,3)$ uses intuition 1 and 3 for reordering the retrieved documents (see Section 4.3).

6.1.1 Results

We present the evaluation efficiency and users' utility results for one-system evaluation in Figure 1 and Figure 2 respectively.

In Figure 1, we find that both $rf(1,2)$ and $rf(1,2,4)$ are much more efficient than *ebase*. $rf(1,2,4)$ performs only a little better than $rf(1,2)$. *ebase* performs similarly as the reordering function at the first few query submissions, because all these functions emphasize the top ranked documents for the first few submissions. However, as the query submission number increases, the benefit of presenting the original ranked list becomes little, because we have collected enough relevance information about the top documents.

In Figure 2, we find that both $rf(1,2)$ and $rf(1,2,4)$ provide similar users' utility as *ebase* for the first few query submissions, and then the utility stays in a little worse level. Users' utility decreases only about 2% by $rf(1,2)$, and 3.5% by $rf(1,2,4)$. Since $rf(1,2)$ provides similar evaluation efficiency as $rf(1,2,4)$ but hurts users' utility much less, $rf(1,2)$ is supposed to be a better choice in practice. In the experiments below, we use $rf(1,2)$ only.

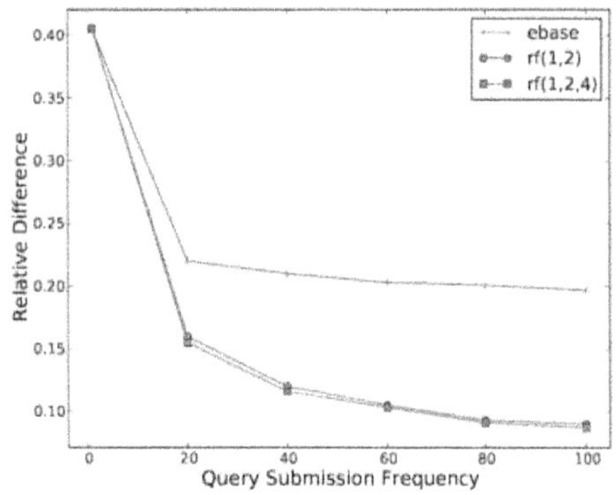

Figure 1: One-system Evaluation: Relative Difference

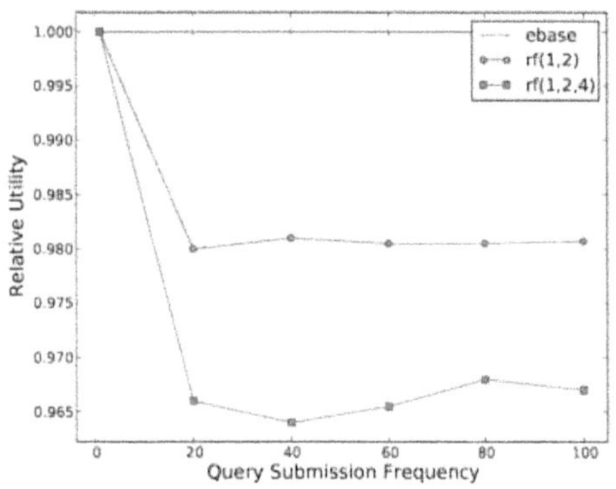

Figure 2: One-system Evaluation: Users' Utility

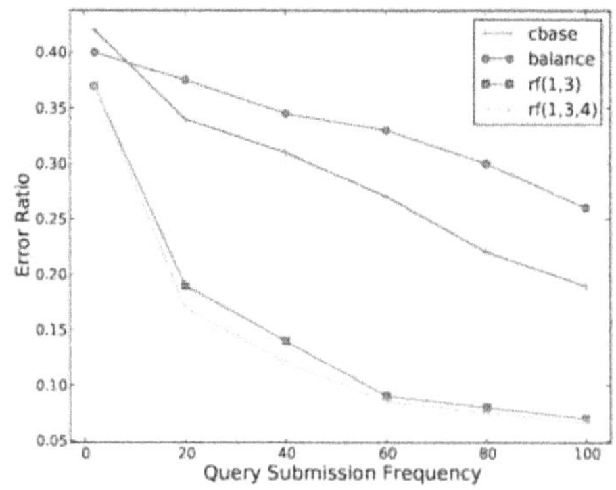

Figure 3: Two-system Comparison: Error Ratio

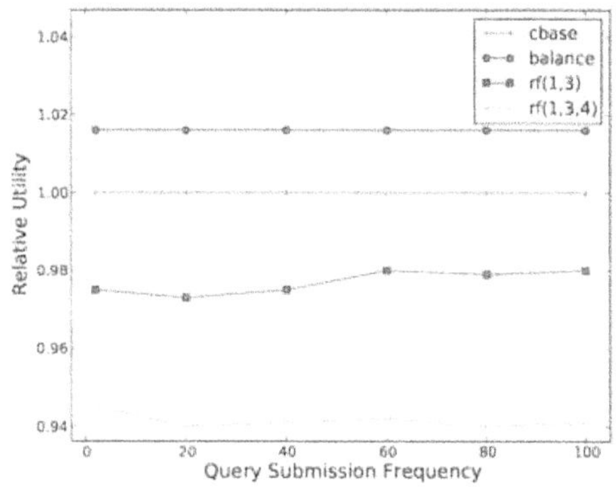

Figure 4: Two-system Comparison: Users' Utility

The accuracy and users' utility results for two-system comparison task is presented in Figure 3 and Figure 4 respectively.

In Figure 3, we find that $rf(1,3,4)$ works best for most cases, $rf(1,3)$ is only a little worse than $rf(1,3,4)$, and both reordering functions work better than the two baselines. *balance* performs better than *cbase* for first few submissions, because it more emphasizes the highly ranked documents. This result is consistent with Radlinski et al.[18]. [18] reported that *balance* strategy can reflect the retrieval systems' performance better than absolute user feedback across the queries. Their experiments were based on the arXiv.org query log, in which each query string should be submitted very few on average. Our results also show that *balance* performs not so well when the query submissions are more because it only collects the top ranked documents' information.

Figure 4 also shows that *balance* can provide a better users' utility than the average of two lists, because each list may miss some relevant documents at the top, but the other contains. $rf(1,3)$ decreases utility by about 2%, and $rf(1,3,4)$ decrease by about 6%. The experimental results suggest that *balance* is a good strategy for better users' utility, and $rf(1,3)$ can evaluate efficiently with little harm.

In conclusion, our findings from the basic experiment are as follows: 1) the reordering functions perform much efficiently than the baselines for both one-system evaluation and two-system comparison task; 2) When using intuition 4, it hurts the users' utility more but the efficiency improvement is not so much, so it suggests to use $rf(1,2)$ for one-system evaluation and $rf(1,3)$ for two-system comparison.

6.2 Multiple Scenarios

The above experimental results show that the proposed reordering functions can perform well on average. The usefulness of the reordering functions may be affected by some other factors such as performance of the evaluated retrieval systems, the measure used for evaluation and click model that employed in the reordering functions. In this section, we explore how these factors affect the efficiency and users' utility of the reordering functions.

6.2.1 Effect of Retrieval Systems' Performance

It would be more informative and useful to compare the performance of reordering functions in various scenarios, such as bad vs. good retrieval performance, and comparing two systems that differ much vs. comparing two similar systems. Thus each such possible scenario should be tested separately to understand the relative strength and weakness of the reordering functions. The following are the different scenarios that we would test in our experiments:

bad vs. good retrieval performance: This can be simulated by controlling the (average) metric (*DCG* is used) score of the ranked list(s).

Comparison of systems with similar or different retrieval performance: This can be simulated by regulating the relative difference in retrieval performance. In

Table 4: Summary of Validation Scenarios

Scenarios	Variation	Parameter Setting
Retrieval	Good	$DCG > 1.5$
Performance	Bad	$DCG \leq 1.5$
System	High	$RDCG \leq 0.3$
Similarity	Low	$RDCG > 0.3$

Table 5: One-system Evaluation: Scenarios

Sys. Perf.	Q. Freq.	Rel. Diff. ebase	Rel. Diff. rf(1,2)	Utility rf(1,2)
Good	20	0.12	0.07(−41.7%)	−2.2%
	100	0.08	0.03(−62.5%)	−2.0%
Bad	20	0.49	0.37(−24.5%)	−1.7%
	100	0.45	0.19(−47.8%)	−1.5%

the experiments, we use the relative difference of DCG score (denoted as $RDCG$, defined in Equation 12 to measure the performance difference, and this conforms to our intuition very well.

$$RDCG(A,B) = \frac{|DCG(A) - DCG(B)|}{\min(DCG(A), DCG(B))} \quad (12)$$

Variations of parameters and the corresponding scenarios are summarized in Table 4. The experimental results are presented in Table 5 and Table 6. The numbers in brackets of *error ratio* or *relative difference* column are relative percentage changes of these values compared to the baseline. In the utility column, the values are relative percentage change compared to the utility of original retrieval result(s).

Our findings are as follows: 1) the proposed reordering functions outperform the baselines in the presented scenarios; 2) Both one-system evaluation and two-system comparison are more difficult for those hard queries. For those queries, the relevant documents are not be highly ranked by the system, so it makes such relevant documents unlikely to be examined. The users' relative utility of reordering function on hard topics are higher. For those hard topics, the original list may rank the relevant documents lower, so the reordering function probably move up those documents and improve the users' utility; 3) The results indicate that two-system comparison problem is quite easy for those very different system pairs, which conforms to the intuition.

6.2.2 Effect of Measures

The inferred relevance information can be interpreted as graded relevance judgment by extending its value range from 0 to 1. We have studied DCG as an IR metric for evaluating retrieval systems. We would further study the effect of other measures.

Table 6: Two-system Comparison: Scenarios

Sys. Perf.	Perf Sim.	Q. Freq.	Err. Ratio cbase	Err. Ratio rf(1,3)	Utility rf(1,3)
Good	Low	20	0.22	0.14(−36.4%)	−2.5%
		100	0.10	0.05(−50.0%)	−2.0%
	High	20	0.08	0.02(−75.0%)	−1.8%
		100	0.02	0.00(−100%)	−1.5%
Bad	Low	20	0.42	0.20(−52.4%)	−8.2%
		100	0.25	0.07(−72.0%)	−8.5%
	High	20	0.18	0.10(−44.4%)	−3.5%
		100	0.05	0.01(−80.0%)	−3.0%

Table 7: One-system Evaluation: Measures

Measures	Q. Freq.	Rel. Diff. ebase	Rel. Diff. rf(1,2)	Utility rf(1,2)
RBP(0.6)	20	0.13	0.12(−7.7%)	−2.1%
	100	0.07	0.06(−14.3%)	−2.0%
RBP(0.95)	20	0.26	0.16(−38.5%)	−1.0%
	100	0.23	0.09(−60.9%)	−0.9%

Table 8: Two-system Comparison: Measures

Measures	Q. Freq.	Err. Ratio cbase	Err. Ratio rf(1,3)	Utility rf(1,3)
RBP(0.6)	20	0.32	0.27(−15.6%)	−2.0%
	100	0.18	0.14(−22.2%)	−2.0%
RBP(0.95)	20	0.33	0.13(−60.6%)	−2.0%
	100	0.20	0.06(−70.0%)	−2.2%

Besides DCG, there are also some other IR metrics based on graded relevance judgments. For example, RBP is a recently proposed graded relevance metric [16] expressed as Equation 13. RBP has no recall component and can adapt to different retrieval applications by adjusting the parameter p.

$$RBP = (1-p)\sum_i R_i \cdot p^{i-1} \quad (13)$$

We would test whether the reordering functions can perform well for predicting score of RBP. To adapt the reordering functions to RBP, we also need to replace the benefit function $w_{1,2}$ and $w_{1,3}$ with the new formulation $w'_{1,2}$ and $w'_{1,3}$, defined in Equation 14 and 15. The derivation is similar to that of DCG.

$$w'_{1,2}(d_i) = p^{2(A_i-1)}\Delta V(r_i) \quad (14)$$

$$w'_{1,3}(d_i) = (p^{A_i-1} - p^{B_i-1})^2 \Delta V(r_i) \quad (15)$$

We conduct two experiments, respectively setting p as 0.95 and 0.6, which have different effects on the ranks. The results are presented in Table 7 and 8 respectively. The results of $RBP(0.95)$ and those of DCG are very similar due to the similar rank weight of DCG and $RBP(0.95)$. However, the performance pattern of using $RBP(0.6)$ is quite different from that of using DCG and $RBP(0.95)$. With $RBP(0.6)$, it benefits less in using the proposed reordering functions compared to the baselines. The metric $RBP(0.6)$ weights very heavily on the top documents, so both the reordering functions and the baseline methods would keep the documents that highly ranked in the original list highly for the query submissions.

From the results, we find that the reordering functions work consistently well with different metrics (with parameter setting) used.

6.2.3 Effect of Click Models

In the reordering framework, a very important component is the click model. First, the document benefit is estimated based on the document relevance inferred by the click model; second, the inferred document relevance is utilized to predict the system performance score directly.

However, different users and their information needs may lead variant clicking behaviors. In practice, a click model used in a search engine may not match the real users' search behavior so well. In this section, we would check whether the proposed reordering functions are robust with a mis-

Table 9: One-system Evaluation: User Models

Click Model	Q. Freq.	Rel. Diff. ebase	Rel. Diff. rf(1,2)	Utility rf(1,2)
DCM	20	0.22	0.16(−27.3%)	−1.8%
	100	0.19	0.09(−52.6%)	−2.2%
CCM (0.97,0.5,0.15)	20	0.23	0.17(−26.1%)	−2.5%
	100	0.19	0.10(−47.4%)	−1.5%

Table 10: Two-system Comparison: User Models

Click Model	Q. Freq.	Err. Ratio cbase	Err. Ratio rf(1,3)	Utility rf(1,3)
DCM	20	0.36	0.16(−55.6%)	−3.0%
	100	0.21	0.06(−71.4%)	−1.9%
CCM (0.97,0.5,0.15)	20	0.34	0.15(−55.9%)	−2.0%
	100	0.19	0.06(−68.4%)	−1.8%

matched click model, i.e., the real users' behavior is more like model M_{user}, but we use a mismatched model $M_{reorder}$ in the reordering framework.

In the experiments, we still use the click chain model with parameters $\alpha_1 = 0.97, \alpha_2 = 0.34, \alpha_3 = 0.23$ to simulate the users' click (M_{user}) exactly same as that used in above experiments, but use another click model ($M_{reorder}$) in the reordering framework to infer the document relevance for reordering documents and evaluating system performance. We use DCM and CCM(0.97,0.5,0.15) as two tested click models ($M_{reorder}$). DCM's parameters are also learned from the same $1M$ sample of click logs. CCM's parameters are set as $\alpha_1 = 0.97, \alpha_2 = 0.5, \alpha_3 = 0.15$. The results from these two models are presented in Table 9 and 10. Comparing the results with the basic results, we find the metric scores are very similar, indicating that the reordering functions are robust with various click models.

7. CONCLUSION

In this paper, we propose a document reordering framework to solve the *efficient evaluation problem* in the context of Web retrieval evaluation based on clickthrough data. Four intuitions are proposed to speed up the relevance information collecting for evaluation purpose, and they are integrated together in an optimizing function. Both our user study and TREC based experiments validate that the reordering framework can efficiently collect relevance information for one-system evaluation and two-system comparison, with little harm to the users' utility. For the reordering functions, the experimental results suggest to use $rf(1,2)$ for one-system evaluation task and $rf(1,2,4)$ for two-system comparison task.

Acknowledgement

This work is supported by NSFC Grant (60933004, 70903008, 61073082) and HGJ Grant 2011ZX01042-001-001.

8. REFERENCES

[1] AGICHTEIN, E., BRILL, E., DUMAIS, S., AND RAGNO, R. Learning user interaction models for predicting web search result preferences. In *SIGIR '06*, pp. 3–10.

[2] BAEZA-YATES, R., GIONIS, A., JUNQUEIRA, F. P., MURDOCK, V., PLACHOURAS, V., AND SILVESTRI, F. Design trade-offs for search engine caching. *ACM Trans. Web 2*, 4 (2008), 1–28.

[3] CARTERETTE, B., ALLAN, J., AND SITARAMAN, R. Minimal test collections for retrieval evaluation. In *SIGIR '06*, pp. 268–275.

[4] CARTERETTE, B., AND JONES, R. Evaluating search engines by modeling the relationship between relevance and clicks. In *NIPS '07*.

[5] CHAPELLE, O., AND ZHANG, Y. A dynamic bayesian network click model for web search ranking. In *WWW '09*, pp. 1–10.

[6] DOU, Z., SONG, R., YUAN, X., AND WEN, J.-R. Are click-through data adequate for learning web search rankings? In *CIKM '08*, pp. 73–82.

[7] DUPRET, G., MURDOCK, V., AND PIWOWARSKI, B. Web search engine evaluation using clickthrough data and a user model. In *Query Log Analysis: Social And Technological Challenges. A workshop at WWW '07)*.

[8] DUPRET, G. E., AND PIWOWARSKI, B. A user browsing model to predict search engine click data from past observations. In *SIGIR '08*, pp. 331–338.

[9] GUO, F., LIU, C., KANNAN, A., MINKA, T., TAYLOR, M., WANG, Y.-M., AND FALOUTSOS, C. Click chain model in web search. In *WWW '09*, pp. 11–20.

[10] GUO, F., LIU, C., AND WANG, Y. M. Efficient multiple-click models in web search. In *WSDM '09*, pp. 124–131.

[11] HUFFMAN, S. B., AND HOCHSTER, M. How well does result relevance predict session satisfaction? In *SIGIR '07*, pp. 567–574.

[12] JÄRVELIN, K., AND KEKÄLÄINEN, J. Cumulated gain-based evaluation of ir techniques. *ACM Trans. Inf. Syst. 20*, 4 (2002), 422–446.

[13] JOACHIMS, T. Unbiased evaluation of retrieval quality using clickthrough data. In *SIGIR Workshop on Mathematical/Formal Methods in Information Retrieval* (2002).

[14] JOACHIMS, T., GRANKA, L., PAN, B., HEMBROOKE, H., RADLINSKI, F., AND GAY, G. Evaluating the accuracy of implicit feedback from clicks and query reformulations in web search. *ACM Trans. Inf. Syst. 25*, 2 (2007).

[15] MIZZARO, S. Measuring the agreement among relevance judges. In *MIRA '99*.

[16] MOFFAT, A., AND ZOBEL, J. Rank-biased precision for measurement of retrieval effectiveness. *ACM Trans. Inf. Syst. 27*, 1 (2008), 1–27.

[17] RADLINSKI, F., AND JOACHIMS, T. Active exploration for learning rankings from clickthrough data. In *KDD '07*, pp. 570–579.

[18] RADLINSKI, F., KURUP, M., AND JOACHIMS, T. How does clickthrough data reflect retrieval quality? In *CIKM '08*, pp. 43–52.

[19] WANG, K., WALKER, T., AND ZHENG, Z. Pskip: estimating relevance ranking quality from web search clickthrough data. In *KDD '09*, pp. 1355–1364.

[20] YILMAZ, E., KANOULAS, E., AND ASLAM, J. A. A simple and efficient sampling method for estimating ap and ndcg. In *SIGIR '08*, pp. 603–610.

[21] YUE, Y., GAO, Y., CHAPELLE, O., ZHANG, Y., AND JOACHIMS, T. Learning more powerful test statistics for click-based retrieval evaluation. In *SIGIR '10*, pp. 507–514.

Unsupervised Query Segmentation Using Clickthrough for Information Retrieval

Yanen Li* [1], Bo-June (Paul) Hsu[2], ChengXiang Zhai[1], Kuansan Wang[2]

[1]Department of Computer Science, University of Illinois at Urbana-Champaign, Urbana, IL 61801
{yanenli2, czhai}@illinois.edu

[2]Microsoft Research, One Microsoft Way Redmond, WA 98052
{paulhsu, kuansan.wang}@microsoft.com

ABSTRACT

Query segmentation is an important task toward understanding queries accurately, which is essential for improving search results. Existing segmentation models either use labeled data to predict the segmentation boundaries, for which the training data is expensive to collect, or employ unsupervised strategy based on a large text corpus, which might be inaccurate because of the lack of relevant information. In this paper, we propose a probabilistic model to exploit clickthrough data for query segmentation, where the model parameters are estimated via an efficient EM algorithm. We further study how to properly interpret the segmentation results and utilize them to improve retrieval accuracy. Specifically, we propose an integrated language model based on the standard bigram language model to exploit the probabilistic structure obtained through query segmentation. Experiment results on two datasets show that our segmentation model outperforms existing segmentation models. Furthermore, extensive experiments on a large retrieval dataset reveals that the results of query segmentation can be leveraged to improve retrieval relevance by using the proposed integrated language model.

Categories and Subject Descriptors

H.3.3 [**Information Storage and Retrieval**]: Information Search and Retrieval—*Query Segmentation and Language Modeling*

General Terms

Algorithms, Performance, Experimentation

*Work done as a summer intern at Microsoft Research

SIGIR'11, July 24–28, 2011, Beijing, China.

Keywords

Query Segmentation, Expectation Maximization Algorithm, Language Modeling, QSLM

1. INTRODUCTION

Since an accurate understanding of the user's query is critical to improving retrieval results, query segmentation is one of the most important tasks in modern information retrieval. For example, accurate query segmentation is the prerequisite for semantic retrieval models, phrase-based query reformulation and automatic relevance feedback. Supervised techniques have been used to solve the query segmentation problem in the past [3, 23]. However, they require lots of segmentation labels which are expensive to collect. An unsupervised approach based on a large text corpus and Wikipedia has been reported to achieve competitive performance [19]; but its accuracy without Wikipedia is still low, partly due to the lack of relevant information about the query structure.

In a modern search engine, there is a large amount of relevant data in the form of clickthroughs. Such data reflects users' implicit preference of documents, and can be leveraged to infer the underlying segmentation of the queries. In this paper, we propose a unsupervised probabilistic model to exploit user clickthroughs for query segmentation. Model parameters are estimated by an efficient EM algorithm. Segmentation results on a standard dataset demonstrate that our model significantly outperforms the EM model in [19] without the use of Wikipedia. Additionally, by combining more data from external resources, such as the Microsoft Web N-gram [22], our model can outperform state-of-the-art baselines.

One of the most important applications for query segmentation is to improve the retrieval models by incorporating query segmentation. Most information retrieval techniques, such as vector space models and language modeling approaches, rely on the bag-of-words assumption that every query term is independent in the relevance computation. But this assumption is over simplified; users have an order in mind when formulating queries to search for information. One of the reasons why bag-of-words based methods remain popular is because data sparsity makes it harder to estimate models imposing term dependencies [4, 5, 18]. Successful query segmentation has a great potential to lead to better retrieval models that can utilize higher-order term dependencies.

However, query segmentation is ambiguous in nature – the same query can be segmented in difference ways by different people. Although several methods for query segmentation have been proposed, surprisingly little research has been performed to address the segmentation ambiguity and incorporate this information into retrieval models. In this paper, we propose a query segmentation model that quantifies the uncertainty in segmentation by probabilistically modeling the query and clicked document pairs. We further incorporate the probabilistic query segmentation into a unified language model for information retrieval. Experiments on a large web search dataset from a major commercial search engine show that the integrated language model with query segmentation (QSLM) outperforms both the BM25 model and other language models.

2. RELATED WORKS

Query segmentation models have been well studied in recent literature [10, 11, 3, 23, 19, 6]. Initially, the mutual information (MI) between adjacent words in a query is employed to segment queries with a cutoff [10, 11].The major drawback of MI based methods is that they are unable to detect multi-word or phrase based dependencies. Compared with MI based models, supervised query segmentation approaches can achieve higher accuracies [3, 23]. For example, by considering every boundary between two consecutive query words as a binary decision variable, Bersgma and Wang [3] trains the weights of a linear decision function with a set of syntactic and shallow semantic features extracted from the labeled data. However, its focus on noun phrase features may not be appropriate for the segmentation of web queries. Furthermore, acquiring training labels demands a great deal of manual effort that may not scale to the web. As another supervised learning approach, Yu and Shi [23] applies conditional random fields to obtain good query segmentation performance. However, it relies on field information features specific to databases, not available for general unstructured web queries. Moreover, the evaluation was conducted only on synthetic data, which is less desirable than real query data.

Tan and Peng [19] introduce a generative model in the unsupervised setting by adopting n-gram frequency counts from a large text corpus and computing the segment scores via expectation maximization (EM). It also utilizes Wikipedia as another term in the minimum description length objective function. Similarly our model in this paper also includes n-gram statistics and applies the EM algorithm to estimate the model parameters. However, we employ clickthrough query-document pairs to improve segmentation accuracy and further refine the retrieval model by utilizing probabilistic query segmentation. Similar probabilistic model is also proposed in [24], but this model focuses in parsing noun phrases thus not generally applicable to web queries.

This work is also closely related to the retrieval models that capture higher order dependencies of query terms. There are several research attempts to incorporate term dependency in query or document to retrieval models [12]. For example, some attempts have been made to add proximity heuristics to the vector space model or generative query LM model [13, 20]. However these methods rely on heuristics, which is not a principled way of incorporating term dependency. More unified higher-order language models have been studied by Srikanth *et al.* (Biterm LM) [18]. However, their assumption that every position is dependent is too strong. In fact, the word dependency is stronger within a semantic unit than across the unit, which is what we assume in our work. LM with query syntactics [5] assumes a structure on the query, but they are too complex to estimate accurately. More important, the query syntactic models usually take only the top (most likely) query structure in the modeling process. However, it is more appropriate to assess the probability for all possible segmentation if multiple structures have comparable probabilities to represent the query.

In addition, search log and clickthrough data have been reported to be able to improve the performance of personalized search [9, 1, 17]. For example, Joachims [9] first proposes to improve the retrieval quality of search engines by learning from the user clickthrough. Shen *et al.* [17] propose a decision-theoretic approach to improve search performance via user feedback. And Agichtein *et al.* [1] demonstrate that web search ranking can be improved by considering user behavior. We add to this line of work a novel way of exploiting the clickthrough data for query segmentation.

3. PROBLEM SETUP

The task of query segmentation is to separate the query words into disjoint segments so that each segment maps to a semantic unit. Given a query $Q = w_1, w_2, ..., w_n$ of length n, a segmentation $S = S_1 S_2 ... S_M$ of length M is consistent with the query Q if $S_m = w_{b_m} w_{b_m+1} ... w_{b_{m+1}-1}$ for $1 = b_1 < b_2 < ... < b_{M+1} = n + 1$. We define $B = b_1, b_2, ..., b_{M+1}$ as the segmentation partition, independent of the actual query words, and $\mathbb{B}_n$ as the set of all possible segmentation partitions consistent with any query of length n. There are a total of 2^{n-1} segmentation partitions in $\mathbb{B}_n$. Note that given a query Q, the segmentation partition B and the query segments S can be uniquely derived from each other.

Because query segmentation is potentially ambiguous, we are interested in assessing the probability of a query segmentation under some probability distribution: $P(S|\theta)$. With such a probabilistic model, we can then select those segmentations with high probabilities and use them to construct models for information retrieval. For example, for the query "*bank of america online banking*", {[*bank of america*] [*online banking*], 0.502}, {[*bank of america online banking*], 0.428} and {[*bank of*] [*america online*] [*banking*], 0.001} are all valid segmentations, where brackets [] are used to indicate segment boundaries and the number at the end is the probability of that particular segmentation. In this example, the first two segmentations are likely segmentations with high probabilities, whereas the last one is a rare segmentation, as reflected by the low probability. In the next section, we discuss how to compute the probability $P(S|Q)$ of a segmentation S given a query Q.

4. QUERY SEGMENTATION

The search log in a modern search engine usually contains a lot of user clickthrough data, where user-issued queries and corresponding clicked documents are recorded. This kind of data contains rich information about users' preferences for each query. By carefully modeling the clickthroughs, we can assess the likelihood of a segmentation structure according to the collective user behavior. Table 1 shows examples of the clicked documents for two real-world queries from the search log. In these examples, although there are variations in the query words and documents, the sub-sequence "bank of america" remains intact in all clicked documents. The evidence strongly suggests that "*bank of america*" should be a segment. This observation motivates us to model the query segmentation using the query and clicked document pairs, a previously unexplored idea.

Table 1: Examples of Query and Clicked Documents

Query	Clicked document title
bank of america invesment	1. bank of america associate banking investments homepage 2. bank of america investment services inc investments overview 3. bank of america associate banking investments banking services ...
credit card bank of america	1. bank of america credit cards contact us overview 2. secured visa credit card from bank of america 3. credit cards overview find the right bank of america credit card for you ...

We now propose an unsupervised query segmentation model using user clickthroughs. We first describe the model for generating queries and will later extend it to query-click document pairs. The process of generating a query can be described as follows:

1. Pick a query length n under a length distribution.
2. Select a segmentation partition $B \in \mathbb{B}_n$, according to a segmentation partition model $P(B|n,\psi)$.
3. Generate query segments S_m consistent with B, according to a segment unigram model $P(S_m|\theta)$.

Recall that given a query Q of length n, the query segments S and the segmentation partition B can be derived from each other. Thus, we can compute the probability of a segmentation as:

$$P(S|Q,\theta,\psi) = P(B|Q,n,\theta,\psi) \tag{1}$$
$$= \frac{P(Q|B,\theta) \cdot P(B|n,\psi)}{\sum_{B' \in \mathbb{B}_n} P(Q|B',\theta) \cdot P(B'|n,\psi)},$$

$$P(Q|B,\theta) = \prod_{m=1}^{M} P(S_m|\theta) \tag{2}$$

where $P(Q|B,\theta)$ is the probability of generating a query Q given segmentation partition B. The $P(B|n)$ can be estimated by an expectation maximization algorithm described in the following section. However, in this paper we set $P(B|n)$ to a particular form by imposing an infinite strong prior that penalizes longer segments:

$$P(B|n,\psi) = \frac{\prod_{m=1}^{M} P(|S_m(B)|\ |\psi)}{\sum_{B' \in \mathbb{B}_n} \prod_{m'=1}^{M(B')} P(|S_{m'}(B')|\ |\psi)} \tag{3}$$

$$P(|S_m(B)|\ |\psi) = e^{-|S_m(B)|^f} \tag{4}$$

where $|S_m(B)|$ is the length of the mth segment specified by B, and f is a factor controlling the segment length penalty. Note that the denominator is constant for a fixed length n. Since the probability of a segmentation is the product of all segment probabilities $P(S_m|\theta)$ and $P(B|n,\phi)$, such a segment length penalty is crucial to counter the bias for longer segments as they result in fewer segments and hence fewer terms in the final product. This need for segment length penalty is also discussed by Peng *et. al* in [14].

To extend the model to observed pairs of the query Q and the clicked document D, we consider Q to be generated from an interpolated model, consisting of the global component $P(S_m|\theta)$ and a document-specific component $P(S_m|\theta_D)$. Specifically, we redefine the query probability given a segmentation partition in Equation (2) as:

$$P(Q|B,\theta,\theta_D) \propto \prod_{m=1}^{M} P(S_m|\theta)P(S_m|\theta_D) \tag{5}$$

Mathematically, this is equivalent to generating each query segment using a log-linear interpolation of the global and document-specific models. Figure 1 illustrates the segmentation partition and the process of generating a query given the model.

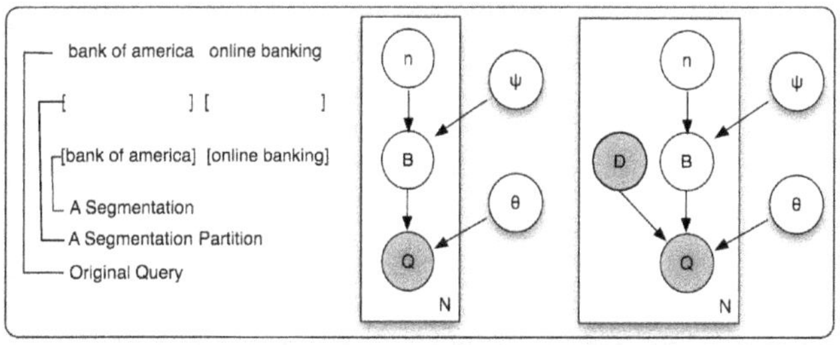

Figure 1: The Generative Model of Segmentation. Left: the query segmentation partition; middle: the process of generating a query Q; right: the process of generating query Q with clicked document D

For $P(S_m|\theta_D)$, we employ a smoothed bigram language model trained from the document D and interpolated with the global document collection statistics θ_C to model the probability of $S_m = w_{b_m} w_{b_m+1} \ldots w_{b_{m+1}-1}$:

$$P(S_m|\theta_D) = \prod_{l=b_m}^{b_{m+1}-1} P(w_l|w_{l-1},\theta_D) \tag{6}$$
$$= \prod_{l=b_m}^{b_{m+1}-1} [(1-\lambda)P_{bi}(w_l|w_{l-1},\theta_D) + \lambda P_{bi}(w_l|w_{l-1},\theta_C)]$$

where

$$P_{bi}(w_l|w_{l-1},\theta_D) = \frac{f^D_{w_{l-1}w_l} + \mu_D \frac{f^D_{w_l}}{|D|}}{f^D_{w_{l-1}} + \mu_D},$$

$$P_{bi}(w_l|w_{l-1},\theta_C) = \frac{f^C_{w_{l-1}w_l} + \mu_C \frac{f^C_{w_l}}{|C|}}{f^C_{w_{l-1}} + \mu_C},$$

λ is the mixture weight, μ_C and μ_D are the bigram backoff weights, and f_{w_l}, $f_{w_{l-1}w_l}$ are the n-gram counts in document D or corpus C.

Overall, we want to estimate $\hat{\theta}$ to maximize the log likelihood of observing all the query-clicked document pairs in the dataset:

$$\log P(\mathbb{Q}|\theta,\theta_D) = \sum_l log \sum_{B\in\mathbb{B}_{n_l}} P(B|n_l) \cdot \prod_{m=1}^{M_l} [P(S_m(Q_l)|\theta) \cdot P(S_m(Q_l)|\theta_{D_l})] \quad (7)$$

With $\hat{\theta}$, we can compute the most probable segmentations for any query according to Equation (1).

4.1 Model Parameter Estimation by EM

Since the joint probability in Equation (7) involves the logarithm of a summation over hidden variables B, there is no exact analytical solution for $\hat{\theta}$. However, we can apply the expectation maximization (EM) algorithm to maximize the joint probability of all observed data. In the E-step, we evaluate the posterior probability of a valid segmentation of Q given the previous model parameter estimate $\theta^{(k-1)}$:

$$P(B|Q,\theta^{(k-1)},\theta_D,\psi) = \frac{P(Q|B,\theta^{(k-1)},\theta_D,\psi) \cdot P(B|n,\psi)}{\sum_{B'\in\mathbb{B}_n} P(Q|B',\theta^{(k-1)},\theta_D,\psi) \cdot P(B'|n,\psi)} \quad (8)$$

where

$$P(Q|B,\theta^{(k-1)},\theta_D,\psi) = \prod_{m=1}^{M} [P(S_m|\theta^{(k-1)}) \cdot P(S_m|\theta_D)]$$

In the M-step, we update the estimate of θ according to:

$$P(w_1...w_r|\theta^{(k)}) = \frac{1}{Z} \cdot \sum_l \sum_{B\in\mathbb{B}_{n_l}} [P(B|Q_l,\theta^{(k-1)},\theta_D,\psi) \cdot \sum_{m=1}^{M_l} \delta(S_m(B,Q_l) = w_1...w_r)] \quad (9)$$

where Z is the normalization factor and $\delta()$ is an indicator function checking if segment S_m is equal to n-gram $w_1...w_r$. For a query of n keywords, a naive computation for the M-step requires summing of all 2^{n-1} possible segmentations, which is computationally impractical for longer queries. Fortunately, it can be computed efficiently using the Baum-Welch algorithm [2].

Here we introduce a graph representation for query segmentation. Given a query Q of length n, all segmentations consistent with Q can be represented by a graph G with $n+1$ nodes. Figure 2 illustrates a graph representation for two valid segmentations of the query "*bank of america online banking*". For a graph with $n+1$ nodes, there are a total of 2^{n-1} ways to connect node 1 to node $n+1$, each corresponding to a valid segmentation. For example, in the upper panel of Figure 2, there is a connection from node 1 to 4, corresponding to a segmentation boundary between *america* and *online*. In this case, the arc from node 1 to 4 corresponds to the segment "bank of america".

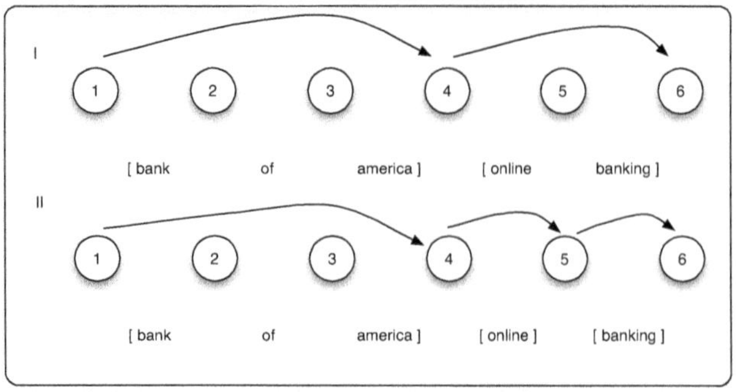

Figure 2: Graph Representation of Segmentations

Using this graph representation, Equation (9) in the M-step can be rewritten as:

$$P(w_1...w_r|\theta^{(k)}) = \frac{\sum_l \sum_i \sum_j \xi_l(i,j) \cdot \delta_l(S_{i\to j} = w_1...w_r)}{\sum_l \sum_i \sum_j \xi_l(i,j)} \quad (10)$$

where $\xi(i,j) = P(S_{i\to j}|Q,\theta^{(k-1)})$ is the probability of the segment S_m represented by the arc from node i to node j for the query Q, $\delta(S_{i\to j} = w_1...w_r)$ is an indicator function with a value of 1 when $S_{i\to j} = w_1...w_r$ and 0 otherwise.

In order to compute $\xi_l(i,j)$, we introduce $\alpha(i) = P(Q,i|\theta^{(t-1)})$, the probability of observing the query Q from the beginning of the graph to node i, and $\beta(j) = P(Q|j,\theta^{(t-1)})$, the probability of observing Q from node j to the end of the graph:

$$\alpha(i) = \sum_{k:k<i} \alpha(k) \cdot P(S_{k\to i}|\theta^{(t-1)}) \cdot e^{-|S_{k\to i}|^f} \cdot P_D(S_{k\to i}),$$

$$\beta(j) = \sum_{k:k>j} \beta(k) \cdot P(S_{j\to k}|\theta^{(t-1)}) \cdot e^{-|S_{j\to k}|^f} \cdot P_D(S_{j\to k}),$$

$$\xi_l(i,j) = \alpha_l(i) \cdot \beta_l(j) \cdot P(S_{i\to j}|\theta^{(t-1)}) \cdot e^{-|S_{i\to j}|^f} \cdot P_{D_l}(S_{i\to j})$$

with the initial condition $\alpha_l(1) = 1, \beta_l(n) = 1$. Algorithm 1 summarizes the steps for estimating θ. For a set of queries with equal length, the computation complexity for each iteration is $O(Ln^2)$, where L is the number of input query-document pairs and n is the number of words in each query. Once the optimal θ is obtained, the probability of a segmentation $P(S|Q,\theta,\psi)$ can be computed by Equation (1).

4.2 Utilizing Other Resources

N-gram statistics from a very large scale of text resources can also be utilized to improve query segmentation. In fact in [19], the biggest improvement in segmentation accuracy is achieved by utilizing information from Wikipedia. In addition, [6] also reports a well-performing naive query segmentation method using Google Web N-gram. Here we propose a simple approach utilizing the Microsoft Web N-gram service. MS Web N-gram is essentially a distribution of n-gram probability θ' over the web. The probability of a segmenta-

Algorithm 1: N-gram concept probability estimation

input : A set of query-clicked document pairs $\mathbb{O} = \{< Q_l, D_l >\}, l \in [1, N]$

output: Optimal estimate of $\theta = \{P(S_m)\}$

Init $P(S_m|\theta^{(0)}) \leftarrow \frac{Count(S_m)}{Count(total\ Ngrams\ in\ query\ collection)}$;

for $t \leftarrow 1$ **to** T **do**

  $P(S_m|\theta^{(t)}) \leftarrow 0$;

  $\xi_{total} \leftarrow 0$;

  for $l \leftarrow 1$ **to** N **do**

    G_l is a graph representing query Q_l, with $n+1$ nodes; $\alpha_l(1) = 1$; $\beta_l(n+1) = 1$;

    for *node* $i \leftarrow 2$ **to** $n+1$ **do**

      $\alpha_l(i) \leftarrow \sum_{k:k<i} \alpha_l(k) \cdot P(S_m|\theta^{(t-1)}) \cdot e^{-|(S_{k\rightarrow i})|^f} \cdot P_{D_l}(S_{k\rightarrow i})$;

    for *node* $j \leftarrow n$ **to** 1 **do**

      $\beta_l(j) \leftarrow \sum_{k:k>j} \beta_l(k) \cdot P(S_{j\rightarrow k}|\theta^{(t-1)}) \cdot e^{-|S_{j\rightarrow k}|^f} \cdot P_{D_l}(S_{j\rightarrow k})$;

    for *node* $i \leftarrow 1$ **to** $n+1$ **do**

      for *node* $j \leftarrow i+1$ **to** $n+1$ **do**

        $\xi_l(i,j) \leftarrow \alpha_l(i) \cdot \beta_l(j) \cdot P(S_{i\rightarrow j}|\theta^{(t-1)}) \cdot e^{-|S_{i\rightarrow j}|^f} \cdot P_{D_l}(S_{i\rightarrow j})$;

        $P(S_m = S_{i\rightarrow j}|\theta^{(t)}) \leftarrow P(S_m = S_{i\rightarrow j}|\theta^{(t)}) + \xi_l(i,j)$;

        $\xi_{total} \leftarrow \xi_{total} + \xi_l(i,j)$;

  $P(S_m|\theta^{(t)}) \leftarrow \frac{P(S_m|\theta^{(t)})}{\xi_{total}}$;

return $\theta = \{P(S_m)\}$;

tion given Q is defined as:

$$P(B|Q,\theta',\psi') \propto P(Q|B,\theta',\psi') \cdot P(B|\psi') \quad (11)$$
$$= \prod_{m=1}^{M} P(S_m|\theta') \cdot P(B|\psi')$$
$$\propto \prod_{m=1}^{M} P(S_m|\theta') \cdot e^{-|S_m(B)|^{f'}}$$

Furthermore, we can combine our query segmentation model with clickthrough and the simple model with Web N-gram into an interpolated model:

$$logP(B|Q,\theta,\theta',\psi,\psi') = (1-\omega) \cdot logP(B|Q,\theta,\psi) + \omega \cdot logP(B|Q,\theta',\psi') \quad (12)$$

we find the setting of $\omega = 0.5, f = 2.0, f' = 2.0$ results in a model with good segmentation accuracy.

5. SEGMENTATION EXPERIMENTS

In this section we report the query segmentation results obtained by our model and other baselines on two datasets. One is from a standard dataset established by previous research, and the other is constructed by ourselves. We also conduct extensive analysis on several aspects of the results.

5.1 Data Preparation and Evaluation Metrics

We use two sets of queries for evaluating the query segmentation models. The first set (Set 1) is a standard query segmentation dataset established by Bergsma and Wang [3], which is also applied in [19]. In this dataset, annotator A, B, and C independently segmented 500 queries which are sampled from the AOL 2006 query log. Among these 500 human queries, the 220 where the 3 judges agree are called the "Intersection" set.

The above segmentation dataset is focused on noun queries. But in this work we are also interested in web queries. Therefore we prepare another set of 1,000 queries sampled from the search log of a major commercial search engine, which we name the 1000-query dataset. We invite three domain experts to segment the queries independently, employing the same evaluation metrics as Set 1. Besides expert annotations, this dataset also has clickthrough information and relevance judgments for the top documents, which is used by subsequent experiments when comparing retrieval models.

To measure the segmentation effectiveness, we report results on three evaluation metrics. (1) Query accuracy: the percentage of queries for which the predicted segmentation matches the gold standard completely; (2) Classification accuracy: the ratio of correctly predicted boundaries in between every two consecutive words; (3) Segment accuracy: how well the predicted segments match the gold standard under the information retrieval measures of precision, recall, and F-score.

As baseline, we include the three models in [19]: Mutual information, EM + corpus (query log), and EM + corpus + Wikipedia. We also include a method using Google Web N-gram [6] and a simple model with MS Web N-gram, as defined in Section 4.2. Our model + clickthrough and our model + clickthrough + MS Web N-gram are included in the comparison. The parameters of our segmentation model is trained on a large set of search log containing about 20 millions query-clicked document pairs.

5.2 Query Segmentation Results

Table 2 shows the results of our model as well as the baseline models on the standard dataset. Columns 3 to 5 represent models without using external data source (basic models), while columns 6 to 9 are models utilizing large external sources, such as Wikipedia and web-scale n-gram (extended models). Among the basic models, our model performs the best according to annotator A, C and the intersection of these annotators. These results are significantly better than the corresponding results by the EM + corpus model in [19]. For the result based on annotator B, our model is comparable to that of [19] (0.571 vs 0.573 on segment F score). For the extended models, simple model + MS Web N-gram performs well, similar to the results for simple model with Google Web N-gram as reported in [6]. It indicates the positive impact of n-gram statistics on query segmentation. However, our model, as well as EM model + Wikipedia in [19] outperforms the simple models consistently in all annotators' judgments; and our extended model performs better than that of [19]. For example, in the intersection judgments, the F score of our model is 0.779, while model in [19] is 0.774. Compared to the simple model + MS Web N-gram, whose intersection F score is 0.728, our model achieves a 7.0% gain on the same measure. It suggests the

Table 3: Results on the 1000-query Dataset

Annotator	Measure	Our Model	Simple Model + MS Web N-gram
A	query accuracy	0.386	0.316
	classify accuracy	0.631	0.538
	segment precision	0.434	0.368
	segment recall	0.540	0.552
	segment F	**0.481**	0.441
B	query accuracy	0.447	0.403
	classify accuracy	0.690	0.619
	segment precision	0.533	0.476
	segment recall	0.602	0.648
	segment F	**0.565**	0.549
C	query accuracy	0.472	0.545
	classify accuracy	0.703	0.749
	segment precision	0.670	0.693
	segment recall	0.582	0.730
	segment F	0.623	**0.713**
Intersection	query accuracy	0.624	0.567
	classify accuracy	0.761	0.642
	segment precision	0.372	0.301
	segment recall	0.405	0.395
	segment F	**0.388**	0.342

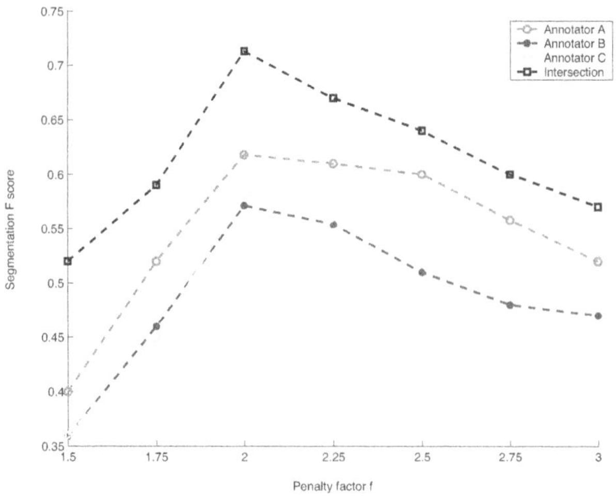

Figure 3: Query Segmentation Performance with Respect to Penalty Factor

effectiveness of our model and the benefit from combining additional large scale N-gram statistics.

5.3 Results on the 1000-query Dataset

We compare our query segmentation model with the simple model + MS Web N-gram on the 1000-query dataset. Table 3 shows the segmentation results on the this set. Although the simple segmentation model with web n-gram works very well in the standard dataset, it performs inferior to our model in the 1000-query dataset. In 2 out of 3 annotator judgments, our model outperforms the simple model. And in the intersection judgments our model also works better than the simple model by 4.6%. Since this dataset is sampled from a set of web search queries, results in this experiment indicate that our model fits web search queries, whose characteristics are different from noun queries, better.

5.4 Effect of the Penalty Factor

The factor f in Equation (4), which controls how much penalty is given to a segment of length $|S_m|$, is important to the our proposed model. We now investigate how the segmentation result changes according to different values of f. For this purpose, we re-run our model (without web n-gram) on the standard dataset with f ranging from 1.5 to 3.0 in steps of 0.25. Figure 3 summarizes the results. There are common trends across annotator A, B, C and their intersection. The F score increases when f increases from 1.5 to 2.0, and decreases afterwards. It suggests that too little penalty (small f) favors long segments and hurts segmentation accuracy, while too much penalty (big f) negatively impacts on the results since it favors segments with very short length. It also indicates that a moderate penalty at $f = 2.0$ is a reasonable choice for the proposed model.

6. INTEGRATED LANGUAGE MODEL

In this section we will introduce the proposed integrated language model with query segmentation (QSLM). We first motivate QSLM with an oracle experiment, then describe the derivation of QSLM, and finally conduct extensive experiments on a large scale web search dataset.

6.1 Oracle Ranker

To motivate the formulation of QSLM, we have carried out an intuitive and interesting experiment. Given an oracle ranker, we let the ranker choose the bigram or unigram language model for each query, whichever gives a better NDCG score. Table 4 lists the result of the oracle ranker compared to other models. As such a simple oracle performs significantly better than either the bigram or unigram language models, it suggests that it may be possible to improve the search ranking if one can successfully emulate the behavior of the Oracle – to accurately predict when to use a unigram model and when to use a bigram model. We will show that query segmentation can help achieve a similar effect.

Table 4: Oracle Ranker

Method	NDCG@1	NDCG@3	NDCG@10
BM25	0.3108	0.3358	0.3986
Unigram LM	0.3117	0.3366	0.3999
Bigram LM	0.3141	0.3380	0.3999
Oracle Ranker	0.3471	0.3628	0.4186

6.2 Integrated Language Model

Given a model for computing the probability of a segmentation S for a query Q, we can exploit this information and develop a new retrieval model incorporating the query segmentation structure. Note that the retrieval model proposed here is independent of the query segmentation technique. We start by formulating the integrated language model with query segmentation based on the probabilistic ranking principle [15]. Specifically, we can rewrite the probability that a document is relevant to a query as follows:

Table 2: Segmentation Performance on the Standard Dataset

Annotator	Measure	MI	[19] EM + Corpus	Our Model	Simple Model + MS Web N-gram	[6] Simple Model + Google Web N-gram	[19] EM + Corpus + Wiki	Our Model + MS Web N-gram
A	query accuracy	0.274	0.414	0.440	0.482	0.536	0.526	0.540
	classify accuracy	0.693	0.762	0.776	0.782	0.807	0.810	0.803
	segment precision	0.469	0.562	0.598	0.645	0.665	0.657	0.669
	segment recall	0.534	0.555	0.639	0.602	0.708	0.657	0.713
	segment F	0.499	0.558	**0.618**	0.622	0.686	0.657	**0.690**
B	query accuracy	0.244	0.440	0.410	0.466	0.380	0.494	0.485
	classify accuracy	0.634	0.774	0.750	0.777	0.752	0.802	0.776
	segment precision	0.408	0.568	0.521	0.568	0.519	0.623	0.591
	segment recall	0.472	0.578	0.631	0.601	0.626	0.640	0.650
	segment F	0.438	**0.573**	0.571	0.584	0.568	**0.631**	0.619
C	query accuracy	0.264	0.416	0.402	0.460	0.454	0.494	0.465
	classify accuracy	0.666	0.759	0.756	0.772	0.772	0.796	0.803
	segment precision	0.451	0.558	0.548	0.597	0.581	0.634	0.624
	segment recall	0.519	0.561	0.619	0.590	0.653	0.642	0.655
	segment F	0.483	0.559	**0.582**	0.594	0.615	0.638	**0.639**
Intersection	query accuracy	0.343	0.528	0.586	0.636	0.627	0.671	0.682
	classify accuracy	0.728	0.815	0.842	0.847	0.851	0.871	0.855
	segment precision	0.510	0.640	0.681	0.736	0.718	0.767	0.770
	segment recall	0.550	0.650	0.747	0.721	0.778	0.782	0.788
	segment F	0.530	0.645	**0.713**	0.728	0.746	0.774	**0.779**

$$
\begin{aligned}
& P(R=1|Q,D) \\
&= \sum_B P(B|Q,D)P(R=1|B,Q,D) \\
&= \sum_B P(B|Q,D)\frac{P(Q|B,D,R=1)P(R=1|B,D)}{\sum_{r=\{0,1\}} P(Q|B,D,R=r)P(R=r|B,D)} \\
&= \sum_B P(B|Q,D)\frac{\frac{P(Q|B,D,R=1)}{P(Q|B,D,R=0)}}{\frac{P(Q|B,D,R=1)}{P(Q|B,D,R=0)} + \frac{P(R=0|B,D)}{P(R=1|B,D)}} \\
&\equiv \sum_B P(B|Q,D)\frac{a}{a+b}
\end{aligned}
$$

where:

$$
a = \frac{P(Q|B,D,R=1)}{P(Q|B,D,R=0)}, \qquad b = \frac{P(R=0|B,D)}{P(R=1|B,D)}.
$$

As the query segmentation is performed independently of the document, $P(B|Q,D) = P(B|Q)$. Furthermore, when a document is irrelevant, we can approximate the query as being generated from the background corpus statistics, independent of the document:

$$
a \approx \frac{P(Q|B,D,R=1)}{P(Q|B,\theta_C)}
$$

Finally, as the relevance of a document is independent of the segmentation partition without knowing the query, we will assume that all document has an equal probability of being relevant. Thus, we can approximate b as the average ratio of irrelevant to relevant documents over a set of queries.

$$
b \approx \frac{P(R=0)}{P(R=1)} \approx \sum_Q \frac{|\text{Irrelevant}(Q)|}{|\text{Relevant}(Q)|}
$$

In this work, we apply a language model approach to estimate the the probability ratio a:

$$
\begin{aligned}
a &\approx \frac{P(Q|B,D,R=1)}{P(Q|B,\theta_C)} \\
&= \prod_{m=1}^{M} \frac{P(S_m|D,R=1)}{P(S_m|\theta_C)} \\
&= \prod_{m=1}^{M} \frac{P(w_{k_m},...,w_{k_{m+1}-1}|\theta_D)}{P(w_{k_m},...,w_{k_{m+1}-1}|\theta_C)} \\
&= \prod_{m=1}^{M} \prod_{i=k_m}^{k_{m+1}-1} \frac{P(w_i|w_{i-1},\theta_D)}{P(w_i|w_{i-1},\theta_C)}
\end{aligned}
$$

For irrelevant documents, the query segments are generated from the an n-gram language model trained from the background corpus. For relevant documents, the query segments are modeled using a smoothed bigram model trained from the document, interpolated with the background corpus. Specifically:

$$
P(w_i|w_{i-1},\theta_C) = \frac{f_{w_{i-1}w_i,C} + \mu_C \frac{f_{w_i,C}}{|C|}}{f_{w_{i-1},C} + \mu_C}, \tag{13}
$$

$$
P_{bi}(w_i|w_{i-1},\theta_D) = \frac{f_{w_{i-1}w_i,D} + \mu_D \frac{f_{w_i,D}}{|D|}}{f_{w_{i-1},D} + \mu_D}, \tag{14}
$$

$$
P(w_i|w_{i-1},\theta_D) = (1-\lambda)P_{bi}(w_i|w_{i-1},\theta_D) + \lambda P(w_i|w_{i-1},\theta_C) \tag{15}
$$

7. RETRIEVAL EXPERIMENTS

In this section we conduct a set of experiments for the QSLM model on the web search task. The main reason why we did not carry out experiments on the TREC datasets is due to the lack of clickthrough data for TREC queries, which is important to our study. In the following sections, we invest several variants of the model and discuss the choice in model parameters.

7.1 Evaluation Metrics and Baselines

We evaluate the retrieval models on a large-scale real world dataset, containing 12,064 English queries sampled from the query log of a major commercial search engine. On average, each query is associated with 74 web documents, with each query-document pair manually assigned a relevance label on a 5-level scale: 0 means that the document D is detrimental to query Q, 4 means that the document D is most relevant to Q. For comparison, we include 3 baseline models in the results: BM25 [16], unigram LM with Dirichlet smoothing [25], and bigram LM as specified in Equation (15). In order to obtain the optimal parameters in our model as well as in the baselines, we divide the whole dataset evenly into a training set and a test set, each containing 6,032 queries, and estimate the parameters from the training set using grid search, as proposed in [21]. The optimal parameters of the models are reported in Table 5. Finally we also list the simple oracle results as reference. The performance of all the retrieval models is measured by mean normalized discounted cumulative gain (NDCG) [7] at truncation levels 1, 3, and 10. We list the dataset statistics in Figure 4 and report detailed results of the retrieval models in Table 6. In Table 6, we report the results by query length. For short queries, there are few variations in the segmentation. Thus, there is little room for improvement by exploiting segmentation information. However, the effect of query segmentation is more pronounced when the query contains 4 or more words, which we consider as a long query. In this case, the NDCGs of BM25 and unigram LM are similar, both outperformed by the bigram LM. However, QSLM's performance (0.3419, 0.3539 and 0.4040) is significantly better than all other models at all levels of NDCG truncation. In fact, we have conducted a paired t-test between QSLM and the other models. At confidence level $\alpha = 0.01$, the difference between QSLM and BM25/unigram LM at all three levels of NDCG truncation is statistically significant. The difference between QSLM and bigram LM at both NDCG@1 and NDCG@3 are significant.

Table 5: Optimal values of parameters

Model	NDCG
Unigram LM	$\mu = 2.702$
Bigram LM	$\mu_C = 425026, \mu_D = 0.51, \lambda = 0.681$
QSLM	$\mu_C = 500213, \mu_D = 0.50, \lambda = 0.90, b = 720$

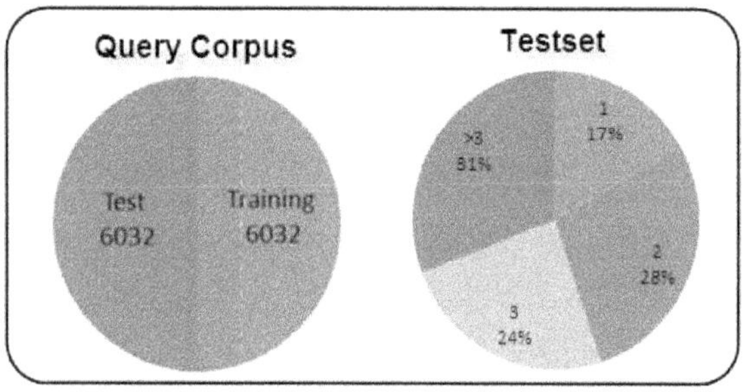

Figure 4: Query Distribution in the Datasets

Table 6: Results of IR Models on Web Search

Length	#Queries	Model	NDCG@1	NDCG@3	NDCG@10
1	1012	BM25	0.2515	0.2773	0.3496
1	1012	Unigram LM	0.2515	0.2767	0.3497
1	1012	Bigram LM	0.2462	0.2737	0.3452
1	1012	QSLM	0.2462	0.2737	0.3452
2	1694	BM25	0.3125	0.3391	0.4068
2	1694	Unigram LM	0.3131	0.3393	0.4076
2	1694	Bigram LM	0.3132	0.3392	0.4074
2	1694	QSLM	**0.3169**	**0.3404**	**0.4078**
2	1694	Oracle Ranker	0.3488	0.3656	0.4266
3	1471	BM25	0.3273	0.3603	0.4226
3	1471	Unigram LM	0.3293	0.3607	0.4242
3	1471	Bigram LM	0.3322	0.3617	0.4244
3	1471	QSLM	**0.3332**	**0.3619**	**0.4251**
3	1471	Oracle Ranker	0.3657	0.3877	0.4423
>3	1855	BM25	0.3287	0.3454	0.3988
>3	1855	Unigram LM	0.3294	0.3476	0.4009
>3	1855	Bigram LM	0.3354	0.3500	0.4009
>3	1855	QSLM	**0.3419**	**0.3539**	**0.4040**
>3	1855	Oracle Ranker	0.3651	0.3752	0.4222

7.2 Alternative Choice of the Bigram Model

As the choice of smoothing methods is critical to language modeling for information retrieval [25], we also test QSLM with an alternative form of bigram model (2-stage smoothed bigram) proposed in [8]:

$$\begin{aligned} P(q_l|q_{l-1},\theta_D) = (1-\lambda_1)[(1-\lambda_2)\frac{f_{q_l,D}+\mu_1/|V|}{|D|+\mu_1} \\ + \quad \lambda_2\frac{f_{q_{l-1}q_l,D}+\mu_2/|V|^2}{f_{q_{l-1},D}+\mu_2}] \\ + \lambda_1[(1-\lambda_3)\frac{f_{q_l,C}+\mu_3/|V|}{|C|+\mu_3} \\ + \quad \lambda_3\frac{f_{q_{l-1}q_l,C}+\mu_4/|V|^2}{f_{q_{l-1},C}+\mu_4}] \end{aligned} \tag{16}$$

$$\begin{aligned} P(q_l|q_{l-1},\theta_C) = (1-\lambda_3)\frac{f_{q_l,C}+\mu_3/|V|}{|C|+\mu_3} \\ + \lambda_3\frac{f_{q_{l-1}q_l,C}+\mu_4/|V|^2}{f_{q_{l-1},C}+\mu_4} \end{aligned} \tag{17}$$

Results in Table 7 show that QSLM with 2-stage smoothed bigram performs slightly better than the original form of smoothed bigram (see Equation (15)) on NDCG3 and NDCG10. However, this smoothed bigram LM has a larger set of parameters to tune than the original bigram LM, from 3 in the original to 7. Therefore, the original form of smoothed bigram model might be more generalizable to other scenarios.

Table 7: QLSM with Difference Bigram Models

Model	NDCG@1	NDCG@3	NDCG@10
QSLM - Bigram Model 1	**0.3419**	0.3539	0.4040
QSLM - Bigram Model 2	0.3404	**0.3549**	**0.4045**

Note: tests are made on 1855 queries of length greater than 3 in the test set.

7.3 Effect of Number of Segmentations

The effectiveness of a retrieval model combined with query segmentation relies on the ability to properly quantify the uncertainty of a segmentation. Ambiguous queries tend to have several segmentations with equal likelihood. So it's necessary to explore how the retrieval model performance changes with respect to the number of segmentations. In this experiment, we run QSLM on long queries from the web search test set (1855 queries) and vary the maximum number of query segmentations from 1 to 10. All segmentations are sorted by their probability. Figure 5 shows the performance trends at NDCG@1, NDCG@3 and NDCG@10. At all three levels of NDCG, it follows a common trend: the results do improve as the number of segmentations increases. In general, the NDCG scores reach a max when the number of segmentations reaches 3 or 4. This demonstrates that we should consider the segmentation probability and incorporate more than one candidate segmentations into the retrieval model. It also illustrates that we can achieve a reasonable result by considering only the top few segmentations.

7.4 Effect of the Penalty Factor on Retrieval

As discussed in Section 5.4, the penalty factor f is important to query segmentation. Here we investigate how

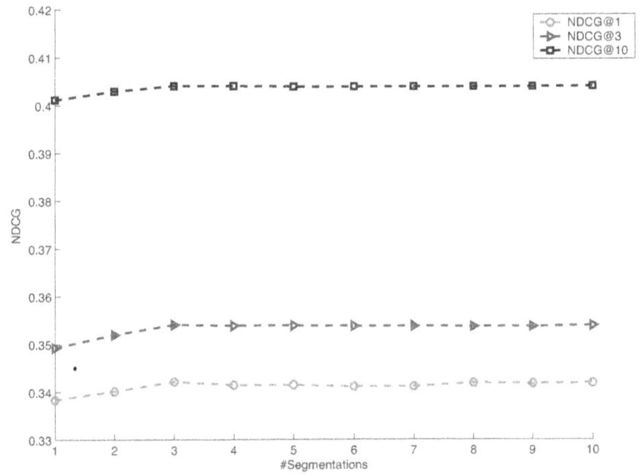

Figure 5: Retrieval Performance with Respect to #Segmentations

this factor impacts the retrieval performance. Towards this goal, we run QSLM on the long queries from the web search test set (1855 queries) with f ranging from 1.5 to 3.5 in steps of 0.25. Figure 6 indicates a very different result from query segmentation: for our retrieval model with query segmentation, the result is not sensitive to the change in f. For example, for NDCG@1, the performance of QSLM increases only slightly from $f = 1.5$ to $f = 2.0$, and decreases slowly afterwards. For NDCG@3 and NDCG@10, the differences in NDCG scores at difference values of f are negligible. The results suggest that our integrated retrieval model is robust to the choice of the penalty factor f.

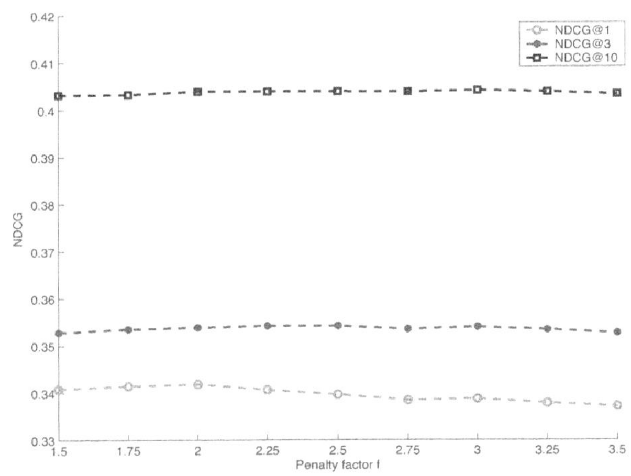

Figure 6: Retrieval Performance with Respect to Penalty Factor

7.5 Comparing to Other Query Segmentation Methods

The formulation of the QSLM model is not constrained by our query segmentation model. Theoretically it can work with query segmentations computed by any other model. It is thus interesting to know whether different query segmentation models will lead to different retrieval results. As mentioned in Section 5.3, we have constructed a 1000-query dataset with expert-labeled segmentations. More importantly, this dataset is randomly sampled from our web search dataset of 12,064 queries. Therefore, there are relevance judgments on each query. In addition to the baselines BM25, unigram LM and bigram LM, we report the results of 3 other models in this experiments: QSLM with query segmentations labeled by three human experts (QSLM^a), QSLM with segmentations computed by simple model + MS Web N-gram (QSLM^b), and QSLM with segmentations computed by our segmentation model with clickthrough only (QSLM^c). Table 8 summarizes the results of these models on 382 long queries. In general, the QSLM models work better than the 3 baselines, no matter what query segmentation model is used. However, the results demonstrate that there are noticeable differences with respect to different segmentation models. Although the simple segmentation model with web n-gram works very well for query segmentation, it is inferior to using human-labeled query segmentations. Meanwhile, QSLM, when coupled with our query segmentation model, works better than the other variants of QSLMs at all NDCG truncation levels. We believe the superior performance of our model is attributed to the appropriate modeling of relevance information in clickthroughs. Such relevance information is embedded in the query segmentations in the users' preferences and subsequently exploited by the integrated language model.

Table 8: IR Models on 1000-query Dataset

Model	NDCG@1	NDCG@3	NDCG@10
BM25	0.3410	0.3525	0.4003
Unigram LM	0.3466	0.3624	0.4057
Bigram LM	0.3626	0.3643	0.4025
QSLM^a	0.3649	0.3656	0.4034
QSLM^b	0.3600	0.3619	0.4020
QSLM^c	**0.3700**	**0.3684**	**0.4058**
Oracle Ranker	0.3929	0.3934	0.4285

Note: tests are made on 382 queries of length greater than 3.

8. CONCLUSIONS

In this paper we propose a novel unsupervised query segmentation model by jointly modeling the query-clicked documents from the search log. Experimental results on two datasets confirm the effectiveness of our model. Furthermore, we develop a unified language model with query segmentation to improve the search ranking. The implicit relevance information in the clickthrough data is the bridge between our query segmentation model and QSLM. Thorough experiments on a large-scale web search dataset show that search relevance can be improved by leveraging the query segmentations. As there is still a large gap in retrieval performance between the oracle ranker and the QSLM model, we plan to further refine the model to reduce gap in the future. Specifically, we would like to explore the use of QSLM as features to other advanced retrieval models [12].

9. ACKNOWLEGEMENTS

This paper is based upon work supported in part by the National Science Foundation under grant CNS-0834709.

10. REFERENCES

[1] E. Agichtein, E. Brill, and S. Dumais. Improving web search ranking by incorporating user behavior information. In *SIGIR '06: Proceedings of the 29th annual international ACM SIGIR conference on Research and development in information retrieval*, pages 19–26, New York, NY, USA, 2006. ACM Press.

[2] L. E. Baum, T. Petrie, G. Soules, and N. Weiss. A Maximization Technique Occurring in the Statistical Analysis of Probabilistic Functions of Markov Chains. *The Annals of Mathematical Statistics*, 41(1):164–171, 1970.

[3] S. Bergsma and Q. I. Wang. Learning noun phrase query segmentation. In *In Proceedings of the 2007 Joint Conference on Empirical Methods in Natural Language Processing and Computational Natural Language Learning (EMNLP-CoNLL)*, pages 819–826.

[4] G. Cao, J.-Y. Nie, and J. Bai. Integrating word relationships into language models. In *Proceedings of the 28th annual international ACM SIGIR conference on Research and development in information retrieval*, SIGIR '05, pages 298–305, New York, NY, USA, 2005.

[5] J. Gao, J.-Y. Nie, G. Wu, and G. Cao. Dependence language model for information retrieval. In *Proceedings of the 27th annual international ACM SIGIR conference on Research and development in information retrieval*, SIGIR '04, pages 170–177, New York, NY, USA, 2004. ACM.

[6] M. Hagen, M. Potthast, B. Stein, and C. Braeutigam. The power of naive query segmentation. In *Proceeding of the 33rd international ACM SIGIR conference on Research and development in information retrieval*, SIGIR '10, pages 797–798, New York, NY, USA, 2010.

[7] K. Järvelin and J. Kekäläinen. Cumulated gain-based evaluation of ir techniques. *ACM Trans. Inf. Syst.*, 20:422–446, October 2002.

[8] S. Javanmardi, J. Gao, and K. Wang. Optimizing two stage bigram language models for ir. In *Proceedings of the 19th international conference on World wide web*, WWW '10, pages 1125–1126, New York, NY, USA.

[9] T. Joachims. Optimizing search engines using clickthrough data. In *KDD '02: Proceedings of the eighth ACM SIGKDD international conference on Knowledge discovery and data mining*, pages 133–142, New York, NY, USA, 2002. ACM Press.

[10] R. Jones, B. Rey, O. Madani, and W. Greiner. Generating query substitutions. In *Proceedings of the 15th international conference on World Wide Web*, WWW '06, pages 387–396, New York, NY, USA, 2006.

[11] T. M. K. M. Risvik and P. Boros. Query segmentation for web search. In *Proceeding of the 12th international conference on World Wide Web*, WWW '03, 2003.

[12] D. Metzler and W. B. Croft. A markov random field model for term dependencies. In *Proceedings of the 28th annual international ACM SIGIR conference on Research and development in information retrieval*, SIGIR '05, pages 472–479, New York, NY, USA, 2005.

[13] G. Mishne and M. de Rijke. Boosting Web Retrieval through Query Operations. In *In Proc. 27th European Conference on Information Retrieval (ECIR '05)*, pages 502–516, 2005.

[14] F. Peng and D. Schuurmans. Self-supervised chinese word segmentation. In *Proceedings of the 4th International Conference on Advances in Intelligent Data Analysis*, IDA '01, pages 238–247, London, UK, 2001. Springer-Verlag.

[15] S. E. Robertson. *The probability ranking principle in IR*, pages 281–286. Morgan Kaufmann Publishers Inc., San Francisco, CA, USA, 1997.

[16] S. E. Robertson and S. Walker. Some simple effective approximations to the 2-poisson model for probabilistic weighted retrieval. In *Proceedings of the 17th annual international ACM SIGIR conference on Research and development in information retrieval*, SIGIR '94, pages 232–241, New York, NY, USA, 1994. Springer-Verlag New York, Inc.

[17] X. Shen, B. Tan, and C. Zhai. Implicit user modeling for personalized search. In *CIKM '05: Proceedings of the 14th ACM international conference on Information and knowledge management*, pages 824–831, New York, NY, USA, 2005. ACM.

[18] M. Srikanth and R. Srihari. Biterm language models for document retrieval. In *Proceedings of the 25th annual international ACM SIGIR conference on Research and development in information retrieval*, SIGIR '02, pages 425–426, New York, NY, USA, 2002.

[19] B. Tan and F. Peng. Unsupervised query segmentation using generative language models and wikipedia. In *Proceeding of the 17th international conference on World Wide Web*, WWW '08, pages 347–356, New York, NY, USA, 2008. ACM.

[20] T. Tao and C. Zhai. An exploration of proximity measures in information retrieval. In *Proceedings of the 30th annual international ACM SIGIR conference on Research and development in information retrieval*, SIGIR '07, pages 295–302, New York, NY, USA, 2007.

[21] M. Taylor, H. Zaragoza, N. Craswell, S. Robertson, and C. Burges. Optimisation methods for ranking functions with multiple parameters. In *Proceedings of the 15th ACM international conference on Information and knowledge management*, CIKM '06, pages 585–593, New York, NY, USA, 2006. ACM.

[22] K. Wang, C. Thrasher, E. Viegas, X. Li, and B.-j. P. Hsu. An overview of microsoft web n-gram corpus and applications. In *Proceedings of the NAACL HLT 2010 Demonstration Session*, HLT-DEMO '10, pages 45–48, Stroudsburg, PA, USA, 2010. Association for Computational Linguistics.

[23] X. Yu and H. Shi. Query segmentation using conditional random fields. In *Proceedings of the First International Workshop on Keyword Search on Structured Data*, KEYS '09, pages 21–26, New York, NY, USA, 2009. ACM.

[24] C. Zhai. Fast statistical parsing of noun phrases for document indexing. In *Proceedings of the fifth conference on Applied natural language processing*, pages 312–319, San Francisco, CA, USA, 1997. Morgan Kaufmann Publishers Inc.

[25] C. Zhai and J. Lafferty. A study of smoothing methods for language models applied to ad hoc information retrieval. In *Proceedings of the 24th annual international ACM SIGIR conference on Research and development in information retrieval*, SIGIR '01, pages 334–342, New York, NY, USA, 2001. ACM.

Collaborative Competitive Filtering: Learning Recommender Using Context of User Choice

Shuang Hong Yang
Georgia Tech
shy@gatech.edu

Bo Long
Yahoo! Labs
bolong@yahoo-inc.com

Alex Smola
Yahoo! Research
smola@yahoo-inc.com

Hongyuan Zha
Georgia Tech
zha@cc.gatech.edu

Zhaohui Zheng
Yahoo! Labs Beijing
zhaohui@yahoo-inc.com

ABSTRACT

While a user's preference is directly reflected in the interactive choice process between her and the recommender, this wealth of information was not fully exploited for learning recommender models. In particular, existing collaborative filtering (CF) approaches take into account only the binary events of user actions but totally disregard the contexts in which users' decisions are made. In this paper, we propose *Collaborative Competitive Filtering* (CCF), a framework for learning user preferences by modeling the choice process in recommender systems. CCF employs a multiplicative latent factor model to characterize the dyadic utility function. But unlike CF, CCF models the user behavior of choices by encoding a local competition effect. In this way, CCF allows us to leverage dyadic data that was previously lumped together with missing data in existing CF models. We present two formulations and an efficient large scale optimization algorithm. Experiments on three real-world recommendation data sets demonstrate that CCF significantly outperforms standard CF approaches in both offline and online evaluations.

Categories and Subject Descriptors: H.3.3 [Information filtering]; I.2.6 [Artificial Intelligence]: Learning

General Terms: Algorithms, Performance

Keywords: Recommender systems, collaborative-competitive filtering, behavior model

1. INTRODUCTION

Recommender systems have become a core component for today's personalized online businesses. With the abilities of connecting various items (e.g., retailing products, movies, News articles, advertisements, experts) to potentially interested users, recommender systems enable online webshops (e.g. Amazon, Netflix, Yahoo!) to expand the marketing efforts from historically a few best-sellings toward a large variety of long-tail (niche) products [4, 25, 9]. Such abilities are endowed by a personalization algorithm for identifying the preference of each individual user, which is at the heart of a recommender system.

Predicting user preference is challenging. Usually, the user and item spaces are very large yet the observations are extremely sparse. Learning from such rare, noisy and largely missing evidences has a high risk of overfitting. Indeed, this *data sparseness* issue has been widely recognized as a key challenge for constructing effective recommender systems.

A straightforward way for building recommender would be to learn each user's preference based on the prior interactions between the user and the recommender system. Typically, such interaction is an "opportunity give-and-take" process (*c.f.* Table 1), where at each interaction:

1) a user u inquires the system (e.g. visits a movie recommendation web site);
2) the system offers a set of (personalized) opportunities (i.e. items) $\mathcal{O} = \{i_1, \dots, i_l\}$ (e.g. recommends a list of movies of potential interest to the user);
3) the user chooses one item $i^* \in \mathcal{O}$ (or more) from these offers and takes actions accordingly (e.g. click a link, rent a movie, view a News article, purchase a product).

Somewhat surprisingly, this interaction process has not been fully-exploited for learning recommenders. Instead, research on recommender systems has focused almost exclusively on recovering user preference by completing the matrix of user actions (u, i^*) while the actual contexts in which user decisions are made are totally disregarded. In particular, Collaborative Filtering (CF) approaches only captures the action dyads (u, i^*) while the contextual dyads (i.e. $\{(u, i)\}$ for all $i \in \mathcal{O}$ and $i \neq i^*$) are typically treated as missing data. For example, the rating-oriented models aim to approximating the ratings that users assigned to items [22, 19, 1, 14]; the recently emerged ranking-oriented algorithms [26, 15] attempt to recover the ordinal ranking information derived from the ratings. Although this matrix-completion formulation of the recommendation problem has led to numerous algorithms which excel at a number of data sets, including the prize-winning work of [14], we argue here that the formulation is inherently flawed — a preference for *Die Hard* given a generic set of movies only tells us that the user appreciates action movies; however, a preference for *Die Hard* over *Terminator* or *Rocky* suggests that the user might favor Bruce

SIGIR'11, July 24–28, 2011, Beijing, China.

User	Offer set	Choice
u_1	$[i_1, i_2, i_3, i_5]$	i_2
u_2	$[i_2, i_3, i_4, i_5]$	i_2
u_3	$[i_1, i_3, i_5, i_6]$	i_5
u_4	$[i_2, i_3, i_4, i_6]$	i_3
u_5	$[i_1, i_3, i_4, i_5]$	i_4
u_6	$[i_1, i_4, i_5, i_6]$	i_6

	i_1	i_2	i_3	i_4	i_5	i_6
u_1	·	1	·		·	
u_2		1	·	·	·	
u_3	·		·		1	·
u_4		·	1	·		·
u_5	·		·	1	·	
u_6	·			·	·	1

Table 1: An example of user-recommender interactions and the derived observation matrix: entries with value "1" denote the action dyads; dyads that are observed without user actions (e.g. offered by the recommender but not picked by the user) are marked with dots ("·"). CF trains only on the 1 entries while the · entries are treated as missing data. CCF distinguishes between unseen entries and entries marked with dots.

Willis over other action heroes. In other words, the context of user choice is vital when estimating user preferences.

When it comes to modeling of user-recommender interactions, an important question arises: what is the fundamental mechanism underlying the user choice behaviors? As reflected by its name, collaborative filtering is based on the notion of "collaboration effects" that *similar items get similar responses from similar users*. This assumption is essential because by encoding the "collaboration" among users or among items or both, CF greatly alleviates the issue of data sparseness and in turn makes more reliable predictions based on the somewhat *pooled* evidences.

It has long been recognized in psychology and economics that, besides the effect of collaboration [5, 20], another mechanism governs users' behavior — *competition* [16, 18, 3]. In particular, items turn to compete with each other for the attention of users; therefore, axiomatically, user u will pick the *best* item i^* (i.e. the one with highest utility) when confronted by the set of alternatives $\mathcal{O}$. For example, consider a user with a penchant for action movies by Arnold Schwarzenegger. Given the choice between *Sleepless in Seattle* and *Die Hard* he will likely choose the latter. However, when afforded the choice between the oeuvres of Schwarzenegger, Diesel or Willis, he's clearly more likely to choose Schwarzenegger over the works of Willis. To capture user's preference more accurately, it is therefore *essential* for a recommender model to take into account such local competition effect. Unfortunately, this effect is absent in a large number of collaborative filtering approaches.

In this paper, we present Competitive Collaborative Filtering (CCF) for learning recommender models by modeling users' choice behavior in their interactions with the recommender system. Similar to matrix factorization approaches for CF, we employ a multiplicative latent factor model to characterize the dyadic utility function (i.e. the utility of an item to a user). In this way, CCF encodes the collaboration effect among users/items just as CF does. But instead of learning only the action dyads (i.e. (u, i^*) or the "1" entries in Table 1), CCF bases the learning of the factorization on the whole user-recommender interaction sessions. It therefore leverages not only the action dyads (u, i^*) but also the dyads in the context without user actions (i.e. (u, i) for all $i \in \mathcal{O}$ and $i \neq i^*$, or the dot entries in Table 1), which were treated as potentially missing data in CF approaches.

To leverage the entire interaction session for latent factor learning, we devise probabilistic models or optimization objectives to encode the local competition effect underlying the user choice process. We present two formulations with different flavors. The first formulation is derived from the *multinomial logit model* that has been widely used for modeling user choice behavior (e.g. choice of brands) in psychology [16], economics [17, 18] and marketing science [11]. The second formulation relates closely to the ordinal regression models in content filtering [12] (e.g. web search ranking). Essentially, both formulations attempt to encodes "local optimality of user choices" to encourage that every opportunity i^* taken by a user u be locally the best in the context of the opportunities $\mathcal{O}$ offered to her. From a machine learning viewpoint, CCF is a hybrid of *local* and *global* learning, where a global matrix factorization model is learned by optimizing a local context-aware loss function. We discuss the implementation of CCF, establish efficient learning algorithms and deliver a package that allows distributed optimization on streaming data.

Experiments were conducted on three real-world recommendation data sets. First, on two dyadic data sets, we show that CCF improves over standard CF models by up to 50+% in terms of offline top-k ranking. Furthermore, on a commercial recommender system, we show that CCF significantly outperform CF models in both offline and online evaluations. In particular, CCF achieves up to 7% improvement in offline top-k ranking and up to 13% in terms of online click rate prediction.

Outline: §2 describes the problem formulation, the backgrounds and motivates CCF. §3 presents the detailed CCF models, learning algorithms and our distributed implementation. §4 reports experiments and results. §5 reviews related work and §6 summarizes the results.

2. PRELIMINARIES

2.1 Problem formulation

Consider the user-system interaction in a recommender system: we have users $u \in \mathcal{U} := \{1, 2, \ldots, U\}$ and items $i \in \mathcal{I} = \{1, 2, \ldots, I\}$; when a user u visits the site, the system recommends a set of items $\mathcal{O} = \{i_1, \ldots, i_l\}$ and u in turn chooses a (possibly empty) subset $\mathcal{D} \subseteq \mathcal{O}$ from $\mathcal{O}$ and takes actions accordingly (e.g. buys some of the recommended products). For ease of explanation, let us temporarily assume $\mathcal{D} = \{i^*\}$, i.e. $\mathcal{D}$ is not empty and contains exactly one item i^*. More general scenarios shall be discussed later.

To build the recommender system, we record a collection of historical interactions in the form of $\{(u_t, \mathcal{O}_t, \mathcal{D}_t)\}$, where t is the index of a particular interaction session. Our goal is to generate recommendations $\mathcal{O}_{\tilde{t}}$ for an incoming visit $\tilde{t}$ of user $u_{\tilde{t}}$ such that the user's satisfaction is maximized. Hereafter, we refer to $\mathcal{U}$ as *user space*, $\mathcal{I}$ as *item space*, $\mathcal{O}_t$ as *offer set* or *context*, $\mathcal{D}_t$ as *decision set*, and i^* as a *decision*.

A key component of a recommender system is a model $r(u, i)$ that characterizes the utility of an item $i \in \mathcal{I}$ to a user $u \in \mathcal{U}$, upon which recommendations for a new inquiry from user u could be done by simply ranking items based on $r(u, i)$ and recommending the top-ranked ones. Collaborative filtering is by far the most well-known method for modeling such dyadic responses.

2.2 Collaborative filtering

In collaborative filtering we are given observations of dyadic responses $\{(u, i, y_{ui})\}$ with each y_{ui} being an observed response (e.g. user's rating to an item, or indication of whether user u took an action on item i). The whole mapping:

$$(u,i) \to y_{ui} \text{ where } u \in \mathcal{U}, i \in \mathcal{I}$$

constitutes a large matrix $Y \in \mathcal{Y}^{|\mathcal{U}|\times|\mathcal{I}|}$. While we might have millions of users and items, only a tiny proportion (considerably less than 1% in realistic datasets) of entries are observable[1].

Collaborative filtering explores the notion of "collaboration effects", i.e., similar users have similar preferences to similar items. By encoding collaboration, CF pools the sparse observations in such a way that for predicting $r(u,i)$ it also borrows observations from other (similar) users/items. Generally speaking, existing CF methods fall into either of the following two categories.

Neighborhood models. A popular class of approaches to CF is based on propagating the observations of responses among items or users that are considered as neighbors. The model first defines a similarity measure between items / users. Then, an unseen response between user u and item i is approximated based on the responses of neighboring users or items [22, 19], for example, by simply averaging the neighboring responses with similarities as weights.

Latent factor models. This class of methods learn predictive latent factors to estimate the missing dyadic responses. The basic idea is to associate latent factors[2], $\phi_u \in \mathbb{R}^k$ for each user u and $\phi_i \in \mathbb{R}^k$ for each item i, and assume a multiplicative model for the dyadic response,

$$p(y_{ui}|u,i) = p(y_{ui}|r_{ui};\Theta),$$

where Θ denotes the set of hyper-parameters, the utility is assumed as a multiplicative function of the latent factors,

$$r(u,i) = \phi_u^\top \phi_i.$$

This way the factors could explain past responses and in turn make prediction for future ones. This model implicitly encodes the Aldous-Hoover theorem [13] for exchangeable matrices – y_{ui} are independent of each other given ϕ_u and ϕ_i. In essence, it amounts to a low-rank approximation of the matrix Y that naturally embeds both users and items into a vector space in which the inner-products directly reflect the semantic relatedness.

To design a concrete model [2, 21, 23], one needs to specify a distribution for the dependence. Afterwards, the model boils down to an optimization problem. For example two commonly-used formulations are:

- **ℓ_2 regression** The most popular learning formulation is to minimize the ℓ_2 loss within an empirical risk minimization framework [14]:

$$\min_\phi \sum_{(u,i)\in\Omega} (y_{ui} - \phi_u^\top \phi_i)^2 + \lambda_{\mathcal{U}} \sum_{u\in\mathcal{U}} ||\phi_u||^2 + \lambda_{\mathcal{I}} \sum_{i\in\mathcal{I}} ||\phi_i||^2,$$

where Ω denotes the set of (u,i) dyads for which the responses y_{ui} are observed, $\lambda_{\mathcal{U}}$ and $\lambda_{\mathcal{I}}$ are regularization weights.

- **Logistic** Another popular formulation [21, 1] is to use logistic regression by optimizing the cross-entropy:

$$\min_\phi \sum_{(u,i)\in\Omega} \log\left[1 + \exp(-\phi_u^\top \phi_i)\right] + \lambda_{\mathcal{U}} \sum_{u\in\mathcal{U}} ||\phi_u||^2 + \lambda_{\mathcal{I}} \sum_{i\in\mathcal{I}} ||\phi_i||^2$$

[1]Note the subtle difference in data representation: while we record entire sessions, CF only records the dyadic responses.
[2]We assume each latent factor ϕ contains a constant component so as to absorb user/item-specific offset into ϕ.

2.3 Motivating discussions

Collaborative filtering approaches have made substantial progresses and are currently the state-of-the-art techniques for recommender system. However, we argue here that CF approaches might be a bit lacking in several aspects. First of all, although data sparseness is a big issue, CF does not fully leverage the wealth of user behavior data. Take the user-recommender interaction process described in §2.1 as an example (c.f. Table 1), CF methods typically use only the action dyad (u, i^*) of each session while other dyads $\{(u,i)|i \in \mathcal{O}, i \neq i^*\}$ are treated missing and totally disregarded, which could be wasteful of the invaluable training resource because these non-action dyads are not totally useless, as shown by the experiments in this paper.

Secondly, most existing CF approaches learn user preference collaboratively by either approximating the dyadic responses $\{y_{ui^*}\}$ [22, 19, 1, 14] or preserving the ordinal ranking information derived from the dyadic responses [26, 15]; none of them models the user choice behavior. Particularly, as users choose from competing alternatives, there is naturally a local competition effect among items being offered in a session. Our work show that this effect could be an important clue for learning user preference.

Because latent factor models are very flexible and could be under-determined (or over-parameterized) even for rather moderate number of users/items. With the above two limitations, CF approaches are vulnerable to over-fitting [1, 14]. Particularly, while most existing CF models might learn consistently on user ratings (numerical value typically with five levels) if given enough training data, they usually perform poorly on binary responses. For example, for the aforementioned interaction process (*c.f.* Table 1), the response y_{ui} is typically a binary event indicating whether or not item i was accepted by the user u. With the non-action dyads being ignored, the responses are exclusively positive observations (either $y_{ui} = 1$ or missing). As a result, we will obtain an overly-optimistic estimator that biases toward positive responses and predicts positive for almost all the incoming dyads (See §4.1 for empirical evidences).

3. COLLABORATIVE COMPETITIVE FILTERING

We present a novel framework for recommender learning by modeling the user-system interaction process. The key insight is that the contexts $\mathcal{O}_t$ in which user's decisions are made should be taken into account when learning recommender models. In practice, a user u could make different decisions when facing different contexts $\mathcal{O}_t$. For instance, an item i would not have been chosen by u if it were not presented to her at the first place; likewise, user u could choose another item if the context $\mathcal{O}_t$ changes such that a better offer (e.g., a more interesting item) is presented to her.

In this section, we describe the framework of collaborative-competitive filtering. We start with some axiomatic views of the user choice behaviors. Following that, we present the learning formulation of CCF. We then develop the optimization algorithms and implementation techniques. We close the section with a discussion of useful extensions.

3.1 Local optimality of user choices

Formally, the individual choice process (i.e. user-recommender interactions) in a recommender system can be viewed as an instance of the *opportunity give-and-take* (GAT) process.

Definition [GAT]: *An opportunity give-and-take process is a process of interactions among an agent u, a system S and a set of opportunities $\mathcal{I}$; at an interaction t:*

- *u is given a set of opportunities $O_t \subset \mathcal{I}$ by S;*
- *u makes the decision by takeing one of the opportunities: $i_t^* \in \mathcal{O}_t$;*
- *Each opportunity $i \in \mathcal{O}_t$ could potentially give u a revenue (utility) of r_{ui} if being taken or 0 otherwise.*

Note that we assume the agent is *a priori* not aware of all the items, and only through the recommender S can she get to know the items, therefore other items that are not in $\mathcal{O}_t$ is unaccessible to u at interaction t. This is reasonable considering that the total number of items in the inventory is usually very large. Moreover, we assume an agent u is a rational decision maker: she knows that her choice of item i will be at the expense of others $i' \in \mathcal{O}_t$, therefore she compares among alternatives before making her choice. In other words, for each decision, u considers both revenue and opportunity cost, and decides which opportunity to take based on the potential profit of each opportunity in $\mathcal{O}$. Specifically, the opportunity cost c_{ui} is the potential loss of u from taking an opportunity i that excludes her to take other opportunities: $c_{ui} = \max\{r_{ui'} : i' \in \mathcal{O} \backslash i\}$; the profit $\pi_{ui} = r_{ui} - c_{ui}$ is the net gain of an decision. By drawing the rational decision theory [16], we present the following principle of individual choice behavior.

Proposition: *A rational decision is a decision maximizing the profit: $i^* = \arg\max_{i \in \mathcal{O}} \pi_{ui}$.*

This proposition implies the constraint of "local optimality of user choice", a local competitive effect restricting that the agent u always chooses the offer that is locally optimal in the context of the offer set $\mathcal{O}_t$.

3.2 Collaborative competitive filtering

The local-optimality principle induces a constraint which could be translated to an objective function for recommender learning:

$$\begin{aligned} &\forall i^* \in \mathcal{D}_t, \quad r_{ui^*} \geqslant \max\{r_{ui} | i \in \mathcal{O}_t \setminus \mathcal{D}_t\} \\ \text{or} \quad & P(i^* \text{ is taken}) = P(r_{ui^*} \geqslant \max\{r_{ui} | i \in \mathcal{O}_t \setminus \mathcal{D}_t\}). \quad (1) \end{aligned}$$

This objective is, however, problematic. First, the inequality constraint restricts the utility function only up to an arbitrary order-preserving transformation (e.g. a monotonically increasing function), and hence cannot yield a unique solution (e.g. point estimation) [17]. Second, optimization based on the induced objective is computationally intractable due to the max operator. To this end, we present two surrogate objectives, which are both computationally efficient and show close connections to existing models.

3.2.1 Softmax model

Our first formulation is based on the random utility theory [16, 17] which has been extensively used for modeling choice behavior in economics [18] and marketing science [11]. In particular, we assume the utility function consists of two components $r_{ui} + e_{ui}$, where: (1) r_{ui} is a deterministic function characterizing the intrinsic interest of user u to item i, for which we use the latent factor model to quantify $r_{ui} = \phi_u^\top \phi_i$; (2) the second part e_{ui} is a stochastic error term reflecting the uncertainty and complexness of the choice process[3]. Furthermore, we assume the error term e_{ui} is an independently and identically distributed Weibull (extreme point) variable:

$$\Pr(e_{ui} \leqslant \epsilon) = e^{-e^{-\epsilon}}.$$

Together with the local-optimality principle, these two assumptions yield the *multinomial logit model* [18, 17, 11]:

$$p(i^* = i | u, \mathcal{O}) = \frac{e^{r_{ui}}}{\sum_{j \in \mathcal{O}} e^{r_{uj}}} \text{ for all } i \in \mathcal{O}. \quad (2)$$

Intuitively, this model enforces the local-optimality constraint by using the *softmax* function as a surrogate of *max*.

Given a collection of training interactions $\{(u_t, \mathcal{O}_t, i_t^*)\}$, the latent factors can be estimated using penalized maximum likelihood via

$$\begin{aligned} \min_{\phi} \sum_t \log\Big[\sum_{i \in \mathcal{O}_t} \exp(\phi_{u_t}^\top \phi_i)\Big] - \phi_{u_t}^\top \phi_{i_t^*} \quad (3) \\ + \lambda_{\mathcal{U}} \sum_{u \in \mathcal{U}} ||\phi_u||^2 + \lambda_{\mathcal{I}} \sum_{i \in \mathcal{I}} ||\phi_i||^2. \end{aligned}$$

While the above formulation is a convex optimization w.r.t. r_{ui} as each of the objective terms in Eq.(3) is strongly concave, it is nonconvex w.r.t. the latent factors ϕ. We postpone the discussion of optimization algorithms to §3.3.

3.2.2 Hinge model

Our second formulation is based on a simple reduction of the local-optimality constraint by noting, from Eq(1), that:

$$\begin{aligned} P(i = i^* | u, \mathcal{O}) &= P((r_{ui^*} - r_{ui}) > (e_{ui} - e_{ui^*}), \ \forall i \in \mathcal{O}) \\ &\leqslant P((r_{ui^*} - \bar{r}_{u\bar{i}}) > (\bar{e}_{u\bar{i}} - e_{ui^*})), \end{aligned}$$

where $\bar{r}_{u\bar{i}} = \frac{1}{|\mathcal{O}|-1} \sum_{i \in \mathcal{O} \setminus i^*} r_{ui}$ is the average potential utility that u could possibly gain from the non-chosen items. Intuitively, the above model encourages that the utility difference between choice and non-chosen items, $r_{ui^*} - \bar{r}_{u\bar{i}}$, to be nontrivially greater than random errors. Based on this notion, we present the following formulation which views the task as a pairwise preference learning problem [12] and uses the non-choices averagely as negative preferences.

$$\begin{aligned} \min_{\theta, \xi} \sum_t \xi_t + \lambda_{\mathcal{U}} \sum_{u \in \mathcal{U}} ||\phi_u||^2 + \lambda_{\mathcal{I}} \sum_{i \in \mathcal{I}} ||\phi_i||^2 \quad (4) \\ \text{s.t.: } r_{ui_t^*} - \frac{1}{|\mathcal{O}_t| - 1} \sum_{i \in \mathcal{O}_t \setminus \{i_t^*\}} r_{ui} \geq 1 - \xi_t \text{ and } \xi_t \geq 0. \end{aligned}$$

This formulation is directly related to the maximum score estimation [17] of the multinomial logit model Eq(2). Intuitively, it directly reflects the insight that user decisions are usually made by comparing alternatives and considering the *difference* of potential utilities. In other words, it learns latent factors by maximizing the marginal utility between user choice and the average of non-choices.

[3]The error term essentially accounts for all the subtle, uncertain and unmeasurable factors that influence user choice behaviors, for example, a user's mood, past experience, or other factors (e.g., whether the decision is made in a hurry, together with her friends, or totally unconsciously)

Again, the optimization is convex w.r.t. r_{ui}, but nonconvex w.r.t. the latent factors, therefore the standard optimization tools such as the large variety of RankSVM [12] solvers are not directly applicable.

3.2.3 Complexity

It is worth noting that our CCF formulations have an appealing linear complexity, $O(|\mathcal{I}| \times |\mathcal{O}|)$, where the offer size $|\mathcal{O}|$ is typically a very small number. For example, Netflix recommends $|\mathcal{O}| = 7$ movies for each visit, and Yahoo! frontpage highlights $|\mathcal{O}| = 4$ hot news for each browser. Therefore, CCF has the same-order complexity as the rating-oriented CF models. Note that the ranking-oriented CF approaches [26, 15] are much more expensive – for each user u, the learning complexity is quadratic $O(|\mathcal{I}|^2)$ as they learn preference of each user by comparing every pair of the items.

3.3 Learning algorithms

As we have already mentioned, due to the use of bilinear terms, both of the two CCF variants are nonconvex optimization problems regardless of the choice of the loss functions. While there *are* convex reformulations for some settings they tend to be computationally inefficient for large scale problems as they occur in industry — the convex formulations require the manipulation of a full matrix which is impractical for anything beyond thousands of users.

Moreover, the interactions between user and items change over time and it is desirable to have algorithms which process this information incrementally. This calls for learning algorithms that are sufficiently efficient and preferably capable to update dynamically so as to reflect upcoming data streams, therefore excluding offline learning algorithms such as classical SVD-based factorization algorithms [14] or spectral eigenvalue decomposition methods [15] that involve large-scale matrices.

We use a distributed stochastic gradient variant with averaging based on the Hadoop MapReduce framework. The basic idea is to decompose the objectives in Eq.(3) or Eq.(4) by running stochastic optimization on sub-blocks of the interaction traces in parallel in the Map phase, and to combine the results for ϕ_i in the Reduce phase.

Stochastic Optimization. We derive a stochastic gradient descent algorithm to solve the optimization described in Eq(3) or Eq(4). The algorithm is computationally efficient and decouplable among different interactions and users, therefore amenable for parallel implementation.

The algorithm loops over all the observations and updates the parameters by moving in the direction defined by negative gradient. Specifically, we can carry out the following update equations on each machine separately:

- For all $i \in \mathcal{O}_t$ do $\phi_i \leftarrow \phi_i - \eta \left[l'(\phi_u^\top \phi_i)\phi_u + \lambda_\mathcal{I} \phi_i\right]$.
- For each u do $\phi_u \leftarrow \phi_u - \eta \left[\sum_{i \in \mathcal{O}_t} l'(\phi_u^\top \phi_i)\phi_i + \lambda_\mathcal{U} \phi_u\right]$.

Here η is the learning rate[4]. The gradients are given by:

$$l'_{\text{Softmax}}(r_{ui}) = \frac{\exp(r_{ui})}{\sum_{j \in \mathcal{O}} \exp(r_{uj})} - \delta_{i,i^*} \quad (5)$$

$$l'_{\text{Hinge}}(r_{ui}) = -\frac{|\mathcal{O}|\,\delta_{i,i^*} - 1}{|\mathcal{O}| - 1} H(1 - r_{ui^*} + \bar{r}_{u\bar{i}}) \quad (6)$$

[4]We carry out an annealing procedure to discount η by a factor of 0.9 after each iteration, as suggested by [14].

where $H(\cdot)$ is the Heaviside function, i.e. $H(x) = 1$ if $x > 0$ and $H(x) = 0$ otherwise.[5]

Feature Hashing. A key challenge in learning CCF models on large-scale data is that the storage of parameters as well as observable features requires a large amount of memory and a reverse index to map user IDs to memory locations. In particular in recommender systems with hundreds of millions of users the memory requirement would easily exceed what is available on today's computers (100 million users with 100 latent feature dimensions each amounts to 40GB of RAM). We address this problem by implementing feature hashing [27] on the space of matrix elements. In particularly, by allowing random collisions and applying hash mapping to the latent factors (i.e. ϕ), we keep the entire representation in memory, thus greatly accelerating optimization.

3.4 Extensions

We now discuss two extensions of CCF to address the fact that in some cases users choose not to respond to an offer at all and that moreover we may have observed features in addition to the latent representation discussed so far.

Sessions without response

In establishing the CCF framework for modeling the user choice behavioral data, we assumed that for each user-system interaction t, the decision set $\mathcal{D}_t$ contains at least one item. This assumption is, however, not true in practice. A user's visit at a recommender system does not always yield an action. For example, users frequently visit online e-commerce website without making any purchase, or browse a news portal without clicking on any advertisement. Actually, such nonresponded visits may account for a vast majority of the traffics that an recommender system receives. Moreover, different users may have different propensities for taking an action. Here, we extend the multinomial logit model to modeling both responded and nonresponded interactions, $(u_t, \mathcal{O}_t, i_t^*)$ and $(u_t, \mathcal{O}_t, \emptyset)$ respectively.

This is accomplished by adding a scalar θ_u for each user u to capture the *action threshold* of user u. We assume that, at an interaction t, user u_t takes an effective action only if she feels that the overall quality of the offers $\mathcal{O}_t$ are good enough and worth the spending of her attention. In keeping with the multinomial logit model this means that

$$p(i^* = i|u, \mathcal{O}) = \frac{\exp(\phi_u^\top \phi_i)}{\exp(\theta_u) + \sum_{j \in \mathcal{O}} \exp(\phi_u^\top \phi_j)} \quad (7)$$

for all $i \in \mathcal{O}$ and the probability of no response is given by the remainder, that is by:

$$\frac{\exp(\theta_u)}{\exp(\theta_u) + \sum_{j \in \mathcal{O}} \exp(\phi_u^\top \phi_j)}.$$

In essence, this amounts to a model where the 'non-response' has a certain reserve utility that needs to be exceeded for a user to respond. We may extend the hinge model in the same spirit (we use a trade-off constant $C > 0$ to calibrate the importance of the non-responses):

[5]In our implementation, we approximate this by the continuous function $\frac{1}{1+e^{-100x}}$. This helps with convergence.

Table 2: Statistics of data sets.

	#user	#item	#dyads	offer size
Social	1.2M	400	29M	-
Netflix-5star	0.48M	18K	100M	-
News	3.6M	2.5K	110M	4

$$\min_{\phi,\xi,\varepsilon,\theta} \sum_t \xi_t + C\sum_t \varepsilon_t + \lambda_{\mathcal{U}} \sum_{u\in\mathcal{U}} ||\phi_u||^2 + \lambda_{\mathcal{I}} \sum_{i\in\mathcal{I}} ||\phi_i||^2$$

$$\text{subject to } r_{u_t i_t^*} - \bar{r}_{u_t \bar{i}} - \theta_u \geqslant 1 - \xi_t \text{ for all } i^* \in \mathcal{D}_t \text{ if } \mathcal{D}_t \neq \emptyset$$
$$\theta_u - r_{u_t i} \geqslant 1 - \varepsilon_t, \quad \forall i \in \mathcal{O}_t \text{ if } \mathcal{D}_t = \emptyset$$
$$r_{ui} = \phi_u^\top \phi_i \text{ and } \xi_t \geqslant 0 \text{ and } \varepsilon_t \geqslant 0 \qquad (8)$$

Content features

In previous sections, we use a plain latent factor model for quantifying utility, i.e. $r_{ui} = \phi_u^\top \phi_i$. A known drawback [1] of such model is that it only captures dyadic data (responses), and therefore generalizes poorly for completely new entities, i.e. unseen users or items, of which the observations are missing at the training stage. Here, we extend the model by incorporating content features. In particular, we assume that, in addition to the latent features ϕs, there exist some observable properties $x_u \in \mathbb{R}^m$ (e.g. a user's self-crafted registration files) for each user u, and $x_i \in \mathbb{R}^n$ (e.g. a textual description of an item) for each item i. We then assume the utility r_{ui} as a function of both types of features (i.e. observable and latent) [28]:

$$r_{ui} \sim p(r_{ui}|\phi_u^\top \phi_i + x_u^\top M x_i)$$

where the matrix $M \in \mathbb{R}^{m\times n}$ provides a bilinear form for characterizing the utility based on the content features of the corresponding dyads. This model integrates both collaborative filtering [14] and content filtering [7]. On the one hand, if the user u or item i has no or merely non-informative observable features, the model degrades to a factorization-style utility model. On the other hand, if we assume that ϕ_u and ϕ_i are irrelevant, for instance, if i or j is totally new to the system such that there is no interaction involving either of them as in a cold-start setting, this model becomes the classical content-based relevance model commonly used in, e.g. webpage ranking [29], advertisement targeting [6], and content recommendation [7].

4. EXPERIMENTS

We report experimental results on two test-beds. First, we evaluate the CCF models with CF baselines on two dyadic data sets with simulated choice contexts. The choice of simulated data generated from CF datasets was made since we are unaware of any *publicly* available datasets directly suitable for CCF. Furthermore, we extend our evaluation to a more strict setting based on user-system interaction session data from a commercial recommender system.

4.1 Dyadic response data

We use dyadic data with binary responses, i.e. $\{(u, i, y_{ui})\}$ where $y_{ui} \in \{1, \text{missing}\}$. We compare different recommender models in terms of their top-k ranking performance.

Social network data. The first data set we used was collected from a commercial social network site, where a user

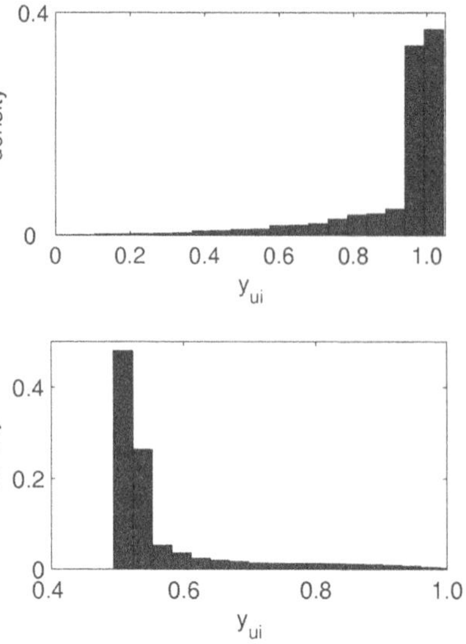

Figure 1: Histograms of the predicted dyadic responses $\{\hat{y}_{ui}\}$: while the predictions by CF (top) are over-optimistically concetrated on positive responses (i.e. predicting "relevant" for all possible dyads), the results obtained by CCF (bottom) demonstrate a more reasonable power-law property.

expresses her preference for an item with an explicit indication of "like". We examine data collected for about one year, involving hundreds of millions of users and a large collection of applications, such as games, sports, news feeds, finance, entertainment, travel, shopping, and local information services. Our evaluation focuses on a random subset consisting of about 400 items, 1.2 million users and 29 million dyadic responses ("like" indications).

Netflix 5 star data. We also report results on a data set derived from the Netflix prize data[6], one of the most famous public data sets for recommendation. The Netflix data set contains 480K users and 18K movies. We derive binary responses by considering only 5-star ratings as "positive" dyads and treating all the others as missing entries.

For both data sets, we randomly split the data into three pieces, one for training, one for testing and the other for validation.

Evaluation metrics. We assess the recommendation performance of each model by comparing the top suggestions of the model to the true actions taken by a user (i.e. "like" or 5-star). We consider three measures commonly used for accessing top-k ranking performance in the IR community:

AP is the *average precision*. AP@n averages the precision of the top-n ranked list of each query (e.g. user).

AR or *average recall* is the average recall of the top-n rank list of each query.

nDCG or *normalized Discounted Cumulative Gain* is the normalized position-discounted precision score. It gives larger credit to top positions.

[6] `http://www.netflixprize.com`. For downloadable codes and more information on Netflix experiment, please visit `http://www.cc.gatech.edu/~syang46/ccf.htm`

Table 3: Top-k ranking performance on two binary dyadic data sets with simulated contexts.

Model		AP@5	AR@5	nDCG@5
Social				
CF	ℓ_2	0.448	0.230	0.475
CF	Logistic	0.449	0.230	0.476
CCF	Softmax	**0.688**	**0.261**	**0.704**
CCF	Hinge	0.686	0.260	0.702
Netflix-5star				
CF	ℓ_2	0.135	0.022	0.145
CF	Logistic	0.135	0.023	0.146
CCF	Softmax	**0.186**	**0.033**	**0.189**
CCF	Hinge	0.185	0.032	0.188

For all the three metrics we use $n = 5$ since most social networks and movie recommendation sites recommend a similar number of items for each user visit.

Evaluation protocol. We compare the two CCF models (i.e. Softmax and Hinge) with the two standard CF factorization models (i.e. ℓ_2 and Logistic) described in §2.2. For dyadic data with binary responses, the Logistic CF model amounts to the state-of-the-art [21, 1].

We adopt a fairly strict top-k ranking evaluation. For each user, we assess the top results out of a total preference ordering of the whole item set. In particular, for each user u, we consider all the items as candidates; we compute the three measures based on the comparison between the ground truth (the set of items in the test set that user u actually liked) and the top-5 suggestions predicted by each model. For statistical consistency, we employ a cross-validation style procedure. We learn the models on training data with parameters tuned on validation data, and then apply the trained models to the test data to assess the performance. All three measures reported are computed on test data only, and they are averaged over five random repeats (i.e. random splits of the data).[7]

To render the data compatible with CCF we simulate a fixed-size pseudo-offer set for each interaction. Specifically, in each step of the stochastic optimization at a positive observation, e.g. $y_{ui} = 1$, we randomly sample a handful set of missing (unobserved) entries $\{y_{ui'}\}_{i'=1:m}$. These sampled dyads are then treated as non-choices, and together with the positive dyad, they are used as the offer set for the current session. In our experiments, we choose $m = 9$ pseudo non-choices; in other words, we assume the offer size $|\mathcal{O}_t|$ $=10$.

Results and analysis. We report the mean scores in Table 3. Since the dataset are fairly large the standard deviations of all values were below 0.001. Consequently we omitted the latter from the results. As can be seen from the table, CCF dramatically outperforms CF baselines on both data sets. In terms of AP@5, the two CCF models gain about 52.8%–53.6% improvements compared to the two CF models on the Social data, and by 37.0%–37.8% on Netflix-5 star. Similar comparisons apply to the nDCG@5 measure. And in terms of the AR@5, CCF models outperform CF competitors by up to 13.5% on Social, and 30% on Netflix-5 star data. All these improvements are statistically highly significant. Note that these results are quite consistent: both CF models perform comparably with each other on both data sets; the performance of the two CCF variants is also comparable; between the two groups, gaps are noticeable.

One argument we made in this paper for motivating our work is that since the CF models disregard the context information and only learns on positive (action) dyads, they almost inevitably yield overly-optimistic predictions (i.e. predicting positive for all possible dyads). We hypothesize that such estimation *bias* is one of the key reasons for the inability of CF models in learning binary dyadic data. As an empirical validation, in Figure 1, we plot the histograms of the predicted dyadic responses $\hat{y}_{ui}$ (i.e. entries of the diffused matrices) obtained by a CF model (ℓ_2) and a CCF model respectively.[8] As we can see, the CF model indeed predicts "positive" for most (if not all) dyads; in contrast, the results obtained by the CCF model demonstrate a more realistic power-law distribution [8].[9]

In reality, since the total number of items in the inventory is too large, each user can only afford to "like" a few items out of the huge amount of alternatives. This power-law property is crucial for information filtering because we are intended to identify a few truly relevant items by *filtering* out many many irrelevant ones. A power-law recommender is desirable in a way analogous to a filter with narrow-bandwidth, which effectively filters out the noises (i.e. irrelevant items) and only let the true signal (i.e. relevant items) pass to the users.

4.2 User-system interaction data

We now move on to a more realistic evaluation by applying CCF to real user-system interaction data. We evaluate CCF in both an offline test and an online test while comparing its results to both CF baselines.

Data. We collected a large-scale set of user-system interaction traces from a commercial News article recommender system. In each interaction, the system offers four personalized articles to the visiting user, and the user chooses one of them by clicking to read that article. The recommendations are dynamically changing over time even during the user's visit. The system regularly logs every click event of every user visit. It also records the articles being presented to users at a series of discrete time points. To obtain a context set for each user-system interaction, we therefore trace back to the closest recording time point right before the user-click, and we use the articles presented at that time point as the offer set for the current session. We collected such interaction traces from logged records of over one month. We use a random subset containing 3.6 million users, 2500 items and over 110 million interaction traces. Learning an effective recommender on this data set is particularly challenging as the article pool is dynamically refreshing, and each article only has a lifetime of several hours — it only appears once within

[7] *Note that the contextual information (the offer set $\mathcal{O}_t$ for each interaction t) is missing for both of the two dyadic data sets.* We use the datasets with simulated contexts. Results on real interaction data are reported in §4.2.

[8] Similar results obtained with other losses.

[9] Note that the distribution starts at around 0.5 instead of 0, which is consistent with our intuitions that there is actually *no* truly "irrelevant" item for a user – any item has potential utility for a user; user choose one over another based on the relative preference rather than absolute utility. This is true especially in this era of information explosion, where a user is typically facing so many alternatives that she can only pick the one she likes *the most* while ignoring the others.

Table 4: **Offline test (top-k ranking performance) on user-system interaction data.**

Model		AP@4	AR@4	nDCG@4
30% Training				
CF	ℓ_2	0.245	0.261	0.255
CF	Logistic	0.246	0.263	0.257
CCF	Softmax	**0.262**	**0.278**	**0.274**
CCF	Hinge	0.261	**0.278**	0.273
50% Training				
CF	ℓ_2	0.250	0.273	0.268
CF	Logistic	0.252	0.276	0.269
CCF	Softmax	**0.266**	**0.285**	**0.278**
CCF	Hinge	0.265	**0.285**	0.277
70% Training				
CF	ℓ_2	0.253	0.275	0.271
CF	Logistic	0.253	0.276	0.274
CCF	Softmax	**0.267**	**0.287**	**0.280**
CCF	Hinge	**0.267**	0.286	**0.280**

a particular day, is pulled out from the pool afterward and never appears again.

Evaluation protocol. We consider the following two evaluation settings, one offline and the other offline.

Offline evaluation Similar to the evaluations presented in §4.1, we evaluate the learned recommender models in terms of the top-k ranking performance on a hold-out test subset. We follow the same configurations in §4.1 and use the three ranking measures, i.e. AP@n, AR@n and nDCG@n as the evaluation metrics. Note that here we use $n = 4$ instead of 5, because it is the default recommendation size used in the news recommender system.

Online evaluation We further conduct an online test. In particular. for each incoming interaction, we use the trained models to predict which item among the four recommendations will be taken by the user. This prediction is of crucial importance because one of the key objectives for a recommender system is to maximize the traffic and monetary revenue by lifting the click-through rate.

Offline test results. In this setting, we train each model on progressive proportions of 30%, 50% and 70% randomly-sampled training data respectively, and evaluate each trained model in terms of offline top-k ranking performance. The results are reported in Table 4. The two CCF models greatly outperform the two CF baselines in all the three evaluation metrics. Specifically, CCF models gain up to 6.9% improvement over the two CF models in terms of average precision; up to 6.5% in terms of average recall, and up to 7.5% in terms of nDCG. We also conducted a t-test with a standard 0.05 significance level, which further indicate that all the improvements obtained by CCF are significant.

It is worth noting that the improvements obtained by CCF compared to CF baselines are especially evident when the training data are sparser (e.g. using only 30% of training data). This observation empirically validates our argument that the contexts contain substantial useful information for learning recommender models especially when the dyadic action responses are scarce.

Table 5: **Online test (predicted click probability) on user-system interaction data.**

Model		30%train	50%train	70%train
Random		0.250		
CF	ℓ_2	0.337	0.343	0.347
CF	Logistic	0.341	0.345	0.347
CCF	Softmax	0.376	0.384	**0.391**
CCF	Hinge	**0.377**	**0.385**	**0.391**

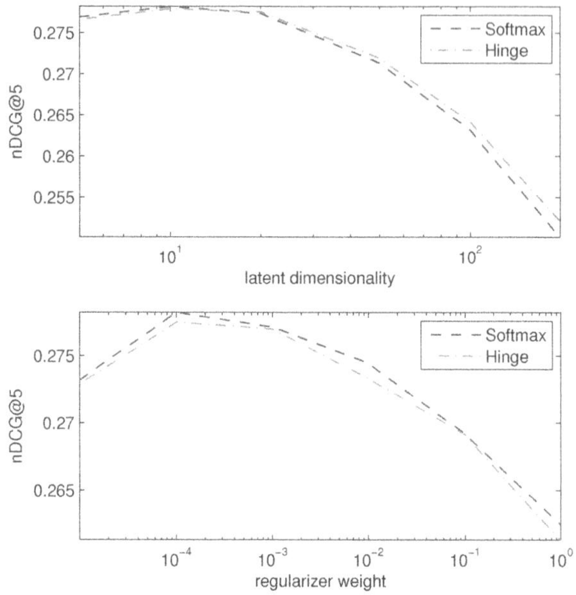

Figure 2: Offline top-k ranking performance (nDCG@5) as a function of latent dimensionality (top) and regularization weight (bottom).

The offline results obtained by CCF are quite satisfactory. For example, the average precision is up to 0.276, which means, out of the four recommended items, on average 1.1 are truly "relevant" (i.e. actually being clicked by the user). This performance is quite promising especially considering that most of the articles in the content pool are transient and subject to dynamically updating.

Online test results. We further evaluate the online performance of each compared model by assessing the predicted click rates. Click-rate is essential for an online recommender system because it is closely-related to both the traffic and the revenue of a webshop. In our evaluation, for each of the incoming visits $(u_t, \mathcal{O}_t, i_t^*)$, we use the trained models to predict the user choice, i.e. we ask the question: "among all the offered items $i \in \mathcal{O}_t$, which one will most likely be clicked?" We use the trained model to rank the items in the offer set, and compare the top-ranked item with the item that was actually taken (i.e. i_t^*) by user u_t. We evaluate the results in terms of the prediction accuracy.

The results are given in Table 5. Because the size of each offer set in the current data set is 4, a random predictor yields 0.25. As seen from the table, while all the four models obtain significantly better predictions than the random predictor, the two CCF models further greatly outperform the two CF models. Specifically, we observe 11.3%–12.7% improvements obtained by CCF models compared to the two CF competitors. These results are quite significant especially considering the dynamic property of the system.

Impact of parameters. The performance of the two CCF models is affected by the parameter settings of the latent dimensionality, k, as well as the regularization weights, $\lambda_{\mathcal{I}}$ and $\lambda_{\mathcal{U}}$. In Figure 2[10], we illustrate how the offline top-k ranking performance changes as a function of these parameters, where we use the same value for both $\lambda_{\mathcal{I}}$ and $\lambda_{\mathcal{U}}$. Here we only reported the results with nDCG@5 measure because the results show similar shapes when other measures (including the click rate) are used. As can be seen from the Figure, the nDCG curves are typically in the inverted U-shape with the optimal values achieved at the middle. In particular, for both the two CCF models, the dimensionality around 20 and regularization weight around 0.0001 yield the best performance, which is also the default parameter setting we used in obtaining our reported results.

Nonresponded sessions. In Section 3.4 we presented two models for encoding nonresponded interactions, e.g. a user visits the News website but does not click any of the recommended articles. These approaches are promising because compared to the responded sessions, the nonresponded ones are typically much more plentiful and if learned successfully, this wealth of information has a potential to alleviating the critical data-sparse issue in recommendation.

Unfortunately, due to the data-logging mechanism of the News recommender system, we were unable to obtain such nonresponded interactions. Instead, for a preliminary test, we conducted evaluation on a small set of *pseudo* nonresponded sessions that are derived from the responded ones. In particular, we hold out a randomly-sampled subset of sessions; for each of these sessions, we hide the item being clicked by the user, and use the remaining items as a nonresponded context set by assuming no click for this set. We augmented this set of derived nonresponded sessions to the training set, and train the model on the combined training data. The results from this preliminary evaluation did not show significant performance improvement. This is likely due to the fact that the surrogate distribution is invalid. A detailed analysis with more realistic data is the subject of future research.

5. RELATED WORK

Although a natural reflection of a user's preference is the process of interaction with the recommender, to our knowledge, this interaction data has not been exploited for learning recommender models. Instead, research on recommender systems has focused almost exclusively on learning the dyadic data. Particularly collaborative filtering approaches only capture the user-item dyadic data with explicit user actions while the context dyads are typically treated missing values. For example, the rating-oriented models aim to approximating the ratings that users assigned to items [22, 19, 1, 14]; whereas the recently proposed ranking-oriented algorithms [26, 15] attempt to recover the ordinal ranking information derived from the ratings.

By exploiting past records of user-item dyadic responses for future prediction based on either *neighborhood based* [22, 19, 15] or *latent factor based* methods [1, 14, 26], collaborative filtering approaches encode the collaboration effect that similar users get similar preference on similar items. In this paper, by leveraging the user-recommender interaction data, we show that much better recommender performance can be obtained when a local-competition effect underlying the user choice behaviors is also encoded.

The multinomial logit model we present is derived based on the random utility theory [16, 17]. The model is well-established and has been widely used for a long time in, e.g. psychology [16], economics [18, 17] and marketing science [11]. Particularly, [11] applied the model to examine the brand choice of households on grocery data; [10] showed this model is theoretically and empirically superior to the ℓ_2 regression model. More recently, the pioneering work of [9] first applied the model to characterize online choices in recommender system and investigated how recommender systems impact sales diversity. Following these steps, this work further employs the model to learn factorization models for recommendation.

The Hinge formulation of CCF shows close connection to the pairwise preference learning approaches widely used in Web search ranking [12]. Our model, however, differs from these content filtering models [12] in that instead of learning a feature mapping as in [12], our model uses the formulation for learning a multiplicative latent factor model.

6. SUMMARY AND FUTURE RESEARCH

We presented a framework for learning recommender by modeling user choice behavior in the user-system interaction process. Instead of modeling only the sparse binary events of user actions as in traditional collaborative filtering, the proposed collaborative-competitive filtering models take into account the contexts in which user decisions are made. We presented two models in this spirit, established efficient learning algorithms and demonstrated the effectiveness of the proposed approaches with extensive experiments on three large-scale real-world recommendation data sets.

There are several promising directions for future research.

Attention budget and position bias. When deriving the CCF model, we admit an assumption that user decides whether to take an offer solely based on the comparison of utilities. This assumption, however, neglects a factor which might be important in practice. In particular, a user might have budgeted attention such that when making choices he only pays attention to a few top-ranked items and totally disregard the others. This *position bias* is evident in both web search ranking and recommendation. We plan to take this into consideration for building choice models.

Recommender strategy and user behavior. A key feature of the current paper is that we assume the recommender adopts a deterministic strategic policy when making recommendations. In practice, a recommender could also adaptively react to the users' actions as well as its own considerations (e.g. inventory constraints, promotion requirement of certain brands). We would like to extend our analysis here to model the interactive process between users and recommender.

Further empirical validation. Due to data collection constraints, some parts of the proposed models are not strictly evaluated in the current paper. We plan to refine the mecha-

[10]Due to heavy computational consumptions, these results are obtained on a relatively small subset of data.

nism for data collection and conduct experiments for further evaluation.

Acknowledgements

Part of this work was supported by NSF Grant IIS-1049694, the 111-Project B07022 and a Yahoo! faculty grant.

7. REFERENCES

[1] D. Agarwal and B.-C. Chen. Regression-based latent factor models. In *15th ACM SIGKDD International conference on Knowledge Discovery and Data Mining*, pages 19–28, 2009.

[2] E. Airoldi, D. M. Blei, S. E. Fienberg, and E. P. Xing. Mixed membership stochastic blockmodels. In *Advances in Neural Information Processing Systems 20*, pages 33–40, 2008.

[3] Y. Bakos and E. Brynjolfsson. Bundling and competition on the internet. *Marketing Science*, 19(1):63–82, 2000.

[4] E. Brynjolfsson, Y. J. Hu, and M. D. Smith. Consumer surplus in the digital economy: Estimating the value of increased product variety at online booksellers. *Management Science*, 49(11):1580–1596, 2003.

[5] D. E. Byrne. *The attraction paradigm.* Academic Press, 1971.

[6] Y. Chen, D. Pavlov, and J. F. Canny. Large-scale behavioral targeting. In *15th ACM SIGKDD international conference on Knowledge Discovery and Data Mining*, pages 209–218, 2009.

[7] W. Chu and S.-T. Park. Personalized recommendation on dynamic content using predictive bilinear models. In *WWW'09: Proceedings of the 18th international conference on World wide web*, pages 691–700, 2009.

[8] M. Faloutsos, P. Faloutsos, and C. Faloutsos. On power-law relationships of the internet topology. In *SIGCOMM'99: Proceedings of the conference on Applications, technologies, architectures, and protocols for computer communication*, pages 251–262, 1999.

[9] D. M. Fleder and K. Hosanagar. Recommender systems and their impact on sales diversity. In *EC'07: Proceedings of the 8th ACM conference on Electronic commerce*, pages 192–199, 2007.

[10] D. H. Gensch and W. W. Recker. The multinomial, multiattribute logit choice model. *Journal of Marketing Research* Vol. 16, No. 1, pp. 124–132. Feb. 1979.

[11] P. M. Guadagni and J. D. Little. A logit model of brand choice calibrated on scanner data. *Marketing Science*, 2(3):203-238, 1983.

[12] R. Herbrich, T. Graepel, and K. Obermayer. Support vector learning for ordinal regression. In *International Conference on Artificial Neural Networks*, pages 97–102, 1999.

[13] O. Kallenberg. *Probabilistic symmetries and invariance principles.* Springer, 2005.

[14] Y. Koren, R. Bell, and C. Volinsky. Matrix factorization techniques for recommender systems. *Computer*, 42(8):30–37, 2009.

[15] N. N. Liu and Q. Yang. Eigenrank: a ranking-oriented approach to collaborative filtering. In *SIGIR'08: Proceedings of the 31st ACM SIGIR conference on Research and development in information retrieval*, pages 83–90, 2008.

[16] R. D. Luce. *Individual choice behavior.* Wiley, 1959.

[17] C. F. Manski. Maximum score estimation of the stochastic utility model of choice. *Journal of Econometrics*, (3):205–228, August 1975.

[18] D. McFadden. Conditional logic analysis of qualitative choice behavior. In *Frontiers of econometrics*, Academic Press, 1974.

[19] M. R. McLaughlin and J. L. Herlocker. A collaborative filtering algorithm and evaluation metric that accurately model the user experience. In *SIGIR'04: Proceedings of the 27th ACM SIGIR conference on Research and development in information retrieval*, pages 329–336, 2004.

[20] M. McPherson, L. S. Lovin, and J. M. Cook. Birds of a feather: Homophily in social networks. *Annual Review of Sociology*, 27(1):415–444, 2001.

[21] K. Miller, T. Griffiths, and M. Jordan. Nonparametric latent feature models for link prediction. In *NIPS'09: Advances in Neural Information Processing Systems 22*, pages 1276–1284, 2009.

[22] B. Sarwar, G. Karypis, J. Konstan, and J. Reidl. Item-based collaborative filtering recommendation algorithms. In *WWW'01: Proceedings of the 10th international conference on World Wide Web*, pages 285–295, 2001.

[23] A. Singh and G. Gordon. A unified view of matrix factorization models. In W. Daelemans, B. Goethals, and K. Morik, editors, *ECML-PKDD'08: European Conference on Machine Learning*, pages 358–373. Springer, 2008.

[24] J. Rennie and N. Srebro. Fast maximum margin matrix factoriazation for collaborative prediction. In *ICML'05: Proceedings of the 22th International Conference on Machine Learning*, 2005.

[25] T. F. Tan and S. Netessine. Is tom cruise threatened? using netflix prize data to examine the long tail of electronic commerce. *Working paper 1361, Wharton school, University of Pennsylvania*, 2010.

[26] M. Weimer, A. Karatzoglou, Q. Le, and A. Smola. Cofirank - maximum margin matrix factorization for collaborative ranking. In *NIPS'07: Advances in Neural Information Processing Systems 20*, pages 1593–1600, 2007.

[27] K. Weinberger, A. Dasgupta, J. Langford, A. Smola, and J. Attenberg. Feature hashing for large scale multitask learning. In *ICML'09: Proceedings of the 26th International Conference on Machine Learning*, pages 1113–1120, 2009. ACM.

[28] S.-H. Yang, B. Long, A. Smola, N. Sadagopan, Z. Zheng, and H. Zha. Like like alike – joint friendship and interest propagation in social networks. In *WWW '11: Proceedings of the 20th international conference on World Wide Web*, 2011.

[29] Z. Zheng, H. Zha, T. Zhang, O. Chapelle, K. Chen, and G. Sun. A General Boosting Method and its Application to Learning Ranking Functions for Web Search. In *NIPS'08: Advances in Neural Information Processing Systems 20.*

CLR: A Collaborative Location Recommendation Framework based on Co-Clustering

Kenneth Wai-Ting Leung
Hong Kong University of Science and Technology
kwtleung@cse.ust.hk

Dik Lun Lee
Hong Kong University of Science and Technology
dlee@cse.ust.hk

Wang-Chien Lee
The Pennsylvania State University
wlee@cse.psu.edu

ABSTRACT

GPS data tracked on mobile devices contains rich information about human activities and preferences. In this paper, GPS data is used in location-based services (*LBSs*) to provide collaborative location recommendations. We observe that most existing LBSs provide location recommendations by clustering the User-Location matrix. Since the User-Location matrix created based on GPS data is huge, there are two major problems with these methods. First, the number of similar locations that need to be considered in computing the recommendations can be numerous. As a result, the identification of truly relevant locations from numerous candidates is challenging. Second, the clustering process on large matrix is time consuming. Thus, when new GPS data arrives, complete re-clustering of the whole matrix is infeasible. To tackle these two problems, we propose the Collaborative Location Recommendation (CLR) framework for location recommendation. By considering activities (i.e., temporal preferences) and different user classes (i.e., *Pattern Users*, *Normal Users*, and *Travelers*) in the recommendation process, CLR is capable of generating more precise and refined recommendations to the users compared to the existing methods. Moreover, CLR employs a dynamic clustering algorithm CADC to cluster the trajectory data into groups of similar users, similar activities and similar locations efficiently by supporting incremental update of the groups when new GPS trajectory data arrives. We evaluate CLR with a real-world GPS dataset, and confirm that the CLR framework provides more accurate location recommendations compared to the existing methods.

Categories and Subject Descriptors

H.2.8 [**Database Management**]: Database Applications—*Data Mining*; H.3.3 [**Information Storage and Retrieval**]: Information Search and Retrieval—*Clustering, Information Filtering*

General Terms

Algorithms, Experimentation

Keywords

Co-Clustering, Collaborative Filtering, Location Recommendation

1. INTRODUCTION

One of the major functions of a location-based service (LBS) is to recommend interesting locations to the users. Most existing LBSs [2] recommend all points of interest (POIs) that are near the users. However, the number of POIs that are close to the user's current position (called the *active location* in this paper) can be numerous. Thus, it is difficult for a user to pick the most relevant suggestions from the large number of recommendations. In order to provide more accurate location suggestions according to the users' interests, many existing LBSs [1], [9], [10], [15] provide location recommendations by first clustering the User-Location matrix, which represents the locations visited by each user, and then making location recommendations based on the user and location clusters. However, a major problem with these methods is that the User-Location matrix created based on GPS data is huge, so the number of recommendations is still very large and the problem of selecting the truly relevant locations remains challenging.

To tackle this problem, we propose the *collaborative location recommendation* (CLR) framework for location recommendation. CLR collects users' GPS trajectory data to discover a set of points of interest (POIs) as candidate locations. Instead of merely considering users and locations represented in a User-Location matrix, we introduce the *Community Location Model* (CLM), which incorporates activities in addition to users and locations. CLM captures the relations between the three important entities, namely, users, activities and locations, in GPS trajectory data with a User-Activity-Location tripartite data structure, which we call CLM graph for simplicity. We argue that activities are important because most users visit locations with the intention to perform some activities (e.g., go to school to study, go to office to work, go to a cinema to watch movie). A novelty of CLM is its ability to derive from GPS trajectories users' temporal preferences through their activities. CLM explores the unique properties among users, activities, and locations to make effective location recommendations. We observe that (1) locations exhibit spatial properties as they contain geographical information; (2) activities exhibit temporal-spatial properties as they represent temporal sequences of visited locations; and (3) users exhibit long-term spatial properties as different users tend to visit different locations according to their long term habits and geographical limits. We argue that, by capturing temporal-spatial information in user activities, the proposed CLM is more effective in discovering similar locations comparing to existing techniques that are based on the User-Location matrix.

In CLR, a co-clustering algorithm *CADC* is employed to cluster the CLM graph in order to obtain high-quality location recommendations. There are a couple of advantages of applying CADC on the CLM graph. First, by exploring the relations between users, activities and locations modeled in CLM, CADC can iteratively

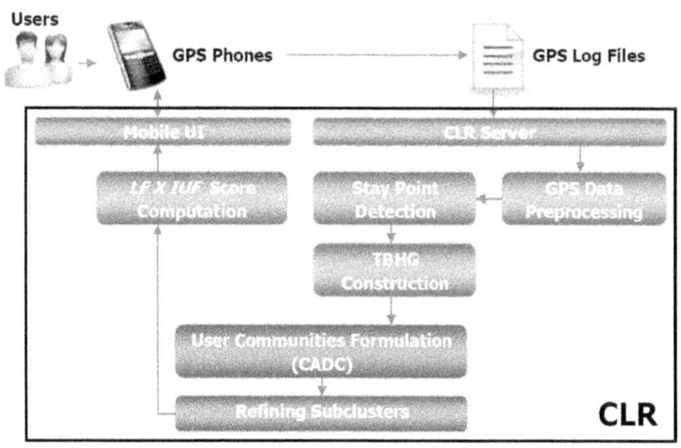

Figure 1: The general process flow of CLR.

cluster different types of similar entities into coherent clusters of similar users, similar activities, and similar locations. Entities in a cluster can be used to discover refined subclusters for making precise recommendations. Moreover, when new GPS trajectory data arrives, CADC can incrementally update the clusters using two separate phases, namely, the *agglomerative phase* and *divisive phase*, without performing the clustering all over again.

While CADC can effectively cluster similar entities together, we observe that the number of similar entities in the same cluster is still too large for making precise recommendations. In order to obtain more precise location recommendations, we introduce two additional steps. First, we propose an *in situ* recommendation refinement method to refine the recommendations for a particular activity performed by a specific user. Second, we introduce *behavioral* refinement, which classifies users into three classes, namely, *Pattern Users*, *Normal Users*, and *Travelers*, according to the sequences of locations that they visited in their activities, and filter out recommendations from different classes of users. Experimental results confirm that recommendations from Travelers are the most accurate among the three classes of users.

In addition to efficient clustering and recommendation refinement, an important issue in CLR is to define an effective ranking function to rank the recommendations according to their relevance. In this paper, we propose a relevance ranking scheme, called $LF \times IUF$ (i.e., Location Frequency × Inverse User Frequency), to rank the location recommendations. The $LF \times IUF$ ranking scheme is inspired by the well-known $TF \times IDF$ scheme in information retrieval. Basically, the interestingness of a location increases proportionally to the number of visits, but is offset by the number of users who have visited the location. The idea is motivated by the observation that a location visited by many users (e.g., a train station or an airport) may not be always an interesting location recommendation.

As discussed, the proposed CLR framework consists of several components, including CADC, CLM, in situ and behavioral refinement methods, and the $LF \times IUF$ ranking scheme. Figure 1 shows the components and the general processing flow in the CLR framework. We conduct an evaluation on the accuracy of the recommendations using a real-world GPS dataset. Experimental results confirm that our approach provides more accurate recommendations comparing to the existing methods based on clustering and collaborative filtering.

The main contributions of this paper are summarized below:

- Unlike methods based on User-Location matrix, we propose the Collaborative Location Model (CLM), which incorporates a new entity type, namely, *activity*, to exploit the relations between activities, users and locations. Activities bring rich temporal-spatial information into CLM to facilitate effective co-clustering.
- To avoid clustering the large trajectory dataset all over again when new GPS data arrives, we adopt a co-clustering method, CADC, which not only discovers similar objects by exploring their similarity ties, but also allows efficient incremental clustering in response to new incoming GPS trajectory data.
- We propose an in situ recommendation refinement method to refine the recommendations corresponding to a location in a particular activity issued by a specific user. We also introduce behavioral refinement to identify three classes of users, namely, *Pattern Users*, *Normal Users* and and *Travelers*, according to the sequence of locations that users visited in their activities, and study the recommendation effectiveness of these three classes of users.
- We devise a new relevance ranking scheme, $LF \times IUF$ (*Location Frequency, Inverse User Frequency*), for recommendation ranking of the locations.
- We implement CLR on the Google Android platform and evaluate the effectiveness of the recommendations using a real-world GPS dataset. The experimental results confirm that CLR provides more accurate recommendations compared to the existing methods.

2. RELATED WORK

Location recommendation is an important feature in location-based services (LBSs). It aims to provide location suggestions that a user may interest in. Different methods have been developed to discover similar locations for recommendation. They can be classified as *similarity-based* and *collaborative-filtering-based (i.e., CF-based)*. Similarity-based recommendations are generated based on the similarities of the candidate locations comparing to the active location (i.e., the current position of a user or a specific location specified by the user). The similarity metrics can be different among different systems. For example, Geodelic generates location recommendations according to the distances of the candidate locations to the active location [3]. Similarly, [5] provides information about the surrounding points of interests (POIs). On Twitter [4], users can identify and provide textual descriptions on their own POIs on a map. They can then search for interesting locations according to the supplied textual descriptions.

On the other hand, CF-based methods make use of the travel histories of a group of similar users (i.e., user-based collaborative filtering) or a set of similar locations (i.e., location-based collaborative filtering) to generate location recommendations. The recommendations are personalized because they are generated according to users who are similar to the active user, or locations that are frequently visited by the active user. In [11], a system was proposed to recommend shops based on users' location data histories. It employs an item-based collaborative filtering algorithm to identify shops for recommendation according to users' movements and geographical conditions of the city. Similarly, in [14], a location-based recommendation system was proposed to suggest locations based on users' current positions and their personal preferences.

More recently, Yu et. al. [16] proposed to mine interesting locations and classical travel sequences from multiple users' GPS trajectory data. They proposed a structure called Tree-Based Hierarchical Graph (TBHG) to model users' GPS trajectory data, and a HIT-based [8] influence model to compute the interestingness scores of locations and authority scores of users. The interestingness scores measure the representativeness of locations, while the authority scores measure the travel experience of users. The two scores are employed to predict a set of interesting locations from experienced users for the location recommendation.

We observe that most of the existing CF-based methods rely on a User-Location rating matrix. The predictions are obtained based on ratings of the same location by similar users (User-based CF), ratings of similar locations made by the same user (Location-based CF), or ratings of similar locations made by similar users (Fusion-based CF). The matrix involved in the CF process is usually huge. Thus, the number of possible candidates to be examined for recommendation can be numerous. Unlike the existing methods, our CLR method introduces *activity* as an additional dimension to obtain more accurate location recommendations by exploiting the temporal-spatial properties in activities. Moreover, we propose a refinement method to recommend locations for a specific user, activity, and location (i.e., according to the current activity performed at the current location by the active user). Therefore, the active user can discover locations that match his/her activities and preferences.

3. COMMUNITY LOCATION MODEL

GPS trajectory data is a sequence of unstructured time-stamped latitude/longitude pairs. In order to organize the unstructured trajectory data into a meaningful data structure to facilitate co-clustering and location recommendation, we propose the *Community Location Model* (CLM) to capture the relations between users, activities, and locations. CLM graphs are input to a co-clustering algorithm presented in Section 4 to discover refined subclusters for location recommendation. In Sections 3.1 and 3.2, we present our method to mine GPS routes and important locations from the GPS trajectory data. CLM is presented in Section 3.3.

3.1 GPS Route

UTC DATE	UTC TIME	LATITUDE	LONGITUDE	ALTITUDE
29/3/2010	2:32:36	22.335950	114.207337	314.721222
29/3/2010	2:32:41	22.335934	114.207505	333.723785
29/3/2010	2:32:46	22.335936	114.207506	335.357819
29/3/2010	2:32:51	22.335932	114.207568	342.328796
29/3/2010	2:32:56	22.335949	114.207525	338.480896
29/3/2010	2:33:01	22.335879	114.207505	336.999359
...	...	...	...	...

(a) Example GPS Points.

(b) Example GPS Route.

Figure 2: Example GPS Points and GPS Route.

A GPS log composes of latitudes, longitudes, speed and time, recorded at a regular time interval. As shown in Figure 2(a), a set of *GPS points* $P = p_1, p_2, ..., p_n$ for user u forms a *GPS route* r^u. Figure 2(b) shows the GPS route constructed using the GPS points in Figure 2(a).

From the GPS log, *stay points* representing geographic regions where activities happen can be discovered. We assume that if a user stays in a particular region for a certain period of time, the region is an important place, e.g., a restaurant that the user visited for breakfast, a classroom where the user attended a lecture, a cinema where the user watched a movie, etc. To detect a stay point from the GPS route, two thresholds, sp_t and sp_d, are used in our study:

- sp_t: the time threshold sp_t dictates the duration the user stays within a stay point s.
- sp_d: the distance threshold sp_d dictates the spatial region the user stays within a stay point s.

Figure 2(b) shows two stay points detected from the GPS route. Note that there could be many stay points in the middle of a route as long as the above thresholds are met.

3.2 Location History

The set of stay points $S = s_1, s_2, ..., s_m$ visited by a user u over a period of time forms the location history LH^u of u. Formally, we define $LH^u = s_1 \rightarrow_{\Delta t_1} s_2 \rightarrow_{\Delta t_2} \cdots \rightarrow_{\Delta t_{m-1}} s_m$, where Δt_k is the time between the leaving time at s_k and the arriving time at s_{k+1}. The location histories of different users can be quite different because of the wide variety of stay points that users can possibly visit. To alleviate this stay point sparsity problem, we employ the tree-based hierarchical graph (*TBHG*) [15] to model the location histories from different users. TBHG is a hierarchical graph containing different-sized location clusters at different levels. The first level consists of all of the users' stay points, which are then hierarchically clustered into location clusters using a divisive clustering algorithms with a distance threshold d. The deeper the level in TBHG, the finer (more precise) the location clusters in that level. Thus, stays points that are physically close to one another will be assigned to the same location clusters at different levels in TBHG. Figure 3 shows an example TBHG constructed in a divisive manner. We observe that the locations in the top level of TBHG are too general for location recommendation, since all of the stay points are grouped into large general location clusters. On the other hand, the locations in the deeper levels of TBHG are too fine-grained for location recommendation, since the location clusters are small resulting in only a few stay points.

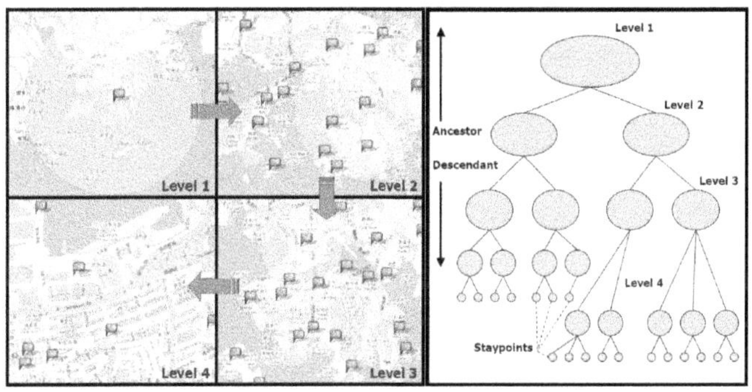

Figure 3: Example TBHG constructed in a divisive manner.

A user's GPS route r^u can be generated using TBHG by finding the locations clusters containing the stay points in r^u and creating edges between the location clusters according to the time sequence of the locations clusters visited by u. Let us first consider that two users are similar if they have visited similar locations. Since deeper levels of the TBHG contain more precise location clusters, if we use them to find similar users we will find fewer but more similar users. On the other hand, the large clusters at the top levels may bring both similar and dissimilar users into a few large clusters, yielding user clusters with low precisions but high recalls.

3.3 Community Location Model

Since GPS trajectories are just sequences of unstructured time-stamped coordinates, we propose the *Community Location Model* (CLM) to organize trajectory data into a meaningful data structure to facilitate co-clustering. A novelty of CLM is the incorporation of activities into the model. Basically, an activity is a segment of GPS trajectory within a certain time frame. Figure 2(b) shows an example of daily activities (i.e., in 24 hours) of a student between her

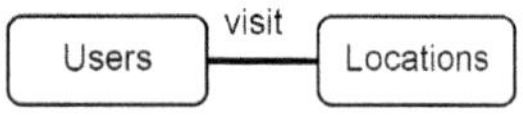

(a) User-Location Model.

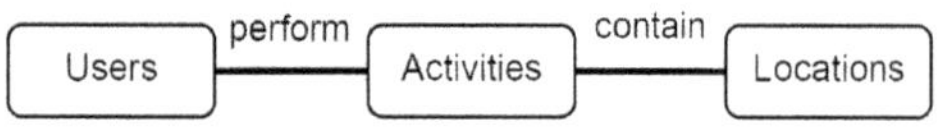

(b) User-Activity and Activity-Location Model.

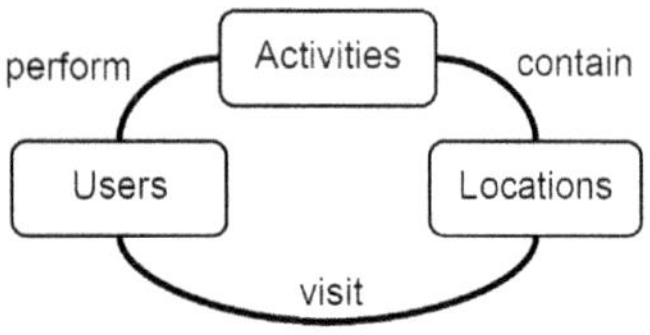

(c) Community Location Model.

Figure 4: Different models for co-clustering.

home (i.e., Ngau Chi Wan) and her university (i.e., HKUST). CLM represents users, activities and locations as three entity types and the relations between the three entity types as binary relations (see Figure 4(c)). An instance of CLM is a User-Activity-Location tripartite graph (called CLM graph), rather than a User-Location matrix, capturing the relations between users, activities and locations in the model. A CLM graph consists of three disjoint node sets representing the sets of users, activities and locations. As described in Section 4, a CLM graph can be clustered with a co-cluster algorithm to form clusters of similar users, similar activities and similar locations. This allows refined clusters to be obtained for location recommendations (also see Section 1).

Figure 5(a) shows an example GPS trajectory data from 5 users with 12 activities on 10 different locations. The arrows in Figure 5(a) represent sequences of location visits in the GPS trajectory data. Figure 5(b) shows the relations between users, activities, and locations in the CLM graph.

We observe that a model that only involves User and Location, as shown in Figure 4(a), is not accurate and effective for clustering relevant locations together, because it does not exploit the temporal-spatial information in Activity. Figure 4(b) shows an alternative model that captures User, Activity, and Location in two separate bipartite graphs. However, it misses the opportunity to exploit long-term spatial properties captured by the direct link between User and Location. On the other hand, CLM exploits all of the spatial properties, temporal-spatial properties, and long-term spatial properties in the co-clustering process. We observe that the three entity types (i.e., User, Activity, and Location) in CLM exhibit different properties that improve the effectiveness of clustering: 1) Location exhibits spatial properties as it contains geographical information; 2) Activity exhibits temporal-spatial properties as it is a temporal sequence of visited locations; and 3) User exhibits long-term spatial properties as different users would visit different locations due to their long term habits or geographical limits.

3.4 Similarity Fusion in CLM

After constructing a CLM graph, we propose to model the similarity between different objects in the CLM graph as follows.

1. Two users are similar if they have similar activity patterns and have visited similar locations.
2. Two activities are similar if they take place in similar sequence of locations and performed by similar users.
3. Two locations are similar if they are visited by similar user and occurred in similar activities.

Formally, we propose the following similarity functions to compute the similarity between pair of users, pair of activities, and pair of locations:

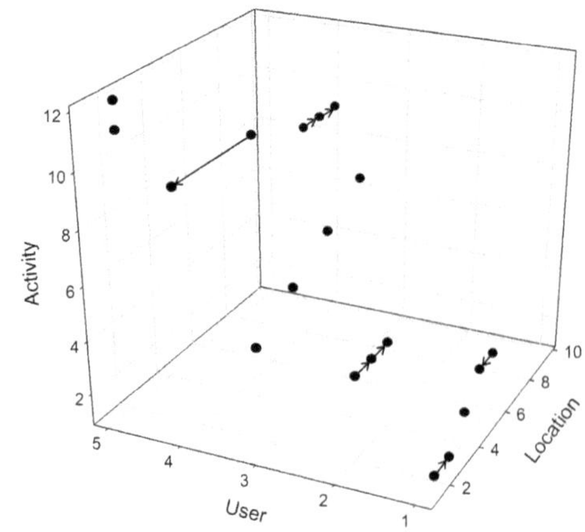

(a) Example location histories from 5 users with 12 activities on 10 locations.

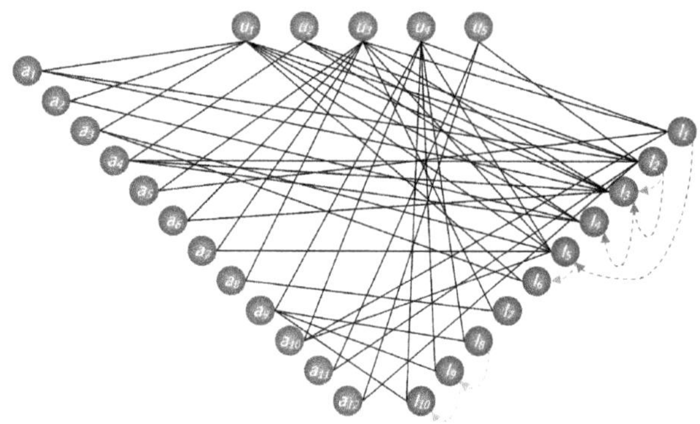

(b) An example tripartite CLM graph G_3.

Figure 5: An Example CLM graph.

$$sim(u_i,u_j)=\frac{\sum_{k=1}^{n}\frac{LCS(a_{(k,u_i)},a_{(k,u_j)})}{max(|a_{(k,u_i)}|,|a_{(k,u_j)}|)}}{n}\alpha_1+\frac{L_{u_i}\cdot L_{u_j}}{\| L_{u_i}\|\| L_{u_j}\|}(1-\alpha_1) \quad (1)$$

$$sim(a_i,a_j)=\frac{LCS(a_i,a_j)}{max(|a_i|,|a_j|)}\alpha_2+\frac{U_{a_i}\cdot U_{a_j}}{\| U_{a_i}\|\| U_{a_j}\|}(1-\alpha_2) \quad (2)$$

$$sim(l_i,l_j)=\frac{U_{l_i}\cdot U_{l_j}}{\| U_{l_i}\|\| U_{l_j}\|}\alpha_3+\frac{A_{l_i}\cdot A_{l_j}}{\| A_{l_i}\|\| A_{l_j}\|}(1-\alpha_3) \quad (3)$$

where $LCS(a_i, a_j)$ is the *longest common subsequence* of a_i and a_j, $a_{(k,u_i)}$ is the activity performed by u_i on day k, $|a_i|$ is the number of locations visited by a_i, L_{u_i} is a weight vector for the set of neighbor location nodes of the user node u_i, and the weight of a location neighbor node $l_{(k,u_i)}$ in L_{u_i} is the weight of the link connecting u_i and $l_{(k,u_i)}$ in the CLM. Similarly, U_{l_i} is a weight vector for the set of neighbor user nodes of the location node l_i, A_{l_i} is a weight vector for the set of neighbor activity nodes of the location node l_i, and A_{l_i} is a weight vector for the set of neighbor activity nodes of the location node l_i, and the weight of an activity neighbor node $a_{(k,l_i)}$ in the weight vector A_{l_i} is the weight of the link connecting l_i and $a_{(k,l_i)}$ in the CLM. Since LCS and cosine similarities lie between [0,1], it is easy to see that the resulting similarities in Equations (1), (2), and (3) also lie between [0,1].

4. DISCOVERING USER COMMUNITIES

In this section, we describe the co-clustering process on GPS trajectory data based on CLM to form clusters of similar users, locations and activities. Traditional agglomerative-only co-clustering algorithms require the tripartite graph to be clustered all over again when new data are inserted into the graph. Thus, it is not suitable for dynamic environments. To alleviate this problem, we adopt the *Community-based Agglomerative-Divisive Clustering* (CADC) algorithm to iteratively cluster different types of entities simultaneously based on CLM.

To begin with, the location histories from all users are used to construct the tripartite CLM graph G_3 (see Figure 5(b)). CADC then clusters G_3 into a new tripartite graph G_3^C, in which the *Users* set is clustered into groups of similar users, and likewise the *Activities* and *Locations* sets are clustered, respectively, into groups of similar activities and similar locations. When new GPS trajectory data arrives, G_3^C is updated with the new data and then incrementally re-clustered using two separate phases, namely, the **agglomerative phase** and **divisive phase**, without re-clustering the whole CLM graph all over again. The agglomerative phase iteratively merges similar clusters, while the divisive phase splits large clusters into small ones to prevent clusters from growing without bound when new data arrives. Figure 6 shows an example of splitting one large user cluster into two smaller, more meaningful ones, when new incoming users arrive. CADC produces clusters of similar users, clusters of similar activities, and clusters of similar locations at the same time. These three types of similar entities will be used in the refinement phase (see Section 5) to obtain more precise subclusters for making recommendation.

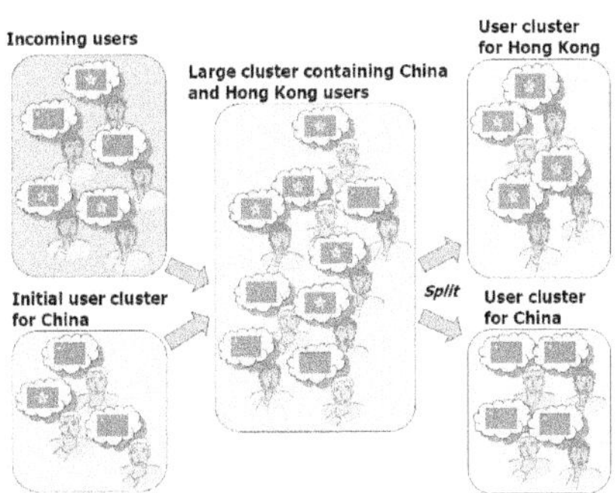

Figure 6: Split of a large cluster into two smaller clusters.

4.1 Agglomerative Phase

The agglomerative phase merges similar entities into clusters. Since we are dealing with tripartite CLM, we extend an agglomerative hierarchical clustering approach for bipartite data structure [6] for the tripartite CLM. Basically, an agglomerative algorithm starts with single entities, and successively merges entities/clusters together. The agglomerative phase of CADC iteratively merges the two most similar users, then the two most similar activities, and then the two most similar locations using the similarity definitions in Equations (1), (2), and (3), respectively. The procedure repeats until no new user, activity or location clusters can be formed by merging.

4.2 Divisive Phase

The divisive phase of CADC splits large clusters into smaller, but tighter ones. It is needed to maintain the coherence of the clusters and to restructure the existing clusters to facilitate incremental update of the affected clusters as new GPS trajectory data arrives. Basically, a divisive algorithm starts with large clusters, and recursively splits the clusters into smaller ones until no new clusters can be formed by splitting. One major problem in the divisive phase is to determine the minimum number of observations (i.e., evidence to perform a split) necessary for the phase to converge. To resolve the problem, the Hoeffding bound [7] is employed to ensure that after n independent observations of a real-valued random variable r with range R, and with confidence $1-\delta$ (where δ is the split threshold), the true mean of r is at least $\overline{r} - \epsilon$, where $\overline{r}$ is the observed mean of the samples and $\epsilon = \sqrt{\frac{R^2 \ln(1/\delta)}{2n}}$.

In the divisive phase, each cluster is assigned with a different ϵ, namely, ϵ_k. The distances between pair of users, pair of activities, and pair of locations are defined, respectively, as the inverse of the similarities defined in Equations (1), (2), and (3).

$$d(u_i,u_j) = (1 - \frac{\sum_{k=1}^{n} \frac{LCS(a_{(k,u_i)}, a_{(k,u_j)})}{max(|a_{(k,u_i)}|, |a_{(k,u_j)}|)}}{n})\beta_1 + \sqrt{\sum_{k=1}^{m} (l_{(k,u_i)} - l_{(k,u_j)})^2 (1-\beta_1)} \quad (4)$$

$$d(a_i,a_j) = \frac{LCS(a_i,a_j)}{max(|a_i|,|a_j|)}\beta_2 + \sqrt{\sum_{k=1}^{m} (u_{(k,a_i)} - u_{(k,a_j)})^2 (1-\beta_2)} \quad (5)$$

$$d(l_i,l_j) = \sqrt{\sum_{k=1}^{n} (u_{(k,l_i)} - u_{(k,l_j)})^2 \beta_3} + \sqrt{\sum_{k=1}^{m} (a_{(k,l_i)} - a_{(k,l_j)})^2 (1-\beta_3)} \quad (6)$$

where $LCS(a_i,a_j)$ is the *longest common subsequence* of a_i and a_j, $a_{(k,u_i)}$ is the activity performed by u_i on day k, $|a_i|$ is the number of locations visited by a_i, $l_{(k,u_i)} \in L_{u_i}$ is the weight of the link connecting u_i and $l_{(k,u_i)}$. Similarly, $u_{(k,l_i)} \in U_{l_i}$ and $a_{(k,l_i)} \in A_{l_i}$.

Assume that two pairs of nodes $d1_n = d(n_i,n_j)$ and $d2_n = d(n_k,n_l)$ are the top-most and second top-most dissimilar nodes in a cluster (based on the distance Equation 4), (5), or (6). Further assume that $\triangle d = d(n_i,n_j) - d(n_k,n_l)$, if $\triangle d > \epsilon_k$, with probability $1-\delta$, the differences between $d(n_i,n_j)$ and $d(n_k,n_l)$ is larger than zero, and pick (n_i,n_j) as the boundary of the cluster when applying Hoeffding bound with $\triangle d$. In the divisive phase, n_i and n_j are selected as the pivots for the splitting, and the clusters are split according to the statistical confidence given by Hoeffding bound. Figure 7 shows an example of splitting a large cluster into two smaller ones.

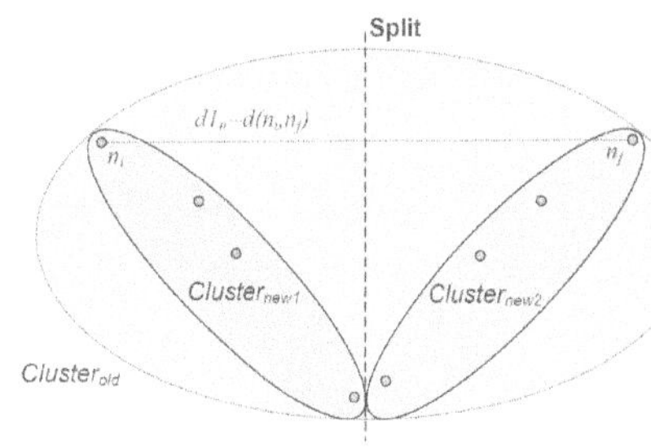

Figure 7: Split $Cluster_{old}$ into $Cluster_{new1}$ and $Cluster_{new2}$.

4.3 The Clustering Algorithm

The clustering algorithm iteratively merges and splits nodes in G_3 until the termination condition is reached. Then the clusters in the final CLM graph G_3^C are output. When new location histories arrive, the new users, activities, and locations are added as singleton nodes to G_3^C and the links between the new nodes are also added to G_3^C. The new graph G_3' is then served as input to the clustering algorithm again. The new nodes are grouped to the correct clusters by the agglomerative phase. If a particular cluster becomes too large because too many new nodes are added to the cluster, the divisive phase will divide the cluster into smaller ones according to the statistical confidence given by Hoeffding bound. These steps are repeated until the termination condition is reached, and the algorithm outputs the final CLM graph.

5. COMMUNITY REFINEMENT

In order to provide high-quality location recommendations to the users, we further refine clusters of users, activities, and locations generated by our CADC co-clustering algorithm. The community refinement component of CLR generates a number of subclusters by intersecting the user, activity, and location clusters in the clustered tripartite graph. Assume that the active user u_a is visiting location l_c when she is performing activity a_b, then we can obtain from the clustered tripartite graph a set of users U_{u_a} similar to u_a, a set of activities A_{a_b} similar to a_b, and a set of locations L_{l_c} similar to l_c. By using the clusters U_{u_a}, A_{a_b}, and L_{l_c} in three different dimensions, we can obtain the following subclusters for location recommendations.

In Situ Refined Subclusters:

- $CADC(L)$: Set of locations similar to location l_c.
- $CADC(U)$: Set of locations visited by users similar to u_a.
- $CADC(A)$: Set of locations where activities similar to a_b are performed.
- $CADC(U, L)$: Set of locations similar to l_c, and visited by users similar to u_a.
- $CADC(U, A)$: Set of locations where activities similar to a_b are performed, and visited by users similar to u_a.
- $CADC(A, L)$: Set of locations similar to l_c where activities similar to a_b are performed.
- $CADC(U, A, L)$: Set of locations similar to l_c, activities similar to a_b are performed, and visited by users similar to u_a.

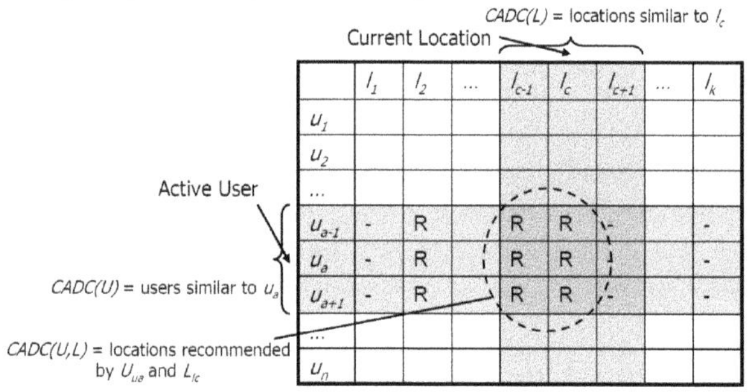

Figure 8: Intersection of $CADC(U)$ and $CADC(L)$ to obtain $CADC(U, L)$.

Figure 8 shows an example of intersecting $CADC(U)$ and $CADC(L)$ to obtain $CADC(U, L)$. $CADC(L)$ can be easily obtained by getting the locations in the clustered CLM graph that are in the same cluster as the active location l_c. However, for $CADC(U)$, we need to get the locations visited by users that are similar to the active user u_a. Thus, we need to first obtain the set of users, $U(u_a)$ and then retrieve locations that have been visited by users in $U(u_a)$, which can be easily obtained by finding the locations nodes that are connected to $U(u_a)$ in the clustered CLM graph. After $CADC(U)$ and $CADC(L)$ are obtained, the locations resulted from $CADC(U)$ are intersected with the locations resulted from $CADC(L)$ to obtain $CADC(U, L)$ as shown in Figure 8.

After determining the subclusters by intersecting $CADC(U)$, $CADC(A)$, and $CADC(L)$, the top k most visited locations in a subclusters will be recommended to the user. The top k locations are picked according to the *Location Frequency (LF)* and *Inverse User Frequency (IUF)*. IUF is taken into account because we find that a location visited by most users may be a general well-known location which is not interesting to the users, and thus its score is penalized by IUF. The following equation is adopted from the well-known $TF \times IDF$ term weighting scheme in information retrieval with LF and IUF replacing, respectively, TF and IDF:

$$score(l) = LF(l) \times IUF(l) \tag{7}$$

where $IUF(l) = \log_2 \frac{\text{total number of users in a subcluster}}{\text{number of users visited} l}$. After computing the scores for all of the locations in a subclusters using Equation (7), the top k locations in a subcluster are recommended to the user.

The in situ subclusters can help filtering out useful important locations for collaborative location recommendations. However, the size of a refined subcluster can still be large, thus resulting in many locations for recommendations. Therefore, we further classify the users into three classes, namely *Pattern Users*, *Normal Users*, and *Travelers*, according to the sequence of locations that they visited in their daily activities, in order to filter out location recommendations from different classes of users. We use the location entropy $S_L(u)$ to measure the randomness of the locations being visited by a user u.

$$S_L(u) = -\sum_{i=1}^{k} p(l_i) \log p(l_i) \tag{8}$$

where k is the total number of locations $L = l_1, l_2, ..., l_k$ that u has visited, $|l_i|$ is the number of daily activities containing the location l_i, $|L| = |l_1| + |l_2| + ... + |l_k|$, and $p(l_i) = \frac{|l_i|}{L}$.

After computing $S_L(u)$ for each user, we can then employ K-Means to classify users into the three classes as follows.

- **Pattern Users:** Users with low location entropies, i.e., they repeat what they do daily, thus having small randomness in the locations they visited.
- **Normal Users:** Users with higher location entropies. They visit more different locations comparing to the pattern users.
- **Travelers:** Users with high location entropies, meaning that they visit many different locations everyday. They can be considered knowledgeable users, since they have good knowledge about different locations.

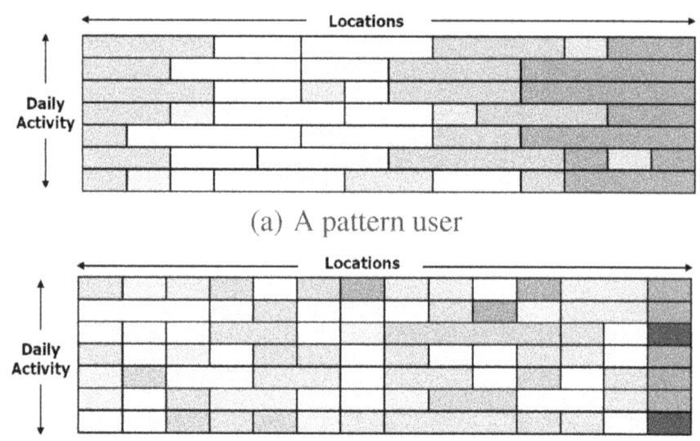

(a) A pattern user

(b) A traveler

Figure 9: Example activities from pattern user and traveler.

Figures 9(a) and 9(b) show example activities from a pattern user and a traveler, respectively, where different colors represent different locations that the users have visited. After classifying the users into Pattern Users, Normal Users, and Travelers, we can then employ them to refine the in situ subclusters into the following behavioral subclusters, each of which only contain one type of users.

Behaviorally Refined Subclusters:

- $PTN(U)$: Set of locations visited by **Pattern** users similar to u_a.
- $PTN(U, L)$: Set of locations similar to l_c and visited by **Pattern** users similar to u_a.
- $PTN(U, A)$: Set of locations performed in activities similar to a_b and visited by **Pattern** users similar to u_a.
- $PTN(U, A, L)$: Set of locations similar to l_c and performed in activities similar to a_b and visited by **Pattern** users similar to u_a.
- $TRL(U)$: Set of locations visited by **Travelers** similar to u_a.

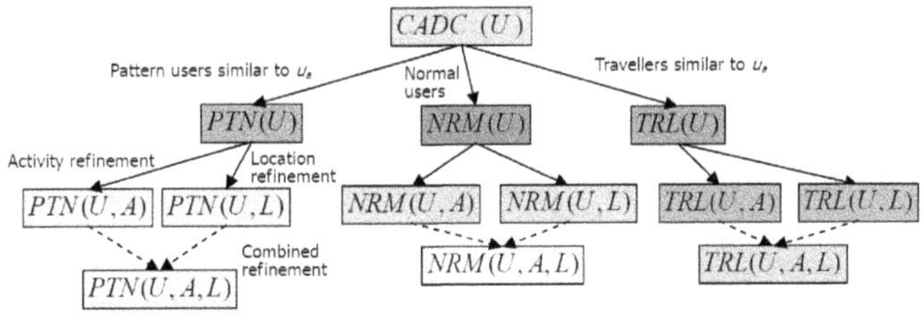

Figure 10: Recommendations from different user classes.

Figure 11: GPS devices used for GPS trajectory data collection.

- $TRL(U, L)$: Set of locations similar to l_c and visited by **Travelers** similar to u_a.
- $TRL(U, A)$: Set of locations performed in activities similar to a_b and visited by **Travelers** similar to u_a.
- $TRL(U, A, L)$: Set of locations similar to l_c and performed in activities similar to a_b and visited by **Travelers** similar to u_a.

After obtaining the refined subclusters according to u_a, a_b, and l_c, the top k locations with the highest $LF \times IUF$ scores in the refined subclusters will be recommended to the active user u_a. In the experiments, we will evaluate and compare the effectiveness of the location recommendations obtained from different in situ and behaviorally refined communities. Figure 10 shows some of the top k location recommendations L^k from different user communities.

6. EXPERIMENTAL RESULTS

In this section, we first present the experimental setup for collecting the GPS trajectory data used in the evaluation of CLR. We then present the methodology used in the evaluation. Then, we evaluate the clustering effectiveness of CADC, the performance of the stay point and location clustering, and the effectiveness of location suggestions.

6.1 Experimental Setup

The GPS trajectory data was collected from 50 different users using the GPS loggers as shown in Figure 11. The users' outdoor trajectories were recorded from September 2009 to May 2010. The GPS loggers were set to record GPS coordinates every second. GPS trajectory data was mainly collected in Hong Kong and China. Figure 12 shows some of the trajectory data collected for the experiments.

6.2 Evaluation Metric

In the experiments, users are asked to evaluate the location recommendations generated by CLR. The top 10 location recommendations generated by CLR are displayed to the users, who are then required to provide ratings to the recommendations according to the criteria as shown in Table 1. Since our top 10 location recommendations are displayed in a ranked list, we employ *normalized discounted cumulative gain (nDCG)* to measure the accuracy of the recommendations. The ratings obtained from a user are used to generate the user's ideal ranking, which are compared against the top 10 location recommendations generated by CLR to obtain the $nDCG$ value of the CLR recommendations. The $nDCG$ of a top 10 recommendation list is computed using the following equations.

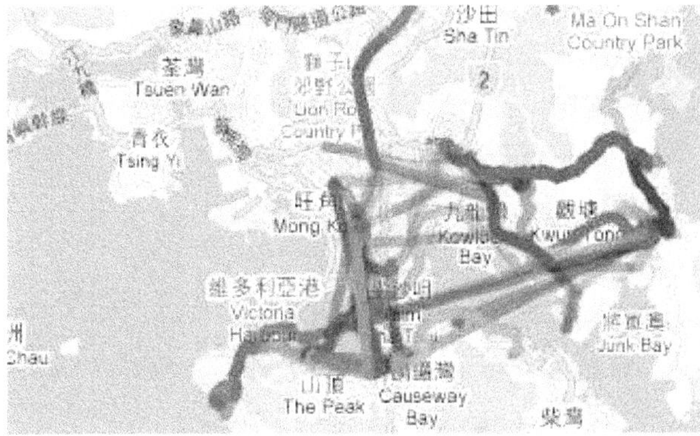

Figure 12: Sample GPS trajectory data collected for the experiments.

Table 1: The rating on the location representativeness

Ratings	Meaning
3	I intended to visit the location
2	I would visit the location if I pass by
1	I have a little chance to visit the location
0	This location is obviously not of my interest

$$DCG = rel_1 + \sum_{i=2}^{10} \frac{rel_i}{log_2 i} \quad (9) \qquad nDCG = \frac{DCG}{IDCG} \quad (10)$$

In CLR, we only consider the top 10 recommendations. Thus, the DCG value of a recommendation list can be computed using Equation (9), where rel_i is the relevance rating of the i-th location in the recommendation list. Then, we normalize the DCG value of the recommendation list with respect to the ideal ranking using Equation (10), where DCG is the DCG value computed from a recommendation list, and $IDCG$ is the DCG value computed from the user's ideal ranking. For example, if the ratings on the top 10 recommendations are [3,2,1,3,2,2,1,0,0,1], then the corresponding $nDCG$ is computed as follow.

$$nDCG = \frac{3 + 2/log2 + 1/log3 + 3/log4 + 2/log5 + 2/log6 + 1/log7 + 1/log10}{3 + 3/log2 + 2/log3 + 2/log4 + 2/log5 + 1/log6 + 1/log7 + 1/log8} = 0.92 \quad (11)$$

$nDCG$ measures the accuracy of a ranked recommendation list generated by CLR. Thus, the higher the $nDCG$ is, the more accurate the recommendations are (i.e., relevant locations are ranked higher in the recommendation list).

6.3 CADC Location Recommendations

We compare CADC against a few state-of-the-art methods, including *Distance*, *SimUser*, *Memory-Based Collaborative Filtering (MemCF)*, *Model-Based Collaborative Filtering (ModelCF)*, and *HITS*.[1] The *Distance* method returns the top 10 locations that are closest to the active location as the location recommendations. The *SimUser* method represents each location with a user vector based on the users who visited the location. It recommends the top 10 locations which have user vectors most similar to the active location's user vector. The *Memory-Based Collaborative Filtering (MemCF)* method is based on the method presented in [13]. We first create a User-Activity-Location matrix to model the relationships between users, activities, and locations. For each missing entry in the matrix, we extract a set of top N similar users, top N similar activities, and top N similar locations, and then use the ratings from the top N entities to predict the value of the missing entry probabilistically. After predicting all of the missing entries, it then recommends the

[1]Hereafter, CADC refers to $CADC(U, A, L)$ as discussed in Section 5 unless stated otherwise.

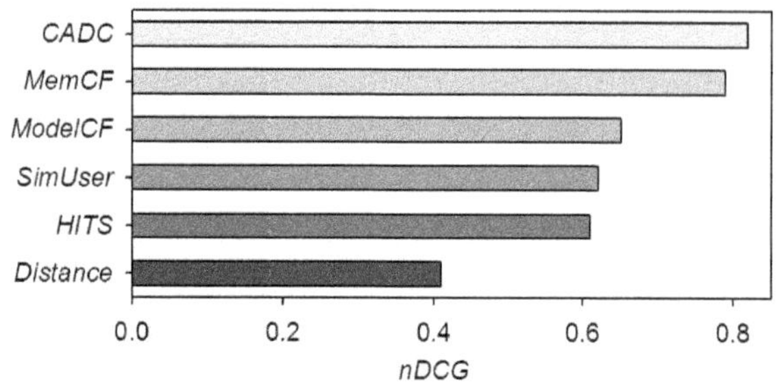

Figure 13: $nDCG$ for Distance, HITS, SimUser, MemCF, ModelCF, and CADC.

top 10 locations that are visited by similar users and where similar activities are performed. In the *Model-Based Collaborative Filtering (ModelCF)* method, we also create a User-Activity-Location matrix but employ a *Higher-Order Singular Value Decomposition (HOSVD)* [12] to predict the missing entries in the matrix. We then return as recommendation the top 10 locations that are visited by similar users and where similar activities are performed. Finally, we also include in the evaluation the *HITS* method proposed in [16]. The HITS method determines a user's authority value using the authority proposition in the hyperlink environment in [8]. The top N users with the highest authority values are picked, and the top 10 locations visited by the top N authority users are returned as location recommendations.

Figure 13 shows the $nDCG$ of CADC and the baseline methods. We observe that the Distance method performs the worst ($nDCG = 0.41$), because the locations that are closest to the active location may not always match the user's spatial interests (i.e., preferences according to the *user* dimension) and the temporal-spatial spatial interests (i.e. preferences according to the *activity* dimension). The HITS method relies only on the recommendations from users with high authority scores. It does not take the user's spatial interests into account. Thus, it performs only slightly better ($nDCG = 0.61$) than the Distance method. The SimUser method considers the user's long term spatial interests. As a result, it yields $nDCG = 0.62$, which is better comparing to the Distance and HITS methods. Both the MemCF and ModelCF methods employ the User-Activity-Location matrix in the collaborative filtering process, thus capturing both the user's long term spatial interests and the temporal-spatial spatial interests. MemCF ($nDCG = 0.79$) performs better than ModelCF ($nDCG = 0.65$), because it performs predictions based on only the truly similar entities (i.e., the top N similar users, top N similar activities, and top N similar locations). Finally, we observe that CADC ($nDCG = 0.82$) performs the best comparing to the other five baseline methods, because the co-clustering method can effectively explore the ties modeled in CLM to iteratively group different types of similar entities simultaneously. The similarity scores are optimized by exploiting similarity fusion to strike a good balance between the similarity scores from different dimensions, thus producing more coherent clusters of similar locations.

6.3.1 CADC Merge Fusion Thresholds α_1, α_2, α_3

We then study the impact of the merge thresholds on CADC's performance by varying the α_1, α_2, and α_3 merge thresholds in Equations (1), (2), and (3), respectively, from 0 to 1 (with 0.1 increments). We obtain the $nDCG$ values under different settings of merge thresholds. When we vary one of the merge thresholds, the other two thresholds are fixed at the optimal values so that only one of the merge thresholds would influence the results. Figure 14(d) shows the $nDCG$ values obtained at different user merge thresholds α_1 from 0 to 1, with α_2 and α_3 fixed at their optimal values (0.4 and 0.6, respectively). We observe that the best $nDCG$ is obtained when $\alpha_1 = 0.5$. This shows that the activity dimension and the location dimension are equally important for identifying similar users. We repeat the experiment on the activity and location merge thresholds (i.e., α_2 and α_3). Similarly, we vary α_2 from 0 to 1, with α_1 and α_3 fixed at their optimal values 0.5 and 0.6, respectively. We observe that the optimal $nDCG$ is obtained when $\alpha_2 = 0.4$. This shows that the sequence of visited locations is more important than the user dimension for identifying similar activities, meaning that two activities performed by two similar users may not always have high similarity to one another (e.g., users u_1 and u_2 are similar because they both live in Clear Water Bay, Hong Kong). However, u_1 can be a housewife, while u_2 can be a student, and they will perform different activities). Finally, we repeat the experiment on α_3 by fixing α_1 and α_2 at 0.5 and 0.4, respectively. The optimal $nDCG$ is achieved when α_3 is at 0.6. This shows that the activity dimension (i.e., the most updated temporal-spatial preferences) is more important than the user dimension (i.e., the long term spatial preferences).

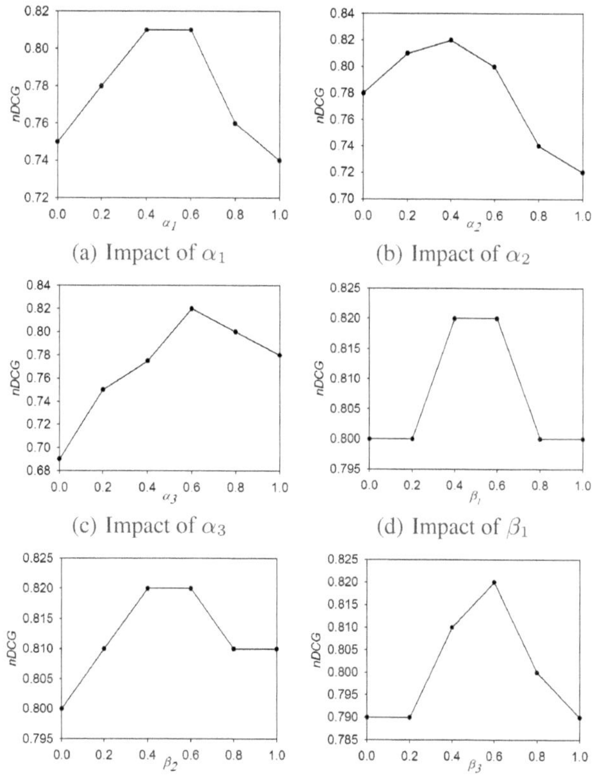

(a) Impact of α_1

(b) Impact of α_2

(c) Impact of α_3

(d) Impact of β_1

(e) Impact of β_2

(f) Impact of β_3

Figure 14: Impact of the merge fusion thresholds α_1, α_2, α_3, and the split fusion thresholds β_1, β_2, and β_3 on CADC.

6.3.2 CADC Split Fusion Thresholds β_1, β_2, β_3

We also study the impact of the split thresholds in CADC by varying the three split thresholds (β_1, β_2, and β_3 in Equations (4), (5), and (6), respectively), from 0 to 1 (with 0.1 increments). As before, when we vary one of the split thresholds, the other two split thresholds are fixed at their optimal values. Figure 14 shows the $nDCG$ values at different split thresholds from 0 to 1. We observe that the $nDCG$ values do not vary much when split thresholds change. This is because we start the CADC algorithm with

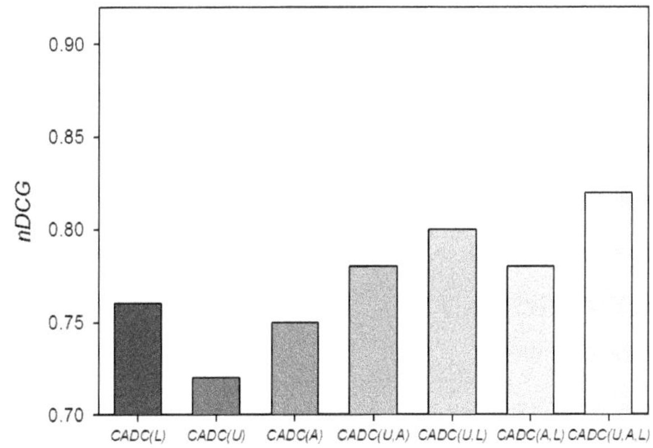

Figure 15: $nDCG$ for the in situ refined communities.

the agglomerative phase to group individual objects together, and we require two objects to be highly similar before they are merged into the same node. Thus, in the divisive phase, only a few splits are required to split the oversize clusters into smaller clusters. We observe that the best $nDCG$ value is obtained when $\beta_1 = 0.5$, $\beta_2 = 0.5$, and $\beta_3 = 0.6$.

6.4 Refined Location Recommendations

6.4.1 *In Situ Refined Recommendations*

We also compare the quality of the location recommendations generated from the refined communities. We first evaluate the in situ refined communities, $CADC(U)$, $CADC(A)$, $CADC(L)$, $CADC(U, A)$, $CADC(U, L)$, $CADC(A, L)$, and $CADC(U, A, L)$, described in Section 5. Figure 15 shows the $nDCG$ values obtained for the in situ refined communities. We observe that the location recommendations generated using only one of the dimensions (i.e., $CADC(U)$ based on only the user dimension, $CADC(A)$ based on only the activity dimension, and $CADC(L)$ based on only the location dimension) are the worst. The $nDCG$ for $CADC(U)$, $CADC(A)$, and $CADC(L)$ are only 0.76, 0.72, and 0.75, respectively. The location recommendations generated using two dimensions (i.e., $CADC(U, A)$ based on the user and activity dimensions, $CADC(U, L)$ based on only the user and location dimensions, and $CADC(A, L)$ based on only the activity and location dimensions) are better than those obtained using one dimension only. $CADC(U, A)$, $CADC(U, L)$, and $CADC(A, L)$ yield $nDCG$ of 0.78, 0.80, and 0.78, respectively. Finally, the location recommendations generated using all the three dimensions (i.e., $CADC(U, A, L)$) are the best. $CADC(U, A, L)$ yields $nDCG = 0.82$, which is the highest value among all of the in situ refined user communities.

6.4.2 *Behaviorally Refined Recommendations*

We also evaluate the quality of the location recommendations generated from using the behaviorally refined communities, $PTN(U)$, $PTN(U, A)$, $PTN(U, L)$, $PTN(U, A, L)$, $TRL(U)$, $TRL(U, A)$, $TRL(U, L)$, and $TRL(U, A, L)$, described in Section 5. Figure 16 shows the $nDCG$ values obtained from the behaviorally refined communities. We observe that the location recommendations obtained from Travelers are better than those obtained from Pattern Users. Consistent with the results obtained for the in situ refined communities, location recommendations generated using only one dimension (i.e., $PTN(U)$ and $TRL(U)$) are not as good as those generated using two dimensions (i.e., $PTN(U, A)$, $TRL(U, A)$, $PTN(U, L)$, and $TRL(U, L)$), and the recommendations generated using all three dimensions (i.e., $PTN(U, A, L)$ and $TRL(U, A, L)$) yield the best $nDCG$ (0.89 and 0.91, respectively).

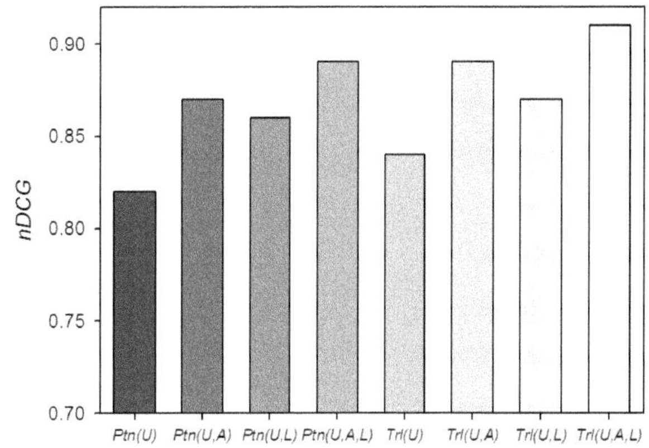

Figure 16: $nDCG$ for the behaviorally refined communities.

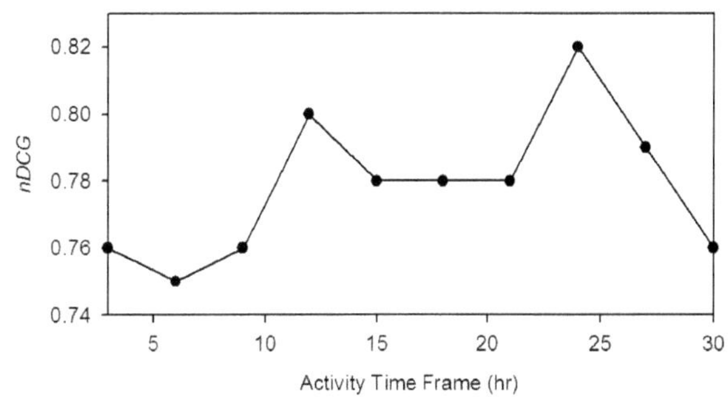

Figure 17: $nDCG$ of CADC with different activity time frames.

Table 2 shows the top 3, 5, and 10 average ratings obtained from the behaviorally refined communities. We observe that the top 5 and 10 average ratings obtained from Travelers are better than those obtained from Pattern Users. This is because Pattern Users usually only visit a few locations in regular patterns. Thus, only a few locations recommended by Pattern Users are useful to other users. On the other hand, Travelers usually travel many different locations. Thus, many of their recommendations are useful to other users, because they are knowledgeable users with experiences in different locations.

6.5 Impact of Activity Length on CLR

As discussed in Section 3.3, an activity is a segment of GPS trajectory within a certain time frame. The length of the time frame can be adjusted to include different numbers of locations associated with an activity (i.e., the longer the time frame, the more locations are associated with an activity). To evaluate the impact of the activity time frame on the accuracy of location recommendations, we repeat the $nDCG$ evaluation on the $CADC(U, A, L)$ method with different time frames. Figure 17 shows the $nDCG$ values of CADC with different activity time frames. We observe that if the time frame is too short (e.g. 3 or 6 hours), the resulting activities will only be associated with a small number of locations. Hence, similar activities cannot be discovered effectively because of the low location overlaps between activities, thus yielding lower $nDCG$ comparing to the optimal value obtained at a 24-hour time frame. On the other hand, if the time frame is too long (e.g. 30 hours), the resulting activities will become too general because of their associations with many different locations. The general activities may bring dissimilar locations together, thus worsening the performance. Finally, we observe that the activity time frame should be either 12 or 24 hours (half-a-day or daily activity), in order to achieve the best performance.

Table 2: The top 3, 5, 10 average ratings for the behaviorally refined communities

	$PTN(U)$	$PTN(U,A)$	$PTN(U,L)$	$PTN(U,A,L)$	$TRL(U)$	$TRL(U,A)$	$TRL(U,L)$	$TRL(U,A,L)$
Top 3	2.34	2.36	2.40	2.43	2.46	2.48	2.48	2.54
Top 5	1.94	1.98	1.96	1.98	2.23	2.25	2.25	2.28
Top 10	1.72	1.72	1.73	1.80	2.08	2.12	2.13	2.18

Table 3: Impact of sp_t on Stay Point Detection

sp_t	# Points	CADC	MemCF	ModelCF	HITS
5mins	2214	0.79	0.75	0.61	0.57
15mins	1297	0.78	0.76	0.62	0.58
30mins	**762**	**0.82**	**0.79**	**0.65**	**0.61**
45mins	497	0.76	0.73	0.64	0.61
60mins	245	0.72	0.71	0.57	0.55

Table 4: Impact of sp_d on Stay Point Detection

sp_t	# Points	CADC	MemCF	ModelCF	HITS
300meters	1863	0.78	0.75	0.63	0.56
500 meters	**762**	**0.82**	**0.79**	**0.65**	**0.61**
800meters	467	0.73	0.71	0.64	0.61

6.6 Impact of sp_t and sp_d on CLR

We also study the influence of the time and distance thresholds (i.e., sp_t and sp_d) on location recommendations. If sp_t and sp_d are too small, we may get locations that lack representativeness (e.g., bus stop, car park, and train station). On the other hand, if sp_t and sp_d are too large, the locations may be too large and too general, leading to difficulty in determining points of interests. To find the optimal time threshold sp_t, we vary sp_t from 5 mins to 60 mins. When we vary sp_t, sp_d is fixed at its optimal value (i.e., $sp_d = 500$ meters). Table 3 shows the $nDCG$ values at different sp_t. We observe that the larger the sp_t, the fewer the number of stay points detected from the users' GPS data. Moreover, CADC yields the best $nDCG$ when $sp_t = 30$ mins by avoiding locations that are too general or too precise.

We repeat the experiment by varying sp_d from 300 meters to 800 meters. When we vary sp_d, sp_t is fixed at its optimal value (i.e., $sp_t = 30$ mins). Table 4 shows the $nDCG$ values at different sp_d. Again, to avoid locations that are too general or too limited, we need to set $sp_d = 500$ meters in order to achieve the best $nDCG$. We observe that the larger the sp_d, the fewer the number of stay points detected from the users' GPS data. Moreover, CADC yields the best $nDCG$ when $sp_t = 500$ meters by avoiding locations that are too general or too precise.

7. CONCLUSIONS

In this paper, we propose the Collaborative Location Recommendation (CLR) framework, which makes location recommendations based on users' GPS trajectory data. We introduce the community location model *(CLM)*, which represents a User-Activity-Location tripartite graph, and employ the CADC co-clustering algorithm to exploit the rich activity information embedded in GPS trajectory data. The idea of online recommendation refinement is also introduced to refine the clusters of similar locations resulted from CADC for a particular activity issued by a specific user in order to obtain high quality location recommendations. Experimental results confirm that our approach can provide more accurate and refined recommendations comparing to the existing methods based on clustering or collaborative filtering.

As for the future work, we plan to incorporate more semantic information in the clustering process to further improve the quality of location recommendations. For example, on Twitter [4], users may provide textual descriptions on their own POIs on a map. Apart from the GPS coordinates, the textual descriptions can also serve as additional information describing the POIs for clustering.

8. REFERENCES

[1] Geolife. http://research.microsoft.com/en-us/projects/geolife/.

[2] Google map. http://maps.google.com/.

[3] Sherpa. http://www.geodelic.com/sherpa/.

[4] Twitter. http://www.twitter.com/.

[5] G. D. Abowd, C. G. Atkeson, J. Hong, S. Long, R. Kooper, and M. Pinkerton. Cyberguide: a mobile context-aware tour guide. *Wireless Networks*, 3(5), 1997.

[6] D. Beeferman and A. Berger. Agglomerative clustering of a search engine query log. In *Proc. of ACM SIGKDD Conference*, 2000.

[7] W. Hoeffding. Probability inequalities for sums of bounded random variables. *JASA*, 58(301), 1963.

[8] J. M. Kleinberg. Authoritative sources in a hyperlinked environment. *JACM*, 46(5), 1999.

[9] Q. Li, Y. Zheng, X. Xie, Y. Chen, W. Liu, and W.-Y. Ma. Mining user similarity based on location history. In *Proc. of SIGSPATIAL GIS Conference*, 2008.

[10] M.-H. Park, J.-H. Hong, and S.-B. Cho. Location-based recommendation system using bayesian user's preference model in mobile devices. In *Proc. of UIC Conference*, 2007.

[11] Y. Takeuchi and M. Sugimoto. Cityvoyager: An outdoor recommendation system based on user location history. In *Proc. of UIC Conference*, 2006.

[12] J. tao Sun, H.-J. Zeng, H. Liu, and Y. Lu. Cubesvd: A novel approach to personalized web search. In *Proc. of WWW Conference*, 2005.

[13] J. Wang, A. P. D. Vries, and M. J. T. Reinders. Unifying user-based and item-based collaborative filtering approaches by similarity fusion. In *Proc. of SIGIR Conference*, 2006.

[14] C.-C. Yu and H.-P. Chang. Personalized location-based recommendation services for tour planning in mobile tourism applications. In *Proc. of EC-Web Conference*, 2009.

[15] V. W. Zheng, Y. Zheng, X. Xie, and Q. Yang. Collaborative location and activity recommendations with gps history data. In *Proc. of WWW Conference*, 2010.

[16] Y. Zheng, L. Zhang, X. Xie, and W.-Y. Ma. Mining interesting locations and travel sequences from gps trajectories. In *Proc. of WWW Conference*, 2009.

Functional Matrix Factorizations for Cold-Start Recommendation

Ke Zhou
College of Computing
Georgia Institute of Technology
Atlanta, GA 30032
kzhou@gatech.edu

Shuang-Hong Yang
College of Computing
Georgia Institute of Technology
Atlanta, GA 30032
shy@gatech.edu

Hongyuan Zha
College of Computing
Georgia Institute of Technology
Atlanta, GA 30032
zha@cc.gatech.edu

ABSTRACT

A key challenge in recommender system research is how to effectively profile *new* users, a problem generally known as *cold-start* recommendation. Recently the idea of progressively *querying* user responses through an *initial interview* process has been proposed as a useful new user preference elicitation strategy. In this paper, we present *functional matrix factorization* (fMF), a novel cold-start recommendation method that solves the problem of initial interview construction within the context of learning user and item profiles. Specifically, fMF constructs a decision tree for the initial interview with each node being an interview question, enabling the recommender to query a user adaptively according to her prior responses. More importantly, we associate latent profiles for each node of the tree — in effect restricting the latent profiles to be a function of possible answers to the interview questions — which allows the profiles to be gradually refined through the interview process based on user responses. We develop an iterative optimization algorithm that alternates between decision tree construction and latent profiles extraction as well as a regularization scheme that takes into account of the tree structure. Experimental results on three benchmark recommendation data sets demonstrate that the proposed fMF algorithm significantly outperforms existing methods for cold-start recommendation.

Categories and Subject Descriptors

H.3.3 [**Information Search and Retrieval**]: Information filtering; I.2.6 [**Artificial Intelligence**]: Learning

General Terms

Algorithms, Performance, Experimentation

Keywords

Recommender systems, Cold-start problem, Collaborative filtering, Decision tree, Functional matrix factorization

SIGIR'11, July 24–28, 2011, Beijing, China.

1. INTRODUCTION

Recommendation systems have become a core component in today's online business world. While E-commerce giants such as Amazon have been greatly benefitted from the abilities of their online recommenders in effectively delivering the *right* items to the *right* people, online startups are increasingly becoming aware of this secret and aggressively sharpening their weapons in order to compete. A key challenge for building an effective recommender system is the well-known cold-start problem — *how to provide recommendations to new users?* While existing *collaborative filtering* (CF) approaches to recommendation perform quite satisfactorily for warm-start users (e.g. users purchasing a lot from an online retailer), it could fail completely for fresh users, simply because the system knows very little about those users in terms of their preferences.

Providing effective cold-start recommendations is of fundamental importance to a recommender system. Offering bad recommendations could risk severely the webshop's revenue, market share and overall reputations, because disappointed customers may turn to other competitors and never come back. This problem is more acute for newly-launched recommender systems (e.g. online startups) because their existing user base is small and attracting more new customers are crucial to their survival. Even for relatively mature recommender systems, a vast majority of the (potential) customers are actually cold-start users - in principle, the population of customers typically follows a power-law distribution w.r.t. the participation frequency such that most customers lie in the long-tail part.

A natural approach to solving the cold-start problem is to elicit new user preferences by query users' responses progressively through an initial interview process [19]. Specifically, at the visit of a new user, the recommender initiates several trials. At each trial, the recommender provides a seed item as a question and ask the user for her opinion; based on the user's responses to the questions, the recommender gradually refines its characterization (i.e. profile) of the user so that it can provide more satisfactory recommendations to the user in the future. A good initial interview process should not be time-consuming: the recommender can only ask a very limited number of questions or otherwise the user will become impatient and leave the system. Equally important, the process should also be effective, i.e. the answers collected from the user should be useful for constructing at least a rough profile for the user. It has been convincingly argued that an effective model for designing the interview process should ask the interview questions adaptively, taking into account the user's responses when asking the next question in the interview process, and decision trees have been found to work especially well for this purpose [7, 19, 20]. As an illustration of movie recommendation, in an interview process depicted in Figure 1, the system asks a new user the question "Do you like the movie Lethal Weapon 4?". The user is allowed to answer with either "Like", "Dislike" or "Unknown". The recommender refines its impression about the user and then direct the user to one of the child nodes and then presents the next interview question according to her previous response. For example, if a user chooses "Like" for "Lethal Weapon 4?" at the root node of Figure 1, she will be directed to the left child node and will be asked the question "Do you like the movie Taxi Driver?"

In this paper, we propose *functional matrix factorization* (fMF), a novel method for the construction of such interview decision trees. We argue that it is more effective to combine the matrix factorization model for collaborative filtering and the decision-tree based interview model into a single framework. Our proposed method is based on the low rank factorization of the incomplete user-item rating matrix with an important twist: it restricts the user profiles to be a *function* of the answers to the interview questions in the form of a decision tree, thus the name functional matrix factorization. The function — playing the role of the initial interview — is in the form of a decision tree with each node being an interview question [7, 20]. Both the decision tree and the item profiles need to be learned; for that we propose an iterative optimization algorithm that alternates between decision tree construction and latent profiles extraction.

Our proposed method tends to explore more effectively the correlation between different items. In particular, the low dimensional user profiles at each node of the decision tree and the item profiles adapt to each other to better fit the training data. Thus, correlation between different items is captured by the low dimensional profiles. As a result, the prediction of ratings can be enhanced by making use of the ratings of different items. Experimental results on three benchmark recommendation data sets, the MovieLens data set, the EachMovie data set and the Netflix data set, demonstrate that the proposed fMF algorithm significantly outperforms existing methods in cold-start recommendation.

Outline: In Section2, we briefly review existing studies for cold-start collaborative filtering. In Section 3, we first introduce matrix factorization for collaborative filtering and then present functional matrix factorization for constructing the interview process for cold-start collaborative filtering by restricting the user profiles to be a function in the form of a decision tree. The learning algorithm based on alternative optimization is then proposed with detailed derivations. Then, we evaluate the proposed method on three data sets and analyze the results in Section 4. Finally we conclude our work and present several future directions in Section 5.

2. RELATED WORK

2.1 Collaborative Filtering

Many studies on recommender systems have been focused on collaborative filtering approaches. These methods can be categorized into memory-based and model-based. The reader is referred to the survey papers [1, 26] for a comprehensive summary of collaborative filtering algorithms.

Recently, matrix factorization becomes a popular direction for collaborative filtering [12, 14, 16, 21, 24]. These methods are shown to be effective in many applications. Specifically, matrix factorization methods usually seek to associate both users and items with latent profiles represented by vectors in a low dimension space that can capture their characteristics. In [22], a convex relaxation for low rank matrix factorization is proposed and applied to collaborative filtering. A probabilistic model for extracting low dimensional profiles is studies in [12], in which latent variables are introduced to capture the users and items and the EM algorithm is used to estimate the parameters. More recently, fueled by the Netflix competition, several improvements have been proposed including the use of regularized SVD [16], and the idea of matrix factorization combined with neighborhood-based methods [14].

2.2 Cold-Start Collaborative Filtering

There have been several studies on the elicitation strategies for new user preferences. The work [18] surveys several guidelines for user preference elicitation. Several models such as [9, 19, 20] constructed the interview process with a static seed set selected based on measures such as informativeness, popularity and coverage. The recent work of [7] proposed a greedy seed selection algorithm by optimizing the prediction performance. Such seed-based methods are not completely satisfactory because the seeds are selected statically in batch, and they do not reflect the user responses during the interview process. In [20], while discussing the IGCN algorithm, it was mentioned the idea of adaptively selecting the interview questions by fitting a decision tree to predefined user clusters. In particular, each node represents an interview question and the user is directed to one of the child nodes according to her response to the parent question. In [8], the authors proposed an algorithm that fits the decision to the users' ratings. This seems to provide a more disciplined approach than that based on the predefined user clusters discussed in IGCN. Our proposed framework goes one step further by integrating the decision tree construction into the matrix factorization framework of collaborative filtering. We should also mention that the decision tree structure used in those methods exhibit interesting resemblance to the Bayesian network approach in [5].

A complimentary line of research for solving the cold-start problem is to utilize the features of users or items. The content features can be used to capture the similarities between users and items and thus reduce the amount of data required to make accurate predictions [2, 3, 10, 15, 23, 25]. For example, the work of [2] utilizes features of items and users as the prior distribution for latent profiles in matrix factorization. Our method is based on the interview process and does not solely rely on features of users and items.

We also want to mention active learning for collaborative filtering [4, 11, 13, 17]. These methods usually select questions that are optimal with respect to some selection criteria, such as the expected value of information or the distance to the true user model. These methods generally are not suitable for interview process since the selection process usually involves optimizing the selection criteria, which is not efficient enough for online interview.

3. FUNCTIONAL MATRIX FACTORIZATION

In this section, we describe the *functional matrix factor-*

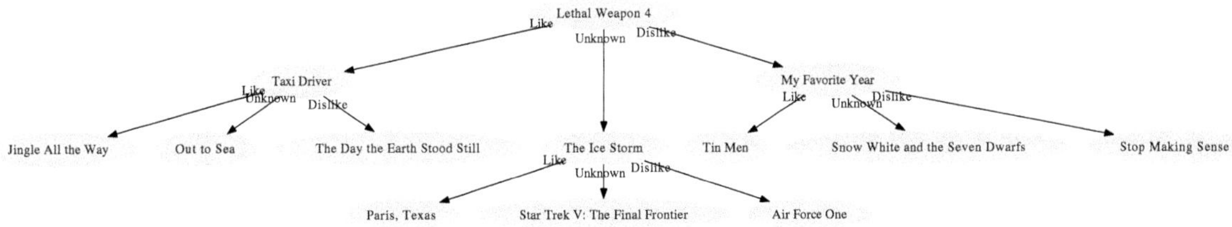

Figure 1: An example for decision trees: Top three levels of a model of depth 6 for MovieLens data set

ization (fMF) method for cold-start collaborative filtering which explores the well-known matrix factorization methods for constructing the interview process. The key innovation is that we parameterize user profiles to be a function of the responses to the possible questions of the interview process and use matrix factorization to compute the profiles.

3.1 Low-Rank Matrix Factorization

Before describing fMF, we first review the matrix factorization method for collaborative filtering. Let r_{ij} denote the rating of user i for item j, where $i = 1, 2, \ldots, N$ and $j = 1, 2, \ldots, M$. In practice, only a small subset of ratings are observed, denoted by $\mathcal{K} = \{r_{ij} \mid (i,j) \in O\}$. The goal of collaborative filtering is to predict the unknown ratings based on ratings in $\mathcal{K}$. Collaborative filtering exploits a basic heuristic that similar users tend to rate similar items in a similar way. One important class of methods for collaborative filtering are based on matrix factorization [12, 24]. Specifically, we associate a K-dimensional vector $u_i \in \mathbb{R}^K$ for each user i and $v_j \in \mathbb{R}^K$ for each item j. The vectors u_i and v_j are usually called user profiles and item profiles since they are intended to capture the characteristics of users and items. The rating r_{ij} of user i for item j can be approximated by a similarity function of u_i and v_j in the low dimensional space, for example, $r_{ij} = u_i^T v_j$.

Given the set of known ratings $\mathcal{K}$, the parameters u_i and v_j can be estimated through fitting the training data by solving the following optimization problem:

$$\min_{u_i, v_j} \sum_{\{(i,j)\} \in O} (r_{ij} - u_i^T v_j)^2.$$

Regularization terms such as the Frobenius norms on the profile vectors can be introduced to avoid overfitting. The problem can be solved by existing numerical optimization methods such as alternating minimization and stochastic gradient descent. In our implementation, we use the alternating optimization for its amenability for the cold-start settings. Specifically, the optimization process performs the following two updates alternatively.

First, for $i = 1, 2, \ldots, N$, minimizing with respect to u_i with all $u_j, j \neq i$ and all v_j fixed:

$$u_i = \operatorname*{argmin}_{u_i} \sum_{(i,j) \in O} (r_{ij} - u_i^T v_j)^2,$$

which is a linear regression problem with squared loss. The closed form solution can be expressed as

$$u_i = \left(\sum_{(i,j) \in O} v_j v_j^T \right)^{-1} \left(\sum_{(i,j) \in O} r_{ij} v_j \right)$$

Then, for $j = 1, 2, \ldots, M$, minimizing with respect to v_j with all $v_i, i \neq j$ and all u_i fixed:

$$v_j = \operatorname*{argmin}_{v_j} \sum_{(i,j) \in O} (r_{ij} - u_i^T v_j)^2,$$

which is also a linear regression problem with similar closed-form solution.

3.2 Functional Matrix Factorization

Now we consider constructing the interview process for cold-start collaborative filtering. Assume that a new user registers at the recommendation system and nothing is known about her. To capture the preferences of the user, the system initiates several interview questions to query the responses from the user. Based on the responses, the system constructs a profile for the user and provides recommendations accordingly.

In the plain matrix factorization model described in Section 3.1, the user profile u_i is estimated by optimizing the ℓ_2 loss on the history ratings r_{ij}. This model does not directly apply to cold-start settings because no rating is observed for the new user prior to the interview process. To build user profiles adaptively according to the user's responses in the course of the interview process, we propose to parameterize the user profile u_i in such a way that the profile u_i is tied to user i's responses in the form of a function, thus the name functional matrix factorization (fMF). More precisely, assume there are P possible *interview questions*. We assume that an answer to a question takes value in the finite set $\{0, 1, \text{Unknown}\}$, representing "Dislike", "Like" and "Unknown", respectively. Furthermore, let a_i denote the P-dimensional vector representing the answers of user i to the P questions. And we tie the profile to the answers by assuming $u_i = T(a_i)$, where T is a function that maps the responses a_i to the user profile $u_i \in \mathbb{R}^k$. To make recommendations for user i, we simply use $r_{ij} = v_j^T T(a_i)$.

Our goal is to learn both T and v_j from the observed ratings $\mathcal{K}$. To this end, substituting $u_i = T(a_i)$ into the low-rank matrix factorization model, we have the following optimization problem:

$$T, V = \operatorname*{argmin}_{T \in \mathcal{H}, V} \sum_{(i,j) \in O} (r_{ij} - v_j^T T(a_i))^2 + \lambda \|V\|^2, \quad (1)$$

where $V = (v_1, \ldots, v_M)$ is the matrix of all item profiles, $\mathcal{H}$ is the space from which the function $T(a)$ is selected and the second term is the regularization term.

Several issues need to be addressed in order to construct the interview process by the above functional matrix factorization. First, the number of all possible interview questions can be quite large (e.g. up to millions of items in movie recommendation); yet a user is only patient enough to answer a few interview questions. Second, the interview process should be adaptive to user's responses, in other words, a follow-up question should be selected based on the user's responses to the previous questions. Therefore, the selection process should be efficient to generate interview questions in real time after the function $T(a)$ is constructed. In addition, since we allow a user to choose "Unknown" to the interview questions, we need to deal with such missing values as well.

Following prior works of [8,20], we use a ternary decision tree to represent $T(a)$. Specifically, each node of the decision tree corresponds to an interview question and has three child nodes. When the user answers the interview question, the user is directed to one of its three child nodes according to her answer. As a result, each user follows a path from the root node to a leaf node during the interview process. A user profile is estimated at each leaf node based on the users' responses, i.e., $T(a)$. The number of interview questions presented to any user is bounded by the depth of the decision tree, generally a small number determined by the system. Also, non-responses to a question can be handled easily in the decision tree with the introduction of a "Unknown" branch.

3.3 Alternative Optimization

The objective function defined in Eq. (1) can be optimized through an alternating minimization process. Specifically, we alternate between the following two steps:

1. Given $T(a)$, we can compute v_j by regularized least square regression. Formally, for each j, we find v_j such that

$$v_j = \underset{v_j}{\operatorname{argmin}} \sum_{(i,j)\in O} (r_{ij} - v_j^T T(a_i))^2 + \lambda \|v_j\|^2.$$

This problem has a closed-form solution given by

$$v_j = \left(\sum_{(i,j)\in O} T(a_i)T(a_i)^T + \lambda I \right)^{-1} \left(\sum_{(i,j)\in O} r_{ij} T(a_i) \right), \quad (2)$$

where I is the identity matrix of appropriate size.

2. Given v_j, we try to fit a decision tree T such that

$$T = \underset{T\in\mathcal{H}}{\operatorname{argmin}} \sum_{(i,j)\in O} (r_{ij} - T(a_i)^T v_j)^2. \quad (3)$$

A critical challenge is that the number of possible trees grows exponentially with the depth of the trees, which can be extremely large even for trees of limited depth. It is therefore computationally extensive to obtain a global optimal solution for the above. We address this problem by proposing an efficient greedy algorithm for finding an approximate solution.

3.4 Decision Tree Construction

Traditional decision tree algorithms such as C4.5 or CART [6] usually minimize objective functions such as classification error and square loss for regression. In our scenario, the objective function is defined in Eq. (3), and we now describe how to build a decision tree in a greedy and recursive fashion to minimize it. Specifically, at each node, we select the best interview question by optimizing the objective defined in Eq. (3) based on the response to this question; the decision tree then splits the user set into three subsets corresponding to the child nodes (i.e. "Like", "Dislike" and "Unknown"). We carry out this procedure recursively until the tree reaches certain depth. In our experiments, the depth is usually set to a small number between 3 and 7.

Formally, starting from the root node, the set of users at current node are partitioned into three disjoint subsets $R_L(p)$, $R_D(p)$ and $R_U(p)$ corresponding to "Like", "Dislike" and "Unknown" of their responses to the interview question p:

$$R_L(p) = \{i | a_{ip} = \text{"Like"}\},$$
$$R_D(p) = \{i | a_{ip} = \text{"Dislike"}\},$$
$$R_U(p) = \{i | a_{ip} = \text{"Unknown"}\}.$$

To find the optimal question p that leads to the best split, we minimize the following objective:

$$\min_p \sum_{i\in R_L(p)} \sum_{(i,j)\in O} (r_{ij} - u_L^T v_j)^2 + \sum_{i\in R_D(p)} \sum_{(i,j)\in O} (r_{ij} - u_D^T v_j)^2 + \sum_{i\in R_U(p)} \sum_{(i,j)\in O} (r_{ij} - u_U^T v_j)^2, \quad (4)$$

where u_L, u_D and u_U are the optimal profiles for users in the child nodes corresponds to the answers of "Like", "Dislike" and "Unknown", respectively:

$$u_L = \underset{u}{\operatorname{argmin}} \sum_{i\in R_L(p)} \sum_{(i,j)\in O} (r_{ij} - u^T v_j)^2,$$
$$u_D = \underset{u}{\operatorname{argmin}} \sum_{i\in R_D(p)} \sum_{(i,j)\in O} (r_{ij} - u^T v_j)^2,$$
$$u_U = \underset{u}{\operatorname{argmin}} \sum_{i\in R_U(p)} \sum_{(i,j)\in O} (r_{ij} - u^T v_j)^2.$$

There also exist closed-form solutions to u_L, u_D and u_D as follows:

$$u_L = \left(\sum_{i\in R_L(p)} \sum_{(i,j)\in O} v_j v_j^T \right)^{-1} \left(\sum_{i\in R_L(p)} \sum_{(i,j)\in O} r_{ij} v_j \right), \quad (5)$$

$$u_D = \left(\sum_{i\in R_D(p)} \sum_{(i,j)\in O} v_j v_j^T \right)^{-1} \left(\sum_{i\in R_D(p)} \sum_{(i,j)\in O} r_{ij} v_j \right), \quad (6)$$

$$u_U = \left(\sum_{i\in R_U(p)} \sum_{(i,j)\in O} v_j v_j^T \right)^{-1} \left(\sum_{i\in R_U(p)} \sum_{(i,j)\in O} r_{ij} v_j \right). \quad (7)$$

After the root node is constructed, its child nodes can be constructed in a similar way, recursively. We summarize our algorithms for functional matrix factorization and decision tree construction in Algorithm 1 and Algorithm, 2 respectively.

Implementation and Computational Complexity. The time complexity for computing v_j with Equation (2) is $O(MK^3)$, where M is the number of items and K is the dimension of the latent space. In order to compute u_L, u_D and u_U at each split, we need to compute the inverse of a square matrix of size K, which takes $O(K^3)$ time. The brute-force approach for generating the matrix itself requires $O(UMK^2)$ time. In order to reduce the time complexity, we observe that the coefficient matrix can be computed based on the sum of ratings, the sum of squares of ratings and the number of ratings for each item within time $O(MK^2)$. With a similar method proposed in [8], the time complexity of computing these statistics of all items is $O(\sum N_i^2)$ for each level of the decision tree, where N_i is the number of ratings by the user i. Thus, the computation complexity for constructing

Algorithm 1 Alternating Optimization for Functional Matrix Factorization

```
Require: The training data K = {r_ij | (i, j) ∈ O}.
Ensure: Estimated decision tree T(a) and item profiles
    v_j, j = 1, 2, ..., M.
  Initialize v_j randomly for j = 1, ..., M.
  while not converge do
    Fit a decision tree T(a) using Algorithm 2.
    Update v_j with Equation (2).
  end while
  return T(a) and v_j, j = 1, 2, ..., M.
```

Algorithm 2 Greedy Decision Tree Construction

```
  function FitTree(UserSet)
  // UserSet: the set of users in current node.
  Calculate u_L, u_D, u_U by Equation (5), (6) and (7) for
    p = 1, ..., P.
  Compute the split criteria L_p by Equation (4) for p =
    1, ..., P.
  Find the best interview question p = argmax_p L_p.
  Split user into three groups R_L(p), R_D(p) and R_U(p).
  if square error reduces after split and depth <
    maxDepth then
    Call FitTree(R_L(p)), FitTree(R_D(p)) and
      FitTree(R_U(p)) to construct the child nodes.
  end if
  return T(a).
  end function
```

the decision tree is $O(D\sum_i N_i^2 + LMK^3 + LM^2K^2)$, where D is the depth of the tree and L represents the number of nodes in the tree. The computation time can be reduced by selecting a subset of items based on some criteria such as the rating variance, and using only the selected items as candidates for the interview questions.

3.5 Hierarchical Regularization

In the above section, u_L, u_D and u_U for each node are estimated by linear regression. When the amount of training data is small, the estimate may overfit the training data. The problem becomes more severe especially for the nodes close to the leaves of the decision tree, because as the split process progresses, users belonging to those nodes become fewer and fewer. To avoid overfitting, regularization terms need to be introduced. Although traditional ℓ_2 regularization can be applied in this case [16], but such approach does not take into account the rich structure of the decision tree.

Here, we propose to apply hierarchical regularization that utilize the structure of the decision tree. Specifically, we shrink the coefficient u of a node toward the one at its parent node. For example:

$$u_L = \underset{u}{\operatorname{argmin}} \sum_{i \in R_L(p)} \sum_{(i,j) \in O} (r_{ij} - u^T v_j)^2 + \lambda_h \|u - u_C\|^2,$$

where u_C is the estimation at the current node and u_L is the estimation at its child node corresponding to the answer "Like" and the parameter λ_h controls the trade-off between training error and regularization. We use $\lambda_h = 0.03$ in our experiments which seems to give good results. The similar idea using parent node as the prior for the child node is also studied in [8], but the ratings for the parent node is used to improve the prediction in the child node.

Table 1: Statistics for Data Sets

Dataset	No. Users	No. Items	No. Ratings
MovieLens	6040	3900	1,000,209
EachMovie	72,916	1628	2,811,983
Netflix	480,189	17,770	104,706,033

4. EXPERIMENTS

In order to evaluate the proposed method for cold-start collaborative filtering, we carry out a set of controlled experiments on three widely used benchmark data sets: MovieLens, EachMovie and Netflix.

4.1 Data sets and Evaluation Metrics

We first briefly describe the data sets.

- The MovieLens[1] data set contains 3900 movies, 6040 users and about 1 million ratings. In this data set, about 4% of the user-movie dyads are observed. The ratings are integers ranging from 1 (bad) to 5 (good).
- The EachMovie data set, collected by HP/Compaq Research, contains about 2.8 million ratings for 1628 movies by 72,916 users. The ratings are integers ranging from 1 to 6.
- The Netflix[2] is one of the largest test bed for collaborative filtering. It contains over 100 million ratings and was split into one training and one test subsets. The training set consists of 100,480,507 ratings for 17,770 movies by 480,189 users. The test set contains about 2.8 million ratings. All the ratings are ranged from 1 to 5.

The performance of an collaborative filtering algorithm will be evaluated in terms of the widely used root mean square error (RMSE) measure, which is defined as follows

$$\text{RMSE} = \left(\frac{1}{|\mathcal{T}|} \sum_{(i,j) \in \mathcal{T}} (r_{ij} - \hat{r}_{ij})^2 \right)^{1/2},$$

where $\mathcal{T}$ represents the set of test ratings, r_{ij} is the ground-truth values for movie j by user i and $\hat{r}_{ij}$ is the predicted value by a collaborative filtering model. We can also normalize the error of each user by the number of their ratings. Our initial results show that the two metrics are consistent in general, so we only report RMSE in our experiments.

4.2 Deriving Interview Responses from User Ratings

The responses a_i of the interview process for user i is required in order to train and evaluate the interview process. Following the standard settings [8,20], we restrict the format of interview questions to be "Do you like item j?" For example, for movie recommendation system, we can ask questions like "Do you like the movie Independence Day?" Then, we can infer the responses for existing users according to their ratings for the corresponding items. For instance, with ratings in 1-5 scale, we assume that the responses a_{ij} of user i to the question "Do you like item j?" can be inferred from her rating r_{ij} as follows:

$$a_{ij} = \begin{cases} 0, & \text{if } (i,j) \in O \text{ and } r_{ij} \le 3 \\ 1, & \text{if } (i,j) \in O \text{ and } r_{ij} > 3 \\ \text{"Unknown"}, & \text{if } (i,j) \notin O \end{cases}$$

[1] http://www.grouplens.org/node/73

[2] http://www.netflixprize.com/

Intuitively, we assume that the user will response 0 (*dislike*) and 1 (*like*) for items she rates with ≤ 3 rating or > 3 rating. If the user did not rate an item selected for the interview process, we assume that she will respond with *unknown*. For EachMovie data set, we use a similar method except setting the threshold to be 4 since its ratings range from 1 to 6.

4.3 Experiment Design

We seek to address the following questions:

1. For new users, how does the proposed algorithm perform? In particular, how effective is the interview process? Moreover, how does the proposed algorithm perform compared to the baseline algorithms?
2. We utilize the ratings from users to simulate their responses to the interview questions in our evaluation. How do missing values in user ratings impact the performance of the proposed algorithm?
3. How does fMF perform in warm-start settings compared to traditional collaborative filtering methods such as plain matrix factorization?
4. How do the parameters impact the performance of the proposed model?

4.4 Cold-Start Performance

We first evaluate the performance of fMF in cold-start settings. For each data set, we split the users into two disjoint subsets, the training set and the test set, containing 75% and 25% users, respectively. The users in the training set are assumed to be warm-start users whose ratings are known by the system. We learn the models and construct the interview process based on these training users. In contrast, the users in the test set are assumed to be cold-start users. The ratings of each user in the test set are partitioned into two sets: the first set is called the *answer set* which is used to generate the user responses in the interview process while the second set is called the *evaluation set* which is used to evaluate the performance after the interview process. The sizes of the answer set and the evaluation set are 75% and 25% of the rated items of each user, respectively. Note that the interview process typically includes only a small number (≤ 7 in our experiments) of questions although the answer set contains 75% of the ratings when deriving the responses for the cold-start users. The evaluation process is summarized in Figure 2.

We compare the performance with two baseline methods, named as Tree and TreeU and briefly described as follows:

- Tree: this is the method proposed in the very recent work of [8]. The method learns a decision tree for initial interview without using latent user/item profiles. It fits the tree based on the ratings of all the items in the inventory. Therefore, at the leaf node, it needs to estimate M ratings for all the M items in the system.

- TreeU: this method learns decision tree and matrix factorization through two separate steps. It first estimates the user profiles and item profiles through plain matrix factorization described in Section 3.1; then, a decision tree is constructed separately using the algorithm of [8] to fit the latent user profiles. The model predicts ratings by using the user profiles from the decision tree and the item profiles from matrix factorization.

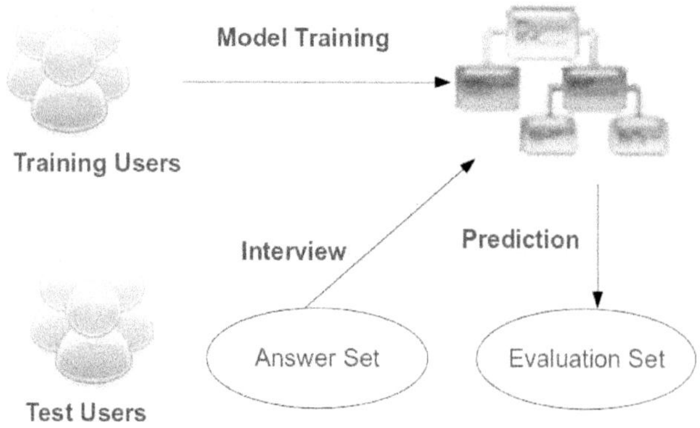

Figure 2: Evaluation process for cold-start users

Our proposed fMF algorithm differs from these two algorithms in that it is a natural integration of both decision tree and matrix factorization.

We use the following parameter settings: For TreeU, we use as default the regularization weight of $\lambda = 0.01$. For Tree and fMF, we apply 4-fold cross validation to determine the parameters.

The results on MovieLens, EachMovie and Netflix data sets are reported in Table 2, Table 3 and Table 4, respectively. Our first observation is that, as expected, the performance is gradually improved (i.e. the RMSE decreases) as the number of interview questions increases. This is true for all three methods, suggesting that these three algorithms are all capable of refining user preference through the interview process. Therefore, all the three methods can be applied to solve the cold-start problem.

Comparing the performance of fMF and Tree, we can see that fMF consistently outperforms Tree in all the three data sets. The improvements are significant according to t-test with significance level $p = 0.05$. This observation illustrate that the interview processes learned by fMF is more effective than those by Tree. We attribute this to the fact that fMF naturally integrates the matrix factorization model into the interview process for cold-start collaborative filtering. In particular, fMF inherits the ability of matrix factorization models in *collaboratively* uncovering the user-item ratings. In contrast, Tree assumes that users/items are independent from one another, and therefore cannot capture the vital collaborative effect.

We can also see that TreeU does not work well, too. Recall that TreeU is a two-stage method — It first extracts the user profiles and item profiles using plain matrix factorization, and then constructs a decision tree on the answers of the interview questions. A possible reason for why it does not perform well is that the user profiles and item profiles obtained from the matrix factorization in warm-start setting usually capture the refined preferences of users and refined characteristics of items. However, in cold-start setting, we are only allowed to ask users a few questions so that the model usually captures only very coarse interests of users. As a result, TreeU usually fails to fit the user profiles from matrix factorization accurately. Thus, its prediction accuracy is relatively low. On the other hand, our method estimates the decision tree and item profiles simultaneously in a combined optimization process. Thus, the user profiles obtained by decision tree and the item profiles can adapt to each other and improve the prediction accuracy.

To provide more comprehensive views of the interview pro-

Table 2: **RMSE on MovieLens data set for cold-start users with respect to the number of interview questions**

No. Questions	3	4	5	6	7
fMF	0.9509	0.9480	0.9437	0.9429	0.9410
Tree	0.9767	0.9683	0.9615	0.9512	0.9523
TreeU	0.9913	0.9887	0.9789	0.9690	0.9657

Table 3: **RMSE on EachMovie data set for cold-start users with respect to the number of interview questions**

No. Questions	3	4	5	6	7
fMF	1.2853	1.2717	1.2715	1.2691	1.2673
Tree	1.2989	1.2842	1.2800	1.2779	1.2750
TreeU	1.3134	1.3009	1.2928	1.2907	1.2905

Table 4: **RMSE on Netflix data set for cold-start user with respect to the number of interview questions**

No. Questions	3	4	5	6	7
fMF	0.9205	0.9189	0.91582	0.9123	0.9121
Tree	0.9320	0.9252	0.9239	0.9228	0.9219
TreeU	0.9422	0.9382	0.9359	0.9322	0.9323

Table 5: **Examples of interview process with 6 questions**

(a) Interview process

Round	Question	Response
1	Being John Malkovich	Dislike
2	Armageddon	Like
3	Maid in Manhattan	Dislike
4	Reservoir Dogs	Like
5	Collateral Damage	Dislike
6	2 Fast 2 Furious	Unknown

(b) Top-5 recommendations

Rank	Movie Title
1	Lord of the Rings: The Return of the King
2	Lord of the Rings: The Two Towers
3	Mobile Suit Gundam: Char's Counterattack
4	Star Wars: Episode V: The Empire Strikes Back
5	Raiders of the Lost Ark

cess, we further look into particular cases. In Table 5 and Table 6, we present the interview process for users in Netflix data set as well as the top-5 recommendations for them after the interview process. From Table 5, we can see that the user chooses "Like" on the movie Armegeddon and Reservoir Dogs, which belong to Fiction and Adventure movies. The recommendation includes Lord of the Rings series and Star Wars. They are quite related to the movie Armegeddon based on their genres. Similarly, the interview process of Table 6 shows that the user likes Drama and Romance movies and the top recommendations for her contain both those two types of movies. Those results illustrate that the recommendations generated by fMF are indeed reasonable.

4.5 The Impact of Non-responses

In our experiments, we utilize the ratings of users to simulate their responses to the interview questions as described in Section 4.2 since the users' responses to the interview questions are not available for the benchmark data sets. In particular, we assume that the user will respond "Unknown"

Table 6: **Examples of interview process with 6 questions**

(a) Interview process

Round	Question	Response
1	Being John Malkovich	Like
2	Armageddon	Dislike
3	What Women Want	Dislike
4	The Royal Tenenbaums	Unknown
5	Pretty Woman	Like
6	Cats: The Ultimate Edition	Unknown

(b) Top-5 recommendations

Rank	Movie Title
1	The Shawshank Redemption
2	Schindler's List
3	Sex and the City: Season 5
4	Sex and the City: Season 4
5	The Usual Suspects

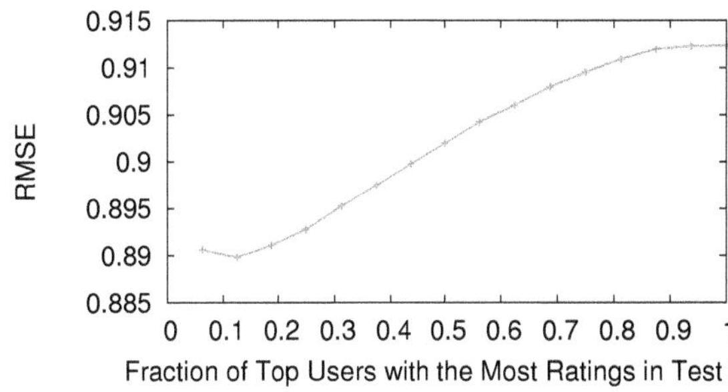

Figure 3: Performance measured by RMSE on Netflix data set with respect to the fraction of users with the most known ratings.

to an interview question if she does not rate the corresponding item. This assumption, however, might be inaccurate in practice. For example, a user's rating to an item might be missing simply because she does not have time to rate it. In this case, the user may actually responds with "Like" or "Dislike" rather than "Unknown" if she is asked to respond to the interview questions. As a result, the missing values in data sets may introduce bias in the training and interview process.[3]

Here, we explore how the missing ratings influence the initial interview process. We investigate the performance of the proposed method on users with different numbers of ratings. To this end, we sort users in the test set by the their numbers of ratings in descending order and then plot, in Figure 3, the performance measured by RMSE with respect to the fraction of users with the most ratings. We can see that the RMSE increases when more users with few ratings are included, which indicates that the performance for users with more ratings is better then the ones with less ratings. This is because that the users with more ratings are less likely to select "Unknown" in our simulation. Thus, they are less likely prone to the influences by the bias introduced by the missing values in the training data.

With this basic understanding, we carry out a set of experiments to investigate the impact of missing values in training

[3]The bias in training data seems to have been largely ignored in previous work.

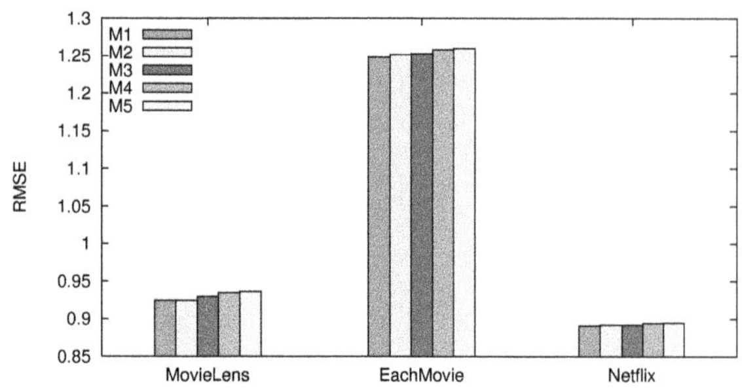

Figure 4: Performance measured by RMSE on three data sets with respect to the fraction of users with the most known ratings.

data. For each of the three data sets, we sort users in training set in descending order. Then, the users in the test set (labeled by MT) is sampled from top 20% users with the most ratings. We only consider the users with sufficiently large number of ratings since we would like to rule out the impact of bias during the interview process and focus on the missing values for training users. We generate five training sets, namely M1 to M5, from the rest of the users in the training set, including the top 20%, 40%, 60%, 80% and 100% of the users that are not selected in the test set, respectively. Again, 75% ratings for each user in MT is used to simulate the interview process and the performance is evaluated on the remaining 25% ratings.

We perform experiments by training the proposed models on M1 to M5 and evaluate them on MT for all three data sets. The results are shown in Figure 4. It can be observed from Figure 4 that the prediction error measured by RMSE increases when more users with few training data are included in the training set. This observation suggests that the performance are indeed affected by the bias introduced by the missing values in training set.

4.6 Warm-Start Performance

In order to answer the third question proposed in Section 4.3, we evaluate the proposed algorithm in warm-start settings and show the relative performance between the cold-start methods and warm-start methods. In particular, we consider the matrix factorization method described as follows:

- MF: The matrix factorization method described in Section 3.1 is included for comparison. We include ℓ_2 regularization to avoid overfitting with $\lambda = 0.01$. The method is not designed for the cold-start problem and thus it requires the user ratings in order to construct user profiles.

We include this method to present a concrete comparisons of the relative performance of the proposed cold-start method and the warm-start methods that are widely studies in previous researches. We compare the proposed algorithm (fMF) with all three methods for warm-start settings: Tree, TreeU and MF. To this end, we perform experiments with different depths of decision trees and report the RMSE of the all the methods over three data sets. For MovieLens and EachMovie data set, we randomly split the ratings for each users into training set and test set and perform 4-fold cross validation. For Netflix data set, we follow the popular evaluation protocol on this data set. Therefore, we train our models on the training set and report the performance on the test set. The performance measured by RMSE with respect to the depths of decision trees is reported in Table 7, Table 8 and Table 9.

We can observe that all the cold-start methods perform worse than the matrix factorization method. This observation is consistent with our expectation because all the three cold-start algorithms are constrained in some ways in order to deal with cold-start users — the goal of the cold-start algorithms is to provide cold-start users with reasonable predictions within a few quick interview questions. For example, the fMF model is restricted in its maximum depth. We should expect comparable performance, if this constraint is eliminated.

As an empirical validation, we further carry out experiments on the MovieLens data set by fitting the decision trees in our model with relatively larger depth. We note that the decision trees of very large depth correspond to interview processes with many questions, which are not proper for initial interview process for cold-start users since users are typically not willing to answer many questions. However, we can show that the performance of the proposed method can be quite close to the matrix factorization method if we relax the constraint and allow the model to use decision trees with large depth. We report the RMSE of fMF with respect to the depth of the decision tree in Figure 5. We also include Tree and MF for comparison. We can see that the RMSE of fMF monotonically decreases as the depth of decision trees increases. Moreover, its performance can be quite close to the matrix factorization method (MF). When the depth of the trees grows, the number of leaf nodes increases. Therefore, there are only a few users at each node. Thus, the user profiles estimated by fMF can be quite close to those by MF. We conclude that our method can be a reasonably good method of general collaborative filtering as well. On the other hand, we can see that the performance of Tree is much worse than MF even with a large number of questions. Moreover, the gap between fMF and Tree becomes larger when the depth of the decision tree grows. This is because Tree predicts the ratings of different items independently at each leaf node, which is not a good model for collaborative filtering in general. We also perform similar experiments with the cold start setting. In this case, the RMSE of fMF decreases with the depth of the decision tree when the depth is not very large (e.g. ≤ 14). We emphasize that the depth of the decision tree is usually set to be a small number since we can not ask a lot of questions to users during the interview process.

4.7 Impact of Model Parameters

There are several parameters that affect the performance of the proposed model. In this section, we carry out experiments to investigate the impacts of these parameters. We only report the results on MovieLens data set as the observations are similar when other data sets are used. By default, the cold-start setting described in Section 4.4 is applied unless otherwise stated.

The parameter K controls the dimension of the user profiles and item profiles for the matrix factorization model. We fix the depth of the decision tree to be 6, and report the performance obtained with different K. The results are depicted in Figure 6. Particularly, as K increases, the factorization model becomes more and more flexible, as a results,

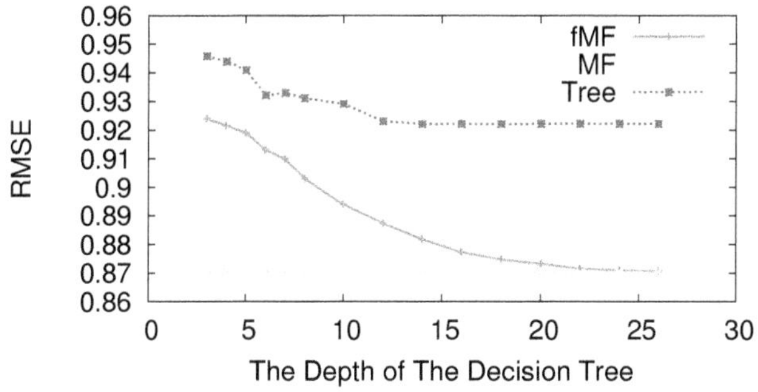

Figure 5: RMSE of fMF, Tree and MF on MovieLens data set with respect to the number of interview questions

Table 7: RMSE on MovieLens data set in warm-start setting

No. Questions	3	4	5	6	7
fMF	0.9240	0.9216	0.9190	0.9134	0.9098
Tree	0.9458	0.9439	0.9409	0.9321	0.9329
TreeU	0.9906	0.9850	0.9771	0.9706	0.9728
MF	0.8702				

Table 8: RMSE on EachMovie data set in warm-start setting

No. Questions	3	4	5	6	7
fMF	1.2548	1.2499	1.2449	1.2366	1.2226
Tree	1.2709	1.2614	1.2664	1.2570	1.2549
TreeU	1.28742	1.2813	1.2790	1.2772	1.2751
MF	1.1790				

Table 9: RMSE on Netflix data set in warm-start setting

No. Questions	3	4	5	6	7
fMF	0.9770	0.9749	0.9721	0.9715	0.9703
Tree	0.9772	0.9761	0.9726	0.9717	0.9713
TreeU	0.9914	0.9879	0.9842	0.9792	0.9752
MF	0.9399				

the RMSE first decreases, and reaches the optima around $K = 20$; thereafter, the model becomes increasingly overparameterized and the performance in turn starts to degrades. For example, the performance with $K = 30$ is worse than the that with $K = 20$. In principle, the optimal K should provide the best trade-off between fitting bias and model complexity.

One of our contributions is that we propose to use hierarchical regularization to avoid overfiting. The impact of the hierarchical regularization is controlled by the parameter λ_h. We evaluate fMF with different values of λ_h on MovieLens data set. The performance obtained by ℓ_2 regularization is also reported for comparison. We can see from Figure 7 that the hierarchical regularization always performs better than the basic ℓ_2 regularization. This observation suggest that hierarchical regularization, by exploiting the structure of the decision tree, provides better regulatory to the functional matrix factorization model.

Another parameter of interest is the regularization weight λ for the item profiles v_j. We vary the value of λ and report the performance measured by RMSE in Figure 8. We can see

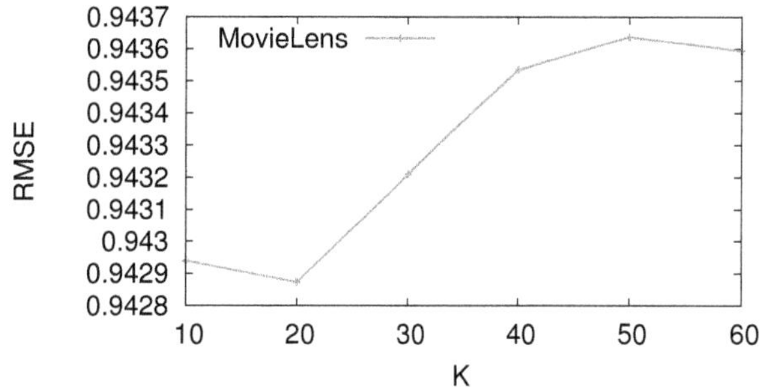

Figure 6: Performance measured by RMSE with respect to different values of K on MovieLens data set. The performance is reported by setting the depth of the decision tree to be 6.

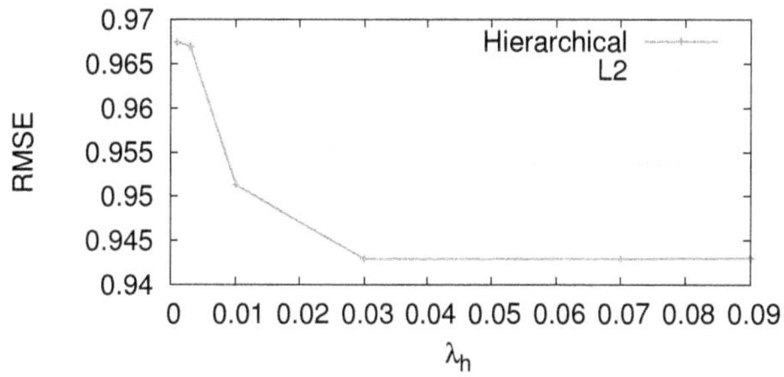

Figure 7: The performance of hierarchical regularization. The performance is reported by setting the depth of the decision tree to be 6.

that the optimal performance is achieved when a moderate λ is used. Especially, the model has a high risk of overfitting if λ is too small.

The learning algorithm of the proposed model is an iterative process. In Figure 9, we plot the both training and test performance measured by RMSE with respect to the number of iterations. We can see that the algorithm converges very quickly, usually within 5 iterations.

5. CONCLUDING REMARKS

The main focus of this paper is on the cold-start problem in recommender systems. We have presented the functional matrix factorization, a framework for simultaneously learning decision tree for initial interview and latent factors for user/item profiling. The proposed fMF algorithm seamlessly integrates matrix factorization for collaborative filtering and decision-tree based interview into one unified framework by reparameterizing the latent profiles as a function of user responses to the interview questions. We have established learning algorithms based on alternating minimization and demonstrated the effectiveness of fMF on real-world recommendation benchmarks.

The current fMF model is based on a basic matrix factorization formulation and does not take into account the content features such as the demographical information of users. For future work, we plan to investigate how to utilize such content features to further enhance the performance of fMF in cold-start recommendations. Moreover, we also plan to conduct in-depth examination on the missing value problem, which seems to introduce considerable bias to the learning process as revealed by our experiments.

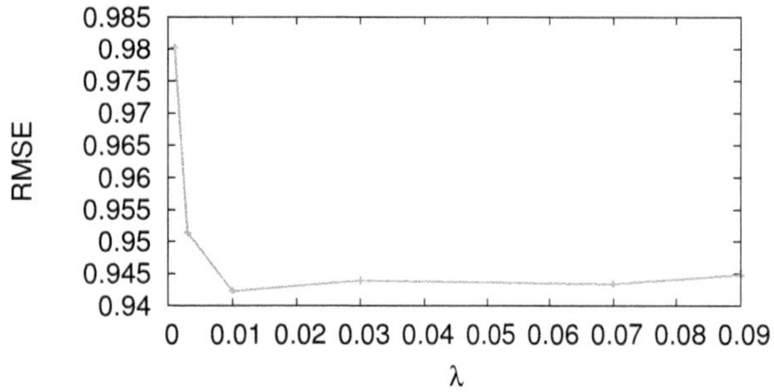

Figure 8: Performance measured by RMSE with respect to different values of λ on MovieLens data set.

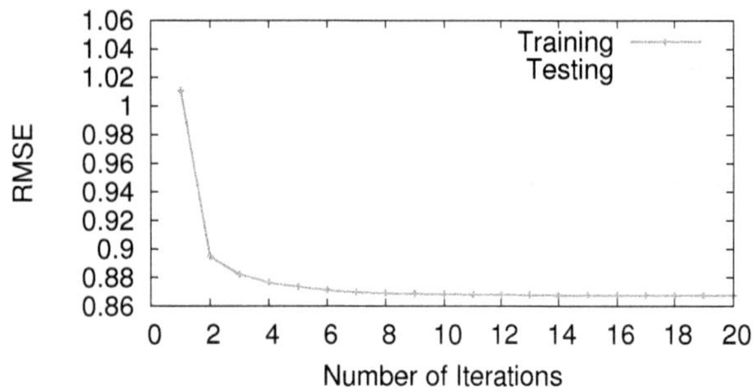

Figure 9: Performance measured by RMSE with respect to the number of iterations on MovieLens data set.

6. ACKNOWLEDGEMENTS

We would like to thank the reviewers for their constructive and insightful comments. Part of this work was supported by NSF Grant IIS-1049694, a Yahoo! faculty grant and 111 Project B07022.

7. REFERENCES

[1] G. Adomavicius and a. Tuzhilin. Toward the next generation of recommender systems: a survey of the state-of-the-art and possible extensions. *IEEE Transactions on Knowledge and Data Engineering*, 17(6):734–749, June 2005.

[2] D. Agarwal and B.-C. Chen. Regression-based latent factor models. *Proceedings of the 15th ACM SIGKDD international conference on Knowledge discovery and data mining - KDD '09*, page 19, 2009.

[3] J. Basilico and T. Hofmann. Unifying collaborative and content-based filtering. *Twenty-first international conference on Machine learning - ICML '04*, page 9, 2004.

[4] C. Boutilier, R. Zemel, and B. Marlin. Active collaborative filtering. In *Proceedings of the Nineteenth Conference on Uncertainty in Artificial Intelligence*, pages 98–106. Citeseer, 2003.

[5] J. Breese, D. Heckerman, C. Kadie, and Others. Empirical analysis of predictive algorithms for collaborative filtering. In *Proceedings of the 14th conference on Uncertainty in Artificial Intelligence*, pages 43–52, 1998.

[6] L. Breiman, J. Friedman, R. Olshen, and C. Stone. *Classification and Regression Trees.* Wadsworth and Brooks, Monterey, CA, 1984.

[7] N. Golbandi, Y. Koren, and R. Lempel. On bootstrapping recommender systems. In *Proceedings of the 19th ACM international conference on Information and knowledge management*, pages 1805–1808. ACM, 2010.

[8] N. Golbandi, Y. Koren, and R. Lempel. Adaptive Bootstrapping of Recommender Systems Using Decision Trees. *WSDM*, 2011.

[9] K. Goldberg, T. Roeder, D. Gupta, and C. Perkins. Eigentaste: A constant time collaborative filtering algorithm. *Information Retrieval*, 4(2):133–151, 2001.

[10] A. Gunawardana and C. Meek. Tied boltzmann machines for cold start recommendations. In *Proceedings of the 2008 ACM conference on Recommender systems*, pages 19–26, New York, New York, USA, 2008. ACM.

[11] A. Harpale and Y. Yang. Personalized active learning for collaborative filtering. In *Proceedings of the 31st annual international ACM SIGIR conference on Research and development in information retrieval*, pages 91–98. ACM, 2008.

[12] T. Hofmann. Latent semantic models for collaborative filtering. *ACM Transactions on Information Systems*, 22(1):89–115, Jan. 2004.

[13] R. Jin and L. Si. A Bayesian approach toward active learning for collaborative filtering. In *Proceedings of the 20th conference on Uncertainty in artificial intelligence*, pages 278–285. AUAI Press, 2004.

[14] Y. Koren. Factor in the neighbors: Scalable and accurate collaborative filtering. *ACM Transactions on Knowledge Discovery from Data (TKDD)*, 4(1):1–24, 2010.

[15] S.-T. Park and W. Chu. Pairwise preference regression for cold-start recommendation. *Proceedings of the third ACM conference on Recommender systems - RecSys '09*, page 21, 2009.

[16] A. Paterek. Improving regularized singular value decomposition for collaborative filtering. In *Proceedings of KDD Cup and Workshop*, volume 2007, pages 5–8. Citeseer, 2007.

[17] D. Pennock, E. Horvitz, S. Lawrence, and C. Giles. Collaborative filtering by personality diagnosis: A hybrid memory-and model-based approach. In *Proceedings of the 16th conference on uncertainty in artificial intelligence*, pages 473–480. Citeseer, 2000.

[18] P. Pu and L. Chen. User-involved preference elicitation for product search and recommender systems. *AI Magazine*, 29(4):93, 2009.

[19] A. Rashid, I. Albert, D. Cosley, S. Lam, S. McNee, J. Konstan, and J. Riedl. Getting to know you: learning new user preferences in recommender systems. In *Proceedings of the 7th international conference on Intelligent user interfaces*, pages 127–134. ACM, 2002.

[20] A. M. Rashid, G. Karypis, and J. Riedl. Learning Preferences of New Users in Recommender Systems: An Information Theoretic Approach. *SIGKDD Workshop on Web Mining and Web Usage Analysis*, 22, Oct. 2008.

[21] S. Rendle, C. Freudenthaler, and L. Schmidt-Thieme. Factorizing personalized Markov chains for next-basket recommendation. *Proceedings of the 19th international conference on World wide web - WWW '10*, page 811, 2010.

[22] J. Rennie and N. Srebro. Fast maximum margin matrix factorization for collaborative prediction. In *Proceedings of the 22nd international conference on Machine learning*, pages 713–719. ACM, 2005.

[23] A. I. Schein, A. Popescul, L. H. Ungar, and D. M. Pennock. Methods and metrics for cold-start recommendations. *Proceedings of the 25th annual international ACM SIGIR conference on Research and development in information retrieval - SIGIR '02*, page 253, 2002.

[24] N. Srebro, J. Rennie, and T. Jaakkola. Maximum-margin matrix factorization. *Advances in neural information processing systems*, 17:1329–1336, 2005.

[25] D. Stern, R. Herbrich, and T. Graepel. Matchbox: large scale online bayesian recommendations. In *Proceedings of the 18th international conference on World wide web*, pages 111–120. ACM, 2009.

[26] X. Su and T. M. Khoshgoftaar. A Survey of Collaborative Filtering Techniques. *Advances in Artificial Intelligence*, 2009(Section 3):1–20, 2009.

Exploiting Geographical Influence for Collaborative Point-of-Interest Recommendation

Mao Ye[1†], Peifeng Yin[1†], Wang-Chien Lee[1†], and Dik-Lun Lee[2‡]
†Department of Computer Science and Engineering, The Pennsylvania State University, PA, USA.
‡Department of Computer Science and Engineering, HKUST, Hong Kong
[1]{mxy177,pzy102,wlee}@cse.psu.edu [2]dlee@cse.ust.hk

ABSTRACT

In this paper, we aim to provide a point-of-interests (POI) recommendation service for the rapid growing location-based social networks (LBSNs), e.g., Foursquare, Whrrl, etc. Our idea is to explore user preference, social influence and geographical influence for POI recommendations. In addition to deriving user preference based on user-based collaborative filtering and exploring social influence from friends, we put a special emphasis on geographical influence due to the spatial clustering phenomenon exhibited in user check-in activities of LBSNs. We argue that the geographical influence among POIs plays an important role in user check-in behaviors and model it by power law distribution. Accordingly, we develop a collaborative recommendation algorithm based on geographical influence based on naive Bayesian. Furthermore, we propose a unified POI recommendation framework, which fuses user preference to a POI with social influence and geographical influence. Finally, we conduct a comprehensive performance evaluation over two large-scale datasets collected from Foursquare and Whrrl. Experimental results with these real datasets show that the unified collaborative recommendation approach significantly outperforms a wide spectrum of alternative recommendation approaches.

Categories and Subject Descriptors

H.3.3 [**Information Search and Retrieval**]: Information Filtering; J.4 [**Computer Applications**]: Social and Behavior Sciences

General Terms

Algorithms, Experimentation.

Keywords

Collaborative Recommendation, Location-based Social Networks, Geographical Influence.

1. INTRODUCTION

With the rapid development of mobile devices, wireless networks and Web 2.0 technology, a number of location-based social networking services, e.g., Loopt[1], Brightkite[2], Foursquare[3] and Whrrl[4], have emerged in recent years.[5] These LBSNs allow users to establish cyber links to their friends or other users, and share tips and experiences of their visits to plentiful point-of-interests (POIs), e.g., restaurants, stores, cinema theaters, etc. In LBSNs, a *POI recommendation* service, aiming at recommending new POIs to users in order to help them explore new places and know their cities better, is an essential function that has received a lot of research momentum recently [25, 26].

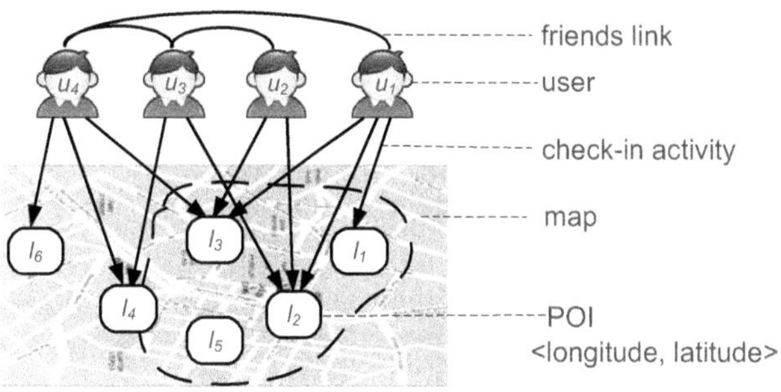

Figure 1: Graph representation of user-user friendship and user-location check-in activity in a LBSN

Indeed, facilitating POI recommendations in LBSNs is a promising and interesting research problem because valuable information such as the "cyber" connections among users as well as the "physical" interactions between users and locations have been captured in the systems. Nevertheless, these information have not been fully explored in prior research studies relevant to POI recommendations. For example, Zheng et. al. have extracted visited locations from GPS trajectory logs of mobile users for location recommendations [25, 26]. However, their studies consider neither the social links between users nor the interactions between users and locations in the recommendation process. In this paper, we aim to exploit the unique geographical implications em-

[1]www.loopt.com
[2]www.brightkite.com
[3]www.foursquare.com
[4]www.whrrl.com
[5]These services are often referred as location based social networks and thus abbreviated as LBSNs in the paper.

bedded in users' interactions with locations, in addition to applying the social influence from users' friends, for POI recommendations in LBSNs.

Users and POIs are two essential types of entities in LBSNs. As illustrated in Figure 1, users in an LBSN, denoted as u_1, u_2, u_3, u_4, are interconnected via social links to form a user social network. Moreover, POIs, denoted as $l_1, l_2, ..., l_6$, are connected with users via their "check-in" activities, which generally reflects the users' tastes on various POIs. Finally, as also logically illustrated in the figure, the POIs, geocoded by ⟨longitude, latitude⟩, are constrained geographically. To make recommendations of POIs to users, obviously the records of previous user check-in activities are very useful. With the availability of such information in LBSNs, an intuitive idea for supporting POI recommendations is to employ the conventional *collaborative filtering (CF)* techniques by treating POIs as the "items" in many successful CF-based recommender systems. The basic argument for this idea is that users' tastes can be deduced by other users who exhibit similar visiting behaviors to POIs in previous check-in activities. Thus, user-based or item-based collaborative filtering techniques may be applicable to POI recommendations. Additionally, the social network of users, which is handily available in the LBSN, can be explored to enhance performance of POI recommendations. Recent studies have argued that social friends tend to share common interests and thus can be used in the process of collaborative filtering for making recommendations [11, 12, 2, 13, 24].

While the ideas above aim to explore the essential information available in LBSNs, i.e., the user-location interactivities and user-user social links, we argue that the geographical influence naturally existing in the activities of users and their geographical proximities cannot be ignored. According to Tobler's First Law of Geography "Everything is related to everything else, but near things are more related than distant things" [19]. Thus, a user intuitively tends to visit nearby POIs. There are two major implications that can be derived from this intuition for POI recommendations: (1) people tend to visit POIs close to their homes or offices; and (2) people may be interested in exploring nearby POIs of a POI that they are in favor of, even if it is far away from home, e.g., a user may explore some restaurants and shops around Time Square when she goes there for a broadway show. Due to the geographical nature of the LBSNs, we believe the geographical influence between users and POIs as well as that amongst POIs are as important as the social influence amongst users, which as indicated earlier may play a positive role for supporting POI recommendations in LBSNs. In short, we are interested in studying the impact of geographical influence and social influence on POI recommendations in LBSNs.

Our approach for supporting POI recommendation service in LBSNs is to develop effective collaborative recommendation techniques that discover POIs of users' interests by incorporating the three complementary factors: i) user preference of POIs; ii) social influence; and iii) geographical influence. Notice that users' implicit preferences of POIs can be derived from their check-in activities on POIs. By considering two users who have checked into a lot of common POIs as similar users, we may discover the implicit preference of a user through the previous check-in activities of her similar users. Recall the example in Figure 1. Since u_1 and u_2 shares many commonly visited POIs, they may be considered as similar users who are assumed to share similar check-in behaviors, i.e., preference of POIs. As a result, l_1 is a good candidate for recommendation to user u_2 since u_1 has visited this POI before. On the other hand, social influence of friends can be incorporated in the recommendation process. For example, when considering l_4 as a recommendations candidate for u_1, the social influence of u_4 on u_1 may contribute to the decision making. Finally, the geographical influence of POIs on nearby POIs can be considered. As shown in the example, since u_2 has visited l_2 and l_3 before, their nearby POIs l_1 and l_5 may be considered positively due to the geographical influence.

As discussed earlier, the conventional item recommendation techniques based on user preference [9, 18, 14, 15, 13] and social influence [12, 13] seem to be applicable for POI recommendation. Nevertheless, their effectiveness on POI recommendations in LBSNs have not been studied. Most importantly, the idea of incorporating the geographical influence between POIs, which is refreshing and promising for POI recommendation, has not been investigated previously. In this paper, we examine the "geographical clustering phenomenon" of user check-in activities in LBSNs and propose a power-law probabilistic model to capture geographical influence among POIs. Accordingly, we realize the targeted collaborative POI recommendation service for LBSNs by incorporating the geographical influence of POIs via Bayesian theory. Finally, we propose a unified location recommendation framework to fuse user preference to POIs along with the social influence among users and the geographical influence among POIs.

In summary, the contributions we made in this research work are four-fold.

- We study the problem of supporting POI recommendation in location-based social networking systems (LBSNs), where POIs are uniquely different from other recommended items in conventional recommender systems because of the fact that "physical" interactions are required between users and POIs. Hence, we investigate the geographical influence between POIs and propose to incorporate geographical influence along with user preference and social influence in the collaborative recommendation techniques we develop for POI recommendations in LBSNs.
- We develop a novel idea to capture the geographical influence by investigating the geographical clustering phenomenon of user check-in activities in LBSNs. We propose to employ a power-law probabilistic model to capture the geographical influence among POIs, and realize our collaborative POI recommendations based on geographical influence via naive Bayesian method.
- We propose a unified recommendation framework for POI recommendations by fusing user preference, social influence and geographical influence to devise a check-in probability prediction model for a given user to visit a POI.
- Finally, we evaluate the proposed recommendation technique over large-scale datasets we collected from two well known LBSNs, i.e., Foursquare and Whrrl. Experimental results show that our proposed collaborative recommendation technique exhibits superior POI recommendation performance against other approaches. Important findings of our evaluation are summarized below.

- Geographical influence shows a more significant impact on the effectiveness of POI recommendations in LBSNs than social influence, improving the recommendation performance by at least 13.8% against social influence.
- Random Walk and Restart [12] may not be suitable for POI recommendation in LBSNs. Based on our analysis over the real data and the experimental results, we find that friends still reflect significantly different preferences and social tie cannot reflect the similarity of check-in behavior among users.
- Item-based collaborative filtering do not provide results comparable to user-based collaborative filtering, because many POIs, in the current state of LBSNs, only show a few user check-ins. Thus item similarity is not as accurate as user similarity.

The rest of this paper is organized as follows. In Section 2, we provide some background on conventional recommendation techniques according to user's own preference and social influence and review related works in the literature. In Section 3, we describe the location recommendation process according to geographical influence. In Section 4, we propose a location recommendation framework, which unifies all three factors together. In Section 5, we perform an empirical study on the different location recommendation algorithms upon two large scale datasets crawled from Foursquare and Whrrl, respectively. Finally, in Section 6, we conclude the paper.

2. PRELIMINARIES

In this section, we first provide background on user-based collaborative filtering and friend-based recommendation, which serve as the building blocks in our fusion approach to exploit user preference and social influence. Next we review some relevant studies in recommender systems.

2.1 User-based Collaborative Filtering

Based on collaborative filtering, users' implicit preference can be discovered by aggregating the behaviors of similar users. Let U and L denote the user set and the POI set in an LBSN, which keeps track of check-in activities in the system. The check-in activity a user $u_i \in U$ has at a POI $l_j \in L$ is denoted as $c_{i,j}$ where $c_{i,j} = 1$ represents u_i has a check-in at l_j before and $c_{i,j} = 0$ means there is no record of u_i visiting l_j. These recorded user check-in activities at POIs are thus used to discover a user's implicit preference of a POI, which can be represented as a probability to predict how likely the user would like to have a check-in at an unvisited POI. We denote this prediction by $\widehat{c}_{i,j}$ and obtain this predicted check-in probability of u_i to l_j as follows.

$$\widehat{c}_{i,j} = \frac{\sum_{u_k} w_{i,k} \cdot c_{k,j}}{\sum_{u_k} w_{i,k}} \tag{1}$$

where $w_{i,k}$ is the similarity weight between users u_i and u_k.

To compute the similarity weights $w_{i,k}$ between users u_i and u_k, several similarity measures can be adopted, e.g., cosine similarity and Pearson correlation. In our study, we choose cosine similarity due to its simplicity. The cosine similarity weight between users u_i and u_k, denoted as $w^U_{i,k}$, is defined as follows.

$$w_{i,k} = \frac{\sum_{l_j \in L} c_{i,j} c_{k,j}}{\sqrt{\sum_{l_j \in L} c^2_{i,j}}\sqrt{\sum_{l_j \in L} c^2_{k,j}}} \tag{2}$$

2.2 Friend-based Collaborative Filtering

Friends tend to have similar behavior because they are friends and might share a lot of common interests, thus leading to correlated check-in behaviors [15, 13]. For example, two friends may hang out to see a movie together sometimes, or a user may go to a restaurant highly recommended by her friends. All those possible reasons suggest that friends might provide good recommendation for a given user due to their potential correlated check-in behavior. In other words, we can turn to user's friends for recommendation, and we call it recommendation based social influence from friends.

POI recommendations based on social influence can be realized by the friend-based collaborative filtering approach as described in [13].

$$\widehat{c}_{i,j} = \frac{\sum_{u_k \in F_i} SI_{k,i} \cdot c_{k,j}}{\sum_{u_k \in F_i} SI_{k,i}} \tag{3}$$

where $\widehat{c}_{i,j}$ is the predicted check-in probability of u_i at l_j, F_i is the friends set of u_i, and $SI_{k,i}$ is *directional* social influence weight u_k has on u_i [14, 15, 13].

On the one hand, we think friends who have closer social tie may have better trust in terms of their recommendation; on the other hand, friends who show more similar check-in behavior should have more similar tastes with the active user, thus suggestions from those friends are more worthy. Thus, in the following, we introduce how to derive the social influence weight by combining the above two aspects.

One way to derive the social influence weight between two friends is based on both of their social connections and similarity of their check-in activities [12].

$$SI_{k,i} = \eta \cdot \frac{|F_k \cap F_i|}{|F_k \cup F_i|} + (1 - \eta) \cdot \frac{|L_k \cap L_i|}{|L_k \cup L_i|} \tag{4}$$

where η is a tuning parameter ranging within $[0, 1]$, and F_k and L_k denote the *friend set* and *POI set* of user u_k, respectively.[6]

Another way of measurement is via the Random Walk with Restart (RWR) technique [20] over the graph that captures both the social connections among users as well as the check-in activities between users and POIs [24]. Starting from a node k, an RWR is performed by randomly following a link to another node at each step. Notice that there is a probability a in every step to restart at node k. By iterating RWR repeatedly until the whole process converges, a stationary (or steady-state) probability for each node can be obtained. The stationary probabilities of nodes give us a long-term visit rate for each user node (e.g., user u_i) given a bias towards a particular starting node (e.g. user u_k). This can be interpreted as the social influence weight user u_k have on u_i, i.e., $SI_{k,i}$.

2.3 Related Work

Content-based and collaborative filtering techniques are two widely adopted approaches for recommender systems [1]. A content-based system selects items for recommendation based on the similarity between item content (e.g., keywords/tags describing the items) and user profile [3, 8, 17].

[6]The friend set of a user refers to the socially connected friends of the user in the LBSN, while her POI set refers to the set of POIs she has check-in activities.

Since it mainly relies on dictionary-bound relations between the terms used in user profiles and item content, implicit associations between users are not considered.

The collaborative filtering systems are divided into two categories, i.e., memory-based and model-based. Memory-based systems can be further classified into *user-based* and *item-based* systems. For user-based systems [9], the similarity between all pairs of users is computed based on their ratings on associated items using some selected similarity measurement such as cosine similarity or Pearson correlation. Based on the user similarity, missing rating corresponding to a given user-item pair can be derived by computing a weighted combination of the ratings upon the same item from similar users. For item-based systems [18], instead of using similarity between users to predict missing rating, predications are made by finding similarly rated items first in order to compute a weighted combination of user ratings upon similar items. On the other hand, the model-based collaborative filtering systems assume that users may form clusters based on their similar behavior in rating items. A model can be learned based on patterns recognized in the rating behaviors of users using machine learning techniques such as clustering algorithms or Bayesian networks [5, 23].

Under the context of social networking systems, social friendship is shown to be beneficial for collaborative filtering based recommendation systems, e.g., memory-based [11, 12] and random walk based [2, 11, 12]. These works argue that social friends tend to share common interests and thus their relationships should be considered in the process of collaborative filtering. Random walk captures a social network as a graph with probabilistic weighted links to represent social relations and thus is able to accurately predict user preferences to items [12] and social influence to other users [24]. On the other hand, social friendship has also been explored in the model-based systems [14, 13]. These work mostly focus on conventional recommendation systems for recommending items such as movies.

Recently, location recommendation and mining has attracted a lot of attentions from the research community [27, 26, 7, 25, 22]. Among them, [27, 26, 7, 25] are mainly focused on GPS datasets which do not consider social relationships among users. In these works, unfortunately, the geographical influence among POIs are not explored [27, 26, 25]. Recently, the correlation of locations in GPS trajectories are explored [7]. In this work, however, locations are still treated as conventional items. As such, the correlations between locations are established through users' activities instead of their geographical influence. [22] is the first research to provide location recommendations services in LBSNs, but with the goal of improving efficiency of location recommendation.

Our study differentiates itself from all these prior works in four aspects: i) the application domain of location-based social networking systems, embracing both social and geographical features in the captured data, is new and unique; ii) the study of social influence and geographical influence in recommender systems for LBSNs is unexplored previously; iii) the proposal of unified collaborative recommendation approach, which incorporates geographical influence along with user preference and social influence, is new and innovative; iv) two large-scale real dataset collected from well known LBSNs, namely, Foursquare and Whrrl datasets, are adopted for performance evaluation.

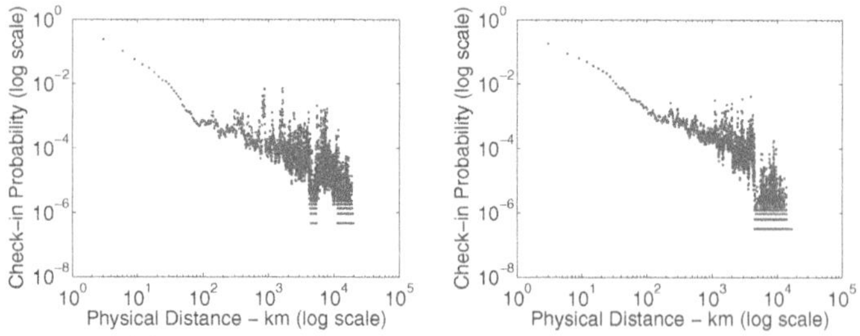

(a) Foursquare (b) Whrrl

Figure 2: Geographical influence probability distribution

3. RECOMMENDATION VIA GEOGRAPHICAL INFLUENCE

As mentioned earlier, the check-in activities of users in LBSNs record their physical interactions (i.e., visits) at POIs, Thus, we argue that the geographical proximities of POIs have a significant influence on users' check-in behavior. To better understand this geographical influence on users, we perform a spatial analysis on real datasets of user check-in activities collected from two well known LBSNs, i.e., Foursquare and Whrrl. Specifically, we aim to study the implication of *distance* on user check-in behavior by measuring how likely two of a user's check-in POIs are within a given distance. To obtain this measurement, we calculate the distances between all pairs of POIs that a user has checked in and plot a histogram (actually probability density function) over the distance of POIs checked in by the same user. As shown in Figure 2, a significant percentage of POIs pairs checked in by the same user appears to be within short distance, indicating a *geographical clustering phenomenon* in user check-in activities.[7] This phenomenon may be attributed to the geographical influence which may be intuitively explained by the following tendencies: (1) people tend to visit POIs close to their homes or offices; and (2) people may be interested in exploring nearby POIs of a POI that they are in favor of, even if it is far away from home. As a result, the POIs visited by the same user tend to be clustered geographically. We believe that this geographical clustering phenomenon in user check-in activities can be exploited for POI recommendations in LBSNs. Thus, in the following, we study and model this geographical influence on user check-in behavior at POIs, aiming to utilize it in POI recommendations.

To achieve our goal, we would like to compute the likelihood that a user u_i would check in both POI l_j and l_k. Based on Figure 2, we intuitively think the check-in probability may follow the power-law distribution. Nevertheless, we observe that the check-in probability of POI pairs visited by the same person over distance is not a standard power-law distribution. Even though the left part of the figure decreases linearly (i.e., decreases exponentially in regular scale) and thus fits power-law distribution very well, the right part may sometimes deviate irregularly (i.e., the probability is high at some points). A reasonable explanation is that users may travel to different places and thus create multiple check-in spatial clusters. Generally speaking, the fact that a user's check-in POIs tend to be in a short distance is confirmed in our data analysis. As mentioned earlier, nearby POIs are more related to each other, which exhibits strong geographical influence. Moreover, the linear portion of the

[7]Note that the figure has been shown in log-log scale.

plot in Figure 2 covers the majority (90%) of the POI pairs. Thus, we propose to use power law distribution to model the check-in probability to the distance between two POIs visited by the same user as follows.

$$y = a \times x^b \tag{5}$$

where a and b are parameters of a power-law distribution, and x and y refer to the distance between two POIs visited by the same user and its check-in probability, respectively.

Equation (5) can transformed into Equation (6) in "log-log" scale to fit a linear model.

$$\log y = w_0 + w_1 \log x \tag{6}$$

Thus, the original power-law distribution can be recovered via the following equation.

$$a = 2^{w_0} \qquad b = w_1 \tag{7}$$

Hence, we can simply apply a linear curve fitting method to realize regression as follows. More specifically, let $y' = \log y$ and $x' = \log x$. We shall fit data as follows

$$y'(x', \mathbf{w}) = w_0 + w_1 \cdot x' \tag{8}$$

where w_0 and w_1 are the linear coefficients, collectively denoted by $\mathbf{w}$. In other words, the model can be learned in form of $\mathbf{w}$. In order to avoid over-fitting, we approach the weight coefficients by least square error method and add a penalty term (i.e., regularization term) to discourage the coefficients from reaching large values as below [6].

$$E(\mathbf{w}) = \frac{1}{2}\sum_{n=1}^{N}\{y'(x'_n, \mathbf{w}) - t_n\}^2 + \frac{\lambda}{2}||\mathbf{w}||^2 \tag{9}$$

where $E(\mathbf{w})$ denotes the loss function, N presents the cardinality of input dataset, t_n is the ground truth corresponding to x'_n, and λ is the regularization term.

Accordingly, the optimal values of a and b form the setting which minimizes the loss function $E(\mathbf{w})$ as below.

$$opt\{a, b\} = \arg\min_{a,b} E(\mathbf{w}) \tag{10}$$

In the following, we introduce a collaborative recommendation method based on the naive Bayesian method to realize POI recommendation in LBSNs. For a given user u_i and its visited POI set L_i, we define the probability that u_i has check-in activities at all locations in L_i by considering the pair-wise distances of POIs in L_i as follows.

$$Pr[L_i] = \prod_{l_m, l_n \in L_i \wedge m \neq n} Pr[d(l_m, l_n)] \tag{11}$$

where $d(l_m, l_n)$ denotes the distance between POIs l_m and l_n, and $Pr[d(l_m, l_n)] = a \times d(l_m, l_n)^b$ which follows the pow-law distribution model we obtained above. Note that here we assume the distances of POI pairs are independent.

Thus, for a given POI l_j (i.e., the recommendation candidate), user u_i, and her visited POI set L_i, we have the likelihood probability for u_i to check in l_j as follows.

$$\begin{aligned} Pr[l_j|L_i] &= \frac{Pr[l_j \cup L_i]}{Pr[L_i]} \\ &= \frac{Pr[L_i] \times \prod_{l_y \in L_i} Pr[d(l_j, l_y)]}{Pr[L_i]} \\ &= \prod_{l_y \in L_i} Pr[d(l_j, l_y)] \end{aligned} \tag{12}$$

To make a POI recommendation, we sort all the POIs in $L - L_i$ in accordance with their $Pr[l_j|L_i]$ ($l_j \in L - L_i$) to return the POI with the highest $Pr[l_j|L_i]$ to the user.

4. UNIFIED COLLABORATIVE POI RECOMMENDATION

In this section, we propose a unified framework to perform collaborative recommendation, which fuses ideas factors of user preference, social influence and geographical influence in POI recommendation. Notice that, different from predicting a POI's rating, we aim to return a ranked list of candidate POIs, which is very similar to conventional information retrieval [4].

4.1 Fusion Framework

As discussed, each factor, i.e., user preference, social influence or geographical influence, can be utilized to realize POI recommendation. Thus, we intuitively can implement three different recommender systems. We propose to use a linear fusion framework to integrate ranked lists provided by the three above-mentioned recommenders into the final ranked list [4, 21]. By integrating multiple recommenders, top-ranked POIs from each of the recommendation algorithms could increase both recall (due to the different highly ranked POIs) and precision (giving that the recommender systems have a high density of user-preferred POIs on top of the results lists.

Let $S_{i,j}$ denote the check-in probability score of user u_i at POI l_j, i.e., the more likely u_i has a check-in activity at l_j, the larger $S_{i,j}$ is. Let $S^u_{i,j}$, $S^s_{i,j}$ and $S^g_{i,j}$ denote the check-in probability scores of user u_i at POI l_j, corresponding to recommender systems based on user preference, social influence and geographical influence, respectively. We have $S_{i,j}$ as follows.

$$S_{i,j} = (1 - \alpha - \beta)S^u_{i,j} + \alpha S^s_{i,j} + \beta S^g_{i,j} \tag{13}$$

where the two weighting parameters α and β ($0 \leq \alpha + \beta \leq 1$) denote the relative importance of social influence and geographical influence comparing to user preference. Here $\alpha = 1$ states that $S_{i,j}$ depends completely on the prediction based on social influence; $\beta = 1$ states that $S_{i,j}$ depends completely on the predication based on geographical influence; while $\alpha = \beta = 0$ states that $S_{i,j}$ counts only on user preference.

4.2 Check-in Probability Score Estimation

According to the above fusion framework, in order to estimate the check-in probability score $S_{i,j}$, we need to predict the check-in probability score of $S^u_{i,j}$, $S^s_{i,j}$ and $S^g_{i,j}$ corresponding to user preference, social influence and geographical influence, respectively. Accordingly, we estimate the check-in probability $p^u_{i,j}$, $p^s_{i,j}$ and $p^g_{i,j}$ for a user u_i to visit a POI l_j in order to obtain $S^u_{i,j}$, $S^s_{i,j}$ and $S^g_{i,j}$, respectively.

First, the predication of $p^u_{i,j}$ can be estimated based on the idea of user-based collaborative filtering as discussed before. More specifically, we utilize the behavior of similar users to realize the predication as Equation (1). Thus we have

$$p^u_{i,j} = \frac{\sum_{u_k} w_{i,k} \cdot c_{k,j}}{\sum_{u_k} w_{i,k}} \tag{14}$$

where $w_{i,k}$ is the similarity weight between users u_i and u_k.

Similarly, the prediction of $p^s_{i,j}$ can be estimated based on based on the idea of friend-based collaborative filtering. Thus, according to Equation (3), we have

$$p^s_{i,j} = \frac{\sum_{u_k \in F_i} SI_{k,i} \cdot c_{k,j}}{\sum_{u_k \in F_i} SI_{k,i}} \tag{15}$$

where F_i is the friends set of u_i, $SI_{k,i}$ is the weight measuring social influence from u_k to u_i.

Finally, $p^g_{i,j}$ can be directly obtained from Equation (12)

$$p^g_{i,j} = Pr[l_j|L_i] = \prod_{l_y \in L_i} Pr[d(l_j, l_y)] \qquad (16)$$

where L_i is the visited POI set of u_i, and $d(l_j, l_y)$ denotes the distance between POIs l_j and l_y.

After we get the check-in probability estimation, we obtain the corresponding scores as follows.

$$S^u_{i,j} = \frac{p^u_{i,j}}{Z^u_i}, \text{ where } Z^u_i = \max_{l_j \in L-L_i}\{p^u_{i,j}\}$$

$$S^s_{i,j} = \frac{p^s_{i,j}}{Z^s_i}, \text{ where } Z^s_i = \max_{l_j \in L-L_i}\{p^s_{i,j}\} \qquad (17)$$

$$S^g_{i,j} = \frac{p^g_{i,j}}{Z^g_i}, \text{ where } Z^g_i = \max_{l_j \in L-L_i}\{p^g_{i,j}\}$$

where Z^u_i, Z^s_i and Z^g_i are normalization terms.

5. EMPIRICAL EVALUATION

In this section, we design and conduct several experiments to compare the recommendation qualities of the proposed collaborative recommendation algorithms with some state-of-the-art recommendation techniques, including collaborative filtering and random walk with restart, and to investigate several interesting questions. Specifically, the design of the experiments aims to achieve the following goals. (1) As our proposed method factors in user preference, social influence from friends and geographical influence from nearby location, we intent to study parameters α and β to understand the roles/weights of the above-mentioned factors in obtaining optimal recommendations. (2) We intend to validate our ideas by comparing the effectiveness of the proposed approach with other state-of-the-art techniques. (3) Due to the growing research interests in social influence from friends, we intend to further study the similarity of check-in behaviors in terms of the strength of "social ties" between two friends. (4) In our proposal, user-based collaborative filtering approach has been employed to discover user preference. We intend to explore the feasibility and necessity of integrating item-based collaborative filtering approach to further enhance the recommendation quality. (5) We would like to understand how data sparsity may affect POI recommendations in LBSNs. (6) How well our techniques deal with cold start users, who do not have many check-in records for discovery of their interests [10].

5.1 Dataset Description

We crawled the websites of Foursquare and Whrrl, two of the most representative LBSNs, for a month to collect two datasets consisting of 153,577 users and 96,229 POIs in Foursquare, and 5,892 users and 53,432 POIs in Whrrl, respectively. Our performance evaluation is conducted on these two large-scale real datasets. After summarizing the check-in records, we get the user-POI check-in matrix densities as 4.24×10^{-5} for Foursquare dataset and 2.72×10^{-4} for Whrrl datasets, respectively. Note that, the effectiveness of recommendation service for sparse dataset (i.e., low density user-POI check-in matrix) is usually not high due to the limited information provided by the dataset. For example, the reported precision in [12] is 0.17 over a pre-prossed dataset with 7.8×10^{-4} density. Thus, in our experiments, we focus on observing the relative performance of algorithms instead of their absolute effectiveness measures, which we expect to improve as the number of LBSN users continues to grow and more check-in activities are logged. To facilitate our evaluation, for each individual user in the datasets, we randomly mark off $x\%$ ($x = 10, 30, 50$ (with 30 as the default value) of all POIs visited by the user. In the experiments, the evaluated POI recommendation algorithms are used to recover the missing user-POI pairs that have been marked off.

5.2 Performance Metrics

A POI recommendation algorithm under evaluation computes a ranking score for each candidate POI (i.e., POI that user has not visited) and returns the top- N highest ranked POIs as recommendations to a targeted user. To evaluate the prediction accuracy, we are interested in finding out how many POIs previously marked off in the preprocessing step recovered in the returned POI recommendations. More specifically, we examine two metrics: (1) the ratio of recovered POIs to the N recommended POIs, and (2) the ratio of recovered POIs to the set of POIs deleted in preprocessing. The former is *precision@N* while the latter is *recall@N*, and collectively referred as *performance@N*. In our experiment, we test the performance when $N = 5, 10, 20$ with 5 as the default value.

5.3 Evaluated Recommendation Approaches

Three factors, namely user preference (U), social influence from friends (S) and geographical influence from POIs (G), are incorporated in our unified collaborative recommendation algorithm, denoted by `USG` in our evaluation. A number of state-of-the-art and new collaborative filtering approaches, some of which can be configured by controlling the weight parameters, $0 < \alpha$, $\beta < 1$, in `USG`, are also evaluated for comparison. In addition of `USG`, the recommendation approaches under evaluation are listed below.

- `user-based CF (denoted by U)` - this is a special case of `USG` by setting both α and β as zeros. In other words, only user preference is considered for recommendation.
- `friend-based CF (denoted by S)` - this is also a special case of `USG`, where $\alpha = 1$. Here, only friends of the targeted user are used in making a specific recommendation. As introduced before, there are two alternative methods to derive the social influence weight between friends. One is to compute the social influence weight based on friends based on Equation(4) [12] and the other is to derive social influence weight between friends using Random Walk and Restart technique [24]. To differentiate these two approaches, we denote them as `S` and $\mathtt{S}_{rwr}$, respectively.
- `GI-based recommendation (denoted by G)` - this approach, considering only the factor of geographical influence, is a special case of `USG` where $\beta = 1$.
- `Random Walk with Restart (denoted by RWR)` - this is a state-of-the-art algorithm recently developed for collaborative item recommendation based on social networks [12]. Users' preferences to items are predicted by Random Walk and Restart over a graph capturing social graph and user-item matrix.
- `User preference/social influence based recommendation (denoted by US)` - this method, considering both user preference and social influence from friends, is a special case of `USG`, where $0 < \alpha < 1$ and $\beta = 0$.
- `User preference/geographical influence based recommendation (denoted by UG)` - this approach, considering both user preference and geographical influ-

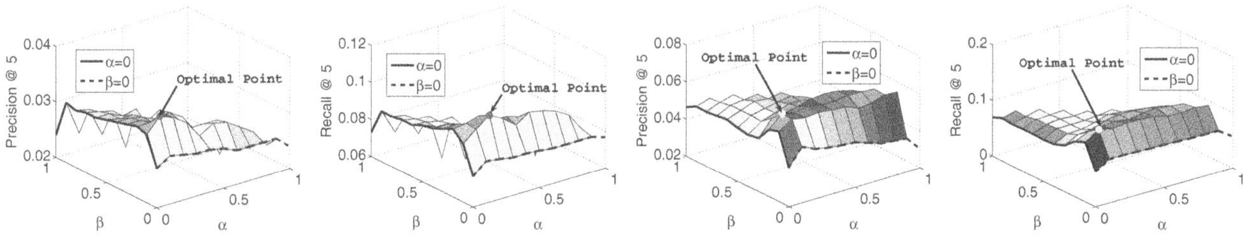

(a) Precision@5 - Foursquare (b) Recall@5 - Foursquare (c) Precision@5 - Whrrl (d) Recall@5 - Whrrl

Figure 3: Tuning parameters

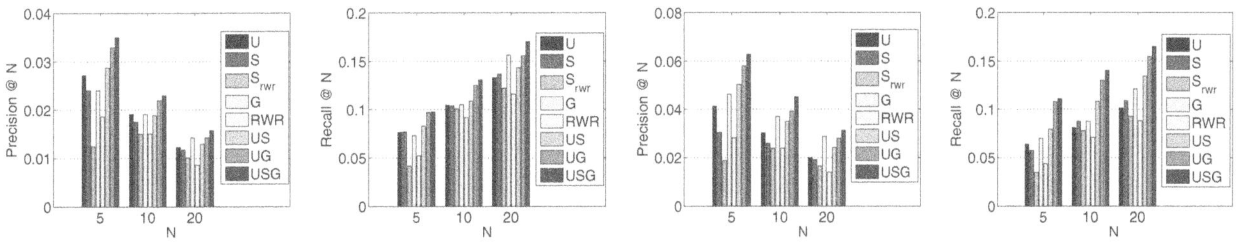

(a) Precision@N - Foursquare (b) Recall@N - Foursquare (c) Precision@N - Whrrl (d) Recall@N - Whrrl

Figure 4: Performance comparison

ence, is a special case of USG, where $0 < \beta < 1$ and $\alpha = 0$.

5.4 Tuning Parameters

As mentioned, two parameters α (for social influence factor) and β (for geographical influence factor) can be controlled to tune the performance of USG and to configure it into other recommendation approaches for evaluation. Here we vary them in USG to understand the roles of user preference, social influence from friends and geographical influence from POIs played in achieving the optimal USG performance. Similarly, we tune α in US and β in UG to findout their optimal settings as well. Figure 3 shows the performance@5 results of USG under different α and β settings, where the best parameter settings are indicated in the figures. The optimal settings for US and UG can also be observed in the figures, i.e., dashed line for US and solid line for UG. Those optimal parameter settings are also summarized in Table 1.

		Precision@5		Recall@5	
		α	β	α	β
Foursquare	US	0.1	–	0.1	–
	UG	–	0.2	–	0.2
	USG	0.1	0.1	0.2	0.1
Whrrl	US	0.1	–	0.1	–
	UG	–	0.1	–	0.1
	USG	0.1	0.2	0.1	0.1

Table 1: Optimal parameter settings

Through this study, we can easily observe that user preference plays a dominate role in contributing to the optimal recommendation, while both social influence and geographical influence are innegligible. More specifically, as shown in Table 1, the factor of user preference contributes at least 70% in making the best recommendation, while both social influence and geographical influence contribute at least 10%.

5.5 Performance Comparison

Next, we compare the effectiveness of the recommendation approaches under evaluation. Figure 4 shows the performance@N ($N = 5, 10, 20$) of all approaches in terms of their best performance (i.e., the performance under the optimal parameter settings). The experiments used both Foursquare and Whrrl datasets. The precision and recall for them are plotted in Figure 4(a) and Figure 4(b), and Figure 4(c) and Figure 4(d), respectively. In these figures, USG always exhibits the best performance in terms of precision and recall under all values of Ns, showing the strength of combines all three factors of user preference, social influence and geographical influence. Notice that both of our real datasets (i.e., Foursquare and Whrrl) have low density. According to the empirical study in [12], the reported precision is about 0.17 over a pre-processed dataset with 7.8×10^{-4} density of user-item matrix. Thus, the measured low precision over our datasets (which are not preprocessed) is reasonable. Most importantly, USG outperforms the baseline approach U (i.e., user-based CF) by about 50% percentage of performance improvement in both datasets.

Between the two alternative social influence measurement methods (i.e., S and S_{rwr}) for friend-based CF, we find S to have much better performance than S_{rwr}. Moreover, RWR shows poor performance for POI recommendation in these experiments. This raises a very interesting question of whether Random Walk and Restart technique is suitable for POI recommendations. In a later section, we shall answer this question by analyzing the correlation between (i) the similarity of check-in behavior among friends and (ii) social ties among friends. For the rest of the experiments, we use S as the component of social influence from friends in US and USG.

Figure 4 also indicates that both social influence and geographical influence can be utilized to perform POI recommendation. As shown, both S and G provide comparable results against U. Notice that, in LBSNs, since the check-

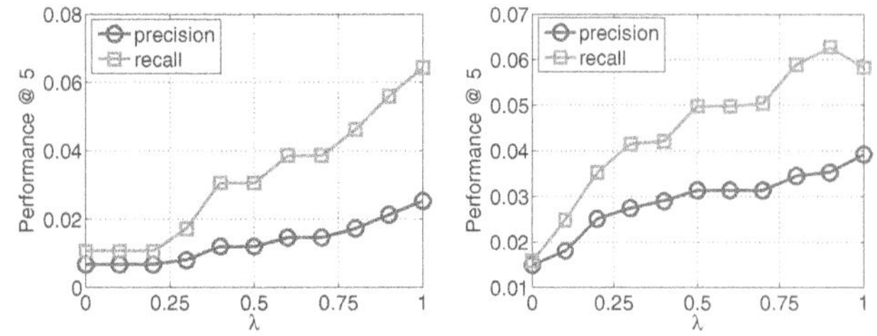

(a) Performance@5 - Foursquare (b) Performance@5 - Whrrl

Figure 5: Fusion of U and L

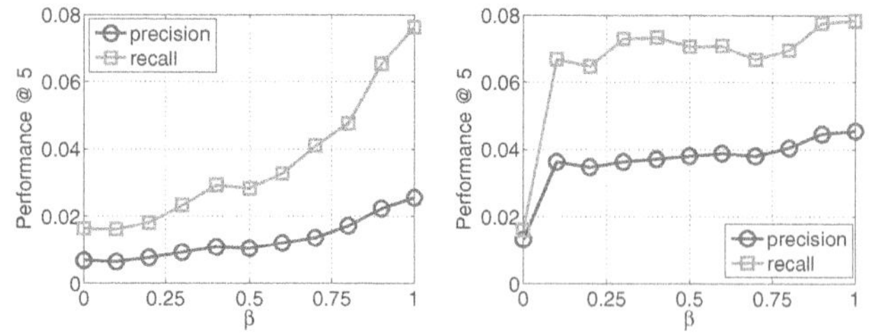

(a) Performance@5 - Foursquare (b) Performance@5 - Whrrl

Figure 6: Fusion of L and G

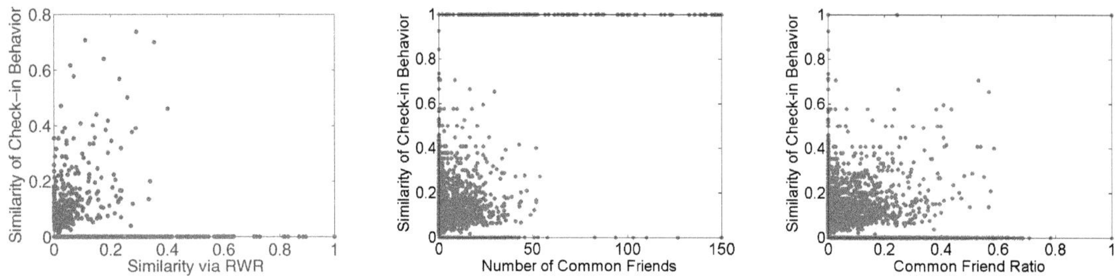

(a) Similarity computed via RWR - Foursquare (b) Number of common friend - Foursquare (c) Common friend ratio - Foursquare

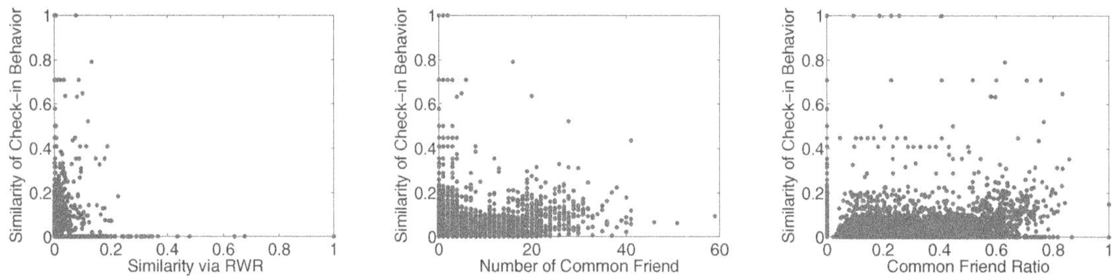

(d) Similarity computed via RWR - Whrrl (e) Number of common friend - Whrrl (f) Common friend ratio - Whrrl

Figure 7: Social tie and its influence implication

in activities involve physical interaction between users and POIs, geographical influence matters a lot, which is confirmed in the study. As shown, G usually outperforms S and sometimes even performs better than U, e.g., when $N = 20$. Also, UG always show better performance than US. This is due to the spatial clustering phenomenon appearing in user check-in activities. Thus, when N is relatively large, there is very good chance to discover most of user's check-in activities based on social influence.

In both Foursquare and Whrrl datasets, we find that when more factors are considered the performance turns out to be better. For example, US is better than U and S, UG is better than U and G, and USG shows the best performance.

5.6 Study on Item-based CF

In addition to user-based CF, item-based CF can also estimate a user's preference to an item, by exploring the similarity between items instead of users [18]. In [21], a CF technique has been proposed to fuse both user-based and item-based similarity to overcome the data sparsity problem [10]. Thus, a potential idea for POI recommendations is to employ the item-based CF (denoted by L). Additionally, geographical influence, which models the influence among POIs, may be seemingly similar to "item similarity" in item-based CF. However, we would like to point out that they are conceptually different and thus should not be mistaken. In this section, we explore the idea of further incorporating L into our framework by examining whether fusing L with U and G respectively into new approaches denoted by UL and GL would outperform U and G alone.

Similar to [21], we introduce a weighting parameter λ in UL. When $\lambda = 1$, UL is reduced to U; and when $\lambda = 0$, L is obtained. Similarly, we introduce a weighting parameter γ in GL. Figure 5 and Figure 6 show the performance of UL and GL on Foursquare and Whrrl datasets under various settings of λ and γ. Surprisingly, these figures show that L brings no advantage at all in enhancing U or L in POI recommendations, indicating item-based CF is not an effective approach in our application. Our explanation is that, at the current stage, POIs in LBSNs may not have been visited by sufficient many users to make item-based CF work well. In other words, the computed similarity between two POIs may not provide a good clue to decide whether a user likes a POI or not. Since U or G alone show much better performance than L, we don't integrate L in our recommendation framework.

5.7 Study on Social Influence

As shown earlier, Random Walk with Restart [12] does not perform well for POI recommendations. To obtain a comprehensive understanding of the reasons behind, we analyze the correlation between the similarity of user check-in behaviors and the user similarity calculated based on Random

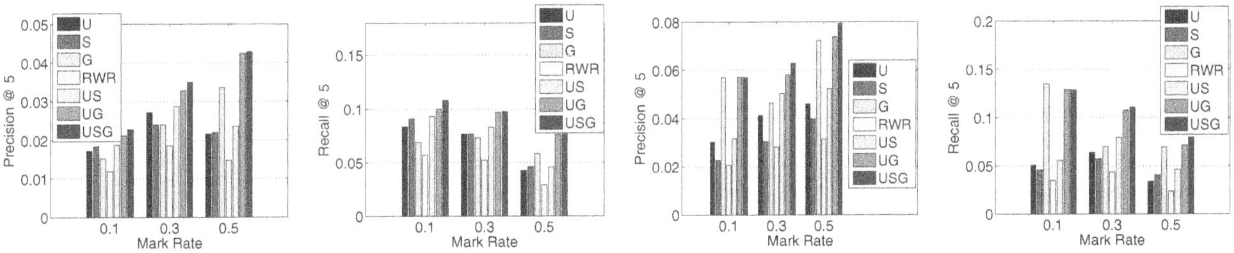

(a) Precision@5 - Foursquare (b) Recall@5 - Foursquare (c) Precision@N - Whrrl (d) Recall@N - Whrrl

Figure 8: Impact of Data Sparsity

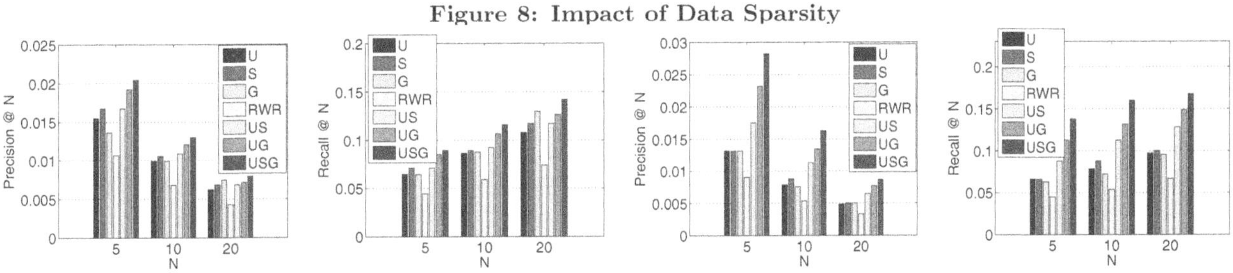

(a) Precision@5 - Foursquare (b) Recall@5 - Foursquare (c) Precision@5 - Whrrl (d) Recall@5 - Whrrl

Figure 9: Performance for cold start users

Walk and Restart. Note that, based on [12], user similarity can be derived from the social graph matrix and user-POI check-in matrix. Figure 7(a) and Figure 7(d) show the plots on Foursquare and Whrrl datasets under the best RWR settings. Both figures show that similar users do not necessarily have high similarity in their check-in behaviors. For example, user pairs with similarity larger than 0.1 usually share nothing in their check-in behavior in both Foursquare and Whrrl datasets. The results indicate that the tastes of a user's friends may actually vary significantly, which has also be discussed in [16] recently. To further verify this finding, we also examine the correlation between the similarity of check-in behaviors between two friends and the strength of their social ties. In our tests, the social tie is defined in two forms: 1) number of common friends (see Figure 7(b) and Figure 7(e) for experimental results) and common friend ratio (see Figure 7(c) and Figure 7(f) for experimental results), where common friend ratio is measured by Jaccard coefficient. For friends who have very strong social tie (i.e., larger number of common friends or larger common friend ratio), we again find their check-in behaviors are not necessarily similar as shown in the figures.

From the above observations, we conclude that friends have different tastes. The similarity in friends' check-in behaviors may not necessarily be reflected in terms of the strength of their social ties. As a matter of fact, in measuring the social influence between friends, we find the factor of check-in behavior to be more important than the factor of social tie. Through our experiments on the `S` algorithm, we find the optimal setting for η in Equation (4) to be smaller than 0.05 in both Foursquare and Whrrl datasets, which indicates the factor of check-in behavior weighs more than the factor of social tie. While `RWR` treats both factors equally, thus degrading the performance in our Foursquare and Whrrl datasets.

5.8 Impact of Data Sparsity

Here, we study how `USG` deals with the data sparsity problem. In order to produce user-POI check-in matrix with different sparsity, we mark off x% = 10%, 30% and 50% of user's check-in activity records from the original check-in datasets for three groups of tests as shown in Figure 8. The larger the mark-off ratio x is, the sparser the user-POI check-in matrix is. As shown, `USG` always exhibits the best performance@5 under all mark-off ratios. Particularly, when the data is very sparse, e.g., x% = 50%, geographical influence plays an extremely important role in recommending interesting POIs to users. The reason is that both users and their social friends have relatively small check-in logs. Thus, the similarity weight or social influence score derived from such sparse data may be misleading. On the other hand, geographical influence, reflecting a global behavior affected by geography, fits the behaviors of most users in LBSNs. Thus, the approaches incorporating geographical influence factor, i.e., `G`, `UG` and `USG`, show great strengths under various data sparsity scenarios.

5.9 Test for Cold Start Users

Finally, we test the performance of POI recommendations for cold start users. Here, we consider those users who have less than 5 check-in activities in the user-POI check-in matrix after removing 30% check-ins as cold start users. As shown in Figure 9, in all cases we tested, `USG` always shows the best performance. Note that in POI recommendations for cold start users, user preference is hard to capture as POIs visited by this user are few. Consequently, `U` shows the worst performance as it only considers user preference. `G`, which explores the spatial clusters of user check-in activities, is also affected. On the other hand, `S` overcomes the lack of user's check-ins as social friends may supply many useful check-ins, potentially useful for POI recommendations. Thus, in this experiment, we find that the recommendation performance of `S` usually works better than `U` and `G` do. Notice that, we find the performance of `G` to be better than `S` in extremely sparse scenario in Figure 8 because in that scenario, social friends' check-in records are very limited as well. Thus, geographical influence prevails due to its applicability to most of the people. However, it is noteworthy that all three factors are very important for the POI recommendations to cold start users, as `USG` is always the best.

6. CONCLUSIONS AND FUTURE WORK

This research attempts to facilitate a POI recommendation service in location-based social networks. Our idea is to incorporate user preference, social influence and geographical influence in the recommendation. In addition to deriving user preference by user-based collaborative filtering and capturing social influence from friends, we model the geographical influence among POIs by employing power law distribution to uncover the spatial clustering phenomenon in user check-in activities. Furthermore, we propose a unified POI recommendation framework, which fuses user preference to a POI with social influence and geographical influence. We conduct a comprehensive performance evaluation over two large-scale real datasets collected from Foursquare and Whrrl. Experimental results show that the unified collaborative recommendation technique is superior to all other recommendation approaches evaluated. Additional findings have been uncovered through analysis of the experimental results, including 1) geographical influence shows a more significant impact on the effectiveness of POI recommendations than social influence; 2) Random Walk and Restart may not be suitable for POI recommendation in LBSNs, because friends exhibit significantly different preferences (i.e., the strength of social ties do not reflect the similarity of check-in behavior among users in LBSNs; 3) Item-base CF is not an effective approach in our application due to insufficient number of visitors to many locations at the current state of LBSNs.

The semantic tags of POIs contain very rich information brought in by LBSN users. As for the next step, we plan to incorporate the semantic tags of POIs to further improve the unified POI recommendation framework we proposed in this paper.

7. REFERENCES

[1] G. Adomavicius and A. Tuzhilin. Toward the Next Generation of Recommender Systems: A Survey of the State-of-the-Art and Possible Extensions. *IEEE TKDE*, 17(6):734–749, 2005.

[2] R. Andersen, C. Borgs, J. T. Chayes, U. Feige, A. D. Flaxman, A. Kalai, V. S. Mirrokni, and M. Tennenholtz. Trust-based recommendation systems: an axiomatic approach. In *WWW*, pages 199–208, 2008.

[3] M. Balabanovic and Y. Shoham. Content-based collaborative recommendation. *CACM*, 40(3):66–72, 1997.

[4] B. T. Bartell, G. W. Cottrell, and R. K. Belew. Automatic combination of multiple ranked retrieval systems. In *SIGIR*, pages 173–181, 1994.

[5] D. Billsus and M. J. Pazzani. Learning collaborative information filters. In *ICML*, pages 46–54, 1998.

[6] C. M. Bishop. *Pattern Recognition and Machine Learning*. 2006.

[7] X. Cao, G. Cong, and C. S. Jensen. Mining significant semantic locations from gps data. *PVLDB*, 3(1):1009–1020, 2010.

[8] A. M. Ferman, J. H. Errico, P. van Beek, and M. I. Sezan. Content-based filtering and personalization using structured metadata. In *JCDL*, page 393, 2002.

[9] J. L. Herlocker, J. A. Konstan, A. Borchers, and J. Riedl. An algorithmic framework for performing collaborative filtering. In *SIGIR*, pages 230–237, 1999.

[10] Z. Huang, H. Chen, and D. D. Zeng. Applying associative retrieval techniques to alleviate the sparsity problem in collaborative filtering. *ACM TOIS*, 22(1):116–142, 2004.

[11] M. Jamali and M. Ester. *TrustWalker*: a random walk model for combining trust-based and item-based recommendation. In *KDD*, pages 397–406, 2009.

[12] I. Konstas, V. Stathopoulos, and J. M. Jose. On social networks and collaborative recommendation. In *SIGIR*, pages 195–202, 2009.

[13] H. Ma, I. King, and M. R. Lyu. Learning to recommend with social trust ensemble. In *SIGIR*, pages 203–210, 2009.

[14] H. Ma, M. R. Lyu, and I. King. Learning to recommend with trust and distrust relationships. In *RecSys*, pages 189–196, 2009.

[15] H. Ma, H. Yang, M. R. Lyu, and I. King. SoRec: social recommendation using probabilistic matrix factorization. In *CIKM*, pages 931–940, 2008.

[16] H. Ma, D. Zhou, C. Liu, M. R. Lyu, and I. King. Recommender Systems with Social Regularization. In *WSDM*, 2011.

[17] P. Melville, R. J. Mooney, and R. Nagarajan. Content-Boosted Collaborative Filtering for Improved Recommendations. In *AAAI/IAAI*, pages 187–192, 2002.

[18] B. M. Sarwar, G. Karypis, J. A. Konstan, and J. Riedl. Item-based collaborative filtering recommendation algorithms. In *WWW*, pages 285–295, 2001.

[19] W. R. Tobler. A Computer Movie Simulating Urban Growth in the Detroit Region. *Economic Geography*, 46:234–240, 1970.

[20] H. Tong, C. Faloutsos, and J.-Y. Pan. Fast Random Walk with Restart and Its Applications. In *ICDM*, pages 613–622, 2006.

[21] J. Wang, A. P. de Vries, and M. J. T. Reinders. Unifying user-based and item-based collaborative filtering approaches by similarity fusion. In *SIGIR*, pages 501–508, 2006.

[22] M. Ye, P. Yin, and W.-C. Lee. Location Recommendation in Location-based Social Networks. In *GIS*, pages 458–461, 2010.

[23] H. Yildirim and M. S. Krishnamoorthy. A random walk method for alleviating the sparsity problem in collaborative filtering. In *RecSys*, pages 131–138, 2008.

[24] Q. Yuan, S. Zhao, L. Chen, S. Ding, X. Zhang, and W. Zheng. Augmenting collaborative recommender by fusing explicit social relationships. In *ACM RecSys-Workshop*, pages 49–56, 2009.

[25] V. W. Zheng, B. Cao, Y. Zheng, X. Xie, and Q. Yang. Collaborative filtering meets mobile recommendation: A user-centered approach. In *AAAI*, 2010.

[26] V. W. Zheng, Y. Zheng, X. Xie, and Q. Yang. Collaborative location and activity recommendations with gps history data. In *WWW*, pages 1029–1038, 2010.

[27] Y. Zheng, L. Zhang, X. Xie, and W.-Y. Ma. Mining interesting locations and travel sequences from gps trajectories. In *WWW*, pages 791–800, 2009.

Why Searchers Switch: Understanding and Predicting Engine Switching Rationales

Qi Guo[1], Ryen W. White[2], Yunqiao Zhang[2], Blake Anderson[2], and Susan T. Dumais[2]
[1] Mathematics and Computer Science, Emory University, Atlanta, GA 30322, USA
[2] Microsoft Corporation, One Microsoft Way, Redmond, WA 98052, USA
qguo3@emory.edu, {ryenw,yuzhan,blakean,sdumais}@microsoft.com

ABSTRACT
Search engine switching is the voluntary transition between Web search engines. Engine switching can occur for a number of reasons, including user dissatisfaction with search results, a desire for broader topic coverage or verification, user preferences, or even unintentionally. An improved understanding of switching rationales allows search providers to tailor the search experience according to the different causes. In this paper we study the reasons behind search engine switching within a session. We address the challenge of identifying switching rationales by designing and implementing client-side instrumentation to acquire in-situ feedbacks from users. Using this feedback, we investigate in detail the reasons that users switch engines within a session. We also study the relationship between implicit behavioral signals and the switching causes, and develop and evaluate models to predict the reasons for switching. In addition, we collect editorial judgments of switching rationales by third-party judges and show that we can recover switching causes *a posteriori*. Our findings provide valuable insights into why users switch search engines in a session and demonstrate the relationship between search behavior and switching motivations. The findings also reveal sufficient behavioral consistency to afford accurate prediction of switching rationale, which can be used to dynamically adapt the search experience and derive more accurate competitive metrics.

Categories and Subject Descriptors
H.3.3 [**Information Storage and Retrieval**]: Information Search and Retrieval–*selection process, search process.*

General Terms
Algorithms, Measurement, Experimentation, Human Factors.

Keywords
Search engine switching, predicting switching rationales.

1. INTRODUCTION
Search engines facilitate rapid access to information on the Web. A user's decision regarding which engine to use most frequently (their primary engine) can be based on factors including reputation, familiarity, effectiveness, interface usability, and satisfaction [18], and can significantly impact their levels of search success [22][24]. Similar factors can influence a user's decision to switch engines, either for a particular query if they are dissatisfied with results or seek broader topic coverage, or for specific task types if another engine specializes in such tasks, or more permanently due to unsatisfactory experiences or relevance changes [23]. The barrier to switching Web search engines is low and multiple engine usage is common. Indeed, prior work in this area suggests that 70% of Web searchers use multiple search engines [24].

Previous work on switching has examined promoting multiple search engine use [24], characterizing both short- and long-term engine switching behavior [22][23], predicting when users will switch [12][15][22], developing metrics for competitive analysis of engines using estimated user preference and user engagement [13], or building conceptual and economic models of search engine choice [17][21]. Despite the economic significance of engine switching to search providers, and its prevalence among search engine users, little is known about users' rationales for switching, the search behaviors that may relate to different rationales, or the features that are most useful in automatically predicting different switching causes. This is in part due to difficulty in reliably identifying switching rationales.

Improved understanding of switching rationales is important and has several applications. If search engines could predict that a searcher was about to switch along with the reason for that switch, they could adapt the search experience accordingly. For example, if a user searching for [*butterfly flight patterns*] is about to switch because they could not find what they were looking for (i.e., the *reason* is dissatisfaction), then the search engine can intervene and provide help such as additional query support. Conversely, if a user searching for [*bellevue apartments*] is about to switch to check for additional offerings (i.e., the *reason* is topic coverage or verification), an intervention could be annoying. Even in offline settings, search providers can improve the search experience through a better understanding of switching rationales. For example, queries resulting in dissatisfaction-related switches can be identified and analyzed to improve search quality.

In this paper, we focus on understanding users' motivations for search engine switching within a single search session. We address the challenge of identifying switching motivations by implementing and deploying a browser extension to capture search interaction and acquire explanations from searchers in situ (i.e., at the time they switch search engines). The in-situ explanations provide first-hand insights about the reasons for switching, and can be used to understand the relationships between patterns of search interaction and the switching causes. We investigate the effect of different interaction features (derived from the query, pre-switch user behavior, and post-switch behavior) on the accuracy of models to automatically predict the reason for a switch.

The main contributions of this paper include:

- The implementation and deployment of client-side instrumentation to collect in-situ searcher explanations that enables the study of session-level switching rationales.
- An in-depth analysis of session-level engine switching rationales and their correlations with behavioral signals.

SIGIR'11, July 24–28, 2011, Beijing, China.

- An investigation and evaluation of predicting switching causes with various session-level behavioral features.

This study is the first research to understand switching causes in-situ and to predict the reasons for search engine switches, laying the groundwork for more extensive future work on engine switching and search satisfaction.

The remainder of this paper is structured as follows. Section 2 outlines previous work on predicting query difficulty, user satisfaction and frustration, and characterizing search engine switching behavior. Section 3 provides an overview of the study. Section 4 describes the design and implementation of our client-side instrumentation for collecting in-situ explanations. In Section 5 we characterize the session-level switching causes, and their correlations with search behavior. In Section 6, we investigate prediction of switching rationales, varying features used. In Section 7, we explore using editorial judgments to approximate the in-situ explanations. We discuss our findings and their implications in Section 8 and conclude in Section 9.

2. RELATED WORK

Three lines of work are most relevant to our research: (i) predicting query performance, (ii) user satisfaction and frustration, and (iii) characterizing and predicting engine switching behavior.

Research on *predicting query performance* has been conducted to understand differences in the quality of search results for different queries. Such predictions can be used to devote additional resources or use alternative methods to improve search results for difficult queries. While it has been shown that using different query representations [4] or retrieval models [3] improves search performance, it is more challenging to accurately predict which methods to use for a particular query.

Measures such as query clarity [7], Jensen-Shannon divergence [6], and weighted information gain [1] have been developed to predict performance on a query (as measured by average precision, for example). Guo *et al.* [10] used interaction features, including switching features, to predict query performance. Leskovec *et al.* [16] used graphical properties of the link structure of the result set to predict the quality of the result set and the likelihood of query reformulation. Teevan *et al.* [20] developed methods to predict which queries could most benefit from personalization. Hassan *et al.* [11] developed methods to predict search success on a session-level. Feild *et al.* [8] developed methods to predict user frustration, and showed that features capable of accurately predicting switching events were also highly predictive of frustration.

Some research has examined *search engine switching behavior*. Early research by Mukhopadhyay *et al.* [17] and Telang *et al.* [21] has used economic models of choice to understand whether people developed brand loyalty to a particular search engine, and how search engine performance (as measured by within-session switching) affected user choice. They found that dissatisfaction with search engine results had both short-term and long-term effects on search engine choice. Juan and Cheng [13] described some more recent research in which they summarize user share, user engagement and user preferences using click data from an Internet service provider. They identify three user classes (loyalists to each of the two search engines studied and switchers), and look at the consistency of engine usage patterns over time.

Heath and White [12] and Laxman *et al.* [15] developed models for predicting switching behavior within search sessions using sequences of user actions (e.g., query, result click, non-result click, switch) and characteristics of the pages visited (type of page and dwell time) as the input features. Heath and White [12] used a simple threshold-based approach to predict a switch action if the ratio of positive to negative examples exceeded a threshold. Using this approach they achieved high precision for low recall levels, but precision dropped off quickly at higher levels of recall. Working with the same data, Laxman *et al.* [15] developed a generative model based on mixtures of episode-generating hidden Markov models and achieved much higher predicative accuracy.

White *et al.* [24] developed methods for predicting which search engine would produce the best results for a query. For each query they represented features of the query, the title, snippets and URLs of top-ranked documents, and the results set, for results from multiple search engines, and learned a model that predicted which engine produced the best results for each query. The model was learned using a large number of queries for which explicit relevance judgments were available. One way in which such results can be leveraged is to promote the use of multiple search engines on a query-by-query basis, using the predictions of the quality of results from multiple engines. White and Dumais [22] characterized search engine switching through a large-scale survey and built predictive models of switching based on features of the pre-switch query, session, and user. White *et al.* [23] modeled long-term engine usage over a six-month period, and identified three user classes: (i) those who do not switch, (ii) those who switch at some time, and (iii) those who switch back and forth between different search engines.

We extend previous work on search engine switching by focusing on *understanding the rationales* for search engine switching in a single search session in depth, and on *predicting switching rationales* given features of the query and pre-/post-switch behavior.

3. STUDY OVERVIEW

We begin by providing definitions used throughout the paper. We then provide an overview of the reasons for engine switching that were identified in previous work, and present the research questions that we address in this paper.

3.1 Definitions

Some terms are formally defined as below.

DEFINITION 1. A *search session* is a sequence of user activities that begins with a query, includes subsequent queries and URL visits, and ends with a period of inactivity. URL visits include both clicks on the search engine result page (SERP clicks) and post-SERP navigation. We used 30 minutes of user inactivity to mark session boundaries; similar timeouts have been used previously to demarcate search sessions in Web log analysis [22].

DEFINITION 2. A *search engine switching event* is a pair of consecutive queries that are issued on different search engines within a single search session. In our definition of a switching event, navigational queries for search engine names (e.g., search on Yahoo! for [*google*], [*google.com*], etc.) are regarded as part of the act of switching and not as the pre- or post-switch query. For example, if a Yahoo! user searches for [*snowshoes*], then for [*google*] and switches to Google, and then searches for [*snowshoe merchants*], then the pre-switch query is [*snowshoes*] (and not [*google*]), and the post-switch query is [*snowshoe merchants*].

DEFINITION 3. A *search goal* is an atomic information need, resulting in one or more related search queries issued to accomplish a single discrete task [11]

3.2 Reasons for Search Engine Switching

In earlier research on characterizing and predicting search engine switching behavior, White and Dumais [22] surveyed 488 users regarding their experiences with search engine switching. They asked respondents to provide retrospective rationales for switching by selecting at least one explanation from a list of possible reasons. For reader reference, in Figure 1 we present the response breakdown reported in their study.

As we can see from the figure, there are three classes of reasons: dissatisfaction (DSAT) with the results in the original engine (dissatisfaction, frustration, expected better results; shown in red in Figure 1 and totaling 57%), verifying or finding additional information (coverage/verification, curiosity; in green and referred to as "Coverage", totaling 26%), and user preferences (destination preferred, destination typically better; in blue, totaling 12%).

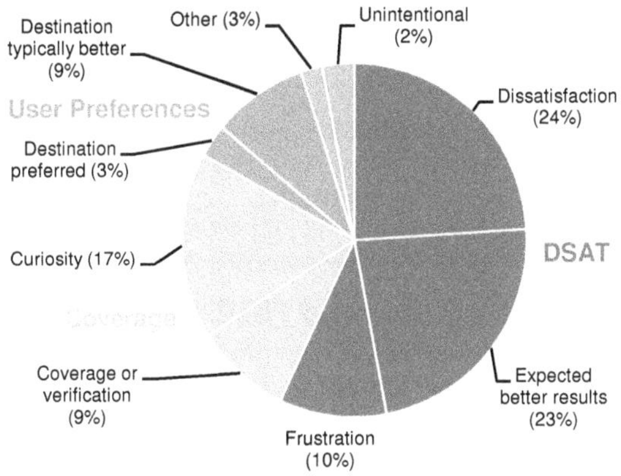

Figure 1. Reasons for search engine switching.

In this study, we collected data about switching rationales at the time the switches happen and develop models to distinguish between DSAT- and coverage-related switches using session-level evidence. We focus on these classes since they are most common, are directly actionable by search providers, and unlike preference-related switching, do not require knowledge of users' long term behavior, which may not be available to the engine at query time.

3.3 Research Questions

Our study answers a number of research questions:

1. Why do searchers switch search engines?
2. Which behavioral signals are associated with different causes?
3. How accurately can we predict the causes of engine switching?

Answers to these questions can help us better understand switching and help search providers improve the user experience in accordance with searchers' motivations for switching or derive more sophisticated competitive metrics for comparing search engines.

4. IDENTIFYING RATIONALES

The first challenge we addressed was collecting switching rationales and their associated search behaviors. One possibility is to design difficult search tasks and ask participants to try to complete these tasks (e.g., [1][8]). For this approach, the challenge lies in the design of tasks that will induce switching behavior naturally. Since switching behavior is rare [22], it is difficult to collect a sufficient amount of switching data in a laboratory setting if participants are not instructed to switch but this will bias the data. Another possibility is to sample from search engine logs and recruit human judges to label sessions. Previous research has demonstrated feasibility in asking human judges to label search success [11]. However, switching rationales are more subjective and personal since they relate not only to searcher goals and result relevance, but also to other factors such as long-term searcher preferences and browser settings. As a result, it is challenging to identify real switching rationales by examining log data alone. Another option is to ask searchers why they switch search engines. White and Dumais [22] asked people to summarize their reasons for switching using a retrospective questionnaire. While this provides some interesting insights, retrospective surveys do not always align with actual behavior and the corresponding behavioral data is not available. Thus, we chose to ask searchers about their switching behavior *in situ* when they switch engines. To obtain these *in-situ* switching assessments we implemented and deployed a browser add-on, called *SwitchWatch*, which presents a short questionnaire to the user at the time of a switch between Google, Yahoo!, or Bing. This questionnaire elicits switching rationales directly from the user at switch time. Figure 2 shows the questionnaire which contains questions about the search task and switching rationale (as described in more detail below).

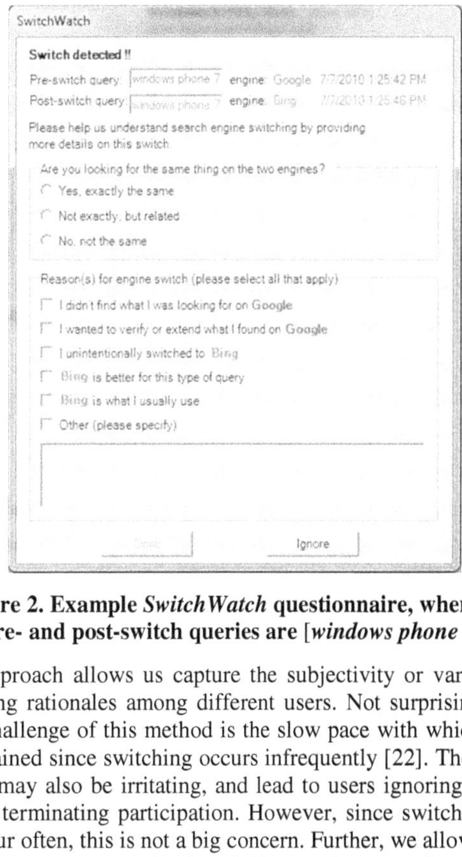

Figure 2. Example *SwitchWatch* questionnaire, where the pre- and post-switch queries are [*windows phone 7*].

This approach allows us capture the subjectivity or variation in switching rationales among different users. Not surprisingly, the main challenge of this method is the slow pace with which labels are obtained since switching occurs infrequently [22]. The pop-up survey may also be irritating, and lead to users ignoring the survey, or terminating participation. However, since switching does not occur often, this is not a big concern. Further, we allow people to ignore the questionnaire (by clicking on the *Ignore* button).

We deployed *SwitchWatch* within Microsoft Corporation for one month to collect sufficient data. We now provide details on its implementation and deployment.

4.1 SwitchWatch Implementation

SwitchWatch was implemented as an add-on for the Internet Explorer browser. Once installed, it started automatically every time a new browser tab was opened and recorded browser activity in that tab to a remote server. For each visited Web page, we recorded the URL, the timestamp, a unique browser window identifier, and an anonymous user identifier. A separate instance of *SwitchWatch* ran for each active browser tab and tab focus/blur events were recorded, allowing us to accurately identify multi-tab usage and Web page dwell times. Intranet and secure (https) URL visits were excluded to help maintain user privacy.

Once an engine switch between two of Google, Yahoo!, and Bing was detected (per definition 2), *SwitchWatch* displayed a questionnaire in the center of the screen occluding part of the active browser window. The questionnaire is shown in Figure 2 for a switch between Google and Bing on query [*windows phone 7*].

As we see in Figure 2, there are two questions shown to users: (i) whether the user changed their search goal (to help determine the extent to which switching was related to goal shifts), and (ii) the cause of the switch. For the first question, the user can pick one response from "exactly the same," "related," and "different" via the radio buttons. For the second question, the user can select multiple reasons that apply. The options include dissatisfaction, coverage, and unintentional. In addition, two options about user habit and preferences are included, namely, "the post-switch engine is better for this type of query" and "the post-switch engine is what I usually use." These response options were selected based on the survey responses in [22], and summarized in Figure 1.An *Ignore* button is also provided to allow users to skip the pop-up if they do not want to interrupt their current task to answer.

4.2 SwitchWatch Deployment

We distributed an invitation to deploy the *SwitchWatch* add-in via email to approximately 2,200 employees within Microsoft Corporation, including colleagues in affiliated groups, interns and 1,000 randomly-selected full-time employees from across the organization. Invitations were sent to employees with a diverse range of occupations, from software engineers and testers, to program managers, paralegals, and administrative staff. 216 employees participated in the study by installing the add-on on their machine, for a response rate of around 10%. Privacy restrictions prevented us from determining the identities or occupations of participants who accepted the invitation to participate. We ran this study for approximately four weeks. In each week, we randomly selected a participant with *SwitchWatch* installed for the week and rewarded them with a 50 USD gift card. There were no other usage requirements to be considered for the prize drawing. Our goal was to retain participants in our study, and make sure that they behaved normally, without forcing them to switch search engines as they may not do normally in their daily search routine.

5. CHARACTERISTICS OF SWITCHING

We now discuss findings on switching characteristics. First, we present the overall summary of search engine switching in the in-situ logs. Second, we discuss how frequently users change search queries and search goals when they switch engines, and the relationship between changing search queries and different switch causes. Finally, we characterize the different switch causes and their associated search behaviors in the session.

5.1 Definitions

We start by providing some definitions used in this section:

- **Same Query (*SQ*):** Identical pre- and post-switch queries.
- **Related Queries (*RQ*):** Pre- query and post-switch query share at least one query term that is not a stop word, but are not *SQ*.
- **Different Queries (*DQ*):** Pre-switch query and post-query do not share any (non-stop-word) terms.
- **Same Goal (*SG*):** User has the same search goal.
- **Related Goals (*RG*):** Search goals related but not same.
- **Different Goals (*DG*):** Search goals are totally different.
- **Ignored:** User dismissed the *SwitchWatch* questionnaire without providing feedback by clicking *Ignore* button.

5.2 Data Overview

We now provide more details on the data that were gathered as part of our experiment. We begin by describing relevant features of the log data gathered by the *SwitchWatch* add-in.

In the in-situ log, 20,554 queries were issued on Google, Yahoo! or Bing by our participants in the four-week duration of the study. Among all the queries, we observed 1029 switches. We excluded 25 switches that were suggestive of users testing *SwitchWatch* (e.g., assessments with queries [*test*], [*hello world*], etc.). As a result, we considered 1,004 instances of search engine switching events, of which 562 (56%) received in-situ assessments. In the remaining 45% of switches, participants clicked *Ignore*, indicating that they did not wish to offer a reason for the switch at that time.

The 1,004 session-level switches in our set comprise only 4.2% of all queries, while 107 (49.5%) of the 216 users who installed the add-in switched search engine within a session at least once (similar to switching rates reported in [22] which was for a much larger and more heterogeneous sample of search engine users).

5.3 Switch Causes and Goal Changes

In this section, we investigate how the changes of search queries and search goals relate to the underlying switching rationales. The inspiration of this analysis came from the observed high percentage of query changes in engine switching events.

5.3.1 Query Changes

We begin by analyzing the breakdown of query changes during engine switching. As described earlier, query change measured by the overlap between pre- and post-switch queries. In our logs, only around 32% of the engine switching events observed had an identical pre- and post-switch query (*SQ*), and approximately 50% of the query pairs shared at least one query term (*SQ+RQ*), the remaining 50% of query pairs comprised different queries *(DQ)*. This raises a question regarding search goal inconsistency during engine switching, something that we explore next.

5.3.2 Goal Changes

We now examine the relationship between changes of search queries and changes of search *goals* (i.e., characterized by *SG, RG,* and *DG* as defined earlier). Table 1 shows the breakdown of user-reported goal changes with respect to query changes. The table shows the percentage of switches where participants clicked *Ignore* and the fraction of remaining judged (non-ignored) queries that received each goal change label.

Almost all (98%) of the switches with the same pre- and post-switch query *(SQ)* share the same search goal (*SG*). In contrast, only 20% switches with related pre- and post-switch queries (*RQ*) are reported as having related goals (*RG*), and only 65% of switches with different pre- and post-switch queries (*DQ*) are reported as having different search goals *(DG)*. This difference is mainly due to the contributions of *RQ* (77% *SG*) and *DQ* (23% *SG*) to switches with same goal. This seems reasonable since users might change the query terms slightly or perhaps make typos when switching with the same search goal. Nevertheless, *SQ* is the best proxy of *SG*, while *RQ* could also be a proxy for *SG* to increase coverage, and *DQ* could be a reasonable proxy of *DG*.

Table 1. Breakdown of goal and query changes.

Query change	Ignored	Goal change [% judged (non-ignored) queries]		
		SG	*RG*	*DG*
All	45%	65%	9%	25%
SQ	27%	98%	1%	1%
RQ	39%	77%	20%	3%
DQ	60%	23%	12%	65%

There are differences in how often the *SwitchWatch* dialog is ignored (by selecting the *Ignore* button) for different query changes. The more related the queries, the more likely users are to provide feedback. The ignore rate of *SQ* switches is 27%, while the ignore rate of *DQ* increases to 60%. Note that we cannot compute the ignore rates for goal changes (*SG*, *RG*, *DG*) since we do not have the search goal information for ignored switches because it was captured explicitly from users by *SwitchWatch.*

5.3.3 Impact on Switch Causes

Now, we study how the change of search queries (as a proxy of search goal change) is related to the underlying switch causes.

As mentioned earlier, the causes were collected via the *SwitchWatch* questionnaires presented to participants when they were about to switch search engines. The candidate set of causes was derived from previous work and included: (i) dissatisfaction with current engine, (ii) additional topic coverage or verification, (iii) unintentional, (iv) post-switch engine was better for this type of task, (v) returning to usual engine, and (vi) other.

In Figure 3 we present the six causes of search engine switching for each class of query changes (*SQ*, *RQ*, *DQ*), and across all switches (*All*). The colors correspond to those used in Figure 1, but unlike Figure 1, these explanations were captured at switch time rather than based on users' recollection of switching events. Focusing on the distribution for *All* in Figure 3, we compare the in-situ reasons and the retrospective reasons reported in Figure 1. There are differences in the figures. For example, dissatisfaction and coverage were less common in-situ than retrospective, and reasons associated with user preferences and unintentional or other reasons were more common in-situ than retrospective. There are some differences in the questions used in the two cases, which make it challenging to map directly between them, as well as a different set of respondents. However, there are some interesting relations, e.g., *dissatisfaction* in Figure 1 includes "dissatisfied" (24%), "expected better" (23%), and "frustrated" (10%), but in Figure 3, dissatisfaction is only "dissatisfied" (26%) and corresponds well with the 24% from the retrospective study. Alternatively, the *SQ* results in Figure 3 correspond well with results in Figure 1. One explanation could be that when people consider switching retrospectively, they focus on *SQ* instances.

There are also different distributions of reasons for switching for the different query relations. The reasons for *SQ* switches are primarily dissatisfaction and coverage, whereas preferences (*usual engine* and *better for task type*) and other (*unintentional* and *other*) are the primary reasons for *DQ*. The reasons for *RQ* lie between these two extremes. Interestingly, as shown in the figure, most of the *DQ* switches are unintentional or indicate a return to respondents' preferred search engine, and only 5% of them were caused by dissatisfaction. This suggests that *DQ* switches may be misleading if used in deriving performance-related metrics, although they are interesting to understand general preferences.

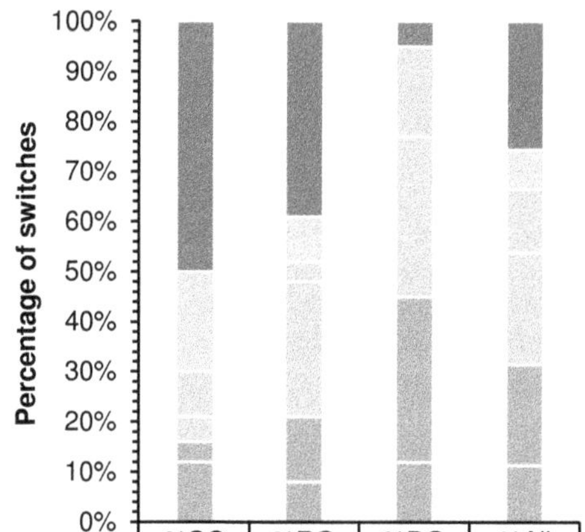

	%SQ	%RQ	%DQ	%All
Dissatisfaction	50	39	5	26
Coverage	20	9	0	8
Other	9	4	18	13
Unintentional	5	27	32	22
Usual engine	4	13	33	20
Better for task type	12	8	12	11

Figure 3. Relationship between query changes and switch causes. Values are shown in the bars in the same order as in the table below the chart.

In contrast, *SQ* has the greatest fraction of queries associated with intentional causes such as dissatisfaction and coverage. Switches caused by dissatisfaction are perhaps the most interesting to a search provider; pre-switch queries are those that the origin engine can improve on in order to retain users, while post-switch queries are important for the destination engine to perform well on in order to gain users. Therefore, we focus on *SQ* switches for later analysis in predicting switching rationales.

In this section we have studied the change of switching queries, search goals, and their connections with the causes of engine switching. We now turn our attention to interaction behaviors associated with different switching motivations. Knowledge of these behaviors may help us predict the reasons behind engine switches given observed session-level search interactions.

5.4 User Behaviors for Same-Query Switches

We study the behaviors surrounding engine switching using the following three groups of features: (i) query, (ii) pre-switch behavior, and (iii) post-switch behavior. These features are useful in characterizing switching and may be useful for predicting switching rationales. All of the features used are described in Table 3, along with the mean and the standard deviation feature values from the in-situ log data for switches associated with dissatisfaction (*DSAT*), *Coverage*, and all other reasons (*Other*). For each feature we perform one-way independent measures analyses of variance (ANOVA) between the three causes of switching, and indicate in the table which paired differences are significantly different with Tukey *post-hoc* testing, for significance with $p < .01$ and $p < .05$. We now describe each feature group in more detail, with reference to Table 2 where appropriate.

Query features derived from the query string itself, include the query length in words and characters, and the time between the pre- and post-switch queries. The longer the query, the more likely the searcher is to be dissatisfied with the search results. Table 2 shows that the number of words in queries associated with dissatisfaction is approximately four, while number of words for switching queries for coverage and other are around three, although the results are not reliable statistically. This is consistent with previous work showing that query length can be an important determinant of search success in Web search [1]. Also included is the time between the pre-switch and post-switch query. The time between the queries is longer for switches associated with dissatisfaction, perhaps because the user is considering all top-ranked search results before making the decision to switch engines.

Pre-switch behavior features from the search interaction before the engine switch include the number of queries (total, unique, and reformulations), the number and rate of clicks broken down by satisfaction and bounce, and the length of the post SERP-trail. Satisfaction with a clicked result (denoted Sat in Table 2) is defined to be a dwell for longer than 30 seconds, as in previous work in this area by Fox *et al.* [9]. Bounces are defined as clicks with a dwell time on the landing page of under 15 seconds, where the searcher returns to the SERP after viewing the landing page. The number of queries is higher for switches associated with coverage, significantly so for the number of queries (*pre_q*). In coverage scenarios, users visit more search results (*pre_c*) and tend to dwell longer on these results (*pre_c_SAT*). We would also expect that the smaller the number of the satisfied clicks and the more *bounces*, the more likely the user is dissatisfied. Trends are in this direction, significantly between the number of bounce clicks (*pre_c_Bounce*) for *DSAT* switches and *Other*. Reformulation rates (*pre_reformRate*) are also somewhat higher for *DSAT* versus *Other*. Also of interest are the number of pages on trails following the SERP click and the number of pages on those trails with the query in their title, the latter of which (*pre_c_containsQ*) appears slightly higher for coverage switches, although not significantly.

Post-switch behavior features correspond to the pre-switch behaviors described earlier in this section. Post-switch behaviors can provide insight into the nature of the search task, and hence potentially the reason for the search engine switch. Interestingly, none of the differences for post-switch behavior were statistically significant. This suggests that post-switch behavior may be less useful for differentiating between switching motivations, something that we will return to later in the paper when we discuss prediction. That said, trends in the findings revealed some similarities to pre-switch behaviors. For example, in switches associated with coverage, there are more queries in the session (*post_q*), and more query reformulation for *DSAT* switches (*post_reform*).

There are noticeable (and some significant) differences in the interaction behavior associated with different switching rationales. In addition to characterizing the interactions associated with the different rationales, we were also interested in whether we could *predict* the reasons behind switching given evidence of searcher interaction behavior within a search session. We now describe our work on predicting engine switching rationales using interactions.

6. PREDICTING SWITCHING CAUSES

We built and evaluated classifiers to predict the reasons for search engine switching. For each reason, we formulate the prediction task as binary classification, where the goal is to predict whether an observed switch is attributable to the reason of interest. We also experimented with multi-class (tertiary) prediction, where the goal was to correctly attribute one of three switching explanations —*DSAT*, *Coverage*, and *Other* (everything else)—to an observed switching event. In this section we describe the results from our

Table 2. Features of search behavior per switching cause. Bolded features exhibit statistically-significant differences. *Dissatisfaction (DSAT)* versus *Other*: ⁿ p<.05; ° p<.01; *Coverage* versus *Other*: ○ p<.05; ● p<.01.

Feature	Mean (stdDev)		
	DSAT	*Coverage*	*Other*
Query features			
q_charLength: Num. chars in switching query	27.3 (±22.5)	18 (±13.5)	18.2 (±12.5)
q_wordLength: Num. words in switching query	4.2 (±3.2)	3.2 (±2.4)	2.9 (±2.0)
q_timeDiff: Time in seconds between the pre-switch and post-switch queries	80.9 (±134)	52.5 (±98.9)	46.7 (±80.1)
Pre-switch features			
***pre_q*●**: Num. queries in session	2.7 (±2.0)	4.0 (±3.5)	2.1 (±1.8)
pre_uniqQ: Num. unique queries in session	2.0 (±1.5)	2.1 (±1.9)	1.4 (±1.0)
pre_reform: Num. query reformulations	1.0 (±1.5)	1.2 (±1.9)	0.4 (±1.0)
pre_uniqQRate: *pre_uniqQ / pre_q*	0.8 (±0.3)	0.7 (±0.3)	0.8 (±0.3)
***pre_reformRate*°** : *pre_reform / pre_q*	0.2 (±0.3)	0.2 (±0.3)	0.1 (±0.2)
pre_c: Num. SERP clicks for related queries	2.0 (±2.9)	2.0 (±2.5)	0.7 (±1.1)
pre_c_Sat: Num. satisfied SERP clicks for related queries	0.8 (±1.7)	1.0 (±1.7)	0.4 (±0.9)
***pre_c_Bounce*°** : Num. bounce SERP clicks for related queries	0.8 (±1.2)	0.6 (±1.0)	0.2 (±0.5)
pre_cRate: *pre_c / pre_q*	0.9 (±2.1)	0.4 (±0.5)	0.3 (±0.4)
pre_c_SatRate: *pre_c_Sat / pre_q*	0.2 (±0.4)	0.3 (±0.4)	0.2 (±0.4)
pre_c_BounceRate: *pre_c_Bounce / pre_q*	0.3 (±0.4)	0.2 (±0.3)	0.2 (±0.4)
pre_t: Num. pages on click trail	1.4 (±2.1)	1.6 (±2.1)	0.5 (±0.9)
pre_c_containsQ: Num. SERP clicks on a search result with title containing at least one non-stop-word query term	0.6 (±2.9)	1.7 (±4.4)	0.4 (±1.8)
Post-switch features			
post_q: Num. queries in session	2.5 (±1.9)	2.9 (±3.7)	2.2 (±2.5)
post_uniqQ: Num. unique queries	1.8 (±1.3)	1.4 (±1.1)	1.3 (±0.8)
post_reform: Num. query reformulations	0.8 (±1.3)	0.5 (±1.1)	0.4 (±0.8)
post_uniqQRate: *post_uniqQ / post_q*	0.8 (±0.3)	0.7 (±0.3)	0.8 (±0.3)
post_reformQRate: *post_reform / post_q*	0.2 (±0.3)	0.1 (±0.2)	0.1 (±0.2)
post_c: Num. SERP clicks for related queries	2.3 (±2.4)	2.1 (±2.8)	1.6 (±2.0)
post_c_Sat: Num. satisfied SERP clicks for related queries	0.9 (±1.2)	0.8 (±1.2)	0.7 (±0.9)
post_c_Bounce: Num. bounce SERP clicks for related queries	1.0 (±1.2)	1.0 (±1.6)	0.7 (±1.0)
post_cRate: *post_c / post_q*	1.0 (±0.4)	0.8 (±0.5)	0.9 (±0.5)
post_c_SatRate: *post_c_Sat / post_q*	0.3 (±0.4)	0.3 (±0.3)	0.3 (±0.4)
post_c_BounceRate: *post_c_Bounce / post_q*	0.3 (±0.4)	0.3 (±0.4)	0.3 (±0.4)
post_t: Num. pages on click trail	2.0 (±2.3)	1.8 (±2.6)	1.2 (±1.8)
post_c_containsQ: Num. SERP clicks on a search result with title containing at least one non-stop-word query term	1.6 (±3.9)	1.3 (±5.9)	3.5 (±8.9)

experiments. We begin by describing the classification algorithm used in the prediction, then describe the evaluation metrics, the models compared in the study, and then the prediction findings.

6.1 Classifiers

We used features described in Table 2 and experimented with a variety of different classification algorithms for predicting switching causes, including decision trees, logistic regression, and naïve Bayes [5], which were the three best performers. The performance of all three methods was similar, and we report on the results of the logistic regression classification here.

6.2 Evaluation Metrics

In evaluating the performance of our predictions, we measure precision (the fraction of predicted instances that were correctly predicted) and recall (the fraction of all true instances that were correctly predicted). We report on the F_β measure, with β set to 0.5, which gives twice as much weight to precision than to recall. Precision is very important in application scenarios for a predictor of switching rationales. In an online scenario, we would want to be highly confident before adapting the search experience based on switch rationale predictions. In an offline scenario, such as studying dissatisfied switches in log data, we need to obtain a set of dissatisfied switches for further analysis. Since there are many switching events in logs, we do not need to classify all switches (have high recall) as long as we can precisely label some.

6.3 Methods Compared

We compare a number of different methods for predicting switching rationales. We used two strong baselines which leverage the marginal distribution and use rules derived manually from a visual inspection of switching events in the logs. The baselines are:

- **Baseline (Prior):** Bases predictions on the class distribution.
- **Baseline (Rule):** Uses rules derived from inspection of switching events in logs. Predict *DSAT* if there is no click before the switch and one or more clicks after the switch; predict *Coverage* if there are clicks before and after the switch; predict *Other* (i.e., all reasons other than dissatisfaction or coverage) if neither of the above rules are triggered.

In addition to these baselines, we also trained binary and tertiary classifiers on varying sets of features described in Table 2:

- **All:** Classifiers trained on all features.
- **Query:** Classifiers trained only using query features.
- **Pre-switch:** Classifiers are trained only using pre-switch behavioral features. These are the features available before engine switching and could be used in combination with a switch predictor (such as that described in [22]) to predict the reason for an anticipated switch.
- **Post-switch:** Classifiers trained only using post-switch behavioral features. This could help the destination engine predict the reason for the incoming switch and adjust the search experience accordingly (e.g., provide diverse results if reason is coverage).

We now present findings on prediction effectiveness using the different feature classes. Given the importance of *SQ* switches to search providers (as discussed earlier in Section 5.3.3), we elected to focus on the set of 354 in-situ *SQ* switches, and used them for training and testing. This is a relatively small set given the fairly intensive *SwitchWatch* deployment effort, primarily because engine switching is a rare event and to maintain reaslism, we did not artificially promote switching in our study. We compare the models via ten-fold cross validation, across 100 randomized experimental runs, and report averages across all runs and folds.

6.4 Binary and Tertiary Predictions

We begin our analysis by comparing the performance of each of the binary classification algorithms with the two baselines, for each of the three classes: *DSAT*, *Coverage*, and *Other*. Table 3 reports the average $F_{0.5}$ values for each switching explanation versus baselines for all features listed in Table 2, and the results of paired t-tests between the models and the baselines.

Table 3. Binary prediction performance (measured via $F_{0.5}$) of *DSAT*, *Coverage*, and *Other*. Significance of differences between models and baselines is marked: Baseline (Prior): △ p<.05, ▲ p<.01; Baseline (Rule): ○ p<.05, ● p<.01.

Method	DSAT	Coverage	Other
Base (Prior)	72.40	27.12	17.40
Base (Rule)	48.84	24.19	20.20
All Features	85.69▲●	47.84▲●	29.01△

The findings presented in Table 3 above show that the prediction model trained with all features significantly outperforms both baselines in the prediction of *DSAT* and *Coverage*, and marginally outperforms the baselines in the prediction of *Other*. The observed gains over the baselines are strong given the limited amount of data available and suggest that there is good predictive signal in the features, espcially for *DSAT* predicitons which are of great interest to search engine providers. Prediction of the *Other* class appears more challenging, perhaps because this class includes several different switching motivations, each of which may have its own associated behavioral patterns.

In addition to the binary classification, we also experimented with multi-class prediction of switch explanation among *three* reasons: *DSAT*, *Coverage*, and *Other*. Multi-class prediction is important because it allows search providers to use a single predictor of switching reasons, potentially reducing training and deployment overhead. Findings from prediction experiments conducted in the same way as above (but this time with three-level judgments) show that the $F_{0.5}$ of a logistic regression model (74.58) exceeded both of the baselines (Prior: 59.46, Rule: 52.80) at $p < .01$. This suggests that multi-class prediction using in-situ data is feasible with these data. However, further work is needed to establish whether a multi-class predictor would outperform a combination of binary classifiers, such as those described above, and study the cost-benefit tradeoffs of each solution.

6.5 Feature Group / Feature Performance

In Table 4 we present the average $F_{0.5}$ metric for how well each model predicts *DSAT* for different sets of features: all features, pre-switch features, query features, and post-switch features.

Table 4. Feature group performance (measured via $F_{0.5}$) for in-situ assessment (*DSAT*).

Group	All	Pre-switch	Query	Post-switch
$F_{0.5}$	85.69	81.12	74.28	78.99

All differences between the four feature groups and the baselines were statistically significant using paired t-tests at $p < .05$. The best predictive performance was attained when all features were used. The most important features learned for those predictions (in descending order of importance) and directionality of their DSAT relationship were *pre_c_SatRate* (–), *pre_c* (+), *pre_uniqQRate* (+), *post_c_containsQ* (+), and *post_reformRate* (–). SERP clicks and query reformulation behavior on both the pre- and post-switch engines may be predictive of user satisfaction, a claim supported by [11]. Factors such as low satisfaction on the pre-switch engine were also good predictors of dissatisfaction-related switching.

Pre-switch features appeared to provide more predictive signal than post-switch features, as was suggested in our earlier analysis of those search behaviors (see Section 5.4). Pre-switch interaction behavior reveals more about searchers' behavior leading up to the switching event, and therefore might provide better quality evidence of the reason behind the switch. In addition, it may also be that there is more variance in what users do following a search engine switch, and that makes features of post-switch behavior less reliable indicators of engine switching rationale.

In-situ assessment affords the capture of switching explanations at switch time from the searcher, and should be an accurate elicitation method for switching rationales. However, it may not always be desirable to deploy such a tool to searchers, especially on a large scale, given interruption costs to users, privacy implications, and the infrastructure required to store large volumes of behavioral data. Therefore, we also explored the use of editorial assessments by third-party judges performing manual log analysis to identify the reasons for search engine switching. Including editorial assessments in our study helps us better understand the judgment correspondence between judges and switching users.

7. EDITORIAL ASSESSMENTS

The main advantages of editorial assessments lie in the large volume of switching data available for analysis and the fact that labels can be obtained faster than the in-situ method. In addition, sessions drawn from logs may be more representative of general Web search activity than those from a subset of searchers who elect to participate in in-situ switch monitoring. The disadvantages of editorial assessment include the possible misinterpretation of switching rationales by third-party human assessors and the cost of human labor involved in performing the assessments. Therefore, in this section we consider the relation between *in situ* judgments by the searcher and those by third-party assessors.

7.1 Log Data

We randomly selected 100 search sessions containing at least one same-query engine switch from the in-situ log data used so far in the paper. Each of these switches was judged by two human assessors and a switching reason was assigned to the first same-query switch in the session. We selected sessions from the in-situ logs so we could directly compare the two judgment methods on the same set of switches. As we will describe later in the section, the judgment task was very intensive. To maintain judgment quality we focused on same-query switches to allow judges to focus on identifying the switching *reason* (rather than goal changes, etc.), restricted judgments to the first same-query switch in each session, and limited the number of judgments per judge to 100.

7.2 Judges

Two human judges performed the editorial assessment task. Both judges are Web search researchers who are familiar with engine switching and search log data. Initial training and discussion was conducted as a pair to help ensure consistency in the labeling. The group examined a few example sessions containing switching events and discussed likely switching motivations.

7.3 Editorial Guidelines

Judges were presented with a spreadsheet containing the 100 sessions to be judged. Each row contained a unique session identifier and the URL of the page visited. If the URL was a search engine result page, the query and engine name were also shown, as were timestamps, and browser and tab identifiers, to help track multi-tasking. Judges answered a few intermediate questions about the search sessions before identifying the reasons for engine switching in order to get acquainted with the searcher's intent and overall experience with the search engine. The intermediate questions included: determining the search goal of the user (based on the taxonomy of search goals proposed by Rose and Levinson [19]), whether the information need requires multiple sources to fulfill, overall success, pre-switch success, and post-switch success. To answer these questions, judges used the information about landing page content and how well it matched query terms as well as the actual sequence of query and click patterns on search results in a session. When determining the reason for the engine switch, the response options included: *Dissatisfaction, Coverage,* and *Other.* Note that we regard unintentional, user habit or user preferences (highlighted as being an important reason in Figure 1) as a subset of *Other* here, since judges may not be able to assess them from log data based solely on a single-session evidence.

Answer options for all questions were presented to judges as drop-down lists in the judgment spreadsheet. Space was also provided for additional comments, although this was seldom used in practice. Judges performed their judgments in isolation and then met to discuss and resolve inconsistencies.

7.4 Judge Agreement

Each judge assessed the same 100 search sessions and each session contained at least one *SQ* switch (that first of which was labeled). The Cohen's kappa (κ) between the two judges for judging switching reasons as *Dissatisfaction*, *Coverage*, and *Other* was 0.78 while κ between judges for *Dissatisfaction* and *Other*, where we merged *Coverage* and *Other* classes, was approximately 0.88. This signifies "substantial" judge agreement for tertiary labeling and "almost perfect" judge agreement for binary labeling [14].

7.5 Switch Causes for Same-Goal Switches

In the case of editorial assessments, we regarded switches with the same query as having the same search goal (given that the analysis in the previous section showed that *SQ* was a reasonable proxy for *SG*). As mentioned earlier, in this analysis we only focus on *Dissatisfaction*, *Coverage*, and *Other* (i.e., all reasons that are not dissatisfaction or coverage).

Overall, there was an 83% agreement between the reasons provided by the third-party judges and the switchers over the same 100 switches used in the analysis presented in this section. The typical disagreements lay in *Coverage* and *Other*, with it being most challenging to differentiate coverage and preference-based switches, which were present in *Other* but not explicitly labeled by judges.

There appears to be reasonable agreement between in-situ and editorial sources on the three main reasons for switching for the *SQ* switches. The editorially-assessed data has a similar distribution to the in-situ data: the percentage of switches associated with dissatisfaction is similar but slightly lower (45% vs. 49%) and the percentage of switches associated with coverage is similar but higher (33% vs. 21%). The differences in coverage estimates may be real, or given fewer assignable switching reasons (three as opposed to six in the in-situ survey), our judges may have over-estimated the amount of switching associated with topic coverage.

7.6 Predicting Switching Causes

Prediction models were constructed using the data provided from the editorial assessment process. In Sections 7.6.1 and 7.6.2 we train *and* test on editorial judgments. However, in Section 7.6.3, we train on editorial judgments and test on in-situ judgments.

7.6.1 Binary and Tertiary Predictions

Baselines were updated to reflect the distributions in the editorial data set. Table 5 shows the average obtained $F_{0.5}$ values. The performance of the prediction model based on all interaction features is reasonable, outperforming both baselines for *DSAT* and *Coverage*, and performing marginally better for *Other*. Performance on predicting DSAT exceeds that of predicting coverage, but the observed gains over the baselines in both cases are lower than we observed for in-situ assessments. One reason for this difference is that less data were available for training and testing the predictive models (i.e., 100 editorial judgments vs. 354 in-situ judgments). To test the extent of this effect, we trained and tested predictive models on the same 100 in-situ switches (using ten-fold cross validation and 100 runs, as before), and observed small differences: the *DSAT* $F_{0.5}$ value with 100 in-situ judgments was 79.43 vs. 85.69 with 354 in-situ judgments. Another reason for the lower performance with editorial assessment could be noisy labels from third-party judges, who may incorrectly interpret logs and would make it challenging to associate reasons with actions.

Table 5. Binary prediction performance (measured via $F_{0.5}$) of *DSAT*, *Coverage*, and *Other*. Train on editorial, test on editorial. Symbol meaning same as Table 3.

Method	*DSAT*	*Coverage*	*Other*
Baseline (Prior)	50.41	35.54	30.16
Baseline (Rule)	54.88	41.90	30.98
All Features	66.16▲●	47.44▲	33.86

In addition to the binary classification, we again experimented with multi-class predictions, this time with the editorial data. The findings showed significant gains in $F_{0.5}$ over baselines (Logistic regression: 64.40, Prior: 50.10, Rule: 45.45) at $p < .01$, suggesting that tertiary prediction using editorial data may also be feasible.

7.6.2 Performance of Feature Groups and Features

In a similar way to Section 6.5, we now examine performance on predicting *DSAT* this time using editorial assessment data. Table 6 summarizes performance for all features, for only query features, and for only pre- and post-switch interaction features.

Table 6. Feature group performance (measured via $F_{0.5}$) for editorial assessment (*DSAT*).

Group	*All*	*Pre-switch*	*Query*	*Post-switch*
$F_{0.5}$	66.16	64.50	57.69	60.12

Once again, prediction performance is worst when using query-only and post-switch features, suggesting that they may be least useful for reliably predicting switch causes. We have already noted that post-switch behavior can be highly variable, making predictions based on it challenging. In addition, in post-assessment debriefings we discovered that judges generally ignored post-switch behavior; something that needs to be resolved in future studies, perhaps by modifying judge instructions.

7.6.3 Predicting In-Situ Judgments

In addition to using the editorial judgments to predict editorial judgments, we can also use the editorial judgments to predict the in-situ judgments, under the assumption that the in-situ judgments are the real ground truth. We re-ran our experiments, again using ten-fold cross validation over 100 runs, but instead of using the editorial judgments for the test fold, we used the associated in-situ judgments. The performance findings are reported in Table 7.

Table 7. Binary prediction performance (measured via $F_{0.5}$) of *DSAT*, *Coverage*, and *Other*. Train on editorial, test on in-situ. Symbol meaning same as Table 3.

Method	DSAT	Coverage	Other
Baseline (Prior)	47.83	32.00	25.05
Baseline (Rule)	50.65	37.17	27.71
All Features	62.76▲●	44.33▲	31.92

The findings show that the performance of the editorial judgments in predicting the in-situ judgments is slightly lower than that obtained when predicting editorial judgments. One explanation is differences in the criteria used by the judge and by the switcher; such inconsistency would lead to poor predictive performance on this task. More work is needed to understand these and other differences noted in this section, primarily because third-party labeling of switching episodes would likely be used in practice.

8. DISCUSSION AND IMPLICATIONS

We have presented an investigation into the causes of search engine switching and the automatic prediction of switching rationales as identified via in-situ and editorial assessments. The study has provided valuable insights into the reasons behind search engine switching and shown that we can predict the motivation behind engine switching with only limited interaction evidence. We found that a large percentage of *DQ* switches are unintentional or preference-related. Therefore, it could be misleading if these switches were included in performance-related analysis and metric derivation. As expected, search goals typically remain constant during *SQ* search engine switches, there are some behavioral patterns (especially in pre-switch behavior) that can reveal different motivations for *SQ* switching, and affording the accurate prediction of different switch rationales. Our findings provide better understanding of switching, and help search engines improve their user experience or derive more accurate competitive metrics.

The findings of the prediction experiments revealed that using the behaviors both before and after the switch lead to the most accurate predictive performance, with accuracy ranging from 65-85% depending on the source of the judgment data. The analysis also showed that the most predictive subset of features were those from interaction preceding the switch. This is promising for the development of real-time support for dissatisfied users, and is in line with the findings of Feild *et al.* [8], who demonstrated value in using recent behavior (including those associated with switching) to predict frustration. In future work, we will experiment further with query features such as type or aggregate clickthrough rate, which have been shown to be effective in predicting query performance and may also be useful in this context [10]. Given that dissatisfaction with the pre-switch engine was the dominant switching rationale, we will also explore the reasons that underlie user dissatisfaction (e.g., lack of diversity, obsolete results, etc.).

The participants in our study were all Microsoft employees. Although we showed some similarities between the switching behavior of these users and those reported in previous work [22], a larger deployment of *SwitchWatch* beyond our organization to a more diverse cohort is needed to further generalize our findings.

This work has a number of practical implications for the design of user-facing search technology. First, predictions of the reasons for switching can be used to dynamically adapt the search experience. Previous work has shown that we can accurately predict *when* a user will switch engine [12][15]. In this research we have shown that we can predict the *reason* behind such switching with good accuracy. Combining these methods would enable us to predict in real-time when a user is going to switch engines because they are dissatisfied. Over time, dissatisfaction-related switches can potentially erode user confidence in the search engine, and ultimately lead to permanent switching. Advanced warning of when switches are likely to occur enables search engines to intervene with an improved experience or offer new capabilities to candidate dissatisfied switchers. Such advanced capabilities include real-time chat with a domain expert or more powerful (but also more computationally-costly) search technologies. Conversely, in cases where the switch is detected by the post-switch engine, perhaps through a toolbar or inspecting the referrer URL, the engine could predict the reason for the switch to them based on post-switch behavior. For example, for incoming switchers dissatisfied with the pre-switch engine, more computational resources could be devoted to ranking. For incoming switchers seeking topic coverage or verification, emphasis could be put on search result diversity.

In addition, search engine companies extensively analyze log data to identify opportunities for improving their service. The ability to predict the reasons for switching allows search engines to compute more accurate competitive metrics that target for improvement of queries frequently leading to dissatisfied switching.

9. CONCLUSIONS AND FUTURE WORK

We have presented a study of the reasons that people switch search engines within sessions. We capture the reasons for switching and associated search behaviors *in-situ* and use the data to develop and evaluate models to automatically predict switching motivations using features of the switching queries and pre- and post-switch behavior. Our findings offer insight into searchers' decision-making processes and demonstrate the relationship between behaviors and switching causes. The findings also reveal sufficient consistency in search behaviors to afford accurate prediction of switching reasons. This could be useful for search providers to improve the search experience for users and derive more accurate competitive metrics. Future work involves studying the different types of dissatisfaction-related switching in more detail, exploring the use of additional features for predictions, creating refined metrics, and deploying switch rationale predictors on a search engine to tailor search experiences to switch rationales.

REFERENCES

[1] Aula, A., Khan, R. M., and Guan, Z. (2010). How does search behavior change as search becomes more difficult? *Proc. CHI*, 35-44.

[2] Bailey, P., White, R.W., Liu, H., and Kumaran, G. (2010). Mining past query trails to label long and rare search engine queries. *ACM TWEB*: 4(15).

[3] Bartell, B.T., Cottrell, G.W., and Belew, R.K. (1994). Automatic combination of multiple ranked retrieval systems. *Proc. SIGIR*, 173–181.

[4] Belkin, N., Cool, C., Croft, W.B., and Callan, J. (1993). The effect of multiple query representations on information retrieval system performance. *Proc. SIGIR*, 339–346.

[5] Bishop, C.M. (2006). *Pattern Recognition and Machine Learning*. New York: Springer.

[6] Carmel, D., Yom-Tov, E., Darlow, A., and Pelleg, D. (2006). What makes a query difficult? *Proc. SIGIR*, 390–397.

[7] Cronen-Townsend, S., Zhou, Y. and Croft, W. B. (2002). Predicting query performance. *Proc. SIGIR*, 299–306.

[8] Feild, H., Allan, J., and Jones, R. (2010). Predicting searcher frustration. *Proc. SIGIR*, 34–41.

[9] Fox, S., Karnawat, K., Mydland, M., Dumais, S.T., and White, T. (2005). Evaluating implicit measures to improve the search experience. *ACM TOIS*, 23(2): 147–168.

[10] Guo, Q., White, R.W., Dumais, S.T., Wang, J., and Anderson, B. (2010). Predicting query performance using query, result, and user interaction features. In *Proc. RIAO*.

[11] Hassan, A., Jones, R., and Klinkner, K.L. (2010). Beyond DCG: User behavior as a predictor of a successful search. *Proc. WSDM*, 221–230.

[12] Heath, A.P. and White, R.W. (2008). Defection detection: Predicting search engine switching. *Proc. WWW*, 1173–1174.

[13] Juan, Y.F. and Chang, C.C. (2005). An analysis of search engine switching behavior using click streams. *Proc. WWW*, 1050–1051.

[14] Landis, J.R. and Koch, G.G. (1977). The measurement of observer agreement for categorical data. *Biometrics*, 33, 159–174.

[15] Laxman, S., Tankasali, V., and White, R.W. (2008). Stream prediction using a generative model based on frequent episodes in event sequences. *Proc. SIGKDD*, 453–461.

[16] Leskovec, J., Dumais, S., and Horvitz, E. (2007). Web projections: Learning from contextual subgraphs of the Web. *Proc. WWW*, 471–480.

[17] Mukhopadhyay, T., Rajan, U., and Telang, R. (2004). Competition between internet search engines. *Proc. HICSS*.

[18] Pew Internet and American Life Project. (2005). *Search Engine Users*. Accessed December 15, 2008.

[19] Rose, D. and Levinson, R. (2004). Understanding user goals in Web search. *Proc. WWW*, 13–19.

[20] Teevan, J., Dumais, S., and Liebling, D. (2008). To personalize or not to personalize: Modeling queries with variation in user intent. *Proc. SIGIR*, 620–627.

[21] Telang, R., Mukhopadhyay, T., and Wilcox, R. (1999). An empirical analysis of the antecedents of internet search engine choice. *Proc. Wkshp on Info. Systems and Economics*.

[22] White, R.W. and Dumais, S.T. (2009). Characterizing and predicting search engine switching behavior. *Proc. CIKM*, 87–96.

[23] White, R.W., Kapoor, A., and Dumais, S.T. (2010). Modeling long-term search engine usage. *Proc. UMAP*, 28–39.

[24] White, R.W., Richardson, M., Bilenko, M., and Heath, A.P. (2008). Enhancing Web search by promoting multiple search engine use. *Proc. SIGIR*, 43–50.

[25] Zhou, Y. and Croft, W.B. (2007). Query performance prediction in Web search environments. *Proc. SIGIR*, 543–550.

Find It If You Can: A Game for Modeling Different Types of Web Search Success Using Interaction Data

Mikhail Ageev*
Research Computing Center
Moscow State University
ageev@mail.cir.ru

Qi Guo Dmitry Lagun Eugene Agichtein
Mathematics and Computer Science Dept.
Emory University
{qguo3,dlagun,eugene}@mathcs.emory.edu

ABSTRACT

A better understanding of strategies and behavior of successful searchers is crucial for improving the experience of all searchers. However, research of search behavior has been struggling with the tension between the relatively small-scale, but controlled lab studies, and the large-scale log-based studies where the searcher intent and many other important factors have to be inferred. We present our solution for performing controlled, yet realistic, scalable, and reproducible studies of searcher behavior. We focus on difficult informational tasks, which tend to frustrate many users of the current web search technology. First, we propose a principled formalization of different types of "success" for informational search, which encapsulate and sharpen previously proposed models. Second, we present a scalable game-like infrastructure for crowdsourcing search behavior studies, specifically targeted towards capturing and evaluating successful search strategies on informational tasks with known intent. Third, we report our analysis of search success using these data, which confirm and extends previous findings. Finally, we demonstrate that our model can predict search success more effectively than the existing state-of-the-art methods, on both our data and on a different set of log data collected from regular search engine sessions. Together, our search success models, the data collection infrastructure, and the associated behavior analysis techniques, significantly advance the study of success in web search.

Primary Classification: H.3.3 [**Information Storage and Retrieval Languages**]: Information Search and Retrieval; *Search process*

General Terms: Experimentation

Keywords: User studies, query log analysis, web search success.

---

* work done while visiting Emory University.

SIGIR'11, July 24–28, 2011, Beijing, China.

1. INTRODUCTION

"Knowledge must come through action." - Sophocles

Searching the web is never a goal in itself: the searchers typically want to obtain the required information quickly and with minimum effort. For many common search tasks, search engines excel at returning the needed information in the first few results, and sometimes directly in the search engine result page (SERP) itself. However, there are difficult search tasks that require significant effort and ingenuity – where only some of the searchers succeed while the majority fails. What makes some searchers successful? What are the key failure modes that tend to result in failed searches? What patterns of searcher behavior can reliably identify a successful search session?

We propose a principled search framework designed to investigate these questions, and present a novel competition-based data collection methodology, to enable empirical study of the different paths to search success. Our approach is based on enticing participants to compete in a game-like setting, to find answers to real informational questions, while tracking the resulting search behavior.

This approach has a number of advantages over previously reported search evaluation methods: i) the information needs are real, well-defined questions selected from community forums such as wiki.answers.com and Yahoo! Answers. ii) the goals (needed information) are known to both the searchers and the assessors, and are well-defined, allowing for objective measures of success; and iii) sufficient amount and diversity of search behavior can be acquired for difficult queries (which are relatively rare among all queries submitted to search engines), thus enabling in-depth study of the behavior characteristics for these difficult and rare queries that were not previously available through passive log analysis.

In summary, our contributions include:

- A flexible and general informational search success model for in-depth analysis of search success and failure for different definitions of success (Section 2).
- A scalable infrastructure for collecting realistic search interaction data with objective success criteria (Section 3).
- Effective machine learning-based techniques for predicting and analyzing different types of search success (Sections 4-6).
- Source code and data are shared with the research community.

Next, we present our search success model, which allows us to formulate hypotheses that motivate our study design, and the experiments described in the rest of the paper.

2. SEARCH SUCCESS MODEL

To better analyze the search process, we propose a simple, yet powerful four-stage *QRAV* (*Q*uery-*R*esult-*A*nswer-*V*erification) model of an informational search success. This model is primarily geared towards analyzing and describing searches with specific, direct information needs, such as those phrased as factoid questions.

We conceptually divide the process of successfully answering factual queries into several parts. First, the user should correctly understand the question and issue a relevant query (*Q* for *Query formulation*). If the query retrieves at least one target document in the top 10 results, we call it a *Good Query*. Then, the user has to find the correct result on a search engine result page (SERP), and click on it to examine the document (*R* for *Result identification*). If a result document contains the correct answer, we call it a *Good URL*, indicated by R^+. Furthermore, we can consider how many clicks away this document was from the SERP, indicated by the subscript. For example, if a document containing a correct answer was the last in the search session, we indicate it as R_L^+. The next step is *extracting* an answer from a document (*A* for *Answer extraction*). Finally, the answer is *verified* that it correctly answers the question and is in fact supported by the document (*V* for *Verification of the answer*).

Thus, the final success of a user in finding an answer to a question depends on successfully performing each stage in the *QRAV* model, represented as $Q^+R^+A^+V^+$. In a case where a user issues a good query and clicks on a good document, but submits an incorrect answer, the outcome would be represented as $Q^+R^+A^+V^-$. Finally, if the success in a particular stage is unknown (or not considered), the "?" mark is used. The model is illustrated graphically in Figure 1, where the states in the process are represented by circles and the arrows represent possible state transitions. Note that some transitions in the model are not possible, e.g., by definition it is not possible to directly go from a bad query (Q^-) to a good result (R^+).

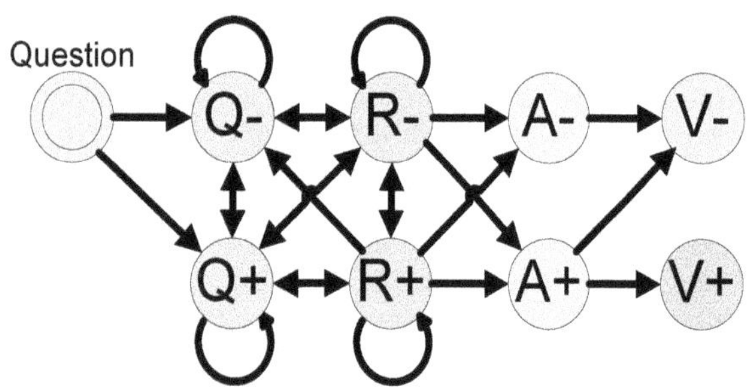

Figure 1: Possible state transitions in QRAV model

Using our *QRAV* model we can describe (and estimate) the success factors at each stage of the search process, and naturally represent previously posed definitions of search success:

- $Q^+R_*^+A^+V^+$: The correct answer was found and validated to be supported by a good document — it is a search success in the strictest sense, most similar to the definition of a correct answer in a TREC question answering track [27].
- $Q^+R_*^+A^+V^?$: An answer was found on a good result, and submitted — which means that the participant was satisfied with the session and believed that she found an answer (but the answer could still be incorrect). This definition of success matches the definition of Aula et al. [2], where the users submitted the answer to a difficult search task, but the answer was not validated.
- $Q^+R_*^+A^?V^?$: A good URL was found — the user visited a relevant page, but did not necessary extract the correct answer. This definition matches the model based on analysis of search engine click logs by independent assessors as in [11].
- $Q^?R_L^+A^?V^?$: A good URL was found *and it was the last in the search session*. This follows the ideas of marginal document *utility* in a search session [9] - after viewing the last document in the search session, the user is satisfied and stops searching.

Having defined our measures of success, we can now analyze the sets of actions (behavior) that correlate with each of the above definitions of success. In other words, at each stage of the process, searchers perform actions, some of which are indicative of a success or failure, or a continuation at one of the *QRAV* stages above. Our study, described next, was designed with the goal of being able to validate, and isolate the success or failure of the searcher at each stage of the process. Using this model we can also analyze the corresponding behavioral clues for *predicting* the success or failure at each stage of the search process.

3. ACQUIRING SEARCH BEHAVIOR DATA

The overall design of the study was modeled on a game, more precisely as a *search competition*: the participants played a game consisting of 10 search tasks (questions) to solve, with a timer displaying the number of seconds remaining, shown to the subject (see Figure 2). The stated goal of the game was to submit the highest possible number of correct answers within the allotted time. Overall, four game rounds were used in this study, with participants recruited and scored separately for each round. The top "players" in each round (typically, those successfully posting a correct answer to 7 or 8 out of the 10 questions) received a bonus payment.

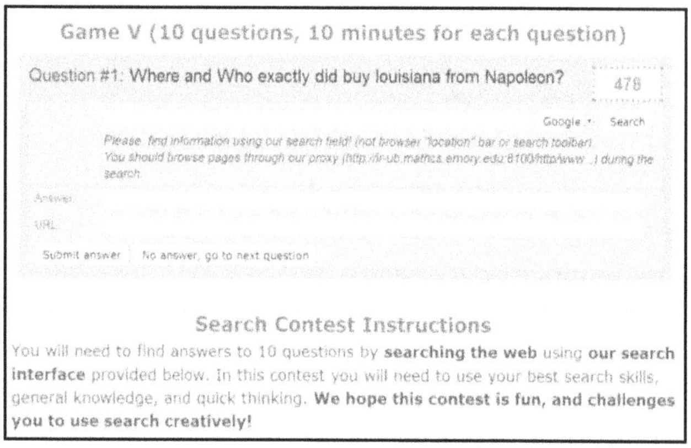

Figure 2. An example search game interface, which has the question, the search query window, and a dropdown box for choosing a search engine to use (Google, Yahoo! Search, or Bing). When the answer is found, the participant submits it together with the supporting URL. The query result page is opened in new tab, allowing natural querying and browsing.

3.1 Search Tasks: Informational Questions

The search tasks were selected from community question answering sites such as wiki.answers.com and Yahoo! Answers by the researchers. The criteria used were that the question should be clearly stated, had a clear answer, and that finding this answer was not a trivial task, that is, the answer was not retrieved simply by submitting the question verbatim to Google, Bing, or Yahoo! Search engines. Overall, 40 such questions were selected, posing (as it turned out) greatly varying levels of difficulty for participants. These questions were randomly split into four game rounds of 10 questions each. A list of questions for an example game is provided in Figure 3.

How many Swedes speak English as a percentage?
When the jominy test was invented?
Which metals float on water?
What is oxygen partial pressure at 5000 feet?
How many Argentine soldiers died in falklands islands war?
What ingredients in cough medicine make you hallucinate?
How do you say welcome in kashmiri?
Am I allowed to carry a parachute onboard as a hand luggage?
What animal is smaller than a bear but it eats a plant called bearberry?
What is the highest peak in western hemisphere?

Figure 3. An list of questions for an example game (the original grammar and spelling are preserved).

3.2 Participants and Study Procedure

Participants were recruited through the Amazon Mechanical Turk (MTurk) website. As a first step, the workers had to solve a *ReCaptcha*[1] puzzle to verify that they are human and not an automated "bot". Then, each participant was directed to the task instructions (describing the game rules), and then clicked on a link to start a game. At that point, a search interface as in Figure 2 appeared, which was to be used for submitting all search queries. The search results appeared either below the search box, or in a different tab (depending on user's normal search preferences), in the original search engine result format. To generate these search results, the queries were submitted (and logged) through our proxy server, which then retrieved and logged the search engine responses and displayed them to the user in the original format.

In order to capture all of the participants' search actions, they were instructed to use only our search interface (and not a separate browser window). After the searcher decided that they found the answer, they were instructed to copy and paste the answer text from the document, together with the supporting URL, into the corresponding fields in the game interface. Each search session (for one question) was completed by either submitting an answer or clicking the "skip question" button to pass to the next question.

Every participant who followed the directions (i.e., used our search interface and submitted at least one answer, regardless of whether the answer was correct or not) was guaranteed the base participation payment of $1. Additionally, the "best" players (i.e., those with the most correct answers found as assessed by the researchers) were promised an additional $1 bonus to stimulate a competitive "feel" of the game. Based on a pilot study used to improve and validate the game design, we found that the bonus feature was crucial to motivate the workers to persist through difficult search tasks. We also found that providing thc bonus option dramatically increased the rate of task completion and reduced the rate of "junk" submissions.

3.3 System Implementation

Our UFindIt game interface was built using Python, Django framework and Apache Web server. The Apache proxy functionality was used by configuring the modules *mod_proxy*, *mod_proxy_html*, and *mod_sed* so that the users could search and browse the Web in a usual way, while the URLs in the html links were automatically replaced. For example, instead of http://site.com/some?params, the HTML links were automatically re-written to request the URL through our proxy.

The behavioral (interaction) events were logged by our proxy and written in the server log. For each user-question session we extracted all the queries, URLs and contents of the visited pages, clicks on search engine result pages, click positions, browsing trails, and the times of all the events.

Our experimental infrastructure and the data used in this study are available for the research community at: http://ir-ub.mathcs.emory.edu/uFindIt/.

4. PREDICTING SEARCH SUCCESS

This section describes the models, features, and algorithms we use for analyzing and predicting the success of searchers.

4.1 Algorithms

Markov Model (MML+Time): As our baseline state-of-the-art model we adapt the Markov Model approach introduced in the reference [11]. As in the original model, the states are the types of visited page — "Q" for SERPs, "R_1" for pages clicked from SERP — or "E" for end-of-session. The only difference from original model is that our data does not contain sponsored-search clicks and search engine-specific links like "related search", but we have information about pages visited from hyperlinks — those pages correspond to additional model state "$R_{>1}$".

The transitions of Markov Model are events of new page visit. Given the session success $B \in \{1,0\}$ (success or fail), the transition probability between two states $s_i, s_i \in \{Q, R_1, R_{>1}, E\}$, is estimated on the training set:

$$P(s_i \to s_j, \Delta t | B) = \frac{N_{s_i,s_j,B}}{N_{s_i,B}} \cdot \Gamma(\Delta t, k, \theta) \quad (1)$$

where $N_{s_i,s_j,B}$ is a frequency of transitions $s_i \to s_j$ in sessions with a given result B, $N_{s_i,B}$ is a frequency of state s_i in those sessions, and Δt is a time delta between events s_i and s_j. The model in reference [11] assumes that Δt has the Gamma distribution $\Gamma(\Delta t, k, \theta)$ with parameters k and θ, estimated from the training set. Parameters k and θ also depend on s_i, s_j, and B.

The trained Markov Model is used to predict session success from the search behavior data. For the sequence of states with known time deltas S=$s_0 \xrightarrow{\Delta t_1} s_1 \xrightarrow{\Delta t_2} \dots \xrightarrow{\Delta t_n} s_n$ the log likelihood of success and failure is estimated as:

$$LL_B(S) = \sum_{i=1}^{n} \log P(s_i \to s_j, \Delta t | B) \quad (2)$$

and the session success is defined as:

$$Pred(B) = \begin{cases} 1 & \text{if } LL_1(S) \geq LL_0(S) \\ 0 & \text{otherwise} \end{cases} \quad (3)$$

[1] www.recaptcha.com

We tested the performance of the Markov Model, with and without the time delta distribution features, and the experiments confirmed that incorporating time delta distribution indeed improves performance. This agrees with the results described in reference [11] and validates our implementation.

Conditional Random Fields (CRF): we use an extension of the Markov Model approach above, by adapting the CRF model [20] for our task. The benefit of CRF is that it allows us to augment the Markov Model with additional *search behavior features*, derived from previous works in references [10, 11, 29], and described next. We use the Mallet[2] implementation of CRF, freely available for research.

A CRF allows us to define a conditional probability $P(y|x,\lambda)$ over the hidden state sequences $y = \{y_1, \ldots, y_n\}$ given a particular observation sequence of n page views $x = \{x_1, \ldots, x_n\}$, and the CRF parameters (λ) that are estimated at training. At training time, the hidden state of an observation (i.e., a page view) can be assigned a "+" or "-" label, depending on whether the user was successful in the task. Alternatively, we can also assign "Q^+", "Q^-", "R^+", "R^-" labels to the intermediate stages in the session to allow more fine-grained modeling. At test time, given an observed page view sequence x', the most likely state sequence y' can be inferred by maximizing the conditional probability $P(y' \mid x', \lambda)$ using the formula:

$$P(y|x,\lambda) = \frac{1}{Z(x)} \exp\left(\sum_j \lambda_j F_j(y,x)\right) \quad (4)$$

where $Z(x)$ is a normalization factor and $F_j(y,x)$ is the jth feature function, which could be either a state feature function or a transition feature function.

An example configuration is shown in Figure 4. Each observation corresponds to a page view (i.e., either a search engine result page, *Query$_i$*; or the landing page of a clicked result, *Result$_i$*), and is represented by a *vector of features* introduced next, (Table 1) such as dwell time on the page, query length in words, and number of queries in a session.

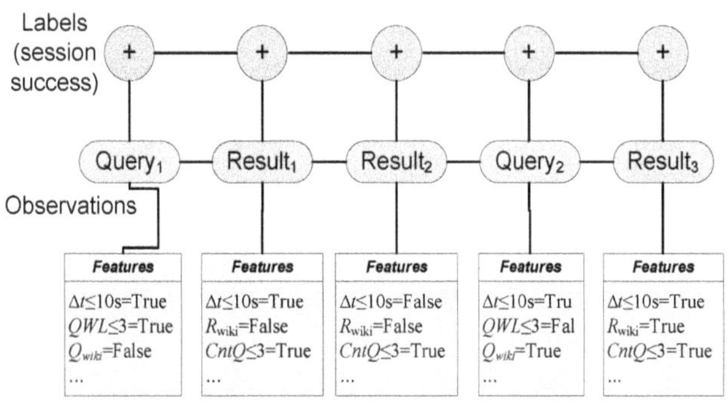

Figure 4. CRF implementation of session-level model. The labels represent overall session success; the observations at each step in the sequence are the features in Table 1.

To experiment with the tradeoff between the precision and recall, we use the *marginal probability* of the last hidden state y_n="+" as the classification confidence, since the last state indicates whether a searcher is successful or not across all potential CRF configurations. The marginal probability is computed by summing over the probabilities of all labeled sequences Y^+ that end with label "+" in their last states, according to the following formula:

$$conf = \sum_{y \in Y^+} P(y|x,\lambda) \quad (5)$$

For our experiments we used the Mallet implementation of CRF, which allows only nominal features. Therefore, we discretize the numeric features using increasingly large thresholds. For numeric features, the used discretization thresholds are shown in the column "Bins". The complete set of behavioral features used for the CRF model is reported in Table 1. We also used aggregated behavioral features for analysis of user success, as described in the next section. The aggregation function is shown in the column "User" for the features that have a reasonable interpretation for describing an individual searcher.

4.2 Search Behavior Representation: Features

We represent searcher behavior by adapting and extending the features introduced in previous studies. Specifically, we use the browsing features from [29]. Additional features, such as session duration and number of viewed pages are adapted from [10]. We also added a feature for the average page trail length.

Feature	*Description*	*CRF Bins*	*User-level Aggregation*
state	Type of visited page $s \in \{Q, R_1, R_{>1}, E\}$, see the Markov		
Δt	Time delta between previous state and current state	≤3s ≤10s ≤30s	$\sum \Delta t$
Q_{engine}	One of {google, bing, yahoo}		
$Q_{abandoned}$	True if there no clicks for the query		
QWL	Query word length	≤3	Avg
Q_{wiki}	True if wikipedia.org is on SERP		
Q_{ADV}	True if the query use advanced query syntax. (i.e., queries that use search operators – quotes, "+" operator, and field operators like "site:" and "allintext:".)		Avg Count
Q_{DT}	Query Deliberation Time - minimum time delta between query and first click		Avg
R_{wiki}	True if visited page is on wikipedia.org		
$R_{Q\_serp\_pos}$	Position of SERP click	≤2 ≤5	Avg
R_{trail}	Length of trail from search engine result page, defined as the number of clicks from SERP	≤1	Avg
ref_{serp} ref_{start}	True if visited page was clicked from the SERP or from the start of a game (these features are extracted from HTTP Referer header, and could catch some patterns of non-linear browsing, when user uses several browser tabs)		
	Session-level aggregates		
CntQ *CntR*	Count of queries and pages in the session	≤1 ≤3	Avg
QPS	$QPS = \frac{CntQ}{\sum \Delta t}$ — average number of Queries submitted by a user Per Second		Avg
CPQ	$CPQ = \frac{CntR}{CntQ}$ — average number of result Clicks Per Query		Avg

Table 1: Behavior features used for CRF. "Q*" features are defined only for SERPs (if the state=Q), "R*" features are defined only for non-SERP pages. Discretization thresholds are shown in the "Bins" column. For the features used in the searcher behavior analysis, the aggregation function is shown in the last column.

[2] Available at: http://mallet.cs.umass.edu/

For the analysis we used only the features that could be reasonably matched to user's search skills or expertise. For example, we hypothesized that highly successful searchers view more results (i.e., *CntR* is higher), use more advanced syntax (i.e., Q_{ADV} is higher), and perform search faster (i.e., the duration of session in seconds — $\sum\Delta t$ is lower). As will be shown in section 5.2, the first two hypotheses are supported by our data, but the third is not. To compute these features, the base feature values in Table 1 are aggregated for each participant according to the rules presented in the last column, and then averaged over all the sessions that the user has completed.

5. RESULTS AND DISCUSSION

This section presents the results of analyzing and predicting search success. First, we describe the participant data and provide descriptive statistics. Then, we contrast the behavior patterns of successful vs. unsuccessful searchers. Then, we analyze the behavior patterns associated with search task difficulty in order to automatically predict search success for the various definitions of success in our model.

5.1 Participant and Search Behavior Data

A total of 200 MTurk participants finished at least one of the game rounds. The user sessions were both automatically and manually checked to detect violations of game rules. For example, some users did not use our search interface, or used unsupported browsers, despite being warned not to do so in the task instructions. We also filtered out the users who did not answer even the easy, effectively trivial questions, as it indicated either poor understanding of the game rules, or an attempt to make a quick buck without effort. After this filtering, 159 users (79.5%) remained in the dataset. Our data for these users consists of 1487[3] search sessions, distributed among 40 distinct questions in 4 game rounds. All these 159 users were paid the base $1 payment. The top 25% of the searchers (ranked by the number of correct answers submitted) were paid an additional $1 bonus. *In total, the user payments cost less than $250.*

Overall, the study participants enjoyed the task, and provided positive comments indicating that the game was interesting (at least, in comparison to the other MTurk tasks), and challenging enough. A sample of users' comments is provided in Figure 5.

"The game was somewhat hard, but I tried my best"

"I enjoyed the search task. But in a few cases defining the proper search term took some time as it had to be refined after the first search. And for that count I may have missed one or two."

"That was pretty interesting and worked well. I felt like I was able to get answers to most of the questions pretty easily."

"Only one was really hard, the Larry Bird one!"

"Little confusing at first... search engines were not very helpful on most without some in depth searching"

Figure 5: Optional feedback submitted by MTurk workers.

Overall, there were from 30 to 50 valid search sessions collected for each question. For each session we extracted the browsing events from our proxy log. Each session was finished by either submitting an answer (87% of sessions), or by passing to the next question. The submitted answers were manually marked as either correct (65% of all sessions) or incorrect. An answer was considered correct if the page of the submitted URL indeed contained the submitted answer. There were 4382 search engine queries in our log data, and 14676 page visits. This data is available at (http://ir-ub.mathcs.emory.edu/uFindIt/).

Additional data statistics, including the overall average session times, number of actions, average query length, and others are reported in Table 2. These statistics largely agree with the published statistics from a similar study of web search success reported by Aula et al. [2]. The small quantitative differences can be expected, as our study focuses on relatively difficult information gathering tasks.

	All sessions	*Successful sessions*	*Unsuccessful sessions*
Count	1487	971	518
Average duration, sec. ($\sum\Delta t$)	215 (223)	182 (176)	276 (384)
Average number of query terms/query (*QWL*)	6.0 (4.8)	5.8 (4.7)	6.6 (5.1)
Average number of queries per session (*CntQ*)	2.9 (6.7)	2.3 (5.0)	4.0 (12.4)
Ratio of queries with operators (Q_{ADV})	0.05 (0.07)	0.05 (0.06)	0.05 (0.13)

Table 2: Descriptive statistics for search sessions collected with the UFindIt game. The corresponding statistics from reference [2] are shown in parentheses.

5.2 Analysis of Successful Searchers

5.2.1 Analysis of Behavioral Features

We use the number of correct answers as a measure of a user's success level. We divide users into three groups, according to different levels of success: HIGH level of success, if the user submitted correct answers to eight or more questions; MEDIUM level for those able to submit correct answers to five to seven questions; and LOW for those submitting correct answers to fewer than five questions.

Feat	User Success Level			LOW vs. HIGH	
	LOW	MEDIUM	HIGH	Effect size d	Power (1–β)
count	34	66	59		
$\sum\Delta t$	216	223	205	0.14	0.15
CntQ	**2.33**	**2.88**	**3.15**	**0.48**	**0.70**
QPS	0.013	0.015	0.016	0.39	0.54
QWL	**7.07**	**5.90**	**5.23**	**1.04**	**1.00**
$R_{Q\_serp\_pos}$	3.58	3.62	3.38	0.19	0.22
CPQ	**0.87**	**1.03**	**1.09**	**0.49**	**0.71**
Q_{DT}	**25**	**15**	**11**	**0.89**	**0.99**
Q_{ADV}	**0.001**	**0.036**	**0.050**	**0.64**	**0.90**
CntR	**2.80**	**3.81**	**3.91**	**0.73**	**0.95**
R_{trail}	**1.13**	**1.20**	**1.28**	**0.55**	**0.79**

Table 3: Comparisons of user behavioral features for different user success levels. Features with significant effect size are shown in bold; observations supported by high statistical power are shaded.

[3] After filtering a small number of empty or broken sessions due to proxy failure or other logging problems.

Specifically, we explore the relationship between searcher success level and the different features of searching behavior. First, we compare the search behavioral features for different success level groups by the mean values. Secondly, we perform independent measures Wilcoxon-Mann-Whitney test for assessing whether the means for LOW and HIGH success-level groups of users differ significantly. We applied Cohen's d-test to determine the effect size for each feature, and evaluate statistical power ($1 - \beta$) using at ($\alpha = 0.05$). Table 3 reports the mean, effect size, and statistical power for browsing features.

Our analysis shows that, as compared to users with LOW success, users with HIGH differ as follows:

- Issue more queries for each question, view more pages, analyze more documents per query, and browse deeper from search engine result pages.
- Issue shorter queries.
- Analyze search result page faster and click faster.
- Use advanced search syntax more frequently.

All three groups of users made a similar effort in terms of amount of working time ($\sum \Delta t$), but successful users exhibited better web search skills, indicated by greater speed.

Our study provides an interesting complement to a larger, but passive log-based study performed by White and Morris [29]. We confirmed empirically their hypothesis that "advanced" users (who use advanced query syntax) indeed are more successful in Web search. Our data agreed with their findings in that HIGH users issued more queries (*CntQ*), but disagreed with the data in [29] on the difference in query length (*QWL*), and the ratio of clicks to queries (*CPQ*). The advanced users analyzed in reference [29] issue longer queries, and perform fewer clicks than LOW users, whereas this difference was not observed in our data. We hypothesize that the disagreements are due to more difficult search tasks in our data, compared to the more common tasks found in a regular search engine log. Other features (such as query deliberation time Q_{DT}, and the number of queries per second QPS) studied both in our research and in [29] are not statistically significant according to both studies.

5.3 Analysis of Search Paths

A similar statistical analysis was performed for the search session success, with different meanings of success following our QRAV model. For this study we approximate the definition of *Good URL* (R^+) and *Good Query* (Q^+) by the partial assessments extracted from our data in the following way: if a URL was submitted by any user as a correct answer, than we consider it to be a *Good URL*, and if a query contains any *Good URLs* on the SERP, than it is considered to be a Good Query. As we have many answers for each question (from 30-50 users), we believe this approach results in a good approximation.

Our data shows that HIGH users, compared to LOW users, had higher scores on different stages of QRAV: they are more likely to issue good query during the session (Q^+), click good documents on result pages (R^+), and submit an answer (A^+).

But the significance of different success levels is non-uniform for different levels of success. LOW users issued good queries in 87% of sessions versus 95% for HIGH users; however, for the LOW users only 42% of the good queries resulted in correct answers as compared to 89% for the HIGH users.

To gain an intuition for the differences in behavior between highly successful searchers (HIGH) and the less successful ones (LOW), consider Figure 6, which summarizes the most likely search paths taken by these user groups, and omits transitions with probability less than 0.1. Interestingly, both HIGH and LOW users tend to submit good queries on the first try (with probabilities of 0.79 and 0.78, respectively). However, LOW users are less likely than HIGH users to *recognize* relevant results (0.38 vs. 0.48). LOW are also more likely to be "stuck" examining bad results (0.53 vs. 0.46), and are very unlikely to transition from bad results to good results ($P<0.1$) or to a good query reformulation ($P<0.1$). In contrast, HIGH users eventually move on from bad results to a good query reformulation ($P=0.17$) or directly to good results ($P=0.12$).

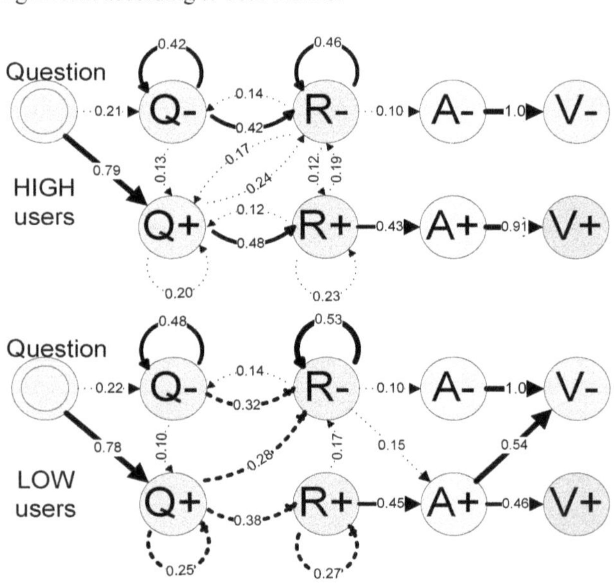

Figure 6: State transition probabilities estimated for users with HIGH and LOW search success ratings. The transition probabilities are indicated by the line weight; transitions with probabilities of less than 0.1 are not shown.

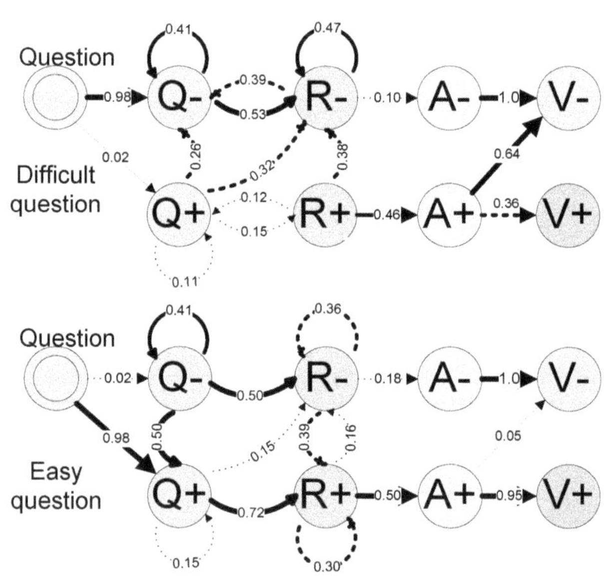

Figure 7: State transition probabilities estimated for all users, for an example difficult and easy question, respectively. The transition probability is indicated by the thickness and number on the transition arcs.

Interesting behavioral differences also exist for "easy" and "difficult" questions (those answered by > 75% and < 25% of participants, respectively). An example of a difficult question is "*When was the jominy test invented?*" For this question, only 8 participants submitted correct answers out of the 44 who attempted this question. The state transitions diagram for this question is shown in Figure 7. It appears that the most difficult aspect of this question is formulating a good search query, with only 2% of the searchers able to formulate a successful query on the first try, and only 29% eventually able to generate a good query reformulation. Furthermore, even after submitting a good query, only 15% of the participants were able to find a relevant document. Once a relevant document is found, 46% of the time a plausible answer was submitted, and 36% of these answers turned out to be valid[4].

In contrast, consider the "easy" question "*What is the highest peak in western hemisphere?*", for which 39 users submitted correct answers out of the 41 who attempted it. The state transitions diagram is also shown in Figure 7. The most probable path for this easy question is the shortest path: $Q^+ \rightarrow R^+ \rightarrow A^+V^+$, which occurs in 37% of the sessions for this question. As another example, for the question "Where and who exactly bought Louisiana from Napoleon?", any reasonable query immediately leads to a document about the history of Louisiana purchase[5]. While the page is definitely relevant, but is relatively long, and it is difficult to extract the correct answer. Some common incorrect answers included "Spain" and "President Jefferson bought Louisiana". In this case, most users found the relevant document (Q^+R^+), but submitted incorrect answers or no answer at all (or $Q^+R^+A^+V^-$ or $Q^+R^+A^-$, respectively).

5.4 Prediction of Search Session Success

In this section we report results on the prediction of session success by using the behavioral features as input. We compare our Conditional Random Fields (CRF) algorithm described in section 4.1 to both the naïve baseline algorithm that always predicts "success" (the majority class), as well as to the state-of-the-art Markov Model method that incorporates time distribution between actions (MML+Time) described in [11] and summarized in section 4.1.

Success Definition	*Baseline*		*MML+Time*		*CRF (All)*		*CRF (Selected)*	
	Acc	*F1*	*Acc*	*F1*	*Acc*	*F1*	*Acc*	*F1*
$Q^?R^+A^+V^+$	0.65	0.40	0.61	0.58	0.68	0.60 (+4%)	0.68	0.62
$Q^?R^?A^+V^?$	0.87	0.47	0.72	0.55	0.86	0.64 (+17%)	0.88	0.66
$Q^?R^+A^?V^?$	0.83	0.45	0.66	0.53	0.80	0.57 (+8%)	0.81	0.59
$Q^?R_L^+A^?V^?$	0.60	0.38	0.59	0.53	0.68	0.66 (+26%)	0.69	0.67

Table 4: Prediction of search session success for different levels of success in QRAV model. Relative improvement against MML+Time model is shown in parenthesis.

We use 4-fold cross-validation in the following manner: for each of the four game rounds we train our model on all sessions from the *other three games*, and apply the trained model to predict the searcher success of the current game. Thus, we have four folds of roughly equal size. For each fold, neither the users nor the questions intersect. We compare algorithms by accuracy and F-measure, macro-averaged over the positive (successful) and negative (unsuccessful) classes. The results are presented in Table 4, which shows that our CRF model exhibits significant improvement over both the baseline and MML+Time models proposed in [11] for all definitions of success except the first one.

5.4.1 *Feature significance*

We now explore the relative significance of behavioral features used for training CRF by using a subset of the features, starting from one feature, and use a greedy search to extend the used subset, one feature at a time, by adding the best of the remaining features. In each step we choose the feature that gives the highest F1 performance of the CRF algorithm for predicting $Q^?R_L^+A^?V^?$ success. The results are shown in Table 5, and the best results obtained by this greedy feature selection for each definition of success are shown in table 4. As we can see, the first, most significant feature (*State*) is the same one as reported in [11] —the search action itself. Interestingly, the time interval between the actions and the choice of the web search engine are the two next most useful features. This makes sense, as the faster searchers are also likely to be more advanced or experienced, and are also more likely to experiment with switching search engines (encouraged by a drop-down box in our search interface). Finally, the position of the search result clicks provides additional indication of the search result quality – which in turn indicates the presence of a good query.

Feature	*F1*	*Accuracy*
State	0.624	0.675
$+\Delta t_{\leq 10}$	0.655 (+5%)	0.680
+Q_engine	0.666 (+1.7%)	0.680
$+R_1$serp_pos$_{\leq 2}$	0.670 (+0.6%)	0.687
$+R_1$serp_pos$_{\leq 5}$	0.671 (+0.1%)	0.686

Table 5: Prediction of search success by the CRF model, when adding one best-performing feature at a time.

We now explore the differences in the performance of the MML variants and our CRF system, for different definitions of search success (Section 2). Figures 8 (a-d) report the precision vs. recall plots of identifying the Successful class. CRF performs best, and significantly better than MML for the definitions proposed in [11] (b) and for the definition proposed in [9] (d). For the other definitions of success (e.g., the most strict one (a)), the improvement of CRF is less striking, while MML variants exhibit performance comparable to the reports in the original study [11].

6. REAL WORLD SUCCESS PREDICTION: A LOG-BASED STUDY

We have shown that our model can successfully predict success of over a hundred participants in the tournament-like setting. Can we use the resulting model, trained on our contest data, to predict search success in a real-world search engine log? To answer this question, we use a large log of web searches performed from hundreds of shared-access workstations in a major university library, and attempt to predict search success using the models trained on our contest data.

[4] Any answer that correctly stated at least the year the Jominy hardness test was invited (1938) was accepted as valid.

[5] http://www.nps.gov/archive/jeff/lewisclark2/circa1804/heritage/louisianapurchase/louisianapurchase.htm

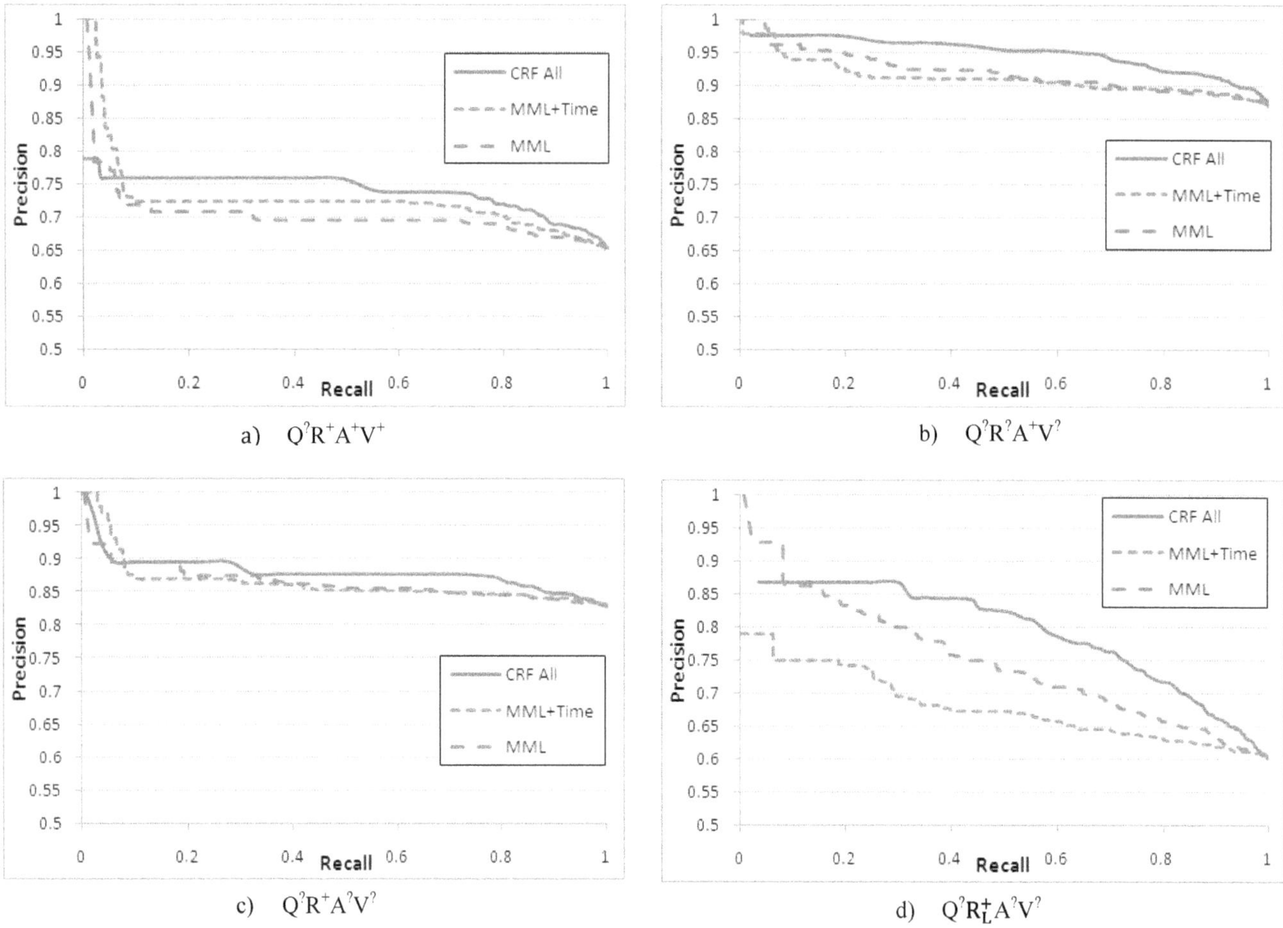

Figure 8. Recall-precision curves for compared algorithms, for different definitions of session success in QRAV model.

6.1 Experimental Setup

The data was collected by instrumenting over 100 shared-use workstations at the Emory University library using the EMU toolkit[6], with participants explicitly opting in to allow the searches to be tracked for library improvements (with roughly 60% opt-in rate). 16,693 search sessions (using almost primarily the Google search engine) were collected over a period of 6 months.

A sample of 175 search sessions consisting of more than one query (and thus more likely to be a non-trivial search) were manually labeled by the researchers to be successful or not, using the methodology and criteria outlined in Hassan et al. [11]. Specifically, the assessors used their best guess of the searcher intent based on the sequence of queries submitted, clicks on the results, and by manual examination of the visited result pages (recorded in the proxy log). 29% of the sessions were labeled as *successful*, 28% as *unsuccessful*, and 43% as *unknown* – where the assessors were not able to infer the searcher intent or determine whether the visited results satisfy the search.

6.2 Methods Compared

We used the CRF trained on all our contest data, using all of the features in Table 2. We trained the algorithms using the two most successful definitions of search success in *QRAV* model, namely $Q^?R^+A^?V^?$ (finding a good document) and $Q^?R^{\ddagger}_{L}A^?V^?$ (finding a good document as last in the search session). Then, the CRF model trained on the UFindIt game data was applied to log data.

6.3 Results and Discussion

Table 7 reports the results of predicting search session success. While the absolute accuracy and F1 values are lower than those on the original search contest data, the predictions significantly and substantially outperform the baseline. This experiment demonstrates that training a success model on search contest data can have significant practical applications, by directly applying the trained models to estimate search success of users of a production search engine.

Training Model: Success Definition	*Baseline*		*CRF (All)*	
	Acc	*F1*	*Acc*	*F1*
$Q^?R^+A^?V^?$	0.51	0.34	**0.55 (+8%)**	**0.52 (+53%)**
$Q^?R^{\ddagger}_{L}A^?V^?$	0.51	0.34	0.53 (+4%)	0.44 (+29%)

Table 7: Prediction of search success for real-world log using CRF trained on contest data, for success definitions in [11] and [9] respectively.

7. RELATED WORK

Our work spans several areas of modeling searcher behavior, including analyzing search log to understand variances in user behavior, evaluating search engine performance, conducting online study using crowd-sourcing approach, and predicting search success and frustration.

[6] http://ir.mathcs.emory.edu/EMU/

Search behavior using general search engine logs has been researched extensively. Jansen et al [16, 17] studied query and search distributions; Beitzel et al. [3], studied topic distribution and other fine-grained properties of a search engine log. Additionally, see [14] for a great overview of search engine log mining in general.

A number of web search evaluation metrics have been proposed. Clarke et al. [4] proposed an evaluation metric based on providing the necessary coverage for the information need. While these metrics provide a good estimate of the quality of the search results, and in turn have been shown to correspond to search effectiveness of users, these do not take into account the search success of a specific user for a session.

There were previous efforts to run a search engine contest to acquire search data. Most notably, the Yandex search engine[7] (a leading web search engine in Russia and Eastern Europe) ran a search contest to evaluate search engine performance, and characteristics of the winner strategies were studied [7, 31]. However, we perform a significantly more in-depth analysis of the search success and behavior and provide a re-usable infrastructure for a very different participant group and higher level of instrumentation detail. Microsoft's Bing search engine recently introduced a search game to improve search engine performance [22], which performed page-centric analysis on which pages were easier or more difficult to find using the Bing search engine.

The previous research closest to the first half of our work is the study of behavioral differences between "expert" users and "novice" users (White and Morris [28]), and the study of behavioral change in difficult search tasks (Aula et al. [2]). White and Morris [28] analyzed search logs of different search engines and defined "expert" searchers as those who use advanced operators in their queries. The authors found several differences in the behavior of expert searchers compared to those who do not use advanced operators. However, the lack of information about user goals and success prevented a more in-depth analysis of the reasons behind the behavioral differences. In our study, we adapt the same criteria to identify advanced users in our data, but, unlike in previous studies, we have well-defined search goals and success definitions, and find interesting similarities and differences. Aula et al. [2] examined the changes of searcher behavior associated with difficult search tasks using data collected from a usability lab study and an online study. To some extent, their approach of online study is similar to ours. However, the users in the previous online study were relatively passive while in our study we provide a competition-like setting to encourage more active search to let the users find best answers possible, which is potentially valuable to understand how advanced searcher behavior can help "novice" users in such difficult tasks and at the same time test the limit of search engine in those difficult tasks. Also, instead of using self-reported success (which could be misleading – as we show in our analysis, some users submit wrong answers that they thought were correct), we defined different types of success in principled way that could be potentially valuable for various applications.

Closest to the second half of our work is the recent work by Hassan et al. [11], which studied the prediction of searcher success on session-level. In their work, the success of a search task is judged by a human assessor using log information, where real search goals are not available, making the judgment potentially noisy. Another related work is by Feild et al. [10] that studied behavioral clues to detect search frustration. The real search goals are known since the data was collected from a user study, but the scale of the data is limited. In our study, we addressed such tension between the relatively small-scale, but controlled lab studies, and the large-scale log-based studies where the searcher goals unknown, by crowd-sourcing the data analysis using a game-like setting. In addition to the relative large scale of our study (hundreds of users) and the known search goals for each task, our study also benefits from the objective and well-defined *search success* metrics that can be used to evaluate whether the searcher goal was actually achieved.

To summarize, the key distinctions of our work compared to previous efforts are: a clear, well-defined QRAV model of search success for informational tasks; an online game-like study framework that enables large-scale user study with clear search goals and realistic search behavior; and an in-depth analysis of searcher behavior that results in more accurate prediction of search success than a previous state-of-the-art model.

8. CONCLUSIONS

We presented a novel methodology for analyzing searcher success in relation to the searcher behavior. What sets our work apart from previous studies is the emphasis on realistic search tasks (extracted from the real user questions on popular community question answering sites), yet allowing for well-defined, objective success criteria. This allowed us to develop a principled fine-grained model of web search success that naturally encompasses previously proposed models. We also developed and validated a competition-based framework for acquiring search behavior data at sufficient scale to allow analysis of successful and unsuccessful searcher behavior, and to train effective models for predicting search success.

Additionally, our study identified important search behavior characteristics that relate to search success. We showed that more successful users are faster and more active in their effort — they issue more queries, clicks, and browse more pages for each question, issue shorter queries, and more actively use query reformulations and advanced query syntax. The key characteristics that distinguish highly successful searchers were the ability to consistently identify relevant documents from a search engine result page, and to extract correct answer from the actual documents. Remarkably, the models trained on our acquired behavior data performed adequately on predicting searcher success based on the regular search engine log.

These findings suggest future directions for collecting real search behavior data in the academia, evaluating search engine performance, and improving search engine result presentation. Other areas for future exploration include personalization of the search success models, developing success metrics for other search intents (e.g., for exploratory search), and extending the contest-based approach to an even larger group of participants. Potential future applications of this work include applying models trained for different success definitions to provide labels for learning-to-rank improvements, and for developing evaluation metrics based on the behavioral metrics developed in this paper.

ACKNOWLEDGMENTS

This work was supported by the National Science Foundation grant IIS-1018321, and by the Yahoo! Faculty Research Engagement Program.

[7] http://www.yandex.com

9. REFERENCES

[1] Azzah Al-Maskari, Mark Sanderson, and Paul Clough. 2007. The relationship between IR effectiveness measures and user satisfaction. In *Proc*. of SIGIR 2007

[2] Anne Aula, Rehan M. Khan, and Zhiwei Guan. How does search behavior change as search becomes more difficult? In Proc. of CHI 2010

[3] Steven M. Beitzel, Eric C. Jensen, Abdur Chowdhury, David Grossman, and Ophir Frieder. 2004. Hourly analysis of a very large topically categorized web query log. In *Proc. of* SIGIR 2004

[4] Charles L.A. Clarke, Maheedhar Kolla, Gordon V. Cormack, Olga Vechtomova, Azin Ashkan, Stefan Büttcher, and Ian MacKinnon. Novelty and diversity in information retrieval evaluation. In *Proc. SIGIR'08*, 659-666, 2008.

[5] Honghua (Kathy) Dai, Lingzhi Zhao, Zaiqing Nie, Ji-Rong Wen, Lee Wang, and Ying Li. 2006. Detecting online commercial intention (OCI). In *Proc.* of WWW 2006

[6] Ali Dasdan, Kostas Tsioutsiouliklis, and Emre Velipasaoglu. 2010. Web search engine metrics: (direct metrics to measure user satisfaction). In *Proc*. of WWW 2010

[7] Dobrov B., Loukachevitch N., Dobrov G., Reznikov Y., Shternov S. Study of Query Transformations in the First Round of Yandex's Cup. In Proc. of "Internet-Mathematics-2005", (in Russian)

[8] D. Downey, S. Dumais, and E. Horvitz. Models of searching and browsing: Languages, studies, and applications. Journal of the American Society for Information Science and Technology (JASIST), 58(6):862--871, 2007

[9] Dupret, G. and Liao, C. A model to estimate intrinsic document relevance from the clickthrough logs of a web search engine. *In Proc. of* WSDM 2010, 181-190

[10] Henry A. Feild, James Allan, and Rosie Jones. Predicting searcher frustration. In Proc. of SIGIR 2010

[11] Ahmed Hassan, Rosie Jones, and Kristina Lisa Klinkner. Beyond DCG: user behavior as a predictor of a successful search. In Proc. of WSDM 2010

[12] Jeff Huang and Efthimis N. Efthimiadis. 2009. Analyzing and evaluating query reformulation strategies in web search logs. In *Proc.* of SIGIR 2009

[13] Scott B. Huffman, Michael Hochster, How well does result relevance predict session satisfaction? In *Proc.* of SIGIR 2007

[14] Bernard J. Jansen, Web Analytics. In *Synthesis Lectures on Information Concepts, Retrieval, and Services*), Morgan & Claypool, 2009

[15] Bernard J. Jansen, Danielle Booth, and Amanda Spink. 2009. Predicting query reformulation during web searching. In *Proc.* of CHI 2009 Extended Abstracts

[16] Bernard J. Jansen, Amanda Spink, and Tefko Saracevic. 2000. Real life, real users, and real needs: a study and analysis of user queries on the web. *Inf. Process. Manage.* 36, 2 (January 2000), 207-227

[17] Bernard J. Jansen and Amanda Spink. 2006. How are we searching the world wide web?: a comparison of nine search engine transaction logs. *Inf. Process. Manage.* 42, 1 (January 2006), 248-263.

[18] Kalervo Järvelin. 2009. Explaining User Performance in Information Retrieval: Challenges to IR Evaluation. In *Proc. of* ICTIR '09

[19] Diane Kelly, Methods for Evaluating Interactive Information Retrieval Systems with Users, Foundations and Trends in Information Retrieval, v.3 n.1—2, p.1-224, January 2009

[20] J. Lafferty, A. McCallum, and F. Pereira. Conditional random Fields: Probabilistic models for segmenting and labeling sequence data. *In Proc.* ICML-01, pages 282-289, 2001.

[21] Chang Liu, Jacek Gwizdka, and Jingjing Liu. 2010. Helping identify when users find useful documents: examination of query reformulation intervals. In *Proceeding of the third symposium on Information interaction in context* (IIiX 2010).

[22] Ma, H. and Chandrasekar, R. and Quirk, C. and Gupta, A. Page hunt: improving search engines using human computation games. *In Proc. of* SIGIR 2009, 746-747

[23] Benjamin Piwowarski, Georges Dupret, and Rosie Jones. 2009. Mining user web search activity with layered bayesian networks or how to capture a click in its context. In *Proc. of* WSDM 2009

[24] Mark Sanderso*n, Monica L*estari Paramita, Paul Clough, and Evangelos Kanoulas. 2010. Do user preferences and evaluation measures line up?. In *Proc.* of SIGIR 2010

[25] Catherine L. Smith and Paul B. Kantor. 2008. User adaptation: good results from poor systems. In *Proc. of* SIGIR 2008.

[26] Andrew Turpin and Falk Scholer. 2006. User performance versus precision measures for simple search tasks. In *Proc.* of SIGIR 2006

[27] E.M. Voorhees, H.T. Dang. Overview of the TREC 2005 Question Answering Track, NIST.

[28] Ryen W. White, Paul N. Bennett, and Susan T. Dumais. 2010. Predicting short-term interests using activity-based search context. In *Proceedings of the 19th ACM international conference on Information and knowledge management* (CIKM 2010)

[29] Ryen W. White and Dan Morris. Investigating the querying and browsing behavior of advanced search engine users. In Proc. of SIGIR 2007.

[30] Ya Xu and David Mease. 2009. Evaluating web search using task completion time. In *Proc.* of SIGIR 2009.

[31] Yandex Internet Search Competitions http://kubok.yandex.ru/organize_eng.html

Measuring Improvement in User Search Performance Resulting from Optimal Search Tips

Neema Moraveji
Stanford University
Stanford, CA 94305
neema@moraveji.org

Daniel Russell
Google
Mountain View, CA 94043
drussell@google.com

Jacob Bien
Stanford University
Stanford, CA 94305
jbien@stanford.edu

David Mease
Google
Mountain View, CA
dmease@google.com

ABSTRACT

Web search performance can be improved by either improving the search engine itself or by educating the user to search more efficiently. There is a large amount of literature describing techniques for measuring the former; whereas, improvements resulting from the latter are more difficult to quantify. In this paper we demonstrate an experimental methodology that proves to successfully quantify improvements from user education. The user education in our study is realized in the form of *tactical search feature tips* that expand user awareness of task-relevant tools and features of the search application. Initially, these tips are presented in an idealized situation: each tip is shown at the same time as the study participants are given a task that is constructed to benefit from the specific tip. However, we also present a follow-up study roughly one week later in which the search tips are no longer presented but the study participants who previously were shown search tips still demonstrate improved search efficiency compared to the control group. This research has implications for search user interface designers and the study of information retrieval systems.

Categories and Subject Descriptors

H.3.3 [**Information storage and retrieval**]: Information Search and Retrieval – *query formulation, search process*, G.3 [**Mathematics of computing**]: Probability and statistics – *experimental design.*

General Terms

Measurement, Design, Experimentation, Human Factors

Keywords

User studies, search interface, experimental design, effectiveness measures, query reformulation, expertise, tactics, tips, suggestions, assistance, efficiency.

1. INTRODUCTION AND MOTIVATION

Research on improving search performance often focuses on the algorithm, input modality, and visualization improvements. However, substantial improvements may also come from research on improving searcher expertise.

Other researchers share this vision [6, 13, 30], and one approach has been to improve pedagogical methods for search instruction [11, 23] and opportunities for modeling expertise of others [28, 31]. Our study tests the idea that educating searchers can produce a large and valuable improvement in search behavior [14].

Search engines have grown increasingly sophisticated and have evolved past the traditional query/response paradigm to include scores of tools and options for specifying queries, targeting certain corpora, visualizing results, browsing result sets, and so on. These tools are often hidden but have the potential to offer tremendous efficiency gains to users who know how to use them appropriately.

Thus, beyond term selection and query formulation, search actions include search techniques, corpus selection, features, and strategies used to solve information needs. We refer to these as search tactics. A tactic is a low-level plan to achieve a search goal, where the goal is simply to solve the present information need [1].

We believe that, in addition to suggesting relevant documents or query reformulations [24], there is high latent value in making relevant search tactics more salient to users. We illustrate this with two studies: first, a study which demonstrates that users can apply search tactics effectively to improve their search performance, and second a study which demonstrates that some improvements are retained when the tactical tips are removed and roughly one week passes. The results of the study are followed by a discussion of implications for designers and researchers of IR systems and expertise.

2. RELATED WORK

Jansen [16] uses the phrase 'automated assistance' in IR systems to refer to specific actions taken by the system to improve search behavior according to some metric. However, we have found in our review that there are multiple, ambiguous and overlapping definitions of automated assistance, including strategies that are presented, tactical advice, feedback on search performance [35], and hints. Jansen and McNeese's taxonomy [17] can be expanded to encompass alternative suggestions. For our purposes, we classify automated assistance into three categories: suggestions for query expansion, search strategies, and search tactics instruction.

2.1 Suggestions for Query Expansion

Suggestions for query expansion are the most popular class of suggestions. Mizzaro [27] provides a review of systems with different automated assistance, all of which aim to influence the user to reformulate or refine his/her query. These include thesaurus systems, automatic reformulation based on semantic analysis, translating natural language queries, and dialog systems to disambiguate queries.

Query suggestions to improve the likelihood of success are seen as most useful in exploratory search for beginning searchers, especially on topics for which they have little knowledge or familiarity [18, 20, 22].

Comparing two techniques that ultimately aim to influence query formulation, Belkin, *et al.* investigated term relevance feedback (meant for manual query reformulation) and Local Context Analysis (meant for automating reformulation), finding that the automatic LCA resulted in fewer user-defined queries, but with no difference in performance for locating document instances within a closed set [3]. Kelly, *et al.* [20] found that specific query suggestions are preferred by searchers over term relevance feedback.

Kelly, *et al.* [19] as well as Capra and Pérez-Quiñones [10] studied how the social dimension of such suggestions can influence their usage, drawing upon theories of social influence. The effect on task efficiency was not measured. Showing information about the popularity and quality of a query suggestion was shown to influence usage, with quality being more important than popularity [19].

The suggestions featured in Brajnik, *et al.*'s [7] FIRE system are primarily aids for query expansion (despite being referred to as strategy suggestions by the authors). They define two classes of such suggestions: "hints" (giving feedback to the user about how the system is interpreting his/her query) and "advice" (executable links to system features to aid query reformulation, such as browsing the thesaurus). In evaluations with 6 users, some found the suggestions in their system "too general" and that, though it sped up their search process, it did not change their search strategy, and participants left believing they would have followed the strategies even without any help.

Like the FIRE system, DAFFODIL [21] was created to give search strategy advice over a closed corpus of scientific literature. It was evaluated with 12 users on an open-ended task. The 16 strategies suggested by DAFFODIL included tactics such as trying alternative spellings of keywords and restricting/broadening the query. Evaluation was done with self-reported Likert assessments that indicated promise for tactical suggestions, but again, task performance was not measured.

Jansen and McNeese [17] found that automated assistance for query expansion resulted in modest performance gains in identifying relevant documents over a closed corpus (using the TREC behavior metric). They found that automated assistance was implemented in 71% of the instances where it was requested (i.e. it was not automatically shown) and that this rate did not depend on expertise.

2.2 Suggesting Strategies

Brajnik, *et al.* [7] summarize search strategies as "the sequence of search statements that identify, restrict, limit a set of retrieved documents to solve an information problem". Belkin, *et al.* [5] classify search strategies into four independent dimensions: method, goal, mode, and resource.

Kriewel and Fuhr [21] argue that an ideal search system would provide useful strategies for completing specific tasks – either by request or proactively helping users improve their search. The goal is to use what we know about search procedures to suggest search strategies.

The system described by Brajnik, *et al.* [7] attempts to infer "critical" situations (such as receiving zero results from a query) and uses a knowledge-based approach to provide strategic suggestions for searching a closed set of scientific literature. Suggestions included scanning related topics or restricting a result set to a particular journal. Again, only 6 participants provided qualitative assessments of how well they thought the system would perform.

2.3 Suggesting Tactics

For search purposes, strategies are longer-term plans that are executed across many moves. By contrast, search tactics are much shorter sequences of moves intended to accomplish a single information goal [2]. Bates defines four types of search tactics [2]: monitoring (keeping the search on track), file structure (identifying desired file type), formulation (aiding query redesign), and term (aiding selection and revision).

In modern search engines, diverse tools are integrated and allow the user to, in effect, use different modes and mediums of search in the same session. Tactical suggestions provide immediate guidance to exploring unfamiliar corpora or visualizations without necessarily focusing on query reformulation.

Examples of modern tactical search suggestions include switching corpora from general webpages to discussion forums or images, changing the input modality from text to voice, changing the visualization of the result set from a list to a map, and changing from keyword to exact phrase terms.

The system presented by Kriewel and Fuhr [21] includes suggestions we would classify as tactical, such as visualizing a social graph of authors, and focusing the query on particular conference proceedings. While these tactics are presented to the user, the description of the system does not include any metric that measures how searcher behavior changes.

For most of the prior work on search suggestions, performance is measured by the TREC standard definition of task success: that is, the proportion of documents identified as relevant to the task, where "relevant" is determined by a group of judges [4]. This is logical because the field is primarily concerned with evaluating IR system performance whereas we are interested in improving user performance. Hence, we instead measure performance in terms of task completion time (TCT) by searchers on the live, unstructured web.

2.4 Summary and Motivation for Present Study

To be sure, query specificity and domain-appropriate term selection remain important components of search expertise. However, this focus on query expansion has neglected other aspects of search expertise, such as task-appropriate tactics based on available search engine features. This area has been understudied for multiple reasons. First, tactical suggestions are not common in closed-corpus systems because query reformulation may be sufficient. Second, IR research systems often test one search engine on one corpus instead of integrating multiple corpora, as is often the case in commercial systems that tie together web, images, video, news, blogs, and other corpora. Third, the tradition of focusing on query reformulation, rather than exploration, has acted as momentum toward features that influence them.

3. EXPERIMENT 1: CAN TACTICAL TIPS IMPROVE SEARCH PERFORMANCE?

A "tactical tip" is a short suggestion for the searcher that suggests a direct action to take to improve the likelihood of successfully solving a search problem. Such a tip does not suggest possible likely documents or query alternatives, but suggests potentially successful approaches to solve the information need. Our experiment seeks to determine if an appropriate tip shown at the moment of need can measurably improve overall searcher performance.

3.1 Experimental Design and Apparatus

To determine this, a controlled user study was conducted where each participant was assigned six directed search tasks. This between-subjects study had one independent variable: availability of a task-relevant tactical tip. The dependent measure was task completion time (TCT), our primary metric for search task performance.

For each trial, the participants in the experiment group were given a search task and were asked to press a 'Start' button after they had read both the task and the tip. The participants in the control group were presented only the task but not the tip. The participants performed the task in other windows or tabs and returned to the user study tab to enter their answer. The screen was then cleared and the next task was displayed.

The user interface for the study displayed the task as shown in Figure 1. For the experiment group, static screenshots illustrating how to use the tip in question were also displayed. For the control group (which saw no tips), only the light blue textbox was displayed.

Each participant varied in the amount of time they spent on the study (for a maximum of 5 minutes per task). All instructions were given textually but participants were unable to copy and paste from the question into a search box because that text was represented as an image. We asked participants to "try their best" but an honorarium was paid regardless of performance.

3.2 Experiment Task Design

The experiment was conducted on the 'open Web' but with specified (directed) tasks [29]. Participants were instructed to use the Firefox browser and the Google search engine, but were permitted to enter any query and view any pages they chose.

We identified six tactical search skills, each of which is designed to be well-served by a particular search tactic: specific query syntax, a feature of the user interface, or narrowing to a particular corpus. (e.g., Skill-2: knowing how to limit searches to a particular file type) Then, for each skill we created two tasks. Tasks 1A and 1B both are more easily solved if the participant has a good grasp of Skill-1, Task 2A and Task 2B with Skill-2, etc. (The set of 6 tips is available at: http://bit.ly/TacticalSearchTips. See Table 1 for the text of the 6 tips as well as the corresponding 12 tasks.)

The tasks were designed with the following requirements: a) the task was judged to be difficult or required a great deal of effort to solve, b) answers to the task can be easily determined to be correct or incorrect and c) the task is well-specified, leaving very little room for misinterpretation.

Participants had a maximum of five minutes to complete each task. They were instructed to give up if they were not able to find (what they believed to be) the correct answer by that time. The time elapsed was shown on the task webpage.

The tasks were purposefully designed to be both difficult to complete and yet still be considered "lookup" tasks, which are characterized by Marchionini [26] as concerning fact retrieval, known item searches, navigation, verification, and question answering.

As shown in Figure 1, the question text was always shown in a light-blue box and, in the tip conditions, the relevant tip was shown below. The tip often (but not always) included screenshots illustrating how to use the feature in question, with callouts to make its functionality immediately apparent.

3.3 Participants

The 491 paid participants (59% female, varied professional and educational backgrounds) in this study are part of a larger pool of people around the U.S. who perform search comparison tasks as part of their normal work flow, selecting tasks from a work-task queue. Participants varied widely in profession and computer expertise. Each participant was randomly assigned to either the experiment (tip shown) group or the control (no tip shown) group.

Figure 1: Task 4A shown here with its tactical tip. This is the layout of the actual instructions the study participant would see. The tip depicted here illustrates the skill searching for videos of certain durations.

We conducted this study in a remote setting for multiple reasons. Participants were able to use the browser and monitor with which they were comfortable. The participants also have a great deal of experience completing tasks of this sort, and so were not subject to strong learning or novelty effects. Because they had a substantial amount of prior practice performing similar tasks, we elected not to run practice trials before beginning the experiment.

3.4 Method

There were roughly 50% of the participants in the experiment and control groups, with around 25% of the population in each of the 4 subgroups: Control-task-set-A, Control-task-set-B, Experiment-task-set-A, Experiment-task-set-B. (The actual numbers vary slightly from group to group due to a small number of abandoned task sets by participants.)

In addition to answer task questions posed, the participants were also asked to rate how successful they thought they were on each task. Each participant was asked to solve all 6 tasks within a maximum of 5 minutes for each task.

Task	Prompt	Search Tip
1A	Imagine you live in Centreville, MD. What library within 15 miles of Centreville has the book *The Person and the Situation* and how far away is it (in miles)?	You can search for books in a local library with Google and see if that book is in a local library by clicking the "Find in a library" link.
1B	Imagine you live in Grand Junction, CO. What is the closest library that carries the book *Arenas of Language Use* and how far is it (in miles)?	(same as 1A)
2A	There are many Microsoft Word files freely available on the web about having good standing posture. Find four (4) different ones and paste the URLs to the 4 files.	You can have Google return only some kinds of files, like Powerpoint and PDF. Use Advanced Search like below or add `filetype:doc` or whatever file type into the search box.
2B	There are many Microsoft Word files freely available on the web about how to correctly cut a dog's nails. Find four (4) different ones and paste the URLs to the 4 files (any dog breed).	(same as 2A)
3A	Which month of 2010 has had the most tweets about Demi Moore so far?	Press 'More' then 'Updates' on the left side of Google search results to see how many Tweets there are that match your keywords.
3B	Which day in July 2010 were there most tweets about George Clooney?	(same as 3A)
4A	Paste the URL of a video about *Surat Thani, Thailand* that is over 21 minutes long.	You can search videos on Google and it will automatically include results from YouTube, Vimeo, and other video sites. You can then sort the list of videos by duration, quality, etc.
4B	Paste the URL of a video about *Nagaland, India* (or people from Nagaland) that is over 50 minutes long.	(same as 4A)
5A	What is the song that contains the lyric *who are you gonna bring the bad things to*?	Putting quotes around your query will search for the exact words in the order you type them.
5B	Find a web page that has the speech that contains the phrase *go in search of the true justice*?	(same as 5A)
6A	Paste 3 URLs that include the full names of people who have the name "Lebron" ... OTHER than Lebron James.	Use the minus sign ('-') to tell Google to REMOVE any results that contain that word.
6B	Paste 3 URLs that include the full names of people who have the name "Mariah" ... OTHER than Mariah Carey.	(same as 6A)

Table 1: Each of the search tasks used. The text of the tips is also shown here, although most tips additionally had screenshots showing the UI (e.g. Figure 1). The complete tips used are available at http://bit.ly/TacticalSearchTips

3.5 Results

Figure 2 shows task completion times for the experiment and control groups for each of the 12 tasks (the box plots were generated using the R package `lattice`).

In these box plots, the black dot, bottom and top of the boxes display the median, 25% and 75% quantiles, respectively. We added black lines to connect the medians for the control and experiment groups for each task.

Comparing the task completion times for the control and experiment groups in Figure 2 shows substantially faster times for the experiment group for each task. For example, the difference in median task completion time between experiment and control is more than 2 minutes for most tasks. Even for Task 5B, which has the smallest difference between groups, the median time is improved by nearly 30 seconds.

In Tasks 1A, 1B, 3A, and 3B the control group fared particularly poorly, with roughly 75% of the participants taking the maximum allowed time (5 minutes). These 4 tasks are especially difficult without the knowledge taught by the two corresponding tactical tips.

The conclusion is that this data supports our original hypothesis—we can measure improvement in search efficiency resulting from search feature tips. Formal verification of the statistical significance of the results is presented later in this paper.

3.6 Discussion

Study participants shown tactical search tips consistently outperformed study participants who were not shown any tips for that task. The tactics present strategies and user interface features but do not suggest relevant documents, media, or answers. We believe that improvements in search performance can be achieved not only from improving retrieval algorithms but also from improving search expertise. The results of this study confirm and quantify this belief: showing searchers tactical tips at a moment just before the skill is to be used reduced search task completion time by roughly 35% for our tasks.

The substantial reduction in task completion time is worth noting. The implication is that providing users with the right tactic at the right time can improve performance dramatically. The larger challenge for IR system designers, then, is to enumerate available tactics and match them with search task behaviors.

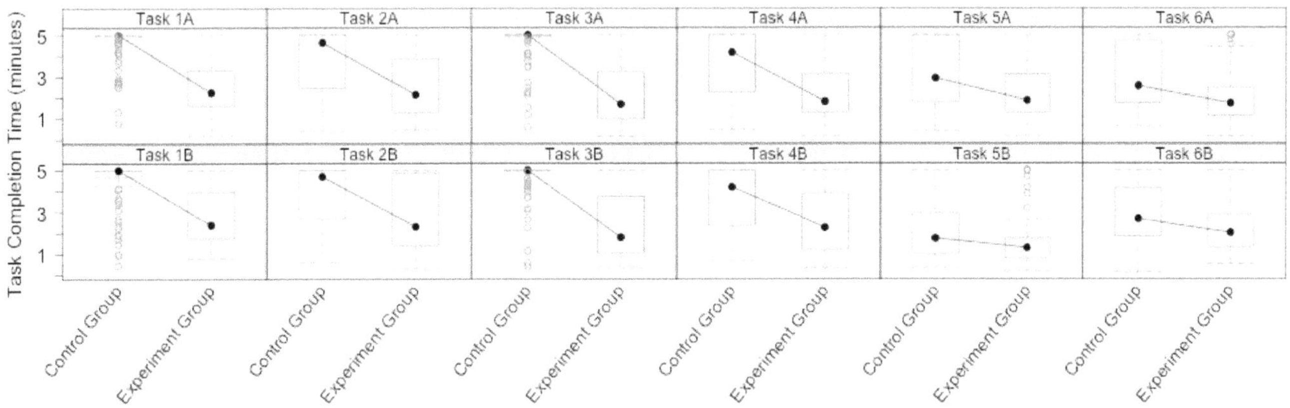

Figure 2: Results of Experiment 1. The experiment group is shown a search tip and the control group is not shown a tip. The task-completion time is substantially faster for the experiment group than the control group for all 12 tasks.

A clear question about these results is, "Are participants actually learning to use the tactic presented in the tip, or are they blindly applying it in a rote manner as cued?" To answer this question, we carried out a follow-up study designed to measure if participants were retaining knowledge of when and how to use the tactics.

4. WEEK 2 EXPERIMENT: ARE INITIAL PERFORMANCE GAINS RETAINED?

We conducted a follow-up experiment roughly one week later to determine if the performance gains shown in the first experiment are maintained. We did this by re-testing both the control and experiment groups with the question variants that they had not seen in Week 1.

4.1 Method

To assess learning effects of the tips in question, we re-assessed the participants from Week 1 using the task variant they had not already seen. In other words, a participant who did Task 6B in Week 1 would be assigned Task 6A in this Week 2 study. This ensures that no participant would see the same task twice. (We note that 146 of the 491 participants from Experiment 1 were unable to participate, which is expected in the normal course of these studies.)

Participants were all retested between 5 and 9 days after they completed the first experiment (timing variation depending on when they decided to take part in each experiment). Participants were unaware that there would be a follow-up study, and not informed that the second set of tasks was connected with the first task set in any way.

4.2 Results

Figure 3 displays box plots for the Week 2 study alongside those from Week 1. In nearly every case (Task 5B being the only exception), the performance improvement (task completion time decrease) from seeing the tip was retained: the skill the participants had learned 5 to 9 days earlier was retained even though there was no stimulus to remind the participants. In fact, the differences between the control and experiment group are almost as large as in Week 1. Thus, the data supports the notion that we can measure retention of the skills learned from the tips. The next section validates the statistical significance of this finding for each task.

In addition to this experiment effect, we can also notice in Figure 3 an interesting effect in the control group from Week 1 to Week 2: namely, participants in the control group improved their performance slightly. This can be attributed to practice and is a common finding in studies of this kind. In fact, by virtue of completing the Week 1 tasks many of the control participants may have discovered, learned or remembered the knowledge that would have been conveyed in the (unseen) tip. This improvement in the control group underscores the importance of using an experimental design that retests the control group in Week 2 in addition to the experiment group.

Task 5B is curiously different in that it is the only task for which the improvement from Week 1 did not carry over from Week 2. Looking at the data in Figure 3, we see that the control group was especially fast with respect to this task (compared to other tasks) in Week 1 and even more so in Week 2. We believe that this task was fairly simple for the participants (especially after having had some practice with the complementary Task 5A in Week 1), which may explain why the improvement relative to the experiment group did not carry over.

5. STATISTICAL MODELING AND INFERENCE

In this section we validate the statistical significance of the findings. Specifically, the data from the Week 1 study suggests that the search tips substantially improve performance for all 12 tasks. Further, the data from the Week 2 study suggest that at least some of the experiment group's advantage over the control group is retained for all tasks except 5B. These findings are valid because it is unlikely to obtain such substantial differences between the control and experiment groups simply by chance given the fairly large participant sample size and the fact that we randomly assigned users to the control and experiment groups. In this section, we formally validate this statement using inference in the context of a statistical model.

The model takes into consideration participant skill variation, the difficulty of each task, and the tip effects for the experiment group. In Week 2 the model also takes into account practice effects for each task as well as the fact that some of the tip effects may be diminished or forgotten for some tasks.

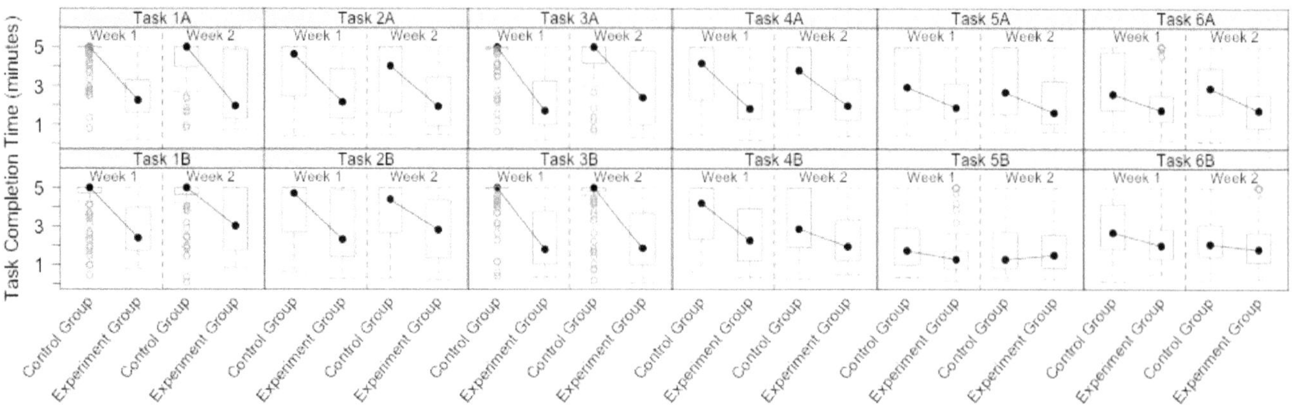

Figure 3: Results of Experiments 1 and 2 (i.e. Week 1 and Week 2). In Week 2 the participants are retested with the task variant they did not see in Week 1. Neither group is shown a search tip in Week 2. The experiment group performs faster than the control group for most tasks, ostensibly due to the memory of the tip from Week 1.

Formally, we will write our model as

$$\mathrm{Log(TCT)}_{ij} = U_i + t_j + d_j + p_j + f_j + \varepsilon_{ij}$$

where the response variable $\mathrm{Log(TCT)}_{ij}$ is the logarithm of the task completion time of user i when doing task j. The logarithm is used because the task completion times are right-skewed, as is done in analogous models employed in task completion time studies (e.g. [25]).

Because the independent variables in this model consist of both fixed effects and random effects, the type of model is known as a mixed effects model. Specifically, the U_i are random user effects that account for individual skill variation [6, 12, 15] and are included because some users are naturally faster than others. We assume that these user effects are independent, zero-mean normal random variables with a common variance. Similarly, the error terms in the model ε_{ij} are also assumed to be independent normal variables with mean zero and a common variance.

The remaining terms t_j, d_j, p_j and f_j are all fixed effects associated with each task j. The terms t_j are the tip effects for the tasks. These are the 12 effects of interest in Week 1. The terms d_j are the difficulties of the 12 tasks. These are not of interest but are essential to include in the model to account for inherent variations in task difficulty. The terms p_j are the 12 practice effects that measure any benefit from practice for each task in Week 2. These are also not of primary interest but are important to include to model the effects of individual practice. Finally, the terms f_j measure the extent to which the benefit of the tips diminishes for each of the 12 tasks for the experiment group in Week 2.

We fit the above model to the data from the 345 participants who completed tasks in both Week 1 and Week 2. We used the R package lme4's implementation of restricted maximum likelihood and the package languageR to generate confidence intervals.

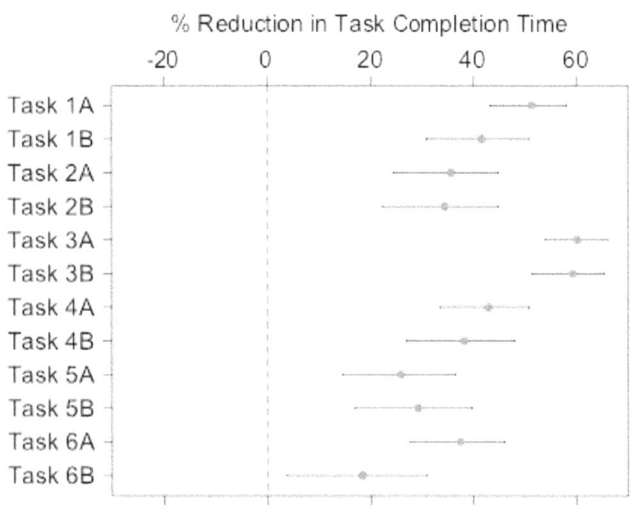

Figure 4: Analysis of Experiment 1 results. The improvement in task completion time (TCT) due to the tip was statistically significant for all 12 tasks. 95% confidence intervals are indicated.

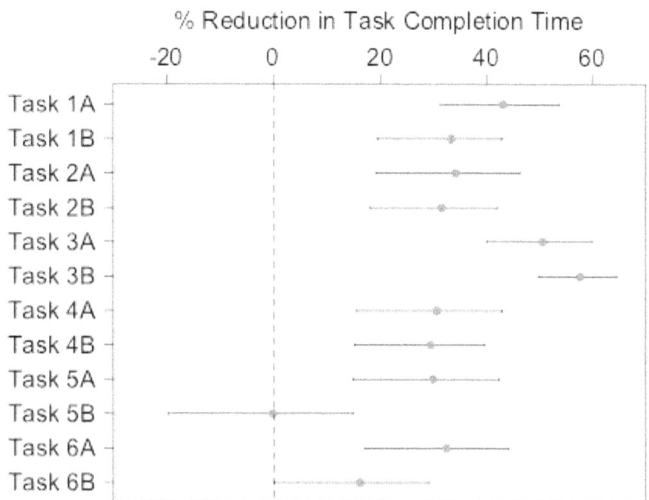

Figure 5: Analysis of Experiment 2 results. The improvement in task completion time (TCT) due to the memory of the tip was statistically significant for all 12 tasks except Task 5B. 95% confidence intervals are indicated.

In Figure 2 we saw that the (Week 1) tip effects appeared to be substantial for all 12 tasks. The model above verifies that indeed all of these effects are statistically significant. Specifically, Figure 4 displays 95% confidence intervals for the percent improvement as a result of the tip for each task. We can see that none of these confidence intervals overlap zero. Again, Tasks 1A, 1B, 3A and 3B show the largest improvement. In particular, Task 3A and 3B are both estimated to have approximately a 60% improvement in efficiency.

In Week 2 the effects of interest are the sum of t_j and f_j for the 12 tasks. In other words, it is of interest to see whether the tip effect remains for each task after the participants have had roughly a week to forget the tip. Figure 3 suggested that the tip benefit does remain except for Task 5B. Again, using the model presented above we can confirm that these effects are indeed statistically significant. This is evidenced by the fact that the 95% confidence intervals shown in Figure 5 do not overlap zero with the exception of 5B. Tasks 3A and 3B show the strongest persistent tip effect.

That the overall performance gains remain for most tasks is understandable given that the tactic in the associated tip is difficult to discover without the tip and that the tasks are fairly easy using the tactic and very difficult without it.. This was a specific design goal of the experiment. In spite of this, inspection of the tasks (shown in Table 1) shows they are feasible tasks.

6. TASK SUCCESS

Up to this point we have considered only the task completion time as our dependent variable. However, in addition to measuring task completion time we also asked the participants to self-report whether or not they felt they had successfully completed each task. In this section we present a brief analysis using the self-reported success rate as the dependent variable.

Figure 6 compares these success rates for the control and experiment groups in both Week 1 and Week 2. We see in the figure that the success rates for the experiment group are higher than those of the control group for all 12 tasks in both weeks. This result is not surprising since we expect the success rates to mirror the task completion time data by virtue of the nature of our experiment.

Figure 6 also shows that overall the experiment group achieved high absolute success rates for all tasks in both weeks, in excess of 80% in most cases. Conversely, the control group did quite poorly for certain tasks such as 1A, 1B, 3A and 3B. Recall that we noted earlier these 4 particular tasks also had the strongest experimental effects in our task completion time analysis.

In order to verify the statistical significance of the experiment versus control differences observed in Figure 6 we fit a model analogous to our previous model for task completion time. The model uses the log odds of the success probability as the response. From analysis of that model we see in both Week 1 and Week 2 all differences are statistically significant except those for Tasks 5B and 6B.

Overall, our conclusion is that the tips presented substantially improve (self-reported) success rate in addition to task completion time.

We will note that we also carried out the same analysis above but instead using an objective measure of success based on what we had predetermined to be "correct" answers for the tasks. That analysis gave even stronger results; however, we chose to present the self-reported success rates here in favor of those results because our predetermined "correct" answers are arguably biased in favor of the search tips. Participants who did not use the tips often found different but possibly correct answers by using alternative search strategies, which we had not considered. We were not able to verify the correctness of their answers in every case. Thus, the self-reported success seemed to be a more fair measure to us.

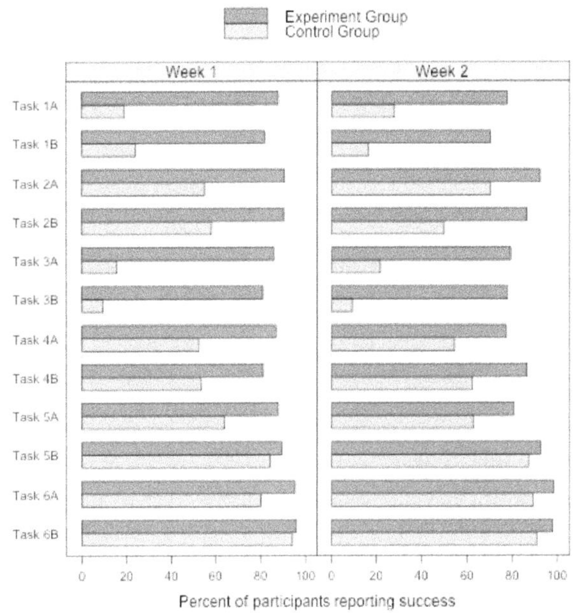

Figure 6: Percent of tasks self-reported as successfully completed. The experiment group consistently reports successful completion of the task.

7. DISCUSSION

These studies demonstrate that we can measure the efficiency gains resulting from relevant search tips, and that these gains persist and continue to be measurable over at least one week, even when the search tips are no longer shown. In the literature on IR systems, few interventions have been able to show such dramatic and sustainable gains in performance strictly by focusing on improving user performance.

A relatively large, diverse sample of users participated in the study, and it was done in an ecologically valid setting. The tasks used in this study were explicitly designed to be both feasible for common use and to show the positive effects of knowing which tactic is appropriate for which task.

We can attribute the performance gains of the experiment group to two possible causes: 1) users learned a new tactic and associated it with a type of task or 2) users were reminded of a previously-known tactic and associated it with a type of task. Both are valid reasons for why tactical suggestions can be useful.

This experiment did not explicitly test the transfer of a learned tactic to another task. Instead, the follow-up study used tasks very closely related to those in the first experiment. The results make no claim of how well users learned to generalize the tactic but rather that certain tactics can be associated with certain, narrow types of tasks.

Prior work points to task [8, 9, 10], search [6], and domain [32, 34] complexity and expertise as some of the contextual factors influencing search performance. The results of our study suggest that providing relevant search tactics may be construed as either augmenting an individual's search expertise (i.e. knowing the tactic well enough to match a task to it) or task expertise (i.e. knowing the task well enough to choose a particular known tactic for it). We propose that such tactical tips are improving upon search expertise rather than that of task or domain. Domain expertise (or topic familiarity) is not particularly relevant and task expertise is not being tested because the tasks are directed lookup tasks that do not require multiple steps or a particular strategy to solve.

The tasks used in this study were explicitly designed to draw out the importance of knowing particular tactics. The use of suggestions should likewise be highly selective in order to maintain a consistent expectation of utility in the user.

Research on improving automated assistance in IR systems tends to improve upon methods of suggesting ways of reformulating queries. The tips used in this study influence users to frame their questions in a new way or to become aware of tactics that are supported by the system and may be useful. From a systems perspective, this requires system designers to be intricately aware of what types of tasks are best-suited for the features supported. Already, search engines are attempting to 'blend' results from different corpora into the standard result set and offer entry points into those corpora (e.g. integrating a few images into a document result set with a prompt for seeing this query in image search).

It is clear that an understanding of a user's level of sophistication and search knowledge is of importance to information retrieval systems, ostensibly to offer appropriate or adaptive feedback and suggestions. For example, White, *et al.* [33] used the presence of advanced search operators in queries as a proxy for expertise. Another indicator may be the use of specific search tactics.

The differences between the control and experiment groups in self-reported successful completion points to the idea that some tactics do not merely improve efficiency, they make some queries possible. For example, participants in Task 3A and 3B who were made aware of the tactic to use the micro-blog searching feature were able to consistently answer this very feasible query while participants who remained ignorant of the tactic simply could not finish it (i.e. gave up after reaching the experiment-imposed maximum of five minutes).

Though the primary goal of IR research is to produce the document the user is seeking, recent cases have been made that move study from document retrieval into exploration of relevant corpora or perspectives on the information need [25]. This shift requires a new perspective on the purpose of automated assistance. Instead of inferring the user's information need as he or she iterates on queries, the system can help the user refine the information need itself. For example, when searching for a book to buy, the search engine could suggest a tactic that shows the locations of libraries nearby given the need to understand a topic. Once ignorant of such a possibility, the user's information need has shifted.

As noted earlier, this study used task completion time as a measure of performance rather than recall or precision. This study was conducted on the open web and the users had the freedom to formulate their own queries or browse as they liked. Our goal is to improve user expertise so we focus on measuring user performance.

The visual and interaction design of tactical tips is an interesting domain of further inquiry. The visual design of the tips used in this study was not constrained by size in any significant way. They also did not incorporate animation or interactivity in any way. The display of the tip would also differ substantially between user-triggered (e.g. [17]) and automatically displayed (as was done in the present study).

7.1 Study Limitations

The following are three major limitations in our study. As explained in [29], we used artificial tasks that were assigned to the participants, not "personal" tasks that were generated by the participants. Second, these results represent a 'best case scenario' where the tips are highly relevant to the task at hand. In practice, it is a much more challenging problem to design the actual user interface so that the tips trigger at the correct time and in the correct context. For this reason our observed improvement in efficiency can be thought of as an upper bound for what could be obtained in practice. Third, we largely ignored task accuracy as a metric for this study in favor of efficiency alone. In a sense, efficiency was a proxy for accuracy because participants were instructed to give up if they hit the five-minute limit.

7.2 Experimental Design

Both experiments presented in this paper (Week 1 and Week 2) used what might be called a simple 2 group "between-subjects" or "case/control" design. Because our treatment effect (learning the skill) is irreversible, we did not have the option of using a standard cross-over design. However, an analogue of the four group cross-over design presented in [25] would have been feasible. We chose not to use that particular design due to its complexity and because the experiment in [25] showed that design was actually slightly worse for estimating experimental effects for the individual tasks, which was the primary interest in our study.

8. CONCLUSION

This study demonstrates that providing tactical search tips, appropriately shown to searchers at the right time, can produce a substantial and measurable improvement in their performance. This gives us hope that further instruction can also have a measurable effect on overall searcher behavior, particularly when extended to strategic instruction and longer-term search behavior on more complex tasks.

9. ACKNOWLEDGEMENTS

The authors would like to thank Esther Wojcicki and Roy Pea for their discussions during the course of the research.

10. REFERENCES

1. Bates, M. J. (1979). Idea tactics. *JASIS*, 30, 280-289.
2. Bates, M. J. (1979). Information search tactics. *JASIS*, 30, 205-214.
3. Belkin, N. J., Cool, C., Head, J., Jeng, J., Kelly, D., Lin, S.-J., Lobash, L., Park, S., Savage-Knepshield, P. A., and Sikora, C. (1999). Relevance feedback versus local context analysis as term suggestion devices. In *TREC Conference: Rutgers' TREC-8 Experience track.*
4. Belkin, N.J., Muresan, G. (2004) Measuring Web search effectiveness: Rutgers at Interactive TREC. *WWW Conference workshop on Measuring Web Effectiveness.*
5. Belkin, N. J., Marchetti, P. G., Cool, C. (1993). Braque: design of an interface to support user interaction in information retrieval. *Info. Processing Mgt.*, 325-344.
6. Bhavnani, S.K. (2001). Important Cognitive Components of Domain-Specific Search Knowledge. *TREC*, 571-578.

7. Brajnik, G., Mizzaro, S., Tasso, C., Venuti, F. (2002). Strategic help in user interfaces for information retrieval. *JASIST,* 53(5), 343–358.

8. Byström, K. (2002). Information and Information Sources in Tasks of Varying Complexity. *JASIST*, 53(7): 581-591.

9. Byström, K., Jarvelin, K. (1995). Task Complexity Affects Information Seeking and Use. *Information Processing and Management*, 31(2): 191-213.

10. Capra, R., Pérez-Quiñones, M.A. (2006). Factors and Evaluation of Refinding Behaviors *SIGIR* Workshop on Personal Information Management, 16-19.

11. Fernández-Luna, J. M., Huete, J. F., Macfarlane, A., Efthimiadis, E. N. (2009). Teaching and learning in information retrieval. *Information Retrieval*. 12, 2 (Apr. 2009), 201-226.

12. Grimes, C., Tang, D., Russell, D. M. (2007). Query logs alone are not enough. *WWW Workshop on Query Log Analysis: Social and Technological Changes*.

13. Gwizdka, J. (2008). Revisiting search task difficulty: Behavioral and individual difference measures. *ASIST*.

14. Hölscher, C. Strube, G. (2000). Web search behavior of Internet experts and newbies. *WWW*, 337-346.

15. Hsieh-Yee, I. (1993). Effects of search experience and subject knowledge on online search behavior: Measuring the search tactics of novice and experienced searchers. *JASIST* 44(3), 161–174

16. Jansen, B. J. (2006). Using temporal patterns of interactions to design effective automated searching assistance systems. *Comm. of the ACM*. 49(4), 72-74.

17. Jansen, B. J. McNeese, M. D. (2005). Evaluating the effectiveness of and patterns of interactions with automated assistance in IR systems. *JASIST*. 56(14), 1480-1503.

18. Jones, R., Rey, B., Madani, O. (2006). Generating query substitutions. *WWW*, 387-396.

19. Kelly, D., Cushing, A., Dostert, M., Niu, X., Gyllstrom, K. (2010). Effects of popularity and quality on the usage of query suggestions during information search. *CHI* 45-54.

20. Kelly, D., Gyllstrom, K., Bailey, E. W. (2009). A comparison of term and query suggestion features for interactive searching. *SIGIR*, 371-378.

21. Kriewel, S. Fuhr, N. (2007). Adaptive search suggestions for digital libraries. *ICADL*, 220-229.

22. Lau, T., Horvitz, E. (1999). Patterns of Search: Analyzing and Modeling Web Query Refinement. *UMAP*, 119-128.

23. Lazonder, A. W. (2003). Principles for Designing Web Searching Instruction. *Education and Information Technologies* 8, 2 (Jun. 2003), 179-193.

24. Liu, Y. and Belkin, N. J. (2008). Query reformulation, search performance, and term suggestion devices in question-answering tasks. *IIiX*, 21-26.

25. Ma, L., Mease, D., Russell, D. M. (2011). A Four Group Cross-Over Design for Measuring Irreversible Treatments on Web Search Tasks. *HICSS*.

26. Marchionini, G. (2006). Exploratory search: From finding to understanding. *Communications of the ACM*, 49(4), p. 41-46.

27. Mizzaro, S. (1996). Intelligent interfaces for information retrieval: A review. Technical Report UDMI/18/96/RR, Department of Mathematics and Computer Science, University of Udine.

28. Moraveji, N. (2010). User interface designs to support the social transfer of web search expertise. *SIGIR*, 915-915.

29. Russell, D., Grimes, C. (2007). Assigned tasks are not the same as self-chosen Web search tasks. *HICSS*.

30. Teevan, J., Alvarado, C., Ackerman. M., Karger, D. (2004). The Perfect Search Engine Is Not Enough: A Study of Orienteering Behavior in Directed Search. *CHI*.

31. Twidale, M. B., Nichols, D. M., Smith, G., and Trevor, J. (1995). Supporting collaborative learning during information searching. *CSCL*, 367-370.

32. White, R., Dumais, S., Teevan, J. (2009). Characterizing the Influence of Domain Expertise on Web Search Behavior. *WSDM*, 132-141

33. White, R., Morris, D. (2007). Investigating the Querying and Browsing Behavior of Advanced Search Engine Users. *SIGIR*, 255-262

34. Wildemuth, B. M. (2004). The effects of domain knowledge on search tactic formulation. *JASIST*, 246-258.

35. Xie, I., & Cool, C. (2009). Understanding help-seeking within the context of searching digital libraries. *JASIST*, 477-494.

ViewSer: Enabling Large-Scale Remote User Studies of Web Search Examination and Interaction

Dmitry Lagun
Mathematics & Computer Science Dept.
Emory University
dlagun@emory.edu

Eugene Agichtein
Mathematics & Computer Science Dept.
Emory University
eugene@mathcs.emory.edu

ABSTRACT

Web search behaviour studies, including eye-tracking studies of search result examination, have resulted in numerous insights to improve search result quality and presentation. Yet, eye tracking studies have been restricted in scale, due to the expense and the effort required. Furthermore, as the reach of the Web expands, it becomes increasingly important to understand how searchers around the world see and interact with the search results. To address both challenges, we introduce ViewSer, a novel methodology for performing web search examination studies remotely, at scale, and without requiring eye-tracking equipment. ViewSer operates by automatically modifying the appearance of a search engine result page, to clearly show one search result at a time as if through a "viewport", while partially blurring the rest and allowing the participant to move the viewport naturally with a computer mouse or trackpad. Remarkably, the resulting result viewing and clickthrough patterns agree closely with unrestricted viewing of results, as measured by eye-tracking equipment, validated by a study with over 100 participants. We also explore applications of ViewSer to practical search tasks, such as analyzing the search result summary (snippet) attractiveness, result re-ranking, and evaluating snippet quality. These experiments could have only be done previously by tracking the eye movements for a small number of subjects in the lab. In contrast, our study was performed with over 100 participants, allowing us to reproduce and extend previous findings, establishing ViewSer as a valuable tool for large-scale search behavior experiments.

Categories and Subject Descriptors

H.4 [**Informational storage and retrieval**]: evaluation, search process.

General Terms

Design, Experimentation, Human Factors.

Keywords

Web search behavior; web search evaluation, remote user studies.

1. INTRODUCTION

Web search engines serve billions of searches a day, providing information for a diverse range of information needs. Understanding and analyzing how users interact with search has emerged as an important area of research. In particular, eye tracking has proven to be an invaluable technology for studying search behavior, providing important insights into search interface design. Yet, despite these advantages, eye tracking studies remain relatively small scale, as they require in-lab participation and supervision, and thus are "too expensive" for day-to-day search evaluation.

This paper proposes a new methodology for *performing large-scale behavioral studies of web search*, while maintaining many of the benefits of the controlled in-lab eye tracking studies of search. For this, we present a specially designed search engine result interface, which we call ViewSer (for Viewport Examination of Web Search Results). ViewSer aims to induce result examination behavior similar to unrestricted viewing, yet allowing us to track precisely the viewed portion of the search result page. For this, ViewSer blurs most of the search result page, except for the search result currently examined (pointed to) by the cursor, which creates a clear "viewport", illustrated in Figure 1. This viewport follows the cursor position, allowing a subject to examine the search results, while the viewport position is tracked.

The kinds of web search evaluation for which ViewSer is designed, focus on evaluating search results individually. Examples of such tasks are: measuring the rates of result examination and estimating snippet attractiveness – valuable for accurate clickthrough interpretation [24] and for learning to rank from click data; and evaluating snippets (result abstracts), e.g., by using the proportion of views to clicks on a result [25], as we demonstrate in this paper. Indeed, in this paper we explore multiple practical applications of ViewSer. As a first task, we show that ViewSer can serve as an effective method to measure and estimate snippet attractiveness - indicating that a snippet tends to "attract" clicks. This in turn can help better interpret clickthrough data for tasks such as learning to rank. Another crucial task is generating and evaluating search result snippets. In this paper we explore an application of ViewSer to detect bad (misleading) snippets which can serve as a valuable feedback to snippet generation algorithms. The contributions of this paper include:

- A novel web search evaluation methodology that could enable large-scale studies of search examination behavior (Section 3).

- A validation of our ViewSer prototype, showing that the search result viewing exhibited by remote participants using our ViewSer interface closely approximates unconstrained search examination (Section 4).
- A demonstration of effectively applying ViewSer to crucial web search tasks of learning to estimate snippet attractiveness, which in turn can be used for result ranking, and for automatically detecting bad (misleading) snippets (Section 5).

This work is just a first step in developing and applying the ideas introduced in this paper. As we continue to refine the ViewSer technology, other applications and evaluation methods will be explored. In summary, we believe that the ViewSer technology will form a crucial component in the future of web search evaluation.

2. RELATED WORK

Our goal is to enable large-scale, remote behavioral studies of web search, focusing on search result examination, normally done with eye-tracking equipment. Thus, our work spans the areas of user studies in IR, search behavior modelling, crowd-sourced IR evaluation, and eye tracking-based evaluation of search.

Crowdsourcing methodology has emerged as a viable way to cheaply obtain human input for a wide range of tasks, including document relevance assessments. One of the most popular web sites providing a marketplace for hiring internet workers is Amazon Mechanical Turk (AMT). Previous efforts studied various aspects of document relevance rating crowd-sourced via AMT, including task completion time, worker's responsiveness, locality and ratings quality in terms of accuracy and inter-rater agreement [2, 21, 6, 20]. Kely et. al. reports an important study of searcher behavior for in-lab and remote participants [19]. In contrast to these studies, our focus is searcher behavior - specifically, search result examination. Somewhat related to our approach, [11] describes crowdsourcing user studies of graphical perception conducted via AMT. However, we are not aware of any published user study of web search examination behavior conducted for hundreds of users in crowdsourcing framework.

Our work is inspired by the emergence of the large-scale, passive logging and analysis of search behavior as an alternative to in-lab studies: the log data has been used for search evaluation [2], for improving search engine ranking [1, 15] among other tasks. However, such log-based studies are a blunt instrument - they are more appropriate for overall search performance evaluation, whereas our proposed methodology enables precise tracking and characterization of searcher behavior, at the level of detail previously only possible with eye tracking studies of search.

To enable this vision, our implementation of ViewSer builds upon the previous work on restricted focus viewing (RFV) described in references [4, 13, 3], where the authors explored the effect of restricted viewing in usability studies of user interfaces. However, our work substantially differs from prior applications of this idea, as our work is, as far as we know, the first to apply this idea to web search. Our approach is also more general, scalable, and efficient compared to previous work: our implementation is based on the Scalable Vector Graphics (SVG) technology natively supported by the Firefox browser, which in turn enables ViewSer to render

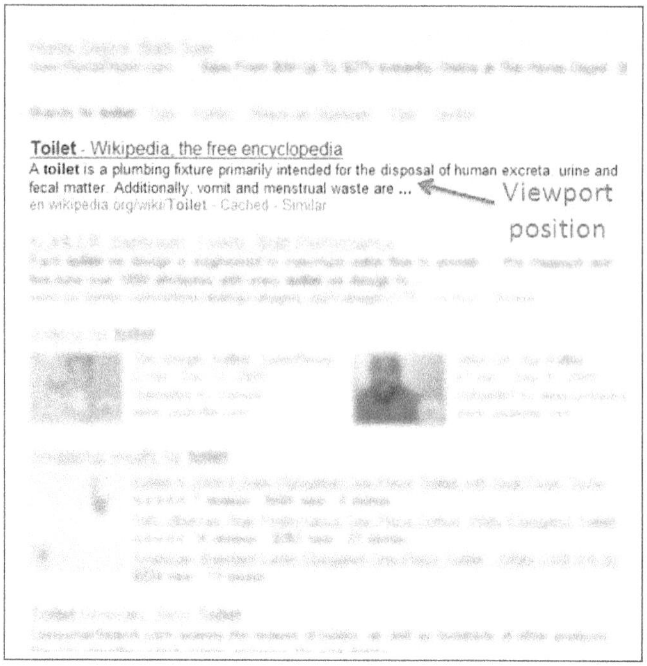

Figure 1: An example of the ViewSer interface displaying a blurred search engine result page (SERP) for the query "toilet", with the viewport revealing the first result.

and blur rich XHTML content such as text formatted with cascade style-sheets, images and videos, while [4] describes an application to image examination.

As we will show, ViewSer has many potential applications to web search. In particular, estimating the "attractiveness" (with respect to clickthrough) of search result summaries, or snippets can improve click interpretation, which is in turn helpful for more accurate ranking models. Previously, Clarke et al. [7] found statistically significant changes in clickthrough patterns due to caption features. The more recent work of [25] confirmed some of the findings of [7] in a different experiment using the concept of "fair pairs". Both of these approaches used methodology based on changes in clickthrough, whereas our work directly measures the searcher examination of the captions, and subsequent behavior. Previous work on snippet evaluation and generation [17] followed a more classical approach, based on explicit labels for snippet quality or language models.

As another application, snippet attractiveness could be useful to improve learning to rank (LTR) from click data, by adjusting the clickthrough counts according to snippet attractiveness. LTR has demonstrated promising results in ranking large scale document collections based on both relevance judgements as well as implicit user feedback, relevant algorithms include [9, 16]. In fact, result attractiveness was already incorporated in click models, though was modelled as an unobservable (hidden) variable [5]. In references [26], snippet presentations features were used as part of user features to better model result examination. Our work is also related to [1], where the authors used features such as query terms, and the browsing and clickthrough statistics, to improve result ranking. In summary, previous models have studied result attractiveness based on changes in click-

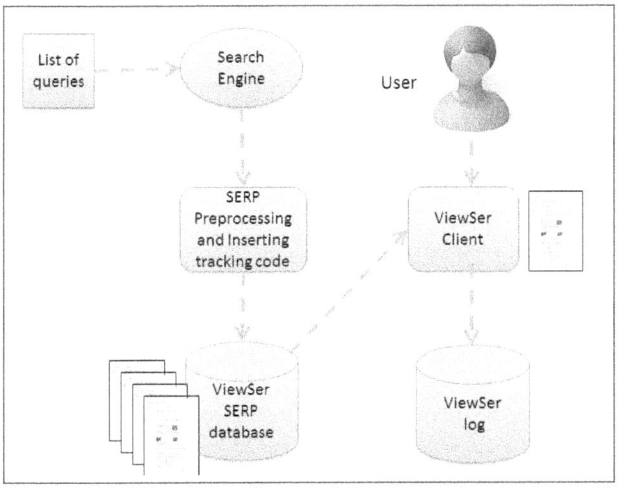

Figure 2: The ViewSer architecture for large-scale search result examination studies.

through patterns or statistical inference based on user clicks. The work described in this paper differs from prior work in that we present and validate a novel methodology for directly measuring result examination. In turn, this enables training models to reproduce and extend previous findings quickly, effectively, and at scale.

3. VIEWSER SYSTEM IMPLEMENTATION

The ViewSer architecture is outlined in Figure 2. First, ViewSer retrieves and pre-processes the search engine result pages (SERPs), by inserting code into each SERP to modify the appearance and to enable tracking of the user interaction events. These SERP pages, and the landing pages of the results (the actual documents) are cached in a database for the subsequent studies, enabling fully reproducible and repeatable experiments. A participant opens one of the pre-processed SERPs, which causes her browser to blur all but one results on the SERP. As the participant moves the viewport around to view the rest of the results, the precise position of the viewport and other searcher interactions are sent to the server and logged for future analysis. The rest of this section describes these steps in more detail.

SERP pre-processing: to emulate the "viewport" of the ViewSer interface, we automatically modified the SERPs by inserting the JavaScript/Scalable Vector Graphics (SVG) code, which is directly supported by the Firefox browser, without requiring any additional plugins or other downloads. The code leaves clear one result region at a time (identified using the HTML DOM tags), and blurs the rest of the SERP. Specifically, the SVG specification is used to describe the blurring effect and incorporate it into regular cascade style sheet class, which can be added to any HTML DOM element in a web page.

More concretely, the fragment of the code in Figure 3, *make-blur*, defines a Gaussian filter for blurring a search result, and can be referenced in a style specification of any HTML element to blur the element's content accordingly. This specific filter is a Gaussian filter with the σ parameter set to 2.5. The second operation performed by make-blur is gray-scaling the element appearance. Conveniently, each search result on a SERP is described within list element

```
<svg:svg>
<svg:filter id="make-blur">
<svg:feGaussianBlur stdDeviation="2.5"/>
<svg:feColorMatrix values="
0.3333  0.3333  0.3333  0       0
0.3333  0.3333  0.3333  0       0
0.3333  0.3333  0.3333  0       0
0       0       0       1       0"/>
```

Figure 3: A fragment of the Support Vector Graphics (SVG) code used by ViewSer to blur HTML elements such as search results.

<LI>. Therefore we modified the style of *<LI>* elements on the SERP, thus blurring all of the results.

ViewSer front-end : Initially, all out-of-focus elements are blurred and discolored to grayscale in order to imitate peripheral vision. Then, when a viewport moves over an element (e.g., a search result), the element's style can be changed back to the original appearance by detecting the onMouseOut event. The SVG-based implementation makes ViewSer scalable for crowdsourcing, as it does not require any additional installation, and responsive by exploiting the optimized native browser support, while allowing precise tracking of the viewing of any HTML element (such as the result position on SERP). These are significant advantages over previously proposed implementations using browser plugins or Java applications [4, 13]. A limitation of ViewSer is that only the complete HTML DOM elements can be revealed, not allowing for partial or gradual occlusion.

Logging the Searcher behavior: To track the viewport movement and other interface events, we injected additional JavaScript code into the SERP shown on the client's machine. This code logged window events such as clicking, scrolling, mouse moves, and finally the hovering events over a search result lasting 200ms or longer (corresponding to the typical duration of a eye movement fixations [23]). These events were buffered and periodically sent to the server via asynchronous HTTP requests for subsequent processing. The ViewSer code and tracking infrastructure is available on the project web-page [1].

4. VALIDATING VIEWSER

To validate the ViewSer technology we performed two main user studies: first, to collect "ground truth" eye tracking data; and second, to collect examination data using our ViewSer interface to compare to the eye-tracking behavior.

4.1 Search Tasks and Study Procedure

We used 25 benchmark search tasks from the WEB Track of the TREC 2009 competition. The goal for each task (the task description) was provided to the participants. For example, the goal of the query "toilet" was stated as: "Find information on buying, installing, and repairing toilets". For each task, the query keywords were submitted to the Google search engine, and the Search Engine Result Pages (SERPs), as well as all the result documents linked from each SERP, were cached. The original SERP layout was not modified (as shown on Figure 1), recreating a realistic search experience for the participants. The participants started with a

[1] http://ir.mathcs.emory.edu/intent/

Query	*Description*
`toilet`	Find information on buying, installing, and repairing toilets.
`mitchell college`	Find information about Mitchell College in New London, CT, such as a prospective student might find useful.
`cheap internet`	I'm looking for cheap (i.e. low-cost) internet service.
`espn sports`	I'm looking for various sports scores and information from the ESPN Sports site.
`euclid`	Find information on the Greek mathematician Euclid.

Table 1: Example queries and descriptions provided to the subjects.

provided SERP for each query, and were instructed to find the needed information with least effort that is, to click only on results that appear relevant. After a subject clicked on a result to examine the document and went back to the SERP, she was asked to rate the document relevance. To be considered a valid response, we required that participants attempt all search tasks, and click and rate at least one result for each task.

4.2 Participants

Eye-tracking group: for this "ground truth" group, ten participants (6 female, 4 male, ages 23.0±1.5, all graduate and undergraduate students and fluent English speakers) were recruited. The eye tracking was performed using a Tobii x60 eye tracker paired with a 17" LCD monitor set to 1280x1024 resolution. The subject's gaze position was sampled at 60 Hz with accuracy of 0.5 degrees. For the two remote studies, participants were recruited through the Amazon Mechanical Turk website, using the standard mechanism of listing our study as an available Human Intelligence Task (HIT).

ViewSer group: The workers were required to use the popular Firefox web browser. They were instructed to view the search results using the ViewSer interface as described above. 203 MTurk workers attempted the remote study. As a first step, the data obtained from MTurk subjects were automatically filtered to discard careless or automated (robot) workers. While the instructions required providing relevance judgements, some workers did not provide relevance judgements, and/or spent less than 1 minute on the whole HIT of 25 queries (presumably, to obtain the payment and move on). After these cases were automatically filtered out, we had valid data from 106 workers (48%).

Unconstrained viewing group: to serve as "control" subjects, we recruited additional 25 MTurk workers. The task was identical to the ViewSer group, except that we removed blurring, allowing for unconstrained viewing of the SERP.

4.3 Results

Our goal was to investigate whether ViewSer indeed induces similar viewing and clickthrough behavior remotely in MTurk subjects, as in the unconstrained viewing setting for the in-lab eye tracking subjects and remote participants. Before presenting quantitative results and analysis, Figure 4 shows an example heatmap of the relative time spent viewing the SERP for the query "toilet", aggregated for all subjects in Eye-tracking group. The first vertical colorbar (a) projects the relative viewing time onto the vertical axis of the SERP for the Eye-tracking group, and the second colorbar (b) for the ViewSer group, showing a noticeable similarity between the most intensely scrutinized search results.

Overall, the ViewSer group required 1 minute and 37 seconds on average (SD=70 seconds) for each search task, compared to 55 seconds on average (SD=20 seconds) for the Eye-tracking group. While the subjects in the ViewSer group took more time for each task, this is to be expected due to more time required to move a mouse pointer. Interestingly, the resulting search behavior patterns of the two groups are remarkably similar otherwise.

ViewSer SERP Examination and Clickthrough: Figure 5 reports the viewing and clickthrough rates for each result rank for the ViewSer group. Each data point indicates the fraction of the result views at each rank position, and the corresponding fraction of the clicks landing on that position, for all searches and participants. The first 3 results were viewed for 93%, 87% , and 78% of the tune, respectively, dropping to 27% for the 10th result. The clickthrough values are correlated with the viewing, with the exception of the results in the last (10th) position, which is slightly more likely to be clicked than the 9th result. These viewing and clickthrough patterns correspond well to the previous studies of unconstrained search result examination behavior [22, 12].

Comparative Analysis of ViewSer vs. Eye-Tracking: Figures 6(a) and 6(b) report the relative viewing times and clickthrough rates for the Eye-Tracking and ViewSer groups, respectively. The values in Figure 6(a) were computed for each subject and query (that is, the viewing time for a particular abstract by a subject was divided by the total viewing time of the corresponding SERP) for an individual query, and then averaged across all queries. The relative viewing time is important, as the longer a searcher's gaze stays on a particular area, more information is processed, and therefore this area receives more attention. Thus, comparing the relative amount of time (attention) spent on examining results through the ViewSer interface, vs. that of the Eye-Tracking group, quantifies the similarity of the viewing behavior of the two groups. Interestingly, ViewSer participants spent more time viewing first results is probably because of higher speed of eye movements compared to hand (mouse) movement, which may increase the likelihood of skipping over the results when viewing the page unconstrained (eye tracking group) compared to requiring to move the mouse to reveal the next result (ViewSer group).

Figure 6(b) reports the relative clickthrough rates for eye tracking and ViewSer participant groups. Each data point corresponds to the percent of all clicks for a query, landing on the corresponding result rank; these values are then averaged across all queries. In other words, the reported clickthrough rates are normalized for each query separately, and then averaged across all queries. We found that ViewSer group exhibits lower clickthrough rates on top results. We hypothesize that this is likely due to ViewSer interface encouraging more careful examination of the results in the top

Figure 4: An example attention heatmap showing the relative viewing time over a SERP for the query „toilet" (Eye-tracking group), and the corresponding colorbar, showing the heatmap density projected onto the vertical axis (a). Overlaid as (b) is the colorbar for the viewing time for the same SERP but for the ViewSer group. This figure illustrates the similar distribution of attention between eye-tracking (a) and ViewSer (b).

positions, resulting in lower rates of "indiscriminate" clicking frequently observed for top-ranked results [1].

Comparative Analysis of Viewing and Clickthrough for Individual Queries: More detailed analysis of the Spearman correlation of viewing and clickthrough behavior for the ViewSer and Eye-Tracking groups for *individual queries* is reported in Figures 7(a) and 7(b), respectively. For the vast majority of queries (over 80%), the correlation of the viewing and clickthrough behavior of the ViewSer and Eye-Tracking groups is over 0.8 and is never below 0.6, indicating that ViewSer provides a close approximation of eye tracking for over 80% of queries, and a moderate approximation for the remainder. To gain additional intuition of the relationship between Eye-tracking and ViewSer behavior for individual queries, we plot the relative viewing time measured using Eye tracking (Y axis) and ViewSer (X axis) for each result for all queries (Figure 8). The color shading indicates the results rank position, where the red color corresponds to rank 1, and the blue color to rank 10. The result viewing times, as measured by the two methods, correlate strongly (r = 0.74). Intuitively, results with higher ranks cluster in the top right quarter as both groups spend more time viewing higher-ranked results, as expected.

Further Analysis: ViewSer vs. Unconstrained Browsing: to validate ViewSer methodology further, namely, to determine whether ViewSer participants examine the SERP differently due to restricting of their peripheral vision, we performed a follow-up study with additional 25 MTurk workers. This final group enjoyed Unconstrained viewing of the SERP, without blurring of out-of-focus results. The clickthrough rates of this group are reported in Figure 9, together with the corresponding ViewSer clickthrough rates. Remarkably, the clickthrough behavior of these groups is similar, with Spearman correlation r = 0.81.

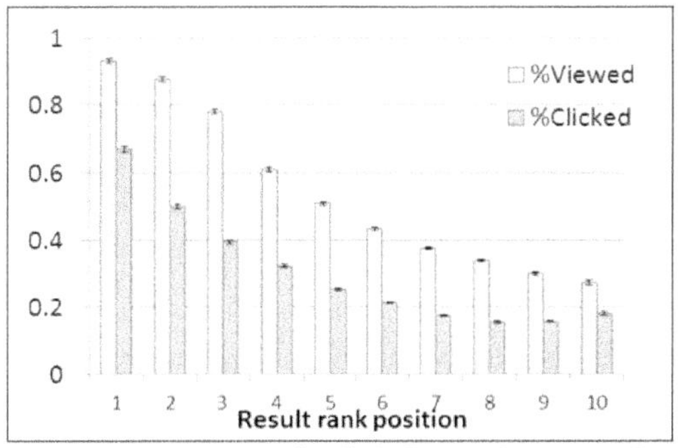

Figure 5: Viewing and clickthrough rates for each rank, aggregated for all queries and participants (ViewSer group).

5. APPLICATIONS TO SEARCH TASKS

This section describes three practical applications of the ViewSer technology to web search. First, Section 5.1 describes collection of relevance rating used in our experiments for this section. Then, we describe how ViewSer could be used to analyze snippet attractiveness (Section 5.2), to improve result ranking (Section 5.3), and to detect misleading snippets (Section 5.4).

5.1 Relevance ratings collection

To validate our findings on a bigger dataset, we collected SERP examination data for an additional 50 queries taken from the HARD track of TREC 2005, resulting in a dataset of 75 queries. Separately from the ViewSer study, we collected comprehensive relevance judgments for all of the results on the first page of results, for all queries in the WEB Track and the HARD Track. The Mechanical Turk workers (MTurk) were recruited to perform the relevance labeling as described above.

To control worker accuracy in ViewSer group we obtained relevance ratings for documents of each query in our collection. Each MTurk HIT was to assess organic (non-sponsored) results for one query. Following the recommendation of [20], the authors labeled 10% of documents as a validation set in order to estimate the worker accuracy and verify the quality of their work. On average, results for each query were rated by 6 workers. Inter-rater agreement, computed with Fleiss Kappa was 0.39, which correspond to fair/moderate agreement. We conjecture that this level of agreement is caused by the difficulty of the tasks and the informational nature of the queries. These ratings were used to compute the worker's accuracy on validation set and to filter workers with low accuracy as unreliable. For the WEB track, 17 of

Table 2: A sample of the snippet features used for estimating snippet attractiveness.

Feature	*Description*
Title (21 features)	
titleQueryTerms	Number of bolded (matched) query terms appeared in title
titleStartsWithQuery	Title starts with phrase match to query
titleQueryMatch	Number of query terms matched by title
titleFirstCapitalLetter	Number of terms with first letter capitalized
titleCapitalizedTerms	Number of capitalized terms in title
titleLengthToQueryLength	Ratio of title length in to query length words
titleHasURL	Equals 1 if title contains URL
titleNonPunctuation	Number of punctuation marks in title
Summary (17 features)	
sumaryPunctuation	Number of punctuation marks in summary
homeInSummary	Feature equals to one if summary contains word home
mapInSummary	Feature equals to one if summary contains map
summarySentanceFragments	Number of sentence fragments delimited by triple dot in the text summary
summaryLinks	Number of links in summary
URL (10 features)	
urlQuery	URL has form www.query.com where the query matches exactly with spaces removed
urlQueryTerms	Number of times query terms matched URL
urlCharacterLength	Length of URL in characters
urlSlashes	Number of slashes (i.e. subdomains) in URL

106 workers were filtered out, and for the HARD track 101 out of 263.

5.2 Application 1: Snippet Attractiveness

In this section we present one possible usage of data collected with ViewSer to analyze snippet attractiveness. The importance of snippet attractiveness as a contributing factor of clickthrough patterns has been explored by a number of researchers [7, 8, 25]. Our work has the advantage that we can directly measure the ratio of the times a snippet was examined to the number of times it was clicked, which call the *COV* ratio. In other words, *COV* is defined as probability of clicking on result given that result was examined. We hypothesize that the *COV* ratio is, in fact, a measure of snippet attractiveness that is independent of the rank position.

Experimental Setup: As a first step, we validate our hypothesis that *COV* is not dependent on the rank position, and in fact can be used as an un-biased estimate of snippet attractiveness. To this end, we calculate Pearson correlation coefficient between the result rank position and number of times the result was examined, clicked, and ratio of these counts. Here we report our comparative analysis of the (*COV*) metric based on data from Eye-tracking and ViewSer groups. We also report Pearson correlation between the *COV* ratio and textual features of the snippets.

As [7, 25] indicate, there exists a strong position bias in the way results are viewed on the SERP - searchers browse the list of results from the top of the page to the bottom, which confirms previous findings [22], and more recently [12]. Such bias puts major obstacles of using click or result viewing time [12] feedback directly in search engine optimization. Different ways of eliminating of the presentation bias in clicks have been studied in [7, 25] as we highlight earlier in the text. In other words, application of additional techniques is required in order to extract useful signals from click data. It is reasonable to expect similar problems with viewing time measured using eye tracking or approximated with mouse hovering [10, 12]. However, our *COV* metric does not correlate with the result rank: the correlation between result rank and COV is 0.05 for the Eye-tracking group and 0.11 for the ViewSer group. This is a remarkable result, indicating that the *COV* ratio does not appear to be affected by result position bias.

Table 3: Snippet feature importance ranked by correlation to attractiveness.

Correlation	*Feature*
0.2009	*titleStartsWithQuery*
0.1195	*summarySentanceFragments*
0.1169	*urlQuery*
0.1118	*titleQueryMatch*
0.1080	*sumaryPunctuation*
0.1060	*homeInSummary*
0.1030	*mapInSummary*

We validated the *COV* ratio measured with ViewSer on our eye tracking data. Figure 10 shows the *COV* ratio broken down by result position. On average we have observed slightly higher *COV* values in ViewSer data in comparison to Eye-tracking. Overall, Pearson correlation coefficient between Eye-tracking and ViewSer groups computed for each individual result was 0.64, which indicates substantial correlation.

In order to understand how *COV* relates to the previous work on estimation of result attractiveness [7, 25], we analyzed the correlation between *COV* and the textual features of the snippets. Table 2 shows example features that we considered. While many of the features used have already been investigated in prior work, we have extended the feature list with features capturing the rich structure of the snippets. For example, the feature *summaryLinks* indicates whether a snippet has additional embedded hyperlinks to

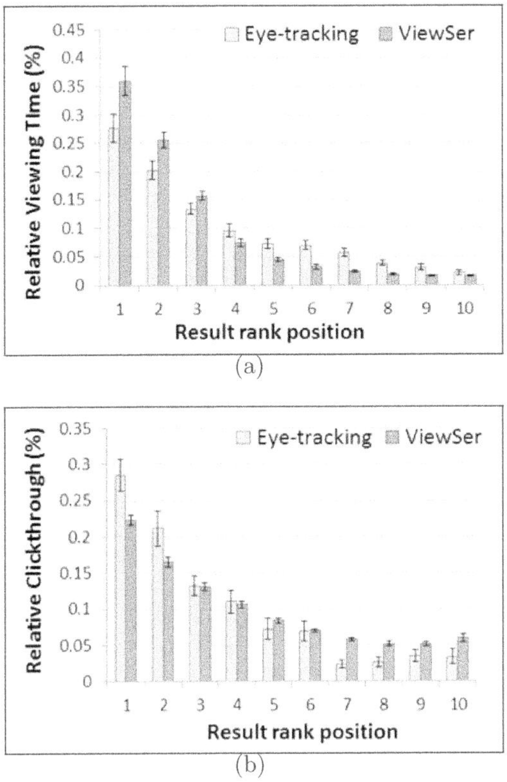

Figure 6: Viewing time (a) and clickthrough rate (b) comparison for the ViewSer and the Eye-Tracking groups, aggregated across all queries and subjects.

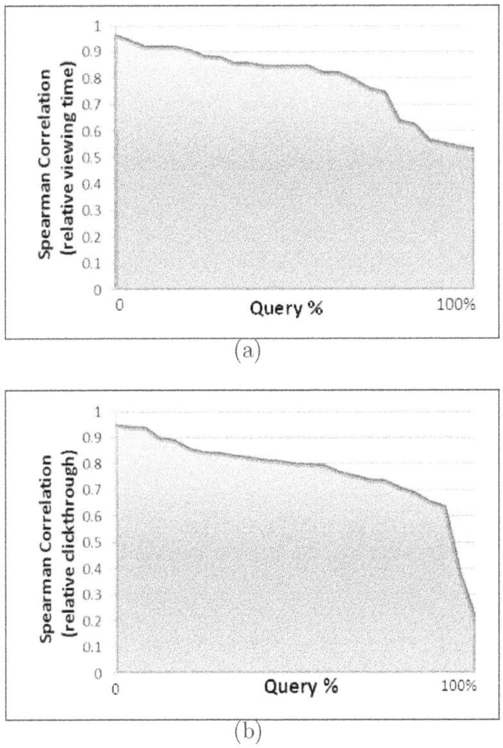

Figure 7: Spearman correlation of the relative viewing time (a) and clickthrough rates (b) for individual queries, for the Eye-tracking and ViewSer groups. The queries are sorted by the correlation coefficient. (mean viewing correlation: 0.79, mean clickthrough correlation: 0.76).

within-site navigation. Another example feature capturing complex snippets is *mapInSummary*, indicating whether a result contains a map with local search results. These features might be useful in predicting result attractiveness, as they can change searcher's SERP examination behavior.

The Table 3 reports the correlation between the *COV* ratio and text features of the snippet. The feature *titleStartWithQuery* has the highest correlation of 0.2. Features *titleStartWithQuery, urlQuery, titleQueryMatch,* and *homeInSummary* have higher correlation with *COV* than other features, which confirms previous findings in references [7, 25].

As we show in the next subsection, using attractiveness as an additional feature can be helpful for important and practical web search tasks.

5.3 Application 2: Result re-ranking

Learning to rank has become a very popular approach to achieve better search results ranking. In this section we investigate whether attractiveness can be used as a feature in learning to rank framework to improve original ranking. Unfortunately, the *COV* statistic as an additional feature measured directly, based on user study, would not be practical for large scale LTR experiments, since it would require collecting viewing data for each individual result. Therefore, we build a regression model to predict result attractiveness based on the textual snippet features. For this purpose we built a regression model predicting *COV* ratio from textual features described in Section 5.2. Thus, we used two additional features for re-ranking: ***COV*** (Click over Views ratio) and ***A***(estimated attractiveness) i.e., the estimated value of *COV* based on textual features.

Experimental Setup: We used the same query and document dataset as described in Section 5.1, providing labeled relevance data for 75 queries and 650 documents. We used *SVM-rank* [16] as the LTR method of choice. To estimate result attractiveness, we used the Gaussian Process regression model with radial basis function kernel. The correlation of the estimated and true COV values was 0.6 (3 fold cross-validation). Improving the estimation of snippet attractiveness will be part of our future work.

Results: Table 4 reports the NDCG [14] averaged across 3 folds for the baseline ranking system (Google) as well as for the re-ranking method, using directly measured *COV* and the the estimated attractiveness (A). The average NDCG of the original ranking was 0.8408. Our first experiment was to train a ranker based on the document position feature and the *COV* ratio, which yielded a significant improvement of 6% over the baseline. This substantial ranking improvement was surprising, given that the search engine was already highly optimized. Following the recommendation of [18], we performed significance test between the original ranking and our system, showing significance at $p < 0.05$. Once attractiveness (A) model was trained on the training data (2 folds) we use it to compute the attractiveness feature for the test fold. As reported in Table 4, the re-ranking performance based on the estimated value of snippet attractive-

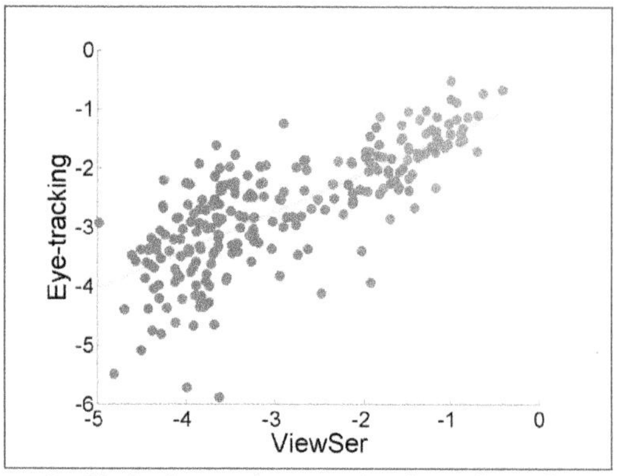

Figure 8: Relative snippet viewing time for top 10 organic results, for Eye-tracking vs. ViewSer (both on logarithmic scale). The color indicates the rank position of the results i.e., the red color corresponds to rank 1, and the blue color corresponds to rank 10. (Pearson $r = 0.74$.)

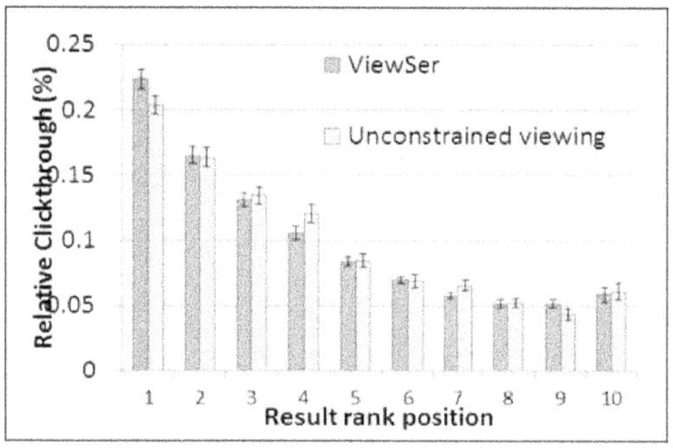

Figure 9: Clickthrough rates for ViewSer and Unconstrained viewing groups (Spearman rank correlation $r = 0.81$).

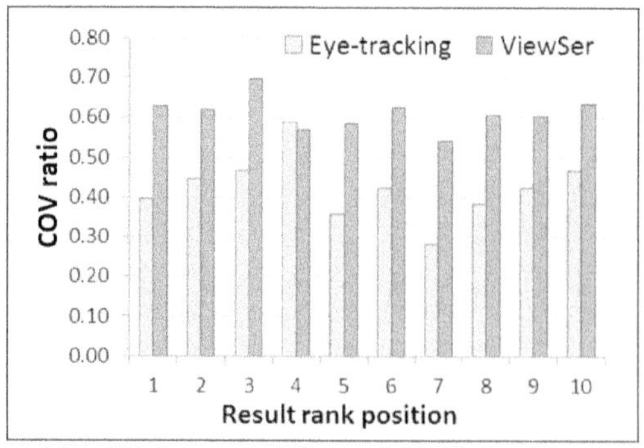

Figure 10: Clicks over Views (*COV*) for Eye-tracking and ViewSer groups, by rank position.

Table 4: Ranking system comparison. P - rank position, *COV* - Clicks over Views, C - clicks, *A* - estimated attractiveness. * indicates significance at $p < 0.05$, ** indicates significance at $p < 0.01$.

Features	NDCG
Baseline (P)	0.8408(−)
P + *COV* (ceiling)	0.8920(+6.09%)**
P +*A*	0.8848(+5.24%)$*$
P + *A* + Clicks	0.8840(+5.14%)*

ness, outperformed the Google baseline ranking by 5.25%, reaching NDCG of 0.8848 and being statistically significant with p<0.05. The slight gap between P + *COV* and P + *A* results is due to the expected regression error, that can be further reduced with more training data or richer features. We also tried to add number of clicks received by document as an additional feature to the ranker, but the performance was slightly lower. Nevertheless, the demonstrated improvements are remarkable, considering the relatively small amount of training data that was required to estimate the snippet attractiveness and in turn improve the ranking over a state-of-the-art Google ranking.

5.4 Application 3: Detecting Bad Snippets

In this section we describe our experiments on detecting bad (i.e., misleading) search snippets. Intuitively, good snippets should clearly summarize the result document so that searcher would be able to understand whether it is worth clicking or not. Specifically, we consider good snippets to be those, that attract clicks on relevant documents, or discourage clicks on non-relevant documents. Conversely, bad snippets would discourage clicks on relevant documents, while attracting clicks on non-relevant documents. More formally, we define snippets to be *Bad* or *Good* based on the snippet *COV* ratio (defined in Section 5.2), and the result relevance (manually labeled as described in Section 5.1):

$$Label(COV, REL) = \begin{cases} Bad & \text{if } (REL \geq 0 \text{ and } COV < \theta_2) \\ & \text{OR } (REL = 0 \text{ and } COV > \theta_1) \\ Good & \text{otherwise} \end{cases}$$

Where the parameters θ_1 and θ_2 are set empirically by manually examining a sample of the snippets and the documents. Thus, *Good* snippets for relevant documents would have higher (i.e., greater than θ_1) *COV* ratio, since a searcher would be more willing to visit the document after examining the snippet. Similarly, a *Good* snippet allows a searcher to identify a non-relevant document, resulting in lower *COV* ratio (i.e., less than θ_2). In contrast, a snippet is considered to be *Bad* if it fails to inform the searcher about the document relevance. Hence, a snippet for a relevant document that exhibits a low *COV* ratio (i.e., less than θ_2) is considered to be *Bad*. We experimented with different values of the θ_1 and θ_2 parameters and determined that the setting θ_1=0.85 and θ_2 =0.35 provides the closest match to our definition, on a subset of the data. With this parameter setting, our dataset contained 589 *Good* snippets and 61 *Bad* snippets.

Figure 12 shows an example of a snippet that appeared in the results to the query "`wildlife extinction`" where the information need was described as *"The spotted owl episode in America highlighted U.S. efforts to prevent the extinction of wildlife species. What is not well known is the effort of other countries to prevent the demise of species native to their countries. What other countries have begun efforts to prevent such declines"*. The snippet summarizes a news article talking about recreating aurochs from reconstructed DNA, which is an attempt to save the specie, so the document was judged as a relevant to the query. However, the text summary of the snippet talks about a seemingly un-

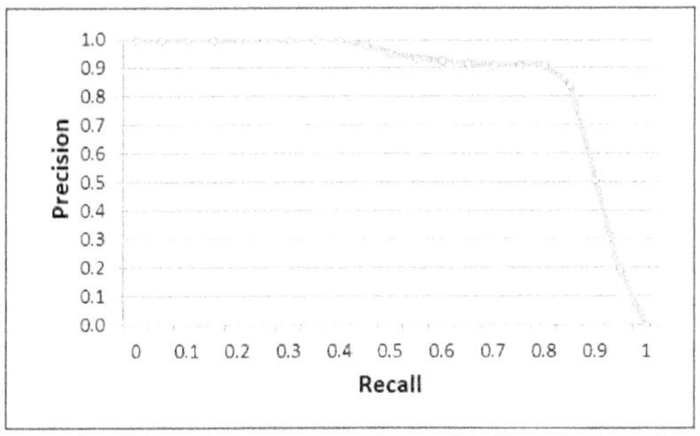

Figure 11: Precision vs. Recall for detecting bad snippets using ViewSer data.

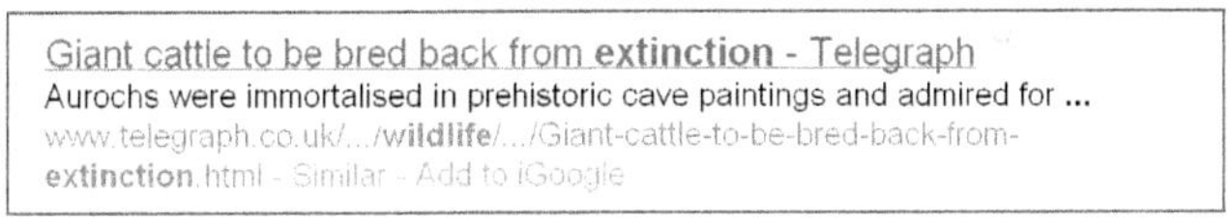

Figure 12: An example of a bad snippet: document is relevant while the COV ratio is low (0.18). This snippet was returned for the query "`wildlife extinction`" at the 4th position. The snippet summarizes a news article talking about recreating aurochs from reconstructed DNA, which is an attempt to save the specie, so the document is relevant to the query. However, text summary of the snippet is not representative, causing searchers to skip the document.

related fact that *"aurochs were immortalized in prehistoric cave paintings"*, which caused many of the searchers to skip this document. Another example of a bad snippet is shown in Figure 13, where a snippet appears relevant, but the actual document is not.

Figure 13: An example of a bad snippet: the document is not relevant while the COV ratio is high (0.85). This snippet was returned for the query "`ship losses`" at the 3rd position. The stated information need was: *"Identify instances in which weather was a main or contributing factor in the loss of a ship at sea"*. The snippet's summary lists relevant keywords, but the actual document does not discuss factors contributing to ship losses.

Experimental Setup: We treat this as a classification problem, where we attempt to predict the snippet label based on the textual features of the snippet, and our estimate of the snippet attractiveness, A, defined in Section 5.2. Specifically, we use the features listed in Table 2, as well as the A feature, as input to classification. We experimented with different classifiers such as Naive Bayes, Logistic Regression, SVM, and others, using 5-fold cross validation.

Results and Discussion: Interestingly, the highest accuracy was achieved by the LogitBoost [9] classifier, resulting in 97.7% accuracy (P = 97.6%, R = 97.7%, F1 = 97.6%, AUC = 93.6%). This improvement is significant over the majority baseline classifier, which had Accuracy of 90.6% (P = 82.1%, R = 90.6%, F1 = 86.2%, AUC = 43.9%). The Precision-Recall curve computed for the LogitBoost classifier is reported in Figure 11, showing that more than 35% of *Bad* snippets can be detected with 100% precision.

As a potential confounding factor, we did not consider whether a snippet contains an answer to the query directly on the SERP, removing the need to click on a document even when it is relevant. While this scenario could potentially violate our definition of a *Good* snippet, for the experiments in this paper, this case is extremely unlikely: the search tasks, especially those from the HARD set, are relatively complex, and are not likely to be answered directly in the snippet. As another research direction, we believe that using only the shallow text features for snippet quality classification leaves significant room for improvement, for example, by incorporating the readability and language model features proposed in [17]. We plan to explore these questions further in our future work.

6. CONCLUSIONS

We presented ViewSer, a novel methodology for crowdsourcing web search behavior evaluation studies. By restricting result viewing to a viewport, ViewSer enables tracking precisely which results are examined on a search engine result page, while preserving the natural result examination and interaction patterns. We validated the ViewSer prototype in a study with over 100 remote participants, recruited through the Amazon MTurk services, showing ViewSer induces similar search behavior compared to the in-lab users monitored using eye tracking. These results indicate that ViewSer could enable large-scale web search behavioral evaluation studies, for the fraction of the cost and effort required to perform these studies in the lab. We have presented three practical applications of ViewSer, namely a new way to learn to estimate snippet attractiveness, which could in turn improve ranking, and an exploratory application to automatically detecting bad (misleading) snippets.

As part of our future work, we plan on improving user click models using examination information collected with ViewSer, as it allows direct observation of result viewing previously only inferred by click models such as [5, 26]. In summary, we believe that ViewSer provides a crucial component that would enable realistic, large-scale, and reproducible behavioral evaluation of web search, which would in turn improve search result presentation (e.g., result summary generation), result ranking, and ultimately the overall web search experience.

ACKNOWLEDGEMENTS: This work has been supported by the NSF grant IIS-1018321 and by the Yahoo! Faculty Research Engagement Program.

7. REFERENCES

[1] E. Agichtein, E. Brill, and S. Dumais. Improving web search ranking by incorporating user behavior information. In *Proceedings of the annual International ACM SIGIR Conference on Research and Development in Information Retrieval*, pages 19–26. SIGIR, 2006.

[2] O. Alonso, D. Rose, and B. Stewart. Crowdsourcing for relevance evaluation. In *ACM SIGIR Forum*, volume 42, pages 9–15. SIGIR, 2008.

[3] R. Bednarik and M. Tukiainen. Validating the restricted focus viewer: A study using eye-movement tracking. *Behavior research methods*, 39(2):274–282, 2007.

[4] A. Blackwell, A. Jansen, and K. Marriott. Restricted focus viewer: a tool for tracking visual attention. *Theory and Application of Diagrams*, pages 575–588, 2000.

[5] O. Chapelle and Y. Zhang. A dynamic bayesian network click model for web search ranking. In *Proceedings of the International Conference on World Wide Web*, pages 1–10. WWW, 2009.

[6] E. Chi, P. Pirolli, and S. Lam. Aspects of augmented social cognition: Social information foraging and social search. In *Proceedings of the International Conference on Online Communities and Social Computing*, pages 60–69. Springer-Verlag, 2007.

[7] C. Clarke, E. Agichtein, S. Dumais, and R. White. The influence of caption features on clickthrough patterns in web search. In *Proceedings of the International ACM SIGIR Conference on Research and Development in Information Retrieval*, pages 135–142. SIGIR, 2007.

[8] E. Cutrell and Z. Guan. What are you looking for?: an eye-tracking study of information usage in web search. In *Proceedings of the ACM SIGCHI Conference on Human Factors in Computing Systems*, pages 407–416. SIGCHI, 2007.

[9] J. Friedman, T. Hastie, and R. Tibshirani. Special invited paper. additive logistic regression: A statistical view of boosting. *The annals of statistics*, 28(2):337–374, 2000.

[10] Q. Guo and E. Agichtein. Towards predicting web searcher gaze position from mouse movements. In *Proceeding of the annual ACM SIGCHI Conference Extended Abstracts on Human factors in Computing Systems*, pages 3601–3606. SIGCHI, 2010.

[11] J. Heer and M. Bostock. Crowdsourcing graphical perception: using mechanical turk to assess visualization design. In *Proceedings of the ACM SIGCHI International Conference on Human Factors in Computing Systems*, pages 203–212. SIGCHI, 2010.

[12] J. Huang, R. W. White, and S. Dumais. No clicks, no problem: using cursor movements to understand and improve search. In *Proceeding of the annual ACM SIGCHI Conference on Human factors in Computing Systems*. SIGCHI, 2011.

[13] A. Jansen, A. Blackwell, and K. Marriott. A tool for tracking visual attention: The restricted focus viewer. *Behavior Research Methods*, 35(1):57–69, 2003.

[14] K. Jarvelin and J. Kekalainen. Cumulated gain-based evaluation of information retrieval techniques. *ACM Transactions on Information Systems (TOIS)*, 20(4):422–446, 2002.

[15] T. Joachims. Optimizing search engines using clickthrough data. In *Proceedings of the ACM SIGKDD International Conference on Knowledge Discovery and Data Mining*, pages 133–142. SIGKDD, 2002.

[16] T. Joachims. Training linear svms in linear time. In *Proceedings of the ACM SIGKDD International Conference on Knowledge Discovery and Data Mining*, pages 217–226. SIGKDD, 2006.

[17] T. Kanungo and D. Orr. Predicting the readability of short web summaries. In *Proceedings of the Second ACM WSDM International Conference on Web Search and Data Mining*, pages 202–211. WSDM, 2009.

[18] G. Kazai, N. Milic-Frayling, and J. Costello. Towards methods for the collective gathering and quality control of relevance assessments. In *Proceedings of the International ACM SIGIR Conference on Research and Development in Information Retrieval*, pages 452–459. SIGIR, 2009.

[19] D. Kelly and K. Gyllstrom. An examination of two delivery modes for interactive search system experiments: remote and laboratory. In *Proceeding of the annual ACM SIGCHI Conference on Human factors in Computing Systems*, pages 1531–1540. SIGCHI, 2011.

[20] A. Kittur, E. Chi, and B. Suh. Crowdsourcing user studies with mechanical turk. In *Proceeding of the annual ACM SIGCHI Conference on Human factors in Computing Systems*, pages 453–456. CHI, 2008.

[21] J. Le, A. Edmonds, V. Hester, and L. Biewald. Ensuring quality in crowdsourced search relevance evaluation. In *Proceedings of the ACM SIGIR Workshop on Crowdsourcing for Search Evaluation (CSE 2010)*, pages 17–20. SIGIR, 2010.

[22] L. Lorigo, M. Haridasan, H. Brynjarsdóttir, L. Xia, T. Joachims, G. Gay, L. Granka, F. Pellacini, and B. Pan. Eye tracking and online search: Lessons learned and challenges ahead. *Journal of the American Society for Information Science and Technology*, 59(7):1041–1052, 2008.

[23] K. Rayner. Eye movements in reading and information processing: 20 years of research. *Psychological bulletin*, 124(3):372, 1998.

[24] K. Wang, N. Gloy, and X. Li. Inferring search behaviors using partially observable markov (pom) model. In *Proceedings of the ACM WSDM International Conference on Web Search and Data Mining*, pages 211–220. WSDM, 2010.

[25] Y. Yue, R. Patel, and H. Roehrig. Beyond position bias: examining result attractiveness as a source of presentation bias in clickthrough data. In *Proceedings of the International Conference on World Wide Web*, pages 1011–1018. WWW, 2010.

[26] Z. Zhu, W. Chen, T. Minka, C. Zhu, and Z. Chen. A novel click model and its applications to online advertising. In *Proceedings of the ACM WSDM International Conference on Web Search and Data Mining*, pages 321–330. WSDM, 2010.

CrowdLogging: Distributed, Private, and Anonymous Search Logging

Henry Feild
Dept. of Computer Science
University of Massachusetts
Amherst, MA 01003
hfeild@cs.umass.edu

James Allan
Dept. of Computer Science
University of Massachusetts
Amherst, MA 01003
allan@cs.umass.edu

Joshua Glatt
Dept. of Computer Science
University of Massachusetts
Amherst, MA 01003
jglatt@cs.umass.edu

ABSTRACT

We describe CrowdLogging, an approach for distributed search log collection, storage, and mining, with the dual goals of preserving privacy and making the mined information broadly available. Most search log mining approaches and most privacy enhancing schemes have focused on centralized search logs and methods for disseminating them to third parties. In our approach, a user's search log is encrypted and shared in such a way that (a) the source of a search behavior artifact, such as a query, is unknown and (b) extremely rare artifacts—that is, artifacts more likely to contain private information—are not revealed. The approach works with any search behavior artifact that can be extracted from a search log, including queries, query reformulations, and query-click pairs. In this work, we: (1) present a distributed search log collection, storage, and mining framework; (2) compare several privacy policies, including differential privacy, showing the trade-offs between strong guarantees and the utility of the released data; (3) demonstrate the impact of our approach using two existing research query logs; and (4) describe a pilot study for which we implemented a version of the framework.

Categories and Subject Descriptors

H.2.8 [**Database Management**]: Database Applications—*data mining*; H.3.3 [**Information Storage and Retrieval**]: Information Search and Retrieval—*search process*; H.3.4 [**Information Storage and Retrieval**]: Systems and software—*distributed systems, user profiles and alert services*

General Terms

Algorithms, Design, Experimentation, Management, Security

Keywords

Distributed query logs, private query log analysis

SIGIR'11, July 24–28, 2011, Beijing, China.

1. INTRODUCTION

Query logs have been a windfall for search engine companies, providing better ranking [15], improved spelling correction [2], more useful query suggestions [5], and generally helping researchers understand how people search [13]. In its simplest form, a query log is the list of queries received by a search engine, along with details of which results the user viewed or clicked. Search providers often enhance the logged information to the extent possible, including asking their users to install "toolbars" on their Web browsers that capture browsing activity across different search providers and all other websites.[1]

With a query log in hand, it is possible to puzzle out not only a great deal about the community of users, but also about individuals: the queries issued and URLs of web pages viewed by each user are connected through an approximate user ID, a browser cookie. It is easy to pull together all the data for a single person, no matter how private or sensitive the information is. The well-known AOL query log incident demonstrated how even anonymizing usernames with random identifiers is not adequate in protecting the identity of individuals: several users were identified by a *New York Times* reporter [4]. User 4417749 was identified through a combination of several infrequent queries conveying private information, such as zip codes and relatives' names. Once that individual was identified, all of her sensitive queries were exposed, in this case providing a disturbingly clear picture of her interests and activities.

The enormous value of query logs, however, means that despite the privacy concerns, many people and organizations are constantly interested in acquiring them. These logs are readily available at large search companies [19, 24, 25], but smaller groups—including academic researchers—have few ways of acquiring such logs. Some logs have been released to the general research community, often after careful efforts to remove all personal information.[2] Unfortunately, not only are the resulting logs artificial (because data is lost), but they are infrequent and short-term snapshots that are adequate only for limited types of research.

To address those issues, we present an approach to capturing and using query logs that (1) provides log access to anyone and (2) provides privacy guarantees that are equal or superior to all existing methods.

[1] http://www.discoverbing.com, http://toolbar.google.com, http://toolbar.yahoo.com
[2] http://ims.dei.unipd.it/websites/LogCLEF/Overview.html

All current search log mining and anonymization models we know of are based on a centralized approach. The entire search log is collected and stored by a single entity, such as a search engine company. This collector can mine the log for its own purposes, of course—and, if they choose, provide some privacy mechanism by which researchers can analyze the data. For example, this privacy mechanism might be query-based, where the researcher poses questions to the collector ("how often has *unusual search* been issued as a query?"), or distribution-based, where the collector creates an anonymized version of the search log, which is then given directly to the researcher.

These centralized approaches work well for collectors that collect their data through a Web service, such as a search engine company. But the drawbacks are considerable: (1) users have virtually no control over their query or click data once it has been collected; (2) shared versions of log data are usually delayed, censored, down-sampled, or modified, thus reducing their utility; and (3) users' privacy is at the mercy of the collector's security capabilities.

We present CrowdLogging, an alternate approach that keeps each user's log on their own machine.[3] In this model, mining tasks are partially handled at each user's site; the results are then relayed to one or more central servers that complete the process. The results of the mining are encrypted in such a way that they can only be decrypted if the data is sufficiently common across many users, making it nearly impossible for a user's private information to be revealed: we will never see the query *ID number 999-99-9999*, because only one person will ever type it in. In addition, the source of log information is stripped, providing a degree of anonymity not normally available—one that means a common but embarrassing query is not connected to any individual: we know that *embarrassing query* was issued by many people, but we do not know who they are.

The combination of these two privacy features yields a data mining system based on distributed, private, and anonymous search logs. There are several advantages of this approach: (1) users have a high degree of control over their collected data, including being able to opt out selectively or entirely; (2) the original, un-anonymized data on each user's computer can be used immediately or with a delay for as many mining tasks as the the user and the security policy allow, and (3) the information collected by the server is either common across many users and disassociated from them all, or is encrypted in such a way that it cannot be determined by someone illegitimately gaining access to the server—or even by someone who has legitimate access to the server, such as by subpoena.

Our contributions include the following: (1) a distributed search log collection, storage, and mining framework, presented in Section 3.1; (2) a comparison of four privacy policies, focusing on the trade-offs between the strength of the guarantees on privacy loss and the utility of the released data, covered in Section 3.2; (3) simulations showing the impact of the framework, using two existing research query logs, described in Section 4; and (4) a pilot study for which we implemented a version of the framework, discussed in Section 5.

[3]It is not necessary that the logs be kept on the user's computer, though doing so maximizes the user's control and the flexibility of the mining tasks and we will focus on that approach in this study.

2. RELATED WORK

The motivation of our work is similar to that of most work on search log anonymization: how can search log information be collected, used, and possibly shared so that the users who are logged will not have private or embarrassing information revealed? Most work in this area has focused on ways to transform a centrally located search log into one that does not violate privacy concerns.

Adar [1] presents two methods for anonymizing a search log in the interest of preserving privacy. First, only queries that are issued by at least t users are kept. Adar uses a secret sharing scheme where queries are encrypted and can only be decrypted if a sufficient number of parts are received. This is similar to Sweeney's k-anonymity work [23] for databases, which assigns a subset of the database's columns to be a quasi-identifier. A row in the database is only released if for each column value in the row's quasi-identifier, there are at least $k-1$ other rows that share the column value.[4] Under Adar's model, a query serves as the quasi-identifier. Adar's second technique anonymizes the identity of users who enter a series of queries that may reveal who they are when taken together, by clustering syntactically related queries from a user's session and releasing each cluster under its own identifier. Our approach uses a similar form of t-anonymity but does not cluster queries, because we do not link a user's various queries: even though individual queries are t-anonymous, there is no guarantee that the syntactic clusters do not contain both identifying and sensitive information when all the queries in the cluster are looked at together. Clustering also rearranges the query log, creating false associations between queries and discarding potentially interesting sequences of queries (e.g., reformulations).

Hong et al. [11] also present a technique for anonymizing search logs. They define k^δ-anonymity, where for every user whose data is listed in the anonymized query log, there are $k-1$ other users that are δ-similar to the user in terms of their data. Their method involves grouping similar users and adding or suppressing data to make user groups appear more similar. The downside to this approach is that some data is permanently discarded and artificial data is added. It is unclear how different types of applications are affected by this anonymization process.

Korolova et al. [16] describe a differentially private method for releasing a query click graph that protects privacy. Their work differs from others in this field in two important ways: (1) the output of their anonymization is a query click graph rather than a search log, and (2) they prove theoretical bounds on the effectiveness of their privacy-protecting scheme, under the assumption that an attacker has an arbitrary amount of outside information. Since *differential privacy* [7] is used, a large amount of data is lost and noise is added, a common trade-off for theoretically sound privacy guarantees. In Section 3.2.3, we show how a portion of their method can be adapted for use as a privacy policy in our framework.

The common thread through these works is that data is permanently lost in the anonymization process, but the

[4]There is extensive work on this type of anonymization in databases, including methods that do not require anonymized sending and that are robust in the presence of malicious participants [26]. Some of those ideas may be applicable in our setting, but our situation is simpler—we have only one "column"—and allows for a simpler apparatus.

loss may be a necessary evil to distribute search logs—particularly to convince legal counsel that the data is sufficiently sanitized. An alternative approach for universities or small organizations providing search is to gather query log information from volunteers. The Community Query Log Project[5] at the Center for Intelligent Information Retrieval was one such attempt to do that. The project distributed a browser toolbar that collected search log information, anonymized the source, and shipped it to a central server. The intent was to review the data to ensure it was sufficiently private and then release it to the research community. Unfortunately, after a year of effort only 34,000 distinct queries were collected—according to the project, the equivalent of six seconds of Google traffic. The project was abandoned in May 2010. A conjecture that motivates our work is that user privacy concerns were a major reasons for poor adoption: the idea was appealing, but people were nervous about participating.

Another body of work attempts to address privacy concerns differently. The TrackMeNot project [12], for example, inserts random queries into the stream of queries issued by a user, with the intent of making it harder for a search engine company to determine a particular user's interests. This provides a degree of privacy, but it makes search logs less useful by inserting additional noise that makes a user's general interests difficult to discern. However, personal or embarrassing queries are still present in the log and TrackMeNot thus does nothing toward making them distributable.

An entirely different approach to making query log information revolves around policy. For example, Bar-Ilan [3] argues for setting up review boards that would allow researchers to use logs under controlled and clearly defined conditions. It is not clear that such a review board would ease privacy concerns sufficiently. Moreover, the limitations such an approach demands would likely disincentivize most researchers.

Our belief is that all of the previous work is problematic in that it rests on the assumption that query logs should be collected in the clear and processed by groups or companies that we trust to store, use, and share the information with our best interests at heart. However, no matter how good their intentions, they may be thwarted by hackers who steal the information [21] or governments that demand access [10].

3. CROWDLOGGING

Our framework, CrowdLogging, consists of three main layers: the system, the privacy policies, and the applications. The system and applications are shown in Figure 1. The privacy policy layer is not explicitly depicted in the figure; it provides constraints on how results are mined, encrypted, aggregated, and released. We describe each of the layers below.

3.1 System

In current search log collection and mining systems (Figure 2), raw browser behavior data is sent from users (by their browsers) to a centralized collector where it is stored. When analysts want to process the data, the collector mines the raw data and then selectively chooses which bits to reveal or suppress in order to respond to the queries posed by analysts. Individual users have no control over how

[5]http://lemurstudy.cs.umass.edu/

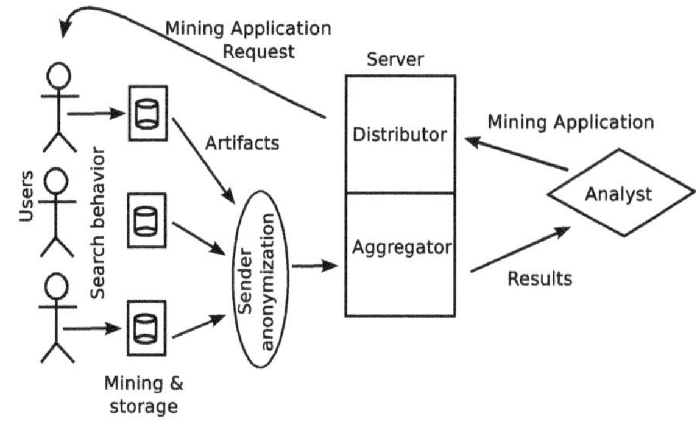

Figure 1: The distributed, private, and anonymous search log mining system.

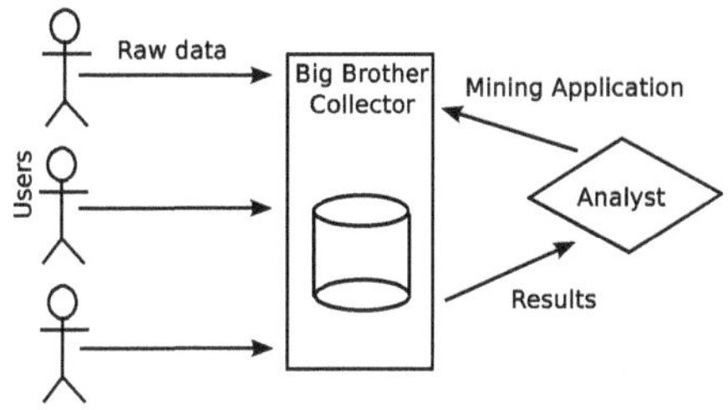

Figure 2: A typical centralized collection, storage, and mining system.

their raw data—which may contain sensitive and identifying information—is used in these mining tasks, and the collector has the ability to look through the raw data at will. Our system moves away from this centralized system model and provides mechanisms for giving users control of their data, keeping their data private, and anonymizing their data.

Distributed. We distribute the storage of raw data to the users that generate the data. A local Web proxy or Web browser extension stores a user's browsing behavior—such as queries submitted to search engines and Web pages visited—to a log located *on that user's computer.* This gives users full control over their raw information—they can remove the log, remove parts of the log, and choose in which mining tasks to participate, depending on the control mechanisms implemented.

Private. In the centralized approach, raw data, such as a query submitted by the user to a search system, is communicated to the collector. In our system, the raw data stays on the users' computers. Only the results of a mining task, which we call *search artifacts*, can leave a user's computer.

To provide privacy, the artifacts are encrypted using a "secret sharing" scheme. Such schemes encrypt an artifact and send with it a piece of the key necessary for decryption. If a sufficient number of distinct key pieces are collected for a particular encrypted artifact, it can be decrypted.

There are different ways to pick which part of the key to include with an encrypted artifact, some of which we will discuss in Section 3.2. In general, the function that generates the key part has four parameters: the artifact, the user's ID, k, and n. k is a number that dictates how many distinct key parts are needed for decryption and n is the number of distinct key parts that are available; $k \leq n$.

A key part generation function that serves as a good example produces different key parts for different combinations of the artifact, user ID, k, and n. This allows an artifact to be decrypted if at least k users generated the same artifact, a specialized version of k-anonymity.

Anonymous. Users' anonymity is protected in two major ways within our system. First, encrypted artifacts are required to go through an anonymizing system before arriving at the aggregation server. This prevents the aggregation server from having the capability of associating potentially identifying information, such as an IP address, with an artifact.

Second, the aggregator provides additional anonymity by not releasing key part information. Depending on how the key part is determined, artifacts from a single user may be linked by part number. Although this connection with the user can be removed, we implement a policy of dropping the part numbers in an abundance of caution. This policy ensures that no information allowing two artifacts to be linked to a single user is released, maintaining users' anonymity.

As with any system, there are security vulnerabilities. We outline these in Section 5.4.

3.2 Privacy policies

In this section, we will describe a sample of privacy policies that are compatible with CrowdLogging. A privacy policy answers four questions: (1) what data can be mined and sent to the server, (2) how it is packaged for sending to the server, (3) how data is aggregated at the server, and (4) what is released to analysts.

3.2.1 Artifact frequency thresholding

We define the artifact frequency thresholding privacy policy (FT_a) to mean that an analyst can access any search artifact mined from the logs of users provided it occurs at least k times. *What can be mined?* There are no constraints on what gets mined from the log. *How does it get packaged?* Each artifact is encrypted and a random key part is assigned. If a particular artifact occurs more than once for a single user, each instance is encrypted with a different key part, though there will be some overlap due to the random generation. *How is data aggregated?* The keys for identical encrypted artifacts are combined; if there are at least k of them, the artifact is decrypted. *What is released?* Pairs of artifacts and counts. If the artifact was decrypted during aggregation, the decrypted form is released. Otherwise, a meaningless string is substituted.

This is a weak privacy policy. A user could enter a query that is both identifying and sensitive k times, causing it to be revealed. Potentially sensitive non-query artifacts could also be extracted. Regardless, the framework allows this policy, and it can be used in conjunction with more private policies, such as artifact frequency differential privacy.

3.2.2 User frequency thresholding

The user frequency thresholding policy (FT_u) is based on k-anonymity as presented by Sweeney [23]. The policy states that an artifact can only be revealed if it is entered by at least k distinct users. *What can be mined?* There are no constraints on what can be mined. *How does it get packaged?* Each artifact must be encrypted and the key part must be such that the same user has the same key part for all instances of the same artifact. *How is data aggregated?* Data is aggregated the same way as under the FT_a policy. *What is released?* The same information is released as under the FT_a policy.

The motivation for FT_u in the context of this work is that an artifact that is extracted from at least k distinct users' logs is not likely to contain sensitive information. For example, consider a particularly sensitive query that contains an individual's name and ID number. It is conceivable that the query will be released under the FT_a policy for a low threshold of k. However, even for a low value of k, it is unlikely that $k-1$ other users will have entered that same sensitive query.

3.2.3 Differential privacy

A drawback of the policies above is that they do not provide any provable guarantee of privacy. A method that has been proposed to quantify privacy loss is differential privacy [7]. The motivation is that, given a database and a query, we want to produce a noisy answer such that the querier has a low probability of determining if any individual was included in the database.

Korolova et al. [16] present a differentially private algorithm for producing a query click graph from a search log. Their algorithm has four steps: (1) take the first d queries from each user; (2) for each query, add some noise to its frequency in the data set and select it for release if it surpasses a threshold K; (3) for released queries, add noise to their frequencies; and (4) release noisy counts for clicks on URLs shown in the top ten results for each query.

There are three major constraints that differential privacy puts on search log mining in order to make the desired guarantees: the number of artifacts mined from a particular user must be limited; Laplace noise must be added to any artifact counts before comparing with the threshold; and each mining job depletes some amount of the privacy quota for a data set, so only one or a small number of mining tasks can be performed on a data set, depending on the parameters.

We present two variations on this algorithm and the formulas behind them to provide additional privacy policies for our framework. In both variations, because our goals are more general, we replace queries with arbitrary search artifacts and we omit the final step of releasing URL click counts.

Artifact frequency differential privacy (DP_a). This algorithm is similar to Korolova et al. [16]: (1) use the first d artifacts from each user; (2) for each artifact, add some noise to its frequency in the data set and select it for release if it surpasses a threshold k_a; (3) for released artifacts, add noise to their frequencies. This provides $(d\ln(\alpha) + d/b_a, \delta)$-differential privacy, where $\alpha = \max\left(\exp(1/b), 1 + \frac{1}{2\exp((k_a-1)/b)-1}\right)$, b is the Laplace noise parameter for step (2), b_a is the Laplace noise parameter for step (3), and $\delta = \frac{d\exp((d-k_a)/b)}{2}$. Because a search artifact can be viewed as a string, just as a query is, the proof for this variation follows directly from the proof presented by Korolova et al. [16]. However, they use K instead of k_a and b_q in place of b_a.[6]

Assuming, as Korolova et al. do, that we want to minimize noise and that $\exp(1/b) \geq 1 + \left(\frac{1}{2\exp((k_a-1)/b)-1}\right)$, we can maximize the threshold k_a by solving $k_a = d\left(1 - \frac{\ln(2\delta/d)}{\epsilon}\right)$, where ϵ is the privacy quota. The implementer needs to

[6]We use this alternative naming to easily differentiate between the two variations we present.

select values for ϵ, δ (less than the inverse of the number of users participating), and d.

What can be mined? Anything can be mined, but only d artifacts can be sent to the server. *How does it get packaged?* Follow the same scheme as for FT_a, except that in addition, an encrypted version of the user ID must be included for the next step. *How is data aggregated?* First, ensure that only d artifacts are present for each user; as a single user may have multiple machines, and the machines do not communicate, it is possible for there to be multiple d-artifact sets sent to the server for the same user ID. Once there are d artifacts per user, data is aggregated the same way as under the FT_a and FT_u policies. *What is released?* The same information is released as under the FT_a and FT_u policies.

User frequency differential privacy (DP_u). This variation differs in step (2) of DP_a: for each artifact, add some noise to *the number of distinct users with that artifact* and release it if that number is at least k_u. Due to the nature of this change, we can modify the proof slightly to obtain a tighter bound on privacy. Specifically, looking at Equation 9 in Korolova et al. [16], we have

$$\frac{1}{2}\sum_{i=1}^{n_y}\exp\left(\frac{M(y_i,D_2)-k_a}{b}\right) \le \frac{d}{2}\exp\left(\frac{d-k_a}{b}\right) \quad (1)$$

where D_2 is a dataset with a single user added, versus D_1, which is the same dataset but with that user removed, $y_1,\ldots,y_{n_y}$ is the set of queries which are unique to D_2, and $M(y_i,D_2)$ returns the frequency of the artifact y_i in D_2. $M(y_i,D_2)$ can return at most d, since a user can only contribute at most d artifacts. However, under the user-frequency model, let $M'(x,D)$ return the number of distinct users associated with an artifact x in D. Thus, $M'(y_i,D_2)$ is at most 1, since y_i is unique to the one user whose data is in D_2 but not D_1. This yields the following, tighter bound:

$$\frac{1}{2}\sum_{i=1}^{n_y}\exp\left(\frac{M'(y_i,D_2)-k_u}{b}\right) \le \frac{d}{2}\exp\left(\frac{1-k_u}{b}\right) \quad (2)$$

This has ramifications for δ, giving us the following optimal user-frequency threshold:

$$k_u = 1 - \frac{d\ln(2\delta/d)}{\epsilon} \quad (3)$$

What can be mined? Anything can be mined, but only d artifacts can be sent to the server. *How does it get packaged?* Follow the same scheme as for FT_u, except that in addition, an encrypted version of the user ID must be included for the next step. *How is data aggregated?* Follow the same procedure as for DP_a. *What is released?* The same information is released as under the other three policies.

3.3 Applications

CrowdLogging allows any mining task—i.e., applications—to be distributed to consenting clients. An application starts with a user's local search log and produces search artifact instances as output, possibly limited by the selected privacy policy. In this section we describe several popular mining applications and show how to implement them in the CrowdLogging framework. We discuss counting queries, query reformulations, query-URL pairs, and learning-to-rank features.

Query frequency mining. We wish to emit all occurrences of queries as search artifacts. Since a query can be submitted to a search engine in many different forms that are semantically identical—e.g., with different spacing or capitalization—we use both the original query and a normalized form that collapses those minor differences. The client therefore sends the server two encrypted pieces of data: the normalized query as the *primary private field* and the original query as the *secondary private field*. The two fields are encrypted with the same key which is derived from the primary private field—that is, the secondary private field will be decryptable only once the primary private field is decryptable, regardless of how many times that particular unnormalized form of the query occurs. The format for the message sent to the server is thus:

$$\langle E(N(query_1)), E(query_1), \textit{key-portion}\rangle$$

where $N(x)$ is a function that returns the normalized version of the string x. When the encrypted artifacts arrive at the server, the server aggregates the tuples based on the primary private key. Once there are a sufficient number of distinct key portions, both private fields can be decrypted. We can then generate and distribute to analysts tuples like:

⟨ "dog food", "DOG FOOD", 1 ⟩
⟨ "dog food", "dog food", 100 ⟩

This is enough information to tell us how frequently a normalized query occurred in the logs as well as the frequency of variations of the query. Depending on the privacy policy, we can aggregate over undecrypted tuples and generate aggregate statistics such as: "5 undecrypted queries were each entered 194 times; 20 undecrypted queries were each entered 195 times." These statistics allow analysts to look at potentially helpful statistics about rare items in a collection without revealing the queries themselves.

Query reformulation mining. The next application we consider is mining query reformulations. Query reformulations occur when a user issues a query and then shortly thereafter tries a different one. Although in many cases the queries are completely unrelated, there are numerous times when they are connected. For example, Jansen et al. report that over half of the users in a 24-hour query log modified their queries [14]. Query reformulations can represent spelling corrections, related words, acronym expansions, or alternate ways of asking the same question.

To find common query reformulations, we can replace the single query in the previous application with a pair of queries, using a tab or other delimiter to separate them—we use a colon in the examples below. The pairs could be restricted to those that are adjacent or to all pairs within a several-minute session. Depending the exact specifications of the application, the pairs might be time-ordered or not. What we send is:

$$\langle E(N(q_{1,1} : q_{1,2})), E(q_{1,1} : q_{1,2}), \textit{key-portion}\rangle$$
$$\langle E(N(q_{2,1} : q_{2,2})), E(q_{2,1} : q_{2,2}), \textit{key-portion}\rangle$$

As in the case of counting queries, the server can count query reformulations and the ones with a sufficient number of distinct key portions can be revealed. If the privacy policy allows for it, this application can be run in tandem with query frequency mining. This allows the server to tabulate how frequent a query is and what percent of its instances are reformulated in a particular way. With this information, the server can derive useful statistics, such as 'the query "dog" is rewritten as "puppy" 50% of the time.' It can also report the most frequent and widely supported reformulations and the proportion of all reformulations they make up.

Compared to non-private query logging, what have we lost? Certain reformulation pairs will be infrequent and so will not be discoverable. For example, we may be able to say that,

"dog"	→	"puppy"	: 50%
"dog"	→	"dog food"	: 20%
"dog"	→	?	: 30%

We cannot know how many additional reformulations are encompassed by the unknown 30%, but we do know the proportion of reformulations for "dog" that we are missing.

Query-URL frequency mining. Another activity that is useful to mine is which pages are clicked on in response to a query and, the flip side, which queries are used frequently to get to a page. Both provide information related to relevance: pages that are probably relevant to the query and words (from queries) that are strongly related to a page.

To discover this information, we use the same approach as for finding query reformulations, except that we provide a query-page pair rather than a query-query pair. The mining mechanism sends the following encrypted search artifact:

$$\langle E(N(q_1 : URL_1)), E(q_1 : URL_1), \textit{key-portion}\rangle$$
$$\langle E(N(q_1 : URL_2)), E(q_1 : URL_2), \textit{key-portion}\rangle$$

where q_i is some query and URL_j is a page (URL) that the user subsequently clicked on, presumably in response to the query. As before, the server does not know who issued the queries that resulted in the clicks. A way to increase the commonality is to reduce the URL to just the domain or a base-level directory.

An obvious variation is to drop the query q_i from the tuple and send only information about pages that are clicked, providing *a priori* measures of popularity for web pages. This would look very similar to the query frequency mining task, but instead of a query, we use a URL.

Learning to rank feature mining. A common setup for a learning to rank (LTR) system is to specify a list of page feature vectors along with a relevance level for an associated query. An LTR system aims to learn how the page features are related to the relevance levels and will place pages with higher relevance levels higher in the ranked list.

One way to support LTR in our approach is as follows. Concatenate a query, a clicked URL, and the list of features as the search artifact. This will yield something like this:

$$\langle E(N(q_1 : URL_1 : f_1 : f_2 \ldots)), E(\ldots), \textit{key-portion}\rangle$$
$$\langle E(N(q_1 : URL_2 : f_1 : f_2 \ldots)), E(\ldots), \textit{key-portion}\rangle$$

where q_i is a query, URL_i is a URL clicked on for a query, and f_i is a feature for a query-URL pair. A pitfall of this approach is that the full list of features are unlikely to be common taken together.

A slightly more robust approach breaks the features into pieces, as follows:

$$\langle E(N(q_1 : URL_1 : \text{F1}{:}f_1)), E(q_1 : URL_1 : \text{F1}{:}f_1), \textit{key-portion}\rangle$$
$$\langle E(N(q_1 : URL_1 : \text{F2}{:}f_2)), E(q_1 : URL_1 : \text{F2}{:}f_2), \textit{key-portion}\rangle$$

Each search artifact consists of a query q_i, a URL URL_i, and one of the features, f_i.

To improve the commonality, the URL could be shortened, as mentioned above. In addition, the features could be mapped into buckets.

4. SIMULATIONS

One of the motivations for query log privacy comes out of the embarrassment caused by AOL's release of query logs. That leads us to explore the impact our approach would have on the users in that log, widely available on the Internet.[7] The log covers three months of activity, from March through May of 2006. It includes more than 10 million unique queries making up 21 million query instances and covers more than 650,000 unique users.

In addition, we analyze the effectiveness of our approach on a 2006 MSN search log. The MSN search logs use session IDs rather than user IDs. This is not ideal as two sessions could originate from a single user, but it offers a different perspective from the AOL log. The log contains a sample of 15 million query instances submitted to the MSN search engine in May 2006, 13 million non-duplicate adjacent queries, 6.6 million distinct queries normalized in casing and spacing, and 7.5 million sessions.

We want to understand how much data would be lost and how well privacy would be protected if the AOL and MSN query logs were collected, stored, and mined using CrowdLogging. To do this, we sort each query log by the anonymized user or session ID, so that we have all of a particular user's queries. We normalize all queries and remove duplicate queries that occurred in succession. We simulate the results of our algorithm on the assumption that each user is a client and there exists some server. We are interested in what information *could have* been discovered given the full log but is no longer available in our distributed and private approach.

Below, we show results for three applications: mining queries, query reformulations, and query-URL pairs. In each case, we analyze the effect that each of the four privacy policies described in Section 3.2 have on the log at large, as well as on one of the exposed AOL users.

There are several parameters that must be set for the differential privacy policies: δ, ϵ, d. Following Korolova et al. [16], we chose $\epsilon = \ln(10)$. Korolova et al. also suggest that $\delta < \frac{1}{n}$, where n is the number of users or sessions contained in the search log. We chose $\frac{1}{n+1}$ for either data set to maximize the amount of privacy that can be safely compromised. The differential privacy policies are constrained to only using d artifacts per user; we have decided to use the most recent d artifacts under the assumption that more recent artifacts are of higher interest than older ones. We used the largest d possible for each value of k.

4.1 Query frequency mining

Given the complete log, all queries can be counted, no matter how rare. We are interested in the portion of queries that are released under our framework as the anonymity threshold increases for the four privacy policies we discussed in Section 3.2. For the AOL log, we show this in Figure 3. The x-axis corresponds to the artifact or user threshold used for each policy. In the AOL logs, the FT_a and FT_u policies release a much larger fraction of the total query impressions compared with the other two policies. This fraction decreases rapidly and then slows, ending around 20% at $k = 160$. In contrast, the two differential privacy policies start off revealing a much smaller portion of total query impressions, but reveal more as k increases. This is because

[7]For example, http://www.atrus.org/hosted/AOL-data.tgz

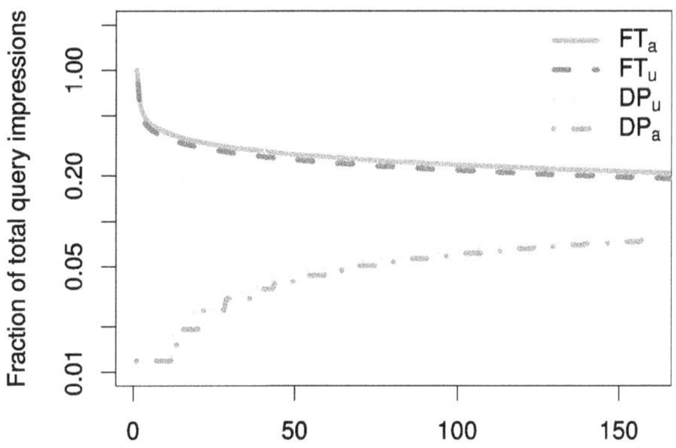

Figure 3: Proportion of total query impressions revealed in the AOL query logs as a function of the four privacy policies.

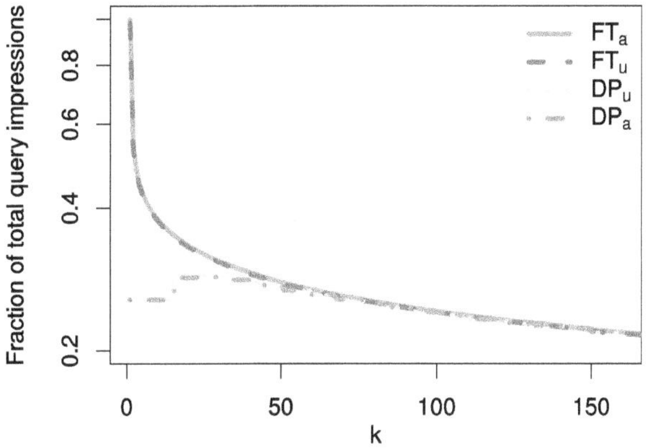

Figure 4: Proportion of total query impressions revealed in the MSN query logs as a function of the four privacy policies.

for any value of k, the differential privacy policies can only use a fixed d queries from each user. As k increases, d increases as well. The DP_u policy releases more queries than DP_a because, for a fixed k, the DP_u can use a larger d than DP_a can.

A similar graph for the MSN log is shown in Figure 4. FT_u and FT_a show a similar trend as on the AOL search log, although the differences between the two is less prominent than in the AOL logs. However, the two differential privacy policies show an initial spike and then follow a non-increasing trend, becoming in sync with the other two policies. This likely has to do with the session-based nature of the MSN log: sessions are generally short and include few queries. Once d exceeds the maximum number of queries in a session, the differential privacy policies are effectively the same as the other two policies. In addition, since sessions are short, it is less likely that a session will produce the same query multiple times, making the query and user frequencies virtually the same.

Due to space constraints, we do not show plots of the fraction of distinct queries under the different policies. For both logs, a very low portion of distinct queries is revealed and the trend under all policies is non-increasing as k increases.

To see how this loss affects an individual, we take a look at the queries of AOL user 4417749, the individual identified by the *New York Times* [4]. User 4417749 entered a total of 239 queries, 224 of which were distinct, meaning the user

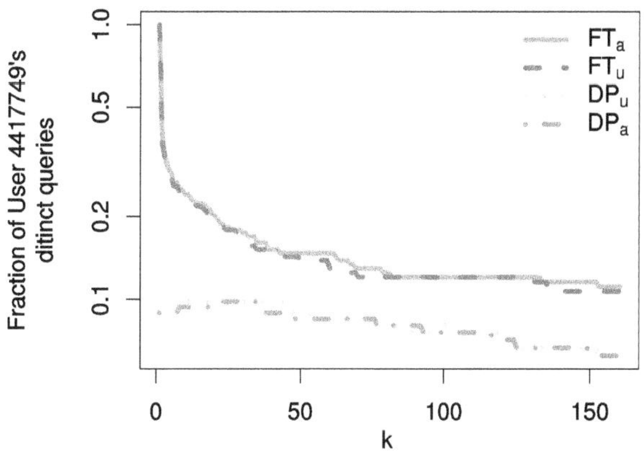

Figure 5: Proportion of distinct queries released for AOL user 4417749 under different privacy policies.

entered very few queries more than once. Figure 5 shows the proportion of the user's distinct queries revealed under each policy.

If we dive into user 4417749's queries and only concentrate on the non-differentially private policies, we see that highly identifiable queries, such as those referencing relatives' names (i.e., same surname) are discarded when $k > 1$. When $k > 2$, we begin to lose queries with location information, such as "gwinnett humane society" and "eugene oregon yellow pages". Queries released with $k \approx 20$ include possibly sensitive queries such as "mini strokes", "paranoia", and "loneliness", though recall that in our framework, those queries would not be associated with the user. When $k > 7500$, we begin to see only the most frequent and generic queries, such as "walmart", "yahoo", and "google".

The differential privacy policies are much more conservative. For a threshold of $1 \leq k \leq 7$, both policies are allowed only one query per user. At this level, both policies suppress virtually all sensitive queries, including queries that could give away location. As k increases, the only queries that remain are the extremely popular ones, like "google". The penalty is that we have access to at most 10% of the queries entered by user 4417749.

4.2 Query reformulation mining

Here we consider adjacent pairs of queries, though again we discard adjacent queries that are identical. We find about 18.7 million unique pairs with 20.4 million instances in the AOL log and 5.1 million distinct pairs with 5.5 million instances in the MSN log.

The portion of total query reformulation instances released from the AOL and MSN logs for varying levels of k under the four policies follow a very similar trend to releasing query impressions. For this reason, we do not provide the graphs. A major difference, however, is the scale: very few query reformulations are released for $k > 1$.

If we use a threshold of $k = 100$, we find that the privacy policies release 233K (FT_a), 196K (FT_u), 44K (DP_u), and 42K (DP_a) queries from the AOL logs—a very low proportion of the overall data set. For MSN, these numbers are smaller: 41k (FT_a), 32k (FT_u), 32k (DP_u), and 31k (DP_a). To have privacy preserved in reformulations, it appears we need to lower our privacy requirements or we need a larger log from which to draw query reformulations.

In the case of AOL user 4417749, we find 237 reformulations. This user never entered the same reformulation twice, and the majority of the reformulations are unique to this user: at $k = 2$ there are only six reformulations that would be revealed under the FT_u policy, and only three reformulations occur more than a few times. Some of the reformulations are spelling mistakes ("lonelyness" → "loneliness", entered by one other user and "oggle" → "google", entered by 225 other users). One is a true conceptual reformulation: "jc penney" → "sears", entered by 46 other users. The "lonelyness" → "loneliness" reformulation is possibly the most sensitive of user 4417749's more widely occurring reformulations, but without knowing the source of reformulations, a researcher using the system would have no idea who entered it, nor would they be able to see what other broadly common queries or reformulations came specifically from the same user.

An interesting phenomenon occurs under the differential privacy policies: the most number of reformulations released by either is exactly one—"oggle" → "google"—and is only released for a short range of k, corresponding to $d = 3$. When $d = 3$, that particular reformulation occurred 22 times across 22 different users. For $d < 3$ and $d > 3$, the number of occurrences of this reformulation is always below the necessary k for both policies.

4.3 Query-URL frequency mining

Finally, we explore the effect of the four privacy policies on query-URL pair mining: how often is a search result URL clicked following a query? The AOL logs consist of 5.4 million distinct and 9.2 million total query-click pairs. The MSN logs have 1.6 million distinct and 2.4 million pairs. On average, each query has just under two associated clicks in both logs.

As k increases, the trend of the the four policies is similar to the one we see in the query frequency graphs. There are moderately fewer query-URL pairs released than query impressions in both search logs, but the difference is not as dramatic as with the query reformulation task. This is in part because there is only a limited set of possible clicks to follow a query, as opposed to the unbounded number of possible reformulations for a query. If k is low enough, the click information will be adequate for some re-ranking approaches under the FT_u and FT_a policies. Similar to the query frequency mining, there are more pairs released for the differential privacy policies as k increases.

AOL user 4417749's released query-URL pairs follow a trend similar to the query impressions released under each of the four policies for this user, though flatter. The user's log consists of 132 distinct and 136 total query-click pairs.

Many of the more popular query-click pairs entered by this user are for navigational queries, such as "google" → "http://www.google.com" and "jcpenny" → "http://www.-jcpenney.com", though some are clearly informational, like "sinus infection" → "http://www.emedicinehealth.com" and "termites" → "http://ianrpubs.unl.edu".

For differential privacy, only the navigational queries entered by AOL user 4417749 are released. At $k = 100$, DP_u and DP_a only release five navigational clicks for the queries: "google", "yahoo", "walmart", "costco", and "blue book" (as in Kelley Blue Book).

4.4 Conclusions of simulations

These simulations show that privacy policies with stronger guarantees have larger utility costs. Some tasks, such as query reformulation mining, will require larger logs for certain policies, such as DP_u and DP_a. However, we can also see that the privacy of the previously identified AOL user would likely have been protected under any of the policies simulated above, in large part due to the fact that artifact linking is explicitly prohibited in the released set.

5. PILOT USER STUDY

To evaluate the practicality of CrowdLogging, we conducted a pilot user study. In this section, we discuss many of the decisions we made in implementing the various components of the system. Then we describe the details of the study itself and provide an analysis of results from three applications we recently deployed on top of the framework. We end with a discussion of system vulnerabilities.

We stress that this study is small and only serves to validate the approach on real web browsers with real data. Collecting enough genuine log data for meaningful analysis is a substantial undertaking that is beyond the scope of this study—though we hope to do so in the future.

5.1 Implementation details

Our implementation, *CrowdLogger*, consists of four components: (1) an extension for the Mozilla Firefox Web browser[8] and (2) a client that together comprise the artifact mining and uploading mechanism; (3) one or more anonymizers, which implement a sender anonymization protocol based on onion routing [9]; and (4) a central server that aggregates the collected artifacts. All components other than the extension communicate using Java remote method invocation (RMI) [18]. We describe each of these components in more detail below.

Firefox extension. In addition to serving as CrowdLogger's user interface, the extension captures a log of the user's search and browsing activity. This process is similar to that of existing search engine toolbars, except that rather than sending log information to a central server, the browser stores it on the user's computer for later processing. The extension is also responsible for polling an application server for new mining tasks, and when available, invoking the client to execute the tasks. Users are prompted before mining tasks are run, giving them control over when their data is used.

Client. Upon being invoked by the extension, the client runs mining tasks on the user's log: it extracts search artifacts from the log, encrypts them using the AES symmetric cipher [6], generates a portion of the decryption key for each artifact by using Shamir's Secret Sharing [22], selects a path of anonymizers to the server, encrypts the encrypted artifacts using the server's and selected anonymizers' RSA public keys [20], and then sends the resulting items to the appropriate anonymizers. Encryption with the server's public key prevents anonymizers from viewing the encrypted search artifacts. The key used as the password for the symmetric cipher must be determined deterministically for each artifact; we set this to be a cryptographic hash value[9] of the artifact's plaintext normalized field, ensuring that every client will encrypt the same artifact in the same manner. The portion of the key passed along with each artifact is dependent on a user-selected pass phrase, thus ensuring that a user never

[8] http://www.mozilla.org/firefox/

[9] For example, using SHA1 [8]

inadvertently provides multiple key parts for the same artifact, even if they participate in experiments across multiple computers. While the network traffic caused by this process is considerable—linear in the number of artifacts—it is comparable to any query logging toolbar and far less than that caused by web services that give real time query suggestions or search results.

Anonymizers. The anonymizers function like the relays of the Tor anonymity network,[10] accepting messages from clients and other anonymizers, unpacking them by decrypting them with its private key, and sending the resulting messages to their next destination, which may be either another anonymizer or the server. As with other anonymizer-based methods, they work by directing traffic through several sites before finally sending it onto its destination. Although such approaches can be compromised with sufficiently advanced monitoring techniques [17] our main goal is that the server cannot extract location information, such as the originating IP address, from connections carrying arriving artifacts.

Server. The server collects anonymized, encrypted data from the clients as directed through the anonymizers. Whenever the server receives a sufficient number of distinct key portions for a given search artifact, it reconstructs the complete key using Shamir's Secret Sharing and decrypts the artifact. The aggregation occurs as described in Section 3.1 for all of the applications we have implemented so far.

5.2 Study details

Once our implementation was complete, we advertised our pilot study to associates via e-mail. Users were asked to accept an informed consent form and were then directed to download the Firefox extension. Upon installing, we asked them to create a user ID or use their existing one, if they had one, and then to register. (The user ID is not associated with any identifying information, so privacy is preserved.) Note that a user could install the extension on multiple computers and register at each location, though the registrations were not linked. The main purpose of the registration was to collect demographic information about the users in the study; it is not part of the framework. The compensation for the study consisted of a weekly drawing for a $20 Amazon.com gift card. Participants were given a greater chance of winning if they referred friends to the study. (Prizes were awarded anonymously since we did not collect participant contact information.)

At the time of submission, the Firefox extension had been downloaded and installed 40 times, with 31 registrations received (some of which were due to the authors).

Our institutional review board approved a version of the system that uses k-anonymity (privacy policy FT_u) with k=5. That means a search artifact must be issued under at least five *distinct* user IDs for it to be decrypted at the server. We are using this study to evaluate our implementation. The pilot study ran for two weeks in January 2011.

5.3 Experiments

We ran the three applications we used for our simulations: query frequency, query reformulation, and query-URL pair mining. For each of the experiments, we compare the four privacy policies to understand what data would be released under each model. Note that most of the data is actually encrypted. However, in our study setup, we know how many people entered a particular artifact and how many instances occurred. The fact that we do not know what the artifact is is inconsequential for our immediate purposes.

[10]http://www.torproject.org/

	Query freq.		Query reform.		Query-click	
k	FT_a	FT_u	FT_a	FT_u	FT_a	FT_u
1	4905	4905	6194	6194	2816	2816
2	1803	46	1783	12	830	9
3	490	13	118	1	288	1
4	402	6	89	1	209	0
5	156	1	36	0	126	0

Table 1: Number of distinct search artifacts released under the FT_u and FT_a privacy policies for three applications run in the implemented framework.

A total of 16 distinct users participated in these experiments from 23 installations. No artifact is shared by more than 8 users, but the trends are evident at $k = 5$, so we analyze k from 1–5. For the differential privacy policies, we use $n = 16$ and $\epsilon = 1/(n + 1)$.

For the query frequency task, 8363 impressions were mined of which 4905 are distinct. A total of 8305 query reformulation instances were extracted from the logs; 6194 were distinct. The query-click pair mining task resulted in 5432 pairs, 2816 of which were distinct. A summary of the amount of data released under the FT_a and FT_u policies for the three applications is shown in Table 1. There is no threshold for which information would be released under either differential privacy method—there were simply too few users for this experiment. For this reason, they are omitted from the table.

The results show that it is possible to implement this system with low overhead on the participants' browsers. Information was collected, aggregated, and decrypted when possible (though our set was small enough that only a control "dummy" query (not included in the statistics in Table 1) and the query "news" appeared often enough to become visible). We are planning a larger study in the future, with support for browsers in addition to Firefox.

5.4 System vulnerabilities

As with any query logging approach, CrowdLogging is vulnerable to certain types of malicious attacks. Attackers could potentially compromise users' computers and steal their search logs, take over one or more of the anonymizers, take over the server, or impersonate user nodes.

The first case applies to all software. If an attacker has access to a user's computer, there is likely much more at stake than the user's search data.

If one or more anonymizers are compromised, the attacker cannot do much, as all of the data is encrypted using the server's RSA public key. If both the anonymizers and the server were attacked simultaneously, then the anonymizers could be re-programmed to keep IP addresses associated with incoming artifacts, potentially revealing users.

If the server is compromised, then a brute-force probing attack can be launched against the artifacts encrypted using the secret sharing scheme. To do this, the attacker must generate a candidate artifact, encrypt it using the sharing scheme, and then compare it with the list of encrypted artifacts. If a match is found, the attacher knows that the candidate artifact is present in the collected data. However, this process is not trivial, so it is unlikely that even a large portion of the collected data would be compromised.

Finally, if attackers impersonate some number of user nodes, they can inject identical artificial data into their logs which may cause specific artifacts to be released that would not otherwise have been released. For example, perhaps the query "bob" was only entered by one legitimate user. If $k = 5$ and there are four attackers that are curious if any other users entered the query "bob", they could add that search to their logs. The artifact "bob" now appears to come from k distinct users and is thus revealed. There is no easy solution to this attack, though we are exploring techniques that might indicate when such an attack is occurring, such as by allowing for trusted users to register and then checking for skew between data submitted by registered and unregistered users.

6. CONCLUSIONS

We presented a novel framework for collecting, storing, and mining search logs in a distributed, private, and anonymous manner called CrowdLogging. The work is motivated jointly by a need to have search logs available to researchers outside of large search companies and a need to instill trust in the users that provide search data. Our framework gives researchers access to up-to-date search data. CrowdLogging also allows users—the individuals who contribute the data that is ultimately mined—an unprecedented amount of control over their data.

We used simulations on two large search logs to show the practicality of several of the privacy policies that are compatible with our framework, including two with theoretically sound privacy guarantees. The simulations show that much of the original data can be ultimately revealed, although the exact amount varies by application and privacy policy.

We showed the viability of the system through a small pilot user study, run over two weeks. This study required a fully functional implementation, which we named CrowdLogger, and demonstrated that all parts of the system work with minimal overhead. A larger study is planned for the future and will further assess the feasibility of using CrowdLogging in realistic settings.

7. ACKNOWLEDGMENTS

We thank Brian Levine for his helpful thoughts about system vulnerabilities and possible defenses. This work was supported in part by the Center for Intelligent Information Retrieval, in part by NSF grant #IIS-0910884, and in part by an NSF Graduate Research Fellowship under grant #DGE-0907995. Any opinions, findings and conclusions or recommendations expressed in this material are the authors' and do not necessarily reflect those of the sponsor.

References

[1] E. Adar. User 4xxxxx9: Anonymizing query logs. In *Query Logs Workshop, WWW*, 2007.

[2] F. Ahmad and G. Kondrak. Learning a spelling error model from search query logs. In *HLT '05*. ACL, 2005.

[3] J. Bar-Ilan. Position paper: Access to query logs—an academic researcher's point of view. In *Query Log Analysis Workshop, WWW*, 2007.

[4] M. Barbaro and T. Zeller Jr. A face is exposed for AOL searcher No. 4417749. *New York Times*, 2006. `http://www.nytimes.com/2006/08/09/technology/09aol.html`.

[5] D. Beeferman and A. Berger. Agglomerative clustering of a search engine query log. In *KDD '00*. ACM, 2000.

[6] J. Daemen and V. Rijmen. *The design of Rijndael: AES–the advanced encryption standard*. Springer Verlag, 2002.

[7] C. Dwork. Differential privacy. *Automata, languages and programming*, pages 1–12, 2006.

[8] P. FIPS. 180-3 Secure Hash Standard (SHS). *Information Technology Laboratory, NIST, Oct*, 2008.

[9] D. Goldschlag, M. Reed, and P. Syverson. Onion routing. *CACM*, 42(2):39–41, 1999.

[10] K. Hafner and M. Richtel. Google resists U.S. subpoena of search data. *New York Times*, 2006. `http://www.nytimes.com/2006/01/20/technology/20google.html`.

[11] Y. Hong, X. He, J. Vaidya, N. Adam, and V. Atluri. Effective anonymization of query logs. In *CIKM '09*, 2009.

[12] D. Howe and H. Nissenbaum. *TrackMeNot: Resisting Surveillance in Web Search*. Oxford Univ. Press, 2009.

[13] B. J. Jansen and A. Spink. How are we searching the World Wide Web? A comparison of nine search engine transaction logs. *Inf. Process. Manage.*, 42(1):248–263, 2006.

[14] B. J. Jansen, A. Spink, and J. Pedersen. A temporal comparison of AltaVista web searching. *JASIST*, 56: 559–570, 2005.

[15] T. Joachims. Optimizing search engines using clickthrough data. In *Proc. of the eighth ACM SIGKDD*, pages 133–142. ACM, 2002. ISBN 158113567X.

[16] A. Korolova, K. Kenthapadi, N. Mishra, and A. Ntoulas. Releasing search queries and clicks privately. In *Proc. of WWW*, pages 171–180, 2009.

[17] S. J. Murdoch and G. Danezis. Low-cost traffic analysis of Tor. In *IEEE Security and Privacy Symposium*, 2005.

[18] Oracle. Java RMI spec. `http://download.oracle.com/javase/6/docs/platform/rmi/spec/rmiTOC.html`.

[19] M. Paşca. Weakly-supervised discovery of named entities using web search queries. In *CIKM '07*. ACM, 2007.

[20] R. L. Rivest, A. Shamir, and L. Adleman. A method for obtaining digital signatures and public-key cryptosystems. *Commun. ACM*, 21(2):120–126, 1978.

[21] M. J. Schwartz. Spam attack captures government data. *Information Week*, 2011. `http://www.informationweek.com/news/security/attacks/showArticle.jhtml?articleID=229000118&cid=RSSfeed_IWK_All#`.

[22] A. Shamir. How to share a secret. *Communications of the ACM*, 22(11):612–613, 1979.

[23] L. Sweeney. k-Anonymity: A Model for Protecting Privacy. *Int. J. Uncertain. Fuzziness Knowl.-Based Syst*, 10(5):557–570, 2002.

[24] S. Wedig and O. Madani. A large-scale analysis of query logs for assessing personalization opportunities. In *KDD '06*. ACM, 2006.

[25] J.-M. Yang, R. Cai, F. Jing, S. Wang, L. Zhang, and W.-Y. Ma. Search-based query suggestion. In *CIKM '08*, 2008.

[26] S. Zhong, Z. Yang, and T. Chen. k-anonymous data collection. *Information Sciences*, 179(17):2948–2963, 2009.

Out of Sight, Not Out of Mind

On the Effect of Social and Physical Detachment on Information Need

Elad Yom-Tov
Yahoo Research
111 W 41st st.
New York, NY 10018
USA
eladyt@yahoo-inc.com

Fernando Diaz
Yahoo Research
111 W 41st st.
New York, NY 10018
USA
diazf@yahoo-inc.com

ABSTRACT

The information needs of users and the documents which answer it are frequently contingent on the different characteristics of users. This is especially evident during natural disasters, such as earthquakes and violent weather incidents, which create a strong transient information need. In this paper we investigate how the information need of users is affected by their physical detachment, as estimated by their physical location in relation to that of the event, and by their social detachment, as quantified by the number of their acquaintances who may be affected by the event. Drawing on large-scale data from three major events, we show that social and physical detachment levels of users are a major influence on their information needs, as manifested by their search engine queries. We demonstrate how knowing social and physical detachment levels can assist in improving retrieval for two applications: identifying search queries related to events and ranking results in response to event-related queries. We find that the average precision in identifying relevant search queries improves by approximately 18%, and that the average precision of ranking that uses detachment information improves by 10%.

Categories and Subject Descriptors

H.3.3 [**Information Search and Retrieval**]: Search process; H.4.3 [**Communications Applications**]: Information browsers

General Terms

performance,experimentation

Keywords

social,physical,distance,information,need

SIGIR'11, July 24–28, 2011, Beijing, China.

1. INTRODUCTION

In today's world, people are ever more informed of news events that take place far from their homes, very shortly after events occur. This is especially true of events which are limited in time and location. The information about these events comes from diverse sources, including media outlets (e.g. television, newspapers, media sites on the web), social media (e.g. Twitter, Facebook), and active seeking of information using web search engines. Their knowledge of the event and its different facets is shaped by external forces (which items are reported by news channels they choose to watch) as much as by their preference for information.

As a motivating example, consider an earthquake event, its different information aspects, and how these might be consumed by users. People close to the event might be interested in emergency services and evacuation procedures. People far from the earthquake may want to know more general details of the earthquake and how they might help people affected by it. Finally, people not in the vicinity of the event, but that have friends or relatives which they think may be affected might seek the names of those injured by the earthquake.

News coverage, which may reflect people's interest in an event, is known to be influenced by the physical distance of consumers from the location of the event. As Chang *et al.* [10] showed, the distance of an event from the USA is one of the most predictive attributes for its media coverage. Furthermore, Wu [30] showed that the volume of media related to news events in Canada and Mexico by USA-based news channels is partially explained by the distance of the events from the closest USA border.

However, while news coverage measures information production with respect to an event, we are interested in more directly measuring people's information demand with respect to an event. Consider the graphs[1] of news coverage, social media coverage, and information seeking for three news events in Figure 1. Although the trends, in general, correlate with each other for a given event, the information-seeking behavior of users is sufficiently different from that of media output to motivate a deeper study of information seeking in isolation.

In this paper, we investigate the information need of individuals in response to special events, both adverse and otherwise, as manifested by active information seeking on the web. We investigate this need as a function of users' relationship to the event, specifically their social detachment

[1]Details of the events and the data are given in Section 4.

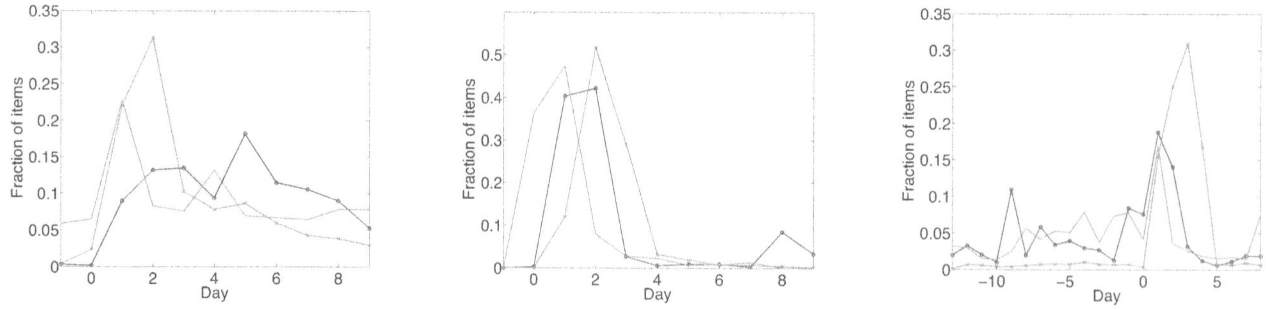

Figure 1: Fraction of mainstream media outlet items (blue, circles), social media items (red) and queries (green, crosses) posted over time in response to the San Bruno (left), New York (middle), and Alaska (right) events. These graphs are best printed in color.

from the event and their geographic distance from it. We show that information need is strongly dependent on social and geographical attachment. We demonstrate that knowledge of social and geographic information can improve retrieval by accurately identifying queries related to an event and consequently retrieving the appropriate documents.

The paper is structured as follows: In Section 2 we survey relevant related work. In Section 3 we enhance a previously-proposed model of information need to account for user characteristics. Section 4 introduces the data we analyzed. In Section 5 we present an analysis of our data and demonstrate the effect of social and geographic detachment levels on information need. Finally, Section 6 demonstrates two information-retrieval applications which benefit from the use of social and geographic detachment.

2. RELATED WORK

Information seeking with respect to news events is gaining increasing attention from the scientific community. Within this area, our work focuses on analyzing the influence of the geographic and social context of the user on querying behavior during an event.

The geographic context of the user has repeatedly been found to have an influence on querying behavior. For example, almost immediate detection of earthquakes in Japan can be performed with very high confidence by tracking the micro-blogging service Twitter [27]. In fact, a service based on Twitter sent alerts within 20 seconds of the events, compared to 6 minutes by the Japan Meteorological Agency. Earthquakes could also be localized by considering the propagation time of earthquakes and the reported location of users. Similarly, Backstrom *et al.*[1] developed a model for pinpointing events based on the location of people querying about them. In this way, both stationary terms (sports teams) and moving events (hurricanes) were pinpointed to within a few kilometers. In both [1] and [27] it was found that the closer people are to an event, the more likely they are to seek information about the event or to report about it. In the context of aggregated search, geographic features of the user as well as those mentioned in the query have been found to be very predictive of user interest in news [15]. Similarly, Hassan *et al.* also found that these geographic features improved general web search [17].

The social context of the user has received somewhat less treatment than geography. Carmel *et al.* [8] demonstrated that, in an intra-organizational setting, the fact that two people are familiar with each other can improve the suggestion of interesting content by serving one person the content which his colleague has marked as interesting. However, that study also concluded that suggesting similar content to similar people can obtain even better results, which may suggest homophily, rather than social connection, is the source of improvement. Teevan *et al.* found that personalizing at the group scale improved effectiveness for group-related queries [28]. The size of a population which can obtain knowledge of an event through their social network has been studied using both empirical data and theoretic models in [5] and [4]. For example, [5] estimated that between one in 17 and one in 140 people knew a person who was directly influenced by the attacks against the World Trade Center on 9/11/2001. Information propagation in electronic social networks in response to a crisis event was studied in [24], where it was shown how students utilized social media to form collective response decisions in response to a shooting incident at Virginia Tech university. We note that our study does not analyze the question of which information is passed via the social network. Instead, given a social network and the location of people, we study which information is of interest to them. In a recent paper, Mendoza *et al.* [20] analyzed the information published and disseminated by users of Twitter during an earthquake in Chile. Their analysis demonstrated that while both rumors and facts related to the earthquake were disseminated, rumors tended to be questioned by users more than facts, which suggests the community filters false information to some extent. Although it is a single event, information regarding the earthquake was disseminated for at least nine days, much longer than observed for many news stories in the public media (as discussed above).

The temporal analysis of news events also received some attention. For example, Leskovec *et al.* showed that media interest in an event peaks within two days and decays somewhat quicker than it arises [18]. Social media outlets have a similar attention timespan, and peak, on average, 2.5 hours later than mainstream media. In the context of aggregated news search, Diaz found—somewhat unsurprisingly—that temporally local variables such as query volume were important in detecting the newsworthiness of a query [11]. In the context of web ranking, researchers have found that a general retrieval model fails for late-breaking news events and specialized query treatment was required to satisfy user intent [12]. This specialized ranker can be further improved by analyzing the discussion of the topic in social media [13].

3. A MODEL OF USER PREFERENCE FOR TOPIC INFORMATION

Define the primal information object as a topic, $T \in \mathcal{T}$, which is information pertinent to a defined subject. Each topic is comprised of two sets: the set of queries users may issue when seeking information about that topic, Q_T, and the set of documents which may satisfy users seeking information about that topic, R_T. Each topic may be partitioned into aspects $\{a_i\} \in T$, $i = 1, 2, \ldots N$, which describe different facets of the topic. Thus, a user may be interested in one or more of a topic's aspects.

Given a user, u, we claim that $P(T|u)$, i.e. the probability of the user's interest in T, and the specific aspects a_i of T which will be of interest to u depend heavily on different properties of u, e.g. $P(a_i|u)$. These properties include a users' demographic information (age, gender, etc), social parameters (circle of friends, acquaintances, and work associates), geographic parameters (location vis-a-vis topic location), as well as other parameters (for example, time of day, exposure to different media, etc).

In this paper we are concerned with two main attributes of users: Their location and social parameters. Specifically, the first property we investigate is $d_{\text{geo}}(u, T)$, which is the geographic distance between the user and epicenter of the event. We term this property the geographic detachment of a user from an event. We hypothesize that $P(T|u)$ is negatively correlated with $d_{\text{geo}}(u, T)$.

The second property we investigate is $a_{\text{soc}}(u, T)$, which is the social affinity between the user and those users geographically close to the epicenter of an event. We term this property social attachment. A simple way of thinking about social affinity is as the number of friends or family close to the event epicenter. We hypothesize that $P(T|u)$ is positively correlated with $a_{\text{soc}}(u, T)$.

Note that both geographic distance and social affinity cannot be defined for every topic. However, for any event which has a clear geographic epicenter these detachment levels can be defined and measured.

4. EXPERIMENTAL SETUP

4.1 Case Studies

In this paper we analyze three events, which are briefly described below:

1. **San Bruno event**: On September 9th, 2010, at 6:11pm local time, a large pipe carrying natural gas exploded in the city of San Bruno (near San Francisco), California. The explosion was registered as a 1.1 magnitude earthquake on the Richter scale. The sound of the explosion led some local residents to initially believe that it was an earthquake or an airplane crash. Eight people died as a result of the explosion, and 38 houses were destroyed.
2. **New York storm**: A violent storm passed through New York city on the 16th September 2010, hitting the boroughs of Queens, Brooklyn, and Staten Island. The storm reached tornado-level in Flushing Meadows (part of Queens), leaving one person dead and causing widespread damage to property.
3. **Alaska elections**: The elections to the USA Senate was held on the 2nd November 2010. The election in Alaska, although part of the electoral process in 33 other USA states, drew significant attention because of a three-way race, which included one candidate who lost the primary elections of her party, but decided to participate in the elections as an independent candidate. She went on to win the elections.

These events were chosen because they were physically localized in their scope and thus have a clear epicenter. Therefore, social and physical detachment are clearly defined for these events. Furthermore, because they are temporally limited, they act as an impulse to the system, and thus create high levels of interest for a relatively short and clearly-defined period.

We determined a radius of influence for each event based on the radius of the community affected. In the case of San Bruno, this was set to 5km, which is roughly the area directly disrupted by the explosion. In New York, we set this radius to 30km, to include all the neighborhoods hit by the storm. The radius for Alaska was set to 500km, to include most of Alaska's population, but not any other state.

4.2 Data

We used two types of data in our study: First, we extracted query-log data of the Yahoo search engine from several days before the event (one day for the first two events, and 10 for the last), until 8 days after the event. For each query we extracted its text, time, a unique identifier of the user who posted it, the results displayed to the user, and the pages he or she selected to view as a result of the query.

The query log was parsed to identify those queries which were likely relevant to the event, using a term-matching scheme. We did this by manually generating a list of keywords for each event. The keywords were drawn from several categories: where the event took place, who was involved in the event, and what happened at the event. We also generated a list of excluded words, to remove irrelevant queries. Queries and keywords were stemmed using a Porter stemmer. A query was considered relevant to the event if keywords from at least two categories were used in the query, and none of the excluded words appearing in it. For example, the list of keywords for the New York event were:

1. **Descriptions**: Tornado, Storm
2. **Location**: New York, NY, NYC, Flushing, Queens, Brooklyn, Statue of Liberty, Staten Island.

We encode data at the granularity of a day in order to remove diurnal effects.

Each user was represented by two measures of separation from the event: A physical separation, measured by his physical distance, where a larger distance indicates a larger separation, and a social separation, measured by the number of contacts local to the event, where a larger number indicates smaller separation.

We used the zip-code given by users at the time of registration with Yahoo to identify their approximate location. An alternative way to determine location could have been

	Number of relevant queries	Number of unique relevant queries	Number of users posting relevant queries
San Bruno	194,184	45,843	79,134
New York	54,678	4,406	34,069
Alaska	281,851	23,921	183,258

Table 1: Query log statistics for the three events

through users' IP address, but as some users use proxy servers, it is not clear that this would be a superior way of measuring location. We computed the physical distance of each user to the event using the Haversine formula.

Finally, we used the list of contacts in the Yahoo Instant Messenger (IM) application as a proxy for users' social network. The number of contacts per person is power-law distributed ($\alpha = -0.99$, $R^2 = 0.93$), with a median of 6 connections per person and an average of 22.7 connections[2]. The list of contacts was used to determine the number of contacts each user had in the area of the event, which are defined as the number of contacts inside the radius of influence of each event. Thus, each query is described by a tuple of its text, time and date, and the physical and social separation of the user who posted it from the event. Table 4.2 provides statistics on the number of queries related to each event which were posted during the days we observed the query log, the number of unique relevant queries, and the number of users which posted these queries.

We quantified the daily media volume of news outlets related to an event by counting the number of document found on Yahoo News[3] every day, which contained all the words used in any of the 50 most popular queries identified in Section 4. Similarly, the volume of social media was measured via the number of Twitter messages which contained the words used in these queries.

5. EMPIRICAL ANALYSIS

5.1 Measuring the Effect of Detachment on Interest in an Event

We begin our analysis by showing how the probability of a user's interest in topics related to the event of interest depend on his geographic and social affinity, that is, we measure $P(T|u)$.

Recall that we are interested in examining the relationship between $P(T|u)$ and our detachment measures. In our analysis we binned users into logarithmically spaced bins according to their geographic detachment from the event, and used the raw social detachment values. Let $\mathcal{U}_{d_{\text{geo}}}$ be the set of users within a distance $d_{\text{geo}} \pm \delta$ of the event; similarly for social affinity. We then, for geographic distance, computed the correlation with $P(T|\mathcal{U}_{d_{\text{geo}}})$, the probability of group interest in T; similarly for social affinity. We define this precisely as,

$$P(T|\mathcal{U}_{d_{\text{geo}}}) = \frac{\sum_{u\in\mathcal{U}_{d_{\text{geo}}}} |Q_u \cap Q_T|}{\sum_{u\in\mathcal{U}_{d_{\text{geo}}}} |Q_u|} \quad (1)$$

Figure 2 shows $P(T|\mathcal{U}_{d_{\text{geo}}})$ related to the San Bruno event as a function of d_{geo} and as a function of a_{soc}. These figures show that interest is correlated with physical and social affinity. Indeed, the fraction of event-related queries decays exponentially as physical detachment weakens, and linearly so in the case of social affinity.

Table 2 shows the correlations between d_{geo} with $P(T|\mathcal{U}_{d_{\text{geo}}})$ for all three events; similarly for social affinity. Additionally, this table shows the polyserial correlation[14] between the log-transformed physical distance and the number of local contacts[4]. The correlation of the two detachment methods is significant, but not very high. This is to be expected, since people closer to an event can be expected to have more local relationships. While both physical detachment and social affinity are significantly correlated with the fraction of event-related queries, physical detachment seems to be a stronger indicator for interest compared to social affinity. This is in line with several studies (for example, [23]) who have found that social attributes are secondary in importance to individual traits. Thus, we conclude that the probability that a user will be interested in an event-related topic is highly correlated with social and geographic detachment.

The events we analyzed are characterized by a strong temporally-limited interest of users. Figure 3 shows the fraction of queries related to the San bruno event as a function of time, partitioned according to the physical distance of users from the event. Day zero marks the day of the explosion. Since the explosion happened in the early hours of the evening, significant interest in the event starts on day 1 and peaks only on day 2. Interest in the event decays rapidly, and could have been faster if not for a spike on day 5, which is likely related to new findings about the event being reported in the media (The New York and Alaska events decay after approximately three days, as seen in Figure 1). Strikingly, as the figure shows, interest in the San Bruno event decays in an identical manner for users independent of whether they were physically close to the event or far from it ($R^2 = 0.95$ between the two time series), though a logical hypothesis would have been that closer users would retain interest in the event for a longer time period. A similar image appears when considering users with no local contacts versus those with many such contacts.

5.2 Measuring the Effect of Detachment on Event Aspects

The fact that users post queries related to an event is, as we demonstrated above, significantly tied to their detachment from that event. However, queries may have been due to different aspects of the topic. Indeed, our hypothesis is that the distribution of aspects is dependent on users' relationship to the event. In this section we identify different aspects of the event-related topics and show how differences in the degree of detachment influence the need for information.

[2]Note that users who were not using the IM application had, by definition, zero connections. Therefore, the average and median number of connections is higher than what would have been obtained using the entire population

[3]`news.yahoo.com`

[4]Polyserial correlation is required because physical distance is a continuous variable, whereas number of local contacts is an ordinal variable

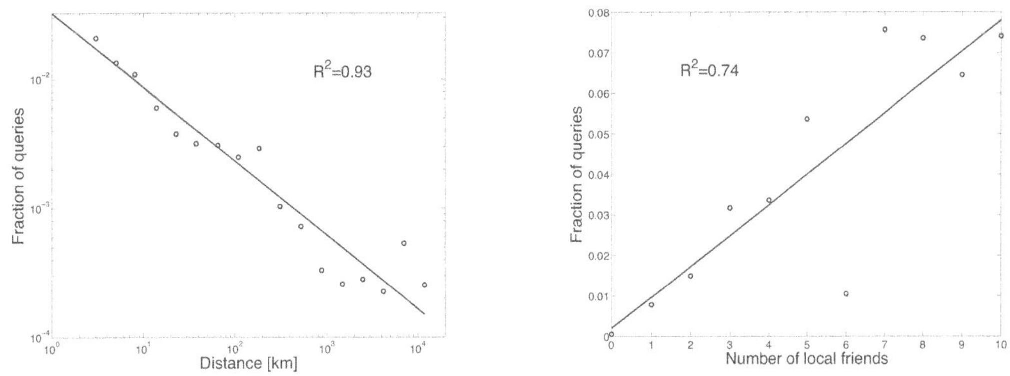

Figure 2: Fraction of queries as a function of the physical distance (left) and the number of local contacts (right). The regression line on the left is an exponential fit with $R^2 = 0.93$ and a linear fit on the right with $R^2 = 0.74$. Note the logarithmic axes of the left figure.

	Polyserial correlation between the physical detachment and social affinity	Correlation (R^2) between the fraction of relevant queries and: physical detachment	social detachment	Slope of the correlation between the fraction of relevant queries and: physical detachment	social detachment
San Bruno	-0.61	0.93	0.74	-0.57	0.008
New York	-0.47	0.71	0.18	-0.33	0.012
Alaska	-0.78	0.60	0.26	-0.22	$8 \cdot 10^{-5}$

Table 2: Correlation between physical and social detachment, and the correlations between binned physical detachment and social affinity with the fraction of queries for all three events. Linear regression was used for the physical detachment, and exponential regression for social affinity. All regression results are statistically significant at $p < 0.01$.

Clusters of queries have been shown in the past to represent different information needs [6, 7]. Therefore, we clustered the queries to identify the different information needs in our data (separately for each event). After stemming and stop-word removal, each query was represented by its TF-IDF model. The queries were then clustered using the k-means algorithm with a cosine similarity measure. The number of clusters was determined by running the algorithm five times using an increasing number of clusters, and using the largest number of clusters which did not generate singleton clusters during any of the five runs. This resulted in 4 clusters for the San Bruno and New York events, and three clusters for the Alaska event. We note that we did not use measures of detachment during clustering.

If the clustering has identified different aspects of the topic, we expect users to have a tendency to post queries which will be part of the same clusters. We measured this hypothesis using the Pearson goodness-of-fit test. This measures, for each user, if the distribution of queries to clusters is significantly different from the same distribution averaged for all users.

We limited this test to users who posted 5 or more queries related to an event so as to obtain good estimates of the distribution. Significance level was determined using a False Detection Rate [2] level of 0.1%.

We found that for the 27% of users of the San Bruno event, 18% of users of the New York event, and 7% of users of the Alaska event had a distribution statistically significantly different from the prior. As a comparison, running this test with randomly permuted data resulted, on average, in less than 0.1% of users who had significantly different distributions. This is a demonstration that the clusters typify different aspects of the event.

Although the clusters were generated using only the text of the query, we found that they created a partition which is statistically significant (Kruskal-Wallis[29], $p < 10^{-5}$) for both social affinity and physical detachment. This suggests that the textual description of an event (or indeed, the aspects of an event sought by different users) is correlated with the detachment level of users.

Figure 4 shows the number of queries from each cluster posted on each day, and the relationship of social and physical detachment on the fraction of queries from each cluster. This figure shows that some clusters have a high preferential physical detachment, for example Cluster 3 in the San Bruno event (Speaman correlation, $\rho = -0.88$), while others, such as Cluster 4 of the San Bruno event have a more pronounced social affinity (Speaman correlation, $\rho = 0.92$). Some of the clusters exhibit weak correlations with detachment levels. These may be a manifestation of an aspect which is commonly queried across geographic or social radii. Interestingly, different clusters have different temporal pat-

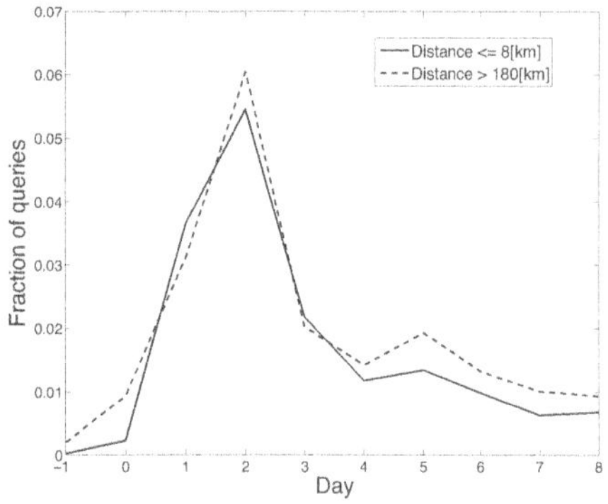

Figure 3: Fraction of event-related queries as a function of time in the San Bruno event, partitioned by the physical distance of users from the event. The fraction of queries for users far from the event was multiplied 50 times, to be on the same scale as users close to the event. Day zero denotes the day of the explosion.

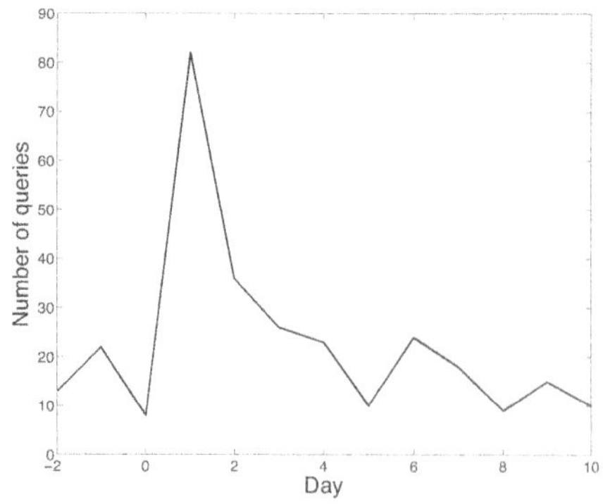

Figure 5: Number of times the query "PG&E" appeared during the San Bruno event.

terns. For example, whereas cluster 1 of the Alaska event has a peak lasting for two days, cluster 2 has a spike lasting only one day.

Therefore, our results indicate that users seek different aspects of information regarding events, and that their interest strongly correlate with their social and geographic detachment. These aspects have different temporal profiles and textual manifestations.

6. APPLICATIONS

6.1 Detecting Queries Related to an Event

Results in previous sections suggest that $P(T|u)$ is strongly related to $d_{\text{geo}}(u,T)$ and $a_{\text{soc}}(u,T)$. Therefore, in this section we use this finding to identify event-related queries. In Section 4, we identified queries relevant to the event using a term-matching method. However, while this method is easy to use in practice, it is likely to miss some queries which used phrases which a human annotator did not consider when generating the list of keywords for term-matching. In this section we show how profiles created using detachment information can be used to identify seemingly queries relevant to the event but which are not in our seed set.

As an example for seemingly unrelated queries, consider the query "PG&E" (Pacific Gas and Electric), which is the name of a local gas company in San Bruno. This query is submitted on regular days, but during the San Bruno event, it was posted with much higher frequency, as shown in Figure 5. It also exhibited a very different distance profile. Detecting these types of queries can be useful for understanding users' information needs, improving retrieval [12], or aggregating news content [11].

As noted above, each query is represented by its text, as well as the time it was submitted, and the physical and social detachment of the user who submitted the query. For popular queries, we can represent each query as the distribution of these three parameters (time, physical attachment, and social attachment). Since in some case there may not be sufficient data to estimate the entire distribution with enough confidence, it may be necessary to resort to sufficient statistics.

Our analysis focused on popular queries, which we defined as those queries which appeared at least 100 times during the event interval. We represented each such query by the number of times it appeared on each day, and the average distance of users who posted this query on that day. This use of averages rather than a distribution allowed us to use queries which appeared relatively few times in the data, while maintaining high confidence in the estimation of the query distribution. Approximately 1M queries appeared at least 100 times for each of the three events.

We compared the representation of the popular queries to that of the clusters of queries identified by term-matching (see Section 5.2 for details of the clustering process). The appearance count was compared using linear correlation, and the average distances using Euclidian distance. A linear predictor was then trained to decide on the weight of each parameter (correlation and distance) in the final scoring of each popular query. Positive (event-related) queries were replicated 100 times to mitigate the effect of their sparseness in the data (approximately 0.5% of queries were event-related).

In our experiments we used five-fold cross validation, to reduce the chance of overfitting. After finding the appropriate weight for each parameter, we measured how well the term-matched queries were identified by the method. The use of term-matched queries as the target queries means our results should be considered an underestimate of the true result.

Term-matched queries are rare in the most popular queries (in the range of 0.1%-0.3%). We therefore report two measures of success in classification: Average precision and lift. For any given fraction of the queries $0 < f < 1$, lift [25] is defined as the ratio between the number of event-related queries among the fraction of T queries that are ranked highest by the proposed system, and the expected number of event-related queries in a random sample from the general query pool of equal size. For example, a lift of 3 at a fraction T = 0.01 means that if we scan the 1% of queries ranked highest by the proposed system, we expect to see

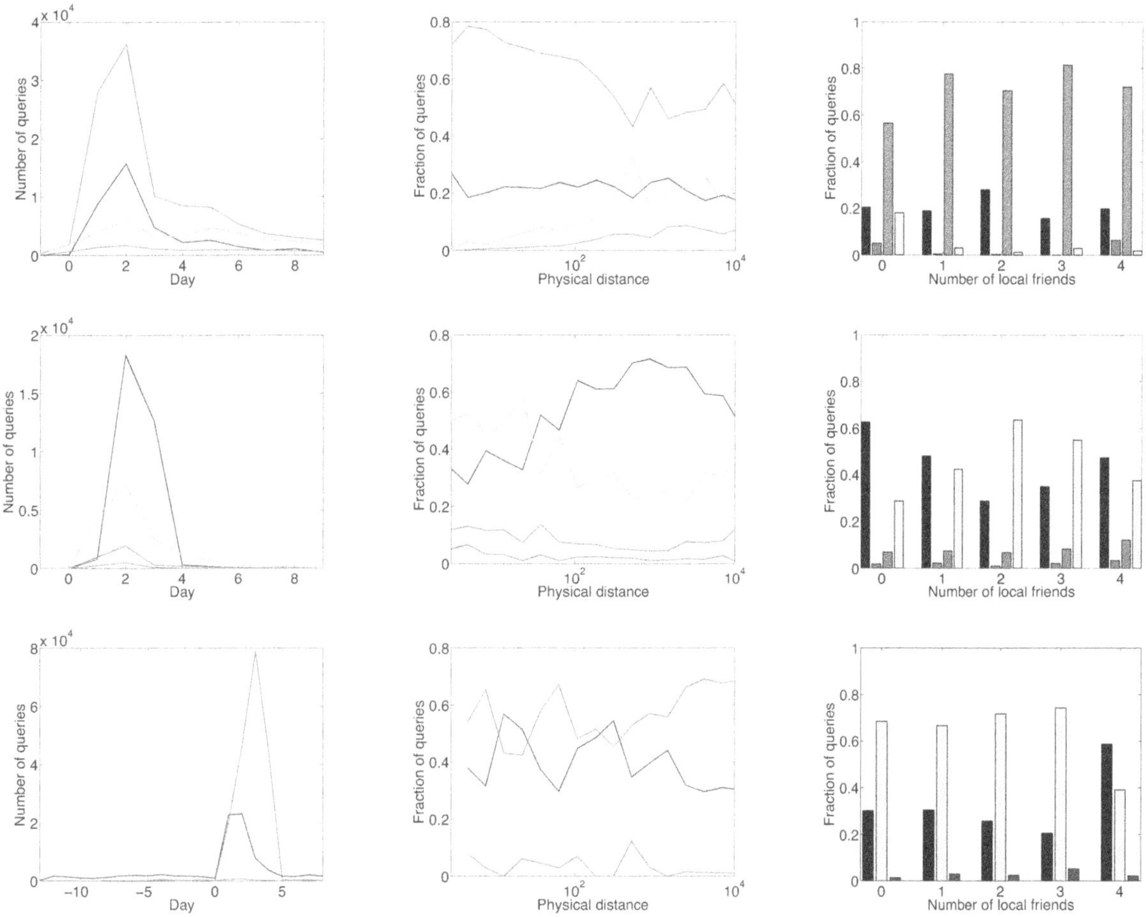

Figure 4: The number of queries from each cluster as a function of time, and the fraction of queries from each cluster as a function of physical and social affinity. Colors denote different clusters: Cluster 1 (blue), Cluster 2 (green), Cluster 3 (red), and Cluster 4 (cyan). Each row presents the data from one event, which are, from top to bottom, San Bruno, New York, and Alaska. These graphs are best printed in color.

three times more event-related queries in this set of queries than in a 0.01-fraction random sample of the queries. Lift measures the precision at a given threshold [9], albeit scaled such that it can be larger than 1.

Table 3 shows the average precision and lift obtained by the system when attempting to identify term-matched queries in the popular queries. The lift is given for 1% of the queries, with and without the use of the physical and social detachment measures. The proposed method accurately identifies the term-matched relevant queries, and improves lift and average precision by 18% over count profiles. This is very useful both for improving query routing and for human annotators to be able to understand the kind of phrases users make use of when searching for information about the event. The detachment profiles improve results (especially in the San Bruno and Alaska cases), though there is no clear preference for use of geographic versus social information. Interestingly, using both social and geographic detachment reduced precision. We attribute this to the sparsity of the positive examples, which accounted for around 0.5% of the data.

Anecdotally, when not using the distance profile, the queries ranked high by the predictor, and which are unrelated to the event, are mostly associated with other news events which peaked in interest around the same time as the event of interest. This is consistent with the use of such features when detecting newsworthy queries in general rather than for a specific topic [11].

In the case of the San Bruno event, we scanned the highest-ranked queries and found that (excluding the term-matched queries) these included mostly names of local news channels, and event-related queries which contained partially-entered words.

Identifying relevant queries in retrospect (using the query profile over the entire time span of the event) is useful for some applications. However, in most cases one would like to identify event-related queries soon after the event begins. Figure 6 shows the lift obtained by our method when considering the data as it is collected. In this experiment, feature vectors for day n were constructed using the data from days -1 to day n (inclusive). As this figure shows, even after only one day of the event, reasonable lift is obtained by our method. This indicates that our method can assist in pinpointing event-related queries soon after they begin.

	Average precision				Lift			
	Count	Physical	Social	All	Count	Physical	Social	All
San Bruno	0.0185	0.0238	0.0119	0.0143	33.7	43.9	50.0	48.0
New York	0.0170	0.0255	0.0117	0.0154	24.5	25.2	25.2	25.2
Alaska	0.0058	0.0051	0.0054	0.0052	11.1	10.4	11.3	10.4

Table 3: Average precision and maximum lift obtained in identifying event-related queries using appearance counts per day (Count) and when additionally using physical and social detachment profiles. The column denoted by "All" represents results when using appearance counts, physical detachment and social detachment information.

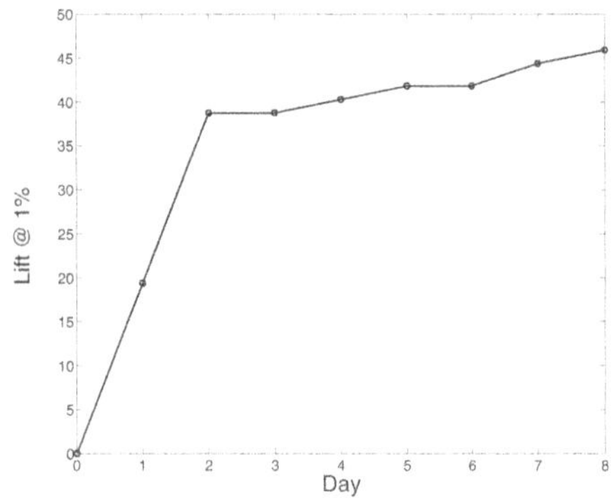

Figure 6: Lift at 1% obtained by using the data from days 0 to N, for the San Bruno event

6.2 Retrieval for Queries Related to Events

In Section 5.2 we demonstrated that detachment affects the aspect of the topic which is sought by users. Therefore, we hypothesize that using the detachment information of users, it should be possible to improve retrieval. Our goal is to identify which pages are likely to be of interest to a user, given her specific detachment information.

One way to use detachment information is to augment queries with attachment data and use a ranking algorithm [22] to find an improved page ranking. While this solution is possible, it should be noted that the distribution of user detachments is far from uniform (there are many more users who are far physically from any event than those close to it). Therefore, a large number of data points as well as care is required when training such a model to provide sufficient weight to examples of sparsely-represented detachment values.

An alternative solution is to partition the data according to detachment metrics, and train a different ranking model for each detachment partition. For example, one model can be trained for those users who are 10km or less from the event, and another model can be trained for those users who are located 10km or more from the event. In the following we take this approach, and build models according to the physical detachment level and/or the social detachment level of users.

We randomly chose approximately 16,000 queries for each of the three events. For each of the queries we extracted the pages presented to users as the search engine results, as well as whether the user clicked each page. A page was considered of interest if it was clicked by the user [16]. We note that our analysis, which was performed after the event, suffers from a certain selection bias by users because the initial ranking of documents was generated by the search engine, over which we had no control. Each page was represented by its rank on the results page (which is a proxy for its perceived importance as estimated by the search engine) and the second-level URL information, e.g., the address `http://news.yahoo.com` would be represented as *news*. This information is important because second-level domains are usually indicative of the type of information on the web site, and are especially useful when distinguishing news and non-news web sites.

Users were partitioned into five groups according to their physical distance from the event, using logarithmical-spaced bins, or to one of three social attachment groups: No local contacts, one local contact, and more than one such contact. We trained one set of models for each detachment type separately and for the combination of the detachment levels. As a baseline, we trained a single model for the entire data (without detachment information). All else being equal, since this model was trained using more data, it could be expected to perform better than the partitioned model. The model used for identifying relevant documents was a decision tree classifier. We used five-fold cross validation in our experimentation, and measured the mean average precision (MAP) and the average precision at the top 5 and top 10 documents (denoted as P@5 and P@10, respectively).

Table 4 shows the results of our experiments. The models which use detachment information obtained a statistically significant improvement over the baseline. Separately, using social detachment gave a larger improvement over the baseline than physical detachment. The improvement in MAP using social detachment information over the baseline was, on average 10%. Improvement in P@5 was 5% and in P@10 2%. Interestingly, using both detachment parameters gave only marginal improvements over social detachment alone. We attribute this to the correlation between the social and physical information, as well as to sparseness of the training data for some models.

We did not find a trend which suggests that the proposed method improves (or decreases) retrieval performance as a function of detachment levels. Rather, gain is distributed across all detachment levels.

Unsurprisingly, the most indicative attributes of models built for users closer to the event featured local news outlets (newspapers and TV channels), whereas for users far from the event these included mostly national news channels and web aggregators such as Yahoo news.

We conclude that the use of detachment information is beneficial in improving retrieval.

	MAP				P@5				P@10			
	Both	Physical	Social	No	Both	Physical	Social	No	Both	Physical	Social	No
San Bruno	0.693	0.692	0.716	0.607	0.182	0.181	0.185	0.164	0.234	0.234	0.236	0.228
New York	0.804	0.794	0.788	0.764	0.128	0.128	0.128	0.128	0.148	0.148	0.148	0.145
Alaska	0.889	0.886	0.898	0.831	0.146	0.146	0.146	0.144	0.167	0.167	0.168	0.167

Table 4: Improvement in retrieval results when using detachment information. Columns denoted by "both" mark models which used both physical and social detachment information. Columns marked by "physical" and "social" denote cases where physical or social detachment information was used, respectively. In all cases and metrics, the use of detachment information improves retrieval in a statistically significant manner ($p < 10^{-2}$, sign test) over the baseline. The differences in MAP when using social, physical, and both measures, are pairwise statistically significant ($p < 10^{-2}$, sign test) except for the use of physical versus both physical and social information. The differences in P@5 and P@10 when using social, physical, and both measures, were not pairwise statistically significant.

7. DISCUSSION

In this paper we investigated the effect of social and geographic detachment of users of information need. We found that the level of detachment has a significant effect on both the level of interest and the type of interest that users have in an event.

The aspects we identified were limited by the fact that only query text was used as their input. In future work, we intend to use more robust clustering and similarity measures [19, 21, 26]. This will allow us to better understand the semantics of aspects, especially as they are understood by the users.

The improvement attained by using social detachment in both applications was markedly better than that of geographic detachment when measured by high-precision metrics (lift, P@5 and P@10). Geographic detachment was better in terms of average precision. We speculate that this is due to the relative sparsity of non-zero social detachment compared to geographic data as well as to the importance of social connections.

Although our sample is limited, our results indicate that highly localized events such as the San Bruno event, tend to be explained better by attachments than events which take place over wider areas such as the other two events. Further research of additional events is required in order to generalize these findings.

An interesting question which arises from our work is the relationship between media (social and commercial) and users' information seeking, as manifested by the query log. The temporal behavior is highly correlated, and includes the appearance of idiosyncratic peaks such as those on day 4 of the San Bruno event. Furthermore, as Figure 1 shows, interest in the Alaska elections is almost entirely limited to dates after the elections themselves. This is surprising, because it indicates that interest in these election is almost solely related to the results of the election and not to candidates' work or people's need for information about voting procedures, etc, prior to the election. This might hint that query log volume is driven to some extent by media interest, but further experimentation is required to validate this link.

Setting the number of local users for finding those who may be influenced by an event was performed in this study using a simple heuristic which is finding all the people in a radius enclosing the urban population which may have been affected by the event. However, if we aim to automate the improvement in search result, the finding of this radius needs to be automated.

One way to estimate the radius of influence is derived in [1]. However, in that study only geographic location was taken into account as influencing the radius of influence. Furthermore, the frequency of queries was posited to decay exponentially as a function of distance. However, our observations are that, because of the location of population centers in relation to the location of an event, the decay in frequency of queries does not follow a simple exponential.

Bernard et al. [3] discussed the question of estimating the number of people who died in an earthquake from an entire population based on sampling a population and determining how many people they knew, first-hand, who had died, as well as the average number of acquaintances each person has (e.g., their immediate social network). Applying this method to our work, the radius of influence can be set to contain the estimated number of affected users, given the other parameters. We plan to verify the utility of this method and, as it is considered a lower bound on the number of affected users, measure how close its estimates are to the ones identified by our heuristic.

8. REFERENCES

[1] Lars Backstrom, Jon Kleinberg, Ravi Kumar, and Jasmine Novak. Spatial variation in search engine queries. In *Proceeding of the 17th international conference on World Wide Web*, WWW '08, pages 357–366. ACM, 2008.

[2] Yoav Benjamini and Yosef Hochberg. Controlling the false discovery rate - a new and powerful approach to multiple testing. *Journal of the Royal Statistical Society B*, 57:289–300, 1995.

[3] H. Russell Bernard, Eugene C. Johnsen, Peter D. Killworth, and Scott Robinson. Estimating the size of an average personal network and of an event subpopulation. In M. Kochen, editor, *The small world*, pages 159–175. 1989.

[4] H. Russell Bernard, Eugene C. Johnsen, Peter D. Killworth, and Scott Robinson. Estimating the size of an average personal network and of an event subpopulation: Some empirical results. *Social science research*, 20:109–121, 1991.

[5] H. Russell Bernard, Peter D. Killworth, Eugene C. Johnsen, Gene A. Shelley, and Christopher McCarty.

Estimating the ripple effect of a disaster. *Connections*, 24(2):18–22, 2001.

[6] David Carmel, Elad Yom-Tov, Adam Darlow, and Dan Pelleg. What makes a query difficult? In *Proceedings of the 29th annual international ACM SIGIR conference on Research and development in information retrieval*, SIGIR '06, pages 390–397. ACM, 2006.

[7] David Carmel, Elad Yom-Tov, and Haggai Roitman. Enhancing digital libraries using missing content analysis. In *Proceedings of the 8th ACM/IEEE-CS joint conference on Digital libraries*, JCDL '08, pages 1–10. ACM, 2008.

[8] David Carmel, Naama Zwerdling, Ido Guy, Shila Ofek-Koifman, Nadav Har'el, Inbal Ronen, Erel Uziel, Sivan Yogev, and Sergey Chernov. Personalized social search based on the user's social network. In *Proceeding of the 18th ACM conference on Information and knowledge management*, CIKM '09, pages 1227–1236, 2009.

[9] Rich Caruana and Alexandru Niculescu-Mizil. Data mining in metric space: an empirical analysis of supervised learning performance criteria. In *Proceedings of the tenth ACM SIGKDD international conference on Knowledge discovery and data mining*, KDD '04, pages 69–78. ACM, 2004.

[10] Tsan-Kuo Chang, Pamela J. Shoemaker, and Nancy Brendlinger. Determinants of international news coverage in the U.S. media. *Communications research*, 14(4):396–414, 1987.

[11] Fernando Diaz. Integration of news content into web results. In *Proceedings of the Second ACM International Conference on Web Search and Data Mining*, 2009.

[12] Anlei Dong, Yi Chang, Zhaohui Zheng, Gilad Mishne, Jing Bai, Ruiqiang Zhang, Karolina Buchner, Ciya Liao, and Fernando Diaz. Towards recency ranking in web search. In *Proceedings of the third ACM international conference on Web search and data mining*, WSDM '10, pages 11–20. ACM, 2010.

[13] Anlei Dong, Ruiqiang Zhang, Pranam Kolari, Jing Bai, Fernando Diaz, Yi Chang, Zhaohui Zheng, and Hongyuan Zha. Time is of the essence: improving recency ranking using Twitter data. In *Proceedings of the 19th international conference on World wide web*, WWW '10, pages 331–340. ACM, 2010.

[14] Fritz Drasgow. Polychoric and polyserial correlations. In S. Kotz and N. Johnson, editors, *The Encyclopedia of Statistics, Volume 7*, pages 68–74. Wiley, 1986.

[15] Ahmed Hassan, Rosie Jones, and Fernando Diaz. A case study of using geographic cues to predict query news intent. In *Proceedings of the 17th ACM SIGSPATIAL International Conference on Advances in Geographic Information Systems*, GIS '09, pages 33–41. ACM, 2009.

[16] Thorsten Joachims. Unbiased evaluation of retrieval quality using clickthrough data. In *SIGIR Workshop on Mathematical/Formal Methods in Information Retrieval*, 2002.

[17] Rosie Jones, Ahmed Hassan, and Fernando Diaz. Geographic features in web search retrieval. In *Proceeding of the 2nd international workshop on Geographic information retrieval*, GIR '08, pages 57–58. ACM, 2008.

[18] Jure Leskovec, Lars Backstrom, and Jon Kleinberg. Meme-tracking and the dynamics of the news cycle. In *Proceedings of the 15th ACM SIGKDD International Conference on Knowledge Discovery and Data Mining*, 2009.

[19] Xiao Li, Ye-Yi Wang, and Alex Acero. Learning query intent from regularized click graphs. In *SIGIR '08: Proceedings of the 31st annual international ACM SIGIR conference on Research and development in information retrieval*, pages 339–346. ACM, 2008.

[20] Marcelo Mendoza, Barbara Poblete, and Carlos Castillo. Twitter under crisis: Can we trust what we RT? In *ACM SIGKDD 2010 Workshop on Social Media Analytics (SOMA)*, 2010.

[21] Donald Metzler, Susan T. Dumais, and Christopher Meek. Similarity measures for short segments of text. In *ECIR*, pages 16–27, 2007.

[22] Ramesh Nallapati. Discriminative models for information retrieval. In *Proceedings of the 27th annual international ACM SIGIR conference on Research and development in information retrieval*, SIGIR '04, pages 64–71, 2004.

[23] Irit Nitzan and Barak Libai. Social effects on customer retention. *Marketing Science Institute working paper*, pages 10–107, 2010.

[24] Leyseia Palen, Sarah Vieweg, Sophia B. Liu, and Amanda Lee Hughes. Crisis in a networked world: Features of computer-mediated communication in the april 16, 2007, Virginia Tech Event. *Social Science Computer Review*, 2009.

[25] Yossi Richter, Elad Yom-Tov, and Noam Slonim. Predicting customer churn in mobile networks through analysis of social groups. In *Proceedings of the SIAM International Conference on Data Mining, SDM 2010*, pages 732–741, 2010.

[26] Mehran Sahami and Timothy D. Heilman. A web-based kernel function for measuring the similarity of short text snippets. In *WWW '06: Proceedings of the 15th international conference on World Wide Web*, pages 377–386. ACM, 2006.

[27] Takeshi Sakaki, Makoto Okazaki, and Yutaka Matsuo. Earthquake shakes Twitter users: real-time event detection by social sensors. In *Proceedings of the 19th international conference on World wide web*, WWW '10, pages 851–860. ACM, 2010.

[28] Jaime Teevan, Meredith Ringel Morris, and Steve Bush. Discovering and using groups to improve personalized search. In *Proceedings of the Second ACM International Conference on Web Search and Data Mining*, WSDM '09, pages 15–24. ACM, 2009.

[29] Graham Upton and Ian Cook. *Oxford dictionary of statistics*. Oxford University Press, 2002.

[30] Haoming Denis Wu. Geographic distance and US newspaper coverage of Canada and Mexico. *International Communication Gazette*, 60(3):253–263, 1998.

Scalable Multi-Dimensional User Intent Identification using Tree Structured Distributions

Vinay Jethava
Chalmers University
Gothenburg, Sweden
jethava@chalmers.se

Liliana Calderón-Benavides
UNAB
Bucaramanga, Colombia
mcalderon@unab.edu.co

Ricardo Baeza-Yates
Yahoo! Research
Barcelona, Spain
rbaeza@acm.org

Chiranjib Bhattacharyya
Indian Institute of Science
Bangalore, India
chiru@csa.iisc.ernet.in

Devdatt Dubhashi
Chalmers University
Gothenburg, Sweden
dubhashi@chalmers.se

ABSTRACT

The problem of identifying user intent has received considerable attention in recent years, particularly in the context of improving the search experience via query contextualization. *Intent* can be characterized by multiple dimensions, which are often not observed from query words alone. Accurate identification of *Intent* from query words remains a challenging problem primarily because it is extremely difficult to discover these dimensions. The problem is often significantly compounded due to lack of representative training sample. We present a generic, extensible framework for learning the multi-dimensional representation of user intent from the query words. The approach models the latent relationships between facets using tree structured distribution which leads to an efficient and convergent algorithm, FastQ, for identifying the multi-faceted intent of users based on just the query words. We also incorporated WordNet to extend the system capabilities to queries which contain words that do not appear in the training data. Empirical results show that FastQ yields accurate identification of intent when compared to a gold standard.

Categories and Subject Descriptors

H.3.3 [**Information Storage and Retrieval**]: *Information Search and Retrieval - Search process*; G.3 [**Probability and Statistics**]: *Probabilistic algorithms*

General Terms

Algorithms, Performance, Theory

Keywords

web search, query intent, facets, Chow-Liu, WordNet, FastQ

1. INTRODUCTION

Identifying user intent[1] behind search queries plays a crucial role in providing a better search experience [16, 29, 28]. The traditional classification of user intent as *navigational*, *transactional* or *informational* has focused on intent as a single dimension [3] or hierarchical extensions [26, 2, 14].

There is a need for a systematic framework to analyze user intent in terms of multiple dimensions (or *facets*) of interest. In fact, if a facet can be predicted well, it is possible to contextualize the answer for a query, triggering a different ranking algorithm or even a completely different user experience. For example, an informational query will rank better information coming from trusted web sites or a time sensitive query may give better ranking to news. Similarly, a local query may trigger a map or a genre specific query may show a particular screen layout. The multiple facets of interest might be correlated, which poses a challenge compared to past approaches [19, 2, 15]. Further, one should be able to predict the user intent for new queries in a reasonably fast manner which can be incorporated into existing search engine technology [8].

This paper tries to model the probabilistic dependencies between the various *dimensions* underlying the user intent of a search query, and then proposes to use the model to identify the *intent* behind the query. Our hope is that by modeling the dependencies well, it might yield a more accurate identification of the underlying intent. We use the set of facets from [4] to illustrate our method. As our model is more complex, we explore the potential of our technique using the minimal set of features available, that is, just the query words. Using more features, such as clicks, would just improve our results.

Our approach immediately raises several challenging questions, namely (a) What kind of models should one use in modeling dependencies? (b) How does one model the joint distribution of query words and the dimensions? and (c) Is it possible to augment the model to cater for unseen query words?

This paper poses the problem of identifying the user's intent behind a query as an *inference problem over a tree structured graphical model*. We argue that the tree structured

[1] In this paper we use intent in a broad sense, including generic and specific intents.

model serves as a natural choice for discovering latent dependencies between several *dimensions* of a query as it is the *simplest* distribution which goes beyond the independence assumption. The associated learning problem is solved by using the Chow-Liu algorithm [6, 21, 27]. In addition, the resultant algorithm should be scalable and preferably online for real world use.

Most of the works available in the literature are based on the analysis of query logs and click-through data. However, the additional information might not be available, or restricted due to privacy concerns. Our method infers the user intent from the query words only, without using click-through documents, web session information, and other meta-data. This shows the potential of the algorithm, as with more features, the performance should improve.

We model the query as a factorial distribution over the observed *query words*, which is equivalent to making the assumption that the impact of a word in the query is independent of the other words. This results in a simplified model which allows an online algorithm for user's intent identification. We also incorporate WordNet [12], a lexical database, to improve the classification accuracy of the user intent of search queries for unseen query words.

In order to perform the identification of the underlying user's needs in the described setting, we introduce *FastQ*, an online distributed algorithm for classifying user intent for search queries. The algorithm dynamically constructs a tree structured factor graph [18] with the appropriate distribution. The intent is inferred by using standard belief propagation (BP) algorithms, and the tree structure of the dynamically constructed factor graph guarantees the convergence of the BP algorithm. Further, the small size of the resulting factor graph corresponding to a search query allows fast (approximate) inference and allows online classification of the user's intent. Experimental timing results show that the method can be incorporated into existing search engine technology [8, 5].

Our Contribution. The main contributions of this work are:

1. We cast the problem of identifying user intent for web search queries as an inference problem; and present a tree structured graphical model for modeling the user intent based on just the query words,

2. The resulting inference is difficult; and we present a scalable, online algorithm *FastQ* for classifying user intent for search queries, and

3. We incorporate WordNet [12], a lexical database, to identify new words present in the search query which are absent in the existing training vocabulary.

4. Our framework is generic and naturally lends itself to extension using other facets or query features, thus enabling its use in other settings.

The rest of this paper is organized as follows: Section 2 outlines previous work related to ours. Section 3 describes our query intent model for the web query classification; and the algorithm for the online query classification; and Section 4 presents our experimental setup and the results obtained. Finally, Section 5 presents our conclusions.

2. RELATED WORK

User's intent. According to Broder's taxonomy [3], the user intents can be *informational, navigational* and *transactional.* Albeit this taxonomy was further extended by Rose & Levinson [26], the original categories are the most widely used, and have been the basis for an important number of studies in the IR area. In the same context, Baeza-Yates *et al.* [2] have proposed that the user intents can be classified as *informational, not-informational* and *ambiguous.* Hu *et al.* [14] have interpreted the user's query intent through the concepts included in Wikipedia; the authors exemplify their proposal throughout the identification of the following intents: travel, personal name, and job finding. More recently, Calderón-Benavides *et al.* [4] have studied the user's intent as a multi-dimensional composition of facets.

Sources to identify the user's intent. In their work, Kang & Kim [17] used information from document content, links and URLs to classify the user's queries into topic relevance task (informational intent), homepage finding task (navigational intent), and service finding task (transactional intent). Lee *et al.* [19] took into account the past user-click behaviour and the anchor link distribution to determine the navigational and informational intents of queries. The content of the documents selected by the users in answer to a query is used in [2]. Liu *et al.* [20] exploited click-through data in order to find navigational and informational/transactional type queries.

Nguyen and Kan [23] defined functional *facets* to describe the user's intent. In their work, Ashkan *et al.* [1] developed a methodology to determine commercial/non-commercial and navigational/informational intent of queries by using ad click-through features, query features, and the content of search engine result pages. In [14], the authors have mapped the user's query intent into the concepts included in Wikipedia, and have represented them through the articles and categories related to each concept.

Recent work on query personalization has focused on modeling the query intent [9, 29, 24, 28] and user behaviour [10, 31]. In particular, Teevan *et al.* [29] investigated the variability in user intent and the relevance search results obtained in terms of implicit relevance measures based on click-through data. They use interdependent sets of features defined using information available in (i) the queries (e.g. *query strings, special syntax*, etc.); (ii) history of similar queries (e.g. #{*queries issued*}, etc.); and (iii) query results (e.g. *click entropy*, etc.). Our work can be viewed as a probabilistic framework for semi-supervised inference of multi-dimensional user intent using *query strings* and the history information available in the queries.

Methods to determine the user's intent. Although early research was based on the manual classification of small sets of queries [3, 26], the use of some of the existing machinery from IR, machine learning, as well as natural language processing techniques have allowed an important progress towards determine the user query intents in bigger datasets. In this context, [17] calculated the probability that the task of a user query is topic relevance (informational queries), or homepage finding (navigational queries), based on the occurrence patterns of the query terms in web pages. Lee et al. [19] made an automatic identification of goals (navigational and informational) through the application of heuristics over clicks made by the users on the results offered by the search engine. In [2] supervised and unsupervised learning methods were applied in order to determine the user goals in context of ODP[2] categories for a set of six thousand queries from a vertical search engine.Jansen *et al.* [15] presented a rule-based automated classification system for queries into hierarchical level of informational, transactional, and navigational intent. However, a clear principle for deriving new rules is not presented and the extension of the rules for a new system of classification or another language is not clear. In [14] they use the Wikipedia link graph to represent the relations among the concept articles and the relations among articles and categories. Such a graph is traversed randomly to obtain a vector with the probabilities that each concept belong to a intent.

Existing methods use multiple features (click-through, weblogs, etc.) to identify the intent either as a simple hierarchy within the framework of *navigational*, *transactional* and *informational* goals. To the best of our knowledge, ours is the first work that identifies user's intent in terms of multiple meaningful dimensions using automated server-side classification. The multi-dimensional based description encapsulates additional information about the user intent in a number of related dimensions, instead of a hierarchical scheme. As a difference to other proposals, in this work the identification of the user's intent does not include click-through data or the document content, but is done by using solely the query words. Additionally, the task of identifying the user intent is performed in an online setting, creating a technology that can be incorporated into existing search engines environments with reasonably fast response time.

3. PROBLEM DEFINITION

3.1 Dimensions of the User's Intent

We chose the multi-dimensional description of user intent presented in [4]. A description of the dimensions, as well as the values that each one of them can take, is presented in Table 1. The multi-dimensional based description encapsulates additional information about the user intent in a number of related dimensions, instead of a hierarchical scheme.

3.2 The Query Classif cation Problem

Let $\check{q} = [q_1, \ldots, q_m]$ denote a query of length $|\check{q}| = m$ consisting of distinct[3] query words $\{q_1, \ldots, q_m\}$. We assume that the user intent can be encapsulated in terms of K facets e.g. *Genre*, *Scope*, etc., where $\mathcal{F}_k$ denote the state space of the kth facet e.g. {*Yes*, *No*} for the facet *Time Sensitivity*.

Given the training data $\mathcal{D} = \{(\check{q}^{(n)}, \vec{f}^{(n)})\}_{1 \le n \le N}$ consisting on N queries $\check{q}^{(n)}$ and the corresponding user intent (in terms of facets) $\vec{f}^{(n)}$, we cast the problem of finding the user intent $\hat{f}^{\dagger} \in \mathcal{F}$ for a new query $\check{q}^{\dagger}$ as an inference problem

$$\hat{f}^{\dagger} = \arg\max_{\vec{f} \in \mathcal{F}} P(\vec{F} = \vec{f} | \check{Q} = \check{q}^{\dagger}, \mathcal{D}) \quad (1)$$

$$= \arg\max_{\vec{f} \in \mathcal{F}} P(\check{Q} = \check{q}^{\dagger} | \vec{F} = \vec{f}, \Lambda) P(\vec{F} = \vec{f} | \Theta) \quad (2)$$

where $\mathcal{F} = \mathcal{F}_1 \times \mathcal{F}_2 \times \ldots \times \mathcal{F}_K$ denotes the state space of facet classifications corresponding to a query; $\Lambda = \Lambda(\mathcal{D})$ and $\Theta = \Theta(\mathcal{D})$ are parameters based on the training data.

[2] http://dmoz.org

[3] Duplicate instances of a word in a query are removed during pre-processing.

Dimension	Values & Meaning
Genre	{*News, Business, Reference, Community*}. It is considered a meta-category that provides a generic context to the user query intent.
Topic	{*Adult & Sex, Arts & Culture, Beauty & Style, Cars & Transportation, Computers & Internet, Education, Entertainment, Music & Games, Finance, Food & Drink, Health, Home & Garden, Industrial Goods & Services, Politics & Government, Religion & belief systems, Science & Mathematics, Social Science, Sports, Technology & Electronic, Travel, Work*}. This list of topics was created by taking the first level categories included in ODP, Yahoo!, and Wikipedia.
Task	{*Informational, Not Informational, Both*} [2]. Considered as the primary need reflected by a query.
Objective	{*Resource, Action*}. Represents the aim of a query, without considering the format of the information to retrieve.
Specificity	{*Specific, Medium, Broad*}. This facet describes how specialized is a query.
Scope	{*Multiple, Unique*}. Shows whether the query contains polysemic words or not.
Authority Sensitivity	{*Yes, No*}. Is the query designed to retrieve authoritative and trusted answers? [23]
Spatial Sensitivity	{*Yes, No*}. Reflects the interest of the user to obtain a resource that is related to a particular spatial location (explicit or not).
Time Sensitivity	{*Yes, No*}. Whether the information to retrieve, involves a date or period of time.

Table 1: The dimensions or *facets* which characterize user intent as in [4].

The following section discusses the choice of Λ and Θ based on the training data; and and then we discuss *FastQ*, a scalable, convergent algorithm for solving the overall inference problem.

3.3 The Query Intent Model

Now we present our generative model for search query $\check{q}$ and corresponding user intent $\vec{f}$ assuming queries and corresponding user intents are drawn from an unknown joint distribution $P(\check{Q} = \check{q}, \vec{F} = \vec{f})$.

A full realization of the joint distribution $P(\check{q}, \vec{f})$ is computationally prohibitive. For example, if the query words are drawn from the vocabulary $\mathcal{V}$ with maximum query length M, there are $\sum_{m=1}^{M} C(|\mathcal{V}|, m)$ possible queries where $C(|\mathcal{V}|, m) = \frac{(|\mathcal{V}|)!}{(|\mathcal{V}|-m)!m!}$; and the facets have $\prod_{i=1}^{K} |\mathcal{F}_i|$ possible states; the full probabilistic modeling would require $O(2^{|\mathcal{V}|} \prod_{i=1}^{K} |\mathcal{F}_i|)$ states. Hence, we use a parametric representation to reduce the dimensionality of the problem.

We assume the dataset $\mathcal{D}$ consists of i.i.d. samples drawn from a joint distribution

$$P(\check{q}^{(n)}, \vec{f}^{(n)} | \Theta, \Lambda) = P(\check{Q} = \check{q}^{(n)} | \vec{F} = \vec{f}^{(n)}, \Lambda) P(\vec{F} = \vec{f}^{(n)} | \Theta) \quad (3)$$

where Θ and Λ are parameters which model the dependencies between the inter-related facets (Θ), and the impact of words of the query on its facet classification (Λ) respectively.

3.3.1 Relationship between Facets

We model the dependencies between the facets using the class of second order product distributions defined on the

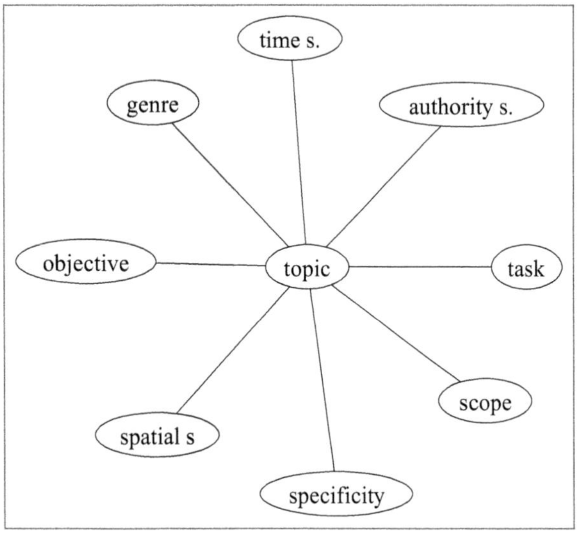

Figure 1: Example spanning tree (T) on facets.

facet variables. Let $\mathcal{T}$ be the set of possible spanning trees defined on the facets. Then, the parameter $\Theta = \Theta_T$ defines a marginal polytope [30] on the spanning tree $T \in \mathcal{T}$. In other words $\Theta_T = \{\Theta_{ij} : (i,j) \in T\} \cup \{\Theta_i : i \in \mathcal{K}\}$ is the set of probability distributions Θ_{ij} defined on the edges of the spanning tree $(i,j) \in T$; and the probability distributions Θ_i defined on the facet variables $i \in \mathcal{K}$ such that

$$\Theta_{ij}(f_i, f_j) \geq 0; \sum_{f_i}\sum_{f_i} \Theta_{ij}(f_i, f_j) = 1 \ \forall (i,j) \in T \quad (4)$$

$$\Theta_i(f_i) \geq 0; \qquad \sum_{f_i} \Theta_i(f_i) = 1 \qquad \forall i \in \mathcal{K} \quad (5)$$

which satisfy the marginal consistency

$$\sum_{f_i \in \mathcal{F}_i} \Theta_{ij}(f_i, f_j) = \Theta_j(f_j) \quad \forall j \in \mathcal{F}_j, (i,j) \in T \quad (6)$$

Then, the probability distribution $P(\vec{F}|\Theta_T)$ is given by

$$P(\vec{F} = \vec{f}|\Theta_T) = \frac{\prod_{(i,j)\in T} \Theta_{ij}(f_i, f_j)}{\prod_{i \in \mathcal{K}} \Theta_i(f_i)^{d_i - 1}} \quad (7)$$

where d_i denotes the degree of the ith facet in the spanning tree T. Figure 1 shows a possible tree structure T defined on the facet variables.

3.3.2 Impact of Query Words on Facets

Now we describe the probability distribution of queries $P(\hat{Q} = \hat{q}|\vec{F} = \vec{f})$ conditioned on the facet variables where $\check{q} = \{q_1, \ldots, q_m\}$ denotes a query of length $|\check{q}| = m$ and $\vec{f} = \{f_1, \ldots, f_K\}$ denotes the facet states. The model assumes the following,

1. Each query has at most M distinct words. This is a valid assumption since, according to [22], nearly 70% of informational queries consists of at most 5 words, and the higher number of terms in not informational queries is 3. In our experimental data $M = 8$.

2. The length of the query $|\check{q}|$ is distributed as $P(|\check{q}| = m) = \beta(m)$ chosen according to [32], such that $\beta(m) \geq 0$ and $\sum_{m=1}^{M} \beta(m) = 1$.

3. The query words are chosen independently conditioned on the facet state $\vec{f}$

$$P(\hat{Q} = \hat{q}|\vec{F} = \vec{f}) = \prod_{w \in \mathcal{V}} P(w \in \check{q}|\vec{F} = \vec{f})^{\mathbf{1}_{w\in\check{q}}} \quad (8)$$

where $\mathcal{V} = \{w : \exists \check{q} \in \mathcal{D} \ni w \in \check{q}\}$ is the vocabulary of words present in the training data.

4. The probability of a word being present in a query $P(w \in \check{q}|\vec{F} = \vec{f})$ conditioned on the joint facet state, $\vec{f}$; can be factorized into a product of probability distributions $P(w \in \check{q}|F_k = f_k)$ of a word w being a query, conditioned on individual facet states f_k

$$P(w \in \check{q}|\vec{F} = \vec{f}) = \prod_{k=1}^{K} \prod_{f \in \mathcal{F}_k} (\lambda^k_{w;f})^{\mathbf{1}_{\vec{f}_k = f}} \quad (9)$$

where $\{\lambda^k_{w;f} \geq 0 : w \in \mathcal{V}, k \in \mathcal{K}, f \in \mathcal{F}_k\}$ is a parameter subject to the constraints

$$\sum_{w \in \mathcal{V}} \lambda^k_{w;f} \ = \ 1 \ \forall k \in \mathcal{K}, f \in \mathcal{F}_k \quad (10)$$

The resulting probability distribution $P(\vec{Q} = \check{q}|\vec{F} = \vec{f}, \Lambda)$ parametrized by Λ is given as

$$P(\check{q}|\vec{f}, \Lambda) \ = \ \frac{\beta(|\check{q}|)e^{\{\sum_{k\in\mathcal{K}, w\in\mathcal{V}} \sum_{f\in\mathcal{F}_k} \log \lambda^k_{w;f} \mathbf{1}_{\check{q}}(w) \mathbf{1}^k_{\vec{f}}(f)\}}}{Z(\vec{f})} \quad (11)$$

where $Z(\vec{f})$ is the normalization function given as

$$Z(\vec{f}) = \sum_{m=1}^{M} \beta(m) \sum_{\check{q}:|\check{q}|=m} \exp(\sum_k \sum_f \sum_w \log \lambda^k_{w;f}) \quad (12)$$

3.3.3 Generative Model

The generative model for a search query and the corresponding user intent is presented in Algorithm 1.

Algorithm 1 The generative model for query $(\check{q}, \vec{f})$

Require: $\mathcal{V}$ {Vocabulary}
Require: Θ_T {Marginal polytope on the facets}
Require: Λ {Conditional word distribution}
  Choose $\vec{f} \sim P(\vec{f}|\Theta_T)$ as in (7) {Facet for query}
  Choose m with $P \sim \beta(\cdot)$ {Query length}
  for $i = 1$ to m **do**
    Choose $q_i \sim P(\cdot|\vec{f})$ as in (11) {Generate word}
    $\check{q} \leftarrow [\check{q}\ q_i]$ {Append word to query}
  end for
  return $(\check{q}, \vec{f})$ {Query and facet classification}

3.4 Estimating the Model Parameters

This section presents the procedure for computing the maximum likelihood estimation (MLE) for the model parameters $\{\Lambda, \Theta_T, T\}$ based on the dataset. The maximum likelihood estimates are obtained as a result of the optimization in

$$\arg\max_{\Lambda,\Theta,T} \sum_{(\check{q}^{(n)}, \vec{f}^{(n)}) \in \mathcal{D}} \log P(\check{q}^{(n)}, \vec{f}^{(n)}|\Theta_T, \Lambda, T) \quad (13)$$

subject to the constraints in (4), (5), (6), (10); where the probability $P(\check{q}^{(n)}, \vec{f}^{(n)}|\Theta_T, \Lambda, T)$ is obtained using (3), (7) and (11). The resulting optimization can be decoupled into separate optimization problems for (Θ^*, T^*) as

$$\begin{aligned}\arg\max_{\Theta, T\in\mathcal{T}} \quad & \textstyle\sum_{\vec{f}^{(n)}} \{ \sum_{(a,b)\in T} \log \Theta_{ab}(f_a^{(n)}, f_b^{(n)}) \\ & \quad - \textstyle\sum_{a\in\mathcal{K}} \log \Theta_a(f_a^{(n)})^{d_a - 1} \} \\ \text{s.t.} \quad & \\ & \textstyle\sum_{f_a, f_b} \Theta_{ab}(f_a, f_b) = 1; \; \Theta_{ab}(f_a, f_b) \geq 0 \; \forall (a,b) \in T \\ & \textstyle\sum_{f_a} \Theta_a(f_a) = 1; \quad \Theta_a(f_a) \geq 0 \quad \forall a \in \mathcal{K} \\ & \textstyle\sum_{f_i \in \mathcal{F}_i} \Theta_{ij}(f_i, f_j) = \Theta_j(f_j) \quad \forall j \in \mathcal{F}_j, (i,j) \in T \end{aligned} \tag{14}$$

and an optimization problem for Λ^* as

$$\begin{aligned}\arg\max_{\Lambda} \quad & \textstyle\sum_{(\breve{q}^{(n)}, \vec{f}^{(n)})\in\mathcal{D}} \{ -\log Z(\vec{f}^{(n)}) \\ & + \textstyle\sum_{k\in\mathcal{K}, f\in\mathcal{F}_k, w\in\mathcal{V}} \log \lambda_{w;f}^k \mathbf{1}_{[w\in\breve{q}^{(n)}]} \mathbf{1}_{[f_k^{(n)}=f]} \} \\ \text{s.t.} \quad & \\ & \lambda_{w;f}^i \geq 0; \quad \forall w \in \mathcal{V}, k \in \mathcal{K}, f \in \mathcal{F}_k \\ & \textstyle\sum_{w\in\mathcal{V}} \lambda_{w;f}^k = 1 \quad \forall k \in \mathcal{K}, f \in \mathcal{F}_k \end{aligned} \tag{15}$$

where $Z(\vec{f}^{(n)})$ is given as (12). Now we solve the optimization problems in (14) and (15).

Notation. We introduce the function $\#(C)$ where C is a valid Boolean expression as the number of queries in dataset $\mathcal{D}$ which satisfy the condition C, i.e. $\#(C) = \sum_{(\breve{q}, \vec{f})\in\mathcal{D}} \mathbf{1}(C)$ where $\mathbf{1}(C)$ is the indicator function, i.e., $\mathbf{1}(C) = 1$ if C is $TRUE$ and 0 otherwise. For example, $\#(w \in \breve{q})$ denotes the number of queries in the dataset $\mathcal{D}$ having query word w; $\#(f_k = f)$ denotes the number of queries for which the kth facet has state f; and so on.

3.4.1 *Estimation of Facet Tree Parameters* (Θ^*, T^*)

The optimization in (14) depends on the facet classifications $\vec{f}^{(n)}$ of the queries in the dataset $\mathcal{D}$, and not on the words $[q_1^{(n)}, \ldots, q_m^{(n)}]$ in the query. Thus, the problem is to fit a second order product distribution to the multivariate data (facets) $\vec{f}^{(n)} \in \mathcal{D}$.

Chow and Liu [6] first investigated the problem of fitting a second order product distribution to multivariate data. They showed that the problem is equivalent to minimizing the Kullback-Liebler divergence [7] between the target distribution on $\mathcal{D}$ and tree based distribution. Their algorithm shows that for the dataset $\mathcal{D}$ and a spanning tree T; the optimal marginal polytope Θ_T^* is given by

$$\Theta_{ij}^*(a,b) = \frac{\#(\vec{f}_i = a, \vec{f}_j = b)}{N} \quad \forall a \in \mathcal{F}_i, b \in \mathcal{F}_j \tag{16}$$

$$\Theta_i^*(a) = \frac{\#(\vec{f}_i = a)}{N} \quad \forall a \in \mathcal{F}_i \tag{17}$$

for edges $(i,j) \in T$. The mutual information $I_{ij}^{\mathcal{D}}$ between facets i and j is given as

$$I_{ij}^{\mathcal{D}} = \sum_{a\in\mathcal{F}_i} \sum_{b\in\mathcal{F}_j} \Theta_{ij}^*(a,b) \log \frac{\Theta_{ij}^*(a,b)}{\Theta_i^*(a)\Theta_j^*(b)} \tag{18}$$

The optimal tree T^* is such that the maximum possible mutual information is encapsulated by its edges.

The algorithm proceeds in two steps, namely, computing the mutual information $I_{ij}^{\mathcal{D}}$ for each pair of facets i and j as in (18); and selecting the top $(K-1)$ edges with the highest mutual information by computing the maximum weight spanning tree for a weighted graph between facets, where each edge between facet i and j has weight $I_{ij}^{\mathcal{D}}$.

3.4.2 *Estimation of Word-Facet Parameters* (Λ^*)

A direct computation of the $\log Z(\vec{f}^{(n)})$ is computationally prohibitive. However, using a variational approach and Jensen's inequality, we can compute an approximate estimate $\hat{\Lambda}^*$ characterized by the conditional distribution of query words conditioned on the facets specification

$$\hat{\lambda}_{w;f}^{k^*} = \frac{\#(w \in \breve{q}, \vec{f}_k = f)}{\#(\vec{f}_k = f)} \tag{19}$$

3.5 User Intent Classif cation

This section presents a fast online procedure for the user intent classification of a test query as:

$$\vec{f}^\dagger = \arg\max_{\vec{f}\in\mathcal{F}} P(\breve{Q} = \breve{q}^\dagger | \vec{F} = \vec{f}, \hat{\Lambda}^*) P(\vec{F} = \vec{f} | \Theta_T^*)$$

A naive solution requires computation of $O(\prod_{i\in\mathcal{K}} \mathcal{F}_i)$ product terms, each having $O(L|\mathcal{K}|)$ multiplications. Further, the computation of $Z(\vec{f})$ for each $\vec{f}$ requires summation over $\mathcal{V}^m$ terms, which is computationally infeasible.

Instead, we perform approximate inference using standard Belief Propagation (BP) on a dynamically constructed factor graph based on the model parameters learnt in Section 3.4. The resulting factor graph is tree structured having K variable nodes and $O(MK)$ factor nodes, and the inference procedure converges in at most K iterations.

3.5.1 *Dynamic Factor Graph*

The factor graph for finding the optimal facet assignment $\vec{f}^\dagger$ for a test query $\breve{q}^\dagger$ consists of two classes of factors, namely,

- factors which model the latent relationship between facets in (7); and
- factors which model the impact of query words on facets based on (9) under the simplifying assumption that there are no latent relationships between facets.

Figure 2 shows the factor graph corresponding to the facet classification. The variable nodes, $F_1, \ldots, F_K$, denote the facet variables which can take possible states in $\mathcal{F}_1, \ldots, \mathcal{F}_K$, respectively. The factors T_i, T_{ij} model the latent relationship between facets, while the factors W_ℓ^i model the impact of the ℓth word of the test query $\breve{q}^\dagger$ affecting the ith facet variable.

The factors, $T^i, i \in \mathcal{K}$ and $T^{ij}, (i,j) \in T^*$ correspond to the latent relationships between the facets in (7). Their beliefs correspond to the parameters (Θ^*, T^*) based on the training data, given as

$$P_{T^i}(F_i = f) = \Theta_i^*(f)^{(1-d_i)} \tag{20}$$

$$P_{T^{ij}}(F_i = f, F_j = f') = \Theta_{ij}^*(f, f') \tag{21}$$

The factors W_ℓ^i model the conditional distribution $\hat{P}(F_k = f | w \in \breve{q})$ under the assumption that all facets are independent of each other.The factors are specified by the beliefs,

$$P_{W_\ell^i}(F_i = f) = \xi_{w;f}^i = \frac{\#(\vec{f}_k = f, w \in \breve{q})}{\#(w \in \breve{q})} \tag{22}$$

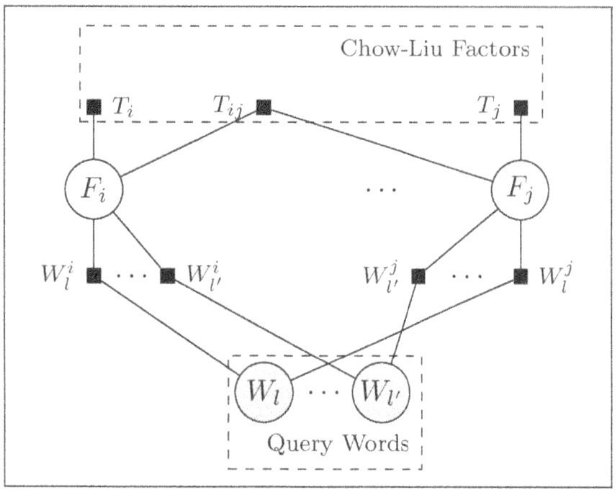

Figure 2: Factor graph for query facet classification. The variable nodes, $F_1, \ldots, F_K$, denote the facets; W_ℓ^i denotes the factor corresponding to the ℓth query word affecting the ith facet variable; and T_i and T_{ij} are the factors corresponding to the Chow-Liu probability distribution on facet variables which capture the facet interdependencies.

where $\xi^k_{w;f}$ is an approximation for $\hat{P}(F_k = f | w \in \check{q})$ obtained as

$$\xi^k_{w;f} \quad \propto \quad P(w \in \check{q} | F_k = f, \hat{\Lambda}^*) \hat{P}^k_1(F_k = f) \qquad (23)$$

and $\hat{P}^k_1(F_k = f) = \frac{\#(\vec{f_k} = f)}{N}$ is the MLE of the probability distribution of the kth facet under simplifying assumption that the each facet is independent of other facets.

The parameter $\Xi^* = \{\xi^k_{w;f} : f \in \mathcal{F}_k, k \in \mathcal{K}, w \in \mathcal{V}\}$ models the impact of the words in a query on the facets. Specifically, $\xi^k_{w;f}$ measures the evidence that the kth facet has value f when the query contains the word w.

We note that the evidence $\xi^k_{w;f}$ in (22) is not defined if the word w is not part of the training vocabulary, i.e., the test query $\check{q}^\dagger$ contains a word w that is not present in the training data $\mathcal{D}$. The following section presents a method for incorporating the influence of new words, i.e. words in the test query which are not present in the vocabulary using the semantic relationships between the words and the existing vocabulary.

3.5.2 WordNet Integration

Let w denote a new word not present in the vocabulary $\mathcal{V}_\mathcal{D}$. Then, the corresponding $\xi^i_{w;f}$ are not defined and the previous algorithm cannot be used. However, a semantically related word w' might be present in the vocabulary $\mathcal{V}_\mathcal{D}$; for which the corresponding $\xi^i_{w';f}$ are defined. It is safe to assume that a strong semantic relationship between the words w and w' will be reflected in the resulting facet classifications, reflected in $\xi^i_{w;f}$ and $\xi^i_{w';f}$. Therefore, it is of interest to be able to relate new words in the query to existing words in vocabulary.

We present a two-step method for integrating the capabilities of WordNet [12], a lexical database, into the facet classification for queries containing new words. We first query WordNet for the related word candidates $W^\perp$ with similarity scores $S^\perp = \{s_{w'} : w' \in W^\perp\}$ for a new query word w using Breadth First Search (BFS) till a maximum search depth L. The second step uses the candidates which are present in the vocabulary $W^\clubsuit = W^\perp \cap \mathcal{V}_\mathcal{D}$ to compute the parameter $\tilde{\xi}^i_{w;f}$. Algorithm 2 presents the heuristic procedure for incorporating related words obtained from WordNet to augment results for a new word.

We note that if the word has no neighbours either in WordNet or in the existing vocabulary, the conditional distribution $P(F_i = \cdot | w \in \check{q}^\dagger)$ is a Dirichlet distribution with parameter $[\frac{\#(F_i = f_1)}{N}, \ldots, \frac{\#(F_i = f_{|\mathcal{F}_i|})}{N}]$. This means that when the test word w has no semantically related neighbours w' with known statistics $\xi^k_{w';f}$, then the conditional distribution is randomly distributed such that, on average, the count statistics for a facet would be same as that found in the training data. However, if there exist neighbours of the word $W^\clubsuit$, that information is incorporated into the conditional distribution for the new word.

Algorithm 2 WordNet integration $\tilde{\xi}_w = F_{\text{WN}}(w)$

Require: L {Maximum depth for BFS}
Require: Ξ^* {Parameter based on $\mathcal{D}$}
Ensure: $w \notin \mathcal{V}_\mathcal{D}$ {New word not present in vocabulary}
Ensure: $\tau^i_f = \frac{\#(f_i = f)}{N}$
  $(W^\perp, S^\perp) \leftarrow BFS(w, L)$ {Related words in WordNet}
  $W^\clubsuit \leftarrow W^\perp \cap \mathcal{V}_\mathcal{D}$ {Related words in vocabulary}
  for $i = 0$ to K **do**
    Initialize $\{\mu^i_1, \ldots, \mu^i_{|\mathcal{F}_i|}\} \sim Dir(\tau^i_{f_1}, \ldots, \tau^i_{f_{|\mathcal{F}_i|}})$
    for all f in $\mathcal{F}_i$ **do**
      $\tilde{\xi}^i_{w;f} = \frac{\mu^i_f + \sum_{w' \in W^\clubsuit} s_{w'} \xi^i_{w';f}}{\sum_{f \in \mathcal{F}_i} (\mu^i_f + \sum_{w' \in W^\clubsuit} s_{w'} \xi^i_{w';f})}$
    end for
  end for
  return $\tilde{\xi}_w = \{\tilde{\xi}^i_{w;f} : i \in \mathcal{K}, f \in \mathcal{F}_i\}$

3.5.3 The FastQ Algorithm

Algorithm 3 FastQ $\hat{f}^\dagger = F(\check{q}^\dagger | \mathcal{D})$

Require: $\check{q}^\dagger$ {Test query}
Require: $\Xi^*, \Theta^*, T^*, \mathcal{V}$ {Parameter from training data $\mathcal{D}$}
  Initialize $G(\mathcal{K}, [])$ {factor graph on facet variables}
  for all (i, j) in T^* **do**
    Add factor T^{ij} s.t. $P_{T^{ij}}(F_i = a, F_j = b) = \Theta^*_{ij}(a, b)$
  end for
  for all i in $\mathcal{K}$ **do**
    Add factor T^i s.t. $P_{T^i}(F_i = a) = \frac{1}{\Theta^*_i(a)^{d_a - 1}}$
  end for
  for $l = 1$ to L **do**
    if $q^\dagger_\ell \in \mathcal{V}$ **then**
      for all i in $\mathcal{K}$ **do**
        Add factor W^i_ℓ s.t. $P_{W^i_\ell}(F_i = f) = \xi^i_{q^\dagger_\ell;f} \forall f \in \mathcal{F}_i$
      end for
    else
      $\tilde{\xi}_{q^\dagger_\ell} = F_{WN}(q^\dagger_\ell)$ {Use WordNet for new query word}
      for all i in $\mathcal{K}$ **do**
        Add factor W^i_ℓ s.t. $P_{W^i_\ell}(F_i = f) = \tilde{\xi}^i_{q^\dagger_\ell;f} \forall f \in \mathcal{F}_i$
      end for
    end if
  end for
  $\hat{f}^\dagger = $ MAX-PROD(G) {Standard BP}
  return $\hat{f}^\dagger = \{f^\dagger_1, \ldots, f^\dagger_K\}$

The overall procedure for facet classification when a new query, $\breve{q}^{\dagger} = \{q_1, \ldots, q_L\}$ is given in Algorithm 3. The algorithm constructs the dynamic factor graph by adding the factors T_i, T_{ij} corresponding to the probability distribution on facets constructed using the Chow-Liu algorithm. Then, if a query word q_ℓ is in the vocabulary $\mathcal{V}$, it adds words to the corresponding word factors, and constructs the word factor W_ℓ^i based on parameter Ξ^*, as in (22). Otherwise, if query word q_ℓ is not in vocabulary $\mathcal{V}$, it constructs the factors W_ℓ^i based on semantically related words in vocabulary $\mathcal{V}$ found using WordNet as in Algorithm 2. The facet assignment $\hat{f}^{\dagger}$ for the test query is computed using a standard implementation of the Max-Product Belief Propagation [18].

CLAIM 1. *The* FastQ *algorithm has the following properties*

(a) The dynamic factor graph is a tree consisting of K variable nodes and $O(MK)$ factor nodes,

(b) The Max-Product Belief Propagation (BP) converges in at most K iterations,

(c) The average time for query classification is $O(K + \bar{c}_{wn}^L)$ where L is the maximum search depth and $\bar{c}_{wn}$ is the average number of semantically related words for a word in WordNet.

PROOF. (a) By construction.

(b) BP converges on trees iterating in at most the number of variable nodes in the tree [18, 30].

(c) The average time spent in WordNet search is $O(\bar{c}_{wn}^L)$ and the BP algorithm takes $O(K)$ time. □

The small size of the constructed factor graph allows an implementation with limited resources. The maximum search depth L in WordNet is a user-controlled parameter which can be reduced to speedup the classification.

3.6 Generalizing the Query Intent Model

This section discusses the procedure for generalizing our model in order to explicitly study some other aspect of user intent. For example, the facet *Medical Sensitive* might be facet of interest relevant to medical search engines such as PubMed [4].

Our query intent model and inference procedure is generic and can be used with other multi-dimensional descriptions of user intent. The requirement is the use of training data which has been classified according to the facet description of interest. Thus, in order to add the facet *Medical Sensitive*, one has to provide the labels for the new facet corresponding to the queries in the training data.

Sometimes, one can avoid the reclassification due to the nature of the data collection procedure. For example, a query having the word *gene* may not be *Medical Sensitive* if the queries are drawn from a generic search engine. However, PubMed queries having the query word *gene* can be assumed to be *Medical Sensitive* (Similar assumptions have been made in [31]). Thus, one can obtain a rough estimate for the normalized influence of words in the query by simply assuming that the queries in PubMed are *Medical Sensitive*, but not in a generic search engine.

[4]http://www.pubmedcentral.nih.gov

Dimension	Overall Agreement	Kappa Coefficient
Time S.	99.23	0.98
Scope	96.74	0.93
Objective	92.54	0.85
Authority S.	84.32	0.69
Topic	68.26	0.66
Task	75.71	0.63
Spatial S.	81.07	0.62
Genre	65.00	0.53
Specificity	55.44	0.33

Table 2: Inter-annotation Agreement and Kappa Coefficient for the dimensions of user's intent.

Alternatively, some of the facets may be known and the remaining might be unknown. For example, if a test query is generated from PubMed, it is safe to assume that the facet *Topic* is *Health* (Similar assumptions have been made in [31]). It is easy to condition on some facets if they are known. The inference for the remaining facets is conditioned [11] over the facet *Topic* having state *Health*.

4. EXPERIMENTAL SETTING

4.1 Dataset

The evaluation data consists of 5,249 queries from a vertical search engine query log in a Spanish speaking country. The sampling of queries took place randomly after calculating the popularity of each query (i.e. the number of times a query was posed), to capture the Zipf's law distribution (in [2] only popular queries were considered). Hence, 15% were taken from to the set of the most popular queries, 15% from the (long) tail set, and the remaining 70% was sampled from the middle set (i.e., queries with average popularity).

The complete collection of queries was manually classified, assigning a value for each of the dimensions described in Section 3.1. Additionally, 10% of the queries (randomly selected) were classified by two judges. In order to measure the consistency of the judges two well known metrics were applied: the Overall Agreement [13] and Kappa Coefficient [25]. The former metric express a score of how much homogeneity, or consensus, there is in the ratings given by judges; however it does not take into account the agreement that would have been expected due solely to chance. In order to overcome this problem, we used the second metric (i.e., the Kappa Coefficient), which is the proportion of agreement between judges after chance agreement is removed from consideration. Table 2 contains the overall agreement of the judges as well as the Kappa coefficient values.

Results from the overall agreement indicate that the consistency of the manual classification is highly satisfactory. In average, the overall agreement is 80%. Eight out of the nine dimensions have reached an overall agreement higher than 65%, which is quite high if we consider the number of dimensions that were assessed, the number of possible values that each dimension can take, as well as the different criteria and the subjectivity of the judges.

In terms of the Kappa coefficient the values obtained reflect a consistency and reliability of the manual classification. The assessment from the judges for all the dimensions is beyond chance, and more over, for three dimensions the agreement was almost perfect.

Training and testing sets. The amount of labelled

% Tr. data	1%			5%			10%			50%		
Model	BASE	WN	FASTQ	BASE	WN	FASTQ	BASE	WN	FASTQ	BASE	WN	FASTQ
author s.	33.48	43.44	**79.85**	42.35	55.41	**79.76**	50.07	61.64	**81.14**	55.97	64.82	**81.70**
genre	30.73	35.51	**51.95**	38.53	43.85	**59.76**	43.18	47.42	**60.63**	50.00	52.47	**65.02**
objective	**81.96**	80.03	73.09	**84.99**	82.51	83.35	**86.03**	83.24	83.01	**86.19**	85.62	85.59
scope	23.51	45.42	**97.56**	37.88	60.75	**97.51**	46.69	67.67	**97.40**	56.51	72.79	**97.28**
spatial s.	45.42	45.15	**59.42**	49.01	49.68	**61.62**	52.82	54.39	**62.14**	56.27	58.32	**67.98**
specificity	75.62	73.55	**77.51**	75.93	74.37	**76.98**	77.24	73.96	**77.51**	77.08	76.41	**78.14**
task	**68.47**	66.61	61.45	**72.60**	69.16	71.02	**75.21**	71.90	71.64	**76.87**	75.78	76.04
time s.	21.25	42.54	**97.98**	35.55	59.32	**98.60**	44.61	64.87	**98.64**	54.37	71.38	**98.43**
topic	11.73	12.85	**14.01**	**21.97**	20.75	19.39	**27.57**	26.90	25.67	34.44	**36.00**	32.90

Table 3: This table compares the classification accuracy (in %) of the user intent dimensions for the different models. The mean accuracies for $N = 10$ trials are shown where fixed number (*% tr data*) of randomly chosen queries were used for training and the remaining data used as test queries. The highest classification accuracy obtained for each facet at given amount of training data (*% tr data*) is highlighted.

data available in most IR scenarios is much smaller than the corresponding test sets. In order to test the models in the low data regime, we have used 1, 5, 10, 50 % of the available queries as training data. We have repeated the experiment for $N = 10$ independent trials where the training samples have been randomly chosen. We report the resulting mean and variance across the trials.

4.2 Models Tested

The two key components of *FastQ* are the modeling of the latent relationships between facets and the incorporation of WordNet lexical database. In order to highlight the impact of the above two factors in the overall results and establish a baseline, we construct two variants of the *FastQ* algorithm described below:

- *BASE*: The model ignores the latent relationships between facets and does not incorporate WordNet to compute the influence of new words in the test query. Thus, the resulting factor graph does not have the factors T_i and T_{ij}; and only has factors W_ℓ^i for the words which are already present in the vocabulary $\mathcal{V}$; ignoring the test query words not present in the vocabulary.
- *WN*: This does not model the latent relationships between facets; but does incorporate WordNet to incorporate the influence of new words in the test query in terms of their semantic neighbours in the existing vocabulary. Thus, the resulting factor graph does not have the factors T_i and T_{ij}; but, has factors, W_ℓ^i for the new words in the test query in addition to factors for known words.

4.3 Results

4.3.1 Classif cation Accuracy

Table 3 presents the classification accuracy of the individual facets. We note that the latent modeling of the facets in *FastQ* improves the accuracy compared to *BASE* and *WN* for the facets: Time Sensitivity, Scope, Spatial Sensitivity, Authority Sensitivity, Genre.

We use the Hamming error to measure the overall accuracy of the prediction, i.e., for a query $\breve{q}^\dagger$ with true facet classification $\vec{f}^\dagger$ and the algorithm prediction $\hat{f}$; the Hamming error $d_H(\vec{f}^\dagger, \hat{f})$ is $d_H(\vec{f}^\dagger, \hat{f}) = \sum_{k=1}^{K} \mathbf{1}_{\hat{f}_k \neq \vec{f}_k^\dagger}$ where $\mathbf{1}_{\hat{f}_k \neq \vec{f}_k^\dagger}$ is 1 if the kth facets are not same; else 0. A low (ideally *zero*) Hamming distance means few (ideally *none*) of the K facets have been incorrectly predicted.

	True	Pred.	P	R	F1
Inf	1382	1584	0.79	0.91	0.85
NotInf	645	635	0.73	0.72	0.72
Both	212	20	0.89	0.08	0.15

Table 4: This table shows the classification (*FastQ*) results for the facet *Task* as Informational (*Inf*), Not Informational (*NotInf*) and Both (*Both*). The table shows precision (P), recall (R) and the F1-score ($F1$) when 50% of the data is used for training and the rest as test queries.

Figure 3(a)-3(c) shows the cumulative distribution of the Hamming errors (number of individually incorrect facets) in the prediction of K facets for 1%, 10% and 50% training data. For example, when 10% of the data is used for training, *FastQ* classifies over 60% of the test queries with at most two mis-classified facets; compared to *WN* (45%) and *BASE* (40%). The modeling of the facet inter-relationships (*FastQ*) improves the overall quality of classification compared to *BASE* and *WN*, especially at low amounts of training data.

We note that FastQ performance compared to BASE is slightly inferior on the facet "Topic", which has 23 possible states. Therefore, accurately modelling the probability distribution requires more data. We note that at 90% training data[5], FastQ does perform better on "Topic" (and all other facets) compared to BASE. We note that in a real world setting, the amount of available data might be greater than a few thousand queries (for example, when using ODP categories). Under such scenario, FastQ will perform better modeling compared to the results shown here.

We attempt to learn a multi-faceted classification of user intent, which is inherently more sophisticated compared to learning the classical notion of user intent as *informational*, *navigational* or *transactional*. However, the closest analogue in our case is the *Task* dimensions whose values are *informational*, *not information* or *both*.

Table 4 shows the classification results for the *Task* dimension when 50% of the queries was used as training data, and the remaining for testing. An average accuracy of 76% is achieved by *FastQ* in the classification of *Task*.

[5]not shown here due to space restriction

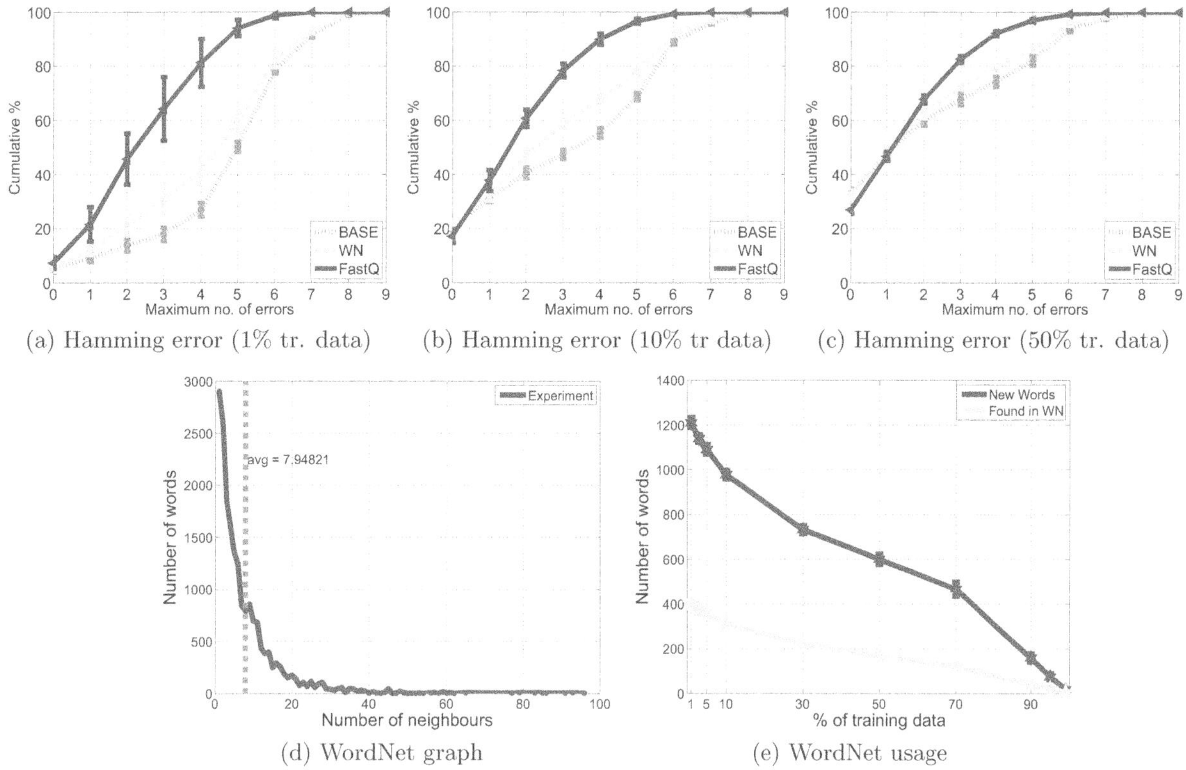

Figure 3: *(a)-(c)* The mean and variance of the Hamming error for the overall facet classification for the models *BASE* (red), *WN* (green) and *FastQ* (blue). *(d)* The histogram showing the number of related words obtained using WordNet for a test query word (blue); and the expected (average) number of related words for a new query word (red). *(e)* This figure shows the mean and variance of the number of new words found in the test data (blue); and the number of words for which related words were found in the training data using WordNet (green); with increasing amount of training data. All figures are based on results obtained from $N = 10$ independent trials.

Method	Size	Accuracy
Topic/homepage [17][‡]	200	91%
FastQ (*Task*)	5249	76%
Rule-based hierarchy [15]	1500000	74%
Query-log based [19]	50	54%
Manual classification [2]	6042	50%

Table 5: Comparison of existing approaches for intent classification with size of the dataset and the classification accuracy. ([‡]Results of [17] are based on TREC test collection.)

Table 5 shows *FastQ* compares favorably to existing methods. We re-iterate the multi-dimensional nature of our work, i.e. *Task* is one of the nine facets which characterize user intent in our case, compared to past approaches.

4.3.2 Impact of WordNet

A comparison of the results in Table 3 and Figure 3(a)-3(c) show the incorporation of WordNet for computing the influence of new words in test query based on semantic neighbours in the existing vocabulary improves the quality of results in *WN* compared to *BASE*, especially at low amounts of training data $(1 - 10\%)$.

Figure 3(e) shows that around 33% of the new words are semantically related to known words in the training data. This might be surprising, but this is explained from the characteristics of the training set that only includes 15% of queries from the head of the query distribution. Thus, incorporating WordNet may allow a better modeling for a significant portion of unseen words in a practical web search scenario.

Figure 3(d) shows the histogram of the number of related words in WordNet, experimentally observed, for a query word that is not present in training data, and its average $\bar{c}_{wn} \simeq 8$. This affects the time spent in search for related candidates of a word not present in training data.

The experiments reported used a breadth first search till maximum depth 3 using the words falling in the *synsets* category. We observed that the similarity scores for the neighbours often is either very close to one, or slightly above zero.

4.3.3 Eff ciency and Scalability

The average time for query classification at WordNet maximum search depth 3 was observed to be 2−3 ms on an AMD Turion64 machine with 4 GB RAM, which is considerably less than the average latency for a search query which is 200 ms [8]. This allows the incorporation of *FastQ* as input to the ranking algorithm of a search engine; using the user intent information to improve the user experience.

In addition, our results show that with a small training set (a few thousand queries), we can get good predictive performance. Hence, with training sets available for large search engines the results might be quite better.

5. CONCLUSIONS AND FUTURE WORK

We have presented an efficient and convergent algorithm for inferring the intent of the web search query, described in terms of multiple facets. Experimental results show that modelling the latent relationships between facets improves the accuracy of prediction. Further, the incorporation of WordNet improves intent classification using the semantic relationships in the language vocabulary.

One possible area of improvement is the usage of multiple semantic relationships, e.g. *synonyms, antonyms, hyponyms,* available in WordNet, which might improve the efficacy of WordNet in intent classification.

Our framework model can be used for fast contextualized ranking of results of a user query with or without clickthrough data. For example, it can be used for a much more refined query classification and clustering. Similarly, the intent classification can be used as input to existing search engine ranking technology [5]. Alternatively, we can use the facet classifications for sorting and displaying the search engine results in a different way creating a new user experience.

In addition, the generality of the framework allows integration of alternative aspects of user intent making it a powerful tool for contextualizing and personalizing search.

6. REFERENCES

[1] A. Ashkan, C. L. Clarke, E. Agichtein, and Q. Guo. Classifying and characterizing query intent. In *Proc. of ECIR*, 578–586, 2009.

[2] R. Baeza-Yates, L. Calderón-Benavides, and C. González-Caro. The intention behind web queries. In *Proc. of SPIRE*, *LNCS* vol. 4209, 98–109, 2006.

[3] A. Z. Broder. A taxonomy of web search. *SIGIR Forum*, 36(2):3–10, 2002.

[4] L. Calderón-Benavides, C. González-Caro, and R. Baeza-Yates. Towards a deeper understanding of the user's query intent. In *Proc. of Query Representation and Understanding Workshop at SIGIR*, 2010.

[5] O. Chapelle and S. S. Keerthi. Efficient algorithms for ranking with SVMs. *Inf. Retr.*, 13(3):201–215, 2010.

[6] C. I. Chow, S. Member, and C. N. Liu. Approximating discrete probability distributions with dependence trees. *IEEE Trans. on Inf. Theory*, 14:462–467, 1968.

[7] T. M. Cover and J. A. Thomas. *Elements of Information Theory.* Wiley, New York, 1991.

[8] J. Dean. Challenges in building large-scale information retrieval systems. WSDM'09 keynote, 2009.

[9] D. Downey, S. Dumais, and E. Horvitz. Heads and tails: Studies of web search with common and rare queries. *Proc. of SIGIR*, 847–848, 2007.

[10] D. Downey, S. Dumais, D. Liebling and E. Horvitz. Understanding the relationship between searchers' queries and information goals. In *Proc. of CIKM*, 449–458, 2008.

[11] F. Eaton and Z. Ghahramani. Choosing a variable to clamp: Approximate inference using conditioned belief propagation. In *Proc. of AISTATS*, 2009.

[12] P.-V. Eds. *EuroWordNet. A multilingual database with lexical semantic networks.* Kluwer Academic, 1998.

[13] G. Hripcsak and A. S. Rothschild. Agreement, the f-measure, and reliability in information retrieval. *JAMIA*, 12(3):296–298, May-Jun 2005.

[14] J. Hu, G. Wang, F. Lochovsky, J. T. Sun, and Z. Chen. Understanding user's query intent with wikipedia. In *Proc. of WWW*, 471–480, 2009.

[15] B. J. Jansen, D. L. Booth, and A. Spink. Determining the informational, navigational, and transactional intent of web queries. *Inf. Process. Manage.*, 44(3):1251–1266, 2008.

[16] B. J. Jansen, A. Spink, and I. Taksa. *Handbook of Research on Web Log Analysis.* Idea Group Inc., 2008.

[17] I.-H. Kang and G. Kim. Query type classification for web document retrieval. In *Proc. of SIGIR*, 64–71, 2003. ACM.

[18] F. R. Kschischang, B. J. Frey, and H.-A. Loeliger. Factor graphs and the sum-product algorithm. *IEEE Trans. on Inf. Theory*, 47:498–519, 1998.

[19] U. Lee, Z. Liu, and J. Cho. Automatic identification of user goals in web search. In *Proc. of WWW*, 391–400, 2005.

[20] Y. Liu, M. Zhang, L. Ru, and S. Ma. Automatic query type identification based on click through information. *LNCS*, 4182:593–600, 2006.

[21] M. Meila. An accelerated chow and liu algorithm: Fitting tree distributions to high-dimensional sparse data. In *Proc. of ICML*, 249–257, 1999.

[22] M. Mendoza and R. Baeza-Yates. A web search analysis considering the intention behind queries. In *Proc. of LA-WEB*, 66–74, 2008.

[23] V. B. Nguyen and M.-Y. Kan. Functional faceted web query analysis. In *Query Log Analysis: Social And Technological Challenges. A workshop at the WWW' 07*, May 2007.

[24] E. Pitler and K. Church. Using word-sense disambiguation methods to classify web queries by intent. In *Proc. of EMNLP*, Jan 2009.

[25] J. J. Randolph. Free-marginal multirater kappa: An alternative to fleiss fixed-marginal multirater kappa. Joensuu Learning and Instruction Symposium, October 2005.

[26] D. E. Rose and D. Levinson. Understanding user goals in web search. In *Proc. of WWW*, 13–19, 2004.

[27] V. Y. F. Tan, A. Anandkumar, L. Tong, and A. S. Willsky. A large-deviation analysis for the maximum likelihood learning of tree structures. In *Proc. of ISIT*, 1140–1144, 2009.

[28] J. Teevan, S. Dumais, and E. Horvitz. Potential for personalization. *ACM Trans. on Computer*, Jan 2010.

[29] J. Teevan, S. Dumais, and D. Liebling. To personalize or not to personalize: modeling queries with variation in user intent. In *Proc. of SIGIR*, 163–170, 2008.

[30] M. J. Wainwright and M. I. Jordan. *Graphical Models, Exponential Families, and Variational Inference.* Now Publishers Inc., Hanover, MA, USA, 2008.

[31] R. White, S. Dumais, and J. Teevan. Characterizing the influence of domain expertise on web search behavior. In *Proc. of WSDM*, 132–141, 2009.

[32] Web query classification. `http://en.wikipedia.org/wiki/Web_query_classification`.

Social Annotation in Query Expansion: a Machine Learning Approach

Yuan Lin, Hongfei Lin, Song Jin, Zheng Ye
School of Computer Science and Technology, Dalian University of Technology
No. 2 LingGong Road GanJingZi District DaLian, China
yuanlin@mail.dlut.edu.cn, hflin@dlut.edu.cn, dutjinsong@gmail.com, zye@mail.dlut.edu.cn

ABSTRACT

Automatic query expansion technologies have been proven to be effective in many information retrieval tasks. Most existing approaches are based on the assumption that the most informative terms in top-retrieved documents can be viewed as context of the query and thus can be used for query expansion. One problem with these approaches is that some of the expansion terms extracted from feedback documents are irrelevant to the query, and thus may hurt the retrieval performance. In social annotations, users provide different keywords describing the respective Web pages from various aspects. These features may be used to boost IR performance. However, to date, the potential of social annotation for this task has been largely unexplored. In this paper, we explore the possibility and potential of social annotation as a new resource for extracting useful expansion terms. In particular, we propose a term ranking approach based on social annotation resource. The proposed approach consists of two phases: (1) in the first phase, we propose a term-dependency method to choose the most likely expansion terms; (2) in the second phase, we develop a machine learning method for term ranking, which is learnt from the statistics of the candidate expansion terms, using ListNet. Experimental results on three TREC test collections show that the retrieval performance can be improved when the term ranking method is used. In addition, we also demonstrate that terms selected by the term-dependency method from social annotation resources are beneficial to improve the retrieval performance.

Categories and Subject Descriptors

H.3.3 [**Information Search and Retrieval**]: Search and Retrieval—*search process, query formulation*

General Terms

Algorithms, Performance, Design, Experimentation

SIGIR'11, July 24–28, 2011, Beijing, China.

Keywords

Query Expansion, Social Annotation, Learning to Rank

1. INTRODUCTION

Queries submitted to search engines always contain very few keywords or phrases, which are generally insufficient to fully describe a user's information need. To solve this problem, query expansion (QE) has been widely used [3, 27, 8, 18]. Among all the methods, pseudo-relevance feedback (PRF) via query expansion has proven to be effective in many information retrieval (IR) tasks [25, 14]. The basic assumption of PRF is that the top-ranked documents in the initial retrieval result contain many useful terms that can help describe the information need better. However, this assumption is often invalid [4] which can result in a negative impact on the retrieval performance. With a rapid development of social communities, a large amount of manually generated annotations, the so-called tags, have emerged which can be a potential resource for query expansion.

In recent years, with the rise of Web 2.0 technologies, social annotations have become a popular way to allow users to contribute descriptive metadata for Web information, such as Web pages and photos. A series of studies have been done on exploring the social annotations for folksonomy [16], recommendation [22], semantic Web [26], Web search [11, 2, 28] etc. Positive impact has been found in these studies. However, it is not clear whether social annotations can be of help as a resource for query expansion. As described in [26], social tags, which link to each other through Web resource, often share similar topics. Thus, a set of tags attached with the same resource (e.g. Web page, photo, production) could help better understand it.

In this paper, we propose a novel query expansion method based on social annotations which are used as the resource of expansion terms. Given a query, a large number of candidate expansion terms (words or phrases) will be chosen to convey users' information needs. We propose a term-dependency method to select the candidate expansion terms based on two term-dependence assumptions of query terms: 1) full independence, 2) sequential dependence. From our initial results of this method, some of the candidate expansion terms are indeed unrelated to the original query. To solve this problem, we develop a novel learning to rank method to rank the candidate terms according to their potential impact on retrieval effectiveness. Once the ranking list is obtained, the top ranked terms will be selected to expand the original query.

The contributions of this paper are as follows: 1) we conduct extensive experiments to evaluate the potential of social annotations as a resource of expansion terms for query expansion, 2) in expansion terms selection process, we investigate two term-dependence assumptions for selecting useful expansion terms from social annotations, 3) according to the impact of expansion terms selected based on these two assumptions, we develop a learning to rank approach for the novel expansion terms ranking: the list of expansion terms pertaining to a query is seemed as an *instance*, and the statistical properties of terms in social annotations are used as the *features* for learning a ranking model.

The remainder of our paper is organized as follows. Section 2 reviews some related work. Section 3 explores the potential of social annotations as a new resource of expansion terms. Section 4 proposes the expansion term ranking method based on the social annotation sample. In Section 5, we report the experimental results and list some discussions about our work. Finally, we conclude the paper and discuss future work in Section 6.

2. RELATED WORK

Automatic query expansion technique has been widely used in IR. Among all the approaches, pseudo-relevance feedback (PRF) has been shown more effective by reformulating the original query using expansion terms from pseudo-relevant documents. Traditional PRF has been implemented in different retrieval models: vector space model [21], probabilistic model [20], relevance model [12], mixture model [32] and so on. Meanwhile, large amounts of research has been conducted to improve traditional PRF by using passages instead of documents [31], by using a local context analysis method [27], by using a query-regularized estimation method [25], by using latent concepts [18], and by using a clustered-based re-sampling method for generating pseudo-relevant documents [14]. These methods follow the basic assumption that the top-ranked documents from an initial search contain many useful terms that can help discriminate relevant documents from irrelevant ones.

Despite the large number of studies, a crucial question is the expansion terms determined in traditional ways from the pseudo-relevant documents are not all useful [4]. Some studies focus on using an external resource for query expansion. They found one of the query expansion failure reasons is the lack of relevant documents in the local collection. Therefore, the performance of query expansion can be improved by using a large external collection. Several external collection enrichment approaches have been proposed, such as search engine query logs [9], some thesauruses (e.g. Wordnet) [7], Wikipedia [29] etc. Our work follows this strategy of a query expansion approach using an external collection as a resource of query expansion terms.

Recently, many researches have focused on the social annotations in large part motivated by their increasing availability across many Web-based applications. P. Mika [19] proposed a tripartite model of actors, concepts and instances for semantic emergence. Heymann et. al [10] found that the social annotation data had a good coverage of interesting pages on the Web. X. Wu et al. [26] explored machine understandable semantics from social annotations in a statistical way and applied the derived emergent semantics to discover and search shared Web bookmarks. Hotho et al. [11] proposed Adapted PageRank and FolkRank to find communities within the folksonomy but have not applied them to Web search. Bao et al. [2] proposed to measure the similarity and popularity of Web pages from Web users' perspective by calculating SocialSimRank and SocialPageRank. Xu et al. [28] proposed a personalized search framework to utilize folksonomy for personalized search. Carman et al. [6] explored how useful tag data might be for improving search results, but they focused mainly on data analysis rather than retrieval experiments.

Different from the above work, we investigate the capability of social annotations in improving the retrieval performance as a promising resource for query expansion.

3. SOCIAL ANNOTATION COLLECTION

In this section, we briefly introduce the advantage of social annotations for our study, and then investigate the potential of the social annotations for filtering irrelevant terms for query expansion.

3.1 Exploiting Social Annotation

In social annotation services like Delicious [26], they allow users to annotate and categorize Web resources with the keywords (called tags). These tags are freely chosen by the users without a pre-defined taxonomy or ontology. A single resource could be annotated with several tags from many disparate users. For example, the tags such as "conference", "research", "acm", "2011", and "sigir" are used by many users to annotate Web page about SIGIR 2011 homepage. As we can see, tags can be the good keywords for describing the respective Web page from various aspects. Moreover, different tags describing the same Web resource are semantically related to some extent.

An annotation typically consists of at least three parts: the URL of the resource (e.g. a Web page), one or more tags, and the user who created the annotation. Thus we abstract it as a triple as follows:

$$\langle user_i, tag_j, url_k \rangle \tag{1}$$

which means that user i has annotated URL k with tag j. In this paper, we focus on what resource annotated with what tags and do not care much about who annotated the resource.

3.2 Social Annotation Data Set

A social annotation service (Delicious) has the potential to give us a great deal of data about Web pages. We collected a sample of Del.icio.us[1] data by crawling its website during March 2009. The data sample consists of 7,063,028 tags on 2,137,776 different URLs with 280,672 different tags.

In our study, we mainly utilize Web pages, tags, and relationship between them. Thus, the social annotation sample is organized as one article per annotation by filtering out the user information. Each article will effectively summarize the most important information of each annotation. Based on our analysis of the social annotation structure, we divide each social annotation article into four fields as shown in Table 1.

Before the experiments, we perform two data preprocessing processes: 1) some tags only reflect personal requirement, such as *"toread"*, *"@read"*, etc. We remove some of them manually. 2) Some users may concatenate several correlative terms to form one tag, e.g. *"java/programming"*,

[1] http://delicious.com

Table 1: Fields of Social Annotation Article

Field	Description
URL	Unique identifier for Web page
Title	Summary of the Web page
Frequency	Annotation frequency of the Web page
Tags	Tags of the Web page annotated

"Iraq_war", *"news-business-finance"*. We split this kind of tags with the help of delimiters.

3.3 Evaluation of Social Annotation Collection

After analyzing a large amount of social annotations, we find that tags are usually semantically related to each other if they are used to annotate the same or related resources for many times. Intuitively, the social annotation collection can be seen as a manually edited thesaurus which provides a wealth of information of relevant terms.

In order to evaluate the potential usefulness of social annotation sample as the expansion term resource, we will consider all the terms extracted from the social annotation sample using the term co-occurrence method.

The term co-occurrence is usually used to measure how often terms appear together in the text window. In our experiment, the text window is defined as one annotation field (e.g. *tags, title*). For a query term q_j and a candidate term t_i in the social annotation sample S, the co-occurrence value is defined as follows:

$$cooc(t_i, q_j) = \frac{\sum_{f \in S} log(tf(t_i|f) + 1.0) \times log(tf(q_j|f) + 1.0)}{log(N)} \quad (2)$$

where N is the sum of articles in social annotation sample S, $tf(.|f)$ is frequency of term appears in field f.

Base on this equation, terms with highest $cooc(t_i, q_j)$ is chosen for the original query term q_j as the candidate expansion terms. The final expansion terms can be selected as follows:

$$\underset{single}{coof}(t_i, Q) = \sum_{q_j \in Q} idf(q_j) idf(t_i) log(cooc(t_i, q_j) + 1.0) \quad (3)$$

where idf is computed as $log(N/df)$, N is the sum of articles in social annotation sample, and df is the number of articles which contain term t.

Inspired by the work of Cao et al. [4], we will test each of these terms to see its impact on the retrieval effectiveness. In order to make the test simpler, we make the following simplifications: 1) Each expansion term is assumed to act on the query independently from other expansion terms; 2) Each expansion term is added into the query with equal weight λ(it is set at 0.01 or -0.01). Based on these simplifications, we measure the performance change due to the expansion term e by the ratio:

$$chg(e) = \frac{MAP(Q \cup e) - MAP(Q)}{MAP(Q)} \quad (4)$$

where $MAP(Q)$ and $MAP(Q \cup e)$ are respectively the MAP of the original query and expanded query (expanded with e).

In our previous work [30], we conducted some preliminary experiments. In our experiment, we set the threshold to 0.005. It means good (or bad) expansion term which can improve (or hurt) the effectiveness should produce a performance change such that $|chg(e)| > 0.005$.

Table 2: Proportions of each group of expansion terms selected from feedback documents

Collection	Good Terms	Neutral Terms	Bad Terms
AP	17.55%	64.01%	18.44%
WSJ	15.83%	66.93%	17.24%
Robust 2004	16.57%	66.05%	17.38%

Table 3: Proportions of each group of expansion terms selected from social annotation sample

Collection	Good Terms	Neutral Terms	Bad Terms
AP	19.05%	59.98%	20.97%
WSJ	18.33%	59.21%	22.46%
Robust 2004	18.47%	60.05%	21.48%

Now, we will examine whether the candidate expansion terms from social annotation sample are good terms. Our verification is made on three TREC collections: AP, WSJ and Robust 2004. We respectively consider 150 queries for each collection and 100 expansion terms for each query with largest probabilities from pseudo-feedback documents and with largest co-occurrence values from social annotation sample. Table 2 and 3 respectively show the proportion of good, bad and neutral expansion terms from feedback documents and social annotation collection for all the queries.

Comparing Table 2 and 3, we can see that the proportion of good terms extracted from social annotation sample is higher than it extracted from pseudo-feedback documents. It means that social annotations have the potential to produce more good terms as the resource for query expansion. From Table 2 and 3, all the proportions of bad terms on all three collections are higher than that of the good ones'. This means while the proportion of good terms increases, social annotation sample indeed introduces more bad terms into the expansion process. The research of Cao et al. [4] shows that the retrieval effectiveness can be much improved if more good expansion terms are added to the original queries. The challenge now is to develop an effective method to correctly select the good terms in the expansion process.

4. EXPANSION TERM RANKING

The challenge to select good terms for query expansion consists of two parts: (1) how to select the candidate expansion terms from the whole social annotation sample, (2) how to distinguish the different importance of these terms.

For the first part, we propose a term-dependency method to select the candidate expansion terms. When the candidate expansion terms selected, we use a novel learning to rank method to rank the candidate terms. Once the ranking list is obtained, the top ranked terms in the list will be selected to expand the original query.

4.1 Term-Dependency Method for Candidate Term Selection

It is well known that the dependencies between terms exist in most queries. For example, in Topic 63 ("machine translation"), occurrences of certain pairs of terms are correlated.

The fact that either one occurs provides strong evidence that the other is also likely to occur.

Eq. (3) assumes that the selection of each query term is determined independently, lacking consideration of latent term relations. Most work on modeling term dependencies in the past has analyzed three different underlying dependence assumptions: *full independence*, *sequential dependence* [23], and *full dependence* [17].

The full independence variant which assumes query terms are independent underlies many retrieval models. Eq. (3) is based on this assumption. The second variant we considered is the sequential dependence. In this variant we assume the dependence between neighboring query terms. Based on this assumption, we generalize Eq. (3) as follows:

$$\underset{bigram}{coof}\,(t_i, Q) = \sum_{j=1}^{n-1} idf(q_j) idf(q_{j+1}) idf(t_i) \\ log(cooc(t_i, q_j) + 1.0) log(cooc(t_i, q_{j+1}) + 1.0) \tag{5}$$

where n is the sum of query terms in original query Q.

The full dependence variant assumes all the query terms are in some way dependent on each other. Under this assumption, each combination of query terms should be considered. In the experiments, the results using this variant are not satisfactory. One of the possible reasons is that some irrelevant term group may be introduced into the term selection procedure.

Therefore, we only consider the first two assumptions and apply the following function with linear interpolation, weighted by a parameter λ.

$$coof(t_i, Q) = (1 - \lambda)\,\underset{single}{coof}\,(t_i, Q) + \lambda\,\underset{bigram}{coof}\,(t_i, Q) \tag{6}$$

Using the term-dependency method, we select the candidate terms with the highest $coof$ scores. For expansion term selection, the term-dependency method will be shown effective in Section 6.

4.2 Term Quality Evaluation

A key idea of our term ranking approach is that one can generalize the knowledge of expansion terms from the past candidate ones to predict effective expansion terms for the novel queries. In order to do this, it requires a method for estimating a candidate term for each training query given examples of its relevant or irrelevant terms.

Intuitively, for query expansion technology, the relevant expansion terms are beneficial to improve the retrieval performance. Inspired by the work of Cao et al. [4], the $chg(e)$ of expansion term e described in Section 3.3 could reflect its potential impact on retrieval effectiveness. Suppose that query q_i has k expansion terms, the relevance label of expansion term e_j $(1 \leq j \leq k)$ is defined as follows:

$$label(e_j) = \begin{cases} 0, chg(e) < 0; \\ 1, chg(e) \geq 0; \end{cases} \tag{7}$$

where $label(e_j) = 1$ reflects term e_j is relevant to query q_i, and $label(e_j) = 0$ reflects term e_j is irrelevant.

In our experiment, we use three TREC collections (see Table 4 in Section 5.1), with 150 queries for each collection. We divide these queries into three groups of 50 queries. In the training dataset, each query has a term list which ranks the candidate expansion terms according to $chg(e)$. To generate the development dataset, we label each term with binary relevance judgments (relevant or irrelevant) according to Eq. (7). For each term in the dataset (training, development or test), we represent it with the features described in the next section.

4.3 Features for Term Ranking

This section describes our current feature set for the expansion term. We utilize the statistical features of single term and also term pair. Each expansion term is represented by a feature vector.

Useful statistical features include those already used in traditional methods such as term frequency (TF), document frequency (DF). In order to capture the relationship between the candidate expansion terms and the original query terms, we consider the co-occurrences of them. The social annotation article described in Section 3.2 consists of four fields (*url, title, frequency, tags*), and we did not use the information in the *url* field in the experiment. Obviously, the importance of a term appearing in the *title* may be different than its appearance in the *tags*. We calculate the statistical features separately in *title*, *tags*, and the whole article. Each expansion term is represented by a feature vector: $[f_1(e), f_2(e), \cdots, f_N(e)]^T$. We will only describe the features in *title* field (f_{title}). The others can be defined similarly.

- Term frequency(TF)

The first features are the classic statistics of term frequency.

$$f_1(e) = tf(e|f_{title}) \tag{8}$$

$$f_4(e) = \frac{tf(e|f_{title})}{\underset{e' \in f_{title}}{max}\; tf(e'|f_{title})} \tag{9}$$

$$f_7(e) = \frac{tf(e|f_{title})}{\sum_{e' \in f_{title}} tf(e'|f_{title})} \tag{10}$$

- Document frequency (DF)

In the experiment, a social annotation article described in Section 3.2 is defined as a document, and *df* of the expansion term e is the number of documents containing e in the specific field. The definitions of *df* features are:

$$f_{10}(e) = df(e|f_{title}) \tag{11}$$

$$f_{13}(e) = \frac{df(e|f_{title})}{\underset{e' \in f_{title}}{max}\; df(e'|f_{title})} \tag{12}$$

$$f_{16}(e) = \frac{df(e|f_{title})}{\sum_{e' \in f_{title}} df(e'|f_{title})} \tag{13}$$

- Co-occurrence with a single query term

The co-occurrence features are used to estimate the relationship between high frequency terms more reliably. Therefore, we define the co-occurrence feature as follows:

$$f_{19}(e) = log\frac{\sum_{i=1}^{n} C(q_i, e|f_{title})}{n} \quad (14)$$

where $C(q_i, e|f_{title})$ is the frequency of co-occurrences of query term q_i and the expansion term e in *title* field.

- Co-occurrence with query term pairs

A stronger co-occurrence relation for an expansion term is with two query terms together. [1] has shown that this type of co-occurrence relation is much better because it can take into account some query contexts.

$$f_{22}(e) = log\frac{\sum_{(q_i,q_j)\in\Omega} C(q_i, q_j, e|f_{title})}{|\Omega|} \quad (15)$$

where Ω is the set of possible query term pairs.

- Term Popularity

The *frequency* field denotes the annotation frequency of Web page, while it also reflects the popularity of Web page. A popular Web page will introduce many more popular tags which may be the good descriptor. Notice that we only develop the distinctive property for terms in *tags* field.

$$f_{25}(e) = \sum_{f_{tags}\in S} frequency(e|f_{tags}) \quad (16)$$

where $frequency(e|f_{tags})$ denotes frequency of the Web page contains the term e in *tags* field.

Our feature space is constructed of statistical features and the unique feature from social annotation sample. Given examples of target term weights paired with corresponding features, the following work is to predict the relevant score of expansion term with given the features. We accomplish this via the ListNet of learning to rank approaches.

4.4 ListNet

ListNet [5] is a feature-based learning to rank approach, which minimizes a listwise ranking loss function based on the probability distribution on permutations. It utilizes result lists as instances in the learning procedure. Based on the neural network model[13], the gradient descent approach[15] is used to minimize the K-L divergence loss. ListNet outputs a linear ranking model that is used to predict the relevance score of a new object. In this paper we use this approach to learning a ranking model for the term ranking.

4.5 Term Ranking Model via ListNet

We now give a general description on learning to rank a set of expansion terms according to their effectiveness.

Assume that, a set of queries $Q = \{q_1, q_2, \cdots, q_m\}$ is given. Each query q_i is associated with a set of possible usable terms $T_i = \{t_{i,1}, t_{i,2}, \cdots, t_{i,n_i}\}$, where $t_{i,j}$ denotes the j-th term is relevant to the i-th query and n_i denotes the sizes of T_i.

Each list of terms T_i is associated with a list of relevance judgment $y_i = \{y_{i,1}, y_{i,2}, \cdots, y_{i,n_i}\}$, where $y_{i,j}$ denotes the extent to which the candidate term $y_{i,j}$ is relevant to the original query q_i. The measure to score the degree is defined as follows:

$$y_{i,j} = \frac{\varphi(q_i \cup t_{i,j}) - \varphi(q_i)}{\varphi(q_i)} \quad (17)$$

where $\varphi(.)$ is a performance measure function, in our experiment, we use MAP as the measure function. The assumption is that the higher performance improvement is observed for the combination of $t_{i,j}$ and q_i the stronger relevance exists between them.

In training, the training set can be denoted as $\Gamma = \{(x_i, y_j)\}_{i=1}^{m}$, where $x_i = \{x_{i,1}, x_{i,2}, \cdots, x_{i,n_i}\}$ is the list of features and $y_i = \{y_{i,1}, y_{i,2}, \cdots, y_{i,n_i}\}$ is the corresponding list of scores. The feature vector $x_{i,j} = \psi(q_i, t_{i,j})$ is created from each query-term pair $(q_i, t_{i,j})$, $i = 1, 2, \cdots, m$ and $j = 1, 2, \cdots, n_i$.

For each feature vector $x_{i,j}$, the ranking function f outputs a score $f(x_{i,j})$. Furthermore, we will obtain a list of scores $z_i = (f(x_{i,1}), \cdots, f(x_{i,n_i})))$ for the list of feature vectors x_i. The objective of learning is formalized as minimization of the total losses with respect to the training data.

$$\sum_{i=1}^{m} L(y_i, z_i) \quad (18)$$

where L is a loss function.

In the term ranking, when a new query q' and its associated terms t' are given, we construct feature vectors x' from them and use the trained ranking function to assign scores to the terms t'. Finally we select the top k terms to expand the original query. We use a learning method for optimizing the loss function based on top *gamma* probability, with Neural Network as model and Gradient Descent as optimization algorithm [5].

Based on the Neural Network model ω, we denote the ranking function as f_ω. For a feature vector $x_{i,j}$, $f_\omega(x_{i,j})$ assigns a score to it. When we use Cross Entropy as metric, the loss function becomes:

$$L(y_j, z_i(f_\omega)) = -\sum_{\forall g\in\xi_\gamma} P_{y_i}(g) log(P_{z_i(f_\omega)})(g) \quad (19)$$

$$P_s(\xi_\gamma(j_1, j_2, \cdots, j_\gamma)) = \prod_{z=1}^{\gamma} \frac{exp(s_{j_z})}{\sum_{l=z}^{n_i} exp(s_{j_l})} \quad (20)$$

$$P_{z_i(f_\omega)}(\xi_\gamma(j_1, j_2, \cdots, j_\gamma)) = \prod_{z=1}^{\gamma} \frac{exp(f_\omega(x_{i,j_z}))}{\sum_{l=1}^{n_i} exp(f_\omega(x_{i,j_l}))} \quad (21)$$

In our experiments, we implemented ListNet with $\gamma = 1$.With some derivation, when $\gamma = 1$ we have:

$$\Delta\omega = \frac{\partial L(y_i, z_i(f_\omega))}{\partial\omega} = -\sum_{j=1}^{n_i} P_{y_i}(x_{i,j})\frac{\partial f_\omega(x_{i,j})}{\partial\omega} + \frac{1}{\sum_{j=1}^{n_i} exp(f_\omega(x_{i,j}))}\sum_{j}^{n_i} exp(f_\omega(x_{i,j}))\frac{\partial f_\omega(x_{i,j})}{\partial\omega} \quad (22)$$

For simplicity, we use a linear Neural Network model in our experiments.

5. EXPERIMENTS

5.1 Experimental Settings

We used three standard TREC collections in our experiments: AP88-90(Associated Press); WSJ87-90(Wall St. Journal); and Robust2004 (the dataset of TREC Robust Track

Table 4: Statistics of Evaluation Datasets

Collection	#Docs	Train Topics	Dev. Topics	Test Topics
AP	242,198	51-100	101-150	151-200
WSJ	173,252	51-100	101-150	151-200
Robust 2004	528,155	301-350	351-400	401-450

Table 5: Performance comparisons of baseline models for all the topics on AP, WSJ, Roust2004 collections

Method	AP	WSJ	Robust 2004
QL	0.2201	0.2270	0.2214
RM	0.2763	0.3272	0.2423

started in 2003). Table 4 shows the details of these collections. For each dataset, we split the topics into three parts: the training data for the rank learner, the development data to estimate the parameters, and the test data.

Retrieval effectiveness is measured in terms of Mean Average Precision (MAP) for top 1000 documents. When an original query Q is given, a set of M candidate expansion terms will be selected from social annotation sample by term-dependency method described in Section 4.1. According to their potential impact on retrieval effectiveness, the ranking model will re-rank the M terms to form a new term ranking list. Once the ranking list is obtained, the top k terms will be selected to form an expansion query Q_{exp}. In the experiments, the Indri 2.6 search engine [24] is used as our basic retrieval system.

5.2 Baseline Models

In the experiments we select three baseline models; one is the query-likelihood language model (**QL**), the second is Lavrenko's relevance model (**RM**) [12] implemented in Indri, the third is the expanded query model by relevance model using the oracle expansion terms selected from documents (**RM+Oracle**). In relevance model RM, it retrieves a set of N documents and forms an expanded query Q_{exp} by adding the top k most likely terms. Note that in RM+Oracle model, we select top k expansion terms with high $chg(e)$ according to Eq. (4) for each query. The expanded query is formed with the following structure:

$$\#weight(\ \lambda_{fb}\ Q_{ori}\quad (1.0 - \lambda_{fb})\ Q_{exp}\ ) \tag{23}$$

For the RM and RM+Oracle methods, we fixed the parameters as follows: $N = 10$, $k = 50$ and $\lambda_{fb} = 0.5$, since we achieve relative good performance under this setting in general.

Table 5 and 6 respectively show the performance (MAP) for all the topics and all the test topics on three TREC collections. Comparing Table 5 and 6, the improvements over the QL model for all the topics and the test topics are on the same levels. In order to facilitate comparison with term ranking model, we only use the test topics to do the retrieval experiments.

As can be seen from Table 6, the relevance model can significantly improve the retrieval performance over the query likelihood language model. Compared with the results of the RM and RM+Oracle methods, the retrieval effectiveness can be much improved if the oracle expansion terms

Table 6: Performance comparisons of baseline models for all the test topics on AP, WSJ, Roust2004 collections

Method	AP	WSJ	Robust 2004
QL	0.2111	0.3364	0.2462
RM	0.2771	0.3906	0.2705
RM+Oracle	0.3201	0.4196	0.3153

are added. This shows the usefulness of correctly selecting the expansion terms with the high potential of improving the retrieval effectiveness. The MAP of the RM+Oracle method represents the upper bound retrieval effectiveness we can expect to obtain using expansion terms extracted from pseudo-relevance documents. These three models serve as the baseline for the following experiments.

6. EVALUATION OF QUERY EXPANSION METHODS BASED ON SOCIAL ANNOTATION COLLECTION

We now turn our attention to our proposed method utilizing the social annotation collection (**SA**) as the resource of query expansion. In order to extract the effective expansion terms from the social annotation collection, we propose an unsupervised method and a supervised learning model.

For the unsupervised method, we investigate the method based on two different term dependence assumptions: *full independence* and *sequential dependence*. In Section 6.1 and 6.2, we evaluate the performance of the unsupervised method, and also demonstrate the social annotation collection could be a good resource for extracting useful expansion terms.

For the supervised learning model, we examine the quality of the term ranking model, and then investigate the performance of the term ranking model for query expansion task.

6.1 Performance of the Method based on Full Independence

We first evaluate the performance of the method based on *full independence* (**SA+FI**). Note that the SA+FI method selects the top k terms with highest co-occurrence according to Eq. (3). From Table 7, we can see that the SA+FI method enhance the retrieval performance over the QL model on all the collections. This indicates that the expansion terms social annotations provided is closely related to the query. Compared with the RM model, the SA+FI method does not work as well as it. Although social annotations may produce more good terms by the SA+FI method, more bad terms is also introduced into the query. That is the most likely reason for the poor performance of the SA+FI method.

The SA+FI method assumes the query terms are independent to each other. Under this assumption, some irrelevant terms may be selected by the SA+FI method. For example, on AP, Topic 159 ("electric car development") scores a mean average precision (MAP) of 0.3100 in the QL model, and in the SA+FI method the MAP of Topic 159 is increased to 0.3657. Using this method, the top ranked expansion terms of Topic 159 are "car", "electric", "development", "program", "energy", "auto", "tool", "design", "green" and "ev". Although the MAP is increased after adding the expansion terms, some irrelevant terms (e.g. "program", "tool", and

Table 7: **Performance comparisons of SA+FI, SA+TD, SA+TDW and SA+Oracle for all the test topics on AP, WSJ, Robust2004 collections.**

Method	AP	WSJ	Robust 2004
SA+FI	0.2380	0.3564	0.2515
SA+TD	0.2562	0.3767	0.2685
SA+TDW	0.2707	0.3885	0.2776
SA+Oracle	0.3537	0.4470	0.3324

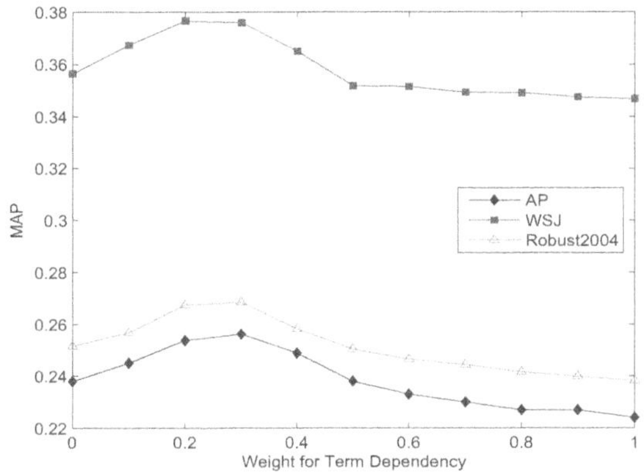

Figure 1: Performance on different weights for SA+TD on AP, WSJ and Robust2004 collections

"design") may also hurt the retrieval performance. To examine the possible impact with the irrelevant terms, we remove the irrelevant terms from the set of expansion terms manually, and add the same number of terms to Topic 159. After this processing, the MAP is increased to 0.4101. We can see that the retrieval performance can be much improved if fewer irrelevant terms are added. Our problem now is to develop an effective method to extract good terms from the social annotation collection.

6.2 Performance of the Method based on Sequential Dependence

In Section 4.1, we take into account the dependencies between query terms, and propose a term-dependency method (**SA+TD**) to select more relevant terms for original queries. The parameter λ in Eq. (6) is used to measure the impact of term-dependency in the term selection phase. When $\lambda = 0$, the term selecting method becomes the SA+FI method. Figure 1 shows the results of assigning different weight on three TREC collections.

As can be seen in Figure 1, the performance is improved when weight λ is at the higher level ($\lambda \leq 0.6$). On the other hand, when $\lambda > 0.5$, the MAP of the SA+TD method is lower than the SA+FI method's. It means the dependencies between query terms can be useful in the term selection process, but it will hurt the performance if much query term dependency information is used. Finally, we set the parameter $\lambda = 0.2$.

In the SA+FI and SA+TD methods, the expansion terms are added into the original query with the same weight. It means all the expansion terms have the same importance with each other. In fact, the co-occurrence of expansion term calculated by Eq. (6) may reflect the importance to the query Q. In the **SA+TDW** method, we will obtain the top k terms for query expansion, whose weights are normalized before being added into original queries. In addition, similar to the RM+Oracle method, we select top k terms with high $chg(e)$ extracted from the social annotation collection to add into the original query, and the results of this method (**SA+Oracle**) represent the upper bound retrieval effectiveness we can expect to obtain using expansion terms extracted from the social annotation collection.

As we can see from Table 7, both the SA+TD and SA+TDW methods achieve better performance than the SA method in the expansion term selection. Term-dependency methods can effectively select relevance terms for the original query. Compared with the two term-dependency methods, the SA+TDW method performs much better. For this method, top k terms with high co-occurrence score are selected to expand the query. This shows that the co-occurrence score could be used to reflect the importance of the expansion term. Using the oracle expansion terms extracted from social annotation collection, the performance can also be much improved than other methods.

Comparing Table 6 and 7, we can see the SA+FI and SA+TD methods do not work as well as the RM model does. On AP and WSJ, the SA+TDW method gets lower performance than the RM model does, but on Robust2004, the performance is improved over the RM model. In a well-tuned relevance model (RM), the expansion terms are weighted according to the distribution they are sampled from collection. That is one of the reasons the SA+TD method gets weak performance. Compared with the results of the SA+Oracle and RM+Oracle methods, the SA+Oracle method achieve better performance. It indicates that the social annotation collection is a good resource for query expansion. Based on these results, the refinement of the expansion term selection process for queries could be expected to further improve retrieval performance. Our goal now is to develop an effective method to select more relevance expansion terms.

6.3 Term Ranking Experiments

Let us now examine the quality of our term ranking model. In ranking performance evaluation, there are many IR evaluation measures: such as Normalized Discounted Cumulative Gain (NDCG) and Mean Average Precision (MAP). In our experiments, we take more attention to the relevance of the top k terms. Therefore, we adopt $P@n$ as the main measures for the performance evaluation of ranking model. The formula of $P@n$ is defined as:

$$P@n = \frac{|relevant\ terms|}{n} \quad (24)$$

i.e., the portion of relevant terms in the top-n result list. $P@n$ is sensitive to the amount of relevance terms returned, and thus is helpful to measure the performance gain on precision of the ranking model.

In our experiment, we use three TREC collections. For each collection, we use 50 queries to training the ranking learner. In training set, each query has a term list which ranks 150 expansion terms according to $chg(e)$ which reflects the term's impact on retrieval effectiveness. To evaluate the performance of ranking learner, according to the methods described in Section 4.2, we label the expansion term e in the development dataset with two levels of relevance judgments: relevance and irrelevance. In test dataset, we rank

Table 8: Term ranking accuracies in terms of $P@n$ on AP, WSJ and Robust2004 collections

Setting		P@10	P@20	P@30
AP	TermList-TD	0.3796	0.3724	0.3653
	TermList-Learning	0.4041	0.3888	0.3952
WSJ	TermList-TD	0.3880	0.3560	0.3500
	TermList-Learning	0.3920	0.3600	0.3647
Robust2004	TermList-TD	0.3612	0.3306	0.3211
	TermList-Learning	0.4061	0.3571	0.3524

the expansion terms order by the co-occurrence score calculated by Eq. (6). This term list is named *TermList-TD*. The *TermList-TD* list could be re-ranked to form a new term list (*TermList-Learning*) by ranking learner. Finally, we represent each expansion term with the features described in section 4.3.

Table 8 shows the performance of our ranking learner on different collections. As mentioned before, an expansion term list (*TermList-TD*) could be obtained according to the co-occurrence score using term-dependency method. Actually, the SA+TD method selected the top k terms from this term list to expand the original query. Our ranking model learns to re-rank the term list produced by term-dependency method to form a new term list (*TermList-Learning*).

From Table 8, for the effective expansion term selection, the ranking learner outperforms the term-dependency method. On AP and Robust2004 datasets, the ranking learner works much better than it works on WSJ dataset. Table 3 shows that the proportion of good terms on WSJ is lower than that on the other two datasets. It may cause that the total of relevance terms in the term list produced by the term-dependency method is lower. This is one of the reasons that the performance on WSJ is not much improved like the other two datasets. In the next section, we will investigate the usefulness of the selected expansion terms from the new re-ranked lists (*TermList-Learning*) for query expansion.

6.4 Performance of Term Ranking Model for Query Expansion

As described in Section 4.5, given a test query, a possible expansion term list is obtained using term-dependency method, and then the ranking learner will re-rank the term lists according to their impact on retrieval effectiveness. The term ranking process performs a further selection of expansion terms from those proposed by term-dependency method. After re-ranking, we use the top ranked terms in the new re-ranked list as the final expansion terms.

For the term re-ranked lists, we mentioned two possible ways to use the term ranking results. The first method (SA+Learning) is to add the top ranked 50 terms with the same weight to original queries. In our term ranking experiments, we are interested to know not only is a term is good, but also the extent to which it is good. The ranking learner will assign a score to all the expansion terms. This score is useful to enhance the weight of an expansion term in the final query model. Therefore, the second method (SA+LearningW) is to add the top 50 terms with different weights, note that their weights are normalized before being interpolated with the original query model.

Table 9 shows the results obtained with both methods. From this table, we can see that both of the two methods

Table 9: Performance comparisons of SAR and SARW for all the test topics on AP, WSJ, Roust2004 collections.

Method	AP	WSJ	Robust 2004
SA+Learning	0.2935	0.4103	0.3033
SA+LearningW	0.3325	0.4145	0.3163

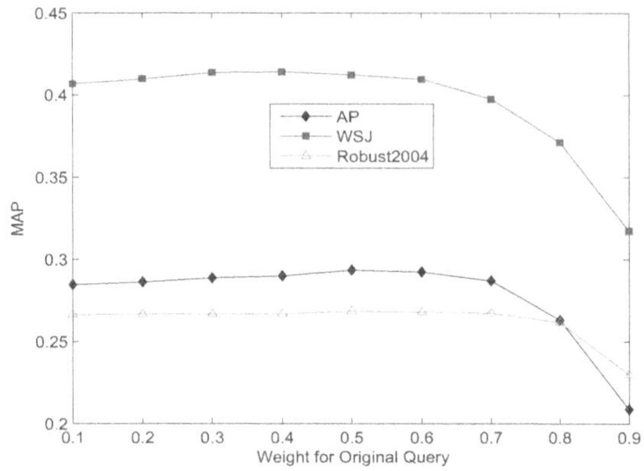

Figure 2: Performance on different weights for SA+TD on AP, WSJ and Robust2004 collections, $k = 50$.

improve the effectiveness. In comparison, although on WSJ and Robust2004 the improvements with the SA+LearningW method are smaller, they are steady on all the three collections.

Comparing Table 7 and 9, the improvements with the SA+Learning and SA+LearningW methods are statistically significant. Our explanation is that, since the term ranking learner performs better (shown in Table 8), some top ranked expansion terms could improve the performance significantly. On the other hand, it means that the relevant expansion terms may be re-ranked in the higher position of the list and the learners have the ability of recommending the most likely terms to the original queries.

Comparing Table 6 and 9, the SA+Learning and SA+LearningW methods outperform the RM model, it shows that the expansion terms selected from re-ranked term lists is more relevance than them extracted from pseudo-relevance documents. Although the the SA+LearningW method does not work well as the RM+Oracle method on AP and WSJ datasets, there is a smaller gap between them. However, on Robust2004 dataset, the SA+LearningW method performs better than the RM+Oracle method. Our explanation is that, for the RM and RM+Oracle methods, the improvement over the QL model on the Robust2004 dataset is not as significant as them on AP and WSJ datasets. It means the pseudo-relevance documents produced more noisy expansion terms for the RM model. It could reduce this influence by using social annotation collection as the resource of expansion terms. However, it is also a difficult task to explore an effective method to mining relevance terms from this new resource. This experiments show that the term ranking model has the ability of selecting more relevant terms for the original queries.

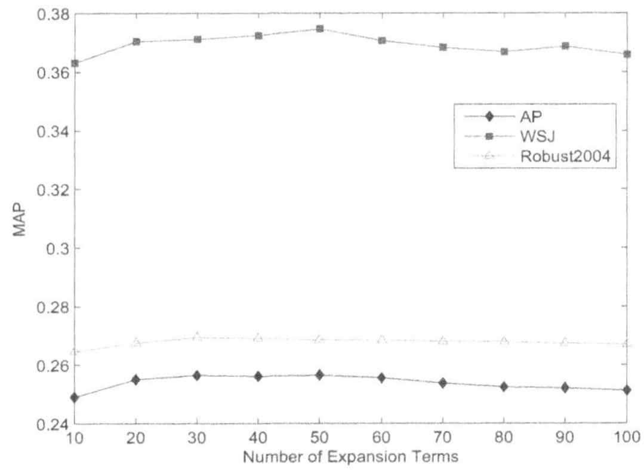

Figure 3: Sensitivity of SA+TD to parameter (k) on AP, WSJ and Robust2004 collections,$\lambda_{fb} = 0.5$.

6.5 Parameter Selection

Both the RM and the SA methods have parameters k and λ_{fb}. We tested these methods with 10 different values of k: the number of expansion terms: 10, 20,..., 100. For λ_{fb}(weight for original query), we tested with 9 different values: 0.1, 0.2,..., 0.9. Figure 2 shows the performance on different weights for original query on AP, WSJ and Robust2004 collections. When λ_{fb} is smaller than 0.6, the performance remains steady. However, when λ_{fb} continues to increase, the performance drops sharply. We conjecture that the main reason is the impact on retrieval effectiveness of expansion terms reduces with λ_{fb} increasing. From another perspective, it also proves the usefulness of expansion terms. Figure 3 shows the sensitivity of SA+TD to k. For the parameter k (the number of expansion terms), when k is around 50, we can achieve the best performance on all collections. When we use more expansion terms for PRF ($k > 50$), the performance changed is not marked. For efficiency, we suggest to choose top 50 terms for query expansion in our proposed method. The results for other methods are similar, and it shows that setting $k = 50$ and $\lambda_{fb} = 0.5$ works best among all the values tested.

7. CONCLUSION

In this paper, we have explored the potential of social annotation as a new resource for query expansion. For TREC topics, we measure the importance of expansion terms according to their impact on the retrieval performance, which selected from social annotation sample. Our experiments show that the expansion terms extracted from social annotation are significantly better than those from the feedback documents, using a simple statistical method. In the expansion term selection phase, in addition to the full independent assumption, the sequential dependence of query terms has been taken into account, which captures more relevant terms that are beneficial to retrieval performance. Another contribution of this paper is that we develop a machine learning approach for query expansion, which learns to rank a set of expansion terms according to their impact on the retrieval performance. We also show that our ranking approach works satisfactorily on the different TREC collections.

This study suggests several interesting research avenues for our future investigations. For the term selection method, because of its weak performance in our experiment the full dependence variant of query terms is not used. In fact, the query context factors could bring significant improvements in retrieval effectiveness. This means that there is still much room to improve the retrieval performance. For the term ranking model, we plan to explore more distinctive features in social annotation sample for the learning process. We leave these limitations as our future work.

8. ACKNOWLEDGMENTS

This work is supported by grant from the Natural Science Foundation of China (No.60673039 and 60973068) , the National High Tech Research and Development Plan of China (No.2006AA01Z151), National Social Science Foundation of China (No.08BTQ025), the Project Sponsored by the Scientific Research Foundation for the Returned Overseas Chinese Scholars, State Education Ministry and The Research Fund for the Doctoral Program of Higher Education (No.20090041110002).

9. REFERENCES

[1] J. Bai, J. Y. Nie, H. Bouchard, and G. Cao. Using query contexts in information retrieval. In *SIGIR '07: Proceedings of the 30st annual international ACM SIGIR conference on Research and development in information retrieval*, pages 15–22. ACM, 2007.

[2] S. Bao, G. Xue, X. Wu, Y. Yu, B. Fei, and Z. Su. Optimizing web search using social annotations. In *WWW '07: Proceedings of the 16th international conference on World Wide Web*, pages 501–510. ACM, 2007.

[3] C. Buckley, G. Salton, J. Allen, and A. Singhal. Automatic query expansion using smart: Trec 3. In *the 3th Text REtrieval Conference (TREC 1994)*, 1994.

[4] G. Cao, J. Y. Nie, and S. Robertson. Selecting good expansion terms for pseudo-relevance feedback. In *SIGIR '08: Proceedings of the 31st annual international ACM SIGIR conference on Research and development in information retrieval*, pages 243–250. ACM, 2008.

[5] Z. Cao, T. Qin, T. Y. Liu, M. F. Tsai, and H. Li. Learning to rank: From pairwise approach to listwise approach. In *ICML '07: Proceedings of the 24th International Conference on Machine Learning*, pages 129–136, 2007.

[6] M. Carman, M. Baillie, R. Gwadera, and F. Crestani. A statistical comparison of tag and query logs. In *SIGIR '09: Proceedings of the 32nd annual international ACM SIGIR conference on Research and development in information retrieval*, pages 123–130. ACM, 2009.

[7] K. Collins-Thompson and J. Callan. Query expansion using random walk models. In *SIGIR '05: Proceedings of the 28th annual international ACM SIGIR conference on Research and development in information retrieval*, pages 704–711. ACM, 2005.

[8] S. Cronen-Townsend, Y. Zhou, and W. B. Croft. A framework for selective query expansion. In *CIKM '04: Proceeding of the 13th ACM conference on Information and knowledge management*, pages 236–237. ACM, 2004.

[9] H. Cui, J. R. Wen, J. Y. Nie, and W. Y. Ma. Query expansion by mining user logs. *IEEE Transactions on knowledge and data engineering*, 15(4):829–839, 2003.

[10] P. Heymann, G. Koutrika, and H. Garcia-Molina. Can social bookmarks improve web search? In *WSDM '08: Proceedings of the First ACM International Conference on Web Search and Data Mining*, pages 195–206. ACM, 2008.

[11] A. Hotho, R. Jaschke, C. Schmitz, and G. Stumme. Information retrieval in folksonomies: Search and ranking. In *ESWC '06: Proceedings of the 3rd European Semantic Web Conference*, pages 411–426, 2006.

[12] V. Lavrenko and W. B. Croft. Relevance based language models. In *SIGIR '01: Proceedings of the 24th annual international ACM SIGIR conference on Research and development in information retrieval*, pages 120–127. ACM, 2001.

[13] Y. LeCun, L. Bottou, G. B. Orr, and K. R. Müller. Efficient backprop. *Neural Networks: Tricks of the Trade*, pages 9–50, 1998.

[14] K. S. Lee, W. B. Croft, and J. Allan. A cluster-based resampling method for pseudo-relevance feedback. In *SIGIR '08: Proceedings of the 31st annual international ACM SIGIR conference on Research and development in information retrieval*, pages 235–242. ACM, 2008.

[15] L. Mason, J. Baxter, P. Bartlett, and M. Frean. Boosting algorithms as gradient descent. In *NIPS '00: Proceedings of the 14th Neural Information Processing Systems*, pages 512–518, 2000.

[16] A. Mathes. Folksonomies - cooperative classification and communication through shared metadata. 2004.

[17] D. Metzler and W. Croft. A markov random field model for term dependencies. In *SIGIR '05: Proceedings of the 28th annual international ACM SIGIR conference on Research and development in information retrieval*, pages 472–479. ACM, 2005.

[18] D. Metzler and W. B. Croft. Latent concept expansion using markov random fields. In *SIGIR '07: Proceedings of the 30th annual international ACM SIGIR conference on Research and development in information retrieval*, pages 311–318. ACM, 2007.

[19] P. Mika. Ontologies are us: A unified model of social networks and semantics. In *ISWC '05: Proceedings of the 4th International Semantic Web Conference*, pages 522–536, 2005.

[20] S. E. Robertson, S. Walker, M. Beaulieu, M. Gatford, and A. Payne. Okapi at trec-4. In *the 4th Text REtrieval Conference (TREC 1996)*, 1996.

[21] J. Rocchio. Relevance feedback in information retrieval. In *The SMART Retrieval System: Experiments in Automatic Document Processing*, pages 313–323, 1971.

[22] Y. Song, Z. Zhuang, H. Li, Q. Zhao, J. Li, W. C. Lee, and C. L. Giles. Real-time automatic tag recommendation. In *SIGIR '08: Proceedings of the 31st annual international ACM SIGIR conference on Research and development in information retrieval*, pages 515–522. ACM, 2008.

[23] M. Srikanth and R. Srihari. Biterm language models for document retrieval. In *SIGIR '02: Proceedings of the 25th annual international ACM SIGIR conference on Research and development in information retrieval*, pages 425–426. ACM, 2002.

[24] T. Strohman, D. Metzler, H. Turtle, and W. B. Croft. Indri: A language model-based search engine for complex queries. In *International conference on Intelligence Analysis*, 2004.

[25] T. Tao and C. Zhai. Regularized estimation of mixture models for robust pseudo-relevance feedback. In *SIGIR '06: Proceedings of the 29th annual international ACM SIGIR conference on Research and development in information retrieval*, pages 162–169. ACM, 2006.

[26] X. Wu, L. Zhang, and Y. Yu. Relevance based language models. In *WWW '06: Proceedings of the 15th international conference on World Wide Web*, pages 417–426. ACM, 2006.

[27] J. Xu and W. Croft. Query expansion using local and global document analysis. In *SIGIR '96: Proceedings of the 19th annual international ACM SIGIR conference on Research and development in information retrieval*, pages 4–11. ACM, 1996.

[28] S. Xu, S. Bao, B. Fei, Z. Su, and Y. Yu. Exploring folksonomy for personalized search. In *SIGIR '08: Proceedings of the 31st annual international ACM SIGIR conference on Research and development in information retrieval*, pages 155–162. ACM, 2008.

[29] Y. Xu, J. F. Jones, and B. Wang. Query dependent pseudo-relevance feedback based on wikipedia. In *SIGIR '09: Proceedings of the 32nd annual international ACM SIGIR conference on Research and development in information retrieval*, pages 59–66. ACM, 2009.

[30] Z. Ye, J. Huang, S. Jin, and H. F. Lin. Exploring social annotation tags to enhance information retrieval performance. In *AMT '10: Proceedings of the 6th International Conferences on Active Media Technology*, pages 255–266, 2010.

[31] D. Yeung, C. Clarke, G. Cormack, T. Lynam, and E. Terra. Model-based feedback in the language modeling approach to information retrieval. In *the 12th Text REtrieval Conference (TREC 2003)*, pages 810–819, 2003.

[32] C. Zhai and J. Lafferty. Model-based feedback in the language modeling approach to information retrieval. In *CIKM '01: Proceeding of the 10th ACM conference on Information and knowledge management*, pages 403–410. ACM, 2001.

Predicting Web Searcher Satisfaction with Existing Community-based Answers

Qiaoling Liu[§], Eugene Agichtein[§], Gideon Dror[†],
Evgeniy Gabrilovich[‡], Yoelle Maarek[†], Dan Pelleg[†], Idan Szpektor[†],
[§]Emory University, Atlanta, GA, USA
[†]Yahoo! Research, Haifa, Israel
[‡]Yahoo! Research, Santa Clara, CA, USA
{qliu26, eugene}@mathcs.emory.edu, {gideondr, gabr, yoelle, dpelleg, idan}@yahoo-inc.com

ABSTRACT

Community-based Question Answering (CQA) sites, such as Yahoo! Answers, Baidu Knows, Naver, and Quora, have been rapidly growing in popularity. The resulting archives of posted answers to questions, in Yahoo! Answers alone, already exceed in size 1 billion, and are aggressively indexed by web search engines. In fact, a large number of search engine users benefit from these archives, by finding existing answers that address their own queries. This scenario poses new challenges and opportunities for both search engines and CQA sites. To this end, we formulate a new problem of predicting the satisfaction of web searchers with CQA answers. We analyze a large number of web searches that result in a visit to a popular CQA site, and identify unique characteristics of searcher satisfaction in this setting, namely, the effects of query clarity, query-to-question match, and answer quality. We then propose and evaluate several approaches to predicting searcher satisfaction that exploit these characteristics. To the best of our knowledge, this is the first attempt to predict and validate the usefulness of CQA archives for external searchers, rather than for the original askers. Our results suggest promising directions for improving and exploiting community question answering services in pursuit of satisfying even more Web search queries.

Categories and Subject Descriptors

H.3.3 [**Information Search and Retrieval**]: Search process

General Terms

Algorithms, Experimentation

Keywords

Searcher satisfaction, community question answering, query clarity, query-question match, answer quality

SIGIR '11, July 24-28, 2011, Beijing, China

1. INTRODUCTION

"Just because Google exists doesn't mean you should stop asking people things." – Alexia Tsotsis [35]

Community-based Question Answering (CQA) sites, such as Yahoo! Answers, Baidu Knows, and Naver Ji-Sik-In, as well as more social-oriented newcomers such as Vark and Quora, have gained substantial popularity over the recent years, effectively filling a niche left by the mainstream Web search engines. People around the globe resort to community help for a variety of reasons, from lack of proficiency in Web search to seeking an answer "with a human touch". Although some of these sites allow for monetary payments in exchange for answering questions (*e.g.*, JustAnswer, or the now discontinued Google Answers), answerers are usually attracted by social reward and less tangible incentives, such as reputation or points, as demonstrated by Raban [23]. The CQA communities are mainly volunteer-driven, and their openness and accessibility appeal to millions of users; for example, the size of Yahoo! Answers surpassed 1 billion answers in 2010[1], and Baidu Knows had over 100 million answered questions as of January 2011[2].

To date, prior studies of community question answering have mainly considered first-order effects, namely, the satisfaction of the original question asker by the posted answers. However, we believe CQA has significant *secondary* benefits, whereas previously answered questions are likely to be useful for future askers of substantially similar or related questions. Indeed, today many additional users already benefit from the public accessibility of CQA archives via all the major web search engines.[3] Existing answers often satisfy information needs of users who submit queries to a Web search engine, obtain results from a CQA site, such as the ones shown in Figure 1, select one of these results, and finally reach a resolved question page on the CQA site, as illustrated in Figure 2.

This scenario poses new challenges and opportunities for both search engines and CQA sites. For search engines, it provides a unique (semi-structured) source of human answers, which are particularly useful for satisfying tail queries [10]. For CQA sites, it creates substantial incoming traffic, which has its own multiple benefits from growing the

[1]http://yanswersblog.com/index.php/archives/2010/05/03/1-billion-answers-served/

[2]`http://zhidao.baidu.com/`, visited on January 19, 2011.

[3]Unfortunately, specific numbers describing the amount of incoming traffic to CQA sites from search engines are not publicly available.

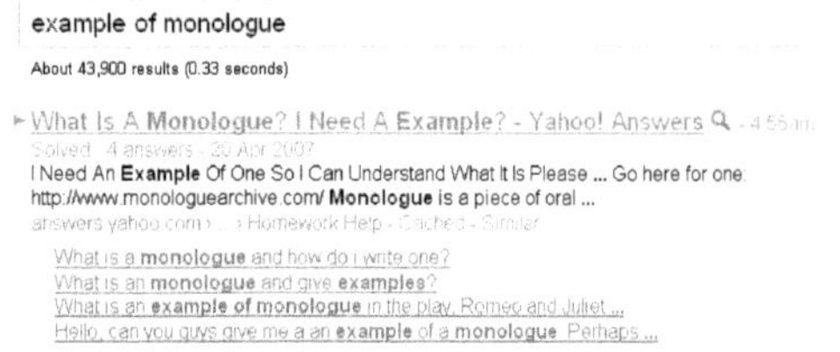

Figure 1: A subset of Google search results including resolved questions from Yahoo! Answers

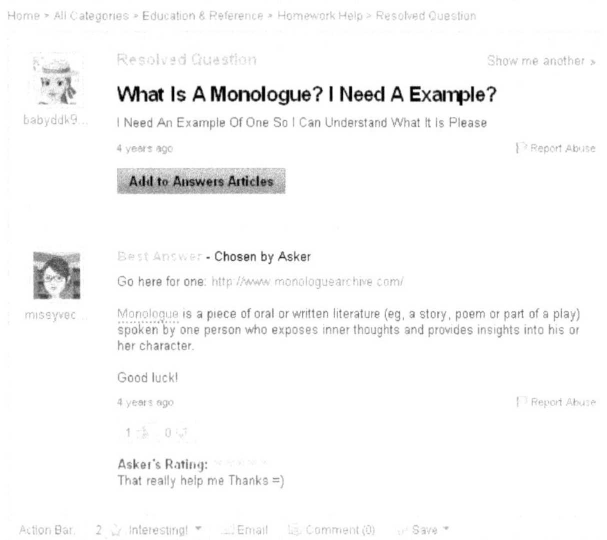

Figure 2: A resolved question on Yahoo! Answers

community to providing advertising revenue. More sophisticated symbiosis is also possible. For example, imagine if a search engine could detect that a user is struggling with a search session (e.g., by using techniques described in [7]). A search engine could then suggest posting a question on a CQA site, optionally suggesting relevant categories for such posting, and could even assist the user in transforming the query into an effective question. But in order to make this vision a reality, it is necessary to understand what it means for a searcher to be satisfied by an existing answer from a CQA archive, and to be able to predict this satisfaction.

This paper proposes and addresses this new problem of predicting the satisfaction of Web searchers with *existing* CQA answers. One way to approach this problem would be to define features of queries, questions, and answers (and possibly pairs thereof), and solve it within the machine learning paradigm. We call this a *direct* approach. This can be done by constructing a labeled dataset of queries and answers, tagged by human judges based on how well they believe a query is satisfied by a given answer.

Since queries are often quite short, and questions, which we view as an intermediate link between queries and answers, are often not much longer, another way to approach the problem is through exogenous knowledge. To this end, we identify three key characteristics of searcher satisfaction, namely, query clarity, query-question match, and answer quality. We then collect separate human labels for each, and build regression models for predicting these characteristics. Learning from these task-specific labels explicitly makes use of domain knowledge about the problem structure, which is not available in the above direct approach. We then use the output of these individual regressors as features in a subsequent regression task, which aims to predict searcher satisfaction. We call this method a *composite* approach. This approach also allows us to better understand how much the performance in the main prediction task can be improved by improving each of the individual regressors (we model this by replacing the intermediate regression predictions with actual human labels). This additional *interpretability* of the model provides further insights into the problem.

We conduct our experimental evaluation using data from one of the leading CQA sites, namely, Yahoo! Answers. We collect human labels for each of the above tasks using Amazon Mechanical Turk. These include labeling searcher satisfaction with a given answer (our main prediction task), as well as intermediate labels for query clarity and query-question match. We gauge the answer quality by using a combination of signals shown to be highly correlated with it [1], namely, the answer length, and the asker and community ratings. The labeled data is publicly available through Yahoo's Webscope program[4].

Since we define a new task (predicting searcher satisfaction with CQA answers), it is difficult to identify a suitable baseline. The closest previously addressed problem, at least in spirit, is *asker satisfaction* - predicting whether the original question asker (on the CQA site) was satisfied with the answers [19]. Intuitively, searcher satisfaction should be related to asker satisfaction. However, as we show later, asker satisfaction and searcher satisfaction appear to be very weakly related, if at all. Hence, an entirely new method is needed to compute *searcher satisfaction*. It is essential to note that, in our scenario, Web search queries are different from the questions originally posted to CQA sites, and more importantly, these queries are issued by different users with different information needs. In fact, the users in these two scenarios are drastically different. Whereas users of the community site are willing to clarify their questions, provide additional details, and even provide feedback to the answerers, Web search users seek immediate satisfaction, and essentially treat existing answers as a static resource.

The main contributions of this paper are threefold. First, we formulate a new problem, namely, predicting *searcher satisfaction* with existing CQA answers. Second, we propose two methods for solving this problem, a direct method and a composite method, which uses the outputs of secondary regressors as features. Finally, we apply our methods to a standard ranking task, where we treat answers as a semi-structured document collection. We show that incorporating our predictor of searcher satisfaction leads to a significant improvement in ordering the answers for a given query. To the best of our knowledge, this is the first attempt to predict and validate the usefulness of CQA archives for external searchers, rather than for the original askers. Our results suggest promising directions for improving and exploiting community question answering services in pursuit of satisfying even more Web search queries.

2. BACKGROUND

Our work spans the areas of filtering, recommending and ranking Community Question Answering (CQA) content,

[4]http://webscope.sandbox.yahoo.com/catalog.php?datatype= Dataset L16 - Yahoo! Answers Query to Question.

and estimating searcher satisfaction with the retrieved CQA content. In this section we first give an overview of the CQA site we chose for our experiments, namely Yahoo! Answers, as it currently holds the largest repository of questions. Then related research will be discussed.

2.1 Yahoo! Answers

With millions of active users, Yahoo! Answers hosts over a billion answers on a wide variety of topics. The system is question-centric: users are interacting by engaging in multiple activities around a specific question. The typical lifecycle of questions is the following: users post new questions and assign them to a predefined category, such as '*Education & Reference > Homework Help*' in the example shown in Figure 2. The new question remains "open" for four days with an option for extension, or can be closed if the asker chooses a best answer earlier. If the question remains unresolved, its status changes from "open" to "in-voting", where other users can vote for a best answer until a clear winner arises. In addition to asking and answering questions, users can also provide feedback by "starring" interesting questions, and rating answers with "thumbs up" or "thumbs down", and voting for best answer as mentioned above. Users can also receive activity updates on questions and follow the activity of other users. Finally, the community is self-moderated, and users can report and block questions and answers that violate the community guidelines (inappropriate language, spam etc.).

We consider here only resolved questions, e.g., questions that have been answered and for which a best answer has been chosen, since they are well indexed by Web Search engines and often have better quality than open or in-voting questions. In addition, we consider only best answers, based on the intuition that an external searcher reaching a Yahoo! Answers page will in most case ignore the other answers. This simplifying assumption is based on the fact that the best answer is prominently displayed below the question (see Figure 2) and users rarely browse results below the fold [22]. A resolved question will thus be represented by a pair *(question, best-answer)* and their associated additional signals such as stars, thumbs-up etc.

An additional type of information that we make use of is the *click data-set*: pairs of queries and the related CQA pages on which users, who issued the queries, clicked within the search results for these queries. In our experiments we utilized a click data-set that consists of pages from Yahoo! Answers that were clicked on within Google's search engine (see Section 4.1.1).

2.2 CQA Quality and Asker Satisfaction

One of the main problems in Yahoo! Answers, and in CQA sites in general, is the high variance in the perceived question and answer quality. Recently, this problem attracted a lot of research attention. Some studies attempted to assess the quality of answers or users [17, 1, 28, 32, 12], or questions [1, 29, 31], and filter or rank them accordingly [33]. Most recently, Horowitz and Kamvar [14] attempted to match questions to possible answerers, aiming at improving the quality of generated answers. Another related effort was estimating the archival value of questions for subsequent recommendation and retrieval [11].

Relatively few studies addressed the satisfaction of a user from the service provided by CQA sites. Most closely related to our work, Agichtein et al. [19] attempted to predict whether the asker of a question will be satisfied with the received answers. Our work goes beyond previous efforts as we propose and empirically evaluate techniques to estimate the satisfaction of *searchers*, as opposed to the original askers and answerers in CQA.

2.3 Web Search Quality and Satisfaction

Significant research has been done on estimating the quality of web search results, and the satisfaction of searchers. Query difficulty has been actively studied in the IR community, [6, 40]. A related problem of query ambiguity can also affect search quality and searcher satisfaction [34]. We adapt these techniques as a first step in predicting searcher satisfaction in CQA, since the latter clearly depends on query interpretation.

Searcher satisfaction in web search was addressed in [15, 8, 13], which utilized query log information for the task, such as relevance measures, as well as user behavior during the search session, including mouse clicks and time spent between user actions. What makes this task such a challenging problem is the large diversity in user goals [26], with a different definition of satisfaction for each, which requires developing unique satisfaction prediction models for the respective information needs. In our work we focus on satisfying types of queries that arguably are the most difficult for a web search engine to satisfy and often require other people to answer [21]. Specifically, we argue that some of these needs can often be satisfied with *existing* answers from CQA archives. Hence, we aim at harnessing the unique structure of such archives for detecting web searcher satisfaction, which is not captured by standard query and session logs.

2.4 Ranking and Recommendation in CQA

Searching CQA archives has been an active area of research, and several retrieval models specialized to CQA content have been proposed, [39, 4]. Such dedicated models are clearly deployed in practice, if only for specialized layout as demonstrated by Google specialized Yahoo! Answers snippets. Examples of other approaches include incorporating category information into retrieval [5], and exploiting the question-answer relationship [36]. While our main focus is on estimating the satisfaction with a *given* retrieved question-answer pair for a query, we adapt and extend these techniques for matching the query to the question and the answer content. Additionally, we show how our work could be applied for effective re-ranking of the retrieved question-answer pairs for a query, resulting in a significant improvement over a state-of-the-art baseline.

In the spirit of XML and semi-structured retrieval [2], it also makes sense to consider document structure in CQA, as has been done for Web Search [25], book retrieval [18] or sponsored search [3]. Thus in the case of Yahoo! Answers, we will consider the resolved question structure and distinguish between a question and its best answer (per our simplifying assumption, cf. Section 2.1), and their associated meta-data, while constructing features for our prediction tasks (see Section 3.2).

3. PREDICTING SEARCHER SATISFACTION

In this section we first introduce the task of predicting searcher satisfaction by a CQA page. Then, we propose approaches for representing and tackling this problem using regression algorithms.

3.1 Problem Description

We now define *searcher satisfaction by a CQA answer*:

Given a search query S, a question Q, and an answer A originally posted in response to Q on a CQA site,

predict whether A *satisfies* the query S.

For example, for a query "example of monologue", the best answer shown in Figure 2 is considered satisfactory because it clearly and comprehensively addresses the search intent.

Thus, instead of a Web search satisfaction task that examines *a (query, Web page)* pair, we consider a different tuple *(query, question, answer)*, where the *(question, answer)* pair has been extracted from the CQA page. The reason for using a more refined representation of *(question, answer)* rather than a full Web page (a Yahoo! Answers page in our case) is mostly for interpretability at a finer level. In practice, when experimenting with Yahoo! Answers in the remainder of this paper, we will use the simplification of considering only the best answer (cf. Section 2.1)[5] as A.

To solve our prediction problem, we propose to break it down into three sub-tasks: *query clarity*, *query-question match* and *answer quality*. More specifically:

- The *query clarity task*, which should not be confused with traditional query difficulty in IR, consists of estimating whether the query may be viewed, and understood, as a question. We hypothesize that if a query is not understandable or ambiguous, a CQA site is unlikely to have an existing satisfactory answer for this query.
- The *query-question match task* consists of estimating whether the question is driven by the same or by a similar enough information need as the query. This is a prerequisite for the answer to have a chance to address the query. Furthermore, since most search result snippets will only show the question title (such as shown in Figure 1), this match is a key driver for the searcher to select a specific CQA page: the question plays the role of a critical intermediary between the query and the answer.
- The *answer quality task* allows estimating the prior quality of the answer, with respect to the original question, and thus relates to the previously studied asker satisfaction task [19]. In our approach, answer quality characteristics are used not as the goal, but rather as additional input for our main task of predicting *searcher satisfaction*.

There are multiple advantages of breaking the main task into subtasks. First, we can better understand and analyze the problem structure, and devise more effective algorithms, as described next. Second, the resulting models become more *interpretable* and informative, by allowing us to analyze performance for each subtask. Finally, answer quality and related prior information (taking advantage of meta-information in particular) may be computed offline within the CQA site using methods such as described in [1].

The searcher satisfaction task seems to be better modeled as a graded task, since we found that it is easier for humans to judge satisfaction as a score within some range (see our human annotation in Section 4.1.2). Therefore, we treat the searcher satisfaction task as a regression problem. To this end, we need to define appropriate features for learning the regressor. We now describe the features used to represent the information in our task, and then formulate our direct and composite approaches.

3.2 Features

By breaking down the main task into three subtasks, we distinguish between query clarity, query-question match, and answer quality features.

Since some of these subtasks were previously studied independently, such as [6, 34, 37] for query clarity, and [19, 1] for answer quality, we leveraged this prior work in the construction of our feature set. We now describe each of the feature groups, while the complete list of features is shown in Table 1.

- *Query clarity features* include query length, click statistics for the query, and query entropy computed based on the click dataset. We also compute a query clarity score based on a language model of the CQA collection, as well as an indicator whether the query starts with a "WH" or other question word.
- *Query-question match features* include match scores computed by popular retrieval models such as cosine similarity, TFIDF, BM25, and KL-divergence language model. For measuring these scores, we treat parts of a CQA page (the question title, question details and the best answer) as separate documents, and match each such part against the query. Additional features include measures of the overlap between the query and question, such as Jaccard coefficient and length ratios, and co-occurrence statistics between the query and the given question from the click data.
- *Answer quality features* are of two types. The first type of features deals with the quality of the answer, and is mainly based on the analysis given in [1]. The second type of features addresses the answer quality as predicting asker satisfaction, which directly maps to our third subtask. To this end, we mostly used the top performing features for predicting asker satisfaction as reported in [19].

Before using these features to build regression models, preprocessing was performed, as described in Section 4.2, to deal with missing values and to normalize the data.

3.3 Direct Approach: Logistic Regression

Our first approach to estimating searcher satisfaction, which we call the *direct approach*, consists of simply training a regressor over all the features defined for a given *(query, question, answer)* tuple. The rationale here is to rely on the power of discriminative learning to optimally use all available features to predict the final target.

While many regression algorithms could be employed for this task, our preliminary experiments with a wide range of models, including Linear Regression, Gaussian Processes, Ridge Regression and Random Forests, indicated Logistic Regression to be the most promising approach due to high variability and non-linear distribution of many of the input features. We now present our adaptation of the "classical" logistic regression algorithm to our problem.

Logistic regression uses the logistic function $f(t) = \exp(t)/(1 + \exp(t))$ to model an output variable restricted to the open set $(0, 1)$. This property makes the logistic function, properly scaled, a natural candidate for modeling our rating targets, all constrained to the range of $(1, 3)$ (see our human annotation in Section 4.1.2).

In what follows, we denote by $(x_i, y) \in R^n \times [1, 3]$, $i =$

[5]Note that the same model could be generalized to considering other, and not necessarily best, answers one at a time if the CQA site could isolate clicks or views of these answers. This is not the case with Yahoo! Answers where all answers are featured one after the other on the same page.

Table 1: Features by subtask

Query clarity features (9 total)
• # of characters in the query. • # of words in the query. • # of clicks following the query. • # of users who issued the query. • # of questions clicked following the query. • Overall click entropy of the query [34]. • User click entropy of the query [37]. • Query clarity score computed based on the language model built with approximately 3 million questions (using title, details and best answer) posted in 2009-2010 [6]. • WH-type of the query (whether it starts with 'what', 'why', 'when', 'where', 'which', 'how', 'is', 'are', 'do').
Query-Question match features (23 total)
• Match scores between the query and the question title/details/best-answer using the cosine/TFIDF/KL-divergence/BM25 retrieval models. • The Jaccard/Dice/Tanimoto coefficient between the query and the question title. • Ratio between the number of characters/words in the query and that in the question title/details. • # of clicks on the question following this/any query. • # of users who clicked the question following this/any query.
Answer quality features (37 total)
• # of characters/words in the answer. • # of unique words in the answer. • Ratio between the number of characters/words of the question (including title and details) and the answer. • # of "thumbs up" minus "thumbs down", divided by the total number of "thumbs" received by the answerer. • # of "thumbs up" minus "thumbs down" received by the answerer. • # of "thumbs up/down" received by the answerer. • Match scores between the answer and the question title/details using cosine/TFIDF/KL-divergence/BM25 retrieval models. • Percentage of users who voted this answer as the best. • # of votes given by the voters for the answer. • Best answer ratio for the answerer. • Avg # of answers attracted by past questions of the asker. • # of answers received by the asker in the past. • Asker's rating of the best answer to her previous question. • Avg past rating by the asker. • Time passed since the asker registered in Yahoo! Answers. • # of previous questions resolved for the asker. • Avg asker rating for best answers in the category. • Avg voter rating for best answers in the category. • Time of day when the question was posted. • Avg # of answers per question in the category. • Time passed since the answerer with most positive votes registered in Yahoo! Answers. • Highest best answer ratio for any answerer of the question. • Avg best answer ratio for all answerers of the question. • Avg # of answers per hour in the category. • Whether the best answer is chosen by the asker. • Asker rating for choosing the answer as best answer.

$1, \ldots, l$, a generic example in the training set, where n is the number of features. We use $f_{w,b}(x_i) = 1 + 2\exp(w^T x_i + b)/(1+\exp(w^T x_i + b))$ as an estimate for the target variable y_i. The parameter vector of the model, w, and the scalar b are obtained by minimizing the squared loss

$$L(w,b) = \frac{1}{2}\sum_{i=1}^{l}\left(f_{w,b}(x_i) - y_i\right)^2 + \frac{\lambda}{2}\|w\|^2 \qquad (1)$$

The second term is introduced for regularization, where λ controls the strength of regularization.

Since there is no closed form solution for the parameters w and b that minimize Equation 1, we resort to Stochastic Gradient Descent [30], a fast and robust optimization method. It is an online algorithm where the parameters, initially random, are being updated using the gradient of the loss. In our case, the update is $b \leftarrow b + \Delta b$ and $w \leftarrow w + \Delta w$, where

$$\Delta b = \eta\,(y_i - f_{w,b}(x_i))\,\frac{\partial f_{w,b}}{\partial w}$$

$$\Delta w = \eta\left((y_i - f_{w,b}(x_i))\,\frac{\partial f_{w,b}}{\partial w} x_i - \frac{\lambda}{l} w\right)$$

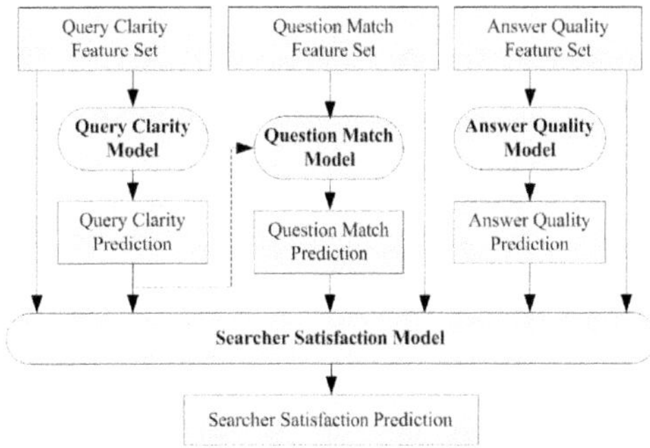

Figure 3: The *composite* approach.

We cycle through random permutations of the observations to achieve convergence. For the learning rate, we use a schedule of the form $\eta = \eta_t = \frac{\eta_0}{t+\tau}$ where $\tau > 0$, and t is the number of update steps taken thus far. The schedule satisfies the Robbins-Monro conditions [24], $\sum \eta_t = \infty$ and $\sum \eta_t^2 < \infty$, hence convergence is guaranteed. In light of the small number of examples in our dataset, we did not attempt to optimize the hyper-parameters of the model. Specifically, since the data is dense and the number of features is much smaller than the number of examples, we used weak regularization $\lambda = 0.01$ in all our experiments. We used moderate values for the learning rate schedule, $\eta_0 = 10$ and $\tau = 10$, and stopped iterating when the training set Mean Squared Error fell below a predefined threshold (0.0001).

3.4 Composite Approach

Our second approach, which we call the *composite approach*, first trains a separate logistic regression model for each of the three subtasks defined above, and then combines their results for main task (predicting searcher satisfaction). Figure 3 depicts the high-level workflow of this approach. In this approach, each regressor is trained using a subset of features relevant for each subtask. Considering that query clarity may affect the question match, we also added query clarity prediction as a feature to the query-question match regressor. Finally, the regression predictions for the three subtasks are provided as features for the final regressor to predict the overall searcher satisfaction.

This composite approach presents several advantages over the direct approach. First, it is more flexible in terms of feature selection. The individual regressors could be trained either on the same feature set, i.e., the large feature vector used in the direct approach, or on different feature sets selected by suitable feature selection methods for each subtask. More importantly, the composite approach can take advantage of the advances made by the research community in each of the sub-tasks, to improve the prediction of overall searcher satisfaction.

4. EXPERIMENTAL SETUP

This section first describes how we assembled a dataset from a sample of Google queries and a log of visits to Yahoo! Answers. We then describe the rating procedure to

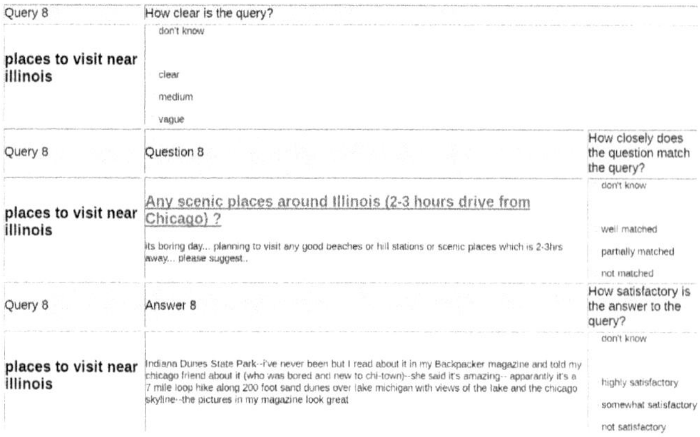

Figure 4: MTurk interface for human labeling.

acquire the "ground truth" for searcher satisfaction, and the characteristics of the resulting data.

4.1 Datasets

4.1.1 *Dataset Preparation*

To explore how searchers are satisfied with the existing answers in CQA sites, we used a large sample of queries issued to Google's search engine from Aug 24, 2010 to Aug 30, 2010 by users who selected as result (by clicking on it) a Yahoo! Answers link. This click dataset contains more than 37M clicks on 6M questions by 20M users following around 20M queries. By analyzing the distribution of this click data, we found that 86% of the queries are issued by only one user; therefore, most of the queries are tail queries.

Since it is hard for human to label searcher satisfaction for such a big dataset, we randomly sampled it to generate a smaller dataset consisting of 614 clicked questions following 457 queries issued by at least two users. These questions and corresponding answers may be biased to satisfy the searchers' information needs, as they are clicked from the search results. To correct this effect, we further issued a random sample of 118 queries to Google's search engine with site restriction to Yahoo! Answers and crawled the top 20 results (all question pages due to the site restriction). Only questions posted in 2009-2010 are kept based on the available associated meta-data. In total, our final dataset comprised of 1681 query-question pairs.

4.1.2 *Human Labeling*

Amazon Mechanical Turk (MTurk) was used to collect human judgments on how an answer satisfies a search query. To better understand the effects of query clarity and query-question match on searcher satisfaction with answers, we also asked the MTurk workers to label how clear the query is and how the question matches the query. Figure 4 shows the interface we used in MTurk. We used 3-scale rating method for all the rating tasks, {clear=1, medium=2, vague=3} for query clarity, {well matched=1, partially matched=2, not matched=3} for question match, and {highly satisfactory=1, somewhat satisfactory=2, not satisfactory=3} for searcher satisfaction. Each MTurk hit consists of 15 *(query, question, answer)* triples as shown in Figure 4, and each hit is labeled by 5-7 workers.

To validate the labels of MTurk workers, we also asked 6 researchers to label the query clarity for all the queries. Then we analyzed the agreement between the researchers and the MTurk workers. We first computed the average rating by researchers as well as by MTurk workers for each query, then used a threshold t to cast each average numerical rating nr into a binary rating br (if $nr <= t$ then br=clear, else br=not clear), and finally we computed the Fleiss's kappa coefficient[9] based on these binary ratings between the two sources. The highest kappa value 0.38 was achieved with a threshold of 1.3 (average agreement=0.70, average majority percentage=0.85). This analysis showed that the ratings from MTurk workers were reasonable.

For query-question match and searcher satisfaction, we only had ratings from the Mechanical Turk. So we used the same threshold strategy to cast each ordinal rating into a binary rating, then computed the Fleiss's kappa coefficient for each MTurk HIT, and finally computed the average kappa value. The highest kappa value (0.34) was achieved with a threshold of 2 for query-question match (average agreement=0.85, average majority percentage=0.91), and the highest kappa value (0.25) was achieved with a threshold of 2 for searcher satisfaction (average agreement=0.76, average majority percentage=0.84).

From the above agreement analysis, we can see that although the kappa coefficient among MTurk workers is not high, possibly due to the careless rating of some MTurk workers, the average rating by all the MTurk workers shows a moderate agreement with researchers. Therefore, we use the average rating by MTurk workers as our ground truth in order to evaluate the prediction of query clarity, query-question match, and searcher satisfaction with answers.

Figure 5 shows the distributions of the resulting ground truth set. The x axis represents the mean over the ratings by all MTurk workers, with 1 standing for the *highest* score, e.g., clear/well-match/highly satisfactory for respectively query clarity/query-question match/searcher satisfaction with answers, and with 3 standing for the *lowest* score for each. The y axis represents the frequency count of ratings in each bucket of x. We can see that all the distributions are skewed, especially the query clarity one due to the bias of the click data. Distribution for question match and searcher satisfaction are more balanced after we add the search engine results. To better understand the relations between the three variables, we computed the Pearson correlation between them and obtained the following result: the correlation between query clarity and searcher satisfaction is 0.1428, and the correlation between question match and searcher satisfaction is 0.6970.

4.2 Data Preprocessing

To make the data more amenable for modeling we used a three-stage preprocessing, performed on each feature:

1. null values have been replaced by the mean value. An example of a null value is the similarity between the query and the question body when the latter is empty;
2. features obtained by counting or summation, such as 'number of characters/words in the query' or 'number of "thumbs up/down" received by the answerer' were log transformed; specifically, we used $x = \log_2(1 + x_{raw})$ instead of the raw values x_{raw};
3. features were shifted and scaled to have a zero mean and a unit variance.

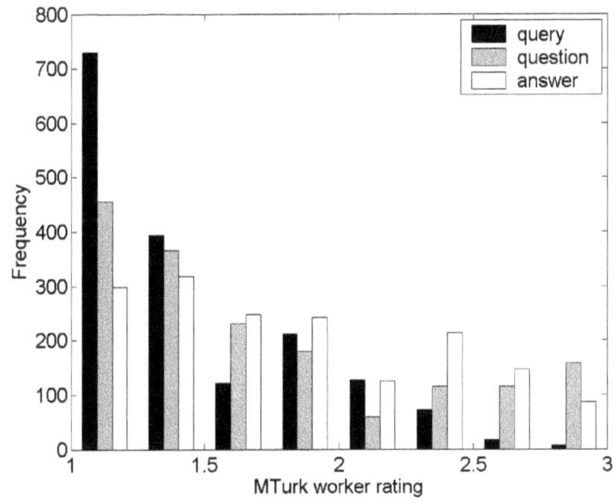

Figure 5: Distributions of the mean ratings of MTurk workers for query clarity, query-question match, and searcher satisfaction with answers.

4.3 Methods Compared

We consider four methods for estimating a searcher's satisfaction on Yahoo! Answers:

• **Google-derived baseline**: As described in Section 4.1.1, we crawled the top 20 results by submitting our queries to Google search, with site restriction to the Yahoo! Answers site. As a result, we obtained a ranked list of question pages for each query from the search engine. The rank of each question page indicates how well this page satisfies the query. Since a search engine ranks results by maximizing searcher's satisfaction with the overall result ordering, we use Google's ranking of question pages as our baseline.

• **Direct approach:** This method implements the logistic regression approach described in Section 3.3.

• **Composite approach:** This method implements the composite approach described in Section 3.4.

• **Composite upper-bound:** We also trained the composite approach with the intermediate predictions for the query clarity and query-question match subtasks replaced with their *human ratings*. Since human judgments are expected to be more reliable than the automatic predictions, this method serves as an upper bound for the possible performance of the fully-automatic composite approach.

4.4 Evaluation Metrics and Setup

Estimating searcher satisfaction: Our main prediction task estimates searcher satisfaction for a query with one given answer, independently of other query-answer pairs. Hence our main evaluation of the direct and composite approaches over all pairs is via root mean squared error (RMSE) and Pearson correlation between predictions and the human judgments. Both RMSE and Pearson correlation are standard performance estimators for regression problems.

When comparing our results to the Google-derived baseline described above, however, we could not use the above metrics, since Google does not divulge an independent score for each query-answer pair. Therefore, we propose to use two different metrics for ranking : (1) Kendall's tau (τ) correlation that has often been used in IR [27] to compare two ranked lists, and (2) the popular NDCG metric often used in IR evaluation [16]. As ground truth, we use the MTurk ratings described above to calculate these metrics as follows:

Kendall's τ: First for each search query s, we identify the set $Q(s)$ of all questions associated with s in our dataset. We then generate the following ranked lists.

1. The ground truth MTurk rating scores between each query s and each question q in $Q(s)$ are used to infer a ranked list L_M.

2. We identify the rank of each question q in $Q(s)$ in the ranked list of question pages featured in our previously described Google-derived baseline. The list of these ranks, that we refer to as L_G, gives us our baseline of ranking of questions by Google for a given query.

3. Similarly the direct and composite approach introduced in the previous section generate a score for each pair (s, q) and these scores induce two ranked lists that we note L_d for the direct approach and L_c for the composite approach.

Kendall's τ correlation is then computed between the ground truth list L_M and each of the system-generated lists L_G, L_d, and L_c. We process the answers $A(s)$ associated with s in the same way, and generate and evaluate the four respective lists in exactly the same manner.

NDCG metric: The ranked lists to compare are generated exactly in the same way as described above for Kendall's τ evaluation. Following Long et al. [20], we do not discretize the ground truth MTurk ratings, and use them directly (in place of relevance) to calculate the gain in the NDCG computation as follows:

$$DCG_p = \sum_{i=1}^{p} \frac{2^{rel_i} - 1}{log_2(1+i)}, nDCG_p = \frac{DCG_p}{IDCG_p}$$

where the relevance values are computed as $rel_i = (3 - r) \in [0, 2]$, where r is the average assessor rating of query-question match or searcher satisfaction, respectively.

Evaluation setup: For training and testing, we use stratified 10-fold cross-validation. This guarantees that the data distribution in each fold is similar to that of the entire dataset.

5. EMPIRICAL EVALUATION

We first present our results for the main task of predicting searcher satisfaction, and compare the direct and the composite approaches. Then, we analyze the performance of the proposed methods to identify key factors that affect the prediction accuracy. Finally, we present the results of applying our models to re-rank CQA answers in search engine results, showing significant improvements of our ranking over Google's.

5.1 Direct vs. Composite Comparison

Table 2 shows the results on predicting searcher satisfaction using our proposed direct and composite approaches. We report the mean ($\pm$ standard deviation) RMSE and Pearson correlation over the ten cross-validation folds.

In the first two rows of Table 2, we see that the composite approach performs better than the direct approach on both

Table 2: Regression results on searcher satisfaction.

Method	Correlation	RMSE
Direct	0.608±0.042	0.222±0.009
Composite	**0.618**±0.054	**0.217**±0.011
Composite upper-bound	0.773±0.029	0.178±0.010

Table 3: Regression results on individual sub-tasks.

Task	Correlation	RMSE
query clarity	0.713±0.028	0.151±0.005
question match	0.702±0.043	0.218±0.014
answer quality	0.213±0.057	0.478±0.015

correlation and RMSE[6] metrics. This difference is statistically significant according to the Wilcoxon two-sided signed ranks test at $p = 0.01$ [38]. This observation is quite intuitive, since the composite approach takes advantage of additional knowledge, which is learned from the human labels for the query clarity and query-question match sub-tasks.

Now consider the last row in Table 2, which reports the upper bound performance of the composite approach. To estimate the upper bound, we replace the individual regressors we trained for the query clarity and query-question match sub-tasks with the *actual* (average) human scores for those tasks, and plug these scores as features into the composite regressor. Evidently, the performance of the composite method can be improved dramatically if its components, namely, the query clarity and the query-question match predictors, are improved. We believe this flexibility of the composite approach constitutes a substantial advantage over the simpler direct approach.

5.2 Analysis and Discussion

Table 3 details the performance of the individual regressors that were combined in the composite approach. Here the query-question match regressor also uses the query clarity prediction as a feature, as explained in Section 3.4. The answer quality regressor is trained using the asker satisfaction ground truth [19] (An asker is considered satisfied iff he selected the best answer and gave at least 3 "stars" for the quality). Again, we report the mean (± standard deviation) RMSE and Pearson correlation over the ten folds.

By analyzing the predictions for searcher satisfaction by the composite regressor, we see that it can predict accurately both when the searcher is satisfied and not satisfied. We show a number of actual examples in Table 4. In the first example (E1), our method is able to correctly detect that the query is a little vague[7], the query-question match is low[8], and the answer is too simple to convince the searcher[9]. On the other hand, in the second example (E2), the query is quite clear and matches the question well, and the answer provides helpful advice to the searcher. Again, our method successfully predicts the overall searcher satisfaction with the answer, as well as individual sub-task scores (query clarity and query-question match).

To better understand the effectiveness of our methods, we also performed error analysis on the 30 cases where the difference between our prediction and the target was larger than 1. We found two cases, E3 and E4 (Table 4), for which our system predicted lower searcher satisfaction than the ground truth. In the other cases, our system predicted higher than actual satisfaction—average prediction of 1.66 versus average ground truth of 2.65. We believe the main reason for these large differences lies in the answer quality. In fact, more than half of the answers are not helpful at all (e.g., E5); other answers show negative opinions towards the askers, or contain ads. Thus, our error analysis confirms the importance of answer quality to searcher satisfaction, and also poses the challenge of more intelligent prediction of answer quality.

[6]Note that lower RMSE values reflect better performance.
[7]Higher values mean *lower* query clarity.
[8]Higher values reflect *poorer* query-question match.
[9]Higher values mean *lower* searcher satisfaction.

Table 5: Mean Kendall's τ and NDCG results on ranking questions and answers for queries.

	Query-question match		Searcher satisfaction	
	τ	NDCG	τ	NDCG
Google	0.359	0.939	0.307	0.905
Direct	–	–	0.434(+41%)	**0.928**(+2.5%)
Comp.	0.301	0.919	**0.437**(+42%)	**0.928**(+2.5%)

5.3 Answer Ranking for Queries

One possible application of predicting searcher satisfaction is using this prediction for ranking CQA pages in Web search. To this end, in Table 5 we compare the quality of ranking produced by our methods to that of Google's ranking of results retrieved from the Yahoo! Answers site. We compared the entire ranked lists of results returned by our methods and by Google to the ranking induced by human (MTurk) labels, therefore, we report different metrics than above, namely, NDCG and Kendall's τ. Our prediction of searcher satisfaction results in improvements over Google's on both metrics. All improvements are statistically significant according to the Wilcoxon double-sided signed ranks test at $p = 0.01$ [38]. Interestingly, Google's ranking of the *questions* (as opposed to answers) for a query is superior, which is to be expected due to additional information Google maybe used for ranking the questions (such as link structure and clicks)—whereas our work focuses on predicting searcher satisfaction with the *answers*, where indeed our methods perform better.

We further analyze these results by plotting the improvements over the Google baseline, for individual queries (Figure 6). Interestingly, it appears that the results do not depend on the number of answers to re-rank. In another experiment (omitted for lack of space), we found that the improvements are not correlated with query length. These results suggest that our methods are robust for a wide range of queries, and are likely to remain stable for other conditions. In summary, our results show that our satisfaction prediction allows our re-ranker to consistently outperform the state-of-the-art Google baseline, and could provide valuable input for other tasks, as we plan to explore in the future.

6. CONCLUSIONS

In this paper we formulated a novel task of predicting searcher satisfaction with answer pages from CQA sites. Prior research mainly concentrated on the first-order effects of community question answering, studying satisfaction of original askers of questions or potential answerers (both on the CQA site itself). In contrast, we study *second-order* effects of CQA archives, which repeatedly benefit many more

Table 4: Sample (query, question, answer) tuples, with predictions and ground truth labels. In the last three columns, lower values are *better* (higher clarity, better match, higher satisfaction).

No	Query	Question	Answer	Query clarity prediction (ground truth)	Query-question match prediction (ground truth)	Search satisfaction prediction (ground truth)
E1	mexican halloween	Is dressing up like a mexican on cinco de mayo or halloween degrading to mexicans?	Not really	1.74 (1.96)	2.04 (1.86)	2.70 (2.71)
E2	how to stop loving someone you shouldn't	How do you stop loving someone you're really not suppose to love?	...Keep your mind occupy with work or school. whatever u can to keep your mind busy...	1.09 (1.14)	1.20 (1.0)	1.16 (1.14)
E3	dtunes source	Ipod touch jailbreak dtunes and installous?	Installous is currently incompatible with the safari download plugin, which is required for dTunes to work...	1.94 (2.03)	2.11 (2.0)	2.01 (1.0)
E4	catsup vs ketchup	The condiment "KETCHUP" where did the name come from?	The most popular theory is that the word ketchup was derived from "koe-chiap" or "ke-tsiap" in the Amoy dialect of China...	1.67 (1.29)	1.85 (2.43)	2.17 (1.14)
E5	how much does it cost to send a letter to canada	How much does it cost to send a letter to canada?	Go to your local post office and ask them.	1.22 (1.26)	1.24 (1.4)	1.89 (3.0)

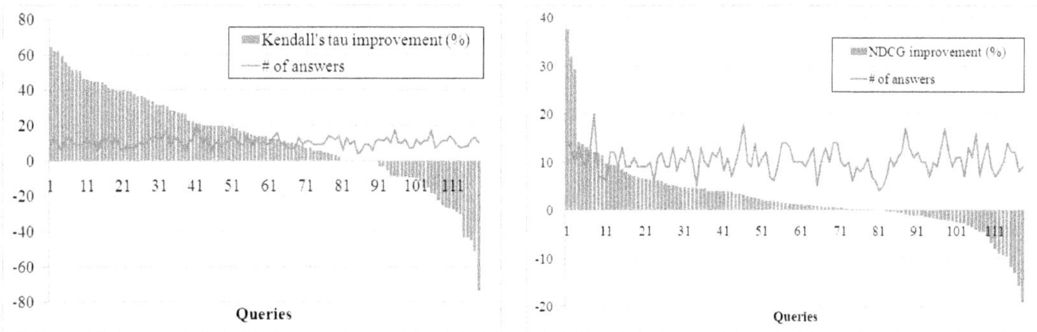

(a) Kendall's τ (b) NDCG

Figure 6: Kendall's τ (a) and NDCG (b) relative improvements of the composite approach over Google's baseline on ranking answers for queries.

Web users when these answers are included in Web search results for a variety of queries. We utilize the unique structure of CQA pages as well as all available community signals (e.g., ratings, thumbs-up) to improve the quality of matching between these pages and Web search queries.

We proposed to break the task of predicting searcher satisfaction into three sub-tasks, namely, predicting query clarity, query-question match, and answer quality. We then formulated two methods for solving the main prediction task. Our *direct* method simply uses all the available features in a single regression model. Our *composite* method first learns three separate regressors for each of the three sub-tasks, and then uses their predictions as features for solving the main task. Predictably, the performance of the composite method is statistically significantly superior to that of the direct method. This can be explained due to its use of additional exogenous knowledge, which is learned from the human labels for each of the sub-tasks while training the three individual regressors. Furthermore, the composite approach is more flexible, and it can immediately benefit as the predictions in individual sub-tasks are improved. Indeed, when we replace the predictions in each sub-task with *actual* human labels, the performance of the composite regressor is dramatically improved.

We believe that modeling the searcher satisfaction with CQA answers has multiple benefits. For example, if a search engine detects that a user is struggling with a search session, it could suggest posting a question on a CQA site, offering help with formulating a natural language question and choosing an appropriate category. On the search engine side, an accurate predictor of searcher satisfaction can be used for improved ranking of CQA results in Web search. Indeed, our results show that this can be achieved. To this end, we compared the quality of ranking of CQA answers produced by our methods with, and demonstrated significant improvements over the quality of the ranking provided by Google's search engine (both compared to the "ideal" ranking generated from the ground truth labels provided by humans).

In our future work, we plan to further investigate the types of queries that are likely to be satisfied by CQA pages. We also plan to improve query-question matching using (monolingual) machine translation models. Another brunch of potential work is to develop semi-supervised or unsupervised methods to predict searcher satisfaction, as large numbers of human labels are hard to obtain. Finally, we intend to study searcher satisfaction with other types of community-generated Web pages that possess interesting structure, such as Facebook pages (subject to appropriate privacy policies).

7. ACKNOWLEDGMENTS

This work was supported by the National Science Foundation grant IIS-1018321 and by the Yahoo! Faculty Research and Engagement Program.

8. REFERENCES

[1] E. Agichtein, C. Castillo, D. Donato, A. Gionis, and G. Mishne. Finding high-quality content in social media. In *Proc. of WSDM*, pages 183–194, 2008.

[2] S. Amer-Yahia and M. Lalmas. XML search: languages, INEX and scoring. *SIGMOD Rec.*, 35:16–23, December 2006.

[3] M. Bendersky, E. Gabrilovich, V. Josifovski, and D. Metzler. The anatomy of an ad: Structured indexing and retrieval for sponsored search. In *WWW'10*, April 2010.

[4] J. Bian, Y. Liu, E. Agichtein, and H. Zha. Finding the right facts in the crowd: factoid question answering over social media. In *WWW '08*, 2008.

[5] X. Cao, G. Cong, B. Cui, C. S. Jensen, and C. Zhang. The use of categorization information in language models for question retrieval. In *CIKM*, 2009.

[6] S. Cronen-Townsend, Y. Zhou, and W. B. Croft. Predicting query performance. In *SIGIR*, 2002.

[7] D. Donato, F. Bonchi, T. Chi, and Y. Maarek. Do you want to take notes?: identifying research missions in Yahoo! Search Pad. In *WWW '10*, 2010.

[8] H. Feild, J. Allan, and R. Jones. Predicting searcher frustration. In *Proc. of SIGIR*, pages 34–41, 2010.

[9] J. L. Fleiss. Measuring nominal scale agreement among many raters. *Psychological Bulletin*, 76(5):378 – 382, 1971.

[10] S. Goel, A. Broder, E. Gabrilovich, and B. Pang. Anatomy of the long tail: Ordinary people with extraordinary tastes. In *WSDM*, 2010.

[11] F. Harper, D. Moy, and J. Konstan. Facts or friends?: distinguishing informational and conversational questions in social Q&A sites. In *CHI*, 2009.

[12] F. M. Harper, D. Raban, S. Rafaeli, and J. A. Konstan. Predictors of answer quality in online q&a sites. In *CHI*, pages 865–874, 2008.

[13] A. Hassan, R. Jones, and K. Klinkner. Beyond DCG: User behavior as a predictor of a successful search. In *Proc. of WSDM*, pages 221–230, 2010.

[14] D. Horowitz and S. Kamvar. The anatomy of a large-scale social search engine. In *WWW*, 2010.

[15] S. B. Huffman and M. Hochster. How well does result relevance predict session satisfaction? In *SIGIR*, pages 567–574, 2007.

[16] K. Järvelin and J. Kekäläinen. Cumulated gain-based evaluation of ir techniques. *ACM Trans. Inf. Syst.*, 20:422–446, October 2002.

[17] J. Jeon, W. B. Croft, J. H. Lee, and S. Park. A framework to predict the quality of answers with non-textual features. In *SIGIR*, 2006.

[18] G. Kazai and A. Doucet. Overview of the INEX 2007 book search track: Booksearch '07. *SIGIR Forum*, 42(1):2–15, 2008.

[19] Y. Liu, J. Bian, and E. Agichtein. Predicting information seeker satisfaction in community question answering. In *SIGIR*, 2008.

[20] B. Long, O. Chapelle, Y. Zhang, Y. Chang, Z. Zheng, and B. L. Tseng. Active learning for ranking through expected loss optimization. In *SIGIR*, pages 267–274, 2010.

[21] M. Morris, J. Teevan, and K. Panovich. A Comparison of Information Seeking Using Search Engines and Social Networks. In *ICWSM*, 2010.

[22] J. Nielsen. User interface directions for the web. *Commun. ACM*, 42:65–72, January 1999.

[23] D. Raban. Self-presentation and the value of information in Q&A web sites. *JASIST*, 60(12):2465–2473, 2009.

[24] H. Robbins and S. Monro. A stochastic approximation method. *Annals of Mathematical Statistics*, 22:400–407, 1951.

[25] S. Robertson, H. Zaragoza, and M. Taylor. Simple BM25 extension to multiple weighted fields. In *Proceedings of CIKM*, pages 42–49, 2004.

[26] D. E. Rose and D. Levinson. Understanding user goals in web search. In *WWW*, pages 13–19, 2004.

[27] M. Sanderson and I. Soboroff. Problems with kendall's tau. In *SIGIR*, 2007.

[28] C. Shah and J. Pomerantz. Evaluating and predicting answer quality in community QA. In *SIGIR*, 2010.

[29] Y.-I. Song, C.-Y. Lin, Y. Cao, and H.-C. Rim. Question utility: A novel static ranking of question search. In *AAAI*, pages 1231–1236, 2008.

[30] J. C. Spall. *Introduction to Stochastic Search and Optimization*. John Wiley & Sons, 2003.

[31] K. Sun, Y. Cao, X. Song, Y.-I. Song, X. Wang, and C.-Y. Lin. Learning to recommend questions based on user ratings. In *CIKM*, pages 751–758, 2009.

[32] M. Surdeanu, M. Ciaramita, and H. Zaragoza. Learning to rank answers on large online qa collections. In *ACL*, pages 719–727, 2008.

[33] M. A. Suryanto, E. P. Lim, A. Sun, and R. H. L. Chiang. Quality-aware collaborative question answering: methods and evaluation. In *WSDM*, 2009.

[34] J. Teevan, S. T. Dumais, and D. J. Liebling. To personalize or not to personalize: modeling queries with variation in user intent. In *SIGIR*, 2008.

[35] A. Tsotsis. Just because Google exists doesn't mean you should stop asking people things. TechCrunch, Oct 2010. http://techcrunch.com/2010/10/23/google-vs-humans/.

[36] X. Wang, X. Tu, D. Feng, and L. Zhang. Ranking community answers by modeling question-answer relationships via analogical reasoning. In *SIGIR*, 2009.

[37] Y. Wang and E. Agichtein. Query ambiguity revisited: clickthrough measures for distinguishing informational and ambiguous queries. In *ACL*, 2010.

[38] F. Wilcoxon. Individual comparisons by ranking methods. *Biometrics Bulletin*, 1:80–83, 1945.

[39] X. Xue, J. Jeon, and W. Croft. Retrieval models for question and answer archives. In *SIGIR*, 2008.

[40] E. Yom-Tov, S. Fine, D. Carmel, and A. Darlow. Learning to estimate query difficulty: including applications to missing content detection and distributed information retrieval. In *SIGIR*, 2005.

Competition-based User Expertise Score Estimation

Jing Liu[†]*, Young-In Song[‡], Chin-Yew Lin[‡]

[†]Harbin Institute of Technology
No. 92, West Da-Zhi St, Nangang Dist.
Harbin, China 150001
jliu@ir.hit.edu.cn

[‡]Microsoft Research Asia
Building 2, No. 5 Dan Ling St, Haidian Dist.
Beijing, China 100190
{yosong, cyl}@microsoft.com

ABSTRACT
In this paper, we consider the problem of estimating the relative expertise score of users in community question and answering services (CQA). Previous approaches typically only utilize the explicit question answering relationship between askers and answerers and apply link analysis to address this problem. The implicit pairwise comparison between two users that is implied in the best answer selection is ignored. Given a question and answering thread, it's likely that the expertise score of the best answerer is higher than the asker's and all other non-best answerers'. The goal of this paper is to explore such pairwise comparisons inferred from best answer selections to estimate the relative expertise scores of users. Formally, we treat each pairwise comparison between two users as a two-player competition with one winner and one loser. Two competition models are proposed to estimate user expertise from pairwise comparisons. Using the NTCIR-8 CQA task data with 3 million questions and introducing answer quality prediction based evaluation metrics, the experimental results show that the pairwise comparison based competition model significantly outperforms link analysis based approaches (PageRank and HITS) and pointwise approaches (number of best answers and best answer ratio) for estimating the expertise of active users. Furthermore, it's shown that pairwise comparison based competition models have better discriminative power than other methods. It's also found that answer quality (best answer) is an important factor to estimate user expertise.

Categories and Subject Descriptors
H.1.2 [**User/Machine Systems**]: Human information processing; H.3.3 [**Information Search and Retrieval**]: Selection process

General Terms
Experimentation

Keywords
Expertise estimation, community question answering, pairwise comparison, competition model

1. INTRODUCTION
Search engines help people search information on the World Wide Web. However, not all human knowledge and experiences can be covered by existing web pages. With the explosive growth of web 2.0 sites, community question and answering services (denoted as CQA) such as Yahoo! Answers[1] and Baidu Zhidao[2], have become important services where people can use natural language rather than keywords to ask questions and seek advice or opinions from real people who have relevant knowledge or experiences. CQA services provide another way to satisfy a user's information needs that cannot be met by traditional search engines. Users are the unique source of knowledge in CQA sites and all users from experts to novices can generate content arbitrarily. Therefore, it is desirable to have a system that can automatically estimate the user expertise score and identify experts who can provide good quality answers. Many applications can benefit from user expertise score estimation, for example, routing questions to experts, extracting good quality answers and creating mechanisms to encourage those identified experts to participate more, etc.

Intuitively, the user expertise score can be estimated from the number of answers per user, the quality of answers, and user interaction. Several models have been proposed to estimate relative expertise scores of users in CQA, for example, analysis of the number of questions and answers [23], analysis of the number of best answers [3], link analysis [14, 23], and modeling user expertise and answer quality simultaneously [2]. Link analysis based approaches [14, 23] utilize question and answering relationships between askers and answerers to estimate the relative expertise score of users. However, answer quality, which is important for estimating user expertise, is not considered in those models. The co-training model [2], which jointly estimates user expertise and answer quality, considers answer quality, but it doesn't model user interaction explicitly. Usually, the best answer is just simply used as an individual feature to estimate user expertise score or answer quality. Despite these past efforts, there is still not a principal way to estimate user expertise score and evaluate results.

In this paper, we propose a general and simple competition-based method to estimate user expertise score. By "general", we mean that our method can be applied to all CQA services that have best answer selection. To the best of our knowledge, all existing CQA services have best answer annotation by their users. By "simple", we mean that our method assumes two simple and intuitive principles: (1) given a question answering thread, it's likely that the expertise score of the best answerer is higher than the asker; (2) Similarly, it's likely that the expertise score of the best answerer is higher than the expertise score of all the other answerers. By applying these two simple principles, we can determine relative expertise scores among users through pairwise comparison between (1) an asker and a best answerer, and between (2) a best

*This work was done when Jing Liu was a visiting student at Microsoft Research Asia.

[1] http://answers.yahoo.com/

[2] http://zhidao.baidu.com/

answerer and all other non-best answerers. Our goal is to explore such general and simple pairwise comparisons to estimate the relative expertise score of users. Each pairwise comparison can be viewed as a two-player competition without tie. In this paper, we present two pairwise comparison based competition models to estimate user expertise score.

For user expertise score evaluation, we use NTCIR-8 CQA task data with 3 million questions and introduce answer quality prediction based evaluation metrics to evaluate our approaches. Our main findings from experiments are that: (a) Our pairwise comparison based competition model significantly outperforms pointwise approaches, including number of answers, number of best answers and best answer ratio; and link-based approaches, including question answering relationship based PageRank and HITS; (b) the pairwise comparison based competition model shows better discriminative power for estimating the relative expertise score of users than other approaches; (c) it's also shown that, as an indicator of answer quality, the best answer is important for estimating user expertise.

This paper is structured as follows. Section 2 discusses related work on user expertise score estimation. Section 3 proposes the notion of pairwise comparisons between users and introduces the competition-based method. Section 4 presents two pairwise comparison based competition models for user expertise estimation. Section 5 introduces the answer quality prediction based evaluation metrics and evaluates the proposed methods. Section 6 concludes this paper and discusses future work.

2. RELATED WORKS

With the rapid increase of CQA sites over recent years, estimating the expertise score of CQA users has become a common task and results in a variety of approaches.

Link analysis based ranking approaches have shown its success in measuring quality of web pages. Two of the most famous link analysis approaches are PageRank [4] and HITS [15]. Early work on estimating expertise score of CQA users employs link analysis technology on the question answering relationship based user graph. In a user graph, each user is viewed as a node. If there is a question answering relationship between two users then there is a directed edge from the asker to the answerer. Zhang et al. [23] proposed the ExpertiseRank model, which is a PageRank-like algorithm, to estimate expertise score of users from online forums. Similar to PageRank, ExpertiseRank considers not only the number of users one has helped, but also whom they helped. By considering askers as hub nodes, and answerers as authority nodes, Jurczyk et al. [14] employed HITS to estimate user expertise score based on the question answering relationship between askers and answerers in CQA. However, answer quality information such as best answer, which reflects asker choices on which answer is correct, useful, readable and informative, is ignored in these works.

Due to the importance of answer quality, many following works incorporate best answer labels into user expertise score estimation. Bian et al. [2] proposed a mutual reinforcement approach for jointly modeling user expertise and answer quality. However, this work does not explicitly model user relationship. It extracted question answering relationship based link information as features. Pal et al. [18] studied user behavior and showed that experts prefer to answer questions that do not already have good answers. This is because experts recognize that they have a higher chance to make more valuable contributions to those questions. Based on this finding, they model users' question selection bias to identify experts. Typically an estimation of user expertise is presented as a ranked list of users with their expertise scores without an explicit indicator of who should be considered as experts. Bouguessa et al. [3] propose a method to solve the problem of determining how many users should be selected as experts from a user list ranked by number of best answers. They also argued that best answer is important to estimate user expertise score.

Besides the question and answering community, user expertise score estimation is also studied in other social networks. Campbell et al. [5] used HITS to compute user expertise score over the user network of e-mail communications. Zhou et al. [24] followed the PageRank paradigm to propose an approach for co-ranking authors and their publications in a heterogeneous network.

Research on user expertise score estimation can benefit a lot of applications. User expertise and other user related information are widely used for evaluating answer quality in CQA [1, 12, 17] and in online forums [7]. Suryanto et al. [22] incorporated user expertise score into question and answer search; they showed that user expertise score can improve question and answer search. Li et al. [16] proposed a framework to route questions to right answerers who are experts and available to answer questions. Horowitz et al. [11] developed a social search engine which routes questions to askers' extended social network, including Facebook and Google Contacts, rather than the question and answering community.

In this paper, our key idea is to propose a competition-based method that explores pairwise comparisons between users inferred from best answer selections, to estimate user expertise score. Each pairwise comparison can be treated as a two-player competition. From a competition-based perspective, expertise score estimation becomes a related problem to the calculation of the statistical skill rating of players or teams in competitive games or sports. The main research works in this area mainly studied ranking players or teams purely based on win-loss results. The most well-known skill rating system is Elo [8], which is designed to calculate the relative skill scores of players in a two-player game. It already has been widely used in many sports including chess, football, and baseball. Elo assumes that the performance of one player in a game is normally distributed around its skill level with a fixed variance and that the probability of each possible outcome of one game is determined by the skill ratings of the two players. TrueSkill [10] extends the Elo with a dynamic variance and targets one main challenge in online games: more than two players or two teams can participate in one game. Mease et al. [18] introduced a penalized maximal likelihood approach to rank NCAA college football teams. Their work also assumes that the intrinsic skill score of one team follows the normal distribution with fixed variance.

To summarize the relation with previous work, our approach (1) incorporates best answer selection to infer pairwise comparison of users, which includes pairwise comparisons between askers and best answerers, non-best answerers and best answerers, and leverages implicit question answering relationships between askers and answerers [14, 23]; (2) proposes a competition-based approach and then applies two-player competition models [10, 18, 6] to estimate the relative expertise score of users.

3. PAIRWISE COMPARISONS OF USERS

CQA is a virtual space where people can ask questions, seek opinions and get experiences from others. When an asker has a problem related to the topic of a certain category, he or she would ask a question within the certain category. Then, there will be several answerers to answer his or her question. To guarantee the quality of content in CQA, the asker must select one answer as the best answer among all the answers he or she received within a fixed number of days after the question was posted. All participants in one question answering thread can be thought of as triplets (a, b, S) consisting of the asker a, the best answerer b whose answer is selected as the best answer, and the set S of all the other answerers who are named as non-best answerers. Figure 1(a) illustrates an example: the asker asked a question and got three answers from three answerers, and the answer posted by the third answerer (Answerer3) was selected as the best answer.

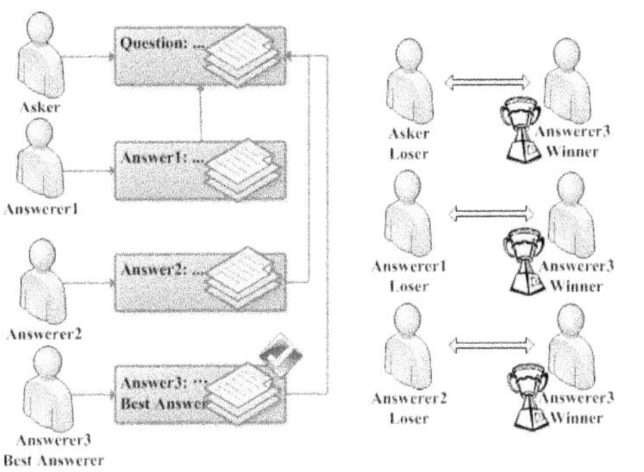

(a) Question answering (b) Pairwise competitions

Figure 1. Example for one question answering thread

Ideally, askers would not select the best answers randomly, but make an informed choice and the selected best answer should have the best quality among all answers. In reality, askers may be careless or subjective; their judgments may be not perfect. However, the best answer selections are still likely to convey some meaningful information. We make the following two intuitive assumptions about best answer selection:

1. Given a question, its best answerer b has a higher expertise level than its asker a. This is pretty straightforward since the best answerer successfully solves the problem that the asker doesn't know.
2. Given a question, its best answerer b has a higher expertise level than all other answerers, i.e. answerers in the set S. This is reasonable since the asker is expected to pick the best answers among all answers assuming the quality of an answer is positively correlated with the expertise level of its provider.

According to this intuition, there are $n = |S| + 1$ pairwise comparisons generated for the question answering thread with the asker a, the best answerer b and the non-best answerer set S. Taking a competition viewpoint, each pairwise comparison can be viewed as a two-player competition with one winner and one loser. Hence, there are n two-player competitions, including one competition between the asker a and the best answerer b, and $|S|$ competitions between the best answerer b and every non-best answerer in the set S. The best answerer b is the winner of each two-player competition, and all other users, including the asker a and all non-best answerers, are losers. Consider again the example from Figure 1. For the given question answering thread, there are three two-player competitions generated, including the one between Asker and Answerer3, the one between Answerer1 and Answerer3, and the one between Answerer2 and Answerer3. Answerer3 is the winner in these three two-player competitions, because his answer is selected as the best answer. Asker, Answerer1 and Answerer2 are all losers in those competitions. Hence, the problem of estimating the relative expert levels of users can be deduced to the problem of learning the relative skills of players from the win-loss results of generated two-player competitions.

Formally, the win-loss results of all two-player competitions generated from the thread q with the asker a, the best answerer b and non-best answerer set S can be represented as the following set:

$$R_q = \{(a \prec b), (s_1 \prec b), (s_2 \prec b), \cdots, (s_{|S|} \prec b)\}, \quad (1)$$

where $j \prec i$ means that user i bests user j.

Using $Q = \{q_1, \cdots, q_{n-1}, q_n\}$ to denote all questions in one category, the win-loss results of all two-player competitions generated from the set Q can be presented as the following set:

$$R = \{(j \prec i) \mid \forall (j \prec i) \in R_{q_i}, i = 1 \cdots |Q|\}. \quad (2)$$

Our problem is to learn the relative skills of players from the set R denoting all the win-loss results. In the next section, we present two competition-based models to solve this problem.

4. COMPETITION BASED MODELS

4.1 TrueSkill

TrueSkill [10] is a Bayesian skill rating system which is designed to calculate the relative skill levels of players in multi-player or multi-player team games. As described in the previous section, our problem is to learn the relative expertise score of users from pairwise competitions without a tie. Hence, we introduce a two-player and no-draw version of TrueSkill to solve our problem.

TrueSkill assumes that the performance of each player in one game follows a normal distribution with its mean μ and its standard deviation σ. μ is the average skill of the player and σ represents a system's uncertainty about its estimation of the player's skill. Intuitively, as a system learns about the skill of one player from more data, the standard deviation σ (uncertainty) will be decreased. TrueSkill assumes that the skill of each player will be slightly changed after each game. This assumption both allows the system to track the skill improvement of players over time and guarantees that the standard deviation σ never decreases to zero. In the TrueSkill paper [10], $\mu - 3\sigma$ is used to rank players to ensure that the top ranked players are highly skilled with high certainty. In this paper, we follow the same approach to rank users.

Before going into details, we give a visual overview of what TrueSkill is. Figure 2 shows a simple example. There are two players: (a) A is an experienced player with a small standard deviation, since the estimation is based on many games and is therefore more certain; (b) B is a new player with a larger standard deviation since the system is not sure about B's skill. Figure 2 (a) shows the skill distributions of two players A and B before a game between them. Figure 2 (b) shows the updated skill distributions of two players after player B wins the new game. From Figure 2 (b), we can see that system makes a big update on the average skill μ of player B, because it considers that player B is probably better than player A based on the outcome of the new game. However, player B's standard deviation σ is still large, because the system is not confident about the estimation on B based on just one more game played by B.

In short, invoking Bayes' theorem, given the current estimated skills (priori probability) of players and the outcome of a new game (likelihood), a TrueSkill model should update its estimation of player skills (posterior probability). Compared to our problem, the outcome of each game is from the set R defined in Equation (2). Taking the set R, whose elements are sorted by time, and setting initial value of average skill μ and standard deviation σ of each player, we can apply TrueSkill to estimate the relative expertise score of each user.

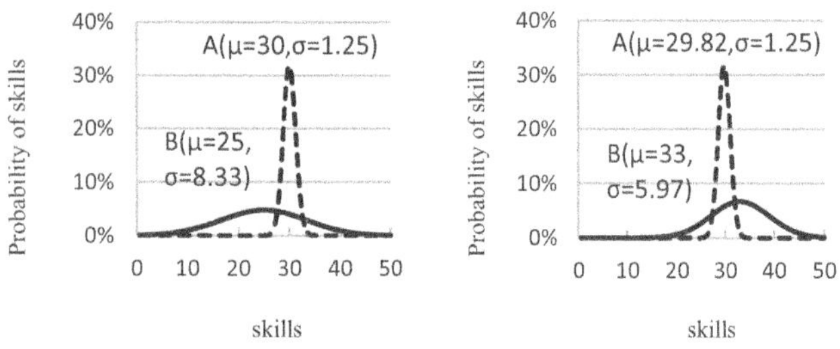

(a) Before the new game (b) After the new game

Figure 2. Example of updating player skill based on the outcome of a new game

The assumptions that updating average skill μ and standard deviation σ are intuitive: (a) the expected outcome is that the player with higher average skill wins the game, causing small updates on average skill μ and standard deviation σ; (b) the unexpected outcome is that the player with lower skill wins the game, causing large updates on average skill μ and standard deviation σ, to make the system more likely to predict the outcomes of future games. According to these assumptions, the equations to update the skills of players and the uncertainty about estimation are as follows:

$$\mu_{winner} = \mu_{winner} + \frac{\sigma_{winner}^2}{c} \cdot v\left(\frac{t}{c}, \frac{\varepsilon}{c}\right), \tag{3}$$

$$\mu_{loser} = \mu_{loser} - \frac{\sigma_{loser}^2}{c} \cdot v\left(\frac{t}{c}, \frac{\varepsilon}{c}\right), \tag{4}$$

$$\sigma_{winner}^2 = \sigma_{winner}^2 \cdot \left[1 - \frac{\sigma_{winner}^2}{c^2} \cdot w\left(\frac{t}{c}, \frac{\varepsilon}{c}\right)\right], \tag{5}$$

$$\sigma_{loser}^2 = \sigma_{loser}^2 \cdot \left[1 - \frac{\sigma_{loser}^2}{c^2} \cdot w\left(\frac{t}{c}, \frac{\varepsilon}{c}\right)\right], \tag{6}$$

where

$$t = \mu_{winner} - \mu_{loser},$$

$$c^2 = 2\beta^2 + \sigma_{winner}^2 + \sigma_{loser}^2,$$

$$v(t, \varepsilon) = \mathcal{N}(t - \varepsilon) / \Phi(t - \varepsilon),$$

$$w(t, \varepsilon) = v(t, \varepsilon) \cdot (v(t, \varepsilon) + t - \varepsilon).$$

Here, $\mathcal{N}(\cdot)$ is the standard normal distribution, $\Phi(\cdot)$ is the cumulative normal distribution, ε is a parameter representing the probability of a draw in one game, and β is a parameter representing the range of skills. For example, the range of skills is large for a chess game, but it's small for gambling. In this paper, we set these two parameters to the value used in the TrueSkill paper [10]. The initial value of average skill μ and standard deviation σ of each player is also the same as the default value used in the TrueSkill paper [10].

The variable t reflects the exceptions on the outcome: (a) the outcome is expected, when t is positive; (b) the outcome is unexpected, when t is negative.

The function $v(t, \varepsilon)$ and $w(t, \varepsilon)$ are weighting factors to average skill μ and standard deviation σ, respectively. These two functions reflect the assumption about updating μ and σ. Figure 3 plots the tendency of function $v(t, \varepsilon)$ for a given ε. It can be observed that: (a) μ will not change too much when t is positive (expected result); (b) μ will change more when t is negative (unexpected result). Similarly, Figure 4 plots the tendency of function $w(t, \varepsilon)$ for a given ε. We can see that: (a) σ will not be changed too much when t is positive (expected result); (b) σ will be changed more when t is negative (unexpected result).

Besides the two weighting functions $v(t, \varepsilon)$ and $w(t, \varepsilon)$, another factor affecting the update on μ and σ is the ratio between the uncertainty of each player (σ_{winner} or σ_{loser}) and the total sum of uncertainties c. The player with a larger uncertainty gets a larger change on both μ and σ.

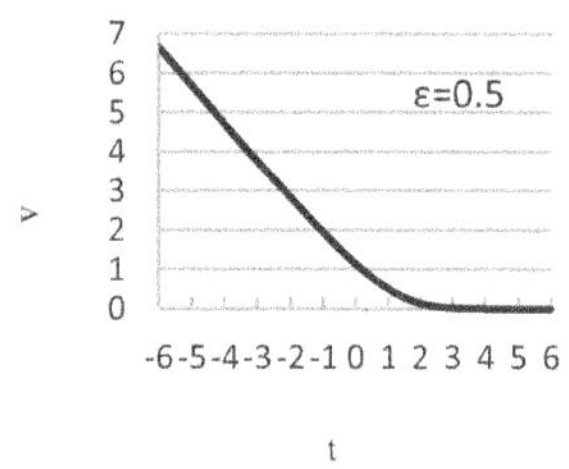

Figure 3. Example curve for function v

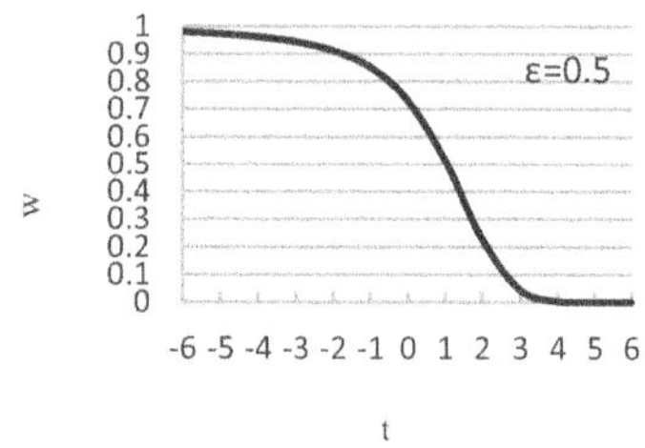

Figure 4. Example curve for function w

4.2 SVM Model

Mease et al. [18] proposed a maximal likelihood approach to rank football teams, which can be solved by a logistic regression model. Inspired by Mease's work, Carterette et al. [6] proposed an SVM model to solve the rank aggregation problem, which combines multiple search results from multiple search engines to produce a better new ranking. In the rank aggregation problem, for a given query, each search engine returns a ranked list of documents $d_1 \prec d_2 \prec d_3 \cdots$, where $d_j \prec d_i$ means that document d_i is ranked higher than document d_j. Each $d_j \prec d_i$ is viewed as a pairwise comparison between two documents (d_i, d_j). The SVM model learns the relevance weight of each document from these extracted pairwise comparisons.

In our problem, the pairwise comparisons of users $(j \prec i) \in R$ can be viewed as pairwise comparisons of documents $d_j \prec d_i$. Thus, we can apply the SVM model proposed by Carterette et al. [6] to learn the relative expertise score of users. The expertise score of each user i is defined as θ_i. In the SVM model, the optimization problem is:

$$\text{minimize } \frac{1}{2}\|\theta\|^2 + C \sum \xi_k \tag{7}$$

$$\text{subject to } y_k(\langle\theta, x_k\rangle + b) \geq 1 - \xi_k; \ \xi_k \geq 0$$

Where $\theta = \{\theta_1, \cdots, \theta_n\}$ and n is the number of all users. Here x_k is a vector of length n associated with a pairwise competition between users, and y is the win-loss result. Given a two-player competition k with the winner i and the loser j, there're two training instances generated: (a) $y_k = 1$, $x_k[i] = 1$, $x_k[j] = -1$; (b) $y'_k = 0$, $x'_k[i] = -1$, $x'_k[j] = 1$. The $\hat{\theta} = (\hat{\theta}_1, \cdots, \hat{\theta}_n)$ that minimize equation (7) are taken as the estimated relative skills of players. In this paper, we use linear kernel SVM LIBLINEAR [9] to solve this optimization problem.

5. EXPERIMENTS

5.1 Data Set

In this paper, we use the NTCIR-8 CQA task data as the experiment data, which is dumped from the Yahoo! Chiebukuro (Japanese Yahoo! Answers) database ranging from April 2004 to October 2005. We choose this corpus because it is the only publically available CQA data with multiple manual answer quality judgments. It contains 3,116,009 questions, 13,477,785 answers including 3,116,008 best answers (one best answer is missed from the data), and 240,784 users. There are 14 categories provided in the data set. Each question belongs to exactly one category. Figure 5 shows the frequency distribution of questions and the frequency distribution of users over the 14 different categories. The NTCIR-8 CQA task organizers sampled 1,500 questions from the entire data set according to the frequency distribution of questions over 14 categories as the test data set. There are 7,443 answers and 6,482 users in the test data set. It includes 1,500 best answers which we denote as BA data. In the testing data, the number of answers per question ranges from 2 to 20.

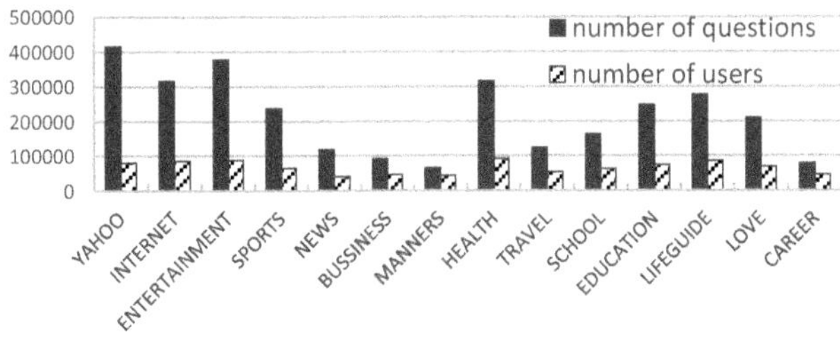

Figure 5. The frequency distribution of questions and users over the 14 top categories

The NTCIR-8 CQA task was originally designed for evaluating answer quality prediction systems. Sakai et al. [20, 21] state that the best answers selected by askers may be biased, and that there may be other good answers besides the best answers. To solve these two problems, NTCIR-8 CQA task organizers hired four assessors to annotate answer quality and assign a graded-relevance score to each answer using a pyramid approach. There are 9 relevance levels from L0 (low) to L8 (high) defined in the testing data. Table 1 shows the number of answers for each relevance level. We shall refer to this ground truth data set as graded answers (GA) data. Table 2 shows the relationship between BA data and GA data. We observe that not all BA are high quality answers based on GA and that there are other good answers besides BA. It also shows that overall BA is still a good answer quality indicator since the number of good BA according to GA is increasing at each higher GA relevance level.

Table 1. Number of answers at each relevance level (GA)

L0	L1	L2	L3	L4	L5	L6	L7	L8	Total
17	32	106	238	1318	1399	1527	1505	1301	7443

Table 2. Number of BAs at each GA relevance level

L0	L1	L2	L3	L4	L5	L6	L7	L8	Total
0	1	7	22	99	156	245	372	598	1500

5.2 Evaluation Metrics

There are two major approaches for the evaluation of user expertise estimation or expert identification: (1) employing traditional information retrieval (IR) evaluation metrics, such as precision, recall and rank correlation etc., to measure system output using a ground truth (an expert set or a user ranked list); (2) evaluating the quality of answers posted by identified experts.

How to get the ground truth is an important problem for the first evaluation approach. Two types of ground truth were used in previous work: (1) an automatically generated user ranked list; (b) a manually annotated expert set. However, both ground truths are not perfect. Jurczyk et al. [14] use several meta-data information sets in CQA to generate a user ranked list as the ground truth, including the average number of votes received by one user, the average number of stars attained by one user, and the best answer ratio of one user. Bian et al. [2] used the top contributor list provided by Yahoo! Answers as the ground truth. The top contributor badge[3] in Yahoo! Answers is automatically computed according to the recent number of best answers and best answer ratio of users. Unfortunately, such an automatic generated ground truth is obtained according to a certain heuristic method, which itself can be viewed as an approach to estimate user expertise level. Thus, the automatic generated ground truth may be not accurate. Pal et al. [18] used an expert set that is annotated by the employees of a CQA site TurboTax as the ground truth. Zhang et al. [23] asked two domain experts to assign an expertise level for each frequent user in an online community according to the posting history of users. However, it's hard to track even a small amount of users in a large online community. The manually annotated expert set may be not up to date or cannot cover all experts in a community.

As discussed previously, Bouguessa et al. [5] consider the problem of how many users should be selected as experts from a user ranking list that is sorted by number of best answers. They proposed an indirect evaluation metric to evaluate their method. They used an automatic answer quality prediction system to evaluate the average quality of answers posted by experts identified by their method. Their assumption is simply that experts are expected to generate high-quality answers. However, automatic answer quality prediction may not be accurate enough.

In this paper, we consider how to estimate the relative expertise scores of users. Therefore, we are interested in evaluating the relative rank of users sorted by their estimated user expertise score. Inspired by Bouguessa's work [3], we assume that the higher the expertise level of a user, the higher the quality of answer provided by the user. Given a testing question, its answers can be sorted by estimated user expertise scores of answerers. Hence, evaluating answer ranking can be a validation of evaluating the relative ranking of users. Additionally, we use a human annotated data set, including GA data and BA data, to evaluate system output, rather than using an automatic answer quality prediction system.

Using BA data, we treat the best answer as the only right answer and evaluate answer ranking with two metrics –Mean Reciprocal Rank (MRR) and Precision@1 (P@1). However, using BA data, we only can do binary judgments. As described previously, there are many other good answers besides the best answers. It's therefore better to use GA data to evaluate. Hence, GA data will be used as the main ground truth.

For GA data, we use two graded-relevance evaluation metrics: nDCG (normalized Discounted Cumulative Gain) and RnDCG (Relatively normalized Discounted Cumulative Gain). In the GA

[3] http://help.yahoo.com/l/us/yahoo/answers/network/contributor.html

data, let the gain values be 0-8 for L0-L8 relevant answers respectively. Let $g(r)$ denote the gain value of the answer ranked at r in a system's output. Similarly, let $g^*(r)$ denote the gain value of the answer ranked at r in the best possible ranking list obtained by sorting all answers in non-ascending order of the gain values. The nDCG score with cutoff n is defined as:

$$\mathrm{nDCG}@n = \frac{\mathrm{systemDCG}@n}{\mathrm{bestDCG}@n}, \quad (8)$$

where

$$\mathrm{systemDCG}@n = \sum_{r=1}^{n} \frac{g(r)}{\log(r+1)},$$

$$\mathrm{bestDCG}@n = \sum_{r=1}^{n} \frac{g^*(r)}{\log(r+1)}.$$

As shown in Table 1, there are 94.7% answers that are equal to or greater than level L4 and that only 0.23% of answers are at level L0 (totally irrelevant). It means that even a bad system can get a high nDCG score. It's different from the standard IR evaluation, because there are much more irrelevant documents in many other IR tasks. Hence, in our particular case, we use a relative normalization approach (RnDCG) to normalize the DCG score (suggested in Sakai et al. [21]), which ensures that the evaluation scores will range fully between 0 and 1 for better differentiating between systems. Let $g^{\Delta}(r)$ denote the gain value of the answer ranked at r in the worst possible ranking list obtained by sorting all answers in non-descending order of the gain values. The RnDCG score with cutoff n can be defined as follows:

$$\mathrm{RnDCG}@n = \frac{\mathrm{systemDCG}@n - \mathrm{worstDCG}@n}{\mathrm{bestDCG}@n - \mathrm{worstDCG}@n}, \quad (9)$$

where

$$\mathrm{worstDCG}@n = \sum_{r=1}^{n} \frac{g^{\Delta}(r)}{\log(r+1)}.$$

In our experiment, we use the entire NTCIR CQA data set (excluding the 1,500 testing questions) as training data to learn the relative expertise score of users for each category. For each testing question within a certain category, all the answers to the question are sorted by the estimated expertise score of their authors. Then, the evaluation metrics for answer ranking can be applied to measure the performances of the user expertise score estimation approaches. In this paper, RnDCG on GA data will be used as the main evaluation metric.

5.3 Baseline Methods

Table 3 lists the user expertise score estimation methods which are evaluated in this paper and their abbreviations. The number of answers and the number of best answers were used as the simplest baselines in [14, 3, 23]. Link analysis approaches can be applied on a question answering relationship based user graph (QA based user graph). In the QA based user graph, there is a directed edge from one asker to its answerer. PageRank and HITS have been applied on the QA based user graph [23, 15]. The QA based user graph assumes that all answers have equal quality. However, the quality of different answers varies drastically in CQA sites [1] as we have observed even at the best answer level in Table 2. Hence, we simply propose to build a user graph based on the question and best answering relationship (QBA based user graph). In the QBA based user graph, there is a directed edge from an asker to its best answerer. The methods running PageRank and HITS on the QBA based user graph are used as the other two baselines.

Table 3. The methods and their abbreviations

Method	Abbrev.
Number of Answers (Sec. 2)	NA
Number of Best Answers (Sec. 2)	NBA
PageRank on QA based user Graph(Sec. 2)	P+QAG
PageRank on QBA based user Graph	P+QBAG
HITS on QA based user Graph(Sec. 2)	H+QAG
HITS on QBA based user Graph	H+QBAG
Best Answer Ratio	BAR
Smoothed Best Answer Ratio	SBAR
TrueSkill (Sec. 4.1)	TS
SVM Model (Sec. 4.2)	SVM

Another simple method we used as a baseline is the best answer ratio (BAR). The BAR of one user u can be computed as follows:

$$BAR(u) = \frac{C(BA; u)}{C(A; u)}, \quad (10)$$

where $C(A; u)$ denotes the number of answers provided by user u, and $C(BA; u)$ denotes the number of best answers provided by user u. To the best of our knowledge, there's no related work using the BAR as a user expertise score estimation method and comparing it with other methods[4]. It was only used as an effective feature to predict answer quality [1, 12, 17].

The BAR might be overestimated or underestimated when $C(A; u)$ is small. For example, given two users A and B, A only posts 1 answer and gets 1 best answer; while B posts 100 answers and has 90 best answers. In this case, A's BAR is higher than B's but we really are not sure that A is really better than B due to the low count of A's answers. In another case, the BAR for a user posting 1 answer and having no best answer is zero, which may be lower than his or her true expertise level. Hence, we propose a smoothed best answer ratio (SBAR) method which considers the number of answers given by a user. It is computed as follows:

$$SBAR(u) = \frac{C(A; u)}{C(A; u) + \alpha} BAR(u) + \frac{\alpha}{C(A; u) + \alpha} BAR_{avg}, \quad (11)$$

where

$$\alpha = \frac{1}{|U|} \cdot \sum_{\forall v \in U} C(A; v), \qquad BAR_{avg} = \frac{1}{|U|} \cdot \sum_{\forall v \in U} BAR(v).$$

Here, $|U|$ denotes the total number of users, α means the average number of answers per user, and BAR_{avg} means the average BAR per user. From Equation (11) we see: if the number of answers posted by a user is small (less than the average number of answers per user), his or her score will be smoothed toward the average score of all users; otherwise it will be close to the maximum likelihood estimation of its BAR.

[4] As discussed in section 5.2, the BAR was used as a method to get the ground truth of user ranking in Jurczyk et al. [14].

Table 4. The performance of all methods on BA and GA data for two user sets.

		GA data						BA data	
	Method	RnDCG@1	RnDCG@3	RnDCG@20	nDCG@1	nDCG@3	nDCG@20	P@1	MRR
Test users with at least 50 answers; 975 selected questions	NA	0.4874	0.5090	0.5035	0.8044	0.9033	0.9455	0.2954	0.5567
	NBA	0.5462	0.5658	0.5577	0.8273	0.9160	0.9516	0.3426	0.5876
	P+QAG	0.5043	0.5184	0.5158	0.8107	0.9050	0.9468	0.3015	0.5604
	P+QBAG	0.5462	0.5631	0.5588	0.8267	0.9153	0.9517	0.3528	0.5964
	H+QAG	0.4866	0.5073	0.5024	0.8044	0.9033	0.9454	0.2974	0.5576
	H+QBAG	0.5424	0.5645	0.5565	0.8268	0.9161	0.9517	0.3426	0.5886
	BAR	0.6684	0.6875	0.6802	0.8767	0.9420	0.9660	0.4349	0.6494
	SBAR	0.6687	0.6885	0.6808	0.8770	0.9425	0.9661	0.4390	0.6519
	TS	0.6738	0.7011	0.6899	0.8779	0.9426	0.9666	0.4349	0.6505
	SVM	**0.6939**	**0.7145**	**0.7061**	**0.8871**	**0.9467**	**0.9688**	**0.4523**	**0.6637**
Test users with at least 1 answer; 1463 selected questions	NA	0.4733	0.4932	0.4905	0.7901	0.8862	0.9409	0.2632	0.5160
	NBA	0.5197	0.5385	0.5338	0.8087	0.8976	0.9460	0.2960	0.5385
	P+QAG	0.4865	0.5012	0.5010	0.7945	0.8872	0.9418	0.2700	0.5193
	P+QBAG	0.5170	0.5395	0.5341	0.8068	0.8972	0.9458	0.3035	0.5457
	H+QAG	0.4738	0.4951	0.4923	0.7903	0.8865	0.9411	0.2659	0.5174
	H+QBAG	0.5175	0.5410	0.5355	0.8086	0.8981	0.9464	0.2973	0.5407
	BAR	0.6534	0.6700	0.6636	0.8659	0.9291	0.9622	**0.3999**	0.6134
	SBAR	0.6585	**0.6812**	**0.6728**	**0.8676**	**0.9316**	**0.9633**	**0.3999**	**0.6155**
	TS	0.6486	0.6636	0.6568	0.8631	0.9272	0.9612	0.3821	0.6018
	SVM	**0.6587**	0.6760	0.6688	**0.8676**	0.9314	0.9629	0.3841	0.6092

5.4 Results

As shown in Table 4, we conduct evaluations on two user sets: (a) the set of all users who posted at least 50 answers in the training data; (b) the set of all users who posted at least 1 answer in the training data.

To test on the first user set, we select a subset of questions from the 1500 testing questions with these two properties: (1) answered by at least two users from the first user set; (2) their best answerers are also from the first user set. It should be noticed that there can be answerers who are not from the first user set (unseen users) and participated the selected testing questions. Hence, in this selected testing question set, the answers posted by unseen users will be removed and only the answers posted by the users from the first user set will be kept. It ensures that only the answers posted by users from the first user set will be evaluated. Then answer quality prediction based evaluation metrics can be applied. There are 975 questions in this selected question set. Similarly, we create another set of testing questions for the second user set. There are 1463 questions in the second selected question set.

The purpose of conducting the first evaluation is to measure the performances of different methods on the set of active users who post many answers. This is because the active users contribute a lot to communities and are the driving force of communities. In our data set, there are 12.5% users who provide more than 50 answers and contribute more than 91.6% answers. Therefore, it would be very beneficial to site owners or CQA researchers to learn more about active users and differentiate between their relative expertise levels. In contrast, the goal of the second evaluation is to measure the performance of different methods on the set of all answerers including the users posting only a few answers. This is because new users that post a small number of answers are the potential new driving force of communities. If a method can well estimate the expertise scores of new users with just a few answers, it would be highly beneficial for online communities.

5.4.1 Answer vs. Best Answer

In this section, we show the effect of using the best answer versus using answer on counting based methods, i.e. NA vs. NBA, and on link analysis based methods, i.e. P+QAG vs. P+QBAG, and H+QAG vs. H+QBAG.

As shown in Table 4, comparing NA with NBA, P+QAG with P+QBAG, and H+QAG with H+QBAG, we found that by incorporating the best answer, the performances of the counting and link analysis based methods are significantly improved in terms of all evaluation metrics on two user sets (Wilcoxon signed-rank test, p-value < 0.01). It partially proves that answer quality (best answer) is important for user expertise score estimation.

As shown in Table 4, P+QAG is slightly better than NA in terms of all evaluation metrics on two different user sets. H+QAG is slightly better than NA in terms of all evaluation metrics on the second user set. However, sometimes it's worse than NA on the first user set. It's similar to what Jurczyk et al. [14] reported: that HITS doesn't perform well sometimes. It's also reported by Zhang et al. [23] that sometimes a relatively simple measure is as good as a complex algorithm such as PageRank. Comparing NBA with P+QBAG and H+QBAG, we come to a similar conclusion that link analysis (or graph) based approaches perform similar to the counting based methods (NA, NBA).

5.4.2 Best Answer Ratio

As we described in section 5.3, to the best of our knowledge, there's no related work comparing such simple, intuitive and strong methods BAR and SBAR with other user expertise estimation methods. As Table 4 shows, it's surprising that simple BAR and SBAR can significantly outperform more complex methods, such as P+QBAG and H+QBAG, in terms of all evaluation metrics on two user sets (Wilcoxon signed-rank test, p-value < 0.01).

Also, we can observe that SBAR is slightly better than BAR in terms of all evaluation metrics on two user sets, since SBAR incorporates smoothing into BAR to avoid over fitting.

Figure 6 shows the distributions of SBAR scores of all answerers in two categories: internet and travel. We observe that the trends of the two distributions are similar (similar trends can be observed in other categories). From Figure 6, we see that the curve denoting the distribution of answerers' SBAR scores can be roughly divided into three parts: short head, long middle, and short tail. The users in the short and sharp head part are the ones with high SBAR scores. The users in the short tail part are the ones with low SBAR scores. One interesting finding is that most of users that fall into the long and flat middle are low frequent users with negative participation patterns. The negative user participation patterns are like the ones highlighted in Figure 6: the negative participation patterns are one answer with zero best answers (1:0), two answers with one best answer (2:1) and two answers with zero best answers (2:0). This reflects Yang et al.'s [13] finding: if an answerer didn't get positive feedback, i.e. selected as the best answer at the initial participation, it is very likely the answerer would stop contributing to a community. Intuitively, a user's BAR score should be highly correlated with continued answering. Because it's likely that only the users who always get positive feedbacks from a community, i.e. selected as the best answer, would like to continuously contribute to the community. However, Yang et al.'s [13] reported that a user's BAR score is just weakly correlated with continued answering. Figure 7 shows the number of answers by users from each bin of SBAR scores. The tail part in Figure 7 tells us the reason is that there were a lot of users who continuously tried to answer questions, even if they always failed.

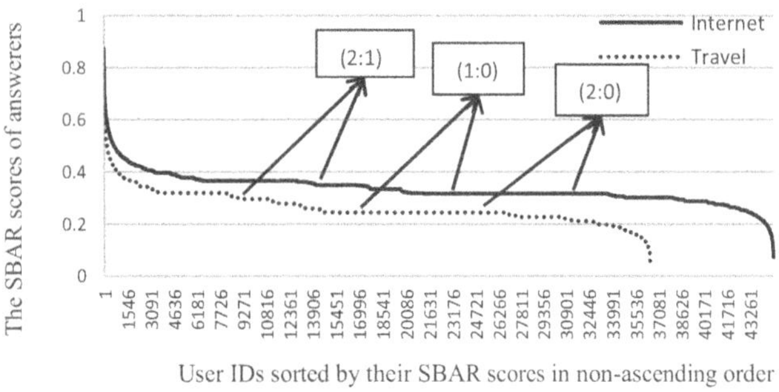

Figure 6. The distribution of answerers' SBAR scores

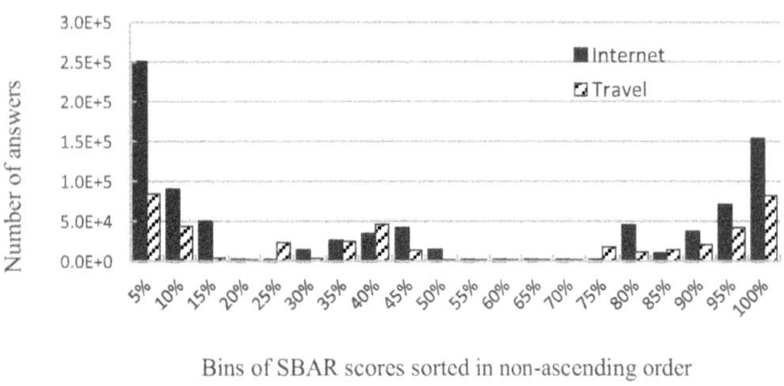

Figure 7. Number of answers for each bin of SBAR scores

From these observations, we find that SBAR can easily distinguish between two user groups: the short head part and the short tail part. However, it doesn't consider interactions between users. If we can take advantage of frequent interactions between high SBAR users and apply competition-based models to estimate relative user expertise score, we might get even better estimation results than using SBAR alone. We show that this can be achieved in the next section.

5.4.3 Best Answer Ratio vs. Competition-based Methods

From the experiment results on the first user set in Table 4, we can see that SVM significantly outperforms TS in terms of all evaluation metrics using GA data (Wilcoxon signed-rank test, in terms of RnDCG@1, RnDCG@3, nDCG@1 and nDCG@3 p-value<0.05; in terms of RnDCG@20 and nDCG@20, p-value<0.01). From the experimental results on the second user set in Table 4, we can see that SVM also outperforms TS in terms of the evaluation metrics using GA data (Wilcoxon signed-rank test, in terms of RnDCG@3, RnDCG@20, nDCG@3 and nDCG@20, p-value<0.01). The reason that SVM can outperform TS is that SVM considers the all pairwise comparisons globally; while TS considers each pairwise comparison one by one. TS was originally designed to track the changes of user skill by assuming that a user's skill will change over time. In our case, a user's expertise level will not change too much within a short period of time.

Comparing BAR and SBAR with TS and SVM on the first user set, we see that SVM significantly outperforms BAR and SBAR in terms of all evaluation metrics using GA data (Wilcoxon signed-rank test, in terms of RnDCG@1 and nDCG@1, p-value<0.05; in terms of RnDCG@3, RnDCG@20, nDCG@3 and nDCG@20, p-value<0.01). Also, it can be observed that TS outperforms BAR and SBAR in terms of all evaluation metrics using GA data (though, it doesn't pass the significant test). It shows that estimating relative user expertise scores of active users can benefit from modeling the interactions between users.

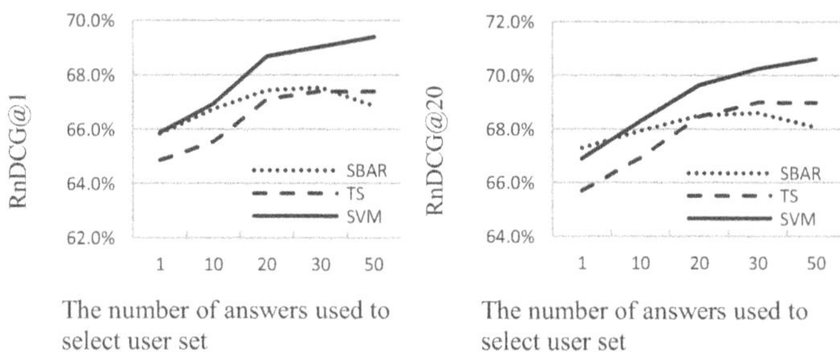

Figure 8. The performance of SBAR, TS and SVM on different user sets, in terms of RnDCG@1 and RnDCG@20

However, it can be observed that SBAR outperforms TS and SVM on the second user set. The reason is that competition-based models (TS and SVM) usually need more data about pairwise comparisons between users to learn well. However, for the low frequent users, there's only a small amount of interaction between them, which may be not enough for a pairwise comparison based competition model to learn the relative expertise scores well. If this is true, it would be interesting to know how active a user needs to be so that competition-based models (TS and SVM) can perform reasonably well and better than the strong baseline SBAR. Hence, we evaluate SBAR, TS and SVM on 5 different user sets selected by different active levels measured by the number of answers posted per user. Figure 8 shows the performance of SBAR, TS and SVM on 5 different user sets, in terms of RnDCG@1 and RnDCG@20, respectively. SVM performs much better than SBAR for the users who posted more than 20 answers. The trend of the TS performance curve is similar. With the increment of the number of answers, the performances of TS and SVM become better.

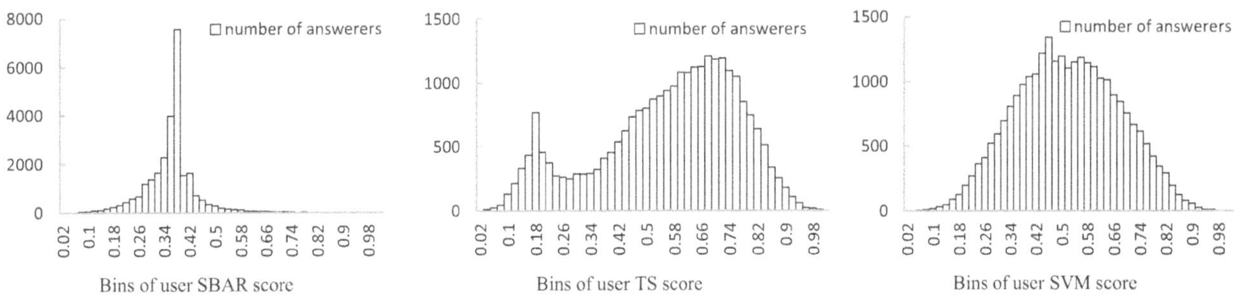

Figure 9. The frequency distributions of user score estimated by three methods (SBAR, TS and SVM) on internet category; only the answerers with at least one best answer are considered, user expertise score has been normalized into [0,1]

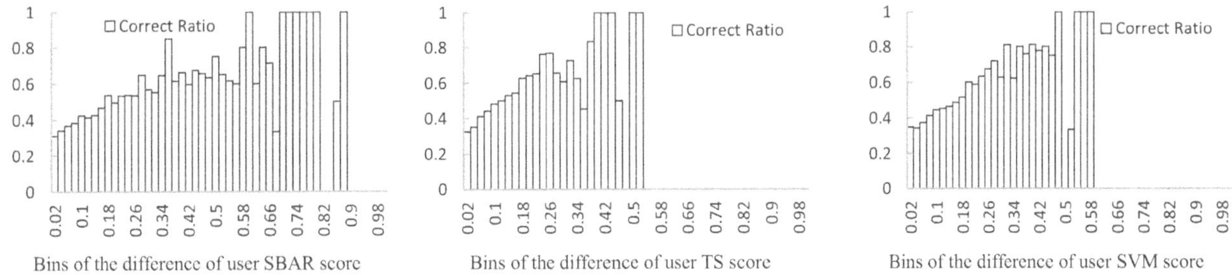

Figure 10. The ratio of correctly predicting pairwise competitions distributed over the difference of two users' expertise estimated by three methods (SBAR, TS and SVM); user expertise score has been normalized into [0,1]

In summary, the experimental results show that pairwise comparison based competition models (TS and SVM) perform better on active user sets. Specifically, SVM significantly outperforms two strong baselines, BAR and SBAR, on active user sets.

Figure 9 shows the frequency distributions of user expertise score estimated by three methods (SBAR, TS and SVM) in the internet category (it's similar in other categories). We make a very interesting observation that the distribution of the SVM score follows a normal distribution, which somewhat reflects our understanding of real world user behavior: (a) the expertise levels of most users are around the average level; (b) there is a small number of users with high expertise levels; (c) also, there is a small number of users with low expertise levels; this is probably due to the fact that users of low expertise are less likely to participate in knowledge sharing communities rather than lack of them. Comparing the score distributions of SBAR, TS, and SVM, we see that the distribution of SBAR score is much sharper.

5.5 Discriminative Power

Given a testing question with n answerers, there are $n(n-1)/2$ pairwise competitions between each two users that can be generated. Let $exp(u)$ denote the expertise score of user u estimated by a given method. Let $rel(a_u)$ denote the relevance level of the answer a provided by user u. For a pairwise competition (u_i, u_j), we say that there are three possible outcomes; (1) u_i is the winner and u_j is the loser when $rel(a_{u_i})$ is larger than $rel(a_{u_j})$; (2) u_i is the loser and u_j is the winner when $rel(a_{u_i})$ is smaller than $rel(a_{u_j})$; (3) it's a tie when $rel(a_{u_i})$ is equal to $rel(a_{u_j})$. We can use the sign of difference between $exp(u_i)$ and $exp(u_j)$ to predict the outcome of the given pairwise competition.

We say the prediction is correct when

$$sgn(exp(u_i) - exp(u_j)) = sgn(rel(a_{u_i}) - rel(a_{u_j})) \quad (12)$$

where

$$sgn(x) = \begin{cases} 1 & if\ x > 0 \\ 0 & if\ x = 0 \\ -1 & if\ x < 0 \end{cases}$$

In this section, we use the first selected question set in Table 4 as the testing data. There are 9,417 pairwise competitions generated. Table 5 shows the performance of SBAR, TS and SVM in predicting the outcome of the generated pairwise competitions. We see that SVM and TS perform better than SBAR.

Table 5. The performance of three methods (SBAR, TS and SVM) to predict the outcome of pairwise competitions

	Incorrect Pairs	Correct Pairs	Error Rate
SBAR	5272	4145	55.98%
TS	5269	4148	55.95%
SVM	**5161**	**4256**	**54.81%**

Furthermore, given a pairwise competition, it's expected that the larger the difference of two users' estimated expertise score, the higher the probability of correct prediction. In contrast to this, it's expected that the smaller the difference, the lower the probability of correct prediction. When the difference is small, it means that the given user expertise score estimation method cannot differentiate between two users well. Discriminative power is defined as the averaged ratio of correct predication at a given difference. Figure 10 shows the discriminative power of three methods (SBAR, TS and SVM) distributed over the difference of two users' expertise scores. Basically, we see that it holds for all three methods that the larger the difference, the higher the ratio of correct prediction. Additionally, we find that when the difference is smaller than a certain number, the ratio of correct predictions will be less than 0.5 (random). If this case happened when we applying user expertise scores on some downstream applications, we could not trust the prediction result by the user expertise score. Hence, the knowledge of the discriminative power of a score method can provide an informed guideline for other downstream applications on how to utilize the estimated user expertise score. For example, only use expertise score information when the score difference is within the discriminative power of the scoring method.

Because the scales of user expertise score output by different methods are different, it's hard to compare the discriminative power of different methods directly. Inspired by R. Herbrich et al. [10], we set six challenge competitions for SBAR, TS, and SVM. Let each method consider which pairwise competitions in the testing data are the most difficult to predict and present them to other methods. Using one user expertise score estimation method (defender), we can sort all 9,417 pairwise competitions in the testing data in non-descending order of the difference between two users' expertise scores and present the top 2,000 pairwise competitions for another user expertise score estimation method (challenger) to predict results. Table 6 shows the success ratio (correct prediction) of each challenger in each challenge competition between two user expertise score estimation methods. We see that SVM beats both TS and SBAR, and TS beats SBAR. It means that the pairwise competition based user expertise estimation method has better discriminative power than SBAR.

Table 6. Comparing the discriminative power of three methods (SBAR, TS and SVM) by using challenging modes

		Challenger		
		SBAR	TS	SVM
Defender	SBAR	N/A	694(34.7%)	**729(36.5%)**
	TS	679(34.0%)	N/A	**724 (36.2%)**
	SVM	**664(33.2%)**	**661 (33.1%)**	N/A

6. CONCLUSTION AND FEATURE WORK

In this paper, we presented two competition-based methods, TS and SVM, to estimate the relative expertise scores of users in CQA. We proposed two simple and intuitive principles and leveraged best answer selection to cast the relative expertise score estimation problem as a problem of relative skill estimation in two-player games where competition-based methods such as TS and SVM can be readily applied to estimate user expertise scores. For evaluation, we introduced an answer quality prediction based evaluation metric and used NTCIR-8 CQA data. We also are the first to introduce the idea of the relation between the discriminative power of scoring methods and their expected performance. Experimental results show that: (1) competition-based models significantly outperform link analysis based methods and pointwise methods; (2) competition-based models have better discriminative power. We also found that competition-based methods perform better when they have enough active users.

Future work may follow two paths: (1) expand the competition-based method into forums by incorporating automatic answer quality prediction; (2) analyze user knowledge to help find subject experts.

7. ACKNOWLEDGEMENT

We would like to thank Tao Qin and Yunbo Cao for their valuable suggestions on this paper, Matt Callcut for his proofreading of this paper, and the anonymous reviewers for their helpful comments on this work.

8. REFERENCES

[1] E. Agichtein, C. Castillo, D. Donato, A. Gionis, and G. Mishne. Finding high-quality content in social media. In *Proc. WSDM*, pages 183–194. 2008.

[2] J. Bian, Y. Liu, D. Zhou, E. Agichtein, and H. Zha. Learning to recognize reliable users and content in social media with coupled mutual reinforcement. In *Proc. WWW*, pages 51–60. 2009.

[3] M. Bouguessa, B. Dumoulin, and S. Wang. Identifying authoritative actors in question-answering forum: the case of Yahoo! answers. In *Proc. SIGKDD*, pages 866–874. 2008.

[4] S. Brin and L. Page. The anatomy of a large-scale hypertextual web search engine. In *Proc. WWW*. 1998.

[5] C. Campbell, P. Maglio, A. Cozzi, and B. Dom. Expertise identification using email communications. In *Proc. CIKM*, pages 528–531. 2003.

[6] B. Carterette and D. Petkova. Learning a ranking from pairwise preferences. In *Proc. SIGIR*, pages 629–630. 2006.

[7] G. Cong, L. Wang, C.-Y. Lin, Y. Song, and Y. Sun. Finding question-answer pairs from online forums. In *Proc. SIGIR*, pages 467–474. 2008.

[8] Elo. *The rating of chessplayers, past and present*. Batsford, 1978.

[9] R.-E. Fan, K.-W. Chang, C.-J. Hsieh, X.-R. Wang, and C.-J. Lin. LIBLINEAR: A library for large linear classification. *Journal of Machine Learning Research*, 9:1871–1874, 2008.

[10] R. Herbrich, T. Minka, and T. Graepel. TrueSkill: A Bayesian skill rating system. In *Proc. NIPS*, 20:569–576, 2007.

[11] D. Horowitz and S. Kamvar. The anatomy of a large-scale social search engine. In *Proc. WWW*, pages 431–440. 2010.

[12] J. Jeon, W. Croft, J. Lee, and S. Park. A framework to predict the quality of answers with non-textual features. In *Proc. SIGIR*, pages 228–235. 2006.

[13] Y. Jiang, W. Xiao, M. Ackerman, and L. Adamic. Activity lifespan: An analysis of user survival patterns in online knowledge sharing communities. In *Proc. AAAI*, 2010.

[14] P. Jurczyk and E. Agichtein. Discovering authorities in question answer communities by using link analysis. In *Proc. CIKM*, pages 919–922. 2007.

[15] J. Kleinberg. Authoritative sources in a hyperlinked environment. *Journal of the ACM (JACM)*, 46(5):604–632, 1999.

[16] B. Li and I. King. Routing Questions to Appropriate Answerers in Community Question Answering Services. In *Proc. CIKM*. 2010.

[17] Y. Liu, J. Bian, and E. Agichtein. Predicting information seeker satisfaction in community question answering. In *Proc. SIGIR*, pages 483–490. 2008.

[18] D. Mease. A penalized maximum likelihood approach for the ranking of college football teams independent of victory margins. *The American Statistician*, 57(4):241–248, 2003.

[19] Pal and J. Konstan. Expert identification in community question answering: exploring question selection bias. In *Proc. CIKM*. 2010.

[20] T. Sakai, D. Ishikawa, and N. Kando. Overview of the NTCIR-8 Community QA Pilot Task (Part II): System Evaluation. In *Proc. NTCIR-8*, pages 433–457, 2010.

[21] T. Sakai, D. Ishikawa, N. Kando, Y. Seki, K. Kuriyama, and C.-Y. Lin. Using Graded-Relevance Metrics for Evaluating Community QA Answer Selection. In *Proc. WSDM*. 2011.

[22] M. Suryanto, E. Lim, A. Sun, and R. Chiang. Quality-aware collaborative question answering: methods and evaluation. In *Proc. WSDM*, pages 142–151. 2009.

[23] J. Zhang, M. Ackerman, and L. Adamic. Expertise networks in online communities: structure and algorithms. In *Proc. WWW*, pages 221–230. 2007.

[24] D. Zhou, S. Orshanskiy, H. Zha, and C. Giles. Co-ranking authors and documents in a heterogeneous network. In *Proc. ICDM*, pages 739–744. 2008.

Learning Online Discussion Structures by Conditional Random Fields

Hongning Wang, Chi Wang, ChengXiang Zhai, Jiawei Han
Department of Computer Science
University of Illinois at Urbana-Champaign
Urbana IL, 61801 USA
{wang296, chiwang1, czhai, hanj}@cs.uiuc.edu

ABSTRACT

Online forum discussions are emerging as valuable information repository, where knowledge is accumulated by the interaction among users, leading to multiple threads with structures. Such replying structure in each thread conveys important information about the discussion content. Unfortunately, not all the online forum sites would explicitly record such replying relationship, making it hard for both users and computers to digest the information buried in a discussion thread.

In this paper, we propose a probabilistic model in the Conditional Random Fields framework to predict the replying structure for a threaded online discussion. Different from previous replying relation reconstruction methods, most of which fail to consider dependency between the posts, we cast the problem as a supervised structure learning problem to incorporate the features capturing the structural dependency and learn their relationship. Experiment results on three different online forums show that the proposed method can well capture the replying structures in online discussion threads, and multiple tasks such as forum search and question answering can benefit from the reconstructed replying structures.

Categories and Subject Descriptors

I.5.1 [**Pattern Recognition**]: Models - Statistical

General Terms

Algorithms, Measurement, Experimentation

Keywords

Threaded Discussion, Replying Relation Reconstruction, Structure Learning

1. INTRODUCTION

As the development of Web 2.0, more and more people take the advantage of online forum discussions to freely share and exchange their mind and knowledge. Valuable knowledge and information on various topics, e.g., sports, health, entertainment and etc., have been accumulated by this collaborative content contribution. More importantly, such knowledge can hardly be found in general web sites and encyclopedia, making forums a unique and valuable resource for extracting useful knowledge to facilitate other information seeking tasks, including forum search [2, 13], question answering [4, 6] and expert finding [21, 8].

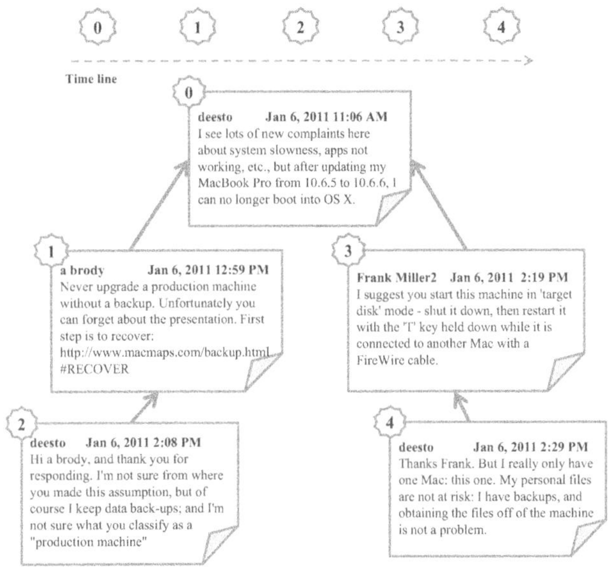

Figure 1: A sample threaded discussion from Apple Discussions

A typical online forum discussion originates from a root post, which initializes a topic for the following discussions, e.g., system failure in Mac OS X in Apple discussions as shown in Figure 1. The followers read existing messages and reply to the post they are informed of or most interested in. From temporal perspective, those replying posts form a chain structure, or thread (as shown in the time line in Figure 1). Replying posts can reply to any preceding post, forming branches of discussion as more users are joining in and making comments. As a result, the discussion thread grows and forms a tree structure from semantic perspective: one post has only one "reply-to" post, while one post can be replied to by multiple posts.

The semantic tree structure is helpful for both human to digest the discussion content and automatic method to ex-

SIGIR'11, July 24–28, 2011, Beijing, China.

tract useful information from it. From user's perspective, it would save a lot of effort to track and get involved in the discussion if the site provides a tree view of the current discussion structure. [13, 5] demonstrate that incorporating the replying relationship boosts the forum retrieval performance; Zhang et al. [21] show that ranking users by their replying relationship would further help to identify the experts in online communities than solely by their post counts.

Nevertheless, such tree structure is not always present in most of online discussion sites. Because phpBB (`http://www.phpbb.com`) and vBulletin (`http://www.vbulletin.com`), which are two most popular softwares to build the online discussion site, do not provide a threaded view as default [13], flat-view online community pages are much more prevalent. In the flat-view systems, the replying relation is not explicitly recorded (some of them contain partial content from the replied post as quotation), and all the posts in one thread are positioned by the chronological order.

In this circumstance, reconstructing the replying relationship from the flat-view discussion forums would be useful. However, this reconstruction task is quite challenging: 1) posts in a discussion thread are temporally dependent upon each other - users always read some of the previous messages before posting; 2) most of the posts are short and highly context dependent, solely examining the post content is inadequate to understand the replying relationship between the posts; 3) rich features are needed to perform better prediction - user's replying habits, friendship and even their online periods are all potential features helpful for analyzing the threaded discussions.

Several approaches have been proposed to address this kind of reconstruction task. A topic modeling based approach is proposed in [11], where the temporal relationship is incorporated into semantic modeling of threaded discussions. In [13], the reconstruction task is converted into a retrieval problem, in which the authors proposed various features to train a Ranking SVM model. Wang et al. [19] utilize a variant of Latent Semantic Analysis (LSA) method to overcome the sparseness in online discussion contents and identify the replying post pairs.

Previous work mainly focused on applying content analysis techniques to identify the replying relation between the posts. However, they do not take other factors, e.g. users interactions and structural dependency, into consideration. In this paper, we cast this replying relationship reconstruction problem as a structural learning task and propose a threadCRF model to solve it in the probabilistic model framework. Various features are incorporated into the proposed threadCRF to capture both long-range and short-range dependencies among the posts. To estimate the relative importance of those features, a supervised learning framework is employed. A set of novel evaluation metrics is introduced to access the quality of structural prediction. Experiment results on three different forum collections, Apple Discussion (`http://discussions.apple.com/`), Google Earth Community (`http://bbs.keyhole.com/`) and CNET forums (`http://forums.cnet.com/`), confirm the effectiveness of the proposed method: structure reconstruction quality gets encouraging improvement over the baseline methods; tasks like forum retrieval and community question answering benefit from the reconstructed replying structure. More importantly, the proposed method is adaptive and generalizes well when trained on different domains.

2. RELATED WORK

Much work has been done recently on extracting information from online forums. Ding et al. [4] extract contexts and answers for the questions from online forums; Shi et al. [15] analyze the user grouping behaviors in online forums; Cong et al. [3] detect the question-answer pairs in the threaded discussions.

Different from the traditional document repository, online forum discussions have their unique internal replying structures, which are crucial for correctly understanding the discussion contents. Xu et al. [20] illustrate as much as 75% of the links in a typical forum page points to noise pages like user profiles, login pages etc., and hence link-based algorithms like PageRank and HITS cannot be used effectively. Besides, they also demonstrate content-induced links are more helpful for ranking forum pages. Seo et al. [13] state that using thread structures to estimate language models improves forum search performance. In [8], Jurczyk et al. show that the linkage pattern can be used to help identify the quality of answers in the online community environment.

However, the replying structure of a threaded discussion is not always available, and some work has been proposed to reconstruct the conversional structures. Shen et al. [14] treat the reconstruction task as a content-based clustering problem and propose to use the clusters of posts as the sub-threads in a threaded discussion. However, this method does not identify the explicit parent-child relations within each cluster. Wang et al. [18] use a graph-based connectivity matrix, in which both content similarity and temporal information are utilized, to recover thread structure. But the parameters are manually tuned in the proposed method. In [11], Lin et al. incorporate the temporal relationship into semantic modeling of threaded discussions based on the statistical topic model. Unfortunately, their model cannot directly predict the replying relationship, and they depend on an additional distance measure in the projected topic space to find the "closest" replying post pairs. In [13], Seo et al. converted this structure prediction task into a ranking problem: each post is considered as a query, and parent candidate posts are considered as the documents to be retrieved. Multiple features are utilized to learn a Ranking SVM model. But because Ranking SVM can only take the post's pairwise interaction into consideration, it fails to directly model the whole discussion structure.

In this paper, various kind of features, from content similarity and posting time gap to user interactions, are introduced in the proposed probabilistic model to capture both the long-range and short-range dependencies within a discussion thread. In addition, to judge the quality of the structure prediction, we design a set of new evaluation metrics, in which we emphasize more about the structure preservability in the good predicted result.

3. PROBLEM DEFINITION

Before introducing the proposed method in detail, we would first define some concepts that would be referred to in later discussions.

Formally, let $T = \{X_0, X_1, \ldots, X_N\}$ be a set of thread discussions from a particular online forum site; each thread X_n consists of m individual posts $\{p_0, p_1, \ldots, p_{m-1}\}$ arranged in the chronological order. In each post p_i of thread X_n, there are 5 attributes: 1) post ID, ranging from [0, m); 2) post content c_i, modeled as a bag of words; 3) author name u_i, the displayed author name for the post; 4) author ID a_i, a unique user identifier in the whole forum; and 5) posting time t_i, the system time stamp when the post is created. In this work, we only assume the above five general post attributes, which should be found in most of the online discussion forum sites; other site-specific attributes, such as post quotations and tree views, are not considered.

Definition (Root Post) Root post is the first post in one discussion thread according to its posting time. It initiates the topic of discussion in this thread.

Definition (Previous Post) Previous post of p_i is the post posted closest in prior to p_i in the chronological order.

Definition (Parent Post) Post p_i is said to be the parent post of p_j if and only if p_j is posted later than p_i and contains an immediate follow-up discussion of p_i. In the threaded-view forum site, this information is indicated by "in response to" or a reply tree. Such pairwise relationship is called "replying to" relation, which is asymmetric.

Definition (Thread Structure) The thread structure defined by the "replying to" relation between posts is strictly a tree: posts in X_n, except for the root post, can only and must have one parent post in X_n. Each path in this tree forms a self-consistent sub-threaded discussion. Such a structure is intuitively demonstrated in Figure 1.

Based on the above definitions, the task of reply relation reconstruction is equivalent to assigning every post p_i in thread X_n a parent post p_{y_i}, which makes every sub-threaded discussion consistent and coherent. We call such parent labeling sequence as Y_n for each X_n.

4. METHOD

Although the "replying to" relation between two posts is defined according to their semantic relations in Section 3, the interaction patterns among the replying posts are far beyond what can be observed merely from the post content. Because most of the posts are very short, content similarity is inadequate to infer the correct replying to relationship. Besides, the involvement of user interactions makes it even harder to predict the replying relation. For example, users are more likely to reply to the post which has replied to him/her before; root post tends to receive more replies than other posts. Another important character of threaded discussion is that the post contents are highly context dependent: the topic focus is evolving during the discussion, so that in order to understand the intension of a certain post it is often necessary to find the conversational information hidden in the related posts. Nevertheless, due to the intra-dependencies among the posts in one thread, such correspondence is not known until we recover the whole replying structure. Thus the difficulty arises from the intuition that every local prediction depends on all the other posts' reply-to assignment in the same thread. On the other hand, the internal dependencies within the replying structure provide regularization over each local prediction, which helps the overall prediction in turn: when we have high confidence on recovering some parts of the thread, the prediction on the less certain parts will become easier with the assumption that the local predictions can be propagated. Intuitively, the assumption holds if we can properly identify the dependency among the predictions. Besides, as there are various types of factors interacting and suggesting different level of dependency, including users, post contents and time, it is hard to determine their relative importance without learning from the data. Therefore, we need an appropriate mechanism to encode the structural dependency among such factors in a systematic way. To achieve this goal, we cast the thread replying relation reconstruction task as a structure learning problem, and propose a thread Conditional Random Field (threadCRF) model to solve it.

4.1 Thread Conditional Random Field

Our main focus in this paper is to exploit the dependencies among the posts, which can facilitate us to better identify the correct structures from the threaded discussion. Probabilistic graphical models provide a systematic methodology to describe and manipulate the short-range and long-range dependencies in both observed data and unknown predictions. By properly defining the features (or potential functions) in the joint/conditional probability, arbitrary dependencies could be encoded and their relative importance can be captured by the feature's weight.

In our reconstruction task, we are more interested in modeling the conditional probability of the replying relationship Y_n given the posts $\{p_0, p_1, \ldots, p_{m-1}\}$ in thread X_n, i.e., $p(Y_n|X_n)$, than their joint probability $p(X_n, Y_n)$. Therefore, Conditional Random Fields (CRFs) [10], which is a family of probabilistic models for sequence segmentation and labeling problems, is the nature choice for solving this problem. By directly modeling the conditional probability, we can flexibly introduce any meaningful features, particularly dependent features of the observed sequence without having to model the distribution of those dependencies.

Following the basic concepts in traditional CRFs, we propose a threadCRF model to capture the dependency among the posts within one thread based on various kinds of features describing the interactions in both posts and authors, and estimate the weights for the designed features in a supervised manner.

In threadCRF, we define the conditional distribution over replying relationship given post sequence X_n as:

$$p(Y_n|X_n) \propto \exp\Big(\sum_{k=1}^{K} \lambda_k f_k(Y_n, X_n)\Big) \tag{1}$$

where $\{f_k(Y_n, X_n)\}_{k=1}^K$ is a set of features defined on the given thread X_n and its parent labeling sequence Y_n; $\{\lambda_k\}_{k=1}^K$ are the weights for the corresponding features.

Thus, given a model $\Theta = \{\lambda_k\}_{k=1}^K$, the replying relation reconstruction task in our threadCRF could be formulated as a Maximum a Posteriori (MAP) inference problem: for each given thread X, we aim to find the optimal replying structure Y', such that,

$$Y' = argmax_{Y \in \mathscr{Y}} p(Y|X, \Theta) \tag{2}$$

where $\mathscr{Y}$ is the set of all the possible replying structures for the given thread X.

Within such a framework, the key challenge is to define a proper set of features by which the dependencies among the posts could be explicitly captured. In this paper, we design

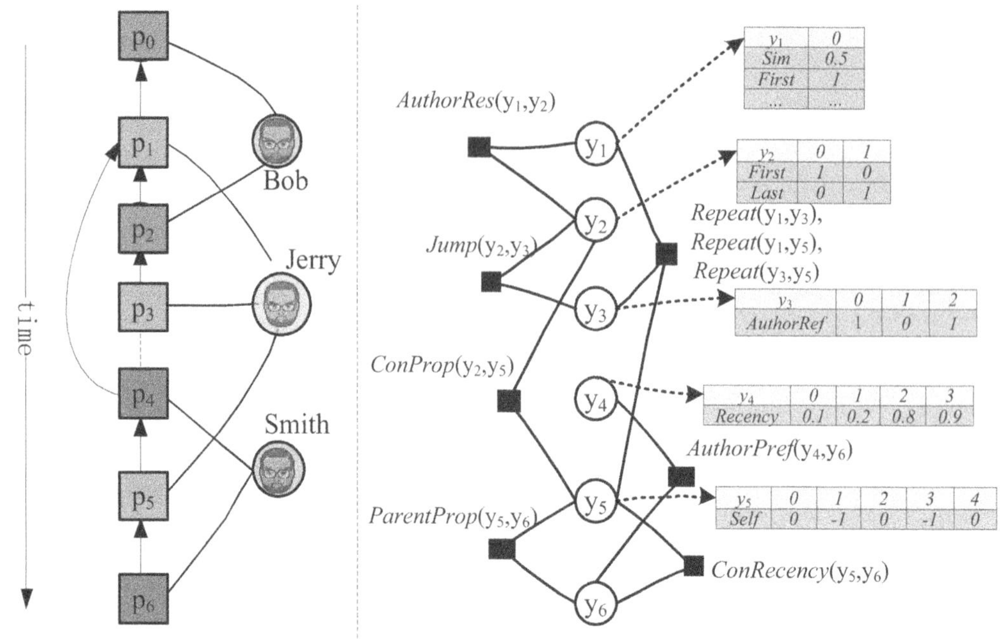

Figure 2: The graphical representation of the proposed threadCRF model, and an illustration of two kinds of features employed. On the left is an example of a threaded discussion; its corresponding factor graph induced by the proposed features is shown on the right. For each node in the factor graph, only a part of related features is shown due to space limit. Node features are listed in the table connected to the related variables by dotted line; edge features are represented by solid rectangles.

features to model both posts' replying patterns and users' interactions in the threaded discussion environment.

4.2 Features

We define two kinds of features, each of which can be formalized by some particular feature functions. The first kind of features depicts the local potential of replying relations, i.e., how likely post p_i replies to p_j if they are close in posting time. Such features can be defined by a function on p_i and its *own* parent assignment p_{y_i}, and outputs a certain confidence measure of this replying pair based on the observed attributes from p_i and p_{y_i}. The second kind of features captures the long-range dependency among the predictions, e.g., users prefer to reply to the post which has replied to him/her before. Such kind of feature functions for posts p_i and p_j not only depends on the observed attributes, but also on the unknown parent assignments for *both* p_i and p_j, since the parent prediction on one of these two posts would affect the parent assignment for the other. Using the language of probabilistic graphical models [9], we treat each post parent assignment as a random variable, and depict the dependency among the features by a factor graph, where the edges are connected by the defined features (as shown in Figure 2). In a factor graph, any complicated dependency can be decomposed into factor functions defined on edges. We can then propagate local predictions along the edges within the graph to find the global optimal prediction.

Previous methods [13] mostly operate on node features, and therefore they are performing isolated predictions for each post. The edge features proposed in this paper are new and can capture more complex dependency than those handled by the node features. Altogether, we propose six node features and seven edge features for our threadCRF. The proposed threadCRF incorporates both kind of features and learns the weights from the given training corpus.

4.2.1 Node features

Node features *only* depend on the observed attributes in post p_i and p_j, i.e., solely from the observed attributes of p_i and p_j, to determine how likely p_i is replying to p_j.

Content Similarity *Sim(y_i)*: the content similarity between post p_i and p_{y_i}. One post tends to reply to another if they are talking about similar topics. We use the standard *TF-IDF* weighted cosine similarity [12], where *IDF* is calculated based on the number of posts containing the word in the given thread.

First Post *First(y_i)*: a binary feature to test if post p_i is replying to the root post. In the threaded discussions, root post initiates the topic for the followers to discuss; as a result, the following posts tend to reply to the root post.

Last Post *Last(y_i)*: a binary feature to test whether post p_i is replying to its previous post. Since in the conversational discussions, authors exchange their ideas in turn. One post in the dialog tends to directly reply to its previous post.

Author Reference *AuthorRef(y_i)*: a binary feature to test whether post p_{y_i}'s author is mentioned in the content of post p_i. In the threaded discussions, especially in the flat-view forum site, to clearly point to the receiver, some posts would directly mention the name of the author of the post he/she is now replying to.

Time Recency *Recency(y_i)*: the time proximity between posting time of post p_i and p_{y_i}. A small time difference between two posts could be an evidence of the replying relationship. We use the time difference between post p_i and the root post to normalize the time difference between the root post and p_{y_i}. We should note the feature ***Recency(y_i)*** is different from ***Last(y_i)***, since ***Recency(y_i)*** is more sensitive to the actual time gap. When ***Recency(y_i)*** approaches 0, it indicates there is a long period of time when no one has followed the previous discussion; as a result, the chance that p_i still replies to p_j would get lower though p_j is p_i's previous post.

Reply to Oneself ***Self(y_i)***: a binary feature to test if post p_i and p_{y_i} are posted by the same author. Since the discussion forum is a place to share and exchange opinions, we assume one author should seldom reply to his/her own post. We should admit that there exist such situations, where the authors want to clarify or expand his/her previous claim. But we believe those cases happen with an arguably small probability and thus assign negative credit for this feature.

4.2.2 Edge features

Edge features are defined over *two* parent assignments y_i and y_j (i>j) together with the observed attributes in p_i and p_j, i.e., (X, Y), to emphasize the dependencies between y_i and y_j. We can either boost or penalize their interactions to reflect our assumptions on the replying structure.

Repeat Reply ***Repeat(y_i, y_j)***: A binary feature to penalize the replying pattern where p_i and p_j reply to the same post, when p_i and p_j are written by the same author. This feature is designed to capture the intuition that users seldom reply to their own posts.

Jumping Reply ***Jump(y_i, y_j)***: A binary feature to penalize the replying pattern where p_i replies to an earlier post p_k by p_j's author a_j rather than its closest preceding post p_j. The intuition behind this feature is that in a conversational discussion, once people get replies from a recent post, he/she is unlikely to jump to an earlier post by the same author to start another conversation.

Author Response ***AuthorRes(y_i, y_j)***: A binary feature to reward the replying from p_i to p_j, if p_j's author a_j has replied to p_i's author a_i before. As the nature of threaded discussion, people discuss with each other in turn and make the conversation evolving. To track this reply/response pattern, we check when p_i replies to the author of p_j, whether post p_j has replied to the author of p_i before.

Author Preference ***AuthorPref(y_i, y_j)***: a binary feature to reward the pattern that post p_i and p_j reply to the same author when p_i and p_j are from one same author. The intention of this feature is to capture the preference of replying pattern between friends against other unknown users, who have not replied to each other before.

Content Propagation ***ConProp(y_i, y_j)***: cosine similarity between post p_i and p_j's parent post p_{y_j}, if p_i is replying to p_j. As we mentioned before, post contents are usually short and highly context dependent. In some cases, people have to borrow some content from one post's parent or even grandparents to understand its topic. To simulate this process, we assume that when p_i is replying to p_j, its content should be somehow similar to p_j's parent's content; in other words, we propagate information from p_j's parent to identify the possibility of p_i is replying to p_j.

Parent Propagation ***ParentProp(y_i, y_j)***: cosine similarity between post p_i and p_j, if they are replying to the same post. Similarity is a symmetric measurement, while replying relation is asymmetric. When two posts are similar to each other, they might be talking about similar topics in a replying relationship, or replying to the same post discussing the parallel aspects. The former is encoded in feature ***Sim(y_i)***, and ***ParentProp(y_i, y_j)*** is designed to catch the latter possibility.

Conversation Recency ***ConRecency(y_i, y_j)***: similar to ***Recency(y_i)*** by assuming a later post has a higher chance to be replied to. But in this feature, we calculate the normalized time gap between three consecutive posts in a conversation: if p_i replies to p_j while p_j replies to p_k, the time gap between p_j and p_k normalized by the time gap between p_i and p_k is used to measure the recency between y_i and y_j in the conversation. The intuition is that ***Recency(y_i)*** only considers the time gap in the whole thread (normalized by parent p_i's posting time to the root), while ***ConRecency(y_i, y_j)*** is designed to capture the recency in each possible subthread discussion. In other words, a newer post tends to join a recently hot discussion in the whole thread.

Table 1: Features for thread reconstruction task

Type	Feature
Node	$\textbf{\textit{Sim}}(y_i = j) = \cos(c_i, c_j)$
	$\textbf{\textit{First}}(y_i) = \begin{cases} 1 & y_i = 0 \\ 0 & \text{otherwise} \end{cases}$
	$\textbf{\textit{Last}}(y_i) = \begin{cases} 1 & y_i = i-1 \\ 0 & \text{otherwise} \end{cases}$
	$\textbf{\textit{AuthorRef}}(y_i = j) = \begin{cases} 1 & c_j \text{ contains } a_i\text{'s name} \\ 0 & \text{otherwise} \end{cases}$
	$\textbf{\textit{Recency}}(y_i = j) = (t_j - t_0)/(t_i - t_0)$
	$\textbf{\textit{Self}}(y_i = j) = \begin{cases} -1 & a_i = a_j \\ 0 & \text{otherwise} \end{cases}$
Edge	$\textbf{\textit{Repeat}}(y_i, y_j) = \begin{cases} -1 & a_i = a_j, y_i = y_j \\ 0 & \text{otherwise} \end{cases}$
	$\textbf{\textit{Jump}}(y_i, y_j) = \begin{cases} -1 & t_{y_i} < t_j, a_{y_i} = a_j, a_{y_j} = a_i \\ 0 & \text{otherwise} \end{cases}$
	$\textbf{\textit{AuthorRes}}(y_i, y_j) = \begin{cases} 1 & a_{y_j} = a_i, y_i = j \\ 0 & \text{otherwise} \end{cases}$
	$\textbf{\textit{AuthorPref}}(y_i, y_j) = \begin{cases} 1 & a_i = a_j, a_{p_i} = a_{p_j} \\ 0 & \text{otherwise} \end{cases}$
	$\textbf{\textit{ConProp}}(y_i, y_j) = \delta(y_i = j)\cos(c_i, c_{p_j})$
	$\textbf{\textit{ParentProp}}(y_i, y_j) = \delta(y_i = y_j)\cos(c_i, c_j)$
	$\textbf{\textit{ConRecency}}(y_i, y_j) = (t_j - t_{y_j})/(t_i - t_{y_j})$

Table 1 summarizes the definitions of these 13 different features, and Figure 2 gives an intuitive illustration of the effects introduced by those features.

The proposed edge features introduce many large-size cliques (in some extreme case the whole thread forms a fully connected graph), which make threadCRF more complex than the commonly used linear chain CRFs[10], skip-chain [16] and even 2D [22] CRFs. Exact inference is intractable in this situation, and we appeal to approximation methods to perform the Maximum a Posteriori inference and model learning.

4.3 Inference and Learning Method

We perform approximate Maximum a Posteriori (MAP) inference for Eq(2) based on a schedule for loopy belief propagation named Tree Reparameterizaton (TRP) [17], which breaks the loops in the induced graph into its spanning trees, and perform exact inference on such generated trees. TRP typically provides quick convergence and more accurate approximation results.

To learn the relative importance of the proposed features, we estimate the weights for each feature in a supervised manner. Given a training set of threads $T = \{X_1, X_2, \ldots, X_N\}$ with ground-truth replying relationship $R = \{Y_1, Y_2, \ldots, Y_N\}$, we need to estimate the optimal model setting $\overline{\Theta} = \{\overline{\lambda_k}\}_{k=1}^{K}$, which maximizes the conditional likelihood defined in Eq(1) over the training set.

The log-likelihood function could be represented as:

$$L_\Theta = \sum_{n=1}^{N} \log p(Y_n|X_n,\Theta) = \sum_i \left[\Theta^T F(Y_n,X_n) - \log Z_\Theta(X_i)\right] \quad (3)$$

where $F(Y_n, X_n)$ are the accumulated feature values defined in Table 1, and $Z_\Theta(X_n) = \sum_Y \exp(\Theta^T F(Y, X_n))$.

To avoid overfitting, we penalize the likelihood with a spherical Gaussian weight prior $\lambda \sim N(0, \sigma^2)$. By taking the derivative of this object function, we get:

$$\nabla L_\Theta = \sum_{n=1}^{N} \left[F(Y_n,X_n) - E_{p_\Theta(Y|X_n)} F(Y,X_n)\right] - \frac{\lambda}{\sigma^2} \quad (4)$$

The first part in Eq(4) is the accumulated empirical feature values in the training set, the second part is the expectation of the features' occurrences in the given training data, which could be efficiently calculated by TRP inferencer, and the last part is the regularization term from the Gaussian prior. This derivative is easy to understand: the maximum likelihood of the training data is reached when the empirical average of the global feature vector equals to its model expectation. L-BFGS algorithm is employed to optimize the object function Eq(3) by the gradient.

5. EXPERIMENTS

5.1 Forum Data Set

We collect 51,716 threads from three different online discussion forums with ground-truth replying relations: Apple Discussion (`http://discussions.apple.com`), Google Earth Community (`http://bbs.keyhole.com`) and CNET (`http://forums.cnet.com`) [5], for evaluation. Apple Discussion and CNET are two computer support forums, where people seek helps for the technical problems they encountered in hardware and software; while Google Earth Community is an entertainment focused forum, where people share interesting findings in the Google Earth software. Apple Discussion and Google Earth threads collections are available at `http://timan.cs.uiuc.edu/downloads.html`.

We perform simple preprocessing on these three collections to refine the evaluation corpus: 1) remove the threads with less than 3 posts, because we don't need to reconstruct the structure for such threads; 2) remove the threads with inconsistent posting time, i.e., earlier post replies to a later one; 3) remove a standard list of stop words [1] and punctuation from each post's content attribute. The basic statistics of the evaluation corpus are shown in Table 2.

Table 2: Summary of evaluation corpus

	#Thread	#User	Max #Posts	Posts /Thread	Tokens /Post
Apple	7,316	11,118	255	6.2	33.3
Google	8,636	6,936	251	7.4	17.6
CNET	15,886	14,382	38	4.9	46.1

From Table 2, we can get a brief sense of the differences between these three collections: 1) in Apple Discussion and CNET, people use more words to explain/answer the problems in their posts, while the posts in Google Earth are much shorter, where people only post links to the attractions they found in Google Earth with very few word descriptions; 2) users discuss more actively in Google Earth (1.25 thread/user) than other forums (0.66 thread/user in Apple Discussion and 1.10 thread/user in CNET).

5.2 Evaluation Criterion

Previous studies on replying relationship reconstruction only employ accuracy on the predicted edges (Acc_{edge}) as the evaluation criterion [11, 19]. However, we argue that such measurement is not sufficient to judge the goodness of the predicted structure: it only evaluates the point-wise predictions on each node, but loses sight on the predicted structure as a whole. We can use the example thread shown in Figure 1 to illustrate the defect in edge accuracy measurement.

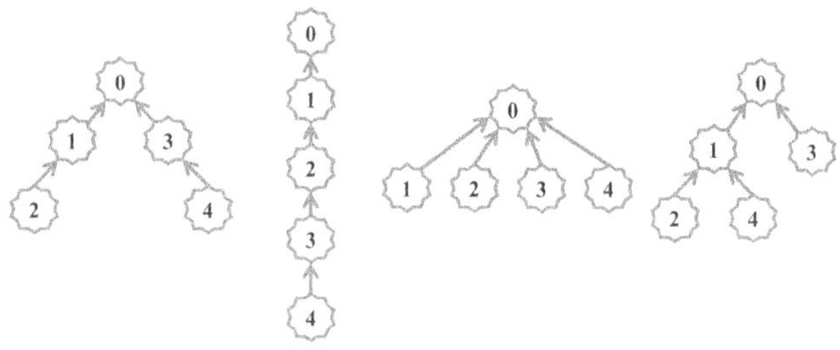

Figure 3: Example reconstruction results for thread shown in Figure 1

Figure 3 lists three different reconstruction results with the ground-truth structure. Both (b) and (d) achieved the same Acc_{edge} of 0.75 (3 out of 4 predictions are correct), which is better than (c)'s Acc_{edge} of 0.5. However, from the point of structural preservation, result (b) (a chain) is quite different from the original structure (a tree), and result (d) is arguably better from this perspective. Besides, when we take the actual discussion content into consideration, structure (b) misleads us: *Frank Miller2* in post 3 is actually replying to *dessto* in post 0 to give a possible solution in his/her first question, rather than to explain *dessto*'s further concern in post 2. Result (b) mistakenly connects post 3 to post 2, which changes the whole context. Therefore, to correctly maintain the discussion context in the scenario of conversational replying reconstruction, a mistake at higher level of the replying tree should incur more serious penalty than the one at a lower level.

To address this problem and more appropriately evaluate the quality of the predicted structure with respect to the ground-truth, we define a set of novel metrics. Formally, suppose $\overline{Y} = \{\overline{y}_0, \ldots, \overline{y}_{m-1}\}$ is the ground-truth structure for thread X, and $Y' = \{y'_0, \ldots, y'_{m-1}\}$ is the prediction. To evaluate how well the discussion context is preserved for each node in the tree, we define path accuracy Acc_{path} as the proportion of correct path from each node to root:

$$\text{Acc}_{path} = \frac{\sum_{i=1}^{m-1} \delta\left[path_{\overline{Y}}(i) = path_{Y'}(i)\right]}{m-1} \quad (5)$$

where $path_{\overline{Y}}(i)$ and $path_{Y'}(i)$ are the set of nodes lying in the path from node i to the root node in ground truth $\overline{Y}$

and prediction Y' respectively. For example, $path_{Y'}(4)$ in Figure 3.(b) is {4,3,2,1,0}.

Acc_{path} measures if we can read from root to a particular post without missing a post, nor meeting an irrelevant one from other branch. To relax the strict whole path matching requirement, we compute the overlap between the path from one node to the root in ground-truth versus in the predicted path, and define path precision P_{path} and recall R_{path} as:

$$P_{path} = \frac{\sum_{i=1}^{m-1} ||path_{\bar{Y}}(i) \subset path_{Y'}(i)||}{m-1} \quad (6)$$

$$R_{path} = \frac{\sum_{i=1}^{m-1} ||path_{Y'}(i) \subset path_{\bar{Y}(i)}||}{m-1} \quad (7)$$

where $||S||$ is the size of set S.

Above path-based metrics emphasize the correct prediction of the nodes with more decedents at higher level of a tree: since we are counting path from every node to the root, higher level nodes will be involved multiple times by its decedents, in that case a mistake at higher levels would incur a more serious penalty.

Another important aspect that should be evaluated is how well a node's local structure is preserved. When one node is a branching node, it's crucial to recover all its child nodes to get the correct track of its sub-trees. For the same sake of allowing inexact match and distinguishing the missing case versus the incorrect-inserting case, we define node precision P_{node} and recall R_{node} as the overlap between the child node set of each node in ground-truth and prediction:

$$P_{node} = \frac{\sum_{i=0}^{m-2} ||child_{\bar{Y}}(i) \subset child_{Y'}(i)||}{m-1} \quad (8)$$

$$R_{node} = \frac{\sum_{i=0}^{m-2} ||child_{Y'}(i) \subset child_{\bar{Y}}(i)||}{m-1} \quad (9)$$

where $child_{\bar{Y}}(i)$ and $child_{Y'}(i)$ are node i's child node set in the corresponding structures. The summation is taken from 0 to m-2 since the last post does not have a child node.

As a commonly used compromise between precision and recall, we also define F-value for the proposed P_{path}, R_{path} and P_{node}, R_{node} as the harmonic mean of these two metrics. Now, we can take the example in Figure 3 to justify the proposed metrics: result (b) achieves Acc_{path} of 0.5, $F1_{path}$ of 0.66 and $F1_{node}$ of 0.75, while result (d) receives Acc_{path} of 0.75, $F1_{path}$ of 0.75 and $F1_{node}$ of 0.75, which is much closer to our intuitive expectation.

When we are evaluating in the corpus level, we could average all the above metrics in the thread level, known as Micro average, or in the whole corpus level, known as Macro average. In the following experiments, we employ both Micro/Marco performance as the evaluation metrics.

5.3 Reply Relation Reconstruction

To compare the effectiveness of the proposed method, we employ several baseline methods: 1) reply to Root Post (FIRST); 2) reply to Previous Post (LAST); 3) ranking by similarity (SIM), in which we use the same cosine similarity measure as ***sim*(y_i)** feature in threadCRF to select the precede most similar post as the parent post. Beside the unsupervised methods, we also use Seo et al.'s supervised Ranking SVM [13] as the baseline, where we use all our node features to train the Ranking SVM model, since Ranking SVM cannot deal with edge features. We use the default parameter setting as in Ranking SVM [7].

Because Apple Discussion and Google Earth are two types of online discussion sites, it would be interesting to compare the methods' performance on these two different domains. We use 75% threads in each collection as the training set and the rest threads for the testing purpose. The reported performance is calculated based on the evaluation criteria proposed in Section 5.2.

Table 3: Prediction performance on Apple

		FIRST	LAST	SIM	Ranking SVM	thread CRF
Acc_{edge}	Micro	0.4241	0.6598	0.5011	0.6977	**0.7350**
	Macro	0.5433	0.6912	0.5999	0.7534	**0.7858**
Acc_{path}	Micro	0.4241	0.4312	0.3918	0.4843	**0.5691**
	Macro	0.5433	0.5632	0.5322	0.6365	**0.6966**
P_{path}	Micro	**1.0000**	0.4312	0.6834	0.6681	0.7254
	Macro	**1.0000**	0.5632	0.7852	0.7780	0.8009
R_{path}	Micro	0.4241	**1.0000**	0.5524	0.7264	0.7559
	Macro	0.5433	**1.0000**	0.6744	0.8176	0.8564
$F1_{path}$	Micro	0.5956	0.6026	0.6110	0.6960	**0.7403**
	Macro	0.7041	0.7206	0.7256	0.7973	**0.8278**
P_{node}	Micro	**0.9097**	0.6598	0.7103	0.7675	0.8228
	Macro	**0.8909**	0.6912	0.7531	0.8090	0.8372
R_{node}	Micro	0.4846	**0.8461**	0.6339	0.8189	0.8315
	Macro	0.5774	0.8571	0.6974	0.8438	**0.8661**
$F1_{node}$	Micro	0.6324	0.7414	0.6699	0.7923	**0.8271**
	Macro	0.7006	0.7653	0.7242	0.8260	**0.8514**

Table 4: Prediction performance on Google

		FIRST	LAST	SIM	Ranking SVM	threadCRF
Acc_{edge}	Micro	0.4897	0.5524	0.5117	0.6285	**0.6308**
	Macro	0.5787	0.6325	0.6122	0.6920	**0.7147**
Acc_{path}	Micro	0.4897	0.3468	0.4016	0.4820	**0.5213**
	Macro	0.5787	0.5178	0.5514	0.6114	**0.6495**
P_{path}	Micro	**1.0000**	0.3468	0.5968	0.7000	0.7679
	Macro	**1.0000**	0.5178	0.7380	0.8157	0.8331
R_{path}	Micro	0.4897	**1.0000**	0.6593	0.6964	0.6745
	Macro	0.5787	**1.0000**	0.7480	0.7530	0.7727
$F1_{path}$	Micro	0.6575	0.5149	0.6265	0.6982	**0.7182**
	Macro	0.7332	0.6823	0.7430	0.7831	**0.8017**
P_{node}	Micro	**0.9231**	0.5524	0.7350	0.7468	0.8013
	Macro	**0.8941**	0.6325	0.7716	0.8001	0.8218
R_{node}	Micro	0.5510	**0.8168**	0.7029	0.7764	0.7523
	Macro	0.6122	**0.8381**	0.7422	0.7849	0.7995
$F1_{node}$	Micro	0.6901	0.6591	0.7186	0.7613	**0.7760**
	Macro	0.7267	0.7210	0.7566	0.7924	**0.8105**

From the results in Table 3 and Table 4, we can find that the proposed threadCRF model outperforms both the unsupervised and supervised baseline methods in these two different collections. The reason heuristic rule-based method FIRST has perfect P_{path} is that all the posts are directly connected to the root post and no other posts can lie in between. The similar reasoning works for LAST's R_{path} performance. However, these two simple heuristics could not capture the real replying structure in the data; as a result, their F1 performance is worse than the supervised learning methods. Besides, we can also find that similarity alone (**SIM**) is far from enough to predict the correct replying structures. The proposed threadCRF works better than Ranking SVM under most of performance metrics: threadCRF improves over 17.65% in Micro Acc_{path} and 9.44% in Marco Acc_{path} against Ranking SVM, which two are the strictest criteria to judge the goodness of the predicted structures. In addition, we perform the paired randomization test with $p<0.05$, which shows the statistical significance of improvements over the Ranking SVM. The comparison results with both the unsupervised heuristic rules and supervised Ranking SVM confirm the benefits of modeling the dependency among the posts in one thread, and the proposed threadCRF model correctly exploits the interactions in both posts and users by the introduced edge features.

When the thread size gets larger, i.e., more than 10 posts, it becomes harder for human to digest and understand the discussion content, and therefore, it is more necessary to perform automatically replying relation reconstruction in this situation. From another perspective, the evaluation performance might be biased by too many short threads, the comparison over long threads will better distinguish different methods' capability. In this experiment, we compare threadCRF with Ranking SVM on the long threads (more than 10 posts) to further investigate the effectiveness of the proposed method. We apply the models trained in previous experiment to analyze their performance only on the testing threads with more than 10 posts. Micro average is used over the selected performance metrics.

Table 5: Prediction performance on long threads

Data Set	Method	Acc_{edge}	Acc_{path}	$F1_{path}$	$F1_{node}$
Apple	RankingSVM	0.6207	0.4523	0.2314	0.7670
	threadCRF	**0.6513***	**0.5686***	**0.3338***	**0.7982***
Google	RankingSVM	**0.5414***	0.2938	0.5521	0.7171
	threadCRF	0.5076	**0.3634***	**0.6025***	**0.7366**

* indicates the improvement is significant ($p<0.05$).

In this testing set, we have 167 threads from Apple Discussion and 226 from Google Earth. Both methods' path-based performance drops compared with the results in Table 3 and Table 4, which is understandable, because the structures are getting more complex. Compared with Ranking SVM's performance, we can discover that threadCRF's performance improves more than that in all the testing cases: 25.71% and 23.67% in terms of Micro Acc_{path} in Apple Discussion and Google Earth accordingly.

5.4 Adaptability Evaluation

Although the proposed threadCRF works in a supervised manner, we want to test its adaptability when we are lack of such labeled training data. There are two scenarios in real situation: 1) we have a small set of labeled thread set from the target forum; 2) we do not any labeled threads from the target forum, but some labeled threads from other forums. In this experiment, we want to investigate our method's capability when applied in both of these two situations.

First, to test the method's dependency on the training data, we variate the training sets during the training phase. We select both Apple Discussion and Google Earth as the evaluation collection and use the same train/test separation as in Section 5.3. The volume of training set is gradually increased from empty to all the training threads. We select Ranking SVM model as the baseline method and compare their Micro Acc_{path} and Micro $F1_{node}$ performance in this experiment. When we have no training samples, we manually set all the features' weights to be 1 for both threadCRF and Ranking SVM.

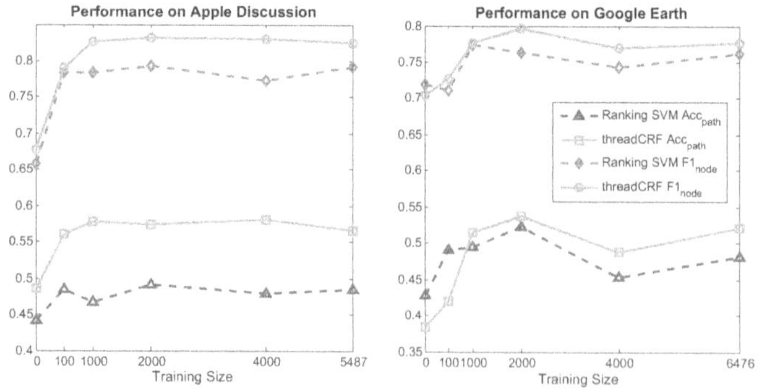

Figure 4: Performance on different training size

From Figure 4, we find with a small training set, 100 labeled threads, threadCRF achieves encouraging performance improvement against the default weight setting. As more training data is available, the performance converges for both methods. Another phenomenon we observe is that threadCRF's performance vibrates over different training sets. The reason is two folds: 1) the employed TRP inferencer in threadCRF is an approximation inference method, the estimated posterior probability varies as starting from different initial points; 2) the variances within the training set introduce noise into the learning phase, similar tendency could also be observed in Ranking SVM's performance.

Second, we perform a cross domain train/test to validate the learning method's generality. In this setting, we evaluate on all the three collections: we randomly select 2,000 threads for training and 2,000 threads for testing from the three data sets accordingly to make the comparison comparable. Besides evaluating the performance on the testing set from the same collections, we also apply the learned model on the other two testing sets from the different domains. Micro Acc_{path} is employed as the evaluation metric and we compare threadCRF with Ranking SVM in this experiment. In Table 6 and Table 7, columns indicate the testing set and rows indicate the training set.

Table 6: Cross domain evaluation on Ranking SVM by Acc_{path}

Train \ Test	Apple	Google	CNET
Apple	0.4730	0.4103	0.5553
Google	0.4757	0.4693	0.4896
CNET	0.4516	0.3724	0.6327

Table 7: Cross domain evaluation on threadCRFs by Acc_{path}

Train \ Test	Apple	Google	CNET
Apple	0.5527	0.4880	0.7172
Google	0.5270	0.4849	0.6919
CNET	0.5057	0.4313	0.6940

From the comparison results in Table 6 and Table 7, we find that threadCRF generalizes better than Ranking SVM in all the three data sets. Because Apple Discussion and

CNET are both computer technical forums, they share some properties in common. Therefore, the threadCRF model trained on Apple Discussion achieves promising performance on CNET, and vice versa. Instead, Google Earth is an entertainment focused forum, where the topics and users' interaction patterns are quite different from the other two forums. Ranking SVM trained on Google Earth doesn't perform as well as the threadCRF on the other two forums: 0.4880 of threadCRF v.s. 0.4103 of Ranking SVM on Apple Discussion and 0.4313 of threadCRF v.s. 0.3724 of Ranking SVM's on CNET. Besides, all the threadCRF's off-diagonal entries are better than Ranking SVM's, which indicates the proposed threadCRF possesses better generality capability than Ranking SVM.

It would be interesting to investigate the weights learned by threadCRF in different collections, from where we can discover interesting patterns in those domains. We normalize the weights from different domains by their corresponding largest weights to make them comparable, and illustrate part of the weights in Table 8.

Table 8: Normalized weights learned by threadCRF

	$\boldsymbol{Sim(y_i)}$	$\boldsymbol{Self(y_i)}$	$\boldsymbol{Repeat(y_i, y_j)}$	$\boldsymbol{AuthorRes(y_i, y_j)}$
Apple	1.0000	0.3102	0.1574	0.0527
Google	0.8441	0.3567	-0.0652	0.1343
CNET	0.5460	0.6218	0.6823	0.3145

From the learned feature weights, we can find $\boldsymbol{Sim(y_i)}$ is the most prominent feature in Apple Discussion. Because the topics in Apple Discussion are relatively more focused, mainly on Apple's products, replying post pairs tend to overlap more in their contents. In CNET, $\boldsymbol{Self(y_i)}$ (reply to oneself), $\boldsymbol{Repeat(y_i, y_j)}$ (repeatedly reply to the same post) and $\boldsymbol{AuthorRes(y_i, y_j)}$ (author response) are all relatively large. This indicates the conversational pattern in CNET is more significant than the other two forums. Another interesting observation is that the weight of $\boldsymbol{Repeat(y_i, y_j)}$ in Google is negative, which means users will reply to the same post they have replied to before. We manually checked the discussions in Google Earth Community and discovered that people repeatedly reply to the same post to provide more links and background of the findings in that post.

5.5 Applications

The replying relationship reconstructed by the proposed threadCRF model can be potentially useful for many further applications. Here we present two sample applications in forum search and community question answering to demonstrate the benefit of reconstructing the replying structure.

5.5.1 Forum Search

Seo et al. [13] demonstrate that using thread structures can lead to significant performance improvement in forum search compared to standard IR methods. In detail, they estimate a post language model by smoothing with the dialogue structure within the ground-truth replying structures.

Following the same line of retrieval model proposed in [13], we compare the retrieval performance on 1) post language model estimated on each individual post; 2) smoothing the post language model by the dialogue structure reconstructed by threadCRF and Ranking SVM; 3) smoothing by the whole thread, in order to justify whether the predicted structures could help the retrieval task.

In the CNET data set, Duan et al. manually selected 30 result documents for 30 different queries under the topic of "Computer & Internet", and annotated them as "relevant" or "irrelevant" [5]. 5-fold cross validation is employed to compare the retrieval performance, where the smoothing parameters in all the language models are exhaustively searched to maximize the MAP metric. MAP, P@1 and P@10 are employed as the evaluation criteria.

Table 9: Forum Search Performance on CNET

	MAP	P@1	P@10
Post Only	0.4893	0.4671	0.3532
Post + Thread	0.4959	0.4643	0.3634
RankingSVM	**0.5084**	0.4999	0.3964
threadCRF	0.5064	**0.5357**	**0.4036**

We can observe that the retrieval model estimated on the reconstructed thread structure generally improves the ranking performance over non-structure smoothing. The reason is that if we directly use all the posts in the thread to smooth the language model without carefully analyzing the semantic relationship between the posts, noise might be introduced into the ranking model and thus affect the retrieval performance, i.e., a degenerated P@1 for Post+Thread.

5.5.2 Community Question Answering

Online forum discussion is a valuable repository for question answering mining tasks. Previous studies on question answering mainly depend on content analysis techniques to find the most probable question-answer pairs [4, 3].

To confirm that the constructed conversational structure can help to detect the answers in the threaded discussion, we choose Apple Discussion as the evaluation collection, in which answer posts are explicitly labeled as "Solved" or "Helpful" by the users who raised the question in the discussion. We use the same train/test split as in Section 5.3.

The first step in question-answer pair extraction task is to identify the questions from the threaded discussion. There are many available techniques to perform such task [3, 6]. To get a clear sense of how the reconstructed structure can help us retrieve the answer posts in a threaded discussion, in this experiment, we assume the question posts are already identified before hand. To achieve it, we filter out the threads without the "Solved" or "Helpful" annotation in the testing set and assume the first post in the left 246 threads are the question posts.

In those question-answering oriented threads, we propose the following criterion to rank all the rest posts in the same thread by:

$$s(p_i) = \begin{cases} \text{child}(p_i) & \text{if root post's author has replied to } p_i \\ 0 & \text{otherwise} \end{cases} \tag{10}$$

Intuitively, we assume a good answer should be the post which the question raiser has replied to, e.g., thanks for the replier or asks for further details, and receives many comments from others.

From Table 10, we can find that the naive content-based method, i.e., rank by similarity, doesn't work in this threaded discussion question answering environment, while replying structure based method achieves promising performance. Be-

Table 10: Performance on answer ranking

	similarity	Ranking SVM	threadCRF
MAP	0.2332	0.3969	**0.4402***
P@1	0.1799	0.6737	**0.6805***

* indicates the improvement is significant ($p<0.05$).

cause most posts in the threads are short, even though they are answering the questions in the previous posts, the content between question post and answer post overlaps little. The structure-based extraction method captures a strong indication for a good answer post from the perspective of user interactions, so that the precision is relatively high.

6. DISCUSSION

In this paper, we proposed a probabilistic graphical model based method, threadCRF, to solve the problem of replying relationship reconstruction in the online threaded discussion forums. By introducing various kind of features, the proposed threadCRF well captures both the long-range and short-range dependency among the posts and better predicts the replying relationship. To judge the quality of the predicted structures, we design a set of novel evaluation metrics. Experiment results on three different forum collections confirm the effectiveness of the proposed method, and the improvement over the baseline methods demonstrates the benefit of modeling the user interaction and long-range dependency in the threaded discussions.

Because the features employed in our method are not strictly limited to forum discussions, and they could be easily adopted to other domains, e.g., replying relationship mining in micro-weblogs, such as Twitter, and user wall posts and comments in social websites, such as Facebook. In addition, other advanced content analysis techniques, e.g., entity reconization/resolution and syntax parsing structure matching, can also be incorporated into our model as features to further enhance the performance.

7. ACKNOWLEDGMENTS

This material is based upon work supported by the National Science Foundation under Grant Numbers IIS-0713581, IIS-0905215, CNS 1028381, and by an AFOSR MURI Grant FA9550-08-1-0265, and the U.S. Army Research Laboratory under Cooperative Agreement No. W911NF-09-2-0053 (NS-CTA). We thank Huizhong Duan for providing the CNet data set and retrieval codes.

8. REFERENCES

[1] Onix text retrieval toolkit stopword list. `http://www.lextek.com/manuals/onix/stopwords1.html`.

[2] S. Bhatia and P. Mitra. Adopting Inference Networks for Online Thread Retrieval. In *Proceedings of the 24th AAAI*, pages 1300–1305, 2010.

[3] G. Cong, L. Wang, C. Lin, Y. Song, and Y. Sun. Finding question-answer pairs from online forums. In *Proceedings of the 31st SIGIR*, pages 467–474, 2008.

[4] S. Ding, G. Cong, C. Lin, and X. Zhu. Using conditional random fields to extract contexts and answers of questions from online forums. *Proceedings of ACL-08: HLT*, pages 710–718, 2008.

[5] H. Duan and C. Zhai. Exploiting Thread Structure to Improve Smoothing of Language Models for Forum Post Retrieval. In *Proceedings of the 33rd ECIR*, 2011.

[6] L. Hong and B. Davison. A classification-based approach to question answering in discussion boards. In *Proceedings of the 32nd SIGIR*, pages 171–178, 2009.

[7] T. Joachims. Optimizing search engines using clickthrough data. In *Proceedings of the 8th KDD*, pages 133–142, 2002.

[8] P. Jurczyk and E. Agichtein. Discovering authorities in question answer communities by using link analysis. In *Proceedings of the 16th CIKM*, pages 919–922, 2007.

[9] D. Koller and N. Friedman. *Probabilistic graphical models*. MIT Press, 2009.

[10] J. Lafferty, A. McCallum, and F. Pereira. Conditional random fields: Probabilistic models for segmenting and labeling sequence data. In *Proceedings of ICML-2001*, pages 282–289, 2001.

[11] C. Lin, J. Yang, R. Cai, X. Wang, and W. Wang. Simultaneously modeling semantics and structure of threaded discussions: a sparse coding approach and its applications. In *Proceedings of the 32nd SIGIR*, pages 131–138, 2009.

[12] G. Salton and C. Buckley. Term-weighting approaches in automatic text retrieval. *Information processing and management*, 24(5):513–523, 1988.

[13] J. Seo, W. Croft, and D. Smith. Online community search using thread structure. In *Proceedings of the 18th CIKM*, pages 1907–1910, 2009.

[14] D. Shen, Q. Yang, J. Sun, and Z. Chen. Thread detection in dynamic text message streams. In *Proceedings of 29th SIGIR*, pages 35–42, 2006.

[15] X. Shi, J. Zhu, R. Cai, and L. Zhang. User grouping behavior in online forums. In *Proceedings of the 15th KDD*, pages 777–786, 2009.

[16] C. Sutton and A. McCallum. *Collective segmentation and labeling of distant entities in information extraction*. 2004.

[17] M. Wainwright, T. Jaakkola, and A. Willsky. MAP estimation via agreement on trees: message-passing and linear programming. *Information Theory, IEEE Transactions on*, 51(11):3697–3717, 2005.

[18] Y. Wang, M. Joshi, W. Cohen, and C. Rosé. Recovering implicit thread structure in newsgroup style conversations. In *ICWSM II*, 2008.

[19] Y. Wang and C. Rosé. Making conversational structure explicit: identification of initiation-response pairs within online discussions. In *Proceedings of HLT-NAACL 2010*, pages 673–676, 2010.

[20] G. Xu and W. Ma. Building implicit links from content for forum search. In *Proceedings of the 29th SIGIR*, pages 300–307, 2006.

[21] J. Zhang, M. Ackerman, and L. Adamic. Expertise networks in online communities: structure and algorithms. In *Proceedings of the 16th WWW*, pages 221–230, 2007.

[22] J. Zhu, Z. Nie, J. Wen, B. Zhang, and W. Ma. 2d conditional random fields for web information extraction. In *Proceedings of the 22nd ICML*, pages 1044–1051, 2005.

Mining Topics on Participations for Community Discovery

Guoqing Zheng†, Jinwen Guo†, Lichun Yang†, Shengliang Xu†,
Shenghua Bao‡, Zhong Su‡, Dingyi Han†, Yong Yu†

†Department of Computer Science and Engineering
Shanghai Jiao Tong University
Shanghai, 200240, China
{gqzheng, guojw, lichunyang, slxu, handy, yyu}@apex.sjtu.edu.cn

‡IBM China Research Laboratory
Beijing, 100094, China
{baoshhua, suzhong}@cn.ibm.com

ABSTRACT

Community discovery on large-scale linked document corpora has been a hot research topic for decades. There are two types of links. The first one, which we call *d2d-link*, indicates connectiveness among different documents, such as blog references and research paper citations. The other one, which we call *u2u-link*, represents co-occurrences or simultaneous **participations** of different users in one document and typically each document from u2u-link corpus has more than one user/author. Examples of u2u-link data covers email archives and research paper co-authorship networks. Community discovery in d2d-link data has achieved much success, while methods for that in u2u-link data either make no use of the textual content of the documents or make oversimplified assumptions about the users and the textual content. In this paper we propose a general approach of community discovery for u2u-link data, i.e., multiple user data, by placing topical variables on multiple authors' participations in documents. Experiments on a research proceeding co-authorship corpus and a New York Times news corpus show the effectiveness of our model.

Categories and Subject Descriptors

H.3.3 [**Information Search and Retrieval**]: Clustering; H.3.3 [**Information Search and Retrieval**]: Retrieval models; H.2.8 [**Database Applications**]: Data mining

General Terms

Algorithms, Experimentation

Keywords

Topics on Participations, Community discovery, Nonparametric statistical model, Hierarchical Dirichlet Process

1. INTRODUCTION

When we talk about linked document data, there are two different types of links. Link of the first one, which we call *d2d-link*, indicates connectiveness between different documents. These kind of data include blog reference data and research paper citation data. Link of the other type, which we call *u2u-link*, represents co-occurrence or simultaneous participations of different users in one document. Usually there are more than one user in each document of this data, so we also call it *Multiple User Data*(MUD). Email archives and research paper co-authorship network fall into this category. Figure 1 gives a sample of a research proceeding corpus, where $u_1, \cdots, u_4$ denote four researchers, and d_1, d_2, d_3 denote three research papers with different colors indicating different research areas. Many methods of community discovery in d2d-link data have been proposed and gain satisfactory results. But as to u2u-link data, rare solutions which combine link information and textual content for community discovery exist. Current approaches either make no use of the textual content of the documents or make oversimplified assumptions about the users as well as the textual content.

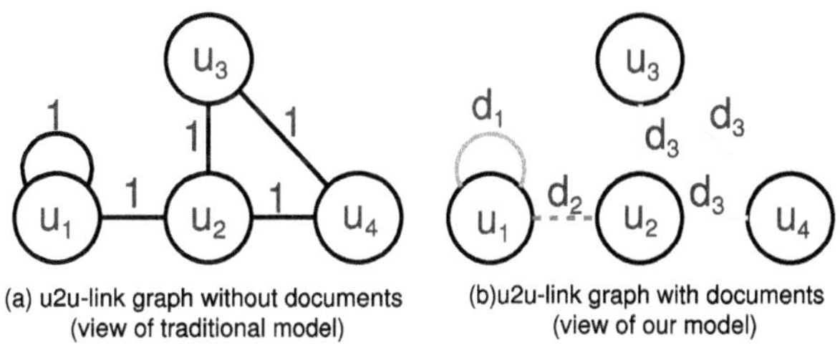

Figure 1: Different views of u2u-link graph(best viewed in color)

One part of traditional methods of community discovery in u2u-link data are performed solely on a u2u-link graph in which the vertices represent the users and the edges indicate links between pairs of authors. A community is typically defined as a subset of users with better connectivity amongst its members than between its members and other users of the graph. The task of community discovery is then to recover such subsets from the given graph. Most of these approaches, including graph cut based methods[21], modularity based methods[16], flow based methods[6] and spectral based methods[20, 1], typically choose an objective function which captures the above intuition of a community and then try to optimize the objective function[9]. These methods only model the links by assigning a certain weight

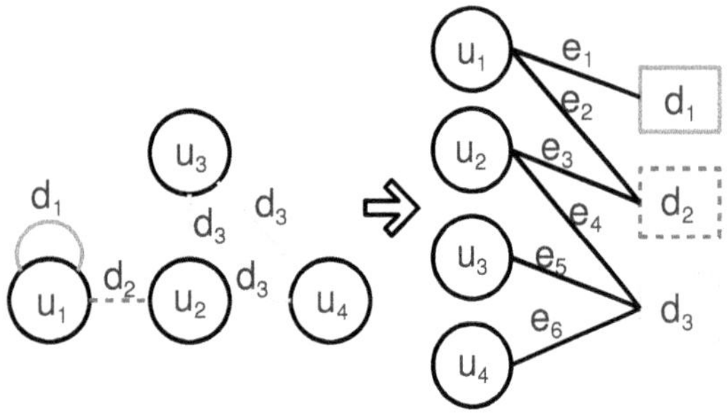

Figure 2: A u2u-link graph and its corresponding participation graph(best viewed in color)

to each link between pairs of users, as the co-authorship network shown in Figure 1(a); though widely applicable and accepted, they make no use of the textual content of the documents and thus give no clue how different authors participate in the documents and what semantics these participations imply. Though some other methods take the textual content into account, they make oversimplified assumptions and thus ignore useful participation information. The NetPLSA model[15] constructs the u2u-link graph as described in Figure 1(a), merges all documents one user participates in into a single document for that user. Thus NetPLSA ignores the various participation information for each user. The Author-Topic(AT) model[22] learns the topic of a document conditioned on the mixture of authors(users) of that document, which implicitly assumes that the distribution over topics of a certain author will not change for all his/her documents. This assumption seems to suffice but it may not fit some real cases such as a researcher switches to another research area and publishes research papers with different topics. A better modeling may exists.

In particular, we propose a Topics-on-Participations(ToP) model for community discovery in u2u-link data. First, we transform the u2u-link graph to an equivalent *participation graph* for clarity, as illustrated in Figure 2. To better exploit the multi-author attribute of each document in the data, we place topical variables on each participation each author get involved in. More specifically, given the u2u-link data, ToP leverages Hierarchical Dirichlet Process(HDP) to introduce hidden topical variables of the participations. Other than the use of participation structure, ToP can look into the documents of the participations in detail to recover sound communities. We first generate the hidden topic variables of the participations and then documents are generated by these according to the hidden variables. Besides, ToP is a nonparametric model, which is a natural outcome of HDP. The setting of community number is a common problem for most of the community discovery algorithms proposed so far. Due to the nonparametric property, ToP is able to automatically select the proper community number according to the observed data.

We evaluate ToP on two real-world datasets, a research proceeding corpus and a New York Times news corpus. The research proceeding corpus consists of paper abstracts from 7 research conferences, i.e. ACL, ICML, SIGGRAPH, SIGIR, SIGKDD, SIGMOD, and WWW during 2005-2009. In total there are 9415 individual authors and 5308 documents. And the New York Times news corpus contains business news mentioning selected sets of companies. As the whole corpus is large, we collect a subset of the corpus, which contains 1677 companies and 2461 documents. Quantitative evaluation on both two datasets shows that ToP outperforms two related community discovery algorithms. Deeper analysis shows that ToP can not only identify the proper number of communities, but also reveal reasonable semantic interpretation for every discovered community.

The main contribution of this paper is two-fold:

- The proposal of ToP which models topics on participations for community discovery in u2u-link data. This modeling makes it possible to mine detailed community information from participations.
- The extensive evaluation on two real-world datasets, verifies the effectiveness of the proposed model. It can automatically detect the proper number of communities, provide a reasonable interpretation of the discovered communities.

The remainder of this paper is organized as follows: Section 2 introduces some related work. Section 3 gives some definitions and formally define the community discovery task. Section 4 presents ToP model in detail. Experimental results as well as some case studies are presented in Section 5. At last, we conclude the paper and discuss about future work in Section 6.

2. RELATED WORK

Much work has been done on community discovery. In this section, we review two lines of work: community discovery in d2d-link data and community discovery in u2u-link data.

2.1 Community Discovery in d2d-link data

In the context of d2d-link data, probabilistic models, such as Latent Dirichlet Allocation(LDA)[3] and its variations, play an important role in uncovering underlying topics from textual data. Zhou et.al [26] successfully extract e-communities based solely on the content of communication documents. Their work gives us a strong support in mining text contents for community discovery. With the aim of taking into account the link information among documents, serveral methods have been proposed. Li et al. in [10] design a sophisticated model for scalable community discovery on textual data with relations. Their model explores the d2d-link graph to detect some community cores and then uses text information to improve community consistency. Cohn and Hofmann combine PLSA and PHITS together and derive a unified model from text contents and citation information of documents under the same latent space [4]. Erosheva et al. apply similar mixed membership model [5] for soft clustering of papers by using text content and references. Liu et al. in [12] propose the Topic-Link LDA model with the intuitive that a link between two documents is determined by both content similarity and author community membership similarity and gain improved results against previous methods. All these approaches captures several aspects of the d2d-link data, but they may be not suitable for community discovery in the u2u-link data.

2.2 Community Discovery in u2u-link data

In the past few decades, many models have been proposed for community discovery in the u2u-link data, but most of these methods are based solely on the u2u-link graph and make no use of the textual content of the documents. Note here, as these methods take into account only the link information and do not consider textual content , they can also be applied to the above mentioned d2d-link data, depending on how a "user" is defined.

Traditionally, community discovery is performed by partition of an u2u-link graph with the aim of optimizing a selected objective function. Many methods have been proposed along this direction, e.g., graph cut based methods, flow based methods, modularity based methods, spectral clustering based direction, etc. Graph cut based methods, including NCut[21], try to find an optimal graph partition with the edge weight between partitions minimized or edge weight inside a partition maximized. Due to the NP-complete complexity of this method, approximate solutions have been proposed. Flake et al.[6] propose approximate algorithms based on network flow ideas to partition the network by solving maximum flow problems, where they define community as a set of entities that has small inter-community cuts and large intra-community cuts. Girvan and Newman[7] introduce *betweenness centrality* to detect communities. After that, Newman and Girvan[16] introduce *modularity* to measure the overall quality of discovered communities. Modularity evaluates how entities in a community connect with other entities in that community and has been adopted by many community detection literature. Modularity can be optimized by using the eigenvectors of the modularity matrix which gives rise to those spectral clustering based methods[20, 1]. McCallum et al. in [14] study a new community discovery task on u2u-link data. Instead of finding densely connected entities, they seek to find out users with similar connection pattern such as similar voting patterns.

Another part of previous work analyzing u2u-link data is based on statistical models[18, 8, 11]. In these models, a latent variable is introduced for each entity to express its potential characteristic and then the models generate the links between them according to the latent variable assignments which are most likely to recover the graph structure[18]. Kemp et al. in [8] extend these models to infinite latent classes. The model can automatically determine the proper latent class number based on the observed graph structure. However, it restricts each entity to only one latent class. Additionally, the discovered class/group in these models is a set of entities which have similar connectivity pattern in the graph, which is quite different from the traditional definition of community, i.e., a densely connected subgraph of the whole network. Because of their general modeling property, these algorithms have been widely adopted, such as biology data analysis [24, 19], co-authorship network analysis [17], Web community identification [6]. Although there are many other great studies in this direction, we do not give a detailed review for each of them because they do not utilize the text information to enhance the community discovery.

In the context of u2u-link data, there have also been some related studies aiming to take advantages of both text contents and the u2u-link structure. Most of these algorithms perform community discovery on a u2u-link graph with text user profiles. In [15], Mei et al. propose a regularized model NetPLSA for discovering more smoothing topics/communities over u2u-link graph by constraining that connected documents that have similar topic distributions. The Author-Topic(AT) model uncovers topics conditioned on the mixture of authors that composed a document[22]. McCallum et al. modeled email archives by a generative process [13]. The proposed Author-Recipient-Topic(ART) model gives each pair of author and recipient a topic distribution instead of a topic distribution per-author. Though their modeling setting shares some similarity with ours, their model is specifically designed for email archives. Different from the above models, our method tries to handle the setting where the text contents are usually associated with more than one user and we aim to quantify the effect of each user's participation contribution to the documents' topical distribution.

3. PROBLEM STATEMENT

In this section, we formally give some definitions and define the task of community discovery from u2u-link data.

Definition 1. **(Participation Graph)**: A participation graph $G = (U \cup \mathcal{D}, E)$ is a bipartite graph where the set of users U and the set of documents $\mathcal{D}$ are two disjoint sets. An edge $e \in E$ connecting user $u \in U$ and document $d \in \mathcal{D}$ indicates that u participates d and we denote this participation with e. So we can construct an equivalent participation graph from every u2u-link data. As we see in Figure 2, we transform a participation graph from the sample u2u-link graph.

Traditionally, a community is a group of users with dense interactions amongst its members than between its members and the remainder of the u2u-link graph. While in our setting, since we have two information sources for community identification, we need to expand the community definition to incorporate both of them, i.e. the topical community.

Definition 2. **(Topical Community)**: A topical community is a soft partition of the users with a multinomial word distribution over the vocabulary $\mathcal{V}$. We denote the topical community space as ϕ_∞. The soft partition means that each user is assigned to each of the communities with a membership weight, i.e. a community distribution. This modeling is natural since it is always the case that a user can belong to multiple communities.

Definition 3. **Task (Community Discovery)**: Given an participation graph G , the task of *Community Discovery* is to find a set of topical communities $\{c_1, c_2, ..., c_K\}$, where the community number K is detected automatically and to calculate the community distribution of each user u, i.e. $\boldsymbol{\theta_u}$.

4. COMMUNITY DISCOVERY MODELING

Briefly speaking, our model looks into the participations, place topical variables on participations and analyzes the latent topics of the documents involved in those participations. In this section, we will introduce our model, the inference method and some basic analysis as well.

4.1 Topics on Participations

Our Topics on Participations(ToP) model first utilizes Hierarchical Dirichlet Process to introduce latent topic variables to each user participation of a document, which forms the modeling for the participation graph part. Then, for the document part, we specify the generation process of a document via a simple topic modeling technique. Finally, we combine the two separate modeling by assuming that they share the same latent topic space.

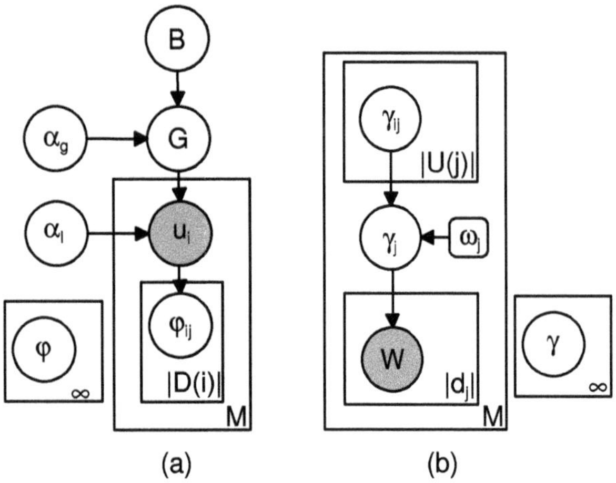

Figure 3: Separated graphical model of ToP. (a) models the participation graph, (b) models the documents.

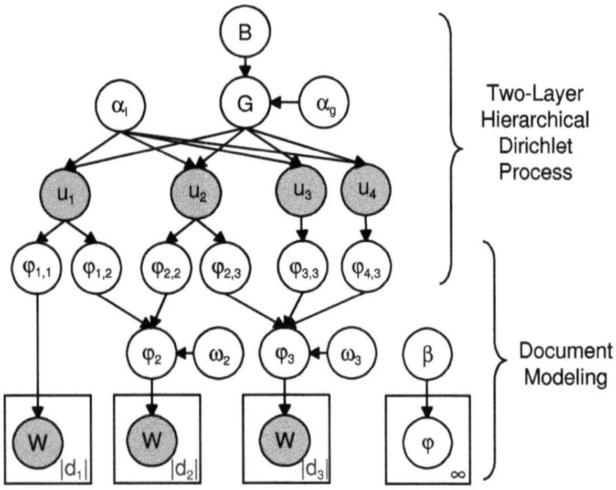

Figure 4: Combined graphical model of ToP for the sample graph in Figure 2 (b)

Participation Graph Modeling. From the participation graph view, we may consider that each user u's participation $e_{u,d}$ in a document d is an evidence indicating the community for the user. In our model, we choose to make it explicit by setting a topical variable for each participation. We call these variables *evidence variables*. Since the community number is typically not known beforehand, $e_{u,d}$ should be a draw from an infinite semantic community space, which will allow the model to learn the community number through the data. Here, we utilize Hierarchical Dirichlet Process to assign evidence variables and build our model.

Figure 3(a) shows the graphical model of our Participation Graph Modeling, where M is the number of users and $|D(i)|$ is the number of documents linked to user i. The outside global Dirichlet Process provides a shared infinite number of variables for all the users' evidence variables. This infinite space brought the non-parametric manner, which enables the model to learn topic number according to the real data. Formally, the Dirichlet process is

$$G|\alpha_g, B \sim DP(\alpha_g, B) \tag{1}$$

where B is the *base measure* and α_g is a positive real number called the *concentration parameter*.

The inside local Dirichlet Process models all participation of a single user in his/her documents. This models the clustering property of a user's participation in documents, i.e. if most publications of a user are related to information retrieval, the next paper of the user will most probably to be about information retrieval again. Formally,

$$U|\alpha_l, G \sim DP(\alpha_l, G) \tag{2}$$

where α_l is a positive real number, called *concentration parameter*. Then, every user's evidence variables are drawn from the infinite space ϕ_∞ as follows:

$$p(\phi_{i,j_{n+1}}|\phi_{i,j_1}, \cdots, \phi_{i,j_n}; \alpha_l) = \frac{\alpha_l G + \sum_{h=1}^{n} \delta(\phi_{i,j_h})}{n + \alpha_l} \tag{3}$$

where ϕ_{i,j_h} denotes the hth evidence variable of U_i, and δ is the atom function. This actually forms a two-layer Hierarchical Dirichlet Process. The specific modeling details and reason of modeling choices can be found in [23].

Document Modeling. To explore the semantics of the text documents, topic modeling is a good choice like PLSA and LDA. Similarly, we set a hidden document model for each document and assume that all the words in that document are drawn from the hidden model. Moreover, since each document is generated by one author or a group of authors, we add a layer that chooses a certain author's topic.

Figure 3(b) shows the graphical model of our Document Modeling, where $|d_j|$ is the number of words in d_j and $|U(j)|$ denotes the number of topic variables connected to γ_j. On the top, γs are the topic variables of all the authors of the document, which are draws from the infinite space γ_∞. Then, ω is the weighting vector parameters for the topic selection process, satisfying $\sum_{h=1}^{|U(j)|} \omega_{j,h} = 1$. The relation of these variables is as

$$p(\gamma_j|\gamma_{(1),j}, \gamma_{(2),j}, \cdots, \gamma_{(|U_j|),j}) = \sum_{h=1}^{|U_j|} \omega_h \delta(\gamma_{(h),j}) \tag{4}$$

where $\gamma_{(h),j}$ denotes the hth evidence variable that connects γ_j. This setting captures the interaction between the authors of the same document by the probability feature that given $\gamma_j = \psi$, the more $\gamma_{(h),j}$ having value ψ, the larger the probability of selecting ψ by γ_j. In other words, the topic variables linked to γ_j tend to agree with each other. Then, we assume that all the words in that document are drawn from the topic model, as the lower part of the Figure 3(b). The joint probability of a document model γ_j and its generated words $\boldsymbol{W}_j$ is:

$$p(W_{j,1}, W_{j,2}, \cdots, W_{j,|\boldsymbol{W}_j|}, \gamma_j) = p(\gamma_j) \prod_{h=1}^{|\boldsymbol{W}_j|} p(W_{j,h}|\gamma_j) \tag{5}$$

where γ_j is a draw from an infinite semantic space γ_∞.

Note that, since the modeling focus is to recover the topic of the links between users, we choose this simpler method (comparing to LDA and PLSA) to model the documents. In fact, this method has also been widely used in language model for information retrieval and naive bayes classifiers because of its light weight yet effective.

Combination of Participation Graph Modeling and Document Modeling. Considering that the community space ϕ_∞ and the document model space γ_∞ are both semantic spaces, we simply unite them into a single space, ϕ_∞. Now, the whole modeling process is finished. To make it clearer, the whole model is shown in Figure 4. Note that the model can not be simplified into box representation and we have to expand the variables. Figure 4 just gives a sample according to the participation graph in Figure 2(b).

4.2 Model Inference

Table 1: the symbols which will be used in model inference

M	the number of users
N	the number of documents
$\boldsymbol{W}_j$	the jth observed document
$D_s(i)$	the set of single-user documents linked to user i
$D_m(i)$	the set of multi-user documents linked to user i
$U(j)$	the set of users linked to document j
$T(i)$	the set of tables in restaurant i
$t_{i,j}$	table index of customer (i,j), $i \in U(j)$, $j \in D(i)$
$k_{t_{i,j}}$	the dish serving on the table that $t_{i,j}$ refers
$k_{i,t}$	$t \in T(i)$, the dish on the tth table in restaurant i
d_j	the mixture component (i.e. dish) index of multi-user document j
$m_{i,k}$	number of tables in restaurant i serving dish k
$n_{i,t,k}$	the number of customers in restaurant i, sitting at table t, eating dish k
$var_.$	a marginal of the variable var, e.g. $m_{i,\cdot}$ denotes the number of tables in restaurant i.
$\boldsymbol{var}$	the set of all var, e.g $\boldsymbol{t}$ denotes the table indices of all the customers
$\boldsymbol{var}^{-s}$	all the var set excluding the upper scripted one, e.g. $\boldsymbol{t}^{-ij}$ denotes all the table indices but t_{ij}

We employ Gibbs sampling for model inference [2]. Firstly, we derive two likelihood expressions for the convenience in the inference derivation later. The conditional density of $\boldsymbol{W}_j$ under mixture component k given all other observed documents is:

$$f_k^{-\boldsymbol{W}_j}(\boldsymbol{W}_j) \tag{6}$$

$$= \frac{\int Mul(\boldsymbol{W}_j|\phi_k) \prod_{j' \neq j, \left\{ \substack{d_{j'}=k, j' \in D_m(\cdot) \\ k_{t_{\cdot,j'}}=k, j' \in D_s(\cdot)} \right\}} Mul(\boldsymbol{W}_{j'}|\phi_k) Dir(\phi_k) d\phi_k}{\int \prod_{j' \neq j, \left\{ \substack{d_{j'}=k, j' \in D_m(\cdot) \\ k_{t_{\cdot,j'}}=k, j' \in D_s(\cdot)} \right\}} Mul(\boldsymbol{W}_{j'}|\phi_k) Dir(\phi_k) d\phi_k}$$

where $Mul()$ denotes multinomial distribution. And the selection probability distribution:

$$s(d_j|k_{t_{\cdot,j}}) = \sum_{i' \in U(j)} \delta(k_{t_{i',j}}) \tag{7}$$

We have set all ω's to be uniform so that these parameters can be omitted. Further note that we will suppress references to the variables in the condition part of a conditional probability except those will used in the probability expression.

There are three sets of hidden variables that need to be sampled: table indices $\boldsymbol{t}$ of customers, mixture component indices $\boldsymbol{d}$ of documents, and dish indices $\boldsymbol{k}$ of tables. We derive the Gibbs sampling expression for each of them.

Sampling $\boldsymbol{t}$. The variable set $\boldsymbol{t}$ should be split to two sets because they are different in sampling. Firstly, if the document j is a single user document, $t_{i,j}$ is sampled by combing the likelihood of generating the observed documents.

$$p(t_{i,j} = t|\boldsymbol{t}^{-i,j}, \boldsymbol{k}) \tag{8}$$
$$\propto \begin{cases} n_{it\cdot} f_{k_{i,t}}^{-\boldsymbol{W}_j}(\boldsymbol{W}_j) & if\ t\ is\ previously\ used \\ \alpha_l p(\boldsymbol{W}_j|\boldsymbol{t}^{-i,j}, t_{i,j} = t^{new}, \boldsymbol{k}) & if\ t = t^{new} \end{cases}$$

where $p(\boldsymbol{W}_j|\boldsymbol{t}^{-i,j}, t_{i,j} = t^{new}, \boldsymbol{k})$ is the liklihood for $t_{i,j} = t^{new}$:

$$p(\boldsymbol{W}_j|\boldsymbol{t}^{-i,j}, t_{i,j} = t^{new}, \boldsymbol{k}) \tag{9}$$
$$= \sum_{k=1}^{K} \frac{m_{\cdot,k}}{m_{\cdot,\cdot} + \alpha_g} f_k^{-\boldsymbol{W}_j}(\boldsymbol{W}_j) + \frac{\alpha_g}{m_{\cdot,\cdot} + \alpha_g} f_{k^{new}}^{-\boldsymbol{W}_j}(\boldsymbol{W}_j)$$

If the sampled value of $t_{i,j}$ is t^{new}, we need to obtain a sample of $k_{i,t^{new}}$:

$$p(k_{i,t^{new}}|\boldsymbol{t}, \boldsymbol{k}^{-i,t^{new}}) \tag{10}$$
$$\propto \begin{cases} m_{\cdot,k} f_k^{-\boldsymbol{W}_j}(\boldsymbol{W}_j) & if\ k\ is\ previously\ used \\ \alpha_g f_{k_{new}}^{-\boldsymbol{W}_j}(\boldsymbol{W}_j) & if\ k = k^{new} \end{cases}$$

Secondly, for $\boldsymbol{t}$ of multi-user documents, we have a similar sampling process but the likelihood function is replaced by the selection function in Equation 7.

$$p(t_{i,j} = t|\boldsymbol{t}^{-ij}, \boldsymbol{k}, \boldsymbol{d}) \tag{11}$$
$$\propto \begin{cases} n_{i,t,\cdot}^{-i,j} s(d_j|k_{t_{\cdot,j}}^{-i}, k_{t_{i,j}} = k_{i,t}) & if\ t\ is\ previously\ used \\ \alpha_l p(d_j|\boldsymbol{t}^{-i,j}, t_{i,j} = t^{new}, \boldsymbol{k}) & if\ t = t^{new} \end{cases}$$

where $p(d_j|\boldsymbol{t}^{-i,j}, t_{i,j} = t^{new}, \boldsymbol{k})$ is:

$$p(d_j|\boldsymbol{t}^{-i,j}, t_{i,j} = t^{new}, \boldsymbol{k}) \tag{12}$$
$$= \sum_{k=1}^{K} \frac{m_{\cdot,k}}{m_{\cdot,\cdot} + \alpha_g} s(d_j|k_{t_{\cdot,j}}^{-i}, k_{t_{i,j}} = k)$$
$$+ \frac{\alpha_g}{m_{\cdot,\cdot} + \alpha_g} s(d_j|k_{t_{\cdot,j}}^{-i}, k_{t_{i,j}} = k^{new})$$

And in the case of choosing t^{new}:

$$p(k_{i,t^{new}}|\boldsymbol{t}, \boldsymbol{k}^{-i,t^{new}}) \tag{13}$$
$$\propto \begin{cases} m_{\cdot,k} s(d_j|k_{t_{\cdot,j}}^{-i}, k_{t_{i,j}} = k) & if\ k\ is\ previously\ used \\ \alpha_g s(d_j|k_{t_{\cdot,j}}^{-i}, k_{t_{i,j}} = k^{new}) & if\ k = k^{new} \end{cases}$$

Sampling $\boldsymbol{d}$. These variables relate only to the selection processes and the multi-user document likelihood. They are thus sampled as

$$p(d_j = k|\boldsymbol{W}_\cdot, \boldsymbol{d}^{-j}, \boldsymbol{t}, \boldsymbol{k}) \tag{14}$$
$$\propto s(d_j = k|k_{t_{\cdot,j}}) f_k^{-\boldsymbol{W}_j}(\boldsymbol{W}_j)$$

Sampling $\boldsymbol{k}$. Since changing $k_{i,t}$ will change the mixture components of all the $t_{i,\cdot}$, the sampling relates to both the selection likelihood and the document likelihood of these variables. So the Gibbs sampling expression is:

$$p(k_{i,t} = k|\boldsymbol{t}, \boldsymbol{k}^{-it}) \tag{15}$$
$$\propto \begin{cases} m_{\cdot,k}^{-it} f_k^{-\boldsymbol{W}_{\{j,j \in D_s(i)\}}}(\boldsymbol{W}_{\{j,j \in D_s(i)\}}) & \text{if } k \text{ is} \\ \prod_{j' \in D_m(i)} s(d_{j'}|k_{t_{\cdot,j'}}^{-i}, k_{t_{i,j'}} = k) & \text{previously used} \\ & \\ \alpha_g f_{k^{new}}^{-\boldsymbol{W}_{j,j \in D_s(i)}}(\boldsymbol{W}_{j,j \in D_s(i)}) & \text{if } k = k^{new} \\ \prod_{j' \in D_m(i)} s(d_{j'}|k_{t_{\cdot,j'}}^{-i}, k_{t_{i,j'}} = k^{new}) & \end{cases}$$

4.3 Model Analysis

Computation Complexity. The computation burden mainly lies in the Gibbs sampling inference part. Due to the sequential sampling process for the unobserved variables $\boldsymbol{t}$, $\boldsymbol{k}$, and $\boldsymbol{d}$, the computation complexity of Gibbs sampling is linear to the total number of the hidden variables. The size of $\boldsymbol{d}$ is the number of documents in $C_1 = D_m(\cdot)$, The size of $\boldsymbol{t}$ is the number of edges in the bipartite link graph $C_2 = \sum_{j=1}^{N} U(j)$. The size of $\boldsymbol{k}$ can be estimated by its expectation $C_3 = \sum_{i=1}^{M} \alpha_l \log(D_m(i) \cup D_s(i))$. Thus, the computation complexity is about $O(C_1 + C_2 + C_3)$.

Parameter Setting Analysis. Although the model is nonparametric, there are still three parameters, two DP concentration parameters α_l and α_g, and one parameter β in the Dirichlet distribution that is set as the base measure for the global DP. The three parameters can be divided to two groups. α_l and α_g control the prior probability of generating new community. Since we have no prior information about the number of communities, they are set to small values, such as 0.1 $\sim$ 1 for $alpha_l$, 1 $\sim$ 10 for $alpha_g$. β controls the impact from the text contents. In typical topic modeling studies, β is always set to around 0.01 so that the text contents can dominate the topic modeling process. While in our setting, β actually controls the balance between the information of text contents and the information of graph structure. The smaller β is the larger the impact of text contents is. We seek to reduce some impact of the text contents so that the graph structure can play a more important role. Therefore, we should set β to a little larger than the usual setting 0.01. From the experiments, we find that 0.01 $\sim$ 0.05 is a suitable interval.

Parameter Estimation. After model training, there may be two sets of mixture components. One set of mixture components are referred by the documents, i.e. either $d_j, j \in D_m(\cdot)$ or $t_{\cdot,j}, j \in D_s(\cdot)$ will refer to them. We call them MC_{ref} for convenience. Accordingly, the others have no referred documents. We call them MC_{nref}. MC_{ref} is influenced by both document contents and graph structure. While MC_{nref} has no influence on the contents. It is originated from the setting that HDP is placed solely on the graph structure, but the text contents information may only agree with the graph information on a subset of the mixture components brought in by HDP. Since MC_{nref} contains no text information, we drop them. The mixture components in MC_{ref} are remained as the final community space. They can be reconstructed by the posterior expectation of them as

$$\hat{\phi}_k = \int \phi_k p(\phi_k|\{\boldsymbol{W}_j|\left\{\begin{array}{l} d_j = k, j \in D_m(\cdot) \\ t_{\cdot,j} = k, j \in D_s(\cdot) \end{array}\right\}\})d\phi_k \tag{16}$$

And the community distribution θ_i of a user i is estimated from the community assignment variables $d_j, j \in D_m(i)$ and $t_{i,j}, j \in D_s(i)$ as

$$\hat{\theta}_i = \frac{1}{|D_m(i)|} \sum_{j \in D_m(i)} \delta(\phi_{k_{d_j}}) + \frac{1}{|D_s(i)|} \sum_{j \in D_s(i)} \delta(\phi_{k_{t_{i,j}}}) \tag{17}$$

Table 2: Statistics of PAPER and NYT

	# of users	# of docs	# of links	# of links/user
PAPER	9415	5308	25034	2.7
NYT	1677	2461	83367	49.7

5. EXPERIMENTS

To test the effectiveness of the proposed ToP model, we apply it to community discovery on two data collections we crawled from the web, a research proceeding corpus and a New York Times news corpus. We perform parameter sensitivity analysis, followed by community semantic analysis. We also compare it with state-of-the-art community discovery algorithms, NCut and NetPLSA, in the experiments.

5.1 Data Collection

We mainly use the research proceeding corpus to evaluate the detailed performance of our model. The dataset contains the abstracts of all papers from 7 research conferences, i.e. ACL, ICML, SIGGRAPH, SIGIR, SIGKDD, SIGMOD, and WWW, between 2005 and 2009. In total, there are 5308 papers and 9415 individual authors. 11913 unique terms appear at least once in the dataset after we preprocess the data by removing common stop words and stemming. We call this corpus PAPER.

ToP model is not limited to discover communities of users. The New York Times news corpus is collected to verify the model's general applicability. We collect a set of companies[1] and their news articles from New York Times. The whole corpus is quite huge. We build a subset of the complete corpus for experiments. The dataset consists of all the articles that mention about at least 3 companies. And hereafter we refer to it as NYT. Table 2 shows some statistics of PAPER and NYT. All the above datasets are publicly available.

5.2 Evaluation Metric

Given two users' community membership distributions, we use the Categorical Clustering Distance(CCD)[25] to compare the quality of these two distributions. This method relates only to users' community membership distributions. So it can be applied to evaluate different algorithms that generate user community distributions with different community dimensions.

Given a test data set consisting of a set of users $U_T = \{u_i|1 \leq i \leq M\}$ with their ideal community membership distributions $\{\theta_i|1 \leq i \leq M\}$ and their computed community membership distributions $\{\hat{\theta}_i|1 \leq i \leq M\}$. The CCD between $\boldsymbol{\theta}$ and $\hat{\boldsymbol{\theta}}$ is given by

$$CCD(\boldsymbol{\theta}, \hat{\boldsymbol{\theta}}) = \min_{w_{k,j}} \sum_{k=1}^{K} \sum_{j=1}^{J} w_{k,j} \sum_{i=1}^{M} |\theta_{i,k} - \hat{\theta}_{i,j}| \tag{18}$$

subject to $w_{k,j} \geq 0, \sum_{k=1}^{K} w_{k,j} = \frac{1}{J}, \sum_{j=1}^{J} w_{k,j} = \frac{1}{K}$ for all k, j, where K and J are the number of communities in $\boldsymbol{\theta}$

[1] http://topics.nytimes.com/topics/news/business/companies/index.html

and $\hat{\boldsymbol{\theta}}$, respectively. Linear programming is used to compute equation (18).CCD is nonnegative and equals zero if and only if the two distributions are identical. The smaller the value is, the closer those two distributions get to each other.

5.3 Ground Truth and Baseline Setting

According to the definition of community in our setting, we build ideal community membership distributions for the above datasets. For the PAPER corpus, we treat each conference as a community and the proportion of the number of papers one author published in each conference as the ideal probability the author belongs to that community. For NYT, those companies are categorized into 10 "sectors" according to New York Times, such as technology, basic material, finance etc. So we treat the categorization as the ideal community membership for those companies.

Two models are selected as baseline for comparison. One is NetPLSA and the other is NCut. Since the two algorithms both run on user link graph, we need to first build such a graph with weights on the links. The weight of a link connecting u_i and u_j is set to be the number of edges that connects u_i and u_j. As these two models are parametric models, the number of communities are set manually. For PAPER, the number of communities of NetPLSA and NCut are both set to be 7, i.e. the number of conferences in the corpus for the reason that these conferences focus on different subjects. This setting method is the same as what the authors of NetPLSA did in their original work. And to NYT, we set the number of communities to be identical to the number of "sectors", i.e., 10, of those companies. For the parameter γ in NetPLSA, we choose the lead-to-optimal-result one for 9 different settings raging from 0.1 to 0.9 with step 0.1.

5.4 Parameter Sensitivity Analysis

We examine different combinations of α_l, α_g and β in the experiment. For each combination of the parameters, we run the inference for 100 iterations. We present the influence of α_l, α_g and β in Figure 5.

From Figure 5, we see that the number of communities detected by our model is not quite sensitive to parameter changes. The number of communities detected from both PAPER and NYT are around 8. Section 5.6 gives explanations why they are not precisely equal to the ideal community number(mainly because of noise). Though not exactly perfect, the number of communities our model detects show the ability of automatically determining the proper number of communities.

5.5 Community Membership Evaluation

On the PAPER dataset, the evaluation result of NCut $CCD = 1351.02$, and we list the evaluation results of NetPLSA regarding to its parameter λ in Table 3. As we see from Table 3, the best CCD value of NetPLSA is 1408.9, which outperforms NCut, so from now on we choose the best evaluation result of NetPLSA as comparison baseline for ToP. In our experiments, we also test different sets of parameters of ToP with α_l varying from 0.1 to 0.5, α_g from 1.0 to 5.0 and β from 0.01 to 0.20. We show part of the detailed evaluation results of ToP with respect to α_l, α_g and β in Figure 6.

With $\alpha_l = 0.2$, $\alpha_g = 5.0$ and $\beta = 0.05$, we get the minimum value of $CCD = 1219.65$ giving a maximum improvement over NetPLSA as

$$\frac{|1219.65 - 1408.9|}{1408.9} \times 100\% = 13.4\%$$

Table 4: Best CCD of NCut, NetPLSA and ToP

	NCut	NetPLSA	ToP
PAPER	1351.02	1408.9	1219.65
NYT	173.9	180.35	141.82

We pick the configuration of α_l, α_g and β which lead to the lowest CCD. Under that configuration, our model detects 8 communities and we make statistics of papers from each conference as shown in Figure 7. Note here that the community membership of a paper is set to be community assignment in the last iteration of Gibbs sampling. We are unable to get this result by using NetPLSA due to its coarse grained modeling of the documents. The horizontal axis represents the communities and the vertical axis represents the percentage of papers from each conference. We also list the top 10 terms for each community discovered by ToP and NetPLSA in Table 5 and Table 6, respectively.

While on the NYT dataset, we only show the best CCD results of NCut, NetPLSA and ToP as shown in Table 4. ToP outperforms both NetPLSA and NCut on NYT. Besides, from the results on NYT, we can see that NCut even outperforms NetPLSA for the reason that it constructs a densely-connected graph on NYT and that NetPLSA neglects too much important network clues to discover proper community structures.

Because ToP models more detailed participation information than NetPLSA, ToP takes longer time to output the community distribution results than NetPLSA does. On the PAPER corpus, NetPLSA takes about $5 \sim 10$s per iteration while ToP takes about $10 \sim 30$s per iteration on a daily workstation depending on the parameters.

5.6 Community Semantic Analysis

From Figure 7, we see that our model discovered 6 major communities and 2 minor communities. We examine the 6 major communities first. Considering both the percentage of papers from each conference appearing in each community and the top 10 terms of every community listed in Table 5, it is easy to see that c_1 well corresponds to the information retrieval community, c_2 is closely related to computer graphics, c_3 is mainly about data mining, c_4 covers the database community, c_5 mainly concerns about computer linguistics, c_6 is closely related to machine learning. Note that papers from WWW scatter around several communities, which is quite reasonable because the WWW conference covers topics in information retrieval, data mining, data management, etc. As to the 4 minor communities, c_7 and c_8 both contain only 1 paper. After an investigation of the data, we find that the authors of the above 2 papers have no co-authorship with the rest authors in the dataset and that the contents of these papers are very dissimilar from others. It is the above two reasons that prevent our model from determining the same number of communities as the ideal one. Let us take the paper belonging to c_7 as an example. *The Portinari project: IR helps art and culture*, a demo paper authored by João Candido Portinari in SIGIR'05, demonstrates a cultural project of collecting and distributing all works of the Brazilian artist Candido Portinari and shows how IR helps accomplish this

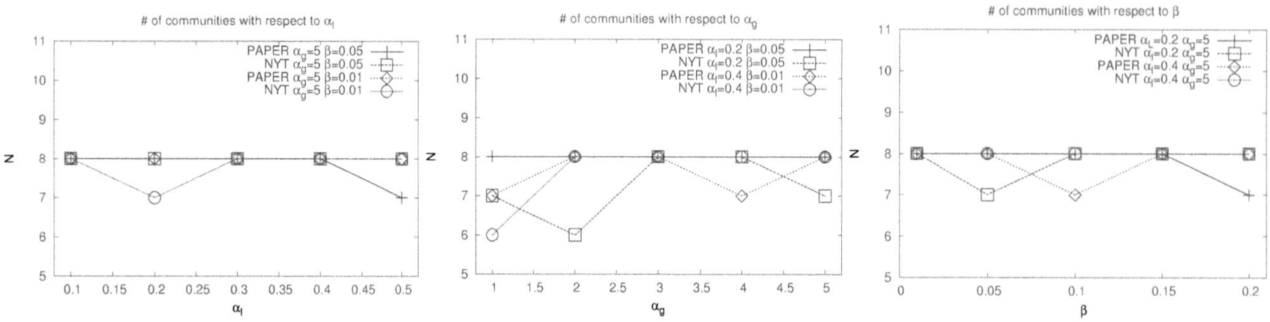

Figure 5: Influence of each parameter on community number

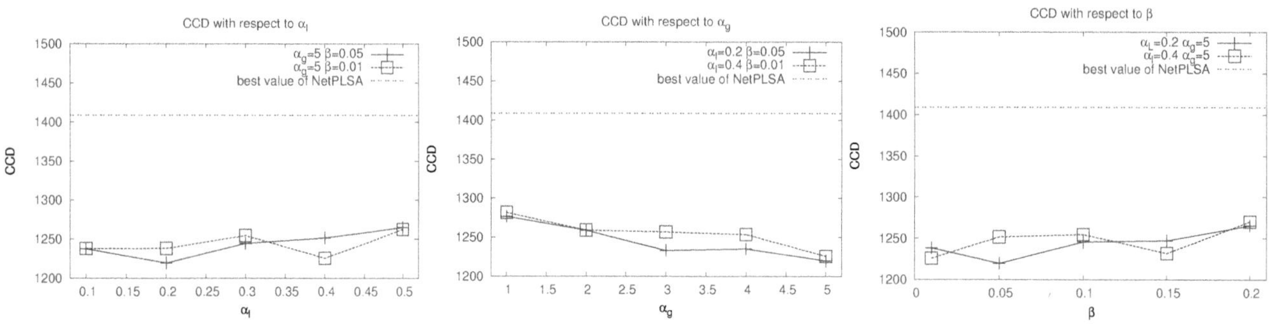

Figure 6: CCD of ToP with respect to each parameter(lower is better)

Table 3: Evaluation result of NetPLSA with respect to the lead-to-optimal-result parameter

λ	0.1	0.2	0.3	0.4	0.5	0.6	0.7	0.8	0.9
$CCD(\boldsymbol{\theta}, \hat{\boldsymbol{\theta}})$	1474.2	1463.8	1435.6	1509.9	1486.5	1408.4	1432.6	1435.7	**1408.9**

Table 5: Top 10 terms extracted by ToP for each community

c_1	c_2	c_3	c_4	c_5	c_6	c_7	c_8
search	imag	data	data	model	learn	portinari	economi
web	model	network	queri	base	algorithm	work	engin
queri	method	algorithm	web	languag	model	paint	perspect
user	motion	mine	system	word	data	brazil	understand
inform	base	pattern	servic	method	method	social	long
model	surfac	graph	applic	approach	problem	project	chang
retriev	present	model	databas	translat	cluster	present	arriv
document	mesh	base	base	system	propos	document	econom
base	time	cluster	user	paper	base	develop	largest
result	algorithm	propos	process	show	classif	import	compani

Table 6: Top 10 terms extracted by NetPLSA

c_1	c_2	c_3	c_4	c_5	c_6	c_7
model	data	data	web	search	system	imag
languag	queri	algorithm	network	queri	user	model
word	databas	learn	user	document	interact	method
base	system	model	social	retriev	visual	motion
translat	applic	problem	content	rank	inform	base
method	process	method	page	inform	model	surfac
approach	xml	cluster	commun	result	base	mesh
text	servic	propos	inform	user	present	light
system	perform	set	data	relev	evalu	time
extract	base	approach	mine	base	content	comput

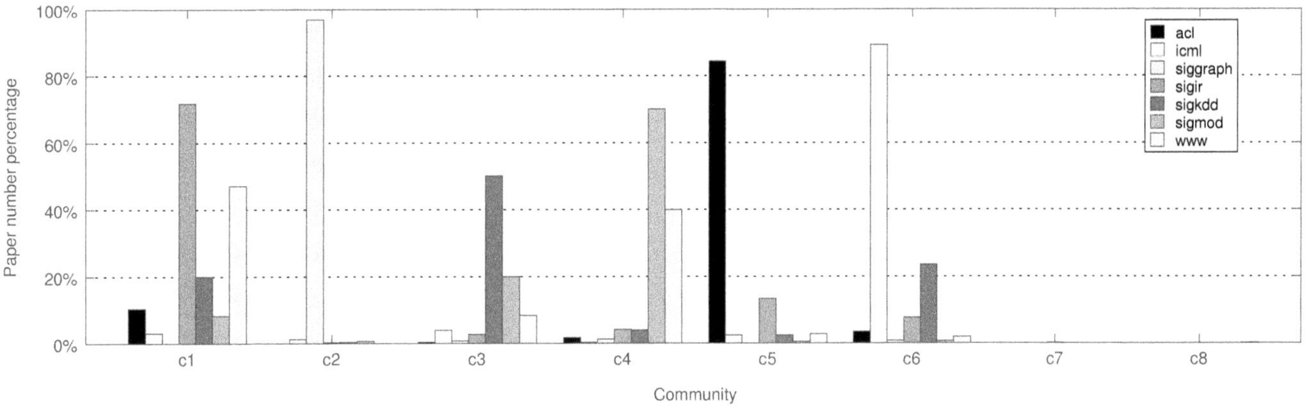

Figure 7: Paper number percentage distribution over community(best viewed in color)

Table 7: Community membership of several active authors

	IR	CG*	DM	DB	CL	ML
W. Bruce Croft	△	△		△	△	
Jamie Callan	△				△	
Chengxiang Zhai	△	△			△	△
James Allan	△	△		△	△	
Andrew McCallum	△				△	△
Kun Zhou		△	△	△		

*CG: Computer Graphics, DB: Database, DM: Data Mining

project and spread the Brazilian culture. The author is actually an isolated point in our co-authorship network. Another example from community c_8, *The New Economy - An Engineer's Perspective*, a keynote by David Brown in WWW'06, tells how mobile communication & computing changes people's daily life and the economy. Also, this author is another isolated point in our co-authorship network.

ToP figures out the community each author gets involved in. Table 7 shows the community membership of several active authors in PAPER. A △ indicates the probability of an author belonging to a community is above some threshold.

From the above analysis, we see that with the number of communities determined automatically, our model has the ability of discovering semantic communities.

5.7 Case Study

This section gives some case studies in the PAPER dataset to show the semantic community discovery ability of ToP. We investigate the PAPER dataset by calculating all the connected components of the co-authorship network and find that there are on average 184 connected components inside the scope of each conference. Also the number of authors who publish papers in more than 2 conferences is 1187. The above two observations imply that the loosely connectd semantic related scenario and densely connected semantic unrelated scenario is common in the PAPER dataset. Thus we show two case studies in each case respectively.

5.7.1 Loosely connected semantic related scenario

For this scenario, we take authors with similar research interests but with neither direct nor indirect co-author relationships to examine our model. That is, they publish paper in the same conference but in different connected components. In this case, we have the following example.

Andrew McCallum and Thomas Hofmann are in two unconnected subgraph in our bipartite graph. Andrew McCallum published nine papers covering topics on data mining in SIGKDD and Thomas Hofmann also contributed one SIGKDD paper *Non-redundant clustering with conditional ensembles* to our dataset. Results of our model successfully assign most of Andrew McCallum's SIGKDD papers and Thomas Hofmann's SIGKDD paper to the same community(c_3 in Figure 7, in which SIGKDD papers make a majority). Therefore, our model can successfully merge loosely connected semantic related communities.

In this scenario, NCut fails to recover this semantic community because it takes no text information into consideration.

5.7.2 Densely connected semantic unrelated scenario

For this seenario, we take authors who have co-author relationships but their co-authored papers are about different research topics to examine our model and we have the following example.

Jerry Scripps, Pang-Ning Tan and Abdol-Hossein Esfahanian together contributed a paper *Measuring the effects of preprocessing decisions and network forces in dynamic network analysis* in SIGKDD'09, while Haibin Cheng and Pang-Ning Tan together contributed a paper *Semi-supervised learning with data calibration for long-term time series forecasting* in SIGKDD'08. It is necessary to mention that there are no records in the PAPER corpus concerning the above 4 authors except these two papers. Therefore, authors of the first paper are densely connected to each other and the same to the authors of the second one. These two author groups share a common vertex (Pang-Ning Tan). Results of ToP assign c_3(Data mining) to the SIGKDD'09 paper and c_6(Machine learning) to the SIGKDD'08 paper, for the reason that the SIGKDD'08 paper mainly focuses on proposing a new learning method. The above analysis shows that our model has successfully split the two densely connected communities whose semantics are not quite related.

While in this scenario, we are unable to recover such detailed community of each paper using NetPLSA due to its coarse grained modeling of the documents by simply merge the above two papers of Pang-Ning Tan into a single document.

6. CONCLUSIONS AND FUTURE WORK

Although community discovery techniques have been developed for decades, there is not much work done in developing general algorithms for u2u-link data while considering textual content information. This paper proposes a principle solution. The main contributions of this paper can be summarized as the following.

1). The proposal of a Topics on Participations(ToP) model for community discovery in u2u-link data. ToP makes it possible for mining detailed information from each participation. Moreover, the proposed model not only captures the structure information induced from the u2u-link graph but also provides a method for automatic selecting proper number of communities.

2). The extensive evaluation on two real-world datasets, which verifies the effectiveness of the proposed model. ToP can automatically detect the proper number of communities, provide a reasonable interpretation of the discovered communities, and outperform the baseline models in mining user community distribution.

There are several potential future directions of this work. First, we will try some other document modeling e.g. PLSA and LDA. Second, we will develop a parallel solution to improve the scalability of our algorithm. Last, by taking temporal dimension into consideration, studying how communities evolve over time also deserves a try.

7. REFERENCES

[1] R. Anderson and K. Lang. Communities from seed sets. In *Proceedings of International Conference on WWW 2006*, pages 475–486, 2006.

[2] C. Andrieun, N. de Freitas, A. Doucet, and M. I. Jordan. An introduction to mcmc for machine learning. *Machine Learning*, 50(1-2):5–43, 2004.

[3] D. M. Blei, A. Y. Ng, and M. I. Jordan. Latent dirichlet allocation. *Journal of Machine Learning Research*, 3:993–1022, 2003.

[4] D. Cohn and T. Hofmann. The missing link - a probabilistic model of document content and hypertext connectivity. In *Proc. of NIPS*, 2001.

[5] E. Erosheva, S. Fienberg, and J. Lafferty. Mixed-membership models of scientific publications. In *Proc. of National Academy of Sciences*, pages 5220–5227, 2004.

[6] G. W. Flake, S. Lawrence, and C. L. Giles. Efficient identification of web communities. In *Proceedings of KDD 2000*, pages 150–160, 2000.

[7] M. Girvan and M. Newman. Community structure in social and biological networks. In *Proceedings of the National Academy of Sciences of the United States of America*, pages 7821–7826, 2002.

[8] C. Kemp, T. L. Griffiths, and J. B. Tenenbaum. Discovering latent classes in relational data, 2004. Technical report.

[9] J. Leskovec, K. J. Lang, and M. W. Mahoney. Empirical comparison of algorithms for network community detection. In *Proceedings of International Conference on WWW 2010*, pages 631–640, 2010.

[10] H. Li, Z. Nie, W.-C. Lee, C. L. Giles, and J.-R. Wen. Scalable community discovery on textual data with relations. In *Proceedings of CIKM 2008*, pages 1203–1212, 2008.

[11] Y. Lin, Y. Chi, S. Zhe, H. Sundaram, and B. L. Tseng. Facetnet: A framework for analyzing communities and their evolutions in dynamic networks. In *Proc. of WWW'08*, pages 685–694, 2008.

[12] Y. Liu, A. Niculescu-Mizil, and W. Gryc. Topic-link lda: Joint models of topic and author community. In *Proc. of ICML'09*, pages 665–672, 2009.

[13] A. McCallum, X. Wang, and A. Corrada-Emmanuel. Topic and role discovery in social networks with experiments on enron and academic email. *Journal of Artificial Intelligence Research*, 30:249–272, 2007.

[14] A. McCallum, X. Wang, and N. Mohanty. Joint group and topic discovery from relations and text. *Statistical Network Analysis: Models, Issues and New Directions*, 2007.

[15] Q. Mei, D. Cai, D. Zhang, and C. Zhai. Topic modeling with network regularization. In *Proc. of WWW'08*, pages 101–110, 2008.

[16] M. Newman and M. Girvan. Finding and evaluating community structure in networks. *Phys Rev E.*, 69(026113), 2004.

[17] M. E. Newman. Coauthorship networks and patterns of scientific collaboration. In *Proc. Nat. Acad. Sci.*, volume 101, Suppl 1, pages 5200–5205, 2004.

[18] K. Nowicki and T. A. Snijders. Estimation and prediction for stochastic blockstructures. *Journal of the American Statistical Association*, 96(455), 2001.

[19] G. Palla, I. Derenyi, I. Farkas, and T. Vicsek. Uncovering the overlapping community structure of complex networks in nature and society. *Nature*, 435:814, 2005.

[20] J. Ruan and W. Zhang. An efficient spectral algorithm for network community discovery and its applications to biological and social networks. In *Proc. of ICDM*, pages 643–648, 2007.

[21] J. Shi and J. Malik. Normalized cuts and image segmentation. *IEEE Transcations of Pattern Analysis and Machine Intelligence*, 22(8):888–905, 2000.

[22] M. Steyvers, P. Smyth, M. Rosen-Zvi, and T. Griffiths. Probabilistic author-topic models for information discovery. In *Proc. of SIGKDD'04*, pages 306–315, 2004.

[23] Y. W. Teh, M. I. Jordan, M. J. Beal, and D. M. Blei. Hierarchical dirichlet processes. *Journal of the American Statistical Association*, 101, 2003.

[24] D. M. Wilkinson and B. A. Huberman. A method for finding communities of related genes. *PNAS*, 101, Suppl 1:5241–5248, 2004.

[25] D. Zhou, J. Li, and H. Zha. A new mallows distance based metric for comparing clusterings. In *Proc. of ICML'05*, pages 1028–1035, 2005.

[26] D. Zhou, E. Manavoglu, J. Li, C. L. Giles, and H. Zha. Probabilistic models for discovering e-communities. In *Proc. of WWW'06*, pages 173–182, 2006.

Authorship Classification: A Discriminative Syntactic Tree Mining Approach*

Sangkyum Kim, Hyungsul Kim, Tim Weninger, Jiawei Han, Hyun Duk Kim
Department of Computer Science
University of Illinois at Urbana-Champaign
Urbana, IL 61801
{kim71, hkim21, weninge1, hanj, hkim277}@illinois.edu

ABSTRACT

In the past, there have been dozens of studies on automatic authorship classification, and many of these studies concluded that the writing style is one of the best indicators for original authorship. From among the hundreds of features which were developed, *syntactic features* were best able to reflect an author's writing style. However, due to the high computational complexity for extracting and computing syntactic features, only simple variations of basic syntactic features such as function words, *POS*(Part of Speech) tags, and rewrite rules were considered. In this paper, we propose a new feature set of k-embedded-edge subtree patterns that holds more syntactic information than previous feature sets. We also propose a novel approach to directly mining them from a given set of syntactic trees. We show that this approach reduces the computational burden of using complex syntactic structures as the feature set. Comprehensive experiments on real-world datasets demonstrate that our approach is reliable and more accurate than previous studies.

Categories and Subject Descriptors

I.2.7 [**Artificial Intelligence**]: Natural Language Processing—*Text Analysis*; H.3.3 [**Information Search and Retrieval**]: Clustering; H.2.8 [**Database Applications**]: Data Mining

*The work was supported in part by the Blue Waters sustained-petascale computing project under the National Science Foundation (award number OCI 07-25070) and the state of Illinois, NDSEG Fellowship, NSF IIS-0905215, NSF-CCF-0905014, U.S. Air Force Office of Scientific Research MURI award FA9550-08-1-0265, and the U.S. Army Research Laboratory under Cooperative Agreement No. W911NF-09-2-0053 (NS-CTA). The views and conclusions contained in this document are those of the authors and should not be interpreted as representing the official policies, either expressed or implied, of the Army Research Laboratory or the U.S. Government. The U.S. Government is authorized to reproduce and distribute reprints for Government purposes notwithstanding any copyright notation here on.

SIGIR '11 July 24-28 2011, Beijing, China

General Terms

Algorithms, Experimentation

Keywords

Authorship Attribution, Text Mining, Text Categorization, Authorship Discrimination, Authorship Classification

1. INTRODUCTION

In computational linguistics and text mining domains, there are three classical classification problems: topic classification, genre classification, and authorship classification. Among these three problems, arguably the most difficult is the classification of documents in terms of their authorship (known as *authorship classification*, authorship attribution and/or authorship discrimination). This problem can be thought of as classifying documents based on the writing styles of the authors. This is a nontrivial problem even for humans: while a human can easily identify the topic and genre of a given document, identifying its authorship is harder. If the documents are in the same topic and genre, the task becomes much harder.

In the era of excessive electronic texts, authorship classification has become more important than ever before with a wide variety of applications. Besides the early works of analyzing the disputed plays of *Shakespeare*(1887) [22] or anonymous documents of *The Federalist Papers*(1964) [24], it could also be used to identify authors of short 'for sale' messages in a newsgroup [36] and even for forensic investigations by identifying authorship of e-mail messages [2]. Detecting plagiarism or copyright infringement of unauthorized reuse of source code by establishing a profile of an author's style is another important application of authorship classification [5].

Existing approaches to authorship classification use various methods to extract effective features, the most common of which include style markers such as function words [9, 33, 1, 12] and grammatical elements such as part of speech (*POS*) tags [3, 11, 35]. Function words are common words (*e.g.* articles, prepositions, pronouns) that have little semantic content of their own but usually indicate a grammatical relationship or generic property. Recently, there have been several papers that claimed function words are more effective than other types of style markers [33, 35, 34].

Unfortunately, research on more complex syntactic structures has not been practical because of the lack of a reliable, automatic tool which retrieves syntactic structures, and be-

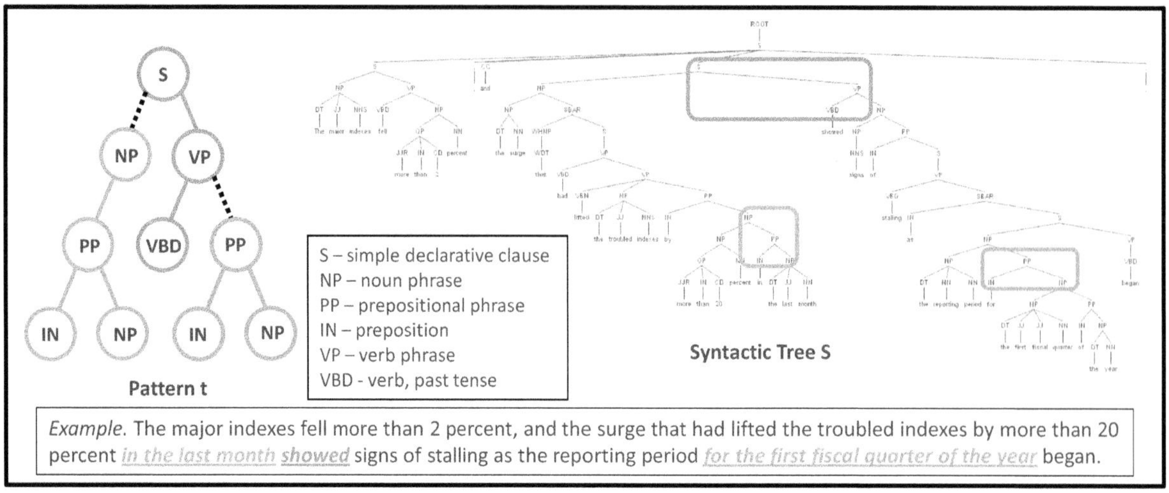

Figure 1: A 2-*ee* subtree t is mined from two *The New York Times* journalists Jack Healy and Eric Dash who worked in the same business department. On average, 21.2% of Jack's sentences contained t while only 7.2% of Eric's sentences contained t.

cause of the high computational cost associated with syntactic structure-based algorithms. Instead, several variations of *POS* tags [9, 11, 15] and rather simple syntactic structures like rewrite rules [3, 11, 15] have been proposed. Among them, bigram *POS* tags and rewrite rules showed reliable performance in various dataset configurations.

Recently, several advanced techniques have been developed which greatly improved the performance of *Natural Language Processing*(*NLP*) tools[1] enabling reliable, highly accurate sentence parsing into a syntactic tree of *POS* tags. A *syntactic tree* is a rooted and ordered tree that is labeled with *POS* tags that represent the syntactic structure of a sentence. Based on the syntactic trees parsed by these tools, we propose a novel syntactic feature set of tree fragments allowing at most k-embedded edges (in short, a k-*ee* subtree). We say there is an embedded edge between two nodes if and only if they are in an ancestor-descendant relationship but not in a parent-child relationship. Compared with previous feature sets that consist of parts of distinct connected subtree components, our new feature set captures the relationship between $k+1$ connected subtree components of a syntactic tree, which leads to a better representation of datasets consisting of long and complex sentences. Figure 1 gives an example of a k-*ee* subtree t for $k = 2$. Pattern t is composed of three smaller subtrees, which are connected by two embedded edges (S,NP) and (VP,PP). The differences in pattern distributions between two authors suggest that a set of k-*ee* subtrees can be utilized as a good feature set for authorship classification.

To reduce the number of features, we only mine a set of frequent and discriminative k-*ee* subtrees, which results in higher accuracy by avoiding overfitting to the training data and by not generating non-discriminative features that often degrade the performance. This task is commonly referred to as pattern-based classification. The original pattern-based classification technique employed a two-step procedure called *generate-and-test* which generates all frequent and closed candidate patterns and then selects the discriminative patterns among them [20]. Unfortunately, it is still intractable to use this *generate-and-test* methodology to get discriminative patterns because there are simply too many candidate patterns.

For this reason, there have been quite a few works which *directly* mine discriminative patterns without generating all candidates [7, 37, 29]. Yet, these existing works cannot be directly applied to our problem setting because they require the feature values to be binary. Instead, we require numeric feature values because a (syntactic) feature can occur multiple times in a document and usually the number of occurrences implies its importance. Existing works are all based on binary-valued features and their theorems and proofs are not easily extendable to numeric-valued features. A recent work ([18]) showed that it has more gain to use numeric values than to discretize them into binary values. It also proposed a new way to directly mining discriminative numeric features by solving a linear programming optimization problem. But all these previous works mine top-1 pattern iteratively until the mined patterns cover the entire data. To cope with this issue, we derive an upper bound of a discriminative score of numeric-valued features, and develop an efficient algorithm that mines in one iteration a set of discriminative patterns to be used for classification purpose.

To validate the utility of our new feature set compared to others, for fair comparisons, we apply the same *SVM* classification algorithm using various feature sets on several real data collections. Because of its high and reliable performance, *SVM* has commonly been used to compare the effectiveness of feature sets [11, 35, 15]. Experimental results demonstrate the effectiveness of the proposed k-*ee* subtree features in comparison to the well-known existing feature sets of function words, *POS* tags, and rewrite rules. We demonstrate that by using k-*ee* subtrees as the feature set we outperform the existing feature sets by 8.23% on average and show that it is significantly better from other approaches by t-test with 95% confidence level.

In summary, the contributions of this paper are as follows:

- We propose a new feature set of k-*ee* subtrees for authorship classification.

[1]We used Stanford Parser (`http://nlp.stanford.edu/software/lex-parser.shtml`), but there are more tools available like **N**atural **L**anguage **T**ool**K**it (NLTK) package (`http://www.nltk.org`).

- We develop an efficient algorithm to directly mine discriminative *k-ee* subtrees, which are not binary but numeric valued features, in one iteration.
- Through comprehensive experiments on various datasets, we demonstrate the utility of our proposed framework to provide an effective solution for the authorship classification problem.

The rest of the paper is organized as follows. Section 2 presents an overview of the related works. In Section 3, we introduce various preliminary concepts and define our new feature set of *k-ee* subtrees. Section 4 explains a *branch-and-bound* framework of discriminative *k-ee* subtree mining. We report experimental results in Section 5, followed by discussions in Section 6 and conclusions in Section 7.

2. RELATED WORKS

There are two main steps involved in any authorship classification algorithm: (1) the feature extraction step and (2) the classification step based on features extracted from the first step.

For the feature extraction step, since the earliest works of the authorship attribution on the plays of *Shakespeare*(1887) [22] and *The Federalist Papers*(1964) [24] that used a small number of common words such as '*and*', '*to*' as a feature set, nearly 1,000 different feature sets have been studied including sentence length, chi-square score, lexical richness [17], vocabulary richness [8], function words [1], word n-grams [27], character n-grams [13], and rewrite rules [3] with lots of controversy on their effectiveness. Even though there is an issue of fair comparison among feature sets because previous works conducted experiments based on their own datasets with different classification methods [33, 28], function words and rewrite rules are generally considered to give reliable and good results. In [35, 34], the authors compared function words with other feature sets (even combination of those feature sets) to show that function words are better than the other feature sets.

Even though many new features have been explored for authorship classification, most of the classification algorithms are simply adapted from other domains' well-known classification algorithms such as *PCA* [16], *k*-nearest neighbor, decision tree, bayesian networks [33], and *SVM* [9, 11, 35, 15]. In [35], a language model based authorship classification framework was proposed, which showed comparable performance to *SVM*. Because of its high and reliable performance, *SVM* has commonly been used to compare the effectiveness of feature sets [11, 35, 15], so in this paper we also use *SVM* for fair comparison between our new feature set and existing feature sets.

While most of the earlier works focused on binary authorship classification problem (classifying documents from two authors) which showed significantly good results, recent works including [2, 19, 21, 33, 35] have brought up the problem of multiple authorship classification (classifying documents from more than two authors). Thus, in this paper, we also show the effectiveness of our proposed *k-ee* subtrees feature set by solving both binary and multiple authorship classification problems.

Our proposed *k-ee* subtrees feature set can be considered to be a variation of tree patterns. In the data mining domain, there have been several studies on tree pattern mining [30, 31, 4]. *TreeMiner* [30] is one of the pioneering frequent tree pattern mining algorithms. For tree classification, rule-based classifiers (*XRules* [31]) and a decision tree based classifier (*Tree*^{2} [4]) were proposed. To the best of our knowledge, mining *k-ee* subtrees has never been discussed before.

3. PRELIMINARIES

Previous authorship attribution approaches adopted function words, *POS* tags, and rewrite rules as a feature set to build a classification model. Even though they achieved good accuracy, there still exists room for a more meaningful feature set to improve the performance. In this section, we describe rewrite rules which are somewhat complex syntactic structures that hold more syntactic information than the other two feature sets. Also, we define our new feature set of *k-ee* subtree patterns.

3.1 Rewrite Rule

In [3], rewrite rules were considered to be building blocks of a syntactic tree, just as words are building blocks of a sentence. Here, a *syntactic tree* is a rooted and ordered tree which is labeled with *POS* tags that represents the syntactic structure of a sentence. Its interior nodes are labeled by non-terminals of the grammar, and the leaf nodes are labeled by terminals.

Compared to previous approaches that utilized function words and *POS* tags, rewrite rules can hold functional structure information of the sentence. In linguistics, a rewrite rule is in the form of "$X \rightarrow Y$" where X is a syntactic category label and Y is a sequence of such labels such that X can be replaced by Y in generating the constituent structure of a sentence. For example, "$NP \rightarrow DT{+}JJ{+}JJ{+}NN$" means that a noun phrase (NP) consists of a determiner (DT) followed by two adjectives (JJ) and a noun (NN).

There is a limit when using rewrite rules as features of a classification model. First, because of the restriction that the entire rule cannot be broken into smaller parts, no similarity between rules are considered. A large number of slightly different rules are all counted as independent features. For instance, a rewrite rule "$NP \rightarrow DT{+}JJ{+}NN$", missing one JJ from the above example, becomes a separate rewrite rule. Second, the expressibility of rewrite rules is limited because they must adhere to a very strict two-level tree structure, which does not allow the entire rule to be broken into smaller parts. For example, the relationships between rewrite rules are missing, which can hold more refined syntactic information. For these reasons, we developed a new feature set of *k-ee* tree patterns that are flexible and complex enough to represent the syntactic structure information of a sentence.

3.2 k-Embedded-Edge Subtree

To overcome the drawbacks of simple syntactic feature sets used in previous approaches, we explore more complex syntactic features. Induced subtrees of a syntactic tree are one of the candidate feature sets whose features are multi-level tree fragments used to model the complex syntactic structure of a sentence. Here, we define a tree t to be an *induced subtree* of a tree s if there exists an identity mapping from t to s preserving all parent-child relationships between the nodes of t. Our pilot experiments showed that a small number of combinations of those induced subtrees could achieve even higher accuracy, which motivated us to define *k-ee* subtrees for our new feature set. Based on this

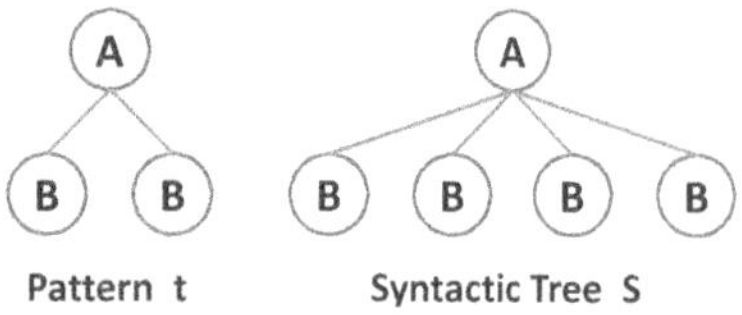

Figure 2: Example of overcounting overlapped *k-ee* subtree occurrences

motivation, we designed a new tree pattern that can capture this phenomenon.

Definition 1. We define an ***embedded*** edge e of a tree s to be a pair of two nodes with an ancestor-descendant relationship. We define a ***k-embedded-edge subtree*** *(shortly,* ***k-ee subtree****)* t of a tree s to be a set of induced subtrees of s that can be connected by at most k embedded edges (not with parent-child relationships) for a user specified value k.

The number of *k-ee* subtrees would be exponential on the number of trees and their sizes. We define a minimum support θ to ensure we only mine general common patterns that will be applicable to test data thus avoiding overfitting. We define the *support* of a feature t (denoted by $sup(t)$) to be the total number of sentences in training data that contains t. We say t is *frequent* if and only if $sup(t) \geq \theta$ for a user-specified minimum support threshold θ.

3.3 Document Representation based on Discriminative k-ee Patterns

The frequency of a pattern in a document (or a set of syntactic trees) is quite important in the sense that it can be a good measure to discriminate the writing styles of different authors. Well-known features like function words, and the *POS* tag-adapted *bag-of-words* approach use the number of occurrences in a document as their frequency measure. However, unlike function words and *POS* tags, *k-ee* subtrees cannot simply adapt the same frequency measure because it generates overlapped occurrences, which would lead to an exaggerated frequency value. Figure 2 is an illustration of this overcounting problem. The syntactic tree S has only one A and four Bs, but the number of occurrences of pattern t becomes 6. More generally, if A has n Bs as its children in S, then the occurrence count of pattern t becomes $O(n^2)$. Since we allow k embedded edges for a *k-ee* subtree, this overcounting problem will be even more amplified.

Our observation that a document is parsed into a set of syntactic trees (of sentences) gave us an insight to define the frequency measure of a *k-ee* subtree in a more natural way by counting the number of syntactic trees of a document that contain the pattern.

Definition 2. We define the ***frequency*** of a *k-ee* subtree t in a document d (denoted by $freq(t, d)$) to be the number of syntactic trees (*i.e.*, parsed sentences) in d that contain t over the total number of sentences in d.

We will discuss how to mine discriminative *k-ee* subtree patterns in the following section (Section 4). For here, suppose we already have them in a set $P = \{t_1, \cdots, t_n\}$. Then, we can express a document d as a vector of their frequencies as $d = (freq(t_1, d), \cdots, freq(t_n, d))$.

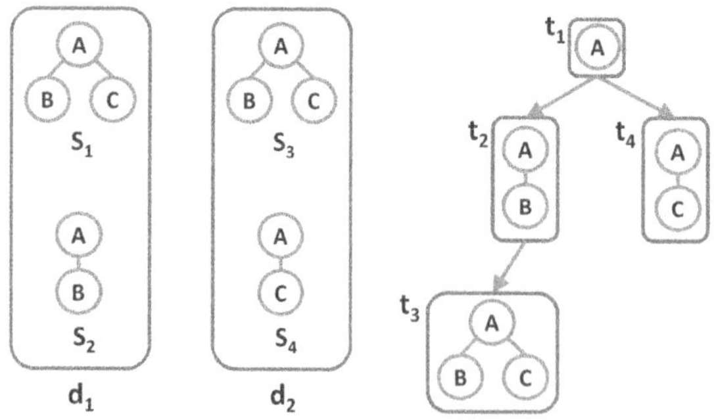

(a) A toy database $\mathcal{D}$ with 2 documents. Each document has 2 syntactic trees.

(b) Pattern growth of *k-ee* subtrees with $\theta = 0.5$ and k=0

Figure 3: Database $\mathcal{D}$ and its frequent *k-ee* subtrees

4. DISCRIMINATIVE K-EE SUBTREE MINING

In the previous section, we introduced *k-ee* subtrees as a new feature set for authorship classification. These patterns hold more expressive syntactic information than other features and are flexible enough to consider partial matchings of syntactic trees, but the number of *k-ee* subtrees is above our control. Therefore, we need to directly mine a small number of discriminative patterns not only to reduce the number of features but also to mine significant patterns which has been shown to improve classification accuracy [6]. In this section, we present a branch-and-bound framework to solve this problem.

4.1 Mining Frequent k-ee Subtrees: Pattern-Growth Approach

We do not generate candidate *k-ee* subtrees and check for frequent attributes. Instead, we find a frequent *k-ee* subtree and extend it by adding a node that is guaranteed to be frequent in a depth-first manner, which enables several pruning techniques for frequent and discriminative pattern mining. We first introduce how to efficiently mine frequent patterns based on pattern-growth approach by using projected database [26, 38], and then explain pruning techniques to mine discriminative patterns.

We illustrate the procedure for pattern-growth approach as follows. First, find a size-1 frequent *k-ee* subtree t in the training dataset $\mathcal{D}$. Second, project the postfix of each occurrence of t in the syntactic trees of $\mathcal{D}$ into a new database $\mathcal{D}_t$. A *postfix* of an occurrence of t in a syntactic tree s is a forest of the nodes of s appearing after the occurrence of t in a pre-order scan of s. Third, find a frequent node v in $\mathcal{D}_t$ that can be attached to the rightmost path of t that forms a *k-ee* subtree. Once v is frequent in $\mathcal{D}_t$, it ensures that the extended pattern is also frequent, so we do not need to scan the whole database $\mathcal{D}$ again. Note that, in this study, we consider a node v attached to t by an (induced) edge different from the one attached by an embedded edge. Fourth, recursively go back to the second step with the extended pattern for every frequent node we find. Note that the projected database of a pattern t keeps shrinking as the mining process moves on and t becomes a bigger superpattern.

EXAMPLE 1. *Figure 3 shows an example of the pattern-growth approach to mine 0-*ee *subtrees from a database $\mathcal{D}$ of four syntactic trees when minimum support threshold is*

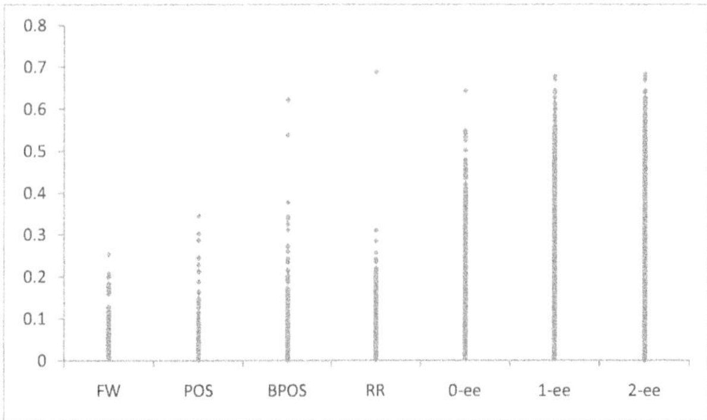

Figure 4: Binned information gain score distribution of various feature sets

0.5. Each pattern is indexed in pattern-generation order. We first search for size-1 frequent patterns, which are t_1, t_5 and t_6. We choose t_1 as a starting point, and find frequent nodes that can be attached to t_1 from its projected database. We find that nodes B and C are frequent, and we extend t_1 to t_2 by adding a node B. Similar procedures are recursively performed until we mine all frequent patterns.

4.2 Binned Information Gain Score

In previous subsections, we presented a *pattern-growth* method to mine frequent patterns, but the resulted patterns may still be too many. Based on the study that the patterns with high discriminative score can improve the classification performance [6], we first evaluate the discriminative power of a *k-ee* subtree. Note that most of the well-known discriminative scores (*e.g.* information gain, fisher score) have upper bound on binary feature values not on numeric feature values [6, 7, 29, 25]. In this subsection, we define a new discriminativeness score, *binned information gain*, and derive its upper bound on the numeric feature values to enable a *branch-and-bound* framework to mine discriminative patterns on numeric feature values.

Definition 3. For a user specified number n, we divide range $[0, 1]$ of the relative sentence frequency per document of t into a partition p of equi-width n bins: $p_1 = [0, \frac{1}{n})$, $p_2 = [\frac{1}{n}, \frac{2}{n})$, $\cdots$, $p_{n-1} = [\frac{n-2}{n}, \frac{n-1}{n})$, $p_n = [\frac{n-1}{n}, 1]$. For a given partition p and m classes $C_1, \cdots, C_m$, we define the *binned conditional entropy* of t by

$$H(C|X) = -\sum_{i=1}^{n} P(X \in p_i) \sum_{k=1}^{m} P(C_k|X \in p_i) \log p(C_k|X \in p_i)$$

and *binned information Gain* of t by $IG(C|X) = H(C) - H(C|X)$ where $H(C) = -\sum_{k=1}^{m} p(C_k) \log p(C_k)$.

A pattern t will have a large binned information gain score if the frequency distribution imbalance between the classes becomes bigger for each bin, which means t is significant to discriminate classes.

Figure 4 presents binned information gain score distributions of various feature sets such as function words (FW), *POS* tags (POS), bigram *POS* tags (BPOS), rewrite rules (RR), and *k-ee* subtrees for k=0, 1, and 2 (0-*ee*, 1-*ee*, and 2-*ee*, respectively). We can easily see that the highest scores are mostly from *k-ee* subtrees, which implies that they can be more meaningful than other features – an assertion we later test in the experiments section.

For a tree pattern t, we denote binned information gain of t by $IG(t)$ and information gain upper bound of t and its superpatterns by $IG_{ub}(t)$. Given a *k-ee* subtree t and a partition p, we define (A, B, p) to be a *frequency distribution* of t where $A = (A_1, \ldots, A_n)$ and $B = (B_1, \ldots, B_n)$ with A_i and B_i being the number of documents in class C_1 and C_2 respectively for each bin p_i of a partition p. Denote (A', B', p) as a frequency distribution of a super pattern t' of t. The following two lemmas describe the properties of (A, B, p) and (A', B', p) that will be used to prove the main theorem to derive the upper bound of binned information gain.

LEMMA 1. *For any $k = 2, \ldots, n$, the following four inequalities hold for a k-ee subtree t and its superpattern t': $\sum_{i=k}^{n} A'_i \leq \sum_{i=k}^{n} A_i$, $\sum_{i=1}^{k-1} A'_i \geq \sum_{i=1}^{k-1} A_i$, $\sum_{i=k}^{n} B'_i \leq \sum_{i=k}^{n} B_i$, and $\sum_{i=1}^{k-1} B'_i \geq \sum_{i=1}^{k-1} B_i$.*

PROOF. Since t' is a superpattern of t, $\sum_{i=k}^{n} A'_i \leq \sum_{i=k}^{n} A_i$ for $k \geq 2$. Therefore, $\sum_{i=1}^{k-1} A_i = |C_1| - \sum_{i=k}^{n} A_i \leq |C_1| - \sum_{i=k}^{n} A'_i = \sum_{i=1}^{k-1} A'_i$ where $|C_i|$ is the number of documents in class C_i. Similar proof for B_i. □

The following lemma shows the condition to get the upper bound of binned information gain for a special case when only the first two bins of frequency distribution are different.

LEMMA 2. *For a given frequency distribution (A, B, p), let (A', B', p) be a frequency distribution with $A'_1 = A_1 + x$, $A'_2 = A_2 - x$ $(0 \leq x \leq A_2)$ and the rest unchanged. If $\frac{A_1}{A_1+B_1} \geq \frac{A_2}{A_2+B_2}$, then (A', B', p) achieves its minimum conditional entropy when $x = A_2$. Otherwise, it achieves its minimum conditional entropy when $x = 0$.*

PROOF. Let $f(x)$ be the conditional entropy of (A',B',p) and N be the total number of documents. Then,

$$\begin{aligned} f(x) &= \frac{A_1+B_1+x}{N}\left(-\frac{A_1+x}{A_1+B_1+x}\log\frac{A_1+x}{A_1+B_1+x}\right. \\ &\quad \left. -\frac{B_1}{A_1+B_1+x}\log\frac{B_1}{A_1+B_1+x}\right) \\ &\quad +\frac{A_2+B_2-x}{N}\left(-\frac{A_2-x}{A_2+B_2-x}\log\frac{A_2-x}{A_2+B_2-x}\right. \\ &\quad \left. -\frac{B_2}{A_2+B_2-x}\log\frac{B_2}{A_2+B_2-x}\right) \\ &\quad +\sum_{i=3}^{n} P(X \in p_i)\sum_{k=1}^{2} P(C_k|X \in p_i)\log p(C_k|X \in p_i) \\ f'(x) &= \frac{1}{N}\log\left(\frac{A_1+B_1+x}{A_1+x}\cdot\frac{A_2-x}{A_2+B_2-x}\right) \end{aligned}$$

If $\frac{A_1}{A_1+B_1} \geq \frac{A_2}{A_2+B_2}$, $f'(x) \leq 0$. Otherwise, $f'(x) > 0$. □

The following theorem describes that the binned information gain upper bound exists and is determined by the frequency distribution of the first two bins.

THEOREM 1. *Given a tree pattern t, its super patterns including itself have a conditional entropy lower bound in the frequency distribution (A', B', p) of one of the following two forms: (1) $A'_1 = A_1 + A_2$, $B'_2 = \sum_{i=2}^{n} B_i$, $B'_1 = B_1$, $B'_i = 0$ $(i = 2, \ldots, n)$ and $A'_i = A_i$ $(i = 3, \ldots, n)$ (2) $B'_1 = B_1 + B_2$, $A'_2 = \sum_{i=2}^{n} A_i$, $A'_1 = A_1$, $A'_i = 0$ $(i = 2, \ldots, n)$ and $B'_i = B_i$ $(i = 3, \ldots, n)$.*

PROOF. Suppose $(\bar{A}, \bar{B}, p)$ is a frequency distribution of a superpattern $\bar{t}$ of t with minimum conditional entropy whose form is in neither cases. Denote $P_i = \frac{\bar{A}_i}{\bar{A}_i+\bar{B}_i}$ and $Q_i = \frac{\bar{B}_i}{\bar{A}_i+\bar{B}_i}$ $(i = 1, \ldots, n)$. By generalizing Lemma 2, either $P_i < P_{i+1}$ or $P_{i+1} = 0$ $(i = 1, \ldots, n-1)$. Symmetrically, either $Q_i < Q_{i+1}$ or $Q_{i+1} = 0$ $(i = 1, \ldots, n-1)$. Then, for all $i = 2, \ldots, n$, either $P_i = 0$ or $Q_i = 0$. ($\because$ Assume $P_i \neq 0$ and $Q_i \neq 0$ for some i. Then, $P_{i-1} < P_i$ and $Q_{i-1} < Q_i$. But, $1 - P_{i-1} = Q_{i-1} < Q_i = 1 - P_i$ which is a contradiction.) Therefore, either $P_2 = 0$ or $Q_2 = 0$. Without loss of generality, say $P_2 = 0$. Then, we can get another distribution $(\bar{A}',\bar{B}',p)$ where $\bar{B}'_2 = \sum_{i=2}^{n} \bar{B}_i$, $\bar{B}'_i = 0$ for $(i = 3, \ldots, n)$, and the rest unchanged from $(\bar{A},\bar{B},p)$. Since its conditional entropy at each bin p_i $(i = 2, \ldots, n)$ becomes 0, it has smaller or the same conditional entropy with $(\bar{A},\bar{B},p)$. By the assumption that $(\bar{A},\bar{B},p)$ has the minimum conditional entropy, their conditional entropy are the same. By Lemma 1, $\bar{A}'_1 \geq A_1 + A_2$ and $\bar{B}'_1 \geq B_1$ ($\because \bar{A}'_2 = 0$ since $P_2 = 0$). If either $\bar{A}'_1 > A_1 + A_2$ or $\bar{B}'_1 > B_1$, then the conditional entropy of $(\bar{A}',\bar{B}',p)$ becomes higher than the conditional entropy of (A',B',p) in the first form of the theorem which is a contradiction to our assumption that the conditional entropy of $(\bar{A},\bar{B},p)$ is minimum. Similar contradiction can be derived when $Q_2 = 0$. □

4.3 Modified Sequential Coverage Method

The binned information gain measure and its upper bound described in Section 4.2 enables a *branch-and-bound* framework, and we can simply perform the feature selection procedure in a traditional *sequential coverage* way as follows ([7, 29]). First, we mine the most discriminative *k-ee* subtree and add it to the feature set. Second, we remove trees that contain the extracted pattern and compute binned information gain scores of the remaining patterns on the updated database. In this way, redundant patterns will have a small chance to be selected. Third, we go back to the first step until either the dataset becomes empty or no more patterns are mined. Once the feature selection procedure is complete, we get a small number of discriminative *k-ee* subtrees. Based on the feature set F of these patterns, we use the document representation described in Section 3.3 to train a classification model.

But this procedure is inefficient when many discriminative patterns need to be mined because the *sequential coverage* method described above is based on iteratively mining one discriminative pattern for each iteration. We observe that the object of iterative approach is to find non-repetitive discriminative patterns. For this purpose, previous works simply applied the decision tree scheme of feature selection either (1) to a sequential coverage method to be used for SVM classification model [7, 29] or (2) to a decision tree classification model directly [10]. The difference between them is that the former recursively mines the dataset that does not contain the pattern, and the latter recursively mines both datasets containing and not containing the pattern. But both approaches need to recompute discriminativeness scores of the patterns on the updated database paying an expensive computational cost, which does not really involve removing repetitive patterns. We propose to use a modified sequential coverage method which does not recompute the binned information gain scores.

4.4 Direct Discriminative k-ee Subtree Mining

In this section, we design a novel algorithm to efficiently mine discriminative patterns in a single iteration. We compute the binned information gain score only once, and apply the sequential coverage method without recomputing the binned information gain scores. Moreover, we propose an efficient way of mining the discriminative patterns in one iteration.

Here, we define some terms and symbols that will be used for the rest of the section. We denote $\mathbf{t} \models \mathbf{s}$ when a *k-ee* subtree t is contained in a tree s. We define $\mathbf{S_t} = \{s \in \mathcal{D} | t \models s\}$ to be a set of trees in a tree dataset $\mathcal{D}$ that contain t. Also, we define $\mathbf{A_t} = \{p : \text{k-ee subtree} | \exists s \in S_t, p = argmax_{p \models s} IG(p)\}$ to be a set of patterns that achieve the highest discriminative score among all patterns in some trees that contain t, and $\mathbf{B_t}$ to be a set of arbitrary patterns from each tree of S_t. We denote $\mathbf{F}$ to be a set of discriminative *k-ee* subtrees in $\mathcal{D}$ mined by the modified sequential coverage method.

The following lemma characterizes discriminative patterns mined by sequential coverage.

LEMMA 3. *For a given tree dataset $\mathcal{D}$,*

$$F = \{t | \exists s \in \mathcal{D} \text{ such that } t = argmax_{p \models s} IG(p)\}.$$

PROOF. By the definition of the modified sequential coverage method mentioned in Section 4.3. □

Lemma 3 explains that the discriminative patterns mined by the modified sequential coverage method are indeed the most discriminative patterns for some trees of $\mathcal{D}$. Based on this observation, we derive a pruning method by *branch-and-bound* approach in the following proposition.

PROPOSITION 1. **(Branch-and-Bound (BB) Pruning)** *If $IG_{ub}(t) < \min_{p \in A_t} IG(p)$, then no superpattern t' of t is in F.*

PROOF. Since $S_t \supseteq S_{t'}$, $IG_{ub}(t) < \min_{p \in A_t} IG(p) \leq \min_{p \in A_{t'}} IG(p)$. That is, t' cannot be the most discriminative pattern for any tree in $S_{t'}$. □

COROLLARY 1. *If $IG_{ub}(t) < \min_{p \in B_t} IG(p)$, then no superpattern t' of t is in F.*

PROOF. By definition of A_t, $IG_{ub}(t) < \min_{p \in B_t} IG(p) \leq \min_{p \in A_t} IG(p)$. □

In case $IG_{ub}(t) = \min_{p \in B_t} IG(p)$, we also skip mining $\mathcal{D}_t$ since any tree containing a superpattern t' of t will also contain another pattern that has higher or the same discriminative score.

Once we know an upper bound of the discriminative score of t's superpatterns, we can use the *BB* pruning method described in Proposition 1. Unfortunately, as alluded to earlier, this is a nontrivial task because the feature values are numeric instead of binary. In Section 4.2, we partitioned the numeric range $[0, 1]$ into a finite number of bins and derived the upper bound of binned information gain score by checking a constant number of cases (at most 2 cases) regardless to the number of bins.

In the mining process, since we do not know A_t, we set B_t to be the set of current best patterns of S_t and apply Corollary 1 as a *BB* pruning condition. For that reason, we maintain current best patterns for each tree.

EXAMPLE 2. *Consider the example from Figure 3. Suppose class c_1 has a document d_1 and class c_2 has a document*

d_2 from a database $\mathcal{D}$. Let the number of bins for binned information gain be 3 (i.e. $n = 3$). We first mine t_1, compute its discriminative score ($IG(t_1) = 0$) and update current B_{t_1} ($B_{t_1} = \emptyset$) by checking t_1. Now, $B_{t_1} = \{t_1\}$. Since $IG_{ub}(t_1) = 1 > \min_{p \in B_{t_1}} IG(p) = 0$, we move on to next pattern t_2 without pruning. We compute t_2's discriminative score ($IG(t_2) = 1$), and update $B_{t_2} = \{t_1\}$ to be $B_{t_2} = \{t_2\}$. Since $IG_{ub}(t_2) = 1 = \min_{p \in B_t} IG(p)$, we can skip generating t_3.

Following the original sequential coverage methodology mentioned in Section 4.3, when a *k-ee* subtree t is generated the trees containing t are removed. But in real classification tasks, we may want to generate multiple patterns to represent a tree to improve accuracy. To address this issue, we use a minimum feature coverage threshold δ introduced in [7], *i.e.*, a tree is removed when it is covered by at least δ discriminative patterns. Lemma 3 and Proposition 1 can easily be adapted with the feature coverage parameter δ by maintaining top-δ patterns for each tree and using δ-th highest discriminative score as a cut-off threshold for each tree.

In summary, we proposed a *branch-and-bound* framework of authorship classification. During the process, the algorithm retains and updates the most discriminative patterns $Opt(s)$ of each tree input, and at the end they become F. The basic framework is to expand the patterns from small to large sizes in pattern-growth approach. Before we expand current pattern t into a larger one, we compute the upper bound of the binned information gain of all superpatterns of t. Based on *BB* pruning described in Corollary 1, if the upper bound value is not greater than the current minimum $Opt(s)$ from all trees (s) containing t, then we can safely skip exploring superpatterns of t.

5. EXPERIMENTS

In this section, we present an empirical evaluation in order to validate the performance of our *k-ee* subtree based authorship classification. We also analyze the effect of the parameters of *k-ee* subtree patterns presented in this paper. The experiments are designed to test the usefulness of *k-ee* subtrees, as a new feature set, for authorship classification.

5.1 Datasets

For the following experiments, we used public data collections extracted from the *TREC* corpus [14] and *The New York Times*[2].

Table 1: Characteristics of data collections

Data	# Authors	Doc	Doc/Author	Sentence	Word
NTNews	4	400	100	19,161	381,450
Movie	4	2,177	415 – 598	51,086	1,299,682
TREC	7	6,336	804 – 1,003	169,767	3,964,865

From *The New York Times* we collected two different types of datasets: news articles and movie reviews. For the news articles, we randomly selected two journalists from the business department, and two other journalists from the health department who were the main contributors in their departments.[3] We collected datasets assuming that the journalists in the same department are likely to write articles on the same topic and genre using similar words.

[2]`http://www.nytimes.com`

[3]Eric Dash and Jack Healy from the business department, and Denise Grady and Gina Kolata from the health department.

For the movie reviews, we used four movie critics from the *The New York Times*. It has three main critics whom we used. We added another randomly selected critic who is one of the major contributors.[4] We collected this data because most of the movies reviewed by the critics overlapped. We assumed movie reviews of the same movie will be on the same topic and genre using similar words.

We also used news articles from the Associated Press (AP) subcollection of the public TREC corpus. The AP collection has over 200,000 documents by more than 2,380 distinct authors. We followed the same experimental configurations as previous works [33, 35] did by using the same datasets from the same seven authors[5] they used. The statistics of each data collection are described in Table 1. Note that the class distributions (or the number of documents per author) are mostly balanced, and in this way we do not have to consider the effect of skewed data.

5.2 Evaluation Methodology

To evaluate the performance, we performed multiclass classification on each data collection using *SVM* with linear kernel. Specifically, we decomposed the multiclass problem into binary problems via one-versus-one method, and paired the authors of each data collection and conducted binary classification on these pairwise datasets. For each dataset, we conducted 5-fold cross validation, and averaged the accuracy as a measure of the performance. For each fold, training data was used to mine the syntactic features and to get a classification model while test data was only used for evaluation purposes. For each training data, we used another 5-fold cross validation to determine appropriate parameter values for the classification model (linear SVM). In this way, our evaluation ensured that there is no information leak from the test data for the classification task.

We used the number of occurrences of each feature as a feature value for the syntactic features except *k-ee* subtrees which used a new frequency measure defined in Definition 2. For the fair comparison, we used the same classifier. In [9, 35], it is shown that *SVM* achieves reliable performance with high accuracy for authorship classification and the choice of the *SVM* kernel has little or no effect on the performance.

5.3 Comparison Feature Sets

To show how effectively our new feature set of *k-ee* subtrees works, we compared the authorship classification performance with other syntactic features such as function words (FW), unigram *POS* tags (POS), bigram *POS* tags (BPOS), and rewrite rules (RR). As for function words, we took the list of 308 function words from [23]. We used 74 *POS* tags from from the stanford parser. 1,088 Bigram *POS* tags were identified from the leaves of syntactic trees. Rewrite rules and *k*-ee subtrees were generated by mining parsed sentences of syntactic *POS*-tagged trees.

In the table 2, we show the average sizes of feature sets for each data collection. To get the number of features of rewrite

[4]The three main critics of *The New York Times* are A. O. Scott, Manohla Dargis, and Stephen Holden. The other critic we used is Jeannette Catsoulis.

[5]The authors are Barry Schweid, Chet Currier, Dave Skidmore, David Dishneau, Don Kendall, Martin Crutsinger, and Rita Beamish.

Table 2: Number of features for *FW*, *POS*, *RR* and *k-ee* feature sets

Data	FW	POS	BPOS	RR	0-ee	1-ee	2-ee
NTNews	308	74	1088	3929	119.2	257.8	453.1
Movie	308	74	1088	9029.2	306.2	575.1	1015.6
TREC	308	74	1088	8278	254.4	570.5	1107

Table 3: Accuracy Comparison on Different Number of Authors and Various Data Collections

Data	# Authors	FW	POS	BPOS	RR	*k-ee*
NTNews	2	92.25	86.67	90.42	89.75	**94.25**
	3	87.08	78.17	83.97	82.17	**90.83**
	4	82.75	71.25	79.45	75.25	**87.75**
Movie	2	93.18	88.99	84.17	92.88	**95.62**
	3	88.03	81.77	82.17	88.45	**92.89**
	4	84.00	76.23	80.25	85.11	**91.30**
TREC	2	93.33	92.43	93.95	95.07	**96.04**
	3	88.63	87.12	89.64	91.49	**93.43**
	4	85.10	83.03	86.30	88.67	**91.50**
	5	82.24	79.71	83.51	86.31	**89.95**
	6	79.80	76.87	81.10	84.26	**88.56**
	7	77.62	74.53	78.92	82.46	**87.37**
Average		86.14	81.40	84.45	86.87	**91.62**

rules and k-ee subtrees, we computed the average value of the number of distinct features of 5-fold training data for each feature set and dataset. As expected, rewrite rules generated much larger number of features than all the other feature sets. It is noticeable that the number of k-*ee* subtrees are far less than the number of bigram *POS* tags and rewrite rules, and sometimes even less than the number of function words. For the rest of the section, we will show that our small sized new feature set of k-*ee* subtrees outperforms all the other feature sets.

5.4 Performance Evaluation

We first show accuracy comparison on various feature sets and then analyze the effect of the parameters of k-ee subtree approach. For the accuracy comparison with other feature sets, we conducted binary authorship classification as well as multiple authorship classification tasks. Table 3 shows the accuracies of those authorship classification tasks for various comparison feature sets and for three different data collections. By default, we used the number of embedded edge $k = 1$, minimum support threshold $\theta = 0$, the number of bins $n = 10$, and minimum feature threshold $\delta = 3$ for discriminative k-ee subtree mining. In Tables 3 and 4, boldface denotes the best result for each dataset.

5.4.1 Overall Effectiveness

Based on the accuracy results in Table 3, our new feature set of k-*ee* subtrees achieved the highest performance of the comparison feature sets. Overall, most feature sets showed high accuracy on binary authorship classification tasks. But when the number of authors was increased, the performance gaps between k-*ee* subtree feature set and all the others became larger.

It is true that bigram *POS* tags and rewrite rules catch deeper insights of an author's writing style since they are more complex and have much larger number of features than *POS* tags. But we conclude that a feature set of k-*ee* subtrees can characterize an author's writing style even better since (1) it allows even more complex syntactic structures than rewrite rules as features, (2) its size is much smaller than the feature set of bigram *POS* tags and rewrite rules, and (3) it achieved better accuracies. Note that the feature set of function words reliably showed reasonable accuracies as previous works mentioned [33, 35, 34]. It achieved better than *POS* tags and sometimes even better than bigram *POS* tags and rewrite rules. This is because function words have two different aspects together (syntactic and lexical) while *POS* tags only have a syntactic aspect. But complex syntactic structures can complement the lack of lexical aspect of the features, since the feature sets of rewrite rules and k-*ee* subtrees showed higher accuracies than function words.

Table 4: Accuracy Comparison on binary authorship classification of *The New York Times* news articles. Two journalists Dash and Healy from the business department are denoted by B_1 and B_2, and two journalists Grady and Kolata from the health department are denoted by H_1 and H_2 respectively.

Author Pair	FW	POS	BPOS	RR	k-ee
(B_1,B_2)	91.5	87	**95**	94	94
(B_1,H_1)	94	85	92	91	**95**
(B_1,H_2)	95.5	92.5	95	**96**	94
(B_2,H_1)	95	92.5	94.5	92.5	**97.5**
(B_2,H_2)	97	95.5	96.5	97.5	**98**
(H_1,H_2)	80.5	67.5	69.5	67.5	**87**
Average	92.25	86.67	90.42	89.75	**94.25**

On average, the feature set of k-*ee* subtrees improved performance over the other feature sets about 8.23% (overall), 6.36% (function word), 12.56% (*POS*), 8.49% (bigram *POS*) and 5.50% (rewrite rule).

We also performed a significance test on the feature sets over k-*ee* subtrees. We used two-tailed t-test on the accuracy results in Table 3, and all their t values (FW:3.18, POS:5.02, BPOS: 4.49, RR: 2.69) indicated that the performance of k-*ee* subtree patterns are significantly different from (or, better than) all the others (95% confidence interval, threshold:2.07).

Note that we could mine k-*ee* subtrees even for minimum support $\theta = 0$, a task rarely done in previous works because too many patterns were generated from the mining process. Further discussions are described in Section 6.1.

5.4.2 Problem Difficulty Analysis

As we explained in Section 5.1, the datasets of *The New York Times* news articles were collected to identify the difficulty of classification problem. We assumed that the journalists from the same departments will be hard to classify because they might use similar terms on the same topic and genre. As expected, classification results in Table 4 show that classifying journalists from different departments was easier than journalists from same departments.

Note that the last row of Table 4 shows extremely worse performance than other cases. We manually analyzed the news articles of H_1 and H_2, and found that their writing styles were quite informal using several quotations which made it the hardest dataset. Even for this hard task, our approach got the highest accuracy with a big gap.

5.4.3 Parameter Analysis

In Figure 5, we analyze the role of each parameter used

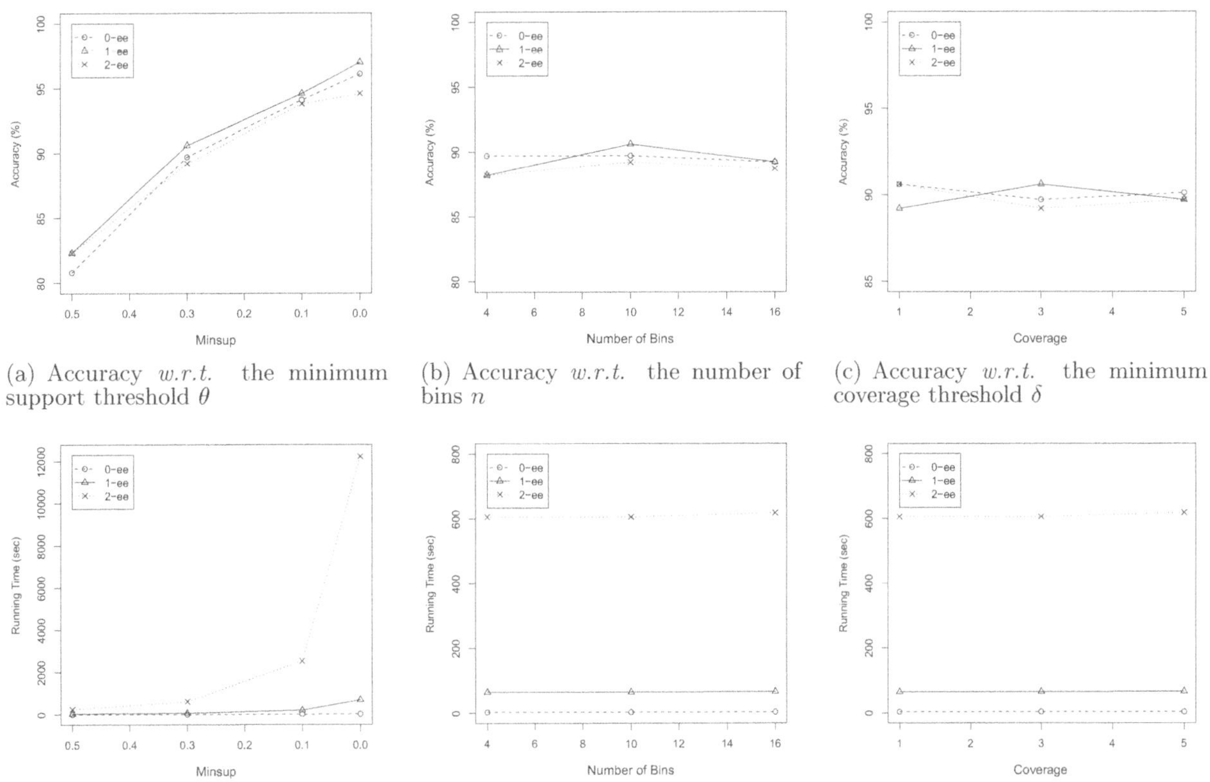

(a) Accuracy *w.r.t.* the minimum support threshold θ

(b) Accuracy *w.r.t.* the number of bins n

(c) Accuracy *w.r.t.* the minimum coverage threshold δ

(d) Running time *w.r.t.* the minimum support threshold θ

(e) Running time *w.r.t.* the number of bins n

(f) Running time *w.r.t.* the minimum coverage threshold δ

Figure 5: Performance Comparisons on Different Parameter Settings

to mine discriminative k-*ee* subtrees. All experiments were conducted for binary classification of two movie critics Stephen Holden and Jeannette Catsoulis. Similar trends could be found from other datasets. For default values, we used $\theta = 0.3$, $n = 10$, and $\delta = 3$. Overall, we found that 1-*ee* subtree feature set showed the best performance. It could be mined with almost in a constant time even with no minimum support threshold. But, when the number of embedded edges increased (*e.g.* $k = 2$), k-*ee* feature set showed worse accuracies because it tended to overfit to the training data. Moreover, it took exponential time to run when minimum support threshold gets smaller. It is good to know that we do not need too complicated syntactic structures (with a high k), because the computation would be too expensive to make our proposed feature set useful.

There are two parameters, n and δ, which are related to our binned information gain score. Based on Figure 5, they did not significantly affect the running time, but somehow affected the accuracy. However, since they achieved the peak within a small range, it was not difficult to optimize their values in our experiments.

6. DISCUSSION

6.1 Minimum Support Threshold

In the experiments, we could put minimum support θ to be 0 to mine discriminative patterns regardless to any minimum support, which is almost impossible for *generate-and-test* methodology that has to generate all patterns. We know that mining frequent pattern is good to avoid overfitting effect, but it is hard to set a correct minimum support threshold value. The authors in [6] show that features with low support have low discriminative power. That is, the discriminative patterns we mine even with no minimum support can be considered to be frequent enough to overcome the overfitting problem.

6.2 Performance of NLP Tools

All current approaches using syntactic features have the same limit of utilizing imperfect natural language processing (*NLP*) tools. For example, to obtain syntactic features (including k-*ee* subtrees), we rely on the performance of *NLP* parsers. It would be a good follow-up work to apply our approach to other informal datasets such as blogs and newsgroups where *NLP* parsers tends to show low performance. We believe our approach will still show reasonably good performance even on those messy datasets with informal wording because the frequent pattern mining will not succumb to parsing errors as shown in Table 4 for (H_1, H_2) author pair.

6.3 Feature Combination

In this paper, we did not consider feature combinations since the main target of this paper is to introduce a new feature set and its effect in authorship classification. In fact, feature combination for authorship classification itself is a different topic with some previous work [32]. Simply applying fixed weights for different feature sets to classify various datasets might not achieve good results because some authors have their own stylistic habits that may be captured in one feature set that is more distinctive than others [35].

7. CONCLUSION

In this paper, we proposed a new syntactic feature set of *k-ee* subtrees to classify documents based on their authorship. To mine *k-ee* subtrees, we developed a direct discriminative *k-ee* subtree mining algorithm via a *branch-and-bound* approach. Our novel algorithm could perform a discriminative score based feature selection procedure to mine discriminative patterns in one step, not iteratively. To directly mine discriminative patterns, we theoretically derived an upper bound of binned information gain score of the numeric feature values.

An experimental study has been performed on public real data collections, which were purposefully chosen to contain the same topics and genres and thus use similar terms. Our *k-ee* subtree-based classification achieved the best results compared to other feature sets. Overall, we conclude that *k*-ee subtrees are meaningful features for authorship classification that achieved high accuracy across various data collections.

8. REFERENCES

[1] S. Argamon and S. Levitan. Measuring the usefulness of function words for authorship attribution. In *ACH/ALLC*, 2005.

[2] Shlomo Argamon, Marin Šarić, and Sterling S. Stein. Style mining of electronic messages for multiple authorship discrimination: first results. In *KDD*, 2003.

[3] H. Baayen, H. van Halteren, and F. Tweedie. Outside the cave of shadows: using syntactic annotation to enhance authorship attribution. *Literary and Linguist Computing*, 11(3):121–132, 1996.

[4] Björn Bringmann and Albrecht Zimmermann. Tree^2 - decision trees for tree structured data. In *PKDD*, 2005.

[5] Steven Burrows, Alexandra L. Uitdenbogerd, and Andrew Turpin. Application of information retrieval techniques for source code authorship attribution. In *DASFAA*, 2009.

[6] Hong Cheng, Xifeng Yan, Jiawei Han, and Chih-Wei Hsu. Discriminative frequent pattern analysis for effective classification. In *ICDE*, 2007.

[7] Hong Cheng, Xifeng Yan, Jiawei Han, and Philip S. Yu. Direct discriminative pattern mining for effective classification. In *ICDE*, 2008.

[8] O. de Vel, A. Anderson, M. Corney, and G. Mohay. Mining e-mail content for author identification forensics. *SIGMOD Record*, 30(4):55–64, 2001.

[9] Joachim Diederich, Jörg Kindermann, Edda Leopold, and Gerhard Paass. Authorship attribution with support vector machines. *Applied Intelligence*, 19(1-2):109–123, 2003.

[10] Wei Fan, Kun Zhang, Hong Cheng, Jing Gao, Xifeng Yan, Jiawei Han, Philip Yu, and Olivier Verscheure. Direct mining of discriminative and essential frequent patterns via model-based search tree. In *KDD*, 2008.

[11] Michael Gamon. Linguistic correlates of style: authorship classification with deep linguistic analysis features. In *COLING*, 2004.

[12] Antonio Miranda García and Javier Calle Martín. Function words in authorship attribution studies. *Literary and Linguistic Computing*, 22(1):49–66, 2007.

[13] Jack Grieve. Quantitative authorship attribution: An evaluation of techniques. *Literary and Linguistic Computing*, 22(3):251–270, 2007.

[14] Donna Harman. Overview of the second text retrieval conference (trec-2). *Information Processing & Management*, 31(3):271–289, 1995.

[15] Graeme Hirst and Ol'ga Feiguina. Bigrams of syntactic labels for authorship discrimination of short texts. *Literary and Linguistic Computing*, 22(4):405–417, 2007.

[16] D. L. Hoover. Statistical stylistics and authorship attribution: an empirical investigation. *Literary and Linguistic Computing*, 16(4):421–444, 2001.

[17] D. L. Hoover. Another perpective on vocabulary richness. *Computers and the Humanities*, 37(2):151–178, 2003.

[18] Hyungsul Kim, Sangkyum Kim, Tim Weninger, Jiawei Han, and Tarek Abdelzaher. Ndpmine: efficiently mining discriminative numerical features for pattern-based classification. In *ECML PKDD*, 2010.

[19] Moshe Koppel, Jonathan Schler, Shlomo Argamon, and Eran Messeri. Authorship attribution with thousands of candidate authors. In *SIGIR*, 2006.

[20] David Lo, Hong Cheng, Jiawei Han, Siau-Cheng Khoo, and Chengnian Sun. Classification of software behaviors for failure detection: a discriminative pattern mining approach. In *KDD*, 2009.

[21] Kim Luyckx and Walter Daelemans. Authorship attribution and verification with many authors and limited data. In *COLING*, 2008.

[22] T. C. Mendenhall. The characteristic curves of composition. *Science*, 11(214):237–246, 1887.

[23] Roger Mitton. Spelling checkers,spelling correctors and the misspellings of poor spellers. *Information Processing and Management*, 23(5):495–505, 1987.

[24] Frederick Mosteller and David L. Wallace. *Inference & Disputed Authorship: The Federalist*. Addison Wesley, 1964.

[25] Siegfried Nijssen, Tias Guns, and Luc De Raedt. Correlated itemset mining in roc space: a constraint programming approach. In *KDD*, 2009.

[26] Jian Pei, Jiawei Han, Behzad Mortazavi-asl, Helen Pinto, Qiming Chen, Umeshwar Dayal, and Mei chun Hsu. Prefixspan: Mining sequential patterns efficiently by prefix-projected pattern growth. In *ICDE*, 2001.

[27] Conrad Sanderson and Simon Guenter. Short text authorship attribution via sequence kernels, markov chains and author unmasking: an investigation. In *EMNLP*, 2006.

[28] Efstathios Stamatatos. A survey of modern authorship attribution methods. *Journal of the American Society for Information Science and Technology*, 60(3):538–556, 2009.

[29] Xifeng Yan, Hong Cheng, Jiawei Han, and Philip S. Yu. Mining significant graph patterns by leap search. In *SIGMOD*, 2008.

[30] Mohammed J. Zaki. Efficiently mining frequent trees in a forest. In *KDD*, 2002.

[31] Mohammed J. Zaki and Charu C. Aggarwal. Xrules: an effective structural classifier for xml data. In *KDD*, 2003.

[32] Ying Zhao and Phil Vines. Authorship attribution via combination of evidence. In *ECIR*, 2007.

[33] Ying Zhao and Justin Zobel. Effective and scalable authorship attribution using function words. In *AIRS*, 2005.

[34] Ying Zhao and Justin Zobel. Searching with style: authorship attribution in classic literature. In *Proceedings of the thirtieth Australasian conference on Computer science*, 2007.

[35] Ying Zhao, Justin Zobel, and Phil Vines. Using relative entropy for authorship attribution. In *AIRS*, 2006.

[36] Rong Zheng, Jiexun Li, Hsinchun Chen, and Zan Huang. A framework for authorship identification of online messages: Writing-style features and classification techniques. *Journal of the American Society for Information Science and Technology*, 57(3):378–393, 2006.

[37] Albrecht Zimmermann and Bjorn Bringmann. Ctc — correlating tree patterns for classification. In *ICDM*, 2005.

[38] Lei Zou, Yansheng Lu, Huaming Zhang, Rong Hu, and Chong Zhou. Mining frequent induced subtrees by prefix-tree-projected pattern growth. In *WAIMW*, 2006.

On Theme Location Discovery for Travelogue Services

Mao Ye[1†*], Rong Xiao[2‡], Wang-Chien Lee[1†], and Xing Xie[2‡]
†Department of Computer Science & Engineering, The Pennsylvania State University, PA, USA.
‡Microsoft Research Asia, Beijing, China.
[1]{mxy177,wlee}@cse.psu.edu [2]{rong,xing.xie}@microsoft.com

ABSTRACT

In this paper, we aim to develop a travelogue service that discovers and conveys various travelogue digests, in form of theme locations, geographical scope, traveling trajectory and location snippet, to users. In this service, theme locations in a travelogue are the core information to discover. Thus we aim to address the problem of *theme location discovery* to enable the above travelogue services. Due to the inherent ambiguity of location relevance, we perform location relevance mining (LRM) in two complementary angles, relevance classification and relevance ranking, to provide comprehensive understanding of locations. Furthermore, we explore the *textual* (e.g., surrounding words) and *geographical* (e.g., geographical relationship among locations) features of locations to develop a co-training model for enhancement of classification performance. Built upon the mining result of LRM, we develop a series of techniques for provisioning of the aforementioned travelogue digests in our travelogue system. Finally, we conduct comprehensive experiments on collected travelogues to evaluate the performance of our location relevance mining techniques and demonstrate the effectiveness of the travelogue service.

Categories and Subject Descriptors

H.3.3 [**Information Storage and Retrieval**]: Information Filtering; I.2.7 [**Artificial Intelligence**]: Natural Language Processing

General Terms

Experimentation

Keywords

classification, ranking, co-training, travelogue services

1. INTRODUCTION

Continued flourish of World Wide Web (WWW) and advance of transportation systems have made *travel*, an integral part of our life, very easy. Particularly, with the advantages of Web 2.0 technology, many people are willing to share their *travelogues*, which record travel experiences, on weblogs, forums and social communities for travels, (e.g., TravelPod[1], IgoUgo[2] and TravelBlog[3]).

Travelogues, which usually contain rich travel information, such as the tours, lodging, meals, expenses, weather conditions, and so on, are highly valuable to a trip planner. Thus, many people turn to on-line travelogue archives or discussion forums to review travelogues well before taking their trips. While reading travelogues may be fun and enjoyable for some, digging into numerous travelogues to find useful trip information is a tedious and boring task for many. Thus, there is a need for developing automatic travelogue mining techniques to convey useful information in a travelogue to its readers in a more effective way.

Generally, there are two kinds of information for a travelogue to be mined; (1) "whereabout" of the travelogue, and (2) "how-about" of the mentioned attractions.

As a travelogue intends to record activities and experiences of its author at locations on a trip (i.e., the whereabout of the trip), a key problem related to (1) concerns extraction of *theme locations*, i.e., locations appeared in a travelogue which are closely relevant to the main themes of the travelogue. Location extraction techniques have been developed in the past [1, 14]. However, due to the nature of human language presentation, locations extracted are not necessarily theme locations of the travelogue. For example, in Figure 1, Siesta Key is very relevant to the theme of this paragraph but Boston is not.

> **Siesta Key** - It is a paradise found in `Sarasota, FL`, located a little over an hour drive south to *Tampa, FL*, and is a favorite gateway spot for many `Florida` locals. I like to spend time there - mainly at beaches and bars ... We got back to *Boston* after one week vocation.

Figure 1: A paragraph in a travelogue for Siesta Key. Relevant locations are in bold, partial relevant locations are in `teletype`, and irrelevant locations are in *italic*.

Another important problem, related to (2) is about extracting specific how-about information regarding theme locations. Hao et. al. [7] pioneered a knowledge discovery technique that extracts general information (e.g., food, surfing, shopping) regarding travel destinations from a corpus of travelogues. However, this technique has mainly focussed on location information extraction without distinguishing

*Part of this work was done when the author was visiting Microsoft Research Asia.

[1]http://www.travelpod.com
[2]http://igougo.com
[3]http://www.travelblog.com

SIGIR '11, July 24-28, 2011, Beijing, China.

whether locations in a travelogue is relevant to its themes or not. As a result, the result is inevitably biased by noisy locations.

To tackle the theme location discovery problem, we propose to extract *textual features* of locations (e.g., surrounding words and syntactic pattern) as well as *geographical features* of locations (e.g., individual location types, structural constraints derived from location ontology) for location relevance mining. With those features, we perform location relevance classification to differentiate relevant theme locations from others in a travelogue. Moreover, we propose a co-training model, by taking advantages of the independent textual and geographical views of the extracted features, to boost classification performance,

Unfortunately, human perception of locations relevant to the themes of a travelogue tends to be fuzzy! Different people may employ different personal criteria to assess relevant theme locations. What's more, the content of a travelogue may sometimes be insufficient for one to decide whether a location is a theme location or not. However, based on the context of a travelogue, we often can still tell whether a location l_A is more relevant than another location l_B to the travelogue, without necessarily deciding whether l_A and l_B are considered as theme locations or not. Based on this observation, we also develop algorithms for location relevance ranking.

Relevance classification and ranking provide two alternative and complementary aspects in our study of location relevance mining. To our best knowledge, there is no existing work addressing the issues of location relevance mining for a given travelogue, not to mention its support for provisioning of various information digests in a travelogue service. Built upon the mining result of location relevance mining, we develop a series of techniques, including theme locations detection, geographical scope calculation, travel trajectory extraction and location snippet extraction, to embody a travelogue service which not only enable trip planners. to find where to go but also what to do. Finally, we conduct a comprehensive set of experiments on collected travelogues to validate our ideas, evaluate the performance of our location relevance mining techniques, and demonstrate the effectiveness of the travelogue service.

The main contributions made in this paper are summarized as follows.

- We identify the problem of theme location discovery in travelogue services. To our best knowledge, this is the first work that explores mining techniques to convey location information in "one" travelogue to its readers in an effective way.
- We develop location relevance classification and ranking techniques, by exploring unique textual and geographical features inherent to travelogues, to discover theme locations effectively.
- Based on the theme locations discovered using our location relevance mining techniques, we develop a series of techniques for extracting various travelogue digests, including theme locations, geographical scope, traveling trajectory and location snippet, in support of the travelogue service we propose.
- Through the performance evaluation conducted on two travelogue corpus (in English and Chinese), we show that the location relevance mining techniques we developed can effectively discover theme locations and demonstrate that the mined theme locations are important for providing high-quality "whereabout" and "how-about" information in a travelogue via the travelogue digests in our travelogue service.

The remainder of the paper is organized as follows. Section 2 introduces the most related literatures. Section 3 provides a overview about location relevance mining for theme location discovery. Section 4 describes the features we extract to perform location relevance study, and Section 5 discusses the detailed algorithms for location relevance mining. Section 6 introduces the techniques to realize travelogue services built upon LRM. Section 7 conducts performance evaluation to validate the proposed location relevance mining techniques and demonstrate the travelogue service. Finally, Section 8 concludes the paper and discusses the future work.

2. RELATED WORK

In this section, we first introduce some existing studies on spatial information retrieval, such as news and travelogues. Then we review techniques related to location relevance mining, followed by a brief summary of semi-supervised learning techniques.

Location-based search has received a lot of interests from both the academia and industry in the past few years. With advances in location extraction techniques [1, 14], spatial interests expressed in text can be learned to support web services for users looking for spatial information [6, 1, 17, 13]. Wang et. al. propose a notion of query dominant location (QDL) to detect the locations truly searched for by queries [17]. On the contrary, Ding et. al., propose to study the geographical extent of spatial web resources that their creators intend to reach [6]. Amitay et. al. propose to assign to each page a (or a few) "geographic focus" in [1]. They identify the focus of a given page by assigning different confidence score for different locations and use hierarchical structure of location terms to summarize locations with high confidence. Silva et. al. [16] propose to use a graph-based approach akin to PageRank to determine a single scopes for each document, based on a geographic knowledge repository. In [13], Aencar et. al. describe strategies for document classification into geography-related categories, using evidence extracted from Wikipedia. Recently, Hao et. al., aiming to provide travelogue services based on summarization of a travelogue corpus, propose to mine location-specific knowledge from a large collection of travelogues using a probabilistic generative model [7]. Different from most existing work, our study enables provisioning of travelogue digests in our travelogue system, and provide new views for users to understand a travelogue.

In this paper, we explore location relevance classification and ranking techniques to address the issues of location relevance mining. While there exist many textual classification techniques such as Support Vector Machine (SVM) [2] and logistic regression [2] and document ranking methods [15, 10, 9, 5] in the literature, the problem of location relevance mining discussed in this paper is very much new, which requires a unique treatment of certain geographical characteristics. For example, Siesta Key is a sibling city of Tampa, while Florida is the state where Siesta Key and Tampa reside. These unique geographical characteristics motivate us to explore interesting location features in devising techniques for location relevance classification and ranking.

In this paper, we follow the semi-supervised learning parad -igm to address the issues of location relevance mining. Semi-supervised learning is desirable for our study because we have obtained a small set of labeled data and a large volume of unlabeled data. The key idea of semi-supervised learning is to enrich labeled training data by labeling unlabeled data via certain learning techniques. Basically, there are three techniques to realize semi-supervise learning, including (1) using the EM (expectation-maximization) algorithm to estimate the parameters of a generative model and the labels of unlabel data [12], (2) defining a graph over the data instances on the basis of certain similarity metric and determining the labels of unlabeled data [3], and (3) using co-training algorithms to exploit the strengthes of multiple learners to label the unlabeled data [4, 8]. In this work, we realize the semi-supervised learning by exploring two independent views, i.e., textual and geographical views, in a co-training approach.

3. THEME LOCATION DISCOVERY - AN OVERVIEW

Theme location discovery aims to discover and assess the theme locations in a given travelogue. The problem of theme location discovery raises two different yet complementary questions: (1) what locations in a travelogue are theme locations? (2) given two locations in a travelogue, which one is more likely to be a theme location?

These two questions are difficult to answer because we don't know exactly what is the main theme of a travelogue perceived by author and readers. However, based on the intention of travelogue writing, we argue that there indeed exist one or more themes in a travelogue, which match well with the purposes/activities/destinations of this trip. To identify the theme locations, one naive approach is to mandate the travelogue authors to supply them or have the readers to label them, but this manual approach is hard to enforce. Moreover, there are already a huge volume of travelogues made available on-line. Therefore, a mining technique that extracts the theme locations for a given travelogue automatically is highly desirable. Based on observations obtained in our preliminary study of labeled travelogues, the theme locations perceived by different people are similar to some extent, even though they may not be the same. Thus, by leveraging the human knowledge, we apply a supervised learning approach to automatically discover theme locations from travelogues using a labeled training dataset. Moreover, as mentioned earlier, we adopt a semi-supervised learning approach to enrich the limited labeled dataset in order to boost the learning performance. To answer the two questions raised above, we study the issues of location relevance for finding the theme locations in two complementary aspects: *location relevance classification* and *location relevance ranking*.

Location relevance classification. The first question can be considered as a classical classification problem by extracting features for each candidate location in the travelogue. However, as we mentioned before, there is an inherent ambiguity among different people in terms of how relevant a candidate location is to the theme of the travelogue. What's more, the content of travelogue is sometimes insufficient to assess whether a location is a theme location or not. For example, in Figure 1, one may assess that Siesta Key is the only theme location; while another person may consider both Sarasota and Florida are also theme locations. Thus, as shown in Figure 2, the main challenge for location relevance classification is where to set a boundary separating theme location from irrelevant locations.

Location relevance ranking. Instead of determining whether a location is a theme location, the second question we aim to answer is whether one location is more relevant than another location to the theme of this trip. As shown in Figure 2, assuming that Siesta Key is the sole theme, we may assess that Tampa is less relevant to the theme location

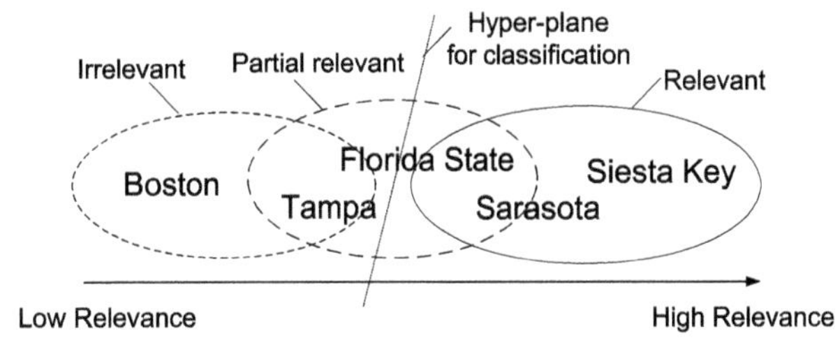

Figure 2: Dilemma in relevant location classification

than Sarasota. In this paper, we adopt two alternative approaches, namely *location likelihood estimation* and *learning to rank*, for location relevance ranking. As discussed in Section 2, while document classification and ranking techniques have been explored for document retrieval, there is an inherent difference between travelogues and documents because locations in a travelogue usually have some interesting relationship, e.g., Siesta Key is a sibling city of Tampa, while Florida is the state which covers Siesta Key and Tampa. Thus, conventional document mining techniques cannot be applied directly to our problem. These unique spatial characteristics motivates us to explore interesting features for location relevance mining.

4. FEATURE EXTRACTION

To perform location relevance mining, it is essential to identify useful features of a location that can help to assess whether the location is relevant to main themes of the travelogue or not. Since travelogues are textual documents recording the authors' experiences in touring places of interests, it naturally contains textual and geographical features. Thus, we identify features associate with locations in these two aspects. Table 1 summarizes the features extracted in our study.

Category	Features
Textual	F_1 : is in title?
	F_2 : number of appearance
	F_3 : bag-of-words
	F_4 : syntactic pattern
Geographical	F_5 : location type
	F_6 : partonomy distance
	F_7 : geographical proximity

Table 1: Features and their categories

On the one hand, for a travelogue, we usually have a title to summarize the theme of the travel. The most relevant locations are usually included there. What's more, interested locations might be mentioned several times in a travelogue, while irrelevant locations appear less frequently. According to this observation, we extract two kinds of features, namely, *is in title?* (denoted as F_1) and *number of appearance* (denoted as F_2), respectively. Besides, surrounding words of a location also provides useful hints. For example, in Figure 1, one may easily understand that "Siesta Key" is the most relevant location name in this paragraph, because important locations are usually heading the paragraphs. Thus for a location in a travelogue, we use its surrounding words to extract *bag-of-word* feature (denoted as F_3) and *syntactic pattern* feature (denoted as F_4) to describe the location. Those above four features are categorized as textual feature.

On the other hand, each location as a physical entity holds geographical properties in the real word. For example, location names referred in a travelogue usually have different location types in location partonomy. As shown in Figure 3, among the locations mentioned in the travelogue in Figure 1, some of them are state name (e.g., Florida), while some are county or township names (e.g., Sarasota and Siesta Key). Location names with smaller scope usually hold higher relevance, otherwise, travelers would not bother to mention them in the travelogue. Thus, we consider the location type to be an important feature, named as *location type* (denoted as F_5).

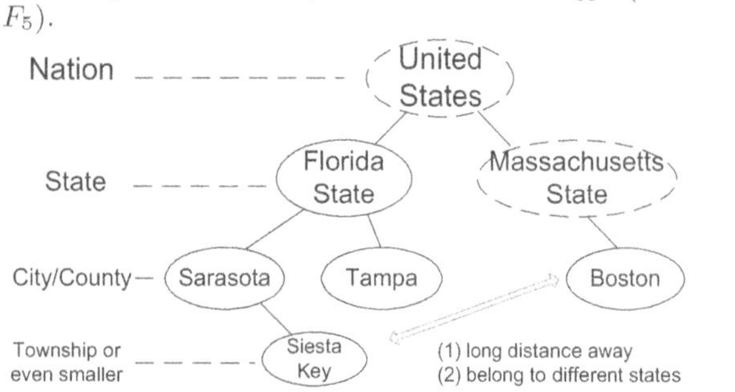

Figure 3: Partonomy hierarchy of locations mentioned in the travelogue shown in Figure 1

Additionally, relevant locations are usually clustered in the partonomy hierarchy of a location ontology. Moreover, people would likely stay in the same state or the same city during the trip. In other words, partonomy distance among the locations provides important information to leverage relevant locations. More specifically, we extract the partonomy distance among locations as feature (denoted as F_6) as follows. Let the partonomy distance (d_{par}) between two locations be the total number of hops in the partonomy hierarchy to their immediate common ancestor. Let l_1 and l_2 be two different locations mentioned in a given travelogue, and l_a be the immediate common ancestor of l_1 and l_2.

$$d_{\text{par}}(l_1, l_2) = hops(l_1, l_a) + hops(l_2, l_a). \quad (1)$$

where $hops(l_x, l_y)$ denotes the number of hops between l_x and l_y along the path of partonomy hierarchy (it equals zero if $l_x = l_y$). For example, in Figure 3, we have the partonomy distance between "Siesta Key" and "Boston" computed as 5, where the immediate common ancestor is "United State".

Finally, if two locations are far away, e.g., Siesta Key and Boston in Figure 3, only one of them could likely be the relevant location for a travelogue. Therefore, we consider geographical proximity (d_{geo}) between two different locations (mentioned in the same travelogue) to be an important feature (denoted as F_7). More specifically, let l_1 and l_2 be two different locations mentioned in a given travelogue, and their latitude and longitude are denoted as (x_1, y_1) and (x_2, y_2) respectively. For simplicity, we use Euclidian distance to present the geographical distance between l_1 and l_2 as follows.

$$d_{\text{geo}}(l_1, l_2) = \sqrt{(x_1 - x_2)^2 + (y_1 - y_2)^2} \quad (2)$$

5. MINING ALGORITHMS

In this section, we introduce algorithms to realize the two mining tasks, namely, *location relevance classification* and *location relevance ranking*, for theme location discovery.

5.1 Location Relevance Classification

Location relevance classification aims to predict whether a location is relevant to the theme of the travelogue or not. As aforementioned, both textual and geographical features are able to assess whether a location is relevant to the theme of a travelogue or not, so we exploit both feature sets of a location to realize location relevance classification. Because of its popularity and good performance in text mining, we adopt SVM to perform supervised classification. Nevertheless, based on our preliminary study, directly applying SVM to perform supervised classification does not produce a good performance. On the one hand, location relevance classification is very challenging due to the inherent ambiguity of location relevance and the limited amount of labeled data available. On the other hand, we noticed that travelogues naturally contains two independent feature sets, i.e., textual and geographical features. Aiming to boost the performance of location relevance classification, we adopt the co-training framework (i.e., semi-supervised learning) as shown in Figure 4 to explore the two feature sets in order to enrich the training set with high-quality newly labeled data in order to obtain a better SVM classifier model. As one of the popular semi-supervised learning algorithms, co-training is a perfectly fit for the classification of location relevance here. It has been shown in [12] that co-training works well under two conditions: (1) each set of features is sufficient for classification, and (2) the two feature sets of each instance are conditionally independent. As both textual and geographical features provide strong hints about whether a location is relevant to the theme location of the travelogue. Based on our preliminary experimentation, we found that the SVM classifiers modeled based on either textual features or geographical features are capable of doing location relevance classification. Moreover, textual and geographical features are proposed to capture the characteristics of a location in totally independent angles, and thus complementary with each other. With both of the above conditions hold, we adopt co-training to boost the performance for location relevance classification.

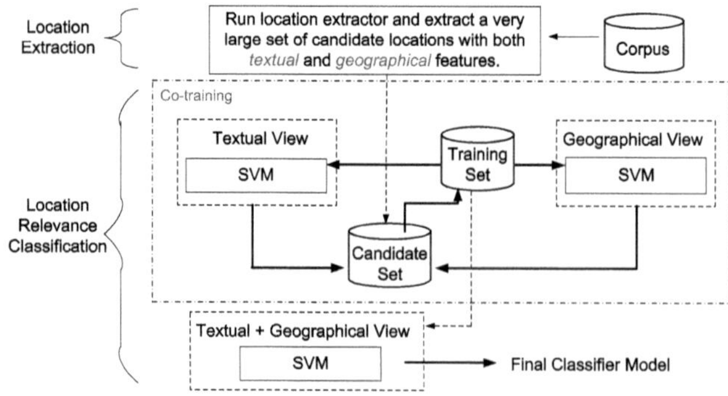

Figure 4: Co-training framework for location relevance classification

Figure 4 illustrates the proposed framework for overall location relevance classification. As shown, the location extraction component in our system scans the travelogue corpus to extract the locations together with their features for each travelogue. The resulted datasets, including *candidate set* and *training set* corresponding to unlabeled and labeled travelogues, are fed to the co-training module to produce a enriched training set (including the original training set plus those high quality newly labeled data) for further classification in the final SVM module (i.e., the bottom box of the figure). Notice that, the final SVM module performs classification in the entire feature space including both textual and geographical features.

Co-training is an iterative process, which typically runs on a large corpus of text documents (i.e., the candidate set) together with a seed training data set (i.e., labeled travelogues here). The main idea of our co-training framework is to explore both textual features and geographical features associated with locations in travelogues to independently and iteratively mine high-quality labels for travelogues. Our co-training algorithm starts with a small number of seed data in the training set. By treating the data instance space in two different views, namely, textual view and geographical view, we have $X = X_t \times X_g$, where X denotes the entire feature space, while X_t and X_g present textual feature space and geographical feature space, respectively. Iterating between these two different views, we use two separate SVMs (one for each view) to decide the labels for those unlabeled travelogues in the candidate set. With newly labeled travelogues, we validate their labels by assigning confidence scores, which are derived based on the distance of a given travelogue to the classification hyperplane learned by SVM. More specifically, the confidence score $s(x)$ for a newly labeled travelogue $x \in X_t$ (or X_g) is calculated as follows.

$$s(x) = |f(x)| = |w^* x + b| \tag{3}$$

where w^* is the optimized hyperplane, while b is the bias term. In order to enrich the training set with high-quality labeled travelogues, we derive a good confidence score threshold θ based on a validation dataset and the current training model learned in each round. As such, only high-quality data (i.e., those newly labeled travelogues with high confidence scores ($s(x) \geq \theta$) are included the training set. As the co-training runs, the training set is enriched continuously until it converges eventually. Finally, a new training dataset larger than the original one is derived from the co-training process. We then adopt SVM to learn upon this new training dataset in the complete feature space (including both textual and geographical features) to obtain the final classifier model.

5.2 Location Relevance Ranking

Location relevance ranking aims to sort locations in accordance with their relevances to the theme of a travelogue. It can be analogized to the problem of document relevance ranking. In location relevance ranking problem, we treat the themes of a travelogue as the query keywords, locations included in the travelogue as candidate documents. However, different from traditional document retrieval, the query keywords (i.e., themes) are implicitly contained in travelogues instead of explicitly specified by users. Here, we introduce two alternative approaches, namely, *location likelihood estimation* and *learning to rank* algorithms to address the ranking problem.

5.2.1 Location Likelihood Estimation

A travelogue is written to record the trip experiences of the author over visited theme locations. Thus, an idea to estimate and rank the relevance of a location in a travelogue to the main themes of the travelogue, motivated by language modeling in information retrieval, is to consider the generation probability of a location in the travelogue. Let l and t denote a location and a travelogue, we use $p(l|t)$ to denote the probability of l appearing in the observed travelogue t. Intuitively, the larger the generation probability of l in t holds, the more relevant l is to the travelogue t. Thus, we define the relevance of location l to a travelogue t as below.

$$\begin{aligned} r(l,t) &= p(l|t) \\ &= \lambda p(l|M_t) + (1-\lambda) p(l|M_c) \\ &= \lambda \frac{tf_{l,t}}{N_t} + (1-\lambda)\frac{tf_l}{N} \end{aligned} \tag{4}$$

where λ is a smoothing factor, and M_t and M_c are the location vocabularies built upon travelogue t and the whole corpus respectively. $tf_{l,t}, tf_l$ are term frequency of location term l appearing in travelogue t and the whole travelogue corpus respectively, and N_t and N are the number of location terms in travelogue t and the whole travelogue corpus, respectively.

5.2.2 Learning to Rank

Recall our example in Figure 1. There are five locations included in the travelogue, but each of them appears only once in the whole document. Based on location likelihood estimate, we may assign them the same rankings, given that smoothing is not applied. Since Siesta Key, Florida, Tampa, and Boston are all popular places, the smoothing technique is not expected to help here. The question is why the location likelihood estimation approach would suggest all those locations to have the same ranks, which is actually against our intuition. The reason is that the language model mainly considers the frequencies of locations, without taking account of other valuable features of given documents, e.g., the surrounding words of locations and the correlation among locations in a travelogue. Thus, we propose an alternative approach, learning to rank model, to realize location relevance ranking by exploiting the textual and geographical feature of the travelogue.

Due to its popularity and simplicity, we adopt Ranking SVM [9], which takes pair-wise relationship of locations in a travelogue to learn a ranking model. Given an input feature space X, where X includes both textual and geographical features, there exists an output space of ranks represented by labels $Y = \{r_1, \cdots, r_q\}$, where q denotes the possible number of ranks. Further, assume that there exists a total order amongst the ranks $r_q \succ r_{q-1} \succ \cdots \succ r_1$, where $\succ$ denotes a preference relationship. Notice that, in this paper, we have three ranks of location relevance, namely "relevant", "partial relevant" and "irrelevant", and the preference relationship in location relevance ranking is "relevant $\succ$ partial relevant $\succ$ irrelevant".

Given a set of ranked instances $Z = \{(x_1, y_1), \cdots, (x_n, y_n)\}$, where n is the number of training instances, $(x_j, y_j)(1 \leq j \leq n)$ is from the space of $X \times Y$. If $y_i > y_j$, we have x_i ranked ahead of x_j, denoted as $x_i \succ x_j$. Assume that F is the set of ranking functions, such that each function $f \in F$ can rank location instances as:

$$x_i \succ x_j \Leftrightarrow f(x_i) > f(x_j) \tag{5}$$

In Ranking SVM, f is assumed to be a linear function [9],

$$f(x) = \langle \omega, x \rangle \tag{6}$$

where ω is weight vector and $\langle \cdot, \cdot \rangle$ denotes inner product. $f(x) = 0$ corresponds to a hyperplane in the feature space,. Thus we have

$$x_i \succ x_j \Leftrightarrow \langle \omega, x_i - x_j \rangle > 0 \tag{7}$$

Given an instance pair x_i and x_j, we create a new instance $x_i - x_j$. If x_i is ranked ahead of x_j, we assign a label $+1$, otherwise -1 to the newly generated instance. As such, we produce a new data set upon which we can build a binary classification model, i.e., the Ranking SVM model. With the Ranking SVM model, and the optimal setting of ω^*, for each location instance x we get its ranking score as $f(x) = \langle \omega^*, x \rangle$.

6. THE TRAVELOGUE SERVICE

In this section, we study how to realize the proposed travelogue service based on the mined location relevance. Particularly, we are interested in conveying theme locations, geographical scope, traveling trajectory and location snippets in a travelogue to the users. Figure 5 illustrates a mock

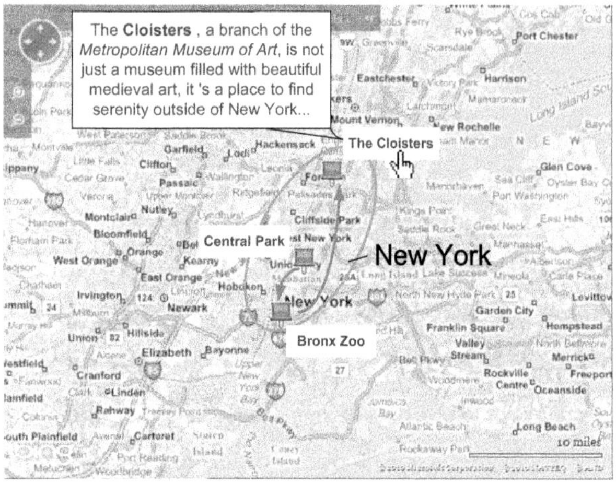

Figure 5: Travelogue service

up of our proposed travelogue service, which provides visualized information for a travelogue over a map. As shown, New York is the geographical scope of the trip. The traveler visited Central Park, Bronx Zoo and The Cloisters in sequence (i.e., three theme locations and a traveling trajectory). By moving the mouse cursor to one of the theme locations, associated location snippet pops out to provide some information. In the following, we present how we use the result of location relevance mining for provisioning of the digests in the travelogue service.

Theme Locations. Locations is an essential entity of travelogues. Anticipating that users would be interested in quickly identifying where the trip activities have happened, we display the theme locations of a travelogue. As we mentioned before, the theme locations can be generated in two ways: i) automatically discovered from the travelogue; and ii) tagged by the travelogue author. Thus, our location relevance classification technique can be used to automatically identify the theme locations. For author-tagged theme locations, we develop a location tag recommendation service to assist the travelogue authors to tag theme locations when they upload their travelogues. Specifically, the location tag recommendation service, presented to the author as a list of ranked theme locations in accordance with their estimated relevances to the theme of the uploaded travelogue, is realized based on the location relevance ranking techniques presented earlier.

Geographical Scope. As a travelogue may cover several theme locations, it is desirable to present the geographical scope of trip activities to its readers. Previous works define geographical scope as a single (or a few) location names to cover *all* locations mentioned in a web page [1, 17]. For our travelogue service, we argue that not all locations are useful for deducing the geographical scope for a travelogue, especially when the noisy locations may produce misleading results. Consider the travelogue in Figure 1, we may argue that its geographical scope should be narrowed down to Florida or even Siesta Key, since both Tampa and Boston are deviating from the theme of this travelogue. Therefore, we follow the ideas in [1] to compute the geographical scope but put our focus on how to derive the input location set, since noisy locations hamper the accuracy of expected geographical scope.

To compute the geographic scope of a travelogue t, we consider only the theme locations L'_t obtained from location relevance classification which effectively purges noisy locations from the entire location set L_t in t.[4] Thus, the geographical scope computing algorithm takes L'_t as input and operates upon the partonomy hierarchy of location ontology (see Figure 3 as an example). First, for each location l in L'_t, we initiate an importance score v_l of l as the number of its appearance in the travelogue. Next, we propagate the influence of l to its parent node l' (and recursively to its ancestor nodes) by adding $v_l \times d$ to v'_l where $0 < d < 1$ is a decay factor. Consider the example in Figure 3, Siesta Key would propagate its influence of importance score to its parent node Sarasota and grand-parent node Florida because the traveler visits Siesta Key and she also stays at Sarasota and Florida. As such, each location in L'_t obtains an importance score that takes influence from its descendants into account. We derive the geographical scope as a location set by adding the theme locations in order of their importance but skipping those with one or more ancestors or decedents already included in the set.

Traveling Trajectory. Traveling trajectory (denoted as T) is extracted based on the result of location relevance classification. Given a travelogue, we obtain a set of theme locations, denoted as $L = \{l_1, l_2, \cdots\}$, from location relevance mining. Given two locations $l_x, l_y \in L$, it is possible that l_x is part of l_y in the partonomy hierarchy. In this case, we exclude l_y from the trajectory. For example, in Figure 3, if Siesta Key and Sarasota are both classified as theme locations, we consider Siesta Key be the reason for the traveler to visit Sarasota. Thus, for trajectory extraction, we highlight the specific point-of-interests and investigate their travel sequence to form a trajectory, which is a subset of L. In other words, locations included in a trajectory are not part of each other. The algorithm for forming POI set is shown in Algorithm 1.

Algorithm 1 POI_SET_FORMATION_ALGORITHM

```
// Input: theme location set L for a given travelogue
POI ← L
for each l_i ∈ T do
    if exists l_j ∈ L such that l_j is part of l_i then
        POI ← POI − {l_i}
    end if
end for
return POI
```

Upon the POI set, we construct a trajectory T based on a simple assumption that the appearance sequence of those location in T is supposed to match well with the travel sequence of the traveler's real trajectory. Thus, we construct the trajectory by sorting locations in the POIs in accordance with the sequence of their appearances in the travelogue to form T. Of course, there still is a room for improvement in forming the trajectory. We plan to further investigate this issue in the future work.

Location Snippet. Location snippet consists of a few (usually one or two) sentences extracted from a travelogue to describe the corresponding location. Given a location l in a travelogue, a desired location snippet is one that includes relevant information about l, e.g., interesting description about some features of l. Based on topic generative model, we may find a word w related to a location l. Specifically, we may derive a probability $p(w|l)$ that models how likely a word w describes a location l for all words in the vocabulary V, which contains all possible words in travelogues [7]. Based on $p(w|l)$, we construct a word set W_l (i.e., a subset of V)

[4] An alternative of L'_t is to use the highest ranked locations obtained from location relevance ranking with some predetermined rank threshold.

which includes informative words regarding l, i.e., word w with high $p(w|l)$ are included in W_l.

Next, for each theme location l, we determine the semantic relevance (SemRel) between l and a candidate snippet s by comparing the "word similarity" between W_l and the set of words in s, denoted as W_s. Intuitively, we can simply use cosine similarity to calculate the distance between W_l and W_s. However, cosine similarity does not capture the latent topic behind of words (e.g., "lunch" and "food" are treated as independent semantically). Thus, we propose to use latent topic distribution to measure the similarity between a location l and a candidate snippet s as follow.

$$\mathrm{SemRel}(l, s) = \frac{\sum_{w_1 \in W_l} \sum_{w_2 \in W_s} \mathrm{TermSim}(w_1, w_2)}{\log(1 + |W_s|)} \quad (8)$$

where

$$\mathrm{TermSim}(w_1, w_2) = \exp\{-\tau D_{JS}(\delta_{w_1} || \delta_{w_2})\}, \quad (9)$$

where δ_w denotes the topic distribution of the word [7], τ is a normalizing factor, and $D_{JS}(p||q)$ denotes the Jensen-Shannon(JS) divergence.

Here please note that, while we only consider the semantic relevance in our selection of representative snippet for a theme location, the geographical relevance has been implicitly taken into consideration in the process of location relevance mining, which effectively purges noisy locations.

7. PERFORMANCE EVALUATION

In this section, we evaluate performance of the proposed location relevance mining techniques and demonstrate the effectiveness of the travelogue service.

7.1 Datasets

There are many sources of travelogues on the Web, ranging from Weblogs such as *Windows Live Spaces* to dedicated travel web-site such as *TravelPod*, *IgoUgo* and *TravelBlog*. We collected approximately 100,000 travelogues in English with location labels fallen in United States to form an English Corpus. Nevertheless, instead of relying on the location labels directly, we implemented a location extractor to extract locations mentioned in these travelogues, yielding 18,000 unique locations. Because some tasks require evaluation by human beings with travel-related background and knowledge, we also built a Chinese Corpus by collecting travelogues from *Ctrip*[5], which consists of 94,000 Chinese travelogues related to around 32,000 locations in China.

7.2 Evaluation on LRM

Here, we first introduce the performance metrics and then present the results of our evaluation on location relevance mining.

7.2.1 Performance Metrics

In the experiments, *Precision* and *Recall* are used to evaluate the performance of location relevance classification; *Normalized Discounted Cumulative Gain (NDCG)* and *Mean Average Precision (MAP)* are used to evaluate the performance of location relevance ranking. Since Precision and Recall are well known metrics, we only discuss NDCG and MAP.

For location relevance ranking problem, given a travelogue t, the NDCG score (NDCG_t) is computed according to the ranked location list L_t (i.e., the output of location relevance ranking), as $\mathrm{NDCG}_t = n_t \sum_{j=1}^{|L_t|} \frac{2^{r_j}-1}{\log(1+j)}$, where r_j is the rank of the location at the j_{th} position of the location list L_t, and n_t is a normalization constant, which is chosen so that a perfect ranking's NDCG score is 1. The final NDCG score is averaged over the scores of all the travelogues. In this paper, the NDCG scores for ranked location lists which include top 1, 3, 5, 7, 9 and 11 locations are reported. MAP stands for the mean of average precisions over all the travelogues. Given a travelogue t and a ranked location list L_t, average precision is defined as $AvePre_t = \sum_{j=1}^{|L_t|} \frac{I(j)(R_j/j)}{R}$, where R and R_j denote the total number of relevant locations and the number of relevant locations before the position $(j+1)$, respectively, and $I(j)$ is an indicator which takes value 1 if the location at position j is relevant and value 0 otherwise.

[5]http://www.ctrip.com

7.2.2 Evaluation Results

An important factor crucial to performance of location relevance classification and ranking is the location features extracted for mining. Thus, to facilitate our studies on impact of extracted features, we form the following four *feature groups*: (1) *baseline* group - we consider "is in title ?" (F_1) and "number of appearance" (F_2) as two basic features, which are frequently used for text mining; (2) *textual* group - we consider all textual features; (3) *geographical* group - we consider all geographical features; (4) *textual+geographical* group - we consider both the textual and geographical features.

As there is no existing dataset for evaluation of location relevance mining, we have to built our own training dataset manually. Since we usually consider a destination in our trip as *relevant locations*, those pass-by/stop-by/nearby locations as *partial relevant location*, and others as *irrelevant locations*, we labeled 1,000 travelogues in the Chinese Corpus for our performance evaluation.

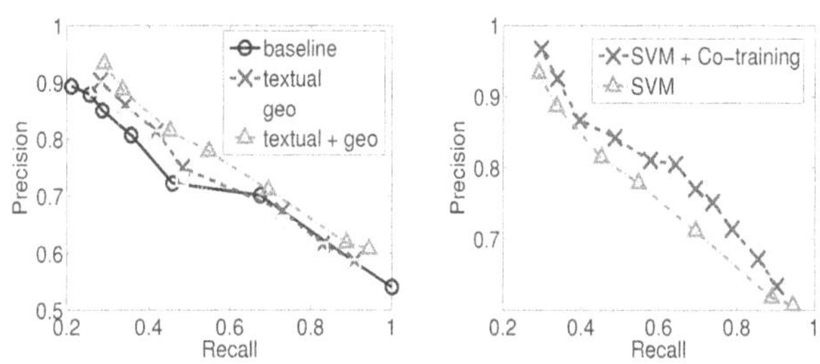

(a) Feature groups (b) Co-training

Figure 6: Location relevance classification

For location relevance classification, we consider relevant locations as positive cases and the other locations as negative cases. Among those 1,000 labeled travelogues, we randomly select 100 travelogues as the test set and the remaining travelogues for training. Figure 6(a) shows the precision-recall curves of location relevance classification with different feature groups. We found that the baseline group (i.e., whether the location appears in the title and the count of locations in a travelogue) already provides strong support for deciding relevant locations. However, classifier using baseline features is effective only to some extent. With more textual features, the location relevance classifier gain improvement. From the figure, we observe that geographical features perform classification very well, showing better performance than baseline features particularly when the precision is higher, as baseline features consider only very limited information. Also shown in Figure 6(a), combining textual and geographical features has the best performance because textual features and geographical features are independent. As a result, combining those two provide more information to assess whether a location is relevance or not.

In this work, co-training approach has been adopted to improve the classification performance (i.e., to combine approximately 1,000 labeled travelogues with approximately 93,000 unlabeled travelogues). In our experiment, we set the labeled data set as *seed* training set. As discussed in Section 5, a confidence threshold θ has been used in our co-training algorithm to derive high-quality labeled training set. Here we estimate θ based on the *precision* threshold value of ρ, which is set as $\rho = 0.95$ in the test. In the co-training process, both textual-feature classifier and geographical-feature classifier are trained as high-precision classifiers (i.e., by setting $\rho = 0.95$). In this experiment, after 4 round of iterations, co-training process terminates. The new training set is then used in classification. We compare the classification results by running the SVM classifier on the original training set (labeled as SVM) and new training set (labeled SVM+Co-Training). Figure 6(b) shows that co-training leads to a better precision-recall performance. As a matter of fact, this improvement can be expected, because both textual features and geographical features can be used to perform the classification task. Moreover, those two are independent and even complementary, so the combination of them enhance the classification performance as shown in Figure 6(a).

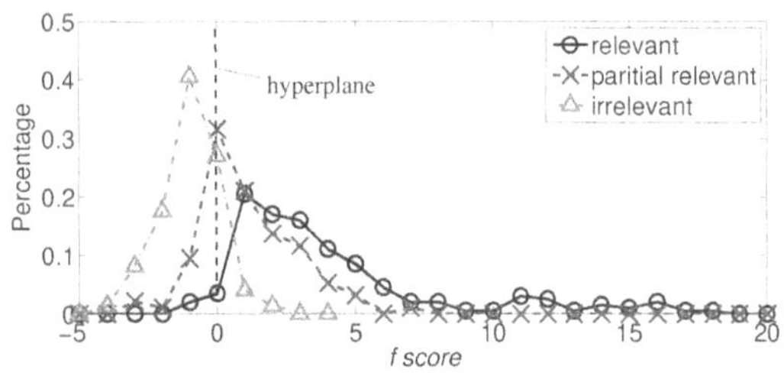

Figure 7: Challenge in location relevance classification

To show the inherent challenges in location relevance classification, we collect a training set with relevant and irrelevant locations, with all partial relevant location filtered out. Let x denotes the feature vector of a location, we calculate $f(x) = w^*x + b$ (denoted as f-score) in the trained SVM model (w^* is the optimized hyperplane, while b is the bias term) for each location in the travelogues of testing dataset. Here, f-score indicates the distance to the classifier hyperplan. Notice that in the test dataset, locations are categorized into three groups, i.e., relevant locations, partial-relevant locations and irrelevant locations. For each group, we plot its f-score distribution in Figure 7. We find that, f-score distribution of partial-relevant location overlaps to some extent with one of relevant locations. This is due to the ambiguity in location relevance perceived by different people. In contrast to the location relevance classification problem, it seems to be easier to rank the relevance of different locations for a given travelogue. In Figure 7, we find the "centers" of the distributions with respect to each location relevance class differ. As shown, the irrelevant location class is positioned in the leftmost part while the relevant location class stands at the rightmost part.

Next, we evaluate the performance of location relevance ranking techniques, including location likelihood estimation (LLE) and learning to rank (L2R), using the same dataset. There are three labeled ranks in our dataset, i.e., relevant, partial relevant and irrelevant. As discussed earlier, NDCG@N and MAP are used as the performance metrics for the experiment.[6]

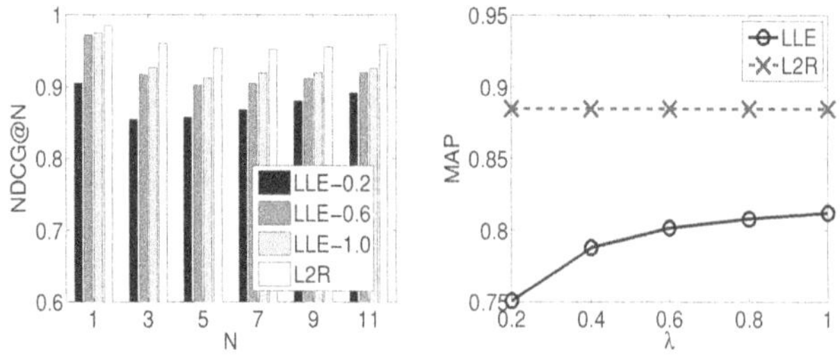

(a) NDCG@N (b) MAP

Figure 8: LLE with varied λ

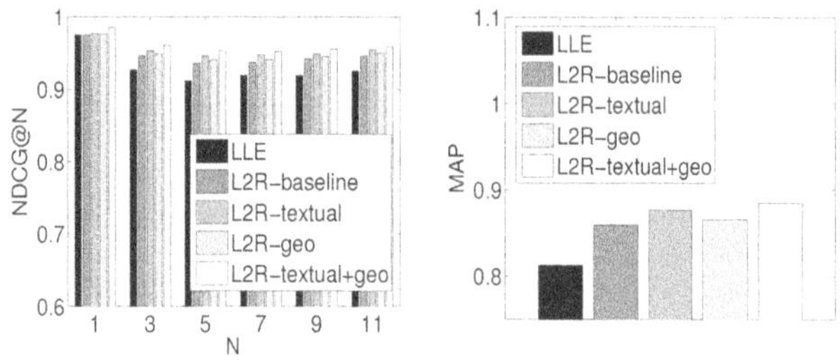

(a) NDCG@N (b) MAP

Figure 9: Improvement with different feature groups

Since there is a smoothing factor λ in the location likelihood estimation, we experimentally find the optimal setting of LLE by tuning λ from 0.2 to 1.0 with a 0.2 step. Interestingly, although LLE is based on the idea of language model, it shows a behavior different from a conventional language model. Specifically, the smoothing parameter in a language model is used to improve the document ranking performance but it has no effect on location relevance ranking, i.e., $\lambda = 1.0$, as shown in our experiments. The is possibly because location relevance ranking is constrained within the given travelogue. As a result, count of a location appearance is much more important than its global popularity.

Next, we show impact of extracted feature groups on LLE and L2R via NDCG@N test (see Figure 9(a)) and MAP test (see Figure 9(b)), respectively. For simplicity, only the best performance (when $\lambda = 1.0$) of LLE is plotted in these two figures. As shown L2R consistently outperforms LLE. Particularly, since LLE is mainly based on word frequency, which is considered as feature F_2, the experiments demonstrate that both textual features and geographical features are indeed effective for improving the performance of location relevance ranking. Also note that the location relevance ranking problem is different from traditional document retrieval problem, where thousands and even millions of candidate documents are to be ranked for a given query. In location relevance ranking, the number of candidate locations in a given travelogue are usually no more than 15. Therefore, it is imperative to ensure all relevant locations ranked higher than the other locations. In the MAP test, we find that the learning to rank approach outperforms the location likelihood estimation approach significantly.

[6]Note that, we only consider relevant locations and other locations in measurement of MAP, since it considers binary cases in ranking performance evaluation.

7.3 Evaluation on the Travelogue Service

Finally, we demonstrate the effectiveness of our travelogue service by evaluating the proposed travelogue digests, including theme locations, geographical scope, traveling trajectory and location snippet.

7.3.1 *Theme Locations*

In our travelogue service, theme locations can be acquired via 1) location relevance classification; or 2) author tagging. The effectiveness of our classification technique has been studied in the last section. On the other hand, author tagging can be assisted by location tag recommendation backed by our location relevance ranking techniques. Here, we evaluate the precision@N and recall@N of tag recommendation (where $N = 1, 3, 5, 7, 9, 11$). Figure 10(a) and Figure 10(b) show that both L2R has a much better performance than LLE (especially when $N = 3$ and 5) in support of location tag recommendation. These results are consistent with the findings in Figure 9(b).

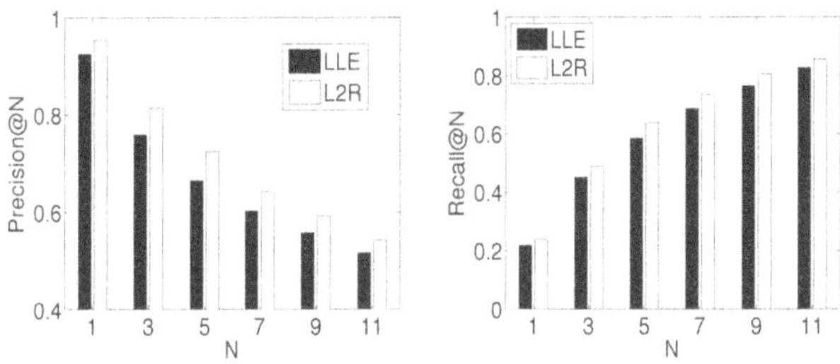

(a) Precision@N (b) Recall@N

Figure 10: Theme location

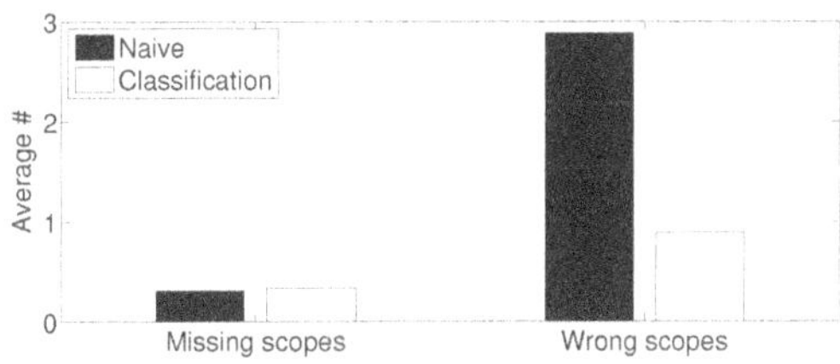

Figure 11: Geographical scope

7.3.2 *Geographical Scope*

Here, we would like to evaluate whether location relevance mining can help improve the accuracy for geographical scope identification. Since there is no existing dataset with labeled geographical scope, we use the travelogues labeled with theme locations to derive the ground truth and use labeled theme locations as inputs for our geographical scope computation algorithm.

We introduce two performance metrics, namely, *average number of missing scopes* (N_m) (i.e., the correct scopes not found) and *average number of wrong scopes* (N_w) (i.e., the scopes found incorrectly) to evaluate the performance. Let $S^* = \{l_1, l_2, \cdots\}$ denote the ground truth scopes for a given travelogue and S be the result we compute. Given two locations l and l', let $r(l, l')$ denote that l is neither ancestor nor descendant of l' in the ontology hierarchy, e.g., $r(\text{Boston}, \text{Florida})$ holds for the example in Figure 3 but $r(\text{Siesta key}, \text{Florida})$ does not. Thus, we have $N_m = |\{l | l \in S^*, \forall l' \in S, r(l, l')\}|$ and $N_w = |\{l | l \in S, \forall l' \in S^*, r(l, l')\}|$.

We compare our approach which takes theme locations as input for geographical scope computation with a naive approach that considers all locations as input. As shown in Figure 11, our approach achieves a much better performance than the naive approach in terms of average number of wrong scopes, while remaining to be competitive in terms of average number of missing scopes. Hence, location relevance mining which helps filter out irrelevant locations can improve the accuracy of geographical scope identification.

7.3.3 *Traveling Trajectory*

In this experiment, we prepared 100 travelogues with labeled traveling trajectories as the ground truth dataset. In order to evaluate the accuracy of our proposed trajectory extraction technique, we introduce a performance metrics, namely *trajectory similarity* ($TS(t_1, t_2)$), which is defined as the graph edit distance [11] between two traveling trajectories t_1 and t_2. Here, we compare our approach with a naive approach that forms a trajectory by considering all locations in a given travelogue as the POI set. As shown in Figure 12, our approach achieves a much better performance since both location relevance classification and POI set formation improve the trajectory extraction accuracy significantly.

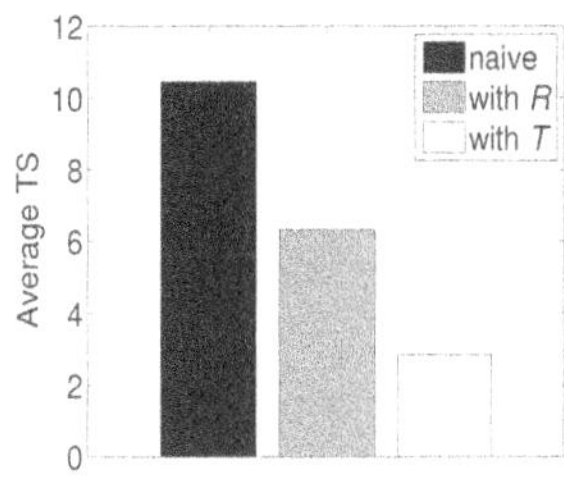

Figure 12: Test on TS

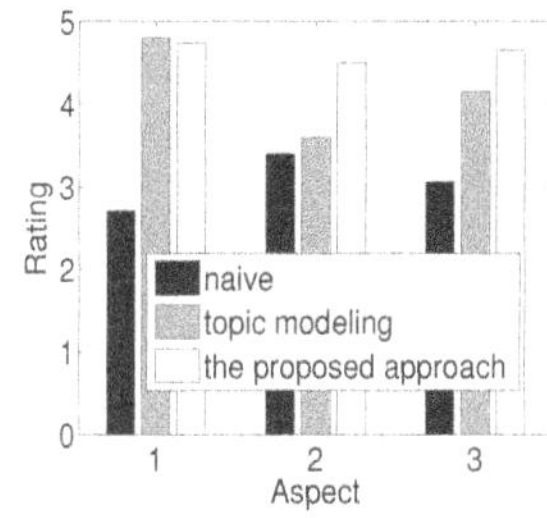

Figure 13: Evaluation on location snippet

7.3.4 *Location Snippets*

Here we evaluate the effectiveness of the extracted location snippets. In [7], sentences/small paragraphs with multiple different locations are ignored due to the lack of location relevance mining techniques. However, those ignored snippets may contain interesting information to the users, because point of interests/locations are usually clustered in geographical proximity and mentioned close by in the text of travelogues. For example, Table 2 shows some interesting location snippets that we extract but missed in [7]. Take the location snippet for "Battery Park" as an example. There are quite a few "noise" locations in the snippet but they provide very informative knowledge about what to and see in Battery Park. In the snippet of "the Cloisters", we find that other locations also provide informative knowledge about where "the Cloisters" locates, i.e., "... around of New York. Located up at 190th Street ...". Finally, travelogue authors often describe locations by comparison, e.g., "Golden Gate Park" vs. "Central Park" in the snippet for "Golden Gate Park".

We conduct a user study to evaluate whether our location snippets are informative in terms of conveying information of the corresponding location. Based on the Chinese corpus, we prepared 20 travelogues, where each travelogue consists of more than 5 locations mentioned. Intuitively, if a small paragraph contains a location name l, then we consider this small paragraph should be describing this location in some way. Thus, a naive approach is to consider those small paragraphs as snippets for the corresponding location involved.

Twenty graduate students were asked to assess the snippets of all 20 travelogues in 1 to 5 ratings in three aspects: namely, (1) geographical-relevance (i.e., to what extent the snippets are describing the corresponding location), (2) comprehensiveness (i.e., to what extent the snippets provide rich information about the themes of the given travelogue), and

focused location	noisy location(s)	snippet
Battery Park	94th Street, Manhattan, the World Trade Center, the Statue of Liberty	Actually , I usually start at the Upper Westside around *94th Street* and go all the way to **Battery Park** at the southern tip of *Manhattan*. **Battery Park** is a great place to end up. The scenery is great with the water, the marina, the *World Trade Center* and the *Statue of Liberty*...
The Cloisters	Metropolitan Museum of Art, New York, 190th Street	**The Cloisters**, a branch of *the Metropolitan Museum of Art*, is not just a museum filled with beautiful medieval art, it 's a place to find serenity around *New York*. Located up at *190th Street*, the Cloisters is a bit of a trek but it's worth it...
Golden Gate Park	NY, Central Park	I call **Golden Gate Park** a smaller version of *NY*'s *Central Park*. It offers so many things to do that I never tire of jogging through it...

Table 2: Location snippet extraction for each individual travelogue.

(3) overall satisfaction. Accordingly, we want to demonstrate whether the proposed method can suggest snippets not only relevant to the corresponding location, but also comprehensive to provide interesting information. For each travelogue, we average all the users' evaluation in all three ratings of each snippet set in a travelogue. Three approaches (i.e., the naive approach, topic modeling approach [7] and the proposed approach) are compared as shown in Figure 13. Since topic modeling approach purges the snippets by deleting those containing multiple locations, it performs the best in terms of geographical relevance. However, our proposed approach also shows very competitive performance in terms of geographic relevance, because our location relevance mining helps to highlight theme locations. For the comprehensiveness, both naive approach and topic modeling approach show worse performance than our proposed approach does. The reason is that our proposed approach includes the location snippet as shown in Table 2, thus providing very comprehensive information against topic modeling approach. Notice that, the naive approach can not differentiate which location is relevant, thus showing the worst performance in the aspect of geographical relevance, and affecting the comprehensiveness consequently. Overall, our proposed approach shows the best performance and user satisfactory.

8. CONCLUSIONS AND FUTURE WORK

In this paper, we develop location relevance mining techniques to discover theme locations of travelogues in support of a proposed travelogue service. Due to inherent ambiguity of location relevance, we perform location relevance mining in two complementary angles, relevance classification and relevance ranking, to provide comprehensive understanding of locations in a travelogue. Furthermore, we explore the *textual* and *geographical* features of locations and adopt a co-training model to improve the classification. Built upon the mining result of location relevance mining, we develop techniques for provisioning of various digests, including theme locations, geographical scope, traveling trajectory and location snippets, in our travelogue service. Finally, we conduct comprehensive experiments on collected travelogues to evaluate the performance of our location relevance mining techniques and demonstrate the effectiveness of the travelogue service.

In the future, we plan to improve the traveling trajectory extraction by considering context provided in travelogue, and utilize location relevance mining techniques to support other travelogue services, such as location-based search.

9. REFERENCES

[1] E. Amitay, N. Har'El, R. Sivan, and A. Soffer. Web-a-where: geotagging web content. In *SIGIR*, 2004.

[2] C. M. Bishop. *Pattern Recognition and Machine Learning*. Springer, 2006.

[3] A. Blum and S. Chawla. Learning from labeled and unlabeled data using graph mincuts. In *ICML*, 2001.

[4] A. Blum and T. M. Mitchell. Combining labeled and unlabeled data with co-training. In *COLT*, 1998.

[5] Z. Cao, T. Qin, T.-Y. Liu, M.-F. Tsai, and H. Li. Learning to rank: from pairwise approach to listwise approach. In *ICML*, 2007.

[6] J. Ding, L. Gravano, and N. Shivakumar. Computing geographical scopes of web resources. In *VLDB*, 2000.

[7] Q. Hao, R. Cai, C. Wang, R. Xiao, J.-M. Yang, Y. Pang, and L. Zhang. Equip tourists with knowledge mined from travelogues. In *WWW*, 2010.

[8] U. Irmak and R. Kraft. A scalable machine-learning approach for semi-structured named entity recognition. In *WWW*, 2010.

[9] T. Joachims. Optimizing search engines using clickthrough data. In *KDD*, 2002.

[10] J. D. Lafferty and C. Zhai. Document language models, query models, and risk minimization for information retrieval. In *SIGIR*, 2001.

[11] M. Neuhaus and H. Bunke. *Bridging the Gap Between Graph Edit Distance and Kernel Machines*. World Scientific Publishing Co., Inc., 2007.

[12] K. Nigam, A. McCallum, S. Thrun, and T. M. Mitchell. Text classification from labeled and unlabeled documents using em. *Machine Learning*, 2000.

[13] R. Odon de Alencar, C. A. Davis, Jr., and M. A. Gonçalves. Geographical classification of documents using evidence from wikipedia. In *GIR*, 2010.

[14] T. Qin, R. Xiao, L. Fang, X. Xie, and L. Zhang. An Efficient Location Extraction Algorithm by Leveraging Web Contextual Information. In *GIS*, 2010.

[15] S. E. Robertson and D. A. Hull. The trec-9 filtering track final report. In *TREC*, 2000.

[16] M. J. Silva, B. Martins, M. S. Chaves, A. P. Afonso, and N. Cardoso. Adding geographic scopes to web resources. *Computers, Environment and Urban Systems*, 30(4):378–399, 2006.

[17] L. Wang, C. Wang, X. Xie, J. Forman, Y. Lu, W.-Y. Ma, and Y. Li. Detecting dominant locations from search queries. In *SIGIR*, 2005.

Effective Sentiment Stream Analysis with Self-Augmenting Training and Demand-Driven Projection

Ismael S. Silva, Janaína Gomide, Adriano Veloso, Wagner Meira Jr., Renato Ferreira
Computer Science Department
Federal University of Minas Gerais
31270-901 Belo Horizonte, Brazil
{ismael.silva, janaina, adrianov, meira, renato}@dcc.ufmg.br

ABSTRACT

How do we analyze sentiments over a set of opinionated Twitter messages? This issue has been widely studied in recent years, with a prominent approach being based on the application of classification techniques. Basically, messages are classified according to the implicit attitude of the writer with respect to a query term. A major concern, however, is that Twitter (and other media channels) follows the data stream model, and thus the classifier must operate with limited resources, including labeled data for training classification models. This imposes serious challenges for current classification techniques, since they need to be constantly fed with fresh training messages, in order to track sentiment drift and to provide up-to-date sentiment analysis.

We propose solutions to this problem. The heart of our approach is a training augmentation procedure which takes as input a small training seed, and then it automatically incorporates new relevant messages to the training data. Classification models are produced on-the-fly using association rules, which are kept up-to-date in an incremental fashion, so that at any given time the model properly reflects the sentiments in the event being analyzed. In order to track sentiment drift, training messages are projected on a demand-driven basis, according to the content of the message being classified. Projecting the training data offers a series of advantages, including the ability to quickly detect trending information emerging in the stream. We performed the analysis of major events in 2010, and we show that the prediction performance remains about the same, or even increases, as the stream passes and new training messages are acquired. This result holds for different languages, even in cases where sentiment distribution changes over time, or in cases where the initial training seed is rather small. We derive lower-bounds for prediction performance, and we show that our approach is extremely effective under diverse learning scenarios, providing gains that range from 7% to 58%.

Categories and Subject Descriptors

H.3.1 [**Information Storage and Retrieval**]: Content Analysis and Indexing; I.5.2 [**Pattern Recognition**]: Classifier Design and Evaluation

General Terms

Algorithms, Experimentation, Performance

Keywords

Sentiment Analysis, Sentiment Drift, Streams, Twitter

1. INTRODUCTION

The rise of text-based social media channels has fueled scientists with torrents of opinionated data about the most diverse topics and entities. This has spurred the proliferation of tools with the ability to analyze the sentiment expressed by the online population which visits and participates in social channels and (micro-)blogs. This population accounts for more than two-thirds of all Internet users [1], and thus sentiment analysis will eventually become a key feature of search engines, which may integrate the aggregate sentiment of the crowd into search results.

Sentiment analysis in these scenarios presents two characteristics that make it more challenging than in other previous researched scenarios. The first is that the task consists of analyzing a humongous amount of messages that are produced continuously by a large and uncontrolled number of users. The second is that these messages tend to be very short, as required by Twitter, but such practice is becoming a trend in other channels. We name this scenario *sentiment streams* and the task *sentiment stream analysis*. In this paper we focus on Twitter, but our techniques may be applicable to any channels that share the same characteristics we just mentioned. Twitter is one of the fastest-growing social media channels, and has proven itself to be an authoritative source for breaking news, some of which concerns events of huge impact world-wide [20]. Sensitive information is created almost in the same time the event is happening in the real world, and it becomes available shortly after it is created. Also, the 140-character limit is very restrictive, not providing enough space for users to explain, elaborate or get distracted from their main point. Twitter is thus a valuable niche for large scale sentiment analysis, and recent years have experienced the emergence of many tools and techniques for this task [26].

There is a growing trend in performing sentiment analysis using classification-related techniques: a process that automatically builds a classification model by learning, from a set of previously labeled messages (i.e., the training data), the underlying characteristics that distinguish one sentiment from another (i.e., happiness, madness, surprise, suspicion). The success of these classifiers rests on their ability to judge attitude by means of textual-patterns present in the messages, which usually appear in the form of (idiomatic) expressions and combinations of words. It is well accepted that the quality of the training data that is provided to the classifier is crucial to its effectiveness. Although there is no consensus on how the training data should be produced, it is commonsense that the cost of manually labeling vast amounts of messages is prohibitive, since the acquisition of these example messages may require the inspection of skilled human annotators. This annotation burden motivated the emergence of a large repertoire of semi-supervised and active learning alternatives [7]. Still, these techniques assume by large that the training data is sampled from a stationary distribution, but time-varying data plays a significant role in sentiment analysis. Twitter, for instance, enables millions of users to tweet at any moment, and thus, variations in sentiment distribution may happen constantly.

We investigate sentiment analysis over Twitter real-time messages. In such scenarios, classifiers must operate with limited computing and training resources. To make things even worse, either sentiment distribution or the characteristics related to certain sentiments may change over time in almost unforeseen ways. This is known as *sentiment drift*, and it makes predictions less accurate as time passes. To prevent deterioration over time the classification model has to be constantly refreshed, meaning that classifiers must be able to automatically incorporate novel information into the training data and update the model on-the-fly, so that the predictions to come can take advantage of up-to-date information immediately. Some well-established classification strategies may become ill-suited in such hard circumstances, while alternate solutions may be more convenient.

We propose to learn sentiments using classification models composed of association rules [2]. After a small training seed is provided to the classifier, it is able to extract these rules which are essentially local mappings relating sentiments to textual-patterns in the messages. Also, two novel features make our classifiers unique in dealing with different settings of sentiment drift, while operating with limited amount of resources:

- They employ a self-augmenting training procedure, which incorporates reliable predictions as new training information, and as a result, the training data is automatically augmented as the message stream passes. The classification model is immediately refreshed by keeping rules up-to-date incrementally, so that the next message in the stream can potentially take advantage of the recently included information. Depending on the stream tightness, the classifiers can also abstain from doubtful predictions, creating a small block of messages that are temporarily waiting for a reliable prediction. These messages for which no reliable prediction is possible with only the training messages available at the time, may benefit from the training information acquired later.
- They perform demand-driven projection, which determines a specific (potentially different) training projection for each message passing through the stream. The training messages that compose each training projection are automatically selected according to the content of the message being analyzed. This incurs in a powerful strategy for tracking different types of sentiment drift, since it removes training messages that are not meaningful to the message being analyzed. We prove that the removed messages are not detrimental to prediction performance, and that the number of rules extracted from each training projection grows polynomially with the size of the vocabulary, no matter the *minimum support* value. This enables the classifier to focus on trending information that is just emerging in the stream, while staying free from a huge amount of meaningless information.

These two features were not coincidentally proposed together. In fact, they have a synergistic effect in the sense that both need each other in order to work properly. The self-augmenting training ability assures the inclusion of new training messages that are necessary to produce up-to-date training projections. At this point, the use of typical computational cost restrictions based on minimum support thresholds would compromise the entire process, since important patterns that are just emerging in the stream would be pruned, and as a result, the classification model would become obsolete and unable to respond to sentiment trends. Therefore, in order to quickly detect the appearance of novel information in the message stream, the classifier must extract rules without employing frequency restrictions based on support. As will be demonstrated, the proposed demand-driven projection approach assures that rules are efficiently extracted from the training projection (i.e., in polynomial time), even without applying restrictions on support. Furthermore, the cost associated with rule extraction is greatly amortized due to a lossless incremental approach, which drastically reduces the number of accesses to the training data.

To evaluate the effectiveness of the proposed classifiers, we performed a systematic set of experiments using sentiment-rich Twitter data collected from three important events in 2010. We employed different different learning scenarios (i.e., different sentiments, different languages, and different training seeds). To validate our claims we derived lower-bounds for classification performance, and the results show that our classifiers are extremely effective under diverse learning scenarios, with gains in prediction performance that range from 7% to 58%.

2. RELATED WORK

The ultimate goal of a classifier is to achieve the best possible prediction performance for the problem at hand. Devising effective classifiers for a specific problem is not a simple task, but there is a body of evidence suggesting that classification offers substantial advantages in several application scenarios, including sentiment analysis [26]. There has been a large amount of prior research in sentiment analysis, especially in the domain of product reviews, movie reviews, and blogs [25]. A variety of classifiers were already evaluated in many different sentiment learning scenarios, such as analyzing brand impact of microbloging [19], or learning consumer confidence and political opinion [9, 23, 24].

More recently, it becomes possible to analyze population sentiment at a large scale. Social channels like Twitter offer the necessary resource: vast amounts of opinionated content [20]. Unfortunately, there is a major bottleneck in the process: the necessity for training examples which are labeled by human annotators. In order to limit human intervention, automated alternatives that use *emoticons* (or tags) [28] and other distant supervision approaches [16] were also proposed, but (1) they are prone to error by definition, (2) they are unable to capture other types of sentiments for which no *emoticon* (or any tag) is associated, and (3) different sentiments may be associated with the same *emoticon* (or the same tag). Ramage et al. [27] characterize users and messages of Twitter using topic models. Their approach is based on labeled latent Dirichlet allocation, which is used to detect topics of words that tend to co-occur in similar tweets and from implied tweet labels (e.g. hashtags, emoticons ad replies). Other alternatives to address the annotation burden include active and semi-supervised learning approaches [7]. However, there is also a major impediment that prevent the application of these approaches: channels such as Twitter follow the data streaming paradigm [4], and thus, (1) classifiers must operate with limited amount of resources, and (2) online sentiment may change over time.

Many techniques have been proposed to handle the issues associated with analyzing data streams. An incremental approach [14] was proposed to focus on streaming data using Hoeffding bounds. Other approaches incrementally update their classification model with new training data to cope with the evolution of the stream [10, 15]. These techniques usually require complex operations to update the model. Also, Wang et. al [31] and Fan [11] proposed ensemble techniques for stream mining.

The above techniques assume that data distribution is smooth, but actually, (concept) drifts are often hidden in the stream. Gama et al. [13] proposed to use a forgetting mechanism based on a sliding window with the most recent observations. Street and Kim [29] proposed a technique based on a ensemble of decision trees to deal with drifting streams. It splits data into batches, fits one decision tree per batch and discards the old models heuristically. Zhu et al. [36] proposed an active learning framework to selectively label instances from drifting streams. The decision tree based technique proposed in [18] keeps the model current while making the most of old data by growing an alternative subtree whenever an old one becomes questionable, and replacing the old with the new when it becomes more accurate to adapt to the current concept. An approach to concept drift [21] was proposed to create and remove weighted experts dynamically corresponding to the changes of performance. An Optional Weight Adjustment method [34, 35] utilizes the most recent data block to detect optional weighted values for the classifier, and applies a kernel mean matching method to minimize the discrepancy of data blocks in the kernel space. Two variants of bagging: ADWIN Bagging and Adaptive-Size Hoeffding Tree (ASHT) Bagging were introduced for tackling non-stationary concepts in data streams [5]. Maloof [22] proposed a new incremental rule learning algorithm, which uses heuristics to adapt the size of training window dynamically.

The advantages of the techniques to be proposed in this paper, when compared against existing techniques, are manifold. Firstly, our classifiers are able to detect exactly the pieces of the training data that must be updated. Consequently, the classification model is updated in a highly efficient way, without wasting computing resources. Secondly, our classifiers are able to project the training data on a demand-driven basis, producing a specific training frame for each message that is analyzed. The messages that compose each frame are automatically selected according to qualitative information present on the message being analyzed. We show that training messages have an expiration time, after which they become totally useless for the sake of classification. Finally, our classifiers are able to abstain from doubtful predictions. The corresponding messages are blocked until more evidence are obtained, and a reliable judgement becomes possible.

3. LEARNING SENTIMENT STREAMS

In this section we present novel classifiers for learning sentiments that are expressed in streams of Twitter messages. We start by discussing classification models based on specialized association rules. Then we describe static models with offline rule extraction, and dynamic models with self-augmenting training and demand-driven projection features.

3.1 Sentiment Stream Analysis

In our context, the task of learning sentiment streams is defined as follows. We have as input a small training seed (referred to as $\mathcal{D}$), which consists of a set of records of the form $< d, s_i >$, where d is a message (represented as a list of terms), and s_i is the sentiment implicit in d. Messages in $\mathcal{D}$ are uniquely identified and the sentiment variable s draws its values from a pre-defined and discrete set of possibilities (e.g., s_1, s_2, ..., s_k). The training seed is used to build functions relating textual patterns in the messages to their corresponding sentiments. A sequence of future messages (referred to as $\mathcal{T}$) consists of records $< t, ? >$ for which only the terms in message t are known, while the sentiment expressed in t is unknown. Classification models obtained from $\mathcal{D}$ are used to score the sentiments for each message in $\mathcal{T}$. However, messages in $\mathcal{T}$ come on streams, so that the classifier must operate with limited computing resources while producing classification models. Also, the classifier must adapt itself due to sentiment drift, being able to acquire new training information as the stream passes, and to select training messages that are relevant to each message in $\mathcal{T}$.

There are countless strategies for devising a classifier for sentiment analysis. The majority of these classification strategies, however, are not well-suited to deal with real-time data coming on streams. Some strategies [6, 8] are specifically devised for offline classification, and this is problematic because producing classification models on-the-fly would be unacceptably costly. Even updating the models in scenarios with high-speed streams would be excessively lengthy. In such hard circumstances, alternate classification strategies may become more convenient. In the following we describe classification models composed of specific association rules, and how these models are used for sentiment-scoring.

Definition 1. A sentiment rule is a specialized association rule $\mathcal{X} \rightarrow s_i$, where the antecedent $\mathcal{X}$ is a set of terms (i.e., a termset), and the consequent s_i is the predicted sentiment. The domain for $\mathcal{X}$ is the vocabulary of $\mathcal{D}$. The cardinality of rule $\mathcal{X} \rightarrow s_i$ is given by the number of terms in the antecedent, that is $|\mathcal{X}|$. The support of $\mathcal{X}$ is denoted as $\sigma(\mathcal{X})$, and is the number of messages in $\mathcal{D}$ having $\mathcal{X}$ as a subset. The confidence of rule $\mathcal{X} \rightarrow s_i$ is denoted as $\theta(\mathcal{X} \rightarrow s_i)$, and is the conditional probability of sentiment s_i given the terms in $\mathcal{X}$, that is, $\theta(\mathcal{X} \rightarrow s_i) = \frac{\sigma(\mathcal{X} \cup s_i)}{\sigma(\mathcal{X})}$.

Offline Rule Extraction

The simplest approach for sentiment learning using sentiment rules is the offline one. A set of rules is extracted from the training data $\mathcal{D}$. These rules compose the classification model.

Definition 2. The classification model is denoted as $\mathcal{R}$, and it is composed of a set of rules $\mathcal{X} \rightarrow s_i$ extracted from $\mathcal{D}$. The model is represented as a pool of entries with the form *<key, data>*, where *key*=$\{\mathcal{X}, s_i\}$ and *data*=$\{\sigma(\mathcal{X}), \sigma(\mathcal{X} \cup s_i), \theta(X \rightarrow s_i)\}$. Each entry in the pool corresponds to a rule, and the key is used to facilitate fast access to the rule properties.

The rule extraction process is divided into two steps: support counting and confidence computation. Once the support $\sigma(\mathcal{X})$ is known, it is straightforward to compute the confidence $\theta(\mathcal{X} \rightarrow s_i)$ for the corresponding rules [33]. There are several smart support-counting strategies [2, 17, 33], and many fast implementations [3] that can be used.

Usually, the support for termsets in $\mathcal{D}$ are computed in a bottom-up way, which starts by scanning all messages in $\mathcal{D}$ and computing the support of each term in isolation (i.e., 1-termsets). In the next iteration, 2-termsets (i.e., termsets of size 2) are enumerated using 1-termsets, and their support values are calculated by accessing the training data. The search for termsets proceeds, and the enumeration process is repeated until the support values for all termsets in $\mathcal{D}$ are finally computed. Obviously, the number of rules increases exponentially with the size of the vocabulary (i.e., the number of distinct terms in $\mathcal{D}$), and computational cost restrictions have to be imposed during rule extraction. Typically, the search space for rules is restricted by pruning rules that do not appear frequently in

$\mathcal{D}$ (i.e., the minimum support approach). While such restrictions make rule extraction feasible, they also lead to lossy classification models, since some rules are pruned and not be included into $\mathcal{R}$.

Sentiment Scoring

Once the classification model $\mathcal{R}$ is extracted from $\mathcal{D}$, rules are collectively used to score sentiments of messages that come later, $\mathcal{T}$. Basically, the model is interpreted as a poll, in which each rule $\{\mathcal{X} \rightarrow s_i\} \in \mathcal{R}$ is a vote given by $\mathcal{X}$ for sentiment s_i. Given a message $t \in \mathcal{T}$, a rule $\mathcal{X} \rightarrow s_i$ is only considered as a valid vote if this rule is applicable to t.

Definition 3. A rule $\{\mathcal{X} \rightarrow s_i\} \in \mathcal{R}$ is said to be applicable to message $t \in \mathcal{T}$ if $\mathcal{X} \subseteq t$. That is, if all terms in $\mathcal{X}$ are present in t.

Not all rules in $\mathcal{R}$ are applicable to a specific message $t \in \mathcal{T}$. Eventually, the model may contain many rules that are not applicable to any message in $\mathcal{T}$. These rules are said to be useless, and the set of all useless rules in $\mathcal{R}$ is denoted as $\mathcal{R}_\emptyset$.

We denote as $\mathcal{R}_t$ the set of all rules in $\mathcal{R}$ that are applicable to message $t \in \mathcal{T}$. Thus, only and all the rules in $\mathcal{R}_t$ are considered as valid votes when scoring sentiments in message t. Therefore, for m future messages in $\mathcal{T} = \{t_1, t_2, \ldots, t_m\}$, the classification model $\mathcal{R}$ can be decomposed as $\{\mathcal{R}_{t_1} \cup \mathcal{R}_{t_2} \cup \ldots \cup \mathcal{R}_{t_m} \cup \mathcal{R}_\emptyset\}$. Rules in $\mathcal{R}_\emptyset$ represent a waste of computational resources, and may pollute the classification model with irrelevant information. Ideally $|\mathcal{R}_\emptyset| = 0$.

Also, we denote as $\mathcal{R}_t^{s_i}$ the subset of $\mathcal{R}_t$ containing only rules predicting sentiment s_i. Votes in $\mathcal{R}_t^{s_i}$ have different weights, depending on the confidence of the corresponding rules. The weighted votes for sentiment s_i are averaged, giving the score for sentiment s_i with regard to message t, as shown in Equation 1:

$$s(t, s_i) = \sum \frac{\theta(\mathcal{X} \rightarrow s_i)}{|\mathcal{R}_t^{s_i}|} \tag{1}$$

Finally, the scores are normalized, as expressed by the scoring function $\hat{p}(s_i|t)$, shown in Equation 2. The scoring function estimates the likelihood of sentiment s_i being the implicit attitude of message t.

$$\hat{p}(s_i|t) = \frac{s(t, s_i)}{\sum_{j=0}^{k} s(t, s_j)} \tag{2}$$

3.2 Self-augmenting Training and Projection

The performance associated with (static) classification models tends to deteriorate over time. This is mainly due to *sentiment drift* [32], which happens when data distribution in $\mathcal{T}$ is different from that in $\mathcal{D}$. The difference usually increases over time, and at some point in time the training data may eventually become meaningless and the classification model obsolete. Drift is commonly observed in streaming environments, being evidenced either when the sentiment distribution shifts, or when the relationship between textual-patterns and sentiments changes [12]. In both cases the need for model adaptation is prevalent in order to track changing-sentiments over time.

Data Inclusion

In order to adapt the classification model accordingly, it is mandatory to gather the most current information emerging in the stream. Latest, most current training messages, may be obtained by exploiting the predictions performed using the sentiment-scoring function shown in Equation 2. These predictions may be used to assign sentiments to messages, generating labeled messages. Further, reliable predictions may be regarded as correct ones and generate reliable labeled messages, which can be included into $\mathcal{D}$.

Definition 4. Given an arbitrary message $t \in \mathcal{T}$, we say that $< t, s_i >$ is a reliable labeled message if $\hat{p}(s_i|t) \geq \delta_{min}$, where δ_{min} is a user-specified threshold ($0.0 < \delta_{min} \leq 1.0$).

The idea is to use δ_{min} as a threshold indicating the minimum reliability necessary to regard labeled message $< t, s_i >$ as a correct one, and, therefore, to include it into the training data $\mathcal{D}$. Intuitively, if reliable predictions are indeed correct ones, then the training data will be continuously augmented with novel training information, keeping the training data up-to-date as the stream evolves. However, the use of support-based pruning during rule extraction prevents the full potential of self-augmenting training, since it is highly probable that the classification model $\mathcal{R}$ will be composed only of the most general rules in $\mathcal{D}$, and most of these rules may be not applicable to future messages carrying trending (i.e., not so frequent) information.

Definition 5. Given a message $t \in \mathcal{T}$, we say that model $\mathcal{R}$ is agnostic to t, if $\mathcal{R}_t = \emptyset$. That is, if $\mathcal{R}$ does not contain rules that are applicable to t. A model $\mathcal{R}$ is said to be gnostic if $\mathcal{R}_t \neq \emptyset$ $\forall t \in \mathcal{T}$.

Unfortunately, an optimal minimum support value that guarantees a gnostic classification model, is unlikely to exist. Therefore, as we discuss in the next section, our rule extraction must be support-free, in order to produce gnostic models, and to exploit the full potential and all the benefits of self-augmenting training.

Online Rule Extraction with Data Projection

So far we have discussed offline rule extraction. Extracting rules on-the-fly, however, offers several advantages. One of these advantages is that the classifiers become able to efficiently extract rules from $\mathcal{D}$ without performing support-based pruning. The idea behind online rule extraction is to avoid completely the extraction of useless rules by projecting the training data on a demand-driven basis. More specifically, rule extraction is delayed until a message $t \in \mathcal{T}$ is given. Then, terms in t are used as a filter which configures the training data $\mathcal{D}$ in a way that only rules that are applicable to t can be extracted. This filtering process produces a projected training data, denoted as $\mathcal{D}_t$, which contains only terms that are present in message t.

Lemma 1. All rules extracted from $\mathcal{D}_t$ are applicable to t.

Proof. Since all training messages in $\mathcal{D}_t$ contain only terms that are present in message t, the existence of a rule $\mathcal{X} \rightarrow s_i$ extracted from $\mathcal{D}_t$, such that $\mathcal{X} \not\subseteq t$, is impossible. ■

Lemma 1 implies that demand-driven training projection assures that $|\mathcal{R}_\emptyset| = 0$, evidencing that only useless rules are not included into the classification model $\mathcal{R}$. The next theorem states that our classifier efficiently extracts rules from $\mathcal{D}$, no matter the minimum-support value (which can be arbitrary low). The key intuition is that the classifier works only on terms that are known to be associated to each other, drastically narrowing down the search space for rules.

Theorem 1. The number of rules extracted from $\mathcal{D}_t$ increases polynomially with the number of distinct terms in $\mathcal{D}$.

Proof. Let n be the number of distinct terms in $\mathcal{D}$. Since an arbitrary message $t \in \mathcal{T}$ contains at most l terms (with $l \ll n$), then any rule applicable to t can have at most l terms in its antecedent. That is, for any rule $\{\mathcal{X} \rightarrow s_i\}$, such that $\mathcal{X} \subseteq t$, $|\mathcal{X}| \leq l$. Consequently, the number of possible rules that are applicable to t is $l + \binom{l}{2} + \ldots + \binom{l}{l} = O(2^l) \ll O(n^l)$. Thus, the number of applicable rules increases polynomially in n. ■

Another advantage provided by demand-driven training projection comes from the fact that the projection also exploits, as a side-effect, the temporal locality associated with terms in $\mathcal{D}$. This is particularly important for dealing with sentiment drift, since by projecting the training data according to the content of a message $t \in \mathcal{T}$, the classifier is essentially concentrating the representative training information in nearly contiguous temporal data frames. However, deciding about the recency of the frame is a tricky issue, since different messages in $\mathcal{T}$ may demand training frames positioned in different points of the stream timeline. That is, some messages in $\mathcal{T}$ may demand more recent training frames, while other messages in $\mathcal{T}$ may demand older ones. Thus, instead of employing a fixed-length temporal training frame for all messages in $\mathcal{T}$, our classifier employs a different frame (i.e., $\mathcal{D}_t$) for each message in $t \in \mathcal{T}$. The recency of the training frame for an arbitrary message t is decided based upon the terms that are in the own message. Since these terms are chronologically related somehow, the projected training data $\mathcal{D}_t$ is likely to contain representative training messages for scoring the sentiments in message t.

Extending Classification Models Dynamically

With online rule extraction, we extend the classification model $\mathcal{R}$ dynamically as messages in $\mathcal{T}$ are processed. Initially $\mathcal{R}$ is empty; a sub-model $\mathcal{R}_{t_i}$ is appended to $\mathcal{R}$ every time the classifier processes a message t_i. Thus, after processing a sequence of m messages $\{t_1, t_2, \ldots, t_m\}$, the model $\mathcal{R}$ is $\{\mathcal{R}_{t_1} \cup \mathcal{R}_{t_2} \cup \ldots \cup \mathcal{R}_{t_m}\}$, and therefore, $\mathcal{R}$ is gnostic to all those m messages.

Producing a sub-model $\mathcal{R}_t$ involves extracting rules from $\mathcal{D}_t$. This operation has a significant computational cost, since it is necessary perform multiple accesses to $\mathcal{D}$. Different messages in $\mathcal{T} = \{t_1, t_2, \ldots, t_m\}$ may demand different sub-models $\{\mathcal{R}_{t_1}, \mathcal{R}_{t_2}, \ldots, \mathcal{R}_{t_m}\}$, but different sub-models may share some rules (i.e., $\{\mathcal{R}_{t_i} \cap \mathcal{R}_{t_j}\} \neq \emptyset$). In this case, memorization is very effective in avoiding work replication, reducing the number of data access operations. Thus, before extracting rule $\mathcal{X} \rightarrow s_i$, the classifier first checks whether this rule is already in $\mathcal{R}$. If an entry is found with a key matching $\{\mathcal{X}, s_i\}$, then the rule in $\mathcal{R}$ is used instead of extracting it from $\mathcal{D}_t$. If it is not found, the rule is extracted from $\mathcal{D}_t$ and then it is inserted into $\mathcal{R}$. The main steps are summarized in Algorithm 1.

Algorithm 1 Online Rule Extraction

Require: message $t \in \mathcal{T}$ and $\mathcal{D}$
Ensure: $\mathcal{R}_t$ and $\mathcal{R}$

1: $\mathcal{D}_t \Leftarrow \mathcal{D}$ projected according to message t
2: $\mathcal{R}_t \Leftarrow$ rules $\{\mathcal{X} \rightarrow s_i\} \notin \mathcal{R}$, extracted from $\mathcal{D}_t$
3: append $\mathcal{R}_t$ to $\mathcal{R}$

Model Maintenance

Entries in the classification model $\mathcal{R}$ may become invalid when reliable labeled messages $< t, s_i >$ are included into $\mathcal{D}$. As a result, $\mathcal{R}$ has to be updated properly. We propose to maintain the model up-to-date incrementally, so that the updated model is exactly the same one that would be obtained by re-constructing it from scratch.

Update speed is a key issue in model maintenance, and a challenge that threatens the efficiency of our approach is that the model may be composed of a potentially large number of rules, and updating all these rules may be unacceptably costly in a streaming environment. Fortunately, not all rules in $\mathcal{R}$ have to be updated.

Lemma 2. The inclusion of a labeled message $< t, s_i >$ into $\mathcal{D}$ does not change the value of $\sigma(\mathcal{X})$, for any termset $\mathcal{X} \not\subset t$.

Proof. Since $\mathcal{X} \not\subset t$, the number of messages in $\mathcal{D}$ having $\mathcal{X}$ as a subset is essentially the same as in $\{\mathcal{D} \cup t\}$. ■

Lemma 3. The inclusion of a labeled message $< t, s_i >$ into $\mathcal{D}$ does not change the value of $\theta(\mathcal{X} \rightarrow s)$, for any rule $\{\mathcal{X} \rightarrow s\} \in \mathcal{R}$ for which $\mathcal{X} \not\subset t, \forall s \in \{s_1, s_2, \ldots, s_k\}$.

Proof. Comes directly from the fact that confidence is invariant under the null-addition operation [30]. ■

From Lemmas 2 and 3, the number of rules that have to be updated due to the inclusion of labeled message $< t, s_i >$, is bounded by the number of possible termsets in t. Since most of the messages that are included into $\mathcal{D}$ contain only a very small fraction of all possible termsets, the inclusion of an arbitrary message t corresponds to a null-addition to most of the rules in $\mathcal{R}$. The following lemma states exactly the rules in $\mathcal{R}$ that have to be updated.

Lemma 4. The only and all the rules in $\mathcal{R}$ that must be updated due to the inclusion of labeled message $< t, s_i >$ are those in $\mathcal{R}_t$.

Proof. All rules $\{\mathcal{X} \rightarrow s_i\} \in \mathcal{R}$ that have to be updated due to the inclusion of $< t, s_i >$ are those for which $\mathcal{X} \subseteq t$. By definition, $\mathcal{R}_t$ contains only and all such rules. ■

Once rules $\{\mathcal{X} \rightarrow s\} \in \mathcal{R}_t$ are retrieved from $\mathcal{R}$, updating the corresponding values for $\sigma(\mathcal{X})$ and $\theta(\mathcal{X} \rightarrow s)$ is a simple operation. It suffices to iterate on $\mathcal{R}_t$ and increment the values of $\sigma(\mathcal{X})$ and $\sigma(\mathcal{X} \cup s)$. The corresponding values for $\theta(\mathcal{X} \rightarrow s)$ are obtained by computing $\frac{\sigma(\mathcal{X} \cup s)}{\sigma(\mathcal{X})}$ $\forall s \in \{s_1, s_2, \ldots, s_k\}$. These steps are summarized in Algorithm 2.

Algorithm 2 Incremental Model Maintenance

Require: labeled message $< t, s_i >$, $\mathcal{D}$, and $\mathcal{R}_i$
Ensure: $\mathcal{R}$

1: **for all** rules $\{\mathcal{X} \rightarrow s\} \in \mathcal{R}_t$ **do**
2: increment $\sigma(\mathcal{X})$
3: increment $\sigma(\mathcal{X} \cup s_i)$
4: $\theta(\mathcal{X} \rightarrow s_i) \Leftarrow \frac{\sigma(\mathcal{X} \cup s_i)}{\sigma(\mathcal{X})}$
5: **end for**

The Sub Judice Strategy

Naturally, some predictions are not reliable enough, given certain values of δ_{min}. An alternative is to abstain from using such doubtful predictions as the classifier does not have enough evidence for a reliable judgement, that is, we do not use the corresponding labeled messages for model building and keep them *sub judice*. As new reliable labeled messages are included into $\mathcal{D}$, new sentiment evidence is exploited, hopefully increasing the reliability of the labeled messages that were previously hold and releasing them. More specifically, when a reliable labeled message is included into $\mathcal{D}$, the classifier re-evaluates all messages that are *sub-judice*. At the end of the process, either doubtful messages become reliable ones (possibly improving prediction performance), or there is no more reliable labeled messages to be included into $\mathcal{D}$ and, therefore, the remaining messages that are *sub-judice* have to be processed normally. The process stops when all messages in $\mathcal{T}$ are processed by the classifier. The main steps are summarized in Algorithm 3.

Algorithm 3 Blocking Doubtful Predictions

Require: message $t \in \mathcal{T}$, δ_{min}
Ensure: $\mathcal{D}$

1: **if** $\hat{p}(s_i|t) < \delta_{min}$
2: keep t *sub judice* until another labeled message is included into $\mathcal{D}$
3: **else**
4: include labeled message $< t, s_i >$ into $\mathcal{D}$
5: **end if**

As will be discussed in the next section, messages in the stream are kept *sub-judice* for a certain period of time, which depends on the application (i.e., minutes, hours, days etc.). After this period, all messages are necessarily processed.

4. EXPERIMENTAL EVALUATION

In this section we empirically analyze the sentiment scoring performance of our classifiers. We employ the mean squared error (MSE) as the basic evaluation measure in our experiments, since we are primarily interested in evaluating sentiment scoring (rather than sentiment prediction). In order to evaluate the scoring performance over the time, we employ the area under the curve (AUC)[1]. We used Multinomial Naive Bayes [4] as baseline, since it is a representative of the state-of-the-art. All datasets used in our experiments were manually labeled by three to five human annotators. Unless otherwise stated, the training seed that is provided to the classifiers are composed by the first 1% of the messages. In the following we describe the datasets, and then we discuss the scoring performance of our classifiers on these datasets[2].

4.1 Brazilian Presidential Elections

The presidential election campaigns were held from June to October 2010. Candidate Dilma Rousseff launched a Twitter page during a public announcement, and she used Twitter as one of the main sources of information for her voters. The campaign attracted more than 500,000 followers and Dilma was the second most cited person on Twitter in 2010. The election came to a second round vote, and Dilma Rousseff won the runoff with 56% of the votes.

Dilma Rousseff Election Campaign. We collected 466,724 Portuguese messages referencing Dilma Rousseff in Twitter during her campaign. We randomly selected 66,643 of these messages, and we annotated them in order to track the population sentiment of approval during this period. Approval varied greatly due to several polemic statements and political attacks, and our goal is to score approval during her campaign. The dataset contains 62,089 distinct terms, and messages are grouped by day (i.e., all messages posted in the same day are placed together in the same group). Messages in the stream come in at a rate of 0.02 messages/sec.

Figure 1 shows a series of results obtained for the evaluation of our classifiers in this dataset. Figure 1-a shows a colored map which allows us to grasp the existence of temporal locality of messages passing in the stream. A message exhibits temporal locality if it is likely to be accessed again in the near future, that is, message $d \in \mathcal{D}$ becomes more likely to be in $\mathcal{D}_{t_i}$ and in $\mathcal{D}_{t_j}$ if $t_i \in \mathcal{T}$ is close in time with $t_j \in \mathcal{T}$. In the figure, messages placed in lighter colored regions are those that appeared in the projected training data of the corresponding message in the x-axis. Messages placed in darker regions, on the other hand, are those that did not appear in the projected training data of the corresponding message in the x-axis. Since messages in the x- and y-axes are chronologically ordered, we can understand how frequently these messages are used over the time. Clearly, messages are gradually less and less used as the stream passes, and future messages tend to demand messages that were just included into $\mathcal{D}$. Also, messages have an expiration time, after which they become useless for the sake of prediction. For instance, the first messages to appear in the stream become meaningless after about 30,000 messages are processed by the classifier. Our classifiers are able to automatically discard such meaningless messages while building classification models.

Figure 1-b shows stacked histograms indicating the percentage of messages in $\mathcal{T}$ that were correctly, wrongly, and not included into $\mathcal{D}$ by varying the value of δ_{min}. As expected, the percentage of messages that are included into $\mathcal{D}$ increases as δ_{min} decreases. This is because message inclusion becomes less restrictive for lower values of δ_{min}. For the same reason, the percentage of messages wrongly included into $\mathcal{D}$ increases as δ_{min} decreases. Figure 1-c shows the same analysis, but allowing the *sub judice* strategy. For this dataset, this strategy was clearly effective, since the percentage of correctly included messages always increases, while the percentage of wrongly included messages always decreases. This is because the *sub judice* strategy makes the classifier able to abstain from doubtful predictions until more evidence is gathered with the inclusion of reliable training information, and this greatly improves scoring performance. For instance, for $\delta_{min} = 0.7$ and using a seed size of 2/100, we observed that, on average, 8% of all messages were kept *sub judice* and 225 messages were inserted into $\mathcal{D}$ at each day (which was the time period for which messages are allowed to be kept *sub-judice*).

Figure 1-d shows the online population approval sentiment over the campaign. We try to approximate sentiment variations using our classifiers. As can be seen, a better sentiment approximation is obtained when the classifier is allowed to perform the *sub judice* strategy. Figure 1-e shows the error area under the curve for different values of δ_{min} and for different training seed sizes. Since our basic performance metric is MSE, the smaller the area under the curve, the better is the performance. As expected, performance increases by increasing the seed size, since in this case more training messages are available. The best performance provided by our classifier ($\delta_{min} = 0.8$) is highly competitive with the performance provided by the baseline. Figure 1-f shows the same analysis, but allowing the classifier to perform the *sub judice* strategy. Most of the results have improved greatly – in some cases the error area decreases by more than 30%, and the resulting performance is much superior than the performance provided by the baseline.

4.2 TIME's Person of the Year

At the end of every year, TIME magazine selects a person, or a

[1]Specifically, we calculate the area under the curve induced by the MSE associated with chunks of messages, that is, messages are grouped by minutes, hours or days depending on the application.
[2]We cannot redistribute the datasets due to Twitter restrictions (`http://dev.twitter.com/pages/api_terms`)

group of persons that has most influenced events during the year. The chosen person for 2010 was Mark Zuckerberg. The reader choice, however, was Julian Assange, with an overwhelming superiority of votes.

Twittersphere Battle: Zuckerberg and Assange. We collected 93,411 English messages referencing Julian Assange and Mark Zuckerberg from 12-15-2010 to 12-21-2010. We randomly selected 5,616 of these messages, and we annotated them in order to track diverse sentiments regarding the magazine's decision. Sentiments include surprise (since the reader choice was pointing to Julian Assange), approval/disapproval, and even fury. The dataset contains 7,294 distinct terms, and messages are grouped by hour. Messages in the stream come in at a rate of 0.02 messages/sec.

Figure 2 shows a series of results obtained for the evaluation of our classifier in this dataset. Figure 2-a shows the effectiveness of training augmentation. The percentage of correctly included messages is approximately the same for δ_{min} values varying from 0.5 to 0.8. However, for $\delta_{min} = 0.8$, no message was wrongly included into $\mathcal{D}$. As a result, the best scoring performance, as shown in Figure 2-b, was obtained with $\delta_{min} = 0.8$. In this case, the area under the curve is essentially the same one obtained by the baseline. However, as the figure also shows, our classifiers obtained much better results when the *sub judice* strategy is allowed. In this case we observed that, on average, 33% of all messages were kept *sub judice* and 60 messages were included into $\mathcal{D}$ at each hour. Figure 2-c shows a X-Y scatter-plot which correlates the moment in time in which a message arrives and the moment in time in which the same message is processed. As shown in the figure, messages are blocked until it becomes possible to perform reliable predictions for them. The first messages to pass through the stream are so doubtful given only the training seed, that the corresponding predictions are kept *sub judice* even for relaxed δ_{min} values (i.e., $\leq$ 0.6). As more labeled messages are included into $\mathcal{D}$, predictions become more reliable, and only predictions with reliability below $\delta_{min} = 0.8$ are kept *sub judice*.

4.3 FIFA World Cup

The 2010 Soccer World Cup involved 32 teams competing for the title. The Brazilian team was defeated by the Dutch team on 07-02-2010, after a controversial match. The Brazilian team scored first, but soon after the Dutch team scored twice and won the match. A specific player, Felipe Melo, had decisive participation (for better or worse) in all three goals.

The Brazilian Defeat. We collected 12,020 messages referencing Felipe Melo. We randomly selected 4,646 of these messages, and we annotated them in order to track the sentiment of appreciation for the participation of Felipe Melo. This resulted in two datasets, the first one containing 3,214 annotated messages in Portuguese (8,101 distinct terms), and the second one containing 1,432 annotated messages in English (4,962 distinct terms). For these datasets, messages are grouped by minute. Messages in the stream come in at a rate of 1.12 messages/sec.

Figures 3 and 4 show a series of results obtained for the evaluation of our classifiers in these datasets. We start by discussing the results regarding the dataset composed of messages in Portuguese. Figure 3-a concerns the temporal locality associated with the messages in this dataset. Old messages are gradually less and less used as the stream passes. For instance, the first messages to appear in the stream become meaningless after about 2,000 messages are processed by the classifier. It is also clear that messages exhibit temporal locality, since, as can be seen, a given message is more likely to be used again in the near future.

Figure 3-b shows the cumulative MSE as the stream passes. The static classifier (i.e., the training data is never augmented with new training messages) offers the worst performance, and the dynamic classifier reaches its maximum performance for $\delta_{min} = 0.5$. This δ_{min} value was used to track appreciation sentiment over time, as shown in Figure 3-c. As can be seen, there was a sudden appreciation increase in the beginning of the match. This is because the queried player, Felipe Melo, made an assistance to a goal. There was also a sudden decrease in appreciation after one hour of match, and this has happened because the same queried player failed two consecutive times, allowing the adversary to score twice, winning the match consequently. As shown in Figure 3-c, the dynamic classifier offers a much better approximation, when compared against the static classifier. The superiority is due to the inclusion of new training messages into $\mathcal{D}$, as shown in Figure 3-d. For $\delta_{min} = 0.5$, the percentage of correctly included messages surpasses 95%.

Figure 3-e shows the error area under the curve obtained for different values of σ_{min}. For most of δ_{min} values, our classifier was able to provide a better performance than the performance provided by the baseline. The performance increases even more if the classifier is allowed to perform the *sub judice* strategy, as shown in the same figure. We finish the analysis of the results obtained for this dataset by inspecting the *sub judice* strategy. Figure 3-f correlates the time in which a message arrives with the time in which the same message is processed. As can be seen, messages are blocked until it becomes possible to perform reliable predictions for them. A large number of messages were blocked exactly just after one hour of match, when there was a sudden sentiment drift. This shows that the *sub judice* strategy is effective for dealing with sentiment drift (as shown in Figure 3-e), even if the drift is huge, such as the one depicted in Figure 3-c.

The last set of experiments concerns the evaluation of the same event, but using the dataset composed of messages in English. Figure 4-a shows the cumulative MSE as the stream passes. Again, the static classifier offers the worst results. Performance improves greatly when $\delta_{min} \leq 0.8$. In these cases, the number of correctly included messages surpasses 92%, as shown in Figure 4-b. As expected, the percentage of wrongly included messages increases as δ_{min} decreases, and thus, the best performance is achieved for $\delta_{min} = 0.7$, as shown in Figure 4-c. Again, the *sub judice* strategy offers a substantial improvement, and when it actually came into action, it is able to decrease the error area by at least 15%.

5. CONCLUSIONS

This paper focused on the important problem of sentiment analysis in streaming environments. We have introduced new classifiers based on sentiment rules. The proposed classifiers are able to exploit reliable predictions in order to augment the training data. The self-augmentation training procedure keeps the classifier up-to-date automatically. Furthermore, sentiment rules are extracted from the training data on a demand-driven basis, by projecting the search space for sentiment rules according to qualitative information in future messages, allowing an efficient extraction. Also, by projecting the training data, the classifier eliminates irrelevant and outdated information from consideration. This happens as a side effect, because messages coming in the stream exhibits temporal locality, and old messages are unlikely to be demanded by recent messages passing through the stream. We also show that training messages have an expiration time, after which they are totally useless for the sake of classification. Our classifier are able to discard from consideration all such meaningless information. A systematic

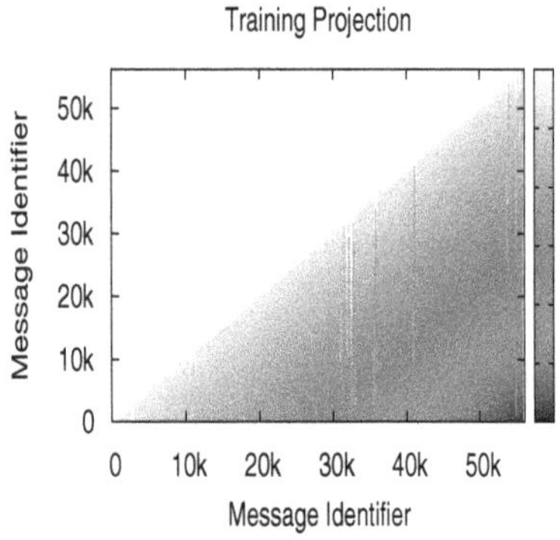

(a) Projected Training Data for each message in $\mathcal{T}$. Given a message x in the x-axis, the figure shows the corresponding $\mathcal{D}_x$ in the y-axis. Lighter colored regions indicate the presence of the corresponding message in $\mathcal{D}_x$.

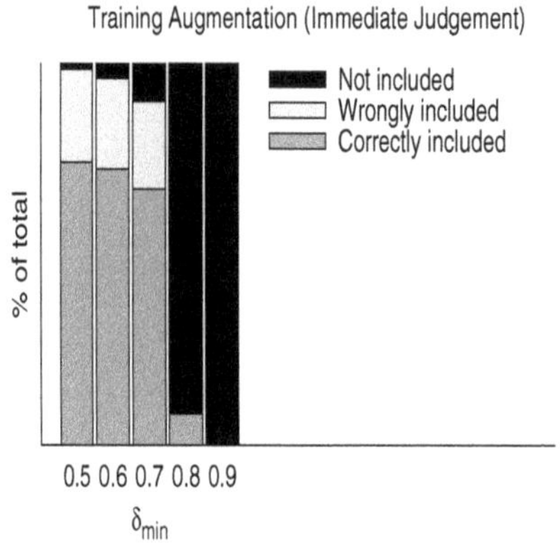

(b) Stacked histograms showing the percentage of messages in $\mathcal{T}$ that were correctly/wrongly/not included into $\mathcal{D}$, for different values of δ_{min} and using seed size of 2/100. No abstention is allowed (i.e., immediate judgement).

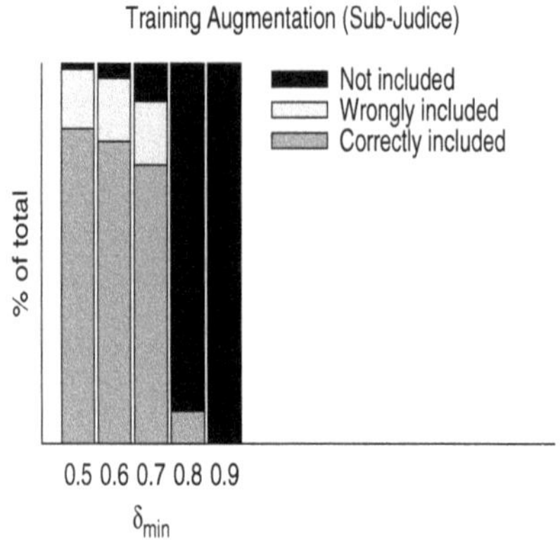

(c) Stacked histograms showing the percentage of messages in $\mathcal{T}$ that were correctly/wrongly/not included into $\mathcal{D}$, for different values of δ_{min} and using seed size of 2/100. Abstention is allowed (*sub judice*).

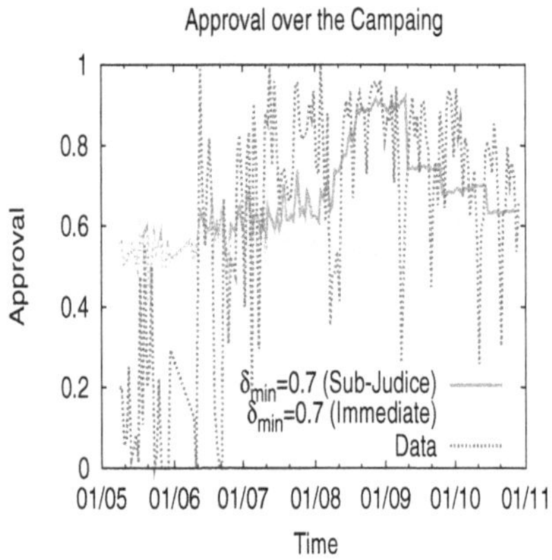

(d) Tracking population approval sentiment over the campaign.

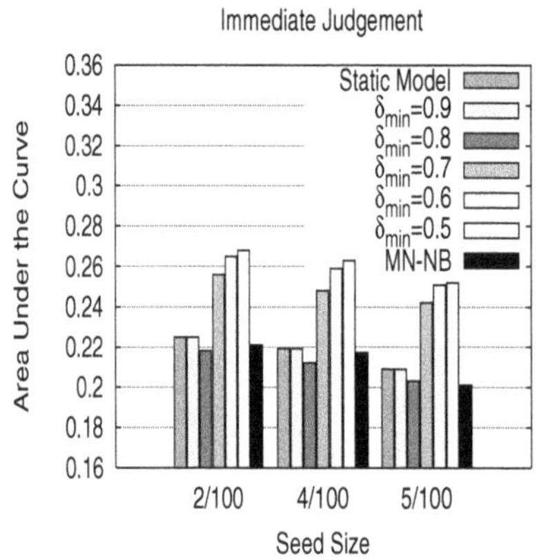

(e) Area under the curve for different values of δ_{min}. Abstention is not allowed (i.e., immediate judgement).

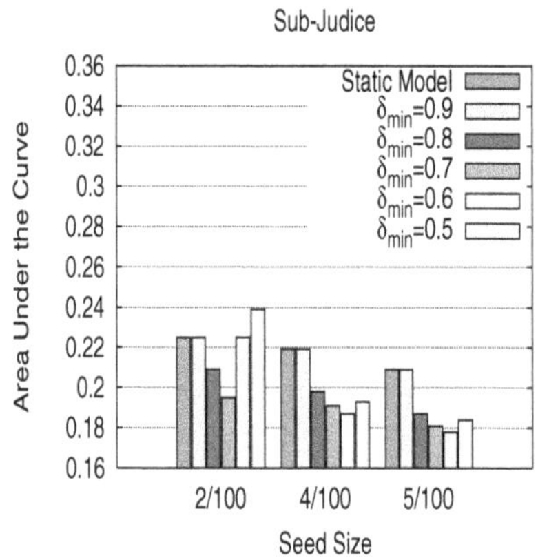

(f) Area under the curve for different values of δ_{min}. Abstention is allowed (i.e., *sub judice*).

Figure 1: Dilma Rousseff's Presidential Campaign (Portuguese).

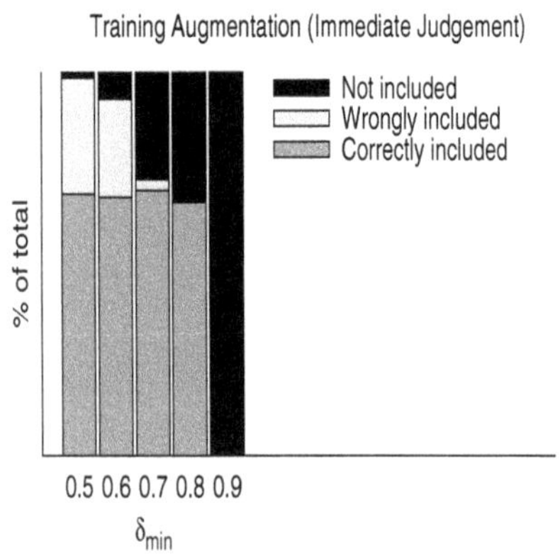

(a) Percentage of messages in $\mathcal{T}$ that were correctly/wrongly/not included into $\mathcal{D}$, for different values of δ_{min}.

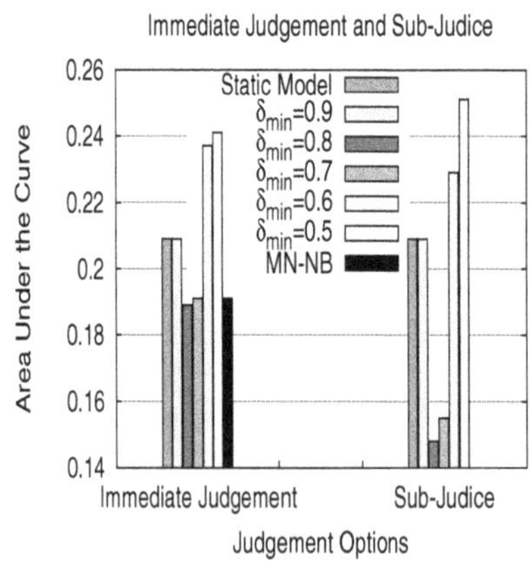

(b) Area under the curve for different values of δ_{min}.

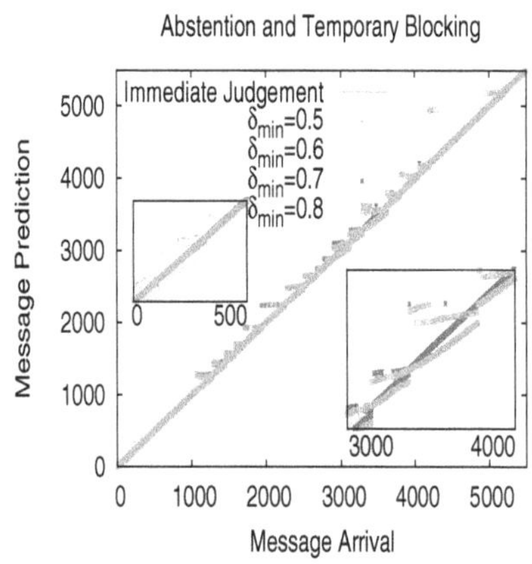

(c) X-Y scatter plot correlating message arrival and prediction, for different values of δ_{min}.

Figure 2: Person of the Year (English).

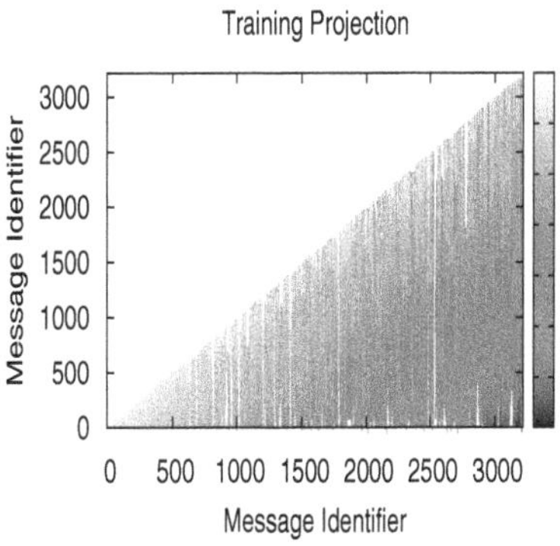

(a) Projected Training Data for each message in $\mathcal{T}$.

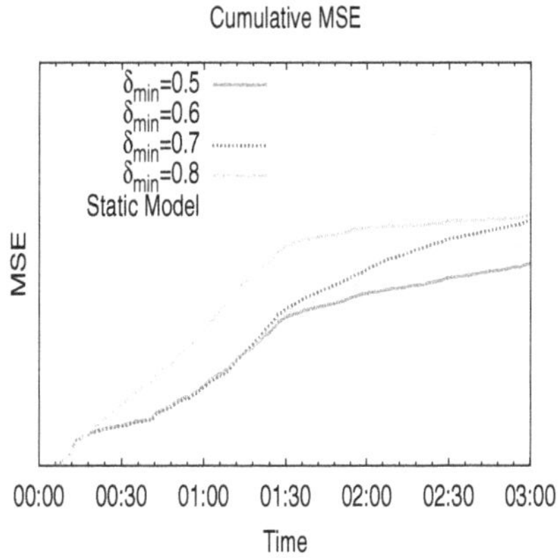

(b) Cumulative MSE for different values of δ_{min}. Messages are grouped by minute, and a MSE value is calculated for each group.

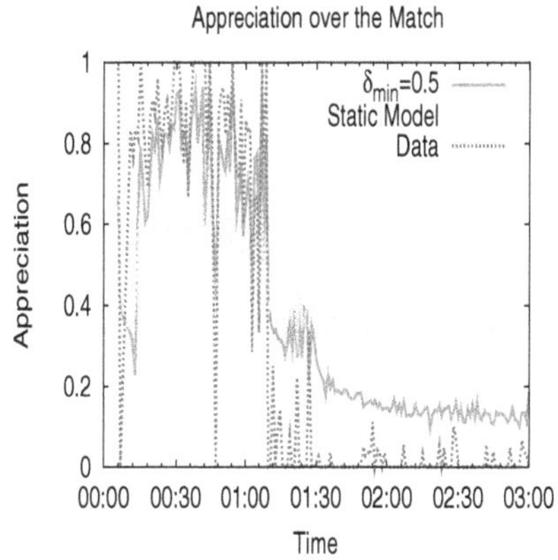

(c) Tracking appreciation sentiment over the match.

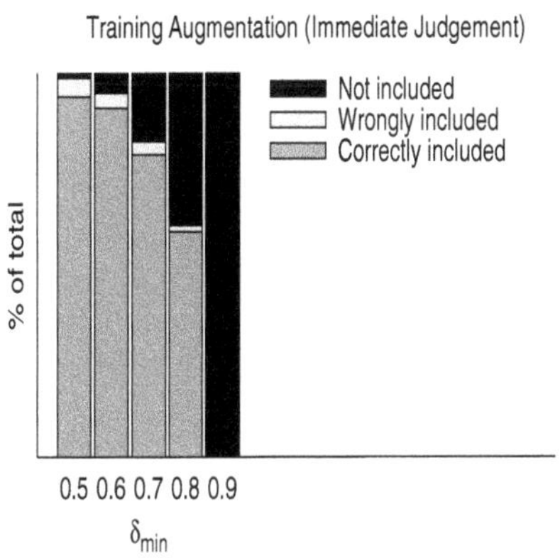

(d) Percentage of messages in $\mathcal{T}$ that were correctly/wrongly/not included into $\mathcal{D}$, for different values of δ_{min}.

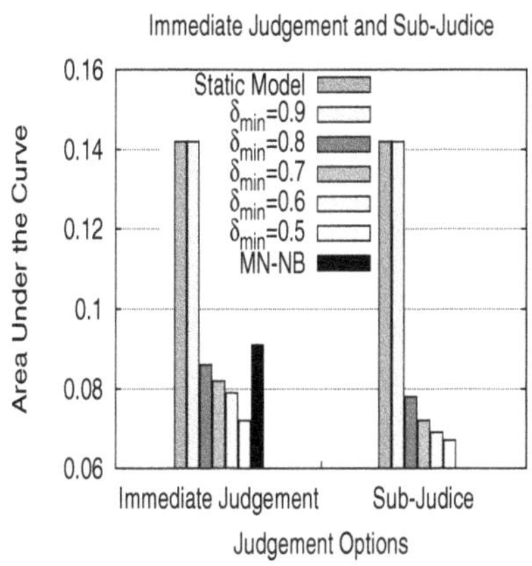

(e) Area under the curve for different values of δ_{min}.

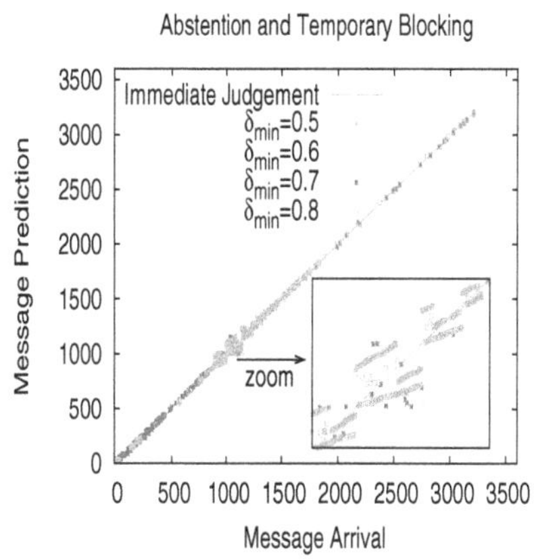

(f) X-Y scatter plot correlating message arrival and prediction, for different values of δ_{min}.

Figure 3: Brazilian Defeat in the FIFA Cup (Portuguese).

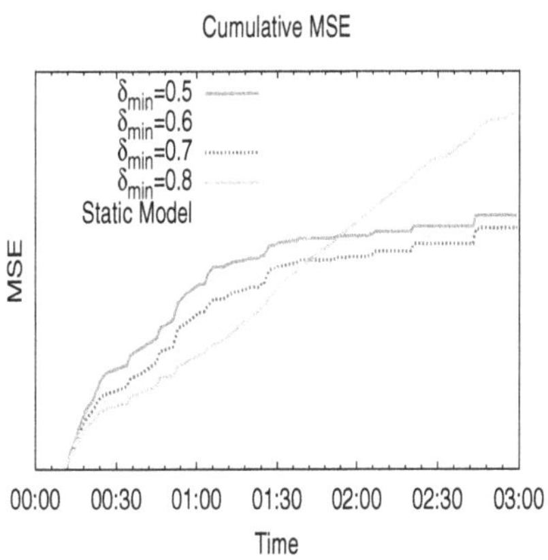

(a) Cumulative MSE for different values of δ_{min}. Messages are grouped by minute, and a MSE value is calculated for each group.

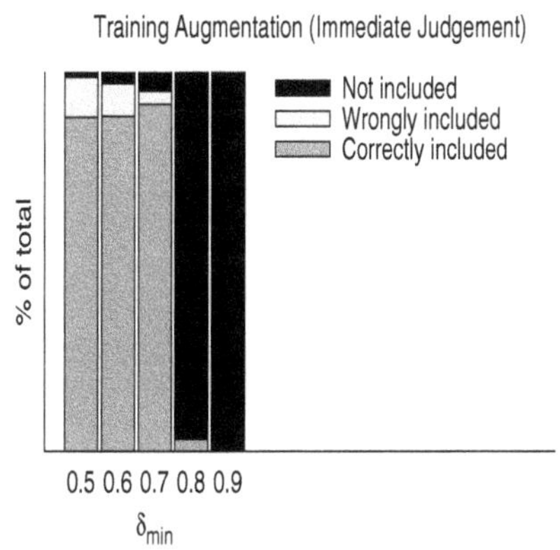

(b) Percentage of messages in $\mathcal{T}$ that were correctly/wrongly/not included into $\mathcal{D}$, for different values of δ_{min}.

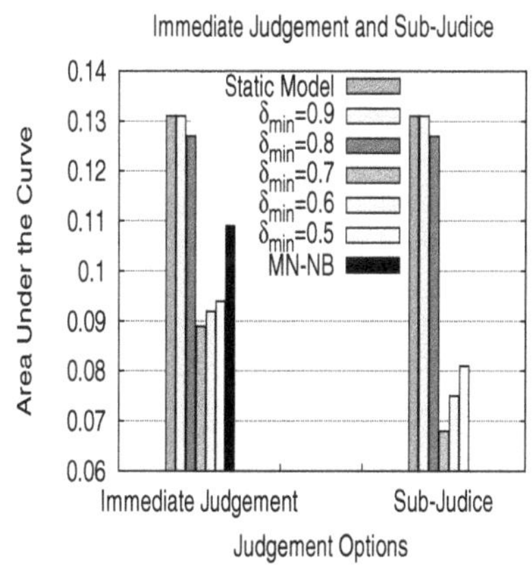

(c) Area under the curve for different values of δ_{min}.

Figure 4: Brazilian Defeat in the FIFA Cup (English).

evaluation involving major 2010 events demonstrated the effectiveness of the proposed classifiers, which were compared against a representative of the state-of-the-art.

We proposed to further improve the prediction performance of these classifiers by introducing the innovative *sub-judice* strategy, which makes the classifiers able to abstain from doubtful predictions, and to temporarily block these predictions until more evidence is gathered due to the inclusion of new reliable training information. Experimental evaluation has shown that the *sub judice* strategy substantially boosts prediction performance providing gains up to 58%.

6. ACKNOWLEDGMENTS

This research was sponsored by UOL (www.uol.com.br) through its UOL Bolsa Pesquisa program process number 20110215215201, CNPq, Capes, Fapemig and Inweb - the Brazilian National Institute of Science and Technology for the Web.

7. REFERENCES

[1] Nielsen online report. social networks & blogs now 4th most popular online activity. 2009.

[2] R. Agrawal, T. Imielinski, and A. Swami. Mining association rules between sets of items in large databases. In *SIGMOD*, pages 207–216. ACM, 1993.

[3] R. Bayardo, B. Goethals, and M. Zaki, editors. *Workshop on Frequent Itemset Mining Implementations*, volume 126, 2004.

[4] A. Bifet and E. Frank. Sentiment knowledge discovery in twitter streaming data. In *Discovery Science*, pages 1–15, 2010.

[5] A. Bifet, G. Holmes, B. Pfahringer, R. Kirkby, and R. Gavalda. New ensemble methods for evolving data streams. In *SIGKDD*, pages 139–148, 2009.

[6] L. Breiman, J. Friedman, R. Olshen, and C. Stone. Classification and regression trees. *Wadsworth Intl.*, 1984.

[7] O. Chapelle, B. Schölkopf, and A. Zien. *Semi-Supervised Learning*. MIT Press, 2006.

[8] C. Cortes and V. Vapnik. Support-vector networks. *Machine Learning*, 20(3):273–297, 1995.

[9] N. Diakopoulos and D. Shamma. Characterizing debate performance via aggregated twitter sentiment. In *CHI*, pages 1195–1198, 2010.

[10] P. Domingos and G. Hulten. Mining high-speed data streams. In *SIGKDD*, pages 71–80, 2000.

[11] W. Fan. Streamminer: A classifier ensemble-based engine to mine concept-drifting data streams. In *VLDB*, pages 1257–1260, 2004.

[12] G. Forman. Tackling concept drift by temporal inductive transfer. In *SIGIR*, pages 252–259, 2006.

[13] J. Gama, R. S. ao, and P. Rodrigues. Issues in evaluation of stream learning algorithms. In *SIGKDD*, pages 329–338, 2009.

[14] J. Gama, R. Rocha, and P. Medas. Accurate decision trees for mining high-speed data streams. In *SIGKDD*, pages 523–528, 2003.

[15] J. Gehrke, V. Ganti, R. Ramakrishnan, and W. Loh. Boat-optimistic decision tree construction. In *SIGMOD*, pages 169–180, 1999.

[16] A. Go, L. Huang, and R. Bhayani. Twitter sentiment classification using distant supervision. In *CS224N Project Report*, 2009.

[17] J. Han, J. Pei, Y. Yin, and R. Mao. Mining frequent patterns without candidate generation: A frequent-pattern tree approach. *Data Mining Knowledge Discovery*, 8(1):53–87, 2004.

[18] G. Hulten, L. Spencer, and P. Domingos. Mining time-changing data streams. In *SIGKDD*, pages 97–106, 2001.

[19] B. Jansen, M. Zhang, K. Sobel, and A. Chowdury. Micro-blogging as online word of mouth branding. In *CHI*, pages 281–290, 2009.

[20] B. Jansen, M. Zhang, K. Sobel, and A. Chowdury. Twitter power: Tweets as electronic word of mouth. *JASIST*, 60(11):2169–2188, 2009.

[21] J. Kolter and M. Maloof. Dynamic weighted majority: an ensemble method for drifting concepts. *Journal of Machine Learning Research*, 8:2755–2790, 2007.

[22] M. A. Maloof. Incremental rule learning with partial instance memory for changing concepts. In *IJCNN*, pages 2764–2769. IEEE, 2003.

[23] B. O'Connor, R. Balasubramanyan, B. Routledge, and N. Smith. From tweets to polls: Linking text sentiment to public opinion time series. In *ICWSM*, pages 122–129, 2010.

[24] A. Pak and P. Paroubek. Twitter as a corpus for sentiment analysis and opinion mining. In *Intl. Conf. on Language Resources and Evaluation*, pages 1320–1326, 2010.

[25] B. Pang, L. Lee, , and S. Vaithyanathan. Thumbs up? sentiment classifcation using machine learning techniques. In *EMNLP*, pages 79–86, 2002.

[26] B. Pang and L. Lee. Opinion mining and sentiment analysis. *Foundations and Trends in Information Retrieval*, 2(1-2):1–135, 2007.

[27] D. Ramage, S. Dumais, and D. Liebling. Characterizing microblogs with topic models. In *ICWSM*, 2010.

[28] J. Read. Using emoticons to reduce dependency in machine learning techniques for sentiment classification. In *ACL Student Research Workshop*, pages 43–48, 2005.

[29] W. Street and Y. Kim. A streaming ensemble algorithm (SEA) for large-scale classification. In *SIGKDD*, pages 377–382, 2001.

[30] P. Tan, V. Kumar, and J. Srivastava. Selecting the right interestingness measure for association patterns. In *SIGKDD*, pages 32–41, 2002.

[31] H. Wang, W. Fan, P. Yu, , and J. Han. Mining concept-drifting data streams using ensemble classifiers. In *SIGKDD*, pages 226–235, 2003.

[32] G. Widmer and M. Kubat. Learning in the presence of concept drift and hidden contexts. *Machine Learning*, 23(1):69–101, 1996.

[33] M. Zaki, S. Parthasarathy, M. Ogihara, and W. Li. New algorithms for fast discovery of association rules. In *SIGKDD*, pages 283–286, 1997.

[34] P. Zhang, X. Zhu, and Y. Shi. Categorizing and mining concept drifting data streams. In *SIGKDD*, pages 812–820, 2008.

[35] P. Zhang, X. Zhu, J. Tan, and L. Guo. Classifier and cluster ensembles for mining concept drifting data streams. In *ICDM*, pages 1175–1180, 2010.

[36] X. Zhu, P. Zhang, X. Lin, and Y. Shi. Active learning from data streams. In *ICDM*, pages 757–762, 2007.

Hypergeometric Language Models for Republished Article Finding

Manos Tsagkias
ISLA, University of Amsterdam
e.tsagkias@uva.nl

Maarten de Rijke
ISLA, University of Amsterdam
derijke@uva.nl

Wouter Weerkamp
ISLA, University of Amsterdam
w.weerkamp@uva.nl

ABSTRACT

Republished article finding is the task of identifying instances of articles that have been published in one source and republished more or less verbatim in another source, which is often a social media source. We address this task as an ad hoc retrieval problem, using the source article as a query. Our approach is based on language modeling. We revisit the assumptions underlying the unigram language model taking into account the fact that in our setup queries are as long as complete news articles. We argue that in this case, the underlying generative assumption of sampling words from a document with replacement, i.e., the multinomial modeling of documents, produces less accurate query likelihood estimates.

To make up for this discrepancy, we consider distributions that emerge from sampling without replacement: the central and non-central hypergeometric distributions. We present two retrieval models that build on top of these distributions: a log odds model and a bayesian model where document parameters are estimated using the Dirichlet compound multinomial distribution.

We analyse the behavior of our new models using a corpus of news articles and blog posts and find that for the task of republished article finding, where we deal with queries whose length approaches the length of the documents to be retrieved, models based on distributions associated with sampling without replacement outperform traditional models based on multinomial distributions.

Categories and Subject Descriptors

H.3.3 [**Information Search and Retrieval**]: Retrieval Models

General Terms

Algorithms, Experiment, Theory

Keywords

Language models, Hypergeometric, Multinomial, Linking, Online news, Social Media

1. INTRODUCTION

Republished article finding (RAF) is the task of identifying instances of articles that have been published in one source and republished more or less verbatim in another. A common instance of the phenomenon occurs with news articles that are being republished by bloggers. The RAF task is important for a number of stakeholders. Publishers of news content are a prime example. For us, the motivation for considering the RAF task comes from the area of online reputation management.

Over the past decade, the web has come to play an increasingly important role in the overall communication strategy of organisations. It continues to offer new opportunities for organisations to directly interact with their customers or audience but it also contains possible threats as online conversations are impossible to control, while the potential impact on an organisation's reputation may be deep and long-lasting. Online reputation management (ORM) is aimed at monitoring the online reputation of an organization, brand or person, by mining news, social media and search engine result pages.

A key aspect of ORM is early detection of news topics that may end up harming the reputation of a given company, brand or person ("customer"), so that public relations activities can be launched to counter such trends. For this purpose it is important to track news stories that talk about an issue that affects the customer. In the blogosphere news stories may be republished for a number of reasons. In our data sets (see Section 4 for details), we have come across instances where bloggers want to share a news item with colleagues or students[1] or where a blogger aims to kick off a discussion around the original news article within his own online community,[2] or where someone uses excerpts from a news article as references in a post where they discuss their own opinion.[3] In addition to this "strict" interpretation of the RAF task (where most or all of a source article is being republished), ORM analysts are also interested in a somewhat looser interpretation, where a key part of a source article (e.g., its lead) is being republished in social media. Republished articles matter to ORM analysts as they may become springboards where intense, possibly negative discussions flare up.

[1]E.g., a very large part of NYT article "A Boy the Bullies Love to Beat Up, Repeatedly" `http://www.nytimes.com/2008/03/24/us/24land.html?_r=1` was republished verbatim in The Kentucky School blog written by the school's teachers, at `http://theprincipal.blogspot.com/2008/03/boy-bullies-love-to-beat-up-repeatedly.html`.

[2]E.g., all of "Financial Russian Roulette" by NYT journalist Paul Krugman was reposted by Mark Thoma (Professor of Economics at University of Oregon) at `http://economistsview.typepad.com/economistsview/2008/09/paul-krugman-fi.html`, with a one sentence commentary by Thoma, followed by about 110 follow-up comments.

[3]See, e.g., "What parts of the agenda would you sacrifice to try to put bushies in jail for torture?" `http://nomoremister.blogspot.com/2009/01/what-parts-of-agenda-would-you.html`.

Having motivated the task of finding republished news articles in the blogosphere, we now turn to addressing the task. At first glance the strict version of the task looks like a duplicate detection task. As we show in Section 5 below, on a strict interpretation of the RAF task, state-of-the-art duplicate detection methods show very reasonable performance in terms of MRR but in terms of MAP they leave room for improvement. Under the more liberal interpretation of the RAF task, the performance of state-of-the-art duplication detection methods drops rapidly, on all metrics.

These initial findings motivate the use of standard information retrieval methods for the RAF task, viewing the original news article as a query to be submitted against an index consisting of, say, blog posts [19, 36]. We follow the latter and focus on language modeling (LM) techniques for the RAF task. Language modeling in IR is usually based on distributions that emerge from *sampling with replacement*, e.g., 2-Poisson, bernoulli, binomial, multinomial [32]. This allows a generative model of language to serve its purpose, namely, to produce infinite amounts of word sequences from a finite word population. However, in the particular case of the RAF task, we are dealing with long (document-size) queries. Here, sampling with replacement can lead to overgeneration of unseen terms; when paired with the long query length, this can have a cumulative and negative effect on performance. It is well-known from general statistics that when the sample size grows close to the population size, i.e., when it is less than 10 times the population, models based on sampling with replacement become less and less accurate [30]. In our case, we consider documents and queries as bags of word level unigrams; unigrams from the document form the population, and unigrams from the query form the sample. In the standard ad hoc retrieval setting, queries tend to be much shorter than documents, i.e., the sample is much smaller than the population. For example, title queries in the TREC Robust 2004 test set have 3 words, while documents are on average 500 words long [37]. However, in the case of our RAF task, the assumption that documents (blog posts) are at least 10 times longer than queries (source news articles) is blatantly violated: in our data set, the former are 800 words long, the latter as many as 700 words: the two are of comparable length.

Our main contribution is an LM-based retrieval model for the RAF task that builds on statistical distributions that emerge from *sampling without replacement*. Documents and queries are considered as urns that contain terms where multiple examples of each term can coexist simultaneously. A document's relevance to an information need, translates into the probability of sampling the query (the source news article) from the document (blog posts). Then, documents are ranked by this probability [33]. A suitable statistical distribution for this model is the *hypergeometric distribution* which describes the number of successes in a sequence of n draws from a finite population without replacement, just as the binomial/multinomial distribution describes the number of successes for draws with replacement.

Our approach to the RAF task consists of deriving a document model and a retrieval model. The document model is based on one of the two multivariate hypergeometric probability distributions we present here: (a) the central hypergeometric distribution and (b) the Wallenius' hypergeometric (also called non-central) distribution. Both can take into account local term weights (such as raw term frequency (TF), while the model based on the Wallenius' distribution also allows one to also incorporate global term weights (such as inverse document frequency (IDF)).

The main research question that we seek to answer is whether distributions based on sampling without replacement provide for a more effective retrieval model for the RAF task than (the usual) distributions based on sampling with replacement. We provide a positive answer to this question and complement the answer with a thorough experimental analysis of our proposed models plus a comparison to existing retrieval models tuned for the RAF task.

The rest of the paper is organized as follows. We present two hypergeometric distributions in Section 2, two retrieval models based on those distributions in Section 3 We present our experimental setup in Section 4, report on results and analysis in Section 5, discuss alternatives in Section 6, present related work in Section 7. and conclude in Section 8.

2. HYPERGEOMETRIC DISTRIBUTIONS

We present two hypergeometric distributions which we will use later for sampling a query from a document: (a) the central hypergeometric, and (b) non-central hypergeometric (also known as Wallenius' hypergeometric distribution). The difference between the two is in how we perform sampling and whether bias in sampling is involved. Under the non-central distribution the probability of drawing a term depends on the outcome of the previous draw, while under the central hypergeometric distribution, terms can be sampled independently [3, 18, 28].

Let us first describe the specific form of language model that we consider in this paper, which builds on the *query unigram model* model proposed in [42]. This model postulates that the relevance of a document to a query can be measured by the probability that the *query is generated by the document*.

Consider a query $\mathbf{q}$ and a document collection C of N documents, $C := \{\mathbf{d}_l\}_{l=1,\ldots,N}$, with both queries and document being represented as vectors of indexed term counts:

$$\begin{aligned}\mathbf{q} &:= (q_1, \ldots, q_i, \ldots, q_V) \in N^V \\ \mathbf{d}_l &:= (d_{l,1}, \ldots, d_{l,i}, \ldots, d_{l,V}) \in N^V\end{aligned}$$

where q_i is the number of times the term i appears in the query and V is the size of the vocabulary. Let us also define the *length* of a query ($n_{\mathbf{q}}$) and of a document (n_l) as the sum of their components: $n_{\mathbf{q}} := \sum_i q_i$ and $n_l := \sum_i d_{l,i}$.

2.1 The central hypergeometric distribution

The *multivariate central hypergeometric distribution* is derived from the observation that since the sampling is done without replacement, the unordered sample is uniformly distributed over the combinations of size $n_{\mathbf{q}}$ chosen from $\mathbf{d}_l$:

$$P_{ch}(\mathbf{q}; n_{\mathbf{q}}, n_l, \mathbf{d}_l) = \frac{\prod_{i=1}^{V} \binom{d_{l,i}}{q_i}}{\binom{n_l}{n_{\mathbf{q}}}}, \tag{1}$$

Terms are sampled independently or simultaneously, reflecting the term independence assumption.

2.2 The non-central hypergeometric distribution

What if terms had an additional property that affected their probability of being sampled, for example, in how many documents they occur? In the urn model, we can think about objects that, except of their different color, can be heavier or bigger than others. This additional property can bias sampling and can be modeled as a weight for each object type. We call this weight ω_i for the ith term in the vocabulary.

Under the *multivariate non-central hypergeometric distribution* the probability of sampling a term depends on the terms sampled so far and also on the remaining terms in the urn. Further, it supports biased sampling allowing for the incorporation of global term weights directly in the probability calculation. The following formula describes the distribution:

$$P_{wh}(\mathbf{q}; n_{\mathbf{q}}, n_l, \mathbf{d}_l) = \left[\prod_i^V \binom{d_{l,i}}{q_i}\right] \int_0^1 \prod_{i=1}^V \left(1 - t^{\omega_i/\Xi}\right)^{q_i} dt \quad (2)$$

where $\Xi = \boldsymbol{\omega} \cdot (\mathbf{n_l} - \mathbf{n_q}) = \sum_{i=1}^V \omega_i (d_{l,i} - q_i)$ regulates the bias of q_i after every draw, and the integral stands for the recursive sampling from time $t = 0$ until all terms are sampled at $t = 1$.

The mathematical derivation, properties and efficient computation methods of the Wallenius' distribution are beyond the scope of this paper. Wallenius [38] provides in-depth information on the characteristics of the non-central distribution and Fog [13] presents efficient methods for sampling from it. The central and non-central hypergeometric distributions are connected in that when $\omega_i = 1$ for all i, then bias is cancelled and the non-central hypergeometric distribution degenerates into the central hypergeometric distribution.

2.3 An example

Now that we have presented the hypergeometric distributions, let us look at an illustrative example on how sampling with and without replacement can lead to different results when the sample size is close to the population size. We start with a query (sample) and we need to calculate the probability of a document (population) to generate the query. In the case of *sampling with replacement*, the probability of sampling a query term t from a document D follows the binomial distribution:[4]

$$binomial(k; n, p) = \binom{n}{k} p^k (1-p)^{n-k} \quad (3)$$

with parameters n, p where n is the number of trials (query size), $p = \frac{\#t_D}{|D|}$ is the probability of a success, namely, the term frequency of t in D, and k is the number of successes, i.e., the term frequency of t in Q. In the case of *sampling without replacement* the probability of sampling a query term t from a document D follows the hypergeometric distribution:

$$hypergeometric(k; m, n, N) = \frac{\binom{m}{k}\binom{N-m}{n-k}}{\binom{N}{n}} \quad (4)$$

with parameters m, n, N where m is the term frequency of t in D, n the number of draws (query size), N the population size (document size), and k the number of successes, namely the term frequency of t in Q.

For our example, we let query Q have 4 terms, each occurring once, and also we define two documents A and B of length 1,000, and 15, respectively which share at least one common term with Q. Let also that query term t occurs 1 time in A and B. The probability of sampling t from A or B when we sample *with* replacement is given by (3) with $k = 1$, $n = 4$, $p_A = 1/1,000$, and $p_B = 1/15$. The calculations result in values of 0.003988 for document A and 0.216810 for B. Similarly, when sampling *without* replacement, we use (4) and set $k = 1$, $m = 1$, $n = 4$, $N_A = 1,000$, and $N_B = 15$. This results in values of 0.004000 for A and in 0.266666 for B. These numbers show that the difference in probability from the two models for document A is negligible ($1.2 \cdot 10^{-5}$) but when the population is close to the sample size (document B), the difference grows three orders of magnitude reaching 0.049. The example illustrates that when queries are of comparable size to the retrieved documents, sampling with replacement can lead to poor likelihood estimates with a cumulative negative effect in the multivariate case, i.e., we calculate probabilities for all query terms.

What is the upshot? It is known that the multinomial approximates the central hypergeometric as the population size remains many times larger than the sample size, i.e., when the document is much longer than the query. In the RAF task, this assumption is violated as queries and documents are expected of roughly the same size. This motivates us to derive retrieval models based on hypergeometric modeling of documents instead of multinomial models.

[4]We use the binomial distribution instead of the multinomial for simplifying the calculations in our example.

3. RETRIEVAL MODELS

Before deriving retrieval models based on hypergeometric modeling of documents, we revisit (1) and (2). We identify three constraints emerging from these equations, which relate to *smoothing* and play a role in the design of a retrieval model:

1. only query terms that occur in the document contribute to the probability,
2. the query should be shorter than the document,
3. the frequency of a query term should be lower than or equal to the term's frequency in the document.

The first constraint is obvious. The other two stem from the fact that is impossible to draw more terms than currently exist in the urn. The second constraint is imposed from the denominator $\binom{n_l}{n_\mathbf{q}}$ which becomes zero when $n_\mathbf{q} > n_l$ and results in infinite probability. The third constraint roots in $\binom{d_{l,i}}{q_i}$ which becomes zero if $q_i > d_{l,i}$ and results in zero probability. In general, $P(\mathbf{q})$ is positive only if

$$\max(0, n_\mathbf{q} + d_{l,i} - n_l) \leq q_i \leq \min(d_{l,i}, n_\mathbf{q}).$$

To address the three constraints listed above, we consider two types of smoothing. The performance of retrieval models that build on top of hypergeometric distributions is sensitive to the employed smoothing strategy, just like other retrieval models are that build on the multinomial or other distributions. In the following two subsections we present two approaches to smoothing. The first approach is somewhat related to relevance feedback and an estimated document model is trained on text from both the query and the document; this approach works for both the central and non-central hypergeometric distribution. The second approach is more elaborate and is based on bayesian inference; this approach works only for the central hypergeometric distribution, as we explain below.

3.1 A log-odds retrieval model

Our first approach to overcome the limitations on q_i, $n_\mathbf{q}$ given a document, is basic in terms that no sophisticated smoothing methods are involved for estimating the parameters of the document model. In a sense, it is remotely related to pseudo-relevance feedback but instead of re-estimating the query model from pseudo-relevant documents, the documents models are complemented with information from the query. One way to visualize the process is to think of a bag with query terms from which we sample the query. Obviously, the probability of sampling the query from the bag is 1. Now, for a document in the collection we add the document terms in the bag and sample the query again. Documents with high vocabulary overlap with the query will result in high probability while documents with only few common terms will result in low probability.

In particular, instead of sampling the query directly from the document, we derive a hypothetical document $\mathbf{d}'$ which is a mixture of the query $\mathbf{q}$ and the document $\mathbf{d}$:

$$\mathbf{d}' := (d'_{l,1}, \ldots, d'_{l,i}, \ldots, d'_{l,V}) \in N^V, \; d'_{l,i} = r_q q_i + r_d d_{l,i}, \quad (5)$$

where r_q, r_d are parameters for regulating the mixture. The length of this hypothetical document is: $n'_l = \sum_i r_q q_i + r_d d_{l,i} = r_q n_{\mathbf{q}} + r_d n_l$.

Now, it holds that $P_.(\mathbf{q}; n_{\mathbf{q}}, n'_l, \mathbf{d}'_l) \in (0, 1]$ because at least some of the terms are always sampled from $\mathbf{d}'_l$ (i.e., those originating from the query), but never all of them because $n_{\mathbf{q}} < n'_l$ by definition of $\mathbf{d}'_l$. The extreme case of $P_.(\mathbf{q}; n_{\mathbf{q}}, n'_l, \mathbf{d}'_l) = 1$ is reached when there is no vocabulary overlap between $\mathbf{d}_l$ and $\mathbf{q}$ and $r_q = 1$, however, this case is hardly encountered in practice because documents without common terms are excluded from ranking.

Document length and the vocabulary intersection between the query and the document both play an important role in the probability outcome, as in other retrieval models. To this end, we normalize the probability given the observation that the probability should maximize when the document is an exact duplicate of the query, i.e., $\mathbf{q} = \mathbf{d}_l$:

$$P_.^{max} = P_.(\mathbf{q}; n_{\mathbf{q}}, (r_q + r_d)n_{\mathbf{q}}, (r_q + r_d)\mathbf{q}). \quad (6)$$

Given this observation, documents able to generate the query with probability close to the maximum should be favored. We express this in the following ranking function:

$$\begin{aligned} Score(Q, D) &= \frac{P_.(\mathbf{q}; n_{\mathbf{q}}, n'_l, \mathbf{d}'_l)}{P_.^{max}} \\ &\propto P_.(\mathbf{q}; n_{\mathbf{q}}, n'_l, \mathbf{d}'_l)). \end{aligned} \quad (7)$$

The denominator can be ignored for ranking since it is constant for all documents. The expression of $P_.^{max}$ holds when we look at finding near or exact duplicates of a query. Under this scenario, query terms are expected to occur in a candidate "duplicate" document in relatively similar frequencies. However, this is hardly true in other settings where retrieved documents can deviate considerably from the query in both vocabulary and term frequencies.

In this respect, the assumption we made for deriving (6), can be too strict. The assumption can be relaxed if we only take into account terms common to the query and to the document and compute the maximum probability based on those. Similarly as before, first we derive a hypothetical document:

$$\mathbf{d}''_l := \{d''_{l,i} : d''_{l,i} = (r_q + r_d)q_i \text{ for } i \in V, q_i > 0, d_{l,i} > 0, \},$$

with length $n''_l = \sum_i d''_{l,i}$. Further, we also reduce the original query to a hypothetical query $\mathbf{q}''$ that consists of terms common to $\mathbf{q}$ and $\mathbf{d}_l$:

$$\mathbf{q}'' := \{q''_i : q_i \text{ for } i \in V, q_i > 0, d_{l,i} > 0, \}.$$

This results in the following definition of maximum probability, previously defined in (6):

$$P_.^{\prime max} = P_.(\mathbf{q}; n_{\mathbf{q}}, n''_l, \mathbf{d}''_l), \quad (8)$$

and the ranking function in (7) becomes:

$$Score(Q, D) = \frac{P_.(\mathbf{q}; n_{\mathbf{q}}, n'_l, \mathbf{d}'_l)}{P_.^{\prime max}}. \quad (9)$$

In this representation, $P_.^{\prime max}$ cannot be ignored because it is dependent on the vocabulary overlap of the query and the document.

3.2 A bayesian retrieval model

A second approach to overcome the limitations on q_i, $n_{\mathbf{q}}$ noted at the start of this section, is to use bayesian inference. Recall that when documents are modeled as a multinomial distribution of terms, and we apply bayes' rule, the conjugate prior distribution to the multinomial is the Dirichlet distribution [41, 42]. Setting the parameters of the Dirichlet distribution accordingly, leads to the well known Dirichlet smoothing method. Here, we follow the same line of reasoning for the multivariate central hypergeometric, and arrive at the *Dirichlet compound multinomial distribution* (DCM, also known as the multivariate Polya distribution) for estimating the parameters of a document model. To the best of our knowledge no closed form is known for the conjugate priors of the non-central hypergeometric distribution; hence, we do not offer a bayesian non-central hypergeometric model.

Now, let us consider that terms $\mathbf{t} = (t_1, \ldots, t_i, \ldots, t_V)$ arise from a multivariate central hypergeometric process where parameter n_N, the vocabulary length, is known ($n_N = \sum_{l=1}^{N} \sum_{i=1}^{V} d_{l,i}$ and $n_N > 0$) and $\theta_l = (\theta_{l,1}, \ldots, \theta_{l,V})$, the vector of term frequencies in the vocabulary that make up the population, are unknown ($0 \le \theta_{l,i} \le n_l$ and $\sum_i \theta_i = n_l$).

Under this model, the probability of generating a particular query q with counts $\mathbf{q}$ is given by:

$$P_{ch}(\mathbf{q}|\theta_l) = \frac{\prod_{i=1}^{V} \binom{\theta_{l,i}}{q_i}}{\binom{n_l}{n_{\mathbf{q}}}}, \quad (10)$$

In the case where documents consist of all vocabulary terms, we can obtain the point estimate $\theta_{l,i} = d_{l,i}$. However, such documents rarely exist. Rather than find a point estimate for the parameter vector θ_l, a distribution over θ_l is obtained by combining a prior distribution over the model parameters $P(\theta_l)$ with the observation likelihood $P(\mathbf{d}_l|\theta_l)$ using Bayes' rule:

$$P(\theta_l|\mathbf{d}_l) = \frac{P(\theta_l)P(\mathbf{d}_l|\theta_l)}{P(\mathbf{d}_l)}, \quad (11)$$

where the observation likelihood is given by:

$$P_{ch}(\mathbf{d}_l|\theta_l) = \frac{\prod_{i=1}^{V} \binom{\theta_{l,i}}{d_{l,i}}}{\binom{n_N}{n_l}}. \quad (12)$$

The conjugate prior of a multivariate hypergeometric process is the DCM with hyperparameters H, an integer greater than zero, and $\alpha = (\alpha_1, \ldots, \alpha_i, \ldots, \alpha_V)$ where $\alpha_i > 0$ and $\sum_{i=1}^{V} \alpha_i = 1$:

$$P(\theta) = \frac{n_l!}{\prod_{i=1}^{V} \theta_i!} \frac{\Gamma(\sum_{i=1}^{V} \alpha_i)}{\prod_{i=1}^{V} \Gamma(\alpha_i)} \frac{\prod_{i=1}^{V} \Gamma(\alpha_i + \theta_i)}{\Gamma(\sum_{i=1}^{V} (\alpha_i + \theta_i))}. \quad (13)$$

where $\theta_i > 0$ and $\sum_i^V \theta i = n_l$. The resulting posterior distribution is also DCM:

$$\begin{aligned} P(\theta|\mathbf{d}_l) &= \frac{(n_V - n_l)!}{\prod_{i=1}^{V} (\theta_i - d_{l,i})!} \\ &\cdot \frac{\Gamma(n_l + \sum_{i=1}^{V} \alpha_i)}{\prod_{i=1}^{V} \Gamma(d_{l,i} + \alpha_i)} \frac{\prod_{i=1}^{V} \Gamma(\alpha_i + \theta_i)}{\Gamma(\sum_{i=1}^{V} (\alpha_i + n_V))}, \end{aligned} \quad (14)$$

with $\theta_i > 0$ and $\sum_{i=1}^{V} \theta_i = H$.

The query likelihood then becomes:

$$P(\mathbf{q}|\mathbf{d}_l) = \int_\theta P(\mathbf{q}|\theta_l) P(\theta_l|\mathbf{d}_l) d\theta_l \quad (15)$$

A standard approximation to the Bayesian predictive distribution $P(\mathbf{q}|\mathbf{d}_l)$ is the use of the maximum posterior (MP) distribution. The approximation consists of replacing the integral in (15) with its maximum value [41, 42]:

$$P_{ch}(\mathbf{q}|\theta_l^{MP}) = \frac{\prod_{i=1}^{V} \binom{\theta_{l,i}^{MP}}{q_i}}{\binom{n_l^{MP}}{n_{\mathbf{q}}}}, \quad (16)$$

Although, there is no closed form solution for the maximum likelihood estimate θ_i of DCM [40], we can use the expected value of

θ_i [20, p.80]:

$$\theta_{l,i}^{MP} = (n_N - n_l)\frac{\alpha_i + d_{l,i}}{\sum_{i=1}^{V}(\alpha_i + d_{l,i})} = (n_N - n_l)\frac{\alpha_i + d_{l,i}}{n_l + \sum_{i=1}^{V}(\alpha_i)},$$

Following [42], we assign $\alpha_i = \mu P(i|C)$ where μ is a parameter and $P(i|C)$ is the probability of the ith term in the collection and the equation above becomes:

$$\theta_{l,i}^{MP} = (n_N - n_l)\frac{d_{l,i} + \mu P(i|C)}{n_l + \mu}. \quad (17)$$

The derivation of DCM from the central hypergeometric distribution is important, because it establishes a similar link to that between multinomial and Dirichlet smoothing. In this respect, the use of DCM is expected to result in positive performance differences over Dirichlet when the sample size is close to the population size but these differences will become smaller when the sample is a small fraction of the population. Indeed, Elkan [12] compared the performance of DCM and the multinomial for document clustering (sample and population are expected to be of comparable size) with results favoring DCM. Xu and Akella [40] introduced a probabilistic retrieval model with experiments on ad hoc retrieval (when the sample is just a fraction of the population size) using Dirichlet and DCM smoothing with results that favour DCM, but small, although statistically significant, differences.

4. EXPERIMENTAL SETUP

We present our research questions, experiments, dataset and evaluation method. For the purpose of finding instances of articles that have been published in one source and republished more or less verbatim in another, we choose to focus on a single target source in our experimental evaluation, namely the blogosphere. This choice is based on the fact that blog posts unlike status updates or microblog posts, can be of arbitrary length and therefore they can be verbatim copies of a news article.

4.1 Experiments

In addressing the RAF problem in both its *strict* and *loose* interpretation, we concentrate on the retrieval effectiveness of the hypergeometric retrieval models for finding how news content propagates in the blogosphere. In this respect our goals are comparable to those of [19, 22, 23, 34]. In particular, we want to know the effectiveness of our log odds hypergeometric retrieval models and of bayesian hypergeometric retrieval model, both for finding republished articles.

To answer these research questions, we compare our methods to seven state-of-the-art retrieval methods listed in Table 1. Among them, simhash is one of the best-performing near-duplicate detection methods [17, 26]; kl has proven successful in plagiarism detection [5]; cosine, probabilistic, and language modeling based methods have performed well in the related topic detection and tracking [2] task.

In our experiments we use the Indri framework for indexing. Each experimental condition returns maximum 1,000 results. For parametric retrieval models we find parameter values that optimize their performance for our dataset. We set $\mu = 1120$ for kl, lm, indri, hgm-central-bayes, $r_q = 1, r_d = 1$ for hgm-central, and hgm-noncentral, and $k_1 = 2.0, b = 0.75$ for bm25f. For hgm-noncentral we set ω_i, to the term's inverse document frequency (IDF).

Table 1: Retrieval models we consider.

Model	Gloss
State-of-the-art models	
simhash	Hamming distance between two simhashes
cosine	Cosine similarity using IDF term weighting
kl	Kullback-Leibler divergence
lm	Unigram language model with Dirichlet smoothing
indri	Language modeling with inference networks and Dirichlet smoothing
bm25f	Okapi BM25F
tf·idf	TFIDF retrieval model
Hypergeometric models	
hgm-central	Log odds retrieval model with multivariate central hypergeometric distribution (9)
hgm-central-bayes	Multivariate central hypergeometric distribution with Dirichlet compound Multinomial smoothing (16)
hgm-noncentral	Log odds retrieval model with multivariate noncentral hypergeometric distribution (16)

4.2 Dataset

The data set that we use as our target social media collection is the Blogs08 collection provided by TREC; the collection consists of a crawl of feeds, permalinks, and homepages of 1.3M blogs during early 2008–early 2009. This crawl results in a total of 28.4M blogs posts (or permalinks). We only used feed data, the textual content of blog posts distributed by feeds and ignored the permalinks. Only using feed data is common practice and requires almost no preprocessing of the data. Extracting posts from the feed data gave us a coverage of 97.7% (27.8M posts extracted). As a second preprocessing step we perform language identification and remove all non-English blog posts from the corpus, leaving us with 16.9M blogs posts. Our index is constructed based on the full content of blog posts.

Our news article dataset is based on the headline collection from the top stories task in TREC 2009. This is a collection of 102,812 news headlines from the New York Times that includes the article title, byline, publication date, and URL. For the purposes of our experiments we extended the dataset by crawling the full body of each of the articles.

4.3 Ground truth and metrics

As there is no standard test collection for the republished article finding task, we created our own.[5] The ideal ground truth for our task would consist of tuples (n, s) consisting of a news article and a social media utterance, where s is a republication of n.

As a proxy, we follow [15, 27, 29] and use blog posts that are explicitly linked to a given news source. Our ground truth is assembled in two phases. First, for each news article we find blog posts that include the article's URL. Second, for each discovered blog post we look for other blog posts that include its URL. The process continues recursively until no more blog posts are discovered. For our experiments we sample headlines with more than ten explicit links and where social media possibly plays a role. For each news article, we take only explicitly linked blog posts within ± 1 day from the article's publication date to reduce the search space.

In the second phase, we removed the explicit links and for each (backlinked) blog post we manually examined whether it is a republication of the news article. In the strict interpretation of the RAF task, the blog post needs to be a copy all of the material from the source news article, possibly interleaved with comments etc.

[5] The ground truth may be retrieved from `http://ilps.science.uva.nl/resource/hypergeometric-lm`

Table 2: Relevance assessments for *strict* and *loose* interpretations of the RAF task.

GT	Topics #	Topics Max length	Topics Min length	Topics Avg. length	Relevant documents #	Relevant documents Max length	Relevant documents Min length	Relevant documents Avg. length	Per topic average
Loose	404	1,723	28	912	5,269	5,362	3	339	13
Strict	160	1,667	324	883	257	2,205	258	774	2

Table 3: System performance for the *strict* interpretation of the RAF on 160 news articles using three hypergeometric models, and seven other retrieval methods. Significance tested against simhash.

runID	P@5	MRR	Rprec	MAP
Baseline				
simhash	0.2838	0.8139	0.6806	0.7794
Hypergeometric retrieval models				
hgm-central	0.3088▲	0.8948▲	0.8160▲	0.8874▲
hgm-central-bayes	0.3100▲	0.8521	0.7390△	0.8429▲
hgm-noncentral	0.3088▲	0.8969▲	0.8098▲	0.8858▲
Other retrieval models				
cosine	0.3088▲	0.8833▲	0.7702▲	0.8691▲
bm25f	0.3075▲	0.8896▲	0.7692▲	0.8713▲
kl	0.3100▲	0.8542	0.7442△	0.8457▲
lm	0.3100▲	0.8500	0.7358	0.8406▲
indri	0.3100▲	0.8479	0.7358	0.8409▲
tf·idf	0.1762▼	0.4524▼	0.2775▼	0.4389▼

In the loose interpretation our assessors made sure that a key part of the source news article was republished in the blog post (e.g., a highly informative title, the news articles's lead or a central paragraph). Two assessors created this ground truth and discussed any differences they encountered until agreement was reached. See Table 2 for details of the resulting test collection; recall that in this paper, news articles are the queries that are submitted against an index of blog posts.

We report on standard IR measures: precision at 5 (P@5), mean reciprocal rank (MRR), mean average precision (MAP), and r-precision (Rprec). Statistical significance is tested using a two-tailed paired t-test and is marked as ▲ (or ▼) for significant differences for $\alpha = .01$, or △ (and ▽) for $\alpha = .05$.

5. RESULTS AND ANALYSIS

In this section, we report on the results of our experiments and conduct an analysis of their outcomes.

Strict interpretation. In our first experiment we study the retrieval effectiveness of our methods with regards to the strict interpretation of the RAF task. To this end, we choose simhash, the state-of-the-art for near-duplicate detection, as our baseline. The performance of three hypergeometric models, and seven retrieval models is listed in Table 3. We see that hgm-central and hgm-noncentral outperform the baseline with statistically significant differences in all metrics. Second and third best (in terms of MAP) come bm25f and cosine similarity with small differences between them; kl, hgm-central-bayes, lm, and indri follow with performance that hovers at the same levels. In general, all methods show strong performance in all metrics, with an exception for tf·idf.

Turning to individual metrics, we find of particular interest Rprec and MAP. For hgm-central Rprec peaks at 0.8160, 20% more than for simhash. In terms of MAP, hgm-central achieves the best score at 0.8874, a 14% improvement over the baseline. With regards to other language modeling based methods, hgm-central outperforms kl, lm, indri (statistically significantly so, in MRR, Rprec, and MAP). In terms of early precision (P@5), all methods show similar performance, which is mainly due to the small number of relevant documents per news article.

To better understand the differences between hgm-central and simhash, we look at per topic differences in average precision. Fig. 1 shows that out of 160 articles, 45 favor the use of hgm-central, and 9 simhash. Manual inspection of the results revealed that hgm-central is able to account for small changes in language: For example, if the title of the republished article had been changed in the blog post, then, according to hgm-central, this blog post will rank lower than a blog post where the title was kept the same as the original. simhash seems unable to capture these differences. This is partially due to its nature which although allows document compression which improves efficiency, it looses in precision. Another finding was the robust ranking capabilities of hgm-central even in lower ranks: blog posts there used only a couple of sentences from the original article. In contrast, ranked lists from simhash were polluted quite early (rank 10), with long documents that are irrelevant to the article, but that do share language with the article; this is in line with findings in [34].

Turning to hgm-central and lm, we find no striking differences in the resulted ranked lists. Differences in MAP are mainly due to how the ground truth is constructed. More specifically, there exist topics for which either method is penalized because the first ranking document is not assessed, however, found relevant after manual inspection. In general, lm was found to rank blog posts higher that contain either short excerpts of the article without commentary, or blog posts that are verbatim copies of the article with lots of commentary. This behavior can be explained by the accumulation of term probabilities using Dirichlet smoothing: probability mass is assigned to terms occurring in the original article. We see that hgm-central counters this problem with the use of P'^{max} which ensures that documents are ranked by how much the blog post "deviates" from the original article.

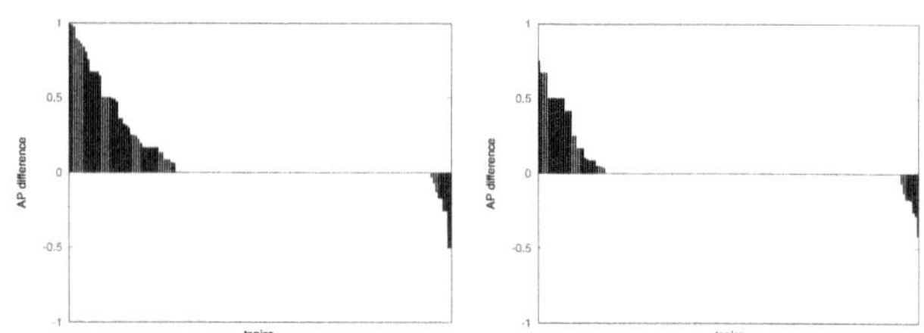

(a) hgm-central vs. simhash (b) hgm-central vs. lm

Figure 1: Per topic difference in average precision (AP) for the strict RAF task.

Loose interpretation. In our second experiment we test retrieval methods with regards to the *loose* interpretation of the RAF task. We set our baseline to hgm-central as it proved the best performing method in the previous experiment. Results in Table 4 show that when we move away from near-duplicates, retrieval effectiveness drops for all methods. hgm-central achieves the best scores overall, followed by bm25f in MRR, and lm, indri, kl in MAP. In this interpretation of the RAF task, simhash, our previous baseline, is one of the least effective along with tf·idf.

Looking at the results in more detail, hgm-central shows ro-

Table 4: **System performance for the *loose* interpretation of the RAF task of 404 news articles using three hypergeometric models, and seven other retrieval methods. Significance tested against hgm-central.**

runID	P@5	MRR	Rprec	MAP
Hypergeometric retrieval models				
hgm-central	0.5446	0.7612	0.4642	0.4413
hgm-central-bayes	0.5411	0.7197▼	0.4708	0.4322▽
hgm-noncentral	0.5550	0.7627	0.4702	0.4093▼
Other retrieval models				
cosine	0.5198▼	0.7379▽	0.4292▼	0.4138▼
bm25f	0.5505	0.7561	0.4662	0.4253▼
kl	0.5426	0.7252▼	0.4603	0.4351
lm	0.5351	0.7165▼	0.4587	0.4366
indri	0.5361	0.7145▼	0.4593	0.4360
simhash	0.2683▼	0.5423▼	0.1692▼	0.1337▼
tf·idf	0.1485▼	0.3084▼	0.1242▼	0.1044▼

bust performance in MRR which is statistically significant over the rest of retrieval methods. hgm-noncentral shows marginally better results in terms of P@5, MRR, and Rprec over hgm-central at the cost of MAP. Finally, we find interesting that bm25f used to outperform language modeling based methods in our first experiment, however, in the current scenario we observe the opposite. This change can be ascribed to the parameter estimation of the models, which is related to the nature of the relevant documents. hgm-central, and hgm-noncentral as parameter free models are not as sensitive to changes in the notion of "relevance."

Document length. Finally, we examine our hypothesis on the effect of document length (population size) and query length (sample size) in retrieval effectiveness between modeling documents as hypergeometric and multinomial distributions of terms. Fig. 2 illustrates the correlation of MAP, MRR, and the length of relevant documents over query length, for hgm-central and lm. Hypergeometric document modeling shows to have strong positive effects in both metrics when document length is up to 0.1 times the query length. As the query and the document length become equal, the differences between the hypergeometric and the multinomial diminish.

Our experimental results demonstrate the utility of hypergeometric retrieval models for the republished article finding task in both its *strict* and *loose* interpretation.

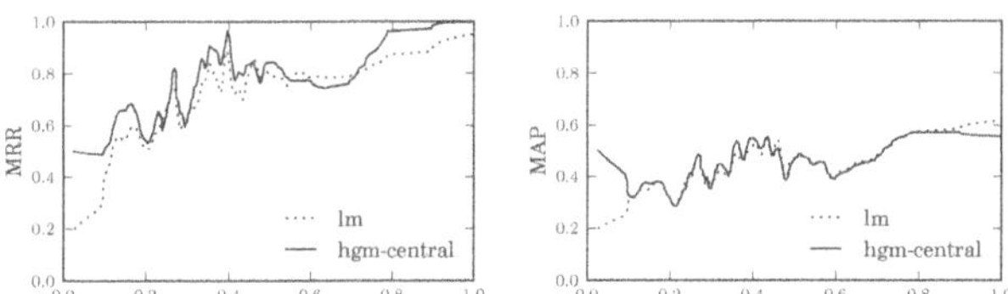

Figure 2: Moving average (window of 30) of MRR (left), and of MAP (right) over the ratio of average relevant document length and query length.

6. DISCUSSION

So far we have examined how different retrieval models perform on the two interpretations of the RAF task. In this section, we take a closer look at the distributions used for document modeling, namely, the multinomial and the hypergeometric and conduct a direct comparison of them by keeping the retrieval model the same and changing the underlying distribution. Further, we study the log odds retrieval model by experimenting with document/query representations, such as TF and TF·IDF, and with different mixture ratios r_q, r_d (see Section 3). Finally, we explore the use of hgm-central, hgm-noncentral and hgm-central-bayes in ad hoc retrieval.

Table 5: **System performance on the *loose* interpretation of the RAF task using the log odds retrieval model and changing the underlying distribution to: multinomial, multivariate central hypergeometric, and multivariate non-central hypergeometric distribution. The parameters r_q, r_d are set to 1. Significance tested against the multinomial.**

runID	P@5	MRR	Rprec	MAP
Log odds retrieval model				
multinomial	0.4297	0.6778	0.3177	0.2723
hgm-central	0.5446▲	0.7612▲	0.4642▲	0.4413▲
hgm-noncentral	0.5550▲	0.7627▲	0.4702▲	0.4093▲
Bayesian retrieval model				
lm	0.5351	0.7165	0.4587	0.4366
hgm-central-bayes	0.5411	0.7197	0.4708△	0.4322

6.1 Hypergeometric vs. multinomial

We are interested in exploring the validity of our hypothesis that hypergeometric document models are superior to multinomial ones when the query size is comparable to document length. We proceed as follows. For each of the two retrieval models we presented, i.e., log odds and bayesian, we create two runs, one using the multivariate hypergeometric distribution and one using the multinomial distribution. Keeping the same retrieval model and smoothing method and varying the underlying distribution, ensures that any observed differences in performance are solely due to the change in the underlying distribution. For our experiments we use the dataset from *loose* interpretation of the RAF task.

Log odds. We use the log odds retrieval model with the parameters r_q, r_d set to 1, and different underlying distributions: multinomial (multinomial), multivariate central hypergeometric (hgm-central), and multivariate non-central hypergeometric (hgm-noncentral). Results in the top half of Table 5 validate our hypothesis. Log-odds document models built on hypergeometric distributions outperform models built on the multinomial distribution. In particular, both hgm-central, and hgm-noncentral outperform multinomial in all metrics with statistically significant differences.

Dirichlet vs DCM. We compare the performance of Dirichlet smoothing on the multinomial distribution (unigram language model) and of DCM on the multivariate central hypergeometric. The smoothing parameter μ was found to peak at 1120 for both models when optimized for MAP. Table 5 (bottom) lists the results. Performance hovers at the same levels for both models, with DCM showing better r-precision with statistically significant difference. This can be attributed to the ability of DCM to capture word burstiness better than the Dirichlet [40] which leads to high early precision.

6.2 Mixture ratios and term weighting

We look at different mixture ratios r_q, r_d for hgm-central and hgm-noncentral; see (5). Table 6 shows that, on average, performance degrades as we deviate from $r_q = 1, r_d = 1$. When $r_d = 2$,

Table 6: System performance using log odds retrieval model and $tf \cdot idf$ for document and query representation, and several mixture ratios r_q, r_d. Significance testing against **hgm-central** with TF, and r_q, r_d set to 1.

runID	Weight	r_q	r_d	P@5	MRR	Rprec	MAP
Mixture ratios r_q, r_d							
hgm-central	TF	1	1	0.5446	0.7612	0.4642	0.4413
hgm-central	TF	1	2	0.5525	0.7576	0.4721▲	0.4382▽
hgm-central	TF	2	1	0.5198▼	0.7251▼	0.4189▼	0.3611▼
hgm-central	TF	3	5	0.5356	0.7338▼	0.4436▼	0.3908▼
hgm-noncentral	TF	1	2	0.5515	0.7536	0.4670	0.4238▼
hgm-noncentral	TF	2	1	0.5173▼	0.7261▼	0.4172▼	0.3620▼
hgm-noncentral	TF	3	5	0.5351	0.7307▼	0.4428▼	0.3886▼
$tf \cdot idf$ representation							
hgm-central	TF·IDF	1	1	0.4238▼	0.7097▼	0.2912▼	0.2435▼
hgm-noncentral	TF·IDF	1	1	0.4861▼	0.7297▼	0.3581▼	0.2901▼

we observe a slight increase for some metrics at the cost of a lower MAP. In particular, hgm-central shows a statistically significant increase in Rprec.

Next, we explore the effect on performance of using global term weights, such as TF·IDF, instead of TF, for the representation of the hypothetical document $\mathbf{d}'$; see (5). The results in Table 6 (bottom) show that the use of TF·IDF leads to a significant decrease in performance for all metrics. Manual inspection reveals that the returned documents are very short, nearly one sentence long. The document size remains small, and comparable to two or three sentences until the end of the rank list. For the topics we examined at, the top ranked document is usually relevant, however, in most cases it is not assessed.

6.3 Ad hoc retrieval

Finally, we look at the performance of our log odds and bayesian retrieval models in ad hoc retrieval. For our experiments, we use TREC-Robust 2004. We formulate our queries using content from the title of each topic. The Dirichlet smoothing parameter μ is set to 1000. Table 7 shows results for indri (baseline), hgm-central-bayes, hgm-central, and hgm-noncentral. We see that hgm-central-bayes shows the same performance as the baseline. Runs based on the log odds retrieval model prove least effective. The reason lies in the value of P'^{max}, which becomes 1 when the query and the document share only one common term–which is common for short queries. Without the normalization factor, and enough information from the query, the performance of the log odds model depends on $\mathbf{d}'$ which is mainly estimated from the document (given the negligible effect from the query due to its short length). To this end, the more elaborate smoothing methods, used in indri, and hgm-central-bayes prove most effective.

The three analyses that we performed in this section establish the following. The hypergeometric distributions are a better choice over the multinomial for modeling documents, when the system has to respond to document long queries. The Dirichlet and DCM smoothing show similar performance, with the later producing better early ranking. Further, retrieval effectiveness benefits the most from document representations that use raw term frequencies (TF), and equal mixture ratios r_q, r_d. Finally, with regards to ad hoc retrieval, retrieval models based on bayesian inference deliver the best performance.

Table 7: System performance on the TREC-ROBUST 2004 collection. Significance tested against **indri**.

runID	P@5	MRR	Rprec	MAP
Title				
indri	0.4570	0.6603	0.2638	0.2221
hgm-central	0.3590▼	0.5406▼	0.2096▼	0.1650▼
hgm-central-bayes	0.4578	0.6603	0.2638	0.2221
hgm-noncentral	0.3597▼	0.5310▼	0.2033▼	0.1571▼

7. RELATED WORK

Our task, republished article finding, is parallel to the tasks of text reuse which, in turn, relates to near-duplicate detection.

Near-duplicate detection. Garcia-Molina et al. [14] introduces the problem of finding document copies across multiple databases. Manku et al. [26] adopt simhash, a document fingerprinting method and hamming distance for efficient near-duplicate detection in web crawling; we used simhash as a baseline in our comparisons. Chang et al. [9] focus on finding event-relevant content using a sliding window over lengths of sentences. Muthmann et al. [31] discover near-duplicates within web forums for grouping similar discussion threads together. They construct a document's fingerprint from a four dimensional vector which consists of domain (in-)dependent text-based features, external links, and semantic features. Kolak and Schilit [23] find popular quoted passages in multiple sources, and use them to link these sources. Abdel-Hamid et al. [1] detect the origin of text segments using shingle selection algorithms. Zhang et al. [43] use two stage approach for finding partial duplicates with applications to opinion mining and enhanced web browsing: sentence level near-duplicate detection (Jaccard distance) and sequence matching; the tasks considered in this paper are similar to ours, however, the authors focus on pruning techniques, while we aim at discovering effective and robust methods, the output of which needs little, if any, further processing.

Text re-use. Broder [8] introduces the mathematical notions of "resemblance" and "containment" to capture the informal notions of "roughly the same" and "roughly contained" and propose efficient methods using document fingerprinting techniques. These notions correspond to our "strict" and "loose" interpretations of the republished article finding task. Seo and Croft [34] compare a set of fingerprinting techniques for text reuse on newswire and blog collections. One of their findings, which we also share, is how text in blogs layout affects the performance of fingerprinting methods. Kim et al. [22] propose an efficient overlap and content reuse detection in blogs and news articles. They find that blog posts contain large amount of exact quotations from the news articles. However, for the particular task, they find that blog posts raise significant challenges against retrieval [21]. Bendersky and Croft [6] consider the issue of text reuse on the web. They address the task using three methods: word overlap, query likelihood, and mixtures models. This work is of particular interest to us, as we focus on better understanding the effectiveness of query likelihood using hypergeometric document models.

Hypergeometric distributions. The univariate central hypergeometric distribution has been firstly used in the past to provide a theoretical framework for understanding performance and evaluation measures in IR [11, 35], and for proving the document-query duality [10].

Wilbur [39] was the first to use the central hypergeometric distribution in a retrieval setting. The vocabulary overlap of two documents is modeled as a hypergeometric distribution for determining the relevance to each other. Wilbur's model initially ignored local and global term weights, such as term frequencies within documents or term document frequency. Term weights are integrated into the final score only later through multiple iterations of the main model. Our retrieval models are able to support local and global term weights in a straightforward manner.

More recently, Bravo-Marquez et al. [7] derived a query reduction method for document long queries using the extended hypergeometric distribution. Amati [3] used the central hypergeometric distribution within the Divergence from Randomness (DFR) framework for deriving the binomial distribution, a readily accepted distribution for the generative model. Amati's model has applications in query expansion [16], pseudo-relevance feedback [4], and enterprise search [24].

8. CONCLUSIONS AND OUTLOOK

We looked at the task of republished article finding (RAF), to discover springboards of discussion in social media related to a news article. Our approach is to find verbatim or near-verbatim copies of the news article building on the language modeling paradigm. Our task is related to near-duplicate detection with the additional challenge that in our scenario, users can inject comments in between excerpts from the original article. To this extent the documents to be retrieved can deviate considerably from the original article.

In the process of tackling the problem, we revisited the assumptions made in unigram language model, namely, using the multinomial distribution for modeling documents. We presented two retrieval models using the hypergeometric distributions, one task-driven (log odds), and one more elaborate using Bayesian inference. In the later, we found that the Dirichlet compound multinomial distribution (DCM) arises naturally for estimating the parameters of a document model. This is an important finding because it links central hypergeometric to DCM as multinomial is linked to Dirichlet. DCM has been derived in the past from hierarchical bayesian modeling techniques as a better model to Dirichlet [12, 25, 40].

Our experiments on finding republished news articles in the blogosphere demonstrate the utility and effectiveness of modeling documents using hypergeometric distributions. We found that our log odds retrieval model is most useful for documents whose size is similar to the query size.

In future work, we envisage to study more in depth different smoothing methods suitable for the hypergeometric distributions and compare them to the multinomial case. Such methods can be challenging to find as they need to meet the requirements set by the hypergeometric distribution, namely, the smoothed estimates need to be larger than those sampled. With regards to the noncentral hypergeometric distribution, we aim at exploring more elaborate ways of incorporating term bias, such as term co-occurence between the document and query. In the long term, we believe that our methods based on hypergeometric distributions hold promise to support grouping of individual news stories into topics, providing support for impact analysis.

Finally, our republished article finding task was formulated in the setting of online reputation management (ORM). ORM is related to search engine optimization, but the two do not coincide and their goals differ widely. ORM gives for a number of recall-oriented retrieval tasks: republished article finding is one, dealing with "creative" name variants and implicit references to a given target in social media is another important example.

Acknowledgments. This research was partially supported by the European Union's ICT Policy Support Programme as part of the Competitiveness and Innovation Framework Programme, CIP ICT-PSP under grant agreement nr 250430, the PROMISE Network of Excellence co-funded by the 7th Framework Programme of the European Commission, grant agreement no. 258191, the DuOMAn project carried out within the STEVIN programme which is funded by the Dutch and Flemish Governments under project nr STE-09-12, the Netherlands Organisation for Scientific Research (NWO) under project nrs 612.061.814, 612.061.815, 640.004.802, 380-70-011, the Center for Creation, Content and Technology (CCCT), the Hyperlocal Service Platform project funded by the Service Innovation & ICT program, the WAHSP project funded by the CLARIN-nl program, and under COMMIT project Infiniti.

9. REFERENCES

[1] O. Abdel-Hamid, B. Behzadi, S. Christoph, and M. R. Henzinger. Detecting the Origin of Text Segments Efficiently. In *Proceedings of the 18th World Wide Web Conference*, pages 61–70, New York, 2009. ACM.

[2] J. Allan, editor. *Topic detection and tracking: event-based information organization*. Kluwer Academic Publishers, Norwell, USA, 2002.

[3] G. Amati. Frequentist and bayesian approach to information retrieval. In M. Lalmas, A. MacFarlane, S. Rüger, A. Tombros, T. Tsikrika, and A. Yavlinsky, editors, *Advances in Information Retrieval*, volume 3936 of *Lecture Notes in Computer Science*, pages 13–24. Springer Berlin / Heidelberg, 2006.

[4] G. Amati. Information theoretic approach to information extraction. In H. Larsen, G. Pasi, D. Ortiz-Arroyo, T. Andreasen, and H. Christiansen, editors, *Flexible Query Answering Systems*, volume 4027 of *Lecture Notes in Computer Science*, pages 519–529. Springer Berlin / Heidelberg, 2006.

[5] A. Barrón-Cedeño, P. Rosso, and J.-M. Benedí. Reducing the plagiarism detection search space on the basis of the kullback-leibler distance. In *Proceedings of the 10th International Conference on Computational Linguistics and Intelligent Text Processing*, CICLing '09, pages 523–534, Berlin, Heidelberg, 2009. Springer-Verlag.

[6] M. Bendersky and W. B. Croft. Finding text reuse on the web. In *Proceedings of the Second ACM International Conference on Web Search and Data Mining*, WSDM '09, pages 262–271, New York, USA, 2009. ACM.

[7] F. Bravo-Marquez, G. L'Huillier, S. Ríos, and J. Velásquez. Hypergeometric language model and Zipf-like scoring function for web document similarity retrieval. In E. Chavez and S. Lonardi, editors, *String Processing and Information Retrieval*, volume 6393 of *Lecture Notes in Computer Science*, pages 303–308. Springer Berlin / Heidelberg, 2010.

[8] A. Broder. On the resemblance and containment of documents. In *Proceedings of the Compression and Complexity of Sequences 1997*, SEQUENCES '97, Washington, USA, 1997. IEEE Computer Society.

[9] H.-C. Chang, J.-H. Wang, and C.-Y. Chiu. Finding event-relevant content from the web using a near-duplicate detection approach. In *IEEE / WIC / ACM International Conference on Web Intelligence*, pages 291–294, Los Alamitos, USA, 2007. IEEE Computer Society.

[10] L. Egghe and R. Rousseau. Duality in information retrieval and the hypergeometric distribution. *Journal of Documentation*, 53(5):488–496, December 1997.

[11] L. Egghe and R. Rousseau. A theoretical study of recall and precision using a topological approach to information retrieval. *Inf. Process. Manage.*, 34:191–218, January 1998.

[12] C. Elkan. Clustering documents with an exponential-family approximation of the dirichlet compound multinomial distribution. In *Proceedings of the 23rd international conference on Machine learning*, ICML '06, pages 289–296, New York, USA, 2006. ACM.

[13] A. Fog. Calculation methods for wallenius' noncentral hypergeometric distribution. *Communications in Statistics - Simulation and Computation*, 37(2):258–273, 2008.

[14] H. Garcia-Molina, L. Gravano, and N. Shivakumar. dscam: Finding document copies across multiple databases. *Parallel and Distributed Information Systems, International Conference*, 1996.

[15] S. Geva and A. Trotman. Inex 2010 Link-The-Wiki Track, 2010. `http://www.inex.otago.ac.nz/`.

[16] B. He and I. Ounis. Combining fields for query expansion and adaptive query expansion. *Information Processing & Management*, 43(5):1294 – 1307, 2007. Patent Processing.

[17] M. Henzinger. Finding near-duplicate web pages: a large-scale evaluation of algorithms. In *Proceedings of the 29th annual international conference on Research and development in information retrieval*, SIGIR '06, pages 284–291, New York, USA, 2006. ACM.

[18] D. Hiemstra and W. Kraaij. Twenty-one at TREC-7: ad-hoc and cross-language track. In *Proceedings of the seventh Text Retrieval Conference (TREC)*, volume 500 of *NIST Special Publications*, pages 227–238. US National Institute of Standards and Technology, 1999.

[19] D. Ikeda, T. Fujiki, and M. Okumura. Automatically linking news articles to blog entries. In *AAAI Spring Symposium*, 2006.

[20] N. L. Johnson, S. Kotz, and N. Balakrishnan. *Discrete Multivariate Distributions*. John Wiley & Sons, New York, 1997.

[21] J. Kim, K. Candan, and J. Tatemura. Organization and tagging of blog and news entries based on content reuse. *Journal of Signal Processing Systems*, 58:407–421, 2010.

[22] J. W. Kim, K. S. Candan, and J. Tatemura. Efficient overlap and content reuse detection in blogs and online news articles. In *Proceedings of the 18th international conference on World wide web*, WWW '09, pages 81–90, New York, USA, 2009. ACM.

[23] O. Kolak and B. N. Schilit. Generating links by mining quotations. In *Proceedings of the nineteenth ACM conference on Hypertext and hypermedia*, HT '08, pages 117–126, New York, USA, 2008. ACM.

[24] C. Macdonald and I. Ounis. Using relevance feedback in expert search. In G. Amati, C. Carpineto, and G. Romano, editors, *Advances in Information Retrieval*, volume 4425 of *Lecture Notes in Computer Science*, pages 431–443. Springer Berlin / Heidelberg, 2007.

[25] R. E. Madsen, D. Kauchak, and C. Elkan. Modeling word burstiness using the dirichlet distribution. In *Proceedings of the 22nd international conference on Machine learning*, ICML '05, pages 545–552, New York, USA, 2005. ACM.

[26] G. S. Manku, A. Jain, and A. Das Sarma. Detecting near-duplicates for web crawling. In *Proceedings of the 16th international conference on World Wide Web*, WWW '07, pages 141–150, New York, USA, 2007. ACM.

[27] R. Mihalcea and A. Csomai. Wikify!: linking documents to encyclopedic knowledge. In *CIKM '07*, pages 233–242.

[28] D. R. H. Miller, T. Leek, and R. M. Schwartz. A hidden markov model information retrieval system. In *Proceedings of the 22nd annual international conference on Research and development in information retrieval*, SIGIR '99, pages 214–221, New York, USA, 1999. ACM.

[29] D. Milne and I. H. Witten. Learning to link with Wikipedia. In *CIKM '08*, pages 509–518, 2008.

[30] D. S. Moore. *The Basic Practice of Statistics*. W. H. Freeman & Co., New York, USA, 2nd edition, 1999.

[31] K. Muthmann, W. M. Barczyński, F. Brauer, and A. Löser. Near-duplicate detection for web-forums. In *Proceedings of the 2009 International Database Engineering & Applications Symposium*, IDEAS '09, pages 142–151, New York, USA, 2009. ACM.

[32] J. M. Ponte and W. B. Croft. A language modeling approach to information retrieval. In *Proceedings of the 21st annual international conference on Research and development in information retrieval*, SIGIR '98, pages 275–281, New York, USA, 1998. ACM.

[33] S. E. Robertson. *The probability ranking principle in IR*, pages 281–286. Morgan Kaufmann Publishers Inc., San Francisco, USA, 1997.

[34] J. Seo and W. B. Croft. Local text reuse detection. SIGIR '08, pages 571–578, New York, USA, 2008. ACM.

[35] W. M. Shaw, R. Burgin, and P. Howell. Performance standards and evaluations in ir test collections: Vector-space and other retrieval models. *Information Processing & Management*, 33(1):15 – 36, 1997.

[36] E. Tsagkias, M. de Rijke, and W. Weerkamp. Linking online news and social media. In *Fourth ACM Web Search and Data Mining (WSDM)*, Hong Kong, February 2011. ACM.

[37] E. M. Voorhees and L. P. Buckland, editors. *Proceedings of the Thirteenth Text REtrieval Conference, TREC 2004, Gaithersburg, Maryland, November 16-19, 2004*, volume Special Publication 500-261, 2004. National Institute of Standards and Technology (NIST).

[38] K. T. Wallenius. Biased sampling; the noncentral hypergeometric probability distribution. Technical report, Stanford University, November 1963.

[39] W. J. Wilbur. Retrieval testing with hypergeometric document models. *J. Am. Soc. Inf. Sci.*, 44:340–351, July 1993.

[40] Z. Xu and R. Akella. A new probabilistic retrieval model based on the dirichlet compound multinomial distribution. In *Proceedings of the 31st annual international conference on Research and development in information retrieval*, SIGIR '08, pages 427–434, New York, USA, 2008. ACM.

[41] H. Zaragoza, D. Hiemstra, and M. Tipping. Bayesian extension to the language model for ad hoc information retrieval. In *Proceedings of the 26th annual international conference on Research and development in informaion retrieval*, SIGIR '03, pages 4–9, New York, USA, 2003. ACM.

[42] C. Zhai and J. Lafferty. A study of smoothing methods for language models applied to ad hoc information retrieval. In *Proceedings of the 24th annual international conference on Research and development in information retrieval*, SIGIR '01, pages 334–342, New York, USA, 2001. ACM.

[43] Q. Zhang, Y. Zhang, H. Yu, and X. Huang. Efficient partial-duplicate detection based on sequence matching. In *Proceeding of the 33rd international conference on Research and development in information retrieval*, SIGIR '10, pages 675–682, New York, USA, 2010. ACM.

Estimation Methods for Ranking Recent Information

Miles Efron
Graduate School of Library & Information Science
University of Illinois, Urbana-Champaign
501 E. Daniel St, Champaign, IL 61820
01-217-265-0825
mefron@illinois.edu

Gene Golovchinsky
FX Palo Alto Laboratory, Inc.
3400 Hillview Ave, #4
Palo Alto, CA 94304
gene@fxpal.com

ABSTRACT
Temporal aspects of documents can impact relevance for certain kinds of queries. In this paper, we build on earlier work of modeling temporal information. We propose an extension to the Query Likelihood Model that incorporates query-specific information to estimate rate parameters, and we introduce a temporal factor into language model smoothing and query expansion using pseudo-relevance feedback. We evaluate these extensions using a Twitter corpus and two newspaper article collections. Results suggest that, compared to prior approaches, our models are more effective at capturing the temporal variability of relevance associated with some topics.

Categories and Subject Descriptors
H.3.3 [**Information Search and Retrieval**]: Retrieval models

General Terms
Algorithms, Experimentation

Keywords
Time, ranking algorithms, information retrieval, microblogs

1. INTRODUCTION
Recency is an important dimension of relevance for many kinds of queries. For these queries, relevant documents must not only be topically appropriate; they must also have been published in the recent past. Though research on *recency queries* is not new, these queries present an especially keen challenge in contemporary IR given the growing popularity of microblogging services such as Twitter [21]. In the context of microblog search, fielding recency queries effectively is of prime importance. This paper proposes three novel approaches to handling recency queries, examining their effectiveness both on microblog data, as well as on more traditional IR data in the form of two TREC news collections.

Previous work has shown how recency can be incorporated into IR [5] [6], particularly under the language modeling framework [15]. In this paper we build on these findings. Our contribution is a group of methods for incorporating temporal information into language modeling IR. Each of the proposed methods relies on Bayesian estimation where we use time as a factor in our retrieval model. In tests, our proposed methods work as effectively as or better than established temporal approaches for recency queries, while mitigating the risk entailed by temporally informed ranking on queries without an explicit recency bias.

SIGIR'11, July 24–28, 2011, Beijing, China.

2. PREVIOUS METHODS FOR INCORPORATING TIME INTO LANGUAGE MODELING IR
This paper's treatment of temporal factors in IR is based on the language modeling approach to document retrieval [18,26]. In particular, we rely on the query likelihood model. Given a query q and a document d we derive a score for d against q that is proportional to the probability that the (multinomial) language model that generated d also generated q:

$$Pr(d|q) \propto Pr(q|d)Pr(d) \quad (1$$

If we momentarily assume that the prior probability distribution is over documents is uniform, we may rank documents in decreasing order of the query's likelihood of generation by the model that generated d. Assuming that this model is a multinomial over words in the indexing language, we have the ranking function:

$$\log Pr(q|d) = \sum_{w \in q} \log Pr(w|d) \quad (2$$

With respect to estimating Pr($w|d$), the application of a smoothing operation has been shown to play a crucial role in successful language modeling IR. Numerous smoothing methods exist [25]. In order to minimize the influence of confounding variables in the following study, we choose the simplest smoothing method: so-called Jelinek-Mercer smoothing, which gives:

$$\hat{P}r(w|d) = (1 - \lambda)\hat{P}r_{ML}(w|d) + \lambda \hat{P}r(w|C) \quad (3$$

where $\hat{P}r_{ML}(w|d)$ is the maximum likelihood estimator, $n(w,d)/n(d)^1$, $\hat{P}r(w|C)$ is the estimated probability of seeing word w in the collection, and λ is a tuning parameter on [0,1].

Using Eq. 2 with estimates from Eq. 3 for *ad hoc* retrieval has shown state-of-the art effectiveness, while easily admitting alterations to the retrieval process.

For instance, in their work on recency queries Li and Croft proposed using the publication date of news articles to inform a prior distribution over documents [15]. Rather than taking $Pr(d)$ in Eq. 1 to be uniform, Li and Croft propose using an exponential distribution:

$$Pr(d|t_d) = r \cdot e^{-r \cdot t_d} \quad (4$$

where t_d is the time in months that has elapsed since document d was published, and r is the rate parameter of the exponential distribution. The intuition of this approach is that newer documents have a higher probability (perhaps of being read) than older documents do. By using Eq. 4 as the document prior in Eq. 1

[1] In our notation, $n(w,d)$ refers to the number of times word w occurs in document d; $n(d)$ is the number of tokens in d.

Li and Croft show significant improvement in retrieval for TREC topics that are explicitly concerned with recent events.

In more recent work, Dakka, Gravano and Ipeirotis augment the standard query likelihood framework to account for time [5]. They approach the problem by considering two types of features for a given document. First, they consider w_d which consists of the lexical terms in document d. Second, they posit t_d which is the timestamp for d. With these definitions in place, we may decompose the likelihood function:

$$Pr(d|q) = Pr(w_d, t_d|q) = Pr(t_d|w_d, q) \cdot Pr(w_d|q) \quad (5$$

Making the simplifying assumption that the temporal relevance of d does not depend on the document's content, w, we drop w from the joint probability in Eq. 5, giving:

$$\begin{aligned} Pr(d|q) &\propto Pr(w_d|q) \cdot Pr(t_w|q) \\ &\propto Pr(q|w_d) \cdot Pr(w_d) \cdot Pr(t_d|q) \end{aligned} \quad (6$$

which is identical to the standard query likelihood model, but with the addition of the probability of observing a time t_d given the query q. Eq. 6 gives a flexible way to add temporal information to document ranking.

3. OVERVIEW: THREE APPROACHES TO TEMPORAL RE-RANKING

In this paper we propose three overarching approaches to incorporating time into retrieval, paying special attention to the matter of recency queries. We offer the following approaches:

1. Query-specific exponential re-ranking
2. Temporally informed smoothing
3. Temporally biased pseudo-relevance feedback

Approach 1. The chief difference between Eq. 6 and the approach offered by Li and Croft is that Eq. 6 allows us to consider not only when a document was published, but also the relationship between that publication time and the query at hand. Under Approach 1 we apply a more aggressive temporal factor if we have evidence that our query is indeed recency-bound. We accomplish this by incorporating query-specific information to estimate the exponential rate parameter r_q to obtain the maximum a posteriori estimate, then applying this result in Eq. 6.

Approach 2. Effectively estimating language models for retrieval requires smoothing, which we accomplish using Eq. 3. This requires choosing a smoothing parameter λ. Typically this value is constant across all documents. However, in the context of recency queries it is plausible that we should smooth older documents' models more aggressively than newer documents. We elaborate on this intuition below. But the thrust of this approach is that each document's model is smoothed more aggressively for documents that are further from the target time associated with the query.

Approach 3. The relevance model framework proposed by Lavrenko and Croft [14] provides a mechanism for using (pseudo) relevance feedback in language modeling IR. A relevance model is typically a multinomial distribution over words giving $Pr(w|R)$. We usually estimate this model by an analysis of the top k documents returned during an initial retrieval. In this setting, $Pr(w|R)$ is estimated by a weighted average of $Pr(w|d)$ in each of the k returned documents. We propose using estimates of $Pr(w|d)$ based on Approach 2 to construct temporally conditioned relevance models.

4. PRELIMINARIES AND CONTEXT

To situate our approaches, we begin with several definitions.

4.1 Representing Time

First we define t_d, the time associated with a document d. Further, we define t^* as the most recent timestamp contained in our corpus C. Alternatively, we can define t^* as *now*. Thus we have:

$$t_d = (t^* - TIMESTAMP(d)) \cdot S \quad (7$$

Here S is a time scale appropriate to the collection, and t_d is the time that has elapsed since d was created. We also use the notation t_0 to refer to the earliest time observed in a corpus. For TREC data, we measure time in fractions of a month; for Twitter data we use fractions of a day.

4.2 Experimental Data and Setup

We evaluated our algorithms using three test collections: a Twitter dataset, TREC AP (disks 1 and 2), and TREC LA/FT (disks 4 and 5) using the lemur toolkit (http://lemurproject.org). We used no stemming or stop-lists (except in one case indicated below).

4.2.1 Twitter Data

We compiled corpus of tweets obtained via the Twitter API. Summary statistics of this corpus appear in Table 1.

Table 1. Summary statistics of Twitter data set.

Number of Tweets	7,168,842		
Number of Tracked Users	9,274		
Earliest Date	18 Jul 2010		
Latest Date	4 Dec 2010		
Queries		Train	Test
	Recency	21	49
	Non-temp.	31	50

The corpus was constructed by choosing an initial group of Twitter users who are, broadly speaking, interested in information retrieval, HCI, data mining, and information science. Full details of this group appear in [20]. The pool of "seed users" consisted of 48 people who posted tweets containing any of eight manually identified keywords during the week surrounding March 24, 2010 (the date of paper notifications for SIGIR 2010). Having identified these "seed" users, we expanded the pool by finding people whom these users follow on Twitter (as of June 2010). The median number of people followed by our seed users was 264; the total was 9,274. Thus the corpus contains a core of "IR community" members, broadened with the extra degree of separation. Having defined our population, we captured all tweets written by this group between July 18 and December 4.

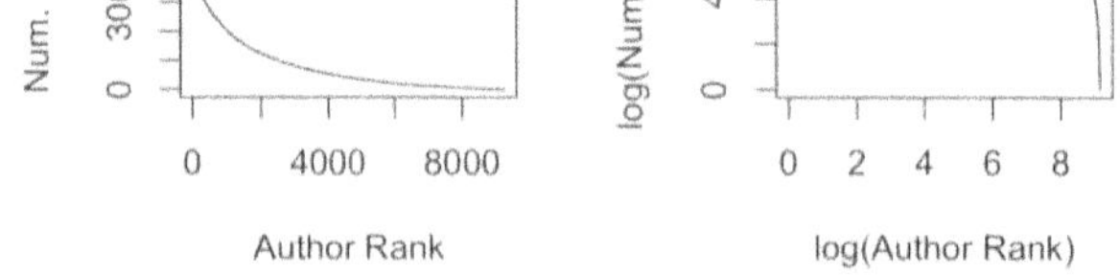

Figure 1. Distribution of Author Tweet Frequency

Figure 1 shows the number of tweets written by each author in our corpus. Somewhat surprisingly, the data do not show as pronounced a power-law distribution as we might expect, suggesting that in fact the contents of the collection was created by a diverse group.

Our retrieval experiments on the Twitter collection were based on a set of test queries which were obtained by asking two users of an experimental Twitter search engine to create queries of two types:

1. Recency Queries: Queries where relevant tweets were necessarily written very recently. These queries were created on December 4, 2010.
2. Non-temporal Queries: Queries where relevant tweets need not be new[2].

Each query author created 25 recency queries and 25 non-temporal queries.

Finally, for each query we obtained relevance judgments via the Amazon Mechanical Turk (AMT) service. We created judgment pools by retrieving n=50 documents using four retrieval models: query likelihood, query likelihood with exponential recency priors, BM25 [19], and KL divergence with pseudo-RF using the relevance model approach [14,24]. These models were chosen in efforts to achieve suitable diversity in the judging pools.

For each judgment we recorded basic demographic information of the judge, a numeric relevance score measured on a three-point Likert scale: 0 (not relevant), 1 (maybe relevant), 2 (relevant), with an option for *I don't know*. Each query/document pair was judged by six workers; queries that received at least one *I don't know* response were omitted. Final numeric relevance scores were obtained by two methods:

- **Averaging:** We counted as relevant documents with an average of at least 1.5 (an admittedly heuristic value).
- **Voting:** The final score was found by a majority vote. However, for a judgment to receive a non-zero score, at least three of the judges needed to agree on its value and none could have given a zero score. Documents that scored 2 were counted as relevant.

For quality control, only AMT workers with 97% or greater approval rates and completion of at least 50 tasks were allowed to participate. Additionally, we omitted judgments that were completed in less time than the first quartile among our sample (seven seconds). This led us to omit 7,843 judgments, leaving a total of 31,454 (also omitting *I don't know* responses).

All judgments for recency queries were gathered on December 5, 2010 so that workers would have suitable context for making their decisions (they were invited to consult the current Twitter stream while making their relevance assessments).

Prior to building our test queries and relevance judgments, we compiled a set of training queries and judgments using the same approach described above, except that the authors themselves created the training queries, and these were created and judged on November 3-4, 2010.

4.2.2 TREC Data

Because recency queries form an important part of many retrieval settings we also tested our approaches on two sets of news text gathered for TREC [7]. Details of the TREC collections are given in Table 2. We used topic titles as the query text.

Table 2. Summary statistics of TREC data sets.

	AP	LA/FT
Documents	AP (disks 1 & 2)	LA Times and Financial Times (disks 4 & 5)
Doc. Count	164,597	342,054
Dates	1 Jan '88 – 31 Dec '89	23 Apr '91 – 31 Dec '94
Topics	101-200	351-450 (test), 301-350 (train)
Recency queries	20 (test only)	24 (test), 17 (train)
Non-temp. queries	72 (test only)	65 (test), 30 (train)

We classified each topic as "recency" or "non-recency" based on the temporal distribution of each query's relevant documents. If at least 2/3 of the relevant documents appear prior to the median document time, the query was considered a candidate for recency status. This was an admittedly *ad hoc* threshold, but it was chosen both for plausibility and in order to generate a suitable number of candidates. We then manually examined each query to determine if it had a *bona fide* temporal dimension to its relevance. Only queries that met the 2/3 criterion and seemed temporally bound were classified as recency queries. [3] All others were called "non-temporal" although they may indeed have temporal qualities aside from recency. Finally, we only retained queries with at least 10 relevant documents. This final number of selected queries for each TREC collection is shown in Table 2. We used TREC topics 301-350 as training data to estimate parameters. The procedure described above yielded 17 recency queries and 33 non-temporal queries, which were evaluated on the LA.FT data.

4.2.3 Baseline Systems

In Section 7 we analyze the effectiveness of our proposed methods of handling recency queries. To contextualize our results, we report comparisons against two baseline systems. The first approach is the simple query likelihood model (QL) of Eq. 2. We also report results obtained by the application of time-based exponential priors (EXP) as outlined by Li and Croft [15]. In our discussion of relevance models, we replace the QL baseline with the Kullback-Leibler divergence (KLD) model [24].

---

[2] In fact, several of our query authors' non-temporal queries did end up showing some temporal bias. In some cases, this was a slight "recency" concern. In other cases, relevant documents tended to cluster around a particular, past time period.

[3] Recency queries: AP (104, 116, 117, 122, 132, 133, 137, 139, 140, 148, 154, 164, 174, 175, 188, 192, 195, 196, 199, 200); FT/LA, train (06,

[3] Recency queries: AP (104, 116, 117, 122, 132, 133, 137, 139, 140, 148, 154, 164, 174, 175, 188, 192, 195, 196, 199, 200); FT/LA, train (06, 307, 311, 316, 319, 320, 321, 324, 326, 329, 331, 334, 337, 339, 340, 345, 346); FT/LA, test (351, 352, 357, 373, 376, 378, 387, 389, 391, 401, 404, 409, 410, 414, 416, 421, 428, 434, 437, 443, 445, 446, 449, 450)

5. TIME AND RETRIEVAL

5.1 Maximum *a posteriori* estimation for exponential re-ranking

In a context such as Twitter, where relevance often has a recency component, rewarding newer documents during retrieval has obvious appeal. On the other hand, a time-only ranking as used by Twitter search fails to capture differences in tweets' relevance to the query. Using an exponential distribution to accomplish a blending of time and language model (Eq. 3) has been shown to be effective in previous research. However, the typical approach to using the exponential distribution as a document prior by definition ignores query-specific concerns. We hypothesize that the aggressiveness of the exponential penalty should hinge on the extent to which a particular query is sensitive to recency.

Assume that we are using Eq. 6 as our document ranking function. We can combine the approaches of Li and Croft and Dakka et al. by letting $Pr(t_d|q)$ follow an exponential distribution. Ignoring the query-independent document prior, we have the ranking function:

$$Pr(d|q) \propto Pr(q|d) \cdot r_q \cdot e^{-r_q \cdot t_d} \qquad (8$$

with an exponential rate parameter r_q. Note that the formalization of Eq. 6 allows us to bring in a query-specific rate parameter. This is important because it has been shown that the performance of an exponential-based age penalty depends strongly on the parameterization of the distribution. Li and Croft found that setting r=0.01 yielded strong performance, while values even slightly larger than this degraded performance significantly.

A second reason that using a query-specific rate parameter is desirable is that a rate parameter leading to improved performance on recency queries appears (on our microblog data) to degrade performance for non-temporal queries. As an example, we tuned the rate parameter for the exponential prior method to r=*0.015* to optimize performance of recency queries on MAP. This parameterization led to the results in Table 3. All comparisons between QL and EXP in are significant at p<0.01 using a randomization test.

These results show two things: For recency queries, applying an exponential prior improves retrieval on our training recency queries, whereas for non-temporal queries, the exponential prior leads to a stark decrease in performance.

Table 3. Retrieval effectiveness using query likelihood and exponential priors. Relevance based on averaging (Sec. 4.2)

	Recency Queries			Non-Temporal Queries		
	MAP	Rprec	NDCG	MAP	Rprec	NDCG
QL	0.321	0.339	0.570	0.424	0.529	0.600
EXP	0.354+	0.373+	0.597+	0.337-	0.439-	0.519-

The decline in performance for non-temporal queries is not surprising, as the temporal re-ranking dilutes the influence of textual similarity in favor of a temporal factor that is presumably not important for these queries.

To compensate, we turn to Eq. 8 to derive an exponential distribution that penalizes older documents to an extent that depends on the strength of evidence that we are dealing with a recency query. We do this in a two-pass approach. That is, we retrieve k documents using QL, estimate r_q based on these, and then re-rank the k documents according to Eq. 8.

For a query q let $T = \{t_1, t_2, \cdots, t_k\}$ be the times associated with the top k documents returned using simple QL (throughout this paper we set k=*500*). With these times in hand we have the maximum likelihood estimator for the exponential rate parameter:

$$\hat{r}_q^{ML} = \frac{1}{\bar{T}} \qquad (9$$

where $\bar{T}$ is the sample mean of T.

For Approach 1, our starting point is the hypothesis that query-specific temporal information can help us arrive at an estimate of the rate parameter that is more appropriate than a one-size-fits all approach. To illustrate this point, we analyzed the MLEs obtained from the recency and non-temporal training queries in our microblog data. We found $\hat{r}_{recency}^{ML} = 0.029$ and that $\hat{r}_{non-temp}^{ML} = 0.017$. The p-value on a one-sided t-test between the MLE rate parameter estimates for recency and non-recency queries was 0.057. In other words, the top documents retrieved for recency queries tended to be newer than documents retrieved for non-temporal queries. This in turn would cause us to penalize older documents more strongly for recency queries, as compared to the penalty applied for non-temporal queries.

In practice, however, we found that the MLEs obtained from our query information led to models that lent too much influence to time, eclipsing lexical query similarity (e.g. 0.029 leads to an overwhelming age penalty). To mitigate this problem, we propose a Bayesian approach, replacing the MLE with the maximum *a posteriori* estimate of r_q.

We note that the conjugate prior of the exponential is the gamma distribution with parameters α and β (our hyperparameters) yields an estimate for the exponential rate parameter [3]:

$$r_q^{MAP} = \frac{\rho + k - 1}{\sigma + \sum_{i=1}^{k} t_i} \qquad (10$$

where ρ and σ are the rate and shape parameters of the geometric distribution, respectively. With this formalization in place we may use r_q^{MAP} in Eq. 8. The summation over the observed document times in the denominator of Eq. 10 should reduce the temporal influence for non-temporally bound queries. We refer to this approach as Bayesian Exponential Ranking (BEX).

5.2 Temporally-smoothed language models

In Section 2 we described the process of smoothing language models for document ranking (Eq. 3). The Jelinek-Mercer approach to smoothing is governed by a smoothing parameter λ that guides the amount of influence that the "background" probability $Pr(w|C)$ plays in the estimation of $Pr(w|d)$. Our second approach to incorporating time into retrieval for recency queries is to smooth older documents' language models more aggressively than newer documents' models. The rationale for this approach is that as documents age, we have less confidence in their precise lexical content. After many months, perhaps an author would use different words to describe the same topic.

We may consider the mixing parameter λ in Eq. 3 as the probability of choosing $Pr(w|C)$. That is, the author chooses the background model with probability λ, otherwise favoring the MLE. Thus the choice of the MLE or the collection language model is (under this interpretation) guided by a binomial distribution with probability parameter λ. Typically we treat this mixing parameter as a heuristic tuning quantity. But we may instead approach it as an estimation problem. With respect to the subject of this paper, we can replace Eq. 3 with:

$$\hat{P}r(w|d) = (1-\lambda_t)\hat{P}r_{ML}(w|d) + \lambda_t \hat{P}r(w|C) \quad (11$$

where we have replaced λ in Eq. 3 with λ_t, a quantity that depends on the time associated with document *d*. The older *d* is (i.e. the larger t_d), the larger λ_t.

To guide this estimation we offer the following scenario. Imagine that at time t^* we want to re-express the content of document *d*. To do so, we generate text from its language model. However, we consider documents in our collection to be of two types: *old* and *new*. If document *d* is "old," we generate a word *w* according to $Pr(w|C)$. If the document is "new" we trust the observed word counts and generate text according to the MLE.

Given this scenario we may understand λ_t as the parameter of a binomial distribution, where a "success" corresponds to finding that *d* is old. To estimate λ_t we have the maximum likelihood estimator:

$$\hat{\lambda}_t^{MLE} = \frac{n(t<t_d)}{n(D)} \quad (12$$

That is, the estimate is the number of documents that are newer than *d* divided by the total number of documents in the collection.

Earlier, however, we took a Bayesian approach to parameter estimation, and we propose doing so again here. Specifically, we assume that we have a prior belief about λ. In the standard language modeling approach we set λ to some constant (in this paper we used λ=0.4). Thus we could say that we believe that λ is likely to be in the vicinity of 0.4. To formalize this intuition, we assume that λ follows a beta distribution (because beta is the conjugate prior of the binomial) with parameters α and β. Again referring the reader to [3] for the derivation, we have the maximum *a posteriori* estimator:

$$\hat{\lambda}_t^{MAP} = \frac{n(t<t_d)+\alpha-1}{n(D)+\beta-\alpha-2} \quad (13$$

For our temporal smoothing query likelihood approach (TSQL), we use the maximum *a postiori* estimate of λ_t of Eq. 11 to estimate $Pr(w|d)$ in the query likelihood model of Eq. 2.

5.3 Temporally conditioned relevance models

A common way to use relevance feedback in language modeling IR relies on Lavrenko and Croft's relevance model formalization [14]. If our query contains *n* tokens $q_1 \dots q_n$ the probability of a word *w* under a relevance model is $Pr(w, q_1 \dots q_n)$. Estimating this conditional probability requires us first to estimate the joint probability $Pr(w, q_1, \dots, q_n)$. For purposes of relevance feedback, the estimation is typically carried out only over the top *k* documents found during an initial retrieval, giving:

$$Pr(w, q_1 \dots q_n) = \sum_{i=1}^{k} Pr(d_i) Pr(w|d_i) \prod_{j=1}^{n} Pr(q_j|d_i) \quad (14$$

This allows us to define the probability of word *w* under the relevance model *R* as:

$$Pr(w|R) = \frac{Pr(w, q_1 \dots q_n)}{Pr(q_1 \dots q_n)} \quad (15$$

From a practical standpoint, relevance feedback typically proceeds by limiting $Pr(w|R)$ to contain non-zero probabilities only for the *f* feedback terms that have the highest values in Eq. 15. Then a second round of retrieval is conducted using the induced relevance model. Typically this is done by ranking documents in increasing order of the Kullback-Leibler divergence between their language models and the relevance model.

Li and Croft proposed integrating recency into relevance models through the quantity $Pr(d_i)$ in Eq. 14. Following their use of document priors, Li and Croft use the exponential distribution for $Pr(d_i)$ using Eq. 4. We refer to this approach as exponential relevance models (EXRM) in contrast to a baseline, non-temporal relevance modeling approach (RM).

However, we propose an alternate approach to incorporating time into relevance models. In many applications, the relevance model of Eq. 15 is interpolated with the original query model before the second retrieval via:

$$\hat{P}r(w|R) = (1-\mu)Pr(w|q) + \mu Pr(w|R) \quad (16$$

where μ is a mixing parameter that plays a role similar to λ in Eq. 3. A large value of μ gives heavy weight to the feedback terms, while a small μ is more conservative, retaining the influence of the original query. (For the RM and EXRM approaches, use Eq. 16 to estimate word probabilities under the relevance model). This is the relevance feedback approach used by the Indri search engine, for instance. Of course, in Eq. 16 μ is another tunable parameter. As in our temporally-smoothed document language models, we propose letting the timestamps of retrieved documents guide the smoothing process, giving more weight to feedback terms when the feedback query retrieves newer documents.

Our approach to setting μ is as follows. Assume we have an initial query *q*. We build a relevance model based on *q* using Eq. 15, performing a second retrieval using the KL divergence method with this relevance model. This yields a vector of feedback document times, $\dot{t}_{fb} = \{t_{fb1}, \cdots, t_{fbk}\}$ where *k* is the number of feedback documents.

In our estimation of μ we are guided by motivation similar to Eq. 12's, asking, for each element of $\dot{t}_{fb}$, how many documents are older? As before, we consider μ in Eq. 16 as a binomial parameter. To estimate this parameter, we begin with maximum likelihood, where success is the observation that a particular feedback document f_{fbi} is newer than a particular document from the collection at large. We thus have the estimate

$$\hat{\mu}^{MLE} = \frac{\sum_{i=1}^{k} n(t>t_{fbi})}{k \cdot n(d)} \quad (17$$

where the sum in the numerator of Eq. 17 is taken over all *k* feedback documents For simplicity we refer to the numerator of Eq. 16 as $S(\dot{t}_{fb})$. This allows us to define the maximum a posteriori estimate of μ:

$$\hat{\mu}^{MAP} = \frac{S(\dot{t}_{fb})+\alpha-1}{k \cdot n(D)+\beta-\alpha-2} \quad (18$$

with hyperparameters α and β. Thus we define our temporally smoothed relevance model as:

$$\hat{P}r(w|R) = (1-\hat{\mu}^{MAP})Pr(w|q) + \hat{\mu}^{MAP} Pr(w|R) \quad (19$$

which we call TSRM.

6. PARAMETERIZATIONS

Using the training data described in Section 3, we tuned the parameters that guide the models that we have proposed. The outcome of this process appears in Table 4. Because optimal values were very close for the TREC and Twitter data, we have chosen a single parameterization for both corpora.

Table 4. Model Parameters. Values chosen or derived for best performance (MAP) on training data.

Param	Description	Eqs.	Value
n	Num. Docs retrieved per query	NA	100
k	Num. top docs. Used for calculations	9, 13	20
r	Rate parameter for exponential priors	4	0.015 (TREC), 0.01 (Twitter)
λ	Parameter for Jelinek-Mercer smoothing	3	0.4
ρ	Effective sample size for exponential MAP estimate (BEX)	9	100
σ	Shape parameter for exponenttial MAP estimate (BEX)	9	Derived
β	Effective sample size for binomial MAP estimate (TSQL, TSRM)	10, 17	2**n(D)* (TSQL) 250 (TSRM)
α	Hyperparameter for binomial MAP estimate (TSQL, TSRM)	10, 17	derived2
μ	Mixing parameter for relevance models (RM, EXRM)	15	0.4
f	Number of expansion terms used in pseudo-RF	NA	10

Throughout this paper we set λ=0.4 in Eq. 3 (for standard smoothing). For time-specific smoothing we choose α and β such that $(\alpha - 1)/(\beta - \alpha - 2) = 0.4$. This makes the time-smoothed models directly comparable to the standard language models smoothed with λ=0.4, leaving only the magnitude of β as a tunable parameter. For simplicity, we take the same approach for estimating μ in Eq. 18. For our query-specific exponential re-ranking, we choose hyperparameters such that $(\rho - 1)/\sigma = 0.015$ for the TREC data and 0.01 for the Twitter data.

To avoid including very common words in expanded queries, we applied a standard stoplist when constructing relevance models. For the TREC data the stopwords consisted of the standard list included with the lemur toolkit. For the Twitter data we supplemented this list with a brief customized stoplist that removed common hostnames, file extensions, etc.

7. EXPERIMENTAL RESULTS

To assess the effectiveness of the proposed temporal retrieval models, we ran experiments using the data sets described in Section 4. Notation and abbreviations that appear in our data reporting are given in Table 5. In the following tables, results of non-temporal baseline runs are shown in grey. Cells marked with + (–) indicate a statistically-significant ($p<0.05$) improvement (decline) versus the related baseline using a randomization test. It is worth noting that in some cases, the score (e.g. MAP) of a run *a* whose improvement over the baseline is larger than run *b*'s does not see statistical significance, while run *b* does. This is due to high variance over the queries for run *a*.

We report three effectiveness metrics, mean average precision (MAP), R-precision (Rprec), and normalized discounted cumulative gain (NDCG) to show the effect of different models with respect to both recall- and precision-based considerations.

The two highlighted rows of Table 5 show our baseline systems (QL and RM). Thus the effectiveness of EXP, BEX, and TSQL is gauged against QL and EXRM and TSQL are compared to RM. We refer to the QL and associated runs as *term-based*, referring to the runs based on relevance models as *feedback runs.*

Table 5. Abbreviations of Experimental Systems. Baseline systems are highlighted in grey.

Abbreviation	Description
QL	Query likelihood (non-temporal)
EXP	Exponential priors as in [15]
BEX	Bayesian exponential ranking
TSQL	Time-smoothed query likelihood
RM	Relevance models (non-temporal)
EXRM	Exponential relevance models as in [15]
TSQL	Time-smoothed relevance models

The starkest result in Table 6 through Table 8 is the difference in performance between recency and non-temporal queries. For recency queries, all three non-feedback models improved MAP for all datasets significantly. Results for R-precision and NDCG were also promising for these runs with all models scoring higher than QL, though only occasionally at statistically significant levels. Moreover, all three models were comparable on recency queries. The difference in effectiveness (on any of our three measures) between EXP and BEX or TSQL was never observed to be statistically significant on the recency queries.

Table 6. Retrieval Effectiveness on TREC AP Data.

	Recency Queries			Non-Temporal Queries		
	MAP	Rprec	NDCG	MAP	Rprec	NDCG
QL	0.198	0.259	0.401	0.150	0.213	0.302
EXP	0.204	0.265	0.408	0.145-	0.208	0.296-
BEX	0.205+	0.265	0.408+	0.147	0.209	0.300
TSQL	0.203+	0.263	0.405	0.148	0.210	0.302
RM	0.267	0.318	0.469	0.192	0.262	0.357
EXRM	0.266	0.317	0.463	0.191	0.262	0.357
TSRM	0.272+	0.323+	0.473+	0.192	0.263+	0.358

However, the picture is quite different when we turn to the non-temporal queries. The method based on exponential document priors saw a statistically significant decline in MAP in comparison with the non-temporal QL for all tested non-temporal queries. Results for R-precision and NDCG are also lower for EXP than for QL in all cases.

Turning to the models proposed in this paper, the BEX approach alleviated the risk of temporal conditioning of search results for in comparison to EXP. As we hypothesized, the rate parameter of the exponential in Eq. 8 was moderated for non-temporal queries, leading to a diminished impact of time in these runs. BEX *did* show declines in performance for recency queries compared to QL. But these declines were less severe than in the case of EXP. Whereas all EXP declines in MAP were statistically significant, only those on the Twitter data were significant for BEX.

The most encouraging result comes from our temporally smoothed query likelihood model (TSQL). TSQL saw a statistically significant decline in performance only once in our experiments (with respect to R-precision on the LA/FT data. In all other cases, the decline in performance incurred by applying temporal smoothing to non-temporal queries was negligible.

The bottom three rows of Table 6 show that relevance feedback hindered retrieval on the Twitter data, with MAP significantly lower for RM than for QL in all cases but one (non-temporal by voting). This poor performance may be due to short documents in the Twitter collection. Thus with respect to relevance feedback models, we focus on the results from Table 7 and Table 8. As Li and Croft found, the EXRM approach shows little improvement over the baseline RM. Several runs, however, show substantial improvement with TSRM. As expected, the bulk of this improvement occurs on recency queries; temporal smoothing appears to have negligible impact on non-temporal queries.

8. DISCUSSION

Two main results emerge from the data reported above: BEX and TSQL improve recency query performance to nearly the same extent as EXP, and BEX and (especially) TSQL are more robust against failure than EXP when applied to non-temporal queries.

Under BEX, bringing query-specific information to specifying the exponential parameter allows recency information to privilege newer documents while tempering this influence for non-temporal queries. Comparing EXP to BEX in Tables 6 and 7 speaks to this.

Table 8. Retrieval Effectiveness on TREC LA/FT Data.

	Recency Queries			Non-Temporal Queries		
	MAP	Rprec	NDCG	MAP	Rprec	NDCG
QL	0.175	0.225	0.324	0.142	0.208	0.306
EXP	0.187+	0.238	0.332	0.134-	0.198-	0.209-
BEX	0.186+	0.241+	0.331+	0.138	0.201-	0.297-
TSQL	0.184+	0.241+	0.326	0.138	0.199-	0.300
RM	0.193	0.244	0.335	0.152	0.222	0.319
EXRM	0.197	0.248	0.340	0.151	0.219-	0.318
TSRM	0.196+	0.244	0.339+	0.152	0.219-	0.318

However, TSQL showed still more robustness and promise. While prior-based methods (EXP and EXRM) gave significant improvements over their baselines four times, TSQL saw 12 significant improvements. Also, EXP and EXRM reduced effectiveness significantly in eleven runs, versus 2 for TSQL (no significant declines for TSQL on MAP). While applying temporal priors to relevance models yielded no discernable improvement over baseline RM, TSRM was able to improve over the baseline RM runs on the TREC data.

8.1 Sensitivity of Models to Parameterizations

Table 4 reminds us that we have defined and set many parameters in the course of this paper. An obvious question is, how sensitive are the proposed methods to the parameterization of their models? Figure 2 shows the effect of changing the parameterization for each of the approaches we have outlined (except relevance feedback). The plotted data are for the recency training queries on both our TREC and Twitter corpora. In each panel, the blue line shows mean average precision as we change the rate parameter for Li and Croft's exponential priors (EXP). The blue solid line shows MAP for the Bayesian estimates of time-sensitive exponentials (BEX). The dashed red line shows the sensitivity of the temporal smoothing method (TSQL). Finally, the horizontal black dotted line is MAP observed for standard query likelihood.

Of special interest in Figure 3 is the behavior of the temporal smoothing model. We can see that while the two methods based on the exponential distribution are highly sensitive to their

Table 7. Retrieval Effectiveness on Twitter Data. Relevance judgments based on averaging and voting methods (Section 4.2)

	Relevance by Averaging						Relevance by Voting					
	Recency Queries			Non-Temporal Queries			Recency Queries			Non-Temporal Queries		
	MAP	Rprec	NDCG	MAP	Rprec	NDCG	MAP	Rprec	NDCG	MAP	Rprec	NDCG
QL	0.340	0.409	0.576	0.336	0.358	0.535	0.325	0.390	0.573	0.276	0.285	0.488
EXP	0.364+	0.420	0.596	0.305-	0.338	0.486-	0.343+	0.411+	0.589	0.244-	0.267-	0.430-
BEX	0.362+	0.421	0.597+	0.317-	0.349	0.499-	0.344+	0.406+	0.591	0.256-	0.274	0.444-
TSQL	0.361+	0.418	0.594	0.335	0.360	0.528	0.347+	0.408+	0.589	0.275	0.287	0.478
RM	0.313	0.399	0.549	0.332	0.367	0.517	0.312	0.383	0.541	0.279	0.298	0.477
EXRM	0.313	0.394	0.538	0.339	0.360	0.526	0.304	0.377	0.534	0.277	0.302	0.477
TSRM	0.315	0.390	0.537	0.337	0.359	0.525	0.306	0.384	0.532	0.277	0.299	0.475

parameterization, TSQL is much less so. In fact, its MAP remains above the baseline QL for all tested parameterizations. We tested parameterizations up to an effective sample size of twenty times $n(D)$. As Eq. 13 shows, so long as we define the hyperparameters such that $\alpha/(\beta-\alpha-1)=0.4$, then as we increase β (the effective sample size) the TSQL model probabilities will simply approach the $\lambda=0.4$ of the standard QL model.

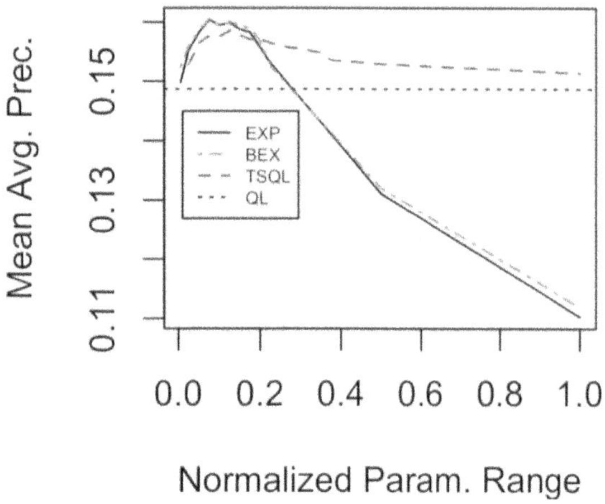

Figure 2. Effect of model parameters on MAP for TREC training data. The x-axis shows the parameters of each model normalized to appear on the same scale.

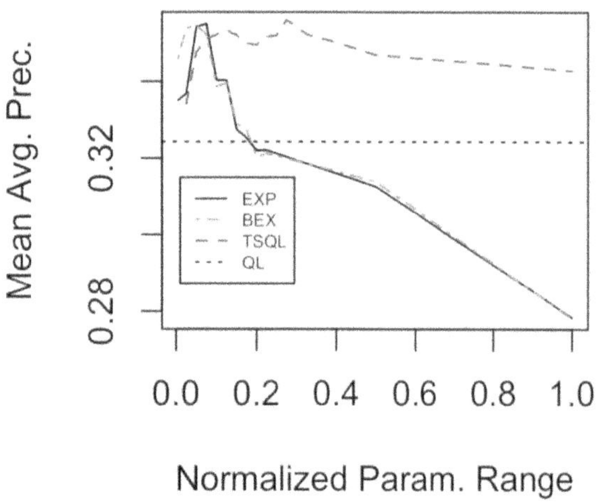

Figure 3. Effect of model parameters on MAP for Twitter training data.

Table 9. Term counts and lengths for documents in Figure 4

	petroleum	exploration	falkland	*n(d)*
FT932-16710	2	1	5	292
FT934-4629	1	2	0	79

8.2 Performance of Time-Smoothed Language Models

In Section 7 we presented evidence that temporal smoothing (TSQL) admits recency considerations into retrieval more effectively than the use of exponential priors (EXP) does. Figure 4 shows the effect of time on the estimated query likelihood, as illustrated by TREC topic 351. We selected two documents, FT932-16710 (the top-ranked document) and FT934-4629 (10th). However, instead of using each document's real timestamp, we replaced its time with the number shown on the x-axis of Figure 4, calculating the time-adjusted query likelihood. This allows us to gauge the change in each document's score as it gets "older."

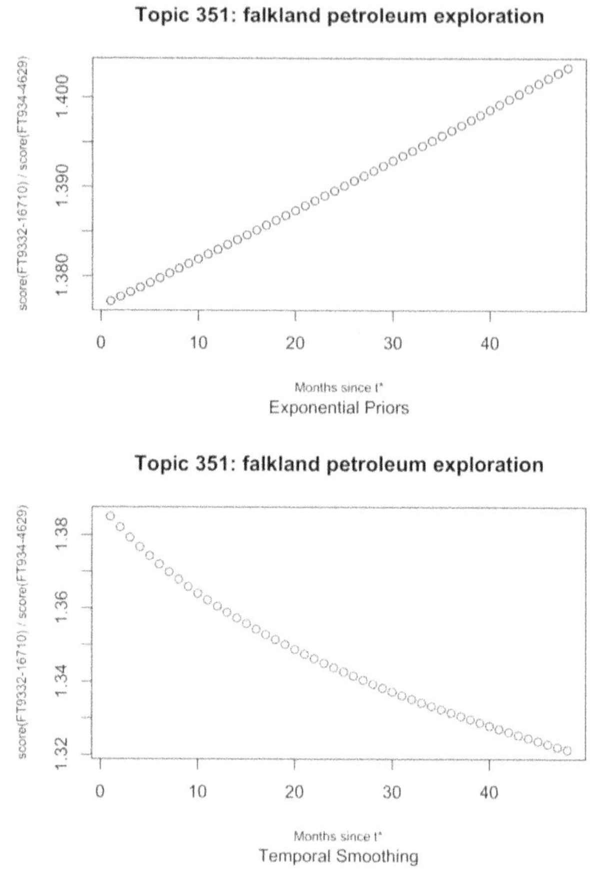

Figure 4. Effect of time on relative document scores using Exponential Priors (EXP, top) and Temporal Smoothing (TSQL, bottom). Points are the ratio of query likelihood at simulated time for documents FT932-16710 and FT934-4629.

Figure 4 shows that time affects document scores quite differently under EXP versus TSQL. As a point of reference, using a constant $\lambda=0.4$, FT932-16710 has a higher likelihood than FT934-4629; the ratio of these quantities is 1.27. Thus all of the ratios in Figure 4 are greater than 1.0. However, as we alter the timestamps on each document—making them appear older—we see that under EXP, the documents become increasingly and linearly *less* similar. On the other hand, temporal smoothing *increases* the similarity between the two documents given that they are "old."

Our interpretation is that TSQL integrates time into scoring in a more realistic way than EXP does. For documents that are "new," TSQL adds stark separation between the documents in Figure 4. But if documents with the same lexical content were older, TSQL's temporal influence diminishes.

9. RELATED WORK

In addition to the work that we have cited in the previous discussion, a great deal of interest has guided research into temporal dimensions of IR. Time, researchers have found, enters into retrieval in several ways—shaping the notion of relevance, constituting a valuable source of evidence in ranking, and helping developers identify suitable algorithms for particular settings.

Temporal factors have been shown to provide leverage in several IR-related problems, including document ranking [6] and query difficulty prediction [8].

Web retrieval has seen particular interest in temporal matters. Change over time raises the matter of page *freshness*, as described in [4]. In other work, it has been shown that changes in Web documents can bear both on how users perceive relevance [20] and how search engines model document contents [1].

A good deal of recent work has analyzed the problem of search in various social settings [13]. Problems such as collaborative and social search [9,11] draw attention to the role that relationships between people play in a variety of search settings. Other work pays specific attention to the social aspects of information seeking in microblog settings [8,16]. More traditional treatments of IR in microblogs is offered in [2,7,10] and [23].

10. FUTURE WORK

The work presented in this paper builds on prior attempts to inject time into queries. We've taken another step toward making time a first-class citizen of the retrieval space, but much remains to be done. The evaluation framework we adopted might be improved by removing some of the arbitrary cutoff parameters, for example.

In addition to recency queries, we might consider queries that prefer older documents. For certain precedence searches (e.g., patent search, trademark search, e-discovery) one might wish to know when certain concepts were first mentioned. The formalisms described here might be inverted to bias the results toward older documents. One challenge is to establish a useful reference point in the past that corresponds to the present in recency queries.

There are other ways of injecting time into search results. We can, for example, represent t_d as a separate dimension in a rank-then-combine approach described by Pickens and Golovchinsky [17]. In this approach time becomes yet another feature on which documents can be ranked. The weight assigned to this dimension can either be calculated analogously to Eq. 12, or can be controlled directly by the user in an exploratory search setting.

Temporal smoothing appears to be an effective way to add time to our consideration during document ranking. However, in this paper we have only pursued a simple application of this idea. In future work it will be of interest to apply the ideas introduced here to other smoothing methods such as Bayesian smoothing with Dirichlet priors. In this case, the temporal influence would guide retrieval in a more complex way than it does using Jelinek-Mercer. This would be especially interesting due to the different nature of the document types we have analyzed. Tweets and news articles obviously differ with respect to length, and thus word frequency. It will be interesting to analyze how temporally informed Dirichlet smoothing bears on such varied documents.

11. CONCLUSION

Though time has long played a role in IR, new problems such as microblog search change the nature of temporal retrieval. In this paper we proposed methods based on Bayesian estimation for incorporating time into language modeling IR. In one approach (BEX), we added a query-specific estimation procedure to the use of an exponential penalty for document age. We also used time to perform document-specific language model smoothing (TSQL). Finally, we used this method to induce temporally smoothed relevance models (TSRM). The methods we propose perform at state of the art effectiveness for recency queries, while showing more robustness than established methods when applied to non-temporal queries.

12. ACKNOWLEDGMENTS

This research was supported in part by a Google academic research award.

13. REFERENCES

[1] Adar, E. Teevan, J., Dumais, S.T., and Elsas, J.L., 2009. The web changes everything: understanding the dynamics of web content. *Proceedings of the Second ACM International Conference on Web Search and Data Mining* (New York, NY, USA, 2009), 282–291.

[2] Bernstein, M. Suh, B., Hong, L., Chen. J., Kairam, S., and Chi, E. 2010. Eddi: Interactive Topic-Based Browsing of Social Status Streams. *UIST 2010: ACM Symposium on User Interface Software and Technology*. (forthcoming) (2010).

[3] Bolstad, W.M. *Introduction to Bayesian Statistics*. Wiley-Interscience.

[4] Dai, N. and Davison, B.D. 2010. Freshness matters. *Proceeding of the 33rd international ACM SIGIR conference on Research and development in information retrieval - SIGIR '10* (Geneva, Switzerland, 2010), 114.

[5] Dakka, W., Gravano, L., Ipeirotis, P., Answering General Time-Sensitive Queries, *IEEE Transactions on Knowledge and Data Engineering*, vol. 99, no. PrePrints, 2010.

[6] Dong, A. Zhang, R., Kolari, P., Bai, J., Diaz, F., Chang, Y., Zheng, Z., and Zha, H. 2010. Time is of the essence: improving recency ranking using Twitter data. *Proceedings of the 19th international conference on World wide web* (New York, NY, USA, 2010), 331–340.

[7] Efron, M. 2010. Hashtag retrieval in a microblogging environment. *Proceeding of the 33rd international ACM SIGIR conference on Research and development in information retrieval* (Geneva, Switzerland, 2010), 787-788.

[8] Efron, M. and Winget, M. 2010. Questions are content: A Taxonomy of Questions in a Microblogging Environment. *Proceedings of the 2010 Annual Meeting of the American Society for Information Science and Technology*. (2010).

[9] Evans, B.M. and Chi, E.H. 2008. Towards a model of understanding social search. *Proceedings of the 2008 ACM conference on Computer supported cooperative work* (San Diego, CA, USA, 2008), 485-494.

[10] Golovchinsky, G. and Efron, M. 2010. Making sense of Twitter search. *Proc. CHI2010 Workshop on Microblogging: What and How Can We Learn From It? April 11, 2010.* (2010).

[11] Horowitz, D. and Kamvar, S.D. 2010. The anatomy of a large-scale social search engine. *Proceedings of the 19th international conference on World wide web* (Raleigh, North Carolina, USA, 2010), 431-440.

[12] Jones, R. and Diaz, F. 2007. Temporal profiles of queries. *ACM Transactions on Information Systems*. 25, 3 (2007), 14-es.

[13] King, I., and Li, J. 2009. Proceeding of the 2nd ACM

workshop on Social web search and mining. (Hong Kong, China, 2009), 70.

[14] Lavrenko, V. and Croft, W.B. 2001. Relevance based language models. *Proceedings of the 24th annual international ACM SIGIR conference on Research and development in information retrieval* (New York, NY, USA, 2001), 120–127.

[15] Li, X. and Croft, W.B. 2003. Time-based language models. *Proceedings of the twelfth international conference on Information and knowledge management - CIKM '03* (New Orleans, LA, USA, 2003), 469.

[16] Morris, M.R., Teevan, J., and Panovich, Katrina. 2010. What do people ask their social networks, and why?: a survey study of status message q&a behavior. *Proceedings of the 28th international conference on Human factors in computing systems* (Atlanta, Georgia, USA, 2010), 1739-1748.

[17] Pickens, J. and Golovchinsky, G. 2008. Ranked feature fusion models for ad hoc retrieval. *Proceeding of the 17th ACM conference on Information and knowledge management* (New York, NY, USA, 2008), 893–900.

[18] Ponte, J.M. and Croft, W.B. 1998. A language modeling approach to information retrieval. *SIGIR 1998: Proceedings of the 21st annual international ACM SIGIR conference on Research and development in information retrieval*. (1998), 275-281.

[19] Robertson, S.E. Walker, S., Jones, S., Hancock-Beaulieu, M.M., and Gatford, M. 1994. Okapi at TREC-3. *In Proceedings of the Third Text REtrieval Conference (TREC 1994)* (1994).

[20] Teevan, J., Dumais, S.T., and Liebling, D.J. 2010. A longitudinal study of how highlighting web content change affects people's web interactions. *Proceedings of the 28th international conference on Human factors in computing systems - CHI '10* (Atlanta, Georgia, USA, 2010), 1353.

[21] Twitter. *http://twitter.com*. Accessed: 12-02-2010.

[22] Voorhees, E.M. 2007. TREC: Continuing information retrieval's tradition of experimentation. *Commun. ACM*. 50, (Nov. 2007), 51–54.

[23] Yang, J. and Leskovec, J. 2011. Temporal variation in online media. *ACM Internation Conference on Web Search and Data Mining (WSDM '11)* (2011).

[24] Zhai, C. and Lafferty, J. 2001. Model-based feedback in the language modeling approach to information retrieval. *CIKM 2001: Proceedings of the tenth international conference on Information and knowledge management*. (2001), 403-410.

[25] Zhai, C. and Lafferty, J. 2004. A Study of Smoothing Methods for Language Models Applied to Information Retrieval. *ACM Transactions on Information Systems*. 2, 2 (2004), 179-214.

[26] Zhai, C. 2008. Statistical Language Models for Information Retrieval A Critical Review. *Found. Trends Inf. Retr.* 2, (Mar. 2008), 137–213.

Query by Document via a Decomposition-Based Two-Level Retrieval Approach

Linkai Weng[†‡], Zhiwei Li[‡], Rui Cai[‡], Yaoxue Zhang[†], Yuezhi Zhou[†], Laurence T. Yang[§], and Lei Zhang[‡]
[†]Dept. Computer Science and Technology, Tsinghua University.
[‡]Microsoft Research Asia.
[§]Dept. Computer Science, St. Francis Xavier University.
[†]wlk02@mails.tsinghua.edu.cn, [†]zyx@moe.edu.cn, [†]zhouyz@mail.tsinghua.edu.cn
[‡]{zli, ruicai, leizhang}@microsoft.com [§]ltyang@gmail.com

ABSTRACT

Retrieving similar documents from a large-scale text corpus according to a given document is a fundamental technique for many applications. However, most of existing indexing techniques have difficulties to address this problem due to special properties of a document query, e.g. *high dimensionality, sparse representation* and *semantic issue.* Towards addressing this problem, we propose a two-level retrieval solution based on a document decomposition idea. A document is decomposed to a compact vector and a few document specific keywords by a dimension reduction approach. The compact vector embodies the major semantics of a document, and the document specific keywords complement the discriminative power lost in dimension reduction process. We adopt locality sensitive hashing (LSH) to index the compact vectors, which guarantees to quickly find a set of related documents according to the vector of a query document. Then we re-rank documents in this set by their document specific keywords. In experiments, we obtained promising results on various datasets in terms of both accuracy and performance. We demonstrated that this solution is able to index large-scale corpus for efficient similarity-based document retrieval.

Categories and Subject Descriptors

H.3.1 [**Information Systems**]: Information Storage and Retrieval—*Content Analysis and Indexing*

General Terms

Algorithms, Performance, Experimentation

Keywords

document decomposition, similarity search, indexing

SIGIR'11, July 24–28, 2011, Beijing, China.

1. INTRODUCTION

In many applications, a fundamental technique is to find similar documents according to a given document from a large-scale text corpus, e.g. a movie recommendation system needs to find similar movies/users to a given movie/user, in both content-based and collaborative filtering scenarios [30]; a blogger wants to know who pirates his blog pages or to do the cross reference; a patent lawyer want to find similar patents as reference cases. Although lots of retrieval technologies have been developed, most of them are designed for short query retrieval, e.g. 2-10 query terms. A document query, e.g. including 2000 query terms, is very different from a short query, as well as corresponding indexing techniques. Following [35], we term this problem as Query By Document (QBD) in this paper.

The QBD problem has three important properties, *high dimensionality, sparse representation* and *semantic issue,* which should be comprehensively considered in the solution. First of all, the document query contains lots of terms, so it is naturally a high-dimension indexing problem. Secondly, the document query is often represented as a language vector, which is quite sparse, and it will incur new challenges when mixed with the high dimension property. At last, a document query often has its inherent semantics, which is quite important information in the similar document matching. This property determines the difference between traditional near-duplicate detection and our QBD problem. The former often focus on the syntax level matching, and try to find exactly the same document only with some minor syntactic difference; the latter, needs to consider the syntactic level matching and semantic level matching together, and try to find related documents from the user perspective.

A simple solution for QBD is a linear scan approach, in which both documents in corpus and a query document are represented by high-dimensional vectors [3], and *cosine* similarity could be adopted to rank documents. However, this solution have two drawbacks: i) for large-scale corpus, its computational cost is unacceptable, ii) direct matching of keywords may encounter some language problems, i.e. *synonymy* and *polysemy* [13], which also loses the important semantic information.

Inverted files is an efficient index structure for large-scale text corpus [39]. In inverted files, words are primary keys, and documents containing the same word are organized as one row of the table. Thus, given a query, documents containing all query terms can be obtained efficiently. For a typical query which contains 2-10 terms, this operation is very efficient [6]. However, inverted files cannot solve the QBD problem. Given a long document query, the computational cost to merge hundreds of rows of the table is unacceptable. Moreover, it is not necessary to require that the returned documents contain all terms of a query document. An optional solution is to select a set of representative words/phrases from the query document, and then search related documents via the inverted files with the constructed "short query" [35]. [35] proposed to score words by TF-IDF weights and mutual-information. However, the selection of representative words largely loses information of a query document, especially the semantic information. Moreover, inverted files cannot solve those language problems we mentioned above.

The QBD essentially is a special high-dimensional indexing (HDI) problem which has been extensively studied in literatures. A basic idea of HDI approaches is to partition a feature space to lots of "bins". If two documents appear in the same bin, they are deemed as similar documents. Typical HDI approaches can be categorized as tree-based, e.g. kd-tree [3], and hash-based approaches, e.g. locality sensitive hashing (LSH) [1]. Due to the well-known curse of dimensionality, tree-based approaches only can be applied to "low" dimensional spaces (say, less than 30) [22]. To find the nearest neighbors in a high-dimensional space by a tree-based approach, we have to perform back-tracking operation frequently in the search process, as will degenerate a such method to be a linear scan. LSH partitions a feature space by a group of carefully designed hash functions. It has been demonstrated to be an effective technique for visual features of images [20]. However, lots of experiments including ours show it is not good at indexing sparse feature vectors, e.g. TF-IDF vectors in QBD problem, because the L_2 distance of sparse features is not as reliable as that of dense features [1][1]. Most of hash-based approaches are designed for detecting near-duplicate documents [18], rather than retrieving similar documents, e.g. shingling algorithms [8] and a random projection-based approach [9].

Dimension reduction (DR) approaches are effective solutions to the QBD problem, e.g. matrix factorization based approaches (e.g. latent semantic indexing (LSI) [13], nonnegative matrix factorization (NMF) [21]), and topic models (e.g. pLSI [19] and LDA [5]), in which high dimensional feature vectors are projected to a low dimensional latent space by minimizing some kinds of reconstruction error. Because the new representations of documents often are dense and compact, many similarity measures, e.g. *cosine* similarity, and HDI approaches, e.g. LSH, work well. Moreover, those language problems, i.e. *synonymy* and *polysemy*, which are often encountered in direct keywords matching-based solutions, can be alleviated [13].

However, DR approaches have an obvious drawback if they are applied to address QBD alone. DR approaches often reduce the discriminative power of document vectors. For example, two news stories, a basketball related and a football related, are likely to be projected to the same or two very near points in the latent space because "sports" are their major semantics (preserved in DR), while basketball and football are their minor semantics (ignored in DR), as shown in Figure 1. These minor semantics exist as residual which is abandoned in a DR process. This observation inspired us that the residual of documents can complement the loss of "characteristics" of documents. For a document, if we can selectively preserve some keywords, which major lead its residual, and along with the compact vector obtained by DR, we can preserve its major semantics as well as most of its discriminative power in a still compact compound representation.

With the above analysis, we proposed a decomposition-based two-level retrieval approach to address the QBD problem in this paper. Firstly, we utilize a principle document decomposition model(DDM)[10] to decompose the original document into three parts of words, i.e. background words, topic related words and document specific words. Background words have no information to distinguish documents, topic related words embody the inter-class differences which are major semantics of a document, and document specific words embody the intra-class differences which are minor but most distinguishing elements of a document. As shown in Figure 1, topic related words are major results of dimension reduction, while document specific words are residual. Then, we design an effective two-level index and rank schema based on the document decomposition results. In the indexing process, the compact and dense topic related vectors can be indexed by a HDI approach, e.g. LSH in this paper, and the document specific keywords can be indexed by inverted/forward files, as shown in Figure 3. In the ranking process, we first get a set of candidate documents by search in LSH index. Documents in this set are likely to talking about the same topics as the query. Then, we re-rank them by their document specific keywords. The top ranked documents are likely to talking about the same details of the same topics. [27] proposed a similar document decomposition idea with a model called PCP based on the PCA, which can also be included in our unified two-stage index and re-rank framework.

The remaining part of the paper is organized as follows. In Section 2, we introduce related works. In Section 3, we continue to introduce our document decomposition idea. Then the two-level index and rank schema is presented in Section 4. A set of practical experiments are conducted and the corresponding results are analyzed in section 5. Finally, conclusions and future work are given in the last Section.

2. RELATED WORKS

Near-duplicate detection is an important related work. It is a classical technique devoting to find duplicate pages or duplicate documents, which are strikingly similar with only some minute difference, e.g. words, fonts, bold types. Near-duplicates are widespread in email, retrieval results, news pages and images. The state-of-the-art solution is considered as the shingling algorithm in [8] and the random projection projection based approach in [9]. Moreover, there are lots of adaptive approaches to satisfy various requirement, such as [24, 11, 12, 14, 18], all of them gain great success in their own scenarios. As mentioned before, the goal of near-duplicate is not exactly the same with our QBD problems, in short, one focus on the syntactic similarity, and the other needs to consider semantic similarity and syntax similarity together. Locality sensitive hashing(LSH) [1] is frequently utilized in near-duplicate detection and is demonstrated effective in the

[1]Even if good parameters for sparse vectors exist, the process to finding them largely depends on designer's experience and extensive experiments.

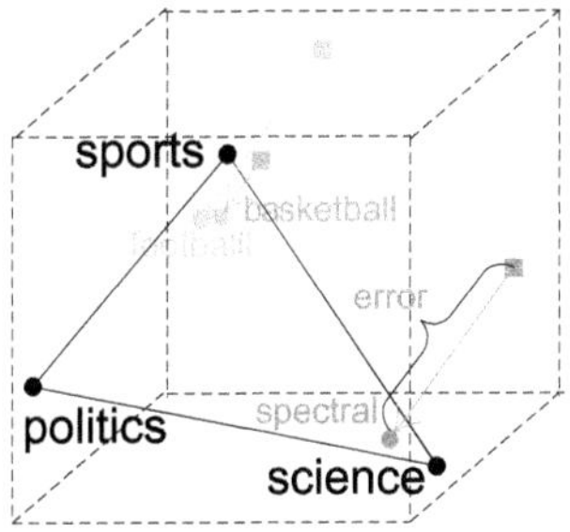

Figure 1: Illustration of the document decomposition idea. The cube denotes a vector space of documents, the triangle is a simplex spanned by three bases, i.e. topics, a rectangle point denotes a document, and a circle point denotes an embedding of a document in the topic simplex. The distance of a document to the simplex is its residual.

compact vector indexing, therefore, our approach adopt LSH to index the compact topic element of document.

Phrase extraction based matching is another related work to QBD problem, which tries to extract some representative phrases from the query document, and then to find related documents containing these representative phrases. Schemas to extract representative phrases are various: [25, 26] utilize statistical information to identify suitable phrases; [16, 33] incorporate the relationships between phrases to identify phrases; [32, 31] apply learning algorithms in the extracting process. [35] is the nowadays phrase extracting based matching approach, which identifies the phrase set by the TF-IDF weight and the mutual information, and then refines the set with the help of phrase association in the wikipedia link graph. Phrase extraction based matching is a quite effective solution to our problem, but the selection of phrases loses much useful information, especially the semantics in the document. In our approach, the document specific words actually are representative phrases which are extracted by a principle language model, and as a complement, the topic elements maintain the semantic information in document.

Topic model based retrieval is also a related work, which often combines topic model element and document language element together. This solution is quite popular nowadays, and [36, 37, 38, 23, 34] are all successful works of this class. The semantic information in document is somewhat complemented in the topic model element, so this solution has been demonstrated effective in many applications. However, there are still two challenges in these existing works: one is that the query is often seen as a bag of words, this assumption is reasonable in the short query scenario, but in our document query application, the semantic structure of the query also needs to be considered; the other one is that when facing the document query scenario with large-scale corpus, the matching efficiency will be a serious issue. To address these two challenges, our approach proposes the document decomposition idea and two-level indexing schema.

3. DOCUMENT DECOMPOSITION

In this section, we present the document decomposition idea and its implementation. It is noted the purpose of decomposing a document is to find a new representation which can be easier indexed.

3.1 Document Decomposition Idea

Our document decomposition idea is originated from dimension reduction approaches. To make the presentation easy to understand, we use LSI to illustrate our basic idea [13]. By LSI, a document, d (a W-dimensional sparse vector, where W is the size of vocabulary), is decomposed to

$$d = \mu + Xw + \epsilon \quad (1)$$

where μ is the mean of features, X is a $W \times k$ matrix, k is the number of principle components ($k \ll W$ for dimension reduction puspose), w is a k-dimensional coefficient vector, and ϵ is a W-dimensional vector. Column vectors of X is a group of so-called base vectors, which span a low-dimensional latent space; w is the projection of a document in the space; ϵ is the residual which is the "distance" of the document to the space. Since, the mean vector, μ, does not contain any discriminative information (i.e. stopwords), it can be removed from the representation of a document. After removing μ, the inner product of a document d in corpus and a query document q could be computed by

$$< d, q >=< Xw_d + \epsilon_d >< Xw_q + \epsilon_q >= w_d^T w_q + \epsilon_d^T \epsilon_q \quad (2)$$

Here, we use a property of LSI decomposition: the residual (ϵ) is orthogonal to principle components (X). Thus, the multiplication of X and ϵ is null. Considering the physical meanings of w and ϵ, we can get an effective approximation to the inner product. For a good LSI decomposition, entries of ϵ usually are very close to zero. Thus, even if we only keep a few large entries of the two ϵ vectors respectively, the inner product of two documents is likely to not changing. However, in this way, we can greatly reduce the storage for documents. To store a raw document vector, d, we need $|d|$ storage cells, where $|d|$ is the length of the document, while to store the new appropriate representation, we only need $k + t$ storage cells, where t is the number of ϵ entries we kept. $k + t$ is much less than $|d|$ in practice. Moreover, in Section 4, we will show that a good property of this approximation enables an efficient indexing solution. In summary, a document is represented by:

$$d \triangleq \{w, \varphi\} \quad (3)$$

where w is a k-dimensional compact vector, and φ is a few keywords.

It is noted that, for short documents, the new representations may increase their storage cost (i.e. $k + t > |d|$). However, we argue that even in this case, the proposed approach has benefits. For a short document, the information containing in it is likely to be insufficient if we only consider words in it alone. In this case, LSI can find complementary information for short documents [29, 34] because they consider all words in the whole corpus. Relationships among words can help short documents to complement their information.

Actually, the document decomposition idea is very general. Any dimension reduction approach, if only it can find the most significant residual words explicitly, can be adopted to implement the idea, e.g. the LSI approach presented above. However, we recommend to implement it by a probabilistic topic model in this paper. Although the computations in the topic model looks much more complex than

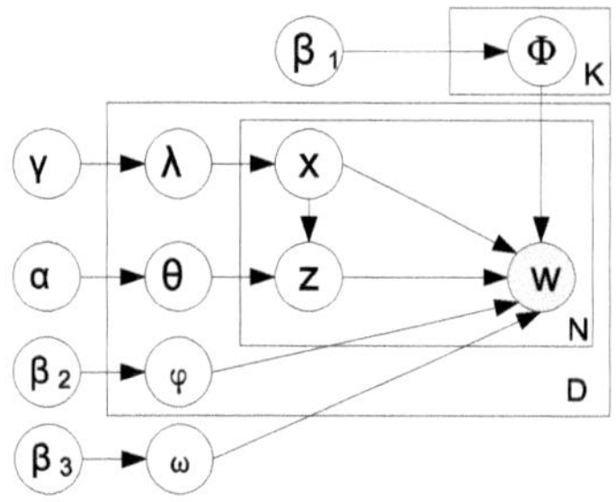

Figure 2: A graphical representation of document decomposition model (DDM).

matrix factorization-based approaches, it can help us better understand the proposed solution[2]. Indeed, the two approaches are equivalent. [15] proved the equivalence of pLSI [19] and non-negative matrix factorization [21].

3.2 A Graphical Model Implementation

A topic model often describes a generative process of a document [5, 19]. It assumes that words of a document are drawn from a set of topic distributions. Document decomposition model (DDM) [10], as shown in Figure 2, is an extension of LDA [5], which is first proposed to model different aspects of a document. The DDM model assumes a document is generated by this process:

1. Draw $\lambda \sim Dirichlet(\gamma)$
2. Draw $\varphi \sim Dirichlet(\beta_2)$
3. Draw $\theta \sim Dirichlet(\alpha)$
4. For each word of the document
   (a) Draw a $x \sim Mult(\lambda)$
   (b) if $x = 1$, draw $z \sim Mult(\theta)$, and then draw a word $w \sim Mult(\phi_z)$
   (c) if $x = 2$, draw a word $w \sim Mult(\varphi)$
   (d) if $x = 3$, draw a word $w \sim Mult(\omega)$

where $Mult$ stands for a multinomial distribution. The key idea of DDM is to use a switch variable x to control the generation of words. x takes value 1, 2 or 3, which controls a word is drawn from either a topic distribution (z and ϕ_z), a document specific distribution (φ), or a corpus background distribution (ω). It provides a nature way to partition a document into three parts of words. Intuitively, a word which widely appears in all documents is likely to be a background/stop word; a word which only appears in a few documents but seldom appears in other documents is likely to be a document specific word; a word which widely appears in documents with a common semantic but seldom appears in other documents without this semantic is likely to be a topic related word. It is interesting to note that document specific words are likely to have the largest TF-IDF values in a document.

From the aspect of matrix factorization, the work of DDM can be understood as simultaneously finding a group of basis vectors ($\phi_{1:K}$, a set of distributions over vocabulary), and coefficients (θ, topic mixture proportion). The conditional probability of a word given a document is computed by

$$p(w|d) = \sum_z p(w|z)p(z|x=1,d)p(x=1|d) \\ + p(w|x=2,d)p(x=2|d) + p(w|x=3,d)p(x=3|d)$$

Thus, the decomposition can be shown in a matrix factorization manner

$$d = \begin{bmatrix} \cdot & \cdot & \cdot \\ \cdot & \phi_{ij} & \cdot \\ \cdot & \cdot & \cdot \end{bmatrix} \begin{bmatrix} \cdot \\ \theta_d \gamma_{d1} \\ \cdot \end{bmatrix} + \begin{bmatrix} \cdot \\ \varphi_d \\ \cdot \end{bmatrix} \gamma_{d2} + \begin{bmatrix} \cdot \\ \omega \\ \cdot \end{bmatrix} \gamma_{d3}$$

This decomposition has the same format as Eq. 1.

3.2.1 Parameter Estimation

To estimate parameters of a graphical model, Expectation Maximization (EM) algorithm is often adopted [19, 5]. However, in DDM, direct optimization to model parameters by EM algorithm is intractable [5, 10]. We adopt Monte Carlo EM [2] instead. In E step, rather than analytically compute the posterior of hidden variables, we draw samples from their posterior distributions. In M-step, we approximate the expectation by a finite sum over samples and maximize the expectation with respect to model parameters. Instead of uisng a full Markov Chain Monte Carlo (MCMC) approach [2], a collapsed Gibbs sampling approach is used to draw samples from posterior [17]. Considering the conditional independencies between variables, we only need to sample hidden variables x and z, while integrate out other hidden variables. The Gibbs sampling equations are easy to obtain

$$p(x_i = 1, z = k|x_{-i}, z_{-i}, w, \Theta) = \\ \frac{\gamma_1 + n^{1,\cdot}_{d,-i}}{\sum_{j=1}^{3} \gamma_j + n^{j,\cdot}_{d,-i}} \times \frac{\alpha_k + n^{1,k}_{d,-i}}{\sum_{j=1}^{K} \alpha_j + n^{1,j}_{d,-i}} \times \frac{\beta_{1,w_i} + n^{1,k}_{-i,w_i}}{\sum_{j=1}^{W} \beta_{1,j} + n^{1,k}_{-i,j}}$$

$$p(x_i = 2|x_{-i}, z_{-i}, w, \Theta) = \frac{\gamma_2 + n^{2,\cdot}_{d,-i}}{\sum_{j=1}^{3} \gamma_j + n^{j,\cdot}_{d,-i}} \times \frac{\beta_{2,w_i} + n^{2,w_i}_{d,-i}}{\sum_{j=1}^{W} \beta_{2,j} + n^{2,\cdot}_{d,-i}}$$

$$p(x_i = 3|x_{-i}, z_{-i}, w, \Theta) = \frac{\gamma_3 + n^{3,\cdot}_{d,-i}}{\sum_{j=1}^{3} \gamma_j + n^{j,\cdot}_{d,-i}} \times \frac{\beta_{3,w_i} + n^{3,w_i}_{\cdot,-i}}{\sum_{j=1}^{W} \beta_{3,j} + n^{3,j}_{\cdot,-i}}$$

where Θ denotes all hyper parameters, i.e. $\alpha, \gamma, \beta_{1,2,3}$, $-i$ means all words except for the current word w_i, $n^{j,k}_{d,-i}$ denotes the number of words generated when $x = j$ and $z = k$ in document d, $n^{j,w_i}_{d,-i}$ denotes the number of times of word w_i generated when $x = j$ in document d, and $n^{1,k}_{-i,w_i}$ denotes the number of times of word w_i assigned to $z = k$. To update hyper-parameters in M step, we adopt the fix-point iteration algorithm proposed in [28].

3.2.2 Inference for Unseen Documents

In practice, we only can learn a model with a small proportion of documents of a large corpus, and then apply it to infer hidden variables of remainder documents. For a retrieval system, we also need to infer latent variables of a query document. For DDM, the inference algorithm is similar as the estimation algorithm. However, model parameters will be fixed to be those obtained in model estimation step. The Gibbs sampling equations are

$$p(x_i = 1, z = k|x_{-i}, z_{-i}, w, \Theta) = \\ \frac{\gamma_1 + n^{1,\cdot}_{d,-i}}{\sum_{j=1}^{3} \gamma_j + n^{j,\cdot}_{d,-i}} \times \frac{\alpha_k + n^{1,k}_{d,-i}}{\sum_{j=1}^{K} \alpha_j + n^{1,j}_{d,-i}} \times \phi_{k,w_i}$$

$$p(x_i = 2|x_{-i}, z_{-i}, w, \Theta) = \frac{\gamma_2 + n^{2,\cdot}_{d,-i}}{\sum_{j=1}^{3} \gamma_j + n^{j,\cdot}_{d,-i}} \times \frac{\beta_{2,w_i} + n^{2,w_i}_{d,-i}}{\sum_{j=1}^{W} \beta_{2,j} + n^{2,\cdot}_{d,-i}}$$

$$p(x_i = 3|x_{-i}, z_{-i}, w, \Theta) = \frac{\gamma_3 + n^{3,\cdot}_{d,-i}}{\sum_{j=1}^{3} \gamma_j + n^{j,\cdot}_{d,-i}} \times \omega_{w_i}$$

[2]The computational cost of the two approaches are almost the same.

It is remarkable that the inferences of latent variables of different documents are independent to each other. From above equations, we can easily verify this fact. Only statistics inside a document take part in the computation of Gibbs sampling, that is, we can distribute documents to different processors and parallel decompose them. Thus, the scalability of DDM is not an issue.

Once we have inferred latent variables of a document, we can easily get its decomposition results. θ is the compact vector as the vector obtained in the LSI-based approach. To find out document specific words of a document, we compute this conditional probability

$$p(x_i = 2|w_i, d) = \frac{p(w_i|x_i = 2, d)p(x_i = 2|d)}{p(w_i|d)} \propto \frac{\varphi_{d,w_i}}{p(w_i|d)}$$

To reduce computation, we approximate the posterior by φ_{d,w_i}. With this probability, we can control the number of document specific words to be an acceptable value, e.g. 15 in our experiments. An advantage of DDM beyond matrix factorization-based approaches is that it can explicitly decompose words of a document to be three categories. This is very helpful when we analyze experimental results.

3.3 Other Implementations

So far we have proposed two mathematically solid approaches to implement the document decomposition idea, but actually we can implement it by many heuristic ways. The only requirement to an approach is that it must be able to get a compound representation of a document like in Eq. 3. We give some examples which will be compared in our experiments.

Under the framework of **topic models**, we need to construct a set of topics($\phi_{1:K}$ of DDM), and then run the inference algorithm of DDM to decompose documents. For this purpose, we can obtain topics by many existing approaches, such as LDA [5] and pLSI [19]. A heuristic but very practicable method is to get topic vectors from web pages of ODP by counting word frequencies in documents of each category. An ODP category may be mapped to a topic or a few topics. These topic vectors are likely to be more reasonable than those got by purely unsupervised models.

Under the framework of **matrix factorization**, we can perform the factorization in many methods, e.g. LSI [13] and NMF [21]. If only we can get a decomposition like Eq. 1, we can extract the co-efficient w as a representation of topic related words and keep the top N largest entries of ϵ as document specific words.

4. INDEXING AND RANKING

We have represented both documents in corpus and a query document by vector pairs $<\theta, \varphi>$, in which θ is a compact vector and φ is a few keywords. In this section, we will present indexing and ranking approaches based on this compound representation.

4.1 Ranking Function

The similarity of two documents is computed by a linear combination of the two components:

$$sim(d, q) = \gamma_{d1}\gamma_{q1} sim(\theta_d, \theta_q) + \gamma_{d2}\gamma_{q2} sim(\varphi_d, \varphi_q) \quad (4)$$

where $\gamma_{.1}$ and $\gamma_{.2}$ mean the word ratios of topic related words and document specific words in a document respectively. They can be got by the inference algorithm. In experiments, we compute $sim(\theta_d, \theta_q)$ and $sim(\varphi_d, \varphi_q)$ by inner products. This simple ranking function does not introduce additional parameters.

If we keep all words in φ (φ is equivalent to the full residual ϵ in Eq. 2), this similarity measure exactly recovers the Eq. 2. Thus, this ranking approach is named as "accurate ranking" in this paper. It defines the upper-bound of retrieval accuracy of the compound representations. In following sections, we will develop an index-based approximation to it, which is required to be as accurate as it but with much lower computational and memory cost.

Similar as Eq. 4, [34] linearly combines probabilities obtained by a traditional language model and a topic model, which achieved best performance in lots of short query retrieval tasks. Without changing its meanings, its ranking function can be rewritten as

$$p(q|d) = \lambda \sum_{w \in q} p(w|d) + (1 - \lambda) \sum_{w \in q} \sum_{z} p(w|z)p(z|d) \quad (5)$$

where z denotes a topic in a LDA model and λ is a coefficient to balance the two terms. By simple derivation, we can prove this function is equivalent to Eq. 4 when the probability $p(w|q) = 1/|q|$ and $p(z|q) = 1/K$. That is, it assumes that the conditional probabilities of different words/topics given the query q are equal. This assumption is reasonable for a short query because we do not have enough information to infer hidden variables only with a few terms. However, for a real document query, we have enough information to infer hidden variables to extract more knowledge from it. Thus, our work can be deemed as an extension of [34] to dealing with long document queries.

4.2 Indexing Scheme

By fully considering the characteristics of the new representations of documents, we designed an efficient indexing structure as shown in Figure 3. We build two separate indices for topic related words (the compact vector θ) and document specific words (φ). The two index are used to approximately compute the similarity given in Eq. 4.

Indexing topic related words. Because topic related words of a document are represented by a compact and dense vector, which is an appropriate data style for LSH, we choose LSH [1] to index them. Previous research [20] and our experiments demonstrated the LSH algorithm is good at indexing compact and dense feature vectors but not good at indexing high-dimensional sparse feature vectors, like TF-IDF features of documents. LSH algorithm will assign a group of hash values to a document. These hash values can be deemed as a new discrete representation of a document. We further adopt inverted list to index them to enable fast similarity computing [20]. Therefore, the memory cost of LSH index is only $L \times D$, where L (e.g. 30 in our experiments) is the number of hash functions of LSH.

Indexing document specific words. Because we can select the most salient document specific words according to the conditional probability $p(x_i = 2|w_i, d)$, we can control the number of document specific words. In experiments, we achieved good retrieval accuracy with only 15 document specific words. Thus, we adopt a simple structure to organize document specific words, i.e. forward list. In the forward list, each entry is a pair <*word id*, *weight*>, in which *weight* is φ_w. Therefore, the memory cost of the forward list index is only $15 \times D$, where D is the number of documents.

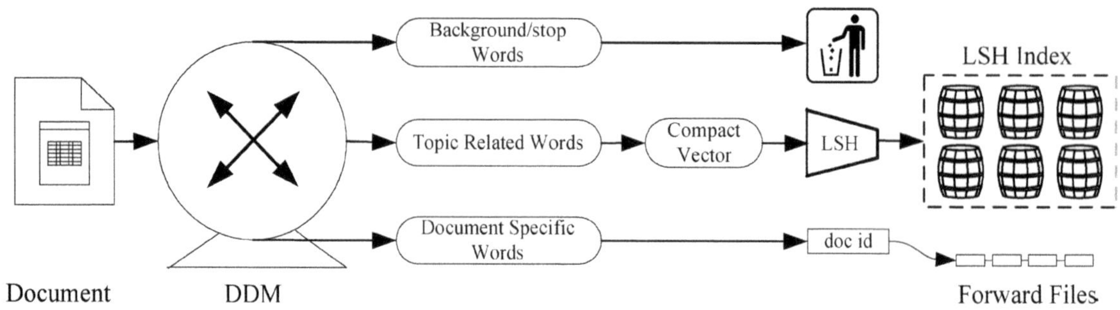

Figure 3: A workflow of our index scheme. The "X" in the centrifuge module motivates the code name of this project, DocX. A centrifuge machine uses centrifugal force for separating substances of different densities, for removing moisture, or for simulating gravitational effects.

4.3 Two-Level Ranking Approach

The functionalities of the two components of the compound representations imply an efficient two-level ranking approach. The similarity $sim(\theta_d, \theta_q)$ distinguish documents belonging to different categories, while $sim(\varphi_d, \varphi_q)$ only is a complement of the first similarity which can further distinguish documents belonging to the same category. Thus, the first similarity is a major component, and the second similarity is a minor component. This observation naturally motivated a two-level ranking approach. In the first stage, we use $sim(\theta_d, \theta_q)$ to select the top k most similar documents as a candidate set. Because we index θ by LSH, we can get a set of related documents much more quickly than a linear scan approach. In the second stage, we use $sim(\varphi_d, \varphi_q)$ to rerank documents in this set. Actually, multiple-level ranking approaches are very popular in IR systems [7].

In our experiments, we set the size of candidate set to 50. The time complexity to respond a query is $30 \times \#collision + 15 \times 50$, where $\#collision$ is the average number of documents in the same bucket in inverted index of LSH. In LSH, $\#collision$ only slightly changes with the increasing of the numbers of documents it indexes [1]. Thus, the solution can answer a query almost in constant time, which is independent to the number of documents the system indexes.

It is noted that, by this index and ranking approach, we only can get an approximate results as the accurate ranking(Eq. 4) because: i) LSH is an approximate nearest-neighbor algorithm; ii) only a few most salient document specific words are kept in index. Although it is an approximate algorithm, its retrieval accuracy is almost as good as the linear ranking in our experiments. The small sacrifice of accuracy significantly shortens the response time and reduces memory cost.

4.4 Scalability

To the best of our knowledge, there are no widely acknowledged criterions on what is a scalable indexing solution. However, the following aspects must be useful when checking the scalability of an indexing solution.

Parallelizable. It implies the indexing of documents must be independent, and its ranking function only uses features within a document and some simple global statistics (e.g. PageRank [6]).

Efficient. The time to building index (e.g. in a few hours) and responding users' queries (e.g. in a few milliseconds) must be acceptable.

Large Capability. Single machine can index several million documents (e.g. Google indexed 5 million pages by one machine in 2003 [4]).

It is easy to check that our indexing and ranking solution can meet these requirements. In our experiments, it takes about 8 hours to decompose 5 million documents and build index by one 3G CPU. The index size of 5 million pages is about 3.5GB (including LSH index, forward files and necessary metadata of documents). The average time to answer a query is about 13ms if the top 50 results are returned. Thus, theoretically, the proposed solution can index any number of documents and provide realtime search service.

5. EXPERIMENTS

We now present the experiment evaluation of our approach. Section 5.1 and Section 5.2 introduce the utilized data sets and the related experiment setup respectively. Section 5.3 evaluates performance of decomposition based approaches, and Section 5.4 evaluates performance of the indexing solution. At last, the scalability issues are discussed in the Section 5.5 to show the efficiency of our approach.

5.1 Data sets

We evaluated the proposed approaches on four datasets shown in Table 1: 20 newsgroups (20NG), Wikipedia pages (Wiki), a randomly selected subset of Wikipedia (SWiki) and a web corpus with 5 million pages (5M) which was randomly sampled from the web TREC'08 corpus. In 20NG, documents belonging to the same category are labeled as relevant documents. Wikipedia organizes documents in a tree structure. If two leaf nodes, i.e. documents, have the same parent or are linked by a "see also" hyperlink, they are labeled as similar documents. SWiki dataset is used to investigate the affection of corpus size to our approaches. For the 5M dataset, we do not have ground truth. The purpose of collecting this dataset is to evaluate scalability of our approaches. In the preprocessing, we performed Porter's stemming and removed words whose document frequencies (DF) are less than 4.

5.2 Experimental Setup

We implemented four baseline approaches: TF-IDF with *cosine* similarity (TFIDF) [3], directly indexing TF-IDF vectors by LSH (LSH) [1], similarity computed only by top N TF-IDF words(TopN) [35], and linearly combining similarity computed by top N TF-IDF words and similarity

Table 1: Details of the four dataset

Dataset	#Train	#Test	#Terms
20NG	11,314	7,532	54,071
Wiki	60,000	1.44 Million	113,748
SWiki	20,000	88,204	98,046
5M	100,000	5 Million	163,871

got by topic mixtures obtained by LDA (TopNLDA) [34]. TopNLDA is one of the state-of-the-art algorithms for web search and also an instantiation of the proposed document decomposition idea. To simplify the notation, we refer to document specific words as DS, and topic related words as TS. We refer to Eq. 4 as DDM, and our index scheme as DDM+Index. We randomly sampled 200 documents from each dataset as queries. In the following experiments, we will adopt the macro-average precision of the top 10 search results for the 200 queries to measure algorithms' performance, which is computed by:

$$\text{Pr}@10 = \frac{1}{N}\sum_{i=1}^{N}\frac{T_i}{10}$$

where N is the number of queries and T_i is the number of related documents in the top 10 search results for the *ith* query.

Our experimental goals include three-fold: 1) performance of the DDM and some practical implementations (rank by Eq. 4); 2) the drop of performance of the index and ranking solution; 3) scalability of the solution.

5.3 Performance of Decomposition-Based Approaches

In this section, we evaluate the best performance that decomposition-based approaches can obtain, which is achieved by Eq. 4.

5.3.1 Results with Different Number of Topics

A common concern about a topic model based algorithm is that the number of topics may significantly affect its performance. How to determine the number of topics is still an open problem. Thus, we run a group of experiments to investigate the effects of topic numbers. In these experiments, we fixed the number of DS words to 15. The results on the three dataset are shown in Figure 4.

The decomposition based approaches significantly outperformed baseline approaches. On the three dataset, the LSH approach almost consistently got the worst results. This fact indicates that LSH is not a good approach to index high-dimensional sparse feature vectors. The accuracy of TS only approach increases with the number of topics, while the accuracy of DS only approach drops. Because in this process more and more DS words will be absorbed into topics, the TS is becoming more and more powerful, while the DS is becoming weaker and weaker. In extreme cases, both DS and TS only approaches degenerate to the TF-IDF approach.

Intuitively, the best results of an approach on the three dataset will be obtained under very different number of topics because the complexities of them are very different. However, we found all their best results were achieved when topic numbers are around 250. The result may be explained by the way we obtain TS and DS words. There are no criterions to define what is a TS word but not a DS word and vice versa. If we increase the number of topics in DDM, some words which previously are classified as DS words will be re-labeled as TS words, and vice versa. Thus, for a dataset, if it can be well represented by the latent space, DS words could be very discriminative or rare words which represent minor semantics of documents, otherwise, DS words will be more like TS words which represent major semantics of documents. Thus, the proposed decomposition-based approaches are not sensitive to dataset or number of topics.

All approaches based on the document decomposition idea outperform the baseline approaches. As we have mentioned, words with largest TF-IDF values are likely to be DS words. However, the TopNLDA got worse accuracy than decomposition based approaches. It is probably because the top N TF-IDF words may be redundant to the topics obtained by LDA, while DDM can decompose a document to two sets of words which are complementary to each other. Moreover, the accuracy of ODP+DS, is close to DDM. This fact further demonstrates the power of the document decomposition idea. Because curves for the two other DDM-based approaches (LDA+DS and LSI+DS) almost overlapped with ODP+DS and DDM, we did not draw them in this figure.

5.3.2 Results with Different Number of DS Words

Theoretically, the number of DS words should be different for different kinds of documents. For example, Wikipedia documents usually are long documents with complex semantics, while documents of 20NG usually are short and simple documents. Thus, DS words for Wikipedia documents should be more than 20NG. However, after we performed experiments we got different answers which are shown in Figure 5. By setting the number of topics to be 250 and the number of DS words to be 15, almost all approaches significantly outperformed baseline approaches. Even when we set the number of DS words to be 5, their performances are better than TopN. The accuracies of TopNLDA is worse than DDM based approaches again. This result could be explained by the reason we discussed in last section. It again demonstrates that DS words are more meaningful than top N TF-IDF words in this ranking framework. Thus, we conclude that 250 topics and 15 DS words are an appropriate setting for a QBD problem.

5.4 Performance of the Indexing Solution

In this section, we evaluate performance of the index solution.

5.4.1 Results with Different Number of Topics

We built index for documents according to the proposed indexing scheme and adopted the two-level ranking approach to rank documents. Because we only evaluate the precision of the top 10 search results, we set the size of candidate set to be 50 in the LSH retrieval step. LSH index has two parameters, i.e. L and k. L is the number of hash functions, which is set to 30; k is the length of hash code, which is set to 6. The results are shown in Figure 6. For all index-based approaches, their curves are only slightly lower than corresponding accurate approaches (the DDM curve). We assert that the two approaches, i.e. DDM and DDM+index, are statistically the same. We run t-test to evaluate this hypothesis. With 99.5% confidence, the hypothesis is true. Therefore, we conclude that the indexing solution is a good approximation to the accurate approaches.

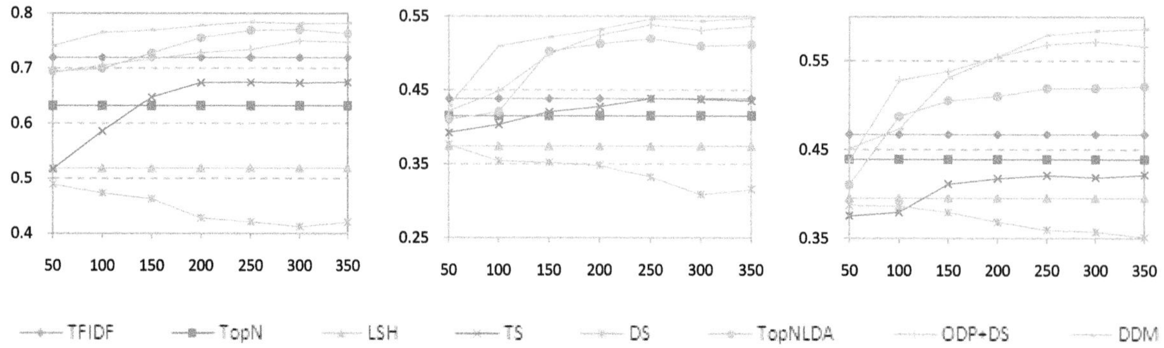

Figure 4: Macro-average Pr@10 change with the number of topics on 20NG, Wiki, and SWiki. TS means that only topic mixtures are used to compute document similarity, DS means that only DS words are used to perform retrieval, and ODP means that topics are got by counting ODP pages.

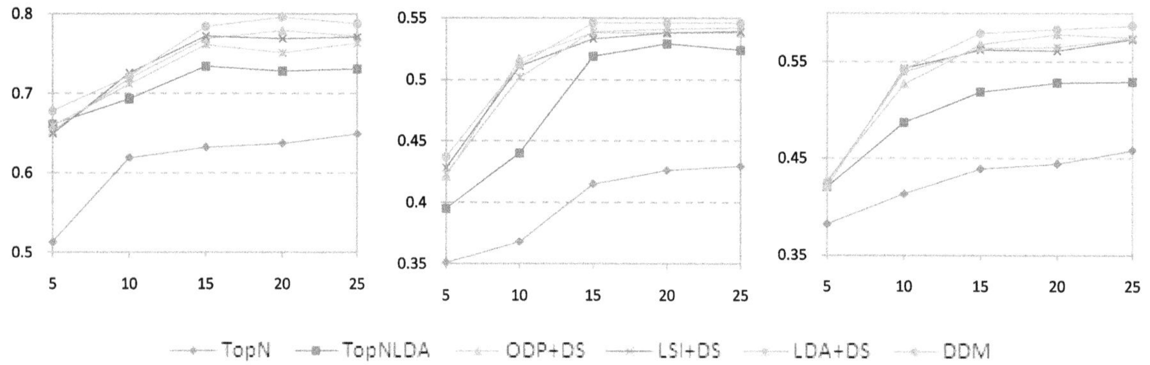

Figure 5: Macro-average Pr@10 change with the number of document specific words on 20NG, Wiki, and SWiki. LSI and LDA mean that topics are obtained by LSI decomposition (3000 documents were used to perform LSI decomposition) and LDA model, respectively

5.4.2 Results with Different Number of DS Words

Figure 7 shows the results with different number of DS words. Curves of DDM and DDM+index almost overlap together at all points. When the number of DS words is bigger than 10, the accuracies of all our approaches are very close. These results further demonstrate that the index solution is a good approximation to the accurate approach.

Combining results of these experiments, we can conclude: 1) DDM outperform other baseline approaches; 2) accuracies of the proposed practical approaches (e.g. ODP+DS) are only slightly worse than DDM; 3) The drop of accuracy of the index solution is acceptable.

5.5 Scalability Issues

The efficiency of a retrieval system could be measured from two-fold, i.e. time and memory cost to build index and answer a query. In our system, a standard index machine is a workstation with a dual-core CPU and 4G bytes RAM, by which we plan to index around 5 million web pages and provide realtime search service. Thus, we mainly measure cost of our approaches under this hardware setting.

5.5.1 Cost of building index

In our system, building index consists of three steps: train a model by a set of documents, infer the left documents and build index as the proposed indexing scheme. The model training is very time-consuming on a large corpus with huge lexicon. It took us about 50 hours to train a model with 100,000 documents (its vocabulary consists of 163,871 terms). Fortunately, we can get the model done once and for ever. The inference time of the three dataset are listed in Table 2. The time for long documents (e.g. Wiki) are slightly longer than short documents (e.g. 20NG). The time per document on all dataset is no longer than 4.5ms. As we have mentioned, the inference could be performed parallel. By a dual-core computer, it takes around 3.2 hours to infer 5 million documents. After we get inferring results, index can be built in around 70 minutes.

Table 2: Inference time for three dataset (#topics=250)

Dataset	#Docs	#Terms	Avg. Time(ms)
20NG	7,532	54,071	3.53
Wiki	1.44 Million	113,748	4.38
5M Pages	5 Million	163,871	4.213

In a real system, index should be able to be loaded in memory to enable fast search [6, 4]. The LSH index size of the 5M (#topics=250, LSH parameters L=30 and k=6 [1, 20]) is around 2.1GB. We use a <*word id*, *weight*> pair to represent a document specific word in the forward files. The size of forward files and lexicon of the 5M is around 800MB. Thus, all index data can be loaded in memory.

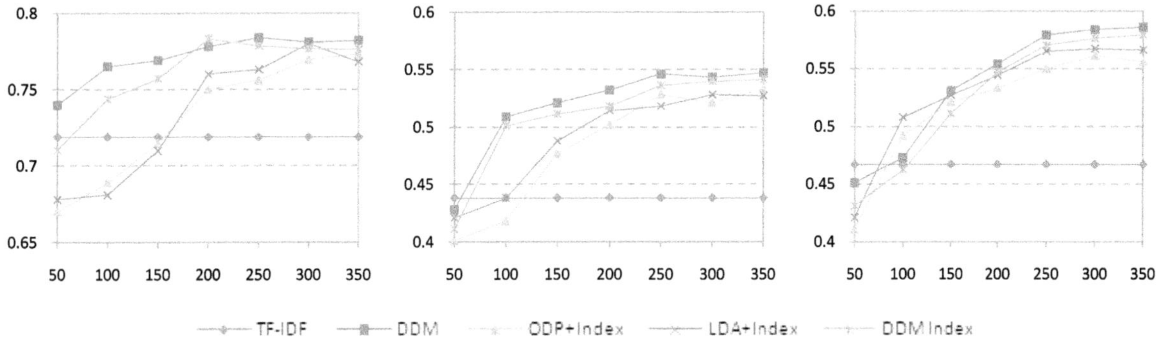

Figure 6: Macro-average Pr@10 of index scheme change with the number of topics on 20NG, Wiki, and SWiki

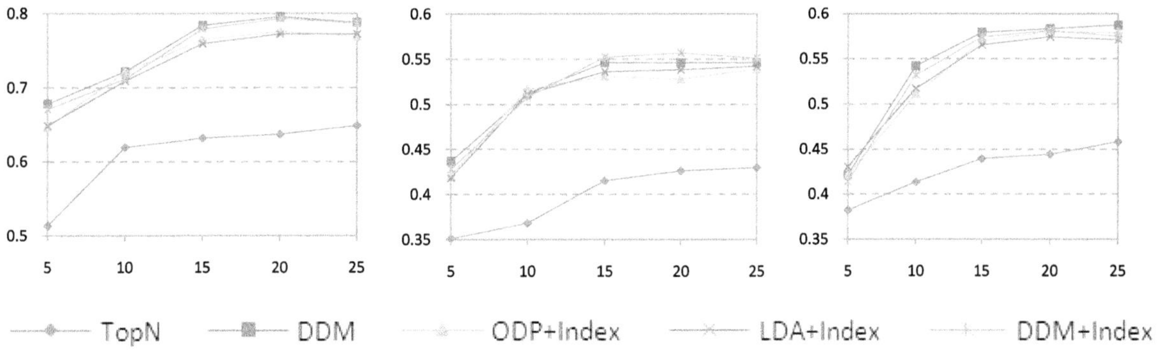

Figure 7: Macro-average Pr@10 of index scheme change with the number of document specific words on 20NG, Wiki, and SWiki

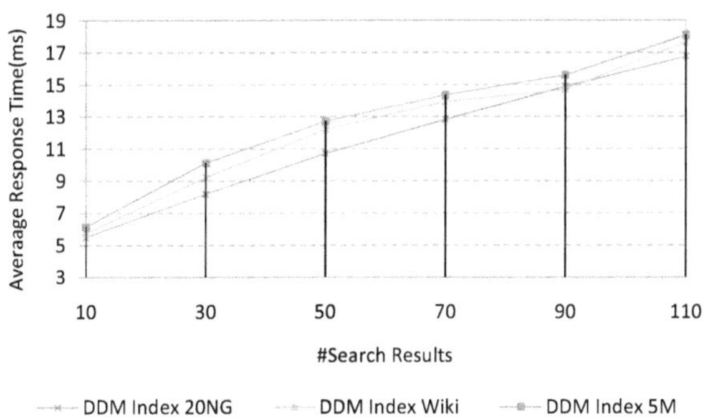

Figure 8: Response time under different size of index

5.5.2 *Time to answer a query*

The average response time as a function of number of returned search results is shown in Figure 8. The response time includes the time to inferring a query document, i.e. about 4ms, and the time for ranking. The response time is almost a constant time, which almost does not increase with the number of documents that the system indexes. If we run accurate ranking algorithm on the 5M pages dataset, the time to answer a query is around 25s. The proposed index solution can accelerate the search speed 100-1000 times, while its results are almost as accurate as the "accurate" ranking approach (Eq. 4). Our system is able to answer more than 20 queries per second.

6. CONCLUSION

We have proposed a solution for large-scale query by document (QBD) application, which essentially is a fast approach to compute nearest neighbors in a high-dimensional sparse feature space. Our theoretic analysis and experimental results demonstrate:

1) The document decomposition idea can solve problems caused by long document queries. Based on this idea, we can represent a document to be a compact vector as well as a few keywords. Retrieval results based on the new representation are better than full text linear scan approach.

2) The indexing and two-level ranking solution significantly reduces both computation and memory cost of the system, while it can provide search results as accurate as the accurate ranking algorithm (Eq. 4). The whole indexing solution is a good trade-off among accuracy, cost and performance.

3) The solution has the same architecture as web search engines. Thus, it can be applied to index large-scale text corpus to support QBD-based applications.

7. REFERENCES

[1] A. Andoni and P. Indyk. Near-optimal hashing algorithms for approximate nearest neighbor in high dimensions. *Commun. ACM*, 51(1):117–122, 2008.

[2] C. Andrieu, N. de Freitas, A. Doucet, and M. I. Jordan. An introduction to mcmc for machine learning. *Machine Learning*, 50(1-2):5–43, 2003.

[3] R. A. Baeza-Yates and B. A. Ribeiro-Neto. *Modern Information Retrieval*. Addison-Wesley, 1999.

[4] L. A. Barroso, J. Dean, and U. Hölzle. Web search for a planet: The google cluster architecture. *IEEE Micro*, 23(2):22–28, 2003.

[5] D. M. Blei, A. Y. Ng, and M. I. Jordan. Latent dirichlet allocation. *JMLR*, 2003.

[6] S. Brin and L. Page. The anatomy of a large-scale hypertextual web search engine. *Computer Networks*, 30(1-7):107–117, 1998.

[7] A. Z. Broder, D. Carmel, M. Herscovici, A. Soffer, and J. Zien. Efficient query evaluation using a two-level retrieval process. In *CIKM*, 2003.

[8] A. Z. Broder, S. C. Glassman, M. S. Manasse, and G. Zweig. Syntactic clustering of the web. *Comput. Netw. ISDN Syst.*, 29(8-13):1157–1166, 1997.

[9] M. S. Charikar. Similarity estimation techniques from rounding algorithms. In *STOC*, pages 380–388, 2002.

[10] C. Chemudugunta, P. Smyth, and M. Steyvers. Modeling general and specific aspects of documents with a probabilistic topic model. In *NIPS*, 2006.

[11] J. Cho, N. Shivakumar, and H. Garcia-Molina. Finding replicated web collections. *SIGMOD Rec.*, 29(2):355–366, 2000.

[12] A. Chowdhury, O. Frieder, D. Grossman, and M. C. McCabe. Collection statistics for fast duplicate document detection. *ACM Trans. Inf. Syst.*, 20(2):171–191, 2002.

[13] S. C. Deerwester, S. T. Dumais, T. K. Landauer, G. W. Furnas, and R. A. Harshman. Indexing by latent semantic analysis. *JASIS*, 41(6):391–407, 1990.

[14] F. Deng and D. Rafiei. Approximately detecting duplicates for streaming data using stable bloom filters. In *SIGMOD '06*, pages 25–36, New York, NY, USA, 2006. ACM.

[15] C. H. Q. Ding, T. Li, and W. Peng. Nonnegative matrix factorization and probabilistic latent semantic indexing: Equivalence chi-square statistic, and a hybrid method. In *AAAI*, 2006.

[16] K. T. Frantzi. Incorporating context information for the extraction of terms. In *ACL'97*, pages 501–503, Morristown, NJ, USA, 1997. Association for Computational Linguistics.

[17] T. L. Griffiths and M. Steyvers. Finding scientific topics. *Proc Natl Acad Sci U S A*, April 2004.

[18] M. R. Henzinger. Finding near-duplicate web pages: a large-scale evaluation of algorithms. In *SIGIR*, 2006.

[19] T. Hofmann. Probabilistic latent semantic indexing. In *SIGIR*, pages 50–57, 1999.

[20] P. Indyk and N. Thaper. Fast image retrieval via embeddings. In *International Workshop on Statistical and Computational Theories of Vision*, 2003.

[21] D. D. Lee and H. S. Seung. Algorithms for non-negative matrix factorization. In *NIPS*, 2000.

[22] T. Liu, A. W. Moore, and A. G. Gray. New algorithms for efficient high-dimensional nonparametric classification. *Journal of Machine Learning Research*, 7:1135–1158, 2006.

[23] X. Liu and W. B. Croft. Cluster-based retrieval using language models. In *SIGIR '04*, pages 186–193, New York, NY, USA, 2004. ACM.

[24] D. P. Lopresti. Models and algorithms for duplicate document detection. In *ICDAR '99*, page 297, Washington, DC, USA, 1999. IEEE Computer Society.

[25] C. D. Manning and H. Schutze. *Foundations of Statistical Natural Language Processing*. The MIT Press, June 1999.

[26] O. Medelyan and I. H. Witten. Thesaurus based automatic keyphrase indexing. In *JCDL '06*, pages 296–297, New York, NY, USA, 2006. ACM.

[27] K. Min, Z. Zhang, J. Wright, and Y. Ma. Decomposing background topics from keywords by principal component pursuit. In *Proceedings of the 19th ACM international conference on Information and knowledge management*, CIKM '10, pages 269–278, New York, NY, USA, 2010. ACM.

[28] T. P. Minka. Estimating a dirichlet distribution. Technical report, Microsoft, 2000.

[29] X. H. Phan, M. L. Nguyen, and S. Horiguchi. Learning to classify short and sparse text & web with hidden topics from large-scale data collections. In *WWW*, 2008.

[30] B. Sarwar, G. Karypis, J. Konstan, and J. Reidl. Item-based collaborative filtering recommendation algorithms. In *WWW'01*, 2001.

[31] T. Tomokiyo and M. Hurst. A language model approach to keyphrase extraction. In *Proceedings of the ACL 2003 workshop on Multiword expressions*, pages 33–40, Morristown, NJ, USA, 2003. Association for Computational Linguistics.

[32] P. D. Turney. Learning algorithms for keyphrase extraction. *Inf. Retr.*, 2(4):303–336, 2000.

[33] O. Vechtomova and M. Karamuftuoglu. Approaches to high accuracy retrieval: Phrase-based search experiments in the hard track. In *TREC*, 2004.

[34] X. Wei and W. B. Croft. Lda-based document models for ad-hoc retrieval. In *SIGIR*, pages 178–185, 2006.

[35] Y. Yang, N. Bansal, W. Dakka, P. Ipeirotis, N. Koudas, and D. Papadias. Query by document. In *WSDM'09*, 2009.

[36] C. Zhai and J. D. Lafferty. Model-based feedback in the language modeling approach to information retrieval. In *CIKM*, pages 403–410, 2001.

[37] Y. Zhang, J. P. Callan, and T. P. Minka. Novelty and redundancy detection in adaptive filtering. In *SIGIR*, pages 81–88, 2002.

[38] Y. Zhang, W. Xu, and J. Callan. Exact maximum likelihood estimation for word mixtures. In *In Text Learning Workshop in ICML'02*, 2002.

[39] J. Zobel and A. Moffat. Inverted files for text search engines. *ACM Comput. Surv.*, 38(2):6, 2006.

Integrating Hierarchical Feature Selection and Classifier Training for Multi-Label Image Annotation

Cheng Jin
School of Computer Science
Fudan University, P. R. China
jc@fudan.edu.cn

Chunlei Yang
Dept of Computer Science
UNC-Charlotte, NC, USA
cyang36@uncc.edu

ABSTRACT

It is well accepted that using high-dimensional multi-modal visual features for image content representation and classifier training may achieve more sufficient characterization of the diverse visual properties of the images and further result in higher discrimination power of the classifiers. However, training the classifiers in a high-dimensional multi-modal feature space requires a large number of labeled training images, which will further result in the problem of *curse of dimensionality*. To tackle this problem, a hierarchical feature subset selection algorithm is proposed to enable more accurate image classification, where the processes for feature selection and classifier training are seamlessly integrated in a single framework. First, a feature hierarchy (i.e., concept tree for automatic feature space partition and organization) is used to automatically partition high-dimensional *heterogeneous* multi-modal visual features into multiple low-dimensional *homogeneous single-modal feature subsets* according to their certain physical meanings and each of them is used to characterize one certain type of the diverse visual properties of the images. Second, principal component analysis (PCA) is performed on each homogeneous single-modal feature subset to select the most representative feature dimensions and a weak classifier is learned simultaneously. After the weak classifiers and their representative feature dimensions are available for all these homogeneous single-modal feature subsets, they are combined to generate an ensemble image classifier and achieve hierarchical feature subset selection. Our experiments on a specific domain of *natural images* have also obtained very positive results.

Categories and Subject Descriptors
I.4.8 [**Image Processing and Computer Vision**]: Scene Analysis-*object recognition*, H.2.8 [**Database Management**]: Database Applications - *image databases.*

General Terms
Algorithms, Measurement, Experimentation

Keywords: Feature hierarchy, SVM image classifier, hierarchical feature selection, boosting.

1. INTRODUCTION

When large-scale image collections come into view, automatic detection of object classes and image concepts may provide more effective solutions for image indexing and retrieval [23, 5, 26, 12]. Image classification is one of the potential solutions for automatic detection of object classes and image concepts from large-scale image collections. Thus achieving more accurate training of the image classifiers plays an important role in supporting multi-label image annotation and semantic image retrieval via keywords [8, 14, 30, 11, 17, 35, 34, 1, 29, 32, 7, 3, 16]. However, the performance of the image classifiers largely depends on two inter-related issues: (1) high-dimensional multi-modal visual features for characterizing the diverse visual properties of the images more sufficiently; (2) effective algorithms for achieving more accurate training of the image classifiers and selecting more representative feature subsets automatically.

Many image classification algorithms have been proposed in the literature [8, 14, 30, 11, 17, 35, 34, 1, 29]. Ideally, using more visual features for image content representation and classifier training has more capacity to characterize various visual properties of the images effectively and efficiently. This may further enhance the classifier's ability on detecting different image concepts and object classes and result in higher classification accuracy. However, learning the image classifiers in a high-dimensional multi-modal feature space requires a large number of labeled training images and generally increases exponentially as the feature dimension increases (i.e., *curse of dimensionality*). When only a limited number of labeled training images are available, there is an urgent need to develop new techniques that are able to achieve accurate training of the image classifiers by using a small number of labeled training images. One promising approach is to select the most representative feature subsets and train the image classifiers simultaneously.

To select the optimal feature subsets for classifier training, many feature selection algorithms have been proposed and they can generally be classified into two categories: *filter* and *wrapper* [33, 18, 13, 28, 20, 24]. A *filter* algorithm separates the procedures for feature selection and classifier training by merely calculating the ranking information for each feature dimension based on its correlation score with the given image concept or object class. On the other hand, a *wrapper* algorithm wraps the procedure for feature selection with the procedure for classifier training. However, both the filter and wrapper approaches ignore the ***feature hierarchy*** and the *heterogeneity* of high-dimensional multi-modal visual features. They perform feature selection directly in the high-dimensional multi-modal feature space and thus they require a large number of labeled training samples to achieve reliable feature selection. Recently, Viola et al. have developed a new feature selection approach by using AdaBoost to train a cascade of linear classifiers [29], which can be treated as a new wrapper-based approach. Each weak classifier depends on only one-dimensional single-modal Harr feature and thus the *correlation* among the multi-modal visual features has been ignored completely.

By incorporating the *feature hierarchy* for automatic feature space partition and organization, our solution is to automatically partition the high-dimensional heterogeneous multi-modal feature space into multiple low-dimensional *homogeneous single-modal feature subsets* according to their certain physical meanings and perform classifier training in each homogeneous single-modal feature subset simultaneously. The **advantages** of our proposed framework include:

(a) Partitioning the high-dimensional heterogeneous multi-modal feature space into multiple low-dimensional homogeneous single-modal feature subsets according to their certain physical meanings can scale up SVM image classifier training significantly because the number of the labeled training images (that are required for classifier training in a low-dimensional homogeneous single-modal feature subset) is reduced dramatically;

(b) Different homogeneous single-modal feature subsets are used to characterize different principal visual properties of the images, thus the corresponding weak classifiers are diverse, complementary and can be combined to generate an ensemble classifier with higher prediction accuracy;

(c) It can support more effective kernel function selection because the geometric property for the distribution of the images in each homogeneous single-modal feature subset can effectively be approximated by using RBF kernel functions;

(d) It can significantly reduce human efforts on labeling large-scale training images by incorporating unlabeled images and feature hierarchy for SVM classifier training, and it is able to boost the image classifiers significantly and result in higher classification accuracy;

(e) It is able to select the most representative feature subsets for different object classes and image concepts and speed up the process for image classification significantly. It also has good scalability with the sizes of the image concepts (object classes) and the feature dimensions.

The major differences between our new approach and the technique proposed in [29] are: (1) feature correlation is exploited to enable more accurate classifier training; (2) ensemble classifier is learned by boosting both the labeled training images and the multi-modal visual features.

This paper is organized as follows: Section 2 introduces our feature extraction framework; Section 3 presents our new framework for joint classifier training and feature selection; Section 4 gives our extensive experimental results on multi-label image annotation; We conclude this paper in Section 5.

2. AUTOMATIC FEATURE EXTRACTION

There are three widely accepted image patterns for image content representation and feature extraction [23]: (a) *region-based approach* by using homogeneous image regions for feature extraction; (b) *scene-based approach* by treating whole image as single visual pattern for feature extraction; (c) *object-based approach* by using image objects for feature extraction.

The major problem for the region-based approach is that there is no accurate correspondence between the image semantics and the homogeneous image regions, and thus the region-based visual features may not be able to detect various image concepts accurately. On the other hand, one single image may consist of multiple object classes, thus the image-based global visual features may not be able to detect the object classes accurately. Using the semantic objects for feature extraction is able to improve the quality of the visual features significantly and result in the image classifiers with higher discrimination power. The major problem for the object-based approach is that automatic object extraction is generally difficult because homogeneous image regions in color or texture do not correspond to the semantic objects directly.

Based on these observations, we believe that it is very important to develop a middle-level framework for achieving semantic-sensitive image content representation, which is able to enhance the quality of the low-level visual features and the discrimination power of the image classifiers. In addition, this middle-level framework should be able to reduce the cost for object extraction and feature extraction. Based on this understanding, we use image Blobs for image content representation and feature extraction. The image blobs are defined as the groups of the neighboring image regions which may have similar color or texture [5].

To detect the image blobs automatically, we use an automatic image segmentation technique that is developed by Deng and Majunanth [6]. The neighboring homogeneous image regions with similar colors or textures are then merged as semantic-sensitive image blobs for image content representation and feature extraction.

After the image blobs are formed, we extract 83-dimensional multi-modal visual features to characterize their multi-modal visual properties of the images. These 83-dimensional heterogeneous multi-modal visual features include: 7-dimensional R,G,B average colors and their variances, 7-dimensional L,U,V average colors and their variances, 62-dimensional texture feature from Gabor filter banks and 7-dimensional Tamura texture. It is worth noting that all these 83-dimensional heterogeneous multi-modal visual features can be organized more effectively by using a ***feature hierarchy***, i.e., multiple homogeneous single-modal feature subsets with certain physical meanings and each feature sunset consists of multiple feature dimensions. To reduce the number of labeled training images that are required for achieving accurate SVM classifier training, all these 83-dimensional *heterogeneous* multi-modal visual features are automatically partitioned into multiple low-dimensional *homogeneous* single-modal feature subsets according to their certain physical meanings. The feature dimensions in the same homogeneous single-modal feature subset share the same physical meaning, and each homogeneous single-modal feature subset is used to characterize one certain type of the diverse visual properties of the images. Obviously, different image concepts and object classes may have different representative feature subsets. Thus it is very important to develop new techniques that are able to select the most representative feature subsets for different image concepts and object classes.

In our experiments, all these 83-dimensional heterogeneous multi-modal feature space are automatically partitioned into ***9*** homogeneous single-modal feature subsets according to their certain physical meanings: 3-dimensional R,G,B average color; 4-dimensional R,G,B color variances; 3-dimensional L,U,V average color; 4-dimensional L,U,V color variances; 2-dimensional average & standard deviation of Gabor filter bank channel energy; 30-dimensional Gabor average channel energy; 30-dimensional Gabor channel energy deviation; 2-dimensional Tamura texture features (coarse & contrast), and 5-dimensional angel histogram derived from Tamura texture. Thus the heterogeneous multi-modal visual features are organized effectively by using two-level *feature hierarchy*: (a) multiple homogeneous single-modal feature subsets with certain physical meanings; (b) multiple visual features for each homogeneous single-modal feature subset that share the same physical meaning.

3. FEATURE SUBSET SELECTION AND CLASSIFIER TRAINING

In order to reduce the number of labeled training images that are required for achieving accurate classifier training, we propose a new framework to enable *hierarchical feature subset selection*, where a weak classifier is learned for each homogeneous single-modal feature subset. Because the dimensions for each homogeneous single-modal feature subset are relatively low, we can use a smaller number of labeled training images to learn the weak classifier accurately. The weak classifiers, which are learned from different homogeneous single-modal feature subsets, are then combined to generate an ensemble classifier for achieving more accurate image classification.

By incorporating the *feature hierarchy* for automatic feature space partition and organization, our lab developed a novel hierarchical algorithm to seamlessly integrate classifier training and hierarchical feature selection in a single framework [11]: (a) The weak classifiers for all these 9 homogeneous single-modal feature subsets are learned simultaneously and principal component analysis (PCA) is used to exploit the feature correlation and select the most representative feature components for each homogeneous single-modal feature subset (i.e., ***in-set feature selection***); (b) The weak classifiers are combined to boost an ensemble classifier, and feature subset selection is achieved by selecting the most effective weak classifiers and the corresponding homogeneous single-modal feature subsets (i.e., ***inter-set feature selection***). Different from [11], which focuses on Grid representation of the feature set, we select features using its self-proved robustness.

Support vector machine (SVM) is used to learn weak classifiers [27, 21, 15, 2], while Adaboost is used to learn the ensemble classifier from combination of weak classifiers [10, 9]. Bagging proposed by Breiman [4] is also a candidate for ensemble classifier learning. Some experiments have shown that AdaBoost sometimes outperforms Bagging. Thus, we use AdaBoost for weak classifier combination.

3.1 Weak Classifier Training

For a given image concept or object class C_j, we use *one-against-all* rule to label the positive training images

Table 1: The optimal parameter pairs $(\bar{C}, \bar{\gamma})$ of the SVM classifiers for some object classes.

object classes	grass	purple flower	red flower
C	10	6	32
$\bar{\gamma}$	1.0	0.5	0.125
object classes	rock	sand field	sky
C	32	8	8192
$\bar{\gamma}$	2	2	0.03125
object classes	snow	water	sunset
C	512	2	8
$\bar{\gamma}$	0.03125	0.5	0.5

$\Omega_{c_j} = \{X_l, Y_l | l = 1, \cdots, N_L\}$ and the negative images. Each labeled training image is represented by (X_l, Y_l), where X_l stands for 83-dimensional blob-based multi-modal visual features , and Y_l, the semantic label. The unlabeled images are denoted as $\overline{Omega}_{c_j}$.

The weak classifier for each homogeneous single-modal feature subset is first learned by using only Ω_{c_j}. For each pairs in Ω_{c_j}, a pair of transformation parameters W and b exists that satisfies $f(X_l) = Y_l(W \cdot \Phi(X_l) + b) \geq +1$, where $\Phi(X_l)$ maps X_l into higher-dimensional space. The kernel function is defined as $\kappa(X_i, X_j) = \Phi(X_i)^T\Phi(X_j)$. The radial basis function (RBF) is selected, $\kappa(X_i, X_j) = exp(-\gamma||X_i - X_j||^2), \gamma > 0$. These two supporting planes have a margin of $2/||W||^2$. The weak SVM classifier is then designed to maximize the margin with the constraints $f(X_l) = Y_l(W \cdot \Phi(X_l) + b) \geq +1$ for the positive images ($Y_l = +1$) and negative ones ($Y_l = -1$).

The margin maximization procedure can be done by the following optimization task with the set of Ω_{c_j}:

$$min \left\{ \frac{1}{2}||W||^2 + C\sum_{l=1}^{N_L} \xi_l \right\} \tag{1}$$

subject to:

$$\forall_{l=1}^{N_L} : Y_l(W \cdot \Phi(X_l) + b) \geq 1 - \xi_l$$

where $\xi_l \geq 0$ is the training error rate, $C > 0$, the penalty parameter and $\frac{1}{2}||W||^2$, the regularization term.

In order to determine the optimal model parameters $(\bar{C}, \bar{\gamma})$ for the weak SVM classifiers, an algorithm was designed as follows: (a) Images in Ω_{c_j} are partitioned into ν groups in equal size, $\nu-1$ groups for classifier training, the residual one for validation. (b) The visual features for each homogeneous single-modal feature subset are firstly normalized to avoid numerical problem. (c) The numeric ranges for C and γ are coarsely partitioned into small pieces with M pairs. $\nu - 1$ groups are used to train the classifier for each pair. When the M classifier models are available, the underlying optimal parameter pair (C, γ) is determined via cross-validation. (d) When (C, γ) at the coarse level is available, a fine partition of the search space around it is used to determine more accurate parameter pair $(\bar{C}, \bar{\gamma})$ in a hierarchical way. (e) With the optimal parameter pair $(\bar{C}, \bar{\gamma})$, the final model for the weak SVM classifier is trained again by using the whole set of training images. Table 1 and 2 shows the optimal parameter pairs $(\bar{C}, \bar{\gamma})$ for some object classes and semantic concepts.

To select the most representative feature components for weak classifier training, for a given homogeneous single-modal

Table 2: The optimal parameter pairs $(\bar{C}, \bar{\gamma})$ of the SVM classifiers for some image concepts.

semantic concepts	mountain view	beach	garden
$\bar{C}$	512	32	312
$\bar{\gamma}$	0.0078	0.125	0.03125
semantic concepts	sailing	skiing	desert
$\bar{C}$	56	128	8
$\bar{\gamma}$	0.625	4	2

feature subset S_j, PCA is used to exploit the feature correlation and enable ***in-set feature selection*** as follows: (1) PCA is used to determine its feature components, which are ranked based on the values of their Eigenvalues. (2) The unrepresentative feature components with small Eigenvalues are sequentially removed from S_j, and the residual ones are used for learning a new weak classifier, which is then tested on the validation image set, and the relevant loss function $L_{S_j}(X_n, Y_n) = |f(X_n) - Y_n|$ is also calculated. (3) the goodness for S_j is defined as:

$$G(S_j) = 1 - \frac{1}{N} \sum_{n=1}^{N} L_{S_j}(X_n, Y_n) \tag{2}$$

(4) The above procedure is performed repeatedly until the goodness of S_j is below a pre-defined threshold. (5) The results will be used as the inputs for ensemble classifier training.

3.2 Classifier Training using Unlabeled Images

In order to achieve accurate image classifiers, it is sometimes too expensive to manually label large amounts of training images. When this is concerned, semi-supervised classifier training becomes a promising solution to take advantage of unlabeled images [15, 2, 19, 25, 31].

To incorporate the unlabeled images $\overline{\Omega_{c_j}}$ for semi-supervised training of the weak SVM classifiers, an ***incremental framework*** was developed to predict labels for images in $\overline{\Omega_{c_j}}$. A hyperplane $< W, b >$ is then estimated by the framework, which separates Ω_{c_j} and $\overline{\Omega_{c_j}}$ with maximum margin [27, 21]. Thus the semi-supervised training of SVM classifier can be formulated as:

$$Min \left\{ \frac{1}{2}||W||^2 + C \sum_{i=1}^{N_L} \xi_i + C^* \sum_{j=1}^{N_u} \xi_j^* \right\} \tag{3}$$

subject to:

$$\begin{cases} \forall_{i=1}^{N_L}: & Y_i[W \cdot \Phi(X_i) + b] \geq 1 - \xi_i, \quad \xi_i > 0 \\ \forall_{j=1}^{N_u}: & Y_j^*[W \cdot \Phi(X_j^*) + b] \geq 1 - \xi_j^*, \quad \xi_j^* > 0 \end{cases} \tag{4}$$

When the number of unlabeled images is small, the training work can be solved simply by trying all possible label assignments for images in $\overline{\Omega_{c_j}}$. However, this will become too expensive and the outlying unlabeled images may mislead the classifiers when the number gets larger.

In order to solve this, an ***incremental framework*** was developed for semi-supervised training of the SVM classifiers, which takes the following major steps: (1) For a given image concept or object class, a weak SVM classifier is first learned from Ω_{c_j} as introduced in Section 3.1. (2) the classifier is then used to predict the labels for images in $\overline{\Omega_{c_j}}$, while the confidence score for the label of the unlabeled

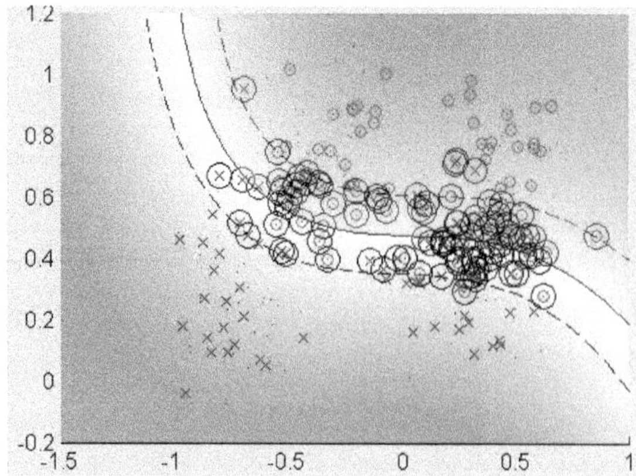

Figure 1: The SVM boundaries that are obtained by a batch-based training approach when all training samples are available at the batch.

image X_j^* is calculated by applying an additional sigmoid function [21]:

$$P(X_j^*) = \frac{1}{1 + e^{\alpha f(X_j^*) + \beta}} \tag{5}$$

where $f(X_j^*)$ is the output of the weak SVM classifier for X_j^*, α and β can be determined by minimizing the negative log-likelihood (NLL) function on the validation image set. The value of $P(X_j^*)$ is used to determine whether or not the unlabeled image X_j^* will be removed from the set through a pre-defined threshold. (3) A new SVM classifier can then be learned incrementally with all the remaining high-confident unlabeled images . (4) Considering the small shift of the hyperplane from previous step, the new SVM classifier is used to predict new labels for these high-confident unlabeled images. Images with inconsistent predicted labels are restored as the unlabeled images. (5) By integrating unlabeled images with consistent predicted labels for incremental classifier training, our incremental algorithm is performed repeatedly until it converges.

A two-dimensional synthetic data set is used to visualize and show the convergence of our incremental framework for semi-supervised SVM classifier training. As discussed in [22], this synthetic data set has two classes with two attributes, each class has a bimodal distribution which is formed by equal mixture of two normal distributions, and two normal distributions share the same covariance matrix. By treating this synthetic data set as an example, we have experimentally obtained the convergence of our incremental framework for semi-supervised SVM classifier training as shown in Fig. 1 and Fig. 2. From our experimental results, one can observe that our incremental framework for semi-supervised SVM classifier training finally converges to the same decision boundaries that are obtained by the batch-based training approach. The theoretical proof of the convergence for incremental SVM classifier training can be found at [27].

3.3 Two-Level Feature Selection and Ensemble Classifier Training

AdaBoost is used for weak classifier combination too enable both a two level feature selection and ensemble classifier training. Feature selection is performed at two different levels simultaneously and accurate image classifiers are learned by using a small number of labeled images. At the first level,

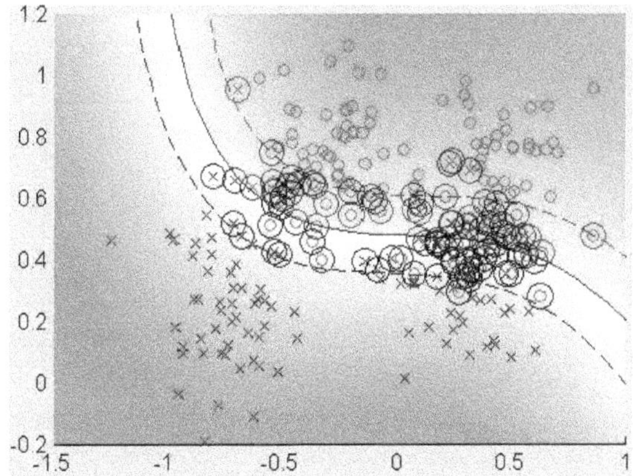

Figure 2: The SVM boundaries that are obtained by our incremental framework for SVM classifier training after it converges.

each visual feature dimension can be treated as a selection unit. PCA is used to select the most representative feature components. At the second level, each homogeneous single-modal feature subset is treated as an individual selection unit, whose *goodness* is measured by estimating the performance of the relevant weak classifier on the cross-validation image set. Thus, the most effective weak classifiers and their corresponding homogeneous single-modal feature subsets form the ***inter-set feature selection*** at the second level.

The process for *inter-set feature selection* at the second level can be treated as a process for ensemble classifier training, where AdaBoost can be used to boost the relevant weak classifiers:

$$H(X) = sign\left\{\sum_{j=1}^{9}\sum_{t=1}^{T}\alpha_t^j f_t^j(X)\right\}, \quad \sum_{j=1}^{9}\sum_{t=1}^{T}\alpha_t^j = 1 \qquad (6)$$

where $f_t^j(X)$ is the weak classifier for the jth homogeneous single-modal feature subset S_j at the tth iteration, and T is the total number of iterations. Higher prediction accuracy can be expected since the ensemble classifier combines the predictions of the weak classifiers and boosts the results. The homogeneous single-modal feature subsets corresponds to the most effective weak classifiers are then selected for image classification.

Compared with previous works, the **advantages** of our proposed work include: (a) Incorporating the feature hierarchy and feature subset selection for SVM classifier training can speed up SVM classifier training significantly because the number of the labeled training images is reduced dramatically for each low-dimensional homogeneous single-modal feature subset; (b) Partitioning the heterogeneous multi-modal feature space into multiple homogeneous single-modal feature subsets automatically can support more effective kernel function selection because the geometric property of the distribution of the images in each homogeneous single-modal feature subset can be effectively approximated by using RBF functions; (c) Incorporating the unlabeled images for semi-supervised SVM classifier training can significantly reduce human efforts on labeling large-scale training images while achieving higher classification accuracy; (d) Our boosting algorithm is able to simultaneously boost both the training images and the feature subsets, thus higher classification accuracy can be obtained; (e) Our proposed classifier training framework is able to select both the most suitable feature subsets for characterizing various visual properties of different image concepts and object classes accurately; (f) Our proposed classifier training framework is scalable with the image concepts (object classes) and the feature dimensions effectively.

4. AUTOMATIC OBJECT DETECTION AND IMAGE CLASSIFICATION

Given a certain test image, its image blobs and the relevant 83-dimensional multi-modal visual features are detected automatically, which are then classified into the most relevant object classes. The neighboring image blobs belongs to the same class are merged into a single region. Based on these object classes, the whole image is then classified into the most relevant image concept and multi-label image annotation can be achieved accurately.

The task of this paper is to detect 19 *object classes* and 15 *image concepts*. After an unlabeled test image is classified, the text keywords for interpreting the object classes and image concepts provide the annotations of the images at the content and concept level respectively. As shown through Fig. 3 to Fig. 6, our multi-label image annotation framework can support more expressive interpretations of the image semantics, and is very attractive to enable multi-modal image retrieval via keywords such that the naive users will have more flexibility to specify their query concepts via various keywords at different semantic levels.

5. ALGORITHM EVALUATION

We evaluate our algorithm on two databases: image database from the Google image search engine with about 30,000 pictures, and Corel image database with more than 3,800 pictures consisting of different image concepts and object classes. For each object class and image concept, only 50 images are labeled for classifier training.

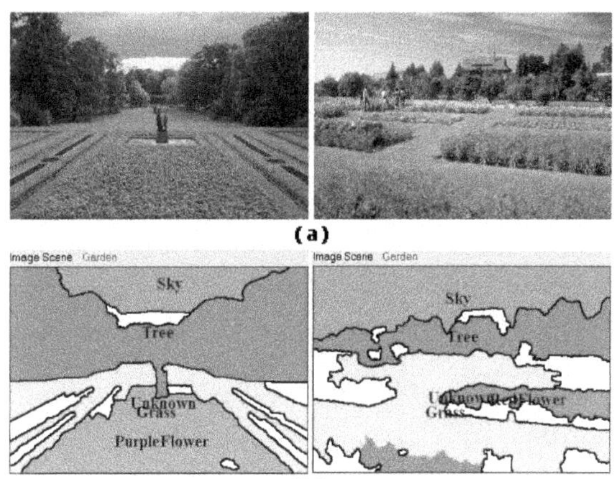

Figure 3: Multi-label image annotation results for the image concept "garden" and the relevant object classes.

With the same number of training images, four sets of comparison experiments are performed to evaluate the effect of our proposed framework for joint feature selection and classifier training using different conditions: (a) Learning the optimal ensemble classifier by using all the weak classifiers and the corresponding homogeneous feature subsets. (b) Performing only the second level of feature selection. (c)

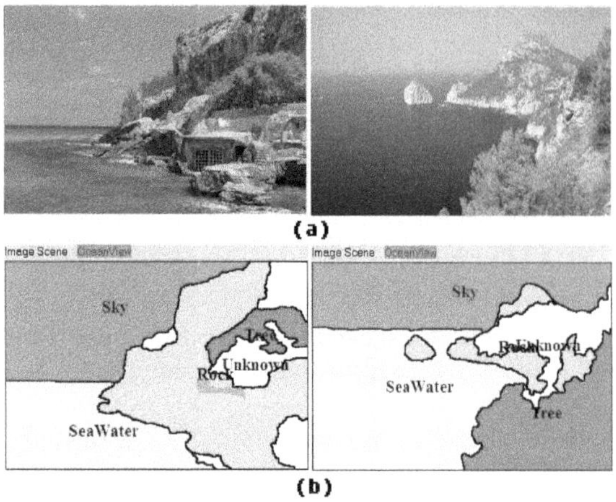

Figure 4: Multi-label image annotation results for the image concept "ocean view" and the relevant object classes.

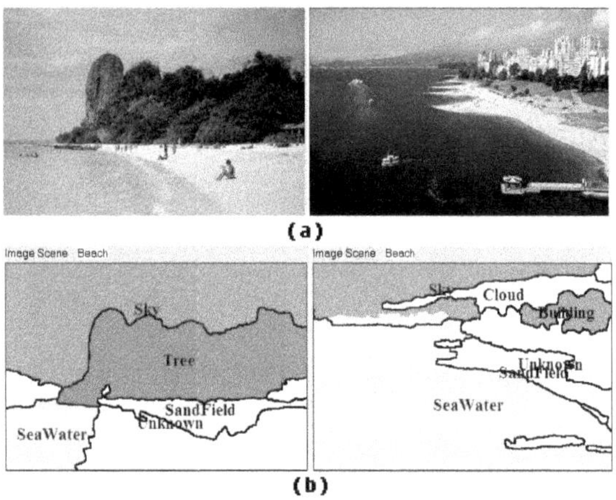

Figure 5: Multi-label image annotation results for the image concept "beach" and the relevant object classes.

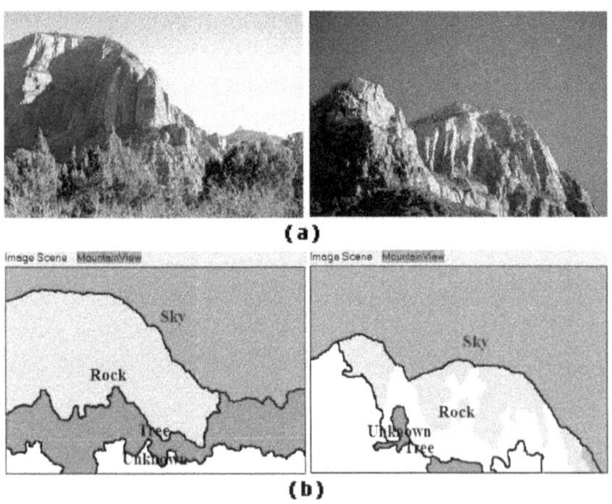

Figure 6: Multi-label image annotation results for the image concept "mountain view" and the relevant object classes.

Performing both the first level (PCA) and the second level of feature selection. (d) Comparing the performance difference between our approach, AdaBoost, and FeatureBoost.

There are 9 homogeneous single-modal feature subsets and the total number of iterations for AdaBoost is $T = 50$. Thus we have obtained $9 \times 50 = 450$ weak SVM classifiers. All

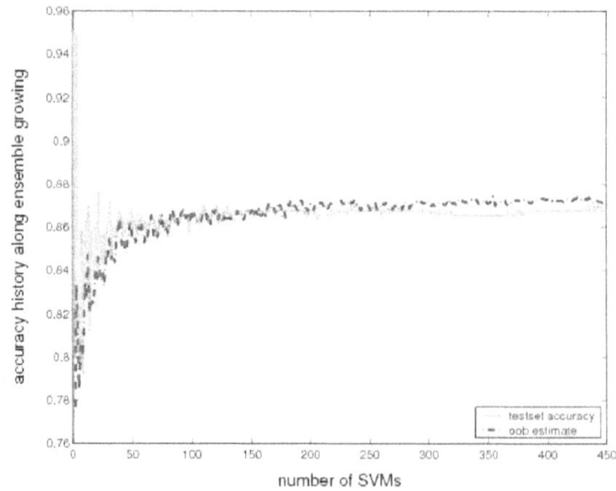

Figure 7: The relationship between the ensemble classifier's performance and the number of weak classifiers for boosting.

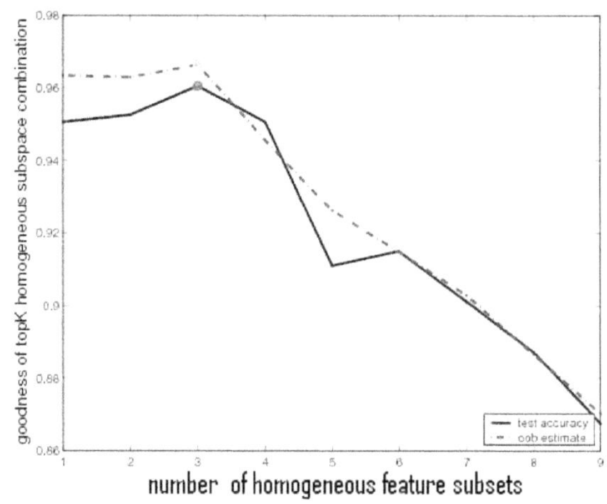

Figure 8: The relationship between the goodness of the ensemble classifier and the number of the selected homogeneous feature subsets.

these weak SVM classifiers can be used to boost the ensemble classifier. Ideally, integrating more weak SVM classifiers for ensemble classifier training may improve the classifier's performance sequentially. For a given object class "sea water", the relationship is obtained between the ensemble classifier's performance and the number of weak SVM classifiers used for ensemble classifier training. As shown in Fig. 7, although adding more weak SVM classifiers may improve accuracy, it is not able to achieve significant improvement after some iterations. This also proves that selecting the most effective weak classifiers and the corresponding homogeneous single-modal feature subsets for image classification can achieve acceptable accuracy. For the same object class "sea water", we have also obtained the optimal number of homogeneous single-modal feature subsets for ensemble classifier training as shown in Fig. 8. It's obvious that only the top 3 homogeneous single-modal feature subsets may boost the classifier's performance significantly.

The performance difference of our ensemble classifier is also evaluated by performing only the second-level feature selection against both levels. As shown in Fig. 9 and Fig. 10, the latter is able to exploit the feature correlation effectively and improve the accuracy of the ensemble classifier significantly.

Table 3: The performance of our classifiers (i.e., precision/recall) for some object classes.

object classes	grass	purple flower	red flower
	83.8% /84.2%	76.9% /75.8%	78.5% /80.2%
object classes	rock	sand field	sky
	75.1% /74.8%	83.2% /78.9%	81.2% /82.6%
object classes	snow	water	sunset
	72.8% /70.2%	80.5% /83.6%	80.2% /81.5%

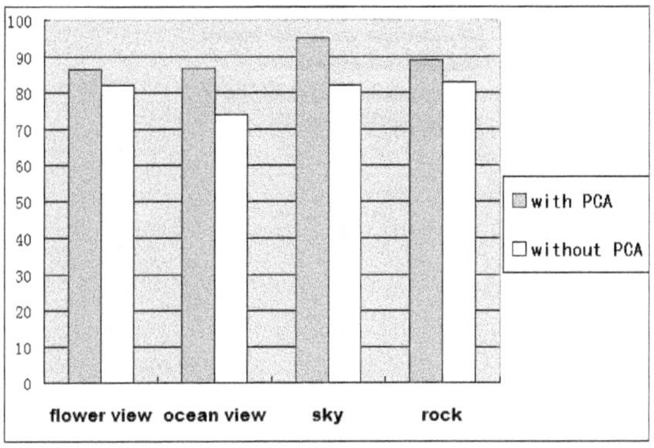

Figure 9: The performance differences of our ensemble classifier (i.e., 100ρ) under different situations.

The performance differences of multiple approaches for ensemble classifier training is shown in Fig. 11 and Fig. 12. With the advantages of both AdaBoost and FeatureBoost, higher classification accuracy can be expected. Results show that our approach can outperform AdaBoost and FeatureBoost. The average performance of our classifiers for some object classes and image concepts are given in Table 3 and Table 4.

The performance of our classifiers is also evaluated with different sizes of unlabeled images for classifier training. Results are shown through Fig. 13 to Fig. 16. It can be observed that if the training set is small, the unlabeled images can improve the classifier's performance significantly. The **reasons** are: (a) The *certain unlabeled images*, originated from the existing image context classes for concept interpretation, are able to improve the underlying SVM decision boundaries. (b) The *informative unlabeled images*, originated from the unknown image context classes, have the capability to provide additional context knowledge for updating the underlying SVM decision boundaries, which

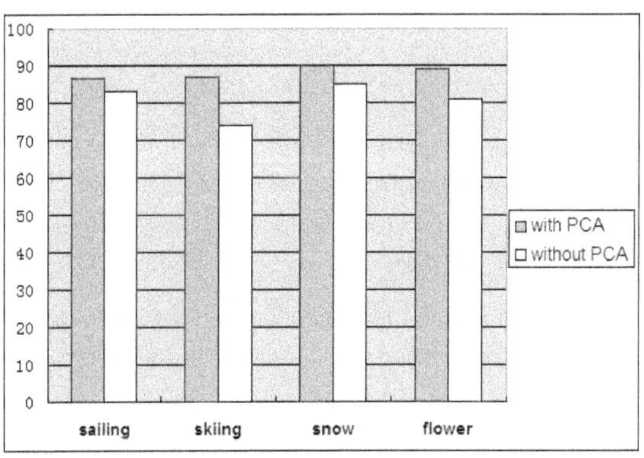

Figure 10: The performance differences of our ensemble classifier (i.e., 100ρ) under different situations.

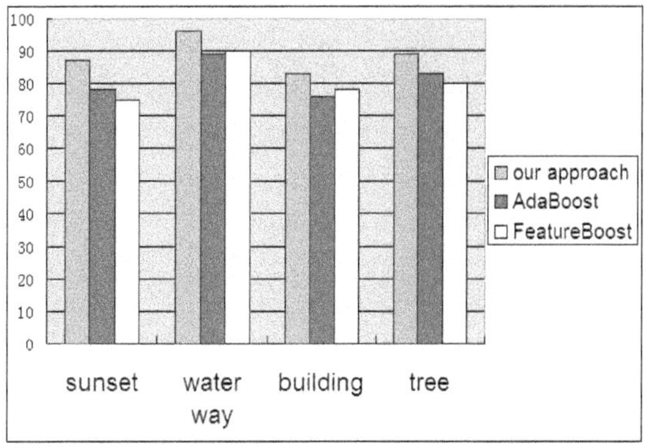

Figure 11: The performance comparison (i.e., 100ρ) for some image concepts and object classes by using different approaches for classifier boosting.

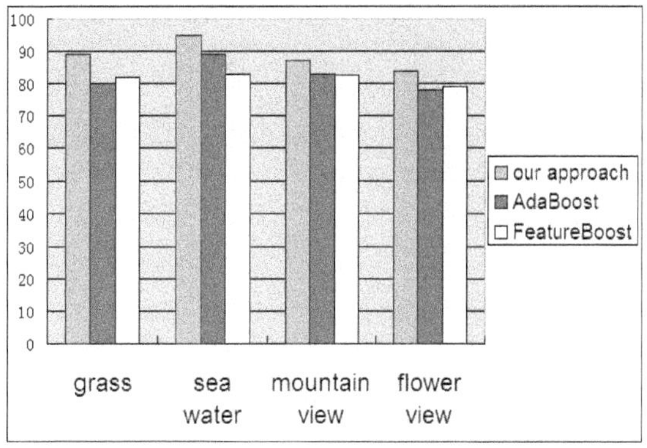

Figure 12: The performance comparison (i.e., 100ρ) for some image concepts and object classes by using different approaches for classifier boosting.

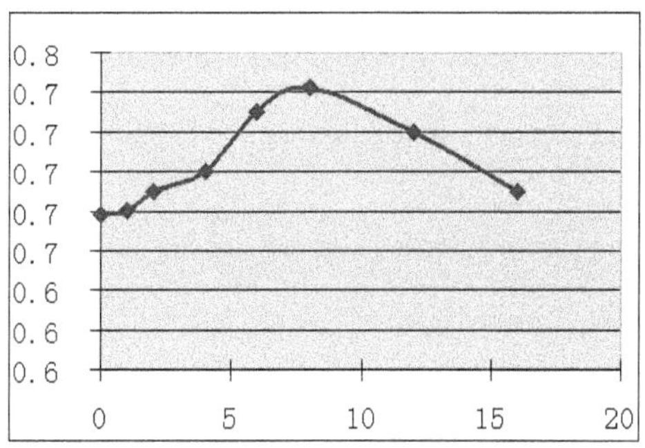

Figure 13: The classification accuracy (i.e., precision ρ) of image concept "beach" with different ratio $\lambda' = \frac{N_u}{N_L}$ between the labeled images and the unlabeled images.

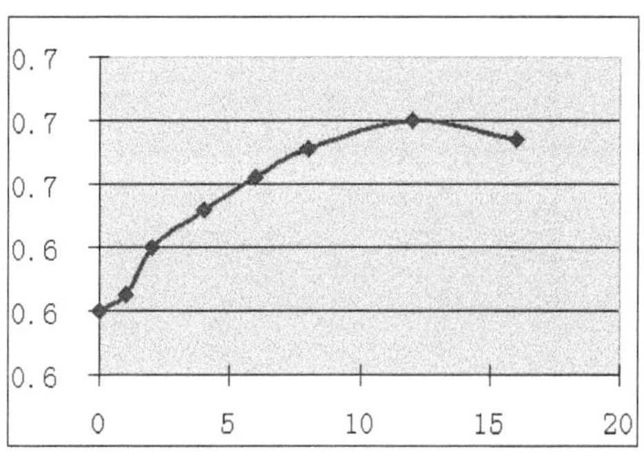

Figure 14: The classification accuracy (i.e., precision ρ) of image concept "garden" with different ratio $\lambda' = \frac{N_u}{N_L}$ between the labeled images and the unlabeled images.

Table 4: **The comparison of our classifiers (i.e., precision/recall) for some image concepts.**

concepts	mountain view	beach	garden
	75.2% /77.2%	85.6% /83.4%	74.6% /72.8%
concepts	sailing	skiing	desert
	70.9% /70.4%	75.3% /75.4%	73.3% /75.2%
concepts	ocean view	waterway	prairie
	71.2% /70.8%	77.8% /74.9%	74.2% /73.6%

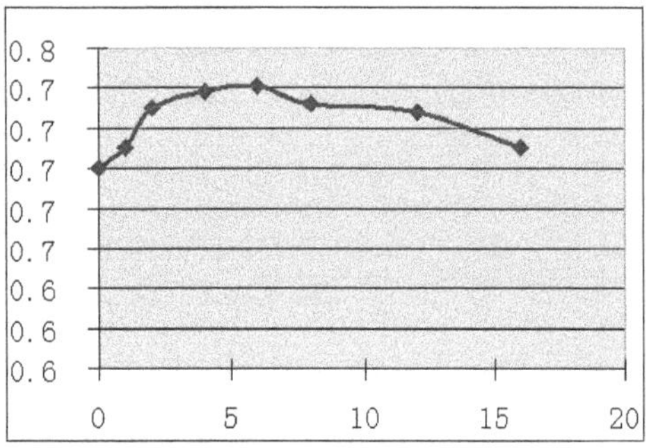

Figure 15: The classification accuracy (i.e., precision ρ) of image concept "mountain view" with different ratio $\lambda' = \frac{N_u}{N_L}$ between the labeled images and the unlabeled images.

will in turn influence the prediction accuracy of the SVM classifiers learned incrementally. (c) The *outlying unlabeled images*, originated from outliers, can be predicted accurately, while misleading effects on classifier training can be eliminated by determining an optimal value of the penalty term C automatically.

When a limited number of labeled images are available and more unlabeled images are involved for semi-supervised classifier training, the classifier's performance will decrease, which is also foreseeable, since large-scale outliers may mislead it.

By using the same number of training samples for classifier training, we have also compared the performance differences between out approach and simply training the classifier directly from the 83-dimensional heterogeneous multi-modal feature space, shown in Fig. 17. It also shows that our approach can obtain higher classification accuracy when labeled training samples are limited.

6. CONCLUSIONS AND FUTURE WORKS

By incorporating the feature hierarchy for ensemble image classifier training, we have proposed a novel approach to enabling hierarchical feature subset selection. By selecting the most effective weak classifiers and the corresponding homogeneous single-modal feature subsets to boost the ensemble image classifier, our proposed framework is able to achieve higher prediction accuracy for image classification and object detection. In addition, our proposed framework has also supported a novel solution for multi-label image annotation and image retrieval via keywords. Our experiments on a specific domain of natural images have also obtained very positive results. Obviously, our proposed algorithm for joint classifier training and feature subset selection can also be applied to other data domains.

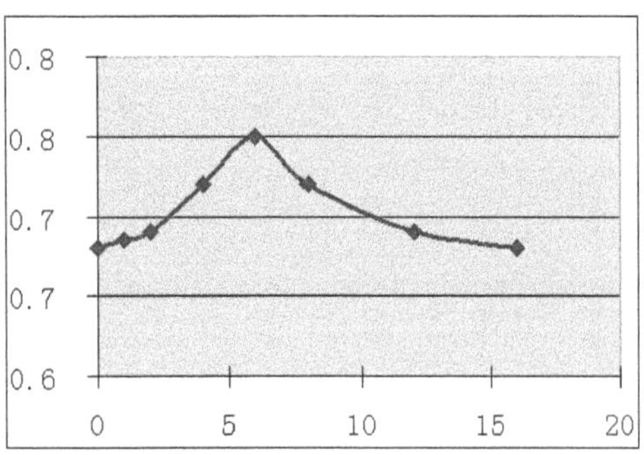

Figure 16: The classification accuracy (i.e., precision ρ) of image concept "skiing" with different ratio $\lambda' = \frac{N_u}{N_L}$ between the labeled images and the unlabeled images.

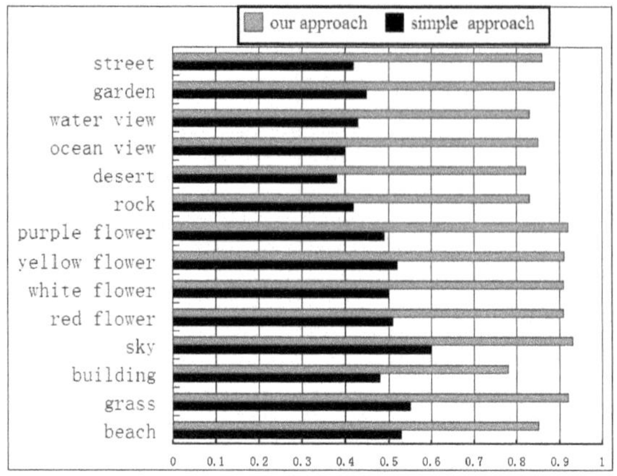

Figure 17: The performance comparison results between our approach and one simple approach for image classifier training.

The main problem for image classification is the large range of possible variations within the same image concept or object class because of various viewing and illumination conditions. Thus it is also very important to develop new techniques that are able to handle the changes of viewing and illumination conditions effectively. By treating various viewing conditions or illumination conditions as the additional selection units, we will label the training images to learn the relevant classifiers under various view or illumination conditions, and our proposed image classifier training technique can be used to combine these classifiers effectively for final prediction and thus it is able to generalize across different viewing and illumination conditions.

7. ACKNOWLEDGMENTS

The authors wish to thank the anonymous reviewers for their helpful comments. This work was partially funded by 973 Program (2010CB327906), Shanghai Leading Academic Discipline Project (B114), Doctoral Fund of Ministry of Education of China (20100071120033), and Shanghai Municipal R&D Foundation (08dz1500109).

8. REFERENCES

[1] K. Barnard and D. Forsyth. Learning the semantics of words and pictures. *ICCV*, pages 408–415, 2001.

[2] K. Bennet and A. Demiriz. Semi-supervised support vector machines. *NIPS*, pages 368–374, 1998.

[3] D. Blei and M. Jordan. Modeling annotated data. *ACM SIGIR*, pages 127–134, 2003.

[4] L. Breiman. Bagging predictors. *Machine Learning*, 24:123–140, 1996.

[5] C. Carson, S. Belongie, H. Greenspan, and J. Malik. Blobworld: Image segmentation using expectation maximization and its application to image querying. *IEEE Trans. on PAMI*, 24:1026–1038, 2002.

[6] Y. Deng and M. Manjunath. Unsupervised segmentation for color-texture regions in images and video. *IEEE Trans. on PAMI*, 23:800–810, 2001.

[7] P. Duygulu, K. Barnard, J. Freitas, and D. Forsyth. Object recognition as machine translation: Learning a lexicon for a fixed image vocabulary. *ECCV*, pages 97–112, 2002.

[8] J. Fan, Y. Gao, and H. Luo. Multi-level annotation of natural scenes using dominant image components and semantic image concepts. *ACM Multimedia*, pages 540–547, 2004.

[9] W. Fan, S. Stolfo, J. Zhang, and P. Chan. Adacost: Misclassification cost-sensitive boosting. *ICML*, pages 99–105, 1999.

[10] Y. Freund and R. Schapire. Experiments with a new boosting algorithm. *ICML*, pages 148–156, 1996.

[11] Y. Gao, J. Fan, H. Luo, X. Xue, and R. Jain. Automatic image annotation by incorporating feature hierarchy and boosting to scale-up svm classifiers. *ACM Multimedia*, pages 901–910, 2006.

[12] K. Ghahremani, C. Shahabi, S. Yao, and R. Zimmermann. Yima: real-time multimedia storage and retrieval. *ACM Multimedia*, pages 668–669, 2002.

[13] J. Jeon, V. Lavrenko, and R. Manmatha. Automatic image annotation and retrieval using cross-media relevance models. *ACM SIGIR*, pages 119–126, 2003.

[14] Y. Jin, L. Khan, L. Wang, and M. Awad. Image annotations by combining multiple evidence and wordnet. *ACM Multimedia*, pages 706–715, 2005.

[15] T. Joachims. Transductive inference for text classification using support vector machines. *ICML*, pages 200–209, 1999.

[16] V. Lavrenko, R. Manmatha, and J. Jeon. A model for learning the semantics of pictures. *NIPS*, pages 553–560, 2003.

[17] A. Makadia, V. Pavlovic, and S. Kumar. A new baseline for image annotation. *ECCV*, pages 316–329, 2008.

[18] D. Modha and W. S. Spangler. Feature weighting in k-means clustering. *Machine Learning*, 52:217–237, 2003.

[19] K. Nigam, A. McCallum, S. Thrun, and T. Mitchell. Text classification from labeled and unlabeled documents using em. *Machine Learning*, pages 103–134, 2000.

[20] J. O'Sullivan, J. Langford, R. Caruana, and A. Blum. Featureboost: A meta learning algorithm that improves model robustness. *ICML*, pages 703–710, 2000.

[21] J. Platt. Probabilistic outputs for support vector machines and comparisons to regularized likelihood methods. *Adavances in Large Margin Classifiers, MIT Press*, 1999.

[22] B. Ripley. Neural network and related methods for classification. *Journal of the Royal Statistical Society, Series B*, 56:409–456, 1994.

[23] A. Smeulders, M. Worring, S. Santini, A. Gupta, and R. Jain. Content-based image retrieval at the end of the early years. *IEEE Trans. on PAMI*, 22:1349–1380, 2000.

[24] C. Sutton, M. Sindelar, and A. McCallum. Feature boosting: Preventing weight undertraining in structured discriminative learning. *CIIR TR-IR-402 University of Masschusetts*, 2005.

[25] M. Szummer and T. Jaakkola. Information regularization with partially labeled data. *NIPS*, pages 1025–1032, 2002.

[26] A. Torralba and A. Oliva. Semantic organization of scenes using discriminant structural templates. *ICCV*, pages 1253–1258, 1999.

[27] V. Vapnik. Statistical learning theory. 1998.

[28] N. Vasconcelos and M. Vasconcelos. Scalable discriminant feature selection for image retrieval and recognition. *CVPR*, pages 770–775, 2004.

[29] P. Viola and M. Jones. Robust real-time face detection. *Intl. J. Computer Vision*, 57:137–154, 2004.

[30] X.-J. Wang, W.-Y. Ma, L. Zhang, and X. Li. Iteratively clustering web images based on link and attribute reinforcements. *ACM Multimedia*, pages 122–131, 2005.

[31] M. Weber, M. Welling, and P. Perona. Unsupervised learning of models for recognition. *ECCV*, pages 18–32, 2000.

[32] C. Yang, M. Dong, and J. Hua. Region-based image annotation using asymmetrical support vector machine-based multiple-instance learning. *CVPR*, pages 2057–2063, 2006.

[33] L. Yu and H. Liu. Feature selection for high-dimensional data: A fast correlation-based filter solution. *ICML*, pages 856–863, 2003.

[34] R. Zhang, Z. Zhang, M. Li, W.-Y. Ma, and H. Zhang. A probabilistic semantic model for image annotation and multi-modal image retrieva. *ICCV*, pages 846–851, 2005.

[35] S. Zhang, J. Huang, Y. Huang, Y. Yu, H. Li, and D. Metaxas. Automatic image annotation using group sparsity. *CVPR*, pages 3312–3319, 2010.

Efficient Manifold Ranking for Image Retrieval

Bin Xu[1], Jiajun Bu[1], Chun Chen[1], Deng Cai[2], Xiaofei He[2], Wei Liu[3], Jiebo Luo[4]

[1]Zhejiang Provincial Key Laboratory of Service Robot
College of Computer Science, Zhejiang University, Hangzhou, China
{xbzju,bjj,chenc,hezhanying}@zju.edu.cn

[2]State Key Lab of CAD&CG, College of Computer Science, Zhejiang University, Hangzhou, China
{dengcai,xiaofeihe}@cad.zju.edu.cn

[3]Columbia University, New York, NY, USA, wliu@ee.columbia.edu

[4]Kodak Research Laboratories, Eastman Kodak Company, Rochester, NY, USA, jiebo.luo@kodak.com

ABSTRACT

Manifold Ranking (MR), a graph-based ranking algorithm, has been widely applied in information retrieval and shown to have excellent performance and feasibility on a variety of data types. Particularly, it has been successfully applied to content-based image retrieval, because of its outstanding ability to discover underlying geometrical structure of the given image database. However, manifold ranking is computationally very expensive, both in graph construction and ranking computation stages, which significantly limits its applicability to very large data sets. In this paper, we extend the original manifold ranking algorithm and propose a new framework named Efficient Manifold Ranking (EMR). We aim to address the shortcomings of MR from two perspectives: scalable graph construction and efficient computation. Specifically, we build an anchor graph on the data set instead of the traditional k-nearest neighbor graph, and design a new form of adjacency matrix utilized to speed up the ranking computation. The experimental results on a real world image database demonstrate the effectiveness and efficiency of our proposed method. With a comparable performance to the original manifold ranking, our method significantly reduces the computational time, makes it a promising method to large scale real world retrieval problems.

Categories and Subject Descriptors

H.3.3 [**Information Search and Retrieval**]: Retrieval models; H.2.8 [**Database Applications**]: Image databases

General Terms

Algorithm, Performance

Keywords

Efficient manifold ranking, image retrieval, graph-based algorithm, out-of-sample

1. INTRODUCTION

Traditional image retrieval systems are based on keyword search, such as Google and Yahoo image search. In these systems, user keyword is matched with the context around an image including the title, manual annotation, web document, etc. These systems don't utilize information from images. However these systems suffer many problems, such as shortage of the text information and inconsistency of the meaning of the text and image.

Content-based image retrieval (CBIR) is a considerable choice to overcome these difficulties. CBIR has drawed a great attention in the past two decades [5, 19, 27]. Different from traditional keyword search systems, CBIR systems utilize the low-level features (color, texture, shape, etc.), automatically extracted from images. This is a vital character for efficient management and search in a large image database. But the low-level features used in CBIR systems are often visually characterized, and with no direct connection with semantic concepts of the images. How to narrow the semantic gap has been the main challenge for CBIR.

Many data sets have underlying cluster or manifold structure. Under such circumstances, the assumption of *label consistency* is reasonable [23, 36]. It means that those nearby data points, or points belong to the same cluster or manifold, are very likely to share the same semantic label. This phenomenon is extremely important to explore the semantic relevance when the label information is unknown. Thus, a good CBIR method should consider low-level features as well as intrinsic structure of the data.

Manifold Ranking (MR) [36,37], a semi-supervised graph-based ranking algorithm, has been widely applied in information retrieval, and shown to have excellent performance and feasibility on a variety of data types, such as the text [28], image [9], and video [34]. The core idea of manifold ranking is to rank the data with respect to the intrinsic structure collectively revealed by a large number of data. By taking the underlying structure into account, manifold ranking assigns each data point a relative ranking score, instead of an absolute pairwise similarity as traditional ways. The score is treated as a distance metric defined on the manifold, which is more meaningful to capturing the semantic relevance degree. He et al. [9] firstly applied manifold ranking to CBIR, and significantly improved image retrieval performance compared with state-of-the-art algorithms.

However, manifold ranking has its own drawbacks to handle large scale data sets – it has expensive computational cost, both in graph construction and ranking computation stages. Particularly, it is costly to handle an out-of-sample query (a new sample). That means original manifold ranking is inadequate for a real world CBIR system, in which the user provided query is always an out-of-sample. It's intolerable for a user to wait a long time to get returns.

In this paper, we extend the original manifold ranking and propose a novel framework named Efficient Manifold Ranking (EMR). We try to address the shortcomings of manifold ranking from two perspectives: the first is scalable graph construction; and the second is efficient computation, especially for out-of-sample retrieval. The main contributions of this paper are as follows. (1) Based on the anchor graph construction [18,35], we design a new form of adjacency matrix and give it an intuitive explanation. (2) By the new form, our method EMR achieves a comparable performance to original manifold ranking but significantly reduces the computational time.

The rest of this paper is organized as follows. In section 2, we briefly discuss some related works and in section 3, we review the manifold ranking algorithm and make a detailed analysis. The proposed approach EMR is described in section 4. In section 5, we present the experiment results on a real world image database. Finally we provide an extension analysis in section 6 and conclusions in section 7.

2. RELATED WORK

In this section, we discuss two most relevant topics to our work: ranking model and content-based image retrieval.

The problem of ranking has recently gained great attentions in both information retrieval and machine learning areas. Conventional ranking models can be content based models, like the Vector Space Model, BM25, and the language modeling [22]; or link structure based models, like the famous PageRank [2] and HITS [15]; or cross media models [13]. Another important category is the learning to rank model, which aims to optimize a ranking function that incorporates relevance features and avoids tuning a large number of parameters empirically [7, 26]. However, many conventional models ignore the important issue of efficiency, which is crucial for a real-time systems, such as a web application. In [29], the authors present a unified framework for jointly optimizing effectiveness and efficiency.

2.1 Graph-based Ranking

In this paper, we focus on a particular kind of ranking model – graph-based ranking. It has been successfully applied in link-structure analysis of the web [2,15] and social networks research [3, 8, 17]. Generally, a graph can be denoted as $G = (V, E, W)$, where V is a set of vertices in which each vertex represents a data point, $E \subseteq V \times V$ is a set of edges connecting related vertices, and W is a adjacency matrix recording the pairwise weights between vertices. The object of a graph-based ranking model is to decide the importance of a vertex in a graph, based on local or global information draw from the graph.

Agarwal [1] proposed to model the data by a weighted graph, and incorporated this graph structure into the ranking function as a regularizer. Guan et al. [8] proposed a graph-based ranking algorithm for interrelated multi-type resources to generate personalized tag recommendation. Liu et al. [17] proposed an automatically tag ranking scheme by performing a random walk over a tag similarity graph. In [3], the authors made the music recommendation by ranking on a unified hypergraph, combining with rich social information and music content. Recently, there have been some papers on speeding up manifold ranking. In [11], the authors partitioned the data into several parts and computed the ranking function by a block-wise way.

2.2 Content-based Image Retrieval

In many cases, we have no more information than the data itself. Without label information, capturing semantic relationship between images is quite difficult. A great amount of researches have been performed for designing more informative low-level features (e.g., SIFT features [20]) to represent images, or better metrics (e.g., DPF [16]) to measure the perceptual similarity, but their performance is restricted by many conditions and is sensitive to the data. Relevance feedback [24] is a powerful tool for interactive CBIR. User's high level perception is captured by dynamically updated weights based on the user's feedback.

Many traditional image retrieval methods focus on the data features too much, and they ignore the underlying structure information, which is of great importance for semantic discovery, especially when the label information is unknown. A good CBIR method should consider the image features as well as the intrinsic structure of the data, in our opinion. Manifold ranking [36,37] ranks data with respect to the intrinsic geometrical structure, which is exactly in line with our consideration.

3. MANIFOLD RANKING REVIEW

In this section, we briefly review the manifold ranking algorithm and make a detailed analysis about its drawbacks. We start form the description of notations.

3.1 Notations and Formulations

Given a set of data $\chi = \{x_1, x_2, \dots, x_n\} \subset R^m$ and build a graph on the data (e.g., kNN graph). $W \in R^{n\times n}$ denotes the adjacency matrix with element w_{ij} saving the weight of the edge between point i and j. Normally the weight can be defined by the heat kernel $w_{ij} = \exp[-d^2(x_i, x_j)/2\sigma^2)]$ if there is an edge linking x_i and x_j, otherwise $w_{ij} = 0$. Function $d(x_i, x_j)$ is a distance metric of x_i and x_j defined on χ, such as the Euclidean distance. Let $r : \chi \to R$ be a ranking function which assigns to each point x_i a ranking score r_i. Finally, we define an initial vector $y = [y1, \dots, y_n]^T$, in which $y_i = 1$ if x_i is a query and $y_i = 0$ otherwise.

The cost function associated with r is defined to be

$$O(r) = \frac{1}{2}(\sum_{i,j=1}^{n} w_{ij}\|\frac{1}{\sqrt{D_{ii}}}r_i - \frac{1}{\sqrt{D_{jj}}}r_j\|^2 + \mu\sum_{i=1}^{n}\|r_i - y_i\|^2), \tag{1}$$

where $\mu > 0$ is the regularization parameter and D is a diagonal matrix with $D_{ii} = \sum_{j=1}^{n} w_{ij}$.

The first term in the cost function is a smoothness constraint, which makes the nearby points in the space have close ranking scores. The second term is a fitting constraint, which means the ranking result should fit to the initial label assignment. If we have more prior knowledge about the relevance or confidence of each query, we can assign different initial scores to the queries. Minimizing the cost function

$O(r)$, we get the optimal r by the following closed form

$$r^* = (I_n - \alpha S)^{-1} y, \quad (2)$$

where $\alpha = \frac{1}{1+\mu}$, I_n is an identity matrix with $n \times n$, and S is the symmetrical normalization of W, $S = D^{-1/2} W D^{-1/2}$. In large scale problems, we prefer to use the iteration scheme:

$$r(t+1) = \alpha S r(t) + (1 - \alpha) y. \quad (3)$$

During each iteration, each point receives information from its neighbors (first term), and retains its initial information (second term). The iteration process is repeated until convergence. When manifold ranking is applied to retrieval (such as image retrieval), after specifying a query by the user, we can use the closed form or iteration scheme to compute the ranking score of each point. The ranking score can be viewed as a metric of the manifold distance which is more meaningful to measure the semantic relevance.

3.2 Analysis

Although manifold ranking has been widely used in many applications and proved effective for multiple resources, it has its own drawbacks to handle large scale data sets, which significantly limits its applicability.

The first is its graph construction method. The kNN graph is quite appropriate for manifold ranking because of its good ability to capture local structure of the data. But the construction cost for kNN graph is $O(kn^2)$, which is expensive in large scale situations. Moreover, manifold ranking, as well as many other graph-based algorithms directly use the adjacency matrix W in their computation. In some cases, it is impossible to keep matrix W as large as $n \times n$ in memory, especially for very large data sets or memory-short environment applications. Thus, we need to find a way to build a graph in both low construction cost and small storage space, as well as good ability to capture underlying structure of the given data set.

The second, manifold ranking has very expensive computational cost because of the matrix inversion operation in equation (2). This has been the main bottleneck to apply manifold ranking in large scale applications. Although we can use the iteration algorithm in equation (3), it is still inefficient in large scale cases and may arrive at a local convergence. Thus, original manifold ranking is inadequate for a real-time retrieval system.

4. EFFICIENT MANIFOLD RANKING

We try to address the shortcomings of original manifold ranking from two main perspectives: scalable graph construction and efficient ranking computation. Particularly, our method can handle the out-of-sample retrieval problem, which is crucial for a real world retrieval system.

4.1 Scalable Graph Construction

To handle scalable data sets, we want the graph construction cost to be linear or near linear with the graph size. That means, for each data point, we can't search the whole graph, like kNN strategy does. To achieve this requirement, we construct an anchor graph [18, 35] and propose a new design of adjacency matrix W.

The definitions of anchor points and anchor graph have appeared in some other works. For instance, in [33], the authors proposed that each data point on the manifold can be locally approximated by a linear combination of its nearby anchor points, and the linear weights become its local coordinate coding. Liu et al. [18] designed the adjacency matrix in a probabilistic measure and used it for scalable semi-supervised learning. This work inspires us much.

4.1.1 Anchor Graph Construction

Now we introduce how to use anchor graph to model the data [18,35]. Suppose we have a data set $\chi = \{x_1, \ldots, x_n\} \subset R^m$ with n samples in m dimensions, and $U = \{u_1, \ldots, u_d\} \subset R^m$ denotes a set of anchors sharing the same space with the data set. Let $f : \chi \to R$ be a real value function which assigns each data point in χ a semantic label. We aim to find a weight matrix $Z \in R^{d \times n}$ that measures the potential relationships between data points in χ and anchors in U. Then we estimate $f(x)$ for each data point as a weighted average of the labels on anchors

$$\widehat{f}(x_i) = \sum_{k=1}^{d} z_{ki} f(u_k), i = 1, \ldots, n, \quad (4)$$

with constraints $\sum_{k=1}^{d} z_{ki} = 1$ and $z_{ki} \geq 0$. Element z_{ki} represents the weight between data point x_i and anchor u_k. We adopt the well known Nadaraya-Watson kernel regression to assign weights smoothly

$$z_{ki} = \frac{K(\frac{|x_i - u_k|}{\lambda})}{\sum_{l=1}^{d} K(\frac{|x_i - u_l|}{\lambda})}, \quad (5)$$

with the *Epanechnikov* quadratic kernel

$$K_\lambda(t) = \begin{cases} \frac{3}{4}(1 - t^2) & \text{if } |t| \leq 1; \\ 0 & \text{otherwise.} \end{cases} \quad (6)$$

The smoothing parameter λ determines the size of the local region in which anchors can affect the target point. It is reasonable to consider that one data point has the same semantic label with its nearby anchors in a high probability. There are many ways to determine the parameter λ. For example, it can be a constant selected by cross-validation from a set of training data. In this paper we use a more robust way to get λ, which uses the nearest neighborhood size s to replace λ, that is

$$\lambda(x_i) = |x_i - u_{[s]}|, \quad (7)$$

where $u_{[s]}$ is the sth closest anchor of x_i.

Specifically, to build the anchor graph, we connect each data point to its s nearest anchors and then assign weights to each connection by the kernel function. So the construction has a total computational complexity $O(sdn)$, where d is the number of anchors. Thus, the number of anchors determines the efficiency of the anchor graph construction. If $d \ll n$, the construction is very fast.

How can we get the anchors? Active learning [25, 32] or clustering methods are considerable choices. For example, we use k-means algorithm and select the centers as anchors. Some fast k-means algorithms [14] can speed up the computation. Random selection is a competitive method which has extremely low selection cost and acceptable performance. Later in our experiments, we compare the performance of using random anchors, fast k-means anchors and normal k-means anchors.

The main feature, also the main advantage of building an anchor graph is separating the graph construction into two stages – an off-line anchor selection stage and an on-line graph construction stage. That means, we can adopt any useful method to select or build the anchors with little concern for their time complexity, while the graph construction is always efficient since it has linear complexity to the date size. Note that we don't have to update the anchors frequently, because informative anchors for a large data set are relatively stable (e.g., the cluster centers), even if a few new samples are added.

4.1.2 Design of Adjacency Matrix

We present a new approach to design the adjacency matrix W and make an intuitive explanation for it. The weight matrix $Z \in R^{d\times n}$ can be seen as a d dimensional representation of the data $X \in R^{m\times n}$, d is the number of anchor points. That is to say, data points can be represented in the new space, no matter what the original features are. This is a big advantage to handle some high dimensional data. Then, with the inner product as the metric to measure the adjacent weight between data points, we design the adjacency matrix to be a low-rank form

$$W = Z^T Z, \tag{8}$$

which means that if two data points are correlative ($W_{ij} > 0$), they share at least one common anchor point, otherwise $W_{ij} = 0$. By sharing the same anchors, data points have similar semantic concepts in a high probability as our consideration. Thus, our design is helpful to explore the semantic relationships in the data.

This formula naturally preserves some good properties of W: sparseness and nonnegativeness. The highly sparse matrix Z makes W sparse, which is consistent with the observation that most of the points in a graph have only a small amount of edges with other points. The nonnegative property makes the adjacent weight more meaningful: in real world data, the relationship between two items is always positive or zero, but not negative. Moreover, nonnegative W guarantees the positive semidefinite property of the graph Laplacian in many graph-based algorithms [18].

In large scale cases, it is expensive to keep the matrix W as large as $n \times n$ in memory, while in our construction, we just need to save the $d \times n$ matrix Z. If $d \ll n$, we can dramatically reduce the memory cost.

4.2 Efficient Computation

After graph construction, the main computational cost for manifold ranking is the matrix inversion in equation (2), whose complexity is $O(n^3)$. So the data size n can not be too large. Although we can use the iteration algorithm, it is still inefficient for large scale cases.

One may argue that the matrix inversion can be done off-line, then it is not a problem for on-line search. However, off-line calculation can only handle the case when the query is already in the graph (an in-sample). If the query is not in the graph (an out-of-sample), for exact graph structure, we have to update the whole graph to add the new query and compute the matrix inversion in equation (2) again. Thus, the off-line computation doesn't work for an out-of-sample query. Actually, for a real CBIR system, user's query is always an out-of-sample.

With the form of $W = Z^T Z$, we can rewrite the equation (2), the main step of manifold ranking, by Woodbury formula as follows. Let $H = ZD^{-\frac{1}{2}}$, and $S = H^T H$, then the final ranking function r can be directly computed by

$$r^* = (I_n - \alpha H^T H)^{-1} y = (I_n - H^T (HH^T - \frac{1}{\alpha} I_d)^{-1} H) y. \tag{9}$$

PROOF. Just check that $(I_n - \alpha H^T H)$ times $(I_n - H^T (HH^T - \frac{1}{\alpha} I_d)^{-1} H)$ gives the identity matrix:

$$\begin{aligned}
&(I_n - \alpha H^T H)(I_n - H^T (HH^T - \tfrac{1}{\alpha} I_d)^{-1} H) \\
&= I_n - \alpha H^T H - (H^T - \alpha H^T H H^T)(HH^T - \tfrac{1}{\alpha} I_d)^{-1} H \\
&= I_n - \alpha H^T H + \alpha H^T (-\tfrac{1}{\alpha} I_d + HH^T)(HH^T - \tfrac{1}{\alpha} I_d)^{-1} H \\
&= I_n - \alpha H^T H + \alpha H^T H \\
&= I_n
\end{aligned}$$

□

By equation (9), the inversion part (taking the most computational cost) changes from a $n \times n$ matrix to a $d \times d$ matrix. If $d \ll n$, this change can significantly speed up the calculation of manifold ranking. Thus, applying our proposed method to a real-time retrieval system is viable, which is a big shortage for original manifold ranking.

During the computation process, we never use the adjacency matrix W. So we don't save the matrix W in memory, but save matrix Z instead. In equation (9), D is a diagonal matrix with $D_{ii} = \sum_{j=1}^{n} w_{ij}$. When $W = Z^T Z$,

$$D_{ii} = \sum_{j=1}^{n} z_i^T z_j = z_i^T v, \tag{10}$$

where z_i is the ith column of Z and $v = \sum_{j=1}^{n} z_j$. Thus we get the matrix D without using W.

A useful trick for computing r^* in equation (9) is running it from right to left. So every time we multiply a matrix by a vector, avoiding the matrix - matrix multiplication. As a result, to compute the ranking function, EMR has a complexity $O(dn + d^3)$.

4.3 EMR for Content-Based Image Retrieval

In this part, we make a brief summary of EMR applied to pure content-based image retrieval. To add more information, we just extend the data features.

First of all, we extract the low-level features of images in the database, and use them as coordinates of data points in the graph. We will further discuss the low-level features in section 5. Secondly, we select representative points as anchors and construct the weight matrix Z by kernel regression with a small neighborhood size s. Anchors are selected off-line and does not affect the on-line process. For a stable data set, we don't frequently update the anchors. At last, after the user specifying or uploading an image as a query, we get or extract its low-level features, update the weight matrix Z, and directly compute the ranking scores by equation (9). Images with highest ranking scores are considered as the most relevant and return to the user.

5. EXPERIMENTAL STUDY

In this section, we show several experimental results and comparisons to evaluate the effectiveness and efficiency of our proposed method EMR on a real world image database. All algorithms in our experiments are implemented in MATLAB 9.0 and run on a computer with 2.0 GHZ(×2) CPU, 8GB RAM.

5.1 Experiments Setup

The image database consisting of 7,700 images from COREL image database. COREL is widely used in many CBIR works [12, 19, 31]. All of the images are from 77 different categories, with 100 images per category. Images in the same category belong to the same semantic concept, such as *beach, bird, elephant* and so on. That is to say, images from the same category are judged relevant and otherwise irrelevant. In Figure 1, we randomly select and show nine image samples from three different categories.

Figure 1: COREL image samples randomly selected from semantic concept beach, bird and elephant.

5.1.1 Evaluation Metric Discussion

There are many measures to evaluate the retrieval results such as *precision*, *recall*, *F measure*, *MAP* and *NDCG* [21]. But for a real CBIR application, especially for a web application, not all the measures are meaningful.

Generally, the image retrieval engine present at most 20 images in a screen without scrolling. Too many images in a screen will confuse the user and drop the experience evidently. Images in the top pages attract the most interests and attentions from the user. So the precision at K metric is significant to evaluate the image retrieval performance.

MAP (Mean Average Precision) provides a single-figure measure of quality across recall levels. Among evaluation measures, MAP has been shown to have especially good discrimination and stability. For a single query, Average Precision is the average of the precision value obtained for the set of top k items existing after each relevant item is retrieved, and this value is then averaged over all queries [21]. That is, if the set of relevant items for a query $q_j \in Q$ is $\{d_1, \ldots, d_{m_j}\}$ and R_{jk} is the set of ranked retrieval results from the top result until you get to item d_k, then

$$MAP(Q) = \frac{1}{|Q|} \sum_{j=1}^{|Q|} \frac{1}{m_j} \sum_{k=1}^{m_j} Precision(R_{jk}). \qquad (11)$$

NDCG is designed for situations of non-binary notions of relevance. It is not suitable here.

5.1.2 Baseline Algorithm

To show EMR's effectiveness, several methods are compared: MR, FMR [11] and SVM for image retrieval (baseline) [25]. Given that the goal of our paper is to improve MR, so the main comparative method is the original MR.

FMR firstly partitions the data into several parts (clustering) and computes the matrix inversion by a block-wise way. It uses the SVD technique which is time consuming. So its computational bottleneck is transformed to SVD. When SVD is accurately solved, FMR equals MR. But FMR uses the approximate solution to speed up the computation. We use 10 clusters and calculate the approximation of SVD with 10 singular values. Higher accuracy requires much more computational time.

SVM can be easily transformed to a query-based ranking algorithm, and has been successfully applied in image retrieval. With the specified relevant/irrelevant (to the query) information, a maximal margin hyperplane is build to separate the relevant from irrelevant images, and then the most relevant images are the ones farthest from the SVM boundary. We use the well known LIBSVM toolbox [4] and select the RBF kernel. The parameters C and g in LIBSVM are 50 and 0.5 respectively.

5.2 Implementation Issues

Here we discuss some important implementation issues for our experiments: low-level features of images and out-of-sample retrieval.

5.2.1 Low-Level Features of Images

Low-level features representation of images is crucial for CBIR. If the low-level features can accurately measure the semantic distance between images, there is no need to design any new retrieval method. Unfortunately, low-level features always fail to capture the high-level semantic concepts. In our opinion, more than the low-level features, a good CBIR method should take the underlying structure of the data into account. In our experiments, we use a 64-dimensional color histogram and a 64-dimensional Color Texture Moment [12, 31] to represent the images.

5.2.2 Out-of-Sample Retrieval

For in-sample data retrieval, we can construct the graph and compute the matrix inversion part of equation (2) offline. But for out-of-sample data, the situation is totally different. In [10], the authors solve the out-of-sample problem by finding the nearest neighbors of the query and using the neighbors as query points. They don't add the query into the graph, therefore their database is static. Moreover, their method may change the query's initial semantic meaning. In contrast, we efficiently update the graph structure and use the new sample as a query for retrieval. The image database can be dynamically updated.

For one instant retrieval, it is unwise to update the whole graph or rebuild the anchors, especially on a large data set. We can adopt fast updating strategies as follows.

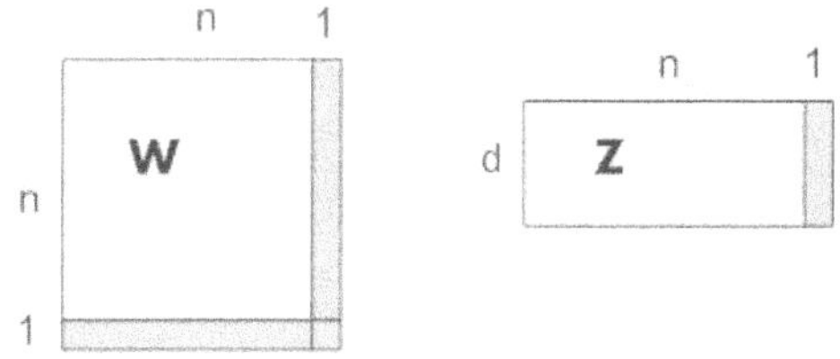

Figure 2: Extend matrix W (MR and FMR) and Z (EMR) in the gray regions for an out-of-sample.

A fast but *inexact* strategy for MR and FMR is leaving the original graph unchanged and adding a new row and a new column to W. But k nearest neighbor relationship is not symmetric, therefore the query's neighbors would lose some local information – its original neighbors' weights decrease relatively and they may have $k+1$ nearest neighbors. While for EMR, each data point is independently computed. We just assign weights between the new query and its nearby anchors. That forms a new column of Z. One point has little effect to the stable anchors in a large data set (e.g., cluster centers). Figure 2 shows the updating strategies.

5.3 Performance

We firstly compare our proposed method EMR with MR, FMR and baseline on COREL database without relevance feedback. Relevance feedback asks users to label some retrieved samples, making the retrieval procedure inconvenient. So if possible, we prefer an algorithm having good performance without relevance feedback. For our method EMR, 1000 k-means anchors are used. Later in the model selection part, we find that using 800 or fewer anchors achieves a close performance.

An important issue needs to be emphasized: although we have the image labels (categories), we don't use them in our algorithm, since in real world applications, labeling is very expensive. The label information can only be used to evaluation and relevance feedback.

At the beginning of the retrieval, we don't have the user specified relevant/irrelevant information. To apply SVM, the pseudo relevance feedback [21] strategy, also known as blind relevance feedback is adopted. We rank the images in the database according to their euclidean distances to the query, and then the nearest ten images are considered as relevant and the farthest ten are irrelevant. With such an approach, we run SVM as normal at the beginning, and the user gets images without any additional interaction.

5.3.1 Average Accuracy

Each image is used as a query and the retrieval performance is averaged. Figure 3 prints the average precision (at 10 to 80) of each method and Table 1 records the average values of recall, F1 score (at 10 to 80), and the values of MAP with all relevant images. It is easy to find that the performance of MR and EMR are very close, while FMR lose a little precision. All the three algorithms are better than the baseline method in the whole range.

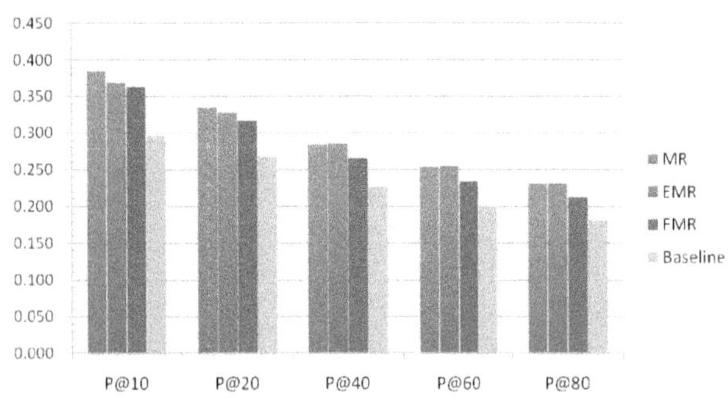

Figure 3: Retrieval precision at top 10 to 80 returns of MR (left), EMR, FMR and Baseline.

Table 1: The average values of Recall, F1 on top 10 to 80, and MAP.

	MR	EMR	FMR	SVM
R@10	0.039	0.037	0.037	0.030
F1@10	0.071	0.068	0.067	0.054
R@20	0.068	0.066	0.064	0.054
F1@20	0.113	0.110	0.106	0.090
R@40	0.115	0.115	0.107	0.092
F1@40	0.163	0.164	0.153	0.130
R@60	0.154	0.155	0.142	0.122
F1@60	0.191	0.193	0.177	0.152
R@80	0.186	0.187	0.172	0.146
F1@80	0.206	0.207	0.190	0.161
MAP	0.190	0.191	0.174	0.143

The anchor points are computed off-line and do not affect the current on-line retrieval system. To speed up the selection, we can use fast k-means strategy or just select random anchors. The fast k-means strategy we used is very simple and effective: setting the number of maximum iterations of k-means to 10 (default 100). Experiments results in Figure 4 show that the performance of fast k-means or random anchors is close to normal k-means anchors. Using random anchors dramatically decreases the anchor points selection cost when the data size is extremely large. Thus, cost and performance are trade-offs in many situations.

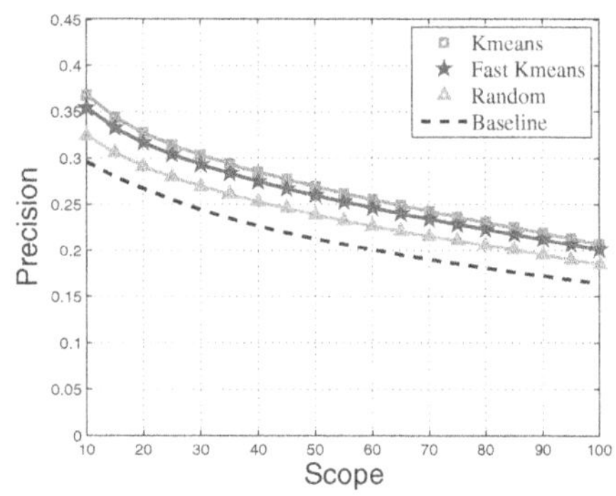

Figure 4: Performance of EMR with random anchors vs. k-means (fast and normal) anchors. Note that using random anchors achieves a close performance to k-means anchors.

To see the performance distribution in the whole data set more concretely, we plot the retrieval precision at top 10 returns for all 77 categories in Figure 5 without relevance feedback. As can be seen, the performance of each algorithm varies with different categories. We find that EMR is fairly close to MR in almost every category, and on some categories, EMR is better than MR. But for FMR, the distribution is totally different.

5.3.2 Response Time for Out-of-Sample

In this section, we compare the response time of MR, FMR and EMR when handling a new sample. We use a serial number of COREL samples, from 1,500 to 7,500, to build the graph and test 100 out-of-samples. The response time (in seconds) for each sample is averaged and showed in Table 2. To test EMR's efficiency in very large data sets,

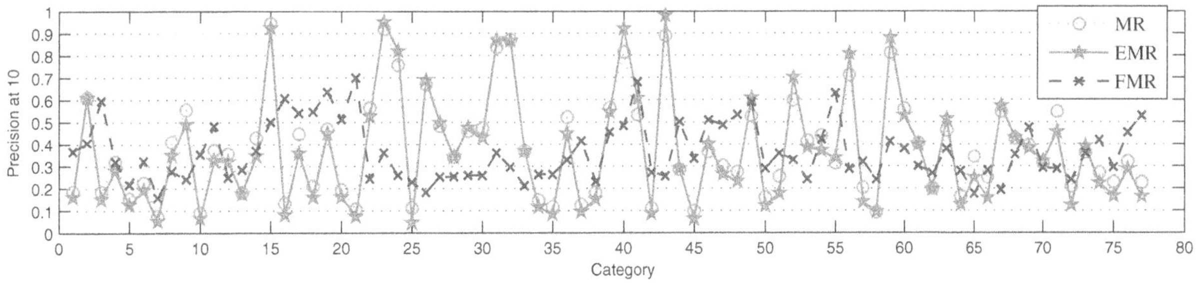

Figure 5: Precision at the top 10 returns of the three algorithms on each category.

we use 50,000 to 200,000 synthetic data in 128 dimensions. Since EMR has a closed form solution, so the response time is reliable and comparable – no matter the data is real or synthetic.

Table 2: Response time in seconds, MR (closed form in MR_c and iteration scheme in MR_{it}), FMR, and EMR (1000 anchors in EMR_{1k} and 800 anchors in EMR_{800}) with different graph size. The last three lines use synthetic data.

Size	MR_c	MR_{it}	FMR	EMR_{1k}	EMR_{800}
1500	1.283	1.685	0.821	0.462	0.264
2500	5.416	5.463	3.014	0.517	0.308
3500	14.233	12.437	7.507	0.576	0.358
4500	29.712	23.355	15.169	0.638	0.402
5500	53.854	39.559	26.866	0.710	0.447
6500	85.319	59.296	42.944	0.769	0.495
7500	129.715	85.916	65.124	**0.833**	**0.542**
50k	-	-	-	**3.869**	**2.700**
100k	-	-	-	**7.375**	**5.201**
200k	-	-	-	**14.534**	**10.183**

When the data size is large, it is extremely costly to save matrix $W \in R^{n \times n}$ in memory for MR and FMR. Even if we could save W in memory, the computational time is too long. But for EMR, we just save the smaller matrix $Z \in R^{d \times n}$, and the time is acceptable.

With different graph size, we fix the number of anchors to 1000 and 800 for convenience. Actually we could use fewer anchors to achieve a good performance in many cases. For MR, we use both the closed form and the iteration scheme. We record the response time of MR by closed form in MR_c and by iteration scheme in MR_{it}. The stop condition for MR_{it} is defined as $\|r^{t+1} - r^t\| < \epsilon$, where t is the iteration step and ϵ is a threshold. We use a very loose threshold 10^{-4}. With smaller threshold, MR_{it} needs more time to converge. We find that, the computational time of MR or FMR increases very fast, while our method increases slowly. Note that the time of extracting low-level features from the query image is not included in the response time, since it is not the focus of our ranking method.

5.3.3 Model Selection

Model selection plays a key role to many machine learning methods. In some cases, the performance of an algorithm may drastically vary by different choices of the parameters, thus we have to estimate the quality of the parameters. In this subsection, we evaluate the performance of our method EMR with different values of the parameters. For each single value, EMR is run independently 10 times and the results are averaged.

There are three parameters in our method EMR: s, α, and N. Parameter s is the neighborhood size in the anchor graph. Small value of s makes the weight matrix Z very sparse. Parameter α is the tradeoff parameter in EMR and MR. Parameter N is the number of anchor points. For convenience, the parameter α is fixed at 0.99, consistent with the experiments performed in [9, 36, 37]

Figure 6 shows the performance of EMR (Precision at 10) by k-means anchors at different values of s. We find that the performance of EMR is not sensitive to the selection of s when $s > 3$. With small s, we can guarantee the matrix Z highly sparse, which is helpful to efficient computation. In our experiments, we just select $s = 5$.

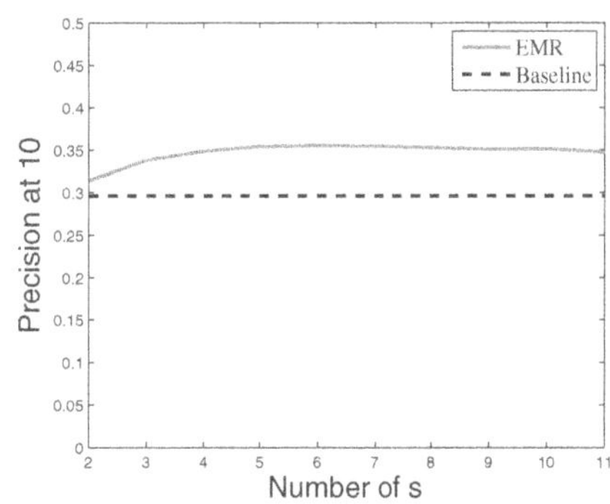

Figure 6: Retrieval precision versus different values of parameter s. The dotted line represents the baseline.

Figure 7(a) shows the performance of EMR (Precision at 10) versus different number of anchors in the whole data set. From the figure, we find that the performance increases very slowly when the number of anchors is larger than 400 (approximately). In previous experiments, we fix the number of anchors to 1000. Actually, a smaller number of anchors, like 800 or 600 anchors, can achieve a close performance. With fewer anchors, the graph construction and out-of-sample retrieval cost will be further reduced. To further investigate how many anchors are required, we evaluate EMR on half of the data set (77 categories, 50 images per category, 3850 images in total) in Figure 7(b). The number of categories is the same and the data size is reduced by half. However

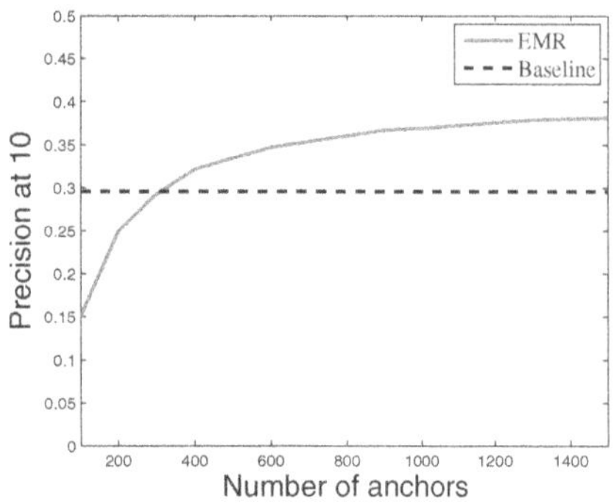

(a) 7700 images

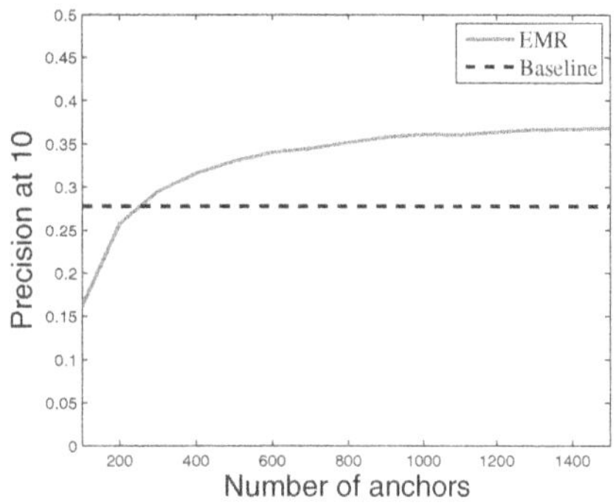

(b) 3850 images

Figure 7: Retrieval precision versus different number of anchor points in (a) 7700 images and (b) 3850 images. The dotted lines represent baseline performance in each case.

the result is similar – the performance increases very slowly when the number of anchors is larger than 400. This demonstrates that the number of required anchors is affected by the underlying structure, but not easily proportional to the size of the data set.

5.3.4 Performance with Relevance Feedback

Relevance Feedback [24] is a powerful interactive technique used to improve the performance of image retrieval systems. With user provided relevant/irrelevant information on the retrieved images, The system can capture the semantic concept of the query more correctly and gradually improve the retrieval precision.

Applying relevance feedback to EMR is extremely simple. We update the initial vector y and recompute the ranking scores. We use an automatic labeling strategy to simulate relevance feedback: for each query, the top 20 returns' ground truth labels (relevant or irrelevant to the query) are used as relevance feedbacks. It is performed for two rounds, since the users have no patience to do more. Images have been labeled in the first round are excluded in the second round. The retrieval performance are plotted in Figure 8. To avoid changing the original query's semantic meaning, the initial scores of the query and the feedbacks are 10 and ± 1 respectively.

By relevance feedback, original MR receives higher improvement than any other methods. But, relevance feedback is designed for real interactive systems in which the data size is always large. Original MR is too slow for these systems. See Table 2, when the data size is 7500, for one out-of-sample retrieval, MR_c needs more than 100 seconds. The meaning of applying relevance feedback to original MR is limited. Our method is a little worse than MR, but it is much faster than MR and better than the rest two. We leave the question of how to make further efforts to EMR's performance by relevance feedback in our future works. In this paper, our focus is to speed up manifold ranking, but not the relevance feedback.

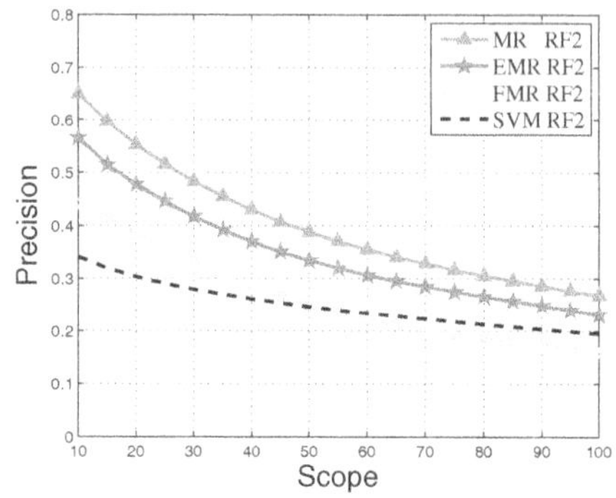

Figure 8: Average precision-scope curves for each methods after two relevance feedbacks.

5.3.5 Case Study

We show two real image retrieval cases in this part to see the performance of EMR intuitively. The first case in Figure 9 succeeds to retrieve relevant images by EMR without relevance feedback. The second case in Figure 10(a) is failed to capture the query's concept at first, but improved greatly after two feedback rounds in Figure 10(b).

An interesting thing is that the distance metric defined by EMR (we name it manifold distance) is very different with traditional metrics (e.g., Euclidean distance) used in many other retrieval methods. Euclidean distance only considers the data similarity, but manifold distance tries to capture the semantic relevance by the underlying structure of the data set. For example, the first retrieved image in the first case is the 34th image retrieved by Euclidean distance.

In the second case, the query is confused with many other concepts, including the oil painting and the elephant. The similar color and texture features make images in those concepts receiving higher ranking scores. At the same time, this case indicates that EMR is confused by the low-level features and misses the dominant concept *antelope* of the query, when there is no manual help. Fortunately, EMR is easy to integrate the label information – after two relevance feedbacks, the concept is captured successfully by EMR.

6. EXTENSION

Many real world applications have highly complex graph structure, like a social network or a web link graph. In such circumstances, the graph is existing and has very large size. If we have rich information about each node, we use EMR for efficient retrieval. But if we have no more information except the graph, how can we accelerate manifold ranking?

Figure 9: A successful content-based image retrieval case by EMR without relevance feedback. The first image with red box is the query, and the rest are the top 10 returns.

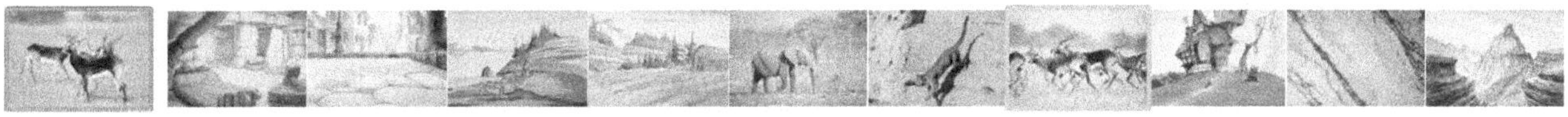

(a) Top 10 returns without relevance feedback. The image with green box is the only one correct.

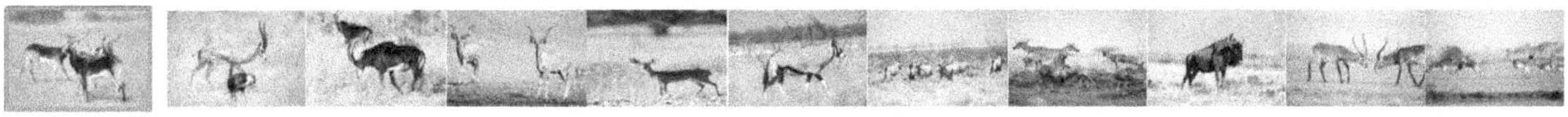

(b) Top 10 returns after two feedback rounds. All images belong to the same category.

Figure 10: A failed case by EMR without relevance feedback, but improved greatly by two feedback rounds. The first image with red box is the query.

Adjacency matrix W is symmetric. Its SVD decomposition is $W = U\Sigma U^T$, where $U \in R^{n\times k}$ and $\Sigma \in R^{k\times k}$. Let $H = D^{-\frac{1}{2}}U$, we can rewrite equation (2) to be

$$r^* = (I_n - H(H^T H - \frac{1}{\alpha}\Sigma^{-1})^{-1}H^T)y, \quad (12)$$

which is very efficient if $k \ll n$. But computing SVD of matrix W requires $O(n^3)$ operations, which is the same with the original matrix inversion. If we can fast decompose W, we save the computational time. Fortunately, W is highly sparse and may have a very low rank. Thus, some fast low-rank matrix approximation methods may help. We can arrange matrix W to be

$$W = \begin{pmatrix} G & W_{21}^T \\ W_{21} & W_{22} \end{pmatrix} \quad \text{and} \quad C = \begin{pmatrix} G \\ W_{21} \end{pmatrix}$$

where G is a $l \times l$ symmetric matrix from W, $l \ll n$. The Nyström method [30] computes SVD of G ($G = U_G\Sigma_G U_G^T$) and approximates singular values and singular vectors of W by $\Sigma = (\frac{n}{l})\Sigma_G$ and $U = \sqrt{\frac{l}{n}}CU_G\Sigma_G^{-1}$. When k singular vectors are used, the cost of this algorithm is $O(l^3 + nlk)$. Another alternative method is the Column-sampling method [6]. It approximates the spectral decomposition of W by using the SVD of C directly ($C = U_C\Sigma_C V_C^T$). That is, $\Sigma = \sqrt{\frac{n}{l}}\Sigma_C$ and $U = U_C$. Its cost is $O(nl^2)$. These two methods both can be used to speed up the computation.

7. CONCLUSIONS AND FUTURE WORK

In this paper, we propose the Efficient Manifold Ranking algorithm which extends the original manifold ranking to handle scalable data sets. We apply EMR to a content-based image retrieval application based on a real world image database. EMR tries to address the shortcomings of original manifold ranking from two perspectives: the first is scalable graph construction; and the second is efficient computation, especially for out-of-sample retrieval. Experimental results demonstrate that EMR is feasible to large scale real world image retrieval systems – it significantly reduces the computational time, as well as the storage space. Actually, our new design of the adjacency matrix can be used to many other graph-based algorithms, and EMR is also feasible to other types of information resources.

In our future work, we will test more visual features and evaluate our method on other databases. Moreover, many social network sites like Flickr allow users to annotate images with free tags, which significantly help us to understand semantic concepts of images. Thus, for images having tag information, we can combine the image features and tag information to improve retrieval performance. Another extension of our work is the distributed computation, an enterprise solution for web scale retrieval systems.

8. ACKNOWLEDGEMENT

This work is supported by Program for New Century Excellent Talents in University (NCET-09-0685).

9. REFERENCES

[1] S. Agarwal. Ranking on graph data. In *Proceedings of the 23rd International Conference on Machine Learning*, pages 25–32, 2006.

[2] S. Brin and L. Page. The anatomy of a large-scale hypertextual Web search engine. *Computer networks and ISDN systems*, 30(1-7):107–117, 1998.

[3] J. Bu, S. Tan, C. Chen, C. Wang, H. Wu, L. Zhang, and X. He. Music recommendation by unified hypergraph: combining social media information and music content. In *Proceedings of the 18th annual ACM international conference on Multimedia*, pages 391–400, 2010.

[4] C.-C. Chang and C.-J. Lin. *LIBSVM: a library for support vector machines*, 2001. Software available at http://www.csie.ntu.edu.tw/ cjlin/libsvm.

[5] R. Datta, D. Joshi, J. Li, and J. Wang. Image retrieval: Ideas, influences, and trends of the new age. *ACM Computing Surveys (CSUR)*, 40(2):1–60, 2008.

[6] A. Frieze, R. Kannan, and S. Vempala. Fast Monte Carlo algorithms for finding low-rank approximations. *Journal of the ACM (JACM)*, 51(6):1025–1041, 2004.

[7] W. Gao, P. Cai, K. Wong, and A. Zhou. Learning to rank only using training data from related domain. In

Proceeding of the 33rd international ACM SIGIR conference on Research and development in information retrieval, pages 162–169. ACM, 2010.

[8] Z. Guan, J. Bu, Q. Mei, C. Chen, and C. Wang. Personalized tag recommendation using graph-based ranking on multi-type interrelated objects. In *Proceedings of the 32nd international ACM SIGIR conference on Research and development in information retrieval*, pages 540–547, 2009.

[9] J. He, M. Li, H. Zhang, H. Tong, and C. Zhang. Manifold-ranking based image retrieval. In *Proceedings of the 12th annual ACM international conference on Multimedia*, pages 9–16, 2004.

[10] J. He, M. Li, H. Zhang, H. Tong, and C. Zhang. Generalized manifold-ranking-based image retrieval. *IEEE Transactions on Image Processing*, 15(10):3170–3177, 2006.

[11] R. He, Y. Zhu, and W. Zhan. Fast Manifold-Ranking for Content-Based Image Retrieval. In *ISECS International Colloquium on Computing, Communication, Control, and Management.*

[12] X. He, D. Cai, and J. Han. Learning a maximum margin subspace for image retrieval. *IEEE Transactions on Knowledge and Data Engineering*, pages 189–201, 2007.

[13] J. Jeon, V. Lavrenko, and R. Manmatha. Automatic image annotation and retrieval using cross-media relevance models. In *Proceedings of the 26th annual international ACM SIGIR conference on Research and development in informaion retrieval*, pages 119–126, 2003.

[14] T. Kanungo, D. Mount, N. Netanyahu, C. Piatko, R. Silverman, and A. Wu. An efficient k-means clustering algorithm: Analysis and implementation. *Pattern Analysis and Machine Intelligence, IEEE Transactions on*, 24(7):881–892, 2002.

[15] J. Kleinberg. Authoritative sources in a hyperlinked environment. *Journal of the ACM (JACM)*, 46(5):604–632, 1999.

[16] B. Li, E. Chang, and C. Wu. DPF-a perceptual distance function for image retrieval. In *International Conference on Image Processing*, volume 2, pages 597–600, 2002.

[17] D. Liu, X. Hua, L. Yang, M. Wang, and H. Zhang. Tag ranking. In *Proceedings of the 18th international conference on World wide web*, pages 351–360, 2009.

[18] W. Liu, J. He, and S. Chang. Large graph construction for scalable semi-supervised learning. In *Proceedings of the 27th International Conference on Machine Learning*, pages 679–686, 2010.

[19] Y. Liu, D. Zhang, G. Lu, and W. Ma. A survey of content-based image retrieval with high-level semantics. *Pattern Recognition*, 40(1):262–282, 2007.

[20] D. Lowe. Object recognition from local scale-invariant features. In *International Conference on Computer Vision*, page 1150, 1999.

[21] C. Manning, P. Raghavan, and H. Schütze. *Introduction to information retrieval.* Cambridge University Press, 2008.

[22] J. Ponte and W. Croft. A language modeling approach to information retrieval. In *Proceedings of the 21st annual international ACM SIGIR conference on Research and development in information retrieval*, pages 275–281. ACM, 1998.

[23] S. Roweis and L. Saul. Nonlinear dimensionality reduction by locally linear embedding. *Science*, 290(5500):2323, 2000.

[24] Y. Rui, T. Huang, M. Ortega, and S. Mehrotra. Relevance feedback: A power tool for interactive content-based image retrieval. *Circuits and Systems for Video Technology, IEEE Transactions on*, 8(5):644–655, 2002.

[25] S. Tong and E. Chang. Support vector machine active learning for image retrieval. In *Proceedings of the 9th ACM international conference on Multimedia*, pages 107–118, 2001.

[26] M. Tsai, T. Liu, T. Qin, H. Chen, and W. Ma. FRank: a ranking method with fidelity loss. In *Proceedings of the 30th annual international ACM SIGIR conference on Research and development in information retrieval*, pages 383–390. ACM, 2007.

[27] R. Veltkamp and M. Tanase. Content-Based Image Retrieval Systems: A Survey. 2002.

[28] X. Wan, J. Yang, and J. Xiao. Manifold-ranking based topic-focused multi-document summarization. In *Proceedings of the 20th International Joint Conference on Artifical Intelligence*, pages 2903–2908, 2007.

[29] L. Wang, J. Lin, and D. Metzler. Learning to efficiently rank. In *Proceeding of the 33rd international ACM SIGIR conference on Research and development in information retrieval*, pages 138–145, 2010.

[30] C. Williams and M. Seeger. Using the Nyström method to speed up kernel machines. In *Advances in Neural Information Processing Systems 13*, 2001.

[31] H. Yu, M. Li, H. Zhang, and J. Feng. Color texture moments for content-based image retrieval. In *International Conference on Image Processing*, volume 3, pages 929–932, 2002.

[32] K. Yu, J. Bi, and V. Tresp. Active learning via transductive experimental design. In *Proceedings of the 23rd international conference on Machine learning*, pages 1081–1088, 2006.

[33] K. Yu, T. Zhang, and Y. Gong. Nonlinear learning using local coordinate coding. *In Advances in Neural Information Processing Systems*, 2009.

[34] X. Yuan, X. Hua, M. Wang, and X. Wu. Manifold-ranking based video concept detection on large database and feature pool. In *Proceedings of the 14th annual ACM International Conference on Multimedia*, pages 623–626, 2006.

[35] K. Zhang, J. Kwok, and B. Parvin. Prototype vector machine for large scale semi-supervised learning. In *Proceedings of the 26th Annual International Conference on Machine Learning*, pages 1233–1240, 2009.

[36] D. Zhou, O. Bousquet, T. Lal, J. Weston, and B. Schölkopf. Learning with local and global consistency. In *Advances in Neural Information Processing Systems*, pages 595–602, 2004.

[37] D. Zhou, J. Weston, A. Gretton, O. Bousquet, and B. Schölkopf. Ranking on data manifolds. In *Advances in Neural Information Processing Systems*, page 169, 2004.

Mining Weakly Labeled Web Facial Images for Search-based Face Annotation

Dayong Wang, Steven C.H. Hoi, Ying He
School of Computer Engineering, Nanyang Technological University, Singapore
{s090023, chhoi, yhe}@ntu.edu.sg

ABSTRACT

In this paper, we investigate a search-based face annotation framework by mining weakly labeled facial images that are freely available on the internet. A key component of such a search-based annotation paradigm is to build a database of facial images with accurate labels. This is however challenging since facial images on the WWW are often noisy and incomplete. To improve the label quality of raw web facial images, we propose an effective Unsupervised Label Refinement (ULR) approach for refining the labels of web facial images by exploring machine learning techniques. We develop effective optimization algorithms to solve the large-scale learning tasks efficiently, and conduct an extensive empirical study on a web facial image database with 400 persons and 40,000 web facial images. Encouraging results showed that the proposed ULR technique can significantly boost the performance of the promising search-based face annotation scheme.

Categories and Subject Descriptors

H.3.3 [**Information Storage and Retrieval**]: Information Search and Retrieval; I.2.6 [**Artificial Intelligence**]: Learning

General Terms

Algorithms, Experimentation

Keywords

web facial images, auto face annotation, unsupervised learning

1. INTRODUCTION

Due to the popularity of various digital cameras and the rapid growth of Internet-based photo sharing, recent years have witnessed an explosion of the number of photos captured and stored by consumers. A large collection of photo images which are usually unlabeled raises a great challenge for end users to browse and search. One possible solution is to tag images manually, which is however time-consuming and often costly for large photo collections.

Instead of annotating images manually, another more salient technique to overcome this challenge is *automated image annotation* [ ], which aims to automatically assign an image some metadata typically in the form of captions or keywords to describe the semantic concepts/objects in the image. Despite being studied extensively [, ,], existing techniques for generic image annotation remain far from practical and satisfactory in real-world applications. Unlike the existing generic image annotation, in this paper, we address a specific sub-topic, i.e., *auto face annotation*, which aims to detect human faces from a photo image and to annotate the human names to the facial image.

Auto face annotation can be beneficial to many real-world applications. For example, with auto face annotation techniques, online photo-sharing sites (e.g., Facebook) can automatically annotate users' uploaded photos to facilitate online photo search and management. Besides, face annotation can also be applied in news video domain to detect important persons appeared in the videos to facilitate news video retrieval and summarization tasks [ ].

Conventional face annotation methods usually adapt existing face recognition techniques by training multi-class face classification models from a collection of human-labeled facial images using supervised machine learning techniques [,]. We refer to such kind of conventional techniques as "model-based face annotation". Such approach is however limited in several aspects. First, it is usually time-consuming and expensive to collect a large amount of human-labeled training facial images. Second, it is usually difficult to generalize the models when new training data or new persons are added, in which an intensive re-training process is usually required. Last but not least, the annotation/recognition performance often scales poorly when the number of persons/classes is very large.

To address the above limitations, in this paper, we investigate a promising search-based framework for auto face annotation, which aims to exploit large amount of weakly labeled facial images that are freely available on the World Wide Web (WWW). Unlike the conventional model-based approaches, the proposed framework is data-driven and model-free, which annotates a novel facial image by a retrieval-based annotation process [ ]. In particular, given a novel facial image for annotation, we first retrieve a set of k most similar facial images from a weakly labeled facial image database, and then label the novel facial image by performing voting on the labels associated with the top k similar facial images.

A key challenge in the above search-based face annotation framework is that labels with web facial images are usually noisy and sometimes may be incomplete due to the nature of image uploading and tagging by WWW users. This is critical as the label quality of the database can considerably affect the final annotation performance of the search-based face annotation process. To overcome this challenge, in this paper, we propose a novel unsupervised label refinement scheme by studying machine learning techniques to enhance the labels purely from the weakly-labeled data without human manual efforts. As a summary, the main contributions in this paper include the following:

- We investigate a promising search-based framework for auto face annotation by mining large amount of weakly labeled facial images freely available on the WWW.
- We propose a novel Unsupervised Label Refinement (ULR) scheme for enhancing label quality via a graph-based and low-rank learning approach.
- We have implemented the proposed search-based face annotation system and conducted an extensive set of experiments, in which encouraging results were obtained.

The rest of this paper is organized as follows. Section 2 reviews the related work. Section 3 gives an overview of the proposed search-based face annotation framework. Section 4 presents the proposed unsupervised label refinement scheme by learning from weakly labeled data. Section 5 discusses our experiments for performance evaluation, and Section 6 concludes this paper.

2. RELATED WORK

Our work is related to several groups of research.

The first group is on the topics of face detection, verification and recognition. Face detection, verification and recognition are classical research problems in computer vision and pattern recognition, which have been extensively studied for many years [,]. Researchers have developed a variety of face databases for the benchmark of face detection and recognition techniques, such as the well-known FERET database [ ]. The traditional studies are often limited for the high-quality databases collected in well-controlled environments. Recent years have observed some emerging benchmark studies of unconstrained face detection and verification techniques on facial images that are collected from the web, such as the LFW benchmark studies [,]. A comprehensive survey on face detection and recognition topics can be found in [,].

The second group of related work is on the topic of face annotation. In general, face annotation can be viewed as an extended face detection and recognition problem. Some studies in literature have attempted to adapt existing face recognition techniques for face annotation tasks by formulating the problem as a supervised face classification task [, , ,]. For example, the work in [ ] adapted the Fisher's linear discriminant analysis method for face annotation, the study in [ ] employed a Bayesian method for face annotation, and the work in [ ] adopted the Support Vector Machines (SVM) to train and predict the probabilities of human names towards transcript matching faces in the videos. Besides the supervised learning approaches, some existing work also attempts to apply semi-supervised learning for face annotation. For example, the work in [ ] proposed a transductive kernel Fisher discriminant for face annotation, which employs both labeled and unlabeled data to train classification models for the annotation tasks. Our work differs from the above existing studies in that our method is model-free by adopting the emerging search-based annotation paradigm for auto face annotation, which is fully data-driven by mining weakly labeled web facial images.

The third group of related work is on the topics of auto image annotation [, ,] and some recent emerging studies on search-based image annotation [, ,]. Conventional image annotation approaches have been studied extensively, which usually apply some existing object recognition techniques to train classification models from human-labeled training images [, ,]. Recently, there is a surge of interests for exploring web image repositories for auto image annotation and object recognition problems using the retrieval-based annotation paradigm [ ]. For example, Russell et al. [ ] developed a large collection of web images with ground truth labels to facilitate object recognition research. Wang et al. [ ] proposed a fast retrieval-based approach for image annotation by studying some efficient hashing technique. Torralba et al. [ ] suggested efficient image search and scene matching techniques for exploring a large-scale web image repository. These studies usually concerned more on efficient indexing and searching techniques, while our work focuses on improving the label quality by machine learning techniques.

The final group of closely related work is about mining web facial images, which aims to leverage noisy web facial images for face recognition [, ,]. For example, Berg et al. [ ] crawled a large number of news pictures and captions from the WWW, and proposed a modified k-means clustering approach for cleaning up noisy web facial images. Recently, Le et al. [ ] proposed a two-step re-ranking scheme to purify text-based retrieval results for some special names. Zhao et al. [ ] proposed a consistency learning method to train face models for famous people by mining the text-image co-occurrence on the web as a weak signal of relevance towards supervised face learning task from a large and noisy training set. Unlike the above existing works that were not designed to optimize the search-based face annotation paradigm, our novel unsupervised label refinement scheme is proposed to optimize the label quality for the search-based face annotation task. Finally, we note that our learning methodology for solving the unsupervised label refinement task is partially inspired by some existing studies in machine learning, including graph-based semi-supervised learning and multi-label learning techniques [, ,].

3. SEARCH-BASED FACE ANNOTATION FRAMEWORK

Figure 1 illustrates the system flow of the proposed search-based face annotation scheme, which consists of the following steps: (1) facial images data collection, (2) face detection and facial feature extraction, (3) high-dimensional facial feature indexing, (4) learning with weakly labeled data, (5) similar face retrieval, (6) face annotation by majority voting from similar faces with their improved labels. The first four steps are conducted before the test phase of a face annotation task, while the last two steps are conducted during the test phase of a face annotation task, which thus should be done very efficiently. We describe each step briefly as follows.

The first step is the collection of facial image data as shown in Figure 1(a), in which we crawled facial images from the WWW by web search engines (e.g., Google) based on a name list that stores the names of persons to be collected. This crawling process produces a collection of facial images, each of them is associated with some human name. Given the nature of web images, these facial images are often noisy, which do not always correspond to the right human name. Thus, we call such kind of web facial images with noisy names as weakly labeled facial image data.

The second step is to pre-process web facial images to extract face-related information, including face region detection and alignment, face region extraction, and facial feature representation. For facial region detection and alignment, we adopt the unsupervised face alignment technique in [ ]. For facial feature representation, we extract the GIST features [ ] to represent the extracted faces. As a result, each face can be represented as a d-dimensional vector.

The third step of the framework is to index the extracted features of the faces by applying some efficient high-dimensional indexing technique to facilitate the task of similar face retrieval in the subsequent step. In our approach, we adopt the Locality-Sensitive Hash-

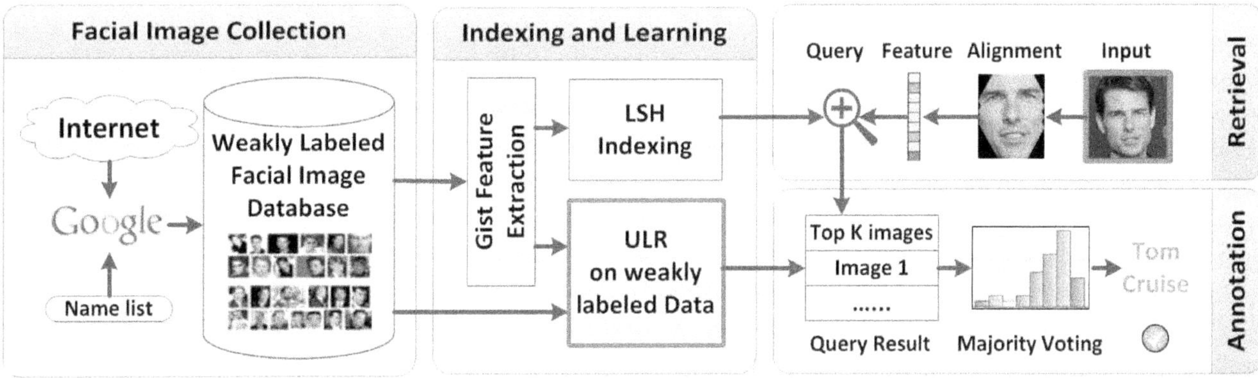

(a) (b) (c)

Figure 1: The system flow of the proposed search-based face annotation scheme. (a) We collect weakly-labeled facial images from WWW using web search engines; (b) We perform face detection and alignment, extract GIST features for the detected faces, and finally apply LSH to index the high-dimensional facial features; after that, we apply the proposed Unsupervised Label Refinement (ULR) method to refine the labels of the facial images; (c) We search for the query facial image to retrieve the top K similar images and use their associated names for voting towards auto annotation.

ing (LSH) [ ], a popular and effective high-dimensional indexing technique for approximate nearest neighbor search.

Besides the indexing step, another key step of our framework is to engage an unsupervised learning scheme to enhance label quality of the weakly labeled facial images. This process is critical to the entire search-based annotation framework since the label quality considerably affects the final annotation performance.

All the above are the processing steps before annotating a query facial image. Next we describe the process of face annotation during the test phase. In particular, given a query facial image for annotation, we first conduct a similar face retrieval process to search for a subset of most similar faces (typically top k similar face examples) from the previously indexed facial database. With the set of top k similar face examples retrieved from the database, the next step is to annotate the facial image with a label (or a subset of labels) by employing a majority voting approach that combines the set of labels associated with these top k similar face examples.

In this paper, we pay our main attention on the key step of the above framework, i.e., the unsupervised learning process to refine labels of the weakly labeled facial images.

4. UNSUPERVISED LABEL REFINEMENT ON WEAKLY LABELED FACIAL IMAGES

In this section, we present a novel Unsupervised Label Refinement (ULR) scheme to refine the labels of web facial image data by learning with weakly labeled data. In the following, we first introduce some preliminaries and notations followed by the problem formulation and the proposed algorithms.

4.1 Preliminaries

We denote by $X \in \mathbb{R}^{n\times d}$ the extracted facial image features, where n and d represent the number of facial images and the number of feature dimensions, respectively. Further we denote by $\Omega = \{n_1, n_2, \ldots, n_m\}$ the list of human names for annotation, where m is the total number of human names. We also denote by $Y \in [0,1]^{n\times m}$ the initial raw label matrix to describe the weak label information, in which the i-th row Y_{i*} represents the label vector of the i-th facial image $\mathbf{x}_i \in \mathbb{R}^d$. In our application, Y is often noisy and incomplete. In particular, for each weak label value Y_{ij}, $Y_{ij} \neq 0$ indicates that the i-th facial image $\mathbf{x}_i$ has the label name n_j, while $Y_{ij} = 0$ indicates that the relationship between i-th facial image $\mathbf{x}_i$ and j-th name is unknown. Note that we usually have $\|Y_{i*}\|_0 = 1$ since each facial image in our database was uniquely collected by a single query.

Following the terminology of graph-based learning methodology, we build a sparse graph by computing a weight matrix $W = [W_{ij}] \in \mathbb{R}^{n\times n}$, where W_{ij} represents the similarity between $\mathbf{x}_i$ and $\mathbf{x}_j$ defined as follows:

$$W_{ij} = \begin{cases} e^{-\frac{\|\mathbf{x}_i - \mathbf{x}_j\|_2^2}{2\sigma^2}} & \text{if } \mathbf{x}_i \in \mathfrak{n}_K(\mathbf{x}_j) || \mathbf{x}_j \in \mathfrak{n}_K(\mathbf{x}_i) \\ 0 & otherwise \end{cases} \quad (1)$$

where $\mathfrak{n}_K(\mathbf{x}_j)$ denotes the $K \ll n$ nearest neighbor list of the data point $\mathbf{x}_j$ based on Euclidean distance.

4.2 Problem Formulation

The goal of the Unsupervised Label Refinement (ULR) task is to learn a refined label matrix $F^* \in \mathbb{R}^{n\times m}$ to improve the initial raw label matrix Y. This is challenging since we have nothing else but the raw label matrix Y and the data examples X themselves. To attack this challenge, we propose a graph-based learning solution based on a key assumption of "label smoothness", i.e., the more similar the visual contents of two facial images, the more likely they share the same labels. The label smoothness principle can be formally formulated as an optimization problem of minimizing the following loss function $E_s(F, W)$:

$$E_s(F, W) = \frac{1}{2}\sum_{i,j=1}^{n} W_{ij}\|F_{i*} - F_{j*}\|_F^2 = tr(F^\top L F) \quad (2)$$

where $\|\cdot\|_F$ denotes the Frobenius norm, W is a weight matrix of a sparse graph built from the n facial images, $L = D - W$ denotes the Laplacian matrix where D is a diagonal matrix with diagonal elements as $D_{ii} = \sum_{j=1}^{n} W_{ij}$, and tr denotes a trace function.

Directly optimizing the above loss function is problematic as it will yield a trivial solution. To tackle this challenge, we notice that the initial raw label matrix usually, though being noisy, still contains some correct and useful label information. Thus, when we optimize to search for the new label matrix F, we shall avoid the solution F being deviated too much from the raw label matrix Y. To this end, we formulate the following optimization task for the unsupervised label refinement problem by including a regularization term $E_p(F,Y)$ to reflect this concern:

$$F^* = \arg\min_{F\geq 0} E_s(F,W) + \alpha \cdot E_p(F,Y) \quad (3)$$

where α is a regularization parameter and $F \geq 0$ enforces F is nonnegative. Next we discuss how to define an appropriate function for $E_p(F,Y)$.

One possible choice of $E_p(F,Y)$ is to simply set $E_p(F,Y) = \|F - Y\|_F^2$. This is however not appropriate as Y is often very sparse, i.e., many elements of Y are zeros due to the incomplete nature of Y. Thus, the above choice is problematic since it may simply force many elements of F to zeros without considering the label smoothness. A more appropriate choice of the regularization should be applied only to those nonzero elements of Y. To this end, we propose the following choice of $E_p(F,Y)$:

$$E_p(F,Y) = \|(F-Y)\circ S\|_F^2 \quad (4)$$

where S is a "sign" matrix $S = [sign(Y_{ij})]$ where $sign(x) = 1$ if $x > 0$ and 0 otherwise, and $\circ$ denotes the Hadamard product (i.e., the entrywise product) between two matrices.

Finally, we notice that the solution of the optimization in (3) is generally dense, which is again not desired since the true label matrix is often sparse. To take the sparsity into consideration, we introduce a sparsity regularizer $E_e(F)$ by following the "exclusive lasso" technique [ ]:

$$E_e(F) = \sum_{i=1}^{n} (\|F_{i*}\|_1)^2 \quad (5)$$

where we introduce an ℓ_1 norm to combine the label weights for the same person with respect to different names, and an ℓ_2 norm to combine the label weights of different persons together. Combining this regularizer and the previous formulation, we have the final formulation as follows:

$$F^* = \arg\min_{F\geq 0} g(F) \quad (6)$$

$$g(F) = E_s(F,W) + \alpha E_p(F,Y) + \beta E_e(F) \quad (7)$$

where $\alpha \geq 0$ and $\beta \geq 0$ are two regularization parameters. The above formulation combines all the terms in the objective function, which we refer it to as "Soft-Regularization Formulation" or "SRF" for short.

Another way to introduce the sparsity is to formulate the optimization by including some convex sparsity constraints, which leads to the following formulation:

$$F^* = \arg\min_{F\geq 0} E_s(F,W) + \alpha E_p(F,Y) \quad (8)$$

$$s.t. \quad \|F_{i*}\|_1 \leq \varepsilon, i = 1, \ldots, n \quad (9)$$

where $\alpha \geq 0$ and $\varepsilon > 1$. We refer to this formulation as "Convex-Constraint Formulation" or "CCF" for short.

It is not difficult to see that the above two formulations are convex, which thus can be solved with global optima by applying convex optimization techniques. Next, we discuss efficient algorithms to solve the above optimization tasks.

4.3 Algorithms

The above optimization tasks belong to convex optimization or more exactly quadratic programming (QP) problems. It seems to be possible to solve them directly by applying generic QP solvers. However, this would be computationally highly intensive since matrix F can be potentially very large, e.g., for a large 400-person database of totally 40,000 facial images in our experiment, F is a 40000×400 matrix that consists of 16 million variables, which is almost infeasible to be solved by any existing generic QP solver.

4.3.1 Algorithm for Soft-Regularization Formulation

We firstly adopt an efficient algorithm to solve the problem in Eq.6, then propose a coordinate descent based approach to improve the scalability. By vectorizing matrix $F \in \mathbb{R}^{n\times m}$ into a column vector $\tilde{\mathbf{f}} = vec(F) \in \mathbb{R}^{(n\cdot m)\times 1}$, we can reformulate $g(F)$ as follows:

$$g(F) = tr(F^\top LF) + \alpha\|(F-Y)\circ S\|_F^2 + \beta\|F\cdot \mathbf{1}\|_F^2 \quad (10)$$

$$= \tilde{\mathbf{f}}^\top Q\tilde{\mathbf{f}} + \mathbf{c}^\top\tilde{\mathbf{f}} + \mathbf{h} \quad (11)$$

where $\circ$ denotes the Hadamard product, $\otimes$ denotes the Kronecker product, $\tilde{\mathbf{y}} = vec(Y)$, $\tilde{\mathbf{s}} = vec(S)$, $\mathbf{1}$ is all one column vector, $U = I_m \otimes L^\top$, $V = (\mathbf{1}^\top \otimes I_n)$, $R = diag(\tilde{\mathbf{s}})$, $Q = U + \alpha R + \beta V^\top V$, $\mathbf{c} = -2\alpha R^\top\tilde{\mathbf{y}}$, $\mathbf{h} = \alpha\tilde{\mathbf{y}}^\top R\tilde{\mathbf{y}}$ and I_k is an identity matrix with dimension $k \times k$.

The above optimization is clearly a QP problem. To solve it efficiently, we adopt an accelerated multi-step gradient algorithm, which converges at $O(\frac{1}{k^2})$, k is the iteration step.

First of all, we reformulate the QP problem as follows:

$$\mathbf{x}^* = \arg\min_{\mathbf{x}} q(\mathbf{x}|Q,\mathbf{c}) = \mathbf{x}^\top Q\mathbf{x} + \mathbf{c}^\top\mathbf{x} \quad \mathbf{s.t.}\ \mathbf{x} \geq 0 \quad (12)$$

We then define a linear approximation function $p_t(\mathbf{x},\mathbf{z})$ for the above function q at point $\mathbf{z}$:

$$p_t(\mathbf{x},\mathbf{z}) = q(\mathbf{z}) + < \mathbf{x}-\mathbf{z}, \nabla q(\mathbf{z}) > + \frac{t}{2}\|\mathbf{x}-\mathbf{z}\|_F^2 \quad (13)$$

where t is the Lipshitz constant of ∇q. In order to achieve the optimal solution $\mathbf{x}^*$, we will update two sequences $\{\mathbf{x}^{(k)}\}$ and $\{\mathbf{z}^{(k)}\}$, recursively. Commonly at each iteration k, the variance $\mathbf{z}^{(k)}$ is named as *search point* and used for constructed combination of the two previous approximate solutions $\mathbf{x}^{(k-1)}$ and $\mathbf{x}^{(k-2)}$. The approximation $\mathbf{x}^{(k)}$ is achieved by the following optimization:

$$\mathbf{x}^{(k+1)} = \arg\min_{\mathbf{x}}\ p_t(\mathbf{x},\mathbf{z}^{(k)}) \quad \mathbf{s.t.}\ \mathbf{x} \geq 0 \quad (14)$$

After ignoring terms that do not depend on $\mathbf{x}$, the former optimization problem Eq.14 could be equally presented as:

$$\min_{\mathbf{x}\geq\mathbf{0}} \mathbf{g}^\top\mathbf{x} + \frac{t}{2}\|\mathbf{x}-\mathbf{z}^{(k)}\|^2 = t\sum_i[\frac{1}{2}(x_i - z_i^{(k)})^2 + \frac{g_i}{t}x_i] \quad (15)$$

where $\mathbf{g} = 2Q\mathbf{z}^{(k)} + \mathbf{c}$. The closed-form solution is given below:

$$x_i = \max(z_i^{(k)} - g_i/t, 0) \quad (16)$$

Finally, Algorithm 1 summarizes the optimization progress.

Algorithm 1: Multi-step Gradient Algorithm for ULR

Input: $Q \in \mathbb{R}^{(n\cdot m)\times(n\cdot m)}$, $\mathbf{c} \in \mathbb{R}^{n\cdot m}$, $t \in \mathbb{R}$
Output: $\mathbf{x}^* \in \mathbb{R}^{n\cdot m}$

begin
- $\alpha_0 = 1$;$k = 1$; $\mathbf{z}^{(0)} = \mathbf{x}^{(0)} = \mathbf{x}^{(-1)} = 0$;
- **repeat**
  - Case SRF : Achieve $\mathbf{x}^{(k)}$ with Eq. 14;
  - Case CCF : Achieve $\mathbf{x}^{(k)}$ with Eq. 19;
  - $\alpha_k = \frac{1+\sqrt{4\alpha_{k-1}^2+1}}{2}$;
  - $\mathbf{z}^{(k)} = \mathbf{x}^{(k)} + \frac{\alpha_{k-1}-1}{\alpha_k}(\mathbf{x}^{(k)} - \mathbf{x}^{(k-1)})$;
  - $k = k + 1$;
- **until** *CONVERGENCE*;

To further improve the scalability, we propose a coordinate descent approach to solving the optimization iteratively. This can take advantages of the power of parallel computation when solving very large-scale problems.

For the proposed coordinate descent approach, at each iteration, we optimize only one label vector F_{i*} by leaving the others $\{F_{j*}|j \neq i\}$ intact. Specifically, at the $(t+1)$-th iteration, we define the following optimization problem for updating $F_{i*}^{(t+1)}$ with $F^{(t)}$:

$$F_{i*}^{(t+1)} = \arg\min_{\mathbf{f}^\top} \Psi(\mathbf{f} \mid F^{(t)}, i) \quad \mathbf{s.t.}\ \mathbf{f} \geq 0 \qquad (17)$$

where the objective function Ψ is defined as follows:

$$\begin{aligned}\Psi(\mathbf{f} \mid F, i) &= L_{ii}\|\mathbf{f}\|^2 + 2\hat{L}_{i*}\hat{F}\mathbf{f} + \alpha\mathbf{z}^\top R\mathbf{z} + \beta\mathbf{f}^\top T\mathbf{f} \\ &= \mathbf{f}^\top\hat{Q}\mathbf{f} + \hat{\mathbf{c}}^\top\mathbf{f} + \hat{\mathbf{h}}\end{aligned}$$

where $\hat{L}_{i*} \in \mathbb{R}^{1\times(n-1)}$ is the i-th row of Laplacian matrix L_{i*} by removing the i-th element L_{ii}, $\hat{F} \in R^{(n-1)\times m}$ is a sub-matrix of F by removing its i-th row F_{i*}, $\mathbf{z} = \mathbf{f} - Y_{i*}^\top$, $R = diag(S_{i*})$, $T = \mathbf{1}\cdot\mathbf{1}^\top$, $\hat{Q} = L_{ii}I_M + \alpha R + \beta T$, $\hat{\mathbf{c}} = 2(\hat{L}_{i*}\hat{F} - \alpha Y_{i*}R)^\top$ and $\hat{\mathbf{h}} = \alpha Y_{i*}RY_{i*}^\top$.

The Eq. 17 is also a smooth QP problem, but much smaller than the original Eq. 10. Similarly, it could be solved efficiently by Algorithm 1. The pseudo-code of the coordinate descent algorithm is summarized in Algorithm 2.

Algorithm 2: Coordinate Descent Algorithm for ULR

Input: $X \in \mathbb{R}^{n\times d}$, $Y \in [0,1]^{n\times m}$
Output: $F^\star \in \mathbb{R}^{n\times m}$

```
begin
    t = 0 and F^(t) = Y;
    repeat
        for i = 1 to n do
            Case SRF: Achieve F_{i*}^(t+1) with Eq. 17;
            Case CCF: Achieve F_{i*}^(t+1) with Eq. 25;
        t = t + 1;
    until CONVERGENCE;
```

4.3.2 Algorithm for Convex-Constraint Formulation

For the convex-constraint formulation, by doing vectorization, we can reformulate Eq. 8 into the following:

$$\min_{\mathbf{x}\geq 0} \mathbf{x}^\top Q^\dagger\mathbf{x} + \mathbf{c}^\top\mathbf{x} \quad \mathbf{s.t.}\ \sum_{k=0}^{m-1} x_{k\cdot n+i} \leq \varepsilon, i = 1,\ldots,n. \quad (18)$$

where $Q^\dagger = U + \alpha R$, $\varepsilon \geq 1$, and all the other symbols are the same as Eq. 10. We also apply the multi-step gradient scheme to solve Eq. 18, however the constraint for the sub-problem is slightly different from Eq. 15, which is defined:

$$\min_{\mathbf{x}\geq 0} \frac{t^\dagger}{2}\|\mathbf{x} - \mathbf{v}\|^2 \quad \mathbf{s.t.}\ \sum_{k=0}^{m-1} x_{k\cdot n+i} \leq \varepsilon, i = 1\ldots,n \qquad (19)$$

where $\mathbf{v} = \mathbf{z}^{(k)} - \frac{1}{t^\dagger}\mathbf{g}^\dagger$, $\mathbf{g}^\dagger = 2Q^\dagger\mathbf{z}^{(k)} + \mathbf{c}$.

We can split the vector $\mathbf{x}$ into a series of sub-vectors $\bar{\mathbf{x}}^i = [x_i, \ldots, x_{(m-1)*n+i}]^\top$, and similarly we can split vector $\mathbf{v}$. Thus, Eq. 19 could be reformulated as:

$$\begin{aligned}\min_{\bar{\mathbf{x}}^0,\bar{\mathbf{x}}^1,\ldots,\bar{\mathbf{x}}^n} \quad & \frac{t^\dagger}{2}\sum_{i=1}^{n}\|\bar{\mathbf{x}}^i - \bar{\mathbf{v}}^i\|^2 \qquad (20)\\ \mathbf{s.t.} \quad & \|\bar{\mathbf{x}}^i\|_1 \leq \varepsilon,\ \bar{\mathbf{x}}^i \geq 0,\ i = 1,\ldots,n.\end{aligned}$$

The above optimization can be decoupled for each sub-vector $\bar{\mathbf{x}}^i$ and solved separately in linear time by following the Euclidean projection algorithm proposed in [ ]. Specifically, we can obtain the optimal solution $\bar{\mathbf{x}}^{i\star}$ for $\bar{\mathbf{x}}^i$ with the following problem:

$$\bar{\mathbf{x}}^{i\star} = \arg\min_{\bar{\mathbf{x}}^i} \|\bar{\mathbf{x}}^i - \bar{\mathbf{v}}^i\|^2 \quad \mathbf{s.t.}\ \|\bar{\mathbf{x}}^i\| \leq \varepsilon; \bar{\mathbf{x}}^i \geq 0. \qquad (21)$$

where $\bar{\mathbf{x}}^{i\star}$ has a linear relationship with the optimal Lagrangian variable $\lambda^\star$, which is introduced by the inequlaity constrain $\|\bar{\mathbf{x}}_i\| \leq \varepsilon$:

$$\bar{x}_j^{i\star} = sign(\bar{v}_j^i) \times \max(|\bar{v}_j^i| - \lambda^\star, 0), j = 1, 2, \ldots m. \qquad (22)$$

where $sign(\cdot)$ is the aforementioned sign function. Suppose $S = \{j|\bar{v}_j^i \geq 0\}$, the optimal $\lambda^\star$ could be obtained:

$$\lambda^\star = \begin{cases} 0 & \sum_{k\in S}|\bar{v}_k^i| \leq \varepsilon, \\ \bar{\lambda} & \sum_{k\in S}|\bar{v}_k^i| > \varepsilon. \end{cases} \qquad (23)$$

where $\bar{\lambda}$ is the unique root of function $f(\lambda)$:

$$f(\lambda) = \sum_{k\in S}\max(|\bar{v}_k^i| - \lambda, 0) - \varepsilon. \qquad (24)$$

$f(\lambda)$ is continuous and monotonically decreasing in $(-\infty, \infty)$. The root $\bar{\lambda}$ can be obtained by the bisection search algorithm in linear time. An improved searching scheme was also proposed in [ ] using the characteristic of function $f(\lambda)$.

Similar to the soft-regularization formulation, we can also adopt the coordinate descent scheme to further improve the scalability. In particular, we define a new update function $\Psi^\dagger$ similar to the aforementioned formula in Eq. 17:

$$F_{i*}^{(t+1)} = \arg\min_{\mathbf{f}^\top} \Psi^\dagger(\mathbf{f} \mid F^{(t)}, i) \quad \mathbf{s.t.}\ \|\mathbf{f}\|_1 \leq \varepsilon, \mathbf{f} \geq 0 \quad (25)$$

where $\Psi^\dagger(\mathbf{f} \mid F, i) = \mathbf{f}^\top\hat{Q}^\dagger\mathbf{f} + \hat{\mathbf{c}}^\top\mathbf{f}$ and all symbols are the same as Eq. 17 except $\hat{Q}^\dagger = L_{ii}I_M + \alpha R$. Eq. 25 is a special case of the optimization problem in Eq. 18, and can be solved efficiently by the same algorithm. Finally, the pseudo codes of the algorithm for the convex-constraint formulation are similar to the previous, as shown in Algorithm 1 and Algorithm 2.

5. EXPERIMENTS

In this section, we conducted extensive experiments to evaluate the performance of the proposed ULR technique for automated face annotation. In the following, we first introduce our experimental testbed, then discuss the comparison schemes and experimental setup, and finally present our experimental results.

5.1 Experiment Testbed

To build our testbed, we first collected a name list consisting of 400 popular actor and actress names downloaded from the **IMDb** website http://www.imdb.com. We collected those names with the billboard: "Most Popular People Born In **yyyy**" of **IMDb**, where **yyyy** is the born year, e.g., the webpage [1] presents all the actor and actresses who were born in 1975 in the popularity order. Our name list covers the actors and actresses who were born between 1950 and 1990. We submitted each name from the list as a query to search for related web images by Google image search engine. The top 200 retrieved web images are crawled automatically. After that we use the OpenCV toolbox to detect the faces and adopt

[1] http://www.imdb.com/search/name?birth_year=1975

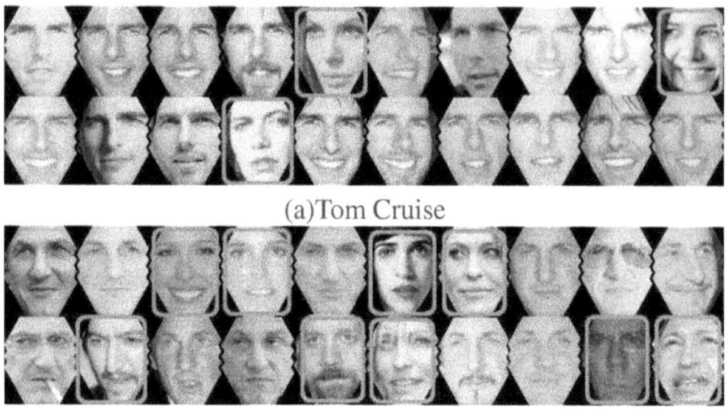

(b)Sean Penn

Figure 2: Two example sets of weakly labeled facial images where wrongly labeled images were highlighted by red boxes: (a) a good case of most images correctly labeled, and (b) a bad case of half of them wrongly labeled.

the DLK algorithm [ ] to align facial images into the same well-defined position. The no-face-detected web images were ignored. As a result, we collected over 40, 000 facial images in our database. We refer to this database as the "retrieval database", which will be used for facial image retrieval during the auto face annotation process. Figure 2 shows two examples in our database.

We also built a "test dataset" by randomly choosing 80 names from our name list. We submitted each selected name as a query to Google and crawled about 100 images from top 200 to 400 search results. Note that we did not consider the top 200 retrieved images since they had already appeared in the retrieval dataset. This aims to examine the generalization performance of our technique for unseen facial images. Since these facial images are often noisy, to obtain ground truth labels for the test dataset, we request our staff to manually examine the facial images and remove the irrelevant facial images for each name. As a result, the test database consists of about 1000 facial images with over 10 faces per person on average.

We run all the experiments on a PC with an Intel(R) Xeon(R) CPU (W3520), 12G memory and MATLAB 2010(b). To handle a very large-scale optimization task of 16-million unknown variables, we adopted the *Parallel Toolbox* in Matlab to exploit the parallel computation power.

5.2 Comparison Schemes and Setup

In our experiments, we implemented all the proposed algorithms for solving the ULR task. We finally adopted the soft-regularization formulation of the proposed ULR technique in our evaluation since it is empirically faster than the convex-constraint formulation according to our implementations. To better examine the efficacy of our technique, we also implemented some baseline annotation method and existing algorithms for comparisons. Specifically, the compared methods in our experiments include the following:

- "ORI": a baseline method that simply adopts the original label information for the search-based annotation scheme, denoted as "ORI" for short.
- "CL": a consistency learning algorithm [ ] proposed to enhance the weakly labeled facial image database, denoted as "CL" for short.
- "MKM": a modified K-means clustering algorithm [ ] proposed to cluster the image database and clean up noise images, denoted as "MKM" for short.
- "ULR": the proposed unsupervised label refinement method, denoted as "ULR" for short.

For a fair comparison to the above approaches, we adopted the same GIST features to represent the facial images. To evaluate their annotation performances, we adopted the *hit rate* at top t annotated results as the performance metric, which measures the likelihood of having the true label among the top t annotated names. For each query facial image, we retrieved a set of top K similar facial images from the database set, and return a set of top T names for annotation by performing a majority voting on the labels associated with the set of top K images.

Further, we discuss parameter settings. For the ULR implementation, we constructed the sparse graph W by setting the number of nearest neighbors to 5 for all cases. In addition, for the two key regularization parameters α and β in the proposed ULR algorithm, we set their values via cross validation. In particular, we randomly divided the test dataset into two equally-sized parts, in which one part was used as validation to find the optimal parameters by grid search, and the other part was used for testing the performance. This procedure was repeated 10 times, and their average performances were reported in our experiments.

5.3 Evaluation of Auto Face Annotation

Table 1 and Figure 3 show the average annotation performance (hit rates) at different T values, in which both mean and standard deviation were reported. Several observations can be drawn from the results.

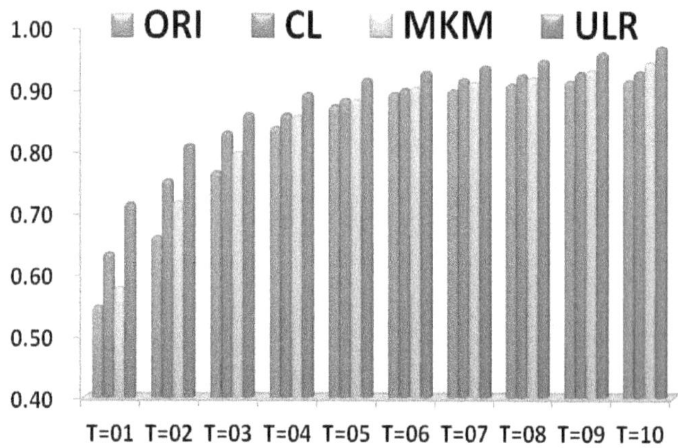

Figure 3: Evaluation of auto face annotation performance in terms of *hit rates* at top T annotated names.

First of all, it is clear that ULR which employs unsupervised learning to refine labels consistently performs better than the ORI baseline using the original weak label, the existing CL algorithm and MKM algorithm. For example, by comparing the hit rate at the first annotated name, ORI, CL and MKM achieved 54.8%, 63.4% and 57.8% respectively, while ULR can significantly boost the hit rate to 71.5%. For the hit rate at top 10 annotated names, the result of ORI, CL and MKM are 91.4% and 92.8% and 94.3% respectively, while ULR can achive a better hit rate 96.8%. The promising result validates the effectiveness of the proposed ULR technique for improving search-based face annotation. Second, when T is small, the hit rate gap, i.e., the hit rate difference between ORI and ULR is more significant, which verifies that the proposed ULR algorithm could efficiently refine the noisy data. Finally, we observed that the annotation performance increases slowly when $T > 5$. In practice, we usually focused on the a small T value since users typically would not be interested in a long list of annotated names.

Table 1: Evaluation of auto face annotation performance in terms of *hit rates* at top T annotated names.

	T=01	T=02	T=03	T=04	T=05
ORI	0.548 $\pm$ 0.013	0.661 $\pm$ 0.011	0.766 $\pm$ 0.009	0.837 $\pm$ 0.010	0.872 $\pm$ 0.010
CL	0.634 $\pm$ 0.012	0.752 $\pm$ 0.010	0.829 $\pm$ 0.010	0.858 $\pm$ 0.010	0.883 $\pm$ 0.009
MKM	0.578 $\pm$ 0.011	0.717 $\pm$ 0.012	0.797 $\pm$ 0.012	0.856 $\pm$ 0.008	0.882 $\pm$ 0.010
ULR	0.715 $\pm$ 0.008	0.809 $\pm$ 0.005	0.859 $\pm$ 0.009	0.892 $\pm$ 0.007	0.916 $\pm$ 0.010
	T=06	**T=07**	**T=08**	**T=09**	**T=10**
ORI	0.892 $\pm$ 0.009	0.898 $\pm$ 0.009	0.907 $\pm$ 0.010	0.912 $\pm$ 0.010	0.914 $\pm$ 0.010
CL	0.899 $\pm$ 0.009	0.916 $\pm$ 0.009	0.922 $\pm$ 0.008	0.926 $\pm$ 0.007	0.928 $\pm$ 0.007
MKM	0.902 $\pm$ 0.009	0.910 $\pm$ 0.009	0.918 $\pm$ 0.009	0.930 $\pm$ 0.009	0.943 $\pm$ 0.008
ULR	0.927 $\pm$ 0.007	0.936 $\pm$ 0.007	0.946 $\pm$ 0.006	0.958 $\pm$ 0.007	0.968 $\pm$ 0.007

5.4 Evaluation on Varied Top-K Retrieved Images and Top-T Annotated Names

This experiment aims to examine the annotation performance under varied values of K and T respectively for top-K retrieved images and top-T annotated names. To ease our discussion, we only show the results of the ULR algorithm. The performance differences between the ULR algorithm and the baseline algorithm as well as the CL algorithm are mostly similar to the observations in the previous experiment. The face annotation performance of varied K and T values are illustrated in Figure 4 and Table 2 where both mean and standard deviation results were reported.

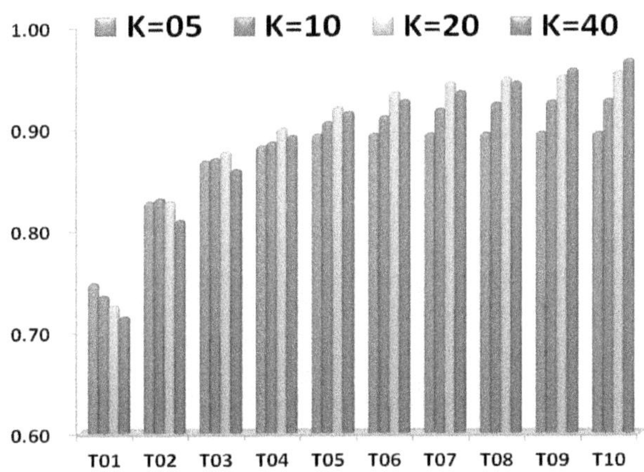

Figure 4: Annotation performance of varied K and T values.

Some observations can be drawn from the experimental results. First of all, when fixing K, we found that increasing T value generally leads to better hit rate results. This is not surprising since generating more annotation results certainly gets a better chance to hit the relevant name. Second, when fixing T, we found that the impact of the K value to the annotation performance fairly depends on the specific T value. In particular, when T is small (e.g., $T = 1$), increasing the K value leads to the decline of the annotation performance; but when T is large (e.g., $T > 5$), increasing the K value often boosts the performance of top-T annotation results. Such results can be explained as follows. When T is very small, e.g., $T = 1$, we prefer a small K value such that only the most relevant images will be retrieved, which thus could lead to more precise results at top-1 annotated results. However, when T is very large, we prefer a relatively large K value since it can potentially retrieve more relevant images and thus can improve the hit rate at top-T annotated results.

Table 2: Annotation performance of varied K and T values.

	T=01	T=02	T=03	T=04	T=05
K=05	0.747 $\pm$ 0.014	0.827 $\pm$ 0.012	0.868 $\pm$ 0.009	0.882 $\pm$ 0.009	0.894 $\pm$ 0.008
K=10	0.735 $\pm$ 0.011	0.831 $\pm$ 0.013	0.870 $\pm$ 0.013	0.886 $\pm$ 0.012	0.906 $\pm$ 0.010
K=20	0.725 $\pm$ 0.011	0.828 $\pm$ 0.010	0.877 $\pm$ 0.012	0.900 $\pm$ 0.010	0.920 $\pm$ 0.011
K=40	0.715 $\pm$ 0.013	0.809 $\pm$ 0.013	0.859 $\pm$ 0.012	0.892 $\pm$ 0.010	0.916 $\pm$ 0.009
	T=06	**T=07**	**T=08**	**T=09**	**T=10**
K=05	0.894 $\pm$ 0.008	0.895 $\pm$ 0.008	0.895 $\pm$ 0.008	0.896 $\pm$ 0.008	0.896 $\pm$ 0.008
K=10	0.911 $\pm$ 0.010	0.919 $\pm$ 0.010	0.924 $\pm$ 0.010	0.927 $\pm$ 0.010	0.928 $\pm$ 0.009
K=20	0.935 $\pm$ 0.007	0.945 $\pm$ 0.007	0.950 $\pm$ 0.006	0.952 $\pm$ 0.006	0.956 $\pm$ 0.006
K=40	0.927 $\pm$ 0.008	0.936 $\pm$ 0.008	0.946 $\pm$ 0.006	0.958 $\pm$ 0.005	0.968 $\pm$ 0.007

5.5 Evaluation on Varied Numbers of Images per Person in Database

This experiment aims to further examine how the annotation performance is affected by the number of facial images per person in building the facial image database. Unlike the previous experiment with top 100 retrieval facial images per person in the database, we created three variants of varied-size databases, which consist of top 50, 75, and 100 retrieval facial images per person, respectively. We denote these three databases as P050, P075, and P100, respectively.

Figure 5 shows the experiment results of average annotation performance. We can draw some observations. First of all, it is clear that the larger the number of facial images per person collected in our database, the better the average annotation performance can be achieved. Second, similar to the previous observations, ULR consistently boosts the annotation performance for all the databases, and achieves the best performance by beating the other competitors for all the cases. Finally, we noticed that enlarging the number of facial images per person in general leads to the increases of computational costs, including time and space costs for indexing and retrieval as well as the ULR learning costs.

5.6 Evaluation of Parameter Sensitivity

There are two key parameters α and β in the ULR algorithm. In the previous experiments, we found the best values by cross validation. In this experiment, we further examine their sensitivity to the annotation performance. Figure 6 shows an evaluation of annotation performance by a grid search on varied values of parameter $\alpha \in [0.1, 0.6]$ and $\beta \in [0, 0.7]$ in one of cross validation experiments. The value of each vertex on the color mesh represents the hit rate gap between ULR and ORI.

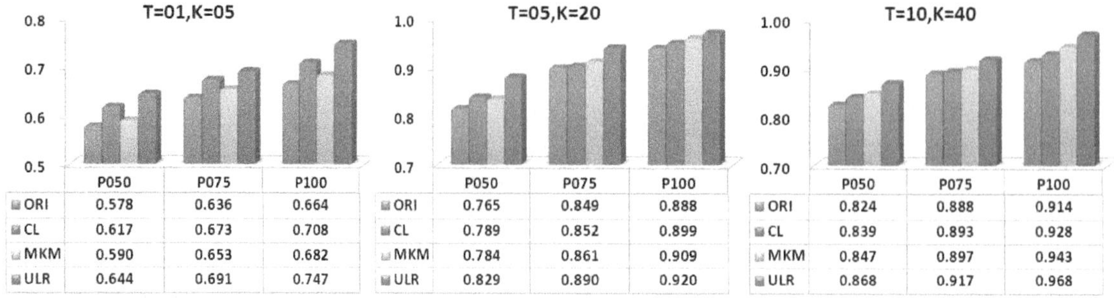

Figure 5: The annotation performance on three different databases, which have different numbers of images per person. Specifically, P050, P075, and P100 denote the databases having the top 50, 75, and 100 retrieval images per person, respectively.

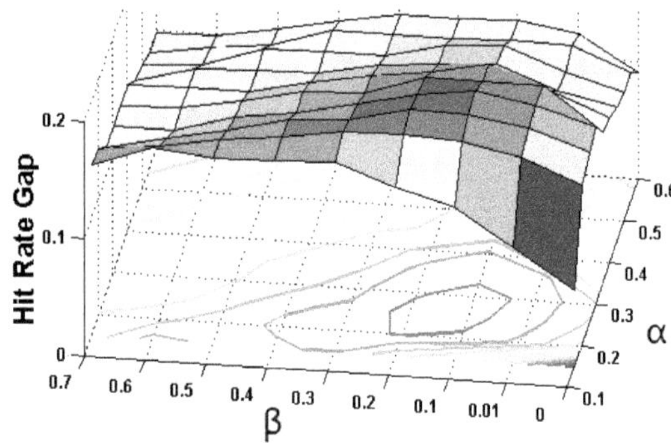

Figure 6: Evaluation of parameter sensitivity with respect to α and β for $T = 1$. The values of the vertex on the color mesh illustrate the hit rate gap between ORI and ULR.

Some observations can be drawn from the results. First, we found that for all α and β values, the proposed ULR scheme always has a positive improvement over ORI with original labels. Second, we found that the best α and β values are about 0.3 and 0.1, respectively. Further, we noticed that it is not difficult to find such good α and β values to get comparable results. Typically, ULR attains fairly good results when choosing $\alpha \in [0.2, 0.4]$ and $\beta \in [0.01, 0.4]$. These results show that ULR is quite robust to the parameters and could always enhance the annotation performance.

5.7 Evaluation of Optimization Efficiency

This section aims to conduct extensive evaluations on the running time cost by the four proposed algorithms. To distinguish the previous four algorithms clearly, in the following subsections, we will refer to the four algorithms by the following abbreviations:

- SRF-MGA: Soft-Regularization Formulation solved by the Multi-step Gradient Algorithm.
- SRF-CDA: Soft-Regularization Formulation solved by the Coordinate Decent Algorithm.
- CCF-MGA: Convex-Constraint Formulation solved by the Multi-step Gradient Algorithm.
- CCF-CDA: Convex-Constraint Formulation solved by the Coordinate Decent Algorithm.

5.7.1 Time Cost Evaluation on Artificial Data

We first compare two algorithms: SRF-MGA and CCF-MGA, which adopt the same gradient-based optimization scheme for two different formulations, as shown in Algorithm 1. We adopted an artificial dataset with varied numbers of classes m = 20, 40, 60, 80, 100 where each class corresponds to a unique Gaussian distribution. We set the number of examples generated from each class as $P = 100$, and the total number of examples $n = 2000, 4000, 6000, 8000, 10000$. The goal of the ULR optimization is to optimize the refined label matrix $F \in \mathbb{R}^{n \times m}$, which has the total number of unknown variables $V = 40000, 160000, 360000, 640000, 1000000$, respectively for each of the above cases. For the iteration number, we set it to 50 for both algorithms.

We randomly generated the artificial datasets and run the algorithms over these random datasets. This procedure was repeated five times. Table 3 show the average running time cost, where the first two columns are the means and their standard deviations obtained by both SRF-MGA and CCF-MGA algorithms, respectively. Figure 7 (a) further illustrates these results. Some observations can be drawn from these results as follows.

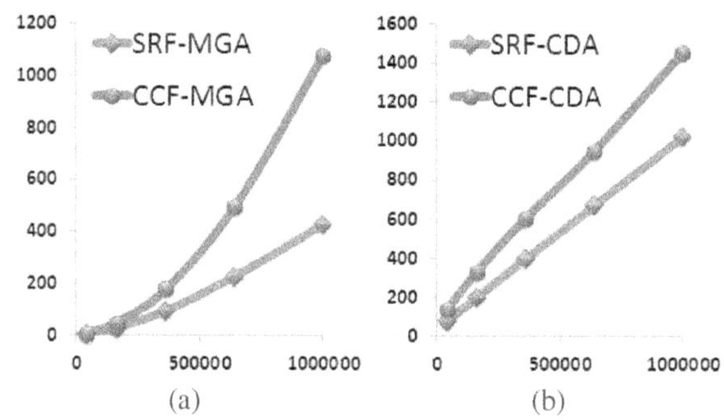

Figure 7: The running time of the proposed four algorithm (SRF-MGA, CCF-MGA, SRF-CDA, CCF-CDA). The group size P is 100. The x-axis presents the number of variables V, The y-axis is the running time(seconds).

First of all, it is clear that increasing the number of variables leads to the increase of the running time cost for both algorithms. Second, by comparing the two algorithms based on two different formulations, we found that the time cost growth rate of SRF-MGA is always slower than that of CCF-MGA, which indicates that SRF-MGA runs always more efficiently than CCF-MGA.

To further compare the difference of their growth rates, we try to fit the running time costs T w.r.t the number of variables V by a function $T = a \times V^b$, where $a, b \in \mathbb{R}$ are two parameters. By fitting the functions using the data shown in Figure 7(a), we obtained $a = 9.04E - 7$ and $b = 1.45$ for SRF-MGA, and $a = 3.70E - 8$ and $b = 1.74$ for CCF-MGA.

We compare running time cost of RF-CDA and CCF-CDA by adopting the similar settings as the previous experiment. For the iteration number, we set the outer-loop iteration number for CDA

Table 3: Average running time (seconds) of the proposed algorithms, where the 2nd rows show the standard deviations.

V	SRF-MGA	CCF-MGA	SRF-CDA	CCF-CDA
40000	4.80	6.76	76.63	136.50
	± 0.15	± 0.06	± 0.07	± 0.09
160000	29.04	49.05	197.92	330.30
	± 0.14	± 0.07	± 0.29	± 37.06
360000	95.43	178.45	399.11	607.20
	± 0.56	± 0.03	± 0.13	± 12.01
640000	228.44	494.29	670.23	950.40
	± 0.23	± 8.60	± 4.60	± 26.46
1000000	428.46	1076.04	1022.70	1457.40
	± 0.04	± 11.99	± 8.94	± 17.68

to 30 and fix the inner iteration number w.r.t. their subproblems to 30. The average running time cost and their standard deviations are illustrated in the last two columns of Table 3 and Figure 7(b).

Firstly, the SRF-based algorithm SRF-CDA spent less time cost than the CCF-based algorithm CCF-CDA. Second, unlike the previous results of the MGA based algorithms, we found that the running time cost grows almost linearly w.r.t the number of variables for both CDA based algorithms. More specifically, by fitting the time cost function $T = a \times V^b$ w.r.t. the number of variables V, we have $a = 3.93E-3$ and $b = 0.90$ for SRF-CDA, and $a = 1.50E-2$ and $b = 0.83$ for CCF-CDA, which show that the time cost growth rates of both algorithms are empirically sublinear. This encouraging result indicates that both CDA based algorithms are efficient and scalable for large-scale datasets.

5.7.2 *Time Cost Evaluation on Real 400-Person Data*

This experiment is to evaluate running time cost of the CDA-based algorithms (SRF-CDA and CCF-CDA) on our 400-person weakly labeled real web facial image dataset. For this real dataset, we have 400 persons and about 100 images for each person, which leads to 40000 images and 16-million unknown variables in our optimization task. We skipped the evaluation of MGA-based algorithms (SRF-MGA and CCF-MGA) since they are computationally too intensive for this large-scale experiment.

We randomly chose $P = \{50, 75, 100\}$ images from each person to build three databases of different sizes. We refer to these databases as $P050$,$P075$ and $P100$, respectively. We set the outer iteration number to 10 for both algorithms, and fixed the inner iteration number for their subproblems to 30. First, we employed the CDA-based algorithms (SRF-CDA and CCF-CDA) directly on those three databases, then we adopted the "*Parallel Computing Toolbox*" in Matlab to speed up the loop structure. We simply used the command "*matlabpool* 4" to estimate 4 local labs for the parallel computing task. The final results are presented in Table 4.

Two observations can be drawn from the above results. First, the same as the previous results, SRF-CDA is faster than CCF-CDA on the real database. Secondly, after applying the "*Parallel Computing Toolbox*", the running time is significantly reduced, which saved roughly two-third of the total time cost.

5.7.3 *Convergence Evaluation*

This experiment is to evaluate the convergence rates of the four different optimization algorithms. In particular, we consider a toy dataset with $m = 100$, $P = 100$, $n = 10000$. Figure 8 show the evaluations on the objective functions of the four different algorithms. For each algorithm, the average running time per iteration was also displayed on each of the figures. Some observations can be drawn from the results.

Table 4: The running time cost (seconds) of SRF-CDA and CCF-CDA algorithms on 400-person retrieval database. The top two rows show the running time cost of algorithms without parallel computing. The last two rows show the results using"*Parallel Computing Toolbox*" in Matlab.

Sequential	P050	P075	P100
SRF-CDA	2726.1 ± 27.9	4078.0 ± 26.3	5506.0 ± 22.7
CCF-CDA	2999.6 ± 33.4	4519.6 ± 34.7	6131.3 ± 31.8
Parallel	P050	P075	P100
SRF-CDA	1072.3 ± 16.6	1556.0 ± 13.2	2022.6 ± 13.3
CCF-CDA	1184.1 ± 18.6	1805.9 ± 21.5	2337.2 ± 11.3

First of all, it is clear that all the algorithms converge quickly. In particular, the two MGA-based algorithms almost converged after 10 iterations, which is slightly slower than the two CDA-based algorithms that almost converged after 8 iterations. Second, with the same formulation, we can see that the final objective values obtained by two different solvers are very close, which validates the correctness of the proposed algorithms. Finally, in terms of time cost per iteration, we found that the algorithms based the SRF formulation are faster than the algorithms based on the CCF formulations. More details about the running time cost comparison are given in the subsequent section.

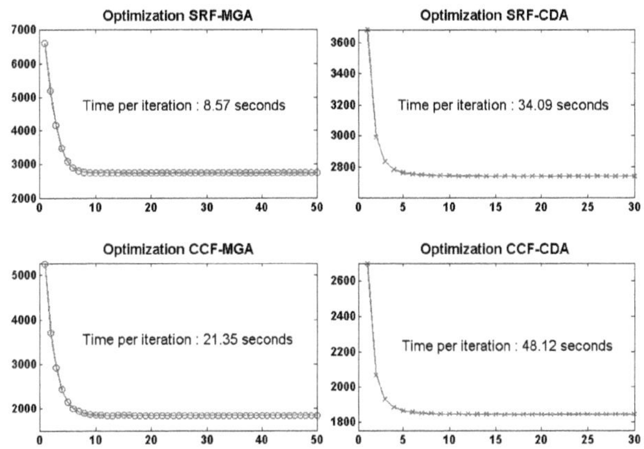

Figure 8: The objective function values of the four different optimization algorithms at each iteration on the toy data with $m = 100$, $P = 100$ and $n = 10000$. The average running time per iteration was also displayed on each of the figures.

6. DISCUSSIONS AND LIMITATIONS

Despite the encouraging results, our work is limited in some aspects. First, in our experiments, we assume each name corresponds to a unique single person, i.e., we do not consider the duplicate name case. This is however possible in reality. Second, we assume the top retrieved web facial images are related to a query human name. This is clearly true for popular human beings, such as movie stars and famous politicians. However, when the query facial image is not a popular person, there may not exist many relevant facial images on the WWW, which is a limitation of all existing data-driven annotation techniques. Third, comparing with the whole WWW, our current facial image database is still not large, though the essential optimization task in our problem is huge. In our future work, we plan to collect a large database, and develop more efficient algorithms to resolve the optimization task.

7. CONCLUSION

This paper investigated a promising search-based face annotation framework for mining weakly labeled facial images freely available on the WWW. To enhance the quality of the noisy and incomplete labels of the web facial images, we proposed a novel Unsupervised Label Refinement (ULR) technique by learning to refine the class labels from the weakly-labeled data. To make the proposed technique feasible for large-scale problems, we presented efficient and scalable optimization algorithms, which successfully solved a ULR optimization task on a real-world web facial image dataset with 400 persons and 40000 facial images by a single PC. From an extensive set of experiments, we found that the proposed technique achieved promising results with about 96% average hit rate of top-10 annotated names over a challenging test set with various web facial images captured in a wild. Our results also indicated that the proposed ULR technique significantly surpassed the other competitors, including the baseline with the original labels and other regular solutions in literature. For the future work, we will further speed up the current solution for very large-scale applications and investigate other machine learning techniques to improve the label refinement task.

Acknowledgement

This work was supported by the Singapore National Research Foundation Interactive Digital Media R&D Program, under research grant NRF2008IDM-IDM004-006.

8. REFERENCES

[1] P. N. Belhumeur, J. P. Hespanha, and D. J. Kriegman. Eigenfaces vs. fisherfaces: Recognition using class specific linear projection. *IEEE Trans. PAMI*, 19(7):711–720, 1997.

[2] T. L. Berg, A. C. Berg, J. Edwards, M. Maire, R. White, Y. W. Teh, E. G. Learned-Miller, and D. A. Forsyth. Names and faces in the news. In *CVPR (2)*, pages 848–854, 2004.

[3] Z. Cao, Q. Yin, X. Tang, and J. Sun. Face recognition with learning-based descriptor. In *CVPR*, pages 2707–2714, San Francisco, CA, 2010.

[4] G. Carneiro, A. B. Chan, P. Moreno, and N. Vasconcelos. Supervised learning of semantic classes for image annotation and retrieval. *IEEE Tran. PAMI*, pages 394–410, 2006.

[5] O. Chapelle, B. Schölkopf, and A. Zien, editors. *Semi-Supervised Learning*. MIT Press, Cambridge, MA, 2006.

[6] W. Dong, Z. Wang, W. Josephson, M. Charikar, and K. Li. Modeling lsh for performance tuning. In *CIKM*, pages 669–678, 2008.

[7] P. Duygulu, K. Barnard, J. de Freitas, and D. A. Forsyth. Object recognition as machine translation: Learning a lexicon for a fixed image vocabulary. In *ECCV*, pages 97–112, 2002.

[8] J. Fan, Y. Gao, and H. Luo. Multi-level annotation of natural scenes using dominant image components and semantic concepts. In *ACM Multimedia*, pages 540–547, 2004.

[9] J. Fan, Y. Gao, H. Luo, and G. Xu. Automatic image annotation by using concept-sensitive salient objects for image content representation. In *SIGIR*, pages 361–368, 2004.

[10] E. Hjelmås and B. K. Low. Face detection: A survey. *Computer Vision and Image Understanding*, 83(3), 2001.

[11] G. B. Huang, M. Ramesh, T. Berg, and E. Learned-Miller. Labeled faces in the wild: A database for studying face recognition in unconstrained environments. Technical Report 07-49, University of Massachusetts, Amherst, October 2007.

[12] J. Jeon, V. Lavrenko, and R. Manmatha. Automatic image annotation and retrieval using cross-media relevance models. In *SIGIR*, pages 119–126, 2003.

[13] D.-D. Le and S. Satoh. Unsupervised face annotation by mining the web. In *IEEE ICDM2008*, pages 383–392, 2008.

[14] J. Liu and J. Ye. Efficient euclidean projections in linear time. In *ICML*, pages 657–664, Montreal, Quebec, Canada, 2009.

[15] P. J. Phillips, H. Moon, S. A. Rizvi, and P. J. Rauss. The feret evaluation methodology for face-recognition algorithms. *IEEE Trans. PAMI*, 22(10):1090–1104, 2000.

[16] B. C. Russell, A. Torralba, K. P. Murphy, and W. T. Freeman. Labelme: A database and web-based tool for image annotation. *Int. J. Comput. Vision*, 77(1-3):157–173, 2008.

[17] S. Satoh, Y. Nakamura, and T. Kanade. Name-it: Naming and detecting faces in news videos. *IEEE MultiMedia*, 6(1):22–35, 1999.

[18] C. Siagian and L. Itti. Rapid biologically-inspired scene classification using features shared with visual attention. *IEEE Trans. PAMI*, 29:300–312, Feb 2007.

[19] Y.-Y. Sun, Y. Zhang, and Z.-H. Zhou. Multi-label learning with weak label. In *AAAI*, 2010.

[20] A. Torralba, Y. Weiss, and R. Fergus. Small codes and large databases of images for object recognition. In *CVPR*, 2008.

[21] C. Wang, L. Zhang, and H.-J. Zhang. Learning to reduce the semantic gap in web image retrieval and annotation. In *SIGIR*, pages 355–362, 2008.

[22] X.-J. Wang, L. Zhang, F. Jing, and W.-Y. Ma. Annosearch: Image auto-annotation by search. In *CVPR*, pages 1483–1490, 2006.

[23] L. Wu, S. C. H. Hoi, R. Jin, J. Zhu, and N. Yu. Distance metric learning from uncertain side information with application to automated photo tagging. In *ACM Multimedia*, pages 135–144, 2009.

[24] P. Wu, S. C. H. Hoi, P. Zhao, and Y. He. Mining social images with distance metric learning for automated image tagging. In *WSDM*, pages 197–206, 2011.

[25] J. Yang and A. G. Hauptmann. Naming every individual in news video monologues. In *ACM Multimedia*, pages 580–587, New York, NY, USA, 2004.

[26] L. Zhang, L. Chen, M. Li, and H. Zhang. Automated annotation of human faces in family albums. In *ACM Multimedia*, pages 355–358, Berkeley, CA, USA, 2003.

[27] M. Zhao, J. Yagnik, H. Adam, and D. Bau. Large scale learning and recognition of faces in web videos. In *FG*, pages 1–7, 2008.

[28] W. Zhao, R. Chellappa, P. J. Phillips, and A. Rosenfeld. Face recognition: A literature survey. *ACM Comput. Surv.*, 35(4):399–458, 2003.

[29] Y. Zhou, R. Jin, and S. C.-H. Hoi. Exclusive lasso for multi-task feature selection. In *JMLR W&C Proceedings (AISTATS2010)*, pages 988–995, Oct 2010.

[30] J. Zhu, S. C. H. Hoi, and L. V. Gool. Unsupervised face alignment by robust nonrigid mapping. In *ICCV*, 2009.

[31] J. Zhu, S. C. H. Hoi, and M. R. Lyu. Face annotation using transductive kernel fisher discriminant. *IEEE Transactions on Multimedia*, 10(1):86–96, 2008.

[32] X. Zhu, Z. Ghahramani, and J. D. Lafferty. Semi-supervised learning using gaussian fields and harmonic functions. In *ICML*, pages 912–919, 2003.

Temporal Index Sharding for Space-Time Efficiency in Archive Search*

Avishek Anand†, Srikanta Bedathur‡, Klaus Berberich†, Ralf Schenkel*

†Max-Planck Institute for Informatics, Saarbrücken, Germany
‡IIIT-Delhi, New Delhi, India
*Saarland University, Saarbrücken, Germany

{aanand,kberberi}@mpi-inf.mpg.de, bedathur@iiitd.ac.in, schenkel@mmci.uni-saarland.de

ABSTRACT

Time-travel queries that couple temporal constraints with keyword queries are useful in searching large-scale archives of time-evolving content such as the web archives or wikis. Typical approaches for efficient evaluation of these queries involve *slicing* either the entire collection [20] or individual index lists [10] along the time-axis. Both these methods are not satisfactory since they sacrifice compactness of index for processing efficiency making them either too big or, otherwise, too slow.

We present a novel index organization scheme that *shards* each index list with *almost zero increase in index size* but still minimizes the cost of reading index entries during query processing. Based on the optimal sharding thus obtained, we develop a practically efficient sharding that takes into account the different costs of random and sequential accesses. Our algorithm merges shards from the optimal solution to allow for a few extra sequential accesses while gaining significantly by reducing the number of random accesses. We empirically establish the effectiveness of our sharding scheme with experiments over the revision history of the English Wikipedia between 2001-2005 ($\approx$ 700 GB) and an archive of U.K. governmental web sites ($\approx$ 400 GB). Our results demonstrate the feasibility of faster time-travel query processing with no space overhead.

Categories and Subject Descriptors

H.3.3 [**Information Search and Retrieval**]: Search process

General Terms

Experimentation, Algorithms, Performance

Keywords

Time-Travel Text Search, Sharding, Slicing, Inverted Index, Web Archives

*Partially supported by the EU within the 7th Framework Programme under contract 258105 "Longitudinal Analytics of Web Archive data (LAWA)"

SIGIR'11, July 24–28, 2011, Beijing, China.

1. INTRODUCTION

Due to the ubiquitous access and ease of location using search engines, much of the human-generated content is available electronically over the Web. This content is constantly evolving with additions, deletions and modifications occurring at very high rates [5, 12, 13, 19]. Search engines continuously crawl and index the Web to keep up with its latest state.

There is a growing awareness, however, that this single-minded pursuit for the latest state of the Web results in losing access to the history of content which could be important in a number of advanced applications. As an answer to this, efforts such as the Internet Archive [3] and European Archive [2] store regular crawls of large portions of the Web for retrospective analysis. Effective querying over these collections requires the use of so-called *time-travel queries* that combine temporal constraints with standard keyword queries. These queries aim to return relevance ordered lists of documents (or, more precisely, document versions) that were "alive" during the specified time interval [10]. For example, on an archive of U.K. government websites, one may pose a query such as inheritance tax @ [2000-2002] to locate documents about inheritance taxation details prevalent during the years 2000-2002. Note that the same query without a temporal constraint would tend to generate results only about latest taxation details and not necessarily from the required time.

Efficient evaluation of these time-travel queries over archives of large collections (such as the Web) is a challenge that we address in this paper. Earlier efforts combined the ideas of index organization in temporal databases with inverted indexes [7, 10, 20], which essentially meant that the time-enriched inverted indexes are *sliced* along the time-axis (or partitioned vertically). Each resulting partition of the index list contains index entries of only those document versions that have a *valid-time interval* overlapping with the time interval of the partition. Answering a time-travel query in such a temporally sliced index involves choosing the correct –much smaller– index partition (or partitions) to evaluate the query.

Though attractive, such an index organization suffers from an index-size blowup incurred during the slicing process, since index entries whose valid-time interval spans across the slicing boundary are replicated. While a careful choice of the slicing boundaries can help to reduce the index blowup [10] in order to achieve acceptable levels of efficiency, 2 to 3 times index size increase is necessary.

1.1 Our Approach

In this paper, we rotate the "knife" of partitioning by 90° and propose to *shard* –or horizontally partition– *each index list* along document identifiers, instead of time (cf. Figure 1). An immediate benefit of this reoriented partitioning is almost *no increase* in the overall index-size (as we show later, only overhead is to maintain a small set of location pointers in each partition). We develop a single-pass greedy algorithm that optimally shards the index list, minimizing the number of index entries read during query processing.

In the resulting sharded index, query processing proceeds by first *opening* all index list shards for each query term, and *seeking* to the right position inside each shard, and, next, sequentially scanning the shard from that position –resulting in one random access followed by a sequential scan. As a random access is at least as expensive as a sequential read (as in disk- and network-based index storage), breaking the index list into too many shards actually degrades performance, even if the abstract processing cost says otherwise. Thus, the practical efficiency of the index organization is achieved only if it is sensitive to the cost ratio of random accesses to sequential accesses. We formulate an optimization framework for tuning the optimal sharding that takes into account the I/O cost ratio of the storage infrastructure and propose a heuristic to combine shards to gain practical runtime efficiency.

In summary, key contributions made in this paper are:

1. A novel temporally sharded index organization for a time-enriched inverted index that overcomes the issue of index-size blowup.
2. An optimal greedy algorithm to shard the index list, so that no time-travel query reads more than the required index entries, thus achieving ideal query processing performance.
3. A framework that achieves practical runtime efficiency by tuning the number of shards that each index list is split into, taking into account the I/O cost ratio of the storage infrastructure. Note that the cost of this is *independent* of the dynamics in the query workload, as it depends only on the storage system parameters.

We performed extensive empirical evaluation on large-scale versioned document collections using real-world keyword queries with temporal constraints at varying granularities. Results of these experiments indicate that our sharded temporal index has a negligible ($\approx 1\%$) increase in index size, but outperforms an optimized implementation of the previous best approach [10].

1.2 Organization

The remainder of this paper is organized as follows: in Section 2, we briefly present the data and time-travel query model that we use in this paper, as well as the time-travel inverted index [10] that we compare our work against. Next, in Section 3, we describe in detail the idea of sharding the inverted index and query processing over the resulting index organization. In Section 4 and in Section 5 we present the details of our idealized sharding and a sharding strategy sensitive to I/O cost ratio respectively. Details of our experimental setup are in Section 7 and the key results are in Section 8. Finally, we discuss previous related work in Section 9, before concluding in Section 10.

2. PRELIMINARIES

2.1 Data and Query Model

We operate on a collection $\mathcal{D}$ of versioned documents. Each document d has a unique identifier id_d and consists of a sequence of its versions, $d = \langle d^1, d^2, \ldots \rangle$, where every version consists of terms drawn from a vocabulary $\mathcal{V}$, i.e., $d^i \subseteq \mathcal{V}$. Furthermore, each document version has an associated valid-time interval $I(d^i) = [\, begin(d^i),\, end(d^i)\,)$ that conveys when the document version d^i existed in the real world. We make the natural assumption that these valid-time intervals for any two versions of the same document are disjoint, i.e.,

$$\forall_{d^i, d^j, i \neq j} I(d^i) \cap I(d^j) = \emptyset\,.$$

A document version that still exists when it is added to the archive is called an *active* version and has $end(d^i) = \infty$.

A time-travel query over $\mathcal{D}$ consists of a set of terms $Q = \{q_1, \ldots, q_m\}$ and a time interval $[b_Q, e_Q]$. When evaluated, this query retrieves the set of document versions that satisfy the keyword query Q and existed at any time during the time interval $[b_Q, e_Q]$. When using the conjunctive boolean model for keyword retrieval, we can write the result as:

$$R(\, Q@[b_Q,\, e_Q]\,) = \left\{ d^k \in \mathcal{D} \mid \forall q \in Q \,:\, q \in d^k \,\wedge\, I(d^k) \cap [b_Q,\, e_Q] \neq \emptyset \right\}.$$

Queries for which $b_Q = e_Q$ holds, so that the query time interval collapses into a single time point, will be referred to as *time-point queries*.

2.2 Index Organization

The index used for handling time-travel queries is based on the established *inverted index* [22], where each term in the vocabulary is associated with a list of entries called an *index list*. Each entry in the index list, $\langle id_d, I(d^i), s \rangle$, consists of a document identifier id_d, the valid-time interval, $I(d^i) = [begin(d^i), end(d^i)]$, and a payload s. Based on the retrieval model employed, the payload can be empty (for boolean retrieval), a scalar value (tf in the document version) or even richer positional information in each version –the index organization supports all these settings. When no confusion arises, we simply use $begin(p)$ and $end(p)$ of an index entry p to refer to the valid-time interval boundaries of the corresponding document version.

This index further supports partitioning of each index list into smaller index lists. This partitioning can be done either along (i) the time-axis, i.e., have all index entries that overlap a contiguous segment of time together, or (ii) the document-identifier dimension. In this work, we call the former partitioning *slicing* and the latter *sharding*.

Index Slicing of [10]

In the time-travel indexing framework proposed by Berberich et al. [10], the time-enriched inverted lists are sliced into several smaller sublists each spanning a specific subinterval of the time axis. As we already mentioned, every entry whose valid-time interval spans the boundaries of more than one slice is replicated in all the slices which overlap (cf. Figure 1). In their paper, the authors also show that the optimal slicing (defined as the setting where any time-travel query reads only those entries that qualify by their valid-time interval) is impractical to achieve due to the resulting blowup (more than 100×) in index size. As an alternative, they formulate an optimization problem which takes as a user-given input, an upper bound κ on the tolerable index-size blowup, and outputs the best slicing satisfying this constraint. The quality of the slicing is determined by the expected number of index entries that are read for any time-travel query.

Another interesting aspect of the above framework is *temporal coalescing*, a way of compressing index lists either in a lossy or non-lossy way. Temporal coalescing merges temporally contiguous entries of the same document into a single index entry, as long as the relative change in the payload s is within a specified threshold ϵ. Although this is somewhat orthogonal to the issue of partitioning, the distribution of valid-time intervals of entries in the index list could vary significantly after performing coalescing.

3. TEMPORAL INDEX SHARDING

The index sharding proposed in this paper, on the other hand, distributes the entries in an index list over disjoint subsets called *shards*, avoiding replication completely (cf. Figure 1). Entries in a shard (and in the original list) are ordered according to their begin times. For each shard we maintain an *impact list* as an additional access structure for efficiently determining the entries whose time segments overlap with a query time interval. This impact list maintains, for every possible begin time of a query time interval, the position in the shard of the earliest entry whose time segment contains the begin time. In other words, the impact list maintains pairs of query begin times (key) and offsets (values) from the shard beginning. Given a query time interval, it is sufficient to start scanning the shard at the position (offset) stored in the impact list, instead of scanning the shard from the beginning. The overall size of each impact list can be reduced by storing only the distinct offset values rather than offsets for all possible query begin-times. A straightforward binary search over the query begin-times gives the correct offset location. For practical granularities of query begin-times such as days, impact lists for the complete index (i.e., for all shards of all terms) can be easily kept in memory.

Query processing follows the established term-at-a-time processing model where index lists are read one after the other and scores of a document version from different lists are merged in memory. For our sharded index, each query term is processed in a sequence of *open-skip-scan* operations, one for each shard:

1. **Open** – Open a shard for a query term.
2. **Skip** – Given the query begin time, lookup offset position from the impact list of the shard and perform a seek to that position. In practice we can combine the open and skip steps into an *open-skip* operation to save an extra I/O operation.
3. **Scan** – Perform sequential reads from this position and terminate when it is certain that rest of the entries do not overlap with the query time interval. As we read the entries sequentially in begin-time order, we can safely terminate when the begin-time of the next entry exceeds the query end-time.

Observe that all the shards for a given term are accessed independently of the temporal constraint in the time-travel query. For a sharded index, merging results from every shard of a index list is not expensive since the shards are disjoint; this is in contrast to the situation for temporally sliced index lists, where entries replicated in different slices must be detected and duplicates removed.

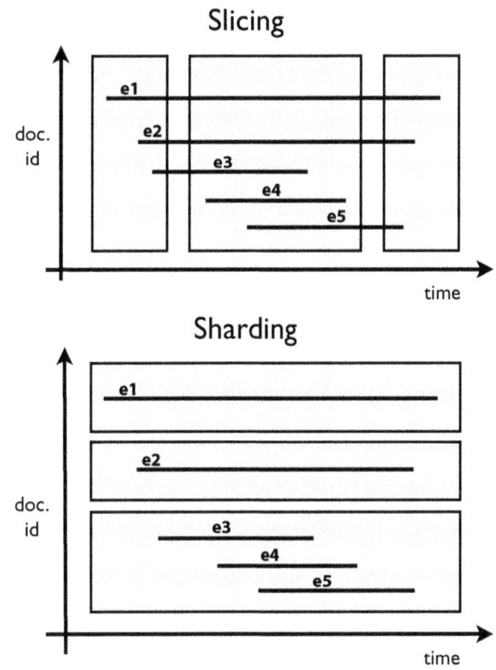

Figure 1: Slicing vs. Sharding of a Index list

4. IDEALIZED INDEX SHARDING

As the entries in each shard are ordered according to their begin times, with the help of the impact list we can easily avoid wasteful reading of entries whose valid-time interval, $I(d^i)$, is before the query begin time. However, this does not guarantee the elimination of all wasteful reads. Consider a situation when two index entries p and q in a shard such that p completely subsumes q, i.e.,

$$begin(p) \leq begin(q) \;\wedge\; end(p) > end(q).$$

Now, the queries with $end(q) \leq b_Q \leq end(p)$ will wastefully read q. This can arbitrarily degrade performance if there are many such entries, for instance, when there is an entry which spans long intervals.

We can avoid any wasteful reads of entries such that no pair of entries from a shard form such a subsumption pattern. In other words, we require that entries in a shard satisfy *staircase property*, defined as follows:

DEFINITION 1 (STAIRCASE PROPERTY). *Given a shard g_i, if we have*

$$\forall p, q \in g_i, begin(p) \leq begin(q) \Rightarrow end(p) \leq end(q)\ ,$$

then we say the shard g_i has the staircase property. □

Clearly, it may be possible to shard a given index list in many different ways so that the staircase property (cf. Figure 2) is satisfied. Since query processing proceeds by open-skip operations for all shards of a term, it is desirable to minimize the number of idealized shards. This can be

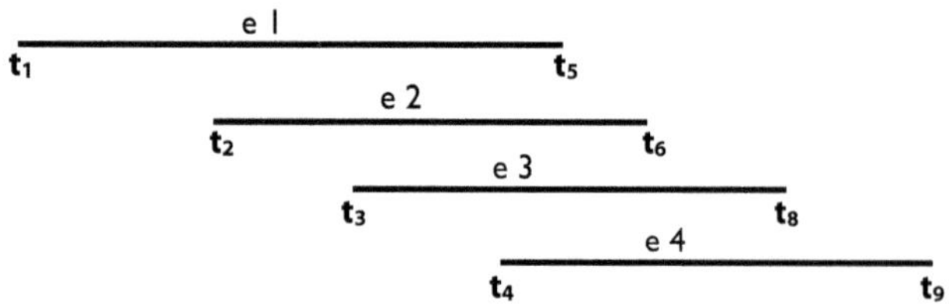

Figure 2: Staircase property

cast into an optimization problem where, given a set of time intervals (corresponding to the valid-time intervals of index entries), minimize the number of shards. Formally,

DEFINITION 2 (IDEALIZED SHARDING). *Given a set of entries L_v for a term v, partition L_v into a* minimal set *of shards $G = \{g_1, \ldots, g_m\}$, $g_i \subseteq L_v$ where:*

$$g_i \cap g_j = \emptyset \qquad \forall g_i, g_j \in G,\ i \neq j \tag{1}$$

$$\bigcup_i g_i = L_v \tag{2}$$

$$\forall g_i \in G \quad : g_i \text{ satisfies the staircase property.} \tag{3}$$

□

4.1 Optimal Algorithm

Algorithm 1 Idealized Sharding Algorithm

Input: L_v sorted in increasing order of begin times
$G_{opt} = \emptyset$ // Idealized sharding

for $i = 1..|L_v|$ **do**
  // Iterate over all entries in the index list for v
  if $\neg\exists g \in G_{opt} : g.end \leq end(L_v[i])$ **then**
    create **new shard** g_{new}
    $g_{new}.end = 0$
    $G_{opt} = G_{opt} \cup \{g_{new}\}$
  end if
  $g_t = \underset{g \in G_{opt}}{argmin}\ (end(L_v[i]) - g.end)$
  $g_t.end = end(L_v[i])$ // Update the end-time of the shard
  $g_t = g_t \cup \{L_v[i]\}$ // Include the current entry into the shard

end for

Output: G_{opt} is the idealized sharding.

Let each shard g_i associated with an index list of begin-time sorted entries have an end-time $g_i.end$, defined as the latest end-time of all the entries in g_i. We employ the greedy algorithm given in Algorithm 1, in which we process all entries of a list L_v in increasing begin-time order. At each iteration, we include an entry e into an existing shard if its inclusion does not violate the *staircase property* of the shard. If there are multiple shards to which e can be assigned, we assign it to the shard with the minimum gap, $end(e) - g_i.end$. If there are currently no shards to which e can be assigned, we start a new shard with e in it. It turns out that the idealized sharding problem maps directly to the problem of decomposing a set of points in a plane into minimum number of ascending chains and essentially uses the same algorithm as in [21].

4.2 Proof of Optimality

We develop the proof for the optimality of Algorithm 1 by first proving a set of three lemmas about key properties of the generated shards. The proofs for the lemmas can be found in the accompanying technical report [4].

The first lemma states that the algorithm produces only shards that have the staircase property.

LEMMA 1 (STAIRCASE PROPERTY). *When Algorithm 1 terminates, every shard created by the algorithm has the staircase property.*

For the next lemma, let the shards created by Algorithm 1 for a list L_v be numbered by their order of creation.

LEMMA 2 (TEMPORAL SUBSUMPTION OF ENTRIES). *For every entry in a shard g_i ($i > 1$) there exists an entry in g_{i-1} which completely subsumes it.*

We introduce the notion of a *stalactite set* of time intervals. A stalactite set S consists of time intervals such that,

$$\forall p, q \in S, begin(p) \leq begin(q) \Rightarrow end(p) > end(q).$$

There may be many such stalactite sets that can be formed using entries from a given index list, L_v. Let us denote the stalactite set of maximum cardinality as $S_{max} : L_v$.

LEMMA 3 (STALACTITE PROPERTY). *The number of shards created by Algorithm 1 for a list L_v is equal to $|S_{max} : L_v|$.*

Now, we can state and prove the optimality of the algorithm.

THEOREM 1. *Algorithm 1 creates an optimal sharding.*

PROOF. It follows from Lemma 1 that every element in $S_{max} : L_v$ has to be a part of a new shards which lower bounds the number of shards to $|S_{max} : L_v|$. Lemma 3, on the other hand, upper bounds the number of shards to $|S_{max} : L_v|$ which proves the optimality of Algorithm 1. □

Further, we show that the algorithm can be implemented efficiently, by making use of the following property of the sharding at any stage during the algorithm:

LEMMA 4 (DESCENDING END TIMES). *If Algorithm 1 created a shard g_i before g_{i+1}, then $g_i.end > g_{i+1}.end$.*

Owing to such an ordering of shard ends, entries can be placed efficiently via a binary search over the shard ends.

5. COST-AWARE MERGING OF SHARDS

Depending on the distribution on valid-time intervals, the idealized sharding introduced in the previous section might generate a large number of shards requiring one *open-seek* operation, involving a random access, for each shard. If the cost of such a random access is high and if the distribution of time intervals gives rise to many idealized shards, query processing performance can degrade. In such cases, it might actually be beneficial to relax the idealized sharding, and reduce the number of shards at the cost of allowing some wasted reads.

In this section, we present an I/O cost-aware technique to selectively merge idealized shards allowing for a controlled amount of wasted reads while reducing the number of random accesses. We introduce a cost model which limits sequential wasted reads due to merging of a set of idealized shards by taking into consideration costs of random accesses and sequential reads of the underlying index infrastructure.

5.1 Cost Model

Let the cost of a random access be C_r, and that of a sequential read be C_s. We allow for a penalty function for a set of idealized shards $\{g_i\}$ as $P(\{g_i\})$ and require it to be bounded by C_r/C_s if the shards should be considered for merging. We refer to this as the *threshold criterion*, i.e,

$$P(\{g_i\}) \leq \frac{C_r}{C_s}$$

An example of such a penalty function is *mean wasted reads*, which is defined as the number of wasted reads incurred during query processing, averaged over all possible query begin time points. Under this penalty function, g_i and g_j can be merged when the mean wasted sequential reads in the *merged shard* is less than the overhead incurred in an open-seek operation. In other words, an open-seek operation to one merged shard accompanied by a few sequential wasted reads is cheaper than two open-seek operations to idealized shards without any wasted reads. As an example, if $C_r/C_s = 100$, then the wasted reading of less than 100 entries, that do not qualify by the temporal constraint, on an average would be more beneficial than performing a random access to an additional shard.

It turns out that due to the specific organization of time intervals in the idealized shards, the total penalty, $P(\{g_i\})$, of merging a set of idealized shards, $\{g_i\}$, can be easily computed from the pairwise penalties of participating idealized shards $P(g_i, g_j)$'s. Also note that $P(g_i, g_i) = 0$. Now, for merging a set of idealized shards $m = \{g_i, g_j, \cdots\}$ the overall penalty $P(m)$ is given by

$$P(m) = \sum_{g_k \in m} P(first(m), g_k)$$

We retain the order in which idealized shards were created, i.e., shards created early have a lower index. Thus $first(m)$ denotes the shard which was created first in m. This can be shown as follows:

For a pair of idealized shards (g_i, g_j) where $i < j$, and for a given query begin-time t, let the set of wasted entries read be $w_{i,j}(t)$. It is easy to see from Lemma 2 that $w_{j,k}(t) \subset w_{i,k}(t)$. Hence, for a set of idealized shards $g_1, g_2, \cdots, g_n$ the $w_{1,2,\cdots,n}(t) = w_{1,n}(t)$, which means that aggregation of multiple idealized shards depends on the idealized shard which is created first. As an example, the penalty incurred due to merging idealized shards {7,10,3,12} would be $P(3,7) + P(3,10) + P(3,12)$.

Computing pairwise penalties: Consider a pair of entries p and q, which belong to different idealized shards, where p is subsumed by q. A read is said to be wasted for each query begin time point lying in the interval $[end(p), end(q))$. The total cost of merging two shards g_i and g_j is the sum of all wasted reads caused from all such pairs of subsumed entries. The average penalty $P(g_i, g_j)$ hence is the total cost of merging the pair of groups divided by all possible query begin time points. Computing wasted reads at each time point can be efficiently implemented by interleaving computation of pairwise wasted reads within Algorithm 1.

5.2 Problem Statement

Given a set of idealized shards G_{opt}, pairwise penalty values $P(g_i, g_j)$ and a threshold C_r/C_s find a set of disjoint merged shards M of *minimum cardinality* such that each of the merged shards respects the *threshold criterion*.

Disjoint merged shards require that no pair of merged shards have an idealized shard in common. We formally define the optimization problem as

$$\min |M| \quad \text{s.t.}$$

$$P(m) \leq C_r/C_s \, , \; m \in M \, ,$$

where m is a merged shard. Observe that the disjoint merging is encoded in the objective function $min|M|$. We refer to the process as **relaxed sharding**.

5.3 Algorithm For Merging Optimal Groups

We present a heuristic algorithm which is shown to perform well in practice in our experimental evaluation. As inputs we expect the set of the idealized shards and the ratio C_r/C_s. We retain the order in which idealized shards were created, i.e., earlier created shards have a lower index.

The pseudo code for merging the idealized shards is presented in Algorithm 2. Every iteration employs a two stage greedy process. The first stage is an *ascending choice phase* in which it chooses all the unmerged/available idealized shards in ascending order of their index until the threshold constraint is violated (lines 11 to 20).

The second stage is a greedy phase (lines 23 to 27) where the remaining capacity is greedily chosen with smallest unmerged shard first (as in the standard greedy approach to the knapsack problem).

6. DEALING WITH INDEX UPDATES

After the initial index building, the archive may grow over time, so that the index needs to be updated. This growth usually comes from a crawler fetching new versions of documents already in the archive, or documents that were unknown before. We therefore make the realistic assumption that the vast majority of updates will either replace an existing active version (setting its end time to the crawl time) or add a new active version (whose begin time is the crawl time, and whose end time is ∞), and assume that the begin time of inserted versions is not smaller than begin times of any version already in the index. Insertions of older versions will be a rare exception, for example caused by merging our archive with another archive; in these cases, we resort to recomputing the index.

We will now explain how the index is maintained under such an update load, mainly by explaining to which (idealized or relaxed) shard a new version is added. Note that the actual techniques for adding new index entries to shards are the same used for updating standard inverted lists, for example in-place updates or logarithmic merging; see [11] for a thorough discussion of such techniques.

We first show how to update idealized shards. Let us assume for the moment that there are no active versions in the index. We then sort the versions to insert by their begin

Algorithm 2 Cost Aware Group Merging

```
Input: G_opt and P(g_i, g_j)
M = ∅    // Merged shards

for i = 1 .. |G_opt| do
   Let g_i ∈ G_opt ∧ g_i ∉ M be next shard in order
   create new shard r_i
   r_i = r_i ∪ {g_i}
   capacity = C_r / C_s

   //ascending choice phase
   for j = i + 1 .. |G_opt| do
      if (P(g_i, g_j) ≤ capacity) ∧ (g_j ∉ M) then
         capacity = capacity − P(g_i, g_j)
         r_i = r_i ∪ {g_j}
      else
         if (g_j ∉ M) ∧ (g_j ∉ r_i) then
            break
         end if
      end if
   end for

   // smallest size first
   while capacity > 0 do
      g_min = argmin_{(g ∈ G_opt) ∩ (g ∉ M)} {P(g_i, g)}
      capacity = capacity − P(g_i, g_min)
      r_i = r_i ∪ {g_min}
   end while
   M = M ∪ r_i
end for

Output: M is the set of merged shards.
```

time and append them to the index by applying Algorithm 1 with them as input, updating and extending the current set of shards. Note that while running the algorithm, we update the (in-memory) impact lists, which can be flushed to disk from time to time by a background process. The resulting set of idealized shards is optimal as the output of the algorithm is the same as if we ran it for all versions (those already in the archive and those added to it) with an initially empty set of shards (the algorithm consumes versions in ascending order of their begin timestamps, and all begin timestamps in the archive are strictly smaller than the begin timestamps of newly added versions).

Active versions make the process more complicated when they are replaced by a newer version; otherwise, they are not touched by the update. Consider an active version d^i of a document d in shard g that is overwritten by a newer version d^{i+1} at time t, setting $end(d^i) = t$. If we just updated $end(d^i)$ and there was at least one other active version in the same shard, we would incur a wasted read of d^i for any query time greater than t. To avoid this, we split shard g into two pieces: The first new shard gets all versions v from g with $begin(v) \leq begin(d^i)$, the second new shard gets the remaining versions. Since versions in shards are sorted by ascending begin timestamp, this can usually be done by simply setting shard boundaries accordingly, without actually moving index entries (which would only be necessary when there are multiple versions with the same begin timestamp, which is very unlikely if the begin time is set to the crawl time). We have to update the impact lists of both new shards, which can be efficiently done on this in-memory data structure. Since versions in the first new shard are unchanged, no wasted reads occur by construction. In the second new shard, wasted reads could only occur when querying for timestamps after $end(d^i)$. Since all begin times of versions other than d^i are larger than $begin(d^i)$, the impact list will point to an index entry after d^i for these queries, avoiding wasted reads. After having updated all end times of active versions that are overwritten, we insert the versions replacing them using the algorithm for updating idealized shards without active versions.

Note that this maintenance procedure can be applied either for batched updates or after each (new or updated) version is read by the crawler.

Updating relaxed shards can be done as follows: When we initially construct the relaxed shards, we store from which idealized shards they were built. When we now insert a (new or updated) version into an idealized shard, we insert it at the same time into its corresponding relaxed shard. This may, of course, result in a set of relaxed shards where for some relaxed shards our cost bound is violated (because the updates incurred too many wasted reads). We therefore compute regularly, for each relaxed shard m, its current aggregated penalty $P(m)$, and recompute all relaxed shards when the maximal or average aggregated penalty gets too large, for example when it exceeds $2 \cdot C_r / C_s$.

7. EVALUATION FRAMEWORK

In this section, we present our experimental setup and the datasets that we use to evaluate our approach in terms of query-processing performance and space consumption.

7.1 Setup

We implemented the sharded index and all our algorithms using Java 1.6. Additionally, we obtained the latest implementation of the sliced index from its authors. All experiments were conducted on Dell PowerEdge M610 servers with 2 Intel Xeon E5530 CPUs, 48 GB of main memory, a large iSCSI-attached disk array, and Debian GNU/Linux (SMP Kernel 2.6.29.3.1) as operating system. Experiments were conducted using the Java Hotspot 64-Bit Server VM (build 11.2-b01).

7.2 Datasets

For our experiments we use the following two real-world datasets.

WIKI The *English Wikipedia revision history* [1], whose uncompressed raw data amounts to 0.7 TBytes, contains the full editing history of the English Wikipedia from January 2001 to December 2005. We indexed all versions of encyclopedia articles excluding versions that were marked as the result of a minor edit (e.g., the correction of spelling errors etc.). This yielded a total of 1,517,524 documents with 15,079,829 versions having a mean (μ) of 9.94 versions per document at standard deviation (σ) of 46.08.

UKGOV This is a subset of the European Archive [2], containing weekly crawls of eleven governmental websites from the U.K. We filtered out documents not belonging to MIME-types `text/plain` and `text/html` to obtain a dataset that totals 0.4 TBytes. This dataset includes 685,678 documents with 17,297,548 versions ($\mu = 25.23$ and $\sigma = 28.38$).

Note that the two datasets represent realistic classes of time-evolving document collections. WIKI is an explicitly versioned document collection, for which all its versions are known. UKGOV is an archive of the evolving Web, for which, due to crawling, we have only incomplete knowledge about its versions. For ease of experimentation, we rounded timestamps in both datasets to day granularity.

7.3 Index Management

Both the sliced and sharded indexes are stored on disk using flat files containing both the lexicon as well as the sliced or sharded index lists. At run time, the lexicon and impact lists are read completely into main memory, and for a given query the appropriate slices or shards are retrieved from the index flat file on disk. For compression we employ 7-bit encoding [17]. Note that such variable-byte encoding is complementary to other compression methods like *temporal coalescing* [10]. We use the following types of indexes in our experimentation:

Sliced Indexes We consider instances of the sliced index that are partitioned following the *space-bound* approach [10]. The parameter κ denotes the space restriction that models the maximum blowup in index size relative to a non-partitioned index. For our experiments we consider four variants of the space-bound approaches i.e., parameter values for $\kappa = \{1.5, 2.0, 2.5, 3.0\}$. These variants are denoted subsequently in the text as SB-1.5, SB-2.0, SB-2.5 and SB-3.0.

Sharded Indexes We consider idealized sharding (IS) and three cost-aware *relaxed sharding* variants with relaxation parameters 10.0, 100.0 and 1000.0 referred to as RS-10, RS-100 and RS-1000. Recall that the relaxation parameter reflects the I/O cost ratio introduced in Section 5. The cost-aware metric is based on the penalty function, *mean wasted reads*, for merging the idealized shards(IS).

Naïve Unpartitioned Index As a second competitor, we build an unpartitioned index with provision for impact lists over ordered begin times referred to as RS-inf. This serves as a proof that our techniques are effective not only because of the impact list construction and a global begin time order.

The average length of the index lists in our sharded index were 496,259 for WIKI and 945,044 for UKGOV. Since sharding causes each index list to be split into multiple shards we briefly look at the size distribution of the above mentioned sharded indexes. For WIKI, idealized sharding (IS) resulted in 79.75 shards per index list (shards/list). This reduces to 32.5 shards/list for RS-10 and further to 11.78 shards/list (RS-100) and 4.71 shards/list (RS-1000). The shard sizes in IS varies from 2% - 8% of the entire index list size, while for RS-10 its 7%-20% and 35%-50% for RS-1000. For UKGOV, IS resulted in 295.8 shards/list. The number of shards/list reduce drastically to 40.63 (RS-10), 14.50 (RS-100) and 4.97 (RS-1000). The shard sizes as a fraction of the entire list vary from 1%-2% (IS) to 7%-8% (RS-10) and finally 4%-44% (RS-1000).

We also evaluate the effect of temporal coalescing [10] on index size and query processing. To this effect we build sharded and sliced indexes with application of temporal coalescing using a parameter $\epsilon = 0.01$. Other than that, we use the same choice of parameters as in the experiments without temporal coalescing.

7.4 Query Workloads and Execution

We compiled two dataset-specific query workloads by extracting frequent queries from the AOL query logs, which were temporarily made available during 2006. For the WIKI dataset we extracted 300 most frequent queries which had a result click on the domain `en.wikipedia.org` and similarly for UKGOV we compiled 50 queries which had result click on `.gov.uk` domains. Both the sliced and sharded index structures are built for terms specific to the query workload. Using these keyword queries, we generated a time-travel query workload with 5 instances each for the following 4 different temporal predicate granularities: day, month, year and queries spanning the full lifetime of the respective document collection.

For query processing we employed conjunctive query semantics i.e., query results contain documents that include all the query terms. We use wall-clock times (in milliseconds) to measure the query processing performance on warm caches using only a single core. Specifically, each query was executed five times in succession and the average of the last four runs was taken for a more stable and accurate runtime measurement.

8. EXPERIMENTAL RESULTS

8.1 Sharding vs Slicing

In the first set of experiments, we compare the performance of sharding and slicing on different query granularities. In the plots presented, runtimes of different variants of both sharded and sliced partitions are shown in milliseconds. Each plot corresponds to a given query granularity – day, month, year or the full life time of the respective collection. C_r/C_s values of disks usually vary in the order of 100 and 1000. Since runtimes for both RS-100 and RS-1000 show low variance throughout all experiments we chose RS-1000 as a reasonable representative for sharding for this comparison.

SB-3.0 is optimized for short time interval queries, because of a higher degree of partitioning, and as expected it performs better than any of its other sliced counterparts ($\kappa = \{1.5, 2.0, 2.5\}$) for day and month queries. In case of WIKI, we see a low difference in query processing times between SB-3.0 (10.63 ms) and RS-1000 (10.26 ms) in case of day queries (Figures 3(a)). The difference is notable for month queries with RS-1000 exhibiting a 19.5% improvement over SB-3.0 (Figure 4(a)). In UKGOV, RS-1000 takes 69.88 ms to process day queries which is almost 40% improvement over SB-3.0 which takes 117.9 ms (Figure 3(b)).

While SB-3.0 is efficient for short time interval queries, they understandably perform worse for longer time intervals because of having to read a larger number of replicated entries inflicted by a higher degree of partitioning. This is shown in Figures 5(a), 6(a), 5(b) and 6(b) where smaller κ valued sliced indexes ($\kappa = \{1.5, 2.0, 2.5\}$) perform better than SB-3.0. In case of WIKI, comparing SB-1.5, which has the best runtimes for year queries and full life time queries, with RS-1000 shows that the latter consistently outperforms in both cases. Query processing times drop by 22.2% (Figure 5(a)) for year queries and by 19% for full lifetime queries (Figure 6(a)). In UKGOV, there is an improvement of almost 29.9% or 279.26 ms(RS-1000 vs SB-1.5) 5(b) for year queries. The full time queries are faster by 931 ms or 21%(RS-1000 vs SB-1.5) as shown in Figure 6(a)

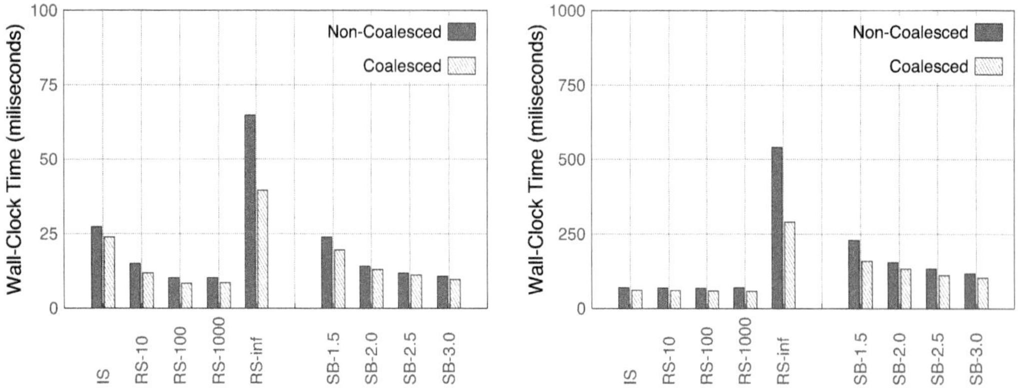

(a) Wikipedia (b) UKGOV

Figure 3: Wall-clock times for day queries

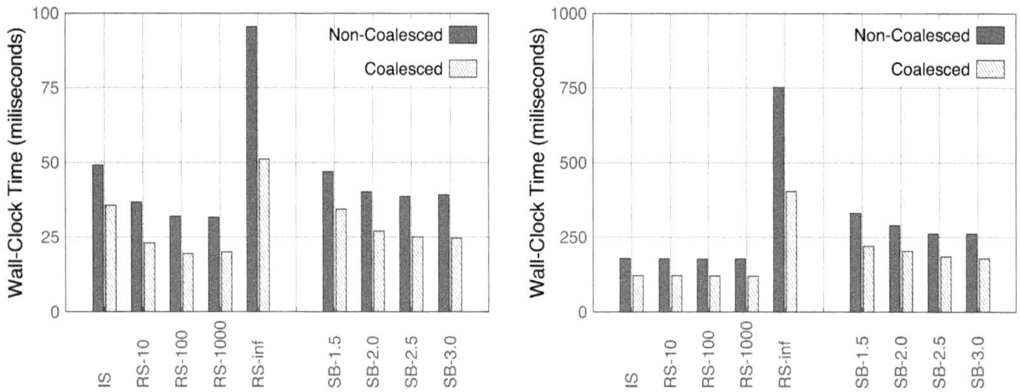

(a) Wikipedia (b) UKGOV

Figure 4: Wall-clock times for month queries

and 6(b) which in absolute terms seems to be a considerable difference.

8.2 Effect of Cost Aware Merging of Shards

The next set of experiments present the effectiveness of cost aware merging of shards. Idealized sharding or IS might be characterized by a high number of shards for certain distributions of document life times. Although query processing on IS results in reading only the relevant entries intersecting with the query time interval, they suffers from inefficiencies due to a large number of random accesses. Especially for disks with $C_r >> C_s$, the open-seek operation on idealized shards might result in considerable overheads.

In WIKI, we see a consistent improvement from IS to RS-1000. This is because idealized sharding admits a fairly large number of shards in this case and thus the I/O costs are dominated by initial random accesses to access these idealized shards. Improvements result from the reduction in the number of shards due to careful merging of idealized shards as presented before in Section 5. Although these reductions might not be significant for queries with larger time intervals, but they reduce query processing time by a sizable fraction for smaller interval queries – day queries improve by 62%(Figure 3(a)) and month queries by 35%(Figure 4(a)). Unlike WIKI, UKGOV does not show any considerable difference in performance which is due to the already low number of initial idealized shards. This indicates that cost-aware merging can be applied as a self-organizing approach depending on the distribution of initial shards.

RS-1000 however outperforms RS-inf by a fairly large margin in all query granularities excepting full-lifetime ones showing the effectiveness of careful sharding of entries. The behavior for full lifetime queries is to be expected because all entries in RS-inf become relevant for such kind of queries and have to be subsequently read.

8.3 Index Sizes

As expected we observe that the size of sharded indexes remain the same as the unsharded index. This is due to the fact that sharding divides the index entries of the unpartitioned lists in a disjoint manner. On the contrary the index entries in a sliced index are subject to replication across slices. The size of the sliced index structures show a direct correlation with the input parameter κ as shown in Figure 7(a). As discussed before, κ regulates the upper bound to the index blowup. The higher the κ the more efficient is the performance of short time interval queries at the expense of a larger index size. However, longer time interval queries are impacted by the higher κ valued indexes due to wasted amount of reads of replicated index entries. Thus the sliced index has to be carefully tuned depending on the time interval of the query workload trading off index size

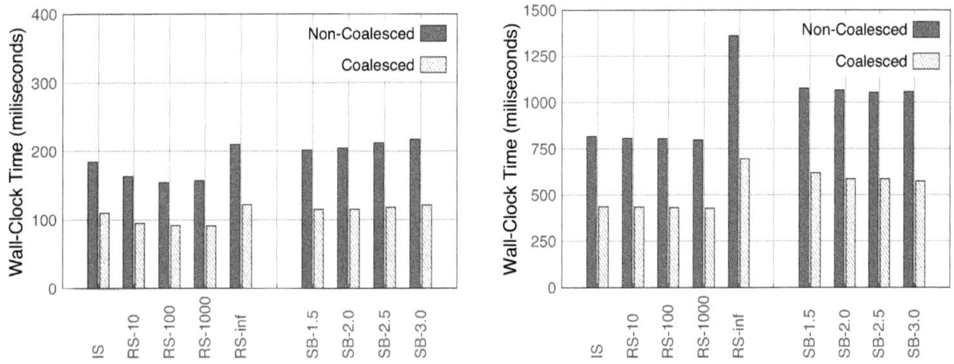

(a) Wikipedia (b) UKGOV

Figure 5: Wall-clock times for year queries

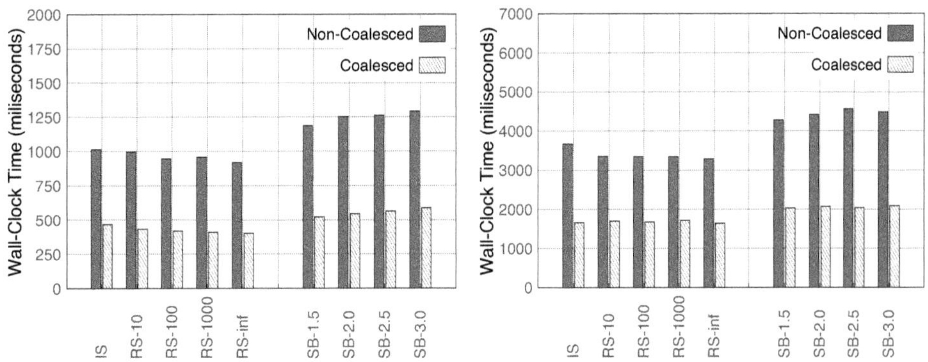

(a) Wikipedia (b) UKGOV

Figure 6: Wall-clock times for full-lifetime queries

and query efficiency. This is not the case with the sharded index where the tradeoff is between number of random accesses and sequential reads, which are local tunable parameters depending on physical characteristics of disks (where the index is stored) irrespective of the query workload. From our experiments we observe that the time taken to build a sharded index is roughly twice the time taken for the standard unpartitioned inverted index. Since the sharded index building process can be easily parallelized, one can efficiently build sharded indexes using a distributed processing platform (e.g., Hadoop).

8.4 Effect of Coalescing

Our experimental results with temporal coalescing of index entries lead to similar results as our experiments on the original, uncoalesced indexes. Independent of the partitioning/sharding used, index size is much smaller than with uncoalesced indexes—up to an order of magnitude for UKGOV and up to a factor of 2 for Wikipedia—and indexes created with sharding are always smaller than those with slicing (Figure 7). The runtime of all methods with temporal coalescing is depicted in Figures 3(a) through 6(b). It is evident that query performance improves with temporal coalescing, with longer time interval queries gaining more than those with smaller time intervals as more entries need to be read. Sharding is still more efficient than slicing, especially with cost-aware merging, and achieves this advantage with indexes of a smaller size.

9. RELATED WORK

Temporal information associated with documents has recently seen increasing attention in information retrieval. One of the earliest known efforts in this direction is by Anick and Flynn [8] who developed a framework for versioning the complete index for historical queries. Recently, Alonso et al. [6] give an overview of relevant research directions. The work on time-travel text search by Berberich et al. [10] is closest to our work in this paper. It introduced the notion of time-travel queries, limiting its discussion to time-point queries. To support this functionality efficiently, index lists from an inverted index are temporally partitioned, in our terminology into slices, providing guarantees on either the space used by the index or query performance. Index entries whose valid-time interval overlaps with multiple of the determined temporal slices are judiciously replicated and put into multiple index lists, thus increasing the overall size of the index. The work by Herscovici et al. [16] focuses on exploiting the redundancy commonly seen in versioned documents to compress the inverted index. Similarly, He et al. [14, 15] consider the problem of efficiently storing inverted indexes on disk using compression; these are orthogonal to our work and could be combined with our sharding techniques.

Research in temporal databases has taken a broader perspective beyond text documents and targeted general class of time-annotated data. Index structures tailored to such data like the Multi-Version B-Tree [9] or LHAM [18] are re-

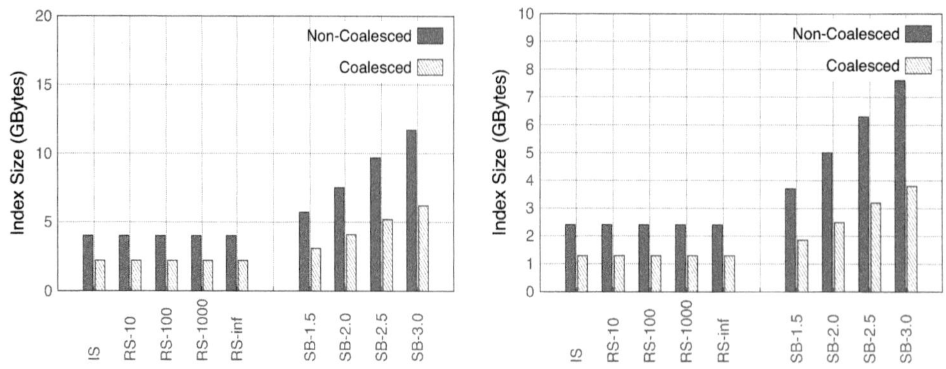

(a) Wikipedia (b) UKGOV

Figure 7: Index sizes

lated to our work, since they also, implicitly or explicitly, rely on a temporal partitioning and replication of data. It is therefore conceivable to apply our proposed techniques in conjunction with one of these index structures.

10. CONCLUSION

This work presents a novel method of index organization based on sharding for solving time-travel queries. Previous approaches traded off space and efficiency of query processing resulting in an index size blowup. Also, there was no single partitioning scheme for a given query time interval granularity. Unlike this, we look at minimizing the I/O during query processing without incurring any overhead in space and are independent of the query workload. We also propose a cost model, which takes into account different I/O costs of the local storage media where the index is stored. The resulting sharding balances sequential read costs and random access costs for efficient query processing. We carried out extensive experiments and show that with no space overhead we consistently perform better than the state-of-art sliced indexes, sometimes even by a factor of 2.

Acknowledgment

We thank the anonymous reviewer for pointing out the connection between Section 4 and the work by Supowit [21].

11. REFERENCES

[1] Wikipedia. `http://en.wikipedia.org/`

[2] European Archive. `http://www.europarchive.org`

[3] Internet Archive. `http://archive.org`

[4] A. Anand, S. Bedathur, K. Berberich and R. Schenkel. Temporal Index Sharding for Space-Time Efficiency in Archive Search. Technical Report MPI-I-2011-5-001, Max-Planck Institute for Informatics, 2010.

[5] E. Adar, J. Teevan, S. T. Dumais, and J. L. Elsas. The web changes everything: understanding the dynamics of web content. In *WSDM*, 2009.

[6] O. Alonso, M. Gertz, and R. Baeza-Yates. On the value of temporal information in information retrieval. *SIGIR Forum*, 41(2):35–41, 2007.

[7] A. Anand, S. Bedathur, K. Berberich, and R. Schenkel. Efficient Temporal Keyword Search over Versioned Text. In *CIKM*, 2010.

[8] P. G. Anick and R. A. Flynn. Versioning a full-text information retrieval system. In *SIGIR*, 1992.

[9] B. Becker, S. Gschwind, T. Ohler, B. Seeger, and P. Widmayer. An asymptotically optimal multiversion b-tree. *VLDB J.*, 5(4), 1996.

[10] K. Berberich, S. Bedathur, T. Neumann, and G. Weikum. A Time Machine for Text Search. In *SIGIR*, 2007.

[11] S. Büttcher, C. L. Clarke, and G. V. Cormack. *Information Retrieval - Implementing and Evaluating Search Engines.* MIT Press, 2010.

[12] F. Douglis, A. Feldmann, B. Krishnamurthy, and J. Mogul. Rate of change and other metrics: a live study of the world wide web. In *USITS*, 1997.

[13] D. Fetterly, M. Manasse, M. Najork, and J. Wiener. A large-scale study of the evolution of web pages. In *WWW*, 2003.

[14] J. He, H. Yan, and T. Suel. Compact full-text indexing of versioned document collections. In *CIKM*, 2009.

[15] J. He, J. Zeng, and T. Suel. Improved index compression techniques for versioned document collections. In *CIKM*, 2010.

[16] M. Herscovici, R. Lempel, and S. Yogev. Efficient indexing of versioned document sequences. In *ECIR*, 2007.

[17] C. D. Manning, P. Raghavan, and H. SchÃijtze. *Introduction to information retrieval.* Cambridge University Press, 2008.

[18] P. Muth, P. E. O'Neil, A. Pick, and G. Weikum. The LHAM Log-Structured History Data Access Method. *VLDB J.*, 8(3-4):199–221, 2000.

[19] A. Ntoulas, J. Cho, and C. Olston. What's New on the Web?: The Evolution of the Web from a Search Engine Perspective. In *WWW*, 2004.

[20] N. Shivakumar and H. Garcia-Molina. Wave-indices: indexing evolving databases. In *SIGMOD*, 1997.

[21] K. J. Supowit. Decomposing a set of points into chains, with applications to permutation and circle graphs. *IPL*, 21(5):249 – 252, 1985.

[22] J. Zobel and A. Moffat. Inverted files for text search engines. *ACM Comput. Surv.*, 38(2), 2006.

Inverted Indexes for Phrases and Strings*

Manish Patil
Department of CS
Louisiana State University
USA
mpatil@csc.lsu.edu

Sharma V. Thankachan
Department of CS
Louisiana State University
USA
thanks@csc.lsu.edu

Rahul Shah
Department of CS
Louisiana State University
USA
rahul@csc.lsu.edu

Wing-Kai Hon
Department of CS
National Tsing Hua University
Taiwan
wkhon@cs.nthu.edu.tw

Jeffrey Scott Vitter
Department of EECS
The University of Kansas
USA
jsv@ku.edu

Sabrina Chandrasekaran
Department of CS
Louisiana State University
USA
schand7@lsu.edu

ABSTRACT

Inverted indexes are the most fundamental and widely used data structures in information retrieval. For each unique word occurring in a document collection, the inverted index stores a list of the documents in which this word occurs. Compression techniques are often applied to further reduce the space requirement of these lists. However, the index has a shortcoming, in that only predefined pattern queries can be supported efficiently. In terms of string documents where word boundaries are undefined, if we have to index all the substrings of a given document, then the storage quickly becomes quadratic in the data size. Also, if we want to apply the same type of indexes for querying phrases or sequence of words, then the inverted index will end up storing redundant information. In this paper, we show the first set of inverted indexes which work naturally for strings as well as phrase searching. The central idea is to exclude document d in the inverted list of a string P if every occurrence of P in d is subsumed by another string of which P is a prefix. With this we show that our space utilization is close to the optimal. Techniques from succinct data structures are deployed to achieve compression while allowing fast access in terms of frequency and document id based retrieval. Compression and speed tradeoffs are evaluated for different variants of the proposed index. For phrase searching, we show that our indexes compare favorably against a typical inverted index deploying position-wise intersections. We also show efficient top-k based retrieval under relevance metrics like frequency and *tf-idf*.

*This work is supported in part by Taiwan NSC Grant 99-2221-E-007-123 (W. Hon) and US NSF Grant CCF–1017623 (R. Shah and J. S. Vitter).

SIGIR'11, July 24–28, 2011, Beijing, China.

Categories and Subject Descriptors

H.3.1 [**Information Storage and Retrieval**]: Content Analysis and Indexing—*Indexing methods*; I.7.3 [**Document and Text Processing**]: Index Generation

General Terms

Algorithms, Experimentation

1. INTRODUCTION

The most popular data structure in the field of Information Retrieval is the inverted index. For a given collection of documents, the index is defined as follows. Each word in this collection is called a *term* and corresponding to each term we maintain a list, called *inverted list*, of all the documents in which this word appears. Along with each document in this list we may store some score which indicates how important the document is with respect to that word. Different variants of the inverted index sort the documents in the inverted lists in a different manner. For instance, the sorting order may be based on the document ids or the scores. Compression techniques are often applied to further reduce space requirement of these lists. However, inverted index has a drawback that it can support queries only on predefined words or terms. As a result, it cannot be used to index documents without well-defined word boundaries.

Different approaches have been proposed to support phrase searching using an inverted index. One strategy is to maintain the position information in the inverted list. That is, for each document d in the inverted list of a word w, we store the positions at which w occurs in d. The positions corresponding to each d in the list can be sorted so as to achieve compression (using encoding functions like gap, gamma, or delta) [15]. To search a phrase, we first search for all the words in the phrase and obtain the corresponding inverted lists. The positions of each word within a document are extracted, so that we can then apply an intersection algorithm to retrieve those documents where these words are appearing in the same order as in the phrase. Another (naive) approach is to store inverted lists for all possible phrases, however, the resulting index size will be very large thus prohibiting its use in practice [38]. Different heuristics are proposed in this respect, such as maintaining the inverted lists only for popular phrases, or maintaining inverted lists of all phrases up to some fixed number (say h) of words. Another approach is called "next-word index" [36, 3, 4, 37], such that corresponding to each term w, a list of all the terms which occurs immediately after w is maintained. This approach will double the space, but it can support searching of any phrase with two words efficiently. Nevertheless, when the phrase goes beyond two words, we have to fall back to the intersection algorithm.

In this paper, we first introduce a variant of inverted index which naturally works for string as well as phrase searching. Our index does not assume any restrictions on the length or the popularity of the phrases. In addition, by avoiding the use of the intersection algorithm we achieve provable bounds for the query answering time with respect to the output size. Furthermore, we show different heuristics and compression techniques to make our index space-efficient. For a collection of English documents, the size of our index for strings and for phrases are ≈ 5 times and ≈ 2 times, respectively, of that of the input data, while it can support document retrievals in 10-40 microseconds per document in ranked order.

2. RELATED WORK

Suffix trees and suffix arrays are efficient data structures which can be used to index a text and support searching for any arbitrary pattern. These data structures can be maintained in linear space and can report all the occurrence of a pattern P in optimal (or nearly optimal) time. The space-efficient versions of suffix trees and suffix arrays are called compressed suffix trees and compressed suffix arrays, respectively, which take space close to the size of the indexed text. From a collection $\mathcal{D}$ of $|\mathcal{D}|$ documents $\{d_1, d_2, ..., d_{|\mathcal{D}|}\}$ of total length n, the problem of reporting documents containing a query pattern P is called the "document listing" problem. This problem was first studied by Matias et al. [21], where they proposed a linear space index with $O(p \log n + |output|)$ query time; here, p denotes the length of the input pattern P and $|output|$ denotes the number of the qualified documents in the output. An index with optimal $O(p + |output|)$ query time was later achieved in [24]. Sadakane [31] showed how to solve the document listing problem using succinct data structures, which take space very close to that of the compressed text. He also showed how to compute the *tf-idf* [2] of each document with the proposed data structures. Similar work was also done by Välimäki and Mäkinen [33] where they derived alternative succinct data structures for the problem.

In many practical situations, we may be interested in only a few documents which are highly relevant to the query. Relevance ranking refers to the ranking of the documents in some order, so that the result returned first is what the user is most interested. This can be the document where the given query pattern occurs most number of times (frequency). The relevance can also be defined by a similarity metric, such as the proximity of the query pattern to a certain word or to another pattern. This problem is modeled as top-k document retrieval, where the task is to retrieve the k highest scoring documents based on some score function. An $O(n \log n)$ words index has been proposed in [16] with $O(p + \log |\mathcal{D}| \log \log |\mathcal{D}| + k)$ query time. Hon et al. [18] proposed a linear-space index ($O(n)$ words) with nearly optimal $O(p + k \log k)$ query time. Yet, the constants hidden in the space bound restricts its use in practice. Culpepper et al. [8] proposed a space-efficient practical index based on wavelet trees [13], but their query algorithm is based on a heuristic, so that it does not guarantee any worst-case query performance.

The most popular ranking function in web search applications is *tf-idf* [2]. Under the *tf-idf* model, Persin et al. [28] give different heuristics to support top-k ranked retrieval when the inverted lists are sorted in decreasing order of the *tf* score. Various generalizations of this are studied by Anh and Moffat [1] under the name "impact ordering". In [25], Navarro and Puglisi showed that wavelet trees can be used for maintaining dual-sorted inverted lists corresponding to a word, where the documents can efficiently be retrieved in score order or in document id order. Recently, Hon et al. [17] proposed an index for answering top-k multi-pattern queries. On a related note, top-k color query problems (with applications in document retrieval) have been studied in [12, 20].

3. PRELIMINARIES

3.1 Suffix Trees and Compressed Suffix Trees

Given a text $T[1...n]$, a substring $T[i...n]$ with $1 \leq i \leq n$ is called a suffix of T. The lexicographic arrangement of all n suffixes of T in a compact trie is known as the *suffix tree* of T [35], where the ith leftmost leaf represents the ith lexicographically smallest suffix. Each edge in the suffix tree is labeled by a character string and for any node u, $path(u)$ is the string formed by concatenating the edge labels from root to u. For any leaf v, $path(v)$ is exactly the suffix corresponding to v. For a given pattern P, a node u is defined as the *locus node* of P if it is the node u closest to the root such that P is a prefix of $path(u)$; such a node can be determined in $O(p)$ time, where p denotes the length of P. The *generalized suffix tree* (GST) is a compact trie which stores all suffixes of all strings in a given collection $\mathcal{D}$ of strings. The drawback of the suffix tree is its huge space consumption, which requires $O(n \log n)$ bits in theory. Yet, it can perform pattern matching in optimal $O(p + |output|)$ time, where $|output|$ is the number of occurrences of P in T. Compressed suffix tree (CST) is a space-efficient version of suffix tree. Several variants of CSTs have been proposed to date [23, 14, 32, 30, 11, 27, 34, 6, 26].

3.2 Range Minimum/Maximum Query (RMQ)

Let $A[1...n]$ be an array of length n. The RMQ index is a linear-space data structure which can return the position and the value of the minimum (maximum) element in any subrange $A[i..j]$ such that $0 \leq i \leq j \leq n$. Although solving RMQ can be dated back from Chazelle's original paper on range searching [7], many simplifications [5] and improvements have been made, culminating in Fischer et al.'s $2n+o(n)$ bit data structure [9, 10]. All these schemes can answer RMQ in $O(1)$ time. We shall use RMQ data structures extensively to report the desired documents while answering our query. The basic result is captured in the following lemma [18]:

LEMMA 1. *Let A be an array of numbers. We can preprocess A in linear time and associate A with a linear-space RMQ data structure such that given a set of t non-overlapping ranges $[L_1, R_1], [L_2, R_2], ..., [L_t, R_t]$, we can find the largest (or the smallest) k numbers in $A[L_1, R_1] \cup A[L_2, R_2] \cup ... \cup A[L_t, R_t]$ in $O(t + k \log k)$ time.*

4. INVERTED INDEX FOR STRINGS AND PHRASES

In traditional inverted indexes, phrase queries are performed by first retrieving the inverted list for each word in the phrase and then applying an intersection algorithm to retrieve those documents in which the words in are appearing in the same order as in the phrase. Unfortunately, there is no efficient algorithm known which performs this intersection in time linear to the size of the output. Another limitation of the traditional inverted indexes is that they do not support string documents where there is no word demarcation (that is, when a query pattern can begin and end anywhere in the document). A naive approach to address these issues is to maintain inverted lists for all possible phrases (or strings). In the next subsection, we introduce a simple index that is based on a suffix tree and augments this with the inverted lists. This index can answer the queries in optimal time, however, the space is a factor of $|\mathcal{D}|$ away from the optimal. As phrase is a special case of a string (that is, string that starts and ends at word boundaries), we will explain our indexes in terms of strings.

4.1 Inverted Lists

Let $\mathcal{D}=\{d_1, d_2, ..., d_{|D|}\}$ be the collection of documents of total length n drawn from an alphabet set Σ, and Δ be the generalized suffix tree of $\mathcal{D}$. Let u be the locus node of a pattern P. Now a naive solution is to simply maintain an inverted list for the pattern corresponding to $path(u)$ for all internal nodes u in Δ. The list associated with a node u consists of pairs of the form $(d_j, score(path(u), d_j))$ for $j = 1, 2, 3, ..., |\mathcal{D}|$, where the score of a document d_j with respect to pattern $P = path(u)$ is given by $score(path(u), d_j)$. We assume that such a score is dependent only on the occurrences of P in the document d_j. An example of such a score metric is frequency, so that $score(P, d_j)$ represents the number of occurrences of pattern P in document d_j. For a given online pattern P, the top-k highest scoring documents can be answered by reporting the first k documents in the inverted list associated with the locus node of P, when the inverted lists are sorted by score order. Since the inverted list maintained at each node can be of length $|\mathcal{D}|$, the total size of this index is $O(n|\mathcal{D}|)$. Though this index offers optimal query time, it stores the inverted list for all possible strings. In the next subsection we show how the inverted lists can be stored efficiently in a total of $O(n)$ space.

4.2 Conditional Inverted Lists

The key idea which leads to $O(n)$ storage for inverted lists is the selection of nodes in the suffix tree for which inverted lists are actually maintained. We begin with the following definitions.

- Maximal String: A given string P is *maximal* for document d, if there is no other string Q such that P is a prefix of Q and every occurrence of P in d is subsumed by Q.
- Conditional Maximal String: Let Q be a maximal string for which P is a prefix and there is no maximal string R such that R is in between P and Q. That is P is a prefix of R and R is a prefix of Q. Then we call Q a *conditional maximal string* of P.

Consider the following sample documents d_1, d_2, and d_3:

- d_1: *This is a cat. This is not a monkey. This is not a donkey.*
- d_2: *This is a girl. This is a child. This is not a boy. This is a gift.*
- d_3: *This is a dog. This is a pet.*

Note that "*This is* " is maximal in d_1 as well as d_2, but not in d_3. The conditional maximal strings of "*This is* " in d_1 are "*This is a cat ... donkey.*" and "*This is not a* ". The conditional maximal strings of "*This is* " in d_2 are "*This is a* " and "*This is not ... gift.*".

LEMMA 2. *The number of maximal strings in a document d_j is less than $2|d_j|$.*

PROOF. Consider the suffix tree Δ_j of document d_j. Then for each maximal string P in d_j, there exists a unique node u in Δ_j such that $path(u) = P$. Thus the number of maximal strings in d_j is equal to the number of nodes in Δ_j. □

LEMMA 3. *For a given pattern P, we have $score(P, d_j) = score(P_i, d_j)$, where P_i is the shortest maximal string in d_j with P as prefix. If such a string P_i does not exist, then $score(P, d_j) = 0$.*

PROOF. As P_i is the shortest maximal string in d_j with P as prefix, every occurrence of a pattern P in d_j is subsumed by an occurrence of pattern P_i. Hence both patterns will have the same score with respect to document d_j, with $score(P, d_j) = 0$ signifying that the pattern P does not occur in d_j. □

LEMMA 4. *For every maximal string Q($\neq$ empty string) in d_j, there exists a unique maximal string P such that Q is a conditional maximal string of P.*

PROOF. Corresponding to each maximal string Q in d_j, there exists a node u in Δ_j (suffix tree of document d_j) such that $Q = path(u)$. The lemma follows by setting $P = path(parent(u))$, where $parent(u)$ denotes the parent of u in Δ_j. □

The number of maximal strings in $\mathcal{D}=\{d_1, d_2, ..., d_{|D|}\}$ is equal to the number of nodes in Δ (Lemma 2). In the context of maximal strings, the index in Section 4.1 maintains inverted lists for all maximal strings in $\mathcal{D}$. However, $score(P, d_j)$ depends only on pattern P and document d_j. This gives the intuition that, for a particular document d_j, instead of having entries in inverted lists corresponding to all maximal strings in $\mathcal{D}$, it is sufficient to include d_j in the inverted lists of only those strings which are maximal in d_j. Thus, for each document d_j, there will be at most $2|d_j|$ entries in all inverted lists, so that the total number of such entries corresponding to all documents is at most $\sum_{j=1}^{|\mathcal{D}|} 2|d_j| = O(n)$. However, the downside of this change is that the simple searching algorithm used in Section 4.1 can no longer serve the purpose. Therefore, we introduce a new data structure called "conditional inverted lists", which is the key contribution of this paper.

From now onwards, we refer to the maximal strings by the pre-order rank of the corresponding node in Δ. That is $P_i = path(u_i)$, where u_i is a node in Δ with pre-order rank i. In contrast to the traditional inverted list, the conditional inverted list maintains $score(P_i, d_j)$ only if P_i is maximal in

d_j. Moreover $score(P_i, d_j)$ is maintained not with P_i, but instead with P_x, such that P_i is a conditional maximal string of P_x in d_j. Therefore, u_x will be a node in the path from root to u_i. Formally, the conditional inverted list is an array of triplets of the form (*string id, document id, score*) sorted in the order of string-ids, where the string-id is pre-order rank of a node in Δ. A key observation is the following: The conditional inverted list of a string P_x has an entry $(i, j, score(P_i, d_j))$ if and only if P_i is a conditional maximal string of P_x in document d_j. From the earlier example, the conditional inverted list of "*This is* " has entries corresponding to the following strings. We assign a *string id* to each of these strings (for simplicity) and let the *score* of a string corresponding to a document be its number of occurrences in that document.

"*This is a cat ... donkey.*" (*string id* $= i_1$, *score* in $d_1 = 1$)
"*This is not a* " (*string id* $= i_2$, *score* in $d_1 = 2$)
"*This is a* " (*string id* $= i_3$, *score* in $d_2 = 3$)
"*This is not a ... gift.*" (*string id* $= i_4$, *score* in $d_2 = 1$)

Since the *string ids* are based on the lexicographical order, $i_3 < i_1 < i_2 < i_4$. Then the conditional inverted list associated with the string "*This is* " is given below. Note that there is no entry for d_3, since "*This is* " is not maximal in d_3.

string id	i_3	i_1	i_2	i_4
document id	d_2	d_1	d_1	d_2
score	3	1	2	1

We also maintain an RMQ (range maximum query) structure over the *score* field in the conditional inverted lists so as to efficiently retrieve documents with highest score as explained later in following subsection.

LEMMA 5. *The total size of conditional inverted lists is* $O(n)$.

PROOF. Corresponding to each maximal string in d_j, there exists an entry in the conditional inverted list with document id j. Hence the number of entries with document id as j is at most $2|d_j|$ and the total size of conditional inverted lists is $O(\sum_{j=1}^{|\mathcal{D}|} 2|d_j|) = O(n)$. □

LEMMA 6. *For any given node u in Δ and any given document d_j associated with some leaf in the subtree of u, there will be exactly one string P_i such that (1) P_i is maximal in d_j, (2) $path(u)$ is a prefix of P_i, and (3) the triplet $(i, j, score(P_i, d_j))$ is stored in the conditional inverted list of a node $u_x \neq u$, where u_x is some ancestor of u.*

PROOF. Since there exists at least one occurrence of d_j in the subtree of u, Statements (1), (2), and (3) can be easily verified from the definition of conditional inverted lists. The uniqueness of P_i can be proven by contradiction. Suppose that there are two strings $P_i^{'}$ and $P_i^{''}$ satisfying all of the above conditions. Then $path(u)$ will be a prefix of $P_i^* = lcp(P_i^{'}, P_i^{''})$, where lcp is the longest common prefix. Then from the one-to-one correspondence that exists between maximal strings and nodes in suffix tree (Lemma 2), it can be observed that the lcp between two maximal strings in a document d_j is also maximal. Thus P_i^* is maximal in d_j and this contradicts the fact that, when $P_i^{'}$ (or $P_i^{''}$) is a conditional maximal string of P_x, there cannot be a maximal string P_i^*, such that P_i^* is a prefix of $P_i^{'}$ and P_x is a prefix of P_i^*. □

4.3 Answering Top-k Queries

Let P be the given online pattern of length p. To answer a top-k query, we first match P in Δ in $O(p)$ time and find the locus node u_i. Let $\ell = i$ and r be the pre-order rank of the rightmost leaf in the subtree of u_i. That is, P_ℓ and P_r represents the lexicographically smallest and largest maximal strings in $\mathcal{D}$ with $path(u_i)$ as a prefix. Then, all maximal strings with P as prefix can be represented by P_z, $\ell \leq z \leq r$. From Lemmas 4 and 6, for each document d_j which has an occurrence in the subtree of u_i, there exists a unique triplet with score $score(P, d_j)$ in the conditional inverted list of some ancestor node u_x of u_i with *string id* $\in [\ell, r]$. Now the top-k documents can be retrieved by first identifying such triplets and then retrieving the k highest scored documents.

Note that the triplets in the conditional inverted lists are sorted according to the string-ids. Hence by performing a binary search of ℓ and r in the conditional inverted list associated with each ancestor of u_i, we obtain t non-overlapping intervals $[\ell_1, r_1], [\ell_2, r_2], ..., [\ell_t, r_t]$, where $t < p$ is the number of ancestors of u_i. Using an RMQ (range maximum query) structure over the *score* field in the conditional inverted lists, the k triplets (thereby documents) corresponding to the k highest scoring documents can be retrieved in $O(t + k \log k)$ time (Lemma 1). Hence the total query time is $O(p) + O(t \log n) + O(t + k \log k) = O(p \log n + k \log k)$.

THEOREM 1. *The String Inverted Index for a collection of documents $\mathcal{D} = \{d_1, d_2, ..., d_{|\mathcal{D}|}\}$ of total length n can be maintained in $O(n)$ space, such that for a given pattern P of length p, the top-k document queries can be answered in $O(p \log n + k \log k)$ time.*

Note that the same structure can be used for document listing problem [24], where we need to list all the documents which has an occurrence of P. This can be answered by retrieving all the documents corresponding to the intervals $[\ell_1, r_1] \cup [\ell_2, r_2] \cup ... \cup [\ell_t, r_t]$ in the conditional inverted lists. Hence the query time is $O(p \log n + docc)$, where $docc$ is the number of documents containing P. If our task is to just find the number of such documents (counting, not listing), we may use $docc = \sum_{i=1}^{t}(r_i - \ell_i)$, and can answer the query in $O(p \log n)$ time.

THEOREM 2. *Given a query pattern P of length p, the document listing queries for a collection of documents $\mathcal{D} = \{d_1, d_2, ..., d_{|\mathcal{D}|}\}$ of total length n can be answered in $O(p \log n + docc)$ time, where docc is the number of documents containing P. The computation of docc (document counting) takes only $O(p \log n)$ time.*

The index described in this section so far is a generalized index for string documents. When word boundaries are well-defined and query patterns will be aligned with word boundaries as well, we can build the inverted index for phrases by replacing the generalized suffix tree with a word suffix tree. A word suffix tree is a trie of all suffixes which start from a word boundary. Now we maintain the conditional inverted lists corresponding to only those strings which start from a word boundary, thus resulting in huge space savings. We call this a phrase inverted index. Theorems 1 and 2 can be rewritten for phrase inverted index as follows.

THEOREM 3. *The Phrase Inverted Index for a collection of documents $\mathcal{D} = \{d_1, d_2, ..., d_{|D|}\}$ with total N suffixes, which start from a word boundary, can be maintained in $O(N)$ space, such that for a given pattern P of length p, the top-k, document listing, and document counting queries can be answered in $O(p \log N + k \log k)$, $O(p \log N + docc)$ and $O(p \log N)$ time, respectively.*

5. PRACTICAL FRAMEWORKS

In Section 4, we introduced the theoretical framework for our index. However, when dealing with the practical performance, the space and time analysis has to be more precise than merely a big-O notation. Consider a collection of English text documents of total length n, where each character can be represented in 8 bits (256 characters, including numbers and symbols corresponding to all ASCII values). Then the text can be maintained in $8n$ bits. The conditional inverted list can consist of at most $2n$ triplets and if each entry in the triplet is 32 bits (word in computer memory), then the total size of the conditional inverted lists can be as big as $(2n \times 3 \times 32)$ bits $= (24 \times 8n)$ bits $= 24 \times (datasize)$. Moreover, we also need to maintain the generalized suffix tree, which takes ≈20-30 times of the text size. Hence the total index size will be $\approx 50 \times (datasize)$. This indicates that the hidden constants in big-O notation can restrict the use of an index in practice especially while dealing with massive data.

In this section, we introduce a practical framework of our index when frequency is used as score metric. That is, $score(P, d_j)$ represents the number of occurrences of pattern P in document d_j. However, the ideas used can also be applied for other measures. Based on different tools and techniques from succinct data structures, we design three practical versions of our index (index-A, index-B, index-C) each successively improving the space requirements. We try to achieve the index compression by not sacrificing too much on the query times. Index-C takes only $\approx 5 \times (datasize)$, and even though it does not guarantee any theoretical bounds on query time, it outperforms the existing indexes [8] for top-k retrieval.

5.1 Index-A

Index-A is a direct implementation of our theoretical index from Section 4 with one change. As suffix tree is being used as an independent component in the proposed index, we replace it by compressed suffix tree (CST) without affecting the index operations and avoid the huge space required for suffix tree. We treat index-A as our base index as it does not modify the conditional inverted lists which form the core of the index.

5.2 Index-B

In this version, we apply different empirical techniques to compress each component of the triplets from the conditional inverted list separately.

- Compressing Document Array: Taking into account that fact that the total number of documents is $|D|$, we use only $\lceil \log |D| \rceil$ bits (instead of an entire word) per entry for the document value.
- Compressing Score Array: When pattern frequency is used as the score metric, score array consists of numbers ranging from 1 to n. The most space-efficient way to store this array would be to use exactly the minimal number of bits for each number with some extra information to mark the boundaries. But this approach may not be friendly in terms of retrieving the values. Our statistical studies showed that more than 90% of entries have frequency values less than 16 (which needs only 4 bits). This leads us to the heuristic for distributing frequency values into four categories: *a*) 1-4 bits, *b*) 5-8 bits, *c*) 9-16 bits, and *d*) 17-32 bits based on the actual number of bits required to represent each value. We use a simple wavelet tree structure [13] which first splits the array into two arrays, one with 1-8 bits and another with 9-32 bits, required per entry. Both arrays are further divided to cover the categories a, b and c, d, respectively. Each of the child nodes can be further divided into two. The values stored at the leaf nodes of the wavelet tree take only as many bits as represented by the category it belongs to. Further, we use rank-select [22, 29] structures on the bit vectors in the wavelet tree for fast retrieval of values.
- Compressing String-id Array: Since the entries in the conditional inverted lists are sorted based on string-id values, we observe that there will be many consecutive entries of the same string-id, each with different document-id. Therefore run-length encoding is a promising technique for string-id compression. In order to support fast retrieval of a particular string-id value, we again maintain additional bit vectors to keep track of which string-id values are stored explicitly and which values are eliminated due to repetition in the conditional inverted lists.

5.3 Index-C

In our final efforts to further reduce the space required for the index, the following two observations play an important role.

- Approximately 50% of the entries from all the conditional inverted lists in the index, have string-id corresponding to leaf node in Δ and have low score value (frequency of one).
- The document array, which is a part of the triplet in the conditional inverted lists, does not contribute in the process of retrieving top-k answers and is used only during reporting to identify the documents with highest score.

It follows from the first observation that pruning the conditional inverted list entries corresponding to leaf nodes would significantly reduce the index space. In particular, we do not store those triplets whose string-id field corresponds to a leaf node in Δ. The downside of this approach is that, the modified index will no longer be able to report the documents with frequency of one. However, this shortcoming can be justified by reductions in space, and algorithmic approach can be employed to retrieve such documents if needed.

From the second observation, we can choose to get rid of the document-id field and incur additional overhead during query time. Briefly speaking, the document-id in the triplet corresponding to an internal node (string-id = pre-order rank of that internal node) is not stored explicitly in the conditional inverted lists. The string-id of a triplet in a conditional inverted list associated with a node u_i is replaced by a pointer which points to another triplet associated with the *highest-descendent* node in the subtree of u_i with the *same* document-id. Now the triplets in the conditional inverted lists are sorted according to the value of this pointers. Retrieval of the document-id can be done in an online fashion by chasing pointers from an internal node up to the leaf corresponding to that document. (Details are deferred to the full paper).

Index-C makes use of both ideas simultaneously. Even though the modifications do not guarantee any theoretical bounds on query time (which can be $O(n)$ in worst case), we observed that index-C performs well in practice.

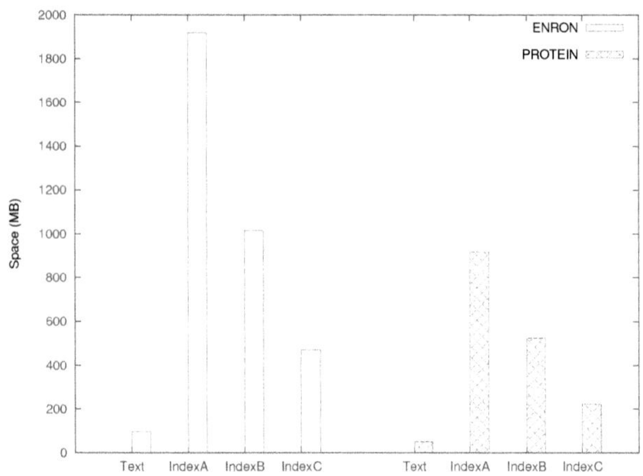

Figure 1: Space comparison of the indexes

6. EXPERIMENTAL ANALYSIS

We evaluated our new index and its compressed variants for space and query time using english texts and protein collections. ENRON is a ≈100MB collection of 48619 email messages drawn from a dataset prepared by the CALO Project (http://www.cs.cmu.edu/~enron/). PROTEIN is a concatenation of 141264 Human and Mouse protein sequences totaling ≈60MB (http://www.ebi.ac.uk/swissprot). We implemented all of the above indexes using the programming language C++, compiled with the g++ compiler version 4.2. Public code libraries at http://www.uni-ulm.de/in/theo/research/sdsl.html and http://pizzachili.dcc.uchile.cl/indexes.html are used to develop some of the components in the indexes. Our experiments were run on an Intel Core 2 Duo 2.26GHz machine with a 4GB RAM. The OS was MAC OS X using version 10.6.5. In the following, we first analyze the space-time tradeoffs for various indexes described in this paper. Then we empirically compare these indexes with the inverted index when word boundaries are well defined and query patterns are aligned on word boundaries.

6.1 Space-Time Tradeoffs

Figure 1 shows the space requirements for the original index and its compressed variants against input text size for both datasets. Reduction in the space requirements for index-B and index-C can be analyzed separately for the three key components of the indexes: Document array, score array and string-id-array. Figure 2 shows the space utilization of these components for each of the proposed indexes. For both document array and score array, even though it is possible to use the theoretically-minimal number of bits required per entry, it would result in a slowdown in the query time due to the lacking of efficient mechanisms for the retrieval of the array values. In index-B, recall that we try to keep the encoding simple and do not compress the data to the fullest extent so as to achieve reasonable compression and restrict query time within acceptable limit simultaneously. In particular, as most of the values in the score (frequency) array (≈ 97% for ENRON, ≈ 98% for PROTEIN) are less than 16, the proposed heuristic for compressing the score array in index-B achieves a very good practical performance. Out of three components, string-id array is the least compressible as its values correspond to the pre-order ranks of nodes in the suffix tree with ranges from 0 to $|T| = n$. We can utilize the fact that string-id array entries for a node are sorted in the increasing order by using difference encoding (such as gap) for efficient compression. However, such a method would naturally incur a query time overhead. Instead, as mentioned in the previous section, index-B makes use of the run-length encoding to represent the consecutive entries with the same string-id value, and was able to eliminate ≈ 30% string-id array entries for ENRON and ≈ 25% string-id array entries for PROTEIN in our experiments. Using these compression techniques, index-B is ≈ 10 times the text as compared to index-A (≈ 20 times text).

Recall that index-C does not store the document id for each entry explicitly to achieve space savings, at the expense of a slightly longer time to report the documents. Space savings are also achieved when we prune the inverted list entries corresponding to the leaf nodes, which account for 50% in ENRON and 55% in PROTEIN of the total number of entries. As a result, index-C improves further on index-B and takes only ≈ 5 times of the text in the space requirement.

For these experiments, 250 queries from ENRON and 125 queries from PROTEIN, which appear in at least 10 documents with frequency 2 or more, are generated randomly for pattern lengths varying from 3 to 10. This therefore forms a total of 2000 and 1000 sample queries for ENRON and PROTEIN, respectively. In addition, we ensure that the selected patterns of length 3 appear in at least 80 documents to observe the practical time in reporting top-k (k = 10, 20, ..., 80) documents. Figure 3 shows the average time required to retrieve $k = 10$ documents with highest score (frequency) for patterns with varying lengths. Average time required for retrieving documents in descending order of score (frequency) for a set of patterns with length 3 is shown in Figure 4 for varying k. These figures show that space savings achieved by the successive variants of our index (with increasing level of compression) will not hurt the query time to a great extent. A nearly linear dependance of query time on pattern length and k can also be observed from these figures. Matching the pattern P in compressed suffix tree Δ and binary search to obtain intervals in conditional inverted list of nodes in compressed suffix tree during top-k retrieval dominates the query time for index-A. Occasional slight drop in the query time for the indexes for increasing pattern length can be attributed to the binary search as it depends on the number of documents in which the query pattern is present. Query

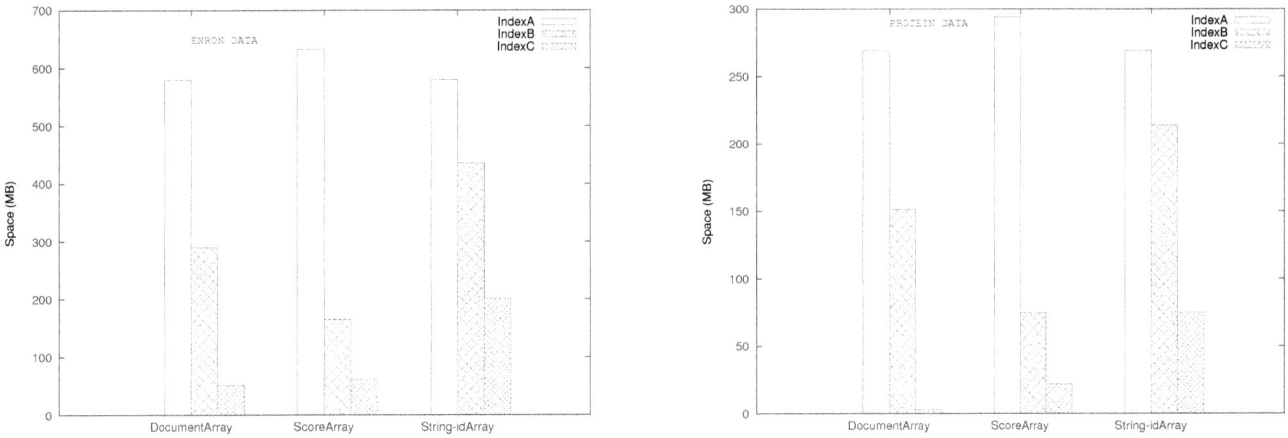

Figure 2: Compression achieved for each of three components in Conditional Inverted Lists

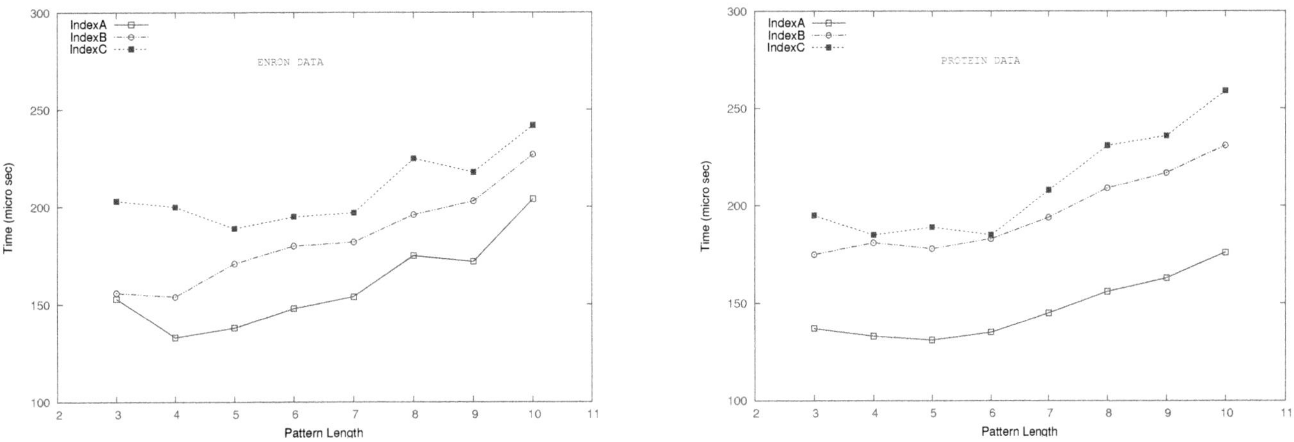

Figure 3: Mean time to report top-10 documents with highest frequency for a set of queries of varying lengths

timings for index-B closely follow to that of index-A, with decoding the score (frequency) values for possible top-k candidates being primarily responsible for the difference. Index-C has an additional overhead of decoding the document-id for each top-k answer to be reported. As a result, the gap in the query time of index-C with the other indexes should gradually increase with k, as is observed in the Figure 4.

6.2 Word/Term Based Search

In this subsection, we compare our phrase indexes with the traditional inverted index, highlighting the advantages of the former ones over the latter one. For a fair comparison, our proposed indexes in this subsection are built on the word suffix tree instead of the generalized suffix tree (Theorem 3) so as to support searching of only those patterns that are aligned with the word boundaries. We begin by comparing the query times. Traditional inverted index are known to be efficient for single-word searching. When the inverted lists are each sorted in descending order of score, ranked retrieval of documents would simply return the initial entries from the list corresponding to the query word. However, for efficient phrase searching, sorting the document lists by document-id (instead of score) would allow faster intersections of multiple lists. Figure 5 shows the time required for retrieving top-10 documents with highest score (frequency)

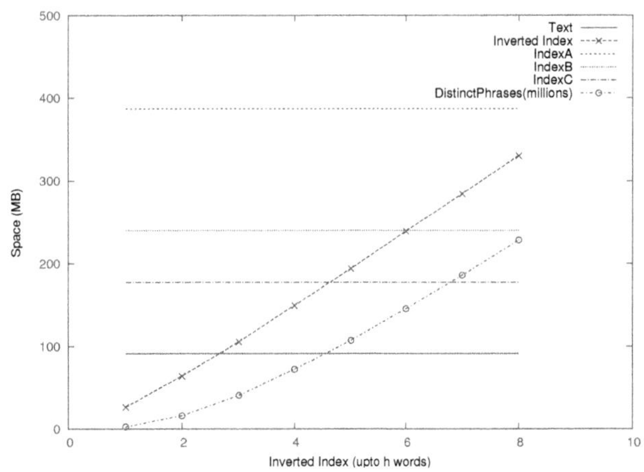

Figure 6: Space for the inverted index up to h words

for a set of phrases consisting of two and three words, respectively. Here, we generated 800 additional queries aligned on english word boundaries from ENRON. Traditional inverted index has its inverted lists sorted according to the document ids as mentioned, and we apply finger binary search [19] for intersecting multiple lists. We do not report the results

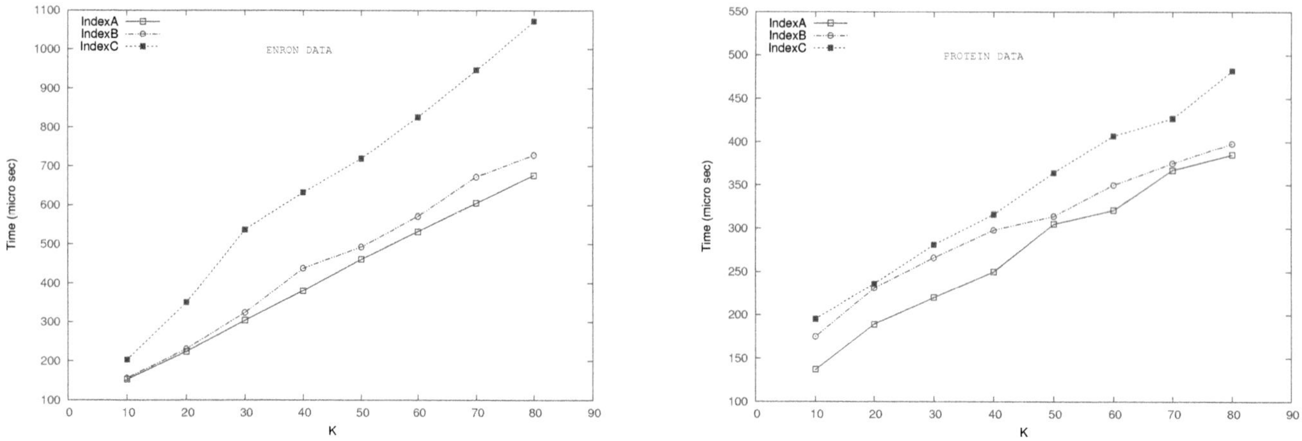

Figure 4: Mean time to report top-k documents with highest frequency for a set of queries with $|P| = 3$

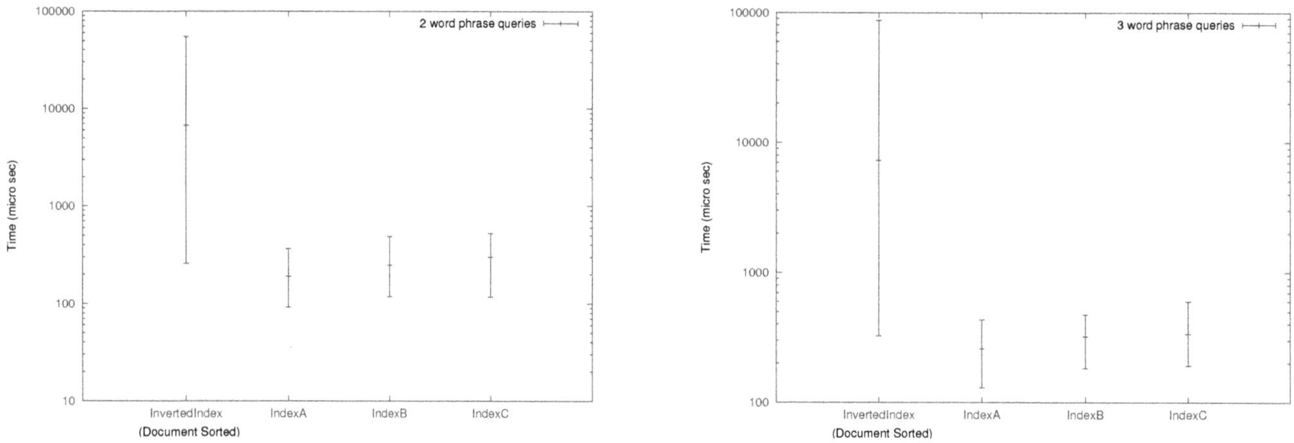

Figure 5: Time (High, Low, Mean) to report top-10 documents with highest frequency for a set of phrase queries with 2 words and 3 words

when inverted lists are sorted by score as the timings were significantly worse. Figure 5 show that our phrase indexes perform much better than the intersection-based retrieval, and the performance degradation in traditional inverted index would become more serious with the increase in words in a phrase query. Query times of our string/phrase indexes show that its query time for reporting top-10 documents is in the range of 100-400 microseconds thus achieving good practical performance.

A key point behind the widespread usage of the inverted index is that it can be stored in little space when compared with the size of input document collection; 20%-60% or more depending on whether it includes the position lists. One way to avoid the intersection of position lists in the phrase queries would be to store inverted list of all phrases up to some fixed number (say h) of words. Such an index still has to reply on intersection for phrases with more than h words. Figure 6 shows the space requirement for this variant of inverted index without the position lists. From the figure, it is clear that the space required for such a solution gradually increases with h and directly depends on the number of distinct phrases in the input text. In contrast, our phrase index supports phrase searching with arbitrary number of words. In the most space-efficient version of our phrase index (index-C), it takes just under 2 times of the input text in space. With gradual increase in space required, the traditional inverted index for phrases up to h words occupies more space than index-C for all $h \geq 5$. It is important to note that the traditional inverted index is maintained as an additional data structure along with the original text, whereas our proposed indexes are self indexes and do not need original text. Thus our phrase index compares favorably against the traditional inverted index for phrase searching in practice.

7. TOP-k TF-IDF QUERIES

In web search engines, *tf-idf* (term frequency–inverse document frequency) [2] is one of the most popular metric for relevance ranking. The query consists of multiple keywords (patterns) say $P_1, P_2, ..., P_m$ and the score of a document d, $score(d)$, is given by

$$score(d) = \sum_{i=1}^{m} tf(P_i, d) \times idf(P_i),$$

where *a)* $tf(P_i, d)$ denotes the number of occurrences of P_i in d, and *b)* $idf(P_i) = \log \frac{|\mathcal{D}|}{1+docc(P_i)}$, with $|\mathcal{D}|$ representing the total number of documents and $docc(P_i)$ representing the number of documents containing pattern P_i. Many other versions of this metric are available in the literature. For top-k document retrieval that is based on the *tf-idf* metric (with multiple query patterns), most of the existing solutions are based on heuristics. When the query consists of a single pattern, the inverted index with document lists sorted in score order can retrieve top-k documents in optimal time. However, for an m-pattern query (a query consisting of m patterns say $P_1, P_2, ..., P_m$), we may need the inverted lists sorted according to the document id as well. In this section, we introduce an exact algorithm and compare the results obtained by applying it to inverted index as well as our index (index-B). Although our algorithm does not guarantee any worst-case query bounds, the focus is to explore the capabilities of our index as a generalized inverted index. Along with our index, we make use of a wavelet tree [13] over the document array for its advantages in offering dual-sorting functionalities. We restrict the query patterns to be words in order to give a fair comparison between our index and the inverted index.

Suppose that N denotes the number of suffixes in the word suffix tree. Let $DA[1...N]$ be an array of document ids, such that $DA[i]$ is the document id corresponding to ith smallest suffix (lexicographically) in the word suffix tree. Note that each entry in DA takes at most $\lceil \log |D| \rceil$ bits to store. Therefore a wavelet tree *W-Tree* of DA can be maintained in $N \log |\mathcal{D}|(1 + o(1))$ bits. Now, given the suffix range $[\ell, r]$ of any pattern P, the term frequency $tf(P, d_j)$ for the document with id j can be computed by counting the number of entries in DA with $DA[i] = j$ and $\ell \leq i \leq r$. This query can be answered in $O(\log |\mathcal{D}|)$ time by exploring the orthogonal range searching functionality of *W-Tree*. Since term frequency in any document can be computed using *W-Tree*, we do not store the score (term frequency) array in index-B. This slightly compensates for the additional space overhead due to *W-Tree*. Inverse document frequency *idf* can be computed using Theorem 3. For simplicity, we describe the algorithm for two pattern queries (P_1 and P_2) as follows, and the algorithm can be easily extended for the general m-pattern queries. Let S_{ans} and S_{doc} be two sets of documents which are set to empty initially, and let d_1^k and d_2^k represents the kth highest scoring document corresponding P_1 and P_2, with *term frequency* as the score function and $score(d) = tf(P_1, d)\ idf(P_1) + tf(P_2, d)\ idf(P_2)$.

$S_{ans} = S_{doc} = \{\}, x = y = 1$
while $|S_{ans}| < k$ **do**
  if $score(d_1^x) \geq score(d_2^y)$ **then**
    $S_{doc} \leftarrow S_{doc} \cup d_1^x$ and $x \leftarrow x + 1$
  else
    $S_{doc} \leftarrow S_{doc} \cup d_2^y$ and $y \leftarrow y + 1$
  end if
  if $|S_{doc}| = 1, 2, 4, 8, 16, ...$ **then**
    $score_{max} = tf(P_1, d_1^x)\ idf(P_1) + tf(P_2, d_2^y)\ idf(P_2)$
    for each $d \in S_{doc}$ **do**
      if $score(d) \geq score_{max}$ and $d \notin S_{ans}$ **then**
        $S_{ans} \leftarrow S_{ans} \cup d$
      end if
    end for
  end if
end while
Choose k documents in S_{ans} with the highest *score* value

The main idea of the algorithm is to maintain a list of candidate top-k documents in the set S_{doc}, and refine the candidate set by moving documents to the set S_{ans} from time to time. Each document in S_{ans} will have score higher than an imaginary $score_{max}$, and the set S_{ans} will always contain the highest scoring documents we have examined so far. The algorithm stops as soon as S_{ans} contains k documents, in which we report the top-k documents from the set.

Experimental Analysis

We compare the performance of our index against the traditional inverted index for answering 2-pattern queries using the algorithm described above. In the traditional inverted index, document lists are sorted either by score (frequency) or document-id. To apply the above heuristic, we need dual-sorted documents lists, where each list is sorted on both score as well as document-id. Score sorted lists support ranked retrieval of documents for individual patterns but *tf-idf* score can not be computed efficiently. If lists are sorted by document-id, though *tf-idf* score computation is faster, document retrieval in ranked order is not efficient. As a result we first duplicate the document lists for each of the pattern P_i and sort them as required. Figure 7 shows the mean time required for retrieving top-k documents for a set of 50 2-pattern queries for ENRON such that each pattern is highly frequent. As observed from the figure, query time for our index increases faster than that of the inverted index.

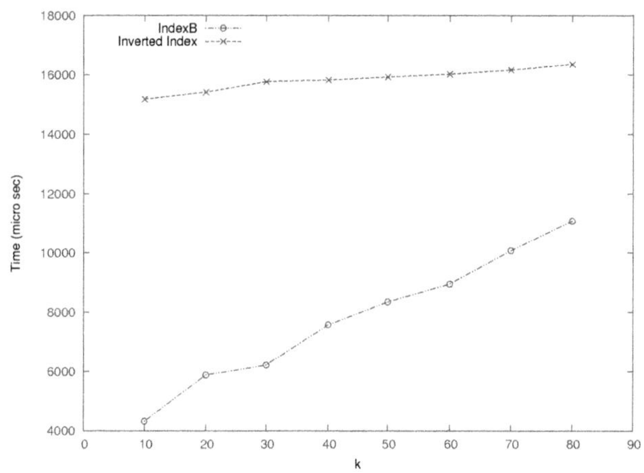

Figure 7: Mean time to report top-k documents for a set of 2-pattern queries

We remark that the major part of the query time used by the inverted index is on re-sorting the the document lists in which the query patterns occur. Thus, if the patterns are not too frequently occurring, the time spent on re-sorting is reduced, and the advantages of our index over the inverted index will vanish. Finally, the size of our index is ≈ 3.1 times of the text size.

8. CONCLUDING REMARKS

This paper introduces the first practical version of inverted index for string documents. The idea is to store lists for a selected collection of substrings (or phrases) in a conditionally sorted manner. Succinct data structures are used to represent these lists so as to reap benefits of dual sorting and achieve good top-k retrieval performance. We show

how top-k *tf-idf* based queries can be executed efficiently. Furthermore, our indexes show a space-time advantage over all of the traditional techniques for searching long phrases. While this is the first prototype, more research will certainly help in deriving structures with great practical impact.

9. REFERENCES

[1] V. Anh and A. Moffat. Pruned Query Evaluation using Pre-computed Impacts. In *ACM SIGIR*, pages 372–379, 2006.

[2] R. Baeza-Yates and B. Ribeiro-Neto. *Modern Information Retrieval*. Addison Wesley, 1999.

[3] D. Bahle, H. E. Williams, and J. Zobel. Compaction Techniques for Nextword Indexes. In *SPIRE*, pages 33–45, 2001.

[4] D. Bahle, H. E. Williams, and J. Zobel. Optimised Phrase Querying and Browsing of Large Text Databases. In *ACSC*, pages 11–19, 2001.

[5] M. A. Bender and M. Farach-Colton. The Level Ancestor Problem Simplified. *Theoretical Computer Science*, 321(1):5–12, 2004.

[6] R. Cánovas and G. Navarro. Practical Compressed Suffix Trees. In *SEA*, pages 94–105, 2010.

[7] B. Chazelle. A Functional Approach to Data Structures and Its Use in Multidimensional Searching. *SIAM Journal on Computing*, 17(3):427–462, 1988.

[8] J. S. Culpepper, G. Navarro, S. J. Puglisi, and A. Turpin. Top-k Ranked Document Search in General Text Databases. In *ESA*, pages 194–205, 2010.

[9] J. Fischer and V. Heun. A New Succinct Representation of RMQ-Information and Improvements in the Enhanced Suffix Array. In *ESCAPE*, pages 459–470, 2007.

[10] J. Fischer, V. Heun, and H. M. Stühler. Practical Entropy-Bounded Schemes for $O(1)$-Range Minimum Queries. In *IEEE DCC*, pages 272–281, 2008.

[11] J. Fischer, V. Mäkinen, and G. Navarro. Faster Entropy-Bounded Compressed Suffix Trees. In *Theoretical Computer Science*, pages 5354–5364, 2009.

[12] T. Gagie, G. Navarro, and S. J. Puglisi. Colored Range Queries and Document Retrieval. In *SPIRE*, pages 67–81, 2010.

[13] R. Grossi, A. Gupta, and J. S. Vitter. High-Order Entropy-Compressed Text Indexes. In *ACM-SIAM SODA*, pages 841–850, 2003.

[14] R. Grossi and J. S. Vitter. Compressed Suffix Arrays and Suffix Trees with Applications to Text Indexing and String Matching. *SIAM Journal on Computing*, 35(2):378–407, 2005.

[15] A. Gupta, W. K. Hon, R. Shah, and J. S. Vitter. Compressed Data Structures: Dictionaries and Data-Aware Measures. *Theoretical Computer Science*, 387(3):313–331, 2007.

[16] W. K. Hon, M. Patil, R. Shah, and S. B. Wu. Efficient Index for Retrieving Top-k Most Frequent Documents. *Journal on Discrete Algorithms*, 8(4):402–417, 2010.

[17] W. K. Hon, R. Shah, S. V. Thankachan, and J. S. Vitter. String Retrieval for Multi-pattern Queries. In *SPIRE*, pages 55–66, 2010.

[18] W. K. Hon, R. Shah, and J. S. Vitter. Space-Efficient Framework for Top-k String Retrieval Problems. In *IEEE FOCS*, pages 713–722, 2009.

[19] F. K. Hwang and S. Lin. A Simple Algorithm for Merging Two Disjoint Linearly Ordered Sets. *SIAM Journal of Computing*, 1(1):31–39, 1972.

[20] M. Karpinski and Y. Nekrich. Top-K Color Queries for Document Retrieval. In *ACM-SIAM SODA*, pages 401–411, 2011.

[21] Y. Matias, S. Muthukrishnan, S. C. Sahinalp, and J. Ziv. Augmenting Suffix Trees, with Applications. In *ESA*, pages 67–78, 1998.

[22] J. I. Munro. Tables. In *FSTTCS*, pages 37–42, 1996.

[23] J. I. Munro, V. Raman, and S. S. Rao. Space Efficient Suffix Trees. In *FSTTCS*, pages 186–196, 1998.

[24] S. Muthukrishnan. Efficient Algorithms for Document Retrieval Problems. In *ACM-SIAM SODA*, pages 657–666, 2002.

[25] G. Navarro and S. J. Puglisi. Dual-Sorted Inverted Lists. In *SPIRE*, pages 309–321, 2010.

[26] E. Ohlebusch, J. Fischer, and S. Gog. CST++. In *SPIRE*, pages 322–333, 2010.

[27] E. Ohlebusch and S. Gog. A Compressed Enhanced Suffix Array Supporting Fast String Matching. In *SPIRE*, pages 51–62, 2009.

[28] M. Persin, J. Zobel, and R. S. Davis. Filtered Document Retrieval with Frequency-Sorted Indexes. *Journal of the American Society for Information Science*, 47(10):749–764, 1996.

[29] R. Raman, V. Raman, and S. S. Rao. Succinct Indexable Dictionaries with Applications to Encoding k-ary Trees and Multisets. In *ACM-SIAM SODA*, pages 233–242, 2002.

[30] L. Russo, G. Navarro, and A. Oliveira. Fully-Compressed Suffix Trees. In *LATIN*, pages 362–373, 2008.

[31] K. Sadakane. Space-Efficient Data Structures for Flexible Text Retrieval Systems. In *ISAAC*, pages 14–24, 2002.

[32] K. Sadakane. Compressed Suffix Trees with Full Functionality. *Theory of Computing Systems*, pages 589–607, 2007.

[33] N. Välimäki and V. Mäkinen. Space-Efficient Algorithms for Document Retrieval. In *CPM*, pages 205–215, 2007.

[34] N. Välimäki, V. Mäkinen, W. Gerlach, and K. Dixit. Engineering a Compressed Suffix Tree Implementation. *ACM Journal of Experimental Algorithmics*, 14, 2009.

[35] P. Weiner. Linear Pattern Matching Algorithms. In *SWAT*, pages 1–11, 1973.

[36] H. E. Williams, J. Zobel, and P. Anderson. What's Next? Index Structures for Efficient Phrase Querying. In *ADC*, pages 141–152, 1999.

[37] H. E. Williams, J. Zobel, and D. Bahle. Fast Phrase Querying with Combined Indexes. *ACM Transactions on Information Systems*, 22(4):573–594, 2004.

[38] J. Zobel and A. Moffat. Inverted Files for Text Search Engines. *ACM Computing Surveys*, 38(2), 2006.

Faster Temporal Range Queries over Versioned Text

Jinru He
CSE Department
Polytechnic Institute of NYU
Brooklyn, NY 11201
jhe@cis.poly.edu

Torsten Suel
CSE Department
Polytechnic Institute of NYU
Brooklyn, NY 11201
suel@poly.edu

ABSTRACT

Versioned textual collections are collections that retain multiple versions of a document as it evolves over time. Important large-scale examples are Wikipedia and the web collection of the Internet Archive. Search queries over such collections often use keywords as well as temporal constraints, most commonly a time range of interest. In this paper, we study how to support such temporal range queries over versioned text. Our goal is to process these queries faster than the corresponding keyword-only queries, by exploiting the additional constraint. A simple approach might partition the index into different time ranges, and then access only the relevant parts. However, specialized inverted index compression techniques are crucial for large versioned collections, and a naive partitioning can negatively affect index compression and query throughput. We show how to achieve high query throughput by using smart index partitioning techniques that take index compression into account. Experiments on over 85 million versions of Wikipedia articles show that queries can be executed in a few milliseconds on memory-based index structures, and only slightly more time on disk-based structures. We also show how to efficiently support the recently proposed stable top-k search primitive on top of our schemes.

Categories and Subject Descriptors

H.3.3 [INFORMATION STORAGE AND RETRIEVAL]: Information Search and Retrieval.

General Terms

Algorithms, Performance.

Keywords

Inverted index, query processing, temporal search, range queries, versioned documents.

1. INTRODUCTION

The major web search engines now have hundreds of millions of users that issue several billion queries per day. Each query needs to be evaluated against the tens of billions of pages covered by the engine, resulting in significant hardware and energy costs. This situation has led to renewed interest in basic query processing architectures and index organizations for large document collections, and a lot of recent research has focused on topics such as index building, index compression, fast index access and traversal, and caching and early termination techniques for fast query processing.

Here, we focus on the special case of versioned document collections. These are collections where each document consists of multiple versions that represent the evolution of the document over time, and the goal is to enable search across the different versions of the documents. Maybe the best-known example of a versioned document collection on the web is Wikipedia, which retains all past versions of all articles, and a lot of researchers have studied the evolution of Wikipedia articles over time. Another important example is the web collection at the Internet Archive, consisting of more than 150 billion web pages that have been crawled since 1996 – or more precisely, 150 billion distinct versions, as many pages were repeatedly crawled over the years. Other examples of versioned collections are revision control systems for source code, document management systems, or versioned file systems that retain all past versions of the files.

Such versioned document collections differ from standard collections in several important ways. First, keeping all past versions results in much larger collections than keeping only the latest version. Second, different versions of the same document are often very similar, but exploiting this redundancy between versions to decrease inverted index size requires specialized index compression techniques. Third, the types of information requests that users have are also different. In particular, many queries have a temporal component, and may ask for relevant documents during a certain time interval. This is the main focus of this paper.

In particular, we are studying how to efficiently support search requests with a temporal restriction (temporal range queries) in versioned document collections. As discussed later, a trivial way to implement such queries is via post filtering, i.e., by traversing the index structures for the complete time range and discarding results outside the query range. Of course, one should hope to actually do much better, by enabling efficient access to only those subsets of the index structures that correspond to the query range.

However, techniques for enabling efficient access to time ranges, usually by partitioning or suitably reordering the index, can result in significant increases in total index size under state-of-the-art versioned index compression techniques, which in turn can slow down processing in both memory-based and disk-based system architectures. Thus, the main

SIGIR'11, July 24–28, 2011, Beijing, China.

challenge we address here is fast temporal range query processing in versioned document collections under state-of-the-art versioned index compression methods.

The remainder of this paper is organized as follows. We first give some background and discuss related work. Then Section 3 lists our main contributions. Section 4 discusses the data sets we use and provides some baseline experimental results. Sections 5 and 6 provide our main contributions, smart partitioning and index reorganization techniques that achieve improved performance for memory- and disk-based indexes. Section 7 shows how to efficiently implement the recently proposed Stable Top-k operator [22] on top of our index. Finally, Section 8 provides some concluding remarks.

2. BACKGROUND AND RELATED WORK

We now provide some background and discuss related work. We start with basics of inverted indexes, and then discuss versioned document collections, versioned index compression, and previous work on range queries.

2.1 Searching Document Collections

There is a vast literature on how to organize and query index structures for standard (i.e., non-versioned) textual document collections. This includes work on compressing index structures using specialized techniques, executing basic forms of Boolean and ranked queries over such collections, and implementing various early termination and tiering strategies that allow ranked query processing without complete index traversal. We refer to the survey of Zobel and Moffat [27] for an overview.

Inverted Indexes: Most current search engines use an *inverted index* structure to support efficient keyword queries [27]. An *inverted index* for a collection of documents is a structure that stores, for each term (word) occurring somewhere in the collection, information about all locations where it occurs. For each term t, the index contains an *inverted list* I_t consisting of a number of *index postings*. Each posting in I_t contains information about the occurrences of t in one particular document d, usually the ID of the document (the docID), the number of occurrences of t in d (the frequency), and possibly other information such as the locations of the occurrences within the document. We assume an index with docIDs and frequencies in this paper.

To a first approximation, ranked query processing in search engines involves traversal of the inverted lists for the query terms, and computation of a score for each document satisfying an initial Boolean filter, usually the AND or OR of the query terms. For efficiency, this score should be computable from the information stored in the inverted index, though in practice often additional features are fetched for a second round of scoring after winnowing of the initial set of candidates. Our techniques here do not depend on the precise scoring function.

Index Compression: The postings in each list are usually sorted by docID and then compressed using any of the techniques in the literature [27]. Most techniques first replace each docID (except the first) by the difference between it and the preceding docID, called *d-gap*, and then encode the d-gaps using a suitable integer compression method. The d-gaps and frequencies are often stored separately, and thus we compress sequences of d-gaps and sequences of frequencies. Inverted lists are usually organized into blocks that can be independently accessed, thus enabling forwards skips during query processing. We use such blocked indexes in our implementations, with a block size of 128 integers.

A large number of inverted index compression techniques have been proposed; see [27] for an overview. Here, we use two techniques that have been previously applied to versioned document collections [12, 13]: *Interpolative Coding* (IPC) [17] and the OPT-PFD method [23] from the PForDelta family of compression schemes [14, 28]. Both methods are especially suitable for compressing clustered (or bursty) sequences of integers, where there are runs of small numbers separated by a few larger numbers. IPC achieves the smallest compressed size but is somewhat slow in decompression, while OPT-PFD has a slightly larger compressed size but allows extremely fast decompression (up to a billion integers per second per core).

2.2 Versioned Document Collections

A versioned document collection D is a set of documents $d_0, \dots d_{n-1}$, where each d_i has m_i versions $d_i^1, d_i^2, \dots, d_i^{m_i}$. We assume a linear history, and do not try to model the case of branches (forks) in the revision history, though we believe most of our ideas could be adapted to this case. Each version has a lifespan associated with it, i.e., a time period where it is valid, and we assume that different versions of the same document have disjoint lifespans.

For an overview of the issues involved in building large scale web archival systems, see [21, 3]. There has been some amount of recent work on indexing and searching of versioned collections. Overall, this work can be split into three subsets, corresponding to different layers of a search architecture for such collections:

- Index compression techniques for versioned collections that exploit the similarity between different versions of a document [4, 15, 8, 25, 5, 12, 13], leading to significantly smaller index sizes and faster index traversal.
- Support for efficient temporal range (or point) queries over versioned collections through suitable index organization and index traversal [5, 2]. Here, the goal is to process queries with temporal constraints (say, for versions that were valid during a certain time interval) faster than a complete traversal of the index followed by subsequent filtering, by allowing efficient access to those index postings that fall into the right time range.
- Implementation of higher-level temporal operators, such as the Stable Top-k operator recently proposed in [22], on top of the index. The idea is that users may be interested in, e.g., documents that were relevant throughout the entire query time interval, or on average very relevant. In general, there may be some aggregation across different versions within the time interval to determine the most suitable documents and versions to return.

We focus here on the middle layer, supporting fast temporal range search. However, we also consider how this interacts with the other two layers. In particular, we will see that a naive approach for range search based on index partitioning can severely affect compressed index size, resulting in significant performance degradation. Thus, one main concern here is on supporting range search while preserving the effectiveness of the lower-level compression methods. We note that this challenge distinguishes the temporal range search problem on versioned document collections from that on non-versioned collections, such as news archives where each article has a publication time or a period of time when it is considered relevant but there is no versioning. (For completeness we also provide some limited experimental results for a non-versioned collection of articles from the New York Times.)

We also consider how to implement higher-level operators on our methods. Here, recent work in [22] proposed algorithms and specialized index structures for one such operator, Stable Top-k. We show in Section 7 that we can in fact implement this operator on top of our unchanged index organizations, with very little overhead, resulting in running times that are faster than those reported in [22] for a specialized index structure on a smaller collection.

2.3 Versioned Index Compression

An inverted index for a versioned collection should allow us to determine which versions of which documents contain a term, and how often. Versioned document collections often use index organizations and compression methods that are somewhat different from those used for standard collections. We now describe three inverted index compression schemes that we use, *Sorted*, *2-DIFF*, and *2R-MSA*, which were shown to achieve very fast query processing speeds in [12, 13].

The *Sorted* method is easy to explain: It simply indexes the versions as if they were separate documents, but assigns docIDs (or really version IDs) such that consecutive versions of the same document receive consecutive IDs. Then either IPC or OPT-PFD is used to compress the resulting inverted lists. This idea of better index compression through proper assignment of docIDs has recently been studied by a number of researchers for the case of standard collections [7, 18, 20, 6, 19, 23], and is also related to the lossy compression approach for versioned indexes proposed in [5].

To describe *2-DIFF* and *2R-MSA*, we need to introduce two-level indexes, first proposed for standard collections in [1], and then applied to versioned collections in [13, 12]. We define the first-level index of a versioned document collection D as an inverted index where the inverted list for a term t contains a posting for document d_i if at least one version d_i^j of d_i contains t. For a term t that occurs in at least one version of d_i, we define the bit vector of t and d_i as an array of m_i bits such that the j-th bit is set to 1 iff version d_i^j contains t. We also define a corresponding frequency vector that has one integer entry for each 1-bit in the bit vector (that is, each version d_i^j containing the term); this entry contains the frequency of the term in the corresponding version.

A two-level index structure for a versioned document collection consists of the first-level index plus a second level storing all the bit and frequency vectors in suitably compressed form. This allows efficient query processing by first running a query on the smaller first-level index, and then fetching and decompressing any necessary bit and frequency vectors. Note that the first level contains only docIDs, and no frequency values. It is compressed using standard index compression techniques such as IPC or PFD, since there is no obvious structure in the data that distinguishes this case from that of a non-versioned collection.

The 2-DIFF and 2R-MSA methods have the same first level structure, as described above, but use different techniques for compressing the vectors in the second level. This is achieved by a transformation that creates virtual document versions on which bit and frequency vectors are defined. For convenience, we assume each document has an initial empty version d_i^0.

Then in 2-DIFF, for each version d_i^j we define a virtual document version d'^j_i consisting of the symmetric difference between d_i^j and the previous version d_i^{j-1}. (Note that in the virtual version, some terms may have a negative frequency.) In 2R-MSA, we create a virtual version $d'^{j,k}_i$ for every $0 < j \leq k \leq m_i$, containing any terms that occur in all versions d_i^j to d_i^k but not in d_i^{j-1} or d_i^{k+1}. (Note that versions are bags, not sets, of terms.) We then keep all non-empty versions. In the case of 2R-MSA, we also reorder (renumber) the virtual versions in decreasing order of size.

Given these virtual versions, we create bit and frequency vectors as defined earlier, and finally we compress these vectors using either IPC or OPT-PFD. We note that 2-DIFF and 2R-MSA are two-level versions of techniques originally proposed in [4] and [15], respectively, with the additional reordering of virtual versions by size in 2R-MSA leading to better compression through clustering. The techniques we present in this paper also apply to other versioned index compression techniques (though the results may vary), and the details of the virtual document definitions above are not really crucial for understanding later sections (as long as the reader understands the concepts of levels, bit vectors, and frequency vectors). Finally, note that we limit ourselves to indexes storing docIDs and frequencies, and the problem of compressing versioned indexes with positions is quite different from the case without positions [25], as it requires working with substrings rather than bags of terms.

2.4 Temporal and Range Search

There is of course a lot of previous work on range search. This includes extensive work by the database community that is focused on numeric or string attributes but that does not look at very large sets of documents and inverted index structures. Work in IR includes support for numerical range constraints [11] (e.g., keyword queries on product catalogs with price or weight constraints), and techniques for geographic or local search [16, 26, 9, 10] (e.g., keyword queries on business listings with location constraints). The main difference is the presence of versioning in our problem, making the previous methods unsuitable.

We define temporal range search as the problem of returning the docIDs, version numbers, and scores of all versions satisfying the keyword as well as temporal range constraints. A simple baseline solution to this problem would first perform a Boolean filter to identify documents satisfying the keyword constraint, then check for the range constraint, and finally fetch the frequencies and compute the scores. In fact, we will implement this method in Section 4, and show that with state-of-the-art index compression and traversal techniques, such an approach is actually reasonably efficient for the collection sizes typically studied in the literature. Note that we do not consider early termination techniques; i.e., we limit ourselves to techniques that must score any version that satisfies the Boolean keyword and range constraints. This means that our results are largely independent of the choice of scoring function, as long as it can be computed from the index data. (We use BM25 in our implementation. Clearly, our methods can be extended to return top-k results, with essentially the same running times.)

However, we should expect to do better than the baseline by exploiting the temporal constraint, if we can organize the index in a way that allows fast access to postings that satisfy this constraint. This idea was evaluated in [5], leading to improvements over the base case through index partitioning along the time axis. However, their work used compression methods that lead to much larger index structures, and thus a slower baseline, than our work. We focus in particular on the trade-offs between index organization and index size for state-of-the-art index compression techniques. Another recent study [2] attempts to accelerate range search by trading off speed and recall; the goal is to retrieve most of the relevant results by selectively searching in only a subset of the index partitions overlapping the query range. However, the results suggest that significant gains in speed can only be obtained with severe decreases in recall, and arguably the same or better trade-offs could also be achieved with existing standard early-termination techniques.

3. OUR CONTRIBUTIONS

In this paper, we describe and evaluate techniques for optimizing the performance of keyword queries with temporal range constraints in versioned collections. In particular, we make the following contributions:

- We evaluate a state-of-the-art implementation of simple baseline methods for searching versioned document collections, establishing the results that need to be beaten by more optimized methods.
- We describe and evaluate document and index partitioning techniques for main memory-based indexes that achieve improved performance over the baseline with only moderate increases in total index size.
- We also study how to organize index structures when the index is partially or completely on disk.
- We show that our methods are fast enough to efficiently support higher level operations, in particular the Stable Top-k operator [22], without the need for specialized index structures.

4. DATA SETS AND BASELINE METHODS

In this section, we perform a careful study of some baseline methods on several data sets. We first introduce the three document sets and the query traces that we used, then describe the baseline methods and their performance, and finish with a discussion of our observations.

4.1 Data Sets and Query Traces

We use versioned collections from Wikipedia and the Internet Archive, and a non-versioned collection with time stamps from the New York Times.

The Wikipedia data (Wiki) consists of 2,401,789 documents with a total of 85,352,299 distinct versions, i.e., about 35 versions per document on average. (We removed versions marked as minor edits.) This is a complete archive of English language Wikipedia articles from January 2001 to January 2008 (more than 1.5 TB in uncompressed form), more than 2 times larger than the set used in [22, 5] and about 10 times larger than that in [13, 12]. The Internet Archive data (IRE) consists of 1,056,981 web pages with 16,680,002 distinct versions from the Irish web domain collected from 1996 to 2006, i.e., about 15 versions per document. In our experiments, we assume that each version here is valid from the time it is fetched to the time a new, distinct version is crawled. The New York Times data (NYT) consists of 1,831,109 news articles from January 1987 to January 2007. Each article has a time stamp indicating the publication date. We assumed that every article had a lifetime of 90 days, as suggested in [2].

We point out that particularly for the Wiki and IRE data sets, versions are not equally distributed over time. In Figure 1 we show the total number of documents and terms (i.e., total postings) in the versions that were valid at certain points in time. We see that both collections experienced significant growth over the total time period, with more content towards the end of the period.

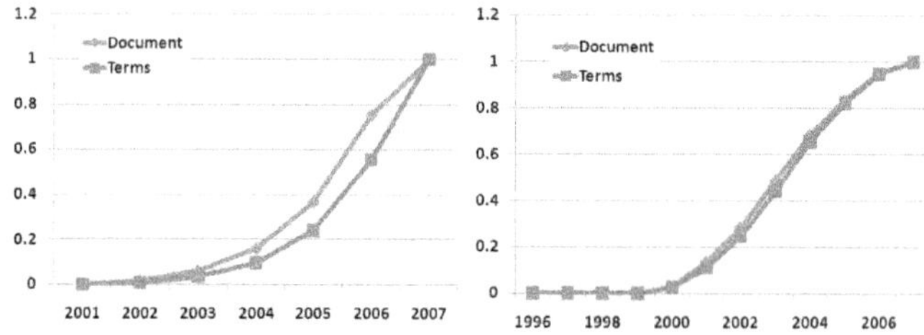

Figure 1: The number of documents and number of terms (i.e., total postings), based on all versions that were valid on a fixed day each year. We show results for Wiki (left) and Ireland (right).

Queries: For each of the three data sets, we compiled query traces using the AOL search query log. For Wiki, we extracted 10,000 queries where the user clicks on a result from the Wikipedia.org domain (following [13]). We also extracted 5,000 and 10,000 queries, respectively, where users clicked on results in the `ie` and `nytimes.com` web domains. Then we assign temporal ranges to these queries by choosing start and end times. The start time is chosen using two different random distributions, (a) uniformly from the total time interval, and (b) biased according to the document distribution shown in Figure 1 so that more queries focus on those times where most of the content resides. We then randomly select an end point such that the expected size of the range is equal to 7 days, 30 days, or one year, to model different granularities for the temporal constraint.

System Setup: All experiments were run on a single core of an Intel Xeon E5520 processor running at 2.26 Ghz. Disk costs were modeled assuming 8 ms access time for each separate access and 50 MB/s sequential transfer rate, which is typical of current low-cost SATA disks.

4.2 Non-Temporal Baseline

We built compressed versioned index structures containing docID and frequency data for our three collections, using existing components described in Section 2. For the non-versioned NYT data set, only the *Sorted* method is applicable; we assigned docIDs according to the time stamps of the articles. We also built a fast query processor using existing components in our group. This processor uses various state-of-the-art techniques such as block-compressed indexes and fast document-at-a-time index traversal. It can execute queries with and without temporal range constraints, and we will later extend it with various improvements. In the following, we provide some benchmark results for our processor that serve as a baseline for later sections.

Index Size: We start by reporting some results for index size and query processing without additional temporal constraints. We first look at the first level of the indexes for Wiki and IRE. In Table 1 we show the total size (in MB) and query processing speed (in millisecs) for the first-level index only, for Wiki and IRE and using IPC and OPT-PFD compression. Queries are chosen from the relevant traces but without range constraints, and we traverse the docID-only postings in the first level to report all documents that contain all query terms (intersection).

	Wiki	Ireland
IPC size (MB)	864	273
IPC speed (ms)	1.0	0.3
PFD size (MB)	1062	394
PFD speed (ms)	0.6	0.1

Table 1: Compressed sizes and query processing speeds for the first-level index structure.

We see from Table 1 that both index sizes and query processing speeds for the first level are quite small. We also see that using IPC rather than OPT-PFD results in decreases in first-level index size, but at the cost of disproportional increases in time. Thus, in the remainder, we choose OPT-PFD for both levels of our index structures. (Results in [13] already suggest using OPT-PFD for the second level.)

Next, we look at total index size (in MB) for the three collections under the different compression schemes, shown in Table 2. We see that, as should be expected from [13], 2-DIFF and 2R-MSA achieve a significantly smaller compressed index size than Sorted, with 2R-MSA doing slightly better than 2-DIFF. In particular, for Wiki with 85 million versions and more than 1.5 TB of uncompressed (though highly redundant) data, we get a complete index size of only about 4 GB, thus allowing the index to be kept completely in main memory on many current machines.

	docID	freq	total
Wiki Sorted	5508	8364	13872
Wiki 2-DIFF	3802	1109	4911
Wiki 2R-MSA	2963	1104	4067
IRE Sorted	1137	856	1993
IRE 2-DIFF	894	282	1176
IRE 2R-MSA	780	170	950
NYT Sorted	453	135	588

Table 2: Compressed index size in MB for docIDs and frequencies using the three compression methods on our data sets.

Non-Temporal Queries: Next, we report results for query processing without temporal range constraints on the full indexes, shown in Table 3. We report the CPU time of query processing (on a single core) assuming the index is in main memory, as well as the disk access and transfer times involved if all inverted lists are located on disk and need to be fetched first (we look at caching of index data further below). For the disk numbers, we use disk access times of 8 ms and a transfer rate of 50 MB/s, and we assume that the first and second levels of each inverted list are next to each other so they can be read with a single seek. (Thus, the access time divided by 8 ms gives the average number of terms per query for each trace, as every list requires a separate access.)

	cpu	disk access	disk transfer	total
Wiki Sorted	18.2	17.4	117	151.1
Wiki 2-DIFF	26.3	17.4	37.2	80.9
Wiki 2R-MSA	27.1	17.4	36.9	81.4
IRE Sorted	0.84	22.9	12.2	35.9
IRE 2-DIFF	1.31	22.9	6.2	30.4
IRE 2R-MSA	1.43	22.9	5.4	29.7
NYT Sorted	0.4	28.2	12.0	40.6

Table 3: CPU and disk cost per query (in ms) under different compression schemes for our three data set.

As we see from Table 3, query processing in main memory is quite fast, with Sorted achieving a time of 18.2 ms on the large Wiki data set. However, Sorted results in much larger index sizes, and this shows itself in the significant costs for retrieving data from disk that make this the slowest method in total cost. For the smaller IRE data set and for NYT, the disk access cost is dominated by access times. But even for Wiki under 2-DIFF and 2R-MSA, access costs are significant compared to transfer costs, implying that we have to avoid optimizations that decrease data transfers at the cost of additional random accesses.

4.3 Basic Temporal Query Processing

We now look at what happens once we add temporal constraints to the queries (while not changing the index organization). We create an additional (relatively small) memory-based table that contains the time ranges of the different versions, allowing efficient lookup given an index posting. We then have two ways to use this table to check the range constraint: We can either first perform the intersection between query terms and then do a lookup for each qualifying version (intersect-first), or we can do a lookup for every posting in the shortest list and then do the intersection with the other terms (check-first), which decreases the cost of the intersection at the cost of more lookups.

In Table 4, we show CPU costs on the three data sets and different compression schemes, assuming a uniform query distribution. In addition to check-first and intersect-first, we also show a method called best-of-both that assumes that each query uses the best approach, giving us an upper bound on what can be achieved by choosing the best for each query. We note that in some cases we see slight improvements over the non-range case, since we do not have to fetch frequency values and compute scores for versions that do not satisfy the range constraint. On the other hand, the cost of doing the simple lookup into the global table is also significant, in some cases more than wiping out the savings. Overall, numbers are similar to the non-range case.

	check-first	intersect-first	best-of-both
Wiki Sorted	16.7	11.2	10.1
Wiki 2-DIFF	29.7	28.1	27.5
Wiki 2R-MSA	30.4	29.2	28.4
IRE Sorted	0.80	0.72	0.7
IRE 2-DIFF	1.32	1.13	1.08
IRE 2R-MSA	1.45	1.33	1.31
NYT Sorted	0.38	0.31	0.29

Table 4: CPU cost of query processing (in ms) under uniform query distribution with range size 30 days.

	bias		uniform	
	2-DIFF	2R-MSA	2-DIFF	2R-MSA
One Week	19.5	20.1	14.8	15.1
30 days	19.9	20.7	15.1	15.4
One Year	22.9	25.8	17.7	21.3

Table 5: CPU costs of query processing with first-level range check, under biased and uniform query distribution for different range sizes.

There is one additional optimization that we can add for two-level methods, without any changes in index organization. As shown in Figure 1, many documents do not exist yet at the beginning of the timeline, as they are only added or crawled later. Thus, after traversing the first level of the index, we could check the documents retrieved in this phase to see if their total lifetime overlaps with the query interval, thus eliminating some documents created only later without fetching the second-level bit vector. However, this means that running times depend more heavily on the query distribution, and in particular on the choice of uniformly chosen versus biased starting point. The uniform model would create a lot of queries that are early in time and thus many documents can be ruled out after the first phase, resulting in faster query processing.

In Table 5 we show CPU costs with this optimization, for queries with expected query range sizes of 7 days, 30 days, and one year, under the uniform and biased query model. We see that the optimization leads to significantly decreased costs for the uniform model, compared to the previous tables. Costs for the biased model are higher, as in every phases of the computation more candidates survive the various range tests. However, we feel that given the distribution shown in Figure 1, the biased model is more appropriate, and thus we choose this model in the following sections.

4.4 Impact of List Caching

So far, we have assumed that the index structure is either completely in main memory, or only on disk. However, this second case is not really realistic for current search systems, which usually cache at least some of the inverted lists in main memory even when the complete index does not fit. Caching is known to provide significant performance boosts [24]. To determine the impact of caching, we implemented a simple caching scheme that selects a static subset of lists to be kept in memory. Lists are selected based on their frequency in a large query trace (disjoint from the actual queries used to measure CPU costs), and based on their size, as small lists are slightly more preferable due to the high cost of random accesses on disk.

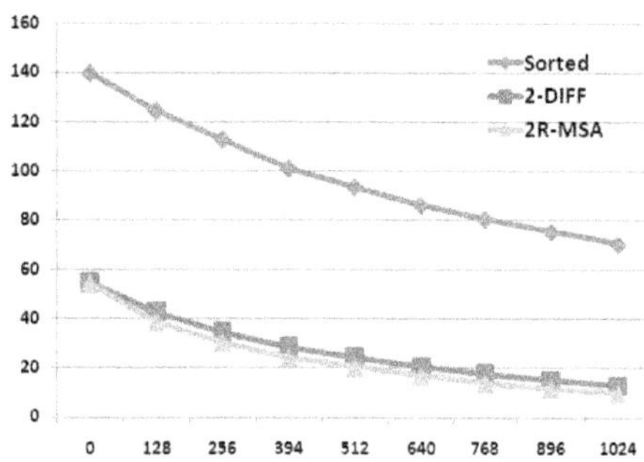

Figure 2: Disk costs in milliseconds per query for different compression methods on the Wiki data set, as cache size is varied between 0 and 1024 MB.

The result are in Figure 2, which shows that disk costs decrease significantly with cache size. With cache size 1024 MB (about 20 to 25% of total index size), the disk cost for 2-DIFF and 2R-MSA has decreased to about 20% of the cost without caching. Also, notice that the relative performance gap of 2-DIFF and 2R-MSA versus Sorted increases as cache size increases – better compression means a higher cache hit rate since a higher percentage of the index fits in the cache, and also less data to fetch when there is a miss. One more observation, not shown due to space constraints, is that the relative cost of disk access times (for seeking the start of an inverted list on disk) increases compared to the transfer cost as cache size increases.

4.5 Discussion

We now briefly discuss the main observations and lessons from this section. First, we observed that using state-of-the-art index compression and traversal techniques, even a baseline query processor is quite efficient, achieving less than 30 ms per query for a memory-based index, and about 80 ms per query for a disk-based index, on the 85 million versions of the Wiki data set. Second, proper compression using two-level techniques makes a significant difference in disk access costs and total index size (the amount of memory we need to buy for the in-memory case). Third, even a small cache in main memory significantly decreases disk access costs. Fourth, even for fairly large data sets, the costs for initiating disk accesses are significant in comparison to the transfer time for sequential reads, particularly with caching. This implies that when we reorganize the index in the next sections to get better performance, it is usually not a good idea to split inverted lists into several pieces that require separate disk reads. Finally, given the results here, we should not expect further improvements by an order of magnitude or more – in the case of a disk-based index, one would expect running times to be lower bounded by $h \cdot t \cdot a$, where h is the cache miss rate (1.0 if there is no caching), t is the average number of terms in a query, and a is the access time (8 ms in our case), assuming a separate seek is needed for any term resulting in a cache miss.

In the next two sections, we will design improved index organizations that decrease both CPU and disk costs. We use the biased query model, and we limit ourselves to the 2-DIFF and 2R-MSA methods as they are much more promising than Sorted.

5. CUTTING DOCUMENTS AND COSTS

We now study how to further decrease the CPU costs of range queries, by suitably splitting documents. Recall that in the previous section, we introduced a first level range check that rules out documents whose lifetime does not intersect the query range. However, the benefits are limited by the properties of the data set. Now suppose we split a document with v versions into two subdocuments, one consisting of the first $v/2$ versions, and the other consisting of the rest. This will increase the size of the first-level index, and the time spent in the first level, as we now have more documents and more postings. It will also increase the size of the second-level index, as we get more, but shorter, bit and frequency vectors that are overall less compressible than the longer vectors we had before (since, in a nutshell, we lose the redundancy between consecutive versions that are separated by subdocument boundaries). However, on the plus side, the first level range checks in our query processor will filter out many more subdocuments that do not overlap the query range.

Thus, we can trade off index size for increased speed, and the question is how to best perform these cuts. One approach is to pick a number of versions s, and greedily partition each document into subdocuments with (at most) b versions each; we call this approach *fix-bits*. However, this means that documents with many versions get split into a large number of subdocuments that each cover only a short period of time, while documents with only a few versions are not cut at all. Decreasing b will exacerbate the first problem, and increasing the latter. Or we can partition by time, and greedily add versions to a subdocument until its lifetime exceeds some fixed amount of time t; we call this *fix-time*. However, this can result in very small subdocuments with only one or two versions for documents with few versions overall, significantly increasing overall index size unless t is chosen quite large. We note that *fix-time* is similar to the time-based index partitioning scheme in [5]; however, we partition each document independently without ever duplicating a version in two partitions. We discuss their method in more detail later.

Finally, we consider a third method that combines these two in an elegant way. If we make the simplifying assumption that query ranges are uniformly chosen (not biased, as we actually use), then the likelihood of a subdocument passing the first level check is roughly proportional to its lifetime.[1] If we assume that the cost of accessing a bit vector in the second level is proportional to its length (number of bits), then the expected cost for the bit vectors of a subdocument, given a query, is proportional to the product of its length in bits and its lifetime. To minimize this, we should chop whenever this product exceeds some threshold p, where the choice of p will determine the blowup in index size. This method avoids the problems of the other schemes discussed above, in that it chops documents with many versions into

[1]Strictly speaking, this depends on both lifetime and query range size.

bigger pieces (but not too big) and documents with fewer versions into smaller pieces (but not too small). We call this *smart* partitioning.

Integrating this into our query processor is easy. We just need to determine the best settings for the parameters b, t, and p in the above methods. In Figure 3 we show the resulting trade-off between total compressed index size and the CPU cost for 30-day range queries, for 2-DIFF and 2R-MSA compression. Figure 4 shows the same for the IRE data. We note that the *smart* partitioning obtains the best trade-off in all cases, with the advantage over the other two methods more pronounced (but absolute improvements more limited) on the IRE data set. We also see that when we make too many partitions, both CPU cost and size increase. For 2-DIFF on Wiki, we see that increasing the index size from 4.9 GB (no chopping) to 5.3 GB already brings down CPU cost from more than 20 to less than 7 ms per query, a very significant improvement.

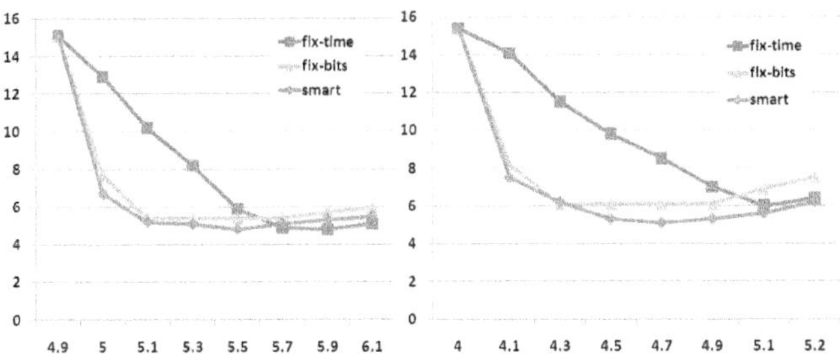

Figure 3: CPU cost per 30-day query under three different document partitioning schemes (in ms) on the y-axis versus total index size (in GB) on the x-axis, on the Wiki data set, for 2-DIFF (left) and 2R-MSA (right).

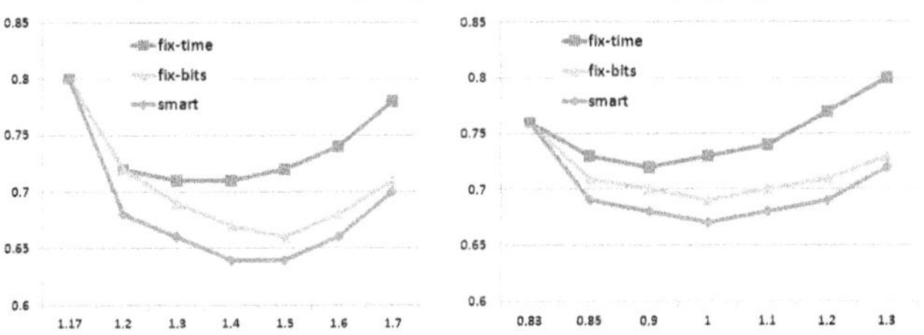

Figure 4: Same as previous figure, on the IRE data set.

We select the parameter p for the smart partitioning that minimizes query processing time. In Table 6, we show the resulting total index sizes and disk costs, plus CPU costs for query ranges of 7 days, 30 days, and one year. We note here that the disk cost is without any caching, that it is independent of query range size as we always fetch the entire inverted list from disk, and that there is a slight increase in disk cost. Overall, we get significant improvements in total cost over Table 5 when the index is in memory, and moderate improvements when it is on disk.

	Wikipedia		Ireland	
	2-DIFF	2R-MSA	2-DIFF	2R-MSA
One Week	6.5	7.3	0.61	0.64
30 days	6.6	7.4	0.62	0.66
One Year	13.8	14.9	0.82	0.85
index size	5532	4727	1418	1024
disk cost	59.1	55.9	29.2	28.9

Table 6: Total index size, disk cost, and CPU cost for various query sizes, under the smart partitioning that minimizes CPU cost.

6. OPTIMIZING DISK ACCESS

In the previous section, we studied methods that decrease the CPU cost of queries through document partitioning. However, the methods do not decrease disk costs, as we still have to fetch the entire inverted list for a query term; in fact, disk cost increased slightly with total index size. In this section, we present methods that optimize disk costs in the case where the index does not fit into main memory. To do so, we need to find ways to partition documents and organize the resulting postings, such that all index postings that intersect with a query range are located in one part of the inverted list; this way, when a list is not in memory, we only need to fetch that part (reducing transfer but not seek time).

6.1 Index Organization Methods

We now describe the different methods that we considered, including the one proposed in [5] and several new ones.

Interval partitioning: This is a version of the technique in [5], which uses a partitioning of the timeline into intervals. For example, for a period of 10 years, we might create 10 partitions, one for each year. We then take the documents and cut them into subdocuments that each fit into one of the partitions. Of course, there will be versions whose lifespan is split between two or more intervals; these will be replicated in each partition, with its lifespan pruned to the interval boundaries. We then assign document IDs to subdocuments such that consecutive docIDs are used within a partition; this organizes each inverted list into partitions that can be accessed separately. It is important to keep each list together in one place on disk – a method that builds independent inverted indexes for each partition would result in much higher disk access costs when queries overlap more than one interval.

Our implementation of this method uses two-level compression and the various other optimizations in our query processor, and thus we would expect faster results than in [5]. However, the method suffers from the same drawbacks as the *fix-time* method in the previous section in that it uses a one-size-fits-all approach for all documents. In addition, the replication of some versions in several intervals will further increase index size. On the plus side, given a query we can fetch all necessary parts of the inverted list in one disk access, by fetching only those partitions of the list with intervals overlapping the query range.

Stencil-Based Methods: To overcome the drawbacks of the *fix-time* and *interval partitioning* methods, we considered using a multi-level hierarchical partitioning of the timeline. Here, level L_0 contains the entire timeline, and we obtain level L_{i+1} from L_i by partitioning each interval in L_i into b subintervals, for some b. Figure 5 shows an example of a 4-level partitioning with $b = 2$ and a timeline of 32 days. We call such a partitioning a stencil; given this we now partition our documents so that each resulting subdocument resides in an interval that fits its range.

We look at two partitioning methods that use the *smart* approach from the previous section. The first one, *partition-first*, just uses the *smart* partitioning to make subdocuments, and then puts each subdocument into the deepest interval in the multi-level partitioning that it fits in. (Thus, we first cut, and then throw into the intervals, with no replication.)

In the second approach, *stencil-first*, we recursively cut documents into subdocuments using the stencil, as follows: Given our current subdocument, we find the deepest interval that it fits in, probably L_0 in the beginning. We then check if the product of lifespan and number of versions is less than p, where p is the parameter for the smart method. If yes, we do not cut it further, and keep it in the current interval. If no, then we cut it into subdocuments that exactly fit into the children of the current interval, and continue. In this case, we need to replicate versions that cross boundaries, as in the single-level case, and we get a more snug fit than in the partition-first case. (Also note that we keep cutting until the product is less than p, while in *smart* we cut as soon as it becomes larger than p; in both cases the idea is to get a cut with product close to p, but now we may have to use a slightly larger p.)

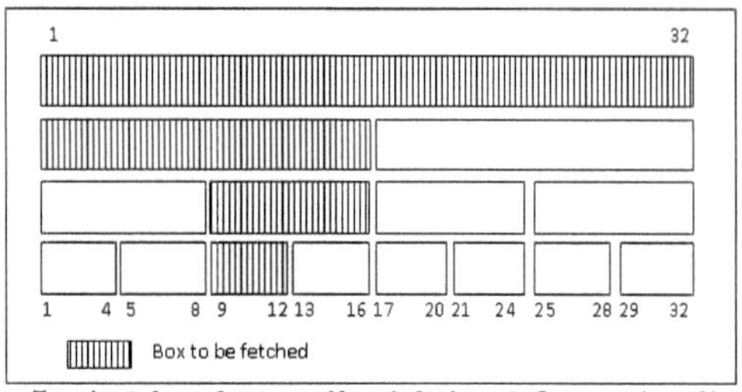

Figure 5: A 4-level stencil with $b = 2$ for a timeline of 32 days. The four shaded partitions need to be fetched for a query with range [9, 11].

Finally, we lay out each inverted list such that the partitions are ordered by an in-order traversal of the multi-level structure. We note that this places the partition corresponding to L_0 in the center, and this partition has to be fetched for any incoming query. Figure 5 shows the four partitions that are fetched for a query with range [9, 11].

Sort-Based Approaches: The next approaches are based on the idea of ordering subdocuments in the lists by assigning docIDs temporally. This is easy to do when each document has a single timestamp or a fixed lifespan t, as in the case of the NYT collection where every article was assumed to be valid for 90 days. If we then assign docIDs by start time, then for a range query $[l, r]$, we only need to fetch and traverse postings for documents with start times between $l - t$ and r, which are located in one consecutive area of the list. However, in our Wiki and IRE data sets, each version has a different lifespan, and of course we cannot afford to store each version by itself, as this would result in a much larger index size. Thus, our goal now is to again partition the documents into subdocuments, such that we can apply the above idea to decrease the amount of list data that we need to retrieve from disk. We look at three policies:

Time-sort is similar to *fix-time* in the previous section. Given a choice of t, we greedily cut into subdocuments with lifespan at most t. If a single version has lifespan larger than t, then we cut and replicate this version. After assigning docIDs based on the start time of each subdocument, given a range query $[l, r]$ we only have to fetch postings with start times between $l - t$ and r.

Smart-sort is based on the *smart* partitioning method from the previous section, that is, we greedily cut whenever the product of lifespan and number of versions in the subdocument becomes larger than some bound p. Then we assign docIDs in the same way as in time-sort. A problem with this is that there is no absolute upper bound t on lifespan, thus making it impossible to translate an incoming range query into a small subset of postings, and this means that usually the entire inverted list will be fetched. We can improve CPU cost by storing for each block of 128 docIDs in the first level of the index the maximum end time of any document in the block. This allows skipping of many such blocks.

Hybrid-sort partitions documents greedily as soon as either of the conditions in time-sort and smart-sort becomes true. Here the idea is to choose t and p such that usually the smart condition will make the cut, with the constraint based on t being triggered as a fuse when the lifespan of a subdocument becomes too large. Thus, we hope to preserve the advantages of smart partitioning while also keeping an absolute upper bound on document lifespan that can be used to fetch only relevant parts of a list from disk.

6.2 Experimental Evaluation

We now evaluate the index size, CPU cost, and disk cost of the six methods, interval, partition-first, stencil-first, time-sort, smart-sort, and hybrid-sort. We use the 2-DIFF compression method, though results for 2R-MSA are similar.

	Wikipedia			Ireland		
	cpu	disk	total	cpu	disk	total
stencil-first	11.4	41.6	53	0.75	27.9	28.7
part.-first	5.6	38.6	44.2	0.56	24.6	25.2
interval	5.9	34.5	40.4	0.57	25.4	26
smart-sort	4.6	61.6	66.4	0.55	32.1	32.7
time-sort	5.8	31.9	37.7	0.51	24.6	25.1
hybrid-sort	4.3	30.3	34.6	0.47	24.5	25

Table 7: CPU costs and disk costs (in ms) for the various methods with best parameter settings, for 30-day queries and 2-DIFF compression.

	Wikipedia			Ireland		
	docIDs	freq	total	docIDs	freq	total
stencil-first	4347	1649	5996	1055	557	1612
part.-first	5677	1365	7042	1552	405	1957
interval	6771	2312	9083	1717	524	2241
smart-sort	4890	1319	6209	1017	413	1430
time-sort	5365	1766	7131	1234	518	1752
hybrid-sort	5300	1738	7038	1224	515	1739

Table 8: Index size (in MB) for the various methods on Wiki and IRE data, using 2-DIFF compression.

Overview of Results: We start with the CPU cost, disk cost (without caching), and total cost per 30-day query, shown in Table 7. The numbers given are for the best choices of various parameters; we investigate some of these choices later. We observe that all methods except smart-sort achieve significant reductions in disk costs versus the earlier sections. The best results are obtained by time-sort and hybrid-sort, followed by interval, and then the multi-level methods partition-first and stencil-first. The interval method suffers from a fair amount of version replication that increases total index size (as shown later). The multi-level methods are limited by the need to fetch the postings located in higher-up intervals in the structure, in particular the root L_0 that is in the middle of the inverted list.

Note that we use a single disk access to fetch all needed partitions of an inverted list; this is the best for our data sets. To do so, we interleave the two index levels. This is simple for stencil and interval, which assign subdocuments to discrete subsets: We just concatenate the first and second level of each subset. For the sort-based methods, we have a slightly more complicated structure. Consider time-sort with parameter t: We store inverted lists in blocks of 128 integers, and interleave blocks from both levels by ordering them by minimum start time. We group the resulting sequence of blocks into chunks of x blocks, and create a table storing for each chunk the minimum start and maximum start of any subdocuments in it. For range query [l,r], we fetch in one access all chunks with minimum start larger than r and maximum start larger than $l-t$ (including any non-qualifying chunks in-between). We define z as the maximum number of first-level blocks between any consecutive second-level blocks. We choose $x >= z$. In all our data we observe $z <= 25$, and we set $x = 40$ in our experiments. Thus, each chunk has at least one first-level and one second-level block. For large z, replicating selected first-level blocks leads to even better results.

It is possible, however, that using more than one disk access in the multi-level methods would result in better performance for even larger index sizes (due to either a larger document collection or inferior index compression techniques).

	Wikipedia			Ireland		
	7	30	365	7	30	365
stencil-first	41.4	41.6	43.6	27.8	27.9	28.2
part.-first	38.3	38.6	42.9	24.4	24.6	25
interval	33.9	34.5	39.5	25.3	25.4	25.7
smart-sort	61.6	61.6	61.6	32.1	32.1	32.1
time-sort	30.6	31.9	36.6	24.6	24.6	25.1
hybrid-sort	29.6	30.3	35.1	24.5	24.5	24.9

Table 9: Disk cost per query for 7-day, 30-day, and one-year queries, on Wiki and IRE with 2-DIFF compression.

	Wikipedia			Ireland		
	7	30	365	7	30	365
stencil-first	10.8	11.4	16.3	0.74	0.75	0.91
part.-first	5.1	5.6	11.1	0.54	0.56	0.81
interval	5.4	5.9	13.7	0.52	0.57	0.84
smart-sort	4.3	4.6	8.9	0.53	0.55	0.86
time-sort	5.2	5.8	11.9	0.49	0.51	0.85
hybrid-sort	3.9	4.3	10.6	0.46	0.47	0.82

Table 10: CPU cost per query for 7-day, 30-day, and one-year queries, on Wiki and IRE with 2-DIFF compression.

Looking at CPU costs in Table 7, we note that most of the techniques also outperform the results in previous sections. In particular, the methods using smart partitioning (smart-sort and hybrid-sort) do extremely well, probably due to a more clustered access pattern into the index during query processing resulting in fewer blocks of OPT-PFD-compressed data to be uncompressed on both index levels.

Next, we look at compressed index size for the various methods, shown in Table 8. We see that interval has the largest index size on both data sets, while stencil-first has the smallest on Wiki (but high CPU and disk costs). All the sort-based methods also perform well. Overall, the results of the two tables suggest that hybrid-sort is the best overall performer, followed by time-sort. However, smart-sort is a good choice when the index is completely in main memory, having lower CPU cost than the smart partitioning in Section 5 with slightly larger index size.

Now we look at how disk costs vary as range query size changes from 7 days to 30 days to 365 days, shown in Table 9. Note that the index structures were optimized for the case of 30 days. As such, we cannot expect queries to become much faster for smaller query ranges. On the other hand, cost increases only moderately for one-year queries. Also, note that for IRE, costs are almost independent of range size as disk costs are dominated by random access times. Corresponding results for CPU cost are shown in Table 10.

Choosing Parameters: Next, we investigate some of the parameter choices we made in the above tables in more detail. For the stencil-based methods, we had to choose the base b and depth d of the multi-level partitioning. We tried various values of b and the simple case of $b = 2$ did overall quite well. In Figure 6 we show the performance of the stencil-first and partition-first methods as we vary the depth d; results suggest choosing 4 or 5 levels for the larger Wiki set and 3 levels for IRE. In Figure 7 we see the total cost as we change the parameter t (the maximum lifespan of a subdocument) used in three methods. We note that t should ideally be chosen somewhat larger than the query size (30 days in this case). For IRE, it can be chosen much larger, but note that the overall timeline in IRE is more than ten years, with fewer versions per document than Wiki.

Impact of Caching: Recall that in real systems, even if the index does not fit in main memory, some significant

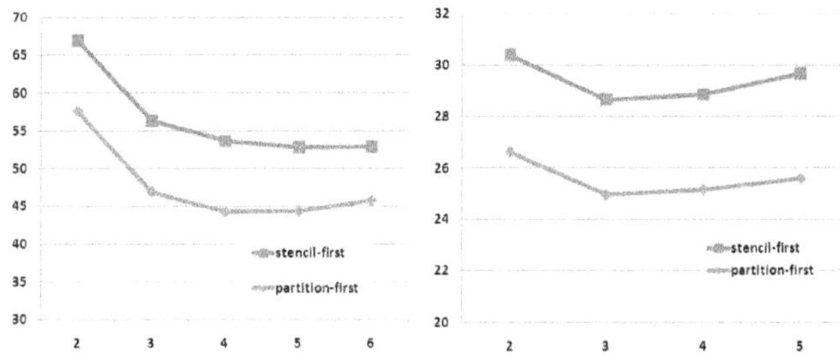

Figure 6: Total cost (in ms) per query for partition-first and stencil-first on the y-axis, as we vary the depth of the partitioning on the x-axis, for 30-day queries for Wiki (left) and IRE (right).

amount of memory is available for list caching, and we saw in Section 4 that this significantly reduces disk costs. In Figure 8, we compare the complete cost per query (CPU cost plus disk cost) of all the algorithms in this section on different cache sizes. We see that, as expected, all methods obtain significant benefits from caching. Overall, hybrid-sort performs best, followed by time-sort and interval. Note that for a cache size of 1024 MB, realistic on most current machines, hybrid-sort is more than three times as fast as the baseline 2-DIFF method from Section 4.

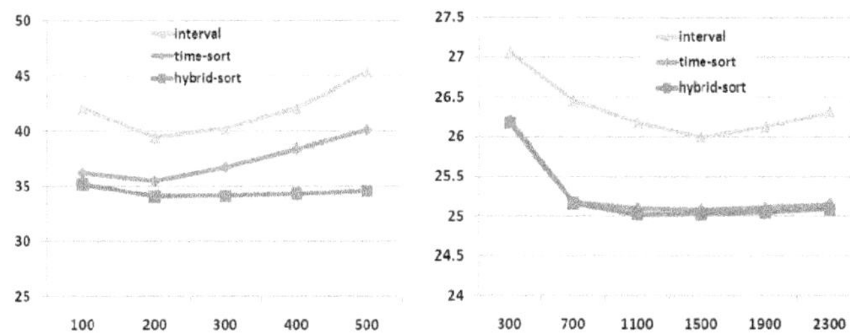

Figure 7: Total cost (in ms) per query for interval, time-sort, and hybrid-sort on the y-axis, as we vary the maximum lifespan (in days) of a subdocument on the x-axis, for Wiki (left) and IRE (right).

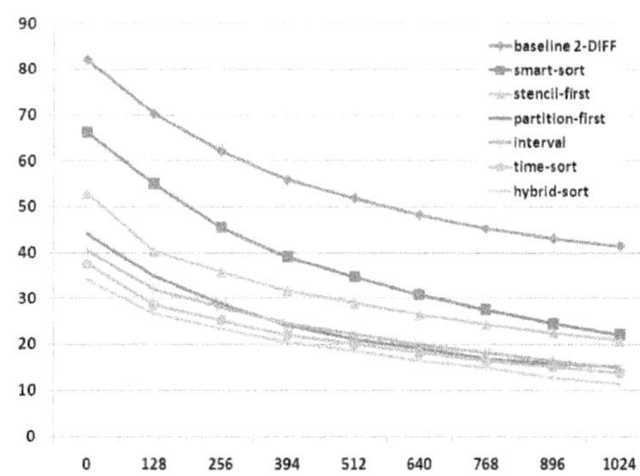

Figure 8: Total cost (CPU plus disk, in ms) per query on the y-axis, for cache sizes ranging from 0 to 1024 MB on the x-axis.

7. AGGREGATE QUERY PROCESSING

Recent work in [22] proposed a new aggregate operator for versioned document collections called Stable Top-k. Given a keyword query, a query range, and a value x, this operator returns all documents that were in the top-k results during at least x% of the query range. In other words, were are looking for documents that were among the most relevant during most of the query range. This is an example of an operator that performs an aggregate computation over several versions that were valid during the query interval; other examples might be documents that are ranked high on average, or documents that scored above a certain threshold score most or all of the time.

U et al. [22] proposed several algorithms for this problem, with the fastest one using an specialized index structure based on R*-trees. In order to explore the efficiency of our range search methods, we decided to implement Stable Top-k on top of our generic mechanism. That is, we use our methods to find all versions that satisfy the keyword and range constraints, and then run a separate (but fairly simple) Stable Top-k algorithm on this result set, which typically consists of a few thousand or few ten thousand versions.

In particular, we implemented a version of the Top-k Bands algorithm in [22], and ran it for different query ranges on Wiki. The results are in Table 11, where we show the additional cost (in ms) for Top-k Bands. We see that this cost is in fact rather small. As it is independent of the method used in the range search, we can get the complete cost by adding the best numbers from this paper. Thus, if the index is completely in main memory, we need to add 4.3 ms for 30-day queries (Table 10), and if it is completely on disk, we need to add 34.4 ms (Table 7). Overall, these results seem to outperform those for the specialized methods in [22], on a data set that is significantly larger. We conclude that generic range search methods can indeed efficiently support aggregate operators such as Stable Top-k.

	stable top-10	stable top-100
7 days	0.6	0.7
30 days	1.3	1.5
1 year	9.5	10.8

Table 11: Additional cost (in ms) of running Top-k Bands on top of our range search, for different query sizes and for $k = 10$ and $k = 100$.

8. CONCLUDING REMARKS

In this paper, we have described and evaluated techniques for efficient temporal range queries in versioned document collections. We evaluated some simple methods to provide a realistic baseline for improvements, and then showed how to decrease CPU and disk costs through suitable index organizations. Finally, we showed that our techniques are fast enough to efficiently support classes of aggregate queries over such collections.

There are several interesting problems that are left open by us. One is about partitioning methods that attempt to minimize index size by maximizing similarity within subdocuments. When cutting a document, we essentially waste the similarity between the two versions separated by the cut. This suggests that we should try to cut whenever a document undergoes significant change. However, this needs to be balanced with the other concerns, the number of versions and the lifespan of the resulting subdocuments, and preliminary experiments by us did not give any nontrivial benefits. A more careful partitioning method based on a suitable model might give some improvements.

While we focused here on versioned collections, we believe that improvements in practice are also possible for non-versioned collections where each document has a timestamp or lifespan associated with it. Finally, we did not consider early-termination techniques for versioned collections, which could compute top-k results without scoring all versions satisfying the keyword and range constraints.

Acknowledgments

This research was supported by NSF Grant IIS-0803605, "Efficient and Effective Search Services over Archival Webs", and by a grant from Google. We also thank the Internet Archive for providing access to the Ireland data set.

9. REFERENCES

[1] I. Altingovde, E. Demir, F. Can, and O. Ulusoy. Incremental cluster-based retrieval using compressed cluster-skipping inverted files. *ACM Trans. on Information Systems*, 26(3), June 2008.

[2] A. Anand, S. Bedathur, K. Berberich, and R. Schenkel. Efficient temporal keyword queries over versioned text. In *Proc. of ACM CIKM Conf.*, 2010.

[3] A. Anand, S. Bedathur, K. Berberich, R. Schenkel, and C. Tryfonopoulos. EverLast: a distributed architecture for preserving the web. In *Proc. of ACM/IEEE JCDL Conf.*, 2009

[4] P. G. Anick and R. A. Flynn. Versioning a full-text information retrieval system. In *Proc. of ACM SIGIR Conf.*, 1992.

[5] K. Berberich, S. Bedathur, T. Neumann, and G. Weikum. A time machine for text search. In *Proc. of ACM SIGIR Conf.*, 2007.

[6] R. Blanco and A. Barreiro. Document identifier reassignment through dimensionality reduction. In *Proc. of European Conf. on Information Retrieval*, 2005.

[7] D. Blandford and G. Blelloch. Index compression through document reordering. In *Proc. of DCC Conf.*,2002.

[8] A. Broder, N. Eiron, M. Fontoura, M. Herscovici, R. Lempel, J. McPherson, R. Qi, and E. Shekita. Indexing shared content in information retrieval systems. In *Proc. of EDBT Conf.*, 2006.

[9] Y.-Y. Chen, T. Suel, and A. Markowetz. Efficient query processing in geographic web search engines. In *Proc. of ACM SIGMOD Conf.*, 2006.

[10] G. Cong, C. S. Jensen, and D. Wu. Efficient retrieval of the top-k most relevant spatial web objects. In *Proc. of Conf. on Very Large Data Bases*, 2009.

[11] M. Fontoura, R. Lempel, R. Qi, and J. Zien. Inverted index support for numeric search. In *Internet Mathematics*,3(2), 153-185, 2006.

[12] J. He, H. Yan, and T. Suel. Compact full-text indexing of versioned document collections. In *Proc. of ACM CIKM Conf.*, 2009.

[13] J. He, J. Zeng, and T. Suel. Improved index compression techniques for versioned document collections. In *Proc. of ACM CIKM Conf.*, 2010.

[14] S. Heman. Super-scalar database compression between RAM and CPU-cache. MS Thesis, Centrum voor Wiskunde en Informatica, Amsterdam, July 2005.

[15] M. Herscovici, R. Lempel, and S. Yogev. Efficient indexing of versioned document sequences. In *Proc. of European Conf. on Information Retrieval*, 2007.

[16] C. B. Jones, A. I. Abdelmoty, D. Finch, and G. Fu. The spirit spatial search engine: Architecture, ontologies and spatial indexing. In *Proc. of Conf. on Geographic Information Science*, 2004.

[17] A. Moffat and L. Stuiver. Binary interpolative coding for effective index compression. *Information Retrieval*, 3:25–47, 2000.

[18] W. Shieh, T. Chen, J. Shann, and C. Chung. Inverted file compression through document identifier reassignment. *Inf. Processing and Management*, 39(1):117–131, 2003.

[19] F. Silvestri. Sorting out the document identifier assignment problem. In *Proc. of European Conf. on Information Retrieval*, 2007.

[20] F. Silvestri, S. Orlando, and R. Perego. Assigning identifiers to documents to enhance the clustering property of fulltext indexes. In *Proc. of ACM SIGIR Conf.*, 2004.

[21] S. Song, J. Jaja. Archiving Temporal Web Information: Organization of Web Contents for Fast Access and Compact Storage. In Technical Report UMIACS-TR-2008-08.

[22] L. U, N. Mamoulis, K. Berberich, and S. Bedathur. Durable top-k search in document archives. In *Proc. of ACM SIGMOD Conf.*, 2010.

[23] H. Yan, S. Ding, and T. Suel. Inverted index compression and query processing with optimized document ordering. In *Proc. of WWW Conf.*, 2009.

[24] J. Zhang, X. Long, and T. Suel. Performance of compressed inverted list caching in search engines. In *Proc. of WWW Conf.*, 2008.

[25] J. Zhang and T. Suel. Efficient search in large textual collection with redundancy. In *Proc. of WWW Conf.*, 2007.

[26] Y. Zhou, X. Xie, C. Wang, Y. Gong, and W.-Y. Ma. Hybrid index structures for location-based web search. In *Proc. of ACM CIKM Conf.*, 2005.

[27] J. Zobel and A. Moffat. Inverted files for text search engines. *ACM Computing Surveys*, 38(2), 2006.

[28] M. Zukowski, S. Heman, N. Nes, and P. Boncz. Super-scalar RAM-CPU cache compression. In *Proc. of ICDE Conf.*, 2006.

Indexing Strategies for Graceful Degradation of Search Quality

Shuai Ding
Polytechnic Institute of NYU
sding@cis.poly.edu

Sreenivas Gollapudi
Microsoft Research
Mountain View, CA, USA
sreenig@microsoft.com

Samuel Ieong
Microsoft Research
Mountain View, CA, USA
saieong@microsoft.com

Krishnaram Kenthapadi
Microsoft Research
Mountain View, CA, USA

Alexandros Ntoulas
Microsoft Research
Mountain View, CA, USA
krishnaram.kenthapadi,antoulas@microsoft.com

ABSTRACT

Large web search engines process billions of queries each day over tens of billions of documents with often very stringent requirements for a user's search experience, in particular, low latency and highly relevant search results. Index generation and serving are key to satisfying both these requirements. For example, the load to search engines can vary drastically when popular events happen around the world. In the case when the load is exceeding what the search engine can serve, queries will get dropped. This results in an ungraceful degradation in search quality. Another example that could increase the query load and affect the user's search experience are ambiguous queries which often result in the execution of multiple query alterations in the back end.

In this paper, we look into the problem of designing robust indexing strategies, i.e. strategies that allow for a graceful degradation of search quality in both the above scenarios. We study the problems of index generation and serving using the notions of document allocation, server selection, and document replication. We explore the space of efficient algorithms for these problems and empirically corroborate with existing theory that it is hard to optimally solve the allocation and selection problems without any replication. We propose a greedy replication algorithm and study its performance under different choices of allocation and selection. Further, we show that under random selection and allocation, our algorithm is optimal.

Categories and Subject Descriptors

H.3.3 [**Information Storage And Retrieval**]: Information Search and Retrieval

General Terms

Search Engine, Index Generation, Index Serve, Performance, Algorithm, Experiment

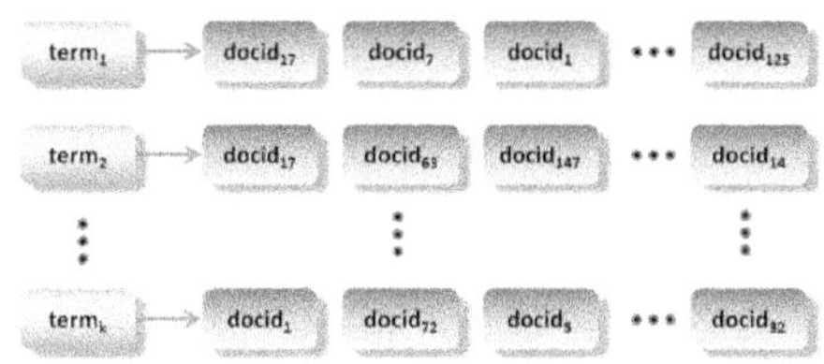

Figure 1: An inverted index over documents and terms

Keywords

Search Quality, Indexing Strategies, Graceful Degradation

1. INTRODUCTION

As the content of the web grows richer, more users rely on search engines to locate relevant information, making search engines one of the most used applications of modern information technology. User experience on a search engine is largely governed by two factors: *latency*, which measures how fast the results are returned to the user, and *accuracy*, which measures how relevant the results are to the query.

The performance of a search index is crucial to a search engine's goal of providing good user experience. Today's commercial search engines employ an inverted index structure that allows efficient retrieval of documents containing a particular term (or word). An inverted index over a collection of terms and the underlying documents consists of a set of inverted lists, one for each term, and often sorted by the relevance of the document for that term [14] (see Figure 1).

The indices of commercial search engines are extremely large and consume a lot of data center resources including CPU, memory, and power. Two important problems involving search indexes that affect search engine performance are:

1. **Index generation**: This problem deals with *allocation* of documents to index servers and building an inverted index on each index server. A naive allocation could be a random assignment of documents to index servers using simple hashing schemes.

2. **Index serving**: At query answering time, each *selected* index server returns a set of top results for the user query, which are then typically aggregated and ranked by a ranking module in the search engine. Under naive allocation, all index servers are typically queried because there is no knowledge of the

index servers to which the top documents for the given query are allocated.

In this paper, we study the inherent trade-off between index selection and allocation strategies on the performance of the index in terms of the quality of the returned search results. More specifically, our goal is to identify strategies that are robust under heavy query loads, i.e. they do not drop queries but instead they allow for a graceful degradation of the quality of results. We begin by observing that under the naive allocation and selection strategies (which we collectively refer to henceforth as indexing strategies), there can be a drop in performance of the system under increased query loads as well as other scenarios such as server failures. Before we proceed to discuss these observations, we need to define what we mean by performance of an index. Generally, a good indexing strategy has to satisfy the following properties even in the presence of unusual spikes in query loads. We will define these notions more formally in Section 2.

(1) **Quality:** The indexing strategy has to surface highly relevant results to user queries.

(2) **High throughput/Low latency:** The indexing strategy should support high throughput of queries.

(3) **Availability:** The documents and the associated inverted index should be available to answer the user queries effectively.

One can clearly observe that the naive indexing strategies do not satisfy all the above properties. Under an unusually high query load, in the absence of any explicit mapping of documents to index servers, all servers need to be queried and therefore there is no way for the search engine but to drop queries that the index cannot handle above its designed peak load. This leads to a drop in the quality of the results since there are queries for which no results are produced. In another scenario when there are node failures, which in principle are common in large distributed systems, property-based allocation (see Section 6) could lead to a drastic drop in quality if the server on which the top documents reside crashes. Often, search engines mitigate this problem by keeping multiple copies of the index (*replication*) at the cost of increased resource usage such as memory and power. In another scenario, all major search engines apply extensive query rewriting techniques[1] to get better search results for the user's queries. Thus, a single user query often results in multiple queries to the index. Again, under the naive selection and allocation strategies, these multiple queries are typically processed *sequentially* on *all* the index server nodes possibly resulting in higher latency for the user query.

One important signal that can be exploited for designing effective indexing strategies is the knowledge of the query workload and the quality of the documents that the search engine typically serves. Both the query frequency and document quality have a direct effect on the indexing strategies. Given the skew typically observed in search query frequencies and the skew in the quality of documents for a given query,[2] one can design more synergistic allocation and selection strategies that can a) gracefully handle high query loads; b) handle node failures; and c) reduce any hot spots (i.e. cases where one or few of the servers see a relatively high fraction of the queries) in the index.

[1]For example, the query 'camera' may be changed to 'digital camera', 'digital photography', 'video camera' and so forth.

[2]Typically observed as a power-law or log-normal distribution.

1.1 Motivation and Objective

Due to the issues with the naive indexing strategies mentioned above, one natural question to ask is: *Can we use less machines in the cluster to answer user queries and also achieve acceptable search quality?* We will show that answers to this question come from more synergistic consideration of allocation and selection strategies. Let us begin by motivating the need for query workload and document-quality aware indexing strategies. Most search engine users only care about the top-k results where k is a number often comparable to the number of index servers available for serving the query results. Therefore, it is likely that only a (small) subset of servers really contribute to serving a query, as explained by the following balls-and-bins argument [13]. Given k balls (top-k results for a query) and n bins (servers in the cluster), the expected number of empty bins after k uniformly random tossings is:

$$n * \left(\frac{n-1}{n}\right)^k \approx \frac{n}{e} \; (when\; k\; equals\; to\; n).$$

In other words, only about 65% of the servers contain a document in the top-k results when k is equal to n. As n grows, the fraction of non-contributing servers also grows. Figure 2 illustrates the growth rate when $k = 10$.

Based on the above observations, we propose the following objective.

> *Given a collection of documents* **D** *and* **n** *servers, find strategies for replication, allocation, and selection such that the quality of results retrieved from* **m** *(* $<$ **n***) servers is maximized.*

1.2 Contribution

In this paper, we address the above index generation problem by considering how to replicate and allocate documents across servers, and the index serving problem by considering how to select servers for query execution. We explore different allocation and selection strategies and their combinations for improved index performance. Overall, in this paper we make the following contributions:

1. We study different allocation and selection strategies for robust indexing. We propose a new selection strategy which outperforms previous selection strategies in search quality.

2. We evaluate our indexing strategies based on speed, quality and availability (or load balancing). Previous work has mostly focused on studying the speed and quality of index. In our work we also study the availability of the results.

3. We study how to employ replication strategies in combination with allocation and selection strategies in order to create indexes with high speed, quality and availability. We study different replication strategies and we propose a greedy replication strategy that is optimal when combined with specific allocation and selection strategies.

4. We experimentally evaluate our indexing strategies on a web dataset of 25.2 million documents. Our results demonstrate that improvement can achieve compared to existing strategies.

The rest of our paper is organized as follows: in Section 2 we discuss the preliminaries and the performance metric for our problem setting. Section 3 and Section 4 study different allocation and selection techniques and their combinations, while Section 5 discusses replication strategies. In Section 6 we present our experimental results and Section 7 discusses the related work. Section 8 concludes.

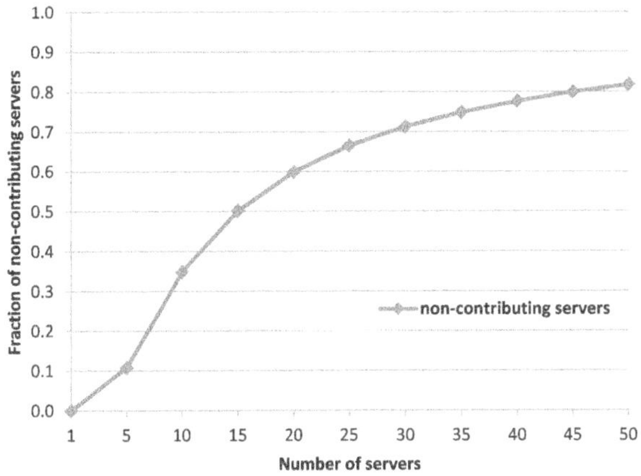

Figure 2: Expected percentage of non-contributing servers. x-axis is the total number of servers, y-axis is the expected percentage of servers which do not contain documents in the top-10 results

2. MODEL

We denote the set of queries by Q, and for each query q, its frequency, or the expected number of times q is queried against the search engine, by $f(q)$. We denote the set of documents to be indexed by D. For each document $d \in D$, there exists a *score* $s(q, d)$ that reflects the relevance of document d is to query q. We treat the scores as input to our problem formulation, and explain the one we used in experiments in the relevant section. For a given query q and a collection of documents $C \subseteq D$, we denote the k documents with the highest score by $B(q, C, k)$. We denote the set of machines, or servers, by $\mathcal{M} = \{M_1, M_2, \ldots, M_n\}$. Documents are stored on these machines.

We study the questions of replication, allocation, and selection in this work. Formally, replication is the question of how many copies of a particular document $d \in D$ we make available across all the servers. We denote this by its replication factor $R(d)$. Allocation is the question of which $R(d)$ servers get assigned a copy of document d. The set of servers that got allocated document d is denoted by $A(d)$, and we view a server M_i as a collection of documents. In particular, this allows us to meaningfully take the union over machines, as this is simply the union of the underlying documents stored in the machines. Both replication and allocation are performed *offline*. Selection is the question of which servers are used to answer a query at *runtime*. Given a query q, and a desired number of servers m, we select $S(q, m)$ to answer the query. Under normal circumstances, we expect $m = n$; however, as motivated previously, due to machine failures or abnormally high query load, we may want to select only a subset of servers to answer a query. Indeed, our focus is on situations where $m < n$, possibly substantially so. A system is determined by the choice of replication, allocation, and selection strategies, (R, A, S).

From the users' perspective, given a query q, the set of top-k documents retrieved when m machines are used is

$$docs(R, A, S, q, m, k) = B(q, \{\cup S(q, m)\}, k) \ .$$

This is determined not only by selection, but also by replication and allocation as they in turn determine what documents are stored on which servers. When it is clear from context, we simply write $docs(q, m, k)$.

Next, we formalize the three desired properties of a system that we outlined in Section 1. We begin with *quality*. For a given query q, we define the quality of the retrieved results by the sum total of the scores of the top-k documents retrieved.

$$qual(q, m, k) = \sum_{d \in docs(q,m,k)} s(q, d) \ .$$

The expected quality of a system, when m servers are used to retrieve top-k results, is given by

$$qual(R, A, S, m, k) = \sum_{q \in Q} f(q) qual(q, m, k) \ .$$

High throughput or *low latency* implies that no index server becomes a hotspot, i.e., a bottleneck, in the presence of query load spikes or server failures. In other words, no index server should be selected to answer queries all the time. We can make this formal by measuring the load of a machine, in terms of the number of queries it has to answer. We define load of the machine as follows.

$$load(M_i, m) = \sum_{q \in Q, M_i \in S(q,m)} f(q) \ .$$

In other words, load of server M_i is determined by the expected number of queries it has to answer. The load of a system is determined by the most loaded machine, i.e.,

$$load(S, m) = \max_i load(M_i, m) \ .$$

Under this definition, a system with smaller load will have lower latency, and all else being equal, we prefer a system with smaller load. Note that load is determined only by selection, and how many machines are used to answer queries.

A useful way of thinking about load is as follows. Consider the baseline of using all servers to answer all queries. The load on each server will then be $\sum_{q \in Q} f(q)$. If we manage to reduce the load on the most loaded machine by half, then we can handle twice the number of queries without an increase in latency. Of course, if this is achieved by selecting only a subset of servers to answer queries, we may suffer from an associated drop in quality. Indeed, this is the subject of investigation in this paper.

Finally, *availability* implies that *most* of the documents should still be accessible during server failures for *any* query. It suggests that machine failures should not lead to drastic decrease in the quality of results. We approximate the potential damage when server M_i fails by the expected contribution of M_i to answering queries. Specifically, we define the value of server M_i in terms of the expected number of top-k documents it contributes, weighted by the number of times the document is replicated, namely,

$$value(M_i, R, m, k) = \sum_{q \in Q} f(q) \sum_{d \in (docs(q,m,k) \cap M_i)} \frac{1}{R(d)} \ .$$

One way to interpret the definition of value of a server is as follows. The baseline is determined by the documents the system retrieves in the absence of machine failures, $docs(q, m, k)$. If a server fails, then it leads to losing certain documents, captured by the set $(docs(q, m, k) \cap M_i)$. For these documents, the actual loss is determined by how many copies of this document is available in the system. The loss is 100% if there is only one copy ($R(d) = 1$), but less if it is replicated more. Hence, we weigh the loss by $\frac{1}{R(d)}$.

The availability of a system is determined by the loss in value in the worst-case failure

$$loss(R, A, S, m, k) = \max_i value(M_i, m, k) \ .$$

Under this definition, a system with smaller loss will have higher availability, and all else being equal, we prefer a system with smaller loss. For simplicity and to ensure that *loss* depends only on replication and allocation, we choose $m = n$ in our computations. Alternative formalization that captures random or multiple failures is possible; the current one is chosen for simplicity and ease of interpretation.

In summary, we are interested in choosing replication, allocation, and selection strategies so as to *maximize quality*, *minimize load*, and *minimize loss*. There are trade-offs among these conflicting objectives, which constitute the focus of this study.

3. DOCUMENT ALLOCATION

Allocation studies the problem of how to assign documents to servers. It plays an important role in determining the availability and the quality of the system. We propose a balanced allocation strategy that exploits the query work load and the document quality.

Instead of assigning documents uniformly at random and achieving good availability in expectation, one can attempt to explicitly minimize the worst-case loss of the system. Recall that to maximize availability, our objective is to:

$$\min loss(R, A, S, m, k) \ .$$

However, optimizing this objective requires knowing the choice of selection strategy. To work around this difficulty, instead of allocating the documents in the top-k results as balanced as possible among the servers, we approximate the value of a document by its expected score to a random query,

$$v(d) = \sum_{q \in Q} f(q)s(q, d)$$

We then want to evenly spread the scores for documents among servers. This is known as the *"makespan problem"* in job scheduling [2, 3]. To this end, we utilize a solution similar to the Longest Processing Time (LPT) algorithm in [8]. More specifically, we allocate the documents greedily to the server with the lowest sum total value of documents. This algorithm is essentially a 4/3 approximation of the optimal [8]. The complete algorithm is given as follows:

```
foreach M_i ∈ 𝓜 do v(M_i) ← 0;
Sort D in descending order of value(d);
foreach d ∈ D do
    Find M_i with smallest v(M_i);
    Assign d to M_i;
    v(M_i) ← v(M_i) + v(d);
end
```

Algorithm 1: BALANCEDALLOCATION Algorithm

Later, in our experimental section we compare the BALANCEDALLOCATION algorithm with two well-known allocation techniques, more specifically random allocation and property-based allocation [10, 11, 16, 19].

4. SERVER SELECTION

Selection studies the problem of which servers are chosen to answer a query. It plays a central role in determining the speed of the system. Together with allocation, they jointly determine the quality of the system. It is typically implemented with two processes: an offline process that precomputes certain statistics, and a runtime process that uses the statistics to select the servers to answer a query at runtime.

If one cares only about quality, the best strategy is to always select all servers. However, this may be infeasible in case of abnormally high workloads as the alternative will be to ignore the queries of some users entirely. In this section, we study selection strategies where the fraction of servers that can be used to answer the query is specified as an input. We propose a selection strategy based on the distribution of document quality for any given query. We approximate the distribution by computing the histogram of term-level scores. In our experimental section, we will compare our proposed selection strategy with those in the literature, i.e. ReDDe [11] and Gloss [9].

In our histogram-based method, we select servers with the highest estimated number of relevant documents to the query. This number is estimated using histogram of term-level scores of each server, similar to [18]. Here, we implicitly assume that the relevance score of a document equals the sum of the scores of the document to terms in the query. For each term t, let $H(t, M_i)$ denote the *histogram* of scores of the documents stored on server M_i for term t. We assume that the histogram is stored at the finest level—a list of scores in decreasing order; in practice, the list is approximated by pairs of (range, count), but the approach can be suitably adapted. We assume that the histogram only stores the non-zero scores, and denote its length by L_t. In the following, we treat the histogram as an array.

Consider some two-term query $q = \{t_1, t_2\}$. Assuming term independence, one can estimate the number of documents on server M_i for which the sum of scores exceed threshold τ using Algorithm 2. The m servers with the highest estimates are selected to answer the query.

```
input : Histograms H(t_1, M_i), H(t_2, M_i), threshold τ
output: Estimated no. of relevant docs ≥ τ on M_i
E({t_1, t_2}, τ, M_i) ← 0;
for i_1 ← 1 to L_{t_1} do
    s_1 ← H(t_1, M_i)[i];
    Search for s_2 in H(t_2, M_i) where s_1 + s_2 ≥ τ;
    Let i_2 be the position of s_2 in H(t_2, M_i);
    E({t_1, t_2}, τ, M_i) ← E({t_1, t_2}, τ, M_i) + i_1 i_2 / |M_i|;
end
return E({t_1, t_2}, τ, M_i)
```

Algorithm 2: HISTOGRAMSELECTION Algorithm

Note that we can perform certain optimizations to speed up the algorithm, such as reducing the search space using the fact that the position in the second histogram is monotonically non-increasing, and to perform early termination when the scores of the remaining documents are too low. The algorithm can easily be generalized to queries with more than two terms.

The algorithm requires an input threshold that can be estimated with the help of the entire histogram for the terms, $H(t_1, D)$ and $H(t_2, D)$. We start with a very high threshold $\overline{\tau}$, and use Algorithm 2 to estimate the number of documents exceeding this threshold for the entire document collection. We repeatedly lower the threshold until the number of documents is at least k, the desired number of documents to return. The threshold is then used in the selection process.

5. ALLOCATING MULTIPLE COPIES

Previous work [10, 9, 16] mainly focuses on indexing strategies which try to use less machines and return good search results, without studying the availability of the index. As discussed before, the availability is a very important factor in designing search engine indexing, especially in a large cluster where disk failure is very common. Given the importance of the index availability, in this section we study different replication strategies. Replication studies the problem of how many copies of each document we make available across all the servers. It plays a key role in determining the availability and the quality of the system. Replication, together with allocation and selection, determines the quality of the system.

We assume that the amount of additional space available for replication is specified by a parameter $C > 0$ (typically C could be a fraction, say, 0.1 or 0.2). The total space available over all servers can accommodate a total of $(1 + C)|D|$ documents. Each server is assumed to have the same capacity, that is, it can accommodate $(1+C)|D|/n$ documents. The goal of replication strategy is to determine the replication function $R()$, so that for each document $d \in D$, $R(d)$ copies are made available across all servers. We require every document to be replicated at least once, that is, $R(d) \geq 1 \ \forall d \in D$. Hence we study how to assign the additional space ($C|D|$) to documents in D. To enable better understanding of replication and for ease of analysis and experimentation, we separate the replication strategy from the allocation strategy, that is, we determine the replication factor of a document independent of which servers would receive the copies of the document. We study four replication strategies below.

We first state and discuss a result that motivates our study of replication.

THEOREM 1. *For a given document replication vector, under random selection, the expected quality of the results returned does not have any dependence on the allocation strategy.*

In other words, the theorem implies that if we use the simple and easy-to-implement strategy of random selection, the allocation strategy does not affect the quality of the results. However, the replication strategy is important since it determines if a top document for a query will be part of the results retrieved and thus indeed affects the quality of the results. As a corollary, when there is no replication ($R(d) = 1 \ \forall d \in D$), if random server selection is used, we can allocate documents with the goal of maximizing availability, that is, minimizing $loss$.

The proof of the theorem follows from the following intuition. Since m different servers are selected at random, for a query and any document d, the probability that it will be included in $docs(q, m, k)$ does not depend on the specific choice of servers where the $R(d)$ copies of d are allocated. In other words, due to the randomness in selection, the probability that there is overlap between the set of m servers randomly selected and the set of $R(d)$ servers where d is allocated depends only on $n, m, R(d)$ and *not* on the specific choices (ids) of the $R(d)$ servers. Thus, under random selection, the allocation strategy does not influence the quality of results.

5.1 Uniform Replication

A naive way to replicate documents is to treat all the documents equally and distribute the additional space equally amongst all documents. First each document is replicated $(1 + \lfloor C \rfloor)$ times, and then with probability $(C - \lfloor C \rfloor)$, each document is allowed an additional copy. When $0 < C < 1$, this process is equivalent to including a second copy of a document with probability C. We call this replication strategy *uniform replication*. As uniform replication strategy is easy and natural to implement, we use it as our baseline in experiments.

5.2 Quality-Based Replication

Instead of treating all the documents equally, we next consider a strategy that gives preference to documents with high *value*. The intuition is that high value documents are more likely to be among the top k results of queries and hence it is desirable to replicate them more often. In quality-based replication, we first assign one copy of every document, and allocate the remaining $C|D|$ space greedily based on the document value, that is, consider the documents in the descending order of value and replicate each such document on all servers until there is no more space available. Recall that the value of a document d is defined as:

$$v(d) = \sum_{q \in Q} f(q)s(q, d) \ .$$

Algorithm QUALITYBIASEDREPLICATION formally describes this replication strategy.

foreach $d \in D$ **do**
  $v(d) \leftarrow \sum_{q \in Q} f(q)s(q, d)$;
end
$w \leftarrow \lfloor \frac{(C-1)|D|}{n-1} \rfloor$;
Let $d_1, d_2, \ldots, d_{|D|}$ represent the documents sorted in the descending order of $v(d)$;
for $i = 1 \ldots w$ **do**
  $R(d_i) \leftarrow n$;
end
$R(d_{w+1}) \leftarrow (C-1)|D| + 1 - (n-1)w$;
for $i = w + 2 \ldots |D|$ **do**
  $R(d_i) \leftarrow 1$;
end

Algorithm 3: QUALITYBIASEDREPLICATION algorithm

5.3 Workload-Aware Replication

In *workload-aware replication*, we assume that the workload is known, and hence the number of available servers (m) to answer a query is also known. To improve upon quality-based replication, instead of replicating a high value document on all servers, we only need to replicate on $n + 1 - m$ servers. Since we select m out of n servers for each query, we are *guaranteed* to select at least one server containing the high value document.

Algorithm WORKLOADAWAREREPLICATION is similar to QUALITYBIASEDREPLICATION, the only difference being that the maximum replication factor is smaller ($n+1-m$ instead of n), hence the available space permits maximal replication of more (high-valued) documents.

foreach $d \in D$ **do**
  $v(d) \leftarrow \sum_{q \in Q} f(q)s(q, d)$;
end
$w \leftarrow \lfloor \frac{(C-1)|D|}{n-m} \rfloor$;
Let $d_1, d_2, \ldots, d_{|D|}$ represent the documents sorted in the descending order of $v(d)$;
for $i = 1 \ldots w$ **do**
  $R(d_i) \leftarrow n + 1 - m$;
end
$R(d_{w+1}) \leftarrow (C-1)|D| + 1 - (n-m)w$;
for $i = w + 2 \ldots |D|$ **do**
  $R(d_i) \leftarrow 1$;
end

Algorithm 4: WORKLOADAWAREREPLICATION algorithm

5.4 Greedy Replication

Our final replication strategy is motivated by the following observation. As more copies of a document become available, intuitively the incremental benefit of an additional copy follows diminishing return. In fact, we implicitly used this fact in workload-aware replication, by observing that beyond $n + 1 - m$ copies, an additional copy of a document carries no benefit.

Formally we analyze the probability that a document replicated $R(d)$ times will be selected (or "hit") when m servers are probed randomly. We observe that this probability depends only on the number of servers n, as well as m and $R(d)$, and hence denote it as $Pr(hit(d)|n, m, R(d))$. Then,

$$Pr(hit(d)|n, m, R(d)) = 1 - \prod_{i=0}^{m-1} \left(1 - \frac{R(d)}{n - i}\right) \quad (1)$$

For given choices of n and m, consider the successive differences in the above probability as $R(d)$ increases, and denote it as: $\delta(R(d)) = Pr(hit(d)|n, m, R(d)) - Pr(hit(d)|n, m, R(d) - 1)$. We remark that $\delta(R(d))$ decreases as $R(d)$ increases. Table 1 shows how the values behave for $n = 10$ and $m = 2$ as $R(d)$ is increased from 1 to 10. For example, it is more beneficial to provide an extra copy when there are just 2 copies as compared to when there are already 7 copies.

Hence given two documents d_1 and d_2 with $v(d_1)$ slightly larger than $v(d_2)$, we prefer their replication counts to be close. Under workload-aware replication, it is possible that d_1 is replicated $n + 1 - m$ times and d_2 just once.

Combining the above desired property with the desire to give preference to high value documents, we devise the following optimization objective for replication.

$$\text{Maximize} \sum_{d \in D} v(d) \cdot Pr(hit(d)|n, m, R(d))$$

$$\text{s.t.} \sum_{d \in D} R(d) \leq (1 + C)|D| \text{ and } R(d) \geq 1 \ \forall d \in D.$$

This optimization problem consists of $|D|$ variables ($R(d)$'s), with an objective function that is extremely non-linear (in fact, has degree m dependence on each variable). Because of this complexity, at first, this problem seems impossible to solve optimally or to even approximate.

We next propose a greedy algorithm and surprisingly show that it achieves the optimal solution. The key insight is to notice that even though $Pr(hit(d)|n, m, R(d))$ is non-linear in $R(d)$, there are only n meaningful choices for $R(d)$ for any document d and thus only n possible values for $Pr(hit(d)|n, m, R(d))$ or $\delta(R(d))$. For each of $C|D|$ steps, the algorithm picks a document with maximum incremental benefit to the objective, that is, with maximum $v(d) \cdot \delta(R(d))$ and assigns an additional copy to the document.

This algorithm can be efficiently implemented by maintaining a binary heap of the incremental gain ($v(d) \cdot \delta(R(d) + 1)$) values for every document. At each step, exactly one document is assigned an additional copy, and thus only its gain value needs to be updated. As this update requires $O(\log |D|)$ steps in the worst case, the algorithm has time complexity $O(C|D| \log |D|)$.

We next show that the greedy algorithm is optimal, i.e., the locally optimal choices gives a globally optimal solution.

THEOREM 2. *Algorithm* GREEDYREPLICATION *finds the optimal replication vector with respect to the replication optimization objective.*

```
Compute the vector (δ(1), δ(2), ..., δ(n)) using Eqn 1;
foreach d ∈ D do
    v(d) ← Σ_{q∈Q} f(q)s(q, d);
    R(d_i) ← 1;
end
for i = 1 ... C|D| do
    Choose the document that can contribute the maximal
    incremental gain to the objective, that is,
    d* ← arg max_{d∈D}(v(d) · δ(R(d) + 1));
    R(d*) ← R(d*) + 1;
end
```

Algorithm 5: GREEDYREPLICATION algorithm

The basic intuition is that the incremental gain in quality by replicating a document decreases as a document is replicated more times. Further, the gain from replicating a document is independent on how many times the other documents are replicated. Therefore, when presented with a choice of documents to replicate, one can proceed greedily. A formal argument is provided below.

PROOF. The proof follows by contradiction. Suppose GREEDYREPLICATION is not optimal, so that the objective evaluated on the solution ALG computed by GREEDYREPLICATION is less than the optimal value. Then for any optimal solution OPT, we can always find two documents $d_1, d_2 \in D$ on which ALG and OPT differ in opposite directions, that is, $R_{OPT}(d_1) \geq R_{ALG}(d_1) + 1$ and $R_{ALG}(d_2) \geq R_{OPT}(d_2) + 1$. If there is more than one optimal solution, we fix OPT as the one with smallest number of copies for d_1.

Define a new valid assignment DIF that differs from OPT on just d_1 and d_2: $R_{DIF}(d_1) = R_{OPT}(d_1) - 1$ (has one less copy of d_1) and $R_{DIF}(d_2) = R_{OPT}(d_2) + 1$ (has one more copy of d_2). It follows that DIF is not optimal, and hence we have:

$$v(d_1) \cdot \delta(R_{OPT}(d_1)) > v(d_2) \cdot \delta(R_{OPT}(d_2) + 1) \quad (2)$$

Since $\delta()$ is a decreasing function, using $R_{OPT}(d_1) \geq R_{ALG}(d_1) + 1$ and $R_{ALG}(d_2) \geq R_{OPT}(d_2) + 1$, we have:

$$v(d_1) \cdot \delta(R_{ALG}(d_1) + 1) \geq v(d_1) \cdot \delta(R_{OPT}(d_1)) \quad (3)$$

$$v(d_2) \cdot \delta(R_{OPT}(d_2) + 1) \geq v(d_2) \cdot \delta(R_{ALG}(d_2)) \quad (4)$$

Combining equations 2, 3 and 4, we get:

$$v(d_1) \cdot \delta(R_{ALG}(d_1) + 1) > v(d_2) \cdot \delta(R_{ALG}(d_2)), \quad (5)$$

implying that when algorithm GREEDYREPLICATION chose to include the last copy of d_2, d_1 would have been a better choice. This is a contradiction since our algorithm is greedy. □

6. EXPERIMENTAL EVALUATION

6.1 Dataset and Performance Metric

In this section we experimentally evaluate the performance of our algorithms on a real-world dataset based on the notions of quality, availability and speed that we discussed earlier. To serve as our collection of documents we used the *Gov2* dataset from TREC's Terabyte Track [1] which consists of 25.2 million Web pages from the `.gov` domain. To serve as our query load for our various policies we used a random subset of the query log of a major search engine comprising 100 thousand queries. In order to have a setting

$R(d)$	1	2	3	4	5	6	7	8	9	10
$Pr(hit(d)\|n, m, R(d))$	0.20	0.37	0.53	0.66	0.77	0.86	0.93	0.97	1.00	1.00
$\delta(R(d))$	0.20	0.17	0.16	0.13	0.11	0.09	0.07	0.04	0.03	0.00

Table 1: Diminishing return observed with more copies of a document ($n = 10$, $m = 2$)

close to that of a realistic search engine, we performed our experiments on a cluster of 50 machines.

The exact ranking function that each search engine employs is closely guarded secret. In this paper we define the score of a document d to query q similar to section 2 as:

$$score(q, d) = \sum_{term\ t\ in\ q} score(t, d)$$

To compute the term relevance we used the BM25 scores [17].

Finally, to measure the quality performance of our policies we used the mean precision at k. That is, for a given allocation, selection, replication policy configuration, we compute the average fraction of top-k documents returned when the policy is applied compared to the top-k when no policy is applied. More formally, for a query load of m queries and for a configuration p:

$$Quality(p) = \frac{1}{m} \sum_{i=1}^{m} \frac{|Res_p(q_i) \cup Res_{OPT}(q_i)|}{|Res_{OPT}(q_i)|}$$

where $Res_p(q_i)$ is the top-k result set of configuration p for query q_i, and $Res_{OPT}(q_i)$ is the top-k result set for query q_i when no policy is applied (i.e. the query is sent to every machine). In our experiments we used $k = 10$.

6.2 Comparison of Allocation Strategies

We compare BALANCEDALLOCATION strategy with two well-known document allocation paradigms.

6.2.1 Random Allocation

A simple allocation strategy is to assign documents uniformly at random to the servers. Random allocation typically achieves good availability as each server receives in expectation the same number of relevant documents for each query. Formally, under random allocation, and assuming that each server has the same probability of serving a query, the expected value of each of the server is the same, i.e., for any two servers M_i and M_j,

$$\mathbb{E}[value(M_i, R, m, k)] = \mathbb{E}[value(M_j, R, m, k)] \ .$$

Since the total value of the system is fixed, this means that the loss is minimized in expectation.

6.2.2 Property-Based Allocation

A popular class of allocation strategies operate by first grouping the documents by certain properties, and then assigning documents with the same (or similar) property value to the same server.

Several property-based allocation strategies have been proposed in the past literature. This includes (1) source-based allocation that is based on treating the domain of a document as its property, used as a baseline for evaluation in [19]; (2) query-driven allocation that is based on grouping together documents that are used to answer similar queries [16]; and (3) topic-based allocation that is based on clustering documents around topics using KL-divergence as the distance function [11, 10].

Property-based allocation strategy typically does not guarantee good availability, as it may happen that many valuable documents get assigned to the same server. To understand better the performance of such allocation strategies, we implemented and compared the source-based allocation method with other allocation strategies in our experiment. This allocation sorts all the pages based on the URLs, then groups consecutive documents and assigns each group to the same server.

6.3 Comparison of Selection Strategies

We compare the HISTOGRAMSELECTION strategy with three strategies, viz., random selection, selection based on a random subset of documents, and a centralized strategy.

6.3.1 Random selection

Random selection is a pure runtime strategy that does not require the storage of any precomputed statistics. Given a query, we randomly select a subset of machines to answer the query.

6.3.2 ReDDe

ReDDe is proposed in [11]. During the offline process, a random sample of documents of about 0.1% of the total size of the collection are drawn, and an index over these samples are computed and stored in a central server. At runtime, given a query, this central index is first queried, and the subset of machines is chosen based on the result to the first query.

6.3.3 Gloss

Gloss is proposed in [9]. During the offline process, for each server, for each term, the average score of the documents for the term for the server is computed and stored in a central server. At runtime a score for each server is computed assuming independence, and the servers with the highest scores are selected.

6.4 Evaluation of Result Quality

We start our experimental evaluation by comparing the quality of results of different combinations of policies. To this end, we first loaded the documents to the cluster of 50 machines using different allocation policies. Then, we ran the queries against the cluster using different combinations of allocation and selection policies. In order to have a consistent view among the runs of the configurations and minimize variations, we evaluated the effect of the work load increase by using the same set of queries over all configurations while restricting our policies to direct each query to a progressively decreasing number of machines (denoting a corresponding increase in the work load). For each combination and selection policies we report the *Quality* metric as defined in the previous section.

We show the results in Figures 3, 4 and 5, each one corresponding to an allocation policy with different lines corresponding to different selection policies. The horizontal axis represents the workload expressed as a multiple of the initial workload when we can afford to use all 50 machines. For example, a workload of 2.0 implies that we have twice the amount of workload and hence we will use half of our machines to answer each query. The vertical axis corresponds to the *Quality* of a given allocation, selection configuration. To better evaluate the performance of our policies we also report the quality of an optimal selection policy (denoted OPT) which selects the best possible combination of machines for a given allocation

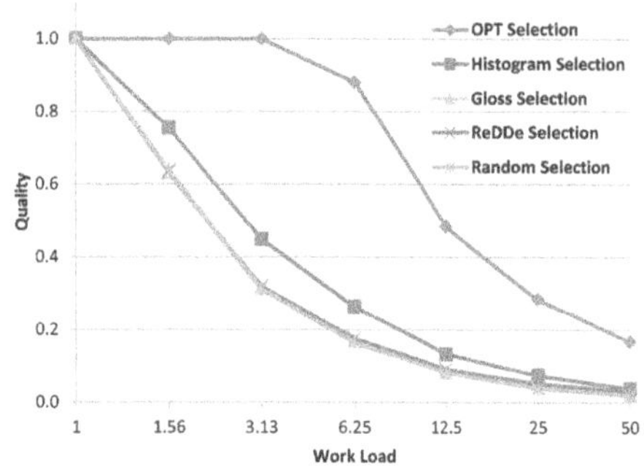

Figure 3: Quality of random allocation with different selection strategies under increasing work load.

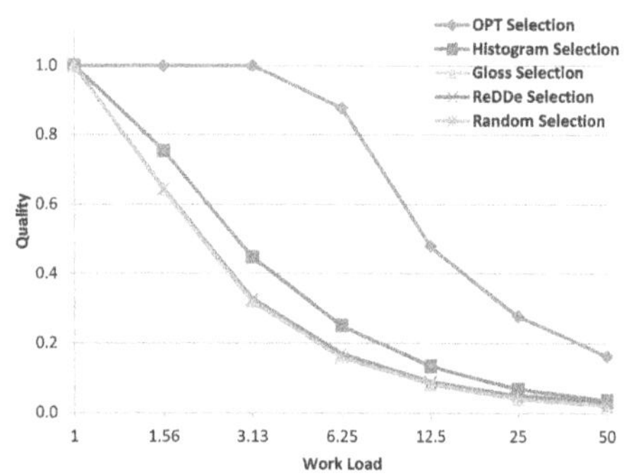

Figure 4: Quality of LPT allocation with different selection strategies under increasing work load.

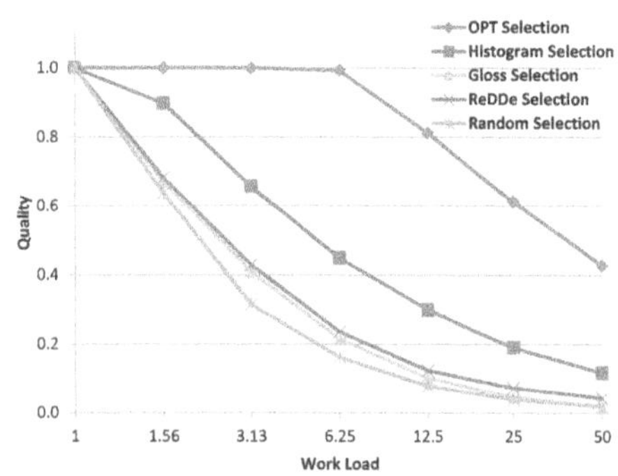

Figure 5: Quality of source-based allocation with different selection strategies under increasing work load.

policy. Also, following [11], for the ReDDe selection policy we used 0.1% of the index to store the necessary statistics.

The general observation regarding the performance of different configurations is that they perform worse than optimal. Additionally, as expected, the achieved quality of the policies decreases as the work load increases. Regarding the random allocation shown in Figure 3, we observe that the Gloss, ReDDe and Random selection policies achieve similar performance. Since documents are evenly spread out among machines, Gloss and ReDDe cannot make good predictions. Our Histogram selection is slightly better overall, but it comes with the additional cost in space and computation time as we discussed in Section 2. Additionally, its performance difference is diminishing as the work load increases.

The LPT allocation policy's goal is to allocate the documents in a very balanced way across all servers. Due to this fact, as we can see from Figure 4, all the selection policies perform similarly to each other. Additionally, their overall performance is slightly worse than the random allocation, which is again an artifact of the more balanced allocation that LPT achieves.

Finally, regarding the Source-based allocation policy shown in Figure 5, we observe that the techniques taking advantage of statistics on the documents on each machine in general outperform the random selection. In this case, ReDDe and Gloss perform similarly with ReDDe slightly better than Gloss. This is due to the fact that Source-based allocation in its attempt to maintain the average score of documents the same across machines may create an imbalance in the number of documents allocated among machines for a given term, which benefits ReDDe.

We also conducted two statistical tests to determine the significance of the differences in quality of the results under different workloads, selection strategy, and allocation strategy. Under a repeated-measure analysis of variance (ANOVA), where each query is treated as a subject that is tested under different combinations of workloads, selection, and allocation, all of these three factors are statistically significant in determining the quality of the retrieved results (at p-value of < 0.0001). Histogram selection and Source-based allocation has especially large positive effect in the quality of the retrieved results across all workloads. Under a paired t-test between all pairs of different conditions, almost all of the differences in the quality of the results are statistically different at p-value of < 0.0001. There are two cases where the results are statistically insignificant: (1) when random selection strategy is paired up with any allocation strategy, which is expected as random selection does not select servers based on statistics of the documents stored; and (2) between random selection and Gloss when allocation is either random or LPT, which is due to both allocation strategy gives rise to servers with close to identical average scores, in which server selection under Gloss is more or less random.

In summary, based on our observations regarding the quality of the different allocation and selection policies we conclude that the Random allocation and Random selection combination is a good candidate due to its simplicity of implementation. Histogram-based selection does perform better than Random selection, however if this particular selection policy is employed it is best combined with Source-based allocation. In the next section we study the availability of these two policies.

6.5 Evaluation of Availability

Another important characteristic of an effective indexing strategy is high availability. Given the scale of search engine indexes, it is important for the system to continue providing good results even under the presence of node failures. In this experiment we study the availability of the indexes created under the various allocation poli-

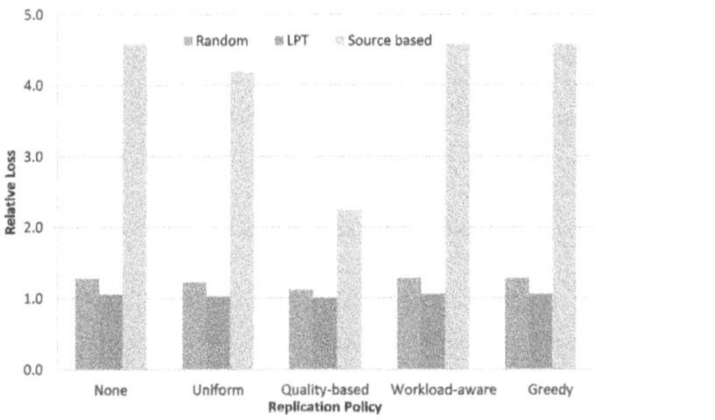

Figure 6: Loss function indicating availability for different allocation and replication policies.

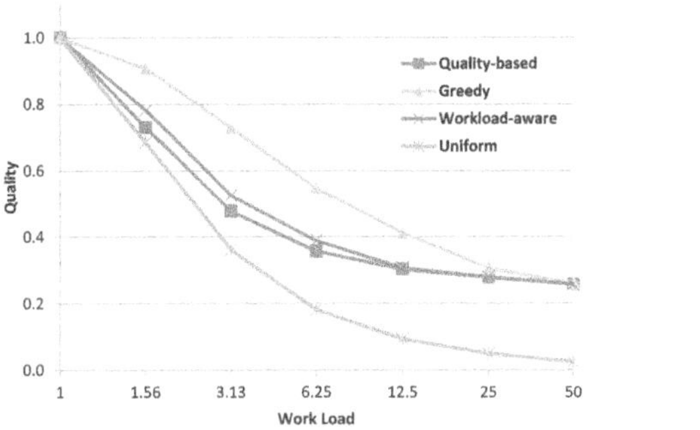

Figure 7: Quality for different replication policies under Random allocation and Random selection.

cies that we used in our previous experiment. To this end, for the three allocation policies, namely Random, LPT and Source-based we computed the loss value for our query set as defined in Section 2. We show the result in the first group of bars of Figure 6. The vertical axis shows the relative loss compared to the average loss across all servers. The higher the value (i.e. the loss), the more concentrated the good documents are in one particular server and thus the lower the availability and the more the system will suffer in the worst case node failure.

From the graph, we observe that the allocation policy with the minimum loss is the LPT allocation policy. This is expected since this particular policy makes an explicit attempt to balance the documents across the machines. The Random allocation policy also achieves reasonably good loss value as it is slightly higher than the LPT. Finally, although the source-based allocation policy was shown to perform very well in terms of quality in our previous experiment, its performance is the worst among the three policies in terms of availability. Its relative loss is almost 4 times higher than that of LPT and Random allocation policies.

6.5.1 *Benefit of Replication*

One way that is typically used to increase availability is the replication of the documents within the index. As additional copies of the same document exist in the system, the availability is expected to be higher since the replicated documents can still be found in case of a node failure. To study this effect, we repeated our availability experiment with the different replication policies that we discussed in Section 5. All replication policies were allowed an additional of 20% (i.e. $C = 0.2$) of the index to be used for replicating documents. We show the relative loss for the Uniform, Quality-based, Workload-aware and Greedy replication policies in the rightmost 4 groups of bars of Figure 6 respectively.

Our first observation comes from the fact that the availability remains almost the same for the Random and LPT allocation policies across the board. The availability of the Source-based allocation is increased when it is combined with the Quality-based replication policy (which also improves slightly the Random allocation). Unfortunately however, the benefits of Source-based allocation in terms of quality are not paired with high availability since it has a loss value twice as high as Random and LPT, even when combined with the best replication policy. On the contrary, the Random allocation with Random selection is more balanced in terms of both quality and availability.

Since we have allowed additional space for replicated documents in our index, we have also affected quality as more versions of the same document are available in the system. To this end, we studied the quality of the Random-allocation and Random-selection combination[3] under different replication policies. We show the results in Figure 7 with the horizontal axis representing workload and the vertical axis the quality as before. We observe that, overall, the quality of the results has increased which is due to the fact that the selection policy can now find more good quality documents. Overall, the Greedy replication policy performs the best.

6.6 Evaluation of Speed

We now turn to study the performance of the different policies in terms of query throughput. One of our main goals in designing an effective indexing mechanism is to be able to accommodate increases in the query load (possibly with some loss in quality) but without suffering delays to the queries served by the system.

To this end, we assume a setting where our system is operating at a query load close to peak capacity and where a selection policy will take charge to select a subset of the machines to serve an incoming query. In our experiment, we set this point to be 1000 queries per second for each of the 50 machines. Then, we increased the incoming query load to the system and we report the number of queries per second directed to the machine that received the maximum number of queries. The higher this number, the higher the expected number of dropped queries since the machine receiving the queries may not be able to serve them.

We report the result on Figure 8. We report our results for the combinations of Random allocation with Random selection, LPT allocation with Histogram selection and Source-based allocation with Histogram selection. Note that the presence of a replication policy does not affect the outcome of our experiment since the same set of machines will be selected. The horizontal axis represents the query load and the vertical axis shows the number of queries per second reaching the most loaded machine under a given query load.

Our first observation is that, overall, as the work load increases the maximum work load at one server remains more or less stable for Random and LPT. For these two policies, about half of the machines got a query load that was higher than the current operating work load of 1000 queries per second. In the case of Source-based, the maximum query load that the busiest machine receives increases proportionally to the increase in the query load in the system. For example, when the work load increases by 6 the maximum query load in the busiest machine increases almost 5 times. Overall, the combination of Random allocation with Random selection performs the best with the maximum load being only 1.4% higher than the current operating work load.

This last observation makes the combination of Random allocation, Random selection and Greedy Replication policies a very good all-around candidate for organizing an index. This combina-

[3]The observations for the remaining policy combinations are similar; we omit the graphs due to space constraints.

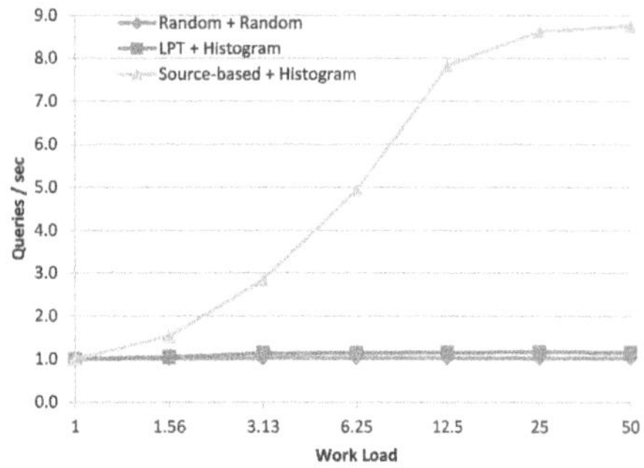

Figure 8: Throughput in thousand queries per second for increasing work loads.

tion is simple to implement and maintain, and it achieves a very good balance between quality, availability and speed.

7. RELATED WORK

In web search literature, there is a plethora of work on document allocation policies across *shards* of index servers. This work can be broadly classified into two categories. One that exploits relationship between documents and the other that is based on relationship between queries. The relationship between documents can be based on either semantic (e.g., *topic-based*) [19] or on other features (e.g., *source-based*) [19]. In their work on document allocation based on topic-based clustering, Xu and Croft [19, 11] used a two-pass K-means clustering algorithm and a KL-divergence distance metric to organize a collection into 100 topical clusters. Several property-based allocation strategies have been proposed in the past literature. This includes a source-based allocation that is based on treating the domain of a document as its property, used as a baseline for evaluation in [19] and a query-driven allocation that is based on grouping together documents that are used to answer similar queries [16].

In the literature related to selection strategies, people have broadly considered exhaustive search and selective search strategies. In the space of selective search strategies, Kulkarni and Callan [11] proposed a two-query approach in which the first query is used to estimate the number of relevant results on each index server. The second query is executed against the servers chosen based on the results of the first query. Gravano and Garcia-Molina [9] proposed a centralized solution for database servers in which a central server keeps appropriate term and server statistics. These statistics are computed offline and at query time, a score for each server is computed assuming independence, and the servers with the highest scores are selected. Ricardo Baeza-Yates et al. studied the feasibility of geographically building multi-site search systems in [4] and B. Barla Cambazoglu etc. proposed query forwarding techniques under geographically distributed indexes [7]. Also in [5] YouSearch is proposed to efficiently search personal web servers.

There has been work on improved load balancing techniques using some degree of replication of documents stored on the servers [12, 6]. Pitoura *et al* [15] have studied the trade-off between load-balancing and latency using replication in P2P systems.

8. CONCLUSIONS

In this study, we explored the space of algorithms for index serving and generation strategies. We measured the performance of our strategies using three natural properties of a search index, *viz.*, quality, latency, and availability. First, we showed that the straightforward random allocation and selection strategies indeed produced good quality results comparable to the more complicated but better strategies such as source-based allocation and histogram selection. Second, we showed the benefit of replication on availability of the search index in surfacing relevant results to the user's query. We empirically showed that without some degree of replication, naive strategies of allocation and selection do not help in producing top-k results with some quality guarantees. In particular, we observed that for a given set of allocation and selection strategies, our greedy replication strategy helps in surfacing the results with the highest quality. Finally, we report that no replication strategy affects the throughput significantly and that the combination of random allocation and selection reduces throughput the least. Overall, we observe that the combination of random allocation and selection combined with greedy replication are a good choice of strategies for index organization.

9. REFERENCES

[1] GOV2 Dataset, TREC Terabyte Track. http://www-nlpir.nist.gov/projects/terabyte/.
[2] Job Shop Scheduling . http://wikipedia.org/wiki/Job_shop_scheduling.
[3] N. Alon, Y. Azar, G. J. Woeginger, and T. Yadid. Approximation schemes for scheduling on parallel machines. *Journal of Scheduling*, 1:55–66, 1998.
[4] R. Baeza-Yates, A. Gionis, F. Junqueira, V. Plachouras, and L. Telloli. On the feasibility of multi-site web search engines. In *CIKM*, 2009.
[5] M. Bawa, R. J. B. Jr., S. Rajagopalan, and E. J. Shekita. Make it fresh, make it quick - searching a network of personal webservers. In *12th International World Wide Web Conference (WWW2003)*, 2003.
[6] J. W. Byers, J. Considine, and M. Mitzenmacher. Simple load balancing for distributed hash tables. In *IPTPS*, pages 80–87, 2003.
[7] B. B. Cambazoglu, E. Varol, E. Kayaaslan, C. Aykanat, and R. Baeza-Yates. Query forwarding in geographically distributed search engines. In *SIGIR*, 2010.
[8] R. L. Graham. Bounds on multiprocessing timing anomalies. *SIAM Journal on Applied Mathematics*, 17:416–429, 1969.
[9] L. Gravano and H. Garcia-molina. Generalizing gioss to vector-space databases and broker hierarchies. In *VLDB*, pages 78–89, 1995.
[10] A. Kulkarni and J. Callan. Document allocation policies for selective searching of distributed indexes. In *CIKM*, 2010.
[11] A. Kulkarni and J. Callan. Topic-based index partitions for efficient and effective selective search. In *SIGIR 2010 Workshop on Large-Scale Distributed Information Retrieval*, 2010.
[12] M. Mitzenmacher. The power of two choices in randomized load balancing. *IEEE Trans. Parallel Distrib. Syst.*, 12(10):1094–1104, 2001.
[13] R. Motwani and P. Raghavan. Randomized algorithms. 1995.
[14] M. Persin, J. Zobel, and R. Sacks-davis. Filtered document retrieval with frequency-sorted indexes. *Journal of the American Society for Information Science*, 47:749–764, 1996.
[15] T. Pitoura, N. Ntarmos, and P. Triantafillou. Replication, load balancing and efficient range query processing in dhts. In *EDBT*, pages 131–148, 2006.
[16] D. Puppin, F. Silvestri, and D. Laforenza. Query-driven document partitioning and collection selection. In *INFOSCALE 2006: Proc. of the first International Conference on Scalable Information Systems*, pages 107–117, 2006.
[17] S. Robertson, H. Zaragoza, and M. Taylor. Simple bm25 extension to multiple weighted fields. In *Proceedings of the thirteenth ACM international conference on Information and knowledge management*, CIKM '04, pages 42–49, 2004.
[18] M. Theobald, G. Weikum, and R. Schenkel. Top-k query evaluation with probabilistic guarantees. In *VLDB*, pages 648–659, 2004.
[19] J. Xu and W. B. Croft. Cluster-based language models for distributed retrieval. In *Proc. of SIGIR*, pages 254–261, 1999.

Incremental Diversification for Very Large Sets: a Streaming-based Approach

Enrico Minack
L3S Research Center
Leibniz Universität Hannover
30167 Hannover, Germany
minack@L3S.de

Wolf Siberski
L3S Research Center
Leibniz Universität Hannover
30167 Hannover, Germany
siberski@L3S.de

Wolfgang Nejdl
L3S Research Center
Leibniz Universität Hannover
30167 Hannover, Germany
nejdl@L3S.de

ABSTRACT

Result diversification is an effective method to reduce the risk that none of the returned results satisfies a user's query intention. It has been shown to decrease query abandonment substantially. On the other hand, computing an optimally diverse set is NP-hard for the usual objectives. Existing greedy diversification algorithms require random access to the input set, rendering them impractical in the context of large result sets or continuous data.

To solve this issue, we present a novel diversification approach which treats the input as a stream and processes each element in an incremental fashion, maintaining a near-optimal diverse set at any point in the stream. Our approach exhibits a linear computation and constant memory complexity with respect to input size, without significant loss of diversification quality. In an extensive evaluation on several real-world data sets, we show the applicability and efficiency of our algorithm for large result sets as well as for continuous query scenarios such as news stream subscriptions.

Categories and Subject Descriptors

H.3.3 [**Information Storage and Retrieval**]: Information Search and Retrieval

General Terms

ALGORITHMS,PERFORMANCE,EXPERIMENTATION

Keywords

Approximation, Diversification, Large sets, Streams

1. INTRODUCTION

A given user query often has a variety of intended meanings or associated information needs. To address this phenomenon, result diversification has been introduced as a technique to reduce the risk that none of the returned items matches the user's information need [25]. A good result set balances relevance and diversity to optimize the probability of user satisfaction. While diversification is an effective means to cater for diverse query interpretations, it is also computationally expensive. To compute an optimally diverse result subset from an input set of relevant items is NP-hard [1, 12]. Therefore, existing approaches use approximation techniques and heuristics to increase the efficiency of diversification [9, 29, 24, 26, 12]. While the computational complexity of state-of-the-art approximation algorithms is usually linear to the input size, they rely on random access to items of the input set. To allow for high performance, the entire input set is hold in main memory, imposing substantial memory requirements on systems processing many user queries in parallel. Further, these algorithms cannot be applied for diversification of result streams, such as results for continuous queries in databases [6, 2], publish/subscribe systems [15, 14] or on Semantic Web data [3]. Diversification of results is impossible for systems that potentially process thousands of queries in parallel when they use algorithms with super-linear runtime and linear memory requirements.

To solve this issue, we present our streaming-based approach which processes items incrementally, maintaining a near-optimal diverse set at any point in time. This approach has linear computation and constant memory complexity with respect to input set size, and naturally fits for streaming applications. It can be used to streamline existing diversification approaches, such as MAXMIN and MAXSUM [12, 9, 10]. Though we reduce memory consumption without compensating with more computation, our evaluation shows that diversification quality does not suffer, while efficiency is increased by orders of magnitude for large sets and streams.

In particular, this work makes the following contributions:

1. We formally define the task of *stream diversification*, which elegantly extends the *set diversification task*.
2. We propose an *incremental diversification framework* suitable to diversify sets and streams.
3. Incremental algorithms for the MAXSUM and MAXMIN diversification problems are provided. With input set size N and output set size k, the algorithms require $O(k^2)$ memory for floating point values, $O(k)$ memory for items, $O(Nk)$ distance computations, and $O(Nk)$ and $O(Nk^2)$ basic arithmetic operations, respectively.
4. While substantially improving diversification efficiency, our algorithms still provide highly diversified sets comparable to state-of-the-art *facility dispersion* approximation algorithms [12].

The remainder of this paper is organized as follows. In the next section, we discuss existing work on set and stream diversification. In Section 3, we provide the formal foundation of diversification. Section 4 presents our main contribution, the incremental diversification framework and two incremental algorithms based on this framework, including a complexity analysis. Their quality and performance is evaluated in Section 5 and compared to state-of-the-art diversification algorithms. Section 6 concludes our work.

2. RELATED WORK

Diversification is studied in many different fields such as biology, ecology, psychology, linguistics, and economics [17]. In media, it manifests itself in a number of dimensions like sub-topic structure, style of writing, sentiment, and ideological perspectives [18]. In the context of Information Retrieval, these aspects should not be regarded as noise or contradictions, but rather as a rich source of information [11].

In [28], Zhai and Lafferty model the Information Retrieval task as a statistical decision problem with the aim to minimize the risk of loss. Here, loss describes how much a result fails to satisfy a user's *information need*. Since this loss is always connected to the relevance of the results, the choice of a specific loss function allows to model different approaches in result set optimization. Traditional Information Retrieval approaches are modeled by a function in which the loss is *independently* estimated for each document. Diversification can be introduced by choosing a function where loss of one document depends on other documents in the result set.

Several such diversification objectives have been proposed and successfully validated. The use of Maximum Marginal Relevance (MMR) was proposed by Carbonell and Goldstein [4], and also used in Zhai et al. [27]. Chen and Karger [5] introduced the *k-call at n* metric: it is 1 if at least k of the top n documents in a result set are deemed relevant, otherwise 0. The aim is to achieve a high average k-call over multiple queries. The choice of a small k leads to higher diversification, a higher k favors relevance. Gollapudi and Sharma [12] express their diversification objectives in terms of facility dispersion optimization problems. In this work, we use their MaxSumDispersion and MaxMinDispersion algorithms as baseline for evaluation. In contrast to [12], only the diversified set is required to be in main memory and the input items are processed incrementally. This allows us to increase the efficiency for large item sets without significant loss of quality, as we show in section 5. Our streaming-based approach is not limited to these two diversification objectives, though, and is independent of any particular relevance and distance measures.

Document similarity is not the only possible source for a diversification objective. Another established approach is to view each document as covering a subset of all possible aspects of the query input [27, 7, 21]. The topical similarity based on the distance in taxonomies (categorical distance) is also used for diversifying product search [12] as well as for book, bookmark, and movie recommendations [29, 26]. Also click rates [23] and query reformulation [21] are valuable sources for effective diversification of Web search results.

As search engine query logs show, there is a fair number of news-related queries [19], suggesting that blog search users have an interest in the blogosphere response to news stories as these develop. To the best of our knowledge, in the context of diversification, this need has only been addressed by Drosou and Pitoura [9]. They propose algorithms that diversify a stream of results using a jumping window approach. The authors argue that an incremental computation of a diverse set of a stream is not possible. While this is true for the *optimal* diverse set, we show that an incremental heuristic approximation is very well possible. Their **SGC** algorithm — a heuristic variant based on a sliding window — is the most similar one in the literature compared to our incremental approach. However, our "window" always starts at the beginning of the stream, providing a diverse set of the entire history, rather than a fixed number of recent items. This allows our algorithm to actively withdraw items from the diverse set to improve its diversity, whereas SGC simply drops diverse items as they leave the window.

Diversification of search results is further considered in the domain of database search. A clustering and weighted sampling approach is used in [24] to obtain a diverse sub-set of results. Greedy algorithms are used in [13] in a similar way as presented here. However, the author does not focus design and evaluation on the streamline character of diversification, and does not consider input streams that are not ordered by relevance (e.g., from continuous queries).

3. DIVERSIFICATION PROBLEMS

In this section, we formally define the problem of diversification and provide the notation for the rest of this paper, mostly following [12]. We first define the classical *Set Diversification* problem, and then extend this notion to the problem of *Stream Diversification* to cover diversification of continuous data.

Set Diversification.

For a given set of results $\mathbf{U} : |\mathbf{U}| = N$ (e.g., search results, news or blog articles matching a user query) we aim to find the set $\mathbf{S}_k \subseteq \mathbf{U} : |\mathbf{S}_k| = k$ that is both relevant *and* diverse. Relevance of a result measures the probability that the user is actually interested in that result ($w : \mathbf{U} \to \mathbb{R}^+$)[1], whereas diversity reflects dissimilarity ((1 - similarity), also denoted distance) of one result to another ($d : \mathbf{U} \times \mathbf{U} \to \mathbb{R}^+$). To simplify the presentation, we assume in the following that d is a metric. Usually, relevance and diversity are conflicting objectives: when the top-k most relevant results do not constitute the maximal diverse set, diversity can only be increased by replacing a top-k result with a less relevant but more dissimilar one. This obviously reduces the overall relevance of the set. The tradeoff between the two measures is captured in a *diversification objective*, a function over a set of items that consolidates the relevance of results $w(\cdot)$ and the diversity between pairs of results $d(\cdot,\cdot)$ into a single measure:

$$f : 2^{\mathbf{U}} \times w \times d \to \mathbb{R} \qquad (1)$$

where $2^{\mathbf{U}}$ denotes the power set of $\mathbf{U}$.

Having the diversification objective at hand, we can define the *diversification problem* as finding the k-size random subset $\mathbf{S}_k \in 2^{\mathbf{U}}$ that maximizes the diversification objective:

$$\mathbf{S}_k^* = \arg \max_{\substack{\mathbf{S}_k \in 2^{\mathbf{U}} \\ |\mathbf{S}_k| = k}} f(\mathbf{S}_k, w(\cdot), d(\cdot,\cdot)) \qquad (2)$$

[1] While result set $\mathbf{U}$ and relevance function w depend on the user query, the explicit introduction of the query itself into this diversification model complicates the notation (cf. [12]).

This optimization is known to be NP-hard [12, 1]. As the number of candidate sets $|\{\mathbf{S}_k \in 2^{\mathbf{U}} : |\mathbf{S}_k| = k\}|$ is $\frac{N!}{(N-k)!}$, an exhaustive exploration of all sets to find the optimal solution is impractical even for small $k \approx 10$ as soon as $N > 20$. Therefore, all proposed diversification approaches use greedy algorithms and/or heuristics to approximate the optimal solution $\mathbf{S}_k^*$ by a near-optimal $\mathbf{S}_k^+$.

Instances of Diversification Objectives and Problems.

Throughout the literature of diversification, there are two popular diversification objectives: SUM[2] and MIN [12, 9]. As the names imply, they are based on the sum or minimum of the two measures w and d. Formally, SUM is defined as

$$f_{\text{SUM}} = (k-1)\sum_{i\in\mathbf{S}_k} w(i) + \lambda \sum_{\substack{i,j\in\mathbf{S}_k\\ i\neq j}} d(i,j) \qquad (3)$$

The first term in Equation 3 sums the relevance scores for each result, the second term sums the distances of all pairs $(i,j) \in \mathbf{S}_k \times \mathbf{S}_k : i \neq j$. Since the first sum runs over k values and the second over $k(k-1)$, this imbalance is compensated by multiplying the first term with $k-1$. In case of $d(\cdot,\cdot)$ being a metric [12, Eq. 1], it suffices to sum over all $\frac{k(k-1)}{2}$ unique unordered pairs and multiply the second term by 2.

The parameter λ allows to balance the influence of relevance and diversity on the objective value. A $\lambda < 1.0$ increases the contribution of relevance, whereas $\lambda > 1.0$ favors item dissimilarity. In order to consider both cases, we use $\lambda = 0.5, 1.0, 2.0$ in our evaluation.

The MIN objective only considers minimum relevance and minimum pairwise distance:

$$f_{\text{MIN}} = \min_{i\in\mathbf{S}_k} w(i) + \lambda \min_{\substack{i,j\in\mathbf{S}_k\\ i\neq j}} d(i,j) \qquad (4)$$

The diversification problems of maximizing the SUM and MIN objectives are referred to as MAXSUM and MAXMIN. These problems can be cast as facility dispersion problems as shown in [12], for which approximation algorithms exist. We briefly summarize these algorithms in the following.

MAXSUMDISPERSION composes the diverse set by selecting $\frac{k}{2}$ pairs of most distant items, with distance defined as $d(i,j)' = w(i) + w(j) + 2\lambda d(i,j)$. If k is odd, the kth item is randomly added to the set. Finding the pair of most distant items is of time complexity $O(N^2)$, thus this algorithm belongs to the complexity class $O(N^2k)$.

Similarly, MAXMINDISPERSION initializes the diverse set with the pair of most distant items, where distance is defined as $d'(i,j) = \frac{1}{2}(w(i)+w(j)) + \lambda d(i,j)$. Then, it adds the item i that maximizes $\min_{j\in\mathbf{S}} d'(i,j)$. After $k-2$ iterations, the diverse set is constructed. Again, finding the pair of most distant items requires $O(N^2)$ distance computations, while the $k-2$ iterations demand $O(Nk)$ operations, summing up to $O(N^2 + Nk)$. As described in [9], the MAXMINDISPERSION algorithm can be improved: instead of selecting the initial two most distant items from the entire input set, it can selected from a uniformly random sample set of size h ($h \ll N$). This has only a small impact on the diversification quality [8], but reduces the complexity to $O(Nk + h^2)$.

[2]The AVG objective bases on *average* relevance and *average* pairwise distance. For a fixed k, it is proportional to the SUM objective and is not separately considered in this work.

Since both algorithms require random access to the input set, it is usually held in memory, yielding to memory complexity of $O(N)$. This makes the application of these algorithms practically infeasible for large sets. In case of data streams, the algorithms need to be executed repeatedly as new items arrive, causing an even higher computational effort. In the following Section 4, we present our incremental approach that solves these issues.

Stream Diversification.

As an extension to the *set diversification problem*, we consider the items of the set to be a sequence or *stream* $\mathbf{S} = (s_1, \dots)$ in the order as retrieved by the respective IR system. For a given query, a traditional document retrieval system provides documents in descending order of relevance. A news or blogs publish/subscribe system provides results matching a continuous query as they are recognized by the system, i.e., ordered by time. We define the diversification problem over a stream $\mathbf{S}$ at each position i in the stream as

$$\mathbf{S}_{k,i}^* = \arg\max_{\substack{\mathbf{S}_k\in 2^{\mathbf{S}_i}\\ |\mathbf{S}_k|=k}} f(\mathbf{S}_k, w(\cdot), d(\cdot,\cdot)) \qquad (5)$$

where $\mathbf{S}_i = \{s_j : j \leq i\}$ is the set of the items at positions $[1,i]$. In other words, for each position i in $\mathbf{S}$, a diversified set $\mathbf{S}_{k,i}^*$ is defined over the subsequence $\mathbf{S}_i = (s_1, s_2, \dots, s_i)$. It can be seen that the set diversification problem is a special case of stream diversification, by viewing the input set $\mathbf{U}$ as stream $\mathbf{S} = (s_1, \dots, s_N)$. Then,

$$\mathbf{S}_k^* \overset{\mathbf{U}=\mathbf{S}_N}{=} \mathbf{S}_{k,N}^* \qquad (6)$$

In contrast to our stream diversification problem, [9, 10] consider a fixed window of recent items for the diversification task. This, for instance, poses a problem for items like news articles or blogs that are not published at a fixed rate. Then, at two different points in time the window covers different periods of time. Further, picking the window size represents an additional optimization problem.

Diversification along a time-ordered stream of results may lead to diversified k-size sets that primarily contain "old" but relevant and highly diverse results while new, similar results are omitted. Such a behavior can be compensated by introducing a decay factor to the relevance function which lowers the item score as its age increases [9]. Function $w_i(s_j)$ is the relevance of item s_j at time i (i.e., when item s_i is observed):

$$w_i(s_j) = w(s_j) * e^{-\alpha t(s_i,s_j)} \qquad (7)$$

with $\alpha = -\frac{\log 0.5}{\log e} t_{1/2}^{-1}$ and $t_{1/2}$ being the half-life time of results' relevances, while $t(s_j, s_i) = \max(t(s_i) - t(s_j), 0)$ provides the time difference between result s_i and s_j if the point in time $t(s_i) > t(s_j)$, or 0 otherwise.

4. INCREMENTAL DIVERSIFICATION

The following section describes our *incremental diversification framework*. It is composed of a generic *incremental diversification algorithm* that employs a general *incremental objective model* to optimize computation. This algorithm efficiently and effectively produces diverse k-size sets in linear time (for fixed k) and over streams in constant time (at each position) with respect to input size. Based on this framework, we develop incremental algorithms for the MAXSUM and MAXMIN diversification objectives.

4.1 Incremental Diversification Framework

Incremental Diversification Algorithm.

The core idea of our incremental diversification algorithm is to process the input as a stream of items and to continuously maintain a diverse subset at each position of the stream. Let $\mathbf{S}^+_{k,i-1}$ be a near-optimal diverse k-element subset of $(s_1, \dots, s_{i-1})$. Then, its successor $\mathbf{S}^+_{k,i}$ is determined as the set with the highest objective among all candidate sets $\mathbf{S}'_{k,i}$ that can be created by replacing at most one element of $\mathbf{S}^+_{k,i-1}$ with s_i.

Formally, this can be defined as

$$\mathbf{S}^+_{k,i} = \underset{\substack{\mathbf{S}'_{k,i} \in 2^{\mathbf{S}^+_{k,i-1} \cup \{s_i\}} \\ |\mathbf{S}'_{k,i}|=k}}{\arg\max} \quad f(\mathbf{S}'_{k,i}, w(\cdot), d(\cdot,\cdot)) \tag{8}$$

To put it differently, two consecutive sets $\mathbf{S}^+_{k,i-1}$ and $\mathbf{S}^+_{k,i}$ with $i \in [k+1, N]$ relate to each other as

$$\mathbf{S}^+_{k,i} = \mathbf{S}^+_{k,i-1} \setminus \{s_j\} \cup \{s_i\} : s_j \in \mathbf{S}^+_{k,i-1} \wedge s_j \notin \mathbf{S}^+_{k,i} \tag{9}$$

if a modification took place, otherwise $\mathbf{S}^+_{k,i} = \mathbf{S}^+_{k,i-1}$. For the first k items, $\mathbf{S}^+_{k,i}$ is trivally defined as $\mathbf{S}^+_{k,i} = \mathbf{S}^+_{k,i-1} \cup \{s_i\} : i \leq k$ with $\mathbf{S}_{k,0} = \emptyset$.

Algorithm 1 specifies this approach in pseudo-code. At the end of each iteration i over $[1, N]$, the algorithm provides the diverse set $\mathbf{S}^+_{k,i}$. In case of streams, this algorithm can continue computation as soon as a new item arrives.

Algorithm 1: Incremental Diversification Algorithm

Input: Set of items $\{s_1, \dots, s_N\}$, size of diverse set k
Output: diverse set of items $\mathbf{S}^+_{k,N}$

1 **for** $i \leftarrow 1$ **to** N **do**
2   **if** $i \leq k$ **then**
3     $\mathbf{S}^+_{k,i} \leftarrow \mathbf{S}^+_{k,i-1} \cup \{s_i\}$;
4   **continue** ;
5   max $\leftarrow f(\mathbf{S}^+_{k,i-1}, w(\cdot), d(\cdot,\cdot))$;
6   $\mathbf{S}^+_{k,i} \leftarrow \mathbf{S}^+_{k,i-1}$;
7   **for** $\forall s_j \in \mathbf{S}^+_{k,i-1}$ **do**
8     $\mathbf{S}'_{k,i} \leftarrow \mathbf{S}^+_{k,i-1} \setminus \{s_j\} \cup \{s_i\}$;
9   *current* $\leftarrow f(\mathbf{S}'_{k,i}, w(\cdot), d(\cdot,\cdot))$;
10   **if** *current* > *max* **then**
11   max $\leftarrow$ *current* ;
12       $\mathbf{S}^+_{k,i} \leftarrow \mathbf{S}'_{k,i}$;
13 **return** $\mathbf{S}^+_{k,N}$;

Additionally, this algorithm can be modified in line 10 to minimize the objective value, rather than maximizing it. This allows to also use the algorithm along with all those diversification objectives that are to be minimized, for instance the MaxCov objective [22].

An important characteristic of this algorithm is that the objective value is computed in the inner loop for k candidate sets $S'_{k,i}$ that, compared to the outcome set of the previous iteration, mutually differ in only one item. In the following, we show how the objective computation can further be optimized by exploiting this fact.

Incremental Objective Model.

The objective value of a set $\mathbf{S}^+_{k,i}$ is computed based on the known objective value of $\mathbf{S}^+_{k,i-1}$. Since both sets relate to each other as defined by Equation 9, only the relevance scores of item s_j (removal) and s_i (addition), as well as the distances $d(s_j, s_l)$ and $d(s_i, s_l) : s_l \in \mathbf{S}^+_{k,i-1} \setminus \{s_j\}$ need to be considered for computation. The incremental diversification algorithm computes the objective of different $\mathbf{S}^+_{k,i}$ by subsequently varying s_j (denoted in line 8 as $\mathbf{S}'_{k,i}$). Therefore, each distance $d(s_i, s_l)$ is reused $k-1$ times in the inner loop and does not need to be recomputed.

4.2 Incremental Sum Objective

The core idea of the incremental Sum objective function exploits the fact that a sum $s = \sum_{i=1}^{n} a_i$ can—instead of recomputing it—be updated when one value $a_j : j \in [1, n]$ gets replaced by a' as $s' = s + a' - a_j$. Equivalently, f_{SUM} in Equation 3 with symmetric distance can be incrementally computed as:

$$\begin{aligned} f_{\text{SUM}}(\mathbf{S}'_{k,i}) = f_{\text{SUM}}(\mathbf{S}^+_{k,i-1}) &+ (k-1)(w(s_i) - w(s_j)) \\ &+ 2\lambda \sum_{\substack{s_l \in \mathbf{S}^+_{k,i-1} \\ s_l \neq s_j}} (d(s_i, s_l) - d(s_j, s_l)) \end{aligned} \tag{10}$$

where $f_{\text{SUM}}(\cdot)$ is a short hand notation for $f_{\text{SUM}}(\cdot, w(\cdot), d(\cdot,\cdot))$.

As the incremental algorithm computes the objective of k different candidate sets $\mathbf{S}'_{k,i}$ with only s_j varying, the algorithm keeps all distances between the elements of $\mathbf{S}^+_{k,i-1}$ in a matrix $\mathbf{D} = (d_{m,n})$ with $d_{m,n} = d(s(m), s(n)) : \forall n, m = 1, \dots, k$. The function $s(\cdot)$ provides the element of the diverse set that corresponds to the index $[1, k]$ of this matrix and the following vectors. The symmetry of $d(\cdot)$ leads to a symmetric matrix $\mathbf{D}$. During the construction of the initial set (line 3 of the algorithm), this matrix is built up for the first k items. From then on, it is updated after the inner loop, as we show later.

The distance between the new item s_i and the items in the current diverse subset, $d(s_i, s(l)) : l = 1, \dots, k$, is reused $k-1$ times for each $s(l)$. Therefore we define the vector $\mathbf{d} = (d_1, \dots, d_k)$ with $d_l = d(s_i, s(l)) : l = 1, \dots, k$. This vector is computed once before the inner loop. We define the sum over all these distances as $\delta_{k,i} = \sum_{n=1}^{k} d_n$.

The vector $\varsigma_{k,i-1} = (\sigma_{1,i-1}, \dots, \sigma_{k,i-1})$ provides the row sums of matrix $\mathbf{D}$: $\sigma_{m,i-1} = \sum_{n=1}^{k} d_{m,n} : m = 1, \dots, k$. Then, Equation 10 can be rewritten as

$$\begin{aligned} f_{\text{SUM}}(\mathbf{S}'_{k,i}) = f_{\text{SUM}}(\mathbf{S}^+_{k,i-1}) \quad &+(k-1)(w(s_i) - w(s_j)) \\ &+2\lambda(\delta_{k,i} - d_j - \sigma_{j,i-1}) \end{aligned} \tag{11}$$

In case $\mathbf{S}^+_{k,i}$ differs from $\mathbf{S}^+_{k,i-1}$ (after the inner loop), the following updates are required: Vector $\varsigma_{k,i}$ is derived from $\varsigma_{k,i-1}$ for all $l = 1, \dots, k$ as

$$\sigma_{l,i} = \begin{cases} \sigma_{l,i-1} + d_l - d_{j,l} & : l \neq j \\ \delta_{k,i} - d_l & : l = j \end{cases} \tag{12}$$

where j refers to the index of s_j as $s(j) = s_j$. Then, matrix $\mathbf{D}$ is updated as $d_{l,j} = d_{j,l} = d_l : l = 1, \dots, k$, and function $s(\cdot)$ is modified so that $s(j) = s_i$. With this strategy, our incremental Sum objective achieves a computation complexity of $O(1)$, while requiring $O(k^2)$ memory.

diversification algorithm	acronym	CPU distances	CPU basic	Memory items	Memory basic
MaxSumDispersion	MSDisp	$O(N^2k)$	$O(N^2k)$	$O(N)$	$O(1)$
MaxSumDispersion cached	MSDisp+	$O(N^2)$	$O(N^2k)$	$O(N)$	$O(N^2)$
MaxSumIncremental	MSInc	$O(Nk)$	$O(Nk)$	$O(k)$	$O(k^2)$
MaxMinDispersion	MMDisp	$O(N^2+Nk)$	$O(Nk)$	$O(N)$	$O(1)$
MaxMinDispersion cached	MMDisp+	$O(N^2)$	$O(Nk)$	$O(N)$	$O(N^2)$
MaxMinDispersion cached (h=2)	MMDisp+h2	$O(Nk+h^2)$	$O(Nk)$	$O(N)$	$O(Nk+h^2)$
MaxMinIncremental	MMInc	$O(Nk)$	$O(Nk^2)$	$O(k)$	$O(k^2)$

Table 1: Complexity in CPU consumption (distance computation and basic operations) and memory consumption (items and basic data types) of different diversification algorithms. Basic operations are arithmetic operations or memory access, basic data types are double precision floating point values.

4.3 Incremental Min Objective

The Min objective defined in Equation 4 bases on the minimum relevance and pairwise distance. Therefore, the objective of each $\mathbf{S}'_{k,i}$ can be computed with the new minimum relevance and distance values of $\mathbf{S}^+_{k,i-1}$ and item s_i.

Similarly to the incremental Sum objective, the pairwise distances between s_i and $s_j \in \mathbf{S}^+_{k,i-1}$ are computed once before the outer loop of the incremental algorithm and are reused to compute the objective of the candidate sets:

$$\min_{s_n \in \mathbf{S}'_{k,i}} w(s_n) = \min\left(\left(\min_{\substack{s_n \in \mathbf{S}^+_{k,i-1}\\ s_n \neq s_j}} w(s_n)\right), w(s_i)\right) \tag{13}$$

$$\min_{\substack{s_n, s_m \in \mathbf{S}'_{k,i}\\ s_n \neq s_m}} d(s_n, s_m) = \min\left(\left(\min_{\substack{n,m \in \{1,\dots,k\}\setminus\{j\}\\ n \neq m}} d_{n,m}\right), \min_{n \in \{1,\dots,k\}\setminus\{j\}} d_n\right) \tag{14}$$

With an ordered vector of all relevances of the diverse set, Equation 13 can be computed in $O(1)$ by comparing the first element (if the respective relevance does not belong to s_j) or the second element (otherwise) of the vector with $w(s_i)$. Equation 14 can be evaluated by finding the smallest distance among $d_{n,m}$ and d_l with $n, m, l \in [1, k]$ that does not belong to s_j. This can be done by a *two-way merge* [16, Sec. 5.2.4] over the ordered vector of all $d_{n,m}$, the ordered vector of all d_l, and the ordered vector of $d_{j,m}$. The result distance is the minimum of the former two vectors that does not appear in the latter one (thus it does not belong to s_j). This operation has a worst-case complexity of $O(k)$, occurring when the k smallest pairwise distances of $\mathbf{S}^+_{k,i-1}$ belong to s_j and all distances to s_i are larger than these. In the best case, when the smallest pairwise distance of $\mathbf{S}^+_{k,i-1}$ does not belong to s_j and is larger than the smallest d_l, (14) has complexity $O(1)$.

4.4 Complexity Analysis

The complexities of our incremental objectives for MaxSum and MaxMin were briefly outlined before. We now analyze the total complexity of our algorithm in detail. The complexities of all algorithms are summarized in Table 1.

The computation and memory complexities are each considered to be compound. The computation contains distance computations and basic arithmetic operations. The former may involve several of the latter, potentially rendering distance computations to be of an order of magnitude slower. Memory consumption is considered a conjunction of memory for items (to be diversified) and memory for basic data types such as double precision floating point values. Again, the former can be orders of magnitude larger than the latter.

As one can see from the pseudo-code, the incremental diversification algorithm has a complexity of $O(Nk)$ set modifications and objective computations. In case of MaxSumIncremental, the structures $\mathbf{D}$, $\mathbf{d}$, $\sigma_{j,i-1}$, and $\delta_{k,i}$ are constructed and updated incrementally outside of the inner loop, requiring $O(k)$ operations for each item. As we have shown, the computation of the objective itself is $O(1)$. Thus, the total computational complexity of MaxSumIncremental is still $O(Nk)$.

The objective computation of MaxMinIncremental has complexity of $O(k)$ in worst-case and $O(1)$ in best-case. The removal and addition of an element from and to the ordered relevance and distances vectors each requires $O(\log k)$ operations. These operations are performed before and after the inner loop, leading to a total complexity of $O(Nk^2)$ and $O(Nk \log k)$, respectively. For both objectives, the memory requirements for maintaining the distance matrix dominates the overall memory complexity, leading to $O(k^2)$. Note that k is usually rather small, according to the "less is more" [5] motto. Thus, our algorithm is essentially linear in the number of items, with a small constant factor determined by k.

5. EXPERIMENTAL EVALUATION

We presented a generic incremental diversification framework, as well as two specific incremental diversification algorithms: MaxMinIncremental and MaxSumIncremental. As shown, computation and memory complexity is reduced compared to their *baseline* algorithms MaxMinDispersion and MaxSumDispersion, at the cost of giving up approximation guarantees. Therefore, the main goal of the experimental evaluation is to show that for real-world data, this does not lead to a decrease in diversification quality for sets and streams. In addition, we measure the performance characteristics of our algorithms and the baseline to confirm analytical results presented in Section 4.4.

5.1 Experimental Setup

Data Sets and Queries.

To show the wide applicability of our algorithms, we evaluated them on three well-known data sets. We opted for data sets that provide us with large result sets and streams — the challenge our incremental diversification algorithms tackle. We used these data sets and queries for evaluation:

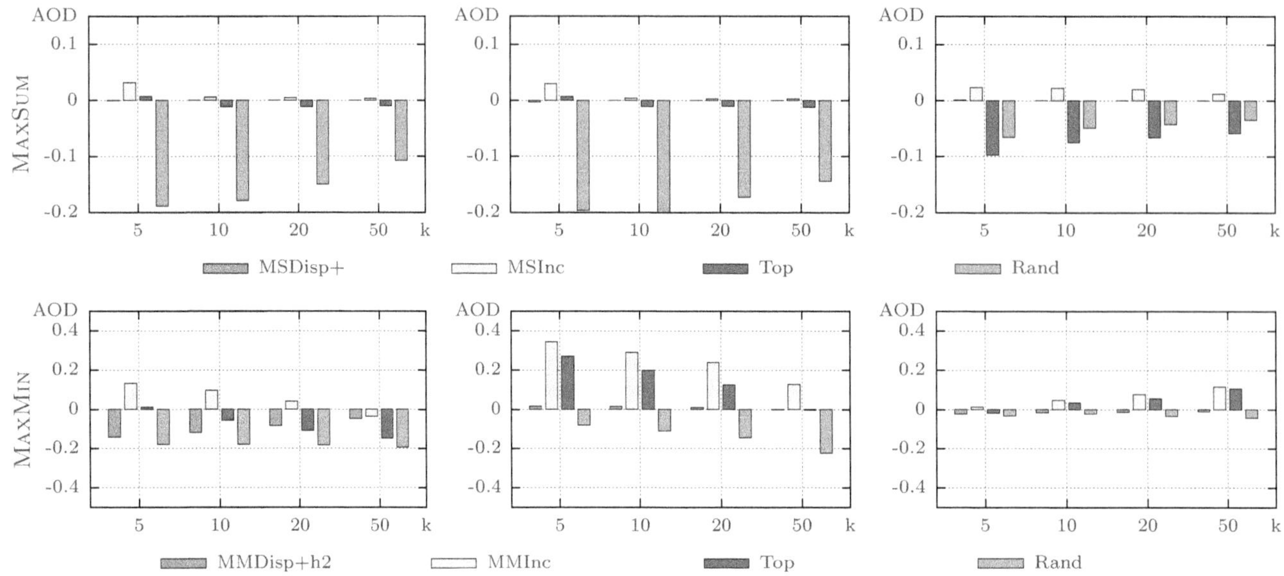

Figure 1: Diversification quality compared to baseline MAXSUMDISPERSION (top) and MAXMINDISPERSION (bottom) on the NYTimes, Blogs08 and DBpedia data set (left to right), with $\lambda = 1$.

NYTimes The *New York Times Annotated Corpus*[3] contains over 1.8 million articles of the New York Times from 1987 until 2007. We obtained over 5,000 user queries from the AOL query log that lead users to `query.nytimes.com` and `topics.nytimes.com`. The publication timestamp renders this data set suitable to generate time-ordered result streams from queries.

Blogs08 The *TREC Blogs 2008 data set*[4] provides over 28 million multi-language blog entries crawled over the period of 2008. We considered a subset of 18 million entries that can be classified[5] as English. As queries, we used the TREC 2008 Blog Track topics of the *opinion search and polarity task*[6]. From these 150 topics, we took the title as a keyword query. The dates of blog retrieval allow us to generate time-ordered streams of blog entries relevant to user queries.

DBpedia The *DBpedia data set v3.5.1*[7] is a semantic data set providing the knowledge of the Wikipedia project as semi-structured data. We used DBpedia as complement to the other two document-centric data sets. Structured result sets and streams may exhibit different characteristics and challenge diversification algorithms differently than unstructured document collection. This data set contains almost 89 million facts extracted from Wikipedia content.

For the DBpedia data set, we aim at generating structured queries that most likely produce long result sets suitable for our evaluation purposes and are likely to be issued. Therefore we exploit frequent structures exposed by the data. From the most frequent types (classes), links between these types, and their most frequent attributes (literal properties), we automatically generated queries containing at most five interconnected typed nodes (resources) and multiple optional unbound attributes. With that approach, we created over 800 queries.

These three data sets are used to generate realistic result sets and streams to put our diversification algorithms under real workload. With a result set ordered by relevance we face the *set diversification* task, ordered by time we tackle the *stream diversification* task.

Relevance and Distance Functions.

The diversification tasks we are focusing on require relevance and distance functions, which are to be defined for each data set individually.

NYTimes/Blogs08 The two document-centric data sets were indexed using the Java Lucene[8] library along with the Snowball stemmer[9]. We use Lucene's normalized relevance score as relevance function. Based on the cosine similarity $CosineSim(\cdot, \cdot)$ of the term frequency vectors, the distance between items is defined as $d(s_i, s_j) = 1 - CosineSim(s_i, s_j)$.

DBpedia The semantic data set is indexed and queried with Java Sesame[10]. After querying, results referring to the same things but with varying values for the attributes were consolidated into a single result with multi-value attributes.

[3]The New York Times Annotated Corpus: `http://corpus.nytimes.com/`.
[4]TREC Web Corpus — BLOGS08: `http://ir.dcs.gla.ac.uk/test_collections/blogs08info.html`.
[5]TextCat Library: `http://textcat.sourceforge.net/`.
[6]Topics for opinion search and polarity task (topics 851–950, 1000–1050): `http://trec.nist.gov/data/blog08.html`.
[7]DBpedia: `http://dbpedia.org/`.
[8]Apache Lucene: `http://lucene.apache.org/java/`.
[9]Snowball Stemmer: `http://snowball.tartarus.org/`.
[10]OpenRDF Sesame: `http://www.openrdf.org/`.

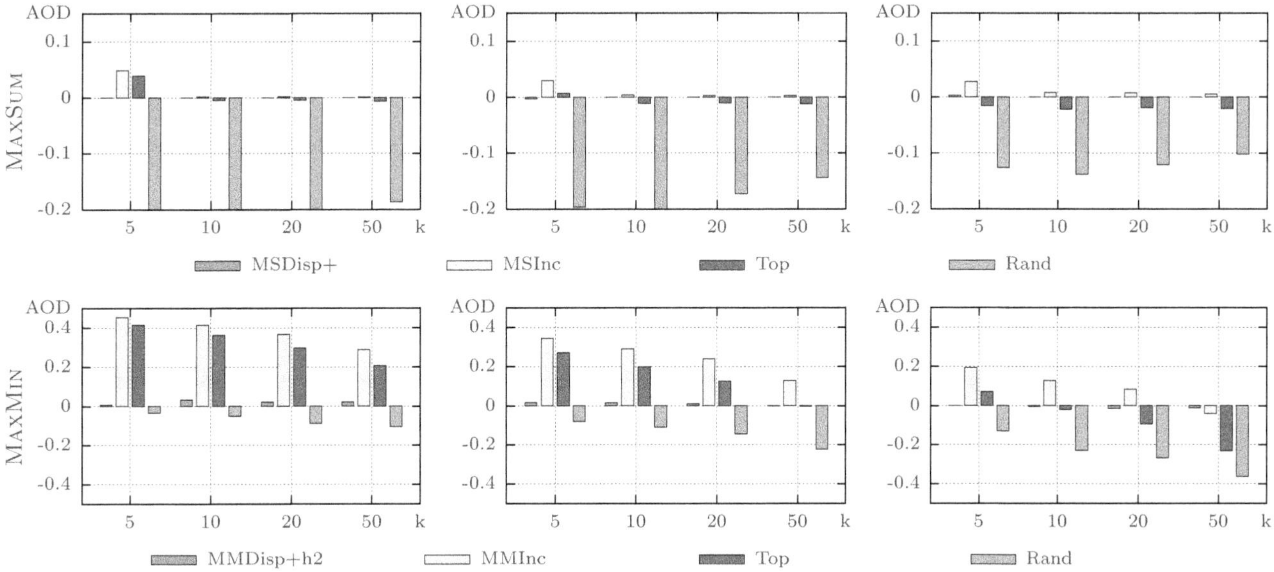

Figure 2: Diversification quality compared to baseline algorithm MAXSUMDISPERSION (top) and MAXMINDISPERSION (bottom) for the Blogs08 data set with $\lambda = 0.5, 1.0, 2.0$ (left to right).

Following [20], we define the distance between two results s_i and s_j as a multi-type-multi-value distance measure:

$$d(s_i, s_j) = \frac{1}{n} \sum_{l=1}^{n} d_l(s_i(a_l), s_j(a_l)) \tag{15}$$

where the query contains the attributes $\mathbf{a} = (a_1, \ldots, a_n)$ and $s_i(a_l)$ refers to the multi-value for attribute a_l of result s_i. Further, the distance $d_l(\mathbf{v_i}, \mathbf{v_j})$ between multi-value $\mathbf{v_i}$ and $\mathbf{v_j}$ of result s_i and s_j for attribute a_l is defined as

$$d_l(\mathbf{v_i} = s_i(a_l), \mathbf{v_j} = s_j(a_l)) = \frac{1}{|\mathbf{v_i}| \cdot |\mathbf{v_j}|} \sum_{t \in \mathbf{v_i}} \sum_{u \in \mathbf{v_j}} d_l(t, u) \tag{16}$$

which corresponds to the average pairwise distance between the values of result s_i and s_j for attribute a_l. The distance between empty multi-values is defined as 1. Obviously, this definition considers two sparse results with disjoint sets of non-empty attributes to be maximally distant (diverse). Consequently, the diversification would favor sets of sparse results, which is unlikely to satisfy users. Therefore, we define relevance as the fraction that reflects the number of attributes of the query that are covered by the result (non-empty). A result that provides values for all attributes obtains relevance 1, whereas results with only a few attribute values get assigned a relevance close to 0. The diversification objective that balances diversity and relevance also balances between sparse and non-sparse results.

The result distance measure can employ different distance measures for different attributes. We use cosine similarity over term frequency vectors for textual values and the absolute difference between numerical values, normalized by the maximum range of the respective attribute.

Evaluation approach.

Our evaluation targets at effectiveness and efficiency of our incremental algorithms compared to baseline algorithms.

Effectiveness Usually, when evaluating diversification approaches, the challenge is to measure result set diversity. Clearly, this measurement must be independent from the diversification objective, which is maximized. A number of established diversity-aware evaluation measures for search approaches exist, e.g., *α-NDCG* [7], *NDCG-IA* [1], and *S-recall* [27].

These measures require sub-topic annotations or relevance judgments which are not available for result set sizes in the order of 10^4 that we evaluate. Fortunately, in our case it is not necessary to directly evaluate the quality of the diversification, because our work approximates already established diversification approaches with validated objective functions [12], and focuses on gains in efficiency, not in diversification quality. Therefore, we only need to assess the approximation quality to validate the effectiveness of our algorithms. For that purpose, a direct comparison of the achieved objective scores instead of using one of the above mentioned quality measures is appropriate.

For comparison, we run each algorithm for all queries, and measure the objective score of the diverse sets. These scores are then normalized to the interval $[0, 1]$ by division by the maximal possible objective value. The difference of an algorithm's and its baseline's normalized objectives renders the *absolute objective difference* (AOD) measure. These are averaged over all queries and used to quantify the loss of quality introduced by streamlining. An AOD value of ± 0.1 expresses an improvement / impairment of 10% within the normalized interval of $[0, 1]$.

Efficiency The algorithm efficiency was measured as follows. The queries were evaluated against the data sets and all results were fetched into memory. Then, the algorithms

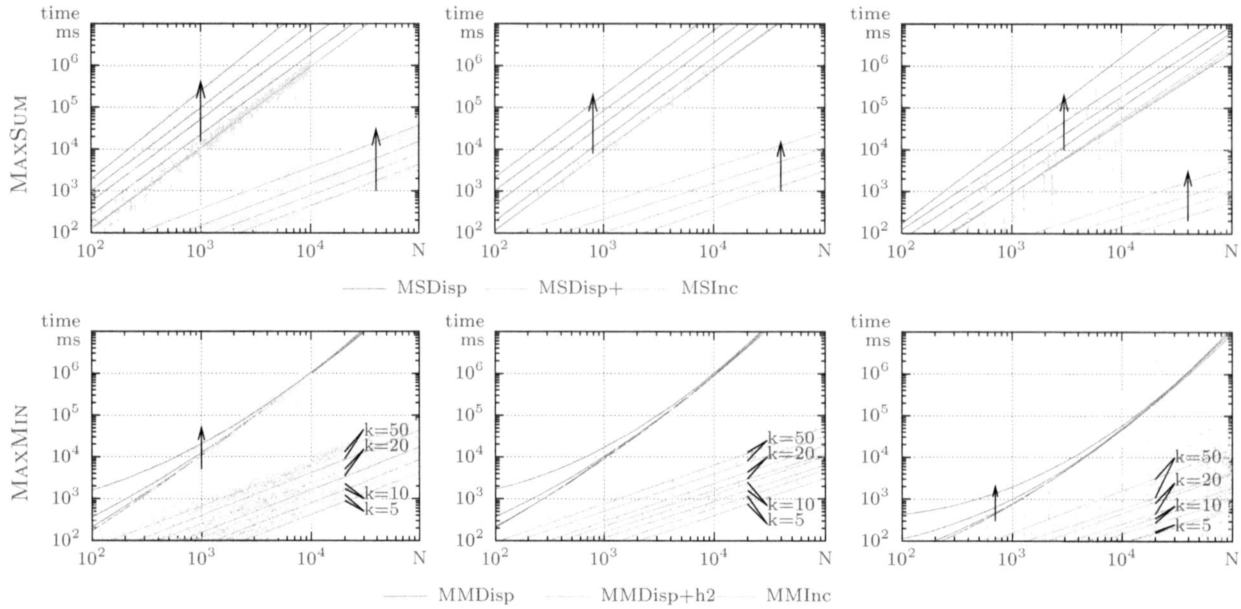

Figure 3: Runtime for MaxSum (top) and MaxMin (bottom) diversification algorithms on the three data sets NYTimes, Blogs08, and DBpedia (left to right) for $k = 5, 10, 20, 50$.

performed the diversification on these in-memory result sets. We only measured the time required for the diversification itself, not taking into account query execution and fetching of the initial result set into memory. The experiments employed the high performance computing cluster with Java™ version 1.6.0_16, employing Intel® Xeon® (X5670, 2.93GHz) processors. Execution time is the actual CPU time consumed by the algorithms, not the "wall clock" time.

Computing the diverse sets of the baseline algorithms is too expensive for very large result sets. Therefore, for MaxSumDispersion we only considered result sets of up to 4,000 elements, for MaxMinDispersion up to 10,000 elements.

In the following, we evaluate effectiveness and efficiency of our incremental algorithms as well as their state-of-the-art non-incremental counterparts for large sets and streams.

5.2 Set Diversification

Algorithms.

For each of the two objectives that we evaluate here, a number of approximation algorithms and variants exist. As baseline algorithms, we consider the facility dispersion based algorithms MaxSumDispersion and MaxMinDispersion [12]. In the following, we refer to these as `MSDisp` and `MMDisp`, respectively. Both can be modified to trade fewer computations against higher memory consumption by caching computed distances. We refer to these as `MSDisp+` and `MMDisp+`, respectively. Further, the variant of `MMDisp+` that initially selects the most distant pair from a h-size random subset of all N items ($h < N$) is also evaluated with $h = 2$ as `MMDisp+h2` [8].

Our incremental algorithms are in the following referred to as `MSInc` and `MMInc`. As *reference algorithms*, we also show the diversity achieved by returning the top-k most relevant items (`Top`), as well as k-random ones (`Rand`).

Diversification Quality.

In Figure 1 we show the difference of the objective score achieved with respect to the baseline algorithm, i.e., the baseline algorithm's score is at 0. For the upper row with the Sum objective, the baseline algorithm is `MSDisp`. The lower row shows results for the Min objective with `MMDisp` as baseline. `MSDisp+` shows the same diversification quality as the baseline, because the only difference is that it caches results and therefore produces identical diverse sets.

For all three data collections, `MSInc` clearly is on par with the baseline. In some instances, the incremental results are even better. Our algorithms *can* be better than the baseline because both approximate the optimal solution. `MSInc` *is* sometimes better because it considers every item in the set, while `MSDisp` only considers items with maximal distance within the remaining item set. For instance, `MSDisp` would add two identical pairs of results with maximal distance to the diverse set, while the second does not increase diversity.

We observe that Min has a higher variation of AOD values. However, also for this objective, the incremental algorithm yields similar or better results than the baseline.

`MSInc` results are more stable over all data sets and configurations than `MMInc`. This might be because for Min the one item with the smallest relevance and distance determines the objective score of the entire set, whereas for Sum all items equally contribute to the final score.

Though `MMDisp+h2` yields reasonable results for Blogs08 and DBPedia, this approach does not work well for the NYTimes collection (Figure 1, bottom left).

Influence of λ.

To investigate the influence of different trade-offs between relevance and distance, we now vary λ between 0.5 and 2.0. The results are shown in Figure 2. For the Sum objective, the approximation quality is not substantially influenced by

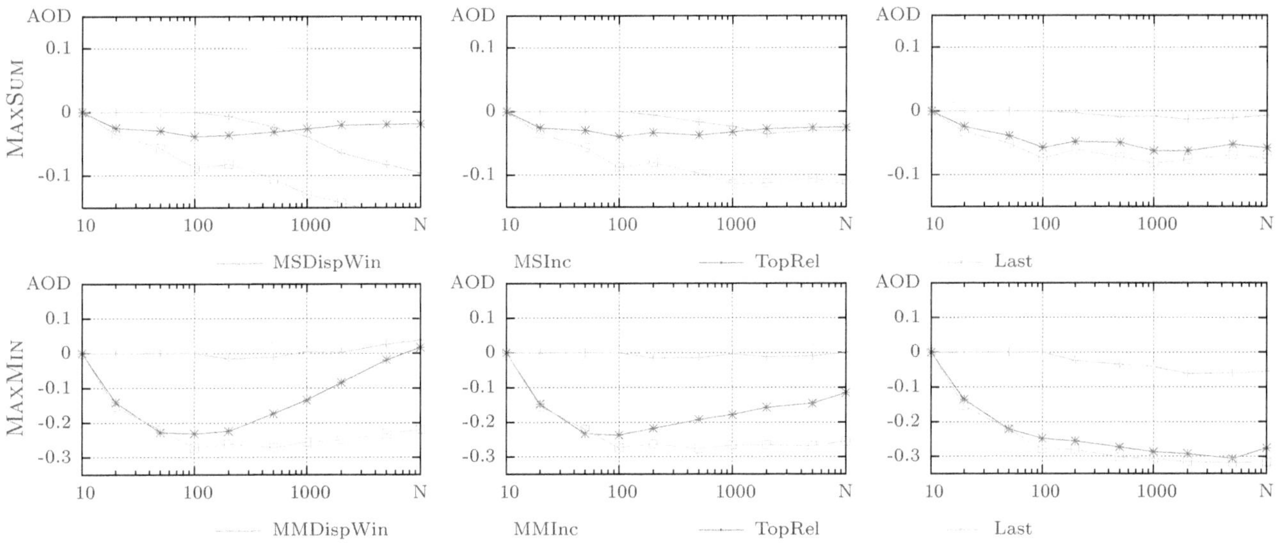

Figure 4: Absolute objective improvements of MAXSUM (top) and MAXMIN (bottom) for the Blogs08 data set with $\lambda = 1.0$ and $k = 10$ for streamline with no decay and decay over $100k$ and $1k$ (from left to right).

the choice of λ. On the other hand, the respective differences for MIN to the baseline algorithm are significantly affected.

For $\lambda = 0.5$, the relevance-only reference `Top` achieves SUM objective scores comparable to the baseline, and for MIN its score is even higher. As expected, for higher λ values the `Top` scores deteriorate soon. We also observe that our incremental algorithms are able to even diversify the top-k results for $\lambda < 1.0$ and always outperform the other variants (except for one case with MIN at $k = 50$ and $\lambda = 2.0$).

Performance Results.

The runtime of our experiments is depicted in Figure 3. Each query is represented by a corresponding dot. In addition, we show fitted regression curves according to Table 1 for these results. Note that results are shown with log-log scales. Here, polynomial complexity classes are displayed as straight lines, with varying slopes according to the degree of complexity, i.e., $O(N^2)$ has a steeper slope than $O(N)$.

All experimental results correspond to the analytical predictions presented in Section 4.4. We see that the extracted queries yield result set sizes from 100 up to 10,000 documents. As expected, processing times of the non-incremental algorithms grow quadratic with this set size.

Computing the distance values for our document collections NYTimes and Blogs08 is equally fast for all documents. In contrast, we observe a high variance for the DBPedia collection (Figure 3, right column). This can be explained by characteristics of the distance function used for the structured data. The performance of this function depends on the number of attributes which varies by an order of magnitude in our query set. Regardless of this variance, the fitting curve matches the analytical curves for this data set, too.

Already for $N = 1{,}000$ and $k = 10$, `MSDisp` requires one minute to compute the diversified set. In contrast, our incremental variant needs only $\approx$100 milliseconds for this set size. `MMInc` has slightly higher response times than `MSInc`, due to the additional k factor in objective computation.

5.3 Stream Diversification

We now evaluate our algorithms against the *stream diversification* task. The experimental setting mimics a stream of results as retrieved from a news or blogs publish/subscribe-system, for example an RSS stream. In contrast to the set-based experiments, items are ordered by timestamp.

Algorithms.

With Equation 5, we define the task of stream diversification as finding at each position of the stream a diverse subset of all items that were observed until that position. As the baseline algorithm, we take all these observed results as a set and obtain the diverse set with the set-based baseline algorithms. This computation turned out to be very expensive. We were unable to process the baseline for streams larger than 10,000 documents while collecting a sufficient amount of measurement points. For that amount, the diversification with $k = 10$ required nearly one hour.

Additional to this baseline, we evaluated a window-variant following the work of Drosou and Pitoura [9] on stream diversification, denoted as `MSDispWin` and `MMDispWin`, respectively. We show the results for a jumping window of 100.

As before, we include two reference algorithms for comparison purposes. The `Last` reference algorithm proposes the k most recent items from a stream as the diverse set, whereas `TopRel` picks the k most relevant items from the stream, ignoring diversity completely.

Optimally, we would compute the diverse set after each new item. However, this is prohibitively expensive for the baseline. Therefore, we distributed ten measuring positions logarithmically over the stream, and computed the results for all algorithms at these positions.

Results. Figure 4 shows the diversification quality for stream data, computed on Blogs08, our largest data set. To evaluate the influence of item relevance decay, the experiments were performed without decay (left column) and with a half-life over $100k$ (middle) and $1k$ (right) items.

As expected, `Last` yields very low objective scores, and `TopRel` is only better for low λ values. `MSInc` / `MMInc` and `MSDispWin` / `MMDispWin` achieve diversification comparable to the baseline, with a slight advantage for our variants.

The baseline algorithm is unusable in practice to perform stream diversification, as mentioned above. `MSDispWin` and `MMDispWin` require on average 250 ms and 80 ms per step. `MSInc` and `MMInc` update the diverse set for each incoming item in virtually no time (< 1 ms time measure accuracy).

We conclude that the windows-based and the incremental variants efficiently allow for stream diversification. `MSInc` and `MMInc` have the advantage that diversification is immediately available for each new incoming item; this would be substantially more expensive for `MSDispWin` and `MMDispWin`.

6. CONCLUSIONS

Diversification is an important strategy to improve user satisfaction in the presence of ambiguous or broad queries. Due to their linear memory complexity, current approximation algorithms cannot be used to diversify large sets of items, or a large number of sets concurrently. Our new incremental approach is linear in computational complexity and constant in memory complexity w.r.t the number of items, and therefore also very well suited for very large sets. As a framework for incremental diversification, our approach is applicable to a wide range of diversification objectives. A thorough evaluation based on three real-world data sets shows that such an incremental computation exhibits the same quality as the baseline algorithm. On the other hand, computation and thus query response time is sped up by several orders of magnitude for sets of a few thousand items and more. In addition, our streaming-based computation enables very efficient diversification of queries over continuous data sources as well, such as news streams or tweets, opening up further applications of diversification.

7. ACKNOWLEDGMENTS

This work was supported by the EU FP7 Integrated Project LivingKnowledge (Contract No. 231126). Experiments were conducted on the high performance computing cluster of the Regional Computing Centre for Lower Saxony (RRZN).

8. REFERENCES

[1] R. Agrawal, S. Gollapudi, A. Halverson, and S. Ieong. Diversifying search results. In *WSDM*, 2009.

[2] S. Babu and J. Widom. Continuous queries over data streams. *SIGMOD Record*, 30(3):109–120, 2001.

[3] D. F. Barbieri, D. Braga, S. Ceri, E. D. Valle, and M. Grossniklaus. C-sparql: Sparql for continuous querying. In *WWW*, 2009.

[4] J. G. Carbonell and J. Goldstein. The use of MMR, diversity-based reranking for reordering documents and producing summaries. In *SIGIR*, 1998.

[5] H. Chen and D. R. Karger. Less is more: probabilistic models for retrieving fewer relevant documents. In *SIGIR*, 2006.

[6] J. Chen, D. J. DeWitt, F. Tian, and Y. Wang. NiagaraCQ: a scalable continuous query system for internet databases. In *ACM SIGMOD*, 2000.

[7] C. L. Clarke, M. Kolla, G. V. Cormack, O. Vechtomova, A. Ashkan, S. Büttcher, and I. MacKinnon. Novelty and diversity in information retrieval evaluation. In *SIGIR*, 2008.

[8] M. Drosou and E. Pitoura. Comparing diversity heuristics. Technical Report TR-2009-05, Comp. Sci. Department, University of Ioannina, Greece, 2009.

[9] M. Drosou and E. Pitoura. Diversity over continuous data. *IEEE Data Eng. Bull.*, 32(4):49–56, 2009.

[10] M. Drosou, K. Stefanidis, and E. Pitoura. Preference-aware publish/subscribe delivery with diversity. In *DEBS*, 2009.

[11] F. Giunchiglia. Managing Diversity in Knowledge. In *IEA/AIE 2006, LNAI 4031*, page 1, 2006.

[12] S. Gollapudi and A. Sharma. An axiomatic approach for result diversification. In *WWW*, 2009.

[13] J. R. Haritsa. The KNDN problem: A quest for unity in diversity. *IEEE Data Eng. Bull.*, 32(4):15–22, 2009.

[14] V. Hristidis, O. Valdivia, M. Vlachos, and P. S. Yu. A system for keyword search on textual streams. In *SDM*, 2007.

[15] U. Irmak, S. Mihaylov, T. Suel, S. Ganguly, and R. Izmailov. Efficient query subscription processing for prospective search engines. In *USENIX*, 2006.

[16] D. E. Knuth. *Sorting and Searching*, volume 3 of *The Art of Computer Programming*. Addison Wesley, 1973.

[17] D. G. McDonald and J. Dimmick. The conceptualization and measurement of diversity. *Communication Research*, 30(1):60–79, 2003.

[18] E. Minack, G. Demartini, and W. Nejdl. Current approaches to search result diversification. In *LivingWeb Workshop at ISWC*, 2009.

[19] G. Mishne and M. de Rijke. A study of blog search. In *ECIR*, 2006.

[20] T.-W. Ryu, , T. wan Ryu, and C. F. Eick. A unified similarity measure for attributes with set or bag of values. In *RSDMGrC*, 1998.

[21] R. L. T. Santos, C. Macdonald, and I. Ounis. Exploiting query reformulations for web search result diversification. In *WWW*, 2010.

[22] D. Skoutas, E. Minack, and W. Nejdl. Dealing with diversity in web search results. In *WebSci10*, 2010.

[23] A. Slivkins, F. Radlinski, and S. Gollapudi. Learning optimally diverse rankings over large document collections. In *ICML*, 2010.

[24] E. Vee, U. Srivastava, J. Shanmugasundaram, P. Bhat, and S. A. Yahia. Efficient computation of diverse query results. In *ICDE*, 2008.

[25] J. Wang and J. Zhu. Portfolio theory of information retrieval. In *SIGIR*, 2009.

[26] C. Yu, L. Lakshmanan, and S. Amer-Yahia. It takes variety to make a world: diversification in recommender systems. In *EDBT*, 2009.

[27] C. Zhai, W. W. Cohen, and J. D. Lafferty. Beyond independent relevance: methods and evaluation metrics for subtopic retrieval. In *SIGIR*, 2003.

[28] C. Zhai and J. D. Lafferty. A risk minimization framework for information retrieval. *Inf. Process. Manage.*, 42(1):31–55, 2006.

[29] C.-N. Ziegler, S. M. McNee, J. A. Konstan, and G. Lausen. Improving recommendation lists through topic diversification. In *WWW*, 2005.

Intent-Aware Search Result Diversif cation

Rodrygo L. T. Santos
rodrygo@dcs.gla.ac.uk

Craig Macdonald
craigm@dcs.gla.ac.uk

Iadh Ounis
ounis@dcs.gla.ac.uk

School of Computing Science
University of Glasgow
G12 8QQ Glasgow, UK

ABSTRACT

Search result diversification has gained momentum as a way to tackle ambiguous queries. An effective approach to this problem is to explicitly model the possible aspects underlying a query, in order to maximise the estimated relevance of the retrieved documents with respect to the different aspects. However, such aspects themselves may represent information needs with rather distinct intents (e.g., informational or navigational). Hence, a diverse ranking could benefit from applying intent-aware retrieval models when estimating the relevance of documents to different aspects. In this paper, we propose to diversify the results retrieved for a given query, by learning the appropriateness of different retrieval models for each of the aspects underlying this query. Thorough experiments within the evaluation framework provided by the diversity task of the TREC 2009 and 2010 Web tracks show that the proposed approach can significantly improve state-of-the-art diversification approaches.

Categories and Subject Descriptors

H.3.3 [**Information Storage and Retrieval**]: Information Search and Retrieval—*retrieval models*

General Terms

Algorithms, Experimentation, Performance

Keywords

Web Search, Relevance, Diversity

1. INTRODUCTION

User queries often carry some degree of ambiguity [38]. On the one hand, genuinely ambiguous queries (e.g., '*zeppelin*') have multiple *interpretations* (e.g., '*airship*', '*band*'). On the other hand, even those queries with a single, clearly defined interpretation might still be underspecified, as it is not clear which *aspects* of this interpretation the user is actually interested in (e.g., '*led zeppelin*'... '*website*'? '*downloads*'? '*biography*'? '*albums*'? '*reunion*'?) [13].

Search result diversification has recently gained attention as a means to tackle query ambiguity. Instead of trying to identify the 'correct' interpretation behind a query, the idea is to diversify the search results, in the hope that different users will find at least one of these results to be relevant to their information need [1]. Differently from the traditional assumption of independent document relevance [30], diversification approaches typically consider the relevance of a document in light of the other retrieved documents. For instance, once users have found the information they are seeking, it is questionable whether documents with the same (or very similar) information will still be of any use [13].

An effective approach to diversifying search results is to *explicitly* account for the various aspects[1] underlying an ambiguous query [1, 7, 33, 36]. By doing so, the problem becomes to select a ranking of documents that collectively provide the maximum relevance with respect to these different aspects. In a real scenario, however, the actual aspects of a query are not known, nor is the relevance of each retrieved document to each query aspect determined with certainty. Moreover, the relevance of a document to a query aspect may depend on the *intent*[2] underlying this aspect (e.g., informational or navigational [4, 31]). Additionally, different aspects could feasibly represent information needs with different intents. For instance, '*website*', '*downloads*', and '*biography*' arguably represent navigational, transactional, and informational aspects of the query '*led zeppelin*', respectively. Similarly, '*albums*' could exemplify a typed query aspect, representing an information need for a list of entities. In the same vein, '*reunion*' might denote a question-answering aspect of the query '*led zeppelin*', regarding whether the legendary rock band have any plans of reuniting in the near future.

Queries with different intents have been shown to benefit from different retrieval models [22]. Likewise, we hypothesise that explicit diversification approaches may benefit from accounting for the intents of different query aspects. For instance, relevance estimations with respect to the '*website*' aspect of the query '*led zeppelin*' could be arguably improved by applying a retrieval model suitable for navigational queries. In this paper, we propose a novel diversification approach, aimed at learning the appropriateness of

SIGIR'11, July 24–28, 2011, Beijing, China.

[1]Unless otherwise noted, through the rest of this paper, we refer to query '*interpretations*' and '*aspects*' indistinctly.

[2]Agrawal et al. [1] use '*intents*' in the sense of what we call '*interpretations*'. We believe our choice is more appropriate in light of the established nomenclature in the literature.

multiple intent-aware retrieval models for each aspect. As a result, the relevance of a document to multiple aspects—i.e., its diversity—can be estimated more effectively.

We thoroughly evaluate our approach in the context of the diversity task of the TREC 2009 and 2010 Web tracks [11, 12]. In particular, we investigate learning strategies that either select the most appropriate retrieval model or merge multiple retrieval models for each query aspect. The results of our investigations attest the effectiveness of both strategies within our proposed intent-aware approach for diversifying Web search results, with significant improvements on top of state-of-the-art diversification approaches.

The remainder of this paper is organised as follows. Section 2 describes related work on search result diversification and search intents. Section 3 further details our main contributions. Section 4 describes our approach for leveraging intent-aware models for diversification. Sections 5 and 6 detail the experimental setup and the evaluation of our approach. Finally, Section 7 presents our conclusions.

2. RELATED WORK

In this section, we provide background on the search result diversification problem and related approaches to this problem. We then set the grounds for our proposed approach by reviewing related work on the use of search intents.

2.1 Search Result Diversif cation

Most of the existing diversification approaches are somehow inspired by the work of Carbonell and Goldstein [5]. The basic idea of their Maximal Marginal Relevance (MMR) method is to iteratively select a document with the highest similarity to the query and lowest similarity to the already selected documents, in order to promote novelty. Subsequent implementations of this idea include the approach of Zhai et al. [41] to model relevance and novelty within a risk minimisation framework. In particular, they promote documents with highly divergent language models from those of the already selected documents. Chen and Karger [10] proposed a probabilistic approach to the related problem of finding at least one relevant result for a given query, by choosing documents under the assumption that those already chosen are not relevant to the query. More recently, Wang and Zhu [39] proposed to diversify a document ranking as a means to reduce the risk of overestimating its relevance. In their work, two documents are compared based on the correlation of their relevance scores.

By assuming that similar documents will cover similar aspects, the aforementioned approaches only consider the aspects underlying a query *implicitly*. An alternative approach consists of *explicitly* modelling these aspects [36]. For instance, Agrawal et al. [1] proposed the IA-Select algorithm for search result diversification. It employs a classification taxonomy over queries and documents to iteratively promote documents that share a high number of classes with the query, while demoting those documents with classes already well represented in the ranking. Similarly, Carterette and Chandar [7] proposed a probabilistic approach to maximise the coverage of the retrieved documents with respect to the aspects of a query, by modelling these aspects as topics identified from the top ranked documents. Recently, Santos et al. [33] introduced the xQuAD probabilistic framework for search result diversification, which explicitly represents different query aspects as 'sub-queries'. They defined a diversification objective based on the estimated relevance of documents to multiple sub-queries, as well as on the relative importance of each sub-query in light of the initial query.

Since our goal is to produce intent-aware relevance estimations given an explicit representation of query aspects, our approach is also set in the context of explicit diversification. Accordingly, in Section 6, we use both IA-Select [1] and xQuAD [33] as a basis for evaluating our approach. In particular, these two approaches represent the state-of-the-art in explicit search result diversification.

2.2 Intents in Information Retrieval

Different information retrieval tasks have benefited from taking into account the intent of a query (e.g., informational, navigational, or transactional [4, 31]). These approaches can be generally categorised based on whether or not they rely on the classification of queries into predefined intents.

Query intent detection approaches first classify a query with respect to a predefined set of intents. A retrieval model specifically trained for the predicted intent is then applied to retrieve documents for the query. For instance, Kang and Kim [22] showed that queries of different intents can benefit from the application of intent-specific retrieval models. A major shortcoming of this approach, however, is the limited accuracy of existing intent detection mechanisms [17].

Instead of classifying a query into a predefined target intent, an alternative is to identify similar queries from a training set, and then to apply a retrieval model appropriate for this set. This approach has an advantage over a classification of queries based on a fixed set of intents, as queries of the same intent often benefit from different retrieval models [17]. For example, Geng et al. [20] proposed an instance-based learning approach using k-nearest neighbour (k-NN) classification to improve Web search effectiveness. In their approach, a k-NN classifier is used to identify training queries similar to an unseen query. A retrieval model is then learned based on the identified queries and applied to the unseen query. A more general approach was proposed by Peng et al. [27]. In their work, multiple ranking functions are chosen from a pool of candidate functions, based on their performance on training queries similar to an unseen query.

Our approach is similar in spirit to the approaches of Kang and Kim [22], Geng et al. [20], and Peng et al. [27]. However, while these approaches focused on inferring the intent of a *query*, we target the problem of inferring the intent underlying different *aspects* of this query. Besides this difference in granularity, our intent-aware approach tackles a different search scenario, namely, search result diversification.

In a similar vein, Santos et al. [34] proposed a selective diversification approach, aimed at tailoring a diversification strategy to the ambiguity level of different queries. In particular, given an unseen query, their approach learns a trade-off between relevance and diversity, based on optimal trade-offs observed for similar training queries. As a result, their approach effectively determines when to diversify the results for an unseen query, and also by how much. Our proposed approach also differs from the approach of Santos et al. [34], in that ours focuses on selecting appropriate retrieval models for different query *aspects*, as opposed to the query itself. More importantly, their approach is orthogonal to ours. In essence, instead of determining *when* to diversify the results for a given query, we tackle the problem of *how* to diversify these results given the identified aspects of this query.

3. CONTRIBUTIONS OF THIS PAPER

The major contributions of this paper are:

1. A novel aspect intent-aware diversification approach, aimed at predicting, for each identified query aspect, the appropriateness of different retrieval models.
2. A thorough evaluation of the proposed approach within the standard experimentation paradigm of the diversity task of the TREC 2009 and 2010 Web tracks.

4. INTENT-AWARE SEARCH RESULT DIVERSIFICATION

As discussed in Sections 1 and 2, different aspects of an ambiguous query can have rather different intents. To illustrate this, consider topic #1 from the diversity task of the TREC 2009 Web track [11], as shown in Figure 1. In this example, different aspects of the query '*obama family tree*' are represented as a set of sub-topics, identified from the query log of a commercial search engine. Moreover, these sub-topics represent aspects with an informational ('inf') or a navigational ('nav') intent, as judged by TREC assessors.

```
<topic number="1" type="faceted">
  <query>obama family tree</query>
  <description>
    Find information on President Barack Obama's family history,
    including genealogy, national origins, places and dates of
    birth, etc.
  </description>
  <subtopic number="1" type="nav">
    Find the TIME magazine photo essay "Barack Obama's Family
    Tree".
  </subtopic>
  <subtopic number="2" type="inf">
    Where did Barack Obama's parents and grandparents come from?
  </subtopic>
  <subtopic number="3" type="inf">
    Find biographical information on Barack Obama's mother.
  </subtopic>
</topic>
```

Figure 1: TREC 2009 Web track, topic #1, along with its corresponding sub-topics.

Inspired by related work in Section 2.2, we hypothesise that diversification approaches can benefit from retrieval models targeted to the intents of different query aspects. For instance, for the query exemplified in Figure 1, a diversification approach could leverage a *navigational intent-aware model* for the first query aspect, and an *informational intent-aware model* for the second and third aspects.

In this work, we propose a supervised learning approach for estimating the appropriateness of multiple intent-aware retrieval models for each query aspect. Given a query q, our goal is to maximise the diversity of the retrieved documents with respect to the aspects underlying this query. Without loss of generality, following an explicit diversification strategy, we can quantify the diversity of a document d given a query q and the other retrieved documents $\mathcal{S}$ as the expected relevance of d with respect to the aspects of q, denoted $\mathcal{A}(q)$:

$$\mathrm{P}(d|\mathcal{S}, q) = \sum_{a \in \mathcal{A}(q)} \mathrm{P}(a|q)\,\mathrm{P}(d|\mathcal{S}, q, a), \qquad (1)$$

where $\mathrm{P}(a|q)$ captures the relative importance of each aspect a given the query q, and $\mathrm{P}(d|\mathcal{S}, q, a)$ denotes the probability of the document d being relevant to this aspect, given how well the documents in $\mathcal{S}$ already satisfy this aspect.

Equation (1) can be seen as a canonical formulation of the objective functions deployed by different explicit diversification approaches in the literature [34]. In particular, these approaches differ primarily in how they represent the set of aspects associated with a query, and in how they estimate the relevance of each document to every identified query aspect. For instance, Agrawal et al. [1] rely on the top-level categories from the Open Directory Project (ODP)[3] for representing query and document classes, and integrate relevance and classification scores for ranking documents. Santos et al. [33] exploit query reformulations from commercial search engines as representations of the different aspects of a query, and directly estimate the relevance of documents to these aspects. Our proposed approach is agnostic to any particular mechanism for generating explicit query aspect representations. Indeed, our only assumption is that different aspects may convey different user intents.

In the interest of keeping the description of our approach general, in the remainder of this section, we adopt an abstract view of aspects and intents.[4] In particular, to formalise our approach, we further derive Equation (1), by marginalising $\mathrm{P}(d|\mathcal{S}, q, a)$ over a target set of intents $\mathcal{I}$:

$$\mathrm{P}(d|q, \mathcal{S}) = \sum_{a \in \mathcal{A}(q)} \mathrm{P}(a|q) \sum_{i \in \mathcal{I}} \mathrm{P}(i|a)\,\mathrm{P}(d|\mathcal{S}, q, a, i), \qquad (2)$$

where $\mathrm{P}(i|a)$ denotes the probability that the aspect a of the initial query q conveys the intent i. Accordingly, $\mathrm{P}(d|\mathcal{S}, q, a, i)$ denotes the relevance of the document d in light of the other retrieved documents $\mathcal{S}$, the query q, the aspect a, and the intent i. Once again, without loss of generality, assuming that different aspects are equally probable (i.e., $\mathrm{P}(a|q) = \frac{1}{|\mathcal{A}(q)|}, \forall a \in \mathcal{A}(q)$),[5] our task becomes two-fold:

1. To infer the probability $\mathrm{P}(i|a)$ of each intent $i \in \mathcal{I}$ given a query aspect $a \in \mathcal{A}(q)$;
2. To learn an appropriate retrieval model $\mathrm{P}(d|\mathcal{S}, q, a, i)$ for each predicted intent $i \in \mathcal{I}$.

In Section 4.1, we propose a classification approach for the first task. For the second task, as described in Section 4.2, we resort to learning-to-rank.

4.1 Inferring the Query Aspect Intents

In order to infer the probability of different intents for a query aspect, we propose a linear classification approach. In particular, given a query aspect a, our goal is to estimate the probability of an intent $i \in \mathcal{I}$ as:

$$\mathrm{P}(i|a) = f(\mathbf{w} \cdot \mathbf{x}_a), \qquad (3)$$

where $\mathbf{x}_a$ is a feature vector representing the aspect a, and $\mathbf{w}$ is a weight vector, which is learned from labelled training data. The function f maps the dot product of the weight and feature vectors into the desired prediction outcome. Alternative regimes for instantiating the function f are described in Section 4.1.1. Section 4.1.2 describes our choices for labelling training data. Lastly, Section 4.1.3 defines the classification space considered in this paper, and describes the query aspect features leveraged for this classification task.

[3] `http://www.dmoz.org`

[4] A concrete instantiation of query aspects and their possible intents is discussed in Section 4.1.3.

[5] For alternatives on how to estimate the likelihood of different query aspects, we refer the reader to [33, 36].

4.1.1 Classification Regimes

We propose two alternative regimes for instantiating the function f in Equation (3): *model selection* and *model merging*. The model selection regime employs a hard classification approach [40]. In particular, this approach treats different intents as mutually exclusive, hence assigning each aspect a single (i.e., the most likely) intent. For instance, for a target set of intents $\mathcal{I} = \{i_1, i_2, i_3\}$, a possible selection outcome could be: $\text{P}(i_1|a) = 1, \text{P}(i_2|a) = 0, \text{P}(i_3|a) = 0$. In this example, the aspect a would be associated with its most likely intent, i_1, and only the retrieval model $\text{P}(d|\mathcal{S}, q, a, i_1)$ would have an impact on the estimated relevance of document d to the aspect a. This classification regime resembles the selective retrieval approaches described in Section 2.2, except that the most appropriate model is selected at the aspect level (as opposed to the query level).

Our second regime, model merging, provides a relaxed alternative to model selection. In particular, it deploys a soft classification approach, in order to obtain a full probability distribution over the considered intents [40]. For the above example, a possible outcome of the model merging classification could be $\text{P}(i_1|a) = 0.6, \text{P}(i_2|a) = 0.3, \text{P}(i_3|a) = 0.1$. In this case, the estimated relevance of a document d to the aspect a would be determined by a linear combination:

$$\begin{aligned}\text{P}(d|\mathcal{S}, q, a) = {} & 0.6 \times \text{P}(d|\mathcal{S}, q, a, i_1) \\ & + 0.3 \times \text{P}(d|\mathcal{S}, q, a, i_2) \\ & + 0.1 \times \text{P}(d|\mathcal{S}, q, a, i_3).\end{aligned}$$

Different classifiers can be deployed to implement both the model selection and model merging regimes. Further details about the specific classifiers that enable both regimes in our investigations are provided in Section 5.3.

4.1.2 Classification Labels

In order to determine the ground-truth intent for different query aspects, we investigate two alternatives. The first one is based on the direct judgement by humans, who base their assessment solely on the observed aspects. However, the differences between query aspects may go beyond their apparent characteristics. For instance, aspects with the same judged intent could still benefit from leveraging different retrieval models [17]. Additionally, judging the intent of different aspects may be costly for large training datasets.

To overcome these limitations, we propose a second alternative for automatically labelling training aspects. Given a training query q with aspects $\mathcal{A}(q)$ and a set of target intents $\mathcal{I}$, with $|\mathcal{A}| = k$ and $|\mathcal{I}| = p$, we devise an oracle selection mechanism. In particular, this oracle mechanism always chooses the best out of the p^k possible selections for the k aspects of q, according to a diversity evaluation metric (e.g., ERR-IA [9], or any of the metrics described in Section 5.4). Although estimating this oracle may be infeasible for large values of k, it can be easily estimated for most practical settings. For instance, the maximum number of aspects per query in the TREC 2009 and 2010 Web tracks is $k = 8$. Moreover, if many more aspects were available for a particular query, less plausible aspects could be discarded without much loss. Indeed, this is precisely what leading Web search engines do when displaying only the top suggestions for a user query, which have been shown to deliver an effective diversification performance [33]. Finally, it is worth noting that this entire labelling process is conducted offline.

4.1.3 Classification Features

So far, we have intentionally described our approach without a strict definition of the classification space. This abstract view of classification instances as query aspects demonstrates the generality of our proposed approach, and its applicability to different explicit diversification approaches in the literature (e.g., [1, 7, 33, 36]). In particular, our proposed approach is not bound to any particular query aspect representation. In fact, any aspect representation that portrays the multitude of information needs underlying an ambiguous query [35] is potentially applicable, as different information needs can convey different user intents.

Nonetheless, to enable our investigations in Section 6, we follow Santos et al. [33, 36] and adopt a concrete representation of query aspects as '*sub-queries*'. In particular, a sub-query can be seen as a keyword-based representation of the information need expressed by a query aspect. In our experiments, we consider two mechanisms for generating sub-queries, as described in Section 5.1. Additionally, limited by the TREC Web test collection used in our experiments [11, 12], we restrict the space of target intents to navigational and informational ones. Based on this representation of aspects and intents, and inspired by research on related query analysis tasks, we devise a large feature set for sub-query intent classification. In particular, these include features computed from the words in the sub-query itself, as well as from the top documents retrieved for this sub-query. In total, we devise 838 features, based on 21 different feature classes. These features are described on the left side of Table 1, and organised into three groups:

Query log features (LOG). Query logs provide valuable evidence for discriminating between informational and navigational intents. To exploit such evidence, we compute several sub-query features based on the 15-million query MSN Search 2006 Query Log. For instance, we count the raw frequency of sub-queries, as navigational sub-queries are generally more popular than informational ones. Likewise, informational sub-queries intuitively require more effort from the users while inspecting the retrieved results. We quantify this in terms of the number of examined results and the time spent in doing so, as well as the click entropy [15].

Query performance predictors (QPP). The intent of a sub-query may be reflected not only on the sub-query itself, but also on the documents retrieved for this sub-query. For instance, a low coherence of the top-retrieved documents could indicate a sub-query with an informational intent. This, in turn, can reflect on the performance of this sub-query when used in a retrieval system. To exploit this intuition, we build upon a large body of research on query performance prediction [6] and leverage both pre- and post-retrieval predictors as sub-query features. In particular, the former are solely based on statistics of the sub-query terms, while the latter also leverage information from the documents retrieved for the sub-query.

Taxonomy-based features (TAX). Informational needs are intuitively broader than navigational ones, in terms of the concepts they cover. To quantify this intuition, we devise different features based on concepts from two different taxonomies derived from Wikipedia: categories and named entities. For the latter, we consider entities of four types: people, organisations, products, and locations. In partic-

Sub-Query Features				Document Features			
Group	Feature Class	Description	Total	Group	Feature Class	Description	Total
LOG	ClickCount	No. of clicks	120	WM	BM25	BM25 score [25]	5
LOG	ClickEntropy	URL-level click entropy [15]	3	WM	DPH	DPH score [25]	5
LOG	HostEntropy	Host-level click entropy	2	WM	LM	LM score (Dirichlet) [25]	5
LOG	QueryFrequency	No. of occurrences	4	WM	PL2	PL2 score [25]	5
LOG	ResultCount	No. of examined results	3	WM	MQT	No. of matching query terms	5
LOG	SessionDuration	Session duration (in sec.)	3	FM	BM25F	BM25F score [25]	1
QPP	AvICTF	Pre-retrieval predictor [21]	1	FM	PL2F	PL2F score [25]	1
QPP	AvIDF	Pre-retrieval predictor [21]	1	DM	MRF	MRF proximity score [25]	8
QPP	AvPMI	Pre-retrieval predictor [21]	1	DM	pBiL	DFR pBiL proximity score [25]	8
QPP	ClarityScore	Post-retrieval predictor [19]	30	LA	Absorbing	Absorbing Model score [28]	1
QPP	EnIDF	Pre-retrieval predictor [21]	1	LA	Edgerecip	No. of reciprocal links [3]	1
QPP	Gamma	Pre-retrieval predictor [21]	2	LA	Inlinks	No. of inlinks	1
QPP	QueryDifficulty	Post-retrieval predictor [2]	30	LA	Outlinks	No. of outlinks	1
QPP	QueryFeedback	Post-retrieval predictor [42]	30	LA	InvPageRank	PageRank transposed score	2
QPP	QueryScope	Pre-retrieval predictor [21]	1	LA	PageRank	PageRank score [26]	1
QPP	TermCount	No. of terms	1	SP	SpamFusion	Spam likelihood [16]	1
QPP	TokenCount	No. of tokens	1	URL	URLDigits	No. of digits in domain and host	2
TAX	ConceptCosine	Cosine over concepts [37]	4	URL	URLComponents	No. of host/path/query components	3
TAX	ConceptCount	No. of concepts [34]	360	URL	URLLength	Length of host/path/query string	3
TAX	ConceptEntropy	Entropy over concepts [37]	120	URL	URLType	Root, subroot, path, file	1
TAX	DisambSenses	No. of disamb. senses [32]	120	URL	URLWiki	Whether URL is from Wikipedia	1
GRAND TOTAL			838				61

Table 1: All features used in this work. Sub-query features (left side) are used for inferring the intents of different query aspects. Document features (right side) are used to produce intent-aware learned models.

ular, we represent the documents retrieved for each sub-query in the space of the concepts from these different taxonomies.[6] Based on this representation, we compute various distributional features, such as the average number of retrieved concepts, the average distance between pairs of documents, and the concept entropy of the entire retrieved list. Additionally, we also quantify the number of ambiguous entities among the top documents retrieved for a sub-query. Our intuition is that the presence of such entities further indicates the broadness of the sub-query [37].

Most of these features are extracted in multiple variants. For instance, retrieval-based features are computed based on five different approaches, as implemented by the Terrier IR platform [25]: Okapi BM25, the Divergence From Randomness (DFR) DPH and PL2 models, a language modelling (LM) approach with Dirichlet smoothing, and a count of the number of matching query terms. Additionally, these features are estimated at six rank cutoffs: 1, 3, 5, 10, 50, and 100. Finally, distributional features (e.g., the number of concepts across the retrieved documents) are summarised using up to four different statistics: mean, standard deviation, median, and maximum. Altogether, these amount to the grand total of 838 features.

4.2 Learning Intent-Aware Retrieval Models

In Section 4.1.1, we proposed two regimes for inferring an intent distribution $P(i|a)$ for each aspect a. In this section, we propose a learning-to-rank approach for producing suitable intent-aware retrieval models for each intent of a.

4.2.1 Model Learning

In order to produce an intent-aware model $P(d|\mathcal{S}, q, a, i)$ for each intent i underlying the aspect a, we once again resort to machine learning. In particular, we deploy a large set of document features, and leave it to a learning-to-rank algorithm to generate retrieval models optimised for different intents. To achieve this goal, each model is learned using the entire feature set, but with a different training set of queries for each target intent. Given the intents considered in our investigation (i.e., informational and navigational), we use two intent-targeted query sets from the TREC 2009 Million Query track [8]. The first set contains 70 informational queries and the second set contains 70 navigational queries, as judged by TREC assessors. As a learning algorithm, we use Metzler's Automatic Feature Selection (AFS) [24]. In particular, AFS learns effective ranking models by directly optimising an IR evaluation metric. In our experiments, it is deployed to optimise mean average precision (MAP).

4.2.2 Document Features

To enable the generation of effective intent-aware retrieval models, we deploy a total of 61 document features, summarised on the right portion of Table 1, and organised into six groups: standard weighting models (WM), field-based models (FM), term dependence models (DM), link analysis (LA), spam (SP), and URL features. As these are all standard features traditionally used in the learning-to-rank literature [29],[7] we refer the interested reader to the descriptions and pointers provided in the table. In particular, each feature is computed for a sample of 5000 documents retrieved by the DFR DPH weighting model for each query. Standard weighting models and term dependence models are deployed with their commonly suggested parameter settings in the literature. Field-based models are trained through simulated annealing [23]. The remaining (query-independent) features are optimised using FLOE [18]. Finally, all feature scores are normalised to lie between 0 and 1 for each query.

Table 2 lists the top 10 features selected by AFS for each of our produced intent-aware models. For each feature, we also show its attained performance in terms of MAP when com-

[6]Category features are computed from documents retrieved from Wikipedia for each sub-query, while entity features are based on documents retrieved from the target collection.

[7]We leave the investigation of features that exploit the dependencies between d and the documents in $\mathcal{S}$ for the future.

	Informational		Navigational	
	Feature	MAP	Feature	MAP
1	DPH	0.2614	DPH	0.2110
2	URLDigits	0.2752	MRF (body)	0.2273
3	PL2 (title)	0.2819	BM25 (title)	0.2408
4	BM25F	0.2915	URLWiki	0.2517
5	pBiL (body)	0.2963	MQT	0.2592
6	pBiL (anchor)	0.2985	URLLength	0.2629
7	Edgerecip	0.3001	Absorbing	0.2666
8	LM (title)	0.3010	InvPageRank	0.2695
9	MQT (body)	0.3017	Inlinks	0.2718
10	MQT	0.3026	pBiL (body)	0.2738

Table 2: Top 10 selected features in the two intent-aware retrieval models used in this paper.

bined with the features selected before it. From the table, we observe that the top selected features are generally intuitive. For instance, DPH (which is used to generate the initial sample of documents for learning) is the top feature for both models. Likewise, as expected, various URL and link analysis features (e.g., URLWiki, URLLength, Absorbing, InvPageRank, Inlinks) are ranked high in the navigational model. Besides producing intuitive intent-aware models, we believe that our data-driven approach based on a large set of features provides a more robust alternative to hand-picking features traditionally associated with a particular intent.

4.3 Summary

In this section, we have introduced a novel supervised learning approach for diversifying the search results in light of the intents of different aspects of an ambiguous query. To enable our investigations in Section 6, we have instantiated our intent-aware diversification approach in light of two target aspect intents, namely, informational and navigational. Given these intents, we have described large feature sets for both inferring the intent distribution of different aspects (Section 4.1), as well as for learning the corresponding intent-aware retrieval models (Section 4.2). Although the choice of appropriate feature sets naturally depends on how learning instances (i.e., aspects) and labels (i.e., intents) are represented [40], it is worth reiterating that our approach is agnostic to these representations. While instantiating it for a different aspect representation or a different set of intents may require devising different features, no modification to the approach itself would be necessary. Moreover, although motivated by the learning tasks at hand, both feature sets in Table 1 comprise features deployed for a variety of different purposes in the literature. As a result, we believe they might be useful for deploying our approach with target intents beyond the two considered in our current investigations.

5. EXPERIMENTAL SETUP

In the next section, we investigate our intent-aware diversification approach proposed in Section 4. In particular, we aim to answer two main research questions:

1. Can we improve diversification performance with our intent-aware *model selection* regime?

2. Can we improve diversification performance with our intent-aware *model merging* regime?

These questions are investigated in Sections 6.1 and 6.2, respectively. In the remainder of this section, we detail the experimental setup that supports these investigations.

5.1 Collection, Queries, and Sub-Queries

Our analysis is conducted within the standard experimentation paradigm provided by the diversity task of the TREC 2009 and 2010 Web tracks [11, 12]—henceforth denoted WT09 and WT10 tasks, respectively. As a document collection, we consider the category-B ClueWeb09 dataset, as used in these tasks. This collection comprises 50 million English documents, aimed to represent the first tier of a commercial search engine index. In our experiments, we index this collection using Terrier [25], after applying Porter's English weak stemmer and without removing stopwords.

The WT09 and WT10 tasks comprise 50 and 48 queries, respectively. As mentioned in Section 4.1.3, for each of these 98 queries, we generate two sets of sub-queries, in order to provide alternative aspect representations for our investigations. The first sub-query set is based on the official sub-topics identified by TREC assessors for each of these queries. In particular, each WT09 query has an average of 3.54 informational and 1.32 navigational aspects, as judged by TREC assessors. For the WT10 queries, these numbers become 2.84 and 1.50, respectively. As TREC only provides a natural language description for each sub-topic, we obtain a shorter, keyword-like version using Amazon's Mechanical Turk. This step was necessary to make these sub-topics better resemble real Web search requests, so as to enable their matching in our query log. Note that this procedure by no means interfere with our conclusions, as these keyword-like sub-topics are uniformly deployed for all tested approaches.

Using the official TREC Web track sub-topics as a sub-query set has two main advantages. Firstly, as discussed in Section 4.1.2, they provide judged intent labels for each sub-query, which can be contrasted to our proposed performance-oriented labelling of training data. Secondly and most important, they provide a controlled environment for evaluating the effectiveness of our approach while isolating the impact of any particular aspect representation. In addition to this 'ground-truth' sub-query set, we also evaluate our approach using an alternative sub-query set. Following Santos et al. [33], for each of the 98 queries, we obtain up to 13 query suggestions from a commercial search engine.

5.2 Diversif cation Approaches

In Section 6, we apply our intent-aware model selection and model merging regimes to two diversification approaches: IA-Select [1] and xQuAD [33]. In particular, both approaches instantiate the general explicit diversification objective described in Equation (1), and hence can directly leverage our intent-aware aspect relevance estimations. Additionally, as discussed in Section 2.1, these approaches are representative of the state-of-the-art in search result diversification. Indeed, a variant of xQuAD was among the top performing approaches in the diversity task of both TREC 2009 and 2010 [11, 12]. In our investigations, both IA-Select and xQuAD diversify the top 1000 documents retrieved by DPH.

5.3 Classif cation Approaches

In Section 4.1, we introduced two regimes for leveraging the inferred intents of different aspects: model selection and model merging. The model selection regime builds upon a hard classification of intents. To enable this regime, we deploy two alternative classifiers. Firstly, we train a support vector machine (SVM) classifier with a polynomial kernel through a sequential minimal optimisation [40]. Our second

		Regime	ERR-IA@20	α-nDCG@20	NRBP	MAP-IA
	DPH		0.1607	0.2097	0.1318	0.0442
WT09 sub-topics	+IA-Select	UNI(INF)	0.2020	0.2472	0.1733	0.0634
	+IA-Select	UNI(NAV)	0.2155	0.2634	0.1885	0.0652
	+IA-Select	SEL(ORA,JUDG)	**0.2166** (7.2,0.5)	**0.2623** (6.1,-0.4)	**0.1859** (7.3,-1.4)	0.0641 (1.1,-1.7)
	+IA-Select	SEL(LOG,JUDG)	0.2090 (3.5,-3.0)	0.2548 (3.1,-3.3)	0.1799 (3.8,-4.6)	0.0657 (3.6,0.8)
	+IA-Select	SEL(SVM,JUDG)	0.2126 (5.2,-1.3)	0.2594 (4.9,-1.5)	0.1834 (5.8,-2.7)	**0.0664** (4.7,1.8)
	+IA-Select	SEL(ORA,PERF)	**0.2782** (37.7▲,29.1▲)	**0.3134** (26.8▲,19.0▲)	**0.2562** (47.8▲,35.9▲)	**0.0724** (14.2▲,11.0▲)
	+IA-Select	SEL(LOG,PERF)	0.2394 (18.5△,11.1△)	0.2780 (12.5△,5.5)	0.2155 (24.4△,14.3△)	0.0688 (8.5▲,5.5)
	+IA-Select	SEL(SVM,PERF)	0.2289 (13.3,6.2)	0.2713 (9.7,3.0)	0.2036 (17.5,8.0)	0.0677 (6.8△,3.8)
	+xQuAD	UNI(INF)	0.1945	0.2423	0.1664	0.0565
	+xQuAD	UNI(NAV)	0.2219	0.2661	0.1954	0.0665
	+xQuAD	SEL(ORA,JUDG)	0.2131 (9.6,-4.0)	**0.2602** (7.4△,-2.2)	0.1826 (9.7,-6.6)	0.0643 (13.8△,-3.3)
	+xQuAD	SEL(LOG,JUDG)	0.2094 (7.7,-5.6)	0.2542 (4.9,-4.5)	0.1801 (8.2,-7.8)	0.0631 (11.7,-5.1)
	+xQuAD	SEL(SVM,JUDG)	**0.2153** (10.7,-3.0)	0.2594 (7.1,-2.5)	**0.1868** (12.3,-4.4)	**0.0671** (18.8,0.9)
	+xQuAD	SEL(ORA,PERF)	**0.2650** (36.2▲,19.4▲)	**0.3025** (24.8▲,13.7▲)	**0.2413** (45.0▲,23.5▲)	0.0688 (21.8▲,3.5▲)
	+xQuAD	SEL(LOG,PERF)	0.2395 (23.1▲,7.9△)	0.2784 (14.9▲,4.6△)	0.2153 (29.4▲,10.2△)	0.0689 (21.9△,3.6)
	+xQuAD	SEL(SVM,PERF)	0.2370 (21.9▲,6.8)	0.2754 (13.7△,3.5)	0.2125 (27.7▲,8.8)	**0.0694** (22.8▲,4.4)
Query suggestions	+IA-Select	UNI(INF)	0.1944	0.2378	0.1676	0.0553
	+IA-Select	UNI(NAV)	0.1978	0.2503	0.1662	0.0610
	+IA-Select	SEL(ORA,PERF)	**0.2736** (40.7▲,38.3▲)	**0.3083** (29.6▲,23.2▲)	**0.2518** (50.2▲,51.5▲)	**0.0687** (24.2▲,12.6▲)
	+IA-Select	SEL(LOG,PERF)	0.2063 (6.1,4.3)	0.2548 (7.1,1.8)	0.1756 (4.8,5.7)	0.0631 (14.1▲,3.4△)
	+IA-Select	SEL(SVM,PERF)	0.2085 (7.3,5.4)	0.2560 (7.7,2.3)	0.1790 (6.8,7.7)	0.0625 (13.0,2.5△)
	+xQuAD	UNI(INF)	0.1766	0.2292	0.1436	0.0545
	+xQuAD	UNI(NAV)	0.2003	0.2485	0.1723	0.0626
	+xQuAD	SEL(ORA,PERF)	**0.2620** (48.4▲,30.8▲)	**0.2985** (30.2▲,20.1▲)	**0.2384** (66.0▲,38.4▲)	**0.0687** (26.1▲,9.7▲)
	+xQuAD	SEL(LOG,PERF)	0.2051 (16.1▲,2.4)	0.2526 (10.2△,1.6)	0.1754 (22.1△,1.8)	0.0636 (16.7▲,1.6)
	+xQuAD	SEL(SVM,PERF)	0.2042 (15.6△,1.9)	0.2526 (10.2,1.6)	0.1743 (21.4△,1.2)	0.0628 (15.2△,0.3)
	WT09 best (uogTrDYCcsB) [11]		0.1922	0.3081	0.1617	0.0592

Table 3: Diversification performance of IA-Select and xQuAD using informational or navigational models uniformly (UNI) or selectively (SEL) according to the WT09 topics, with the WT10 topics used for training.

classifier performs a multinomial logistic regression with a ridge estimator [40]. In both cases, the single most likely intent is chosen for each aspect, in a typical selective fashion. In order to enable our second regime, model merging, we fit the output of the SVM classifier to a logistic regression model, hence obtaining a full probability distribution over intents for each aspect underlying the query [40]. In order to cope with the high dimensionality of our sub-query feature set, classification is performed after a dimensionality reduction via principal component analysis [40]. All classification tasks are performed using the Weka suite.[8]

5.4 Evaluation and Training Procedure

We report our results based on the official evaluation metrics in the diversity task of the TREC 2010 Web track [12]: ERR-IA [9], α-nDCG [13], NRBP [14], and MAP-IA [1]. The first three metrics implement a cascade user model, which penalises redundancy by assuming an increasing probability that users will stop inspecting the results as they find their desired information. The fourth metric is based on a simpler model, which rewards a high coverage of query aspects, without directly penalising redundancy.

Our evaluation ensures a complete separation between training and test settings. In particular, we use the WT09 and WT10 queries interchangeably as training and test, in a cross-year evaluation fashion (i.e., we train on WT09 and test on WT10, and vice versa). This training procedure renders our results on the WT10 queries directly comparable to those of participant systems in TREC 2010. For the reported results on the WT09 queries, however, we note that TREC 2009 participant systems naturally did not have access to WT10 queries for training. This training procedure is used for the classification approaches described in Section 5.3, as well as for xQuAD's diversification trade-off parameter λ [33]. As for IA-Select, it is a parameter-free diversification approach, and hence requires no training.

[8]http://www.cs.waikato.ac.nz/ml/weka/

6. EXPERIMENTAL EVALUATION

In this section, we evaluate our intent-aware diversification approach, in order to answer the two research questions stated in Section 5. In particular, Section 6.1 investigates the effectiveness of our *model selection* regime, while Section 6.2 analyses the effectiveness of the *model merging* regime. Both regimes were described in Section 4.1.1.

6.1 Intent-Aware Model Selection

Our primary goal in this experiment is to assess the effectiveness of our model selection regime for search result diversification. As described in Section 4.1.1, this regime selects the most likely between an informational and a navigational intent-aware retrieval model for each aspect. As a baseline, we consider a simple regime that uniformly deploys one of the informational or navigational models for all aspects, regardless of the intents of these aspects. To validate our findings, as described in Section 5.2, we test both our model selection regime as well as the baseline uniform regime applied to two diversification approaches: IA-Select and xQuAD. Additionally, these diversification approaches are deployed using two different aspect representations: the official TREC Web track sub-topics and query suggestions from a search engine, as discussed in Section 5.1. Moreover, we test variants of our model selection regime. Each variant is denoted SEL($\mathcal{C}$,$\mathcal{L}$), where $\mathcal{C}$ and $\mathcal{L}$ denote a classifier and a set of classification training labels, respectively. In particular, $\mathcal{C}$ can be one of three classifiers: an oracle (ORA), which simulates a perfect classification accuracy, and the logistic regression (LOG) and support vector machine (SVM)

		Regime	ERR-IA@20	α-nDCG@20	NRBP	MAP-IA
	DPH		0.1952	0.2620	0.1509	0.0469
WT10 sub-topics	+IA-Select	UNI(INF)	0.2485	0.3261	0.2011	0.0717
	+IA-Select	UNI(NAV)	0.2866	0.3465	0.2490	0.0729
	+IA-Select	SEL(ORA,JUDG)	0.2829 (13.8,-1.3)	0.3496 (7.2,0.9)	0.2428 (20.7,-2.5)	**0.0763** (6.4,4.7)
	+IA-Select	SEL(LOG,JUDG)	0.2797 (12.6,-2.4)	0.3442 (5.6,-0.7)	0.2396 (19.1,-3.8)	0.0730 (1.8,0.1)
	+IA-Select	SEL(SVM,JUDG)	**0.2897** (16.6△,1.1)	**0.3535** (8.4,2.0)	**0.2485** (23.6△,-0.2)	0.0750 (4.6,2.9)
	+IA-Select	SEL(ORA,PERF)	**0.3791** (52.6▲,32.3▲)	**0.4228** (29.7▲,22.0▲)	**0.3491** (73.6▲,40.2▲)	**0.0859** (19.8▲,17.8▲)
	+IA-Select	SEL(LOG,PERF)	0.3117 (25.4▲,8.8▲)	0.3710 (13.8▲,7.1▲)	0.2734 (36.0▲,9.8△)	0.0773 (7.8,6.0△)
	+IA-Select	SEL(SVM,PERF)	0.3044 (22.5▲,6.2)	0.3638 (11.6△,5.0)	0.2667 (32.6▲,7.1)	0.0765 (6.7,4.9)
	+xQuAD	UNI(INF)	0.2472	0.3241	0.2007	0.0715
	+xQuAD	UNI(NAV)	0.2905	0.3479	0.2535	0.0754
	+xQuAD	SEL(ORA,JUDG)	0.2699 (9.2,-7.1)	0.3408 (5.2,-2.0)	0.2245 (11.9,-11.4)	0.0782 (9.4,3.7)
	+xQuAD	SEL(LOG,JUDG)	0.2708 (9.5,-6.8)	0.3346 (3.2,-3.8)	0.2333 (16.2,-8.0)	0.0743 (3.9,-1.5)
	+xQuAD	SEL(SVM,JUDG)	**0.2913** (17.8△,0.3)	**0.3512** (8.4,0.9)	**0.2546** (26.9△,0.4)	**0.0793** (10.9,5.2)
	+xQuAD	SEL(ORA,PERF)	**0.3616** (46.3▲,24.5▲)	**0.4119** (27.1▲,18.4▲)	**0.3294** (64.1▲,29.9▲)	**0.0864** (20.8▲,14.6▲)
	+xQuAD	SEL(LOG,PERF)	0.3090 (25.0▲,6.4)	0.3664 (13.1△,5.3)	0.2726 (35.8▲,7.5)	0.0791 (10.6,4.9)
	+xQuAD	SEL(SVM,PERF)	0.3098 (25.3▲,6.6)	0.3680 (13.5△,5.8)	0.2707 (34.9▲,6.8)	0.0798 (11.6△,5.8)
Query suggestions	+IA-Select	UNI(INF)	0.2468	0.3135	0.2053	0.0652
	+IA-Select	UNI(NAV)	0.2826	0.3419	0.2454	0.0677
	+IA-Select	SEL(ORA,PERF)	**0.3677** (49.0▲,30.1▲)	**0.4174** (33.1▲,22.1▲)	**0.3343** (62.8▲,36.2▲)	**0.0774** (18.7▲,14.3▲)
	+IA-Select	SEL(LOG,PERF)	0.2942 (19.2▲,4.1)	0.3523 (12.4△,3.0)	0.2575 (25.4△,4.9)	0.0715 (9.7▲,5.6△)
	+IA-Select	SEL(SVM,PERF)	0.2945 (19.3▲,4.2)	0.3530 (12.6▲,3.2)	0.2586 (26.0▲,5.4)	0.0722 (10.7△,6.6△)
	+xQuAD	UNI(INF)	0.2456	0.3110	0.2025	0.0600
	+xQuAD	UNI(NAV)	0.2579	0.3211	0.2174	0.0597
	+xQuAD	SEL(ORA,PERF)	**0.3554** (44.7▲,37.8▲)	**0.4078** (31.1▲,27.0▲)	**0.3210** (58.5▲,47.7▲)	**0.0768** (28.0▲,28.6▲)
	+xQuAD	SEL(LOG,PERF)	0.2743 (11.7△,6.4)	0.3375 (8.5△,5.1)	0.2349 (16.0△,8.0)	0.0716 (19.3▲,19.9▲)
	+xQuAD	SEL(SVM,PERF)	0.2805 (14.2▲,8.8△)	0.3435 (10.5△,7.0)	0.2418 (19.4▲,11.2)	0.0730 (21.7▲,22.3▲)
	WT10 best (uogTrB67xS) [12]		0.2981	0.4178	0.2616	0.0737

Table 4: Diversification performance of IA-Select and xQuAD using informational or navigational models uniformly (UNI) or selectively (SEL) according to the WT10 topics, with the WT09 topics used for training.

classifiers described in Section 5.3. As for the classification labels $\mathcal{L}$, as described in Section 4.1.2, we consider both human judgements (JUDG) as well as the selection with best diversification performance (PERF) on the training data.

Tables 3 and 4 compare the aforementioned variants of our model selection regime to the baseline uniform regime on the WT09 and WT10 queries, respectively, in terms of the four metrics described in Section 5.4: ERR-IA@20, α-nDCG@20, NRBP, and MAP-IA. In parentheses, we show the percent improvement of each variant of our model selection regime compared to the uniform regime that uses the informational (UNI(INF)) or the navigational (UNI(NAV)) model, respectively. Significant improvements are measured by the Wilcoxon signed-rank test. In particular, the symbols ▲ (▼) and △ (▽) denote a significant increase (decrease) at the $p < 0.01$ and $p < 0.05$ levels, respectively. Lastly, the bottom row in Tables 3 and 4 shows the performance of the top performing category-B system in the WT09 and WT10 tasks [11, 12], respectively, hence providing a further reference value for evaluating our intent-aware approach.

From Tables 3 and 4, we first note that the uniform application of an informational or a navigational model provides a strong baseline performance. The uniform application of the navigational model, in particular, performs at least comparably to the best performing TREC system in both the WT09 and WT10 tasks. To see whether our model selection regime can improve upon this strong baseline, we first look at the performance of this regime using an oracle classifier. The results show that a massive improvement can be attained by selecting the most appropriate model for each aspect (as opposed to uniformly using a single model for all aspects) for both IA-Select and xQuAD, when the performance-oriented labels (PERF) are used for training. On the WT09 queries (Table 3), compared to the strongest uniform setting (i.e., UNI(NAV)) in terms of ERR-IA@20, improvements can be as high as 29.1% for IA-Select and 19.4% for xQuAD using the Web track sub-topics as sub-queries, and are always significant. When using query suggestions, the potential improvements are 38.3% and 30.8%, respectively. On the WT10 queries (Table 4), similar figures are observed: 32.3% and 24.5% gain for IA-Select and xQuAD, respectively, using the Web track sub-topics; 30.1% and 37.8% using query suggestions. Once again, all improvements are statistically significant. Human judgements, in contrast, provide a supotimal labelling criterion, as denoted by the lower performance attained when using the JUDG labels. Indeed, even an oracle classifier, which always choses the correct intent according to these judgements (i.e., the SEL(ORA,JUDG) regime), cannot improve over applying the navigational model uniformly. As discussed in Section 4.1.2, this further confirms our intuition that the appropriateness of an intent-aware retrieval model for a given aspect cannot be effectively judged purely on the basis of the apparent characteristics of this aspect.

Besides showing a strong potential for improving diversification performance, as demonstrated using an oracle classifier (i.e., the SEL(ORA,PERF) regime), our intent-aware approach is also effective in a practical deployment based on standard classifiers. Indeed, Tables 3 and 4 show that our model selection regime using both logistic regression (LOG) and support vector machine (SVM) classifiers with PERF labels always improves compared to a uniform regime, often significantly. For instance, on the WT09 queries (Table 3) and considering the Web track sub-topics as aspect representations, compared to the stronger UNI(NAV) baseline, improvements in terms of ERR-IA@20 are as high as 11.1% for IA-Select (SEL(LOG,PERF)) and 7.9% for xQuAD (SEL(LOG,PERF)). On the WT10 queries (Table 4), improvements are as high as 8.8% for IA-Select (SEL(LOG,PERF))

		Regime	ERR-IA@20	α-nDCG@20	NRBP	MAP-IA
WT09	DPH		0.1607	0.2097	0.1318	0.0442
	+IA-Select	SEL(SVM,JUDG)	0.2126	0.2594	0.1834	0.0664
	+IA-Select	MRG(SVM,JUDG)	**0.2224** (4.6)	**0.2661** (2.6)	**0.1930** (5.2)	**0.0670** (0.9)
	+IA-Select	SEL(SVM,PERF)	**0.2289**	**0.2713**	**0.2036**	0.0677
	+IA-Select	MRG(SVM,PERF)	0.2206 (-3.6)	0.2644 (-2.5)	0.1922 (-5.6)	**0.0681** (0.6)
	+xQuAD	SEL(SVM,JUDG)	0.2153	0.2594	0.1868	0.0671
	+xQuAD	MRG(SVM,JUDG)	**0.2212** (2.7)	**0.2638** (1.7)	**0.1936** (3.6)	**0.0676** (0.7)
	+xQuAD	SEL(SVM,PERF)	0.2370	0.2754	**0.2125**	**0.0694**
	+xQuAD	MRG(SVM,PERF)	**0.2371** (0.0)	**0.2759** (0.2)	0.2117 (-0.4)	0.0692 (-0.3)
WT10	DPH		0.1952	0.2620	0.1509	0.0469
	+IA-Select	SEL(SVM,JUDG)	0.2897	0.3535	0.2485	0.0750
	+IA-Select	MRG(SVM,JUDG)	**0.2946** (1.7▵)	**0.3579** (1.2▵)	**0.2537** (2.1▵)	**0.0755** (0.7)
	+IA-Select	SEL(SVM,PERF)	0.3044	0.3638	0.2667	0.0765
	+IA-Select	MRG(SVM,PERF)	**0.3069** (0.8)	**0.3663** (0.7)	**0.2690** (0.9)	**0.0769** (0.5)
	+xQuAD	SEL(SVM,JUDG)	0.2913	0.3512	0.2546	0.0793
	+xQuAD	MRG(SVM,JUDG)	**0.2960** (1.6)	**0.3544** (0.9)	**0.2594** (1.9)	**0.0798** (0.6)
	+xQuAD	SEL(SVM,PERF)	**0.3098**	**0.3680**	**0.2707**	0.0798
	+xQuAD	MRG(SVM,PERF)	0.2997 (-3.3)	0.3592 (-2.4)	0.2622 (-3.1)	**0.0819** (2.6)

Table 5: Diversification performance of IA-Select and xQuAD using informational or navigational models selectively (SEL) or through merging (MRG). WT09 and WT10 results are shown on the top and bottom halves, respectively. As in Tables 3 and 4, WT09 results are trained on WT10 topics, and vice versa.

and 6.6% for xQuAD (SEL(SVM,PERF)). Similar improvements across the other reported metrics are consistently observed. When query suggestions are used as aspect representations, although improvements are less pronounced, they are consistent and can still be significant.

Overall, the results in this section answer our first research question, by showing that diversification performance can be significantly improved by leveraging the most appropriate intent-aware retrieval model for each query aspect. Our model selection regime using performance-oriented classification labels is particularly effective, significantly improving upon a uniform regime comparable to the top performing systems of the TREC 2009 and 2010 Web tracks [11, 12]. Furthermore, the consistency of our observations for two state-of-the-art diversification approaches and according to multiple evaluation metrics attests the robustness of the model selection regime. In the next section, we contrast this regime against the alternative model merging regime.

6.2 Intent-Aware Model Merging

After demonstrating the effectiveness of selecting a single model for each query aspect, in this experiment, we investigate whether deploying a model merging regime could bring further improvements. For this investigation, we focus our attention to the TREC Web track sub-topics as an aspect representation. As discussed in Section 5.1, this representation allows for assessing the effectiveness of our merging regime across the two proposed training labelling alternatives, JUDG and PERF. The results based on query suggestions using PERF labels lead to identical conclusions and are hence omitted for brevity. In particular, Table 5 shows the diversification performance of IA-Select and xQuAD under the model merging regime (MRG), in contrast to their performance under the model selection regime (SEL), which serves as our baseline in this investigation. Similarly to Tables 3 and 4, percent differences between these two regimes are shown in parentheses, alongside one of the aforementioned symbols to denote the significance (or lack thereof) of such differences. As discussed in Section 5.3, both regimes are based on predictions made by an SVM classifier. In particular, the model merging regime is enabled by fitting the SVM predictions to a logistic regression model.

From Table 5, we observe that the model merging regime can improve upon the model selection regime in most cases, particularly on the WT10 queries (bottom half of Table 5). However, the merging regime can also underperform compared to the selection regime, when PERF labels are used for IA-Select and xQuAD, on WT09 and WT10, respectively. Nevertheless, significant differences are only observed when IA-Select is deployed under the MRG(SVM,JUDG) regime on the WT10 queries. These results answer our second research question, by showing that merging multiple intent-aware models can be at least as effective as selecting the single most likely model. Moreover, we believe that the merging regime can offer additional benefits for an intent-aware diversification. For one, it can help attenuate the harm of selecting the wrong model for a particular sub-query. Additionally, it provides a natural upper-bound for the selection regime. Indeed, model selection is a special instance of model merging, with a mutually exclusive probability distribution.

7. CONCLUSIONS

In this paper, we have introduced a novel intent-aware approach for search result diversification. Given the possible intents underlying the aspects of a query, our approach learns the appropriateness of retrieval models targeted to each of these intents. These models are then leveraged selectively or combined in a merging fashion in order to refine the estimation of the relevance of the retrieved documents with respect to each query aspect. In particular, our approach builds upon a general explicit diversification model, which makes it seamlessly deployable by existing approaches in the literature. Indeed, thorough experiments in the context of the TREC 2009 and 2010 Web tracks demonstrate that our approach is general and significantly improves the effectiveness of two state-of-the-art diversification approaches.

Our data-driven approach for learning both intent-aware retrieval models and their appropriateness for a given aspect opens up promising directions. In particular, the full potential of our approach could be further exploited by building upon a larger pool of intent-aware retrieval models (e.g., with, say, a transactional model [4]), as well as features capturing dependencies between the retrieved documents.

8. REFERENCES

[1] R. Agrawal, S. Gollapudi, A. Halverson, and S. Ieong. Diversifying search results. In *WSDM*, pages 5–14, 2009.

[2] G. Amati, C. Carpineto, G. Romano, and F. U. Bordoni. Query difficulty, robustness and selective application of query expansion. In *ECIR*, pages 127–137, 2004.

[3] L. Becchetti, C. Castillo, D. Donato, S. Leonardi, and R. Baeza-Yates. Link-based characterization and detection of Web spam. In *AIRWeb*, 2006.

[4] A. Broder. A taxonomy of Web search. *SIGIR Forum*, 36(2):3–10, 2002.

[5] J. Carbonell and J. Goldstein. The use of MMR, diversity-based reranking for reordering documents and producing summaries. In *SIGIR*, pages 335–336, 1998.

[6] D. Carmel and E. Yom-Tov. Estimating the query difficulty for information retrieval. In *SIGIR*, page 911, 2010.

[7] B. Carterette and P. Chandar. Probabilistic models of ranking novel documents for faceted topic retrieval. In *CIKM*, pages 1287–1296, 2009.

[8] B. Carterette, V. Pavluz, H. Fangx, and E. Kanoulas. Million Query track 2009 overview. In *TREC*, 2009.

[9] O. Chapelle, D. Metlzer, Y. Zhang, and P. Grinspan. Expected reciprocal rank for graded relevance. In *CIKM*, pages 621–630, 2009.

[10] H. Chen and D. R. Karger. Less is more: Probabilistic models for retrieving fewer relevant documents. In *SIGIR*, pages 429–436, 2006.

[11] C. L. A. Clarke, N. Craswell, and I. Soboroff. Overview of the TREC 2009 Web track. In *TREC*, 2009.

[12] C. L. A. Clarke, N. Craswell, I. Soboroff, and G. V. Cormack. Overview of the TREC 2010 Web track. In *TREC*, 2010.

[13] C. L. A. Clarke, M. Kolla, G. V. Cormack, O. Vechtomova, A. Ashkan, S. Büttcher, and I. MacKinnon. Novelty and diversity in information retrieval evaluation. In *SIGIR*, pages 659–666, 2008.

[14] C. L. A. Clarke, M. Kolla, and O. Vechtomova. An effectiveness measure for ambiguous and underspecified queries. In *ICTIR*, pages 188–199, 2009.

[15] P. Clough, M. Sanderson, M. Abouammoh, S. Navarro, and M. Paramita. Multiple approaches to analysing query diversity. In *SIGIR*, pages 734–735, 2009.

[16] G. V. Cormack, M. D. Smucker, and C. L. A. Clarke. Efficient and effective spam filtering and re-ranking for large Web datasets. *Inf. Retr.*, 2011.

[17] N. Craswell and D. Hawking. Overview of the TREC 2004 Web track. In *TREC*, 2004.

[18] N. Craswell, S. Robertson, H. Zaragoza, and M. Taylor. Relevance weighting for query independent evidence. In *SIGIR*, pages 416–423, 2005.

[19] S. Cronen-Townsend, Y. Zhou, and W. B. Croft. Predicting query performance. In *SIGIR*, pages 299–306, 2002.

[20] X. Geng, T.-Y. Liu, T. Qin, A. Arnold, H. Li, and H.-Y. Shum. Query dependent ranking using k-nearest neighbor. In *SIGIR*, pages 115–122, 2008.

[21] B. He and I. Ounis. Query performance prediction. *Inf. Syst.*, 31(7):585–594, 2006.

[22] I.-H. Kang and G. Kim. Query type classification for Web document retrieval. In *SIGIR*, pages 64–71, 2003.

[23] S. Kirkpatrick, C. D. Gelatt, and M. P. Vecchi. Optimization by simulated annealing. *Science*, 220(4598):671–680, 1983.

[24] D. A. Metzler. Automatic feature selection in the Markov random field model for information retrieval. In *CIKM*, pages 253–262, 2007.

[25] I. Ounis, G. Amati, V. Plachouras, B. He, C. Macdonald, and C. Lioma. Terrier: A high performance and scalable information retrieval platform. In *SIGIR, OSIR Workshop*, 2006.

[26] L. Page, S. Brin, R. Motwani, and T. Winograd. The PageRank citation ranking: Bringing order to the Web. Technical Report 1999-66, Stanford, 1999.

[27] J. Peng, C. Macdonald, and I. Ounis. Learning to select a ranking function. In *ECIR*, pages 114–126, 2010.

[28] V. Plachouras, I. Ounis, and G. Amati. The static absorbing model for the Web. *J. Web Eng.*, 4(2):165–186, 2005.

[29] T. Qin, T.-Y. Liu, J. Xu, and H. Li. LETOR: A benchmark collection for research on learning to rank for information retrieval. *Inf. Retr.*, 13(4):346–374, 2010.

[30] S. E. Robertson. The probability ranking principle in IR. *J. Doc.*, 33(4):294–304, 1977.

[31] D. E. Rose and D. Levinson. Understanding user goals in Web search. In *WWW*, pages 13–19, 2004.

[32] M. Sanderson. Ambiguous queries: Test collections need more sense. In *SIGIR*, pages 499–506, 2008.

[33] R. L. T. Santos, C. Macdonald, and I. Ounis. Exploiting query reformulations for Web search result diversification. In *WWW*, pages 881–890, 2010.

[34] R. L. T. Santos, C. Macdonald, and I. Ounis. Selectively diversifying Web search results. In *CIKM*, pages 1179–1188, 2010.

[35] R. L. T. Santos and I. Ounis. Diversifying for multiple information needs. In *ECIR, DDR Workshop*, pages 37–41, 2011.

[36] R. L. T. Santos, J. Peng, C. Macdonald, and I. Ounis. Explicit search result diversification through sub-queries. In *ECIR*, pages 87–99, 2010.

[37] R. Song, Z. Luo, J.-Y. Nie, Y. Yu, and H.-W. Hon. Identification of ambiguous queries in Web search. *Inf. Process. Manage.*, 45(2):216–229, 2009.

[38] K. Spärck-Jones, S. E. Robertson, and M. Sanderson. Ambiguous requests: Implications for retrieval tests, systems and theories. *SIGIR Forum*, 41(2):8–17, 2007.

[39] J. Wang and J. Zhu. Portfolio theory of information retrieval. In *SIGIR*, pages 115–122, 2009.

[40] I. H. Witten and E. Frank. *Data Mining: Practical Machine Learning Tools*. 2005.

[41] C. Zhai, W. W. Cohen, and J. Lafferty. Beyond independent relevance: Methods and evaluation metrics for subtopic retrieval. In *SIGIR*, pages 10–17, 2003.

[42] Y. Zhou and W. B. Croft. Query performance prediction in web search environments. In *SIGIR*, pages 543–550, 2007.

Parameterized Concept Weighting in Verbose Queries

Michael Bendersky
Dept. of Computer Science
U. of Massachusetts
Amherst, MA
bemike@cs.umass.edu

Donald Metzler
Information Sciences Institute
U. of Southern California
Marina del Rey, CA
metzler@isi.edu

W. Bruce Croft
Dept. of Computer Science
U. of Massachusetts
Amherst, MA
croft@cs.umass.edu

ABSTRACT

The majority of the current information retrieval models weight the query concepts (e.g., terms or phrases) in an unsupervised manner, based solely on the collection statistics. In this paper, we go beyond the unsupervised estimation of concept weights, and propose a parameterized concept weighting model. In our model, the weight of each query concept is determined using a parameterized combination of diverse importance features. Unlike the existing supervised ranking methods, our model learns importance weights not only for the explicit query concepts, but also for the latent concepts that are associated with the query through pseudo-relevance feedback. The experimental results on both newswire and web TREC corpora show that our model consistently and significantly outperforms a wide range of state-of-the-art retrieval models. In addition, our model significantly reduces the number of latent concepts used for query expansion compared to the non-parameterized pseudo-relevance feedback based models.

Categories and Subject Descriptors

H.3.3 [**Information Storage and Retrieval**]: Information Search and Retrieval

General Terms

Algorithms, Experimentation

Keywords

Parameterized concept weighting, query expansion

1. INTRODUCTION

Term weighting is a classical information retrieval problem that has been studied for decades. However, despite significant advances, a majority of the most widely used information retrieval models, including language modeling [29] and BM25 [30], still weight the importance of query concepts (e.g., terms or phrases) in a simple, unsupervised manner. Such unsupervised estimates of concept importance tend to be based solely on global collection statistics, as evidenced by the standard *inverse document frequency* (IDF) measure of a term's importance.

However, such unsupervised estimates of concept importance have two major shortcomings that can degrade retrieval effectiveness. First, these estimates are rigid and inflexible, due to their dependency on a single global statistic (e.g., IDF). Such dependency does not take into account the influence of a wide range of factors beyond document frequency on the importance of a query concept. Flexible query term weighting is particularly important for verbose queries that often contain a mix of key and complementary concepts [5, 14].

Second, most of the importance weighting research has been applied to single terms (i.e., unigrams). Relatively little research has been done to investigate the appropriateness of IDF and other unsupervised importance weights for multiple-term concepts, including bigrams, phrases, and other proximity expressions. In fact, recent work by Macdonald and Ounis suggests that global statistics do not play as important of a role for such concepts [22]. This research highlights the need for improved understanding of possible alternatives for estimating the importance of multiple-term concepts.

To overcome the shortcomings of unsupervised concept weighting, a number of researchers have recently proposed to incorporate flexible supervised concept importance weighting into the Markov Random Field model [18, 6, 23]. In particular, the weighted sequential dependence model (`WSD`) proposed by Bendersky et al. [6] models the importance weight of the query concepts (including query terms, exact phrases and proximity matches) as a linear combination of document-independent features, such as the number of times the concept occurred as a Wikipedia title, its frequency within a query log, and its global frequency within a large web crawl. The `WSD` model provides a flexible way of estimating importance and can be effectively optimized using existing learning to rank approaches.

The main shortcoming of the `WSD` model [6], and its variants [31, 37], is that the weighting is performed exclusively on the concepts that explicitly occur within the query and disregards the *latent* concepts associated with the information need underlying the query (e.g., the concepts distilled by state-of-the-art query expansion approaches such as relevance model [16] or latent concept expansion [24]). Therefore, the question of how to seamlessly and effectively in-

SIGIR'11, July 24–28, 2011, Beijing, China.

Query Terms	Query Bigrams	Expansion Terms
.1064 patrol	.0257 civil air	.0639 cadet
.1058 civil	.0236 air patrol	.0321 force
.1046 training	.0104 training participants	.0296 aerospace
.0758 participants	.0104 participants receive	.0280 cap

Table 1: Explicit and latent concepts with the highest importance weight for the query "What is the current role of the civil air patrol and what training do participants receive?".

tegrate these latent concepts within a supervised concept weighting model still remains open.

To address this question, in this paper, we propose a novel *parameterized query expansion* model. The proposed model provides an effective alternative to the standard unsupervised weighting for both single terms and multiple-term concepts. In addition, the model generalizes the current supervised concept weighting approaches [6, 18, 31, 35, 37] and provides a *unified* framework for weighting both explicit and latent query concepts.

As an illustrative example of the parameterized query expansion in action, consider the verbose query

> "What is the current role of the civil air patrol and what training do participants receive?"

Table 1 shows the most important explicit query concepts (i.e., the query terms and bigrams) and the most important latent concepts (i.e., the expansion terms) learned by our model. Note that the weights assigned by our model are different from the weights that would be assigned by IDF alone. For instance, while the term *air* has higher IDF than the term *training*, it is deemed less important for the query. In addition, while the term *air* is not important on its own, it is significant in the context of the bigram *air patrol*.

In the case of the query in Table 1, the parameterized query expansion model improves the retrieval effectiveness by 64% over the standard query-likelihood model [29], by 21% over the `WSD` model [6], and by 8% over the latent concept expansion model [24]. As the evaluation in Sec. 5 demonstrates, these gains in retrieval effectiveness are consistent across queries and collections.

This paper has three primary contributions. First, we describe a novel parameterized query expansion model. Parameterized query expansion provides a flexible framework for modeling the importance of both explicit and latent query concepts. As we show, this framework is a generalization and unification of current state-of-the-art concept weighting [6, 18, 31] and query expansion [24, 15] models. Second, we describe a novel two-stage optimization technique for parameterized query expansion. This technique leverages learning to rank approaches for effective estimation of the explicit and latent concepts importance weights. Finally, we carry out a detailed empirical evaluation that demonstrates the state-of-the-art effectiveness of the proposed model. Our evaluation shows that the approach is particularly beneficial for verbose queries, but is also highly effective for short keyword queries.

The remainder of this paper is laid out as follows. First, Sec. 2 details the process of concept weight parameterization. Then, Sec. 3 describes query expansion with parameterized concept weights. Related work is covered in Sec. 4. Experimental evaluation is provided in Sec. 5. Finally, Sec. 6 concludes the paper and describes directions for future work.

2. PARAMETERIZED CONCEPT WEIGHTING

Given a query Q, we assume that there exists a set of *concepts* related to the underlying information need. In this paper, we use a very broad definition of a concept. A concept is defined as *any syntactic expression that can be matched within a document.*

Clearly, there are a multitude of concept types that can potentially be associated with the information need: individual words, exact phrases, unordered phrases, etc. It is important to note that these concept types can be either explicitly present in the query (e.g., query terms or phrases), or latent (e.g., concepts that are associated with the information need via the process of query expansion).

Formally, we use $\mathcal{T}$ to denote the set of all possible concept types (explicit and latent) associated with the information need underlying the query Q. Then, to assign a score to document D in response to the query Q, we use a linear weighted combination of matches in document D of all concepts types in $\mathcal{T}$ as follows:

$$sc(Q, D) = \sum_{T \in \mathcal{T}} \sum_{\kappa \in T} \lambda_\kappa f(\kappa, D). \quad (1)$$

This ranking function consists of two components: a concept matching function $f(\kappa, D)$ that computes how related κ is to D, and a concept importance weight λ_κ that indicates the importance of κ. We now discuss how these two components are computed.

2.1 Matching function $f(\kappa, D)$

The concept matching function $f(\kappa, D)$ assigns a score to the matches of concept κ in the document D. The function can take various forms, but in information retrieval applications it is commonly a monotonic function, i.e., its value increases with the number of times concept κ matches document D.

Throughout the remainder of this paper we assume that the matching function $f(\kappa,D)$ takes the form

$$f(\kappa, D) = \log \frac{tf_{\kappa,D} + \mu \frac{tf_{\kappa,\mathcal{C}}}{|\mathcal{C}|}}{|D| + \mu}. \quad (2)$$

where $tf_{\kappa,D}$ and $tf_{\kappa,\mathcal{C}}$ are the number of concept occurrences in the document and the collection, respectively; μ is a free parameter; $|D|$ is the number of terms in D, and $|\mathcal{C}|$ is the total number of terms in the collection.

The matching function in Eq. 2 is exactly the log of the language modeling estimate for concept κ with Dirichlet smoothing [39]. We use the language modeling estimate as a concept matching function since it is convenient and efficient to compute and exhibits state-of-the-art retrieval performance in other concept-based retrieval models [23, 24]. However, Eq. 1 can also be implemented using other matching functions such as BM25 [30] or DFR [3].

2.2 Importance weight λ_κ

Parameter λ_κ assigns a document-independent importance weight to each concept κ associated with the information need. Based on Eq. 1, the score for document D increases as it matches more of the important concepts associated with the information need. Therefore, correct estimation of the concept importance weight λ_κ is a crucial aspect of the ranking function in Eq. 1. There are several possible approaches for determining concept importance.

One common approach is tying the weights λ_κ of all the concepts of the same type T. This approach is commonly used in the bag-of-words models [29, 3, 30], as well as models that incorporate multiple concept types [23, 28, 10]. Concept weight tying is equivalent to the assumption that all the concepts of the same type are equally important for expressing the query intent. Such an assumption can be potentially detrimental for retrieval performance, especially for complex verbose queries, which combine a large number of concepts of different types [5].

Accordingly, we would like to relax the uniform importance assumption and estimate the weights λ_κ. Clearly, separately estimating a single weight for each concept κ is infeasible, since the number of possible concepts is exponential in the size of the vocabulary.

Instead, we parameterize a concept of type T using a set of importance features Φ^T, which is associated with each concept of the type T. Thus, a concept weight, λ_κ, can be represented as a linear weighted combination of importance features

$$\lambda_\kappa = \sum_{\varphi \in \Phi^T} w_\varphi \varphi(\kappa). \quad (3)$$

Although a linear form of the importance weighting function is used to simplify parameter estimation (see Sec. 3.3), there is no reason why more complex functional forms could not be used instead.

2.3 Parameterized Ranking Function

Having specified the concept matching function and the parameterized concept weight, we are now ready to derive the final parameterized form of our ranking function. Plugging the parameterized concept weight λ_κ from Eq. 3 into Eq. 1, we get

$$sc(Q,D) = \sum_{T \in \mathcal{T}} \sum_{\varphi \in \Phi^T} w_\varphi \sum_{\kappa \in T} \varphi(\kappa) f(\kappa, D). \quad (4)$$

From Eq. 4 it is evident that $sc(Q,D)$ is in fact linear in w_φ. This observation simplifies the optimization of Eq. 4, since many current learning to rank techniques [19] can be readily applied to efficiently and effectively optimize a linear ranking function.

Recently, there has been some work on ranking with parameterized concept weights [5, 6, 18, 35]. There are two main limitations in the existing work that we address in this paper.

First, the previous work does not take the holistic view presented in this paper, and optimizes weights for a predetermined concept type. For instance, Bendersky and Croft [5] apply parameterized weights only to the noun phrase concepts, Lease [18] applies it only to the query terms, and Svore et al. [35] only to the query term spans [33].

Second, the aforementioned previous work focuses on the surface form of the query, rather than its underlying information need. Therefore, it is only applicable to the concepts that are explicitly present in the query, and not to the latent concepts that are obtained through query expansion. In contrast, in this paper we propose a novel *parameterized query expansion* model that applies parameterized concept weighting to both the explicit and the latent query concepts.

3. PARAMETERIZED QUERY EXPANSION

In this section, we provide a detailed description of the *parameterized query expansion* retrieval model. This model is an implementation of the general parameterized concept weighting model defined in Sec. 2. It jointly weights several types of both explicit and latent concepts associated with the query. To fully describe the parameterized query expansion model (also referred to as PQE), in Sec. 3.1 we detail the concept types used by the model; in Sec. 3.2 we describe the set of features that determine the concept importance; finally, in Sec. 3.3 we outline the process of optimizing the retrieval effectiveness of the parameterized ranking function.

3.1 Concept Types

In this section, we define the set of concept types $\mathcal{T}$ used by the parameterized query expansion retrieval model. Recall that the choice of $\mathcal{T}$ will determine the structure of the parameterized ranking function in Eq. 4. PQE draws from two sources of evidence for deriving the concepts in $\mathcal{T}$. The first source is the set of words $(q_1, q_2, \ldots, q_{|Q|})$ that appear in the query Q. The second source is the set of latent concepts – concepts that are associated with the query Q through the process of pseudo-relevance feedback. Overall, $\mathcal{T}$ consists of the following concept types.

(1) *QT-concepts.* The query term (QT) concepts are simply the individual query words q_i. This is the most common concept type in information retrieval, which is used both in bag-of-words models [29, 30] and models that incorporate multiple concept types [23, 27, 10].

(2) *PH-concepts.* The phrase (PH) concepts are combinations of query terms that are matched as *exact phrases* in the document. Exact phrase matching has often been used for improving the performance of retrieval methods [9, 38]. Most recently, it has been shown that using query bigrams for exact phrase matching is a simple and efficient method for improving the retrieval performance in large scale web collections [23, 27, 28]. Following this finding, we define the PH-concepts as adjacent query word pairs $(q_i q_{i+1})$.

(3) *PR-concepts.* Similarly to the PH-concepts, the proximity (PR) concepts are defined over adjacent query word pairs $(q_i q_{i+1})$. In order to match the document, both of the individual words in a PR-concept must occur in any order within a *window of fixed length.* In this paper, we fix the window size to 8 words, following some previous work on proximity matching [23, 24, 28].

(4) *ET-concepts.* The expansion (ET) concepts are defined as the top-K terms associated with the query through the process of pseudo-relevance feedback. There is an abundance of literature on query expansion using pseudo-relevance feedback, most recent of which includes, among many others, work by Lavrenko and Croft [16], Tao and Zhai [36], Cao et al. [8], and Lv an Zhai [21]. In this paper we use the *latent concept expansion* (LCE) technique, first proposed by Metzler and Croft [24]. This technique has several important advantages, including state-of-the art performance [24, 15] and the ability to leverage information about arbitrary concepts to improve the quality of query expansion.

To obtain the initial set of ET-concepts using LCE, we first rank documents in the collection using Eq. 4 including only the concept types manifested in the query itself (QT-concepts, PH-concepts and PR-concepts). Then, all the terms in the pseudo-relevant set of documents $\mathcal{R}$ (top ranked

Feature	Description
GF(κ)	Frequency of κ in Google n-grams
WF(κ)	Frequency of κ in Wikipedia titles
QF(κ)	Frequency of κ in a search log
CF(κ)	Frequency of κ in the collection
DF(κ)	Document frequency of κ in the collection
AP(κ)	A priori concept weight

Table 2: Concept importance features Φ^T.

documents) are weighted by

$$w_{LCE}(\kappa) = \sum_{D \in \mathcal{R}} \exp\left(\gamma_1 sc(Q,D) + \gamma_2 f(\kappa, D) - \gamma_3 \log \frac{tf_{\kappa,\mathcal{C}}}{|\mathcal{C}|}\right), \tag{5}$$

where γ_i's are free parameters. Finally, K terms with the highest w_{LCE} weights, are added to the set of ET-concepts.

As evident from Eq. 5, w_{LCE} combines three key features to rank a concept: document relevance (manifested by the document score $sc(Q,D)$), score of the concept in the pseudo-relevance set $\mathcal{R}$ (manifested by the matching function $f(\kappa,D)$), and the inverse collection frequency (ICF) of the concept ($-\log \frac{tf_{\kappa,\mathcal{C}}}{|\mathcal{C}|}$). The ICF factor dampens the weights of very common words, thereby improving the quality of the initial set of ET-concepts.

Latent concept expansion can be adopted to include any arbitrary concept type for query expansion. However, in this paper we limit the expansion to individual terms. First, this focus improves the overall efficiency of the PQE model. Second, previous work found no significant benefits when additional types of latent concepts (such as bigrams) were associated with the query in addition to terms alone [24].

3.2 Concept Importance Features

As described in Sec. 2, in order to derive the ranking function $sc(Q, D)$ (Eq. 4), we associate a separate set of importance features Φ^T with each concept type T = (QT, PH, PR, ET). As these features depend only on the concept itself, they can leverage the statistics of the underlying document collection as well as the statistics of external data sources to achieve a potentially more accurate concept weighting.

Following previous work [5, 6, 37], in this paper we use three such external data sources: (i) a large collection of web n-grams, (ii) a sample of a search log, and (iii) Wikipedia. Some of these data sources provide better coverage of terms, while others provide more focused sources of information for determining concept importance. Although there are numerous additional data sources that could be potentially used, we intentionally limit our attention to these three sources as they are available for research purposes, and can be used to reproduce the reported results.

The first source, the Google n-grams corpus[1], contains the frequency counts of English n-grams generated from approximately 1 trillion word tokens. We expect these counts to provide a more accurate frequency estimator, especially for smaller corpora, where some concept frequencies may be underestimated due to the collection size.

In addition, we use a large sample of a search log consisting of approximately 15 million queries[2]. We use this data source to estimate how often a concept occurs in user queries. Intuitively, we assume a positive correlation between an importance of a concept for retrieval and the frequency with which it occurs in queries formulated by the search engine users.

Finally, our third external data source is a snapshot of Wikipedia article titles[3]. Due to the large volume and the high diversity of topics covered by Wikipedia, we assume that important concepts will often appear in its article titles.

For each concept type, we derive five simple frequency features based on these three external sources, as well as the underlying document collection (see Table 2). Note that the parameterized concept weighting in Eq. 3 does not restrict us to this particular set of features, and any additional importance features can be associated with each concept type. However, in this paper, we limit our attention to these five features, since they can be efficiently computed and cached even for large-scale web collections [37], and are suitable for operational retrieval systems.

In addition to the frequency features, Table 2 lists a sixth feature, AP(κ), which is an a priori concept weight (a weight assigned to the concept by default). AP(κ) is set to 1 for query-based concept types (QT, PH, PR), and to w_{LCE} (Eq. 5) for the ET-concepts.

The features in Table 2 are computed for each of the four concept types, resulting in 24 features overall. For each such feature φ, we need to estimate the parameter w_φ (see Eq. 4). This estimation process is described in the next section.

3.3 Concept Weight Optimization

To estimate the free parameters w_φ associated with the concept importance features in the ranking function in Eq. 4, we rely on a large and growing body of literature on the learning to rank methods for information retrieval (see Liu [19] for a survey). In this section, we first discuss the coordinate ascent (CA) algorithm [25], which we choose as a base optimization algorithm (Sec. 3.3.1). Then, in Sec. 3.3.2 we discuss the adaption of the CA algorithm for the parameterized query expansion.

3.3.1 Coordinate Ascent

As previously discussed, the ranking function in Eq. 4 is linear w.r.t. w_φ. Therefore, as a base algorithm for optimizing the parameters in Eq. 4 we make use of the coordinate ascent (CA) algorithm proposed by Metzler and Croft [25].

The CA algorithm iteratively optimizes a target metric (in our case, retrieval metric such as MAP) by performing a series of one-dimensional line searches. It repeatedly cycles through each of the parameters w_φ, holding all other parameters fixed while optimizing it. This process is performed iteratively over all parameters until the gain in the target metric is below a certain threshold. Although we use the CA algorithm primarily for its simplicity, efficiency and effectiveness, any other learning to rank approach that estimates the parameters for linear models such as RankSVM [13] or RankNet [7] can be adopted as well.

3.3.2 Optimization with Pseudo-Relevance Feedback

In contrast to most other learning to rank approaches, which usually consider only the concepts that explicitly occur in the query, the parameterized query expansion combines evidence from the query itself and the pseudo-relevance feedback in response to the query. Therefore, the setting of

[1]Available as LDC Catalog # LDC2006T13

[2]Available as a part of Microsoft 2006 RFP dataset.

[3]Available at http://download.wikimedia.org/enwiki/

(a) **Training Phase**

(a1) $\mathbf{Q} \leftarrow$ *Train queries*
(a2) $\mathcal{T} \leftarrow (\mathtt{QT_Q}, \mathtt{PH_Q}, \mathtt{PR_Q})$
(a3) $\mathcal{W}'_\Phi \leftarrow \mathtt{CA}(\mathbf{Q}, \mathcal{T})$
(a4) $\mathcal{R}'_\mathbf{Q} \leftarrow \mathtt{Rank}(\mathbf{Q}, \mathcal{T}, \mathcal{W}'_\Phi)$
(a5) $\mathtt{ET_Q} \leftarrow \mathtt{LCE}(\mathbf{Q}, \mathcal{R}'_\mathbf{Q})$
(a6) $\mathcal{T} \leftarrow (\mathtt{QT_Q}, \mathtt{PH_Q}, \mathtt{PR_Q}, \mathtt{ET_Q})$
(a7) $\mathcal{W}_\Phi \leftarrow \mathtt{CA}(\mathbf{Q}, \mathcal{T})$

(b) **Testing Phase**

(b1) $\mathbf{Q} \leftarrow$ *Test queries*
(b2) $\mathcal{T} \leftarrow (\mathtt{QT_Q}, \mathtt{PH_Q}, \mathtt{PR_Q})$
(b3) $\mathcal{R}'_\mathbf{Q} \leftarrow \mathtt{Rank}(\mathbf{Q}, \mathcal{T}, \mathcal{W}_\Phi)$
(b4) $\mathtt{ET_Q} \leftarrow \mathtt{LCE}(\mathbf{Q}, \mathcal{R}'_\mathbf{Q})$
(b5) $\mathcal{T} \leftarrow (\mathtt{QT_Q}, \mathtt{PH_Q}, \mathtt{PR_Q}, \mathtt{ET_Q})$
(b6) $\mathcal{R}_\mathbf{Q} \leftarrow \mathtt{Rank}(\mathbf{Q}, \mathcal{T}, \mathcal{W}_\Phi)$

Figure 1: Algorithms for (a) training and (b) testing phases of the parameterized query expansion model.

the importance feature weights associated with the query-based concept types (QT, PH, PR), will have a direct effect on the quality of the ET-concepts set, obtained through pseudo-relevance feedback.

To address this challenge, we propose a novel two-stage optimization technique for estimating the set of free parameters $\mathcal{W}_\Phi$ in the PQE retrieval model. While simple, this two-stage technique is effective for learning robust weights for both explicit and latent query concepts, as well as improving the quality of the set of ET-concepts.

The algorithm in Fig. 1 provides a schematic overview of this two-stage optimization. At the first stage of the training phase (Fig. 1 (a)), we include only the explicit concept types for optimizing the weights $\mathcal{W}_\Phi$ (line *a3*) and ranking with Eq. 4 (line *a4*). This initial ranking is used to obtain a large initial pool of ET-concepts[4] using latent concept expansion, as described in Eq. 5 (line *a5*).

At the second stage of the training phase, we include both explicit and latent concepts for ranking with Eq. 4 (line *a6*). A second round of the CA algorithm is then performed in order to re-estimate the weights $\mathcal{W}_\Phi$ for all concept types (line *a7*). To make the optimization process more efficient, at each iteration of the CA algorithm, we use only a small set of the top-K ET-concepts from the initial large pool[5]. At each iteration, the top-K ET-concepts are updated based on the current setting of the $\mathcal{W}_\Phi$.

The training phase concludes after the second round of the CA algorithm is completed. At this point, the weights $\mathcal{W}_\Phi$ are optimized (in terms of the target retrieval metric) for the training queries. We then use a held-out set of test queries to evaluate the performance of the optimized weights $\mathcal{W}_\Phi$ (Fig. 1 (b)).

4. RELATED WORK

Importance weighting of query concepts is one of the key challenges of information retrieval research. However, the majority of commonly used bag-of-words retrieval models (including, among many others, BM25 [30] and language modeling [11, 29, 39]) still use unsupervised term weighting based on global collection statistics, which resembles the term weighting proposed by Luhn [20] in 1958.

Recently, researchers began investigating techniques for supervised weighting of the terms and concepts in the query [5, 6, 18, 31, 35]. However, these investigations mostly focus only on assigning importance weights to a subset of predetermined concept types.

[4]We set the size of the large pool to 100 concepts.
[5]We limit the size of this small set to 10 concepts.

Name	# Docs	Topic Numbers
ROBUST04	528,155	301-450, 601-700
WT10g	1,692,096	451-550
GOV2	25,205,179	701-850

Table 3: Summary of TREC collections and topics used for evaluation in Sec. 5.

⟨*title*⟩	dam removal
⟨*desc*⟩	Where have dams been removed and what has been the environmental impact?

Figure 2: An example of ⟨*title*⟩ and ⟨*desc*⟩ portions of a TREC topic #752.

For instance, Lease [18] focuses on term weighting, Bendersky and Croft [5] on noun phrases, and Svore et al. [35] on query term spans. In addition, these supervised techniques take into account only the explicit query concepts and disregard the latent concepts that can be associated with the query via expansion. The parameterized query expansion method proposed in this paper addresses these limitations.

Another field of research which is relevant to this paper is pseudo-relevance feedback. While there is a large number of successful pseudo-relevance feedback based retrieval models (e.g., [8, 16, 24, 21, 38]), most of them employ unsupervised weighting for both explicit and latent concepts. A notable exception is the work by Cao et al. [8] which uses binary classification to determine the importance of the expansion terms. Unlike Cao et al. [8], the proposed parameterized query expansion method takes a more holistic approach, and assigns importance weights to *both* explicit and latent concepts.

5. EVALUATION

This section describes the details of our experimental evaluation. First, in Sec. 5.1, we describe the experimental setup used for the evaluation. Then, in Sec. 5.2, we compare the performance of the parameterized query expansion (PQE) method to the performance of several standard non-parameterized retrieval methods. Further analysis, comparisons and in-depth discussion of the results are provided in Sec. 5.3.

5.1 Experimental Setup

The retrieval experiments described in this paper are implemented using Indri, an open-source search engine [34]. The structured query language implemented in the Indri search engine natively supports multiple concept types, including exact phrases and proximity matches. The Indri query language also supports custom term weighting schemes. As a result, Indri provides a flexible and convenient platform for evaluating the performance of our method.

Table 3 presents a summary of the TREC corpora used in our experiments. The corpora vary both by type (ROBUST04 is a newswire collection, while WT10g and GOV2 are web collections), number of documents, and number of available topics, thereby providing a diverse experimental setup for assessing the robustness of the proposed retrieval method.

During indexing and retrieval, both documents and queries are stemmed using the Porter stemmer. Stopword removal is performed on both documents and queries using the stan-

		Concept Types			
		QT	PH	PR	ET
Non-parameterized methods	QL	$\mathcal{N}$			
	SD	$\mathcal{N}$	$\mathcal{N}$	$\mathcal{N}$	
	RM	$\mathcal{N}$			$\mathcal{N}$
	LCE	$\mathcal{N}$	$\mathcal{N}$	$\mathcal{N}$	$\mathcal{N}$
Parameterized methods	WSD	$\mathcal{P}$	$\mathcal{P}$	$\mathcal{P}$	
	WRM	$\mathcal{P}$			$\mathcal{P}$
	PQE	$\mathcal{P}$	$\mathcal{P}$	$\mathcal{P}$	$\mathcal{P}$

Table 4: Summary of the evaluated retrieval methods. Each cell indicates whether the weights for the concept type are parameterized according to Eq. 3 ($\mathcal{P}$) or not ($\mathcal{N}$). An empty cell indicates that the concept type is not used by the retrieval method.

dard INQUERY stopword list [2]. The free parameter μ in the concept matching function $f(\kappa,D)$ (see Eq. 2) is set to 2,500, according to the default Indri configuration of the Dirichlet smoothing parameter.

The optimization of the PQE method is done using 3-fold cross-validation with mean average precision (MAP) as the target metric of the CA algorithm (see Sec. 3.3.2). The statistical significance of differences in the performance of PQE with respect to other retrieval methods is determined using a two-sided Fisher's randomization test with 50,000 permutations and $\alpha < 0.05$.

As was shown in previous work [4, 5, 6, 18], the impact of concept weighting techniques varies significantly across queries of different length. In general, more verbose queries are expected to benefit more from concept weighting, since they are more likely to contain concepts of varying importance. Thus, to test the performance of the proposed methods across multiple query lengths, we treat the ⟨*title*⟩ and the ⟨*desc*⟩ portions of TREC topics as two separate sets of queries in our experiments. The ⟨*title*⟩ and the ⟨*desc*⟩ query convey the same information need for the same topic, but differ in their structure. The ⟨*title*⟩ query is a short keyword query, while the ⟨*desc*⟩ query is a verbose natural language description of the information need. Fig. 2 shows an example of ⟨*title*⟩ and ⟨*desc*⟩ queries for TREC topic #752.

5.2 General Evaluation

Our initial evaluation compares the retrieval performance of the *parameterized query expansion* (PQE) retrieval method (described in Sec. 3) to the performance of several standard baseline methods that do not employ concept weight parameterization.

First, we compare the retrieval performance of the PQE method to the performance of the query likelihood (QL) [29] and sequential dependence model (SD) [23] retrieval methods. These baselines do not perform query expansion, and differ in the choice of the query-based concept types that they use. QL is a standard bag-of-words method. In contrast, the SD method uses, in addition to query terms, both PH-concepts and PR-concepts (which are described in Sec. 3.1). The SD method has consistently demonstrated state-of-the-art retrieval effectiveness in a variety of search tasks, and especially for search over large web collections [23]. Top performing submissions at several TREC tracks have used SD: Terabyte Track 2004-2006 [26], Million Query Track 2007-2008 [1] and Web Track 2009 [32].

Second, we compare the performance of PQE to the performance of two retrieval methods that perform pseudo-relevance feedback (PRF) for query expansion: the RM3 variant of the relevance model (RM) [16] and Latent Concept Expansion (LCE) [24]. Both of these methods are known to improve retrieval performance over methods that do not employ query expansion. Analogously to the QL and SD methods, the RM and LCE methods differ in their choice of the query-based concept types. RM is a bag-of-words model, while LCE uses both PH-concepts and PR-concepts. Both PRF-based methods use individual terms (i.e., unigrams) for query expansion.

Both RM and LCE exhibit highly competitive retrieval performance. Particularly, the LCE method is among the most effective PRF-based methods for large-scale web collections [23, 15]. Lease [17] has recently affirmed its effectiveness at the TREC Relevance Feedback track.

To ensure competitive baseline performance, the free parameters in the PRF-based methods – such as the number of documents used for pseudo-relevance feedback, the query weight in the RM method and the γ parameters in the LCE method (see Eq. 5) – are set using 3-fold cross-validation, analogously to the PQE method. To maintain reasonable efficiency, especially for the large web collection GOV2, we limit the number of expansion terms to 10 for all the PRF-based methods presented in Table 5.

Overall, the four baselines described above differ in their choice of concept types. In contrast to the PQE method, they do not parameterize the concept weights. Table 4 summarizes the choice of concepts and weight parameterization by these methods (as well as two additional methods that will be discussed in Sec. 5.3). For instance, we can see from Table 4 that LCE and PQE share the same concept types, but differ in the parameterization of the concept weights.

5.2.1 Baseline Comparisons

Table 5 compares the retrieval effectiveness of the four baselines to the retrieval effectiveness of PQE, both for ⟨*title*⟩ and ⟨*desc*⟩ queries. Effectiveness is measured using both an early precision metric (prec@20), and the mean average precision of the entire ranked list of 1,000 documents (MAP).

First, it is clear from Table 5 that methods that use multiple concept types (SD, LCE, PQE) are superior to the methods that use terms alone (QL, RM). This result holds for all the collections, for both prec@20 and MAP.

Second, the LCE method, which uses both multiple explicit query concept types and latent expansion concepts, outperforms the SD method, which uses the query concepts alone. This result is consistent with previous work [24], and demonstrates the positive effect of query expansion, even when multiple query concept types are used.

Finally, we compare the proposed method, PQE, to the four baselines. In all 12 comparisons (three collections, two metrics and two query types), our method outperforms all the baselines, in most cases to a statistically significant degree. There are two key elements that contribute to the success of the PQE retrieval method.

First, similarly to LCE, PQE combines multiple explicit concept types with expansion concepts. This combination leads to a very substantial improvement over the standard bag-of-words methods. For instance, for ⟨*desc*⟩ queries on the GOV2 collection, PQE achieves 24% and 17% improvement in MAP over QL and RM, respectively.

⟨*title*⟩	ROBUST04		WT10g		GOV2	
	prec@20	MAP	prec@20	MAP	prec@20	MAP
QL	34.86	24.43	23.99	19.39	50.41	29.56
SD	36.31^{q}	25.90^{q}	23.84	20.63	55.34^{q}	32.24^{q}
RM[10]	36.67^{q}	27.19^{qs}	24.04	19.71	51.15^{s}	30.07
LCE[10]	38.39^{qs}_{r}	28.93^{qs}_{r}	24.95	21.09^{qs}_{r}	55.10^{q}_{r}	33.63^{qs}_{r}
PQE[10]	$\mathbf{39.02}^{qs}_{r}$	$\mathbf{29.16}^{qs}_{r}$ *(+12.6/+0.80)*	$\mathbf{26.31}^{qs}_{rl}$	$\mathbf{21.19}^{qs}_{r}$ *(+2.7/+0.50)*	$\mathbf{56.66}^{q}_{r}$	$\mathbf{34.84}^{qs}_{rl}$ *(+8.1/+3.6)*

⟨*desc*⟩	ROBUST04		WT10g		GOV2	
	prec@20	MAP	prec@20	MAP	prec@20	MAP
QL	33.05	24.22	26.35	18.87	47.62	25.66
SD	34.94^{q}	25.65^{q}	27.45	19.82	50.67^{q}	27.94^{q}
RM[10]	35.04^{q}	25.92^{q}	27.15	20.49^{q}	48.42	27.11^{q}
LCE[10]	37.57^{qs}_{r}	28.10^{qs}_{r}	28.50	21.26	52.52^{qs}_{r}	30.66^{qs}_{r}
PQE[10]	$\mathbf{38.98}^{qs}_{rl}$	$\mathbf{29.40}^{qs}_{rl}$ *(+11.6/+4.6)*	$\mathbf{29.90}^{qs}_{rl}$	$\mathbf{22.17}^{qs}$ *(+11.8/+4.3)*	$\mathbf{54.70}^{qs}_{rl}$	$\mathbf{31.68}^{qs}_{rl}$ *(+13.4/+3.3)*

Table 5: Retrieval effectiveness comparison with all the baselines. Statistically significant differences are marked using the first letter in the title of the retrieval method under comparison. Best result per column is marked by boldface. The numbers in parenthesis indicate improvement over SD and LCE methods, respectively.

Second, unlike all the standard baselines in Table 5, the PQE method applies parameterized concept weighting to both explicit and latent concepts. The parameterized concept weighting leads to significant improvements over all the non-parameterized baselines, including those that use multiple concept types. In most cases, these improvements are statistically significant for both metrics, and they are consistent across different collections.

On average, for ⟨*desc*⟩ queries, there is a 12.2% gain in MAP over SD, and 4.1% gain over LCE. Note that when comparing PQE and LCE methods, the concept weight parameterization is the only factor that contributes to the effectiveness gain, since these two methods share the same concept types (as demonstrated in Table 4).

5.2.2 Robustness

In Table 5 we have shown that the PQE method significantly improves the overall performance compared to two state-of-the-art PRF-based methods (RM and LCE). In this section, we analyze the *robustness* of PQE, compared to these two methods. Following previous work [24], we define the robustness of the method as the number of queries improved or hurt (and by how much – in terms of MAP) as the result of the application of the method. A highly robust expansion technique will significantly improve many queries and only minimally hurt a few.

Fig. 3 provides an analysis of the robustness of RM, LCE and PQE for the ⟨*desc*⟩ queries[6]. The histograms in Fig. 3 show, for various ranges of relative decreases/increases in MAP, the number of queries that were hurt/improved with respect to the QL baseline.

Fig. 3 unequivocally demonstrates that PQE is more robust compared to the other two methods. For instance, for the GOV2 collection, PQE improves the performance of 75% of the queries w.r.t. QL, compared to 64% and 68% of the queries improved by RM and LCE respectively. Similar improvements are observed for the other two collections.

In addition, the PQE method is much less likely to significantly hurt the performance, compared to the other two methods. For instance, for the ROBUST04 collection, PQE decreases performance by more than 25% for only 24 (out of 250) queries, compared to 33 and 34 queries with such a decrease for the RM and LCE methods, respectively.

[6]The robustness of these methods for the ⟨*title*⟩ queries is similar, and is omitted due to space constraints.

5.2.3 Graded Relevance Judgments

In Table 5 and Fig. 3, we have evaluated the retrieval methods using binary relevance judgments — documents are either assumed relevant or non-relevant. However, graded relevance judgments (i.e., categorical judgments with more than two degrees of relevance) are becoming more widely used, especially for evaluating web search tasks. Accordingly, in addition to the binary metrics, we use the normalized discounted cumulative gain (nDCG) metric, which takes into account multiple relevance grades, to evaluate the retrieval effectiveness for the GOV2 collection, which has graded relevance judgments available.

Table 6 shows the nDCG at the top 20 results, as well as the nDCG of the entire ranked list for the PQE method along with the two most effective baselines from Table 5 (SD and LCE). The results in Table 6 are in agreement with the results for the binary metrics in Table 5.

PQE is the most effective among the three methods, in most cases to a statistically significant degree. It is interesting to note that while it is often the case that query expansion methods do not have a significant positive effect on early precision [21, 24], PQE shows significant improvements over the SD method for prec@20 and nDCG@20 metrics for both ⟨*title*⟩ and ⟨*desc*⟩ queries.

5.2.4 ⟨title⟩ and ⟨desc⟩ Queries

While most of the previous concept weighting techniques specifically target verbose natural language queries [5, 12, 14, 18], the parameterized concept weighting described in Sec. 2 is more general, and can be applied to any type of query. Table 5 and Table 6 show that PQE outperforms the other methods for both ⟨*title*⟩ and ⟨*desc*⟩ queries.

Intuitively, however, we expect that the parameterized concept weighting will be more beneficial for longer, more complex queries, which may contain more concepts of varying importance. Overall, the results in Table 5 and Table 6

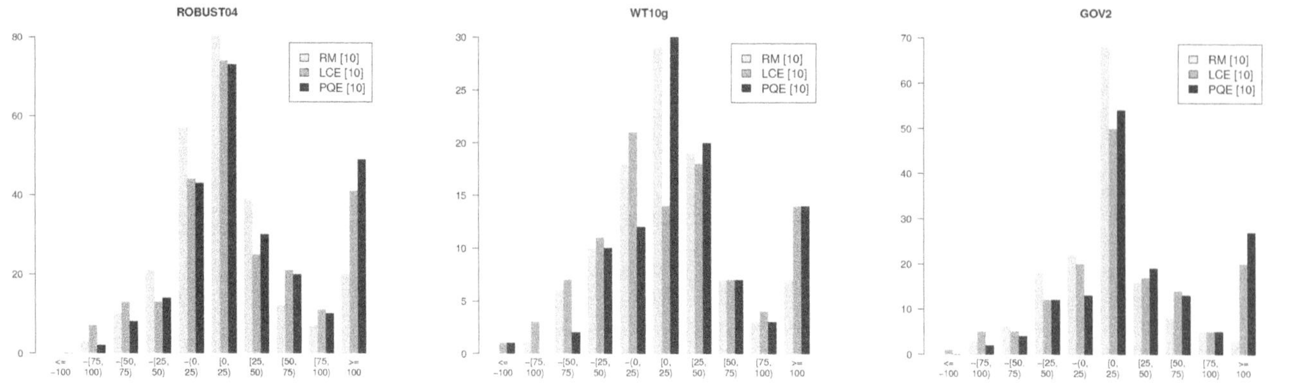

Figure 3: Robustness of RM[10], LCE[10] and PQE[10] methods for the ⟨*desc*⟩ queries w.r.t. the QL method.

⟨*title*⟩	GOV2	
	nDCG@20	nDCG@1000
SD	44.54	60.48
LCE[10]	43.70	61.29
PQE[10]	**45.20**$_l$ *(+1.5/+3.4)*	**62.32**^s_l *(+3.0/+1.7)*

⟨*desc*⟩	GOV2	
	nDCG@20	nDCG@1000
SD	41.15	54.45
LCE[10]	41.66	56.41
PQE[10]	**43.30**^s_l *(+5.2/+3.9)*	**57.60**^s_l *(+5.8/+2.1)*

Table 6: Retrieval effectiveness evaluation (nDCG@k) for the GOV2 collection with graded relevance judgments. Statistically significant differences are marked using the first letter in the title of the retrieval method under comparison. Best result per column is marked by boldface. The numbers in parenthesis indicate improvement over SD and LCE methods, respectively.

confirm this intuition. The gains attained by the parameterized concept weighting for ⟨*desc*⟩ queries are, on average, higher than those attained for ⟨*title*⟩ queries. For instance, the average gain in MAP of the PQE method over the LCE method is 1.7% for the ⟨*title*⟩ queries, compared to 4.1% for the ⟨*desc*⟩ queries.

It is important to note, however, that the effectiveness gains achieved by the PQE method are consistent, and in many cases statistically significant, for both ⟨*title*⟩ and ⟨*desc*⟩ queries. This showcases the applicability of the parameterized concept weighting employed by the PQE method for a variety of search scenarios, apart from verbose natural language queries.

5.3 Further analysis

In the remainder of this section, we provide a deeper analysis of the various aspects of the PQE method. In Sec. 5.3.1 we compare the performance of PQE to the performance of some previously proposed parameterized retrieval methods. In Sec. 5.3.2 we compare the effectiveness of PQE with a small number of expansion concepts to the effectiveness of non-parameterized PRF-based methods that use an increasingly large number of expansion concepts. Finally, in Sec. 5.3.3 we compare PQE with two recently published methods for query expansion that employ concept weighting.

5.3.1 Parameterized Retrieval Methods

In Sec. 5.2 we have compared the performance of the PQE method to the performance of four standard retrieval methods that do not perform any parameterized concept weighting. In this section, we compare PQE with two additional retrieval methods, both of which employ parameterized concept weighting. These parameterized retrieval methods differ in their choice of the concept types.

The first method is WSD, proposed by Bendersky et al. [6]. This method is a parameterized version of the standard SD method. The second method, WRM is the parameterized version of the RM method. It is conceptually similar to the PQE method, however it only uses unigram concepts (QT and ET-concepts).

Table 4 summarizes the concepts and the parameterization of the WSD and WRM methods. We compare the effectiveness of these two methods to the effectiveness of the PQE method in Table 7.

First, we note that the three parameterized retrieval methods WSD, WRM, and PQE outperform their non-parameterized counterparts (SD, RM and LCE, respectively). In most cases these performance gains are statistically significant. For instance, WSD attains a 5.5% gain over SD, and WRM attains a 10.3% gain over RM for the ⟨*desc*⟩ queries. Moreover, analogously to the PQE method, these gains, while consistent for all queries, are, on average, larger for the ⟨*desc*⟩ queries.

Second, we note that PQE is, overall, the best-performing parameterized retrieval method. The only exception is the WT10g collection, where WSD and PQE are statistically indistinguishable. On average, PQE attains 4.7% gain over WSD and 3.5% gain over WRM for the ⟨*desc*⟩ queries (and much higher gains for the ROBUST04 and GOV2 collections, specifically).

5.3.2 Number of Expansion Concepts

In Table 5, we have limited ourselves to the efficient setting of using solely the top ten ET-concepts for query expansion. In this section, we study the effect of increasing

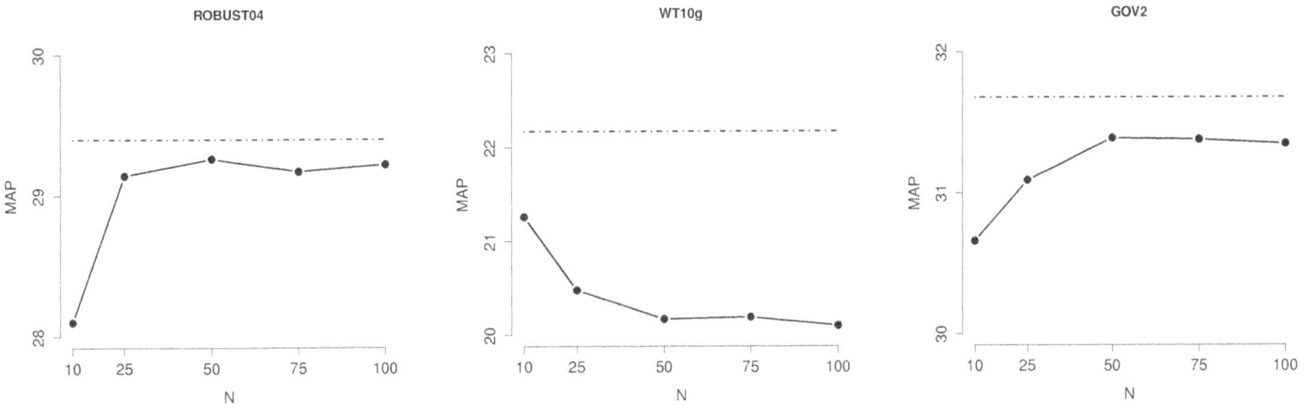

Figure 4: Effect of increasing the number of expansion concepts (N) on the retrieval effectiveness (MAP) of the ⟨*desc*⟩ queries. Solid line — the effectiveness of LCE[N]. Dotted line — the effectiveness of PQE[10].

⟨*title*⟩	ROBUST04	WT10g	GOV2
`WSD`	26.16	**21.48**	33.13
`WRM[10]`	27.35	19.86	31.08
`PQE[10]`	$\mathbf{29.16}^{s}_{r}$	21.19_{r}	$\mathbf{34.84}^{s}_{r}$

⟨*desc*⟩	ROBUST04	WT10g	GOV2
`WSD`	27.49	**22.60**	29.46
`WRM[10]`	27.77	22.46	29.89
`PQE[10]`	$\mathbf{29.40}^{s}_{r}$	22.17	$\mathbf{31.68}^{s}_{r}$

Table 7: Retrieval effectiveness (MAP) of the parameterized retrieval methods. Statistically significant differences are marked using the second letter in the title of the retrieval method under comparison. Best result per column is marked by boldface.

the number of expansion concepts. Particularly, we are interested in addressing the question of whether the addition of expansion concepts in the non-parameterized PRF-based methods (e.g., `LCE`) can compensate for their lack of accurate concept weighting.

Fig. 4 shows the effect of increasing the number of expansion concepts used by the `LCE` retrieval method on its retrieval effectiveness for the ⟨*desc*⟩ queries[7] for all test collections. Fig. 4 demonstrates that adding expansion terms improves the effectiveness of `LCE` in some cases (but worsens it in the case of WT10g). However, adding more `ET`-concepts to `LCE` is still inferior to the fixed setting of using the top ten `ET`-concepts in the `PQE` method, while significantly increasing the query latency.

Fig. 4 demonstrates the importance of parameterized concept weighting for creating both effective and efficient retrieval methods that can scale to large web collections. Compared to the non-parameterized retrieval methods, `PQE` provides a more accurate estimate of concept importance. Moreover, since the features that are used to determine the importance of a concept can be pre-computed and cached (see Sec. 3.2), `PQE` effectively and efficiently filters out the less important expansion concepts and minimizes the query execution time.

[7]The results for the ⟨*title*⟩ queries are similar, and are omitted due to space constraints.

		Topics	MAP	Source
(a)	`MIX+SOFT-10`	351-400	21.25	*Table 11* [8]
	`PQE[10]`		**21.97**	
(b)	`PRM1`	801-850	33.22	*Table 2* [21]
	`PQE[10]`		**37.41**	

Table 8: Additional comparisons with: (a) Cao et al. [8]; (b) Lv and Zhai [21]. Best result per comparison is marked by boldface.

5.3.3 Additional Comparisons

In this section, we compare the performance of the `PQE` retrieval method to the performance of two recently proposed query expansion methods that employ concept weighting and proximity information. The first method was proposed by Cao et al. [8], and uses binary classification to weight expansion terms. The second method was proposed by Lv and Zhai [21], and leverages term proximities for expansion term weighting. While less general than the approach proposed here, these two methods also focus on concept weighting, and hence we briefly compare their performance to `PQE`.

For comparison, we use the MAP results reported in the papers by Cao et al. [8] and Lv and Zhai [21], for a subset of topics overlapping with our evaluation. The reported results are for the ⟨*title*⟩ queries only, since these queries are also used in the papers under consideration. Table 8 reports the comparison between the `PQE` method and these two methods. While we cannot draw statistical significance conclusions, since we have no information on individual query performance, we can see from Table 8 that `PQE` is the best performing method in both comparisons.

In all the cases in Table 8 similar query and document processing was applied (Porter stemming, INQUERY stopwords removal, setting of smoothing parameters and number of expansion terms), and similar baselines were reported. Hence, we can confidently attribute the performance gains to the effectiveness of our method, even when compared to other state-of-the-art query expansion methods that use concept weighting and proximity information.

6. CONCLUSIONS

In this paper, we introduced a novel framework for query expansion with parameterized concept weighting. Parameterized query expansion generalizes and unifies several of the current state-of-the-art concept weighting and query expansion approaches.

Unlike many common retrieval models that use unsupervised concept weighting based on a single global statistic, parameterized query expansion leverages a number of publicly available sources such as Wikipedia and a large collection of web n-grams, to achieve a more accurate concept importance weighting. This importance weighting is applied to both explicit query concepts (terms, exact phrases and proximity matches) as well as latent concepts, which are associated with the query using pseudo-relevance feedback.

An empirical evaluation on newswire and web TREC corpora unequivocally demonstrates the state-of-the-art effectiveness of the parameterized query expansion. Our method consistently outperforms a number of strong baseline methods, which use term dependencies and pseudo-relevance feedback with a larger number of latent concepts. It also achieves significant gains over methods that use parameterized concept weighting, but do not perform query expansion. The highest effectiveness gains are demonstrated for verbose natural language queries, but parameterized query expansion is beneficial for the keyword queries as well.

Overall, our findings demonstrate that the parameterized query expansion is an effective and flexible framework that can seamlessly incorporate multiple concept types. Accordingly, in future work, we intend to introduce additional types of concepts into the parameterized query expansion framework, including multiple-term expansion concepts, named entities, and non-adjacent query term pairs.

7. ACKNOWLEDGMENTS

This work was supported in part by the Center for Intelligent Information Retrieval and in part by ARRA NSF IIS-9014442. Any opinions, findings and conclusions or recommendations expressed in this material are the authors' and do not necessarily reflect those of the sponsor.

8. REFERENCES

[1] J. Allan, J. Aslam, B. Carterette, V. Pavlu, and E. Kanoulas. Million Query Track 2008 overview. In *Proc. of TREC*, 2008.

[2] J. Allan, M. E. Connell, W. B. Croft, F. F. Feng, D. Fisher, and X. Li. INQUERY and TREC-9. In *Proc. of TREC-9*, pages 551–562, 2000.

[3] G. Amati and C. J. Van Rijsbergen. Probabilistic models of information retrieval based on measuring the divergence from randomness. *ACM Transactions on Information Systems (TOIS)*, 20(4):357–389, October 2002.

[4] N. Balasubramanian, G. Kumaran, and V. R. Carvalho. Exploring reductions for long web queries. In *Proc. of SIGIR*, pages 571–578, 2010.

[5] M. Bendersky and W. B. Croft. Discovering key concepts in verbose queries. In *Proc. of SIGIR*, pages 491–498, 2008.

[6] M. Bendersky, D. Metzler, and W. B. Croft. Learning concept importance using a weighted dependence model. In *Proc. of WSDM*, pages 31–40, 2010.

[7] C. Burges, T. Shaked, E. Renshaw, A. Lazier, M. Deeds, N. Hamilton, and G. Hullender. Learning to rank using gradient descent. In *Proc. of ICML*, pages 89–96, 2005.

[8] G. Cao, J.-Y. Nie, J. Gao, and S. Robertson. Selecting good expansion terms for pseudo-relevance feedback. In *Proc. of SIGIR*, pages 243–250, 2008.

[9] J. Fagan. Automatic phrase indexing for document retrieval. In *Proc. of SIGIR*, pages 91–101, 1987.

[10] J. Gao, H. Qi, X. Xia, and J.-Y. Nie. Linear discriminant model for information retrieval. In *Proc. of SIGIR*, pages 290–297, 2005.

[11] D. Hiemstra. Term-specific smoothing for the language modeling approach to information retrieval: the importance of a query term. In *In Proc. of SIGIR*, pages 35–41, 2002.

[12] S. Huston and W. B. Croft. Evaluating verbose query processing techniques. In *Proc. of SIGIR*, pages 291–298, 2010.

[13] T. Joachims. Optimizing search engines using clickthrough data. In *Proc. of KDD*, pages 133–142, 2002.

[14] G. Kumaran and V. R. Carvalho. Reducing long queries using query quality predictors. In *Proc. of SIGIR*, pages 564–571, 2009.

[15] H. Lang, D. Metzler, B. Wang, and J.-T. Li. Improved latent concept expansion using hierarchical markov random fields. In *Proc. of CIKM*, pages 249–258, 2010.

[16] V. Lavrenko and W. B. Croft. Relevance Models in Information Retrieval. In W. B. Croft and J. Lafferty, editors, *Language modeling for Information Retrieval*, pages 11–56. Kluwer, 2003.

[17] M. Lease. Incorporating relevance and pseudo-relevance feedback in the markov random field model. In *Proc. of TREC*, 2008.

[18] M. Lease. An improved markov random field model for supporting verbose queries. In *Proc. of SIGIR*, pages 476–483, 2009.

[19] T.-Y. Liu. Learning to Rank for Information Retrieval. *Foundations and Trends in Information Retrieval*, 3(3), 2009.

[20] H. Luhn. The Automatic Creation of Literature Abstracts. *IBM Journal of Research and Development*, 2(2):159, 1958.

[21] Y. Lv and C. Zhai. Positional relevance model for pseudo-relevance feedback. In *Proc. of SIGIR*, pages 579–586, 2010.

[22] C. Macdonald and I. Ounis. Global statistics in proximity weighting models. In *Proc. of the SIGIR Web N-Gram Workshop*, 2010.

[23] D. Metzler and W. B. Croft. A Markov random field model for term dependencies. *Proc. of SIGIR*, pages 472–479, 2005.

[24] D. Metzler and W. B. Croft. Latent concept expansion using markov random fields. *Proc. of SIGIR*, pages 311–318, 2007.

[25] D. Metzler and W. B. Croft. Linear feature-based models for information retrieval. *Information Retrieval*, 10(3):257–274, 2007.

[26] D. Metzler, T. Strohman, and W. B. Croft. Indri at TREC 2005: Terabyte track. In *Proc. of TREC*, 2005.

[27] G. Mishne and M. de Rijke. Boosting Web Retrieval Through Query Operations. In *Proc. of ECIR*, pages 502–516, 2005.

[28] J. Peng, C. Macdonald, B. He, V. Plachouras, and I. Ounis. Incorporating term dependency in the DFR framework. In *Proc. of SIGIR*, pages 843–844, 2007.

[29] J. M. Ponte and W. B. Croft. A language modeling approach to information retrieval. In *Proc. of SIGIR*, pages 275–281, 1998.

[30] S. E. Robertson and S. Walker. Some simple effective approximations to the 2-Poisson model for probabilistic weighted retrieval. In *Proc. of SIGIR*, pages 232–241, 1994.

[31] L. Shi and J.-Y. Nie. Using various term dependencies according to their utilities. In *Proc. of CIKM*, pages 1493–1496, 2010.

[32] M. D. Smucker, C. Clarke, and G. V. Cormack. Experiments with ClueWeb09: Relevance feedback and web tracks. In *Proc. of TREC*, 2009.

[33] R. Song, M. Taylor, J.-R. Wen, H.-W. Hon, and Y. Yu. Viewing term proximity from a different perspective. In *Proc. of ECIR*, pages 346–357, 2008.

[34] T. Strohman, D. Metzler, H. Turtle, and W. B. Croft. Indri: A language model-based search engine for complex queries. In *Proc. of IA*, 2004.

[35] K. M. Svore, P. H. Kanani, and N. Khan. How good is a span of terms?: exploiting proximity to improve web retrieval. In *Proc. of SIGIR*, pages 154–161, 2010.

[36] T. Tao and C. Zhai. An exploration of proximity measures in information retrieval. In *Proc. of SIGIR*, pages 295–302, 2007.

[37] L. Wang, D. Metzler, and J. Lin. Ranking under temporal constraints. In *Proc. of CIKM*, pages 79–88, 2010.

[38] J. Xu and W. B. Croft. Query expansion using local and global document analysis. *Proc. of SIGIR*, pages 4–11, 1996.

[39] C. Zhai and J. Lafferty. A study of smoothing methods for language models applied to information retrieval. *ACM Transactions on Information Systems*, 22(2):179–214, 2004.

UPS: Efficient Privacy Protection in Personalized Web Search

Gang Chen, He Bai, Lidan Shou, Ke Chen, and Yunjun Gao
Dept. of Computer Science, Zhejiang University
Hangzhou, China
cg@zju.edu.cn, baihe.zju@gmail.com, should@zju.edu.cn, chenk@zju.edu.cn, gaoyj@zju.edu.cn

ABSTRACT

In recent years, personalized web search (PWS) has demonstrated effectiveness in improving the quality of search service on the Internet. Unfortunately, the need for collecting private information in PWS has become a major barrier for its wide proliferation. We study privacy protection in PWS engines which capture personalities in user profiles. We propose a PWS framework called UPS that can generalize profiles in for each query according to user-specified privacy requirements. Two predictive metrics are proposed to evaluate the privacy breach risk and the query utility for hierarchical user profile. We develop two simple but effective generalization algorithms for user profiles allowing for query-level customization using our proposed metrics. We also provide an online prediction mechanism based on query utility for deciding whether to personalize a query in UPS. Extensive experiments demonstrate the efficiency and effectiveness of our framework.

Categories and Subject Descriptors

H.3.3 [**Information Search and Retrieval**]: Search process; H.3.m [**Miscellaneous**]; D.2.8 [**Software Engineering**]: Metrics—*complexity measures, performance measures*

General Terms

Experimentation, Measurement

Keywords

Personalized, Privacy, Metric, Utility, Trade-off

1. INTRODUCTION

Personalized web search (PWS) is a general category of search techniques which provide search results tailored for individual user needs. As a price, user information has to be collected and analyzed to figure out the user intention behind the issued query. The solutions to PWS can generally be categorized into two types, namely *click-log-based* methods and *profile-based* ones. Although there are pros and cons for both types [5], the *profile-based* PWS has demonstrated more effectiveness in improving the quality of web search recently, with increasing usage of personal and behavior information to profile its users, which is usually gathered implicitly from query history [22, 19, 21], browsing history [20, 17], click-through data [16, 12, 5], bookmarks [10], user documents [22, 27] and so forth. Unfortunately, this implicitly collected personal data can easily reveal a gamut of the user's private life. Privacy issues rising from the lack of protection for such data, for instance the AOL query logs scandal[7], not only cause panic among individual users, but also dampen the data-publisher's enthusiasm in offering personalized service. In fact, privacy concerns have become the major barrier for wide proliferation of PWS services.

To address this privacy threat, researchers of profile-based PWS have to consider two contradicting effects during the search process. On one hand, they attempt to improve the search quality with the personalization utility of the user profile. On the other hand, they need to hide the privacy existing in the user profile to minimize the risk of privacy breach. A few previous studies [27, 9] suggest that people may compromise privacy if the personalization yields them profitability in service quality. In an ideal case, significant gain in personalization would be easily traded with only a small portion, often referred to as a *generalization*, of the user profile. Thus, user privacy can be protected without compromising the personalized search quality.

Unfortunately, these previous works do not address privacy protection in PWS adequately. The problems with the existing methods are explained in the following observations.

(1) *The existing works in privacy protection of PWS generalizes each user profile for only once off line, and then use Such profile to personalize all queries from a same user indiscriminatingly.* The "one profile fits all" strategy certainly has drawbacks given a variety of queries. One evidence reported in [5] is that profile-based personalization may not even help to improve the search quality for some ad-hoc queries, though exposing user profile to a server could put the user's privacy at risk. Therefore, a query-oriented decision on generalization degree, and even on whether personalize the search or not, would help to provide flexible service. To the best of our knowledge, no previous work has supported such feature.

(2) *The current solutions do not take into account the customization of privacy requirements, probably making some user profiles to be over-generalized while some others insufficiently generalized.* For example, in [27], all the sensitive topics are detected using an absolute metric called surprisal based on the information theory, assuming that the interests with less user document support are more sensitive. However, this assumption may not be correct. If a user has a large number of documents about "sex", the surprisal of this topic may lead to a conclusion that "sex" is very general and not

SIGIR'11, July 24–28, 2011, Beijing, China.

sensitive, despite the truth which is opposite. Unfortunately, few prior work can effectively address individual privacy needs during the generalization.

(3) *Many personalization techniques require iterative user interactions when creating personalized search results.* For example, some click-based metrics as *rank scoring* [2] and *average rank* [12], etc., are used to refine the search results through multiple query iterations. This paradigm is however infeasible as user profile generalization is needed for protecting privacy for each query. This inevitably pose a new challenge in terms of efficiency. Thus we need predictive metrics for the search quality and breach risk after personalization, without incurring iterative user interaction.

To solve the above problems, our approach customizes profile generalization on two levels, namely the *user-level* and the *query-level*. The *user-level* customization allows users to specify personalized privacy requirements. The *query-level* customization varies the generalization granularity based on the contents of the query. Meanwhile, our approach guarantees the efficiency during the generalization as it has to be applied online.

We perform the online generalization based on two conflicting metrics, namely the *query utility* and the *risk of privacy disclosure*, defined for user profiles, which are captured in a hierarchical taxonomy. The basic idea is to maintain the complete user profile on the client side, and exploit the semantic information contained in the taxonomy to model user-specified privacy requirements. Given a query, a local search wrapper employs a generalization algorithm which attempts to strike a balance between the two metrics, while respecting the privacy requirements. The output is then exposed to the server to personalize the search results. Our main contributions are summarized as following.

- We propose a PWS framework called UPS (literally for User customizable Privacy-preserving Search) that can generalize profiles for each query according to user-specified privacy requirements.
- We propose two predictive metrics to evaluate the privacy breach risk and the query utility for hierarchical user profile.
- We develop two simple but effective generalization algorithms for user profiles allowing for query-level customization using our proposed metrics.
- We provide an online mechanism based on query utility for deciding whether to personalize a query in UPS.
- Extensive experiments demonstrate the efficiency and effectiveness of our UPS framework.

The rest of this paper is organized as follows. Section 2 reviews the related work, focusing on PWS and its privacy preservation. Section 3 briefly describes the UPS architecture. Section 4 introduces the user profile data and gives the problem statement. The generalization techniques used in UPS are proposed in Section 5. The experimental results and findings are reported in Section 6. Finally, Section 7 concludes the paper.

2. RELATED WORKS

In this section, we overview the related works. We focus on the literature of profile-based personalization and privacy protection in PWS system.

2.1 Profile-Based Personalization

Previous works on profile-based PWS mainly focus on improving the search utility. The basic idea of these works is to tailor the search results by referring to, often implicitly, a user profile that reveals an individual information goal. In the remainder of this subsection, we review the previous solutions to PWS on two aspects, namely the *representation* of profiles, and the *measure* of the effectiveness of personalization.

Many profile representations are available in the literature to facilitate different personalization strategies. Earlier techniques utilize term lists/vectors [20] or bag of words[22] to represent their profile. However, most recent works build profiles in hierarchical structures due to their stronger descriptive ability, better scalability, and higher access efficiency. The majority of the hierarchical representations are constructed with existing weighted topic hierarchy/graph, such as ODP[1] [5, 4, 19, 11], Wikipedia[2] [6, 14], etc. Another work in [27] builds the hierarchical profile automatically via term-frequency analysis on the user data. In our proposed UPS framework, we do not focus on the implementation of the user profiles. Actually, our framework can potentially adopt any hierarchical representation based on a taxonomy of knowledge.

As for the performance measures of PWS in the literature, Normalized Discounted Cumulative Gain (nDCG) [8] is a common measure of the effectiveness of an information retrieval system. It is based on a human-graded relevance scale of item-positions in the result list, and is therefore known for its high cost in explicit feedback collection. To reduce the human involvement in performance measuring, researchers also propose other metrics of personalized web search that rely on clicking decisions, including *Average Precision* [1, 27], *Rank Scoring* [2], and *Average Rank* [19, 12]. We use the *Average Precision* metric, proposed by [5], to measure the effectiveness of the personalization in UPS. Meanwhile, our work is distinguished from previous studies as it also proposes two predictive metrics, namely *search utility* and *risk of privacy disclosure*, on a profile instance without requesting for user feedback.

2.2 Privacy Protection in PWS System

Generally there are two classes of privacy protection problems for PWS. One class includes those treat privacy as the identification of an individual, as described in [18]. The other includes those consider the sensitivity of the data, particularly the user profiles, exposed to the PWS server.

Typical works in the literature of protecting user identifications (class one) try to solve the privacy problem on different levels, including the *pseudo-identity*, the *group identity*, *no identity*, and *no personal information*. Solution to the first level is proved to fragile[7]. The third and fourth levels are impractical due to high cost in communication and cryptography. Therefore, the existing efforts focus on the second level. Both [26] and [28] provide online anonymity on user profiles by generating a group profile of k users. Using this approach, the linkage between the query and a single user is broken. In [3], the useless user profile (UUP) protocol is proposed to shuffle queries among a group of users who issue them. As a result any entity cannot profile a certain individual. These works all assume the existence of a trustworthy third-party anonymizer, which is not readily available over the Internet at large.

The solutions in class two do not require third-party assistance. In these solutions, users only trust themselves and cannot tolerate the exposure of their complete profiles an anonymity server. In [9], Krause et al. employ statistical techniques to learn a probabilistic model, and then use this model to generate the near-optimal partial profile. One main limitation in this work is that it builds the user profile as a finite set of attributes, and the probabilistic model is trained through predefined frequent queries. These assumptions are impractical in the context of PWS. Xu et al. proposed a privacy pro-

[1]Open Directory Project (ODP), http://dmoz.org/

[2]Wikipedia, the Free Encyclopedia, http://www.wikipedia.org/

tection solution for PWS based on hierarchical profiles [27]. Using a user-specified threshold, a generalized profile is obtained in effect as a rooted subtree of the complete profile. Unfortunately, this work does not address the query utility, which is crucial for the service quality of PWS. For comparison, our approach takes both the privacy requirement and the query utility into account.

A more important property which distinguishes our work from [27] is that we provide *personalized privacy protection* in PWS. The concept of personalized privacy protection is first introduced by Xiao et al. [24] in Privacy-Preserving Data Publishing (PPDP). A person can specify the degree of privacy protection for her/his sensitive values by specifying "guarding nodes" in the taxonomy of the sensitive attribute. Motivate by this, we allow users to customize privacy needs in their hierarchical user profiles.

Aside from the above works, a couple of recent studies have raised an interesting question which concerns the privacy protection in PWS. The works in [5, 23] have found that personalization may have different effects on different queries. Queries with larger *click-entropies*, namely distinct queries, are expected to benefit more from personalization, while those with smaller values (ambiguous ones) are not. Moreover, the latter may even cause privacy disclosure. Therefore, the need for personalization becomes questionable for such queries. Teevan et al. [23] collect a set of features of the query to classify queries by their click-entropy. While these works are motivative in questioning whether to personalize or not to, they assume the availability of massive user query logs (on the server side) and user feedback. In our UPS framework, we differentiate distinct queries from ambiguous ones based on a client-side solution using the predictive query utility metric.

3. OVERVIEW OF UPS

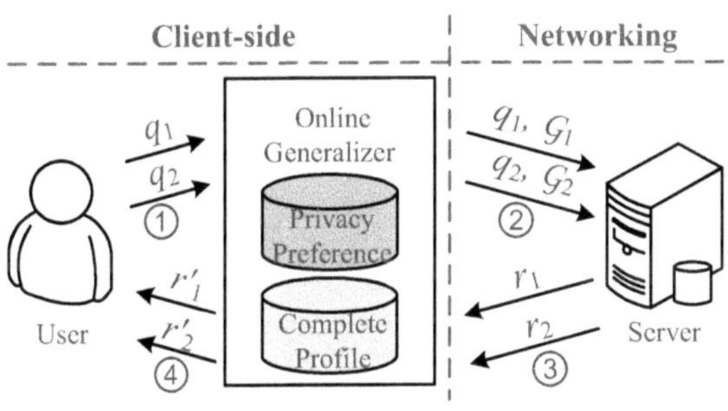

Figure 1: System architecture of UPS

The UPS framework consists of a non-trusty search engine server and a number of clients. As illustrated in Figure 1, each client user accessing the search service trusts no one but himself/herself. The key facility for privacy protection is an *online generalizer* implemented as a search proxy running on the client machine itself. The proxy maintains both the complete *user profile*, in a hierarchy of nodes with semantics, and the *user-specified (customized) privacy requirements* represented as a set of *forbidden nodes*.

The search process is described as following. (1) When a user issues a query q_i on the client, the proxy generalizes the user profile according to both the *user-specified privacy requirements* and the *query content*. The former is used for user-level customization while the latter is for query-level customization. The output of this run-time step is a generalized user profile $\mathcal{G}_i$ satisfying the privacy requirements. (2) Subsequently the query and the generalized user profile are sent together to the PWS server for personalized search. (3) The search results are personalized with the profile and delivered back to the query proxy. (4) Finally, the proxy either presents the raw results to the user, or reranks them with the complete user profile.

In the next section, we shall focus on the novel techniques in (1) representing user profile in a hierarchical taxonomy; (2) generalizing the profile according to customized privacy requirements; (3) optimzing the generalization.

4. DATA STRUCTURE AND PROBLEM DEFINITION

In this section, we first introduce the structure of user profile in UPS. Then we describe the techniques to generalize a user profile. Finally, we present the attack model and formulate the problem of privacy protection in user profile generalization.

4.1 User Profile

Consistent with many previous works in personalized Web services, each user profile in UPS adopts a hierarchical tree structure. Each node in the tree is selected from a taxonomy repository. For ease of presentation, Table 1 summarizes all the symbols used in this paper.

Table 1: Symbols and Descriptions

Symbol	Description
$root(\mathcal{T})$	The root of the tree $\mathcal{T}$
$subtr(n,\mathcal{T})$	The subtree rooted on n within $\mathcal{T}$
$paren(n,\mathcal{T})$	The parent of n within $\mathcal{T}$
$C(n,\mathcal{T})$	Children of n within $\mathcal{T}$
$S(\mathcal{T})$	All nodes to build the tree $\mathcal{T}$
$P(n,\mathcal{T})$	All nodes on the path from root of $\mathcal{T}$ to n

We start by introducing two assumptions to formalize our definition of user profile:

ASSUMPTION 1. *There exists a public accessible taxonomy repository, denoted as $\mathcal{R}$, which represents the entire topic domain (of human knowledge) as a huge topic hierarchy.*

Specifically, given any topic t detected with human knowledge, we can find a corresponding node (also referred to as t) within $\mathcal{R}$. Moreover, the subtree $subtr(t,\mathcal{R})$ is recognized as the taxonomy accompanying topic t.

ASSUMPTION 2. *Every node t within the taxonomy repository $\mathcal{R}$ is labeled with a coefficient called* succession ratio, *denoted by $t.succ$, which describes how likely a topic can be narrowed down from its parent node. Formally,* succession ratio *is defined as:*

$$t.succ = \begin{cases} Pr(t) = 1, & t = root(\mathcal{R}) \\ Pr(t|paren(t,\mathcal{R})), & t \neq root(\mathcal{R}). \end{cases} \quad (1)$$

The above assumptions can be used to define a probability model which is crucial for defining the user profile. If both assumptions are satisfied, $\mathcal{R}$ can be mapped to a weighted partition strategy on the probability space of the topic domain. Then, every topic inside $\mathcal{R}$ can be considered as a random event. The root of $\mathcal{R}$ represents the domain itself, and its probability is obviously 100%. For any other topic t, the probability can be calculated by multiplying the succession ratio when traversing the path from the root to t.

$$\begin{aligned} Pr(t) &= t.succ \times Pr(paren(t,\mathcal{R})) \\ &= \prod_{s\in P(t,\mathcal{T})} s.succ \end{aligned} \quad (2)$$

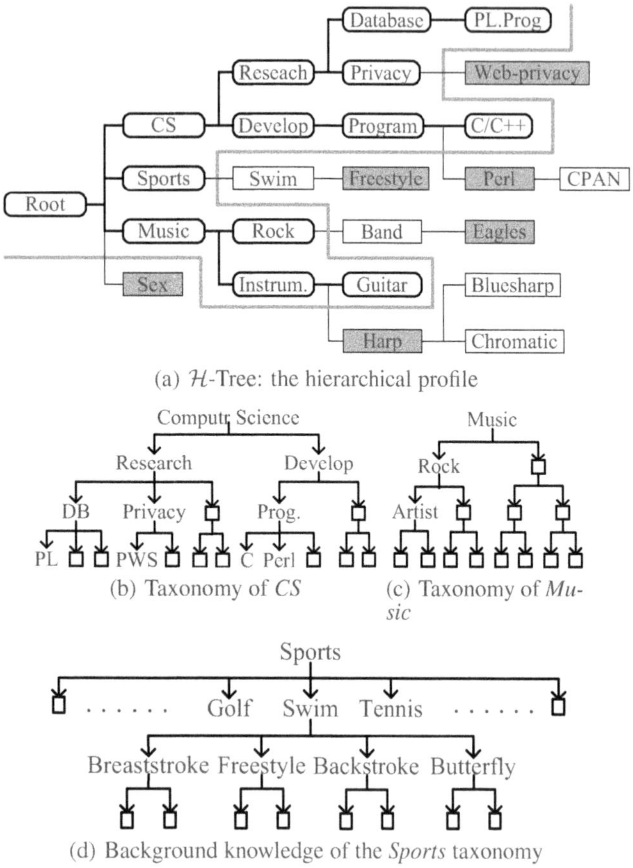

Figure 2: Taxonomy-based user profile

Before giving the formal definition of user profile, we also need to introduce the notion of rooted subtree.

DEFINITION 1. (ROOTED SUBTREE) *Given two trees $\mathcal{T}_1$ and $\mathcal{T}_2$, the predicate "$\mathcal{T}_1$ is a rooted subtree of $\mathcal{T}_2$" is* TRUE *if there exists a node set $D \subseteq S(\mathcal{T}_2)$ that, $\mathcal{T}_1$ is generated by removing the subtree set $\{subtr(t, \mathcal{T}_2) | t \in D\}$ from $\mathcal{T}_2$. We use $\mathcal{T}_1 = rsubtr(\mathcal{T}_2, D)$ to denote that $\mathcal{T}_1$ is a rooted subtree of $\mathcal{T}_2$ by removing node set D.*

Now we can formalize the user profile as follows:

DEFINITION 2. (USER PROFILE/$\mathcal{H}$-TREE) *Given a taxonomy repository $\mathcal{R}$, a user profile $\mathcal{H}$ is a* rooted subtree *generated from the taxonomy repository $\mathcal{R}$. i.e., the predicate "$\mathcal{H}$ is a rooted subtree of $\mathcal{R}$" is* TRUE.

As Definition 2 states, user profile $\mathcal{H}$ is a hierarchical representation of user's interests, in the form of a subset selected (no matter implicitly or explicitly) from the entire topic domain denoted by the repository $\mathcal{R}$. Hence, $\mathcal{H}$ inherits all its node features from $\mathcal{R}$, including the succession ratios of all nodes in $\mathcal{H}$.

A diagram of a sample $\mathcal{H}$-Tree is illustrated in Figure 2(a). We can observe that the user is mainly interested in *Computer Science* and *Music*, because the major portion of this profile is made up of fragments from taxonomies of *CS* and *Music*, as shown in Figure 2(b) and 2(c) respectively. Some other taxonomies also serve in comprising the profile, for example *Sports* and *Sex*. Note that the irrelevant parts of the tree are omitted.

4.2 Customized Privacy Requirements

Customized privacy requirements are given by specifying a number of so-called *forbidden-nodes*. This process is also called *forbidding* in our work.

Given a user profile $\mathcal{H}$, a user can easily specify his/her privacy preference by selecting in $\mathcal{H}$ a number of sensitive topics (nodes) which are not allowed to appear in the generalized profile. These *forbidden-nodes* indicate the customized privacy requirements of the user and will not be disclosed to the server.

DEFINITION 3. (FORBIDDEN-NODE SET/$F(U)$) *Given a user U and his/her profile $\mathcal{H}$, the Forbidden-Node Set, denoted as $F(U)$, is the set of sensitive topics specified by U that satisfies the following two constraints:*
1)$F(U) \subseteq S(\mathcal{H})$.
2)$\forall f1, f2 \in F(U)$ $(f1 \neq f2)$, $f1$ cannot present in the subtree of $f2$, i.e., $subtr(f2, \mathcal{H})$.

In the sample profile shown in Figure 2(a), user U specifies $F(U)$ = {*PWS-privacy*, *Freestyle*, *Perl*, *Eagles*, *Harp*, *Sex*} as the forbidden-node set, which is highlighted in dark color in $\mathcal{H}$. Apparently, all the subtrees rooted at any nodes in $F(U)$ must also be removed in the generalized profile. For example, both *Bluesharp* and *Chromatic* under *Harp* should be removed. This is because an adversary can easily infer the forbidden-nodes from them given the knowledge of the public accessible taxonomy repository $\mathcal{R}$.

Note that there are some special cases for $F(U)$ which do not require generalization. Specifically, $F(U) = \emptyset$ implies that U is willing to release the entire $\mathcal{H}$, while $F(U) = \{root(\mathcal{H})\}$ means that U will not disclose any personal information for PWS.

4.3 Generalizing User Profile

Specifying a forbidden-node set $F(U)$ may not be enough for privacy protection, as rooted subtree $rsubtr(\mathcal{H}, F(U))$ may still lead to severe privacy disclosure. In the profile shown in 2(a), the user forbids *Freestyle* to conceal his/her swimming stroke from others. Thus, the output of a forbidding operation on the profile only releases its parent node *Swim*. Unfortunately, an adversary may probably infer *Freestyle*, because in the background knowledge of Swim (Figure 2(d)), Freestyle is a main branch besides the other three. If all styles are equally distributed, the probability of leakage is 25%. In contrast, suppose that node Swim has numerous sibling nodes in the background knowledge of the Sports taxonomy, if we remove node *Swim*, making node *Sports* a leaf node of the generalized profile, the output would provide much stronger protection to the user's privacy. The reason is that the probability of the forbidden-node leakage (Freestyle) becomes much smaller now. The process of removing nodes which cause large probabilities of forbidden-node leakage is called *pruning*.

As another example, the parent node of Harp, namely Instrument, does not need to be pruned because the latter owns a large number of child nodes in the background knowledge. To save space, we do not plot the background knowledge of the taxonomy under node Instrument.

By performing the forbidding and pruning procedures, we can obtain a generalized user profile defined as follows.

DEFINITION 4. (GENERALIZED PROFILE/$\mathcal{G}$-TREE) *A generalized profile is a rooted subtree obtained in effect by removing a node set $X(U)$ from $\mathcal{H}$, i.e., $rsubtr(\mathcal{H}, X(U))$, where $X(U)$ satisfies*
1) $\forall f \in F(U)$, $\exists x \in X(U)$ and $f \in S(subtr(x, \mathcal{H}))$,
2) $\forall x1, x2 \in X(U)$ $(x1 \neq x2)$, $x1$ cannot present in the subtree of $x2$, i.e., $subtr(x2, \mathcal{H})$.

The nodes in $X(U)$ define a *guarding boundary* in $\mathcal{H}$. In our running example, $X(U)$ = {*PWS-privacy*, *Perl*, *Swim*, *Band*, *Harp*, *Sex*}, and is visualized as the red curve in Figure 2(a).

4.4 Attack Model and Problem Definition

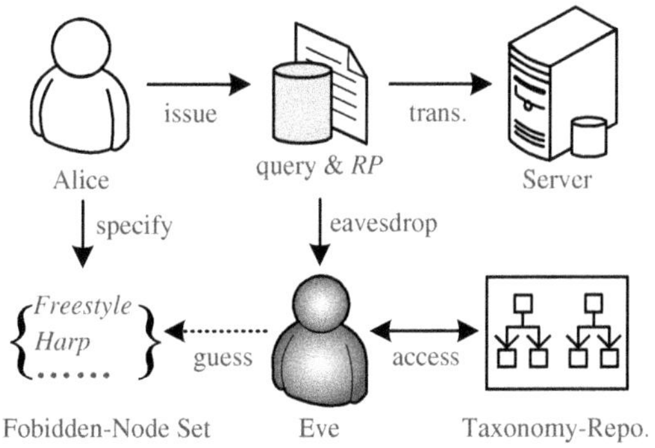

Figure 3: Attack model of personalized web search

Based on the above discussions, we can hereby define the attack and formulate the optimization problem for generalizing user profile. Our work aims at providing protection against a typical kind of privacy attack, namely *eavesdropping*. Consider the scenario shown in Figure 3. To corrupt Alice's privacy, the eavesdropper Eve successfully intercepts the communication between Alice and the PWS-server through some measures, such as *man-in-the-middle* attack, invading the server, etc. Consequently, whenever Alice issues a query, the entire copy of the query together with a run-time generalized profile $\mathcal{G}$ will be captured by Eve. Based on $\mathcal{G}$, Eve will attempt to rebuild the original $\mathcal{H}$ and predict the Forbidden-Node Set of Alice, with the background knowledge from the public-accessible taxonomy repository $\mathcal{R}$.

It is worth mentioning that, in our attack model, Eve is regarded as an adversary satisfying the following assumptions.

Knowledge-bounded The background knowledge of the adversary should be limited to the taxonomy repository $\mathcal{R}$. Both the profile $\mathcal{H}$ and privacy are defined based on $\mathcal{R}$. This makes the profile-base generalization is incapable of resisting an adversary holding knowledge beyond such scope.

Session-bounded None of previous captured information is available for tracing the same victim in a long duration. In other words, the eavesdropping will be started and ended within a single query session.

These assumptions seem strong, but are reasonable in practice. This is due to the fact that majority of privacy attacks on the Web are undertaken by some automatic programs for sending targeted (spam) advertisements to a large amount of PWS-users. These programs rarely act as a real person that collects prolific information of a specific victim for a long time as the latter is much more costly. Subsequently, the privacy disclosure can be simplified to the exposure of user-specified Forbidden-Nodes, and can be measured by the probability the adversary touch any Forbidden-Node ($\forall f \in F(U)$) of an individual, provided that the generalized profile ($\mathcal{G}$) for a given query q is intercepted. Thus, the privacy protection of personalized web search is to minimize this probability.

Meanwhile, it is always important to minimize the loss of utility when generalizing the user profile for privacy protection. For instance, in the running example of Fig 2(a), if we prune node *Sports* instead of *Swim* from (G), the privacy of U will be protected. However, this operation should be avoided because it will introduce considerable ambiguity if U queries for something related to the *freestyle* stroke (maybe the server will respond with items about improvised hip-hop). We now define the problem of privacy-preserving generalization in UPS as follows. Our definition relies on both the metric of privacy and the one of utility,

PROBLEM 1. (δ-RISK PROFILE GENERALIZATION) *Given a user profile $\mathcal{H}$ with Forbidden-Node Set $F(U)$ specified, a query q, metric of privacy $risk(q, \mathcal{G})$, metric of utility $util(q, \mathcal{G})$ and a user specified threshold δ, the optimal privacy-preserving generalization is to find an optimal instance of $\mathcal{G}$ (denoted as $\mathcal{G}*$), which satisfies the following Equation 3.*

$$\mathcal{G}* = \underset{\mathcal{G}}{\operatorname{argmax}}(util(q, \mathcal{G})), \quad risk(q, \mathcal{G}) < \delta \tag{3}$$

Where δ is the user-tolerant upper bound of the probability the attacker can touch his/her privacy. Note that metrics $risk(q, \mathcal{G})$ and $util(q, \mathcal{G})$ only depends on the instance of $\mathcal{G}$ and the issued query q as they are implemented to predict the privacy risk and personalization utility of $\mathcal{G}$ over q, without any user feedback. More details of these metrics will be presented in Section 5.2.

5. IMPLEMENTATION AND OPTIMIZATION

In this section, we present our implementation of privacy-preserving generalization in UPS. The generalization is implemented in two phases, namely the *offline* and *online* phases. We shall first describe the key techniques in each phase briefly. Second, we discuss the problem of measuring utility and privacy online based on the query and generalized profile. Third, we propose two efficient heuristic algorithms to find the near-optimal trade-off between the utility and the user privacy during generalization. Finally, some extra issues are discussed.

5.1 Implementation of Generalization

In our solution, we initialize the client proxy (generalizer) by generating the complete user profile and his/her privacy preference during the offline processing. In the run-time, when a query is issued, the proxy computes a generalized $\mathcal{G}$-profile on the fly. Specifically, our solution consists of the following steps:

Offline-1. Hierarchical profile construction The first step of the offline processing is to build the user profile in a topic hierarchy $\mathcal{H}$ that reveals user interests. To construct the profile, we first transform various types of user data into a set of plain-text documents, denoted as $D(U)$. Then we initialize $\mathcal{H}$ as a single root node. Given a public accessible taxonomy repository $\mathcal{R}$ (e.g., ODP, Wikipedia, etc), we detect the topic t in $\mathcal{R}$ for every document $d \in D(U)$, and insert the vector of t into $\mathcal{H}$. At last, the profile of U is created when all the user documents are processed. It should be noted that this step is replaceable and thus it is open to all available solutions if only the generated profile satisfy Definition 2.

Algorithm 1: InitSensitivityLabels(t)

Input: A profile node t in $\mathcal{H}$

if $\|\mathcal{C}(t, \mathcal{H})\| > 0$ **then**
  foreach *node* $i \in \mathcal{C}(t, \mathcal{H})$ **do**
    InitSensitivityLabels(i);
  $t.sen \leftarrow \sum_{i \in \mathcal{C}(t,\mathcal{H})} i.sen \times i.succ$;

Offline-2. Integration of customized privacy requirements This step detects the risk (severity) of U's privacy corruption for the exposure of every node t in $\mathcal{H}$ according to $F(U)$, denoted as $t.sen$. First, for each node $t \in S(\mathcal{H})$, we need to prepare for the initial value of its sensitivity based on the following rule. If $t \in F(U)$, then $t.sen$ is initialized to 1.0. Otherwise, $t.sen$ is initialized to 0.0 as it is safe for sharing it. Second, our framework computes and labels the sensitivity of each node in $\mathcal{H}$ as Equation 4, following bottom-up fashion. This is achieved by invoking the recursive routine $InitSensitivityLabels$ on $root(\mathcal{H})$, as shown in Algorithm 1.

$$t.sen = Pr(F(U)|t) = \sum_{x \in F(U)} Pr(x|t) \tag{4}$$

When the above two steps are finished, we have obtained the profile $\mathcal{H}$ with privacy preference $F(U)$ ready, which sets up the basis for the *Online* processing. When a query q is issued, the online customized generalization consists of the following two steps:

Online-1. Query-topic mapping. Typically, a user profile $\mathcal{H}$ contains a variety of topics. To process query-level customized generalization on it, we need to extract the topic domain detected from the query, and use it as an early-pruning strategy to reduce the search space in the user profile. Following this idea, we employ a mapping strategy denoted by $\mathcal{M}_{\mathcal{R}}(.)$, which depends on $\mathcal{R}$, to assign the query q to the related topic domain $\mathcal{M}_{\mathcal{R}}(q)$, where each topic can be found as a node in $\mathcal{R}$. Moreover, each topic $t \in \mathcal{M}_{\mathcal{R}}(q)$ is associated with a weight $t.gain$, quantifying the relevancy between q and t. Since the number of related topics of different queries might be different. For fairness these weights are normalized as $t.gain = Pr(t|q)$. Thus, the greater $t.gain$ is, the higher possibility q covers the topic t. As the mapping strategy used here is also replaceable, different solutions can be adopted. The details of query-topic mapping will be presented in Section 5.4.

Online-2. Cost-based generalization. On the topic domain bounded by q and $\mathcal{H}$ in the previous step, the Online Generalizer solves Problem 1 in a cost-based manner. The details of this technique will also be given in Section 5.3.

5.2 The Metrics Used in Generalization

Before looking into the generalization algorithm, we need to handle a major challenge for designing the algorithm. That is how to construct an appropriate metrics, namely $util(q, \mathcal{G})$ and $risk(q, \mathcal{G})$, to predict the personalization utility and the privacy risk on issuing a query q with a selected instance of $\mathcal{G}$ effectively. We will analyze these two metrics separately at first.

The purpose of the utility metric is to predict the potential gain (in revealing the user's information goal) of the query q on a generalized profile $\mathcal{G}$. Different from the similar problem proposed by Krause. et. al [9], we do not have appropriate probabilistic tools to model the user's target intention. However, we can transform this utility prediction into the estimation of the discriminating power of a given query q (together with $\mathcal{G}$) under the assumption below.

ASSUMPTION 3. *When a PWS-strategy is given ,the search quality is only determined by the discriminating power of the query on the exposed profile.*

Intuitively, the *fewer* topics a query covers, the *more specific* these topics are, and the *more* discriminating power the query has. Based on this observation, we formalize the utility of a given q and $\mathcal{G}$ with the tool *Mutual Information*, i.e., $I_{\mathcal{G}}(Q;T)$ in Equation 5, which estimates how much knowing q reduces the uncertainty about the topic domain bounded by $\mathcal{G}$.

$$\begin{aligned} I_{\mathcal{G}}(Q;T) &= \sum_{q \in Q} \sum_{t \in S(\mathcal{G})} Pr(t,q) \log \left(\frac{Pr(t,q)}{Pr(t)\,Pr(q)} \right) \\ &= \sum_{q \in Q} Pr(q) \sum_{t \in S(\mathcal{G})} Pr(t|q) \log \left(\frac{Pr(t|q)}{Pr(t)} \right) \end{aligned} \tag{5}$$

Moreover, as our solution focuses on query-level customized generalization, the query set Q contains only one query q and thus $Pr(q) = 1$. As a result, Equation 5 can be simplified as

$$\begin{aligned} util(q, \mathcal{G}) &= I_{\mathcal{G}}(Q;T) = I_{\mathcal{G}}(q;T) \\ &= \sum_{t \in S_q(\mathcal{G})} Pr(t|q) \log \left(\frac{Pr(t|q)}{Pr(t)} \right) \\ &= D_{\mathrm{KL}}(Pr(t|q) \| Pr(t)) \end{aligned} \tag{6}$$

Notice that in Equation 6, $S_q(\mathcal{G})$ is a special topic set constructed as follows: $\forall t \in \mathcal{M}_{\mathcal{R}}(q)$, (i) if $t \in S(\mathcal{G})$, t is added to $S_q(\mathcal{G})$; otherwise (ii) walk through the path to t to reach the farthest topic t' within $\mathcal{G}$, and then add t' to $S_q(\mathcal{G})$. In this case, we need to add the quota of $t.gain$ to $t'.gain$. For example, assume that "Root/Sports/Football" is a related topic of the query issued by the owner of $\mathcal{H}$-profile in Figure 2(a), the corresponding topic that can be added to $S_q(\mathcal{G})$ is "Root/Sport".

The cost model of privacy is recognized by the overall identification of an individual's sensitive topics. For simplicity, we treat the confidentiality of $F(U)$ as a rigid target. That is, the exposure of any single Forbidden-Node $x \in F(U)$ is recognized as a privacy corruption. Then, the overall cost model over $\mathcal{G}$ is modeled as the maximum of the probability to reveal any Forbidden-Node with any topic t in $\mathcal{G}$ exposed. Using sensitivity labeled on each topic in $\mathcal{G}$ during **Offline-2**, we can define the privacy cost with the metric $risk(q, \mathcal{G})$ in Equation 7.

$$\begin{aligned} risk(q, \mathcal{G}) &= \max_{t \in S_q(\mathcal{G})} \sum_{x \in F(U)} Pr(x|t) \\ &= \max_{t \in S_q(\mathcal{G})} t.sen \end{aligned} \tag{7}$$

We have described how we can quantify the utility $util(q, \mathcal{G})$ for any given instance of generalized profile $\mathcal{G}$, and its associated privacy cost $risk(q, \mathcal{G})$. Using these two predictive metrics, the framework UPS can embody the generalization self-adaptively. Intuitively, our goal is to find a $\mathcal{G}$, that maximizes $util(q, \mathcal{G})$ while keeping $risk(q, \mathcal{G})$ under the threshold δ, as defined in Problem 1.

5.3 The Optimization Algorithms

Basically, finding the optimal generalization needs to evaluate metrics $util$ and $risk$ on all possible candidates. Due to the huge space of possible topics determined by the repository $\mathcal{R}$, the main challenge here is to reduce the computational hardness. Suppose $\mathcal{H}$ is a tree having depth n and an average fanout of m. As all rooted subtrees of $\mathcal{H}$ are candidates of $\mathcal{G}$, the number of candidates grows exponentially with $m * n$, as shown in Equation 8.

$$O(m,n) = \begin{cases} a_0 = 0, & n = 0, \\ a_n = (a_{n-1}+1)^m, & n > 0. \end{cases} \approx O(2^{m*n}) \tag{8}$$

It can be proven that finding the optimal generalization candidate is NP-hard, as it is a reduction from another NP-hard problem proposed in [9]. In [9], Krause et al. model the user profile as a finite set of personal attributes $V = \{v_1, v_2, ...v_n\}$, and quantify the utility (of predicting the user's target) and the risk (of identifying the user) over a given set $A \subseteq V$. They then propose the problem of selecting an optimal subset $A*$ of attributes to reveal (known as *Attribute Selection*), which maximally an aggregative metrics considering both the utility and the risk as much as possible. Krause et al. have proven that this is an NP-hard search problem, which can be reduced to our problem.

THEOREM 1. *Finding Optimal δ-Risk Profile Generalization (Problem 1) is NP-hard.*

PROOF. The reduction is quite straightforward: Given an instance of set V in *Attribute Selection*, we construct a corresponding instance of the hierarchal profile $\mathcal{H}$ in *Profile Generalization* by simply considering all the attributes of V as leaves and assigning $root(\mathcal{H})$ as the parent to them. In this depth-2 hierarchy, for each leaf v, its $v.gain$ and $v.sen$ are specified with definitions in *Attribute Selection*. Obviously, the output instance of $G*$ in *Profile Generalization* is also the solution to *Attribute Selection* since $G*$ is another depth-2 hierarchy having set $A*$ as leaves. □

Algorithm 2: GreedyUtility($\mathcal{H}$, $\mathcal{M}_\mathcal{R}(q)$, δ)

Input: profile $\mathcal{H}$; topic domain $\mathcal{M}_\mathcal{R}(q)$; threshold δ
Output: generalized profile $\mathcal{G}*$ satisfying δ-privacy

1 Calculate $clarity(q)$ with Equation 9;
2 **if** $clarity(q) < \mu$ **then**
3 Let $u_{max} \leftarrow -\infty$;
4 Let $\mathcal{G}* \leftarrow \emptyset$;
5 Let $\mathcal{G} \leftarrow rsubtr(\mathcal{H}, F(U))$;
6 Generate $S_q(\mathcal{G})$ by imposing $\mathcal{M}_\mathcal{R}(q)$ on $\mathcal{G}$;
7 Rebuild $\mathcal{G}$ from $S_q(\mathcal{G})$;
8 **while** $\mathcal{G} \neq root(\mathcal{R})$ **do**
9 **if** $risk(q, \mathcal{G}) < \delta$ *and* $util(q, \mathcal{G}) > u_{max}$ **then**
10 $\mathcal{G}* \leftarrow \mathcal{G}$;
11 $u_{max} \leftarrow util(q, \mathcal{G})$;
12 Let $x \leftarrow \text{argmax}_{t \in S_q(\mathcal{G})}\ util(q, rsubtr(\mathcal{G}, \{t\}))$;
13 $\mathcal{G} \leftarrow rsubtr(\mathcal{G}, \{x\})$;
14 Update $S_q(\mathcal{G})$ by replacing x with $paren(x, \mathcal{G})$;
15 $paren(x, \mathcal{G}).gain \leftarrow paren(x, \mathcal{G}).gain + x.gain$;
16 Normalize $t.gain$ among $\forall t \in S_q(\mathcal{G})$;
17 **return** $\mathcal{G}*$;
18 **return** $root(\mathcal{R})$ as $\mathcal{G}*$;

In view of the computational hardness in finding the optimal generalization, we propose a greedy search algorithm, called GreedyUtility, to approximate this optimization. Algorithm 2 presents the pseudo-code of the algorithm.

The loop on line 8-16 is the core component of the algorithm. The basic idea is as follows: The algorithm iteratively chooses a topic t from the candidate set $S_q(\mathcal{G})$ when a further generalization, namely removing t from $\mathcal{G}$, can obtain the highest gain in the personalization utility performance $util(q, \mathcal{G})$. The iteration does not terminate until $\mathcal{G}$ is generalized to the single root. The intermediate instance of $\mathcal{G}$ with maximum $util$ and $risk$ under the threshold δ is recorded as $\mathcal{G}*$. Obviously, the search space of this algorithm is bounded to the number of nodes in the profile, i.e. $O(m^n)$, for a profile with average depth n and fanout m.

The time complexity of Algorithm 2 looks poor as it needs to greedily traverse through the generalization space to find the global optimal $\mathcal{G}$. Fortunately, this cost is significantly offset by the benefit of employing query-topic mapping. when we employ the related topic domain $\mathcal{M}_\mathcal{R}(q)$ (output of Query-topic mapping) to rebuild $\mathcal{G}$, the search space of the algorithm is reduced to $S_q(\mathcal{G})$. Since $\mathcal{G}*$ is initialized with the topics in $S_q(\mathcal{G})$, a considerable number of irrelevant branches (topics) at upper levels of $\mathcal{H}$ are pruned. Thus the initial number of leaves in $\mathcal{G}$ becomes very limited. As a result, the necessary number of iterations is reduced significantly after this process.

An additional optimization implemented in Algorithm 2 is the *clarity prediction*, namely to make online decision of whether to personalize a query. This is based on an observation that a great number of queries are distinct enough to describe the users' information needs without ambiguity. For such queries, personalization may be unnecessary, and profile-based personalization will contribute little or even harm the quality of service, as demonstrated in [5]. We use the proposed predictive query utility to detect such queries. Formally, each query is given a clarity measure over the taxonomy repository.

$$clarity(q) = util(q, \mathcal{R}) = I_\mathcal{R}(q; T) \quad (9)$$

In the algorithm, if $clarity(q) > \mu$, where μ is a system parameter, we skip the generalization and do not send the personalized profile to the server.

Algorithm 2, GreedyUtility, is the direct approximate solution to the Problem 1, which is based on the observation that users usually prefer to constrain the risk of privacy disclosure during the generalization and try to maximize the query utility. Moreover, GreedyUtility can resist adversaries without the *Session-bounded* constant, if the user does not increase the threshold δ.

We also propose another algorithm, GreedyPerformance, which simply tries to find $\mathcal{G}*$ that maximizes an aggregative metric $perf$ combined with $util$ and $risk$ (instead of only $util$ in GreedyUtility). GreedyPerformance is only used in experiment to analyze the trade-off between the utility and the privacy. The aggregative metric $perf$ will be presented in Section 6.2;

5.4 Extra Issues in Generalization

As mentioned in Section 5.1, step Offline-1 and Online-1 can both be replaced by alternative methods. However, the effectiveness of the UPS framework depends largely on the taxonomy repository being used. We recommend to employ hands-on and well-defined concept categorizations, such as ODP [4, 19], Wikipedia [6, 14] etc. For other methods not based on such taxonomies [27], we can extract the repository by mining the topic distribution among the documents stored in the server. Nevertheless, this simulation is expensive to process.

Meanwhile, our framework assumes the availability of *succession ratio* information within the repository $\mathcal{R}$, which has been supported by many solutions, e.g., the tree-profile of [27], where each node is associated with a set of supporting documents covering its topic. The *succession ratio* of a topic t (i.e., $t.succ$) can be instanced as the proportion of t's supporting documents in the supporting documents of t's parent. In fact, even if these succession ratios are absent in the repository, we can easily simulate them. One straightforward method is to use the topological structure of the taxonomy itself. For instance, Swim only has four children in the taxonomy of Swim, as shown in Figure 2(d), and hence $Freestyle.succ$ can be simply calculated as $1/4 = 0.25$. Similarly, succession ratios of *Breaststroke*, *Backstroke* and *Butterfly* can be computed.

As for the mapping strategy used in Online-1, different solutions can be adopted. While some strategies [15, 13] assigns weights to all candidates in $\mathcal{M}_{\mathcal{R}}(q)$, others do not. In the latter situation, we can simply share weights equally among the related topics, i.e., for $|\mathcal{M}_{\mathcal{R}}(q)| = n, \forall t \in \mathcal{M}_{\mathcal{R}}(q), t.gain = Pr(t|q) = 1/n$. In addition, to solutions without the ready-to-use repository, the alternative of mappings is to use the term-distance between the query and topic label. Nevertheless, such mapping strategy is unstable because it suffers from the common limitation of term-based profile, such as *irrelevant words*, *polysomy*, and *synonymy* etc.

6. EXPERIMENTAL RESULTS

In this section, we present the experimental results of UPS. We conduct three experiments on UPS. In the first experiment, we study the detailed results of the metrics in each iteration of the proposed algorithms. Second, we look at the effectiveness of the proposed Query-Topic Mapping techniques. In the third experiment, we study the effectiveness of Clarity Prediction technique and the search quality of UPS.

6.1 Experimental Setup

The UPS framework is implemented on a PC with a Pentium Dual-Core 2.50GHz CPU and 2GB main memory, running Microsoft Windows XP. All the algorithms are implemented in Java.

To evaluate the UPS framework, we use the AOL search query data as our dataset, which is the most recent published data we could find. The AOL search query data contains over 20 million queries and 30 million clicks of 650k users over 3 months (March 1, 2006 to May 31, 2006). The data format of each record is as follows:

$$\{AnonID,\ Query,\ QueryTime[,\ ItemRank,\ ClickURL]\}$$

Where the first 3 fields stand for the user of the identifier $AnonID$ issued the $Query$ at the timestamp $QueryTime$, and the last 2 optional fields appear when the user further click the URL $ClickURL$ at the position $ItemRank$ in the rank list returned by AOL over $Query$. We extract query logs of 50 distinct users (with #clicks $\geqslant$ 2000) to build 50 user profiles. For each user, the user profile is built with the documents dumped from all $ClickURL$ in his/her log. In the original AOL-data, the $ClickURL$ field is truncated to the domain name (e.g. www.une.edu/mwwc/ becomes www.une.edu) except the URL is of the protocol *https*. As a result, we have to recover the full URLs by means of *REPLAY*. That is, to re-issue the $Query$ of the AOL-records to some designate search engines and then retrieve the URLs match $ClickURL$. We processed *REPLAY* respectively on top-100 results returned by Yahoo and ODP, and 40% (#clicks $\geqslant$ 800) and 25% (#clicks $\geqslant$ 500) full URLs is recovered. 80% of recovered documents are used to build profile and the rest are used as the test set.

We utilize the ODP Web Directory as the public accessible taxonomy repository $\mathcal{R}$. Note that the replaceable components of the framework (i.e. Offline-1 and Online-1) are both implemented using it. To build the complete user profile, each clicked document recovered from *REPLAY*, is mapped to a deep ODP category[3] using the method proposed by [25] and all these generated category vectors are combined together to form the profile $\mathcal{H}$. Additionally, the number of pages mapped to a specific ODP category can indicate the user's personal preference on it. Finally, for each profile, we randomly choose no more than 5 topics (with depth >= 3) as the Forbidden-Nodes.

During the Online process, we issue every query form the test set to a local search engine on the dump of ODP hierarchy [4] indexed with Luecene. The query-topic mapping of Online-1 is implemented by analyzing the statistics of ODP categories labeled on the returned documents, and the relevance weight of each topic, i.e., $t.gain$, is represented with the category frequency. After that the optimal generalized profile $\mathcal{G}*$ is used to re-rank the result list of the test query, the search quality can be evaluated on the ranked lists before and after personalization.

6.2 Experiment 1: Micro Results of Queries

In this experiment, we analyze and compare the effect of the generalization on queries with different *clarity*, and study the trade-off between utility and privacy in the GreedyPerformance algorithm. As mentioned in Section 5.3, GreedyPerformance use an aggregative metric $perf$ which is defined with both $util$ and $risk$ as follows:

$$perf(q, \mathcal{G}) = util(q, \mathcal{G}) - \lambda * risk(q, \mathcal{G}), \qquad (10)$$

where λ can be considered a privacy-to-utility conversion factor. We can find different solutions of $\mathcal{G}*$ by varying λ. In effect, a small λ leads to solutions with higher utility and higher cost, whereas a large values of λ incurs solutions with lower utility and lower privacy cost. The algorithm GreedyPerformance is only used to validate the feasibility to trade-off between the two contradicting metrics of utility and privacy. This idea is borrowed from [9].

All queries are clustered by their *clarity* values into three groups using the 1-dimensional k-means algorithm. These three groups are called *Distinct Queries*, *Medium Queries*, and *Ambiguous Queries*, in descending order of their respective clarity values. These groups can be specified according to the following empirical rules obtained by splitting the boundaries between two neighboring clusters.

- Distinct Queries for $clarity(q) > 9.3$.
- Medium Queries for $6.9 < clarity(q) \leq 9.3$.
- Ambiguous Queries for $clarity(q) \leq 6.9$.

As the results of queries within the same group display similar trends in this experiment, we only plot the results of three representative queries ("Wikipedia" for Distinct Queries, "Freestyle" for Medium Queries, and "Program" for Ambiguous Queries) in Figure 4. To facilitate the comparison, all results in this experiment are generated by using a particular user profile, that is, the entire repository $\mathcal{R}$. We simply use the related topics set $\mathcal{M}_{\mathcal{R}}(q)$ to be $F(U)$.

As Figure 4(a) shows, the utilities of all three samples show a diminishing-returns property during generalization, especially the ambiguous one (i.e. "Program"). This indicates that the higher-level topics in the profile are more effective in improving the search quality during the personalization, while the lower-level ones are less. This property has also been reported in [9, 27].

In addition, we observe the following results in Figure 4(a). First the distinct queries (i.e. "Wikipedia") require much fewer iterations than the ambiguous ones. Second, the diminishing-returns properties of the utility of ambiguous queries are more apparent, while the utility of distinct queries increases almost linearly in most iterations. The reason of such results is that the distinct queries have fewer related topics (usually less than 3 in our experiment) than the ambiguous ones, and these topics are more specific. This significantly contributes to their $clarity$.

In Figure 4(b), the risk first declines rapidly, but the decrease slows down as more specific profile information becomes hidden. Figure 4(c) illustrates the trade-off pattern between the *utility* and

[3] To focus on the pure English categories, we filtered all categories under "*Top/World*" and "*Top/Adult/World*".

[4] URL: http://rdf.dmoz.org/rdf/content.rdf.u8.gz

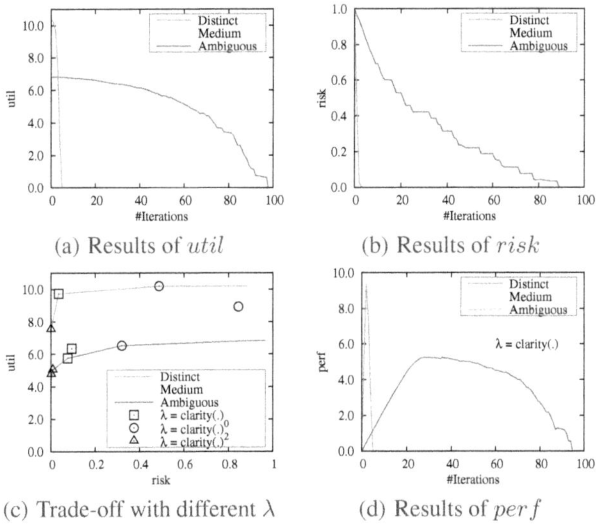

(a) Results of *util* (b) Results of *risk*

(c) Trade-off with different λ (d) Results of *perf*

Figure 4: Results of queries during each iteration in GreedP

risk measures. For all the queries, we observe an interesting finding that there is an apparent "knee" on their trade-off curve when $\lambda \approx clarity(q)$. Before this tuning point, small concessions on privacy can bring great promotion on utility; while after that, any tiny increase of utility will lead to enormous increase in risk. Hence, at this knee, we can achieve near-maximal utility at near-minimum cost. Therefore, we plot $perf$ with $\lambda = clarity(q)$ in Figure 4(d) for the three samples. The generalization finds out the near-optimal trade-off for all of them within limited iterations. The maximum value of overall performance of distinct queries is larger than the other groups since they have better utility.

6.3 Experiment 2: Effectiveness of Query-Topic Mapping

We first verify the effectiveness of query-topic mapping in our generalization algorithms. To facilitate the comparison, we simulate two typical user profiles: one named *diverse* is obtained by merging the subtrees of the related topics of the three queries groups (namely Distinct, Medium, and Ambiguous); the other named *similar* is obtained by randomly choosing three specific topics (low-level nodes) that are close in the taxonomy.

Table 2: Average Number of Iterations in Generalization

Profile	Query Group	GreedyP/U	Opti-QTM	Optimal
diverse	Distinct	8.73	19.41	1.32×10^{26}
	Medium	29.68	8.20×10^5	1.32×10^{26}
	Ambiguous	95.29	1.44×10^{18}	1.32×10^{26}
similar	Distinct	5.47	12.55	8.99×10^{11}
	Medium	17.13	1.56×10^4	8.99×10^{11}
	Ambiguous	49.97	1.15×10^9	8.99×10^{11}

Table 2 lists the average number of iterations of different algorithms, where *Opti-QTM* and *Optimal* stand for the exhaustive algorithms (with or without Query-Topic Mapping respectively) to find the optimal generalized profile. We can find that the original search space of *Optimal* is so huge that it is impractical to process the exhaustion on a complete profile. The introduction of Query-Topic Mapping reduces the search space significantly in *Opti-QTM*. However, the efficiency of exhaustion is still intolerable when $\|S_q(\mathcal{H})\|$ is large. Our greedy algorithms further reduce the search space to the size of the rebuilt profile (with $S_q(\mathcal{H})$ as leaves), therefore ensuring the efficiency of online generalization.

6.4 Experiment 3: Results of Clarity Prediction and Search Quality

In this experiment, we demonstrate the effectiveness of the proposed Clarity Prediction technique, and evaluate the real search quality on commercial search engines using our UPS framework. The search results is re-ranked with the generalized profile output by $GreedyUtility$ over 50 target users. The final search quality is evaluated using the Average Precision (denoted as $\mathcal{AP}$) of the click records of the users. $\mathcal{AP}$ is defined as

$$\mathcal{AP} = \sum_{i=1}^{n} \frac{i}{l_i.rank}/n \qquad (11)$$

where l_i is the ith relevant link identified for a query, and n is the number of relevant links.

For each test query, the framework computes the Borda fusion[5] of the *UPRank* τ_u and the original rank τ_o as the personalized ranking, and then evaluate the $\mathcal{AP}$ of the search results on both the fusion and the original ranking. UPRank is defined as the descending order of link l sorted by the $uscore$, which is the weighted sum over topics reserved in profile $\mathcal{G}*$, where the weight $rel(l,t)$ is the relevance between the link and the profile topic [25]. The $uscore$ is given by

$$uscore(l) = \sum_{t \in S_q(\mathcal{G}*)} rel(l,t). \qquad (12)$$

Figure 5 shows the average $\mathcal{AP}$ of the ranks before (Original) and after (Fusion) personalization (GreedyUtility with $\delta = 0.1$ and *clarity prediction* feature disabled) on the test queries respectively on Yahoo and ODP. From both results we can observe that improvements of the search quality for Medium Queries and Ambiguous Queries are much more significant than that of Distinct Queries. In particular, the personalization on Distinct Queries of Yahoo results reduces the average performance from 73.4% to 63.6%. This is because some irrelevant profile topics (noises) are added. The results demonstrate that profile-based personalization is more suitable for queries with small $clarity(q)$. Therefore, clarity prediction is an effective technique to determine whether personalization can improve the search quality of a given query.

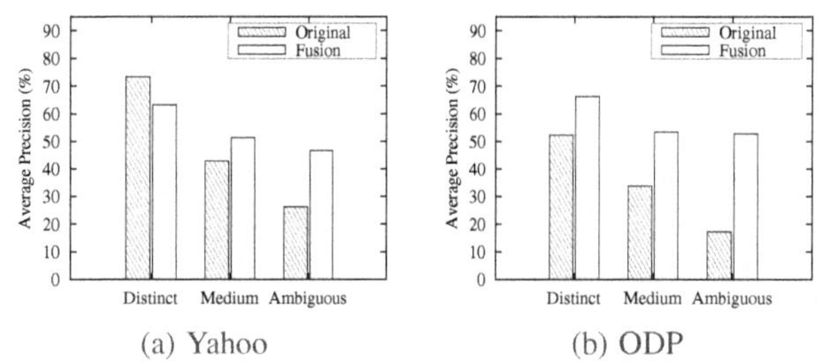

(a) Yahoo (b) ODP

Figure 5: Effectiveness of clarity prediction

Figure 6 shows the results of search quality by varying the δ threshold. It is observed that the average precision of FusionRank increases rapidly when δ grows from 0.0 to 0.1. Then, further increasing δ (in effect exposing more specific topics) will only improve the search quality marginally. Moreover, the $\mathcal{AP}$ of FusionRank based on Yahoo (Figure 6(a)) has a dramatic drops when $\delta >= 0.3$.

A comparison between the personalization results of ODP and Yahoo reveals that, although the original ODP-Rank ($\mathcal{AP} = 37.3\%$)

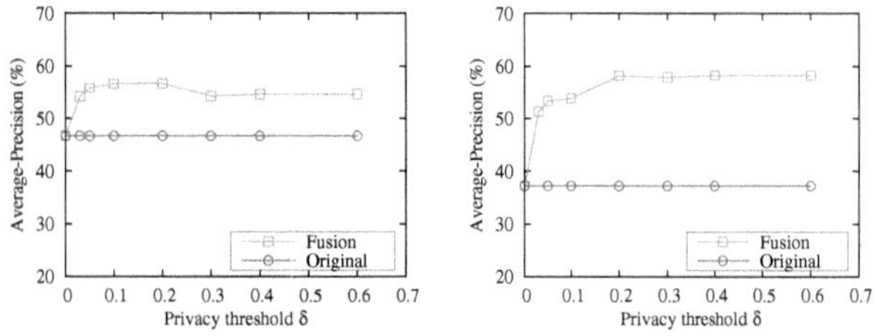

(a) Yahoo (b) ODP

Figure 6: Results of personalized search performance

is much worse than the original Yahoo-Rank ($\mathcal{AP} = 46.7\%$), personalization on ODP will generate better ranking than that on Yahoo. The reason for this maybe is that the document-distribution of ODP over all the available topics is expectedly more consistent with its own taxonomy repository, which has been used to implement our framework.

7. CONCLUSIONS

This paper presented a client-side privacy protection framework called UPS for personalized Web search. UPS could potentially be adopted by any PWS which captures user profiles in a hierarchical taxonomy. The framework allowed users to specify customized privacy requirements via the hierarchical profiles. In addition, UPS also performed online generalization on user profiles to preserve the personal privacy without compromising the search quality. We proposed two greedy algorithms, namely GreedyUtility and GreedyPerformance, for the online generalization. The GreedyUtility algorithm could maximize the query utility while maintaining the disclosure probability below a user-specified threshold. The GreedyPerformance algorithm could be used to strike a balance between the disclosure risk and the search quality. We also designed a novel method for deciding whether to personalize a query on-the-fly. This method was distinguished from the existing approaches as it completely relied on the client-side utility estimation of the query. Our experimental results revealed that UPS could achieve quality search results while preserving user's customized privacy requirements. The results also confirmed the effectiveness and efficiency of our solution.

For future work we will try to resist adversaries with boarder background knowledge, such as richer relationship among topics (e.g., exclusiveness, sequentiality, etc.), or capability to capture a series of k requests from the victim. We will also seek more sophisticated method to build the user profile, and better metrics to predict the performance (especially the utility) of UPS.

8. ACKNOWLEDGMENTS

This work is supported in part by the National Science Foundation of China (NSFC Grant No. 60803003, 60970124).

9. REFERENCES

[1] R. Baeza-Yates and B. Ribeiro-Neto. *Modern Information Retrieval*. Addison Wesley Longman, 1999.

[2] J. S. Breese, D. Heckerman, and C. M. Kadie. Empirical analysis of predictive algorithms for collaborative filtering. In *UAI*, pages 43–52, 1998.

[3] J. Castellí-Roca, A. Viejo, and J. Herrera-Joancomartí. Preserving user's privacy in web search engines. *Comput. Commun.*, 32(13-14):1541–1551, 2009.

[4] P. A. Chirita, W. Nejdl, R. Paiu, and C. Kohlschütter. Using odp metadata to personalize search. In *SIGIR*, 2005.

[5] Z. Dou, R. Song, and J.-R. Wen. A large-scale evaluation and analysis of personalized search strategies. In *WWW*, pages 581–590, 2007.

[6] E. Gabrilovich and S. Markovich. Overcoming the brittleness bottleneck using wikipedia: Enhancing text categorization with encyclopedic knowledge. In *AAAI*, 2006.

[7] K. Hafner. *Researchers Yearn to Use AOL Logs, but They Hesitate*. New York Times, August 23, 2006.

[8] K. Järvelin and J. Kekäläinen. Ir evaluation methods for retrieving highly relevant documents. In *SIGIR*, pages 41–48, 2000.

[9] A. Krause and E. Horvitz. A utility-theoretic approach to privacy in online services. *J. Artif. Intell. Res. (JAIR)*, 39:633–662, 2010.

[10] J. Pitkow, H. Schütze, T. Cass, R. Cooley, D. Turnbull, A. Edmonds, E. Adar, and T. Breuel. Personalized search. *Commun. ACM*, 45(9):50–55, 2002.

[11] A. Pretschner and S. Gauch. Ontology-based personalized search and browsing. In *ICTAI '99*, 1999.

[12] F. Qiu and J. Cho. Automatic identification of user interest for personalized search. In *WWW*, pages 727–736, 2006.

[13] G. Qiu, K. Liu, J. Bu, C. Chen, and Z. Kang. Quantify query ambiguity using odp metadata. In *SIGIR*, 2007.

[14] K. Ramanathan, J. Giraudi, and A. Gupta. Creating hierarchical user profiles using wikipedia. *HP Labs*, 2008.

[15] P. Schönhofen. Identifying document topics using the wikipedia category network. *WIAS*, 7(2):195–207, 2009.

[16] X. Shen, B. Tan, and C. Zhai. Context-sensitive information retrieval using implicit feedback. In *SIGIR*, 2005.

[17] X. Shen, B. Tan, and C. Zhai. Implicit user modeling for personalized search. In *CIKM*, 2005.

[18] X. Shen, B. Tan, and C. Zhai. Privacy protection in personalized search. *SIGIR Forum*, 41(1):4–17, 2007.

[19] M. Spertta and S. Gach. Personalizing search based on user search histories. In *WI*, 2005.

[20] K. Sugiyama, K. Hatano, and M. Yoshikawa. Adaptive web search based on user profile constructed without any effort from users. In *WWW*, 2004.

[21] B. Tan, X. Shen, and C. Zhai. Mining long-term search history to improve search accuracy. In *KDD*, 2006.

[22] J. Teevan, S. T. Dumais, and E. Horvitz. Personalizing search via automated analysis of interests and activities. In *SIGIR*, pages 449–456, 2005.

[23] J. Teevan, S. T. Dumais, and D. J. Liebling. To personalize or not to personalize: modeling queries with variation in user intent. In *SIGIR*, pages 163–170, 2008.

[24] X. Xiao and Y. Tao. Personalized privacy preservation. In *SIGMOD*, 2006.

[25] D. Xing, G.-R. Xue, Q. Yang, and Y. Yu. Deep classifier: automatically categorizing search results into large-scale hierarchies. In *WSDM*, pages 139–148, 2008.

[26] Y. Xu, K. Wang, G. Yang, and A. W.-C. Fu. Online anonymity for personalized web services. In *CIKM*, pages 1497–1500, 2009.

[27] Y. Xu, K. Wang, B. Zhang, and Z. Chen. Privacy-enhancing personalized web search. In *WWW*, pages 591–600, 2007.

[28] Y. Zhu, L. Xiong, and C. Verdery. Anonymizing user profile for personalized web search. In *WWW*, pages 1225–1226, 2010.

Handling Data Sparsity in Collaborative Filtering using Emotion and Semantic Based Features

Yashar Moshfeghi
School of Computing Science
University of Glasgow
Glasgow, UK
yashar@dcs.gla.ac.uk

Benjamin Piwowarski
School of Computing Science
University of Glasgow
Glasgow, UK
bpiwowar@dcs.gla.ac.uk

Joemon M. Jose
School of Computing Science
University of Glasgow
Glasgow, UK
jj@dcs.gla.ac.uk

ABSTRACT

Collaborative filtering (CF) aims to recommend items based on prior user interaction. Despite their success, CF techniques do not handle *data sparsity* well, especially in the case of the *cold start* problem where there is no past rating for an item. In this paper, we provide a framework, which is able to tackle such issues by considering item-related emotions and semantic data. In order to predict the rating of an item for a given user, this framework relies on an extension of Latent Dirichlet Allocation, and on gradient boosted trees for the final prediction. We apply this framework to movie recommendation and consider two emotion spaces extracted from the movie plot summary and the reviews, and three semantic spaces: actor, director, and genre. Experiments with the 100K and 1M MovieLens datasets show that including emotion and semantic information significantly improves the accuracy of prediction and improves upon the state-of-the-art CF techniques. We also analyse the importance of each feature space and describe some uncovered latent groups.

Categories and Subject Descriptors: H.3.3 Information Storage and Retrieval - *Information Search and Retrieval - Information Filtering*
General Terms: Performance, Experimentation
Keywords: Semantic, Emotion, Collaborative Recommendation, Collaborative Filtering

1. INTRODUCTION

Recommender systems attempt to alleviate users' information overload by filtering documents that are not relevant to the users' interests [1]. Amongst these, collaborative filtering (CF) systems are the most widely used [19]. CF techniques recommend an item to a user by considering data gathered from other users [7]. Examples of such systems are Amazon.com for products, and Netflix[1] for movies.

[1] http://www.netflixprize.com/

SIGIR'11, July 24–28, 2011, Beijing, China.

In this work, we propose a novel approach for CF by integrating semantic and emotion information along with the rating information. This is motivated by the fact that a user likes a movie for a set of latent reasons, e.g. due to style of its direction. This information can improve the CF system prediction accuracy, especially when data is sparse, i.e. when there is not enough data available (e.g. ratings) to be used by standard CF techniques. Data sparsity is a well-known problem for CF systems [1] and in the extreme case of the so-called "cold start" problem, there is no rating for new users or items, making the prediction process impossible.

From a technical perspective, for each semantic (e.g. actor) and emotion (e.g. plot summary emotion) space we propose to construct latent groups of users. In order to do so, we extend a well-known model-based approach, namely Latent Dirichlet Allocation (LDA) [2]. In each space, we propose a methodology to compute the probability that a given user likes an item. Finally, in order to predict a rating, the information about the different spaces is aggregated using standard machine learning techniques.

Our work also is one of the few that explores the use of emotion in IR. Emotion is being proposed as a good feature to use in IR experiments [21]. Recent advances in psychology and linguistics make emotion extraction from textual documents feasible, thus making it appropriate to consider emotional features in IR. Despite their potential important role, emotions are seldom used in CF. In this work, we extracted emotions using the OCC[2] model (Section 3.1), and developed a sophisticated psycho-linguistic model to extract emotions expressed in movie reviews and plot summaries. We use these as a new source of information that indicates whether a movie will be liked or not by any user.

Finally, from an experimental point of view, we have conducted extensive experiments where we vary the sparsity of the dataset and compare our models to two state-of-the-art CF approaches. Furthermore we present preliminary experiments in an item cold start scenario and analyse qualitatively the latent spaces uncovered by our extended LDA approach.

The rest of the paper is organised as follows: Section 2 discusses related works in CF and emotion extraction techniques, our approach is described in Section 3, experiment methodology in Section 4, results in Section 5, and finally the discussion and conclusion in Section 6.

[2] OCC stands for the creators of the model, Ortony, Clore and Collins.

2. BACKGROUND

2.1 Collaborative Filtering Categories

CF techniques mostly make use of users' past ratings to predict user's level of interest for an item. Despite their success they face issues of scalability and sparsity [1].

The scalability problem refers to the quantity of data, i.e. the number of users and items: many CF algorithms fail to scale to big datasets. This issue is further stressed by the fact that in real-world systems, new items and new users appear every day, therefore generating a huge amount of data.

The sparsity problem refers to the situations where the ratio of unrated items to rated ones is high therefore not providing enough information for CF systems for their predictions. Data sparsity can be down to many factors. Firstly, judging is a cognitively expensive activity [6]. Secondly, there are unpopular or unseen items [17]. Finally, in special cases, known as the *cold start* problem (i.e. new user and/or new item), no ratings are available at all. In the following, we discuss how previous works in CF have tackled these two challenges.

CF systems can be divided into memory- and model-based approaches [1]. In a memory-based approach, recommendation is made by determining the nearest neighbours of a user and/or item, and then aggregating the ratings of these neighbours. These CF techniques have the advantage of being better adapted to users with unusual tastes, but they are impractical to use [7] due to scalability issues since calculating the neighbourhood for users and/or items can be time consuming, especially in real life (i.e. commercial) datasets.

Model-based techniques learn a user and/or item model from data [7] and are able to scale to large datasets; the model proposed in this paper lies in this category. There are many different model-based approaches such as regression models [27] based on user and item features or clustering of user and/or items, but the most successful ones are based on dimensionality reduction techniques because they deal better with data sparsity. We rely on such techniques in this work.

Dimensionality reduction techniques find lower dimensional latent topics from a higher dimensional information space. The most well known of these approaches are Latent semantic indexing (LSI), Principal Component Analysis (PCA), or probabilistic approaches like the probabilistic LSI (pLSI) [8], nonparametric probabilistic Principal Component Analysis (NPCA) and LDA [2]. A downside of reducing the dimension is that important information (i.e. ratings) that can be useful for predicting unusual user-item ratings may also be discarded [30].

In order to deal with different feature spaces, we base our work on LDA, which can be extended for our purposes and has been shown to be competitive compared to state-of-the-art CF techniques, outperforming the unigram model and pLSI [2]. This approach is also the base of many state-of-the-art CF systems such as the URP model by Marlin [14]. LDA will assign high probabilities to movies that are liked *and* judged by many users thus favouring popularity over the fact of being liked. This "popularity" problem becomes worse when feature spaces are used since some features can be present in just a few movies (e.g. a user likes an actor who has played only in a few not so popular movies). In this work, we show how an extension of LDA can overcome this problem.

In order to cope with data sparsity, it is necessary to resort to external sources of information. This becomes mandatory when dealing with the cold start problem, since the absence of rating hinders the possibility of using CF techniques that rely only on rating information.

A common approach is to use the representation of users and items to predict ratings. For instance, [25] first uses these representations along with a user profile to create new ratings and then applies the standard CF techniques on the denser data. However, in these approaches, the similarity between item and user is based on the actual representations of their contents and not on the latent relation among them.

A second approach tries to use this external information by capturing the latent relationship between items and users. Mobasher [19] uses a memory-based approach that takes advantage of an ontology and of a latent semantic model. However, creating and maintaining the ontology is a very laborious task. Park and Chu [24] use regression techniques where user demographical information and the item metadata are used as features. However, the user demographic information is unreliable in general and, more importantly, in their approach users are not characterised by the movies they rated. Finally, Moshfeghi et al. [20] proposed to use a memory-based approach where the neighbourhood of an item in semantic spaces was used to predict the rating. However, in our work, we use a model-based technique, which can scale to large datasets and also considers both semantic and emotion information.

2.2 Emotion and Collaborative Filtering

Emotions are considered to be important factors influencing overall human effectiveness including the rational tasks such as reasoning, decision-making, communication and interaction [9]. In recent years there has been an increasing amount of research in both academia and industry to enable computers to detect emotions [3]. This is due to the utility of emotion information in applications such as those in affective computing, opinion mining, market analysis and human computer interaction. For example, Winoto and Tang [29] investigated the effect of user mood on their ratings and consequently modified a collaborative recommender system to depend on user mood. However, mood is difficult to gather since it either needs explicit feedback or relies on unreliable and invasive techniques (e.g. face detection). Fortunately, due to advances in NLP, we now have reliable tools to extract emotion data from textual sources [28]. Our approach exploits such techniques to extract emotional information and apply it in CF algorithms.

Text does not only contain topical but also emotional information. In fact, text contains clues to emotions related to what the writer wants to transmit or what his or her mood was at the time of writing [28]. Emotions extracted from text were first used in a sentiment analysis task [28]. The essential issue in sentiment analysis is to identify the positive (favourable) or negative (unfavourable) opinion towards the topic of a text. Sentiments extracted from movie reviews have been used to infer unknown ratings of users [23, 5]. Existing approaches (using sentiment in CF) are complementary to our work. For example using sentiment as a substitute for ratings [11] or relying on sentiment expressed over movie aspects (e.g. actors in the movie are good/bad) in order to provide opinionated ratings [10] could be used likewise in our work.

Other than using sentiments, none of the works exploit the much richer emotion information for collaborative filtering. In psycholinguistic and its practical applications, emotion sensing requires a significantly more detailed text analysis, since emotions are a finer-grained version of sentiment. We believe that this extra information is useful for CF.

There are multiple views on what emotions are and how they can be represented [9]. Ekman regards emotion as psychosomatic states and categorises them into six discrete categories[3] [3]. Some commercial systems follow this approach in order to classify emails [12]. The alternative OCC model [22] is considered to be more informative than Ekman's by the cognitive psychological community. It specifies 22 emotion types (joy, distress, happy-for, sorry-for, resentment, gloating, hope, fear, satisfaction, fears-confirmed, relief, disappointment, shock, surprise, pride, shame, admiration, reproach, gratification, remorse, gratitude and anger) and two cognitive states (love and hate), based on the valence reaction to agents, events and objects. One of the state-of-the-art emotion extraction methods was introduced by Shaikh et al. [28]. It adapts the OCC model for textual documents employing natural language processing techniques for emotion extraction. We use this method to identify emotions in text.

Given the improvement of emotion extraction systems and the overwhelming engagement of users in providing user-generated content and evidence on the role of emotion in decision making, we firmly believe that it is now appropriate to exploit emotions in recommendation. In contrast to previous work, we do not use sentiments to infer rating associated to a user review, but we instead use emotions as another source of information about an item, and show in the experiments that emotion information extracted from movie reviews and plot summaries can be useful to tackle the data sparsity problem.

3. APPROACH

In our approach, we postulate that CF techniques can be improved by taking into account item semantic and emotion information. In this section we describe our framework showing how it can be applied to movie recommendation.

We first suppose that a movie can be described as a set of features in a so-called feature space s. For example, in the actor space, a movie is described by the set of actors that played in the movie. The different spaces that we consider are further described in Section 3.1.

For a given space s, we first evaluate the probability that a user u, defined by his/her past ratings, likes the movie m that is described by a feature f (e.g. De Niro played in the movie):

$$P(+|f,u,s) \tag{1}$$

where $+$ denotes the event that a user likes a movie. In Section 3.2, we show how LDA was extended in order to compute this value.

As a movie is described by a set of features (e.g. actors in the actor space) and thus it is necessary to aggregate the probability in Eq. (1) over these features, i.e. to estimate the probability that a movie m is liked by user u:

$$P(+|m,u,s) \tag{2}$$

We show in Section 3.3 a way to estimate Eq. (2) given the different probabilities calculated with Eq. (1) for each possible feature where the presence of a feature independently influences the relevance of an item.

Because the underlying characteristics of feature spaces vary, they provide different, and hopefully complementary views on the same object. Therefore we chose to use a machine learning approach to combine the prediction made on individual spaces (Section 4.3.2). The performance of each individual feature space, and discussion of whether they complement each other is in Section 4.

3.1 Feature Spaces

In this paper, we considered three types of feature spaces. The first and simplest type of feature space is movie space where we consider the movie itself as a feature. In this space, the probability of a movie to be liked is directly given by Eq. (1) where f is the movie at hand. It is the space on which most of the CF systems are based since it relates movie and users by their ratings.

The second type of feature space is semantic. In this work, we consider three such spaces, namely actor, director and genre spaces, since they are readily available on the Web and are likely to be good predictors for user ratings. A movie is represented as the set of features that characterise the movie in each of these spaces. For example, in the actor space, the movie *Dr. Mabuse: The Gambler* is associated with the list of its actors, i.e. Rudolf Klein-Rogge, Aud Egede Nissen, etc.

Finally the last type of feature space is the emotion space where for each movie, emotion features are constructed based on the emotion extracted from its reviews or plot summaries. In order to extract emotions from text, we used our implementation[4] of Shaikh et al. [28] which is considered as the state-of-the-art method. Since the extraction is sentence-based, the following explains the method of aggregating the detected emotions for movie related texts.

Both movie reviews and plot summaries are composed of a set of texts, which in turn are composed of a set of sentences. Let T denotes the set of texts associated to a movie (either reviews or plot summaries), and S_t the set of sentences associated to a text $t \in T$.

The emotion classifier of Shaikh et al. [28] makes a binary decision about each emotion for a sentence, i.e. decides whether the emotion is present or not. For each sentence k of a text t, we can use this classifier to construct a vector of 24 components, each of those associated with one of the 22 emotions and two cognitive states (see Section 2.2). Each component can take the value 0 (the emotion is not present in the sentence) or 1 (the emotion is present).

In order to represent the emotions in a text $t \in T$, we sum the emotion vectors of the sentences in t. Since we want to give equal importance to each text, we normalise the values by dividing by the number of sentences. Then, for a set of texts T we sum the vectors corresponding to the individual texts and normalise again, this time by the number of texts.

[3]Specifically happiness, sadness, fear, anger, disgust and surprise

[4]This is due to the fact that some components of Shaikh et al.'s system are not available. Our implementation achieve a better performance than the Liu et al. [13] system, which is considered as another state-of-the-art emotion extraction method [28]

Formally an emotion vector for a set of texts T is defined as

$$emotions(T) = \frac{1}{|T|}\sum_{t\in T}\frac{1}{|S_t|}\sum_{k\in S_t} emotions(k) \quad (3)$$

Since we use a LDA model (see Section 3.2) we eventually need to discretize the components of the emotion vector. As the distribution of values for each emotion can be very different we used a non-parametric way of discretizing by assigning to each value its corresponding quartile.

For example, if the values of the component corresponding to the emotion "fear" are distributed evenly in the four quartiles $[0, 0.3)$, $[0.3, 0.4)$, $[0.4, 0.75)$ and $[0.75, 1]$, then a value of 0.32 for fear would be transformed into 2. From an LDA perspective, this would in turn be represented by "fear-2".

3.2 Building Latent Spaces

In this section, we show how to estimate the probability that a movie is liked or disliked because of a feature. We build upon LDA [2] which is a generative probabilistic model for discrete data collection mainly used for textual corpora.

LDA represents documents as a distribution probability over latent topics, where each latent topic is a distribution over words. Documents that have similar topics should share the same latent topic distribution. This can be paralleled with CF where users who share the same ratings for the same items have related interests, and should thus be in the same *latent groups* that are defined by a similar distribution over features.

In the LDA approach to CF described[5] in [2], a user is defined by a probability distribution over a set of latent groups. Each group in turn defines a probability distribution over the movies that are liked by the users represented by this group. It is then possible to compute the probability that a user likes a movie by marginalising over the different possible latent groups. More formally, LDA defines the probability to observe a series of movies $\mathcal{M}_u^+ = (m_1, \ldots, m_n)$ liked by a user u:

$$p\left(\mathcal{M}_u^+|\alpha,\beta\right) = \int p\left(\theta|\alpha\right)\left(\prod_{i=1}^{n}\sum_{z=1}^{T} p\left(z|\theta\right)p\left(m_i|\beta_z\right)\right)\mathrm{d}\theta \quad (4)$$

where T is the number of latent groups, θ follows Dirichlet distribution of hyper-parameters α, z (the latent group) follows a multinomial distribution given by θ and finally the probability of liking a movie m given the latent set of users z follows a multinomial distribution given by β_z. The model is fully specified by the α and the β_z for each possible latent group z. Those hyper-parameters are learnt by maximising the likelihood of the dataset (Section 4.3.1).

However, one of the problems of LDA is that it gives high probabilities to popular movies. Let us illustrate this problem with an example. First, consider two movies judged the same number of times. The probability given by LDA will rank the two movies in order of their probability to be liked. But, if the first movie has been judged by all the users and liked half of the time, it will have the same probability as another movie judged by only half of the users but liked all the time. This is not desirable.

This LDA limitation is due to the fact that in the movie space, LDA assigns high probabilities to movies that are liked *and* judged by many users. Thus the probability assigned to a movie m for a given latent group does not correspond to the probability that this movie would be liked by a user of this latent group, but rather to the probability that if we pick at random a movie liked by a user of this latent group, it will be m. Formally, LDA gives us the joint probability $P(+, m|u, s)$ instead of the conditional probability $P(+|m, u, s)$.

This "popularity" problem becomes worse when using feature spaces because some features can be presented in just a few movies (like an actor who has played only in a few not so popular movies).

We propose to alleviate this problem by considering negative information (i.e in movie space, movies that have been disliked, or in semantic or emotion space, features that appear in a movie that has been disliked). That is, we define LDA as a generative process of a series of couples feature-decision $\mathcal{F}_{u,s} = ((f_1, d_1), \ldots, (f_n, d_n))$ where f_i is a feature and d_i its associated decision, either "liked" (+) or "disliked" (-):

$$p\left(\mathcal{F}_{u,s}|\alpha,\beta\right) = \int p\left(\theta|\alpha\right)\left(\prod_{i=1}^{n}\sum_{z=1}^{T} p\left(z|\theta\right)p\left(f_i, d_i|\beta_z\right)\right)\mathrm{d}\theta$$

Let us illustrate how the set of couples is computed in the actor space. Assume that a user has (i) liked a movie with actors a, b and c; (ii) disliked a movie with actors a and b; (iii) liked a movie with actors a and d. This user would be represented by the couples $(a,+)$, $(b,+)$, $(c,+)$, $(a,-)$, $(b,-)$, $(a,+)$ and $(d,+)$.

Besides addressing the popularity problem, this approach also has two advantages. First, we consider more information to learn the LDA latent groups, since negative information is used. Second, user groups reflect not only features (e.g. actors) that appear in the movies they like, but also in the movies they don't like, thus providing richer information.

The LDA model is used to compute the posterior distribution of whether the feature f indicates a movie liked (+) or disliked (-) given the past user interaction $\mathcal{F}_{u,s}$ and the learnt parameters α and β, that is

$$P(\pm, f|u, s) = p\left(\pm, f|\mathcal{F}_{u,s}, s, \alpha, \beta\right)$$

In the next section, this probability is used to derive the final formula corresponding to a movie being liked in a feature space.

3.3 Probability Estimation based on a Feature Space

This section presents our methodology for calculating the probability that a movie is liked given a user and corresponding movie features. Our approach is based on a simple "averaging" method where the probability that the movie is liked is the expectation that the movie is liked because of each of its features. We also tried other forms of aggregation but preliminary results suggested that they would not improve over this simple method.

The probability $P(+|m, u, s)$ that user u likes movie m in

[5]To ease the reading, we adapted here the notations and concepts. For example, we refer to latent topics as *latent groups* since we are performing LDA on non textual information.

the feature space s can be written as

$$P(+|m,u,s) = \sum_{f\in F} P(+,f|m,u,s) = \sum_{f\in F} P(+|f,u,s)P(f|m,s) \quad (5)$$

where F is the set of possible features for a given movie and where we assumed that (i) features are examined one at a time to make a decision about whether a movie is liked or not. In this case, f and f' are disjoint events whenever $f \neq f'$; (ii) when the feature is known the judgment does not depend any more on the movie, i.e. $P(+|f,m,u,s) = P(+|f,u,s)$; (iii) when there is no judgment involved, the fact that a given user and a given movie are independent, i.e. $P(u,m) = P(u)P(m)$; (iv) the fact that a movie has a given feature is independent from the user, i.e. $P(f|m,u,s) = P(f|m,s)$.

Eq. (5) reduces to the estimation of two quantities: the probability of considering the feature f given a movie m and a space s, i.e. $P(f|m,s)$, and the probability that a user u likes a movie given that it has the feature f, i.e. $P(+|f,u,s)$.

The latter probability is straightforward to estimate, since the probability $P(+|f,u,s)$ can be rewritten as

$$P(+|f,u,s) = \frac{P(+,f|u,s)}{P(+,f|u,s)+P(-,f|u,s)} \quad (6)$$

where $P(\pm,f|u,s)$ is the probability that the feature f occurs in a movie that is liked (or disliked) by the user u in the space s, which is given by our extended LDA.

Note that when only a few observations are available for a given movie the estimations given by Eq. (6) can be unreliable. This is especially true when the data sparsity is high. We tried different smoothing techniques, and report the best performing one, the Laplace smoothing:

$$P(+|f,u,s) = \frac{P(+,f|u,s)+\epsilon}{P(+,f|u,s)+P(-,f|u,s)+2\epsilon} \quad (7)$$

The ϵ value is set to $0.001 \times |s|^{-1}$ where $|s|$ is the number of features of space s. This scaling was necessary in order to adapt to the different spaces where the number of features can vary greatly.

With respect to the probability $P(f|m,s)$, unless we have an a priori reason to give more importance to a feature (e.g. to give a higher importance to the main actors), we can assume a uniform distribution over the feature present in the movie m in the space s. Denoting $F(m,s)$ the set of features present in movie m in the space s and $\#F(m,s)$ the set cardinality, the probability $P(f|m,s)$ is $\frac{1}{\#F(m,s)}$ if f is a feature of space s for the movie m and 0 otherwise.

Putting the derived quantities back into Eq. (5), the final prediction formula is

$$P(+|m,u,s) = \sum_{f\in F(m,s)} \frac{1}{\#F(m,s)} \frac{P(+,f|u,s)+\epsilon}{P(f|u,s)+2\epsilon} \quad (8)$$

Note that in the case of the movie space, each movie is defined by one distinct feature and the sum reduces to one term.

Finally, to compute the final rating prediction for a given item we combine the information from the different spaces as given by Eq. (8), using boosted trees (see Section 4.3.2).

4. EXPERIMENTS

4.1 Test Collection

Our approach is evaluated on two MovieLens datasets [26] containing 100,000 ratings for 1682 movies from 943 users (100K dataset) and 1 million ratings for 3900 movies from 6040 users (1M dataset) respectively. In both datasets, there are at least 20 movie ratings per user. The rating scale takes values from 1 (not liked) to 5 (most liked).

We extracted the information needed to define the different semantic and emotion spaces from the IMDb website[6]. We considered the genre, the actors, and the director as our semantic spaces. Emotion extracted from plot summaries and movie reviews was used to define our emotion spaces.

4.2 Evaluation Protocols

The variability of our results was studied by performing a 10-fold cross validation where each time we used 70% of the users to train the LDA (Section 4.3.1), and 20% to identify the number of latent groups for LDA and to train the boosted trees based on LDA output (Section 4.3.2). The remaining 10% was used for performing the test.

In order to study the impact of sparsity on our models, following the standard methodology, we randomly removed some ratings from the training set so that the maximum number of rated items per user is below a given threshold (10, 20 and no limit, coined "full"), where 10 represents the highest sparsity and full the lowest.

The last processing step divides, for each user, the set of rated items into two. One set is used to represent the past history of the user, i.e. to compute the user representation in the various feature latent spaces. The second set of items are held out, and their predicted rating is computed with each model before being compared to the real value in order to measure the performance of the model. We considered the following two splitting methodologies:

Random For each user, we randomly divide the items in two. In doing so, some users might have rated an item that is held out for testing for another user.

Cold Start 10% of the items that have been rated by the test users were randomly selected to be the held out set for *all* users. In order to ensure that it is a cold start, we also removed the ratings of these items in the whole training set.

Metrics.

To measure the performance of the models, we used three different metrics. First, we report a measure of the average error made at the rating level. Two of the most widely used metrics of collaborative filtering, namely MSE (Mean Squared Error) and MAE (Mean Average Error) belong to this category. Results were similar for both, and in this paper, we only report the former due to space limits.

The goal of CF is often to return the relevant items to the user, such as the top rated movies. The performance of a CF algorithm with respect to those movies is better measured by mean average precision (MAP). Due to limited space, we do not include the complete results, but instead report the cases where MAP had a different behaviour than MSE.

[6]The Internet Movie Database (IMDb, http://www.imdb.com/)

Evaluation Methodology.

We tested the performance of our models with different combinations of the features spaces, i.e. Movie (M), Director (D), Actor (A), Genre (G) , Review Emotion (R) and Plot Summary Emotion (P) spaces. The configuration M is similar to LDA, but as explained in Section 3.2, does make use of negative information.

In the first set of experiments, we investigated the effect of each individual space. These models are represented by the initial Letter associated to each space (M, G, A, D, R or P).

In the second set of experiments, we investigated the effect of a combination of spaces. We experimented by using, besides the movie space, only emotion spaces (MPR), semantic spaces (MGAD) and all the spaces (MGADPR).

Finally, we used three different baselines. First, as a threshold, we report the performance of a constant rating estimator that returns the mean of the ratings in the training set. Second, for comparison we also report the performance of the original LDA approach (identified as LDA) along with our model on movie space (identified as M). Third, as a much stronger baseline, we report the performance of nonparametric probabilistic principal component analysis (NPCA) presented by Yu et al. [31], which has been shown to outperform other state-of-the-art approaches in the literature.

In the cold start situation, systems that rely on past item ratings cannot predict ratings for the items that do not provide such information (e.g. new items). This means, we will not be able to employ NPCA, original LDA, or our model based on movie space (M) to address the cold start problem. In the cases where the M space is combined with others, we simply removed the space M, leading to combinations based on emotions (PR), semantic spaces (GAD) and all the spaces (GADPR). It can be argued that the review emotion space (R) should not be used when we are dealing with the cold start problem. However, in our experiments, we consider the reviews as a movie feature rather than a user feature since any individual who is not part of the CF system can give these reviews. Moreover, we are interested to see the effect of utilising the review emotion space when there is no rating available for a movie.

4.3 Optimising Parameters

4.3.1 LDA

We described how we use LDA in Section 3.2. In order to train the LDA model, we need binary relevance judgments, and two sets of hyper-parameters, namely the number of latent groups T and the initial α and β.

With respect to the transformation into binary values, ratings of 3 (neutral) were discarded and we mapped 1-2 to negative, and 4-5 to positive.

We set the initial values of α and β as proposed by Misra et al. [18]. The number of latent groups has great influence on the performance of the LDA approach. We used the standard methods to find the right number of latent groups in dimensionality reduction techniques based on the likelihood over a held out set of training data [18].

In this paper, for each space and dataset, we tried several different quantities of latent groups, namely 3, 5, 10, 20, 35, 50, 100, 120, and 150. The maximum number of latent groups was set to 150 for computational reasons. The number of latent groups was selected by maximising the likelihood of observations over the second subset of the training set.

4.3.2 Boosted Tree

In order to predict the final rating, we use the standard machine learning technique of gradient boosted trees [4]. The features given to the boosted trees are a set of probabilities given by Eq. (8), one for each of the different spaces used in a given model, the output is a predicted rating between 1 and 5.

Note that even in the case of single space-based models, e.g. M, G or A, boosted trees are still useful since they map the probability of a movie to be liked to the rating scale. In order to ensure a fair comparison, we also used boosted trees to predict a final rating for the LDA-based model.

The parameters used for our experiment were found during preliminary experiments. We set the maximum number of trees to 2000, a maximum tree depth of 3 and a gaussian cost function that directly optimises the MSE. We used 65% of the data to train the boosted trees leaving 35% to control for over-fitting.

5. RESULTS & DISCUSSION

In Section 5.1 we analyse the results for models based on individual and multiple spaces, and discuss the latent groups discovered by LDA in Section 5.2.

5.1 Quantitative Study of the Performance of the Models

Figure 1a (random split) and 1b (cold start split) show the box plots for the MSE measure, for the two test collections (100K and 1M) and for different levels of sparsity (10, 20, and full). Each box plot reports, over the 10 cross validation sets, five important pieces of information namely the minimum, first, second (median), third, and maximum quartiles[7]. We performed a paired t-test between measures obtained for each user to check the significance of the difference with the baseline (M in Figure 1a and mean in Figure 1b). We use (*) and (**) to denote the fact that a model had results different from that of the baseline in all the cross validation sets with the confidence levels ($p < 0.05$) and ($p < 0.01$) respectively.

Main results.

With respect to models based on several feature spaces, we observed that the proposed model combining all spaces (MGADPR) consistently and significantly outperformed other models, including NPCA (shown in Figure 1a). With low sparsities, it has a better median and similar variance, and with high sparsities, it has a slightly better median but a much lower variance. This shows that substantial performance improvements can be achieved by integrating multiple sources of information for predicting ratings.

We can see that the model using movie space (M) has a slightly better performance (statistically significant) than original LDA (identified as LDA in Figure 1a) with complete data (1M, Full). However, in case of high sparsity, this model performed poorly. Hence for this space, popularity is important when data is sparse. We did not observe the same pattern for the models using semantic or emotion

[7]Further information can be found in [16].

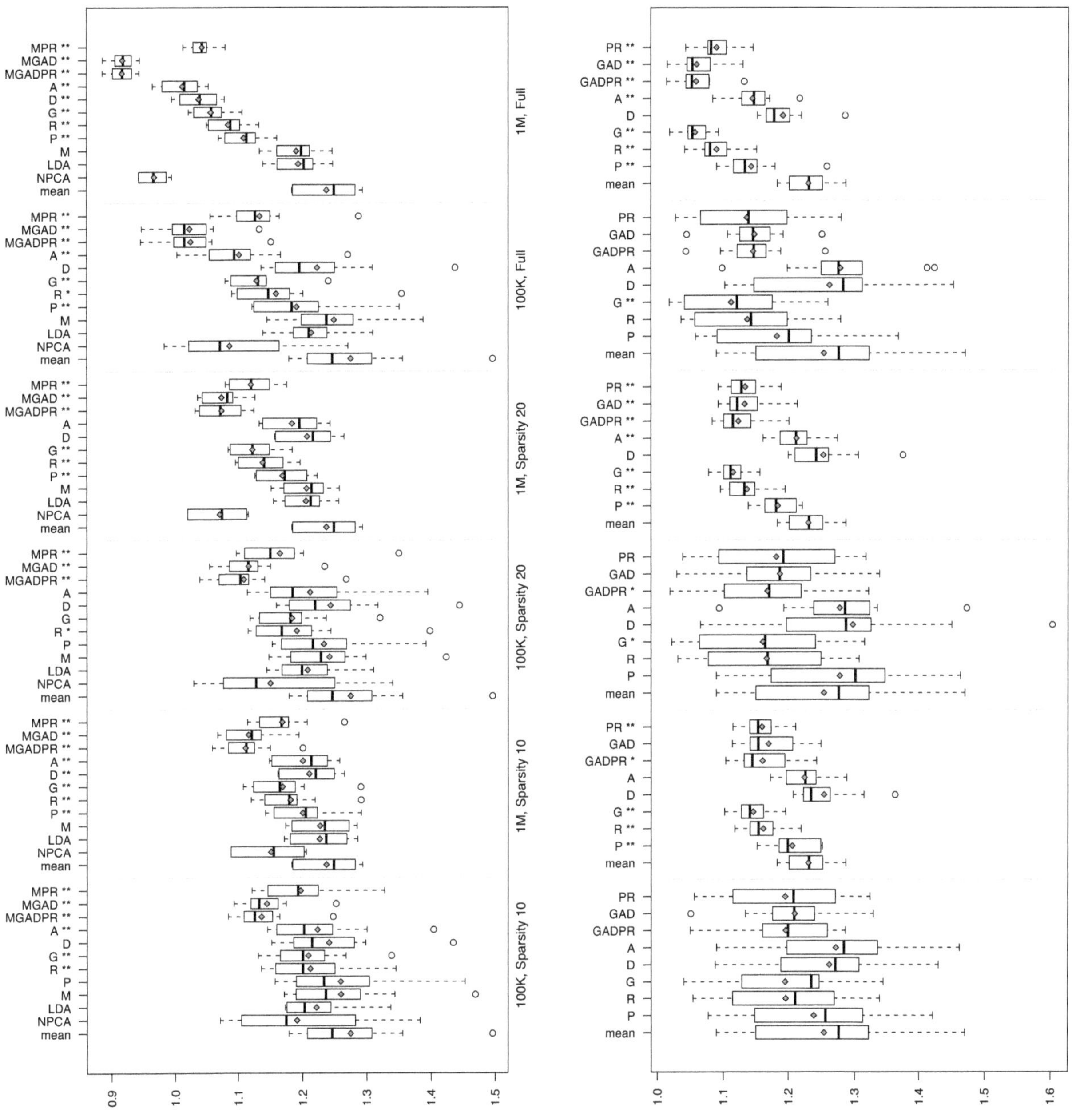

(a) Random split

(b) Cold start split

Figure 1: Box plot of MSE for different sparsities (no sparsity, sparsity=20, sparsity=10) and datasets (100K, 1M). The lower the value, the better the performance. The diamond represents the mean of each model.

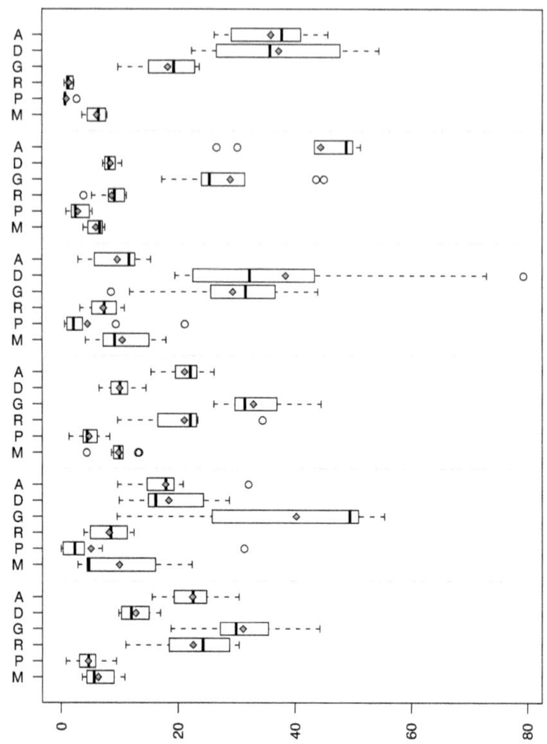

Figure 2: Box plot of the importance of each space in MGADPR model calculated by boosted trees for different sparsities (no sparsity, sparsity=10) , and datasets (100K, 1M). The higher the value, the higher the importance. The diamond represents the mean of each model.

space. In preliminary experiments (not reported here), the models based on our extended LDA (with negative and positive information) did outperform those based on the original LDA model. The improvement of our model, with semantic or emotion spaces, is significantly better than original LDA model.

Cold start.

The state-of-the-art methods discussed in this paper do not handle the cold start problem and we therefore consider the mean of ratings as our baseline. In Figure 1b we present how our proposed approach performs in the case of the cold start problem. There is an overall increase of 0.1 in MSE for GADRP over the baseline, and this holds for different level of sparsity. The comparison between the model using emotion spaces (i.e PR) and the one using semantic spaces (i.e. GAD) shows a comparable performance between them (sparsity "full" and 20), but with high sparsity (10), emotion space based models are performing better.

MAP and MSE.

By comparing the MAP (not shown here) and MSE performances, we can distinguish systems that are good at predicting the rating on average from those that improve the top ranking. We observed that movie and actor feature spaces do perform well at predicting top ranked items (at the price of a higher variability in the 100K dataset). The models based on emotions and to some extent genre (G) do not perform well in terms of MAP compared to the other spaces. This means that while they are useful to predict accurate ratings, they are not good predictors for highly rated items.

Analysing Feature Spaces.

Let us now analyse the performance of each feature space separately. In the case of the full scenario for the 1M dataset, we have a clear ordering of the different spaces based on their performance. As shown in Figure 1a, this order is actor, director genre, plot summary emotion, movie review emotion and finally movie space. When the sparsity of the database increases, the best performing spaces (i.e. actor and director) degrades more than the others. This is due to the fact that these spaces have many more features (i.e. the number of actors or directors is many more than the number of genres), and hence are more likely to lack information when sparsity increases. In the extreme case of the cold start problem, director and actor spaces performed the worst. Another interesting finding is that emotions are useful in sparse scenarios, and especially in cold start situations, as shown by the comparison of movie review emotion with genre spaces (Figure 1b).

In addition, the comparison between the model using emotion spaces (i.e MPR) and the one using semantic spaces (i.e. MGAD) shows a superiority of the latter one in low sparsity situations (Full in Figure 1a). Emotion spaces add an extra dimension of information in high sparsity scenarios as shown with sparsities of 10 and 20 (random and cold start splits) since they decrease MSE and the variance of the performance measure.

Finally, in order to investigate further the importance of the feature spaces, we used the measure of relative influence proposed by Friedman et al. [4] for boosted trees. Each of the features is given an importance between 0 and 100, so that the sum over features equals 100. The importance of a variable reflects how important the drop in performance would be, if the feature was to be removed. We report the box plot of the relative influence over the 10 cross validations for the model (MGADPR) in Figure 2.

We can observe different relative influences depending on the amount of data. In the 1M dataset with no sparsity (1M, Full in Figure 2), the most important spaces are actor, director, and then genre, and movie. This means that emotion spaces are not important when the data provides sufficient information to predict the rating of the movie based on more direct indicators like the actors in the movie.

However, at the other extreme, i.e. the most sparse scenario (100K, 10 in Figure 2), actor, director and movie space do not influence the decision making process of boosted trees as much as the movie review emotion space and genre do. Again we observe that the movie review emotion space acquires more importance than plot summary emotion space.

It can also be observed that there is a connection between the number of different features in a feature space and the use of this feature space for different volumes of data. For example, genre and emotion spaces have less features in comparison to the other ones, and are more likely to be used when there is not much data (i.e. ratings) to train from.

To investigate whether emotions do bring more information than sentiments, we performed experiments using a sentiment feature space[8] instead of emotion feature space (following the methodology in Section 3.1). The improvement is lower, but not significantly, than the one obtained over emotion feature space . However, the usefulness of the emotion feature space is illustrated in the next section where users' latent groups implicitly (through LDA) were created based on the emotions extracted from external movie reviews.

5.2 Analysis of Latent Groups

In this subsection we illustrate the latent groups discovered by LDA with some examples for two of the most important semantic spaces (i.e. actor and genre) and the emotion spaces. Here, we used the data learnt by LDA with the full data (1M, no sparsity) for better interpretability.

We first selected the most important latent groups based on the expectation of the probability $P(z)$ over the set of training users. For each of these latent groups, we calculated the top and bottom five features f for $p(+|f,s)$ and reported them in Table 1. Note that the number after each feature in the table for movie review (R) and plot summary (P) emotion spaces, corresponds to the discretised quartile to which it belongs (Section 3.1), and ranges from 1 to 4. We now discuss our findings, based on the analysis of several latent groups beyond those presented in the table.

In the actor space, we observe that in most of the latent groups, the important actors (i.e. those who play the main role) are separated from other actors (e.g. supporting actors). This is due to the fact that these actors were consistently liked whereas the supporting actors also play in the movies that a user has not liked. The second observation is that the actors who are categorised together in a latent group either play in the same movies or the same genre, or belong to the same period of time. LDA hence did correctly put together actors into coherent latent groups.

In the genre space, we observe that the features within latent groups are also related. For example, the genres with respectively the highest and the lowest probability do define distinct types of genre profiles, and the top movies related to this latent group perfectly match the liked genres.

In the movie review emotion space, we observe that the features within the latent group indicate those movies for which users expressed disappointment or dissatisfaction. By looking at the reviews given for the top movies for this latent group one can observe supporting comments such as "The movie had nothing to do with the title." and "It played off more as a B movie." for *Soft Toilet Seats* and "The story doesn't hit you over the head explaining events like most films" for *New Rose Hotel*. However, positive comments with high ambiguity such as "I saw this movie when I was very young and at first never really understood it." and "I mistake it for a Disney movie a lot of the time but who can blame me" can be considered as reproach and therefore the referring movie (in this case *The Swan Princess*) considered in the same group. Therefore, if a user has an unusual taste and likes the movies that the majority of people don't like then more such movies will be recommended to him or her. This feature is unique to this space. On the other hand, if the interest of the user is similar to the crowd, then the recommendation will also be common to that of the crowd such as the movies *Sneakers*, *Amistad*, and *A Simple Plan* for another important latent group.

[8]The sentiment values were extracted based on the work presented in [15].

In the plot summary emotion space, we observe that the features within latent groups meaningfully select movies based on the emotion interpretation of their storyline. For instance, the top latent group corresponds to the movies that have a twist of story or surprising (or shocking) emotion. This makes the plot summary different from genre space. This can be seen better by looking at the top movies for this latent group. For example, "her character is to be killed off" or "Her life begins to fall apart" for the movie *The Killing of Sister George* or "A ... mother ... facing divorce is thrust back in time ... Given the chance to change the course of her life ..." for the movie *Peggy Sue Got Married*, and "John Shaft ... first finds himself up against ... the leader of the black crime mob ... finally working with [him] against the white mafia ..." for the movie *Shaft*.

In order to gain further insight on the relationship between the different feature spaces, we calculated the Pearson's correlation of the predicted ratings for the model based on single features spaces. We observed that genre and emotion spaces (especially reviews that have a correlation around 0.8 for the complete dataset) had the highest correlation at different levels of sparsity. This is an interesting observation as the information present in these spaces is of a very different nature. However, it can be argued that the emotion expressed in the movie reviews are influenced the most by the genre of the movie. Other spaces had rather low correlations (below 0.4), showing that they are more likely to be complementary. A final observation is that correlation decreases when sparsity increases confirming the observation that considering different feature spaces is important in high sparsity situations.

6. CONCLUSIONS

In this paper we studied the effect of emotion and semantic spaces in improving the performance of a model-based CF system, and analysed the effect of sparsity and dataset sizes in rating prediction accuracy and recommendation precision. We observed that movie and actor spaces are the most and least sensitive spaces to sparsity and dataset size. We also observe that the model that uses all spaces is the best performing model over all sparsities and datasets performing better than a state-of-the-art CF system.

The LDA approach to CF was adapted to cluster semantic movie information as well as emotion information based on users' ratings. We proposed to include negative information (movies that have been disliked) into the LDA generation process and for each feature space we calculated the probability that a movie is liked (or not) given a user. Based on this, we predicted a rating using boosted trees.

The results show that emotional features consistently play a role in improving the recommendation quality in comparison to the scenario where only the movie space (i.e. the baseline) is used. Furthermore the effectiveness of emotion spaces increases with the sparsity of the dataset, especially in a cold start situation. This indicates that emotion spaces encapsulate a potential source of information. A comparison between the improvement achieved in MSE and MAP values shows that emotion spaces are more effective in predicting the actual ratings than detecting top rated movies. We also observed that movie review emotion space and genre space based models predict similar ratings, but it is important to note that emotion features are the outcome of an emotion extraction system and not manually created metadata as is

Table 1: The five highest and lowest probability features and the five highest probability of being a feature in a liked movie for the most important latent groups in actor, genre and movie review emotion spaces (No sparsity - 1M dataset)

Space	Features with the highest & lowest probability	Movies with the highest probability
Actor	**Highest:** Tommy Lee Jones, Samuel L. Jackson, Sean Connery, Fred Dalton Thompson, James Earl Jones **Lowest:** K. Baltz, P. T. Vince, E. Izzard, A. Dick, S. Lawrence	In the Line of Fire, Die Hard, The Mask of Zorro, U.S. Marshalls, Twister
Genre	**Highest:** Adventure, Crime, Musical, Mystery, Sci-Fi **Lowest:** Comedy, War, Documentary, Action, Western	The Man in the Iron Mask, Brenda Starr, Let's Get Harry, The Avengers, Indiana Jones and the Temple of Doom
Movie Review Emotion	**Highest:** reproach-1, reproach-4, surprise-1, distress-1, reproach-2 **Lowest:** distress-3, joy-2, joy-3, sorry-for-2, resentment-2	Above the Rim, Power 98, Soft Toilet Seats, New Rose Hotel, The Swan Princess
Plot Summary Emotion	**Highest:** surprise-1, shock-3, surprise-2, gloating-4, distress-3 **Lowest:** joy-1, hate-3, joy-3, hate-2, surprise-3	Peggy Sue Got Married, The French Connection, Shaft, Blast from the Past, The Killing of Sister George

the case for genre, thus they do not require costly and time consuming human intervention.

Emotion extracted from the movie plot summary and movie review emotion spaces affect system performance differently. We believe that this is due to the richer emotional content in opinionated movie reviews than the relatively more objective plot summary texts. It is also important to consider that there is much room for improving the accuracy of emotion extraction techniques.

In future work, we would like to improve our predictions for sparse datasets, relying more on semantic and emotion spaces. In order to do so, we plan to (1) investigate more sophisticated ways to aggregate feature probabilities for semantic and emotion spaces, in order to account for the variance (uncertainty) and importance of each feature (e.g. distinguish between main and secondary actors); (2) investigate the effect of semantic and emotion spaces in other domains such as books and products and (3) more importantly, we plan to continue working on utilising emotions extracted from text to improve the performance of information retrieval tasks such as novelty, diversification and personalisation.

7. REFERENCES

[1] G. Adomavicius and A. Tuzhilin. Toward the next generation of recommender systems: a survey of the state-of-the-art and possible extensions. *TKDE'05*, June 2005.

[2] D. M. Blei, A. Y. Ng, and M. I. Jordan. Latent dirichlet allocation. *JMLR'03*, 2003.

[3] P. Ekman and H. Oster. Facial Expressions of Emotion. *Annual Reviews in Psychology*, 1979.

[4] J. H. Friedman. Greedy function approximation: A gradient boosting machine. *The Annals of Statistics*, 2001.

[5] A. B. Goldberg and X. Zhu. Seeing stars when there aren't many stars: graph-based semi-supervised learning for sentiment categorisation. *TextGraphs-1*, 2006.

[6] M. Hancock-Beaulieu and S. Walker. An evaluation of automatic query expansion in an online library catalogue. *J. Doc.*, 1992.

[7] T. Hofmann. Collaborative filtering via gaussian probabilistic latent semantic analysis. *SIGIR'03*, 2003.

[8] T. Hofmann. Latent semantic models for collaborative filtering. *ACM TOIS*, 2004.

[9] C. Izard. *The Psychology of Emotions*. Plenum Publishing Corporation, 1991.

[10] N. Jakob, S. H. Weber, M. C. Müller, and I. Gurevych. Beyond the stars: exploiting free-text user reviews to improve the accuracy of movie recommendations. *TSA '09*, 2009.

[11] C. Leung, S. Chan, and F. Chung. Integrating collaborative filtering and sentiment analysis: A rating inference approach. *ECAI'06*, 2006.

[12] H. Liu, H. Lieberman, and T. Selker. A model of textual affect sensing using real-world knowledge. *IUI'03*, 2003.

[13] H. Liu, T. Selker, and H. Lieberman. Visualizing the affective structure of a text document. *CHI'03*, 2003.

[14] B. Marlin. Modeling user rating profiles for collaborative filtering. *NIPS'04*, 2004.

[15] S. M. A. Masum, H. Prendinger, and M. Ishizuka. Sentiment assessment of text by analyzing linguistic features and contextual valence assignment. *AAAI'08*, 2008.

[16] R. McGill, J. Tukey, and W. Larsen. Variations of box plots. *American Statistician*, 1978.

[17] P. Melville, R. J. Mooney, and R. Nagarajan. Content-boosted collaborative filtering for improved recommendations. *AAAI'02*, 2002.

[18] H. Misra, O. Cappé, and F. Yvon. Using lda to detect semantically incoherent documents. *CoNLL'08*, 2008.

[19] B. Mobasher, X. Jin, and Y. Zhou. Semantically Enhanced Collaborative Filtering on the Web. *LNCS*, 2004.

[20] Y. Moshfeghi, D. Agarwal, B. Piwowarski, and J. M. Jose. Movie Recommender: Semantically Enriched Unified Relevance Model for Rating Prediction in Collaborative Filtering. *ECIR'09*, 2009.

[21] Y. Moshfeghi and J. M. Jose. Role of emotional features in collaborative recommendation. *ECIR'11*, 2011.

[22] A. Ortony, G. Clore, and A. Collins. *The cognitive structure of emotions*. Cambridge University Press, 1990.

[23] B. Pang and L. Lee. Seeing stars: Exploiting class relationships for sentiment categorization with respect to rating scales. *ACL'05*, 2005.

[24] S.-T. Park and W. Chu. Pairwise preference regression for cold-start recommendation. *RecSys'09*, 2009.

[25] D. Pennock, E. Horvitz, S. Lawrence, and C. Giles. Collaborative filtering by personality diagnosis: A hybrid memory-and model-based approach. *UAI'00*, 2000.

[26] P. Resnick, N. Iacovou, M. Suchak, P. Bergstrom, and J. Riedl. Grouplens: an open architecture for collaborative filtering of netnews. *CSCW'94*, 1994.

[27] B. Sarwar, G. Karypis, J. Konstan, and J. Reidl. Item-based collaborative filtering recommendation algorithms. *WWW'01*, 2001.

[28] M. A. M. Shaikh, H. Prendinger, and M. Ishizuka. A Linguistic Interpretation of the OCC Emotion Model for Affect Sensing from Text. *Affective Information Processing*, 2009.

[29] P. Winoto and T. Y. Tang. The role of user mood in movie recommendations. *Expert Systems with Applications*, 2010.

[30] G.-R. Xue, C. Lin, Q. Yang, W. Xi, H.-J. Zeng, Y. Yu, and Z. Chen. Scalable collaborative filtering using cluster-based smoothing. *SIGIR'05*, 2005.

[31] K. Yu, S. Zhu, J. Lafferty, and Y. Gong. Fast nonparametric matrix factorisation for large-scale collaborative filtering. *SIGIR'09*, 2009.

Fast Context-aware Recommendations with Factorization Machines

Steffen Rendle
Social Network Analysis
University of Konstanz
78457 Konstanz, Germany
steffen.rendle@uni-konstanz.de

Zeno Gantner, Christoph Freudenthaler, Lars Schmidt-Thieme
Information Systems and Machine Learning Lab
University of Hildesheim
31141 Hildesheim, Germany
{gantner,freudenthaler,schmidt-thieme}@ismll.de

ABSTRACT

The situation in which a choice is made is an important information for recommender systems. Context-aware recommenders take this information into account to make predictions. So far, the best performing method for context-aware rating prediction in terms of predictive accuracy is *Multiverse Recommendation* based on the Tucker tensor factorization model. However this method has two drawbacks: (1) its model complexity is exponential in the number of context variables and polynomial in the size of the factorization and (2) it only works for categorical context variables. On the other hand there is a large variety of fast but specialized recommender methods which lack the generality of context-aware methods.

We propose to apply *Factorization Machines* (FMs) to model contextual information and to provide context-aware rating predictions. This approach results in fast context-aware recommendations because the model equation of FMs can be computed in linear time both in the number of context variables and the factorization size. For learning FMs, we develop an iterative optimization method that analytically finds the least-square solution for one parameter given the other ones. Finally, we show empirically that our approach outperforms *Multiverse Recommendation* in prediction quality and runtime.

Categories and Subject Descriptors

H.3.3 [**Information Systems**]: Information Search and Retrieval—*Information filtering*; I.2.6 [**Artificial Intelligence**]: Learning—*Parameter Learning*

General Terms

Algorithms, Experimentation, Measurement, Performance

Keywords

Context-Aware Recommender System, Factorization Machine, Rating Prediction, Tensor Factorization

1. INTRODUCTION

Rating prediction in recommender systems relies primarily on the information of *how* (which rating, e.g. on a scale from 1 to 5 stars) *who* (which user) rated *what* (which item, e.g. movie, news article, or product). There are many methods that take additional data about the *who* (demographic information about the user, age, profession, gender) or the *what* (item attributes like movie genres or keywords from the product description) into account.

Besides such data about the entities involved in the rating events, there is possibly also information about the *situation* in which the rating event happens, e.g. the current location, the time, who is nearby, or the current mood of the user. Such situational information is usually called *context*. Because it is known from decision psychology that the setting and the mood of a person do influence their behavior, it is desirable to exploit context information in recommender systems. *Context-aware rating prediction* relies on the information of *how who* rated *what* in *which context* (see also figure 1).

Classical recommender system methods do not take context information into account. Some approaches perform pre- or post-processing of the data to make standard methods context-aware. While such ad-hoc solutions may work in practice, they have the shortcoming that all steps in the process need supervision and fine-tuning. Methods that integrate all kinds of input data into one model are more practical in this respect, as well as theoretically more elegant. Currently, the most flexible and strongest approach in terms of prediction accuracy is *Multiverse Recommendation* [5] that relies on Tucker decomposition and allows to work with any categorical context. However, for real-world scenarios its computational complexity is too high as it is in $O(k^m)$ where k is the dimensionality of the factorization and m the number of modes/variables involved.

In this paper, we propose a context-aware rating predictor that is based on *Factorization Machines* (FM) [14]. FMs include and can mimic the most successful approaches in recommender systems including matrix factorizion [18], SVD++ [6] or PITF [15]. We show how FMs can be applied to a wide variety of context domains including categorical, set categorical or real-valued domains. Besides this flexibility in modeling, the complexity of FMs is linear both in k and m which allows fast prediction and learning with context-aware data. For learning the model parameters of FMs, we propose a new algorithm that is based on alternating least squares (ALS). Our algorithm directly finds the optimal solution for one model parameter given all the other ones and a joint optimum is found within a few iterations. Like for stochastic gradient descent (SGD), the complexity for one iteration of our ALS algorithm is in $O(|S|\, m\, k)$ where $|S|$ is the number of training examples. The main advantage of our new ALS algorithm over SGD is that no learning rate has to be determined. This is very important in practice, because the quality of SGD learning relies largely on a good learning rate and thus an expensive search has to be done. This is not necessary for ALS.

In our experiments, we show empirically that context-aware FMs can capture context information and improve predictive accuracy. Furthermore, FMs outperform the state-of-the-art method *Multiverse Recommendation* both in prediction quality and largely in runtime.

1. In contrast to other context-aware rating predictors, FMs are easily applicable to a wide variety of contexts. We show how to generate feature vectors for context of categorical, set categorical and real-valued domains.

2. We develop a new learning algorithm for FMs that directly computes the least-square solution of a model parameter given the remaining parameters. The advantage of our ALS algorithm over SGD is that it works without a learning rate.

3. Compared to the state-of-the-art context-aware rating prediction method *Multiverse Recommendation*, FMs have a linear complexity and empirically provide a better prediction quality in much less time.

2. CONTEXT-AWARE RATING PREDICTION

We first describe the standard rating prediction task and then extend it to context-aware rating prediction. Next we show how this task can be expressed as a regression task from real-valued feature vectors under extreme sparsity. We also discuss shortly why standard regression models are not effective in this setting.

2.1 Rating prediction

Standard rating prediction can be defined as a regression task over users $U = \{u_1, u_2, \ldots\}$ and items $I = \{i_1, i_2, \ldots\}$, where a target function $y : U \times I \to \mathbb{R}$ has to be estimated. The target function represents the rating, e.g. $y(u,i)$ is the rating of user u for item i. We denote the observed part of y by $S \subset U \times I$; i.e. for all $(u,i) \in S$, we know the rating $y(u,i)$ in advance. The task of rating prediction is to estimate a function $\hat{y}$ that can predict $\hat{y}(u,i)$ for any user-item combination.

2.2 Context

In context-aware recommender systems, it is assumed that some additional information is available that influences the rating behavior. We define a context as a variable $c \in \mathcal{C}$. Examples are the mood the user was in when (s)he rated an item (e.g. $\mathcal{C} = \{happy, sad, \ldots\}$), the time at which a rating was given (e.g. $\mathcal{C} = \mathbb{R}^+$), the last items seen (e.g. $\mathcal{C} = \mathcal{P}(I)$) or the location (e.g. $\mathcal{C} = \mathbb{R}^2$).

2.3 Context-aware rating prediction

If multiple contexts $\mathcal{C}_3, \ldots, \mathcal{C}_m$ are allowed the task is to estimate the following rating function:

$$y : U \times I \times \mathcal{C}_3 \ldots \times \mathcal{C}_m \to \mathbb{R} \tag{1}$$

Note that we start the index of the context variables with 3 because from a technical point of view, users and items can be seen as the first and second 'context'.

Figure 2 shows an example for context-aware data on the left side. There are users U in mood $\mathcal{C}_3$ watching movies I together with other users $\mathcal{C}_4$:

$$U = \{\boldsymbol{A}lice, \boldsymbol{B}ob, \boldsymbol{C}harlie\}$$
$$I = \{\boldsymbol{TI}tanic, \boldsymbol{N}otting\ \boldsymbol{H}ill, \boldsymbol{S}tar\ \boldsymbol{W}ars, \boldsymbol{S}tar\ \boldsymbol{T}rek\}$$
$$\mathcal{C}_3 = \{\boldsymbol{S}ad, \boldsymbol{N}ormal, \boldsymbol{H}appy\}$$
$$\mathcal{C}_4 = \mathcal{P}(U)$$

The first tuple in Fig. 2 states that ***A**lice* rated ***TI**tanic* with 5 stars and that she has watched this movie with ***C**harlie* while she was ***H**appy*.

3. RELATED WORK

Most research in recommender systems focus on context-unaware methods that analyze only the user-item interaction. Here matrix factorization approaches (e.g. [18, 6]) have become very popular as they usually outperform traditional k-nearest neighbor methods (e.g. [17]). There is also research in incooperating meta-data like user or item attributes into the prediction, like Stern et al. [19] who extend a matrix factorization model. However, meta-data often yields in only little or no improvement over strong baseline methods for rating prediction if enough feedback data is present [12]. The difference between such user/ item attributes and context is that attributes are attached only to either an item or user (e.g. a genre is attached to a movie) whereas context is attached to the whole rating event (e.g. the mood of a user when rating an item).

In contrast to the huge literature on standard recommender systems, there is only little research on context-aware recommender systems. The most basic approaches are contextual pre-filtering and post-filtering where a standard context-unaware recommender system is applied and the data is either preprocessed based on the context of interest before applying the recommender or the results are postprocessed [11]. Examples for pre-processing are item-splitting [3] or the multidimensional model of Adomavicius et al. [1] which is based on OLAP cubes. More sophisticated approaches use all the context and user-item information simultaneously to make predictions. Oku et al. [9] use SVMs for context-aware predictions – which have limitations in sparse applications like recommender systems as no 2-way interaction between items and users can be estimated directly [14]. Li et al. [8] suggest to see context as a user feature which is dynamic, i.e. can change. There is also some research on context-aware recommendation systems for item prediction [16], which is a ranking task instead of a regression task like the problem we are dealing with in this paper.

3.1 Multiverse Recommendation

Recently, Karatzoglou et al. [5] have proposed to apply the Tucker decomposition [20] to factorize the tensor over user, items and all categorical context variables directly. They called their approach *Multiverse Recommendation* and have shown empirically that their approach results in better prediction accuracy than item-splitting [3] and the OLAP approach [1]. In our evaluation, we will compare our *Factorization Machine* approach to *Multiverse Recommendation.*

As both our approach and *Multiverse Recommendation* are based on factorization models, we shortly recapitulate their approach and highlight the differences. Their model equation is the Tucker Decomposition, which decomposes an m-mode tensor into a smaller core tensor $\mathcal{B}$ and one factor matrix $\mathbf{V}^{(m)}$ per mode. For context-aware recommender systems, the first mode is the user, the second the item and the remaining $m-2$ modes are the context variables. The model equation can be written as:

$$\hat{y}(u, i, c_3, \ldots, c_m) := \sum_{f_1}^{k_1} \cdots \sum_{f_m}^{k_m} b_{f_1,\ldots,f_m} v_{u,f_1}^{(U)} v_{i,f_2}^{(I)} \prod_{l=3}^{m} v_{c_l,f_l}^{\mathcal{C}_l},$$

with

$$\mathcal{B} \in \mathbb{R}^{k_1 \times \ldots \times k_m}, \quad \mathbf{V}^{(U)} \in \mathbb{R}^{|U| \times k_1}$$
$$\mathbf{V}^{(I)} \in \mathbb{R}^{|I| \times k_2}, \quad \mathbf{V}^{(\mathcal{C}_l)} \in \mathbb{R}^{|\mathcal{C}_l| \times k_l}.$$

The major drawback of this model is that its computational complexity is in $O(\prod_{l=1}^{m} k_l)$. Assuming factorization dimensions of equal size, i.e. $k := k_l$, this means a computational complexity of $O(k^m)$. Thus the complexity of computing one context-aware rating is exponential in the number of modes and polynomial in the number of factors. This leads to both poor learning and poor prediction runtime as soon as the number of factors growths. In Figure 5 we compare the learning runtime of *Multiverse Recommendation* empirically to our FM approach. A second limitation of *Multiverse Recommendation* in comparison to our approach is that only categorical context can be modeled – e.g. categorical set variables or real-valued variables are not possible. Finally, in the related task of item or tag recommendation (which is a ranking task), it has been shown that often it is better to factorize several lower variable interactions (e.g. pairwise ones [15]) instead of one m-ary relation (like the Tucker Decomposition). The reason is that under high sparsity, factorized pairwise relations can be estimated well but factorized m-ary relations are harder to estimate. Our FM approach follows this idea and models all nested interactions up to pairwise ones.

3.2 Attribute-aware Recommendation

In contrast to the little work on general context-aware methods, there is much more research on attribute-aware or specialized recommender systems. For example [19] or [2] present extensions of the matrix factorization model that can handle user and item attributes. There are also several works on taking time-effects into account, e.g. [7, 21]. However, all of these approaches are designed only for specific problems and cannot handle the general problem setting of context-aware recommendation that we examine in this work. For sure for specific and important problems (e.g. time-aware or attribute-aware recommendation) it is beneficial to investigate specialized methods that are supposed to be the best models for a certain problem, but on the other hand also research on general methods like context-aware recommenders is important as they offer the largest flexibility and may serve as (strong) baselines for specialized models.

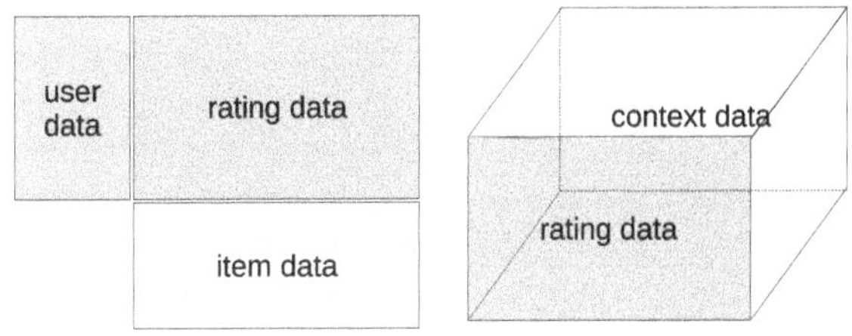

Figure 1: Attribute-aware methods can take additional information about the user or the item separately into account (left), whereas context-aware methods are more general and can analyze data that is simultaneously attached to all 'modes', i.e. the whole rating event (right).

3.3 Alternating Least Square Optimization

For the model class of matrix factorization, Bell and Koren [4] proposed an ALS method that alternates between optimizing all user factors and all item factors. As the whole factor matrix of all users (resp. items) is optimized jointly, the computation complexity is $O(k^3)$. This complexity issue of standard ALS is the reason why SGD approaches are more popular in the recommender system literature than ALS. Pilászy et al. [13] have proposed to optimize the factors within each user (resp. item) one after the other which results in an ALS algorithm constant in k, i.e. $O(k)$ because the matrix inversion is avoided. The general idea of optimizing one factor at a time is the same idea that we apply for our ALS algorithm for FMs. Both approaches [4, 13] work only for matrix factorizations and thus cannot handle any context like our proposed FMs which model all interactions. Furthermore our ALS algorithm also learns the global bias and basic 1-way effects.

4. CONTEXT-AWARE RATING PREDICTION WITH FMS

FMs are a generic model class that subsumes and can mimic several of the most successful recommender systems, among them matrix factorization [18], SVD++ [6] or PITF [15]. We shortly recapitulate the FM model and then show in detail how it can be applied to context-aware data and what happens inside an FM using such context-aware data. In the second main part, we propose a new fast alternating least square (ALS) optimization algorithm that makes FM much easier applicable compared to SGD algorithms because it works without any learning rate.

4.1 Rating Prediction with FMs

A factorization machine (FM) [14] models all interactions between pairs of variables with the target, including nested ones, by using factorized interaction parameters[1]:

$$\hat{y}(\mathbf{x}) := w_0 + \sum_{i=1}^{n} w_i\, x_i + \sum_{i=1}^{n} \sum_{j=i+1}^{n} \hat{w}_{i,j}\, x_i\, x_j \tag{2}$$

where $\hat{w}_{i,j}$ are the factorized interaction parameters between pairs:

$$\hat{w}_{i,j} := \langle \mathbf{v}_i, \mathbf{v}_j \rangle = \sum_{f=1}^{k} v_{i,f} \cdot v_{j,f} \tag{3}$$

and the model parameters Θ that have to be estimated are:

$$w_0 \in \mathbb{R}, \quad \mathbf{w} \in \mathbb{R}^n, \quad \mathbf{V} \in \mathbb{R}^{n \times k} \tag{4}$$

That means w_0 is the global bias, w_i models the interaction of the i-th variable to the target and $\hat{w}_{i,j}$ models the factorized interaction of a pair of variables with the target. Note also that unlike other factorization models like matrix factorization or PARAFAC, FMs can work with any continuous input data $\mathbf{x}$.

In [14] it has also been shown that an FM (eq. 2) can be computed very efficiently in $O(k \cdot m(\mathbf{x}))$ as it is equivalent to:

$$\hat{y}(\mathbf{x}) = w_0 + \sum_{i=1}^{n} w_i\, x_i + \frac{1}{2} \sum_{f=1}^{k} \left(\left(\sum_{i=1}^{n} v_{i,f}\, x_i \right)^2 - \sum_{i=1}^{n} v_{i,f}^2\, x_i^2 \right) \tag{5}$$

For the task of regression, the most widely used loss function is square loss. To prevent overfitting it is common to add a regularization term – usually L2. In total, we use the following regularized least square criterion for optimization:

$$\text{RLS-OPT} = \sum_{(\mathbf{x},y) \in S} (\hat{y}(\mathbf{x}) - y)^2 + \sum_{\theta \in \Theta} \lambda_{(\theta)}\, \theta^2 \tag{6}$$

where $\lambda_{(\theta)}$ is a regularization (hyper-)parameter for the model parameter θ. In general, the regularization term can be chosen individually for each model parameter. But in practice it makes sense to use the same regularization parameters for similar model parameters – in our experiments we use: $\lambda_{(w_0)} = 0$ as there is no need to regularize the global bias; the same $\lambda_{(\mathbf{w})}$ for all parameters $w_i \in \mathbf{w}$ and the same $\lambda_{(\mathbf{V})}$ for all parameters $v_{i,f} \in \mathbf{V}$.

4.2 Context-aware FMs

A wide variety of context-aware data can be transformed into such a prediction task using real valued feature vectors $\mathbf{x} \in \mathbb{R}^n$ (see figure 2, right side for an example). We will show possible mappings $\mathbf{z} : \mathcal{C} \to \mathbb{R}^{n_z}$ for different kinds of domains:

- **Categorical domain**: A categorical variable domain $\mathcal{C}$ like users U, items I, or mood can be transformed into a real-valued vector $\mathbf{z}$ using one indicator variable per categorical level. E.g. in our example the mood domain $\mathcal{C}_3$ has three states, so we can express ***Alice***'s mood ***Happy*** with the vector $\mathbf{z}$(***Happy***) $= (0, 0, 1)$, or if she is in a ***Sad*** context with: $\mathbf{z}$(***Sad***) $= (1, 0, 0)$.

- **Categorical set domain**: if the realization of a variable can be sets of categorical variables (e.g. ***Alice*** has watched ***Star Wars*** with ***Bob*** and ***Charlie***), the transformation can be made by using one indicator variable per context level. E.g. $\mathbf{z}$({***Bob***, ***Charlie***}) $= (0, 0.5, 0.5)$; here we suggest to normalized $\mathbf{z}$ for non-empty context values such that all vectors sum up to 1. This makes sure that all vectors have the same weight which is often desirable.

- **Real valued domains**: If a domain is already a number (e.g. $\mathcal{C} \subseteq \mathbb{R}$), we can directly use the real number as feature, e.g. $\mathbf{z}(3.141) = 3.141$.

The final feature vector $\mathbf{x}$ can be obtained by concatenating the single mappings:

$$\mathbf{x}(u, i, c_3, \ldots, c_m) = (\mathbf{z}_1(u), \mathbf{z}_2(i), \mathbf{z}_3(c_3), \ldots, \mathbf{z}_m(c_m)) \tag{7}$$

This data vectors $\mathbf{x}$ are then the input for the FM (eq. 2).

Example.

Figure 2 shows a complete example how to transform the context-aware data of section 2.3 into a prediction problem from real-valued features. The example contains the categorical domains user U, item I and mood $\mathcal{C}_3$ as well as a set-categorical domain, the friends the movie has been watched with, $\mathcal{C}_4$. To get an insight of how an FM will work, we investigate shortly the model equation of an FM applied to this data[2]. When we look at the feature vector $\mathbf{x}$ of our example, one can see that most of them are 0 and thus the FM model equation can be rewritten as:

$$\begin{aligned}\hat{y}(\mathbf{x}(u, i, c_3, c_4)) &= w_0 + w_i + w_u + w_{c_3} + \sum_{t \in c_4} x_t\, w_t \\ &+ \langle \mathbf{v}_i, \mathbf{v}_u \rangle + \langle \mathbf{v}_i, \mathbf{v}_{c_3} \rangle + \langle \mathbf{v}_i, \sum_{t \in c_4} x_t\, \mathbf{v}_t \rangle \\ &+ \langle \mathbf{v}_u, \mathbf{v}_{c_3} \rangle + \langle \mathbf{v}_u, \sum_{t \in c_4} x_t\, \mathbf{v}_t \rangle + \langle \mathbf{v}_{c_3}, \sum_{t \in c_4} x_t\, \mathbf{v}_t \rangle\end{aligned}$$

That means the FM model contains the bias term for the individual item i, user u, mood c_3 and the average bias of the co-watchers c_4. Furthermore it factorizes all pairwise interactions between these four variables. Comparing the FM model with the standard matrix factorization model (e.g. [18]) for the user u and the item i, one can see that the FM contains also exactly this factorization: $\langle \mathbf{v}_i, \mathbf{v}_u \rangle$. Additionally, it factorizes all pairwise interactions with all context variables. This shows how FMs automatically include one of the best performing recommender system models, the matrix factorization model.

4.3 Fast Learning

As the model equation of FMs can be calculated in linear time (see eq. 5), it is straightforward to develop a stochastic gradient descend (SGD) optimization algorithm for a variety of loss functions. However SGD requires to find a good learning rate which is big enough to have convergence after a reasonable amount of iterations and small enough that the gradient steps are made towards the minimum which is especially important in latter iteration stages. In the following,

[1]We restrict our discussion to 2-way FMs ($d = 2$).

[2]Please note that we do this analysis only to explain what happens implicitly in the FM – nothing has to be done explicitly when applying an FM. The end-user (domain expert) has only to specify the input features (i.e. the $\mathbf{x}$ vector) and run a generic FM tool with this data.

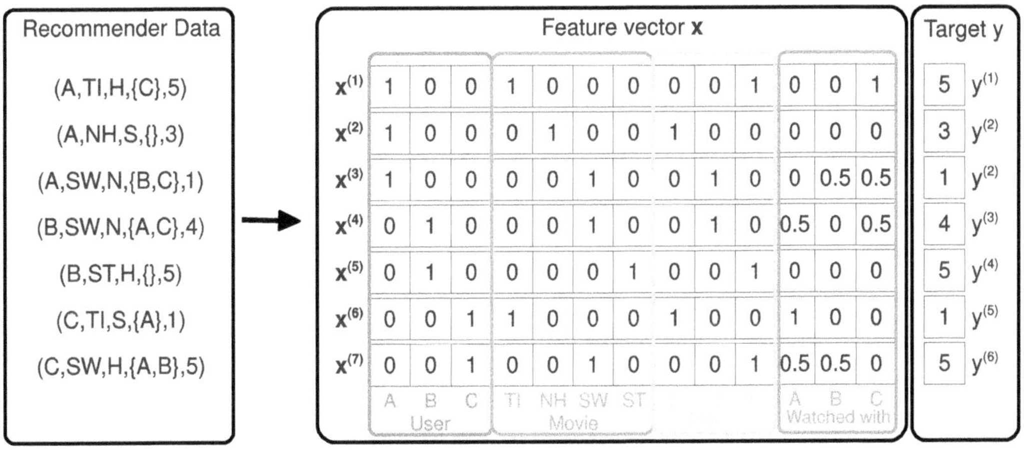

Figure 2: Context-aware recommendation data (left side) is transformed into a prediction problem from real-valued features (right side) by encoding the categorical and set categorical variables (left side) with indicator variables (right side). Here in the feature vector x, the first three values indicate the user, the next four ones the movie, the next three ones the mood and the last three ones the other users a movie has been watched with.

we suggest a new alternating least square (ALS) learning algorithm that finds the optimal value for a model parameter given the remaining ones.

4.3.1 Alternating Least Square

The analytical least-square solution for a model parameter can be found for FMs because they are linear functions (in each model parameter) and there is an analytic solution for every linear function. We will show this in the following two lemmas.

LEMMA 1 (LINEARITY IN θ). *An FM is a linear function with respect to every single model parameter $\theta \in \Theta$ and thus can be reexpressed as:*

$$\hat{y}(\mathbf{x}|\theta) = g_{(\theta)}(\mathbf{x}) + \theta\, h_{(\theta)}(\mathbf{x}) \tag{8}$$

where $g_{(\theta)}$ and $h_{(\theta)}$ are independent of the value[3] *of the parameter θ.*

PROOF. We proof this by stating g and h explicitly for the model parameters. For the global bias w_0, the FM can be rewritten as:

$$\hat{y}(\mathbf{x}|w_0) = w_0 \underbrace{1}_{h_{(w_0)}(\mathbf{x})} + \underbrace{\sum_{i=1}^{n} w_i\, x_i + \sum_{i=1}^{n}\sum_{j=i+1}^{n} \hat{w}_{i,j}\, x_i\, x_j}_{g_{(w_0)}(\mathbf{x})}$$

for w_l:

$$\hat{y}(\mathbf{x}|w_l) = w_l \underbrace{x_l}_{h_{(w_l)}(\mathbf{x})} + \underbrace{w_0 + \sum_{i=1, i\neq l}^{n} w_i\, x_i + \sum_{i=1}^{n}\sum_{j=i+1}^{n} \hat{w}_{i,j}\, x_i\, x_j}_{g_{(w_l)}(\mathbf{x})}$$

[3]The functions g and h are indexed with the **name** of the parameter θ because their form depends on the variable θ (e.g. is different for w_0 and w_l) but they do not depend on the **value** of θ.

And for the factorized 2-way interactions $v_{l,f}$:

$$\hat{y}(\mathbf{x}|v_{l,f}) := v_{l,f} \overbrace{x_l \sum_{i=1, i\neq l} v_{i,f}\, x_i}^{h_{(v_{l,f})}(\mathbf{x})} \underbrace{+ w_0 + \sum_{i=1}^{n} w_i\, x_i + \sum_{i=1}^{n}\sum_{j=i+1}^{n} \sum_{\substack{f'=1 \\ (f'\neq f)\vee(l\notin\{i,j\})}}^{k} v_{i,f'}\, v_{j,f'}\, x_i\, x_j}_{g_{(v_{l,f})}(\mathbf{x})}$$

□

REMARK 1. *For linear decomposable functions like $\hat{y}$ of an FM, the function $h_{(\theta)}(x)$ is the gradient of $\hat{y}$ with respect to θ:*

$$h_{(\theta)}(\mathbf{x}) = \frac{\partial}{\partial\theta}\hat{y}(\mathbf{x}|\theta) \tag{9}$$

Differentiating $\hat{y}$ leads directly to this result.

LEMMA 2 (OPTIMAL VALUE FOR θ). *The regularized least-square solution of a single parameter θ for a linear model $\hat{y}(\mathbf{x}|\theta)$ is:*

$$\theta = -\frac{\sum_{(\mathbf{x},y)\in S} \left(g_{(\theta)}(\mathbf{x}) - y\right) h_{(\theta)}(\mathbf{x})}{\sum_{(\mathbf{x},y)\in S} h^2_{(\theta)}(\mathbf{x}) + \lambda_{(\theta)}} \tag{10}$$

PROOF. To gain the regularized least-square solution analytically, the first derivative of the optimization criterion (eq. 6) w.r.t. θ has to be found:

$$\frac{\partial}{\partial\theta}\text{RLS-OPT} = \sum_{(\mathbf{x},y)\in S} 2\,(\hat{y}(\mathbf{x}) - y)\, h_{(\theta)}(\mathbf{x}) + 2\,\lambda_{(\theta)}\,\theta$$

The minimum is where this derivative is 0:

$$\sum_{(\mathbf{x},y)\in S} 2\,(\hat{y}(\mathbf{x})-y)\,h_{(\theta)}(\mathbf{x}) + 2\,\lambda_{(\theta)}\,\theta = 0$$

$$\Leftrightarrow \sum_{(\mathbf{x},y)\in S} \left(g_{(\theta)}(\mathbf{x})-y\right)\,h_{(\theta)}(\mathbf{x}) + \sum_{(\mathbf{x},y)\in S} \theta\, h^2_{(\theta)}(\mathbf{x}) + \lambda_{(\theta)}\,\theta = 0$$

$$\Leftrightarrow \theta = -\frac{\sum_{(\mathbf{x},y)\in S}\left(g_{(\theta)}(\mathbf{x})-y\right)h_{(\theta)}(\mathbf{x})}{\sum_{(\mathbf{x},y)\in S} h^2_{(\theta)}(\mathbf{x}) + \lambda_{(\theta)}}$$

□

4.3.2 Learning Algorithm

Lemma 2 with the gradients $h_{(\theta)}$ (see remark 1 and eq. (10)) allows to analytically find the optimal value of each model parameter θ of the FM given the remaining model parameters. A joint optimum of all model parameters Θ can be found iteratively by calculating the optimum of each model parameter one after another and repeating this several times. In figure 3 such an algorithm is sketched – the meaning and purpose of e and q will be explained later. First the model parameters are initialized, where the 0- and 1-way interactions (w_0 and w_l) can be initialized with 0 and the factorization parameters with small 0-centered random values. In the main loop the parameters are optimized one after the other. The idea here is to optimize first lower interactions and then higher ones because for lower interactions more data is observed and thus their estimates are more reliable. Within the factors of the 2-way interactions, first all features of the first factor dimension are optimized, then the features of the second factor dimension, etc. This allows the f-th factor to find the residuals for the 1st to $(f-1)$th factor dimensions. This optimization main loop is repeated several times until convergence to the joint optimum of all model parameters.

4.3.3 Fast Calculation

Straightforward computation of the optimum for each parameter with eq. (10) would mean to calculate g and h for each training example and in each parameter update. Now, we show how to calculate the values efficiently for FMs. This involves three improvements: (1) precomputing error terms, (2) precomputing h-terms for 2-way interactions and (3) using the sparsity in S. In total, this will lead to an update algorithm where a full iteration over all parameters is in $O(|S|\,\overline{m}_S\,k)$ – i.e. linear in the number of non-zero elements in the whole dataset and the number of factors.

Precomputing error terms.

The first bottleneck in updating the parameter θ with eq. (10) is calculating $(g_{(\theta)}(\mathbf{x})-y)$ for each training case $(\mathbf{x},y)\in S$. Obviously, a trivial computation of this is in $O(m(\mathbf{x})\,k)$.

Now we will show, how to compute this in constant time $O(1)$ if the error is known. Lets define for each training case, the error[4] $e(\mathbf{x},y|\Theta)$ of the model given the model parameter as:

$$e(\mathbf{x},y|\Theta) := \hat{y}(x|\Theta) - y \qquad (11)$$

This allows to rewrite:

$$g_{(\theta)}(\mathbf{x}) - y = e(\mathbf{x},y|\Theta) - \theta\, h_{(\theta)}(\mathbf{x}) \qquad (12)$$

[4]Actually, e is not the error, but e^2 is. Nevertheless, we use the term *error* for convenience.

procedure LEARNALS(S)
  $w_0 \leftarrow 0$ ▷ Initialize the model parameters
  $\mathbf{w} \leftarrow (0,\ldots,0)$
  $\mathbf{V} \sim \mathcal{N}(0,\sigma)$
  for $(\mathbf{x},y)\in S$ **do** ▷ Precompute e and q
    $e(\mathbf{x},y|\Theta) \leftarrow \hat{y}(\mathbf{x},y) - y$
    for $f\in\{1,\ldots,k\}$ **do**
      $q(\mathbf{x},f|\Theta) \leftarrow \sum_{i=1}^{n} v_{i,f}\,x_i$
    end for
  end for
  repeat ▷ Main optimization loop
    $w_0^* \leftarrow -\frac{\sum_{(\mathbf{x},y)\in S}(e(\mathbf{x},y|\Theta)-w_0)}{|S|+\lambda_{(w_0)}}$ ▷ global bias
    $e(\mathbf{x},y|\Theta) \leftarrow e(\mathbf{x},y|\Theta) + (w_0^* - w_0)$
    $w_0 \leftarrow w_0^*$
    for $l\in\{1,\ldots,n\}$ **do** ▷ 1-way interactions
      $w_l^* \leftarrow -\frac{\sum_{(\mathbf{x},y)\in S}(e(\mathbf{x},y|\Theta)-w_l\,x_l)x_l}{\sum_{(\mathbf{x},y)\in S} x_l^2+\lambda_{(w_l)}}$
      $e(\mathbf{x},y|\Theta) \leftarrow e(\mathbf{x},y|\Theta) + (w_l^* - w_l)\,x_l$
      $w_l \leftarrow w_l^*$
    end for
    for $f\in\{1,\ldots,k\}$ **do** ▷ 2-way interactions
      for $l\in\{1,\ldots,n\}$ **do**
        $v_{l,f}^* \leftarrow -\frac{\sum_{(\mathbf{x},y)\in S}(e(\mathbf{x},y|\Theta)-v_{l,f}\,h_{(v_{l,f})}(\mathbf{x}))h_{(v_{l,f})}(\mathbf{x})}{\sum_{(\mathbf{x},y)\in S} h^2_{(v_{l,f})}(\mathbf{x})+\lambda_{(v_{l,f})}}$
        $e(\mathbf{x},y|\Theta) \leftarrow e(\mathbf{x},y|\Theta) + (v_{l,f}^* - v_{l,f})h_{(v_{l,f})}(\mathbf{x})$
        $q(\mathbf{x},f|\Theta) \leftarrow q(\mathbf{x},f|\Theta) + (v_{l,f}^* - v_{l,f})h_{(v_{l,f})}(\mathbf{x})$
        $v_{l,f} \leftarrow v_{l,f}^*$
      end for
    end for
  until stopping criterion is met
  return $w_0, \mathbf{w}, \mathbf{V}$
end procedure

Figure 3: Alternating least algorithm that optimizes the model parameters w_0, $\mathbf{w}$ and $\mathbf{V}$ for least-square in $O(|S|\,\overline{m}_{|S|}\,k)$ time (see section 4.3.3) where $|S|$ are the number of training examples and $\overline{m}_{|S|}$ the average number of non-zero elements in an input vector $\mathbf{x}$.

Which can be used in the nominator of eq. (10). We store the error in a vector $\mathbf{e}\in\mathbb{R}^{|S|}$ over all training examples and precompute it at the beginning. After changing the value of a model parameter from θ to θ^*, the error also changes. This change on the error can be computed analytically by:

$$e(x,y|\Theta^*) = e(x,y|\Theta) + (\theta^* - \theta)\,h_{(\theta)}(\mathbf{x}) \qquad (13)$$

where Θ^* is the set of all model parameters where only the value of θ has changed to θ^*.

Precomputing h-terms.

After storing error terms, the computation complexity only depends on the complexity of the $h_{(\theta)}$-functions. For the parameters w_0 and w_i, the complexity of $h_{(\theta)}$ is constant, thus also computing the terms within the sums of the nominator and denominator as well as the error update is in constant time. But for the factorized parameters, computing h contains a loop over all variables. We will show now how to compute this in constant time. First, we can reformulate $h_{(v_{l,f})}$ as:

$$h_{(v_{l,f})}(\mathbf{x}) = x_l \sum_{i=1}^{n} v_{i,f}\, x_i - x_l^2\, v_{l,f}$$
$$= x_l\, q(\mathbf{x}, f|\Theta) - x_l^2\, v_{l,f} \quad (14)$$
$$(15)$$

with

$$q(\mathbf{x}, f|\Theta) := \sum_{i=1}^{n} v_{i,f}\, x_i \quad (16)$$

This term q is independent of l and can be precomputed for each training case and factor in a matrix $\mathbf{Q} \in \mathbb{R}^{|S|\times k}$. With a precomputation of the q-terms, the h-function can be computed in constant time with eq. (14). When updating a parameter $v_{l,f}$ to $v_{l,f}^*$, we have to update the corresponding q-term as well. This can be done in constant time with:

$$q(\mathbf{x}, f|\Theta^*) = q(\mathbf{x}, f|\Theta) + (v_{l,f}^* - v_{l,f})\, x_l \quad (17)$$

Again Θ^* are the new parameters after the value of $v_{l,f}$ changed to $v_{l,f}^*$, while the rest of the parameters keep unchanged.

Sparsity in S.

With the two enhancements described so far, the computation of each term within the sums of the nominator and denominator of the update rules eq. (10) can be calculated in constant time. Now, we investigate the overall complexity. First, for the w_0 parameter, the optimization complexity is $O(|S|)$. Secondly, for each update (eq. (10)) of the 1- and 2-way interactions of the l-th parameter, one has to loop only over training examples where h is nonzero – these are the training examples where $x_l \neq 0$. Thus the complexity for updating a 1-way or 2-way parameter is in $O(m_l)$[5]. In total there are n 1-way and $n\,k$ 2-way parameters, so the complexity for one whole iteration (i.e. updating all parameters) is $O(\sum_{l=1}^{n} m_l\, k) = O(\sum_{(\mathbf{x},y)\in S} m(\mathbf{x})\, k) = O(|S|\, \overline{m}_{|S|}\, k)$.

5. EVALUATION

In this section, we empirically investigate if the greater model flexibility and better runtime of FMs comes to the price of less prediction quality compared to the state-of-the-art context-aware method *Multiverse Recommendation*. Furthermore we want to examine the sensitivity of SGD to the choice of the learning rate and if our ALS optimization can successfully work without this hyperparameter.

5.1 Methodology

Datasets. Even though the problem of context-aware rating prediction is highly relevant in practice, there are only a few publicly available datasets: the *Food* dataset [10], the *Adom.* dataset [1] as well as the *Yahoo! Webscope* dataset[6] enriched with context-aware information by [5]. The *Food* dataset contains 6360 ratings (1 to 5 stars) by 212 users for 20 menu items where one context variable captures if the situation in which the user rates is virtual or real (i.e. if (s)he imagines to be hungry or (s)he really is) and the second one how hungry the user is. The *Adom.* dataset contains 1524 rating events (1 to 15 stars) for movies with five context variables about companion, the weekday and other time information. For the *Yahoo! Webscope* dataset (221367 rating events) we follow [5] and apply their method to generate datasets with an increasing number of dependency of the target on the context – we generate 9 datasets for $\alpha = \beta \in \{0.1, \ldots, 0.9\}$.

Methods. We compare context-aware FMs to *Multiverse Recommendation*. Note that *Multiverse Recommendation* has been shown to outperform other context-aware recommender systems on the *Yahoo! webscope*, *Food* and *Adom.* dataset [5]. As context-unaware baseline we use FMs (*FM (nocontext)*) where only the user and item variables are used generating the feature vectors which is equivalent to matrix factorization with bias terms (see [14] for a proof) which is one of the strongest context-**un**aware recommender algorithms. All models are optimized for regularized least-squares (eq. 6). The FMs are optimized with our proposed ALS algorithm. *Multiverse Recommendation* is learned with an SGD algorithm similar to the one proposed in [5].

Protocol. We remove a 5% sample from each dataset which is used as validation set for tuning the hyperparameters for optimal MAE. After hyperparameter search, we make a 5-fold cross validation on the remaining 95% of the dataset – i.e. the validation set for hyperparameter tuning is not used any more. We report the mean RMSE and MAE over the 5 experiments. All methods are implemented in C++ and were run on the same hardware.

Experimental Reproducibility. Our FM implementation with ALS optimization, a *Multiverse Recommendation* implementation and the dataset generation scripts can be downloaded from our website[7].

5.2 Results

5.2.1 ALS vs. SGD Learning

In figure 4, we compare the test error of an SGD implementation to our ALS-approach on the Webscope dataset[8]. The leftmost figure shows the prediction quality on the test set after each iteration. The two plots on the right side show the minimal RMS error on the test set for several learning rates after 10 and 100 iterations. One can see that the prediction quality of SGD depends largely on the learning rate and the number of iterations that is chosen. If the SGD learning rate is chosen too large (e.g., here 0.01), the quality of ALS cannot be reached. With a small learning rate one can reach the quality of ALS – provided that the number of iterations is large enough (see rightmost graphs) and that one stops learning near the minimum (see leftmost graph) on a validation set to prevent overfitting.

This experiment shows that SGD needs a careful and time-consuming search for the learning rate. In contrast to this, ALS requires no such search because it does not have this

[5]Remind that m_l is the number of training cases in S where $x_l \neq 0$ which is usually low in our sparse setting

[6]`http://research.yahoo.com/Academic_Relations` ydata-ymovies-user-movie-ratings-content-v1_0

[7]`http://www.libfm.org/`

[8]The model is a context-aware FM with $k = 64$; the regularization parameters have been tuned individually for each learning method.

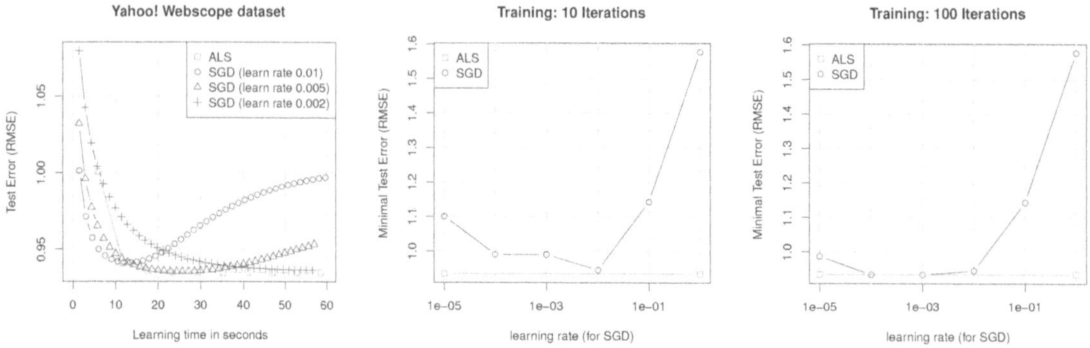

Figure 4: On the left side test error curves are plotted for three choices of learning rates. The two plots on the right show the best RMSE found after 10 and 100 iterations respectively for several choices of learning rates. This shows that for applying typical stochastic gradient descent (SGD) algorithms an appropriate learning rate has to be found. Usually an expensive search over hyperparameters is performed. Our ALS algorithm works without such a hyperparameter.

hyperparameter. With regard to prediction quality, SGD can perform as good as ALS but only with the right choice of the learning rate. This makes ALS clearly favorable in application.

5.2.2 Runtime

One of the main disadvantages of *Multiverse Recommendation* for practical use is that the computation complexity of the model is in $O(k^m)$ which is an issue for both learning and prediction. That means even for standard non-context-aware recommender systems, the runtime is quadratic in the dimensionality of the factorization k and for context-aware problems at least cubic. This makes it hard to apply for larger number of factors k. In contrast to this, the computational complexity of factorization machines is linear in both k and m: $O(k\,m)$.

In this experiment, we compare the runtime for one full iteration over all training examples of *Multiverse Recommendation* to context-aware FMs. As dataset, we used *Yahoo! Webscope* with $m = 4$. To show the polynomial growth of the runtime with an increasing number of the dimensionality factorization, we run both models with $k \in \{1, 2, 4, 8, 16, 32, 64, 128\}$ – for *Multiverse Recommendation* the maximal k we use was 32. In figure 5, the results are reported. These empirical results match to the theoretical complexity analysis. The runtime of the FM is linear and one full iteration over all training examples can be made for example in about 11 seconds (for $k = 128$) whereas the complexity of *Multiverse Recommendation* growths with k^4 such that the runtime for $k = 16$ is already 30 minutes and for $k = 32$ about 8 hours.

5.2.3 Prediction Quality

Finally, we want to investigate if the flexibility and fast runtime of context-aware FMs comes to the price of poor prediction quality compared to the *Multiverse Recommendation* method. Therefore we compare the prediction quality on the *Food*, *Adom* and *Webscope* dataset[9]. Figure 6 shows that context-aware FMs and *Multiverse Recommendation* have comparable prediction quality for the *Food* and *Adom.* datasets. Furthermore, both methods outperform the context-unaware method (here equivalent to a matrix factorization model).

[9]For the *Adom.* dataset our implementation of *Multiverse Recommendation* performed much worse than reported in [5]. Thus in favor of *Multiverse Recommendation* we report their (better) MAE value.

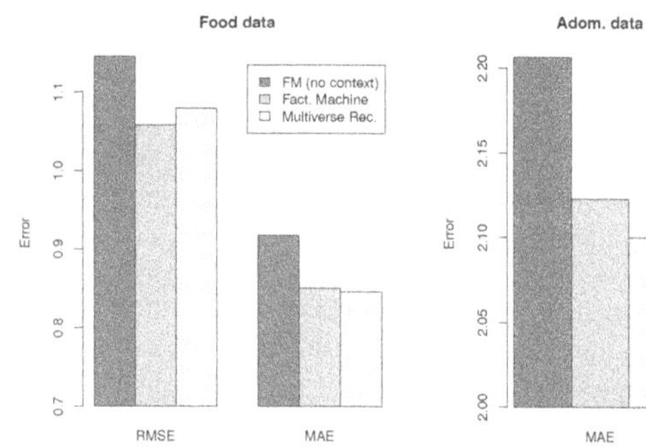

Figure 6: The context-aware methods *Multiverse Recommendation* [5] and our proposed context-aware *Factorization Machine* benefit from incooperating the context-information into the rating prediction.

In a third experiment, we investigate the artificially enriched *Yahoo! Webscope* dataset (see [5]) with an increasing influence of context variables on the rating. Figure 7 shows that both context-aware FM and *Multiverse Recommendation* benefit from ratings that have a stronger dependence on the context. In contrast to this, the prediction quality of context-unaware FM gets worse when the rating depends stronger on the context because for context-unaware FMs the context is unobserved and thus they cannot explain this dependency.

Comparing both context-aware methods among each other, one can see that FMs throughout generate much better predictions than *Multiverse Recommendation*. E.g. for RMSE the difference is about 0.10 to 0.15 points whereas for MAE it is about 0.08 to 0.10 points. This matches to results from the related area of tag recommendation, where a pairwise interaction model (PITF) outperforms the Tucker decomposition empirically in sparse problems [15]. Note that the

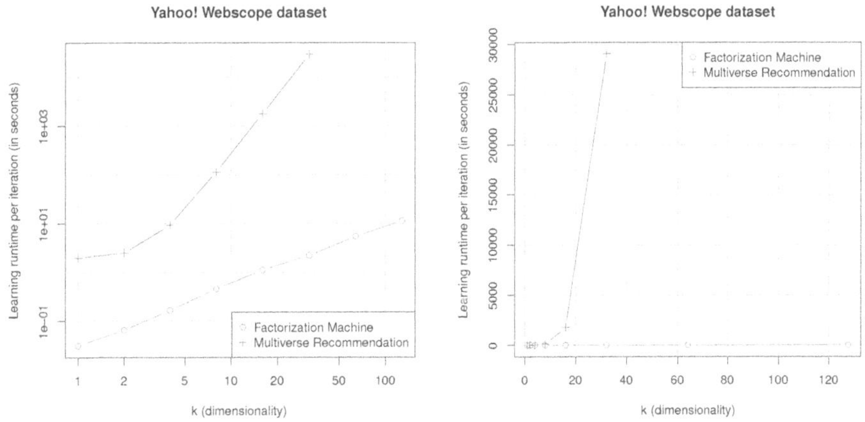

Figure 5: Learning runtime in seconds for one iteration over the whole training dataset (the left side is in log-log scale). The runtime of the *Factorization Machine* is linear in the number of latent factors k whereas for *Multiverse Recommendation* [5] it is polynomial (here $O(k^4)$). E.g. for a factorization size of $k = 16$ ($k = 32$), one iteration with the FM takes only 1.1 second (2.2 seconds), whereas for *Multiverse Recommendation* it takes about 30 minutes (8 hours).

Multiverse Recommendation model is the Tucker decomposition and the FM includes all possible pairwise interactions (like PITF).

5.2.4 Summary

Our experiments have shown that context-aware FMs are able to take contextual information into account to enhance predictions like the state-of-the-art method *Multiverse Recommendation*. In terms of runtime, FMs are linear which makes them applicable to a large dimensionality of factors, many context-variables and many observations. In contrast to this *Multiverse Recommendation* cannot handle a large number of factorization dimensions or modes. The advantage in terms of runtime is not traded in for prediction quality. Instead, on the dense datasets (*Food* and *Adom.*) the prediction quality of both methods is comparable whereas FMs outperform *Multiverse Recommendation* largely in sparse settings (*Yahoo! Webscope*). Finally, ALS optimized FMs are easily applicable as they do not require an expensive search for the learning rate like SGD optimized FMs or *Multiverse Recommendation*.

6. CONCLUSION

In this paper, we have shown how to apply factorization machines to the task of context-aware recommender systems. FMs are easily applicable to a wide variety of context by specifying only the input data. This allows them to solve scenarios where standard tensor factorization approaches cannot be applied (e.g. categorical set domains, real-valued domains). We have developed a new learning algorithm for FMs that analytically solves the least-square problem for each model parameter independently. This is especially helpful in practice as no learning rate has to be specified like in SGD approaches. Compared to *Multiverse Recommendation* which is the best-performing method for context-aware rating prediction so far, our approach achieves much faster runtime both in training and prediction ($O(k\, m)$ instead of $O(k^m)$) as well as a better prediction quality. To summarize, context-aware FMs combine the flexibility to be applied in many different scenarios and high prediction accuracy due to factorized interactions with fast and scalable computation due to the linear model complexity.

7. ACKNOWLEDGMENTS

We would like to thank Hideki Asoh, Gediminas Adomavicius and Alexander Tuzhilin for sharing their data sets.

8. REFERENCES

[1] G. Adomavicius, R. Sankaranarayanan, S. Sen, and A. Tuzhilin. Incorporating contextual information in recommender systems using a multidimensional approach. *ACM Transactions on Information Systems*, 23(1):103–145, 2005.

[2] D. Agarwal and B.-C. Chen. Regression-based latent factor models. In *KDD '09: Proceedings of the 15th ACM SIGKDD international conference on Knowledge discovery and data mining*, pages 19–28, New York, NY, USA, 2009. ACM.

[3] L. Baltrunas and F. Ricci. Context-based splitting of item ratings in collaborative filtering. In *RecSys '09: Proceedings of the third ACM conference on Recommender systems*, pages 245–248, New York, NY, USA, 2009. ACM.

[4] R. M. Bell and Y. Koren. Scalable collaborative filtering with jointly derived neighborhood interpolation weights. In *Proceedings of the 7th IEEE International Conference on Data Mining (ICDM 2007), October 28-31, 2007, Omaha, Nebraska, USA*, pages 43–52. IEEE Computer Society, 2007.

[5] A. Karatzoglou, X. Amatriain, L. Baltrunas, and N. Oliver. Multiverse recommendation: n-dimensional tensor factorization for context-aware collaborative filtering. In *RecSys '10: Proceedings of the fourth ACM conference on Recommender systems*, pages 79–86, New York, NY, USA, 2010. ACM.

[6] Y. Koren. Factorization meets the neighborhood: a multifaceted collaborative filtering model. In *KDD '08: Proceeding of the 14th ACM SIGKDD international*

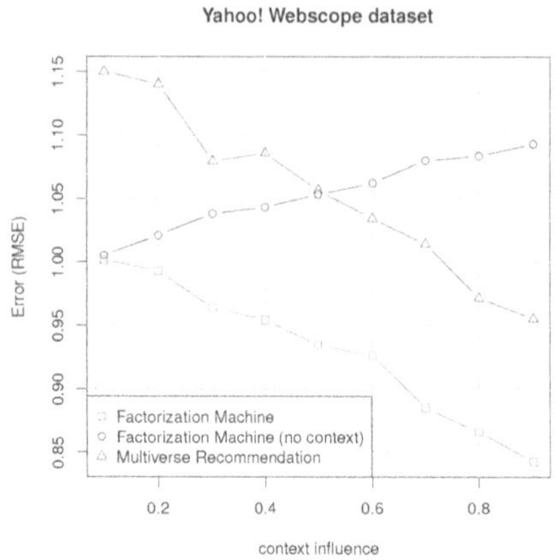

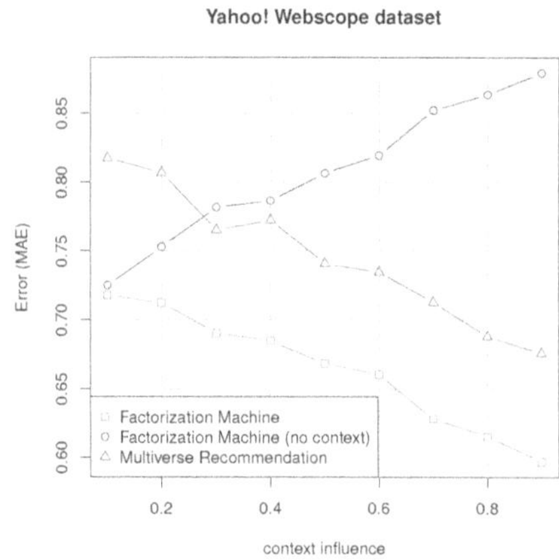

Figure 7: Prediction error with an increasing influence of the context on the rating. Context-aware FMs largely outperform *Multiverse Recommendation* [5] in quality. Secondly, context-aware FMs profit from an increasing influence of the context on the rating whereas non-contextaware FMs suffer from having no data (context) to explain the shift in the ratings.

conference on Knowledge discovery and data mining, pages 426–434, New York, NY, USA, 2008. ACM.

[7] Y. Koren. Collaborative filtering with temporal dynamics. In *KDD '09: Proceedings of the 15th ACM SIGKDD international conference on Knowledge discovery and data mining*, pages 447–456, New York, NY, USA, 2009. ACM.

[8] Y. Li, J. Nie, Y. Zhang, B. Wang, B. Yan, and F. Weng. Contextual recommendation based on text mining. In *Proceedings of the 23rd International Conference on Computational Linguistics: Posters*, COLING '10, pages 692–700, Stroudsburg, PA, USA, 2010. Association for Computational Linguistics.

[9] K. Oku, S. Nakajima, J. Miyazaki, and S. Uemura. Context-aware svm for context-dependent information recommendation. In *MDM '06: Proceedings of the 7th International Conference on Mobile Data Management*, page 109, Washington, DC, USA, 2006. IEEE Computer Society.

[10] C. Ono, Y. Takishima, Y. Motomura, and H. Asoh. Context-aware preference model based on a study of difference between real and supposed situation data. In *UMAP '09: Proceedings of the 17th International Conference on User Modeling, Adaptation, and Personalization*, pages 102–113, Berlin, Heidelberg, 2009. Springer-Verlag.

[11] U. Panniello, A. Tuzhilin, M. Gorgoglione, C. Palmisano, and A. Pedone. Experimental comparison of pre- vs. post-filtering approaches in context-aware recommender systems. In *RecSys '09: Proceedings of the third ACM conference on Recommender systems*, pages 265–268, New York, NY, USA, 2009. ACM.

[12] I. Pilászy and D. Tikk. Recommending new movies: even a few ratings are more valuable than metadata. In *RecSys '09: Proceedings of the third ACM conference on Recommender systems*, pages 93–100, New York, NY, USA, 2009. ACM.

[13] I. Pilászy, D. Zibriczky, and D. Tikk. Fast als-based matrix factorization for explicit and implicit feedback datasets. In *RecSys '10: Proceedings of the fourth ACM conference on Recommender systems*, pages 71–78, New York, NY, USA, 2010. ACM.

[14] S. Rendle. Factorization machines. In *Proceedings of the 10th IEEE International Conference on Data Mining*. IEEE Computer Society, 2010.

[15] S. Rendle and L. Schmidt-Thieme. Pairwise interaction tensor factorization for personalized tag recommendation. In *WSDM '10: Proceedings of the third ACM international conference on Web search and data mining*, pages 81–90, New York, NY, USA, 2010. ACM.

[16] A. Said, S. Berkovsky, and E. W. De Luca. Putting things in context: Challenge on context-aware movie recommendation. In *CAMRa2010: Proceedings of the RecSys '10 Challenge on Context-aware Movie Recommendation*, New York, NY, USA, 2010. ACM.

[17] B. Sarwar, G. Karypis, J. Konstan, and J. Reidl. Item-based collaborative filtering recommendation algorithms. In *Proceedings of the 10th international conference on World Wide Web*, pages 285–295, New York, NY, USA, 2001. ACM Press.

[18] N. Srebro, J. D. M. Rennie, and T. S. Jaakola. Maximum-margin matrix factorization. In *Advances in Neural Information Processing Systems 17*, pages 1329–1336. MIT Press, 2005.

[19] D. H. Stern, R. Herbrich, and T. Graepel. Matchbox: large scale online bayesian recommendations. In *Proceedings of the 18th international conference on World wide web*, WWW '09, pages 111–120, New York, NY, USA, 2009. ACM.

[20] L. Tucker. Some mathematical notes on three-mode factor analysis. *Psychometrika*, 31:279–311, 1966.

[21] L. Xiong, X. Chen, T.-K. Huang, J. Schneider, and J. G. Carbonell. Temporal collaborative filtering with bayesian probabilistic tensor factorization. In *Proceedings of the SIAM International Conference on Data Mining (SDM 2010)*, pages 211–222. SIAM, 2010.

Filtering Semi-Structured Documents Based on Faceted Feedback

Lanbo Zhang, Yi Zhang
School of Engineering
University of California, Santa Cruz
Santa Cruz, CA 95064 USA
{lanbo, yiz}@soe.ucsc.edu

Qianli Xing*
Department of Computer Science and Technology
Tsinghua University, Beijing 100084 China
xingqianli@gmail.com

ABSTRACT

Existing adaptive filtering systems learn user profiles based on users' relevance judgments on documents. In some cases, users have some prior knowledge about what features are important for a document to be relevant. For example, a Spanish speaker may only want news written in Spanish, and thus a relevant document should contain the feature "Language: Spanish"; a researcher working on HIV knows an article with the medical subject "Subject: AIDS" is very likely to be interesting to him/her.

Semi-structured documents with rich faceted metadata are increasingly prevalent over the Internet. Motivated by the commonly used faceted search interface in e-commerce, we study whether users' prior knowledge about faceted features could be exploited for filtering semi-structured documents. We envision two faceted feedback solicitation mechanisms, and propose a novel user profile learning algorithm that can incorporate user feedback on features. To evaluate the proposed work, we use two data sets from the TREC filtering track, and conduct a user study on Amazon Mechanical Turk. Our experimental results show that user feedback on faceted features is useful for filtering. The new user profile learning algorithm can effectively learn from user feedback on faceted features and performs better than several other methods adapted from the feature-based feedback techniques proposed for retrieval and text classification tasks in previous work.

Categories and Subject Descriptors

H.3.3 [**Information Storage and Retrieval**]: Information Search and Retrieval

General Terms

Algorithms, Experimentation

*This work was done while this author was a visiting student at UC Santa Cruz

Keywords

Adaptive Filtering, Content-Based Filtering, User Feedback, Faceted Feedback, Labeled Features, Semi-structured Documents, Document Facets

1. INTRODUCTION

Information filtering systems process a document stream and recommend relevant documents to individual users. Existing filtering approaches are generally categorized into content-based filtering and collaborative filtering. This paper focuses on the content-based adaptive filtering. In content-based filtering, the system assumes documents with similar content to what a user liked before are likely to be relevant. In adaptive filtering, potentially relevant documents must be delivered immediately, thus the system has no time to accumulate and rank a set of documents as a traditional retrieval system does. An adaptive filtering system usually makes a binary decision to accept or reject a newly arrived document for each individual user.

A content-based filtering system maintains a user profile for each user to represent his/her information need(s). Assuming a user provides some examples of relevant documents initially, the user profile is created based on these examples and/or the initial user query. While filtering, the profile is updated based on periodic feedback from the user. Largely influenced by the TREC filtering track, almost all existing content-based filtering approaches learn user profiles based on user-labeled documents. The documents could be news, technical reports, emails, or messages. In commercial recommender systems such as Amazon, eBay, etc., the labeled documents could be the descriptions of a set of user-rated items.

Similar to many other IR applications, a filtering system usually involves a large number of document features, including terms and facet-value pairs (such as "Author: Stephen Hawking"), etc. Usually, only a limited number of features are useful for determining whether a document is relevant or not. In many cases, users have some prior knowledge about what features are important, especially if the semantic meanings of the features are clear. For example, a researcher interested in HIV has the knowledge that the facet-value pair "MeSH: AIDS" is an important feature and the documents containing this feature are very likely to be relevant. Besides, users may want to put constraints on some facets of the delivered documents, such as format, authors, language, etc. For example, a Chinese reader may only want news articles written in Chinese.

In this paper, we explore how to exploit users' prior knowledge about document features for the filtering task. Specifically, we focus on the filtering of semi-structured documents, which usually contain a number of faceted features (i.e., facet-value pairs). There are three major reasons why we think user feedback on faceted features (i.e., faceted feedback) is promising. First, users might be able to provide reliable feedback on document facets. Compared with isolated terms, common document facets including format, authors, language, topics, subjects, prices, genres, etc., usually represent clear semantic concepts and thus are easier for users to understand. Similar to e-commerce users, filtering system users might be able to provide reliable feedback on facet-value pairs. Second, semi-structured documents with faceted features are increasingly prevalent. Due to several advantages offered by semi-structured documents, many publishers and information providers are creating documents in structured or semi-structured format. The development of text mining techniques (classification, clustering, information extraction, etc.) has made it possible to create facets for text documents automatically. The Semantic Web effort, social tagging web sites, and the Open Directory Project also provide a good way to create faceted features using the power of folksonomy. Besides, for certain document types (pictures, movies, products, etc.), faceted features are usually more accessible and informative than terms. Third, faceted search has gained great success in e-commerce over past years, and most popular online retailers, such as Amazon and eBay, now provide faceted search interfaces for buyers to narrow down products by putting constraints on a group of merchandise facets, such as category, price, brand, size, etc. This strengthens our belief that users are willing and able to give reliable feedback on faceted features in order to achieve a better experience.

To use faceted feedback for filtering, we need to answer three important research questions. First, how to select a small number of feature candidates for users to provide feedback. There are usually a large number of facet-value pairs in the whole corpus and it is important not to overwhelm users with too many candidates. Considering that a filtering system may have collected some labeled documents over time, we propose a feature candidate selection method based on both labeled and unlabeled documents. Secondly, how to design the user interface to help users provide reliable feedback. We envision two alternative user interaction mechanisms and compare their performances in this paper. Thirdly, given different types of feedback from the user including relevance feedback on documents and faceted feedback on features, how to learn the user profile. In this paper, we propose a semi-supervised user profile learning algorithm that can integrate two types of user feedback in a unified framework. We also implement some other methods by adapting techniques proposed for retrieval and text classification tasks and compare our algorithm with these methods.

The major contributions of this paper include: 1) we evaluate the usage of user feedback on faceted features for the filtering task and the experimental results show that faceted feedback is useful, especially in the cold-start scenario, where the filtering process starts with few or no relevant documents; 2) we propose a user profile learning algorithm that can learn from user feedback on both instances and features. The experimental results show that this algorithm performs consistently well and seems more robust than some other methods used for retrieval and text classification tasks; and 3) we envision and compare two user interaction mechanisms for soliciting user feedback on faceted features and observe no significant difference with respect to filtering performances between these two mechanisms.

2. RELATED WORK

Previous research on content-based filtering is largely influenced by the Filtering Track in TREC 4-11 [11] [12] [6] [7] [8] [19] [17] [18], where the task is to identify documents relevant to a specific topic from a document stream. Almost all research on content-based filtering is based on learning from labeled documents, and to our knowledge, this is the first work that aims to use user feedback on features for the filtering task.

Although using user feedback on features is not studied in the context of filtering, there is some related work about using feature feedback for retrieval and text-related learning tasks such as text classification.

Relevance feedback [20] has been shown to be an effective way to help retrieval systems improve retrieval performance. Besides the commonly used relevance feedback mechanism in which users are asked to judge whether a document is relevant or not, there has been some work on soliciting user feedback on document features. The term-based feedback mechanism, in which users are asked to identify relevant terms, has been studied by several researchers [5, 22, 2, 9, 10]. Recently, faceted feedback has been proposed for users to identify suitable faceted constraints on semi-structured documents to help improve retrieval performance [25].

There has been some recent interest in incorporating user-labeled features into text classification [14, 16, 15, 4]. Most research in this area involves asking users to label terms, and exploring how to learn a classifier from labeled terms. Liu et al. [14] ask human annotators to identify highly predictive terms from term clusters. The unlabeled instances are then soft-labeled according to their cosine similarity to the pseudo-instances that only contain user-identified features. Raghavan, Madani, and Jones [16] interleave user feedback on instances and features in a unified learning framework called tandem learning. Their experiments demonstrate that humans can provide accurate information about features, and that it takes one fifth as long to label features as to label instances. Raghavan and Allan [15] provide several methods for training SVMs with labeled features, including adjusting the parameters of labeled features, creating pseudo-instances that only contain labeled features, and soft-labeling unlabeled instances. Dayanic et al. [3] combine domain knowledge with training examples in a Bayesian framework. The domain knowledge is used to specify a prior distribution for the parameters of a logistic regression model. Druck et al. [4] propose a semi-supervised learning algorithm that uses labeled features to constrain the model's predictions on unlabeled instances based on generalized expectation criteria.

This paper differs from the prior work by focusing on a different task: adaptive information filtering. Some of the techniques we tried in this paper are motivated by the prior work. The new user profile learning algorithm proposed in this paper is motivated by [4], however, with significant differences. First, our algorithm is designed to incorporate two types of user feedback, that is, to learn from labeled instances and features simultaneously in order to fit the filtering task where users may provide mixed types of feedback.

In our algorithm, we use a unified loss function to combine user feedback on both instances and features. Secondly, our model is designed to capture the sufficiency and necessity of user-labeled features. The assumption of our model is users can identify important features and an important feature should have a high correlation with the document label. To measure this correlation, we propose the concepts of sufficiency and necessity and explicitly capture them in our algorithm.

3. FACETED FEEDBACK FOR FILTERING

In this paper, each metadata field of semi-structured documents is called a document facet, such as "Date", "Author", "People", "Source", "Topic", "Location", etc. A document may be assigned with one or several values on a particular facet. We call a facet (f) with a specific value (v) a facet-value pair (f: v) or a faceted feature. Examples of faceted features are "Date: 2010-12-25", "Author: Stephen Hawking", "Region: United States", etc. Faceted features convey important information about documents which may not be clearly expressed in document texts, for example, the "Date" of a news article. In some cases, this information is crucial in determining the relevance of a document. For example, a user may only want news on a topic reported recently rather than years ago. To help explore user information needs, it is reasonable to ask users for feedback on faceted features. In this paper, "user feedback on faceted features" is sometimes called "faceted feedback" for short.

3.1 User Interaction Mechanism

In a typical feature-based feedback mechanism, users are asked to identify "relevant" features from a group of candidates. However, the definition of "relevance" of a feature is usually not well-defined. Instead, we expect users to select features that are predictive of document labels (*relevant* or *non-relevant*), or from a mathematical point of view, the correlation between a relevant feature and the document label should be high. To help understand how users can identify the relevant features, we roughly categorize relevant features into the following two groups:

1. ***sufficient features***: a feature is ***sufficient*** if all documents with this feature are relevant. We define the ***sufficiency*** of a feature (f) as the probability that a document is relevant ($y = 1$) when this document has this feature ($f = 1$), that is $P(y = 1|f = 1)$. Sufficient features should have $P(y = 1|f = 1)$ equal or close to 1.

2. ***necessary features***: a feature is ***necessary*** if all relevant documents in the whole corpus must have this feature. We define the ***necessity*** of a feature (f) as the probability that a document has this feature ($f = 1$) when this document is relevant ($y = 1$), that is $P(f = 1|y = 1)$. Necessary features should have $P(f = 1|y = 1)$ equal or close to 1.

According to the definition of correlation in statistics, $P(y = 1|f = 1)$ and $P(f = 1|y = 1)$ are the only two factors that account for the correlation between a feature and the document label.

We envision two interaction mechanisms for soliciting user feedback on features. In the first mechanism, the system asks users to identify "relevant" features from a group of feature candidates. In the second mechanism, the system asks users to specifically identify which features are likely to be sufficient and which are likely to be necessary. If the user thinks the existence of a faceted feature is strong evidence of a document being relevant, the feature is probably sufficient. For example, the facet-value pair "MeSH: AIDS" is probably a sufficient feature for the researcher interested in HIV. On the other hand, if the user thinks a relevant document should meet some faceted constraint as specified by a faceted feature, the feature is probably necessary. For example, the facet-value pair "Language: Spanish" is probably a necessary feature for the Spanish speaker who only wants news articles written in Spanish.

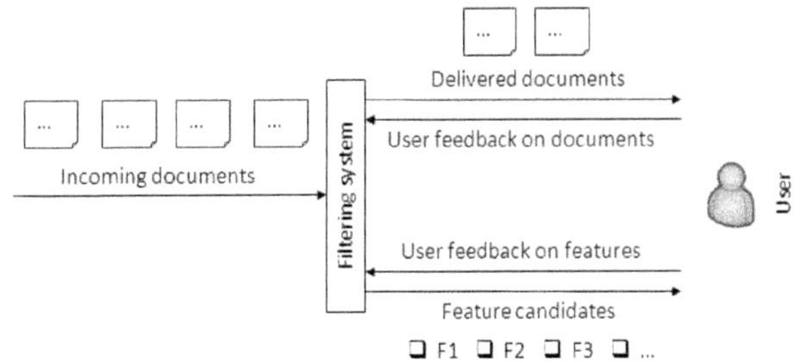

Figure 1: Two types of user feedback in a filtering system

3.2 Incorporating User Feedback on Features

We envision a filtering system that integrates two types of user feedback: 1) relevance feedback on documents; and 2) user feedback on features (Figure 1). Whenever a new document arrives, the system determines whether to deliver it to a user based on how well this document matches the user profile. At any time, the system can suggest a set of probably relevant features based on the current user profile. Users can choose to provide relevance feedback on delivered documents or to identify relevant features from the feature candidates. Whenever the system receives any type of feedback from the user, it updates the user's profile accordingly.

4. FEATURE CANDIDATE SELECTION

When asking for feature-based feedback, it is important not to overwhelm users with too many feature candidates. In this section, we focus on how to select a small number of feature candidates. Intuitively, good feature candidates should: 1) have a high probability of being chosen by the user; and 2) provide substantial information for user profile learning. In this paper, we focus on the first aspect and leave the second to our future work.

There has been much previous work on feature selection for text classification [23], and most of the existing approaches are based on the availability of labeled documents. However, in the scenario of filtering, the number of user-labeled documents is usually small or even zero, especially at the early stage of a filtering process, which is known as the cold-start problem [21]. Thus, we need a feature selection method that fits the filtering task better.

We propose a method for feature selection based on the current user profile, a set of user-labeled documents (**L**), and a set of unlabeled documents (**C**). The first step is to classify all unlabeled documents into a positive set $\mathbf{C}^+$ and a negative set $\mathbf{C}^-$ according to the current user profile. Then existing feature selection methods can be adapted here based on the set of user-labeled relevant documents ($\mathbf{L}^+$), the set of user-labeled non-relevant documents ($\mathbf{L}^-$), the set of positively classified documents ($\mathbf{C}^+$), and the set of negatively classified documents ($\mathbf{C}^-$).

Motivated by the well known TF*IDF method, we use the following scoring function to rank features for feature selection:

$$\text{score}(f) = (\alpha \text{N}(f, \mathbf{L}^+) + \beta \text{N}(f, \mathbf{C}^+)) * \text{IDF}(f) \quad (1)$$

where $\text{N}(f, \mathbf{L}^+)$ is the number of relevant documents that contain feature f (similarly for $\text{N}(f, \mathbf{C}^+)$), $\text{IDF}(f)$ is the Inverse Document Frequency of feature f, α and β are the corresponding weights. The intuition behind this ranking function is a feature occurring rarely in the whole corpus (thus has a high IDF) while frequently in the relevant ($\mathbf{L}^+$) and probably relevant documents ($\mathbf{C}^+$) is highly predictive of the document label.

5. USER PROFILE LEARNING: THE GENERALIZATION CONSTRAINT MODEL

In a filtering system with feature-based feedback enabled, the user profile learning algorithm should be able to learn from user feedback on both instances and features simultaneously. In this section, we introduce the Generalization Constraint Model (GCM), which incorporates user-labeled features as constraints on model generalization.

5.1 Notations

We define the notations that will be used later as follows:

- y: the label of a document. $y = 1$ means "relevant" and $y = -1$ "non-relevant".
- f: the indicator of whether a feature appears or not, $f = 1$ means "appear" and $f = -1$ "not appear".
- $\boldsymbol{\theta}$: the model parameter (i.e., user profile vector).
- $\mathbf{d}_i$: the vector representation of document i.
- $\mathbf{C}$: the set of unlabeled documents.
- $\mathbf{C}_f$: the set of documents in $\mathbf{C}$ where a particular feature appears ($f = 1$) or not ($f = -1$).
- $\mathbf{L}$: the set of user-labeled documents.
- $\mathbf{F}_s$: the set of features labeled as "sufficient" by the user.
- $\mathbf{F}_n$: the set of features labeled as "necessary" by the user.

5.2 Modeling Sufficiency and Necessity

The assumption of our model is a user selects a feature because this feature has a high sufficiency and/or necessity. To make use of user feedback on features, we need to model a feature's sufficiency $P(y = 1|f = 1)$ and necessity $P(f = 1|y = 1)$.

Logistic regression has been shown to work well for adaptive filtering [24]. We use logistic regression to model the probability of a document label (y) given the document vector ($\mathbf{d}_i$) and the user profile ($\boldsymbol{\theta}$):

$$P(y|\mathbf{d}_i, \boldsymbol{\theta}) = \frac{1}{1 + \exp(-y\boldsymbol{\theta}^{\mathbf{T}}\mathbf{d}_i)} \quad (2)$$

Assume that the probability of a document's label (y) is independent with any feature (f) given the user profile ($\boldsymbol{\theta}$):

$$P(y|\mathbf{d}_i, f, \boldsymbol{\theta}) = P(y|\mathbf{d}_i, \boldsymbol{\theta})$$

Assume the probability of a document vector ($\mathbf{d}_i$) is independent with the user profile ($\boldsymbol{\theta}$) given a feature (f):

$$P(\mathbf{d}_i|f, \boldsymbol{\theta}) = P(\mathbf{d}_i|f)$$

Then the sufficiency of a feature given the user profile could be derived as follows:

$$\begin{aligned} P(y|f, \boldsymbol{\theta}) &= \sum_{\mathbf{d}_i \in \mathbf{C}} P(y|\mathbf{d}_i, f, \boldsymbol{\theta}) P(\mathbf{d}_i|f, \boldsymbol{\theta}) \\ &= \sum_{\mathbf{d}_i \in \mathbf{C}} P(y|\mathbf{d}_i, \boldsymbol{\theta}) P(\mathbf{d}_i|f) \\ &= \sum_{\mathbf{d}_i \in \mathbf{C}_f} \frac{P(y|\mathbf{d}_i, \boldsymbol{\theta})}{|\mathbf{C}_f|} \end{aligned} \quad (3)$$

where $|\mathbf{C}_f|$ denotes the total number of documents in $\mathbf{C}_f$. $P(y|d_i, \theta)$ can be calculated using the current user profile.

According to Bayes' theorem, the necessity of a feature given the user profile could be derived as follows:

$$\begin{aligned} P(f|y, \boldsymbol{\theta}) &= \frac{P(f, y|\boldsymbol{\theta})}{P(y|\boldsymbol{\theta})} = \frac{P(f, y|\boldsymbol{\theta})}{\sum_{f=+/-1} P(f, y|\boldsymbol{\theta})} \\ &= \frac{P(y|f, \boldsymbol{\theta}) P(f|\boldsymbol{\theta})}{\sum_{f=+/-1} P(y|f, \boldsymbol{\theta}) P(f|\boldsymbol{\theta})} \\ &= \frac{P(y|f, \boldsymbol{\theta}) P(f)}{\sum_{f=+/-1} P(y|f, \boldsymbol{\theta}) P(f)} \end{aligned} \quad (4)$$

where $P(f|\boldsymbol{\theta}) = P(f)$ since f and $\boldsymbol{\theta}$ are independent with each other. $P(f)$ can be estimated according to the occurrence number of f in the whole corpus.

5.3 Reference Distributions

A feature labeled as "necessary" by the user should have a high necessity, and a feature labeled as "sufficient" should have a high sufficiency. To quantify the necessity and sufficiency of user-labeled features, we introduce two Bernoulli distributions as the reference distributions: $T_{y|f}$ and $T_{f|y}$. For sufficient features, the distribution $P(y|f, \boldsymbol{\theta})$ should be close to the distribution $T_{y|f}$; and for necessary features, the distribution $P(f|y, \boldsymbol{\theta})$ should be close to the distribution $T_{f|y}$. We use KL divergence to measure the distances between $P_{y|f,\boldsymbol{\theta}}$ and $T_{y|f}$ (Equation 5), and $P_{f|y,\boldsymbol{\theta}}$ and $T_{f|y}$ (Equation 6).

$$\mathbf{D}_{\text{KL}}(P_{y|f,\boldsymbol{\theta}}, T_{y|f}) = \sum_{y=+/-1} P(y|f, \boldsymbol{\theta}) \log \frac{P(y|f, \boldsymbol{\theta})}{T(y|f)} \quad (5)$$

$$\mathbf{D}_{\text{KL}}(P_{f|y,\boldsymbol{\theta}}, T_{f|y}) = \sum_{f=+/-1} P(f|y, \boldsymbol{\theta}) \log \frac{P(f|y, \boldsymbol{\theta})}{T(f|y)} \quad (6)$$

The parameters of the reference distributions $T_{y|f}$ and $T_{f|y}$ could be tuned using a parameter tuning set. We did not use the special distribution $T(y = 1|f = 1) = 1$ for sufficient features and the special distribution $T(f = 1|y =$

$1) = 1$ for necessary features since users usually do not have enough knowledge to accurately distinguish if a feature is exactly sufficient/necessary or not. While tuning the parameters in our experiments, we found these special distributions are far from optimal and the optimal values of $T(f = 1|y = 1)$ and $T(y = 1|f = 1)$ tend to be relatively low.

The parameters of the reference distributions should be facet-dependent, since the reliability of user feedback on different facets may differ significantly. Some facets, such as "Time", "Location", and "People", represent very clear concepts and are easy for users to understand. While some other facets, such as "Topic", usually do not have a clear definition and different users may disagree on what values a document should have on these facets. User feedback on the first class of facets is usually more credible than that on the second class. Thus we may want to use different reference distributions for features of different facets. In our experiments, the parameters of reference distributions of different facets are tuned on a parameter tuning set, and we find the optimal reference distributions for different facets are significantly different.

5.4 Integrating Two Types of Feedback

We propose to use a unified loss function to combine user feedback on both instances and features. Given user-labeled documents $\mathbf{L}$, user-identified sufficient features $\mathbf{F}_s$, and user-identified necessary features $\mathbf{F}_n$, the loss function is:

$$\begin{aligned} L(\boldsymbol{\theta}) = & -\lambda_1 \sum_{\mathbf{d}_i \in \mathbf{L}} \log P(y_i|\mathbf{d}_i, \boldsymbol{\theta}) \\ & + \lambda_2 \sum_{f_j \in \mathbf{F}_s} \mathbf{D}_{\mathrm{KL}}(P_{y_j|f_j,\boldsymbol{\theta}}, T_{y_j|f_j}) \\ & + \lambda_3 \sum_{f_k \in \mathbf{F}_n} \mathbf{D}_{\mathrm{KL}}(P_{f_k|y_k,\boldsymbol{\theta}}, T_{f_k|y_k}) \\ & + \lambda_4 \|\boldsymbol{\theta}\|^2 \end{aligned} \quad (7)$$

where the first item corresponds to user feedback on documents, the second and third items correspond to user feedback on features, and the fourth item handles regularization. λ_1, λ_2, λ_3, and λ_4 are pre-set parameters that could be tuned on the parameter tuning set.

The user profile $\boldsymbol{\theta}^*$ can be obtained by minimizing the loss function:

$$\boldsymbol{\theta}^* = \arg\min_{\boldsymbol{\theta}} L(\boldsymbol{\theta}) \quad (8)$$

Gradient-based optimization algorithms, such as conjugate gradient descent, could be used to find the optimal user profile $\boldsymbol{\theta}^*$.

6. EXPERIMENTAL METHODOLOGY

6.1 Experimental Goals

We design a series of experiments to evaluate the proposed ideas and methods. Specifically, our experiments are designed to answer the following questions:

- Is user feedback on faceted features useful for filtering?
- Can the Generalization Constraint Model proposed in section 5 effectively learn user profiles from user feedback on both instances and features?
- Which user interaction mechanism for soliciting faceted feedback proposed in Section 3.1 is better?
- How does the Generalization Constraint Model compare with other methods with the similar goal?

To answer the first and second questions, we conduct a user study on Amazon Mechanical Turk to collect user feedback on faceted features. Then we run adaptive filtering experiments using the proposed user profile learning algorithm and see whether filtering performances could be improved compared with no faceted feedback. To answer the third question, we design two user interfaces with different tasks: one is to ask users to select relevant features and the other is to ask users to select necessary and sufficient features respectively. To answer the fourth question, we implement several methods originally proposed for learning from labeled features for search or text classification task, and compare them with the proposed algorithm on the adaptive filtering task.

6.2 Data Sets

We use two data sets from the TREC filtering track for the adaptive filtering experiments.[1]

The **OHSUMED** data set is used in the TREC 2000 filtering track [19]. This data set consists of a medical corpus, 63 topics (information needs), and the corresponding document relevance judgments. The corpus contains a total of 348,566 medical articles selected from a subset of 270 medical journals covering years from 1987 to 1991. Each document of this corpus has some metadata fields including MeSH (Medical Subject Headings), Author, Date, etc., from which we can create faceted features. In our experiments, we chose to use the MeSH field, which is perhaps the most informative metadata field for the information needs in this data set.

The **RCV1** data set is used in the TREC 2002 filtering track [18]. We only use the first 50 topics of this track to simulate user information needs[2]. The RCV1 (Reuters Corpus Volume 1) corpus [13] contains about 810,000 Reuters news stories published from 1996-08-20 to 1997-08-19. Each document of this corpus has some metadata, and we choose to use three metadata fields (Topic, geographical Region, and Industry) to create faceted features.

6.3 Filtering Settings

The filtering settings in our experiments are similar to those of the adaptive filtering task in the TREC filtering track, however, there are some changes. For each user, the filtering system starts with an initial query, some (or zero) relevant document samples, and a set of unlabeled documents for training. Before the filtering process starts, the user is asked to provide the first-round faceted feedback. Then the system starts filtering the testing documents in the order of document publishing date. During the filtering process, relevance judgments on delivered documents are available for user profile learning in order to simulate

[1]We are not using recommendation data sets like MovieLens, where faceted features are available as well, since it is hard to collect user feedback on faceted features due to the lack of well-defined user information needs.

[2]The prior research shows that the other topics do not match real user information needs well.

users' immediate relevance feedback on documents. If one-third of the testing documents are processed and at least two documents have been delivered, the system will present the second-round feature candidates to the user for faceted feedback refinement and incorporate the user's faceted feedback immediately. By setting the second-round user interaction, we want to evaluate whether users are able to improve the quality of their feedback during the filtering process.

The user profile is updated whenever some user feedback is available. We also change the number of initially known relevant documents to see if faceted feedback is more useful when fewer relevant documents are initially known and if it is no longer useful when more relevant documents are available.

6.4 Faceted Feedback Collection

To evaluate whether real users are able to provide useful feedback on features for the filtering task, we conduct a user study on Amazon Mechanical Turk. Mechanical Turk is an online marketplace for work, where requesters can publish tasks that require human intelligence and workers can choose to work on the tasks to get paid. Researchers have compared TREC assessors with Mechanical Turk workers, and demonstrated that Mechanical Turk workers are a good source for IR evaluation [1].

In our user study, Mechanical Turk workers are recruited to act as real filtering users and provide faceted feedback. To avoid careless workers and ensure the quality of the study, we restrict the qualified workers who can work on our tasks to those in the United States[3] and have an approval rate of over 95% and more than 50 approved submissions on Mechanical Turk. Since the OHSUMED data set contains a lot of medical terms, we require that workers have common sense in medicine in order to be qualified to work on this data set.

We design two tasks for each query: the first task (**Task I**) is to ask the user to select "relevant" features, and the second (**Task II**) is to ask users to select "necessary" and "sufficient" features respectively. Equation 1 is used to rank features and we keep the top 20 ones as feature candidates. For each individual query, we recruit ten workers with half of them working on the first task and half of them on the second task. The users working on the first task are only asked to provide one round of feedback, and users working on the second task are asked to provide two rounds of feedback. For the first-round feedback, the topic statement (including Title, Description, and Narrative) and a group of feature candidates (we use 10 in our experiments) are shown to the user; and for the second-round feedback, a set of delivered documents are additionally shown to help users refine their feedback. In Task II, users were given the explanations of sufficient and necessary features (including examples of these two types of features). For each task, results of all five users are used and the average performance will be reported.

6.5 Document and User Profile Representation

For each document vector, we use term features, faceted features, along with a dummy variable always equal to 1. Specifically, we use the following formula to compute a document vector $\mathbf{d}$:

$$\mathbf{d}(i) = \frac{\mathrm{tf}(i,\mathbf{d})}{\mathrm{tf}(i,\mathbf{d}) + 0.5 + 1.5 * \frac{\mathrm{length}(\mathbf{d})}{\mathrm{avgDocLength}}} * \frac{\log \frac{N+0.5}{\mathrm{df}(i)}}{\log(N+1)} \quad (9)$$

In Equation 9, $\mathrm{tf}(i,\mathbf{d})$ is the frequency of feature i in document $\mathbf{d}$. For a faceted feature, we assume its frequency is 1 if it occurs in a document, otherwise 0. $\mathrm{df}(i)$ is the document frequency of feature i, N is the total number of documents. At any time of the filtering process, only documents that have been processed are considered for the computation of all statistics in Equation 9.

Both term features and faceted features are used in user profiles. To ensure a number of faceted features are kept in the user profile, we select term features and faceted features separately. For each user profile, we allow the maximum number of term features to be 30 and the maximum number of faceted features to be 10. We use the Rocchio method [20] to determine which features will be kept in the user profile. For faceted features, we assume user-labeled faceted features are contained in the original query when applying the Rocchio method.

6.6 Evaluation Metrics

In the TREC-9, TREC-10 and TREC-11 filtering tracks, the following utility function was used [18]:

$$\mathrm{T9U} = \mathrm{T10U} = \mathrm{T11U} = 2R^+ - N^+ \quad (10)$$

where R^+ is the number of relevant documents delivered, and N^+ is the number of non-relevant documents delivered. A normalized version of T11SU was also used in TREC-11:

$$\mathrm{T11SU} = \frac{\max(\frac{\mathrm{T11U}}{\mathrm{MaxU}}, \mathrm{MinNU}) - \mathrm{MinNU}}{1 - \mathrm{MinNU}} \quad (11)$$

where $\mathrm{MaxU} = 2 * (R^+ + R^-)$ is the maximum possible utility and $\mathrm{MinNU} = -0.5$.

We use **T11SU** as the major evaluation measure, and all algorithms are designed to optimize this measure (if applicable). We will also report the results on **T11U**, Macro-**Precision**, and Macro-**Recall**.

6.7 More Details

For each data set, we split the query topics into two equal-size sets for parameter tuning and testing respectively. The parameters of all reference distributions and $\lambda_1, \lambda_2, \lambda_3, \lambda_4$ in Equation 7 are tuned on the parameter tuning set by maximizing the metric T11SU. For simplicity, we manually set $\alpha = 2, \beta = 1$ in Equation 1 to give a higher weight to the frequency in user-labeled relevant documents ($\mathbf{L}^+$).

7. EXPERIMENTAL RESULTS

7.1 The Overall Performance

The performances with and without faceted feedback are compared in Table 1. For each data set, we tried several runs starting with 0/1/2 relevant documents respectively. The baseline runs ("rDocs = 0/1/2") learn user profiles from only relevance judgments on documents using Norm-2 regularized logistic regression. To ensure the baseline methods are well implemented, we compared the performances of the baseline runs with those reported in previous work [26, 19, 18], and found our performances are comparable to them.

[3]This limits the users to be native English speakers or those familiar with English.

For each run with faceted feedback ("with FFb"), the Generalization Constraint Model is used to learn user profiles from both relevance judgments on documents and user feedback on faceted features. For runs included in Table 1, we use two rounds of user feedback collected in Task II, where users are asked to select necessary and sufficient features respectively.

According to Table 1, we have the following findings: 1) **Faceted feedback can help improve filtering performances.** We find filtering performances are improved on both data sets when using faceted feedback. 2) **Faceted feedback is more valuable when fewer relevant documents are initially available.** All measures are improved significantly[4] when no relevant document is initially available on OHSUMED. Most measures are improved significantly when one relevant document is initially available on OHSUMED and zero or one relevant document is initially available on RCV1. On both data sets, only slight improvements are observed for most measures when starting with two relevant documents. This is not surprising since faceted feedback can provide less additional information when more relevant documents are initially available.

Table 1: Adaptive filtering performances with and without faceted feedback. (Docs/Q) is the average number of delivered documents for each user profile. "↑" indicates a statistically significant improvement over the corresponding baseline.

OHSUMED					
Setting	**T11SU**	**T11U**	**Prec**	**Rec**	**Docs/Q**
rDocs: 0	0.335	1.36	0.193	0.092	8.4
with FFb	0.371↑	6.68↑	0.322↑	0.185↑	16.3
rDocs: 1	0.358	3.81	0.271	0.190	18.4
with FFb	0.371	7.90↑	0.339↑	0.255↑	23.4
rDocs: 2	0.359	7.97	0.300	0.288	27.6
with FFb	0.370	6.68	0.349↑	0.303	25.6
RCV1					
Setting	**T11SU**	**T11U**	**Prec**	**Rec**	**Docs/Q**
rDocs: 0	0.379	11.92	0.315	0.149	17.5
with FFb	0.415↑	29.24	0.389	0.232↑	31.8
rDocs: 1	0.445	29.28	0.367	0.275	32.4
with FFb	0.481↑	42.40	0.455↑	0.352↑	42.1
rDocs: 2	0.502	48.60	0.483	0.389	47.9
with FFb	0.504	50.28	0.504	0.404	50.5

7.2 Filtering Algorithm Comparison

There have been some methods for learning from labeled features proposed in previous work. We adapt some of them to the adaptive filtering task and compare them with the proposed Generalization Constraint Model (GCM). These methods include:

- **Boolean Strategy**: The Boolean model has been used in many IR applications, such as faceted search in e-commerce. It seems a natural choice to only deliver documents that contain user-specified features. In our experiments, we tried two runs of Boolean model: BOOL(A) and BOOL(O). BOOL(A) requires a document to have all user-specified features (AND) in order to be delivered, and BOOL(O) requires a document to have at least one of the user-specified features (OR). Before applying the Boolean filter, the Norm-2 regularized logistic regression is used for the first-round filtering and only the accepted documents will be considered in the Boolean filter.
- **Feature Selection**: This method relies on user feedback to do feature selection and only user-selected features will be used in the user profile. The Norm-2 regularized logistic regression is then used to learn user profiles. Feature selection has been shown to be an important step in many IR applications including filtering. This method assumes that user-selected features are important for document classification; however, it leaves the feature-weight learning work to the learning algorithm.
- **Pseudo-Relevant Document**: This method generates a pseudo-relevant document based on user-selected features. In our experiments, we tried two runs: "Pseudo-D" and "Pseudo-Q". "Pseudo-D" treats all user-selected features as a pseudo-relevant document. "Pseudo-Q" combines user-selected features with the topic statement. Since documents in our data sets contain two types of features (terms and facet-value pairs) and only user feedback on faceted features is collected, it seems a more reasonable choice to treat the topic statement together with user-selected faceted features as a pseudo-relevant document.
- **Feature Prior**: This method assumes user-selected features follow a special prior distribution. In [3], the authors use Bayesian logistic regression to incorporate domain knowledge for text classification. In our experiments, we assume user-selected features follow a prior distribution with a special mean, while all other features follow a prior with mean 0. The special mean is tuned on the parameter tuning set.
- **Generalized Expectation Criteria (GEC)**: This method is proposed in [4] for text classification task. The labeled features are used directly to constrain the model's predictions on unlabeled instances and the soft constraints are expressed using generalized expectation criteria. The assumption of this method is a document containing a labeled feature has a high probability of belonging to the corresponding class(es). In other words, labeled features are assumed sufficient for the corresponding class(es). Unlike the GCM proposed in this paper, GEC assumes no labeled instances are available, and does not try to capture the necessity of user-labeled features. In our experiments, we modify GEC by adding an item corresponding to labeled instances to the objective function used in [4] and compare it with GCM.

For all above methods and our method (GCM), user feedback collected in Task I is used; no relevant documents are initially known; and the Norm-2 regularized logistic regression is used as the underlying filtering algorithm, if necessary. For our method (GCM), we assume user-selected features are both necessary and sufficient.

[4]We use t-tests with threshold p-value 0.05 for all significance tests in this paper.

Table 2 compares the performances of different methods. Although widely used in the e-commerce domain, the Boolean models (BOOL(A) and BOOL(O)) do not work well on both data sets. No significant improvement is achieved and Recall is hurt significantly on RCV1. This result is consistent with the findings reported in [25] for document retrieval task. Using user feedback for feature selection (FS) improves the performances, but not significantly. Using user feedback as a pseudo-relevant document (Pseudo-D) does not work well on both data sets and hurts the measure we are focusing on (T11SU). This is not surprising in our experimental settings: we use both term and faceted features while the pseudo-relevant document contains only faceted features. Conversely, we can understand why "Pseudo-Q" performs better, though no significant improvement is observed on RCV1. The "Prior" method significantly improves Recall, but the improvements on other measures are not significant. The Generalized Expectation Criteria (GEC) works well on RCV1, however, not significantly better than the baseline on OHSUMED. This is probably because OHSUMED has fewer relevant documents and feature necessity (which is not captured by GEC) is more important for a document to be relevant on this data set. According to Table 2, most existing methods do not perform consistently better than the baseline on the filtering data sets. Encouragingly, our model (GCM) significantly outperforms the baseline on both data sets.

Table 2: Adaptive filtering performances using different user profile learning algorithms. T11SU is the measure all algorithms try to optimize (if applicable).

OHSUMED					
Algrthm	**T11SU**	**T11U**	**Prec**	**Rec**	**Docs/Q**
Baseline	0.335	1.36	0.193	0.092	8.4
BOOL(A)	0.348	1.61	$0.796^{\uparrow}$	0.032	2.1
BOOL(O)	0.335	1.32	0.219	0.079	7.1
FS	0.339	3.23	0.226	0.106	12.0
Pseudo-D	$0.302^{\downarrow}$	2.71	0.221	$0.200^{\uparrow}$	23.9
Pseudo-Q	$0.362^{\uparrow}$	$4.81^{\uparrow}$	$0.278^{\uparrow}$	$0.160^{\uparrow}$	14.0
Prior	0.344	7.58	0.220	$0.166^{\uparrow}$	19.3
GEC	0.341	3.61	0.233	0.081	9.7
GCM	$0.363^{\uparrow}$	$6.13^{\uparrow}$	$0.275^{\uparrow}$	$0.156^{\uparrow}$	14.4
RCV1					
Algrthm	**T11SU**	**T11U**	**Prec**	**Rec**	**Docs/Q**
Baseline	0.379	11.92	0.315	0.149	17.5
BOOL(A)	0.351	4.16	$0.579^{\uparrow}$	$0.048^{\downarrow}$	4.7
BOOL(O)	0.388	15.64	0.362	0.155	17.5
FS	0.386	14.36	0.315	0.167	20.4
Pseudo-D	0.365	24.68	0.286	$0.235^{\uparrow}$	40.0
Pseudo-Q	0.397	23.60	0.360	0.187	25.6
Prior	0.414	28.88	0.357	$0.240^{\uparrow}$	32.3
GEC	$0.409^{\uparrow}$	24.80	0.351	$0.223^{\uparrow}$	30.5
GCM	$0.413^{\uparrow}$	27.44	$0.395^{\uparrow}$	$0.215^{\uparrow}$	29.3

7.3 User Interaction Mechanism Comparison

Two user interaction mechanisms (used in Task I and II respectively) are compared and the filtering performances using two mechanisms are reported in Table 3. The run "Rel" corresponds to Task I in which users are asked to select relevant features and only the first-round user feedback is used; "NS(1r)" corresponds to Task II in which users are asked to select sufficient and necessary features respectively and only the first-round feedback is used; and "NS(1&2r)" uses both two rounds of user feedback collected in Task II. All runs start with zero relevant documents. The Generalization Constraint Model (GCM) is used for all runs except the "Baseline". For the run "Rel", we assume all user-selected features are both necessary and sufficient when applying the GCM.

Table 3 shows that users can provide useful feedback with both interaction mechanisms. It is somewhat surprising that there is no significant difference between "Rel" and "NS(1r)". Table 4 shows two query examples with two users' feedback collected in Task I and II respectively. In general, the necessary features the user selected look reasonable; however, the sufficient features are not. This is probably because very few facet-value pairs are sufficient (or approximately sufficient) on our data sets (especially on RCV1), while users tend to choose some results so their results are not rejected on Mechanical Turk.

We also compared "NS(1r)" and "NS(1&2r)" to see if the quality of user feedback can be improved during the filtering process. However, we did not observe significant improvement on "NS(1&2r)" over "NS(1r)". There are two possible explanations: 1) the additional information provided to users does not help them improve feedback quality significantly; or 2) faceted feedback is no longer useful when a few documents have been labeled.

Table 3: Adaptive filtering performances using different user interaction mechanisms. Baseline: no faceted feedback used; Rel: faceted feedback collected in Task I is used; NS(1r): 1st round faceted feedback collected in Task II is used; NS(1&2r): two rounds of faceted feedback collected in Task II are used. "↑" indicates a significant improvement over the "Baseline". No significant difference is observed between "Rel" and "NS(1r)", and "NS(1r)" and "NS(1&2r)".

OHSUMED					
Setting	**T11SU**	**T11U**	**Prec**	**Rec**	**Docs/Q**
Baseline	0.335	1.36	0.193	0.092	8.4
Rel	$0.363^{\uparrow}$	$6.13^{\uparrow}$	$0.275^{\uparrow}$	$0.156^{\uparrow}$	14.4
NS(1r)	$0.366^{\uparrow}$	$5.35^{\uparrow}$	$0.314^{\uparrow}$	$0.186^{\uparrow}$	14.9
NS(1&2r)	$0.371^{\uparrow}$	$6.68^{\uparrow}$	$0.322^{\uparrow}$	$0.185^{\uparrow}$	16.3
RCV1					
Setting	**T11SU**	**T11U**	**Prec**	**Rec**	**Docs/Q**
Baseline	0.379	11.92	0.315	0.149	17.5
Rel	$0.413^{\uparrow}$	27.44	$0.395^{\uparrow}$	$0.215^{\uparrow}$	29.3
NS(1r)	$0.409^{\uparrow}$	23.08	0.352	$0.213^{\uparrow}$	27.8
NS(1&2r)	$0.415^{\uparrow}$	29.24	0.389	$0.232^{\uparrow}$	31.8

8. CONCLUSIONS AND FUTURE WORK

Users of filtering systems might be willing to interact with the system and provide some feedback in order to gain a

Table 4: Examples of faceted feedback. Rel: a user's faceted feedback in Task I; NS: a user's 2nd round faceted feedback in Task II. N: necessary features; S: sufficient features.

Title: 35 yo with advanced metastatic breast cancer **Description**: chemotherapy advanced for advanced metastatic breast cancer		
Rel		MeSH: Breast Neoplasms MeSH: Neoplasm Metastasis MeSH: Combined Modality Therapy
NS	N	MeSH: Breast Neoplasms MeSH: Female MeSH: Antineoplastic Agents, Combined
	S	MeSH: Breast Neoplasms MeSH: Neoplasm Metastasis MeSH: Antineoplastic Agents
Title: Tourism Great Britain **Description**: Retrieve documents pertaining to tourism into Great Britain and the efforts being undertaken to increase it.		
Rel		Region: UNITED KINGDOM Industry: AIR TRANSPORT Topic: TRAVEL AND TOURISM
NS	N	Region: UNITED KINGDOM Topic: TRAVEL AND TOURISM
	S	Topic: ECONOMICS Industry: HOTELS AND ACCOMMODATION

better long-term experience. Existing content-based adaptive filtering systems learn user profiles mainly based on users' relevance feedback on documents. We propose to exploit user feedback on faceted features for filtering semi-structured documents. We propose a feature candidate selection method fitting to the filtering task, and a user profile learning algorithm that can incorporate user feedback on both instances and features.

We evaluate our work on two filtering data sets from the TREC filtering track and conduct a user study to collect faceted feedback on Amazon Mechanical Turk. The experimental results show that user feedback on faceted features is useful for filtering, especially in the cold-start settings that few or no relevant documents are provided before the filtering process starts. The Generalization Constraint Model we proposed is a semi-supervised learning algorithm and can explicitly model the two key factors (necessity and sufficiency) that account for the correlation between a user-labeled feature and the document label. The experimental results show that GCM performs consistently well on two data sets and seems more robust than several other methods. We also compared two user interaction mechanisms for soliciting user feedback on faceted features and found no significant difference with respect to filtering performances. It is also observed that user feedback refinement in our experiments is not quite useful.

This is the first step to exploiting faceted feedback for filtering semi-structured documents, and the techniques proposed are far from optimal. The feature candidate selection method used in this paper focuses on selecting features with a high probability of being chosen by the user. However, a good feature candidate should also bring as many learning benefits if its label is known. In our future work, we will explore active learning techniques for faceted feature candidate selection. Also, we will pay attention to the specialties of faceted features. For example, features on different document facets are not equally informative for a particular information need. In this paper, we manually choose important metadata fields (facets) for our experiments, and it is still an open question how to automatically identify useful facets for users to provide feedback.

How to use feedback on features is an important question in retrieval, text classification and filtering, and this problem has not been well researched. Existing work in this direction mainly uses some simple approaches. For example, adjusting the weights of user-labeled features using heuristics, converting labeled features to pseudo-labeled instances, etc. The Generalization Constraint Model proposed in this paper performs well on the filtering task, and can also be adapted for retrieval and text classification tasks in the future.

Terms are the dominating features on the data sets used in this paper, and we expect that faceted feedback will be even more useful in applications where faceted features are dominating, such as product/coupon/discount email alerts sent from Groupon.com. Evaluation on these applications is a direction we will be going with our future work.

9. ACKNOWLEDGEMENTS

This work was funded by National Science Foundation IIS-0713111, IIS-0953908, UCSC/LANL ISSDM, and China Scholarship Council. Any opinions, findings, conclusions or recommendations expressed in this paper are the authors', and do not necessarily reflect those of the sponsors.

10. REFERENCES

[1] O. Alonso and S. Mizzaro. Can we get rid of trec assessors? using mechanical turk for relevance assessment. In *Proceedings of the SIGIR 2009 Workshop on the Future of IR Evaluation*, 2009.

[2] P. Anick. Using terminological feedback for web search refinement: a log-based study. In *SIGIR '03: Proceedings of the 26th annual international ACM SIGIR conference on Research and development in informaion retrieval*, pages 88–95, New York, NY, USA, 2003. ACM.

[3] A. Dayanik, D. D. Lewis, D. Madigan, V. Menkov, and A. Genkin. Constructing informative prior distributions from domain knowledge in text classification. In *Proceedings of the 29th annual international ACM SIGIR conference on Research and development in information retrieval*, SIGIR '06, pages 493–500, New York, NY, USA, 2006. ACM.

[4] G. Druck, G. Mann, and A. McCallum. Learning from labeled features using generalized expectation criteria. In *Proceedings of the 31st annual international ACM SIGIR conference on Research and development in information retrieval*, SIGIR '08, pages 595–602, New York, NY, USA, 2008. ACM.

[5] D. Harman. Towards interactive query expansion. In *SIGIR '88: Proceedings of the 11th annual international ACM SIGIR conference on Research and*

development in information retrieval, pages 321–331, New York, NY, USA, 1988. ACM.

[6] D. A. Hull. The trec-6 filtering track: Description and analysis. *Proceedings of the Sixth Text Retrieval Conference (TREC-6), USA,*, 1997.

[7] D. A. Hull. The trec-7 filtering track: description and analysis. In *Proceedings of TREC-7, 7th Text Retrieval Conference*, 1998.

[8] D. A. Hull and S. Robertson. The trec-8 filtering track final report. In *Proceedings of the 8th Text Retrieval Conference (TREC-8), USA,*, 1999.

[9] D. Kelly and X. Fu. Elicitation of term relevance feedback: an investigation of term source and context. In *Proceedings of the 29th annual international ACM SIGIR conference on Research and development in information retrieval*, SIGIR '06, pages 453–460, New York, NY, USA, 2006. ACM.

[10] D. Kelly, K. Gyllstrom, and E. W. Bailey. A comparison of query and term suggestion features for interactive searching. In *Proceedings of the 32nd international ACM SIGIR conference on Research and development in information retrieval*, SIGIR '09, pages 371–378, New York, NY, USA, 2009. ACM.

[11] D. D. Lewis. The trec-4 filtering track. In *The 4th Text REtrieval Conference (TREC-4)*, 1995.

[12] D. D. Lewis. The trec-5 filtering track. In *The Fifth Text REtrieval Conference (TREC-5)*, 1996.

[13] D. D. Lewis, Y. Yang, T. Rose, and F. Li. Rcv1: A new benchmark collection for text categorization research. 2004.

[14] B. Liu, X. Li, W. S. Lee, and P. S. Yu. Text classification by labeling words. In *Proceedings of the 19th national conference on Artifical intelligence*, AAAI'04, pages 425–430. AAAI Press, 2004.

[15] H. Raghavan and J. Allan. An interactive algorithm for asking and incorporating feature feedback into support vector machines. In *Proceedings of the 30th annual international ACM SIGIR conference on Research and development in information retrieval*, SIGIR '07, pages 79–86, New York, NY, USA, 2007. ACM.

[16] H. Raghavan, O. Madani, and R. Jones. Active learning with feedback on features and instances. *J. Mach. Learn. Res.*, 7:1655–1686, December 2006.

[17] S. Robertson and I. Soboroff. The trec 2001 filtering track report. In *Proceedings of the Tenth Text REtrieval Conference (TREC-10)*, 2001.

[18] S. Robertson and I. Soboroff. The trec 2002 filtering track report. In *Proceedings of the Eleventh Text REtrieval Conference (TREC-11)*, 2002.

[19] S. E. Robertson and D. A. Hull. The trec-9 filtering track final report. In *Proceedings of the 9th Text Retrieval Conference (TREC-9), USA,*, 2000.

[20] J. J. Rocchio. Relevance feedback in information retrieval. 1971.

[21] A. I. Schein, A. Popescul, L. H. Ungar, and D. M. Pennock. Methods and metrics for cold-start recommendations. In *Proceedings of the 25th annual international ACM SIGIR conference on Research and development in information retrieval*, SIGIR '02, pages 253–260, New York, NY, USA, 2002. ACM.

[22] B. Tan, A. Velivelli, H. Fang, and C. Zhai. Term feedback for information retrieval with language models. In *SIGIR '07: Proceedings of the 30th annual international ACM SIGIR conference on Research and development in information retrieval*, pages 263–270, New York, NY, USA, 2007. ACM.

[23] Y. Yang and J. O. Pedersen. A comparative study on feature selection in text categorization. In *Proceedings of the Fourteenth International Conference on Machine Learning*, ICML '97, pages 412–420, San Francisco, CA, USA, 1997. Morgan Kaufmann Publishers Inc.

[24] Y. Yang, S. Yoo, J. Zhang, and B. Kisiel. Robustness of adaptive filtering methods in a cross-benchmark evaluation. In *Proceedings of the 28th annual international ACM SIGIR conference on Research and development in information retrieval*, SIGIR '05, pages 98–105, New York, NY, USA, 2005. ACM.

[25] L. Zhang and Y. Zhang. Interactive retrieval based on faceted feedback. In *Proceeding of the 33rd international ACM SIGIR conference on Research and development in information retrieval*, SIGIR '10, pages 363–370, New York, NY, USA, 2010. ACM.

[26] Y. Zhang. Using bayesian priors to combine classifiers for adaptive filtering. In *Proceedings of the 27th annual international ACM SIGIR conference on Research and development in information retrieval*, SIGIR '04, pages 345–352, New York, NY, USA, 2004. ACM.

Learning Relevance from Heterogeneous Social Network and Its Application in Online Targeting

Chi Wang*
UIUC
chiwang1@illinois.edu

Rajat Raina
Facebook
rajatr@fb.com

David Fong†
Stanford University
clfong@stanford.edu

Ding Zhou
Facebook
dzhou@fb.com

Jiawei Han
UIUC
hanj@illinois.edu

Greg Badros
Facebook
badros@fb.com

ABSTRACT

The rise of social networking services in recent years presents new research challenges for matching users with interesting content. While the content-rich nature of these social networks offers many cues on "interests" of a user such as text in user-generated content, the links in the network, and user demographic information, there is a lack of successful methods for combining such heterogeneous data to model interest and relevance. This paper proposes a new method for modeling user interest from heterogeneous data sources with distinct but unknown importance. The model leverages links in the social graph by integrating the conceptual representation of a user's linked objects. The proposed method seeks a scalable relevance model of user interest, that can be discriminatively optimized for various relevance-centric problems, such as Internet advertisement selection, recommendation, and web search personalization.

We apply our algorithm to the task of selecting relevant ads for users on Facebook's social network. We demonstrate that our algorithm can be scaled to work with historical data for all users, and learns interesting associations between concept classes automatically. We also show that using the learnt user model to predict the relevance of an ad is the single most important signal in our ranking system for new ads (with no historical clickthrough data), and overall leads to an improvement in the accuracy of the clickthrough rate prediction, a key problem in online advertising.

Categories and Subject Descriptors

H.2.8 [**Database Management**]: Database Applications—*Data Mining*

*This work was done while the author was at Facebook.
†This work was done while the author was at Facebook.

SIGIR'11, Jul 24–28, 2011, Beijing, China.

General Terms

Algorithms, Experimentation, Economics

Keywords

Online Advertising, Heterogeneous Social Networks, Cognitive Relevance, Clickthrough Prediction

1. INTRODUCTION

Social networking services such as Facebook, Youtube, Twitter and MySpace have attracted hundreds of millions of users and become part of the Internet mainstream and an important part of our daily lives. Compared to traditional interest-based online communities, social networking services offer an additional network layer on top of user interest, as they center around people and their connections [6]. Social network users do not usually state their interest explicitly, but instead make connections, including direct connections with other users and groups, and implicit connections formed by interactions—such as commenting or clicking behavior—with user-generated content and other entities in the network, as shown in Figure 1. These connections provide valuable information about a user's interest, but are typically of varying importance and quality. The ability to infer a coherent model of users' interests from the heterogeneous parts of the network has the potential to provide personalized recommendation and more relevant advertisement targeting [23, 8].

Although the ideas developed in this paper can be applied to recommendation and other content matching tasks, we focus on the specific task of serving relevant advertisements to users in a social network. The foundation of pay-per-click advertising systems is a system for predicting the clickthrough rate (CTR) of an ad for a given user or query. Typically, such predictions are based on a machine learning model that uses various hand-crafted features, and is trained on historical click data. Features employed in current social networking sites mainly inherit the keyword-targeting prototype that is successful in search engine advertising, and demography-targeted advertising that is prevalent in traditional brand advertising. However, the characteristics of social networking sites are not fully exploited by these methods. On one hand, the large amounts of data about user activity and social context are unique in social network services and offer the opportunity for better inference of personalized interests than traditional methods. For example,

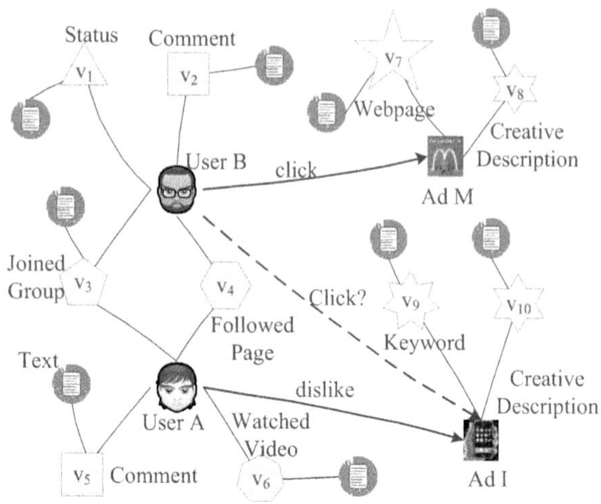

Figure 1: An example of user-ad-source heterogeneous network. Users are linked to different types of objects. These objects typically have associated text information. Ads are also linked to different type of objects with supporting text. We know some ads are clicked and some are shown but not clicked, for a small fraction of user-ad pairs, and we need to predict clicks for other user-ad pairs.

we can use user-generated content as contextual signals for content-based advertising. On the other hand, it is nontrivial to utilize these data. First, not all the contents have strong contextual relevance. For example, when users check friends' news or talk with friends, their intent is usually not related to business. Thus we cannot simply concatenate all the text from linked objects to augment a user's profile. Second, if we use keyword or concept matching to measure the relevance independently of the targeting problem, simply counting the exact matching concepts or even related concepts in the taxonomy cannot capture the latent signal—for example, an ad about Photographers[1] is better targeted to users interested in Weddings, rather than users interested in Photography.

In this paper, we formulate and tackle the problem of relevance learning for online targeting in heterogeneous social networks. To develop a better relevance model in the context of a heterogeneous social network, we propose a framework for CTR prediction based on a variant vector space model. First, for dimensionality reduction, we use semantically meaningful concepts to abstract the interest of users and the topic of ads, such as "Cartoon Movie" and "Music Bands and Artists", and thus both user and ad can be represented by a concept vector where each component is the weight for corresponding topic. Second, rather than a simplified view of a friendship social graph, we use the multi-typed networks to characterize user interaction with pages, groups, and other entities. These nodes have text content from which we can extract concepts, and serve as concept sources to their linked objects. Then user interests and other target content can be summarized from the concept classes of linked source nodes. Finally, to quantitatively distinguish the level of importance of different types of nodes in the network, and to systematically capture the intuition that a user concept may match multiple ad concepts with different association weights, we develop a generic user model to learn the weight for heterogeneous linked sources and the association between every pair of user concept and target concept jointly. The model can be applied on top of any concept extraction method.

We demonstrate a series of offline and online experiments that validate our hypothesis: 1) our model is capable of finding hidden associations between user concepts and ad concepts, such as Photographers with Weddings; 2) finding concept class associations and source importance weighting mutually enhance each other in terms of resolving the mismatching between user concept space and ad concept space; and 3) demography and keywords matching help with targeting, but not as precisely as our jointly learnt user model.

[1]We use capitalized phrases to represent a concept class.

2. RELATED WORK

2.1 Online Advertising and User Modeling

Online advertisement targeting and ranking have been widely studied in the context of search-based and content-based targeting, *e.g.*, Google AdWords and AdSense. Search-based targeting, or sponsored search can be thought of as a document retrieval problem, where the ads are the "documents" to be retrieved given a search query. Content-based targeting, a.k.a., contextual advertising, is a sister technology to sponsored search, where the ad retrieval is based on a webpage. Studies on such models show that the vocabulary mismatch problem is critical [9, 20, 7]. Motivated by that, we represent user interests and ads with vectors in a space of concept classes—which is significantly lower dimensional than the space of possible keywords—and learn a weighted matching function based on click history data. There are only a few recent published studies on user-centric targeting in the context of social network sites, perhaps due to the lack of data from widely-used social network sites. Bao *et al.* [4] proposed a influence-based diffusion model for targeting on implicit-relationship Q&A websites with little user-generated content. In comparison, we study a social network site with abundant user-generated content.

In terms of modeling user interests for search and recommendation systems, most works concentrate on one type of user generated data, while on a heterogeneous social network various sources can be used to analyze a user's behavior. Examples include user interaction history during web search [3], user generated tags [21], and browsing behavior in quasi-social networks [19]. A recent work by Wen *et al.* [24] studied users in social networks where there are multiple types of data. However, they assign each source an empirical weight when combining them and study the interest independently of the targeting task, while our model learns the weights from history data and can optimize the relevance measure towards different tasks.

Recent researchers also start to leverage social cues to enhance user interest modeling. Most of them augment the interest of one user from other users. Piwowarski and Zaragoza [18], White *et al.* [25] combine the interests of other users that visit the same page. Likewise, in collaborative filtering tasks it is assumed that those who had similar opinions on a set of items tend to agree again on other items [13, 14]. Konstas *et al.* [16] shows that incorporation of friendship and social tagging can improve the performance of a music recommendation system. Nevertheless their random-walk-based approach suffer from the scalability issue in large social networks. Distinct with these works, we do not explicitly reply on the friendship link to propagate interests, as previous studies already suggest that explicit relationships are not good indicators of the nature of user interactions[4] and the quality of inferring user interests from their friends varies [24]. Instead, we use links to other entity nodes to propagate interests. These nodes include the interaction with friends such as wallposts, as well as similar behaviors such as liking a page or joining a group. In this way we will not propagate the interests between one and his friends who never have interaction, while the users who share more similar linked objects will have more interest augmentation to each other through the training process.

2.2 Concept Extraction

User interests and ad contents can be extracted by unsupervised or supervised methods. Compared to the classification-based methods, unsupervised topic models such as Latent Dirichlet Allocation [5] are not restricted to a predefined set of labels, but are harder to use and modify when working with thousands of possible topics. With the development of knowledge representation language [11], domain specific ontologies can be constructed and used to label web content according to a concept taxonomy. Supervised learning based on a reference ontology can achieve a good semantic representation of user interests [22, 10], and has the advantages that it is scalable and the results corresponding to a predefined ontology are easy to interpret.

3. PROBLEM STATEMENT

We consider the task of predicting the clickthrough rate for a user on a target object recommended to the user. In our discussions, we assume the target object to be an ad.

Formally, our input is a heterogeneous network $G = (V, E)$. The set of vertices V can be partitioned into user nodes V^u, ad nodes V^a and their various linked source nodes: $V = V^u \cup V^a \cup \Lambda^u \cup \Lambda^a$, where $\Lambda^u = \cup_{i=1}^{n_u} \Lambda_i^u$ and $\Lambda^a = \cup_{j=1}^{n_a} \Lambda_j^a$ are the respective sources. Each user node $v_x \in V^u$ can be linked to one or more source nodes in $\Lambda_i^u, 1 \le i \le n_u$; each ad node $v_y \in V^a$ can be linked to one or more source node in $\Lambda_j^a, 1 \le j \le n_a$; and each source node $v_z \in \Lambda^u \cup \Lambda^a$ has some text associated with it. In principle we can define source types based on both object type and link type. In this work, we regard each type of object as a type of source, and assume there are two types of links, positive and negative, *e.g.*, "like" and "dislike". The linked sources accordingly have positive or negative contributions to the concepts of the linked user or ad node. For some user and ad node pairs, we know the existence of past impressions and whether the user clicked the ad. For any given pair of user node and ad node, our task is to predict the probability that the user will click on the ad.

Our output will serve as a feature in a machine learning model, to be trained with many different features. To enable an ad ranking system to examine the relevance between any user and any ad inside a large-scale social network in real time, we need to represent user interest and ad content in a concise yet semantically meaningful way allowing efficient measure of the relevance. We use clustered concept classes that are more precise cognitive unit than terms to summarize a user's interest. These concepts also serve as a common representation for integrating information across different

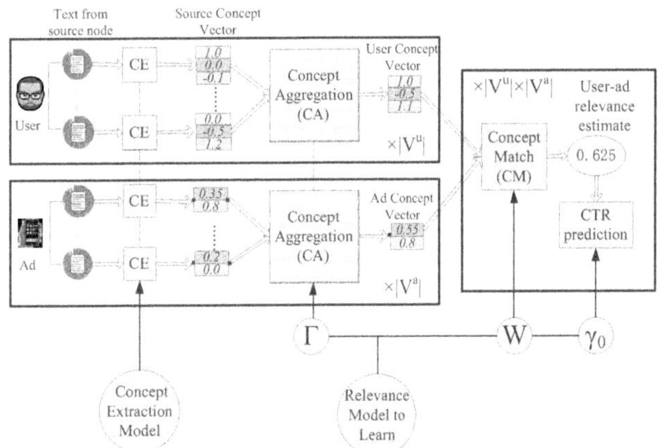

Figure 2: The pipeline of our relevance feature generation for CTR prediction and the model to learn

sources.

Figure 2 outlines the pipeline for our relevance prediction. We first give some definitions.

- *Concept Space.* A concept space is a d-dimensional real number space $\mathbb{R}^d$ that encodes some cognitive classification system such as ontology. Each dimension represents a concept class in the system. For example, in a human-edited Web directory [2], each category in the directory can be used as a concept class.
- *Concept Vector.* A concept vector is a vector in the concept space defined above that represents the cognitive property of an object. The component in each dimension indicates how strong the object is associated with the corresponding concept. For example, (Movie:0.5, Soccer:0.3) is a short representation of a sparse concept vector where all the weights are zero except for two concepts. For generality we allow user concept vector and ad concept vector to be in different concept spaces.
- *Concept Extraction(CE).* Given a source node's associated text, output its concept vector $\mathbf{c}$ in certain concept space.
- *Concept Aggregation(CA).* Given a user or an ad v_x, and the set of linked source nodes S_x—for each node $v_i \in S_x$, the corresponding concept vectors are already extracted as $\mathbf{c}_i$—output a concept vector $\mathbf{c}$ for this user or ad.
- *Concept Matching(CM).* Given a pair of user concept vector $\mathbf{u}$ and ad concept vector $\mathbf{a}$, produce a real value feature f to predict the likelihood of the user clicking the ad.

The pipeline of CE→ CA → CM allows user concept vector and ad concept vector be extracted and aggregated offline, and stored in high speed medium. The online feature computation can be efficient with fast access to the concept vector and fast vector matching algorithm. The three modules are tuned in the following manner. First, we choose a supervised concept extraction model. Then we learn the parameters in the rest two models and test them on click data. In this paper we focus on how to learn a good relevance prediction model that manipulates the concept aggregation and matching module for better CTR prediction.

Table 1: **Examples of the text concept extraction model used for the experiments. There are tens of thousands of possible concepts, and so the output concept vector is very sparse (tens of nonzero dimensions typically after thresholding).**

Input text	Sample concepts with weights
Get low cost car insurance.	`Business/Financial_Services/Insurance/Automotive,0.36;` `Home/Personal_Finance/Insurance,0.30;...`
I am cooking for mom today.	`Home/Cooking,0.20;` `Home/Family/Parenting/Mothers,0.16;...`

4. LEARNING RELEVANCE

We first briefly describe our concept extraction method. Then we discuss several baseline methods for relevance prediction, followed by our solution.

4.1 A Handcrafted Relevance Estimate

Learning Concepts. The task of concept extraction is to transform given text into the most salient topics that occur in the text. A variety of text modeling approaches are possible here, including categorization approaches that classify text into a pre-defined ontology of topics, and topic modeling approaches that automatically find semantically meaningful clusters [5]. While our methods are applicable to any finite vector representation of users and ads, for concreteness, we present results using a categorization approach. Using labeled webpage data from a reference ontology, we trained a large-vocabulary, bag-of-words based linear text classifier that accepts an arbitrary text input, and attempts to predict the strength of association with each label in the ontology. We use each label as a possible concept class, and use the predicted strength as the weight on that concept, thus transforming any input text into a concept vector. This model is not the focus of the paper, and we simply illustrate the method by examples in Table 1.

A baseline for Relevance Prediction. Based on the output of the concept extraction model above, we have a simple method to aggregate the concept vectors and measure the relevance between users and ads. For each user and each ad, we can use unweighted sum of the concept vectors extracted from all linked sources. Then we compute the cosine similarity of two concept vectors as the baseline feature for prediction.

There are several problems with this baseline feature. First of all, the different type of sources should have different prediction power of users' interests in ads. For example, greetings between friends may not be as useful as shared links to a movie or clicks on a previous ad. It is natural to assume that weighted sum of the concept vector from different sources is a better strategy for relevance inference. However, empirical assignment of source weights is not straightforward. It is not obvious whether the group a user belongs to should have higher weight than the posts on the wall. Not everyone publishes status messages, but most have profiles. Different sources have different level of quality, coverage and relevance to business. To find the best weighting we need to learn from the data.

Second, the cosine similarity metric needs to be improved due to the following reasons: 1) different concept may have different power for distinguishing the interest, *e.g.*, top level node Society *VS.* leaf node Society/Relationships/Dating; 2) the intuition that one user concept can match multiple ad concepts (e.g., the video game FIFA Series can match the computer game or the sport soccer) and vice versa; and 3) user concept space and ad concept space are not necessarily identical. So a better measure should allow one user concept to match different ad concepts and vice versa, and does not require they are in the same concept space. This measure is even harder to handcraft, but can be learnt from data.

Now we have two more improved methods, one to learn source weights and the other to learn a better measure. A natural question is can we combine the two to obtain an even better model, and whether they interact with each other. Our intuition is that better assessment of source importance should help us find a better measure; and the better matching function should also facilitate the noise reduction and quality of integration from different sources. Based on that intuition we develop a joint model to integrate the learning of these two parts, and it incorporates all the above means as special cases.

4.2 Jointly Learning Source Weights and Concept Association

Based on above analysis, we add unknown parameters to the aggregation and matching model. Our relevance model consists of both aggregation and matching, and we will learn the parameters for them together from training data. For aggregation, we combine the user concept vector from each source by weighted summation,

$$\mathbf{u}_x = \sum_{i=1}^{n_u} \sum_{v_j \in \Lambda_i^u \cap S_x} \gamma_i^u \mathbf{c}_j = \sum_{i=1}^{n_u} \gamma_i^u \mathbf{s}_i^x = \mathbf{U}_x \mathbf{\Gamma}_u \quad (1)$$

where $\mathbf{c}_j$ is the concept vector from the node v_j, S_x is the set of source nodes linked with user v_x, and γ_i^u is the weight for the i-th type of user source. For simplification we let $\mathbf{s}_i^x = \sum_{v_j \in \Lambda_i^u \cap S_x} \mathbf{c}_j \in \mathbb{R}^{d_u}$ be the sum of concept vectors from the i-th type source. Then we have the matrix representation $\mathbf{U}_x \mathbf{\Gamma}_u$, where $\mathbf{\Gamma}_u = (\gamma_1^u, \dots, \gamma_{n_u}^u)^T$ and $\mathbf{U}_x = (\mathbf{s}_1^x, \dots, \mathbf{s}_{n_u}^x)$. Likewise the ad concept vector will be

$$\mathbf{a}_y = \sum_{i=1}^{n_a} \sum_{v_j \in \Lambda_i^a \cap S_y} \gamma_i^a \mathbf{c}_j = \sum_{i=1}^{n_a} \gamma_i^a \mathbf{t}_i^y = \mathbf{A}_y \mathbf{\Gamma}_a \quad (2)$$

where $\mathbf{t}_i^y = \sum_{v_j \in \Lambda_i^a \cap S_y} \mathbf{c}_j \in \mathbb{R}^{d_a}$, $\mathbf{\Gamma}_a = (\gamma_1^a, \dots, \gamma_{n_a}^a)^T$, and $\mathbf{A}_y = (\mathbf{t}_1^y, \dots, \mathbf{t}_{n_a}^y)$. And for concept vector matching we allow any user concept in user concept space $\mathbb{R}^{d_u}$ to match any ad concept in ad concept space $\mathbb{R}^{d_a}$, with a pairwise weight $w_{i,j}$. Formally, we have the definition for the normalized bilinear form similarity sim as follows:

$$\begin{aligned} sim(\mathbf{u}_x, \mathbf{a}_y) &= \frac{1}{\|\mathbf{u}_x\| \, \|\mathbf{a}_y\|} \sum_{i=1}^{d_u} \sum_{j=1}^{d_a} w_{i,j} u_{x,i} a_{y,j} \\ &= \frac{1}{\|\mathbf{u}_x\| \, \|\mathbf{a}_y\|} \mathbf{u}_x^T \mathbf{W} \mathbf{a}_y \end{aligned} \quad (3)$$

where $u_{x,i}$ is the i-th component of the vector $\mathbf{u}_x$ and $a_{y,j}$ is the j-th component of the vector $\mathbf{a}_y$. Here $\|.\|$ is the L2 normal number of the vector, and $\mathbf{W} = [w_{i,j}]_{d_u \times d_a}$ is the transformation matrix as it transforms a user concept vector $\mathbf{u}_x$ into ad concept space $\mathbf{u}_x \mathbf{W} \in \mathbb{R}^{d_a}$. $\mathbf{W}$ virtually defines a bilinear form from $\mathbb{R}^{d_u} \times \mathbb{R}^{d_a} \longrightarrow \mathbb{R}$.

Substituting Eq. (1) and Eq. (2) into Eq. (3), we have a new relevance feature by using weighted sources and normalized bilinear form similarity,

$$f(x, y) = \frac{1}{\|\mathbf{U}_x\mathbf{\Gamma}_u\| \, \|\mathbf{A}_y\mathbf{\Gamma}_a\|}\mathbf{\Gamma}_u^T\mathbf{U}_x^T\mathbf{W}\mathbf{A}_y\mathbf{\Gamma}_a \quad (4)$$

We model the probability that a user x will click on an ad y as a generalized linear model in $f(x, y)$. Specifically, using the sigmoid function $g(x) = \frac{1}{1+\exp(-x)}$, we assume:

$$p(\text{user } x \text{ clicks ad } y) = g(f(x, y) + \gamma_0) \quad (5)$$

We can now collect historical data (x_i, y_i, z_i) on user x_i being shown ad y_i, with $z_i = 1$ when this resulted in a click (and $z_i = 0$ otherwise). We learn the unknown parameters in the model by maximizing the discriminative likelihood of this data:

$$L = \sum_{i=1}^{N} \log g((2z_i - 1)(f(x_i, y_i) + \gamma_0)) \quad (6)$$

where N is the number of training examples.

We have three sets of parameters to learn: the user source weights, the ad source weights, and the transformation matrix. Since our concept extraction model can produce tens of thousands distinct concepts, the above learning problem can have hundreds of millions of free parameters. Using a stochastic gradient descent algorithm, we can scan the training data once and iteratively update the three sets of parameters one set after another, as shown in Algorithm 1. Given a training example (x, y, z) from training data, the error in our prediction is given by $z - p(\text{user } x \text{ clicks ad } y)$, or simply $z - p$. We can derive the following gradient descent update rules:

$$\Delta\gamma_0 = r_0(z - p) \quad (7)$$

$$\Delta\mathbf{\Gamma}_u = \frac{r_1(z - p)}{\|\mathbf{u}_x\| \, \|\mathbf{a}_y\|}\mathbf{U}_x^T(I - \frac{\mathbf{u}_x\mathbf{u}_x^T}{\|\mathbf{u}_x\|^2})\mathbf{W}\mathbf{a}_y \quad (8)$$

$$\Delta\mathbf{\Gamma}_a = \frac{r_2(z - p)}{\|\mathbf{u}_x\| \, \|\mathbf{a}_y\|}\mathbf{A}_y^T(I - \frac{\mathbf{a}_y\mathbf{a}_y^T}{\|\mathbf{a}_y\|^2})\mathbf{W}^T\mathbf{u}_x \quad (9)$$

$$\Delta\mathbf{W} = \frac{r_3(z - p)}{\|\mathbf{u}_x\| \, \|\mathbf{a}_y\|}\mathbf{u}_x\mathbf{a}_y^T \quad (10)$$

where r_k is the learning rate for k-th set of parameters. Intuitive choices are $r_0 < r_1 = r_2 < r_3$ because the number of parameters in 3rd set is significantly larger than the first two sets.

The optimization problem is convex if we have only one set of parameters $\mathbf{W}$; in that case it is identical to logistic regression. However, when $\mathbf{\Gamma}_u$ and $\mathbf{\Gamma}_a$ are introduced the objective function is not convex. The gradient descent algorithm converges to a local maximum. The advantage of our stochastic gradient descent algorithm is that a single update is very efficient. We do not need to update all the parameters at each iteration, but just a small fraction of related ones. Assuming the user concept vector and ad concept vector contain l_u and l_a concepts with nonzero weights, only $(l_u l_a + n_u + n_a)$ parameters need be updated. Eq. (8) and (9) dominate the computation time. By storing $\mathbf{W}$ in a big hash table, the $\mathbf{u}_x^T\mathbf{W}\mathbf{a}_y$ can be computed in $O(l_u l_a)$ time. The complexity for training on one sample is $O((n_u + n_a)l_u l_a)$.

The algorithm applies to any general concept vector space. It can learn features of user-ad matching even when the user vector and ad vector are in different spaces. For example, to

Algorithm 1: Learning without regularization.

Input: number of sources n_u, n_a, user concept space $\mathbb{R}^{d_u}$, ad concept space $\mathbb{R}^{d_a}$, learning rates r_0,r_1,r_2,r_3,overall CTR c_0.
Data: training set $T = \{(z_{x,y}, \mathbf{U}_x, \mathbf{A}_y)\}$
Output: γ_0
Result: $\mathbf{W}, \mathbf{\Gamma}_u, \mathbf{\Gamma}_a$

Initialize all $w_{i,j} \leftarrow 0, 1 \le i \le d_u, 1 \le j \le d_a$;
Initialize all $\gamma_i^u, \gamma_j^a \leftarrow 1, 1 \le i \le n_u, 1 \le j \le n_a$;
Initialize $\gamma_0 \leftarrow c_0$;
repeat
    foreach *training example* $(z_{x,y}, \mathbf{U}_x, \mathbf{A}_y)$ **do**
1.1 $z \leftarrow z_{x,y}$;
        Combine user sources $\mathbf{u}_x \leftarrow \mathbf{U}_x\mathbf{\Gamma}_u$;
        Combine ad sources $\mathbf{a}_y \leftarrow \mathbf{A}_y\mathbf{\Gamma}_a$;
        Compute prediction p according to Eq. (5);
1.2   Update γ_0, $\mathbf{\Gamma}_u$, $\mathbf{\Gamma}_a$, $\mathbf{W}$ according to Eq. (7)-(10);
    end
until *convergence*;

learn the relevance between user demography and ad concepts, we can let each component of the user vector represent a demography group, and learn the transformation matrix $\mathbf{W}$. Without source weight to learn, the objective function is convex and the algorithm converges to global optimum.

We further suggest regularizing the transformation matrix $\mathbf{W}$ for two reasons. First, such regularization has been shown to reduce overfitting and improve generalization to future data, especially in problems with very large numbers of free parameters [17]. Second, the online computation for *sim* is more expensive than the dot product. It takes $O(l_u l_a)$ time even if we assume the lookup of an element in $\mathbf{W}$ takes $O(1)$ time, while the dot product only requires $O(l_u + l_a)$ time if we use the sorted sparse vector as data structure. To optimize it we can precompute the vector $\mathbf{u}_x^T\mathbf{W}$ and $\|\mathbf{u}_x\|$ for every user, and just do dot product for online computation. Using the L1 regularizer provides a principled way to reduce the number of nonzeros in $\mathbf{W}$.

With L1 regularization term, we now minimize the following objective function:

$$L' = -L + C\sum_{i,j}|w_{i,j}| = -L + C\|\mathbf{W}\|_1 \quad (11)$$

where large values of $C > 0$ produce fewer number of nonzeros in $\mathbf{W}$, at the potential cost of modeling power.

As before, we can use gradient descent algorithm, with an extra step to clip values at zero. The update rule becomes

$$\Delta\mathbf{W} = \frac{r_3(z - p)}{\|\mathbf{u}_x\| \, \|\mathbf{a}_y\|}\mathbf{u}_x\mathbf{a}_y^T - r_3C * sgn(\mathbf{W}) \quad (12)$$

Algorithm 2 shows the new online learning algorithm. We partition the training data to m chunks, and do the regularization after every $k = N/m$ examples. The complexity depends on the number of nonzero terms in $\mathbf{W}$, say n_w. The running time for training on N samples with m chunks is $O(N(n_u + n_a)l_u l_a + mn_w)$. In our data l_u, l_a, n_u and n_a are constants in the same order of magnitude as 10. n_w remains almost constant, although in the order of magnitude 10^6. So the training time grows linearly with the sample size with these constraints.

Algorithm 2: Learning with an L1 regularizer

Input: # of sources n_u, n_a, user and ad concept space $\mathbb{R}^{d_u}$, $\mathbb{R}^{d_a}$, learning rates r_0,r_1,r_2,r_3, overall CTR c_0, threshold t, regularization step m.
Data: training set $T = \{(z_{x,y}, \mathbf{U}_x, \mathbf{A}_y)\}$
Output: γ_0
Result: $\mathbf{W}, \mathbf{\Gamma}_u, \mathbf{\Gamma}_a$

```
Initialize all w_{i,j} ← 0, 1 ≤ i ≤ d_u, 1 ≤ j ≤ d_a;
Initialize all γ^u_i, γ^a_j ← 1, 1 ≤ i ≤ n_u, 1 ≤ j ≤ n_a;
Initialize γ_0 ← c_0;
k ← ⌊|T|/m⌋;
Separate training set into k chunks of m examples;
repeat
    for i = 1; i <= k; i++ do
        foreach (z_{x,y}, U_x, A_y) ∈ i-th chunk do
            Execute 1.1 to 1.2 in Algorithm 1;
        end
    end
    foreach w_{i,j} ∈ W do
        w_{i,j} ← w_{i,j} − sgn(w_{i,j}) * t;
        if |w_{i,j}| < t then //filter small weight
            w_{i,j} ← 0;
        end
    end
until convergence;
```

5. EXPERIMENTS

We conduct experiments on Facebook's large-scale online advertising system. First, we do preliminary analyses on the baseline relevance feature, and show its potential and problems in clickthrough prediction. Then we use our model to learn variant relevance features, compare them and verify our assumptions with a series of performance studies and decompositional analyses. Finally, we test the performance of our feature when working together with other features and show its improvement to offline clickthrough prediction. Due to business confidentiality, we report only relevant performance when showing experimental results.

5.1 Experiment Setup

Data Sets. We test our approaches on a sample of ads clickthrough data recorded on `facebook.com`. We sample historical click data anonymously from a small fraction of the 500 million monthly active users, and use the ad impressions seen by these users for training. Users are connected with about 50 different kinds of objects that are treated as the concept sources; ads have 4 concept sources in our setup. We use only non-private sources from users for concept extraction—*e.g.*, chat logs or user messages are never looked at. On average a user is connected to 80 community pages, groups and events, and create 90 pieces of content each month [1]. For offline analysis, we use anonymized click data from the user sample, gathered over one week. Since the positive examples (clicks) have low rates and can lead to biased estimates [15], we reduce the imbalance with a downsampling strategy similar to previous work [7].

Concept Extraction Model. For our experiments, we use the publicly available topic hierarchy in DMOZ Open Directory Project [2] as labeled concept classes, and use the documents linked to each class to train a concept classifier. The classifier is named ODP. The second concept extraction model is a pseudo concept model that uses demography group instead of classified concepts for user concept space (while using the ODP concepts for the ads). We use it to show the generality of our learning algorithm. ODP has tens of thousands concept classes in total, and DEMO contains hundreds of demography groups, classified by country, age, gender, education, political stand and relationship status. For ODP, the concept vectors are high-dimensional though sparse, leading to millions of learning parameters to be learnt in the transformation matrix $\mathbf{W}$.

Relevance Model. We have presented algorithms for two sorts of learnt parameters: the weights $\mathbf{\Gamma}_a, \mathbf{\Gamma}_u$ on each heterogeneous source, and the transformation matrix $\mathbf{W}$. As a demonstration, we compare with our relevance feature against various baselines:

- f: Our relevance feature using weighted sources + learnt pseudo bilinear form similarity.
- cos: Baseline model with unweighted sources + a plain cosine similarity feature, or in other words, a uniform diagonal transformation matrix.
- $wcos$: Weighted sources + cosine similarity .
- $f_{unweighted}$: Unweighted sources + learnt similarity.
- f_{sparse}: Weighted sources + transformation matrix learnt with sparse coding.

For each baseline, the parameters (source weights or transformation matrix) were relearnt by adding the relevant constraint to the optimization problem.

5.2 Preliminary study of Baseline Features

We first explore the value provided by the baseline feature cos in CTR prediction. Using labeled ads impression data, we compute the baseline feature and bucketize the impressions according to feature values. The i-th bucket ($0 \leq i < 100$) contains all the impressions with feature value $cos \in [\frac{i}{100}, \frac{i+1}{100})$. For all the impressions in each bucket, we plot the average CTR divided by average estimated CTR(ECTR), which is given by an existent ranking system without cognitive relevance feature. A perfect system should always have CTR/ECTR=1. The farther CTR/ECTR is from 1, the more the estimate should be adjusted. We see from Figure 3(a) that if we use unweighted sources and exact concept match, the feature value has a positive correlation with CTR/ECTR. It suggests that tuning up and down the CTR estimation for high and low relevance feature respectively can improve the accuracy.

We repeat this for the feature cos obtained by using user concept vectors from each single source. Figure 3(b) shows the regression trend of CTR/ECTR with cosine similarity. The larger slope indicates a stronger prediction power for that source. The prediction power varies a lot from source to source, and unweighted combination of all sources is even worse than using a certain source in this rough estimate. Figure 3(c) shows the coverage of the cosine similarity for all user-ad impressions during a week. As we can see from Figure 3(c), for each source no more than 40% of the total impressions have at least one matching concept; even we use all sources, only half of total impressions are "covered" in this sense. The low coverage of nonzero similarity values provides another motivation to improve the similarity metric beyond the analysis in Section 4.1, while the observation that every

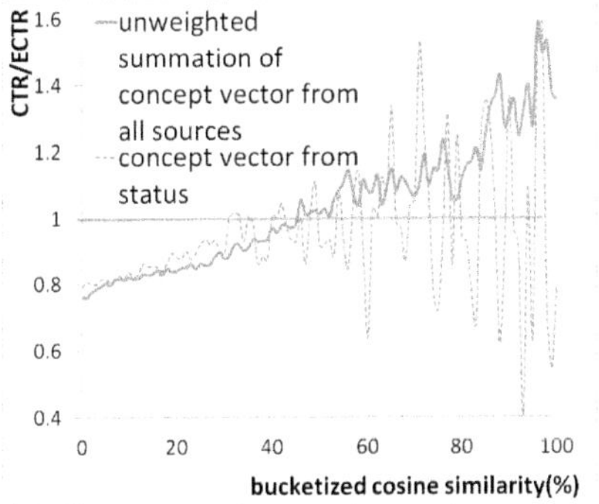

(a) Cosine similarity pivots the correction to the estimated CTR; unweighted summation causes noisy pivoting effect

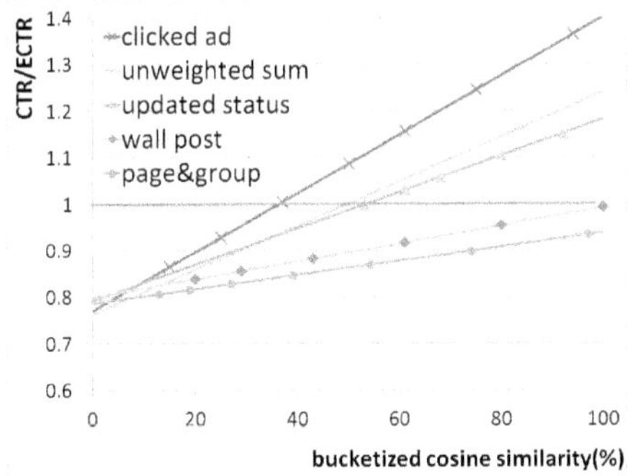

(b) Using concept vector from different sources to do relevance matching has different pivoting power

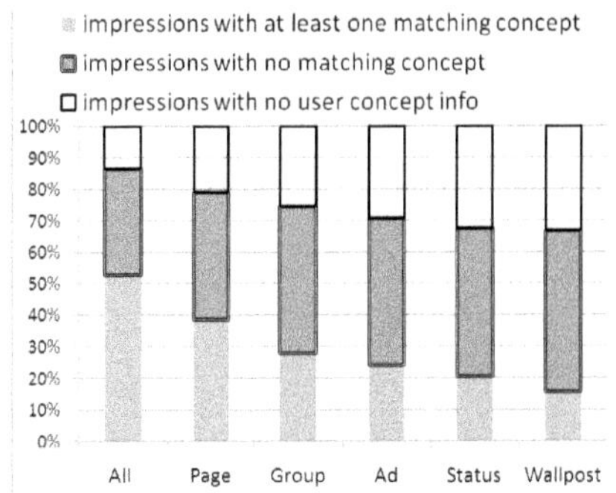

(c) Impression coverage by cosine similarity values, using concept vectors from different sources

Figure 3: Potential CTR prediction improvement by cosine similarity feature. Sources vary in the power of relevance matching and the coverage of the ad impressions where they can suggest an exact concept match.

Table 2: logloss(*)/logloss(cos) for different relevance feature, where logloss is the deviation w.r.t. randomness. Higher values indicate that the model does a better job in predicting clickthroughs from input concept data.

Iteration	logloss deviation wrt randomness (ratio to cos)			
	$wcos$	$f_{unweighted}$	f	f_{sparse}
100K	2.6	4.4	**5.6**	**5.6**
200K	2.8	5.7	**6.9**	**6.9**
500K	2.7	6.7	**8.1**	8.0
1M	2.9	7.7	**9.5**	9.4
2M	2.9	8.8	**10.9**	10.8
test	3.8	11.2	**14.3**	13.7

source has unequal power and coverage suggests we should assign different weights to different sources.

5.3 Analysis of Our Relevance Model

This section presents the results of our learning algorithm for source weights and transformation matrix. First we compare the error reduction of by variant relevance models on the same test set. We then analyze the learnt model parameters to interpret the benefits of our method, and present interesting discoveries.

5.3.1 Learning Results

We applied the algorithms described in Section 4.2 to clickthrough data collected anonymously over 4 days from 1 million sampled users, and test on the next 3 days. In our implementation, we used a fixed learning rate, and chose other algorithm parameters using validation error.

Table 2 shows the percentage logloss reduction obtained by our algorithm (left) and various baselines, where the logloss reduction is measured compared to random guessing with the empirical click rate c_0, and displayed as a ratio of the logloss reduction achieved by cos. The baseline feature cos is only slightly better than random guessing, due to its low coverage and the lack of ability to match distinct but related concept classes. The cosine similarity with weighted sources ($wcos$) has as 4 times large logloss improvement as unweighted sources, but has the same coverage

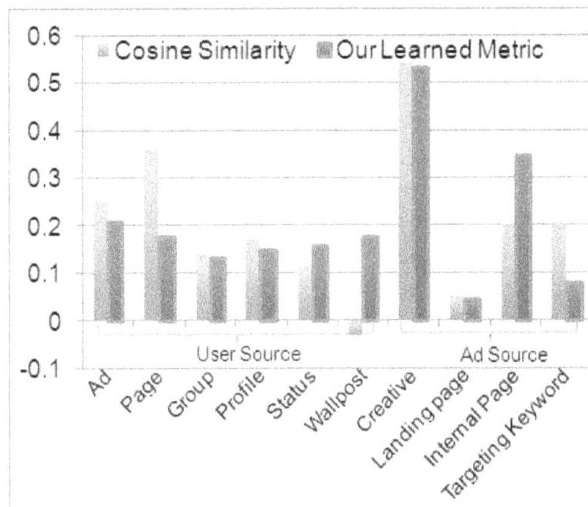

Figure 4: Weights of concept source for two settings: cosine similarity and normalized bilinear form similarity.

problem. The normalized bilinear form similarity can solve that problem and the logloss reduction is 10-fold larger than cos. With our jointly learnt model, the logloss reduction can be further improved, gaining a 14-fold of cos. Finally, the learning results with sparse coding demonstrate that we can reduce the number of nonzero parameters we need to store by 73-80%, thus reducing the overheads of feature computation, with only a small effect (within 5%, relatively) on the observed logloss performance. That speeds up the online feature computation by 53 times.

5.3.2 Source Weights

The learned weights of concept sources for cosine similarity and the learnt bilinear form similarity are shown in Figure 4. Some sources are entitled nearly zero weight due to extremely low coverage, and we omit it and only show the major sources, 6 for users (the ads they clicked before, the pages they are linked to, the groups they join, their profile interests, status updates and wallposts) and 4 for ads (descriptions created by the advertiser, linked pages outside Facebook, Facebook pages and keywords for targeting).

It is not surprising that "clicked ads" rank high as a user source, because it is the target we want to predict. We also observe that page concepts get higher source weight than

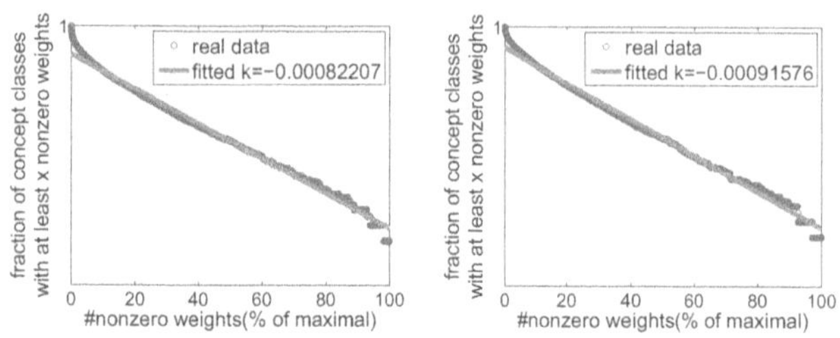

(a) #nonzero weights/row (b) #nonzero weights/col

Figure 5: Nonzero elements distribution in the transformation matrix, y axis in log scale

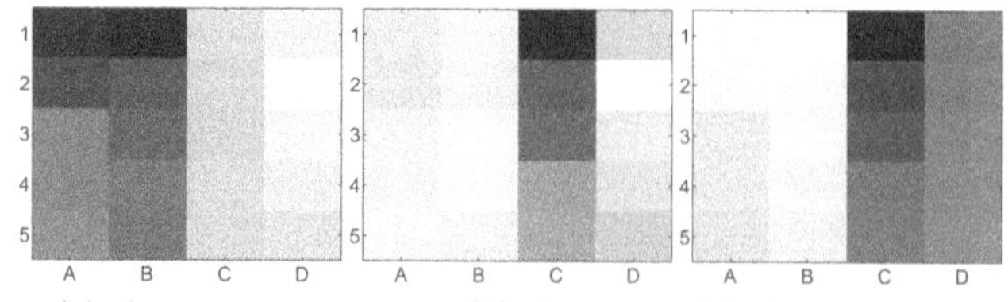

(a) $f_{unweighted}$ (b) f (c) f-$f_{unweighted}$

ac	A - Trading Card Games	B - Rabbits Personal Pages	C - Shrek Series	D - Entertainment Weblogs
uc1	Music	Music	Arts	Music/ Styles
uc2	Christianity	Society	Animation Movies	Society
uc3	Movies	Video Games	Humor	Humor
uc4	Music/ Styles	Online Communities	Cartoons	Movies
uc5	Parenting Weblogs	Music/ Styles	Movies	Animation Movies

Figure 6: The different transformation matrices for unweighted sources and weighted sources. 4 groups of user-ad concept association are shown by gray scale, black=1, white=-1. In each group 5 associate user concepts for a fixed ad concept are chosen.

group concepts, which might imply that the groups are not necessarily formed by interests, while pages better reflect the collective interests of their users. For ad concepts, the dominant source is the ad creative text, the visible part to the user. However, the other sources add extra information, beyond what is achievable just using the creative text. For ads that link to a known onsite object (e.g., ads about a music artist), the concepts for that object strongly indicate good ad concepts. Further, important information can be gleaned by looking at the landing page for the ad, as well as the targeting criteria provided by the advertisers. Taken together, these results validate our hypothesis that important semantic information can be obtained by looking at many heterogeneous sources of information, even though the sources have varying levels of noise.

An interesting observation is that if we change the concept matching function, the importance of sources varies qualitatively. For example, if we only allow exact concept matching with cosine similarity, some textual content such as wallposts are noisy and are assigned low source weights, indicating that exact concept match is not appropriate for them. However, the improved similarity metric can handle this problem by changing the association weight between the implicit interests and related classes of ads. When we allow matching across concept classes with our transformation matrix, we are able to use all of these sources successfully.

5.3.3 *Transformation Matrix*

To better understand the output of the learning algorithm, we now examine the learned transformation matrix $\mathbf{W}$. The i-th row of this matrix corresponds to the i-th user concept, and the j-th column to the j-th ad concept. The weight on (i, j) is used to match the i-th user concept to the j-th ad concept. For ODP, the learned matrix is sparse and contains 3% (which is already millions) nonzero parameter values, with extremely skewed density in various rows and columns of the matrix. The number of nonzero weights in each row and each column both satisfy power-law distributions (Figure 5). On average, each row and column contains several hundred nonzero values—which means that a user or ad concept can potentially match several hundred concepts.

Figure 6 visualizes three 5-by-4 matrices to show the typical difference between the transformation matrix learned with unweighted sources and weighted sources for ODP. The 4 columns divide the association into 4 groups. In each group we fix the ad concept class, and select 5 user concept classes whose association weight with that ad concept disagree in the two cases. Along each column, say column A, we have 5 cells now corresponding to 5 user-ad concept pair from (uc_{A1}, ac_A) to (uc_{A5}, ac_A). Each cell in the grid is dyed according to the association weight. Dark color means positive association and light means negative. See the table below the figures for a map. In general, the association weight given by f looks more meaningful because it amplifies the concepts from cleaner source and shrinks the concepts from noisier source. For example, the interests in music have nothing much to do with ads of trading card games or personal pages with rabbits $(A1, B1, A4, B5)$; the interests in animation movies and humors apparently signal a tendency to click ads about Shrek Series $(C2, C3)$. This suggests that transformation matrix can be better learned if the importance of concept sources are better distinguished.

From the analyses from above two sections, we conclude is that source weighting and non-exact matching mutually enhance each other and an integrate combination of them lead to higher quality of prediction. Thus our algorithm for learning them jointly, instead of separately picking the source weights and the matrix $\mathbf{W}$, is expected to be crucial.

5.3.4 *Case Study*

The values in the learned transformation matrix capture various statistical associations between the user and ad concept classes. Table 3 shows some extreme cases from which we can interpret the user-ad relevance captured by the matrix. Eight categories of such cases are studied. We present four of them due to space limitation. For each category, we give examples from different concept extraction models. The first category we show is about a single ad concept class which is related to many user concept classes. Turn-based strategic video games are associate with more than 70% user interests, and Christianity denominations relate to almost every demography group. Ads with such concepts have diversely targeted users. The other 3 categories we show in Table 3 are about concept pairs which have very strong or

Table 3: Interpreting the transformation matrix

Characteristics	*CE*	*Example:#related concepts(%)*
Ad concepts associated with most user concepts	ODP	Turn Based Video Games: 71
	DEMO	Christianity Denominations: 97
Characteristics	*CE*	*Example: association weight*
Strong positive associations	ODP	Browser Based Casinos →Facebook Platform:0.59
	DEMO	Female→Dance:0.74, Male→Guitar:0.72
Strong negative associations	ODP	Birthdays→ Online Games:-0.72, Arts→ Society:-0.52
	DEMO	Female→Sexuality Politics:-0.76, US → Mah Jongg:-0.46
Identical but weak associations	ODP	US Colleges:-0.20, Poker Personal Pages:-0.18,

Table 4: Relative variance reduction achieved when a feature is added to test feature set. High values for important features.

Test feature set	$wcos$	f	f_{DEMO}
F_0 = user-ad relevance feature	0.12	**0.34**	0.008
$F_1 = F_0$ + user click bias	0.03	**0.06**	0.002

very weak associations. Strong associations could be either positive or negative, *e.g.*, females favor dance while males like guitar; US people do not like Mahjongg, which is a popular gambling game in Asia. Some user concepts have weak association weight with the identical ad concept. That actually reflects a mismatch when we use cosine similarity—though the concept of colleges in US can be found in many user pages and profiles, it does not imply that these users will like ads about colleges in US. On the contrary, such ads will attract people who have not been in US colleges.

There are also several hard-to-interpret results, such as the negative association between birthdays and online games. Such results may either reflect unexpected input statistics, or might be influenced by the imperfectness of concept extraction, or bias in the training set (as the training samples are generated by an optimized ranking system).

5.4 Cognitive Relevance for Targeting

To compare our relevance feature with previously studied or commonly used features, such as keyword-based, clustering-based and friendship-based relevance features, we train new CTR prediction models using two different configurations of features for test purpose. In one configuration (called F_0), we include all existing features in an ad ranking system that capture inferred user-ad relevance (and are thus meaningful even for new ads). This checks the additional relevance value brought by our new feature. In the second configuration (called F_1), we additionally include features that capture the bias of different users to click on ads and the past clicking behavior of users. This helps check that the observed gains from our relevance features cannot be explained solely by capturing a user's past clicks with hand-crafted features. In each case, we experiment with training a model with and without our new relevance feature. We evaluate the importance of each feature by variance reduction achieved [12], and the improvement of logloss reduction when each of them is added to the test feature sets.

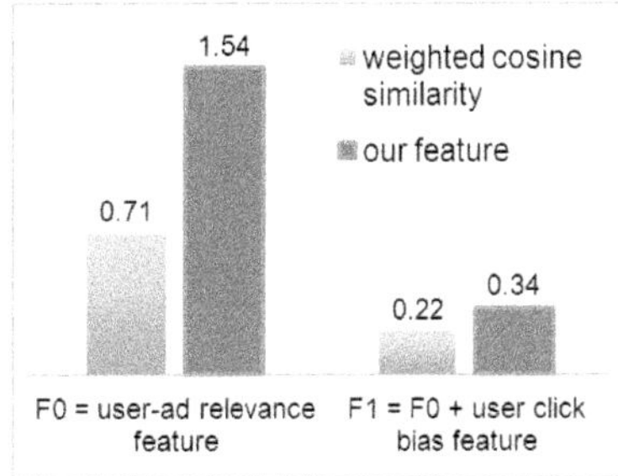

Figure 7: Improvement of logloss reduction (%) by cognitive relevance over test feature sets F_0 and F_1

Table 4 shows the approximate importance for each feature given by training and testing a CTR prediction model over one week of click data (60% for training and 40% for test) for a fraction of users. Among all the inferred relevance features between a user and an ad, the feature generated by our learned model ranks highest and is twice as important as the second highest. When we include user-click-bias features in our comparison, we find our feature still outperforms all individual non-historical features and most historical features as well (not shown in the table). Weighted cosine similarity has importance 1/3 and 1/2 of f in the two cases and also ranks high, but demography relevance is of one order lower importance weight. As a consequence, our feature brings a significant improvement in logloss reduction, while demography feature has improvement lower than 0.1% (and thus not plotted in Figure 7). The relevance feature is especially useful for the challenge of ranking newly created ads, for which historical click data is not available—the feature thus forms an apriori idea of the quality of an ad for each user. When an ad has been shown for an extended period of time, it is possible to collect actual clickthrough information for that ad from a large sample of users, and it is likely that the apriori relevance feature will be less significant.

5.4.1 *Online experiment results*

As a final evaluation, we test the performance improvement achievable by adding the new feature to the ad ranking system that uses the existing optimized features. We randomly select about 5M users and partition them into two equal large groups. The first group G_0 are targeted by the ranking system trained with all previous features, but without our new relevance features (F_2); the other group G_1 are targeted by a retrained ranking system with the exact concept match feature ($wcos$) and our final relevance feature (f) added. As expected, our relevance features help improve the underlying ads metrics in these online experiments. For example, for the impressions with our relevance feature f larger than a relevance threshold, we observe that the CTR is improved by at least 30% across the board.

For post-experiment analysis, we placed the new feature values into 100 percentile buckets, such that each bucket contains an equal number of impressions. We compare the CTR improvement of G_1 over G_0 by showing observed CTR in G_1 for different values of the feature bucket as a multiplier of the overall CTR of G_0 . For a strongly predictive feature, we expect the feature value to be very indicative of the actually observed CTR in the system. From Figure 8 we find that the two features we added have comparable power when measuring relevance for those impressions with

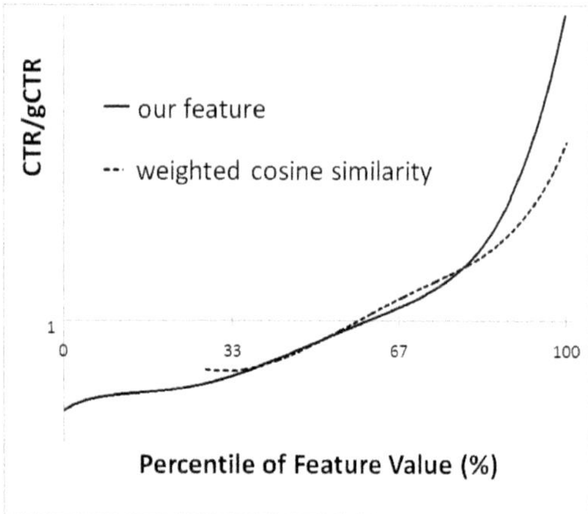

Figure 8: The CTR boost observed (as a ratio of average CTR in the control group G_0) when we add our new relevance feature f and the baseline feature $wcos$ to test feature set. The plot shows that high values of our relevance feature are indicative of possible clicks, and low values are indicative of poor relevance or low clicks. The absolute values of the y-axis labels are hidden for confidentiality.

"moderate" relevance (from 40% to 70%), but our feature is much stronger in finding highly relevant user-ad pairs and boosting CTR for them. Unlike the exact match similarity, which is zero for a large percentage of impressions (more than 30% as seen from Figure 3(c) and 8, when no exact concept matches are found), our feature is also good at ranking them and finding ad impressions that are likely to have low-relevance, and get lower clicks than expected.

6. CONCLUSION AND FUTURE WORK

In this study we aim for relevance based targeting in large scale social network sites. We infer user interests and ad concepts from heterogeneous sources and links, and develop user-ad relevance feature based on weighted matching between any pair of concept classes. We learn both the link weights and matching matrix from click data, and find they mutually enhance each other. Experimental results reveal insights into user preferences in online social networks and suggest valuable potential for more relevant targeting.

We have made some simplifying assumptions in this study that can be relaxed in future work. For example, we do not model temporal aspects of user-generated content, and do not personalize weights on various sources. The method can be applied on top of richer concept extraction models, which should help provide a clearer signal of concept associations. Finally, for more complex models, parallel learning algorithms and better data infrastructure can be studied to facilitate the offline learning and online ranking.

7. ACKNOWLEDGEMENTS

Chi Wang was supported in part by the U.S. National Science Foundation under grant IIS-09-05215, and by the Army Research Laboratory under Cooperative Agreement Number W911NF-09-2-0053 (NS-CTA). The authors thank Andrei Alexandrescu, Wenjie Fu, Hong Ge, John Hegeman, Nuwan Senaratna, Tao Xu and members of the Facebook ads engineering team for their insights and their work on building parts of the system described in this paper, and Zhenhui Li and Quanquan Gu for valuable discussions.

8. REFERENCES

[1] *Facebook Statistics*, `http://www.facebook.com/press/info.php?statistics`.
[2] *The Open Directory Project (ODP)*, `http://www.dmoz.org`.
[3] E. Agichtein, E. Brill, and S. Dumais. Improving web search ranking by incorporating user behavior information. In *SIGIR '06*.
[4] H. Bao and E. Y. Chang. Adheat: an influence-based diffusion model for propagating hints to match ads. In *WWW '10*.
[5] D. M. Blei, A. Y. Ng, and M. I. Jordan. Latent dirichlet allocation. *Journal of Machine Learning Research*, 3:993–1022, 2003.
[6] D. Boyd and N. B. Ellison. Social network sites: Definition, history, and scholarship. *Journal of Computer-Mediated Communication*, 13(1), 2007.
[7] D. Chakrabarti, D. Agarwal, and V. Josifovski. Contextual advertising by combining relevance with click feedback. In *WWW '08*.
[8] P. Chatterjee, D. L. Hoffman, and T. P. Novak. Modeling the clickstream: Implications for web-based advertising efforts. *Marketing Science*, 22, 2003.
[9] M. Ciaramita, V. Murdock, and V. Plachouras. Online learning from click data for sponsored search. In *WWW '08*.
[10] M. Daoud, L. Tamine, M. Boughanem, and B. Chebaro. Learning implicit user interests using ontology and search history for personalization. In *WISE'07: Proceedings of the 2007 international conference on Web information systems engineering*.
[11] D. Fensel, F. van Harmelen, I. Horrocks, D. L. McGuinness, and P. F. Patel-Schneider. Oil: An ontology infrastructure for the semantic web. *IEEE Intelligent Systems*, 16, 2001.
[12] J. H. Friedman. Greedy function approximation: A gradient boosting machine. *Annals of Statistics*, 29, 2001.
[13] D. Goldberg, D. Nichols, B. M. Oki, and D. Terry. Using collaborative filtering to weave an information tapestry. *Commun. ACM*, 35, 1992.
[14] Q. Gu, J. Zhou, and C. H. Q. Ding. Collaborative filtering: Weighted nonnegative matrix factorization incorporating user and item graphs. In *SDM*, 2010.
[15] G. King and L. Zeng. Logistic regression in rare events data. *Political Analysis*, 9:137–163, 2001.
[16] I. Konstas, V. Stathopoulos, and J. M. Jose. On social networks and collaborative recommendation. In *SIGIR '09*.
[17] A. Y. Ng. Feature selection, l1 vs. l2 regularization, and rotational invariance. In *ICML '04: Proceedings of the twenty-first international conference on Machine learning*.
[18] B. Piwowarski and H. Zaragoza. Predictive user click models based on click-through history. In *CIKM '07*.
[19] F. Provost, B. Dalessandro, R. Hook, X. Zhang, and A. Murray. Audience selection for on-line brand advertising: privacy-friendly social network targeting. In *KDD '09*.
[20] B. Ribeiro-Neto, M. Cristo, P. B. Golgher, and E. Silva de Moura. Impedance coupling in content-targeted advertising. In *SIGIR '05*.
[21] A. Shepitsen, J. Gemmell, B. Mobasher, and R. Burke. Personalized recommendation in social tagging systems using hierarchical clustering. In *RecSys '08*.
[22] D. Vallet, M. Fernández, P. Castells, P. Mylonas, and Y. Avrithis. Personalized information retrieval in context. In *3rd International Workshop on Modeling and Retrieval of Context*, 2006.
[23] C. Wang, P. Zhang, R. Choi, and M. D'Eredita. Understanding consumers attitude toward advertising. In *Eighth Americas Conference on Information Systems*, pages 1143–1148, 2002.
[24] Z. Wen and C.-Y. Lin. On the quality of inferring interests from social neighbors. In *KDD '10*.
[25] R. W. White, P. Bailey, and L. Chen. Predicting user interests from contextual information. In *SIGIR '09*.

Author Index

www.ingramcontent.com/pod-product-compliance
Ingram Content Group UK Ltd.
Pitfield, Milton Keynes, MK11 3LW, UK
UKHW051455290926
15471UKWH00008B/1218

9 781450 312516